Medical and Health Information Directory

Volume 3:
Health Services

ISSN 0749-9973

TWENTY-EIGHTH EDITION

Medical and Health Information Directory

A Guide to Organizations, Agencies, Institutions, Programs, Publications, Services, and Other Resources Concerned with Clinical Medicine, Basic Biomedical Sciences, and the Technological and Socioeconomic Aspects of Health Care

Volume 3:

Health Services
Including Clinics, Treatment Centers, Care Programs, and Counseling/Diagnostic Services

Part 2

Chapters 20-28

Donna Batten
Project Editor

GALE
CENGAGE Learning

Detroit • New York • San Francisco • New Haven, Conn • Waterville, Maine • London

GALE
CENGAGE Learning

Medical and Health Information Directory, 28th Edition, Volume 3

Project Editor: Donna Batten

Editorial Support Services: Emmanuel Barrido

Composition and Electronic Capture: Gary Oudersluys

Manufacturing: Rita Wimberley

For product information and technology assistance, contact us at
Gale Customer Support, 1-800-877-4253.
For permission to use material from this text or product,
submit all requests online at **www.cengage.com/permissions.**
Further permissions questions can be emailed to
permissionrequest@cengage.com

Gale
27500 Drake Rd.
Farmington Hills, MI, 48331-3535

ISBN-13: 978-1-4144-7877-7 ISBN-10: 1-4144-7877-1 (set)
ISBN-13: 978-1-4144-7878-4 ISBN-10: 1-4144-7878-X (vol. 1 set)
ISBN-13: 978-1-4144-7879-1 ISBN-10: 1-4144-7879-8 (vol. 1, part 1)
ISBN-13: 978-1-4144-7880-7 ISBN-10: 1-4144-7880-1 (vol. 1, part 2)
ISBN-13: 978-1-4144-7881-4 ISBN-10: 1-4144-7881-X (vol. 1, part 3)
ISBN-13: 978-1-4144-7882-1 ISBN-10: 1-4144-7882-8 (vol. 1, part 4)
ISBN-13: 978-1-4144-7883-8 ISBN-10: 1-4144-7883-6 (vol. 2 set)
ISBN-13: 978-1-4144-7884-5 ISBN-10: 1-4144-7884-4 (vol. 2, part 1)
ISBN-13: 978-1-4144-7885-2 ISBN-10: 1-4144-7885-2 (vol. 2, part 2)
ISBN-13: 978-1-4144-7886-9 ISBN-10: 1-4144-7886-0 (vol. 3 set)
ISBN-13: 978-1-4144-7887-6 ISBN-10: 1-4144-7887-9 (vol. 3, part 1)
ISBN-13: 978-1-4144-7888-3 ISBN-10: 1-4144-7888-7 (vol. 3, part 2)
ISBN-13: 978-1-4144-7889-0 ISBN-10: 1-4144-7889-5 (vol. 3, part 3)
ISBN-13: 978-1-4144-7890-6 ISBN-10: 1-4144-7890-9 (vol. 3, part 4)

ISSN 0749-9973

Printed in the United States of America
1 2 3 4 5 17 16 15 14 13

Contents

Descriptive Listings

Introduction

Volume 3 of the *Medical and Health Information Directory (MHID)*, a three-part softcover resource, is now in its twenty-eighth edition. *MHID* is a convenient one-stop source of information on clinics, treatment centers, care programs, and counseling/diagnostic services. It directs health care professionals and the public alike to a wide variety of health services in the United States, including:

- AIDS Programs
- Amyotrophic Lateral Sclerosis Clinics
- Audiology & Speech/Language Services
- Cancer Programs
- Community & Migrant Health Centers
- Cystic Fibrosis Centers
- Clinical Programs for the Developmentally Disabled
- Domestic Violence and Sexual Assault Programs
- Eating Disorders Clinics
- Family Planning Services
- Genetic Services Centers
- Headache Clinics
- Home Health Care Agencies
- Hospices
- In Vitro Fertilization Clinics
- Kidney Dialysis & Transplant Services
- Mental Health Services
- Multiple Sclerosis Centers & Clinics
- Organ & Tissue Banks
- Pain Management Programs
- Runaway & Homeless Youth Centers
- Sickle Cell Anemia Centers
- SIDS Information & Counseling Programs
- Sleep Disorders Centers & Laboratories
- Substance Abuse Services
- Suicide Prevention & Crisis Intervention Centers

Comprehensive Coverage

There are many published and unpublished directories of service agencies that provide specialized health care in the United States; however, these directories are usually limited in coverage to a single health issue or to a particular geographic area. In contrast, Volume 3 of *MHID* is broad in scope, presenting resources, a significantly larger compilation of programs that provide treatment and care for, or information on, a wide range of medical and health-related conditions and issues on a national level.

Content and Arrangement

Volume 3 consists of Descriptive Listings and an Alphabetical Name and Keyword Index.

- The Descriptive Listings are organized within 35 chapters, according to type of health service, as outlined on the "Contents" pages.
- The Alphabetical Name and Keyword Index speeds access to Volume 3 entries through a consolidated listing of all clinics, treatment centers, care programs, and counseling/diagnostic services included in the book.

For additional information on the content, arrangement, and indexing of Volume 3, consult the "User's Guide" following this introduction.

Method of Compilation

The twenty-eighth edition of Volume 3 represents a complete revision and updating of all material presented in the previous edition, incorporating thousands of changes to addresses, telephone numbers, personnel, and other key details.

Many sources were used to update this edition, including federal and state government documents and publications, and lists and directories supplied by numerous national organizations.

Companion Volumes Profile Organizations and Information Resources

The companion volumes in this set complement Volume 3's coverage of health services:

- **Volume 1** covers organizations, agencies, and institutions
- **Volume 2** covers publications, libraries, and other information resources

Together, these volumes provide complete coverage of the medical and health care information and delivery system.

Available in Electronic Formats

Licensing. The *Medical and Health Information Directory* is available for licensing. The complete database is provided in a fielded format and is deliverable on such media as disk or CD-ROM. For more information, contact Gale's Business Development Group at 1-800-877-GALE, or visit us on our web site at http://gale.cengage.com/bizdev.

Online. The Directory is also available online as part of the *Gale Directory Library*. For more information, call 1-800-877-GALE.

Comments Welcome

We encourage users to bring new or unlisted resources to our attention. Every effort will be made to include them in subsequent editions of *MHID*. Comments and suggestions for improving the directory are also welcome. Please contact:

Medical and Health Information Directory
Gale
27500 Drake Rd.
Farmington Hills, MI 48331-3535
Telephone: (248)699-GALE
Toll-Free: (800)877-4253
Fax: (248)699-8865

Volume 3 of the *Medical and Health Information Directory (MHID)* consists of a main body of Descriptive Listings grouped within separate chapters by type of health service, and an Alphabetical Name and Keyword Index, which provides a convenient alphabetical listing of all clinics, treatment centers, care programs, and counseling/diagnostic services included in Volume 3. Each section is described below.

Listings are numbered sequentially within 35 separate chapters, as outlined on the "Contents" pages. Details on the content, arrangement, indexing, and sources for each chapter are provided in the following descriptions.

AIDS Programs

- Scope: Clinical research programs sponsored by the National Institute of Allergy and Infectious Diseases (NIAID) at sites across the country to evaluate promising therapies, drugs, and vaccines for people infected with the human immunodeficiency virus (HIV), the cause of AIDS. The chapter comprises three sections: 1) AIDS Clinical Trials Units (ACTU), 2) Community Programs for Clinical Research on AIDS (CPCRA), and 3) AIDS Vaccine Evaluation Units. ACTUs, which conduct large, multi-center studies at U.S. universities and medical centers, evaluate therapies for all aspects of HIV disease in adults and children. CPCRA studies bring clinical trials to HIV-infected patients in such community settings as hospitals, health centers, private practices and clinics, and drug treatment facilities. They complement studies in the ACTUs by focusing on how to use available treatments most effectively and determining the long-term consequences of different treatments. AVEUs conduct clinical trials of experimental vaccines to prevent HIV infection.
- Entries Include: Institution and/or program name, address, telephone number, fax number, e-mail address, and web site.
- Arrangement: Geographical by states, then alphabetical by institution/program names within each state.
- Indexed by: Institution or program names.
- Source: The National Institute of Allergy and Infectious Diseases (National Institutes of Health, U.S. Department of Health and Human Services).

Amyotrophic Lateral Sclerosis Clinics

- Scope: Clinics certified by the ALS Association that specialize in the care and treatment of people suffering from Amyotrophic Lateral Sclerosis (ALS).
- Entries Include: Institution and/or program name, address, telephone number, fax number, e-mail address, web site, and contact name.
- Arrangement: Geographical by states, then alphabetical by institution/program names within each state.
- Indexed by: Institution or program names.
- Source: List provided by the ALS Association (1275 K St. NW, Ste. 1050, Washington, DC 20005; 800-782-4747; http://www.alsa.org).

Arthritis & Musculoskeletal Diseases Centers

- Scope: Multipurpose Arthritis and Musculoskeletal Diseases Centers that conduct research on the causes, treatment, and prevention of arthritis and musculoskeletal diseases. With grant support from the National Institute of Arthritis and Musculoskeletal and Skin Diseases (NIAMS), these centers develop and carry out programs in basic and/or clinical research, epidemiology and health services research, and research related to professional, patient, and public education.
- Entries Include: Institution name, address, and telephone number.
- Arrangement: Geographical by states, then alphabetical by institution names within states.
- Indexed by: Institution names.
- Source: The National Institute of Arthritis and Muscu-

loskeletal and Skin Diseases (National Institutes of Health, U.S. Department of Health and Human Services).

Audiology and Speech/Language Services

- Scope: Services for the deaf and hearing-impaired comprising two sections: 1) Educational Programs, including residential and day schools that offer pre-school through secondary-level education for deaf children, and 2) Rehabilitation Programs that provide clinical services in audiology, speech-language pathology, or both.
- Entries Include: Organization or institution name, address, telephone number, fax number, e-mail address, and web site.
- Arrangement: Geographical by states and cities, then alphabetical by organization or institution names within cities.
- Indexed by: Organization or institution names.
- Source: Original research by the editorial staff.

Services for the Blind and Sight Impaired

- Scope: Institutions in two sections: 1) Educational Programs for blind and visually impaired children, pre-school through high school, and 2) Libraries for the Blind and Physically Handicapped. Libraries are part of a national network established by The Library of Congress to provide free recorded and Braille materials to persons who are unable to read or use standard printed materials because of visual or physical impairment.
- Entries Include: Institution name, address, telephone number, fax number, e-mail address, and web site.
- Arrangement: Educational Programs are geographical by states, then alphabetical by institution names within states. Libraries for the Blind and Physically Handicapped are geographical by states, then alphabetical by library names within states.
- Indexed by: Institution names.
- Source: National Library Service for the Blind and Physically Handicapped (a service of the Library of Congress) and original research by the editorial staff.

Brain and Spinal Cord Injury Programs

- Scope: Institutions that provide services for brain and spinal cord injured persons. Included, among others, are programs administered by the Spinal Cord Injury Service of the U.S. Department of Veterans Affairs and programs that receive funding as model spinal cord injury systems from the National Institute on Disability and Rehabilitation Research (NIDRR).
- Entries Include: Parent institution and/or program name, address, and telephone number, as well as a notation identifying programs supported by NIDRR.
- Arrangement: Geographical by states, then alphabetical by institution/program names within states.
- Indexed by: Parent institution and/or program names.
- Source: Original research by the editorial staff.

Burn Care Services

- Scope: Hospitals that offer specialized burn care services.
- Entries Include: Institution name, address, telephone number, fax number, e-mail address, and the number of designated burn care beds in each hospital.
- Arrangement: Geographical by states, then alphabetical by institution names within states.
- Indexed by: Institution names.
- Source: Original research by the editorial staff.

Cancer Programs

- Scope: Hospital cancer programs approved by the Commission on Cancer of the American College of Surgeons.
- Entries Include: Institution name, address, and telephone number.
- Arrangement: Geographical by states and cities, then alphabetical by institution names within cities.
- Indexed by: Institution names.
- Source: *Commission on Cancer Approved Cancer Programs* (published by the American College of Surgeons, 633 N. St. Clair St., Chicago, IL 60611, http://www.facs.org, 800-621-4111) and the National Cancer Institute, National Institutes of Health, U.S. Department of Health and Human Services.

Community & Migrant Health Centers

- Scope: Community and/or migrant health centers that receive funding through two federal grant programs administered by the Bureau of Primary Health Care (Health Resources and Services Administration, Public Health Service, U.S. Department of Health and Human Services). Community health centers provide basic primary medical services to persons located in rural and urban areas with financial, geographic, or cultural barriers to care. Migrant health centers provide a comprehensive range of primary health services to migrant and seasonal farm workers and their dependents.

- Entries Include: Organization name, address, telephone number, and the type of funding (community health center, migrant health center, or both) provided to each grantee organization.
- Arrangement: Geographical by states and cities, then alphabetical by organization names within cities.
- Indexed by: Organization names.
- Source: Original research by the editorial staff.

Cystic Fibrosis Centers

- Scope: Centers affiliated with the Cystic Fibrosis Foundation. These centers, located at institutions throughout the country, specialize in diagnosis and comprehensive care for children and young adults who suffer from the disease.
- Entries Include: Institution name, address, telephone number, and fax number.
- Arrangement: Geographical by states, then alphabetical by institution names within states.
- Indexed by: Institution names.
- Source: List provided by the Cystic Fibrosis Foundation (6931 Arlington Rd., 2nd Floor, Bethesda, MD 20814; 800-FIGHT-CF; http://www.cff.org).

Clinical Programs for the Developmentally Disabled

- Scope: Programs that provide comprehensive diagnosis/evaluation, counseling, treatment, and follow-up services to children and adults who have or are at risk of having a developmental disability, including intellectual disabilities, cerebral palsy, epilepsy, autism, or other conditions closely related to mental retardation.
- Entries Include: Institution and/or program name, address, and telephone number.
- Arrangement: Geographical by states, then alphabetical by institution/program names within states.
- Indexed by: Institution or program names.
- Source: Original research by the editorial staff.

Domestic Violence and Sexual Assault Programs

- Scope: Community resources nationwide for victims of domestic violence. Each of these programs offers some or all of the following services: shelters for battered women and their children, 24-hour crisis lines, information and referrals, support groups, counseling, and legal advocacy.
- Entries Include: Parent organization and/or program name, address, telephone number, fax number, e-mail address and, for most, crisis phone number(s) (24-hour hotlines, unless noted otherwise).
- Arrangement: Geographical by states and cities, then alphabetical by organization/program names within cities.
- Indexed by: Parent organization and/or program names.
- Source: Original research by the editorial staff.

Down Syndrome Clinics

- Scope: Clinics that specialize in the care and treatment of people suffering from Down Syndrome.
- Entries Include: Institution and/or program name, address, telephone number, and contact name.
- Arrangement: Geographical by states, then alphabetical by organization names within states.
- Indexed by: Institution or program names.
- Source: List provided by the National Down Syndrome Congress (30 Mansell Ct., Ste. 108, Roswell, GA 30076; 800-232-NDSC; http://www.ndsccenter.org).

Eating Disorders Clinics

- Scope: Clinics that specialize in the care and treatment of people suffering from Eating Disorders.
- Entries Include: Institution and/or program name, address, telephone number, fax number, e-mail address, and web site.
- Arrangement: Geographical by states, then alphabetical by organization names within states.
- Indexed by: Institution or program names.
- Source: Original research by the editorial staff.

Family Planning Services

- Scope: Offices, affiliates, and chapters of the Planned Parenthood Federation of America.
- Entries Include: Organization name, address, telephone number, and fax number.
- Arrangement: Geographical by states, then alphabetical by organization name within states.
- Indexed by: Organization names.
- Source: Directory provided by the Planned Parenthood Federation of America (434 W. 33rd St., New York, NY 10001; (212)541-7800; http://www.plannedparenthood.org).

Genetic Services Centers

- Scope: Clinical genetic services centers that offer comprehensive diagnostic services, medical management, counseling, and follow-up care for a range of genetic conditions. (Specialized clinics and programs, such as those for cystic fibrosis, hemophilia, and sickle cell anemia, are covered in separate chapters of this publication.)

- Entries Include: Institution name, address, telephone number, fax number, e-mail address, and web site.
- Arrangement: Geographical by states then alphabetical by institution names within states.
- Indexed by: Institution names.
- Source: Original research by the editorial staff.

Headache Clinics

- Scope: Clinics that specialize in the treatment of migraine headaches.
- Entries Include: Institution name, address, telephone number, fax number, web site, and contact person.
- Arrangement: Geographical by states then alphabetical by institution names within states.
- Indexed by: Institution names.
- Source: List provided by the National Migraine Association (100 N Union St., Ste. B, Alexandria, VA 22314; (703) 349-1929; http://www.migraines.org)

Hemophilia Centers

- Scope: Federally funded hemophilia treatment facilities.
- Entries Include: Parent institution and/or center name, address, telephone number, fax number, email address, and web site.
- Arrangement: Geographical by states, then alphabetical by institution/center names within states.
- Indexed by: Parent institution and/or center names.
- Source: Maternal and Child Health Bureau (Health Resources and Services Administration, U.S. Department of Health and Human Services).

Home Health Care Agencies

- Scope: Home health agencies accredited by The Joint Commission, formerly named the Joint Commission on Accreditation of Healthcare Organizations. These hospitals, public health departments, and various for-profit and nonprofit organizations provide skilled nursing, home health aids, and other therapeutic services in patients' own homes.
- Entries Include: Parent organization and/or agency name, address, telephone number, contact person, and current accreditation status.
- Arrangement: Geographical by states and cities, then alphabetical by organization/agency names within cities.
- Indexed by: Parent organization and/or agency names.
- Source: List provided by The Joint Commission (One Renaissance Blvd., Oakbrook Terrace, IL 60181; (630) 792-5000; http://www.jointcommission.org).

Hospices

- Scope: Hospices that are Medicare certified. These organizations, which may be independent units, sponsored by hospitals, or affiliated with home health care agencies, focus on managing the pain and discomfort of terminally ill persons and provide emotional support to family members as well. Services usually take place in the home, but are sometimes provided in hospital or nursing home units.
- Entries Include: Parent organization and/or hospice name, address, and telephone number.
- Arrangement: Geographical by states and cities, then alphabetical by organization names within cities.
- Indexed by: Parent organization and/or hospice names.
- Source: Original research by the editorial staff.

In Vitro Fertilization Clinics

- Scope: Clinics that specialize in in vitro fertilization procedures.
- Entries Include: Organization and/or facility name, address, telephone number, and contact person.
- Arrangement: Geographical by state, then alphabetical by organization and/or facility name within state.
- Indexed by: Organization and/or facility name.
- Source: Original research by the editorial staff.

Kidney Dialysis & Transplant Services

- Scope: Facilities approved by the Centers for Medicare and Medicaid Services, U.S. Department of Health and Human Services, to provide kidney dialysis and transplant services under the Medicare program.
- Entries Include: Parent organization and/or facility name, address, telephone number, and the number of dialysis treatment stations at each facility.
- Arrangement: Geographical by states and cities, then alphabetical by organization/facility names within cities.
- Indexed by: Parent organization and/or facility names.
- Source: *National Listing of Medicare Providers Furnishing Kidney Dialysis and Transplant Services*

(published by the Office of Clinical Standards and Quality, Centers for Medicare and Medicaid Services, U.S. Department of Health and Human Services).

Mental Health Services

- Scope: Governmental, public, or private organizations, agencies, and institutions that provide services to persons with mental disorders. The chapter comprises three sections: 1) Multiservice Mental Health Organizations, which provide two or more of the following care services: inpatient, residential, partial care (day/evening), outpatient, and residential supportive care; 2) Psychiatric Hospitals, which provide 24-hour inpatient care to mentally ill persons; and 3) Residential Treatment Centers for Emotionally Disturbed Children, which serve children and adolescents under age 18.
- Entries Include: Organization, agency, or institution name, address, telephone number, and toll-free and fax numbers.
- Arrangement: Geographical by states and cities, then alphabetical by organization/agency/institution names within each of the sections noted above.
- Indexed by: Organization, agency, or institution names.
- Source: Original research by the editorial staff.

Multiple Sclerosis Centers & Clinics

- Scope: MS Comprehensive Care Centers and MS Care Centers. The Comprehensive Care Centers, established throughout the country by neurologists specializing in the field of MS, provide a broad range of services to meet the medical, psychosocial, educational and rehabilitation needs of people with multiple sclerosis and their families. The Care Clinics are affiliated with local chapters of the National Multiple Sclerosis Society. Many are also part of the Consortium of MS Centers, which has established guidelines for the type and quality of programs needed.
- Entries Include: Organization or institution name, address, and telephone number.
- Arrangement: Geographical by states, then alphabetical by organization/institution names within states.
- Indexed by: Organization or institution names.
- Source: List provided by the National Multiple Sclerosis Society (733 3rd Ave., 3rd Floor, New York, NY 10017; 800-FIGHT-MS; http://www.nmss.org).

Muscular Dystrophy Clinics

- Scope: Clinics sponsored by the Muscular Dystrophy Association at hospitals nationwide to provide diagnostic examinations, as well as follow-up care, to patients afflicted with any of the 40 neuromuscular diseases covered by the association's programs.
- Entries Include: Institution name, address, telephone number, toll-free number, fax number, e-mail address, and web site.
- Arrangement: Geographical by states, then alphabetical by institution names within states.
- Indexed by: Institution names.
- Source: Original research by the editorial staff.

Organ and Tissue Banks

- Scope: Tissue and organ banks that obtain, evaluate, and distribute eye tissue for use in corneal transplantation, research, and education; and blood cord banks.
- Entries Include: Parent organization and/or eye bank name, address, telephone number, fax number, e-mail address, and web site.
- Arrangement: Geographical by states, then alphabetical by organization names within states.
- Indexed by: Parent organization and/or bank names.
- Source: Original research by the editorial staff.

Pain Management Programs

- Scope: Inpatient and/or outpatient centers and clinics concerned with improving the quality of life for persons suffering acute chronic pain (i.e., headaches, backaches, arthritis, etc.).
- Entries Include: Parent organization and/or program name, address, and telephone number.
- Arrangement: Geographical by states, then alphabetical by organization/program names within states.
- Indexed by: Parent organization and/or program names.
- Source: Original research by the editorial staff.

Runaway & Homeless Youth Centers

- Scope: Grantees that receive federal funding through the Runaway and Homeless Youth Program administered by the U.S. Administration on Children, Youth and Families. These community-based centers provide a range of services, including temporary shelter, counseling, legal aid, and referrals to medical care.

- Entries Include: Organization name, address, telephone number, fax number, e-mail address, and web site.
- Arrangement: Geographical by states, then alphabetical by organization names within states.
- Indexed by: Organization names.
- Source: Original research by the editorial staff.

Sickle Cell Anemia Centers

- Scope: Sickle cell programs, including comprehensive sickle cell centers funded by the National Heart, Lung, and Blood Institute, as well as programs located in Veterans Affairs Medical Centers.
- Entries Include: Institution name, address, telephone number, and fax number.
- Arrangement: Geographical by states, then alphabetical by institution names within states.
- Indexed by: Institution names.
- Source: Lists provided by the U.S. Department of Veterans Affairs and the National Heart, Lung, and Blood Institute (National Institutes of Health, U.S. Department of Health and Human Services).

SIDS Information & Counseling Programs

- Scope: State agencies and programs funded by the Maternal and Child Health Bureau (Public Health Service, U.S. Department of Health and Human Services) to disseminate public information and counsel families affected by SIDS (Sudden Infant Death Syndrome).
- Entries Include: Agency and/or program name, address, and telephone number.
- Arrangement: Geographical by states, then alphabetical by agency/program names within states.
- Indexed by: Agency and/or program names.
- Source: Original research by the editorial staff.

Sleep Disorders Centers & Laboratories

- Scope: Accredited members of the American Academy of Sleep Medicine, including centers which provide full diagnostic and treatment services for all types of sleep-related disorders, and laboratories which specialize only in sleep-related breathing disorders.
- Entries Include: Parent institution and/or center/laboratory name, address, telephone number, and fax number.
- Arrangement: Geographical by states, then alphabetical by institution or center/laboratory names within states.
- Indexed by: Parent institution and/or center/laboratory names.
- Source: Membership roster provided by the American Academy of Sleep Medicine (2501 N. Frontgate Rd., Darien, IL 60561; (630) 737-9790; http://www.aasmnet.org).

Sports Medicine Clinics

- Scope: Organizations and institutions that provide a variety of services aimed at the diagnosis, treatment, and prevention of injuries resulting from participation in professional or recreational sports.
- Entries Include: Organization or institution name, address, telephone number, e-mail address, and web site.
- Arrangement: Geographical by states and cities, then alphabetical by organization/institution names within cities.
- Indexed by: Organization or institution names.
- Source: Original research by the editorial staff.

Substance Abuse Services

- Scope: Federal, state, local, and privately-funded organizations, agencies, and organizations that provide alcoholism and/or drug abuse treatment services.
- Entries Include: Organization, agency, or institution name, address, telephone number, toll-free and fax numbers, e-mail address and web site.
- Arrangement: Geographical by states and cities, then alphabetical by organization/agency/institution names within cities.
- Indexed by: Organization, agency, or institution names.
- Source: Substance Abuse and Mental Health Services Administration, U.S. Department of Health and Human Services.

Suicide Prevention & Crisis Intervention Centers

- Scope: Organizations that provide suicide prevention and crisis intervention services.
- Entries Include: Parent organization and/or center name, address, business telephone number, and one or more crisis phone numbers. (Most crisis lines are available 24 hours a day, seven days a week, unless otherwise noted.)
- Arrangement: Geographical by states and cities, then alphabetical by organization/center names within cities.

- Indexed by: Parent organization and/or center names.
- Source: Original research by the editorial staff.

Veterans Services

- Scope: Veterans services comprising three sections: 1) Veterans Affairs Medical Centers; 2) Post-Traumatic Stress Disorder (PTSD) Programs that provide a variety of inpatient, outpatient, and residential treatment services to veterans suffering from PTSD or co-existing PTSD/substance abuse; and 3) Vietnam Vet Centers that provide a broad range of psychological and vocational counseling, as well as other assistance to Vietnam-era veterans and their families. (Other veterans services covered in separate Volume 3 chapters include sickle cell anemia programs, spinal cord injury programs, and substance abuse treatment programs.)
- Entries Include: Facility name, address, and telephone number.
- Arrangement: Geographical by states and cities, then alphabetical by facility names within each of the sections noted above.
- Indexed by: Facility names.
- Source: Lists provided by the U.S. Department of Veterans Affairs.

Alphabetical Name and Keyword Index

The Alphabetical Name and Keyword Index provides access to all clinics, treatment centers, care programs, and counseling/diagnostic services included in Volume 3. Index references are to book entry numbers rather than to page numbers.

Many of the entries in Volume 3 use a hierarchical organization name structure, with a parent organization and often intermediate sub-units preceding the specific unit name. The Alphabetical Name and Keyword Index offers access to all multiple-part organization names via the parent organization name. Some entries are also referenced under the specific unit name and some under a significant intermediate unit name. Multiple parts of names are separated in index citations by a bullet (•). If several entries have the same parent organization, as is the case with many of the health services listed in Volume 3, the related units appear as a group under the name of the parent organization.

Alphabetizing Rules

In both the descriptive listings chapters and the index, organization names are sorted on a word-by-word basis, so that "New York Easter Seal Society" comes before "Newark Beth Israel Medical Center." Initial articles ("A," "An," or "The") are ignored for sorting purposes. Conjunctions, articles, and most prepositions elsewhere in the names are also not considered in alphabetizing. In addition:

- Numbers are sorted as if spelled-out and interfiled alphabetically with other non-number words.
- Abbreviations such as "U.S.," "St.," "Mt.," "Ft.," and "Dr." are sorted as if spelled-out and interfiled with names in which the full version of those words are used.
- Personal names are sorted under the first name, or initial, within the descriptive listings chapters. In the index, they can be accessed under both the first and last names.

Act.	Acting
Adj.	Adjutant
Admin.	Administrator
AFB	Air Force Base
AK	Alaska
AKA	Also Known As
AL	Alabama
Alt. Contact	Alternate Contact
Apt.	Apartment
AR	Arkansas
Assoc.	Associate
Asst.	Assistant
Ave.	Avenue
AZ	Arizona
Bldg.	Building
Blvd.	Boulevard
Br.	Branch
CA	California
Cat. No.	Catalogue Number
CEO	Chief Executive Officer
Chf.	Chief
Chm.	Chairman
Cir.	Circle
Clghse.	Clearinghouse
c/o	Care of
CO	Colorado
Co.	Company
Coll.	Collection
Comdr.	Commander
Commun.	Communication
Coord.	Coordinator
Corp.	Corporation
Couns.	Counselor
CT	Connecticut
Ct.	Court
Ctr.	Center
DC	District of Columbia
DE	Delaware
Dept.	Department
Desc	Description
Dir.	Director
Dr.	Drive
E.	East
Educ.	Education
Exec.	Executive
Expy.	Expressway
Ext.	Extension
First Pub	First Published
FL	Florida
Flr.	Floor
Fnded	Founded
Freq	Frequency
Frmly	Formerly
Ft.	Fort
Fwy.	Freeway
GA	Georgia
Gen.	General
Geo. Dist.	Geographical Distribution
GU	Guam
Hd.	Head
HI	Hawaii
Hwy.	Highway
IA	Iowa
ID	Idaho
IL	Illinois
IN	Indiana
Inc.	Incorporated
Info.	Information
KS	Kansas
KY	Kentucky
LA	Louisiana
Lang	Language
Lib.	Library
Libn.	Librarian
Ln.	Lane
MA	Massachusetts
MD	Maryland
ME	Maine
Med.	Medical
Mem	Members
Mgr.	Manager
MI	Michigan
MN	Minnesota
MO	Missouri
MS	Mississippi
MT	Montana
Mt.	Mount
N.	North
Natl.	National
NC	North Carolina
ND	North Dakota
NE	Nebraska, Northeast
NH	New Hampshire
NJ	New Jersey
No.	Number
NV	Nevada
NW	Northwest
NY	New York
Off.	Officer
OH	Ohio
OK	Oklahoma
OR	Oregon
PA	Pennsylvania
Pgs	Pages
Pkwy.	Parkway
Pl.	Place
Plz.	Plaza
PO Box	Post Office Box
PR	Puerto Rico
Pres.	President
Prog.	Program
Pub	Publication
RD	Rural Delivery
Rd.	Road
Ref.	Reference
Reg.	Regional
Res.	Research
RFD	Rural Free Delivery
RI	Rhode Island
Rm.	Room
RR	Rural Route
Rte.	Route
S.	South

SC	South Carolina
Sci.	Science
SD	South Dakota
SE	Southeast
Sec.	Secretary
Sect.	Section
Serv.	Service
Soc.	Social
Spec.	Specialist
Sq.	Square
Sr.	Senior
St.	Saint, Street
Sta.	Station
Ste.	Suite, Sainte
Subscript	Subscription(s)
Supv.	Supervisor
SW	Southwest
Telecom	Telecommunications
Ter.	Terrace
TN	Tennessee
Tpke.	Turnpike
Trl.	Trail
TX	Texas
Univ.	University
U.S.	United States
U.S. Dist	U.S. Distributor
UT	Utah
VA	Virginia
VI	Virgin Islands
VP	Vice President
VT	Vermont
W.	West
WA	Washington
WV	West Virginia
WY	Wyoming

Chapter 20
Hospices

The hospice programs listed below are arranged geographically by the states and cities in which they are located, then alphabetically by organization names within cities. Consult the "User's Guide" located at the front of this directory for additional information.

ALABAMA

Alabaster

18839 ■ Family Comfort Hospice of Alabaster, LLC
567 1st St. N
Alabaster, AL 35007
Ph: (205)663-5614

18840 ■ New Beacon--Alabaster
122 7th Ave. NE
Alabaster, AL 35007
Ph: (205)620-3508
Free: 800-789-0975
Fax: (205)620-6181
URL: http://www.newbeacon.org

Albertville

18841 ■ Hospice of Marshall County
408 Martling Rd.
Albertville, AL 35951
Ph: (256)891-7724
Free: 888-334-9336
Fax: (256)891-7754
E-mail: info@hospicemc.org
URL: http://www.hospicemc.org

18842 ■ Southeast Hospice Network, LLC--Marshall County
202 E McKinney Ave.
Albertville, AL 35950
Ph: (256)894-8266
Fax: (256)894-8265
URL: http://southeasthospicenetwork.com/contactus.php

Anadlusia

18843 ■ Comfort Care Hospice
1805 E 3 Knotch St., Ste. 3
Anadlusia, AL 36420
Ph: (334)427-4000
Free: 866-427-4001
Fax: (334)427-4004
URL: http://www.comfortcarehospice.org

Anniston

18844 ■ Hope Hospice, inc.--Anniston
PO Box 5578
Anniston, AL 36205
Ph: (256)820-3995
Free: 256-820-3997
E-mail: gtallent@hopehospiceinc.com
URL: http://hopehospiceinc.com/

18845 ■ New Beacon--Anniston
818 Leighton Ave.
Anniston, AL 36207
Ph: (256)236-5334
Free: 800-283-5334
Fax: (256)231-4558
URL: http://www.newbeacon.org/page/show/183626-new-beacon-anniston

Athens

18846 ■ Hospice of Athens Limestone County
405 S Marion St.
Athens, AL 35611
Ph: (256)232-5017
Fax: (256)230-0085
E-mail: info@athenslimestonehospice.org
URL: http://www.athenslimestonehospice.org

Attalla

18847 ■ Gadsden Regional Hospice
82 Industrial Blvd.
Attalla, AL 35954
Ph: (256)538-7460
Fax: (256)538-5905
URL: http://www.gadsdenregional.com/Pages/home.aspx

Auburn

18848 ■ Bethany House of East Alabama Medical Center
1171 Gatewood Dr.
Auburn, AL 36830
Ph: (334)826-0032
Fax: (334)826-2018
URL: http://www.hospiceeamc.org/

18849 ■ Hospice of East Alabama Medical Center (EAMC)
665 Opelika Rd.
Auburn, AL 36830
Ph: (334)826-1899
Fax: (334)826-0756
URL: http://www.hospice.eamc.org/

Bay Minette

18850 ■ County Community Hospice of Baldwin County
311 D'Olive St.
Bay Minette, AL 36507
Ph: (251)937-7330
Fax: (251)973-6674
URL: http://www.comhospice.com/default.asp?ID=2

Birmingham

18851 ■ Care First Hospice
1400 Urban center Ste. 240
Birmingham, AL 35209
Ph: (205)313-2801
Fax: (205)313-2801
URL: http://www.carefirst-al.com/hospice.html

18852 ■ Countryside Hospice Care--Birmingham
13521 Shelby County 280, Ste. 253
Birmingham, AL 35242
Free: 866-292-9538
Fax: (205)991-9191
URL: http://www.solamorhispice.com

18853 ■ Holistic Health Care
1500 1st Ave. N
Birmingham, AL 35203
Ph: (205)314-3420
Fax: (205)314-3421
URL: http://www.wellness.com/

18854 ■ Hope Hospice, Inc.--Birmingham
1100 E Park Dr., Ste. 303
Birmingham, AL 35235
Ph: (205)583-4673
Free: 888-583-HOPE
Fax: (205)583-4674
URL: http://www.hopehospiceinc.com

18855 ■ Hospice Compassus-Financial Support Center
3500 Blue Lake Dr.
Birmingham, AL 35243
Ph: (205)970-3888
Fax: (205)970-6677
E-mail: info@aatshospicecom.com
URL: http://www.hospicecompassus.com/

18856 ■ Hospice Services of Alabama
2367 Lakeside Dr.
Birmingham, AL 35244
Ph: (205)682-9996
Free: 888-682-9996
Fax: (205)682-9994
URL: http://www.hsofal.com/

18857 ■ New Beacon, Inc.--Birmingham
201 Office Park Dr. Ste. 100
Birmingham, AL 35223
Ph: (205)939-8799
Free: 888-653-8314
Fax: (205)939-8709
E-mail: dcox@newbeacon.org
URL: http://www.newbeacon.org/page/show/183628-new-beacon-birmingham
Formerly: Unity Hospice Services, Inc.

18858 ■ Odyssey Healthcare of Birmingham, Inc.
2000B S Bridge Pkwy., Ste. 150
Birmingham, AL 35209
Ph: (205)870-4340
Free: 877-637-9432
Fax: (205)870-9928
URL: http://www.odsyhealth.com

18859 ■ UAB Center for Palliative Care
1530 3rd Ave. S, CPM 3
Birmingham, AL 35294
Ph: (205)975-0826
Fax: (205)996-6873
URL: http://www.palliative.uab.edu

Brewton

18860 ■ Comfort Care Hospice of Brewton
722 Douglas Ave.
Brewton, AL 36426
Ph: (251)867-6232
Free: 877-867-6232
Fax: (251)867-6234
URL: http://www.comfortcarehospice.org

18861 ■ Covenant Hospice, Inc.--Brewton
1023 Douglas Ave.
Brewton, AL 36426-1586
Ph: (251)867-6993
Free: 800-541-3072
Fax: (251)867-5850
URL: http://www.covenanthospice.org

Brownsboro

18862 ■ Amedisys Hospice Care of Brownsboro
5767 Cove Commons Dr., Ste. A
Brownsboro, AL 35714
Ph: (256)288-0094
Fax: (256)288-0121
URL: http://www.amedisys.com/

Centre

18863 ■ Cherokee Hospice
775 Cherokee Plaza
Centre, AL 35960
Ph: (256)927-1144
URL: http://www.nursing-homes-care.com/directory/hh/cherokee-home-health-41.html

Cullman

18864 ■ Comfort Care Hospice of Cullman
2035 Alabama Hwy. 157
Cullman, AL 35058
Ph: (256)739-2588
Free: 866-739-2588
Fax: (256)775-1260
URL: http://www.comfortcarehospice.org

18865 ■ Gentiva Hospice--Cullman
1213 Cullman Shopping Center SW
Cullman, AL 35055
Ph: (256)737-7234
Fax: (256)737-7356
URL: http://www.gentiva.com/hospice/hospice_locations.php#al
Formerly: Wiregrass Hospice--Cullman.

18866 ■ Hospice of Cullman County
402 4th Ave. NE
Cullman, AL 35055
Ph: (256)739-2486
Fax: (256)737-0985
URL: http://www.hospiceofcullmancounty.org/

18867 ■ Life Care Hospice, Inc.
21 Beachgrove Road
Cullman, AL 35058
Ph: (256)734-1170
Free: 886-734-1170
Fax: (256)734-7576
URL: http://www.lifecarehospice.com

18868 ■ Omega Hospice of Cullman
101 2nd Ave. SE
Cullman, AL 35055
Ph: (256)737-1793
Fax: (256)737-3765
E-mail: info@omegahospicecares.com
URL: http://omegahospicecares.com/

Dadeville

18869 ■ Lake Martin Hospice
201 Mariarden Rd.
Dadeville, AL 36853
Ph: (256)825-7821
E-mail: tstephens@lakemartinhospital.com
URL: http://www.lakemartinhospital.com/hospice.html

Daphne

18870 ■ Covenant Hospice Inc.--Daphne
1040 Stanton Rd.
Daphne, AL 36526-7585
Ph: (251)626-5255
Free: 866-626-5255
Fax: (251)626-5922
URL: http://www.covenanthospice.org

Decatur

18871 ■ Aseracare Hospice--Decatur
219 E Moulton St.
Decatur, AL 35601
Ph: (256)350-8688
Free: 877-350-8688
Fax: (256)350-9890
URL: http://hospice.aseracare.com/home.aspx

18872 ■ Hospice of the Valley--Decatur
240 Johnson St. SE
Decatur, AL 35601
Ph: (256)350-5585
E-mail: cdobson@hospiceofthevalley.net
URL: http://www.hospiceofthevalley.net

Demopolis

18873 ■ Comfort Care Hospice LLC
935 U.S. Hwy. 80 W
Demopolis, AL 36732
Ph: (334)289-2106
Free: 888-737-9931
Fax: (334)289-2693
E-mail: mtatum@comfortcarehospice.org
URL: http://www.comfortcarehospice.org

Dothan

18874 ■ Covenant Hospice--Dothan
104 Rock Bridge Rd.
Dothan, AL 36303
Ph: (334)794-7847
URL: http://www.covenanthospice.org/Dothan/

18875 ■ Gentiva Hospice-Dothan
2740 Headland Ave.
Dothan, AL 36303
Ph: (334)944-2290
Fax: (334)699-3041
URL: http://www.gentiva.com/
Formerly: Wiregrass Hospice--Dothan, A Gentiva Company.

Elba

18876 ■ First Choice Hospice, Inc.
832 N Troy Hwy.
Elba, AL 36323
Ph: (334)897-0650
Fax: (334)897-0019

Enterprise

18877 ■ Dayspring Hospice, LLC
PO Box 311246
Enterprise, AL 36331
Ph: (334)347-2999
Free: 888-615-6646
Fax: (334)347-2980
URL: http://www.dayspringhospice.com/Photo-Pages/Volunteer-Valentines-Party/1328 3028_TATMU/1/965109008_W3vR6/Small

18878 ■ Gentiva Hospice-Enterprise
557 Glover Ave.
Enterprise, AL 36330-2024
Ph: (334)347-3353
URL: http://www.gentiva.com/
Formerly: Wiregrass Hospice Enterprise.

Eufaula

18879 ■ Gentiva Hospice - Eufaula
335 Macon Ave.
Eufaula, AL 36027-1827
Ph: (334)687-7641
Fax: (334)687-2823
URL: http://www.gentiva.com/
Formerly: Wiregrass Hospice, Eufaula.

Evergreen

18880 ■ Evergreen Medical Center Hospice
110 Lewis St.
Evergreen, AL 36401
Ph: (251)578-2939
URL: http://www.evergreenmedical.org/hospice.htm

Fayette

18881 ■ Hospice of Fayette Medical Center
1653 Temple Ave. N
Fayette, AL 35555
Ph: (205)932-5966
Fax: (205)932-8054
URL: http://www.dchsystem.com/body.cfm?id=37861

Florence

18882 ■ Gentiva Hospice-Florence
2530 Florence Dr., Ste. B
Florence, AL 35630
Ph: (256)764-0873
Fax: (256)766-6898
URL: http://www.gentiva.com

18883 ■ Hospice of the Shoals
115 Fairground Rd.
Florence, AL 35630-1283
Ph: (256)767-6699
Free: 866-767-6699
Fax: (256)767-3116
E-mail: dpruitt@hofts.org
URL: http://www.hospiceoftheshoals.org

Foley

18884 ■ Amedisys Hospice Care of Foley
1628 N McKenzie St., Ste. 103
Foley, AL 36525
Ph: (251)971-1436
Free: 866-392-6951
Fax: (251)971-3326
URL: http://www.amedisys.com/hospice_locations.cfm?id=1

18885 ■ AseraCare Hospice-Foley
1113 A McKenzie St.
Foley, AL 36535
Ph: (251)943-6094
Free: 866-411-0539
Fax: (251)943-6097
URL: http://hospice.aseracare.com/home.aspx

18886 ■ Community Hospice of Baldwin County
2770 S McKenzie St., Ste. C
Foley, AL 36535
Ph: (251)943-5015
Fax: (251)943-3986
E-mail: info@comhospice.com
URL: http://www.comhospice.com/default.asp?ID=2

Fultondale

18887 ■ Family Comfort Hospice-Fultondale
341 Walker Chapel Plaza, Ste. 105
Fultondale, AL 35068
Ph: (205)502-5959
Fax: (202)502-5966
URL: http://www.fchospice.com/

Gadsden

18888 ■ Comfort Care Hospice of Gadsden
500 S 5th St.
Gadsden, AL 35901
Ph: (256)547-3050
Free: 888-547-3050
Fax: (256)547-3322
URL: http://www.comfortcarehospice.org/hospice

18889 ■ New Beacon--Gadsden
244 S 4th St.
Gadsden, AL 35901
Ph: (256)549-5011
Fax: (256)549-5018
URL: http://www.newbeacon.org/page/show/183631-new-beacon-gadsden

Greenville

18890 ■ Comfort Care Hospice of Greenville
501 E Commerce St.
Greenville, AL 36037
Ph: (334)383-9688
Free: 866-383-9688
Fax: (334)383-9788
URL: http://www.comfortcarehospice.org/hospice

Hamilton

18891 ■ AseraCare Hospice-Hamilton
1215 Military St. S
Hamilton, AL 35570
Ph: (205)921-9091
Free: 888-373-5446
Fax: (205)952-9714
URL: http://hospice.aseracare.com/home.aspx

Homewood

18892 ■ Amedisys Hospice Care of Birmingham
2204 Lakeshore Dr., Ste. 110
Homewood, AL 35209
Ph: (205)868-9221
Free: 800-977-1859
URL: http://www.amedisys.com/

18893 ■ Amedisys Hospice Services--Homewood
2204 Lakeshore Dr., Ste. 110
Homewood, AL 35209
Ph: (205)868-0147
Free: 800-977-1859
Fax: (205)803-4126
URL: http://www.amedisys.com/hospice.cfm

Hoover

18894 ■ Evercare Hospice and Palliative Care--Hoover
33 Inverness Center Pkwy.
Hoover, AL 35242
Ph: (205)437-8655
Free: 800-985-3305
Fax: (205)437-8510
URL: http://www.evercarehospice.com/

18895 ■ Helping Hands Hospice--Hoover
400 Emery Dr.
Hoover, AL 35244
Ph: (205)444-0126
Fax: (205)444-0128
E-mail: administrator@helpinghandshospice.net
URL: http://www.helpinghandshospice.net/

Hunstville

18896 ■ Heartlite Hospice Care
2411 Alabama Street
Hunstville, AL 35801
Ph: (256)532-2397
Free: 877-259-1754
Fax: (256)259-1790
E-mail: heartlitalabama@aol.com
URL: http://www.heartlitehospicecare.com/

Huntsville

18897 ■ Gentiva Hospice-Huntsville
303 Williams Ave. SW, Ste. 116
Huntsville, AL 35801
Ph: (256)519-8808
Fax: (256)519-8809
URL: http://www.gentiva.com/
Formerly: Wiregrass Hospice, Huntsville.

18898 ■ Hospice Family Care
3304 Westmill Dr.
Huntsville, AL 35805
Ph: (256)650-1212
Free: 888-619-8000
Fax: (256)880-2929
E-mail: info@hospicefamilycare.org
URL: http://www.hospicefamilycare.org

18899 ■ Hospice of North Alabama, LLC
3311 Bob Wallace Ave. SW, No. 101
Huntsville, AL 35805
Ph: (256)533-4300
Free: 800-314-9863
Fax: (256)533-4122
E-mail: info@hospiceofnorthalabama.com
URL: http://www.hospiceofnorthalabama.com/

Jackson

18900 ■ AseraCare Hospice - Jackson
4115 North College Avenue
P.O. box 1281
Jackson, AL 36545
Ph: (251)246-4113
Free: 877-208-4113
Fax: (251)246-4888
URL: http://hospice.aseracare.com/

18901 ■ AseraCare/Hospice South Jackson
4115 N College Ave.
Jackson, AL 36545-1281
Ph: (251)246-4113
Free: 877-208-4113
URL: http://hospice.aseracare.com/

Jacksonville

18902 ■ Countryside Hospice Care-Jacksonville
320 Branscomb Dr. SW
Jacksonville, AL 36265
Free: 866-235-3909
Fax: (256)782-3590
URL: http://www.countrysidehospice.com/locations.html

Jasper

18903 ■ Gentiva Hospice - Jasper
4330 Hwy. 78 E
Jasper, AL 35501
Ph: (205)384-3882
Fax: (205)384-3733
URL: http://www.gentiva.com/
Formerly: Wiregrass Hospice - Jasper.

18904 ■ New Beacon of Jasper
302 Blackwell Dairy Rd.
Jasper, AL 35504
Ph: (205)387-9339
Fax: (205)387-8226
URL: http://www.newbeacon.org

18905 ■ Southeast Hospice Network
4330 Hwy. 78 E, Ste. 120-121
Jasper, AL 35501
Ph: (205)387-2300
Fax: (205)387-2301
URL: http://www.southeasthospicenetwork.com/

Livingston

18906 ■ Legacy Hospice, Inc. Livingston
216 S Washington St.
Livingston, AL 35470
Free: 877-652-6167
Fax: (205)652-9110
E-mail: corporate@legacyhospice.net
URL: http://www.legacyhospice.net/

Mobile

18907 ■ AseraCare/Hospice South of Mobile, LLC
3280 Dauphin St.
Mobile, AL 36606
Ph: (251)343-0989
Free: 877-580-3700
Fax: (251)343-0792
URL: http://hospice.aseracare.com/

18908 ■ Covenant Hospice, Inc.--Mobile
3201 Dauphin St., Ste. D
Mobile, AL 36606
Ph: (251)478-8671
URL: http://www.covenanthospice.org/Mobile/

18909 ■ Gentiva Hospice-Mobile
824 Western American Circle
Mobile, AL 36609
Ph: (251)340-6387
Fax: (251)340-6392
URL: http://www.gentiva.com/hospice/hospice_locations.php#al

18910 ■ Infirmary Hospice Care
3290 Dauphin St., Ste. 505
Mobile, AL 36606
Ph: (251)435-7460
Fax: (251)435-7499
URL: http://www.infirmaryhospice.org/

18911 ■ Odyssey HealthCare of Mobile
2800 Dauphin St., Ste. 103
Mobile, AL 36606-2477
Ph: (251)478-9900
Free: 877-637-9432
Fax: (251)478-9902
E-mail: info@odsyheath.com
URL: http://www.odsyhealth.com/default.asp

Monroeville

18912 ■ AseraCare-Monroeville
1979 Hwy. 21 Bypass
Monroeville, AL 36461-0276
Ph: (251)575-3409
Free: 877-273-3409
Fax: (251)575-2023
URL: http://www.aseracare.com

Montgomery

18913 ■ Amedisys Hospice of Montgomery
8160 Decker La.
Montgomery, AL 36117
Ph: (334)395-7789
Fax: (334)395-7882
URL: http://www.amedisys.com/hospice.cfm

18914 ■ Baptist Hospice
301 Interstate Park Dr., Ste. 301
Montgomery, AL 36109
Ph: (334)395-5000
Free: 866-910-9597
Fax: (334)395-5012
E-mail: hospiceinfo@baptistfirst.org
URL: http://www.baptistfirst.org/services/hospice

18915 ■ Gentiva Hospice, Montgomery
7075 Haleyon Park Dr. Ste. 202
Montgomery, AL 36117-8026
Ph: (334)260-0015
Fax: (334)260-0603
URL: http://www.gentiva.com/
Formerly: Wiregrass Hospice, Montgomery.

18916 ■ Hospice of Montgomery
1111 Holloway Pk.
Montgomery, AL 36117
Ph: (334)279-6677
Fax: (334)279-2223
URL: http://www.hospiceofmontgomery.org

18917 ■ Southeast Hospice Network-Montgomery
3001 Zelda Rd., Ste. 300
Montgomery, AL 36106
Ph: (334)260-2916
Fax: (334)260-2918
URL: http://www.southeasthospicenetwork.com/contactus.php

18918 ■ VistaCare--Montgomery
700 Interstate Pk. Dr., Ste. 705
Montgomery, AL 36109
Ph: (334)260-0015
Free: 877-559-1010
Fax: (334)260-0603
E-mail: lisa.bond@vistacare.com
URL: http://www.vistacare.com

Moulton

18919 ■ Comfort Care Hospice of Moulton
11227 Alabama Hwy 157, Ste. M
Moulton, AL 35650
Ph: (256)905-0280
Free: 866-905-0280
Fax: (256)905-0284
URL: http://www.comfortcarehospice.org

Oneonta

18920 ■ New Beacon of Oneonta
1901-C 2nd Ave. E
Oneonta, AL 35121
Ph: (205)274-0549
Free: 888-653-8314
Fax: (205)625-5726
URL: http://www.newbeacon.org

Oxford

18921 ■ Gentiva Hospice--Oxford
1825 Day St.
Oxford, AL 36203
Ph: (256)831-2964
Fax: (256)835-1417
URL: http://www.gentiva.com/
Formerly: Wiregrass Hospice.

Pelham

18922 ■ Comfort Care Hospice
245 Cahaba Valley Pkwy., Ste. 110
Pelham, AL 35124
Ph: (205)663-6887
Free: 877-231-0321
Fax: (205)663-6874
URL: http://www.comfortcarehospice.org

18923 ■ Southeast Hospice Network-Pelham
2050 Oak Mountain Dr., Ste. 1-2
Pelham, AL 35124
Ph: (205)621-9970
Fax: (205)621-9972
URL: http://www.southeasthospicenetwork.com/contactus.php

Pell City

18924 ■ Lakeside Hospice, Inc.
PO Box 544
Pell City, AL 35125-0544
Ph: (205)884-1111
Free: 800-427-3993
Fax: (205)884-1114
URL: http://www.lakesidehospice.org

Phenix City

18925 ■ VistaCare--Phenix City
3615 S Railroad St., Ste. 3
Phenix City, AL 36867
Ph: (334)298-8988
Free: 888-534-5295
Fax: (334)298-9535
E-mail: diane.bush@vistacare.com
URL: http://www.vista-care.com
Diane Bush, Executive Director

Rainbow City

18926 ■ Amedisys Hospice-Rainbow City
115 W Grand Ave., Ste. 70
Rainbow City, AL 35906
Ph: (256)442-0771
Free: 866-466-8460
URL: http://www.amedisys.com/hospice_locations.cfm?id=1

Rainsville

18927 ■ ABC Hospice
PO Box 1486
Rainsville, AL 35986
Free: 866-847-8660
URL: http://www.abchospice.com/

Roanoke

18928 ■ Countryside Hospice-Roanoke
3355 Hwy 431, Ste. 3
Roanoke, AL 36274
Free: 888-307-2560
Fax: (334)863-4999
URL: http://www.countrysidehospice.com/locations.html

Scottsboro

18929 ■ Comfort Care Hospice of Scottsboro
102 Micah Way Ste. 1100
Scottsboro, AL 35769
Ph: (256)259-0906
Free: 877-259-0906
Fax: (256)259-0907
URL: http://www.comfortcarehospice.org

18930 ■ New Beacon of Scottsboro
112 College St.
Scottsboro, AL 35768
Ph: (256)574-4622
Free: 800-239-7766
Fax: (256)259-3772
URL: http://www.newbeacon.org

Selma

18931 ■ Cahaba Hospice Inc.
410 Church St.
Selma, AL 36701-4545
Ph: (334)418-0566
Free: 888-418-0570
Fax: (334)418-0570
E-mail: patm@cahabahospice.com
URL: http://www.cahabahospice.com
Patricia Moten, Executive Director

Southside

18932 ■ Lawley Premier Hospice Care
1250 Hwy. 77
Southside, AL 35907
Ph: (256)413-4473
Fax: (256)413-7358
E-mail: dedramoore@lawleydrug.com
URL: http://www.lawleypremierhospicecare.com/
Dee Moore, Director

Sylacauga

18933 ■ American HomeCare Hospice
3235 Old Sylacauga Hwy.
Sylacauga, AL 35151
Ph: (256)245-9212
Free: 866-558-6789
Fax: (256)245-9213
E-mail: heavensapp@charterinternet.com
URL: http://www.americanhomecarehospice.com

18934 ■ Coosa Valley Hospice
315 W Hickory St.
Sylacauga, AL 35150
Ph: (256)401-4545
URL: http://www.cvhealth.net/
Glenn C. Sisk, Chief Executive Officer

Talladega

18935 ■ Comfort Care Hospice LLC
702 E Battle St., Ste. C
Talladega, AL 35160
Ph: (256)761-1250
Free: 800-761-1250
Fax: (256)761-1766
URL: http://www.comfortcarehospice.org

Tallassee

18936 ■ Community Hospice Care--Tallahassee
805 Friendship Rd.
Tallassee, AL 36078
Ph: (334)283-6541
Fax: (334)283-4258
E-mail: info@chal.org
URL: http://www.chal.org

Troy

18937 ■ Hospice Advantage--Troy
413 S Brundidge St.
Troy, AL 36081
Ph: (334)566-4357
Free: 800--HOSPICE
URL: http://www.hospiceadvantage.net/
Formerly: Lighthouse Hospice of Alabama.

Trussville

18938 ■ Alabama Regional Hospice Care
413 Main St. Ste. D
Trussville, AL 35173
Ph: (205)655-0753

Tuscaloosa

18939 ■ Amedisys Hospice of Tuscaloosa
500 Towncenter Blvd., Ste. B
Tuscaloosa, AL 35406
Ph: (205)345-4907
Free: 866-719-6866
Fax: (205)345-4713
URL: http://www.amedisys.com/hospice.cfm

18940 ■ AseraCare Hospice-Northport--Tuscaloosa
971 Fairfax Pk.
Tuscaloosa, AL 35406
Ph: (205)391-4539
Free: 877-491-9678
Fax: (205)391-4625
E-mail: ask@aseracare.com
URL: http://hospice.aseracare.com/home.aspx

18941 ■ Hospice of West Alabama
3851 Loop Rd.
Tuscaloosa, AL 35404
Ph: (205)523-0101

Free: 877-362-7522
Fax: (205)523-0102
URL: http://www.hospiceofwestalabama.com/index.php?option=com_frontpage&Itemid=1

Valley

18942 ■ Chattahoochee Hospice
6 Medical Park N
Valley, AL 36854-3665
Ph: (334)756-8043
Free: 800-770-8043
Fax: (334)756-8059
URL: http://www.chattahoocheehospice.com/

Wetumpka

18943 ■ Comfort Care Hospice-Wetumpka
629 Coosa River Pkwy.
Wetumpka, AL 36092
Ph: (334)514-0244
Free: 888-514-0244
Fax: (334)514-0241
URL: http://www.comfortcarehospice.org/hospice

18944 ■ Hospice Advantage-Wetumpka
4253 Wetumpka Hwy
Wetumpka, AL 36110
Ph: (334)512-6112
Fax: (334)512-1013
URL: http://www.helpingheartshospice.com
Formerly: Helping Hearts Hospice, LLC.

Winfield

18945 ■ Hospice of Northwest Alabama Inc.
PO Box 1216
Winfield, AL 35594-1216
Ph: (205)487-8140
Fax: (205)487-8740

ALASKA

Anchorage

18946 ■ Amedisys Hospice of Anchorage
3903 Arctic Blvd., Ste. 102
Anchorage, AK 99503
Ph: (907)272-0204
Free: 877-816-8792
Fax: (907)272-1151
URL: http://www.amedisys.com/hospice.cfm

18947 ■ Hospice of Anchorage
2612 E Northern Lights Blvd.
Anchorage, AK 99508
Ph: (907)561-5322
Fax: (907)561-0334
E-mail: info@hospiceofanchorage.org
URL: http://www.hospiceofanchorage.org
Donna Stephens, Executive Director

18948 ■ Providence Hospice--Anchorage
3435 East Tudor Road
Anchorage, AK 99507
Ph: (206)464-2255
Fax: (907)212-2374
URL: http://www.providence.org/alaska/services/palliative/default.htm

Fairbanks

18949 ■ Hospice of the Tanana Valley
2001 Gillam Way
Fairbanks, AK 99701
Ph: (907)474-0311
Fax: (907)452-7643
URL: http://www.hospicetv.org/

Juneau

18950 ■ Hospice and Home Care of Juneau
419 6th St.
Juneau, AK 99801-1072
Ph: (907)463-6100
Fax: (907)463-3835
E-mail: hospice@juneau.com
URL: http://www.ccsjuneau.org/15,hospice

Wasilla

18951 ■ Mat-Su Regional Hospice
950 E Bogard Rd., Ste. 132
Wasilla, AK 99654
Ph: (907)352-4800
Fax: (907)352-4801
E-mail: g.stocker@msrmc.com
URL: http://www.matsuregional.com/Pages/home.aspx

ARIZONA

Avondale

18952 ■ Hospice of Arizona--Avondale
1830 N 95th Ave., Ste. 110
Avondale, AZ 85037
Ph: (602)678-1313
Fax: (602)535-0834
E-mail: infoaz@americanhospice.com
URL: http://www.americanhospice.com/arizona

Bullhead City

18953 ■ Mohave Hospice
2755 Silver Creek Rd.
Bullhead City, AZ 86442
Ph: (928)763-3620
Fax: (928)704-8850

Casa Grande

18954 ■ Casa Grande Inpatient Unit
950 N Arizona Rd.
Casa Grande, AZ 85222
Ph: (520)374-2130
Fax: (520)374-2155

18955 ■ Hospice Compassus--Casa Grande
1675 E Monument Plaza Circle
Casa Grande, AZ 85122
Ph: (520)421-7143
Free: 800-320-6384
Fax: (520)421-7315
E-mail: contactusAZCAS@hospicecom.com
URL: http://www.hospicecompassus.com/pg-hospice-compassus-locations.html?s=AZ&pi d=36
Formerly: RTA Hospice and Palliative Care.

Chandler

18956 ■ Chandler Regional Medical Center
475 S Dobson Rd.
Chandler, AZ 85224
Ph: (480)728-3491
URL: http://www.chandlerregional.org/Medical_Services/053183

18957 ■ East Valley Hospice
1351 N Alma School Rd., Ste. 250
Chandler, AZ 85224
Ph: (480)895-5434
Fax: (480)305-5782
E-mail: info@evhospice.com
URL: http://www.evhospice.com/

Cottonwood

18958 ■ Verde Valley Community Hospice
859 Cove Parkway
Cottonwood, AZ 86326
Ph: (928)634-1073
Fax: (928)634-1401

Dewey

18959 ■ Hospice of the Pines
13175 E Hwy. 169
Dewey, AZ 86327
Ph: (928)632-0111
Free: 877-632-0111
Fax: (928)632-0333

Flagstaff

18960 ■ Hospice Compassus-Flagstaff
1000 N Humphrey's St., Ste. 220
Flagstaff, AZ 86001
Ph: (928)763-6433
Free: 888-880-4782
Fax: (928)763-6437
URL: http://www.hospicecompassus.com/pg-hospice-compassus-locations.html?s=AZ&pi d=39

18961 ■ Northland Hospice and Palliative Care
425 N Switzer Canyon Dr., Ste. A
Flagstaff, AZ 86002
Ph: (928)779-1227
Fax: (928)779-5884
E-mail: hospice@northlandhospice.org
URL: http://www.northlandhospice.org

18962 ■ Olivia White Hospice Home
752 N Switzer Canyon Dr.
Flagstaff, AZ 86001
Ph: (928)226-1915
Fax: (928)779-5884
URL: http://www.northlandhospice.org/subjects/oliviawhite/hospicehome.htm

Gilbert

18963 ■ Gilbert Inpatient Unit
13639 Ray Road
Gilbert, AZ 85296
Ph: (480)461-3144
Fax: (480)844-9711

Green Valley

18964 ■ Valor Hospice Care and Palliative Care
1131 S LaCanada Dr., Ste. 103
Green Valley, AZ 85614
Ph: (520)339-0200
Free: 877-615-3996
Fax: (520)399-3036
URL: http://www.valorhospicecare.com/valor/

Kingman

18965 ■ Kingman Regional Medical Center Hospice
3269 Stockton Hill Rd.
Kingman, AZ 86409
Ph: (928)692-4680
Fax: (928)692-2733
E-mail: tradler@azkmc.com
URL: http://www.azkrmc.com/hospice.php

Lake Havasu City

18966 ■ Hospice of Havasu
365 S Lake Havasu Ave.
Lake Havasu City, AZ 86403
Ph: (928)453-2111
Free: 888-468-2111
E-mail: niannone@hospicehavasu.org
URL: http://www.hospicehavasu.org

Lakeside

18967 ■ Hospice Compassus-Lakeside
1789 W Commerce Dr.
Lakeside, AZ 85929
Ph: (928)368-4400
Free: 888-273-0782
Fax: (928)368-4424
URL: http://www.hospicecompassus.com/pg-hospice-compassus-locations.html?s=AZ&pi d=40
Formerly: RTA Hospice & Palliative Care.

Mesa

18968 ■ Allegiance Hospice Care Agency
761 E University Dr.
Mesa, AZ 85203
Ph: (480)834-4325
Fax: (480)834-4396

18969 ■ Hospice Family Care, Inc-Mesa
1550 S Alma School Rd., Ste. 102
Mesa, AZ 85210-2074
Ph: (480)889-1113
Fax: (480)388-3073
E-mail: intake@hfc-az.com
URL: http://www.hfc-az.com

18970 ■ Hospice of the Southwest
450 N Dobson Rd., Ste. 108
Mesa, AZ 85202
Ph: (480)456-9300
Fax: (480)456-9696
E-mail: info@hospiceofthesouthwest.com
URL: http://www.hospiceofthesouthwest.com/

18971 ■ Odyssey HealthCare of Phoenix-Mesa Inpatient
6215 E Arbor Ave.
Mesa, AZ 85206
Ph: (480)218-9000
Free: 877-637-9432
Fax: (480)218-9014
URL: http://www.odsyhealth.com

Peoria

18972 ■ Hospice Family Care-Peoria
9045 W Athens Rd.
Peoria, AZ 85382
Ph: (623)876-9100
URL: http://www.hfc-az.com/

Phoenix

18973 ■ Affinity - Hospice of Life--Phoenix
2501 W Dunlap Ave., Ste. 125
Phoenix, AZ 85021
Ph: (602)253-2273
Fax: (602)253-1999
URL: http://www.affinityhospice.com

18974 ■ Cornerstone Hospice Inc.--Phoenix
7310 N 16th St., Ste. 230
Phoenix, AZ 85020
Ph: (602)263-0925
Fax: (602)263-0929
E-mail: ellenduncan@msn.com
URL: http://www.cornerstonehospice.net/

18975 ■ Covenant Southwest Hospice
3877 N 7th St., Ste. 280
Phoenix, AZ 85014
Ph: (602)507-6718
URL: http://covenantsouthwesthospice.com/

18976 ■ Desert Oasis Hospice
20815 N 25th Pl. Ste. A106
Phoenix, AZ 85050
Ph: (602)424-4204
Fax: (602)424-4208
E-mail: info@desertoasishospice.com
URL: http://www.desertoasishospice.com/

18977 ■ Evercare Hospice and Palliative Care--Phoenix
3141 N 3rd Ave.
Phoenix, AZ 85013
Ph: (602)749-5900
Free: 866-658-4658
Fax: (602)749-5999
URL: http://www.evercarehospice.com

18978 ■ Hearts for Hospice--Phoenix
5225 N Central Ave., Ste. 100
Phoenix, AZ 85012-1400
Ph: (602)265-3333
URL: http://www.heartsforhospice.com/home.php

18979 ■ Highway Christian Hospice Inc.
67 E Weldon Ave., Ste. 317
Phoenix, AZ 85012-2045
Ph: (602)274-1952
Fax: (602)274-2338
E-mail: hch1996@earthlink.net
URL: http://www.highwaychristianhospice.com/

18980 ■ Hospice of Arizona--Phoenix
19820 N 7th Ave., Ste. 130
Phoenix, AZ 85021
Ph: (602)678-1313
Fax: (602)242-2178
E-mail: infoaz@americanhospice.com
URL: http://www.americanhospice.com/arizona

18981 ■ Hospice Inspiris
2025 N 3rd St., Ste. 205
Phoenix, AZ 85004
Ph: (602)712-1000
Free: 800-395-5188
Fax: (602)712-0012
URL: http://www.hospiceinspiris.com/

18982 ■ Hospice of the West LLC
21410 N 19th Ave.
Phoenix, AZ 85027

18983 ■ Infinity Hospice Care--Phoenix
5110 N 40th St., Ste. 107
Phoenix, AZ 85016
Ph: (602)381-0375
Free: 866-381-0375
Fax: (602)381-0385
URL: http://www.infinityhospicecare.com

18984 ■ Odyssey Healthcare of Phoenix
202 E Earll Dr., Ste. 160
Phoenix, AZ 85012
Ph: (602)279-0677
Free: 877-637-9432
Fax: (602)279-1085
E-mail: info@odsyhealth.com
URL: http://www.odsyhealth.com

18985 ■ Premier Hospice & Palliative Care
3737 N 7th St., Ste. 203
Phoenix, AZ 85014
Ph: (602)274-7572
URL: http://www.premierhospiceaz.com/

18986 ■ Prime Care Hospice, LLC
4225 W Glendale Ave.
Phoenix, AZ 85051
Ph: (623)847-2323
Fax: (623)847-2626

18987 ■ Serenity Hospice and Palliative Care
7227 N 16th St., Ste. 170
Phoenix, AZ 85020
Ph: (602)216-2273
URL: http://www.serenityhospiceaz.com/

18988 ■ Serenity House--Phoenix
4122 N 17th St.
Phoenix, AZ 85016
Ph: (602)216-2273
URL: http://www.serenityhospiceaz.com/In-PatientUnit.html

18989 ■ VistaCare Hospice--Phoenix
202 E Earll Dr., Ste. 160
Phoenix, AZ 85012
Ph: (602)648-6911
Free: 800-851-3522
Fax: (602)648-6912
E-mail: shana.hudson@vistacare.com
URL: http://www.vistacare.com
Norma McGee, Executive Director

Prescott

18990 ■ Hospice Family Care Inc-Prescott
110 E. Sheldon
Prescott, AZ 86301
Free: 888-534-5222
E-mail: intake@hfc-az.com
URL: http://www.hfc-az.com/

Sedona

18991 ■ Hospice Compassus--Sedona
70 Bell Rock Plz., Ste. A
Sedona, AZ 86351
Ph: (928)284-0180
Fax: (928)284-9352
URL: http://www.rtahospice.org/content.cfm?id=6&pid=0&s=AZ
Formerly: RTA Hospice and Palliative Care.

Sells

18992 ■ Tohono O'odham Hospice
Fereral Rte. 15, Milepost 9
HC01 Box 9100
Sells, AZ 85634
Ph: (520)361-1800
E-mail: admissions@toltc.org
URL: http://www.toltc.org/hospice.html

Sierra Vista

18993 ■ Valor Hospice Care--Sierra Vista
500 E Fry Blvd., Ste. L-11
Sierra Vista, AZ 85635
Free: 877-615-3996
URL: http://www.valorhospice.com/

Tempe

18994 ■ Grace Hospice--Tempe
4515 S McClintock Dr., Ste. 210
Tempe, AZ 85282
Ph: (480)775-2599
Fax: (480)775-3714
URL: http://www.gracehospiceaz.com/

Tubac

18995 ■ Soulistic Hospice
26 Tubac Rd., Ste. C2
Tubac, AZ 85646
Ph: (520)398-2333
Fax: (520)398-9524
URL: http://www.soulistichospice.org/

Tucson

18996 ■ Carondelet Hospice and Palliative Care
630 N Alvernon Way, Ste. 361
Tucson, AZ 85711
Ph: (520)205-7700
Fax: (520)205-7598
E-mail: hospice@carondelet.org
URL: http://www.carondelet.org
Formerly: Carondelet Hospice Services.

18997 ■ Casa De La Luz Hospice
400 W Magee Rd.
Tucson, AZ 85704
Ph: (520)544-9890
Fax: (520)544-9894
URL: http://www.casahospice.com

18998 ■ Casa De La Luz Hospice--Tucson Inpatient Unit
5830 N Fountains Ave.
Tucson, AZ 85741
Ph: (520)575-6425
Fax: (520)575-6429
URL: http://www.casahospice.com/services.html#inpatient

18999 ■ Evercare Hospice and Palliative Care--Tucson
17 W Wetmore
Tucson, AZ 85705
Ph: (520)407-8000
Free: 877-233-2902
Fax: (520)748-5120
URL: http://www.evercarehospice.com

19000 ■ Heartland Hospice Care-Tucson
3112 N Swan Rd.
Tucson, AZ 85712
Ph: (520)325-2790
Free: 800-427-1902
Fax: (520)325-2746
URL: http://www.hcr-manorcare.com/tabId/67/default.aspx?FacilityID=4604&City=tucson&State=AZ&PostalCode=&CareTypes=99134

19001 ■ Hospice Family Care-Tucson
3703 N Swan Rd.
Tucson, AZ 85718
Ph: (520)790-9299
Free: 800-839-3288
E-mail: intake@hfc-az.com
URL: http://www.hfc-az.com/

19002 ■ Kanmar Place
400 W Magee Rd.
Tucson, AZ 85704-3802
Ph: (520)544-9890
Fax: (520)544-9894
URL: http://www.casahospice.com/kanmar.html

19003 ■ Odyssey Healthcare of Tucson
5210 E Williams Cir., Ste. 300
Tucson, AZ 85711
Ph: (520)577-0270
Free: 877-637-9432
Fax: (520)577-0450
URL: http://www.odsyhealth.com/

19004 ■ Tucson Medical Center Hospice
5301 E Grant Rd.
Tucson, AZ 85712
Ph: (520)327-5461
URL: https://www.tmcaz.com/TucsonMedicalCenter/Hospice/Hospice_Services

19005 ■ Valor Hospice Care--Tucson
1860 E River Rd., Ste. 200
Tucson, AZ 85718
Ph: (520)615-3996
Free: 877-615-3996
Fax: (520)615-3998
URL: http://valorhospicecare.com/

Willcox

19006 ■ Charles William Leighton, Jr. Hospice
521 W Maley Pl.
Willcox, AZ 85644
Ph: (520)384-5878
Fax: (520)384-4127

Yuma

19007 ■ Hospice Compassus-Yuma
1025 W 24th St., Ste. 15
Yuma, AZ 85364
Ph: (928)344-6100
Fax: (928)317-0311
E-mail: contactusAZYUM@hospicecom.com
URL: http://www.hospicecompassus.com

19008 ■ Hospice of Yuma
1824 S 8th Ave.
Yuma, AZ 85364
Ph: (928)343-2222
Free: 877-343-2226
Fax: (928)343-0688
E-mail: wecare@hospiceofyuma.com
URL: http://www.hospiceofyuma.com

ARKANSAS

Batesville

19009 ■ Caring Hands Hospice--Batesville
2000 Harrison, Ste. E
Batesville, AR 72501
Ph: (870)698-0505
Free: 800-822-8232
URL: http://www.approvehomemedical.com/caring-hands-hospice.htm

Berryville

19010 ■ St. John's Hospice-Berryville
804 W Freeman, Ste. 4
Berryville, AR 72616
Ph: (870)423-5255
Free: 800-827-3355
URL: http://www.stjohns.com/homecarehospice/

Cabot

19011 ■ Arkansas Hospice - Cabot
3022 S 2nd St.
Cabot, AR 72023
Ph: (501)748-3333
Free: 866-941-5656
URL: http://www.arkansashospice.org/

Camden

19012 ■ Ouachita County Medical Center Hospice
726 California Ave. SW
Camden, AR 71701
Ph: (870)836-1301
Fax: (870)836-1371
URL: http://www.ouachitamedcenter.com/Hospice+Services/41.html

Cherokee Village

19013 ■ Caring Hands Hospice--Cherokee Village
9 Choctaw Trace
Cherokee Village, AR 72529
Ph: (870)257-3006
Fax: (870)257-3012
URL: http://www.caringhandshospice.net/

Conway

19014 ■ Arkansas Hospice Conway
1014 Markham St., Ste. 1
Conway, AR 72032-
Free: 888-879-5401
URL: http://www.arkansashospice.org

Dardanelle

19015 ■ Arkansas Department of Health Area III Hospice
719 N 59th St.
Dardanelle, AR 72834
Ph: (501)229-1496
Fax: (479)229-2386
URL: http://www.adhhomecare.org/

El Dorado

19016 ■ Life Touch Hospice
2301 Champagnolle Rd.
El Dorado, AR 71730
Ph: (870)862-0337
Free: 866-378-0388
URL: http://www.lifetouchhospice.org/

Fayetteville

19017 ■ Washington Regional Hospice
34 W Colt Sq.
Fayetteville, AR 72703
Ph: (479)713-7385
Free: 888-611-1094
Fax: (479)444-7120
URL: http://www.wregional.com/body.cfm?id=106

Forrest City

19018 ■ Arkansas Department of Health - Forrest City
413 N Division
Forrest City, AR 72335
Ph: (870)633-1340
Fax: (870)633-6988
URL: http://www.adhhomecare.org/locationdetail.php?OfficeLink=HL39

19019 ■ Patient's Choice Hospice-Forrest City
310 N Forrest
Forrest City, AR 72335-3313
Ph: (870)633-4613
Fax: (870)633-0935
URL: http://www.lhcgroup.com/

Fort Smith

19020 ■ Area Agency on Aging
524 Garrison Ave.
Fort Smith, AR 72901
Ph: (479)783-5550
Free: 800-737-1827
E-mail: areaagency@agingwest.org
URL: http://www.agingwest.org/

19021 ■ Hospice Peachtree/dba Peachtree Hospice LLC--Rogers Ave., Fort Smith
4300 Rogers Ave., Ste. 33
Fort Smith, AR 72903
Ph: (479)494-0100
Free: 800-752-0444
Fax: (479)494-0102
URL: http://www.peachtreehospice.com

19022 ■ Hospice Peachtree/dba Peachtree Hospice LLC--Towson Ave., Fort Smith Palliative Care Unit
1001 Towson Ave.
Fort Smith, AR 72903
Ph: (479)494-0100
Free: 800-752-0444
Fax: (479)494-0102
URL: http://www.peachtreehospice.com/

19023 ■ Mercy Hospice Inpatient Unit--Fort Smith
7301 Rogers Ave.
Fort Smith, AR 72903
Ph: (479)314-1150
Fax: (479)314-1152
URL: http://www.stedwardmercy.com/services/mercy_hospice.asp

19024 ■ Saint Edward Mercy Medical Center Hospice
5401 Ellsworth Rd.
Fort Smith, AR 72917-7000
Ph: (479)314-1150
Free: 800-225-9743
Fax: (479)314-1152
URL: http://www.stedwardmercy.com/services/mercy_hospice.asp

Harrison

19025 ■ Hospice of the Hills--Harrison
825 N Spring St.
Harrison, AR 72601
Ph: (870)414-4141
Fax: (870)365-2461
E-mail: kathy.brown@narmc.net
URL: http://www.narmc.com/services/hospice_hills.htm

Holiday Island

19026 ■ Patient's Choice Hospice-Holiday Island
2 Parkcliff Dr.
Holiday Island, AR 72631
Ph: (479)253-6203

Free: 888-303-9549
Fax: (479)253-7687
URL: http://www.lhcgroup.com/Facilities/FacilitiesDisplay.asp?p1=1485&p2=Y&SM=Y& Sort=

Hot Springs

19027 ■ Levi Hospice
300 Prospect Ave.
Hot Springs, AR 71901-4003
Ph: (501)624-1281
Free: 800-264-5384
Fax: (501)622-3500
E-mail: levi@levihospital.com
URL: http://www.levihospital.com

Hot Springs National Park

19028 ■ Arkansas Hospice Hot Springs Unit
628 Malvern Ave.
Hot Springs National Park, AR 71903
Free: 888-818-9992
URL: http://www.arkansashospice.org

Jonesboro

19029 ■ Flo and Phil Jones Hospice House St. Bernard's Development Foundation
1148 E Matthews Ave.
Jonesboro, AR 72401
Ph: (870)336-5009
Fax: (870)336-5016
E-mail: kbobbitt@sbrmc.org
URL: http://www.stbernardsfoundation.org/view/180

19030 ■ Saint Bernard's Hospice--Jonesboro
225 E Jackson
Jonesboro, AR 72401
Ph: (870)972-4100
URL: http://www.stbernards.info/departments-services/extended-care/hospice/

Little Rock

19031 ■ Arkansas Department of Health Hospice-Little Rock
5800 W 10th St.
Little Rock, AR 72204-1749
Ph: (501)661-2951
Free: 800-482-5400
Fax: (501)280-4595
URL: http://www.adhhomecare.org/locationdetail.php?OfficeLink=HL98

19032 ■ Arkansas Hospice Little Rock Inpatient Center
St. Vincent Doctors Hospital
6101 St. Vincent Cir.
Little Rock, AR 72205-5340
Ph: (501)522-6274
URL: http://www.arkansashospice.org

19033 ■ Odyssey HealthCare of Little Rock
10800 Financial Centre Pkwy., Ste. 380
Little Rock, AR 72205
Ph: (501)223-8868
Free: 866-407-9132
Fax: (501)217-4975
URL: http://www.odsyhealth.com/site.asp?id=24

Magnolia

19034 ■ Arkansas Department of Health Hospice VI
207 W Calhoun
Magnolia, AR 71753
Ph: (870)234-7183
Fax: (870)235-3755
URL: http://www.healthyarkansas.com

19035 ■ Serenity Hospice, LLC--Magnolia
222 N Pine, Ste. 2
Magnolia, AR 71753
Ph: (870)901-0500
URL: http://www.serenityhospice.net/

Malvern

19036 ■ Arkansas Department of Health Hospice--Malvern
2204 E Sullenberger
Malvern, AR 72104
Ph: (501)332-6996
Fax: (501)332-6989
URL: http://www.adhhomecare.org/locationdetail.php?OfficeLink=HL68

Mena

19037 ■ Mena Regional Hospice
601 Highway 71 N, Ste. BB
Mena, AR 71953-4394
Ph: (479)394-1134
Fax: (479)394-1134
URL: http://www.lhcgroup.com/Hospice/Mena/

Mount Ida

19038 ■ Arkansas Department of Health Hospice IV-Mtount Ida
346 Luzerne
Mount Ida, AR 71957
Ph: (870)867-3138
Fax: (870)867-3656
URL: http://www.adhhomecare.org/locationdetail.php?OfficeLink=HL81

Mountain Home

19039 ■ CMC Hospice
400 S College, Ste. 2
Mountain Home, AR 72653-3991
Ph: (870)424-4000
Fax: (870)424-4072
URL: http://lhcgroup.com/Facilities/FacilitiesDisplay.asp?p1=2240&p2=Y&SM=Y&Sort =

19040 ■ Hospice House--Mountain Home
774 Long St.
Mountain Home, AR 72653
Ph: (870)508-1200

19041 ■ Hospice of the Ozarks
701 Burnett Dr.
Mountain Home, AR 72653
Ph: (870)508-1771
Fax: (870)508-1777
URL: http://www.baxterregional.org/programs_and_services/64-hospice-services

Mountain View

19042 ■ Arkansas Department of Health Hospice X
204 Whitfield St.
Mountain View, AR 72560
Ph: (870)269-3308
Fax: (870)269-3368
URL: http://www.healthyarkansas.com/hospice.pdf

North Little Rock

19043 ■ Arkansas Hospice North Little Rock
14 Parkstone Circle
North Little Rock, AR 72116
Ph: (877)713-2348
Fax: (501)748-3334
URL: http://www.arkansashospice.org/locations.html

19044 ■ Arkansas Hospice--North Little Rock
14 Parkstone Circle
North Little Rock, AR 72116
Ph: (501)748-3333
Free: 877-713-2348
URL: http://www.arkansashospice.org/

Pine Bluff

19045 ■ Arkansas Hospice, Inc-Pine Bluff
2501 W 28th St.
Pine Bluff, AR 71603
Free: 800-596-6195
Fax: (870)850-6221
URL: http://www.arkansashospice.org

19046 ■ Hospice Angels
3801 Camden Rd.
Chapel Village 1, Ste. 12
Pine Bluff, AR 71603
Ph: (870)534-4847
Free: 800-537-0585
Fax: (870)534-4884
E-mail: hospice@ipa.net
URL: http://www.hospiceangelsar.com/

Russellville

19047 ■ Arkansas Department of Health Hospice-Russellville
1509 E Main, Ste. 6
Russellville, AR 72834
Ph: (479)890-4834
Fax: (479)968-8738
URL: http://www.adhhomecare.org/locationdetail.php?OfficeLink=HLA0

19048 ■ Arkansas Hospice Russellville
2405 E Parkway, Ste. 3
Russellville, AR 72802
Ph: (479)498-2050
Free: 888-498-2050
Fax: (479)498-2053
URL: http://www.arkansashospice.org

Searcy

19049 ■ NEA Hospice of Arkansas
106 Spring St.
Searcy, AR 72143
Ph: (501)279-7955
Fax: (501)279-2049
E-mail: info@neahospice.com
URL: http://neahospice.com/nea2_002.htm

Springdale

19050 ■ Circle of Life Hospice--Springdale
901 Jones Rd.
Springdale, AR 72762
Ph: (479)750-6632
Free: 800-495-5511
E-mail: mmckinney@nwacircleoflife.org
URL: http://www.nwacircleoflife.com

19051 ■ Earlene Howard Hospice House
901 Jones Rd.
Springdale, AR 72762
Ph: (479)750-6632
Free: 800-495-5511
E-mail: sthomason@nwacircleoflife.org
URL: http://www.nwacircleoflife.org/about/contact.html

Texarkana

19052 ■ Arkansas Department of Health Hospice-Texarkana
503 Walnut
Texarkana, AR 71854
Ph: (870)773-2108
Fax: (870)773-3292
URL: http://www.adhhomecare.org/locationdetail.php?OfficeLink=HLA7

19053 ■ Hospice Peachtree/dba Peachtree Hospice, LLC - Arkansas
4425 Jefferson Blvd., Ste. 104
Texarkana, AR 71854
Ph: (870)773-4353
Free: 866-210-4418
Fax: (870)773-4418
E-mail: jpetrus@pthfs.com
URL: http://www.peachtreehospice.com

West Memphis

19054 ■ Arkansas Department of Health Hospice 9 - East Crittenden County HU
901 N 7th St.
West Memphis, AR 72301

Ph: (870)732-3764
Fax: (870)733-0860
URL: http://www.adhhomecare.org/locationdetail.php?OfficeLink=HLB5

19055 ■ Unity Hospice Care LLC--West Memphis
202 N Rhodes
West Memphis, AR 72301
Ph: (870)735-2824
Fax: (870)735-2584

CALIFORNIA

Anaheim

19056 ■ Hospice Care of the West
505 N Euclid, Ste. 480
Anaheim, CA 92801
Free: 800-405-1159
Fax: (714)817-9585
E-mail: info@hospicecareofthewest.com
URL: http://www.hospicecareofthewest.com/

19057 ■ New Haven Hospice Care, Inc.
1700 E Lincoln Ave., Ste. 202
Anaheim, CA 92805
Ph: (714)774-2498
Fax: (714)774-2485
E-mail: info@newhavenhospicecare.org
URL: http://www.newhavenhospicecare.org/

Apple Valley

19058 ■ Community Hospice of Victor Valley
16147 Kamana Rd.
Apple Valley, CA 92307
Ph: (760)946-4730
Fax: (760)242-0566
E-mail: chad.talley@chvv.net
URL: http://www.chvv.net

Auburn

19059 ■ Sutter Auburn Faith Hospice
11795 Education St., Ste. 224
Auburn, CA 95602
Ph: (530)886-6650
Fax: (530)886-6661
URL: http://sutterauburnfaith.org/services/

Bakersfield

19060 ■ Hoffmann Hospice--Bakersfield
8501 Brimhall Rd., Bldg. 100
Bakersfield, CA 93312
Ph: (661)410-1010
Fax: (661)410-1110
URL: http://www.hoffmannhospice.org/content/main.php

19061 ■ Mercy Hospitals of Bakersfield
2215 Truxtun Ave.
Bakersfield, CA 93301
Ph: (661)632-5000
URL: http://www.mercybakersfield.org/index.htm

19062 ■ Odyssey HealthCare of Bakersfield
5001 E Commercenter Dr., Ste. 140
Bakersfield, CA 93309
Ph: (661)324-1232
Free: 866-691-9868
Fax: (661)324-0931
URL: http://www.odsyhealth.com

19063 ■ Optimal Hospice Care-Bakersfield
1675 Chester Avenue Ste. 401
Bakersfield, CA 93309
Ph: (661)716-4000
Free: 888-597-6115
Fax: (661)716-4004
URL: http://www.optimalcares.com/

Banning

19064 ■ Visiting Nurse Association of the Inland Counties-Banning
264 N Highland Springs Ave., Bldg. 4, Ste. A
Banning, CA 92220
Ph: (951)845-8439
Fax: (951)769-1038
URL: http://www.vna-ic.org/

Barstow

19065 ■ Visiting Nurse Association of the Inland Counties-Barstow
222 E. Main St., Suite 112
Barstow, CA 92311
Ph: (760)256-2016
Fax: (760)256-2302
URL: http://www.vna-ic.org/

Bellflower

19066 ■ Tesca Hospice, Inc.
8514 E Artesia Blvd.
Bellflower, CA 90706
Ph: (562)272-6677
Fax: (562)272-0150
URL: http://www.tescahospice.com/

Bishop

19067 ■ Hospice of the Owens Valley
155 Pioneer Ln.
Bishop, CA 93514-2557
Ph: (760)873-3742
Fax: (760)873-3742

Camarillo

19068 ■ Camarillo Hospice
400 Rosewood Ave. Ste. 102
Camarillo, CA 93010
Ph: (805)389-6870
Fax: (805)389-0296
E-mail: info@camarillohospice.org
URL: http://www.camarillohospice.org

19069 ■ Vitas Innovative Hospice Care-LA & Ventura County
333 N Lantana St.
Camarillo, CA 93010
URL: http://www.vitas.com/

Campbell

19070 ■ Odyssey HealthCare of Northern California
1500 Hamilton Ave., Ste. 212
Campbell, CA 95008
Ph: (408)626-4868
Free: 877-637-9432
Fax: (408)626-4869
URL: http://www.odsyhealth.com

Carlsbad

19071 ■ Hospice of the North Coast
5441 Avenida Encinas, Ste. A
Carlsbad, CA 92008
Ph: (760)431-4100
Fax: (760)431-4133
E-mail: hnc@hospicenorthcoast.org
URL: http://www.hospicenorthcoast.org

Cathedral City

19072 ■ VITAS Innovative Hospice Care of the Inland Empire
Satellite Office
35325 Date Palm Dr., Ste. 204
Cathedral City, CA 92234
Ph: (760)321-2273
Free: 866-418-4827
Fax: (760)321-7149
URL: http://www.vitas.com

Cerritos

19073 ■ Trinity Care Hospice
17315 Studebaker Rd., Ste. 101
Cerritos, CA 90703
Ph: (562)809-2150
Free: 866-210-1055
Fax: (562)402-3336
URL: http://www.trinitycarehospice.org

Chester

19074 ■ Sierra Hospice
150 Brentwood Dr.
Chester, CA 96020-0095
Ph: (530)258-3412
Fax: (530)258-3104
E-mail: sierrahospice@frontier.com
URL: http://www.sierrahospice.com/

Chico

19075 ■ Butte Home Health and Hospice
10 Constitution Dr.
Chico, CA 95973
Ph: (530)895-0462
Free: 800-655-0462
Fax: (530)895-9623
URL: http://www.buttehomehealth.com

19076 ■ Enloe Hospice
1531 Esplanade
Chico, CA 95926
Ph: (530)332-7300
URL: http://www.enloe.org/guide_to_services/home-care_and_hospice.asp

Citrus Heights

19077 ■ First Call Home Care & Hospice
6929 Sunrise Blvd., Ste. 180
Citrus Heights, CA 95610
Ph: (915)725-2580
Fax: (916)725-2511
E-mail: fc@fchosp.com
URL: http://www.fchosp.com/

Claremont

19078 ■ Inland Hospice Association
233 W Harrison Ave.
Claremont, CA 91711
Ph: (909)399-3289
Fax: (909)626-4369
E-mail: info@inlandhospice.org
URL: http://www.inlandhospice.org
James Covey, Executive Director

19079 ■ Visiting Nurse Association & Hospice of Southern California
150 W First St., Ste. 270
Claremont, CA 91711
Ph: (909)624-3574
Free: 800-969-4862
Fax: (909)624-1559
URL: http://www.vnasocal.org/

Colton

19080 ■ Charter Hospice/dba Reche Canyon Rehabilitation and Health Care Center
1012 E Cooley Dr., Ste. G
Colton, CA 92324
Ph: (909)825-2969
Fax: (909)825-8751

Commerce

19081 ■ Bella Vida Hospice
5900 S Eastern Ave., Ste. 156
Commerce, CA 90040
Ph: (323)825-4501
Fax: (323)825-4480
URL: http://www.bellavidahospice.org/en/

Concord

19082 ■ Aseracare Hospice--Concord
1001 Galaxy Way, Ste. 101
Concord, CA 94520
Ph: (925)798-5791
Free: 800-928-8841
Fax: (925)363-4394
URL: http://hospice.aseracare.com/home.aspx

19083 ■ Evercare Hospice & Palliative Care--Concord
2300 Clayton Rd.
Concord, CA 94520
Ph: (925)246-7600
Free: 877-416-8555
Fax: (925)602-2822
URL: http://www.evercarehospice.com/

19084 ■ Sutter VNA and Hospice--Concord
4071 Port Chicago Hwy., Ste. 120
Concord, CA 94520
Ph: (925)363-4120
Fax: (877)472-0312
URL: http://www.suttervnaandhospice.org

Covina

19085 ■ Holy Family Hospice Care
310 E Rowland St.
Covina, CA 91723
Ph: (626)974-8984
Fax: (626)967-9956

19086 ■ VITAS Innovative Hospice Care of San Gabriel Cities
1343 N Grand Ave.
Covina, CA 91724-3467
Ph: (626)918-2273
URL: http://www.vitas.com

Cupertino

19087 ■ Kaiser Permanente Hospice
10050 N Wolfe Rd.
Cupertino, CA 95014
Ph: (408)342-6699
Fax: (408)342-6646
URL: https://www.kaiserpermanente.org/

Davis

19088 ■ Yolo Hospice
1909 Galileo Ct., Ste. A
Davis, CA 95618
Ph: (530)758-5566
Free: 800-491-7711
Fax: (530)758-5122
E-mail: djena@yolohospice.org
URL: http://www.yolohospice.org
Doug Jena, Executive Director

Diamond Springs

19089 ■ Snowline Hospice of El Dorado County, Inc.
6520 Pleasant Valley Rd.
Diamond Springs, CA 95619
Ph: (530)621-7820
Free: 916-817-2338
Fax: (530)621-4503
URL: http://www.snowlinehospice.org

Dublin

19090 ■ Hope Hospice--Dublin
6377 Clark Ave., Ste. 100
Dublin, CA 94568
Ph: (925)829-8770
Free: 800-HOS-PICE
Fax: (925)829-0868
E-mail: info@hopehospice.com
URL: http://www.hopehospice.com

Emeryville

19091 ■ Sutter VNA and Hospice--Emeryville
1900 Powell St., Ste. 300
Emeryville, CA 94608
Ph: (510)450-8596
Free: 866-652-9178
Fax: (510)450-8532
URL: http://www.suttervnaandhospice.org/locations/locations_emeryville.html

Encino

19092 ■ Skirball Hospice
6345 Balboa Blvd., Ste. 213
Encino, CA 91335
Ph: (818)774-3000
Fax: (818)774-3020
E-mail: skirballhospice@jha.org
URL: http://www.jha.org/about/skirball.asp

19093 ■ Vitas Innovative Hospice Care of San Fernando Valley
16030 Ventura Blvd.
Encino, CA 91436
Ph: (818)385-0273
Free: 800-757-4242
Fax: (818)971-3497
URL: http://www.vitas.com

Escondido

19094 ■ The Elizabeth Hospice
150 W Crest St.
Escondido, CA 92025
Ph: (760)737-2050
Free: 800-797-2050
URL: http://www.elizabethhospice.org

Eureka

19095 ■ Hospice of Humboldt
2010 Myrtle Ave.
Eureka, CA 95501
Ph: (707)445-8443
Fax: (707)445-2209
E-mail: info@hospiceofhumboldt.org
URL: http://www.hospiceofhumboldt.org

Fairfield

19096 ■ North Bay Hospice and Bereavement
5140 Business Center Dr.
Fairfield, CA 94534
Ph: (707)646-3595
Fax: (707)429-6846
URL: http://www.northbay.org/NorthBayHospice-Bereavement.aspx

19097 ■ Vitas Innovative Hospice Care-Solano County
2480 Hillborn Rd., Ste. 105
Fairfield, CA 94534
URL: http://www.vitas.com/

Fallbrook

19098 ■ Fallbrook Hospice
624 E Elder St.
Fallbrook, CA 92028
Ph: (760)728-1191
URL: http://www.fallbrookhospital.com/Services/Pages/Hospice.aspx

Folsom

19099 ■ Mercy Hospice--Folsom
1650 Creekside Dr.
Folsom, CA 95630
Ph: (916)983-7400
URL: http://www.mercyfolsom.org/Medical_Services/Mercy_Home_Care/MHFV2_M120682

Fresno

19100 ■ AseraCare Hospice-Fresno
650 W Alluvial Ave.
Fresno, CA 93711
Ph: (559)447-2540
Free: 866-693-0093
Fax: (559)447-2559
URL: http://hospice.aseracare.com/home.aspx

19101 ■ Hinds Hospice--Fresno
1616 W Shaw Ave.
Fresno, CA 93711-3513
Ph: (559)248-8591
Free: 800-400-4677
Fax: (559)248-8580
URL: http://www.hindshospice.org/

19102 ■ Hinds Hospice Home Inpatient Services
1416 W Twain Ave.
Fresno, CA 93711
Ph: (559)222-0793
Free: 800-440-4677
Fax: (559)222-4782
URL: http://www.hindshospice.org/

19103 ■ Optimal Hospice Care-Fresno
6770 N West Ave., Ste. 105
Fresno, CA 93711
Ph: (559)320-4000
Free: 877-882-6423
Fax: (559)320-4004
URL: http://www.optimalcares.com/

19104 ■ Optimal Hospice Care-Fresno
6770 N West Ave., Ste. 105
Fresno, CA 93711
Ph: (559)320-4000
Free: 877-882-6423
Fax: (559)320-4004
URL: http://www.optimalcares.com/

19105 ■ Saint Agnes Hospice
1303 E Herndon Ave.
Fresno, CA 93720-3309
Ph: (559)450-3000
E-mail: hospice@samc.com
URL: http://www.samc.com/UMAP.asp?ID=1324

Garden Grove

19106 ■ Hospice Journey of California
10507 Garden Grove Blvd.
Garden Grove, CA 92843
Ph: (714)260-0226
Fax: (714)260-0228
URL: http://hospicejourneyofcalifornia.com/

19107 ■ Odyssey Healthcare of Orange County
7077 Orangewood Ave., Ste. 201
Garden Grove, CA 92841
Ph: (714)934-4520
Free: 877-637-9432
Fax: (714)934-4515
URL: http://www.odsyhealth.com

Glendora

19108 ■ Community Care Hospice
222 W Foothill Blvd.
Glendora, CA 91741
Ph: (626)335-9759
Free: 888-339-5888
Fax: (626)335-5040

Grass Valley

19109 ■ Hospice of the Foothills
11270 Rough and Ready Hwy.
Grass Valley, CA 95945
Ph: (530)272-5739
Fax: (530)272-0328
URL: http://www.hospiceofthefoothills.org

Hanford

19110 ■ Hanford Community Medical Center Adventist Health Home Care
460 Kings County Dr., Ste. 101
Hanford, CA 93230-4328
Ph: (559)585-3425
Fax: (559)582-3420
URL: http://www.adventisthealthcv.com/services_homecare.html

Hayward

19111 ■ Odyssey HealthCare, Inc.
22320 Foothill Blvd.
Hayward, CA 94541
Ph: (510)582-8434
Fax: (510)582-8490

Healdsburg

19112 ■ North County Hospice St. Joseph Health System-Synoma County
205 East St.
Healdsburg, CA 95448
Ph: (707)431-1135
Fax: (707)431-1139
URL: http://www.stjosephhealth.org/Services/Hospice/Default.aspx

Hemet

19113 ■ Ramona VNA & Hospice
890 W Stetson Ave., Ste. A
Hemet, CA 92543
Ph: (951)658-9288
Free: 800-588-7862
Fax: (951)679-3944
E-mail: info@ramonavna.org
URL: http://www.ramonavna.org

Hollister

19114 ■ Central Coast VNA and Hospice--Hollister
341 Tres Pinos Rd., Ste. 103-A
Hollister, CA 95023
Ph: (831)372-6668
E-mail: vnainfo@ccvna.com
URL: http://www.ccvna.com/

Hughson

19115 ■ Alexander Cohen Hospice House
2201 Euclid Ave.
Hughson, CA 95326
Ph: (209)883-3250
Fax: (209)883-3270
URL: http://www.hospiceheart.org/patients/achh/index.htm

Inglewood

19116 ■ Los Angeles Hospice Care Inc.
301 N Prairie Ave., Ste. 310
Inglewood, CA 90301
Ph: (310)674-4940

Irvine

19117 ■ Vitas Innovative Hospice Care of Orange County
220 Commerce
Irvine, CA 92602-1323
Ph: (714)921-2273
Free: 800-486-6157
Fax: (714)734-2780
URL: http://www.vitas.com

Jackson

19118 ■ Hospice of Amador
1500 S Hwy. 49, Ste. 205
Jackson, CA 95642-2652
Ph: (209)223-5500
Fax: (209)223-4964
E-mail: info@hospiceofamador.org
URL: http://www.hospiceofamador.org/

Joshua Tree

19119 ■ Hospice of Morongo Basin
61675 29 Palms Hwy.
Joshua Tree, CA 92252-2389
Ph: (760)366-1308
Fax: (760)366-1935
E-mail: hospiceofmb@gmail.com
URL: http://www.hospiceofmorongobasin.org/

King City

19120 ■ Central Coast VNA and Hospice--King City
809 Broadway St.
King City, CA 93930
Ph: (831)385-1014
Fax: (831)385-8428
E-mail: vnafoundation@ccvna.com
URL: http://www.ccvna.com/

La Mesa

19121 ■ LakeView Home
9472 Loren Dr.
La Mesa, CA 91942
Ph: (619)668-6995
Fax: (619)668-5954

19122 ■ Sharp HospiceCare
8881 Fletcher Pkwy., Ste. 336
La Mesa, CA 91942-3134
Ph: (619)667-1900
Free: 800-827-4277
Fax: (619)667-1916
E-mail: info@sharp.com
URL: http://www.sharp.com/hospice/index.cfm

La Mirada

19123 ■ Hospice of Presbyterian
15050 Imperial Hwy.
La Mirada, CA 90638-1301
Ph: (562)947-3668
URL: http://www.whittierpres.com
Remarks: Intake phone number: (626)397-3600.

Laguna Hills

19124 ■ Hospice Care of California
23521 Paseo de Valencia, Ste. 108
Laguna Hills, CA 92653
Ph: (949)454-0207
Free: 800-889-3227
Fax: (714)577-9679
E-mail: ahablitzel@hospicecareofca.org
URL: http://www.hospicecareofca.org/

19125 ■ Hospice of Saddleback Valley
23521 Paseo de Valencia, Ste. 100
Laguna Hills, CA 92653
Ph: (949)460-1600
Fax: (949)462-3171
E-mail: emakres@memoriacare.org
URL: http://www.memorialcare.org/saddleback/services/hospice/index.cfm

Lake Isabella

19126 ■ Optimal Hospice Care-Lake Isabella
6504 Lake Isabella Blvd., Ste. E
Lake Isabella, CA 93240
Ph: (760)379-5038
Free: 888-597-6115
Fax: (760)379-5951
URL: http://www.optimalcares.com/

19127 ■ Optimal Hospice Care-Lake Isabella
6504 Lake Isabella Blvd., Ste. E
Lake Isabella, CA 93240
Ph: (760)379-5038
Free: 888-597-5951
Fax: (760)379-5951
URL: http://www.optimalcares.com/

Lakeport

19128 ■ Hospice Services of Lake County
1717 S Main St.
Lakeport, CA 95453-5668
Ph: (707)263-6222
Free: 800-900-8820
Fax: (707)263-4045
E-mail: kgarvey@lakecountyhospice.org
URL: http://www.lakecountyhospice.org

Lakewood

19129 ■ Admiral Hospice Care
4010 Watson Plaza Dr., Ste. 120
Lakewood, CA 90712
Ph: (562)429-1500
Fax: (562)429-1599
E-mail: jmercado@admiralhospicecare.com
URL: http://www.admiralhospice.com/
Josie Jones, President

Larkspur

19130 ■ Hospice By the Bay-Larkspur
17 E Sir Francis Drake Blvd.
Larkspur, CA 94939
Ph: (415)927-2273
Fax: (415)925-1004
URL: http://www.hospicebythebay.org

Long Beach

19131 ■ Miller Children's Hospital
2801 Atlantic Ave.
Long Beach, CA 90806
Ph: (562)933-5437
Fax: (562)933-8016
URL: http://www.millerchildrenshospitallb.org/index.php

19132 ■ ZG International Healthcare Division/dba Pacific Oasis Hospice
2750 E Spring St., Ste. 240
Long Beach, CA 90806
Ph: (562)981-3600
Fax: (562)981-9300

Los Angeles

19133 ■ Cedars - Sinai Medical Center
8700 Beverly Blvd.
Los Angeles, CA 90048
Ph: (310)423-3277
Fax: (310)423-9525
URL: http://www.csmc.edu

19134 ■ Los Angeles Hospice
3807 Wilshire Blvd., Ste. 1228
Los Angeles, CA 90010-3101
Ph: (213)351-1030
Free: 888-578-8885
Fax: (213)351-1032
URL: http://www.losangeleshospice.com/

19135 ■ Roze Room Hospice--Los Angeles
5455 Wilshire Blvd., Ste. 810
Los Angeles, CA 90036
Ph: (323)938-1155
Free: 800-828-9017
Fax: (323)938-9558
E-mail: lena@rozeroomhospice.org
URL: http://www.rozeroomhospice.org

19136 ■ Roze Room Hospice of Ventura
5455 Wilshire Blvd., Ste. 810
Los Angeles, CA 93003
Ph: (323)938-1155
Free: 800-828-9017
Fax: (323)938-9558
E-mail: lena@rozeroomhospice.org
URL: http://www.roseroomhospice.org

19137 ■ Verdugo Hospice Care Center
4170 Verdugo Rd.
Los Angeles, CA 90065
Ph: (323)257-5715
Free: 800-599-9930
Fax: (323)257-5447
E-mail: info@verdugohospice.com
URL: http://www.verdugohospice.com/

Mariposa

19138 ■ John C. Fremont Healthcare District Hospice
PO Box 216
Mariposa, CA 95338-0216
Ph: (209)966-3800
Free: 877-359-4504
Fax: (209)966-3778
E-mail: jcfadm@jcfhospital.com
URL: http://www.jcfhospital.com

Martinez

19139 ■ Kaiser Permanente--Martinez
200 Muir Rd.
Martinez, CA 94553
Ph: (925)313-4540
Fax: (925)372-1448

Marysville

19140 ■ Inland Valley Hospice
319 G St.
Marysville, CA 95901-5813
Ph: (916)749-4368

Merced

19141 ■ Bristol Hospice - California LLC
1170 W Olive Dr., Ste. B
Merced, CA 95348
Ph: (209)384-1415
Fax: (209)384-1449
URL: http://www.bristolhospice.com/

19142 ■ Hinds Hospice--Merced
410 W Main St., Ste. A
Merced, CA 95341
Ph: (209)383-3123
Fax: (209)383-5308
URL: http://www.hindshospice.org
Formerly: Hospice of Merced.

Modesto

19143 ■ Community Hospice--Modesto
4368 Spyres Way
Modesto, CA 95356
Ph: (209)578-6300
Free: 866-645-4567
Fax: (209)541-3294
E-mail: heart@hospiceheart.org
URL: http://www.hospiceheart.org

19144 ■ Optimal Hospice Care-Modesto
122 W Granger Ave.
Modesto, CA 95350
Ph: (209)338-3000
Fax: (209)338-3020
URL: http://www.optimalcares.com/

19145 ■ Optimal Hospice Care-Modesto
122 W Granger Ave.
Modesto, CA 95350
Ph: (209)338-3000
Fax: (209)338-3020
URL: http://www.optimalcares.com/

Monterey

19146 ■ Central Coast VNA and Hospice--Monterey
5 Lower Ragsdale Dr.
Monterey, CA 93940-5740
Ph: (831)372-6668
Fax: (831)648-7726
E-mail: vnainfo@ccvna.com
URL: http://www.ccvna.com/

19147 ■ Heartland Hospice Services--Monterey
2511 Garden Rd., Ste. B-200
Monterey, CA 93940
Ph: (831)373-8442
Free: 800-427-1902
Fax: (831)373-8444
E-mail: careline@hcr-manorcare.com
URL: http://www.hcr-manorcare.com

19148 ■ Hospice of the Central Coast
23625 Holman Hwy.
Monterey, CA 93940
Ph: (831)624-5311
Free: 888-45C-HOMP
E-mail: information@chomp.org
URL: http://www.chomp.org/what-we-do/hospice/index.aspx

Moorpark

19149 ■ Moorpark Health Care Center
4762 Maureen Ln.
Moorpark, CA 93021-7126
Ph: (805)517-1620
Fax: (805)517-1621
E-mail: info@mhcchome.com
URL: http://www.tlchomehospice.com
Formerly: Tender Loving Care Facility.

19150 ■ Tender Loving Care Home Hospice--Moorpark
5400 Atlantis Ct.
Moorpark, CA 93021
Ph: (805)517-1620
Fax: (805)517-1621
E-mail: tlc@tlchomehospice.com
URL: http://www.tlchomehospice.com

Mount Shasta

19151 ■ Mercy Hospice - Mount Shasta
914 Pine St.
Mount Shasta, CA 96067-2143
Ph: (530)926-6111
Fax: (530)926-9396
URL: http://www.mercymtshasta.org/Medical_Services/077980

Murrieta

19152 ■ Hospice of the Valleys--Murrieta
25240 Hancock Ave., Ste. 120
Murrieta, CA 92562
Ph: (951)200-7800
Fax: (951)973-7763
E-mail: info@hovsc.org
URL: http://www.hospiceofthevalleys.org

19153 ■ Visiting Nurse Association of the Inland Counties-Murrieta
39815 Alta Murrieta Dr., Ste. C4
Murrieta, CA 92563
Ph: (951)894-5330
Fax: (951)894-5348
URL: http://www.vna-ic.org/

Napa

19154 ■ Hospice of Napa Valley and Adult Day Services
414 S Jefferson St.
Napa, CA 94559-4515
Ph: (707)258-9080
Free: 800-451-4664
Fax: (707)258-9096
E-mail: info@napavalleyhospice-ads.org
URL: http://www.napavalleyhospice-ads.org/

Newark

19155 ■ Vitas Innovative Hospice Care of San Francisco Bay Area
39899 Balentine Dr., Ste. 161
Newark, CA 94560
Ph: (510)438-9602
Free: 866-258-4827
Fax: (510)360-4816
URL: http://www.vitas.com

Newport Coast

19156 ■ Crystal Cove Hospice
356 White Cap Lane
Newport Coast, CA 92657

Oakland

19157 ■ Asian Network Hospice
212 9th St., Ste. 205
Oakland, CA 94607
Ph: (510)268-1118
Fax: (510)268-9905
URL: http://www.anphc.com

19158 ■ Pathways Home Health and Hospice--Oakland
333 Hegenberger Rd., Ste. 700
Oakland, CA 94621
Ph: (510)632-4390
Free: 888-900-0811
Fax: (510)632-3334
URL: http://www.pathwayshealth.org

Orange

19159 ■ Heartland Home Health Care and Hospice--Orange
725 W Town & Country Rd., Ste. 130
Orange, CA 92868
Ph: (714)558-2366
Free: 866-539-9320
Fax: (714)558-0230
URL: http://www.hcr-manorcare.com

19160 ■ Seasons Hospice & Palliative Care--Orange
750 The City Drive, Ste. 120
Orange, CA 92868
Free: 877-508-0644
URL: http://honoringlife-offeringhope.org/

Palm Desert

19161 ■ Visiting Nurse Association of the Inland Counties-Palm Desert
42-600 Cook St., Ste. 202
Palm Desert, CA 92211
Ph: (760)674-0451
Fax: (760)776-1612
URL: http://www.vna-ic.org/

Palm Springs

19162 ■ Desert Hospital Hospice of the Desert Communities
1150 N Indian Canyon Dr.
Palm Springs, CA 92262-4872
Ph: (760)323-6511
Fax: (760)323-6580
URL: http://www.desertmedctr.com/en-US/Pages/default.aspx

19163 ■ Family Hospice Care
255 N El Cielo Rd., Ste. 300
Palm Springs, CA 92262
Ph: (760)674-3344
Free: 877-799-6463
Fax: (760)674-3372
E-mail: info@familyhospicecare.com
URL: http://www.familyhospicecare.com/

Palmdale

19164 ■ Hoffmann Hospice--Palmdale
655 West Ave. Q, Ste. A
Palmdale, CA 93551
Ph: (661)272-2355
Fax: (661)272-4588
URL: http://www.hoffmannhospice.org

Palo Alto

19165 ■ Veterans Hospice and Palliative Care Center-Palo Alto
3801 Miranda Ave.
Palo Alto, CA 94304
Ph: (650)493-5000
Fax: (650)849-0260
URL: http://www.paloalto.va.gov/

Panorama City

19166 ■ Los Angeles Hospice North Branch
8121 Van Nuys Blvd., Ste. 528
Panorama City, CA 91402
Ph: (818)785-3970
E-mail: amy@lahospice.com
URL: http://www.losangeleshospice.com/

Pasadena

19167 ■ Seasons Hospice & Palliative Care of California, LLC--Pasadena
2700 E Foothill Blvd., Ste. 300
Pasadena, CA 91107
Free: 866-278-7500
Fax: (626)463-7307
URL: http://www.seasons.org/

Petaluma

19168 ■ Hospice of Petaluma
416 Payran St.
Petaluma, CA 94952-5907
Ph: (707)778-6242
Fax: (707)778-0144
URL: http://www.memorialhospice.org/hospice_petaluma.aspx
Formerly: Memorial Hospice.

Pleasant Hill

19169 ■ Hospice of the East Bay--Pleasant Hill
3470 Buskirk Ave.
Pleasant Hill, CA 94523
Ph: (925)887-5678
Fax: (925)887-5679
E-mail: webmaster@hospiceeastbay.org
URL: http://www.hospicecc.org/ProgramsServices/BrunsHouse.aspx
Formerly: Hospice and Palliative Care of Contra Costa - Bruns House.

Portervills

19170 ■ Optimal Home Health
661 N Prospect
Portervills, CA 93257
Ph: (559)782-7670
Free: 800-924-2252
Fax: (559)782-7674
URL: http://www.optimalhomehealth.com/

Poway

19171 ■ Horizon Hospice--Poway
13053 Poway Rd., Ste. A
Poway, CA 92064
Ph: (858)748-3030
Free: 800-304-4430
Fax: (858)748-3747
URL: http://www.horizonhospicesandiego.com/

Rancho Mirage

19172 ■ Odyssey HealthCare of Palm Springs
71-777 San Jacinto Dr., Ste. 102
Rancho Mirage, CA 92270
Ph: (760)346-2816
Free: 866-346-2816
Fax: (760)341-5620

Red Bluff

19173 ■ Saint Elizabeth Hospice--Red Bluff
1425 Vista Way
Red Bluff, CA 96080
Ph: (530)528-4207
Fax: (530)528-4216
URL: http://redbluff.mercy.org/index.htm

Redding

19174 ■ Mercy Hospice--Redding
2175 Rosaline Ave.
Redding, CA 96001
Ph: (530)225-6000
URL: http://redding.mercy.org/Medical_Services/052026

Ridgecrest

19175 ■ Optimal Hospice Care-Ridgecrest
1653 Triangle Dr.
Ridgecrest, CA 93555
Ph: (760)446-4790
Fax: (760)499-9269
URL: http://www.optimalcares.com/

19176 ■ Ridgecrest Regional Hospice
1653 Triangle Dr., Ste. B
Ridgecrest, CA 93555
Ph: (760)499-3617
Fax: (760)499-3614
URL: http://www.rrh.org/hospice

Riverside

19177 ■ Care Alternatives Hospice--Riverside
7344 Magnolia Ave., Ste. 245
Riverside, CA 92504
Ph: (951)353-8006
Free: 866-821-1212
Fax: (951)353-8106
URL: http://www.carealt.com

19178 ■ Heartland Home Healthcare and Hospice--Riverside
1700 Iowa Ave., Ste. 230
Riverside, CA 92507
Ph: (909)369-8604
Free: 866-539-9320
Fax: (909)715-4594
E-mail: careline@hcr-manorcare.com
URL: http://www.hcr-manorcare.com

19179 ■ Visiting Nurse Association of the Inland Counties
6235 River Crest Dr., Ste. L
Riverside, CA 92507
Ph: (951)656-3153
Fax: (951)656-4795
URL: http://www.vna-ic.org

Roseville

19180 ■ Bristol Hospice Sacramento
2140 Professional Dr., Ste. 210
Roseville, CA 95661
Ph: (916)782-5511
Fax: (916)782-5635
URL: http://www.bristolhospice.com/aboutus.html

19181 ■ Sutter VNA and Hospice--Roseville
1836 Sierra Gardens Dr., Ste. 130
Roseville, CA 95661
Ph: (916)797-7850
Free: 866-652-9178
Fax: (916)781-6447
URL: http://www.suttervnaandhospice.org

Sacramento

19182 ■ Sutter VNA and Hospice--Sacramento
7300 Folsom Blvd., Ste. 100
Sacramento, CA 95826
Ph: (916)388-6255
Free: 866-652-9178
Fax: (916)381-5135
URL: http://www.suttervnaandhospice.org

19183 ■ UC Davis Hospice
3630 Business Dr.
Sacramento, CA 95820
Ph: (916)734-2458
Free: 800-268-9232
Fax: (916)454-1903
URL: http://www.ucdmc.ucdavis.edu/homecare/hospice/

19184 ■ VITAS Innovative Hospice Care of Sacramento Valley and Foothalls
3841 N Freeway Blvd., Ste. 210
Sacramento, CA 95834
Ph: (916)925-7010
Free: 866-554-4827
Fax: (916)566-2250
URL: http://www.vitas.com

Salinas

19185 ■ Central Coast VNA Hospice--Salinas
6 Quail Run Circle, Ste. 101
Salinas, CA 93907
Ph: (831)372-6668
Fax: (831)758-3849
URL: http://www.ccvna.com/

San Bernardino

19186 ■ Odyssey HealthCare of Riverside
225 W Hospitality Ln., Ste. 102
San Bernardino, CA 92408
Ph: (909)888-5000
Free: 877-637-9432
Fax: (909)888-4040
URL: http://www.odsyhealth.com

19187 ■ Pacific Hospice
1998 N Arrowhead Ave.
San Bernardino, CA 92405
Ph: (909)882-8466
Fax: (909)882-9203
E-mail: phospice@aol.com
URL: http://www.pacifichospice.org/

19188 ■ Vitas Innovative Hospice Care of the Inland Empire
1845 Business Ctr. Dr., Ste. 120
San Bernardino, CA 92408-3467
Ph: (909)386-6000
Free: 800-394-6774
Fax: (909)386-6004
URL: http://www.vitas.com

19189 ■ Vitas Innovative Hospice Care-Inland Empire
1845 Business Center Dr.
San Bernardino, CA 92408
Ph: (909)386-6000
URL: http://www.vitas.com/

19190 ■ VNA and Hospice of Southern California
412 E Vanderbilt Way, Ste. 100
San Bernardino, CA 92408
Ph: (909)384-0737
Free: 800-556-0219
Fax: (909)885-8301
URL: http://www.vnasocal.org

San Diego

19191 ■ Avalon Hospice and Palliative Care
3914 Murphy Canyon Rd., Ste. A226
San Diego, CA 92123
Ph: (858)751-0315
Fax: (858)560-0435
E-mail: contact@asvalonhospice.com
URL: http://www.avalonhospice.com

19192 ■ LightBridge Hospice
5280 Carroll Canyon Rd., Ste. 310
San Diego, CA 92121
Ph: (858)458-2992
Fax: (858)458-3655
URL: http://www.lightbridgehospice.com/

19193 ■ Odyssey HealthCare of San Diego
9444 Balboa Ave., Ste. 290
San Diego, CA 92123
Ph: (858)565-2499
Free: 877-637-9432
Fax: (858)565-2548
URL: http://www.odsyhealth.com

19194 ■ San Diego Hospice and The Institute for Palliative Medicine
4311 3rd Ave.
San Diego, CA 92103-1407
Ph: (619)688-1600
Free: 866-688-1600
Fax: (619)688-9665
E-mail: info@sdhospice.org
URL: http://www.sdhospice.org

19195 ■ Sharp Hospice Care
8695 Spectrum Center Blvd.
San Diego, CA 92123
Ph: (858)499-4000
Free: 800-681-9188
Fax: (858)499-5938
URL: http://www.sharp.com/hospice/

19196 ■ Silverado Hospice of San Diego
3750 Convoy St., Ste. 200A
San Diego, CA 92111
Free: 888-355-7961
Fax: (858)565-1646
URL: http://www.silveradosenior.com/hospice_care

19197 ■ VITAS Innovative Hospice Care of San Diego
9655 Granite Ridge Dr., Ste. 300
San Diego, CA 92123-2674
Ph: (858)499-8901
Free: 800-966-8705
Fax: (858)503-4785
URL: http://www.vitas.com

San Francisco

19198 ■ American CareQuest, Inc.
1426 Fillmore St., Ste. 210
San Francisco, CA 94115
Ph: (415)885-9100
Fax: (415)885-9107
E-mail: info@americancarequest.com
URL: http://www.americancarequest.com/

19199 ■ Hospice By the Bay-San Francisco
1902 Van Ness Ave., 2nd Fl.
San Francisco, CA 94109
Ph: (415)626-5900
Fax: (415)925-1004
URL: http://www.hospicebythebay.org

19200 ■ Pathways Home Health and Hospice--San Francisco
395 Oyster Point Blvd., Ste. 128
San Francisco, CA 94109-4822
Ph: (650)634-0133
Free: 888-755-7855
Fax: (650)871-0991
E-mail: info@pathwayshealth.org
URL: http://www.pathwayshealth.org

19201 ■ Self-Help HomeCare and Hospice
407 Sansome St.
San Francisco, CA 94111
Ph: (415)677-7628
Fax: (415)398-5903
URL: http://www.selfhelpelderly.org/services/hospice.php

19202 ■ Sutter VNA and Hospice--San Francisco
1625 Van Ness Ave., Ste. 4-A
San Francisco, CA 94109
Ph: (415)600-0460
Fax: (415)600-0461
URL: http://www.suttervnaandhospice.org/

19203 ■ Zen Hospice Project
273 Page St.
San Francisco, CA 94102-5616
Ph: (415)913-7682
Fax: (415)236-6298
E-mail: guesthouse@zenhospice.org
URL: http://www.zenhospice.org

San Jose

19204 ■ Concierge Health Care Services
333 W San Carlos St., Ste. 1680
San Jose, CA 95110
Ph: (408)287-5007
Fax: (408)287-0505
E-mail: info@hcconcierge.com
URL: http://www.hcconcierge.com/

19205 ■ Hospice of the Valley--San Jose
4850 Union Ave.
San Jose, CA 95124
Ph: (408)559-5600
Fax: (408)559-3462
E-mail: request@hospicevalley.org
URL: http://www.hospicevalley.org

San Juan Capistrano

19206 ■ Silverado Hospice-San Juan Capistrano
San Juan Capistrano, CA 92675
Free: 888-245-4338
Fax: (949)240-9977
E-mail: slutz@silveradohospice.com
URL: http://www.silveradosenior.com/hospice/Orange_County_CA/zip_92675/silverado _senior_living/2585

San Leandro

19207 ■ George Mark Children's House
2121 George Mark Ln.
San Leandro, CA 94578
Ph: (510)346-4624
Fax: (510)346-4620
E-mail: info@georgemark.org
URL: http://www.georgemark.org

San Luis Obispo

19208 ■ Hospice Partners of the Central Coast
227 South St., Ste. R
San Luis Obispo, CA 93401
Ph: (805)782-8608
Free: 800-801-8019
Fax: (805)782-8614
E-mail: hpccinfo@wilshirehcs.org
URL: http://www.hospicepartners.org

San Mateo

19209 ■ Mission Hospice of San Mateo County
1670 S Amplhett Blvd., Ste. 300
San Mateo, CA 94403
Ph: (650)554-1000
Fax: (650)554-1001
E-mail: dwilson@missionhospice.org
URL: http://www.missionhospice.org
Dwight Wilson, Chief Executive Officer

19210 ■ Sutter VNA and Hospice--San Mateo
700 S Claremont St., Ste. 220
San Mateo, CA 94402
Ph: (650)685-2830
Fax: (650)347-2769
URL: http://suttervnaandhospice.org

Santa Barbara

19211 ■ Hospice of Santa Barbara Inc.
2050 Alameda Padre Sierra, Ste. 100
Santa Barbara, CA 93103
Ph: (805)563-8820
Fax: (805)563-8821
E-mail: info@hospiceofsantabarbara.org
URL: http://www.hospiceofsantabarbara.org

19212 ■ Serenity House--Santa Barbara
900 Calle de Los Amigos
Santa Barbara, CA 93105-5451
Ph: (805)965-5555
E-mail: info@vnhcsb.org
URL: http://www.vnhcsb.org
Formerly: Leigh Block House.

19213 ■ Visiting Nurse and Hospice Care of Santa Barbara
222 E Canon Perdido St.
Santa Barbara, CA 93101
Ph: (805)965-5555
Fax: (805)690-6259
E-mail: info@vnhcsb.org
URL: http://www.vnhcsb.org/

Santa Clara

19214 ■ Heartland Home Healthcare and Hospice--Santa Clara
2005 De La Cruz Blvd., Ste. 271
Santa Clara, CA 95050-3013
Ph: (408)450-7850
Free: 800-427-1902
Fax: (408)486-8282
E-mail: careline@hcr-manorcare.com
URL: http://www.hcr-manorcare.com/tabld/67/default.aspx?FacilityID=4687&City=&State=&PostalCode=95050&CareTypes=99134

19215 ■ Optimal Hospice Care-Bay Area
3375 Scott Blvd., Ste. 310
Santa Clara, CA 95054
Ph: (408)207-9222
Fax: (408)207-9227
URL: http://www.optimalcares.com/

19216 ■ Optimal HospiceCare-Bay Area
3375 Scott Blvd., Ste. 310
Santa Clara, CA 95054
Ph: (408)207-9222
Fax: (408)207-9227
URL: http://www.optimalcares.com/component/option,com_contact/task,view/contact_ id,18/Itemid,3/

Santa Fe Springs

19217 ■ Hospice Care of California
14111 Freeway Dr., Ste. 321
Santa Fe Springs, CA 90670
Free: 800-889-3227
Fax: (562)407-9354
E-mail: ahablitzel@hospicecareofca.org
URL: http://www.hospicecareofca.org/
Ann Hablitzel, Executive Director

Santa Maria

19218 ■ Marian Hospice
1400 E Church St.
Santa Maria, CA 93454-6917
Ph: (805)739-3000
Fax: (805)739-3829
E-mail: diana.vea@chw.edu
URL: http://www.marianmedicalcenter.org/Medical_Services/184026

Santa Monica

19219 ■ Hospice Partners of Southern California
3250 Ocean Park Blvd., Ste. 100-C
Santa Monica, CA 90405
Ph: (310)264-8413
Fax: (310)829-6032
E-mail: hpscinfo@wilshirehcs.org
URL: http://www.hospicepartnerssc.org/

Santa Rosa

19220 ■ Heartland Home Healthcare and Hospice--Santa Rosa
2455 Bennett Valley Rd., Ste. B214
Santa Rosa, CA 95404-5663
Ph: (707)523-0111
Free: 800-427-1902
E-mail: careline@hcr-manorcare.com
URL: http://www.hcr-manorcare.com

19221 ■ Sutter VNA and Hospice--Santa Rosa
1110 N Dutton Ave.
Santa Rosa, CA 95401-4606
Ph: (707)535-5700
Fax: (707)542-5742
URL: http://www.suttervnaandhospice.org

Scotts Valley

19222 ■ Hospice of Santa Cruz County
940 Disc Dr.
Scotts Valley, CA 95066
Ph: (831)430-3000
Fax: (831)430-9272
URL: http://www.hospicesantacruz.org

Signal Hill

19223 ■ Alpenglow Hospice, Inc.
3200 E 19th St.
Signal Hill, CA 90755-1244
Ph: (562)494-7687
Fax: (877)220-2481
E-mail: jpimentel@alpenglowhospice.com
URL: http://www.alpenglowhospice.com/

Simi Valley

19224 ■ Silverado Hospice--Simi Valley
5775 E Los Angeles Ave.
Simi Valley, CA 93063
Ph: (805)577-1818
Free: 888-252-3143
Fax: (805)577-8019
URL: http://www.silveradosenior.com/hospice/LA_Ventura_County_CA/zip_93063/silve rado_senior_living/2587

19225 ■ Solara Hospice & Palliative Care
1919 Williams St., Ste. 330
Simi Valley, CA 93065
Ph: (805)578-3536
Fax: (805)578-3518
E-mail: sun.needell@solarhospice.com
URL: http://solarahospice.com/

Solana Beach

19226 ■ Hospice by the Sea--Solona Beach
312 S Cedros Ave., Ste. 250
Solana Beach, CA 92075
Ph: (858)794-0195
Fax: (858)794-0147
E-mail: kathiejackson@hospicebythesea.com
URL: http://www.hospicebythesea.org

Sonoma

19227 ■ Hospice By the Bay-Sonoma
190 W Napa St.
Sonoma, CA 95476
Ph: (415)935-7504
Fax: (415)935-7590
URL: http://www.hospicebythebay.org

Sonora

19228 ■ Sonora Regional Home Health & Hospice of the Sierra
20100 Cedar Rd. N
Sonora, CA 95370
Ph: (209)536-5700
Fax: (209)532-3238
E-mail: wheelehc@ah.org
URL: http://www.adventisthealth.org/healthservices/goDocDocument.asp?CN=244&DID= 247

South Lake Tahoe

19229 ■ Barton Hospice
2092 Lake Tahoe Blvd.
South Lake Tahoe, CA 96150
Ph: (530)543-5581
Fax: (530)541-2653
URL: http://www.bartonhealth.org

Stockton

19230 ■ Asercare Hospice
2529 W March Ln.
Stockton, CA 95207
Ph: (209)474-8349
Free: 866-740-7157
Fax: (209)474-8356
URL: http://www.aseracare.com

19231 ■ Catholic Healthcare West
1800 N California St.
Stockton, CA 95204
Ph: (209)943-2000
URL: http://www.chwhealth.org/index.htm

19232 ■ Hospice of San Joaquin
3888 Pacific Ave.
Stockton, CA 95204
Ph: (209)957-3888
Fax: (209)957-3986
E-mail: webmaster@hospicesj.org
URL: http://www.hospicesj.org

Sun City

19233 ■ Hope Hospice and Healthcare, Inc.
29798 Haun Rd., Ste. 102
Sun City, CA 92586
Ph: (951)679-8872
Fax: (951)679-7882

Sunnyvale

19234 ■ Pathways Home Health and Hospice--Sunnyvale
585 N Mary Ave.
Sunnyvale, CA 94085
Ph: (408)730-5100
Fax: (408)730-8726
E-mail: info@pathwayshealth.org
URL: http://www.pathwayshealth.org

Thousand Oaks

19235 ■ Hospice of the Conejo
80 E Hillcrest Dr., Ste. 204
Thousand Oaks, CA 91360
Ph: (805)495-2145
Fax: (805)495-3092
E-mail: hospice@adnetsol.com
URL: http://www.hospiceoftheconejo.org/

Torrance

19236 ■ Cherish Hospice, Inc.
2340 Plaza Del Amo
Torrance, CA 90501
Ph: (310)320-1677
Fax: (310)320-1258

19237 ■ Torrance Memorial Home Health and Hospice
3330 Lomita Blvd.
Torrance, CA 90505-5002
Ph: (310)784-3739
Fax: (310)784-3717
URL: http://www.torrancememorial.org

19238 ■ TrinityCare Hospice
2601 Airport Dr., Ste. 230
Torrance, CA 90505
Ph: (310)530-3800
Free: 800-535-8446
Fax: (310)257-3557
URL: http://www.trinitycarehospice.org

19239 ■ VITAS Innovative Hospice Care of Coastal Cities
990 W 190th St., Ste. 120
Torrance, CA 90502-1014
Ph: (714)921-2273
Free: 800-966-7757
URL: http://www.vitas.com

19240 ■ Ziba Hospice
21151 S Western Ave.
Torrance, CA 90501
Ph: (310)328-4865
Fax: (310)328-4309
E-mail: info@zibahospice.com
URL: http://zibahospice.com/

Truckee

19241 ■ Tahoe Forest Hospice
10121 Pine Ave.
Truckee, CA 96160
Ph: (530)587-6011
Fax: (530)582-3211
E-mail: information@tfhd.com
URL: http://www.tfhd.com/

Turlock

19242 ■ Hospice of Emanuel
1850 Colorado Ave.
Turlock, CA 95382
Ph: (209)664-2550
Fax: (209)664-2425
URL: http://www.emanuelmedicalcenter.org/

Union City

19243 ■ Kaiser Hayward Hospice Program
30116 Eigenbrodt Way
Union City, CA 94587
Ph: (510)675-5777
Fax: (510)675-5778
URL: http://www.kaiserpermanente.org

Van Nuys

19244 ■ Providence TrinityCare Hospice
16600 Sherman Way
Van Nuys, CA 91406
Ph: (818)779-0120
Fax: (818)779-0678
URL: http://www.trinitycarehospice.org

Ventura

19245 ■ Livingston Memorial VNA
1996 Eastman Ave., Ste. 101
Ventura, CA 93003
Ph: (805)642-0239
Free: 800-223-4862
Fax: (805)642-2320
URL: http://www.lmvna.org

Victorville

19246 ■ Visiting Nurse Association of the Inland Counties-Victorville
12421 Hesperia Rd., Ste. 11
Victorville, CA 92395
Ph: (760)241-3564
Fax: (760)241-7055
URL: http://www.vna-ic.org/

Visalia

19247 ■ Kaweah Delta Health Care District Hospice of Tulare County, Inc.
900 W Oak Ave.
Visalia, CA 93291
Ph: (559)733-0642
Fax: (559)733-0658
URL: http://www.kaweahdelta.org/giving/hospice.asp

19248 ■ Optimal Hospice
5429 Avenida de los Robles, Ste. D
Visalia, CA 93291
Ph: (559)741-7220
Free: 888-474-7224
Fax: (559)635-4869
URL: http://www.optimalcares.com

19249 ■ Optimal Hospice Care-Visalia
5429 Avenida de los Robles, Ste. D
Visalia, CA 93291
Ph: (559)741-7220
Free: 888-474-7224
Fax: (559)635-4869
URL: http://www.optimalcares.com/

Vista

19250 ■ Seasons Hospice & Palliative Care of California-San Diego, LLC
973 Vale Terrace, Ste. 108
Vista, CA 92084
Ph: (760)643-0400
Free: 877-643-0401
Fax: (760)643-0402
URL: http://honoringlife-offeringhope.org/

Walnut Creek

19251 ■ VITAS Innovative Hospice Care of the East Bay
365 Lennon Ln., Ste. 140
Walnut Creek, CA 94598
Ph: (925)930-9373
Fax: (925)945-3850
URL: http://www.vitas.com

West Covina

19252 ■ Citrus Valley Hospice
820 N Phillips Ave.
West Covina, CA 91791
Ph: (626)859-2263
URL: http://www.cvhp.org/

19253 ■ Heartland Home Health Care and Hospice--West Covina
1000 Lakes Dr., Ste. 225
West Covina, CA 91790-2900
Ph: (626)918-1207
Free: 866-539-9320
Fax: (626)918-4918
E-mail: careline@hcr-manorcare.com
URL: http://www.hcr-manorcare.com

19254 ■ Odyssey Healthcare of Los Angeles
1900 W Garvey South Ave., Ste. 200
West Covina, CA 91790
Ph: (626)851-4000
Free: 877-637-9432
Fax: (626)851-4041
E-mail: info@odsyhealth.com
URL: http://www.odsyhealth.com

Westlake Village

19255 ■ Buena Vista Hospice
143 Trunfo Rd., No. 103
Westlake Village, CA 91361
Ph: (805)777-1133
Fax: (805)777-1132
E-mail: info@bvhospice.com
URL: http://www.buenavistahospicecare.com

Willits

19256 ■ Phoenix Hospice
Home Care and Hospice Services, Mendocino County
1 Madrone St.
Willits, CA 95490-4225
Ph: (707)459-1818
Fax: (707)459-9298

Yreka

19257 ■ Madrone Hospice Inc./Adult Day Healthcare Services
255 Collier Cir.
Yreka, CA 96097
Ph: (530)842-3160
Fax: (530)842-6412
URL: http://www.madronehospice.org

Yuba City

19258 ■ Fremont-Rideout Hospice
939 Live Oak Blvd.
Yuba City, CA 95991
Ph: (530)790-3006
URL: http://www.frhg.org/hospital.aspx?pid=25&id=30

Yucca Valley

19259 ■ Visiting Nurse Association of the Inland Counties-Yucca Valley
56300 29 Palms Hwy., Ste. 105
Yucca Valley, CA 92284
Ph: (760)365-4271
Fax: (760)365-1754
URL: http://www.vna-ic.org/

COLORADO

Alamosa

19260 ■ Hospice del Valle
514 Main St.
Alamosa, CO 81101-2644
Ph: (719)589-9019
Fax: (719)589-5094

Aurora

19261 ■ Affinity Hospice of Life--Aurora
2121 S Blackhawk St., Ste. 110
Aurora, CO 80014
Ph: (303)745-3197
Fax: (303)750-4573
URL: http://www.affinityhospice.com

19262 ■ Kaiser Permanente--Aurora
2550 S Parker Rd.
Aurora, CO 80014
Ph: (303)636-3325
Fax: (303)636-3358

Basalt

19263 ■ Hospice of the Valley-Basalt
PO Box 3768
Basalt, CO 81621
Ph: (970)927-6650
Fax: (970)927-6659

Boulder

19264 ■ Family Hospice--Boulder
1790 30th St., Ste. 308
Boulder, CO 80301
Ph: (303)440-0205
Fax: (303)440-0209
E-mail: familyhospice@familyhospice.net
URL: http://www.familyhospice.net

Canon City

19265 ■ Fremont Regional Hospice
1439 Main St.
Canon City, CO 81212
Ph: (719)275-4315
Fax: (719)275-8315
URL: http://www.fremontregionalhospice.com/

19266 ■ Sangre De Cristo Hospice- West
601 Greenwood Ave.
Canon City, CO 81212
Ph: (719)275-1261
Fax: (719)275-1805
E-mail: info@sangredecristohospice.org
URL: http://www.pueblohospice.org

Collbran

19267 ■ Hospice and Palliative Care of Western Colorado
PO Box 294
Collbran, CO 81624-0294
Ph: (970)487-3844
Fax: (970)487-3422
URL: http://www.hospicewco.com/i4a/pages/index.cfm?pageid=1

Colorado Springs

19268 ■ Evercare Hospice and Palliative Care--Colorado Springs
5450 Tech Center Dr.
Colorado Springs, CO 80919
Ph: (719)265-1100
Free: 866-840-9253
Fax: (719)265-1101
URL: http://www.evercarehospice.com

19269 ■ Odyssey Healthcare of Colorado Springs
5526 N Academy Blvd., Ste. 108
Colorado Springs, CO 80918
Ph: (719)573-4166
Free: 877-637-9432
Fax: (719)573-4164
E-mail: info@odsyhealth.com
URL: http://www.odsyhealth.com
Formerly: Hospice of the Comforter.

19270 ■ Pikes Peak Hospice and Palliative Care of Colorado Springs, Inc.
825 E Pikes Peak Ave., Ste. 600
Colorado Springs, CO 80903-3624
Ph: (719)633-3400
Fax: (719)633-3800
URL: http://www.pikespeakhospice.org

19271 ■ Solamor Hospice--Colorado Springs
655 Southpointe Ct., No. 201
Colorado Springs, CO 80906
Ph: (719)226-0091
Fax: (719)226-7900
URL: http://www.solamorhospice.com/

Cortez

19272 ■ Hospice of Montezuma
1345 S Broadway
Cortez, CO 81321-0740
Ph: (970)565-4400
Fax: (970)565-9543
E-mail: office@hospiceofmontezuma.org
URL: http://www.hospiceofmontezuma.org

Delta

19273 ■ Hospice and Palliative Care of Western Colorado
195 Stafford Ln.
Delta, CO 81416
Ph: (970)874-6823
Free: 877-867-5744
Fax: (970)874-6903
URL: http://www.hospicewco.com

Denver

19274 ■ Colorado Community Hospice/Interlink Healthcare Services
3501 W 23rd Ave.
Denver, CO 80211
Ph: (303)546-7921
Fax: (303)238-4293
URL: http://www.coloradocommunityhospice.org/

19275 ■ Denver Hospice
501 S Cherry St., Ste. 700
Denver, CO 80246
Ph: (303)321-2828
Fax: (303)321-7171
URL: http://www.thedenverhospice.org

19276 ■ Namaste Comfort Care
1633 Fillmore St., Ste. 300
Denver, CO 80206
Ph: (303)860-9915
Fax: (303)860-9914
E-mail: namaste@comfortnow.org
URL: http://www.namastehospice.com/

19277 ■ VNA Hospice at Home
390 Grant St.
Denver, CO 80203
Ph: (303)698-2121
Fax: (866)613-9489
URL: http://www.vnacolorado.org/Services/HospiceAtHome.aspx

Englewood

19278 ■ Evercare Hospice and Palliative Care--Englewood
6455 S Yosemite St.
Englewood, CO 80111
Ph: (303)714-2400
Free: 888-437-4673
Fax: (303)714-2396
URL: http://www.evercarehospice.com

19279 ■ Hospice of Saint John-Inverness Drive
8 Inverness Dr. E, Ste. 250
Englewood, CO 80112
Ph: (303)232-7900
Fax: (303)232-3614

Erie

19280 ■ Front Range Hospice
685 Briggs St., Ste. 200
Erie, CO 80516
Ph: (303)957-3101
Fax: (303)957-3113
E-mail: info@frhospice.com
URL: http://www.frontrangehospice.com/

Estes Park

19281 ■ Hospice of the Estes Valley
555 Prospect Ave.
Estes Park, CO 80517-2740
Ph: (970)586-2273
Fax: (970)586-3895

Evergreen

19282 ■ Mount Evans Hospice, Inc.
3081 Bergen Peak Dr.
Evergreen, CO 80439
Ph: (303)674-6400
Fax: (303)674-8813
E-mail: info@mtevans.org
URL: http://www.mtevans.org

Fort Collins

19283 ■ Pathways Hospice - Community Care for Northern Colorado
305 Carpenter Rd.
Fort Collins, CO 80525-6927
Ph: (970)663-3500
Fax: (970)663-1180
E-mail: info@pathways-care.org
URL: http://www.pathways-care.org/
Formerly: Hospice of Larimer County, Inc.

Grand Junction

19284 ■ Hospice and Palliative Care of Western Colorado
2754 Compass Dr., Ste. 377
Grand Junction, CO 81506
Ph: (970)241-2212
Fax: (970)257-2400
E-mail: info@hospicewco.com
URL: http://www.hospicewco.com

Greeley

19285 ■ Hospice Inpatient Unit
1801 16th St.
Greeley, CO 80631
Ph: (970)475-0041
Fax: (970)475-0040
URL: http://www.hpcnc.org

19286 ■ Hospice and Palliative Care of Northern Colorado, Inc.
2726 W 11th St. Rd.
Greeley, CO 80634
Ph: (970)352-8487
Fax: (970)475-0037
URL: http://www.hpcnc.org

Greenwood Village

19287 ■ Agape Hospice Services
6041 S Syracuse Way, Ste. 220
Greenwood Village, CO 80111
Ph: (720)482-1988
Free: 877-771-1231
Fax: (720)482-1990
URL: http://www.agape-healthcare.com

Gunnison

19288 ■ Hospice and Palliative Care of the Gunnison Valley
805 W Tomichi Ave.
Gunnison, CO 81230
Ph: (970)641-4254
Fax: (970)641-4874
E-mail: hospice@glc-co.org
URL: http://gunnisonhospice.org/

Hot Sulphur Springs

19289 ■ Heart of the Mountains Hospice, Inc.
613 First St.
Hot Sulphur Springs, CO 80451
Ph: (970)725-3378
E-mail: hospice@co.grand.co.us
URL: http://www.grandcountyhospice.org/

La Junta

19290 ■ Arkansas Valley Hospice
118 W 4th St.
La Junta, CO 81050
Ph: (719)384-8827
Fax: (719)384-2045
URL: http://www.grandcountyhospice.org/

Lafayette

19291 ■ Hospice Care of Boulder/Broomfield Counties
2594 Trailridge Dr. E
Lafayette, CO 80026
Ph: (303)449-7740
Fax: (303)604-5393
E-mail: info@hospicecareonline.org
URL: http://www.hospicecareonline.org

Lakewood

19292 ■ Hospice of Saint John Foundation, Inc.
1320 Everett Ct.
Lakewood, CO 80215
Ph: (303)232-7900
Fax: (303)232-3614
E-mail: scooper@hospiceofsaintjohn.org
URL: http://www.hospiceofsaintjohn.org
Steven Cooper, President

Lamar

19293 ■ Lamar Area Hospice Association
108 W Olive St.
Lamar, CO 81052
Ph: (719)336-2100
Fax: (719)336-3845

Longmont

19294 ■ HospiceCare of Boulder and Broomfield Counties-Longmont
2130 Mountain View Ave., Ste. 201
Longmont, CO 80501
Ph: (303)449-7740
Fax: (303)604-5393
URL: http://www.hospicecareonline.org

Louisville

19295 ■ Hospice of Boulder and Broomfield Counties
Care Center
1855 Plaza Dr.
Louisville, CO 80027
Ph: (303)449-7744
Fax: (303)926-3931
URL: http://hospicecareonline.org/

Loveland

19296 ■ Pathways Hospice - Community Care for Northern Colorado
Care Center at McKee
2000 N Boise
Loveland, CO 80538
Ph: (970)593-6062
Fax: (970)593-6063
URL: http://www.pathways-care.org/Pathway_Services/Places-of-Care.php
Formerly: Hospice of Larimer County.

Mead

19297 ■ Halcyon Hospice & Palliative Care
PO Box 177
Mead, CO 80542
Ph: (970)535-0870
Fax: (303)329-0870
E-mail: info@halcyonhospice.org
URL: http://www.halcyonhospice.org/

Montrose

19298 ■ Hospice and Palliative Care of Western Colorado
645 S 5th St.
Montrose, CO 81402
Ph: (970)240-7734
Free: 866-310-8900
Fax: (970)240-7263
URL: http://www.hospicewco.com

Pueblo

19299 ■ Frontier Hospice--Pueblo
503 N Main, Ste. 103
Pueblo, CO 81003
Ph: (719)544-5891
Free: 877-544-5891
Fax: (719)544-5895
E-mail: lrussell@frontierhospiceco.com
URL: http://www.frontierhospiceco.com

19300 ■ Joni Fair Hospice House
1207 Pueblo Blvd. Way
Pueblo, CO 81005
Ph: (719)542-0032
E-mail: info@sangredecristohospice.org
URL: http://www.pueblohospice.org/house.html

19301 ■ Sangre de Cristo Hospice and Palliative Care
1207 Pueblo Blvd. Way
Pueblo, CO 81005-2175
Ph: (719)542-0032
Fax: (719)542-1413
E-mail: info@sangredecristohospice.org
URL: http://pueblohospice.org

Salida

19302 ■ Angel of Shavano Hospice
8044 W Highway 50
Salida, CO 81201
Ph: (719)539-2467
Fax: (719)530-0166
E-mail: marji.ackermann@hrrmc.net

Springfield

19303 ■ Southeast Colorado Hospital
200 E 10th St.
Springfield, CO 81073
Ph: (719)523-4057
E-mail: stirmer@sechosp.org
URL: http://www.sechosp.org/hospice.htm

Steamboat Springs

19304 ■ Northwest Colorado Visiting Nurse Association
940 Central Park Dr., Ste. 101
Steamboat Springs, CO 80487-8816
Ph: (970)879-1632
Fax: (970)870-1326
URL: http://www.nwcovna.info/
Formerly: Hospice and Palliative Care Services of Northwest Colorado.

Sterling

19305 ■ Hospice of the Plains Inc. - Sterling Office
100 Broadway, Ste. 1-A
Sterling, CO 80751
Ph: (970)526-7901
Fax: (970)526-7902
E-mail: contact@hospiceoftheplains.org
URL: http://hospiceoftheplains.org/

Walsenburg

19306 ■ Sangre De Cristo Hospice & Palliative Care-South Office
124 W 8th St.
Walsenburg, CO 81089
Ph: (719)738-2588
Fax: (719)738-2588
URL: http://www.pueblohospice.org/walsenburg.html

Westminster

19307 ■ Heartland Home Health Care and Hospice--Westminster
8774 Yates Dr., No. 100
Westminster, CO 80031
Ph: (303)926-1001
Fax: (303)926-1030
URL: http://www.hcr-manorcare.com

Wheat Ridge

19308 ■ Exempla Lutheran Medical Center
3210 Lutheran Pkwy.
Wheat Ridge, CO 80033
Ph: (303)425-7200
Fax: (303)403-7295
E-mail: hospice@exempla.org
URL: http://www.exempla.org/hospice

19309 ■ VistaCare Hospice-Wheatridge
4350 Wadsworth Blvd., Ste. 250
Wheat Ridge, CO 80033
Ph: (303)639-9243
Fax: (303)639-9238
E-mail: aokane@odsyhealth.com
URL: http://www.vistacare.com/

Windsor

19310 ■ AccentCare-Windsor
1180 Main St., Ste. 9
Windsor, CO 80550
Ph: (970)346-9700
Fax: (970)346-9710
URL: http://www.accentcare.com/

Woodland Park

19311 ■ Prospect Home Care and Hospice
16222 Hwy. 24, Ste. 120
Woodland Park, CO 80863
Ph: (719)687-0549
Fax: (719)687-8558
URL: http://www.prospecthch.org

Wray

19312 ■ Hospice of the Plains, Inc. - Wray Office
1017 W 7th St.
Wray, CO 80758
Ph: (970)332-4116
Fax: (970)332-4102
URL: http://hospiceoftheplains.org/

CONNECTICUT

Bristol

19313 ■ Hospice of Bristol Hospital
222 Main
Bristol, CT 06010
Ph: (860)585-4752
Fax: (860)585-1756
E-mail: info@bristolhospital.org
URL: http://www.bristolhospital.org/

Brookfield

19314 ■ Masonicare Home Health & Hospice--Brookfield
777 Federal Rd.
Brookfield, CT 06804
Ph: (203)775-0675
URL: http://www.masonicare.org/healthcare_services/ctvna/locations.asp

Danbury

19315 ■ Danbury Hospital CARES Program-2 South
24 Hospital Ave.
Danbury, CT 06810
Ph: (203)739-6662
Fax: (203)739-8678
URL: http://www.danburyhospital.org/

19316 ■ Regional Hospice of Western Connecticut, Inc.
405 Main St.
Danbury, CT 06810-4710
Ph: (203)739-8300
Fax: (203)739-8301
E-mail: regionalhospice@danhosp.ort
URL: http://www.regionalhospicect.org

Danielson

19317 ■ Masonic Home Health & Hospice
20 Furnace Ave.
Danielson, CT 06239-3027
Ph: (860)774-1366
Free: 800-528-6664
URL: http://www.masonicare.org/healthcare_services/ctvna.asp
Formerly: Hospice and Palliative Care of Connecticut/Connecticut VNA's Hospice.

East Hartford

19318 ■ Masonicare Home Health & Hospice--East Hartford
111 Founders Plz., Ste. 200
East Hartford, CT 06108
Ph: (860)528-2273
Fax: (860)290-6775
URL: http://www.masonicare.org/healthcare_services/ctvna.asp
Formerly: Connecticut VNA's Hospice.

East Lynne

19319 ■ Masonicare Home Health and Hospice--East Lynne
Latimer Brook Commons
339 Flanders Rd., Ste. 215
East Lynne, CT 06333
Ph: (860)691-4630
Fax: (860)859-4140
URL: http://www.masonicare.org/

Glastonbury

19320 ■ VITAS Innovative Hospice Care of Hartford
628 Hebron Ave., Ste. 300
Glastonbury, CT 06033
Ph: (860)920-6000
Fax: (860)920-6050
URL: http://www.vitas.com

19321 ■ Vitas Innovative Hospice Care of Hartford
628 Hebron Ave., Ste. 300
Glastonbury, CT 06033
Ph: (860)920-6000
Fax: (860)920-6050
URL: http://www.vitas.com/

Greenwich

19322 ■ Greenwich Hospital Home Hospice
5 Perryridge Rd.
Greenwich, CT 06830
Ph: (203)863-3000
Fax: (203)863-3888
E-mail: Maria.Marini@greenwichhospital.org
URL: http://www.greenhosp.org/medicalservices_homehospice.asp

Hartford

19323 ■ Saint Francis Hospital Medical Center Home Care & Hospice
114 Woodland St.
Hartford, CT 06105-1230
Ph: (860)714-4000
Free: 800-613-8817
Fax: (860)714-8033
URL: http://www.stfranciscare.org

19324 ■ VNA Health Care Hospice and Palliative Care
103 Woodland St.
Hartford, CT 06105-1233
Ph: (860)249-4862
Free: 800--HOMECAR
Fax: (860)246-8734
URL: http://www.vnahealthcare.org

Mansfield Center

19325 ■ Hospice of Eastern Connecticut
34 Ledgebrook Dr.
Mansfield Center, CT 06250-1664
Ph: (860)456-7288
Fax: (860)423-5702
E-mail: sueb@vnaeast.org
URL: http://www.vnaeast.org/

Meriden

19326 ■ Franciscan Hospice Care
267 Finch Ave.
Meriden, CT 06451
Ph: (203)238-1441
Fax: (203)686-0807
E-mail: info@franciscanhc.org
URL: http://www.franciscanhc.org

Middlebury

19327 ■ VITAS Innovative Hospice Care of Waterbury
1579 Straits Tnpke., Unit C
Middlebury, CT 06762

Ph: (203)437-3111
Fax: (203)437-3150
URL: http://www.vitas.com

Middletown

19328 ■ Middlesex Hospice and Palliative Care
28 Crescent St.
Middletown, CT 06457-3654
Ph: (860)358-6100
Free: 800-664-5031
URL: http://www.midhosp.org/go/85A7BF29-0A67-45B9-2C7BD778DDB7F960/

Milford

19329 ■ SolAmor Hospice--Milford
4 Oxford Rd., E4
Milford, CT 06460
Ph: (302)301-0489
Fax: (302)201-0632
URL: http://www.solamorhospice.com/

Mystic

19330 ■ Beacon Hospice
12 Roosevelt Ave.
Mystic, CT 06355
Free: 800-536-5601
Fax: (800)-536-5620
E-mail: info@beaconhospice.com
URL: http://www.beaconhospice.com/

New Milford

19331 ■ New Milford Visiting Nurse Association Hospice
68 Park Ln.
New Milford, CT 06776-2325
Ph: (860)354-2216
Free: 860-354-2216
Fax: (860)350-2852
E-mail: info@newmilfordvna.org
URL: http://www.newmilfordvna.org

Norwalk

19332 ■ Masonicare Home Health & Hospice-Norwalk
535 Connecticut Ave.
Norwalk, CT 06854
Ph: (203)831-8882
Fax: (203)866-6191
URL: http://www.masonicare.org/healthcare_services/ctvna/norwalk.asp

Norwich

19333 ■ Hospice of Southeastern Connecticut
227 Dunham St.
Norwich, CT 06360
Ph: (860)848-5699
Free: 877-654-4035
Fax: (860)848-6898
E-mail: information@hospicesect.org
URL: http://www.hospicesect.org

19334 ■ Masonicare Home Health & Hospice--Norwich
12 Case St.
Norwich, CT 06360
Ph: (860)859-4133
Fax: (860)859-4140
URL: http://www.masonicare.org/healthcare_services/ctvna.asp
Formerly: Connecticut VNA's Hospice.

Oxford

19335 ■ Hospice at Home Program of VNS of Connecticut
84 Oxford Rd.
Oxford, CT 06478
Ph: (203)888-9706
Fax: (203)888-9806
E-mail: mchudwick@vnsct.org
URL: http://www.vnsct.com/hospice.htm

Plainville

19336 ■ Hospice and Palliative Care Program of VNA of Central Connecticut, Inc.
56 W Main St.
Plainville, CT 06062
Ph: (860)793-3000
Fax: (860)793-1922
E-mail: Karenp@vnacc.com
URL: http://www.vnacc.org

Putnam

19337 ■ Hospice of Northeastern Connecticut
Day Kimball Home Care and Hospital
320 Pomfret St., Rte. 44
Putnam, CT 06260-1836
Ph: (860)928-0422
Free: 800-664-2442
Fax: (860)963-2259
URL: http://www.daykimball.org

Salisbury

19338 ■ Salisbury Visiting Nurse Association, Inc.
30A Salmon Kill Rd.
Salisbury, CT 06068
Ph: (860)435-0816
Fax: (860)435-4852
E-mail: info@salisburyvna.org
URL: http://www.salisburyvna.org

Sharon

19339 ■ Hospice of Northwest Connecticut--Hospital Hill Road
Sharon Healthcare Center
27 Hospital Hill Rd.
Sharon, CT 06069-0625
Ph: (860)364-1002
Fax: (860)364-9830
URL: http://www.sharonhospital.com/page.cfm?page_id=222

19340 ■ Hospice of Northwest Connecticut--Law Road
Sharon Health Care Center
1 Law Rd.
Sharon, CT 06069
Ph: (860)364-1796
Fax: (860)364-9830
URL: http://www.sharonhospital.com/page.cfm?page_id=222

Simsbury

19341 ■ Farmington Valley VNA Hospice Program
8 Old Mill Ln.
Simsbury, CT 06070
Ph: (860)651-3539
Free: 800-842-9710
URL: http://www.vnavalleycare.org
Formerly: Hospice of Farmington Valley, Valley Care.

19342 ■ McLean Homecare and Hospice
75 Great Pond Rd.
Simsbury, CT 06070
Free: 860-658-3700
Fax: (860)408-1319
URL: http://www.mcleancare.org/hospice.shtml

Stamford

19343 ■ Richard L. Rosenthal Hospice Residence
100 Shelburne Rd.
Stamford, CT 06902
Ph: (203)276-3003
Fax: (203)355-4044
URL: http://www.hospitalsoup.com/listing/7105-richard-l-rosenthal-hospice-reside nce

19344 ■ Visiting Nurse and Hospice Care of Southwest Connecticut
1266 E Main St.
Stamford, CT 06902-4108
Ph: (203)276-3000
Fax: (203)276-3001
URL: http://www.vnhcsw.org

Stratford

19345 ■ VITAS Innovative Hospice Care of Fairfield
Merritt 8 Corporate Park
99 Hawley La., Ste. 1204
Stratford, CT 06614
Ph: (203)455-3300
Fax: (203)455-3350
URL: http://www.vitas.com

Torrington

19346 ■ Hospice at Home - A Program Visiting Nurse Services of Connecticut
62 Commercial Blvd.
Torrington, CT 06790-3097
Ph: (860)482-6419
Fax: (860)482-8347
URL: http://www.vnsct.com

Trumbull

19347 ■ Hospice at Home-A Program of VNS of CT
40 Lindeman Dr.
Trumbull, CT 06611
Ph: (203)330-0520
Fax: (203)396-0520
URL: http://www.vnsct.com/

Vernon

19348 ■ North Central Hospice/Visiting Nurse and Health Services of Connecticut Inc.
8 Keynote Dr.
Vernon, CT 06066
Ph: (860)872-9163
Fax: (860)872-3030
E-mail: info@vnhsc.org
URL: http://www.vnhsc.org

Wallingford

19349 ■ Masonicare Home Health & Hospice--Wallingford
33 N Plains Industrial Rd.
Wallingford, CT 06492
Ph: (203)679-5888
Fax: (203)269-7619
URL: http://www.masonicare.org/healthcare_services/ctvna.asp
Formerly: Hospice and Palliative Care of Connecticut.

Watertown

19350 ■ Hospice Program of VNA Health at Home Inc.
27 Siemon Company Dr.
Watertown, CT 06795
Ph: (860)274-7531
Free: 888-274-7531
Fax: (860)274-4173
URL: http://www.vnahealthathome.org

West Hartford

19351 ■ Hebrew Health Care
1 Abrahms Blvd.
West Hartford, CT 06117
Ph: (860)523-3800
Fax: (860)920-1806
URL: http://www.hebrewhealthcare.org/

Wilton

19352 ■ Visiting Nurse & Hospice of Fairfield County
PO Box 489
Wilton, CT 06897
Ph: (203)762-8958
Free: 800-898-HOME
Fax: (203)761-8889
E-mail: info@visitingnurse.net
URL: http://www.visitingnurse.net/

Winsted

19353 ■ Hospice of Foothills Visiting Nurse/Home Care
Foothills Hospice
32 Union St.
Winsted, CT 06098-1521
Ph: (860)379-8561
Fax: (860)738-7479
E-mail: winsted.vna@snet.net
URL: http://www.vnaa.org/VNAA/vna/Foothills_Visiting_Nurse___Home_Care_Inc,CTWINS.aspx

DELAWARE

Dover

19354 ■ Delaware Hospice
Dover Office
911 S DuPont Hwy.
Lotus Plaza
Dover, DE 19901
Ph: (302)678-4444
Free: 800-838-9800
Fax: (302)678-4451
E-mail: mkane@delawarehospice.org
URL: http://www.dehospice.org/

Milford

19355 ■ Delaware Hospice-Milford
100 Patriots Way
Milford, DE 19963
Ph: (302)856-7717
Fax: (302)422-7315
URL: http://www.delawarehospice.org/

19356 ■ Vitas Innovative Hospice Care-Delaware
1016 N Walnut St.
Milford, DE 19963
Ph: (305)374-4143
Fax: (305)350-6784
URL: http://www.vitas.com/

Newark

19357 ■ Heartland Home Health Care and Hospice--Newark
256 Chapman Rd., Ste. 102
Newark, DE 19702
Ph: (302)737-7080
Fax: (302)737-7282
URL: http://www.hcr-manorcare.com

19358 ■ Seasons Hospice and Palliative Care-Newark
220 Continental Dr., Ste. 101
Newark, DE 19713
Ph: (302)533-3800
Fax: (302)553-3801
URL: http://honoringlife-offeringhope.org/

19359 ■ VITAS Innovative Hospice Care of Delaware
100 Commerce Dr.
Newark, DE 19713
Ph: (302)451-4000
Fax: (302)451-4050
URL: http://www.vitas.com

Wilmington

19360 ■ Compassionate Care Hospice of Delaware
702B Kirkwood Hwy.
Wilmington, DE 19805
Ph: (302)993-9090
Free: 800-219-0092
Fax: (302)993-9094
URL: http://cchnet.net/

19361 ■ Delaware Hospice, Inc.--Wilmington
3515 Silverside Rd.
Wilmington, DE 19810
Ph: (302)478-5707
Free: 800-838-9800
Fax: (302)479-2586
E-mail: mkane@delawarehospice.org
URL: http://www.dehospice.org/

19362 ■ Heartland Hospice House of Delaware
5661 Ochletree Ln.
Wilmington, DE 19808
Ph: (302)737-7080
Fax: (302)235-0461
URL: http://www.hcr-manorcare.com/

19363 ■ Odyssey Healthcare of Wilmington
1407 Foulk Rd., Ste. 200
Wilmington, DE 19803
Ph: (302)479-7500
Free: 877-637-9432
Fax: (302)479-5720
E-mail: info@odsyhealth.com
URL: http://www.odsyhealth.org

DISTRICT OF COLUMBIA

Washington

19364 ■ Capital Hospices--Washington DC
4401 Connecticut Ave. NW, Ste. 700
Washington, DC 20008-2322
Ph: (202)244-8300
Free: 800-869-2136
Fax: (202)244-1413
URL: http://www.capitalhospice.org/

19365 ■ Providence Hospital Palliative Care Service
1150 Varnum St. NE
Washington, DC 20017
Ph: (202)269-7051
Fax: (202)269-7661
URL: http://www.provhosp.org/About_us/HFacilities/CarrollM/ProfRes/Pall_Care.htm

19366 ■ VITAS Innovative Hospice Care of Greater Washington
1200 First St., NE, Ste. 320
Washington, DC 20002
Ph: (202)415-5400
URL: http://www.vitas.com

FLORIDA

Altamonte Springs

19367 ■ Hospice of the Comforter Horizons Bereavement Center
480 W Central Pkwy.
Altamonte Springs, FL 32714
Ph: (407)682-0808
Fax: (407)682-5737
URL: http://www.hospiceofthecomforter.org

Arcadia

19368 ■ Tidewell Hospice and Palliative Care-Arcadia
919 N Arcadia Ave.
Arcadia, FL 34266
Ph: (863)231-3350
Fax: (863)231-3346
E-mail: info@tidewell.org
URL: http://www.tidewell.org/locations.html

Auburndale

19369 ■ Good Shepherd Hospice of Mid-Florida
105 Arneson Ave.
Auburndale, FL 33823
Ph: (863)297-1880
Fax: (863)965-5601
URL: http://www.goodshepherdhospice.org

Aventura

19370 ■ VITAS Inpatient Hospice Unit Aventura Medical Center
20900 Biscayne Blvd., 7th Fl.
Aventura, FL 33180
Ph: (305)682-7274
Fax: (305)937-6919
URL: http://www.vitas.com

Bartow

19371 ■ Good Shepherd Hospice--Bartow
1239 E Main St., Ste. 1
Bartow, FL 33830
Ph: (863)533-0203
Fax: (863)292-4096
URL: http://www.goodshepherdhospice.org

Bay Pines

19372 ■ Bay Pines VA Healthcare System
10000 Bay Pines Blvd.
Bay Pines, FL 33744
Ph: (727)398-6661
Free: 888-820-0230
URL: http://www.baypines.va.gov/

Beverly Hills

19373 ■ Hospice of Citrus County Inc.--Beverly Hills
PO Box 641270
Beverly Hills, FL 34464-1270
Ph: (352)527-9200
Fax: (352)527-0386
E-mail: caring@hospiceofcitruscounty.org
URL: http://www.hospiceofcitruscounty.org

19374 ■ HPH Hospice - Citrus Office
3545 N Lecanto Hwy.
Beverly Hills, FL 34465
Ph: (352)527-4600
Free: 800-697-1799
Fax: (352)527-4507
URL: http://www.hph-hospice.org/locations
Formerly: Hernando Pasco Hospice - Citrus Office.

Boca Raton

19375 ■ Hospice By the Sea
Boca Care Center
1531 W Palmetto Park Rd.
Boca Raton, FL 33486
Ph: (561)395-5031
Free: 800-633-2577
E-mail: info@hbts.org
URL: http://www.hbts.org/

Boynton Beach

19376 ■ Hospice of Palm Beach County--Boynton Beach
Bethesda Memorial Hospice and Palliative Care Center
2815 S Seacrest Blvd.
Boynton Beach, FL 33435
Ph: (561)364-2463
Free: 888-848-5200
Fax: (561)364-2464
URL: http://www.hpbc.com/about/units-offices.shtml#regional

19377 ■ VITAS Innovative Hospice Care of the Palm Beaches
1901 S Congress Ave.
Boynton Beach, FL 33426
Ph: (561)364-1479
Fax: (561)734-6342
URL: http://www.vitas.com

19378 ■ VITAS Innovative Hospice Care of the Palm Beaches
1901 S Congress Ave., Ste. 420
Boynton Beach, FL 33426
Ph: (561)364-1479
Fax: (561)734-6342
URL: http://www.vitas.com/Aboutus/Locations/Florida/tabid/184/Default.aspx

Bradenton

19379 ■ Tidewell Hospice Administration--Education and Human Resources
6310 Capital Dr., Ste. 100
Bradenton, FL 34202
Ph: (941)552-5900
Fax: (941)552-5988
URL: http://tidewell.org/locations.html

19380 ■ TideWell Hospice and Palliative Care-West Office
Administrative Office
3355 26th St. W
Bradenton, FL 34205
Ph: (941)782-4933
URL: http://www.tidewell.org/locations.html

Brooksville

19381 ■ Hernando Hospice Care Center
12242 Cortez Blvd.
Brooksville, FL 34613
Ph: (352)544-1181
Fax: (352)597-4132
URL: http://www.hph-hospice.org/carecenters/hernando-care-center
Formerly: Hernando-Pasco Hospice.

19382 ■ HPH Hospice - East Hernando Office
698 S Broad St.
Brooksville, FL 34601
Ph: (352)796-2611
Free: 866-486-8771
Fax: (352)796-7703
URL: http://www.hphospice.org
Formerly: Hernando Pasco Hospice.

19383 ■ HPH Hospice
West Hernando Office
12260 Cortez Blvd.
Brooksville, FL 34601
Ph: (352)597-1882
Fax: (352)597-4667
URL: http://www.hph-hospice.org/
Formerly: Hernando-Pasco Hospice.

Carrabelle

19384 ■ Big Bend Hospice, Inc.
Carrabelle Office
207 Ave. B SE
Carrabelle, FL 32322
Ph: (850)697-2074
Fax: (850)697-3165
URL: http://www.bigbendhospice.org

Chiefland

19385 ■ Haven Hospice--Chiefland
311 NE 9th St.
Chiefland, FL 32626
Ph: (352)493-2333
Free: 800-727-1889
Fax: (352)493-0553
URL: http://www.havenhospice.org

Clearwater

19386 ■ Suncoast Hospice--Clearwater
5771 Roosevelt Blvd.
Clearwater, FL 33760
Ph: (727)586-4432
Fax: (727)523-4125
URL: http://www.thehospice.org
Formerly: Hospice of the Florida Suncoast.

Clermont

19387 ■ Mike Conley Hospice House
2100 Oakley Seaver Blvd.
Clermont, FL 34711
Free: 888-728-6234
URL: http://cshospice.org/?about_us/inpatient-care/hospice-houses.html

Crawfordville

19388 ■ Big Bend Hospice, Inc.
Wakulla Office
2889 Crawfordville Hwy.
Crawfordville, FL 32327
Ph: (850)926-9412
Fax: (850)926-9431
URL: http://www.bigbendhospice.org

Crestview

19389 ■ Covenant Hospice--Crestview
Crescent Park Medical Complex
370 W Redstone Dr.
Crestview, FL 32536
Ph: (850)682-3628
Free: 800-541-3072
URL: http://www.covenanthospice.org/crestview/

19390 ■ Emerald Coast Hospice--Crestview
131 Redstone Ave., Ste. 110
Crestview, FL 32536
Ph: (850)689-0300
Fax: (850)689-0307
URL: http://www.gentiva.com/hospice/hospice_locations.php#fl
Formerly: Hospice of the Emerald Coast.

Dade City

19391 ■ East Pasco Hospice Care Center
37439 Clinton Ave.
Dade City, FL 33525
Ph: (352)567-6837
Fax: (352)567-1898
URL: http://www.hph-hospice.org/locations

19392 ■ East Pasco Hospice House
James P. Gills Hospice House
37441 Clinton Ave.
Dade City, FL 33525
Ph: (352)521-3500
Fax: (352)521-6791
URL: http://www.hph-hospice.org/locations

19393 ■ Gulfside Regional Hospice House at Edwinola
37826 Sky Ridge Circle
Dade City, FL 33525
Ph: (813)780-1235
Fax: (813)780-6801
URL: http://www.grhospice.org

19394 ■ HPH Hospice
East Pasco Office
37445 Clinton Ave.
Dade City, FL 33525
Ph: (352)518-1400
Free: 800-486-8790
Fax: (813)788-5119
URL: http://www.hph-hospice.org/locations
Formerly: Hernando Pasco Hospice.

Dayton Beach

19395 ■ Hospice of the Palm Coast
149 S Ridgewood Ave., Ste. 600
Dayton Beach, FL 32114
Ph: (386)248-2380
Fax: (386)248-2388
URL: http://www.odsyhealth.com

Edgewater

19396 ■ Halifax Health-Hospice of Volusia Flagler
Southeast Volusia Care Center
4140 S Ridgewood
Edgewater, FL 32141
Ph: (386)425-8950
URL: http://www.halifaxhealth.org/locations/hospiceofvolusiaflagler.aspx

Fort Lauderdale

19397 ■ Catholic Hospice--Fort Lauderdale
2900 W Cypress Creek Rd., Ste. 7
Fort Lauderdale, FL 33309
Ph: (954)676-5465
Fax: (954)676-5466
E-mail: specialcare@catholicshospice.org
URL: http://www.catholichospice.org/

19398 ■ Florida Medical Center
Hospice Inpatient Unit
5000 W Oakland Park Blvd., 3 W
Fort Lauderdale, FL 33313
Ph: (954)730-2794
Free: 800-938-4827
URL: http://www.vitas.com

19399 ■ Hospice Care of Southeast Florida, Inc.
309 SE 18th St.
Fort Lauderdale, FL 33316
Ph: (954)467-7423
Free: 800-372-1757
E-mail: broward@hospicecareflorida.org
URL: http://www.hospicecareflorida.org

19400 ■ VITAS Innovative Hospice Care of Broward County
5420 NW 33rd Ave., Ste. 100
Fort Lauderdale, FL 33309
Ph: (954)486-4085
Free: 800-938-4827
Fax: (954)777-5328
URL: http://www.vitas.com

19401 ■ VITAS Inpatient Hospice Unit
Florida Medical Center
5000 W Oakland Park Blvd.
Fort Lauderdale, FL 33313
Ph: (954)730-2794
Fax: (954)730-2793
URL: http://www.vitas.com

19402 ■ VITAS Inpatient Hospice Unit
Fort Lauderdale Nursing and Rehabilitation
2000 E Commercial Blvd.
Fort Lauderdale, FL 33308
Ph: (954)343-9499
Fax: (954)343-9498
URL: http://www.vitas.com

Fort Myers

19403 ■ Hope Healthcare Services
9470 Health Park Circle
Fort Myers, FL 33908
Ph: (239)482-4673
Fax: (239)482-7298
E-mail: email@hopehcs.org
URL: http://www.hopehcs.org/

19404 ■ Hope Hospice and Community Services, Inc.
9470 Health Park Cir.
Fort Myers, FL 33908
Ph: (239)482-4673
Free: 800-835-1673
Fax: (239)482-2488
URL: http://www.hopehospice.org
Formerly: Hope Hospice and Palliative Care.

Fort Pierce

19405 ■ St. Lucie Hospice House
5090 Dunn Rd.
Fort Pierce, FL 34981
Ph: (772)462-8900
Fax: (772)467-1751

19406 ■ Treasure Coast Hospice - Saint Lucie Hospice House
5090 Dunn Rd.
Fort Pierce, FL 34981
Ph: (772)462-8900
Free: 800-299-4677
URL: http://www.tchospice.org/
Formerly: Hospice House of the Treasure Coast.

19407 ■ Treasure Coast Hospices--Fort Pierce
2500 Virginia Ave., Ste. 202
Fort Pierce, FL 34981
Ph: (772)419-0460
URL: http://www.tchospices.org

Fort Walton Beach

19408 ■ Hospice of the Emerald Coast-Ft. Walton
340 Beal Pkwy. NW, Ste. B
Fort Walton Beach, FL 32548-3924
Ph: (850)862-3240
Fax: (850)862-7976
URL: http://www.gentiva.com/location_finder/

19409 ■ Regency Hospice of Northwest Florida
11 Racetrack Rd., Ste. G
Fort Walton Beach, FL 32547
Ph: (850)226-4166
Fax: (850)226-6932
URL: http://www.regencyhospice.com/

Gainesville

19410 ■ Haven Hospice--Gainesville
4200 NW 90th Blvd.
Gainesville, FL 32606
Ph: (352)378-2121
Free: 800-727-1889
URL: http://www.havenhospice.org

Haines City

19411 ■ Good Shepherd Hospice--Haines City
218 S Dixie Dr.
Haines City, FL 33844
Ph: (863)419-8884
Free: 800-355-8170
Fax: (863)419-4718
URL: http://www.goodshepherdhospice.org

Hollywood

19412 ■ Hospice By the Sea Hollywood Inpatient Unit
3600 Washington St.
Hollywood, FL 33021
Ph: (954)985-6394
Free: 800-392-3188
Fax: (954)986-6104
URL: http://www.hospicebythesea.org

Hudson

19413 ■ HPH Hospice Care Center North Pasco Office
12107 Majestic Blvd.
Hudson, FL 34667-2455
Ph: (727)863-7971
Free: 800-486-8784
Fax: (727)868-9261
URL: http://www.hph-hospice.org/
Formerly: Hernando Pasco Hospice Care Center.

19414 ■ Hudson Hospice House
12139 Majestic Blvd.
Hudson, FL 34667
Ph: (727)863-5900
Fax: (727)819-8025
URL: http://www.hph-hospice.org/hospice-houses/west-pasco-hospice-house

Inverness

19415 ■ Hospice of Citrus County Care Unit
Citrus Memorial Hospital
502 W Highland Blvd.
Inverness, FL 34452
Ph: (352)560-6277
Fax: (352)560-6279
E-mail: caring@hospiceofthenaturecoast.org
URL: http://www.hospiceofthenaturecoat.org/

19416 ■ Hospice of Citrus County, Inc.--Inverness
326 S Line Ave.
Inverness, FL 34452
Ph: (352)560-0105
Fax: (352)560-0143
E-mail: caring@hospiceofcitruscounty.org
URL: http://www.hospiceofcitruscounty.org/

Jacksonville

19417 ■ Acosta-Rua Center for Caring
5450 Ramona Blvd.
Jacksonville, FL 32205
Ph: (904)268-5200
Fax: (904)596-6036
URL: http://www.communityhospice.com/

19418 ■ Anne and Donald McGraw Center for Caring
4715 Worrall Way
Jacksonville, FL 32224
Ph: (904)268-5200
Fax: (904)596-6036
URL: http://www.communityhospice.com/

19419 ■ Community Hospice of Northeast Florida
4266 Sunbeam Rd.
Jacksonville, FL 32257
Ph: (904)268-5200
Fax: (904)596-6036
URL: http://www.communityhospice.com/

19420 ■ George and Margaret Morris Center for Caring
Shanda Jacksonville Pavilion, 6th Fl.
580 W 8th St.
Jacksonville, FL 32209
Ph: (904)244-1651
Free: 800-274-6614
Fax: (904)596-6036
URL: http://www.communityhospice.com

19421 ■ Haven Hospice-Jacksonville
8301 Cypress Plaza Dr., Ste. 119
Jacksonville, FL 32256
Ph: (904)733-9818
Free: 866-733-9818
Fax: (904)733-8864
URL: http://www.havenhospice.org/

19422 ■ Heartland Hospice Services--Jacksonville
8130 Baymeadows Way W, Ste. 201
Jacksonville, FL 32256
Ph: (904)737-2553
Fax: (904)737-2631
URL: http://www.hcr-manorcare.com/Home/tabid/36/Default.aspx

Key West

19423 ■ Hospice of the Florida Keys
1319 William St.
Key West, FL 33040
Ph: (305)294-8812
Fax: (305)294-9348
E-mail: cburchard@hospicevna.com
URL: http://www.hospicevna.com

Kissimmee

19424 ■ VITAS Innovative Hospice Care of Central Florida Kissimmee Satellite Ofc.
1200 N Central Ave., Ste. 200
Kissimmee, FL 34741
Ph: (305)374-4143
Fax: (305)350-6784
URL: http://www.vitas.com/

Lake City

19425 ■ Haven Hospice Lake City - Suwannee Valley Hospice Care Center
6037 W US Hwy. 90
Lake City, FL 32055
Ph: (386)752-9191
Free: 800-759-6357
Fax: (386)752-4118
URL: http://www.havenhospice.org

Lakeland

19426 ■ Good Shepherd Hospice--Lakeland
115 S Missouri Ave., Ste. 500
Lakeland, FL 33815
Ph: (863)682-0027
Free: 800-464-3994
Fax: (863)682-3006
URL: http://www.goodshepherdhospice.org

19427 ■ Lakeland Regional Medical Center
1324 Lakeland Hills Blvd.
Lakeland, FL 33805
Ph: (863)687-1100
Fax: (863)284-1848
URL: http://lrmc.com/

Largo

19428 ■ Suncoast Hospice--Largo
11701 S Belcher Rd.
Largo, FL 33773-5135
Ph: (727)586-4432
Fax: (727)581-5846
URL: http://www.thehospice.org
Formerly: Hospice of the Florida Suncoast.

Lecanto

19429 ■ Hospice of Citrus County, Inc.--Lecanto
3350 W Audubon Park Path
Lecanto, FL 34461
Ph: (352)746-6578
Free: 866-642-0962
Fax: (352)746-7254
E-mail: caring@hospiceofcitruscounty.org
URL: http://www.hospiceofcitruscounty.org

Madison

19430 ■ Big Bend Hospice Inc. Madison Office
225 SW Smith St.
Madison, FL 32340

Ph. (850)878-5310
Fax: (850)973-8105
URL: http://www.bigbendhospice.org

Maitland

19431 ■ VITAS Innovative Hospice Care of Central Florida
2201 Lucien Way, Ste. 100
Maitland, FL 32751
Ph: (407)875-0028
Fax: (407)691-4574
URL: http://www.vitas.com/

Marianna

19432 ■ Gentiva Hospice of the Emerald Coast-Marianna
2491 Commercial Park Dr.
Marianna, FL 32448-2521
Ph: (850)526-1932
Fax: (850)526-1938
URL: http://www.gentiva.com/
Formerly: Hospice of the Emerald Coast.

Melbourne

19433 ■ VITAS Innovative Hospice of Brevard County
4450 West Eau Gallie Blvd., Ste. 250
Melbourne, FL 32934
Ph: (321)751-6671
Free: 800-938-4827
Fax: (321)751-6998
URL: http://www.vitas.com

Miami

19434 ■ Aventura Medical Center
20900 Biscayne Blvd., 7th Fl.
Miami, FL 33180
Ph: (305)682-7274
URL: http://www.vitas.com/Aboutus/Locations/Florida/tabid/184/Default.aspx

19435 ■ Catholic Hospice-Miami
9415 SW 72nd St., Ste. 111
Miami, FL 33173
Ph: (305)822-2380
Fax: (305)824-0665
E-mail: specialcare@catholichospice.org
URL: http://www.catholichospice.org/contact

19436 ■ Douglas Gardens Hospice, Inc.
5200 NE 2nd Ave.
Miami, FL 33137
Ph: (305)762-3883
Fax: (305)762-1558
URL: http://www.douglasgardenshospice.org/

19437 ■ Odyssey HealthCare-Miami
6161 Blue Lagoon Dr., Ste. 170
Miami, FL 33126
Ph: (786)388-1400
Fax: (786)388-1401
URL: http://www.odsyheatlth.com

19438 ■ VITAS Innovative Hospice Care of Miami - Dade Satellite Office
18001 Old Cutler Rd., Ste. 454
Miami, FL 33157
Ph: (786)573-1379
Fax: (786)573-7870
URL: http://www.vitas.com

19439 ■ VITAS Inpatient Hospice Unit Hialeah Hospital
651 E 25th St., 2nd Fl.
Miami, FL 33013
Ph: (305)835-4444
Fax: (305)835-4681
URL: http://www.vitas.com

19440 ■ VITAS Inpatient Hospice Unit North Shore Medical Center
1100 NW 95th St., 2nd Fl.
Miami, FL 33150
Ph: (305)835-6164
Fax: (305)696-1945
URL: http://www.vitas.com

Miami Lakes

19441 ■ Catholic Hospice--Miami Lakes
14875 NW 77 Ave., Ste. 100
Miami Lakes, FL 33014
Ph: (305)822-2380
Free: 800-533-3933
Fax: (305)824-0665
E-mail: specialcare@catholichospice.org
URL: http://www.catholichospice.org

Milton

19442 ■ Covenant Hospice, Inc.--Milton
5907 Berryhill Rd.
Milton, FL 32570
Ph: (850)202-5930
Free: 866-898-5930
Fax: (850)202-5932
URL: http://www.covenanthospice.org

Mims

19443 ■ VITAS Innovative Hospice Care of Brevard County-N Brevard
2431 Taylor St.
Mims, FL 32754
Ph: (305)374-4143
Fax: (305)350-6784
URL: http://www.vitas.com/

Monticello

19444 ■ Big Bend Hospice, Inc. Monticello Office
205 N Mulberry St.
Monticello, FL 32344
Ph: (850)997-2827
Fax: (850)997-1511
E-mail: admissions@bigbendhospice.org
URL: http://www.bigbendhospice.org

Naples

19445 ■ Avow Hospice
1095 Whippoorwill La.
Naples, FL 34105
Ph: (239)261-4404
Fax: (239)261-8683
URL: http://www.avowhospice.org/

19446 ■ VITAS Innovative Hospice Care-Collier
4980 Tamiami Trail N, Ste. 102
Naples, FL 34109
Ph: (239)649-2300
URL: http://www.vitas.com/

New Port Richey

19447 ■ Gulfside Regional Hospice. Inc.--New Port Richey
6117 Trouble Creek Rd.
New Port Richey, FL 34653-5240
Ph: (727)845-5707
Free: 800-561-4883
Fax: (727)845-7254
E-mail: info@grhospice.org
URL: http://www.gulfsideregionalhospice.org/

19448 ■ HPH Hospice - Central West Pasco
6807 Rowan Rd.
New Port Richey, FL 34653
Ph: (727)848-7160
Free: 866-727-7160
Fax: (727)849-9630
URL: http://www.hph-hospice.org/locations
Formerly: Hernando Pasco Hospice.

19449 ■ Marliere Hospice Care Center
6801 Rowan Rd.
New Port Richey, FL 34653
Ph: (727)848-7160
Free: 866-727-7160
Fax: (727)849-9630
URL: http://www.hph-hospice.org/locations

19450 ■ Newport Richey Hospice House
6230 Lafayette St.
New Port Richey, FL 34652
Ph: (727)841-6316
Fax: (727)842-7143
URL: http://www.gulfsideregionalhospice.org/locations.html
Formerly: Gulfside Regional Hospice House.

Niceville

19451 ■ Covenant Hospice, Inc.--Niceville
101 Hart St.
Niceville, FL 32578
Ph: (850)729-1800
Free: 866-729-1800
Fax: (850)729-7883
URL: http://www.covenanthospice.org

Ocala

19452 ■ Estelle's House
2897 SE 62nd St.
Ocala, FL 34480
Ph: (352)629-4556
Fax: (352)629-7155
URL: http://www.hospiceofmarion.com/estelles-house.html

19453 ■ Hospice of Marion County
3231 SW 34th Ave.
Ocala, FL 34474-8489
Ph: (352)873-7400
Free: 888-482-5018
Fax: (352)873-7435
URL: http://www.hospiceofmarion.com/

19454 ■ Legacy House
9505 SW 110th St.
Ocala, FL 34481
Ph: (352)291-5100
Fax: (352)291-5005
URL: http://www.hospiceofmarion.com/legacy-house.html

19455 ■ Odyssey Hospice-Ocala
1320 SE 25th Loop, Ste. 101
Ocala, FL 34471
Ph: (352)622-9331
Fax: (352)622-6418
URL: http://www.odsyhealth.com/default.asp

19456 ■ Sylvia's House
2895 SE 62nd St.
Ocala, FL 34480
Ph: (352)629-1313
Fax: (352)629-9553
URL: http://www.hospiceofmarion.com/sylvias-house.html

Okeechobee

19457 ■ Hospice of Okeechobee
411 SE 4th St.
Okeechobee, FL 34974
Ph: (863)467-2321
Free: 888-332-9067
Fax: (863)467-8330
E-mail: director@hospiceofokeechobee.com
URL: http://www.hospiceofokeechobee.org/

19458 ■ Treasure Coast Hospices--Okeechobee
1203 Parrott Ave.
Okeechobee, FL 34974
Ph: (863)763-0707
Fax: (863)763-3870
URL: http://www.tchospice.org/

Orange City

19459 ■ Halifax Health Hospice of Volusia/Flagler West Volusia Care Center
1625 Veterans Memorial Pkwy.
Orange City, FL 32763
Ph: (386)584-7600
Fax: (386)851-7625
URL: http://www.halifaxhealth.org/locations/hospiceofvolusiaflagler.aspx

Orlando

19460 ■ Samaritan Care Hospice
1300 N Semoran Blvd., Ste. 210
Orlando, FL 32807
Ph: (407)514-1300
Fax: (407)514-1301
E-mail: eva.sylvester@fundltc.com
URL: http://www.samcarehospice.com/

Ormond Beach

19461 ■ Florida Hospital Memorial Hospice Care
770 W Granada Blvd., Ste. 304
Ormond Beach, FL 32174
Ph: (386)671-2138
Free: 800-404-1133
Fax: (386)672-0314
E-mail: fhmshospicecare@fhms.org
URL: http://www.fhhospicecare.org/

19462 ■ Florida Hospital Oceanside Inpatient Unit
264 S Atlantic Ave.
Ormond Beach, FL 32176
Ph: (386)672-4161
Fax: (386)673-5063
URL: http://www.floridahospitalmemorial.org/

19463 ■ Hospice of Volusia/Flagler
555 W Granada Blvd., Ste. H-8
Ormond Beach, FL 32174
Ph: (386)673-7770
Free: 800-272-2717
Fax: (386)673-9945
URL: http://www.hovf.org/locations.aspx

Palatka

19464 ■ Roberts Hospice Care Center
6400 St. Johns Ave.
Palatka, FL 32177-6817
Ph: (386)328-7100
Free: 800-568-6551
Fax: (386)328-8172
URL: http://www.havenhospice.org/locations_palatka.html?hh=3
Formerly: Hospice of North Central Florida/Hospice of the Lakes.

Palm Bay

19465 ■ William Childs Hospice House
381 Medplex Pkwy.
Palm Bay, FL 32907
Ph: (321)434-8400
Fax: (321)952-0494
URL: http://www.health-first.org/hospitals_services/hospice_house.cfm

Palm Beach Gardens

19466 ■ Hospice of Palm Beach County, Inc-Palm Beach Gardens Medical Center
3360 Burns Rd.
Palm Beach Gardens, FL 33410
Ph: (561)625-5080
Fax: (561)863-2955
E-mail: info@hpbc.com
URL: http://www.hpbc.com/about/units-offices.shtml#regional

Palm Coast

19467 ■ Hospice of Volusia/Flager
7 Florida Park Dr.
Palm Coast, FL 32135
Ph: (386)446-0300
Free: 800-272-2717
URL: http://www.hospicevolusiaflagler.org

19468 ■ Stuart F. Meyer Hospice House
150 Memorial Medical Pkwy.
Palm Coast, FL 32164
Ph: (386)586-1500
Fax: (386)586-1510
URL: http://www.fhhospicecare.org/AboutHospice/Inpatientcareunits/StuartFMeyerHo spiceHouse.aspx

Palm Harbor

19469 ■ Suncoast Hospice House Brookside
164 W Lake Rd.
Palm Harbor, FL 34684
Ph: (727)523-2101
Fax: (727)523-4125
URL: http://www.thehospice.org/find_care/hospice_houses.aspx

19470 ■ Suncoast Hospice North Community Center--Palm Harbor
2675 Tampa Rd.
Palm Harbor, FL 34684-3109
Ph: (727)586-4432
Fax: (727)581-5846
URL: http://www.thehospice.org
Formerly: Hospice of the Florida Suncoast.

Palmetto

19471 ■ Ellenton GIP
4151 37th St. E
Palmetto, FL 34221
Ph: (941)845-3000
Fax: (941)723-3255

19472 ■ Tidewell Hospice of Southwest Florida - East Office
4151 37th St. E
Palmetto, FL 34221
Ph: (941)845-3000
Free: 800-959-4291
Fax: (941)721-8252
E-mail: info@tidewell.org
URL: http://tidewell.org/index.html

Panama City

19473 ■ Covenant Hospice, Inc.--Panama City
107 W 19th St.
Panama City, FL 32405
Ph: (850)785-3040
Free: 866-785-3040
Fax: (859)785-2552
URL: http://www.covenanthospice.org/PanamaCity/

19474 ■ Gentiva Hospice--Panama City
2925 Martin Luther King Blvd.
Panama City, FL 32405-4411
Ph: (850)769-0055
Fax: (850)769-0321
URL: http://www.gentiva.com/
Formerly: Hospice of the Emerald Coast.

Pembroke Pines

19475 ■ VITAS Inpatient Hospice Unit Memorial Hospital Pembroke
7800 Sheridan St.
Pembroke Pines, FL 33024
Ph: (954)963-8003
Fax: (954)986-8318
URL: http://www.vitas.com

Pensacola

19476 ■ Covenant Hospice, Inc.--Pensacola
2001 N Palafox St.
Pensacola, FL 32501
Ph: (850)202-0840
URL: http://www.covenanthospice.org/
Formerly: Hospice of Northwest Florida.

19477 ■ Emerald Coast Hospice-Pensacola
1555 N. Pala Fox street
Pensacola, FL 32504
Ph: (850)438-2201
Free: 800-531-9513
Fax: (850)474-7289
URL: http://www.gentiva.com/hospice/hospice_locations.php#fl

19478 ■ Joyce Goldenberg Hospice Inpatient Residence
10075 Hillview Dr.
Pensacola, FL 32514-5469
Ph: (850)484-3529
Free: 800-541-3072
Fax: (850)484-2770
URL: http://www.covenanthospice.org/

Perry

19479 ■ Big Bend Hospice, Inc. Perry Office
107 E Green St.
Perry, FL 32347
Ph: (850)838-3096
Fax: (850)838-1406
URL: http://www.bigbendhospice.org

Pinellas Park

19480 ■ Hospice House-Woodside
6770 102nd Ave.
Pinellas Park, FL 33782-2909
Ph: (727)586-4432
URL: http://www.thehospice.org/

Port Charlotte

19481 ■ Tidewell Hospice and Palliative Care Port Charlotte Office
1144 Veronica St.
Port Charlotte, FL 33952
Ph: (941)979-4300
Free: 800-959-4291
E-mail: info@tidewell.org
URL: http://tidewell.org/index.html
Formerly: Hospice of Southwest Florida.

19482 ■ Tidewill Hospice and Palliative Care Port Charlotte House
1158 Veronica St.
Port Charlotte, FL 33952
Ph: (941)979-4355
Free: 800-959-4291
E-mail: info@tidewell.org
URL: http://tidewell.org/locations.html

Port Orange

19483 ■ Hospice of Volusia/Flagler
3800 Woodbriar Trl.
Port Orange, FL 32129
Ph: (386)322-4701
Free: 800-272-2717
Fax: (386)322-4702
URL: http://www.hfch.org/

Port Saint Lucie

19484 ■ Treasure Coast Hospice North
10360 S Federal Hwy.
Port Saint Lucie, FL 34952
Ph: (772)335-7862
Fax: (772)403-4518
URL: http://www.tchospice.org/
Formerly: Hospice of Martin and Saint Lucie, Inc.

Punta Gorda

19485 ■ Tidewell Hospice Inc-Punta Gorda
900 Tamiami Trail, Unite 111
Punta Gorda, FL 33950
Ph: (941)205-0200
E-mail: info@tidewell.org
URL: http://www.tidewell.org/locations.html

Quincy

19486 ■ Big Bend Hospice, Inc.
Quincy Office
105 N Jackson St.
Quincy, FL 32351
Ph: (850)875-4973
Fax: (850)627-1338
URL: http://www.bigbendhospice.org

Ruskin

19487 ■ LifePath Hospice and Palliative Care--Ruskin
Sun City Center Community Resource Center
3725 Upper Creek Dr.
Ruskin, FL 33573
Ph: (813)634-7621
Free: 800-634-7621
Fax: (813)633-3861
URL: http://www.lifepath-hospice.org

Saint Augustine

19488 ■ Haven House Hospice-St. Augustine
200 Southpark Blvd., Ste. 207
Saint Augustine, FL 32086
Ph: (904)810-2377
URL: http://www.havenhospice.org/

Sarasota

19489 ■ Tidewell Hospice and Palliative Care Administrative Office
5955 Rand Blvd.
Sarasota, FL 34238
Ph: (941)552-7500
Free: 800-959-4291
E-mail: info@tidewell.org
URL: http://tidewell.org/locations.html
Formerly: Hospice of Southwest Florida.

19490 ■ Tidewell Hospice and Palliative Care, Inc.
Sarasota Team Administrative Office
1751 Mound St.
Sarasota, FL 34236
Ph: (941)487-3100
Free: 800-959-4291
Fax: (941)929-2373
E-mail: info@tidewell.org
URL: http://tidewell.org/locations.html

Sebring

19491 ■ Cornerstone Hospice-Sebring
231 US Hwy. 27 N
Village Fountain Plaza
Sebring, FL 33870
Ph: (863)382-4563
Free: 800-503-5756
Fax: (863)295-7909
URL: http://cshospice.org/

19492 ■ Good Shepherd Hospice Inc-Sebring
4418 Sun 'N Lake Blvd.
Sebring, FL 33872
Ph: (863)402-1066
Free: 888-748-1066
Fax: (863)402-0230
URL: http://www.goodshepherdhospice.org/locations/

Stuart

19493 ■ Harper House/Hay - Madeira House Hospice
1000 SE Rhunke St.
Stuart, FL 34994
Ph: (772)419-0460
URL: http://www.tchospice.org

19494 ■ Treasure Coast Hospices-South
1201 SE Indian St.
Stuart, FL 34997
Ph: (772)403-4500
Free: 800-299-4677
Fax: (772)403-4513
URL: http://www.tchospice.org
Formerly: Hospice of Martin and Saint Lucie, Inc.

Summerfield

19495 ■ Tuscany House
17395 SE 109th Terrace Rd.
Summerfield, FL 34491
Ph: (352)307-3417
Fax: (352)245-2938
URL: http://www.hospiceofmarion.com

Sumterville

19496 ■ Lane Purcell House
2294 CR 526 E
Sumterville, FL 33585
Ph: (352)343-1341
Free: 888-728-6234
Fax: (352)742-1618
URL: http://cshospice.org/?about_us/inpatient-care/hospice-houses.html

Sun City Center

19497 ■ Hospice House--Sun City Center
908 American Eagle Blvd.
Sun City Center, FL 33573-5228
Ph: (813)634-9000
Free: 800-209-2200
URL: http://www.goodshepherdhospice.org

Tallahassee

19498 ■ Big Bend Hospice, Inc.
Tallahassee Office
1723 Mahan Center Blvd.
Tallahassee, FL 32308
Ph: (850)878-5310
Free: 800-772-5862
Fax: (850)309-1638
URL: http://www.bigbendhospice.org

19499 ■ Covenant Hospice--Tallahassee
1545 Raymond Diehl Rd., Ste. 102
Tallahassee, FL 32308
Ph: (850)575-4998
Free: 800-541-3072
Fax: (850)386-9161
URL: http://www.covenanthospice.org/

Tamarac

19500 ■ University Medical Center Hospice
VITAS Inpatient Hospital Unit
7201 N University Dr.
Tamarac, FL 33321
Ph: (954)724-6290
Fax: (954)726-2705
URL: http://www.vitas.com

Tampa

19501 ■ Life Path Hospice
3010 W Azeele St.
Tampa, FL 33609
Ph: (813)877-2200
Free: 800-209-2200
Fax: (813)872-7037
URL: http://www.lifepath-hospice.org/

Tavares

19502 ■ Cornerstone Hospice & Palliative Care-Tavares
2455 Lane Park Rd.
Tavares, FL 32778
Ph: (352)343-1341
Free: 888-728-6234
Fax: (866)303-1184
URL: http://cshospice.org/index.php
Formerly: Hospice of Lake and Sumter/Cornerstone Hospice.

19503 ■ Frank & Helen DeScipio Hospice House-Tavares
2445 Lane Park Rd.
Tavares, FL 32778
Ph: (352)343-1341
Fax: (352)742-1618
URL: http://cshospice.org/?about_us/inpatient-care/hospice-houses.html

Tavernier

19504 ■ HospiceCare of Southeast Florida, Inc.
91256 Overseas Hwy.
Tavernier, FL 33070
Ph: (305)852-3223
Free: 866-221-3574
Fax: (305)852-8223
E-mail: monroe@hospicecareflorida.org
URL: http://www.hospicecareflorida.org

19505 ■ VITAS Innovative Hospice Care of Dade-Monroe Tavernier
90290 Overseas Hwy., Ste. 101
Tavernier, FL 33070
Ph: (305)374-4143
Fax: (305)350-6784
URL: http://www.vitas.com/Aboutus/Locations/Florida/tabid/184/Default.aspx

Temple Terrace

19506 ■ LifePath Hospice and Palliative Care--Temple Terrace
11150 N. 53rd Street
Temple Terrace, FL 33616
Ph: (863)908-7650
Fax: (863)402-0230
URL: http://www.lifepath-hospice.org

Titusville

19507 ■ Hospice of Saint Francis, Inc.
1250-B Gruman Pl.
Titusville, FL 32780
Ph: (321)269-4240
Free: 866-269-4240
Fax: (321)269-5428
E-mail: hosf@hospiceofstfrancis.com
URL: http://hospiceofstfrancis.com

Trinity

19508 ■ Gulfside Center for Hospice Care at Trinity
2144 Welbilt Blvd.
Trinity, FL 34655
Ph: (727)376-3658
Fax: (727)375-5259
URL: http://www.grhospice.org/locations.html

Venice

19509 ■ Tidewell Hospice and Palliative Care Venice House
220 Wexford Blvd.
Venice, FL 34293-4463
Ph: (941)441-2000
Free: 800-959-4291
E-mail: info@tidewell.org
URL: http://tidewell.org/locations.html
Formerly: Hospice of Southwest Florida.

Vero Beach

19510 ■ Visiting Nurse Association Corporate Headquarters
1110 35th Ln.
Vero Beach, FL 32960-6549
Ph: (772)567-5551
Free: 800-749-5760
Fax: (772)569-4174
URL: http://www.vnatc.com/home/pages/ContactUs.cfm
Formerly: Visiting Nurse Association Hospice of Indian River County.

19511 ■ VNA Hospice House-Vero Beach
901 37th St.
Vero Beach, FL 32960-6504
Ph: (772)978-5600
Free: 800-749-5760
Fax: (772)567-9938
URL: http://www.vnatc.com/home/pages/ContactUs.cfm
Formerly: Visiting Nurse Association Hospice of Indian River County.

Viera

19512 ■ Wuesthoff Hospice & Palliative Care
8060 Spyglass Hill Rd.
Viera, FL 32940
Ph: (321)253-2222
Free: 800-259-2007
E-mail: judy.powers@wuesthoff.org
URL: http://www.brevardhospice.org/

West Melbourne

19513 ■ Hospice of Health First, Inc.
1900 Dairy Rd.
West Melbourne, FL 32904-4046
Ph: (321)952-0494
Free: 888-434-3730
E-mail: info@health-first.org
URL: http://www.health-first.org/

West Palm Beach

19514 ■ Hospice of Palm Beach County, Inc.--West Palm Beach
5300 East Ave.
West Palm Beach, FL 33407-2387
Ph: (561)848-5200
Free: 888-848-5200
Fax: (561)863-2955
E-mail: info@hpbc.com
URL: http://www.hpbc.com/

19515 ■ VITAS Innovtive Hospice Care of Palm Beach Satellite Office
4360 Northlake Blvd., Ste. 114
West Palm Beach, FL 33410
Ph: (305)374-4143
Fax: (305)350-6784
URL: http://www.vitas.com/Aboutus/Locations/Florida/tabid/184/Default.aspx

Winter Haven

19516 ■ Cornerstone Hospice-Winter Haven
2590 Havendale Blvd. NW
Winter Haven, FL 33881
Ph: (863)291-5560
Free: 800-503-5756
Fax: (863)295-7909
URL: http://cshospice.org/?contact-us/directions.html

Winter Park

19517 ■ VITAS Inpatient Hospice Unit HCR Manor Care
2075 Loch Lomond Dr.
Winter Park, FL 32792
Ph: (407)670-6400
Fax: (407)640-6430
URL: http://www.vitas.com

19518 ■ Winter Park
200 N Lakemont
Winter Park, FL 32792
Ph: (407)599-6044
Fax: (407)599-6045
URL: http://www.winterparkhospital.com

Zephyrhills

19519 ■ Gulfside Regional Hospice Inc.--Zephyrhills
5760 Dean Dairy Rd.
Zephyrhills, FL 33542
Ph: (813)377-1265
URL: http://www.grhospice.org/locations.html

GEORGIA

Albany

19520 ■ Albany Community Hospice
2332 Lake Park Dr.
Albany, GA 31707
Ph: (229)312-7050
Free: 800-417-0057
Fax: (229)312-7055
URL: http://www.albanycommunityhospice.com/

19521 ■ Englewood Hospice Care, Inc.
507 N Jefferson St.
Albany, GA 31705
Ph: (229)435-2109
Fax: (229)435-0729
E-mail: ewhealth@bellsouth.net
URL: http://englewoodhealthsystems.com/hospice.htm

Alpharetta

19522 ■ Omega Health Care of Georgia
8560 Holcomb Bridge Rd., Ste. 110
Alpharetta, GA 30022
Ph: (678)240-4190
Fax: (678)240-4189
URL: http://www.omega-healthcare.com/web/Locations/tabid/58/Default.aspx

Americus

19523 ■ Phoebe Sumter Hospice
1048 E Forsyth St.
Americus, GA 31709
Ph: (229)924-6011
Fax: (229)928-1322
URL: http://www.phoebesumter.org/getpage.php?name=focusonliving

Athens

19524 ■ Hospice Advantage-Athens
135 Athens W Pkwy.
Athens, GA 30606
Ph: (706)354-1707
Fax: (706)354-1708
URL: http://www.hospiceadvantage.net/

19525 ■ Odyssey Healthcare of Athens
855 Gaines School Rd., Ste. G
Athens, GA 30605
Ph: (706)549-5736
Free: 877-637-9432
Fax: (706)208-1530
URL: http://www.odsyhealth.com/

19526 ■ Silverleaf Hospice
435 Hawthorne Ave. Ste. 500
Athens, GA 30606
Ph: (706)546-0286
Fax: (706)546-0289
URL: http://silverleafhospice.com/999/index.php?page/Home.html

Atlanta

19527 ■ Altus Healthcare and Hospice, Inc.
1 Dunwoody Park, Ste. 128
Atlanta, GA 30338
Ph: (770)730-8405
Fax: (770)730-8408
URL: http://www.altushospice.com/

19528 ■ AseraCare Hospice--Atlanta
30 Perimeter Park Dr., Ste. 201
Atlanta, GA 30341
Ph: (770)698-8785
Free: 800-974-4677
Fax: (770)698-9775
URL: http://hospice.aseracare.com/home.aspx

19529 ■ Compassionate Healthcare Mgmt Group Inc/dba Compassionate Hospice of North GA
1801 Peachtree St., Ste. 100
Atlanta, GA 30309
Ph: (678)651-1440
Fax: (678)651-1470
URL: http://www.chcmg.com/

19530 ■ First Quality Healthcare
3915 Cascade Rd. SW, Ste. 105
Atlanta, GA 30331-8512
Ph: (404)696-4126
Fax: (404)696-1429
E-mail: info@firstqualityhealthcare.net
URL: http://www.firstqualityhealthcare.net/

19531 ■ Guardian Hospice of Atlanta
4360 Chamblee Dunwoody Rd., Ste. 535
Atlanta, GA 30341
Ph: (770)458-1624
Free: 877-458-1624
Fax: (770)458-2390
URL: http://www.guardianhospice.us/

19532 ■ Hospice Atlanta-Visiting Nurse Health System
1244 Park Vista Dr. NE
Atlanta, GA 30319
Ph: (404)869-3000
Fax: (404)869-3099
URL: http://www.vnhs.org/services/hospice.aspx

19533 ■ Odyssey HealthCare of Georgia
2302 Parklake Dr. NE, Ste. 150
Atlanta, GA 30345
Ph: (678)937-1800
Free: 877-637-9432
Fax: (678)937-1901
URL: http://www.odsyhealth.com/

19534 ■ VistaCare Center at Wesley Woods
Bud Terrace Bldg., 6th Fl.
1833 Clifton Rd. NE
Atlanta, GA 30329
Ph: (404)638-3600
Fax: (404)633-3611
E-mail: mdellorso@odsyhealth.com
URL: http://www.vistacare.com/

19535 ■ VITAS Hospice, Atlanta Metro
1575 Northside Dr. NW, Ste. 470
Atlanta, GA 30318
Ph: (404)250-1806
Fax: (404)875-4363
URL: http://www.vitas.com

19536 ■ Weinstein Hospice-Yad V'Lev
3150 Howell Mill Rd. NW
Atlanta, GA 30351
Ph: (404)352-4308
Fax: (404)351-0182
E-mail: info@weinsteinhospice.org
URL: http://www.weinsteinhospice.com/

Augusta

19537 ■ Alliance Hospice
3685 Old Petersburg Rd., Ste. 145
Augusta, GA 30907
Ph: (706)447-2461
Free: 877-440-2461
Fax: (706)447-2465
URL: http://www.alliancehospice.com

19538 ■ Heartland Hospice Services--Augusta
1365 Interstate Pkwy.
Augusta, GA 30909
Ph: (706)860-7374
Fax: (706)860-9410
URL: http://www.hcr-manorcare.com

19539 ■ Odyssey Hospice-Augusta
3508 Professional Circle, Ste. A
Augusta, GA 30907
Ph: (706)210-5900
Fax: (706)228-1601
URL: http://www.odsyhealth.com

19540 ■ Regency Hospice-Augusta
2919 Professional Pkwy., Ste. A
Augusta, GA 30907
Ph: (706)868-4422
Fax: (706)868-4424
URL: http://www.regencyhospice.com

19541 ■ Trinity Hospice-Augusta
2260 Wrightsboro Rd.
Augusta, GA 30904
Ph: (706)481-7000
URL: http://www.trinityofaugusta.com/Pages/home.aspx

Austell

19542 ■ Wellstar Community Hospice
4040 Hospital W Dr.
Austell, GA 30106-8117
Ph: (770)732-6710
Fax: (770)732-6732
URL: http://www.wellstar.org/ws_content/ws_medical_services.aspx?id=274&menu_id=78

Bainbridge

19543 ■ Gentiva Hospice, Bainbridge
430 E Shotwell St.
Bainbridge, GA 39819-4058
Ph: (229)246-1941
Fax: (229)246-1991
URL: http://www.gentiva.com/
Formerly: Wiregrass Hospice, Bainbridge.

19544 ■ Hospice of Southwest Georgia--Bainbridge
1323 E Shotwell St.
Bainbridge, GA 39819
Ph: (229)246-9965
Free: 800-290-6567
Fax: (229)246-9644
URL: http://bainbridgega.com/bainbridge/hospice.shtml

Baxley

19545 ■ Hospice of South Georgia, Inc.--Baxley
37 Tippins St.
Baxley, GA 31513
Ph: (912)366-1733
E-mail: sheryl.boinski@sgmc.org
URL: http://www.hospiceofsouthgeorgia.org/

Bogart

19546 ■ VistaCare Hospice-Bogart
150 Ben Burton Rd.
Bogart, GA 30622
Ph: (706)369-9888
Free: 877-228-9888
Fax: (706)369-9793
E-mail: dzadorozny@vistacare.com
URL: http://www.vistacare.com/search_results.asp

Brunswick

19547 ■ Heartland Hospice Services--Brunswick
1109 Fountain Lake Dr.
Brunswick, GA 31525
Ph: (912)261-8760
Fax: (912)261-8931
URL: http://www.hcr-manorcare.com/

19548 ■ Hospice of the Golden Isles
1692 Glynco Pkwy.
Brunswick, GA 31525
Ph: (912)265-4735
Free: 866-275-6801
Fax: (912)265-6100
URL: http://www.hospice.me/

Calhoun

19549 ■ At Peace Hospice Care
216B Newtown Rd.
Calhoun, GA 30701
Ph: (706)602-4975
Free: 877-444-0330
Fax: (706)602-4976
URL: http://atpeacehospicecare.com/

Carrollton

19550 ■ Tanner Hospice Care
101 Clinic Ave.
Carrollton, GA 30117
Ph: (770)214-2355
URL: http://www.tanner.org/Main/Hospice.aspx

Cartersville

19551 ■ Amedisys Hospice Care of Cartersville
1217 Joe Frank Harris Pkwy. SE
Cartersville, GA 30120
Ph: (770)382-0114
Free: 866-313-1217
Fax: (770)382-1393
URL: http://www.amedisys.com/hospice.cfm

19552 ■ Heartland Hospice Care-Cartersville
20 Collins Dr., Ste. A
Cartersville, GA 30121
Ph: (770)382-0721
Fax: (770)382-1263
URL: http://www.hcr-manorcare.com/

19553 ■ Omega Health Care of NW Georgia
27 Maple Ridge Dr., Ste. A
Cartersville, GA 30121-2293
Ph: (770)382-5055
Fax: (770)382-7488
E-mail: chide@omega-healthcare.com
URL: http://www.omega-healthcare.com/web/

19554 ■ Regency Hospice, LLC--Cartersville
20 B Fox Chase
Cartersville, GA 30120
Ph: (770)382-7175
Fax: (770)382-4927
URL: http://www.regencyhospice.com

College Park

19555 ■ Divine Hospice Care
Bldg. G, Ste. 150
5532 Old National Hwy.
College Park, GA 30349
Ph: (404)762-6880

Columbus

19556 ■ Columbus Hospice of Alabama
7020 Moon Rd.
Columbus, GA 31909
Ph: (706)569-7992
Fax: (706)569-8560
E-mail: m.smajd@columbushospice.com
URL: http://www.columbushospice.com/

19557 ■ VistaCare-Columbus Georgia
100 Brookstone Centre Pkwy.
Columbus, GA 31904
Ph: (706)653-0835
Fax: (706)653-8067
E-mail: Tamika.nicholson@vistacare.com
URL: http://www.vistacare.com/search_results.asp

Dalton

19558 ■ Amedisys Hospice Services--Dalton
1510 N Thorton Ave., Ste. 200
Dalton, GA 30720
Ph: (706)259-2518
Free: 877-353-5915
Fax: (706)259-3159
URL: http://www.amedisys.com/hospice.cfm
Formerly: Adventa Hospice Services.

19559 ■ Hamilton Medical Center Hospice
1209 Memorial Dr.
Dalton, GA 30722
Ph: (706)278-2848
Fax: (706)277-7443
URL: http://www.hamiltonhealth.com

19560 ■ Heartlite Hospice Care-Dalton
1011 Abutment Rd., Ste. 108
Dalton, GA 30721
Ph: (706)272-1035
Free: 800-420-2638
Fax: (706)272-1036
URL: http://www.heartlitehospicecare.com/

Decatur

19561 ■ Odyssey HealthCare of Atlanta Inpatient
2362 Lawrenceville Hwy
Decatur, GA 30033
Ph: (404)235-7600
Fax: (404)235-7614
URL: http://www.odsyhealth.com/default.asp

Douglasville

19562 ■ VistaCare--Douglasville
6458 Spring St., Ste. 100
Douglasville, GA 30134
Ph: (770)489-4225
Free: 877-455-9295
Fax: (770)489-8471
URL: http://www.vistacare.com/locations/site.asp?199

Dublin

19563 ■ Hospice of Laurens County
205 N Franklin St.
Dublin, GA 31040-1344
Ph: (478)272-8333
Fax: (478)272-1695
E-mail: hospicelc@bellsouth.net
URL: http://www.hospiceoflaurenscounty.net/

East Ellijay

19564 ■ Hospice Advantage, Inc-East Ellijay
583 Highland Crossing, Ste. 210
East Ellijay, GA 30540
Ph: (706)635-1060
Fax: (706)635-1061
URL: http://www.hospiceadvantage.net/

Fayetteville

19565 ■ Harbor Grace Hospice
500 W Lanier Ave., Ste. 401
Fayetteville, GA 30214
Ph: (678)962-5850
Fax: (678)962-5855
URL: http://www.harborgracehospice.com/

19566 ■ Heartland Hospice--Fayetteville
115 Huntington Park Dr.
Fayetteville, GA 30214
Ph: (770)461-1658
URL: http://www.hcr-manorcare.com/

19567 ■ Hospice Advantage-Fayetteville
101 Yorktown Dr., Ste. 223
Fayetteville, GA 30214
Ph: (678)817-4180
Fax: (678)817-4178
URL: http://www.hospiceadvantage.net/

Fitzgerald

19568 ■ Blue-Gray Community Hospice
815 S Main St.
Fitzgerald, GA 31750
Ph: (229)424-7330
Fax: (229)423-3930
URL: http://www.dorminymedical.net

Fort Oglethorpe

19569 ■ Hutcheson Hospice
100 Mitchell Rd.
Fort Oglethorpe, GA 30742-3683
Ph: (706)866-9854
URL: http://www.hutcheson.org/?pageid=8

Gainesville

19570 ■ Hospice of Northeast Georgia Medical Center
2150 Limestone Pkwy.
Gainesville, GA 30501
Ph: (770)219-8888
Free: 888-572-3900
Fax: (770)219-8887
URL: http://www.nghs.com/Hospice.aspx?id=122
Formerly: Hand in Hand Hospice.

Griffin

19571 ■ Brightmoor Hospice, Inc.
3223 Newnan Rd.
Griffin, GA 30224
Ph: (770)467-9930
Fax: (770)467-9932
URL: http://www.brightmoorhospice.com/

19572 ■ VistaCare--Griffin
242 O'Dell Rd., Unit 4
Griffin, GA 30224
Ph: (770)229-1670
Free: 866-311-6286
Fax: (770)229-9136
URL: http://www.vistacare.com/locations/site.asp?203

Hiawassee

19573 ■ Regency Hospice--Hiawassee
236 S Main St.
Hiawassee, GA 30546
Ph: (706)896-1251
Fax: (706)896-1843
URL: http://www.regencyhospice.com/

Jasper

19574 ■ Georgia Mountains Hospice
70 Caring Way
Jasper, GA 30143-1960
Ph: (706)253-4100
Free: 800-692-7199
Fax: (706)253-4101
URL: http://www.gmhospice.org/

Jesup

19575 ■ Hospice of South Georgia, Inc.--Jesup
117 Drennon Dr.
Jesup, GA 31545-0011
Ph: (912)588-0080
Free: 866-675-9855
Fax: (912)588-0082
E-mail: information@hopiceoga.org
URL: http://hospicesoga.org/

Kennesaw

19576 ■ Amedisys Hospice-Kennesaw
1701 Barrett Lakes Blvd., Ste. 280
Kennesaw, GA 30144
Ph: (770)423-1316
Free: 866-921-1668
Fax: (770)423-1316
URL: http://www.amedisys.com/hospice_locations.cfm?id=4

19577 ■ Hospice Advantage, Inc.--Kennesaw
1925 Vaughn Rd. NW, Ste. 200
Kennesaw, GA 30144
Ph: (770)218-1997
Free: 800--HOSPICE
Fax: (770)218-1975
URL: http://www.hospiceadvantage.net

La Fayette

19578 ■ Countryside Hospice Care--La Fayette
106 Pearl Dr., Unit 107
La Fayette, GA 30728-2924
Free: 800-660-7381
Fax: (706)638-7545
URL: http://www.countrysidehospice.com

Lagrange

19579 ■ West Georgia Hospice
1510 Vernon Rd.
Lagrange, GA 30240-4131
Ph: (706)845-3905
Free: 888-368-3905
Fax: (706)812-2650
URL: http://www.wghealth.org/hospice.html

Lawrenceville

19580 ■ Amedisys Hospice-Lawrenceville
575 Old Norcross Rd., Ste. J
Lawrenceville, GA 30046
Ph: (678)442-7338
Free: 866-693-6866
Fax: (678)442-7410
URL: http://www.amedisys.com/hospice_locations.cfm?id=4

19581 ■ Heathfield Hospice-Lawrenceville
1075 Old Norcross Rd., Ste. S
Lawrenceville, GA 30046
Ph: (678)985-3300
Fax: (770)995-3898
URL: http://www.gentiva.com/location_finder/

19582 ■ VistaCare--Lawrenceville
1000 Hurricane Shoals Rd. NE, Ste. D1200
Lawrenceville, GA 30043
Ph: (678)225-5014
Free: 800-324-7917
Fax: (678)226-2135
URL: http://www.vistacare.com/locations/site.asp?210

Macon

19583 ■ Evercare Hospice & Palliative Care-Macon
4875 Riverside Dr.
Macon, GA 31210
Ph: (478)812-9299
Fax: (478)812-9270
URL: http://www.evercarehospice.com/where_to_find_us.jsp#Georgia

19584 ■ Heartland Hospice Services--Macon
200 Northside Crossing
Macon, GA 31210
Ph: (478)477-0101
URL: http://www.hcr-manorcare.com/

19585 ■ Hospice Care Options, Inc.
1125 Walnut St.
Macon, GA 31201
Ph: (478)743-3033
Free: 800-563-8680
Fax: (478)746-4550
URL: http://www.hcoga.com/agency-locations-and-service-area.da

19586 ■ Hospice of Central Georgia
3780 Eisenhower Pkwy.
Macon, GA 31206
Ph: (478)633-5660
Free: 800-211-1084
Fax: (478)781-3348
E-mail: info@hospiceofcentralgeorgia.org
URL: http://www.hospiceofcentralgeorgia.com/index.asp

Marietta

19587 ■ Gentiva Healthcare-Marietta
1395 S Marietta Pkwy., Ste. 910
Marietta, GA 30067
Ph: (770)951-6100
Free: 888--GENTIVA
Fax: (770)541-3689
URL: http://www.gentiva.com/hospice/index.php
Formerly: Healthfield Hospice - North Atlanta.

19588 ■ Heritage Hospice, Inc.--Marietta
1290 Kennestone Cir., Ste. A-213
Marietta, GA 30066
Ph: (770)423-5959
Fax: (770)432-5944
URL: http://www.heritage-hospice.com

Mcdonough

19589 ■ Embracing Hospice-South Office
2340 Patrick Henry Pkwy.
Mcdonough, GA 30253
Ph: (678)961-2160
Fax: (678)961-2161
E-mail: infoga@americanhospice.com
URL: http://www.hospitalsoup.com/listing/10055-embracing-hospice-emory

Newnan

19590 ■ Amedisys Hospice Care of Newnan
1825 Hwy. 34 E, Ste. 2200
Newnan, GA 30265
Ph: (770)502-3667
Free: 866-694-5374
Fax: (770)502-3657
URL: http://www.amedisys.com/hospice.cfm

19591 ■ VistaCare--Newnan
1585 Hwy. 34 E
Newnan, GA 30265
Ph: (770)251-1367
Free: 800-324-8145
Fax: (770)251-8324
URL: http://www.vistacare.com
Michelle Stone, Executive Director

Norcross

19592 ■ Evercare Hospice and Palliative Care--Norcross
3720 Davinci Ct.
Norcross, GA 30092
Ph: (770)417-2018
Fax: (770)417-2020
URL: http://www.evercarehospice.com/

Rome

19593 ■ Floyd Heyman Hospice Care
304 Turner McCall Blvd.
Rome, GA 30165
Ph: (706)509-5000
Fax: (706)509-3201
E-mail: contactus@floyd.org
URL: http://www.floyd.org/hospice/index.htm

19594 ■ Transition Hospice Care
540 Broad St., Ste. B
Rome, GA 30161
Ph: (706)378-2272
Free: 877-781-2273
Fax: (706)378-3019
E-mail: info@transitionshc.com
URL: http://www.transitionshc.com

Roswell

19595 ■ Creative Hospice Care
10888 Crabapple Rd.
Roswell, GA 30075
Ph: (678)966-0077
Fax: (770)797-9930
URL: http://www.homesteadhospice.net

Savannah

19596 ■ Hospice Savannah, Inc.
PO Box 13190
Savannah, GA 31416
Ph: (912)355-2289
Free: 888-355-4911
Fax: (912)355-2376
URL: http://www.hospicesavannah.org/

19597 ■ Island Hospice - Savannah
3 W Perry St.
Savannah, GA 31401
Ph: (912)629-2727
Fax: (912)629-2729
URL: http://www.thagroup.org

19598 ■ Odyssey Healthcare of Savannah
5105 Paulsen St., Ste. 225D
Savannah, GA 31405
Ph: (912)352-8200
Free: 877-637-9432
Fax: (912)352-8283
E-mail: info@odsyhealth.com
URL: http://www.odsyhealth.com/

19599 ■ Spanish Oaks Hospice
8510 Whitfield Ave.
Savannah, GA 31406
Ph: (912)356-0233
Fax: (912)356-0193

Snellville

19600 ■ Embracing Hospice Inpatient Unit
2160 Fountain Dr.
Snellville, GA 30078
Ph: (678)344-9494
Fax: (678)344-5757
E-mail: infoga@americanhospice.com
URL: http://www.embracinghospicecare.com/

Social Circle

19601 ■ Abbey Hospice
215 Azalea Ct.
Social Circle, GA 30025
Ph: (770)464-5858
Fax: (770)464-5870
E-mail: info@abbeyhospice.com
URL: http://www.abbeyhospice.com

Statesboro

19602 ■ Ogeechee Area Hospice
200 Donehoo St.
Statesboro, GA 30458
Ph: (912)764-8441
Free: 800-236-1142
Fax: (912)489-8247
E-mail: customerRelations@oahospice.org
URL: http://www.ogeecheeareahospice.org/

Stockbridge

19603 ■ Gentiva Hospice--Stockbridge
216 Business Center Dr.
Stockbridge, GA 30281
Ph: (678)289-6044
Fax: (678)565-3408
URL: http://www.gentiva.com/
Formerly: Healthfield Hospice.

19604 ■ VITAS Inpatient Hospice Unit-Stockbridge
931 Rock Quarry Rd.
Stockbridge, GA 30281
Ph: (305)374-4143
Fax: (305)350-6784
URL: http://www.vitas.com/

Thomaston

19605 ■ Thomaston Hospice, Inc.
316 W Gordon St.
Thomaston, GA 30286
Ph: (706)647-2273
Fax: (706)646-3858
URL: http://www.thomastonhospice.com/

Thomasville

19606 ■ Hospice of Southwest Georgia--Thomasville
818 Gordon Ave.
Thomasville, GA 31792-6611
Ph: (229)227-5520
Free: 800-290-6567
Fax: (229)227-5526
URL: http://www.archbold.org/Content/Default/1/15/0/services/hospice.html

Tifton

19607 ■ Hospice of Tift Area
104-1 W 8th St.
Tifton, GA 31794
Ph: (229)353-6330
Free: 800-648-1935
Fax: (229)353-6338
URL: http://www.hospice-of-tiftarea.com/body.cfm?id=52&SubDomain=true

Union City

19608 ■ Southwest Christian Care Hospice
7225 Lester Rd.
Union City, GA 30291
Ph: (770)969-8354
Fax: (770)969-1940
URL: http://www.swchristiancare.org

Valdosta

19609 ■ Hospice of South Georgia--Valdosta
205 Woodrow Wilson Dr.
Valdosta, GA 31602
Ph: (229)249-4100
Fax: (229)249-4102
URL: http://www.hospiceofsouthgeorgia.org
Formerly: South Georgia Medical Center, Hospice of South Georgia.

19610 ■ Langdale Hospice House
2263 Pineview Dr.
Valdosta, GA 31602
Ph: (229)249-4100
Free: 866-810-3354
URL: http://www.hospiceofsouthgeorgia.org/LHH.html

Vidalia

19611 ■ Serenity Hospice Care-Vidalia
304 W First St.
Vidalia, GA 30474
Ph: (912)537-1410

19612 ■ Southern Community Hospice Inc. Community Hospice
904 Mt. Vernon Rd.
Vidalia, GA 30474
Ph: (912)537-0063
Free: 800-477-4758
Fax: (912)537-2005

Villa Rica

19613 ■ Oak Brook Hospice
660 W Bankhead Hwy., Ste. E
Villa Rica, GA 30180
Ph: (678)840-4333
Fax: (678)840-5090
E-mail: info@oakbrookhospice.com
URL: http://www.oakbrookhospice.com/contactus.html

Warner Robins

19614 ■ Heart of Georgia Hospice
103 Westridge Dr.
Warner Robins, GA 31088-8111
Ph: (478)953-5161
Fax: (478)953-5232
URL: http://www.heartofgahospice.org/
Formerly: Hospice of Houston County.

19615 ■ Vista Care-Warner Robins
319 Margie Dr.
Warner Robins, GA 31088
Ph: (478)953-1016
Free: 888-493-8779
Fax: (478)953-1044
E-mail: Jessica.kitchens@vistacare.com
URL: http://www.vistacare.com

Watkinsville

19616 ■ St. Mary's Hospice=Watkinsville
1021 Jamestown Blvd.
Watkinsville, GA 30677
Ph: (706)389-2273
Fax: (706)389-2259
URL: http://www.stmarysathens.org

HAWAII

Hilo

19617 ■ Hospice of Hilo
1011 Waianuenue Ave.
Hilo, HI 96720-2019
Ph: (808)969-1733
Fax: (808)969-4863
E-mail: hospice@hospiceofhilo.org
URL: http://www.hospiceofhilo.org/

Honolulu

19618 ■ Bristol Hospice, Hawaii LLC
Waterfront Plaza Four
500 Ala Moana Blvd., Ste. 4-545 & 547
Honolulu, HI 96814
Ph: (808)536-8012
Fax: (808)536-8013

19619 ■ Hospice Hawaii Inc.
860 Iwilei Rd.
Honolulu, HI 96817-5018
Ph: (808)924-9255
Fax: (808)922-9161
E-mail: info@hospicehawaii.org
URL: http://www.hospicehawaii.org/

19620 ■ Hospice Hawaii, Inc. Palolo House
2449 10th Ave.
Honolulu, HI 96816
Ph: (808)732-6354
Fax: (808)732-6375
URL: http://www.hospicehawaii.org/

19621 ■ Saint Francis Hospice Program Sister Maurueen Keleher Center
24 Puiwa Rd.
Honolulu, HI 96817-1127
Ph: (808)595-7566
Fax: (808)595-6996
URL: http://www.stfrancishawaii.org/About/Pages/SisterMaureenKeleher.aspx

Kailua

19622 ■ Hospice Hawaii Kailua House
566 Papalani St.
Kailua, HI 96734
Ph: (808)262-4055
Fax: (808)263-9767
E-mail: info@hospicehawaii.org
URL: http://www.hospicehawaii.org/

Kailua Kona

19623 ■ Hospice of Kona
75-5925 Walua Rd.
Kailua Kona, HI 96740
Ph: (808)324-7700
Fax: (808)331-0767
URL: http://www.hospiceofkona.org
Victoria Calvin, Director

Kamuela

19624 ■ North Hawaii Hospice, Inc.
65-1328 Kawaihae Rd.
Kamuela, HI 96743
Ph: (808)885-7547
Fax: (808)885-5592
E-mail: nhh.office@northhawaiiantel.net
URL: http://www.northhawaiihospice.org

Kaunakakai

19625 ■ Hospice Hawaii, Inc. Molokal
PO Box 408
Kaunakakai, HI 96748
Ph: (808)553-4310
Fax: (808)553-3183
URL: http://www.hospicehawaii.org/

Lihue

19626 ■ Kauai Hospice
4457 Pahee St.
Lihue, HI 96766
Ph: (808)245-7277
Fax: (808)245-5006
E-mail: info@kauaihospice.org
URL: http://www.kauaihospice.org/

Wailuku

19627 ■ Hospice Maui
400 Mahalani St.
Wailuku, HI 96793-2547
Ph: (808)244-5555
Fax: (808)244-5557
E-mail: hospice@maui.net
URL: http://www.hospicemaui.org/

IDAHO

Boise

19628 ■ A Better Way Home
12345 W Mercedes St.
Boise, ID 83713
Ph: (208)322-4663
Fax: (208)322-6087
URL: http://www.betterwayid.com/

19629 ■ Four Rivers Hospice
7941 W Rifleman St.
Boise, ID 83706
Ph: (208)367-7343
Free: 866-750-9109
Fax: (208)367-4566
URL: http://www.amedisys.com/hospice_locations.cfm
Formerly: Four Rivers HH and Hospice.

19630 ■ Life's Doors Hospice
420 S Orchard St.
Boise, ID 83705
Ph: (208)344-6500
Fax: (208)344-6590
E-mail: info@lifesdoors.com
URL: http://www.lifesdoors.com/

19631 ■ Phillippi Cottage
1121 S. Phillippi
Boise, ID 83705
Ph: (208)344-6500
Fax: (208)344-6590
URL: http://www.lifesdoors.com/phillipi.htm

19632 ■ Saint Luke's Hospice--Bosie
325 W Idaho St.
Boise, ID 83702
Ph: (208)381-2721
URL: http://www.stlukesonline.org/boise/specialties_and_services/hospice/

Burley

19633 ■ Intermountain Healthcare Hospice
1501 Hiland Ave.
Burley, ID 83318-2682
Ph: (208)678-8844
Free: 800-527-1118
Fax: (208)678-6314
URL: http://intermountainhealthcare.org/hospitals/cassia/Pages/home.aspx

Caldwell

19634 ■ Hearth 'n Home Hospice & Palliative Care-Caldwell
822 S 10th Ave.
Caldwell, ID 83605
Ph: (208)454-0262
Free: 800--HOSPICE
Fax: (208)454-0232
URL: http://www.heartnhomehospice.com/Office_Caldwell.php
Minda Jacobson, Executive Director

Chubbuck

19635 ■ Access Home Care and Hospice--Chubbuck
190 W Burnside Ave., Ste. E
Chubbuck, ID 83202
Ph: (208)637-2273
Fax: (208)637-8867
E-mail: info@accesshomecareandhospice.com
URL: http://accesshomecareandhospice.com/

Coeur D Alene

19636 ■ Applegate HomeCare and Hospice--Coeur D Alene
700 W Ironwood Dr., Ste. 300
Coeur D Alene, ID 83814
Ph: (208)765-2273
Fax: (208)666-0289
URL: http://www.applegatehomecare.com/Pages/About.aspx

Eagle

19637 ■ Boise Memorial Hospice
600 E State St., Ste. 300
Eagle, ID 83616
Ph: (208)938-4100
Fax: (208)938-4564
URL: http://www.boisememorialhospice.com/

Emmett

19638 ■ Heart 'n Home Hospice & Palliative Care-Emmett
306 S Washington
Emmett, ID 83617
Ph: (208)365-2099
Fax: (208)365-2902
URL: http://www.heartnhomehospice.com/

19639 ■ XI Hospice, Inc-Emmett Branch
1015 S Johns Ave.
Emmett, ID 83617
Ph: (208)365-6303
Fax: (208)365-6330

19640 ■ XI Hospice Inc-Meridian Branch
1717 N Crestmont Dr.
Emmett, ID 83646
Ph: (208)887-6200
Fax: (208)887-6224

Fruitland

19641 ■ Heart 'n Home Hospice and Palliative Care--Fruitland
1100 NW 12th St.
Fruitland, ID 83619
Ph: (208)452-2663
Free: 866-278-3662
Fax: (208)452-2665
URL: http://www.heartnhomehospice.com/
Sandy Bowen, Executive Director

Grangeville

19642 ■ Syringa General Hospital Hospice Program
607 W Main St.
Grangeville, ID 83530
Ph: (208)983-1700
Free: 800-772-5137
Fax: (208)983-0863
URL: http://www.syringahospital.org

Hayden

19643 ■ Hospice of North Idaho
9493 N Government Way
Hayden, ID 83835
Ph: (208)772-7994
Free: 800-388-4677
Fax: (208)772-5916
E-mail: hospice@honi.org
URL: http://www.honi.org/

Idaho Falls

19644 ■ Hands of Hope Hospice, Inc.
1379 E 17th St.
Idaho Falls, ID 83404
Ph: (208)523-7441
Fax: (208)542-0528
E-mail: info@handsofhopehospice.com
URL: http://www.handsofhopehospice.com/

19645 ■ Hospice of Eastern Idaho, Inc.
1810 Moran St.
Idaho Falls, ID 83401-4337
Ph: (208)529-0342
Fax: (208)529-6981
E-mail: hei@ida.net
URL: http://www.hospiceofeasternidaho.com/

19646 ■ Solace Health Care
Idaho Falls, ID 83401
Ph: (208)757-8444
Fax: (208)965-8351

Jerome

19647 ■ Hospice Visions Hospice Home
539 E 100 S
Jerome, ID 83338
Ph: (208)324-3763

Ketchum

19648 ■ Hospice of the Wood River Valley
507 1st Ave. N
Ketchum, ID 83340-4320
Ph: (208)726-8464
Fax: (208)726-7686
E-mail: hospice@hwrv.svcoxmail.com
URL: http://www.hpcwrv.org

Lewiston

19649 ■ Family Hospice
Saint Joseph Regional Medical Center
1250 Idaho St.
Lewiston, ID 83501
Ph: (208)799-5275
Fax: (208)799-5343
URL: https://www.sjrmc.org/services/family-hospice/

Meridian

19650 ■ Harrison's Hope...A Caring Place
1979 N Locust Grove
Meridian, ID 83646
Ph: (208)947-6800
Fax: (208)947-6806
E-mail: contact@harrisonshope.com
URL: http://www.harrisonshope.com/

19651 ■ Heart 'n Home Hospice-Meridian
3557 E Overland Rd.
Meridian, ID 83642
Ph: (208)288-1143
Fax: (208)288-1145
URL: http://www.heartnhomehospice.com/

19652 ■ Hearts for Hospice--Meridian
3090 Gentry Way, Ste. 150
Meridian, ID 83642
Ph: (208)389-2276
Fax: (208)389-2282
E-mail: infohearts@heartsforhospice.com
URL: http://www.heartsforhospice.com

19653 ■ Horizon Home Health and Hospice Inc.
900 N Linder Rd.
Meridian, ID 83642
Ph: (208)888-7877
Fax: (208)888-7987
URL: http://www.horizonhh.com/

19654 ■ Legacy Hospice Meridian
680 S Progress Ave., Ste. 2A
Meridian, ID 83642
Ph: (208)888-3669
Fax: (208)898-3675
URL: http://www.legacyhomecare.com/

Nampa

19655 ■ Journeys Hospice, Inc.
223 E Amity Ave.
Nampa, ID 83686
Ph: (208)461-3035
Fax: (208)466-0693
E-mail: journeys@journeys-hospice.com
URL: http://www.journeys-hospice.com/

Payette

19656 ■ XL Hospice, Inc.--Payette
2480 Hwy 52
Payette, ID 83661
Ph: (208)642-9222
Free: 800-574-5911
Fax: (208)652-9224
E-mail: sarah@xlhospice.com
URL: http://www.xlhospice.com/

Resburg

19657 ■ Rexburg Home Health and Hospice
280 E Maine
Resburg, ID 83440
Ph: (208)356-6688
Fax: (208)359-9725
URL: http://www.theaspengroup.net/locations.html

Saint Maries

19658 ■ Hospice of Benewah County
702 W College Ave.
Saint Maries, ID 83861
Ph: (208)245-5734
Fax: (208)245-5734

Salmon

19659 ■ Hospice of Salmon Valley
506 Van Dreff St.
Salmon, ID 83467
Ph: (208)756-6122
Fax: (208)756-6126

Sandpoint

19660 ■ Bonner Community Hospice
PO Box 1448
Sandpoint, ID 83864-0877
Ph: (208)265-1179
Fax: (208)265-1085
URL: http://www.bonnergeneral.org/index.php?option=com_content&view=article&id=88:hospice&catid=63:medical-services&Itemid=155

Twin Falls

19661 ■ Hospice Visions
209 Shoup Ave. W
Twin Falls, ID 83301
Ph: (208)735-0121
Free: 800-735-0121
Fax: (208)735-0661
E-mail: tvg@thevisionsgroup.org
URL: http://www.thevisionsgroup.org/

ILLINOIS

Addison

19662 ■ Family Centered Hospice
2171 Executive Dr., Ste. 450
Addison, IL 60101
Ph: (630)317-3300
Free: 866-320-3300
Fax: (630)317-3310
URL: http://www.familyhhs.com/hospiceServices.php

Alton

19663 ■ BJC Hospice at Alton
1 Professional Dr., Ste. 180
Alton, IL 62002
Ph: (618)463-7100
Free: 800-916-7541
Fax: (618)463-7127
URL: http://www.bjchospice.org/

Arlington Heights

19664 ■ Monarch Hospice & Palliative Care
3115 N Wilke Rd., Ste. H
Arlington Heights, IL 60004
Ph: (847)885-1818
Free: 800--HOSPICE
Fax: (847)797-8263
URL: http://www.monarchhospice.com/

Aurora

19665 ■ VNA of Fox Valley: VNA Hospice
400 N Highland Ave.
Aurora, IL 60506
Ph: (630)978-2532
Fax: (630)978-1129
URL: http://www.vnafoxvalley.com/hospice.html

Barrington

19666 ■ Hospice of Northeastern Illinois
Pepper Family Hospice Home and Center for Care
405 Lake Zurich Rd.
Barrington, IL 60010
Ph: (847)381-5599
Free: 800-425-4444
Fax: (847)381-8042
URL: http://www.hospiceanswers.org/

Belleville

19667 ■ Family Hospice--Belleville
5110 W Main St.
Belleville, IL 62226
Ph: (618)277-1800
Fax: (618)277-1074
E-mail: info@familyhospice.org
URL: http://www.familyhospice.org

19668 ■ Hospice of Southern Illinois Inc.--Belleville
305 S Illinois St.
Belleville, IL 62222
Ph: (618)235-1703
Free: 800-233-1708
Fax: (618)235-3130
E-mail: info@hospice.org
URL: http://www.hospice.org/

19669 ■ Passages Hospice-Belleville
134 N 28th St.
Belleville, IL 62226
Ph: (618)234-7078
Fax: (618)257-7266
E-mail: info@passageshospice.com
URL: http://www.passageshospice.com/

Bloomington

19670 ■ OSF Hospice, Bloomington
2200 E Washington St.
Bloomington, IL 61704
Ph: (309)662-3311
URL: http://www.osfstjoseph.org

19671 ■ Passages Hospice-Bloomington
315 N Prairie St.
Bloomington, IL 61701
Ph: (309)828-8139
Fax: (309)827-4878
E-mail: info@passageshospice.com
URL: http://www.passageshospice.com/

Blue Island

19672 ■ MetroSouth Hospice
12935 Gregory St.
Blue Island, IL 60406
Ph: (708)385-0372
Fax: (708)835-1702
E-mail: info@metrosouthmedicalcenter.com
URL: http://www.metrosouthmedicalcenter.com/pg-hospice-care.html

Bourbonnais

19673 ■ Hospice of Kankakee Valley, Inc.
482 Main St. NW
Bourbonnais, IL 60914
Ph: (815)939-4141
E-mail: main@hkvcares.org
URL: http://www.hkvcares.org

Burbank

19674 ■ A Touch of Grace Hospice
8250 S Cicero Ave.
Burbank, IL 60459
Ph: (708)499-3400
Fax: (708)499-3404
E-mail: info@touchofgrace.net
URL: http://www.atouchofgracehospice.com/

Canton

19675 ■ Graham Hospital Hospice Unit
210 W Walnut St.
Canton, IL 61520
Ph: (309)647-5240
Fax: (309)649-5197
URL: http://www.grahamhospital.org/CareAtHome/

Carol Stream

19676 ■ CNS Hospice
690 E North Ave.
Carol Stream, IL 60188
Ph: (630)665-7000
URL: http://www.cdh.org/ClinicalServices.aspx?id=9056

Carrollton

19677 ■ The Blessing Hospice-Greene County
330 5th St.
Carrollton, IL 62016
Ph: (217)942-3775
Fax: (217)942-9057
URL: http://www.blessinghospital.org/pages/default.asp?NavID=586

Carthage

19678 ■ The Blessing Hospice-Hancock County
403 S Adams, Rm. L106
Carthage, IL 62321
Ph: (217)357-3221
Fax: (217)357-6011
URL: http://www.blessinghospital.org/pages/default.asp?NavID=586

Casey

19679 ■ Lincolnland Hospice of Sarah Bush Lincoln--Casey
412 NW 3rd St.
Casey, IL 62420-1014
Ph: (217)932-4061
Free: 800-454-4055
URL: http://www.sblhs.org/body.cfm?id=436

Champaign

19680 ■ Carle Hospice
206A W Anthony Dr.
Champaign, IL 61822
Ph: (217)383-3488
Free: 800-239-3620
URL: http://www.carlehomehealthservices.com/hospice/

19681 ■ Provena Hospice-Champaign
Hospice & Transitions Program
1501 Interstate Dr., Ste. C
Champaign, IL 61822
Ph: (217)353-3400
URL: http://www.provena.org/lifeconnections/

Chicago

19682 ■ Holy Cross Hospital Hospice Unit Seasons Hospice Inc.
2701 2 68th St., 3rd Fl.
Chicago, IL 60629
Free: 800-570-8809
URL: http://www.honoringlife-offeringhope.org/cont_illi.html

19683 ■ Horizon Hospice Inc.--Chicago
833 W Chicago Ave.
Chicago, IL 60642
Ph: (312)733-8900
Free: 866-733-6028
Fax: (312)733-8952
E-mail: info@horizonhospice.org
URL: http://www.horizonhospice.org/

19684 ■ Northwestern Memorial Hospital Palliative Care and Home Hospice Program
676 N Saint Clair
Chicago, IL 60611
Ph: (312)926-4600
Fax: (312)926-4922
URL: http://www.nmh.org/nmh/home.htm

19685 ■ Odyssey HealthCare of Chicago South
7601 S Kostner Ave., Ste. 400
Chicago, IL 60652
Ph: (773)767-9100
Free: 877-637-9432
Fax: (773)767-9101
E-mail: info@odsyhealth.com
URL: http://www.odsyhealth.com/

19686 ■ VITAS Innovative Hospice Care Chicagoland Central Satellite Office
1340 S Damen Ave., Ste. 200A
Chicago, IL 60608
Ph: (312)997-7200
Free: 866-388-4827
Fax: (312)997-7250
URL: http://www.vitas.com/

19687 ■ VITAS Mercy Hospital Hospice--Chicago Inpatient Unit
2525 S Michigan Ave., 6th Fl.
Chicago, IL 60616
Ph: (312)567-5622
Free: 800-938-4827
Fax: (312)328-7748
URL: http://www.vitas.com

19688 ■ Weiss Memorial Hospital Hospice Care
4646 N Marine Dr.
Chicago, IL 60640
Ph: (773)878-8700
Free: 800-503-1234
URL: http://www.weisshospital.com/medical-services/special-services/hospice.aspx

Chicago Heights

19689 ■ VITAS Saint James Hospital Hospice Inpatient Unit
1423 Chicago Rd.
Chicago Heights, IL 60411
Ph: (708)709-2005
Free: 800-938-4827
Fax: (708)709-2004
URL: http://www.vitas.com/

Danville

19690 ■ Carle Home Care & Hospice-Danville
2300 N Vermillion St.
Danville, IL 61832
Free: 800-239-3620

DeKalb

19691 ■ DeKalb County Hospice
2727 Sycamore Rd.
DeKalb, IL 60115
Ph: (815)756-3000
Fax: (815)758-0962
E-mail: khagen@kishospital.org
URL: http://www.dekalbcountyhospice.org

Decatur

19692 ■ Decatur Memorial Hospice
2300 N Edward St.
Decatur, IL 62526
Ph: (217)876-8121
E-mail: customers@dmhhs.org
URL: http://www.dmhcares.org/services/homehealth/hospice.aspx

Des Plains

19693 ■ Seasons Hospice, Inc.--Des Plains
606 Potter Rd.
Des Plains, IL 60016
Ph: (847)375-2721
Free: 800-570-8809
Fax: (847)759-9448
E-mail: seasons_il@seasons.org
URL: http://honoringlife-offeringhope.org/
Formerly: Seasons Hospice and Palliative Care, Inc.

Dixon

19694 ■ Hospice of the Rock River Valley
264 Illinois Rte. 2
Dixon, IL 61021-9111
Ph: (815)288-3673
Free: 800-646-9242
Fax: (815)288-1181
E-mail: carolyn@hospicerockriver.org
URL: http://www.hospicerockriver.org/

19695 ■ KSB Hospice
215 E First St.
Dixon, IL 61021
Ph: (815)288-5531
URL: http://www.ksbhospital.com/index.php?option=com_content&task=view&id=69&Itemid=80

Downers Grove

19696 ■ Advocate Hospice--Downers Grove
1441 Branding Ln., Ste. 310
Downers Grove, IL 60515-5624
Ph: (630)963-6800
Free: 800-564-2025
Fax: (630)963-6877
URL: http://www.advocatehealth.com/body.cfm?id=58

Effingham

19697 ■ Lincolnland Hospice of Sarah Bush Lincoln--Effingham
405 S Banker, Ste. 204
Effingham, IL 62401-2570
Ph: (217)347-0363
Free: 800-454-4055
Fax: (217)347-3647
URL: http://www.sblhs.org/body.cfm?id=436

Elgin

19698 ■ Passages Hospice--Elgin
134 N McLean Blvd.
Elgin, IL 60123
Ph: (847)695-1431
Fax: (847)329-9215
E-mail: info@passageshospice.com
URL: http://www.passageshospice.com/

19699 ■ Provena Hospice
77 N Airlite St.
Elgin, IL 60123-4912
Ph: (847)622-3467
URL: http://www.provena.org/

Fairview Heights

19700 ■ Heartland Home Health Care and Hospice--Fairview Heights
333 Salem Pl.
Fairview Heights, IL 62208
Ph: (618)632-0304
Fax: (618)632-0364
URL: http://www.hcr-manorcare.com

Freeport

19701 ■ FHN Hospice
1045 W Stephenson St.
Freeport, IL 61032
Ph: (815)599-7240
Free: 877-873-3621
Fax: (815)233-3549
E-mail: wecare@fhn.org
URL: http://www.fhn.org/specialtyCare.asp?ID=24

Galesburg

19702 ■ Harbor Light Hospice-Galesburg
1865 N Henderson St., Ste. 10
Galesburg, IL 61401
Ph: (309)343-3030
Free: 800-419-0542
Fax: (309)343-3047
URL: http://www.harborlighthospice.com/

Geneva

19703 ■ Fox Valley Hospice
200 Whitfield Dr.
Geneva, IL 60134
Ph: (630)232-2233
Fax: (630)232-0023
E-mail: info@foxvalleyhospice.net
URL: http://www.fvvh.org/

Glen Ellyn

19704 ■ Harbor Light Hospice Glen Ellyn
800 Roosevelt Rd., Bldg. C, Ste. 206
Glen Ellyn, IL 60137
Ph: (630)942-0100
Free: 800-419-0542
Fax: (630)942-0118
E-mail: infoge@harborlighthospice.com
URL: http://www.harborlighthospice.com/

Glenview

19705 ■ Midwest Palliative and Hospice Care Center--Glenview
2050 Claire Court
Glenview, IL 60025
Ph: (847)467-7423
Fax: (847)556-1611
URL: http://www.midwestpalliativeandhospicecare-center.org/

Granite City

19706 ■ Gateway Regional Hospice-Granite City
2100 Madison Ave.
Granite City, IL 62040
Ph: (618)798-3399
Fax: (618)798-3564
URL: http://www.chs.net/hospitals/map.html

Greenville

19707 ■ Bond County Hospice
503 S Prairie St.
Greenville, IL 62246
Ph: (618)664-5020
URL: http://www.bchd.us/

Hanover Park

19708 ■ Alexian Brothers Hospice
1515 E Lake St., Ste. 206
Hanover Park, IL 60133
Ph: (630)233-5100
Fax: (630)233-5101
E-mail: homehealth@alexian.net
URL: http://www.alexianbrothershealth.org/services/hospice/index.aspx

Harvey

19709 ■ Ingalls Hospice & Palliative Care
1 Ingalls Dr.
Harvey, IL 60426
Ph: (708)331-1360
Fax: (708)915-3115
URL: http://www.ingalls.org/

Hillside

19710 ■ Heartland Hospice Services--Hillside
4415 W Harrison St., Ste. 403
Hillside, IL 60162
Ph: (708)236-1246
Free: 888-733-3750
URL: http://www.hcr-manorcare.com/
Formerly: Hospice Partners.

Hinsdale

19711 ■ St. Thomas Hospice
119 E Ogden Ave.
Hinsdale, IL 60521
Ph: (630)856-6990
Fax: (630)856-6999
URL: http://www.keepingyouwell.com/CareAndServices/Hospice.aspx

Joliet

19712 ■ Joliet Area Community Hospice
250 Water Stone Cir.
Joliet, IL 60431
Ph: (815)740-4104
Free: 800-360-1817
Fax: (815)740-4107
E-mail: info@joliethospice.org
URL: http://www.joliethospice.org/

19713 ■ VITAS Innovative Hospice Care of Chicagoland-S Joliet
3033 W Jefferson
Joliet, IL 60435
Ph: (815)730-8670
Fax: (815)730-8756
URL: http://www.vitas.com/Aboutus/Locations/Illinois/tabid/189/Default.aspx

LaSalle

19714 ■ VITAS Innovative Hospice Care-LaSalle
105 Marquette St.
LaSalle, IL 61301
Ph: (305)374-4143
Fax: (305)350-6784
URL: http://www.vitas.com/Aboutus/Locations/Illinois/tabid/189/Default.aspx

Lansing

19715 ■ Hospice of the Calumet Area Inc.
3224 Ridge Rd., Ste. 202
Lansing, IL 60438
Ph: (708)895-8332
Fax: (219)922-1947
E-mail: info@hospicecalumet.org
URL: http://www.hospicecalumet.org/

Libertyville

19716 ■ Condell Medical Center Hospice
115 W Church St.
Libertyville, IL 60048
Ph: (847)816-8848
Fax: (847)816-9051
URL: http://www.condell.org/home-services/hospice_volunteer_ops.php

19717 ■ Midwest Palliative and Hospice Care Center--Libertyville
904B S Milwaukee Ave.
Libertyville, IL 60048
Free: 800-331-5484
Fax: (847)556-1611
URL: http://www.midwestpalliativeandhospicecare-center.org/
Formerly: Palliative Care Center and Hospice of the North Shore.

Lombard

19718 ■ Merit Hospice Services LLC
1300 S Main St.
Lombard, IL 60148
Ph: (630)652-7900
Free: 877-748-2202
Fax: (630)652-7948
URL: http://www.merithomehealth.com

19719 ■ VITAS Innovative Hospice Care of Chicagoland Northwest
580 Waters Edge, Ste. 100
Lombard, IL 60148
Ph: (630)495-8484
Free: 866-310-2273
Fax: (630)495-1598
URL: http://www.vitas.com

Loves Park

19720 ■ OSF Hospice-Loves Park
9951 Rock Cut Crossing
Loves Park, IL 61111
Ph: (815)921-8780
Free: 800-673-5288
Fax: (815)921-8781
URL: http://www.osfhomecare.org/

Macomb

19721 ■ McDonough District Hospital The MDH Hospice
525 E Grant St.
Macomb, IL 61455
Ph: (309)836-1543
Free: 800-690-2132
Fax: (309)836-1545
E-mail: info@mdh.org
URL: http://www.mdh.org/

Marion

19722 ■ Hospice of Southern Illinois Inc.--Marion
204 Halfway Rd.
Marion, IL 62959-1665
Ph: (618)997-3030
Free: 800-233-1708
Fax: (618)998-0680
E-mail: info@hospice.org
URL: http://www.hospice.org

Mattoon

19723 ■ Lincolnland Hospice of Sarah Bush Lincoln--Mattoon
700 Broadway Ave. E
Mattoon, IL 61938-4671
Ph: (217)235-0660
Free: 800-345-3191
URL: http://www.sblhs.org/body.cfm?id=436

Melrose Park

19724 ■ Gottlieb Home Health Services/Hospice
701 W North Ave.
Melrose Park, IL 60160-1612
Ph: (708)450-5072
Fax: (708)681-1136
URL: http://www.gottliebhospital.org/

Metropolis

19725 ■ Lourdes Hospice--Metropolis
616 Market St.
Metropolis, IL 62960
Ph: (618)524-3757
Free: 800-595-3647
URL: http://www.lourdes-pad.org/hospice.asp

Moline

19726 ■ Trinity Visiting Nurse and Homecare Association-Moline
106 19th St.
Moline, IL 61265
Ph: (563)742-4700
Fax: (563)742-4705
URL: http://www.vnaa.org/vnaa/vna/Trinity_Visiting_Nurse_and_Homecare_Asso,ILRIS L.aspx?p=8

Morris

19727 ■ Grundy Community Hospice
518 W Illinois Ave.
Morris, IL 60450
Ph: (815)942-8525
Fax: (815)942-4934
URL: http://www.grundyhospice.org/

Normal

19728 ■ BroMenn Hospice
1304 Franklin Ave.
Normal, IL 61761
Ph: (309)454-1400
URL: http://www.advocatehealth.com/body.cfm?id=2029

North Chicago

19729 ■ North Chicago VA Medical Center
3001 Green Bay Rd.
North Chicago, IL 60064
Ph: (847)688-1900
Free: 800-393-0865
URL: http://www.northchicago.va.gov/

Oak Lawn

19730 ■ Little Co. of Mary Home Based Services
9800 Southwest Hwy.
Oak Lawn, IL 60453
Ph: (708)229-4663
Fax: (708)499-5975
URL: http://lcmh.org/body.cfm?xyzpdqabc=0&id=14&action=detail&ref=42

Olney

19731 ■ Hospice of Southeastern Illinois
800 E Locust St.
Olney, IL 62450-2553
Ph: (618)395-2131
Free: 800-375-9343
Fax: (618)392-2517
URL: http://www.richlandmemorial.com

Olympia Fields

19732 ■ Horizon Hospice & Palliative Care-Olympia Fields
3420 Vollmer Rd.
Olympia Fields, IL 60461
Ph: (708)283-8150
Free: 888-865-8073
Fax: (708)283-8973
E-mail: info@horizonhospice.org
URL: http://www.horizonhospice.org/

Oregon

19733 ■ Ogle County Hospice Association
421 Pines Rd.
Oregon, IL 61061
Ph: (815)732-2499
Free: 888-421-3100
Fax: (815)732-6077
E-mail: director@oglecohospice.net
URL: http://www.oglecountyhospice.org/

Ottawa

19734 ■ CHO Hospice-Ottawa
1601 Mercury Cir.
Ottawa, IL 61350
Ph: (815)433-6096
Fax: (815)431-5582
URL: http://www.ottawaregional.org/

Palatine

19735 ■ Heartland Hospice Services--Palatine
220 N Smith St., Ste. 420
Palatine, IL 60067
Ph: (847)991-0176
Free: 888-733-3750
Fax: (847)991-2194
URL: http://www.hcr-manorcare.com

Palos Heights

19736 ■ Palos Community Hospital Hospice
12251 S 80th Ave.
Palos Heights, IL 60463
Ph: (708)923-4000
E-mail: webmaster@paloscomm.org
URL: http://www.paloscommunityhospital.org/

Park Ridge

19737 ■ Advocate Hospice-Park Ridge
205 W Touhy
Park Ridge, IL 60068
Ph: (847)318-1072
Fax: (847)384-3696
URL: http://www.advocatehealth.com

19738 ■ Rainbow Hospice Inc.
444 N Northwest Hwy., Ste. 145
Park Ridge, IL 60068
Ph: (847)685-9900
Fax: (847)685-6390
E-mail: info@rainbowhospice.org
URL: http://www.rainbowhospice.org/

Pecatonica

19739 ■ Hospice Care of America-Pecatonica
520 Main St., Ste. A
Pecatonica, IL 61063
Ph: (815)239-1000
Fax: (815)239-2200
E-mail: info@hospicecareofamerica.com
URL: http://www.hospicecareofamerica.com/

Peoria

19740 ■ Harbor Light Hospice--Peoria
2000 W Pioneer Pkwy.
Peoria, IL 61615
Ph: (309)689-9760
Free: 800-419-0542
Fax: (309)689-9764
E-mail: infope@hospiceharborlight.com
URL: http://www.hospiceharborlight.com/

19741 ■ Hospice Compassus-Peoria
2000 W Pioneer Pkwy., Ste. 24
Peoria, IL 61615
Ph: (309)691-0280
Fax: (309)691-0392
E-mail: contactusILPEO@hospicecom.com
URL: http://www.hospicecompassus.com/index.cfm

19742 ■ Methodist Medical Center Hospice Services
Glen Oak Medical Plaza
221 NE Glen Oak Ave., Ste. 200
Peoria, IL 61636
Ph: (309)672-5746
URL: http://www.mymethodist.net/services/hospice.aspx

19743 ■ OSF Hospice-Peoria
2265 Altofer Dr.
Peoria, IL 61615
Ph: (309)344-3161
Free: 800 673-5288
Fax: (309)683-7752
URL: http://www.osfhomecare.org/hospice/about-hospice-care.html

Peru

19744 ■ Illinois Valley Hospice
1305 6th St.
Peru, IL 61354
Ph: (815)224-1307
Fax: (815)224-1665
URL: http://www.ivch.org/

Pittsfield

19745 ■ The Blessing Hospice-Pike County
967 W Washington
Pittsfield, IL 62363-1355
Ph: (217)285-5274
Fax: (217)285-1358
URL: http://www.blessinghospital.org/

Pontiac

19746 ■ OSF HomeCare
608 N Ladd
Pontiac, IL 61764-1745
Ph: (815)844-6982
Fax: (815)842-2150
URL: http://www.osfhomecare.org/

Quincy

19747 ■ The Blessing Hospice--Quincy
PO Box 7005
Quincy, IL 62305-7005
Ph: (217)228-5521
Fax: (217)223-5521
URL: http://www.blessinghospital.org/

Rockford

19748 ■ Heartland Hospice Services--Rockford
6885 Vistagreen Way
Rockford, IL 61107
Ph: (815)282-2279
Fax: (815)227-5093
URL: http://www.hcr-manorcare.com/tabId/68/Default.aspx?City=&State=&PostalCode=61107&CareTypes=99134

19749 ■ Hospice Care of America
483 N Mulford Rd.
Rockford, IL 61114
Ph: (815)316-2700
Free: 888-206-9972
Fax: (815)316-2702
E-mail: info@hospicecareofamerica.com
URL: http://www.hospicecareofamerica.com/

19750 ■ Northern Illinois Hospice and Grief Center
4215 Newburg Rd.
Rockford, IL 61108
Ph: (815)398-0500
Fax: (815)398-0588
URL: http://www.northernillinoishospice.org/
Formerly: Northern Illinois Hospice Association.

19751 ■ VNA Hospice of Rockford Hospice of Rockford
4223 E State St.
Rockford, IL 61108
Ph: (815)971-3550
Fax: (815)971-9964
E-mail: vnaweb@rhsnet.org
URL: http://www.rhsnet.org/aboutus-vna.aspx

Skokie

19752 ■ CovenantCare at Home-Skokie
5700 Old Orchard Rd.
Skokie, IL 60077
Ph: (773)878-4583
Fax: (773)878-5222
URL: http://www.covenantcareathome.org/

19753 ■ Midwest Palliative and Hospice Care Center--Skokie
The Knox Bldg.
9701 Knox Ave., 3rd Fl.
Skokie, IL 60076
Ph: (847)467-7423
Free: 800-331-5484
Fax: (847)675-8205
URL: http://www.midwestpalliativeandhospicecare-center.org/
Formerly: Palliative Care Center and Hospice of the North Shore.

19754 ■ NorthShore University HealthSystem Home and Hospice Services
4901 Searle Pkwy.
Skokie, IL 60076
Ph: (847)982-4367
Fax: (847)982-4282
URL: http://www.northshore.org/

South Holland

19755 ■ Providence Hospice-South Holland
16300 Louis Ave.
South Holland, IL 60473
Ph: (708)331-0400
Fax: (708)877-4818
URL: http://www.providlifeservices.com

Spring Valley

19756 ■ Saint Margaret's Hospice
600 E 1st St.
Spring Valley, IL 61362
Ph: (815)664-1429
Fax: (815)664-1140
E-mail: stmarg@aboutsmh.org
URL: http://www.aboutsmh.org

Springfield

19757 ■ Hospice Care of Sangamon
319 E Madison, Ste. 3N
Springfield, IL 62701
Ph: (217)525-3733
Fax: (217)525-3739
URL: http://www.sangamoncountyhospice.com/

19758 ■ Memorial Home Services: Hospice
720 N Bond St.
Springfield, IL 62702-4915
Ph: (217)788-9337
Free: 800-342-4862
Fax: (217)757-7322

Tinley Park

19759 ■ VITAS Innovative Hospice Care of Chicagoland S-Tinley Pk.
8525 W 183rd St.
Tinley Park, IL 60487
Ph: (708)781-4400
Fax: (708)781-4364
URL: http://www.vitas.com/

Vandalia

19760 ■ Fayette County Health Department Hospice-Vandalia
509 W Edwards St.
Vandalia, IL 62471
Ph: (618)283-1044
Fax: (619)288-5038
E-mail: fchd@fayettehealthdept.org
URL: http://www.fayettehealthdept.org/

Virginia

19761 ■ Cass-Schuyler Area Hospice
331 S Main St.
Virginia, IL 62691
Ph: (217)452-3057
Fax: (217)452-7245

Watseka

19762 ■ Iroquois Memorial Hospice
200 E Fairman Ave.
Watseka, IL 60970
Ph: (815)432-0185
Free: 800-242-2731
Fax: (815)432-6199
E-mail: info@iroquoismemorial.com
URL: http://www.iroquoismemorial.com/index.cfm?pageID=89

Waukegan

19763 ■ Star Hospice of Vista Health
2645 Washington St.
Waukegan, IL 60085
Ph: (847)360-2220
Fax: (847)625-6180
URL: http://www.vistahealth.com/Pages/home.aspx
Formerly: Provena Hospice.

Westchester

19764 ■ Generations Healthcare, LLC
4 Westbrook Corporate Ctr.
Westchester, IL 60154
Ph: (708)409-3040
Fax: (708)409-3041
E-mail: csabeckis@generationshospice.com
URL: http://www.generationshospice.com/

Willowbrook

19765 ■ Seasons Hospice and Palliative Care, Inc. - Willowbrook Office
621 Plainfield Rd.
Willowbrook, IL 60527
Free: 800-570-8809
Fax: (630)654-9301
URL: http://honoringlife-offeringhope.org/

INDIANA

Angola

19766 ■ Cameron Home Health Care and Hospice
416 E Maumee St.
Angola, IN 46703
Ph: (260)665-2141
Free: 800-942-9583
Fax: (260)665-8608
URL: http://www.cameronmch.com

Berne

19767 ■ Family Hospice and Palliative Care-Berne
265 W Water St.
Berne, IN 46711
Ph: (260)589-8598
Fax: (260)589-8079
URL: http://www.fhpc-in.org/

Bloomington

19768 ■ Bloomington Hospital Home Health and Hospice
333 E Miller Dr.
Bloomington, IN 47402
Ph: (812)353-9818
Free: 800-206-5200
Fax: (812)353-9630
URL: http://www.bloomingtonhospital.org

Columbia City

19769 ■ Parkview Home Health & Hospice--Columbia City
333 N Oak St.
Columbia City, IN 46725
Ph: (269)373-9800
Free: 800-363-9977
Fax: (260)373-9947
URL: http://www.parkview.com/HealthServices/AdditionalServices/HHandH/Pages/Hosp iceCare.aspx

Columbus

19770 ■ Hospice of South Central Indiana, Inc.--Columbus
2626 E 17th St.
Columbus, IN 47201-5417
Ph: (812)314-8000
Fax: (812)314-8153
URL: http://www.hospiceofsouthcentralindiana.org/

Cumberland

19771 ■ American Home Health and Hospice-Cumberland
7506 W US 40
Cumberland, IN 46229
Ph: (866)917-6500
Fax: (317)542-0424
E-mail: infor@americanhomehealthcare.us
URL: http://www.americanhomehealthcare.us/

Danville

19772 ■ Advocate Hospice-Danville
2605 E Main St.
Danville, IN 46122
Ph: (317)745-5147
Fax: (317)745-5936
E-mail: advocate.hospice@comcast.net
URL: http://www.advocatehospice.com/

19773 ■ Day By Day Hospice
1668 E Main St.
Danville, IN 46122
Ph: (317)745-4673
Free: 800-564-7029
Fax: (317)745-5264
E-mail: info@daybydayhospice.com
URL: http://www.daybydayhospice.com

Elkhart

19774 ■ Center for Hospice and Palliative Care - Elkhart
22579 Old US 20E
Elkhart, IN 46516
Ph: (574)264-3321
Free: 800-413-9083
Fax: (574)264-5892
URL: http://www.centerforhospice.org/
Formerly: Hospice of Elkhart County.

Evansville

19775 ■ Heritage Hospice, Inc.--Evansville
1201 W Buena Vista Rd., Ste. A
Evansville, IN 47715
Ph: (812)429-0721
URL: http://www.heritagehospice.org

19776 ■ St. Mary's Medical Center
3700 Washington Ave.
Evansville, IN 47750
Ph: (812)485-7227
Fax: (812)485-7227
URL: http://www.stmarys.org/body.cfm?id=17

19777 ■ VistaCare-Evansville
323 Metro Ave.
Evansville, IN 47715
Ph: (812)962-3340
Free: 888-799-1201
Fax: (812)962-1141
URL: http://www.vistacare.com/

Fishers

19778 ■ Community Visiting Nurse Association Hospice
9894 E 121st St.
Fishers, IN 46037
Ph: (317)621-4700
Fax: (317)621-4710
URL: http://vnaa.org/vnaa/searches/findVNA.aspx?k=IN

Fort Wayne

19779 ■ Heartland Home Health Care and Hospice--Fort Wayne
1315 Directors Row, Ste. 200
Fort Wayne, IN 46808-1284
Ph: (260)484-7622
Free: 877-484-7622
Fax: (260)484-7619
E-mail: careline@hcr-manorcare.com
URL: http://www.hcr-manorcare.com

19780 ■ Parkview Home Health & Hospice--Fort Wayne
1900 Carew St.
Fort Wayne, IN 46805-5361
Ph: (260)373-9800
Free: 800-363-9977
Fax: (260)373-9947
URL: http://www.parkview.com/

19781 ■ Visiting Nurse & Hospice Home-Ft. Wayne
5910 Homestead Rd.
Fort Wayne, IN 46814
Ph: (260)435-3222
Fax: (260)435-3235
URL: http://www.vnhh.org/

Fowler

19782 ■ Serenity Hospice-Fowler
103 S Grant Ave.
Fowler, IN 47944
Ph: (765)884-7000
Fax: (765)884-7001
URL: http://www.serenity-hospice.com/

Franklin

19783 ■ Americare Hospice
1150 N Main St., Ste. A
Franklin, IN 46131
Ph: (317)736-0055
Fax: (317)346-6049
URL: http://www.americarehome.com/

Greensburg

19784 ■ Hospice of South Central Indiana-Decatur
1201 N Lincoln St.
Greensburg, IN 47240
Ph: (812)662-6375
Fax: (812)662-6539
URL: http://www.hospiceofsouthcentralindiana.org/

Greenwood

19785 ■ Saint Francis Hospice--Greenwood
438 S Emerson Ave.
Greenwood, IN 46143
Ph: (317)865-2092
Free: 800-782-6731
Fax: (317)859-2622
URL: http://www.stfrancis-indy.org/

Hammond

19786 ■ Blue Skies Hospice, Inc.
2714 169th St.
Hammond, IN 46323
Ph: (219)554-0688
Fax: (219)933-1773
URL: http://www.blueskieshospice.com/

Huntington

19787 ■ Parkview Home Health & Hospice-Huntington
2806 Theater Ave.
Huntington, IN 46750
Ph: (219)358-5271
Fax: (219)358-5272
URL: http://www.parkview.com/Pages/default.aspx

Indianapolis

19788 ■ Amedisys Hospice Services-Indianapolis
9101 Wesleyan Rd., Ste. 305
Indianapolis, IN 46268
Ph: (317)870-9901
Free: 866-647-0683
Fax: (317)870-9921
URL: http://www.amedisys.com/hospice_locations.cfm?id=5

19789 ■ AseraCare Hospice--Indianapolis
8460 Bearing Dr.
Indianapolis, IN 46268
Ph: (317)871-8500
Free: 800-371-2034
Fax: (317)871-0819
URL: http://www.aseracare.com/

19790 ■ Clarion Health Hospice
1815 N Capitol
Indianapolis, IN 46202
Ph: (317)962-0800
Fax: (317)962-5229
E-mail: webmaster@clarian.org
URL: http://www.clarian.org/

19791 ■ Harbor Light Hospice-Indianapolis
Cedar Green Office Park
7164 Graham Rd., Ste. 150
Indianapolis, IN 46250
Ph: (317)849-5600
Free: 888-849-5670
Fax: (317)849-5686
E-mail: infoin@harborlighthospice.com
URL: http://www.harborlighthospice.com/Indiana/contact.html

19792 ■ Heartland Home Health Care and Hospice Inc.--Indianapolis
931 E 86th St.
Indianapolis, IN 46240-1852
Ph: (317)251-3012
Free: 800-558-6928
Fax: (317)251-3016
E-mail: careline@hcr-manorcare.com
URL: http://www.hcr-manorcare.com

19793 ■ Odyssey HealthCare of Central Indiana
5303 Lakeview Pkwy. S Dr.
Indianapolis, IN 46268
Ph: (317)299-5060
Free: 877-637-9432
Fax: (317)299-5540
E-mail: info@odsyhealth.com
URL: http://www.odsyhealth.com

19794 ■ Saint Vincent Hospice
8450 N Payne Rd., Ste. 100
Indianapolis, IN 46268
Ph: (317)338-4040
Free: 888-780-7284
Fax: (317)338-4044
URL: http://www.stvincent.org/ourservices/hospice/hospiceservices/default.htm

19795 ■ St. Vincent Hospice
2001 W 86th St.
Indianapolis, IN 46260
Ph: (317)338-4060
Free: 888-780-7284
URL: http://www.stvincent.org/Hospice.aspx

19796 ■ Seasons Hospice and Palliative of Indiana LLC
8350 S Emerson Ave., Ste. 140
Indianapolis, IN 46237
Ph: (317)885-4200
Free: 800-570-8809
Fax: (317)885-4220
E-mail: info@seasons.org
URL: http://www.honoringlife-offeringhope.org/

19797 ■ VA Medical Center, HPHC-Indianapolis
1481 W 10th St.
Indianapolis, IN 46202
Ph: (317)554-0000
URL: http://www.va.gov/

19798 ■ Visiting Nurse Services/Hospice Central Indiana
4701 N Keystone Ave.
Indianapolis, IN 46205
Ph: (317)722-8229
Free: 800-248-6540
Fax: (317)722-8240
URL: http://www.vnsi.org/

19799 ■ VistaCare--Indianapolis
6431 S East St.
Indianapolis, IN 46227
Ph: (317)788-0300
Free: 800-480-9408
Fax: (317)788-8760
URL: http://www.vistacare.com/

Kendalville

19800 ■ Parkview Home Health & Hospice--Kendalville
1836 Ida Red Rd.
Kendalville, IN 46755
Ph: (260)373-9800
Free: 800-363-9977
URL: http://www.parkview.com/healthservices/additionalservices/hhandh/pages/welc ome2.aspx

Kokomo

19801 ■ Amedisys Hospice-Kokomo
2761 Albright Rd., Bldg. B
Kokomo, IN 46902
Ph: (765)864-0134

Free: 877-604-5283
Fax: (765)864-0182
URL: http://www.amedisys.com/hospice_locations.cfm?id=5

19802 ■ Guardian Angel Hospice-Kokomo
513 W Lincoln Rd.
Kokomo, IN 46902
Ph: (765)453-7702
Fax: (765)452-2944
E-mail: info@guardianangelhospice.com
URL: http://www.guardianangelhospice.com/

Lafayette

19803 ■ Guardian Angel Hospice-Lafayette
1221 Creasy Lane
Lafayette, IN 47905
Ph: (765)453-7702
Fax: (765)452-2944
E-mail: info@guardianangelhospice.com
URL: http://www.guardianangelhospice.com/

19804 ■ Saint Elizabeth Hospice--Lafayette
1415 Salem St., Ste. 202 W
Lafayette, IN 47904
Ph: (765)423-6224
Free: 800-755-5650
Fax: (765)449-5192
URL: http://www.ste.org/DesktopDefault.aspx?tabid=182

19805 ■ Serenity Hospice-Lafayette
1221 S Creasy La., Ste. H
Lafayette, IN 47905
Ph: (765)446-9100
Free: 866-616-1201
Fax: (765)446-7137
URL: http://www.serenity-hospice.com/

Lawrenceburg

19806 ■ Dearborn County Hospital Home Health & Hospice
600 Wilson Creek Rd.
Lawrenceburg, IN 47025-1004
Ph: (812)537-1010
Free: 800-676-5428
Fax: (812)537-8436
URL: http://www.dch.org/

Logansport

19807 ■ Guardian Angel Hospice-Logansport
1050 W Market St.
Logansport, IN 46947
Ph: (574)722-5551
Fax: (574)722-5554
E-mail: info@guardianangelhospice.com
URL: http://www.guardianangelhospice.com

Marion

19808 ■ Guardian Angel Hospice-Marion
118 E 4th St.
Marion, IN 46952
Ph: (765)453-7702
Fax: (765)453-7825
E-mail: info@guardianangelhospice.com
URL: http://www.guardianangelhospice.com

19809 ■ New Hope Hospice--Marion
1385 N Baldwin Ave.
Marion, IN 46952
Ph: (765)677-0684
Free: 800-299-8003
Fax: (765)677-0689
URL: http://www.newhopehospice.com/

19810 ■ VAMC: Northern Indiana Health Care System-Marion Campus
1700 E 38th St.
Marion, IN 46953
Ph: (765)674-3321
URL: http://www.northernindiana.va.gov/

19811 ■ Visiting Nurse & Hospice Home
205 S Washington St.
Marion, IN 46952
Ph: (765)668-0885
Fax: (765)668-0889

Merrillville

19812 ■ Harbor Light Hospice--Merrillville
500 W Lincoln Hwy., Ste. F
Merrillville, IN 46410
Ph: (219)793-1200
Free: 800-237-4242
Fax: (219)793-9292
E-mail: Infome@harborlighthospice.com
URL: http://www.hospiceharborlight.com

Michigan City

19813 ■ VNA HomeCare, Hospice-Michigan City
901 S Woodland Ave.
Michigan City, IN 46360
Ph: (219)872-3331
URL: http://www.laportehealth.org/patients/services/home_care/index.cfm

Mishawaka

19814 ■ Center for Hospice Care
4220 Edison Lakes Pkwy.
Mishawaka, IN 46545
Ph: (574)243-3100
Fax: (574)243-3134
URL: http://www.centerforhospice.org/

Mitchell

19815 ■ Hoosier Uplands Home Health and Hospice
500 W Main St.
Mitchell, IN 47446
Ph: (812)849-4447
Free: 800-827-2219
Fax: (812)849-0547
E-mail: jeremiah@hoosieruplands.org
URL: http://www.hoosieruplands.org/

Mooresville

19816 ■ Americare Hospice-Mooresville
233 E High St., Unit 16
Mooresville, IN 46158
Ph: (317)834-8436
Fax: (317)834-8437
URL: http://www.americarehome.com/

Muncie

19817 ■ Ball Memorial Hospice
2401 W University Ave.
Muncie, IN 47303
Ph: (765)747-4273
Fax: (765)751-5008
URL: http://www.accesschs.org/ball_memorial_hospital/

Munster

19818 ■ Hospice of the Calumet Area
600 Superior Ave.
Munster, IN 46321
Ph: (219)922-2732
Fax: (219)922-1947
E-mail: info@hospicecalumet.org
URL: http://www.hospicecalumet.org
Formerly: The William J. Riley Memorial Residence.

19819 ■ William J Riley Memorial Residence
511 Otis Bowen Dr.
Munster, IN 46321
Ph: (219)922-2732
Fax: (219)922-1947
E-mail: info@hospicecalumet.org
URL: http://www.hospicecalumet.org/hospice-house/

New Albany

19820 ■ Hospice of Southern Indiana
624 E Market St.
New Albany, IN 47150
Ph: (812)945-4596
Free: 800-895-5633
Fax: (812)945-4733
E-mail: smiller@hospices.org
URL: http://www.hosparus.org/
Formerly: Hospice and Palliative Care.

New Castle

19821 ■ Covenant Hospice--New Castle
1029 S 14th St.
New Castle, IN 47362
Ph: (765)529-6672
Free: 877-757-1357
Fax: (765)529-7094
E-mail: info@covenant-hospice.org
URL: http://www.covenant-hospice.com
Brett Karanovich, Chief Executive Officer

Newburgh

19822 ■ AseraCare Hospice-Evansville
3775 Haley Dr.
Newburgh, IN 47630
Ph: (812)858-1032
Free: 800-404-0289
Fax: (812)858-1601
URL: http://hospice.aseracare.com/home.aspx

North Vernon

19823 ■ Hospice of Jennings County
245 Norris Ave.
North Vernon, IN 47265
Ph: (812)346-5944
Free: 800-841-4938
URL: http://www.hospiceofsouthcentralindiana.org/locations/hospice_of_jennings_c ounty.php

Plymouth

19824 ■ Center for Hospice and Palliative Care - Plymouth
112 S Center St., Ste. C
Plymouth, IN 46563
Ph: (574)935-4511
Free: 800-413-9083
Fax: (574)935-4589
URL: http://www.centerforhospice.org
Formerly: Marshall County Hospice.

Portland

19825 ■ State of the Heart Home Health and Hospice
1237 SR 67
Portland, IN 47371
Ph: (260)726-3220
Free: 800-417-7535
Fax: (800)527-0514
E-mail: jaytc@stateoftheheartcare.org
URL: http://www.stateoftheheartcare.org

Rensselaer

19826 ■ Jasper County Hospital Home Health Care/Hospice
1104 E Grace St.
Rensselaer, IN 47978
Ph: (219)866-5141
Free: 888-511-5141
Fax: (219)866-2236
E-mail: wmaster@jchh.com
URL: http://www.jchh.com/Hospice.html

Richmond

19827 ■ AceraCare Hospice-Richmond
1400 Industries Rd., Ste. 201
Richmond, IN 47374
Ph: (765)962-1949

Free: 877-234-8583
Fax: (765)935-4067
URL: http://hospice.aseracare.com/home.aspx

19828 ■ Reid Hospital and Health Care Services Hospice
1100 Reid Pkwy.
Richmond, IN 47374-1908
Ph: (765)983-3000
Free: 888-983-3344
Fax: (765)983-3254
URL: http://www.reidhospital.org/index.cfm?pageID=37

Rochester

19829 ■ Hope Hospice Inc.--Rochester
1476 W 18th St.
Rochester, IN 46975
Ph: (574)224-4673
Free: 888-737-4673
Fax: (574)224-4444
E-mail: danpurkey@hopehospicefc.com
URL: http://www.hopehospicefc.com/
Formerly: Hope Hospice of Fulton County.

Rockport

19830 ■ Spencer County Hospice
225 Main St.
Rockport, IN 47635
Ph: (812)649-9151
Fax: (812)649-5186
E-mail: spcohospice@psci.net
URL: http://www.psci.net/spcohospice/

Seymour

19831 ■ Schneck Medical Center Hospice
411 W Tipton St.
Seymour, IN 47274
Ph: (812)522-2349
Free: 800-234-9222
E-mail: info@schneckmed.org
URL: http://www.schneckmed.org/

Shelbyville

19832 ■ Hospice of South Central Indiana-Shelby County
425 E Washington St., Ste. B
Shelbyville, IN 46176
Ph: (317)392-4560
Free: 800-841-4938
URL: http://www.hospiceofsouthcentralindiana.org/locations/hospice_of_shelby_cou nty.php

South Bend

19833 ■ Center for Hospice and Palliative Care, Inc.
111 Sunnybrook Ct.
South Bend, IN 46637
Ph: (574)243-3100
Free: 800-413-9083
Fax: (574)243-3134
URL: http://www.centerforhospice.org

19834 ■ Harbor Light Hospice--South Bend
4330 Miami St.
South Bend, IN 46614
Ph: (574)291-5030
Free: 574-291-5039
E-mail: Infosb@harborlighthospice.com
URL: http://www.harborlighthospice.com/Indiana/index.html

Sullivan

19835 ■ Home Health and Hospice of Sullivan County
817 N Section St., Ste. A
Sullivan, IN 47882
Ph: (812)268-0431
URL: http://www.schosp.com/

Terre Haute

19836 ■ Hospice of the Wabash Valley
400 8th Ave.
Terre Haute, IN 47804
Ph: (812)232-7611
Free: 800-844-7610
URL: http://www.uhhg.org/vnahospice/

19837 ■ VistaCare--Terre Haute
3401 S 4th St.
Terre Haute, IN 47802
Ph: (812)478-3250
Free: 866-871-0014
Fax: (812)478-2470
URL: http://www.vistacare.com
Heather Lumsdon, Executive Director

Valparaiso

19838 ■ Arthur B. and Ethel V. Horton VNA Hospice Center
2401 Valley Dr.
Valparaiso, IN 46383
Ph: (219)462-5195
Fax: (219)462-6020
E-mail: webmaster@vnaportercounty.org
URL: http://www.vnaportercounty.org/new%20hospice%20center.htm

19839 ■ AseraCare Hospice-Valparaiso
332 W US Hwy 30
Valparaiso, IN 46385
Ph: (219)462-6398
Free: 877-234-8583
Fax: (765)935-4067
URL: http://www.aseracare.com

Warsaw

19840 ■ Kosciuske Home Care & Hospice
1515 Provident Dr., Ste. 250
Warsaw, IN 46580
Ph: (574)372-3401
Free: 866-359-3403
E-mail: info@koshomecare.org
URL: http://www.koshomecare.org
Formerly: KCH Homecare & Hospice.

Washington

19841 ■ Helping Hearts Hospice
Davies Community Hospital
1314 E Walnut St.
Washington, IN 47501
Ph: (812)254-2760
Free: 888-872-0564
Fax: (812)254-8957
E-mail: msmith@dchosp.org
URL: http://www.dchosp.org/daviess.nsf/View/Hospice

IOWA

Albia

19842 ■ Care Initiatives Hospice-Albia
4 S Main St.
Albia, IA 52531-2041
Ph: (641)932-3488
Free: 877-577-8222
Fax: (641)932-3486
URL: http://www.careinitiativeshospice.org/

19843 ■ Hospice of Monroe County-Albia
Monroe County Hospital
6580 165th St.
Albia, IA 52531
Ph: (641)932-1701
E-mail: info@mchalbia.com
URL: http://www.mchalbia.com/

Algona

19844 ■ Hospice of the Heartland--Algona
1515 S Phillips St.
Algona, IA 50511-3649
Ph: (515)295-2451
Free: 800-603-8433
Fax: (515)295-5256
URL: http://www.krhc.com

Amana

19845 ■ Essence of Life Hospice
3207 220th Tr.
Amana, IA 52203
Ph: (319)622-3195
Free: 877-622-3195
Fax: (319)622-3330
E-mail: essencehospice@southslope.net
URL: http://www.essencehospice.com/

Ames

19846 ■ Homeward Hospice
1111 Duff Ave.
Ames, IA 50010
Ph: (515)239-2011
Free: 877-469-0079
Fax: (515)956-6050
URL: http://www.mgmc.org/

Atlantic

19847 ■ CCMH HomeCare/Hospice, Inc.
Cass County Memorial Hospital
1501 E 10th St.
Atlantic, IA 50022-7480
Ph: (712)243-8006
Fax: (712)243-7416
E-mail: info@casshealth.org
URL: http://www.casshealth.org/

Bettendorf

19848 ■ Genesis Hospice
2535 Maplecrest Rd., Ste. 4
Bettendorf, IA 52722
Ph: (563)421-5500
Free: 866-862-2862
Fax: (563)421-5425
URL: http://www.genesishealth.com/services/home_health_hospice/index.aspx

19849 ■ Trinity Pathway Hospice
4500 Utica Rd.
Bettendorf, IA 52722
Ph: (563)742-4700
Free: 877-242-8899
Fax: (563)742-4705
URL: http://trinityqc.com/body.cfm?id=252

Boone

19850 ■ Hospice of Central Iowa-Boone
811 Story St.
Boone, IA 50036-2712
Ph: (515)432-4060
Free: 800-334-1052
Fax: (515)432-4076
URL: http://www.hospiceofcentraliowa.org/

Carroll

19851 ■ Saint Anthony Regional Hospice
311 S Clark St.
Carroll, IA 51401
Ph: (712)794-5555
URL: http://www.stanthonyhospital.org/

Cedar Falls

19852 ■ Care Initiative Hospice-Waterloo
6915 Chancellor Dr., Ste. A
Cedar Falls, IA 50613
Ph: (319)232-6148

Free: 877-577-3999
Fax: (319)232-6823
URL: http://www.careinitiativeshospice.org/where_we_are_waterloo.html

Cedar Rapids

19853 ■ Care Initiatives Hospice-Cedar Rapids
5005 Bowling St., SW, Ste. C
Cedar Rapids, IA 52404
Ph: (310)390-4161
Fax: (319)390-6923
URL: http://www.careinitiativeshospice.org/where_we_are.html

19854 ■ Hospice Compassus--Cedar Rapids
3409 Cedar Heights Dr.
Cedar Rapids, IA 50613
Ph: (319)362-2500
Fax: (319)362-2501
E-mail: contactusIACR@hospicecom.com
URL: http://www.amenityhospice.com
Formerly: Amenity Hospice.

19855 ■ Saint Luke's Hospital Hospice
290 Blairs Ferry Rd. NE, Ste. 100
Cedar Rapids, IA 52406
Ph: (319)369-7744
Fax: (319)368-5531
URL: http://www.stlukescr.org/our-services/all-other-services/hospice/

Centerville

19856 ■ Hospice of Central Iowa, Centerville
103 E Van Buren St.
Centerville, IA 52544
Ph: (641)856-5502
Free: 800-500-2614
Fax: (641)856-5362
URL: http://www.hospiceofcentraliowa.org

Chariton

19857 ■ Circle of Life Hospice--Chariton
1010 N 7th St.
Chariton, IA 50049
Ph: (641)774-2339
Free: 866-774-2339
Fax: (641)774-5267
E-mail: info@cofhomecare.com
URL: http://cofhomecare.com/colabout.html

Clarion

19858 ■ Hospice for Wright County
115 1st St. SE
Clarion, IA 50525-1401
Ph: (515)532-3461
Free: 800-944-1713
Fax: (515)532-3762
URL: http://www.wrightcounty.org/_1newsite/Departments/Public_Health/Offices/Office2.as p

Council Bluffs

19859 ■ AseraCare Hospice--Council Bluffs
508 E Broadway
Council Bluffs, IA 51503-4413
Ph: (712)325-1751
Free: 800-591-2273
Fax: (712)325-1895
URL: http://www.aseracare.com

19860 ■ Hospice with Heart, Inc.
300 W Broadway, Ste. 114
Council Bluffs, IA 51503-6528
Ph: (712)325-6802
E-mail: hospice@hospicewithheart.org
URL: http://www.hospicewithheart.org/

Cresco

19861 ■ Howard County Community Hospice
327 8th Ave. W
Cresco, IA 52136
Ph: (563)547-2989
Fax: (563)547-4223
URL: http://www.rhshc.com/

Creston

19862 ■ Greater Regional Hospice
1715 W Prairie St.
Creston, IA 50801-1054
Ph: (641)782-3528
Free: 888-424-0485
Fax: (641)782-3541
URL: http://www.greaterregional.org/services.php?cdf=50
Formerly: Green Valley Hospice Greater Comm Hospital.

Davenport

19863 ■ Beacon of Hope Hospice Inc.--Davenport
1020 W 35th St.
Davenport, IA 52806
Ph: (563)391-6933
Free: 888-932-2732
Fax: (563)391-5104
URL: http://www.yourtrustedpartner.com/bohdlocation.htm

19864 ■ Heartland Hospice Services--Davenport
2322 E Kimberly Rd.
Davenport, IA 52807
Ph: (563)359-3540
Free: 888-733-3750
Fax: (563)359-9092
E-mail: careline@hcr-manorcare.com
URL: http://www.hcr-manorcare.com

19865 ■ Hospice Compassus-Davenport
1850 E 53rd St., Ste. 1
Davenport, IA 52807
Free: 877-377-1607
E-mail: contactusiadav@hospicecom.com
URL: http://www.hospicecompassus.com/

Decorah

19866 ■ Winneshiek Medical Center Hospice
901 Montgomery St.
Decorah, IA 52101-2325
Ph: (563)382-9671
Fax: (563)387-3116
E-mail: webmaster@winmedical.org
URL: http://www.winmedical.org/healthservices.php?hsid=15
Formerly: Hospice of Winneshiek County.

Denison

19867 ■ Crawford County Home Health Hospice and Public Health
105 N Main St.
Denison, IA 51442
Ph: (712)263-3303
Fax: (712)263-4033
URL: http://www.crawfordcountyhealth.com/eminder.asp

Des Moines

19868 ■ Kavannagh House on 56th St.
Hospice of Central Iowa
900 56th St.
Des Moines, IA 50312
Ph: (515)255-0857
Fax: (515)255-8401
E-mail: tdale@hospiceofcentraliowa.org
URL: http://www.hospiceofcentraliowa.org/index.cfm?page=2
Formerly: Kavanagh House Hospice.

19869 ■ Mercy Hospice--Des Moines
603 E 12th St.
Des Moines, IA 50309-5515
Ph: (515)643-8400
Fax: (515)643-0973
E-mail: ediehl@mercydesmoines.org
URL: http://www.mercydesmoines.org/comm_resources/hospice.cfm

19870 ■ Taylor House
3401 E Douglas Ave.
Des Moines, IA 50317
Ph: (515)557-3111
Fax: (515)557-3157
URL: http://www.intrusthealth.org/body.cfm?id=42

Dubuque

19871 ■ Heartland Hospice Care-Dubuque
1660 Embassy W Dr.
Dubuque, IA 52002
Ph: (563)584-9223
Fax: (563)584-9030
URL: http://www.hcr-manorcare.com/tabid/67/default.aspx?FacilityID=4618

19872 ■ Hospice of Dubuque
2255 John F Kennedy Rd.
Dubuque, IA 52002-2846
Ph: (563)582-1220
Free: 815-747-3622
Fax: (563)582-8089
E-mail: info@hospiceofdubuque.org
URL: http://www.hospiceofdubuque.com/

Emmetsburg

19873 ■ Hospice of Palo Alto County
3210 1st St.
Emmetsburg, IA 50536
Ph: (712)852-5422
Fax: (712)852-5573
URL: http://www.pachs.com/services/hospice.shtml

Fort Dodge

19874 ■ Paula J. Baber Hospice Home
2630 9th Ave. S
Fort Dodge, IA 50501
Ph: (515)574-8500
URL: http://www.trmc.org/baber-hospice-home.cfm

19875 ■ Trinity Hospice
802 Kenyon Rd.
Fort Dodge, IA 50501
Ph: (515)574-6420
Fax: (515)574-6985
URL: http://www.trmc.org/hospice.cfm
Formerly: Hopsice of Fort Dodge.

Fort Madison

19876 ■ Lee County Health Department Hospice
2218 Ave. H
Fort Madison, IA 52627
Ph: (319)372-5225
Free: 800-458-6672
Fax: (319)372-4373
E-mail: healthdepartment@leecounty.org
URL: http://www.leecounty.org/Services/Health/Home_Care_Hospice/HomeCare.html

Greenfield

19877 ■ Care Initiatives Hospice--Greenfield
122 Public Square
Greenfield, IA 50849
Ph: (641)743-2264
Free: 877-577-8555
Fax: (641)743-2268
URL: http://www.careinitiativeshospice.org/

Grinnell

19878 ■ Grinnell Regional Hospice
210 4th Ave.
Grinnell, IA 50112-1898
Ph: (641)236-2418
Fax: (641)236-2956
URL: http://www.grmc.us/services/hospice.html

Grundy Center

19879 ■ Cedar Valley Hospice--Grundy Center
310 E Ave. G
Grundy Center, IA 50638
Ph: (319)824-3868
Free: 888-878-3868
Fax: (319)824-3125
E-mail: cedarvalleyhospice@cvhospice.org
URL: http://www.cvhospice.org

Ida Grove

19880 ■ Horn Hospice
Horn Memorial Hospital
701 E Second St.
Ida Grove, IA 51445
Ph: (712)364-3311
Fax: (712)364-4065
E-mail: harm@hornmemorialhospital.org
URL: http://www.hornmemorialhospital.org/getpage.php?name=hospice

Independence

19881 ■ Cedar Valley Hospice--Independence
801 1st St. E
Independence, IA 50644
Ph: (319)334-6960
Free: 888-273-8957
Fax: (319)334-7313
URL: http://www.cvhospice.org/

Iowa City

19882 ■ Iowa City Hospice
1025 Wade St.
Iowa City, IA 52240-6626
Ph: (319)351-5665
Free: 800-897-3052
Fax: (319)351-5729
E-mail: info@iowacityhospice.com
URL: http://www.iowacityhospice.com/

19883 ■ Iowa City VA Medical Center
601 Hwy. 6 W
Iowa City, IA 52246
Ph: (319)338-0581
Fax: (319)688-3854
URL: http://www.iowacity.va.gov/

19884 ■ University of Iowa Community HomeCare
UI Community HomeCare Inc.
2949 Sierra Court SW
Iowa City, IA 52240
Ph: (319)337-8522
Free: 888-262-6469
Fax: (319)337-8524
E-mail: kaefringbr@healthcare.uiowa.edu
URL: http://www.uihealthcare.com/depts/uihomecare/index.html

Johnston

19885 ■ Childserve Homecare Service
5406 Merle Hay Rd.
Johnston, IA 50131
Ph: (515)727-8750
URL: http://www.childserve.org/index.php/homecare-service

19886 ■ Mercy Hospice-Johnston
5820 Winwood Dr.
Johnston, IA 50131
Ph: (515)643-6150
Fax: (515)643-6149
E-mail: ediehl@mercydesmoines.org
URL: http://www.mercydesmoines.org/comm_resources/hospice_johnston.cfm

Knoxville

19887 ■ Hospice of Central Iowa Knoxville
213 E Main St., Ste. 103
Knoxville, IA 50138
Ph: (641)842-4312
Free: 800-350-9209
Fax: (641)842-3246
E-mail: ttassell@hospiceofcentraliowa.org
URL: http://www.hospiceofcentraliowa.org

Lake City

19888 ■ Stewart Memorial Community Hospital
Community Hospice
1301 W Main St.
Lake City, IA 51449
Ph: (712)464-3171
Free: 800-262-2614
Fax: (712)464-3269
E-mail: info@stewartmemorial.org
URL: http://www.stewartmemorial.org

Le Mars

19889 ■ Hospice of Siouxland North
Hwy. 3 E
Floyd Valley Hospital
Le Mars, IA 51031
Ph: (712)546-4848
Free: 800-383-4545
Fax: (712)233-1123
E-mail: thousandj@hospicemail.com
URL: http://www.hospiceofsiouxland.org

Manchester

19890 ■ Hospice of Comfort
Regional Medical Center
PO Box 359
Manchester, IA 52057
Ph: (563)927-7303
Fax: (563)927-7444
URL: http://www.regmedctr.org/page.php?id=18&title=Hospice_of_Comfort#

Mapleton

19891 ■ Burgess Hospice
111 S 5th St.
Mapleton, IA 51034

Maquoketa

19892 ■ Hospice of Jackson County, Inc.
511 W Quarry St.
Maquoketa, IA 52060
Ph: (563)652-0123
Fax: (563)652-2181
E-mail: hospice@qwest.net
URL: http://www.hospiceofjacksoncounty.com/

Marshalltown

19893 ■ Iowa River Hospice
502 Plaza Heights Rd.
Marshalltown, IA 50158
Ph: (641)753-7704
Free: 800-827-4521
E-mail: rhospice@marshallnet.com
URL: http://www.iowariverhospice.org

Mason City

19894 ■ Hospice of North Iowa
232 2nd St. SE
Mason City, IA 50401-3906
Ph: (641)422-6200
Free: 800-297-4719
Fax: (641)422-6253
URL: http://www.mercynorthiowa.com/services/hospice/index.shtml

Milford

19895 ■ Lakes Regional Hospice
1003 21st St.
Milford, IA 51351
Ph: (712)338-9998
URL: http://www.lakeshealth.org/services/details.asp?ID=11

Monticello

19896 ■ Above & Beyond Home Health Care
116 N Cedar St.
Monticello, IA 52310
Ph: (319)465-4637
Fax: (319)465-3491

Mount Ayr

19897 ■ Hospice of Central Iowa Mount Ayr
107 S Fillmore St.
Mount Ayr, IA 50854-1823
Ph: (641)464-2088
Free: 888-464-7222
Fax: (641)464-2009
E-mail: kstackhouse@hospiceofcentraliowa.org
URL: http://www.hospiceofcentraliowa.org/

Mount Pleasant

19898 ■ Hospice of Central Iowa-Mount Pleasant
204 S Jefferson St., Ste. 103
Mount Pleasant, IA 52641
Ph: (319)385-4472
Free: 888-385-4472
URL: http://www.hospiceofcentraliowa.org/index.cfm?page=2

Muscatine

19899 ■ Unity Health Care Home Care & Hospice
1609 Cedar St.
Muscatine, IA 52761
Ph: (563)263-3325
Fax: (563)263-6202
URL: http://www.unityiowa.org/contact_us.php

Newton

19900 ■ Hospice of Jasper County
204 N 4th Ave. E
Newton, IA 50208-3135
Ph: (641)787-3074
Fax: (641)791-4819
E-mail: info@skiffmed.com
URL: http://www.skiffmed.com/jasperhospice.asp?id=1060730211

Onawa

19901 ■ Burgess Hospice
1600 Diamond St.
Onawa, IA 51040
Ph: (712)423-9324
Fax: (712)423-9188
E-mail: sjohnston@burgesshc.org
URL: http://www.burgesshc.org
Formerly: Burgess Memorial Hospice.

Orange City

19902 ■ Orange City Home Health Hospice
400 Central Ave. NW
Orange City, IA 51041
Ph: (712)737-5279
Free: 800-808-6264
Fax: (712)737-5258
URL: http://ochealthsystem.org/home-health-hospice/

Osceola

19903 ■ Hospice of Central Iowa--Osceola
715 W McLane St.
Osceola, IA 50213
Ph: (641)342-2888
Fax: (641)342-2889
URL: http://www.hospiceofcentraliowa.org

Oskaloosa

19904 ■ Mahaska Hospice
1225 C Ave. E
Oskaloosa, IA 52577
Ph: (641)672-3260
Fax: (641)672-3490
URL: http://www.mahaskahealth.org/index.php/outpatient-services/home-health-serv ices

Ottumwa

19905 ■ Good Samaritan Society Home Health and Hospice
1 Oak Ridge Rd.
Ottumwa, IA 52501
Ph: (641)684-9309
Fax: (641)684-9308
URL: http://www.good-sam.com

19906 ■ Hospice of Wapello
312 E Alta Vista Ave.
Ottumwa, IA 52501-1413
Ph: (641)682-0684
Free: 800-806-4967
Fax: (641)684-9209
E-mail: hospice@pcsia.net
URL: http://www.hospice-ottumwa.com

Pella

19907 ■ Hospice of Pella-Comfort House
505 Union St.
Pella, IA 50219
Ph: (641)620-5050
Fax: (641)620-5080
E-mail: info@aatspellahealth.org
URL: http://www.pellahealth.org/services/hospice.php

Perry

19908 ■ Hospice of Central Iowa - Perry
402 12th St.
Perry, IA 50220
Ph: (515)465-4705
Free: 888-206-0080
Fax: (515)465-5560
E-mail: lhoger@hospiceofcentraliowa.org
URL: http://www.hospiceofcentraliowa.org
William P. Havekost, Director

Pocahontas

19909 ■ Pocahontas Community Hospital Hospice
606 NW 7th St.
Pocahontas, IA 50574-1028
Ph: (712)335-3430
Fax: (712)335-3431
URL: http://www.pocahontashospital.org/services.html

Sac City

19910 ■ Loring Family Hospice
211 Highland Ave.
Sac City, IA 50583
Ph: (712)662-7105
Free: 800-344-3767
Fax: (712)662-3284
URL: http://www.loringhospital.org/body.cfm?id=28

Sheldon

19911 ■ Sanford Home Health and Hospice-Sheldon
PO Box 250
Sheldon, IA 51201
Ph: (712)324-6420
Fax: (714)324-6445
URL: http://www.sanfordsheldon.org/

Sibley

19912 ■ Avera McKennan Branch Hospice and Palliative Care
115 Cedar Ln.
Sibley, IA 51249-0258
Ph: (712)754-4611
Fax: (712)754-4612
URL: http://www.avera.org/mckennan/services/hospice/index.aspx
Formerly: Oscola Community Hospice.

Sioux Center

19913 ■ CHEARS Homehealth & Hospice
30 19th St. SW
Sioux Center, IA 51250
Ph: (712)722-8108
Free: 800-722-1922
Fax: (712)722-1294
URL: http://www.averamckennan.org/amck/regional-facilities/siouxcenter/services/homeheal th.aspx

Sioux City

19914 ■ Care Initiatives Hospice-Sioux City
3500 S Lakeport St.
Sioux City, IA 51106
Ph: (712)239-1226
Fax: (712)239-1514
URL: http://www.careinitiativeshospice.org/who_we_are_team.aspx

19915 ■ Hospice of Siouxland
4300 Hamilton Blvd.
Sioux City, IA 51104
Ph: (712)233-4144
Free: 800-383-4545
Fax: (712)233-1123
E-mail: thounsandj@hospicemail.com
URL: http://www.hospiceofsiouxland.org

Spencer

19916 ■ Hospice of Northwest Iowa
1200 1st Ave. E
Spencer, IA 51301
Ph: (712)264-6380
Fax: (712)264-6470
URL: http://www.spencerhospital.org

Storm Lake

19917 ■ Storm Lake Area Hospice
Buena Vista Regional Medical Center
1525 W 5th St.
Storm Lake, IA 50588
Ph: (712)749-2747
Free: 888-712-5433
Fax: (712)749-2750
URL: http://www.bvrmc.org/getpage.php?name=hospice

Urbandale

19918 ■ Iowa Health Home Care-Intrust
11333 Aurora Ave.
Urbandale, IA 50322
Ph: (515)557-3128
Fax: (515)557-3290
URL: http://www.iowahealthhomecare.org/

W Burlington

19919 ■ Great River Hospice
1306 S Washington Rd.
W Burlington, IA 52655
Ph: (319)768-3350
Fax: (319)768-3366
URL: http://www.greatrivermedical.org/

Washington

19920 ■ Hospice of Washington County--Washington
948 E 11th St.
Washington, IA 52353
Ph: (319)653-7321
Free: 888-966-6608
Fax: (319)653-4057
E-mail: dignity@lisco.com
URL: http://www.hospicewashingtoncounty.org/

Waterloo

19921 ■ Cedar Valley Hospice-Waterloo
2101 Kimball Ave., Ste. 401
Waterloo, IA 50704
Ph: (319)272-2002
Free: 800-617-1972
Fax: (319)272-2038
E-mail: cedarvalleyhospice@cvhospice.org
URL: http://www.cvhospice.org

Waverly

19922 ■ Cedar Valley Hospice-Waverly
207 20th St. NW
Waverly, IA 50677
Ph: (319)352-1274
Free: 877-485-7081
Fax: (319)352-9001
E-mail: cedarvalleyhospice@cvhospice.org
URL: http://www.cvhospice.org
Formerly: Bremer Butler Hospital.

Webster City

19923 ■ Hospice/Respite Care of Hamilton County
821 Seneca St.
Webster City, IA 50595
Ph: (515)832-9565
Fax: (515)832-9660
E-mail: dhiggins@hamiltoncountypublichealth.com
URL: http://www.hamiltoncountypublichealth.com

West Des Moines

19924 ■ Bright Kavannagh House
Hospice of Central Iowa
1821 W Grand
West Des Moines, IA 50265
Ph: (512)255-0857
Fax: (515)274-1137
E-mail: tdale@hospiceofcentraliowa.org
URL: http://www.hospiceofcentraliowa.org/index.cfm?page=2

19925 ■ Hospice of Central Iowa
The Bright Center
401 Railroad Pl.
West Des Moines, IA 50265-4730
Ph: (515)274-3400
Free: 800-806-9934
Fax: (515)274-1137
E-mail: nhaskins@hospiceofcrntraliowa.org
URL: http://www.hospiceofcentraliowa.org

Winterset

19926 ■ Middle River Hospice
300 W Hutchings St.
Winterset, IA 50273
Ph: (515)462-2373
Fax: (515)462-5008
URL: http://www.madisonhealth.com

KANSAS

Abilene

19927 ■ Hospice of Dickinson County
511 NE 10th St.
Abilene, KS 67410
Ph: (785)263-6630
Fax: (785)263-6636
URL: http://www.mhsks.org/

Beloit

19928 ■ Solomon Valley Hospice
400 W 8th St.
Beloit, KS 67420-0399
Ph: (785)738-3342
Fax: (785)738-3224
E-mail: pjones@mchks.com
URL: http://www.mchks.com/Directory.aspx?DID=27

Clay Center

19929 ■ Meadowlark Hospice
709 Liberty St.
Clay Center, KS 67432
Ph: (785)632-2225
Fax: (785)632-3257
E-mail: mhospice@ccmcks.org
URL: http://www.ccmcks.org/hospice/mhospice.html

Coffeyville

19930 ■ Harry Hynes Memorial Hospice--Coffeyville
2404 W 8th St.
Coffeyville, KS 67337
Ph: (620)251-1640
Fax: (620)251-2130
URL: http://www.hynesmemorial.org/

Dodge City

19931 ■ Hospice of the Prairie Inc.
200 4th Cir.
Dodge City, KS 67801
Ph: (620)227-7209
Fax: (620)227-7429
E-mail: hopi@sbcglobal.net
URL: http://www.hospiceoftheprairie.com

El Dorado

19932 ■ Amedisys Hospice-El Dorado
2733 W Central Ave.
El Dorado, KS 67042
Ph: (316)322-8115
Free: 866-708-6560
Fax: (316)322-8125
URL: http://locations.amedisys.com/states.cfm?id=26

19933 ■ AseraCare Hospice-Wichita
112 W Pine
El Dorado, KS 67042
Ph: (316)322-7017
Free: 877-234-6692
Fax: (316)322-8710
URL: http://hospice.aseracare.com/hospice-care.aspx

Emporia

19934 ■ Hand in Hand Homecare and Hospice
1015 Industrial Rd.
Emporia, KS 66801-1581
Ph: (620)340-6177
Free: 800-334-6215
Fax: (620)340-6178
E-mail: info@handinhandhospice.org
URL: http://www.handinhandhospice.org

Garden City

19935 ■ Saint Catherine Home Care Services
602 N 6th St.
Garden City, KS 67846-5509
Ph: (620)272-2519
Free: 800-281-4077
Fax: (620)272-2664
URL: http://www.stcath-hosp.org

Hays

19936 ■ Palliative Care/Lifeline of Hays Medical Center
2220 Canterbury Dr.
Hays, KS 67601
Ph: (785)623-6200
Free: 800-990-0731
Fax: (785)623-5465
E-mail: snoll@haysmed.com
URL: http://www.haysmed.com
Formerly: Hays Home Health and Hospice Center.

Hiawatha

19937 ■ Hospice of Northeast Kansas-Multi-County
PO Box 182
Hiawatha, KS 66434
Ph: (785)742-7192
Fax: (785)742-4237
E-mail: nekmulti@rainbow.net
URL: http://nekhealth.tripod.com/

Holton

19938 ■ Holton Community Hospital Home Health and Hospice
1110 Columbine Dr.
Holton, KS 66436-8824
Ph: (785)364-2116
Fax: (785)364-2860
URL: http://www.rhrjc.org/index_flash.php

Hutchinson

19939 ■ Hospice of Reno County, Inc.
1600 N Lorraine, Ste. 203
Hutchinson, KS 67501
Ph: (620)665-2473
Free: 800-267-6891
Fax: (620)669-5959
URL: http://www.hospicerenocounty.com

Iola

19940 ■ Allen County Hospice Allen County Hospital
101 S First St.
Iola, KS 66749
Ph: (620)365-1000
URL: http://www.allencountyhospital.com/

Junction City

19941 ■ Hospice at Geary Community Hospital
1310 W Ash
Junction City, KS 66441
Ph: (785)762-2653
Fax: (785)238-2685
URL: http://www.gchks.org/

Lansing

19942 ■ Sunflower Health Care, Inc.--Lansing
112 S Main St.
Lansing, KS 66043
Ph: (913)680-0800
Fax: (913)680-0804
E-mail: jsaporito@omega-healthcare.com
URL: http://omega-healthcare.com/web/Default.aspx?alias=omega-healthcare.com/web /sunflower

Lawrence

19943 ■ Hospice Care in Douglas County
200 Maine St.
Lawrence, KS 66044
Ph: (785)843-3738
Free: 800-264-3739
Fax: (785)843-0757
URL: http://www.vna-ks.org/

Leawood

19944 ■ Continua Hospice-Kansas
13002 State Line Rd.
Leawood, KS 66209
Ph: (913)905-0255
Fax: (913)339-9775
E-mail: homehealthinformation@continuaHH.com
URL: http://www.continuahh.com/

Manhattan

19945 ■ Home Care and Hospice, Inc
3801 Vanesta Dr.
Manhattan, KS 66503
Ph: (785)537-0688
Free: 800-748-7474
Fax: (785)537-1309
E-mail: cnolte@hcandh.org
URL: http://www.homecareandhospice.org

Newton

19946 ■ Harry Hynes Memorial Hospice-Newton
606 n Main St., Ste. 202
Newton, KS 67114
Ph: (316)283-1103
Free: 800-767-4965
E-mail: hospice@hynesmemorial.org
URL: http://www.hynesmemorial.org/

Olathe

19947 ■ Hospice of Olathe Medical Center
20333 W 151st St., TDB2
Olathe, KS 66061-5350
Ph: (913)324-8515
Free: 800-264-4315
Fax: (913)324-8597
URL: http://www.olathehealth.org/About-Us/Hospice

Oskaloosa

19948 ■ Hospice of Jefferson County
1212 Walnut St.
Oskaloosa, KS 66066
Ph: (785)863-2447
Fax: (785)863-3323
URL: http://health.jfcountyks.com/

Overland Park

19949 ■ Care Alternatives of Kansas
9393 W 110th St., Bldg. 51
Corporate Woods Ste. 500
Overland Park, KS 66210
Ph: (913)323-6847
Free: 866-821-1212
Fax: (913)323-6848
URL: http://health.jfcountyks.com/

19950 ■ Catholic Community Hospice--Overland Park
9740 W 87th St.
Overland Park, KS 66212
Ph: (913)621-5090
Fax: (913)342-1472
URL: http://catholiccommunityhospice.com/

19951 ■ Hospice Advantage, Inc-Overland Park
6340 Glenwood St.
Overland Park, KS 66202
Ph: (913)859-9582
Free: 800--HOSPICE
Fax: (913)859-9536
URL: http://health.jfcountyks.com/

19952 ■ Kansas City Hospice & Palliative Care--Overland Park
10100 W 87th St., Ste. 100
Overland Park, KS 66212
Ph: (913)894-8228
Fax: (913)894-8446
URL: http://www.kansascityhospice.org/

Parsons

19953 ■ Harry Hynes Memorial Hospice-Parsons
3106 Main St.
Parsons, KS 67357
Ph: (620)423-3863
Fax: (620)423-0441
E-mail: hospice@hynesmemorial.org
URL: http://www.hynesmemorial.org/

Phillipsburg

19954 ■ Hospice Services, Inc.
424 8th St.
Phillipsburg, KS 67661-0116
Ph: (785)543-2900
Free: 800-315-5122
Fax: (785)543-5688
E-mail: hospice@ruraltel.net
URL: http://www.hospicenwks.net/

Pittsburg

19955 ■ Hospice Compassus-Pittsburg
200 E Centennial Ste. 2
Pittsburg, KS 66762
Ph: (620)232-9898
Fax: (620)232-9896
E-mail: contactusKSPIT@hospicecom.com
URL: http://www.hospicecompassus.com/loc-KSPIT.html

Pratt

19956 ■ South Wind Hospice
496 Yucca La.
Pratt, KS 67124
Ph: (620)672-7553
Free: 888-731-7553
Fax: (620)672-7554
E-mail: swhospic@pratt.net
URL: http://www.southwindhospice.com

Sabetha

19957 ■ Nemaha County Home Health and Hospice
14th and Oregon
Sabetha, KS 66534
Ph: (785)284-0203
Fax: (785)284-1517
E-mail: lkey@sabethahospital.com
URL: http://www.sabethahospital.com/

Salina

19958 ■ Hospice of Salina, Inc.
730 Holly La.
Salina, KS 67402-2238
Ph: (785)825-1717
Fax: (785)825-4949
E-mail: hospice@srhc.com
URL: http://www.hospiceofsalina.org

Shawnee Mission

19959 ■ VITAS Innovative Hospice Care of Kansas City-Shawnee Mission
10000 W 75th St.
Shawnee Mission, KS 66204
Ph: (913)772-1631
Fax: (913)722-2326
URL: http://www.vitas.com/

Stilwell

19960 ■ Sunflower Health Care, Inc-Stilwell
7398 W 162nd Terrace
Stilwell, KS 66085
Ph: (913)897-1104
Fax: (913)897-1103
E-mail: bpatterson@omega-healthcare.com
URL: http://omega-healthcare.com/web/Default.aspx?alias=omega-healthcare.com/web /sunflower

Topeka

19961 ■ Catholic Community Hospice-Topeka
234 S Kansas Ave.
Topeka, KS 66603
Ph: (785)357-5107
Free: 877-621-5090
Fax: (785)233-7234
URL: http://catholiccommunityhospice.com/

19962 ■ Heart of America Hospice--Kansas
3715 SW 29th St., Ste. 100
Topeka, KS 66614
Ph: (785)228-0400
Fax: (785)228-9049
URL: http://www.heartofamericahospice.com/

19963 ■ Heartland Hospice Services--Topeka
2231 SW Wanamaker Rd., Ste. 202
Topeka, KS 66604-1779
Ph: (785)271-6500
Free: 800-214-0282
Fax: (785)271-8229
URL: http://www.hcr-manorcare.com/

19964 ■ Heartland Hospice Services--Topeka
2231 SW Wanamaker Rd.
Topeka, KS 66614
Ph: (785)271-6500
Fax: (785)271-8229
URL: http://www.heartlandhospice.com

19965 ■ Midland Hospice Care
200 SW Frazier Cir.
Topeka, KS 66606-2800
Ph: (785)232-2044
Free: 800-491-3691
Fax: (785)232-5567
URL: http://www.midlandcareconnection.org/Page.aspx?pid=614

Wamego

19966 ■ PRN Home Health and Hospice-Wamego
1010 Lincoln Ave.
Wamego, KS 66547
Ph: (785)456-7764
Fax: (785)456-7194
URL: http://www.prnhomehealthhospice.com/

Wichita

19967 ■ Amedisys Hospice Services-Wichita
250 W Douglas, Ste. 101
Wichita, KS 67202-3113
Ph: (316)945-0459
Free: 866-334-7790
Fax: (316)945-9897
URL: http://www.amedisys.com/hospice_locations.cfm

19968 ■ Good Shepherd Hospice-Wichita
439 N McLean Blvd., Ste. 100
Wichita, KS 67203
Ph: (316)616-2277
Free: 877-598-2277
E-mail: infowichita@goodshepherdhospice.com
URL: http://www.goodshepherdhospice.com/

19969 ■ Harry Hynes Memorial Hospice--Wichita
313 S Market St.
Wichita, KS 67202
Ph: (316)265-9441
Free: 800-767-4965
Fax: (316)265-6066
URL: http://www.hynessmemorial.org

19970 ■ Heartland Home Health Care and Hospice--Wichita
3210 W Kellogg Dr.
Wichita, KS 67213
Ph: (316)788-7626
Fax: (316)788-7072
E-mail: careline@hcr-manorcare.com
URL: http://www.hcr-manorcare.com

19971 ■ National Hospice/dba Promises Kept Hospice
9415 E Harry St., Ste. 403
Wichita, KS 67207
Ph: (316)686-5999
Fax: (316)686-5634

19972 ■ Rivercross Hospice--Wichita
251 S Whittier St.
Wichita, KS 67207
Ph: (316)260-9690
Free: 877-291-9690
Fax: (316)440-5562
E-mail: info@rivercrosshospice.com
URL: http://www.rivercrosshospice.com/

KENTUCKY

Ashland

19973 ■ Community Hospice--Ashland
1538 Central Ave.
Ashland, KY 41101
Ph: (606)329-1890
Free: 800-926-6184
Fax: (606)329-0018
E-mail: hospice@chospice.org
URL: http://www.chospice.org

Bardstown

19974 ■ Hospice of Nelson County Flaget Memorial Hospital
4305 New Shepherdsville Rd.
Bardstown, KY 40004
Ph: (502)350-5570
Fax: (502)349-1292
URL: http://www.sjhlex.org/body.cfm?id=1674

Berea

19975 ■ Hospice Care Plus, Inc.
208 Kidd Dr.
Berea, KY 40403
Ph: (859)986-1500
Free: 800-806-5492
Fax: (859)986-2546
URL: http://www.hospicecp.org

Campbellsville

19976 ■ Hospice of Central Kentucky-Campbellsville
Green River Plaza, Ste. 5
295 Campbellsville Bypass
Campbellsville, KY 42718
Ph: (270)789-4247

Free: 800-859-8782
Fax: (270)789-4248
URL: http://www.hosparus.org/

Corbin

19977 ■ Hospice of the Bluegrass-Corbin
1020 Cumberland Falls Hwy.
Corbin, KY 40701
Ph: (606)523-3090
Fax: (606)523-3045
E-mail: info@hospicebg.org
URL: http://www.hospicebg.org/

Cynthiana

19978 ■ Hospice of the Bluegrass--Cynthiana
1317 U.S. Hwy. 62E
Cynthiana, KY 41031
Ph: (859)234-6462
Free: 800-756-6005
Fax: (859)234-8671
E-mail: acox@hospicebg.org
URL: http://www.hospicebg.com
Amy Cox, Executive Director

Danville

19979 ■ Heritage Hospice--Danville
120 Enterprise Dr.
Danville, KY 40422
Ph: (859)236-2425
Free: 800-203-6633
URL: http://www.heritagehospice.com

Dixon

19980 ■ Saint Anthony's Hospice-Dixon
1255 US 41-A S
Dixon, KY 42409-0305
Ph: (270)639-6501
Fax: (270)639-6505
URL: http://www.stanthonyshospice.org/

Edgewood

19981 ■ Hospice Care of St. Elizabeth Healthcare
483 S Loop Dr.
Edgewood, KY 41017
Ph: (859)301-4600
Fax: (859)301-4601
URL: http://www.stelizabeth.com/

Elizabethtown

19982 ■ Hospice of Central Kentucky-Elizabethtown
105 Diecks Dr.
Elizabethtown, KY 42702
Ph: (270)737-6300
Free: 800-686-9577
Fax: (270)737-4053
URL: http://www.hosparus.org/
Formerly: Hospice and Palliative Care of Central Kentucky.

Florence

19983 ■ Hospice of Northern Kentucky
7388 Turfway Rd.
Florence, KY 41042
Ph: (859)441-6332
Free: 800-200-5408
Fax: (859)441-2032
E-mail: info@hospicebg.com
URL: http://www.hospicebg.com

Frankfort

19984 ■ Hospice of the Bluegrass--Frankfort
208 Steele St.
Frankfort, KY 40601
Ph: (502)223-1744
Free: 800-926-1302
Fax: (502)223-7788
E-mail: info@hospicebg.com
URL: http://www.hospicebg.com

Glasgow

19985 ■ T.J. Samson Community Hospice Home Care Program
1301 N Race St.
Glasgow, KY 42143
Ph: (270)651-4430
Fax: (270)651-4862
E-mail: tjsamson@tjsamson.org
URL: http://www.tjsamson.org

Harlan

19986 ■ Mountain Heritage Hospice
168 Village Center Rd., Ste. 160
Harlan, KY 40831
Ph: (606)573-6111
Free: 800-371-6112
Fax: (606)573-7964
E-mail: info@hospicebg.com
URL: http://www.hospicebg.com

Hartford

19987 ■ Hospice of Ohio County
1211 Old Main St.
Hartford, KY 42347
Ph: (270)298-7411
Fax: (270)298-9937
URL: http://www.ohiocountyhospital.com/DepartmentsServices.cfm?pageId=28

Hazard

19988 ■ Hospice of the Bluegrass--Hazard
3115 N Main St., Ste. 101
Hazard, KY 41071
Ph: (606)439-2111
Free: 800-560-1101
Fax: (606)439-4198
E-mail: info@hospicebg.com
URL: http://www.hospicebg.com
Formerly: Mountain Community Hospice.

Henderson

19989 ■ Saint Anthony's Hospice--Henderson
2410 S Green St.
Henderson, KY 42420
Ph: (270)826-2326
Free: 866-380-2326
Fax: (270)831-2169
URL: http://www.stanthonyshospice.org/

Hopkinsville

19990 ■ Pennyroyal Hospice
220 Burley Ave.
Hopkinsville, KY 42240
Ph: (270)885-6428
Fax: (270)885-4901
URL: http://www.pennyroyalhospice.com

Lexington

19991 ■ Central Baptist Hospital
1740 Nicholasville Rd.
Lexington, KY 40503
Ph: (859)260-2116
Fax: (859)260-4349
URL: http://www.centralbap.com/

19992 ■ Hospice of the Bluegrass--Lexington
2312 Alexandria Dr.
Lexington, KY 40504
Ph: (859)276-5344
Free: 800-876-6005
Fax: (859)223-0490
E-mail: info@hospicebg.com
URL: http://www.hospicebg.com

19993 ■ Hospice of the Bluegrass-St Joseph In-Patient Unit
1 Saint Joseph Dr.
Lexington, KY 40504
Ph: (859)313-2770
Fax: (859)278-1264
URL: http://www.hospicebg.com/stjoseph.html

London

19994 ■ Tri-County Hospice--London
740 E Laurel Rd.
London, KY 40744
Ph: (606)877-3950
Free: 800-241-2208
Fax: (606)877-3956
URL: http://www.sjhlex.org/body.cfm?id=1006

Louisville

19995 ■ Hosparus Grief Counseling Center
3532 Ephraim McDowell Dr.
Louisville, KY 40205
Ph: (502)456-5451
Free: 888-345-8197
Fax: (502)456-9701
E-mail: mdunlap@hospices.org
URL: http://www.hosparus.org/
Formerly: Bridges Center, Alliances of Community Hospices.

19996 ■ Hospice of Louisville--Ephraim McDowell Drive
3532 Ephraim McDowell Dr.
Louisville, KY 40205
Ph: (502)456-6200
Free: 800-264-0521
Fax: (502)456-6655
URL: http://www.hosparus.org/
Formerly: Hospice and Palliative Care of Louisville.

19997 ■ Hospice of Louisville Norton Healthcare Pavilion Inpatient
315 E Broadway, 6th Flr.
Louisville, KY 40202
Ph: (502)629-3600
Fax: (502)629-3638
URL: http://www.hosparus.org/
Formerly: Hospice and Palliative Care of Louisville.

19998 ■ Kosair Children's Hospital, Hearts & Hands Palliative Care Program
231 E Chestnut St.
Louisville, KY 40202
Ph: (502)629-7516
Fax: (502)629-5057
URL: http://nortonhealthcare.com/home_kosair.cfm?id=628

19999 ■ Peoplefirst Rehabilitation
680 S 4th St., Ste. 1
Louisville, KY 40202
Ph: (502)596-7300
Free: 800-545-0749
E-mail: rehabclinicalservices@peoplefirstrehab.com
URL: http://www.peoplefirstrehab.com

Madisonville

20000 ■ Green River Hospice
418 N Scott St.
Madisonville, KY 42431
Ph: (270)326-4660
Fax: (270)326-4779
URL: http://www.troverfoundation.org/

Maysville

20001 ■ Hospice of Hope
909 Kenton Station Dr.
Maysville, KY 41056
Ph: (606)759-4050
Free: 800-928-4848
URL: http://www.hospiceofhope.com

Monticello

20002 ■ Hospice of Lake Cumberland-Monticello
1219 N Main St.
Monticello, KY 42633
Ph: (606)343-5026
Fax: (606)343-5045
URL: http://www.hospicelc.org/

Morehead

20003 ■ Saint Claire Home Care/Hospice
304 W 2nd St.
Morehead, KY 40351
Ph: (606)783-6812
Free: 800-264-0616
Fax: (606)783-6828
URL: http://www.st-claire.org/svs_hhs_02.php

Morganfield

20004 ■ Saint Anthony's Hospice--Morganfield
203 W McElroy St.
Morganfield, KY 42437
Ph: (270)389-2254
Fax: (270)639-6505
URL: http://www.stanthonyshospice.org/

Murray

20005 ■ Murray-Calloway County Hospital
803 Poplar St.
Murray, KY 42071
Ph: (270)767-2108
Fax: (270)767-2149
URL: https://www.murrayhospital.org/

20006 ■ Murray-Calloway County Hospital Hospice
803 Poplar St.
Murray, KY 42071
Ph: (270)767-2108
Free: 800-822-1840
Fax: (270)767-2149
URL: http://www.murrayhospital.org/body.cfm?xyzpdqabc=0&id=7&action=detail&ref=74

Nicholasville

20007 ■ Hospice of the Bluegrass - Jessamine County
109 Shannon Pkwy.
Nicholasville, KY 40356
Ph: (859)887-2696
Free: 800-279-0750
Fax: (859)885-1474
E-mail: info@hospicebg.com
URL: http://www.hospicebg.com

Owensboro

20008 ■ Hospice of Western Kentucky
3419 Wathens Crossing
Owensboro, KY 42301
Ph: (270)926-7655
Fax: (270)685-0516
URL: http://hospiceofwky.org/

Paducah

20009 ■ Lourdes Hospice--Paducah
1530 Lone Oak Rd.
Paducah, KY 42003
Ph: (270)444-2444
URL: http://www.elourdes.com/

Paintsville

20010 ■ Community Hospice-Paintsville
869 US Hwy. 23 N
Paintsville, KY 41240
Ph: (606)297-1095
Fax: (606)297-2178
E-mail: hospice@chospice.org
URL: http://www.chospice.org
Susan Hunt, Executive Director

Pikeville

20011 ■ Hospice of the Bluegrass-Pikeville
101 Hibbard St.
Pikeville, KY 41501
Ph: (606)437-3700
Fax: (606)437-3737
URL: http://www.hospicebg.org/

Richmond

20012 ■ Compassionate Care Center
350 Isaacs La.
Richmond, KY 40475
Ph: (859)626-9292
Fax: (859)626-9272

Shelbyville

20013 ■ Hospice of Louisville--Main Street
540 Main St.
Shelbyville, KY 40065
Ph: (502)647-2400
Free: 800-264-0521
URL: http://www.hosparus.org/
Formerly: Hospice and Palliative Care of Louisville.

Somerset

20014 ■ Hospice of Lake Cumberland
100 Parkway Dr.
Somerset, KY 42503-3450
Ph: (606)679-4389
Free: 800-937-9596
Fax: (606)678-0191
E-mail: keroberts@hospicelc.org
URL: http://www.hospicelc.org/

Winchester

20015 ■ Hospice East
407 Shoppers Dr.
Winchester, KY 40391
Ph: (859)744-9866
Fax: (859)744-1971
E-mail: carolr@hospiceeast.com
URL: http://www.hospiceeast.com/
Carol W. Richardson, Executive Director

LOUISIANA

Alexandria

20016 ■ Guardian Hospice Care, LLC-Alexandria
5212 Rue Verdun
Alexandria, LA 71303
Ph: (318)484-4418
Free: 866-909-2315
Fax: (313)484-2732
E-mail: jwray@guardianhospicecare.com
URL: http://www.guardianhospicecare.com/

20017 ■ Hospice Compassus-Alexandria
3212 Industrial St.
Alexandria, LA 71301
Ph: (318)442-5002
Fax: (318)442-5009
E-mail: contactusLAALX@hospicecom.com
URL: http://www.hospicecompassus.com/

Baton Rouge

20018 ■ Amedisys Hospice of Baton Rouge
13702 Coursey Blvd.
Baton Rouge, LA 70817
Ph: (225)751-4599
Fax: (225)751-4579
URL: http://www.amedisys.com

20019 ■ Clarity Hospice of Baton Rouge
8116 One Calais Ave.
Baton Rouge, LA 70809
Ph: (225)291-4700
Fax: (225)291-4242

20020 ■ Hospice Associates-Baton Rouge
8119 Picardy Ave.
Baton Rouge, LA 70809
Ph: (225)218-1300
Fax: (225)218-1400
E-mail: info@hospiceassociates.com
URL: http://www.hospiceassociates.com/

20021 ■ Hospice of Baton Rouge
9063 Siegen Ln., Ste. A
Baton Rouge, LA 70810
Ph: (225)767-4673
Fax: (225)769-8113
E-mail: info@hospicebr.org
URL: http://www.hospicebr.org

20022 ■ Hospice Compassus-Baton Rouge
8280 YMCA Plaza Dr., Bldg. 3, Ste. B
Baton Rouge, LA 70810
Ph: (225)768-0866
Fax: (225)768-0923
E-mail: contactuslabr@hospicecom.com
URL: http://www.hospicecompassus.com/

20023 ■ Hospice in His Care, LLC
3233 S Sherwood Forest Blvd.
Baton Rouge, LA 70816
Ph: (225)214-0010
Fax: (225)490-4237

Bogalusa

20024 ■ Camellia Home Health and Hospice--Bogalusa
1616 S Columbia St., Stes. C and D
Bogalusa, LA 70427
Ph: (985)735-0410
Free: 888-735-0410
Fax: (985)735-0342
URL: http://www.camelliahealth.com/

Denham Springs

20025 ■ Generations Hospice Service Corp.
32948 LA Hwy. 16
Denham Springs, LA 70726-2937
Ph: (225)791-7775
Fax: (225)791-7719
URL: http://www.generationshospice.org/

Dubach

20026 ■ Hospice of Caring Hearts
463 Pea Ridge Rd.
Dubach, LA 71235-3357
Ph: (318)255-2033
Fax: (318)255-2077
URL: http://www.hospiceofcaringhearts.com/

Gonzales

20027 ■ Amedisys Hospice-Gonzales
1124 S Burnside Ave., Bldg. 300-B
Gonzales, LA 70737
Ph: (225)644-3616
Free: 877-370-3581
Fax: (225)644-3683
URL: http://www.amedisys.com/

Greenwell Springs

20028 ■ Health Care Options, Inc-Greenwell Springs
6639 Sullivan Rd., Ste. B
Greenwell Springs, LA 70739
Ph: (225)261-7915
Free: 800-895-1392
URL: http://www.healthcareoptionsinc.com/hospice.htm

Hammond

20029 ■ Vital Hospice-Hammond
19184 Dr John Lambert Dr.
Hammond, LA 70403
Ph: (985)340-3184
Fax: (985)340-3966
URL: http://www.vitalhcgroup.com/vital-hospice

Houma

20030 ■ Amedisys Hospice-Houma
1403 Saint Charles St., Ste. 103
Houma, LA 70360
Ph: (985)872-0292
Free: 877-364-4909
Fax: (985)872-0293
URL: http://www.amedisys.com/

20031 ■ Haydel Memorial Hospice
1011 Verret St.
Houma, LA 70360
Ph: (985)665-1020
Fax: (985)655-1023
E-mail: info@haydelhospice.com
URL: http://haydelhospice.com/privacy.php

Lafayette

20032 ■ Heart of Hospice LLC--Lafayette
201 W Vermilion St.
Lafayette, LA 70501
Ph: (337)232-8159
Fax: (337)232-8160
URL: http://www.heartofhospice.net/

20033 ■ Hospice of Acadiana, Inc.
2600 Johnston St., Ste. 200
Lafayette, LA 70503
Ph: (337)232-1234
Free: 800-738-2226
Fax: (337)232-1297
URL: http://www.hospiceacadiana.com

20034 ■ St. Theresa's Hospice and Palliative Care
100 General Mouton Ave.
Lafayette, LA 70501
Ph: (337)232-0262
Fax: (337)232-0266

Lake Charles

20035 ■ Odyssey Healthcare of Lake Charles
814 W McNeese St., Ste. 100
Lake Charles, LA 70605
Ph: (337)562-3200
Free: 877-637-9432
Fax: (337)478-9501
E-mail: info@odsyhealth.com
URL: http://www.odsyhealth.com

Mamou

20036 ■ Louisiana Hospice of Mamou
908 Cherry St.
Mamou, LA 70554
Ph: (337)468-0364
Fax: (337)468-0549
URL: http://www.lhcgroup.com/hospice/mamou/

Mandeville

20037 ■ Hospice Associates-Mandeville
600 Mariners Plaza, Ste. 611
Mandeville, LA 70448
Ph: (985)951-7071

20038 ■ Hospice of Saint Tammany
4410 Hwy. 22
Mandeville, LA 70471
Ph: (985)871-5976
Fax: (985)871-5977
URL: http://www.stph.org

20039 ■ Lakeshore Hospice
2659 N Causeway Blvd.
Mandeville, LA 70471
Ph: (985)871-9272
Fax: (985)871-9766

20040 ■ Life Source Services, LLC
1305 W Causeway App. Ste. 115
Mandeville, LA 70471
Ph: (985)674-0907
Fax: (985)624-7736

Marksville

20041 ■ Hospice Care of Avoyelles Parish
302 S Preston St.
Marksville, LA 71351-3038
Ph: (318)253-4248
Fax: (318)253-4818

Metairie

20042 ■ Amedisys Hospice-Metairie
3501 N Causeway Blvd., Ste. 225
Metairie, LA 70002
Ph: (504)832-9363
Free: 877-604-5276
Fax: (504)832-9368
URL: http://www.amedisys.com/

20043 ■ Guardian Hospice, Inc.--Metairie
825 Little Farms, Ste. D
Metairie, LA 70003
Ph: (504)737-2244
Fax: (504)737-2045
URL: http://www.guardianhospice.com/

20044 ■ Hospice Associates of Greater New Orleans Area
3941 Houma Blvd., Ste. 1A
Metairie, LA 70006
Ph: (504)457-2200
Fax: (504)457-2207
E-mail: info@hospiceassociates.com
URL: http://www.hospiceassociates.com/

20045 ■ Odyssey Hospice of New Orleans
2800 Veterans Blvd., Ste. 180
Metairie, LA 70002
Ph: (504)830-7600
Free: 877-637-9432
Fax: (504)830-7666
E-mail: info@odsyhealth.com
URL: http://www.odsyhealth.com

Minden

20046 ■ Agape Northwest Hospice Group-Minden
203 Pearl St.
Minden, LA 71055
Ph: (318)371-1140
Fax: (318)371-1142
E-mail: agapeminden@gambleguestcare.com
URL: http://agapehospicegroup.com/

Monroe

20047 ■ Hospice Compassus-Monroe
2213 Justice St.
Monroe, LA 71201
Ph: (318)322-0062
Fax: (318)322-3355
URL: http://www.hospicecompassus.com/

20048 ■ Hospice Family Alliance, LLC
111 Hudson La., Ste. B
Monroe, LA 71201
Ph: (318)329-9300
Fax: (318)329-9658

20049 ■ Patient Choice Hospice and Palliative Care
1101 Hudson La., Ste. D
Monroe, LA 71201
Ph: (318)322-2235
Free: 866-460-6930
Fax: (318)410-1513
URL: http://www.lhcgroup.com/Facilities/FacilitiesDisplay.asp?p1=1427&p2=Y&SM=Y& Sort=

New Iberia

20050 ■ AAA Home Health and Hospice
2111 Hwy. 14
New Iberia, LA 70560
Ph: (337)367-0940
Fax: (337)365-0970
E-mail: info@aaahomehealth.com
URL: http://www.aaahomehealth.com/

New Orleans

20051 ■ Hospice Compassus-New Orleans
2424 Edenborn Ave.
New Orleans, LA 70001
Ph: (504)834-1655
Fax: (504)834-1677
URL: http://www.hospicecompassus.com/

New Roads

20052 ■ Pointe Coupee Hospice
350 Hospital Rd.
New Roads, LA 70760
Ph: (225)638-5717
Fax: (225)638-5849
URL: http://www.pchhh.org/contact-us

Oberlin

20053 ■ Brighton Bridge Hospice, LLC
PO Box 279
Oberlin, LA 70655
Ph: (337)639-9200
Fax: (337)639-3032
E-mail: contact@brightonbridge.com
URL: http://www.brightonbridge.com/

Opelousas

20054 ■ Hospice Care of Avoyelles Parish-Opelousas
614 S Main St.
Opelousas, LA 70570
Ph: (337)-9423622
Fax: (337)942-3623

Pineville

20055 ■ VAMC Alexandria VA Medical Center
2495 Shreveport Hwy., 71 N
Pineville, LA 71360
Ph: (318)473-0010
Fax: (318)483-5029
URL: http://www.va.gov/502alexandria/

River Ridge

20056 ■ River Region Hospice, LLC
507 Upstream St.
River Ridge, LA 70123
Ph: (504)739-1205
Fax: (503)739-3993
URL: http://www.riverregionhospice.com/

Ruston

20057 ■ Agape Hospice Group-Ruston
1503 Goodwin Rd., Ste. 101
Ruston, LA 71270
Ph: (318)513-1112
Fax: (318)513-2240
E-mail: agaperuston@gambleguestcare.com
URL: http://agapehospicegroup.com/

Shreveport

20058 ■ Agape Hospice Care of Shreveport, LLC
806 Brook Hollow Dr.
Shreveport, LA 71105
Ph: (318)861-2150
Free: 866-404-2100
Fax: (318)861-2157
E-mail: agapeshreveport@gambleguestcare.com
URL: http://agapehospicegroup.com/

20059 ■ Circle of Life Hospice-Shreveport
900 Pierremont Rd., Ste. 110
Shreveport, LA 71106
Ph: (318)869-4012
Fax: (318)869-4024
E-mail: circleoflifeinc@bellsouth.net
URL: http://www.circleoflifehospiceinc.com/

20060 ■ Hospice Compassus-Shreveport
8660 Fern Ave.
Shreveport, LA 71105
Ph: (318)524-1046
Fax: (318)524-2166
E-mail: contactusLASHR@hospicecom.com
URL: http://www.hospicecompassus.com/loc-LASHR.html

20061 ■ Hospice of Shreveport/Bossier
3829 Gilbert
Shreveport, LA 71104
Ph: (318)865-7177
Free: 800-824-4672
URL: http://www.hospicesb.com/

20062 ■ Life Path Hospice Care Services, LLC
8720 Quimper Pl., Ste. 100
Shreveport, LA 71105
Ph: (318)222-5711
Fax: (318)222-5715
E-mail: lifepath3@bellsouth.net
URL: http://www.lifepathhospicecare.com

20063 ■ Odyssey HealthCare of Shreveport
8508 Line Ave., Ste. A
Shreveport, LA 71106
Ph: (318)868-8788
Free: 877-637-9432
Fax: (318)868-9788
E-mail: info@odsyhealth.com
URL: http://www.odsyhealth.com

20064 ■ Willis Knighton Hospice of Louisiana
600 E Flournoy Lucas Rd.
Shreveport, LA 71115
Ph: (318)212-2000
Fax: (318)212-2189
URL: http://www.wkhs.com/Hospice/Home.aspx

West Monroe

20065 ■ Agape Hospice Group-West Monroe
510 Trenton St., Ste. 100
West Monroe, LA 71291
Ph: (318)387-1115
Fax: (318)317-1122
E-mail: agapewestmonroe@gambleguestcare.com
URL: http://agapehospicegroup.com/

MAINE

Auburn

20066 ■ Androscoggin Home Care & Hospice--Auburn
236 Stetson Rd.
Auburn, ME 04210
Ph: (207)333-6300
Free: 866-482-7131
Fax: (207)333-6309
URL: http://www.ahch.org/

Augusta

20067 ■ Beacon Hospice, Inc-Augusta
45 Commerce Dr.
Augusta, ME 04330
Ph: (207)621-1212
Fax: (207)621-1215
URL: http://www.beaconhospice.com/

Bangor

20068 ■ Bangor Area Visiting Nurses
885 Union St., Ste. 220
Bangor, ME 04401-3092
Ph: (207)973-6550
Fax: (207)973-6557
E-mail: vnaa@vnaa.org
URL: http://www.vnaa.org/vnaa/vna/Bangor_Area_Visiting_Nurses,MEBANG.aspx

20069 ■ Community Health and Counseling Services--Bangor
42 Cedar St.
Bangor, ME 04402
Ph: (207)947-0366
Fax: (207)990-5826
URL: http://www.chcs-me.org

20070 ■ St. Joseph Hospice
900 Broadway
Bangor, ME 04401
Ph: (207)907-1810
Free: 800-646-5000
URL: http://www.stjoeshealing.org/

Belfast

20071 ■ Hospice Volunteers of Waldo County
PO Box 772
Belfast, ME 04915
Ph: (207)930-2677
Fax: (207)338-2367

20072 ■ Kno-Wal-Lin Home Care Visiting Nurse Associations of America
147 Waldo Ave., Ste. 6
Belfast, ME 04915-6922
Ph: (207)338-2002
Free: 800-540-0561
Fax: (207)338-2206
URL: http://www.vnaa.org/vnaa/vna/Kno_Wal_Lin_Home_Care,MEROCK02.aspx

20073 ■ Waldo County Healthcare, Inc.
118 Northport Ave.
Belfast, ME 04915
Ph: (207)338-2500
Free: 800-649-2536
URL: http://www.wcgh.org/services-programs/home-health-hospice/

Brunswick

20074 ■ Chans Hospice Care
60 Baribeau Dr.
Brunswick, ME 04011
Ph: (207)729-6782
Fax: (207)721-3007
E-mail: chans@midcoasthealth.com
URL: http://www.chanshomehealthcare.com/

Damariscotta

20075 ■ Miles Home Health and Hospice
40 Belvedere Rd.
Damariscotta, ME 04543
Ph: (207)563-4592
Fax: (207)563-8652
URL: http://www.mileshealthcare.org/miles_body.cfm?id=515

Dover Foxcroft

20076 ■ Community Health and Counseling Services-Dover
14 Summer St.
Dover Foxcroft, ME 04426
Ph: (207)564-2267
Fax: (207)564-7814
E-mail: dnelson@chcs-me.org
URL: http://www.chcs-me.org/

20077 ■ Pine Tree Hospice
883 W Main St.
Dover Foxcroft, ME 04426
Ph: (207)564-4346
Fax: (207)564-4400
E-mail: wecare@pinetreehospice.org
URL: http://www.pinetreehospice.org

Eddington

20078 ■ New Hope Hospice--Eddington
1344 Main Rd.
Eddington, ME 04428
Ph: (207)843-7521
Free: 877-346-4337
Fax: (207)843-6645
E-mail: lelhajj@newhopehospice.org
URL: http://www.newhopehospice.org/

Lewiston

20079 ■ Androscoggin Home Care & Hospice--Lewiston
15 Strawberry Ave.
Lewiston, ME 04240
Ph: (207)777-7740
Free: 800-482-7412
Fax: (207)777-7748
URL: http://www.ahch.org
Formerly: Hospice of Androscoggin Home Health.

20080 ■ Beacon Hospice-Lewiston
55 Lisbon St., Ste. 2600
Lewiston, ME 04240
Ph: (207)782-4242
URL: http://www.beaconhospice.com/

Lincoln

20081 ■ Community Health and Counseling Services-Lincoln
Rte. 155 Enfield Rd.
Lincoln, ME 04457
Ph: (207)794-2001
URL: http://www.chcs-me.org/home5.html

Machias

20082 ■ Community Health and Counseling Services-Machias
7 E Main St.
Machias, ME 04654
Ph: (207)225-8311
Fax: (207)255-8199
URL: http://www.chcs-me.org/

Newcastle

20083 ■ Kno-Wal-Lin Home Care Hospice Program
605 Rte. 1, Ste. 2
Newcastle, ME 04553
Ph: (207)563-5119
Free: 800-540-0561
Fax: (207)563-8651
URL: http://www.penbayhealthcare.org/penbayhealthcare/services/Kno-Wal-Lin_Home_Care

Rockland

20084 ■ Kno-Wal-Lin Home Care, Hospice Program
170 Pleasant St.
Rockland, ME 04841

Ph: (207)594-9561
Free: 800-540-9561
Fax: (207)594-1461
URL: http://www.penbayhealthcare.org/penbayhealthcare/services/Kno-Wal-Lin_Home_Care

Scarborough

20085 ■ SolAmor Hospice-Allegiance Hospice-South Portland
23 Spring Street Ste. C
Scarborough, ME 04074
Ph: (207)761-6967
Fax: (207)772-6240
URL: http://www.solamorhospice.com/content/locations/default.aspx

Scarborough

20086 ■ Gosnell Memorial Hospice House
11 Hunnewell Rd.
Scarborough, ME 04074
Ph: (207)289-3600
Fax: (207)833-1506
E-mail: info@hospiceofsouthernamine.org
URL: http://www.hospiceofsouthernmaine.org/care-settings/gosnell/index.html

20087 ■ Hospice of Southern Maine
180 US Rte. 1
Scarborough, ME 04074
Ph: (207)289-3640
Fax: (207)883-1040
E-mail: info@hospiceofsouthernmaine.org
URL: http://www.hospiceofsouthernmaine.org/

South Portland

20088 ■ Beacon Hospice, Inc.--South Portland
54 Atlantic Pl.
South Portland, ME 04106
Ph: (207)772-0929
Fax: (207)883-2383
URL: http://www.beaconhospice.com

20089 ■ VNA Home Health Care
50 Foden Rd.
South Portland, ME 04106-1709
Ph: (207)780-8624
Free: 800-757-3326
Fax: (207)756-8676
URL: http://www.vnahomehealth.org

Waterville

20090 ■ HealthReach HomeCare and Hospice
10 Water St., Ste. 307
Waterville, ME 04901
Ph: (207)861-6200
Free: 877-561-7299
E-mail: info@healthreach.org
URL: http://www.mainegeneral.org/body.cfm?id=19

20091 ■ Hospice Volunteers of Waterville Area
PO Box 200
Waterville, ME 04903-0200
Ph: (207)873-3615
Fax: (207)873-5094
E-mail: hospiceinfo@hvwa.org
URL: http://www.hvwa.org

York

20092 ■ Beacon Hospice-York
42 Brickyard Ct.
York, ME 03909
Ph: (207)351-3020
URL: http://www.beaconhospice.com/

MARYLAND

Annapolis

20093 ■ Hospice of the Chesapeake--Annapolis
445 Defense Hwy.
Annapolis, MD 21401
Ph: (410)987-2003
Fax: (443)837-1505
URL: http://www.hospicechesapeake.org/

Baltimore

20094 ■ Amedisys Hospice of Greater Chesapeake
8003 Corporate Dr., Ste. G
Baltimore, MD 21236
Ph: (410)931-8195
Free: 877-370-3612
Fax: (410)931-2864
URL: http://www.amedisys.com/hospice_locations.cfm?id=8

20095 ■ Amedisys Hospice Services--Baltimore
Upper Chesapeake/Saint Joseph Home Care
8003 Corporate Dr., Ste. G
Baltimore, MD 21236
Ph: (410)931-0990
Free: 877-640-1809
Fax: (410)931-2144
URL: http://www.amedisys.com/hospice_locations.cfm
Formerly: Harford Hospice.

20096 ■ Heartland Hospice Services--Baltimore
4 E Rollings Crossroads, Ste. 307
Baltimore, MD 21228-6210
Ph: (410)719-8670
Free: 866-834-1528
E-mail: careline@hcr-manorcare.com
URL: http://www.hcr-manorcare.com

20097 ■ John Hopkins Children's Center
Rubenstein 2019
Baltimore, MD 21287
Ph: (410)614-4750
Fax: (410)614-1673
URL: http://www.hopkinschildrens.org/

20098 ■ Joseph Richey Hospice, Inc.
838 N Eutaw St.
Baltimore, MD 21201
Ph: (410)523-2150
Fax: (410)523-1146
E-mail: info@josephrichey.com
URL: http://www.josephricheyhospice.org

20099 ■ Professional Healthcare Resources
1501 S Edgewood St.
Baltimore, MD 21227
Ph: (410)368-2825
Fax: (410)368-8449
E-mail: intake@phri.com
URL: http://www.phri.com/

20100 ■ Union Memorial Hospital Palliative Care
201 E University Pkwy.
Baltimore, MD 21278
Ph: (410)554-6497
URL: http://www.unionmemorial.org/body.cfm?id=556168

Beltsville

20101 ■ Heartland Hospice Services--Beltsville
12304 Baltimore Ave.
Beltsville, MD 20705
Ph: (240)264-1692
Fax: (240)264-1696
URL: http://www.hcr-manorcare.com/

Catonsville

20102 ■ Heartland Hospice Services--Catonsville
4 E Rolling Crossroads
Catonsville, MD 21228
Ph: (410)719-8670
Fax: (410)719-0241
URL: http://www.hcr-manorcare.com

Centreville

20103 ■ Hospice of Queen Anne's, Inc.
255 Comet Dr.
Centreville, MD 21617
Ph: (443)262-4100
Fax: (443)758-5471
URL: http://www.hospiceofqueenannes.org/

Chestertown

20104 ■ Chester River Home Care and Hospice
0602 Church Hill Rd.
Chestertown, MD 21620-2318
Ph: (410)778-1049
Free: 877-778-1049
Fax: (410)778-7399
URL: http://www.chesterriverhealth.org

Cumberland

20105 ■ Western Maryland Health System-Hospice Services
12500 Willowbrook Rd.
Cumberland, MD 21502
Ph: (240)964-7000
E-mail: webmaster1@wmhs.com
URL: http://www.wmhs.com/index.php?option=com_content&view=article&id=116&Itemid =169

Easton

20106 ■ Shore Home Care and Hospice
121 Federal St.
Easton, MD 21601
Ph: (410)820-6052
Fax: (410)820-7284
URL: http://www.shorehealth.org/services/shc/

20107 ■ Talbot Hospice Foundation
586 Cynwood Dr.
Easton, MD 21601-3805
Ph: (410)822-6681
Fax: (410)822-5376
E-mail: info@talbothospice.org
URL: http://www.talbothospice.org

Elkridge

20108 ■ Evercare Hospice & Palliative Care--Elkridge
6095 Marshalee Dr.
Elkridge, MD 21075
Ph: (410)379-3599
Fax: (410)379-3554
URL: http://www.evercarehospice.com/

Elkton

20109 ■ Northern Chesapeake Hospice
Seasons VNA Hospice and Palliative Care
113 N Bridge St., 3rd Fl.
Elkton, MD 21921
Free: 800-898-4862
E-mail: season_ce@seasons.org
URL: http://honoringlife-offeringhope.org/

Frederick

20110 ■ Hospice of Frederick County
Division of Frederick Memorial Hospital
516 Trail Ave., Ste. C
Frederick, MD 21701
Ph: (240)566-3030
Fax: (240)566-3040
URL: http://www.hospiceoffrederickco.com

Hagerstown

20111 ■ Hospice of Washington County Inc.--Hagerstown
747 Northern Ave.
Hagerstown, MD 21742
Ph: (301)791-6360
URL: http://www.hospiceofwc.org

Harwood

20112 ■ John and Arloine Mandrin Chesapeake Hospice House
3675 Solomons Island Rd.
Harwood, MD 20776
Ph: (410)798-0791
Fax: (410)798-1541

Hunt Valley

20113 ■ Gilchrist Hospice Care
11311 McCormick Rd.
Hunt Valley, MD 21031
Ph: (443)849-8200
Fax: (443)849-8284
E-mail: lmulligan@gilchristhospice.org
URL: http://www.gilchristhospice.org/

La Plata

20114 ■ Hospice of Charles County
PO Box 1703
La Plata, MD 20646
Ph: (301)934-1268
Free: 888-934-1268
Fax: (301)934-3910
E-mail: info@hospiceofcharlescounty.org
URL: http://www.hospiceofcharlescounty.org

Landover

20115 ■ Hospice of the Chesapeake--Landover
8724 Jericho City Dr.
Landover, MD 20785
Ph: (301)499-4500
Fax: (301)499-7876
URL: http://www.hospicechesapeake.org

Largo

20116 ■ Capital Hospice-Largo
9200 Basil Ct.
Largo, MD 20774
Ph: (301)883-0866
URL: http://www.capitalhospice.org/network/locations.asp

Linthicum Heights

20117 ■ Tate Foundation Chesapeake Hospice House
817 S Camp Meade Rd.
Linthicum Heights, MD 21090-3032
Ph: (410)691-0201
Free: 800-745-6132
URL: http://www.hospicechesapeake.org/tate-hospice-house

Mr. Airy

20118 ■ Kline Hospice House
7000 Kimmel Rd.
Mr. Airy, MD 21771
Ph: (301)829-0459

Oakland

20119 ■ Hospice of Garrett County
69 Wolf Acres Dr.
Oakland, MD 21550
Ph: (301)334-5151
Fax: (301)334-5800
URL: http://www.hospiceofgarrettcounty.org/

Olney

20120 ■ Montgomery General Hospital
18109 Prince Philip Dr., Ste. 325
Olney, MD 20832
Ph: (301)570-7400
Fax: (301)570-7420
URL: http://www.montgomerygeneral.org/

Prince Frederick

20121 ■ Calvert Hospice
PO Box 838
Prince Frederick, MD 20678
Ph: (410)535-0892
Fax: (410)535-5677
E-mail: calverthospice@chesapeake.net
URL: http://www.calverthospice.org

Randallstown

20122 ■ Seasons Hospice and Palliative Care, Inc-Randallstown
5401 Old Court Rd.
Randallstown, MD 21133
Ph: (410)701-4565
Fax: (410)701-4561
E-mail: info@seasons.org
URL: http://www.honoringlife-offeringhope.org/

Rockville

20123 ■ Casey House
Montgomery Hospice Inpatient Facility
6001 Muncaster Mill Rd.
Rockville, MD 20855
Ph: (240)361-6800
Fax: (240)631-6809
URL: http://www.montgomeryhospice.org/

20124 ■ Jewish Social Service Agency Hospice
6123 Montrose Rd.
Rockville, MD 20852
Ph: (301)881-3700
Fax: (301)770-0901
E-mail: info@jssa.org
URL: http://www.jssa.org

20125 ■ Montgomery Hospice
1355 Piccard Dr., Ste. 100
Rockville, MD 20850
Ph: (301)921-4400
Fax: (301)921-4433
URL: http://www.montgomeryhospice.org

Salisbury

20126 ■ Coastal Hospice & Home Care
2604 Old Ocean City Rd.
Salisbury, MD 21804
Ph: (410)742-8732
Fax: (410)548-5669
URL: http://www.coastalhospice.org

Westminster

20127 ■ Carroll Hospice
292 Stoner Ave.
Westminster, MD 21157
Ph: (410)871-8044
Free: 888-224-2580
Fax: (410)871-7242
URL: http://www.carrollhospitalcenter.org

White Marsh

20128 ■ Community Hospice of Maryland
9940 Franklin Sq. Dr., Ste. K
White Marsh, MD 21236
Free: 866-234-7742
Fax: (866)410-2780
URL: http://www.communityhospices.org

MASSACHUSETTS

Amherts

20129 ■ Fisher Home for End-of-Life Care
1165 N Pleasant St.
Amherts, MA 01002
Ph: (413)549-0115
Free: 866-549-0115
Fax: (413)549-1694
E-mail: fisherhome@croker.com
URL: http://www.fisherhome.org

Attleboro

20130 ■ Hospice of Community VNA
10 Emory St.
Attleboro, MA 02703
Ph: (508)222-0118
Free: 800-220-0110
Fax: (508)226-1012
E-mail: info@communityvna.com
URL: http://communityvna.com

Bedford

20131 ■ Affinity Hospice Of Life--Bedford
14 Crosby Dr.
Bedford, MA 01803
Ph: (781)275-1184
Fax: (781)275-1644
URL: http://www.affinityhospice.com/

Bourne

20132 ■ Solamor Hospice--Bourne
123 Waterhouse Rd., Ste. 5
Bourne, MA 02532
Ph: (508)833-7710
Fax: (508)833-7780
URL: http://www.solamorhospice.com/

Brighton

20133 ■ Caritas Good Samaritan Hospice
310 Allston St.
Brighton, MA 02135
Ph: (617)566-6242
Fax: (617)566-3055
E-mail: cgsmcmail@cchcs.org
URL: http://www.caritaschristi.org/Good_Samaritan/Home_Page/Good_Samaritan_Home_ Page

Brockton

20134 ■ Hospice of Boston Inc./Hospice of Greater Brockton
500 Belmont St.
Brockton, MA 02301
Ph: (508)583-0383
Fax: (508)583-1193
E-mail: info@hospicecapecod.org
URL: http://www.hospiceboston-brockton.com

Charlestown

20135 ■ Beacon Hospice, Inc-Charlestown
529 Main St.
Charlestown, MA 02129
Ph: (617)242-4872
Fax: (617)241-5784
E-mail: info@beaconhospice.com
URL: http://www.beaconhospice.com/

Charlton

20136 ■ Overlook VNA and Hospice--Charlton
88 Masonic Home Rd.
Charlton, MA 01507
Ph: (508)434-2200
Fax: (508)434-2397
URL: http://www.masonichealthsystem.org/index.tpl?ng_view=3

Chelsea

20137 ■ Dr. Matthew S. Shwartz Hospice and Palliative Care
285 Commandants Way
Chelsea, MA 02150
Ph: (617)889-0779
Fax: (617)889-8745
URL: http://www.hospicefed.org/hospice_pages/hospices/shwartz.html

Danvers

20138 ■ Hospice of the North Shore
75 Sylvan St.
Danvers, MA 01923
Ph: (978)774-7566
Fax: (978)774-8700
E-mail: info@hns.org
URL: http://www.hns.org

20139 ■ Kaplan Family Hospice House
78 Liberty St.
Danvers, MA 01923
Ph: (978)774-4566
Fax: (978)774-8700
URL: http://www.hns.org/Kaplan_House.aspx

20140 ■ VNACare Hospice, Inc.
5 Federal
Danvers, MA 01923
Ph: (978)777-6100
URL: http://www.vnacarenetwork.org/

Everett

20141 ■ Hospice Services of Massachusetts
391 Broadway
Everett, MA 02149
Ph: (617)381-7015
Fax: (617)381-7579
URL: http://www.hospiceservicesofma.com/

Fairhaven

20142 ■ Community Nurse and Hospice Care
62 Center St.
Fairhaven, MA 02719
Ph: (508)992-6278
Fax: (508)996-0781
E-mail: jfagan@communitynurse.com
URL: http://www.communitynurse.com
Jane Stankiewicz, President

20143 ■ Southcoast Hospice
200 Mill Rd.
Fairhaven, MA 02719
Ph: (508)984-0200
Free: 800-587-0541
Fax: (508)984-0215
URL: http://www.southcoast.org

Fall River

20144 ■ Beacon Hospice and Palliative Care-Fall River
182 N Main St.
Fall River, MA 02720
Ph: (508)324-1900
Fax: (508)324-4672
URL: http://www.beaconhospice.com/Locations/Massachusetts+-+Fall+River+/default

20145 ■ Hospice Outreach
502 Bedford St.
Fall River, MA 02720-
Ph: (508)673-1589
Free: 888-423-8001
Fax: (508)678-5093
URL: http://www.vnasm.org

Framingham

20146 ■ Brookhaven Hospice, LLC-Framingham
6 Beech St.
Framingham, MA 01702
Ph: (508)820-4800
Fax: (508)820-4809
E-mail: info@brookhavenhospice.com
URL: http://www.brookhavenhospice.com/

20147 ■ MetroWest Hospice
85 Lincoln St.
Framingham, MA 01702
Ph: (508)383-7000
Fax: (508)820-0811
URL: http://www.mwmc.com/home-care-hospice.aspx

20148 ■ MetroWest Hospice-Framingham
85 Lincoln St.
Framingham, MA 01702
Ph: (508)383-7000
Fax: (508)626-8053
URL: http://www.hospicefed.org/hospice_pages/hospices/metro.html#

Gardner

20149 ■ Gardner VNA Hospice
34 Pearly Ln.
Gardner, MA 01440
Ph: (978)632-1230
Free: 800-382-7305
Fax: (978)632-4513
URL: http://www.gardnervna.org/

Greenfield

20150 ■ Hospice of Franklin County
329 Conway St.
Greenfield, MA 01301
Ph: (413)774-2400
Fax: (413)774-2455
E-mail: info@hospiceefc.org
URL: http://www.hospicefc.org/

Haverhill

20151 ■ Beacon Hospice & Palliative Care-Haverhill
350 Main St.
Haverhill, MA 01830
Ph: (978)524-9510
URL: http://www.beaconhospice.org

Holyoke

20152 ■ Hospice Life Care
113 Hampden St.
Holyoke, MA 01040
Ph: (413)533-3923
Fax: (413)536-4513
URL: http://www.holyokevna.org/

Hyannis

20153 ■ Hospice & Palliative Care of Cape Cod, Inc.
765 Attucks Ln.
Hyannis, MA 02601
Ph: (508)957-0200
Free: 800-642-2423
Fax: (508)957-0229
E-mail: info@hospicecapecod.org
URL: http://www.hospicecapecod.org

Lawrence

20154 ■ Merrimack Valley Hospice
360 Merrimack St.
Lawrence, MA 10843
Ph: (978)552-4501
Fax: (978)552-4543
URL: http://www.merrimackvalleyhospice.org/

Leominster

20155 ■ HealthAlliance Home Health and Hospice
25 Tucker Dr.
Leominster, MA 01453
Ph: (978)728-0621
Fax: (978)728-0655
E-mail: homehealth@healthalliance.com
URL: http://www.healthalliancehomehealthandhospice.org/

Longmeadow

20156 ■ Spectrum Home Health and Hospice Care
770 Converse St.
Longmeadow, MA 01106
Ph: (413)567-4600
Fax: (413)567-3782
E-mail: info@jewishgeriatric.org
URL: http://www.jewishgeriatric.org/spectrum.html

Lowell

20157 ■ Allegiance Hospice Group, Inc.
67 Middle St.
Lowell, MA 01852
Ph: (978)275-9660
Free: 877-255-4623
Fax: (978)275-9663
URL: http://www.allegiancehospice.com/

20158 ■ Saints Memorial Medical Center
2 Hospital Dr.
Lowell, MA 01852
Ph: (978)458-1411
Fax: (978)934-8357
E-mail: cwi@saintsmed.org
URL: http://www.saintsmedicalcenter.com/

20159 ■ VNA Hospice of Greater Lowell
336 Central St.
Lowell, MA 01853-1065
Ph: (978)459-9343
Free: 800-349-8585
Fax: (978)459-0981
E-mail: community@vnalowell.org
URL: http://www.vnalowell.org

Malden

20160 ■ Hallmark Health Visiting Nurse Association and Hospices, Inc.
178 Savin St.
Malden, MA 01248
Ph: (781)338-7877
Fax: (781)338-7880
URL: http://www.hallmarkhealth.org/

Marlborough

20161 ■ Care Alternatives--Marlborough
181 Cedar Hill Rd.
Marlborough, MA 01752
Ph: (866)508-8390
Fax: (508)229-8435
URL: http://www.carealt.com/

Middleton

20162 ■ Solamor Hospice-Middleton
161 S Main St.
Middleton, MA 01949
Ph: (978)777-8222
Fax: (405)602-6481
URL: http://www.solamorhospice.com/

Nantucket

20163 ■ Hospice Care of Nantucket
57 Prospect St.
Nantucket, MA 02554
Ph: (508)825-8325
Fax: (508)825-8301
E-mail: hospice@ackhosp.org
URL: http://www.hospiceofnantucket.org

Natick

20164 ■ Natick VNA, Inc.
209 W Central St., Ste. 313
Natick, MA 01760
Ph: (508)653-3081
Fax: (508)653-8276
URL: http://www.natickvna.org/

Needham

20165 ■ VNA Care Hospice, Inc.
Stanley Tippett House
175 Highland Street
Needham, MA 02494
Ph: (617)661-4944
Free: 800-728-1862
Fax: (617)876-2526
URL: http://www.vnacarenetwork.org/services/tippett.html

Newton

20166 ■ Hospice of the Good Shepherd
2042 Beacon St.
Newton, MA 02468
Ph: (617)969-6130
Fax: (617)928-1450
URL: http://www.hospicegoodshepherd.org/

20167 ■ Seasons Hospice and Palliative Care of Massachusetts, LLC
275 Grove St.
Newton, MA 02366
Ph: (866)670-9449
Fax: (866)855-1993
E-mail: info@seasons.org
URL: http://www.seasons.org/

North Adams

20168 ■ VNA & Hospice of Northern Berkshire Inc.
535 Curran Memorial Hwy.
North Adams, MA 01247
Ph: (413)458-8042
Fax: (413)662-6815
E-mail: vnahnb@bcn.net
URL: http://www.nbhealth.org/index.php?nav_id=46

North Bridge

20169 ■ Salmon Hospice
45 Beaumont Dr.
North Bridge, MA 01590
Ph: (508)266-6402
Fax: (508)266-6403

North Chatham

20170 ■ Broad Reach Hospice and Palliative Care
390 Orleans Rd.
North Chatham, MA 02650
Ph: (508)945-4611
E-mail: info@broadreachhealth.org
URL: http://www.broadreachhealth.org/hospice_care.htm

North Dartmouth

20171 ■ Overlook VNA and Hospice--North Dartmouth
41 State Rd.
North Dartmouth, MA 02747
Ph: (508)990-8160
Fax: (508)990-8166
URL: http://www.masonichealthsystem.org/index.tpl?&ng_view=3

Northampton

20172 ■ VNA & Hospice (VNAH) of Cooley Dickinson
168 Industrial Dr.
Northampton, MA 01060
Ph: (413)584-1060
Fax: (413)586-3912
URL: http://www.vnaandhospice.org/

Northbridge

20173 ■ Salmon Hospice Care-Northbridge
42 Beaumont Dr.
Northbridge, MA 01534
Ph: (508)266-6403
Fax: (508)266-6403

Norwell

20174 ■ Norwell VNA and Hospice
91 Longwater Circle
Norwell, MA 02061
Ph: (781)659-4512
Fax: (781)659-0150
URL: http://www.nvna.org/

Norwood

20175 ■ Caritas Good Samaritan Hospice
3 Edgewater Dr.
Norwood, MA 02062
Ph: (781)769-8282
Fax: (781)762-0718
URL: http://www.caritasgoodsamaritanhospice.org/

Oak Bluffs

20176 ■ Hospice of Martha's Vineyard
1 Hospital Way
Oak Bluffs, MA 02557-2549
Ph: (508)693-0189
Fax: (508)693-7229
E-mail: hospice@vineyard.net
URL: http://www.hospice.vineyard.net

Palmer

20177 ■ Quaboag Valley Hospice
42 B Wright St.
Palmer, MA 01069
Ph: (413)283-9715
Fax: (413)283-8084
URL: http://www.winghealth.org/wingip.cfm?id=3296

Pittsfield

20178 ■ Guardian Hospice of MA
75 S Church St.
Pittsfield, MA 01201
Ph: (781)341-1775
Fax: (781)341-1775
URL: http://www.hospicefed.org/hospice_pages/hospices/guardian.html

20179 ■ HospiceCare in the Berkshires, Inc.
369 South St.
Pittsfield, MA 01202
Ph: (413)443-2994
Fax: (413)443-7814
URL: http://www.hcib.org/page.php?PageID=2095&PageName=Home

Plymouth

20180 ■ Cranberry Hospice
36 Cordage Park Cir.
Plymouth, MA 02360
Ph: (508)746-0215
Fax: (508)830-2399
URL: http://www.jordanhospital.org/body.cfm?xyzpdqabc=0&id=7&action=detail&ref=2 9

Randolph

20181 ■ Old Colony Hospice
1 Credit Union Way
Randolph, MA 02368
Ph: (781)341-4145
Fax: (781)297-7345
URL: http://www.oldcolonyhospice.org/

Raynham

20182 ■ Hospice Care of Greater Taunton
244 N Main St.
Raynham, MA 02767
Ph: (508)822-1447
Free: 888-423-8001
Fax: (508)880-3367
URL: http://www.vnasm.org

Shirley

20183 ■ Hospice of Nashoba Nursing Service
2 Shaker Rd., Ste. D225
Shirley, MA 01464
Ph: (978)425-6675
Free: 800-698-3307
Fax: (978)425-6671
URL: http://www.nashoba.org/

Shrewsbury

20184 ■ Solamor Hospice-Shrewsbury
415 Boston Turnpike
Shrewsbury, MA 01545
Ph: (508)845-2379
Fax: (508)845-9670
URL: http://www.solamorhospice.com/content/locations/default.aspx

Somerset

20185 ■ Clifton Hospice Services, LLC
PO Box 25
Somerset, MA 02726
Ph: (508)675-7583
Fax: (508)677-1436

South Dennis

20186 ■ VNA of Cape Cod Hospice
434 Rte. 134
South Dennis, MA 02660
Ph: (508)957-7710
Free: 800-631-3900
URL: http://www.vnacapecod.org

Southborough

20187 ■ VistaCare Hospice-Southborough
2 Willow St., Ste. 102
Southborough, MA 01745
Ph: (508)229-0912
Free: 877-691-5800
Fax: (508)229-2376
URL: http://www.vistacare.com/locations/site.asp?159

20188 ■ VNA Care Hospice, Inc.-Southborough
333 Turnpike Rd.
Southborough, MA 01772
Ph: (508)786-0693
URL: http://www.vnacarenetwork.org/

Waltham

20189 ■ Evercare Hospice, Inc.--Waltham
950 Winter St.
Waltham, MA 02451
Ph: (781)472-8640
Fax: (781)472-8747
URL: http://www.evercarehospice.com

20190 ■ Life Choice Hospice--Waltham
460 Totten Pond Rd., Ste. 390
Waltham, MA 02451
Ph: (781)487-2201
Fax: (617)232-3743
E-mail: info@lifechoicehospice.com
URL: http://www.lifechoicehospice.com/contact.html

20191 ■ Partners HealthCare at Home-Hospice Care
281 Winter St.
Waltham, MA 02451
Ph: (781)894-1100
Fax: (781)736-0908
URL: http://www.partnershomecare.org/hospice.htm

Wareham

20192 ■ Hospice Services of Massachusetts
577 Main St.
Wareham, MA 02571
Ph: (508)291-0049
Fax: (508)291-8009
E-mail: contact@hospiceservicesofma.com
URL: http://www.hospiceservicesofma.com/

Wayland

20193 ■ Wayside Hospice/Parmenter VNA & Comm Care
266 Cochituate Rd.
Wayland, MA 01778
Ph: (508)358-3000
Free: 800-506-2295
Fax: (508)358-3005
URL: http://www.parmenter.org

Wellesley

20194 ■ AseraCare Hospice-Wellesley Hills
40 Washington St.
Wellesley, MA 02481
Ph: (781)235-0203
Fax: (781)235-4754
URL: http://hospice.aseracare.com/home.aspx

Westfield

20195 ■ Noble Visiting Nurse and Hospice Services
77 Mill St.
Westfield, MA 01085-5400
Ph: (413)562-7049
Fax: (413)568-9434
E-mail: nvnhs@noblehealth.org
URL: http://www.noblehospice.org/

Westwood

20196 ■ VistaCare--Westwood
690 Canon St., Ste. 220
Westwood, MA 02090
Ph: (781)407-9900
Free: 877-691-5800
Fax: (781)407-9975
URL: http://www.vistacare.com

Worcester

20197 ■ AseraCare Hospice--Worcester
Worcester, MA
Ph: (781)235-0203
Free: 800-310-4282
Fax: (781)235-4754
URL: http://hospice.aseracare.com/home.aspx

20198 ■ Holy Trinity Hospice
1183 Main St.
Worcester, MA 01608
Ph: (508)791-8200
Fax: (508)791-8205
URL: http://www.holytrinityhospice.org/

20199 ■ Jewish HealthCare Center/dba Jewish Home Hosice
629 Salisbury St.
Worcester, MA 01609
Ph: (508)713-0532
Fax: (508)713-0554
E-mail: adminast@jewishhealthcarecenter.com
URL: http://www.jewishhealthcarecenter.com/

20200 ■ Notre Dame Hospice
557 Plantation St.
Worcester, MA 01605
Ph: (508)852-5505
Fax: (508)852-1162
E-mail: info@nortredamehospice.org
URL: http://www.notredamehospice.org/

20201 ■ UMASS Memorial Hospice
650 Lincoln St.
Worcester, MA 01605-2011
Ph: (508)754-0052
Free: 800-300-0202
Fax: (508)854-8227
URL: http://www.winghealth.org/medicalcenterip.cfm?id=3277

20202 ■ VNA Care Hospice, Inc-Rose Monahan Hospice Home
10 Judith Rd.
Worcester, MA 01602
Ph: (508)421-5120
Fax: (508)421-5122
URL: http://www.vnacm.org

20203 ■ VNA Care Hospice Inc.--Worcestser
120 Thomas St.
Worcester, MA 01608-1223
Ph: (508)751-6880
Free: 800-521-5539
Fax: (781)890-6627
URL: http://www.vnacarenetwork.org/

Yarmouthport

20204 ■ Beacon Hospice and Palliative Care-Hyannis Office
259 Willow St., Ste. 2
Yarmouthport, MA 02675
Ph: (508)778-1622
Fax: (508)778-1625
URL: http://www.beaconhospice.com/BeaconShines/default.aspx

MICHIGAN

Ada

20205 ■ Hospice of Michigan-Grand Rapids
989 Spaulding SE
Ada, MI 49301
Ph: (616)454-1426
Fax: (616)356-5230
URL: http://www.hom.org/

Adrian

20206 ■ Hospice of Lenawee
415 Mill Rd.
Adrian, MI 49221
Ph: (517)263-2323
Fax: (517)263-1279
URL: http://www.hospiceoflenawee.org

Allegan

20207 ■ Wings of Hope Hospice and Palliative Care, Inc.
530 Linn St.
Allegan, MI 49010-1525
Ph: (269)686-8659
Free: 800-796-2676
Fax: (269)686-9643
URL: http://www.alleganhospice.com

Allen Park

20208 ■ Henry Ford Hospice-Kaleidoscope Kids & Henry Ford Hospice Wayne Team
17333 Federal Dr.
Allen Park, MI 48101
Ph: (313)874-6400
Fax: (313)874-6032
URL: http://www.henryfordhealth.org/

Alma

20209 ■ MidMichigan Home Care--Alma
175 E Warwick Dr.
Alma, MI 48801
Ph: (989)466-3214
Fax: (989)463-6933
URL: http://www.midmichigan.org/

Alpena

20210 ■ Hospice of Michigan Alpena
112 W Chisholm St.
Alpena, MI 49707
Ph: (989)354-5258
Free: 800-968-9794
Fax: (989)356-6931
URL: http://www.hom.org

20211 ■ Hospice of the Sunrise Shore
109 N 2nd Ave.
Alpena, MI 49707
Ph: (517)358-1156
Free: 800-664-8587
Fax: (517)358-1702
URL: http://www.vitalcare.org

Ann Arbor

20212 ■ Arbor Hospice and Home Care--Ann Arbor
2366 Oak Valley Dr.
Ann Arbor, MI 48103
Ph: (734)662-5068
Fax: (734)662-2330
E-mail: info@arborhospice.org
URL: http://www.arborhospice.org

20213 ■ Heartland Home Healthcare and Hospice--Ann Arbor
3840 Packard Rd.
Ann Arbor, MI 48108-2280
Ph: (734)973-1145
Free: 888-973-1145
Fax: (734)973-1241
E-mail: careline@hcr-manorcare.com
URL: http://www.hcr-manorcare.com

20214 ■ VAMC: VA Ann Arbor Healthcare System
2215 Fuller Rd.
Ann Arbor, MI 48105
Free: 800-361-8387
URL: http://www.annarbor.va.gov/

Battle Creek

20215 ■ Battle Creek VA Medical Center
5500 Armstrong Rd.
Battle Creek, MI 49037
Ph: (269)966-5600
Free: 888-214-1247
URL: http://www.battlecreek.va.gov/

20216 ■ Lifespan Good Samaritan Hospice
5470 Glenn Cross Rd.
Battle Creek, MI 49015
Ph: (269)979-6440
Fax: (269)660-6324
URL: http://www.bchealth.com/services/lifespan/hospice.shtml

20217 ■ Lifespan, Inc.
166 E Goodale Ave.
Battle Creek, MI 49037
Ph: (269)660-3600
Fax: (269)660-3760
URL: http://lifespancares.org/

Bay City

20218 ■ Heartland Home Health Care and Hospice--Bay City
1426 Straits Dr.
Bay City, MI 48706
Ph: (989)667-3440

Free: 800-427-1902
Fax: (989)667-3437
E-mail: careline@hcr-manorcare.com
URL: http://www.hcr-manorcare.com

20219 ■ Hospice Advantage, Inc-Bay City
401 Center Ave.
Bay City, MI 48078
Ph: (989)893-0500
Fax: (989)893-0200
URL: http://www.hospiceadvantage.net/

Benton Harbor

20220 ■ Lakeland Hospice
2550 Meadowbrook Rd., Ste. 110
Benton Harbor, MI 49022
Ph: (269)985-4433
Fax: (269)985-4494
URL: http://www.lakelandhealth.org/

Bessemer

20221 ■ Superior Home Nursing and Hospice
210 N Moore St.
Bessemer, MI 49911-1052
Ph: (906)667-0200
Fax: (906)667-0020
URL: http://www.wupdhd.org/?page_id=29

Big Rapids

20222 ■ Hospice of Michigan Big Rapids
400 Perry Ave.
Big Rapids, MI 49307
Ph: (231)796-7371
Free: 888-247-5701
Fax: (231)796-4841
URL: http://www.hom.org

Bingham Farms

20223 ■ In-House Hospice Solutions
30400 Telegraph Rd.
Bingham Farms, MI 48025
Free: 800-311-5365
Fax: (248)799-6130
URL: http://www.in-househospice.com/activek/content.asp?sapp=inhouse&s=&catid=3

Bloomfield Hills

20224 ■ Mercy Hospice--Bloomfield Hills
281 Enterprise Ct.
Bloomfield Hills, MI 48302-0312
Ph: (248)858-7735
Free: 800-832-1155
Fax: (248)858-8323
URL: http://www.trinityhomehealth.com/locations/
Formerly: Cranbrook Hospice Care.

Byron Center

20225 ■ Faith Hospice at Trillium Woods
8214 Pfeiffer Farms Dr.
Byron Center, MI 49315
Ph: (616)235-5100
Fax: (616)235-5050
URL: http://faithhospicecare.org/

Cadillac

20226 ■ Mercy Hospice Cadillac
7985 Mackinaw Tr.
Cadillac, MI 49601
Ph: (231)779-9550
Fax: (231)779-9554
URL: http://www.trinity-health.org/index.htm

Caro

20227 ■ Heartland Home Health Care and Hospice--Caro
1796 W Carol Rd., Ste. C
Caro, MI 48273
Ph: (989)872-4452
Fax: (989)872-2887
URL: http://www.hcr-manorcare.com/Home/Hospice-Care/tabid/142/Default.aspx

Cass City

20228 ■ Hospice Advantage--Cass City
5986 E Cass City Rd.
Cass City, MI 48726
Ph: (989)872-5852
Fax: (989)872-5853
URL: http://www.hospiceadvantage.com

Charlevoix

20229 ■ Hospice of Northwest Michigan
220 W Garfield Ave.
Charlevoix, MI 49720
Ph: (231)547-7448
Free: 800-678-4780
Fax: (231)547-1164
E-mail: info@hospicenwm.org
URL: http://www.hospicenwm.org/
Formerly: Northwest Michigan Community Health Agency.

Cheboygan

20230 ■ Hospice of the Straits
761 Lafayette Ave.
Cheboygan, MI 49721
Ph: (231)627-4774
Free: 800-342-7711
Fax: (231)627-8771
URL: http://www.vitalcare.org/

Clare

20231 ■ MidMichigan Home Care-Clare
1432 McEwan St.
Clare, MI 48617
Ph: (989)802-5958
Fax: (989)802-5056
URL: http://www.midmichigan.org/

Clinton Township

20232 ■ Hospice of Henry Ford Health System
Saint Joseph's Team
16931 19 Mile Rd.
Clinton Township, MI 48038
Ph: (586)263-2840
Free: 800-492-9909
Fax: (586)263-2895
E-mail: pciecha1@henryfordhealth.org
URL: http://www.henryfordhealth.org

Clinton Twp.

20233 ■ In-House Hospice Solutions
23885 Denton
Clinton Twp., MI 48036
Ph: (586)468-8580
Fax: (586)468-8034
E-mail: info@in-househospice.com
URL: http://www.in-househospice.com/activek/content.asp?s=&catid=42

Coldwater

20234 ■ Branch County Home Health and Hospice
Community Health Center
274 E Chicago St.
Coldwater, MI 49036
Ph: (517)279-5420
Free: 888-530-5331
Fax: (517)279-5429
E-mail: marketing@chcbc.com
URL: http://www.chcbc.com

Detroit

20235 ■ Henry Ford Hospice-Detroit Campus
2799 W Grand Blvd.
Detroit, MI 48202
Ph: (313)916-7926
Fax: (313)916-9378
URL: http://www.henryfordhealth.org

20236 ■ Hospice of Michigan Detroit
400 Mack Ave.
Detroit, MI 48201
Ph: (313)578-6200
Free: 877-207-0039
Fax: (313)578-6377
URL: http://www.hom.org

20237 ■ John D. Dingell VA Medical Center
4646 John R St.
Detroit, MI 48201
Ph: (313)576-3997
Fax: (313)576-1092
URL: http://www.detroit.va.gov/

Escanaba

20238 ■ OSF Hospice
901 N Lincoln Rd.
Escanaba, MI 49829
Ph: (906)786-4456
Fax: (906)786-3693
URL: http://www.osfhomecare.org/hospice/
Formerly: OSF Bay de Noc Hospice.

Flint

20239 ■ Avalon Hospice
2360 Stonebridge Dr.
Flint, MI 48532-5406
Ph: (810)733-7250
Free: 877-637-9432
Fax: (810)733-8424
E-mail: info@avalonhospice.org
URL: http://www.avalonhospice.org

20240 ■ Heartland Home Health Care and Hospice--Flint
1321 S Linden Rd.
Flint, MI 48532
Ph: (810)230-1318
Free: 888-427-6818
Fax: (810)230-1619
URL: http://www.hcr-manorcare.com

Frankenmuth

20241 ■ Lutheran Home Care Hospice of Hope
9710 Junction Rd., Ste. A
Frankenmuth, MI 48734
Ph: (989)652-4663
Free: 800-645-4421
Fax: (989)652-3279
E-mail: hospiceofhope@lhminc.org
URL: http://www.lhminc.org

Gladwin

20242 ■ Hospice of Gladwin Area
PO Box 557
Gladwin, MI 48624
Ph: (989)426-4464
Fax: (989)426-3057
URL: http://www.hospiceofgladwinarea.com

20243 ■ MidMichigan Home Care-Gladwin
1277 E Cedar Ave.
Gladwin, MI 48624
Ph: (989)246-2510
Fax: (989)246-2507
URL: http://www.midmichigan.org

Goodrich

20244 ■ Genesys Hospice-Goodrich
7280 S State Rd.
Goodrich, MI 48438
Ph: (810)636-5000
Fax: (810)636-5019
URL: http://www.genesys.org/GRMCWeb.nsf/0/D5624CFFD79B111C8525727B0067C712

Grand Rapids

20245 ■ Faith Hospice--Grand Rapids
2100 Raybrook St. SE, Ste. 300
Grand Rapids, MI 49546
Ph: (616)235-5100
Fax: (616)235-5050
URL: http://www.faithhospicecare.org/
Formerly: Hospice of Holland Home.

20246 ■ Heartland Home Health Care and Hospice--Grand Rapids
500 Cascade West Pkwy. SE
Grand Rapids, MI 49546
Ph: (616)956-0636
Free: 888-427-7311
Fax: (616)956-7617
E-mail: careline@hcr-manorcare.com
URL: http://www.hcr-manorcare.com

20247 ■ In-House Hospice Solutions-Grand Rapids
4403 Cascade Rd. SE, Ste. 5
Grand Rapids, MI 49546
Free: 866-967-2100
Fax: (616)974-8300
E-mail: info@in-househospice.com
URL: http://www.in-househospice.com/activek/content.asp?sapp=inhouse&s=&catid=3

20248 ■ Spectrum Health Hospice and Palliative Care
4500 Breton Ave. SE
Grand Rapids, MI 49508
Ph: (616)391-4200
Fax: (616)391-4230
URL: http://www.spectrum-health.org/body_locations.cfm?id=638&action=detail&ref= 2279

Grayling

20249 ■ Mercy Home Care, Grayling and Houghton Lake
324 Meadows Dr.
Grayling, MI 49738
Ph: (989)348-4383
Free: 877-217-9899
E-mail: thhsgeneral@trinity-health.org
URL: http://www.trinityhomehealth.org/cms/Michigan-Home-Care-Agencies/mercy-home -care-grayling.html
Don Melerant, Executive Director

Hancock

20250 ■ Aspirus Superior Home Health Hospice--Hancock
540 Depot St.
Hancock, MI 49930-2031
Ph: (906)482-7382
Fax: (906)482-9410
URL: http://www.wupdhd.org/?page_id=2283
Formerly: Superior Home Nursing and Hospice.

Hillsdale

20251 ■ Hospice of Hillsdale County
124 S Howell St.
Hillsdale, MI 49242-2011
Ph: (517)437-5252
Fax: (517)437-5253
E-mail: hospiceofhillsdalecounty@gmail.com
URL: http://www.hospiceofhillsdalecounty.org

Holland

20252 ■ Hospice of Holland
270 Hoover Blvd.
Holland, MI 49423
Ph: (616)396-2972
Fax: (616)396-2808
URL: http://www.hollandhospice.org

20253 ■ Hospice House of Holland
445 104th Ave.
Holland, MI 49423
Ph: (616)396-2972
Fax: (616)396-2808
URL: https://www.hollandhospice.org/careathospice-house/directions/

Howell

20254 ■ In-House Hospice Solutions-Howell
3469 W Grand River, Ste. 101
Howell, MI 48843
Ph: (517)540-9721
Fax: (517)540-9726
URL: http://www.in-househospice.com/activek/content.asp?sapp=inhouse&s=&catid=3

Ionia

20255 ■ The Ionia Area Hospice
601 E Washington St.
Ionia, MI 48846
Ph: (616)527-0681
Fax: (616)527-3655
URL: http://www.hospiceoflansing.org

Iron River

20256 ■ Northstar Home Care & Hospice-Iron River
1300 W Ice Lake Rd.
Iron River, MI 49935
Ph: (906)265-9189
URL: http://www.northstarhs.org/getpage.php?name=locations&

Ironwood

20257 ■ Regional Hospice Services-Ironwood Team
N10561 Grandview Ln.
Ironwood, MI 49938
Ph: (906)932-2525
Fax: (906)932-8046
E-mail: hospice@ncis.net
URL: http://regionalhospice.org/

Jackson

20258 ■ Allegiance Hospice Home
1 Jackson Sq.
100 E Michigan Ave.
Jackson, MI 49201
Ph: (517)841-6982
Free: 888-821-3256
Fax: (517)841-6986
URL: http://www.allegiancehealth.org/content.aspx?id=348

20259 ■ Great Lakes Hospice
900 Cooper St.
Jackson, MI 49202
Ph: (517)780-9500
Free: 800-379-1600
Fax: (517)780-9700
URL: http://www.greatlakeshomehealth.com/

Kalamazoo

20260 ■ Borgess Visiting Nurse & Hospice
348 N Burdick St.
Kalamazoo, MI 49007
Ph: (269)343-1396
Free: 800-343-1396
Fax: (269)382-8686
URL: http://www.borgess.com/default.aspx?pId=73

20261 ■ Hospice Care of Southwest Michigan
222 N Kalamazoo Mall
Kalamazoo, MI 49007
Ph: (269)345-0273
Fax: (269)345-8522
E-mail: hospice@hospiceswmi.org
URL: http://www.hospiceswmi.org

20262 ■ In-House Hospice Services-Kalamazoo
5360 Holiday Terrace, Ste. 24A
Kalamazoo, MI 49009
Free: 877-353-7200
Fax: (269)353-3323
URL: http://www.in-househospice.com/activek/content.asp?sapp=inhouse&s=&catid=3

20263 ■ Rose Arbor-Residential Hospice Facility
5473 Croyden Ave.
Kalamazoo, MI 49009
Ph: (269)345-0273
Fax: (269)345-8750
E-mail: hospice@hospiceswmi.org
URL: http://www.hospiceswmi.org

Lambertville

20264 ■ Erie West Hospice & Palliative Care LLC-Lambertville
3333 Sterns Rd.
Lambertville, MI 48144
Ph: (734)568-6917
Fax: (734)568-6921
E-mail: marketing@eriwesthospice.com
URL: http://www.eriewesthospice.com/

20265 ■ Hospice of Northwest Ohio-Lambertville
8132 Secor Rd.
Lambertville, MI 48144
Ph: (734)568-6801
E-mail: bsharek@hospicenwo.org
URL: http://www.hospicenwo.org/index.php?gclid=CM-Y7Ja4vqUCFYHb4AodSgjqYQ

Lanse

20266 ■ Aspirus Superior Home Health & Hospice-Lanse
303 Baraga Ave.
Lanse, MI 49946-1409
Ph: (906)524-6142
Fax: (906)524-6144
URL: http://www.wupdhd.org/?page_id=2283
Formerly: Superior Home Nursing and Hospice.

Lansing

20267 ■ Hospice Advantage, Inc-Lansing
801 S Waverly Rd.
Lansing, MI 48917
Ph: (517)886-8470
Fax: (517)886-8471
URL: http://www.hospiceadvantage.net/

20268 ■ The Hospice of Lansing
4052 Legacy Pkwy., Ste. 200
Lansing, MI 48911
Ph: (517)882-4500
Fax: (517)882-3010
URL: http://www.hospiceoflansing.org

20269 ■ Hospice of Lansing-Residence
3411 Stoneleigh Dr.
Lansing, MI 48910
Ph: (517)882-1663
Fax: (517)882-1612
URL: http://www.hospiceoflansing.org

Lapeer

20270 ■ A-One Hospice, Inc.
404 W Nepessing St., Ste. D
Lapeer, MI 48446
Ph: (810)667-9200
Fax: (810)667-7106

Livonia

20271 ■ Angela Hospice Home Care Inc.
Angela Hospice Care Center
14100 Newburgh Rd.
Livonia, MI 48154-5010
Ph: (734)464-7810
Free: 866-464-7810
Fax: (734)464-6930
E-mail: president@angelahospice.org
URL: http://www.angelahospice.org

Madison Heights

20272 ■ Hospice of Henry Ford Health System
655 W 13 Mile Rd.
Madison Heights, MI 48071
Ph: (248)588-2468
Fax: (248)588-4210
URL: http://www.henryfordhealth.org

20273 ■ Seasons Hospice and Palliative Care of Michigan, Inc.
27355 John R
Madison Heights, MI 48071
Ph: (248)291-2698
Fax: (248)291-2697
E-mail: info@seasons.org
URL: http://honoringlife-offeringhope.org/

Marlette

20274 ■ United Hospice Service
2770 Main St.
Marlette, MI 48453-1141
Ph: (989)635-4143
Free: 800-635-7490
Fax: (989)635-4145
E-mail: mrhinfo@mrhcares.org
URL: http://www.marletteregionalhospital.org/service-hospice.html

Marquette

20275 ■ Lake Superior Hospice Association
914 W Baraga
Marquette, MI 49855
Ph: (906)225-7760
Fax: (906)225-7765
URL: http://www.lakesuperiorhospice.com/

20276 ■ Upper Peninsula Home Health, Hospice, and Private Duty
1414 W Fair Ave., Ste. 44
Marquette, MI 49855-2675
Ph: (906)225-4545
Fax: (906)225-7543
URL: http://www.uphomehealth.com

Mason

20277 ■ Heartland Home Health Care and Hospice--Mason
825 S Cedar
Mason, MI 48854-2400
Ph: (517)244-0404
Free: 888-670-7448
Fax: (517)676-7057
E-mail: careline@hcr-manorcare.com
URL: http://www.hcr-manorcare.com

Midland

20278 ■ MidMichigan Visiting Nurse Hospice
3007 N Saginaw Rd.
Midland, MI 48640-4555
Ph: (989)633-1426
Free: 800-852-9350
Fax: (989)633-1440
URL: http://www.midmichigan.org

Monroe

20279 ■ Mercy Memorial Hospice of Monroe
718 N Monroe St.
Monroe, MI 48162
Ph: (734)240-8400
Free: 800-636-3610
Fax: (734)240-8950
URL: http://www.mercymemorial.org/serv_hospice.php

Mount Pleasant

20280 ■ Woodland Hospice and Morey Bereavement Center
2597 S Meridian Rd.
Mount Pleasant, MI 48858
Ph: (989)773-6137
Fax: (989)773-1072
URL: http://www.woodlandhospice.com/

Muskegon

20281 ■ Bob & Merle Scolnick Hospice House
888 Terrace St.
Muskegon, MI 49440
Ph: (231)726-5026
Fax: (231)722-4992

20282 ■ Hackley Visiting Nurse and Hospice Services, Inc.
888 Terrace St.
Muskegon, MI 49440
Ph: (231)726-5025
Free: 800-499-5025
Fax: (231)726-4958
URL: http://www.vns-muskegon.org

20283 ■ Hospice of Muskegon-Oceana/dba Harbor Hospice
The Leila and Cyrus Poppen Hospice Residence
100 W Western Ave., Ste. 400
Muskegon, MI 49444
Ph: (231)728-3442
Free: 800-497-9559
Fax: (231)798-7359
E-mail: info@yourhospice.org
URL: http://www.yourhospice.org

Newberry

20284 ■ Bay Shore Home Nursing/LMAS District Health Department
14150 County Road 428
Newberry, MI 49868
Ph: (906)789-1284
Fax: (906)789-1445

Oak Park

20285 ■ Hospice of the Visiting Nurse Association of Southeast Michigan
25900 Greenfield Rd.
Oak Park, MI 48237
Ph: (248)967-9611
Free: 800-882-5720
Fax: (248)967-8338
URL: http://www.vna.org

Ontonagon

20286 ■ Aspirus Superior Home Health Hospice-Ontonagon
408 Copper St.
Ontonagon, MI 49953-1158
Ph: (906)884-4485
Fax: (906)884-2358
URL: http://www.westernuphealth.org
Formerly: Superior Home Nursing and Hospice.

Paw Paw

20287 ■ Hospice Care of Southwest Michigan
801 Hazen St., Ste. A
Paw Paw, MI 49045
Ph: (269)423-6015
Fax: (269)423-7364
URL: http://www.hospiceswmi.org/

Petoskey

20288 ■ Hospice of Little Traverse Bay
1 Hiland Dr.
Petoskey, MI 49770
Ph: (231)487-4825
Fax: (231)487-4228
URL: http://www.hospiceltb.org/

Plymouth

20289 ■ Arbor Hospice-Western Wayne
40500 Ann Arbor Rd. E
Plymouth, MI 48170
Ph: (734)656-0031
Fax: (734)254-0985
URL: http://www.arborhospice.org/

Port Huron

20290 ■ Blue Water Hospice
1430 Military St., Ste. A
Port Huron, MI 48060
Ph: (810)982-8809
Free: 800-959-4131
Fax: (810)984-4090
URL: http://www.vnabwh.com

Portage

20291 ■ Heartland Home Care and Hospice--Portage
8075 Creekside Dr.
Portage, MI 49204
Ph: (269)324-5705
Fax: (269)324-1815
URL: http://www.hcr-manorcare.com/Home/CareatHome/tabid/141/Default.aspx

Rochester

20292 ■ Guardian Angel Hospice Care
1715 Northfield Dr.
Rochester, MI 48309
Ph: (248)293-2441
Fax: (248)852-2175

Saginaw

20293 ■ Covenant VNA Hospice
500 S Hamilton St.
Saginaw, MI 48602-1511
Ph: (517)799-6020
Free: 800-862-4968
Fax: (517)799-6062
E-mail: info@vna-saginaw.org
URL: http://www.covenanthealthcare.com/body_vna.cfm?id=556733

20294 ■ Hospice of Michigan-Saginaw
3995 Fashion Sq. Blvd.
Saginaw, MI 48603
Ph: (517)732-2151
Fax: (517)731-2897
URL: http://www.hom.org/

20295 ■ James E. Cartwright Care Center
3443 Hospital Rd.
Saginaw, MI 48603
Ph: (989)583-0250
Fax: (989)583-0251
URL: http://www.covenanthealthcare.com/body_vna.cfm?id=506&oTopID=506

20296 ■ VAMC: Aleda E. Lutz VA Medical Center
1500 Weiss St.
Saginaw, MI 48602
Ph: (988)497-2500
URL: http://www.saginaw.va.gov/

Saint Joseph

20297 ■ Hospice at Home-St. Joseph
4025 Health Pk. La.
Saint Joseph, MI 49085
Ph: (269)429-7100
Fax: (269)429-1307
E-mail: info@hospiceathonecares.org
URL: http://www.hospiceathomecares.org/

Sault Sainte Marie

20298 ■ Hospice of Chippewa County Chippewa County Health Department
508 Ashmun St., Ste. 120
Sault Sainte Marie, MI 49783
Ph: (906)635-1566
Fax: (906)253-1466
URL: http://www.chippewahd.com/chippewahd/site/default.asp

South Haven

20299 ■ Hospice at Home-South Haven
5055 Blue Star Hwy.
South Haven, MI 49090
Ph: (269)637-3825
Fax: (269)637-6777
E-mail: info@hospiceathonecares.org
URL: http://hospiceathomecares.org/

Southfield

20300 ■ Barbara Ann Karmanos Cancer Institute Hospice
24601 Northwestern Hwy.
Southfield, MI 48075-2473
Ph: (248)827-1592
Free: 800-527-6266
Fax: (248)827-0972
URL: http://www.karmanos.org

20301 ■ Heartland Home Healthcare and Hospice--Southfield
28588 Northwestern Hwy., Ste. 600
Southfield, MI 48076
Ph: (248)948-1019
Free: 877-329-1001
Fax: (248)945-3333
E-mail: careline@hcr-manorcare.com
URL: http://www.hcr-manorcare.com

20302 ■ Henry Ford Hospice Residence-Oakland
26900 Franklin Rd.
Southfield, MI 48034
Ph: (248)353-6019
Fax: (248)353-6389
URL: http://www.henryford.com/body.cfm?id=38919

20303 ■ Hospice Advantage, Inc-Southfield
21415 Civic Center Dr.
Southfield, MI 48076
Ph: (248)684-7634
Fax: (248)684-9514
URL: http://www.hospiceadvantage.net/

20304 ■ Hospice Compassus-Southfield
24445 Northwestern Hwy.
Southfield, MI 48075
Ph: (245)355-9900
Fax: (248)355-5705
E-mail: contactusMIDET@hospicecom.com
URL: http://www.samaritancarehospice.com/index.cfm

20305 ■ Hospice of Michigan-Southfield
26957 Northwestern Hwy.
Southfield, MI 48033
Ph: (734)769-4212
Fax: (734)971-1980
URL: http://www.hom.org/

20306 ■ Odyssey Healthcare of Detroit
25925 Telegraph Rd., Ste. 102
Southfield, MI 48034
Ph: (248)356-5070
Free: 877-637-9432
Fax: (248)356-6292
E-mail: info@odsyhealth.com
URL: http://www.odsyhealth.com

20307 ■ Universal Hospice Care Inc.
24315 Northwestern Hwy., Ste. 102
Southfield, MI 48075
Ph: (248)799-9225
Fax: (248)799-9223
E-mail: info@universalhospicecare.com
URL: http://www.universalhospicecare.com/

20308 ■ VITAS Innovative Hospice Care of Southeast Michigan
26261 Evergreen Rd.
Southfield, MI 48076
Ph: (248)204-6300
Fax: (248)204-6250
URL: http://www.vitas.com/Aboutus/Locations/Michigan/tabid/191/Default.aspx

Southgate

20309 ■ Affinity-Hospice of Life--Southgate
15450 Northline Rd.
Southgate, MI 48195
Ph: (734)284-4315
Fax: (734)284-6125
URL: http://www.affinityhospice.com/

Spring Lake

20310 ■ Hospice of North Ottawa Community
18525 Woodland Ridge Dr.
Spring Lake, MI 49456
Ph: (616)846-2015
Fax: (616)846-7227
URL: http://www.noch.org/heartwood_detail.aspx?id=124

St. Ignace

20311 ■ LMAS Home Health & Hospice of Mackinac County
749 Hombach
St. Ignace, MI 49781
Ph: (906)643-7700
Fax: (906)643-7719
URL: http://www.lmasdhd.org/

Sturgis

20312 ■ Hospice of Sturgis
1613 E Chicago
Sturgis, MI 49091
Ph: (269)651-2348
Free: 800-891-1332
Fax: (269)651-3891
URL: http://www.sturgishospital.com

Traverse City

20313 ■ Munson Hospice House
450 Brook St.
Traverse City, MI 49684
Ph: (231)935-6520
Fax: (231)935-8536
E-mail: info@smhc.net
URL: http://www.munsonhealthcare.org/

20314 ■ Munson Hospice and Palliative Care
1105 6th St.
Traverse City, MI 49684-2349
Ph: (231)935-8482
Free: 800-252-2065
Fax: (231)935-8536
E-mail: contact@mhc.net
URL: http://www.munsonhealthcare.org

Troy

20315 ■ William Beaumont Hospice
1200 Stephenson Hwy.
Troy, MI 48083-1115
Ph: (248)743-9400
Fax: (248)743-9410
URL: http://www.beaumonthospitals.com/hospice

Warren

20316 ■ Henry Ford Hospice-Warren
13251 E 10 Mile
Warren, MI 48089-2076
Ph: (586)759-0874
Fax: (586)759-1745
URL: http://www.henryfordhealth.org/body.cfm?id=37995

West Branch

20317 ■ Heartland Home Health Care and Hospice-West Branch
PO Box 667
West Branch, MI 48661
Ph: (989)345-0651
Fax: (989)345-0964
URL: http://www.hcr-manorcare.com/

20318 ■ Hospice of Helping Hands
335 E Houghton Ave.
West Branch, MI 48661-1127
Ph: (989)345-3500
Free: 800-992-6592
Fax: (989)345-2991
URL: http://www.hospiceofhelpinghands.com/

Westland

20319 ■ Community Hospice Inc.--Westland
32932 Warren Rd., Ste. 100
Westland, MI 48185-3095
Ph: (734)522-4244
Free: 800-444-0425
Fax: (734)522-2099

Wyandotte

20320 ■ Hospice of Henry Ford - Downriver
1927 Eureka Rd.
Wyandotte, MI 48192-6009
Ph: (734)246-6963
URL: http://www.henryfordhealth.org

Ypsilanti

20321 ■ Saint Joseph Mercy Hospice
Washtenaw Medical Arts Bldg.
3075 Clark Rd., Ste. 200
Ypsilanti, MI 48197
Ph: (734)327-3400
Free: 888-418-5572
Fax: (734)327-3274
E-mail: svecc@trinity-health.org
URL: http://www.stjoeshealth.org/body_annarbor.cfm?id=168&fr=true

20322 ■ St. Joseph Mercy Hospice
3075 Clark Rd.
Ypsilanti, MI 48197
Ph: (734)327-3200
Fax: (734)327-3464
URL: http://www.sjmercyhealth.org/default.cfm?id=1

MINNESOTA

Albany

20323 ■ Albany Area Hospice
300 3rd Ave.
Albany, MN 56307
Ph: (320)845-6120
Fax: (320)845-6147
URL: http://www.albanyareahospital.com/Hospice.htm

Albert Lea

20324 ■ Crossroads Community Hospice
404 W Fountain St.
Albert Lea, MN 56007-2437
Ph: (507)373-2384
Free: 800-245-3065
Fax: (507)377-6451

Alexandria

20325 ■ Hospice of Douglas County
725 elm St.
Alexandria, MN 56308
Ph: (320)763-6018
Fax: (320)763-4127
URL: http://hospicedouglascounty.org/

Appleton

20326 ■ Rice Hospice - Appleton
30 S Behl St.
Appleton, MN 56208
Ph: (320)231-4450
Free: 800-336-7423
E-mail: kben@rice.willmar.mn.us
URL: http://www.ricehospice.com/

Auston

20327 ■ Austin Medical Center Homecare and Hospice
1000 1st Dr. NW
Auston, MN 55912
Ph: (507)434-1416
Fax: (507)434-1276
URL: http://www.mayohealthsystem.org/mhs/live/page.cfm?pp=locations/serviceoutput.cfm&orgid=AMC&nav=Ser&id=200000000048

Bagley

20328 ■ Clearwater Hospice
212 Main Ave., N
Bagley, MN 56621
Ph: (218)694-6581
Fax: (218)694-6594

Baudette

20329 ■ Lakewood Hospice
600 Main Ave. S
Baudette, MN 56623-2855
Ph: (218)634-1795
Free: 800-245-9483
Fax: (218)634-3490
URL: http://www.lakewoodhealthcenter.org/

Bemidji

20330 ■ North Country HomeCare & Hospice
3525 Pine Ridge Ave. NW
Bemidji, MN 56601-5115
Ph: (218)333-5665
Fax: (218)333-5642
E-mail: sdobbelstein@nchs.com
URL: http://www.nchs.com

Benson

20331 ■ Rice Hospice - Benson
2125 Minnesota Ave.
Benson, MN 56215
Ph: (320)843-1308
Fax: (320)843-1306
E-mail: gben@rice.willmar.mn.us
URL: http://www.ricehospice.com/contactus.htm

Bloomington

20332 ■ AseraCare Hospice - Bloomington
8585 W 78th St., No. 320
Bloomington, MN 55438
Ph: (952)943-0009
Free: 800-314-1021
Fax: (952)943-1187
URL: http://www.aseracare.com/

20333 ■ HealthPartners-Hospice and Palliative Care
8101 34th Ave. S
Bloomington, MN 55420
Ph: (952)883-6877
Fax: (952)883-7288
URL: http://www.healthpartners.com/public/

Blue Earth

20334 ■ United Hands Hospice
520 S Galbraith St.
Blue Earth, MN 56013
Ph: (507)526-7388
Free: 888-295-2642
Fax: (507)526-2467
URL: http://www.uhd.org/location-blueearth.php

Breckenridge

20335 ■ Riveredge Hospice
2400 St. Francis Dr.
Breckenridge, MN 56520
Ph: (218)643-0467
Fax: (218)643-0865
URL: http://www.sfcare.org/body.cfm?id=29

Cambridge

20336 ■ St. Jude Hospice--Cambridge
160 N Birch
Cambridge, MN 55008
Ph: (763)689-3735
Fax: (763)689-4435
URL: http://www.saintjudehospice.com/

Chaska

20337 ■ Marie Steiner Kelting Hospice Home
9120 Shady Oaks Rd.
Chaska, MN 55318
Ph: (952)442-6030
Fax: (952)442-6542
URL: http://www.ridgeviewmedical.org/Services/ServiceDetails.aspx?ServiceId=92

Crosby

20338 ■ HomeHealth Partnership
320 E Main St.
Crosby, MN 56441
Ph: (218)546-2311
Fax: (218)546-4313

Dawson

20339 ■ Rice Hospice - Dawson
1282 Walnut St.
Dawson, MN 56232-2333
Ph: (320)769-4793
Fax: (320)769-4576
E-mail: duls@rice.willmar.mn.us
URL: http://www.ricehospice.com/

Detroit Lakes

20340 ■ Hospice of the Red River Valley/Detroit Lakes
1102 W River Rd.
Detroit Lakes, MN 56501
Ph: (218)847-9493
Free: 800-237-4629
Fax: (218)846-1446
URL: http://www.hrrv.org

Duluth

20341 ■ Saint Luke's Hospice, Duluth
220 N 6th Ave. E
Duluth, MN 55805
Ph: (218)249-6100
Free: 800-321-3790
Fax: (218)249-6116
URL: http://www.slhduluth.com/hospital/other-services/hospice/

20342 ■ SMDC Hospice & Palliative Care-Duluth/Superior Hospice
330 E 2nd St.
Duluth, MN 55805
Ph: (218)786-4020
Free: 800-500-8604
E-mail: hospice@smdc.org
URL: http://www.stmarysduluth.org/otherservices/hospice/hospice.htm

20343 ■ Solvay Hospice House
801 Baylis St.
Duluth, MN 55811
Ph: (218)529-3400
Fax: (218)529-3419
E-mail: solvay@smdc.org
URL: http://www.solvayhospicehouse.org/

Edina

20344 ■ N.C. Little Memorial Hospice
7019 Lynmar Ln.
Edina, MN 55435
Ph: (952)928-9394
Fax: (052)925-3578
E-mail: director@lieelehospice.org
URL: http://www.littlehospice.org/
Robert J. Solheim, Director

Fairmont

20345 ■ Fairmont Medical Center Hospice
800 Medical Center Dr.
Fairmont, MN 56031
Ph: (507)238-8600
Fax: (507)238-8671
URL: http://www.mayohealthsystem.org/mhs/live/page.cfm?pp=locations/locationhome.cfm&nav=Hom&OrgID=FC

Faribault

20346 ■ Faribault Area Hospice
200 State Ave.
Faribault, MN 55021
Ph: (507)332-4834
Fax: (507)332-4829
URL: http://www.hospiceride.com/

Fergus Falls

20347 ■ Lakeland Hospice and Home Care
1505 Pebble Lake Rd., Ste. 400
Fergus Falls, MN 56538
Ph: (218)998-1400
Free: 888-820-7885
Fax: (218)998-1420
E-mail: information @lakelandhospicehomecare.org
URL: http://www.lakelandhospice.org

Fosston

20348 ■ First Care Hospice-Fosston
900 Hilligoss Blvd., SE
Fosston, MN 56542
Ph: (218)435-2672
Fax: (218)435-2175
URL: http://www.firstcare.org/index.aspx

Glenwood

20349 ■ Glacial Ridge Hospice-Glenwood
10 4th Ave. SE
Glenwood, MN 56334
Ph: (320)634-2221
Free: 866-667-4747
Fax: (320)634-2244
URL: http://www.glacialridge.org/

Grand Marais

20350 ■ North Shore Health Care Foundation
501 E 5th St., Ste. 107
Grand Marais, MN 55604
Ph: (218)387-9076
Fax: (218)387-9076
URL: http://www.northshorehealthcarefoundation.org/

Grand Rapids

20351 ■ St. Mary's Hospice and Palliative Care-Grand Rapids
202 NE 3rd St.
Grand Rapids, MN 55744
Ph: (218)327-8780
Free: 800-650-8520
URL: http://www.stmarysduluth.org/otherservices/hospice/itascateam.htm

Granite Falls

20352 ■ Rice Hospice - Granite Falls
345 10th Ave.
Granite Falls, MN 56241-1442
Ph: (320)564-6239
Fax: (320)564-2169
E-mail: Michele.Prekker@rice.willmar.mn.us
URL: http://www.ricehospice.com/

Hallock

20353 ■ Kittson County Hospice
1010 S Birch Ave.
Hallock, MN 56728
Ph: (218)843-3612
Fax: (218)843-2311

Hendricks

20354 ■ Good Shepherd Hospice--Hendricks
503 E Lincoln St.
Hendricks, MN 56136
Ph: (507)275-3134
Fax: (507)275-3104

Hibbing

20355 ■ North Star Hospice
1101 E 37th St., Ste. 27
Hibbing, MN 55746-0174
Ph: (218)262-6982
Fax: (218)262-1723
URL: http://www.range.fairview.org

Hutchinson

20356 ■ Connect Care Hospice
710 Park Island Dr. SW
Hutchinson, MN 55350
Ph: (320)234-5031
Free: 800-454-8616
Fax: (320)234-5032
E-mail: info@connectcaremn.org
URL: http://www.connectcaremn.org/

International Falls

20357 ■ North Star Hospice-International Falls
900 3rd St.
International Falls, MN 56649
Ph: (218)283-7058
Fax: (218)283-7050

Lakeville

20358 ■ Minnesota Community Hospice
18472 Kenyon Ave.
Lakeville, MN 55044
Ph: (952)435-6828
Fax: (952)435-6933
E-mail: Jackie.mnhospice@frontiernet.net
URL: http://mncommunityhospice.com/

Litchfield

20359 ■ Litchfield Area Hospice
218 N Holcombe Ave.
Litchfield, MN 55355-2257
Ph: (320)693-7367
Fax: (320)693-7418
URL: http://www.augustanahomes.org

Little Falls

20360 ■ Unity Family Home Care & Hospice
015 2nd St. SE
Little Falls, MN 56345
Ph: (320)631-5575
Fax: (320)632-1354
URL: http://www.stgabriels.com/UFHospice.html
Formerly: Hospice of Morrison County, Unity Family Home Care.

Luverne

20361 ■ Cottage of Hospice
217 N Oakley St.
Luverne, MN 56156
Ph: (507)283-9356
Fax: (507)449-0024

20362 ■ Hospice of Sanford Hospital Luverne
1600 N Kniss Ave.
Luverne, MN 56156
Ph: (507)283-2321
Fax: (507)283-2091
URL: http://www.luvernecommunityhospital.org
Formerly: Hospice of Luverne Community Hospital.

Mankato

20363 ■ Saint Peter Area Hospice/ Immanuel-Saint Joseph's Mayo HS Program
1400 Madison Ave., Ste. 324A
Mankato, MN 56002
Ph: (507)385-2618
E-mail: Loeffler.Stephanie@mayo.edu
URL: http://www.mayohealthsystem.org

Marshall

20364 ■ Prairie Home Hospice
300 S Bruce St.
Marshall, MN 56258
Ph: (507)537-9247
Fax: (507)537-9258
URL: http://www.prairiehomehospice.org

Minneapolis

20365 ■ Children's Hospital and Clinics Home Care and Hospice
2525 Chicago Ave.
Minneapolis, MN 55404-4518
Ph: (612)813-6000
Fax: (612)813-6358
URL: http://www.childrensmn.org/web/hospice/008386.asp

20366 ■ Fairview Homecare and Hospice
2450 26th Ave. S
Minneapolis, MN 55406
Ph: (612)721-2491
Free: 866-827-5039
Fax: (612)728-2400
URL: http://www.fairview.org/hospice/

Montevideo

20367 ■ Rice Hospice - Montevideo
824 N 11th St.
Montevideo, MN 56265-1629
Ph: (320)269-8877
Fax: (320)269-8186
E-mail: jbus@rice.willmar.mn.us
URL: http://www.ricehospice.com/

New Ulm

20368 ■ Allina Homecare, Hospice and Palliative Care-New Ulm
1324 Fifth St. N
New Ulm, MN 56073
Ph: (507)233-1555
URL: http://www.allina.com/ahs/home.nsf/

Nisswa

20369 ■ Good Samaritan Society Home Care and Hospice
25372 Smiley Rd. Nisswa Sq.
Nisswa, MN 56468
Ph: (218)963-9452
Fax: (218)963-9746
URL: http://www.good-sam.com/

Northfield

20370 ■ Northfield Hospice
2000 North Ave.
Northfield, MN 55057
Ph: (507)646-1314
Fax: (507)646-6877
E-mail: info@northfieldhospital.org
URL: http://www.northfieldhospital.org/medical/hospice.htm

Oakdale

20371 ■ BJM Hospice, LLC/dba St. Jude Hospice
7200 Hudson Blvd.
Oakdale, MN 55128
Ph: (651)735-3656
Fax: (651)735-0126
URL: http://www.saintjudehospice.com/

Olivia

20372 ■ Renville County Hospice
611 Fairview Ave. E
Olivia, MN 56277-4213
Ph: (320)523-1261
Fax: (320)523-3571
E-mail: wennerg@rchospital.com
URL: http://rchospital.com/

Onamia

20373 ■ Mille Lacs Home Care Hospice
200 N Elm St.
Onamia, MN 56359
Ph: (320)532-2802
Fax: (320)532-4325
URL: http://www.malhealth.org

Ortonville

20374 ■ Rice Hospice - Ortonville/Graceville
450 Eastvold Ave.
Ortonville, MN 56278
Ph: (320)839-4124
Fax: (320)839-4107
E-mail: Lois.Banken@rice.willmar.mn.us
URL: http://www.ricehospice.com/

Owatonna

20375 ■ Allina Homecare, Hospice & Palliative Care--Homestead House
2350 26th St. NW
Owatonna, MN 55060
Ph: (507)446-0936
Fax: (507)455-2207
URL: http://www.allina.com/ahs/home.nsf/

Paynesville

20376 ■ Rice Hospice - Paynesville
200 1st St. W
Paynesville, MN 56362
Ph: (320)243-7768
Fax: (320)243-1541
E-mail: clun@rice.willmar.mn.us
URL: http://www.ricehospice.com/contactus.htm

Plymouth

20377 ■ Hospice of Twin Cities
10405 6th Ave. N, Ste. 250
Plymouth, MN 55441
Ph: (763)531-2424
Free: 800-364-2478
Fax: (763)531-2422
E-mail: schaidp@hospiceofthetwincities.com
URL: http://www.hospiceofthetwincities.com
Pam Schaid, Executive Director

Princeton

20378 ■ Fairview Homecare and Hospice-Princeton Area Hospice
110 S 6th Ave.
Princeton, MN 55371
Ph: (763)389-1923
URL: http://www.fairview.org/

20379 ■ Fairview Lakes Hospice
110 S 6th Ave.
Princeton, MN 55013
Ph: (612)721-2491
Free: 866-827-5039
URL: http://www.fairview.org/homecare/

Redwood Falls

20380 ■ Redwood Area Hospital Hospice
100 Fallwood Rd.
Redwood Falls, MN 56283
Ph: (507)637-4579
Fax: (507)697-6015
URL: http://www.redwoodareahospital.org/Clinical%20Services/Hospice/hospice.htm

Rochester

20381 ■ Heartland Hospice Services--Rochester
3143 Superior Dr.
Rochester, MN 55901
Ph: (507)292-1170
Fax: (507)292-1169
URL: http://www.hcr-manorcare.com

20382 ■ Mayo Hospice Program
200 First St. SW
Rochester, MN 55905
Ph: (507)284-4002
Fax: (507)284-0220

20383 ■ Seasons Hospice
1811 Greenview Pl. SW, Ste. 110
Rochester, MN 55902
Ph: (507)285-1930
Fax: (507)288-7251
E-mail: contact@seasonshospice.org
URL: http://www.seasonshospice.org/

Roseau

20384 ■ LifeCare Medical Center
715 Delmore Dr.
Roseau, MN 56751-1534
Ph: (218)463-2500
Fax: (218)463-1266
E-mail: jpahlen@lifecaremc.com
URL: http://lifecaremedicalcenter.org/services/hospice.html
Formerly: Northern Communities Hospice.

Roseville

20385 ■ Heartland Home Health Care and Hospice--Roseville
2685 Long Lake Rd.
Roseville, MN 55113-2504
Ph: (651)633-6522
Free: 800-666-7919
Fax: (651)633-5733
E-mail: careline@hcr-manorcare.com
URL: http://www.hcr-manorcare.com

20386 ■ Presbyterian Homes Hospice, Inc.
2845 Hamline Ave.
Roseville, MN 55113
Ph: (651)631-6123
Fax: (651)631-6108

Saint Cloud

20387 ■ Heartland Hospice Services--Saint Cloud
605 Franklin Ave. NE
Saint Cloud, MN 56304
Ph: (651)633-6522
Fax: (651)633-5733
URL: http://www.hcr-manorcare.com

20388 ■ Saint Cloud Hospital Hospice/Homecare
48 29th Ave. N
Saint Cloud, MN 56303
Ph: (320)259-9375
Fax: (320)240-3266
URL: http://www.centracare.com/

Saint Louis Park

20389 ■ Methodist Hospital Hospice
6500 Excelsior Blvd.
Saint Louis Park, MN 55426
Ph: (952)993-6087
Fax: (952)993-5081
URL: http://www.parknicollet.com/methodist/

Saint Paul

20390 ■ Allina Hospice and Palliative Care
1055 Westgate Dr., Ste. 100
Saint Paul, MN 55114
Ph: (651)635-9173
Free: 800-261-0879
Fax: (651)628-2999
URL: http://www.allina.com/hospice

20391 ■ Regions Hospital
640 Jackson St.
Saint Paul, MN 55101
Ph: (651)254-3456
URL: http://www.regionshospital.com/

20392 ■ Saint Mary's Hospice--Saint Paul
2076 St. Anthony Ave.
Saint Paul, MN 55104
Ph: (651)789-5030
Fax: (651)789-0078

Sauk Centre

20393 ■ Saint Michael's Hospice
425 Elm St. N
Sauk Centre, MN 56378
Ph: (320)352-2221
Fax: (320)352-5150
E-mail: mblaske@stmichaelshospital.org
URL: http://www.stmichaelshospital.org

St. Louis Park

20394 ■ Sholom Care and Johnson Hospice
3630 Phillips Pkwy.
St. Louis Park, MN 55426
Ph: (952)939-1515
Fax: (952)933-1485
E-mail: bruppe@sholom.com
URL: http://www.sholom.com/

Stillwater

20395 ■ Lakeview Hospice
927 Churchill St. W
Stillwater, MN 55082
Ph: (651)430-3320
Free: 800-732-1422
Fax: (651)275-5775
E-mail: geriw@lakeview.org
URL: http://www.lakeview.org

Tyler

20396 ■ Ridgeview Hospice
240 Willow St.
Tyler, MN 56178
Ph: (507)247-5973
Fax: (507)247-2390

Virginia

20397 ■ Hospice SMDC & Palliative Care-East Range Team
901 9th St. N
Virginia, MN 55792-3349
Ph: (218)748-7975
Free: 877-851-2213
Fax: (218)748-7991
URL: http://www.stmarysduluth.org/otherservices/hospice/hospice.htm

Waconia

20398 ■ Ridgeview Home Care
113 W Main St.
Waconia, MN 55387
Ph: (952)442-6030
Free: 800-967-4751
Fax: (952)442-6542
URL: http://www.ridgeviewmedical.org/Services/ServiceDetails.aspx?ServiceId=62

Wadena

20399 ■ Tri-County Hospice--Wadena
415 N Jefferson St.
Wadena, MN 56482
Ph: (218)631-7460
Fax: (218)631-7588
URL: http://www.tricountyhospital.org/

Warren

20400 ■ Altru Hospice--Warren
North Valley Health Center
508 N Minnesota St.
Warren, MN 56762
Ph: (218)745-6565
Fax: (218)745-6568
URL: http://www.altru.org/body.cfm?id=537

Willmar

20401 ■ Rice Hospice--Willmar
301 Becker Ave. SW
Willmar, MN 56201
Ph: (320)231-4450
Fax: (320)231-4864
URL: http://www.ricehospice.com

Winona

20402 ■ Winona Area Hospice Services
175 E Wabasha St.
Winona, MN 55987
Ph: (507)457-4468
Fax: (507)457-4168
URL: http://www.winonahealth.org/

MISSISSIPPI

Amory

20403 ■ Heritage Hospice, Inc.--Amory
231 N Main St.
Amory, MS 38821

Ph: (662)257-9811
Fax: (662)257-9817
URL: http://www.heritagehospice.net/philosophy.htm

Batesville

20404 ■ Baptist Homecare and Hospice-North Mississippi
PO Box 1429
Batesville, MS 38606
Ph: (662)578-5402
Fax: (662)578-8410

20405 ■ Mid-Delta Hospice--Batesville
441 Hwy. 6 E, Ste. 1
Batesville, MS 38606
Free: 800-737-6985
URL: http://www.middelta.com/

20406 ■ Unity Hospice Care--Batesville
319 Hwy. 51 N
Batesville, MS 38606
Ph: (662)578-9555
Fax: (662)578-9556
E-mail: psherman@unityhospicecare.org
URL: http://www.unityhospicecare.org/

Belzoni

20407 ■ Mid-Delta Hospice--Belzoni
502 N Hayden St.
Belzoni, MS 39038
Ph: (662)247-1254
Free: 800-543-9055
Fax: (662)247-4924
URL: http://www.middelta.com

Carthage

20408 ■ Hospice in His Hands--Carthage
242 Thaggard Rd.
Carthage, MS 39051
Ph: (601)298-1004
Free: 866-598-1004
Fax: (601)298-1001
URL: http://www.hospiceinhishands.com

Charleston

20409 ■ Mid-Delta Hospice-Charleston
15 S Square St.
Charleston, MS 38921
Ph: (662)647-3428
Fax: (662)647-9456
URL: http://www.middelta.com/

Clarksdale

20410 ■ Mid-Delta Hospice--Clarksdale
222 Issaquena Ave.
Clarksdale, MS 38614
Ph: (662)624-4910
Free: 800-809-5202
Fax: (662)624-4372
URL: http://www.middelta.com
Formerly: Mid-South Hospice.

Cleveland

20411 ■ Mid-Delta Hospice-Cleveland
300-B South St.
Cleveland, MS 38732
Ph: (662)843-3550
Fax: (662)843-2345
URL: http://www.middelta.com/

Collinsville

20412 ■ Hometown Hospice--Collinsville
8366 Hwy. 19 N
Collinsville, MS 39325-9395
Ph: (601)626-7277
Free: 877-626-7277
Fax: (601)626-8988

Columbia

20413 ■ Camellia Home Health and Hospice--Columbia
1445 Hwy 98 E
Columbia, MS 39429
Ph: (601)731-1707
Fax: (601)731-5063
URL: http://www.camelliahealth.com/

Columbus

20414 ■ Baptist Memorial Hospice - Columbus
2520 5th St. N
Columbus, MS 39703
Ph: (662)243-1173
Free: 800-544-8762
Fax: (662)243-2094
URL: http://www.baptistonline.org/services/medical/homecare/agencies.asp

Corinth

20415 ■ AseraCare Hospice-Corinth
209 Alcorn Dr.
Corinth, MS 38834
Ph: (662)665-9185
Fax: (662)665=9604
URL: http://hospice.aseracare.com/home.aspx

20416 ■ Magnolia Regional Health Center Home Health and Hospice Agency
2034 E Shiloh Rd.
Corinth, MS 38834
Ph: (662)293-1405
Free: 800-843-7553
Fax: (662)286-4242
E-mail: info@mrhc.org
URL: http://www.mrhc.org

D'Iberville

20417 ■ Gulf Coast Hospice--D'Iberville
4107 Popps Ferry Rd.
D'Iberville, MS 39540
Ph: (228)354-9636
Fax: (228)354-9637

Flowood

20418 ■ Gentiva Home Health Care-Flowood
106 Riverview Dr.
Flowood, MS 39232
Ph: (601)362-7801
Fax: (601)362-7811
URL: http://www.gentiva.com/hospice/

20419 ■ Odyssey HealthCare-Flowood
2001 Airport Rd. N, Ste. 304
Flowood, MS 39232
Ph: (601)973-3550
Free: 866-973-3550
Fax: (601)973-3551
URL: http://www.odsyhealth.com/default.asp

Gautier

20420 ■ Hospice of Light
2101 Hwy. 90
Gautier, MS 39553
Ph: (228)497-2400
Free: 888-497-2404
Fax: (228)497-9035
E-mail: kennon.barton@mysrhs.com
URL: http://www.mysrhs.com/medical-specialties/hospice-of-light

Greenville

20421 ■ Mid-Delta Hospice--Greenville
1707 S Colorado
Greenville, MS 38703
Ph: (662)335-1065
Fax: (662)335-1068
URL: http://www.middelta.com/

Greenwood

20422 ■ Mid-Delta Hospice-Greenwood
1907 Hwy. 82 W
Greenwood, MS 38930
Ph: (662)453-2256
Fax: (662)455-5184
URL: http://www.middelta.com/

20423 ■ Unity Hospice Care, Inc.--Greenwood
805 W Park Ave., Ste. 5C
Greenwood, MS 38930-2832
Ph: (662)451-7776
Fax: (662)451-7991

Grenada

20424 ■ Unity Hospice Care, Inc-Grenada
1300 Sunset Dr.
Grenada, MS 38901
Ph: (662)226-4246
Fax: (662)226-1097
E-mail: psherman@unityhospicecare.org
URL: http://www.unityhospicecare.org/

Gulfport

20425 ■ Memorial Hospice
4500 13th St.
Gulfport, MS 39502-1810
Ph: (228)867-4160
Fax: (228)867-4166
URL: http://www.gulfportmemorial.com

20426 ■ Odyssey HealthCare of Gulf Coast
9414 Three Rivers Rd., Ste. 3
Gulfport, MS 39503
Ph: (228)864-0065
Free: 877-637-9432
Fax: (228)864-0076
URL: http://www.odsyhealth.com

Hattiesburg

20427 ■ Camellia Home Health and Hospice--Hattiesburg
133 Mayfair Rd.
Hattiesburg, MS 39402
Ph: (601)264-8691
Free: 800-783-8691
Fax: (601)264-8692
URL: http://www.camelliahealth.com/
Formerly: Quality Hospice of the Gulf Coast.

20428 ■ Deaconess Hospice-Hattiesburg
108 Lundy La.
Hattiesburg, MS 39402
Ph: (601)261-4010
Fax: (601)261-4018
URL: http://www.deaconesshomecare.com/index.php/hospice-services

20429 ■ Hospice Division of South MS Home HLT-Hattiesburg
108 Lundy Ln.
Hattiesburg, MS 39404-5788
Ph: (601)261-4010

Indianola

20430 ■ Mid-Delta Hospice-Indianola
501 Catchings Ave.
Indianola, MS 38751
Ph: (662)887-3130
Fax: (662)887-6824
E-mail: intake@mail.middelta.com
URL: http://www.middelta.com/

Jackson

20431 ■ Camellia Home Health and Hospice--Jackson
225 Katherine Dr.
Jackson, MS 39232
Ph: (601)939-6428

Free: 866-375-0582
URL: http://www.camelliahealth.com/

Laurel

20432 ■ ComfortCare Hospice
PO Box 607
Laurel, MS 39441
Free: 800-300-3443
Fax: (601)339-6275
E-mail: lgavin@scrmc.com
URL: http://www.scrmc.com

20433 ■ ComfortCare Hospice
PO Box 607
Laurel, MS 39441
Ph: (601)422-0054
Fax: (601)339-6275
URL: http://www.scrmc.com/

Lexington

20434 ■ Mid-Delta Hospice--Lexington
106 Court Sq.
Lexington, MS 39095
Ph: (662)247-1254
Free: 800-773-8858
Fax: (662)247-4924
E-mail: intake@mail.middelta.com
URL: http://www.middelta.com/

Magee

20435 ■ Hospice In His Hands-Magee
521 5th St. SW
Magee, MS 39111-3948
Ph: (601)849-5903
Free: 866-849-5903
Fax: (601)849-5346
E-mail: info@hospiceinhishands.com
URL: http://www.hospiceinhishands.com

McComb

20436 ■ Hospice Compassus-McComb
140 N 5th St.
McComb, MS 39648
Ph: (601)250-0884
Fax: (601)684-3097
E-mail: info@hospicecom.com
URL: http://www.hospicecompassus.com/

Meridian

20437 ■ Harper's Hospice Care, Inc.
1703 24th Ave.
Meridian, MS 39301
Ph: (601)483-4134
Free: 866-763-5613
Fax: (601)483-4831
E-mail: hhcare@bellsouth.net
URL: http://www.harpershospice.com

20438 ■ Hospice Compassus-Meridian
725 Front St. Ext.
Meridian, MS 39301
Ph: (601)483-5200
Fax: (601)483-5050
E-mail: contactusMSMER@hospicecom.com
URL: http://www.hospicecompassus.com/

Natchez

20439 ■ Hospice Compassus-Natchez
300 Highland Blvd., Ste. G
Natchez, MS 39120
Ph: (601)442-6600
Free: 800-629-4147
Fax: (601)442-6466
E-mail: contactusMSNAT@hospicecom.com
URL: http://www.hospicecompassus.com/

Olive Branch

20440 ■ A and E Hospice, Inc.
aka Unity Hospice Care, LLC-Olive Branch
6810 Crumpler Blvd., Ste. 101
Olive Branch, MS 38654
Ph: (662)893-5662
Fax: (662)893-4032
E-mail: bseals@unityhospicecare.org
URL: http://www.unityhospicecare.org/contactus.asp

20441 ■ Spring Valley Hospice, LLC
7139 Commerce Dr., Ste. B-2
Olive Branch, MS 38654
Ph: (662)890-5554
Fax: (662)890-5746
URL: http://www.springvalleyhospice.com/

Oxford

20442 ■ North Mississippi Hospice of Oxford
104 Skyline Dr.
Oxford, MS 38655
Ph: (662)234-0140
Free: 877-234-0140
Fax: (662)234-0176
E-mail: info@nmshospice.com
URL: http://nmshospice.com/index.html

20443 ■ Unity Hospice Care, LLC--Oxford
317 Heritage Dr.
Oxford, MS 38655
Ph: (662)238-7771
Fax: (662)238-7775
E-mail: bseals@unityhosicecare.org
URL: http://www.unityhospicecare.org/

Philadelphia

20444 ■ AseraCare/Hospice South of Philadelphia LLC
250 Canal Pl.
Philadelphia, MS 39350
Ph: (601)656-8388
Fax: (601)650-9474
URL: http://www.aseracare.com/

20445 ■ Quality Hospice Care, Inc.
340 Byrd Ave.
Philadelphia, MS 39350
Ph: (601)656-5252
Fax: (601)656-5253

Port Gibson

20446 ■ Memorial Hospice--Port Gibson
409 McComb Ave.
Port Gibson, MS 39150

Senatobia

20447 ■ AseraCare/Hospice Senatobia
144 Norfleet Dr., Ste. A
Senatobia, MS 38668
Ph: (662)562-7607
Free: 800-748-9245
Fax: (662)562-7679
URL: http://www.aseracare.com/

Southaven

20448 ■ North Mississippi Hospice of Oxford/Southaven
120 Guthrie Dr.
Southaven, MS 38671
Ph: (662)342-9745
Fax: (662)342-0441
E-mail: info@nmshospice.com
URL: http://www.nmshospice.com/

20449 ■ Unity Hospice Care, LLC--Southaven
3964 Goodman Rd.
Southaven, MS 38672
Ph: (662)893-5662
Fax: (662)893-5664
E-mail: bseals@unityhospicecare.org
URL: http://www.unityhospicecare.org/

Starkville

20450 ■ Gentiva Home Health Care-Starkville
1099 Start Rd.
Starkville, MS 39760
Ph: (662)323-6777
Fax: (662)323-6780
URL: http://www.gentiva.com/hospice/

20451 ■ Unity Hospice Care, LLC-Starkville
1085 Stark Rd.
Starkville, MS 39759
Ph: (662)338-0007
Fax: (662)338-0025
E-mail: bseals@unityhospicecare.org
URL: http://www.unityhospicecare.org

Tupelo

20452 ■ Amedisys Hospice-Tupelo
144 S Thomas St., Ste. 105
Tupelo, MS 38801
Ph: (662)620-1050
Fax: (662)620-1007
URL: http://www.amedisys.com/

20453 ■ AseraCare Hospice-Tupelo
PO Box 3478
Tupelo, MS 38803
Ph: (662)840-3780
Free: 800-565-7180
Fax: (662)680-4592
URL: http://hospice.aseracare.com/home.aspx

20454 ■ Gentiva Home Health Care-Tupelo
101 N Industrial Rd.
Tupelo, MS 38801
Ph: (662)844-9725
Fax: (662)680-3685
URL: http://www.gentiva.com/location_finder/

20455 ■ North Mississippi Medical Center Hospice
422A E President St.
Tupelo, MS 38801
Ph: (662)377-3612
Free: 800-843-3375
Fax: (662)377-2537
URL: http://www.nmhs.net

20456 ■ Residence Hospice Care, Inc.
398 E Main St., Ste. 135
Tupelo, MS 38804
Ph: (662)840-4064
Fax: (662)840-4074
E-mail: info@residencehospiceinc.org
URL: http://www.residencehospiceinc.org/

20457 ■ St. Jude Hospice-Tupelo
3166 W Jackson St., Ste. 2
Tupelo, MS 38801
Ph: (662)841-5910
Free: 800-467-7423
Fax: (662)841-5910
URL: http://www.saintjudehospice.com/

20458 ■ Sanctuary Hospice House, Inc.
5159 W Main St.
Tupelo, MS 38803
Ph: (662)844-2111
Fax: (662)844-2354
E-mail: office@sanctuaryhospicehouse.com
URL: http://www.sanctuaryhospicehouse.com/

20459 ■ Unity Hospice Care-Tupelo
1413 W Main St.
Tupelo, MS 38801
Ph: (662)844-2870
Fax: (662)844-2871
E-mail: bseals@unityhospicecare.org
URL: http://www.unityhospicecare.org/

Union

20460 ■ Hospice Direct, Inc.
PO Box 218
Union, MS 39365
Ph: (601)774-2727
Fax: (601)774-2728

Verona

20461 ■ Darlington Oaks
107 Skeet Dr.
Verona, MS 38879
Ph: (662)566-4011
Fax: (662)566-4044
URL: http://www.darlingtonoaks.com/

Walnut Grove

20462 ■ Helping Hands Hospice, Inc.--Walnut Grove
Hospice in His Hands
PO Box 387
Walnut Grove, MS 39189
Free: 866-621-0119
Fax: (601)267-6690
URL: http://www.hospiceinhishands.com

Waveland

20463 ■ Hospice Compassus-Waveland
141 Hwy. 90
Waveland, MS 39576
Ph: (615)377-7022
Fax: (615)373-4457
E-mail: contactusMSGC@hospicecom.com
URL: http://www.hospicecompassus.com/

Yazoo City

20464 ■ Mid-Delta Hospice-Yazoo City
522 Grand Ave.
Yazoo City, MS 39194
Ph: (662)247-1254
Fax: (662)247-4924
E-mail: intake@mail.middelta.com
URL: http://www.middelta.com/

MISSOURI

Bethany

20465 ■ Harrison County Hospice
PO Box 425
Bethany, MO 64424
Ph: (660)425-6324
Fax: (660)425-6939
E-mail: onealm@alpha.mopublic.org
URL: http://www.hchdhealth.org/hospice.htm

Blue Springs

20466 ■ Hospice Advantage, Inc-Blue Springs
1201 NW Jefferson St.
Blue Springs, MO 64015
Ph: (816)228-2500
Fax: (816)228-2539
URL: http://www.hospiceadvantage.net/

Bowling Green

20467 ■ Community Loving Care Hospice, LLC
914 W Main St.
Bowling Green, MO 63334
Ph: (573)324-9828
Fax: (573)324-3026
URL: http://www.clchospice.com/

20468 ■ Pike County Home Health and Hospice
19 N Main Cross St.
Bowling Green, MO 63334
Ph: (573)324-2111
Fax: (573)324-5517
URL: http://www.pikecountyhealth.org/hospice.html

Branson

20469 ■ Access Hospice Care
800 Hwy. 248
Branson, MO 65616
Ph: (417)332-3511
Fax: (417)332-3512

20470 ■ Hospice Compassus-Branson
3044 Shepherd of the Hills Expy., Ste. 200
Branson, MO 65616
Ph: (417)335-2004
Fax: (417)335-2012
URL: http://www.hospicecompassus.com/

Butler

20471 ■ Heartland Hospice Services--Butler
612 W Fort Scott St.
Butler, MO 64730
Ph: (660)679-4300
Fax: (660)679-0700
URL: http://www.hcr-manorcare.com/

Cameron

20472 ■ Comfort Care Hospice
1005 W 3rd St.
Cameron, MO 64429-1564
Ph: (816)632-4411
Fax: (816)632-4505
URL: http://www.cameronregional.org/

Cape Girardeau

20473 ■ Southeast Hospice
10 Doctor's Park
Cape Girardeau, MO 63703
Ph: (573)335-6208
Free: 888-397-0646
Fax: (573)334-8754
URL: http://www.southeastmissourihospital.com/content/hospice.htm

Chesterfield

20474 ■ Pathways Community Hospice
14805 N Outer 40 Rd.
Chesterfield, MO 63017
Ph: (636)733-7399
Fax: (636)733-7398
URL: http://www.delmargardens.com/pathways/

Clinton

20475 ■ Twin Lakes Hospice
725 E Ohio St.
Clinton, MO 64735
Ph: (660)890-2014
Free: 800-328-5446
Fax: (660)890-2018
E-mail: hospice@iland.net
URL: http://www.twinlakeshospice.com

Columbia

20476 ■ Boone Hospital Home Care
601 Business Loop 70 W
Parkade Ctr., Ste. 280
Columbia, MO 65201
Ph: (573)875-0555
Fax: (573)875-0606
URL: http://www.boone.org/bhc/?booneorg=/bhc/cms/1/bhhc/index.html

20477 ■ Option Care/Missouri River Hospice
1410 Heriford Dr.
Columbia, MO 65202
Ph: (573)635-5643
Free: 800-456-0417
Fax: (573)635-6652
URL: http://www.missouririverhospice.org/

20478 ■ Preferred Hospice of Missouri Central
1900 N Providence Rd.
Columbia, MO 65202
Ph: (573)499-4540
Fax: (405)470-4454
URL: http://www.preferredhospice.com/

Dexter

20479 ■ AseraCare Hospice-Dexter
1615 W Business US Hwy. 60, Ste. A
Dexter, MO 63841
Ph: (573)624-3655
Fax: (573)624-4323
URL: http://www.aseracare.com/

Farmington

20480 ■ BJC Hospice at Parkland
757 Weber Rd.
Farmington, MO 63640
Ph: (314)872-5050
Fax: (314)273-0834
URL: http://www.bjchospice.org/

20481 ■ Presbyterian Hospice of Mid-America
412 Cayce St.
Farmington, MO 63640
Ph: (573)756-7066
Fax: (573)756-7991
E-mail: info@pmma.org
URL: http://www.presbyterianmanors.org/

Fayette

20482 ■ Howard County Home Health and Hospice
101 Furr St.
Fayette, MO 65248
Ph: (660)248-2100
Free: 866-748-2100
Fax: (660)248-3347
E-mail: swiehardt@hchhh.org
URL: http://www.hchhh.org

Fenton

20483 ■ Alternative Hospice
1749 Gilsinn La.
Fenton, MO 63026
Ph: (636)343-3839
Fax: (636)343-6367
URL: http://www.alternativehospice.com/

Fredericktown

20484 ■ Safe Harbor Hospice, Inc.
101 Kingsbury Blvd.
Fredericktown, MO 63645
Ph: (573)783-7625
Fax: (573)783-2126
URL: http://www.safeharborhospice.com/

Hannibal

20485 ■ The Blessing Hospice - Hannibal
2 Melgrove Ln., Ste. 101
Hannibal, MO 63401
Ph: (573)221-5669
Fax: (573)221-5177
URL: http://www.blessinghospital.org/pages/default.asp?NavID=586

Independence

20486 ■ Groves Community Hospice
1515 W White Oak St.
Independence, MO 64050
Ph: (816)896-1096
Fax: (816)521-4737
E-mail: donnag@thegroves.com
URL: http://www.thegroves.com/

20487 ■ Kansas City Hospice & Palliative Care--Independence
14500 E 42nd St., Ste. 240
Independence, MO 64055
Ph: (816)468-5700
Fax: (816)468-1720
URL: http://www.kansascityhospice.org/

20488 ■ VITAS Innovative Hospice Care--Independence
4041 S Lynn Ct. Dr.
Independence, MO 64055
Ph: (816)447-3201
Fax: (816)447-3220
URL: http://www.vitas.com/

Jefferson City

20489 ■ Hospice Compassus-Jefferson City
600 Monroe St.
Jefferson City, MO 65101
Ph: (573)556-3547
Fax: (573)556-6597
URL: http://www.hospicecompassus.com/

Joplin

20490 ■ Avalon Hospice-Joplin
2000 Maiden La.
Joplin, MO 64804
Ph: (417)782-6811
Fax: (417)782-6854
URL: http://www.avalon-hospice.com/page/show/195982-avalon-hospice-missouri

20491 ■ Hospice Compassus-Joplin
2650 E 32nd St.
Joplin, MO 64804
Ph: (417)623-8272
Fax: (417)623-7280
URL: http://www.hospicecompassus.com/

Kansas City

20492 ■ AseraCare Hospice--Kansas City
11020 NW Ambassador Dr., Ste. 305
Kansas City, MO 64153
Free: 877-878-3900
Fax: (816)880-9933
URL: http://www.aseracare.com/

20493 ■ Care Alternatives of Missouri LLC
1420 NW Vivion Rd.
Kansas City, MO 64118
Ph: (816)548-8111
Fax: (816)548-8110
URL: http://www.carealt.com/

20494 ■ Good Shepherd Hospice--Kansas City
7611 Stateline Rd.
Kansas City, MO 64114
Ph: (816)822-2292
Free: 800-687-9808
URL: http://www.goodshepherdhospices.com/

20495 ■ Grace Hospice--Kansas City
9233 Ward Pkwy., Ste. 201
Kansas City, MO 64114
Ph: (816)444-4611
Free: 866-878-4611
Fax: (816)444-9480
URL: http://www.gracehospicekc.com

20496 ■ Heartland Hospice Services--Kansas City
1001 E 101st Terr.
Kansas City, MO 64131-3367
Ph: (816)943-1798
Free: 800-666-7919
Fax: (816)941-3881
E-mail: careline@hcr-manocare.com
URL: http://www.hcr-monorcare.com

20497 ■ Kansas City Hospice House
12000 Wornall Rd.
Kansas City, MO 64145
Ph: (816)941-1000
Fax: (816)531-8231
URL: http://www.kansascityhospice.org/Hospice-House-HHOverview/Index.htm

20498 ■ Kansas City Hospice & Palliative Care--Kansas City
9221 Ward Pkwy.
Kansas City, MO 64114
Ph: (816)363-2600
Fax: (816)523-0068
URL: http://www.kansascityhospice.org/

20499 ■ Odyssey HealthCare of Kansas City
800 E 101st Terr.
Kansas City, MO 64131
Ph: (816)333-1980
Free: 877-637-9432
Fax: (816)333-2421
E-mail: info@odsyhealth.com
URL: http://www.odsyhealth.com

20500 ■ Saint Luke's Hospice--Kansas City
3100 Broadway St.
Kansas City, MO 64111
Ph: (816)756-1160
Free: 888-303-7576
Fax: (816)756-2596
URL: http://www.saintlukeshealthsystem.org/

Kirksville

20501 ■ Hospice of Northeast Missouri
201 S Baltimore St., Ste. C
Kirksville, MO 63501-4520
Ph: (660)627-9711
Fax: (660)627-7005
E-mail: hospiceofnm@cableone.net
URL: http://www.hospiceofnortheastmissouri.org/

Lees Summit

20502 ■ Omega Health Care--Lees Summit
3171 NE Carnegie
Lees Summit, MO 64064
Ph: (816)268-4130
Fax: (816)268-4134
URL: http://www.omega-healthcare.com/web/

20503 ■ Village Hospice
400 NW Murray Rd.
Lees Summit, MO 64081
Ph: (816)525-0986
Fax: (816)251=8019

Liberty

20504 ■ Hospice Advantage, Inc.--Liberty
16 Westwoods Dr.
Liberty, MO 64068
Ph: (816)883-2075
Fax: (816)883-2076
URL: http://www.hospiceadvantage.net/

Macon

20505 ■ Hospice Compassus-Macon
303 Missouri
Macon, MO 63552
Ph: (615)377-7022
Fax: (615)373-4457
URL: http://www.hospicecompassus.com/

Marshall

20506 ■ Fitzgibbon - Mary Montgomery Hospice
2305 S 65 Hwy.
Marshall, MO 65340-2106
Ph: (660)831-3293
Fax: (660)831-3316
E-mail: info@fitzgibbon.org
URL: http://www.fitzgibbon.org/homehealth.htm

Maryland Hts.

20507 ■ Evercare Hospice & Palliative Care-Maryland Hts.
13655 Riverport Dr.
Maryland Hts., MO 63043
Ph: (314)592-3670
Fax: (314)592-3681
URL: http://www.evercarehospice.com/

Moberly

20508 ■ HomeCare of Mid-Missouri
102 W Reed St.
Moberly, MO 65270-1555
Ph: (660)263-1517
Fax: (660)263-8033
E-mail: homecare@mcmsys.com
URL: http://www.villageprofile.com/missouri/moberly/health212/

Monett

20509 ■ Hospice Compassus-Monett
845 Hwy 60
Monett, MO 65708
Ph: (417)235-9097
Fax: (417)235-5276
URL: http://www.hospicecompassus.com/

Mountain Grove

20510 ■ Hospice Compassus-Mountain Grove
807 N Main
Mountain Grove, MO 65711
Ph: (417)926-4146
Fax: (417)926-6123
URL: http://www.hospicecompassus.com/

North Kansas City

20511 ■ NorthCare Hospice & Palliative Care
2900 Clay Edwards Dr.
North Kansas City, MO 64116
Ph: (816)691-5119
Fax: (816)346-7119
E-mail: drcanderson@northcarehospice.org
URL: http://www.northcarehospice.org/
Dr. Clay Anderson, Director

Osage Beach

20512 ■ Hospice Compassus-Osage Beach
4681 Hwy. 54
Osage Beach, MO 65065
Ph: (573)348-1566
Fax: (573)348-1567
E-mail: contactusMOOSB@hospicecom.com
URL: http://www.hospicecompassus.com/

Osceola

20513 ■ Hospice Compassus-Osceola
270 Chestnut
Osceola, MO 64776
Ph: (417)646-2650
Fax: (417)646-2675
E-mail: contactusMOOSC@hospicecom.com
URL: http://www.hospicecompassus.com/

Park Hills

20514 ■ Hospice Care Inc.--Park Hills
PO Box 1000
Park Hills, MO 63601
Ph: (573)431-0162
Free: 800-876-0162
URL: http://www.hospicecare-inc.org/

Platte City

20515 ■ Three Rivers Hospice, Inc.
700 Branch St., Ste. 4
Platte City, MO 64079
Ph: (816)431-2333

Free: 866-478-7898
Fax: (816)431-2334
URL: http://www.3rivershospice.com/

Riverside

20516 ■ Kendallwood Hospice-Riverside
2908 NW Vivion Rd.
Riverside, MO 64150
Ph: (816)587-1000
Fax: (816)587-3000
URL: http://www.kendallwoodhospice.com/

Rolla

20517 ■ Phelps Regional Homecare
575A Blues Lake Pkwy.
Rolla, MO 65401
Ph: (573)264-2425
Fax: (573)364-3993
URL: http://www.pcrmc.com/services/

Saint Joseph

20518 ■ Hands of Hope Hospice
137 N Belt Hwy.
Saint Joseph, MO 64506
Ph: (816)271-7190
Free: 800-443-1143
Fax: (816)271-7672
URL: http://www.heartland-health.com/body.cfm?id=189&action=detail&ref=4

Saint Louis

20519 ■ Faith Hospice, Inc.--Saint Louis
4150 Crescent Dr.
Saint Louis, MO 63129
Ph: (314)892-4441
Fax: (314)892-4478

20520 ■ Heartland Home Health Care and Hospice--Saint Louis
12101 Woodcrest Executive Dr.
Saint Louis, MO 63141
Ph: (314)453-0990
Free: 800-338-6667
Fax: (314)453-0290
E-mail: careline@hcr-manorcare.com
URL: http://www.hcr-manorcare.com

20521 ■ Odyssey HealthCare of St. Louis
2055 Craigshire Rd., Ste. 410
Saint Louis, MO 63146
Ph: (314)275-6100
Free: 877-637-9432
Fax: (314)275-6101
E-mail: info@odsyhealth.com
URL: http//www.odsyhealth.com

20522 ■ Saint Anthony's Hospice--Saint Louis
10016 Kennerly Rd.
Saint Louis, MO 63128-2106
Ph: (314)525-7370
Fax: (314)525-7375
URL: http//www.stanthonyshospice.com

20523 ■ Unity Health Hospice
Saint John's Mercy Hospice
1000 Des Peres Rd.
Saint Louis, MO 63131
Ph: (314)729-4400
Fax: (314)729-4412
URL: http://www.stjohnsmercy.org/services/hospice/

20524 ■ VITAS Healthcare Corporation-Saint Louis
1807 Park 270 Dr., Ste. 110
Saint Louis, MO 63146
Ph: (314)682-3400
URL: http://www.vitas.com/

20525 ■ VNA Hospice Care-Saint Louis
11440 Olive Blvd., Ste. 200
Saint Louis, MO 63141
Ph: (314)918-7171
Fax: (314)918-8054
URL: http://www.stjohnsmercy.org/services/hospice/

Saint Peters

20526 ■ Nurses & Company Home Health & Hospice
115 Piper Hill Dr.
Saint Peters, MO 63376
Ph: (636)926-3722
Fax: (636)926-3872
URL: http://www.nursesandco.com/

Springfield

20527 ■ Hospice Compassus-Springfield
2135 S Eastgate Ave.
Springfield, MO 65809
Ph: (417)841-4800
Fax: (417)882-0371
E-mail: contactusMOSPR@hospicecom.com
URL: http://www.hospicecompassus.com/

20528 ■ Hospice Compassus-Springfield
1465 E Primrose
Springfield, MO 65804
Ph: (417)882-0453
Fax: (417)882-1245
E-mail: contactusMOSPR@hospicecom.com
URL: http://www.hospicecompassus.com/

20529 ■ Omega Health Care of SW Missouri, Inc.
2041 S Stewart Ave.
Springfield, MO 65804
Ph: (417)886-6995
Fax: (417)886-7129
E-mail: gmarvin@omega-healthcare.com
URL: http://www.omega-healthcare.com/

20530 ■ St. John's Hospice Care--Springfield
1570 W Battlefield
Springfield, MO 65807
Ph: (471)820-7550
Fax: (417)820-7426
URL: http://stjohns.com/

Sullivan

20531 ■ BJC Hospice at Sullivan
153 E Springfield Rd.
Sullivan, MO 63080
Ph: (573)468-3630
Fax: (573)860-4038
URL: http://www.bjc.org

Warrensburg

20532 ■ Johnson County Hospice Care
429 Burkarth Rd.
Warrensburg, MO 64093
Ph: (660)747-6121
Fax: (660)747-6087
URL: http://www.johnsoncountyhealth.org/

Warsaw

20533 ■ Twin Lakes Hospice-Warsaw
304 Main St.
Warsaw, MO 65355
Ph: (660)438-9700
E-mail: hospice@iland.net
URL: http://www.twinlakeshospice.com/

Wentzville

20534 ■ Community Loving Care Hospice, LLC
251 E Pearce Blvd.
Wentzville, MO 63385-1529
Ph: (636)639-6280
Free: 800-252-3649
Fax: (636)639-6317
URL: http://www.clchospice.com

MONTANA

Anaconda

20535 ■ Anaconda Pintler Hospice
108 0ak St.
Anaconda, MT 59711
Ph: (406)563-7030
Fax: (406)563-7030

Big Timber

20536 ■ Hearts & Hands Hospice
Pioneer Medical Center
PO Box 1337
Big Timber, MT 59011
Ph: (406)932-4603
Fax: (406)932-4628

Billings

20537 ■ Journey Hospice
712 Carbon street
Billings, MT 59102
Ph: (406)794-1546
Fax: (406)248-3626
E-mail: journeyhospice@hotmail.com
URL: http://www.Journeyhospice.org

20538 ■ Riverstone Health Hospice Services
123 S 27th
Billings, MT 59101
Ph: (406)651-6441
Fax: (406)247-3303
URL: http://riverstonehealth.org/

20539 ■ Rocky Mountain Hospice--Billings
2110 Overland Ave.
Billings, MT 59102
Ph: (406)294-0785
Fax: (406)294-0788
E-mail: sherinaeissler@rockymountainhospice.com
URL: http://www.rockymountainhospice.com/

Bozeman

20540 ■ Hospice of Southwest Montana
1600 Ellis St.
Bozeman, MT 59715
Ph: (406)585-1099
Fax: (406)585-1073
URL: http://www.bozemandeaconess.org/

Butte

20541 ■ Easter Seal/Highlands Hospice
3703 Harrison Ave.
Butte, MT 59701
Ph: (406)533-0020
Fax: (406)533-0019
URL: http://esgw-nrm.easterseals.com/site/PageServer?pagename=NRMM_hospice

20542 ■ Rocky Mountain Hospice-Butte
19 Discovery Dr.
Butte, MT 59701
Ph: (406)494-6114
Fax: (406)294-6115
E-mail: traceytharp@rockymountainhospice.com
URL: http://www.rockymountainhospice.com/

Choteau

20543 ■ Peace Hospice of Montana/Teton
PO Box 455
Choteau, MT 59422
Ph: (406)466-3575
Fax: (406)466-3576
E-mail: benefis@benefis.org
URL: http://www.benefis.org/pages/default.asp?NavID=215&PageCat=peace

Dillon

20544 ■ Barrett Hospital and Healthcare
90 Hwy. 91 S
Dillon, MT 59725
Ph: (406)683-9221
Fax: (406)683-9216
E-mail: tclarno@barretthospital.org
URL: http://www.barretthospital.org/getpage.php?name=facilities

Great Falls

20545 ■ Benefis Peace Hospice of Montana
2800 11th Ave. S, Ste. 23
Great Falls, MT 59405
Ph: (406)455-3040
Fax: (406)455-3070
E-mail: benefis@benefis.org
URL: http://www.benefis.org/pages/default.asp?NavID=215&PageCat=peace

Hamilton

20546 ■ Marcus Daly Center for Hospice & Palliative Care
1200 Westwood Dr.
Hamilton, MT 59840
Ph: (406)363-6503
Fax: (406)363-2866
URL: http://www.mdmh.org/index_flash.php

Havre

20547 ■ Bear Paw Hospice
Hospice Program
30 W 13th St.
Havre, MT 59501
Ph: (406)262-1444
Fax: (406)262-1629
URL: http://www.nmhcare.org/?id=26

Helena

20548 ■ Frontier Home Health and Hospice
800 Front St.
Helena, MT 59601
Ph: (406)433-4140
Fax: (406)447-3144
E-mail: Helena@frontierhhh.com
URL: http://www.frontierhhh.com/

20549 ■ Hospice of Saint Peter's Hospital
2475 E Broadway St.
Helena, MT 59601
Ph: (406)444-2244
Fax: (406)447-2540
E-mail: pstebbins@stpetes.org
URL: http://www.stpetes.org/html/Services/hospice.php

Kalispell

20550 ■ Home Options Hospice
175 Commons Loop, Ste. 100
Kalispell, MT 59901
Ph: (406)751-4200
Fax: (406)257-0355

Libby

20551 ■ Saint John's Hospice
350 Louisiana Ave.
Libby, MT 59923
Ph: (406)293-0180
Fax: (406)293-2262
E-mail: info@sjlh.com
URL: http://www.sjlh.com

Livingston

20552 ■ Livingston Hospice Care
504 S 13th St.
Livingston, MT 59047
Ph: (406)222-5030

Miles City

20553 ■ Holy Rosary Healthcare
2600 Wilson St.
Miles City, MT 59301
Ph: (406)233-2600
Free: 800-843-3820
Fax: (406)233-7134
URL: http://www.hrh-mt.org/body.cfm?id=43

Missoula

20554 ■ Hospice of Missoula
800 Kensington Ave.
Missoula, MT 59801
Ph: (406)543-4408
Fax: (406)543-4418
URL: http://www.hospiceofmissoula.com/

20555 ■ Partners in Home Care-Hospice
2687 Palmer St.
Missoula, MT 59808-1710
Ph: (406)728-8848
Free: 888-729-8848
Fax: (406)327-3727
URL: http://www.partnersinhomecare.org/index.aspx/services/hospice

Plains

20556 ■ Clark Fork Valley Hospital-Hospice
10 Kruger Rd.
Plains, MT 59859
Ph: (406)826-4873
Fax: (406)826-4880
URL: http://www.cfvh.org/default.aspx

Plentywood

20557 ■ Sheridan Memorial Hospice
440 W Laurel Ave.
Plentywood, MT 59254
Ph: (406)765-3703
Fax: (406)765-3800
URL: http://www.sheridanmemorial.net/

Red Lodge

20558 ■ Beartooth Hospice
600 W 21st St.
Red Lodge, MT 59068
Ph: (406)446-0050
Fax: (406)446-0084

Ronan

20559 ■ Lake County Home Health and Hospice
711 Main St. SW
Ronan, MT 59864
Ph: (406)883-7300
Fax: (406)676-5243

Scobey

20560 ■ Daniels Memorial HomeHealth/Hospice
105 5th Ave. E
Scobey, MT 59263
Ph: (406)487-2296
Fax: (406)487-2471

Stevensville

20561 ■ Aspen House of Montana
107 Bell Xing W
Stevensville, MT 59870
Ph: (406)642-3010
Fax: (406)642-3582
URL: http://www.aspenhospice.com/

NEBRASKA

Alliance

20562 ■ Prairie Haven Hospice Alliance
Regional West Health Services--Alliance
2409 Box Butte Ave.
Alliance, NE 69301
Ph: (308)762-6500
Free: 877-699-7794
Fax: (308)762-2298
URL: http://www.rwmc.net/body.cfm?id=35

Beatrice

20563 ■ AseraCare Hospice-Beatrice
200 N 24th St., Ste. A
Beatrice, NE 68310
Ph: (262)646-1761
Fax: (262)646-5634
URL: http://hospice.aseracare.com/home.aspx

Bellevue

20564 ■ Hillcrest Home Care
1820 Hillcrest Dr.
Bellevue, NE 68005
Ph: (402)934-2226
Fax: (402)682-6563
URL: http://www.hillcresthealth.com/services/home-care

Chadron

20565 ■ Chadron Comm Hospital/Home Health Hospice
825 Centennial Dr.
Chadron, NE 69337
Ph: (308)432-5521
Fax: (308)432-0411
URL: http://www.chadronhospital.com/

Columbus

20566 ■ Columbus Community Hospital
4600 38th St.
Columbus, NE 68601
Ph: (402)562-9622
Fax: (402)563-9622
E-mail: info@columbushosp.org
URL: http://www.columbushosp.org/

Cozad

20567 ■ Central Plains Hospice
Cozad Community Health System
300 E 12th St.
Cozad, NE 69130
Ph: (308)784-2261
Free: 800-243-9872
Fax: (308)784-4691
URL: http://cozadhealthcare.com/index.php?option=com_content&task=view&id=11&Itemid=10

Fremont

20568 ■ Fremont Area Medical Center
450 E 23rd St.
Fremont, NE 68025
Ph: (402)941-7333
Fax: (402)727-3892
URL: http://www.famc.org/

Grand Island

20569 ■ AseraCare Hospice-Grand Island
1203 Allen Dr.
Grand Island, NE 68803
Ph: (402)228-6262
Free: 877-858-5319
Fax: (402)228-6267
URL: http://www.aseracare.com/

20570 ■ Respect My Wishes
Saint Francis Medical Center Hospice
Grand Island Coalition for End of Life Care
Grand Island, NE 68803
Ph: (308)384-4600
Free: 800-353-4894
E-mail: info@respectmywishes.org
URL: http://www.respectmywishes.org/

Hastings

20571 ■ Mary Lanning Hospice
715 N St. Joseph Ave.
Hastings, NE 68901
Ph: (402)460-5868
Fax: (402)461-5091
E-mail: lflorian@mlmh.org
URL: http://www.mlmh.org/

Kearney

20572 ■ AseraCare Hospice-Kearney
4111 4th Ave.
Kearney, NE 68847
Ph: (308)698-0580
Fax: (308)698-0585
URL: http://www.aseracare.com/

20573 ■ Good Samaritan Hospice--Kearney
2501 30th Ave.
Kearney, NE 68847-2926
Ph: (308)865-7090
Fax: (308)865-2923
URL: http://www.gshs.org/

Lexington

20574 ■ Tri-County Hospital Hospice
PO Box 980
Lexington, NE 68850-0980
Ph: (308)324-8300
Fax: (308)324-8613
E-mail: bhoulden@tricountyhospital.com
URL: http://www.tricountyhospital.com

Lincoln

20575 ■ AseraCare Hospice--Lincoln
1600 S 70th St., Ste. 201
Lincoln, NE 68506
Ph: (402)488-1363
Fax: (402)488-5976
URL: httpp://www.aseracare.com

20576 ■ HoriSun Hospice, Inc.
3883 Normal Blvd., Ste. 108
Lincoln, NE 68510-2645
Ph: (402)484-6444
Free: 877-412-1181
Fax: (402)484-6464
URL: http://www.horisunhospice.com/

20577 ■ Hospice of Tabitha
4720 Randolph St.
Lincoln, NE 68510
Ph: (402)486-8575
Free: 800-418-9335
Fax: (402)486-8578
E-mail: clientservices@tabitha.org
URL: http://www.tabitha.org/services/home_based_s/hospice.html

20578 ■ Saint Elizabeth Hospice St. Elizabeth Regional Medical Center--Lincoln
245 S 84th St.
Lincoln, NE 68510
Ph: (402)486-7043
Fax: (402)219-5060
E-mail: prizzo@stez.org
URL: http://www.saintelizabethonline.com

McCook

20579 ■ Community HealthCare and Hospice--McCook
407 W 5th
McCook, NE 69001
Ph: (308)344-8356
Fax: (308)344-1515
E-mail: communityhospital@chmccook.org
URL: http://www.chmccook.org/

Norfolk

20580 ■ AseraCare Hospice-Norfolk
1909 Vicki La.
Norfolk, NE 68701
Ph: (402)379-4158
Free: 866-300-3479
Fax: (402)379-4080
URL: http://www.aseracare.com

North Platte

20581 ■ Great Plains Regional Medical Center
1021 S Cottonwood St.
North Platte, NE 69103
Ph: (308)696-7434
Free: 877-343-1288
Fax: (308)696-7407
URL: http://www.gprmc.com/body.cfm?id=54&action=detail&ref=11

O'Neil

20582 ■ AserCare Hospice-O'Neil
131 N 4th St.
O'Neil, NE 68763
Ph: (402)336-3988
Free: 866-503-4609
Fax: (402)336-2271
URL: http://www.aseracare.com/

Omaha

20583 ■ Alegent Health Hospice
7070 Spring St.
Omaha, NE 68106-3519
Ph: (402)898-8000
Free: 800-829-1099
Fax: (402)898-8090
E-mail: hospicecaringcircles@alegent.org
URL: http://www.alegent.com/body.cfm?id=5395

20584 ■ AseraCare Hospice--Omaha
8710 Fredrick Ave.
Omaha, NE 68124
Ph: (402)926-2680
Free: 800-536-6288
Fax: (402)926-2347
URL: http://www.aseracare.com/

20585 ■ Children's Hospital and Medical Center
8200 Dodge St.
Omaha, NE 68114-4113
Ph: (402)955-5400
Free: 800-437-0272
URL: http://www.childrensomaha.org
Gary Perkins, President
Beds: 108.

20586 ■ Methodist Home Health and Hospice
8601 W Dodge Rd., Ste. 138
Omaha, NE 68114-3457
Ph: (402)354-3200
Free: 800-239-3065
Fax: (402)354-3320
URL: http://www.methodisthospice.com/

20587 ■ Odyssey HealthCare of Omaha
444 Regency Pkwy. Dr., Ste. 200
Omaha, NE 68114
Ph: (402)397-0990
Free: 877-637-9432
Fax: (402)397-5290
E-mail: info@odsyhealth.com
URL: http://www.odsyhealth.com

20588 ■ Visiting Nurse Association of the Midlands Hospice
12565 W Center Rd., Ste. 100
Omaha, NE 68144
Ph: (402)342-5566
Free: 800-456-8869
Fax: (402)930-4110
E-mail: info@thevnacares.org
URL: http://thevnacares.org/index.htm

Pender

20589 ■ Hospice of Siouxland Nebraska
200 Valley View Dr.
Pender, NE 68047
Ph: (402)385-0199
Free: 800-383-4545
Fax: (402)385-2281
URL: http://www.hospiceofsiouxland.org

Scottsbluff

20590 ■ Prairie Haven Hospice Alliance Regional West Health Services--Scottsbluff
2 W 42nd St., Ste. 2300
Scottsbluff, NE 69361-0615
Ph: (308)630-1149
Free: 877-699-7794
Fax: (308)630-1886
URL: http://www.rwmc.net/body.cfm?id=35

Sidney

20591 ■ Memorial Health Center Hospice & Palliative Care
645 Osage St.
Sidney, NE 69162-1714
Ph: (308)254-5825
Fax: (308)254-4225
URL: http://www.memorialhealthcenter.org/services/homehealth/index.html

Wahoo

20592 ■ CRMT, Inc. Hospice and Home Healthcare of Saunders County
141 E 5th St.
Wahoo, NE 68066
Ph: (402)443-4798
Fax: (402)443-1586

York

20593 ■ AseraCare Hospice Care of Nebraska
1100 Lincoln Ave., Ste. B1
York, NE 68467
Ph: (402)362-7733
Free: 888-225-2115
Fax: (402)362-7747
URL: http://www.aseracare.com/
Formerly: Hospice Care of Nebraska.

NEVADA

Elko

20594 ■ Horizon Hospice--Elko
790 Commercial St., Ste. 200
Elko, NV 89801
Ph: (775)778-0612
Fax: (775)777-3648

Fallon

20595 ■ XL Hospice Corp.--Fallon
139 Keddie St.
Fallon, NV 89406
Ph: (775)423-9511
Free: 800-574-5911
Fax: (208)642-9224
E-mail: xlhospice@fmtc.com
URL: http://www.xlhospice.com/about.html

Henderson

20596 ■ Medical Services of America Home Health and Hospice
2520 St. Rose Pkwy.
Henderson, NV 89074
Ph: (702)568-1176
Fax: (702)568-1194
URL: http://www.medicalservicesofamerica.com/

20597 ■ New Hope Hospice of Nevada
8 Sunset Way, Ste. 101
Henderson, NV 89014
Ph: (702)736-8180
Fax: (702)736-8056

20598 ■ St. Rose Dominican Hospitals-Rose de Lima Campus
102 E Lake Mead Pkwy.
Henderson, NV 89015
Ph: (702)616-6559
Free: 800-225-3414
URL: http://www.strosehospitals.org/Medical_Services/182213

Las Vegas

20599 ■ Affinity-Hospice of Life--Las Vegas
2700 E Sunset Rd.
Las Vegas, NV 89120
Ph: (702)380-1006
Fax: (702)380-1142
URL: http://www.affinityhospice.com/

20600 ■ Comfort Hospice Care-Las Vegas
6655 W Sahara Ave.
Las Vegas, NV 89146
Ph: (702)489-4412
Fax: (702)489-4381
E-mail: Carolcable@comforthospicecare.com
URL: http://www.comforthospicecare.com/

20601 ■ Compassioncare Hospice
4440 S Arville Ste. 12
Las Vegas, NV 89103
Ph: (702)636-0200
Fax: (702)636-2208
URL: http://www.compassioncarehospice.com/

20602 ■ Creekside Hospice
3675 Pecos McLeod, Ste. 900
Las Vegas, NV 89121
Ph: (702)650-7669
Fax: (702)650-7670
E-mail: info@creeksidehospice.net
URL: http://www.creeksidehospice.net

20603 ■ Family Home Hospice UnitedHealthcare Nevada
1701 W Charleston Blvd.
Las Vegas, NV 89102
Ph: (702)671-1111
Fax: (702)383-9826
URL: http://www.uhcnevada.com/body.cfm?id=27

20604 ■ Hospice of Las Vegas
5765 S Rainbow Blvd., Ste. 111
Las Vegas, NV 89118
Ph: (702)853-9063
Fax: (702)853-9066
E-mail: customerservice@hospiceoflasvegas.org
URL: http://hospiceoflasvegas.org/

20605 ■ Infinity Hospice Care--Las Vegas
7251 W Charleston Blvd.
Las Vegas, NV 89117
Ph: (702)880-7002
Fax: (702)880-9444
E-mail: info@InfinityHospiceCare.com
URL: http://www.infinityhospicecare.com/

20606 ■ Nathan Adelson Hospice - North West
3391 N Buffalo Rd.
Las Vegas, NV 89129
Ph: (702)733-0320
Fax: (702)983-3907
URL: http://www.nah.org

20607 ■ Nathan Adelson Hospice--Swenson Street, Las Vegas
4141 S Swenson St.
Las Vegas, NV 89119
Ph: (702)733-0320
Fax: (702)796-3196
URL: http://www.nah.org

20608 ■ Odyssey Healthcare of Las Vegas
4011A McLeod Dr.
Las Vegas, NV 89121
Ph: (702)693-4904
Free: 877-637-9432
Fax: (702)693-4925
E-mail: info@odsyhealth.com
URL: http://www.odsyhealth.com

20609 ■ Solari Hospice Care
5550 S Jones Blvd.
Las Vegas, NV 89118
Ph: (702)870-0000
Free: 800-825-1705
Fax: (702)870-9500
E-mail: lasvegas@solarihospice.net
URL: http://www.solarihospice.com/

Laughlin

20610 ■ New Hope Hospice-Laughlin National Hospice Management, Inc.
3650 S Pointe Cir., Ste. 112
Laughlin, NV 89029
Ph: (702)298-4673
Fax: (702)298-3921
URL: http://www.yourtrustedpartner.com/nhhllocation.htm

Mesquite

20611 ■ Virgin Valley Hospice-Mesquite
315 Calais Dr.
Mesquite, NV 89027
Ph: (702)228-0282
Free: 888-867-8405
Fax: (435)673-0436
URL: http://www.virginvalleyhomecare.com/types-of-home-care/hospice/

North Las Vegas

20612 ■ VA Southern NV Healthcare System
PO Box 360001
North Las Vegas, NV 89036
Ph: (702)248-0439
Fax: (702)636-4025
URL: http://www.lasvegas.va.gov/

Pahrump

20613 ■ Nathan Adelson Hospice - Pahrump
1480 E Calvada Blvd.
Pahrump, NV 89048
Ph: (775)751-6700
Free: 888-281-8646
Fax: (775)751-6699
URL: http://www.nah.org

Reno

20614 ■ Circle of Life Hospice Inc.--Reno
1575 Delucchi Ln., Ste. 214
Reno, NV 89502
Ph: (775)827-2298
Fax: (775)824-3860
E-mail: deb@colhospice.com
URL: http://www.colhospice.com

20615 ■ St. Mary's Hospice of Northern Nevada
18653 Wedge Pkwy.
Reno, NV 89511
Ph: (775)770-3081
Fax: (775)770-6904
URL: http://www.saintmarysreno.org/index.htm

Sparks

20616 ■ VistaCare-Sparks
1625 E Prater Way
Sparks, NV 89434
Ph: (775)825-5008
Fax: (775)825-5140
URL: http://www.vistacare.com/

Winnemucca

20617 ■ Humboldt Volunteer Hospice
705 E 4th St.
Winnemucca, NV 89445
Ph: (775)625-4263
Fax: (775)623-6218
E-mail: hvh@humboldthospice.com
URL: http://humboldtvolunteerhospice.community.officelive.com/default.aspx

NEW HAMPSHIRE

Berlin

20618 ■ Androscoggin Valley Hospital Home Health & Hospice
50 Page Hill Rd.
Berlin, NH 03570
Ph: (603)326-5870
Fax: (603)326-5881
URL: http://www.avhnh.org/

Concord

20619 ■ Concord Regional VNA Hospice Services
30 Pillsbury St.
Concord, NH 03302
Ph: (603)224-4093
Free: 800-924-8620
Fax: (603)228-7360
E-mail: mary.deveau@crvna.org
URL: http://www.crvna.org/services/hospice.php

Dover

20620 ■ Wentworth Homecare & Hospice, LLC
113 New Rochester Rd., Ste. 4
Dover, NH 03820
Ph: (603)742-7921
Fax: (603)742-3835
URL: http://www.wdhospital.com/body.cfm?id=183

Exeter

20621 ■ Rockingham VNA & Hospice
137 Epping Rd.
Exeter, NH 03833-1550
Ph: (603)772-2981
Free: 800-540-2981
Fax: (603)778-1250
URL: http://www.exeterhospital.com/about-exeter/rockingham-vna-hospice/

Franklin

20622 ■ Franklin VNA & Hospice
75 Chestnut St.
Franklin, NH 03235
Ph: (603)934-3454
Fax: (603)934-2222
URL: http://www.vnafnh.org/

Keene

20623 ■ Beacon Hospice-Keene
391 west Street
Keene, NH 03431
Ph: (603)357-8523
Free: 877-357-8523
Fax: (603)357-8526
URL: http://www.beaconhospice.com/
Bridgette Martel, Director

20624 ■ Home Healthcare, Hospice and Community Services
312 Marlboro St.
Keene, NH 03431
Ph: (603)352-2253
Free: 800-541-4145
Fax: (603)358-3904
E-mail: info@hcsservices.org
URL: http://www.hcsservices.org

Laconia

20625 ■ Community Health and Hospice
780 N Main St.
Laconia, NH 03246
Ph: (603)524-8444
Free: 800-244-8549
Fax: (603)524-8217
URL: http://www.chhnh.org

Lancaster

20626 ■ Weeks Medical Center-Home Health and Hospice Services
278 Main St.
Lancaster, NH 03584
Ph: (603)788-5020
Fax: (603)788-5068

Lebanon

20627 ■ Dartmouth Hitchcock Medical Center
One Medical Center Dr.
Lebanon, NH 03756
Ph: (603)650-5402
Fax: (603)650-8699
URL: http://www.dartmouth-hitchcock.org/about_dh/dhmc.html

Littleton

20628 ■ North Country Home Health and Hospice Agency
536 Cottage St.
Littleton, NH 03561
Ph: (603)444-5317
Free: 800-371-5317
Fax: (603)837-9451
URL: http://www.nchin.org/members.html
Gail Tomlinson, Executive Director

Londonderry

20629 ■ Amedisys Hospice of Londonderry
1 E Commons
Londonderry, NH 03053
Ph: (603)421-0414
Free: 866-230-3143
Fax: (603)421-3143
URL: http://www.amedisys.com/hospice_locations.cfm?id=28

Manchester

20630 ■ SolAmor Hospice-Manchester
340 Granite St., 2nd Fl.
Manchester, NH 03102
Ph: (603)606-7974
Fax: (603)606-7988
URL: http://www.solamorhospice.com/

20631 ■ VNA Home Health and Hospice Services, Inc.--Manchester
33 S Commercial St., Ste. 401
Manchester, NH 03104
Ph: (603)622-3781
Free: 800-624-6084
Fax: (603)641-4082
E-mail: info@manchestervna.org
URL: http://www.manchestervna.org

Merrimack

20632 ■ Community Hospice House--Merrimack
210 Naticook Rd.
Merrimack, NH 03054
Ph: (603)595-5688
Fax: (605)494-5609
E-mail: info@hhc.org
URL: http://www.hhhc.org/community_hospice_house/

20633 ■ Home Health and Hospice Care
80 Continental Blvd.
Merrimack, NH 03054
Ph: (603)424-3822
Free: 800-887-5973
Fax: (603)429-1844
E-mail: info@hhc.org
URL: http//www.hhhc.org

Nashua

20634 ■ Home Health & Hospice Care
22 Prospect St.
Nashua, NH 03060
Ph: (603)882-2941
Fax: (603)883-1515
E-mail: info@hhc.org
URL: http://www.hhhc.org/

20635 ■ Saint Joseph Hospital Palliative Care
172 Kinsley St.
Nashua, NH 03060
Ph: (603)882-3000
URL: http://stjosephhospital.com/Palliative-Medicine

New London

20636 ■ Lake Sunapee Region VNA Hospice and Palliative Care
107 Newport Rd.
New London, NH 03257
Ph: (603)526-4077
Fax: (603)526-4272
E-mail: info@lakesunapeevna.org
URL: http://www.lakesunapeevna.org
Formerly: Lake Sunapee Home Care and Hospice.

Newport

20637 ■ Connecticut Valley Home Care/Hospice
958 John Stark Hwy.
Newport, NH 03773
Ph: (603)543-6800
Fax: (603)863-8383
E-mail: info@vrh.org
URL: http://www.vrh.org/medical-services/a-i/home-care/default.aspx

North Conway

20638 ■ Visiting Nurse and Hospice Care Services of Northern Carroll
46 Seavey St.
North Conway, NH 03860-5355
Ph: (603)356-7006
Fax: (603)447-6766
URL: http://vnsncc.org/

North Hampton

20639 ■ Solamor Hospice-North Hampton
65 Lafayette Rd.
North Hampton, NH 03862
Ph: (603)964-5183
Fax: (603)964-5280
URL: http://www.solamorhospice.com/

Plymouth

20640 ■ Pemi-Baker Home Health and Hospice
101 Boulder Point Dr.
Plymouth, NH 03264
Ph: (603)536-2232
Fax: (603)536-2189
E-mail: cengelbert@pbhha.org
URL: http://www.pemibakerhomehealth.org/
Chandra Engelbert, Executive Director

Portsmouth

20641 ■ Amedisys Hospice-Portsmouth
95 Brewery La.
Portsmouth, NH 03801
Ph: (603)431-5442
Fax: (603)431-5484
URL: http://www.amedisys.com/hospice.cfm

20642 ■ New Hampshire Palliative Care Services, LLC
550 Lincoln Ave.
Portsmouth, NH 03801
Ph: (603)969-0815
Fax: (603)436-8690

West Lebanon

20643 ■ VNA and Hospice of VT/NH--West Lebanon
66 Benning St.
West Lebanon, NH 03784
Ph: (603)298-8399
Free: 888-300-8853
Fax: (603)298-0407
URL: http://www.vnavnh.org/

Wolfeboro

20644 ■ VNA-Hospice of Southern Carroll County
240 S Main St.
Wolfeboro, NH 03894-1620
Ph: (603)569-2729
Free: 888-242-0655
Fax: (603)569-2409
E-mail: intake@vnahospice.net
URL: http://www.vnahospice.net/

NEW JERSEY

Bayonne

20645 ■ Bayonne Visiting Nurse Association and Hospice
325 Broadway
Bayonne, NJ 07002
Ph: (201)339-2500
Fax: (201)437=2918
E-mail: bvna@aol.com
URL: http://www.bvna.org/

Bloomfield

20646 ■ Hospice of New Jersey--Bloomfield
400 Broadacres Dr.
Bloomfield, NJ 07003
Ph: (973)893-0818
Fax: (973)893-0828
URL: http://www.hospicenj.com/new_jersey

Brick

20647 ■ Meridian Nursing and Rehabilitation at Brick
Meridian Health
415 Jack Martin Blvd.
Brick, NJ 08724
Ph: (732)206-8000
Free: 800-560-9990
URL: http://www.meridianhealth.com/index.cfm/services/nursingrehab/Brick/index.c fm

Bridgeton

20648 ■ South Jersey Healthcare Hospice Inpatient Center
333 Irving Ave.
Bridgeton, NJ 08302

Ph: (856)575-4280
Fax: (888)200-7799
URL: http://www.sjhs.com/content/sjhhospiceinpatientcenter.htm

Burlington

20649 ■ Masonic Hospice Services
902 Jacksonville Rd.
Burlington, NJ 08016
Ph: (609)589-4444
Fax: (609)386-0414
E-mail: hospice@njmasonic.org
URL: http://www.njmasonic.org/Hospice/tabid/80/Default.aspx

Cherry Hill

20650 ■ Lighthouse Hospice--Cherry Hill
1040 N Kings Hwy., Ste. 100
Cherry Hill, NJ 08034
Ph: (856)414-1155
Free: 888-467-7423
Fax: (856)414-1313
E-mail: sandie@lighthousehospice.net
URL: http://www.lighthousehospice.net

Clark

20651 ■ Homeside Hospice LLC
67 Walnut Ave., Ste. 205
Clark, NJ 07066
Ph: (732)381-3444
Fax: (732)381-3445
E-mail: homesidehospice@aol.com
URL: http://www.homesidehospice.com/

Cranbury

20652 ■ Embracing Hospice Care of New Jersey West, LLC
109 S Main St., Ste. 23
Cranbury, NJ 08512
Ph: (609)662-9800
Fax: (609)448-7227
URL: http://www.embracinghospicecare.org/

Eatontown

20653 ■ VITAS Innovative Hospice Care of New Jersey Shore
1 Meridan Rd.
Eatontown, NJ 07724
Ph: (732)389-0066
Free: 866-338-4827
Fax: (732)389-2007
URL: http://www.vitas.com

Edison

20654 ■ Barbara E. Cheung Memorial Hospice
1 Roosevelt Dr.
Edison, NJ 08837
Ph: (732)321-9335
Fax: (732)321-0836
E-mail: frank.damiani@rossevelthealth.org
URL: http://www.mciauth.com/roosevelt.htm

20655 ■ Haven Hospice JFK Medical Center
65 James St.
Edison, NJ 08820-3947
Ph: (732)321-7769
Fax: (732)205-1478
URL: http://www.jfkmc.org/departments-and-clinical-services/medical-services/hav en-hospice

Egg Harbor Twp.

20656 ■ Holy Redeemer Home Care NJ Shore-Hospice--Egg Harbor Township
6550 Delilah Rd.
Egg Harbor Twp., NJ 08234
Ph: (609)761-0300
Fax: (609)761-0261
URL: http://www.holyredeemer.com/Main/Home.aspx

Elizabeth

20657 ■ Father Hudson House
111 Dehart Pl.
Elizabeth, NJ 07202-1224
Ph: (908)353-6060
Fax: (908)353-4504
E-mail: info@centerforhope.com
URL: http://www.centerforhope.com/hudson.htm

Englewood

20658 ■ Hospice of Englewood Hospital
75 E Demarest Ave.
Englewood, NJ 07631
Ph: (201)894-3333
Fax: (201)541-2730
URL: http://www.englewoodhospital.com/ms_home-health_hospice.asp

Ewing

20659 ■ Greenwood House Hospice
53 Walter St.
Ewing, NJ 08628
Ph: (609)718-0589
Fax: (609)883-6011
E-mail: rgoldstein@greenwoodhouse.org
URL: http://www.greenwoodhouse.org/services
Richard Goldstein, Executive Director

Flemington

20660 ■ Hunterdon Hospice
2100 Wescott Dr.
Flemington, NJ 08822
Ph: (908)788-6600
Fax: (908)788-6651
E-mail: aeboyle@att.net
URL: http://www.hunterdonhealthcare.org/services/home_care/hospice.asp

Hackensack

20661 ■ Inpatient Hospice Program of Hackensack University Medical Center
336 Prospect Ave.
Hackensack, NJ 07601
Ph: (201)678-5810
Fax: (201)487-1982
URL: http://www.humc.com/hospice/index.html

Jersey City

20662 ■ Hudson Hospice Volunteers, Inc.
93 Clerk St.
Jersey City, NJ 07305-4323
Ph: (201)433-6225
Fax: (201)433-2928
URL: http://www.hudsonhospicevolunteers.com/

Livingston

20663 ■ VITAS Innovative Hospice Care of New Jersey North
70 S Orange Ave.
Livingston, NJ 07039
Ph: (973)994-4738
Fax: (973)422-5385
URL: http://www.hudsonhospicevolunteers.com/

Long Branch

20664 ■ Saint Barnabas Hospice and Palliative Care Center at Monmouth Medical Center
300 2nd Ave.
Long Branch, NJ 07740
Ph: (732)923-6226
Fax: (732)923-6469
URL: http://www.saintbarnabas.com/hospitals/hospice/monmouth/index.html

Manahawkin

20665 ■ Southern Ocean Hospice
1140 Rte. 72W
Manahawkin, NJ 08050
Ph: (609)489-0252
Fax: (609)978-3171
URL: http://www.southernoceanmedicalcenter.com/

Marlton

20666 ■ Samaritan Hospice
5 Eves Dr., Ste. 300
Marlton, NJ 08053-3101
Ph: (856)596-1600
Free: 800-229-8183
Fax: (856)596-7881
E-mail: info@samaritanhospice.org
URL: http://www.samaritanhospice.org

Millburn

20667 ■ Atlantic Homecare and Hospice
33 Bleeker St.
Millburn, NJ 07041
Ph: (973)379-8440
Free: 800-350-2771
Fax: (973)379-8498
E-mail: ahch.information@atlantichealth.org
URL: http://www.atlantichealth.org/Atlantic/Patient+Care+Services/Hospice

Moorestown

20668 ■ The Hospice of Moorestown VNA
300 Harper Dr.
Moorestown, NJ 08057
Ph: (856)552-1300
Free: 877-862-4663
Fax: (856)552-1301
E-mail: services@moorestownvna.org
URL: http://www.moorestownvna.org

Morristown

20669 ■ Visiting Nurse Association of Northern New Jersey
175 South St.
Morristown, NJ 07960
Ph: (973)451-4109
Fax: (973)539-9802
URL: http://www.vnannj.org/

Mount Holly

20670 ■ Samaritan Hospice Inpatient Center
175 Madison Ave. S
Mount Holly, NJ 08060
Ph: (609)845-2200
Fax: (609)845-2209
E-mail: info@samaritanhospice.org
URL: http://www.samaritanhospice.org/

Mount Laurel

20671 ■ VITAS Innovative Hospice Care of New Jersey West
521 Fellowship Rd., Ste. 110
Mount Laurel, NJ 08054
Ph: (856)778-0222
Free: 866-528-4827
Fax: (856)778-8036
URL: http://www.vitas.com/

Neptume

20672 ■ Meridian Home Care
1340 A Campus Pkwy.
Neptume, NJ 07753
Ph: (732)751-3700
Fax: (732)751-3751
URL: http://www.meridianathome.com/hospice-care

Newton

20673 ■ Karen Ann Quinlan Hospice - Northwest New Jersey
99 Sparta Ave.
Newton, NJ 07860
Ph: (973)383-0115
Free: 800-882-1117
Fax: (973)383-6889
E-mail: info@karenannquinlanhospice.org
URL: http://www.karenannquinlanhospice.org

Paramus

20674 ■ Valley Hospice--Paramus
15 Essex Rd.
Paramus, NJ 07652
Ph: (201)291-6000
Free: 800-994-6610
Fax: (201)291-6230
URL: http://www.valleyhealth.com/Valley_HomeCare.aspx?id=42

Pennsville

20675 ■ Memorial Hospice--Pennsville
390 N Broadway
Pennsville, NJ 08070
Ph: (856)678-8500
Fax: (856)678-6991
URL: http://www.mhschealth.com/

Piscataway

20676 ■ Odyssey HealthCare of New Jersey
242 Old New Brunswick Rd., Ste. 140
Piscataway, NJ 08854
Ph: (732)562-8800
Free: 877-637-9432
Fax: (732)562-8686
E-mail: info@odsyhealth.com
URL: http://www.odsyhealth.com

Pleasantville

20677 ■ Atlanticare Hospice
PO Box 1626
Pleasantville, NJ 08232
Ph: (609)272-2424
Free: 888-744-0523
Fax: (609)272-2414
URL: http://www.atlanticare.org/healthservices/hospice.php
Formerly: Atlantic City Medical Center Hospice.

Rahway

20678 ■ Robert Wood Johnson University Hospital
Rahway Hospital Hospice
865 Stone St.
Rahway, NJ 07065
Ph: (732)499-6169
URL: http://www.rwjuhr.com/new/departments.html

Red Bank

20679 ■ Riverview Medical Center Hospice-Redbrook Cancer Center
1 Riverview Plaza
Red Bank, NJ 07701
Ph: (732)741-2700
Free: 800-560-9990
URL: http://www.riverviewmedicalcenter.com/RMC/waystogive/meridianathomehospice/ index.cfm

Runnemede

20680 ■ Holy Redeemer Hospice
150 Ninth Ave.
Runnemede, NJ 08078
Free: 800-255-8986
Fax: (856)312-2580

Scotch Plains

20681 ■ Center for Hope Hospice and Palliative Care
1900 Raritan Rd.
Scotch Plains, NJ 07076-2963
Ph: (908)889-7780
Fax: (908)889-5172
E-mail: info@centerforhope.com
URL: http://www.centerforhope.com

20682 ■ Peggy Coloney's House at Hope Village
Center for Hope Hospice & Palliative Care
1900 Raritan Rd.
Scotch Plains, NJ 07076-2963
Ph: (908)288-0500

Somerset

20683 ■ Martin and Edith Stein Hospice
49 Veronica Ave.
Somerset, NJ 08873
Ph: (732)227-1212
Fax: (732)227-1722
URL: http://www.wilfcampus.org/steinhospice

Somerville

20684 ■ Community Care Hospice-Somerville
110 W End Ave.
Somerville, NJ 08876
Ph: (908)725-9355
Fax: (908)725-1033
URL: http://www.communityvna.org/

Stratford

20685 ■ VITAS Inpatient Hospice Unit at Kennedy Memorial Hospitals Unv Med Ctr Stratford
18 E Laurel Rd., 3rd Fl.
Stratford, NJ 08084
Ph: (305)374-4143
Fax: (305)350-6784
URL: http://www.vitas.com/Aboutus/Locations.aspx

Swainton

20686 ■ Holy Redeemer Hospice-Cape May Branch
1601 Rt 9 N
Swainton, NJ 08210
Ph: (609)465-2080
Fax: (609)463-6121

Teaneck

20687 ■ Holy Name Home Care/Hospice
725 Teaneck Rd.
Teaneck, NJ 07666
Ph: (201)833-3740
Fax: (201)227-6063
URL: http://www.holyname.org/ForSeniors/hospice.asp

Thorofare

20688 ■ Heartland Hospice Services--Thorofare
800 Jessup Rd., Ste. 807
Thorofare, NJ 08086
Ph: (856)251-0707
Free: 800-427-1902
Fax: (856)251-9937
E-mail: careline@hcr-manorcare.com
URL: http://www.hcr-manorcare.com

Tinton Falls

20689 ■ VNA of Central Jersey Hospice Program
1100 Wayside Rd.
Tinton Falls, NJ 07712
Ph: (732)493-2220
Free: 800-862-3330
URL: http://www.vnacj.org/

Toms River

20690 ■ Holy Redeemer Home Care NJ Shore-Hospice--Toms River
1228 Rte. 37 W
Toms River, NJ 08755
Ph: (609)339-4811
Fax: (732)288-7055

20691 ■ Hospice of New Jersey--Toms River
40 Bey Lea Rd.
Toms River, NJ 08753
Ph: (732)818-3460
Fax: (732)818-3465
URL: http://www.americanhospice.com/new_jersey

20692 ■ Solamor Hospice-Toms River
1415 Hooper Ave.
Toms River, NJ 08753
Free: 866-411-9555
Fax: (732)341-7492
URL: http://www.solamorhospice.com/

20693 ■ Van Dyke Hospice & Palliative Care Center
99 Rte. 37 W
Toms River, NJ 08755
Ph: (732)818-6800
Free: 800-338-3131
Fax: (732)818-6823
E-mail: edorick@sbhcs.com
URL: http://www.saintbarnabas.com/hospitals/hospice/index.html
Formerly: Community Medical Center.

Totowa

20694 ■ Passaic Valley Hospice
783 Riverview Dr.
Totowa, NJ 07512
Ph: (973)256-4636
Fax: (973)256-9463
URL: http://www.vhsofnj.com/

Trenton

20695 ■ Capital Health System
446 Bellevue Ave.
Trenton, NJ 08618
Ph: (609)394-4000
URL: http://www.capitalhealth.org/

20696 ■ VNA of Mercer County Hospice
171 Jersey St.
Trenton, NJ 08603
Ph: (609)695-3461
Fax: (609)503-6083
URL: http://www.vnahomecare.org

Wall

20697 ■ Embracing HospiceCare of New Jersey
2101 Hwy. 34, Ste. B
Wall, NJ 07719
Ph: (732)974-2545
Free: 888-541-1800
Fax: (732)974-1666
URL: http://www.embracinghospicecare.org/

West Orange

20698 ■ Saint Barnabas Hospice and Pall Care Ctr at Newark Beth Israel Medical Center
95 Old Short Hills Rd.
West Orange, NJ 07052
Ph: (973)926-8400
Fax: (073)923-1602

20699 ■ Saint Barnabas Hospice and Palliative Care Center--West Orange
95 Old Short Hills Rd.
West Orange, NJ 07052
Ph: (973)322-4800
Fax: (973)322-4795
URL: http://www.sbhcs.com/hospitals/hospice/

Woodbury

20700 ■ Alliance Hospice-Woodbury
901 A Mantua Pike
Woodbury, NJ 08096
Ph: (856)666-9400
Fax: (856)686-9406
URL: http://www.alliancehospice.com/

NEW MEXICO

Alamogordo

20701 ■ Home Health Agency of Alamogordo
PO Drawer 29
Alamogordo, NM 88311
Ph: (505)437-3500
Fax: (505)437-2399

Albuquerque

20702 ■ Ambercare Hospice, Inc.--Albuquerque
2129 Osuna Rd. NE
Albuquerque, NM 87113
Ph: (505)244-0046
Fax: (505)243-8408
E-mail: ambercareabq@ambercare.com
URL: http://ambercare.com

20703 ■ Heartland Hospice Services--Albuquerque
4001 Indian School Rd. NE, Ste. 300
Albuquerque, NM 87110
Ph: (505)323-1464
Fax: (505)323-1465
E-mail: careline@hcr-manorcare.com
URL: http://www.hcr-manorcare.com

20704 ■ Heritage Home Healthcare and Hospice
3721 Rutledge Rd. NE
Albuquerque, NM 87110
Ph: (505)262-6455
Fax: (505)262-6456
URL: http://www.heritagehomehealthcare.com/

20705 ■ Hospice Compassus-Albuquerque
6000 Uptown Blvd.
Albuquerque, NM 87110
Ph: (505)332-0847
Fax: (505)332-9629
URL: http://www.hospicecompassus.com/

20706 ■ Hospice De La Luz
3812 Academy Pkwy. N NE
Albuquerque, NM 87109
Ph: (505)217-2490
Fax: (505)873-1060
E-mail: bmontoya@hospicedelaluz.com
URL: http://hospicedelaluz.com/

20707 ■ Hospice of the Sandias, LLC
105 Hospital Loop NE
Albuquerque, NM 87109
Ph: (505)881-5342
Fax: (505)348-1006
URL: http://www.hospiceofthesandias.com

20708 ■ Odyssey HealthCare of New Mexico
5600 Wyoming Blvd. NE
Albuquerque, NM 87109
Ph: (505)884-8857
Fax: (505)884-8895
URL: http://www.odsyhealth.com/default.asp

20709 ■ Presbyterian Hospice
Kaseman Hospital
8300 Constitution Pl. NE
Albuquerque, NM 87110
Ph: (505)559-1133
Fax: (505)559-6067
URL: http://www.phs.org/PHS/programs/homecare-hospice/index.htm

20710 ■ SolAmor Hospice--Albuquerque
5700 Harper NE, Ste. 300
Albuquerque, NM 87109
Ph: (505)821-2500
Fax: (505)821-2505
URL: http://www.solamorhospice.com/

20711 ■ University of New Mexico Hospice Department
1650 University NE
Albuquerque, NM 87102-1726
Ph: (505)272-6700
Fax: (505)272-6735
URL: http://hospitals.unm.edu/mariposa/index.shtml

20712 ■ VistaCare--Albuquerque
5639 Jefferson St. NE
Albuquerque, NM 87109
Ph: (505)449-3400
Free: 888-605-1969
Fax: (505)821-5449
URL: http://www.vistacare.com

20713 ■ VistaCare Center at Lovelace
601 Dr. Martin Luther King Ave. NE
Albuquerque, NM 87102
Ph: (505)727-3153
Fax: (505)727-3158
URL: http://www.vistacare.com/

Belen

20714 ■ Ambercare Hospice Inc.--Belen
420 N Main St.
Belen, NM 87002
Ph: (505)861-0060
Fax: (505)861-0045
E-mail: ambercareabq@ambercare.com
URL: http://www.ambercare.com

Carlsbad

20715 ■ Home Care Connection Hospice
513 S Canal St.
Carlsbad, NM 88220
Ph: (505)887-6050
Fax: (575)887-8908
E-mail: abock@thehomecare.net
URL: http://www.thehomecare.net/

20716 ■ Lakeview Christian Hospice Care
1300 N Canal St.
Carlsbad, NM 88220
Ph: (505)887-0933
Free: 877-922-7300
Fax: (505)885-7738
URL: http://www.lakeviewchristian.com/hospice.html

20717 ■ Landsun Hospice
1815 Westridge Rd.
Carlsbad, NM 88220-3507
Ph: (575)234-5830
Free: 800-274-9966
Fax: (575)234-5850
URL: http://landsunhomes.com/Hospice.html

20718 ■ VistaCare--Carlsbad
611 N Canal St.
Carlsbad, NM 88220
Ph: (505)887-1835
Free: 800-530-4851
Fax: (505)887-6967
E-mail: info@vistacare.com
URL: http://www.vistacare.com

Clovis

20719 ■ Hospice of the Sandias, LLC-Clovis
516 Mitchell St.
Clovis, NM 88101
Ph: (575)935-5683
Fax: (575)935-5685
URL: http://www.hospiceofthesandias.com/

20720 ■ VistaCare-Clovis
2708 N Prince St.
Clovis, NM 88101
Ph: (505)762-7067
Fax: (505)762-2563
URL: http://www.vistacare.com/

Deming

20721 ■ Mimbres Valley Hospice
113 N Pearl St.
Deming, NM 88030
Ph: (505)544-4663
Fax: (505)544-4665

Farmington

20722 ■ Basin Home Health and Hospice
200 N Orchard Ave.
Farmington, NM 87401
Ph: (505)325-8231
Fax: (505)325-4516
E-mail: itdept@BasinHomeHealth.com
URL: http://www.basinhomehealth.com

Hobbs

20723 ■ Starr Hospice
1601 N Turner St.
Hobbs, NM 88240
Ph: (575)393-7007
Free: 866-473-STAR
Fax: (505)391-8666
E-mail: support@starcareonline.com
URL: http://www.starcareonline.com/

20724 ■ VistaCare--Hobbs
1515 Calle Sur
Hobbs, NM 88240
Ph: (505)392-2060
Free: 800-658-6844
Fax: (505)392-2807
E-mail: info@vistacare.com
URL: http://www.vista-care.com

Las Cruces

20725 ■ Ambercare Hospice Inc-LasCruces
850 N Telshor
Las Cruces, NM 88011
Ph: (575)556-8409
E-mail: ambercareabq@ambercare.com
URL: http://ambercare.com/hospice/

20726 ■ Mesilla Valley Hospice Inc.
299 E Montana Ave.
Las Cruces, NM 88005
Ph: (575)525-5757
Fax: (575)527-2204
E-mail: info@myhospice.org
URL: http://www.mvhospice.org

Los Alamos

20727 ■ Los Alamos VNS Hospice
116 Central Park Sq.
Los Alamos, NM 87544
Ph: (505)662-2525
Fax: (505)662-7390
URL: http://www.lavns.com

Mora

20728 ■ Esperanza Home Health Care/Hospice
PO Box 270
Mora, NM 87732
Ph: (575)387-2215
Free: 800-858-9754
Fax: (575)387-9047
E-mail: Esperanza@nnmt.net
URL: http://www.esperanzahomehealth.com/

Roswell

20729 ■ Roswell Hospice HomeCare and Hospice
Family HomeCare Services, Inc.
1107 S Main St.
Roswell, NM 88202
Ph: (575)623-8000
Fax: (575)624-8566
URL: http://roswellhomecareandhospice.com/

20730 ■ VistaCare-Roswell
400 N Pennsylvania Ave.
Roswell, NM 88201
Ph: (575)627-1145
Fax: (575)627-1150
URL: http://www.vistacare.com/

Santa Fe

20731 ■ Ambercare Hospice-Santa Fe
550-D St. Michael's Dr.
Santa Fe, NM 87505
Ph: (505)244-0046
Fax: (505)243-8408
E-mail: ambercareabq@ambercare.com
URL: http://ambercare.com/

Silver City

20732 ■ Gila Regional Medical Center Hospice
1313 E 32nd St.
Silver City, NM 88061-7251
Ph: (575)574-4000
Free: 877-763-1065
Fax: (575)538-9714
URL: http://www.grmc.org/medical_services_tmp.php?CID=11

20733 ■ Horizon Hospice Inc-Silver City
1260 E 32nd St.
Silver City, NM 88061
Ph: (575)534-1800
Fax: (575)388-2742

Taos

20734 ■ Mountain Home Health Hospice
630 Paseo Del Sur 180
Taos, NM 87571
Ph: (575)758-4786
Fax: (575)758-0560

Tucumcari

20735 ■ Helping Hands Hospice--Tucumcari
615 S 2nd St.
Tucumcari, NM 88401
Ph: (575)461-0099
Free: 800-662-8840
Fax: (575)461-3621

NEW YORK

Albany

20736 ■ Community Hospice of Albany County
445 New Karner Rd.
Albany, NY 12205
Ph: (518)724-0200
Free: 800-678-0711
Fax: (518)724-0299
URL: http://www.communityhospice.org

20737 ■ Community Hospice Inn
St. Peter's Hospital
315 S Manning Blvd.
Albany, NY 12208
Ph: (518)525-1563
Fax: (518)525-1936
URL: http://www.communityhospice.org

Albion

20738 ■ Hospice of Orleans, Inc.
14080 Rt. 31 W
Albion, NY 14411
Ph: (585)589-0809
Fax: (585)589-5304
URL: http://www.hospiceoforleans.org

Amsterdam

20739 ■ Community Hospice of Amsterdam
246 Manny's Corners Rd.
Amsterdam, NY 12010
Ph: (518)843-5412
Fax: (518)843-9057
URL: http://www.communityhospice.org

Auburn

20740 ■ Hospice of the Finger Lakes
1130 Corporate Dr.
Auburn, NY 13021
Ph: (315)255-2733
Fax: (315)252-9080
E-mail: tkline@hospiceofthefingerlakes.org
URL: http://www.hospiceofthefingerlakes.org

Binghamton

20741 ■ Our Lady of Lourdes Hospital
169 Riverside Dr.
Binghamton, NY 13905
Ph: (607)798-5515
Fax: (607)798-7681
URL: http://www.lourdes.com/

Bronx

20742 ■ Calvary Hospital Hospice
1740 Eastchester Rd.
Bronx, NY 10461-2300
Ph: (718)518-2465
Free: 866-888-6680
E-mail: ndagostino@calvaryhospital.org
URL: http://www.calvaryhospital.org/site/pp.asp?c=ktJUJ9MPIsE&b=3226197

20743 ■ VNSNY Hospice Care-Bronx
1200 Waters Pl.
Bronx, NY 10461
Ph: (718)536-3785
Fax: (718)863-8357
URL: http://www.vnsny.org/

Brooklyn

20744 ■ Caring Hospice Services of New York, LLC
3071 Ave. U
Brooklyn, NY 11229
Ph: (718)743-4600
Free: 877-743-4600
Fax: (718)743-6400
URL: http://www.caringhospice.com

20745 ■ Metropolitan Jewish Hospice and Palliative Care Program
6323 7th Ave.
Brooklyn, NY 11220
Ph: (718)921-7948
Fax: (718)759-3640

20746 ■ VNSNY Hospice Care-Brooklyn
1630 E 15th St.
Brooklyn, NY 11229
Ph: (718)787-3150
URL: http://www.vnsny.org/

Canandaigua

20747 ■ Compassionate Care Inc.
400 S Main St.
Canandaigua, NY 14424
Ph: (585)394-0660
Fax: (585)396-3357

Castle Point

20748 ■ VA Hudson Valley Health Care System
Rte. 90
Castle Point, NY 12511
Ph: (845)831-2000
Fax: (914)788-4320
URL: http://www.hudsonvalley.va.gov/

Catskill

20749 ■ Community Hospice of Columbia/Greene
47 Liberty St.
Catskill, NY 12414
Ph: (518)943-5402
Fax: (518)943-0776
URL: http://www.communityhospice.org

Cheektowaga

20750 ■ Center for Hospice and Palliative Care-Cheektowaga
225 Como Park Blvd.
Cheektowaga, NY 14227
Ph: (716)686-1900
Fax: (716)686-8181
URL: http://www.hospicebuffalo.com/

Cobleskill

20751 ■ Catskill Area Hospice and Palliative Care, Inc.--Cobleskill
795 E Main St., Ste. 11
Cobleskill, NY 12043
Ph: (518)234-7611
Fax: (518)234-7612
URL: http://www.cahpc.org

Corning

20752 ■ Southern Tier Hospice and Palliative Care
11751 E Corning Rd.
Corning, NY 14830
Ph: (607)962-3100
Free: 800-734-1570
Fax: (607)962-4300
E-mail: info@sthospice.org
URL: http://www.sthospice.org

Cortland

20753 ■ Caring Community Hospice of Cortland
11 Kennedy Pkwy.
Cortland, NY 13045
Ph: (607)753-9105
Fax: (607)758-7668
E-mail: hospice@oddyssey.net
URL: http://www.cortlandhospice.org/

Delhi

20754 ■ Catskill Area Hospice and Palliative Care, Inc-Delhi
116 Main St.
Delhi, NY 13753
Ph: (607)746-2668
Fax: (607)746-7035
URL: http://www.cahpc.org/

East Elmhurst

20755 ■ VNSNY Hospice Care-Queens
7520 Astoria Blvd., Ste. 220
East Elmhurst, NY 11370
Ph: (718)888-6960
URL: http://www.vnsny.org/

Geneva

20756 ■ Ontario-Yates Hospice
756 Pre Emption Rd.
Geneva, NY 14456

Ph: (315)789-9821
Fax: (315)789-5768
URL: http://www.flvns.org/

Gloversville

20757 ■ Mountain Valley Hospice--Gloversville
108 Steele Ave.
Gloversville, NY 12078
Ph: (518)725-4545
Fax: (518)725-8066
E-mail: info@mountainvalleyhospice.com
URL: http://www.mountainvalleyhospice.com

Hudson Falls

20758 ■ Washington County Hospice & Palliative Care Program
415 Lower Main St.
County Annex Bldg.
Hudson Falls, NY 12839
Ph: (518)746-2400
Free: 800-624-4221
Fax: (518)746-2410
E-mail: info@hospicare.org
URL: http://www.health.state.ny.us/facilities/hospice/county/washington.htm
Formerly: Hospice of Washington County.

Ithaca

20759 ■ Hospicare and Palliative Care Services of Tompkins County
172 E King Rd.
Ithaca, NY 14850
Ph: (607)272-0212
Fax: (607)272-0237
E-mail: info@hospicare.org
URL: http://www.hospicare.org

Lakewood

20760 ■ Hospice Chautauqua County
20 W Fairmount Ave.
Lakewood, NY 14750
Ph: (716)753-5383
Fax: (716)753-5253
URL: http://www.hospicechautco.org/

Liverpool

20761 ■ Hospice of Central New York
990 7th N St.
Liverpool, NY 13088
Ph: (315)634-1100
Fax: (315)634-1111
E-mail: info@hosicecny.org
URL: http://www.hospicecny.org/
Formerly: Hospice & Palliative Care Associates.

Lockport

20762 ■ Hospice and Palliative Care Group, Inc.
Niagara Hospice
4675 Sunset Dr.
Lockport, NY 14094
Ph: (716)439-4417
Fax: (716)439-6035
E-mail: info@niagarahospice.com
URL: http://www.niagarahospice.org

Lowville

20763 ■ Lewis County Hospice
7785 N State St.
Lowville, NY 13367
Ph: (315)376-5230
Fax: (315)376-5435
URL: http://www.lewiscountypublichealth.com/hospice.html

Melville

20764 ■ Good Shepherd Hospice--Melville
24 Old Country Rd.
Melville, NY 11777
Ph: (631)645-6300
URL: http://www.goodshepherdhospice.net
Formerly: Saint Charles Hospice.

20765 ■ Good Shepherd Hospice--Melville
245 Old Country Rd.
Melville, NY 11747
Ph: (631)465-6300
Fax: (634)564-6513
URL: http://www.goodshepherdhospice.net/

20766 ■ Hospice Care Network-Hospice Inn
70 Pinelawn Rd.
Melville, NY 11747
Ph: (631)773-6706
Fax: (631)773-6714
URL: http://www.hospice-care-network.org/HospiceWeb/hospice-inn.cfm

Middletown

20767 ■ Hospice of Orange & Sullivan Counties, Inc.--Middletown
90 Crystal Run Rd.
Middletown, NY 10941
Ph: (846)92-5571
Fax: (845)692-6678
URL: http://www.hospiceoforange.com/

Montrose

20768 ■ VAMC: Franklin Deleno Roosevelt Campus of the VA Hudson Valley Healthcare System
2094 Albany Post Rd.
Montrose, NY 10548
Ph: (914)737-4400
Fax: (914)788-4320
URL: http://www2.va.gov/directory/guide/facility.asp?id=92

Mt. Morris

20769 ■ Livingston County Hospice
2 Livingston County Campus
Mt. Morris, NY 14510
Ph: (585)243-7290
E-mail: pking@co.livingston.ny.us
URL: http://www.hpcanys.org/county.asp?ID=26

New City

20770 ■ United Hospice of Rockland, Inc.
11 Stokum Ln.
New City, NY 10956-3505
Ph: (845)634-4974
Fax: (845)634-7549
E-mail: info@hospiceofrockland.org
URL: http://www.hospiceofrockland.org

New Hartford

20771 ■ Hospice and Palliative Care, Inc.--New Hartford
4277 Middle Settlement Rd.
New Hartford, NY 13413
Ph: (315)735-6484
Free: 800-317-5661
Fax: (315)793-8852
E-mail: info@hospicecareinc.org
URL: http://www.hospicecareinc.org/

New York

20772 ■ Elizabeth Seton Pediatric Center
590 Ave. of the Americas
New York, NY 10011
Ph: (646)459-3600
Fax: (646)459-3636
E-mail: info@setonpediatric.org
URL: http://www.setonpediatric.org/

20773 ■ Jacob Perlow Hospice
39 Broadway
New York, NY 10006
Ph: (212)649-8908
Fax: (212)649-5573
URL: http://hospicenyc.org/

20774 ■ Pax Christi Hospice
170 W 12th St.
New York, NY 10011
Ph: (718)876-1022
Fax: (718)876-1803

20775 ■ Shirley Goodman/Himan Brown Residence
1844 Second Ave.
New York, NY 10128
Ph: (212)360-3176
URL: http://www.vnsny.org/our-services/by-life-event/hospice/residences/

20776 ■ VNSYNY Hospice Care - New York City
1250 Broadway
New York, NY 10001
Ph: (212)609-1920
Free: 800-675-0391
Fax: (212)290-3933
URL: http://www.vnsny.org

Newburgh

20777 ■ Hospice of Orange & Sullivan Counties, Inc.--Newburgh
800 Stony Brook Ct.
Newburgh, NY 12550
Ph: (845)561-6111
Free: 800-924-0157
Fax: (845)561-2179
URL: http://www.hospiceoforange.com

20778 ■ Kaplan Family Hospice
One Sunrise La.
Newburgh, NY 12550
Ph: (845)561-6111
Free: 800-924-0157
Fax: (845)561-2179
URL: http://www.hospiceoforange.com/residence.htm#

Norwich

20779 ■ Hospice of Chenango County
21 Hayes St.
Norwich, NY 13815
Ph: (607)334-3556
Fax: (607)334-3688
E-mail: hospice@hospicechenango.org
URL: http://www.hospicechenango.org

Olean

20780 ■ HomeCare and Hospice
1225 W State St.
Olean, NY 14760-2135
Ph: (716)372-5735
Free: 800-339-7011
URL: http://www.homecare-hospice.org/
Formerly: Comstock Hospice Care Network.

Oneonta

20781 ■ Catskill Area Hospice and Palliative Care Inc.--Oneonta
1 Birchwood Dr.
Oneonta, NY 13820
Ph: (607)432-6773
Fax: (607)432-7741
URL: http://www.cahpc.org

Oswego

20782 ■ Oswego County Hospice
70 Bunner St.
Oswego, NY 13126
Ph: (315)349-8259
Fax: (315)349-8269
URL: http://www.co.oswego.ny.us/health/hospice.html

Patchogue

20783 ■ Brookhaven Memorial Hospital Medical Center Hospice
105 W Main St.
Patchogue, NY 11772
Ph: (631)687-2960
Fax: (631)687-2970
E-mail: communityrelations@bmhmc.org
URL: http://www.brookhavenhospital.org/Services/Specialized_Services/Hospice

Plattsburgh

20784 ■ Hospice of the North Country
358 Tom Miller Rd.
Plattsburgh, NY 12901
Ph: (518)561-8465
Free: 800-639-6430
Fax: (518)561-3182
E-mail: mcolmenero-macmillan@hospice.org
URL: http://www.hospicenc.org/

Port Henry

20785 ■ High Peaks Hospice & Palliative Care, Inc.
4322 Main St.
Port Henry, NY 12974
Ph: (518)546-9850
Fax: (518)546-9853
E-mail: kathysauers@highpeakshospice.com
URL: http://www.highpeakshospice.com/

Potsdam

20786 ■ Hospice and Palliative Care of Saint Lawrence Valley, Inc.
6805 US Hwy. 11
Potsdam, NY 13676
Ph: (315)265-3105
Fax: (315)265-0323
E-mail: info@hospiceslv.org
URL: http://www.hospiceslv.org

Poughkeepsie

20787 ■ Hospice, Inc.
374 Violet Ave.
Poughkeepsie, NY 12601
Ph: (845)473-2273
Fax: (845)454-5015
E-mail: hospiceinfo@hospiceinc.org
URL: http://seriousillness.org/slc/services/index.php

Rensselaer

20788 ■ Community Hospice of Rensselaer County
295 Valley View Blvd.
Rensselaer, NY 12144
Ph: (518)285-8150
Fax: (518)285-8192
URL: http://www.communityhospice.org

Rochester

20789 ■ Elizabeth G. and Jennifer J. Hildebrant Hospice Care Center
2652 Ridgeway Ave.
Rochester, NY 14626
Ph: (585)436-3462
Fax: (585)214-1136

20790 ■ Lifetime Care Hospice
3111 Winton Rd. S
Rochester, NY 14623
Ph: (585)214-1146
Fax: (585)214-1136
URL: http://hospiceinfohospitalpiceinc.org

20791 ■ Palliative Center for Caring
1500 Portland Ave.
Rochester, NY 14621
Ph: (585)697-6603

Saranac Lake

20792 ■ High Peaks Hospice
309 Country Rte. 47, Ste. 3
Saranac Lake, NY 12983
Ph: (518)891-0606
Free: 877-324-1686
Fax: (518)891-0657
E-mail: marievannortwick@highpeakshospice.com
URL: http://www.highpeakshospice.com/

Saratoga Springs

20793 ■ Community Hospice of Saratoga
179 Lawrence St.
Saratoga Springs, NY 12866
Ph: (518)581-0800
Fax: (518)581-9460
URL: http://www.communityhospice.org

Schenectady

20794 ■ Community Hospice of Schenectady
1411 Union St.
Schenectady, NY 12308-3009
Ph: (518)377-8846
Fax: (518)377-8868
URL: http://www.communityhospice.org

Sleepy Hollow

20795 ■ Phelps Hospice, Phelps Memorial Hospital Center
701 N Broadway
Sleepy Hollow, NY 10591
Ph: (914)366-3325
Fax: (914)366-1538
E-mail: msernatinger@pmhc.us
URL: http://www.phelpshospital.org/clinical_specialties_services/hospice.php

Smithtown

20796 ■ St. Catherine of Siena Hospital
50 Rte. 25A
Smithtown, NY 11787
Ph: (631)862-3646
Fax: (631)862-3749
URL: http://www.stcatherines.chsli.org/

Staten Island

20797 ■ University Hospice
256 Mason Ave.
Staten Island, NY 10305
Ph: (718)226-6450
Fax: (718)226-6607
URL: http://www.siuh.edu/hospice/

Tuckahoe

20798 ■ Jansen Hospice and Palliative Care
69 Main St.
Tuckahoe, NY 10707
Ph: (914)961-2818
Fax: (914)961-8654
URL: http://jansenhospice.org/

Vestal

20799 ■ Lourdes Hospice-Vestal
4102 Old Vestal Rd.
Vestal, NY 13850
Ph: (607)584-9154
Fax: (607)352-1738
E-mail: info@lourdes.com
URL: http://www.lourdes.com/

Watertown

20800 ■ Hospice of Jefferson County
425 Washington St.
Watertown, NY 13601
Ph: (315)788-7323
Fax: (315)788-9653
E-mail: foundation@jeffhospice.org
URL: http://www.jeffhospice.org

Webster

20801 ■ Visiting Nurse Hospice
2180 Empire Blvd.
Webster, NY 14580
Ph: (585)787-2233
E-mail: info@vnsnet.com
URL: http://www.vnsnet.com/

20802 ■ Webster Comfort Care Home, Inc.
700 Holt Rd.
Webster, NY 14580-9162
Ph: (585)872-5290
Fax: (585)872-7521
E-mail: wcch@webstercomfortcare.ort
URL: http://www.webstercomfortcare.org

West Islip

20803 ■ Good Samaritan Hospital
1000 Montauk Hwy.
West Islip, NY 11795
Ph: (631)376-3736
Fax: (631)376-3743
URL: http://www.good-samaritan-hospital.org/index.php

Westhampton Beach

20804 ■ East End Hospice
481 Westhampton-Riverhead Rd.
Westhampton Beach, NY 11978
Ph: (631)288-8400
E-mail: info@eeh.org
URL: http://www.eeh.org

White Plains

20805 ■ Hospice and Palliative Care of Westchester
311 North St., Ste. 204
White Plains, NY 10605
Ph: (914)682-1484
Fax: (914)559-3092
E-mail: info@hospiceofwestchester.com
URL: http://www.hospiceofwestchester.com

NORTH CAROLINA

Ahoskie

20806 ■ University Health Systems Hospice Care
521 Myers St. W
Ahoskie, NC 27910-3811
Ph: (252)332-3392
Free: 877-816-0474
Fax: (252)332-5705
E-mail: bhoggard@uhseast.com
URL: http://www.uhseast.com/hospice/

Albemarle

20807 ■ Hospice of Stanly County
960 N 1st St.
Albemarle, NC 28001
Ph: (704)983-4216
Free: 800-230-4236
Fax: (704)983-6662
E-mail: ahowell@hospiceofstanly.org
URL: http://www.hospiceofstanly.org

Asheboro

20808 ■ Hospice of Randolph County
416 Vision Dr.
Asheboro, NC 27204
Ph: (336)672-9300
Fax: (336)672-0868
E-mail: info@hospiceofrandolph.org
URL: http://www.hospiceofrandolph.org

Asheville

20809 ■ Care Partners Hospice and Palliative Care
68 Sweeten Creek Rd.
Asheville, NC 28803
Ph: (828)277-4800
Fax: (828)255-2880
URL: http://www.carepartners.org/pagedisplay.cfm-?mainpage=6

20810 ■ John F. Keever Solace Center
85 Zillicoa St.
Asheville, NC 28813
Ph: (828)255-0231
Fax: (828)255-2880
E-mail: info@carepartners.org
URL: http://www.carepartners.org/pagedisplay.cfm?mainpage=6&subpage=25

Bayboro

20811 ■ Hospice of Pamlico County
11146 State Hwy. 55 E
Bayboro, NC 28515
Ph: (252)745-5171
Fax: (252)745-7025

Boone

20812 ■ High Country Health Care System Hospice--Boone
400 Shadowline Dr.
Boone, NC 28607
Ph: (828)264-9155
Fax: (828)264-9154
E-mail: hospice@hchealth.net
URL: http://www.highcountryhospice.org/

Brevard

20813 ■ Transylvania Regional Hospital Hospice
1266 Asheville Hwy.
Brevard, NC 28712
Ph: (828)883-5254
Fax: (828)883-5363
URL: http://www.trhospital.org

Burgaw

20814 ■ Liberty Home Care and Hospice-Burgaw
904-B S Walker St.
Burgaw, NC 28425
Ph: (910)259-1150
Free: 800-200-9339
Fax: (910)259-1155
URL: http://www.libertyhomecare.com/details.as-p?ID=19

20815 ■ Lower Cape Fear Hospice and LifeCare Center=Burgaw
308 S Campbell St.
Burgaw, NC 28425
Ph: (910)259-2827
Fax: (910)796-7901
URL: http://www.hospiceandlifecarecenter.org/

Burlington

20816 ■ Amedisys Hospice-Burlington
1111 Huffman Mill Rd.
Burlington, NC 27215
Ph: (336)584-4440
Fax: (336)584-4404
URL: http://www.amedisys.com/hospice_locations.cfm?id=10
Formerly: Tender Loving Care Home Care and Hospice.

20817 ■ Hospice & Palliative Care Center of Alamance Caswell
914 Chapel Hill Rd.
Burlington, NC 27215-6715
Ph: (336)532-0100
Free: 800-588-8879
Fax: (336)532-0058
E-mail: servingyou@hospiceac.org
URL: http://www.hospiceac.org
Formerly: Hospice of Alamance Caswell.

20818 ■ Liberty Home Care and Hospice-Burlington
2563 Eric Ln., Ste. F
Burlington, NC 27215
Ph: (336)226-4053
Free: 866-304-7236
Fax: (336)226-0297
URL: http://www.libertyhomecare.com/details.as-p?ID=26

Burnsville

20819 ■ Hospice of Yancey County
856 George's Fork Rd.
Burnsville, NC 28714
Ph: (828)682-9675
Fax: (828)682-4713
E-mail: info@hospiceofyancey.org
URL: http://www.hospiceofyancey.org

Chapel Hill

20820 ■ Community Home Care and Hospice-Chapel Hill
1777 N Fordham Blvd., Ste. 107
Chapel Hill, NC 27514-5810
Ph: (919)933-0137

20821 ■ UNC Hospice--Chapel Hill
1101 Weaver Dairy Rd.
Chapel Hill, NC 27514
Ph: (919)843-1667
E-mail: unchospice@unch.unc.edu
URL: http://www.unchealthcare.org/site/hospice

Charlotte

20822 ■ Hospice at Charlotte
1420 E 7th St.
Charlotte, NC 28204
Ph: (704)375-0100
Fax: (704)375-8623
E-mail: information@hospiceatcharlotte.org
URL: http://www.hpccr.org

20823 ■ Presbyterian Hospice and Palliative Care
200 Hawthorne La.
Charlotte, NC 28233
Ph: (704)384-6478
Fax: (704)384-8182
URL: http://www.presbyterian.org

Clayton

20824 ■ Community Home Care and Hospice-Clayton
962 Hwy. 42 W
Clayton, NC 27520
Ph: (919)989-7276

Clinton

20825 ■ Advantage Hospice and Home Care--Clinton
358 N East Blvd.
Clinton, NC 28328
Ph: (910)296-0346
Fax: (910)299-0458

20826 ■ Community Home Care and Hospice-Clinton
216 Beaman St.
Clinton, NC 28328

20827 ■ Home Health and Hospice Care-Clinton
1023 Beaman St.
Clinton, NC 28328
Ph: (910)592-1421
Fax: (910)592-7392
E-mail: info@3hc.org
URL: http://www.3hc.org/

20828 ■ Liberty Home Care and Hospice-Clinton
1206 Southwest Blvd.
Clinton, NC 28328-4628
Ph: (910)592-8367
URL: http://www.libertyhomecare.com/listHos.asp

Clyde

20829 ■ Haywood Regional Medical Center Hospice
560 Leroy George Dr.
Clyde, NC 28721-7408
Ph: (828)452-8811
Fax: (828)452-7078
URL: http://www.haymed.org

Columbus

20830 ■ Hospice of the Carolina Foothills Inc.
130 Forest Glen Dr.
Columbus, NC 28722
Ph: (828)894-7000
Free: 800-617-7132
Fax: (828)894-2254
E-mail: info@hocf.org
URL: http://www.hocf.org

Dallas

20831 ■ Gaston Hospice, Inc-Robin Johnson House
5005 Shepherds Way Dr.
Dallas, NC 28034
Ph: (704)922-4211
Fax: (704)865-0590
E-mail: gastonhospice@gmh.org
URL: http://www.gastonhospice.org/

Dobson

20832 ■ Joan and Howard Woltz Hospice Home
945 Zephyr Rd.
Dobson, NC 27017
Ph: (336)356-5000
Fax: (336)356-5001
URL: http://www.woltzhospicehome.org/

Dunn

20833 ■ Hospice of Harnett County, Inc.
111-A N Ellis Ave.
Dunn, NC 28334
Ph: (910)892-1213
Fax: (910)892-1229
E-mail: info@harnetthospice.org
URL: http://harnetthospice.org/

20834 ■ Liberty Home Care and Hospice-Dunn
105 Hunt Valley Dr.
Dunn, NC 28334
Ph: (910)892-6427
Free: 800-829-6426
Fax: (910)892-1592
URL: http://www.libertyhomecare.com/

Durham

20835 ■ Community Home Care and Hospice-Durham
1738 Hillandale Rd.
Durham, NC 27705
Ph: (919)806-5040

20836 ■ Duke Home Care and Hospice
4321 Medical Park Dr., Ste. 101
Durham, NC 27704-2199
Ph: (919)620-3853
Free: 800-599-9339
Fax: (919)620-9188
URL: http://www.dhcc.dukehealth.org
Formerly: Duke Health Community Care, dba Duke Community Hospice Services.

20837 ■ Duke Home Care & Hospice-Hock Family Pavilion
4023 N Roxboro Rd.
Durham, NC 27707
Ph: (919)613-6738
URL: http://dhch.duhs.duke.edu/

20838 ■ Duke University Center for Palliative Care
2424 Hock Plaza
Durham, NC 27705
Ph: (919)668-7215
Fax: (919)668-1300
URL: http://www.duke.edu

20839 ■ Liberty Home Care and Hospice Services-Durham
3414 N Duke St., Ste. 201
Durham, NC 27704
Ph: (919)479-7393
Free: 866-674-4191
Fax: (919)479-7393
URL: http://www.libertyhomecare.com/details.asp?ID=36

Elizabeth City

20840 ■ Albemarle Hospice
PO Box 189
Elizabeth City, NC 27907
Ph: (252)338-4066
Free: 800-478-0477
Fax: (252)338-3767
E-mail: gsp@ppcc.dst.nc.us
URL: http://www.ahc-nc.org

20841 ■ Community Home Care and Hospice--Elizabeth City
1601 N Road St., Ste. B
Elizabeth City, NC 27909
Ph: (252)335-4594

Elizabethtown

20842 ■ Lower Cape Fear Hospice and Life Care Center
Bladen County Office
101 S Craig St.
Elizabethtown, NC 28337
Ph: (910)862-3111
Free: 800-735-6354
Fax: (910)862-3148
E-mail: hospice.lifecarecenter@lcfh.org
URL: http://www.hospiceandlifecarecenter.org

Elkin

20843 ■ Mountain Valley Hospice and Palliative Care-Elkin
688 N Bridge St.
Elkin, NC 28621
Ph: (336)526-2650
Fax: (336)526-2370
URL: http://www.mtnvalleyhospice.org/

Engelhard

20844 ■ Community Home Care and Hospice-Engelhard
33460 US 264, No. 3
Engelhard, NC 27824
Ph: (252)925-7159

Erwin

20845 ■ Community Home Care and Hospice--Erwin
400 E H Street
Erwin, NC 28339
Ph: (910)892-7548

Fayetteville

20846 ■ Advantage Hospice and Home Care-Fayetteville
1708 Owen Dr.
Fayetteville, NC 28304
Ph: (910)223-3107

20847 ■ Carol S. Roberson Hospice Center
2431 Legion Rd.
Fayetteville, NC 28306
Ph: (910)429-7000

20848 ■ Community Home Care and Hospice--Fayetteville
5301 Morganton Rd.
Fayetteville, NC 28314
Ph: (910)323-9816
Free: 800-569-1348
Fax: (910)487-6725

20849 ■ Home Health and Hospice Care-Fayetteville
2504 Raeford Rd.
Fayetteville, NC 28305
Ph: (910)860-7858
Fax: (910)860-8279
E-mail: info@3hc.org
URL: http://www.3hc.org/

Flat Rock

20850 ■ Four Seasons Hospice and Palliative Care
571 S Allen Rd.
Flat Rock, NC 28731
Ph: (828)692-6178
E-mail: ccomeaux@nchospice.com
URL: http://www.fourseasonscfl.org/

20851 ■ Four Seasons Hospice and Palliative Care
Elizabeth House
581 S Allen Rd.
Flat Rock, NC 28731
Ph: (828)692-6178
Free: 866-466-9734
Fax: (828)692-9867
URL: http://www.fourseasonscfl.org/

Forest City

20852 ■ Hospice of Rutherford County
374 Hudlow Rd.
Forest City, NC 28043-0336
Ph: (828)245-0095
Free: 800-218-2273
Fax: (828)245-5389
URL: http://www.hospiceofrutherford.org/

Franklinton

20853 ■ Tender Loving Care Home Care and Hospice-Franklinton
Amedisys Home Health Services
3320 US 1 Hwy.
Franklinton, NC 27525
Ph: (919)496-1900
Fax: (919)496-7052

Garner

20854 ■ Amedisys Hospice of Garner
220 N Fidelity Ct.
Garner, NC 27529
Ph: (919)773-4865
Free: 866-773-8797
Fax: (919)773-4985
URL: http://www.amedisys.com/

20855 ■ Tender Loving Care Home Care and Hospice-Garner
Amedisys Home Health Services
220 New Fidelity Ct.
Garner, NC 27529
Ph: (919)773-4865
Fax: (919)773-4985

Gastonia

20856 ■ Gaston Hospice County Inc.
258 E Garrison Blvd.
Gastonia, NC 28054
Ph: (704)861-8405
Fax: (704)865-0590
E-mail: gastonhospice@gmh.org
URL: http://www.gastonhospice.org

Goldsboro

20857 ■ 3HC - Goldsboro
2402 Wayne Memorial Dr.
Goldsboro, NC 27534
Ph: (919)735-1386
Free: 800-879-4442
Fax: (919)731-4985
E-mail: info@3hc.org
URL: http://www.3hc.org/locations.html
Formerly: Home Health and Hospice Care - Goldsboro.

20858 ■ Community Home Care and Hospice--Goldsboro
1201 Wayne Memorial Dr.
Goldsboro, NC 27534

20859 ■ Home Health and Hospice Care-Goldsboro
2402 Wayne Memorial Dr.
Goldsboro, NC 27534
Ph: (919)735-1386
Fax: (919)731-4985
E-mail: swiehardt@hchhh.org
URL: http://www.hchhh.org/

20860 ■ Kitty Askins Hospice Center
107 Handley Park Ct.
Goldsboro, NC 27534
Ph: (919)735-5887
Fax: (919)735-5948
E-mail: info@3hc.org
URL: http://www.3hc.org/locations.html

Greensboro

20861 ■ Beacon Place
2502 Summit Ave.
Greensboro, NC 27405
Ph: (336)621-5301
Fax: (336)375-2348
E-mail: csmith@hospicegso.org
URL: http://www.hospicegso.org/index.php?option=com_content&task=view&id=14&Itemid=31

20862 ■ Hospice & Palliative Care of Greensboro
2500 Summit Ave.
Greensboro, NC 27405-4522
Ph: (336)621-2500
Fax: (336)621-4516
E-mail: csmith@hospicegso.org
URL: http://www.hospicegso.org
Formerly: Hospice at Greensboro.

20863 ■ Kids Path
Hospice and Palliative Care of Greensboro
2504 Summit Ave.
Greensboro, NC 27405-4522
Ph: (336)544-5437
Fax: (336)544-2270
E-mail: mtaylor@hospicegso.org
URL: http://www.hospicegso.org/index.php?option=com_content&task=view&id=15&Itemid=32

20864 ■ Moses Cone Health System
1200 N Elm St.
Greensboro, NC 27401
Ph: (336)832-2770
Fax: (336)832-8192
URL: http://www.mosescone.com/

Greenville

20865 ■ Community Home Care and Hospice-Greenville
3740 S Evans St., Ste. E
Greenville, NC 27834
Ph: (252)321-1528

20866 ■ Home Health and Hospice Care
1880 W Arlington Blvd.
Greenville, NC 27834
Ph: (919)758-8212
Fax: (919)758-1384
URL: http://www.3hc.org/

Henderson

20867 ■ Community Home Care and Hospice-Henderson
1242 Dabney Dr.
Henderson, NC 27536
Ph: (252)430-7760

High Point

20868 ■ Hospice of the Piedmont--High Point
1801 Westchester Dr.
High Point, NC 27262
Ph: (336)889-8446
Fax: (336)889-3450
E-mail: info@hospice-careconnection.org
URL: http://www.hospice-careconnection.org

Highlands

20869 ■ Highlands-Cashiers Hospice
190 Hospital Dr.
Highlands, NC 28741
Ph: (828)526-1402
Fax: (828)526-1402
E-mail: info@hchospital.org
URL: http://www.hchospital.org/inside/hospice/hospice.htm

Hillsborough

20870 ■ Duke Community Hospice Services At the Meadowlands
1001 Corporate Dr.
Hillsborough, NC 27278
Ph: (919)644-0764
Fax: (919)644-0932
URL: http://dhch.duhs.duke.edu/modules/dhchospice/index.php?id=7

Huntersville

20871 ■ Levine & Dickson Hospice House
Hospice & Palliative Care
11900 Vanstory Dr.
Huntersville, NC 28078
Ph: (704)375-0100
Fax: (704)335-3599
URL: http://www.hpccr.org/patients-info-levine-dickson-house.cfm

Jacksonville

20872 ■ Continuum Home Care and Hospice
3391 Henderson Dr. Ext.
Jacksonville, NC 28546
Ph: (910)989-2682
Fax: (910)989-2691
URL: http://www.continuumhch.com/

20873 ■ Liberty Home Care and Hospice-Jacksonville
1700 Country Club Rd.
Jacksonville, NC 28546
Ph: (910)346-4800
Free: 800-800-0614
Fax: (910)346-5870
URL: http://www.libertyhomecare.com/

Jefferson

20874 ■ High Country Health Care System-Hospice--Jefferson
392 Hwy. 88 E
Jefferson, NC 28640
Ph: (336)246-6443
Fax: (336)246-8504
E-mail: hospice@hchealth.net
URL: http://www.highcountryhospice.org/

Kannapolis

20875 ■ Hospice & Palliative Care of Cabarrus County
5003 Hospice La.
Kannapolis, NC 28081
Ph: (704)935-9434
Fax: (704)935-9435
E-mail: info@hpccc.org
URL: http://www.hpccc.org/

Kenansville

20876 ■ Carolina East Home Care and Hospice/Duplin Home Care and Hospice
PO Box 887
Kenansville, NC 28349
Ph: (910)296-0819
Free: 800-537-2908
Fax: (910)296-0482
E-mail: info@carolinaeast.org
URL: http://www.carolinaeast.org

Kinston

20877 ■ Community Home Care and Hospice--Kinston
701 Doctors Dr.
Kinston, NC 28501
Ph: (252)527-2201

20878 ■ Continuum Home Care & Hospice of Lenior County
704 M. Plaza Blvd.
Kinston, NC 28501
Ph: (252)527-3784
Fax: (252)527-5360
URL: http://continuumhch.com/

Laurinburg

20879 ■ Hospice of Scotland County
610 Lauchwood Dr.
Laurinburg, NC 28353
Ph: (910)276-7176
Free: 877-276-7176
Fax: (910)277-1941
E-mail: cswanson@caldwellhospice.org
URL: http://www.hospiceofscotlandcounty.org
Cathy Swanson, Executive Director

20880 ■ Morrison Manor
Hospice of Scotland County
PO Box 1033
Laurinburg, NC 28353
Ph: (910)276-7176
Fax: (910)277-1941
URL: http://www.scotlandhospice.org/getpage.php?name=manor&sub=Static

Leland

20881 ■ Community Home Care and Hospice--Leland
117 Village Rd., Ste. E
Leland, NC 28451
Ph: (910)371-6427

Lenoir

20882 ■ Caldwell Hospice and Palliative Care, Inc.
902 Kirkwood St. NW
Lenoir, NC 28645
Ph: (828)754-0101
Fax: (828)757-3335
URL: http://www.caldwellhospice.org

Lexington

20883 ■ Hospice of Davidson County
200 Hospice Way
Lexington, NC 27292
Ph: (336)475-5444
Free: 800-768-4677
URL: http://www.hospiceofdavidsoncounty.org

Lillington

20884 ■ E. Carlton Powell Hospice Center
185 Pine State St.
Lillington, NC 27546
Ph: (910)893-5394

Lincolnton

20885 ■ Hospice of Lincoln County
107 N Cedar St.
Lincolnton, NC 28092
Ph: (704)732-6146
Fax: (704)736-0264
E-mail: fortner@hospiceatcharlotte.com
URL: http://www.hospiceatcharlotte.com/lincoln-county.cfm

Louisburg

20886 ■ Community Home Care Hospice-Louisburg
928 N Main St.
Louisburg, NC 27549
Ph: (919)496-1206

Lumberton

20887 ■ Community Home Care and Hospice-Lumberton
2402 N Roberts Ave.
Lumberton, NC 28358
Ph: (910)618-9866

20888 ■ Liberty Home Care and Hospice-Lumberton
705 A Wesley Pines Rd.
Lumberton, NC 28358
Ph: (910)738-4512
Free: 800-356-3296
Fax: (910)738-4631
URL: http://www.libertyhomecare.com/details.asp?ID=3

20889 ■ Southeastern Hospice
Southeastern Region Medical Center
1100 Pine Run Dr.
Lumberton, NC 28358
Ph: (910)671-4803
Fax: (910)671-6450
URL: http://www.srmc.org/

Manteo

20890 ■ Dare Home Health and Hospice
PO Box 1000
Manteo, NC 27954
Ph: (252)475-5028
Fax: (252)473-9814
URL: http://www.co.dare.nc.us/depts/health/hhhome.htm

Marion

20891 ■ Hospice of McDowell County Inc.
575 Airport Rd.
Marion, NC 28752
Ph: (828)652-1318
Fax: (828)659-1631
E-mail: hospice@hospiceofmcdowell.org
URL: http://hospiceofmcdowell.org

Maysville

20892 ■ Home Health and Hospice Care-Maysville
204 main St.
Maysville, NC 28555
Ph: (910)743-2800
Fax: (910)743-2321
E-mail: info@3hc.org
URL: http://www.3hc.org/

Mocksville

20893 ■ Hospice & Palliative CareCenter of Davie County
377 Hospital St.
Mocksville, NC 27208
Ph: (336)753-0212
Fax: (336)753-5576
URL: http://hospicecarecenter.org/

Monroe

20894 ■ Community Home Care and Hospice--Monroe
2661 W Roosevelt Blvd., Ste. 104-107
Monroe, NC 28110-0454
Ph: (704)225-1498

20895 ■ Hospice of Union County--Monroe
700 W Roosevelt Blvd.
Monroe, NC 28110
Ph: (704)292-2100
Fax: (704)292-2190
E-mail: mlinker@houc.org
URL: http://www.houc.org/

Mooresville

20896 ■ Hospice and Palliative Care of Iredell County
150 Fairview Rd.
Mooresville, NC 28117
Ph: (704)633-0051
Fax: (704)633-1963
E-mail: hoic@hoic.org
URL: http://www.hoic.org

Morehead City

20897 ■ Community Home Care and Hospice-Morehead City
3328 D Bridges St.
Morehead City, NC 28557
Ph: (252)240-1142

20898 ■ Hospice of Carteret County
3500 Arendell St.
Morehead City, NC 28557-1619
Ph: (252)808-6085
Fax: (252)808-6573
URL: http://www.ccgh.org/services/hospice/

Mount Airy

20899 ■ Mountain Valley Hospice and Palliative Care--Mount Airy
401 Technology Ln.
Mount Airy, NC 27030
Ph: (336)789-2922
Free: 888-789-2922
Fax: (336)789-0856
URL: http://www.mtnvalleyhospice.org/
Formerly: Hospice of Surry County, Inc.

New Bern

20900 ■ Community Home Care and Hospice-New Bern
1423 S Glenburnie Rd., Ste. A
New Bern, NC 28562
Ph: (252)367-1380

20901 ■ Continuum Home Care & Hospice of Craven County
1505 Glenburnie Ave.
New Bern, NC 28562
Ph: (252)638-6821
Fax: (252)638-6844
URL: http://continuumhch.com/

Newton

20902 ■ Palliative Care Center and Hospice of Catawba Valley
3975 Robinson Rd.
Newton, NC 28658-9715
Ph: (828)466-0466
Fax: (828)466-8862
URL: http://www.hospiceofcatawbavalley.org/

Pembroke

20903 ■ Native Angels Hospice-Pembroke
201 E Livermore Dr.
Pembroke, NC 28372
Ph: (910)272-6400
Free: 800-718-1541
Fax: (910)521-0976
URL: http://www.nativeangels.biz/

Pinehurst

20904 ■ FirstHealth Hospice and Palliative Care
5 Aviemore Dr.
Pinehurst, NC 28374-9797
Ph: (910)715-6000
Free: 866-861-7485
Fax: (910)715-6032
URL: http://www.firsthealth.org

Pittsboro

20905 ■ UNC Hospice--Pittsboro
480 Hillsboro St.
Pittsboro, NC 27312-1077
Ph: (919)542-5545
Free: 877-715-0606
Fax: (919)542-6232
E-mail: unchospice@unch.unc.edu
URL: http://www.unchealthcare.org/site/hospice?searchterm=hospice
Formerly: Hospice of Chatham County.

Raeford

20906 ■ Liberty HomeCare & Hospice-Raeford
336 S Main St.
Raeford, NC 28376
Ph: (910)875-8198
Fax: (910)875-8862
URL: http://www.libertyhomecare.com/

Raleigh

20907 ■ Community Home Care and Hospice-Raleigh
7714 Chapel Hill Rd.
Raleigh, NC 27607
Ph: (919)233-1100

20908 ■ Heartland Home Health Care and Hospice--Raleigh
3200 Atlantic Ave., Ste. 100
Raleigh, NC 27604-1009
Ph: (919)981-6238
Fax: (919)235-0770
E-mail: careline@hcr-manorcare.com
URL: http://www.hcr-manorcare.com/

20909 ■ Hospice of Wake County
250 Hospice Circle
Raleigh, NC 27607
Ph: (919)828-0890
URL: http://www.hospiceofwake.org

20910 ■ Liberty Home Care and Hospice-Raleigh
3200 Spring Forest Rd.
Raleigh, NC 27616
Ph: (919)850-4303
URL: http://www.libertyhomecare.com/

Roanoke Rapids

20911 ■ Community Home Care and Hospice-Roanoke Rapids
112 Long Circle
Roanoke Rapids, NC 27870
Ph: (252)535-1605

Rockingham

20912 ■ Community Home Care and Hospice-Rockingham
1015 Fayetteville Rd.
Rockingham, NC 28379
Ph: (910)865-2871

20913 ■ Richmond County Hospice/Hospice Haven
1119 N US Hwy. 1
Rockingham, NC 28379
Ph: (910)997-4464
Fax: (910)997-4484
URL: http://www.richmondcountyhospice.com

Rocky Mount

20914 ■ Community Home Care and Hospice-Asheboro
5301 Morganton Rd.
Rocky Mount, NC 27804
Ph: (252)557-1742
E-mail: info.hospice@community-companies.com
URL: http://www.communityhch.com/

20915 ■ Community Home Care and Hospice--Rocky Mount
3124 Zebulon RD.
Rocky Mount, NC 27804-2425
Ph: (252)442-4918
E-mail: foundation@community-companies.com
URL: http://www.communityhch.com/

Roxboro

20916 ■ Home Health and Hospice of Person County
355 S Madison Blvd.
Roxboro, NC 27573
Ph: (336)597-2542
Fax: (336)597-3367
URL: http://health.personcounty.net/pchd/

Salisbury

20917 ■ Hospice & Palliative CareCenter of Rowan County
12 Klumac Rd.
Salisbury, NC 28144
Ph: (704)633-5447
Fax: (704)633-5576
URL: http://hospicecarecenter.org/

Sanford

20918 ■ Community Home Care and Hospice--Sanford
809 Wicker St.
Sanford, NC 27330
Ph: (919)718-5417

20919 ■ Liberty HomeCare and Hospice-Sanford
1005 Carthage St.
Sanford, NC 27331
Ph: (919)774-9522
Free: 800-767-9522
Fax: (919)774-8560
URL: http://www.libertyhomecare.com/

Seven Springs

20920 ■ Carolina East Home Care and Hospice--Seven Springs
PO Box 240
Seven Springs, NC 28578
Ph: (252)569-0019
Fax: (252)569-0025
E-mail: info@carolinaeast.org
URL: http://www.carolinaeast.org/

Shelby

20921 ■ Hospice of Cleveland County-Wendover
The Kathleen Dover Hamrick Hospice House
953 Wendover Heights Dr.
Shelby, NC 28150
Ph: (704)487-7108
Fax: (704)487-7218
URL: http://www.hospicecares.cc/wendover.htm

20922 ■ Hospice and Palliative Care - Cleveland County
951 Wendover Heights Dr.
Shelby, NC 28150-3565
Ph: (704)487-4677
Fax: (704)481-8050
URL: http://www.hospicecares.cc/index.htm

Siler City

20923 ■ Community Home Care and Hospice--Siler City
1414 E 11th St.
Siler City, NC 27344
Ph: (919)663-1244

20924 ■ Liberty HomeCare and Hospice-Silery /City
401 E Third St.
Siler City, NC 27344
Ph: (919)742-4843
Free: 800-775-4746
Fax: (919)742-5337
URL: http://www.libertyhomecare.com/

Smithfield

20925 ■ Home Health and Hospice Care - Smithfield
723 S 3rd St.
Smithfield, NC 27577
Ph: (919)934-0664
Free: 800-283-4442
Fax: (919)934-9046
E-mail: info@3hc.org
URL: http://www.3hc.org/locations.html

20926 ■ Johnston Memorial Home Care & Hospice
PO Box 1376
Smithfield, NC 27577
Ph: (919)938-7560
Fax: (919)989-2129
E-mail: careline@johnstonhealth.org
URL: http://www.johnstonmemorial.org

20927 ■ Secu Hospice House-Smithfield
426 Hospital Rd.
Smithfield, NC 27577
Ph: (919)209-5100
Fax: (919)209-5150
E-mail: secufoundation@ncsecu.org
URL: https://www.ncsecufoundation.org/Hospice-House.html

Sparta

20928 ■ High Country Health Care System-Alleghany County
81-A W Doughton St.
Sparta, NC 28675
Ph: (336)372-5352
Fax: (336)372-5352
E-mail: hospice@hchealth.net
URL: http://www.highcountryhospice.org/

Spruce Pine

20929 ■ Hospice and Palliative Care Center of Mitchell County
236 Hospital Dr.
Spruce Pine, NC 28777
Ph: (828)765-5677
Fax: (828)765-5680
URL: http://www.hospicemc.com

Statesville

20930 ■ Community Home Care and Hospice-Statesville
225 Davie Ave.
Statesville, NC 28677
Ph: (704)871-8036

20931 ■ Gordon Hospice House
2341 Simonton Rd.
Statesville, NC 28625
Ph: (704)761-2399
URL: http://www.hoic.org/gordon_house.asp

20932 ■ Hospice of Iredell County
2347 Simonton Rd.
Statesville, NC 28625
Ph: (704)873-4719
Fax: (704)872-1810
E-mail: hoic@hoic.org
URL: http://www.hoic.org

Supply

20933 ■ Liberty HomeCare & Hospice Services-Supply
1120 Ocean Hwy. W
Supply, NC 28462
Ph: (910)754-8134
Free: 800-800-0618
Fax: (910)754-2096
URL: http://www.libertyhomecare.com/

20934 ■ Lower Cape Fear Hospice and Life Care Center--Supply
Brunswick County Office
10 Doctors Cir., Ste. 4
Supply, NC 28462-4089
Ph: (910)796-7900
Free: 800-733-1476
Fax: (910)796-7901
E-mail: hospice.lifecarecenter@lcfh.org
URL: http://www.hospiceandlifecarecenter.org

Swansboro

20935 ■ Community Home Care and Hospice-Swansboro
714 W Corbett Ave.
Swansboro, NC 28584
Ph: (910)346-2334

Sylva

20936 ■ Westcare Home Health and Hospice
68 Hospital Rd.
Sylva, NC 28779
Ph: (828)586-7000
URL: http://64.85.191.80/services/hospice

Tarboro

20937 ■ Community Home Care and Hospice--Tarboro
1702 Howard Ave.
Tarboro, NC 27886
Ph: (252)823-1155

20938 ■ Edgecombe HomeCare & Hospice
PO Box 100
Tarboro, NC 27886
Ph: (252)641-7522
Free: 888-404-3424
Fax: (252)641-7004
URL: http://www.edgecombecountync.gov/health/home-hospice.aspx

20939 ■ University Health Systems Home Health and Hospice
111 Hospital Dr.
Tarboro, NC 27886
Ph: (252)641-1002
Free: 877-816-0474
URL: http://www.uhseast.com/hospice/

Taylorsville

20940 ■ Hospice and Home Care of Alexander County Inc.
50 Lucy Echerd Ln.
Taylorsville, NC 28681
Ph: (828)632-5026
Free: 877-615-5026
Fax: (828)632-3707
E-mail: tonya@alexanderhospicehomecare.org
URL: http://www.hospiceandhomecarealexander.org
Tonya Roland, Executive Director

Thomasville

20941 ■ Liberty HomeCare & Hospice-Thomasville
1007 Lexington Ave.
Thomasville, NC 27886
Ph: (336)472-1080
Free: 800-272-5283
Fax: (336)472-1080
URL: http://www.libertyhomecare.com/

Troy

20942 ■ Community Home Care and Hospice-Troy
120 N Main St.
Troy, NC 27371
Ph: (910)572-1693

Valdese

20943 ■ Burke Hospice and Palliative Care, Inc.
1721 Enon Rd.
Valdese, NC 28690-9314
Ph: (828)879-1601
Fax: (828)879-3500
E-mail: info@burkehospice.org
URL: http://new.burkehospice.org/

Wadesboro

20944 ■ Anson Community Hospice
PO Box 744
Wadesboro, NC 28170
Ph: (704)695-1595
Fax: (704)695-1596

20945 ■ Hospice of Union County--Wadesboro
205 W Morgan St.
Wadesboro, NC 28170
Ph: (704)694-4880
Fax: (704)694-3550
E-mail: mlinker@houc.org
URL: http://www.houc.org/
Mike Linker, Executive Director

20946 ■ Liberty HomeCare & Hospice-Wadesboro
921 E Caswell St.
Wadesboro, NC 28170
Ph: (704)694-5002
Free: 800-473-5912
Fax: (704)694-6419
URL: http://www.libertyhomecare.com/

Wallace

20947 ■ Community Home Care and Hospice--Wallace
312 E Southerland St.
Wallace, NC 28466
Ph: (910)275-0121

Walnut Cove

20948 ■ Hospice & Palliative CareCenter of Stokes County
PO Box 863
Walnut Cove, NC 27052
Ph: (336)591-1124
Fax: (336)591-4063
URL: http://www.hospicecarecenter.org/

Washington

20949 ■ Community Home Care and Hospice--Washington
814 Washington Plaza Shopping Center
Washington, NC 27889
Ph: (252)946-0312

Wentworth

20950 ■ Hospice of Rockingham County, Inc.
2150 Hwy. 65
Wentworth, NC 27375
Ph: (336)427-9022
Fax: (336)427-9030
E-mail: hospicerc@triadbiz.rr.com
URL: http://www.hospiceofrockinghamcounty.com

Whiteville

20951 ■ Community Home Care and Hospice--Whiteville
16 White's Crossing Plaza, Ste. B
Whiteville, NC 28472
Ph: (910)642-5009

20952 ■ Liberty HomeCare & Hospice-Whiteville
46 McNeill Plaza
Whiteville, NC 28472
Ph: (910)642-5808
Free: 800-800-9617
Fax: (910)640-1374
URL: http://www.libertyhomecare.com/

20953 ■ Lower Cape Fear Hospice and Life Care Center
Columbus County Angel House Hospice Care Center
206 Warrior Tr. Rd.
Whiteville, NC 28472
Ph: (910)642-9051
Free: 800-735-6354
Fax: (910)642-0223
URL: http://www.hospiceandlifecarecenter.org

Wilmington

20954 ■ Katherine and Duncan Phillips LifeCare & Counseling Center
1414 Physicians Dr.
Wilmington, NC 28401
Ph: (910)796-7900
Free: 800-733-1476
Fax: (910)796-7901
URL: http://www.hospiceandlifecarecenter.org

20955 ■ Wilmington Hospice Care Center
1406 Physicians Dr.
Wilmington, NC 28401
Ph: (910)762-9422
Free: 800-501-3501
Fax: (910)762-9423
URL: http://www.hospiceandlifecarecenter.org

Wilson

20956 ■ Community Home Care and Hospice-Wilson
1604 Forest Hills Rd. W
Wilson, NC 27893-3409
Ph: (252)291-5353

20957 ■ Home Health and Hospice Care-Wilson
2305 Wellington Dr. SW Ste. C
Wilson, NC 27893
Ph: (252)291-4400
Fax: (252)237-4396
URL: http://www.3hc.org/

20958 ■ WilMed Hospice
1705 Tarboro St. SW
Wilson, NC 27893
Ph: (252)399-8924
Fax: (252)399-7369
URL: http://www.wilmed.org/hospice.asp

Winston Salem

20959 ■ Hospice and Palliative Care Center
101 Hospice Ln.
Winston Salem, NC 27103
Ph: (336)768-3972
Fax: (336)659-0461
URL: http://www.hospicecarecenter.org

20960 ■ Kate B. Reynolds Hospice Home
101 Hospice La.
Winston Salem, NC 27103
Ph: (336)760-1114
Fax: (336)774-1690
URL: http://www.hospicecarecenter.org/programsKate.aspx

Winterville

20961 ■ AseraCare Hospice-Winterville
4051 S Memorial Dr.
Winterville, NC 28590
Ph: (252)353-3326
Fax: (252)353-3331
E-mail: ask@aseracare.com
URL: http://hospice.aseracare.com/home.aspx

Yadkinville

20962 ■ Mountain Valley Hospice and Palliative Care--Yadkinville
208 N Jackson St.
Yadkinville, NC 27055
Ph: (336)679-2466
Fax: (336)679-4734
E-mail: info@mtnvalleyhospice.org
URL: http://www.mtnvalleyhospice.org/

NORTH DAKOTA

Ashley

20963 ■ Ashley Medical Center Hospice
612 Center Ave. N
Ashley, ND 58413
Ph: (701)288-3433
Fax: (701)288-3938
URL: http://www.amctoday.org/hospice.html

Bismarck

20964 ■ Saint Alexius Home Care and Hospice
1120 E Main Ave.
Bismarck, ND 58501
Ph: (701)530-4500
Fax: (701)530-4572
URL: http://www.st.alexius.org
Formerly: Saint Alexius Hospice.

Carrington

20965 ■ Health Center Presentation Hospice of Carrington
800 N 4th St.
Carrington, ND 58421-1217
Ph: (701)652-3141
Fax: (701)652-3595
URL: http://www.carringtonhealthcenter.net/artman/publish/printer_20.shtml.htm

Cavalier

20966 ■ Altru Hospice-Cavalier
201 E 3rd Ave. S
Cavalier, ND 58220
Ph: (701)780-5888
Fax: (701)780-5849
URL: http://www.altru.org/body.cfm?id=537

Devils Lake

20967 ■ Mercy Hospice--Devils Lake
1031 7th St. NE
Devils Lake, ND 58301
Ph: (701)662-2131
Fax: (701)662-9681
URL: http://www.mercyhospitaldl.com/Hospice.htm/

Dickinson

20968 ■ Heartland Hospice--Dickinson
30 7th St. W
Dickinson, ND 58601-4335
Ph: (701)456-4378
Fax: (701)456-4809
E-mail: stjoesinfo@catholichealth.net
URL: http://www.stjoeshospital.org/Hospice.htm

Fargo

20969 ■ Hospice of the Red River Valley--Fargo
1701 38th St. SW
Fargo, ND 58103-4499
Ph: (701)356-1500
Free: 800-237-4629
Fax: (701)356-1592
URL: http://www.hrrv.org

Grafton

20970 ■ Altru Home Services of Unity Medical Center - Grafton
164 W 13th St.
Grafton, ND 58237-1826
Ph: (701)352-9399
Fax: (701)352-9377
URL: http://www.altru.org/body.cfm?id=537&oTopID=537

Grand Forks

20971 ■ Altru Hospice--Grand Forks
1380 S Columbia Rd.
Grand Forks, ND 58201
Ph: (701)780-5888
Fax: (701)780-5849
URL: http://www.altru.org

20972 ■ Hospice of the Red River Valley - Grand Forks
3001 A 32nd Ave. S
Grand Forks, ND 58201
Ph: (701)772-3172
Free: 877-550-1112
Fax: (701)772-3530
URL: http://www.hrrv.org/

Hazen

20973 ■ Sakakawea Hospice
510 8th Ave. NE
Hazen, ND 58545
Ph: (701)748-7380
Fax: (701)748-6004
E-mail: lknoll@sakmedcenter.org
URL: http://www.wrtc.com/sshhc

Jamestown

20974 ■ Jamestown Hospital Hospice
419 5th St. NE
Jamestown, ND 58401
Ph: (701)253-4833
Free: 800-281-8888
Fax: (701)253-4837
E-mail: billk@jamestownhospital.com
URL: http://www.jamestownhospital.com

Lisbon

20975 ■ Hospice of the Red River Valley/Lisbon
415 Main St.
Lisbon, ND 58054
Ph: (701)683-4649
Free: 800-237-4629
Fax: (701)683-5412
URL: http://www.hrrv.org

Mandan

20976 ■ Medcenter One Home Health and Hospice
910 18th St. NW
Mandan, ND 58554
Ph: (701)323-8400
Fax: (701)323-8409
URL: http://www.medcenterone.com/

Mayville

20977 ■ Hospice of the Red/River Valley/Mayville Ofc.
24 Main St. E
Mayville, ND 58257
Ph: (701)786-2393
Free: 888-817-4629
Fax: (701)786-2448
URL: http://www.hrrv.org

McVille

20978 ■ Altru Home Services-McVille
200 N Main St.
McVille, ND 58254
Ph: (701)322-4328
Fax: (701)322-4408

Minot

20979 ■ Trinity Hospice Agency
PO Box 5020
Minot, ND 58702
Ph: (701)857-5082
Free: 800-862-0005
Fax: (701)857-5079
URL: http://www.trinityhealth.org

Park River

20980 ■ Altru Home Services-Park River
115 Vivian St. W
Park River, ND 58270
Ph: (701)284-4548
Fax: (701)284-4584
E-mail: tnelson@altru.org
URL: http://www.altru.org/body.cfm?id=1428

Rugby

20981 ■ Heart of America Hospice--Rugby
800 S Main Ave.
Rugby, ND 58368
Ph: (701)776-5455
Fax: (701)776-5448
E-mail: CHickman@hamc.com
URL: http://www.hamc.com/

Valley City

20982 ■ Hospice of the Red River Valley/Valley City
202 S Central Ave.
Valley City, ND 58072-3325
Ph: (701)845-1781
Free: 800-237-4629
Fax: (701)845-1799
URL: http://www.hrrv.org

Williston

20983 ■ Mercy Hospice--Williston
1301 15th Ave. W
Williston, ND 58801
Ph: (701)774-7430
Fax: (701)774-7465
URL: http://www.mercy-williston.org/ServiceDisplay.aspx?ID=29

Wishek

20984 ■ Prairieview Hospice
1007 4th Ave. S
Wishek, ND 58495
Ph: (701)452-3113
Fax: (701)452-2179
URL: http://www.wishekhospital.com/

OHIO

Akron

20985 ■ Hospice & Palliative Care of Visiting Nurse Service
3358 Ridgewood Rd.
Akron, OH 44333
Ph: (330)665-1455
Fax: (330)668-4670
URL: http://www.vnsa.com/

20986 ■ Hospice of Summa
444 N Main St.
Akron, OH 44310
Ph: (330)379-9438
Fax: (330)379-5177
URL: http://www.vnsa.com/

20987 ■ In-House Hospice Solutions-Akron
1530 W Market St.
Akron, OH 44313
Free: 888-260-9835
Fax: (330)343-2370
URL: http://www.vnsa.com/

20988 ■ Senior Independence of Akron/Canton
1815 W Market St., Ste. 303
Akron, OH 44313
Ph: (330)873-3468
Fax: (330)873-3465
URL: http://seniorindependence.org/hospice.asp

Ashland

20989 ■ Hospice of North Central Ohio, Inc.--Ashland
1050 Dauch Dr.
Ashland, OH 44805
Ph: (419)281-7107
Free: 800--HOSPICE
Fax: (419)281-8427
E-mail: hospice@bright.net
URL: http://www.hospiceofnorthcentralohio.org

Ashtabula

20990 ■ Hospice of Ashtabula County
1166 Lake Ave.
Ashtabula, OH 44004
Ph: (440)997-6619
Fax: (440)997-6478
URL: http://www.hospicewr.org

Barberton

20991 ■ Barberton Hospice and Palliative Care
527 W Tuscarawas Ave.
Barberton, OH 44203
Ph: (330)861-0400
E-mail: hospice@hospiceofmedina.org
URL: http://www.hospiceofmedina.org/barberton/barberton.aspx

Beachwood

20992 ■ Montefiore Hospice
1 David N. Myers Pkwy.
Beachwood, OH 44122
Ph: (216)360-9080
Free: 877-855-1877
Fax: (216)910-2299
E-mail: info@montefiorecare.org
URL: http://www.montefiorecare.org

Bowling Green

20993 ■ Bridge Home Health and Hospice
1069 Klotz Rd.
Bowling Green, OH 43402
Ph: (419)352-9808
Free: 800-982-3306
URL: http://www.heritagecorner.com/bridge-hospice/

Brooklyn Heights

20994 ■ VITAS Innovative Hospice Care of Cleveland
600 E Granger Rd., Ste. 100
Brooklyn Heights, OH 44131
Ph: (216)706-2100
URL: http://www.vitas.com/Aboutus/Locations/Ohio/tabid/194/Default.aspx

Cambridge

20995 ■ Hospice of Guernsey, Inc.
PO Box 1165
Cambridge, OH 43725
Ph: (740)432-7440
Free: 800-283-0316
Fax: (740)432-7424
E-mail: hospiceofguernsey@firewireinternet.com
URL: http://www.hospiceofguernsey.com/

Canfield

20996 ■ Senior Independence-Canfield
6715 Tippecanoe Rd.
Canfield, OH 44406
Ph: (330)533-4350
Fax: (330)533-4650
URL: http://seniorindependence.org/

Canton

20997 ■ Aultman Hospice Program
2821 Woodlawn NW
Canton, OH 44708
Ph: (330)479-4805
Free: 800-628-4302
Fax: (330)479-4803
URL: http://www.aultman.org/

20998 ■ Hospice of Stark County
3611 Whipple Ave. NW
Canton, OH 44718
Ph: (330)493-0126
Free: 877-733-0010
E-mail: hospice@myhospice.org
URL: http://www.myhospice.org

Carrollton

20999 ■ Hospice of Carroll County
1040 Trump Rd. NW, Ste. B
Carrollton, OH 44615
Ph: (330)627-4796
Free: 877-339-3035
Fax: (330)627-7235
E-mail: hospice@myhospice.org
URL: http://www.myhospice.org

Cincinnati

21000 ■ Heartland Hospice Services--Cincinnati
3800 Red Bank Rd., D
Cincinnati, OH 45150
Ph: (513)831-5800
Fax: (513)831-5159
URL: http://www.hcr-manorcare.com/Home/Hospice-Care/tabid/142/Default.aspx

21001 ■ Hospice of Cincinnati
4360 Cooper Rd.
Cincinnati, OH 45242
Ph: (513)891-7700
URL: http://www.hospiceofcincinnati.org/

21002 ■ Hospice of Cincinnati - Western Hills Unit
3131 Queen City Ave.
Cincinnati, OH 45238
Ph: (513)891-7700
URL: http://www.hospiceofcincinnati.org/western_hills.shtml

21003 ■ Hospice of Southwest Ohio
7625 Carmargo Rd.
Cincinnati, OH 45243
Ph: (513)770-0820
Fax: (513)770-0848
URL: http://www.hswo.org/

21004 ■ Odyssey HealthCare of Cincinnati
4350 Glendale-Milford
Cincinnati, OH 45242
Ph: (513)554-6300
Fax: (513)554-6301
E-mail: info@odsyhealth.com
URL: http://www.odsyhealth.com/default.asp

21005 ■ Star Shine Hospice of Children's Hospital
3333 Burnet Ave
Cincinnati, OH 45229
Ph: (513)636-4663
Fax: (513)636-7152
E-mail: starshine@cchmc.org
URL: http://www.cincinnatichildrens.org/svc/alpha/s/hospice/default.htm

21006 ■ VAMC: Cincinnati
3200 Vine St.
Cincinnati, OH 45220
Ph: (513)861-3100
Fax: (513)475-6471
URL: http://www.cincinnati.va.gov/

21007 ■ Vitas Healthcare Corp.
11500 Northlake Dr., Ste. 400
Cincinnati, OH 45249
Ph: (513)742-6310
URL: http://www.vitas.com

21008 ■ VITAS Innovative Hospice - Inpatient Unit--Cincinnati
151 W Galbraith Rd.
Cincinnati, OH 45216
Free: 800-779-4922
URL: http://www.vitas.com

Circleville

21009 ■ Berger Hospice Care
600 N Pickaway St.
Circleville, OH 43113
Ph: (740)474-2126
Fax: (740)420-8675
E-mail: pr@bergerhealth.com
URL: http://www.bergerhealth.com

Cleveland

21010 ■ Hospice of the Western Reserve-Cleveland Office
19201 Villaview Rd.
Cleveland, OH 44119
Ph: (216)383-2222
Fax: (216)481-4940
URL: http://www.hospicewr.org

21011 ■ Hospice of the Western Reserve Inc. Hospice House--Cleveland
300 E 185th St.
Cleveland, OH 44119
Ph: (216)383-2222
Free: 800-707-8922
Fax: (216)383-5298
URL: http://www.hospicewr.org

21012 ■ Hospice of the Western Reserve, Inc. - University Circle Office
10645 Euclid Ave.
Cleveland, OH 44106
Ph: (216)231-8650
Fax: (216)231-8291
URL: http://www.hospicewr.org

21013 ■ Louis B. Stokes Cleveland VA Medical Center
10701 E. Blvd.
Cleveland, OH 44106
Ph: (216)791-3800
Fax: (216)707-6450
URL: http://www.cleveland.va.gov/

Clyde

21014 ■ Hospice of Memorial Hospital
430 S Main St.
Clyde, OH 43410
Ph: (419)547-6419
Free: 800-413-1555
Fax: (419)547-9459
E-mail: webmaster@fremontmemorial.org
URL: http://www.fremontmemorial.org/hospice

Columbus

21015 ■ Acclaim Hospice and Palliative Care
2800 Corporate Exchange Dr.
Columbus, OH 43232
Ph: (614)890-8900

21016 ■ Heartland Home Health Care and Hospice-Columbus
6500 Busch Blvd.
Columbus, OH 43229
Ph: (614)840-9856
Fax: (614)433-0641
URL: http://www.hcr-manorcare.com/Home/CareatHome/tabid/141/Default.aspx

21017 ■ Heartland Hospice Services--Columbus
6500 Busch Blvd., Ste. 210
Columbus, OH 43229
Ph: (614)840-9856
Free: 800-427-1902
Fax: (614)433-0641
E-mail: careline@hcr-manorcare.com
URL: http://www.hcr-manorcare.com

21018 ■ Home Reach Hospice
3595 Olentangy River Rd.
Columbus, OH 43214-3440
Ph: (614)566-5377
Free: 888-389-6231
Fax: (614)566-4391
E-mail: hospice@ohiohealth.com
URL: http://www.ohiohealth.com/body.cfm?id=407

21019 ■ VITAS Innovative Hospice Care--Columbus
655 Metro Place South
Columbus, OH 43017
Free: 800-815-8482
Fax: (800)920-8482
URL: http://www.vitas.com/

Dayton

21020 ■ Dayton Veterans Affairs Hospice and Palliative Care
4100 W 3rd St.
9 N Hospice Unit
Attn 110 HP
Dayton, OH 45428-9000
Ph: (937)268-6511
Fax: (937)262-2131
E-mail: hayes.kathleen_a@dayton.va.gov
URL: http://www.va.gov/

21021 ■ Evercare Hospice & Palliative Care-Dayton
130 W Second St., Ste. 400
Dayton, OH 45402
Ph: (937)226-8611
Fax: (888)810-8182
URL: http://www.evercarehospice.com/

21022 ■ Heartland Home Health Care and Hospice--Dayton
3131 S Dixie Dr., Ste. 221
Dayton, OH 45439
Ph: (937)299-6980
E-mail: careline@hcr-manorcare.com
URL: http://www.hcr-manorcare.com

21023 ■ Hospice of Dayton Inc.
324 Wilmington Ave.
Dayton, OH 45420
Ph: (937)256-4490
Free: 800-653-4490
Fax: (937)256-5951
E-mail: ddailey@hospiceofdayton.org
URL: http://www.hospiceofdayton.org

21024 ■ Odyssey Healthcare of Dayton
3085 Woodman Dr.
Dayton, OH 45420
Ph: (937)298-2800
Fax: (937)298-2801
URL: http://www.odsyhealth.com/default.asp

21025 ■ Senior Independence-Dayton
6520 Poe Ave.
Dayton, OH 45414
Ph: (937)415-5666
Fax: (937)415-5690
URL: http://seniorindependence.org/

21026 ■ VITAS Inpatient Hospice Unit at One Elizabeth Place
One Elizabeth Place NW
Dayton, OH 45408
Ph: (306)374-4143
Fax: (305)350-6784
URL: http://www.vitas.com/

Dover

21027 ■ Hospice of Tuscarawas County, Inc.
201 W 3rd St.
Dover, OH 44622
Ph: (330)343-7605
Free: 800-947-7284
Fax: (330)343-3542
E-mail: hospice@myhospice.org
URL: http://www.hospiceoftusc.org

Elyria

21028 ■ New Life Hospice--Elyria
5255 N Abbe Rd.
Elyria, OH 44035
Ph: (440)934-1458
Free: 800-770-5767
Fax: (440)934-1567
URL: http://www.community-health-partners.com

Fairlawn

21029 ■ AseraCare Hospice-Akron
2820 W Market St.
Fairlawn, OH 44333
Ph: (330)835-3813
Fax: (330)835-4594
URL: http://www.aseracare.com/

Findlay

21030 ■ Bridge Home Health and Hospice
15100 Birchaven Ln.
Findlay, OH 45840
Ph: (419)423-5351
Free: 800-982-3306
URL: http://www.bvhealthsystem.org/?id=32&sid=1

Fremont

21031 ■ Heartland Hospice Service Inc-Fremont
905 W State St.
Fremont, OH 43420
Ph: (419)355-9204
Fax: (888)427-6630
URL: http://www.hcr-manorcare.com/

Galion

21032 ■ HomeCare Matters Home Health & Hospice
1220 N Market St.
Galion, OH 44833
Ph: (419)468-7985
Fax: (419)468-9211
E-mail: hcmoffice@rrohio.com
URL: http://www.homecarematters.org/

Greenville

21033 ■ State of the Heart Home Health and Hospice
1350 N Broadway
Greenville, OH 45331
Ph: (937)548-2999
Free: 800-417-7535
Fax: (937)548-7144
E-mail: darketc@stateoftheheartcare.org
URL: http://www.stateoftheheartcare.org

Hamlton

21034 ■ Hospice of Hamilton
1010 Eaton Ave.
Hamlton, OH 45013
Ph: (513)895-1270
Fax: (513)895-1271
URL: http://www.hospiceofcincinnati.org/care_centers.shtml

Highland Heights

21035 ■ Harbor Light Hospice-Highland Heights
734-C Alpha Dr.
Highland Heights, OH 44143
Ph: (440)269-1888
Fax: (440)269-1988
URL: http://www.harborlighthospice.com/

Independence

21036 ■ Heartland Home Health Care and Hospice--Independence
4807 Rockside Rd., Ste. 110
Independence, OH 44131
Ph: (216)520-0765
E-mail: careline@hcr-manorcare.com
URL: http://www.hcr-manorcare.com

21037 ■ Hospice of Cleveland Clinic
6801 Brecksville Rd., Ste. 10
Independence, OH 44131-5032
Ph: (216)444-9819
Free: 800-263-0403
Fax: (216)520-1973
URL: http://my.clevelandclinic.org/services/palliative_medicine/hospice/default

Ironton

21038 ■ Community Hospice-Ironton
2122 S 9th St.
Ironton, OH 45638
Ph: (740)532-2524
Free: 800-717-1050
E-mail: hospice@chospice.org
URL: http://www.chospice.org/

Kenton

21039 ■ Hardin County Hospice
15 N Detroit St., Ste. 4000
Kenton, OH 43326
Ph: (419)673-1897
Free: 800-823-1897
Fax: (419)674-4463
E-mail: hch@hardincountyhospice.org
URL: http://www.hardincountyhospice.org/

Lakewood

21040 ■ Hospice of the Western Reserve-Lakewood
14601 Detroit Ave.
Lakewood, OH 44107
Ph: (216)227-9048
Fax: (216)227-9232
URL: http://www.hospicewr.org/

Lancaster

21041 ■ FairHope Hospice and Palliative Care, Inc.
282 Sells Rd.
Lancaster, OH 43130
Ph: (740)654-7077
Fax: (740)654-6321
E-mail: admin@fairhopehospice.org
URL: http://www.fairhopehospice.org

Lima

21042 ■ Saint Rita's Hospice
959 W North St.
Lima, OH 45805
Ph: (419)226-9064

Logan

21043 ■ Hospice of Hocking County
393 W Front St.
Logan, OH 43138
Ph: (740)380-1186
Fax: (740)385-6816
E-mail: admin@fairhopehospice.org
URL: http://fairhopehospice.org/

London

21044 ■ Loving Care Hospice
56 S Oak St.
London, OH 43140
Ph: (740)852-7755
Free: 800-313-6458
Fax: (740)852-7762
URL: http://www.lovingcare.us/

Lorain

21045 ■ Hospice of the Western Reserve, Inc-Lorain
2173 N Ridge Road E
Lorain, OH 44055
Ph: (440)284-2999
Fax: (440)284-3812
E-mail: jzink@hospicewr.org
URL: http://www.hospicewr.org/about/

21046 ■ New Life Hospice Center of St. Joseph
3700 Kolbe Rd.
Lorain, OH 44053
Ph: (440)934-1458
Fax: (440)934-5767
URL: http://www.mercyonline.org/

Mansfield

21047 ■ Hospice of North Central Ohio, Inc.--Mansfield
371 Cline Ave.
Mansfield, OH 44906
Ph: (419)524-9200
Free: 800--HOSPICE
Fax: (419)522-8400
URL: http://www.hospiceofnorthcentralohio.org/index.cfm

21048 ■ MedCentral Hospice
335 Glessner Ave.
Mansfield, OH 44903-2269
Ph: (419)526-8442
Fax: (419)756-2298
URL: http://www.medcentral.org/body.cfm?id=200

Marietta

21049 ■ Home Nursing Service and Hospice Marietta Memorial Hospital
210 N Seventh St., Ste. 300
Marietta, OH 45750
Ph: (740)374-9100
URL: http://www.mmhospital.org/homehealth

Marion

21050 ■ Marion General Hospital Quality of Life Hospice
278 Barks Rd., W
Marion, OH 43302-7367
Ph: (740)383-8930
Fax: (740)383-8764
URL: http://www.mariongeneral.com/index.php?page=hospicecare

Marysville

21051 ■ Loving Care Hospice-Marysville
113 S Main St.
Marysville, OH 43040
Ph: (937)644-1928
E-mail: lovecare@gn.net

Mason

21052 ■ Acclaim Home Health Services, Inc.
4770 Duke Dr., Ste. 195
Mason, OH 45040
Ph: (513)336-6133
Fax: (513)336-6134
URL: http://www.ahhsi.com/index.php

Maumee

21053 ■ Odyssey HealthCare of Toledo
1745 Indian Wood Cir., Ste. 200
Maumee, OH 43537
Ph: (419)887-6700
Free: 877-637-9432
Fax: (419)887-6701
E-mail: info@odsyhealth.com
URL: http://www.odsyhealth.com

Mayfield Heights

21054 ■ Odyssey HealthCare of Cleveland
6140 Parkland Blvd., Ste. 105
Mayfield Heights, OH 44124
Ph: (440)995-1740
Free: 877-637-9432
Fax: (440)995-1741
E-mail: info@odsyhealth.com
URL: http://www.odsyhealth.com

Medina

21055 ■ Hospice of Medina County
797 N Court St.
Medina, OH 44256
Ph: (330)722-4771
Free: 800-700-4771
Fax: (330)722-5266
E-mail: hospice@hospiceofmedina.org
URL: http://www.hospiceofmedina.org

Mentor

21056 ■ Hospice of the Western Reserve, Inc.--Mentor
5786 Heisley Rd.
Mentor, OH 44060
Ph: (440)951-8692
Fax: (440)975-0655
URL: http://www.hospicewr.org

Middletown

21057 ■ Hospice Care of Middletown Inc.
1001 Grove St., Ste. 800
Middletown, OH 45044
Ph: (513)424-2273
Free: 800-653-4490
Fax: (513)424-5450
URL: http://www.yourhometownhospice.org/

Millersburg

21058 ■ Holmes County Hospice
931 Wooster Rd.
Millersburg, OH 44654
Ph: (330)674-5035
Free: 877-674-5035
Fax: (330)674-2528
URL: http://www.holmeshealth.org/hospice.htm

Moraine

21059 ■ VITAS Innovative Hospice Care of Cincinnati Dayton Satellite
3055 Kettering Blvd.
Moraine, OH 45439-1989
Ph: (937)223-2312
Fax: (937)223-8027
URL: http://www.vitas.com/

Mount Gilead

21060 ■ Hospice of Morrow County, Inc.
228 South St.
Mount Gilead, OH 43338
Ph: (419)946-9822
Fax: (419)946-9971
E-mail: hospicemc@redbird.net
URL: http://www.hospicemorrowcounty.org/

Mount Orab

21061 ■ Hospice of Hope
215 Hughes Blvd.
Mount Orab, OH 45154
Ph: (937)444-4900
Fax: (937)444-4966
E-mail: Kavin@hohope.org
URL: http://www.hospiceofhope.com/

Mount Vernon

21062 ■ Hospice of Knox County
17700 Coshocton Rd.
Mount Vernon, OH 43050-3420
Ph: (740)397-5188
Fax: (740)397-5189
E-mail: general@hospiceofknox.org
URL: http://www.hospiceofknox.org

Munroe Falls

21063 ■ Harbor Light Hospice--Munroe Falls
25 S Main St.
Munroe Falls, OH 44262
Ph: (866)779-7470
Fax: (330)686-5902
URL: http://www.harborlighthospice.com/

Napoleon

21064 ■ Hospice of Henry County
1843 Oakwood Ave.
Napoleon, OH 43545-9243
Ph: (419)599-5612
Fax: (419)599-1714
E-mail: homecare@henry-net.com
URL: http://www.henrycohd.org/

Newark

21065 ■ Hospice of Licking County, Inc./Hospice of Central Ohio
2269 Cherry Valley Rd.
Newark, OH 43055
Ph: (740)344-0311
Free: 800-804-2505
Fax: (740)344-6577
URL: http://www.hospiceofcentralohio.org/

North Canton

21066 ■ Mercy Medical Center Hospice
7568 Whipple Ave. NW
North Canton, OH 44720-6922
Ph: (330)649-4380
Fax: (330)649-4399
URL: http://www.cantonmercy.org/

Olmsted Falls

21067 ■ Hospice Care Center of the Renaissance
26376 John Rd.
Olmsted Falls, OH 44138
Ph: (216)444-2288
Fax: (216)520-1973
URL: http://www.hospicewr.org/

Ottawa

21068 ■ Putnam County HomeCare & Hospice
139 Court St.
Ottawa, OH 45875
Ph: (419)523-4449
Fax: (419)523-6328
URL: http://www.pchh.net

Parma

21069 ■ Continuum Care Hospice
12380 Plaza Dr., Ste. 102
Parma, OH 44130
Ph: (216)898-8444
Fax: (216)362-0677
E-mail: continuumcarehospice@lhshealth.com
URL: http://www.continuumcarehospice.com/contact/

21070 ■ Holy Family Hospice
6707 State Rd.
Parma, OH 44134
Ph: (440)888-7722
Fax: (440)866-6040
URL: http://www.holyfamilyhome.com/

Pataskala

21071 ■ Hospice of Central Ohio
621 W Broad St.
Pataskala, OH 43062
Ph: (740)927-0069
Fax: (740)927-6647
URL: http://www.hospiceofcentralohio.org/

Perrysburg

21072 ■ Hospice of Northwest Ohio--Perrysburg
30000 E River Rd.
Perrysburg, OH 43551
Ph: (419)661-4001
Fax: (419)661-4015
E-mail: director@hospicenwo.org
URL: http://www.hospicenwo.org

Poland

21073 ■ Hospice of the Valley Hospice House--Poland
9803 Sharrott Rd.
Poland, OH 44514
Ph: (330)788-1992
Fax: (330)788-1998
URL: http://www.hospiceofthevalley.com/

Portsmouth

21074 ■ Heartland Home Health Care and Hospice--Portsmouth
35 Bierly Rd., Ste. 2
Portsmouth, OH 45662
Ph: (740)351-0565
Fax: (740)351-0575
E-mail: careline@hcr-manorcare.com
URL: http://www.hcr-manorcare.com

21075 ■ Hospice of Southern Ohio
2201 25th St.
Portsmouth, OH 45662
Ph: (740)356-2600
E-mail: rubyt@somc.org
URL: http://www.somc.org/about/facilities/hospice/index.asp

Saint Clairsville

21076 ■ Medi Home Health and Hospice--Saint Clairsville
68150 Bayberry Dr.
Saint Clairsville, OH 43950
Free: 800-845-5850
Fax: (888)342-6190

21077 ■ Tender Loving Care Home Care and Hospice--Saint Clairsville
Amedisys Home Health Services
52171 National Rd. E
Saint Clairsville, OH 43950
Ph: (740)526-0624
Fax: (740)526-0617

Saint Marys

21078 ■ Grand Lake Hospice
1122 E Spring
Saint Marys, OH 45885
Ph: (419)394-7434
Fax: (419)394-6503
URL: http://www.grandlakehealth.org/

Sandusky

21079 ■ Stein Hospice Service Inc.
1200 Sycamore Line
Sandusky, OH 44870
Free: 800-625-5269
Fax: (419)625-5761
E-mail: steinhospice@steinhospice.org
URL: http://www.steinhospice.org

Seaman

21080 ■ Hospice of Hope-Ohio Valley Inpatient Center
230 Medical Park Dr.
Seaman, OH 45679
Ph: (937)386-3030
Fax: (937)386-3049
E-mail: kavin@hohope.org
URL: http://www.somc.org/about/facilities/hospice/index.asp

Sidney

21081 ■ Wilson Hospice
Wilson Memorial Hospital
915 Michigan St. W
Sidney, OH 45356
Ph: (937)498-4777
Fax: (937)498-4669
URL: http://www.wilsonhospital.com/index.cfm/m/3/s/66.cfm

Springfield

21082 ■ Community Mercy Hospice
Community Mercy Health Partners
444 W Harding Rd.
Springfield, OH 45504
Ph: (937)390-9665
Fax: (937)390-2363
E-mail: jmharris@health-partners.org
URL: http://www.ehealthconnection.com/regions/springfield/content/Community_Merc y_Hospice_Home.asp

Steubenville

21083 ■ Valley Hospice--Steubenville
380 Summit Ave.
Steubenville, OH 43952
Ph: (740)284-4440
Free: 877-284-4441
Fax: (740)284-4478
E-mail: knichols@valleyhospice.org
URL: http://www.valleyhospice.org

Strongsville

21084 ■ Hospice Services of Southwest General
18659 Drake Rd.
Strongsville, OH 44136-7059
Ph: (440)816-5000
Fax: (440)816-5038
URL: http://www.swgeneral.com

Sylvania

21085 ■ Visiting Nurse Hospice & Health Care
5455 Monroe St.
Sylvania, OH 443560
Ph: (419)824-7400
Fax: (419)882-8307
URL: http://www.promedica.org/

Tiffin

21086 ■ Community Hospice Care--Tiffin
181 E Perry St.
Tiffin, OH 44883-2312
Ph: (419)447-4040
Free: 800-834-8100
Fax: (419)447-4657
E-mail: info@communityhospicecare.com
URL: http://www.communityhospicecare.com

Toledo

21087 ■ Ashanti Hospice and Palliative Care
Sunset Retirement Communities
4020 Indian Rd., Ste. A
Toledo, OH 43606
Ph: (419)724-1047
Fax: (419)724-1048
URL: http://www.sunset-communities.org/ashanti.php

21088 ■ Heartland Home HealthCare and Hospice--Toledo
3450 W Central Ave., Ste. 230
Toledo, OH 43606
Ph: (419)531-0440
E-mail: careline@hcr-manorcare.com
URL: http://www.hcr-manorcare.com

21089 ■ Hospice of Northwest Ohio--Toledo
800 S Detroit Ave.
Toledo, OH 43609
Ph: (410)661-4001
Fax: (419)661-4015
E-mail: bsharek@hospicenwo.org
URL: http://www.hospicenwo.org/

21090 ■ Virginia Clifford Hospice Center
Hospice of Northwest Ohio
800 S Detroit Ave.
Toledo, OH 43609
Ph: (419)661-4001
Fax: (419)661-4015
E-mail: bsharek@hospicenwo.org
URL: http://www.hospicenwo.org/index.php?src=gendocs&ref=Care_Hospice&category=services

Troy

21091 ■ Hospice of Miami County, Inc.
Summit Professional Bldg.
550 Summit Ave., Ste. 101
Troy, OH 45373
Ph: (937)335-5191
Fax: (937)335-8841
URL: http://www.homc.org

Upper Sandusky

21092 ■ Hospice of Wyandot County
320 W Maple St., Ste. C
Upper Sandusky, OH 43351
Ph: (419)294-5787
Fax: (419)294-4721

Warrensville Heights

21093 ■ Hospice of the Western Reserve, Inc.--Warrensville Heights
4670 Richmond Rd., Ste. 200
Warrensville Heights, OH 44128
Ph: (216)283-3140
Fax: (216)283-3181
URL: http://www.hospicewr.org

Waverly

21094 ■ InCare At Home Health and Hospice
681 E Third St.
Waverly, OH 45690
Ph: (740)947-3010
Fax: (740)947-3510
URL: http://www.traditionshealth.org/

West Chester

21095 ■ Evercare Hospice and Palliative Care--West Chester
9050 Centre Pointe Dr.
West Chester, OH 45069
Ph: (513)682-4040
Free: 888-437-4673
Fax: (513)682-4044
URL: http://www.evercarehospice.com

Westerville

21096 ■ Harbor Light Hospice--Westerville
751 Brookeedge Plaza Dr.
Westerville, OH 43081
Ph: (614)891-6378
Fax: (614)884-0540
E-mail: Infoco@harborlighthospice.com
URL: http://www.harborlighthospice.com/

Westlake

21097 ■ Harbinger Hospice
1119 Bassett Rd.
Westlake, OH 44145
Ph: (440)899-7659
Free: 866-745-7142
Fax: (440)899-9029
E-mail: harbingerhospice@mindspring.com
URL: http://www.harbingerhospice.com

21098 ■ Hospice of the Western Reserve Inc.--Westlake
29101 Health Campus Dr., Ste. 400
Westlake, OH 44145
Ph: (440)892-6680
Fax: (440)892-6690
URL: http://www.hospicewr.org

Wilmington

21099 ■ Community Care Hospice, Inc.
200 R Gordon Dr.
Wilmington, OH 45177
Ph: (937)382-5400
Free: 877-903-5400
Fax: (937)382-3898
URL: http://www.communitycarehospice.com

Wintersville

21100 ■ Charity Hospice, Inc.
PO Box 2483
Wintersville, OH 43953
Ph: (740)264-2280
Fax: (740)264-2290
URL: http://www.charityhospice.org/

Wooster

21101 ■ Hospice and Palliative Care of Greater Wayne County
2525 Back Orrville Rd.
Wooster, OH 44691
Ph: (330)264-4899
Free: 800-884-6547
Fax: (330)264-4874
E-mail: hospice@wchospice.org
URL: http://www.wchospice.org

Xenia

21102 ■ Hospice of the Miami Valley
46 N Detroit St.
Xenia, OH 45385
Ph: (937)458-6028
Fax: (937)458-6021
URL: http://www.charityhospice.org/

Youngstown

21103 ■ Hospice of the Valley--Youngstown
5190 Market St.
Youngstown, OH 44512
Ph: (330)788-1992

Free: 800-640-5180
Fax: (330)788-1998
E-mail: Mary_Foster@hmis.org
URL: http://www.hospiceofthevalley.com

21104 ■ MVI HospiceCare Inc.
4891 Belmont Ave.
Youngstown, OH 44505
Ph: (330)759-9487
Free: 800-449-4684
Fax: (330)759-9564
URL: http://www.mvihomecare.com

Zanesville

21105 ■ Genesis Hospice and Palliative Care
713 Forest Ave.
Zanesville, OH 43701
Ph: (740)454-5365
Free: 800-953-7673
Fax: (740)454-7592
URL: http://www.genesishcs.org

OKLAHOMA

Ada

21106 ■ Halo Hospice
701 N Broadway Ave.
Ada, OK 74820
Ph: (580)332-8009
Fax: (580)332-8387

Anadarko

21107 ■ Faith Hospice of SW Oklahoma
602 W Virginia St.
Anadarko, OK 73005
Ph: (405)247-9526
Fax: (405)247-9558
URL: http://www.faithhospices.com/

Ardmore

21108 ■ Cross Timbers Hospice
207 C St. NW
Ardmore, OK 73401
Ph: (580)223-0655
Free: 800-498-0655
Fax: (580)223-3267
E-mail: hospice@crosstimbershospice.org
URL: http://www.crosstimbershospice.org

21109 ■ Faith Hospice of Southern Oklahoma LLC
1122 Walnut Dr.
Ardmore, OK 73401
Ph: (580)226-4620
Fax: (580)226-4591
URL: http://www.faithhospices.com/

Bartlesville

21110 ■ Carter Healthcare and Hospice--Bartlesville
3081 SE Washington Blvd.
Bartlesville, OK 74006
Ph: (918)333-1400
Fax: (918)333-1403
E-mail: sales@carterhealthcare.net
URL: http://comfortinghandshospice.com/

21111 ■ Comforting Hands Hospice
2450 SE Washington Blvd.
Bartlesville, OK 74006
Ph: (918)331-0003
Fax: (918)331-9556
URL: http://comfortinghandshospice.com/

21112 ■ Rivercross Hospice--Bartlesville
922 SE Frank Phillips Blvd.
Bartlesville, OK 74003
Ph: (918)338-4381
Fax: (918)270-2867
E-mail: info@rivercrosshospice.com
URL: http://www.rivercrosshospice.com/

Bethany

21113 ■ Frontier Hospice--Bethany
3908 N Peniel Ave.
Bethany, OK 73008
Ph: (405)789-2913
Fax: (405)789-2558
URL: http://www.americanhospice.com/

Blackwell

21114 ■ Image Hospice Faith Hospice Services
114 S Main
Blackwell, OK 74631
Ph: (580)363-3793
URL: http://www.imagehomecare.com/

Broken Arrow

21115 ■ Angelic Hospice-Broken Arrow
3790 S Elm Place
Broken Arrow, OK 74011
Ph: (918)622-3800
Fax: (918)622-1574
E-mail: bainfo@angelichospice.com
URL: http://www.angelichospice.com/

21116 ■ Hometown Hospice-Broken Arrow
804 S Main St.
Broken Arrow, OK 74012
Ph: (918)251-6441
Fax: (918)251-6602

Chickasha

21117 ■ Lifeline Hospice, Inc.
1701 W Iowa
Chickasha, OK 73023
Ph: (405)224-4891
Fax: (405)224-3083
URL: http://www.chickashalifeline.com/

Clinton

21118 ■ Carter Health Care and Hospice--Clinton
230 S 30th
Clinton, OK 73701
Ph: (580)323-5330
Fax: (580)323-5446
E-mail: sales@carterhealthcare.net
URL: http://www.carterhealthcare.net/

21119 ■ Integris Western Oklahoma Hospice
100 N 30 St.
Clinton, OK 73601
Ph: (580)323-2363
Free: 888-951-2277
Fax: (580)332-0821
URL: http://integrisok.com/clinton

Duncan

21120 ■ Chisholm Trail Hospice/Svc of Duncan Regional Hospital
2000 W Elk Ave.
Duncan, OK 73534-2000
Ph: (580)251-8764
Free: 877-252-5300
Fax: (580)251-8760
E-mail: info@duncanregional.com
URL: http://www.duncanregional.com/body.cfm?id=41

El Reno

21121 ■ Russell-Murray Hospice
221 S Bickford
El Reno, OK 73036
Ph: (405)262-3088
Free: 888-262-4487
Fax: (405)262-3082
URL: http://russellmurrayhospice.com

Enid

21122 ■ Carter Healthcare and Hospice--Enid
2324 W Garriot Rd.
Enid, OK 73701
Ph: (580)482-5600
URL: http://www.carterhealthcare.net

21123 ■ Hospice Circle of Love
314 S 3rd St.
Enid, OK 73701-5736
Ph: (580)234-2273
Fax: (580)234-1990
E-mail: chadc@hospicecircleoflove.com
URL: http://www.hospicecircleoflove.com

Grove

21124 ■ Good Shepherd Hospice--Grove
2084 S Main St.
Grove, OK 74344
Ph: (918)786-6182
Free: 800-787-2226
Fax: (918)786-6185
E-mail: infogrove@goodshepherdhospice.com
URL: http://www.goodshepherdhospice.com

Guthrie

21125 ■ Companion Hospice, LLC
1314 E Oklahoma
Guthrie, OK 73044
Ph: (405)282-3980
Fax: (405)282-3981
URL: http://www.companionhospice.net

Henryetta

21126 ■ Heritage Hospice LLC--Henryetta
114 S 4th St.
Henryetta, OK 74437
Ph: (918)652-3919
Free: 888-838-3919
Fax: (918)652-2619
URL: http://www.heritagehospicellc.com

Lawton

21127 ■ Hospice of Southwest Oklahoma
1930 NW Ferris Ave., Ste. 5
Lawton, OK 73507
Ph: (580)248-5885
Free: 800-897-4652
Fax: (580)355-2446
E-mail: juli.ricken@hospiceofswok.org
URL: http://www.hospiceoflawton.org
Juli Ricken, Director

McAlester

21128 ■ Heartland Hospice Services--McAlester
210 E Camanche
McAlester, OK 74501
Ph: (918)302-0700
Fax: (918)302-0707
E-mail: careline@hcr-manorcare.com
URL: http://www.hcr-manorcare.com

21129 ■ Hospice of McAlester
PO Box 1333
McAlester, OK 74502
Ph: (918)423-3911
Fax: (918)423-4241
E-mail: info@hospicemc.org
URL: http://hospicemc.org/

Miami

21130 ■ Heaven and Earth Hospice Christian Health Care
3 S Main St.
Miami, OK 74354

Ph: (918)451-9325
Fax: (918)451-9127
E-mail: info@c-healthcare.com
URL: http://www.c-healthcare.com/content/view/81/47/

21131 ■ Integris Regency Hospice
115 S Main
Miami, OK 74354
Ph: (918)542-1226
Fax: (918)540-3812

Muskogee

21132 ■ Good Neighbor Hospice
1122 N Main St.
Muskogee, OK 74401
Ph: (918)681-4988
Fax: (918)681-4995
E-mail: jgaddy@goodneighborhospice.com
URL: http://goodneighborhospice.com/

21133 ■ Hometown Hospice--Muskogee
2307 S York St.
Muskogee, OK 74403-8876
Ph: (918)681-4440
Free: 866-681-4440
Fax: (918)681-4428
URL: http://www.hometownhospice.com/

21134 ■ Professional Home Hospice
1320 N Mill St., Ste. 124
Muskogee, OK 74401
Ph: (918)683-9400
Free: 866-683-9400
Fax: (918)683-9444

21135 ■ Solamor Hospice--Muskogee
222 S 32nd St.
Muskogee, OK 74401
Ph: (918)686-6899
Fax: (918)686-6890
URL: http://www.solamorhospice.com/

Noble

21136 ■ Hospice By Loving Care
312 Cherry St.
Noble, OK 73068
Ph: (405)872-1515
Free: 888-768-4856
Fax: (405)872-7478
URL: http://www.lovingcarehealth.com

Norman

21137 ■ Carter Healthcare and Hospice--Norman
828 N Porter
Norman, OK 73071
Ph: (405)329-6660
E-mail: sales@carterhealthcare.net
URL: http://www.carterhealthcare.net/

21138 ■ Faith Hospice of Oklahoma
611 24th Ave SW
Norman, OK 73069
Ph: (405)321-2257
URL: http://www.faithhospices.com/

21139 ■ Heartland Hospice Services--Norman
1100 N Porter Ave., Ste. 104
Norman, OK 73071
Ph: (405)579-8565
Fax: (405)579-0192
E-mail: careline@hcr-manorcare.com
URL: http://www.hcr-manorcare.com

Oklahoma City

21140 ■ Alleve Hospice
8524 S Western Ave., Ste. 105
Oklahoma City, OK 73139
Ph: (405)605-7787
Fax: (405)605-7789
E-mail: allevehospice@coxinet.net
URL: http://www.allevehospice.com/

21141 ■ Autumn Bridge Hospice
3500 NW 39 St.
Oklahoma City, OK 73112
Ph: (405)440-2440
Fax: (405)449-2441
E-mail: questions@autumnbridgehospice.com
URL: http://www.autumnbridgehospice.com

21142 ■ Choice Hospice
One NW 64th
Oklahoma City, OK 73116
Ph: (405)879-3470
Fax: (405)879-1625
E-mail: choice@choicehealthcare.net
URL: http://www.choicehealthcare.net/index.html

21143 ■ City Hospice
3714 N Portland Ave.
Oklahoma City, OK 73112-2924
Ph: (405)942-8999
Fax: (405)942-0047
E-mail: info@cityhospice.org
URL: http://cityhospice.org/default.aspx

21144 ■ Community Hospice of Oklahoma
3555 NW 58th St., Ste. 900
Oklahoma City, OK 73112
Ph: (405)917-0650

21145 ■ Excell Hospice
1200 SW 104th St.
Oklahoma City, OK 73139
Ph: (405)631-0521
Fax: (405)631-2661
URL: http://www.excellhomecare.net

21146 ■ Full Life Hospice, LLC
Centerpointe Resources, Inc.
4001 N Classen Blvd.
Oklahoma City, OK 73118
Ph: (405)418-2659
Fax: (405)488-1009
URL: http://www.centerpointeresources.com/html/hospice.php

21147 ■ Good Shepherd Hospice--Oklahoma City
4350 Will Rogers Pkwy., Ste 400
Oklahoma City, OK 73108
Ph: (405)943-0903
Free: 800-687-9808
E-mail: InfoOKC@GoodShepherdHospice.com
URL: http://www.goodshepherdhospice.com

21148 ■ Hospice of Oklahoma County
4334 NW Expressway St., Ste. 106
Oklahoma City, OK 73116
Ph: (405)848-8884
Fax: (405)841-4899
E-mail: Nancy.Willard@integrisok.com
URL: http://www.hospiceokcounty.com

21149 ■ Interim Healthcare
5600 N May Ave., Ste. 145
Oklahoma City, OK 73112
Ph: (405)848-3555
Fax: (405)842-4629
URL: http://www.interimhealthcare.com/

21150 ■ Mercy at Home-Hospice
Mercy Health System of Oklahoma
4401 W Memorial Rd.
Oklahoma City, OK 73134
Ph: (405)232-4663
Fax: (405)752-3666
URL: http://www.mercyok.net/mhc/medicalservices/hospice/default.asp

21151 ■ Mission Hospice, LLC
2525 NW Expwy., Ste. 312
Oklahoma City, OK 73112
Ph: (405)848-3779
Free: 888-644-3526
Fax: (405)848-8481
URL: http://www.missionhospicellc.com

21152 ■ Physicians Choice in Care, LLC
1131 E Britton Rd.
Oklahoma City, OK 73131
Ph: (405)936-9433
Fax: (405)936-9435

21153 ■ Quality Life Hospice
7845 N Robinson Ave., Ste. H4
Oklahoma City, OK 73116
Ph: (405)767-9033
Fax: (405)767-9931
URL: http://www.qualitylifehospice.com/

21154 ■ Solamor Hospice-Oklahoma City
1900 NW Expwy., Ste. 320
Oklahoma City, OK 73118
Ph: (405)604-9113
Fax: (405)602-6481
URL: http://www.solamorhospice.com/

21155 ■ Sooner Hospice
2212 NW 50th St., Ste. 143C
Oklahoma City, OK 73112
Ph: (405)608-0555
Fax: (405)608-0557
E-mail: soonerhospice@coxinet.net
URL: http://www.soonerhospice.com/

21156 ■ Valir Hospice, LLC
825 N Broadway
Oklahoma City, OK 73102
Ph: (405)609-3636
Fax: (405)609-3698
E-mail: hospice@valir.com
URL: http://www.soonerhospice.com/

Owasso

21157 ■ Hope Hospice--Owasso
8291 N Owasso Expwy.
Owasso, OK 74055
Ph: (918)272-3060
Fax: (918)272-3617
URL: http://www.hopehospiceok.com/

Ponca City

21158 ■ Hospice of North Central Oklahoma, Inc.
1904 N Union St., Ste. 103
Ponca City, OK 74601-1542
Ph: (580)762-9102
Free: 800-814-9102
Fax: (580)762-9111
E-mail: gwood@hospiceofnco.com
URL: http://www.hospiceofnorthcentraloklahoma.com/

Poteau

21159 ■ Advantage Home Health & Hospice
20775 292nd St.
Poteau, OK 74953
Ph: (918)647-0653
Fax: (918)647-0654

21160 ■ Peachtree Hospice, Poteau, LLC
PO Box 460
Poteau, OK 74953
Ph: (918)647-7008
Fax: (918)647-7168
E-mail: jpetrus@pthfs.com
URL: http://www.peachtreehospice.com/

21161 ■ Professional Home Hospice
206 Oak St.
Poteau, OK 74953
Ph: (918)649-1378
Free: 888-647-1378
Fax: (918)649-1278

Pryor

21162 ■ Integris Hospice of Mayes County
111 N Bailey
Pryor, OK 74361
Ph: (918)825-1600
Fax: (918)824-6319

Purcell

21163 ■ Hospice By Loving Care-Purcell
301 W Main St.
Purcell, OK 73080
Ph: (405)527-1117
Fax: (405)527-8899
URL: http://www.professionalhomehospice.com/

Shawnee

21164 ■ Heartland Home Health Care and Hospice--Shawnee
3700 N Kickapoo
Shawnee, OK 74804
Ph: (405)214-6442
Fax: (405)214-6404
E-mail: careline@hcr-manorcare.com
URL: http://www.hcr-manorcare.com

Stillwater

21165 ■ Judith Karman Hospice Inc.
915 S Main St.
Stillwater, OK 74076
Ph: (405)377-8012
Fax: (405)624-9007
E-mail: hospice@judithkarmanhospice.org
URL: http://www.judithkarmanhospice.org

Tahlequah

21166 ■ Carter Healthcare and Hospice--Tahlequah
200 E Harris Circle, Ste. A
Tahlequah, OK 74464
Ph: (918)458-0663
Fax: (918)453-9109
E-mail: sales@carterhealthcare.net
URL: http://www.carterhealthcare.net/

21167 ■ Carter Healthcare and Hospice--Tahlequah
200 E Harris Circle, Ste. A
Tahlequah, OK 74464
Ph: (918)458-0663
Fax: (918)453-9109
E-mail: sales@carterhealthcare.net
URL: http://www.carterhealthcare.net/

21168 ■ Hospice of the Cherokee
1 Plaza S
Tahlequah, OK 74464
Ph: (918)458-5080
Fax: (918)458-5103
URL: http://www.cnhhs.org/

Tulsa

21169 ■ Carter Health Care and Hospice--Tulsa
2846 E 101st St.
Tulsa, OK 74137
Ph: (918)425-4000
Fax: (918)425-0780
URL: http://www.carterhealthcare.net/

21170 ■ Good Shepherd Hospice--Tulsa
6218 S Lewis Ave., Ste. 1110
Tulsa, OK 74136
Ph: (918)743-5067
Free: 800-687-6269
E-mail: InfoTulsa@GoodShepherdHospice.com
URL: http://www.goodshepherdhospice.com/

21171 ■ Grace Hospice of Oklahoma, LLC
6400 S Lewis, Ste. 1000
Tulsa, OK 74153
Ph: (918)744-7223
Free: 800-659-0307
Fax: (918)744-7240
E-mail: avah@gracehospice.com
URL: http://www.gracehospice.com
Ava Caughrean, Executive Director

21172 ■ Hospice of Green Country Inc.
2121 S Columbia Ave., Ste. 200
Tulsa, OK 74114
Ph: (918)747-2273
Fax: (918)747-2573
URL: http://www.hospiceofgreencountry.org

21173 ■ Infinity Care of Tulsa
6914 S Yorktown, Ste. 115
Tulsa, OK 74136
Ph: (918)392-0800
Fax: (918)392-0808
URL: http://www.infinitycare.com

OREGON

Ashland

21174 ■ Ashland Community Hospital Hospice & Palliative Care Services
1970 Ashland St.
Ashland, OR 97520
Ph: (541)522-9900
Fax: (541)552-9905
URL: http://www.ashlandhospital.org/

Astoria

21175 ■ Lower Columbia Hospice
486 12th St.
Astoria, OR 97103
Ph: (503)338-6230
Fax: (503)338-7590
E-mail: info@columbiamemorial.org
URL: http://www.ashlandhospital.org/

Baker City

21176 ■ Heart 'n Home Hospice & Palliative Care-Baker City
1405 Campbell St.
Baker City, OR 97814
Ph: (541)524-7688
Fax: (541)524-7682
URL: http://www.heartnhomehospice.com/

Beaverton

21177 ■ Odyssey HealthCare of Portland
8625 SW Cascade Ave.
Beaverton, OR 97008
Ph: (503)574-2900
Fax: (503)574-2901
URL: http://www.odsyhealth.com

21178 ■ Providence Hospice and Palliative Care West
3601 SW Murray Blvd.
Beaverton, OR 97005
Ph: (503)215-4321
Fax: (503)574-9480
E-mail: janice.potts@providence.org

21179 ■ Signature Hospice--Beaverton
7100 Scholls Ferry Rd.
Beaverton, OR 97008
Free: 800-936-4756
Fax: (503)682-3989

Bend

21180 ■ Hospice House-Bend
2075 NE Wyatt Ct.
Bend, OR 97701
Ph: (541)383-4102
Fax: (541)388-4102
URL: http://www.partnersbend.org/services/Hospice-House/

21181 ■ Partners in Care Hospice
2075 NE Wyatt Ct.
Bend, OR 97701
Ph: (541)382-5882
Fax: (541)382-2960
URL: http://www.partnersbend.org/
Formerly: Central Oregon Hospice.

Brookings

21182 ■ Curry County Home Health/Hospice
306 Wharf
Brookings, OR 97415
Ph: (541)469-0405
E-mail: homecare@co.curry.or.us
URL: http://www.co.curry.or.us/homehealth/cchhh.htm

Burns

21183 ■ Harney County Home Health/Hospice
415 N Fairview Ave.
Burns, OR 97720
Ph: (541)573-8360
Fax: (541)573-8389
E-mail: cherylk1@centurytel.net
URL: http://www.co.harney.or.us/homehealth.html

Coos Bay

21184 ■ Pacific Home Health and Hospice
455 S 4th St.
Coos Bay, OR 97420
Ph: (541)266-7008
Fax: (541)266-7008

21185 ■ South Coast Hospice
1620 Thompson Rd.
Coos Bay, OR 97420
Ph: (541)269-2986
Fax: (541)269-0576
E-mail: sch@schospice.org
URL: http://www.schospice.org

Corvallis

21186 ■ Benton Hospice Service
2350 NW Professional Dr.
Corvallis, OR 97330
Ph: (541)757-9616
Free: 800-898-9616
Fax: (541)757-1760
E-mail: bhs@bentonhospice.org
URL: http://www.bentonhospice.org

Eugene

21187 ■ Cascade Health Solutions
2650 Suzanne Way
Eugene, OR 97408
Ph: (541)228-3008
Fax: (541)228-3182
E-mail: blaughhunn@cascadehealth.org
URL: http://www.cascadehealth.org/home_health_hospice/

21188 ■ Hospice of Sacred Heart
1121 Fairfield Ave.
Eugene, OR 97402
Ph: (541)461-7550
Fax: (541)461-7697
E-mail: info@peacehealthlabs.org
URL: http://www.peacehealth.org

21189 ■ Signature Hospice-Eugene
195 Silver Lane
Eugene, OR 97404
Ph: (541)689-3508
Free: 866-306-4279
Fax: (541)461-0571
URL: http://www.signaturehospice.com/ME2/Audiences/Default.asp?AudID=BA2C88D6EA584FC7B7247DBF7D3D3EAB

Florence

21190 ■ Peace Harbor Hospice
310 9th St.
Florence, OR 97439
Ph: (541)997-3418
Fax: (541)997-8290
URL: http://www.peacehealth.org/

Gold Beach

21191 ■ Curry County Home Health/Hospice
29984 Ellensburg Ave.
Gold Beach, OR 97444
Ph: (541)247-7084
Free: 800-535-9472
Fax: (800)535-2117
E-mail: kentl@co.curry.or.us
URL: http://www.co.curry.or.us/homehealth/cchhh.htm

Grants Pass

21192 ■ Lovejoy Hospice
939 SE 8th St.
Grants Pass, OR 97526
Ph: (541)474-1193
Free: 888-758-8569
Fax: (541)474-3035
E-mail: info@lovejoyhospice.org
URL: http://www.lovejoyhospice.org

Heppner

21193 ■ Pioneer Memorial Home Health and Hospice
PO Box 9
Heppner, OR 97836
Ph: (541)676-2946
Fax: (541)676-9017
E-mail: michaelb@mocohd.org
URL: http://www.morrowcountyhealthdistrict.org/PMHH.html

Hermiston

21194 ■ Vange John Memorial Hospice
1050 W Elm St.
Hermiston, OR 97838
Ph: (541)667-3542
Fax: (541)667-3541
URL: http://www.gshealth.org/

Hillsboro

21195 ■ Hospice of Washington County--Hillsboro
900 SE Oak St.
Hillsboro, OR 97123
Ph: (503)648-9565
Fax: (503)648-1282
E-mail: christine@hospicewc.org
URL: http://www.hospicewc.org

Hood River

21196 ■ Heart of Hospice, LLC--Hood River
205 Wasco Loop
Hood River, OR 97031
Ph: (541)386-1942
Fax: (541)386-1728
E-mail: info@heartofhospice.org
URL: http://www.heartofhospice.org/

21197 ■ Hospice of the Gorge
1630 Woods Ct.
Hood River, OR 97031
Ph: (541)387-6449
Free: 800-955-3911
Fax: (541)386-6700
E-mail: info@hospiceofthegorge.org
URL: http://www.hospiceofthegorge.org/

John Day

21198 ■ Blue Mountain Hospice
170 Ford Rd.
John Day, OR 97845
Ph: (541)575-1648
Fax: (541)575-3506
E-mail: bmhadm@centurytel.net
URL: http://www.bluemountainhospital.org/getpage.php?name=index

Klamath Falls

21199 ■ High Desert Hospice LLC
2894 Greensprings Dr.
Klamath Falls, OR 97601
Ph: (541)882-1636
Fax: (541)882-1799
E-mail: jflorez1@hdhweb.com
URL: http://www.hdhweb.com/

21200 ■ Klamath Hospice, Inc.
4745 S 6th St.
Klamath Falls, OR 97603
Ph: (541)882-2902
Free: 877-882-2902
Fax: (541)882-1992
E-mail: mail@klamathhospice.org
URL: http://www.klamathhospice.org

La Grande

21201 ■ Grande Ronde Hospital Home Care Services
PO Box 3290
La Grande, OR 97850
Ph: (541)963-1453
Fax: (541)963-1872
URL: http://www.grh.org/

La Pine

21202 ■ Newberry Hospice
51681 Huntington Rd.
La Pine, OR 97739
Ph: (541)536-7399
Fax: (541)536-9312
E-mail: hdta@endnet.com
URL: http://newberryhospice.com/

Lakeview

21203 ■ Lakeview Home Health and Hospice
700 South J
Lakeview, OR 97630
Ph: (541)947-7296
Fax: (541)947-3133
URL: http://www.lakehealthdistrict.org/getpage.php?name=home&sub=Home

Madras

21204 ■ Mountain View Hospital District Hospice
470 NE A St.
Madras, OR 97741
Ph: (541)475-3882
Fax: (541)475-0602
E-mail: mvhd@mvhd.org
URL: http://www.cascadehealthcare.org/Mountain-View/index.aspx

McMinnville

21205 ■ Legacy Hospice McMinnville
2275 NE McDaniel Ln.
McMinnville, OR 97128
Ph: (503)472-9685
Fax: (503)434-9052
URL: http://www.legacyhealth.org/

Medford

21206 ■ Asante Home Care and Hospice dba Rogue Valley Medical Center Home Health Agency
2825 E Barnett Rd.
Medford, OR 97504-8127
Ph: (541)789-7000
Free: 800-888-6579
Fax: (541)608-5239
E-mail: kadkison@asante.org
URL: http://www.asante.org

21207 ■ Providence Hospice-Medford
2033 Commerce Dr.
Medford, OR 97504
Ph: (541)732-6500
Free: 800-804-2017
E-mail: cindy.hunter@providence.org
URL: http://www.providence.org/medford/services/cancer/hospice-care.htm

Oregon City

21208 ■ Willamette Falls Hospice
1505 Division St.
Oregon City, OR 97045
Ph: (503)655-7581
Fax: (503)655-7585
URL: http://www.willamettefallshospital.org/hospice.html

Portland

21209 ■ Adventist Health Hospice--Portland
5835 NE 122nd Ave., Ste. 135
Portland, OR 97230
Ph: (503)251-6192
Fax: (503)251-6080
E-mail: AHNW@ah.org
URL: http://www.adventisthealthnw.com/Hospice.asp

21210 ■ Hospice Care of the Northwest
1500 NE Irving St., Ste. 200
Portland, OR 97232
Ph: (877)263-7776
Fax: (877)263-7778
E-mail: administrator@hospicecarenw.com
URL: http://www.hospicecarenw.com/

21211 ■ House Call Providers
4531 SE Belmont, Ste. 250
Portland, OR 97215
Ph: (503)988-5303
Fax: (503)988-5112
E-mail: koconnor@housecallproviders.org
URL: http://www.housecallproviders.org/

21212 ■ Kaiser Permanente Continuing Care
2701 NW Vaughn St., Ste. 140
Portland, OR 97210
Ph: (503)499-5200
Fax: (503)499-5213
URL: https://www.kaiserpermanente.org/

21213 ■ Legacy Hopewell House Hospice
6171 SW Capitol Hwy.
Portland, OR 97239
Ph: (503)224-7890
Free: 800-903-5118
URL: http://www.legacyhealth.org/body.cfm?id=710

21214 ■ Legacy Hospice Services
815 NE Davis
Portland, OR 97232
Ph: (503)220-1000
Free: 800-896-6287
URL: http://www.co.clackamas.or.us/socialservices/rguide/info1668aa.html

21215 ■ Providence Hospice--Portland
1235 NE 47th Ave., Ste. 148
Portland, OR 97213-2100
Ph: (503)215-2273
Fax: (503)215-4846
URL: http://providence.org/Oregon/Programs_and_Services/Hospice/default.htm

21216 ■ Serenity Palliative Care and Hospice
6975 SW Sandburg St.
Portland, OR 97223
Ph: (503)639-0600
Fax: (503)639-0699
URL: http://www.serenityhospice.org/

Prineville

21217 ■ Pioneer Memorial Hospice-Prineville
1201 N Elm St.
Prineville, OR 97554
Ph: (541)447-2510
Fax: (541)447-2514
URL: http://www.cascadehealth.org/

Redmond

21218 ■ Hospice of Redmond, Sisters, and Grant County
732 SW 23rd St.
Redmond, OR 97756
Ph: (541)548-7483
Free: 877-244-0858
Fax: (541)548-1507
E-mail: hospice@bendcable.com
URL: http://www.redmondhospice.org

Roseburg

21219 ■ Amedisys Hospice of Roseburg
2510 NW Edenbower Blvd.
Roseburg, OR 97471
Ph: (541)440-2530
Fax: (541)440-2530
URL: http://www.amedisys.com/

21220 ■ Mercy Hospice--Roseburg
2400 NW Stewart Pkwy.
Roseburg, OR 97470
Ph: (541)677-2384
Fax: (541)677-2498
URL: http://www.mercyrose.org/services/hospice.html

Salem

21221 ■ Hospice Care of the NOrthwest
2290 Commercial St., SE
Salem, OR 97302
Ph: (503)595-2260
Fax: (503)595-2265
URL: http://hospicecarenw.com/

21222 ■ Odyssey HealthCare-Pacific Northwest
707 13th St. SE, Ste. 299
Salem, OR 97301
Ph: (503)362-3040
Free: 877-637-9432
Fax: (503)362-3480
URL: http://www.odsyhealth.com/default.asp

21223 ■ Willamette Valley Hospice
1015 3rd St.
Salem, OR 97304
Ph: (503)588-3600
Free: 800-555-2431
Fax: (503)363-3891
E-mail: info@wvh.org
URL: http://www.wvh.org

Sandy

21224 ■ Mount Hood Hospice
39641 Scenic St.
Sandy, OR 97055
Ph: (503)668-5545
Fax: (503)668-7951
E-mail: inquire@Mthoodhospice.org
URL: http://www.mthoodhospice.com

The Dalles

21225 ■ Hospice of The Gorge-The Dalles Office
751 Myrtle St.
The Dalles, OR 97058
Ph: (541)296-3228
Fax: (541)298-4204
E-mail: info@hospiceofthegorge.org
URL: http://www.hospiceofthegorge.org/

Tigard

21226 ■ Signature Hospice-Tigard
7070 SW Fir Loop
Tigard, OR 97223
Free: 800-936-4756
Fax: (503)682-3989
URL: http://www.4signatureservice.com/ME2/Audiences/Default.asp?AudID=28783D6C89554B83A22EC6267CBF883E

Tillamook

21227 ■ Adventist Health/Hospice--Tillamook
1015 3rd St.
Tillamook, OR 97141-3430
Ph: (503)815-2458
Fax: (503)815-2288
E-mail: wheelehc@ah.org
URL: http://www.adventisthealth.org/healthservices/goDocDocument.asp?DID=254

Warrenton

21228 ■ Lower Columbia Hospice Adult Foster Care Home
Lower Columbia Hospice
91848 HW 104
Warrenton, OR 97146
Ph: (503)861-1725
Fax: (503)338-6240

Wilsonville

21229 ■ Signature Hospice-Wilsonville
25117 SW Parkway
Wilsonville, OR 97070
Free: 800-936-4756
Fax: (503)682-3989
URL: http://www.4signatureservice.com/ME2/Audiences/Default.asp?AudID=28783D6C89554B83A22EC6267CBF883E

PENNSYLVANIA

Allentown

21230 ■ Arcadia Hospice
7248 Tilghman St.
Allentown, PA 18106
Ph: (610)336-8000
Fax: (610)336-8001
E-mail: info@arcadiahospice.com
URL: http://www.arcadiahospice.com/

21231 ■ AseraCare Hospice-Allentown
5920 Hamilton Blvd.
Allentown, PA 18106
Ph: (610)562-3873
Fax: (610)562-3904
URL: http://www.aseracare.com/

21232 ■ Diakon Hospice Saint John--Allentown
798 Hausman Rd.
Allentown, PA 18104
Ph: (610)391-2300
Fax: (610)391-2301
E-mail: bergstroml@diakon.org
URL: http://www.diakon.org/hospice/

21233 ■ Heartland Home Health Care and Hospice--Allentown
881 Marcon Blvd., Ste. 3700
Allentown, PA 18109
Ph: (610)432-1022
E-mail: careline@hcr-manorcare.com
URL: http://www.hcr-manorcare.com

21234 ■ Lehigh Valley Hospice
2166 S 12th St.
Allentown, PA 18103
Ph: (610)402-7300
URL: http://www.lvhn.org/hospice

21235 ■ Sacred Heart Hospice-Allentown
2268 S 12th St.
Allentown, PA 18103
Ph: (610)871-2802
Fax: (610)871-5918
E-mail: dspengle@shh.org
URL: http://www.shh.org/

Altoona

21236 ■ AseraCare Hospice-Altoona
1015 Logan Blvd.
Altoona, PA 16602
Ph: (814)941-2900
Fax: (814)941-0600
URL: http://www.aseracare.com/

21237 ■ Home Nursing Agency Hospice
102 Chestnut Ave.
Altoona, PA 16601
Ph: (814)946-5411
Free: 800-445-6262
Fax: (814)941-1648
E-mail: help@homenursingagency.com
URL: http://www.homenursingagency.com

Ambler

21238 ■ ACTS Hospice
812 N Bethlehem Pike
Ambler, PA 19002
Ph: (267)350-7200
Fax: (267)464-1594
URL: http://www.actsretirement.org/

Bala Cynwyd

21239 ■ Wissahickon Hospice
150 Monument Rd., Ste. 300
Bala Cynwyd, PA 19004
Ph: (610)617-2400
Free: 800-789-PENN
Fax: (610)617-2409
URL: http://www.pennmedicine.org/homecare/

Belle Vernon

21240 ■ ANOVA Hospice and Palliative Care Services LLC
1580 Broad Ave. Ext.
Belle Vernon, PA 15012
Ph: (724)929-3200
Fax: (724)929-3817
E-mail: info@anovahomehealth.com
URL: http://www.anovahomehealth.com/anova_Hospice_Palliative_Services.html

Bensalem

21241 ■ Immediate Homecare and Hospice
2920 Olga Ave.
Bensalem, PA 19020
Ph: (215)638-2223
Fax: (215)638-3439
URL: http://www.immediatehomecareinc.com/

Bethlehem

21242 ■ St. Luke's Hospice-Bethlehem
1510 Valley Center Pkwy., Ste. 200
Bethlehem, PA 18017
Ph: (610)954-1100
Fax: (610)954-2820
E-mail: infolink@slhn.org
URL: http://St.Luke'sHospice-Bethlehem

Bloomsburg

21243 ■ Berwick Hospice
6850 Lows Rd.
Bloomsburg, PA 17815
Ph: (570)759-5153
Fax: (570)759-5490

21244 ■ Columbia Montour Home Hospice
410 Glenn Ave., Ste. 200
Bloomsburg, PA 17815
Ph: (570)784-1723
Free: 800-349-4702
Fax: (570)784-8512
URL: http://www.bloomhealth.net/cmhhh/hospice_maria.htm

Blue Bell

21245 ■ Heartland Home Health Care and Hospice--Blue Bell
460 Northtown Rd.
Blue Bell, PA 19422
Ph: (610)941-6700
Fax: (610)941-6440
URL: http://www.hcr-manorcare.com/

21246 ■ Heartland Hospice Care-Philadelphia
460 Norristown Rd., Ste. 101
Blue Bell, PA 19422
Ph: (610)941-6700
Fax: (888)427-6630
URL: http://www.hcr-manorcare.com/tabId/68/Default.aspx?City=&State=&PostalCode=19422&CareTypes=99134

21247 ■ Odyssey Health Care of Philadelphia
512 Township Line Rd., Bldg. 2
Blue Bell, PA 19422
Ph: (215)619-7710
Free: 877-637-9432
Fax: (215)619-7635
E-mail: info@odsyhealth.com
URL: http://www.odsyhealth.com/

21248 ■ VistaCare-Blue Bell
512 Township Line Rd.
Blue Bell, PA 19422
Ph: (610)825-0333
Fax: (610)825-3444
URL: http://www.vistacare.com/

21249 ■ VITAS Innovative Hospice Care of Philadelphia
1740 Walton Rd., Ste. 100
Blue Bell, PA 19422
Ph: (610)260-6020
Free: 800-209-1080
Fax: (610)230-4980
URL: http://www.vitas.com

Bradford

21250 ■ McKean County Visiting Nurse Association Hospice
116 Interstate Pkwy.
Bradford, PA 16701-1257
Ph: (814)368-4143
Free: 800-342-5862
Fax: (814)362-4306
URL: http://www.brmc.com/index.aspx?id=18&tabid=34

Brookville

21251 ■ AseraCare Hospice-Brookville
231 Allegheny Blvd.
Brookville, PA 15825
Ph: (814)849-8819
Fax: (814)849-7709
URL: http://www.aseracare.com/

Butler

21252 ■ Albert Gallatin Home Care and Hospice Services--Butler
240 Pullman Sq.
Butler, PA 16001
Ph: (724)431-4170
Free: 877-274-9306
Fax: (724)431-3175
URL: http://www.amedisys.com/hospice_locations.cfm?id=25

21253 ■ VAMC: VA Butler Healthcare
325 New Castle Rd.
Butler, PA 16001
Ph: (724)285-2763
Fax: (724)285-2755
URL: http://www.butler.va.gov/

21254 ■ VNA Hospice, Western PA
154 Hindman Rd.
Butler, PA 16001
Ph: (724)282-6806
Fax: (724)282-1509
URL: http://www.vna.com/services/hospice-services

Camp Hill

21255 ■ Odyssey Health Care of Harrisburg
4660 Trindle Rd., Ste. 204
Camp Hill, PA 17011
Ph: (717)612-1200
Free: 877-637-9432
Fax: (717)612-1201
E-mail: info@odsyhealth.com
URL: http://www.odsyhealth.com

Canonsburg

21256 ■ Albert Gallatin Home Care and Hospice Services--Canonsburg
2215 Hill Church Houston Rd.
Canonsburg, PA 15317
Ph: (724)873-7330
Fax: (724)873-8202

Carbondale

21257 ■ Home Health Care Professionals & Hospice Inc.
299 Canaan St.
Carbondale, PA 18407
Ph: (270)281-3310
Free: 888-675-2400
Fax: (570)281-3310
URL: http://www.hhcpinc.com/

Carlisle

21258 ■ Hospice of Central PA--Carlisle
17 E High St., Ste. 102
Carlisle, PA 17013
Ph: (717)241-0014
Free: 866-779-7374
Fax: (717)241-0047
E-mail: info@hospiceofcentralpa.org
URL: http://www.hospiceofcentralpa.org/contact.htm

Carmichaels

21259 ■ Hospice Care Corporation-Carmichaels
102 Carmichaels Plz.
Carmichaels, PA 15320
Ph: (304)966-2656
Fax: (304)966-2677
URL: http://www.hospicecarecorp.org/

Carnegie

21260 ■ Harmony Hospice LLC-Carnegie
811 Washington Ave.
Carnegie, PA 15106
Ph: (412)276-4700
Fax: (412)276-0473
E-mail: info@harmonyhospice.com
URL: http://www.harmonyhospice.com/

Chadds Ford

21261 ■ Heartland Home Health Care and Hospice-Chadds Ford
5 Christy Dr.
Chadds Ford, PA 19317
Ph: (484)840-0811
Fax: (484)840-0818
URL: http://www.hcr-manorcare.com/

Chambersburg

21262 ■ Lutheran Home Care Services Inc.
2700 Luther Dr.
Chambersburg, PA 17202
Ph: (717)264-8178
Free: 800-840-9081
Fax: (717)264-6347
E-mail: info@lutheranhomecare.org
URL: http://www.lutheranhomecare.org/

Clarks Summit

21263 ■ AseraCare Hospice-Clarks Summit
749 Northern Blvd.
Clarks Summit, PA 18411
Ph: (570)319-3670
Fax: (570)586-6054
URL: http://www.aseracare.com/

Clearfield

21264 ■ Clearfield Hospital Hospice
438 W Front St.
Clearfield, PA 16830-1419
Ph: (814)768-2012
Free: 800-281-8000
Fax: (814)768-2458
URL: http://www.clearfieldhosp.org/dept-svc/hospice/Hospice.aspx

Danville

21265 ■ Columbia Montour Home Hospice Bloomburg Health System
1 Maria Hall Dr.
Danville, PA 17821
Ph: (570)784-1723
Fax: (570)784-8512
E-mail: info@bloomhealth.org
URL: http://www.bloomhealth.net/cmhhh/hospice_maria.htm

Darby

21266 ■ VITAS Innovative Hospice Care Mercy Fitzgerald Hospital
1500 Lansdowne Ave.
Darby, PA 19023
Ph: (610)237-5010
URL: http://www.vitas.com
Formerly: Mercy Health Hospice Program.

Doylestown

21267 ■ Doylestown Hospital Hospice
595 W State St.
Doylestown, PA 18901
Ph: (215)345-2671
Fax: (267)880-1393
URL: https://www.dh.org/body.cfm?id=83

Dresher

21268 ■ Life Choice Hospice--Dresher
200 Dryden Rd.
Dresher, PA 19025
Free: 800-557-7570
Fax: (215)893-1740
URL: http://www.lifechoicehospice.com/

East Stroudsburg

21269 ■ VNA Hospice of Monroe County
502 Independence Rd.
East Stroudsburg, PA 18301

Ph: (570)421-5390
Fax: (570)421-7423
E-mail: info@vnahospiceofmc.org
URL: http://www.vnahospiceofmc.org

Easton

21270 ■ Easton Hospital Hospice
3421 Nightingale Dr.
Easton, PA 18045
Ph: (610)258-7189
Fax: (610)258-5178
URL: http://www.easton-hospital.com/Services/Pages/Home%20Health%20and%20Hospice%20Services.aspx

Elizabethtown

21271 ■ Masonic Villages
One Masonic Dr.
Elizabethtown, PA 17022
Ph: (717)367-1121
Fax: (717)351-4978
E-mail: pr@masonicvillagespa.org
URL: http://www.masonicvillagespa.org/

Erie

21272 ■ AseraCare Hospice--Erie
1600 Peninsula Dr., Ste. 14
Erie, PA 16505
Ph: (814)836-5255
Fax: (814)833-3152
URL: http://www.aseracare.com/

21273 ■ Great Lakes Home Healthcare and Hospice
1700 Peach St., Ste. 244
Erie, PA 16501-2134
Ph: (814)877-6120
Fax: (814)877-6032
URL: http://www.hamot.org/

21274 ■ Heartland Hospice Services--Erie
719 Indiana Dr.
Erie, PA 16505
Ph: (814)878-5990
Fax: (814)878-5996
URL: http://www.hcr-manorcare.com/tabid/67/default.aspx?FacilityID=4703

21275 ■ Hospice of Metropolitan Erie
202 E 10th St.
Erie, PA 16503-1008
Ph: (814)456-6689
Fax: (814)456-8219
URL: http://www.hospiceerie.org

21276 ■ Lakeland Area Hospice
2221 A Peninsula Dr.
Erie, PA 16506
Ph: (814)838-0511
Fax: (815)838-0517

Forty Fort

21277 ■ VNA Hospice of Northeast Pennsylvania
900 Rutter Ave.
Forty Fort, PA 18704
Ph: (615)465-7000
URL: http://www.vnahospice.org/homehealth.htm

Franklin

21278 ■ VNA of Venango County, Inc.
491 Allegheny Blvd.
Franklin, PA 16323
Ph: (814)432-6555
Fax: (814)432-6588
E-mail: vnaa@vnaa.org
URL: http://vnaa.org/vnaa/vna/VNA_of_Venango_County,PAOILC.aspx

Ft. Washington

21279 ■ Care Alternatives--Fort Washington
501 Office Center Dr.
Ft. Washington, PA 19034
Ph: (215)542-2100
Fax: (215)542-2103
URL: http://www.carealt.com/

Gettysburg

21280 ■ Lutheran Home Care Services
260 W High St.
Gettysburg, PA 17325
Ph: (717)334-6208
Free: 800-840-9081

Greensburg

21281 ■ Excela Health Hospice
134 Industrial Pk. Rd., Ste. 1600
Greensburg, PA 15601
Ph: (724)689-1910
Free: 877-771-1234
Fax: (724)689-1457
URL: http://www.excelahealth.org/services_hh.asp

Harrisburg

21282 ■ AseraCare Hospice - Harrisburg
75 S Houcks Rd.
Harrisburg, PA 17109
Free: 800-551-4466
Fax: (717)541-4470
URL: http://www.aseracare.com

21283 ■ Homeland Hospice
2300 Vartan Way
Harrisburg, PA 17110
Ph: (717)221-7890
Fax: (717)221-7891
E-mail: nbaer@homelandhospice.org
URL: http://www.homelandcenter.org/hospice/

21284 ■ Hospice of Central PA--Harrisburg
1320 Linglestown Rd.
Harrisburg, PA 17110
Ph: (717)732-1000
Fax: (717)234-0375
E-mail: info@hospiceofcentralpa.org
URL: http://www.hospiceofcentralpa.org/

Hazle Twp.

21285 ■ Diakon Hospice Saint John-Hazle Twp.
1201 B N. Church St.
Hazle Twp., PA 18202
Ph: (610)682-1439
Fax: (570)453-5202
E-mail: bergstroml@diakon.org
URL: http://www.diakon.org/HOSPICE/

Hermitage

21286 ■ Sharon Regional Health System Hospice and Palliative Care
2320 Highland Rd.
Hermitage, PA 16148
Ph: (724)983-3878
Fax: (724)983-5949
URL: http://www.sharonregional.com/

Honesdale

21287 ■ Diakon Hospice Saint John-Honesdale
416 Main St.
Honesdale, PA 18431
Ph: (570)251-8712
Fax: (570)251-8716
E-mail: bergstroml@diakon.org
URL: http://www.diakon.org/HOSPICE/

Indiana

21288 ■ Family Hospice and Palliative Care Service of the VNA Indiana County
850 Hospital Rd., Ste. 3000
Indiana, PA 15701
Ph: (724)463-6340
E-mail: marionreott@hotmail.com
URL: http://www.vnaindianacounty.com

Jeannette

21289 ■ Hospice of Westmoreland
600 Jefferson Ave.
Jeannette, PA 15644
Ph: (724)527-1435
Fax: (724)527-2450

Johnstown

21290 ■ AseraCare Hospice-Johnstown
706 Eisenhower Blvd.
Johnstown, PA 15904
Ph: (866)921-1710
Fax: (814)269-4177
URL: http://www.aseracare.com/

21291 ■ Conemaugh Regional Hospice
315 Locust St., Ste. 5E
Johnstown, PA 15901
Ph: (814)534-6100
Fax: (888)553-5503
E-mail: emailus@conemaugh.org
URL: https://www2.conemaugh.org/template_article.aspx?id=3360

Kennett Sq.

21292 ■ Genesis Health Care
101 E State St.
Kennett Sq., PA 19348
Ph: (610)925-4060
Free: 800-944-7776
Fax: (610)925-4000
E-mail: info@genesishcc.com
URL: http://www.genesishcc.com/

King of Prussia

21293 ■ Hospice Inspiris-King of Prussia
1006 W 8th Ave.
King of Prussia, PA 19406
Ph: (610)265-2066
Fax: (610)265-2766
URL: http://www.hospiceinspiris.com/

21294 ■ Seasons Hospice and Palliative Care of Pennsylvania
700 S Henderson Rd., Ste. 225
King of Prussia, PA 19406
Ph: (888)839-7410
Fax: (619)768-7701
E-mail: info@seasons.org
URL: http://www.honoringlife-offeringhope.org/cont_penn.html

Knox

21295 ■ Clarion Forest VNA Hospice
305 Main St.
P0 Box 668
Knox, PA 16232
Ph: (814)797-1492
Free: 800-428-1481
URL: http://www.cfvna.org/

Lancaster

21296 ■ Heartland Home Health and Hospice--Lancaster
217 Granite Run Dr., Ste. 200
Lancaster, PA 17601
Ph: (717)581-1450
URL: http://www.hcr-manorcare.com

21297 ■ Hospice of Lancaster County
685 Good Dr.
Lancaster, PA 17604-4125
Ph: (717)295-3900
Fax: (717)391-9582
E-mail: info@hospiceoflancaster.org
URL: http://www.hospiceoflancaster.org

Langhorne

21298 ■ St. Mary's Medical Center-Langhorne
1201 Langhorne Newtown Rd.
Langhorne, PA 19047
Ph: (215)710-4616
Fax: (215)710-2851
URL: http://www.stmaryhealthcare.org/

Lemont Furnace

21299 ■ Fayette Home Care and Hospice
110 Youngstown Rd.
Lemont Furnace, PA 15456
Ph: (724)430-6833
Fax: (724)430-6850
URL: http://www.fayettehomecare.net/

Lewisburg

21300 ■ Evangelical Hospice
1 Hospital Dr.
Lewisburg, PA 17837
Ph: (570)522-2550
Free: 800-377-3826
E-mail: information@evanhospital.com
URL: http://www.evanhospital.com

Mars

21301 ■ Celtic Hospice and Palliative Care Services LLC
150 Scharberry La.
Mars, PA 16046
Ph: (724)625-4280
Free: 800-355-8894
Fax: (800)931-4288
E-mail: info@celtichealthcare.com
URL: http://celtichealthcare.com/pallative-hospice.php

Masontown

21302 ■ Albert Gallatin Home Care and Hospice Services--Masontown
Amedisys Home Health Services
2181 McClellandtown Rd.
Masontown, PA 15461
Ph: (724)583-2680
Free: 866-583-9675
Fax: (724)583-2685
URL: http://www.amedisys.com/hospice_locations.cfm?id=25

Meadville

21303 ■ Hospice of Crawford County
464 Pine St.
Meadville, PA 16335
Ph: (814)333-5403
Fax: (814)333-5407

Monongahela

21304 ■ Albert Gallatin Home Care and Hospice Services--Monogahela
Amedisys Home Health Services
100 Stoops Dr.
Monongahela, PA 15063
Ph: (724)483-4109
Fax: (724)483-4015
URL: http://www.amedisys.com/hospice_locations.cfm?id=25

21305 ■ ViaQuest Inc.
610 Park Ave.
Monongahela, PA 15063
Ph: (724)258-2580
Fax: (724)258-2568
URL: http://www.viaquestinc.com/hc_services.html

Monroeville

21306 ■ Cedards Hospice Home
4363 Northern Pike
Monroeville, PA 15146
Ph: (412)229-3960
Fax: (412)373-2685
URL: http://www.cedarscommunityhospice.com/hospice_center.html

Mountville

21307 ■ AseraCare Hospice--Mountville
315 Primrose Ln., Ste. 101
Mountville, PA 17554
Ph: (717)285-2039
Fax: (717)285-7761
URL: http://www.aseracare.com

New Castle

21308 ■ Celtic Healthcare of Lawrence
1000 S Mercer St., 1st Fl.
New Castle, PA 16101
Free: 800-355-8894
Fax: (724)656-4170
E-mail: info@celtichealthcare.com
URL: http://www.celtichealthcare.com/

21309 ■ Celtic Hospice and Palliative Care
1000 S Mercer St., lst Fl.
New Castle, PA 16101
Free: 800-355-8894
Fax: (724)656-4170
E-mail: info@celtichealthcare.com
URL: http://celtichealthcare.com/pallative-hospice.php

21310 ■ Jameson Hospice of Lawrence County
Jameson Hospital North Campus
1211 Wilmington Ave.
New Castle, PA 16105
Ph: (724)658-9001
Fax: (724)656-4241
URL: http://jamesonhealth.org/hospice-end-of-life-care

Norristown

21311 ■ Montgomery Hospital Hospice Program
25 W Fornance St.
Norristown, PA 19401
Ph: (610)272-1080
Fax: (610)272-0163
URL: http://www.montgomeryhospital.org/homecare-hospice-services-182.html

North East

21312 ■ Community Nursing Services of Northeast
7 Park St.
North East, PA 16428
Ph: (814)725-4300
Fax: (814)725-4664
URL: http://www.northeastnurses.com

North Wales

21313 ■ Hospice of the Madlyn & Leonard Abramson Center for Jewish Life
1425 Horsham Rd.
North Wales, PA 19454
Ph: (215)371-1393
Fax: (215)371-3035
URL: http://www.abramsoncenter.org/

Olyphant

21314 ■ VNA Hospice and Palliative Care Center of Lackawanna County
301 Delaware Ave.
Olyphant, PA 18447
Ph: (570)383-5180
Free: 800-936-7671
Fax: (570)383-5189
E-mail: vnahospice@teisprint.com
URL: http://www.vnahospice.org

Oxford

21315 ■ Brandywine River Valley Hospice
121 Bell Tower La.
Oxford, PA 19363
Ph: (610)998-1700
Fax: (610)998-1799

Peckville

21316 ■ AseraCare Hospice-Mid Valley Hospital
1400 Main St.
Peckville, PA 18452
Ph: (570)586-4579
Fax: (570)583-5711
URL: http://www.aseracare.com/

Philadelphia

21317 ■ Friends Hospice
706 W Girard Ave.
Philadelphia, PA 19123
Ph: (215)925-6848
Fax: (215)925-6846
E-mail: info@friendshospice.org
URL: http://www.friendshospice.org

21318 ■ Holy Redeemer Home Care and Hospice
12265 Townsend Rd.
Philadelphia, PA 19154-1201
Ph: (215)671-9200
Free: 800-346-6462
URL: http://www.holyredeemer.com/Main/Public/HospiceServices1.aspx

21319 ■ Hospice of the VNA of Greater Philadelphia
3300 Henry Ave., 5th Fl.
Philadelphia, PA 19129
Ph: (215)581-2046
Fax: (215)581-2049
E-mail: hospice@vnaphilly.org
URL: http://www.vnaphilly.org

21320 ■ Nazareth Hospital Hospice
Inpatient Unit - VITAS
Holy Family Bldg., 2nd Fl.
2601 Holme Ave.
Philadelphia, PA 19152
Ph: (215)209-1080
Free: 800-938-4827
Fax: (215)335-6648
URL: http://www.vitas.com

21321 ■ Palliative Care Services
Fox Chase Cancer Center
333 Cottman Ave.
Philadelphia, PA 19111
Ph: (215)728-3011
Fax: (215)728-5270
URL: http://www.fccc.edu

21322 ■ Saint Agnes Medical Center Hospice
Inpatient Unit - VITAS
1900 S Broad St.
Philadelphia, PA 19145
Ph: (215)339-4320
Free: 800-938-4827
Fax: (215)339-5521
URL: http://www.vitas.com/

21323 ■ VITAS - Frankfort Hospital Hospice Inpatient Unit
4900 Frankford Ave., 3rd Fl.
Philadelphia, PA 19124
Ph: (215)831-2563
Free: 800-938-4827
Fax: (215)831-2560
URL: http://www.vitas.com

Pittsburgh

21324 ■ AseraCare Hospice--Pittsburgh
1500 Ardmore Blvd., Ste. 501
Pittsburgh, PA 15221
Ph: (412)271-2273
Fax: (412)271-3611
URL: http://www.aseracare.com

21325 ■ Bethany Hospice Services
6 Parkway Ctr., Ste. 100
Pittsburgh, PA 15220
Ph: (412)921-2209
Free: 877-781-2221
E-mail: info@bethanyhospice.com
URL: http://www.bethanyhospice.com

21326 ■ Family Hospice & Palliative Care
50 Moffett St.
Pittsburgh, PA 15243
Ph: (412)572-8800
Fax: (412)572-8826
E-mail: rsciullo@familyhospice.com
URL: http://www.familyhospice.com
Formerly: Family Hospice.

21327 ■ Forbes Hospice
4800 Friendship Ave.
Pittsburgh, PA 15224
Ph: (412)325-7200
Free: 800-381-8080
Fax: (412)325-7303
URL: http://www.wpahs.org/hospice/

21328 ■ Gateway Health Care, Hospice and Palliative Care Services
9380 McKnight Rd., Ste. 201
Pittsburgh, PA 15237
Ph: (412)536-2020
Free: 877-878-2244
Fax: (412)536-2021
E-mail: info@gatewayhospice.com
URL: http://www.gatewayhospice.com

21329 ■ Heartland Home Health Care and Hospice--Pittsburgh
750 Holiday Dr., Ste. 110
Pittsburgh, PA 15220
Ph: (412)928-2126
Fax: (412)928-2127
E-mail: careline@hcr-manorcare.com
URL: http://www.hcr-manorcare.com
Formerly: In Home Health.

21330 ■ Hope Hospice Inc.--Pittsburgh
3292 Babcock Blvd.
Pittsburgh, PA 15237-2839
Ph: (412)367-3685
Free: 877-367-3685
URL: http://www.hopehospicepgh.org

21331 ■ Interim HealthCare Hospice of Western PA, Inc.
1789 S Braddock Ave., Ste. 220
Pittsburgh, PA 15218
Ph: (412)371-3726
Fax: (412)243-4313
URL: http://www.interimhealthcare.com/pittsburghpa/

21332 ■ Odyssey HealthCare of Pennsylvania
190 Bilmar Dr., Ste. 200
Pittsburgh, PA 15205
Ph: (412)920-5500
Free: 877-637-9432
Fax: (412)920-5515
E-mail: info@odsyhealth.com
URL: http://www.odsyhealth.com

21333 ■ Sivitz Jewish Hospice
200 JHF Dr.
Pittsburgh, PA 15217
Ph: (412)422-5700
Free: 866-395-9086
Fax: (412)422-4547
E-mail: dgritzer@jaapgh.org
URL: http://www.jaapgh.org/services_sivitz.asp

Pittston

21334 ■ Heartland Homecare and Hospice--Pittston
38 N Main St.
Pittston, PA 18640
Ph: (570)654-0220
Fax: (570)654-0360
URL: http://www.hcr-manorcare.com/

Plains

21335 ■ Amedisys Hospice Care of Plains
672 N River St.
Plains, PA 18705
Ph: (570)829-0880
Fax: (570)829-0889
URL: http://www.amedisys.com/

Pottstown

21336 ■ Tri County Hospice
13 Armand Hammer Blvd.
Pottstown, PA 19464
Ph: (610)327-7216
Fax: (610)327-7562
URL: http://www.pottstownmemorial.com/Services/Pages/Home%20Care.aspx

21337 ■ Visiting Nurses Association of Pottstown and Vicinity
1963 E High St.
Pottstown, PA 19464
Ph: (610)327-5700
Free: 888-862-2911
Fax: (610)327-5701
URL: http://www.vnapottstown.org

Pottsville

21338 ■ Covenant Home Care-Pottsville
1510 Hwy 61 S
Pottsville, PA 17901
Ph: (570)385-5522
Fax: (570)385-5287
URL: http://www.covenanthc.org/

Punxsutawney

21339 ■ Family Hospice of Punxsutawney VNA of Indiana County
Station Square Ste. 15
RR #5, Box 27E
Punxsutawney, PA 15767
Ph: (814)938-2385
Free: 800-272-7943
Fax: (724)465-3182
URL: http://vnaa.org/vnaa/vna/Family___Hospice_of_Punxsutawney,PAINDI04.aspx

Reading

21340 ■ Covenant Home Care-Berks County
2615 Perkiomen Ave.
Reading, PA 19606
Ph: (610)779-6432
Free: 800-726-8761
Fax: (610)779-5002
URL: http://www.covenanthc.org/content/about/

Roaring Spring

21341 ■ Nason Hospital Hospice
108 Nason Dr.
Roaring Spring, PA 16673
Ph: (814)224-6218
Fax: (814)224-6248
URL: http://nasonhospital.com/

Saint Marys

21342 ■ Community Nurses, Inc.
757 Johnsonburg Rd.
Saint Marys, PA 15857
Ph: (814)781-1415
Free: 800-841-9397
Fax: (814)781-6917
E-mail: info@communitynurses.org
URL: http://www.communitynurses.org/

Scottdale

21343 ■ Albert Gallatin Home Care and Hospice Services--Scottdale Amedisys Home Health Services
109 Crossroads Rd.
Scottdale, PA 15683
Ph: (724)626-2194
Fax: (724)626-2768
URL: http://www.amedisys.com/hospice_locations.cfm?id=25

Scranton

21344 ■ Inpatient Unit at Community Medical Center
1800 Mulberry St.
Scranton, PA 18510
Ph: (570)969-7111
Fax: (570)969-7120

Scranton Ave.

21345 ■ Mercy Hospice-Scranton
746 Jefferson Ave.
Scranton Ave., PA 18510
Ph: (570)961-0725
Fax: (570)340-5484
URL: http://www.health-partners.org/

Sellersville

21346 ■ Grand View Hospital Hospice
700 Lawn Ave.
Sellersville, PA 18960
Ph: (215)453-4210
Fax: (215)453-4328
URL: http://www.gvh.org/homepage.cfm?id=1

Sharon

21347 ■ Sharon Regional Health System
2320 Highland Rd.
Sharon, PA 16146
Ph: (724)938-3878
Free: 866-852-3960
E-mail: dgarrett@ atssrhs-pa.org
URL: http://www.sharonregional.com/hospice.asp

Somerset

21348 ■ In Touch Hospice Program Somerset Hospital
1474 N Center Ave.
Somerset, PA 15501
Ph: (814)443-5047
Fax: (814)443-5269

State College

21349 ■ Centre Crossings Hospice
2437 Commercial Blvd., Ste. 6
State College, PA 16801
Ph: (814)237-7400
Fax: (814)237-2900

Stroudsburg

21350 ■ Stroudsburg Hospice
296 E Brown St.
Stroudsburg, PA 18301
Ph: (615)465-7000

Susquehanna Twp.

21351 ■ Carolyn Croxton Slane Residence
1701 Linglestown Rd.
Susquehanna Twp., PA 17110
Ph: (717)732-1000
Free: 866-779-7374
E-mail: residence@hospiceofcentralpa.org
URL: http://www.hospiceofcentralpa.org

Titusville

21352 ■ Hospice of Crawford County
310 N Monroe St.
Titusville, PA 16354
Ph: (814)827-0330
Fax: (814)827-0371

Towanda

21353 ■ Guthrie Home Care DBA Guthrie Hospice
RR 1, Box 154
Towanda, PA 18848
Ph: (570)265-8615
Free: 800-4-GUTHRI
Fax: (570)265-5208
URL: http://www.guthrie.org/services/homecare

21354 ■ Memorial Hospital Hospice
1 Hospital Dr.
Towanda, PA 18848
Ph: (570)268-2374
Fax: (570)265-0932
E-mail: info@memorialhospital.org
URL: http://www.memorialhospital.org/Hospice.html

Uniontown

21355 ■ Albert Gallatin Home Care and Hospice--Uniontown
20 Highland Park Dr., Ste. 302
Uniontown, PA 15401
Ph: (724)438-6660
Free: 800-245-4144
Formerly: Albert Gallatin Hospice Program.

Warminster

21356 ■ Abington Hospice at Warminster-Hospice Volunteer Office
225 Newtown Rd.
Warminster, PA 18979
Ph: (215)441-6834
URL: http://www.amh.org/

Warren

21357 ■ Hospice of Warren County
2 Crescent Pk. W
Warren, PA 16365
Ph: (814)723-2455
Fax: (814)723-6259
E-mail: hospiceofwarren@wgh.org
URL: http://www.hospiceofwarrencounty.com

Washington

21358 ■ Hospice Care of the Washington Hospital
10 Leet St.
Washington, PA 15301-3382
Ph: (724)250-4500
Fax: (724)250-4558
E-mail: info@washingtonhospital.org
URL: http://www.washingtonhospital.org/hospice_new.htm

Wellsboro

21359 ■ Laurel Home Health / Hospice
24 Walnut St.
Wellsboro, PA 16901
Ph: (570)723-0760
Free: 800-808-5287
Fax: (570)723-0789
URL: http://www.laurelhs.org

West Chester

21360 ■ Neighborhood Hospice
400 E Marshall St.
West Chester, PA 19380
Ph: (610)696-6511
Free: 800-848-1155
Fax: (610)344-7064
URL: http://www.nvnacc.com/

West Grove

21361 ■ Willow Tree Hospice
100 Sycamore Dr.
West Grove, PA 19390
Ph: (610)869-2201
Fax: (610)869-2011
E-mail: info@willowtreehospice.com
URL: http://www.willowtreehospice.com/

Wilkes Barre

21362 ■ Hospice of the Sacred Heart
600 Baltimore Dr.
Wilkes Barre, PA 18702
Ph: (570)706-2400
Fax: (570)970-9717
E-mail: wecare@hospicesacredheart.org
URL: http://www.hospicesacredheart.org/

Williamsport

21363 ■ Susquehanna HomeCare & Hospice
1100 Grampian Blvd.
Williamsport, PA 17701
Ph: (570)320-7691
Fax: (570)320-7898
URL: http://www.susquehannahealth.org/

Willow Grove

21364 ■ Hospice Compassus-Willow Grove
711 York Rd.
Willow Grove, PA 19090
Ph: (215)653-7310
Fax: (215)653-7340
URL: http://www.samaritancarehospice.com/index.cfm

Windber

21365 ■ Windber Hospice
600 Somerset Ave.
Windber, PA 15963
Ph: (814)467-3646
Fax: (814)467-3466
E-mail: rberkey@windbercare.org
URL: http://www.windbercare.org/windberhospice/index.asp

Wyndmoor

21366 ■ Keystone Care, LLC
8765 Stenton Ave.
Wyndmoor, PA 19038
Ph: (215)836-2440
Fax: (215)836-2448
URL: http://www.keystonecare.com

Wyomissing

21367 ■ Diakon Hospice Saint John-Wyomissing
1030 Reed Ave.
Wyomissing, PA 19610
Ph: (610)320-7980
Fax: (610)320-7974
URL: http://www.diakon.org/Hospice/

21368 ■ Heartland Home Health Care and Hospice--Wyomissing
4 Park Plaza, Ste. 105
Park Rd.
Wyomissing, PA 19610
Ph: (610)373-6898
Free: 800-427-1902
Fax: (610)373-6098
E-mail: careline@hcr-manorcare.com
URL: http://www.hcr-manorcare.com/

York

21369 ■ AseraCare Hospice--York
44 Bowman Rd.
York, PA 17404
Ph: (717)845-8599
Free: 888-273-0935
Fax: (717)718-4463
URL: http://www.aseracare.com

21370 ■ Heartland Home Health Care and Hospice-York
3417C Concord Rd.
York, PA 17402
Ph: (717)840-1002
Fax: (717)840-1690
URL: http://www.hcr-manorcare.com/

21371 ■ VNA Home Health and Hospice-Wellspan
540 S George St.
York, PA 17401
Ph: (717)812-4433
Fax: (717)812-8189
URL: http://www.wellspan.org/

21372 ■ White Rose Hospice Memorial Hospital
1412 6th Ave.
York, PA 17403
Ph: (717)849-5642
Fax: (717)849-5630
URL: http://www.mhyork.org/Services/White-Rose-Hospice.aspx

21373 ■ York Hospital Department of Palliative Care
1001 S George St.
York, PA 17403
Ph: (717)851-3467
Fax: (717)851-4184
URL: http://www.wellspan.org/

PUERTO RICO

Adjuntas

21374 ■ Servicios de Hospicio de Adjuntas
46 Calle Rodulfo Gonzalez
Adjuntas, PR 00601
Ph: (787)829-2953
Fax: (787)829-1093
URL: http://pr-adjuntas.doctors.at/dr/servicios-de-hospicio-de-adjuntas

Arecibo

21375 ■ Hospicio La Paz Inc.
152 Rodriguez Irizarry St.
Arecibo, PR 00612-4625
Ph: (787)878-1548
Free: 800-981-0032
Fax: (787)880-0832

Bayamon

21376 ■ Healthkeepers Hospice, Inc.
Calle 1 B-14 Urb Santa Cruz
Bayamon, PR 00961-6922
Ph: (787)786-4626
Fax: (787)786-4676

21377 ■ Servicios Suplementarios De Salud, Inc.
Ave Carlos Andaluz, X-48
Bayamon, PR 00956
Ph: (787)780-4010

Ponce

21378 ■ Hospicio La Guadalupe Inc.
PO Box 7699
Ponce, PR 00732
Ph: (787)259-8210
Fax: (787)259-0206
E-mail: hospigua@prtc.net

21379 ■ Hospicio San Judas
PO Box 7750
Ponce, PR 00732
Ph: (787)840-8356
Free: 866-740-8356
Fax: (787)842-0797

RHODE ISLAND

East Providence

21380 ■ Beacon Hospice-East Providence
1 Catamore Blvd.
East Providence, RI 02914
Ph: (401)438-0008
Fax: (401)438-2252
URL: http://www.beaconhospice.com/

Lincoln

21381 ■ Visiting Nurse Association of Greater Rhode Island
Six Blackstone Valley Place
Lincoln, RI 02865
Free: 800-696-7991
Fax: (401)762-7300
E-mail: ccc@vnsgri.org
URL: http://www.vnsgri.org/

Newport

21382 ■ Hospice at Visiting Nurse Service of Newport Bristol County
21 Chapel St.
Newport, RI 02840
Ph: (401)682-2100
Fax: (401)682-2887

North Smithfield

21383 ■ The Suite at St. Antoine
10 Rhodes Ave.
North Smithfield, RI 02896
Ph: (401)767-3500
Free: 800-696-7991
URL: http://www.stantoine.net/residence.htm

Pawtucket

21384 ■ Hospice of Nursing Placement, Inc.
334 East Ave.
Pawtucket, RI 02860
Ph: (401)728-6500
Fax: (401)728-6509
URL: http://www.nursingplacement.com/hnp.html

Portsmouth

21385 ■ Hospice at Visiting Nurse Service of Newport Bristol County
1184 E Main Rd.
Portsmouth, RI 02871
Ph: (401)682-2100
Free: 800-456-1195
Fax: (401)682-2111
URL: http://www.vnsri.com

Providence

21386 ■ Home and Hospice Care of RI Philip Hulitar Inpatient Center
1085 N Main St.
Providence, RI 02904
Ph: (401)351-5570
Free: 877-322-1678
Fax: (401)351-2813
URL: http://www.hhcri.org

Warwick

21387 ■ Odyssey Health Care of Rhode Island
2374 Post Rd., Ste. 206
Warwick, RI 02886
Ph: (401)738-1492
Free: 877-637-9432
Fax: (401)738-4029
E-mail: info@odsyhealth.com
URL: http://www.odsyhealth.com

SOUTH CAROLINA

Abbeville

21388 ■ Hospice Care of South Carolina-Abbeville
103 W Pickens St.
Abbeville, SC 29620
Ph: (864)366-2273
Fax: (864)366-2276
E-mail: erin.richardson@hospicecare.net
URL: http://www.hospicecare.net/
Erin Richardson, Director

Aiken

21389 ■ Hospice Care of South Carolina-Aiken
946 Millbrooke Ave., Ste. A
Aiken, SC 29803
Ph: (803)649-9201
Fax: (888)732-8116
E-mail: shanna.blackmon@hospicecare.net
URL: http://www.hospicecare.net/
Shanna Blackmon, Director

21390 ■ Liberty Home Care & Hospice
610 Aldrich St., NE
Aiken, SC 29801
Ph: (803)643-0001
Free: 888-858-7114
Fax: (803)649-0490
URL: http://www.libertyhomecare.com/

21391 ■ Regency Hospice--Aiken
105 Summerwood Way, Ste. D
Aiken, SC 29803
Ph: (803)648-2117
Fax: (803)648-9107
URL: http://www.regencyhospice.com

21392 ■ Trinity Home Services-Aiken Center for Hospice and Palliative Care
690 Medical Park Dr.
Aiken, SC 29801
Ph: (803)643-0001
Fax: (803)648-7045

Anderson

21393 ■ Hallmark Hospice, LLC
117 Broadbent Way
Anderson, SC 29625
Ph: (864)224-6757
Fax: (864)224-8688
URL: http://www.solarishc.com/

21394 ■ Hospice of the Upstate
1835 Rogers Rd.
Anderson, SC 29621
Ph: (864)224-3358
Free: 800-261-8636
Fax: (864)328-1132
E-mail: office@hospicehouse.ne
URL: http://www.hospicehouse.net

Barnwell

21395 ■ Hospice Care of South Carolina-Barnwell
27 Hugh St.
Barnwell, SC 29812
Ph: (803)541-7114
Fax: (888)470-2963
E-mail: jeffp@hospicecare.net
URL: http://www.hospicecare.net
Jeff Plummer, Director

Bishopville

21396 ■ Hospice Care of South Carolina-Bishopville
121 N Main St.
Bishopville, SC 29010
Ph: (803)484-6869
Fax: (888)847-6103
E-mail: michelle.wrona@hospicecare.net
URL: http://www.hospicecare.net
Michelle Wrona, Director

Bluffton

21397 ■ Hospice Care of the Lowcountry, Inc.
PO Box 3827
Bluffton, SC 29910
Ph: (843)706-2296
Fax: (843)706-4095
URL: http://www.hospicecarelc.org/

21398 ■ Tidewater Hospice
10 Buckingham Plantation Dr.
Bluffton, SC 29910
Ph: (843)757-9388
Fax: (866)527-0937
E-mail: Living@TidewaterHospice.com
URL: http://www.tidewaterhospice.com/

Camden

21399 ■ Kershaw Health Hospice
2001 W Dekalb St.
Camden, SC 29020
Ph: (803)425-1916
Fax: (803)713-1650
URL: http://www.kershawhealth.org/services/hospice.aspx

Charleston

21400 ■ A Caring Heart Hospice
6296 Rivers Ave., Ste. 307
Charleston, SC 29406
Ph: (843)225-2300
Fax: (843)225-2301

21401 ■ Heartland Hospice Services--Charleston
1064 Gardner Rd.
Charleston, SC 29407
Ph: (843)766-7646
Fax: (843)766-9766
E-mail: careline@hcr-manorcare.com
URL: http://www.hcr-manorcare.com

21402 ■ Odyssey HealthCare of Charleston
5965 Core Rd.
Charleston, SC 29406
Ph: (843)554-4048
Fax: (843)747=6407
URL: http://www.odsyhealth.com

21403 ■ Winyah Community Hospice
1027 Physicians Dr.
Charleston, SC 29414
Ph: (843)554-7161
Fax: (843)554-7830

Chesterfield

21404 ■ Hospice of Chesterfield County, Inc.
PO Box 293
Chesterfield, SC 29709
Ph: (843)623-9155
Free: 800-572-9322
Fax: (843)623-3833
URL: http://www.hospiceofchesterfieldcounty.com/

Clinton

21405 ■ Hospice Care of South Carolina
100 Plaza Circle
Clinton, SC 29325
Ph: (864)833-3002
Fax: (864)833-3006

21406 ■ Hospice of Laurens County Inc.
1304 Springdale Dr.
Clinton, SC 29325
Ph: (864)833-6287
Free: 800-465-4454
Fax: (864)833-0556
E-mail: hospice@backroads.com
URL: http://www.hospiceoflaurenscounty.com

Columbia

21407 ■ Columbia IP-Portsbridge
141 Stoneridge Dr.
Columbia, SC 29210
Ph: (803)939-2788
Fax: (803)939-4640

21408 ■ Gentiva Hospice--Columbia
534 St. Andrews Rd.
Columbia, SC 29210
Ph: (803)213-9980
Fax: (803)213-9989
URL: http://www.gentiva.com/hospice/hospice_locations.php

21409 ■ Harmony Care Hospice
100 Ashland Park La., Ste. K
Columbia, SC 29210
Ph: (803)223-6544
Fax: (803)223-6550
E-mail: info@harmonycarehospice.com
URL: http://www.harmonycarehospice.com/

21410 ■ Heartstrings Hospice, Inc.
115 Blarney Dr.
Columbia, SC 29223
Ph: (803)699-3233
Free: 877-599-3233
Fax: (803)699-3919
URL: http://www.heartstringshospice.com/

21411 ■ Hospice Care of Tri-County--Columbia
166 Stone Ridge Dr., Ste. 100
Columbia, SC 29210
Ph: (803)750-8697
Fax: (803)750-8695
URL: http://www.msa-corp.com/companies/hospice-careoftricounty.aspx

21412 ■ Palmetto Health Hospice--Columbia
1400 Pickens St.
Columbia, SC 29202
Ph: (803)296-3100
Free: 800-238-1884
Fax: (803)296-3320
URL: http://www.palmettohealth.org/body.cfm?id=1371

21413 ■ Regency Hospice-Columbia
140 Stoneridge Dr.
Columbia, SC 22910
Ph: (803)765-0099
Fax: (803)765-0091
URL: http://www.gentiva.com/hospice/hospice_locations.php

21414 ■ Winyah Community Hospice Care - Columbia
305 Stoneridge Dr., Ste. B
Columbia, SC 29210
Ph: (803)794-2515
Free: 877-794-2515
Fax: (803)794-2514

Conway

21415 ■ Heartland Hospice Services--Conway
1500 Main St.
Conway, SC 29526
Ph: (843)248-2061
Fax: (843)381-0934
URL: http://www.hcr-manorcare.com/

21416 ■ Hospice Care of South Carolina-Horry
1320-G Hwy. 501 Business
Conway, SC 29526
Ph: (843)347-2200
Fax: (888)277-8781
E-mail: adinan@hospicecare.net
URL: http://www.hospicecare.net/

21417 ■ Mercy Care-Treasures of the Heart
1227 16th Ave.
Conway, SC 29526
Ph: (843)488-0906
URL: http://www.mercyhospice.org/

21418 ■ Solaris Hospice Myrtle Beach
National HealthCare Corporation
124 Professional Pk. Dr.
Conway, SC 29526
Ph: (843)349-4400
Fax: (843)349-4401
URL: http://www.nhccare.com/search.cfm

Dillon

21419 ■ Community Home Care and Hospice--Dillon
805 N 8th Ave.
Dillon, SC 29536
Ph: (843)841-1135
URL: http://www.communityhch.com/

Edgefield

21420 ■ Hospice Care of South Carolina-Edgefield
211 A Norris St.
Edgefield, SC 29824
Ph: (803)637-1901
Fax: (888)264-6183
E-mail: thomas.sample@hospicecare.net
URL: http://www.hospicecare.net/
Thomas Sample, Director

Esley

21421 ■ Hospice Care of South Carolina-Pickens
900 E Main St.
Esley, SC 29640
Ph: (864)850-1100
Fax: (888)521-3837
E-mail: Judith.witthoeft@hospicecare.net
URL: http://www.hospicecare.net/
Judith Witthoeft, Director

Fairfax

21422 ■ Hospice Care of South Carolina-Hampton-Allendale
761 Allendale-Fairfax Hwy.
Fairfax, SC 29827
Ph: (803)702-4252
Fax: (888)868-9810
E-mail: johnnieb@hospicecare.net
URL: http://www.hospicecare.net/
Johnnie Benson, Director

Florence

21423 ■ Carolinas Hospice
121 E Cedar St.
Florence, SC 29501
Ph: (843)629-6800
Fax: (843)629-6870
URL: http://www.carolinashospital.com/medical-services/community-health/carolina s-hospice.asp

21424 ■ McLeod Hospice
McLeod Regional Medical Center
1203 E Cheves St.
Florence, SC 29501-4449
Ph: (843)777-2564
Free: 800-768-4556
URL: http://www.mcleodhealth.org/MRMC/hospice.cfm

21425 ■ Winyah Community Hospice Care--Florence
Amedisys
217 Dozier Blvd.
Florence, SC 29501
Ph: (843)656-0820
Free: 877-656-0820
Fax: (866)669-7957
URL: http://www.amedisys.com/hospice_locations.cfm?id=13

Gaffney

21426 ■ Hospice Care of South Carolina-Cherokee
1612 N Limestone St.
Gaffney, SC 29341
Ph: (864)487-3166
Fax: (888)526-2413
E-mail: amandak@hospicecare.net
URL: http://www.hospicecare.net
Amanda Knowles, Director

Garden City

21427 ■ Regency Hospice-Myrtle Beach
11943 Grand Haven Dr.
Garden City, SC 29576
Ph: (843)651-2335
Fax: (843)651-2385
URL: http://www.regencyhospice.com/

Georgetown

21428 ■ Hospice Care of South Carolina-Georgetown
722 N Fraser St., Unit C
Georgetown, SC 29440
Ph: (843)520-4400
Fax: (888)534-0427
E-mail: adinan@hospicecare.com
URL: http://www.hospicecare.net/
Adina Norton, Director

21429 ■ Tidelands Community Hospice, Inc.
2591 N Fraser St.
Georgetown, SC 29440
Ph: (843)546-3410
Free: 888-922-3410
Fax: (843)527-6964
URL: http://www.tidelandshospice.org

Greenville

21430 ■ Abundant Life Hospice
744 E Stove Ave.
Greenville, SC 29601
Ph: (864)370-9707
Fax: (864)370-9706
E-mail: www.all.employees@lifewithdignity.net
URL: https://sites.google.com/a/lifewithdignity.net/www/

21431 ■ Gentiva Hospice Greenville
430 Roper Mountain Rd., Ste. E
Greenville, SC 29615
Ph: (864)329-0588
Fax: (864)329-0986
URL: http://www.gentiva.com/hospice/hospice_locations.php#sc
Formerly: Wiregrass Hospice Greenville.

21432 ■ Hospice Care of South Carolina-Greenville
1 Caledon Ct., Ste. 1-A
Greenville, SC 29615
Ph: (864)235-0344
Fax: (888)317-3645
E-mail: kayburns@hospicecare.net
URL: http://www.hospicecare.net/
Kay Burns, Director

21433 ■ St. Francis Health System
317 Saint Francis Dr.
Greenville, SC 29601
Ph: (864)255-1000
Fax: (864)255-1349
URL: http://www.saintfrancis.com/

21434 ■ Solaris Hospice-Greenville
National HealthCare Corporation
111 Smith Hines Rd., Ste. D
Greenville, SC 29607
Ph: (864)297-7444
URL: http://www.nhccare.com/search.cfm

21435 ■ VistaCare--Brendan Way, Greenville
15 Brendan Way, Ste. 100
Greenville, SC 29615-2347
Ph: (864)297-3164
Free: 866-779-6855
Fax: (864)297-3159
URL: http://www.vistacare.com

21436 ■ Winyah Community Hospice Care--Greenville
Amedisys
880 Pleasantburg Dr., Unit A & F
Greenville, SC 29607
Ph: (864)335-0455
Free: 866-381-2085
Fax: (864)335-0456
URL: http://www.amedisys.com/

Greenwood

21437 ■ Hospice Care of South Carolina-Greenwood
231 Hampton Ave., Ste. A
Greenwood, SC 29646
Ph: (864)227-2555
Fax: (888)539-6827
E-mail: erin.richardson@hospicecare.net
URL: http://www.hospicecare.net/
Erin Richardson, Director

21438 ■ HospiceCare of the Piedmont, Inc.
408 W Alexander Ave.
Greenwood, SC 29646
Ph: (864)227-9393
Fax: (864)227-9377
E-mail: info@hospicepiedmont.org
URL: http://www.hospicepiedmont.org

Greer

21439 ■ Lutheran Hospice-Upstate
218A Trade St.
Greer, SC 29652
Ph: (864)848-1777
Free: 888-547-2562
Fax: (864)877-3441
E-mail: info@lutheranhospice.org
URL: http://www.lutheranhospice.org

Hardeeville

21440 ■ Island Hospice--Hardeeville
300 New River Pkwy.
Hardeeville, SC 29927
Ph: (843)208-3660
Fax: (843)208-3668

Hartsville

21441 ■ LifeCare Hospice of South Carolina, LLC
202 S Second St.
Hartsville, SC 29551
Ph: (843)332-2221
Fax: (843)332-2242

Hilton Head Island

21442 ■ Palmetto Coastal
PO Box 23349
Hilton Head Island, SC 29925
Ph: (843)305-0209
Fax: (843)726-9251

Kingstree

21443 ■ Hospice Care of South Carolina-Williamsburg
131 N Academy St.
Kingstree, SC 29556
Ph: (843)355-3105
Fax: (888)534-3274
E-mail: rebeccab@hospicecare.net
URL: http://www.hospicecare.net/
Rebecca Bradford, Director

Lancaster

21444 ■ Hospice Care of South Carolina-Lancaster
412 N White St., Ste. A
Lancaster, SC 29720
Ph: (803)285-2014
Fax: (888)853-6575
E-mail: janiceb@hospicecare.net
URL: http://www.hospicecare.net/
Janice Broach, Director

21445 ■ Hospice of Lancaster
902 W Meeting St.
Lancaster, SC 29720
Ph: (803)286-1472
Free: 800-488-2567
Fax: (803)286-1378

Landrum

21446 ■ Smith Phayer Hospice House
Hospice of the Carolina Foothills
260 Fairwinds Rd.
Landrum, SC 29356
Ph: (864)457-9100
Fax: (864)457-9130
URL: http://www.hocf.org/services/house.php

Loris

21447 ■ Mercy Care-Loris
4265 Suggs St., Ste. 110
Loris, SC 29569
Ph: (843)848-6480
Fax: (843)347-5535
E-mail: info@mercycare.org
URL: http://www.mercyhospice.org/mercy-care-services.cfm?page=11

McCormick

21448 ■ Hospice Care of South Carolina-McCormick
203 S Main St.
McCormick, SC 29835
Ph: (864)852-6015
Fax: (888)748-4017
E-mail: erin.richardson@hospicecare.net
URL: http://www.hospicecare.net/
Erin Richardson, Director

Moncks Corner

21449 ■ Solaris Hospice-Charleston
National HealthCare Corporation
3751 S Live Oak Dr., Ste. E
Moncks Corner, SC 29461
Ph: (843)402-0614
Fax: (843)402-0893
URL: http://www.nhccare.com/search.cfm

Mount Pleasant

21450 ■ Carolina Hospice Care, Inc.
410 Mill St.
Mount Pleasant, SC 20464
Ph: (843)849-5910
Fax: (843)881-9603
E-mail: info@carolinahospicecare.com
URL: http://carolinahospice.com

21451 ■ Lutheran Hospice-Low Country
1885 Rifle Range Rd., Ste. 46
Mount Pleasant, SC 29464
Ph: (843)856-4735
Free: 800-940-9177
E-mail: info@lutheranshopice.org
URL: http://www.lutheranhospice.org

Mt Pleasant

21452 ■ Hospice Center
Hospice of Charleston-Gentiva
676 Wando Pk. Blvd.
Mt Pleasant, SC 29464
Ph: (843)529-3100
Fax: (843)725-7959
E-mail: rosina.feagin@gentiva.com
URL: http://www.hospiceofcharlestonfoundation.org/programs/hospice_center.html

Mt. Pleasant

21453 ■ Hospice of Charleston
676 Wando Pk. Blvd.
Mt. Pleasant, SC 29464
Ph: (843)529-3100
Free: 800-617-6152
Fax: (843)529-3111
E-mail: rosina.feagin@gentiva.com
URL: http://www.hospiceofcharleston.com/

Myrtle Beach

21454 ■ Mercy Care-Myrtle Beach
PO Box 50640
Myrtle Beach, SC 29579
Ph: (843)347-5500
Fax: (843)347-5535
URL: http://www.mercyhospice.org/

Newberry

21455 ■ Palmetto Health Hospice--Newberry
1400 Camelia Ave.
Newberry, SC 29108
Ph: (803)405-0808
Fax: (803)405-9766
URL: http://www.palmettohealth.org/body.cfm?id=1371

Nichols

21456 ■ Shepherd Care Hospice
210 S Nichols St.
Nichols, SC 29581
Ph: (843)526-1186
Fax: (843)526-1389
URL: http://www.palmettohealth.org/body.cfm?id=1371

North Augusta

21457 ■ Alliance Hospice
802 E Martintown Rd.
North Augusta, SC 29841

Ph: (803)441-0174
Fax: (803)441-0177
E-mail: info@alliancehospice.com
URL: http://www.alliancehospice.com/

Orangeburg

21458 ■ Winyah Community Hospice Care-Orangeburg
Amedisys
1180 Boulevard St., Ste. A & B
Orangeburg, SC 29115
Ph: (803)534-2750
Free: 877-400-0933
Fax: (803)534-3319
URL: http://www.amedisys.com/

Pawley's Island

21459 ■ Winyah Community Hospice Care-Pawleys Island
Amedisys
137 Professional Ln., Unit A
Pawley's Island, SC 29585
Ph: (843)979-0304
Free: 877-652-0093
Fax: (843)979-0228
URL: http://www.amedisys.com/hospice_locations.cfm?id=13

Port Royal

21460 ■ Friends of Caroline Hospice
1110 13th St.
Port Royal, SC 29935
Ph: (843)525-6257
Fax: (843)525-9418
E-mail: carolinehosp@islc.net
URL: http://www.carolinehospice.org

Prosperity

21461 ■ Hospice Care of South Carolina-Newberry
600 N Wheeler Ave.
Prosperity, SC 29127
Ph: (803)364-0625
Fax: (888)808-4173
E-mail: thomas.sample@hospicecare.net
URL: http://www.hospicecare.net/
Thomas Sample, Director

Rock Hill

21462 ■ Hospice Care of South Carolina-York
1230 Ebenezer Rd.
Rock Hill, SC 29732
Ph: (803)324-6288
Fax: (888)832-2156
E-mail: donna.bryant@hospicecare.net
URL: http://www.hospicecare.net/
Donna Bryant, Director

21463 ■ Hospice and Community Care
PO Box 993
Rock Hill, SC 29731
Ph: (803)329-1500
Free: 800-895-2273
Fax: (803)329-5935
E-mail: info@hospicecommunitycare.org
URL: http://www.hospicecommunitycare.org

21464 ■ Regency Hospice-Rock Hill
420 S Herlong Ave., Ste. 104
Rock Hill, SC 29732
Ph: (803)328-2141
Fax: (803)327-9256
URL: http://thomas.samplehospitalpicecare.net

21465 ■ Wayne T Patrick Hospice House
Hospice & Community Care
2275 India Hook Rd.
Rock Hill, SC 29732
Ph: (803)329-1600
Fax: (803)324-6354
E-mail: info@hospicecommunitycare.org
URL: http://www.hospicecommunitycare.org/Patrick-Hospice-House.php

Saluda

21466 ■ Hospice of South Carolina-Saluda
404 Batesburg Hwy.
Saluda, SC 29138
Ph: (864)445-0111
Fax: (888)804-6675
E-mail: thomas.sample@hospicecare.net
URL: http://www.hospicecare.net/
Thomas Sample, Director

Seneca

21467 ■ OMH Hospice of the Foothills
390 Keowee School Rd.
Seneca, SC 29672
Ph: (864)882-8940
Fax: (864)882-7240
URL: http://www.oconeemed.org/

Simpsonville

21468 ■ Heartland Hospice Services--Simpsonville
421 SE Main St.
Simpsonville, SC 29681
Ph: (864)963-0045
Fax: (864)963-0899
URL: http://www.hcr-manorcare.com/

21469 ■ Open Arms Hospice
St. Francis Hospital
1836 W Georgia Rd.
Simpsonville, SC 29680
Ph: (864)688-1700
Fax: (864)688-1705
URL: http://www.stfrancishealth.org/our-services-open-arms-hospice.html

Spartanburg

21470 ■ Hospice Care of South Carolina-Spartanburg
1989 S Pine St.
Spartanburg, SC 29302
Ph: (864)595-1123
Fax: (888)824-9645
E-mail: deedee.mitchell@hospicecare.net
URL: http://www.hospicecare.net/
Dee Dee Mitchell, Director

21471 ■ Hospice Compassus-Spartanburg
500 Jeff Davis Dr.
Spartanburg, SC 29303
Ph: (864)542-2536
Fax: (877)447-2273
E-mail: contactusSCSPG@hospicecom.com
URL: http://www.hospicecompassus.com/loc-SC-SPG.html

21472 ■ Winyah Community Hospice Care-Spartanburg
Amedisys
818-a E Main St.
Spartanburg, SC 29302
Ph: (864)541-7159
Free: 866-951-1240
Fax: (864)541-7163
URL: http://www.amedisys.com/hospice_locations.cfm?id=13

Summerville

21473 ■ Palmetto Health Hospice-Summerville
1815 Old Trolley Rd.
Summerville, SC 29485
Ph: (843)821-4011
Fax: (843)821-4339
URL: http://www.palmettohealth.org/

Sumter

21474 ■ Hospice Care of Tri-County--Sumter
2560 Tahoe Dr.
Sumter, SC 29150
Ph: (803)905-7720
Fax: (803)905-7631

Walterboro

21475 ■ Hospice Care of South Carolina-Colleton
134 Bells Hwy.
Walterboro, SC 29488
Ph: (843)782-3900
Fax: (888)871-3076
E-mail: johnnieb@hospicecare.net
URL: http://www.hospicecare.net/
Johnnie Benson, Director

21476 ■ Winyah Community Hospice Care--Walterboro
Amedisys
203-A & 203-B Eddie Chasteen Dr.
Walterboro, SC 29488
Ph: (843)549-5166
Free: 866-549-5166
Fax: (843)549-5177
URL: http://iweb.nhpco.org/iweb/Membership/MemberDirectorySearch.aspx?pageid=3257&showTitle=1

West Columbia

21477 ■ Solaris Hospice-West Columbia
National HealthCare Corporation
3955 Southeastern Way, Ste. 1-A
West Columbia, SC 29169
Ph: (803)794-4141
URL: http://www.nhccare.com/

White Rock

21478 ■ Lutheran Hospice--White Rock
PO Box 805
White Rock, SC 29177
Ph: (803)749-7770
Fax: (803)479-7774
E-mail: info@lutheranhospice.org
URL: http://www.lutheranhospice.org

SOUTH DAKOTA

Aberdeen

21479 ■ Avera St. Luke's North Plains Hospice
305 S State St.
Aberdeen, SD 57401
Ph: (605)622-5200
Fax: (605)622-5201
URL: http://www.avera.org/st-lukes-hospital/services/hospice/index.aspx

Brookings

21480 ■ Brookings Hospital Hospice
300 22nd Ave.
Brookings, SD 57006
Ph: (605)696-7700
Fax: (605)696-7731
URL: http://www.brookingshospital.org

Flandreau

21481 ■ Avera McKennan Hospice and Palliative Care-Flandreau
214 N Prairie
Flandreau, SD 57028
Ph: (605)997-2433
URL: http://www1.avera.org/amck/regionalfacilities/flandreaumedical/services/ser vices.aspx

Huron

21482 ■ Huron Regional Medical Center Home Care Agency
172 4th St. SE
Huron, SD 57350
Ph: (605)353-6520
Fax: (605)353-6300
E-mail: info@huronregional.org
URL: http://www.huronregional.org

Madison

21483 ■ Madison Community Hospice Avera McKennan Branch
917 N Washington Ave.
Madison, SD 57042
Ph: (605)256-8640
URL: http://www.avera.org/mckennan/services/hospice/hospice-locations.aspx

Miller

21484 ■ Hand County Memorial Hospital Avera
300 W 5th St.
Miller, SD 57362
Ph: (605)853-2421
Fax: (605)853-0333
URL: http://www.avera.org/

Mitchell

21485 ■ Mitchell Community Hospice at Avera Queen of Peace
525 N Foster St.
Mitchell, SD 57301-2966
Ph: (605)995-2268
Fax: (605)995-5624
URL: http://www.averaqueenofpeace.org/aqop/services/hospice/index.aspx

Parkston

21486 ■ St. Benedict Hospice Avera St. Benedict Health Center
401 W Glynn Dr.
Parkston, SD 57366
Ph: (605)928-7368
URL: http://www1.avera.org/aqop/astb/services/hospice/index.aspx

Pierre

21487 ■ Saint Mary's Hospice--Pierre
801 E Sioux Ave.
Pierre, SD 57501
Ph: (605)224-3218
Fax: (605)224-3213
URL: http://www.st-marys.com/outpatientservices_hospice.htm

Rapid City

21488 ■ Hospice of the Hills--Rapid City
224 Elk St.
Rapid City, SD 57701
Ph: (605)719-7780
Fax: (605)719-7719
URL: http://www.regionalhealth.com/Our-Services/Hospice-Care/Hospice-of-the-Hill s.aspx
Marcia Taylor, Director

Sioux Falls

21489 ■ AseraCare Hospice-Sioux Falls
4101 S Westport Ave.
Sioux Falls, SD 57106
Ph: (605)361-0700
Fax: (605)361-9476
URL: http://www.aseracare.com/

21490 ■ Avera McKennan Hospice and Palliative Care
800 E 21st St.
Sioux Falls, SD 57117
Ph: (605)322-7705
Fax: (605)322-7713
URL: http://www.averamckennan.org

21491 ■ Avera McKennan Hospice and Palliative Care-Sioux Falls
800 E 21st St.
Sioux Falls, SD 57117
Ph: (605)322-7705
Fax: (605)322-7715
URL: http://www.avera.org/mckennan/index.aspx

21492 ■ Compassionate Care Hospice of the MidWest
5200 S Cliff Ave., Ste. 103
Sioux Falls, SD 57108
Ph: (605)338-2066
Fax: (605)371-3754
URL: http://www.avera.org/mckennan/index.aspx

21493 ■ Good Samaritan Society-Luther Manor
4800 W 57th St.
Sioux Falls, SD 57108
Ph: (605)336-1997
Fax: (605)362-3319
URL: http://www.good-sam.com/communities/showLocation.asp?backlink=/services/sho wService.asp?id=18&id=233

21494 ■ Sanford Hospice
2710 W 12th St.
Sioux Falls, SD 57104
Ph: (605)328-4440
Fax: (605)328-5963
URL: http://www.sanfordhealth.org
Formerly: Sioux Valley Hospice.

Spearfish

21495 ■ Hospice of the Northern Hills Spearfish Regional Hospital
1440 N Main St.
Spearfish, SD 57783-1505
Ph: (605)644-4444
Free: 800-276-8920
Fax: (605)644-4241
URL: http://www.regionalhealth.com/Our-Locations/Regional-Hospitals/Spearfish-Re gional-Hospital/Health-Services/Hospice.aspx

Wessington Springs

21496 ■ Springs Hospice Avera Weskota Memorial Medical Center
608 1st St NE
Wessington Springs, SD 57382
Ph: (605)539-1201
Fax: (605)539-1844
URL: http://www1.avera.org/aqop/averaweskota/index.aspx

Yankton

21497 ■ Avera Sacred Heart Hospice
501 Summit St.
Yankton, SD 57078
Ph: (605)668-8309
Fax: (605)668-8338
URL: http://www.averasacredheart.com/ash/services/hospice/index.aspx

TENNESSEE

Algood

21498 ■ Caris Healthcare--Algood
2525 Hwy. 111 N
Algood, TN 38506
Ph: (931)537-3430
Fax: (931)537-2340
URL: http://www.carishealthcare.com/

Athens

21499 ■ Amedisys Hospice Services--Athens
614 Congress Pkwy. N
Athens, TN 37303
Ph: (423)507-8755
Free: 866-890-2977
Fax: (423)507-8748
URL: http://www.amedisys.com/
Formerly: Adventa Hospice Services.

21500 ■ Avalon Hospice of Athens
740 Tell St., Ste. 300
Athens, TN 37303
Ph: (423)745-1730
Free: 877-745-1730
Fax: (423)745-1730
URL: http://www.avalon-hospice.com/page/show/148949-avalon-athens

Bristol

21501 ■ Wellmont Hospice House
280 Steeles Rd.
Bristol, TN 37620
Ph: (423)844-5252
Free: 877-230-NURSE
Fax: (423)844-6379
URL: http://www.wellmont.org/Hospitals/Facilities/Wellmont-Hospice-House.aspx

Camden

21502 ■ Tennessee Quality Hospice--Camden
207B Hwy. 641 N
Camden, TN 38320
Ph: (734)584-9500
Free: 866-584-9500
URL: http://www.tnhomecare.com/

Chattanooga

21503 ■ Amedisys Hospice, Inc.--Chattanooga
Bldg. 500A
7161 Lee Hwy., Ste. 400
Chattanooga, TN 37421
Ph: (423)499-0018
Free: 800-951-2561
Fax: (423)499-4342
URL: http://www.amedisys.com/hospice.cfm
Formerly: Housecall Hospice; Adventa Hospice, Inc.

21504 ■ Caris Healthcare--Chattanooga
5959 Shallowford Rd.
Chattanooga, TN 37421
Ph: (423)855-9018
Fax: (423)899-6056
URL: http://www.carishealthcare.com/

21505 ■ Hospice of Chattanooga
4411 Oakwood Dr.
Chattanooga, TN 37416
Ph: (423)892-4289
Free: 800-267-6828
Fax: (423)892-8301
URL: http://www.hospiceofchattanooga.org

Clarksville

21506 ■ AseraCare Hospice-Clarksville
1539 C Ashland City Bypass
Clarksville, TN 37040
Ph: (931)551-4100
Fax: (931)551-8710
URL: http://www.aseracare.com/

21507 ■ Gateway Hospice
1606 Haynes St.
Clarksville, TN 37043
Ph: (931)502-3600
Fax: (931)502-3624
URL: http://www.todaysgateway.com/Pages/home.aspx

Cleveland

21508 ■ Family HomeCare and Hospice
175 24th St. NW
Cleveland, TN 37311
Ph: (423)559-6092
Fax: (423)559-6093

21509 ■ Home Health Care of East Tennessee Inc.
1796 Mount Vernon Dr. NW
Cleveland, TN 37311
Ph: (423)472-9585
Free: 800-545-0418
Fax: (423)614-7118

21510 ■ Hospice of Cleveland
2145 Keith St. NW
Cleveland, TN 37311
Ph: (423)476-3696

Columbia

21511 ■ Caris Healthcare, LP--Columbia
1412 Trotwood Ave.
Columbia, TN 38401
Ph: (931)388-1615
Free: 800-467-7423
Fax: (931)388-1617
URL: http://www.carishealthcare.com/

21512 ■ Hospice Compassus-Columbia
1412 Trotwood Ave.
Columbia, TN 38401-4968
Ph: (931)381-4090
Fax: (931)381-4037
URL: http://www.hospicecompassus.com/

Cookeville

21513 ■ Gentiva Hospice-Cookeville
851 S Willow Ave.
Cookeville, TN 38501
Ph: (931)528-5133
Fax: (931)372-0249
URL: http://www.gentiva.com/hospice/

Cordova

21514 ■ AseraCare Hospice-Memphis
320 Walnut Bend S
Cordova, TN 38018
Ph: (901)309-1855
Fax: (901)309-5066
URL: http://www.aseracare.com/

Covington

21515 ■ Baptist Home Care and Hospice-Tipton
1618-C Hwy. 51 S
Covington, TN 38019
Ph: (901)476-0333
Fax: (901)476-4333
URL: http://www.baptistonline.org/

Crossville

21516 ■ Caris HealthCare, LP-Crossville
60 Ridley St., Ste. 127
Crossville, TN 38555
Ph: (931)456-8970
Free: 877-456-8970
Fax: (931)456-7783
URL: http://www.carishealthcare.com/

21517 ■ Hospice of Cumberland County, Inc.
30 E Adams St.
Crossville, TN 38555
Ph: (931)484-4748
Fax: (931)456-7882
URL: http://www.cumberlandhospice.com

Dickson

21518 ■ Avalon Hospice-Dickson
714 E College St.
Dickson, TN 37055
Ph: (615)889-5995
URL: http://www.avalon-hospice.com/

21519 ■ Caris Healthcare-Dickson
114 Hwy. 70 E
Dickson, TN 37055
Ph: (615)441-5296
Fax: (615)446-8381
URL: http://www.carishealthcare.com/

Elizabethton

21520 ■ Amedisys Hospice, Inc.--Elizabethtown
167 Hudson Dr.
Elizabethton, TN 37643
Ph: (423)547-0852
Free: 800-774-1404
Fax: (423)543-6449
URL: http://www.amedisys.com/hospice_locations.cfm
Formerly: Adventa Hospice, Inc.

Fayetteville

21521 ■ Hospital Home Health and Hospice
1797 Wilson Pkwy.
Fayetteville, TN 37334
Ph: (931)433-8088
Free: 800-498-8085
Fax: (931)433-8086
E-mail: debbie.kilpatrick@lchealthsystem.com
URL: http://www.lchealthsystem.com/lchs.nsf/view/homehealthhospice

Franklin

21522 ■ Guardian Hospice--Franklin
800 Crescent Centre Dr.
Franklin, TN 37067
Ph: (615)771-8979
Fax: (615)771-7933
URL: http://www.guardianhomecare.us/

21523 ■ Willowbrook Hospice, Inc.
381 Riverside Dr., Ste. 440
Franklin, TN 37064
Ph: (615)791-8499
Free: 800-790-8499
Fax: (615)595-9775
URL: http://www.willowbrookhealth.com

Germantown

21524 ■ Unity Hospice Care, LLC-Germantown
3085 Fountainside Dr.
Germantown, TN 38138
Ph: (901)756-7322
Fax: (901)756-7085
E-mail: bseals@unityhospice.org
URL: http://www.unityhospicecare.org/

Greeneville

21525 ■ Caris Healthcare-Greenville
225 W Summer St.
Greeneville, TN 37743
Ph: (865)694-4988
Fax: (856)694-7878
URL: http://www.carishealthcare.com/greenville.php

Greenville

21526 ■ Amedisys Hospice of Greenville
127 Serral Dr.
Greenville, TN 37745
Ph: (423)638-2707
Fax: (423)638-4732
URL: http://www.amedisys.com/

Huntingdon

21527 ■ Baptist Memorial Homecare & Hospice
631 R B Wilson Dr.
Huntingdon, TN 38344
Ph: (731)986-3220
Fax: (931)986-2134
URL: http://www.bmhcc.org/

Jackson

21528 ■ AseraCare Hospice-Jackson
250 N Parkway Blvd.
Jackson, TN 38305
Ph: (731)660-4283
Fax: (731)660-2043
URL: http://www.aseracare.com/

21529 ■ Hospice of West Tennessee
1804 US Hwy. 45 Bypass, Ste. 100
Jackson, TN 38305
Ph: (731)664-4220
Fax: (731)664-4231
E-mail: hospice@wth.org
URL: http://www.hospicewth.org/body.cfm?id=198&SubDomain=true

21530 ■ Tennessee Quality Hospice--Jackson
29 N Star Dr.
Jackson, TN 38305
Ph: (731)584-9500
Free: 866-971-0986
Fax: (731)584-4080
URL: http://www.tnhomecare.com/

Knoxville

21531 ■ Amedisys Hospice, Inc.--Knoxville
1420 Dutch Valley Rd., Ste. C
Knoxville, TN 37918-1424
Ph: (865)689-7123
Free: 800-380-7509
Fax: (865)689-8445
URL: http://www.amedisys.com/hospice_locations.cfm
Formerly: Adventa Hospice, Inc.

21532 ■ Covenant Homecare/Hospice--Knoxville
3001 Lake Brook Blvd., Ste. 101
Knoxville, TN 37909
Ph: (865)374-0600
Free: 888-719-8087
Fax: (865)374-0870
URL: http://www.covenanthealth.com/?id=179&sid=1

21533 ■ Saint Mary's Hospice Services Mercy Health Partners--Knoxville
7447 Andersonville Pke.
Knoxville, TN 37938-4238
Ph: (865)925-5500
Fax: (865)925-9147
E-mail: lcollier@mercy.com
URL: http://www.mercy.com/hospice.asp

Maryville

21534 ■ Blount Memorial Hospital Hospice
1095 E Lamar Alexander Pkwy.
Maryville, TN 37804
Ph: (865)977-5702
Fax: (865)977-4787
URL: http://www.blountmemorial.org/body.cfm?id=110

McKenzie

21535 ■ AseraCare Hospice-McKenzie
1939 A Cedar St.
McKenzie, TN 38201
Ph: (731)352-1340
Fax: (731)352-5563
URL: http://www.aseracare.com/

Memphis

21536 ■ Amedisys Hospice of Memphis
1355 Lynnfield Rd.
Memphis, TN 38119
Ph: (901)680-0378
Fax: (901)818-4894
URL: http://www.amedisys.com

21537 ■ Baptist Trinity Homecare and Hospice
6141 Walnut Grove Rd.
Memphis, TN 38120
Ph: (901)767-6767
Free: 800-727-6416
Fax: (901)762-4410
E-mail: info.memphis@bmhcc.org
URL: http://www.baptistonline.org/services/medical/homecare/trinity.asp

21538 ■ Methodist Alliance Hospice
6423 Shelby View Dr., Ste. 103
Memphis, TN 38134
Ph: (901)516-1600
Free: 800-968-8326
Fax: (901)380-8170
URL: http://www.methodisthealth.org/methodist/Healthcare+Services/Hospice+%26+Palliative+Care

21539 ■ Odyssey HealthCare of Memphis
5350 Poplar Ave., Ste. 850
Memphis, TN 38119
Ph: (901)818-5600
Free: 877-637-9432
Fax: (901)818-5640
URL: http://www.odsyhealth.com

Milan

21540 ■ Caris Health Care, LP--Milan
5120 Telecom Dr., Ste. B
Milan, TN 38358
Ph: (731)686-3723
Free: 800-467-7423
Fax: (731)686-8745
URL: http://www.carishealthcare.com

Monteagle

21541 ■ Amedisys Hospice of South Pittsburg
1045 W Main St., Ste. D
Monteagle, TN 37356
Ph: (931)924-5014
Free: 866-890-2081
Fax: (931)924-5013
URL: http://www.amedisys.com/hospice_locations.cfm

Morristown

21542 ■ Amedisys Hospice--Morristown
1423 W Morris Blvd.
Morristown, TN 37813
Ph: (423)587-9484
Free: 800-659-2633
Fax: (423)587-9408
URL: http://www.amedisys.com/hospice_locations.cfm
Formerly: Adventa Hospice, Inc.

21543 ■ Smoky Mountain Home Health & Hospice-Morristown
506 W Morris Blvd.
Morristown, TN 37813
Ph: (423)581-8140
Fax: (423)581-8131
URL: http://www.smokyhhc.org/

Murfreesboro

21544 ■ Alive Hospice - Murfreesboro Office
1639 Medical Center Pkwy., Ste. 202
Murfreesboro, TN 37129
Ph: (800)327-1085
Fax: (615)321-8902
E-mail: info@alivehospice.org
URL: http://www.alivehospice.org/locations-murfreesboro.php
Formerly: Hospice of Murfreesboro.

21545 ■ Caris Healthcare, LP--Murfreesboro
242 Heritage Park Dr., Ste. 101
Murfreesboro, TN 37129
Ph: (615)217-8720
Free: 800--HOSPICE
Fax: (615)217-8728
URL: http://www.carishealthcare.com

Nashville

21546 ■ Alive Hospice, Inc.
1718 Patterson St.
Nashville, TN 37203
Ph: (615)327-1085
Free: 800-327-1085
Fax: (615)321-8902
E-mail: info@alivehospice.org
URL: http://www.alivehospice.org

21547 ■ Alive Hospice at St. Thomas Hospital
4220 Harding Road
Nashville, TN 37205
Ph: (615)222-5151
Fax: (615)222-5152
E-mail: info@alivehospice.org
URL: http://www.alivehospice.org/locations-st-thomas.php

21548 ■ AseraCare Hospice - Nashville
441 Donelson Pike
Nashville, TN 37214
Ph: (615)316-2243
Free: 866-448-1803
Fax: (615)316-7687
URL: http://www.aseracare.com

21549 ■ Avalon Hospice-Nashville
2525 Perimeter Place Dr., Ste. 121
Nashville, TN 37214
Ph: (615)889-5995
URL: http://www.avalon-hospice.com/

21550 ■ Caris Healthcare, LP--Nashville
2525 Perimeter Place Dr., Ste. 131
Nashville, TN 37214
Free: 800-467-7423
URL: http://www.carishealthcare.com

21551 ■ Odyssey HealthCare of Nashville
1400 Donelson Pike, Ste. B-5
Nashville, TN 37217
Ph: (615)365-1009
Free: 877-637-9432
Fax: (615)366-2419
E-mail: info@odsyhealth.com
URL: http://www.odsyhealth.com

Newport

21552 ■ Smoky Mountain Home Health & Hospice, Inc. Corporate Office
222 Heritage Blvd.
Newport, TN 37821
Ph: (423)623-0233
Free: 800-338-7844
E-mail: homehealth@smokyhhc.com
URL: http://www.smokyhhc.org/

Sevierville

21553 ■ Caris Healthcare--Sevierville
816 Middle Creek Rd.
Sevierville, TN 37862
Ph: (865)453-0321
Fax: (865)453-3745
URL: http://www.carishealthcare.com/

Sneedville

21554 ■ Hancock County Home Health and Hospice Agency
147 Court St.
Sneedville, TN 37869
Ph: (423)733-4032
Fax: (423)733-2681

Somerville

21555 ■ Caris Healthcare, LP--Somerville
17410 Hwy. 64
Somerville, TN 38068
Free: 800-467-7423
URL: http://www.carishealthcare.com/somerville.php

Springfield

21556 ■ Caris Healthcare-Springfield
2308 A Memorial Blvd.
Springfield, TN 37172
Ph: (615)384-3833
Fax: (615)384-3287
URL: http://www.carishealthcare.com/

21557 ■ North Crest Hospice
101 E Mooreland Dr.
Springfield, TN 37172
Ph: (615)384-9425
Fax: (615)384-9468
E-mail: info@northcrest.com
URL: http://www.northcrest.com/HospitalServices/ByDepartment/Hospice/tabid/94/De fault.aspx

Sweetwater

21558 ■ Amedisys-Sweetwater
665 New Hwy. 68, Ste. B
Sweetwater, TN 37874
Ph: (423)351-0233
Fax: (423)562-8209
URL: http://www.amedisys.com/

Tazewell

21559 ■ Claiborne Home Health Care
409 Cawood Rd.
Tazewell, TN 37879
Ph: (423)626-4272
Free: 800-541-7367
Fax: (423)626-2086
URL: http://www.claibornehospital.org/home_health.htm

Tullahoma

21560 ■ AseraCare Hospice - Tullahoma
414 Wilson Ave.
Tullahoma, TN 37388
Ph: (931)393-4482
Free: 866-488-1804
Fax: (931)361-3049
URL: http://www.aseracare.com

21561 ■ Hospice Compassus-Tullahoma
936 N Jackson
Tullahoma, TN 37388
Ph: (931)455-9118
Fax: (931)455-0863
E-mail: contactusTNTUL@hospicecom.com
URL: http://www.hospicecompassus.com/loc-TNTUL.html

Union City

21562 ■ Baptist Home Care and Hospice--Union City
PO Box 621
Union City, TN 38281-0621
Ph: (731)884-8617
Fax: (731)884-8626
URL: http://www.bmhcc.org/services/medical/home-care/

Waynesboro

21563 ■ Tennessee Quality Hospice--Waynesboro
540 Hwy 64 E
Waynesboro, TN 38485
Ph: (931)722-2785
Free: 866-692-8156
Fax: (931)722-2787
URL: http://www.tnhomecare.com/

TEXAS

Abilene

21564 ■ Hendrick Hospice Care
1682 Hickory St.
Abilene, TX 79601
Ph: (325)677-8516
Free: 800-622-8516
Fax: (325)675-5031
E-mail: dstephenson@ehendrick.org
URL: http://www.hendrickhospice.org

21565 ■ Hospice of the Big Country Inc.
4601 Hartford St.
Abilene, TX 79605
Ph: (915)793-5450
Free: 800-588-0300
Fax: (915)793-5459
URL: http://www.westtexasrehab.org/our-services/big-country-hospice.html

21566 ■ Sears Methodist Hospice
3233 S Willis
Abilene, TX 79605-6649
Ph: (325)692-4500
URL: http://www.sears-methodist.org/content/view/30/92/

21567 ■ Solaris Hospice-Abilene
4150 S Danville Dr.
Abilene, TX 79605
Ph: (325)692-2271
Free: 888-376-5274
Fax: (325)692-2931
URL: http://www.solarisfamily.com/areasserved

Amarillo

21568 ■ BSA Hospice
721 N Tyler
600 N Tyler
Amarillo, TX 79107
Ph: (806)212-8028
Free: 800-315-6209
URL: http://www.bsahs.org/body.cfm?id=554

21569 ■ Hospice Care of the Southwest
6600 Killgrove Dr. Ste. 110
Amarillo, TX 79106
Ph: (806)356-0026
Free: 866-654-2941
Fax: (806)358-3114
URL: http://www.hospicesouthwest.com

21570 ■ Odyssey HealthCare of Amarillo
6900 W I-40 W, Ste. 150
Amarillo, TX 79106
Ph: (806)372-7696
Free: 877-637-9432
Fax: (806)372-2825
E-mail: info@odsyhealth.com
URL: http://www.odsyhealth.com

21571 ■ Vista Care--Amarillo
6900 I-40 W, Ste. 150
Amarillo, TX 79106
Ph: (806)372-7696
Free: 866-488-6862
Fax: (806)372-2825
URL: http://www.vistacare.com

Andrews

21572 ■ Home Hospice-Andrews
801 N Main, Ste. G
Andrews, TX 79714
Ph: (432)524-5139
Free: 877-524-2784
Fax: (432)524-2784
URL: http://www.homehospicewtx.com/

Arlington

21573 ■ Freedom Hospice-Arlington
1907 Ascension Blvd., Ste. 200
Arlington, TX 76006
Ph: (817)265-0151
Fax: (817)265-0145
E-mail: info@freedom-hospice.com
URL: http://www.freedom-hospice.com/

21574 ■ Tender Heart Hospice Care-Arlington
3210 W Park Row
Arlington, TX 76013
Ph: (817)265-0089
Fax: (817)265-0089
URL: http://tenderhearthh.com/

Austin

21575 ■ Angel Heart Hospice, LLC
8213-A Shoal Creek Blvd., Ste. 104
Austin, TX 78757
Ph: (512)342-8288
Free: 866-655-8288
Fax: (512)342-8122
E-mail: info@angelhearthospice.com
URL: http://www.angelhearthospice.com

21576 ■ Doug's House Project Transitions, Inc.
PO Box 4826
Austin, TX 78765
Ph: (512)454-8646
Fax: (512)454-5039
E-mail: info@projecttransitions.org
URL: http://www.resolutionshospice.com/

21577 ■ Heart to Heart Hospice of Austin
4029 S Capital of Texas Hwy.
Austin, TX 78704
Ph: (512)707-2600
Fax: (512)322-9969
E-mail: zellis@hearttohearthospice.com
URL: http://www.hearttohearthospice.com/

21578 ■ Hospice Austin
4107 Spicewood Springs Rd., Ste. 100
Austin, TX 78759
Ph: (512)342-4700
Free: 800-445-3261
Fax: (512)795-9053
E-mail: info@hospiceaustin.org
URL: http://www.hospiceaustin.org

21579 ■ Hospice Austin's at Christopher House
2820 E Martin Luther King Jr. Blvd.
Austin, TX 78702-1544
Ph: (512)322-0747
Free: 800-445-3261
Fax: (512)477-7970
E-mail: info@hospiceaustin.org
URL: http://www.hospiceaustin.org

21580 ■ Lighthouse Hospice-Austin
8701 N Mopac, Ste. 420
Austin, TX 78759
Ph: (512)349-0402
Fax: (512)349-0114
URL: http://www.lighthouse-hospice.com/

21581 ■ Odyssey HealthCare of Austin
4201 W Parmer Ln., Ste. 100
Austin, TX 78727
Ph: (512)310-0214
Free: 877-637-9432
Fax: (512)310-9328
E-mail: info@odsyhealth.com
URL: http://www.odsyhealth.com

21582 ■ Resolutions Hospice-Austin
401 A Heron Dr.
Austin, TX 78734
Ph: (512)343-5555
Fax: (713)528-6444
URL: http://www.resolutionshospice.com/

21583 ■ Texas Home Health Hospice--Austin
3520 Executive Center Dr.
Austin, TX 78731
Ph: (512)372-4194
Free: 800-917-0833
Fax: (512)372-4351
URL: http://www.mytexashospice.com/

21584 ■ VistaCare--Austin
7800 Shoal Creek Blvd., Ste. 130W
Austin, TX 78757
Ph: (512)453-4144
Free: 800-444-2405
Fax: (512)453-4165
URL: http://www.vistacare.com

Bastrop

21585 ■ AseraCare Hospice-Bastrop
1015 Main St.
Bastrop, TX 78602
Ph: (512)308-9148
Fax: (512)308-9174
URL: http://www.aseracare.com/

Baytown

21586 ■ Faith Community Hospice, LLC
4721 Garth, Ste. H
Baytown, TX 77521
Ph: (281)422-0414
Free: 877-422-0414
Fax: (281)422-9605
E-mail: info@faithcommunityhospice.com
URL: http://www.faithcommunityhospice.com

21587 ■ Hospice Compassus-Baytown
1610 James Bowie Dr., Ste. A105
Baytown, TX 77520
Ph: (281)837-9200
Free: 877-575-7245
Fax: (281)827-9201
E-mail: contactusTXBAY@hospicecom.com
URL: http://www.hospicecompassus.com/

Beaumont

21588 ■ Hospice of Texas
2900 North St., Ste. 100
Beaumont, TX 77702
Ph: (409)832-4582
Free: 800-550-7476
Fax: (409)832-6345
URL: http://www.hospiceoftexas.com

21589 ■ Odyssey HealthCare of Beaumont
550 Fannin St., Ste. 1230
Beaumont, TX 77701
Ph: (409)212-0020

Free: 877-637-9432
Fax: (409)212-0022
E-mail: info@odsyhealth.com
URL: http://www.odsyhealth.com

21590 ■ Texas Home Health Hospice--Beaumont
5683 Eastex Fwy.
Beaumont, TX 77706
Ph: (409)899-1152
Fax: (409)898-0155
URL: http://www.mytexashospice.com/

Bedford

21591 ■ Heritage Hospice of Texas
1321 Brown Trail
Bedford, TX 76022
Ph: (817)268-2643
Fax: (817)282-1062

Bellaire

21592 ■ Houston Solari Hospice Care
6800 W Loop S, Ste. 250
Bellaire, TX 77401
Ph: (713)664-7120
Fax: (713)644-7190
URL: http://www.solarihospice.com/go2/solari-hospice-home.cfm

Big Spring

21593 ■ Crossroads Hospice
421 S Main St.
Big Spring, TX 79720
Ph: (432)263-5300
Fax: (432)263-5301

21594 ■ Home Hospice--Big Spring
111 E 7th St., Ste. A
Big Spring, TX 79720-2442
Ph: (432)264-7599
Fax: (432)264-7597
URL: http://www.homehospicewtx.com/

21595 ■ Odyssey HealthCare of Big Spring
1003 E FM 700
Big Spring, TX 79720
Ph: (432)263-5999
Fax: (432)263-9998
URL: http://www.odsyhealth.com/default.asp

Bowie

21596 ■ Solaris Hospice inc-Bowie
800 Hwy 59 N
Bowie, TX 76230
Ph: (940)872-8080
Fax: (940)872-8082
URL: http://www.solarisfamily.com/

Breckenridge

21597 ■ Solaris Hospice Inc-Breckenridge
1226 W Walker
Breckenridge, TX 76424
Ph: (254)559-5473
Free: 888-376-5274
Fax: (254)559-5515
URL: http://www.solarisfamily.com/

Brenham

21598 ■ Hospice Brazos Valley-Brenham
302 E Blue Bell Rd.
Brenham, TX 77833
Ph: (979)277-9525
Fax: (979)277-9575
URL: http://www.hospicebrazosvalley.org/contact.html

Brownsville

21599 ■ Odyssey HealthCare of South Texas
2501 Paredes Line Rd.
Brownsville, TX 78526
Ph: (956)504-5298
Free: 877-637-9432
Fax: (956)504-9265
E-mail: info@odsyhealth.com
URL: http://www.odsyhealth.com

Brownwood

21600 ■ Lighthouse Hospice-Brownwood
107 E South Park Dr.
Brownwood, TX 76801
Ph: (325)643-5718
Free: 866-678-0505
Fax: (325)643-6249
URL: http://www.lighthouse-hospice.com/

21601 ■ Solaris Hospice, Inc.
413 Center Ave.
Brownwood, TX 76801
Ph: (325)641-1630
Fax: (325)641-1639
URL: http://solarisfamily.com/areasserved

Bryan

21602 ■ Hospice Brazos Valley Inc-Bryan
502 W 26th St.
Bryan, TX 77803
Ph: (979)821-2266
Fax: (979)821-0041
URL: http://www.hospicebrazosvalley.org/

Burleson

21603 ■ Accolade Hospice-Burleson
308 E Renfro
Burleson, TX 76028
Ph: (817)426-3870
Free: 877-426-3870
Fax: (817)426-3812
URL: http://www.accoladehomecare.com/

21604 ■ Emery J. Lilge Hospice House
301 Medical Park Cir.
Burleson, TX 76028
Ph: (817)615-2150
Free: 800-226-0373
Fax: (817)615-2159
E-mail: scolston@chot.org
URL: http://www.chot.org

Burnet

21605 ■ Seton Highland Lakes Hospice
PO Box 1219
Burnet, TX 78611
Ph: (512)756-8003
Fax: (512)756-8046

Canadian

21606 ■ Hemphill County Hospice
1020 S 4th St.
Canadian, TX 79014-3315
Ph: (806)323-6422
Fax: (806)323-8061
URL: http://www.hch.dst.tx.us/hospice/hospice.htm

Carthage

21607 ■ Heartsway Hospice of Northeast Texas
437 W Panola St.
Carthage, TX 75633
Ph: (903)690-9924
Fax: (903)295-1680
E-mail: care@heartswayhospice.org
URL: http://www.heartswayhospice.org/

Cleburne

21608 ■ Community Hospice of Texas
1208 W Henderson St., Ste. B
Cleburne, TX 76033
Ph: (817)556-3100
Fax: (817)648-0275
URL: http://www.chot.org/

College Station

21609 ■ Texas Home Health Hospice--College Station
1605 Rock Prairie Rd.
College Station, TX 77845
Ph: (979)268-7472
Fax: (979)268-7475
URL: http://www.mytexashospice.com/

Conroe

21610 ■ Lighthouse Hospice-Conroe
200 River Pointe
Conroe, TX 77304
Ph: (281)290-7727
Fax: (281)290-8460
URL: http://www.lighthouse-hospice.com/

21611 ■ Odyssey Health Care of Conroe
100 I-45 N, Ste. 300
Conroe, TX 77301
Ph: (936)788-7707
Free: 877-637-9432
Fax: (936)788-7708
E-mail: info@odsyhealth.com
URL: http://www.odsyhealth.com

21612 ■ Odyssey House Inpatient Facility
233 I-45 S
Conroe, TX 77304
Ph: (936)539-1400
Fax: (936)539-1402
E-mail: info@odsyhealth.com
URL: http://www.odsyhealth.com

Corpus Christi

21613 ■ Nurses on Wheels Hospice
1101 3rd St.
Corpus Christi, TX 78404-2311
Ph: (361)814-1669
Fax: (361)850-7577
E-mail: mdgarcia@nursesonwheelsinc.com
URL: http://www.nursesonwheelsinc.com

21614 ■ Odyssey Healthcare of Corpus Christi
5350 S Staples St., Ste. 400
Corpus Christi, TX 78411
Ph: (361)992-2700
Free: 877-637-9432
Fax: (361)992-2703
E-mail: info@odsyhealth.com

21615 ■ VistaCare--Corpus Christi
4320 S Padre Island Dr., Ste. B
Corpus Christi, TX 78411
Ph: (361)854-1540
Free: 888-878-1540
Fax: (361)980-8661
URL: http://www.vista-care.com

Corsicana

21616 ■ Hospice of Cedar Lake--Vital Signs
625 N Maine
Corsicana, TX 75110
Ph: (903)874-4745
Free: 800-259-2043
Fax: (903)489-2044
URL: http://www.cedarlakenursing.com/

Crockett

21617 ■ Pineywoods Hospice Inc
2205 E Goliad, Ste. 104
Crockett, TX 75835
Ph: (936)546-0457
Fax: (936)327-7561
E-mail: info@apwhhc.com
URL: http://www.apineywoods.com/

Dallas

21618 ■ Autumn Journey Hospice
5347 Spring Valley Rd.
Dallas, TX 75254
Ph: (972)233-0525
Fax: (214)447-9480
E-mail: wecare@autumnjourneyhospice.com
URL: http://www.autumnjourneyhospice.com

21619 ■ Century Hospice
4101 McEwen Dr., Ste. 500
Dallas, TX 75244
Ph: (972)239-0907
Fax: (972)239-0908
E-mail: Admin@centuryhospice.com
URL: http://www.centuryhospice.com/

21620 ■ Community Hospice of Texas
1341 W Mockingbird La.
Dallas, TX 75247
Ph: (214)920-8450
Fax: (214)920-8496
URL: http://www.chot.org/

21621 ■ Heartland Home Health Care and Hospice--Dallas
8700 N Stemmons Fwy., Ste. 144
Dallas, TX 75247-3729
Ph: (214)630-9070
Free: 866-243-7713
Fax: (214)630-9071
E-mail: careline@hcr-manorcare.com
URL: http://www.hcr-manorcare.com

21622 ■ Hospice Compassus-Dallas
12222 Merit Dr., Ste. 1240
Dallas, TX 75251
Ph: (248)355-9900
Fax: (248)355-5705
E-mail: contactusTXDAL@hospicecom.com
URL: http://www.hospicecompassus.com

21623 ■ Hospice Plus
3100 McKinnon
Dallas, TX 75201
Ph: (214)343-7900
Fax: (214)343-2900
E-mail: info@hospiceplus.net
URL: http://www.hospiceplus.net/

21624 ■ Lion Hospice, Inc.
5401 N Central Expressway, Ste. 222
Dallas, TX 75205
Ph: (214)261-0140
Free: 877-774-3352
Fax: (214)261-0141
E-mail: Dallas@lionhospice.com
URL: http://www.lionhospice.com/

21625 ■ Odyssey HealthCare of North Texas
5440 Harvest Hill Rd.
Dallas, TX 75230
Ph: (972)720-0999
Free: 877-637-9432
Fax: (972)720-1115
E-mail: info@odsyhealth.com
URL: http://www.odsyhealth.com

21626 ■ St. Michael's Hospice Corporation
10214 Inwood Rd.
Dallas, TX 75229
Ph: (214)866-0233
Fax: (214)866-0232

21627 ■ Seasons Hospice & Palliative Care-Dallas
8610 Greenville Ave.
Dallas, TX 75243
Ph: (214)528-2200
Free: 866-570-6484
Fax: (214)355-4097
E-mail: info@seasons.org
URL: http://honoringlife-offeringhope.org/

21628 ■ VistaCare--Dallas
7557 Rambler Rd., Ste. 112
Dallas, TX 75231
Ph: (214)231-3914
Free: 800-375-4677
Fax: (214)630-4032
URL: http://www.vistacare.com

21629 ■ VITAS Innovative Hospice Care of Dallas
8585 Stemmons Fwy., Ste. 700
Dallas, TX 75247
Ph: (972)661-2004
Free: 800-664-2004
Fax: (972)448-6542
URL: http://www.vitas.com

De Soto

21630 ■ Elysian Hospice, LLC
1636 N Hampton Rd.
De Soto, TX 75115
Ph: (972)224-1876
Fax: (972)224-1494
E-mail: info@elysianhospice.com
URL: http://elysianhospice.com/

21631 ■ Twinber Hospice Care
509 N Hampton Rd.
De Soto, TX 75115
Ph: (972)274-2803
Free: 877-278-2903
Fax: (972)274-4009
E-mail: twinber@twinberinc.com
URL: http://www.twinberinc.com/HospiceHome.html

Decatur

21632 ■ Integracare Hospice--Decatur
1451 W Business 380, Bldg. 4
Decatur, TX 76234
Ph: (940)627-2888
Free: 877-494-2211
Fax: (940)627-9627
URL: http://www.integracarehh.com/

21633 ■ Solaris Hospice, Inc.
2205 S Fm 51, Ste. 400
Decatur, TX 76234
Ph: (940)627-1011
Free: 888-376-5274
Fax: (940)627-7803
URL: http://www.solarishc.com

Del Rio

21634 ■ Val Verde Regional Medical Center Hospice
801 N Bedell Ave.
Del Rio, TX 78840
Ph: (830)774-4580
Free: 888-774-4580
Fax: (830)774-2485
E-mail: info@vvrmc.org
URL: http://www.vvrmc.org

Dublin

21635 ■ Community Care Services Hospice
118 E Live Oak St., Ste. 104
Dublin, TX 76446
Ph: (254)445-4675
Free: 800-454-4677
Fax: (254)445-2972

Dumas

21636 ■ Memorial Hospice--Dumas
224 E 2nd St.
Dumas, TX 79029
Ph: (806)935-4884
Fax: (806)935-2251
URL: http://www.mchd.net/getpage.php?name=hospice

Eagle Pass

21637 ■ Fort Duncan Home Health and Hospice Care
3147 Megan St.
Eagle Pass, TX 78852
Ph: (830)757-0966
Free: 888-278-4053
Fax: (830)757-0976
URL: http://ephospice.com/

Eastland

21638 ■ Lighthouse Eastland
957 E Main
Eastland, TX 76448
Ph: (254)629-1268
Free: 800-950-0363
Fax: (254)629-8698
URL: http://www.lighthouse-hospice.com/

El Paso

21639 ■ Circle of Hope Hospice of VNA
4171 N Mesa St., Ste. 500
El Paso, TX 79902
Ph: (915)543-6243
E-mail: lblack@vnaelpaso.com
URL: http://www.vnaelpaso.com

21640 ■ Hospice of El Paso Inc.
1750 Curie Dr.
El Paso, TX 79902
Ph: (915)532-5699
Fax: (915)532-7822
E-mail: hospice@hospiceelpaso.com
URL: http://www.hospiceelpaso.org

21641 ■ La Mariposa Hospice at Providence Hospital
1250 Cliff Dr., Ste. 5E
El Paso, TX 79902
Ph: (915)577-7870
Fax: (915)577-7969
URL: http://www.sphn.com/en-US/Pages/default.aspx

21642 ■ Odyssey HealthCare of El Paso
7500 Viscount
El Paso, TX 79925
Ph: (915)778-9058
Free: 877-637-9432
Fax: (915)778-9053
E-mail: info@odsyhealth.com
URL: http://www.odsyhealth.com

Ennis

21643 ■ Family First Hospice
109 SW Main St.
Ennis, TX 75119
Ph: (972)878-2273
Free: 866-834-3700
Fax: (972)878-2278
URL: http://www.familyfirsthospice.com/

Fairfield

21644 ■ THEE Hospice Home Health Hospice
714 E Commerce
Fairfield, TX 75840

Ph: (903)389-9821
Fax: (903)389-9826
E-mail: information@homehealthhospice.com
URL: http://homehealthhospice.com/index.php?option=com_content&task=view&id=13&Itemid=28

Floresville

21645 ■ Nurses In Touch Community Hospice
1815 10th St.
Floresville, TX 78114
Ph: (830)216-7111
Free: 800-441-9938
Fax: (830)216-7115
URL: http://www.nursesintouch.com

Flower Mound

21646 ■ Ardent Hospice
3020 Broadmoor La.
Flower Mound, TX 75022
Ph: (469)293-1515
Fax: (469)293-1530
E-mail: administrator@ardenthospice.com
URL: http://www.ardenthospice.com/

Fort Worth

21647 ■ Alpha-Omega Hospice
PO Box 162041
Fort Worth, TX 76161-2041
Ph: (817)238-0770
Fax: (817)238-0786
URL: http://www.alphaomegahospice.com/

21648 ■ Bridgeway Hospice
150 W Magnolia
Fort Worth, TX 76104
Ph: (817)332-0400
Fax: (817)332-0411

21649 ■ Community Hospice of Texas
6100 Western Pl., Ste. 500
Fort Worth, TX 76107
Ph: (817)870-2795
Free: 800-226-0373
Fax: (817)989-3220
E-mail: dswart@chot.org
URL: http://www.chot.org

21650 ■ Covenant Hospice and Palliative Care--Fort Worth
3221 Collinsworth St., Ste. 160
Fort Worth, TX 76107
Ph: (817)735-8741
Free: 866-790-8136
Fax: (817)735-8836
E-mail: office@covenantcare.net
URL: http://www.covenantcare.net

21651 ■ Heart to Heart Hospice of Fort Worth, LLC
5608 Malvey Ave.
Fort Worth, TX 76107
Ph: (972)731-9700
Fax: (972)731-9708
URL: http://www.hearttohospice.com/

21652 ■ Hospice House West
1111 Summit Ave.
Fort Worth, TX 76102
Ph: (817)870-9995
Fax: (917)870-9996
URL: http://www.chot.org

21653 ■ Odyssey Healthcare of Fort Worth
2630 W FWY, Ste. 102
Fort Worth, TX 76102
Ph: (817)338-1512
Free: 877-637-9432
Fax: (817)339-2577
E-mail: info@odsyhealth.com
URL: http://www.odsyhealth.com

21654 ■ Seasons Hospice & Palliative Care of Texas
5237 N Riverside Dr.
Fort Worth, TX 76137
Ph: (817)887-0017
Free: 866-746-0009
Fax: (817)665-2145
E-mail: info@seasons.org
URL: http://www.seasons.org/

21655 ■ Universal Home Health and Hospices Services
1208 Country Club Ln.
Fort Worth, TX 76112
Ph: (817)451-1404
Free: 877-337-0757
Fax: (817)451-2204
E-mail: ana@universal-health.com
URL: http://www.universal-health.com

21656 ■ VITAS Baylor All Saints Medical Center
Hospice Inpatient Unit
1400 8th Ave.
Fort Worth, TX 76104
Ph: (817)922-4570
Free: 800-938-4827
Fax: (817)922-4575
URL: http://www.vitas.com

21657 ■ VITAS Innovative Hospice Care of Fort Worth
2501 Parkview Dr., Ste. 600
Fort Worth, TX 76102
Ph: (817)870-7000
Free: 800-938-4827
Fax: (817)870-7090
URL: http://www.vitas.com

Fredericksburg

21658 ■ Greater Hill Country Hospice
Hill Country Memorial Hospice
808 Reuben St.
Fredericksburg, TX 78624
Ph: (830)997-1335
Free: 800-859-3169
Fax: (830)997-3547
URL: http://www.hcmhs.org/Main/Hospice.aspx

Gainesville

21659 ■ Home Hospice of Cooke County
1001 E Broadway
Gainesville, TX 76240
Ph: (940)665-9891
Free: 888-233-7455
Fax: (940)665-8607
E-mail: info.cooke@homehospice.org
URL: http://www.homehospice.org

Georgetown

21660 ■ Hospice Austin-Williamson City
1101 Williams Dr.
Georgetown, TX 78628
Ph: (512)342-4700
Fax: (512)795-9053
E-mail: info@hospiceaustin.org
URL: http://www.hospiceaustin.org/site/pp.asp?c=bdJPITMyA&b=5613561

21661 ■ Lighthouse Hospice-Georgetown
2913 Williams Dr.
Georgetown, TX 78628
Ph: (512)942-6247
Free: 866-678-0505
Fax: (512)868-1132
URL: http://www.lighthouse-hospice.com/

21662 ■ Wesleyan Hospice-Georgetown
508 Leander Rd.
Georgetown, TX 78626
Ph: (512)863-8848
Fax: (512)863-3117
E-mail: hospice@wesleyanhomes.org
URL: http://www.wesleyanhomnes.org
Cheryl Frederick, Director

Gilmer

21663 ■ Legacy Hospice-Gilmer
100 Jefferson
Gilmer, TX 75644
Ph: (903)680-2334
Fax: (903)680-2338
E-mail: contact @legacyhospice.com
URL: http://legacyhospice.com/

Graham

21664 ■ Solaris Hospice-Graham
509 Elm St.
Graham, TX 76450
Ph: (940)521-0922
Fax: (940)521-9722
URL: http://www.solarisfamily.com/

Grand Saline

21665 ■ Autumn Woods Hospice Care
Country Trails Hospice
PO Box 588
Grand Saline, TX 75140
Ph: (903)962-7597
Fax: (903)962-3406
URL: http://www.awhospice.com/

Grapevine

21666 ■ Integracare Hospice-Grapevine
2559 SW Grapevine Pkwy.
Grapevine, TX 76051
Ph: (817)310-4921
Fax: (817)310-4990
URL: http://www.integracarehh.com/

Greenville

21667 ■ VistaCare--Terrell Road, Greenville
2824 Terrell Rd., Ste. 500
Greenville, TX 75402
Ph: (903)454-1107
Free: 800-856-2420
Fax: (903)454-2177
URL: http://www.vista-care.com

Gun Barrel City

21668 ■ Caring Hearts Hospice--Gun Barrel City
1837 W Main
Gun Barrel City, TX 75156
Ph: (903)887-4788
Fax: (903)887-7288

Hallettsville

21669 ■ Hospice of South Texas, Hallettsville
404 N Texana
Hallettsville, TX 77964
Ph: (361)798-2077
Free: 800-685-5268
Fax: (361)798-2176
E-mail: hospice@hospice-vic.org
URL: http://www.hospice-vic.org

Houston

21670 ■ Advanced Care Hospice-Houston
Q-Staff
17300 Saturn La., Ste. 111
Houston, TX 77058

Ph: (281)204-8944
Fax: (281)204-8941
E-mail: info@advancedcarehospice.com
URL: http://www.qstaff-hospice.com/

21671 ■ AseraCare Hospice--Houston
1235 N Loop West, Ste. 215
Houston, TX 77008
Ph: (713)864-2626
Free: 888-646-8696
Fax: (713)864-9476
URL: http://www.aseracare.com

21672 ■ Buckner Hospice Houston
1321 Park Bayou Dr.
Houston, TX 77077
Ph: (281)493-6800
Fax: (281)493-6807
E-mail: tcooper@buckner.org
URL: http://www.bucknerretirement.org/hospice.shtml

21673 ■ Evercare Hospice & Palliative Care-Houston
9702 Bissonnet
Houston, TX 77036-8000
Ph: (713)219-6490
Free: 888-303-6166
Fax: (713)219-6491
URL: http://www.evercarehospice.com/where_to_find_us.jsp#Texas

21674 ■ Gulf Coast Hospice of Houston
9555 W Sam Houston Pkwy. S
Houston, TX 77099
Ph: (713)772-2700
Fax: (713)772-2708
URL: http://gchospice.com/

21675 ■ Heart to Heart Hospice of Greater Houston
2929 Briarpark Dr., Ste. 320
Houston, TX 77042
Ph: (713)984-2100
Free: 866-984-4455
Fax: (713)984-2171
E-mail: jturner@hearttohearthospice.com
URL: http://www.hearttohearthospice.com/

21676 ■ Hospice Compassus-Houston
1770 St. James Pl., Ste. 330
Houston, TX 77056
Ph: (713)850-8853
Free: 877-575-7152
Fax: (713)850-8850
E-mail: contactusTXHOUS@hospicecom.com
URL: http://www.hospicecompassus.com/loc-TX-HOUS.html

21677 ■ Memorial Hermann Hospice
16538 Air Center Blvd.
Houston, TX 77032
Ph: (281)784-7520
Fax: (281)540-7535
E-mail: webmaster@memorialhermann.org
URL: http://www.memorialhermann.org/servicesand-programs/hospicecare/content.aspx ?id=1266

21678 ■ Methodist Hospital
6565 Fannin St.
Houston, TX 77030
Ph: (713)790-3311
URL: http://www.methodisthealth.com/

21679 ■ Odyssey Health Care of Houston
2636 S Loop W, Ste. 210
Houston, TX 77054
Ph: (713)592-5600
Free: 888-592-5602
Fax: (713)592-5604
E-mail: info@odsyhealth.org
URL: http://www.odsyhealth.org

21680 ■ Resolutions Hospice-Houston
8305 Knight Rd.
Houston, TX 77054
Ph: (832)588-6083
Fax: (713)383-4447
E-mail: jbodine@rhospice.com
URL: http://www.resolutionshospice.com/

21681 ■ Silverado Hospice-Houston
13810 Champions Forest Dr.
Houston, TX 77069
Ph: (281)397-8800
Free: 888-494-6958
Fax: (281)397-8813
URL: http://www.silveradosenior.com/hospice/Houston/zip_77069/silverado_senior_l iving/2588

21682 ■ Texas Home Health Hospice--Houston
7676 Hillmont St., Ste. 300
Houston, TX 77040
Ph: (512)372-4194
Free: 800-917-0833
URL: http://www.txhha.com/

21683 ■ VistaCare--Houston
13325 Hargrave Rd., Ste. 230
Houston, TX 77070
Ph: (713)290-1746
Free: 800-541-0417
Fax: (713)290-1829
URL: http://www.vistacare.com
Wayne Jeske, Exec.Dir.

21684 ■ VITAS Innovative Hospice Care of Houston
4848 Loop Central Dr.
Houston, TX 77081
Ph: (713)663-7777
Free: 800-628-8081
Fax: (713)663-4990
URL: http://www.vitas.com

21685 ■ VITAS Innovative Hospice Care of Houston
North Satellite Office
3845 FM 1960 Rd. W, Ste. 390
Houston, TX 77068
Ph: (713)663-4900
URL: http://www.vitas.com

Hunstville

21686 ■ 1st Choice Hospice, LLC
PO Box 1137
Hunstville, TX 77342
Ph: (936)295-7100
Fax: (936)295-7102

Hurst

21687 ■ Bishop Hospice
2712 N Hurstview Dr.
Hurst, TX 76054
Ph: (817)514-2232
Fax: (817)281-6717
E-mail: info@bishophospice.com
URL: http://www.bishophospice.com

21688 ■ Heartland Hospice Services--Hurst
1845 Precinct Line Rd., Ste. 107
Hurst, TX 76054
Ph: (817)849-8880
Fax: (817)849-8884
URL: http://www.hcr-manorcare.com

Irving

21689 ■ Compassionate Hands Hospice
6500 N Beltline Rd., Ste. 180
Irving, TX 75063
Ph: (972)870-9991
Free: 888-870-9991
Fax: (972)870-9993
E-mail: InfoDallas@CompassionateHandsHospice.com
URL: http://www.compassionatehandshospice.com/

21690 ■ Faith Hospice--Irving
6100 Colwell Blvd., Ste. 225
Irving, TX 75039
Ph: (972)401-9090
Fax: (214)413-1525
URL: http://www.faithpresbyterianhospice.org/

21691 ■ VITAS Inpatient Hospice Unit Hearthstone Assisted Living
2425 Texas Dr.
Irving, TX 75062
Ph: (972)659-6900
Fax: (972)669-6932
URL: http://www.vitas.com/

Jasper

21692 ■ Lakes Area Hospice
254 Ethel St.
Jasper, TX 75951
Ph: (409)384-5995
Free: 800-661-9047
Fax: (409)384-9655
E-mail: hospice@lakesareahospice.org
URL: http://www.lakesareahospice.org/

Katy

21693 ■ Resolutions Hospice-Katy
21720 Kingsland Blvd., Ste. 304
Katy, TX 77450
Ph: (281)579-5690
Fax: (713)383-4447
E-mail: jbodine@rhospice.com
URL: http://www.resolutionshospice.com/

Kerrville

21694 ■ Peterson Hospice
Hill Country Memorial Hospice
1121 Broadway
Kerrville, TX 78028-3514
Ph: (830)258-7799
URL: http://www.petersonrmc.com/

21695 ■ VistaCare--Kerrville
1001 Water St., Ste. B-100
Kerrville, TX 78028
Ph: (830)792-6200
Free: 800-444-1317
Fax: (830)792-6204
URL: http://www.vista-care.com

La Grange

21696 ■ Hospice Brazos Valley Inc-La Grange
1048 N Jefferson
La Grange, TX 78945
Ph: (979)968-6913
Fax: (979)968-6843
URL: http://www.hospicebrazosvalley.org/

Lake Jackson

21697 ■ Helping Hands & Hearts Hospice
412 Plantation Dr.
Lake Jackson, TX 77566
Ph: (979)297-3775
Fax: (979)297-2774
E-mail: handsandhearts@sbcglobal.net
URL: http://www.brazoriacountyhospice.org/

21698 ■ Hospice Care Team, Inc.--Lake Jackson
107 West Way, Ste. 29
Lake Jackson, TX 77566
Ph: (979)297-6043

Free: 800-545-8738
Fax: (979)297-4752
URL: http://www.hospicecareteam.org

Laredo

21699 ■ Laredo Hospice
213 W Village Blvd., Ste. 3
Laredo, TX 78041
Ph: (956)718-3000
Fax: (967)722-3006
URL: http://laredohospice.com/

League City

21700 ■ Hospice Compassus-League City
1100 Gulf Fwy. S, Ste. 122
League City, TX 77573
Ph: (281)316-7777
Free: 877-575-7250
Fax: (281)316-7778
E-mail: contactusTXLEA@hospicecom.com
URL: http://www.hospicecompassus.com/

Lewisville

21701 ■ Heart to Heart Hospice-Lewisville
1500 Waters Ridge Dr.
Lewisville, TX 75057
Ph: (817)731-9700
Fax: (817)731-9708
E-mail: rwatson@hearttohearthospice.com
URL: http://www.hearttohearthospice.com/

21702 ■ Mercy Hospice-Lewisville
417 Oak Bend
Lewisville, TX 75067
Ph: (972)459-9992
Fax: (972)459-9911

Linden

21703 ■ Peachtree Hospice, LLC-Texas
PO Box 1538
Linden, TX 75563
Ph: (903)791-6255
Fax: (903)791-6256
E-mail: jpetrus@pthfs.com
URL: http://www.peachtreehospice.com/

Littlefield

21704 ■ Legacy of Love Hospice
125 W Marshall Howard Blvd.
Littlefield, TX 79339
Ph: (806)385-9329
Fax: (806)385-9340
E-mail: legacyoflovehospice@valornet.com
URL: http://legacyoflovehospice.com/

Livingston

21705 ■ Hospice Care of the Southwest
317 W Church St.
Livingston, TX 77351
Ph: (936)327-9991
Fax: (936)327-9995
URL: http://hospicesouthwest.com/

21706 ■ Polk County Office
1601 US Hwy 59 Loop N
Livingston, TX 77351
Ph: (936)327-8888
Fax: (936)327-8890

Longview

21707 ■ Beacon Hospice-Longview
5016 Gilmer Rd.
Longview, TX 75608
Ph: (903)553-0035
Fax: (903)553-0065
E-mail: wecare@beaconhospice.net
URL: http://www.beaconhospice.net/

21708 ■ Heart's Way Hospice of Northeast Texas
1306 Pine Tree Rd.
Longview, TX 75604
Ph: (903)295-1680
Free: 800-371-1016
Fax: (903)295-1690
E-mail: rebeccav@heartswayhospice.org
URL: http://www.heartswayhospice.org

21709 ■ Legacy Hospice Longview
1121 Judson Rd., Ste. 184B
Longview, TX 75601
Ph: (903)291-1160
Fax: (903)753-0988
E-mail: ccclegacyhospice@yahoo.com
URL: http://www.legacyhospice.com/

21710 ■ Texas Home Health Hospice--Longview
500 E Loop 281
Longview, TX 75305
Ph: (903)234-0943
Fax: (903)328-9068

Lubbock

21711 ■ Accolade Hospice-Lubbock
510 Indiana Ave.
Lubbock, TX 79413
Ph: (806)791-2100
Free: 866-725-2111
Fax: (806)293-2944
URL: http://www.accoladehomecare.com/Home.aspx

21712 ■ Hospice of Lubbock
1102 Slide Rd.
Lubbock, TX 79416
Ph: (806)795-2751
Free: 800-658-2648
Fax: (806)795-8464
URL: http://www.hospiceoflubbock.com

21713 ■ Hospice of the South Plains
1401 9th St.
Lubbock, TX 79401
Ph: (806)747-9484
Fax: (806)747-9497

21714 ■ Integracare Hospice-Lubbock
1312 Texas Ave.
Lubbock, TX 79401
Ph: (806)472-6900
Free: 866-702-7917
Fax: (806)788-5571
URL: http://www.integracarehh.com/locations-integracare.html

21715 ■ Odyssey HealthCare of Lubbock
1717 Norfolk Ave.
Lubbock, TX 79416
Ph: (806)741-0707
Fax: (806)741-0708
E-mail: info@odsyhealth.com
URL: http://www.odsyhealth.com/default.asp

21716 ■ VistaCare/Carillion
Carillion House
1717 Norfolk Ave. Ste. A
Lubbock, TX 79416
Ph: (806)784-3824
Free: 800-499-3464
Fax: (806)791-5800
URL: http://www.vista-care.com

Lufkin

21717 ■ Heart to Heart Hospice-Lufkin
1320 S John Redditt
Lufkin, TX 75904
Ph: (936)699-6001
Fax: (936)699-6009
E-mail: jkendrick@hearttohearthospice.com
URL: http://www.hearttohearthospice.com/

21718 ■ Hospice in the Pines
116 S Raguet St.
Lufkin, TX 75904
Ph: (936)632-1514
Free: 800-324-8557
Fax: (936)632-1582
E-mail: nshaw@hospiceinthepines.com
URL: http://www.hospiceinthepines.com

21719 ■ A Pineywoods Hospice, Inc.
103A Carriage Dr.
Lufkin, TX 75904
Ph: (936)634-1617
Fax: (936)634-7967

Mexia

21720 ■ Providence Hospice--Mexia
107 E Palestine Pl.
Mexia, TX 76667
Ph: (254)472-0779
Free: 866-279-4728
E-mail: lcampbell@chot.org
URL: http://www.providencehospice.org

Midland

21721 ■ Home Hospice--Midland
901 W Missouri Ave.
Midland, TX 79701
Ph: (432)570-0700
Free: 888-570-0701
Fax: (432)570-0866
URL: http://www.homehospicewtx.com

21722 ■ Hospice of Midland Inc.
911 W Texas Ave.
Midland, TX 79701
Ph: (432)682-2855
Free: 800-339-1180
Fax: (432)682-2989
E-mail: hospicemidland@hospiceofmidland.org
URL: http://www.hospiceofmidland.com

Mineral Wells

21723 ■ Integracare Hospice--Mineral Wells
937 FM 1821 N, Ste. A
Mineral Wells, TX 76067
Ph: (940)325-5255
Free: 800-966-7455
Fax: (940)325-5258
URL: http://www.integracarehh.com/locations-integracare.html

21724 ■ Solaris Hospice Inc-Mineral Wells
101 Holly Hill Rd.
Mineral Wells, TX 76067
Ph: (940)325-0059
Free: 888-376-5274
Fax: (940)325-5000
URL: http://www.solarisfamily.com/areasserved

Mission

21725 ■ Selah Hospice Care, Inc.
1601 E Griffin Pkwy.
Mission, TX 78572
Ph: (956)424-3377
Fax: (956)424-3476
E-mail: info@selahcare.com
URL: http://www.selahcare.com/

Mount Pleasant

21726 ■ Cypress Basin Hospice
207 Morgan St.
Mount Pleasant, TX 75456-0544
Ph: (903)577-1510
Free: 888-429-2966
Fax: (903)577-9377
E-mail: info@cbhospice.org
URL: http://www.cbhospice.org

New Braunfels

21727 ■ Hope Hospice--New Braunfels
611 N Walnut Ave.
New Braunfels, TX 78130
Ph: (830)625-7500
Free: 800-499-7501
Fax: (830)606-1388
E-mail: info@hopehospice.net
URL: http://www.hopehospice.net
Formerly: Hospice New Braunfels.

North Richland Hills

21728 ■ Hospice Compassus-North Richland Hills
7001 Blvd. 26, Ste. 500
North Richland Hills, TX 76180
Ph: (817)590-9623
Free: 800-873-4618
Fax: (817)590-1603
E-mail: contactusTXNRH@hospicecom.com
URL: http://www.hospicecompassus.com/loc-TXFTWTH.html

Odessa

21729 ■ Home Hospice--Odessa
516 N Texas
Odessa, TX 79761
Ph: (432)580-9990
Fax: (432)580-9989
URL: http://www.homehospicewtx.com/

21730 ■ Hospice House of Home Hospice
903 N Sam Houston
Odessa, TX 79761
Ph: (432)580-0067
Fax: (432)337-2538
URL: http://www.homehospiceodessa.com

21731 ■ Star Hospice
620 N Grant Ave., Ste. 100
Odessa, TX 79761
Ph: (432)580-7707
Free: 866-360-STAR
Fax: (432)580-7937
URL: http://starcareonline@starcareonline.com

Olney

21732 ■ Solaris Hospice Inc-Olney
1001 W Main, Ste. 4
Olney, TX 76374
Ph: (940)564-2471
Free: 888-376-5274
Fax: (940)564-2476
URL: http://www.solarisfamily.com/

Orange

21733 ■ Southeast Texas Hospice
PO Box 2385
Orange, TX 77631-2385
Ph: (409)886-0622
Free: 800-749-3497
Fax: (409)886-0623
E-mail: sth@exp.net
URL: http://www.setxhospice.com

Pampa

21734 ■ BSA Hospice
Baptist St. Anthony's Health System
800 N Sumner St.
Pampa, TX 79065-5233
Ph: (806)665-6677
Free: 800-658-6985
Fax: (806)665-8423
URL: http://www.bsahs.org/body.cfm?id=1149

Paris

21735 ■ Legacy Hospice-Paris
2675 NE Loop 286
Paris, TX 75460
Ph: (903)784-1147
Fax: (903)784-1532
E-mail: ccclegacyhospice@yahoo.com
URL: http://legacyhospice.com/contact.html

Perryton

21736 ■ Hospice of Ochiltree General Hospital
2309 S Cedar
Perryton, TX 79070
Ph: (806)435-2122
Fax: (806)435-3704
E-mail: sheryn.watts@cohs.net
URL: http://www.ochiltreehospital.com/page8.html
Sheryn Watts, Director

Plainview

21737 ■ Area Community Hospice, Inc.
3109 Olton Rd.
Plainview, TX 79072
Ph: (806)293-2732
Fax: (806)293-2755
E-mail: areacommunity@achospice.com
URL: http://www.areacommunityhospice.com/

Rockport

21738 ■ AIM Hospice
703 E Concho St.
Rockport, TX 78382
Ph: (361)729-0507
Free: 800-854-2674
Fax: (361)727-2354
E-mail: info@aimhospice.org
URL: http://www.aimhospice.org

San Angelo

21739 ■ Hospice of San Angelo, Inc.
36 E Twohig Ave., Ste. 1100
San Angelo, TX 76903
Ph: (325)658-6524
Fax: (325)658-8895
E-mail: info@hospiceofsanangelo.org
URL: http://www.hospiceofsanangelo.org/

21740 ■ VistaCare--San Angelo
402 N Bryant Blvd.
San Angelo, TX 76903
Ph: (325)481-0123
Free: 800-362-7567
Fax: (325)481-3211
URL: http://www.vistacare.com

San Antonio

21741 ■ Air Force Village Home Health & Hospice
4917 Ravenswood Dr.
San Antonio, TX 78227
Free: 800-724-5771
URL: http://www.airforcevillages.com/hospice-care-veterans-military/

21742 ■ Alamo Hospice
114 W. Glenview, Ste. 100
San Antonio, TX 78228
Ph: (210)444-2244
Fax: (210)227-5714
URL: http://www.airforcevillages.com/hospice-care-veterans-military/

21743 ■ Harbour Hospice of Bexar County, LLC
12915 Jones-Maltsberger
San Antonio, TX 78247
Ph: (210)403-9911
Fax: (210)403-9926
E-mail: agorchow@harbourhospice.org
URL: http://harbourhospice.org/

21744 ■ Heart to Heart Hospice of San Antonio, LLC
8918 Tesoro Dr., Ste. A
San Antonio, TX 78217
Ph: (210)824-4113
Fax: (210)824-4994
E-mail: jroost@bethanyhospicecare.com
URL: http://www.hearttohearthospice.com/

21745 ■ Heartland Home Health Care and Hospice--San Antonio
5368 Fredericksburg Rd., Ste. 300
San Antonio, TX 78229
Ph: (210)340-0499
Fax: (210)615-1177
E-mail: careline@hcr-manorcare.com
URL: http://www.hcr-manorcare.com

21746 ■ Hospice Compassus--San Antonio
4204 Woodcock Dr., Ste. 240
San Antonio, TX 78228
Ph: (210)731-0505
Free: 800-662-9213
Fax: (210)731-0223
E-mail: contactusTXSAN@hospicecom.com
URL: http://www.hospicecompassus.com/loc-TX-SAN.html

21747 ■ Hospice Inspiris, LLC
5835 Callighan Rd., Ste. 400
San Antonio, TX 78288
Ph: (210)684-3900
Free: 866-937-4186
Fax: (610)684-3905
URL: http://www.hospiceinspiris.com/

21748 ■ Odyssey Healthcare of San Antonio
4440 Piedras Dr., Ste. 125
San Antonio, TX 78228
Ph: (210)733-1212
Free: 877-637-9432
Fax: (210)733-1331
E-mail: info@odsyhealth.com
URL: http://www.odsyhealth.com

21749 ■ VistaCare--San Antonio
4242 Woodcock Dr., Ste. 101
San Antonio, TX 78228-1325
Ph: (210)738-8141
Free: 800-836-6727
Fax: (210)738-3507
URL: http://www.vistacare.com

21750 ■ VITAS Innovative Hospice Care of San Antonio
5430 Fredericksburg Rd.
San Antonio, TX 78229
Ph: (210)348-4300
Free: 800-278-4827
Fax: (210)348-4380
URL: http://www.vitas.com

21751 ■ VITAS Inpatient Unit--San Antonio
8109 Fredericksburg, 3rd Fl.
San Antonio, TX 78229
Ph: (210)575-0600
Free: 800-278-4827
Fax: (210)575-0610
URL: http://www.vitas.com

San Benito

21752 ■ Amenity Hospice, Inc.
625 N Sam Houston Rd.
San Benito, TX 78586
Ph: (956)361-5100
Fax: (956)361-5106

San Marcos

21753 ■ Central Texas Medical Center Hospice
1315 IH-35 N
San Marcos, TX 78666-7113
Ph: (512)754-6159

Free: 800-927-9004
Fax: (512)754-1657
URL: http://www.ctmc.org/CareAndServices/Hospice.aspx
Formerly: Hospice of Central Texas.

21754 ■ VistaCare-San Marcos
1911 Corporate Dr.
San Marcos, TX 78666
Ph: (512)392-9138
Free: 866-840-2887
Fax: (512)392-9148
E-mail: Adam.Currie@vistacare.com
URL: http://www.vistacare.com/locations/site.asp?228
Adam Currie, Executive Director

Seminole

21755 ■ Memorial Hospice-Seminole
209 NW 8th St.
Seminole, TX 79360
Ph: (432)758-5811
Fax: (432)758-4884
URL: http://www.semmem.com/hospice.php

Sequin

21756 ■ Guadalupe Regional Hospice Guadalupe Regional Medical Center
1215 E Court St.
Sequin, TX 78155
Ph: (830)401-7561
Fax: (830)379-4441
E-mail: rghaynes@grmedcenter.com
URL: http://www.grmedcenter.com/patient_care/#hospice

Seven Points

21757 ■ Lighted Pathways Health Services, Inc.
PO Box 43731
Seven Points, TX 75143
Free: 903-432-9055
Fax: (903)432-9455
E-mail: lightedpathways@yahoo.com
URL: http://www.lightedpathwayshospice.com/

Sherman

21758 ■ Home Hospice of Grayson County
505 W Center St.
Sherman, TX 75090
Ph: (903)868-9315
Free: 888-233-7455
Fax: (903)893-2772
E-mail: info.grayson@homehospice.org
URL: http://www.homehospice.org

Springtown

21759 ■ Solaris Hospice Inc-Springtown
417 E Hwy. 199, Ste. 2
Springtown, TX 76082
Ph: (817)523-5604
Free: 888-376-5274
Fax: (817)523-7947
URL: http://www.solarisfamily.com/areasserved

Stafford

21760 ■ Memorial Hermann Hospice South
11929 W Airport, Ste. 150
Stafford, TX 77477
Ph: (281)325-5650
Fax: (281)565-5220
E-mail: webmaster@memorialhermann.org
URL: http://www.memorialhermann.org/servicesand-programs/hospicecare/content.aspx ?id=1266

Stephenville

21761 ■ Universal Health Care Hospice
1523 W Lingleville Rd.
Stephenville, TX 76401
Ph: (254)918-7420
Free: 800-466-3227
E-mail: debbie@universal-health.com
URL: http://www.universal-health.com/hospice.html
Debbie Schutkowski, Executive Director

Sugar Land

21762 ■ Silverado Hospice of Houston
2205 Williams Trace Blvd.
Sugar Land, TX 77478
Ph: (281)565-2900
Free: 866-493-0675
Fax: (281)565-2901
URL: http://www.silveradosenior.com/hospice/Houston/zip_77478/silverado_senior_l iving/2589

Sulphur Springs

21763 ■ Legacy Hospice-Sulphur Springs
1409 College St., Ste. C
Sulphur Springs, TX 75482
Ph: (903)335-8901
Fax: (903)335-8904
E-mail: ccclegacyhospice@yahoo.com
URL: http://www.legacyhospice.com/contact.html

Temple

21764 ■ Scott & White Home Care and Hospice Agency
2401 S 31st St.
Temple, TX 76508
Ph: (254)724-2111
Free: 800-792-3710
Fax: (254)724-1667
E-mail: appointments@swmail.sw.org
URL: http://www.sw.org/web/patientsAndVisitors/iw-content/public/hospice/en_us/ht ml/hospice.jsp

21765 ■ VistaCare--Temple
2626B S 37th St.
Temple, TX 76504
Ph: (254)742-2000
Free: 800-643-3139
Fax: (254)742-2023
URL: http://www.vistacare.com
Formerly: VistaCare Family Hospice of Temple.

Texarkana

21766 ■ Hospice of Texarkana, Inc.
803 Spruce St.
Texarkana, TX 75501
Ph: (903)794-4263
Fax: (903)774-1108
URL: http://www.hospiceoftexarkana.org/home.htm

21767 ■ Lester Dierksen Memorial Hospice
6500 N Summer Hill Rd.
Texarkana, TX 75503
Ph: (903)793-6350
Fax: (903)793-6354

21768 ■ Serenity Hospice-Texarkana
4508 Texas Blvd.
Texarkana, TX 75501
Ph: (903)255-0430
URL: http://www.serenityhospice.net/

Texas City

21769 ■ Hospice Care Team, Inc.--Texas City
1708 N Amburn Rd.
Texas City, TX 77591
Ph: (409)938-0070
Free: 800-545-8738
Fax: (409)938-1509
E-mail: info@hospicecareteam.org
URL: http://www.hospicecareteam.org

Tomball

21770 ■ Lighthouse Hospice-Tomball
14011 Park Dr., Ste. 201
Tomball, TX 77377
Ph: (281)290-7727
Free: 888-290-7727
Fax: (281)290-8460
URL: http://www.lighthouse-hospice.com/

21771 ■ Sunset Hospice, Inc-Tomball
1420 Rudel St.
Tomball, TX 77401
Ph: (281)290-7600
Fax: (281)290-7603
E-mail: SunsetHospice@yahoo.com
URL: http://www.sunsethospice.com/

Tyler

21772 ■ Hospice of East Texas
4111 University Blvd.
Tyler, TX 75701
Ph: (903)266-3400
Free: 800-777-9860
URL: http://www.hospiceofeasttexas.org

21773 ■ Odyssey HealthCare of East Texas
Wadel-Connally Bldg.
112 E Line St.
Tyler, TX 75702
Ph: (903)533-8383
Free: 877-637-9432
Fax: (903)533-8388
URL: http://www.odyssey-healthcare.com/site.asp?id=158&SiteBrand=ODYSSEY&ReferType=&ReferBrand=Odyssey

21774 ■ Serenity Hospice-Tyler
120 E South Town, Ste. 200
Tyler, TX 75703
Ph: (903)509-0301
Fax: (903)509-5971
E-mail: contactus@legacyhospice.com
URL: http://www.legacyhospice.com/

Uvalde

21775 ■ Uvalde Memorial Home Health & Hospice Services
1025 Garner Field Rd.
Uvalde, TX 78801
Ph: (830)278-6251
Fax: (830)278-8529
E-mail: j.buckner@umhtx.org
URL: http://www.umhtx.org

Victoria

21776 ■ Hospice of South Texas--Victoria
605 E Locust Ave.
Victoria, TX 77901
Ph: (361)572-4300
Free: 800-874-6908
Fax: (361)570-8742
E-mail: hospice@hospice-vic.org
URL: http://www.hospiceofsouthtexas.org

Waco

21777 ■ Hillcrest Community Hospice
3000 Herring Ave.
Waco, TX 76708
Ph: (254)202-5150
Fax: (254)752-5180
URL: http://www.hillcrest.net/

21778 ■ Providence Hospice--Waco
4830 Lakewood Dr.
Waco, TX 76710
Ph: (254)399-9099
Fax: (254)399-8397
URL: http://www.providencehospice.org/

21779 ■ Texas Home Health Hospice--Quincy
7503 Bosque Blvd.
Waco, TX 76712
Ph: (254)756-0404
Free: 866-382-0404
Fax: (254)757-1468
URL: http://www.mytexashospice.com/

21780 ■ VistaCare--Waco
510 N Valley Mills Dr., Ste. 703
Waco, TX 76710
Ph: (254)399-0963
Free: 800-311-6831
Fax: (254)399-8200
URL: http://www.vistacare.com

Waxahachie

21781 ■ Odyssey HealthCare of Waxahachie
2001 Bates, Ste. 400
Waxahachie, TX 75167
Ph: (972)938-9888
Free: 877-637-9432
Fax: (972)938-9838
E-mail: info@odsyhealth.com
URL: http://www.odsyhealth.com

Whitney

21782 ■ Hospice of the Heart Inc.
210 N Bosque St.
Whitney, TX 76692
Ph: (254)694-6009
Free: 800-773-3245
Fax: (254)694-9926
E-mail: hoth@valornet.com
URL: http://www.lakewhitneychamber.com/OnePagers/Hospice_of_the_heart.htm

Wichita Falls

21783 ■ Hospice of Wichita Falls Inc.
4909 Johnson Rd.
Wichita Falls, TX 76310
Ph: (940)691-0982
Free: 800-378-2822
Fax: (940)687-1294
E-mail: hospice@hospiceofwf.org
URL: http://www.hospiceofwf.org

21784 ■ Solaris Hospice Inc-Wichita Falls
2910 Kemp
Wichita Falls, TX 76308
Ph: (940)322-3344
Fax: (940)322-3349
URL: http://www.solarisfamily.com/

Yoakum

21785 ■ Accolade Hospice--Yoakum
222 W Grand
Yoakum, TX 77995
Ph: (361)293-9099
Free: 877-293-9099
Fax: (361)293-9098
URL: http://www.accoladehomecare.com

UTAH

American Fork

21786 ■ Applegate HomeCare and Hospice-American Fork
28 S 1100 E
American Fork, UT 84003
Ph: (801)763-0101
Fax: (801)763-0111
URL: http://www.applegatehomecare.com/Pages/Home.aspx

21787 ■ Hearts for Hospice--American Fork
677 Quality Dr., Ste. 201
American Fork, UT 84003
Ph: (801)772-0243
Fax: (801)772-0978
E-mail: infohearts@heartsforhospice.com
URL: http://www.heartsforhospice.com/

Bountiful

21788 ■ Applegate Homecare and Hospice-Bountiful
425 Medical Dr.
Bountiful, UT 84010
Ph: (801)296-2245
Fax: (801)296-2257
URL: http://www.applegatehomecare.com/Pages/Home.aspx

21789 ■ Aspire Hospice
420 W 1500 S
Bountiful, UT 84010
Ph: (801)292-0296
Fax: (801)294-5601
URL: http://www.aspirehealthcare.org/

Brigham City

21790 ■ Alpine Hospice-Brigham City
95 N 100E
Brigham City, UT 84302
Ph: (435)734-1300
Fax: (435)734-9384
URL: http://www.alpinehomecare.com/

21791 ■ Integrity Hospice LLC-Brigham City
64 S 100 W
Brigham City, UT 84302
Ph: (435)757-8368
Free: 888-922-2739
Fax: (435)734-9819
URL: http://integrityhomecare.org/hospice-care

Cedar City

21792 ■ Intermountain Homecare-Cedar City
1333 N Main St.
Cedar City, UT 84721
Ph: (435)716-5349
Fax: (435)716-5361
URL: http://intermountainhealthcare.org/services/homecare/hospice/Pages/home.asp x

21793 ■ Southern Utah Hospice--Cedar City
337 S Main, Ste. 210
Cedar City, UT 84720
Ph: (435)586-9400
Fax: (435)865-1539
URL: http://www.nursingathome.com/

Delta

21794 ■ Intermountain Homecare-Delta
126 S White Sage Ave.
Delta, UT 84624
Ph: (801)977-9900
Free: 800-527-1118
Fax: (801)977-9956
URL: http://intermountainhealthcare.org/services/homecare/hospice/Pages/home.asp x

Fillmore

21795 ■ Intermountain Homecare-Fillmore
25 N Main St.
Fillmore, UT 84631
Ph: (801)977-9900
Fax: (801)977-9956
URL: http://intermountainhealthcare.org/services/homecare/hospice/Pages/home.asp x

Garden City

21796 ■ Access Home Care and Hospice--Garden City
96 W Logan Rd., Ste. 2
Garden City, UT 84028
Ph: (435)946-2620
Fax: (435)946-2605
URL: http://www.accesshomecareandhospice.com/

Gunnison

21797 ■ Gunnison Valley Hospital
45 E 100 N
Gunnison, UT 84634
Ph: (435)528-3955
Fax: (435)528-2188
URL: http://www.gvhospital.org/

Heber City

21798 ■ Alpine Hospice-Heber
135 S Main, Ste. 206
Heber City, UT 84032
Ph: (435)654-1464
Fax: (435)657-1612
URL: http://www.gvhospital.org/

21799 ■ Applegate HomeCare and Hospice--Heber City
345 W 600 S
Heber City, UT 84032
Ph: (435)654-5983
Fax: (435)654-9110
URL: http://www.applegatehomecare.com/Pages/Home.aspx

21800 ■ Intermountain Homecare-Heber City
175 N Main
Heber City, UT 84032
Ph: (435)657-4323
Fax: (435)654-2576
URL: http://intermountainhealthcare.org/services/homecare/hospice/Pages/home.asp x

Hildale

21801 ■ Southern Utah Hospice-Hildale
1280 W Utah Ave.
Hildale, UT 84784
Ph: (435)874-2333
Fax: (435)874-2334
URL: http://www.nursingathome.com/

Hurricane

21802 ■ Southern Utah Hospice--Hurricane
51 N 1000 West, Ste. 6
Hurricane, UT 84737
Ph: (435)635-9300
Fax: (435)635-9306
URL: http://www.nursingathome.com

Kanab

21803 ■ Southern Utah Hospice--Kanab
60 South 100 E
Kanab, UT 84741
Ph: (435)644-2200
URL: http://www.nursingathome.com

Layton

21804 ■ Comfort Hospice Care-Layton
124 S Fairfield Rd., Ste. B
Layton, UT 84041
Ph: (801)547-0812
Fax: (801)547-0818
E-mail: Carolcable@comforthospicecare.com
URL: http://www.comforthospicecare.com/

21805 ■ Symbii Home Health and Hospice--Layton
1916 N 700 W
Layton, UT 84041
Ph: (801)444-0221
Fax: (801)444-2658
URL: http://www.symbiihealth.com/

Logan

21806 ■ Access Home Care and Hospice--Logan
74 W 100 N
Logan, UT 84321
Ph: (435)755-6599
Fax: (435)755-6548
URL: http://www.accesshomecareandhospice.com/

21807 ■ Intermountain Homecare--Logan
1400 N 550 East
Logan, UT 84341
Ph: (435)716-5477
Fax: (435)716-5361
URL: https://intermountainhealthcare.org/services/homecare/hospice/Pages/home.as px
Formerly: IHC Hospice of Cache Valley.

Moab

21808 ■ Community Nursing Services-Moab
1030 S Bowling Alley La., Ste. 1
Moab, UT 84532
Ph: (435)259-0466
Free: 866-220-1712
Fax: (435)259-0467
URL: http://cns-cares.org/

Mount Pleasant

21809 ■ Intermountain Homecare-Mt. Pleasant
130 W Main
Mount Pleasant, UT 84647
Ph: (801)977-9900
Fax: (801)977-9956
URL: http://intermountainhealthcare.org/services/homecare/hospice/Pages/home.asp x

Murray

21810 ■ Alpine Hospice--Murray
990 W 5370 South
Murray, UT 84123
Ph: (801)747-5500
Fax: (801)747-5587
URL: http://www.alpinehospice.com/locations.asp

21811 ■ Community Nursing Services--Murray
383 W Vine St., Ste. 300
Murray, UT 84123
Ph: (801)233-6100
Free: 800-486-2186
Fax: (801)233-6110
E-mail: lweagle@cnsvna.org
URL: http://www.cnsvna.org

21812 ■ Haven Hospice--Murray
5292 S College Dr.
Murray, UT 84123
Ph: (801)676-6000
Fax: (801)676-6001
URL: http://www.superiorhomecare.com/

21813 ■ Summit Home Health & Hospice
5882 S 900 E, Ste. 101
Murray, UT 84121
Ph: (801)542-7150
Fax: (801)542-7154
URL: http://www.summithomehealth.com/

21814 ■ Superior Hospice-Murray
184 E 5900 S
Murray, UT 84107
Ph: (801)254-3200
Free: 800-466-3227
Fax: (801)254-8680
URL: http://www.superiorhomecare.com/

Nephi

21815 ■ Central Valley Hospice
152 W 1500 N
Nephi, UT 84648
Ph: (435)623-3051
Fax: (435)623-3059

Ogden

21816 ■ Applegate HomeCare and Hospice--Ogden
1492 E Ridgeline Dr.
Ogden, UT 84405
Ph: (801)621-4027
Fax: (801)399-9740
URL: http://www.applegatehomecare.com/Pages/Home.aspx

21817 ■ Community Nursing Services-Ogden
425 E 5350 S, Ste. 110
Ogden, UT 84403
Ph: (801)476-0088
Fax: (801)476-0099
URL: http://cns-cares.org/

21818 ■ Hearts for Hospice--Ogden
942 Chamber St., No. 16
Ogden, UT 84403
Ph: (801)475-6222
Free: 888-772-0243
Fax: (891)475-6061
URL: http://www.heartsforhospice.com

21819 ■ Hospice Care of Northern Utah, LLC
986 E 1200 N
Ogden, UT 84404
Ph: (801)552-8270
Fax: (801)621-5434

21820 ■ Intermountain Hospice--Ogden
3776 Wall Ave.
Ogden, UT 84405
Ph: (801)399-1400
Fax: (801)621-2531
URL: http://intermountainhealthcare.org/Pages/home.aspx

21821 ■ VistaCare--Ogden
425 E 5350 S, Ste. 155
Ogden, UT 84405
Ph: (801)475-5300
Free: 877-475-5300
Fax: (801)475-5235
URL: http://www.vistacare.com

Orem

21822 ■ Alpine Hospice - Orem
259 Sorem Blvd.
Orem, UT 84058
Ph: (801)221-0669
Fax: (801)225-1529
URL: http://www.alpinehospice.com/locations.asp

21823 ■ IHC Hospice
1165 S 800 East
Orem, UT 84097
Ph: (801)225-0584
Free: 800-888-9225
URL: http://intermountainhealthcare.org/services/homecare/hospice/Pages/home.asp x

Providence

21824 ■ Alpine Hospice - Logan
227 N Spring Creek Pkwy.
Providence, UT 84332
Ph: (435)753-7001
Fax: (435)753-7088
URL: http://www.alpinehospice.com/locations.asp

Richfield

21825 ■ IHC Hospice--Richfield
70 E 1000 N, Ste. B
Richfield, UT 84701
Ph: (435)893-0371
Free: 800-777-4971
Fax: (435)893-0383
URL: http://intermountainhealthcare.org/Pages/home.aspx

Roosevelt

21826 ■ Uintah Basin Hospice
26 W 200 N, Ste. 78-15
Roosevelt, UT 84066
Ph: (435)722-2418
Free: 800-874-8244
E-mail: info@ubmc.org
URL: http://www.ubmc.org

Saint George

21827 ■ Applegate HomeCare and Hospice-St. George
1490 E Foremaster Dr., Ste. 340
Saint George, UT 84790
Ph: (435)628-1569
Fax: (435)634-9480
URL: http://www.applegatehomecare.com/Pages/Home.aspx

21828 ■ Rocky Mountain Hospice-St. George
230 N 1680 E
Saint George, UT 84790
Ph: (435)753-6699
Free: 800-574-7666
URL: http://www.rmcare.com/

21829 ■ Southern Utah Hospice--Saint George
640 E 700 South
Saint George, UT 84790
Ph: (435)673-8666
Fax: (435)673-0436
URL: http://www.nursingathome.com

21830 ■ Zion's Way Hospice
912 W 1600 S
Saint George, UT 84770
Ph: (435)688-0648
Fax: (435)688-0715
E-mail: jlabrum@zionswayhospice.com
URL: http://www.zionswayhospice.com/

Salt Lake City

21831 ■ Affinity Hospice of Life--Salt Lake City
4141 Highland Dr.
Salt Lake City, UT 84124
Ph: (801)973-0217
Fax: (801)973-0246
URL: http://www.affinityhospice.com/locationdetails.php?id=258

21832 ■ Applegate HomeCare and Hospice-Salt Lake City
5330 S 900 E
Salt Lake City, UT 84117
Ph: (801)261-3023
Fax: (801)262-2872
URL: http://www.applegatehomecare.com/Pages/Home.aspx

21833 ■ Bristol Hospice-Salt Lake City
670 E 3900 S, Ste. 210
Salt Lake City, UT 84107
Ph: (801)924-0867
Fax: (801)747-3864
URL: http://www.bristolhospice.com/

21834 ■ Care Source Hospice
1624 E 4500 South
Salt Lake City, UT 84117
Ph: (801)266-7200
Fax: (801)266-7004
URL: http://www.ecaresource.com

21835 ■ Community Nursing Services-Corporate Office
383 W Vine St., Ste. 300
Salt Lake City, UT 84123
Ph: (801)233-6100
Free: 800-486-2186
Fax: (801)233-6110
URL: http://www.cns-cares.org/

21836 ■ Good Shepherd Home Health and Hospice
5383 S 900 E
Salt Lake City, UT 84117
Ph: (801)277-6474
Fax: (801)277-6475
URL: http://www.goodshepherdhc.com/

21837 ■ HCS Hospice Specialists
3949 S 700 E
Salt Lake City, UT 84107
Ph: (801)293-8700
Fax: (801)293-8701
E-mail: info@hospicespecialists.com
URL: http://www.hospicespecialists.com/

21838 ■ Hearts for Hospice--Salt Lake City
111 East 5600 S, No. 110
Salt Lake City, UT 84107
Ph: (801)288-0670
Free: 888-772-0243
URL: http://www.heartsforhospice.com/home.php

21839 ■ IHC Hospice--Salt Lake City
2250 S 1300 West
Salt Lake City, UT 84119
Ph: (801)977-9900
Free: 800-527-1118
URL: http://intermountainhealthcare.org/Pages/home.aspx

21840 ■ Inspiration Hospice-Salt Lake City
835 E 4800 S
Salt Lake City, UT 84107
Ph: (801)281-1314
Fax: (801)281-1450
E-mail: info@inspirationhospice.com
URL: http://www.inspirationhospice.com/

21841 ■ Lighthouse Hospice-Salt Lake City
6794 S 1300 E
Salt Lake City, UT 84121
Ph: (801)562-2273
Fax: (801)569-2449
E-mail: keith@lighthousehospice.biz
URL: http://www.lighthousehospice.biz/

21842 ■ Millcreek Home Health and Hospice
1398 E Luck La.
Salt Lake City, UT 84106
Ph: (801)463-2478
Fax: (801)486-0961
URL: http://www.millcreek-online.com/
Nan Green, Executive Director

21843 ■ Silverado Hospice of Utah-Salt Lake City
860 E 4500 S
Salt Lake City, UT 84117
Ph: (801)506-1500
Free: 866-522-8125
Fax: (801)506-1501
URL: http://www.silveradosenior.com/hospice_care

21844 ■ University of Utah Palliative Care
50 N Medical Dr., Ste. 4B120
Salt Lake City, UT 84132
Ph: (801)581-7818
Fax: (801)585-9166
URL: http://healthcare.utah.edu/internalMedicine/generalMedicine/palliative.html

21845 ■ VistaCare-Salt Lake City
1111 Brickyard Rd.
Salt Lake City, UT 84106
Ph: (801)467-7772
Free: 866-317-8921
Fax: (801)467-7799
E-mail: TArnold@odsyhealth.com
URL: http://www.vistacare.com/locations/site.asp?224
Trisha Arnold, Executive Director

Sandy

21846 ■ Access Home Care and Hospice--Sandy
9565 S 700 E, Ste. 201
Sandy, UT 84070
Ph: (801)495-3090
Fax: (801)495-3088
URL: http://www.accesshomecareandhospice.com/

21847 ■ Symbii Home Health and Hospice-Salt Lake City
45 W 10000 S
Sandy, UT 84070
Ph: (891)433-0344
Fax: (801)433-0075
URL: http://www.symbiihealth.com/

South Ogden

21848 ■ VistaCare-South Ogden
425 E 5350 S
South Ogden, UT 84405
Ph: (801)475-5300
Free: 877-475-5300
Fax: (801)475-5235
E-mail: unknown@odsyhealth.com
URL: http://www.vistacare.com/locations/site.asp?216

Tooele

21849 ■ Mountain West Hospice
Mountain West Medical Center
1887 N Aaron Dr.
Tooele, UT 84074
Ph: (435)882-4163
URL: http://www.mountainwestmc.com/Our%20Services/Pages/Home%20Care%20and%20Hosp ice%20Services.aspx

VERMONT

Barre

21850 ■ Central Vermont Home Health and Hospice Inc.
600 Granger Rd.
Barre, VT 05641
Ph: (802)223-1878
Free: 800-286-1219
Fax: (802)223-5897
URL: http://www.cvhhh.org/

Bennington

21851 ■ VNA and Hospice of Southwestern Vermont Healthcare
160 Benmont Ave.
Bennington, VT 05201-5004
Ph: (802)442-5502
Free: 800-496-5400
Fax: (820)442-4919
URL: http://svhealthcare.org

Brattleboro

21852 ■ Brattleboro Area Hospice
191 Canal St.
Brattleboro, VT 05301
Ph: (802)257-0775
Free: 800-579-7300
Fax: (802)254-8652
E-mail: brattleborohospice@adelphia.net
URL: http://www.brattleborohospice.org

Colchester

21853 ■ Hospice of the Champlain Valley
1110 Prim Rd., Ste. 1
Colchester, VT 05446
Ph: (802)860-4410
Fax: (802)860-4466
E-mail: means@vnacares.org
URL: http://www.vnacares.org/

Enosburg Falls

21854 ■ Franklin County Home Health Agency
44 Center St.
Enosburg Falls, VT 05450
Ph: (802)933-8387
Fax: (802)933-6105
E-mail: info@fchha.org
URL: http://www.fchha.org/hospice.htm

Morrisville

21855 ■ Lamoille Home Health and Hospice
54 Farr Ave.
Morrisville, VT 05661-9181
Ph: (802)888-4651
Fax: (802)888-7822
E-mail: vahha@comcast.net
URL: http://www.vnavt.com/lamoi.htm

Norwich

21856 ■ Bayada Hospice
309 Main St., Ste. 1
Norwich, VT 05055
Ph: (802)526-2380
Fax: (802)526-2518
E-mail: mco@bayada.com
URL: http://bayada.com/

Rutland

21857 ■ Rutland Area VNA & Hospice
7 Albert Cree Dr.
Rutland, VT 05702
Ph: (802)775-0568
Fax: (802)775-2304
URL: http://www.ravnah.org/

Saint Johnsbury

21858 ■ Caledonia Home Health Care and Hospice
Northern Counties Health Care
161 Sherman Dr.
Saint Johnsbury, VT 05819-0383
Ph: (802)748-8116
Free: 800-924-8116
Fax: (802)748-3285
E-mail: brendas@nchcvt.org

Springfield

21859 ■ VNA and Hospice of VT/NH-Springfield
38 Pleasant St.
Springfield, VT 05156
Ph: (802)885-2503
Free: 800-575-5162

Williston

21860 ■ Vermont Respite House
99 Allen Brook La.
Williston, VT 05446
Ph: (802)879-0943
Fax: (802)860-4466
E-mail: keegan@vnacares.org
URL: http://www.vnacares.org/health-care-services/end-of-life-care/vermont-respi te-house

VIRGINIA

Abingdon

21861 ■ Hospice of Southwest Virginia--Abingdon
Wythe County Community Hospital
301 Valley St. NE
Abingdon, VA 24210
Ph: (276)623-1440
Free: 866-312-5946
Fax: (276)628-4877
URL: http://www.wcch.org/getpage.php?name=hospice&sub=Services

21862 ■ Hospice Support Services of Washington County
PO Box 1172
Abingdon, VA 24212
Ph: (276)676-7220
Fax: (276)676-4394
URL: http://www.hospicewashingtoncounty.org/support.html

Alexandria

21863 ■ Capital Hospice--Alexandria
5568 General Washington Dr., Ste. A215
Alexandria, VA 22312
Ph: (703)333-6960
Free: 800-869-2136
URL: http://www.capitalhospice.org/

21864 ■ National Hospice and Palliative Care Organization (NHPCO)
1731 King St., Ste. 100
Alexandria, VA 22314
Ph: (703)837-1500
Free: 800-658-8898
Fax: (703)837-1233
E-mail: nhpco_info@nhpco.org
URL: http://www.nhpco.org
J. Donald Schumacher, President
Description: Represents hospice organizations and individuals interested in the promotion of the hospice concept and program of care. Promotes standards of care in program planning and implementation. Monitors health care legislation and regulation relevant to hospice care. Sponsors professional liaison and peer group networking. Collects data for demonstrating definitive national trends in the hospice movement. Compiles statistics. Conducts educational and training programs in numerous aspects of hospice care for administrators and care-givers. Maintains nonlending library of hospice-related books. Operates helpline to assist public in identifying hospice programs in their area.

Annandale

21865 ■ Professional Healthcare Resources
7619 Little River Turnpike, Ste. 600
Annandale, VA 22003
Ph: (703)379-9012
Free: 866-243-1234
Fax: (866)845-0762
E-mail: intake@phri.com
URL: http://www.phri.com/

Arlington

21866 ■ Capital Hospice--Arlington Halquist Memorial Inpatient Center
4715 15th St. N
Arlington, VA 22205-2640
Ph: (703)525-7070
Free: 800-869-2136
Fax: (703)525-7313
URL: http://www.capitalhospice.org/

Bedford

21867 ■ Bedford Hospice Care
815 Summit St.
Bedford, VA 24523-2636
Ph: (540)587-6592
Free: 800-422-8482
Fax: (540)587-4105
URL: http://www.carilion.com

Bristol

21868 ■ Caris HealthCare-Bristol
1701 Euclid Ave., Ste. H
Bristol, VA 24201
Free: 877-342-3456
URL: http://www.carishealthcare.com/

Charlottesville

21869 ■ Hospice House--Charlottesville
501 Park St.
Charlottesville, VA 22902
Ph: (434)817-6900

21870 ■ Hospice of the Piedmont--Charlottesville
675 Peter Jefferson Pkwy., Ste. 300
Charlottesville, VA 22911
Ph: (434)817-6900
Free: 800-975-5501
Fax: (434)245-0187
E-mail: info@hopva.org
URL: http://www.hopva.org

Chesapeake

21871 ■ Medi Home Health and Hospice-Chesapeake
1112 B Eden Way N
Chesapeake, VA 23320
Ph: (757)420-7192

21872 ■ Sentara Hospice Program
535 Independence Pkwy., Ste. 200
Chesapeake, VA 23320
Ph: (757)549-5744
Fax: (757)549-5685
URL: http://www.sentara.com/Services/HomeCare/Pages/HospiceProgram.aspx

Christiansburg

21873 ■ Good Samaritan Hospice Inc-Christiansburg
1160 Moose Dr. NW
Christiansburg, VA 24073
Ph: (540)381-3171
E-mail: info@goodsamhospice.org
URL: http://www.goodsamhospice.com/

Clifton Forge

21874 ■ Mountain Regional Hospice
537 Main St.
Clifton Forge, VA 24422
Ph: (540)862-8820
Fax: (540)862-8822
URL: http://www.mrhpco.com

Colonial Heights

21875 ■ Crater Community Hospice Inc.
840 W Roslyn Rd., Ste. E
Colonial Heights, VA 23834-3547
Ph: (804)526-4300
Fax: (804)526-4337
URL: http://www.cratercommunityhospice.org/index.shtml

Covington

21876 ■ Sentara Hospice Program-Covington
214 W Main St.
Covington, VA 24426
Ph: (540)965-9260
Fax: (540)962-7113
URL: http://www.sentara.com/Services/HomeCare/Pages/HospiceProgram.aspx

Culpeper

21877 ■ Hospice of the Rapidan
1200 Sunset Ln.
Culpeper, VA 22701
Ph: (540)825-4840
Fax: (540)825-7752
E-mail: kclements@hotr.org
URL: http://www.hotr.org

Danville

21878 ■ Liberty Home Care & Hospice
500 Piney Forest Rd.
Danville, VA 24541
Ph: (434)799-2308
Free: 866-240-6147
Fax: (434)799-2356
URL: http://www.libertyhomecare.com/details.asp?ID=1

Fairfax

21879 ■ Evercare Hospice & Palliative Care--Fairfax
4000 Legato Rd.
Fairfax, VA 22033
Ph: (703)896-7700
Fax: (703)383-3450
URL: http://www.evercarehospice.com/

21880 ■ Heartland Home Health Care and Hospice--Fairfax
3900 Jermantown Rd., Ste. 460
Fairfax, VA 22030
Ph: (703)273-8693
Fax: (703)273-8694
E-mail: careline@hcr-manorcare.com
URL: http://www.hcr-manorcare.com

Falls Church

21881 ■ Capital Hospice--Falls Church
2900 Telestar Ct.
Falls Church, VA 22042
Ph: (703)538-2065
Free: 866-545-6964
URL: http://www.capitalhospice.org

21882 ■ Goodwin House Hospice
3440 S Jefferson St.
Falls Church, VA 22041
Ph: (703)820-1488
E-mail: llateana@goodwinhouse.org
URL: http://www.goodwinhouse.org
Linda Lateana, Executive Director

Farmville

21883 ■ Centra Hospice of the Hills
713 Oak St.
Farmville, VA 23901
Ph: (434)315-2885
Fax: (434)200.7468
URL: http://www.centrahealth.com/

21884 ■ Hospice of Central Virginia--Farmville
202 Clark St.
Farmville, VA 23901
Ph: (434)392-9666
Fax: (434)392-8954
URL: http://www.hospiceva.com/

Fishersville

21885 ■ AMC Hospice of the Shenandoah
64 Sports Medicine Dr.
Fishersville, VA 22939
Ph: (540)332-4909
Fax: (540)332-4991
E-mail: hospice@augustahealth.com
URL: http://www.augustahealth.com/hospice

Franklin

21886 ■ Southampton Memorial Hospice
100 Fairview Dr.
Franklin, VA 23851
Ph: (757)562-5887
Fax: (757)516-0090
URL: http://www.smhfranklin.com/pages/home.aspx

Fredericksburg

21887 ■ Mary Washington Home Health and Hospice
5012 Southpoint Pkwy.
Fredericksburg, VA 22407
Ph: (540)741-1667
Free: 800-257-1667
Fax: (540)741-1841
URL: http://www.medicorp.org/hospice.mgi

Galax

21888 ■ Mountain Valley Hospice and Palliative Care-Galax
606A E Stuart Dr.
Galax, VA 24333
Ph: (276)236-3939
Fax: (276)236-4843
URL: http://www.mtnvalleyhospice.org/

21889 ■ Twin County Hospice
Twin County Regional Healthcare
PO Box 106
Galax, VA 24333
Ph: (276)236-0973
Free: 800-295-3342
Fax: (276)236-6455
URL: http://www.tcrh.org/services/hospice/default_hospice.asp

Glen Allen

21890 ■ Hospice Community Care-Glen Allen
10128 W Broad St., Ste. J
Glen Allen, VA 23060
Ph: (804)290-0951
Free: 800-409-9094
Fax: (804)290-0952
E-mail: info@hospicecommunity.com
URL: http://www.hospicecommunity.com/Virginia/index.html

Gloucester

21891 ■ Riverside Walter Reed Hospice
7358 Main St.
Gloucester, VA 23061
Ph: (804)693-1111
Fax: (804)693-8816
URL: http://www.riversideonline.com/homecare/hospice.cfm

Hampton

21892 ■ Sentara Home Care & Hospice-Hampton
3713 Magruder Blvd., Ste. G
Hampton, VA 23666
Ph: (757)766-2600
Fax: (757)766-1728
URL: http://www.sentara.com/Pages/default.aspx

Harrisonburg

21893 ■ Rockingham Memorial Hospital Hospice
235 Cantrell Ave.
Harrisonburg, VA 22801
Ph: (540)433-4429
Fax: (540)433-4193
URL: http://www.rmhonline.com

Leesburg

21894 ■ Capital Hospice--Leesburg
209 Gibson St. NW, Ste. 202
Leesburg, VA 20176
Ph: (703)777-7866
Free: 800-869-2136
Fax: (703)771-8904
URL: http://www.capitalhospice.org/

Lexington

21895 ■ Rockbridge Area Hospice
315 Myers St.
Lexington, VA 24450
Ph: (540)463-1848
Fax: (540)463-5219
URL: http://www.rockbridgeareahospice.org/

Lynchburg

21896 ■ Centra Health Hospice of the Hills
3300 Rivermont Ave.
Lynchburg, VA 24501
Ph: (434)200-3204
Fax: (434)200-7468
URL: http://lgh.centrahealth.com/services/hospice-of-the-hills

Manassas

21897 ■ Capital Hospice--Manassas
10530 Linden Lake Plz.
Manassas, VA 20109
Ph: (703)392-6707
Free: 800-869-2136
Fax: (703)392-5116
URL: http://www.capitalhospice.org/

Newport News

21898 ■ Heartland Hospice Services--Newport News
11835 Fishing Point Dr.
Newport News, VA 23606
Ph: (757)594-8215
Fax: (757)594-8530
URL: http://www.hcr-manorcare.com/

21899 ■ Hospice Community Care-Newport News
1064 Loftis Blvd.
Newport News, VA 23606
Ph: (757)594-0288
Fax: (757)594-0388
URL: http://www.harborlight.com/

21900 ■ Riverside Hospice
12420 Warwick Blvd.
Newport News, VA 23606-4207
Ph: (757)594-2745
Fax: (757)594-3227
URL: http://www.riversideonline.com/homecare/hospice.cfm

Norfolk

21901 ■ Odyssey HealthCare of Hampton Roads
6363 Center Dr., Ste. 201
Norfolk, VA 23502
Ph: (757)461-0600
Free: 877-637-9432
Fax: (757)461-0610
E-mail: info@odsyhealth.com
URL: http://www.odsyhealth.com

21902 ■ Personal Touch Home Care and Hospice
5505 Robin Hood Rd., Ste. C1
Norfolk, VA 23573
Ph: (757)855-1355
Fax: (757)855-1199
E-mail: swalton@pthomecare.com
URL: http://www.pthomecare.com/pages/index.cfm?CFID=2009246&CFTOKEN=17721874

21903 ■ Sentara Home Care and Hospice Services
6015 Poplar Hall Dr., Ste. 101
Norfolk, VA 23502
Ph: (757)538-9324
URL: http://www.sentara.com/Services/HomeCare/Pages/HomeCareServices.aspx

Onancock

21904 ■ Hospice and Palliative Care of the Eastern Shore
165 Market St.
Onancock, VA 23417
Ph: (757)787-3310
Fax: (757)787-3320
E-mail: kagar@hpces.org
URL: http://www.hpces.org/
Karen Agar, Executive Director

Petersburg

21905 ■ Crater Community Hospice, Inc
3916 S Crater Rd.
Petersburg, VA 23805
Ph: (804)526-4300
Fax: (804)526-4337
E-mail: info@cratercommunityhospice.org
URL: http://www.cratercommunityhospice.org/index.shtml

Portsmouth

21906 ■ Bon Secours Hospice--Portsmouth
3636 High St.
Portsmouth, VA 23707
Ph: (757)889-2273
Fax: (757)397-6457
E-mail: june_hecker@bshsi.org
URL: http://www.bonsecourshamptonroads.com/our-services-home-health-care-hospice -and-palliative-care.html/

21907 ■ Edmarc Hospice for Children
516 London St.
Portsmouth, VA 23704
Ph: (757)967-9251
Fax: (757)967-9124
URL: http://www.edmarc.org

Radford

21908 ■ Carilion Hospice Service, NRV
707 Randolph St.
Radford, VA 24141
Ph: (540)633-9370
Fax: (540)633-9377
URL: http://www.carilion.com

Reston

21909 ■ Evercare Hospice & Palliative Care--Reston
12018 Sunrise Valley Dr.
Reston, VA 20191
Ph: (571)262-5200
Free: 888-245-1384
Fax: (571)521-7249
URL: http://www.evercarehospice.com/index.jsp

Richlands

21910 ■ Legacy Hospice
Preferred Hospice
1963 2nd St.
Richlands, VA 24641
Ph: (276)596-9181
Free: 866-596-9181
Fax: (276)596-9182
URL: http://www.legacyhospicecare.org/

Richmond

21911 ■ AseraCare Hospice-Richmond
8001 Franklin Farms Dr.
Richmond, VA 23229
Ph: (804)282-4364
Free: 866-691-8959
Fax: (804)288-4734
URL: http://www.aseracare.com/

21912 ■ Bon Secours Hospice--Richmond
8580 Magellan Pkwy., Bldg. 4
Richmond, VA 23227
Ph: (804)627-5200
Free: 866-664-6344
URL: http://www.bshsi.com

21913 ■ Care Alternatives of Virginia, LLC
6802 Paragon Pl., Ste. 103
Richmond, VA 23230
Ph: (804)673-1330
Free: 866-821-1212
Fax: (804)673-2778
URL: http://www.carealt.com/abouthospice.asp

21914 ■ Heartland Home Health Care and Hospice, Inc.--Richmond
1504 Santa Rosa Rd., Ste. 114
Richmond, VA 23229
Ph: (804)288-0235
Fax: (804)288-4380
E-mail: carolino@hcr-manorcare.com
URL: http://www.hcr-manorcare.com

21915 ■ Hospice of Central Virginia--Richmond
7231 Forest Ave., Ste. 100
Richmond, VA 23226
Ph: (804)281-0451
Free: 800-501-0451
Fax: (804)281-0954
URL: http://www.americanhospice.com

21916 ■ Hunter Holmes McGuire Veterans Affairs Hospice Unit
1201 Broad Rock Blvd.
Richmond, VA 23224
Ph: (804)675-5448
Fax: (804)675-5386
URL: http://www2.va.gov/directory/guide/facility.asp?id=112

21917 ■ Medi Home Health and Hospice--Richmond
8100 3 Chopt Rd.
Richmond, VA 23229
Ph: (804)282-4301
Fax: (804)282-4303
URL: http://www.msa-corp.com

21918 ■ Odyssey HealthCare of Richmond
8000 Franklin Farms Dr., Ste. 100
Richmond, VA 23229
Ph: (804)282-4617
Free: 877-637-9432
Fax: (804)282-4535
E-mail: info@odsyhealth.com
URL: http://www.odsyhealth.com

Roanoke

21919 ■ Carilion Hospice Services-Roanoke
1917 Franklin Rd. SW, Ste. B
Roanoke, VA 24014
Ph: (540)224-4753
Free: 800-964-9300
Fax: (540)983-1181
URL: http://www.carilion.com

21920 ■ Good Samaritan Hospice--Roanoke
2408 Electric Rd.
Roanoke, VA 24018
Ph: (540)776-0198
Free: 888-466-7809
Fax: (540)776-0841
E-mail: info@goodsamhospice.org
URL: http://www.goodsamhospice.org

21921 ■ Medi Home Health and Hospice--Roanoke
5369 Peters Creek Rd.
Roanoke, VA 24019
Ph: (540)278-1322
URL: http://www.msa-corp.com

Rocky Mount

21922 ■ Carilion Hospice Services of Franklin County
180 Floyd Ave.
Rocky Mount, VA 24151
Ph: (540)489-6503
Fax: (540)489-6540
URL: http://www.carilion.com

Rural Retreat

21923 ■ Virginia's Hospice Care
544 N Main St.
Rural Retreat, VA 24368
Ph: (276)686-6321
Free: 888-776-8869
Fax: (276)686-6160

Salem

21924 ■ Amedisys Hospice, Inc.--Salem
1312 W Main St.
Salem, VA 24153
Ph: (540)378-5281
Free: 800-394-8720
Fax: (540)378-6005
URL: http://www.amedisys.com
Formerly: Adventa Hospice, Inc.

South Boston

21925 ■ Halifax Regional Hospice
2204 Wilborn Ave.
South Boston, VA 24592
Ph: (434)517-3339
Free: 800-423-1276
Fax: (434)517-3105
URL: http://www.hrhs.org/servicesHospice.html

South Hill

21926 ■ CMH Community Hospice
300 E Ferrel St.
South Hill, VA 23970
Ph: (434)447-3151
Fax: (434)447-2565

Springfield

21927 ■ Greenspring Village Hospice
7410 Spring Village Dr.
Springfield, VA 22150
Ph: (703)923-3122
Fax: (703)923-3129

Stuart

21928 ■ Mountain Valley Hospice and Palliative Care--Stuart
22099 Jeb Stuart Hwy.
Stuart, VA 24171
Ph: (276)694-4416
Fax: (276)694-4308
URL: http://www.mtnvalleyhospice.org/

21929 ■ R.J. Reynolds Patrick County Memorial Hospital Hospice of Patrick County
835 Woodland Dr.
Stuart, VA 24171
Ph: (276)694-8614
Fax: (276)694-8655
E-mail: pcrissman@rjhospital.com
URL: http://www.co.patrick.va.us/businesses.cfm?pg=9&catID=66

Tappahannock

21930 ■ Hospice of Central Virginia--Tappahannock
1328 Tappahannock Blvd.
Tappahannock, VA 22560
Ph: (804)443-4090
Fax: (804)443-4150
E-mail: info@americanhospice.com
URL: http://hospiceva.iarbiz.com/4YKhoj7EQjM=

21931 ■ Riverside Tappahannock Hospice
618 Hospital Rd.
Tappahannock, VA 22560-5000
Ph: (804)443-6130
Fax: (804)443-6129
URL: http://www.riversideonline.com/

Vienna

21932 ■ Odyssey HealthCare of Arlington Virginia
8229 Boone Blvd., Ste. 510
Vienna, VA 22182
Ph: (703)821-9200
Free: 888-921-9200
Fax: (703)821-9700
E-mail: info@odsyhealth.com
URL: http://www.odsyhealth.com

21933 ■ VITAS Innovative Hospice Care of Northern VA
1604 Spring Hill Dr.
Vienna, VA 22182
Ph: (703)270-4300
Fax: (703)788-6687
URL: http://www.vitas.com

Virginia Beach

21934 ■ Heartland Home Health Care and Hospice--Virginia Beach
5029 Corporate Woods Dr., Ste. 200
Virginia Beach, VA 23462
Ph: (757)490-9323
E-mail: careline@hcr-manorcare.com
URL: http://www.hcr-manorcare.com

Williamsburg

21935 ■ Sentara Home Care & Hospice
1100 Professional Dr.
Williamsburg, VA 23185
Ph: (757)549-5744
Fax: (757)259-6479
URL: http://www.sentara.com/Services/HomeCare/Pages/HospiceProgram.aspx

Winchester

21936 ■ Blue Ridge Hospice
333 W Cork St., 4th Fl.
Winchester, VA 22601
Ph: (540)536-5210
Fax: (540)678-0584
E-mail: hospice@blueridgehospice.org
URL: http://www.blueridgehospice.org

Wytheville

21937 ■ Hospice of Southwest Virginia--Wytheville
600 W Ridge Rd.
Wytheville, VA 24382-1044
Ph: (276)228-1710
E-mail: info@wcch.org
URL: http://www.wcch.org

WASHINGTON

Bellevue

21938 ■ Group Health/Home & Community Services
2100 124th Ave. NE, Ste. 110
Bellevue, WA 98005-1934
Ph: (425)556-6346
Free: 888-954-2509
Fax: (425)556-6335
URL: http://www.ghc.org/

Bremerton

21939 ■ Hospice of Kitsap County
570 Lebo Blvd.
Bremerton, WA 98310

Ph: (360)698-4611
Fax: (360)377-2817
E-mail: info@hospicekc.org
URL: http://www.hospicekc.org/
Dr. Jennifer Ekin, President

Centralia

21940 ■ Assured Home Health & Hospice Visiting Nurse Associations of America
1821 Cooks Hill Rd.
Centralia, WA 98531
Ph: (360)330-2640
Free: 800-833-9404
Fax: (360)807-7790
URL: http://vnaa.org/vnaa/vna/Assured_Home_Health___Hospice,wacent.aspx

Chehalis

21941 ■ Providence Sound Home Care and Hospice
500 NE Washington Ave.
Chehalis, WA 98532-2126
Ph: (360)459-8311
Free: 800-869-8695
URL: http://www.providence.org/swsa

Clarkston

21942 ■ Tri State Hospital Home Health and Hospice
1100 Highland Ave.
Clarkston, WA 99403
Ph: (509)758-2568
Free: 800-200-6292
Fax: (509)758-3413
E-mail: rpeters@tristatehospital.org
URL: http://www.tristatehospital.org

Ellensburg

21943 ■ Home Care of Kittitas Valley
401 E Mt. View Ave.
Ellensburg, WA 98926
Ph: (509)962-7438
Free: 800-734-5326
Fax: (509)925-8450
URL: http://www.kvch.com/

Everett

21944 ■ Providence Hospice and Home Care of Snohomish County
2731 Wetmore, Ste. 500
Everett, WA 98201
Ph: (425)261-4800
Fax: (425)261-4850
E-mail: phhc@providence.org
URL: http://www.providence.org/everett/hospice_and_home_care/default.htm

Goldendale

21945 ■ Klickitat Valley Health, Home Health & Hospice
310 S Roosevelt Ave.
Goldendale, WA 98620
Ph: (509)773-0380
Fax: (509)773-0384
E-mail: homehealth@kvhealth.net
URL: http://www.kvhealth.net/home_health.html

Hoquiam

21946 ■ Harbors Home Health & Hospice
201 7th St.
Hoquiam, WA 98550
Ph: (360)532-5454
Free: 800-772-1319
Fax: (360)533-0999
E-mail: dee@myhhhh.org
URL: http://www.myhhhh.org

Kennewick

21947 ■ Tri-Cities Chaplaincy
2108 W Entiat Ave.
Kennewick, WA 99336
Ph: (509)783-7416
Fax: (509)735-7850
E-mail: info@tricitieschaplaincy.org
URL: http://www.tricitieschaplaincy.org

Kirkland

21948 ■ Evergreen Hospice Services
12822 124th Ln. NE
Kirkland, WA 98034
Ph: (425)899-1040
Fax: (425)899-1099
URL: http://www.evergreenhealthcare.org

Liberty Lake

21949 ■ Family Home Care and Hospice
22820 E Appleway
Liberty Lake, WA 99019
Ph: (509)755-4902
Fax: (509)473-4953
URL: http://www.familyhomecare.org/

Longview

21950 ■ Community Home Health & Hospice-Longview
1035 11th Ave.
Longview, WA 98632
Ph: (360)425-8510
Free: 800-378-8510
Fax: (360)425-4667
URL: http://www.chhh.org/

Moses Lake

21951 ■ Central Basin Home Health & Hospice
311 W 3rd Ave.
Moses Lake, WA 98837
Ph: (509)765-1856
Free: 800-765-1856
Fax: (509)765-3323

Mountlake Terrace

21952 ■ Swedish Visiting Nurse Services
6100 219th St. SW
Mountlake Terrace, WA 98043
Ph: (206)386-6602
Fax: (425)744-2497
URL: http://www.swedish.org/Services/Home-Care/Home-Care-Services/Hospice-Pallia tive-Care

Mt. Vernon

21953 ■ Hospice of the Northwest
819 S 13th St.
Mt. Vernon, WA 98274
Ph: (360)814-5550
Free: 800-894-5877
Fax: (360)814-5591
E-mail: Hospice_info@hospicenw.org
URL: http://www.hospicenw.org/onlineresources.cfm

Olympia

21954 ■ Providence Sound Home Care & Hospice
3432 S Bay Rd. NE
Olympia, WA 98506
Ph: (206)459-8311
Fax: (206)493-4657
URL: http://www.providence.org/swsa

Omak

21955 ■ Amedisys Hospice of Omak
800 S Jasmine St., Ste. 3
Omak, WA 98841
Ph: (509)422-8621
Free: 877-422-8621
Fax: (509)422-0131
URL: http://www.amedisys.com/hospice_locations.cfm?id=35

Port Townsend

21956 ■ Jefferson Health Care Hospice
834 Sheridan St.
Port Townsend, WA 98368
Ph: (360)385-2200
Free: 800-244-8917
Fax: (360)379-2242
URL: http://www.jeffersonhealthcare.org/web/Services/HomeHealthHospice/tabid/65/ Default.aspx

Renton

21957 ■ Providence Health & Services
2001 Lind Ave. SW
Renton, WA 98507
Ph: (425)254-5468

Seattle

21958 ■ Kline Galland Hospice Services Kline Galland Home
7500 Seward Park Ave. S
Seattle, WA 98118
Ph: (296)725-8800
Fax: (206)722-5210
E-mail: jeffc@klinegalland.org
URL: http://www.klinegalland.org/gallandHome.html
Jeff Cohen, President

21959 ■ Providence Hospice of Seattle
425 Pontius Ave. N, Ste. 300
Seattle, WA 98109
Ph: (206)320-4000
Free: 888-782-4445
Fax: (206)320-2280
E-mail: Lyn.Miletich@providence.org
URL: http://www2.providence.org/kingcounty/facilities/providence-hospice-of-seat tle/Pages/default.aspx

Silverdale

21960 ■ Hospice of Kitsap County
3100 Bucklin Hill Rd.
Silverdale, WA 98383
Ph: (360)698-4611
Fax: (360)692-1893
E-mail: info@hospicekc.org
URL: http://www.hospiceofkitsapcounty.org

Spokane

21961 ■ Horizon Hospice--Spokane
123 W Cascade Way, Ste. E
Spokane, WA 99208
Ph: (509)489-4581
Fax: (509)482-0717
E-mail: lguske@aol.com
URL: http://www.seriousillness.org/spokane/services/

21962 ■ Hospice of Spokane
121 S Arthur
Spokane, WA 99201
Ph: (509)456-0438
Free: 888-459-0438
Fax: (509)532-8863
E-mail: info@hospiceofspokane.org
URL: http://www.hospiceofspokane.org

Sunnyside

21963 ■ Lower Valley Hospice
3920 Outlook Rd.
Sunnyside, WA 98944-9202
Ph: (509)837-1676

Free: 800-474-6008
Fax: (509)837-2878
E-mail: info@lowervalleyhospice.org
URL: http://www.lowervalleyhospice.org/?page_id=39

Tacoma

21964 ■ Group Health/Home Health & Hospice
950 Pacific Ave.
Tacoma, WA 98402
Ph: (253)274-4618
Fax: (253)274-4601

21965 ■ Multicare Hospice of Tacoma
3901 S Fife St.
Tacoma, WA 98415
Ph: (253)301-6400
Free: 888-516-4504
Fax: (253)301-6528
URL: http://www.multicare.org

Tukwila

21966 ■ Highline Hospice
12844 Military Rd. S
Tukwila, WA 98168
Ph: (206)439-9095
Fax: (206)433-1031
E-mail: commrelations@highlinemedical.org
URL: http://www.highlinemedicalcenter.org/health-care-services/health-hospice/hos pice.htm

University Pl.

21967 ■ Franciscan Hospice
2901 Bridgeport Way W
University Pl., WA 98466
Ph: (253)534-7000
Fax: (253)534-7099
URL: http://www.hospice.fhshealth.org/

Vancouver

21968 ■ Community Home Health & Hospice
14508 NE 20th Ave.
Vancouver, WA 98686
Ph: (360)253-4626
Fax: (360)253-4859
URL: http://www.chhh.org/

21969 ■ Hospice of Southwest
100 E 33rd St., Ste. 201
Vancouver, WA 98661
Ph: (360)696-5100
Fax: (360)696-5038
URL: http://www.swmedicalcenter.com/body.cfm?id=3076

Walla Walla

21970 ■ Jonathan M. Wainwright Memorial VA Medical Center
77 Wainwright Dr.
Walla Walla, WA 99362
Ph: (509)525-5200
URL: http://www.wallawalla.va.gov/

21971 ■ Walla Walla Community Hospice
1067 Isaacs Ave.
Walla Walla, WA 99362
Ph: (509)525-5561
Fax: (509)525-3517
E-mail: info@wwhospice.org
URL: http://www.wwhospice.org

Wenatchee

21972 ■ Central Washington Hospital Home Health and Hospice
Central Washington Hospital
1201 S Miller St.
Wenatchee, WA 98801
Ph: (509)665-6049
Fax: (509)665-6038
E-mail: contactus@cwhs.com
URL: http://www.cwhs.com/hcs/Hospice.aspx

WEST VIRGINIA

Anmoore

21973 ■ Amedisys Hospice Care-Anmoore
Casino Dr., Ste. 102
Anmoore, WV 26323
Ph: (304)622-1297
Free: 877-277-8574
Fax: (304)622-0978
URL: http://www.amedisys.com/hospice_locations.cfm?id=20

Arthurdale

21974 ■ Hospice Care Corporation--Arthurdale
Rt. 92 S
Arthurdale, WV 26520-0760
Ph: (304)864-0884
Free: 800-350-1161
Fax: (304)864-6306
URL: http://www.hospicecarecorp.org/offices.shtml#Preston

Baldwin

21975 ■ ADORAY Home Health and Hospice
2231 Hwy 12, Ste. 201
Baldwin, WV 54002
Ph: (715)684-5020
Free: 800-359-0174
Fax: (715)684-5033
URL: http://www.adoray.org/

Beckley

21976 ■ Bowers Hospice House Hospice of Southern West Virginia
454 Cranberry Dr.
Beckley, WV 25801
Ph: (304)255-6404
Free: 800-900-6404
Fax: (304)255-6494
E-mail: info@hospiceofsouthernwv.org
URL: http://www.hospiceofsouthernwv.org/house.asp

Belington

21977 ■ Mountain Hospice--Belington
1600 Crim Ave.
Belington, WV 26250
Ph: (304)823-3922
Free: 888-763-7789
Fax: (304)823-3926
URL: http://www.mountainhospice.com

Berkeley Springs

21978 ■ Hospice of the Panhandle-Morgan County
270 N Washington St.
Berkeley Springs, WV 25411
Ph: (304)258-0790
Fax: (304)258-0793
URL: http://www.hospiceotp.org/

Bluefield

21979 ■ Amedisys Hospice Care-Bluefield
Rt. 2, Box 182
Bluefield, WV 24701
Ph: (304)327-0600
Fax: (304)327-0611
URL: http://www.amedisys.com/

Bridgeport

21980 ■ People's Hospice
327 Medical Park Dr.
Bridgeport, WV 26330
Ph: (304)624-2424
Fax: (304)622-9458
URL: http://www.uhcwv.org/

Buckhannon

21981 ■ Saint Joseph's House
1 Amalia Dr.
Buckhannon, WV 26201
Ph: (304)473-6800
Fax: (304)473-6815
URL: http://www.stj.net/index.php/services/home_health_hospice/

Burnsville

21982 ■ Hospice Care Corporation-Burnsville
PO Box 323
Burnsville, WV 26335
Ph: (304)853-2279
Fax: (304)457-3941
URL: http://www.hospicecarecorp.org/

Chapmanville

21983 ■ Dignity Hospice of Southern WV
557 Main St.
Chapmanville, WV 25508
Ph: (304)855-4764
Free: 800-297-8076
Fax: (304)831-6001
URL: http://www.dignityhospice.org

Charleston

21984 ■ Hubbard Hospice House
1001 Kennawa Dr.
Charleston, WV 25311
Ph: (304)768-8523
Free: 800-560-8523
URL: http://www.hospicecarewv.org

21985 ■ Kanawha Hospice Care--Charleston
1606 Kanawha Blvd. W
Charleston, WV 25312
Ph: (304)768-8523
Free: 800-560-8523
Fax: (304)768-8627
E-mail: contactus@hospicecarewv.org
URL: http://www.hospicecarewv.org/

Davis

21986 ■ Mountain Hospice-Davis
385 William Ave.
Davis, WV 26260
Free: 888-763-7789
URL: http://www.mountainhospice.com/

Elkins

21987 ■ Hospice Care Inpatient Unit-Elkins
169 Diamond St.
Elkins, WV 26241
Ph: (304)637-0618
Fax: (304)637-0805
URL: http://www.hospicecarecorp.org/

21988 ■ Mountain Hospice-Elkins
2 First St.
Elkins, WV 26241
Ph: (304)636-0556
Fax: (304)636-1450
URL: http://www.mountainhospice.com/

Fairmont

21989 ■ Hospice Care Corporation--Fairmont
1406 Country Club Rd.
Fairmont, WV 26554
Ph: (304)363-3815
Fax: (304)366-2054
URL: http://www.hospicecarecorp.org/

Franklin

21990 ■ Mountain Hospice-Franklin
PO Box 416
Franklin, WV 26807
Ph: (304)358-3585
Fax: (304)358-3586
URL: http://www.mountainhospice.com/

Grafton

21991 ■ Hospice Care Corporation-Grafton
7 Harmon Center
Grafton, WV 26354
Ph: (304)265-6340
Fax: (304)265-6384
URL: http://www.hospicecarecorp.org/

Huntington

21992 ■ Emogene Dolin Jones Hospice House
Hospice of Huntington
3100 Staunton Rd.
Huntington, WV 25702
Ph: (304)781-8400
Free: 866-821-0353
URL: http://www.hospiceofhuntington.org/hospice-services/emogene-dolin-jones-hos pice-house/

21993 ■ Hospice of Huntington
1101 6th Ave.
Huntington, WV 25701
Ph: (304)529-4217
Free: 800-788-5480
Fax: (304)523-6051
URL: http://www.hospiceofhuntington.org

Lewisburg

21994 ■ Kanawha Hospice Care-Lewisburg
223 Maplewood Ave.
Lewisburg, WV 24901
Ph: (304)645-2700
Free: 800-237-0842
Fax: (304)645-3188
E-mail: gbv@hospicecarewv.org
URL: http://www.hospicecarewv.org/

Madison

21995 ■ Kanawha Hospice Care-Madison
467 Main St.
Madison, WV 25130
Ph: (304)369-0183
Free: 800-560-8523
E-mail: contactus@hospicecarewv.org
URL: http://www.hospicecarewv.org/

Martinsburg

21996 ■ Hospice of the Panhandle
122 Waverly Ct.
Martinsburg, WV 25403
Ph: (304)264-0406
Free: 800-345-6538
Fax: (304)264-0409
URL: http://www.hospiceotp.org

Morgantown

21997 ■ Hospice Care Corporation--Morgantown
3363 University St.
Morgantown, WV 26505
Ph: (304)599-4200
Fax: (304)599-1125
URL: http://www.hospicecarecorp.org

21998 ■ Morgantown Hospice
PO Box 4222
Morgantown, WV 26504-4222
Ph: (304)285-2777
Free: 866-317-2777
Fax: (304)285-1456
URL: http://www.morgantownhospice.com/

21999 ■ Tender Loving Care Home Care and Hospice--Morgantown
Amedisys Home Health Services
246 Cheat Rd., Ste. 3
Morgantown, WV 26508
Ph: (304)292-4868
Free: 866-934-6229
Fax: (304)292-4867
URL: http://www.amedisys.com/

Parkersburg

22000 ■ Amedisys Hospice Care of Parkersburg
417 Grand Park Dr., Ste. 206
Parkersburg, WV 26101
Ph: (304)424-6270
Fax: (304)424-6274
URL: http://www.amedisys.com/

Parsons

22001 ■ Hospice Care Corporation-Parsons
303 First St.
Parsons, WV 26287
Ph: (304)478-2680
Fax: (304)478-3851
URL: http://www.hospicecarecorp.org/

Petersburg

22002 ■ Grant Memorial Hospital Hospice
Rts. 28/55 Hospital Dr.
Petersburg, WV 26847
Ph: (304)257-1026
Fax: (304)257-2093
URL: http://www.grantmemorial.com/

Philippi

22003 ■ Hospice Care Corporation--Philippi
50 S Main St.
Philippi, WV 26416
Ph: (304)457-2141
Fax: (304)457-3941
URL: http://www.hospicecarecorp.org

Princeton

22004 ■ Hospice Compassus-Princeton
1033 Stafford Dr.
Princeton, WV 24740
Ph: (304)431-2000
Free: 800-626-5277
Fax: (304)431-2002
E-mail: contactusWVBLU@hospicecom.com
URL: http://www.hospicecompassus.com/loc-WVPRIN.html

Summersville

22005 ■ Kanawha Hospice Care-Summersville
1129 Broad St.
Summersville, WV 26651
Ph: (304)768-8253
Fax: (304)768-8627
URL: http://hospicecarewv.org/

Welch

22006 ■ Hospice Compassus-Welch
66 Elkins St.
Welch, WV 24801
Ph: (304)436-2300
Free: 866-612-1929
Fax: (304)436-2306
E-mail: contactusWVWEL@hospicecom.com
URL: http://www.hospicecompassus.com/loc-WVWEL.html

Wheeling

22007 ■ Tender Loving Care Home Care and Hospice--Wheeling
Amedisys Home Health Care
1251 Warwood Ave. Ste. A
Wheeling, WV 26003
Ph: (304)217-3300
Free: 866-327-3204
Fax: (304)217-3306
URL: http://www.amedisys.com/hospice.cfm

22008 ■ Valley Hospice--Wheeling
308 Mount St. Joseph Rd.
Wheeling, WV 26003
Ph: (304)242-1977
Free: 877-242-1977
Fax: (304)242-0278
URL: http://www.valleyhospice.org

WISCONSIN

Antigo

22009 ■ LeRoyer Hospice
112 E 5th Ave.
Antigo, WI 54409
Ph: (715)623-2331
Fax: (715)623-9440

Appleton

22010 ■ Hospice At Cherry Meadows
2600 Heritage Woods Dr.
Appleton, WI 54915-1484
Ph: (920)969-0919
Free: 800-984-5554
Fax: (920)969-0020

22011 ■ ThedaCare at Home
3000 E College Ave.
Appleton, WI 54915
Ph: (920)730-3497
Free: 800-236-4101
Fax: (920)969-0020
URL: http://www.thedacare.org/ThedacareWeb/

Ashland

22012 ■ Regional Hospice Services Inc.--Ashland
2101 Beaser Ave.
Ashland, WI 54806
Ph: (715)685-5151
Fax: (715)685-6404
E-mail: hospice@ncis.net
URL: http://www.regionalhospice.org

Baraboo

22013 ■ Home Health United Hospice
1111 8th St.
Baraboo, WI 53913
Ph: (608)242-1516
Fax: (866)553-0711
E-mail: info@hhuvns.org
URL: http://www.homehealthunited.org/

Beaver Dam

22014 ■ Hillside Homecare/Hospice
Beaver Dam Community Hospitals, Inc.
709 S University Ave
Beaver Dam, WI 53916
Ph: (920)887-4050
Fax: (920)887-6815
E-mail: HomeHealthcareHospice@bdch.org
URL: http://bdch.com/Services/HillsideCommunity/Hospice/default.asp

Beloit

22015 ■ Beloit Regional Hospice
655 3rd St., Ste. 200
Beloit, WI 53511
Ph: (608)363-7421

Free: 877-363-7421
Fax: (608)363-7426
E-mail: info@beloitregionalhospice.com
URL: http://www.beloitregionalhospice.com

Black River Falls

22016 ■ Black River Hospice
711 W Adams St.
Black River Falls, WI 54615
Ph: (715)284-1365
Fax: (715)284-3699
URL: http://www.blackriverhospital.com/

Burlington

22017 ■ Odyssey HealthCare of Milwaukee
197 W Chestnut St.
Burlington, WI 53105
Ph: (214)922-9711
Fax: (214)-922-9752
URL: http://www.odsyhealth.com/default.asp

Chilton

22018 ■ Calumet County Health Department Hospice Program
206 Court St.
Chilton, WI 53014
Ph: (920)849-1432
Fax: (920)849-1476

Chippewa Falls

22019 ■ Saint Joseph's Home Health & Hospice
2661 County Hwy. 1
Chippewa Falls, WI 54729
Ph: (715)726-3485
Fax: (715)726-3601
E-mail: info@sjcf.hshs.org
URL: http://www.stjoeschipfalls.com/our_services/home_hospice.phtml

De Pere

22020 ■ Heartland Home Health Care and Hospice-De Pere
1145 W Main Ave., Ste. 205
De Pere, WI 54115
Ph: (920)336-6455
Fax: (920)336-6646
URL: http://www.hcr-manorcare.com/

22021 ■ Unity Hospice
2366 Oak Ridge Circle
De Pere, WI 54115
Ph: (715)524-3635
Fax: (920)338-8111
URL: http://www.unityhospice.org/

Dodgeville

22022 ■ Uplands Hills Home Care and Hospice
800 Compassion Way
Dodgeville, WI 53533
Ph: (608)930-8000
Free: 877-876-2680
Fax: (608)930-7250
URL: http://www.uplandhillshealth.org/index.php

Fond Du Lac

22023 ■ Agnesian Healthcare-Hospice Home of Hope
400 County Rd. K
Fond Du Lac, WI 54935
Ph: (920)906-1000
Fax: (920)906-1013
URL: http://www.agnesian.com/

22024 ■ Heartland Home Health and Hospice-Fond Du Lac
63 W Pioneer Rd.
Fond Du Lac, WI 54935
Free: 800-216-5708
URL: http://www.hcr-manorcare.com/

22025 ■ Hospice Advantage-Fond Du Lac
79 N Pioneer Rd.
Fond Du Lac, WI 54935
Ph: (920)922-1560
Fax: (920)922-1563
URL: http://www.hospiceadvantage.net/

22026 ■ Hospice Advantage, Inc-Fond Du Lac
79 N Pioneer Rd.
Fond Du Lac, WI 54935
Ph: (920)922-1560
Fax: (920)922-1563
URL: http://www.hospiceadvantage.net/

Friendship

22027 ■ Hospice Touch Tomah Memorial Hospital
1874 Hwy. 13
Friendship, WI 53950
Ph: (608)374-0250
Fax: (608)374-0256
E-mail: tmh@tomahhospital.org
URL: http://www.tomahhospital.org/content/detail.cfm?pageid=24

Green Bay

22028 ■ AseraCare Hospice - Green Bay
1294 Lombardi Ave.
Green Bay, WI 54304
Ph: (479)201-5184
Fax: (479)478-2903
URL: http://www.aseracare.com/

22029 ■ Aurora Visiting Nurse Association Hospice
Green Bay Branch
931 Discovery Rd.
Green Bay, WI 54311-8002
Free: 877-268-9138
Fax: (920)288-5151
URL: http://www.aurorahealthcare.org/services/vna/offices.asp
Formerly: Visiting Nurse Association of Wisconsin.

Green Lake

22030 ■ Hospice Hope
745 South St.
Green Lake, WI 54941
Ph: (920)294-6220
Fax: (920)294-6238
URL: http://www.agnesian.com/specialty_home.html#hoshope

Hartford

22031 ■ Aurora VNA Hospice Jackson Branch
69 Sell Dr.
Hartford, WI 53027
Ph: (262)677-1451
Fax: (262)677-1451
URL: http://www.aurorahealthcare.org/

Hayward

22032 ■ Regional Hospice
Hayward Team
15910 W Company Lake Rd.
Hayward, WI 54843
Ph: (715)634-6433
Fax: (715)634-5737
URL: http://www.regionalhospice.org/

Janesville

22033 ■ HospiceCare Inc.
3001 W Memorial Dr.
Janesville, WI 53548
Ph: (608)755-1871
Free: 888-563-5374
Fax: (608)755-5710
E-mail: hci@hospicecareinc.com
URL: http://www.hospicecareinc.com

Jefferson

22034 ■ Rainbow Hospice Care Inc.
147 W Rockwell St.
Jefferson, WI 53549
Ph: (920)674-6255
Free: 888-493-8276
Fax: (920)674-5288
URL: http://www.rainbowhospicecare.org

Kaukauna

22035 ■ St. Paul Elder Services
316 E 14th St.
Kaukauna, WI 54130
Ph: (920)766-6189
Fax: (920)759-0534
URL: http://www.stpaulelders.org/

La Crosse

22036 ■ Franciscan Skemp Hospice
Mayo Health Clinic
212 S Eleventh St.
La Crosse, WI 54601
Ph: (608)791-9790
Free: 800-362-5454
Fax: (608)791-9548
URL: http://www.mayohealthsystem.org/

22037 ■ Gunderson Lutheran At Home Hospice
1900 South Ave.
La Crosse, WI 54602
Ph: (608)791-8435
Free: 800-848-5443
Fax: (608)791-8415
E-mail: webmaster@gundluth.org
URL: http://www.gundluth.org/?id=498&sid=1

Lake Geneva

22038 ■ Aurora VNA Hospice-Lake Geneva
500 Interchange N
Lake Geneva, WI 53147
Ph: (262)249-5860
Fax: (262)249-5870
URL: http://www.aurorahealthcare.org/

Lancaster

22039 ■ Grant County Hospice
111 S Jefferson St.
Lancaster, WI 53813
Ph: (608)273-6416
Fax: (608)723-6501
URL: http://www.co.grant.wi.gov/

Madison

22040 ■ HospiceCare Inc.
5395 E Cheryl Pkwy.
Madison, WI 53711
Ph: (608)276-4660
Free: 800-553-4289
Fax: (608)276-4380
E-mail: hci@hospicecareinc.com
URL: http://www.hospicecareinc.com

Maintowoc

22041 ■ Manitowoc County Community Hospice
HomeCare Health Services & Hospice
1004 Washington St.
Maintowoc, WI 54220

Ph: (920)684-7155
Fax: (920)684-8653
URL: http://homecarehealth.org/

Manitowoc

22042 ■ Holy Family Memorial Hospice
600 York St.
Manitowoc, WI 54220-2020
Ph: (920)320-6535
URL: http://www.hfmhealth.org/?id=60&sid=1

Marinette

22043 ■ Unity Hospice-Marinette
700 Owena St.
Marinette, WI 54143
Ph: (715)582-1050
Free: 800-990-9249
Fax: (920)338-8111
URL: http://www.unityhospice.org/

Mauston

22044 ■ Hospice Touch Tomah Memorial Hospital-Mauston
1050 Division
Mauston, WI 53948
Ph: (608)374-0250
Fax: (608)374-0256
URL: http://www.tomahhospital.org/

Medford

22045 ■ Hope Hospice and Palliative Care-Medford
537 W Broadway Ave.
Medford, WI 54451
Ph: (715)748-3434
Fax: (715)748-1268
E-mail: hhospice@newnorth.net
URL: http://www.hhospice.com/

Milwaukee

22046 ■ Aurora Health Care-Milwaukee
3000 W Montana St.
Milwaukee, WI 53215
Ph: (414)647-3000
URL: http://www.aurorahealthcare.org/

22047 ■ Heartland Home Health Care and Hospice--Milwaukee
1233 N Mayfair Rd.
Milwaukee, WI 53226
Ph: (262)641-0778
Fax: (262)641-2720
URL: http://www.hcr-manorcare.com/

22048 ■ Odyssey HealthCare-Milwaukee
10150 W National Ave., Ste. 200
Milwaukee, WI 53227
Ph: (414)546-3200
Free: 888-280-3332
Fax: (414)546-3401
URL: http://www.odsyhealth.com/site.asp?id=26

22049 ■ Ruth Hospice
Village at Manor Park
7500 W Dean Rd.
Milwaukee, WI 53223
Ph: (414)607-4254
Fax: (414)371-7383
URL: http://www.vmpcares.com/

22050 ■ VITAS Inpatient Hospice Unit at the Lutheran Home
7500 W North Ave., 3rd Fl.
Milwaukee, WI 53213
Ph: (414)457-6710
URL: http://www.vitas.com/

22051 ■ Wheaton Franciscan Home Health and Hospice
5000 W Chambers St.
Milwaukee, WI 53210
Ph: (414)447-2000
E-mail: webmaster@wfhc.org
URL: http://www.mywheaton.org/programs/home_health/index.asp

Monroe

22052 ■ Monroe Clinic Hospice
515 22nd Ave.
Monroe, WI 53566
Ph: (608)324-1230
Free: 800-367-8406
Fax: (608)324-1302
URL: http://www.monroeclinic.org/

Phillips

22053 ■ Flambeau Home Health & Hospice
133 N Lake Ave.
Phillips, WI 54555
Ph: (715)339-4371
Free: 800-206-9322
Fax: (715)339-4477
URL: http://citehealth.com/home-care-agencies/wisconsin/cities/phillips/flambeau -home-health-hospice

Pleasant Prairie

22054 ■ Hospice Alliance
10220 Prairie Ridge Blvd.
Pleasant Prairie, WI 53158
Ph: (262)652-4400
Free: 800-830-8344
Fax: (262)652-4516
E-mail: hospice@hospicealliance.net
URL: http://www.hospicealliance.net

Rice Lake

22055 ■ Lakeview Medical Center Home Health Care & Hospice
1100 N Main St.
Rice Lake, WI 54868
Ph: (715)236-6265
Fax: (715)236-6578
E-mail: harm.sandy@lakeviewmedical.org
URL: http://www.lakeviewmedical.com

Shawano

22056 ■ Shawano Community Hospice
309 N Bartlett St.
Shawano, WI 54166
Ph: (715)524-2169
Fax: (715)524-7140
URL: http://shawanomed.org/HealthServices/ServiceDirectory/tabid/56/Default.aspx

Sheboygan

22057 ■ Saint Nicholas Hospice
Matthews Oncology Association
3100 Superior Ave.
Sheboygan, WI 53081
Ph: (920)457-5770
Fax: (920)457-5951
URL: http://www.stnicholashospital.org/
Formerly: Community Home Hospice.

Spooner

22058 ■ Regional Hospice - Spooner Team
819 Ash St.
Spooner, WI 54801-1201
Ph: (715)635-9077
Fax: (715)635-9078
URL: http://www.regionalhospice.org/

Stevens Point

22059 ■ Ministry Home Care
Hospice Services - Stevens Point
2501 Main St., Ste. A
Stevens Point, WI 54481
Ph: (715)346-5355
Free: 800-398-7897
Fax: (715)345-1304
E-mail: info@ministryhomecare.org
URL: http://www.ministryhomecare.org
Formerly: Hospice of Portage County.

Tomah

22060 ■ The Hospice Touch Tomah Memorial Hospital
321 Butts Ave.
Tomah, WI 54660
Ph: (608)374-0250
Fax: (608)374-0256
E-mail: touch@tomahhospital.org
URL: http://www.tomahhospital.org/services/2-hospice.html

Wausau

22061 ■ Aspirus Comfort Care and Hospice Services
Aspirus Wausau Hospital
333 Pine Ridge Blvd.
Wausau, WI 54401
Ph: (715)847-2121
Free: 800-283-2881
URL: http://www.aspirus.org/ourServices/index.cfm?catID=1&subCatID=1&pageID=1

Wauwatosa

22062 ■ VITAS Innovative Hospice Care of Milwaukee
2675 North Mayfair Rd., Ste. 480
Wauwatosa, WI 53226
Ph: (414)257-2600
Free: 888-821-6500
Fax: (414)454-3133
URL: http://www.vitas.com

West Allis

22063 ■ Season's Hospice and Palliative Care of Wisconsin, Inc.
6737 W Washington St., Ste. 2150
West Allis, WI 53214
Free: 800-379-5105
E-mail: info@seasons.org
URL: http://honoringlife-offeringhope.org/

West Bend

22064 ■ Cedar Community Hospice
5595 County Rd. Z
West Bend, WI 53095
Ph: (262)306-2100
Fax: (262)306-2689
URL: http://www.cedarcommunity.org

Woodruff

22065 ■ Seasons of Life Hospice Home
Ministry Home Care
Dr. Kate Hospice
8951 Woodruff Rd.
Woodruff, WI 54568
Ph: (715)356-8805
Free: 800-234-3542
Fax: (715)358-5907
E-mail: info@ministryhomecare.org
URL: http://www.ministryhealth.org/MinistryHomeCare/HospiceHomes11/SeasonsofL1.n ws

WYOMING

Buffalo

22066 ■ Susie Bowling Lawrence Hospice
Johnson County Healthcare Center
497 W Lott St.
Buffalo, WY 82834

Ph: (307)684-5521
Fax: (307)684-5385
URL: http://www.buffalohealthcare.vcn.com/JCHC_Hospice.htm

Casper

22067 ■ Central Wyoming Hospice Program/Cara Lou Chapman Hospice Home
319 S Wilson St.
Casper, WY 82601
Ph: (307)577-4832
Fax: (307)577-4841
E-mail: cwhp@cwhp.org
URL: http://www.cwhp.org

Cheyenne

22068 ■ United Medical Center Hospice
6000 Sycamore Rd.
Cheyenne, WY 82009
Ph: (307)633-7016
Fax: (307)633-7085
E-mail: comments@crmcwy.org
URL: http://www.umcwy.org

Gillette

22069 ■ Campbell County Memorial Hospital Hospice
PO Box 3011
Gillette, WY 82717-3011
Ph: (307)685-6230
Fax: (307)685-6210
URL: http://www.ccmh.net/Services/Home_Care_Services/Hospice.aspx

Laramie

22070 ■ Hospice of Laramie
1262 N 22nd St., Unit A
Laramie, WY 82072-5307
Ph: (307)745-9254
Fax: (307)742-5967
URL: http://www.hospiceoflaramie.com/

Moorcroft

22071 ■ Treasured Memories Hospice
PO Box 189
Moorcroft, WY 82721
Ph: (307)756-3344
Fax: (307)756-3394
URL: http://www.treasuredmemorieshospice.com/

Rock Springs

22072 ■ Hospice of Sweetwater County
809 Thompson St., Ste. D
Rock Springs, WY 82901
Ph: (307)362-1990
Fax: (307)352-6769

Sheridan

22073 ■ Hospice of the Big Horns
1401 W 5th St.
Sheridan, WY 82801
Ph: (307)672-1083
Fax: (307)672-2585
E-mail: mhschc@sheridanhospital.org
URL: http://www.sheridanhospital.org

Chapter 21
In Vitro Fertilization Clinics

Listed below are hospitals and medical centers that specialize in in-vitro fertilization services. Entries are sorted geographically by states and provinces, then alphabetically by institution names within states and provinces. For additional information, see the "User's Guide" located at the front of this directory.

ALABAMA

22074 ■ Alabama Fertility Specialists
2700 Hwy. 280, Ste. 370E
Birmingham, AL 35223
Ph: (205)874-0000
Fax: (205)874-7021
URL: http://www.alabamafertility.com/

22075 ■ ART Fertility Program of Alabama
2006 Brookwood Medical Center Dr., Ste. 508
Birmingham, AL 35209
Ph: (205)870-9784
Free: 800-476-9784
URL: http://www.artprogramal.com
Kathryn L. Honea, Director

22076 ■ Center for Reproductive Medicine - Alabama
3 Mobile Infirmary Cir., No. 213
Mobile, AL 36607
Ph: (251)438-4200
E-mail: info@infertilityalabama.com
URL: http://www.infertilityalabama.com
George Koulianos, Director

22077 ■ Huntsville Reproductive Medicine, PC
185 Chateau Dr., Ste. 301
Huntsville, AL 35801
Ph: (256)213-2229
Fax: (256)213-9978
E-mail: patientservices@hsvrm.com
URL: http://www.huntsvilleivf.com
Dr. Andrew J. Harper, Director

22078 ■ University of Alabama at Birmingham
Department of Obstetrics and Gynecology
In Vitro Fertilization Program
2000 6th Ave. S
Birmingham, AL 35205
Ph: (205)801-8000

22079 ■ University of South Alabama
Department of Obstetrics and Gynecology
Reproductive Endocrinology Division
In Vitro Fertilization Program
307 University Blvd. N, CC/CB326
Mobile, AL 36688
Ph: (251)415-1496
E-mail: brizk@jaguarl.usouthal.edu
URL: http://www.southalabama.edu/usahealthsystem/obgyn/mission.html

ALASKA

22080 ■ Midwest Center for Reproductive Health
Denali OB/GYN
4001 Dale St., Ste. 105
Anchorage, AK 99508
Ph: (907)222-9930
Fax: (907)222-9931
URL: http://home.gci.net/~denali/

ARIZONA

22081 ■ Advanced Fertility Care--Scottsdale
9819 N 95th St., Ste. 105
Scottsdale, AZ 85258
Ph: (480)874-2229
Free: 866-668-0921
Fax: (480)874-2231
E-mail: info@advancedfertilitycare.com
URL: http://www.advancedfertilitycare.com/

22082 ■ Advanced Fertility Care--Tempe
2055 E Southern Ave., Ste. C
Tempe, AZ 85282
Ph: (480)413-2229
Free: 866-668-0921
Fax: (480)413-2228
E-mail: info@advancedfertilitycare.com
URL: http://www.advancedfertilitycare.com/

22083 ■ Arizona Associates for Reproductive Health
8573 E Princess Dr., Ste. 101
Scottsdale, AZ 85255
Ph: (480)946-9900
Fax: (480)946-9914
URL: http://www.azarh.com/

22084 ■ Arizona Center for Fertility Studies
8997 E Desert Cove Ave.
2nd Floor
Scottsdale, AZ 85260
Ph: (480)630-0212
Fax: (480)860-6819
E-mail: drjsn@acfs2000.com
URL: http://www.acfs2000.com

22085 ■ Arizona Center for Reproductive Endocrinology and Infertility
5190 E Farness Dr., No. 114
Tucson, AZ 85712
Ph: (520)326-0001
Dr. Timothy Gelety, Director

22086 ■ Fertility Treatment Center--Glendale
Northwest Valley Office
6320-B W Union Hills Dr., Ste. 2700
Glendale, AZ 85308
Ph: (623)385-7350
URL: http://www.fertilitytreatmentcenter.com

22087 ■ Fertility Treatment Center--Scottsdale
8415 N Pima Rd., Ste. 290
Scottsdale, AZ 85258
Ph: (480)998-9876
URL: http://www.fertilitytreatmentcenter.com/
Dr. Daniel F. Rychlik, Director

22088 ■ Fertility Treatment Center--Tempe
ASU Research Park
Reproductive Medical Institute Complex
2155 E Conference Dr., Ste. 115
Tempe, AZ 85284
Ph: (480)831-2445
URL: http://www.fertilitytreatmentcenter.com/
Dr. H. Randall Craig, Director

22089 ■ IVF Phoenix
Bldg. I
9817 N 9th St., Ste. 105
Scottsdale, AZ 85258
Ph: (602)765-2229
Fax: (602)493-6641
E-mail: info@ivfphoenix.com
URL: http://www.ivfphoenix.com/
Dr. John L. Couvaras, Director

22090 ■ Reproductive Health Center
4518 E Camp Lowell Dr.
Tucson, AZ 85712
Ph: (520)733-0083
URL: http://www.ivftucson.com

22091 ■ Reproductive Health Center, Inc.
4518 E Camp Lowell Dr.
Tucson, AZ 85712
Ph: (520)733-0083
Free: 866-906-7761
Fax: (520)733-0771
URL: http://www.ivftucson.com/

22092 ■ Southwest Fertility Center--Mesa
1520 S Dobson Rd., Ste. 215
Mesa, AZ 85202
Ph: (602)956-7481
URL: http://www.southwestfertilitycenter.com
Dr. Sujatha Gunnala, Director

22093 ■ Southwest Fertility Center--Phoenix
3125 N 32nd St., Ste. 200
Phoenix, AZ 85018
Ph: (602)956-7481
URL: http://www.southwestfertilitycenter.com

ARKANSAS

22094 ■ Arkansas Fertility and Gynecology Associates
9101 Kanis Rd., Ste. 300
Little Rock, AR 72205
Ph: (501)801-1200
Free: 877-801-5353
Fax: (501)801-1207
E-mail: Fertilitydoc@obgynmail.com
URL: http://www.arkansasfertility.com

22095 ■ University of Arkansas
IVF Program
5800 W 10th St., Ste. 705
Little Rock, AR 72204

Ph: (501)296-1800
Fax: (501)296-1722
E-mail: mangle@uams.edu
URL: http://www.uams.edu/obgyn/infertility/ivf.asp

CALIFORNIA

22096 ■ Advanced Fertility Associates
1111 Sonoma Ave., Ste. 214
Santa Rosa, CA 95405
Ph: (707)575-5831
Fax: (707)575-4379
E-mail: info@afamd.com
URL: http://www.afamd.com/
Dr. Jennifer Ratcliffe, Director

22097 ■ Alta Bates In Vitro Fertilization Program
2999 Regent St., Ste. 101A
Berkeley, CA 94705
Ph: (510)649-0440
Fax: (510)649-8700
E-mail: abivf@pacbell.net
URL: http://www.abivf.com

22098 ■ ART Reproductive Center
450 N Roxbury Dr., Ste. 520
Beverly Hills, CA 90210
Ph: (310)246-4621
URL: http://www.artreproductivecenter.com
Dr. Mark Surrey, Director

22099 ■ California Center for Reproductive Health
16550 Ventura Blvd., Ste. 400
Encino, CA 91436
Ph: (818)907-1571
Fax: (818)907-1574
URL: http://www.center4reproduction.com
Dr. Eliran Mor, Director

22100 ■ California Fertility Partners
11818 Wilshire Blvd., Ste. 300
Los Angeles, CA 90825
Ph: (310)828-4008
Fax: (310)828-3310
E-mail: gringler@aol.com
URL: http://www.lainfertility.com

22101 ■ California IVF: Davis Fertility Center, Inc.
1550 Drew Ave. Ste. 100
Davis, CA 95618
Ph: (530)771-0177
Fax: (530)771-0135
E-mail: info@californiaivf.com
URL: http://www.californiaivf.com/
Dr. Ernest J. Zeringue, Director

22102 ■ Center for Fertility and Gynecology
18370 Burbank Blvd., Ste. 301
Tarzana, CA 91356
Ph: (818)881-9800
Fax: (818)881-1857
URL: http://www.vermesh.com

22103 ■ Fertility and Gynecology Center IVF Clinic
9833 Blue Larkspur Ln.
Monterey, CA 93940
Free: 877-733-4483
URL: http://www.montereybayivf.com/
Dr. Edward Ramirez, Director

22104 ■ Fertility Physicians of Northern California
2581 Samaritan Dr., Ste. 309
San Jose, CA 95124
Ph: (408)356-5000
Free: 800-597-2234
Fax: (408)356-8954
E-mail: info@fpnc.com
URL: http://www.fpnc.com
Formerly: Fertility and Reproductive Health Institute of Northern California.

22105 ■ Garfield Fertility Center
320 S Garfield Ave., Ste. 226
Alhambra, CA 91801
Ph: (626)943-9536
Fax: (626)943-9529
Brian C. Su, Director

22106 ■ Huntington Reproductive Center--Fullerton
1950 Sunnycrest Dr., Ste. 2400
Fullerton, CA 92835
Ph: (714)738-4200
Free: 866-472-4483
Fax: (714)738-4496
URL: http://www.havingbabies.com

22107 ■ Huntington Reproductive Center--Laguna Hills
23961 Calle de la Magdalena, Ste. 503
Laguna Hills, CA 92653
Ph: (949)472-9446
Free: 866-472-4483
Fax: (949)472-3739
URL: http://www.havingbabies.com

22108 ■ Huntington Reproductive Center--Pasadena
333 S Arroyo Pkwy., 3rd Fl.
Pasadena, CA 91105
Ph: (626)440-9161
Free: 866-472-4483
Fax: (626)440-0138
URL: http://www.havingbabies.com

22109 ■ Huntington Reproductive Center--Tarzana
5525 Etiwanda Ave., Ste. 311
Tarzana, CA 91356
Ph: (818)996-2188
Free: 866-472-4483
Fax: (818)996-2111
URL: http://www.havingbabies.com/

22110 ■ Huntington Reproductive Center--West Los Angeles
11500 Olympic Blvd., Ste. 504
West Los Angeles, CA 90064
Ph: (310)481-0881
Free: 866-472-4483
Fax: (310)481-9017
URL: http://www.havingbabies.com/

22111 ■ Huntington Reproductive Center--Westlake Village
1220 La Venta Ave., Ste. 103
Westlake Village, CA 91361
Ph: (805)374-1737
Free: 866-472-4483
Fax: (805)374-1736
URL: http://www.havingbabies.com

22112 ■ IGO Medical Group of San Diego In Vitro Fertilization Program
9339 Genesee Ave., Ste. 220
San Diego, CA 92121
Ph: (858)455-7520
Fax: (858)554-1312
E-mail: igo@igomed.com
URL: http://www.igomed.com

22113 ■ Laurel Fertility Care
1700 California St., Ste. 570
San Francisco, CA 94109
Ph: (415)673-9199
Free: 888-442-3888
Fax: (415)673-8796
URL: http://www.laurelivf.com/
Formerly: Fertility Associates of the Bay Area.

22114 ■ Loma Linda University Center for Fertility and In Vitro Fertilization
11370 Anderson St., Ste. 3950
Loma Linda, CA 92354
Ph: (909)558-2851
Fax: (909)558-2450
E-mail: lomalindaivf@yahoo.com
URL: http://www.llu.edu/lluhc/fertility
J. Corselli, Director

22115 ■ Marin Reproductive Medical Associates
1100 S Eliseo Dr., Ste. 107
Greenbrae, CA 94904
Ph: (415)464-8688
Fax: (415)464-8042

22116 ■ Napa Valley Fertility Center--Greenbrae
350 Bon Air Rd., Ste. 300
Greenbrae, CA 94904
Ph: (707)259-1955
URL: http://www.napavalleyfertility.com/NVFC-home.html

22117 ■ Napa Valley Fertility Center--Napa
1175 Trancas St.
Napa, CA 94558
Ph: (707)259-1955
URL: http://www.napavalleyfertilitycenter.com/NVFC/NVFC-home.html

22118 ■ Napa Valley Fertility Center--Sonoma
596 1st St. E
Sonoma, CA 95476
Ph: (707)259-1955
URL: http://www.napavalleyfertility.com/NVFC/home.html

22119 ■ Northern California Fertility Medical Center
1130 Conroy Ln., Ste. 100
Roseville, CA 95661
Free: 866-773-2229
Fax: (916)773-8391
URL: http://www.ncfmc.com/

22120 ■ Pacific Fertility Center
55 Francisco St., Ste. 500
San Francisco, CA 94133
Ph: (415)834-3000
Free: 888-834-3095
Fax: (415)834-3099
E-mail: info@pacificfertility.com
URL: http://www.pacificfertilitycenter.com

22121 ■ Pacific Reproductive Center
3720 Lomita Blvd., Ste. 200
Torrance, CA 90505
Ph: (310)376-7000
Fax: (310)373-0319
URL: http://www.4afamily.com/
Dr. Rifaat Salem, Director

22122 ■ Reproductive Partners Medical Group
240 S La Cienega Blvd., Ste. 350
Beverly Hills, CA 90211
Ph: (310)855-2229
E-mail: reproduce@earthlink.net
URL: http://www.reproductivepartners.com

22123 ■ Reproductive Science Center of the San Francisco Bay Area
3160 Crow Canyon Rd., Ste. 150
San Ramon, CA 94583
Ph: (925)452-4711
Fax: (925)901-1481
E-mail: drgalen@drgalen.com
URL: http://www.drgalen.com
Dr. Donald Galen, Director
Formerly: Center for Reproductive Science of the San Francisco Bay Area.

22124 ■ San Diego Fertility Center
11515 El Camino Real, Ste. 100
San Diego, CA 92130
Ph: (858)794-6363
Fax: (858)794-6360
E-mail: whummel@sdfertility.com
URL: http://www.sdfertility.com
Dr. William Hummel, Director

22125 ■ Santa Monica Fertility Specialists
2825 Santa Monica Blvd., Ste. 100
Santa Monica, CA 90404
Ph: (310)566-1470
Free: 866-991-1990
Fax: (310)566-1485
URL: http://www.santamonicafertility.com

22126 ■ Scripps Clinic Fertility Center
10666 N Torrey Pines Rd.
La Jolla, CA 92037
Ph: (858)554-8630
Fax: (858)554-9092
E-mail: jrakoff@scrippsclinic.com
URL: http://www.scrippsclinic.com

22127 ■ Sher Institutes for Reproductive Medicine--Chino Hills
2140 Grand Ave.
Chino Hills, CA 91206
Ph: (909)548-0810
Fax: (909)548-0530
E-mail: losangeles@haveababy.com
URL: http://www.haveababy.com/SIRM/aboutSIRM/centers/losangeles.html
Dr. Brian Acacio, Director

22128 ■ Sher Institutes for Reproductive Medicine--Sacramento
2288 Auburn Blvd., Ste. 204
Sacramento, CA 95821
Ph: (916)568-2125
E-mail: sacramento@haveababy.com
URL: http://www.haveababy.com/SIRM/aboutSIRM/centers/losangeles.html
Dr. Robert Greene, Director

22129 ■ Southern California reproductive Center--Lancaster
44105 N 15th St., Ste. 304
Lancaster, CA 93534
Ph: (661)253-3633
URL: http://scrcivf.com

22130 ■ Southern California Reproductive Center--Beverly Hills
450 N Roxbury Dr., Ste. 500
Beverly Hills, CA 90210
Ph: (310)277-2393
URL: http://www.scrcivf.com

22131 ■ Southern California Reproductive Center Medical Group
2320 Bath St., Ste. 307
Santa Barbara, CA 93105
Ph: (805)569-1950
Fax: (800)600-6944
URL: http://www.scrcivf.com

22132 ■ Southern California Reproductive Center--San Luis Obispo
35 Casa St., Ste. 220
San Luis Obispo, CA 93401
Ph: (805)569-1950
URL: http://www.scrcivf.com

22133 ■ Southern California Reproductive Center--Santa Monica
2001 Santa Monica Blvd., Ste. 770W
anta Monica, CA 90404
Ph: (310)829-4781
URL: http://www.scrcivf.com

22134 ■ Southern California Reproductive Center--Valencia
27871 Smyth Dr., Ste. 102
Valencia, CA 91355
Ph: (661)253-3633
URL: http://www.scrcivf.com

22135 ■ Southern California Reproductive Center--Ventura
4080 Loma vista Rd., Ste. P
Ventura, CA 93003
Ph: (805)658-9112
URL: http://www.scrcivf.com

22136 ■ Specialty Care for Women
1255 East St., Ste. 201
Redding, CA 96001
Ph: (530)244-9052

22137 ■ Stanford University Reproductive Endocrinology and Infertility Clinic
900 Welch Rd., Ste. 15
Palo Alto, CA 94304
Ph: (650)498-7911
Fax: (650)723-6175
E-mail: fertilitycenter@stanfordmed.edu
URL: http://www.stanfordivf.org

22138 ■ Tyler Medical Clinic In Vitro Fertilization Program
9301 Wilshire Blvd., Ste 208
Beverly Hills, CA 90210
Ph: (310)278-7590
Fax: (310)278-7599
E-mail: info@tylermedicalclinic.com
URL: http://www.tylermedicalclinic.com
Dr. Peyman Saadat, Director

22139 ■ University of California, Davis Fertility Center
2521 Stockton Blvd., Ste. 4200
Sacramento, CA 95817
Ph: (916)734-6106
Free: 800-2-UCDAVIS
Fax: (916)734-6150
E-mail: fertility@ucdmc.ucdavis.edu
URL: http://www.ucdmc.ucdavis.edu/fertility/

22140 ■ University of California, San Francisco Center for Reproductive Health
2356 Sutter St., 7th Fl.
San Francisco, CA 94115
Ph: (415)353-7475
Fax: (415)353-7744
E-mail: info@ucsfivf.org
URL: http://www.ucsfivf.org
Dr. Linda Giuduce, Director

22141 ■ USC Fertility
1127 Wilshire Blvd., Ste. 1400
Los Angeles, CA 90017
Ph: (213)975-9990
URL: http://uscfertility.org

22142 ■ Walnut Creek Fertility
240 La Casa Via, Ste. 100
Walnut Creek, CA 94598
Ph: (925)932-2565

22143 ■ Women's Specialty and Fertility Center
722 Medical Center E, Ste. 105
Clovis, CA 93611
Ph: (559)299-7700

22144 ■ Zouves Fertility Center
901 Campus Dr., Ste. 214
Daly City, CA 94015
Free: 800-800-1160
Fax: (650)301-4923
E-mail: Info@GoIVF.com
URL: http://www.goivf.com/
Dr. Christos Zouves, Director

COLORADO

22145 ■ Colorado Center for Reproductive Medicine--Denver
Rose Medical Center
4545 E 9th Ave., Ste. 420
Denver, CO 80220
Ph: (303)355-2555
URL: http://www.colocrm.com

22146 ■ Colorado Center for Reproductive Medicine--Lone Tree
10290 RidgeGate Cir.
Lone Tree, CO 80124
Ph: (303)788-8300
Fax: (303)788-8310
E-mail: ccrm@colocrm.com
URL: http://www.colocrm.com
Dr. William B. Schoolcraft, Director

22147 ■ Colorado Center for Reproductive Medicine--Louisville
Avista Adventist Hospital
Avista 2 Medical Plz., Ste. 240
80 Health Park Dr.
Louisville, CO 80027
Ph: (303)665-0150
URL: http://www.colocrm.com

22148 ■ Colorado Reproductive Endocrinology
4600 E Hale Pkwy., Ste. 350
Denver, CO 80220
Ph: (303)321-7115
Free: 888-817-0124
Fax: (303)321-9519
E-mail: susantrout@coloradofertility.com
URL: http://www.coloradofertility.com
Dr. Susan W. Trout, Director

22149 ■ Conceptions Reproductive Associates--Lafayette
300 Exempla Cir., Ste. 370
Lafayette, CO 80026
Ph: (303)449-1084
Fax: (303)449-1039
URL: http://www.conceptionsrepro.com

22150 ■ Conceptions Reproductive Associates--Littleton
271 W County Line Rd.
Littleton, CO 80129
Ph: (303)794-0045
Fax: (303)794-2054
E-mail: info@conceptionsrepro.com
URL: http://www.conceptionsrepro.com
Dr. Bruce H. Albrecht, Director

22151 ■ Fertility Center of Colorado
6160 Tuft Blvd., Ste. 210
Colorado Springs, CO 80923
Ph: (719)636-0080
Fax: (719)636-3030
E-mail: cscrhlab@aol.com
URL: http://www.fertilitycentercolorado.com
Dr. Eric H. Silverstein, Director

22152 ■ Reproductive Genetics In Vitro
Bldg. 3, Ste. 400
6000 E Evans Ave.
Denver, CO 80222
Ph: (303)399-5393
Free: 800-399-5577
Fax: (303)399-9160
E-mail: info@reprogen.com
URL: http://www.reprogen.com
Dr. George P. Henry, Director

22153 ■ Reproductive Medicine and Fertility Center
265 Parkside Dr., Ste. 200
Colorado Springs, CO 80910
Ph: (719)475-2229
Fax: (719)475-2227
E-mail: info@475-baby.com
URL: http://www.475-baby.com
Dr. Paul C. Magarelli, Director

22154 ■ Rocky Mountain Center for Reproductive Medicine
1080 E Elizabeth
Fort Collins, CO 80524
Ph: (970)493-6353
Free: 800-624-9035
Fax: (970)493-6366
E-mail: embryologist@drbachus.com
URL: http://www.drbachus.com
Dr. Kevin E. Bachus, Director

22155 ■ Rocky Mountain Fertility Center
9235 Crown Crest Blvd.
Parker, CO 80138
Ph: (303)999-3877
Fax: (303)999-3878
URL: http://www.rockymountainfertility.com
Dr. Deborah Smith, Director

22156 ■ University of Colorado
Advanced Reproductive Medicine
4125 Briargate Pkwy., Ste. 350
Colorado Springs, CO 80920
Ph: (719)314-3333
Fax: (719)314-3344
URL: http://www.coloradospringsinfertility.org

22157 ■ University of Colorado Health Sciences Center
Advanced Reproductive Medicine
1635 Aurora Ct., Ste. 3400
Aurora, CO 80045
Ph: (720)848-1690
Free: 888-899-7441
Fax: (720)848-1678
URL: http://www.ucarm.org
Dr. William D. Schlaff, Director

CONNECTICUT

22158 ■ Center for Advanced Reproductive Services
Hartford Fertility and Reproductive Endocrinology Center
100 Retreat Ave., Ste. 900
Hartford, CT 06112
Ph: (860)525-8283
Fax: (860)525-1930

22159 ■ Connecticut Fertility Associates - Bridgeport
4920 Main St., Ste. 301
Bridgeport, CT 06606
Ph: (203)373-1200
Fax: (203)375-6516
E-mail: askus@CtFertility.com
URL: http://www.connecticutfertility.com/bport.html

22160 ■ Connecticut Fertility Associates - Norwalk
148 East Ave., Ste. 2C
Norwalk, CT 06851
Ph: (203)855-1200
Fax: (203)866-3668
E-mail: askus@ctfertility.com
URL: http://www.connecticutfertility.com

22161 ■ New England Fertility Institute
1275 Summer St., No. 201
Stamford, CT 06905
Ph: (203)325-3200
Fax: (203)323-3130
E-mail: mwelch@nefertility.com
URL: http://www.nefertility.com

22162 ■ Park Avenue Fertility and Reproductive Medicine
5520 Park Ave., Ste. 103
Trumbull, CT 06611
Ph: (203)372-6700
Fax: (203)372-6706
E-mail: administration@parkavefertility.com
URL: http://www.parkavefertility.com

22163 ■ Reproductive Medicine Associates of Connecticut
10 Glover Ave.
Norwalk, CT 06850
Ph: (203)750-7400
Free: 800-865-5431
Fax: (203)846-9579
E-mail: info@rmact.com
URL: http://www.rmact.com
Dr. Fikry Salib, Director

22164 ■ Stamford Hospital
Reproductive Endocrinology and Infertility
Shelburne & W Broad Sts.
Stamford, CT 06904
Ph: (203)325-7559
Fax: (203)325-7259
E-mail: fginsburg@stamhealth.org
URL: http://www.stamfordhospital.org
Dr. Frances W. Ginsburg, Director

22165 ■ University of Connecticut Health Center--Farmington
The Center for Advanced Reproductive Services
Dowling South Bldg., 3rd Fl.
263 Farmington Ave.
Farmington, CT 06030-6224
Ph: (860)679-4580
Fax: (860)679-1499
E-mail: fertilitycenter@uconn.org
URL: http://www.fertilitycenter-uconn.org
Dr. John C. Nulsen, Director

22166 ■ University of Connecticut Health Center--Hartford
Center for Advanced Reproductive Services
100 Retreat Ave., Ste. 900
Hartford, CT 06106
Free: 866-525-8283
URL: http://www.uconnfertility.com

22167 ■ Yale Reproductive Endocrinology and Infertility--Guilford
385 Church St., Ste. 102
Guilford, CT 06437
Ph: (203)785-4708
Free: 877-925-3483
URL: http://www.yalefertilitycenter.org

22168 ■ Yale Reproductive Endocrinology and Infertility--Westport
125 A Kings Hwy., N
Westport, CT 06880
Ph: (203)341-8899
URL: http://www.yalefertilitycenter.com

22169 ■ Yale University
IVF Program
Reproductive Endocrinology & Infertility
150 Sargent Dr., 2nd Fl.
New Haven, CT 06511
Ph: (203)785-4708
Free: 877-YALE-IVF
Fax: (203)764-5619
E-mail: pasquale.patrizio@yale.edu
URL: http://www.yalerei.org
Dr. Pasquale Patrizio, Director

DELAWARE

22170 ■ Delaware Institute for Reproductive Medicine
4745 Ogletown-Stanton Rd., Ste. 111
Newark, DE 19713
Ph: (302)738-4600
Fax: (302)738-3508
E-mail: jbrussell@ivf-success.com
Dr. Jeffrey B. Russell, Director
Formerly: Medical Center of Delaware, Reproductive Endocrinology and Fertility Center.

DISTRICT OF COLUMBIA

22171 ■ ART Institute of Washington, Inc.
Bldg. 2, Rm. 4304
6900 Georgia Ave. NW
Washington, DC 20307
Ph: (202)782-9537
Fax: (202)782-4833
URL: http://www.wramc.amedd.army.mil/departments/gyn/r
Dr. James H. Segars, Director

22172 ■ Columbia Fertility Associates
2440 M St. NW, Ste. 401
Washington, DC 20037
Ph: (202)293-6567
Fax: (202)778-6190
URL: http://columbiafertilityassociates.com/
Dr. Safa M. Rifka, Director

22173 ■ Dominion Fertility--Washington
1145 19th st., NW, Ste. 410
Washington, DC 20036
Ph: (703)920-3890
URL: http://www.dominionfertility.com

22174 ■ George Washington University
In Vitro Fertilization Program
22nd St. NW & I St. NW, 5th Fl.
Washington, DC 20037
Ph: (202)741-2500
Fax: (202)741-2518
E-mail: adubey@mfa.gwu.edu
URL: http://www.gwdocs.com/1132534780717.html
Dr. Paul R. Gindoff, Director

22175 ■ James A. Simon, MD, PC
In Vitro Fertilization Clinic
1850 M St. NW, Ste. 450
Washington, DC 20036
Ph: (202)293-1000
Fax: (202)463-6150
E-mail: jsimon@whrc.net
URL: http://www.jamesasimonmd.com
Dr. James A. Simon, Director

22176 ■ Shady Grove Fertility--Washington
2021 K St. NW, Ste. 701
Washington, DC 20006
Ph: (202)296-2595
Fax: (202)296-2835
URL: http://www.shadygrovefertility.com
Dr. Eric A. Widra, Director

FLORIDA

22177 ■ Assisted Fertility Program of North Florida
3627 University Blvd. S, Ste. 450
Jacksonville, FL 32216
Ph: (904)398-1473
Free: 800-777-4831
E-mail: artnorthflorida@aol.com
URL: http://www.assistedfertility.org
Dr. Marwan Shaykh, Director
Formerly: First Coast Assisted Fertility Program.

22178 ■ Boca Fertility
875 Meadows Rd., No. 334
Boca Raton, FL 33486
Ph: (561)368-5500
Fax: (561)368-4793
E-mail: frontdesk@bocafertility.com
URL: http://www.bocafertility.com
Dr. Moshe R. Peress, Director
Formerly: Fertility Institute, Boca Raton.

22179 ■ Center for Advanced Reproductive Endocrinology
201 N Pine Island Rd.
Plantation, FL 33324
Ph: (954)584-2273

Free: 866-246-2273
Fax: (954)587-9630
E-mail: info@care-life.com
URL: http://www.care-life.com
Dr. Mick Abae, Director

22180 ■ Center for Reproductive Medicine--Orlando
3435 Pinehurst Ave.
Orlando, FL 32804
Ph: (407)740-0909
Free: 800-343-6331
Fax: (407)740-7262
E-mail: info@ivforlando.com
URL: http://www.ivforlando.com
Dr. Mike Abae, Director

22181 ■ Fertility Center and Applied Genetics of Florida
5664 Bee Ridge Rd., No. 103
Sarasota, FL 34233
Ph: (941)342-1568
Fax: (941)342-8296
E-mail: drpabon@comcast.net
URL: http://www.drpabon.com
Dr. Julio E. Pabon, Director

22182 ■ Fertility Center of Assisted Reproduction and Endocrinology
5931 Brick Ct.
Winter Park, FL 32792
Ph: (407)672-1106
Free: 866-322-7310
Fax: (407)678-2790
E-mail: info@myfertilitycare.com
URL: http://www.myfertilitycare.com
Dr. Mark P. Trolice, Director

22183 ■ The Fertility Experts
2454 McMullen Booth Rd., Ste. 601
Clearwater, FL 33759
Ph: (727)796-7705
Fax: (727)796-8764
URL: http://www.thefertilityexperts.com

22184 ■ Fertility & IVF Center of Miami
8950 N Kendall Dr., Ste. 103
Miami, FL 33176
Ph: (305)596-4013
Free: 866-483-2229
Fax: (305)596-4557
E-mail: info@yahoo.com
URL: http://www.miami-ivf.com
Dr. Michael H. Jacobs, Director

22185 ■ Fertility and Reproductive Medicine Center for Women
95 Bulldog Blvd., Ste. 204
Melbourne, FL 32901
Ph: (321)724-4410
Fax: (321)956-9957
E-mail: chamoun@aol.com
Dr. Diran Chamoun, Director

22186 ■ Florida Institute for Reproductive Medicine
836 Prudential Dr., No. 902
Jacksonville, FL 32207
Ph: (904)399-5620
Fax: (904)399-5645
URL: http://www.firmjax.com
Dr. Kevin L. Winslow, Director

22187 ■ Florida Institute for Reproductive Sciences and Technologies
Weston Regional Healthpark
2300 N Commerce Pkwy., Ste. 313
Weston, FL 33326
Ph: (954)217-3456
Fax: (954)217-3462
E-mail: FIRSTivf@aol.com
URL: http://www.FIRSTivf.net
Dr. Minna Ruth Selub, Director

22188 ■ IVF Florida Reproductive Associates
2960 N SR 7, Ste. 300
Margate, FL 33063
Ph: (954)247-6200
Fax: (954)247-6262
URL: http://www.ivfflorida.com
Dr. David I. Hoffman, Director

22189 ■ Jacksonville Center for Reproductive Medicine
7051 Southpoint Pkwy., Ste. 200
Jacksonville, FL 32216
Ph: (904)493-2229
Fax: (904)396-4546
E-mail: info@jcrm.org
URL: http://www.jcrm.org
Dr. Michael D. Fox, Director

22190 ■ New Leaders in Fertility and Endocrinology
4400 Bayou Blvd., Ste. 36
Pensacola, FL 32504
Ph: (850)857-3733
Fax: (850)857-0670
E-mail: newfertility@aol.com
URL: http://www.fertilityleaders.com/
Dr. Barry A. Ripps, Director

22191 ■ Palm Beach Fertility Center
9291 Glades Rd., Ste. 202
Boca Raton, FL 33434
Ph: (561)477-7728
Free: 800-953-BABY
Fax: (561)477-7035
E-mail: admin9970@earthlink.net
URL: http://www.palmbeachfertility.com
Dr. Mark S. Denker, Director

22192 ■ Palmetto Fertility Center of South Florida
7100 W 20th Ave., Ste. 205
Miami, FL 33016
Ph: (303)558-0808
Fax: (303)558-0806
E-mail: info@fertilitymiami.com
URL: http://www.palmettoivf.com
Dr. Michael D. Graubert, Director

22193 ■ Reproductive Health Associates, PA
2695 Ulmerton Rd.
Clearwater, FL 33762
Ph: (727)572-5300
Fax: (727)572-5022
Dr. Catherine L. Cowart, Director

22194 ■ Reproductive Medicine Group
5245 E Fletcher Ave., Ste. 1
Tampa, FL 33617
Ph: (813)914-7304
URL: http://www.floridafertility.com
Dr. Marc Bernhisel, Director

22195 ■ The Reproductive Medicine Group--Brandon
612 Medical Care Dr.
Brandon, FL 33511
Ph: (813)661-9114
URL: http://floridafertility.com

22196 ■ The Reproductive Medicine Group--Clearwater
3165 McMullen Booth Rd., Bldg. F, Ste. 2
Clearwater, FL 33761
Ph: (727)724-0702
URL: http://floridafertility.com

22197 ■ South Florida Institute for Reproductive Medicine--Miami
7300 SW 62nd Pl., 4th Fl.
Miami, FL 33143
Ph: (305)662-7901
Fax: (305)662-7910
E-mail: ivfmd@ivfmd.com
URL: http://www.ivfmd.com
Dr. Maria Bustillo, Director

22198 ■ South Florida Institute for Reproductive Medicine--Naples
1280 Creekside St., Ste. 105
Naples, FL 34108
Ph: (305)662-7901
URL: http://www.ivfmd.com

22199 ■ Southwest Florida Fertility Center
15730 New Hampshire Ct.
Fort Myers, FL 33908
Ph: (239)561-3430
Fax: (239)561-6980
URL: http://www.swflfertility.com
Dr. Jacob L. Glock, Director

22200 ■ Specialists in Reproductive Medicine and Surgery
Bldg. 53
12611 World Plz. Ln.
Fort Myers, FL 33907
Ph: (239)275-8118
Fax: (239)275-5914
E-mail: fertility@dreamababy.com
URL: http://www.dreamababy.com
Dr. Craig R. Sweet, Director

22201 ■ University Fertility Associates
7171 N Dale Mabry Hwy., Ste. 401
Tampa, FL 33614
Ph: (813)933-9166
URL: http://www.universityfertilityassociates.com
Formerly: Fertility Institute of W Florida.

22202 ■ University of Florida Shands Hospital Women's Health, Magnolia Parke In Vitro Fertilization Program
3951 NW 48th Terr., Ste. 101
Gainesville, FL 32606
Ph: (352)265-6200
Fax: (352)265-0281
E-mail: williams@obgyn.ufl.edu
URL: http://www.shands.org/find/service/invitro.asp
Dr. R. Stan Williams, Director

22203 ■ University of Miami Infertility Center
Cedars Medical Center
1400 NW 12th Ave., Ste. 5
Miami, FL 33136
Ph: (305)243-8642
Fax: (305)324-0363
URL: http://umic.miami.edu
Dr. George R. Attia, Director

GEORGIA

22204 ■ Atlanta Center for Reproductive Medicine
1800 Howell Mill Rd., Ste. 675
Atlanta, GA 30318
Ph: (770)928-2276
Fax: (770)592-2092
E-mail: info@acrm.com
URL: http://www.atlantainfertility.com
Dr. James P. Toner, Director

22205 ■ Emory Reproductive Center
550 Peachtree St. NE, Ste. 1800
Atlanta, GA 30308
Ph: (404)778-3401
Fax: (404)686-4956
URL: http://www.emoryivf.org
Dr. Donna R. Session, Director

22206 ■ Georgia Reproductive Specialists
5445 Meridian Mark Rd., Ste. 270
Atlanta, GA 30342
Ph: (404)843-2229
Fax: (404)843-0812
URL: http://www.ivf.com/
Dr. Carolyn R. Kaplan, Director

22207 ■ MCG Reproductive Medicine and Inferility Assocites
618 Ponder Pl., Ste. 2
Evans, GA 30809
Ph: (706)722-4434
Fax: (706)722-9647
URL: http://www.ivfaugusta.com
Dr. Ana A. Murphy, Chairman

22208 ■ MCG Reproductive Medicine and Infertility Associates
810 Chafee St.
Augusta, GA 30904
Ph: (706)722-4434
Fax: (706)722-9647
E-mail: aemmi@mcg.edu
Dr. Adelina M. Emmi, Director

22209 ■ Medical Center of Georgia Central Georgia Fertility Institute
4075 Elnora Dr.
Macon, GA 31210
Ph: (478)757-7888
Free: 888-824-7890
Fax: (478)757-7887
Dr. William J. Butler, Director

22210 ■ Reproductive Biology Associates--Atlanta
1150 Lake Hearn Dr., Ste 400
Atlanta, GA 30342
Ph: (404)257-1900
URL: http://www.rba-online.com
Dr. Daniel B. Shapiro, Director

22211 ■ Reproductive Biology Associates--Fayetteville
1267 Highway 54 W, Ste. 3200
Fayetteville, GA 30214
Ph: (678)366-2154
URL: http://www.rba-online.com

22212 ■ Reproductive Biology Associates--Lawrenceville
500 Medical Center Blvd., Ste. 330
Lawrenceville, GA 30046
Ph: (770)277-3361
URL: http://www.rba-online.com

22213 ■ Reproductive Biology Associates North Crescent Medical Center
11975 Morris Rd., Ste. 220
Alpharetta, GA 30005
Ph: (770)426-8822
URL: http://rba-online.com

22214 ■ Servy Institute for Reproductive Endocrinology
812 Chafee Ave.
Augusta, GA 30904
Ph: (706)724-0228
Fax: (706)722-2387
E-mail: eservy@yahoo.com
URL: http://www.servyinstitute.com/
Dr. Edouard J. Servy, Director
Formerly: Augusta Reproductive Associates.

HAWAII

22215 ■ Advanced Reproductive Center of Hawaii
1319 Punahou St., Ste. 520
Honolulu, HI 96826
Ph: (808)949-6611
Fax: (808)949-6610
E-mail: drhuang@archawaii.com
URL: http://archawaii.com/
Dr. Christopher T.F. Huang, Director

22216 ■ Fertility Institute of Hawaii
Medical Arts Bldg.
407 Uluniu St., Ste. 312
Kailua, HI 96734
Ph: (808)262-0544
Fax: (808)262-3744
URL: http://www.ivfcenterhawaii.com

22217 ■ Fertility Institute of Hawaii Hale Pawa'a
1401 S Beretania St., Ste. 250
Honolulu, HI 96814
Ph: (808)545-2800
Fax: (808)262-3744
URL: http://ivfcenterhawaii.com

22218 ■ Hawaii Center for Reproductive Medicine and Surgery
642 Ulukahiki St., Ste. 300
Kailua, HI 96734
Ph: (808)261-4166
Fax: (808)261-4086
URL: http://www.hawaiireproductivecenter.com/
Dr. Celia E. Dominguez, Director

22219 ■ Pacific In Vitro Fertilization Institute
1319 Punahou St., Ste. 980
Honolulu, HI 96826
Ph: (808)946-2226
Free: 866-944-0440
Fax: (808)943-1563
E-mail: info@pacificinvitro.com
URL: http://www.pacificinvitro.com
Dr. Thomas S. Kosasa, Director

22220 ■ Tripler Army Medical Center Department of Obstetrics and Gynecology Reproductive Endocrinology Infertility
1 Jarrett White Rd.
Honolulu, HI 96859
Ph: (808)433-6845
Fax: (808)433-1552
URL: http://www.tamc.amedd.army.mil/offices/obgyn/rei.htm

IDAHO

22221 ■ Idaho Center for Reproductive Medicine
111 Main St., Ste. 100
Boise, ID 83702
Ph: (208)342-5900
Fax: (208)342-2088
URL: http://www.idahofertility.com/
Dr. Russell A. Foulk, Director

ILLINOIS

22222 ■ Advanced Fertility Center of Chicago
30 Tower Ct., Ste. F
Gurnee, IL 60031
Ph: (847)662-1818
Fax: (847)662-3001
E-mail: nurse@advancedfertility.com
URL: http://www.advancedfertility.com
Dr. Richard Sherbahn, Director

22223 ■ Advanced Reproductive Health Center
1 E Erie St.
Chicago, IL 60611
Free: 866-IVF-CHGO
URL: http://www.chicago-ivf.com/

22224 ■ The Center for Human Reproduction
2825 N Halsted St.
Chicago, IL 60657
Ph: (773)472-4949
Fax: (773)935-3691
URL: http://www.centerforhumanreprod.com

22225 ■ Fertility Centers of Illinois--River North IVF
900 N Kingsbury, RW 6
Chicago, IL 60610
Ph: (312)222-8200
Fax: (312)494-1692
URL: http://www.fcionline.com
Dr. Angeline Beltsos, Director

22226 ■ Fertility Centers of Illinois, S.C.
8651 W 159th St., Ste. 5
Orland Park, IL 60462
Ph: (708)633-1999
Fax: (708)633-1888
E-mail: infertilitydoc@mediaonc.net
URL: http://www.fcionline.com/aboutus_orlandpark.htm

22227 ■ Friberg Medical Associates Chicago Women's Wellness Center
845 N Michigan Ave.
Chicago, IL 60611
Ph: (312)642-6777
Fax: (312)642-8383
E-mail: Info@FribergMedical.com
URL: http://www.fribergmedical.com/
Dr. Jan Friberg, Director

22228 ■ Highland Park IVF Center
767 Park Ave. W, Ste. B400
Highland Park, IL 60035
Ph: (847)266-3535
Fax: (847)266-8838
Dr. Edward L. Marut, Director
Formerly: Fertility Centers of Illinois, S.C.

22229 ■ Hinsdale Center for Reproduction
121 N Elm St.
Hinsdale, IL 60521
Ph: (630)856-3535
Fax: (630)856-3545
E-mail: info@hinsdale-ivf.com
URL: http://www.hinsdale-ivf.com
Dr. Jay H. Levin, Director

22230 ■ InVia Fertility
Doctors Bldg. 2, Ste. 406
1585 N Barrington Rd.
Hoffman Estates, IL 60194
Ph: (847)884-8884
Fax: (847)884-8093
E-mail: info@karandeivf.com
URL: http://www.inviafertility.com/
Dr. Vishvanath C. Karande, Director
Formerly: Karande and Associates.

22231 ■ IVF1
636 Raymond Dr., Ste. 303
Naperville, IL 60563
Ph: (630)357-6540
Fax: (630)357-6435
E-mail: rsm@ivf1.com
URL: http://www.ivf1.com
Dr. Randy S. Morris, Director

22232 ■ Midwest Fertility Center In Vitro Fertilization Program
4333 Main St.
Downers Grove, IL 60515
Ph: (630)810-0212
Free: 800-244-0212
Fax: (630)810-1027
E-mail: fertility@IVF.us
URL: http://www.midwestfertilitycenter.com
Dr. Amos E. Madanes, Director
Formerly: Midwest Infertility Center.

22233 ■ North Shore Fertility
4250 Dempster
Skokie, IL 60076
Ph: (847)763-8850
Fax: (847)763-8851
URL: http://www.northshorefertility.com
Dr. Susan A. Davies, Director

22234 ■ Northwestern Memorial Hospital
251 E Huron St.
Chicago, IL 60611
Ph: (312)695-7269
Free: 877-926-4664
Fax: (312)926-8244
URL: http://www.nmh.org/nmh/prentice/infertility.htm
Dr. Edmond Confino, Director

22235 ■ Oak Brook Fertility Center
2425 W 22nd St., No. 102
Oak Brook, IL 60523
Free: 866-759-5832
E-mail: wpdmowski@oakbrookfertility.com
URL: http://www.oakbrookfertility.com
Dr. W. Paul Dmowski, Director

22236 ■ Reproductive Endocrinology Associates--Springfield
340 W Miller St.
Springfield, IL 62702
Ph: (217)523-4700
Fax: (217)523-9025
URL: http://www.drmcrae-reproendoassoc.yourmd.com
Dr. Mary Ann McRae, Director

22237 ■ Reproductive Health and Fertility Center
973 Featherstone Rd., Ste. 100
Rockford, IL 61107
Ph: (815)986-3737
Free: 877-373-7552
URL: http://www.wemakefamilies.com/
Dr. Chiravudh Sawetawan, Director

22238 ■ Reproductive Health Specialists
744 Essington Rd.
Joliet, IL 60435
Ph: (815)730-1100
Fax: (815)730-1066
E-mail: info@reproductivespecialist.com
URL: http://www.reproductivespecialist.com
Dr. Marek W. Piekos, Director

22239 ■ Rinehart Center for Reproductive Medicine
2500 Ridge Ave., Ste. 200
Evanston, IL 60201
Ph: (847)869-7777
Fax: (847)869-7782
E-mail: rinehartcenter@ameritech.net
URL: http://www.illinoisivf.com/
Dr. John S. Rinehart, Director

22240 ■ Rinehart--Coulam Center
3825 Highland Ave., Ste. 2M
Downers Grove, IL 60515
Ph: (630)960-2570
Fax: (630)960-2694
E-mail: Rinehart@ameritech.net
URL: http://www.illinoisivf.com
Dr. John S. Rinehart, Director

22241 ■ Rush--Copley Center for Reproductive Health
2020 Ogden Ave., No. 250
Aurora, IL 60504
Ph: (630)978-6254
Fax: (630)499-2487
URL: http://www.rushcopley.com/rcmg/reproductive_health/welcome/aspx
Dr. Zvi Binor, Director

22242 ■ Rush Presbyterian-Saint Luke's Medical Center
Rush Center for Advanced Reproductive Care
In Vitro Fertilization Program
1725 W Harrison
Chicago, IL 60612
Ph: (312)942-6609
E-mail: contact_rush@rush.edu
URL: http://www.rush.edu/rumc/page-1099918806892.html

22243 ■ Sher Institutes for Reproductive Medicine--Peoria
5401 N Knoxville, Ste. 110
Peoria, IL 61614
Ph: (309)689-0411
Fax: (309)789-0784
E-mail: centralil@haveababy.com
URL: http://www.haveababy.com/SIRM/aboutSIRM/centers/centralillinois.html
Dr. Natalie Schultz, Director

22244 ■ University of Chicago Hospitals
Reproductive Endocrinology and Infertility
Department of OB/GYN, MC 2050
5841 S Maryland Ave., Rm. MC-2050
Chicago, IL 60637
Ph: (773)834-1167
Fax: (773)702-5848
URL: http://www.chicagofertility.org
Dr. Anthony J. Caruso, Director

22245 ■ University of Illinois, Chicago
Reproductive Endocrinology and Infertility
1801 W Taylor St., Ste. 4A
Chicago, IL 60612
Ph: (312)996-9820
Free: 800-842-1002
Fax: (312)355-3161
E-mail: mpucci1@uic.edu
URL: http://www.uicivf.org
Dr. Humberto Scoccia, Director

INDIANA

22246 ■ Advanced Fertility Group
1222 Professional Blvd.
Evansville, IN 47714
Ph: (812)469-4920
Fax: (812)469-4930
URL: http://www.advancedfertilitygroup.com
Dr. William L. Gentry, Director

22247 ■ Associated Fertility and Gynecology
7910 W Jefferson, No. 301
Fort Wayne, IN 46804
Ph: (260)432-6250
Fax: (260)436-7220
URL: http://www.afg-ivf.com/
Dr. Shelby O. Cooper, Director

22248 ■ Bonaventura Reproductive Medicine
11725 Illinois St., Ste. 345
Carmel, IN 46032
Ph: (317)814-4570
Fax: (317)814-4571
E-mail: ldoc8@aol.com
URL: http://www.bonaventurafertility.com/
Dr. Leo M. Bonaventure, Director

22249 ■ Family Beginnings
8435 Clearvista Pl., Ste. 104
Indianapolis, IN 46256
Ph: (317)595-3665
Fax: (317)595-3666
URL: http://www.www.ivf-indiana.com
Dr. James G. Donahue, Director

22250 ■ Jarrett Fertility Group LLC
11725 Illinois St., Ste. 515
Carmel, IN 46032
Ph: (317)814-4110
Free: 888-674-0101
Fax: (317)814-4114
E-mail: info@jarrettfertility.com
URL: http://www.jarrettfertility.com
Dr. John C. Jarrett, Director

22251 ■ Midwest Fertility Specialists
12188-A N Meridian, Ste. 250
Carmel, IN 46032
Ph: (317)571-1637
Free: 800-218-3012
Fax: (317)571-9483
E-mail: lreuter@ivfmidwest.com
URL: http://www.midwestfertility.com
Dr. Laura M. Reuter, Director

22252 ■ Reproductive Care of Indiana
201 Pennsylvania Pkwy., Ste. 310
Indianapolis, IN 46280
Ph: (317)817-1800
Fax: (317)817-1810
URL: http://www.reprocareindiana.com
Dr. Michael A. Henry, Director

22253 ■ Reproductive Endocrinology Associates--Indianapolis
2020 W 86th St., No. 310
Indianapolis, IN 46260
Ph: (317)872-1515
Fax: (317)879-2784
E-mail: dcline3192@msn.com
URL: http://www.reproductivehope.com
Dr. Donald L. Cline, Director

22254 ■ University Hospital--Indianapolis
Department of Obstetrics and Gynecology
In Vitro Fertilization Program
Department of OB/GYN
550 N University Blvd., Rm. 2440
Indianapolis, IN 46202
Ph: (317)274-4875
Fax: (317)278-3787
E-mail: mshepar@iupui.edu
URL: http://www.iuwhc.com/Infertility_Services.asp.htm
Dr. Marguerite Shepard, Director

22255 ■ Women's Specialty Health Centers
9660 E 146th St., Ste. 300
Noblesville, IN 46060
Ph: (317)774-1200
Free: 866-322-2263
Fax: (317)774-1222
URL: http://www.familyjoy.net
Dr. David S. McLaughlin, Director

IOWA

22256 ■ Mid Iowa Fertility Clinic
1371 NW 121st St.
Clive, IA 50325
Ph: (515)222-3060
Free: 888-306-3060
Fax: (515)222-9563
E-mail: admin@midiowafertility.com
URL: http://www.midiowafertility.com
Dr. Donald C. Young, Director

22257 ■ University of Iowa Hospitals and Clinics--Davenport
Reproductive Endocrinology and Infertility Clinic
Mississippi Valley Medical Plz.
3400 Dexter Ct., Ste. 100
Davenport, IA 52807
Ph: (563)355-2244
URL: http://www.uihealthcare.com/depts/med/obgyn/infertility

22258 ■ University of Iowa Hospitals and Clinics--Iowa City
Reproductive Endocrinology and Infertility Clinic
200 Hawkins Dr.
Iowa City, IA 52242
Ph: (319)356-8483
Fax: (319)384-8353
URL: http://www.uihealthcare.com/depts/med/obgyn/infertility/
Dr. Bradley Van Voorhis, Director

KANSAS

22259 ■ The Center for Reproductive Medicine
9220 E 29th St., Ste. 102
Wichita, KS 67226
Ph: (316)687-2112
Fax: (316)687-1260
E-mail: grainger@southwest.net
URL: http://www.cfrm.net/
Formerly: University of Kansas Wichita, The Center for Reproductive Medicine.

22260 ■ Midwest Reproductive Center
Doctors Bldg.
20375 W 151st St., Ste. 403
Olathe, KS 66061

Ph: (913)780-4300
URL: http://www.midwestreproductive.com

22261 ■ Reproductive Resource Center
120 W 106th St., Ste. 120
Overland Park, KS 66215
Free: 877-221-2323
Fax: (913)894-0841
URL: http://www.rrc-gkc.com/

22262 ■ Reproductive Resource Center of Greater Kansas City
12200 W 106th St., Ste. 120
Overland Park, KS 66215
Ph: (913)894-2323
Fax: (913)894-0841
URL: http://www.rrc-gkc.com

22263 ■ University of Kansas Medical Center
Women's Reproductive Center
Center for Advanced Reproductive Medicine
3901 Rainbow Blvd., 5th Fl.
Kansas City, KS 66160
Ph: (913)588-6276
Fax: (913)588-6258
URL: http://www.kumc.edu/carm

KENTUCKY

22264 ■ University of Louisville
OB/GYN Associates
Fertility Center
315 E Broadway
Louisville, KY 40202
Ph: (502)271-5999
Fax: (502)271-5994
E-mail: lovivf@aol.com
URL: http://kyinfertility.com
Albert Arnull, Director
Formerly: Norton Hospital, Fertility Program.

LOUISIANA

22265 ■ Fertility and Endocrine Associates
4121 Dutchmans Ln., Ste. 414
Louisville, LA 40207
Ph: (502)897-2144
E-mail: info@ivfkentucky.com
URL: http://www.ivfkentucky.com/lrc.html
Dr. Robert J. Homm, Director

22266 ■ Fertility Institute--Baton Rouge
8595 Picardy Ave., Ste. 240
Baton Rouge, LA 70809
Ph: (985)892-7621
Free: 800-433-9009
E-mail: info@fertilityinstitute.com
URL: http://www.fertilityinstitute.com

22267 ■ Fertility Institute--Metairie
4770 S I-10 Service Rd. W, Ste. 201
Metairie, LA 70001
Ph: (985)892-7621
Free: 800-375-0048
Fax: (985)892-9245
URL: http://www.fertilityinstitute.com

22268 ■ Fertility Institute of New Orleans
800 N Causeway Blvd., Ste. 2C
Mandeville, LA 70448
Ph: (985)892-7621
URL: http://www.fertilityinstitute.com

22269 ■ Fertility & Women's Health Center of Louisiana
Lake Charles Memorial Hospital
1900 Gauthier Rd.
Lake Charles, LA 70605
Free: 888-467-2229
URL: http://www.fertilityanswers.com

22270 ■ Fertility & Women's Health Center of Louisiana
Rapides regional Medical Center
501 Medical Center Dr., Ste. 4C
Alexandria, LA 71301
Free: 888-467-2229
URL: http://www.fertilityanswers.com

22271 ■ Ochsner Elmwood Medical Center
Bldg. A, 1st Fl.
1221 S Clearview Pkwy.
Jefferson, LA 70121
Ph: (504)842-4366
URL: http://www.ochsner.org/

22272 ■ Tulane University Hospital and Clinic Fertility Clinic
1415 Tulane Ave.
New Orleans, LA 70112
Ph: (504)988-2341
Free: 800-588-5800
Fax: (504)584-1680
URL: http://www.tuhc.com

22273 ■ Women's Hospital
Physician's Tower I, Ste. 670
9000 Airline Hwy.
Baton Rouge, LA 70815
Ph: (225)926-6886

MAINE

22274 ■ Boston IVF
Bangor Women's HealthCare
Webber West Bldg.
417 State St., Ste. 442
Bangor, ME 04401
Ph: (207)945-6206
URL: http://www.www.bostonivf.com

22275 ■ Boston IVF, Inc
Central Maine Medical Center
300 Main St.
Lewiston, ME 04240
Ph: (207)795-0111
URL: http://www.bostonivf.com
Dr. Alan S. Penzias, Director

22276 ■ Maine Medical Partners
Division of Reproductive Endocrinology and Infertility
778 Main St., Ste. 2
South Portland, ME 04106
Ph: (207)775-1255
Free: 877-858-2483
Fax: (207)775-1299
URL: http://www.mainecrh.org/

MARYLAND

22277 ■ Center for Reproductive Medicine - Maryland
9711 Medical Center Dr.
Rockville, MD 20850
Ph: (301)424-1904

22278 ■ Fertility Center of Maryland
110 West Rd., Ste. 102
Towson, MD 21204
Ph: (410)296-6400
Free: 800-405-4IVF
Fax: (410)296-6405
URL: http://www.fertilitycentermd.com
Dr. Santiago Padilla, Director

22279 ■ Fertility Center of Maryland
2014 S Tollgate Rd., Ste. 107
Bel Air, MD 21015
Ph: (410)296-6400
URL: http://www.fertilitycentermd.com

22280 ■ Genetics and IVF Institute
11300 Rockville Pike, Ste. 612
Bethesda, MD 20852
Ph: (301)357-8866
Free: 800-552-4363

22281 ■ George Washington University
Medical Faculty Associates
Fertility Center
4825 Bethesda Ave., Ste. 300
Bethesda, MD 20815
Free: 888-WASH-IVF
URL: http://www.washivf.com/

22282 ■ Johns Hopkins Fertility Center & IVF Program
Div. Of Reproductive Endocrinology & Infertility
Fertility Center
10753 Falls Rd., Ste. 335
Lutherville, MD 21093
Ph: (410)616-7140
URL: http://www.hopkinsmedicine.org/fertility
Howard Zacur, Director
Formerly: Howard and Georgeanna Jones Service.

22283 ■ Mid-Atlantic Fertility Centers
10215 Fernwood Rd., Ste. 301A
Bethesda, MD 20817
Ph: (301)897-8850
Fax: (301)897-8040
URL: http://www.midatlanticfertility.com
Dr. Rafat A. Abbasi, Director
Formerly: Montgomery Fertility Institute.

22284 ■ Shady Grove Fertility Center--Annapolis
2000 Medical Pkwy., Ste. 308
Annapolis, MD 21401
Ph: (410)224-5500
Fax: (410)224-4272
URL: http://www.shadygrovefertility.com

22285 ■ Shady Grove Fertility Center--Baltimore
419 W Redwood St., Ste. 500
Baltimore, MD 21015
Ph: (410)328-2304
Fax: (410)510-1062
URL: http://www.shadygrovefertility.com

22286 ■ Shady Grove Fertility Center--Bel Air
201 Plumtree Rd., Ste. 201
Bel Air, MD 21015
Ph: (410)569-0545
Fax: (410)510-1062
URL: http://www.shadygrovefertility.com

22287 ■ Shady Grove Fertility Center--Frederick
Patriot Medical Center
45 Thomas Johnson Dr., Ste. 107
Frederick, MD 21044
Ph: (301)631-1180
Fax: (301)631-1299
URL: http://www.shadygrovefertility.com

22288 ■ Shady Grove Fertility Center--Rockville
Reproductive Science Center
15001 Shady Grove Rd., Ste. 400
Rockville, MD 20850
Ph: (301)340-1188
Free: 888-761-1967
Fax: (301)340-1612
E-mail: news@fshadygrovefertility.com
URL: http://www.shadygrovefertility.com
Dr. Michael Levy, Director

22289 ■ Shady Grove Fertility Center--Towson
6569 N Charles St.
Towson, MD 21204
Ph: (410)512-8300

Free: 888-761-1967
Fax: (410)512-8390
E-mail: info@fshadygrovefertility.com
URL: http://www.shadygrovefertility.com/
Formerly: Greater Baltimore Medical Center.

MASSACHUSETTS

22290 ■ Baystate Reproductive Medicine
3300 Main St.
Springfield, MA 01199-1112
Ph: (413)794-7045
Fax: (413)794-7345
URL: http://www.baystatehealth.com/brm
Dr. Daniel R. Grow, Director
Formerly: Baystate In Vitro Fertilization.

22291 ■ Boston IVF--Brookline
1 Brookline Pl., Ste. 302
Brookline, MA 02445
Ph: (617)735-9000
Free: 888-300-2483
Fax: (617)738-8993
URL: http://www.bostonivf.com

22292 ■ Boston IVF - Metro West
115 Lincoln St., 3rd Fl.
Farmington, MA 01702
Ph: (781)434-6500
URL: http://www.bostonivf.com

22293 ■ Boston IVF
Mount Auburn Hospital
300 Mount Auburn St.
Cambridge, MA 02238
Ph: (781)434-6500
URL: http://www.bosonivf.com

22294 ■ Boston IVF
South Shore Center
2300 Crown colony Dr., Ste. 104
Quincy, MA 02169
Ph: (617)793-1100
URL: http://www.bostonivf.com

22295 ■ Boston IVF
Waltham Center
130 2nd Ave.
Waltham, MA 02451
Ph: (781)434-6500
URL: http://www.bostonivf.com

22296 ■ Boston IVF--Worcester
123 Summer St., Ste. 250
Worcester, MA 01608
Ph: (781)434-6500
URL: http://www.bostonivf.com

22297 ■ Brigham and Women's Hospital
Center for Assisted Reproductive Medicine
75 Francis St., Ste. ASB1-3
Boston, MA 02115
Ph: (617)732-4285
URL: http://nsmc.partners.org/web/service/womens_reproductive_medicine
Dr. Mitchell Rein, Director

22298 ■ Cardone Reproductive Medicine and Infertility
2 Main St., Ste. 150
Stoneham, MA 02180
Ph: (781)438-9600
Fax: (781)438-9601
URL: http://www.cardonerepromed.com/
Dr. Vito R.S. Cardone, Director

22299 ■ Fertility Centers of New England--Reading
20 Pond Meadow Dr., Ste. 101
Reading, MA 01867
Ph: (877)FCNE-IVF
URL: http://www.fertilitycenter.com

22300 ■ Fertility Solutions--Cambridge
330 Mount Auburn St.
Cambridge, MA 02138
Free: 877-813-0159
URL: http://www.fertilitysolutionsne.com

22301 ■ Fertility Solutions--Dedham
45 Stergis Way
Dedham, MA 02026
Free: 877-813-0159
URL: http://www.fertilitysolutionsne.com

22302 ■ Fertility Solutions--Peabody
1 Essex Center Dr.
Peabody, MA 01960
Free: 877-813-0159
URL: http://www.fertilitysolutionsne.com

22303 ■ Fertility Solutions--Woburn
12 Alfred St., Ste. 330
Woburn, MA 01801
Free: 877-813-0159
URL: http://www.fertilitysolutionsne.com

22304 ■ Reproductive Science Center
1 Forbes Rd.
Lexington, MA 02421
Free: 800-858-4832
URL: http://www.rscnewengland.com
Dr. Samuel C. Pang, Director

22305 ■ Reproductive Science Center of New England--Milford
14 Prospect St.
Milford, MA 01757
Free: 800-858-4832
URL: http://www.rscnewengland.com

22306 ■ Tufts Medical Center
Department of Obstetrics and Gynecology
Division of Reproductive Endocrinology and Infertility
Tufts Medical Center, No. 036
800 Washington St.
Boston, MA 02111
Ph: (617)636-0053
URL: http://www.tuftsmedicalcenter.org/OurServices/ReproductiveEndocrinologyandI nfertilityold/default

MICHIGAN

22307 ■ Center for Reproductive Medicine and Surgery
300 Park St., Ste. 460
Birmingham, MI 48009
Ph: (248)593-6990
URL: http://www.reproductive-medicine.com
Dr. Michael S. Mersol-Barg, Director

22308 ■ The Fertility Center--Grand Rapids
3230 Eagle Park Dr. NE, Ste. 100
Grand Rapids, MI 49525
Ph: (616)988-2229
Free: 877-904-4483
URL: http://www.fertilitycentermi.com/
Formerly: Michigan Reproductive and IVF Center.

22309 ■ The Fertility Center--Kalamazoo
5659 Stadium Dr.
Kalamazoo, MI 49009
Ph: (269)324-5100
Free: 877-500-1658
Fax: (269)324-5041
URL: http://www.fertilitycentermi.com

22310 ■ The Fertility Center--Lansing
1200 E Michigan Ave., Ste. 700
Lansing, MI 48912
Ph: (616)988-2229
Free: 877-904-4448
Fax: (616)988-2010
URL: http://www.fertilitycentermi.com

22311 ■ Hurley Medical Center
Center for Reproductive Medicine
1 Hurley Plaza, Ste. 209
Flint, MI 48503
Free: 866-750-4111
E-mail: reprod1@hurleymc.com
URL: http://www.hurleymc.com/?id=158&sid=1

22312 ■ IVF Michigan, PC--Ann Arbor
3145 Clark Rd., Ste 301
Ann Arbor, MI 48197
Ph: (734)434-4766
Free: 866-844-2888
E-mail: Dr.Ayers@MidwestIVF.com
URL: http://ivf-michigan.com
Formerly: Ann Arbor Reproductive Medicine Associates.

22313 ■ IVF Michigan, PC--Brighton
2300 Genoa Business Park, Ste. 180
Brighton, MI 48114
Ph: (819)225-3390
Free: 866-844-2888
E-mail: Dr.Ayers@MidwestIVF.com
URL: http://www.ivf-michigan.com/

22314 ■ IVF Michigan, PC--Dearborn
5728 Schaefer Rd., Ste. 203
Dearborn, MI 48126
Ph: (313)582-4333
Free: 866-844-2888
E-mail: Dr.Ayers@MidwestIVF.com
URL: http://ivf-michigan.com

22315 ■ IVF Michigan, PC--Flint
2 Hurley Plaza, Ste. 209
Flint, MI 48503-5904
Ph: (810)257-9714
Free: 866-844-2888
E-mail: Dr.Ayers@MidwestIVF.com
URL: http://ivf-michigan.com

22316 ■ IVF Michigan, PC--Rochester Hills
3950 S Rochester Rd., Ste. 2300
Rochester Hills, MI 48307
Ph: (248)844-8845
Free: 866-844-2888
E-mail: Dr.Ayers@MidwestIVF.com
URL: http://ivf-michigan.com

22317 ■ IVF Michigan, PC--Saginaw
5400 Mackinaw Rd., Ste. 4100
Saginaw, MI 48604
Ph: (517)792-8771
Free: 866-844-2888
E-mail: Dr.Ayers@MidwestIVF.com
URL: http://ivf-michigan.com

22318 ■ Michigan Center for Fertility and Women's Health
4700 13 Mile Rd.
Warren, MI 48092
Ph: (586)576-0431
Fax: (586)576-0924
URL: http://www.micenterforfertility.com/

22319 ■ Oakwood Healthcare System--Clinton Township
43900 Garfield Rd.
Clinton Township, MI 48038
Ph: (586)416-1800
URL: http://www.oakwood.org/?id=301&sid=5

22320 ■ Oakwood Healthcare System--Dearborn
Center for Reproductive Medicine
18181 Oakwood Blvd., Ste. 109
Dearborn, MI 48124
Ph: (313)299-6650
URL: http://www.oakwood.org/?id=301&sid=5

22321 ■ Sparrow Health System
Sparrow Fertility Services
1200 E Michigan Ave., Ste. 355
Lansing, MI 48912-1811
Ph: (517)364-5780
Fax: (517)364-5785
E-mail: fertilitycenter@sparrow.org
URL: http://www.sparrow.org/fertilityservices/services.asp

22322 ■ University of Michigan Medical Center - OB/GYN
Infertility Center
Briarwood Bldg. 1
475 Market St., Ste. B, 1st Fl.
Ann Arbor, MI 48108
Ph: (734)936-7030
Fax: (734)936-7371
URL: http://www2.med.umich.edu

22323 ■ Wayne State University Physicians Group
26400 W 12 Mile Rd., Ste. 140
Southfield, MI 48034
Ph: (248)352-8200
URL: http://www.infertilityupg.com

22324 ■ West Michigan Reproductive Institute
Assisted Reproductive Technology Program
885 Forest Hill Ave. SE
Grand Rapids, MI 49546
Ph: (616)942-5180
Fax: (616)942-2450

22325 ■ William Beaumont Hospital
In Vitro Fertilization Program
3535 W 13 Mile Rd., Ste. 344
Royal Oak, MI 48073
Ph: (248)551-0515
URL: http://www.beaumonthospitals.com/thyroid-endocrine-fertility-testing

MINNESOTA

22326 ■ Abbott Northwestern Hospital
Center for Reproductive Medicine
2828 Chicago Ave. S, Ste. 400
Minneapolis, MN 55407
Ph: (612)863-5390
Fax: (612)863-2697
E-mail: michelle.dalbec@ivfminnesota.com
URL: http://www.ivfminnesota.com

22327 ■ Mayo Clinic
Reproductive Endocrinology & Infertility
200 First St. SW
Rochester, MN 55905
Ph: (507)284-9792
URL: http://www.mayoclinic.org/reproductive-medicine

22328 ■ MeritCare Bemidji
MeritCare Reproductive Medicine
1233 34th St. NW
Bemidji, MN 56601
Ph: (218)333-5000
URL: http://www.meritcare.com/medicalservices/specialties/repromed/index.aspx

22329 ■ Midwest Center for Reproductive Health
CentraCare Women's and Children's Clinic
1900 CentraCare Cir., Ste. 2300
Saint Cloud, MN 56303
Ph: (320)654-3630
Fax: (320)654-3677
URL: http://www.centracare.com/clinics/women_child/index.html

22330 ■ Midwest Center for Reproductive Health
Duluth Clinic
400 E 3rd St.
Duluth, MN 55805
Ph: (218)786-3282
Fax: (218)786-3274
URL: http://www.smdc.org

22331 ■ Midwest Center for Reproductive Health
Mankato Clinic
1230 E Main St.
Mankato, MN 56002
Ph: (507)389-8539
Fax: (507)625-3973
URL: http://www.mankato-clinic.com

22332 ■ Reproductive Medicine and Infertility Associates
2101 Woodwinds Dr., Ste. 100
Woodbury, MN 55125
Ph: (651)222-6050
Free: 800-440-7359
Fax: (651)222-5975
E-mail: dawn@rmia.com
URL: http://www.rmia.com
Dr. Jacques P. Stassart, Director

22333 ■ University of Minnesota
Department of Obstetrics and Gynecology
Reproductive Medicine Center
Riverside Professional Bldg.
606 24th Ave. S, Ste. 500
Minneapolis, MN 55454
Ph: (612)372-7050
URL: http://www.umphysicians.umn.edu/clinics_min_objectname_Reproductive_Medicin e_Center.html

MISSISSIPPI

22334 ■ Mississippi Fertility Institute
Woman's Specialty Center
501 Marshal St., No. 600
Jackson, MS 39202
Ph: (601)948-6540
Free: 800-696-7059
URL: http://www.ivfmississippi.com

22335 ■ University of Mississippi Medical Center
In Vitro Fertilization Program
2500 N State St.
Jackson, MS 39216
Ph: (601)815-1080
Free: 866-330-9805
E-mail: bcoward@ob-gyn.umsmed.edu
URL: http://obgyn.umc.edu/cs-ivf.html
Randall S. Hines, Director

MISSOURI

22336 ■ Infertility Center of Saint Louis at Saint Luke's Hospital
224 S Woods Mill Rd., Ste. 730
Saint Louis, MO 63017
Ph: (314)576-1400
Fax: (314)576-1442
URL: http://www.infertile.com
Dr. Sherman J. Silber, Director

22337 ■ Midwest Woman's Healthcare
2790 Clay Edwards Dr., Ste. 625
Kansas City, MO 64116
Ph: (816)421-3115

22338 ■ Saint Luke's Hospital
Infertility Center of Saint Louis
224 S Woods Mill Rd., Ste. 730
Saint Louis, MO 63017
Ph: (314)576-1400
Fax: (314)576-1442
URL: http://www.infertile.com
Dr. Sherman J. Silber, Director

22339 ■ Sher Institutes for Reproductive Medicine--Creve Coeur
456 N New Ballas, Ste. 101
Creve Coeur, MO 63141
Ph: (314)983-9000
URL: http://www.haveababy.com/index_stl.cfm?&city=stl&site=stl
Dr. Peter Ahlering, Director

22340 ■ Washington University School of Medicine
Barnes--Jewish Hospital
Division of Reproductive Endocrinology and Infertility
4444 Forest Park Ave., Ste. 3100
Saint Louis, MO 63108
Ph: (314)286-2400
Fax: (314)286-2455
URL: http://www.infertility.wustl.edu

NEBRASKA

22341 ■ Heartland Center for Reproductive Medicine
7308 S 142nd St.
Omaha, NE 68138
Ph: (402)717-4200
Free: 877-831-3227
Fax: (402)717-4230
E-mail: dlubrant@heartlandfertility.com
URL: http://www.heartlandfertility.com

NEVADA

22342 ■ The Fertility Center--Las Vegas
8851 W Sahara Ave., Ste. 100
Las Vegas, NV 89117
Ph: (702)254-1777
Free: 800-509-7174
Fax: (702)254-1213
E-mail: info@fertilitycenterlv.com
URL: http://www.fertilitycenterlv.com

22343 ■ Nevada Center for Reproductive Medicine
645 Sierra Rose Dr., Ste. 205
Reno, NV 89511
Ph: (775)828-1200
URL: http://www.nevadafertility.com/

22344 ■ Nevada Fertility CARES
653 Town Center Dr., Ste. 206
Las Vegas, NV 89144
Ph: (702)341-6616
Fax: (775)828-1785

22345 ■ Red Rock Fertility Center
6420 Medical Center St., Ste. 100
Las Vegas, NV 89148
Ph: (702)262-0079
Fax: (702)685-6910
URL: http://www.lasvegasfertility.com

22346 ■ Sher Institute for Reproductive Medicine--Las Vegas
3121 S Maryland Pkwy., No. 300
Las Vegas, NV 89118
Ph: (702)892-9696
Free: 866-317-2229
Fax: (702)892-9666
E-mail: lasvegas@haveababy.com
URL: http://www.haveababy.com/SIRM/aboutSIRM/centers/lasvegas.html

NEW HAMPSHIRE

22347 ■ Dartmouth-Hitchcock Medical Center
In Vitro Fertilization Program
1 Medical Center Dr.
Lebanon, NH 03756-0001
Ph: (603)650-5000

22348 ■ EverGreen Women's Health Care Fertility Services
280 Main St., Ste. 131
Nashua, NH 03060
Ph: (603)577-FERT
E-mail: office@evergreenfertility.com
URL: http://www.evergreenfertility.com

22349 ■ Fertility Centers of New England
Bldg. C, Unit 1
875 Greenland Rd.
Portsmouth, NH 03801
Free: 877-FCNE-IVF
URL: http://www.fertilitycenter.com/

22350 ■ Fertility Centers of New England--Bedford
169 S River Rd., Ste. 11
Bedford, NH 03110
Free: 877-FCNE-IVF
URL: http://www.fertilitycenter.com/

NEW JERSEY

22351 ■ Cooper Center for In Vitro Fertilization
8002 E Greentree Commons
Marlton, NJ 08053
Ph: (856)751-5575
Fax: (856)751-7289
URL: http://www.ccivf.com/in-vitro_fert.html

22352 ■ Diamond Institute for Infertility and Menopause
89 Millburn Ave.
Millburn, NJ 07041
Ph: (973)761-5600
Free: 800-992-8941
Fax: (973)761-5100
URL: http://www.diamondinstitute.com/
Dr. Arie Birkenfeld, Director

22353 ■ Hackensack University Medical Center
University of Medicine and Dentistry of New Jersey
New Jersey Medical School
Division of Reproductive Endocrinology and Infertility
30 Prospect Ave.
Hackensack, NJ 07601
Ph: (201)336-8108
Dr. Andrea Vidali, Director
Formerly: University of Medicine and Dentistry of New Jersey, New Jersey Medical School, In Vitro Fertilization Program.

22354 ■ Institute for Reproductive Medicine and Science at Saint Barnabas Medical Center
Department of Obstetrics and Gynecology
In Vitro Fertilization Program
94 Old Short Hills Rd.
E Wing, Ste. 403
Livingston, NJ 07039
Ph: (973)322-8286
Free: 877-456-4IVF
Fax: (973)322-8890
URL: http://www.sbivf.com

22355 ■ IVF New Jersey
81 Veronica Ave.
Somerset, NJ 08873
Free: 866-447-6411
Fax: (732)545-1164
URL: http://www.ivfnj.com

22356 ■ Reproductive Medicine Associates of New Jersey
2 Industrial Way W
Eatontown, NJ 07724
Ph: (732)935-1002
URL: http://www.rmanj.com

22357 ■ Reproductive Medicine Associates of New Jersey
25 Rockwood Place, Ste. 125
Englewood, NJ 07631
Ph: (201)569-7773
URL: http://www.rmanj.com

22358 ■ Sher Institutes for Reproductive Medicine--Bedminster
Bedminster Medical Plz.
1 Robertson Dr.
Bedminster, NJ 07921
Ph: (908)781-0666
Free: 877-798-2229
Fax: (908)781-6377
E-mail: newjersey@haveababy.com
URL: http://www.haveababy.com/SIRM/aboutSIRM/centers/newjersey.html
Dr. Al Peters, Director

22359 ■ Sher Institutes for Reproductive Medicine--Greater Lehigh Valley
201 Strykers Rd., Ste. 4
Phillipsburg, NJ 08865
Free: 888-591-2229
URL: http://www.haveababy.com/SIRM/aboutSIRM/centers/greaterlehighvalley.html
Dr. Al Peters, Director

22360 ■ South Jersey Fertility Center--Egg Harbor Township
2500 English Creek Ave., Ste. 225
Egg Harbor TWP, NJ 08234
Ph: (609)813-2192
URL: http://www.sjfert.com

22361 ■ South Jersey Fertility Center--Forked River
730 Lacey Rd., Ste. G-09
Forked River, NJ 08731
Ph: (609)693-5049
URL: http://www.sjfert.com

22362 ■ South Jersey Fertility Center--Marlton
400 Lippincott Dr., No. 130
Marlton, NJ 08053
Ph: (856)596-2233
Fax: (856)596-2411
URL: http://www.sjfert.com/

22363 ■ University of Medicine and Dentistry of New Jersey
Robert Wood Johnson Medical School
Center for Advanced Reproductive Medicine and Infertility
Durham Center
4 Ethel Rd., Ste. 405A
Edison, NJ 08817
Ph: (732)339-9300
Fax: (732)339-9400
URL: http://www.infertilitydocs.com

22364 ■ Women's Fertility Center
106 Grand Ave.
Englewood, NJ 07631
Ph: (201)569-6979
E-mail: info@njfertility.com
URL: http://www.njfertility.com/

NEW MEXICO

22365 ■ Center for Reproductive Medicine of New Mexico
201 Cedar St. SE, Ste. S1-20
Albuquerque, NM 87106
Ph: (505)247-3333
Free: 866-WANT-IVF
E-mail: repromednm@aol.com
URL: http://infertility-ivf.com
Formerly: Presbyterian Hospital In Vitro Fertilization Program.

22366 ■ Reproductive Medicine and Fertility Center
Bldg. 2, Ste. 240
2701 Frontier NE Surge
Albuquerque, NM 87106
Free: 877-457-2229
URL: http://www.475-baby.com

22367 ■ Southwest Fertility Services
1720 Wyoming NE
Albuquerque, NM 87112
Ph: (505)271-9651

NEW YORK

22368 ■ Advanced Fertility Services
1625 3rd Ave.
New York, NY 10128
Ph: (212)369-8700
Fax: (212)722-5587
URL: http://www.infertilityny.com

22369 ■ Batzofin Fertility Services
16 E 40th St., 2nd Fl.
New York, NY 10016
Ph: (212)679-2289
Fax: (212)679-2288
E-mail: jbatzofin@batzofinfertility.com
URL: http://www.batzofinfertilityservices.com
Dr. Joel Batzofin, Director

22370 ■ Brooklyn/Westside Fertility Center Fertility Center
55 Central Park W
New York, NY 10023
Ph: (212)721-4597
Fax: (212)721-4598
E-mail: drdov@aol.com
Formerly: St. Lukes/Roosevelt In Vitro Fertilization Program, Central Park West.

22371 ■ Columbia University
The Center for Women's Reproductive Care
1790 Broadway, 2nd Fl.
New York, NY 10019
Ph: (646)756-8282
Fax: (646)756-8220
E-mail: AM2028@columbia.edu
URL: http://www.columbiafertility.org
Dr. Mark V. Sauer, Director
Formerly: Sloane Hospital for Women, In Vitro Fertilization Program.

22372 ■ Connecticut Fertility Associates--New York
110 E 55th St., 9th Fl.
New York, NY 10022
Ph: (212)754-1200
Fax: (212)754-1200
URL: http://www.connecticutfertility.com/nyc.html

22373 ■ Cornell University Medical College
The Center for Reproductive Medicine and Infertility
1305 York Ave.
New York, NY 10021
Ph: (646)962-CRMI
Free: 888-703-3456
Fax: (212)746-8208
E-mail: ivf@nyp.org
URL: http://www.ivf.org
Dr. Zev Rosenwaks, Director

22374 ■ Infertility & Invitro Fertilization Medical Associates of WNY, PLLC
4510 Main St.
Snyder, NY 14226
Ph: (716)839-3057
Fax: (716)839-1477
URL: http://www.buffaloivf.com

22375 ■ Institute for Reproductive Health and Infertility
1561 Long Pond Rd., Ste. 410
Rochester, NY 14626
Ph: (585)453-7760
Fax: (585)453-7771

22376 ■ Island Reproductive Services
1110 South Ave., Ste. 305
Staten Island, NY 10314
Ph: (718)761-6000
Fax: (718)761-6066
URL: http://www.islandreproductive.com/
Dr. Eric Knochenhauer, Director

22377 ■ Long Island In Vitro Fertilization
Bldg. 19, Ste. 70
2500 Nesconset Hwy., Rte. 347
Stony Brook, NY 11790
Ph: (631)331-7575
Fax: (631)331-1332
E-mail: info@longislandivf.com
URL: http://www.longislandivf.com

22378 ■ Montefiore's Institute of Reproductive Medicine and Health
141 S Central Ave.
Dobbs Ferry, NY 10530
Ph: (914)997-1060
URL: http://www.montefiore.org/services/coe/women-shealth/invitro

22379 ■ Mount Sinai Medical Center
RMA of NY
635 Madison Ave., 10th Fl.
New York, NY 10022
Ph: (212)756-5777
Fax: (212)756-5770
URL: http://www.rmany.com
Al Copperman, Director

22380 ■ New York Methodist Hospital
Fertility Institute
506 6th St.
Brooklyn, NY 11215
Ph: (718)775-3443
Fax: (718)780-5085
URL: http://www.kofinasfertility.com

22381 ■ New York University
Fertility Center
660 1st Ave. (at 38th St.)
New York, NY 10016
Ph: (212)263-8990
URL: http://www.nyufertilitycenter.org/ivf/

22382 ■ North Shore University Hospital
In Vitro Fertilization Program
Center for Human Reproduction
300 Community Dr.
Manhasset, NY 11030
Ph: (516)562-2229
Fax: (516)562-1710
URL: http://www.northshorelijivf.com

22383 ■ Reproductive Medicine Associates of New York
21 Laurel Ave.
Cornwall, NY 12512
Ph: (914)997-6200
URL: http://www.rmany.com

22384 ■ Reproductive Medicine Associates of New York--Garden City
400 Garden City Plaza, Ste. 107
Garden City, NY 11530
Ph: (516)746-3633
URL: http://www.rmany.com

22385 ■ Reproductive Medicine Associates of New York--New York
635 Madison Ave., 10th Fl.
New York, NY 10022
Ph: (212)756-5777
URL: http://www.rmany.com

22386 ■ Reproductive Medicine Associates of New York--White Plains
Garden Level, Ste. G
15 N Broadway
White Plains, NY 10601
Ph: (914)997-6200
URL: http://www.rmany.com

22387 ■ Sher Institutes for Reproductive Medicine--Long Island
800 Woodbury Rd., Ste. G
Woodbury, NY 11797
Ph: (516)584-8710
Fax: (516)584-8711
E-mail: longisland@haveababy.com
URL: http://www.haveababy.com/SIRM/aboutSIRM/centers/newyork.html
Dr. Jeffrey Braverman, Director

22388 ■ Sher Institutes for Reproductive Medicine--New York
425 5th Ave.
New York, NY 10016
Ph: (646)792-7476
Free: 866-747-6692
Fax: (646)274-0600
E-mail: newyork@haveababy.com
URL: http://www.haveababy.com/SIRM/aboutSIRM/centers/newyork.html
Dr. Geoffrey Sher, Director

22389 ■ Sher Institutes for Reproductive Medicine--Westchester
3020 Westchester Ave., Ste. 304
Purchase, NY 10577
Ph: (914)696-7476
Fax: (914)606-7314
E-mail: longisland@haveababy.com
URL: http://www.haveababy.com/SIRM/aboutSIRM/centers/newyork.html
Dr. Drew Tortoriello, Director

NORTH CAROLINA

22390 ■ Advanced Reproductive Concepts
9800 W Kincey Ave., Ste. 160
Huntersville, NC 28078
Ph: (704)947-9000
Fax: (704)992-1900
URL: http://www.affordable-ivf.com
Dr. Mark L. Jutras, Director

22391 ■ Chapel Hill Fertility Center
109 Conner Dr., Ste. 2200
Chapel Hill, NC 27514
Ph: (919)968-4656
Fax: (919)967-8637
E-mail: drberger@tubalreversal.com
URL: http://www.chapelhillfertility.com

22392 ■ Duke Fertility Center
5704 Fayetteville Rd.
Durham, NC 27713
Ph: (919)572-4673
URL: http://dukefertilitycenter.org

22393 ■ Duke University Medical Center
In Vitro Fertilization Program
PO Box 5704
Durham, NC 27710
Ph: (919)684-5327
Fax: (919)681-7904
E-mail: couch004@atmc.duke.edu
URL: http://www.duke.edu/

22394 ■ Piedmont Reproductive Endocrinology Group
675 Biltmore Ave., Ste. H
Asheville, NC 28803
Ph: (828)210-8284
Free: 866-725-7734
Fax: (828)350-7516
URL: http://www.pregonline.com/

22395 ■ Wake Forest University Baptist Medical Center
Center for Reproductive Medicine
131 Miller St., 2nd Fl.
Winston Salem, NC 27157
Ph: (336)716-6476
Fax: (336)716-0194
URL: http://www1.wfubmc.edu/ivf/IVF+-+ART/ivf.htm

22396 ■ Wake Forest University Baptist Medical Center
Center for Reproductive Medicine
Prudential Carolinas Realty Bldg.
802 Green Valley Rd., Ste. 106
Greensboro, NC 27408
Ph: (336)716-6476
Fax: (336)716-0194
URL: http://www1.wfubmc.edu/ivf/IVF+-+ART/ivf.htm

NORTH DAKOTA

22397 ■ MeritCare Reproductive Medicine
1111 Harwood Dr. S
Fargo, ND 58103
Ph: (701)234-2700
Free: 800-437-4010
URL: http://www.meritcare.com/medicalservices/specialties/repromed/index.aspx

22398 ■ Midwest Center for Reproductive Health
Innovis Health
3000 32nd Ave. S
Fargo, ND 58103
Ph: (701)364-4550
Fax: (701)364-4551
URL: http://www.innovishealth.com

22399 ■ Midwest Center for Reproductive Health
Mid Dakota Clinic
1000 E Rosser
Bismarck, ND 58501
Ph: (701)530-6074
Fax: (701)530-6430
URL: http://www.middakotaclinic.com

OHIO

22400 ■ Bethesda Center for Reproductive Health and Fertility
10506 Montgomery Rd., Ste. 303 & 305
Cincinnati, OH 45242
Ph: (513)745-1675
Free: 800-634-1222
Fax: (513)745-1676
E-mail: bethesda_center@trihealth.com
URL: http://www.bethesdafertility.com

22401 ■ Cleveland Clinic--Beachwood
26900 Cedar Rd., Ste. 220S
Beachwood, OH 44122
Ph: (216)839-3150
URL: http://www.clevelandclinic.org

22402 ■ Cleveland Clinic--Canfield
6674 Tippecanoe Rd., No. 3
Canfield, OH 44406
Ph: (330)702-1950
URL: http://www.clevelandclinic.org

22403 ■ Cleveland Clinic--Solon
29800 Bainbridge Rd.
Solon, OH 44139
Ph: (440)519-6800
URL: http://www.clevelandclinic.org

22404 ■ Cleveland Clinic--Strongsville
16761 South Park Center
Strongsville, OH 44136
Ph: (440)878-2500
URL: http://www.clevelandclinic.org

22405 ■ Fertility Center of Northwest Ohio
2142 N Cove Blvd.
Toledo, OH 43606
Ph: (419)291-8830
URL: http://www.promedica.org/default.aspx?PageID=620

22406 ■ Institute for Reproductive Health
3805 Edward Rd., Ste. 450
Cincinnati, OH 45209
Ph: (513)924-5550
E-mail: sawadalla@aol.com
URL: http://www.cincinnatifertility.com/
Dr. Sherif Awadalla, Director

22407 ■ IVF Michigan, PC--Toledo
6711 Monroe St., Bldg. 3, Ste. A
Toledo, OH 43620
Ph: (419)885-8080
Free: 866-844-2888
E-mail: Dr.Ayers@MidwestIVF.com
URL: http://ivf-michigan.com

22408 ■ Miami Valley Hospital
Fertility Program
1 Wyoming St.
Dayton, OH 45409-2711
Ph: (937)208-2120
Fax: (937)208-8357
E-mail: jeschneider@mvh.org
URL: http://www.miamivalleyhospital.com/maternity.htm

22409 ■ Reproductive Gynecology Labs, LLC
In Vitro Fertilization/Andrology Center
95 Arc St., Ste. 250
Akron, OH 44304
Ph: (330)375-7722
Fax: (330)253-6708
URL: http://reproductivegynecologyinc.liveonatt.com/RGL%20Lab%20Services.nxg
Formerly: Akron City Hospital In Vitro Fertilization Center.

22410 ■ University Hospitals Health System
MacDonald Fertility and IVF Program
11100 Euclid, Ste. 120
Cleveland, OH 44106
Ph: (216)844-1514
Fax: (216)844-7098
E-mail: infertility@uhhs.com
URL: http://fertilityandivf.com/

OKLAHOMA

22411 ■ Center for Reproductive Health--Oklahoma City
1000 N Lincoln Blvd., No. 300
Oklahoma City, OK 73104
Ph: (405)271-9200
Fax: (405)271-9222
Dr. Gilbert G. Haas, Director

22412 ■ Henry G Bannett Jr. Fertility Center
Integris Baptist Medical Canter
3433 NW 56th, Bldg. B
Oklahoma City, OK 73112
Ph: (405)949-6060
URL: http://www.integris-health.com

22413 ■ Tulsa Center for Fertility & Women's Health
115 E 15th St.
Tulsa, OK 74119
Ph: (918)584-2870
Free: 888-944-1440
Fax: (918)587-3602
URL: http://www.fertilitytulsa.com/
Formerly: Hillcrest Fertility Center.

OREGON

22414 ■ OHSU, Eugene
Center for Health and Healing
In Vitro Fertilization Program
3303 SW Bond
Portland, OR 97239
Ph: (503)418-3700
E-mail: fertlab@ohsu.edu
URL: http://www.fertilityoregon.com
Dr. Ken Burry, Director
Formerly: The Fertility Center at Women's Care.

22415 ■ Oregon Reproductive Medicine
2222 NW Lovejoy St., Ste. 304
Portland, OR 97210
Ph: (503)274-4994
Free: 877-567-4994
Fax: (503)274-4946
URL: http://www.oregonreproductivemedicine.com

PENNSYLVANIA

22416 ■ Abington Reproductive Medicine
Price Medical Bldg.
1245 Highland Ave., Ste. 404
Abington, PA 19001
Ph: (215)887-2010
URL: http://www.abington-repromed.com
Formerly: Abington Memorial Hospital, Toll Center for Reproductive Sciences.

22417 ■ Center for Fertility and Reproductive Endocrinology
1 Monroe Center
3824 Northern Pike, Ste. 800
Monroeville, PA 15146
Ph: (412)641-1600
URL: http://www.upmc.com/HospitalFacilities/Hospitals/Magee?ObGynServices/Fertil ity/Pages/Fertility.aspx

22418 ■ Center for Fertility and Reproductive Endocrinology--Butler
901 E Brady St.
Butler, PA 16001
Ph: (724)285-9200
URL: http://www.upmc.com/HospitalFacilities/Hospitals/Magee?ObGynServices/Fertil ity/Pages/Fertility.aspx

22419 ■ Center for Fertility and Reproductive Endocrinology--Hermitage
875 N Hermitage Rd.
Hermitage, PA 16148
Ph: (724)347-4851
URL: http://www.upmc.com/HospitalFacilities/Hospitals/Magee?ObGynServices/Fertil ity/Pages/Fertility.aspx

22420 ■ Center for Fertility and Reproductive Endocrinology--Johnstown
348 Budfield St.
Johnstown, PA 15904
Ph: (412)641-1600
URL: http://www.upmc.com/HospitalFacilities/Hospitals/Magee?ObGynServices/Fertil ity/Pages/Fertility.aspx

22421 ■ Cooper Institute for Reproductive Hormonal Disorders
7447 Old York Rd.
Melrose Park, PA 19027
Ph: (215)635-4400
Fax: (215)635-2304
URL: http://www.ccivf.com/
Dr. Jerome H. Check, Director

22422 ■ Family Fertility Center
95 Highland Ave., Ste. 100
Bethlehem, PA 18017
Ph: (610)868-8600
URL: http://www.familyfertility.com
Dr. H. Christina Lee, Director

22423 ■ Hospital of the University of Pennsylvania
Reproductive Endocrinology and Infertility
In Vitro Fertilization Program
3701 Market St., Ste. 800
Philadelphia, PA 19104
Ph: (215)662-2971
Fax: (215)349-5512
E-mail: ccoutifaris@obgyn.upenn.edu
URL: http://www.uphs.upenn.edu/obgyn/divisions/rei.htm
Dr. Christos Coutifaris, Director

22424 ■ Infertility Solutions
1275 S Cedar Crest Blvd., Ste. 3
Allentown, PA 18103
Ph: (610)776-1217
Free: 877-258-2217
Fax: (610)776-4149
URL: http://www.infertilitysolutions.com
Dr. Bruce Rose, Director

22425 ■ Jefferson Medical College
Women's Medical Specialties
In Vitro Fertilization Program
834 Chestnut St., Rm. 400
Philadelphia, PA 19107
Ph: (215)955-4018
Fax: (215)923-1089
E-mail: lori.glatsky@jefferson.edu
URL: http://www.jeffersonhospital.org/obgyn/article4548.html
Larry I. Barmat, Director

22426 ■ Reproductive Science Institute
945 Chesterbrook Blvd.
Chesterbrook, PA 19087
Ph: (610)981-6000
Fax: (610)964-0536
E-mail: rsidoc@aol.com
URL: http://www.rsiinfertility.com

22427 ■ RMA of Philadelphia
625 Clark Ave., Ste. 17B
King of Prussia, PA 19406
Ph: (215)654-1544
URL: http://www.rmaphiladelphia.com

22428 ■ RMA of Philadelphia
320 Middletown Blvd., Ste. 303
Langhorne, PA 19047
Ph: (267)852-0780
URL: http://www.rmaphiladelphia.com

22429 ■ West Penn Allegheny Health System
Jones Institute for Reproductive Medicine of Eastern Medical School
4800 Friendship Ave.
Pittsburgh, PA 15224
Free: 866-305-6637
URL: http://www.jonesinstitutepittsburgh.org
Dr. Scott W. Kauma, Director

22430 ■ Women's Clinic, Ltd.
Infertility/In Vitro Fertilization Program
301 S 7th Ave., Ste. 245
West Reading, PA 19611
Ph: (610)374-2214
URL: http://infertilitypa.com/ivf.htm

RHODE ISLAND

22431 ■ Fertility Solutions--Providence
758 Eddy St, 2nd Fl.
Providence, RI 02903
Free: 877-813-0159
URL: http://www.fertilitysolutionsne.com

22432 ■ Reproductive Science Center of New England--Providence
134 Thurbers Ave., Ste. 207
Providence, RI 02905
Free: 800-858-4832
URL: http://www.rscnewengland.com

22433 ■ Women and Infants Hospital In Vitro Fertilization Program
101 Dudley St.
Providence, RI 02905
Ph: (401)274-1100
E-mail: wihinfo@atwswihri.org
URL: http://www.womenandinfants.com/body.cfm?id=164

SOUTH CAROLINA

22434 ■ Advanced Fertility and Reproductive Endocrinology Institute
2728 Sunset Blvd., Ste. 305
West Columbia, SC 29169
Ph: (803)939-1515
Free: 866-293-2273
URL: http://www.ivfwecare.com
Dr. Gail F. Whitman-Ella, Director

22435 ■ Greenville Hospital System Center for Women's Medicine Reproductive Endocrinology and Infertility
890 W Faris Rd., Ste. 470
Greenville, SC 29605
Ph: (864)455-1600
E-mail: tprice@ghs.org
URL: http://www.ghs.org/Content.aspx?id=81312
Dr. Bruce A. Lessey, Director
Formerly: Reproductive Endocrinology Associates.

22436 ■ Piedmont Reproductive Endocrinology Group
17 Caledon Ct., Ste. C
Greenville, SC 29615
Ph: (864)990-7734
Fax: (864)232-7099
URL: http://www.pregonline.com
Dr. John F. Payne, Director

22437 ■ Southeastern Fertility Center--Charleston
1375 Hospital Dr.
Charleston, SC 29464
Ph: (843)881-3900
URL: http://www.sefertility.com

SOUTH DAKOTA

22438 ■ Sanford Women's Health Sanford Clinic Fertility and Reproductive Endocrinology
1500 W 22nd St.
Sioux Falls, SD 57105
Ph: (605)328-7700
E-mail: info@sanfordwomenshealth.org
URL: http://www.obgynltd.org/services/index.php?id=13
Dr. Keith A. Hansen, Director

TENNESSEE

22439 ■ Center for Reproductive Health--Nashville
2410 Patterson St., Ste. 401
Nashville, TN 37203
Ph: (615)321-8899
Fax: (615)321-8877
URL: http://www.65.17.201.92

22440 ■ Fertility Resources Center Appalachian Fertility and Endocrinology Center
2204 Pavilion Dr., Ste. 307
Kingsport, TN 37660
Ph: (423)392-6330
Fax: (423)392-6053
E-mail: realgamete@aol.com

TEXAS

22441 ■ Baylor College of Medicine Texas Center for Reproductive Health
Barnett Tower
Baylor Medical Plz.
3600 Gaston Ave., Ste. 504
Dallas, TX 75246
Ph: (214)821-2274
Fax: (214)821-2373
URL: http://www.txcrh.com/
Dr. J. Michael Putnam, Director

22442 ■ Center for Assisted Reproduction
1701 Park Place Ave.
Bedford, TX 76022
Free: 866-284-5289
URL: http://www.embryo.net
Dr. Kevin Doody, Director

22443 ■ Center for Reproduction and Women's Health Care
7400 Fannin St., Ste. 1180
Houston, TX 77054
Ph: (713)790-9900
Fax: (713)790-9901
URL: http://www.houstonfertilityspecialist.com
Dr. Robert B. McWilliams, Director

22444 ■ Center of Reproductive Medicine
3701 Kirby Dr., Ste. 840
Houston, TX 77098
Ph: (281)332-0073
Fax: (281)557-5837
URL: http://www.infertilitytexas.com
Dr. Vicki Schnell, Director

22445 ■ Center of Reproductive Medicine
3560 Delaware, Ste. 402
Beaumont, TX 77706
Ph: (409)898-1603
URL: http://www.infertilitytexas.com

22446 ■ Center for Reproductive Medicine--Webster
1015 Medical Center Blvd., Ste. 2100
Webster, TX 77598
Ph: (281)332-0073
URL: http://www.infertilitytexas.com

22447 ■ Center for Women's Medicine Fertility Clinic
17198 St. Luke's Way, Ste. 410
The Woodland, TX 77384
Ph: (713)467-4488
URL: http://www.infertilityanswers.com

22448 ■ Cooper Institute for Advanced Reproductive Medicine
Methodist Health Center
16651 SW Fwy., Ste. 200
Sugar Land, TX 77479
Ph: (713)771-9771
URL: http://cooperinst.jimdo.com/
Dr. C. James Chuong, Director

22449 ■ Dallas fertility Associates
5477 Glen Lakes Dr., Ste. 200
Dallas, TX 75231
Ph: (214)363-5965
URL: http://dfwivf.com

22450 ■ Fertility Center of San Antonio
4499 Medical Dr., Ste. 200
San Antonio, TX 78229
Ph: (210)692-0577
Free: 800-708-1869
Fax: (210)692-1210
E-mail: info@fertilitysa.com
URL: http://www.fertilitysa.com

22451 ■ Fertility Specialists of Houston
7900 Fannin St.
Houston, TX 77054
Ph: (713)512-7900
URL: http://www.fshivf.com/
Dr. George M. Grunert, Director

22452 ■ Houston Fertility Institute
Tomball Regional Hospital
605 Holderreith Blvd.
Tomball, TX 77375
Ph: (281)357-1881
Fax: (281)237-1436
URL: http://www.hfi-ivf.com

22453 ■ Houston Infertility Clinic
9055 Katy Fwy., Ste. 450
Houston, TX 77024
Ph: (713)862-6181
URL: http://www.infertilityivfhouston.com/
Dr. Sonja Kristiansen, Director

22454 ■ Houston IVF
929 Gessner, Ste. 2300
Houston, TX 77024
Ph: (713)465-1211
Fax: (713)550-1475
URL: http://www.houstonivf.net/
Dr. Dorothy Roach, Director

22455 ■ IVF Plano
6300 W Parker Rd., No.G28
Plano, TX 75093
Ph: (972)612-2500
Fax: (972)612-9601
URL: http://www.ivfplano.com

22456 ■ North Houston Center for Reproductive Medicine
530 Wells Fargo Dr., Ste. 116
Houston, TX 77090
Ph: (281)444-4784
Free: 800-444-0812
Fax: (281)444-0429
URL: http://www.nhcrm.com/

22457 ■ Presbyterian Hospitals of Dallas/Plano In Vitro Fertilization Program
8160 Walnut Hill, Ste. 328
Dallas, TX 75231
Ph: (214)363-5965
Fax: (214)363-0639
E-mail: mmorton@phscare.org
URL: http://www.dfwivf.com/

22458 ■ Reproductive Medicine Associates of Texas--Austin
2911 Medical Arts bldg. 17
Austin, TX 78705
Ph: (512)479-7979
Fax: (512)479-7985
URL: http://www.tmatx.com

22459 ■ Reproductive Medicine Associates of Texas--Medical Drive, San Antonio
4330 Medical Dr., Ste. 200
San Antonio, TX 78229
Ph: (210)337-8453
Fax: (210)337-8452
URL: http://www.rmatx.com

22460 ■ Reproductive Medicine Associates of Texas--Stone Oak Parkway, San Antonio
19296 Stone Oak Pkwy.
San Antonio, TX 78258
Ph: (210)337-8453
Fax: (210)337-8452
URL: http://www.rmatx.com

22461 ■ Scott and White Clinic
Department of Obstetrics and Gynecology
In Vitro Fertilization Program
2401 S 31st St.
Temple, TX 76508
Ph: (254)724-2738
URL: http://www.sw.org/
Formerly: Texas A&M University.

22462 ■ Sher Institutes for Reproductive Medicine--Dallas
7777 Forest Ln., Ste. C-638
Dallas, TX 75230
Ph: (972)566-6686
Free: 877-656-6670
URL: http://www.haveababy.com/SIRM/aboutSIRM/centers/dallas.html
Dr. Walid Saleh, Director

22463 ■ Texas Fertility Center--Austin
6500 N Mopac, bldg. 1, Ste. 1200
Austin, TX 78731
Ph: (512)451-0149
URL: http://www.txfertility.com

22464 ■ Texas Fertility Center--Rock Round
16040 Park Valley Dr., Bldg. 1, Ste. 201
Rock Round, TX 78681
Ph: (512)451-0149

22465 ■ Texas Tech Health Sciences Center
Texas Tech Medical Center
3601 4th St., Stop 8340
Lubbock, TX 79430
Ph: (806)743-4342
URL: http://www.ttuhsc.edu/amarillo/som/OB/residency/#ie

22466 ■ University of Texas Medical Branch--Dickinson
Department of Obstetrics and Gynecology
In Vitro Fertilization Program
1804 FM 646 W, Ste. N
Dickinson, TX 77539
Ph: (281)335-1942
Free: 800-509-2229
E-mail: mnagaman@utmb.edu
URL: http://www.utmb.edu/whc/services/InfertilityRelatedServices.html

22467 ■ University of Texas Medical Center--Dallas
Department of Obstetrics and Gynecology
In Vitro Fertilization Program
5323 Harry Hines Blvd.
Dallas, TX 75390
Ph: (214)648-4747
Fax: (214)648-8066
URL: http://www8.utsouthwestern.edu

UTAH

22468 ■ Reproductive Care Center
10150 Petunia Way
Sandy, UT 84092
Ph: (801)878-8888
Fax: (801)878-8890
URL: http://www.fertilitydr.com

22469 ■ University of Utah
Reproductive Endocrinology and Infertility Division
50 N Medical Dr., No. 2355
Salt Lake City, UT 84132
Ph: (801)581-3834
URL: http://medicine.utah.edu/obgyn/UCRM/REI/About_Us/index.htm
Dr. Mark Gibson, Chief

VERMONT

22470 ■ Vermont Center for Reproductive Medicine
Women's Health Care Service/FAMC
111 Colchester Ave.
Burlington, VT 05401
Ph: (802)847-0986
URL: http://www.fahc.org/Womens_Health/Womens_IVF/index.html
Dr. Julia V. Johnson, Director

VIRGINIA

22471 ■ Assisted Fertility Program
1900 Electric Rd.
Salem, VA 24153
Ph: (540)772-3220
Fax: (540)772-3229
URL: http://www.assistedfertility.com
Dr. Marwan M. Shaykh, Director

22472 ■ Dominion Fertility--Arlington
46 S Glebe Rd., Ste. 301
Arlington, VA 22204
Ph: (703)920-3890
Fax: (703)892-6037
E-mail: info@dominionfertility.com
URL: http://www.dominionfertility.com
Dr. Michael DiMattina, Director

22473 ■ Dominion Fertility--Loudon
4055 Riverside Pkwy, Ste. 220
Loudon, VA 20176
Ph: (703)920-3890
URL: http://www.dominionfertility.com

22474 ■ Dominion Fertility--Reston
1800 Town Center Dr., Ste. 222
Reston, VA 20190
Ph: (703)920-3890
URL: http://www.dominionfertility.com

22475 ■ Genetics and IVF Institute
3015 Williams Dr.
Fairfax, VA 22031
Ph: (703)698-7355
Free: 800-552-4363
Fax: (703)698-0418
E-mail: givf@givf.com
URL: http://www.givf.com

22476 ■ George Washington University
Medical Faculty Associates
Fertility Center
8233 Old Courthouse Rd., Ste. 150
Vienna, VA 22182
Free: 888-WASH-IVF
URL: http://www.washivf.com/

22477 ■ Jones Institute for Reproductive Medicine
601 Colley Ave.
Norfolk, VA 23507
Ph: (757)446-7100
Free: 800-51J-ONES
Fax: (757)446-7544
URL: http://www.jonesinstitute.org
Dr. Sergio Oehninger, Director

22478 ■ Medical College of Virginia
OBGYN
1101 E Marshall St.
MCV Station, Box 980034
Richmond, VA 23298
Ph: (804)828-7877
Fax: (804)828-0573
E-mail: dwstoval@hsc.vca.edu
URL: http://www.obgyn.vcu.edu

22479 ■ Muasher Center for Fertility and IVF
8501 Arlington Blvd., Ste. 500
Fairfax, VA 22031
Ph: (703)542-3610
Fax: (703)876-6317
URL: http://www.mcfivf.com
Dr. Suheil Muasher, Director

22480 ■ Northridge Reproductive Medicine and Surgery
Fertility Clinic
1215 Lee St.
Charlottesville, VA 22908
Ph: (434)924-0211
URL: http://www.healthsystem.virginia.edu/internet/maps/services_detail.cfm?id=5 7

22481 ■ Richmond Center for Fertility and Endocrinology
IVF Program
7603 Forest Ave., Ste.301
Richmond, VA 23229
Ph: (804)285-9700
Free: 800-222-1014
Fax: (804)285-9745
E-mail: info@eggdoc.com
URL: http://www.eggdoc.com
Formerly: Henrico Doctors' Hospital, IVF/GIFT/ZIFT Program.

22482 ■ Shady Grove Fertility--Leesburg
19500 Sanridge Way, Ste. 280
Leesburg, VA 20176
Ph: (703)723-1757
Free: 888-761-1967
Fax: (703)723-1269
URL: http://www.shadygrovefertility.com
Dr. Naveed Khan, Director

22483 ■ Virginia Center for Reproductive Medicine
11150 Sunset Hills Rd., Ste. 100
Reston, VA 20190
Ph: (703)437-7722
URL: http://www.vcrmed.com
Dr. Fadi I. Sharara, Director

22484 ■ Virginia IVF and Andrology
9030 Stony Point Pkwy., Ste. 390
Richmond, VA 23235
Ph: (804)323-9980
Fax: (804)323-9984
URL: http://vaivf.com
Dr. Dennis W. Matt, Director

22485 ■ Washington Fertility Center
4316 Evergreen Ln.
Annandale, VA 22003
Ph: (703)658-3100
Fax: (703)658-3103
E-mail: frhc@erols.com
URL: http://www.washingtonfertility.com
Formerly: Institute for Reproductive Medicine.

WASHINGTON

22486 ■ Bellingham IVF and Fertility Care
2980 Squalicum Pkwy., Ste. 103
Bellingham, WA 98225
Ph: (360)715-8124
Free: 800-860-3967
Fax: (360)715-8126
E-mail: info@bellinghamivf.com
URL: http://www.bellinghamivf.com

22487 ■ Gyft Clinic
In Vitro Fertilization Program
502 South M St.
Second Floor
Tacoma, WA 98405
Ph: (253)475-5433
Fax: (253)473-6715
E-mail: gclinic@qwestoffice.net
URL: http://www.gyftclinic.com

22488 ■ Overlake Reproductive Health
12303 NE 130th Lane, Ste. 400
Kirland, WA 98034
Ph: (425)646-4700
Fax: (425)646-1076
URL: http://www.fertileweb.com

22489 ■ Washington Center for Reproductive Medicine
1370 116th Ave. NE, Ste. 100
Bellevue, WA 98004
Ph: (425)462-6100
Free: 866-937-2229
URL: http://www.seattleivf.com

WEST VIRGINIA

22490 ■ Wake Forest Center for Reproductive Medicine--Beckley, West Virginia
410 Carriage Dr.
Beckley, WV 25801
Ph: (336)716-6476
URL: http://www1.wfubmc.edu/ivf/IVF+-+ART/ivf.htm

22491 ■ West Virginia University Center for Reproductive Medicine
1322 Pineview Dr.
Morgantown, WV 26505
Ph: (304)598-3100
Dr. Kevin McGinnis, Director

WISCONSIN

22492 ■ Reproductive Specialty Center
2350 N Lake Dr., Ste. 504
Milwaukee, WI 53211
Ph: (414)289-9668
URL: http://www.reproductivecenter.com

22493 ■ Saint Luke's Medical Center POB Advanced Institute of Fertility
2801 W Kinnickinnic River Pkwy., Ste. 535
Milwaukee, WI 53215
Ph: (414)645-5437
Free: 800-829-BABY
Fax: (414)645-5401
E-mail: info@aiof.com
URL: http://www.aiof.com
Dr. K. Paul Katayama, Director

22494 ■ University of Wisconsin Women's Endocrinology & Reproductive Clinic
In Vitro Fertilization Program
600 Highland Ave., Ste. H-4/630
Madison, WI 53719
Ph: (608)265-0300

22495 ■ Wisconsin Fertility Institute
3146 Deming Way
Middleton, WI 53562
Ph: (608)824-0075
Fax: (608)829-0748
URL: http://www.wisconsinfertility.com
Dr. David Olive, Director

Chapter 22
Kidney Dialysis & Transplant Services

The facilities listed below are approved to provide kidney dialysis and transplant services. Entry arrangement is geographical by states and cities, then alphabetical by facility names within cities. Consult the "User's Guide" located at the front of this directory for further information.

ALABAMA

Alabaster

22496 ■ Fresenius Medical Care--Shelby
1022 1st St. N, Ste. 101
Alabaster, AL 35007
Free: 866-434-2597
URL: http://www.ultracare-dialysis.com/
Dialysis Stations: 12. **Formerly:** Alabama Dialysis Services--Shelby.

Alexander City

22497 ■ Fresenius Medical Care - Alexander City
3368 Hwy. 280 Bypass, Ste. G1
Alexander City, AL 35010
Free: 866-434-2597
URL: http://www.ultracare-dialysis.com/
Dialysis Stations: 9. **Formerly:** Physicians Choice Dialysis - Alexander City.

Andalusia

22498 ■ Fresenius Medical Care--Andalusia
403 W Bypass
Andalusia, AL 36420
Free: 866-434-2597
URL: http://www.ultracare-dialysis.com/
Dialysis Stations: 10. **Formerly:** Renal Care Group.

Athens

22499 ■ Athens Dialysis DaVita
15953 Athens Limestone Dr.
Athens, AL 35613
Free: 800-244-0582
URL: http://www.davita.com/home/locations/index.cfm?state=al
Dialysis Stations: 12.

Atmore

22500 ■ DaVita Atmore Dialysis Center
807 E Craig St.
Atmore, AL 36502
Free: 800-424-6589
Fax: (251)446-1950
URL: http://www.davita.com
Dialysis Stations: 10.

Auburn

22501 ■ Fresenius Medical Care of Auburn
211 E University Dr.
Auburn, AL 36832
Free: 866-434-2597
URL: http://www.ultracare-dialysis.com/
Dialysis Stations: 10.

Bay Minette

22502 ■ Fresenius Medical Care--Bay Minette
2505 Hand Ave.
Bay Minette, AL 36507
Free: 866-434-2597
URL: http://www.ultracare-dialysis.com/
Dialysis Stations: 10.

Bessemer

22503 ■ DaVita--Bessemer
901 Westlake Mall, Ste. 101
Bessemer, AL 35020
Free: 800-424-6589
Fax: (205)424-3408
URL: http://www.davita.com
Dialysis Stations: 16. **Formerly:** Gambro Healthcare.

Birmingham

22504 ■ Children's Hospital of Alabama Dialysis Center/Solid Organ Transplant Clinic
1600 7th Ave. S
Birmingham, AL 35233
Ph: (205)939-6631
Fax: (205)558-2319
URL: http://www.chsys.org/body.cfm?id=137&action=detail&ref=35
Dialysis Stations: 7.

22505 ■ DaVita--Birmingham Central Dialysis Facility
728 Richard Arrington Blvd. S
Birmingham, AL 35233
Free: 800-424-6589
Fax: (205)297-9190
URL: http://www.davita.com
Dialysis Stations: 32. **Formerly:** Gambro Healthcare.

22506 ■ DaVita--Birmingham East Dialysis Facility
1105 E Park Dr.
Birmingham, AL 35235
Free: 800-424-6589
Fax: (205)836-5157
URL: http://www.davita.com
Dialysis Stations: 20. **Formerly:** Gambro Healthcare.

22507 ■ DaVita--Birmingham Home Training Dialysis
2101 7th Ave. S
Birmingham, AL 35233
Free: 800-424-6589
Fax: (205)322-5758
URL: http://www.davita.com
Dialysis Stations: 2. **Formerly:** Gambro Healthcare.

22508 ■ DaVita--Birmingham North Dialysis Facility
1917 32nd Ave. N
Birmingham, AL 35207
Free: 800-424-6589
Fax: (205)297-9058
URL: http://www.davita.com
Dialysis Stations: 24.

22509 ■ Dialysis Clinic, Inc.--Birmingham
8713 Parkway E
Birmingham, AL 35206
Ph: (205)838-5400
URL: http://www.dciinc.org
Dialysis Stations: 16.

22510 ■ Diversified Specialty Institutes Norwood Clinic Dialysis Unit
1424 N Carraway Blvd.
Birmingham, AL 35234
Ph: (205)502-5300
Free: 866-293-0394
URL: http://www.dsi-corp.com/usa.html
Dialysis Stations: 20. **Formerly:** National Renal Institutes/Fresenius Medical Care.

22511 ■ Fresenius Medical Care--Birmingham
2131 Magnolia Ave. S
Birmingham, AL 35205
Free: 866-434-2597
URL: http://www.ultracare-dialysis.com/
Dialysis Stations: 12. **Formerly:** Alabama Dialysis Services--Southside.

22512 ■ Fresenius Medical Care--Birmingham
3918 Montclair Rd., Ste. 110
Birmingham, AL 35213
Free: 866-434-2597
URL: http://www.ultracare-dialysis.com/
Dialysis Stations: 24. **Formerly:** Alabama Dialysis Services--Montclair.

22513 ■ Fresenius Medical Care--Birmingham
708 Cotton Ave. SW
Birmingham, AL 35211
Free: 866-434-2597
URL: http://www.ultracare-dialysis.com/
Dialysis Stations: 34. **Formerly:** Alabama Dialysis Services--Birmingham.

22514 ■ Fresenius Medical Care--West
633 Lomb Ave.
Birmingham, AL 35211
Free: 866-434-2597
URL: http://www.ultracare-dialysis.com/
Dialysis Stations: 24. **Formerly:** Alabama Dialysis Services--West.

Boaz

22515 ■ DaVita--Boaz
Dialysis Facility
16 Central Henderson Rd.
Boaz, AL 35957
Free: 800-424-6589
Fax: (256)840-1951
URL: http://www.davita.com
Dialysis Stations: 10. **Formerly:** Gambro Healthcare.

Brewton

22516 ■ Dialysis Affiliates of South Alabama
1205 Belleville Ave.
Brewton, AL 36426
Ph: (251)867-3650
Dialysis Stations: 10.

Camden

22517 ■ Fresenius Medical Care--Wilcox County
Dialysis Services
229 Camden Bypass
Camden, AL 36726
Free: 866-434-2597
URL: http://www.ultracare-dialysis.com/
Dialysis Stations: 10.

Center Point

22518 ■ DaVita
Center Point Dialysis
2337 1st St. NE
Center Point, AL 35215
Free: 800-424-6589
Fax: (205)853-0933
URL: http://www.davita.com

Clanton

22519 ■ Fresenius Medical Care--Clanton
275 Health Center Dr.
Clanton, AL 35045
Free: 866-434-2597
URL: http://www.ultracare-dialysis.com/
Dialysis Stations: 10. **Formerly:** Alabama Dialysis Services--Clanton.

Cullman

22520 ■ Dialysis Clinic, Inc.--Cullman
1734 Eva Rd. NE
Cullman, AL 35055
Ph: (256)734-3055
URL: http://www.dciinc.org
Dialysis Stations: 16.

Dadeville

22521 ■ Fresenius Medical Center - Dadeville
52 Waterworks Dr.
Dadeville, AL 36853
Free: 866-434-2597
URL: http://www.ultracare-dialysis.com/
Dialysis Stations: 15.

Daphne

22522 ■ Home Dialysis Options of Baldwin County
Baldwin County At Home
27880 N Main St., Ste. A
Daphne, AL 36526
Free: 800-424-6589
URL: http://www.davita.com

Decatur

22523 ■ Dialysis Clinic, Inc.--Decatur
1601 6th Ave. SE
Decatur, AL 35601
Ph: (256)350-8882
URL: http://www.dciinc.org
Dialysis Stations: 24.

22524 ■ Home Dialysis of North Alabama
1216 Sommerville Rd. SE
Decatur, AL 35601
Ph: (256)340-0012
Dialysis Stations: 1.

Demopolis

22525 ■ DaVita--Demopolis
Dialysis Facility
511 S Cedar St.
Demopolis, AL 36732
Free: 800-424-6589
Fax: (334)289-7038
URL: http://www.davita.com
Dialysis Stations: 12. **Formerly:** Gambro Healthcare.

Dothan

22526 ■ DaVita
Wiregrass Kidney Center
1450 Ross Clark Cir.
Dothan, AL 36301
Free: 800-424-6589
Fax: (334)792-8912
URL: http://www.davita.com

22527 ■ Dialysis Clinic, Inc.--Dothan
1546 E Main St.
Dothan, AL 36301
Ph: (334)793-3519
URL: http://www.dciinc.org
Dialysis Stations: 31.

22528 ■ Dialysis Clinic, Inc.--Dothan Dialysis Facility
1557 E Main St.
Dothan, AL 36301
Ph: (334)793-3519
URL: http://www.gambro.com
Dialysis Stations: 18. **Formerly:** Gambro Healthcare--Dothan.

22529 ■ Dothan Dialysis
216 Graceland Dr.
Dothan, AL 36305
Free: 800-424-6589
Fax: (334)793-2404
URL: http://www.davita.com

Enterprise

22530 ■ Dialysis Clinic, Inc.--Enterprise
3861 Salem Rd.
Enterprise, AL 36330
Ph: (334)347-8233
URL: http://www.dciinc.org
Dialysis Stations: 16.

Eufaula

22531 ■ DaVita--Eufaula
220 S Orange St.
Eufaula, AL 36027
Free: 800-424-6589
URL: http://www.davita.com
Dialysis Stations: 10. **Formerly:** Gambro Healthcare.

Eutaw

22532 ■ DaVita--Greene County Dialysis
544 US Hwy. 43 S
Eutaw, AL 35462
Free: 800-424-6589
URL: http://www.davita.com
Dialysis Stations: 10. **Formerly:** Gambro Healthcare.

Fairfield

22533 ■ Fresenius Medical Care--Fairfield
6508 E J Oliver Blvd.
Fairfield, AL 35064
Free: 866-434-2597
URL: http://www.ultracare-dialysis.com/
Dialysis Stations: 12. **Formerly:** Alabama Dialysis Services--Fairfield.

Fairhope

22534 ■ Fresenius Medical Care--Eastern Shore
Dialysis Facility
124 Professional Park Dr.
Fairhope, AL 36532
Free: 866-434-2597
URL: http://www.ultracare-dialysis.com/
Dialysis Stations: 24.

Fayette

22535 ■ DaVita Fayette/Tuscaloosa
Dialysis Center
2450 Temple Ave. N
Fayette, AL 35555
Free: 800-424-6589
Fax: (205)932-8332
URL: http://www.davita.com
Dialysis Stations: 10. **Formerly:** Gambro Healthcare.

Florence

22536 ■ DaVita--Florence Dialysis
422 E Dr. Hicks Blvd.
Florence, AL 35630
Free: 800-424-6589
Fax: (256)767-3728
URL: http://www.davita.com

22537 ■ DaVita--Renaissance
1840 Darby Dr.
Florence, AL 35630
Free: 800-424-6589
URL: http://www.davita.com

Foley

22538 ■ DaVita
South Baldwin Dialysis Center
150 W Peachtree St.
Foley, AL 36535
Free: 800-424-6589
URL: http://www.davita.com
Dialysis Stations: 13.

22539 ■ Fresenius Medical Care--Foley
230 E Fern Ave.
Foley, AL 36545
Free: 866-434-2597
URL: http://www.ultracare-dialysis.com/
Dialysis Stations: 10.

Fort Payne

22540 ■ Fresenius Medical Care--Fort Payne
2202 Jordan Rd. SW, Ste. 100
Fort Payne, AL 35968
Free: 866-434-2597
URL: http://www.ultracare-dialysis.com/
Dialysis Stations: 12. **Formerly:** Alabama Dialysis Services--Fort Payne.

Gadsden

22541 ■ DaVita--Gadsden
Dialysis Center
409 S 1st St.
Gadsden, AL 35901
Free: 800-424-6589
URL: http://www.davita.com
Dialysis Stations: 24. **Formerly:** Gambro Healthcare.

Gardendale

22542 ■ Fresenius Medical Care--Gardendale
592 Fieldstown Rd., Ste. 102
Gardendale, AL 35071
Free: 866-434-2597
URL: http://www.ultracare-dialysis.com/
Dialysis Stations: 12.

Georgiana

22543 ■ Dialysis Clinic Inc.--Georgiana
715 Meeting St.
Georgiana, AL 36033
Ph: (334)376-0277
URL: http://www.dciinc.org
Dialysis Stations: 10.

22544 ■ Dialysis Clinic, Inc.--Georgiana
715 Meeting St.
Georgiana, AL 36033
Ph: (334)376-0277
URL: http://www.dciinc.org
Dialysis Stations: 10.

Greenville

22545 ■ Fresenius Medical Care--Camellia Dialysis Facility
108 LV Stabler Dr.
Greenville, AL 36037
Free: 866-434-2597
URL: http://www.ultracare-dialysis.com/
Dialysis Stations: 8.

Gulf Shores

22546 ■ DaVita--Gulf Shores
3947 Gulf Shores Pkwy.
Gulf Shores, AL 36542
Free: 800-424-6589
URL: http://www.davita.com

22547 ■ Patient First Dialysis
6642 Hwy. 59
Gulf Shores, AL 36542
Ph: (251)968-2585
E-mail: info@patientfirstdialysis.com
URL: http://www.patientfirstdialysis.com/
Dialysis Stations: 10.

Guntersville

22548 ■ Fresenius Medical Care--Lakeview
45 Medical Park Dr., Ste. A
Guntersville, AL 35976
Free: 866-434-2597
URL: http://www.ultracare-dialysis.com/
Dialysis Stations: 17.

Hamilton

22549 ■ Fresenius Medical Care--Hamilton, Alabama
1256 Military St. S
Hamilton, AL 35570
Free: 866-434-2597
URL: http://www.ultracare-dialysis.com/
Dialysis Stations: 7. **Formerly:** Alabama Dialysis Services--Hamilton.

Hoover

22550 ■ Fresenius Medical Care--Hoover
2104 Lorna Ridge La.
Hoover, AL 35216
Free: 866-434-2597
URL: http://www.ultracare-dialysis.com/
Dialysis Stations: 12.

Huntsville

22551 ■ Fresenius Medical Care/Chase Dialysis Center
1849 Keats Dr. NW
Huntsville, AL 35810
Free: 866-434-2597
URL: http://www.ultracare-dialysis.com/
Dialysis Stations: 20.

22552 ■ Fresenius Medical Care/Discovery Dialysis
1131 Eagletree Ln., Ste. 100
Huntsville, AL 35801
Free: 866-434-2597
URL: http://www.ultracare-dialysis.com/
Dialysis Stations: 17.

22553 ■ Fresenius Medical Care - Huntsville
2325 Pansy St., Ste. C
Huntsville, AL 35801
Free: 866-434-2597
URL: http://www.ultracare-dialysis.com/
Dialysis Stations: 32.

22554 ■ Fresenius Medical Care--North Alabama
1311 N Memorial Pkwy., Ste. 200
Huntsville, AL 35801
Free: 866-434-2597
URL: http://www.ultracare-dialysis.com/
Dialysis Stations: 22.

22555 ■ Fresenius Medical Care--Parkway Dialysis Center
1311 N Memorial Pkwy., Ste. 100
Huntsville, AL 35801
Free: 866-434-2597
URL: http://www.ultracare-dialysis.com/
Dialysis Stations: 15.

Jackson

22556 ■ Fresenius Medical Care - Tombigbee
215 Walker Springs Rd.
Jackson, AL 36545
Free: 866-434-2597
URL: http://www.ultracare-dialysis.com/
Dialysis Stations: 24.

Jacksonville

22557 ■ PCD Jacksonville
331 Henry Rd. SW
Jacksonville, AL 36265
Ph: (256)435-3161
Dialysis Stations: 12.

Jasper

22558 ■ Diversified Specialty Institutes--Walker County
589 Hwy. 78 W
Jasper, AL 35501
Ph: (205)221-1056
Free: 866-293-0394
URL: http://www.dsi-corp.com/usa.home
Dialysis Stations: 12.

22559 ■ Fresenius Medical Care--Walker
3510 3rd St. N
Jasper, AL 35501
Free: 866-434-2597
URL: http://www.ultracare-dialysis.com/
Dialysis Stations: 16. **Formerly:** Alabama Dialysis Services--Walker.

Lafayette

22560 ■ Fresenius Medical Care - Chambers
802 Hospital St.
Lafayette, AL 36862
Free: 866-434-2597
URL: http://www.ultracare-dialysis.com/
Dialysis Stations: 16.

Madison

22561 ■ Fresenius Medical Care--Odyssey Dialysis
40 Hughes Rd.
Madison, AL 35758
Free: 866-434-2597
URL: http://www.ultracare-dialysis.com/
Dialysis Stations: 15.

Midfield

22562 ■ Fresenius Medical Care--Midfield Dialysis
613 Bessemer Super Hwy.
Midfield, AL 35228
Free: 866-434-2597
URL: http://www.ultracare-dialysis.com/engine/
Dialysis Stations: 24.

Mobile

22563 ■ Fresenius Medical Care--Dauphin Island Parkway Dialysis Facility
2381 Dauphin Island Pkwy.
Mobile, AL 36605
Free: 866-434-2597
URL: http://www.ultracare-dialysis.com/
Dialysis Stations: 20.

22564 ■ Fresenius Medical Care--East Mobile
1217 Government St.
Mobile, AL 36604
Free: 866-434-2597
URL: http://www.ultracare-dialysis.com/
Dialysis Stations: 17.

22565 ■ Fresenius Medical Care--Jaguar
575 Stanton Rd.
Mobile, AL 36617
Free: 866-434-2597
URL: http://www.ultracare-dialysis.com/
Dialysis Stations: 26.

22566 ■ Fresenius Medical Care--Mobile
2620 Old Shell Rd.
Mobile, AL 36606
Free: 866-434-2597
URL: http://www.ultracare-dialysis.com/
Dialysis Stations: 24.

22567 ■ Fresenius Medical Care--Port City Dialysis Center
201 St. Joseph St., Ste. F
Mobile, AL 36602
Free: 866-434-2597
URL: http://www.ultracare-dialysis.com/
Dialysis Stations: 20.

22568 ■ Fresenius Medical Care--Toulminville Dialysis Facility
2056 Dr. Martin Luther King Jr. Ave.
Mobile, AL 36617
Free: 866-434-2597
URL: http://www.ultracare-dialysis.com/
Dialysis Stations: 19.

22569 ■ Fresenius Medical Care--University of South Alabama Dialysis Facility
1925 Health Services Dr.
Mobile, AL 36688
Free: 866-434-2597
URL: http://www.ultracare-dialysis.com/
Dialysis Stations: 20.

22570 ■ Fresenius Medical Care--West Mobile Dialysis Facility
6601 Wall St., Ste. A
Mobile, AL 36695
Free: 866-434-2597
URL: http://www.ultracare-dialysis.com/
Dialysis Stations: 20.

Monroeville

22571 ■ Fresenius Medical Care--Whetstone Dialysis Facility
676 S Alabama Ave.
Monroeville, AL 36460
Free: 866-434-2597
URL: http://www.ultracare-dialysis.com/
Dialysis Stations: 11. **Formerly:** Dialysis Facility of Monroeville.

Montgomery

22572 ■ Dialysis Clinic, Inc.--Montgomery
544 S McDonough St.
Montgomery, AL 36104
Ph: (334)265-9190
URL: http://www.dciinc.org
Dialysis Stations: 24.

22573 ■ Fresenius Medical Care - Capitol City
255 S Jackson St.
Montgomery, AL 36104
Free: 866-434-2597
URL: http://www.ultracare-dialysis.com/
Dialysis Stations: 34.

22574 ■ Fresenius Medical Care--Montgomery Baptist Dialysis Facility
1400 Narrow Ln. Pkwy.
Montgomery, AL 36111
Free: 866-434-2597
URL: http://www.ultracare-dialysis.com/
Dialysis Stations: 25.

22575 ■ Physicians Choice Dialysis--East Montgomery
DaVita
6890 Winton Blount Blvd.
Montgomery, AL 36117
Free: 800-424-6589
Fax: (334)260-9496
URL: http://www.DaVita.com
Dialysis Stations: 13.

22576 ■ Physicians Choice Dialysis--Montgomery
DaVita
1001 Forest Ave.
Montgomery, AL 36106
Free: 800-424-6589
Fax: (334)269-0024
URL: http://www.davita.com
Dialysis Stations: 31.

Moulton

22577 ■ Dialysis Clinic, Inc.--Moulton
1962 Main St.
Moulton, AL 35650
Ph: (256)974-1400
URL: http://www.dciinc.org
Dialysis Stations: 10.

Muscle Shoals

22578 ■ Muscle Shoals Dialysis
DaVita
712 State St.
Muscle Shoals, AL 35661
Free: 800-424-6589
URL: http://www.davita.com
Dialysis Stations: 10.

Northport

22579 ■ DaVita--Northport Dialysis Center
2401 Hospital Dr.
Northport, AL 35476
Free: 800-424-6589
Fax: (205)339-8807
URL: http://www.davita.com
Dialysis Stations: 10. **Formerly:** Gambro Healthcare.

Oneonta

22580 ■ Fresenius Medical Care--Oneonta
150 Gilbreath Dr., Ste. 1
Oneonta, AL 35121
Free: 866-434-2597
URL: http://www.ultracare-dialysis.com/
Dialysis Stations: 8. **Formerly:** ADS Oneonta.

Opelika

22581 ■ DaVita--Opelika
2340 Pepperell Pkwy.
Opelika, AL 36801
Free: 800-424-6589
URL: http://www.davita.com
Dialysis Stations: 10,.

22582 ■ Fresenius Medical Care--Opelika Dialysis Facility
2609 Village Professional Dr., Ste. 2
Opelika, AL 36802
Free: 866-434-2597
URL: http://www.ultracare-dialysis.com/
Dialysis Stations: 25.

Oxford

22583 ■ Renal Advantage Inc. Care Centers--Snow St.--Oxford
711 Snow St.
Oxford, AL 36203
Ph: (256)835-5914
URL: http://www.renaladvantage.com
Dialysis Stations: 25.

Ozark

22584 ■ DaVita--Ozark Dialysis Center
214 Hospital Ave.
Ozark, AL 36360
Free: 800-424-6589
Fax: (334)774-1828
URL: http://www.davita.com
Dialysis Stations: 13. **Formerly:** Gambro Healthcare.

Pelham

22585 ■ Fresenius Medical Care--Cahaba Valley
120 Cahaba Valley Pkwy., Ste. 150
Pelham, AL 35124
Free: 866-434-2597
URL: http://www.ultracare-dialysis.com/
Dialysis Stations: 24. **Formerly:** Alabama Dialysis Services--Cahaba Valley.

Pell City

22586 ■ Dialysis Clinic, Inc.--Pell City
2805 Dr. John Haynes Dr.
Pell City, AL 35125
Ph: (205)884-4240
URL: http://www.dciinc.org
Dialysis Stations: 10.

22587 ■ Fresenius Medical Care--Pell City
2804 Dr. John Haynes Dr.
Pell City, AL 35125
Free: 866-434-2597
URL: http://www.ultracare-dialysis.com/
Dialysis Stations: 10. **Formerly:** Alabama Dialysis Services--Pell City.

Phenix City

22588 ■ Dialysis Clinic, Inc.--Phenix City
1611 21st Court
Phenix City, AL 36867
Ph: (334)448-4840
URL: http://www.dciinc.org
Dialysis Stations: 12.

22589 ■ Phenix City Dialysis Center
DaVita
1900 Opelika Rd.
Phenix City, AL 36867
Free: 800-424-6589
Fax: (334)298-1943
URL: http://www.davita.com
Dialysis Stations: 20.

Prattville

22590 ■ Fresenius Medical Care--Prattville
692 Covered Bridge Pkwy.
Prattville, AL 36066
Free: 866-434-2597
URL: http://www.ultracare-dialysis.com/
Dialysis Stations: 10.

22591 ■ Physicians Choice Dialysis--Prattville
DaVita
1815 Glynwood Dr.
Prattville, AL 36066
Free: 800-424-6589
URL: http://www.davita.com
Dialysis Stations: 16.

Prichard

22592 ■ Fresenius Medical Care--Prichard Dialysis Facility
4016 St. Stephens Rd.
Prichard, AL 36613
Free: 866-434-2597
URL: http://www.ultracare-dialysis.com/
Dialysis Stations: 24.

Rainbow City

22593 ■ DaVita--Rainbow City
2800 Rainbow Dr.
Rainbow City, AL 35906
Free: 800-424-6589
URL: http://www.davita.com
Dialysis Stations: 16. **Formerly:** Gambro Healthcare.

Roanoke

22594 ■ Renal Advantage Inc--Roanoke Roanoke Dialysis Clinic
4459 US Hwy. 431
Roanoke, AL 36274
Ph: (334)863-8365
URL: http://www.renaladvantage.com
Dialysis Stations: 13. **Formerly:** National Renal Alliance.

Russellville

22595 ■ DaVita--Russellville Dialysis Facility
14897 Hwy. 43
Russellville, AL 35653
Free: 800-424-6589
Fax: (256)332-8959
URL: http://www.davita.com
Dialysis Stations: 10. **Formerly:** Gambro Healthcare.

Scottsboro

22596 ■ Fresenius Medical Care--Scottsboro
20988 John T. Reid Hwy
Scottsboro, AL 35768
Free: 866-434-2597
URL: http://www.ultracare-dialysis.com/
Dialysis Stations: 16.

Selma

22597 ■ Fresenius Medical Care - Dallas County
200 S Park Pl.
Selma, AL 36701
Free: 866-434-2597
URL: http://www.ultracare-dialysis.com/
Dialysis Stations: 21.

22598 ■ Fresenius Medical Care - Selma
905 Medical Center Pkwy.
Selma, AL 36701
Free: 866-434-2597
URL: http://www.ultracare-dialysis.com/
Dialysis Stations: 26.

22599 ■ Fresenius Medical Care--Valley Creek
201 Lincoln Ln.
Selma, AL 36701
Free: 866-434-2597
URL: http://www.ultracare-dialysis.com/
Dialysis Stations: 16. **Formerly:** Physicians Choice Dialysis of Selma.

Semmes

22600 ■ Fresenius Medical Care--Magnolia Grove
7940 Moffett Rd.
Semmes, AL 36575
Free: 866-434-2597
URL: http://www.ultracare-dialysis.com/
Dialysis Stations: 20. **Formerly:** BMA--Magnolia.

Sheffield

22601 ■ DaVita--Sheffield Dialysis Center
1120 S Jackson Hwy., Ste. 107
Sheffield, AL 35660
Free: 800-424-6589
Fax: (256)381-8199
URL: http://www.davita.com
Dialysis Stations: 12. **Formerly:** Gambro Healthcare.

Sylacauga

22602 ■ DaVita--Sylacauga Dialysis Facility
331 James Payton Blvd.
Sylacauga, AL 35150
Free: 800-424-6589
Fax: (256)249-2786
URL: http://www.davita.com
Dialysis Stations: 13. **Formerly:** Gambro Healthcare.

22603 ■ Fresenius Medical Care--Sylacauga
314 W Spring St.
Sylacauga, AL 35150
Free: 866-434-2597
URL: http://www.ultracare-dialysis.com/
Dialysis Stations: 12. **Formerly:** Alabama Dialysis Services--Sylacauga.

Talladega

22604 ■ DaVita--Talladega
726 Battle St. E
Talladega, AL 35160
Free: 800-424-6589
Fax: (256)362-2356
URL: http://www.davita.com

22605 ■ PCD Talladega Fresenius Medical Care
805 North St., E
Talladega, AL 35160
Free: 866-434-2597
URL: http://www.ultracare-dialysis.com/
Dialysis Stations: 17. **Formerly:** Renal Care Group.

22606 ■ Renal Advantage Inc--Talladega
717 Stone Ave.
Talladega, AL 35160
Ph: (256)362-4449
URL: http://www.renaladvantage.com
Dialysis Stations: 19. **Formerly:** National Renal Alliance.

Thomasville

22607 ■ Fresenius Medical Care--Thomasville, Alabama
30230 Hwy. 43
Thomasville, AL 36784
Free: 866-434-2597
URL: http://www.ultracare-dialysis.com/
Dialysis Stations: 20.

Troy

22608 ■ Fresenius Medical Care - Troy
606 Botts Ave.
Troy, AL 36081
Free: 866-434-2597
URL: http://www.ultracare-dialysis.com/
Dialysis Stations: 15.

Tuscaloosa

22609 ■ DaVita--Tuscaloosa Dialysis Facility
805 Old Mill St.
Tuscaloosa, AL 35401
Free: 800-424-6589
Fax: (205)752-6566
URL: http://www.davita.com
Dialysis Stations: 19. **Formerly:** Gambro Healthcare.

22610 ■ DaVita--Tuscaloosa University Dialysis Center
220 15th St.
Tuscaloosa, AL 35401
Free: 800-424-6589
Fax: (205)345-5071
URL: http://www.davita.com
Dialysis Stations: 24. **Formerly:** Gambro Healthcare.

22611 ■ Tuscaloosa Nephrology Associates Home Dialysis
535 Jack Warner Pkwy. NE, Ste. K
Tuscaloosa, AL 35404
Ph: (205)556-5541
Dialysis Stations: 0.

Tuskegee

22612 ■ Fresenius Medical Care--Tuskegee Dialysis Facility
802 E Martin Luther King Hwy.
Tuskegee, AL 36083
Free: 866-434-2597
URL: http://www.ultracare-dialysis.com/
Dialysis Stations: 20.

Valley

22613 ■ Fresenius Medical Care--Langdale Dialysis Facility
8 Medical Park
Valley, AL 36854
Free: 866-434-2597
URL: http://www.ultracare-dialysis.com/
Dialysis Stations: 12.

Wetumpka

22614 ■ DaVita Physicians Choice Dialysis--Elmore County
515 Hospital Dr.
Wetumpka, AL 36092
Free: 800-424-6589
URL: http://www.davita.com
Dialysis Stations: 10.

Winfield

22615 ■ Fresenius Medical Care Northwest Alabama Kidney Center
638 Tahoe Rd.
Winfield, AL 35594
Free: 866-434-2597
URL: http://www.ultracare-dialysis.com/engine/
Dialysis Stations: 10.

ALASKA

Anchorage

22616 ■ Fresenius Medical Care--Anchorage
3950 Laurel St.
Anchorage, AK 99508
Free: 866-434-2597
URL: http://www.ultracare-dialysis.com/
Dialysis Stations: 35. **Formerly:** Alaska Kidney Center.

22617 ■ Liberty Dialysis--Anchorage
901 E Dimond Blvd.
Anchorage, AK 99515
Ph: (907)522-9009
URL: http://www.libertydialysis.com

22618 ■ Liberty Dialysis--Anchorage Home Program
901 E Dimond Blvd.
Anchorage, AK 99515
Ph: (907)868-4845
URL: http://www.libertydialysis.com

Fairbanks

22619 ■ Fresenius Medical Care--Fairbanks
1863 Airport Way
Fairbanks, AK 99701
Free: 866-434-2597
URL: http://www.ultracare-dialysis.com/
Dialysis Stations: 17. **Formerly:** Renal Care Group.

Juneau

22620 ■ Fresenius Medical Care--Juneau
9109 Mendenhall Rd., Ste. 6
Juneau, AK 99801
Free: 866-434-2597
URL: http://www.ultracare-dialysis.com/
Dialysis Stations: 9. **Formerly:** Renal Care Group.

Wasilla

22621 ■ Fresenius Medical Care--Wasilla
3787 E Meridian Loop
Wasilla, AK 99654
Free: 866-434-2597
URL: http://www.ultracare-dialysis.com/
Dialysis Stations: 12. **Formerly:** RCG Mat Su.

ARIZONA

Apache Junction

22622 ■ Fresenius Medical Care--Apache Junction Dialysis Center
11540 E University Dr., Ste. 109
Apache Junction, AZ 85220
Ph: (480)357-5572
Free: 866-434-2597
URL: http://www.ultracare-dialysis.com/
Dialysis Stations: 24. **Formerly:** Renal Care Group.

Avondale

22623 ■ Diversified Specialty Institutes Avondale Dialysis Center
13055 W McDowell Rd., Ste. 101F
Avondale, AZ 85392
Ph: (623)935-5460
URL: http://www.dsi-corp.com
Dialysis Stations: 24.

22624 ■ Fresenius Medical Care - Avondale Dialysis
10750 W McDowell Rd., Ste. E-500
Avondale, AZ 85323
Ph: (623)643-9334
Free: 866-434-2597
URL: http://www.ultracare-dialysis.com/
Dialysis Stations: 20.

Bullhead City

22625 ■ Fresenius Medical Care--Bullhead City Dialysis Center
2650 Miracle Mile
Bullhead City, AZ 86442
Ph: (928)763-5550
Free: 866-434-2597
URL: http://www.ultracare-dialysis.com/
Dialysis Stations: 23.

Casa Grande

22626 ■ Fresenius Medical Care--Casa Grande Dialysis Facility
695 E Cottonwood Ln.
Casa Grande, AZ 85122
Ph: (520)836-2566
Free: 866-434-2597
URL: http://www.ultracare-dialysis.com/
Dialysis Stations: 16. **Formerly:** RenalWest.

22627 ■ Western Skies Dialysis Inc.
1041 N Arizona Rd.
Casa Grande, AZ 85222
Ph: (520)836-5883
Dialysis Stations: 16.

Chandler

22628 ■ Fresenius Medical Care - Chandler
912 W Chandler Blvd, Bld. A-D
Chandler, AZ 85225
Free: 866-434-2597
URL: http://www.ultracare-dialysis.com/
Dialysis Stations: 24. **Formerly:** Renal Care Group.

22629 ■ Ocotillo Dialysis DaVita
975 W Chandler Heights, Ste. 101
Chandler, AZ 85248
Free: 800-424-6589
URL: http://www.davita.com
Dialysis Stations: 12.

Chinle

22630 ■ DaVita--Chinle
c/o U.S. Public Health Service Indian Hospital
US Hwy. 191
Chinle, AZ 86503
Free: 800-424-6589
Fax: (928)674-5461
URL: http://www.davita.com
Dialysis Stations: 26.

Cottonwood

22631 ■ Diversified Specialty Institutes Cottonwood Dialysis Center
203 S Candy Ln., Ste. 11A & B
Cottonwood, AZ 86326
Ph: (928)639-0014
URL: http://www.dsi-corp.com
Dialysis Stations: 10.

Douglas

22632 ■ Dialysis Clinic Inc.--Douglas
99 E 16th St.
Douglas, AZ 85607
Ph: (520)364-2204
Fax: (520)364-2296
URL: http://www.dciinc.org
Dialysis Stations: 12.

Flagstaff

22633 ■ Flagstaff Dialysis Center Fresenius Medical Care
5200 E Cortland Blvd., Ste. A1
Flagstaff, AZ 86004
Free: 866-434-2597
URL: http://www.ultracare-dialysis.com/
Dialysis Stations: 12.

Florence

22634 ■ Santan Dialysis Fresenius Medical Care
PO Box 2370
Florence, AZ 85132
Free: 866-434-2597
URL: http://www.ultracare-dialysis.com/
Dialysis Stations: 12.

Gilbert

22635 ■ DaVita--Gilbert
5222 E Baseline, Ste. 104
Gilbert, AZ 85234
Ph: (480)832-6996
Free: 800-424-6589
URL: http://www.davita.com
Dialysis Stations: 24. **Formerly:** Gambro Healthcare.

22636 ■ Fresenius Medical Care--Mesa Dialysis Center
1525 N Gilbert Rd., No. 121
Gilbert, AZ 85234
Ph: (480)497-1127
Free: 866-434-2597
URL: http://www.ultracare-dialysis.com/
Dialysis Stations: 12.

Glendale

22637 ■ Brookwood Dialysis Clinic DaVita
8910 N 43rd Ave., Ste. 107
Glendale, AZ 85302
Ph: (623)937-2735
Free: 800-424-6589
URL: http://www.davita.com
Dialysis Stations: 24.

22638 ■ DaVita Arrowhead Lakes Dialysis Center
20325 N 51st Ave., Bldg. 11, Ste. 186
Glendale, AZ 85308
Ph: (623)533-6521
Free: 800-424-6589
URL: http://www.davita.com
Dialysis Stations: 24.

22639 ■ Fresenius Medical Care--Arrowhead Dialysis
16844 N 59th Ave.
Glendale, AZ 85306
Ph: (602)439-8200
Free: 866-434-2597
URL: http://www.ultracare-dialysis.com/
Dialysis Stations: 13.

22640 ■ Fresenius Medical Care--Dialysis Center of Glendale
5957 W Northern Ave., No. 108
Glendale, AZ 85301
Ph: (623)435-1155
Free: 866-434-2597
URL: http://www.ultracare-dialysis.com/
Dialysis Stations: 18.

22641 ■ Fresenius Medical Care--Glendale
5750 W Thunderbird Rd., Ste. G-750
Glendale, AZ 85306
Ph: (602)439-9502
Free: 866-434-2597
Dialysis Stations: 24. **Formerly:** RCG--Glendale.

22642 ■ Glendale Family Health Center
5141 W Lamar Rd.
Glendale, AZ 85301
Ph: (623)344-6781
URL: http://www.mihs.org/ourfacility/glendale.html
Dialysis Stations: 9.

Goodyear

22643 ■ Fresenius Medical Care--Goodyear
500 N Bullard Ave., Ste. C-34
Goodyear, AZ 85338
Ph: (623)925-8955
Free: 866-434-2597
URL: http://www.ultracare-dialysis.com/engine/
Dialysis Stations: 24.

22644 ■ Fresenius Medical Care--Palm Valley Dialysis Services
13657 W McDowell Rd., Ste. 106
Goodyear, AZ 85338
Free: 866-434-2597
URL: http://www.ultracare-dialysis.com/
Dialysis Stations: 12.

Kayenta

22645 ■ DaVita--Kayenta
US Highway 163 N
Kayenta, AZ 86033
Ph: (928)697-8182
Free: 800-424-6589
URL: http://www.davita.com
Dialysis Stations: 18.

Kingman

22646 ■ Fresenius Medical Care Kingman Dialysis
1739 E Beverly Ave., Ste. 208
Kingman, AZ 86401
Ph: (928)681-4300
Free: 866-434-2597
URL: http://www.ultracare-dialysis.com/engine/
Dialysis Stations: 11.

22647 ■ Kingman Kidney Clinic Inc. Dialysis Facility
4055 Stockston Hill Rd., Ste. 15
Kingman, AZ 86409
Ph: (928)692-6500
Dialysis Stations: 15.

Lake Havasu City

22648 ■ Fresenius Medical Care--Lake Havasu City Dialysis Facility
1761 McCulloch Blvd., Ste. G
Lake Havasu City, AZ 86403
Ph: (928)680-4748
Free: 866-434-2597
URL: http://www.ultracare-dialysis.com/
Dialysis Stations: 12. **Formerly:** Renalwest.

Laveen

22649 ■ Gila River Dialysis Center West Gila River Health Care
9721 W Pecos Rd.
Laveen, AZ 85339
Ph: (602)271-7950
URL: http://www.grhc.org/getpage.php?name=dia
Dialysis Stations: 20.

Mammoth

22650 ■ Fresenius Medical Care--Mammoth
14786 S Hwy. 77
Mammoth, AZ 85618
Ph: (520)487-0150
Free: 866-434-2597
URL: http://www.ultracare-dialysis.com/
Dialysis Stations: 12. **Formerly:** Renal Care Group.

Maricopa

22651 ■ Renal Care Group--AK-Chin Dialysis Facility
16536 N Maricopa Rd.
Maricopa, AZ 85239
Free: 866-434-2597
URL: http://www.ultracare-dialysis.com/
Dialysis Stations: 12. **Formerly:** Renal Care Group.

Mesa

22652 ■ DaVita Central Mesa Dialysis Center
1134 E University Dr., Ste. 101
Mesa, AZ 85203
Ph: (480)464-3851
Free: 800-424-6589
URL: http://www.davita.com
Dialysis Stations: 24.

22653 ■ DaVita Mountain Vista Dialysis Center
10238 E Hampton Ave., Ste. 108
Mesa, AZ 85209
Ph: (480)357-0366
Free: 800-424-6589
URL: http://www.davita.com
Dialysis Stations: 24.

22654 ■ Diversified Specialty Institutes Mesa Dialysis Center
1337 S Gilbert Rd., Ste. 109
Mesa, AZ 85204
Ph: (480)926-1906
URL: http://www.dsi-corp.com
Dialysis Stations: 16.

22655 ■ Diversified Specialty Institutes Southwest Mesa Dialysis Center
1457 W Southern Ave., Ste. D-19
Mesa, AZ 85202
Ph: (480)894-5411
URL: http://www.dsi-corp.com
Dialysis Stations: 24.

22656 ■ Fresenius Medical Care--East Valley
135 S Power Rd., No. 103
Mesa, AZ 85206
Free: 866-434-2597
URL: http://www.ultracare-dialysis.com/
Dialysis Stations: 36. **Formerly:** RCG-East Valley.

22657 ■ Fresenius Medical Care Mesa
1337 S Gilbert Rd., Ste. 106
Mesa, AZ 85204
Ph: (480)926-9222
Free: 866-434-2597
URL: http://www.ultracare-dialysis.com/
Dialysis Stations: 1. **Formerly:** RCG--Home Dialysis of Mesa.

22658 ■ Fresenius Medical Care--Red Mountain Dialysis Services
1211 N Country Club Dr., Ste. A-4
Mesa, AZ 85201
Ph: (480)833-7440
Free: 866-434-2597
URL: http://www.ultracare-dialysis.com/
Dialysis Stations: 13.

Miami

22659 ■ Fresenius Medical Care--Globe Dialysis Facility
2250 US Hwy. 60, Ste. O-2
Miami, AZ 85539
Ph: (928)425-2624
Free: 866-434-2597
URL: http://www.ultracare-dialysis.com/
Dialysis Stations: 16. **Formerly:** Renal Care Group.

Nogales

22660 ■ DaVita--Nogales Dialysis Center
1231 W Target Range Rd.
Nogales, AZ 85621
Ph: (520)287-6597
Free: 800-424-6589
URL: http://www.davita.com
Dialysis Stations: 13. **Formerly:** Gambro Healthcare.

Parker

22661 ■ Fresenius Medical Care--Parker Dialysis Center
Agency Rd.
Parker, AZ 85344
Free: 866-434-2597
URL: http://www.ultracare-dialysis.com/
Dialysis Stations: 10. **Formerly:** BMA of Parker.

Payson

22662 ■ DaVita Rim Country
809 W Longhorn Rd., Ste. E
Payson, AZ 85541
Ph: (928)474-7000
Free: 800-424-6589
URL: http://www.davita.com
Dialysis Stations: 6.

Peoria

22663 ■ Fresenius Medical Care Phoenix Artificial Kidney Center
13090 N 94th Dr., Ste. 100
Peoria, AZ 85381
Free: 866-434-2597
URL: http://www.ultracare-dialysis.com/
Dialysis Stations: 21.

Peridot

22664 ■ Fresenius Medical Care--San Carlos
PO Box 748
Peridot, AZ 85542
Ph: (928)475-5987
Free: 866-434-2597
URL: http://www.ultracare-dialysis.com/
Dialysis Stations: 16. **Formerly:** Renal Care Group.

Phoenix

22665 ■ Banner Good Samaritan Transplant Services Banner Health
1300 N 12th St., Ste. 404
Phoenix, AZ 85006
Ph: (602)839-7000
URL: http://www.bannerhealth.com

22666 ■ DaVita--Estrella
8410 W Thomas Rd., Bldg. 1, Ste. 100
Phoenix, AZ 85037
Ph: (623)247-0808
Free: 800-424-6589
URL: http://www.davita.com
Dialysis Stations: 24. **Formerly:** Southwest Kidney Institute.

22667 ■ DaVita Maryvale Dialysis Center
4845 W McDowell Rd., Ste. 10A
Phoenix, AZ 85035
Ph: (602)278-8349
Free: 800-424-6589
URL: http://www.davita.com
Dialysis Stations: 24.

22668 ■ DaVita--Papago Dialysis Center
1401 N 24th St., Ste. 2
Phoenix, AZ 85008
Ph: (602)392-0668
Free: 800-424-6589
URL: http://www.davita.com
Dialysis Stations: 6.

22669 ■ DaVita--Phoenix
337 E Coronado Rd., Ste. 101
Phoenix, AZ 85004
Ph: (602)253-9006
Free: 800-424-6589
URL: http://www.davita.com
Dialysis Stations: 24. **Formerly:** Southwest Kidney Institute.

22670 ■ DaVita Raven Dialysis Center
3540 E Baseline Rd., Ste. 110
Phoenix, AZ 85042
Ph: (602)431-2110
Free: 800-424-6589
URL: http://www.davita.com

22671 ■ Diversified Specialty Institutes Northeast Phoenix Dialysis Center
3305 E Greenway Rd., Ste. 1
Phoenix, AZ 85032
Ph: (602)765-3919
URL: http://www.dsi-corp.com
Dialysis Stations: 16.

22672 ■ Diversified Specialty Institutes South Phoenix Dialysis Center
4621 S Central Ave.
Phoenix, AZ 85040
Ph: (602)304-1977
URL: http://www.dsi-corp.com
Dialysis Stations: 20.

22673 ■ Fresenius Medical Care Arcadia Dialysis Center
2702 N 44th St., Ste. 107B
Phoenix, AZ 85008
Ph: (602)955-7475
Free: 866-434-2597
URL: http://www.ultracare-dialysis.com/
Dialysis Stations: 12.

22674 ■ Fresenius Medical Care--Awhatukee
4629 E Chandler Blvd., Ste. 100
Phoenix, AZ 85048
Ph: (480)785-2270
Free: 866-434-2597
URL: http://www.ultracare-dialysis.com/
Dialysis Stations: 16. **Formerly:** Renal Care Group.

22675 ■ Fresenius Medical Care Central Phoenix Dialysis
3421 N 7th Ave.
Phoenix, AZ 85013
Free: 866-434-2597
URL: http://www.ultracare-dialysis.com/
Dialysis Stations: 16.

22676 ■ Fresenius Medical Care--Desert Valley Dialysis
15846 N Cave Creek Rd., No. 2
Phoenix, AZ 85032
Free: 866-434-2597
URL: http://www.ultracare-dialysis.com/
Dialysis Stations: 16.

22677 ■ Fresenius Medical Care Dialysis Services of Deer Valley
21241 N 23rd Ave., Ste. 11
Phoenix, AZ 85027
Ph: (623)869-6089
Free: 866-434-2597
URL: http://www.ultracare-dialysis.com/
Dialysis Stations: 19.

22678 ■ Fresenius Medical Care--Estrella Dialysis Center
5546 W Roosevelt Rd., No. 1
Phoenix, AZ 85043
Ph: (602)352-0724

Free: 866-434-2597
URL: http://www.ultracare-dialysis.com/
Dialysis Stations: 22.

22679 ■ Fresenius Medical Care--Maryvale Dialysis Facility
4522 W Indian School Rd., Ste. B1-3
Phoenix, AZ 85031
Ph: (623)247-0695
Free: 866-434-2597
URL: http://www.ultracare-dialysis.com/
Dialysis Stations: 16. **Formerly:** Renal Care Group.

22680 ■ Fresenius Medical Care--North Phoenix Home
1957 W Dunlap Ave., Ste. 6C
Phoenix, AZ 85021
Ph: (602)943-1763
Free: 866-434-2597
URL: http://www.ultracare-dialysis.com/
Dialysis Stations: 19.

22681 ■ Fresenius Medical Care--South Mountain Dialysis Center
26 E Baseline Rd., Ste. 142
Phoenix, AZ 85040
Ph: (602)268-8158
Free: 866-434-2597
URL: http://www.ultracare-dialysis.com/
Dialysis Stations: 17.

22682 ■ Fresenius Medical Care--South Phoenix Dialysis Services
1021 S 7th Ave., Ste. 108
Phoenix, AZ 85007
Free: 866-434-2597
URL: http://www.ultracare-dialysis.com/
Dialysis Stations: 18.

22683 ■ Maricopa Medical Center Dialysis Center
2525 E Roosevelt
Phoenix, AZ 85008
Ph: (602)344-1601
URL: http://www.mihs.org/about-us/
Dialysis Stations: 10.

22684 ■ Mayo Clinic Hospital--Kidney Transplant--Phoenix
5777 E Mayo Blvd.
Phoenix, AZ 85054
Ph: (480)342-1233
URL: http://www.mayoclinic.org/mchospital-sct/
Dialysis Stations: 0.

22685 ■ Phoenix Children's Hospital Dialysis Center
1920 E Cambridge Rd., Ste. 102
Phoenix, AZ 85016
Ph: (602)546-3220
URL: http://www.phoneixchildrens.com/medical-specialties/nephrology.html
Dialysis Stations: 6.

22686 ■ Phoenix Children's Hospital Renal Transplant Center
1919 E Thomas Road
Phoenix, AZ 85016
Ph: (602)546-0965
URL: http://www.phoenixchildrens.com/medical-specialties/transplant/
Dialysis Stations: 0.

Polacca

22687 ■ DaVita--Hopi Dialysis Center
PO Box 964
Polacca, AZ 86042
Ph: (928)737-5490
Free: 800-424-6589
URL: http://www.davita.com
Dialysis Stations: 11.

Prescott

22688 ■ Diversified Specialty Institutes--Prescott
980 Willow Creek Rd., No. 101
Prescott, AZ 86301
Ph: (928)776-9459
URL: http://www.dsi-corp.com
Dialysis Stations: 12. **Formerly:** RCG--Prescott.

22689 ■ Yavapai Dialysis Fresenius Medical Care
3605 Ranch Dr.
Prescott, AZ 86303
Free: 866-434-2597
URL: http://www.ultracare-dialysis.com/
Dialysis Stations: 9.

Queen Creek

22690 ■ Fresenius Medical Care Southeast Valley Dialysis
22715 S Ellsworth Rd., Bldg. D
Queen Creek, AZ 85142
Ph: (480)677-2463
Free: 866-434-2597
URL: http://www.ultracare-dialysis.com/
Dialysis Stations: 16. **Formerly:** Renal Care Group.

Sacaton

22691 ■ Gila River Dialysis East
565 W Seed Farm Rd.
Sacaton, AZ 85247
Ph: (602)271-7901
URL: http://www.grhc.org/getpage.php?name=clinics
Dialysis Stations: 40.

Safford

22692 ■ Fresenius Medical Care--Safford Dialysis Facility
1250 S 20th Ave.
Safford, AZ 85546
Ph: (928)428-1400
Free: 866-434-2597
URL: http://www.ultracare-dialysis.com/
Dialysis Stations: 16. **Formerly:** Renal Care Group.

Scottsdale

22693 ■ Camelback Dialysis Center DaVita
7321 E Osborn Dr.
Scottsdale, AZ 85251
Ph: (480)970-0924
Free: 800-424-6589
URL: http://www.davita.com
Dialysis Stations: 8.

22694 ■ DaVita--Desert Mountain Dialysis
9220 E Mountain View, Ste. 105
Scottsdale, AZ 85258
Ph: (480)391-2241
Free: 800-424-6589
URL: http://www.davita.com
Dialysis Stations: 24.

22695 ■ DaVita--Scottsdale Dialysis Center
4725 N Scottsdale Rd., Ste. 100
Scottsdale, AZ 85251
Ph: (480)994-1445
Free: 800-424-6589
URL: http://www.davita.com
Dialysis Stations: 30.

22696 ■ Fresenius Medical Care--North Scottsdale Dialysis Facility
16101 N 82nd St., Ste. 6-7
Scottsdale, AZ 85260
Ph: (480)607-2953
Free: 866-434-2597
URL: http://www.ultracare-dialysis.com/
Dialysis Stations: 13. **Formerly:** Bio Medical Applications of Scottsdale.

22697 ■ Fresenius Medical Care - Salt River Dialysis Center
10301 E Osborn Rd., Bldg. 14
Scottsdale, AZ 85256
Ph: (480)362-1044
Free: 866-434-2597
URL: http://www.ultracare-dialysis.com/
Dialysis Stations: 16. **Formerly:** Renal Care Group.

22698 ■ Fresenius Medical Care - Scottsdale
1495 N Hayden, Ste. D1-D4
Scottsdale, AZ 85257
Ph: (480)949-7844
Free: 866-434-2597
URL: http://www.ultracare-dialysis.com/
Dialysis Stations: 12. **Formerly:** Renal Care Group.

Sells

22699 ■ DaVita--Sells
PO Box 3030
Sells, AZ 85634
Ph: (520)383-1701
Free: 800-424-6589
URL: http://www.davita.com
Dialysis Stations: 20. **Formerly:** Gambro Healthcare Sells.

Show Low

22700 ■ Fresenius Medical Care--Show Low Dialysis Facility
1500 S White Mountain Blvd., No. 204
Show Low, AZ 85901
Ph: (928)532-8430
Free: 866-434-2597
URL: http://www.ultracare-dialysis.com/
Dialysis Stations: 12. **Formerly:** Renal Care Group.

Sierra Vista

22701 ■ Sierra Vista Dialysis DaVita
629 N Hwy. 90, Ste. 6,7
Sierra Vista, AZ 85635
Free: 800-424-6589
URL: http://www.davita.com
Dialysis Stations: 20.

Sun City

22702 ■ DaVita--Palm Brook Dialysis Center
14664 N Del Webb Blvd.
Sun City, AZ 85351
Ph: (623)583-6550
Free: 800-424-6589
URL: http://www.davita.com
Dialysis Stations: 20.

22703 ■ Desert Dialysis Services Inc.--Sun City
13000 N 103rd Ave., Ste. 66
Sun City, AZ 85351
Ph: (623)583-3131
Dialysis Stations: 20.

22704 ■ Fresenius Medical Care--Sun City Dialysis Facility
10050 W Bell Rd., Ste. 29-31
Sun City, AZ 85351
Ph: (623)815-1770
Free: 866-434-2597
URL: http://www.ultracare-dialysis.com/
Dialysis Stations: 12. **Formerly:** Renal Care Group.

Sun City West

22705 ■ DaVita Westbrook Dialysis
13907 W Camino Del Sol
Sun City West, AZ 85375
Ph: (623)214-7088
Free: 800-424-6589
URL: http://www.davita.com
Dialysis Stations: 16.

22706 ■ Fresenius Medical Care - Granite Valley
14510 W Shumway Dr., Ste. 100
Sun City West, AZ 85375
Ph: (623)546-2718
Free: 866-434-2597
URL: http://www.ultracare-dialysis.com/
Dialysis Stations: 18.

Sun Lakes

22707 ■ Fresenius Medical Care--Sun Lakes Dialysis Facility
9666 E Riggs Rd., Ste. 143
Sun Lakes, AZ 85248
Ph: (480)883-1301
Free: 866-434-2597
URL: http://www.ultracare-dialysis.com/
Dialysis Stations: 16. **Formerly:** Renal Care Group.

Surprise

22708 ■ DaVita--Surprise
14674 W Mountain View Blvd.
Surprise, AZ 85374
Ph: (623)546-6120
Free: 800-424-6589
URL: http://www.davita.com
Dialysis Stations: 4.

22709 ■ Fresenius Medical Care--Sun City West Dialysis
12213 W Bell Rd., No. 110
Surprise, AZ 85374
Ph: (623)583-8865
Free: 866-434-2597
URL: http://www.ultracare-dialysis.com/
Dialysis Stations: 18.

Tempe

22710 ■ DaVita--Tempe
2149 E Warner Rd., Ste. 110
Tempe, AZ 85284
Ph: (480)610-6170
Free: 800-424-6589
URL: http://www.davita.com
Dialysis Stations: 24. **Formerly:** Southwest Kidney Dialysis.

22711 ■ Diversified Specialty Institutes Tempe Dialysis Center
8820 S Kyrene Rd.
Tempe, AZ 85284
Ph: (480)893-2299
URL: http://www.dsi-corp.com
Dialysis Stations: 12.

22712 ■ Fresenius Medical Care--Tempe Dialysis Facility
1449 W Southern Ave.
Tempe, AZ 85282
Ph: (480)967-6360
Free: 866-434-2597
URL: http://www.ultracare-dialysis.com/
Dialysis Stations: 20. **Formerly:** Renal Care Group.

Tuba City

22713 ■ DaVita--Tuba City Dialysis Unit
500 Edgewater Dr.
Tuba City, AZ 86045
Ph: (928)283-4525
Free: 800-424-6589
URL: http://www.davita.com
Dialysis Stations: 26.

Tucson

22714 ■ DaVita--Northwest Tucson
2945 W Ina Rd., Ste. 105
Tucson, AZ 85741
Ph: (520)797-0049
Free: 800-424-6589
URL: http://www.davita.com
Dialysis Stations: 18.

22715 ■ DaVita--Pasqua Yaqui Dialysis Center
7490 S Camino De Oeste
Tucson, AZ 85757
Ph: (520)879-6161
Free: 800-424-6589
Fax: (520)790-3174
URL: http://www.davita.com
Dialysis Stations: 13. **Formerly:** Gambro Healthcare.

22716 ■ DaVita Tucson Central Dialysis
2901 E Grant Rd.
Tucson, AZ 85716
Ph: (520)325-3408
Free: 800-424-6589
URL: http://www.davita.com
Dialysis Stations: 12.

22717 ■ DaVita--Tucson East Dialysis Center
6420 E Broadway, No. C-300
Tucson, AZ 85710
Ph: (520)790-2775
Free: 800-424-6589
URL: http://www.davita.com
Dialysis Stations: 27. **Formerly:** Gambro Healthcare.

22718 ■ DaVita--Tucson South Center
2024 E Irvington
Tucson, AZ 85714
Ph: (520)573-0200
Free: 800-424-6589
URL: http://www.davita.com
Dialysis Stations: 30. **Formerly:** Gambro Healthcare.

22719 ■ DaVita--Tucson South Dialysis Center
3662 S 16th Ave.
Tucson, AZ 85713
Ph: (520)882-9665
Free: 800-424-6589
URL: http://www.davita.com
Dialysis Stations: 30. **Formerly:** Gambro Healthcare.

22720 ■ DaVita--Tucson West
1780 W Anklam Rd.
Tucson, AZ 85745
Free: 800-424-6589
URL: http://www.davita.com
Dialysis Stations: 34. **Formerly:** Gambro Healthcare.

22721 ■ Dialysis Clinic Inc.--Desert Dialysis Center
2022 E Prince Rd.
Tucson, AZ 85719
Ph: (520)327-0007
Fax: (520)806-0986
URL: http://www.dciinc.org
Dialysis Stations: 19.

22722 ■ Fresenius Medical Care Northwest Tucson Dialysis
6261 N La Cholla Blvd., Ste. 181
Tucson, AZ 85741
Ph: (520)297-1490
Free: 866-434-2597
URL: http://www.ultracare-dialysis.com/engine/
Dialysis Stations: 20.

22723 ■ Fresenius Medical Care--West Tucson
100 W Grant Rd.
Tucson, AZ 85705
Ph: (520)624-0266
Free: 866-434-2597
URL: http://www.ultracare-dialysis.com/engine/
Dialysis Stations: 24.

22724 ■ Midvale Park Dialysis Fresenius Medical Care
1430 Valencia Rd., Ste. 1
Tucson, AZ 85746
Free: 866-434-2597
URL: http://www.ultracare-dialysis.com/
Dialysis Stations: 24.

22725 ■ Rita Ranch Dialysis DaVita
7355 S Houghton Rd., Ste. 101
Tucson, AZ 85747
Free: 800-424-6589
URL: http://www.davita.com
Dialysis Stations: 12.

22726 ■ South Tucson Dialysis Fresenius Medical Care
2802 S 6th Ave.
Tucson, AZ 85713
Free: 866-434-2597
URL: http://www.ultracare-dialysis.com/
Dialysis Stations: 24.

22727 ■ UAHSC Transplant
PO Box 245003
Tucson, AZ 85724
Ph: (520)694-7365
Dialysis Stations: 0.

Whiteriver

22728 ■ Fresenius Medical Care--Whiteriver Dialysis Facility
102 W Hospital Dr.
PO Bpx 1899
Whiteriver, AZ 85941
Free: 866-434-2597
URL: http://www.ultracare-dialysis.com/
Dialysis Stations: 16. **Formerly:** Renal Care Group.

Winslow

22729 ■ Fresenius Medical Care--Winslow Dialysis Center Ltd.
1313 E 3rd St.
Winslow, AZ 86047
Ph: (928)289-3318
Free: 866-434-2597
URL: http://www.ultracare-dialysis.com/
Dialysis Stations: 9.

Yuma

22730 ■ DaVita--South Yuma Dialysis Center
7179 E 31st Place.
Yuma, AZ 85365
Free: 800-424-6589
URL: http://www.davita.com
Dialysis Stations: 20. **Formerly:** Gambro Healthcare.

22731 ■ DaVita--Yuma
2130 W 24th St.
Yuma, AZ 85364
Free: 800-424-6589
URL: http://www.davita.com
Dialysis Stations: 30. **Formerly:** Gambro Healthcare.

ARKANSAS

Benton

22732 ■ Arkansas Renal Systems Nephrology Associates, P.A.
1200 N Main, Ste. 2
Benton, AR 72222

Ph: (501)663-0490
Fax: (501)663-5948
URL: http://arkansasrenal.com/clinics.htm
Dialysis Stations: 12.

22733 ■ Fresenius Medical Care--Benton Dialysis Facility
2101 Congo Rd.
Benton, AR 72015
Ph: (501)776-1418
Free: 866-434-2597
URL: http://www.ultracare-dialysis.com/
Dialysis Stations: 16. **Formerly:** Renal Care Group.

Bentonville

22734 ■ Benton County Dialysis Center
801 SE Plaza Ave., Ste. 1
Bentonville, AR 72712
Ph: (479)273-7340
URL: http://www.wregional.com/body.cfm?id=458
Dialysis Stations: 17

22735 ■ Benton County Dialysis & PD Center
1104 SE 30th St.
Bentonville, AR 72712
Ph: (479)657-6220
Dialysis Stations: 17.

22736 ■ DaVita--Bentonville
1104 SE 30th St.
Bentonville, AR 72712
Ph: (479)657-6229
Free: 800-424-6589
URL: http://www.davita.com
Dialysis Stations: 21. **Formerly:** Kidney Centers.

Blytheville

22737 ■ Fresenius Medical Care--Blytheville Dialysis Facility
1001 E Moultrie
Blytheville, AR 72315
Free: 866-434-2597
URL: http://www.ultracare-dialysis.com/
Dialysis Stations: 15.

Camden

22738 ■ Arkansas Nephrology Services Ouachita Valley Kidney Center
1114 Washington NW
Camden, AR 71701
Ph: (870)837-1330
URL: http://www.arkneph.com/ovkc.html
Dialysis Stations: 29.

Conway

22739 ■ Arkansas Renal Systems Nephrology Associates, P.A.
824 N Creek Dr.
Conway, AR 72032
Ph: (501)327-1001
Fax: (501)327-2126
URL: http://arkansasrenal.com/
Dialysis Stations: 10. **Formerly:** Central Arkansas Dialysis.

22740 ■ Fresenius Medical Care--Conway
201 Skyline Dr., Ste. 32
Conway, AR 72032
Free: 866-434-2597
URL: http://www.ultracare-dialysis.com/
Dialysis Stations: 10. **Formerly:** RCG--Conway.

Crossett

22741 ■ Arkansas Nephrology Services Ashley Kidney Center Dialysis Facility
1019 Fred Lagrone Dr.
Crossett, AR 71635
Ph: (870)305-1225
URL: http://www.arkneph.com/akc.html
Dialysis Stations: 18.

El Dorado

22742 ■ Arkansas Nephrology Services South Arkansas Kidney Center--El Dorado Dialysis Facility
620 W Grove St.
El Dorado, AR 71730
Ph: (870)862-8788
Fax: (870)862-5756
URL: http://www.arkneph.com/sakc.html
Dialysis Stations: 34.

Fayetteville

22743 ■ DaVita - Fayetteville
509 E Millsap, Ste. 111
Fayetteville, AR 72703
Ph: (479)443-6688
Free: 800-424-6509
URL: http://www.davita.com
Dialysis Stations: 9. **Formerly:** Regional Kidney Centers.

22744 ■ North Hills Dialysis
107 E Monte Painter Dr.
Fayetteville, AR 72703
Ph: (479)463-7000
Fax: (479)587-8421
URL: http://www.wregional.com/body.cfm?id=458
Dialysis Stations: 19. **Formerly:** Fayetteville Dialysis Clinic.

Forrest City

22745 ■ Fresenius Medical Care--Saint Francis County Dialysis Services
210 Barrow Hill Rd.
Forrest City, AR 72335
Free: 866-434-2597
URL: http://www.ultracare-dialysis.com/
Dialysis Stations: 22.

Helena

22746 ■ Fresenius Medical Care--Helena
108 D Anna Pl.
Helena, AR 72342
Free: 866-434-2597
URL: http://www.ultracare-dialysis.com/
Dialysis Stations: 18. **Formerly:** Renal Care Group.

Hope

22747 ■ Hempstead County Dialysis Unit
1803 S Laurel
Hope, AR 71801
Ph: (870)777-4040
Dialysis Stations: 10.

22748 ■ Hope Dialysis Center
407 W 16th St.
Hope, AR 71801
Ph: (870)777-1700
Dialysis Stations: 11.

Hot Springs

22749 ■ Arkansas Nephrology Services Hot Springs Dialysis
1 Mercy Ln., Ste. 103
Hot Springs, AR 71913
Ph: (501)624-0153
URL: http://www.arkneph.com/hs.html
Dialysis Stations: 21.

22750 ■ Arkansas Nephrology Services Ouachita Regional Dialysis Center
1900 Malvern Ave., Ste. 102
Hot Springs, AR 71901
Ph: (501)624-0196
URL: http://www.arkneph.com/ordc.html
Dialysis Stations: 24.

22751 ■ Hot Springs Diagnostic Associates Arkansas Nephrology Services, Ltd.
1900 Malvern, Ste. 304
Hot Springs, AR 71901
Ph: (501)321-9803
URL: http://www.arkneph.com/centers.htm
Dialysis Stations: 20.

Jacksonville

22752 ■ Central Arkansas Dialysis--Jacksonville
202 John Hardin Dr.
Jacksonville, AR 72076
Ph: (501)982-2224
Fax: (501)982-4220
Dialysis Stations: 9. **Formerly:** Renal Systems Inc.

22753 ■ DaVita--Jacksonville Dialysis Centers of Arkansas
400 T. P. White Dr.
Jacksonville, AR 72076
Ph: (501)241-1300
Free: 800-424-6589
URL: http://www.davita.com
Dialysis Stations: 8.

Jonesboro

22754 ■ Saint Bernards Regional Medical Center Dialysis Center
540 E Washington
Jonesboro, AR 72401
Ph: (870)972-4477
URL: http://www.sbrmc.com/departments-services/clinical/dialysis-center/
Dialysis Stations: 22.

Little Rock

22755 ■ Arkansas Children's Hospital Outpatient Dialysis Clinic
1 Children's Way
Little Rock, AR 72202
Ph: (501)364-1100
URL: http://www.archildrens.org/

22756 ■ Arkansas Children's Hospital Transplant Center
1 Children's Way
Little Rock, AR 72202
Ph: (501)364-1813
URL: http://www.arkchildrens.org/about/special.asp#nephrology
Dialysis Stations: 4.

22757 ■ Baptist Health Med. Ctr. Dialysis Center
9601 I 630, Exit 7
Little Rock, AR 72205
Ph: (501)202-2364
URL: http://www.baptist-health.com/default.asp
Dialysis Stations: 9.

22758 ■ Baptist Health Medical Center Dialysis Facility
9601 I-630, Exit 7
Little Rock, AR 72205
Ph: (501)202-2364
URL: http://www.baptist-health.com
Dialysis Stations: 9.

22759 ■ DaVita - Little Rock Dialysis
5800 W 10th St., Ste. 510
Little Rock, AR 72204
Ph: (501)661-7930
Free: 800-424-6589
URL: http://www.davita.com
Dialysis Stations: 17. **Formerly:** DVA Renal Healthcare.

22760 ■ Fresenius Medical Care--Little Rock Dialysis
10310 W Markham, Ste. 100
Little Rock, AR 72205
Ph: (501)225-3890
Free: 866-434-2597
URL: http://www.ultracare-dialysis.com/
Dialysis Stations: 20. **Formerly:** Renal Care Group.

22761 ■ Midtown Dialysis Center
No. 2 Lile Court, Ste. 102
Little Rock, AR 72205
Ph: (501)221-3123
Dialysis Stations: 24.

22762 ■ St. Vincent Infirmary Dialysis Center
No. 2 St. Vincent Circle
Little Rock, AR 72205
Ph: (501)552-2140
URL: http://www.stvincenthealth.com
Dialysis Stations: 8.

22763 ■ University of Arkansas for Medical Sciences--Transplant Kidney/Nephrology
Transplant Surgery Slot 520-4
Little Rock, AR 72205
Ph: (501)686-6644
URL: http://www.uamshealth.com/kidney
Dialysis Stations: 0.

Magnolia

22764 ■ Southwest Arkansas Dialysis--Magnolia
225 N Dudney
Magnolia, AR 71753
Ph: (870)234-1322
Fax: (870)234-1366
Dialysis Stations: 9.

McCrory

22765 ■ Dialysis Clinic Inc.--McCrory
139 W Hwy. 64, Ste. 100
McCrory, AR 72101
Ph: (870)731-0220
Fax: (870)731-0223
URL: http://www.dciinc.org
Dialysis Stations: 9.

McGehee

22766 ■ US Renal Care Kidney Center of McGehee
610 W Holly St.
McGehee, AR 71654
Ph: (870)222-6700
Fax: (870)222-6203
URL: http://www.usrenalcare.com/
Dialysis Stations: 11.

Mena

22767 ■ Mena Dialysis Center Arkansas Nephrology Services
1200 Crestwood Cir.
Mena, AR 71953
Ph: (479)394-8085
Fax: (479)394-2164
URL: http://www.arkneph.com/mdc.html
Dialysis Stations: 16.

Monticello

22768 ■ Fresenius Medical Care--Monticello Dialysis Facility
774 Jordan Dr.
Monticello, AR 71655
Free: 866-434-2597
URL: http://www.ultracare-dialysis.com/
Dialysis Stations: 16. **Formerly:** Renal Care Group.

Mountain Home

22769 ■ RVM-Renal Center of Mountain Home
200 E 8th St., Ste. 101
Mountain Home, AR 72653
Ph: (870)508-6500
Fax: (870)508-6550
E-mail: info@renalventures.com
URL: http://www.renalventures.com/
Dialysis Stations: 20. **Formerly:** Baxter County Regional Medical Center.

Newport

22770 ■ Newport Dialysis Center
1912 McClain Pratt Sq.
Newport, AR 72112
Ph: (870)523-2607
Dialysis Stations: 9.

North Little Rock

22771 ■ Arkansas Nephrology Services Springhill Dialysis Center
Springhill Medical Plaza
3401 Springhill Dr., Ste. 190
North Little Rock, AR 72117
Ph: (501)945-3669
URL: http://www.arkneph.com/
Dialysis Stations: 17.

22772 ■ DaVita--North Little Rock
4505 E McCain Blvd.
North Little Rock, AR 72117
Ph: (501)945-2323
Free: 800-424-6589
URL: http://www.davita.com
Dialysis Stations: 12.

Paragould

22773 ■ US Renal Care of Northeastern Arkansas - Paragould
No. 1 Medical Plaza Dr., Ste. 201
Paragould, AR 72450
Ph: (870)215-0187
Fax: (871)215-5320
URL: http://www.usrenalcare.com
Dialysis Stations: 13.

Pine Bluff

22774 ■ Fresenius Medical Care--Jefferson County Dialysis Facility
2801 Olive St., Ste. 19
Pine Bluff, AR 71603
Ph: (870)534-2233
Free: 866-434-2597
URL: http://www.ultracare-dialysis.com/
Dialysis Stations: 22. **Formerly:** Renal Care Group.

22775 ■ US Renal Care Pine Bluff Dialysis Center
2302 W 28th, Ste. C
Pine Bluff, AR 71603
Ph: (870)534-7400
Fax: (870)541-0845
URL: http://www.usrenalcare.com
Dialysis Stations: 24. **Formerly:** USRC of Southeast Arkansas.

22776 ■ US Renal Care of SEA Pine Bluffs Dialysis
2302 W 28th St., Ste. C
Pine Bluff, AR 71603
Ph: (870)534-7400
Fax: (870)541-0845
URL: http://www.usrenalcare.com
Dialysis Stations: 24.

Russellville

22777 ■ Arkansas Nephrology Services River Valley Dialysis Center Dialysis Facility
3121 W 2nd Court
Russellville, AR 72801
Ph: (479)968-4687
URL: http://www.arkneph.com/rvkc.html
Dialysis Stations: 20.

Searcy

22778 ■ Central Arkansas Dialysis--Searcy
3208 Langley St.
Searcy, AR 72143
Ph: (501)268-4400
Dialysis Stations: 16. **Formerly:** Renal Systems Inc.

Siloam Springs

22779 ■ DaVita--Siloam Springs
500 S Mt. Olive St., Ste. 107
Siloam Springs, AR 72761
Free: 800-424-6589
Fax: (479)524-0769
URL: http://www.davita.com
Dialysis Stations: 8. **Formerly:** Siloam Springs Dialysis Center.

22780 ■ Dialysis Center of Siloam Springs
2125 E Main St., Ste. 12
Siloam Springs, AR 72761
Ph: (479)524-5214
URL: http://www.wregional.com/body.cfm?id=458
Dialysis Stations: 11.

Springdale

22781 ■ DaVita - Springdale
708 Quandt Ave.
Springdale, AR 72764
Free: 800-424-6589
Fax: (479)750-7059
URL: http://www.davita.com
Dialysis Stations: 16. **Formerly:** Regional Kidney Centers.

Stuttgart

22782 ■ Fresenius Medical Care--Stuttgart Dialysis Center
2202 S Main St.
Stuttgart, AR 72160
Ph: (870)673-8823
Free: 866-434-2597
URL: http://www.ultracare-dialysis.com/
Dialysis Stations: 16. **Formerly:** Renal Care Group.

22783 ■ US Renal Care of SEA
805 W Madison
Stuttgart, AR 72160
Ph: (870)673-0008
URL: http://www.usrenalcare.com
Dialysis Stations: 15.

Texarkana

22784 ■ Vamana Inc. in Texarkana
422 Beech St.
Texarkana, AR 71854
Ph: (870)773-1111
Dialysis Stations: 11.

West Memphis

22785 ■ Fresenius Medical Care--East Arkansas Dialysis Facility
310 S Rhodes
West Memphis, AR 72301
Free: 866-434-2597
URL: http://www.ultracare-dialysis.com/
Dialysis Stations: 25. **Formerly:** BMA of East Arkansas.

Wynne

22786 ■ Saint Bernard's - Wynne
310 S Falls Blvd.
Wynne, AR 72396
Ph: (870)208-1170
URL: http://www.stbernards.info/
Dialysis Stations: 6.

CALIFORNIA

Alhambra

22787 ■ Alhambra Community Dialysis Unit
2300 W Valley Blvd.
Alhambra, CA 91803
Ph: (626)458-4726
Dialysis Stations: 21.

22788 ■ San Gabriel Dialysis
Fresenius Medical Care
1801 W Valley Blvd., Ste. 102
Alhambra, CA 91803
Free: 866-434-2597
URL: http://www.ultracare-dialysis.com/
Dialysis Stations: 38.

22789 ■ San Gabriel Valley Peritoneal Dialysis
Fresenius Medical Care
1801 W Valley Blvd., Ste. 204
Alhambra, CA 91803
Free: 866-434-2597
URL: http://www.ultracare-dialysis.com/
Dialysis Stations: 6.

Anaheim

22790 ■ Anaheim Dialysis
DaVita
1107 W La Palma Ave.
Anaheim, CA 92801
Ph: (714)502-2400
Free: 800-424-6589
URL: http://www.davita.com
Dialysis Stations: 25. **Formerly:** Gambro.

22791 ■ Anaheim Hills Dialysis Center
4201 E La Palma Ave.
Anaheim, CA 92807
Ph: (714)996-2900
Dialysis Stations: 21.

22792 ■ Fresenius Medical Care--North Orange County
Dialysis Facility
511 N Brookhurst St., Ste. 100
Anaheim, CA 92801
Ph: (714)778-0488
Free: 866-434-2597
URL: http://www.ultracare-dialysis.com/
Dialysis Stations: 18.

Antioch

22793 ■ DaVita
Antioch Dialysis Center
3100 Delta Fair Blvd.
Antioch, CA 94509
Ph: (925)743-5000
Free: 800-424-6589
Fax: (925)753-5055
URL: http://www.davita.com
Dialysis Stations: 20.

22794 ■ Fresenius Medical Care--Buchanan Road, Antioch
Dialysis Facility
2386 Buchanan Rd.
Antioch, CA 94509
Ph: (925)756-2490
Free: 866-434-2597
URL: http://www.ultracare-dialysis.com/
Dialysis Stations: 15.

Apple Valley

22795 ■ Victor Valley Dialysis
DaVita
16049 Kamana Rd.
Apple Valley, CA 92307
Ph: (760)242-8311
Free: 800-424-6589
URL: http://www.davita.com
Dialysis Stations: 22. **Formerly:** Gambro.

Atwater

22796 ■ DaVita--Atwater
Dialysis Center
580 E Bellevue Rd.
Atwater, CA 95301
Ph: (209)357-3770
Free: 800-424-6589
URL: http://www.davita.com
Dialysis Stations: 10. **Formerly:** Gambro Healthcare.

Auburn

22797 ■ DaVita--Auburn
Dialysis Facility
3126 Professional Dr., No. 100
Auburn, CA 95603
Ph: (530)886-8221
Free: 800-424-6589
URL: http://www.davita.com
Dialysis Stations: 16. **Formerly:** Gambro Healthcare.

Azusa

22798 ■ Azusa Dialysis Center, LLC
312 N Azusa Ave.
Azusa, CA 91702
Ph: (626)633-1500
Dialysis Stations: 24.

Bakersfield

22799 ■ Bakersfield Dialysis Center
DaVita
5143 Office Park Dr.
Bakersfield, CA 93309
Ph: (661)325-4741
Free: 800-424-6589
URL: http://www.davita.com
Dialysis Stations: 76.

22800 ■ Brimhall Dialysis
DaVita
8501 Brimhall Rd., Bldg. 500
Bakersfield, CA 93311
Ph: (661)387-6603
Free: 800-424-6589
URL: http://www.davita.com
Dialysis Stations: 20.

22801 ■ Fresenius Medical Care--Bakersfield
8625 Liberty Pk. Dr., Ste. 102
Bakersfield, CA 93311
Free: 866-434-2597
URL: http://www.ultracare-dialysis.com/
Dialysis Stations: 25.

22802 ■ Northeast Bakersfield Dialysis
DaVita
3761 Mall View Rd.
Bakersfield, CA 93306
Ph: (661)872-9836
Free: 800-424-6589
URL: http://www.davita.com
Dialysis Stations: 12. **Formerly:** Gambro Healthcare.

22803 ■ Pegasus Dialysis, LLC
3101 Pegasus Dr., Ste. 100
Bakersfield, CA 93308
Ph: (661)615-4200
Dialysis Stations: 21.

22804 ■ White Lane Dialysis
DaVita
7701 White Ln., Ste. D
Bakersfield, CA 93309
Ph: (661)396-7158
Free: 800-424-6589
URL: http://www.davita.com
Dialysis Stations: 20. **Formerly:** Bakersfield South Dialysis.

Baldwin Park

22805 ■ Advanced Dialysis Center--Baldwin Park
3932 Downing Ave.
Baldwin Park, CA 91706
Ph: (626)856-3333
Dialysis Stations: 18.

22806 ■ Baldwin Park Medical Center
Peritoneal Dialysis Unit
Kaiser Permanente
1011 Baldwin Pk. Blvd.
Baldwin Park, CA 91706
Ph: (626)851-1011
URL: https://health.kaiserpermanente.org/wps/portal/facility/100167
Dialysis Stations: 2.

Banning

22807 ■ Banning Dialysis
DaVita
6090 W Ramsey St.
Banning, CA 92220
Ph: (951)845-4494
Free: 800-424-6589
URL: http://www.davita.com
Dialysis Stations: 16.

Barstow

22808 ■ Desert Cities Dialysis of Barstow
655 S 7th St.
Barstow, CA 92311
Ph: (760)256-3918
Dialysis Stations: 16.

Beaumont

22809 ■ Renal Advantage Inc.--Beaumont
1536 E 6th St.
Beaumont, CA 92223
Ph: (951)769-5072
URL: http://www.renaladvantage.com
Dialysis Stations: 24.

Bellflower

22810 ■ Bellflower Dialysis Center
DaVita
15736 Woodruff Ave.
Bellflower, CA 90706
Ph: (562)804-3099
Free: 800-424-6589
URL: http://www.davita.com
Dialysis Stations: 20.

22811 ■ Fresenius Medical Care - Bellflower
10116 Rosecrans Ave.
Bellflower, CA 90706
Ph: (562)920-2070
Free: 866-434-2597
URL: http://www.ultracare-dialysis.com/
Dialysis Stations: 36.

Benicia

22812 ■ Benicia Dialysis Center
DaVita
560 1st St., Bldg. D-103
Benicia, CA 94510
Ph: (707)745-1488
Free: 800-424-6589
URL: http://www.davita.com
Dialysis Stations: 14. **Formerly:** Vivra Renal Care.

Berkeley

22813 ■ Berkeley Dialysis Center DaVita
2920 Telegraph Ave.
Berkeley, CA 94705
Ph: (510)649-9870
Free: 800-424-6589
URL: http://www.davita.com
Dialysis Stations: 23. **Formerly:** Gambro Healthcare.

22814 ■ Fresenius Medical Care - Berkeley
2895 7th St.
Berkeley, CA 94710
Ph: (510)843-0627
Free: 866-434-2597
URL: http://www.ultracare-dialysis.com/
Dialysis Stations: 24.

Beverly Hills

22815 ■ Beverly Hills Dialysis Center DaVita
50 N La Cienega Blvd., Ste. 300
Beverly Hills, CA 90211
Ph: (310)289-1613
Free: 800-424-6589
URL: http://www.davita.com
Dialysis Stations: 30.

Bishop

22816 ■ Toiyabe Dialysis Center
44 Tu Su Ln.
Bishop, CA 93514
Ph: (760)873-7611
Dialysis Stations: 8.

Blythe

22817 ■ Fresenius Medical Care--Blythe Desert Dialysis Facility
737 W Hobson Way
Blythe, CA 92225
Ph: (760)922-4415
Free: 866-434-2597
URL: http://www.ultracare-dialysis.com/
Dialysis Stations: 13.

Brawley

22818 ■ Fresenius Medical Care--Brawley
751 Legion Rd., Ste. 100
Brawley, CA 92227
Ph: (760)344-3766
Free: 866-434-2597
URL: http://www.ultracare-dialysis.com/
Dialysis Stations: 20.

Brea

22819 ■ Brea Dialysis Center DaVita
595 Tamarack, Ste. A & B
Brea, CA 92821
Ph: (714)990-0110
Free: 800-424-6589
URL: http://www.davita.com
Dialysis Stations: 21.

Brentwood

22820 ■ Fresenius Medical Care of Brentwood
4510 O'Hara Ave., Ste. B
Brentwood, CA 94513
Ph: (925)513-7135
Free: 866-434-2597
URL: http://www.ultracare-dialysis.com/
Dialysis Stations: 18.

Burbank

22821 ■ DaVita--Burbank Dialysis Center
1211 N San Fernando Rd.
Burbank, CA 91504
Ph: (818)842-5576
Free: 800-424-6589
Fax: (818)845-4299
URL: http://www.davita.com
Dialysis Stations: 24. **Formerly:** Gambro.

22822 ■ Fresenius Medical Care Burbank Dialysis
2031 Alameda Ave., Ste. 202
Burbank, CA 91506
Ph: (818)845-3830
Free: 866-434-2597
URL: http://www.ultracare-dialysis.com/
Dialysis Stations: 21.

Burlingame

22823 ■ Burlingame Dialysis Center
1720 El Camino Real, Ste. 12
Burlingame, CA 94010
Ph: (650)696-3680
Dialysis Stations: 13.

Calexico

22824 ■ Fresenius Medical Care--Calexico Desert Dialysis Facility
408 E 3rd St., Ste. A
Calexico, CA 92231
Ph: (760)357-2400
Free: 866-434-2597
URL: http://www.ultracare-dialysis.com/
Dialysis Stations: 18.

Camarillo

22825 ■ DaVita--Dialysis Center of Camarillo
2438 N Ponderosa Dr., Ste. C-101
Camarillo, CA 93010
Ph: (805)764-0171
Dialysis Stations: 18.

22826 ■ Fresenius Medical Care--Camarillo Dialysis Center
3801 Las Posas Rd., Ste. 103
Camarillo, CA 93010
Ph: (805)388-2449
Free: 866-434-2597
URL: http://www.ultracare-dialysis.com/
Dialysis Stations: 15.

Canyon Country

22827 ■ Canyon Country Dialysis Center, LLC
18520 Via Princessa, Bldg. C-1
Canyon Country, CA 91387
Ph: (661)298-5300
Dialysis Stations: 15.

Carmichael

22828 ■ Manzanita Dialysis Center DaVita
4005 Manzanita Ave., Ste. 17 & 18
Carmichael, CA 95608
Ph: (916)483-3241
Free: 800-424-6589
URL: http://www.davita.com
Dialysis Stations: 21.

Carson

22829 ■ Carson Artificial Kidney Center, LLC
1309 E Carson St.
Carson, CA 90745
Ph: (310)513-1427
Dialysis Stations: 16.

22830 ■ Fresenius Medical Care - Carson
20710 S Leapwood Ave., Ste. F
Carson, CA 90746
Ph: (310)323-8997
Free: 866-434-2597
URL: http://www.ultracare-dialysis.com/
Dialysis Stations: 11.

Ceres

22831 ■ DaVita--Ceres
1768 Mitchell Rd., Ste. 308
Ceres, CA 95307
Ph: (209)538-9853
Free: 800-424-6589
URL: http://www.davita.com
Dialysis Stations: 12.

Cerritos

22832 ■ Cerritos Dialysis Center, LLC
19222 Pioneer Blvd., Ste. 101
Cerritos, CA 90703
Ph: (562)924-9990
Dialysis Stations: 21.

Chico

22833 ■ Chico Dialysis Center DaVita
530 Cohasset Rd.
Chico, CA 95926
Ph: (530)895-8966
Free: 800-424-6589
URL: http://www.davita.com
Dialysis Stations: 20.

22834 ■ RAI Ceres Ave Chico Renal Advantage, Inc.
3011 Ceres Ave.
Chico, CA 95926
Ph: (530)343-5279
URL: http://www.renaladvantage.com
Dialysis Stations: 20. **Formerly:** Gambro Healthcare of Chico.

22835 ■ Renal Advantage Inc. Care Centers--Chico
3011 Ceres Ave., Ste. 125
Chico, CA 95973
Ph: (530)343-5279
URL: http://www.renaladvantage.com
Dialysis Stations: 20.

22836 ■ South Chico Dialysis Center DaVita
2345 Forest Ave.
Chico, CA 95928
Ph: (530)894-2180
Free: 800-424-6589
URL: http://www.davita.com
Dialysis Stations: 18.

Chino

22837 ■ DaVita--Chino Dialysis Facility
4445 Riverside Dr.
Chino, CA 91710
Ph: (909)464-0347
Free: 800-424-6589
URL: http://www.davita.com
Dialysis Stations: 24. **Formerly:** Gambro.

Chula Vista

22838 ■ Fresenius Medical Care--Balboa--Marina Bay
630 Bay Blvd., Ste. 101
Chula Vista, CA 91910
Free: 866-434-2597
URL: http://www.ultracare-dialysis.com/
Dialysis Stations: 31.

22839 ■ Fresenius Medical Care--Marina Bay
Fresenius Medical Care
630 Bay Blvd., Ste. 101
Chula Vista, CA 91910
Ph: (619)420-6725
Free: 866-434-2597
URL: http://www.fmcna.com/fmcna/index.htm
Dialysis Stations: 31. **Formerly:** Gambro.

22840 ■ Home Dialysis Therapies of San Diego - South
678 3rd Ave., Ste. 210
Chula Vista, CA 91910
Ph: (619)422-0003
URL: http://www.homedialysistherapies.com
Dialysis Stations: 1.

22841 ■ RAI--Broadway--Chula Vista
Renal Advantage Inc.
1181 Broadway, Ste. 5
Chula Vista, CA 91911
Ph: (619)585-0016
URL: http://www.renaladvantage.com
Dialysis Stations: 30. **Formerly:** DaVita--Mission Dialysis Center of Chula Vista.

22842 ■ Renal Advantage Inc. Care Centers--Broadway--Chula Vista
1181 Broadway, Ste. 5
Chula Vista, CA 91911
Ph: (619)585-0016
URL: http://www.renaladvantage.com
Dialysis Stations: 30.

Citrus Heights

22843 ■ Antelope Dialysis Center
DaVita
6406 Tupelo Dr., Ste. A
Citrus Heights, CA 95621
Ph: (916)721-1800
Free: 800-424-6589
URL: http://www.davita.com
Dialysis Stations: 12.

City of Industry

22844 ■ Mohan Dialysis Center of Industry
15757 E Valley Blvd.
City of Industry, CA 91744
Ph: (626)333-3801
Dialysis Stations: 32.

Clearlake

22845 ■ Clearlake Dialysis Center
DaVita
14400 Olympic Dr.
Clearlake, CA 95422
Ph: (707)994-9785
Free: 800-424-6589
URL: http://www.davita.com
Dialysis Stations: 12.

Clovis

22846 ■ Community Dialysis Center--Clovis
685 Medical Center Dr. W, No. 105X
Clovis, CA 93611
Ph: (559)324-4030
URL: http://www.communitymedical.org/137.htm
Dialysis Stations: 12.

Colton

22847 ■ Arrowhead Regional Medical Center
400 N Pepper Ave.
Colton, CA 92324
Ph: (909)580-3911
URL: http://www.arrowheadmedcenter.org
Dialysis Stations: 8.

22848 ■ Renal Advantage Inc.--Colton
1275 West C St.
Colton, CA 92324
Ph: (909)430-0930
URL: http://www.renaladvantage.com
Dialysis Stations: 20. **Formerly:** Gambro.

Colusa

22849 ■ Colusa Indian Health Clinic Dialysis
3710 Hwy. 45, Ste. A
Colusa, CA 95932
Ph: (530)458-3707
URL: http://www.colusa-nsn.gov/Health-Clinic/Health-Clinic.html
Dialysis Stations: 6.

Compton

22850 ■ Mobile Dialysis Services, Inc.--Compton
801 W Compton Blvd.
Compton, CA 90220
Ph: (310)637-9026
Dialysis Stations: 36.

Concord

22851 ■ Concord Dialysis Center
DaVita
2300 Stanwell Dr., Ste. C
Concord, CA 94520
Ph: (925)677-7492
Free: 800-424-6589
URL: http://www.davita.com
Dialysis Stations: 21.

Corona

22852 ■ DaVita--Corona Dialysis Center
1820 Fullerton Ave., Ste. 180
Corona, CA 92881
Ph: (951)736-6660
Free: 800-424-6589
URL: http://www.davita.com
Dialysis Stations: 14. **Formerly:** California Kidney Center.

Costa Mesa

22853 ■ Costa Mesa Dialysis
DaVita
1590 Scenic Ave.
Costa Mesa, CA 92626
Ph: (714)540-9401
Free: 800-424-6589
URL: http://www.davita.com
Dialysis Stations: 24.

22854 ■ Costa Mesa Dialysis
DaVita
1590 Scenic Ave.
Costa Mesa, CA 92626
Free: 800-424-6589
URL: http://www.davita.com
Dialysis Stations: 24.

22855 ■ Newport Mesa Dialysis Services
Avantis Renal Therapy
1175 Baker St., Ste. B
Costa Mesa, CA 92626
Ph: (714)641-5808
URL: http://www.avantusrenaltherapy.com/
Dialysis Stations: 16.

Covina

22856 ■ Citrus Dialysis Center
315 N 3rd Ave., Ste. 104
Covina, CA 91723
Ph: (626)331-0133
Dialysis Stations: 22.

22857 ■ Mohan Dialysis Center of Covina
158 W College St.
Covina, CA 91723
Ph: (626)859-2522
Dialysis Stations: 18.

Cudahy

22858 ■ DaVita--Premier Dialysis Center
7612 Atlantic Ave.
Cudahy, CA 90201
Ph: (323)562-5511
Free: 800-424-6589
URL: http://www.davita.com
Dialysis Stations: 36.

Culver City

22859 ■ Fresenius Medical Care - Culver City Dialysis
9432 Venice Blvd.
Culver City, CA 90232
Ph: (310)836-2237
Free: 866-434-2597
URL: http://www.ultracare-dialysis.com/
Dialysis Stations: 24.

22860 ■ Intensive Renal Care
9808 Venice Blvd., Ste. 200
Culver City, CA 90232
Ph: (310)841-0500
Dialysis Stations: 18.

Cupertino

22861 ■ Satellite Dialysis
Cupertino Dialysis Center
10596 N Tantau Ave.
Cupertino, CA 95014
Ph: (408)517-5777
URL: http://www.satellitehealth.com/
Dialysis Stations: 42.

Daly City

22862 ■ Daly City Dialysis Center
DaVita
1498 Southgate Ave.
Daly City, CA 94015
Ph: (650)755-4751
Free: 800-424-6589
URL: http://www.davita.com
Dialysis Stations: 34. **Formerly:** Gambro Healthcare.

22863 ■ Westlake Daly City Dialysis Center
DaVita
2201 Junipero Sierra Blvd., Ste. A
Daly City, CA 94014
Free: 800-424-6589
URL: http://www.davita.com
Dialysis Stations: 24.

Delano

22864 ■ DaVita
Delano Dialysis
905 Main St.
Delano, CA 93215
Ph: (661)721-2483
Free: 800-424-6589
URL: http://www.davita.com
Dialysis Stations: 17.

Dixon

22865 ■ DaVita
Joy of Dixon Dialysis Center
1640 N Lincoln St.
Dixon, CA 95620
Ph: (707)693-8301
Free: 800-424-6589
URL: http://www.davita.com
Dialysis Stations: 11.

22866 ■ Dixon Dialysis Services--N Lincoln Street
125 N Lincoln St., Ste. B
Dixon, CA 95620
Ph: (707)678-6433
Dialysis Stations: 12.

Downey

22867 ■ DaVita--Downey Dialysis Center
8630 Florence Ave.
Downey, CA 90240
Ph: (562)923-6741
Free: 800-424-6589
URL: http://www.davita.com
Dialysis Stations: 19.

22868 ■ DaVita
Downey Landing Dialysis Center
11611 Bellflower Blvd.
Downey, CA 90241
Ph: (562)862-0001
Free: 800-424-6589
URL: http://www.davita.com
Dialysis Stations: 25.

22869 ■ Downey Regional Dialysis Center, LLC
8333 Iowa St., Ste. 100
Downey, CA 90241
Ph: (562)923-5901
Dialysis Stations: 21.

22870 ■ Kaiser Foundation Hospital Medical Center--Downey
Kaiser Permanente
CAPD Dept.--Basement
Downey, CA 90242
Ph: (562)657-9170
URL: https://www.kaiserpermanente.org/
Dialysis Stations: 6.

East Los Angeles

22871 ■ DaVita
Doctors Dialysis of East Los Angeles
950 S Eastern Ave.
East Los Angeles, CA 90022
Ph: (323)262-2229
Free: 800-424-6589
URL: http://www.davita.com
Dialysis Stations: 32.

22872 ■ East Los Angeles Dialysis Center
5830 E Whittier Blvd.
East Los Angeles, CA 90022
Ph: (323)887-8545
Dialysis Stations: 40.

22873 ■ Fresenius Medical Care--East Los Angeles
5220 E Telford
East Los Angeles, CA 90022
Ph: (323)269-2091
Free: 866-434-2597
URL: http://www.ultracare-dialysis.com/engine/

El Cajon

22874 ■ Fresenius Medical Care--East County Dialysis Center
570 N 2nd St.
El Cajon, CA 92021
Ph: (619)588-7500
Free: 866-434-2597
URL: http://www.ultracare-dialysis.com/
Dialysis Stations: 24.

22875 ■ Renal Advantage Inc.--Fletcher Parkway, El Cajon
858 Fletcher Pkwy.
El Cajon, CA 92020
Ph: (619)442-4122
URL: http://www.renaladvantage.com
Dialysis Stations: 22. **Formerly:** DaVita--Mission Dialysis Center of El Cajon.

El Centro

22876 ■ Fresenius Medical Care--El Centro Desert Valley Dialysis Center
110 S 5th St.
El Centro, CA 92243
Ph: (760)353-0353
Free: 866-434-2597
URL: http://www.ultracare-dialysis.com/
Dialysis Stations: 20.

22877 ■ Fresenius Medical Care--Imperial County
397 Ross Ave.
El Centro, CA 92243
Ph: (760)353-3323
Free: 866-434-2597
URL: http://www.ultracare-dialysis.com/
Dialysis Stations: 12.

22878 ■ Imperial Valley Home Therapies
Fresenius Medical Care
2205 W Ross Ave., Ste. 3
El Centro, CA 92243
Free: 866-434-2597
URL: http://www.ultracare-dialysis.com/
Dialysis Stations: 0.

El Cerrito

22879 ■ El Cerrito Dialysis Center
DaVita
10690 San Pablo Ave.
El Cerrito, CA 94530
Ph: (510)528-9590
Free: 800-424-6589
URL: http://www.davita.com
Dialysis Stations: 20. **Formerly:** Gambro Healthcare.

El Monte

22880 ■ DaVita--Rosemead Springs Dialysis
DaVita
3212 Rosemead Blvd.
El Monte, CA 91731
Ph: (626)280-2080
Free: 800-424-6589
URL: http://www.davita.com
Dialysis Stations: 16.

Elk Grove

22881 ■ Elk Grove Dialysis
DaVita
9281 Office Park Cir., No. 105
Elk Grove, CA 95758
Ph: (916)691-0480
Free: 800-424-6589
URL: http://www.davita.com
Dialysis Stations: 21.

22882 ■ RAI Elk Grove Blvd.
Renal Advantage Inc.
8139 Elk Grove Blvd., Ste. 200
Elk Grove, CA 95758
Ph: (916)478-3520
URL: http://www.renaladvantage.com
Dialysis Stations: 24. **Formerly:** Gambro Healthcare.

22883 ■ West Elk Grove Dialysis Center
DaVita
2208 Kausen Dr., Ste. 100
Elk Grove, CA 95758
Ph: (916)683-5992
Free: 800-424-6589
URL: http://www.davita.com
Dialysis Stations: 22.

Emeryville

22884 ■ Wellbound of Emeryville
Satellite Healthcare
2000 Powell St., Ste. 140
Emeryville, CA 94608
Ph: (510)985-9660
URL: http://www.satellitehealth.com/
Dialysis Stations: 4.

Encinitas

22885 ■ Encinitas Dialysis
DaVita
332 Santa Fe Dr., Ste. 100
Encinitas, CA 92024
Ph: (769)632-2323
Free: 800-424-6589
URL: http://www.davita.com
Dialysis Stations: 15. **Formerly:** Scripps Dialysis Center; Gambro Dialysis Center.

Encino

22886 ■ South Valley Dialysis
DaVita
17815 Ventura Blvd., Ste. 100
Encino, CA 91316
Ph: (818)757-4520
Free: 800-424-6589
URL: http://www.davita.com
Dialysis Stations: 25.

Escondido

22887 ■ DaVita--Escondido Home Training
635 E Grand Ave.
Escondido, CA 92025
Free: 800-424-6589
URL: http://www.davita.com
Dialysis Stations: 1. **Formerly:** Gambro.

22888 ■ Escondido Dialysis
DaVita
203 E 2nd Ave.
Escondido, CA 92025
Ph: (760)743-4401
Free: 800-424-6589
URL: http://www.davita.com
Dialysis Stations: 19. **Formerly:** Gambro.

Eureka

22889 ■ BMA Eureka
Fresenius Medical Care
2765 Timber Ridge Ln.
Eureka, CA 95503
Ph: (707)445-2033
Free: 866-434-2597
URL: http://www.ultracare-dialysis.com/
Dialysis Stations: 15.

Exeter

22890 ■ DaVita--Exeter
DaVita
1116 W Visalia Rd., Ste. 106
Exeter, CA 93221
Ph: (559)592-1025
Free: 800-424-6589
URL: http://www.davita.com
Dialysis Stations: 12.

Fairfield

22891 ■ Fairfield Dialysis Center
DaVita
4660 Central Way
Fairfield, CA 94534
Ph: (707)863-7369
Free: 800-424-6589
URL: http://www.davita.com
Dialysis Stations: 32.

22892 ■ RAI Chadbourne
Renal Advantage Inc.
490 Chadbourne Rd., Ste. D
Fairfield, CA 94534
Ph: (707)434-9088
URL: http://www.renaladvantage.com
Dialysis Stations: 21. **Formerly:** Gambro Healthcare Solano.

Fontana

22893 ■ Fontana Dialysis
DaVita
17950 Foothill Blvd.
Fontana, CA 92335
Ph: (909)356-9664
Free: 800-424-6589
URL: http://www.davita.com
Dialysis Stations: 28.

22894 ■ Kaiser Foundation Hospital Medical Center--Fontana
Kaiser Permanente
Peritoneal Dialysis Unit
9961 Sierra Ave.
Fontana, CA 92335
Ph: (909)427-4253
URL: http://www.kaiserpermanente.com
Dialysis Stations: 4.

22895 ■ RAI--Juniper Ave--Fontana
Renal Advantage Inc.
10557 Juniper Ave., Ste.
Fontana, CA 92337
Ph: (909)854-4336
URL: http://www.renaladvantageb.com
Dialysis Stations: 24.

Fort Bragg

22896 ■ Dialysis Clinic Inc.
Fort Bragg Dialysis
512 Cypress St.
Fort Bragg, CA 95437
Ph: (707)964-1610
URL: http://www.dciinc.org
Dialysis Stations: 10.

Foster City

22897 ■ Foster City Dialysis Center
DaVita
1261 E Hillside Blvd., Ste. 2
Foster City, CA 94404
Ph: (650)638-9301
Free: 800-424-6589
URL: http://www.davita.com
Dialysis Stations: 16.

Fountain Valley

22898 ■ Renal Advantage Inc.--Fountain Valley
Dialysis Center
17197 Newhope St., Stes. A-D
Fountain Valley, CA 92708
Ph: (714)241-0196
URL: http://www.renaladvantage.com
Dialysis Stations: 24. **Formerly:** Gambro.

Fremont

22899 ■ Fresenius Medical Care--Fremont
Dialysis Facility
39505 Paseo Padre Pkwy.
Fremont, CA 94538
Ph: (510)659-1240
Free: 866-434-2597
URL: http://www.ultracare-dialysis.com/
Dialysis Stations: 24.

Fresno

22900 ■ Ash Tree Dialysis
DaVita
2666 N Grove Industrial Dr., Ste. 106
Fresno, CA 93727
Free: 800-424-6589
URL: http://www.davita.com
Dialysis Stations: 36.

22901 ■ Community Dialysis Center
285 N Fresno St.
Fresno, CA 93701
Ph: (559)459-3901
Dialysis Stations: 23.

22902 ■ DaVita
Ash Tree Dialysis, PD & At Home
2666 N Grove Industrial Dr., Ste. 106
Fresno, CA 93727
Free: 800-424-6589
URL: http://www.davita.com
Dialysis Stations: 36. **Formerly:** Fresno Dialysis Clinic.

22903 ■ DaVita
Fresno At Home and PD Center
568 E Herndon Ave.
Fresno, CA 93720
Ph: (559)448-0127
Free: 800-424-6589
URL: http://www.davita.com

22904 ■ Fresno Dialysis Center
DaVita
1111 E Warner Ave.
Fresno, CA 93710
Ph: (559)439-1845
Free: 800-424-6589
URL: http://www.davita.com
Dialysis Stations: 26. **Formerly:** Gambro.

22905 ■ North Fresno Dialysis
Fresenius Medical Care
6737 N Willow, Bldg. C
Fresno, CA 93712
Free: 866-434-2597
URL: http://www.ultracare-dialysis.com/
Dialysis Stations: 20.

22906 ■ Palm Bluff Dialysis Center
DaVita
770 W Pinedale
Fresno, CA 93711
Ph: (559)438-8512
Free: 800-424-6589
URL: http://www.davita.com
Dialysis Stations: 25. **Formerly:** Gambro Healthcare.

22907 ■ San Joaquin Valley Dialysis Center
3636 N 1st St., No. 144
Fresno, CA 93726
Ph: (559)221-6311
Dialysis Stations: 22.

Fullerton

22908 ■ DaVita - Crossroads Dialysis Center
3214 Yorba Linda Blvd.
Fullerton, CA 92831
Ph: (714)577-6940
Free: 800-424-6589
URL: http://www.davita.com
Dialysis Stations: 24.

22909 ■ Fullerton Dialysis
Davita
238 Orangefair Mall Ave.
Fullerton, CA 92832
Ph: (714)447-3045
Free: 800-424-6589
URL: http://www.davita.com
Dialysis Stations: 25.

Garden Grove

22910 ■ RAI--Garden Grove Blvd.--Garden
Renal Advantage Inc.
12555 Garden Grove Blvd., Ste. 100
Garden Grove, CA 92843
Ph: (714)741-7255
URL: http://www.renaladvantage.com
Dialysis Stations: 13.

22911 ■ RAI-Harbor Blvd.--Garden Grove
Renal Advantage Inc.
12761 Harbor Blvd., Ste. 1-3
Garden Grove, CA 92840
Ph: (714)539-3122
URL: http://www.renaladvantage.com
Dialysis Stations: 26.

Gardena

22912 ■ Pacific Gateway Dialysis, LLC
Innovative Dialysis Systems
1149 W 190th St., Ste 1004
Gardena, CA 90248
Ph: (310)965-0830
URL: http://www.idsdialysis.com
Dialysis Stations: 21.

22913 ■ Pacific South Bay Dialysis Inc.
Beach Cities Dialysis--Gardena
1045 W Redondo Beach Blvd., Ste. 105
Gardena, CA 90247
Ph: (310)515 0788
URL: http://www.idsdialysis.com
Dialysis Stations: 17.

Gilroy

22914 ■ Satellite Dialysis--Gilroy
7800 Arroyo Circle, Ste. B
Gilroy, CA 95020
Ph: (408)848-5410
URL: http://www.satellitehealth.com/
Dialysis Stations: 24.

Glendale

22915 ■ Glendale Dialysis
DaVita
1000 E Palmer Ave.
Glendale, CA 91205
Ph: (818)241-6382
Free: 800-424-6589
URL: http://www.davita.com
Dialysis Stations: 22.

22916 ■ Glendale Kidney Center
Dialysis Facility
1427 S Glendale Ave.
Glendale, CA 91205
Ph: (818)662-0222
Dialysis Stations: 19.

22917 ■ North Glendale Dialysis
DaVita
1505 Wilson Terrace, Ste. 190
Glendale, CA 91206
Free: 800-424-6589
URL: http://www.davita.com
Dialysis Stations: 36.

Glendora

22918 ■ Mohan Dialysis Center of Glendora
638 S Glendora Ave.
Glendora, CA 91740
Ph: (626)914-5553
Dialysis Stations: 21.

22919 ■ RAI--Foothill Blvd.--Glendora
Renal Advantage Inc.
120 W Foothill Blvd.
Glendora, CA 91740
Ph: (626)335-7551
URL: http://www.renaladvantage.com
Dialysis Stations: 32. **Formerly:** DaVita.

Granada Hills

22920 ■ Kidney Care Center of the North Valley
16907 Devonshire Blvd.
Granada Hills, CA 91344
Ph: (818)366-4600
Fax: (818)366-4606
URL: http://www.idsdialysis.com
Dialysis Stations: 20.

Grass Valley

22921 ■ Grass Valley Dialysis Center
DaVita
360 Crown Point Circle, Ste. 210
Grass Valley, CA 95949
Ph: (530)477-0734
Free: 800-424-6589
URL: http://www.davita.com
Dialysis Stations: 8. **Formerly:** Sierra Hemodialysis.

Greenbrae

22922 ■ Satellite Dialysis--Greenbrae
Satellite Healthcare
565 Sir Francis Drake Blvd.
Greenbrae, CA 94904
Ph: (415)924-8622
URL: http://satellitehealth.com
Dialysis Stations: 23.

Hacienda Heights

22923 ■ Hacienda Dialysis Center
2020 S Hacienda Blvd., Ste. G
Hacienda Heights, CA 91745
Ph: (626)968-9558
Dialysis Stations: 20.

Hanford

22924 ■ Hanford At Home Dialysis
DaVita
900 N Douty St., Ste. A
Hanford, CA 93230
Ph: (559)587-9014
Free: 800-424-6589
URL: http://www.davita.com

22925 ■ Hanford Dialysis
DaVita
402 W Eighth St.
Hanford, CA 93230
Ph: (559)582-5462
Free: 800-424-6589
URL: http://www.davita.com
Dialysis Stations: 20.

Harbor City

22926 ■ Fresenius Medical Care - South Bay
1221 W Pacific Coast Hwy.
Harbor City, CA 90710
Ph: (310)539-1221
Free: 866-434-2597
URL: http://www.ultracare-dialysis.com/
Dialysis Stations: 25.

Hawthorne

22927 ■ DaVita--Sunrise Dialysis Center
13039 Hawthorne Blvd.
Hawthorne, CA 90250
Ph: (310)644-4087
Free: 800-424-6589
URL: http://www.davita.com
Dialysis Stations: 25.

Hayward

22928 ■ Hayward Dialysis Center
DaVita
21615 Hesperian Blvd., Ste. F
Hayward, CA 94541
Ph: (610)780-9094
Free: 800-424-6589
URL: http://www.davita.com
Dialysis Stations: 30.

22929 ■ Kaiser Hospital ESRD PD Unit
27303 Sleepy Hollow
Hayward, CA 94545
Ph: (510)784-2079
URL: http://www.kaiserpermanente.org
Dialysis Stations: 4.

22930 ■ South Hayward Dialysis Center
DaVita
254 Jackson St.
Hayward, CA 94544
Ph: (510)583-1255
Free: 800-424-6589
URL: http://www.davita.com
Dialysis Stations: 24.

Hemet

22931 ■ DaVita--Diamond Valley Dialysis Center
1030 E Florida Ave.
Hemet, CA 92543
Ph: (951)766-4581
Free: 800-424-6589
URL: http://www.davita.com
Dialysis Stations: 12. **Formerly:** Vivra Renal Care.

Hesperia

22932 ■ Hesperia Dialysis Center
DaVita
14135 Main St., Ste. 501
Hesperia, CA 92345
Ph: (760)947-7405
Free: 800-424-6589
URL: http://www.davita.com
Dialysis Stations: 20.

Huntington Beach

22933 ■ Huntington Beach Dialysis
DaVita
16892 Bolsa Chica Ave., Ste. 100
Huntington Beach, CA 92649
Ph: (714)846-2102
Free: 800-424-6589
URL: http://www.davita.com
Dialysis Stations: 10. **Formerly:** USHAWL, Inc.--Orange County Dialysis West; Gambro.

Indio

22934 ■ Kidney Institute of the Desert
81715 Dr. Carreon Blvd., Ste. B2
Indio, CA 92201
Ph: (760)347-8181
Dialysis Stations: 20.

22935 ■ RAI--Monroe--Indio
Renal Advantage Inc.
46-767 Monroe St., Ste. 101
Indio, CA 92201
Ph: (760)347-3986
URL: http://www.renaladvantage.com
Dialysis Stations: 18.

Inglewood

22936 ■ Airport Dialysis
DaVita
4632 W Century Blvd.
Inglewood, CA 90304
Ph: (310)677-4262
Free: 800-424-6589
URL: http://www.davita.com
Dialysis Stations: 28. **Formerly:** Gambro.

22937 ■ Angel Kidney Care of Inglewood, Inc.
994 S. La Brea Ave.
Inglewood, CA 90301
Ph: (310)671-2420
URL: http://www.angelkidneycare.com/
Dialysis Stations: 20.

22938 ■ Fresenius Medical Care--Inglewood Dialysis Facility
336 E Hillcrest Ave., Ste. 100
Inglewood, CA 90301
Ph: (310)673-3656
Free: 866-434-2597
URL: http://www.ultracare-dialysis.com/
Dialysis Stations: 21.

22939 ■ Fresenius Medical Care - West Los Angeles
301 N Prairie Ave., Ste. 100
Inglewood, CA 90301
Ph: (310)674-9640
Free: 866-434-2597
URL: http://www.ultracare-dialysis.com/
Dialysis Stations: 21.

22940 ■ Imperial Dialysis
DaVita
2738 W Imperial Hwy.
Inglewood, CA 90303
Ph: (323)779-5399
Free: 800-424-6589
URL: http://www.davita.com
Dialysis Stations: 30.

22941 ■ Inglewood Dialysis
DaVita
125 E Arbor Vitae
Inglewood, CA 90301
Ph: (310)677-6114
Free: 800-424-6589
URL: http://www.davita.com
Dialysis Stations: 41. **Formerly:** Gambro Healthcare.

22942 ■ RAI--Centinela--Inglewood
Renal Advantage Inc.
1416 Centinela Ave.
Inglewood, CA 90302
Ph: (310)673-6865
URL: http://www.renaladvantage.com
Dialysis Stations: 25. **Formerly:** DaVita--Pacific Coast Dialysis Center.

Irvine

22943 ■ RAI--Laguna Canyon--Irvine
Renal Advantage Inc.
16255 Laguna Canyon Rd.
Irvine, CA 92618
Ph: (949)727-4495
URL: http://www.renaladvantage.com
Dialysis Stations: 24. **Formerly:** DaVita.

Irwindale

22944 ■ Fresenius Medical Care--Irwindale
12711 Ramona Blvd., Ste. 111
Irwindale, CA 91706
Ph: (626)856-3944
Free: 866-434-2597
URL: http://www.ultracare-dialysis.com/
Dialysis Stations: 31.

King City

22945 ■ Mee Memorial Hospital-Dialysis
809 Broadway
King City, CA 93930
Ph: (831)385-6034
URL: http://www.meememorial.com
Dialysis Stations: 9.

La Harbra

22946 ■ Quotidian Dialysis
1055 E La Harbra Blvd., Ste. 6
La Harbra, CA 90631
Ph: (562)694-8520
URL: http://www.quotidiandialysis.org/
Dialysis Stations: 1.

La Mesa

22947 ■ Fresenius Medical Care Dialysis Center
5995 Severin Dr.
La Mesa, CA 91942

Ph: (619)462-9992
Free: 866-434-2597
URL: http://www.ultracare-dialysis.com/
Dialysis Stations: 24.

La Palma

22948 ■ La Palma Dialysis Center, LLC
5451 La Palma Ave., Ste. 35
La Palma, CA 90623
Ph: (714)523-5970
Dialysis Stations: 12.

La Puente

22949 ■ La Puente Dialysis Center
California Kidney Specialists
14557 Temple Ave.
La Puente, CA 91744
Ph: (626)917-1719
Fax: (626)917-2914
URL: http://www.californiakidneyspecialists.com/
Dialysis Stations: 24.

LaGrange

22950 ■ LaGrange Dialysis Clinic
140 Old Mill Rd.
LaGrange, CA 30241
Ph: (706)884-6825
Dialysis Stations: 22.

Laguna Hills

22951 ■ Saddleback Dialysis
DaVita
23141 Plaza Pointe Dr.
Laguna Hills, CA 92653
Ph: (949)588-9211
Free: 800-424-6589
URL: http://www.davita.com
Dialysis Stations: 25. **Formerly:** Gambro.

Lake Elsinore

22952 ■ DaVita--Lake Elsinore Dialysis Center
32291 Mission Tr.
Lake Elsinore, CA 92530
Ph: (951)674-5050
Free: 800-424-6589
URL: http://www.davita.com
Dialysis Stations: 18.

Lakeport

22953 ■ Lakeport Dialysis Center
DaVita
804 Eleventh St.
Lakeport, CA 95453
Ph: (707)263-7132
Free: 800-424-6589
URL: http://www.davita.com
Dialysis Stations: 12.

Lakewood

22954 ■ DaVita - Lakewood Dialysis Center
4611 Silva St.
Lakewood, CA 90712
Ph: (562)633-7441
Free: 800-424-6589
URL: http://www.davita.com
Dialysis Stations: 30.

Lancaster

22955 ■ DaVita
Antelope Valley Dialysis
1759 W Ave. J, Ste. 102
Lancaster, CA 93534
Ph: (661)942-6400
Free: 800-424-6589
URL: http://www.davita.com
Dialysis Stations: 30.

22956 ■ Fresenius Medical Care--Antelope Valley
44950 Valley Central Way, Ste. 108
Lancaster, CA 93536
Ph: (661)729-5680
Free: 866-434-2597
URL: http://www.ultracare-dialysis.com/
Dialysis Stations: 22.

Lincoln

22957 ■ RAI Lincoln Dialysis
Renal Advantage Inc.
Bldg. 11
811 Sterling Pkwy.
Lincoln, CA 95648
URL: http://www.renaladvantage.com
Dialysis Stations: 21.

Livermore

22958 ■ Livermore Dialysis Center
DaVita
3201 Doolan Rd., Ste. 175
Livermore, CA 94551
Free: 800-424-6589
URL: http://www.davita.com
Dialysis Stations: 24.

Lodi

22959 ■ Lodi Dialysis Center
DaVita
1610 W Kettleman Ln., Ste. D
Lodi, CA 95242
Ph: (209)334-9888
Free: 800-424-6589
Fax: (209)333-0888
URL: http://www.davita.com
Dialysis Stations: 21.

22960 ■ Tokay Dialysis Center
DaVita
312 S Fairmont Ave., Ste. A
Lodi, CA 95240
Ph: (209)369-5418
Free: 800-424-6589
URL: http://www.davita.com
Dialysis Stations: 12.

22961 ■ Tokay Home Dialysis Center
DaVita
777 S Ham Dr., Ste. L
Lodi, CA 95242
Ph: (209)333-8909
Free: 800-424-6589
URL: http://www.davita.com

Loma Linda

22962 ■ Loma Linda University Kidney Center
11375 Anderson St.
Loma Linda, CA 92354
Ph: (909)558-4225
URL: http://www.llu.edu
Dialysis Stations: 20.

22963 ■ Loma Linda University Medical Center
Childrens Hospital
11234 Anderson St., Rm. 4219
Loma Linda, CA 92354
Ph: (909)558-8218
URL: http://lomalindahealth.org
Dialysis Stations: 7.

Lomita

22964 ■ Pacific Dialysis Services Inc.
1830 Lomita Blvd.
Lomita, CA 90717
Ph: (310)530-7796
URL: http://www.idsdialysis.com
Dialysis Stations: 21.

Lompoc

22965 ■ Lompoc Artificial Kidney Center
Dialysis Facility
127 W Pine Ave.
Lompoc, CA 93436
Ph: (805)740-2000
Dialysis Stations: 18.

Long Beach

22966 ■ Bixby Knolls Dialysis
DaVita
3744 Long Beach Blvd.
Long Beach, CA 90807
Ph: (562)424-1403
Free: 800-424-6589
URL: http://www.davita.com
Dialysis Stations: 23.

22967 ■ DaVita--Long Beach
3111 Long Beach Blvd.
Long Beach, CA 90807
Ph: (562)426-5155
Free: 800-424-6589
URL: http://www.davita.com
Dialysis Stations: 26.

22968 ■ Fresenius Medical Care--Long Beach Dialysis Center
440 W Ocean Blvd.
Long Beach, CA 90802
Ph: (562)432-4444
Free: 866-434-2597
URL: http://www.ultracare-dialysis.com/
Dialysis Stations: 16.

22969 ■ Fresenius Medical Care--North Long Beach
145 W Victoria St.
Long Beach, CA 90805
Ph: (310)639-3122
Free: 866-434-2597
URL: http://www.ultracare-dialysis.com/
Dialysis Stations: 13.

22970 ■ Long Beach Dialysis Center
1045 Atlantic Ave., Ste. 108
Long Beach, CA 90813
Ph: (562)435-3637
URL: http://www.idsdialysis.com
Dialysis Stations: 24.

22971 ■ Long Beach Harbor (UCLA) Dialysis Center
DaVita
1075 E Pacific Coast Hwy.
Long Beach, CA 90806
Ph: (562)599-1511
Free: 800-424-6589
URL: http://www.davita.com
Dialysis Stations: 12.

22972 ■ Nephron Dialysis Center of Lakewood, LLC
5820 Downey Ave.
Long Beach, CA 90805
Ph: (562)663-0788
Dialysis Stations: 25.

22973 ■ West Coast Dialysis Center, LLC
3780 Kilroy Airport Way, Ste. 110
Long Beach, CA 90806
Ph: (562)989-3010
URL: http://www.idsdialysis.com
Dialysis Stations: 23.

Los Alamitos

22974 ■ Los Alamitos Hemodialysis Center
3810 Katella Ave.
Los Alamitos, CA 90720
Ph: (562)598-9527
Dialysis Stations: 32.

Los Angeles

22975 ■ Baldwin Hills Dialysis Center
3705 S La Brea Ave.
Los Angeles, CA 90016
Ph: (323)293-4488
Dialysis Stations: 17.

22976 ■ California Kidney Care Center
1400 S Grand Ave., Ste. 105
Los Angeles, CA 90015
Ph: (213)867-1111
Dialysis Stations: 20.

22977 ■ Century City Dialysis Center
DaVita
10630 Santa Monica Blvd.
Los Angeles, CA 90025
Free: 800-424-6589
URL: http://www.davita.com
Dialysis Stations: 25.

22978 ■ Children's Hospital of Los Angeles Dialysis and TX Program
Division of Nephrology
4650 Sunset Blvd., Box 40
Los Angeles, CA 90027
Ph: (323)361-2295
URL: http://www.childrenshospitalla.org
Dialysis Stations: 10.

22979 ■ DaVita
Carabello Dialysis Center
757 E Washington Blvd.
Los Angeles, CA 90021
Ph: (213)745-2860
Free: 800-424-6589
URL: http://www.davita.com
Dialysis Stations: 24.

22980 ■ DaVita--Crescent Heights Dialysis Center
8151 Beverly Blvd.
Los Angeles, CA 90048
Ph: (323)655-6226
Free: 800-424-6589
URL: http://www.davita.com
Dialysis Stations: 20.

22981 ■ DaVita--East Los Angeles Plaza Dialysis Facility
1700 Cesar Chavez Blvd., Ste. L100
Los Angeles, CA 90033
Ph: (323)261-0484
Free: 800-424-6589
URL: http://www.davita.com
Dialysis Stations: 33. **Formerly:** Gambro--White Memorial.

22982 ■ DaVita--Kenneth Hahn Plaza Dialysis Center
11854 S Wilmington Ave.
Los Angeles, CA 90059
Ph: (323)567-5077
Free: 800-424-6589
URL: http://www.davita.com
Dialysis Stations: 20.

22983 ■ DaVita--Los Angeles Dialysis Center
2250 S Western Ave.
Los Angeles, CA 90018
Ph: (323)733-2260
Free: 800-424-6589
URL: http://www.davita.com
Dialysis Stations: 17.

22984 ■ DaVita--Los Angeles Downtown Dialysis Facility
2021 S Flower St.
Los Angeles, CA 90007
Free: 800-424-6589
URL: http://www.davita.com
Dialysis Stations: 27. **Formerly:** Gambro.

22985 ■ DaVita--TRC--USC Kidney Center
2310 Alcazar St.
Los Angeles, CA 90033
Ph: (323)441-9966
Free: 800-424-6589
URL: http://www.davita.com
Dialysis Stations: 43. **Formerly:** Total Renal Care/University of Southern California Kidney Center.

22986 ■ DaVita--Washington Plaza Dialysis Center
516 E Washington Blvd.
Los Angeles, CA 90015
Ph: (213)749-2433
Free: 800-424-6589
URL: http://www.davita.com
Dialysis Stations: 24.

22987 ■ Florence Dialysis Center
351 W Florence Ave.
Los Angeles, CA 90003
Ph: (323)789-5690
URL: http://www.dialysisflorence.com/
Dialysis Stations: 32.

22988 ■ Fresenius Medical Care--Mid-Wilshire
3545 Wilshire Blvd., Ste. 100-103
Los Angeles, CA 90010
Ph: (213)382-8864
Free: 866-434-2597
URL: http://www.ultracare-dialysis.com/engine/
Dialysis Stations: 17.

22989 ■ Hollywood Dialysis Center
DaVita
5108 Sunset Blvd.
Los Angeles, CA 90027
Ph: (323)913-4010
Free: 800-424-6589
URL: http://www.davita.com
Dialysis Stations: 20.

22990 ■ Kaiser Foundation Hospital Medical Center--Sunset
Kaiser Permanente
Dialysis Unit
4700 Sunset Blvd., 2nd Fl.
Los Angeles, CA 90027
Ph: (323)783-4479
URL: http://www.kaiserpermanente.org
Dialysis Stations: 30.

22991 ■ Kaiser Foundation Hospital Medical Center--West Los Angeles
Kaiser Permanente
Acute Dialysis Center
6041 Cadillac Ave., Ste. 2-W
Los Angeles, CA 90034
Ph: (323)857-3245
URL: http://www.kaiserpermanente.org
Dialysis Stations: 3.

22992 ■ Kidney Center of Los Angeles
1125 W 6th St., Ste. 101
Los Angeles, CA 90017
Ph: (213)481-3041
URL: http://www.idsdialysis.com
Dialysis Stations: 22.

22993 ■ Los Angeles Community Dialysis South
1801 S La Cienega Blvd.
Los Angeles, CA 90035
Ph: (310)840-5688
Dialysis Stations: 20.

22994 ■ RAI--Compton--Los Angeles
Renal Advantage Inc.
11859 Compton Ave.
Los Angeles, CA 90059
Ph: (323)563-1140
URL: http://www.renaladvantage.com
Dialysis Stations: 25. **Formerly:** Gambro.

22995 ■ RAI--East Olympic--Los Angeles
Renal Advantage Inc.
5714 E Olympic Blvd.
Los Angeles, CA 90022
Ph: (323)887-0841
URL: http://www.renaladvantage.com
Dialysis Stations: 24.

22996 ■ Saint Vincent Dialysis Center, Inc.
201 S Alvarado St., Ste. 220
Los Angeles, CA 90057
Ph: (213)484-7425
Dialysis Stations: 17.

22997 ■ St. Vincent Medical Center--Renal TX
2200 W Third St., Ste. 500
Los Angeles, CA 90057
Ph: (213)484-5551
URL: http://www.stvincentmedicalcenter.com/Pages/default.aspx
Dialysis Stations: 0.

22998 ■ Tower Dialysis
DaVita
8635 W 3rd St., Ste. 560-W
Los Angeles, CA 90048
Ph: (310)855-1742
Free: 800-424-6589
URL: http://www.davita.com
Dialysis Stations: 25. **Formerly:** Gambro Healthcare.

22999 ■ UCLA Medical Center--Pediatrics, Renal TX
UCLA Health System
PO Box 951796
Los Angeles, CA 90095
Ph: (310)825-6836
URL: http://www.uclahealth.org/body.cfm?id=453&action=detail&limit_department=29&limit_division=1044&limit_program=0
Dialysis Stations: 0.

23000 ■ University Park Dialysis Center
DaVita
3986 S Figueroa St.
Los Angeles, CA 90037
Ph: (213)749-8297
Free: 800-424-6589
URL: http://www.davita.com
Dialysis Stations: 20.

23001 ■ USC University Hospital, Renal TX
1510 San Pablo St., HCC 200
Los Angeles, CA 90033
Ph: (323)442-5908
URL: http://www.uscuniversityhospital.org/uscuh/services/transplant-programs

23002 ■ Westside Dialysis Center
Innovative Dialysis Systems
300 S Robertson Blvd.
Los Angeles, CA 90048
Ph: (310)385-8683
URL: http://www.idsdialysis.com
Dialysis Stations: 24. **Formerly:** Gambro Healthcare.

23003 ■ Wilshire Dialysis Center
DaVita
1212 Wilshire Blvd.
Los Angeles, CA 90017
Ph: (213)482-5181
Free: 800-424-6589
URL: http://www.davita.com
Dialysis Stations: 19.

Los Banos

23004 ■ Los Banos Dialysis Center
DaVita
221 I St.
Los Banos, CA 93635
Ph: (209)826-7280

Free: 800-424-6589
URL: http://www.davita.com
Dialysis Stations: 11. **Formerly:** Gambro Healthcare.

Los Gatos

23005 ■ Fresenius Medical Care--Los Gatos
14651 S Bascom, Ste. 100
Los Gatos, CA 95032
Ph: (408)358-3791
Free: 866-434-2597
URL: http://www.ultracare-dialysis.com/
Dialysis Stations: 12.

Lynwood

23006 ■ DaVita--Imperial Care Dialysis Center
4345 E Imperial Hwy.
Lynwood, CA 90262
Ph: (310)900-0333
Free: 800-424-6589
URL: http://www.davita.com
Dialysis Stations: 31.

23007 ■ DaVita
Kidney Dialysis Care Unit
3600 E Martin Luther King Jr. Blvd.
Lynwood, CA 90262
Ph: (310)639-6320
Free: 800-424-6589
URL: http://www.davita.com
Dialysis Stations: 32.

Madera

23008 ■ DaVita
Almond Wood Dialysis Clinic
501 E Almond Ave.
Madera, CA 93637
Ph: (559)664-9252
Free: 800-424-6589
URL: http://www.davita.com
Dialysis Stations: 22.

Manteca

23009 ■ Manteca Dialysis Center
DaVita
1156 S Main St.
Manteca, CA 95337
Ph: (209)823-3078
Free: 800-424-6589
URL: http://www.davita.com
Dialysis Stations: 8. **Formerly:** Gambro Healthcare.

23010 ■ Yosemite Street Dialysis Center
DaVita
1650 W Yosemite Ave.
Manteca, CA 95337
Ph: (209)824-5552
Free: 800-424-6589
URL: http://www.davita.com
Dialysis Stations: 21.

Martinez

23011 ■ Kaiser Permanente--Martinez
200 Muir Rd., Hacienda Bldg., 2nd Fl.
Martinez, CA 94553
Ph: (925)372-1445
URL: https://health.kaiserpermanente.org/wps/portal/facility/100167
Dialysis Stations: 8.

Marysville

23012 ■ Marysville Dialysis Center
DaVita
1015 8th St.
Marysville, CA 95901
Ph: (530)741-9801
Free: 800-424-6589
URL: http://www.davita.com
Dialysis Stations: 15.

McKinleyville

23013 ■ Fresenius Medical Care --McKinleyville
1550 Heartland Dr.
McKinleyville, CA 9519
Free: 866-434-2597
URL: http://www.ultracare-dialysis.com/
Dialysis Stations: 15.

Menlo Park

23014 ■ Wellbound of Menlo Park
Satellite Healthcare
927 Hamilton Ave.
Menlo Park, CA 94025
Ph: (650)566-0180
URL: http://www.satellitehealth.com/
Dialysis Stations: 4.

Merced

23015 ■ North Merced Dialysis Center
DaVita
3150 G St., Ste. A
Merced, CA 95340
Ph: (209)723-0439
Free: 800-424-6589
URL: http://www.davita.com
Dialysis Stations: 20. **Formerly:** Gambro Healthcare.

23016 ■ Satellite Dialysis--Merced
Satellite Health
3376 North Hwy. 59, Ste. I
Merced, CA 95348
Ph: (209)383-7370
URL: http://www.satellitehealth.com/
Dialysis Stations: 25.

Milpitas

23017 ■ Satellite Dialysis--Milpitas
Satellite Healthcare
1860 Milmont Dr.
Milpitas, CA 95035
Ph: (408)935-0600
URL: http://satellitehealth.com
Dialysis Stations: 24.

23018 ■ Wellbound of Milpitas LLC
Satellite Healthcare
180 Milmont Dr.
Milpitas, CA 95035
Ph: (408)935-0550
URL: http://www.satellitehealth.com
Dialysis Stations: 0.

Mission Hills

23019 ■ Fresenius Medical Care--Mission Hills
11550 Indian Hills Rd., Ste. 100
Mission Hills, CA 91345
Ph: (818)898-1724
Free: 866-434-2597
URL: http://www.ultracare-dialysis.com/
Dialysis Stations: 22.

23020 ■ Holy Cross Renal Center
Hemodialysis Inc.
14901 Rinaldi St., Ste. 100
Mission Hills, CA 91345
Ph: (818)365-6961
Fax: (818)365-3061
URL: http://www.hemodialysis-inc.com/
Dialysis Stations: 52.

Mission Viejo

23021 ■ Fresenius Medical Care--Mission Viejo
23681 Via Linda, Ste. E
Mission Viejo, CA 92691
Ph: (949)587-0163
Free: 866-434-2597
URL: http://www.ultracare-dialysis.com/
Dialysis Stations: 18.

23022 ■ Mission Viejo Dialysis
DaVita
27640 Marguerite Pkwy.
Mission Viejo, CA 92692
Ph: (949)347-2433
Free: 800-424-6589
URL: http://www.davita.com
Dialysis Stations: 20. **Formerly:** Gambro.

Modesto

23023 ■ Modesto Kidney Center, LLC
Innovative Dialysis Systems
305 E Granger Ave., Ste. 102
Modesto, CA 95350
Ph: (209)574-6800
URL: http://www.idsdialysis.com
Dialysis Stations: 17.

23024 ■ Parkway Kidney Center
Innovative Dialysis Systems
2200 Plaza Pkwy., Ste. B1-B4
Modesto, CA 95350
Ph: (209)574-6818
URL: http://www.idsdialysis.com
Dialysis Stations: 24.

23025 ■ Satellite Dialysis--Central Modesto
Satellite Healthcare
1315 10th St., Ste. 300
Modesto, CA 95354
Ph: (209)238-4087
URL: http://www.satellitehealth.com/
Dialysis Stations: 25.

23026 ■ Satellite Dialysis--Modesto
Satellite Health
3500 Coffee Rd., Ste. 21
Modesto, CA 95355
Ph: (209)578-0691
URL: http://www.satellitehealth.com/
Dialysis Stations: 25.

23027 ■ Wellbound of Modesto
Satellite Healthcare
1315 10th St., Ste. 100
Modesto, CA 95354
Ph: (209)238-4080
URL: http://www.satellitehealth.com/
Dialysis Stations: 4.

Monrovia

23028 ■ Mountain View Dialysis Center, Inc.
900 S Mountain Ave.
Monrovia, CA 91016
Ph: (626)932-1810
Dialysis Stations: 24.

Montclair

23029 ■ DaVita--Montclair Dialysis Center
5050 Palo Verde St., Ste. 100
Montclair, CA 91763
Ph: (909)625-0339
Free: 800-424-6589
URL: http://www.davita.com
Dialysis Stations: 20.

Montebello

23030 ■ Doctor's Dialysis Center of Montebello
DaVita
1721 W Whittier Blvd.
Montebello, CA 90640
Ph: (323)722-1116
Free: 800-424-6589
URL: http://www.davita.com
Dialysis Stations: 28.

23031 ■ Montebello Artificial Kidney Center
3404 W Beverly Blvd.
Montebello, CA 90640
Ph: (323)728-7580
Dialysis Stations: 24.

23032 ■ Montebello Dialysis Center LLC
111 W Beverly Blvd., Ste. A
Montebello, CA 90640
Ph: (323)278-5555
Fax: (323)278-5554
URL: http://www.idsdialysis.com
Dialysis Stations: 15.

23033 ■ Peritoneal Dialysis Center of America, Inc.
3112 W Beverly Blvd.
Montebello, CA 90640
Ph: (323)722-2053
Dialysis Stations: 0.

Monterey

23034 ■ Monterey Peninsula Dialysis Innovative Dialysis Systems
2066 N Fremont Blvd.
Monterey, CA 93940
Ph: (831)655-6950
URL: http://www.idsdialysis.com
Dialysis Stations: 18. **Formerly:** Clinishare Dialysis Network.

Monterey Park

23035 ■ DaVita--Garfield Hemodialysis Center
118 Hilliard Ave.
Monterey Park, CA 91754
Ph: (626)288-5796
Free: 800-424-6589
URL: http://www.davita.com
Dialysis Stations: 25.

23036 ■ DaVita--Monterey Park Dialysis Center
2560 Corporate Pl., Bldg. D, Ste. 100-101
Monterey Park, CA 91754
Ph: (323)780-8787
Free: 800-424-6589
URL: http://www.davita.com
Dialysis Stations: 28.

23037 ■ San Gabriel Regional Dialysis Training Center
809 S Atlantic Blvd., Ste. 103
Monterey Park, CA 91754
Ph: (626)576-8556
URL: http://www.idsdialysis.com
Dialysis Stations: 2.

Moreno Valley

23038 ■ DaVita Canyon Springs Dialysis
22555 Alessandro Blvd.
Moreno Valley, CA 92553
Free: 800-424-6589
URL: http://www.davita.com
Dialysis Stations: 32.

23039 ■ DaVita--Valley View Dialysis
26900 Cactus Ave.
Moreno Valley, CA 92555
Ph: (951)247-2844
Free: 800-424-6589
URL: http://www.davita.com
Dialysis Stations: 34.

Mountain View

23040 ■ El Camino Dialysis Center
Oak Pavillion 110
2490 Grant Rd.
Mountain View, CA 94040
Ph: (650)940-7015
Dialysis Stations: 25.

23041 ■ Palo Alto Center Palo Alto Medical Foundation
701 E El Camino
Mountain View, CA 94040
Ph: (650)934-7400
URL: http://www.pamf.org/paloalto/
Dialysis Stations: 0.

Murrieta

23042 ■ DaVita--Murrieta Dialysis Center
25100 Hancock Ave., Ste. 101-103
Murrieta, CA 92562
Ph: (951)698-7860
Free: 800-424-6589
URL: http://www.davita.com
Dialysis Stations: 13.

Napa

23043 ■ Napa Dialysis Center DaVita
3900-C Bel Aire Plz., Ste. C
Napa, CA 94558
Ph: (707)253-8938
Free: 800-424-6589
URL: http://www.davita.com
Dialysis Stations: 20.

23044 ■ Napa Valley Dialysis
1100 Trancas St., Ste. 267
Napa, CA 94558
Ph: (707)224-6533
Dialysis Stations: 10.

National City

23045 ■ Fresenius Medical Care--National City Dialysis Center
303 W 26th St.
National City, CA 91950
Ph: (619)474-8151
Free: 866-434-2597
URL: http://www.ultracare-dialysis.com/
Dialysis Stations: 22.

Newark

23046 ■ Fresenius Medical Care--Ardenwood Dialysis Facility
37478 Cedar Blvd., Ste. A
Newark, CA 94560
Ph: (510)744-0790
Free: 866-434-2597
URL: http://www.ultracare-dialysis.com/
Dialysis Stations: 12.

Newport Beach

23047 ■ Newport Beach Dialysis Renal Research Institute
3333 W Pacific Coast Hwy., Ste. 101
Newport Beach, CA 92663
Ph: (949)631-0107
Dialysis Stations: 16.

Norco

23048 ■ Norco Dialysis Center DaVita
1901 Town and Country Dr., Ste. 100
Norco, CA 92860
Ph: (951)738-0185
Free: 800-424-6589
URL: http://www.davita.com
Dialysis Stations: 20.

North Highlands

23049 ■ DaVita North Highlands Dialysis Center
4986 Watt Ave., Ste. F
North Highlands, CA 95660
Ph: (916)344-0183
Free: 800-424-6589
URL: http://www.davita.com
Dialysis Stations: 15.

North Hollywood

23050 ■ North Hollywood Dialysis DaVita
12126 Victory Blvd.
North Hollywood, CA 91606
Ph: (818)980-5070
Free: 800-424-6589
URL: http://www.davita.com
Dialysis Stations: 28.

Northridge

23051 ■ Kidney Dialysis Center of Northridge, LLC
18546 Roscoe Blvd., Ste. 108
Northridge, CA 91324
Ph: (818)886-3771
Fax: (818)886-5734
URL: http://208.127.9.175/KCI/DialysisCenters/KD-CNR.aspx
Dialysis Stations: 24.

Norwalk

23052 ■ DaVita--Norwalk Dialysis Center
12375 E Imperial Hwy.
Norwalk, CA 90650
Ph: (562)929-7430
Free: 800-424-6589
URL: http://www.davita.com
Dialysis Stations: 17.

Oakdale

23053 ■ Oakdale Kidney Center LLC Dialysis Facility
1405 West F St., Ste. B
Oakdale, CA 95361
Ph: (209)848-5780
URL: http://www.idsdialysis.com
Dialysis Stations: 10.

Oakland

23054 ■ DaVita--Alameda County Dialysis Center
10700 Macarthur Blvd., Ste. 14A
Oakland, CA 94605
Ph: (510)633-9844
Free: 800-424-6589
URL: http://www.davita.com
Dialysis Stations: 19. **Formerly:** Gambro Healthcare.

23055 ■ Oakland Dialysis Center DaVita
5354 Claremont Ave.
Oakland, CA 94618
Ph: (510)597-0104
Free: 800-424-6589
URL: http://www.davita.com
Dialysis Stations: 40. **Formerly:** Gambro Healthcare.

23056 ■ Oakland Peritoneal Dialysis Center DaVita
2633 Telegraph, No. 115
Oakland, CA 94612
Ph: (510)267-0819
Free: 800-424-6589
URL: http://www.davita.com
Dialysis Stations: 0.

23057 ■ RAI Bancroft
Renal Advantage Inc.
7200 Bancroft Ave., Ste. 220
Oakland, CA 94605
Ph: (510)553-1333
URL: http://www.renaladvantage.com
Dialysis Stations: 26.

23058 ■ RAI-East Bay-Oakland
Renal Advantage Inc.
3012 Summit St., Ste. 6630
Oakland, CA 94609
Ph: (510)893-2060
URL: http://www.renaladvantage.com
Dialysis Stations: 27.

23059 ■ RAI Oakland Home Program 1
Renal Advantage Inc.
2710 Telegraph Ave., Ste. 205
Oakland, CA 94612
Ph: (510)452-8302
URL: http://www.renaladvantage.com

23060 ■ RAI Peralta
Renal Advantage Inc.
2757 Telegraph Ave.
Oakland, CA 94612
Ph: (510)835-0154
URL: http://www.renaladvantage.com
Dialysis Stations: 27. **Formerly:** DaVita Dialysis.

23061 ■ Renal Advantage Inc. Care Centers--Bancroft
6955 Foothill Dr., Ste. 220
Oakland, CA 94605
Ph: (510)553-1333
URL: http://www.renaladvantage.com
Dialysis Stations: 26.

23062 ■ Renal Advantage Inc. Care Centers--East Bay--Oakland
3012 Summit St., Ste. 6630
Oakland, CA 94609
Ph: (510)893-2060
URL: http://www.renaladvantage.com
Dialysis Stations: 27.

Oceanside

23063 ■ North Coast Kidney Center
Fresenius Medical Care
3300 Vista Way, Ste. A
Oceanside, CA 92056
Ph: (760)721-4344
Free: 866-434-2597
URL: http://www.ultracare-dialysis.com/
Dialysis Stations: 30.

23064 ■ Renal Advantage Inc.--Oceanside
2227 El Camino Real, Ste. B
Oceanside, CA 92054
Ph: (760)757-1838
URL: http://www.renaladvantage.com
Dialysis Stations: 12. **Formerly:** DaVita--Mission Dialysis Center of Oceanside.

Ontario

23065 ■ DaVita
Ontario Dialysis
1950-A Grove Ave., Ste. 101
Ontario, CA 91761
Ph: (909)930-5566
Free: 800-424-6589
URL: http://www.davita.com
Dialysis Stations: 20.

23066 ■ Dialysis Center of Ontario
Renal Carepartners
2850 Inland Empire Blvd., Ste. C
Ontario, CA 91761
Ph: (909)476-2638
E-mail: info@renalcp.com
URL: http://www.renalcp.com
Dialysis Stations: 18.

23067 ■ Ontario Dialysis Inc.
1001 W Sixth St., Ste. A
Ontario, CA 91762
Ph: (909)984-0320
Dialysis Stations: 32.

Orange

23068 ■ DaVita--Main Place Dialysis Center
972 Town & Country Rd.
Orange, CA 92868
Ph: (714)836-0155
Free: 800-424-6589
URL: http://www.davita.com
Dialysis Stations: 21.

23069 ■ Saint Joseph Hospital Kidney Dialysis Denter
St. Joseph Health System
Sr. Elizabeth Bldg.
1100 W Stewart Dr.
Orange, CA 92868
Ph: (714)771-8033
URL: http://www.sjo.org/Clinical_Services/Kidney_Dialysis_Center.aspx
Dialysis Stations: 41.

23070 ■ Satellite Dialysis of Orange
Satellite Healthcare
1518 W La Veta Ave.
Orange, CA 95354
Ph: (714)285-9675
URL: http://www.satellitehealth.com/
Dialysis Stations: 24.

23071 ■ UCI Medical Center,Renal TX
UC Irvine Healthcare
101 City Dr.
Orange, CA 92868
Ph: (714)456-7890
URL: http://www.healthcare.uci.edu/ts.asp

23072 ■ UCI Renal Dialysis Center
101 City Drive, Bldg. 51
Orange, CA 92868
Ph: (714)456-5555
Dialysis Stations: 20.

Orangevale

23073 ■ Orangevale Dialysis Center
DaVita
9267 Greenback Ln., Ste. A-2
Orangevale, CA 95662
Ph: (916)988-5666
Free: 800-424-6589
URL: http://www.davita.com
Dialysis Stations: 20.

Oroville

23074 ■ Oroville Dialysis Clinic
Dialysis Clinic Inc.
3012 Olive Hwy.
Oroville, CA 95966
Ph: (530)532-6800
URL: http://www.dciinc.org
Dialysis Stations: 15.

Oxnard

23075 ■ Fresenius Medical Care--Channel Islands
Dialysis Center
2679 S Saviers Rd., Ste. B
Oxnard, CA 93033
Ph: (805)486-2929
Free: 866-434-2597
URL: http://www.ultracare-dialysis.com/
Dialysis Stations: 20.

23076 ■ Fresenius Medical Care--Oxnard
Dialysis Facility
1801 Holser Walk, Ste. 310
Oxnard, CA 93030
Ph: (805)988-3339
Free: 866-434-2597
URL: http://www.ultracare-dialysis.com/
Dialysis Stations: 21.

Palm Desert

23077 ■ RAI--Corporate Way--Palm Desert
Renal Advantage Inc.
41-501 Corporate Way
Palm Desert, CA 92260
Ph: (760)346-7588
URL: http://www.renaladvantage.com
Dialysis Stations: 21. **Formerly:** DaVita.

Palm Springs

23078 ■ Palm Springs Dialysis
DaVita
1061 N Indian Canyon Dr.
Palm Springs, CA 92262
Ph: (760)325-0909
Free: 800-424-6589
URL: http://www.davita.com
Dialysis Stations: 20.

Palmdale

23079 ■ East Palmdale Dialysis Center
2710 E Palmdale Blvd.
Palmdale, CA 93550
Ph: (661)456-1500
Dialysis Stations: 20.

23080 ■ High Desert Hemodialysis Inc.
1007 West Ave. M-14, Ste. B
Palmdale, CA 93551
Ph: (661)265-7810
Dialysis Stations: 10.

23081 ■ Palmdale Regional Dialysis Center
DaVita
1643 E Palmdale Blvd.
Palmdale, CA 93550
Ph: (661)540-0925
Free: 800-424-6589
URL: http://www.davita.com
Dialysis Stations: 24.

Palo Alto

23082 ■ Lucile Packard Stanford Pediatric Transplant
Lucile Packard Children's Hospital at Stanford
703 Welch Rd., Ste. H2
Palo Alto, CA 94304
Ph: (650)498-5480
URL: http://www.lpch.org/clinicalSpecialtiesServices/COE/Transplant/IndexTranspl antProgram.html
Dialysis Stations: 0.

23083 ■ Lucille Packard Stanford Ped Transplant
703 Welch Rd., Ste. 100
Palo Alto, CA 94304
Ph: (650)498-5480
Fax: (650)497-8718
URL: http://www.lpch.org/

Panorama City

23084 ■ Kidney Center of Panorama City
Dialysis Facility
14860 Roscoe Blvd., Ste. 101
Panorama City, CA 91402
Ph: (818)901-9822
Dialysis Stations: 15.

Paramount

23085 ■ DaVita--Paramount Dialysis Center
8319 Alondra Blvd.
Paramount, CA 90723
Ph: (562)634-9774
Free: 800-424-6589
URL: http://www.davita.com
Dialysis Stations: 34.

Pasadena

23086 ■ DaVita--Eaton Canyon Dialysis
2551 E Washington Blvd.
Pasadena, CA 91107
Ph: (626)798-8896
Free: 800-424-6589
URL: http://www.davita.com
Dialysis Stations: 30.

23087 ■ Huntington Dialysis Center
Hemodialysis Inc.
806 S Fair Oaks Ave.
Pasadena, CA 91105
Ph: (626)792-0548
URL: http://www.hemodialysis-inc.com/
Dialysis Stations: 48.

23088 ■ Pasadena Dialysis Center
Liberty Dialysis
1111 S Arroyo Pkwy., Ste. 150
Pasadena, CA 91105
Ph: (626)441-9500
URL: http://www.libertydialysis.com
Dialysis Stations: 24.

Petaluma

23089 ■ Fresenius Medical Care--Petaluma Dialysis Facility
715 S Point Blvd., Ste. A
Petaluma, CA 94954
Ph: (707)765-9379
Free: 866-434-2597
URL: http://www.ultracare-dialysis.com/
Dialysis Stations: 17.

Pismo Beach

23090 ■ Kidney Dialysis Center of Pismo Beach
320 James Way, Ste. 110
Pismo Beach, CA 93449
Ph: (805)556-0577
Dialysis Stations: 14.

Pittsburg

23091 ■ Fresenius Medical Care
Diablo Renal Services--Pittsburg
2155 Loveridge Rd.
Pittsburg, CA 94565
Free: 866-434-2597
URL: http://www.ultracare-dialysis.com/
Dialysis Stations: 15.

Placerville

23092 ■ Placerville Dialysis Center
DaVita
3964 Missouri Flat Rd., Ste. J
Placerville, CA 95667
Ph: (530)626-6097
Free: 800-424-6589
URL: http://www.davita.com
Dialysis Stations: 12.

Pleasant Hill

23093 ■ Fresenius Medical Care
Diablo Renal Services--Concord
Dialysis Facility
508-D Contra Costa Blvd.
Pleasant Hill, CA 94523
Ph: (925)798-8844
Free: 866-434-2597
URL: http://www.ultracare-dialysis.com/
Dialysis Stations: 22.

Pleasanton

23094 ■ Pleasanton Dialysis Center
DaVita
5720 Stoneridge Mall Rd., No. 160
Pleasanton, CA 94588
Ph: (925)737-0120
Free: 800-424-6589
URL: http://www.davita.com
Dialysis Stations: 20.

Pomona

23095 ■ Garey Dialysis Center
Renal Advantage Inc.
150 E Arrow Hwy.
Pomona, CA 91767
Ph: (909)593-5863
URL: http://www.renaladvantage.com
Dialysis Stations: 29.

23096 ■ Pomona Dialysis
DaVita
2111 N Garey Ave.
Pomona, CA 91767
Free: 800-424-6589
URL: http://www.davita.com
Dialysis Stations: 28.

Porterville

23097 ■ Porterville Hemodialysis Facility
385 N Pearson Dr.
Porterville, CA 93257
Ph: (559)781-5551
Dialysis Stations: 20.

23098 ■ Sierra View District Hospital Dialysis Center
283 N Pearson Dr.
Porterville, CA 93257
Ph: (559)791-3900
URL: http://www.sierra-view.com/
Dialysis Stations: 32.

Rancho Cordova

23099 ■ Sunrise Community Dialysis Center
DaVita
2951 Sunrise Blvd., Ste. 145
Rancho Cordova, CA 95742
Ph: (916)631-3606
Free: 800-424-6589
URL: http://www.davita.com
Dialysis Stations: 12.

23100 ■ Sunset Dialysis Center
DaVita
3071 Gold Canal Dr.
Rancho Cordova, CA 95670
Ph: (916)638-8429
Free: 800-424-6589
URL: http://www.davita.com
Dialysis Stations: 24.

Rancho Cucamonga

23101 ■ Fresenius Medical Care--Rancho Cucamonga
Dialysis Services
10532 Acadia St., Ste. B-2 & B-3
Rancho Cucamonga, CA 91730
Ph: (909)987-8887
Free: 866-434-2597
URL: http://www.ultracare-dialysis.com/
Dialysis Stations: 25.

Rancho Mirage

23102 ■ The Kidney Institute--Eisenhower Medical Center
Dialysis Facility
Probst Bldg., Ste. 103
39000 Bob Hope Dr.
Rancho Mirage, CA 92270
Ph: (760)837-9696
URL: http://www.healthcare.uci.edu/nps.asp
Dialysis Stations: 20.

Red Bluff

23103 ■ Red Bluff Dialysis
DaVita
2455 Sister Mary Columba Dr.
Red Bluff, CA 96080
Ph: (052)7-0052
Free: 800-424-6589
URL: http://www.davita.com
Dialysis Stations: 15.

Redding

23104 ■ DCI Redding
180 Northpoint Dr.
Redding, CA 96003
Ph: (530)246-1140
Fax: (530)246-1128
URL: http://www.dciinc.org
Dialysis Stations: 24.

23105 ■ Redding Dialysis Center & At Home
DaVita
1876 Park Marina Dr.
Redding, CA 96001
Ph: (530)246-7474
Free: 800-424-6589
URL: http://www.davita.com
Dialysis Stations: 28.

23106 ■ Redding Dialysis Center
DaVita
1876 Park Marina Dr.
Redding, CA 96001
Free: 800-424-6589
URL: http://www.davita.com
Dialysis Stations: 28.

Redlands

23107 ■ RAI--Indiana Court--Redlands
Renal Advantage Inc.
Dialysis Center
1210 Indiana Court
Redlands, CA 92374
Ph: (909)792-8880
Fax: (909)798-4154
URL: http://www.renaladvantage.com
Dialysis Stations: 18. **Formerly:** Gambro.

Redondo Beach

23108 ■ Pacific South Bay Dialysis Inc.
Coastal Dialysis Center
514 N Prospect Ave.
Redondo Beach, CA 90277
Ph: (310)379-6671
URL: http://www.idsdialysis.com
Dialysis Stations: 7. **Formerly:** Gambro Healthcare--South Bay.

Redwood City

23109 ■ Satellite Dialysis--Redwood City
1410 Marshall St.
Redwood City, CA 94063
Ph: (650)366-0789
URL: http://satellitehealth.com
Dialysis Stations: 25.

Reedley

23110 ■ Fresenius Medical Care--Reedley
1421 N Acacia
Reedley, CA 93654
Ph: (559)637-1676
Free: 866-434-2597
URL: http://www.ultracare-dialysis.com/
Dialysis Stations: 9.

Rialto

23111 ■ RAI--North Riverside--Rialto
Renal Advantage Inc.
1850 N Riverside Ave., Ste. 150
Rialto, CA 92376
Ph: (909)879-1185
URL: http://www.renaladvantage.com
Dialysis Stations: 21. **Formerly:** DaVita.

Ridgecrest

23112 ■ Indian Wells Valley Dialysis Center
DaVita
212 S Richmond Rd.
Ridgecrest, CA 93555
Ph: (760)371-7506
Free: 800-424-6589
URL: http://www.davita.com
Dialysis Stations: 12.

Riverside

23113 ■ DaVita--Riverside Dialysis Center
4361 Latham St., Ste. 100
Riverside, CA 92501
Ph: (951)682=2700
Free: 800-424-6589
URL: http://www.davita.com
Dialysis Stations: 32.

23114 ■ Fresenius Medical Care--Riverside Dialysis Services
3470 La Sierra Ave., Ste. E
Riverside, CA 92503
Ph: (951)343-7700
Dialysis Stations: 26.

23115 ■ Kaiser Foundation Hospital Medical Center--Riverside
Kaiser Permanente
10800 Magnolia Ave., Module 1X
Riverside, CA 92505
Ph: (951)353-4887
URL: http://www.kaiserpermanente.com
Dialysis Stations: 4.

23116 ■ Magnolia West Dialysis & At Home
DaVita
11161 Magnolia Ave., Ste. B
Riverside, CA 92505
Ph: (951)351-8090
Free: 800-424-6589
URL: http://www.davita.com
Dialysis Stations: 2.

23117 ■ Riverside Community Hospital Transplant Center
4000 14th St., Ste. 214
Riverside, CA 92501
Ph: (951)684-1415
URL: http://www.rchc.org/CustomPage.asp?guidCustomContentID=C2E8782B-8729-40F88B FC-608D6982CC27
Dialysis Stations: 0.

23118 ■ Riverside PD Central
DaVita
3660 Park Sierra, Ste. 108
Riverside, CA 92505
Ph: (951)687-3900
Free: 800-424-6589
URL: http://www.davita.com
Dialysis Stations: 8.

Rocklin

23119 ■ RAI Fairway Rocklin
Renal Advantage Inc.
Comprehensive Renal Services
6000 Fairway Dr., No. 14
Rocklin, CA 95677
Ph: (916)624-3871
URL: http://www.renaladvantage.com
Dialysis Stations: 14.

Rosemead

23120 ■ Metropolitan Dialysis Center LLC
Innovative Dialysis Systems
3100 Del Mar Ave.
Rosemead, CA 91770
Ph: (626)288-7860
URL: http://www.idsdialysis.com/facilities.html
Dialysis Stations: 18.

23121 ■ Rosemead Dialysis Center
7403 Hellman Ave.
Rosemead, CA 91770
Ph: (626)280-6161
Fax: (626)280-7887
Dialysis Stations: 17.

Roseville

23122 ■ RAI Harding Blvd.
Renal Advantage Inc.
218 Harding Blvd.
Roseville, CA 95678
Ph: (916)786-2728
URL: http://www.renaladvantage.com
Dialysis Stations: 15. **Formerly:** Sierra Hemodialysis; Gambro Healthcare.

23123 ■ RAI Secret Ravine Pkwy.
Renal Advantage Inc.
Bldg. D, Ste. 130
1451 Secret Ravine Pkwy.
Roseville, CA 95661
Ph: (916)773-4000
URL: http://www.renaladvantage.com
Dialysis Stations: 20. **Formerly:** Gambro Healthcare--Placer.

Sacramento

23124 ■ Alhambra Dialysis Center
DaVita
1315 Alhambra Blvd., Ste. 100
Sacramento, CA 95816
Ph: (916)457-8252
Free: 800-424-6589
URL: http://www.davita.com
Dialysis Stations: 20.

23125 ■ Alhambra Dialysis Center
DaVita
1315 Alhambra Blvd., Ste. 100
Sacramento, CA 95816
Free: 800-424-6589
URL: http://www.davita.com
Dialysis Stations: 20.

23126 ■ DaVita
South Sacramento Dialysis Center
7000 Franklin Blvd., No. 880
Sacramento, CA 95823
Ph: (916)427-2561
Free: 800-424-6589
URL: http://www.davita.com
Dialysis Stations: 18.

23127 ■ DCI Madison Dialysis Clinic
5222 Madison Ave.
Sacramento, CA 95841
Ph: (916)338-6644
Dialysis Stations: 12.

23128 ■ DCI Rancho Dialysis Clinic
10294 Rockingham Dr.
Sacramento, CA 95827
Ph: (916)857-1819
Dialysis Stations: 16.

23129 ■ DCI/University Dialysis Clinic
1771 Stockton Blvd.
Sacramento, CA 95816
Ph: (916)453-0803
URL: http://www.dciinc.org/
Dialysis Stations: 24.

23130 ■ Florin Dialysis Center
DaVita
7000 Stockton Blvd.
Sacramento, CA 95823
Ph: (916)424-3990
Free: 800-424-6589
Fax: (916)424-3799
URL: http://www.davita.com
Dialysis Stations: 31.

23131 ■ Natomas Dialysis
DaVita
30 Goldenland Ct.
Sacramento, CA 95834
Ph: (916)285-6452
Free: 800-424-6589
URL: http://www.davita.com
Dialysis Stations: 24.

23132 ■ Southgate Dialysis
Dialysis Clinic Inc.
7231 E Southgate Dr.
Sacramento, CA 95823
Ph: (916)395-7585
URL: http://www.dciinc.org/
Dialysis Stations: 19.

23133 ■ Sutter Medical Center Transplant
Sutter Health
5151 F St.
Sacramento, CA 95819
Ph: (916)733-8133
URL: http://www.sutterhealth.org/medicalspecialties/transplants/adv_transplant_s mc.html
Dialysis Stations: 0.

23134 ■ UC Davis Medical Center Transplant
2315 Stockton Blvd., Rm. 1018
Sacramento, CA 95817
Free: 800-821-9912
URL: http://www.ucdmc.ucdavis.edu/transplant/
Dialysis Stations: 0.

23135 ■ University Dialysis Center--Sacramento
DaVita
777 Campus Common Rd., Ste. 100
Sacramento, CA 95825
Ph: (916)920-0877
Free: 800-424-6589
URL: http://www.davita.com
Dialysis Stations: 21.

23136 ■ Wellbound of Sacramento
Satellite Health
2610 El Paseo Ln., Ste. F19
Sacramento, CA 95821
Ph: (916)486-8005
URL: http://www.satellitehealth.com/
Dialysis Stations: 4.

Salinas

23137 ■ Salinas Dialysis Center
DaVita
955 Blanco Cir., Ste. C
Salinas, CA 93901
Ph: (831)758-6222
Free: 800-424-6589
URL: http://www.davita.com
Dialysis Stations: 34.

San Bernardino

23138 ■ DaVita
Citrus Valley Dialysis & At Home
894 Hardt St.
San Bernardino, CA 92408
Ph: (909)388-6608
Free: 800-424-6589
URL: http://www.davita.com
Dialysis Stations: 20.

23139 ■ Fresenius Medical Care--Loma Linda
269 E Caroline St., Ste. A
San Bernardino, CA 92408
Ph: (909)514-1008
Free: 866-434-2597
URL: http://www.ultracare-dialysis.com/
Dialysis Stations: 24.

23140 ■ Fresenius Medical Care--San Bernardino
636 E Brier Dr., Ste. 150
San Bernardino, CA 92408
Ph: (909)890-9508
Free: 866-434-2597
URL: http://www.ultracare-dialysis.com/
Dialysis Stations: 21.

23141 ■ Mountain Vista Dialysis Center
DaVita
4041 University Pkwy.
San Bernardino, CA 92407
Free: 800-424-6589
URL: http://www.davita.com
Dialysis Stations: 24.

23142 ■ Renal Advantage Inc.--North Waterman
San Bernardino Dialysis Center
1500 N Waterman Ave.
San Bernardino, CA 92404
Ph: (909)381-1591
URL: http://www.renaladvantage.com
Dialysis Stations: 32. **Formerly:** Gambro.

23143 ■ San Bernardino Valley Home Dialysis Center
1500 N Waterman Ave., Ste. B
San Bernardino, CA 92404
Ph: (909)381-1595
Dialysis Stations: 0.

San Diego

23144 ■ College Dialysis
DaVita
6535 University Ave.
San Diego, CA 92115
Ph: (619)287-8796
Free: 800-424-6589
URL: http://www.davita.com
Dialysis Stations: 20. **Formerly:** DaVita--University.

23145 ■ DaVita--Carmel Mountain
9850 Carmel Mountain Rd., Ste. A-D
San Diego, CA 92154
Ph: (858)538-1083
Free: 800-424-6589
URL: http://www.davita.com
Dialysis Stations: 16. **Formerly:** Gambro.

23146 ■ DaVita--San Diego East
292 Euclid Ave., Ste. 100
San Diego, CA 92114
Ph: (619)262-7225
Free: 800-424-6589
URL: http://www.davita.com
Dialysis Stations: 21. **Formerly:** Gambro.

23147 ■ DaVita--San Diego South Dialysis Center
995 Gateway Center Way, Ste. 101
San Diego, CA 92102
Ph: (619)262-1960
Free: 800-424-6589
URL: http://www.davita.com
Dialysis Stations: 17. **Formerly:** Gambro.

23148 ■ FMC Balboa--Kearny Mesa Dialysis Center
Fresenius Medical Care
7907 Ostrow St., Ste. A
San Diego, CA 92111
Ph: (858)571-0232
Free: 866-434-2597
URL: http://www.ultracare-dialysis.com/
Dialysis Stations: 28.

23149 ■ Fresenius Medical Care/Chula Vista Dialysis Center, South
2252 Verus St., Ste. D
San Diego, CA 92154
Ph: (619)429-9201
Free: 866-434-2597
URL: http://www.ultracare-dialysis.com/
Dialysis Stations: 30.

23150 ■ Fresenius Medical Care/Dialysis Services of College
4660 El Cajon Blvd., Ste. 110
San Diego, CA 92115
Ph: (619)516-4803
Free: 866-434-2597
URL: http://www.ultracare-dialysis.com/
Dialysis Stations: 12.

23151 ■ Fresenius Medical Care/Dialysis Services of Paradise
6919 Paradise Valley Rd.
San Diego, CA 92139
Ph: (619)475-2872
Free: 866-434-2597
URL: http://www.ultracare-dialysis.com/
Dialysis Stations: 20.

23152 ■ Fresenius Medical Care/Gateway Dialysis Center, East
720 Gateway Center Dr., Ste. B
San Diego, CA 92102
Ph: (619)264-4100
Free: 866-434-2597
URL: http://www.ultracare-dialysis.com/
Dialysis Stations: 24.

23153 ■ Fresenius Medical Care--Hillcrest Dialysis Services
3960 Third Ave.
San Diego, CA 92103
Ph: (619)299-3900
Free: 866-434-2597
URL: http://www.ultracare-dialysis.com/
Dialysis Stations: 20.

23154 ■ Fresenius Medical Care--Kearney Mesa Dialysis Center
7927 Ostrow St., Ste. A
San Diego, CA 92111
Ph: (858)571-0232
Free: 866-434-2597
URL: http://www.ultracare-dialysis.com/
Dialysis Stations: 28.

23155 ■ Fresenius Medical Care--La Jolla
4765 Carmel Mountain Rd., Ste. 100
San Diego, CA 92130
Ph: (858)793-0058
Free: 866-434-2597
URL: http://www.ultracare-dialysis.com/
Dialysis Stations: 24.

23156 ■ Fresenius Medical Care--Rancho
11031 Via Frontera, Ste. C
San Diego, CA 92127
Ph: (858)385-0700
Free: 866-434-2597
URL: http://www.ultracare-dialysis.com/
Dialysis Stations: 16.

23157 ■ Fresenius Medical Care--San Ysidro Dialysis Center
3010 Del Sol Blvd.
San Diego, CA 92154
Ph: (619)429-9690
Free: 866-434-2597
URL: http://www.ultracare-dialysis.com/
Dialysis Stations: 20.

23158 ■ Home Dialysis Therapies of San Diego--North
10672 Wexford St., Ste. 250
San Diego, CA 92131
Ph: (858)549-3400
URL: http://www.homedialysistherapies.com/
Dialysis Stations: 1.

23159 ■ Home Dialysis Therapies of San Diego--North
10672 Wexford St., Ste. 250
San Diego, CA 92131
Ph: (858)549-3400
URL: http://www.homedialysistherapies.com/
Dialysis Stations: 1.

23160 ■ Rady Children's Hospital of San Diego
3020 Childrens Way, MC 5115
San Diego, CA 92123
Ph: (858)966-8882
URL: http://www.rchsd.org/
Dialysis Stations: 3.

23161 ■ Renal Advantage Inc.--Mission Gorge San Diego
7007 Mission Gorge Rd., 1st Fl.
San Diego, CA 92120
Ph: (619)229-1070
URL: http://www.renaladvantage.com
Dialysis Stations: 33. **Formerly:** DaVita Mission Dialysis Center of San Diego.

23162 ■ San Ysidro Dialysis
DaVita
1445 30th St., Ste. A
San Diego, CA 92154
Ph: (619)575-3901
Free: 800-424-6589
URL: http://www.davita.com
Dialysis Stations: 16. **Formerly:** Gambro.

23163 ■ Sharp Memorial Hospital Renal Transplant
7901 Frost St.
San Diego, CA 92123
Ph: (858)939-3400
URL: http://www.sharp.com/transplant/index.cfm
Dialysis Stations: 0.

23164 ■ UCSD Medical Center
Dialysis Program
200 W Arbor Dr., Mail Code 878
San Diego, CA 92103
Ph: (619)543-5646
URL: http://health.ucsd.edu/specialties/nephrology/
Dialysis Stations: 18.

23165 ■ UCSD Medical Center--Renal Transplant
200 W arbor Dr., MC8745
San Diego, CA 92103
Ph: (619)574-8612
URL: http://health.ucsd.edu/specialties/transplant.asp
Dialysis Stations: 0.

San Dimas

23166 ■ San Dimas Dialysis Center Inc.
1335 Cypress St., Ste. 102
San Dimas, CA 91773
Ph: (909)542-2802
Dialysis Stations: 32.

San Fernando

23167 ■ Fresenius Medical Center--San Fernando
Dialysis Center
451 S Brand Blvd., Ste. 100
San Fernando, CA 91340
Ph: (818)837-9980
Free: 866-434-2597
URL: http://www.ultracare-dialysis.com/
Dialysis Stations: 25.

San Francisco

23168 ■ California Pacific MC Dialysis
2333 Buchanan St.
San Francisco, CA 94120
Ph: (415)600-3258
Dialysis Stations: 30.

23169 ■ CPMC Davies Campus
Dialysis Unit
South Tower, 2nd Fl.
45 Castro St.
San Francisco, CA 94114
Ph: (415)600-5075
Dialysis Stations: 16.

23170 ■ Kaiser Hospital Hemodialysis
2425 Geary Blvd., Rm. 1251
San Francisco, CA 94115
Ph: (415)833-3430
URL: http://www.kaiserpermanente.org
Dialysis Stations: 7.

23171 ■ Pediatric Dialysis Unit at UCSF
400 Parnassus, Rm. A127
San Francisco, CA 94143
Ph: (415)353-2425
URL: http://www.ucsfhealth.org/childrens/speical/d/101533.html
Dialysis Stations: 5.

23172 ■ RAI Cesar Chavez
Renal Advantage Inc.
1750 Cesar Chavez St., Ste. A
San Francisco, CA 94124
Ph: (415)206-9775
URL: http://www.renaladvantage.com
Dialysis Stations: 32. **Formerly:** Potrero Hill Dialysis Center.

23173 ■ RAI Haight
Renal Advantage Inc.
1800 Haight St.
San Francisco, CA 94117
Ph: (415)752-9886
URL: http://www.renaladvantage.com
Dialysis Stations: 17. **Formerly:** Community Hemodialysis.

23174 ■ RAI Ocean Avenue
Renal Advantage Inc.
1738 Ocean Ave.
San Francisco, CA 94112
Ph: (415)406-1090
URL: http://www.renaladvantage.com
Dialysis Stations: 24.

23175 ■ San Francisco Dialysis Center
Dialysis Center & At Home
DaVita
1499 Webster St.
San Francisco, CA 94115
Ph: (415)928-9003
Free: 800-424-6589
URL: http://www.davita.com
Dialysis Stations: 30.

23176 ■ San Francisco General Hospital
Renal Center
1001 Potrero Bldg. 100, Rm. 340B
San Francisco, CA 94110
Ph: (415)206-8242
URL: http://medschool.ucsf.edu/sfgh/
Dialysis Stations: 13.

23177 ■ SF Chinatown Dialysis Center
DaVita
636 Clay St.
San Francisco, CA 94111
Ph: (415)291-8992
Free: 800-424-6589
URL: http://www.davita.com
Dialysis Stations: 22.

23178 ■ UC Chronic Dialysis--Mount Zion
1675 Scott St.
San Francisco, CA 94115
Ph: (415)885-7421
Fax: (415)885-7396
URL: http://www.ucsfhealth.org/clinics/dialysis_center_at_mount_zion/
Dialysis Stations: 14.

23179 ■ UCSF Kidney Transplant Center
400 Parnassus Ave., Box 0116
San Francisco, CA 94143
Ph: (415)353-1551
URL: http://www.ucsfhealth.org/kidneytransplant/
Dialysis Stations: 0.

23180 ■ Wellbound of San Francisco
Satellite Healthcare
1166 Post St., Ste. 201
San Francisco, CA 94109
Ph: (415)474-1309
URL: http://www.satellitehealth.com/

San Gabriel

23181 ■ San Gabriel Nephrology Services LLC
801 S San Gabriel Blvd.
San Gabriel, CA 91776
Ph: (626)285-1830
Dialysis Stations: 36.

San Jose

23182 ■ Aborn Dialysis Center
DaVita
3162 S White Rd.
San Jose, CA 95148
Free: 800-424-6589
URL: http://www.davita.com
Dialysis Stations: 18.

23183 ■ Cornerhouse Dialysis Center
DaVita
2005 Naglee Ave.
San Jose, CA 95128
Ph: (408)998-0183
Free: 800-424-6589
URL: http://www.davita.com
Dialysis Stations: 15.

23184 ■ Evergreen Dialysis Services
2240 Tully Rd.
San Jose, CA 95122
Ph: (408)238-9100
Dialysis Stations: 33.

23185 ■ Fresenius Medical Care--San Jose
6850 A Santa Teresa Blvd.
San Jose, CA 95119
Free: 866-434-2597
URL: http://www.ultracare-dialysis.com/
Dialysis Stations: 24.

23186 ■ Rose Garden Dialysis Center
El Camino Hospital
999 W Taylor St.
San Jose, CA 95126
Ph: (408)494-1000
Dialysis Stations: 16.

23187 ■ San Jose At Home
DaVita
4400 Stevens Creek Blvd., Ste. 50
San Jose, CA 95129
Ph: (408)985-2011
Free: 800-424-6589
URL: http://www.davita.com
Dialysis Stations: 4.

23188 ■ Santa Clara Valley Renal Care Center
2220 Moorpark Ave.
San Jose, CA 95128
Ph: (408)885-5730
Dialysis Stations: 25.

23189 ■ Satellite Dialysis--East San Jose
2121 Alexian Dr., Ste. 118
San Jose, CA 95116
Ph: (408)258-8720
URL: http://www.satellitehealth.com/
Dialysis Stations: 56.

23190 ■ Satellite Dialysis--Santa Teresa
Satellite Health
7019 Realm Dr.
San Jose, CA 95119
Ph: (408)229-1110
URL: http://www.satellitehealth.com/
Dialysis Stations: 25.

23191 ■ Satellite Dialysis--South San Jose
Satellite Healthcare
393 Blossom Hill Rd., Ste. 110
San Jose, CA 95123
Ph: (408)629-9802
URL: http://satellitehealth.com
Dialysis Stations: 25.

23192 ■ Satellite Dialysis--White Road
Satellite Health
1450 S White Road, Ste. 30
San Jose, CA 95127
Ph: (408)272-9810
URL: http://www.satellitehealth.com/
Dialysis Stations: 25.

23193 ■ Wellbound of San Jose
Satellite Healthcare
1525 Meridian Ave., Ste. 101
San Jose, CA 95125
Ph: (408)269-3600
URL: http://www.satellitehealth.com/
Dialysis Stations: 4.

San Juan Capistrano

23194 ■ San Juan Capistrano South Dialysis
DaVita
31736 Rancho Viejo Rd., Ste. B
San Juan Capistrano, CA 92675
Ph: (949)240-1454
Free: 800-424-6589
URL: http://www.davita.com
Dialysis Stations: 18. **Formerly:** Gambro.

23195 ■ San Juan Capistrano South Dialysis
DaVita
31736 Rancho Viejo Rd., Ste. B
San Juan Capistrano, CA 92675
Free: 800-424-6589
URL: http://www.davita.com
Dialysis Stations: 18.

San Leandro

23196 ■ DaVita
East Bay Peritoneal Dialysis
13939 E 14th St., Ste. 110
San Leandro, CA 94578
Ph: (510)614-1380
Free: 800-424-6589
URL: http://www.davita.com
Dialysis Stations: 4.

23197 ■ RAI E. 14th
Renal Advantage Inc.
198 E 14th St.
San Leandro, CA 94577
Ph: (510)430-8311
URL: http://www.renaladvantage.com
Dialysis Stations: 21. **Formerly:** Total Renal Care.

23198 ■ San Leandro Dialysis
Renal Advantage Inc. Care Centers
15555 E 14th St., Ste. 520
San Leandro, CA 94578
Ph: (510)317-6510
URL: http://www.renaladvantage.com
Dialysis Stations: 24.

23199 ■ Wellbound of South Leandro
Satellite Healthcare
1040 Davis St., Ste. 101
San Leandro, CA 94577
Ph: (510)383-9602
Fax: (510)383-9631
URL: http://www.satellitehealth.com
Dialysis Stations: 25.

San Luis Obispo

23200 ■ Kidney Dialysis Center of San Luis Obispo
1043 Marsh St.
San Luis Obispo, CA 93401
Ph: (805)543-1013
Dialysis Stations: 20. **Formerly:** Renal Care Center of San Luis Obispo.

San Marcos

23201 ■ San Marcos Dialysis Center
DaVita
2135 Montiel Rd., Bldg. G
San Marcos, CA 92069
Ph: (760)975-0170
Free: 800-424-6589
URL: http://www.davita.com
Dialysis Stations: 20.

San Mateo

23202 ■ Mills Dialysis Center
100 S San Mateo Dr.
San Mateo, CA 94401
Ph: (650)696-4931
Dialysis Stations: 19.

23203 ■ Wellbound of San Mateo
Satellite Healthcare
2000 S El Camino Real, 2nd Fl.
San Mateo, CA 94403
Ph: (650)377-0882
URL: http://www.satellitehealth.com/
Dialysis Stations: 24.

San Pablo

23204 ■ San Pablo Dialysis Center
DaVita
14020 San Pablo Ave.
San Pablo, CA 94806
Ph: (510)234-0835
Free: 800-424-6589
URL: http://www.davita.com
Dialysis Stations: 22.

San Rafael

23205 ■ Northgate Dialysis Center
DaVita
650 Las Gallinas Ave.
San Rafael, CA 94903
Ph: (415)444-0376
Free: 800-424-6589
URL: http://www.davita.com
Dialysis Stations: 13.

23206 ■ Northgate Dialysis Center
DaVita
650 Las Gallinas Road
San Rafael, CA 94903
Free: 800-424-6589
URL: http://www.davita.com
Dialysis Stations: 13.

Sanger

23207 ■ Sanger Sequoia Dialysis Center
DaVita
2517 Jensen Ave., Bldg. B
Sanger, CA 93657
Free: 800-424-6589
URL: http://www.davita.com
Dialysis Stations: 16.

Santa Ana

23208 ■ DaVita--Santa Ana Dialysis Center
1820 E Deere Ave.
Santa Ana, CA 92705
Ph: (949)251-1221
Free: 800-424-6589
URL: http://www.davita.com
Dialysis Stations: 26.

23209 ■ DaVita--Tustin Dialysis Center
2090 N Tustin Ave., Ste. 100
Santa Ana, CA 92705
Ph: (714)835-2450
Free: 800-424-6589
URL: http://www.davita.com
Dialysis Stations: 24.

23210 ■ Fresenius Medical Care--South Orange County
Dialysis Facility
2020 E 1st St., Ste. 110
Santa Ana, CA 92705
Ph: (714)972-1236
Free: 866-434-2597
URL: http://www.ultracare-dialysis.com/
Dialysis Stations: 26.

23211 ■ St. Joseph Hospital Dialysis Center--Santa Ana
2212 E 4th St., Ste. 2212
Santa Ana, CA 92705
Ph: (714)571-7850
URL: http://www.sjo.org/Clinical_Services/Kidney_Dialysis_Center.aspx
Dialysis Stations: 30.

23212 ■ Western Medical Center Santa Ana Renal Transplant
1001 N Tustin Ave.
Santa Ana, CA 92705
Ph: (714)953-3653
URL: http://www.westernmedicalcenter.com/Hospital-Services/KidneyTransplantation
Dialysis Stations: 0.

Santa Barbara

23213 ■ Fresenius Medical Care--Santa Barbara
Community Dialysis Center
222 Pesetas Ln.
Santa Barbara, CA 93110
Ph: (805)964-7873
Free: 866-434-2597
URL: http://www.ultracare-dialysis.com/
Dialysis Stations: 14.

23214 ■ Santa Barbara Artificial Kidney Center LLC
1704 State St.
Santa Barbara, CA 93101
Ph: (805)682-9942
Dialysis Stations: 16.

Santa Clara

23215 ■ Kaiser Permanente--Santa Clara
710 Lawrence Expwy., No. 460
Santa Clara, CA 95051
Ph: (408)851-4560
URL: http://www.kaiserpermanente.org
Dialysis Stations: 0.

Santa Cruz

23216 ■ Satellite Dialysis--Santa Cruz
Satellite Healthcare
2128 Soquel Ave., Ste. 1
Santa Cruz, CA 95062
Ph: (831)425-0727
URL: http://satellitehealth.com
Dialysis Stations: 20.

Santa Fe Springs

23217 ■ Fresenius Medical Care--Norwalk East
13063 Rosecrans Ave.
Santa Fe Springs, CA 90670
Ph: (562)404-7400
Free: 866-434-2597
URL: http://www.ultracare-dialysis.com/engine/
Dialysis Stations: 18.

23218 ■ Sante Fe Springs Regiona Dialysis Center
10012 Norwalk Blvd., Ste. 190
Santa Fe Springs, CA 90670
Ph: (562)903-8281
Dialysis Stations: 24. **Formerly:** Santa Fe Community Hemodialysis Center Inc.

Santa Maria

23219 ■ Central Coast Kidney Disease Center
1401 E Main St.
Santa Maria, CA 93454
Ph: (805)349-8600
Dialysis Stations: 17.

Santa Monica

23220 ■ DaVita--Mar Vista
2020 Santa Monica Blvd., Ste. 100 & 120
Santa Monica, CA 90404
Free: 800-424-6589
URL: http://www.davita.com
Dialysis Stations: 20.

23221 ■ Santa Monica Dialysis
DaVita
1260 15th St., Ste. 102
Santa Monica, CA 90404
Ph: (310)393-4744
Free: 800-424-6589
URL: http://www.davita.com
Dialysis Stations: 22. **Formerly:** Gambro, Inc.

Santa Paula

23222 ■ Fresenius Medical Care--Santa Paula Dialysis Facility
242 E Harvard Blvd.
Santa Paula, CA 93060
Ph: (805)525-1500
Free: 866-434-2597
URL: http://www.ultracare-dialysis.com/
Dialysis Stations: 16.

23223 ■ Regional Kidney Center Inc.
Kidney Care of Santa Paula
253 March St.
Santa Paula, CA 93060
Ph: (805)525-3977
Dialysis Stations: 10.

Santa Rosa

23224 ■ BMA Santa Rosa
Fresenius Medical Care
1020 2nd St.
Santa Rosa, CA 95404
Ph: (707)527-5350
Free: 866-434-2597
URL: http://www.ultracare-dialysis.com/
Dialysis Stations: 16.

23225 ■ Fresenius Medical Care Santa Rosa North
487 Aviation Blvd., Ste. 110
Santa Rosa, CA 95403
Ph: (707)568-1755
Free: 866-434-2597
URL: http://www.ultracare-dialysis.com/
Dialysis Stations: 13.

23226 ■ Satellite Dialysis--Santa Rosa
Satellite Healthcare
2301 Circadian Way, Ste. C
Santa Rosa, CA 95401
Ph: (707)526-0717
URL: http://www.satellitehealth.com/
Dialysis Stations: 48.

23227 ■ Wellbound of Santa Rosa
Satellite Healthcare
2301 Circadian Way, Ste. B
Santa Rosa, CA 95407
Ph: (707)541-3410
URL: http://www.satellitehealth.com/
Dialysis Stations: 0.

Selma

23228 ■ Selma Dialysis Center
DaVita
2711 Cinema Way, Ste. 111
Selma, CA 93662
Free: 800-424-6589
URL: http://www.davita.com
Dialysis Stations: 16.

Sherman Oaks

23229 ■ Regional Kidney Center, Inc.
Kidney Center of Sherman Oaks, Inc.
4955 Van Nuys Blvd., Ste. 111
Sherman Oaks, CA 91403
Ph: (818)285-5913
Dialysis Stations: 18.

Simi Valley

23230 ■ Dialysis Center of Simi Valley, Inc.
DaVita
2950 N Sycamore Dr., Ste. 100
Simi Valley, CA 93065
Ph: (805)584-2411
URL: http://www.idsdialysis.com
Dialysis Stations: 15.

23231 ■ Simi Dialysis Center LLC
1407 E Los Angeles Ave., Ste. G
Simi Valley, CA 93065
Ph: (805)306-0578
Dialysis Stations: 12.

Soledad

23232 ■ Soledad Dialysis Center
DaVita
901 Los Coches Dr.
Soledad, CA 93960
Ph: (831)678-4310
Free: 800-424-6589
URL: http://www.davita.com
Dialysis Stations: 18.

Sonora

23233 ■ Satellite Dialysis--Sonora
Satellite Healthcare
136 E Columbia Way
Sonora, CA 95370
Ph: (209)532-3072
URL: http://satellitehealth.com
Dialysis Stations: 9.

South El Monte

23234 ■ DaVita--Greater El Monte Dialysis Center
1938 Tyler Ave., Ste. J-168
South El Monte, CA 91733
Ph: (626)350-6692
Free: 800-424-6589
URL: http://www.davita.com
Dialysis Stations: 14.

23235 ■ Greater Los Angeles Dialysis Inc.
11204 E Rush St.
South El Monte, CA 91733
Ph: (626)582-1121
Dialysis Stations: 17.

South San Francisco

23236 ■ Satellite Dialysis--South San Francisco
Satellite Healthcare
205 Kenwood Way
South San Francisco, CA 94080
Ph: (650)616-7788
URL: http://satellitehealth.com
Dialysis Stations: 24.

23237 ■ Westborough Dialysis Center
DaVita
925 El Camino Real
South San Francisco, CA 94080
Ph: (650)624-5433
Free: 800-424-6589
URL: http://www.davita.com
Dialysis Stations: 5.

Stanford

23238 ■ Stanford Hospital & Clinics Transplant Services
Boswell Clinic, A160
300 Pasteur Dr.
Stanford, CA 94305
Ph: (650)725-9891
URL: http://stanfordhospital.org/clinicsmedServices/COE/transplant/kidney/
Dialysis Stations: 0.

Stockton

23239 ■ Delta Sierra Dialysis Center
DaVita
555 W Benjamin Holt Dr., No. 200
Stockton, CA 95207
Ph: (209)473-2294
Free: 800-424-6589
URL: http://www.davita.com
Dialysis Stations: 13.

23240 ■ RAI North California
Renal Advantage Inc.
2350 N California St.
Stockton, CA 95204
Ph: (209)943-0854
URL: http://www.renaladvantage.com
Dialysis Stations: 15. **Formerly:** Gambro Healthcare of Stockton.

23241 ■ RAI West March
Renal Advantage Inc.
3115 W March Ln., Ste. A
Stockton, CA 95219
Ph: (209)955-7527
URL: http://www.renaladvantage.com
Dialysis Stations: 36. **Formerly:** Gambro Healthcare of San Joaquin.

23242 ■ Satellite Dialysis of Stockton
Satellite Healthcare
1801 E March Ln., Ste. A-100
Stockton, CA 95210
Ph: (209)473-6890
URL: http://www.satellitehealth.com/
Dialysis Stations: 25.

23243 ■ Stockton Home Dialysis Center
DaVita
545 E Cleveland St., Ste. A
Stockton, CA 95204
Ph: (209)944-9055
Free: 800-424-6589
URL: http://www.davita.com
Dialysis Stations: 0. **Formerly:** Gambro Healthcare.

23244 ■ Stockton Kidney Clinic
DaVita
1523 E March La., Ste. 200
Stockton, CA 95210
Free: 800-424-6589
URL: http://www.davita.com
Dialysis Stations: 13.

23245 ■ Wellbound of Stockton LLC
Satellite Healthcare
3555 Deer Park Dr., Ste. 140
Stockton, CA 95219
Ph: (209)955-5630
URL: http://www.satellitehealth.com/
Dialysis Stations: 0.

Sunnyvale

23246 ■ Satellite Dialysis--Sunnyvale
Satellite Healthcare
155 N Wolfe Rd.
Sunnyvale, CA 94086
Ph: (408)617-1887
URL: http://satellitehealth.com
Dialysis Stations: 25.

Temecula

23247 ■ DaVita--Temecula Dialysis Center
40945 County Center Dr., Ste. G
Temecula, CA 92591
Ph: (951)296-9744
Free: 800-424-6589
URL: http://www.davita.com
Dialysis Stations: 18. **Formerly:** California Kidney Center.

Temple City

23248 ■ Temple City Dialysis Facility, Inc.
9945 Lower Asuza Rd.
Temple City, CA 91780
Ph: (626)442-3400
Dialysis Stations: 18.

Templeton

23249 ■ Kidney Dialysis Center of Templeton LLC
Kidney Center Inc.
1310 Las Tablas Rd., Ste. 103
Templeton, CA 93465
Ph: (805)434-3473
URL: http://www.kidneycenter.com/Dialysis_Facilities/Dialysis_Centers.htm
Dialysis Stations: 16.

Thousand Oaks

23250 ■ Fresenius Medical Care--Conejo Valley Renal Center
227 W Janss Rd., Ste. 115
Thousand Oaks, CA 91360
Ph: (805)496-6071
Free: 866-434-2597
URL: http://www.ultracare-dialysis.com/
Dialysis Stations: 15.

23251 ■ Regional Kidney Center Inc.
Kidney Center of Thousand Oaks, Inc.
375 Rolling Oaks Dr., Ste. 100
Thousand Oaks, CA 91361
Ph: (805)557-1036
Dialysis Stations: 15.

Torrance

23252 ■ DaVita--TRC/Harbor, University of California, Los Angeles
Dialysis Facility & At Home
21602 S Vermont Ave.
Torrance, CA 90502
Ph: (310)533-0413
Free: 800-424-6589
URL: http://www.davita.com
Dialysis Stations: 30.

23253 ■ LAC Harbor--UCLA Medical Center
1000 W Carson St.
Torrance, CA 90509
Ph: (310)222-2462
URL: http://www.humc.edu/
Dialysis Stations: 5.

23254 ■ LAC Harbor--UCLA Medical Center
Box 429 (Hemodialysis)
Torrance, CA 90509
Ph: (310)222-2462
URL: http://www.humc.edu/
Dialysis Stations: 5.

23255 ■ Pacific South Bay Dialysis Inc.
Beach Cities Dialysis--Torrance
20911 Earl St., Ste. 160
Torrance, CA 90503
Ph: (310)371-4244
Fax: (310)371-2166
URL: http://www.idsdialysis.com
Dialysis Stations: 9.

23256 ■ Skypark Dialysis
Innovative Dialysis Systems
3295 Skypark Dr.
Torrance, CA 90505
Ph: (310)539-5091
URL: http://www.idsdialysis.com
Dialysis Stations: 12. **Formerly:** Pacific Gateway.

Tracy

23257 ■ Satellite Dialysis--Tracy
Satellite Healthcare
2156 W Grant Line Rd., Ste. 150
Tracy, CA 95377
Ph: (209)832-4899
URL: http://www.satellitehealth.com/
Dialysis Stations: 25.

23258 ■ Tracy Dialysis Center
DaVita
425 Beverly Pl., Ste. A
Tracy, CA 95376
Ph: (209)839-0398
Free: 800-424-6589
Fax: (209)839-7009
URL: http://www.davita.com
Dialysis Stations: 12. **Formerly:** Gambro Healthcare.

Tulare

23259 ■ Tulare Dialysis
DaVita
545 E Tulare Ave.
Tulare, CA 93274
Ph: (559)688-8991
Free: 800-424-6589
URL: http://www.davita.com
Dialysis Stations: 16. **Formerly:** Gambro.

Turlock

23260 ■ DaVita
Turlock Dialysis Center
50 W Syracuse Ave.
Turlock, CA 95380
Free: 800-424-6589
URL: http://www.davita.com
Dialysis Stations: 16.

23261 ■ Satellite Dialysis--Turlock
Satellite Healthcare
1729 N Olive, No. 9
Turlock, CA 95382
Ph: (209)667-4888
URL: http://satellitehealth.com
Dialysis Stations: 25.

Tustin

23262 ■ RAI--East First Street--Tustin
Renal Advantage Inc.
535 E 1st St.
Tustin, CA 92780
Ph: (714)730-1428
URL: http://www.renaladvantage.com
Dialysis Stations: 25. **Formerly:** Gambro.

Ukiah

23263 ■ Pear Tree Dialysis Center
DaVita
126 N Orchard
Ukiah, CA 95482
Ph: (707)467-9000
Free: 800-424-6589
URL: http://www.davita.com
Dialysis Stations: 12. **Formerly:** Gambro Healthcare.

Union City

23264 ■ Union City Dialysis Center
DaVita
32930 Alvarado-Niles Rd., No. 300
Union City, CA 94587
Ph: (510)489-6996
Free: 800-424-6589
URL: http://www.davita.com
Dialysis Stations: 38.

Upland

23265 ■ Upland Dialysis
DaVita
600 N 13th Ave.
Upland, CA 91786
Ph: (909)946-3802
Free: 800-424-6589
URL: http://www.davita.com
Dialysis Stations: 24.

Vacaville

23266 ■ Creekside Dialysis Center
DaVita
141 Parker St.
Vacaville, CA 95688
Ph: (707)453-1325
Free: 800-424-6589
URL: http://www.davita.com
Dialysis Stations: 12.

23267 ■ Vacaville Dialysis Clinic
DaVita
941 Merchant St.
Vacaville, CA 95688
Ph: (707)449-6485
Free: 800-424-6589
URL: http://www.davita.com
Dialysis Stations: 15.

Valencia

23268 ■ Santa Clarita Kidney Center
Innovative Dialysis Systems
23861 W McBean Pkwy., Ste. E-11
Valencia, CA 91355
Ph: (661)222-7370
URL: http://www.idsdialysis.com
Dialysis Stations: 15.

Vallejo

23269 ■ Carquinez Dialysis Center
DaVita
125 Corporate Pl., Ste. C
Vallejo, CA 94590
Ph: (707)556-3637
Free: 800-424-6589
URL: http://www.davita.com
Dialysis Stations: 21.

23270 ■ Vallejo Dialysis Center
DaVita
121 Hospital Dr.
Vallejo, CA 94589
Ph: (707)553-9174
Free: 800-424-6589
URL: http://www.davita.com
Dialysis Stations: 19.

23271 ■ Wellbound of Vallejo
Satellite Healthcare
480 Redwood St., Ste. 40
Vallejo, CA 94590
Ph: (707)556-3070
URL: http://www.satellitehealth.com/
Dialysis Stations: 4.

Van Nuys

23272 ■ DaVita--Valley Dialysis Center
16149 Hart St.
Van Nuys, CA 91406
Ph: (818)787-0990
Free: 800-424-6589
URL: http://www.davita.com
Dialysis Stations: 23.

23273 ■ Kidney Center of Van Nuys
14624 Sherman Way, Ste. 106
Van Nuys, CA 91405
Ph: (818)994-2333
Dialysis Stations: 14.

Ventura

23274 ■ Fresenius Medical Care--Ventura
4567 Telephone Rd., Ste. 101
Ventura, CA 93003
Ph: (805)658-9211
Free: 866-434-2597
URL: http://www.ultracare-dialysis.com/
Dialysis Stations: 27.

23275 ■ Kidney Center Inc.
Kidney Dialysis Center of Ventura LLC
2705 Loma Vista Rd., Ste. 101
Ventura, CA 93003
Ph: (805)643-7549
Dialysis Stations: 20.

Victorville

23276 ■ Desert Cities Dialysis Center
12675 Hesperia Rd.
Victorville, CA 92392
Ph: (760)241-8063
Dialysis Stations: 30.

Visalia

23277 ■ DaVita--Tri-Counties Home Training
433 S Bridge St.
Visalia, CA 93277
Ph: (559)734-0836
Free: 800-424-6589
URL: http://www.davita.com
Dialysis Stations: 2. **Formerly:** Gambro.

23278 ■ Gateway Home Dialysis
1120 N Chinowth
Visalia, CA 93291
Ph: (559)622-9844
Dialysis Stations: 1. **Formerly:** Visalia Dialysis Center.

23279 ■ Kaweah Delta Dialysis Facility
5040 W Tulare Ave.
Visalia, CA 93277
Ph: (559)624-3600
URL: http://www.kaweahdelta.org/services/renal.asp
Dialysis Stations: 26.

23280 ■ Visalia Dialysis
DaVita
1031 N Demaree Rd.
Visalia, CA 93291
Ph: (559)732-8149
Free: 800-424-6589
URL: http://www.davita.com
Dialysis Stations: 16. **Formerly:** Gambro.

Vista

23281 ■ Fresenius Medical Care--Buena Creek
950 Hacienda Dr.
Vista, CA 92081
Free: 866-434-2597
URL: http://www.ultracare-dialysis.com/
Dialysis Stations: 20.

23282 ■ Fresenius Medical Care--Oceanside
950 Hacienda Dr.
Vista, CA 92081
Free: 866-434-2597
URL: http://www.ultracare-dialysis.com/

Walnut Creek

23283 ■ Fresenius Medical Care--Walnut Creek
365 Lennon Ln., No. 160
Walnut Creek, CA 94598
Ph: (925)947-4545
Free: 866-434-2597
URL: http://www.ultracare-dialysis.com/
Dialysis Stations: 20. **Formerly:** Bio-Medical Applications of Walnut Creek.

23284 ■ Walnut Creek Dialysis Center & At Home
DaVita
4061 N Wiget Ln.
Walnut Creek, CA 94598
Ph: (925)979-9732
Free: 800-424-6589
URL: http://www.davita.com
Dialysis Stations: 3.

23285 ■ Walnut Creek Dialysis Center
DaVita
404 N Wiget La.
Walnut Creek, CA 94598
Free: 800-424-6589
URL: http://www.davita.com
Dialysis Stations: 24.

Watsonville

23286 ■ Satellite Dialysis--Watsonville
Satellite Healthcare
40 Penny Ln., Ste. 1
Watsonville, CA 95076
Ph: (831)728-8855
URL: http://satellitehealth.com
Dialysis Stations: 21.

West Covina

23287 ■ DaVita--Covina Dialysis Center
1547 W Garvey Ave. N
West Covina, CA 91790
Ph: (626)960-9404
Free: 800-424-6589
URL: http://www.davita.com
Dialysis Stations: 17.

23288 ■ Fresenius Medical Care--West Covina Kidney Center
Dialysis Facility
1540 W Covina Pkwy., Ste. 101
West Covina, CA 91790
Ph: (626)337-8007
Free: 866-434-2597
URL: http://www.ultracare-dialysis.com/
Dialysis Stations: 20.

23289 ■ Queens Dialysis Unit, Inc.
1135 S Sunset Ave., Ste. 103
West Covina, CA 91790
Ph: (626)337-4245
Dialysis Stations: 21.

West Hills

23290 ■ San Fernando West Kidney Center
7230 Medical Center Dr., Ste. 101
West Hills, CA 91307
Ph: (818)888-4730
Dialysis Stations: 12.

West Sacramento

23291 ■ West Sacramento Dialysis Clinic
DaVita
3450 Industrial Blvd., Ste. 100
West Sacramento, CA 95691
Ph: (916)371-4947
Free: 800-424-6589
URL: http://www.davita.com
Dialysis Stations: 21.

Westminster

23292 ■ RAI--Goldenwest--Westminster
Renal Advantage Inc.
15330 Goldenwest St.
Westminster, CA 92683
Ph: (714)373-1543
URL: http://www.renaladvantage.com
Dialysis Stations: 24.

23293 ■ RAI--Hospital Circle--Westminster
Renal Advantage Inc.
290 Hospital Circle
Westminster, CA 92683
Ph: (714)895-3698
URL: http://www.renaladvantage.com
Dialysis Stations: 16. **Formerly:** Gambro Healthcare.

23294 ■ Westminster South Dialysis
DaVita
14014 Magnolia St.
Westminster, CA 92683
Ph: (714)897-5659
Free: 800-424-6589
URL: http://www.davita.com
Dialysis Stations: 12. **Formerly:** Gambro Healthcare.

Whittier

23295 ■ DaVita - Whittier Dialysis Center
10055 Whittwood Dr., Ste. A
Whittier, CA 90603
Ph: (562)947-1808
Free: 800-424-6589
URL: http://www.davita.com
Dialysis Stations: 18.

23296 ■ Intercommunity Dialysis Center
12291 E Washington Blvd., Ste. 410
Whittier, CA 90606
Ph: (562)696-1841
Dialysis Stations: 31.

23297 ■ Whittier Kidney Dialysis Center
16417 E Whittier Blvd.
Whittier, CA 90603
Ph: (562)947-8999
Dialysis Stations: 29.

Windsor

23298 ■ Satellite Dialysis--Windsor
Satellite Healthcare
911 Medical Center Plz., Ste. 16
Windsor, CA 95492
Ph: (707)836-1091
URL: http://satellitehealth.com
Dialysis Stations: 12.

Woodland

23299 ■ Woodland Dialysis Services, LLC
35 W Main St.
Woodland, CA 95695
Ph: (530)668-4503
Dialysis Stations: 13.

Woodland Hills

23300 ■ Fresenius Medical Care--Woodland Hills
Dialysis Center
19836 Ventura Blvd., Ste. C
Woodland Hills, CA 91364
Ph: (818)713-9040
Free: 866-434-2597
URL: http://www.ultracare-dialysis.com/
Dialysis Stations: 21. **Formerly:** Kaiser Hospital Dialysis Center.

23301 ■ Kaiser Permanente--Woodland Hills Dialysis Center
5601 DeSoto Ave.
Woodland Hills, CA 91365
Ph: (818)719-3610
URL: http://www.kaiserpermanente.com
Dialysis Stations: 2.

Yorba Linda

23302 ■ Kaiser Foundation Hospital Medical Center--Anaheim
Kaiser Permanente
PD Unit
Peritoneal Dialysis Unit
22550 E Savi Ranch Pkwy.
Yorba Linda, CA 92887
Ph: (714)685-3785
URL: http://www.kaiserpermanente.com
Dialysis Stations: 1.

Yuba City

23303 ■ Plumas Street Dialysis Center
640 Plumas St.
Yuba City, CA 95991
Ph: (530)673-6656
Dialysis Stations: 15.

23304 ■ Yuba City Dialysis Center
DaVita
1525 Plumas Ct., Ste. A
Yuba City, CA 95991
Ph: (530)671-3652
Free: 800-424-6589
URL: http://www.davita.com
Dialysis Stations: 24.

Yucaipa

23305 ■ Yucaipa Dialysis Center
DaVita
33487 Yucaipa Blvd.
Yucaipa, CA 92399
Ph: (909)797-6200
Free: 800-424-6589
URL: http://www.davita.com
Dialysis Stations: 12.

Yucca Valley

23306 ■ Hi-Desert Dialysis
DaVita
58457 Twenty-Nine Palms Hwy., Ste. 102
Yucca Valley, CA 92284
Ph: (760)228-2045
Free: 800-424-6589
URL: http://www.davita.com
Dialysis Stations: 14. **Formerly:** Gambro Healthcare.

COLORADO

Alamosa

23307 ■ Alamosa Dialysis
DaVita
612 Del Sol Dr.
Alamosa, CO 81101
Ph: (719)589-2022
Free: 800-424-6589
URL: http://www.davita.com
Dialysis Stations: 12.

Arvada

23308 ■ Arvada Dialysis Center
DaVita
9950 W 80th Ave., Ste. 25
Arvada, CO 80005
Ph: (303)456-9556
Free: 800-424-6589
URL: http://www.davita.com
Dialysis Stations: 16. **Formerly:** Western Dialysis Center of Arvada.

23309 ■ Kidney Center of Arvada
American Renal Associates
5265 Vance St.
Arvada, CO 80002
Ph: (303)403-1127
Fax: (303)403-1128
URL: http://www.americanrenal.com
Dialysis Stations: 21.

Aurora

23310 ■ Aurora Dialysis
DaVita
1411 S Potomac, Ste. 100
Aurora, CO 80012
Ph: (303)368-1911
Free: 800-424-6589
URL: http://www.davita.com
Dialysis Stations: 27.

23311 ■ Aurora Dialysis
Fresenius Medical Care
962 Potamac Cir.
Aurora, CO 80011
Ph: (303)340-1398
Free: 866-434-2597
URL: http://www.ultracare-dialysis.com/
Dialysis Stations: 24. **Formerly:** Renal Care Group.

23312 ■ The Children's Hospital Kidney Center
13123 E 16th Ave., Box 328
Aurora, CO 80045
Ph: (720)777-6263
URL: http://www.thechildrenshospital.org/
Dialysis Stations: 9.

23313 ■ East Aurora Dialysis
DaVita
482 S Chambers Rd.
Aurora, CO 80017
Ph: (303)696-1137
Free: 800-424-6589
URL: http://www.davita.com
Dialysis Stations: 28.

23314 ■ University of Colorado Hospital--Dialysis
12605 E 16th Ave., Box F774
Aurora, CO 80045
Ph: (720)848-9700
URL: http://www.uch.edu/
Dialysis Stations: 10.

Boulder

23315 ■ Boulder Dialysis
DaVita
2880 Folsom St., Ste. 110
Boulder, CO 80304
Ph: (303)440-5600
Free: 800-424-6589
URL: http://www.davita.com
Dialysis Stations: 14. **Formerly:** Western Dialysis Center of Boulder.

Brighton

23316 ■ DaVita Brighton Dialysis
4700 E Bromley Ln., Ste. 103
Brighton, CO 80601
Ph: (303)659-2511
Free: 800-424-6589
URL: http://www.davita.com
Dialysis Stations: 12.

Canon City

23317 ■ Canon City Dialysis
Fresenius Medical Care
2245 Fremont Dr.
Canon City, CO 81212
Ph: (719)276-8404
Free: 866-434-2597
URL: http://www.ultracare-dialysis.com/
Dialysis Stations: 12.

Castle Rock

23318 ■ Liberty Dialysis--Castle Rock
4352 Trail Boss Dr.
Castle Rock, CO 80104
Ph: (303)389-5626
URL: http://www.libertydialysis.com
Dialysis Stations: 13.

Colorado Springs

23319 ■ Liberty Dialysis--Colorado Springs Central
1910 E Lelaray St.
Colorado Springs, CO 80909
Ph: (719)380-4878
URL: http://www.libertydialysis.com
Dialysis Stations: 26.

23320 ■ Liberty Dialysis--North Colorado Springs
2180 Hollowbrook Dr.
Colorado Springs, CO 80918
Ph: (719)593-2999
URL: http://www.libertydialysis.com
Dialysis Stations: 16.

23321 ■ Liberty Dialysis--South Colorado Springs
2508 Airport Rd.
Colorado Springs, CO 80909
Ph: (719)227-7455
URL: http://www.libertydialysis.com
Dialysis Stations: 18.

23322 ■ North Colorado Springs Dialysis
Davita
6071 E Woodmen Rd., Ste. 100/120
Colorado Springs, CO 80923
Ph: (719)638-1223
Free: 800-424-6589
URL: http://www.davita.com
Dialysis Stations: 15.

23323 ■ Pikes Peak Dialysis Center
DaVita
2002 Lelaray St., Ste. 130
Colorado Springs, CO 80909
Free: 800-424-6589
URL: http://www.davita.com
Dialysis Stations: 43.

23324 ■ Printers Place Dialysis Center
DaVita
2802 International Circle
Colorado Springs, CO 80910
Ph: (719)630-0602
Free: 800-424-6589
URL: http://www.davita.com
Dialysis Stations: 16.

23325 ■ Reliant Renal Care--Colorado Springs
Dialysis Facility
1605 N Union Blvd., No. 100
Colorado Springs, CO 80909
Ph: (719)447-0818
URL: http://www.reliantrenalcare.com/
Dialysis Stations: 16.

Commerce City

23326 ■ Commerce City Dialysis
DaVita
6320 Holly St.
Commerce City, CO 80022
Ph: (303)853-4300
Free: 800-424-6589
URL: http://www.davita.com
Dialysis Stations: 18.

Cortez

23327 ■ Four Corners Dialysis Clinic--Cortez
DaVita
610 E Main St., Ste. C
Cortez, CO 81321
Ph: (970)565-4302
Free: 800-424-6589
URL: http://www.davita.com
Dialysis Stations: 16.

Denver

23328 ■ Belcaro Dialysis
Davita
755 S Colorado Blvd.
Denver, CO 80246
Ph: (303)777-2844
Free: 800-424-6589
URL: http://www.davita.com
Dialysis Stations: 14.

23329 ■ Central Denver Dialysis
Fresenius Medical Care
765 S Broadway
Denver, CO 80209
Ph: (303)765-1699
Free: 866-434-2597
URL: http://www.ultracare-dialysis.com/
Dialysis Stations: 24. **Formerly:** RCG Central Denver.

23330 ■ Children's Hospital Kidney Center
13123 E 16th Ave
Denver, CO 80218
Ph: (720)777-6263
URL: http://www.thechildrenshospital.org/conditions/kidney_urinary/kidney/index
Dialysis Stations: 9.

23331 ■ Denver Dialysis
DaVita
2900 Downing St., Ste. C
Denver, CO 80205
Ph: (303)292-0303
Free: 800-424-6589
URL: http://www.davita.com
Dialysis Stations: 16.

23332 ■ Lowry Dialysis Center
DaVita
7465 E 1st Ave., Unit A
Denver, CO 80230
Ph: (303)367 0046
Free: 800-424-6589
URL: http://www.davita.com
Dialysis Stations: 26.

23333 ■ Park Hill Dilaysis
Fresenius Medical Care
7606 E 36th Ave.
Denver, CO 80238
Free: 866-434-2597
URL: http://www.ultracare-dialysis.com/
Dialysis Stations: 20.

23334 ■ Rocky Mountain Dialysis
Fresenius Medical Care
4600 Hale Pkwy., Ste. 120
Denver, CO 80220
Ph: (303)320-6894
Free: 866-434-2597
URL: http://www.ultracare-dialysis.com/
Dialysis Stations: 30. **Formerly:** RCG Rocky Mountain.

23335 ■ South Denver Dialysis
DaVita
850 E Harvard Ave., Ste. 60
Denver, CO 80210
Ph: (303)744-0559
Free: 800-424-6589
URL: http://www.davita.com
Dialysis Stations: 16. **Formerly:** Renal Treatment Center--South Denver.

Durango

23336 ■ Durango Dialysis Center
DaVita
72 Suttle St., Unit D
Durango, CO 81303
Ph: (970)385-8608
Free: 800-424-6589
URL: http://www.davita.com
Dialysis Stations: 8.

Englewood

23337 ■ Englewood Dialysis
DaVita
3247 S Lincoln St.
Englewood, CO 80110
Ph: (303)761-0600
Free: 800-424-6589
URL: http://www.davita.com
Dialysis Stations: 18.

23338 ■ Lonetree Dialysis
DaVita
9777 Mt. Pyramid Ct., Ste. 140
Englewood, CO 80112
Ph: (303)662-0466
Free: 800-424-6589
URL: http://www.davita.com
Dialysis Stations: 12.

Fort Collins

23339 ■ Northern Colorado Kidney Center
Fresenius Medical Care
1213 Riverside
Fort Collins, CO 80524
Ph: (970)493-7575
Free: 866-434-2597
URL: http://www.ultracare-dialysis.com/
Dialysis Stations: 20.

Fountain

23340 ■ Fountain Dialysis Center
DaVita
6910 Bandley Dr., Ste. 100
Fountain, CO 80817
Ph: (719)393-0190
Free: 800-424-6589
URL: http://www.davita.com
Dialysis Stations: 13.

Grand Junction

23341 ■ DCI--Grand Junction
2748 Crossroads Blvd.
Grand Junction, CO 81506
Ph: (970)255-0900
Dialysis Stations: 17.

23342 ■ Grand Junction Dialysis Center & At Home
DaVita
710 Wellington Ave., No. 20
Grand Junction, CO 81501
Ph: (970)263-8573
Free: 800-424-6589
URL: http://www.davita.com
Dialysis Stations: 18. **Formerly:** Saint Mary's Hospital.

23343 ■ Mesa County Dialysis
DaVita
561 25 Road, Ste. D
Grand Junction, CO 81505
Free: 800-424-6589
URL: http://www.davita.com
Dialysis Stations: 15.

Greeley

23344 ■ Willow Station Dialysis
Fresenius Medical Care - Greeley
2343 27th St., No. 503
Greeley, CO 80631
Ph: (970)330-6100
Free: 866-434-2597
URL: http://www.ultracare-dialysis.com/
Dialysis Stations: 25.

La Junta

23345 ■ LaJunta Dialysis
Fresenius Medical Care
1116 Carson Ave.
La Junta, CO 81050
Ph: (719)383-2300
Free: 866-434-2597
URL: http://www.ultracare-dialysis.com/
Dialysis Stations: 8.

Lafayette

23346 ■ Kidney Center of Lafayette
American Renal Associates
2655 Crescent Dr., Ste. C
Lafayette, CO 80026
Ph: (720)890-4661
Fax: (720)890-4662
URL: http://www.americanrenal.com
Dialysis Stations: 24.

Lakewood

23347 ■ DaVita Lakewood Dialysis Center
DaVita
1750 Pierce St.
Lakewood, CO 80214
Ph: (303)238-6111
Free: 800-424-6589
URL: http://www.davita.com
Dialysis Stations: 18.

23348 ■ Kidney Center of Lakewood
American Renal Associates
6166 W Alameda Ave.
Lakewood, CO 80226
Ph: (303)922-6371
Fax: (303)922-6372
URL: http://www.americanrenal.com
Dialysis Stations: 21.

Lamar

23349 ■ Lamar Dialysis
Fresenius Medical Care
108 W Lee Ave.
Lamar, CO 81052
Ph: (719)336-1170
Free: 866-434-2597
URL: http://www.ultracare-dialysis.com/
Dialysis Stations: 12.

Littleton

23350 ■ Littleton Dialysis
Davita
209 W County Line Rd.
Littleton, CO 80129
Ph: (303)730-7540
Free: 800-424-6589
URL: http://www.davita.com
Dialysis Stations: 17.

Longmont

23351 ■ Kidney Center of Longmont
American Renal Associates
1960 Ken Pratt Blvd., Ste. A
Longmont, CO 80501
Ph: (303)485-7100
Fax: (303)485-7099
URL: http://www.americanrenal.com
Dialysis Stations: 20.

23352 ■ Longmont Dialysis
DaVita
1715 Iron Horse Dr., Ste. 170
Longmont, CO 80501
Ph: (303)485-4084
Free: 800-424-6589
URL: http://www.davita.com
Dialysis Stations: 18.

Loveland

23353 ■ Loveland Dialysis
Fresenius Medical Care
2940 Ginnala Dr.
Loveland, CO 80538
Ph: (970)663-9155
Free: 866-434-2597
URL: http://www.ultracare-dialysis.com/
Dialysis Stations: 20. **Formerly:** Loveland Dialysis.

Montrose

23354 ■ Montrose Dialysis
Dialysis Clinic, Inc.
945 S 4th St.
Montrose, CO 81401
Ph: (970)240-3302
Dialysis Stations: 10.

Parker

23355 ■ Parker Dialysis Center
DaVita
10371 S Park Glenn Way, Ste. 180
Parker, CO 80138
Ph: (303)840-0541
Free: 800-424-6589
URL: http://www.davita.com
Dialysis Stations: 12.

Pueblo

23356 ■ Liberty Dialysis--Pueblo
850 Eagleridge Blvd.
Pueblo, CO 81008
Ph: (719)253-5980
URL: http://www.libertydialysis.com
Dialysis Stations: 18.

23357 ■ Pueblo Dialysys
Fresenius Medical Care
41 Montbello Rd., Ste. 200
Pueblo, CO 81001
Ph: (719)545-1575
Free: 866-434-2597
URL: http://www.ultracare-dialysis.com/
Dialysis Stations: 33. **Formerly:** Qualicenters--Pueblo.

23358 ■ Pueblo South Dialysis
Fresenius Medical Care
3426 Lake Ave., Ste. 110
Pueblo, CO 81004
Ph: (719)564-2442
Free: 866-434-2597
URL: http://www.ultracare-dialysis.com/
Dialysis Stations: 20.

Pueblo West

23359 ■ Pueblo West Dialysis
Fresenius Medical Care
73 N Aspen Ski Way
Pueblo West, CO 81007
Free: 866-434-2597
URL: http://www.ultracare-dialysis.com/
Dialysis Stations: 13.

Sterling

23360 ■ The James Harrigan Center Dialysis
615 Fairhurst
Sterling, CO 80751
Ph: (970)521-3208
Dialysis Stations: 12.

Thornton

23361 ■ DaVita - Thornton
8800 Fox Dr.
Thornton, CO 80260
Ph: (303)430-7020
Free: 800-424-6589
URL: http://www.davita.com
Dialysis Stations: 24.

Trinidad

23362 ■ Reliant Renal Care--Trinidad
400 Benedicta Ave., Ste. C
Trinidad, CO 81082
Ph: (719)845-0003
URL: http://www.reliantrenalcare.com/
Dialysis Stations: 12.

Walsenburg

23363 ■ Walsenburg Dialysis
Fresenius Medical Care
23450 Hwy. 160
Walsenburg, CO 81089
Free: 866-434-2597
URL: http://www.ultracare-dialysis.com/
Dialysis Stations: 12.

Westminster

23364 ■ Kidney Center of Westminster
American Renal Associates
8410 Decatur St., Ste. 200
Westminster, CO 80031
Ph: (303)430-6518
Fax: (303)430-6519
URL: http://www.americanrenal.com
Dialysis Stations: 24.

23365 ■ North Metro Denver Dialysis
DaVita
12365 Huron St., Ste. 500
Westminster, CO 80234
Ph: (303)451-9093
Free: 800-424-6589
URL: http://www.davita.com
Dialysis Stations: 17.

23366 ■ Westminster Dialysis
DaVita
9053 Harlan St., No. 90
Westminster, CO 80030
Ph: (303)427-2400
Free: 800-424-6589
URL: http://www.davita.com
Dialysis Stations: 22.

CONNECTICUT

Bloomfield

23367 ■ Bloomfield Dialysis
DaVita
29 Griffin Rd. S
Bloomfield, CT 06002
Ph: (860)243-5389
Free: 800-424-6589
URL: http://www.davita.com
Dialysis Stations: 16. **Formerly:** Gambro Healthcare.

Branford

23368 ■ Branford Dialysis
DaVita
249 W Main St.
Branford, CT 06405
Ph: (203)481-8531
Free: 800-424-6589
URL: http://www.davita.com
Dialysis Stations: 13. **Formerly:** Gambro Healthcare.

23369 ■ Shoreline Dialysis Center
Avantis Renal Therapy
34 E Industrial Rd.
Branford, CT 06405
Ph: (203)315-8113
URL: http://www.avantusrenaltherapy.com/
Dialysis Stations: 16.

Bridgeport

23370 ■ Bridgeport Dialysis
DaVita
900 Madison Ave.
Bridgeport, CT 06606
Ph: (203)335-0191
Free: 800-424-6589
URL: http://www.davita.com
Dialysis Stations: 51. **Formerly:** Gambro Healthcare.

Bristol

23371 ■ Fresenius Medical Care - Dialysis Services of Forestville
135 Middle St.
Bristol, CT 06010
Ph: (860)584-2155
Free: 866-434-2597
URL: http://www.ultracare-dialysis.com/
Dialysis Stations: 20.

Danbury

23372 ■ Danbury Hospital
Nelson A. Gelfman Dialysis Unit
111 Osborne St., Ste. 211
Danbury, CT 06810
Ph: (203)739-7382
URL: http://www.danburyhospital.org/
Dialysis Stations: 19.

East Hartford

23373 ■ East Hartford Dialysis Center
Fresenius Medical Care
200 Pitkin St.
East Hartford, CT 06108
Ph: (860)282-6266
Free: 866-434-2597
URL: http://www.ultracare-dialysis.com/
Dialysis Stations: 24.

Enfield

23374 ■ Enfield Dialysis Center
Fresenius Medical Care
113 Elm St.
Enfield, CT 06082
Free: 866-434-2597
URL: http://www.ultracare-dialysis.com/
Dialysis Stations: 13.

Fairfield

23375 ■ Black Rock Dialysis
DaVita
427 Stillson Rd.
Fairfield, CT 06824
Ph: (203)382-9566
Free: 800-424-6589
URL: http://www.davita.com
Dialysis Stations: 16.

23376 ■ Liberty Dialysis--Fairfield
500 Kings Hwy.
Fairfield, CT 06825
Ph: (203)583-8875
URL: http://www.libertydialysis.com
Dialysis Stations: 18.

Farmington

23377 ■ University of Connecticut Dialysis Center
230 Farmington Ave.
Farmington, CT 06032
Ph: (860)678-1459
URL: http://health.uchc.edu/clinicalservices/kidney/index.htm
Dialysis Stations: 20.

Hartford

23378 ■ Fresenius Medical Care--Hartford
3580 Main St.
Hartford, CT 06120
Ph: (860)560-4054
Free: 866-434-2597
URL: http://www.ultracare-dialysis.com/
Dialysis Stations: 19.

23379 ■ Hartford Dialysis
DaVita
675 Tower Ave.
Hartford, CT 06112
Ph: (860)242-0735
Free: 800-424-6589
URL: http://www.davita.com
Dialysis Stations: 24. **Formerly:** Saint Francis Hospital Dialysis Center; Gambro Healthcare.

23380 ■ Hartford Hospital
Dialysis Unit
80 Seymour St., JB7/JB8
Hartford, CT 06102

Ph: (860)545-2070
URL: http://www.harthosp.org
Dialysis Stations: 40.

23381 ■ Hartford Hospital Transplant Services
80 Seymour St., JB7/JB8
Hartford, CT 06102
Ph: (860)545-2070
URL: http://www.harthosp.org/transplant/KidneyTransplantation/default.aspx
Dialysis Stations: 40.

Manchester

23382 ■ Manchester Dialysis Center
Dialysis Clinic Inc.
319 Main St.
Manchester, CT 06040
Ph: (860)432-9499
URL: http://www.dciinc.org
Dialysis Stations: 31.

Meriden

23383 ■ Central Connecticut Dialysis Center
Fresenius Medical Care
377 Research Pkwy.
Meriden, CT 06450
Ph: (203)639-2880
Free: 866-434-2597
URL: http://www.ultracare-dialysis.com/
Dialysis Stations: 23.

Middletown

23384 ■ Middlesex Dialysis Center LLC
DaVita
100 Main St.
Middletown, CT 06457
Free: 800-424-6589
URL: http://www.davita.com
Dialysis Stations: 19.

Milford

23385 ■ Milford Dialysis
DaVita
470 Bridgeport Ave.
Milford, CT 06460
Ph: (203)882-9013
Free: 800-424-6589
URL: http://www.davita.com
Dialysis Stations: 14. **Formerly:** Gambro Healthcare.

New Britain

23386 ■ Hospital of Central Connecticut - Dialysis Unit
100 Grand St.
New Britain, CT 06050
Ph: (860)224-5011
URL: http://thocc.org
Dialysis Stations: 22. **Formerly:** New Britain General Hospital.

New Haven

23387 ■ New Haven Dialysis
DaVita
100 Church St. S, Ste. C
New Haven, CT 06519
Ph: (203)785-8885
Free: 800-424-6589
URL: http://www.davita.com
Dialysis Stations: 36. **Formerly:** Gambro Healthcare.

23388 ■ New Haven Home Dialysis
Fresenius Medical Care
136 Sherman Ave.
New Haven, CT 06511
Free: 866-434-2597
URL: http://www.ultracare-dialysis.com/
Dialysis Stations: 4.

23389 ■ St. Raphael Dialysis Center--New Haven
Hospital of St. Raphael
137 Water St.
New Haven, CT 06511
Ph: (203)772-2421
URL: http://www.srhs.org/body.cfm?id=169
Dialysis Stations: 28.

23390 ■ Yale-New Haven Organ Transplant Center
Yale-New Haven Hospital
Transplant & Immunology Section
New Haven, CT 06520
Ph: (203)785-2565
URL: http://www.ynhh.org/transplantation-center/default.aspx
Dialysis Stations: 0.

New London

23391 ■ New London Dialysis
DaVita
5 Shaw's Cove, Ste. 100
New London, CT 06320
Ph: (860)701-1357
Free: 800-424-6589
URL: http://www.davita.com
Dialysis Stations: 22. **Formerly:** Gambro Healthcare.

Newington

23392 ■ Dialysis Center of Newington
Fresenius Medical Care
375 Willard Ave.
Newington, CT 06111
Ph: (860)667-3898
Free: 866-434-2597
URL: http://www.ultracare-dialysis.com/
Dialysis Stations: 17.

North Haven

23393 ■ Liberty Dialysis--North Haven
510 Washington Ave.
North Haven, CT 06473
Ph: (203)234-7071
URL: http://www.libertydialysis.com
Dialysis Stations: 18.

23394 ■ North Haven Dialysis Center
Hospital of St. Raphael
266 State St., Ste. 2
North Haven, CT 06473
Ph: (203)230-1946
URL: http://www.srhs.org/body.cfm?id=109
Dialysis Stations: 18.

North Windham

23395 ■ Windham Dialysis Center
DaVita
375 Tuckie Rd.
North Windham, CT 06256
Ph: (860)456-1677
Free: 800-424-6589
URL: http://www.davita.com
Dialysis Stations: 7. **Formerly:** Rockville General Hospital Dialysis Unit in North Windham.

Norwalk

23396 ■ South Norwalk Dialysis
DaVita
31 Stevens St.
Norwalk, CT 06856
Ph: (203)838-6017
Free: 800-424-6589
URL: http://www.davita.com
Dialysis Stations: 22. **Formerly:** Gambro Healthcare.

Norwich

23397 ■ Norwich Dialysis
DaVita
113 Salem Tpke.
Norwich, CT 06360
Ph: (860)887-1632
Free: 800-424-6589
URL: http://www.davita.com
Dialysis Stations: 16.

Orange

23398 ■ Liberty Dialysis--Orange
240 Indian River Rd., Ste. D
Orange, CT 06477
Ph: (203)891-8992
URL: http://www.libertydialysis.com
Dialysis Stations: 19.

Plantsville

23399 ■ Fresenius Medical Care of Southington
341 West St.
Plantsville, CT 06479
Ph: (860)621-3557
Free: 866-434-2597
URL: http://www.ultracare-dialysis.com/
Dialysis Stations: 19.

Rocky Hill

23400 ■ Physicians Dialysis Inc.
DaVita
30 Waterchase Dr.
Rocky Hill, CT 06067
Ph: (860)563-6000
Free: 800-424-6589
URL: http://www.davita.com
Dialysis Stations: 24.

Shelton

23401 ■ Shelton Dialysis
DaVita
750 Bridgeport Ave.
Shelton, CT 06484
Ph: (203)925-9520
Free: 800-424-6589
URL: http://www.davita.com
Dialysis Stations: 16. **Formerly:** Gambro Healthcare.

Stamford

23402 ■ Stamford Dialysis
DaVita
30 Commerce Rd.
Stamford, CT 06902
Ph: (203)358-9969
Free: 800-424-6589
URL: http://www.davita.com
Dialysis Stations: 25. **Formerly:** Gambro Healthcare.

23403 ■ Stamford Dialysis
DaVita
30 Commerce Rd.
Stamford, CT 06902
Free: 800-424-6589
URL: http://www.davita.com
Dialysis Stations: 25.

Torrington

23404 ■ Torrington Dialysis
DaVita
Joseph Marcantonio Kidney Center
780 Litchfield, Ste. 100
Torrington, CT 06790
Free: 800-424-6589
URL: http://www.davita.com
Dialysis Stations: 19.

Vernon Rockville

23405 ■ Vernon Dialysis Center
DaVita
460 Hartford Tpke.
Vernon Rockville, CT 06066
Ph: (860)896-1537
Free: 800-424-6589
URL: http://www.davita.com
Dialysis Stations: 22. **Formerly:** Rockville General Hospital.

Waterbury

23406 ■ Greater Waterbury Dialysis
DaVita
209 Highland Ave.
Waterbury, CT 06708
Ph: (203)574-7933
Free: 800-424-6589
URL: http://www.davita.com
Dialysis Stations: 30. **Formerly:** Gambro Healthcare.

23407 ■ Waterbury Heights Dialysis
DaVita
150 Mattatuck Heights Rd.
Waterbury, CT 06705
Ph: (203)419-0488
Free: 800-424-6589
URL: http://www.davita.com
Dialysis Stations: 16.

DELAWARE

Dover

23408 ■ Bayhealth Medical Center--Kent General Campus
640 S State St.
Dover, DE 19901
Ph: (302)744-7322
URL: http://www.bayhealth.org
Dialysis Stations: 7.

23409 ■ Fresenius Medical Care--Central Delaware
Blue Hen Corporate Center
655 Bay Rd., Ste. 4M
Dover, DE 19901
Ph: (302)678-5718
Free: 866-434-2597
URL: http://www.ultracare-dialysis.com/
Dialysis Stations: 25.

23410 ■ Fresenius Medical Care--Greentree
97 Commerce Way, Ste. 104
Dover, DE 19904
Ph: (302)674-1919
Free: 866-434-2597
URL: http://www.ultracare-dialysis.com/
Dialysis Stations: 16.

Georgetown

23411 ■ Fresenius Medical Care--Mid Sussex County
34 Georgetown Pl.
Georgetown, DE 19947
Ph: (302)854-0230
Free: 866-434-2597
URL: http://www.ultracare-dialysis.com/
Dialysis Stations: 21.

Lewes

23412 ■ Beebe Medical Center
Dialysis Center
424 Savannah Rd.
Lewes, DE 19958
Ph: (302)645-3643
URL: http://www.beebemed.org
Dialysis Stations: 2.

Middletown

23413 ■ Fresenius Medical Care of Middletown
104 Sleepy Hollow Dr., Ste. 100
Middletown, DE 19709
Ph: (302)449-1601
Free: 866-434-2597
URL: http://www.ultracare-dialysis.com/
Dialysis Stations: 12.

Milford

23414 ■ Fresenius Medical Care--Milford
656-D N Dupont Hwy.
Milford, DE 19963
Ph: (302)424-0552
Free: 866-434-2597
URL: http://www.ultracare-dialysis.com/
Dialysis Stations: 25. **Formerly:** Bio-Medical Applications of Milford.

New Castle

23415 ■ Fresenius Medical Care Dialysis Services--First State, Inc.
608 Ferry Cutoff St.
New Castle, DE 19720
Ph: (302)328-9044
Free: 866-434-2597
URL: http://www.ultracare-dialysis.com/
Dialysis Stations: 24.

Newark

23416 ■ Christiana Care Health System Renal Transplant
Medical Arts Pavilion 2, Ste. 2224
4735 Ogletown-Stanton Rd.
Newark, DE 19718
Ph: (302)623-3866
Free: 866-682-6792
URL: http://www.christianacare.org/kidneytransplant
Dialysis Stations: 0.

23417 ■ Christiana Hospital Hemodialysis Unit
Christiana Care Health System
4755 Ogleton-Stanton Rd.
Newark, DE 19718
Ph: (302)733-1001
URL: http://www.christianacare.org
Dialysis Stations: 17.

23418 ■ Fresenius Medical Care--Christiana Dialysis Facility
University Plaza Shopping Center
63 University Plz.
Newark, DE 19702
Ph: (302)453-8834
Free: 866-434-2597
URL: http://www.ultracare-dialysis.com/
Dialysis Stations: 20.

Rehoboth Beach

23419 ■ Fresenius Medical Care of Rehoboth, Inc.
Dialysis Facility
20699 Coastal Hwy., Ste. 3
Rehoboth Beach, DE 19971
Ph: (302)226-9330
Free: 866-434-2597
URL: http://www.ultracare-dialysis.com/
Dialysis Stations: 16.

Seaford

23420 ■ Fresenius Medical Care--Seaford
23006 Sussex Hwy.
Seaford, DE 19973
Ph: (302)268-3152
Free: 866-434-2597
URL: http://www.ultracare-dialysis.com/
Dialysis Stations: 16.

23421 ■ Liberty Dialysis--Seaford
600 Health Services Dr.
Seaford, DE 19973
Ph: (302)262-0852
URL: http://www.libertydialysis.com
Dialysis Stations: 16.

Smyrna

23422 ■ Fresenius Medical Care--Smyrna
210 Stadium St., Rte. 13
Smyrna, DE 19977
Ph: (302)659-5220
Free: 866-434-2597
URL: http://www.ultracare-dialysis.com/
Dialysis Stations: 16.

Wilmington

23423 ■ Alfred I. DuPont Hospital for Children's Dialysis Center
Transplant/Dialysis Center
1600 Rockland Rd.
Wilmington, DE 19899
Ph: (302)651-5374
URL: http://www.nemours.org/hospital/de/aidhc.html
Dialysis Stations: 6.

23424 ■ Fresenius Medical Care--Brandywine Dialysis Facility
303 A St.
Wilmington, DE 19801
Ph: (302)658-7469
Free: 866-434-2597
URL: http://www.ultracare-dialysis.com/
Dialysis Stations: 25.

23425 ■ Fresenius Medical Care--Newport Pike
605 W Newport Pke.
Wilmington, DE 19804
Ph: (302)633-6228
Free: 866-434-2597
URL: http://www.ultracare-dialysis.com/
Dialysis Stations: 16.

23426 ■ Fresenius Medical Care--North Wilmington
4000 Washington St.
Wilmington, DE 19802
Ph: (302)762-2903
Free: 866-434-2597
URL: http://www.ultracare-dialysis.com/
Dialysis Stations: 17.

23427 ■ Fresenius Medical Care--Riverside Park
700 W Lea Blvd.
Riverside Medical Arts Complex, Ste. G2
Wilmington, DE 19802
Ph: (302)762-8585
Free: 866-434-2597
Dialysis Stations: 26.

23428 ■ Fresenius Medical Care of Wilmington, Inc.
Dialysis Services
St. Francis Hospital, Ste. 404
7th & Clayton St.
Wilmington, DE 19806
Ph: (302)421-9177
Free: 866-434-2597
URL: http://www.ultracare-dialysis.com/
Dialysis Stations: 17.

23429 ■ Liberty Dialysis--Wilmington
913 Delaware Ave.
Wilmington, DE 19806
Ph: (302)429-0142
URL: http://www.libertydialysis.com
Dialysis Stations: 19.

DISTRICT OF COLUMBIA

Washington

23430 ■ BMA--Columbia Heights Fresenius Medical Care
106 Irving St. NW, Ste. 1400
Washington, DC 20010
Ph: (202)829-0060
Free: 866-434-2597
URL: http://www.ultracare-dialysis.com/
Dialysis Stations: 35.

23431 ■ BMA Dupont Circle Fresenius Medical Care
11 DuPont Circle NW, Ste. LL-100
Washington, DC 20036
Ph: (202)483-0176
Free: 866-434-2597
URL: http://www.ultracare-dialysis.com/
Dialysis Stations: 30.

23432 ■ Capitol Dialysis American Renal Associates
140 Q St. NE
Washington, DC 20002
Ph: (202)636-9411
URL: http://www.americanrenal.com
Dialysis Stations: 29.

23433 ■ Children's National Medical Center Dialysis Unit
111 Michigan Ave. NW, Rm. 3130
Washington, DC 20010
Ph: (202)476-5148
URL: http://www.childrensnational.org
Dialysis Stations: 6.

23434 ■ Children's National Medical Center--Transplant
Dept. of Nephrology W Wing 1.5
Washington, DC 20010
Ph: (202)476-5058
URL: http://www.childrensnational.org/DepartmentsandPrograms/default.aspx?Id=227&Type=Program&Name=KidneyTransplantation
Dialysis Stations: 0.

23435 ■ DaVita--Brentwood Dialysis Facility
1231 Brentwood Rd. NE
Washington, DC 20018
Ph: (202)636-3711
Free: 800-424-6589
URL: http://www.davita.com
Dialysis Stations: 24. **Formerly:** Gambro Healthcare - Brentwood.

23436 ■ DaVita--Eighth Street Dialysis Facility
300 8th St. NE
Washington, DC 20002
Ph: (202)543-9105
Free: 800-424-6589
URL: http://www.davita.com
Dialysis Stations: 24. **Formerly:** Gambro Healthcare - Eighth Street.

23437 ■ DaVita--George Washington Southeast Dialysis Unit
3857-A Pennsylvania Ave. SE
Washington, DC 20020
Free: 800-424-6589
URL: http://www.davita.com
Dialysis Stations: 15. **Formerly:** Gambro Healthcare - Southeast.

23438 ■ DaVita--K Street Dialysis
2131 K St. NW
Washington, DC 20037
Ph: (202)223-8453
Free: 800-424-6589
URL: http://www.davita.com
Dialysis Stations: 25.

23439 ■ DaVita--Lee Street Dialysis Facility
5155 Lee St. NE
Washington, DC 20019
Ph: (202)398-1047
Free: 800-424-6589
URL: http://www.davita.com
Dialysis Stations: 20.

23440 ■ East River Park Dialysis Center Fresenius Medical Care
3929 Minnesota Ave. NE
Washington, DC 20019
Ph: (202)397-2700
Free: 866-434-2597
URL: http://www.ultracare-dialysis.com/
Dialysis Stations: 18.

23441 ■ Fresenius Medical Care BMA--Northeast Washington
817 Varnum St. NE
Washington, DC 20017
Free: 866-434-2597
URL: http://www.ultracare-dialysis.com/
Dialysis Stations: 20.

23442 ■ Georgetown University Hospital Renal Dialysis Unit
3800 Reservoir Rd. NW, 2nd Main
Washington, DC 20007
Ph: (202)444-3664
URL: http://www.georgetownuniversityhospital.org
Dialysis Stations: 5.

23443 ■ Georgetown University Hospital Renal Dialysis Unit/Transplant
3800 Reservoir Rd., NW
Washington, DC 20007
Ph: (202)444-3664
URL: http://www.georgetownuniversityhospital.org/
Dialysis Stations: 5.

23444 ■ Grant Park Dialysis daVita
5000 Nannie Helen Burroughs Ave. NE
Washington, DC 20019
Ph: (202)399-7700
Free: 800-424-6589
URL: http://www.davita.com
Dialysis Stations: 12.

23445 ■ Greater Southeast Community Dialysis Center Fresenius Medical Care
1350 Southern Ave. SE
Washington, DC 20032
Ph: (202)561-0828
Free: 866-434-2597
URL: http://www.ultracare-dialysis.com/
Dialysis Stations: 12.

23446 ■ Howard University Hospital Renal Dialysis Unit
2041 Georgia Ave. NW
Washington, DC 20060
Ph: (202)865-7365
URL: http://www.howard.edu
Dialysis Stations: 21.

23447 ■ Total Renal Care--Georgetown on the Potomac DaVita
3223 K St. NW, Ste. 110
Washington, DC 20007
Ph: (202)333-5211
Free: 800-424-6589
URL: http://www.davita.com
Dialysis Stations: 12.

23448 ■ Union Plaza Dialysis Center DaVita
810 1st St. NE, Ste. 100
Washington, DC 20002
Ph: (202)842-3127
Free: 800-424-6589
URL: http://www.davita.com
Dialysis Stations: 15.

23449 ■ Washington Hospital Center Section of Nephrology
110 Irving St. NW, Rm. 2A66
Washington, DC 20010
Ph: (202)877-5645
URL: http://www.whcenter.org/body.cfm?id=555638
Dialysis Stations: 20.

23450 ■ Washington Nursing Dialysis DaVita
2425 25th St. SE
Washington, DC 20020
Free: 800-424-6589
URL: http://www.davita.com
Dialysis Stations: 9.

FLORIDA

Alachua

23451 ■ Fresenius Medical Care Dialysis Services--Alachua
11550 Research Cir.
Alachua, FL 32615
Ph: (386)418-2235
Free: 866-434-2597
URL: http://www.ultracare-dialysis.com/
Dialysis Stations: 15.

Altamonte Springs

23452 ■ BMA--North Orlando Fresenius Medical Care Dialysis Facility
750 S North Lake Blvd., Ste. 1024
Altamonte Springs, FL 32701
Ph: (407)831-7070
Free: 866-434-2597
URL: http://www.ultracare-dialysis.com/
Dialysis Stations: 12.

Apopka

23453 ■ Apopka Artificial Kidney Center Fresenius Medical Care
1065 W Orange Blossom Trl.
Apopka, FL 32712
Ph: (607)880-2121
Free: 866-434-2597
URL: http://www.ultracare-dialysis.com/
Dialysis Stations: 16.

23454 ■ Apopka Dialysis DaVita
640 Executive Park Ct.
Apopka, FL 32703
Ph: (407)389-8980
Free: 800-424-6589
URL: http://www.davita.com
Dialysis Stations: 24. **Formerly:** Dialysis Services Central Florida.

Arcadia

23455 ■ Arcadia Dialysis Center Davita
1341 E Oak St.
Arcadia, FL 34266
Ph: (863)491-8550
Free: 800-424-6589
URL: http://www.davita.com
Dialysis Stations: 15.

Atlantis

23456 ■ Fresenius Medical Care--Atlantis
5503 S Congress Ave., Ste. 101
Atlantis, FL 33462
Ph: (561)967-0633

Free: 866-434-2597
URL: http://www.ultracare-dialysis.com/
Dialysis Stations: 21. **Formerly:** Atlantis Dialysis Center.

Ave Maria

23457 ■ Ave Maria Dialysis
DaVita
5340 Useppa Dr., Ste. 101
Ave Maria, FL 34142
Free: 800-424-6589
URL: http://www.davita.com
Dialysis Stations: 16.

Bartow

23458 ■ Bartow Dialysis
DaVita
1190 E Church St.
Bartow, FL 33830
Ph: (863)533-1601
Free: 800-424-6589
URL: http://www.davita.com
Dialysis Stations: 17. **Formerly:** Gambro Healthcare.

Belle Glade

23459 ■ Renal Care Center--Belle Glade
Fresenius Medical Care
933 SE 1st St.
Belle Glade, FL 33430
Ph: (561)996-0602
Free: 866-434-2597
URL: http://www.ultracare-dialysis.com/
Dialysis Stations: 27.

Boca Raton

23460 ■ American Renal Associates
1905 Clint Moore Rd., Ste. 211
Boca Raton, FL 33496
Ph: (561)893-6878
URL: http://www.americanrenal.com
Dialysis Stations: 21. **Formerly:** Boca/Delray Renal Associates Inc.

23461 ■ American Renal Associates - South Boca Raton Dialysis LLC
905 Clint Moore Rd.
Boca Raton, FL 33496
Ph: (561)893-6878
URL: http://www.americanrenal.com
Dialysis Stations: 6.

23462 ■ Boca Raton Artificial Kidney Center
DaVita
998 NW 9th Ct.
Boca Raton, FL 33486
Ph: (561)392-3940
Free: 800-424-6589
URL: http://www.davita.com
Dialysis Stations: 14.

23463 ■ Pinnacle Dialysis of Boca Raton
DaVita
2900 N Military Trl., Ste. 195
Boca Raton, FL 33431
Ph: (561)241-6667
Free: 800-424-6589
URL: http://www.davita.com
Dialysis Stations: 27.

23464 ■ Renal Associates of Boca Raton, Inc.
1905 Clint Moore Rd., Ste. 211
Boca Raton, FL 33496
Ph: (561)893-6878
Free: 800-446-5013
E-mail: info@bocaratondialysis.com
URL: http://www.bocaratondialysis.com
Dialysis Stations: 21.

23465 ■ West Boca Dialysis Center
Fresenius Medical Care
19801 Hampton Dr.
Boca Raton, FL 33434
Ph: (561)488-0202
Free: 866-434-2597
URL: http://www.ultracare-dialysis.com/
Dialysis Stations: 19.

Bonita Springs

23466 ■ Bonita Springs Dialysis
DaVita
9134 Bonita Beach Rd.
Bonita Springs, FL 34135
Ph: (239)949-0444
Free: 800-424-6589
URL: http://www.davita.com
Dialysis Stations: 16. **Formerly:** Gambro Healthcare.

23467 ■ Naples AKC--North Collier Branch
Fresenius Medical Care
3465 Bonita Beach Rd., No. 9
Bonita Springs, FL 34134
Ph: (239)495-8883
Free: 866-434-2597
URL: http://www.ultracare-dialysis.com/
Dialysis Stations: 14.

Boynton Beach

23468 ■ BMA--Boynton Beach
Fresenius Medical Care
3451 Woolbright Rd.
Boynton Beach, FL 33436
Ph: (561)737-8970
Free: 866-434-2597
URL: http://www.ultracare-dialysis.com/
Dialysis Stations: 12.

23469 ■ Boynton Beach Dialysis Center
Fresenius Medical Care
3925 W Boynton Beach Blvd., No. 110
Boynton Beach, FL 33436
Ph: (561)740-4025
Free: 866-434-2597
URL: https://www.ultracare-dialysis.com/
Dialysis Stations: 21.

23470 ■ Fresenius Medical Care--Boynton Beach Gulf Stream
3925 W Boynton Beach Blvd., Ste. 110
Boynton Beach, FL 33436
Free: 866-434-2597
URL: http://www.ultracare-dialysis.com/

23471 ■ Fresenius Medical Care - North Boynton Beach Dialysis Services
4965 Lechalet Blvd.
Boynton Beach, FL 33436
Ph: (561)734-5585
Free: 866-434-2597
URL: http://www.ultracare-dialysis.com/
Dialysis Stations: 17.

23472 ■ Universal Kidney Center of Boynton Beach
4895 Windward Passage Dr., Ste. 5
Boynton Beach, FL 33436
Ph: (561)740-1981
URL: http://www.universalkidneycenter.com
Dialysis Stations: 21.

Bradenton

23473 ■ Bradenton Artificial Kidney Center
Fresenius Medical Care
5902 Pointe West Blvd.
Bradenton, FL 34209
Ph: (941)792-3290
Free: 866-434-2597
URL: http://www.ultracare-dialysis.com/
Dialysis Stations: 21.

23474 ■ Bradenton Dialysis Center LLC
American Renal Associates
5837 W 21st Ave.
Bradenton, FL 34209
Ph: (303)403-1127
URL: http://www.americanrenal.com
Dialysis Stations: 16.

23475 ■ Bradenton Dialysis
DaVita
3501 Cortez Rd. W
Bradenton, FL 34210
Ph: (941)727-4209
Free: 800-424-6589
URL: http://www.davita.com
Dialysis Stations: 17. **Formerly:** Gambro Healthcare.

23476 ■ Southwest Florida Dialysis Center
Renal Carepartners
520 Manatee Ave. E
Bradenton, FL 34208
Ph: (941)747-5500
URL: http://www.renalcp.com
Dialysis Stations: 24.

Brandon

23477 ■ Brandon Artificial Kidney Center
Fresenius Medical Care
634 Oakfield Dr.
Brandon, FL 33511
Ph: (813)661-3815
Free: 866-434-2597
URL: http://www.ultracare-dialysis.com/
Dialysis Stations: 16.

23478 ■ Brandon Dialysis Center
Diversified Specialty Institutes
731 W Lumsden Rd.
Brandon, FL 33511
Ph: (813)661-7474
URL: http://www.dsi-corp.com

23479 ■ Brandon East Dialysis
DaVita
114 E Brandon Blvd.
Brandon, FL 33511
Ph: (813)657-2783
Free: 800-424-6589
URL: http://www.davita.com
Dialysis Stations: 20. **Formerly:** Gambro Healthcare.

Cape Coral

23480 ■ Cape Coral South Dialysis
DaVita
3046 Del Prado Blvd. S, Ste. 4A
Cape Coral, FL 33904
Ph: (239)549-0339
Free: 800-424-6589
URL: http://www.davita.com
Dialysis Stations: 18.

Casselberry

23481 ■ Casselberry Dialysis
DaVita
4970 S US Hwy. 17/92
Casselberry, FL 32707
Free: 800-424-6589
URL: http://www.davita.com
Dialysis Stations: 20.

Celebration

23482 ■ Celebration Dialysis
DaVita
1154 Celebration Blvd.
Celebration, FL 34747
Ph: (407)566-1780
Free: 800-424-6589
URL: http://www.davita.com
Dialysis Stations: 20.

Century

23483 ■ Fresenius Medical Care--Century
6001 Industrial Blvd.
Century, FL 32535
Ph: (850)256-4727
Free: 866-434-2597
URL: http://www.ultracare-dialysis.com/
Dialysis Stations: 13. **Formerly:** Renal Care Group.

Chipley

23484 ■ Chipley Dialysis
DaVita
877 3rd St., Ste. 2
Chipley, FL 32428
Ph: (850)638-7783
Free: 800-424-6589
URL: http://www.davita.com
Dialysis Stations: 14. **Formerly:** Community Dialysis Center.

Citra

23485 ■ Ocala Regional Kidney Center North
DaVita
2620 W Hwy. 316
Citra, FL 32113
Ph: (352)591-4680
Free: 800-424-6589
URL: http://www.davita.com
Dialysis Stations: 15.

Clearwater

23486 ■ Belleair Dialysis Center
Fresenius Medical Care
617 Lakeview Rd., Ste. B
Clearwater, FL 33756
Free: 866-434-2597
URL: http://www.ultracare-dialysis.com/
Dialysis Stations: 20.

23487 ■ BMA--Clearwater
Fresenius Medical Care
2565 Enterprise Rd.
Clearwater, FL 33763
Ph: (727)796-9122
Free: 866-434-2597
URL: http://www.ultracare-dialysis.com/
Dialysis Stations: 16.

23488 ■ FMC--Belleair Home Therapies
Kidney Group of Clearwater LLC
617 Lakeview Rd., Ste. C
Clearwater, FL 33756
Ph: (727)441-8590
Dialysis Stations: 2.

23489 ■ Renal Advantage Inc. Care Centers - Clearwater
1124 Lakeview Rd., Ste. 1
Clearwater, FL 33756
Ph: (727)461-5477
URL: http://www.renaladvantage.com
Dialysis Stations: 20

23490 ■ Renal Advantage Inc. Care Centers--Clearwater
29296 US Hwy. 19 N, Ste. 1
Clearwater, FL 33761
Ph: (727)785-9036
URL: http://www.renaladvantage.com
Dialysis Stations: 21.

Clermont

23491 ■ Fresenius Medical Care --Clermont
312 Mowhawk Rd.
Clermont, FL 34715
Ph: (352)243-1200
Free: 866-434-2597
URL: http://www.ultracare-dialysis.com/
Dialysis Stations: 16. **Formerly:** Renal Care Group.

Clewiston

23492 ■ Fresenius Medical Care Dialysis Services--Clewiston
851 W Ventura Ave.
Clewiston, FL 33440
Ph: (863)983-8855
Free: 866-434-2597
URL: http://www.ultracare-dialysis.com/
Dialysis Stations: 10.

Cooper City

23493 ■ Embassy Lakes Artificial Kidney Center
DaVita
11011 Sherida St.
Cooper City, FL 33026
Free: 800-424-6589
URL: http://www.davita.com
Dialysis Stations: 16.

Coral Gables

23494 ■ Coral Gables Kidney Center
DaVita
3280 Ponce de Leon Blvd.
Coral Gables, FL 33126
Ph: (305)448-9888
Free: 800-424-6589
URL: http://www.davita.com
Dialysis Stations: 20.

Coral Springs

23495 ■ Complete Dialysis Care
DaVita
7850 W Sample Rd.
Coral Springs, FL 33065
Free: 800-424-6589
URL: http://www.davita.com
Dialysis Stations: 24.

Crestview

23496 ■ Nephrology Center of Crestview
Fresenius Medical Care
129 Redstone Ave., Ste. B
Crestview, FL 32539
Ph: (850)682-4726
Free: 866-434-2597
URL: http://www.ultracare-dialysis.com/
Dialysis Stations: 16. **Formerly:** Renal Care Group/ Nephrology Center of Crestview.

23497 ■ North Okaloosa Dialysis Center
DaVita
320 W Redstone Ave.
Crestview, FL 32536
Ph: (850)683-5700
Free: 800-424-6589
URL: http://www.davita.com
Dialysis Stations: 15.

Crystal River

23498 ■ Crystal River Dialysis Center & At Home
DaVita
7435 W Gulf to Lake Hwy.
Crystal River, FL 34429
Free: 800-424-6589
URL: http://www.davita.com
Dialysis Stations: 16.

23499 ■ Crystal River Dialysis Center
DaVita
7435 W Gulf to Lake Hwy.
Crystal River, FL 34429
Free: 800-424-6589
URL: http://www.davita.com
Dialysis Stations: 16.

Davenport

23500 ■ Davenport Dialysis Center
DaVita
45597 US Hwy. 27
Davenport, FL 33897
Ph: (863)419-7408
Free: 800-424-6589
URL: http://www.davita.com
Dialysis Stations: 12.

Davie

23501 ■ Renal Care Partners Home Program
4970 SW 52nd St., No. 304
Davie, FL 33314
Ph: (954)791-7301
URL: http://www.renalcp.com/
Dialysis Stations: 10.

23502 ■ Universal Kidney Center of Davie
11570 State Rd. 84
Davie, FL 33325
Ph: (054)727-9100
URL: http://www.universalkidneycenter.com
Dialysis Stations: 21.

23503 ■ University Artificial Kidney Center LLC
Regional KRU Medical Ventures
7950 SW 30th St.
Davie, FL 33328
Ph: (954)577-2778
URL: http://www.krumed.com/
Dialysis Stations: 15.

Daytona Beach

23504 ■ Daytona Beach Dialysis
American Renal Associates
578 Health Blvd.
Daytona Beach, FL 32114
Ph: (386)258-7322
URL: http://www.americanrenal.com
Dialysis Stations: 20.

23505 ■ Daytona South Dialysis
DaVita
1801 S Nova Rd., Ste. 306
Daytona Beach, FL 32119
Free: 800-424-6589
URL: http://www.davita.com
Dialysis Stations: 16.

23506 ■ Dialysis Care Center of Daytona
American Renal Associates
720 Clyde Morris Blvd.
Daytona Beach, FL 32114
Ph: (386)947-9872
URL: http://www.americanrenal.com
Dialysis Stations: 17.

De Funiak Springs

23507 ■ Fresenius Medical Care--De Funiak Springs
43 Shoemaker Dr.
De Funiak Springs, FL 32433
Ph: (850)892-2119
Free: 866-434-2597
URL: http://www.ultracare-dialysis.com/
Dialysis Stations: 17.

Deerfield Beach

23508 ■ AKC of Deerfield Beach
DaVita
1983 W Hillsboro Blvd.
Deerfield Beach, FL 33442
Ph: (954)426-3350
Free: 800-424-6589
URL: http://www.davita.com
Dialysis Stations: 16.

Defuniak Springs

23509 ■ Defuniak Springs Dialysis
DaVita
1045 US Hwy. 331 S
Defuniak Springs, FL 32435
Ph: (850)892-1345
Free: 800-424-6589
URL: http://www.davita.com
Dialysis Stations: 12.

Deland

23510 ■ Deland Dialysis
DaVita
350 E New York Ave.
Deland, FL 32724
Ph: (386)738-2570
Free: 800-424-6589
URL: http://www.davita.com
Dialysis Stations: 18.

Delray Beach

23511 ■ Boynton/North Delray Dialysis
Davita
2655 W Atlantic Ave.
Delray Beach, FL 33445
Ph: (561)279-2626
Free: 800-424-6589
URL: http://www.davita.com
Dialysis Stations: 22. **Formerly:** Gambro Healthcare - North Delray.

23512 ■ Delray Beach Dialysis Center LLC
American Renal Associates
5130 Linton Blvd., Ste. G4
Delray Beach, FL 33484
Ph: (561)498-5959
URL: http://www.americanrenal.com
Dialysis Stations: 16.

23513 ■ Renal Carepartners--Delray Beach
15300 Jog Rd., Unit 104
Delray Beach, FL 33486
Ph: (561)499-1878
Fax: (561)499-8978
URL: http://www.renalcp.com
Dialysis Stations: 20.

Deltona

23514 ■ BMA--Deltona
Fresenius Medical Care
1200 Deltona Blvd., Ste. 53
Deltona, FL 32725
Ph: (386)574-0225
Free: 866-434-2597
URL: http://www.ultracare-dialysis.com/
Dialysis Stations: 14.

Destin

23515 ■ Fresenius Medical Care--Highway 90, Destin
7720 US Hwy. 90, Ste. 150
Destin, FL 32550
Free: 866-434-2597
URL: http://www.ultracare-dialysis.com/
Dialysis Stations: 12. **Formerly:** Renal Care Group.

23516 ■ Fresenius Medical Care--Highway 98, Destin
7720 US Hwy. 98 W
Destin, FL 32550
Free: 866-434-2597
URL: http://www.ultracare-dialysis.com/
Dialysis Stations: 12. **Formerly:** Renal Care Group.

Dunedin

23517 ■ Gulf Breeze Dialysis Center & At Home
DaVita
1519 Main St.
Dunedin, FL 34698
Free: 800-424-6589
URL: http://www.davita.com
Dialysis Stations: 25.

23518 ■ Gulf Coast Dialysis Center Inc.
1121 Overcash Dr.
Dunedin, FL 34698
Ph: (727)733-1112
URL: http://www.gulfcoastdialysiscenter.com/

Fernandina Beach

23519 ■ Amelia Island Dialysis
DaVita
1525 Lime St., Ste. 120
Fernandina Beach, FL 32034
Ph: (904)491-1998
Free: 800-424-6589
URL: http://www.davita.com
Dialysis Stations: 12. **Formerly:** Regional--RTC Southeast, LP.

Fort Lauderdale

23520 ■ Broward Dialysis
DaVita
1500 N Federal Hwy., No. 100
Fort Lauderdale, FL 33304
Ph: (954)396-8990
Free: 800-424-6589
URL: http://www.davita.com
Dialysis Stations: 21. **Formerly:** Gambro Healthcare - Broward County.

23521 ■ Dialysis Services Fort Lauderdale
Fresenius Medical Care
3863 W Broward Blvd.
Fort Lauderdale, FL 33312
Free: 866-434-2597
URL: http://www.ultracare-dialysis.com/

23522 ■ East Fort Lauderdale Dialysis Center LLC
DaVita
1301 S Andrews Ave., Ste. 101
Fort Lauderdale, FL 33315
Ph: (954)761-1273
Free: 800-424-6589
URL: http://www.davita.com
Dialysis Stations: 18.

23523 ■ Fort Lauderdale Artificial Kidney Center
6606 N Federal Hwy.
Fort Lauderdale, FL 33308
Ph: (954)776-6056
Dialysis Stations: 18.

23524 ■ Fort Lauderdale Renal Associates
DaVita
6264 N Federal Hwy.
Fort Lauderdale, FL 33308
Ph: (954)776-3791
Free: 800-424-6589
URL: http://www.davita.com
Dialysis Stations: 22.

23525 ■ Universal Kidney Center, Inc.
Dialysis Facility
4875 NE 20th Terr.
Fort Lauderdale, FL 33308
Ph: (954)958-9300
URL: http://www.universalkidneycenter.com
Dialysis Stations: 15.

Fort Myers

23526 ■ BMA--South Ft. Myers
Fresenius Medical Care
Dialysis Facility
9400 Gladiolus Dr., Ste. 200
Fort Myers, FL 33908
Ph: (239)482-6700
Free: 866-434-2597
URL: http://www.ultracare-dialysis.com/
Dialysis Stations: 12.

23527 ■ Fort Meyers South Dialysis
DaVita
8570 Granite Court
Fort Myers, FL 33908
Ph: (239)482-0080
Free: 800-424-6589
URL: http://www.davita.com
Dialysis Stations: 16. **Formerly:** Gambro Healthcare - Fort Myers South.

23528 ■ Fort Myers Dialysis
DaVita
2133 Winkler Ave.
Fort Myers, FL 33901
Ph: (239)939-0213
Free: 800-424-6589
URL: http://www.davita.com
Dialysis Stations: 34. **Formerly:** Gambro Healthcare.

23529 ■ Fort Myers North Dialysis
DaVita
16101 N Cleveland Ave.
Fort Myers, FL 33908
Ph: (239)656-4403
Free: 800-424-6589
URL: http://www.davita.com
Dialysis Stations: 12. **Formerly:** Gambro Healthcare.

Fort Pierce

23530 ■ Bright Dialysis
DaVita
1801 S 23rd St., Ste. 1
Fort Pierce, FL 34950
Ph: (772)460-6199
Free: 800-424-6589
URL: http://www.davita.com
Dialysis Stations: 22.

23531 ■ RAI Care Centers--Fort Pierce
Renal Advantage Inc.
2501 Ohio Ave.
Fort Pierce, FL 34950
Ph: (772)465-6551
URL: http://www.renaladvantage.com
Dialysis Stations: 25.

Fort Walton Beach

23532 ■ DaVita
Fort Walton Beach Dialysis Center & At Home
1110 Hospital Rd., Ste. A
Fort Walton Beach, FL 32547
Ph: (850)862-6989
Free: 800-424-6589
URL: http://www.davita.com
Dialysis Stations: 12.

23533 ■ RCG--Ft Walton Beach
Fresenius Medical Care
Dialysis Facility
925 Mar Walt Dr., Ste. 3
Fort Walton Beach, FL 32547
Ph: (850)864-4411
Free: 866-434-2597
URL: http://www.ultracare-dialysis.com/
Dialysis Stations: 38. **Formerly:** Renal Care Group.

Gainesville

23534 ■ BMA--Gainesville East
Fresenius Medical Care
720 SW 2nd Ave., Ste. 250
Gainesville, FL 32601
Ph: (352)335-1751
Free: 866-434-2597
URL: http://www.ultracare-dialysis.com/
Dialysis Stations: 19.

23535 ■ BMA--Gainesville
Fresenius Medical Care
1775 NW 80th Blvd.
Gainesville, FL 32606
Ph: (352)332-8998
Free: 866-434-2597
URL: http://www.ultracare-dialysis.com/
Dialysis Stations: 21.

23536 ■ Shands at Univ. of Florida Outpatient Dialysis
Adult Dialysis
2409 SW Archer Rd.
Gainesville, FL 32608
Ph: (352)265-6890
URL: http://www.shands.org
Dialysis Stations: 29.

23537 ■ University of Florida Dialysis
Dialysis Clinic Inc.
3850 NW 83rd St., Ste. 101
Gainesville, FL 32606
Ph: (352)337-6021
Fax: (352)337-6028
URL: http://www.dciinc.org
Dialysis Stations: 12.

Haines City

23538 ■ RAI Care Centers--Haines City
Renal Advantage Inc.
110 Patterson Rd.
Haines City, FL 33844
Ph: (863)422-0800
URL: http://www.renaladvantage.com
Dialysis Stations: 18.

Hallandale Beach

23539 ■ Aventura Kidney Center
DaVita
22 SW 11th St.
Hallandale Beach, FL 33009
Ph: (954)458-0887
Free: 800-424-6589
URL: http://www.davita.com
Dialysis Stations: 12.

Hawthorne

23540 ■ Fresenius Medical Care Dialysis Services--Hawthorne
5837 SE US Hwy. 301
Hawthorne, FL 32640
Ph: (352)481-2664
Free: 866-434-2597
URL: http://www.ultracare-dialysis.com/
Dialysis Stations: 15.

Hialeah

23541 ■ Advanced Dialysis Institute, Inc.
7150 W 20th Ave., Ste. 109
Hialeah, FL 33016
Ph: (305)827-8399
Dialysis Stations: 15.

23542 ■ BMA--Hialeah
Fresenius Medical Care
7170 W 20th Ave.
Hialeah, FL 33016
Ph: (305)825-2046
Free: 866-434-2597
URL: http://www.ultracare-dialysis.com/
Dialysis Stations: 27.

23543 ■ DaVita
Flamingo Park Kidney Center
Dialysis Facility
901 E 10th Ave., Bay 17
Hialeah, FL 33010
Ph: (305)884-5677
Free: 800-424-6589
URL: http://www.davita.com
Dialysis Stations: 21.

23544 ■ Hialeah Artificial Kidney Center
DaVita
2750 W 68th St., No. 207
Hialeah, FL 33016
Ph: (305)557-6545
Free: 800-424-6589
URL: http://www.davita.com
Dialysis Stations: 10.

Hilliard

23545 ■ Hilliard Dialysis Center LLC
American Renal Associates
551858 US Hwy. 1, No. 118
Hilliard, FL 32046
Ph: (904)845-2612
URL: http://www.americanrenal.com
Dialysis Stations: 12.

Hollywood

23546 ■ Embassy Lakes Artificial Kidney Center
DaVita
11011 Sheridan St.
Hollywood, FL 33026
Free: 800-424-6589
URL: http://www.davita.com

23547 ■ Hollywood Artificial Kidney Center
Regional--KRU Medical Ventures
1150 N 35th Ave., Ste. 100
Hollywood, FL 33021
Ph: (954)894-7500
URL: http://www.krumed.com/
Dialysis Stations: 17.

23548 ■ Memorial Regional Hospital Dialysis Unit
3501 Johnson St.
Hollywood, FL 33021
Ph: (954)985-5860
URL: http://www.memorialregional.com
Dialysis Stations: 11.

23549 ■ Miramar Kidney Center
DaVita
2501 Dykes Rd., Ste. 200
Hollywood, FL 33027
Free: 800-424-6589
URL: http://www.davita.com
Dialysis Stations: 16.

23550 ■ Regional--KRU Medical Ventures
Hallandale Artificial Kidney Center
2655 Hollywood Blvd.
Hollywood, FL 33020
Ph: (954)925-9909
URL: http://www.krumedicalventures.com
Dialysis Stations: 22.

23551 ■ Renal Care Partners at Memorial West, LLC
601 N Flamingo Rd., Ste. 109
Hollywood, FL 33028
Ph: (954)362-5010
URL: http://www.renalcp.com/Memorial_West_FL.html
Dialysis Stations: 16.

23552 ■ South Broward Artificial Kidney Center
DaVita
4401 Hollywood Blvd.
Hollywood, FL 33021
Ph: (954)962-2211
Free: 800-424-6589
URL: http://www.davita.com
Dialysis Stations: 30.

23553 ■ Universal Kidney Centers--Pembroke Pines Miramar
18004 NW 6th St.
Hollywood, FL 33029
Ph: (954)433-9400
URL: http://www.universalkidneycenters.com/pembroke_pines_universal_kidney_cente r.html
Dialysis Stations: 21.

Homestead

23554 ■ Fresenius Medical Care--Naranja
26585 S Dixie Hwy.
Homestead, FL 33032
Ph: (305)257-1031
Free: 866-434-2597
URL: http://www.ultracare-dialysis.com/
Dialysis Stations: 16.

23555 ■ Homestead Artificial Kidney Center
Fresenius Medical Care
99 NE 8th St.
Homestead, FL 33030
Ph: (305)245-0241
Free: 866-434-2597
URL: http://www.ultracare-dialysis.com/
Dialysis Stations: 25.

Hudson

23556 ■ Bayonet Point--Hudson Kidney Center
DaVita
14144 Nephron Ln.
Hudson, FL 34667
Ph: (727)863-5459
Free: 800-424-6589
URL: http://www.davita.com
Dialysis Stations: 16.

23557 ■ Gulf Coast Kidney Center--Hudson
14153 Yosemite Dr., Ste. 102
Hudson, FL 34667
Ph: (727)862-0603
Dialysis Stations: 8.

Inverness

23558 ■ Inverness Dialysis Center
Fresenius Medical Care
1510 Hwy. 41 N
Inverness, FL 34450
Ph: (352)637-0500
Free: 866-434-2597
URL: http://www.ultracare-dialysis.com/
Dialysis Stations: 17.

Jacksonville

23559 ■ American Renal Associates--Jacksonville
1725 Oakhurst Ave., Ste. 100
Jacksonville, FL 32208
Ph: (303)403-1127
URL: http://www.americanrenal.com
Dialysis Stations: 20.

23560 ■ American Renal Associates--West Jacksonville
425 N Lee St., Ste. 103
Jacksonville, FL 32204
Ph: (904)598-2711
URL: http://www.americanrenal.com
Dialysis Stations: 29.

23561 ■ BMA--Jacksonville
Fresenius Medical Care
1715 Kings Ave.
Jacksonville, FL 32207
Ph: (904)396-7203
Free: 866-434-2597
URL: http://www.ultracare-dialysis.com/
Dialysis Stations: 18.

23562 ■ BMA--Saint Johns
Fresenius Medical Care
3132 St. John's Bluff Rd. S
Jacksonville, FL 32246
Ph: (904)641-0806
Free: 866-434-2597
URL: http://www.ultracare-dialysis.com/
Dialysis Stations: 15.

23563 ■ Dialysis Clinic Inc--Gateway
5258-10 Norwood Ave.
Jacksonville, FL 32208
Ph: (904)764-6381
URL: http://www.dciinc.org
Dialysis Stations: 24.

23564 ■ Dialysis Clinic Inc.--Jacksonville
757 Union St. W
Jacksonville, FL 32202
Ph: (904)354-0409
Fax: (904)354-0415
URL: http://www.dciinc.org
Dialysis Stations: 32.

23565 ■ Dialysis Clinic, Inc. of Southpoint
4221 Southpoint Blvd.
Jacksonville, FL 32216
Ph: (904)296-6362
Fax: (904)296-6473
URL: http://www.dciinc.org
Dialysis Stations: 24.

23566 ■ First Coast Dialysis Center
Fresenius Medical Care
5730 Bowden Rd., Ste. 110
Jacksonville, FL 32216
Ph: (904)419-0273
Free: 866-434-2597
URL: http://www.ultracare-dialysis.com/
Dialysis Stations: 18.

23567 ■ Fresenius Medical Care
Duval Kidney Center
1107 Myra St., Ste. 101
Jacksonville, FL 32204
Ph: (904)354-3333
Free: 866-434-2597
URL: http://www.ultracare-dialysis.com/
Dialysis Stations: 17.

23568 ■ Fresenius Medical Care--Jacksonville
10614 Lem Turner Rd.
Jacksonville, FL 32218
Ph: (904)768-8576
Free: 866-434-2597
URL: http://www.ultracare-dialysis.com/
Dialysis Stations: 27.

23569 ■ Fresenius Medical Care--Mandarin
9143 Philips Hwy., Ste. 110
Jacksonville, FL 32256
Ph: (904)538-0270
Free: 866-434-2597
URL: http://www.ultracare-dialysis.com/
Dialysis Stations: 16.

23570 ■ Fresenius Medical Care--Oceanway
12961 N Main St., Ste. 305
Jacksonville, FL 32218
Ph: (904)757-7425
Free: 866-434-2597
URL: http://www.ultracare-dialysis.com/
Dialysis Stations: 12.

23571 ■ Jacksonville Beach Dialysis
Fresenius Medical Care
1711 5th St.
Jacksonville, FL 32250
Ph: (904)247-9974
Free: 866-434-2597
URL: http://www.ultracare-dialysis.com/
Dialysis Stations: 17.

23572 ■ Jacksonville South Dialysis Center and At Home
DaVita
14965 Old Saint Augustine Rd., Ste. 114
Jacksonville, FL 32258
Ph: (904)880-9494
Free: 800-424-6589
URL: http://www.davita.com
Dialysis Stations: 16.

23573 ■ Mayo Clinic Florida
Outpatient Dialysis
Jacksonville, FL 32224
Ph: (904)296-5631
URL: http://www.mayoclinic.org/jacksonville/
Dialysis Stations: 24.

23574 ■ Normandy Village Dialysis Center
American Renal Associates
7764 Normandy Blvd.
Jacksonville, FL 32221
Ph: (904)781-7272
URL: http://www.americanrenal.com
Dialysis Stations: 19.

23575 ■ Regency Dialysis Center
DaVita
9535 Regency Sq. Blvd. N
Jacksonville, FL 32225
Ph: (904)725-0526
Free: 800-424-6589
URL: http://www.davita.com
Dialysis Stations: 16.

23576 ■ Shands Jacksonville
Dialysis Clinics Inc.
ESRD
655 W 8th St.
Jacksonville, FL 32209
Ph: (904)244-5448
URL: http://www.dciinc.org
Dialysis Stations: 40.

Jupiter

23577 ■ Jupiter Kidney Center LLC
American Renal Associates
1701 Military Tr., Ste. 140
Jupiter, FL 33458
Ph: (303)403-1127
URL: http://www.americanrenal.com
Dialysis Stations: 19.

Key West

23578 ■ Fresenius Medical Care--Key West
Dialysis Facility
1122 N Roosevelt Blvd.
Key West, FL 33040
Ph: (305)294-8453
Free: 866-434-2597
URL: http://www.ultracare-dialysis.com/
Dialysis Stations: 14.

Kissimmee

23579 ■ Central Florida Kidney Center--Osceola
2220 E Irlo Bronson Memorial Hwy., Ste. 6
Kissimmee, FL 34744
Ph: (407)870-1880
URL: http://cfkc.net/
Dialysis Stations: 17.

23580 ■ Kissimmee Dialysis
DaVita
Dialysis Facility
802 N John Young Pkwy.
Kissimmee, FL 34741
Free: 800-424-6589
URL: http://www.davita.com
Dialysis Stations: 25. **Formerly:** Gambro Healthcare - Kissimmee.

Lady Lake

23581 ■ Laurel Manor Dialysis Center at the Villages
DaVita
1950 Laurel Manor Dr.
Lady Lake, FL 32162
Free: 800-424-6589
URL: http://www.davita.com

23582 ■ Ocala Regional Kidney Center--South
DaVita
Dialysis Facility
13940 U.S Hwy. 441, Bldg. 400
Lady Lake, FL 32159
Ph: (352)751-1240
Free: 800-424-6589
URL: http://www.davita.com
Dialysis Stations: 25.

Lake City

23583 ■ BMA--Lake City
Fresenius Medical Care
1445 SW Main Blvd., Ste. 120
Lake City, FL 32025
Ph: (386)755-4990
Free: 866-434-2597
URL: http://www.ultracare-dialysis.com/
Dialysis Stations: 25.

Lake Wales

23584 ■ Lake Wales Dialysis
DaVita
Dialysis Facility
1125 Bryn Mawr Ave.
Lake Wales, FL 33853
Ph: (863)679-9851
Free: 800-424-6589
URL: http://www.davita.com
Dialysis Stations: 12.

23585 ■ RAI Care Centers--Lake Wales Renal Treatment Center
Dialysis Facility
1348 State Rd. 60-E
Lake Wales, FL 33853
Ph: (863)676-9510
Dialysis Stations: 15.

Lake Worth

23586 ■ Renal Care Center--Wellington
Fresenius Medical Care
Dialysis Facility
9835 Lake Worth Rd., Ste. 13
Lake Worth, FL 33467
Ph: (561)969-7799
Free: 866-434-2597
URL: http://www.ultracare-dialysis.com/
Dialysis Stations: 19.

Lakeland

23587 ■ Lakeland Dialysis
DaVita
515 E Bella Vista St.
Lakeland, FL 33805
Ph: (863)688-5463
Free: 800-424-6589
URL: http://www.davita.com
Dialysis Stations: 16.

23588 ■ Lakeland South Dialysis & At Home
DaVita
Dialysis Facility
5050 S Florida Ave., Ste. 1
Lakeland, FL 33813
Ph: (863)648-1719
Free: 800-424-6589
URL: http://www.davita.com
Dialysis Stations: 16.

23589 ■ Watson Clinic Kidney Center Dialysis Facility
1550 Lakeland Hills Blvd.
Lakeland, FL 33805
Ph: (863)680-7560
URL: http://www.watsonclinic.com/
Dialysis Stations: 25.

Largo

23590 ■ Bay Breeze Dialysis Clinic inc
DaVita
11465 Ulmerton Rd.
Largo, FL 33778
Ph: (727)581-9894
Free: 800-424-6589
URL: http://www.davita.com
Dialysis Stations: 20.

23591 ■ RAI Care Centers--Largo
Renal Advantage Inc.
Dialysis Facility
12505 Starkey Rd., Ste. B
Largo, FL 33773
Ph: (727)531-8227
URL: http://www.renaladvantage.com
Dialysis Stations: 21. **Formerly:** Gambro Healthcare - Seminole.

Lauderhill

23592 ■ Florida Kidney Center
Fresenius Medical Care
7309 W Oakland Park Blvd.
Lauderhill, FL 33319
Ph: (954)578-7678
Free: 866-434-2597
URL: http://www.ultracare-dialysis.com/
Dialysis Stations: 32.

Leesburg

23593 ■ Lake Dialysis
DaVita
221 N 1st St.
Leesburg, FL 34748
Ph: (352)326-8100
Free: 800-424-6589
URL: http://www.davita.com
Dialysis Stations: 16.

23594 ■ Lake Griffin East Dialysis
DaVita
401 E North Ave.
Leesburg, FL 34748
Ph: (352)315-0062
Free: 800-424-6589
URL: http://www.davita.com
Dialysis Stations: 16. **Formerly:** Physician's Renal Care of Leesburg.

23595 ■ Leesburg Dialysis Center
DaVita
801 E Dixie Ave., No. A-108
Leesburg, FL 34748
Ph: (352)728-1153
Free: 800-424-6589
URL: http://www.davita.com
Dialysis Stations: 17.

Lehigh Acres

23596 ■ Lehigh Acres Dialysis
DaVita
2719 4th St. W
Lehigh Acres, FL 33971
Ph: (239)479-5251
Free: 800-424-6589
URL: http://www.davita.com
Dialysis Stations: 16. **Formerly:** Gambro Healthcare - Lehigh Acres.

Live Oak

23597 ■ Fresenius Medical Care Dialysis Services--Live Oak
10543 Suwannee Plz. Blvd.
Live Oak, FL 32060
Ph: (386)364-6604
Free: 866-434-2597
URL: http://www.ultracare-dialysis.com/
Dialysis Stations: 21.

Longwood

23598 ■ Central Florida Kidney Center--Longwood
Dialysis Facility
745 W State Rd. 434, Ste. A
Longwood, FL 32750
Ph: (407)332-4448
URL: http://cfkc.net/
Dialysis Stations: 15.

MacClenny

23599 ■ Fresenius Medical Care--MacClenny
244 N 3rd St.
MacClenny, FL 32063
Ph: (904)259-9660
Free: 866-434-2597
URL: http://www.ultracare-dialysis.com/
Dialysis Stations: 13.

Madison

23600 ■ Four Freedoms Dialysis
DaVita
289A SW Range Ave.
Madison, FL 32340
Ph: (850)973-3852
Free: 800-424-6589
URL: http://www.davita.com
Dialysis Stations: 16. **Formerly:** Gambro Healthcare.

Margate

23601 ■ Complete Dialysis Care and At Home Davita
7850 W Sample Rd.
Margate, FL 33065
Free: 800-424-6589
URL: http://www.davita.com

23602 ■ NW Broward Artificial Kidney Center
Fresenius Medical Care
2514 N State Rd. 7
Margate, FL 33063
Free: 866-434-2597
URL: http://www.ultracare-dialysis.com/
Dialysis Stations: 21.

23603 ■ Universal Kidney Center of Margate--Coral Springs
Fresenius Medical Care
2514 N State Rd. 7
Margate, FL 33063
Ph: (954)968-8500
Free: 866-434-2597
URL: http://www.ultracare-dialysis.com/
Dialysis Stations: 30.

Marianna

23604 ■ Marianna Dialysis Center
DaVita
2930 Optimist Dr.
Marianna, FL 32448
Free: 800-424-6589
URL: http://www.davita.com
Dialysis Stations: 21.

23605 ■ Renal Treatment Center--Marianna
DaVita
2930 Optimist Dr.
Marianna, FL 32448
Free: 800-424-6589
URL: http://www.davita.com
Dialysis Stations: 21.

Melbourne

23606 ■ Fresenius Medical Care--Brevard
4940 Stack Blvd., Ste. C3-7
Melbourne, FL 32901
Ph: (321)952-1181
Free: 866-434-2597
URL: http://www.ultracare-dialysis.com/
Dialysis Stations: 20. **Formerly:** Renal Care Group.

23607 ■ Melbourne Dialysis
DaVita
2235 S Babcock St.
Melbourne, FL 32901
Ph: (321)956-6252
Free: 800-424-6589
URL: http://www.davita.com
Dialysis Stations: 16. **Formerly:** Gambro Healthcare.

23608 ■ Melbourne Kidney Center
1400 S Apollo Blvd.
Melbourne, FL 32901
Ph: (321)724-0461
URL: http://www.melbournekidney.com/
Dialysis Stations: 28.

23609 ■ North Melbourne Dialysis Inc.
14 Suntree Pl., Ste. 102
Melbourne, FL 32940
Ph: (321)253-9033
Dialysis Stations: 10.

Merritt Island

23610 ■ RAI-S Courtenay--Merritt Island
Renal Advantage Inc.
245 S Courtenay Pkwy., Bldg. A
Merritt Island, FL 32952
Ph: (321)452-0020
URL: http://www.renaladvantage.com
Dialysis Stations: 32. **Formerly:** Brevard Kidney & Hypertension Center.

Miami

23611 ■ Aventura Dialysis Center
American Renal Associates
19010 NE 29th Ave.
Miami, FL 33180
Ph: (305)692-9006
URL: http://www.americanrenal.com
Dialysis Stations: 16.

23612 ■ BMA--Cutler Ridge
Fresenius Medical Care
18942 S Dixie Hwy.
Miami, FL 33157
Ph: (305)252-7575
Free: 866-434-2597
URL: http://www.ultracare-dialysis.com/
Dialysis Stations: 19.

23613 ■ BMA--Kendall
Fresenius Medical Care
9193 SW 72nd St., Ste. 100-B
Miami, FL 33173
Ph: (305)279-2010
Free: 866-434-2597
URL: http://www.ultracare-dialysis.com/
Dialysis Stations: 30.

23614 ■ BMA--Metropolitan Miami
Fresenius Medical Care
5550 W Flagler St.
Miami, FL 33134
Ph: (785)388-1305
Free: 866-434-2597
URL: http://www.ultracare-dialysis.com/
Dialysis Stations: 15.

23615 ■ BMA--South Miami
Fresenius Medical Care
8770 SW 144th St.
Miami, FL 33176
Ph: (305)255-3100
Free: 866-434-2597
URL: http://www.ultracare-dialysis.com/
Dialysis Stations: 22.

23616 ■ BMA--West Date
Fresenius Medical Care
2791 SW 137th Ave.
Miami, FL 33175
Ph: (305)207-2388
Free: 866-434-2597
URL: http://www.ultracare-dialysis.com/
Dialysis Stations: 16.

23617 ■ Center for Kidney Disease
DaVita
1190 NW 95th St., Ste. 208
Miami, FL 33150
Ph: (305)691-2144
Free: 800-424-6589
URL: http://www.davita.com
Dialysis Stations: 21.

23618 ■ Dade Dialysis Center
Fresenius Medical Care
1601 NW 8th Ave.
Miami, FL 33136
Ph: (305)324-1727
Free: 866-434-2597
URL: http://www.ultracare-dialysis.com/
Dialysis Stations: 27.

23619 ■ Florida Renal Center
DaVita
3500 NW 7th St.
Miami, FL 33125
Ph: (305)649-4448
Free: 800-424-6589
URL: http://www.davita.com
Dialysis Stations: 20.

23620 ■ Fresenius Medical Care--The Glades
16740 SW 88th St.
Miami, FL 33196
Free: 866-434-2597
URL: http://www.ultracare-dialysis.com/
Dialysis Stations: 17.

23621 ■ Greater Miami Dialysis
DaVita
Dialysis Facility
160 NW 176th St., No. 100
Miami, FL 33169
Ph: (305)653-6033
Free: 800-424-6589
URL: http://www.davita.com
Dialysis Stations: 20. **Formerly:** Gambro Healthcare - Greater Miami.

23622 ■ Interamerican Dialysis Center & At Home
DaVita
7815 Coral Way, Ste. 115
Miami, FL 33155
Ph: (305)261-4823
Free: 800-424-6589
URL: http://www.davita.com
Dialysis Stations: 24.

23623 ■ Jackson Memorial Hospital
Pediatric Dialysis Unit
1611 NW 12th Ave.
Miami, FL 33136
Ph: (305)585-5372
URL: http://www.jhsmiami.org
Dialysis Stations: 8.

23624 ■ Jackson Memorial Hospital Transplant Center
1801 NW 9th Ave.
Miami, FL 33136
Ph: (305)355-5000
URL: http://www.jhsmiami.org/landing.cfm?id=7
Dialysis Stations: 0.

23625 ■ John Cunio Dialysis Center
Fresenius Medical Care
2561 Coral Way
Miami, FL 33145
Ph: (305)860-8111
Free: 866-434-2597
URL: http://www.ultracare-dialysis.com/
Dialysis Stations: 25.

23626 ■ Kidney Spa LLC
219 NW 12th Ave., Ste. C4
Miami, FL 33128
Ph: (305)329-2900
Dialysis Stations: 18.

23627 ■ Kidney Treatment Center--Miami
13500 N Kendall Dr., No. 131
Miami, FL 33186
Ph: (305)388-5222
Dialysis Stations: 22.

23628 ■ Miami Artificial Kidney Center, LLC
KRU Medical Ventures
Dialysis Facility
9175 SW 87th Ave.
Miami, FL 33176
Ph: (305)273-3830
URL: http://www.krumed.com/
Dialysis Stations: 18.

23629 ■ Miami Campus Dialysis
DaVita
1500 NW 12th Ave., Ste. 106
Miami, FL 33136
Ph: (305)324-8891
Free: 800-424-6589
URL: http://www.davita.com
Dialysis Stations: 33. **Formerly:** Gambro Healthcare - Miami.

23630 ■ Miami Children's Hospital Dialysis Unit
6125 SW 31st St.
Miami, FL 33155
Ph: (305)669-6479
URL: http://www.mch.com
Dialysis Stations: 4.

23631 ■ Miami East Dialysis
DaVita
1250 NW 7th ST., Ste. 106
Miami, FL 33125
Ph: (305)547-1496
Free: 800-424-6589
URL: http://www.davita.com
Dialysis Stations: 16. **Formerly:** Gambro Healthcare.

23632 ■ North Beach Dialysis Center
17801 NW 2nd Ave., Ste. 229
Miami, FL 33169
Ph: (305)653-7222
Dialysis Stations: 22.

23633 ■ West Kendall Dialysis Center
Fresenius Medical Care
12000 SW 131st Ave.
Miami, FL 33186
Ph: (305)254-4840
Free: 866-434-2597
URL: http://www.ultracare-dialysis.com/
Dialysis Stations: 25.

Miami Beach

23634 ■ South Beach Dialysis
DaVita
4701 N Meridian Ave.
Miami Beach, FL 33140
Ph: (305)534-2240
Free: 800-424-6589
URL: http://www.davita.com
Dialysis Stations: 22. **Formerly:** Gambro Healthcare.

Miami Lakes

23635 ■ Miami Lakes Artificial Kidney Center
DaVita
14600 NW 60th Ave.
Miami Lakes, FL 33014
Ph: (786)639-0496
Free: 800-424-6589
URL: http://www.davita.com
Dialysis Stations: 18.

Miami Shores

23636 ■ Florida Dialysis Institute
9999 NE 2nd Ave., Ste. 119
Miami Shores, FL 33138
Ph: (786)621-4888
Dialysis Stations: 19.

Middleburg

23637 ■ Middleburg Dialysis LLC
American Renal Associates
2070 Palmetto St., Ste. B-1
Middleburg, FL 32068
Ph: (904)406-5560
URL: http://www.americanrenal.com
Dialysis Stations: 16.

Milton

23638 ■ DaVita
Santa Rosa Dialysis Center
5819 Hwy. 90
Milton, FL 32583
Ph: (850)623-8299
Free: 800-424-6589
URL: http://www.davita.com
Dialysis Stations: 12. **Formerly:** West Florida Medical Center.

23639 ■ Nephrology Center of Milton
Fresenius Medical Care
5934 Berry Hill Medical Park Dr., No. 2
Milton, FL 32570
Ph: (850)626-9448
Free: 866-434-2597
URL: http://www.ultracare-dialysis.com/
Dialysis Stations: 17. **Formerly:** Renal Care Group/Nephrology Center of Milton.

Minneola

23640 ■ Fresenius Medical Care--Clermont
312 Mohawk Rd.
Minneola, FL 34715
Free: 866-434-2597
URL: http://www.ultracare-dialysis.com/

Mount Dora

23641 ■ Mount Dora Dialysis
DaVita
2735 Old Hwy 441
Mount Dora, FL 32757
Ph: (352)383-7022
Free: 800-424-6589
URL: http://www.davita.com
Dialysis Stations: 22. **Formerly:** Lake Superior Renal Care.

Naples

23642 ■ ARA--Naples Dialysis Center LLC
4529 Executive Dr.
Naples, FL 34119
Ph: (239)566-7180
URL: http://www.americanrenal.com
Dialysis Stations: 20.

23643 ■ BMA--South Collier
Fresenius Medical Care
12703 Tamiami Trail E, No. 121
Naples, FL 34113
Ph: (239)732-5333
Free: 866-434-2597
URL: http://www.ultracare-dialysis.com/
Dialysis Stations: 16.

23644 ■ Kidney Institute of Naples
Naples Nephrology
878 109th Ave. N
Naples, FL 34108
Ph: (239)596-3044
URL: http://www.naplesnephrology.com/kidneyinstitute.html
Dialysis Stations: 0.

23645 ■ Naples Artificial Kidney Center
Fresenius Medical Care
3699 Airport Pulling Rd. N
Naples, FL 34105
Ph: (239)263-0802
Free: 866-434-2597
URL: http://www.ultracare-dialysis.com/
Dialysis Stations: 15.

23646 ■ Naples Dialysis Center
DSI Corp
6625 Hillway Cir.
Naples, FL 34112
Ph: (239)775-9454
URL: http://www.dsi-corp.com/usa.html
Dialysis Stations: 19.

23647 ■ Naples Dialysis
DaVita
Dialysis Facility
661 9th St. N
Naples, FL 34102
Ph: (239)659-5202
Free: 800-424-6589
URL: http://www.davita.com
Dialysis Stations: 15. **Formerly:** Gambro Healthcare - Naples.

23648 ■ North Naples Dialysis LLC
1750 SW Health Pkwy.
Naples, FL 34109
Ph: (239)594-8758
URL: http://www.northnaplesdialysis.com/
Dialysis Stations: 20.

Navarre

23649 ■ Fresenius Medical Care --Navarre
8888 Navarre Pkwy.
Navarre, FL 32566
Ph: (850)515-0810
Free: 866-434-2597
URL: http://www.ultracare-dialysis.com/
Dialysis Stations: 16. **Formerly:** Renal Care Group.

New Port Richey

23650 ■ DaVita
New Port Richey Kidney Center & At Home
7421 Ridge Rd.
New Port Richey, FL 34652
Free: 800-424-6589
URL: http://www.davita.com
Dialysis Stations: 16.

23651 ■ Gulf Coast Kidney Center--New Port Richey
Physicians Dialysis
4802 Grand Blvd.
New Port Richey, FL 34652
Ph: (727)862-0603
E-mail: info@physiciansdialysis.com
URL: http://www.dialysischoice.com/
Dialysis Stations: 11.

New Smyrna Beach

23652 ■ New Smyrna Beach Artificial Kidney Center
KRU Medical Ventures
821 State Rd. 44
New Smyrna Beach, FL 32168
Ph: (386)409-8855
URL: http://www.krumed.com/
Dialysis Stations: 11.

23653 ■ New Smyrna Beach Dialysis
DaVita
Dialysis Facility
110 S Orange St.
New Smyrna Beach, FL 32168
Ph: (386)409-0025
Free: 800-424-6589
URL: http://www.davita.com
Dialysis Stations: 13. **Formerly:** Gambro Healthcare - New Smyrna Beach.

North Miami

23654 ■ Miami North Dialysis
DaVita
860 NE 125th St.
North Miami, FL 33161
Ph: (305)893-7887
Free: 800-424-6589
URL: http://www.davita.com
Dialysis Stations: 17. **Formerly:** Gambro Healthcare - Miami North.

North Miami Beach

23655 ■ Miami Regional Dialysis Center Inc.
American Renal Associates
100 NW 170th St., Ste. 106
North Miami Beach, FL 33169
Ph: (305)650-8822
URL: http://www.americanrenal.com
Dialysis Stations: 26.

23656 ■ Venture Dialysis Center
DaVita
16855 NE 2nd Ave., Ste. 205
North Miami Beach, FL 33162
Free: 800-424-6589
URL: http://www.davita.com
Dialysis Stations: 12.

North Port

23657 ■ Palm Breeze Dialysis
DaVita
14942 Tamiami Trail, Ste. G
North Port, FL 34287
Free: 800-424-6589
URL: http://www.davita.com
Dialysis Stations: 16.

Oakland Park

23658 ■ Advanced Dialysis Center of Ft. Lauderdale
911 E Oakland Park Blvd.
Oakland Park, FL 33334
Ph: (954)318-7000
URL: http://www.advanced-dialysis.com/
Dialysis Stations: 23.

Ocala

23659 ■ Ocala Regional Kidney Center--East
DaVita
2870 SE 1st Ave.
Ocala, FL 34471
Ph: (352)351-9140
Free: 800-424-6589
URL: http://www.davita.com
Dialysis Stations: 32.

23660 ■ Ocala Regional Kidney Center--West
DaVita
9401 SW Hwy. 200, Ste. 600
Ocala, FL 34481
Free: 800-424-6589
URL: http://www.davita.com
Dialysis Stations: 28.

23661 ■ Ocala Regional Kidney Centers - Home Dialysis
DaVita
2860 SE 1st Ave.
Ocala, FL 34471
Ph: (352)622-8758
Free: 800-424-6589
URL: http://www.davita.com
Dialysis Stations: 10.

Ocoee

23662 ■ Ocoee Dialysis
DaVita
11140 W Colonial Dr., Ste. 5
Ocoee, FL 34761
Ph: (407)877-0626
Free: 800-424-6589
URL: http://www.davita.com
Dialysis Stations: 18. **Formerly:** Gambro Healthcare - Ocoee.

Okeechobee

23663 ■ Renal Care Center--Okeechobee
Fresenius Medical Care
Dialysis Facility
201 SW 16th St.
Okeechobee, FL 34974
Ph: (863)467-7654
Free: 866-434-2597
URL: http://www.ultracare-dialysis.com/
Dialysis Stations: 12.

Opa Locka

23664 ■ Miami Gardens Dialysis
DaVita
3363 NW 167th St.
Opa Locka, FL 33056
Ph: (305)627-9311
Free: 800-424-6589
URL: http://www.davita.com
Dialysis Stations: 16.

Orange City

23665 ■ DaVita
Orange City Dialysis
Dialysis Facility
242 Treemonte Dr., Bldg. II
Orange City, FL 32763
Free: 800-424-6589
URL: http://www.davita.com
Dialysis Stations: 16. **Formerly:** Gambro Healthcare - Orange City.

Orange Park

23666 ■ Northeast Florida Dialysis Center
American Renal Associates
2020 Kingsley Ave., Ste. B
Orange Park, FL 32073
Ph: (904)272-7331
URL: http://www.americanrenal.com
Dialysis Stations: 16.

23667 ■ Northeast Florida Dialysis Center
American Renal Associates
2141 Lock Rand Blvd., Ste. 113
Orange Park, FL 32073
Ph: (303)403-1127
URL: http://www.americanrenal.com
Dialysis Stations: 24.

23668 ■ Orange Park Kidney Center
Fresenius Medical Care
2061 Professional Center Dr.
Orange Park, FL 32073
Ph: (904)276-3311
Free: 866-434-2597
URL: http://www.ultracare-dialysis.com/
Dialysis Stations: 13.

Orlando

23669 ■ BMA--West Orlando
Fresenius Medical Care
Dialysis Facility
5600 W Colonial Dr., Ste. 101
Orlando, FL 32808
Ph: (407)297-3777
Free: 866-434-2597
URL: http://www.ultracare-dialysis.com/
Dialysis Stations: 20.

23670 ■ Central Florida Kidney Center
203 Ernestine St.
Orlando, FL 32801
Ph: (407)843-6110
URL: http://cfkc.net/
Dialysis Stations: 40.

23671 ■ Central Florida Kidney Center--Vineland
4301 Vineland Rd., No. E-17
Orlando, FL 32811
Ph: (407)425-4415
Dialysis Stations: 12.

23672 ■ Central Orlando Dialysis
DaVita
2548 N Orange Blossom Trl., Ste. 400
Orlando, FL 32804
Ph: (407)246-5081
Free: 800-424-6589
URL: http://www.davita.com
Dialysis Stations: 24.

23673 ■ DaVita--Orlando Home Training
116 Sturtevant St.
Orlando, FL 32806
Free: 800-424-6589
URL: http://www.davita.com
Dialysis Stations: 2. **Formerly:** Gambro Healthcare.

23674 ■ Florida Hospital
Dialysis Unit
601 E Rollins St.
Orlando, FL 32803
Ph: (407)303-1956
URL: http://www.floridahospital.com
Dialysis Stations: 7.

23675 ■ Fresenius Medical Care--East Orlando
Dialysis Facility
2200 N Alafaya Trl., Ste. 600
Orlando, FL 32826
Ph: (407)282-1506
Free: 866-434-2597
URL: http://www.ultracare-dialysis.com/
Dialysis Stations: 17.

23676 ■ Orlando Artificial Kidney Center
Fresenius Medical Center
3100 Clay Ave., Ste. 100
Orlando, FL 32804
Ph: (407)898-4815
Free: 866-434-2597
URL: http://www.ultracare-dialysis.com/
Dialysis Stations: 25.

23677 ■ Orlando Dialysis
DaVita
14050 Town Loop Blvd., Ste. 104
Orlando, FL 32837
Ph: (407)858-9458
Free: 800-424-6589
URL: http://www.davita.com
Dialysis Stations: 15.

23678 ■ Orlando Downtown Dialysis
DaVita
Dialysis Facility
116 Sturtevant St.
Orlando, FL 32806
Free: 800-424-6589
URL: http://www.davita.com
Dialysis Stations: 23. **Formerly:** Gambro Healthcare - Orlando.

23679 ■ Orlando East Dialysis
DaVita
1160 S Semoran Blvd., Ste. C
Orlando, FL 32807
Ph: (407)823-9533
Free: 800-424-6589
URL: http://www.davita.com
Dialysis Stations: 15. **Formerly:** Gambro Healthcare - Orlando East Dialysis.

23680 ■ Orlando Home Training Dialysis
DaVita
116 Sturtevant Ave., Ste. 2
Orlando, FL 32806
Free: 800-424-6589
URL: http://www.davita.com
Dialysis Stations: 4. **Formerly:** Gambro Healthcare.

23681 ■ Orlando North Dialysis
DaVita
5135 Adanson St., Ste. 700
Orlando, FL 32804
Ph: (407)539-3998
Free: 800-424-6589
URL: http://www.davita.com
Dialysis Stations: 16. **Formerly:** Gambro Healthcare - Orlando North.

23682 ■ Orlando Park Dialysis
DaVita
5397 W Colonial Dr., Ste. 120
Orlando, FL 32808
Free: 800-424-6589
URL: http://www.davita.com
Dialysis Stations: 16.

23683 ■ Orlando Southwest Dialysis
DaVita
Dialysis Facility
6925 Lake Ellenor Dr., Ste. 650
Orlando, FL 32809
Ph: (407)852-1751
Free: 800-424-6589
URL: http://www.davita.com
Dialysis Stations: 18. **Formerly:** Gambro Healthcare - Orlando Southwest.

Ormond Beach

23684 ■ Ormond Beach Dialysis
DaVita
495 S Nova Rd., Ste. 109
Ormond Beach, FL 32174
Ph: (386)676-2405
Free: 800-424-6589
URL: http://www.davita.com
Dialysis Stations: 17. **Formerly:** Gambro Healthcare - Ormond Beach.

Palatka

23685 ■ BMA--Palatka
Fresenius Medical Care
Dialysis Facility
6541 St. John Ave.
Palatka, FL 32177
Ph: (386)328-6600
Free: 866-434-2597
URL: http://www.ultracare-dialysis.com/
Dialysis Stations: 27.

Palm Bay

23686 ■ Palm Bay Kidney Center
Melbourne Kidney Centers
220 Medplex Pkwy. NE
Palm Bay, FL 32907
Ph: (321)722-2709
URL: http://www.melbournekidney.com/
Dialysis Stations: 18.

Palm Beach Gardens

23687 ■ North Palm Beach Dialysis Center
DaVita
3375 Burns Rd., Ste. 101
Palm Beach Gardens, FL 33410
Ph: (561)775-8700
Free: 800-424-6589
URL: http://www.davita.com
Dialysis Stations: 19.

Palm Coast

23688 ■ Dialysis Care Center of Palm Coast
American Renal Associates
515 Palm Coast Pkwy. SW
Palm Coast, FL 32137
Ph: (386)447-4477
URL: http://www.americanrenal.com
Dialysis Stations: 16.

23689 ■ Palm Coast Dialysis
DaVita
13 Kingswood Dr., Ste. A
Palm Coast, FL 32137
Ph: (376)445-4445
Free: 800-424-6589
URL: http://www.davita.com
Dialysis Stations: 18. **Formerly:** Gambro Healthcare - Palm Coast.

Palm Springs

23690 ■ DaVita
Lake Worth Dialysis and At Home
2459 S Congress Ave.
Palm Springs, FL 33406
Free: 800-424-6589
URL: http://www.davita.com

Palmetto

23691 ■ Palmetto Artificial Kidney Center
Fresenius Medical Care
627 10th St. E
Palmetto, FL 34221
Ph: (941)729-4858
Free: 866-434-2597
URL: http://www.ultracare-dialysis.com/
Dialysis Stations: 20.

Panama City

23692 ■ Coastal Kidney Centers LLC
DaVita
510 N McArthur Ave.
Panama City, FL 32401
Ph: (850)914-0824
Free: 800-424-6589
URL: http://www.davita.com
Dialysis Stations: 28.

23693 ■ Panama City Dialysis Center
DaVita
615 Hwy. 231
Panama City, FL 32405
Ph: (850)785-1233
Free: 800-424-6589
URL: http://www.davita.com
Dialysis Stations: 37.

Panama City Beach

23694 ■ West Beach Dialysis Center
DaVita
16201 Panama City Beach Hwy., Ste. 102
Panama City Beach, FL 32413
Ph: (850)233-0837
Free: 800-424-6589
URL: http://www.davita.com

Pembroke

23695 ■ Johnson Dialysis Center
7763 Johnson St.
Pembroke, FL 33024
Ph: (954)962-9640
Dialysis Stations: 16.

Pembroke Pines

23696 ■ Pembroke Pines Artificial Kidney Center
KRU Medical Ventures
12145 Pembroke Rd.
Pembroke Pines, FL 33082
Ph: (954)435-2553
URL: http://www.krumed.com/
Dialysis Stations: 22.

Pensacola

23697 ■ Fresenius Medical Care--Baptist North
1040 E Nine Mile Rd.
Pensacola, FL 32514
Free: 866-434-2597
URL: http://www.ultracare-dialysis.com/
Dialysis Stations: 19. **Formerly:** Renal Care Group.

23698 ■ Fresenius Medical Care--West Pensacola
8187 W Fairfield Dr., Ste. 7A
Pensacola, FL 32506
Free: 866-434-2597
URL: http://www.ultracare-dialysis.com/
Dialysis Stations: 25. **Formerly:** Renal Care Group.

23699 ■ Nephrology Center of Pensacola
Fresenius Medical Care
1717 NE St., Ste. 501
Pensacola, FL 32501
Free: 866-434-2597
URL: http://www.ultracare-dialysis.com/
Dialysis Stations: 36. **Formerly:** Renal Care Group/Nephrology Center of Pensacola.

23700 ■ RCG--Sacred Heart Adult Dialysis
Fresenius Medical Care
5401 Corporate Woods Dr., Ste. 850
Pensacola, FL 32504
Ph: (850)484-8646
Free: 866-434-2597
URL: http://www.ultracare-dialysis.com/
Dialysis Stations: 16. **Formerly:** Renal Care Group-Sacred Heart.

23701 ■ Sacred Heart Pediatric Dialysis
Fresenius Medical Care
5151 N 9th Ave.
Pensacola, FL 32504
Ph: (850)416-7426
URL: https://www.ultracare-dialysis.com
Dialysis Stations: 7.

23702 ■ Sacred Heart Pediatric
Fresenius Medical Care
Depaul Bldg., 3rd Fl.
5151 N 9th Ave.
Pensacola, FL 32504
Free: 866-434-2597
URL: http://www.ultracare-dialysis.com/engine/

23703 ■ West Florida Dialysis
DaVita
8333 N Davis Hwy.
Pensacola, FL 32514
Ph: (850)474-8424
Free: 800-424-6589
URL: http://www.davita.com
Dialysis Stations: 27.

23704 ■ West Pensacola Dialysis Center
DaVita
598 N Fairfield Dr.
Pensacola, FL 32506
Ph: (850)453-6066
Free: 800-424-6589
URL: http://www.davita.com
Dialysis Stations: 16.

Perry

23705 ■ Perry Dialysis
DaVita
118 W Main
Perry, FL 32347
Ph: (850)584-6012
Free: 800-424-6589
URL: http://www.davita.com
Dialysis Stations: 16. **Formerly:** Gambro Healthcare.

Pinellas Park

23706 ■ Fresenius Medical Care--Pinellas Park
7901 US Hwy. 19 N
Pinellas Park, FL 33781
Ph: (727)544-5916
Free: 866-434-2597
URL: http://www.ultracare-dialysis.com/
Dialysis Stations: 20.

Plant City

23707 ■ Plant City Dialysis
DaVita
1211 W Reynolds St., Ste. 1
Plant City, FL 33563
Ph: (813)752-2136
Free: 800-424-6589
URL: http://www.davita.com
Dialysis Stations: 17. **Formerly:** Gambro Healthcare.

Plantation

23708 ■ BMA--Plantation
Fresenius Medical Care
Dialysis Facility
849 N Nob Hill Rd.
Plantation, FL 33324
Ph: (954)382-0151
Free: 866-434-2597
URL: http://www.ultracare-dialysis.com/
Dialysis Stations: 15.

23709 ■ Fresenius Medical Care Dialysis Services--Fort Lauderdale
3863 W Broward Blvd.
Plantation, FL 33312
Ph: (954)321-7772
Free: 866-434-2597
URL: http://www.ultracare-dialysis.com/
Dialysis Stations: 21.

23710 ■ Pine Island Kidney Center
DaVita
1871 N Pine Island Rd.
Plantation, FL 33322
Ph: (954)916-8958
Free: 800-424-6589
URL: http://www.davita.com
Dialysis Stations: 15.

23711 ■ Plantation Dialysis
DaVita
7061 Cypress Rd., Ste. 103
Plantation, FL 33317
Ph: (954)832-2100
Free: 800-424-6589
URL: http://www.davita.com
Dialysis Stations: 25.

Pompano Beach

23712 ■ Artificial Kidney Center--Broward
DaVita
1011 E Atlantic Blvd.
Pompano Beach, FL 33060
Ph: (954)942-5115
Free: 800-424-6589
URL: http://www.davita.com
Dialysis Stations: 24.

23713 ■ Fresenius Medical Care--Coral Springs
850 Riverside Dr.
Pompano Beach, FL 33071
Free: 866-434-2597
URL: http://www.ultracare-dialysis.com/
Dialysis Stations: 28.

Port Charlotte

23714 ■ Gulf Coast Dialysis Inc.
DaVita
3300 Tamiami Trl., Ste. 101A
Port Charlotte, FL 33952
Ph: (941)625-9985
Free: 800-424-6589
URL: http://www.davita.com
Dialysis Stations: 1.

23715 ■ Port Charlotte Artificial Kidney Center
DaVita
4300 Kings Hwy., Ste. 406-D17
Port Charlotte, FL 33980
Ph: (941)625-2822
Free: 800-424-6589
URL: http://www.davita.com
Dialysis Stations: 21.

Port Richey

23716 ■ New Port Richey Kidney Center
DaVita
7421 Ridge Rd.
Port Richey, FL 34668
Free: 800-424-6589
URL: http://www.davita.com
Dialysis Stations: 28.

Port Saint Lucie

23717 ■ BMA--Port Saint Lucie
Fresenius Medical Care
1680 SE Lyngate Dr., No. 101
Port Saint Lucie, FL 34952
Ph: (772)335-5240
Free: 866-434-2597
URL: http://www.ultracare-dialysis.com/
Dialysis Stations: 16.

23718 ■ Fresenius Medical Care--Tradition
1748 SW St. Lucia W Blvd.
Port Saint Lucie, FL 34986
Free: 866-434-2597
URL: http://www.ultracare-dialysis.com/
Dialysis Stations: 13.

23719 ■ Goldtree Kidney Center LLC
American Renal Associates
1407 Southeast Goldtree Dr., Ste. A
Port Saint Lucie, FL 34952
Ph: (303)403-1127
URL: http://www.americanrenal.com
Dialysis Stations: 15.

23720 ■ RAI Care Centers--Port Saint Lucie
Renal Advantage Inc.
8661 S US Hwy. 1
Port Saint Lucie, FL 34952
Ph: (772)807-7229
URL: http://www.renaladvantage.com
Dialysis Stations: 22.

Punta Gorda

23721 ■ Renal Advantage Inc.--Punta Gorda Dialysis Facility
355 Dupont St.
Punta Gorda, FL 33950
Ph: (941)505-0777
URL: http://www.renaladvantage.com
Dialysis Stations: 16.

Quincy

23722 ■ Quincy Dialysis
DaVita
878 Strong Rd.
Quincy, FL 32351
Ph: (850)875-1570
Free: 800-424-6589
URL: http://www.davita.com
Dialysis Stations: 22.

Royal Palm Beach

23723 ■ Western Community Dialysis Center LLC
American Renal Associates
11301 Okeechobee Blvd.
Royal Palm Beach, FL 33411
Ph: (303)403-1127
URL: http://www.americanrenal.com
Dialysis Stations: 18.

Ruskin

23724 ■ Sun City Center
DaVita
775 Cortaro Dr.
Ruskin, FL 33573
Ph: (813)633-2847
Free: 800-424-6589
URL: http://www.davita.com
Dialysis Stations: 17.

Saint Augustine

23725 ■ Fresenius Medical Care--Saint Augustine
1680 Osceola Elementary Rd., Ste. B
Saint Augustine, FL 32084
Ph: (904)824-6191
Free: 866-434-2597
URL: http://www.ultracare-dialysis.com/
Dialysis Stations: 17.

23726 ■ KRU Medical Ventures
Saint Augustine Kidney Center
264 Southpark Cir. E
Saint Augustine, FL 32086
Ph: (904)808-0445
Fax: (904)808-0446
URL: http://www.krumed.com
Dialysis Stations: 19.

23727 ■ Saint Augustine Artificial Kidney Center
KRU Medical Ventures
264 South Park Circle E
Saint Augustine, FL 32086
Ph: (904)808-0445
Fax: (904)808-0446
URL: http://www.krumed.com/
Dialysis Stations: 19.

Saint Cloud

23728 ■ St. Cloud Dialysis
DaVita
4750 Old Canoe Creek Rd.
Saint Cloud, FL 34769
Ph: (407)498-0018
Free: 800-424-6589
URL: http://www.davita.com
Dialysis Stations: 20. **Formerly:** Nephrology Consultants Dialysis Center.

Saint Petersburg

23729 ■ All Children's Hospital Dialysis Dialysis Center
501 6th St. S
Saint Petersburg, FL 33701
Ph: (727)767-4166
URL: http://www.allkids.org
Dialysis Stations: 6.

23730 ■ Fresenius Medical Care--South Saint Petersburg
650 34th St. S
Saint Petersburg, FL 33711
Ph: (727)321-2527
Free: 866-434-2597
URL: http://www.ultracare-dialysis.com/
Dialysis Stations: 24.

23731 ■ Pinellas West Shore Dialysis
DaVita
3451 66th St. N
Saint Petersburg, FL 33710
Free: 800-424-6589
URL: http://www.davita.com
Dialysis Stations: 12.

23732 ■ Renal Advantage Inc.--Saint Petersburg
1101 9th St. N
Saint Petersburg, FL 33701
Ph: (727)895-1472
URL: http://www.renaladvantage.com
Dialysis Stations: 21. **Formerly:** Bay Area Dialysis Center - Saint Petersburg.

23733 ■ Saint Petersburg Dialysis
DaVita
Dialysis Facility
1117 Arlington Ave. N
Saint Petersburg, FL 33705
Ph: (727)896-9029
Free: 800-424-6589
URL: http://www.davita.com
Dialysis Stations: 20. **Formerly:** Gambro Healthcare - Saint Petersburg.

23734 ■ St. Petersburg South Dialysis
DaVita
Dialysis Facility & At Home
2850 34th St. S
Saint Petersburg, FL 33711
Ph: (727)864-4050
Free: 800-424-6589
URL: http://www.davita.com
Dialysis Stations: 20. **Formerly:** Gambro Healthcare.

Sanford

23735 ■ Fresenius Medical Care--Sanford Dialysis Facility
419 E First St.
Sanford, FL 32771
Ph: (407)688-6765
Free: 866-434-2597
URL: http://www.ultracare-dialysis.com/
Dialysis Stations: 21.

23736 ■ Sanford Dialysis
DaVita
1701 W 1st St.
Sanford, FL 32771
Ph: (407)268-9425
Free: 800-424-6589
URL: http://www.davita.com
Dialysis Stations: 24.

Sarasota

23737 ■ NNA Kidney Dialysis Center--Sarasota
Fresenius Medical Care
1630 Tuttle Ave.
Sarasota, FL 34239
Ph: (941)373-9270
Free: 866-434-2597
URL: http://www.ultracare-dialysis.com/
Dialysis Stations: 24. **Formerly:** Renal Care Group/ NNA Kidney Dialysis Center.

23738 ■ Sarasota Physicians Dialysis Center
1921 Waldemere St., Ste. 107
Sarasota, FL 34239
Ph: (941)917-6444
Dialysis Stations: 37.

Sebastian

23739 ■ Sebastian Dialysis
DaVita
1424 U.S Hwy. 1, Ste. C
Sebastian, FL 32958
Ph: (772)589-9182
Free: 800-424-6589
URL: http://www.davita.com
Dialysis Stations: 16. **Formerly:** Gambro Healthcare - Sebastian.

Sebring

23740 ■ BMA--Avon Park
Fresenius Medical Care
4833 Sun-N-Lakes Blvd.
Sebring, FL 33872
Ph: (863)385-1850
Free: 866-434-2597
URL: http://www.ultracare-dialysis.com/
Dialysis Stations: 14.

23741 ■ Highlands Dialysis Center
American Renal Associates
4245 Sun N Lake Blvd.
Sebring, FL 33872
Ph: (863)382-9443
URL: http://www.americanrenal.com
Dialysis Stations: 11.

23742 ■ Renal Care Center--Sebring
Fresenius Medical Care
40 Medical Center Ave.
Sebring, FL 33870
Ph: (863)385-7351
Free: 866-434-2597
URL: http://www.ultracare-dialysis.com/
Dialysis Stations: 17.

Seminole

23743 ■ Seminole Dialysis Center
10755 Park Blvd. N
Seminole, FL 33772
Ph: (727)393-5551
Dialysis Stations: 17.

South Daytona

23744 ■ Daytona South Dialysis--South Daytona
DaVita
1801 S Nova Rd.
South Daytona, FL 32119
Free: 800-424-6589
URL: http://www.davita.com

Spring Hill

23745 ■ Hernando Kidney Center
DaVita
2985 Landover Blvd.
Spring Hill, FL 34608
Ph: (352)683-3630
Free: 800-424-6589
URL: http://www.davita.com
Dialysis Stations: 34.

Starke

23746 ■ Fresenius Medical Care--Starke
444 W Madison St.
Starke, FL 32091
Free: 866-434-2597
URL: http://www.ultracare-dialysis.com/
Dialysis Stations: 26.

23747 ■ Fresenius Medical Care--Starke
444 W Madison St.
Starke, FL 32091
Free: 866-434-2597
URL: http://www.ultracare-dialysis.com/
Dialysis Stations: 26.

Stuart

23748 ■ Treasure Coast Kidney Center--North
Fresenius Medical Care
Dialysis Facility
2348 SE Ocean Blvd.
Stuart, FL 34996
Ph: (772)286-2470
Free: 866-434-2597
URL: http://www.ultracare-dialysis.com/
Dialysis Stations: 20.

Sun City

23749 ■ Sun City Dialysis Center
American Renal Associates
952 Cypress Village Blvd.
Sun City, FL 33573
Ph: (813)642-9209
URL: http://www.americanrenal.com
Dialysis Stations: 14.

Tallahassee

23750 ■ Tallahassee Dialysis
DaVita
Dialysis Facility
1607 Physicians Dr.
Tallahassee, FL 32308
Ph: (850)878-8776
Free: 800-424-6589
URL: http://www.davita.com
Dialysis Stations: 30. **Formerly:** Gambro Healthcare - Tallahassee.

23751 ■ Tallahassee South Dialysis
DaVita
Dialysis Facility
2410 S Adams St.
Tallahassee, FL 32301
Ph: (850)224-8757
Free: 800-424-6589
URL: http://www.davita.com
Dialysis Stations: 20. **Formerly:** Gambro Healthcare - Tallahassee South.

23752 ■ West Tallahassee Dialysis
DaVita
Dialysis Facility & At Home
2645 W Tennessee St., Ste. 8 & 14
Tallahassee, FL 32304
Ph: (850)574-0239
Free: 800-424-6589
URL: http://www.davita.com
Dialysis Stations: 20.

Tamarac

23753 ■ Tamarac Artificial Kidney Center
DaVita
7140-48 W McNab Rd.
Tamarac, FL 33321
Ph: (954)720-5336
Free: 800-424-6589
URL: http://www.davita.com
Dialysis Stations: 19.

23754 ■ Tamarac Kidney Center
Fresenius Medical Care
7059 NW 88th Ave.
Tamarac, FL 33321
Free: 866-434-2597
URL: http://www.ultracare-dialysis.com/
Dialysis Stations: 24.

Tampa

23755 ■ Advanced Renal Care
3614 W Kennedy Blvd., Ste. A
Tampa, FL 33609
Ph: (813)874-2700
URL: http://arcrenal.com
Dialysis Stations: 14.

23756 ■ BMA--Tampa
Fresenius Medical Care
Dialysis Facility
3242 Henderson Blvd., No. 200
Tampa, FL 33609
Ph: (813)872-0933
Free: 866-434-2597
URL: http://www.ultracare-dialysis.com/
Dialysis Stations: 16.

23757 ■ BMA--Ybor City
Fresenius Medical Care
1602 N 21st St.
Tampa, FL 33605
Ph: (813)247-5720
Free: 866-434-2597
URL: http://www.ultracare-dialysis.com/
Dialysis Stations: 16.

23758 ■ Carrollwood Artificial Kidney Center
Fresenius Medical Care
4553 Gunn Hwy.
Tampa, FL 33624
Free: 866-434-2597
URL: http://www.ultracare-dialysis.com/
Dialysis Stations: 21.

23759 ■ DaVita--Central Tampa
South Bldg.
4204 N MacDill Ave.
Tampa, FL 33607
Free: 800-424-6589
URL: http://www.davita.com
Dialysis Stations: 20. **Formerly:** Gambro Healthcare.

23760 ■ Fresenius Medical Care--Carrollwood
Westwood Plz. Shopping Center
4553 Gunn Hwy.
Tampa, FL 33624
Free: 866-434-2597
URL: http://www.ultracare-dialysis.com/
Dialysis Stations: 16.

23761 ■ Fresenius Medical Care--North Tampa
4450 Fletcher Ave., Ste. D
Tampa, FL 33613
Ph: (813)979-9081
Free: 866-434-2597
URL: http://www.ultracare-dialysis.com/
Dialysis Stations: 24. **Formerly:** Renal Care Group.

23762 ■ Greater Tampa Home at Home
DaVita
4204 N MacDill Ave.
Tampa, FL 33607
Free: 800-424-6589
URL: http://www.davita.com
Dialysis Stations: 20.

23763 ■ National Renal Institutes--Tampa Central
4705 N Armenia Ave.
Tampa, FL 33603
Ph: (813)353-8100
Dialysis Stations: 20.

23764 ■ Suncoast Dialysis Center
3500 E Fletcher Ave., Ste. 122
Tampa, FL 33613
Ph: (813)972-3722
Dialysis Stations: 8.

23765 ■ Tampa General Hospital
Pediatric Dialysis
2 Columbia Dr.
Tampa, FL 33601
Ph: (813)844-4210
URL: http://www.tgh.org
Dialysis Stations: 7.

23766 ■ Tampa General Hospital Transplant Center
409 Bayshore Blvd.
Tampa, FL 33606
Ph: (813)349-6509
URL: http://www.tgh.org/transplantation.htm
Dialysis Stations: 0.

23767 ■ University of South Florida Dialysis Center
10770 N 46th St., No. A100
Tampa, FL 33617
Ph: (813)632-7918
URL: http://health.usf.edu
Dialysis Stations: 29.

23768 ■ West Tampa Dialysis
DaVita
Dialysis Facility
4515 George Rd., Ste. 300
Tampa, FL 33634
Ph: (813)884-4008
Free: 800-424-6589
URL: http://www.davita.com
Dialysis Stations: 22. **Formerly:** Gambro Healthcare - West Tampa.

Temple Terrace

23769 ■ Temple Terrace Dialysis
DaVita
Dialysis Facility
11306 53rd St.
Temple Terrace, FL 33617
Ph: (813)989-2062
Free: 800-424-6589
URL: http://www.davita.com
Dialysis Stations: 24. **Formerly:** Gambro Healthcare - Temple Terrace.

The Villages

23770 ■ Laural Manor Dialysis Center
DaVita
1950 Laurel Manor Dr., Ste. 190
The Villages, FL 32162
Free: 800-424-6589
URL: http://www.davita.com
Dialysis Stations: 16.

Titusville

23771 ■ Dialysis and Kidney Center of North Brevard
830 Century Medical Dr., Unit C
Titusville, FL 32796
Ph: (321)269-6270
Dialysis Stations: 12.

23772 ■ Titusville Dialysis and Kidney Center
American Renal Associates
801 Garden St.
Titusville, FL 32796
Ph: (321)567-0122
URL: http://www.americanrenal.com
Dialysis Stations: 14.

Trenton

23773 ■ Suwannee River Kidney Center
Fresenius Medical Care
319 W Wade St.
Trenton, FL 32693
Ph: (352)463-2008
Free: 866-434-2597
URL: http://www.ultracare-dialysis.com/
Dialysis Stations: 25.

University Park

23774 ■ Lakewood University Dialysis Center
Diversified Specialty Institutes
8131 Cooper Creek Blvd.
University Park, FL 34201
Ph: (941)359-0676
URL: http://www.dsi-corp.com
Dialysis Stations: 11.

Venice

23775 ■ Dialysis Center--Venice
DaVita
816 Pinebrook Rd.
Venice, FL 34292
Ph: (941)486-9057
Free: 800-424-6589
URL: http://www.davita.com
Dialysis Stations: 23.

23776 ■ Venice Kidney Center
Fresenius Medical Care
1120 Indian Hills Blvd.
Venice, FL 34293
Ph: (941)493-5969
Free: 866-434-2597
URL: http://www.ultracare-dialysis.com/
Dialysis Stations: 16. **Formerly:** Renal Care Group.

Vero Beach

23777 ■ Indian River Dialysis
DaVita
2150 45th St.
Vero Beach, FL 32967
Ph: (772)567-2529
Free: 800-424-6589
URL: http://www.davita.com
Dialysis Stations: 16.

23778 ■ Renal Care Center--Vero Beach
Fresenius Medical Care
Dialysis Facility
1515 Indian River Blvd., Ste. A-101
Vero Beach, FL 32960
Ph: (772)778-4917
Free: 866-434-2597
URL: http://www.ultracare-dialysis.com/
Dialysis Stations: 23.

West Palm Beach

23779 ■ Atlantic Kidney Centers KKC
American Renal Associates
4700 Congress Ave., Ste. 104
West Palm Beach, FL 33407
Ph: (561)845-2888
URL: http://www.americanrenal.com
Dialysis Stations: 14.

23780 ■ Dialysis Association of the Palm Beaches
DaVita
2611 Poinsettia Ave.
West Palm Beach, FL 33407
Ph: (561)833-0759
Free: 800-424-6589
URL: http://www.davita.com
Dialysis Stations: 20.

23781 ■ Fresenius Medical Care Dialysis Services--West Palm Beach
2000 Continental Dr., Ste. A
West Palm Beach, FL 33407
Ph: (561)840-4141
Free: 866-434-2597
URL: http://www.ultracare-dialysis.com/
Dialysis Stations: 15.

23782 ■ Fresenius Medical Care--Royal Palm Beach
6901 Okeechobee Blvd., Ste. D-19
West Palm Beach, FL 33411
Ph: (561)616-3335
Free: 866-434-2597
URL: http://www.ultracare-dialysis.com/
Dialysis Stations: 12.

23783 ■ Fresenius Medical Care--West Palm
1522 N Dixie Hwy.
West Palm Beach, FL 33401
Ph: (561)833-5355
Free: 866-434-2597
URL: http://www.ultracare-dialysis.com/
Dialysis Stations: 19. **Formerly:** Renal Care Group.

23784 ■ Lake Worth Dialysis
DaVita
2459 S Congress Ave., Ste. 100
West Palm Beach, FL 33406
Free: 800-424-6589
URL: http://www.davita.com
Dialysis Stations: 25.

23785 ■ Saint Mary's Hospital Dialysis Unit
901 45th St.
West Palm Beach, FL 33407
Ph: (561)882-6470
URL: http://www.stmarysmc.com
Dialysis Stations: 22.

Weston

23786 ■ Weston Dialysis Center
DaVita
2685 Executive Park Dr.
Weston, FL 33331
Ph: (954)389-1290
Free: 800-424-6589
URL: http://www.davita.com
Dialysis Stations: 15.

Winter Garden

23787 ■ Central Florida Kidney Center--Winter Garden
741 S Dillard St.
Winter Garden, FL 34787
Ph: (407)654-9127
URL: http://cfkc.net/
Dialysis Stations: 21.

23788 ■ Winter Garden Dialysis
DaVita
1221 Winter Garden Vineland Rd.
Winter Garden, FL 34787
Ph: (407)877-0364
Free: 800-424-6589
URL: http://www.davita.com
Dialysis Stations: 16. **Formerly:** Central Florida Kidney Center.

Winter Haven

23789 ■ Renal Advantage Inc. Care Centers--Winter Haven
400 Security Square
Winter Haven, FL 33880
Ph: (863)294-7887
URL: http://www.renaladvantage.com
Dialysis Stations: 20.

23790 ■ Security--Winter Haven Square
Renal Advantage Inc.
Dialysis Facility
120 Bates Ave. SW, Ste. 170
Winter Haven, FL 33880
Ph: (863)294-7887
URL: http://www.renaladvantage.com
Dialysis Stations: 16.

23791 ■ Winter Haven Dialysis
DaVita
Dialysis Center
1625 Martin Luther King Dr.
Winter Haven, FL 33881
Free: 800-424-6589
URL: http://www.davita.com
Dialysis Stations: 20. **Formerly:** Gambro Healthcare - Winter Haven.

Winter Park

23792 ■ Fresenius Medical Care Dialysis Services - Winter Park
6848 Aloma Ave.
Winter Park, FL 32792
Ph: (407)673-5191
Free: 866-434-2597
URL: http://www.ultracare-dialysis.com/
Dialysis Stations: 16.

23793 ■ Winter Park Dialysis
DaVita
3727 N Goldenrod Rd.
Winter Park, FL 32792
Ph: (407)657-5262
Free: 800-424-6589
URL: http://www.davita.com
Dialysis Stations: 12.

23794 ■ Winter Park Hemodialysis
DaVita
4100 Metric Dr., Ste. 300
Winter Park, FL 32792
Ph: (407)681-7600
Free: 800-424-6589
URL: http://www.davita.com
Dialysis Stations: 24.

Ybor City

23795 ■ East Tampa Dialysis
DaVita
1701 E 9th Ave.
Ybor City, FL 33605
Free: 800-424-6589
URL: http://www.davita.com
Dialysis Stations: 16.

Zephyrhills

23796 ■ Wesley Chapel Dialysis
DaVita
2255 Green Hedges Way
Zephyrhills, FL 33544
Free: 800-424-6589
URL: http://www.davita.com
Dialysis Stations: 6.

23797 ■ Zephyrhills Dialysis
DaVita
Dialysis Facility
6610 Stadium Dr.
Zephyrhills, FL 33542
Ph: (813)788-4887

Free: 800-424-6589
URL: http://www.davita.com
Dialysis Stations: 20. **Formerly:** Gambro Healthcare - Zephyrhills.

GEORGIA

Adel

23798 ■ Dialysis Corporation of America of Adel
203 E Robinson St.
Adel, GA 31620
Ph: (229)896-4529
URL: http://www.dialysiscorporation.com
Dialysis Stations: 14.

Albany

23799 ■ Clark Home Training Center Dialysis Clinic Inc.
1210 N Jefferson St.
Albany, GA 31701
Ph: (229)888-3996
URL: http://www.dciinc.org
Dialysis Stations: 3.

23800 ■ Dialysis Clinic, Inc.--Albany
1200 N Jefferson St.
Albany, GA 31701
Ph: (229)888-3996
URL: http://www.dciinc.org
Dialysis Stations: 25.

23801 ■ Dialysis Clinic Inc.--Albany West Town
1921 W Oakridge Dr.
Albany, GA 31721
Ph: (229)435-9295
URL: http://www.dciinc.org
Dialysis Stations: 25.

23802 ■ Dialysis Clinic Inc.--East Albany
1314 Radium Springs Rd.
Albany, GA 31702
Ph: (229)434-1175
URL: http://www.dciinc.org
Dialysis Stations: 21.

Alma

23803 ■ Dialysis Facility of Alma, Inc.
415 S Dixon St.
Alma, GA 31510
Ph: (912)632-8010
Dialysis Stations: 17.

Americus

23804 ■ Americus Dialysis DaVita Dialysis Center
227 N Lee St.
Americus, GA 31709
Ph: (229)928-2257
Free: 800-424-6589
URL: http://www.davita.com
Dialysis Stations: 19. **Formerly:** Gambro Healthcare.

Arlington

23805 ■ Dialysis Clinic, Inc.--Arlington
585 Martin Luther King, Jr. Dr.
Arlington, GA 39813
Ph: (229)725-4888
URL: http://www.dciinc.org
Dialysis Stations: 12.

Athens

23806 ■ Athens East Dialysis DaVita
2026 S Milledge Ave., Ste. A2
Athens, GA 30605
Ph: (706)549-3297
Free: 800-424-6589
URL: http://www.davita.com
Dialysis Stations: 19.

23807 ■ Athens Kidney Center Dialysis Facility
1440 N Chase St.
Athens, GA 30601
Ph: (706)227-2110
URL: http://www.athenskidneycenter.com/
Dialysis Stations: 18.

23808 ■ Athens West Dialysis DaVita
2047 Prince Ave., Ste. A
Athens, GA 30606
Ph: (706)546-0054
Free: 800-424-6589
URL: http://www.davita.com
Dialysis Stations: 38. **Formerly:** Gambro Healthcare.

23809 ■ Classic City Dialysis
2485 Jefferson Rd.
Athens, GA 30606
Ph: (706)850-7400
Dialysis Stations: 12.

23810 ■ Fresenius Medical Care--Clarke County
5105 Jefferson Rd.
Athens, GA 30606
Free: 866-434-2597
URL: http://www.ultracare-dialysis.com/
Dialysis Stations: 26. **Formerly:** RCG Clarke County Dialysis.

Atlanta

23811 ■ Atlanta Dialysis DaVita Dialysis Facility
567 North Ave., Ste. 200
Atlanta, GA 30308
Ph: (404)853-1695
Free: 800-424-6589
URL: http://www.davita.com
Dialysis Stations: 28. **Formerly:** Gambro Healthcare.

23812 ■ Atlanta Midtown Dialysis DaVita
489 Peachtree St., Ste. 100
Atlanta, GA 30308
Ph: (404)249-9199
Free: 800-424-6589
URL: http://www.davita.com
Dialysis Stations: 22. **Formerly:** Gambro Healthcare.

23813 ■ Atlanta West Dialysis DaVita Dialysis Center
2538 Martin Luther King Jr. Dr. SW
Atlanta, GA 30311
Ph: (404)699-1300
Free: 800-424-6589
Fax: (404)699-1144
URL: http://www.davita.com
Dialysis Stations: 20. **Formerly:** Gambro Healthcare.

23814 ■ Bakers Ferry Dialysis DaVita
3645 Bakers Ferry Rd.
Atlanta, GA 30331
Ph: (404)691-1932
Free: 800-424-6589
URL: http://www.davita.com
Dialysis Stations: 18.

23815 ■ Buckhead Dialysis
1575 Northside Dr. NE
Atlanta, GA 30318
Ph: (404)351-8266
Dialysis Stations: 17.

23816 ■ Central Atlanta Dialysis Center Fresenius Medical Care
22 Executive Park W NE, Ste. 2200
Atlanta, GA 30329
Free: 866-434-2597
URL: http://www.ultracare-dialysis.com/
Dialysis Stations: 24.

23817 ■ Children's Healthcare of Atlanta--Egleston
1405 Clifton Rd. NE
Atlanta, GA 30322
Ph: (404)785-6121
URL: http://www.choa.org/
Dialysis Stations: 9.

23818 ■ Children's Healthcare of Atlanta/Egleston Dialysis Unit
1405 Clifton Rd. NE
Atlanta, GA 30322
Ph: (404)785-6121
URL: http://www.choa.org/default.aspx?id=960
Dialysis Stations: 9.

23819 ■ Dialysis Clinic, Inc. of Atlanta--Piedmont Home Dialysis
120 Piedmont Ave., Ste. 100
Atlanta, GA 30303
Ph: (404)230-2967
URL: http://www.dciinc.org
Dialysis Stations: 0.

23820 ■ Dialysis Clinic Inc.--Crawford
240 Ponce De Leon Ave. NE
Atlanta, GA 30308
Ph: (404)888-4539
URL: http://www.dciinc.org
Dialysis Stations: 28.

23821 ■ Dialysis Clinic Inc.--Crawford
240 Ponce de Leon Ave. NE
Atlanta, GA 30308
Ph: (404)888-4530
Fax: (404)888-4539
URL: http://www.dciinc.org
Dialysis Stations: 28.

23822 ■ Dialysis Clinic Inc. Home Dialysis
120 Piedmont Ave., Ste. 300
Atlanta, GA 30303
Ph: (404)230-2873
URL: http://www.dciinc.org

23823 ■ Dialysis Clinic Inc.--Northside
870 Northside Dr., Ste. 400
Atlanta, GA 30318
Ph: (404)230-2966
URL: http://www.dciinc.org
Dialysis Stations: 27.

23824 ■ Dialysis Clinic Inc.--Northside
870 Northside Dr. NW, Ste. 300
Atlanta, GA 30318
Ph: (404)888-4520
Fax: (404)888-4529
URL: http://www.dciinc.org
Dialysis Stations: 23.

23825 ■ East Atlanta Dialysis DaVita
1308 Moreland Ave. SE
Atlanta, GA 30316
Free: 800-424-6589
URL: http://www.davita.com
Dialysis Stations: 23. **Formerly:** Gambro Healthcare Atlanta.

23826 ■ Emory Dialysis at Greenbriar
2841 Greenbriar Pkwy., SW
Atlanta, GA 30331
Ph: (404)778-1001
URL: http://www.emoryhealthcare.org/
Dialysis Stations: 17.

23827 ■ Emory Dialysis--Northside
Emory Healthcare
610 Northside Dr., NW
Atlanta, GA 30318
Ph: (404)778-1050
URL: http://www.emoryhealthcare.org/dialysis/index.html
Dialysis Stations: 41.

23828 ■ Ford Factory Square Dialysis
DaVita
567 North Ave., NE, Ste. 100
Atlanta, GA 30308
Free: 800-424-6589
URL: http://www.davita.com
Dialysis Stations: 25.

23829 ■ Fresenius Medical Care--Atlanta Downtown
231 NW 14th St.
Atlanta, GA 30318
Free: 866-434-2597
URL: http://www.ultracare-dialysis.com/
Dialysis Stations: 21. **Formerly:** Holton Dialysis Clinic.

23830 ■ Fresenius Medical Care--Perimeter Dialysis Center
5825 Glenridge Dr., Ste. 150, Bldg. 3
Atlanta, GA 30328
Free: 866-434-2597
URL: http://www.ultracare-dialysis.com/
Dialysis Stations: 21.

23831 ■ Fresenius Medical Care--Sandy Springs
Bldg. 200
7840 Roswell Rd., Ste. 210
Atlanta, GA 30350
Free: 866-434-2597
URL: http://www.ultracare-dialysis.com/
Dialysis Stations: 21.

23832 ■ Home Dialysis of North Atlanta, Inc.
980 Johnson Ferry Rd.
Atlanta, GA 30342
Ph: (404)835-5081
Dialysis Stations: 2.

23833 ■ Lake Hearn Dialysis
DaVita
1150 Lake Hearn Dr., Ste. 100
Atlanta, GA 30342
Free: 800-424-6589
URL: http://www.davita.com
Dialysis Stations: 16.

23834 ■ Lindbergh Dialysis Center
2695 Buford Hwy., Ste. 108
Atlanta, GA 30324
Ph: (404)315-0605
Dialysis Stations: 10.

23835 ■ Linden Dialysis
DaVita
121 Linden Ave.
Atlanta, GA 30308
Free: 800-424-6589
URL: http://www.davita.com
Dialysis Stations: 20. **Formerly:** DaVita-Midtown Dialysis Facility.

23836 ■ Loring Heights Dialysis
DaVita
1575 Northside Dr.
Atlanta, GA 30318
Free: 800-424-6589
URL: http://www.davita.com
Dialysis Stations: 20. **Formerly:** Gambro Healthcare.

23837 ■ Piedmont Dialysis
DaVita
105 Collier Rd. NW, B Level
Atlanta, GA 30309
Free: 800-424-6589
Fax: (404)352-8376
URL: http://www.davita.com
Dialysis Stations: 21. **Formerly:** Gambro Healthcare.

23838 ■ Piedmont Hospital Transplant
1968 Peachtree Rd., NW
Atlanta, GA 30309
Ph: (404)605-3730
URL: http://www.piedmonthospital.org/oth/Page.asp?PageID=OTH000167
Dialysis Stations: 0.

23839 ■ Ralph McGill Dialysis
DaVita
448 Ralph McGill Blvd. NE
Atlanta, GA 30312
Free: 800-424-6589
URL: http://www.davita.com
Dialysis Stations: 21.

23840 ■ Renal Carepartners of Dunwoody
7840 Roswell Rd., Ste. 310
Atlanta, GA 30350
Ph: (770)518-2662
URL: http://www.renalcp.com
Dialysis Stations: 6.

23841 ■ South Fulton Dialysis
DaVita
2685 Metropolitan Pkwy. SW
Atlanta, GA 30315
Free: 800-424-6589
Fax: (404)761-2618
URL: http://www.davita.com
Dialysis Stations: 20. **Formerly:** Gambro Healthcare.

23842 ■ Southern Adamsville Dialysis
DaVita
3651 Bakers Ferry Rd. SW
Atlanta, GA 30331
Free: 800-424-6589
URL: http://www.davita.com
Dialysis Stations: 12.

23843 ■ Southwest Atlanta Dialysis Center
DaVita
3620 Martin Luther King Jr. Dr. SW
Atlanta, GA 30331
Free: 800-424-6589
URL: http://www.davita.com
Dialysis Stations: 34.

Augusta

23844 ■ American Renal Associates--Augusta, LLC
1000 Telfair St.
Augusta, GA 30901
Ph: (706)774-0130
URL: http://www.americanrenal.com
Dialysis Stations: 30.

23845 ■ American Renal Associates--South Augusta Clinic
1649 Gordon Hwy.
Augusta, GA 30906
Ph: (706)796-1236
URL: http://www.americanrenal.com
Dialysis Stations: 30.

23846 ■ Fresenius Medical Care of Augusta Inc.
1109 Medical Center Dr., Ste. 195
Augusta, GA 30909
Free: 866-434-2597
URL: http://www.ultracare-dialysis.com/
Dialysis Stations: 21.

23847 ■ Fresenius Medical Care--New Bailie
914 New Bailie St.
Augusta, GA 30912
Free: 866-434-2597
URL: http://www.ultracare-dialysis.com/
Dialysis Stations: 24.

23848 ■ Fresenius Medical Care--Walton Way, New Bailie
1717 Walton Wy.
Augusta, GA 30904
Free: 866-434-2597
URL: http://www.ultracare-dialysis.com/
Dialysis Stations: 24.

23849 ■ Nephrology Center--South Augusta
DaVita
Dialysis Facility
1631 Gordon Hwy., Store 1B
Augusta, GA 30906
Free: 800-424-6589
URL: http://www.davita.com
Dialysis Stations: 19.

23850 ■ RAI Peach Orchard Rd.--Augusta
3206 Peach Orchard Rd.
Augusta, GA 30906
Free: 866-434-2597
URL: http://www.renaladvantage.com/
Dialysis Stations: 16. **Formerly:** Fresenius Medical Care Dialysis Services--South Augusta.

23851 ■ South Augusta Dialysis Center
Renal Advantage Inc.
2841 Deans Bridge Rd.
Augusta, GA 30906
Ph: (706)790-5909
URL: http://www.renaladvantage.com
Dialysis Stations: 21. **Formerly:** National Renal Alliance.

23852 ■ Wylds Road Dialysis
DaVita
1815 Wylds Road
Augusta, GA 30909
Free: 800-424-6589
URL: http://www.davita.com
Dialysis Stations: 20.

Austell

23853 ■ Cobb Dialysis
DaVita
3865 S Medical Park Dr.
Austell, GA 30106
Free: 800-424-6589
URL: http://www.davita.com
Dialysis Stations: 25. **Formerly:** Cobb Nephrology Dialysis Center.

23854 ■ Colonial Springs Dialysis
DaVita
2840 East West Connector
Austell, GA 30106
Free: 800-424-6589
URL: http://www.davita.com
Dialysis Stations: 15.

23855 ■ Diversified Specialty Institutes--Austell
3642 Marathon Circle
Austell, GA 30106
Ph: (770)439-4170
URL: http://www.dsi-corp.com
Dialysis Stations: 12.

23856 ■ Fresenius Medical Care--South Cobb
1886 Stallion Pkwy.
Austell, GA 30106
Free: 866-434-2597
URL: http://www.ultracare-dialysis.com/
Dialysis Stations: 30.

Bainbridge

23857 ■ Decatur County Dialysis Center
700 Gordon Ave.
Bainbridge, GA 39819
Ph: (229)243-0280
Dialysis Stations: 19.

23858 ■ Fresenius Medical Care--Bainbridge
703 E Shotwell St.
Bainbridge, GA 39819
Free: 866-434-2597
URL: http://www.ultracare-dialysis.com/
Dialysis Stations: 16. **Formerly:** South Georgia Dialysis Services.

Barnesville

23859 ■ Barnesville Dialysis
783 Hwy. 341 S
Barnesville, GA 30204
Ph: (770)358-1142
Dialysis Stations: 10.

Baxley

23860 ■ Baxley Dialysis DaVita
539 Fair St.
Baxley, GA 31513
Ph: (912)366-0202
Free: 800-424-6589
URL: http://www.davita.com
Dialysis Stations: 13. **Formerly:** Gambro Healthcare.

Blairsville

23861 ■ Union County Dialysis--Georgia
334 Appalachian Ave.
Blairsville, GA 30512
Ph: (706)835-1925
Dialysis Stations: 17.

Bremen

23862 ■ Fresenius Medical Care--Breman
108 Redding Dr.
Bremen, GA 30110
Free: 866-434-2597
URL: http://www.ultracare-dialysis.com/
Dialysis Stations: 16.

Brunswick

23863 ■ Brunswick Dialysis DaVita Dialysis Facility & At Home
53 Scranton Connector
Brunswick, GA 31525
Ph: (912)264-8657
Free: 800-424-6589
URL: http://www.davita.com
Dialysis Stations: 24. **Formerly:** Gambro Healthcare.

23864 ■ Fresenius Medical Care--Golden Isles
475 Gateway Center Blvd.
Brunswick, GA 31525
Free: 866-434-2597
URL: http://www.ultracare-dialysis.com/
Dialysis Stations: 24.

23865 ■ South Brunswick Dialysis DaVita
4420 Altama Ave., Ste. 19
Brunswick, GA 31520
Free: 800-424-6589
URL: http://www.davita.com
Dialysis Stations: 20. **Formerly:** Gambro Healthcare.

Buena Vista

23866 ■ DaVita--Buena Vista Dialysis Facility
349 Geneva Rd.
Buena Vista, GA 31803
Free: 800-424-6589
URL: http://www.davita.com
Dialysis Stations: 10.

Buford

23867 ■ Buford Dialysis & At Home DaVita
1550 Buford Hwy., Ste. 1E
Buford, GA 30518
Free: 800-424-6589
URL: http://www.davita.com
Dialysis Stations: 12.

Cairo

23868 ■ Grady County Dialysis Facility
1182 5th St. SE
Cairo, GA 31728
Ph: (229)377-9606
Dialysis Stations: 12.

Calhoun

23869 ■ Dialysis Corporation of America of Calhoun
105 Professional Pl.
Calhoun, GA 30701
Ph: (706)624-4497
URL: http://www.dialysiscorporation.com
Dialysis Stations: 15.

Camilla

23870 ■ Mitchell County Dialysis Center
251 US 19 N
Camilla, GA 31730
Ph: (229)336-5874
Dialysis Stations: 12.

Canton

23871 ■ Diversified Specialty Institutes--Canton
260 Hospital Rd.
Canton, GA 30114
Ph: (678)880-3939
URL: http://www.dsi-corp.com
Dialysis Stations: 19. **Formerly:** National Renal Institutes.

23872 ■ Fresenius Medical Care--North Georgia
411 Hospital Rd.
Canton, GA 30114
Free: 866-434-2597
URL: http://www.ultracare-dialysis.com/
Dialysis Stations: 14.

Carrollton

23873 ■ Carroll County Dialysis Fresenius Medical Care
157 Clinic Ave., Ste. 102
Carrollton, GA 30117
Free: 866-434-2597
URL: http://www.ultracare-dialysis.com/
Dialysis Stations: 26.

Cartersville

23874 ■ Diversified Specialty Institutes Cartersville Dialysis Center, LLC
203 S Tennessee St.
Cartersville, GA 30120
Ph: (678)721-9090
URL: http://www.dsi-corp.com
Dialysis Stations: 13. **Formerly:** Regional Preferred Medical Group.

23875 ■ Fresenius Medical Care--Cartersville Dialysis Facility
14 Roving Rd. SE
Cartersville, GA 30121
Free: 866-434-2597
URL: http://www.ultracare-dialysis.com/
Dialysis Stations: 16.

Cedartown

23876 ■ Cedartown Dialysis DaVita Dialysis Facility
325 West Ave.
Cedartown, GA 30125
Free: 800-424-6589
URL: http://www.davita.com
Dialysis Stations: 16. **Formerly:** Gambro Healthcare.

23877 ■ Harbin Clinic Cedartown Dialysis
14 Cherokee Rd.
Cedartown, GA 30125
Ph: (770)748-2567
URL: http://www.harbinclinic.com/locations-cedartown
Dialysis Stations: 16.

Chatsworth

23878 ■ Fresenius Medical Care--Murray Dialysis
108 Hospital Dr.
Chatsworth, GA 30705
Free: 866-434-2597
URL: http://www.ultracare-dialysis.com/
Dialysis Stations: 14.

Claxton

23879 ■ Claxton Dialysis Center Fresenius Medical Care Dialysis Center
312 N River St.
Claxton, GA 30417
Free: 866-434-2597
URL: http://www.ultracare-dialysis.com/
Dialysis Stations: 16.

Clayton

23880 ■ Fresenius Medical Care--Clayton
108 Plaza Way
Clayton, GA 30525
Free: 866-434-2597
URL: http://www.ultracare-dialysis.com/
Dialysis Stations: 11.

College Park

23881 ■ Fresenius Medical Care--Atlanta
1720 Phoenix Pkwy.
College Park, GA 30349
Free: 866-434-2597
URL: http://www.ultracare-dialysis.com/
Dialysis Stations: 18.

23882 ■ Fresenius Medical Care--College Park
2545 Sullivan Rd.
College Park, GA 30337
Free: 866-434-2597
URL: http://www.ultracare-dialysis.com/
Dialysis Stations: 18. **Formerly:** College Park Dialysis Center.

Columbus

23883 ■ Columbus Dialysis--Bradley Park Drive
DaVita
6228 Bradley Park Dr., Ste. B
Columbus, GA 31904
Free: 800-424-6589
URL: http://www.davita.com
Dialysis Stations: 28.

23884 ■ Community Dialysis Center of Columbus, LLC
1120 13th St.
Columbus, GA 31901
Ph: (706)507-0004
Dialysis Stations: 17.

23885 ■ Dialysis Clinic Inc.--Boxwood Place
1711 Boxwood Pl.
Columbus, GA 31906
Ph: (706)565-8392
URL: http://www.dciinc.org
Dialysis Stations: 28.

23886 ■ Dialysis Clinic, Inc.--Columbus
710 Front Ave.
Columbus, GA 31901
Ph: (706)323-2415
URL: http://www.dciinc.org
Dialysis Stations: 27.

23887 ■ Dialysis Clinic Inc.--North Columbus
2424-B Warm Springs Rd.
Columbus, GA 31904
Ph: (706)322-1959
URL: http://www.dciinc.org
Dialysis Stations: 38.

23888 ■ Fresenius Medical Care--Chattahoochee Valley
2042 Wynnton Rd.
Columbus, GA 31906
Free: 866-434-2597
URL: http://www.ultracare-dialysis.com/
Dialysis Stations: 15.

23889 ■ Fresenius Medical Care--Muscogee County
Dialysis Center
1851 Manchester Expy.
Columbus, GA 31904
Free: 866-434-2597
URL: http://www.ultracare-dialysis.com/
Dialysis Stations: 16.

23890 ■ Fresenius Medical Care--River City
2443 Brookstone Center Pkwy.
Columbus, GA 31904
Free: 866-434-2597
URL: http://www.ultracare-dialysis.com/
Dialysis Stations: 17.

23891 ■ West Georgia Dialysis & At Home
DaVita
1216 Stark Ave.
Columbus, GA 31906
Free: 800-424-6589
URL: http://www.davita.com
Dialysis Stations: 20.

Commerce

23892 ■ Commerce Kidney Center
592 Ridge Way Rd., Ste. A
Commerce, GA 30529
Ph: (706)335-6665
Dialysis Stations: 15.

Conyers

23893 ■ Conyers Dialysis
DaVita
1501 Milstead Rd. NE
Conyers, GA 30012
Free: 800-424-6589
URL: http://www.davita.com
Dialysis Stations: 13.

23894 ■ Fresenius Medical Care--Conyers Dialysis Facility
1285 Wellbrook Cir. NE
Conyers, GA 30012
Free: 866-434-2597
Dialysis Stations: 14.

Cordele

23895 ■ Cordele Dialysis
DaVita
Dialysis Center and At Home
1013 E 16th Ave.
Cordele, GA 31015
Free: 800-424-6589
URL: http://www.davita.com
Dialysis Stations: 17.

23896 ■ Crisp Regional Hospital Dialysis Unit
902 N 7th St.
Cordele, GA 31015
Ph: (229)276-3212
URL: http://www.crispregional.org
Dialysis Stations: 18.

Covington

23897 ■ Covington Renal Center
Diversified Specialty Institutes
4179 Baker St.
Covington, GA 30014
Ph: (770)385-4015
URL: http://www.dsi-corp.com
Dialysis Stations: 17.

23898 ■ Fresenius Medical Care--Covington Dialysis Facility
7215 Industrial Blvd.
Covington, GA 30014
Free: 866-434-2597
URL: http://www.ultracare-dialysis.com/
Dialysis Stations: 20.

23899 ■ Fresenius Medical Care Dialysis Services of Newton
11415 Brown Bridge Rd.
Covington, GA 30016
Free: 866-434-2597
URL: http://www.ultracare-dialysis.com/
Dialysis Stations: 11.

Cumming

23900 ■ Cumming Dialysis
DaVita
911 Marketplace Blvd., Ste. 3
Cumming, GA 30041
Free: 800-424-6589
URL: http://www.davita.com
Dialysis Stations: 12. **Formerly:** Gambro Healthcare.

23901 ■ Fresenius Medical Care--Cumming
1070 Buford Hwy.
Cumming, GA 30041
Free: 866-434-2597
URL: http://www.ultracare-dialysis.com/
Dialysis Stations: 15.

Dahlonega

23902 ■ Renal Carepartners--Dahlonega
73 Maxwell Ln., Ste. 3
Dahlonega, GA 30533
Ph: (706)482-0590
Fax: (706)482-0594
URL: http://www.renalcp.com
Dialysis Stations: 17.

Dallas

23903 ■ Paulding Dialysis
DaVita
4019 Johns Rd.
Dallas, GA 30132
Free: 800-424-6589
URL: http://www.davita.com
Dialysis Stations: 10. **Formerly:** Paulding Nephrology Center.

Dalton

23904 ■ Fresenius Medical Care Dalton
1009 Professional Blvd.
Dalton, GA 30720
Free: 866-434-2597
URL: http://www.ultracare-dialysis.com/
Dialysis Stations: 22.

Dawson

23905 ■ Dialysis Clinic, Inc.--Dawson
806 Forrester Dr. SE
Dawson, GA 39842
Ph: (229)995-2433
URL: http://www.dciinc.org
Dialysis Stations: 19.

Decatur

23906 ■ DaVita
Snapfinger Center
5255 Snapfinger Park Dr., Ste. 110
Decatur, GA 30035
Free: 800-424-6589
URL: http://www.davita.com
Dialysis Stations: 20. **Formerly:** Lithonia Dialysis Center.

23907 ■ Decatur Dialysis Center
DaVita
1987 Candler Rd.
Decatur, GA 30032
Free: 800-424-6589
URL: http://www.davita.com
Dialysis Stations: 20.

23908 ■ Dialysis Clinic Inc.--Dekalb
558 Medlock Rd.
Decatur, GA 30030
Ph: (404)371-0499
URL: http://www.dciinc.org
Dialysis Stations: 12.

23909 ■ Dialysis of Lithonia
DaVita
2485 Park Central Blvd.
Decatur, GA 30035
Free: 800-424-6589
URL: http://www.davita.com
Dialysis Stations: 16.

23910 ■ East DeKalb Dialysis Center
DaVita
2801 Candler Rd.
Decatur, GA 30034
Free: 800-424-6589
URL: http://www.davita.com
Dialysis Stations: 17. **Formerly:** Georgia Nephrology LLC.

23911 ■ Eastlake Dialysis
DaVita
1757 Candler Rd. SE
Decatur, GA 30032
Free: 800-424-6589
URL: http://www.davita.com
Dialysis Stations: 20. **Formerly:** Gambro Healthcare.

23912 ■ Emory Dialysis at Candler
Emory Healthcare
2726 Candler Rd.
Decatur, GA 30034

Ph: (404)778-1025
URL: http://www.emoryhealthcare.org
Dialysis Stations: 38.

23913 ■ Fresenius Medical Care--Decatur
2721 Irwin Way
Decatur, GA 30030
Free: 866-434-2597
URL: http://www.ultracare-dialysis.com/
Dialysis Stations: 21.

23914 ■ Fresenius Medical Care of Dekalb Gwinnett Inc.
497 Winn Way, Ste. 160
Decatur, GA 30030
Free: 866-434-2597
URL: http://www.ultracare-dialysis.com/
Dialysis Stations: 20.

23915 ■ Fresenius Medical Care Dialysis Center--Snapfinger
5250 Snapfinger Park Dr.
Decatur, GA 30035
Free: 866-434-2597
URL: http://www.ultracare-dialysis.com/
Dialysis Stations: 21.

23916 ■ Fresenius Medical Care--Snapfinger
5250 Snapfinger Park Dr.
Decatur, GA 30035
Free: 866-434-2597
URL: http://www.ultracare-dialysis.com/
Dialysis Stations: 21.

23917 ■ Southern Lane Dialysis
DaVita
1840 Southern Ln.
Decatur, GA 30033
Free: 800-424-6589
URL: http://www.davita.com
Dialysis Stations: 16. **Formerly:** Gambro Healthcare.

Demorest

23918 ■ Fresenius Medical Care--Habersham
735 N Historic Hwy. 441
Demorest, GA 30535
Free: 866-434-2597
URL: http://www.ultracare-dialysis.com/
Dialysis Stations: 11.

Douglas

23919 ■ Douglas Dialysis
DaVita
190 Westside Dr., Ste. A
Douglas, GA 31533
Free: 800-424-6589
URL: http://www.davita.com
Dialysis Stations: 20. **Formerly:** Gambro Healthcare.

Douglasville

23920 ■ Arbor Place Dialysis
DaVita
9559 Hwy. 5, Ste. 1
Douglasville, GA 30135
Ph: (678)391-0949
Free: 800-424-6589
URL: http://www.davita.com
Dialysis Stations: 12.

23921 ■ Douglasville Dialysis
DaVita
3899 Longview Dr.
Douglasville, GA 30135
Free: 800-424-6589
URL: http://www.davita.com
Dialysis Stations: 20. **Formerly:** Gambro HealthcareelaHe.

23922 ■ Fresenius Medical Care--Douglas County
4645 Timber Ridge. Rd.
Bldg. 200, Ste. 140
Douglasville, GA 30135
Free: 866-434-2597
URL: http://www.ultracare-dialysis.com/
Dialysis Stations: 17. **Formerly:** Regional Preferred Medical Group.

Dublin

23923 ■ Laurens County--Dublin
DaVita
2400 Bellevue Rd.
Dublin, GA 31021
Free: 800-424-6589
URL: http://www.davita.com
Dialysis Stations: 26. **Formerly:** Gambro Healthcare.

23924 ■ Shamrock Dialysis
DaVita
1016 Claxton Dairy Rd., Ste. 1A
Dublin, GA 31021
Free: 800-424-6589
URL: http://www.davita.com
Dialysis Stations: 14.

Duluth

23925 ■ Duluth Dialysis Center
3770 Howell Ferry Road
Duluth, GA 30096
Ph: (678)495-0420
Dialysis Stations: 16.

23926 ■ Medlock Bridge Dialysis
DaVita
10680 Medlock Bridge Rd., Ste. 103
Duluth, GA 30097
Free: 800-424-6589
URL: http://www.davita.com
Dialysis Stations: 16.

East Point

23927 ■ Atlanta South Dialysis
DaVita
Dialysis Facility
3158 SE Main St., Ste. A
East Point, GA 30344
Free: 800-424-6589
Fax: (404)761-0622
URL: http://www.davita.com
Dialysis Stations: 18. **Formerly:** Gambro Healthcare.

23928 ■ East Point Dialysis
DaVita
2669 Church St.
East Point, GA 30344
Free: 800-424-6589
URL: http://www.davita.com
Dialysis Stations: 28.

23929 ■ Trinity Dialysis Clinic
1354 Cleveland Ave.
East Point, GA 30344
Ph: (404)763-0405
Dialysis Stations: 20.

Eastman

23930 ■ Fresenius Medical Care of Eastman
1078 Plaza Ave.
Eastman, GA 31023
Free: 866-434-2597
URL: http://www.ultracare-dialysis.com/
Dialysis Stations: 21.

Elberton

23931 ■ Elberton Dialysis Facility Inc.
DaVita
894 Elbert St.
Elberton, GA 30635
Free: 800-424-6589
URL: http://www.davita.com
Dialysis Stations: 18.

Ellijay

23932 ■ DaVita Ellijay Dialysis
449 Industrial Blvd., Ste. 240
Ellijay, GA 30540
Free: 800-424-6589
URL: http://www.davita.com
Dialysis Stations: 5.

23933 ■ Fresenius Medical Care - Ellijay
941 Progress Rd., Box 2
Ellijay, GA 30540
Free: 866-434-2597
URL: http://www.ultracare-dialysis.com/
Dialysis Stations: 15.

Evans

23934 ■ Fresenius Medical Care--Evans
3000 McCrary Ct.
Evans, GA 30809
Free: 866-434-2597
URL: http://www.ultracare-dialysis.com/
Dialysis Stations: 21.

Fayetteville

23935 ■ Dialysis Clinic, Inc.--Fayetteville
155 Brandywine Blvd.
Fayetteville, GA 30214
Ph: (770)716-6940
URL: http://www.dciinc.org
Dialysis Stations: 23.

23936 ■ Fayetteville Dialysis
DaVita
1279 Hwy. 54 W
Fayetteville, GA 30214
Free: 800-424-6589
URL: http://www.davita.com
Dialysis Stations: 13. **Formerly:** Gambro Healthcare.

Fitzgerald

23937 ■ Dialysis Corporation of America--Fitzgerald
402 S Grant St.
Fitzgerald, GA 31750
Ph: (229)409-2221
URL: http://www.dialysiscorporation.com
Dialysis Stations: 12.

Forest Park

23938 ■ DaVita
Forest Park Dialysis Center
380 Forest Pkwy.
Forest Park, GA 30297
Free: 800-424-6589
URL: http://www.davita.com
Dialysis Stations: 18.

Forsyth

23939 ■ Fresenius Medical Care Dialysis Services--Forsyth
91 Martin Luther King Dr.
Forsyth, GA 31029
Free: 866-434-2597
URL: http://www.ultracare-dialysis.com/
Dialysis Stations: 13.

Fort Oglethorpe

23940 ■ Dialysis Clinic, Inc.--Fort Oglethorpe
201 Thomas Rd., Ste. A
Fort Oglethorpe, GA 30742
Ph: (706)861-6668
Fax: (706)861-6088
URL: http://www.dciinc.org
Dialysis Stations: 17.

Fort Valley

23941 ■ DaVita--Fort Valley
557 Bluebird Blvd.
Fort Valley, GA 31030
Free: 800-424-6589
URL: http://www.davita.com
Dialysis Stations: 13.

23942 ■ Fresenius Medical Care of Fort Valley
135 Avera Dr.
Fort Valley, GA 31030
Free: 866-434-2597
URL: http://www.ultracare-dialysis.com/
Dialysis Stations: 10.

Gainesville

23943 ■ Fresenius Medical Care--Gainesville
1856 Thompson Bridge Rd., Ste. 101
Gainesville, GA 30501
Free: 866-434-2597
URL: http://www.ultracare-dialysis.com/
Dialysis Stations: 25. **Formerly:** Renal Care Group of Gainesville.

23944 ■ Fresenius Medical Care--Lake Lanier
2565 Thompson Bridge Rd.
Gainesville, GA 30501
Free: 866-434-2597
URL: http://www.ultracare-dialysis.com/
Dialysis Stations: 10. **Formerly:** Renal Care Group-Lake Lanier.

23945 ■ Gainesville Dialysis & At Home
DaVita
2545 Flintridge Rd.
Gainesville, GA 30501
Free: 800-424-6589
URL: http://www.davita.com
Dialysis Stations: 15.

Garden City

23946 ■ Fresenius Medical Care - Chatham Dialysis Center
113 Minus Ave.
Garden City, GA 31408
Free: 866-434-2597
URL: http://www.ultracare-dialysis.com/
Dialysis Stations: 16.

Gray

23947 ■ Renal Advantage Inc.
Gray Dialysis Center
1002 Boulder Dr.
Gray, GA 31032
Ph: (478)986-3066
URL: http://www.renaladvantage.com
Dialysis Stations: 18. **Formerly:** National Renal Alliance.

Greensboro

23948 ■ Greensboro Dialysis Facility LLC
1220 Siloam Rd.
Greensboro, GA 30642
Ph: (706)453-7222
Dialysis Stations: 15.

Griffin

23949 ■ DaVita Inc./Griffin Dialysis Center
731 S 8th St.
Griffin, GA 30224
Free: 800-424-6589
URL: http://www.davita.com
Dialysis Stations: 24.

23950 ■ Iris City Dialysis
DaVita
521 N Expressway, Ste. 1509
Griffin, GA 30223
Free: 800-424-6589
URL: http://www.davita.com
Dialysis Stations: 18.

23951 ■ Spalding County Dialysis
1570 Williamson Rd.
Griffin, GA 30224
Ph: (770)467-8116
Dialysis Stations: 20.

Grovetown

23952 ■ Nephrology Centers of America--Grovetown
442 Park 20 West Dr.
Grovetown, GA 30813
Ph: (706)860-0831
Dialysis Stations: 16. **Formerly:** Park West Dialysis Center.

Hapeville

23953 ■ Renal Care Partners--Hapeville
800 Virginia Ave.
Hapeville, GA 30354
Ph: (678)681-3949
URL: http://www.renalcp.com
Dialysis Stations: 18.

Hawkinsville

23954 ■ Dialysis Corporation of America of Hawkinsville
292 Industrial Blvd., Ste. 100
Hawkinsville, GA 31036
Ph: (478)892-8008
Fax: (478)892-8040
URL: http://www.dialysiscorporation.com
Dialysis Stations: 16.

23955 ■ Hawkinsville Dialysis Center
Rte. 4 Box 8015 Industrial Blvd.
Hawkinsville, GA 31036
Ph: (478)892-8008
Dialysis Stations: 16.

Hinesville

23956 ■ Hinesville Dialysis
DaVita
522 EG Miles Pkwy.
Hinesville, GA 31313
Free: 800-424-6589
URL: http://www.davita.com
Dialysis Stations: 16. **Formerly:** Gambro Healthcare.

23957 ■ Magnolia Oaks Dialysis
DaVita
2377 Hwy. 196 W.
Hinesville, GA 31313
Free: 800-424-6589
URL: http://www.davita.com
Dialysis Stations: 15.

Hiram

23958 ■ Fresenius Medical Care--Hiram
3919 Atlanta Hwy.
Hiram, GA 30141
Free: 866-434-2597
URL: http://www.ultracare-dialysis.com/
Dialysis Stations: 16.

Hogansville

23959 ■ Hogansville Dialysis Clinic
Renal Advantage Inc.
1002 Williams St.
Hogansville, GA 30230
Ph: (706)637-4028
URL: http://www.renaladvantage.com
Dialysis Stations: 17. **Formerly:** National Renal Alliance.

Jackson

23960 ■ DaVita Grovepark Dialysis Center
794 McDonough Rd., Ste. 103
Jackson, GA 30233
Free: 800-424-6589
URL: http://www.davita.com
Dialysis Stations: 12.

Jesup

23961 ■ Jesup Dialysis
DaVita
301 Peachtree St.
Jesup, GA 31545
Free: 800-424-6589
URL: http://www.davita.com
Dialysis Stations: 16. **Formerly:** Gambro Healthcare.

Jonesboro

23962 ■ DaVita--Jonesboro Dialysis Center
129 King St.
Jonesboro, GA 30236
Free: 800-424-6589
URL: http://www.davita.com
Dialysis Stations: 20.

23963 ■ Fresenius Medical Care--Clayton County
Dialysis Facility
335 Upper Riverdale Rd., Ste. A-1
Jonesboro, GA 30236
Free: 866-434-2597
URL: http://www.ultracare-dialysis.com/
Dialysis Stations: 21. **Formerly:** Renal Care Group.

23964 ■ Spivey Peritoneal, Home Dialysis Center & At Home
DaVita
1423 Stockbridge Rd., Ste. B
Jonesboro, GA 30236
Free: 800-424-6589
URL: http://www.davita.com
Dialysis Stations: 2.

La Fayette

23965 ■ Dialysis Clinic, Inc.--LaFayette
614 Patterson Rd.
La Fayette, GA 30728
Ph: (706)638-6553
URL: http://www.dciinc.org
Dialysis Stations: 16.

LaGrange

23966 ■ West George Dialysis--LaGrange
Renal Advantage Inc.
140 Glenn Bass Rd.
LaGrange, GA 30240
Ph: (706)884-6825
URL: http://www.renaladvantage.com
Dialysis Stations: 33. **Formerly:** West Georgia Health Systems Inc.

Lawrenceville

23967 ■ Fresenius Medical Care--Duluth/Lawrenceville
1115 Herrington Rd.
Lawrenceville, GA 30044
Free: 866-434-2597
URL: http://www.ultracare-dialysis.com/
Dialysis Stations: 19.

23968 ■ Fresenius Medical Care--Lawrenceville
350 Philip Blvd. NW
Lawrenceville, GA 30045
Free: 866-434-2597
URL: http://www.ultracare-dialysis.com/
Dialysis Stations: 17. **Formerly:** Renal Care Group.

23969 ■ Gwinnett Dialysis Facility
605 Old Norcross Rd.
Lawrenceville, GA 30045
Ph: (770)962-1231
Dialysis Stations: 21.

23970 ■ Sugarloaf Dialysis
DaVita
1705 Belle Meade Ct., Ste. 110
Lawrenceville, GA 30043
Free: 800-424-6589
URL: http://www.davita.com
Dialysis Stations: 20. **Formerly:** Lawrenceville Dialysis.

Lithia Springs

23971 ■ Sweetwater Dialysis
DaVita
7117 S Sweetwater Rd.
Lithia Springs, GA 30122
Free: 800-424-6589
URL: http://www.davita.com
Dialysis Stations: 17. **Formerly:** Douglas Nephrology Center.

Lithonia

23972 ■ Fresenius Medical Care--Lithonia
2701 Evans Mill Rd.
Lithonia, GA 30058
Free: 866-434-2597
URL: http://www.ultracare-dialysis.com/
Dialysis Stations: 20.

23973 ■ Fresenius Medical Care--South Dekalb/Rockdale
6085 Hillandale Dr.
Lithonia, GA 30058
Free: 866-434-2597
URL: http://www.ultracare-dialysis.com/
Dialysis Stations: 20.

Loganville

23974 ■ Loganville Dialysis Center
3977 Atlanta Hwy., Ste. 104-105
Loganville, GA 30052
Ph: (678)639-1633
Dialysis Stations: 10.

Louisville

23975 ■ Dialysis Services--East Georgia
Fresenius Medical Care
1069 Peachtree St.
Louisville, GA 30434
Free: 866-434-2597
URL: http://www.ultracare-dialysis.com/
Dialysis Stations: 11.

23976 ■ Nephrology Centers of America--Louisville
1201 Peachtree St.
Louisville, GA 30434
Ph: (478)625-3311
Dialysis Stations: 16.

Mableton

23977 ■ Mableton Dialysis
1330 Veterans Memorial Hwy. SW, Ste. 1380
Mableton, GA 30126
Ph: (770)485-1773
Dialysis Stations: 17.

Macon

23978 ■ DaVita Dialysis of Middle Georgia
747 Second St.
Macon, GA 31201
Free: 800-424-6589
URL: http://www.davita.com
Dialysis Stations: 19.

23979 ■ East Macon Dialysis Center & At Home
DaVita
165 Emery Hwy., Ste. 101
Macon, GA 31217
Free: 800-424-6589
URL: http://www.davita.com
Dialysis Stations: 24.

23980 ■ Eisenhower Pkwy. Dialysis Center
Renal Advantage Inc.
2525 Second St.
Macon, GA 31201
Ph: (478)738-0420
URL: http://www.renaladvantage.com
Dialysis Stations: 26. **Formerly:** National Renal Alliance.

23981 ■ Fresenius Medical Care--Macon
280 Clinton St.
Macon, GA 31217
Free: 866-434-2597
URL: http://www.ultracare-dialysis.com/
Dialysis Stations: 20.

23982 ■ Fresenius Medical Care - South Macon Dialysis
2500 2nd St.
Macon, GA 31206
Free: 866-434-2597
URL: http://www.ultracare-dialysis.com/
Dialysis Stations: 20.

23983 ■ Kidney Dialysis Center LLC
DaVita
640 Martin Luther King Jr. Blvd.
Macon, GA 31201
Free: 800-424-6589
URL: http://www.davita.com
Dialysis Stations: 24. **Formerly:** Dialysis Treatment Centers of Macon.

23984 ■ Pine Street Dialysis
Fresenius Medical Care
745 Pine St.
Macon, GA 31210
Free: 866-434-2597
URL: http://www.ultracare-dialysis.com/
Dialysis Stations: 18.

23985 ■ RAI Hemlock St.--Macon
Renal Advantage Inc.
657 Hemlock St., Ste. 100
Macon, GA 31201
Ph: (478)742-8001
URL: http://www.renaladvantage.com
Dialysis Stations: 22. **Formerly:** National Renal Alliance.

Madison

23986 ■ Madison Kidney Center
1311 Atlanta Hwy., Ste. A
Madison, GA 30650
Ph: (706)752-1113
Dialysis Stations: 12.

Marietta

23987 ■ Cobb County Dialysis Center
Diversified Specialty Institutes
506 Roswell St.
Marietta, GA 30060
Ph: (770)426-5110
URL: http://www.dsi-corp.com
Dialysis Stations: 16. **Formerly:** Regional Preferred Medical Group.

23988 ■ Fresenius Medical Care--Marietta
1277 Kennestone Cir., Ste. 600
Marietta, GA 30066
Free: 866-434-2597
URL: http://www.ultracare-dialysis.com/
Dialysis Stations: 25.

23989 ■ Fresenius Medical Care--North Cobb
1392 Bells Ferry Rd.
Marietta, GA 30066
Free: 866-434-2597
URL: http://www.ultracare-dialysis.com/
Dialysis Stations: 25.

23990 ■ Kennestone Dialysis and At Home
DaVita
200 Cobb Pkwy. N
Marietta, GA 30062
Free: 800-424-6589
URL: http://www.davita.com
Dialysis Stations: 18.

Martinez

23991 ■ Renal Advantage Inc. Crossroads--Augusta
1719 Magnolia Way
Martinez, GA 30907
Ph: (706)228-7253
URL: http://www.renaladvantage.com
Dialysis Stations: 17.

McDonough

23992 ■ McDonough Dialysis Facility
Davita
114 Dunn St.
McDonough, GA 30253
Free: 800-424-6589
URL: http://www.davita.com
Dialysis Stations: 24.

23993 ■ South Henry Dialysis Center
1095 Henry Pkwy. Connector
McDonough, GA 30252
Ph: (678)688-3507
Dialysis Stations: 16.

Metter

23994 ■ Candler County Dialysis
DaVita
325 Cedar Rd.
Metter, GA 30439
Free: 800-424-6589
URL: http://www.davita.com
Dialysis Stations: 20. **Formerly:** Gambro Healthcare.

Milledgeville

23995 ■ DaVita Inc.--Milledgeville
400 S Wayne St.
Milledgeville, GA 31061
Free: 800-424-6589
URL: http://www.davita.com
Dialysis Stations: 12.

23996 ■ Medical Kidney Services of Central Georgia
521 W Montgomery St., Ste. 14-A
Milledgeville, GA 31061
Ph: (478)453-2031
Dialysis Stations: 12.

Millen

23997 ■ Fresenius Medical Care--Millen Dialysis Facility
242 N Masonic St.
Millen, GA 30442
Free: 866-434-2597
URL: http://www.ultracare-dialysis.com/
Dialysis Stations: 11.

Monroe

23998 ■ Fresenius Medical Care--Walton
299 Plaza Dr.
Monroe, GA 30655
Free: 866-434-2597
URL: http://www.ultracare-dialysis.com/
Dialysis Stations: 11.

23999 ■ Walton Dialysis Center
710 Breedlove Dr.
Monroe, GA 30655
Ph: (770)207-0850
Dialysis Stations: 21.

Montezuma

24000 ■ Montezuma Dialysis
DaVita
114 DeVaughn Ave.
Montezuma, GA 31063
Free: 800-424-6589
URL: http://www.davita.com
Dialysis Stations: 12. **Formerly:** Gambro Healthcare.

Monticello

24001 ■ Monticello Dialysis Center
Renal Advantage Inc.
1393 Funderburg Dr.
Monticello, GA 31064
Ph: (706)468-1240
URL: http://www.renaladvantage.com
Dialysis Stations: 12. **Formerly:** National Renal Alliance.

Moultrie

24002 ■ Colquitt Regional Medical Center Dialysis
3131 S Main St.
Moultrie, GA 31768
Ph: (229)985-3420
E-mail: info@colquittregional.com
URL: http://www.colquittregional.com/
Dialysis Stations: 25.

24003 ■ Moultrie Dialysis Center
DaVita
2419 S Main St.
Moultrie, GA 31768
Free: 800-424-6589
URL: http://www.davita.com
Dialysis Stations: 10.

Newnan

24004 ■ DaVita Newnan Dialysis
1565 E Hwy. 34
Newnan, GA 30265
Free: 800-424-6589
URL: http://www.davita.com
Dialysis Stations: 18.

24005 ■ Newnan Dialysis Services
Renal Advantage Inc.
101 Werz Industrial Dr.
Newnan, GA 30263
Ph: (770)251-7896
URL: http://www.renaladvantage.com
Dialysis Stations: 19. **Formerly:** National Renal Alliance.

Norcross

24006 ■ Fresenius Medical Care--Norcross
4650 Jimmy Carter Blvd., Ste. 111-113
Norcross, GA 30093
Free: 866-434-2597
URL: http://www.ultracare-dialysis.com/
Dialysis Stations: 17. **Formerly:** Regional Preferred Medical Group, Norcross Dialysis Center.

Palmetto

24007 ■ Renal Advantage Inc.--Palmetto
500 Walnut Way
Palmetto, GA 30268
Ph: (770)463-1442
URL: http://www.renaladvantage.com
Dialysis Stations: 18.

Perry

24008 ■ Perry Dialysis Center
DaVita
1027 Keith Dr.
Perry, GA 31069
Free: 800-424-6589
URL: http://www.davita.com
Dialysis Stations: 11. **Formerly:** Kidney Care of Perry.

Pooler

24009 ■ Pooler Dialysis
DaVita
54 Traders Way
Pooler, GA 31322
Free: 800-424-6589
URL: http://www.davita.com
Dialysis Stations: 14.

Quitman

24010 ■ Brooks County Dialysis Facility
101 E Davis St.
Quitman, GA 31643
Ph: (229)263-6340
Dialysis Stations: 12.

Rincon

24011 ■ Fresenius Medical Care--Rincon
604 Towne Park W
Rincon, GA 31326
Free: 866-434-2597
URL: http://www.ultracare-dialysis.com/
Dialysis Stations: 11.

Riverdale

24012 ■ DaVita--Southern Crescent Dialysis Center
275 Upper Riverdale Rd. SW, Ste. B
Riverdale, GA 30274
Free: 800-424-6589
URL: http://www.davita.com
Dialysis Stations: 20.

24013 ■ South Atlanta Kidney Care Dialysis Facility LLC
195 Upper Riverdale Rd., Ste. A
Riverdale, GA 30274
Ph: (770)994-0171
Dialysis Stations: 0.

Rome

24014 ■ Harbin Clinic Dialysis Center
172 Three Rivers Dr. NE
Rome, GA 30161
Ph: (706)234-6905
Dialysis Stations: 21.

24015 ■ Rome Dialysis
DaVita
15 John Maddox Dr.
Rome, GA 30165
Free: 800-424-6589
URL: http://www.davita.com
Dialysis Stations: 23. **Formerly:** Gambro Healthcare.

Roswell

24016 ■ Fresenius Medical Care--Alpharetta
1260A Upper Hembree Rd., Ste. A
Roswell, GA 30076
Free: 866-434-2597
URL: http://www.ultracare-dialysis.com/
Dialysis Stations: 17.

24017 ■ North Fulton Dialysis
DaVita
1250 N Meadow Pkwy.
Roswell, GA 30076
Free: 800-424-6589
URL: http://www.davita.com
Dialysis Stations: 9. **Formerly:** Gambro Healthcare.

Royston

24018 ■ Dialysis Corporation of America--Royston
611 Cook St.
Royston, GA 30662
Ph: (706)245-0817
URL: http://www.dialysiscorporation.com
Dialysis Stations: 18.

Saint Marys

24019 ■ St. Mary's Dialysis
DaVita
2714 Osborne Rd.
Saint Marys, GA 31558
Free: 800-424-6589
URL: http://www.davita.com
Dialysis Stations: 16. **Formerly:** Gambro Healthcare.

Sandersville

24020 ■ RAI S Harris St.--Sandersville
614 S Harris St.
Sandersville, GA 31082
Free: 866-434-2597
URL: http://www.renaladvantage.com/
Dialysis Stations: 21. **Formerly:** Fresenius Medical Care of Sandersville Inc.

Savannah

24021 ■ Abercorn Dialysis
DaVita
Dialysis Center
11706 Mercy Blvd., Bldg. 9
Savannah, GA 31419
Ph: (912)961-6006
Free: 800-424-6589
URL: http://www.davita.com
Dialysis Stations: 12. **Formerly:** Kidney Treatment Center of Savannah; Gambro Healthcare--Savannah, Southside.

24022 ■ Coastal Dialysis Center
Fresenius Medical Care
1460 E Victory Dr.
Savannah, GA 31404
Free: 866-434-2597
URL: http://www.ultracare-dialysis.com/
Dialysis Stations: 43.

24023 ■ Derenne Dialysis
DaVita
5303 Montgomery St.
Savannah, GA 31405
Free: 800-424-6589
URL: http://www.davita.com
Dialysis Stations: 26. **Formerly:** Gambro Healthcare--Savannah Montgomery.

24024 ■ Renal Advantage Inc.--Savannah Dialysis Facility
1020 Drayton St.
Savannah, GA 31401
Ph: (912)233-6067
URL: http://www.renaladvantage.com
Dialysis Stations: 26. **Formerly:** Savannah Dialysis Center.

24025 ■ Williams Street Dialysis
DaVita
2812 Williams St.
Savannah, GA 31404
Free: 800-424-6589
URL: http://www.davita.com
Dialysis Stations: 12. **Formerly:** Dialysis Services Group--Savannah, East; Gambro Healthcare.

Smyrna

24026 ■ Fresenius Medical Care--Smyrna
2700 Highlands Pkwy., Ste. A
Smyrna, GA 30082
Free: 866-434-2597
URL: http://www.ultracare-dialysis.com/
Dialysis Stations: 21. **Formerly:** Smyrna Dialysis Center LLC.

Snellville

24027 ■ DaVita--Snellville
2135 Main St. E
Snellville, GA 30078
Free: 800-424-6589
URL: http://www.davita.com
Dialysis Stations: 16.

24028 ■ Fresenius Medical Care of Snellville Inc.
Dialysis Facility
2096 McGee Rd.
Snellville, GA 30078
Free: 866-434-2597
URL: http://www.ultracare-dialysis.com/
Dialysis Stations: 11.

24029 ■ Snellville Dialysis Center
2290 Oak Rd.
Snellville, GA 30078
Ph: (678)879-1231
Dialysis Stations: 15.

Springfield

24030 ■ Effingham North Dialysis
DaVita
301 N Pine St.
Springfield, GA 31329
Free: 800-424-6589
URL: http://www.davita.com
Dialysis Stations: 12. **Formerly:** Gambro Healthcare.

Statesboro

24031 ■ East Georgia Regional Dialysis Center & At Home
DaVita
450 Georgia Ave., Ste. A
Statesboro, GA 30458
Free: 800-424-6589
URL: http://www.davita.com
Dialysis Stations: 17.

24032 ■ Fresenius Medical Care--Bulloch County
1355 Brampton Ave.
Statesboro, GA 30458
Free: 866-434-2597
URL: http://www.ultracare-dialysis.com/
Dialysis Stations: 22.

24033 ■ Nephrology Center of Statesboro
DaVita
4B College Plaza
Statesboro, GA 30458
Free: 800-424-6589
URL: http://www.davita.com
Dialysis Stations: 18.

Stockbridge

24034 ■ Henry Dialysis Center
Fresenius Medical Care
1365 Rock Quarry Rd., Ste. 100
Stockbridge, GA 30281
Free: 866-434-2597
URL: http://www.ultracare-dialysis.com/
Dialysis Stations: 21. **Formerly:** Renal Care Group.

24035 ■ North Henry Dialysis
DaVita
5627 N Henry Blvd., Ste. I-1
Stockbridge, GA 30281
Free: 800-424-6589
URL: http://www.davita.com
Dialysis Stations: 16.

24036 ■ Stockbridge Dialysis Clinic LLC
3580 Cameron Pkwy.
Stockbridge, GA 30281
Ph: (678)565-6228
Dialysis Stations: 20.

Stone Mountain

24037 ■ Fresenius Medical Care--Stone Mountain
5723 Memorial Dr.
Stone Mountain, GA 30083
Free: 866-434-2597
URL: http://www.ultracare-dialysis.com/
Dialysis Stations: 19. **Formerly:** Regional Preferred Medical Group.

24038 ■ Mountain Park Dialysis
DaVita
5235 Memorial Dr.
Stone Mountain, GA 30083
Free: 800-424-6589
URL: http://www.davita.com
Dialysis Stations: 12.

24039 ■ Nova Dialysis Clinic
5329 Memorial Dr., Ste. B
Stone Mountain, GA 30083
Ph: (678)904-7010
E-mail: info@novadialysis.com
URL: http://www.novadialysis.com/
Dialysis Stations: 20.

Summerville

24040 ■ Harbin Clinic Summerville Dialysis Center
12541 Hwy. 27
Summerville, GA 30747
Ph: (706)857-4050
URL: http://www.harbinclinic.com/locations-summerville
Dialysis Stations: 17.

Suwanee

24041 ■ North Gwinnett Dialysis
Fresenius Medical Care
185 Old Peachtree Rd. NW
Suwanee, GA 30024
Free: 866-434-2597
URL: http://www.ultracare-dialysis.com/
Dialysis Stations: 20. **Formerly:** Renal Care Group.

Swainsboro

24042 ■ RAI Medical Center Dr.--Swainsboro
3 Medical Center Dr.
Swainsboro, GA 30401
Ph: (478)237-8186
Free: 866-434-2597
URL: http://www.renaladvantage.com/
Dialysis Stations: 10. **Formerly:** Fresenius Medical Care--Swainsboro.

Sylvester

24043 ■ Dialysis Clinic, Inc.--Sylvester
102 Pineview Dr.
Sylvester, GA 31791
Ph: (229)776-0250
URL: http://www.dciinc.org
Dialysis Stations: 12.

Thomaston

24044 ■ Thomaston Dialysis
DaVita
1075 Hwy. 19 N
Thomaston, GA 30286
Free: 800-424-6589
URL: http://www.davita.com
Dialysis Stations: 17.

Thomasville

24045 ■ Fresenius Medical Care--Thomasville, Georgia
300 W Jackson St.
Thomasville, GA 31792
Free: 866-434-2597
URL: http://www.ultracare-dialysis.com/
Dialysis Stations: 16. **Formerly:** Renal Care Group/Renex Dialysis Clinics.

24046 ■ Southwest Georgia Dialysis
201 Old Albany Rd.
Thomasville, GA 31792
Ph: (229)227-5000
Dialysis Stations: 41.

Thomson

24047 ■ Fresenius Medical Care - Thomson Dialysis
1020 W Hill St.
Thomson, GA 30824
Free: 866-434-2597
URL: http://www.ultracare-dialysis.com/
Dialysis Stations: 21.

Tifton

24048 ■ Tift Regional Medical Center Dialysis Center
1010 Edgefield Dr.
Tifton, GA 31794
Ph: (229)556-6350
URL: http://www.tiftregional.com/
Dialysis Stations: 22.

24049 ■ Tifton Dialysis
DaVita
624 Love Ave.
Tifton, GA 31794
Free: 800-424-6589
URL: http://www.davita.com
Dialysis Stations: 14.

Toccoa

24050 ■ Fresenius Medical Care--Toccoa
929 Falls Rd.
Toccoa, GA 30577
Free: 866-434-2597
URL: http://www.ultracare-dialysis.com/
Dialysis Stations: 17. **Formerly:** Renal Care Group.

Tucker

24051 ■ Fresenius Medical Care Tucker Dialysis Center
4845 LaVista Rd.
Tucker, GA 30084
Free: 866-434-2597
URL: http://www.ultracare-dialysis.com/
Dialysis Stations: 16.

24052 ■ Northlake Dialysis
DaVita
1350 Montreal Rd.
Tucker, GA 30084
Free: 800-424-6589
URL: http://www.davita.com
Dialysis Stations: 20. **Formerly:** Comprehensive Renal Care of Northlake LLC.

24053 ■ Tucker Dialysis
DaVita
4434 Hugh Howell Rd.
Tucker, GA 30084
Free: 800-424-6589
URL: http://www.davita.com
Dialysis Stations: 16.

Union City

24054 ■ Union City Dialysis
DaVita
6851 Shannon Pkwy.
Union City, GA 30291
Free: 800-424-6589
URL: http://www.davita.com
Dialysis Stations: 16.

Valdosta

24055 ■ DCA of Central Valdosta
Dialysis Corporation of America
506 N Patterson St.
Valdosta, GA 31601
Ph: (229)219-0099
URL: http://www.dialysiscorporation.com/
Dialysis Stations: 18.

24056 ■ DCA of South Georgia
Dialysis Corporation of America
3564 N Crossing Circle
Valdosta, GA 31602
Ph: (229)249-3222
URL: http://www.dialysiscorporation.com/
Dialysis Stations: 21.

24057 ■ Dialysis Corporation of America--Central Valdosta
506 N Patterson St.
Valdosta, GA 31602
Ph: (229)219-0099
URL: http://www.dialysiscorporation.org
Dialysis Stations: 18.

24058 ■ Dialysis Corporation of America--South Georgia
Dialysis Facility
3564 N Crossing Circle
Valdosta, GA 31602
Ph: (229)249-3222
URL: http://www.dialysiscorporation.org
Dialysis Stations: 21.

24059 ■ Oak Street Dialysis
DaVita
Dialysis Center
2704 N Oak St., Bldg. H
Valdosta, GA 31602
Free: 800-424-6589
URL: http://www.davita.com
Dialysis Stations: 23. **Formerly:** Gambro Healthcare--Valdosta.

24060 ■ RAI Kings Way--Valdosta
Renal Advantage Inc.
4358 Kings Way
Valdosta, GA 31602
Ph: (706)444-4444
URL: http://www.renaladvantage.com
Dialysis Stations: 18. **Formerly:** National Renal Alliance.

24061 ■ Renal Advantage Inc.--Valdosta
1115 S Patterson St.
Valdosta, GA 31601
Ph: (229)242-9610
URL: http://www.renaladvantage.com
Dialysis Stations: 22.

Vidalia

24062 ■ American Renal Associates Vidalia Clinic LLC
906 E 1st St.
Vidalia, GA 30474
Ph: (912)538-8908
URL: http://www.americanrenal.com
Dialysis Stations: 21.

24063 ■ Nephrology Center of Vidalia
DaVita
1806 Edwina Dr.
Vidalia, GA 30474
Free: 800-424-6589
URL: http://www.davita.com
Dialysis Stations: 21.

24064 ■ Toombs County Dialysis
Fresenius Medical Care
105 Melvin Page Pl.
Vidalia, GA 30474
Free: 866-434-2597
URL: http://www.ultracare-dialysis.com/
Dialysis Stations: 12.

24065 ■ Vidalia First Street Dialysis
DaVita
906 E First St.
Vidalia, GA 30474
Free: 800-424-6589
URL: http://www.davita.com
Dialysis Stations: 21.

Villa Rica

24066 ■ Fresenius Medical Care--Villa Rica
130 Prospector Dr.
Villa Rica, GA 30180
Free: 866-434-2597
URL: http://www.ultracare-dialysis.com/
Dialysis Stations: 16.

Warner Robins

24067 ■ Dialysis Center of Middle Georgia
DaVita
509 N Houston Rd.
Warner Robins, GA 31093
Free: 800-424-6589
URL: http://www.davita.com
Dialysis Stations: 10.

24068 ■ Dialysis Services of Houston County
Fresenius Medical Care
816 Duke Ave.
Warner Robins, GA 31093
Free: 866-434-2597
URL: http://www.ultracare-dialysis.com/
Dialysis Stations: 16.

24069 ■ Fresenius Medical Care--Warner Robins
Dialysis Facility
118 Osigian Blvd.
Warner Robins, GA 31088
Free: 866-434-2597
URL: http://www.ultracare-dialysis.com/
Dialysis Stations: 21.

Washington

24070 ■ Washington Dialysis Facility
DaVita
154 Washington Plz.
Washington, GA 30673
Free: 800-424-6589
URL: http://www.davita.com
Dialysis Stations: 17.

Waycross

24071 ■ DaVita--Waycross
308 Carswell Ave.
Waycross, GA 31501
Free: 800-424-6589
URL: http://www.davita.com
Dialysis Stations: 16.

24072 ■ Dialysis Facilities Inc.--Waycross
220 Uvalda St.
Waycross, GA 31501
Ph: (912)285-2487
Dialysis Stations: 19.

Waynesboro

24073 ■ Nephrology Center of Waynesboro
163 S Liberty St.
Waynesboro, GA 30830
Ph: (706)554-4668
Dialysis Stations: 20.

Winder

24074 ■ Barrow County Dialysis Center
189 W Athens St., Ste. 9
Winder, GA 30680
Ph: (770)868-8517
Dialysis Stations: 14.

Woodstock

24075 ■ DaVita Woodstock Dialysis
2001 Professional Pkwy., Ste. 100
Woodstock, GA 30188
Free: 800-424-6589
URL: http://www.davita.com
Dialysis Stations: 16.

24076 ■ Fresenius Medical Care--Woodstock
110 Londonderry Ct., Ste. 100
Woodstock, GA 30188
Free: 866-434-2597
URL: http://www.ultracare-dialysis.com/
Dialysis Stations: 16.

Wrightsville

24077 ■ Wrightsville Dialysis
DaVita
511 W Elm St.
Wrightsville, GA 31096
Free: 800-424-6589
URL: http://www.davita.com
Dialysis Stations: 12. **Formerly:** Gambro Healthcare.

GUAM

Dededo

24078 ■ Renal Centers of Guam
600 Harmon Loop Ste. 104
Dededo, GU 96929
Ph: (671)637-3068
Dialysis Stations: 20.

Hagatna

24079 ■ Guam Renal Care
Dialysis Facility
265 Chalan Santo Papa
Hagatna, GU 96910
Ph: (671)475-3600
URL: http://www.idsdialysis.com
Dialysis Stations: 21.

Tamuning

24080 ■ Guam Dialysis Center--Tamuning
Guam Medical Plaza
633 Governor Carlos Camacho Rd.
Tamuning, GU 96913
Ph: (671)646-3516
URL: http://www.idsdialysis.com
Dialysis Stations: 22.

24081 ■ Guam Memorial Hospital Dialysis Center
850 Gov. Carlos Camacho Rd.
Tamuning, GU 96913
Ph: (671)647-2237
URL: http://www.gmha.org
Dialysis Stations: 13.

HAWAII

Aiea

24082 ■ Dialysis Services of Pearlridge
Fresenius Medical Care
98-1005 Moanalua Rd., Ste. 420
Aiea, HI 96701
Free: 866-434-2597
URL: http://www.ultracare-dialysis.com/
Dialysis Stations: 48.

Ewa Beach

24083 ■ Leeward Dialysis Facility
Liberty Dialysis
91-2137 Fort Weaver Rd.
Ewa Beach, HI 96706
Ph: (808)671-3042
URL: http://www.libertydialysis.com
Dialysis Stations: 24.

Hilo

24084 ■ Hilo Dialysis
Liberty Dialysis Hawaii
140 Rainbow Dr.
Hilo, HI 96720
Ph: (808)935-3422
URL: http://www.libertydialysis.com
Dialysis Stations: 24.

Honolulu

24085 ■ Fresenius Medical Care--Aloha Dialysis Center
1520 Liliha St., 1st Fl.
Honolulu, HI 96817
Free: 866-434-2597
URL: http://www.ultracare-dialysis.com/
Dialysis Stations: 20.

24086 ■ Hawaii Medical Center--East
Transplant Institute
Honolulu, HI 96720
Ph: (808)547-6228
URL: http://www.hawaiimedcent.com/
Dialysis Stations: 0.

24087 ■ Honolulu Dialysis Center
Fresenius Medical Care
Dialysis Center
226 N Kuakini St., 2nd Fl.
Honolulu, HI 96817
Free: 866-434-2597
URL: http://www.ultracare-dialysis.com/
Dialysis Stations: 48.

24088 ■ Kaimuki Dialysis
Liberty Dialysis
3625 Harding Ave.
Honolulu, HI 96816
Ph: (808)735-2585
URL: http://www.libertydialysis.com
Dialysis Stations: 24.

24089 ■ Kapahulu Dialysis Center
Fresenius Medical Care
750 Palani Ave.
Honolulu, HI 96816
Free: 866-434-2597
URL: http://www.ultracare-dialysis.com/
Dialysis Stations: 24.

24090 ■ Siemsen Dialysis Facility
Liberty Dialysis
2226 Liliha St., Ste. 226
Honolulu, HI 96817
Ph: (808)585-4600
URL: http://www.libertydialysis.com
Dialysis Stations: 74.

Kailua Kona

24091 ■ Liberty Dialysis--Kona
78-6831 Alii Dr., Ste. 336
Kailua Kona, HI 96740
Ph: (808)322-2131
URL: http://www.libertydialysis.com
Dialysis Stations: 12.

Kamuela

24092 ■ North Hawaii Dialysis
Liberty Dialysis
67-1123 Mamalahoa Hwy., No. 112
Kamuela, HI 96743
Ph: (808)930-2001
URL: http://www.libertydialysis.com
Dialysis Stations: 9.

Kaneohe

24093 ■ Fresenius Medical Care--Ko'Olau
47-388 Hui Iwa St.
Kaneohe, HI 96744
Free: 866-434-2597
URL: http://www.ultracare-dialysis.com/
Dialysis Stations: 24.

24094 ■ Windward Dialysis Center
Fresenius Medical Care
45-480 Kaneohe Bay Dr., No. D09
Kaneohe, HI 96744
Free: 866-434-2597
URL: http://www.ultracare-dialysis.com/
Dialysis Stations: 24.

Kapolei

24095 ■ Fresenius Medical Care Dialysis Services of Kapolei
555 Farrington Hwy.
Kapolei, HI 96707
Free: 866-434-2597
URL: http://www.ultracare-dialysis.com/
Dialysis Stations: 24.

Kaunakakai

24096 ■ Molokai Dialysis Facility
Liberty Dialysis
PO Box 1917
Kaunakakai, HI 96748
Ph: (808)553-8088
URL: http://www.libertydialysis.com
Dialysis Stations: 6.

Lahaina

24097 ■ Kahana Dialysis
Liberty Dialysis Hawaii
10 Hoohui Rd., Ste. 100
Lahaina, HI 96761
Ph: (808)669-6628
URL: http://www.libertydialysis.com
Dialysis Stations: 12.

Lanai City

24098 ■ Lanai Community Dialysis
Fresenius Medical Care
628 7th St.
Lanai City, HI 96763
Free: 866-434-2597
URL: http://www.ultracare-dialysis.com/
Dialysis Stations: 3.

Lihue

24099 ■ Kauai Dialysis Facility
Liberty Dialysis
3224 Elua St.
Lihue, HI 96766
Ph: (808)245-3770
URL: http://www.libertydialysis.com
Dialysis Stations: 11.

Wahiawa

24100 ■ Wahiawa Dialysis Center
Fresenius Medical Care
850 Kilani Ave.
Wahiawa, HI 96786
Free: 866-434-2597
URL: http://www.ultracare-dialysis.com/
Dialysis Stations: 24.

Waianae

24101 ■ Waianae Dialysis
Liberty Dialysis
86-080 Farrington Hwy., Ste. 101
Waianae, HI 96792
Ph: (808)696-0216
URL: http://www.libertydialysis.com
Dialysis Stations: 16.

Wailuku

24102 ■ Maui Dialysis Facility
Liberty Dialysis
105 Maui Lani Pkwy.
Wailuku, HI 96793
Ph: (808)244-9600
URL: http://www.libertydialysis.com
Dialysis Stations: 48.

Waipahu

24103 ■ Waipahu Dialysis
Liberty Dialysis
94-450 Mokuola St., Ste. 109
Waipahu, HI 96797
Ph: (808)697-2200
URL: http://www.libertydialysis.com
Dialysis Stations: 24.

IDAHO

Blackfoot

24104 ■ DaVita
Snake River Dialysis Center and PD
1491 Parkway Dr.
Blackfoot, ID 83221
Free: 800-424-6589
URL: http://www.davita.com

24105 ■ Idaho Kidney Center--Blackfoot
Liberty Dialysis
98 Poplar
Blackfoot, ID 83221
Ph: (208)782-2220
URL: http://www.libertydialysis.com
Dialysis Stations: 6.

Boise

24106 ■ Table Rock Dialysis Center
DaVita
5610 W Gage St., Ste. B
Boise, ID 83706

Free: 800-424-6589
URL: http://www.davita.com
Dialysis Stations: 25. **Formerly:** Saint Alphonsus Nephrology Center--Boise.

Burley

24107 ■ Burley Dialysis Center
DaVita
741 N Overland Ave.
Burley, ID 83318
Free: 800-424-6589
URL: http://www.davita.com
Dialysis Stations: 12. **Formerly:** Saint Alphonsus Nephrology Center--Burley.

Caldwell

24108 ■ Caldwell Dialysis Center
DaVita
821 S Smeed Pkwy.
Caldwell, ID 83605
Free: 800-424-6589
URL: http://www.davita.com
Dialysis Stations: 12.

Coeur D'Alene

24109 ■ Fresenius Medical Care--North Idaho Dialysis Facility
Kootenai Medical Center
2100 Ironwood Court, Ste. A
Coeur D'Alene, ID 83814
Free: 866-434-2597
URL: http://www.ultracare-dialysis.com/
Dialysis Stations: 12. **Formerly:** Renal Care Group/Inland Northwest Renal Care Group.

Hayden

24110 ■ Liberty Dialysis--Hayden
8556 Wayne Dr.
Hayden, ID 83835
Ph: (208)762-7760
URL: http://www.libertydialysis.com
Dialysis Stations: 16.

Idaho Falls

24111 ■ Liberty Dialysis--Idaho Falls
2381 E Sunnyside Rd.
Idaho Falls, ID 83404
Ph: (208)523-8500
URL: http://www.libertydialysis.com
Dialysis Stations: 20.

24112 ■ University of Utah Dialysis Program
Gem State Regional Dialysis Center
2225 Teton Plaza, Ste. A
Idaho Falls, ID 83404
Ph: (208)522-4831
URL: http://www.utahinternalmedicine.com
Dialysis Stations: 22.

Lewiston

24113 ■ Tri-State Dialysis Center
730 21st St.
Lewiston, ID 83501
Ph: (208)746-8280
Dialysis Stations: 13.

Meridian

24114 ■ Liberty Dialysis--Meridian
3525 E Louise Dr., Ste. 100
Meridian, ID 83642
Ph: (208)846-8335
URL: http://www.libertydialysis.com
Dialysis Stations: 15.

24115 ■ Treasure Valley Dialysis Center
DaVita
3525 E Louise Dr., Ste. 155
Meridian, ID 83642
Free: 800-424-6589
URL: http://www.davita.com
Dialysis Stations: 9.

Montpelier

24116 ■ Bear Lake Dialysis Center
164 S 5th St.
Montpelier, ID 83254
Ph: (208)847-1630
Dialysis Stations: 7.

Moscow

24117 ■ Fresenius Medical Care--Palouse
723 Main St.
Moscow, ID 83843
Free: 866-434-2597
URL: http://www.ultracare-dialysis.com/
Dialysis Stations: 10.

24118 ■ Moscow Dialysis Center
DaVita
212 Rodeo Dr., Ste. 110
Moscow, ID 83843
Free: 800-424-6589
URL: http://www.davita.com
Dialysis Stations: 8.

Nampa

24119 ■ Liberty Dialysis--Nampa
280 W Georgia Ave.
Nampa, ID 83686
Ph: (208)463-8558
URL: http://www.libertydialysis.com
Dialysis Stations: 12.

24120 ■ Nampa Dialysis Center
DaVita
Dialysis Center
846 Park Centre Wy.
Nampa, ID 83651
Free: 800-424-6589
URL: http://www.davita.com
Dialysis Stations: 15. **Formerly:** Saint Alphonsus Nephrology Center.

Pocatello

24121 ■ Gate City Dialysis Center
DaVita
2001 Bench Rd.
Pocatello, ID 83201
Free: 800-424-6589
URL: http://www.davita.com
Dialysis Stations: 18. **Formerly:** Portneuf Nephrology Center.

24122 ■ Idaho Kidney Center - Pocatello
Liberty Dialysis
444 Hospital Way, No. 600
Pocatello, ID 83201
Ph: (208)478-5600
URL: http://www.libertydialysis.com
Dialysis Stations: 20.

Ponderay

24123 ■ Idaho Panhandle Dialysis
Fresenius Medical Care
204 N Triangle Dr.
Ponderay, ID 83852
Free: 866-434-2597
URL: http://www.ultracare-dialysis.com/
Dialysis Stations: 13.

Post Falls

24124 ■ Post Falls Dialysis Unit
Fresenius Medical Care
1300 E Mullan, Ste. 1200
Post Falls, ID 83854
Free: 866-434-2597
URL: http://www.ultracare-dialysis.com/
Dialysis Stations: 12. **Formerly:** Renal Care Group.

Rexburg

24125 ■ Yellowstone Dialysis Center
University of Utah
Dialysis Program
1165 Summers Ave.
Rexburg, ID 83440
Ph: (208)656-0378
URL: http://healthcare.utah.edu/dialysis/
Dialysis Stations: 9.

Sandpoint

24126 ■ Liberty Dialysis--Sandpoint
1210 Washington Ave.
Sandpoint, ID 83864
Ph: (208)263-4488
URL: http://www.libertydialysis.com
Dialysis Stations: 12.

Twin Falls

24127 ■ Twin Falls Dialysis Center
DaVita
Dialysis Center & At Home
1840 Canyon Crest Dr.
Twin Falls, ID 83301
Free: 800-424-6589
URL: http://www.davita.com
Dialysis Stations: 15. **Formerly:** Saint Alphonsus Nephrology Center.

ILLINOIS

Aledo

24128 ■ Aledo Kidney Center, LLC
409 NW 9th Ave.
Aledo, IL 61231
Ph: (309)582-2227
Dialysis Stations: 6.

Alsip

24129 ■ Alsip Dialysis Center
Fresenius Medical Care
12250 S Cicero, Ste. 105
Alsip, IL 60803
Free: 866-434-2597
URL: http://www.ultracare-dialysis.com/
Dialysis Stations: 16.

Alton

24130 ■ Alton Dialysis
DaVita
3511 College Ave.
Alton, IL 62002
Free: 800-424-6589
URL: http://www.davita.com
Dialysis Stations: 12. **Formerly:** Gambro Healthcare.

Antioch

24131 ■ Fresenius Medical Care--Depot, Antioch
311 Depot, Ste. H
Antioch, IL 60002
Free: 866-434-2597
URL: http://www.ultracare-dialysis.com/
Dialysis Stations: 12.

Arlington Heights

24132 ■ Northwest Kidney Center
Diversified Specialty Institutes
17 W Golf Rd.
Arlington Heights, IL 60005
Ph: (847)437-2188
URL: http://www.dsi-corp.com
Dialysis Stations: 18.

Aurora

24133 ■ Aurora Dialysis Center
Fresenius Medical Care
455 Mercy Ln.
Aurora, IL 60506
Free: 866-434-2597
URL: http://www.ultracare-dialysis.com/
Dialysis Stations: 14.

24134 ■ Fox Valley Dialysis
1300 Waterford Dr.
Aurora, IL 60504
Ph: (630)236-1300
URL: http://www.foxvalleydialysis.com/
Dialysis Stations: 26.

Belleville

24135 ■ Metro East Dialysis & At Home
DaVita
5105 W Main St.
Belleville, IL 62226
Free: 800-424-6589
URL: http://www.davita.com
Dialysis Stations: 36. **Formerly:** Renal Care of Illinois Inc.

Benton

24136 ■ Benton Dialysis
DaVita
1151 Rt. 14 W
Benton, IL 62812
Free: 800-424-6589
URL: http://www.davita.com
Dialysis Stations: 13.

Berwyn

24137 ■ Fresenius Medical Care--Berwyn
2601 S Harlem Ave., 1st Fl.
Berwyn, IL 60402
Free: 866-434-2597
URL: http://www.ultracare-dialysis.com/
Dialysis Stations: 28. **Formerly:** Renal Care Group.

Bloomington

24138 ■ Fresenius Medical Care--Central Illinois Bloomington Home
1404 Eastland Dr., Unit 103
Bloomington, IL 61701
Free: 866-434-2597
URL: http://www.ultracare-dialysis.com/
Dialysis Stations: 0. **Formerly:** Renal Care Group.

24139 ■ Fresenius Medical Care--McLean County
1505 Eastland Medical Dr., Lower Level
Bloomington, IL 61701
Free: 866-434-2597
URL: http://www.ultracare-dialysis.com/
Dialysis Stations: 20. **Formerly:** Midwest Kidney Center.

Blue Island

24140 ■ Blue Island Dialysis Center
Fresenius Medical Care
12200 S Western, Ste. 119-120
Blue Island, IL 60406
Free: 866-434-2597
URL: http://www.ultracare-dialysis.com/
Dialysis Stations: 24.

Bolingbrook

24141 ■ Bolingbrook Dialysis
Fresenius Medical Care
329 Remington Blvd., Ste. 110
Bolingbrook, IL 60440
Free: 866-434-2597
URL: http://www.ultracare-dialysis.com/
Dialysis Stations: 20.

Bourbonnais

24142 ■ Kankakee County Dialysis and At Home
DaVita
581 William R. Latham Sr. Dr., Ste. 104
Bourbonnais, IL 60914
Free: 800-424-6589
URL: http://www.davita.com
Dialysis Stations: 12.

Breese

24143 ■ Breese Dialysis
Renal Advantage Inc.
160 N Main St.
Breese, IL 62230
Ph: (618)526-7370
Dialysis Stations: 8.

Buffalo Grove

24144 ■ Buffalo Grove Dialysis
Diversified Specialty Institutes
1291 W Dundee Rd.
Buffalo Grove, IL 62230
Ph: (847)253-9400
URL: http://www.dsi-corp.com
Dialysis Stations: 14.

Burbank

24145 ■ Fresenius Medical Care Dialysis Services of Burbank
4811 W 77th St.
Burbank, IL 60459
Free: 866-434-2597
URL: http://www.ultracare-dialysis.com/
Dialysis Stations: 22.

Canton

24146 ■ Fresenius Medical Care--Canton
210 W Walnut St.
Canton, IL 61520
Free: 866-434-2597
URL: http://www.ultracare-dialysis.com/
Dialysis Stations: 8. **Formerly:** Midwest Kidney Center.

Carbondale

24147 ■ Fresenius Medical Care--Carbondale
725 S Lewis Ln.
Carbondale, IL 62901
Free: 866-434-2597
URL: http://www.ultracare-dialysis.com/
Dialysis Stations: 22.

Carpentersville

24148 ■ Quality Renal Care--Carpentersville
2203 Randall Rd.
Carpentersville, IL 60110
Ph: (847)426-6456
Dialysis Stations: 13.

Centralia

24149 ■ Centralia Dialysis
DaVita
1231 State Rte. 161 E
Centralia, IL 62801
Free: 800-424-6589
URL: http://www.davita.com
Dialysis Stations: 14. **Formerly:** Nephroplex Dialysis of Centralia.

Champaign

24150 ■ Illini Renal Dialysis & At Home
Davita
507 E University
Champaign, IL 61820
Free: 800-424-6589
URL: http://www.davita.com
Dialysis Stations: 10. **Formerly:** Gambro Healthcare--Champaign.

Chester

24151 ■ Fresenius Medical Care--Randolph County
Dialysis Facility
102 Memorial Dr.
Chester, IL 62233
Free: 866-434-2597
URL: http://www.ultracare-dialysis.com/
Dialysis Stations: 7.

Chicago

24152 ■ Austin Community Kidney Center
Fresenius Medical Care
4800 W Chicago Ave., 2nd Fl.
Chicago, IL 60651
Free: 866-434-2597
URL: http://www.ultracare-dialysis.com/
Dialysis Stations: 16.

24153 ■ Beverly Dialysis
DaVita
8109 S Western Ave.
Chicago, IL 60620
Free: 800-424-6589
URL: http://www.davita.com
Dialysis Stations: 10.

24154 ■ Chicago Dialysis Center
Fresenius Medical Care
820 W Jackson St.
Chicago, IL 60607
Free: 866-434-2597
URL: http://www.ultracare-dialysis.com/
Dialysis Stations: 33.

24155 ■ Chicago Westside Dialysis
Fresenius Medical Care
1340 S Damen Ave., Ste. 100
Chicago, IL 60608
Free: 866-434-2597
URL: http://www.ultracare-dialysis.com/
Dialysis Stations: 31.

24156 ■ Children's Dialysis Center
DaVita
2611 N Halsted St.
Chicago, IL 60614-2304
Free: 800-424-6589
URL: http://www.davita.com
Dialysis Stations: 6.

24157 ■ Childrens Memorial Hospital Transplant Program
2300 Childrens Plaza, Box 57
Chicago, IL 60614
Ph: (773)975-8644
URL: http://www.childrensmemorial.org/depts/siragusa/kidney/overview.aspx
Dialysis Stations: 0.

24158 ■ Circle Medical Management
Dialysis Facility
1426 W Washington Blvd.
Chicago, IL 60607
Ph: (312)829-1424
URL: http://www.cmmdialysis.com/
Dialysis Stations: 26.

24159 ■ Dialysis Services of Congress Parkway
Fresenius Medical Care
3410 W Van Buren St.
Chicago, IL 60624
Free: 866-434-2597
URL: http://www.ultracare-dialysis.com/
Dialysis Stations: 30.

24160 ■ Emerald Dialysis
DaVita
710 W 43rd St.
Chicago, IL 60647
Free: 800-424-6589
URL: http://www.davita.com
Dialysis Stations: 24.

24161 ■ Fresenius Medical Care--Bridgeport
825 W 35th St.
Chicago, IL 60609
Free: 866-434-2597
URL: http://www.ultracare-dialysis.com/
Dialysis Stations: 27.

24162 ■ Fresenius Medical Care--Garfield
5401 S Wentworth
Chicago, IL 60609
Free: 866-434-2597
URL: http://www.ultracare-dialysis.com/
Dialysis Stations: 22. **Formerly:** RCG.

24163 ■ Fresenius Medical Care--Lakeview/Thorek Hospital
4008 N Broadway Ave., Ste. 1200
Chicago, IL 60613
Free: 866-434-2597
URL: http://www.ultracare-dialysis.com/
Dialysis Stations: 10.

24164 ■ Fresenius Medical Care--Neomedica--Loop
557 W Polk St., Ste. 203
Chicago, IL 60607
Free: 866-434-2597
URL: http://www.ultracare-dialysis.com/
Dialysis Stations: 24.

24165 ■ Fresenius Medical Care--Neomedica--Marquette Park
6535 S Western Ave.
Chicago, IL 60636
Free: 866-434-2597
URL: http://www.ultracare-dialysis.com/
Dialysis Stations: 14.

24166 ■ Fresenius Medical Care--Neomedica--North Kilpatrick
4800 N Kilpatrick Ave.
Chicago, IL 60630
Free: 866-434-2597
URL: http://www.ultracare-dialysis.com/
Dialysis Stations: 20. **Formerly:** Neomedica Dialysis Center North.

24167 ■ Fresenius Medical Care--Neomedica--South
9200 S Chicago Ave.
Chicago, IL 60617
Free: 866-434-2597
URL: http://www.ultracare-dialysis.com/
Dialysis Stations: 36.

24168 ■ Fresenius Medical Care--Neomedica--South Shore Dialysis Center
2420 E 79th St.
Chicago, IL 60649
Free: 866-434-2597
URL: http://www.ultracare-dialysis.com/
Dialysis Stations: 16.

24169 ■ Fresenius Medical Care--Northwestern
Olson Pavillion, Ste., 4-200
710 N Fairbanks Ct.
Chicago, IL 60611
Free: 866-434-2597
URL: http://www.ultracare-dialysis.com/
Dialysis Stations: 44.

24170 ■ Fresenius Medical Care--Prairie
1717 S Wabash Ave.
Chicago, IL 60616
Free: 866-434-2597
URL: http://www.ultracare-dialysis.com/
Dialysis Stations: 27.

24171 ■ Fresenius Medical Care--Rogers Park Dialysis Facility
2277 W Howard St.
Chicago, IL 60645
Free: 866-434-2597
URL: http://www.ultracare-dialysis.com/
Dialysis Stations: 20. **Formerly:** Renal Care Group.

24172 ■ Fresenius Medical Care--Roseland Dialysis
132 W 111th St.
Chicago, IL 60628
Free: 866-434-2597
URL: http://www.ultracare-dialysis.com/
Dialysis Stations: 12.

24173 ■ Fresenius Medical Care--Southside Dialysis Center
3134 W 76th St.
Chicago, IL 60652
Free: 866-434-2597
URL: http://www.ultracare-dialysis.com/
Dialysis Stations: 39.

24174 ■ Fresenius Medical Care--West Belmont Dialysis Center
4943 W Belmont Ave.
Chicago, IL 60641
Free: 866-434-2597
URL: http://www.ultracare-dialysis.com/
Dialysis Stations: 10.

24175 ■ Fresenius Medical Care--West Metro Dialysis Center
1044 N Mozart, 3rd Fl.
Chicago, IL 60622
Free: 866-434-2597
URL: http://www.ultracare-dialysis.com/
Dialysis Stations: 30.

24176 ■ Garfield Kidney Center
3250 W Franklin Blvd.
Chicago, IL 60624
Ph: (773)638-1160
Dialysis Stations: 16.

24177 ■ Greenwood Dialysis Center
Fresenius Medical Care
1111 E 87th St., Ste. 700
Chicago, IL 60619
Free: 866-434-2597
URL: http://www.ultracare-dialysis.com/
Dialysis Stations: 28.

24178 ■ Jackson Park Dialysis Center
Fresenius Medical Care
7531 S Stony Island
Chicago, IL 60649
Free: 866-434-2597
URL: http://www.ultracare-dialysis.com/
Dialysis Stations: 24.

24179 ■ John H. Stroger Jr. Hospital of Cook County
Division of Nephrology
Hektoen Bldg.
627 S Wood St., Ste. 639
Chicago, IL 60612
Ph: (312)864-4600
URL: http://www.cchil.org/dom/nephrology.html
Dialysis Stations: 6.

24180 ■ Kennedy Home Dialysis
DaVita
5509 N Cumberland, Ste. 515
Chicago, IL 60656
Free: 800-424-6589
URL: http://www.davita.com
Dialysis Stations: 5.

24181 ■ Lake Park Chronic Hemodialysis Unit
University of Chicago Medical Center
1531 E Hyde Park Blvd.
Chicago, IL 60615
Ph: (773)702-1531
URL: http://www.uchospitals.edu/specialties/nephrology/
Dialysis Stations: 19.

24182 ■ Lake Shore Bone & Joint Institute
Northwestern Memorial Hospital
3691 Willowcreek Rd. Ste. 100
Chicago, IL 60611
Ph: (312)695-0828
URL: http://www.nmh.org/nm/location+clinics+specialty+services
Dialysis Stations: 0.

24183 ■ Lincoln Park Dialysis
DaVita
3157 N Lincoln Ave.
Chicago, IL 60657-3111
Free: 800-424-6589
URL: http://www.davita.com
Dialysis Stations: 22. **Formerly:** Lincoln Park Nephrology Association.

24184 ■ Little Village Dialysis
DaVita
2335 W Cermak Rd.
Chicago, IL 60608
Free: 800-424-6589
URL: http://www.davita.com
Dialysis Stations: 16.

24185 ■ Logan Square Dialysis Services Inc.
DaVita
2659 N Milwaukee Ave.
Chicago, IL 60647
Free: 800-424-6589
URL: http://www.davita.com
Dialysis Stations: 20.

24186 ■ Loop Dialysis Center
Diversified Specialty Institutes
1101 S Canal St., Lower Level
Chicago, IL 60607
Ph: (312)341-2543
URL: http://www.dsi-corp.com
Dialysis Stations: 28.

24187 ■ Midway Dialysis
Fresenius Medical Care
6201 W 63rd St.
Chicago, IL 60638
Free: 866-434-2597
URL: http://www.ultracare-dialysis.com/
Dialysis Stations: 12.

24188 ■ Montclare Dialysis
DaVita
7009 W Belmont Ave.
Chicago, IL 60634
Free: 800-424-6589
URL: http://www.davita.com
Dialysis Stations: 16.

24189 ■ Mount Greenwood Dialysis
DaVita
3401 W 111th St.
Chicago, IL 60655
Free: 800-424-6589
URL: http://www.davita.com
Dialysis Stations: 16.

24190 ■ Mount Sinai Hospital and Medical Center
Renal Unit
1500 S California Ave.
Chicago, IL 60608
Ph: (773)257-6686
URL: http://www.sinai.org
Dialysis Stations: 11.

24191 ■ Nephron Dialysis Center Ltd.
5140 N California Ave., Ste. 510
Chicago, IL 60625
Ph: (773)293-2100
Dialysis Stations: 12.

24192 ■ Northcenter Dialysis
Fresenius Medical Care
2620 W Addison St.
Chicago, IL 60657
Free: 866-434-2597
URL: http://www.ultracare-dialysis.com/
Dialysis Stations: 12.

24193 ■ Resurrection Medical Center
Outpatient Dialysis Center
7435 W Talcott Ave.
Chicago, IL 60631
Ph: (773)792-9920
URL: http://www.reshealth.org
Dialysis Stations: 14.

24194 ■ Ross Dialysis--Englewood
Fresenius Medical Care
6333 S Green St.
Chicago, IL 60621
Free: 866-434-2597
Dialysis Stations: 20. **Formerly:** Midwest Renal Care, Inc.

24195 ■ Ross Dialysis--Englewood
Fresenius Medical Care
6333 S Green St.
Chicago, IL 60621
Free: 866-434-2597
URL: http://www.ultracare-dialysis.com/
Dialysis Stations: 20.

24196 ■ Rush University Medical Center
Pediatric Dialysis Unit
1725 W Harrison St., Ste. 710
Chicago, IL 60612
Ph: (312)942-3695
E-mail: contact_rush@rush.edu
URL: http://www.rush.edu/rumc/page-1099918800681.html
Dialysis Stations: 5.

24197 ■ Scottsdale Dialysis Center
Diversified Specialty Institutes
4651 W 79th St., Ste. 100
Chicago, IL 60652
Ph: (773)582-8911
URL: http://www.dsi-corp.com
Dialysis Stations: 32.

24198 ■ Skyline Home Dialysis
DaVita
7009 W Belmont Ave.
Chicago, IL 60634
Free: 800-424-6589
URL: http://www.davita.com
Dialysis Stations: 0.

24199 ■ Stony Island Dialysis
DaVita
8725 S Stony Island Ave.
Chicago, IL 60617
Ph: (773)834-5830
Free: 800-424-6589
URL: http://www.davita.com
Dialysis Stations: 24.

24200 ■ Summit Medical Care
1310A W 18th St., Ste. A
Chicago, IL 60608
Ph: (312)491-9700
Dialysis Stations: 0.

24201 ■ University of Chicago--Woodlawn
1164 E 55th St.
Chicago, IL 60615
Ph: (773)702-3399
URL: http://www.uchospitals.edu/specialties/nephrology/
Dialysis Stations: 19.

24202 ■ University of Illinois Hospital Dialysis
1859 W Taylor, UIMCC MC 794
Chicago, IL 60612
Ph: (312)413-5202
URL: http://uillinoismedcenter.org/content.cfm/nephrology_services
Dialysis Stations: 26.

24203 ■ Uptown Chicago Dialysis
Fresenius Medical Care
4720 N Marine Dr.
Chicago, IL 60640
Free: 866-434-2597
URL: http://www.ultracare-dialysis.com/
Dialysis Stations: 12.

24204 ■ Woodlawn Pediatric Home Program
DaVita
5841 S Maryland Ave., Rm. L-26
Chicago, IL 60637
Ph: (773)702-9010
Free: 800-424-6589
URL: http://www.davita.com
Dialysis Stations: 5.

Chicago Heights

24205 ■ Chicago Heights Dialysis
DaVita
177-B W Joe Orr Rd.
Chicago Heights, IL 60612
Free: 800-424-6589
URL: http://www.davita.com
Dialysis Stations: 16.

Crestwood

24206 ■ Direct Dialysis
14255 S Cicero Ave.
Crestwood, IL 60445
Ph: (708)824-9200
Dialysis Stations: 6.

24207 ■ Fresenius Medical Care--Crestwood Dialysis Facility
4861-73 W Cal Sag Rd.
Crestwood, IL 60445
Free: 866-434-2597
URL: http://www.ultracare-dialysis.com/
Dialysis Stations: 32. **Formerly:** Renal Care Group.

Crystal Lake

24208 ■ Crystal Lake Dialysis Center
American Renal Associates
6298 Northwest Hwy., Ste. 300
Crystal Lake, IL 60014
Ph: (815)477-0825
URL: http://www.americanrenal.com
Dialysis Stations: 9.

Danville

24209 ■ Danville Dialysis Services, LLC
910 W Clay St.
Danville, IL 61832
Ph: (217)446-1111
Dialysis Stations: 19.

Decatur

24210 ■ Decatur East Wood Dialysis & At Home
DaVita
794 E Wood St.
Decatur, IL 62523
Free: 800-424-6589
URL: http://www.davita.com
Dialysis Stations: 16. **Formerly:** Gambro Healthcare.

24211 ■ Fresenius Medical Care--Decatur
1830 S 44th St.
Decatur, IL 62521
Free: 866-434-2597
URL: http://www.ultracare-dialysis.com/
Dialysis Stations: 12. **Formerly:** Renal Care Group.

24212 ■ Fresenius Medical Care--Decatur East Home Dialysis
302 W Hay St., Ste. 207
Decatur, IL 62526
Free: 866-434-2597
URL: http://www.ultracare-dialysis.com/
Dialysis Stations: 0. **Formerly:** Renal Care Group.

24213 ■ Macon County Dialysis
DaVita
1090 W McKinley
Decatur, IL 62526
Free: 800-424-6589
URL: http://www.davita.com
Dialysis Stations: 21.

Deerfield

24214 ■ Deerfield Dialysis Center
Fresenius Medical Care
405 Lake Cook Rd., Ste. A13
Deerfield, IL 60015
Free: 866-434-2597
URL: http://www.ultracare-dialysis.com/
Dialysis Stations: 12.

Dixon

24215 ■ Dixon Dialysis Center--W 2nd Street
101 W 2nd St.
Dixon, IL 61021
Ph: (815)284-0555
Dialysis Stations: 8.

24216 ■ Dixon Kidney Center
DaVita
1131 N Galena Ave.
Dixon, IL 61021
Free: 800-424-6589
URL: http://www.davita.com
Dialysis Stations: 8.

Downers Grove

24217 ■ Downers Grove Dialysis Center
Fresenius Medical Care
Dialysis Center
3825 Highland Ave., Ste. 102
Downers Grove, IL 60515
Free: 866-434-2597
URL: http://www.ultracare-dialysis.com/
Dialysis Stations: 19.

DuQuoin

24218 ■ Fresenius Medical Care--DuQuoin
4 W Main St.
DuQuoin, IL 62832
Free: 866-434-2597
URL: http://www.ultracare-dialysis.com/
Dialysis Stations: 10.

East Alton

24219 ■ Fresenius Medical Care--Southwest Illinois
No. 7 Eastgate Plz.
East Alton, IL 62024
Free: 866-434-2597
URL: http://www.ultracare-dialysis.com/
Dialysis Stations: 19.

East Peoria

24220 ■ Affiliated Home Dialysis, LLC--East Peoria
2500 N Main St., Ste. 1A
East Peoria, IL 61611
Ph: (309)698-1095
URL: http://www.affiliateddialysis.com/inner/service_offerings.htm
Dialysis Stations: 2.

24221 ■ East Peoria Dialysis
Fresenius Medical Care
3300 N Main
East Peoria, IL 61611
Free: 866-434-2597
URL: http://www.ultracare-dialysis.com/
Dialysis Stations: 24. **Formerly:** Renal Care Group.

Edwardsville

24222 ■ Edwardsville Dialysis
DaVita
235 S Buchanan St.
Edwardsville, IL 62025
Free: 800-424-6589
URL: http://www.davita.com
Dialysis Stations: 8.

Effingham

24223 ■ Effingham Dialysis
DaVita
904 Medical Park Dr., Ste. 1
Effingham, IL 62401
Free: 800-424-6589
URL: http://www.davita.com
Dialysis Stations: 16.

Elk Grove

24224 ■ Affiliated Home Dialysis--Elk Grove
1014 Bonaventure Dr.
Elk Grove, IL 60007
Ph: (847)352-4711
URL: http://www.affiliateddialysis.com/inner/service_offerings.htm#link1
Dialysis Stations: 1.

Elk Grove Village

24225 ■ Elk Grove Home Dialysis Center
Fresenius Medical Care
901 Biesterfield Rd., Ste. 401
Elk Grove Village, IL 60007
Free: 866-434-2597
URL: http://www.ultracare-dialysis.com/
Dialysis Stations: 0.

24226 ■ Fresenius Medical Care--Elk Grove Dialysis Center
901 Biesterfield Rd., Ste. 400
Elk Grove Village, IL 60007
Free: 866-434-2597
URL: http://www.ultracare-dialysis.com/
Dialysis Stations: 28.

Elmhurst

24227 ■ Dupage Peritoneal Dialysis Services
Fresenius Medical Care
501 W Lake St., Ste. 201
Elmhurst, IL 60126
Free: 866-434-2597
URL: http://www.ultracare-dialysis.com/
Dialysis Stations: 0.

24228 ■ PRS, LLC
188 Industrial Dr., Ste. 100
Elmhurst, IL 60126
Ph: (630)359-3249
Dialysis Stations: 1.

Evanston

24229 ■ Evanston Northwestern Healthcare
NorthShore Medical Group--Evanston
2650 Ridge Rd., Rm. 1420
Evanston, IL 60201
Ph: (847)570-1588
URL: http://www.northshore.org/
Dialysis Stations: 5.

24230 ■ Evanston Renal Center
Diversified Specialty Institutes
1715 Central St.
Evanston, IL 60201
Ph: (847)491-1214
URL: http://www.dsi-corp.com
Dialysis Stations: 18.

24231 ■ Fresenius Medical Care--Mid-America Evanston
2953 Central St., 1st Fl.
Evanston, IL 60201
Free: 866-434-2597
URL: http://www.ultracare-dialysis.com/
Dialysis Stations: 20. **Formerly:** Renal Care Group.

Evergreen Park

24232 ■ Fresenius Medical Care--Evergreen Park
9730 S Western Ave., Ste. 150
Evergreen Park, IL 60805
Free: 866-434-2597
URL: http://www.ultracare-dialysis.com/
Dialysis Stations: 27.

Fairfield

24233 ■ DaVita--Wayne County
303 NW 11th St., Ste. 1
Fairfield, IL 62837
Free: 800-424-6589
URL: http://www.davita.com
Dialysis Stations: 8.

Fairview Heights

24234 ■ Fairview Heights Dialysis
Renal Advantage Inc.
821 Lincoln Hwy.
Fairview Heights, IL 62208
Ph: (618)632-9550
URL: http://www.renaladvantage.com
Dialysis Stations: 20. **Formerly:** Gambro Healthcare.

Freeport

24235 ■ Freeport Dialysis Satellite Dialysis
1028 Kunkle Blvd.
Freeport, IL 61032
Free: 800-424-6589
URL: http://www.davita.com
Dialysis Stations: 10.

Galesburg

24236 ■ Western Illinois Kidney Center
695 N Kellogg St., 4th Fl.
Galesburg, IL 61401
Ph: (309)345-4580
Dialysis Stations: 11.

Geneseo

24237 ■ Quad Cities Kidney Center - Geneseo
600 N College Ave., Ste. 150
Geneseo, IL 61254
Ph: (309)945-1787
Dialysis Stations: 6.

Geneva

24238 ■ Tri Cities Dialysis LLC
306 Randall Rd.
Geneva, IL 60134
Ph: (630)262-1306
Dialysis Stations: 18.

Glendale Heights

24239 ■ Glendale Heights Dialysis Center
Fresenius Medical Care
520 E North Ave.
Glendale Heights, IL 60139
Free: 866-434-2597
URL: http://www.ultracare-dialysis.com/
Dialysis Stations: 17.

Glenview

24240 ■ Glenview Dialysis Center
Fresenius Medical Care
4248 Commercial Wy.
Glenview, IL 60025
Free: 866-434-2597
URL: http://www.ultracare-dialysis.com/
Dialysis Stations: 20.

Granite City

24241 ■ Granite City Dialysis Center
DaVita
9 American Village
Granite City, IL 62040
Free: 800-424-6589
URL: http://www.davita.com
Dialysis Stations: 20.

Gurnee

24242 ■ Fresenius Medical Care--Neomedica--Gurnee
101 S Greenleaf, Ste. B
Gurnee, IL 60031
Free: 866-434-2597
URL: http://www.ultracare-dialysis.com/
Dialysis Stations: 14.

Harrisburg

24243 ■ Fresenius Medical Care--Saline County
Dialysis Facility
275 Small St.
Harrisburg, IL 62946
Free: 866-434-2597
URL: http://www.ultracare-dialysis.com/
Dialysis Stations: 15.

Harvey

24244 ■ Community Dialysis of Harvey
16641 S Halsted St., Ste. A
Harvey, IL 60426
Ph: (708)210-9500
Dialysis Stations: 16.

Hazel Crest

24245 ■ DSI--Hazelcrest
Diversified Specialty Institutes
3470 W 183rd St.
Hazel Crest, IL 60429
Free: 866-434-2597
E-mail: info@dsi-corp.com
URL: http://www.dsi-corp.com/
Dialysis Stations: 16. **Formerly:** Renal Care Group.

24246 ■ Fresenius Medical Care--Hazel Crest
17524 Carriage Wy.
Hazel Crest, IL 60429
Free: 866-434-2597
URL: http://www.ultracare-dialysis.com/
Dialysis Stations: 16.

Highland Park

24247 ■ Highland Park Hospital
Northshore University HealthSystem
777 Park Ave. W
Highland Park, IL 60035
Ph: (847)432-8000
URL: http://www.northshore.org/locations/highland-park-hospital/
Dialysis Stations: 20.

Hoffman Estates

24248 ■ Fresenius Medical Care--Hoffman Estates
3150 W Higgins Rd., Ste. 190
Hoffman Estates, IL 60195
Free: 866-434-2597
URL: http://www.ultracare-dialysis.com/
Dialysis Stations: 17.

24249 ■ Fresenius Medical Care--Neomedica--Hoffman Estates
3150 W Higgins Rd., Ste. 190
Hoffman Estates, IL 60195
Free: 866-434-2597
URL: http://www.ultracare-dialysis.com/
Dialysis Stations: 17.

Jacksonville

24250 ■ DaVita
Jacksonville Dialysis
Dialysis Facility
Doctors Plz., Ste. 11
1515 W Walnut St.
Jacksonville, IL 62650
Free: 800-424-6589
URL: http://www.davita.com
Dialysis Stations: 14. **Formerly:** Gambro Healthcare - Jackson.

Jerseyville

24251 ■ JCH Dialysis LLC
917 S State
Jerseyville, IL 62052
Ph: (618)498-9532
Dialysis Stations: 7.

Joliet

24252 ■ Home Dialysis Network
Fresenius Medical Care
95 129th Infantry Dr.
Joliet, IL 60435
Free: 866-434-2597
URL: http://www.ultracare-dialysis.com/

24253 ■ Silver Cross Hospital
1200 Maple Rd.
Joliet, IL 60432
Ph: (815)740-7144
URL: http://www.silvercross.org
Dialysis Stations: 14.

24254 ■ Silver Cross Renal Center West
1051 Essington Rd., Ste. 160
Joliet, IL 60431
Ph: (815)729-9240
Dialysis Stations: 29.

24255 ■ Sun Health Inc.
Dialysis Facility
2121 Oneida St., Ste. 104
Joliet, IL 60435
Ph: (815)744-9300
Dialysis Stations: 17.

Kankakee

24256 ■ Provena Saint Mary's Hospital Dialysis Center
455 W Court St., Ste. 100
Kankakee, IL 60901
Ph: (815)937-2470
URL: http://provena.org/stmarys
Dialysis Stations: 24.

Kewanee

24257 ■ Fresenius Medical Care--Kewanee
230 W South St.
Kewanee, IL 61443
Free: 866-434-2597
URL: http://www.ultracare-dialysis.com/
Dialysis Stations: 7. **Formerly:** Midwest Kidney Center.

Lake Bluff

24258 ■ Fresenius Medical Care--Lake Bluff
101 Waukegan Rd., Ste. 700
Lake Bluff, IL 60044
Free: 866-434-2597
URL: http://www.ultracare-dialysis.com/
Dialysis Stations: 16.

Lake Villa

24259 ■ Lake Villa Dialysis & At Home
DaVita
37809 N Illinois, Rt. 59
Lake Villa, IL 60046
Free: 800-424-6589
URL: http://www.davita.com
Dialysis Stations: 12.

Libertyville

24260 ■ Lake County Dialysis Services Inc.
DaVita
918 S Milwaukee Ave.
Libertyville, IL 60048
Free: 800-424-6589
URL: http://www.davita.com
Dialysis Stations: 16.

Lincoln

24261 ■ Lincoln Dialysis
DaVita
2100 W 5th St.
Lincoln, IL 62656
Free: 800-424-6589
URL: http://www.davita.com
Dialysis Stations: 14. **Formerly:** Gambro Healthcare - Lincoln.

Lincolnwood

24262 ■ Center for Renal Replacement LLC
7301 N Lincoln Ave., Ste. 205
Lincolnwood, IL 60712
Ph: (847)675-5555
Fax: (847)675-7019
URL: http://www.crrdialysis.com/
Dialysis Stations: 16.

Litchfield

24263 ■ Litchfield Dialysis
DaVita
915 St. Francis Way
Litchfield, IL 62056
Free: 800-424-6589
URL: http://www.davita.com
Dialysis Stations: 11. **Formerly:** Gambro Healthcare - Litchfield.

Lockport

24264 ■ Lockport Home Dialysis and At Home
DaVita
16626 W 159th St., Ste. 703
Lockport, IL 60441
Free: 800-424-6589
URL: http://www.davita.com
Dialysis Stations: 3.

Lombard

24265 ■ Lombard Home Therapies
Fresenius Medical Care
1980 Springer
Lombard, IL 60148
Free: 866-434-2597
URL: http://www.ultracare-dialysis.com/
Dialysis Stations: 1.

Macomb

24266 ■ Fresenius Medical Care--Macomb
523 E Grant St.
Macomb, IL 61455
Free: 866-434-2597
URL: http://www.ultracare-dialysis.com/
Dialysis Stations: 5.

Manteno

24267 ■ Manteno Dialysis Center
Kankakee Valley Dialysis
1 E Division St.
Manteno, IL 60950
Ph: (815)468-1000
URL: http://kvdndialysis.com/mantano-dialysis-center.html
Dialysis Stations: 15.

Marengo

24268 ■ Quality Renal Care, LLC--Marengo
910 Greenlee St., Ste. B
Marengo, IL 60152
Ph: (815)568-5800
Dialysis Stations: 10.

Marion

24269 ■ Fresenius Medical Care--Williamson County
900 Skyline Dr., Ste. 200
Marion, IL 62959
Free: 866-434-2597
URL: http://www.ultracare-dialysis.com/
Dialysis Stations: 11.

24270 ■ Marion Dialysis & At Home
DaVita
324 S 4th St.
Marion, IL 62959
Free: 800-424-6589
URL: http://www.davita.com
Dialysis Stations: 13.

Markham

24271 ■ Diversified Specialty Institutes--Markham
3053-3055 W 159th St.
Markham, IL 60426
Ph: (708)333-3516
URL: http://www.dsi-corp.com
Dialysis Stations: 22.

Maryville

24272 ■ Maryville Dialysis & At Home
DaVita
2136-B Vadalabene Dr.
Maryville, IL 62062
Free: 800-424-6589
URL: http://www.davita.com
Dialysis Stations: 12.

24273 ■ Maryville Home Dialysis
DaVita
2136 Vadalabene Dr.
Maryville, IL 62062
Free: 800-424-6589
URL: http://www.davita.com
Dialysis Stations: 2.

Matteson

24274 ■ Olympia Fields Dialysis Center & At Home
DaVita
4557-B W Lincoln Hwy.
Matteson, IL 60443
Free: 800-424-6589
URL: http://www.davita.com
Dialysis Stations: 24.

Mattoon

24275 ■ Mattoon Dialysis
DaVita
200 Richmond Ave. E
Mattoon, IL 61938
Free: 800-424-6589
URL: http://www.davita.com
Dialysis Stations: 16. **Formerly:** Gambro Healthcare - Mattoon.

Maywood

24276 ■ Foster McGaw Hospital of Loyola--Transplant
Loyola University Health System
2160 S First Ave., Bldg. 54, Rm. 203
Maywood, IL 60153
Ph: (708)216-3454
URL: http://www.luhs.org/programs/kidney/kidney_home.htm
Dialysis Stations: 0.

24277 ■ University Hospital Loyola Dialysis Center
Bldg. 102, Rm. 3661
1201 Roosevelt Rd.
Maywood, IL 60153
Ph: (708)531-7050
URL: http://www.loyolamedicine.org
Dialysis Stations: 30. **Formerly:** Foster McGaw Hospital of Loyola.

McHenry

24278 ■ Fresenius Medical Care of McHenry
4312 W Elm St.
McHenry, IL 60050
Free: 866-434-2597
URL: http://www.ultracare-dialysis.com/
Dialysis Stations: 12.

Melrose Park

24279 ■ Fresenius Medical Care--Neomedica--Melrose Park Dialysis Center
1111 Superior St., Ste. 204
Melrose Park, IL 60160
Free: 866-434-2597
URL: http://www.ultracare-dialysis.com/
Dialysis Stations: 18.

24280 ■ North Avenue Dialysis Center
Fresenius Medical Care
911 W North Ave.
Melrose Park, IL 60160
Free: 866-434-2597
URL: http://www.ultracare-dialysis.com/
Dialysis Stations: 20.

Merrionette Park

24281 ■ Fresenius Medical Care--Merrionette Park
11630 S Kedzie
Merrionette Park, IL 60803
Free: 866-434-2597
URL: http://www.ultracare-dialysis.com/
Dialysis Stations: 16. **Formerly:** Renal Care Group.

Metropolis

24282 ■ Fresenius Medical Care of Metropolis
20 Hospital Dr.
Metropolis, IL 62960
Free: 866-434-2597
URL: http://www.ultracare-dialysis.com/
Dialysis Stations: 8.

Mokena

24283 ■ Mokena Dialysis
Fresenius Medical Care
8910 W 192nd St., Ste. A & B
Mokena, IL 60448
Free: 866-434-2597
URL: http://www.ultracare-dialysis.com/
Dialysis Stations: 14.

Moline

24284 ■ Quad Cities Kidney Center Ltd.
400 John Deere Rd.
Moline, IL 61265
Ph: (309)762-5570
Dialysis Stations: 30.

Morris

24285 ■ Fresenius Medical Care--Morris
1401 Lakewood Dr., Ste. B
Morris, IL 60450
Free: 866-434-2597
URL: http://www.ultracare-dialysis.com/
Dialysis Stations: 8. **Formerly:** RCG Central Illinois.

24286 ■ Silver Cross Renal Center Morris
1551 Creek Dr.
Morris, IL 60450
Ph: (815)942-3995
Dialysis Stations: 9.

Mount Vernon

24287 ■ Mount Vernon Dialysis & At Home
DaVita
1800 Jefferson Ave.
Mount Vernon, IL 62864
Free: 800-424-6589
URL: http://www.davita.com
Dialysis Stations: 14. **Formerly:** Nephroplex Dialysis of Mount Vernon.

Naperville

24288 ■ Naperville Dialysis Center
Fresenius Medical Care
Dialysis Center
100 Spalding Dr., Ste. 108
Naperville, IL 60566
Free: 866-434-2597
URL: http://www.ultracare-dialysis.com/
Dialysis Stations: 15.

24289 ■ Naperville North Dialysis Center
Fresenius Medical Care
516 W 5th Ave.
Naperville, IL 60563
Free: 866-434-2597
URL: http://www.ultracare-dialysis.com/
Dialysis Stations: 12.

Niles

24290 ■ Big Oaks Dialysis
DaVita
5623 W Touhy Ave.
Niles, IL 60714
Free: 800-424-6589
URL: http://www.davita.com
Dialysis Stations: 12.

24291 ■ Fresenius Medical Care - Niles
9371 N Milwaukee Ave.
Niles, IL 60714
Free: 866-434-2597
URL: http://www.ultracare-dialysis.com/
Dialysis Stations: 32.

24292 ■ Fresenius Medical Care--Niles Dialysis Center
9371 Milwaukee Ave.
Niles, IL 60714
Free: 866-434-2597
URL: http://www.ultracare-dialysis.com/
Dialysis Stations: 32.

Norridge

24293 ■ Fresenius Medical Care--Norridge Dialysis Center
4701 N Cumberland Ave., Ste. 15/18A
Norridge, IL 60656
Free: 866-434-2597
URL: http://www.ultracare-dialysis.com/
Dialysis Stations: 18.

Oak Lawn

24294 ■ Stony Creek Dialysis
DaVita
9115 S Cicero Ave.
Oak Lawn, IL 60453
Free: 800-424-6589
URL: http://www.davita.com
Dialysis Stations: 12. **Formerly:** Diamond Dialysis--Oak Lawn.

Oak Park

24295 ■ Fresenius Medical Care--Oak Park Dialysis Unit
733 W Madison St.
Oak Park, IL 60302
Free: 866-434-2597
URL: http://www.ultracare-dialysis.com/
Dialysis Stations: 32.

24296 ■ Fresenius Medical Care--West Suburban Dialysis Center
518 N Austin, Ste. 5000
Oak Park, IL 60302
Free: 866-434-2597
URL: http://www.ultracare-dialysis.com/
Dialysis Stations: 46.

24297 ■ Maple Avenue Kidney Center
Rush Medical Office Bldg.
610 S Maple Ave., Ste. 4100
Oak Park, IL 60304
Ph: (708)660-4100
URL: http://www.mapleavenuekidneycenter.com/
Dialysis Stations: 12.

Olney

24298 ■ Olney Dialysis Center
DaVita
117 N Boone St.
Olney, IL 62450
Free: 800-424-6589
URL: http://www.davita.com
Dialysis Stations: 7.

Olympia Fields

24299 ■ Fresenius Medical Care--South Suburban
2609 W Lincoln Hwy.
Olympia Fields, IL 60461
Free: 866-434-2597
URL: http://www.ultracare-dialysis.com/
Dialysis Stations: 27. **Formerly:** RCG.

Orland Park

24300 ■ Fresenius Medical Care--Orland Park Dialysis Facility
9160 W 159th St.
Orland Park, IL 60462
Free: 866-434-2597
URL: http://www.ultracare-dialysis.com/
Dialysis Stations: 18. **Formerly:** Renal Care Group.

Oswego

24301 ■ Fresenius Medical Care--Oswego
1051 Station Dr.
Oswego, IL 60543
Free: 866-434-2597
URL: http://www.ultracare-dialysis.com/
Dialysis Stations: 11.

Ottawa

24302 ■ Ottawa Dialysis
Fresenius Medical Care
1601 Mercury Cir., Ste. 3
Ottawa, IL 61350
Free: 866-434-2597
URL: http://www.ultracare-dialysis.com/
Dialysis Stations: 10. **Formerly:** Midwest Kidney Center.

Pekin

24303 ■ Fresenius Medical Care--Central Illinois Pekin
600 S 13th St.
Pekin, IL 61554
Free: 866-434-2597
URL: http://www.ultracare-dialysis.com/
Dialysis Stations: 9. **Formerly:** Midwest Kidney Center.

Peoria

24304 ■ DaVita
Peoria At Home
719 Main St.
Peoria, IL 61602
Free: 800-424-6589
URL: http://www.davita.com

24305 ■ Fresenius Medical Care--Peoria Downtown
Dialysis Facility
410 W Romeo B Garrett Ave.
Peoria, IL 61605
Free: 866-434-2597
URL: http://www.ultracare-dialysis.com/
Dialysis Stations: 32. **Formerly:** Midwest Kidney Center.

24306 ■ Fresenius Medical Care--Peoria North
10405 N Juliet Ct.
Peoria, IL 61615
Free: 866-434-2597
URL: http://www.ultracare-dialysis.com/
Dialysis Stations: 15. **Formerly:** RCG.

24307 ■ St. Francis Medical Center
530 NE Glen Oak Ave.
Peoria, IL 61637
Ph: (309)655-2000
URL: http://www.osfsaintfrancis.org/
Dialysis Stations: 0.

Pittsfield

24308 ■ DaVita Pittsfield II
640 W Washington St.
Pittsfield, IL 62363
Ph: (217)285-2113
Free: 800-424-6589
Dialysis Stations: 5.

Plainfield

24309 ■ Fresenius Medical Care--Plainfield
2320 Michas Dr.
Plainfield, IL 60586
Free: 866-434-2597
URL: http://www.ultracare-dialysis.com/
Dialysis Stations: 12.

Pontiac

24310 ■ Fresenius Medical Care--Pontiac
804 W Madison St.
Pontiac, IL 61764
Free: 866-434-2597
URL: http://www.ultracare-dialysis.com/
Dialysis Stations: 9. **Formerly:** Renal Care Group.

Quincy

24311 ■ Quincy Medical Group
Peritoneal Dialysis Center
1025 Maine St.
Quincy, IL 62301
Ph: (217)222-6550
Dialysis Stations: 0.

Rock Island

24312 ■ Quad Cities Kidney Center--Rock Island, LLC
2623 17th St.
Rock Island, IL 61201
Ph: (309)786-1400
Dialysis Stations: 12.

Rockford

24313 ■ Churchview Dialysis Center
DaVita
5970 Churchview Dr.
Rockford, IL 61107
Free: 800-424-6589
URL: http://www.davita.com
Dialysis Stations: 24. **Program(s):** Support Groups.

24314 ■ Rockford Dialysis
DaVita
3339 N Rockton Ave.
Rockford, IL 61103
Free: 800-424-6589
URL: http://www.davita.com
Dialysis Stations: 19.

24315 ■ Rockford Dialysis
Dialysis Center of America, Inc.
1302 E State St.
Rockford, IL 61104
Ph: (815)968-5794
Dialysis Stations: 12.

24316 ■ Roxbury Dialysis Center & At Home
DaVita
622 Roxbury Rd.
Rockford, IL 61108
Free: 800-424-6589
URL: http://www.davita.com
Dialysis Stations: 16.

Rolling Meadows

24317 ■ Fresenius Medical Care--Neomedica--Rolling Meadows
4180 Winnetka Ave.
Rolling Meadows, IL 60008
Free: 866-434-2597
URL: http://www.ultracare-dialysis.com/
Dialysis Stations: 24.

Round Lake Heights

24318 ■ Fresenius Medical Care--Neomedica--Round Lake
401 W Nippersink
Round Lake Heights, IL 60073
Free: 866-434-2597
URL: http://www.ultracare-dialysis.com/
Dialysis Stations: 16.

Rushville

24319 ■ Rushville Dialysis
DaVita
112 Sullivan Dr.
Rushville, IL 62681
Free: 800-424-6589
URL: http://www.davita.com
Dialysis Stations: 7.

Sandwich

24320 ■ Sandwich Dialysis LLC
Fresenius Medical Care
1310 N Main St., Ste. 105
Sandwich, IL 60548
Free: 866-434-2597
URL: http://www.ultracare-dialysis.com/
Dialysis Stations: 8.

Sauget

24321 ■ Sauget Dialysis Center
DaVita
2061 Goose Lake Rd.
Sauget, IL 62206
Free: 800-424-6589
URL: http://www.davita.com
Dialysis Stations: 16.

Schaumburg

24322 ■ Schaumburg Dialysis Center
Diversified Specialty Institutes
1156 S Roselle Rd.
Schaumburg, IL 60193
Ph: (847)524-4310
URL: http://www.dsi-corp.com
Dialysis Stations: 14.

Shelbyville

24323 ■ Shelbyville Community Dialysis
410 S Heinlein Dr.
Shelbyville, IL 62565
Ph: (217)774-1527
Dialysis Stations: 8.

Silvis

24324 ■ Quad Cities Kidney Center Silvis LLC
880 Crosstown Ave.
Silvis, IL 61282
Ph: (309)792-3517
Dialysis Stations: 12.

Skokie

24325 ■ Skokie Dialysis
Fresenius Medical Care
9801 Woods Dr.
Skokie, IL 60077
Free: 866-434-2597
URL: http://www.ultracare-dialysis.com/
Dialysis Stations: 14. **Formerly:** RCG.

24326 ■ Wellbound/Satellite Dialysis
Evanston Dialysis Center
8950 Gross Point Rd., Ste. 300
Skokie, IL 60077
Ph: (847)965-1901
URL: http://www.satellitehealth.com/

South Barrington

24327 ■ South Barrington Dialysis Center
American Renal Associates
33 W Higgins Rd., Ste. 920-945
South Barrington, IL 60010
Ph: (847)783-6832
URL: http://www.americanrenal.com
Dialysis Stations: 10.

South Holland

24328 ■ Diversified Specialty Institutes--South Holland
16136 S Park Ave.
South Holland, IL 60473
Ph: (708)331-0200
URL: http://www.dsi-corp.com
Dialysis Stations: 20.

24329 ■ Fresenius Medical Care--Neomedica--South Holland Dialysis Center
17225 S Paxton Ave.
South Holland, IL 60473
Free: 866-434-2597
URL: http://www.ultracare-dialysis.com/
Dialysis Stations: 17.

Spring Valley

24330 ■ Fresenius Medical Care--Spring Valley
12 B Wolfer Industrial Dr.
Spring Valley, IL 61362
Free: 866-434-2597
URL: http://www.ultracare-dialysis.com/
Dialysis Stations: 16. **Formerly:** Midwest Kidney Center.

Springfield

24331 ■ Memorial Medical Center Transplant and Dialysis Center
701 N 1st St.
Springfield, IL 62781
Ph: (217)788-3840
URL: https://www.memorialmedical.com/Default.aspx
Dialysis Stations: 11.

24332 ■ Renal Advantage Inc.--Centre West Springfield
1112 Centre W Dr.
Springfield, IL 62704
Ph: (217)787-3310
URL: http://www.renaladvantage.com
Dialysis Stations: 14. **Formerly:** DaVita--Lincolnland.

24333 ■ Springfield Central Dialysis & At Home
DaVita
932 N Rutledge
Springfield, IL 62702
Free: 800-424-6589
URL: http://www.davita.com
Dialysis Stations: 21. **Formerly:** Gambro Healthcare.

24334 ■ Springfield Montvale Dialysis
DaVita
2930 Montvale Dr., Ste. A
Springfield, IL 62704
Free: 800-424-6589
URL: http://www.davita.com
Dialysis Stations: 17. **Formerly:** Gambro Healthcare - Montvale.

Sterling

24335 ■ Whiteside Dialysis Facility
DaVita
2600 N Locust St., Ste. D
Sterling, IL 61081
Free: 800-424-6589
URL: http://www.davita.com
Dialysis Stations: 15.

Streator

24336 ■ Fresenius Medical Care--Streator
2356 N Bloomington St.
Streator, IL 61364
Free: 866-434-2597
URL: http://www.ultracare-dialysis.com/
Dialysis Stations: 8.

24337 ■ Fresenius Medical Care--Streator
2356 N Bloomington St.
Streator, IL 61364
Free: 866-434-2597
URL: http://www.ultracare-dialysis.com/
Dialysis Stations: 8.

Sycamore

24338 ■ Sycamore Dialysis & At Home
DaVita
2200 Gateway Dr.
Sycamore, IL 60178
Free: 800-424-6589
URL: http://www.davita.com
Dialysis Stations: 12.

Taylorville

24339 ■ Taylorville Dialysis
DaVita
901 W Spresser
Taylorville, IL 62568
Free: 800-424-6589
URL: http://www.davita.com
Dialysis Stations: 10. **Formerly:** Gambro Healthcare - Taylorville.

Urbana

24340 ■ Champaign--Urbana Dialysis Center
Fresenius Medical Care
1405 W Park St.
Urbana, IL 61801
Free: 866-434-2597
URL: http://www.ultracare-dialysis.com/
Dialysis Stations: 25.

Vandalia

24341 ■ Vandalia Dialysis
DaVita
301 Mattes Ave.
Vandalia, IL 62471
Free: 800-424-6589
URL: http://www.davita.com
Dialysis Stations: 8.

Villa Park

24342 ■ Fresenius Medical Care--Villa Park
200 E North Ave.
Villa Park, IL 60181
Free: 866-434-2597
URL: http://www.ultracare-dialysis.com/
Dialysis Stations: 24. **Formerly:** Renal Care Group.

Waterloo

24343 ■ Renal Advantage Hamacher--Waterloo
509 Hamacher Rd., Ste. 206
Waterloo, IL 62298
Ph: (618)939-9003
URL: http://www.renaladvantage.com

Waukegan

24344 ■ Diversified Specialty Institutes--Waukegan Home Program
1616 Grand Ave., Ste. F
Waukegan, IL 60085
Ph: (847)360-9621
URL: http://www.dsi-corp.com
Dialysis Stations: 0.

24345 ■ Diversified Specialty Institutes--Waukeka Renal Center
1616 Grand Ave., Ste. C
Waukegan, IL 60085
Ph: (847)662-5111
URL: http://www.dsi-corp.com
Dialysis Stations: 24.

West Chicago

24346 ■ Fresenius Medical Care of DuPage West
450 E Roosevelt Rd.
West Chicago, IL 60185
Free: 866-434-2597
URL: http://www.ultracare-dialysis.com/
Dialysis Stations: 16.

24347 ■ West Chicago Dialysis Center
Fresenius Medical Care
1850-63 Neltnor Blvd.
West Chicago, IL 60185
Free: 866-434-2597
URL: http://www.ultracare-dialysis.com/
Dialysis Stations: 12.

Westchester

24348 ■ Fresenius Medical Care--Westchester Dialysis Center
2400 Wolf Rd., Ste. 101A
Westchester, IL 60154
Free: 866-434-2597
URL: http://www.ultracare-dialysis.com/
Dialysis Stations: 24.

24349 ■ Fresenius Medical Care--Westchester Home
2400 Wolf Rd., Ste. 101-B
Westchester, IL 60154
Free: 866-434-2597
URL: http://www.ultracare-dialysis.com/
Dialysis Stations: 0.

Willowbrook

24350 ■ Fresenius Medical Care--Willowbrook
6300 S Kingery Hwy., Ste. 408
Willowbrook, IL 60527
Free: 866-434-2597
URL: http://www.ultracare-dialysis.com/
Dialysis Stations: 20.

Woodridge

24351 ■ Woodridge Home Dialysis and At Home
DaVita
7425 Janes Ave.
Woodridge, IL 60517
Free: 800-424-6589
URL: http://www.davita.com
Dialysis Stations: 6.

Yorkville

24352 ■ Yorkville Dialysis Center LLC
1400 N Beecher Rd.
Yorkville, IL 60560
Ph: (630)553-6952
Dialysis Stations: 8.

INDIANA

Anderson-

24353 ■ Fresenius Medical Care--Anderson
1903 E 60th St.
Anderson-, IN 46013
Free: 866-434-2597
URL: http://www.ultracare-dialysis.com/
Dialysis Stations: 21.

Auburn

24354 ■ Fresenius Medical Care--Dekalb County
1144 W 15th St.
Auburn, IN 46706
Free: 866-434-2597
URL: http://www.ultracare-dialysis.com/
Dialysis Stations: 12. **Formerly:** Renal Care Group/ Northeast Indiana Kidney Center-Auburn.

24355 ■ Quad Counties Dialysis Center Diversified Specialty Institutes
528 N Grandstaff Dr.
Auburn, IN 46706
Ph: (260)927-0100
URL: http://www.dsi-corp.com/
Dialysis Stations: 10. **Formerly:** National Renal Institutes--Quad Counties Dialysis Center.

Batesville

24356 ■ DaVita--Batesville Dialysis
232 State Rd. 129
Batesville, IN 47006
Free: 800-424-6589
URL: http://www.davita.com
Dialysis Stations: 12.

Bedford

24357 ■ Fresenius Medical Care--Lawrence County Dialysis Unit
1520 23rd St., Ste. C
Bedford, IN 47421
Free: 866-434-2597
URL: http://www.ultracare-dialysis.com/
Dialysis Stations: 12. **Formerly:** Dunn Memorial Hospital, Dialysis Unit.

Bloomington

24358 ■ Bloomington Dialysis Fresenius Medical Care
575 S Patterson Dr.
Bloomington, IN 47403
Free: 866-434-2597
URL: http://www.ultracare-dialysis.com/
Dialysis Stations: 24. **Formerly:** Renal Care Group.

24359 ■ Hoosier Hills Dialysis DaVita
143 S Kingston Dr.
Bloomington, IN 47408
Free: 800-424-6589
URL: http://www.davita.com
Dialysis Stations: 16.

Bluffton

24360 ■ Fresenius Medical Care--Wells County
1100 S Main St.
Bluffton, IN 46714
Free: 866-434-2597
URL: http://www.ultracare-dialysis.com/
Dialysis Stations: 8.

Carmel

24361 ■ Carmel Dialysis DaVita
180 E Carmel Dr.
Carmel, IN 46032
Free: 800-424-6589
URL: http://www.davita.com
Dialysis Stations: 12.

24362 ■ Fresenius Medical Care--Carmel
12400 N Meridian St.
Carmel, IN 46032
Free: 866-434-2597
URL: http://www.ultracare-dialysis.com/
Dialysis Stations: 12.

Chesterton

24363 ■ Liberty Dialysis--Duneland-Coffee Creek
3100 Village Point, Ste. 101
Chesterton, IN 46304
Ph: (219)395-8020
URL: http://www.libertydialysis.com
Dialysis Stations: 19.

Columbus

24364 ■ Fresenius Medical Care--Columbus Bartholomew Dialysis Facility
2325 18th St., Ste. 120
Columbus, IN 47201
Free: 866-434-2597
URL: http://www.ultracare-dialysis.com/
Dialysis Stations: 15. **Formerly:** Renal Care Group.

Connersville

24365 ■ Fresenius Medical Care--Connersville
6049 Industrial Ave. N
Connersville, IN 47331
Free: 866-434-2597
URL: http://www.ultracare-dialysis.com/
Dialysis Stations: 12. **Formerly:** Renal Care Group.

Corydon

24366 ■ Corydon Dialysis Center DaVita
1937 B Old Hwy. 135 N
Corydon, IN 47112
Free: 800-424-6589
URL: http://www.davita.com
Dialysis Stations: 12.

24367 ■ Fresenius Medical Care--Corydon
1141 Hospital Dr., Ste. B-1
Corydon, IN 47112
Free: 866-434-2597
URL: http://www.ultracare-dialysis.com/
Dialysis Stations: 12.

Crawfordsville

24368 ■ Liberty Dialysis--Crawfordsville
1710 Lafayette Rd.
Crawfordsville, IN 47933
Ph: (765)359-1613
URL: http://www.libertydialysis.com
Dialysis Stations: 10. **Formerly:** Montgomery County Dialysis.

Crown Point

24369 ■ Fresenius Medical Care--Crown Point
851 W Burrell Dr.
Crown Point, IN 46307
Free: 866-434-2597
URL: http://www.ultracare-dialysis.com/
Dialysis Stations: 24.

Daleville

24370 ■ Ball Dialysis--Daleville Renal Advantage Inc.
14520 W Davis Dr.
Daleville, IN 47334
Ph: (765)378-1735
URL: http://www.renaladvantage.com
Dialysis Stations: 12. **Formerly:** National Renal Alliance.

Danville

24371 ■ Fresenius Medical Care--Hendricks County Danville Dialysis Facility
1594 E Main St., Ste. A
Danville, IN 46122
Free: 866-434-2597
URL: http://www.ultracare-dialysis.com/
Dialysis Stations: 21.

Decatur

24372 ■ Fresenius Medical Care--Tri-Counties Dialysis Center
817 S 13th St.
Decatur, IN 46733
Free: 866-434-2597
URL: http://www.ultracare-dialysis.com/
Dialysis Stations: 10.

Dyer

24373 ■ Fresenius Medical Care--Dyer
2150 Gettler St., Ste. 105
Dyer, IN 46311
Free: 866-434-2597
URL: http://www.ultracare-dialysis.com/
Dialysis Stations: 24.

East Chicago

24374 ■ DaVita--East Chicago Dialysis Facility
4320 Fir St., Ste. 404
East Chicago, IN 46312
Free: 800-424-6589
URL: http://www.davita.com
Dialysis Stations: 11.

24375 ■ East Chicago Dialysis Center Fresenius Medical Care
1207 E Chicago Ave.
East Chicago, IN 46312
Free: 866-434-2597
URL: http://www.ultracare-dialysis.com/
Dialysis Stations: 14.

Elkhart

24376 ■ Regional Nephrology Inc.--Elkhart
700 Waterbury Park Dr.
Elkhart, IN 46517
Ph: (574)294-4444
Dialysis Stations: 24.

Elwood

24377 ■ Fresenius Medical Care--Elwood
1805 S Anderson
Elwood, IN 46036
Free: 866-434-2597
URL: http://www.ultracare-dialysis.com/
Dialysis Stations: 12.

Evansville

24378 ■ East Evansville Dialysis, PD & At Home DaVita
1312 Professional Blvd., Ste. 100
Evansville, IN 47714
Free: 800-424-6589
URL: http://www.davita.com
Dialysis Stations: 26.

24379 ■ Fresenius Medical Care--Ohio Valley Dialysis Center
230 Bellemeade Ave.
Evansville, IN 47713
Free: 866-434-2597
URL: http://www.ultracare-dialysis.com/
Dialysis Stations: 18.

24380 ■ North Evansville Dialysis DaVita
1151 W Buena Vista
Evansville, IN 47710
Free: 800-424-6589
URL: http://www.davita.com
Dialysis Stations: 24.

Fort Wayne

24381 ■ Central Fort Wayne Dialysis Center
Diversified Specialty Institutes
1940 Bluffton Rd.
Fort Wayne, IN 46809
Ph: (260)478-2659
URL: http://www.dsi-corp.com
Dialysis Stations: 20. **Formerly:** NRI/Dialysis of Central Fort Wayne.

24382 ■ DuPont Dialysis
Fresenius Medical Care
10204 E DuPont Circle Dr.
Fort Wayne, IN 46825
Free: 866-434-2597
URL: http://www.ultracare-dialysis.com/
Dialysis Stations: 12. **Formerly:** Renal Care Group.

24383 ■ Fresenius Medical Care--Fort Wayne Jefferson
7836 W Jefferson Blvd., St. LL10
Fort Wayne, IN 46804
Free: 866-434-2597
URL: http://www.ultracare-dialysis.com/
Dialysis Stations: 24.

24384 ■ Lake Avenue Dialysis Center
3909 Lake Ave.
Fort Wayne, IN 46805
Ph: (260)420-7666
Dialysis Stations: 24.

24385 ■ Lake Avenue Dialysis Center
Diversified Specialty Institutes
3909 Lake Ave., Ste. 4
Fort Wayne, IN 46805
Ph: (260)420-2666
Fax: (260)424-2036
URL: http://www.dsi-corp.com
Dialysis Stations: 24. **Formerly:** Fresenius Medical Care--Lake Avenue Dialysis Center.

24386 ■ Lutheran Hospital of Indiana Transplant
Lutheran Health Network
7950 W Jefferson Blvd., MOB II, Ste. 200
Fort Wayne, IN 46804
Ph: (260)435-6275
URL: http://www.lutheranhospital.com/interior.php?t=140
Dialysis Stations: 0.

24387 ■ South Anthony Dialysis Center
Diversified Specialty Institutes
7017 S Anthony Blvd.
Fort Wayne, IN 46816
Ph: (260)447-2220
URL: http://www.dsi-corp.com
Dialysis Stations: 14. **Formerly:** Fresenius Medical Care.

Frankfort

24388 ■ Liberty Dialysis--Frankfort
1300 S Jackson St.
Frankfort, IN 46041
Ph: (765)656-3377
URL: http://www.libertydialysis.com
Dialysis Stations: 6. **Formerly:** Saint Elizabeth Dialysis at Clinton County.

Franklin

24389 ■ DaVita--Franklin Dialysis & At Home
1140 W Jefferson St., Ste. A
Franklin, IN 46131
Free: 800-424-6589
URL: http://www.davita.com
Dialysis Stations: 14.

24390 ■ Fresenius Medical Care--Franklin, Indiana
1159 W Jefferson St., Ste. 201
Franklin, IN 46131
Free: 866-434-2597
URL: http://www.ultracare-dialysis.com/
Dialysis Stations: 12.

Gary

24391 ■ DaVita--Gary
Comprehensive Renal Care
4802 Broadway
Gary, IN 46408
Free: 800-424-6589
URL: http://www.davita.com
Dialysis Stations: 40.

24392 ■ Fresenius Medical Care - Northwest Indiana Dialysis
3290 Grant St.
Gary, IN 46408
Free: 866-434-2597
URL: http://www.ultracare-dialysis.com/
Dialysis Stations: 23.

24393 ■ Northwest Indiana Dialysis
Fresenius Medical Care
3290 Grant St.
Gary, IN 46408
Free: 866-434-2597
URL: http://www.ultracare-dialysis.com/
Dialysis Stations: 24.

Goshen

24394 ■ Fresenius Medical Care Nephrology--Goshen
2257 Karisa Dr.
Goshen, IN 46526
Free: 866-434-2597
URL: http://www.ultracare-dialysis.com/
Dialysis Stations: 25.

Greencastle

24395 ■ Fresenius Medical Care--Greencastle
316 Medic Way
Greencastle, IN 46135
Free: 866-434-2597
URL: http://www.ultracare-dialysis.com/
Dialysis Stations: 13.

Greendale

24396 ■ Lawrenceburg Dialysis Center
DaVita
555 E Eads Pkwy., Ste. 200
Greendale, IN 47025
Free: 800-424-6589
URL: http://www.davita.com
Dialysis Stations: 12.

Greenfield

24397 ■ Fresenius Medical Care--Greenfield
1051 N State St.
Greenfield, IN 46140
Free: 866-434-2597
URL: http://www.ultracare-dialysis.com/
Dialysis Stations: 12. **Formerly:** Renal Care Group.

Greensburg

24398 ■ Greensburg Dialysis and At Home
DaVita
1531 N Commerce E Dr.
Greensburg, IN 47240
Free: 800-424-6589
URL: http://www.davita.com
Dialysis Stations: 12.

24399 ■ Tree City Dialysis
Fresenius Medical Care
999 N Michigan Ave.
Greensburg, IN 47240
Free: 866-434-2597
URL: http://www.ultracare-dialysis.com/
Dialysis Stations: 12.

24400 ■ Tree City Dialysis
Fresenius Medical Care
999 N Michigan Ave.
Greensburg, IN 47240
Free: 866-434-2597
URL: http://www.ultracare-dialysis.com/
Dialysis Stations: 12.

Greenwood

24401 ■ DaVita
Indy South Dialysis and At Home
972 Emerson Pkwy., Ste. E
Greenwood, IN 46143
Free: 800-424-6589
URL: http://www.davita.com
Dialysis Stations: 12.

24402 ■ Dialysis Services of Greenwood
Renal Advantage Inc.
125 Airport Pkwy., Ste. 140
Greenwood, IN 46143
Ph: (317)883-1280
URL: http://www.renaladvantage.com
Dialysis Stations: 18. **Formerly:** Fresenius Medical Care.

Hammond

24403 ■ DaVita--Hammond
222 Douglas St.
Hammond, IN 46320
Free: 800-424-6589
URL: http://www.davita.com
Dialysis Stations: 32.

24404 ■ Fresenius Medical Care--Saint Margaret Dialysis Center
Campus Dialysis Unit
5454 Hohman Ave.
Hammond, IN 46320
Free: 866-434-2597
URL: http://www.ultracare-dialysis.com/
Dialysis Stations: 24.

24405 ■ Liberty Dialysis--Hammond
7214 Calumet Ave.
Hammond, IN 46324
Ph: (219)228-4477
URL: http://www.libertydialysis.com
Dialysis Stations: 16.

Hobart

24406 ■ Fresenius Medical Care--Hobart
1330 S Wisconsin St.
Hobart, IN 46342
Free: 866-434-2597
URL: http://www.ultracare-dialysis.com/
Dialysis Stations: 24.

Huntington

24407 ■ Dialysis of Huntington
Diversified Specialty Institutes
3040 W Park Dr.
Huntington, IN 46750
Ph: (260)355-0250
URL: http://www.dis-corp.com
Dialysis Stations: 18. **Formerly:** NRI.

24408 ■ Fresenius Medical Care--Huntington
2859 N Park Ave.
Huntington, IN 46750
Free: 866-434-2597
URL: http://www.ultracare-dialysis.com/
Dialysis Stations: 12. **Formerly:** RCG.

Indianapolis

24409 ■ Clarian Center--Methodist Campus
Indiana University Health
I-65 at 21st St.--5H
Indianapolis, IN 46202
Ph: (317)962-2266
URL: http://iuhealth.org/methodist/contact-locations
Dialysis Stations: 12.

24410 ■ Clarian Health Partners
Adult Dialysis Center
Methodist Hospital
I-65 at 21st St.
Indianapolis, IN 46206
Ph: (317)920-3400
URL: http://www.clarian.org
Dialysis Stations: 16.

24411 ■ Clarian Home Dialysis
Indiana University Health
8803 N Meridian St., Ste. 150
Indianapolis, IN 46260
Ph: (317)963-6850
URL: http://iuhealth.org/kidney/
Dialysis Stations: 6.

24412 ■ Clarian IU
Dialysis Center
550 N University Blvd., Rm. UH1115
Indianapolis, IN 46202
Ph: (317)274-3436
URL: http://www.medicine.indiana.edu
Dialysis Stations: 31.

24413 ■ Clarian IU
Indianapolis University Hospital
Clarian Health Partners
550 N University Blvd., Rm. UH1115
Indianapolis, IN 46202
Ph: (317)944-4283
URL: http://iuhealth.org/
Dialysis Stations: 31.

24414 ■ DaVita--Wishard
1001 W 10th St., Rm. W5703
Indianapolis, IN 46202
Free: 800-424-6589
URL: http://www.davita.com
Dialysis Stations: 3.

24415 ■ Dialysis Clinic Inc.--Indianapolis
Wishard Memorial Hospital, D-508
1001 W 10th St.
Indianapolis, IN 46202
Ph: (317)630-8569
Fax: (317)630-8435
URL: http://www.dciinc.org

24416 ■ Dialysis Clinic, Inc.--Indianapolis
1719 W 10th St.
Indianapolis, IN 46222
Ph: (317)631-2005
URL: http://www.dciinc.org
Dialysis Stations: 27.

24417 ■ Dialysis Institute of Indiana
Fresenius Medical Care
2480 N Meridian St.
Indianapolis, IN 46208
Free: 866-434-2597
URL: http://www.ultracare-dialysis.com/
Dialysis Stations: 40.

24418 ■ Dialysis Institute of Northwest Indianapolis
Renal Advantage Inc.
6488 Corporate Dr.
Indianapolis, IN 46278
Ph: (317)328-9667
URL: http://www.renaladvantage.com
Dialysis Stations: 16. **Formerly:** NRI.

24419 ■ Diversified Specialty Institutes--Marion County
Bldg. B
3834 S Emerson Ave.
Indianapolis, IN 46203
Ph: (317)787-3171
URL: http://www.dsi-corp.com
Dialysis Stations: 24. **Formerly:** NRI.

24420 ■ Fresenius Medical Care--Circle City
1420 N Senate Ave., Ste. 100
Indianapolis, IN 46202
Free: 866-434-2597
URL: http://www.ultracare-dialysis.com/
Dialysis Stations: 20.

24421 ■ Fresenius Medical Care--Indianapolis East
6635 E 21st St., Ste. 400
Indianapolis, IN 46219
Free: 866-434-2597
URL: http://www.ultracare-dialysis.com/
Dialysis Stations: 24. **Formerly:** RCG.

24422 ■ Fresenius Medical Care
Indianapolis East Home
1315 N Arlington Ave., Ste. 240
Indianapolis, IN 46219
Free: 866-434-2597
URL: http://www.ultracare-dialysis.com/

24423 ■ Fresenius Medical Care Indianapolis East Home Dialysis
1315 N Arlington Ave., Ste. 240
Indianapolis, IN 46219
Free: 866-434-2597
URL: http://www.ultracare-dialysis.com/
Dialysis Stations: 0. **Formerly:** RCG.

24424 ■ Fresenius Medical Care--Indianapolis North
1717 W 86th St., Ste. 500
Indianapolis, IN 46260
Free: 866-434-2597
URL: http://www.ultracare-dialysis.com/
Dialysis Stations: 21. **Formerly:** RCG.

24425 ■ Fresenius Medical Care--Indianapolis South
Dialysis Facility
1350 E County Line Rd., Ste. L
Indianapolis, IN 46227
Free: 866-434-2597
URL: http://www.ultracare-dialysis.com/
Dialysis Stations: 13. **Formerly:** Renal Care Group.

24426 ■ Fresenius Medical Care--Indianapolis West
Dialysis Facility
805 Beachway Dr., Ste. 100
Indianapolis, IN 46224
Free: 866-434-2597
URL: http://www.ultracare-dialysis.com/
Dialysis Stations: 18. **Formerly:** Renal Care Group.

24427 ■ Fresenius Medical Care--Midtown-Indiana
Dialysis Facility
3007 Dr. Andrew J. Brown Ave.
Indianapolis, IN 46205
Free: 866-434-2597
URL: http://www.ultracare-dialysis.com/
Dialysis Stations: 18. **Formerly:** Renal Care Group.

24428 ■ Fresenius Medical Care--Shadeland Station
7155 Shadeland Station, Ste. 130
Indianapolis, IN 46256
URL: http://www.ultracare-dialysis.com/
Dialysis Stations: 24. **Formerly:** RCG.

24429 ■ St. Vincent Hospital Transplant Services
8333 NAAB Rd., Ste. 300
Indianapolis, IN 46260
Ph: (317)338-6701
URL: http://www.stvincent.org/Transplant.aspx
Dialysis Stations: 0.

24430 ■ Westview Dialysis & At Home
DaVita
3749 Commercial Dr.
Indianapolis, IN 46222
Free: 800-424-6589
URL: http://www.davita.com
Dialysis Stations: 17.

Jasper

24431 ■ Jasper Dialysis
DaVita
721 W 13th St., Ste. 105
Jasper, IN 47546
Free: 800-424-6589
URL: http://www.davita.com
Dialysis Stations: 13. **Formerly:** Regional Kidney Care of Jasper.

Jeffersonville

24432 ■ Fresenius Medical Care - Southern Indiana
525 Broadway St.
Jeffersonville, IN 47130
Free: 866-434-2597
URL: http://www.ultracare-dialysis.com/
Dialysis Stations: 20.

Kendallville

24433 ■ Kendallville Dialysis Center
Diversified Specialty Institutes
602 Sawyer Rd.
Kendallville, IN 46755
Ph: (260)599-0423
URL: http://www.dsi-corp.com
Dialysis Stations: 20.

Knox

24434 ■ Duneland Dialysis--Knox
Liberty Dialysis
1008 S Edgewood Dr.
Knox, IN 46534
Ph: (574)772-2480
URL: http://www.libertydialysis.com
Dialysis Stations: 9.

Kokomo

24435 ■ Fresenius Medical Care--Kokomo
2350 S Dixon Rd., Ste. 450
Kokomo, IN 46902
Free: 866-434-2597
URL: http://www.ultracare-dialysis.com/
Dialysis Stations: 24. **Formerly:** Renal Care Group.

24436 ■ Liberty Dialysis--Kokomo
3760 S Reed Rd.
Kokomo, IN 46902
Ph: (765)864-1669
URL: http://www.libertydialysis.com
Dialysis Stations: 15.

La Porte

24437 ■ Duneland Dialysis--La Porte
Liberty Dialysis
1007 Lincolnway
La Porte, IN 46350
Ph: (219)326-6362
URL: http://www.libertydialysis.com
Dialysis Stations: 8.

24438 ■ Regional Nephrology Inc.--LaPorte
2910 Monroe St.
La Porte, IN 46350
Ph: (219)324-0944
Dialysis Stations: 12.

Lafayette

24439 ■ Fresenius Medical Care--Lafayette
915 Mezzanine Dr.
Lafayette, IN 47905
Free: 866-434-2597
URL: http://www.ultracare-dialysis.com/
Dialysis Stations: 12.

24440 ■ Liberty Dialysis--Lafayette II
1020 N 18th St.
Lafayette, IN 47904
Ph: (765)420-8000
URL: http://www.libertydialysis.com
Dialysis Stations: 32.

24441 ■ Wellbound of Lafayette
2 Executive Dr., Ste. B
Lafayette, IN 47905
Ph: (765)446-1627
URL: http://www.satellitehealth.com/
Dialysis Stations: 4.

Lawrenceburg

24442 ■ DaVita--Lawrenceburg Dialysis LLC
555 Eads Pkwy., Ste. 200
Lawrenceburg, IN 47025
Ph: (812)537-5750
URL: http://www.davita.com
Dialysis Stations: 12.

Lebanon

24443 ■ Lebanon Dialysis
Liberty Dialysis
2485 N Lebanon St.
Lebanon, IN 46052
Ph: (765)485-0533
URL: http://www.libertydialysis.com
Dialysis Stations: 9. **Formerly:** Witham Health Services.

Linton

24444 ■ Fresenius Medical Care--Linton
Dialysis Center
Lonetree Rd.
RR1, Box 996
Linton, IN 47441
Free: 866-434-2597
URL: http://www.ultracare-dialysis.com/
Dialysis Stations: 7. **Formerly:** Renal Care Group.

Logansport

24445 ■ Fresenius Medical Care--Logansport
1333 Smith St.
Logansport, IN 46947
Free: 866-434-2597
URL: http://www.ultracare-dialysis.com/
Dialysis Stations: 12. **Formerly:** Renal Care Group.

Madison

24446 ■ DaVita--Madison
Dialysis Facility
220 Clifty Dr., Unit K
Madison, IN 47250
Free: 800-424-6589
URL: http://www.davita.com
Dialysis Stations: 9.

24447 ■ Fresenius Medical Care--Madison
1708 Cragmont St.
Madison, IN 47250
Free: 866-434-2597
URL: http://www.ultracare-dialysis.com/
Dialysis Stations: 12.

Marion

24448 ■ Grant County Dialysis
Fresenius Medical Care
1797 W Kem Rd.
Marion, IN 46952
Free: 866-434-2597
URL: http://www.ultracare-dialysis.com/
Dialysis Stations: 24. **Formerly:** RCG.

Martinsville

24449 ■ Fresenius Medical Care--Morgan County
2200 John Wooden Dr., Ste. 106
Martinsville, IN 46151
Free: 866-434-2597
URL: http://www.ultracare-dialysis.com/
Dialysis Stations: 10.

Merrillville

24450 ■ DaVita - Merrillville Dialysis & PD
9223 Taft St.
Merrillville, IN 46410
Free: 800-424-6589
URL: http://www.davita.com
Dialysis Stations: 16.

24451 ■ Merrillville Dialysis Center
Fresenius Medical Care
Dialysis Center
8670 Broadway
Merrillville, IN 46410
Free: 866-434-2597
URL: http://www.ultracare-dialysis.com/
Dialysis Stations: 26.

Michigan City

24452 ■ Comprehebsive Renal Care--Michigan City
DaVita
9836 W 400 N
Michigan City, IN 46360
Free: 800-424-6589
URL: http://www.davita.com
Dialysis Stations: 16.

Mishawaka

24453 ■ Fresenius Medical Care--Nephrology Mishawaka Home
710 Park Pl.
Mishawaka, IN 46545
Ph: (574)273-6777
URL: https://www.ultracare-dialysis.com
Dialysis Stations: 26. **Formerly:** Nephrology Inc.--Mishawaka.

24454 ■ Nephrology Physicians LLC
710 Park Pl.
Mishawaka, IN 46545
Ph: (574)273-6767
URL: http://www.nephinc.com/home-hemodialysis.asp
Dialysis Stations: 2.

Monticello

24455 ■ Liberty Dialysis--Monticello
810 S 6th St.
Monticello, IN 47960
Ph: (574)583-3576
URL: http://www.libertydialysis.com
Dialysis Stations: 12. **Formerly:** White County Satellite Dialysis Unit.

Muncie

24456 ■ Ball Acute Muncie
Renal Advantage Inc.
2401 University Ave.
Muncie, IN 47373
Ph: (765)747-3504
URL: http://www.renaladvantage.com
Dialysis Stations: 7.

24457 ■ Ball Dialysis--Renaissance
3400 W Community Dr.
Muncie, IN 47304
Ph: (765)287-8621
Dialysis Stations: 0.

24458 ■ Fresenius Medical Care--Muncie
4021 W Kilgore Ave.
Muncie, IN 47304
Free: 866-434-2597
URL: http://www.ultracare-dialysis.com/
Dialysis Stations: 24.

24459 ■ North Granville Dialysis Clinic
Renal Advantage Inc.
3001 N Granville Ave.
Muncie, IN 47303
Ph: (765)288-3740
URL: http://www.renaladvantage.com
Dialysis Stations: 16.

24460 ■ RAI North St--Muncie
Renal Advantage Inc.
Dialysis Unit
2705 W North St.
Muncie, IN 47303
Ph: (765)747-3020
URL: http://www.renaladvantage.com
Dialysis Stations: 30. **Formerly:** National Renal Institute.

Munster

24461 ■ Comprehensive Renal Care--Munster
Davita
8317 Calumet Ave., Ste. A
Munster, IN 46321
Free: 800-424-6589
URL: http://www.davita.com
Dialysis Stations: 16.

24462 ■ Fresenius Medical Care--Neomedica--Munster
Dialysis Facility
314 Ridge Rd.
Munster, IN 46321
Free: 866-434-2597
URL: http://www.ultracare-dialysis.com/
Dialysis Stations: 16.

New Albany

24463 ■ Fresenius Medical Care--Floyd County
Dialysis Facility
1919 State St., Ste. 150
New Albany, IN 47150
Free: 866-434-2597
URL: http://www.ultracare-dialysis.com/
Dialysis Stations: 14.

24464 ■ New Albany Dialysis
DaVita
2669 Charlestown Rd., Ste. F
New Albany, IN 47150
Free: 800-424-6589
URL: http://www.davita.com
Dialysis Stations: 12.

New Castle

24465 ■ Renal Advantage Inc.--New Castle
101 Emerson Ave.
New Castle, IN 47362
Ph: (765)521-0938
URL: http://www.renaladvantage.com
Dialysis Stations: 21.

New Haven

24466 ■ Canal Dialysis
Fresenius Medical Care
1308 Minnich Rd.
New Haven, IN 46774
Free: 866-434-2597
URL: http://www.ultracare-dialysis.com
Dialysis Stations: 12. **Formerly:** RCG - Northeast Indiana Kidney Center - New Haven; Fresenius Medical Care.

Noblesville

24467 ■ Fresenius Medical Care--Noblesville Dialysis Facility
165 Sheridan Rd.
Noblesville, IN 46060
Free: 866-434-2597
URL: http://www.ultracare-dialysis.com
Dialysis Stations: 12. **Formerly:** Renal Care Group - Noblesville.

North Vernon

24468 ■ North Vernon Dialysis
DaVita
2340 N State Hwy. 7, Ste. A
North Vernon, IN 47265
Free: 800-424-6589
URL: http://www.davita.com
Dialysis Stations: 10.

Peru

24469 ■ Peru Dialysis
Fresenius Medical Care
25 W 2nd St.
Peru, IN 46970
Free: 866-434-2597
URL: http://www.ultracare-dialysis.com/
Dialysis Stations: 12.

Plainfield

24470 ■ Diversified Specialty Institutes--Plainfield
8110 Network Dr.
Plainfield, IN 46168
Ph: (317)838-8089
URL: http://www.dsi-corp.com
Dialysis Stations: 24.

Plymouth

24471 ■ Fresenius Medical Care Nephrology--Marshall County
2855 Miller Dr., Ste. 209
Plymouth, IN 46563
Free: 866-434-2597
URL: http://www.ultracare-dialysis.com/
Dialysis Stations: 12.

Portage

24472 ■ Fresenius Medical Care--Portage Dialysis Center
5972 U.S Hwy. 6
Portage, IN 46368
Free: 866-434-2597
URL: http://www.ultracare-dialysis.com/
Dialysis Stations: 14.

24473 ■ Portage Dialysis
DaVita
5823 US Hwy. 6
Portage, IN 46368
Free: 800-424-6589
URL: http://www.davita.com
Dialysis Stations: 16.

Porter

24474 ■ DaVita--Chesterton
711 Plaza Dr., Ste. 6
Porter, IN 46304
Free: 800-424-6589
URL: http://www.davita.com
Dialysis Stations: 12.

Princeton

24475 ■ Princeton Dialysis
DaVita
2227 Sherman Dr.
Princeton, IN 47670
Free: 800-424-6589
URL: http://www.davita.com
Dialysis Stations: 12.

Richmond

24476 ■ Fresenius Medical Care--Richmond
940 Chester Blvd.
Richmond, IN 47374
Free: 866-434-2597
URL: http://www.ultracare-dialysis.com/
Dialysis Stations: 24. **Formerly:** Renal Care Group.

Rushville

24477 ■ Rush County Dialysis
DaVita
1400 N Cherry St.
Rushville, IN 46173
Free: 800-424-6589
URL: http://www.davita.com
Dialysis Stations: 8.

Saint John

24478 ■ Saint John Dialysis
DaVita
10033 Wicker Ave., Unit 6
Saint John, IN 46373
Free: 800-424-6589
URL: http://www.davita.com
Dialysis Stations: 16.

Salem

24479 ■ DaVita
Salem Dialysis Center
1201 N Jim Day Rd., Ste. 103
Salem, IN 47167
Free: 800-424-6589
URL: http://www.davita.com
Dialysis Stations: 12.

24480 ■ Dialysis Services of Salem
Fresenius Medical Care
102 Connie Ave., Ste. 104
Salem, IN 47167
Free: 866-434-2597
URL: http://www.ultracare-dialysis.com/
Dialysis Stations: 8.

Scottsburg

24481 ■ Diversified Specialty Institutes--Scottsburg Dialysis Facility
1451 N Gardner St.
Scottsburg, IN 47170
Ph: (812)752-2949
Fax: (812)752-4156
URL: http://www.dsi-corp.com
Dialysis Stations: 12. **Formerly:** Fresenius Medical Care.

24482 ■ Scott County Dialysis
Fresenius Medical Care
130 N Westavia Blvd.
Scottsburg, IN 47170
Free: 866-434-2597
URL: http://www.ultracare-dialysis.com/
Dialysis Stations: 12.

Seymour

24483 ■ Fresenius Medical Care--Seymour
200 E 3rd St.
Seymour, IN 47274
Free: 866-434-2597
URL: http://www.ultracare-dialysis.com/
Dialysis Stations: 12. **Formerly:** Renal Care Group.

Shelbyville

24484 ■ DSI--Blue River Valley Dialysis Facility
2309 S Miller St., Ste. 100
Shelbyville, IN 46176
Ph: (317)398-0486
URL: http://www.dsi-corp.com/
Dialysis Stations: 12. **Formerly:** Shelbyville Kidney Center.

24485 ■ Fresenius Medical Care--Shelbyville, Indiana Dialysis Facility
2500 Parkway Dr.
Shelbyville, IN 46176
Free: 866-434-2597
URL: http://www.ultracare-dialysis.com/
Dialysis Stations: 12. **Formerly:** Renal Care Group.

South Bend

24486 ■ Regional Nephrology Inc.--Blackthorn
6201 Nimtz Pkwy.
South Bend, IN 46628
Ph: (574)246-7000
Dialysis Stations: 24.

Spencer

24487 ■ Fresenius Medical Care--Spencer Dialysis Center
11 Crane Ave.
Spencer, IN 47460
Free: 866-434-2597
URL: http://www.ultracare-dialysis.com
Dialysis Stations: 9. **Formerly:** Renal Care Group.

Tell City

24488 ■ CRC-tell City Dialysis Center
DaVita
1602 Main St.
Tell City, IN 47586
Free: 800-424-6589
URL: http://www.davita.com
Dialysis Stations: 12.

Terre Haute

24489 ■ Fresenius Medical Care--Terre Haute
315 E Springhill Dr.
Terre Haute, IN 47802
Free: 866-434-2597
URL: http://www.ultracare-dialysis.com/
Dialysis Stations: 17. **Formerly:** Renal Care Group.

24490 ■ Fresenius Medical Care--Terre Haute North
351 Maiden La.
Terre Haute, IN 47804
Free: 866-434-2597
URL: http://www.ultracare-dialysis.com/
Dialysis Stations: 24.

24491 ■ Fresenius Medical Care--Wabash Valley
4001 E Wabash Ave.
Terre Haute, IN 47803
Free: 866-434-2597
URL: http://www.ultracare-dialysis.com/
Dialysis Stations: 2. **Formerly:** Dialysis Center of Wabash Valley.

Valparaiso

24492 ■ DaVita--ValParaiso Dialysis Facility
606 E Lincoln Way
Valparaiso, IN 46383
Free: 800-424-6589
URL: http://www.davita.com
Dialysis Stations: 22.

Vincennes

24493 ■ Vincennes Dialysis & At Home DaVita
700 Willow St., Ste. 101
Vincennes, IN 47591
Free: 800-424-6589
URL: http://www.davita.com
Dialysis Stations: 20.

Warsaw

24494 ■ Fresenius Medical Care--Warsaw
3334 Lake City Hwy.
Warsaw, IN 46580
Free: 866-434-2597
URL: http://www.ultracare-dialysis.com/
Dialysis Stations: 12. **Formerly:** RCG-Northeast Indiana Kidney Center.

Washington

24495 ■ Daviess County Dialysis DaVita
310 NE 14th St.
Washington, IN 47501
Free: 800-424-6589
URL: http://www.davita.com
Dialysis Stations: 10.

Winchester

24496 ■ RAI Greenville Ave--Winchester Renal Advantage Inc.
409 Greenville Ave.
Winchester, IN 47394
Ph: (765)584-8000
URL: http://www.renaladvantage.com
Dialysis Stations: 12. **Formerly:** National Renal Alliance.

IOWA

Algona

24497 ■ North Iowa Mercy Dialysis Center--Algona
1515 S Phillips
Algona, IA 50511
Ph: (515)295-2451
Dialysis Stations: 5.

Ames

24498 ■ Mary Greeley Medical Center--Ames
2322 E 13th St.
Ames, IA 50010
Ph: (515)239-6800
URL: http://www.mgmc.org
Dialysis Stations: 17.

Atlantic

24499 ■ Atlantic Dialysis DaVita
1500 E 10th St., Ste. B
Atlantic, IA 50022
Free: 800-424-6589
URL: http://www.davita.com
Dialysis Stations: 6.

Bettendorf

24500 ■ Quad Cities Kidney Center - Bettendorf LLC
4480 Utica Ridge Rd.
Bettendorf, IA 52722
Ph: (563)344-9977
Dialysis Stations: 9.

Carroll

24501 ■ Saint Anthony's Regional Hospital Dialysis Unit
311 S Clark St.
Carroll, IA 51401
Ph: (712)792-8278
URL: http://www.stanthonyhospital.org
Dialysis Stations: 12.

Cedar Rapids

24502 ■ Mercy Medical Center Cedar Rapids Dialysis Unit
701 10th St. SE
Cedar Rapids, IA 52403
Ph: (319)398-6432
URL: http://www.mercycare.org
Dialysis Stations: 8.

24503 ■ Mercy Medical Center Dialysis--Mercy Plaza
5264 Council St. NE, Ste. 200
Cedar Rapids, IA 52402
Ph: (319)398-6423
URL: http://www.mercycare.org
Dialysis Stations: 33.

Centerville

24504 ■ Mercy Medical Center - Centerville
1 St. Joseph's Dr.
Centerville, IA 52544
Ph: (641)437-3516
URL: http://www.mercycenterville.org
Dialysis Stations: 10.

Charles City

24505 ■ North Iowa Mercy Dialysis Center--Charles City
707 Gilbert St.
Charles City, IA 50616
Ph: (641)228-3567
Dialysis Stations: 8.

Clinton

24506 ■ Mercy Medical Center--Clinton Dialysis Facility
1410 N 4th St.
Clinton, IA 52732
Ph: (563)244-3683
URL: http://www.mercyclinton.com
Dialysis Stations: 13. **Formerly:** Samaritan Health System.

Corydon

24507 ■ Wayne County Hospital ESRD ESRD
417 S East St.
Corydon, IA 50060
Ph: (641)872-2260
URL: http://www.waynecountyhospital.org
Dialysis Stations: 5.

Council Bluffs

24508 ■ Council Bluffs Dialysis Center DaVita
300 W Broadway, No. 150
Council Bluffs, IA 51503
Free: 800-424-6589
URL: http://www.davita.com
Dialysis Stations: 24. **Formerly:** Gambro Healthcare.

Creston

24509 ■ Creston Dialysis DaVita
1700 W Townline Rd., Ste. 2B
Creston, IA 50801
Free: 800-424-6589
URL: http://www.davita.com
Dialysis Stations: 8. **Formerly:** Kidney Care.

Davenport

24510 ■ Genesis Medical Center, East Rusholme St.
1227 E Rusholme St.
Davenport, IA 52803
Ph: (563)421-6440
URL: http://www.genesishealth.com
Dialysis Stations: 24.

24511 ■ Quad Cities Kidney Center--Davenport
120 W Locust St.
Davenport, IA 52803
Ph: (563)323-3300
Dialysis Stations: 19.

Decorah

24512 ■ Mayo Dialysis Center--Decorah
901 Montgomery St.
Decorah, IA 52101
Ph: (563)382-1961
URL: http://www.mayoclinic.org
Dialysis Stations: 4.

Des Moines

24513 ■ Central Des Moines Dialysis DaVita
1215 Pleasant St., Ste. 106
Des Moines, IA 50309
Free: 800-424-6589
URL: http://www.davita.com
Dialysis Stations: 20. **Formerly:** Kidney Care Inc.

24514 ■ Dialysis Services Des Moines South Fresenius Medical Care
6651 SW 9th St.
Des Moines, IA 50315
Free: 866-434-2597
URL: http://www.ultracare-dialysis.com/
Dialysis Stations: 19.

24515 ■ East Des Moines Dialysis & At Home DaVita
1301 Pennsylvania Ave., Ste. 208
Des Moines, IA 50316
Free: 800-424-6589
URL: http://www.davita.com
Dialysis Stations: 17.

24516 ■ Fresenius Medical Care Dialysis Services Des Moines
1111 6th Ave.
Des Moines, IA 50314
Free: 866-434-2597
URL: http://www.ultracare-dialysis.com/
Dialysis Stations: 21. **Formerly:** Mercy Hospital Medical Center.

24517 ■ Riverpoint Dialysis DaVita
501 SW 7th St., Ste. B
Des Moines, IA 50309
Free: 800-424-6589
URL: http://www.davita.com
Dialysis Stations: 16.

Dubuque

24518 ■ Tri-State Dialysis--Dubuque
1500 Delhi St., No. 2100
Dubuque, IA 52001
Ph: (563)589-4033
Dialysis Stations: 32.

24519 ■ Tri-State Dialysis--Dubuque
Dubuque Internal Medicine
1515 Delhi St.
Dubuque, IA 52001
Ph: (563)589-4033
URL: http://www.dubuqueinternalmed.com/services.phtml
Dialysis Stations: 32.

Fairfield

24520 ■ Southeastern Renal Dialysis,L.C.--Fairfield
2000 S Main St.
Fairfield, IA 52556
Ph: (641)469-3313
Dialysis Stations: 10.

Fort Dodge

24521 ■ Trinity Regional Medical Center
821 S 25th St.
Fort Dodge, IA 50501
Ph: (515)574-6200
URL: http://www.trmc.org
Dialysis Stations: 16.

Fort Madison

24522 ■ Southeastern Renal Dialysis--Fort Madison
4703 Ave. L
Fort Madison, IA 52627
Ph: (319)372-7829
Dialysis Stations: 12.

Grinnell

24523 ■ University of Iowa Hospital and Clinics--Grinnell
803 Broad St.
Grinnell, IA 50112
Ph: (641)236-7419
URL: http://www.grmc.us/
Dialysis Stations: 10.

Harlan

24524 ■ Harlan Dialysis
DaVita
1213 Garfield Ave.
Harlan, IA 51537
Free: 800-424-6589
URL: http://www.davita.com
Dialysis Stations: 6. **Formerly:** NHS-Harlan Renal Dialysis.

Hospers

24525 ■ Northwest Iowa Dialysis Center
112 Sunset Dr.
Hospers, IA 51238
Ph: (712)752-8330
Dialysis Stations: 8.

Independence

24526 ■ Covenant--Mercycare Dialysis--Independence
Wheaton Franciscan Healthcare
1600 1st St. E
Independence, IA 50644
Ph: (319)272-5000
URL: http://www.covhealth.com
Dialysis Stations: 12.

Iowa City

24527 ■ University of Iowa Hospital & Clinics Dialysis
200 Hawkins Dr.
Iowa City, IA 52242
Ph: (319)356-3047
URL: http://www.uihealthcare.org/otherservices.aspx?id=1666
Dialysis Stations: 16.

24528 ■ University of Iowa Hospital and Clinics
Transplant/Dialysis Center
W336-4AZ
200 Hawkins Dr.
Iowa City, IA 52242
Ph: (319)356-3047
URL: http://www.grmc.us/
Dialysis Stations: 16.

24529 ■ VA Medical Center Transplant--Iowa City
Hwy 6, 5 S
Iowa City, IA 52246
Ph: (319)338-0581
URL: http://www.iowacity.va.gov/Transplant/
Dialysis Stations: 0,.

Iowa Falls

24530 ■ Mary Greeley Medical Center--Iowa Falls
Iowa Falls Dialysis Center
701 Washington Ave., Ste. D
Iowa Falls, IA 50126
Ph: (641)648-5241
URL: http://www.mgmc.org
Dialysis Stations: 8.

Keokuk

24531 ■ Southeastern Renal Dialysis LC--Lee County
Dialysis Facility
1419 Morgan St.
Keokuk, IA 52632
Ph: (319)524-2105
Dialysis Stations: 10.

Manchester

24532 ■ Tri-State Dialysis--Manchester
709 W Main St.
Manchester, IA 52057
Ph: (563)927-7370
Dialysis Stations: 12.

24533 ■ Tri-State Dialysis--Manchester
709 W Main
Manchester, IA 52057
Ph: (563)927-7370
Dialysis Stations: 12.

Maquoketa

24534 ■ Maquoketa Kidney Center LLC
700 W Grove St.
Maquoketa, IA 52060
Ph: (563)652-4051
Dialysis Stations: 8.

Marengo

24535 ■ Marengo Memorial Hospital
Dialysis Unit
300 W May St.
Marengo, IA 52301
Ph: (319)642-8052
URL: http://www.marengohospital.org
Dialysis Stations: 6.

Marshalltown

24536 ■ Mary Greeley Medical Center--Marshalltown
Marshalltown Dialysis
3120 S 2nd
Marshalltown, IA 50158
Ph: (641)752-1819
URL: http://www.mgmc.org
Dialysis Stations: 7.

Mason City

24537 ■ Mercy Dialysis Center--Mason City
1000 4th St. SW
Mason City, IA 50401
Ph: (641)422-7961
URL: http://www.mercynorthiowa.com
Dialysis Stations: 16.

Mount Ayr

24538 ■ Ringgold County Hospital
Dialysis Unit
504 N Cleveland
Mount Ayr, IA 50854
Ph: (641)464-4468
E-mail: info@rchmtayr.org
URL: http://www.rchmtayr.org/hospdept.html#dialysis
Dialysis Stations: 7.

Mount Pleasant

24539 ■ Southeastern Renal Dialysis LC--Mount Pleasant
Saunders Park
507 S White St.
Mount Pleasant, IA 52641
Ph: (319)385-6720
Dialysis Stations: 12.

Muscatine

24540 ■ University of Iowa Hospital and Clinics--Muscatine
Muscatine Outreach Dialysis
3465 Mulberry Ave.
Muscatine, IA 52761
Ph: (563)262-9303
URL: http://www.grmc.us
Dialysis Stations: 12.

Newton

24541 ■ Newton Dialysis
DaVita
204 N 4th Ave. E, Ste. 134
Newton, IA 50208
Free: 800-424-6589
URL: http://www.davita.com
Dialysis Stations: 8.

North Liberty

24542 ■ University of Iowa Hospital and Clinics--North Liberty
Outreach Dialysis Unit
5 Lions Dr.
North Liberty, IA 52317
Ph: (319)626-2174
URL: http://www.grmc.us
Dialysis Stations: 12.

Onawa

24543 ■ Dialysis Clinic, Inc.--Onawa
1620 Diamond St. Place
Onawa, IA 51040
Ph: (712)433-9720
URL: http://www.dciinc.org
Dialysis Stations: 12.

Ottumwa

24544 ■ Fresenius Medical Care--Ottumwa
Dialysis Facility
1110 N Quincy Ave., Ste. 44
Ottumwa, IA 52501
Free: 866-434-2597
URL: http://www.ultracare-dialysis.com/
Dialysis Stations: 14.

Pella

24545 ■ Pella Regional Health Center
Dialysis Unit
404 Jefferson St.
Pella, IA 50219

Ph: (641)628-6695
URL: http://www.pellahealth.org
Dialysis Stations: 9.

Perry

24546 ■ Perry Dialysis
DaVita
610 10th St.
Perry, IA 50220
Ph: (515)465-2657
Dialysis Stations: 8.

Shenandoah

24547 ■ Shenandoah Dialysis
DaVita
300 Pershing Ave.
Shenandoah, IA 51601
Ph: (712)246-5220
Dialysis Stations: 12. **Formerly:** Nebraska Health System.

Sioux City

24548 ■ Midwest Dialysis
Fresenius Medical Care
4000 Indian Hills Dr.
Sioux City, IA 51108
Free: 866-434-2597
URL: http://www.ultracare-dialysis.com/
Dialysis Stations: 16.

24549 ■ Siouxland Dialysis
Fresenius Medical Care
2530 Glenn Ave.
Sioux City, IA 51106
Free: 866-434-2597
URL: http://www.ultracare-dialysis.com/
Dialysis Stations: 25.

Spencer

24550 ■ Milton & Ethyl Warner Dialysis Unit--Spencer
Spencer Municipal Hospital
1200 1st Ave. E
Spencer, IA 51301
Ph: (712)264-6464
URL: http://www.spencerhospital.org
Dialysis Stations: 8.

Spirit Lake

24551 ■ Warner Dialysis Center
3150 18th St.
Spirit Lake, IA 51360
Ph: (712)336-2910
Dialysis Stations: 12.

Storm Lake

24552 ■ Renal Center of Storm Lake, LLC
Dialysis Facility
1426 N Lake Ave.
Storm Lake, IA 50588
Ph: (712)732-6900
URL: http://www.renalventures.com/map_ia.html
Dialysis Stations: 16.

Vinton

24553 ■ Mercy Dialysis--Vinton
Covenant--Mercycare, Inc.
Dialysis Unit
502 N 9th Ave.
Vinton, IA 52349
Ph: (319)472-6359
URL: http://www.covhealth.com
Dialysis Stations: 6.

Washington

24554 ■ University of Iowa Hospital and Clinics--Washington
Dialysis Unit
414 E Polk St.
Washington, IA 52353
Ph: (319)653-4171
URL: http://www.grmc.us
Dialysis Stations: 6.

Waterloo

24555 ■ Black Hawk Dialysis
DaVita
3421 W 9th St.
Waterloo, IA 50702
Ph: (319)272-8700
URL: http://www.davita.com
Dialysis Stations: 25. **Formerly:** Covenant Medical Center.

24556 ■ Cedar Valley Dialysis Center
DaVita
1661 W Ridgeway Ave.
Waterloo, IA 50701
Free: 800-424-6589
URL: http://www.davita.com
Dialysis Stations: 24.

Waverly

24557 ■ Covenant Waverly Dialysis Center
2020 3rd Ave. NW
Waverly, IA 50677
Ph: (319)268-3575
URL: http://www.covhealth.com
Dialysis Stations: 9.

Webster City

24558 ■ Trinity Regional Medical Center Dialysis--Webster City
1610 Collins St., Ste. D
Webster City, IA 50595
Ph: (515)832-1667
Dialysis Stations: 7.

West Burlington

24559 ■ Southeastern Renal Dialysis LC--West Burlington
1213 S Gear
West Burlington, IA 52655
Ph: (319)758-0691
Dialysis Stations: 12.

West Des Moines

24560 ■ DaVita
West Des Moines Dialysis
6800 Lake Dr., No. 185
West Des Moines, IA 50266
Free: 800-424-6589
URL: http://www.davita.com
Dialysis Stations: 10. **Formerly:** Kidney Care East Iowa.

West Union

24561 ■ West Union Dialysis Center
DaVita
405 Hwy. 150 N
West Union, IA 52175
Free: 800-424-6589
URL: http://www.davita.com
Dialysis Stations: 16. **Formerly:** Cedar Valley Dialysis.

KANSAS

Chanute

24562 ■ Fresenius Medical Care--Chanute
Dialysis Facility
703 S Plummer
Chanute, KS 66720
Free: 866-434-2597
URL: http://www.ultracare-dialysis.com
Dialysis Stations: 12. **Formerly:** Renal Care Group - Chanute.

Concordia

24563 ■ Fresenius Medical Care--Concordia
1100 Highland Dr.
Concordia, KS 66901
Ph: (785)243-6132
Dialysis Stations: 8.

Derby

24564 ■ Renal Treatment Center--Derby
DaVita
Dialysis Facility
250 W Red Powell Dr.
Derby, KS 67037
Free: 800-424-6589
URL: http://www.davita.com
Dialysis Stations: 18.

Dodge City

24565 ■ Fresenius Medical Care--Dodge City
Dialysis Facility
204 Ross Blvd.
Dodge City, KS 67801
Free: 866-434-2597
URL: http://www.ultracare-dialysis.com
Dialysis Stations: 12. **Formerly:** Renal Care Group - Dodge City.

El Dorado

24566 ■ Susan B. Allen Dialysis Center
Fresenius Medical Care
701 W Central
El Dorado, KS 67042
Free: 866-434-2597
URL: http://www.ultracare-dialysis.com/
Dialysis Stations: 12. **Formerly:** Renal Care Group/ Susan B. Allen Dialysis Center.

Emporia

24567 ■ Fresenius Medical Care--Emporia
Dialysis Facility
Newman Memorial County Hospital
1201 W 12th St.
Emporia, KS 66801
Free: 866-434-2597
URL: http://www.ultracare-dialysis.com
Dialysis Stations: 8. **Formerly:** Renal Care Group - Emporia.

Garden City

24568 ■ Renal Treatment Centers--Garden City
DaVita
401 N Main St.
Garden City, KS 67846
Free: 800-424-6589
URL: http://www.davita.com
Dialysis Stations: 10.

Great Bend

24569 ■ Fresenius Medical Care--Great Bend
Dialysis Facility
3904 6th St.
Great Bend, KS 67530
Free: 866-434-2597
URL: http://www.ultracare-dialysis.com
Dialysis Stations: 12. **Formerly:** Renal Care Group - Great Bend.

Hays

24570 ■ Fresenius Medical Care--Hays
Dialysis Facility
2905 Canterbury Dr.
Hays, KS 67601

Free: 866-434-2597
URL: http://www.ultracare-dialysis.com
Dialysis Stations: 13. **Formerly:** Renal Care Group - Hays.

Horton

24571 ■ Horton Dialysis
DaVita
1901 Euclid Ave.
Horton, KS 66439
Free: 800-424-6589
URL: http://www.davita.com
Dialysis Stations: 8.

Hutchinsomn

24572 ■ Hutchinson Clinic Renal Dialysis Center
1701 E 23rd St.
Hutchinsomn, KS 67502
Ph: (620)513-3740
Dialysis Stations: 5.

Hutchinson

24573 ■ Dialysis Center of Hutchinson
1901 N Waldrom
Hutchinson, KS 67502
Ph: (620)694-4099
Dialysis Stations: 17.

24574 ■ Fresenius Medical Care--Reno County
1900 E 23rd Ave.
Hutchinson, KS 67502
Free: 866-434-2597
URL: http://www.ultracare-dialysis.com/
Dialysis Stations: 17.

Independence

24575 ■ Independence Dialysis Center
DaVita
801 W Myrtle
Independence, KS 67301
Free: 800-424-6589
URL: http://www.davita.com
Dialysis Stations: 12.

Junction City

24576 ■ Saline County Dialysis--Junction City
Dialysis Facility
1106 St. Mary's Rd.
Junction City, KS 66441
Ph: (785)238-3213
Dialysis Stations: 8.

Kansas City

24577 ■ Renal Advantage Inc.--Kansas City
6401 Parallel Pkwy.
Kansas City, KS 66102
Ph: (913)299-1044
URL: http://www.renaladvantage.com

24578 ■ Wyandotte Central Dialysis
DaVita
3737 State Ave., No. 100
Kansas City, KS 66102
Free: 800-424-6589
URL: http://www.davita.com
Dialysis Stations: 12.

24579 ■ Wyandotte County Dialysis
DaVita
4837 State Ave.
Kansas City, KS 66102
Free: 800-424-6589
URL: http://www.davita.com
Dialysis Stations: 17.

24580 ■ Wyandotte West Dialysis
DaVita
Dialysis Facility
8919 Parallel Pkwy., Ste. 121
Kansas City, KS 66112
Free: 800-424-6589
URL: http://www.davita.com
Dialysis Stations: 12. **Formerly:** Gambro Healthcare.

Lawrence

24581 ■ Kansas Dialysis Services--Lawrence
330 Arkansas St., Ste. 100
Lawrence, KS 66044
Ph: (785)843-2000
Dialysis Stations: 13.

Leavenworth

24582 ■ Leavenworth Dialysis
DaVita
501 Oak St.
Leavenworth, KS 66048
Free: 800-424-6589
URL: http://www.davita.com
Dialysis Stations: 12.

Leawood

24583 ■ Bio-Medical Applications of Leawood
Fresenius Medical Care
Dialysis Facility
11313 Ash St.
Leawood, KS 66211
Free: 866-434-2597
URL: http://www.ultracare-dialysis.com/
Dialysis Stations: 9.

Lenexa

24584 ■ Johnson County Dialysis
DaVita
10453 W 84th Terr.
Lenexa, KS 66214
Free: 800-424-6589
URL: http://www.davita.com
Dialysis Stations: 24.

24585 ■ Lenexa Dialysis & At Home
DaVita
8630 Halsey
Lenexa, KS 66215
Free: 800-424-6589
URL: http://www.davita.com
Dialysis Stations: 17.

Liberal

24586 ■ Fresenius Medical Care--Liberal
2319 N Kansas Ave.
Liberal, KS 67905
Free: 866-434-2597
URL: http://www.ultracare-dialysis.com/
Dialysis Stations: 17. **Formerly:** Renal Care Group - Liberal.

Maize

24587 ■ Maize Dialysis Center
DaVita
10001 W Grady Ave.
Maize, KS 67101
Free: 800-424-6589
URL: http://www.davita.com
Dialysis Stations: 24.

Manhattan

24588 ■ Kansas Dialysis Services--Manhattan
Bldg. B, Ste. 266
1133 College Ave.
Manhattan, KS 66502
Ph: (785)565-9500
Dialysis Stations: 12.

Newton

24589 ■ Fresenius Medical Care--Newton, Kansas
Dialysis Facility
625 Medical Center Dr.
Newton, KS 67114
Free: 866-434-2597
URL: http://www.ultracare-dialysis.com
Dialysis Stations: 12. **Formerly:** Renal Care Group - Newton.

24590 ■ Newton Dialysis Center
DaVita
1223 Washington Rd.
Newton, KS 67114
Free: 800-424-6589
URL: http://www.davita.com
Dialysis Stations: 12.

Olathe

24591 ■ Olathe Dialysis
DaVita
732 W Frontier Ln.
Olathe, KS 66061
Free: 800-424-6589
URL: http://www.davita.com
Dialysis Stations: 12. **Formerly:** Gambro Healthcare.

Ottawa

24592 ■ Kansas Dialysis Services--Ottawa
1320 S Ash, Ste. 206
Ottawa, KS 66607
Ph: (785)242-5300
Dialysis Stations: 10.

Parsons

24593 ■ Parsons Dialysis Center
DaVita
Renal Treatment Centers
1902 S Hwy. 59, Bldg. B
Parsons, KS 67357
Free: 800-424-6589
URL: http://www.davita.com
Dialysis Stations: 12. **Formerly:** Renal Treatment Center.

Pittsburg

24594 ■ Fresenius Medical Care--Pittsburg
2824 N Broadway
Pittsburg, KS 66762
Free: 866-434-2597
URL: http://www.ultracare-dialysis.com/
Dialysis Stations: 17. **Formerly:** Renal Care Group.

Pratt

24595 ■ Pratt Dialysis Center
DaVita
203 Watson, Ste. 110
Pratt, KS 67124
Free: 800-424-6589
URL: http://www.davita.com
Dialysis Stations: 12.

Sabetha

24596 ■ Kansas Dialysis Services--Sabetha
106 N 12th St.
Sabetha, KS 66534
Ph: (785)284-0100
Dialysis Stations: 10.

Salina

24597 ■ Saline County Dialysis--Salina
700 E Iron
Salina, KS 67402
Ph: (785)823-6460
Dialysis Stations: 31.

Topeka

24598 ■ Fresenius Medical Care--Topeka
920 SW Washburn Ave., No. 200
Topeka, KS 66606
Free: 866-434-2597
URL: http://www.ultracare-dialysis.com/
Dialysis Stations: 14.

24599 ■ Kansas Dialysis Services--Topeka
634 SW Mulvane, No. 300
Topeka, KS 66606
Ph: (785)234-2277
Dialysis Stations: 51.

Westwood

24600 ■ University of Kansas Medical Center Dialysis Unit
4720 Rainbow Blvd., Ste. 200
Westwood, KS 66205
Ph: (913)588-6065
URL: http://www.kumc.edu
Dialysis Stations: 28.

Wichita

**24601 ■ DaVita
East Wichita Dialysis Center**
320 N Hillside
Wichita, KS 67214-4918
Free: 800-424-6589
URL: http://www.davita.com
Dialysis Stations: 24. **Formerly:** Renal Treatment Center--East Wichita.

24602 ■ Fresenius Medical Care--Wichita Dialysis Facility
1007 N Emporia
Wichita, KS 67214
Free: 866-434-2597
URL: http://www.ultracare-dialysis.com
Dialysis Stations: 31. **Formerly:** Renal Care Group - Wichita.

24603 ■ Fresenius Medical Care--Wichita East
9341 E 21st St. N
Wichita, KS 67206
Free: 866-434-2597
URL: http://www.ultracare-dialysis.com/
Dialysis Stations: 16.

24604 ■ Fresenius Medical Care--Wichita West
750 N Socora, Ste. 500
Wichita, KS 67212
Free: 866-434-2597
URL: http://www.ultracare-dialysis.com/
Dialysis Stations: 12. **Formerly:** Renal Care Group.

**24605 ■ Northeast Wichita Dialysis Center
DaVita**
2630 N Webb Rd., Bldg. 100, Ste. 100
Wichita, KS 67226
Free: 800-424-6589
URL: http://www.davita.com
Dialysis Stations: 12.

**24606 ■ Pediatrics Dialysis Service at Wesley
Fresenius Medical Care**
550 N Hillside Ave.
Wichita, KS 67214
Free: 866-434-2597
URL: http://www.ultracare-dialysis.com/
Dialysis Stations: 4.

24607 ■ Via Christi Regional Medical Center--Transplant
929 N St. Francis
Wichita, KS 67214
Ph: (316)268-5890
URL: http://www.via-christi.org/
Dialysis Stations: 0.

**24608 ■ Wichita Dialysis Center & At Home
DaVita**
909 N Topeka
Wichita, KS 67214
Free: 800-424-6589
URL: http://www.davita.com
Dialysis Stations: 23.

Winfield

**24609 ■ DaVita
Renal Treatment Centers--Winfield
Dialysis Facility**
1315 E 4th Ave.
Winfield, KS 67156
Free: 800-424-6589
URL: http://www.davita.com
Dialysis Stations: 12.

KENTUCKY

Ashland

24610 ■ Fresenius Medical Care--Ashland Dialysis Facility
432 16th St.
Ashland, KY 41101
Free: 866-434-2597
URL: http://www.ultracare-dialysis.com/
Dialysis Stations: 24.

Barbourville

24611 ■ Renal Advantage Inc.--Barbourville
315 Hospital Dr.
Barbourville, KY 40906
Ph: (606)545-6600
URL: http://www.renaladvantage.com

Bardstown

**24612 ■ Bardstown Dialysis
DaVita**
210 W John Fitch Ave.
Bardstown, KY 40004
Free: 800-424-6589
URL: http://www.davita.com
Dialysis Stations: 10.

24613 ■ Fresenius Medical Care--Bardstown
317 Kentucky Home Sq., Ste. 3
Bardstown, KY 40004
Free: 866-434-2597
URL: http://www.ultracare-dialysis.com/
Dialysis Stations: 12.

Bowling Green

24614 ■ Bowling Green Kidney Center
1834 Lyda Ave.
Bowling Green, KY 42104
Ph: (270)782-1318
Dialysis Stations: 19.

Cadiz

24615 ■ Fresenius Medical Care--Trigg County
2484 Main St.
Cadiz, KY 42211
Free: 866-434-2597
URL: http://www.ultracare-dialysis.com/
Dialysis Stations: 12.

Campbellsville

24616 ■ Fresenius Medical Care--Campbellsville
107 Medical Pk. Dr.
Campbellsville, KY 42718
Free: 866-434-2597
URL: http://www.ultracare-dialysis.com/
Dialysis Stations: 13.

**24617 ■ Taylor County Dialysis
Davita**
101 Kingswood Dr.
Campbellsville, KY 42718
Ph: (270)789-4100
URL: http://www.davita.com
Dialysis Stations: 16.

Central City

**24618 ■ Dialysis Specialists of Central City
Fresenius Medical Care**
222 Phillip Stone Way
Central City, KY 42330
Free: 866-434-2597
URL: http://www.ultracare-dialysis.com/
Dialysis Stations: 14.

Cold Spring

**24619 ■ Cold Spring Dialysis
DaVita**
430 Crossroads Blvd.
Cold Spring, KY 41076
Ph: (859)441-3981
Dialysis Stations: 12.

Corbin

24620 ■ Dialysis Clinic, Inc.--Corbin
500 S Main St.
Corbin, KY 40701
Ph: (606)523-1070
URL: http://www.dciinc.org
Dialysis Stations: 16.

Covington

**24621 ■ 12th St. Covington Dialysis
DaVita**
1500 James Simpson Jr. Way, Ste. 1100
Covington, KY 41011
Free: 800-424-6589
URL: http://www.davita.com
Dialysis Stations: 17.

Crestview Hills

**24622 ■ Crestview Hills Dialysis
DaVita**
400 Centre View Blvd.
Crestview Hills, KY 41017
Free: 800-424-6589
URL: http://www.davita.com
Dialysis Stations: 23. **Formerly:** Gambro Healthcare.

Cynthiana

24623 ■ Fresenius Medical Care--Cynthiana
994 US Hwy. 27 S, Ste. 6
Cynthiana, KY 41031
Free: 866-434-2597
URL: http://www.ultracare-dialysis.com/
Dialysis Stations: 13.

Danville

24624 ■ Dialysis Clinic, Inc.--Danville
475 Whirlaway Dr.
Danville, KY 40422
Ph: (859)236-5982
URL: http://www.dciinc.org
Dialysis Stations: 21.

24625 ■ Fresenius Medical Care - Danville
975 Hustonville Rd., Ste. 1
Danville, KY 40422
Free: 866-434-2597
URL: http://www.ultracare-dialysis.com/
Dialysis Stations: 12.

Elizabethtown

24626 ■ DaVita--Woodland Dialysis Center
912 Woodland Dr., Ste. C
Elizabethtown, KY 42701
Free: 800-424-6589
URL: http://www.davita.com
Dialysis Stations: 29.

24627 ■ Fresenius Medical Care--Hardin County
1324 Woodland Dr., Ste. B
Elizabethtown, KY 42701
Free: 866-434-2597
URL: http://www.ultracare-dialysis.com/
Dialysis Stations: 12.

Florence

24628 ■ Fresenius Medical Care--Boone County
7205 Dixie Hwy.
Florence, KY 41402
Free: 866-434-2597
URL: http://www.ultracare-dialysis.com/
Dialysis Stations: 13.

24629 ■ Turfway Dialysis & PD
DaVita
11 Spiral Dr., Ste. 15A
Florence, KY 41042
Free: 800-424-6589
URL: http://www.davita.com
Dialysis Stations: 16.

Frankfort

24630 ■ Dialysis Clinic, Inc.--Frankfort
1038 Burlington Ln., Ste. B, C, & D
Frankfort, KY 40601
Ph: (502)223-5918
URL: http://www.dciinc.org
Dialysis Stations: 20.

24631 ■ Fresenius Medical Care--Frankfort
608 Chamberlin Ave.
Frankfort, KY 40601
Free: 866-434-2597
URL: http://www.ultracare-dialysis.com/
Dialysis Stations: 16.

Georgetown

24632 ■ Renal Advantage Inc.--Georgetown
98 Mary Lynn Dr.
Georgetown, KY 40324
Ph: (502)867-3855
URL: http://www.renaladvantage.com

Glasgow

24633 ■ Glasgow Kidney Center
205 Professional Park Dr.
Glasgow, KY 42141
Ph: (270)651-7776
Dialysis Stations: 15.

24634 ■ T.J. Samson Kidney Care
930 Happy Valley Rd.
Glasgow, KY 42141
Ph: (270)651-7124
Dialysis Stations: 12.

Grayson

24635 ■ Fresenius Medical Care--Grayson
286 State Hwy. 1947
Grayson, KY 41143
Free: 866-434-2597
URL: http://www.ultracare-dialysis.com/
Dialysis Stations: 15.

Greenup

24636 ■ Fresenius Medical Care--Greenup
965 Townhill Plz.
Greenup, KY 41144
Free: 866-434-2597
URL: http://www.ultracare-dialysis.com/
Dialysis Stations: 13.

Hagerhill

24637 ■ DaVita--Paintsville Dialysis
4750 Hwy. 321 S
Hagerhill, KY 41222
Free: 800-424-6589
URL: http://www.davita.com
Dialysis Stations: 12.

Harlan

24638 ■ Fresenius Medical Care--Harlan
136 Village Center Rd.
Harlan, KY 40831
Free: 800-434-2597
URL: http://www.ultracare-dialysis.com/
Dialysis Stations: 17.

Hazard

24639 ■ Fresenius Medical Care--Hazard Dialysis Facility
516 Village Ln.
Hazard, KY 41701
Free: 866-434-2597
URL: http://www.ultracare-dialysis.com/
Dialysis Stations: 16.

Henderson

24640 ■ Gardenside Dialysis
DaVita
70 N Gardenmile Rd.
Henderson, KY 42420
Free: 800-424-6589
URL: http://www.davita.com
Dialysis Stations: 15. **Formerly:** Renal Kidney Care of Henderson.

Hopkinsville

24641 ■ Christian County Dialysis
DaVita
200 Burley Ave.
Hopkinsville, KY 42240
Free: 800-424-6589
URL: http://www.davita.com
Dialysis Stations: 13. **Formerly:** Gambro Healthcare.

24642 ■ Hopkinsville Dialysis & At Home
DaVita
Dialysis Center
1914 S Virginia St.
Hopkinsville, KY 42240
Free: 800-424-6589
URL: http://www.davita.com
Dialysis Stations: 17. **Formerly:** Gambro Healthcare - Hopkinsville.

Jackson

24643 ■ Fresenius Medical Care of Jackson
1550 US Hwy. 15 S
Jackson, KY 41339
Free: 866-434-2597
URL: http://www.ultracare-dialysis.com/
Dialysis Stations: 12.

Kuttawa

24644 ■ Fresenius Medical Care--Kuttawa
95 Lakeshore Dr.
Kuttawa, KY 42055
Free: 866-434-2597
URL: http://www.ultracare-dialysis.com
Dialysis Stations: 10. **Formerly:** National Nephrology Associates - Lourdes Dialysis of Kuttawa.

La Grange

24645 ■ Fresenius Medical Care--Oldham County
2100 Button Ln., Ste. 105
La Grange, KY 40031
Free: 866-434-2597
URL: http://www.ultracare-dialysis.com/
Dialysis Stations: 16.

24646 ■ La Grange Dialysis Center
DaVita
240 Parker Dr.
La Grange, KY 40031
Free: 800-424-6589
URL: http://www.davita.com
Dialysis Stations: 12.

Lebanon

24647 ■ Fresenius Medical Care--Lebanon Marion County
703 E Main St., Ste. 2
Lebanon, KY 40033
Free: 866-434-2597
URL: http://www.ultracare-dialysis.com/
Dialysis Stations: 10.

Leitchfield

24648 ■ Leitchfield Dialysis
DaVita
912 Wallace Ave., Ste. 106
Leitchfield, KY 42754
Free: 800-424-6589
URL: http://www.davita.com
Dialysis Stations: 10.

Lexington

24649 ■ Dialysis Clinic, Inc.--Lexington
100 Venture Court
Lexington, KY 40511
Ph: (859)252-7712
URL: http://www.dciinc.org
Dialysis Stations: 32.

24650 ■ Dialysis Clinic Inc.--Southland
2374 Professional Heights Dr.
Lexington, KY 40503
Ph: (859)967-0400
URL: http://www.dciinc.org
Dialysis Stations: 23.

24651 ■ Fresenius Medical Care--Lexington East
1101 Winchester Rd., Ste. 100
Lexington, KY 40505
Free: 866-434-2597
URL: http://www.ultracare-dialysis.com/
Dialysis Stations: 16. **Formerly:** Renal Care Group/Kentucky Renal Care Group.

24652 ■ Fresenius Medical Care--Lexington North
1610 Leestown Rd., Ste. 180
Lexington, KY 40511
Free: 866-434-2597
URL: http://www.ultracare-dialysis.com/
Dialysis Stations: 25. **Formerly:** Renal Care Group.

24653 ■ Fresenius Medical Care--Lexington South
171 N Eagle Creek Dr., Ste. 110
Lexington, KY 40509
Free: 866-434-2597
URL: http://www.ultracare-dialysis.com/
Dialysis Stations: 16. **Formerly:** Renal Care Group.

24654 ■ Hamburg Dialysis
DaVita
1745 Alysheba Way, Ste. 110
Lexington, KY 40509

Free: 800-424-6589
URL: http://www.davita.com
Dialysis Stations: 12.

24655 ■ Kentucky Children's Hospital
800 Rose St., MN-109
Lexington, KY 40536
Ph: (859)257-1552
URL: http://ukhealthcare.uky.edu/kch/
Dialysis Stations: 0.

24656 ■ Kentucky Nephrology
1101 Winchester Rd., Ste. 200
Lexington, KY 40505
Ph: (859)225-4595
Dialysis Stations: 3.

24657 ■ Nalco, LLC
Dialysis Center
1591 Winchester Rd., Ste. 102
Lexington, KY 40505
Ph: (859)299-3379
Dialysis Stations: 3.

London

24658 ■ London Dialysis Clinic
Renal Advantage Inc.
775 N Laurel Rd.
London, KY 40741
Ph: (606)862-8888
URL: http://www.renaladvantage.com
Dialysis Stations: 12. **Formerly:** Renal Health Dialysis Center.

Louisa

24659 ■ Louisa--Fort Gay Regional Dialysis
2145 Hwy. 2565
Louisa, KY 41230
Ph: (606)638-3403
Dialysis Stations: 15.

Louisville

24660 ■ DaVita--Louisville Dialysis
8037 Dixie Hwy.
Louisville, KY 40258
Free: 800-424-6589
URL: http://www.davita.com
Dialysis Stations: 20.

24661 ■ DSI--Louisville
Dialysis Facility
635 S 3rd St.
Louisville, KY 40202
Ph: (502)561-1314
URL: http://www.dsi-corp.com
Dialysis Stations: 16. **Formerly:** Renal Care Group.

24662 ■ Fresenius Medical Care/Dialysis Services of Audubon
2355 Poplar Level Rd., Ste. G 2-10
Louisville, KY 40217
Free: 866-434-2597
URL: http://www.ultracare-dialysis.com/
Dialysis Stations: 25.

24663 ■ Fresenius Medical Care--East Louisville
Dialysis Facility
5620 Bardstown Rd.
Louisville, KY 40291
Free: 866-434-2597
URL: http://www.ultracare-dialysis.com/
Dialysis Stations: 12.

24664 ■ Fresenius Medical Care--Northeast Louisville
3701 Chamberlain La.
Louisville, KY 40241
Free: 866-434-2597
URL: http://www.ultracare-dialysis.com/
Dialysis Stations: 12.

24665 ■ Fresenius Medical Care--South Central Louisville
8319 Preston Hwy., Ste. C,D.E
Louisville, KY 40219
Free: 866-434-2597
URL: http://www.ultracare-dialysis.com/
Dialysis Stations: 16.

24666 ■ Fresenius Medical Care--South Louisville
Dialysis Facility
1514 Crum Ln.
Louisville, KY 40216
Free: 866-434-2597
URL: http://www.ultracare-dialysis.com/
Dialysis Stations: 24.

24667 ■ Fresenius Medical Care--Suburban Louisville
Dialysis Facility
3991 Dutchmans Ln., Ste. G-02
Louisville, KY 40207
Free: 866-434-2597
URL: http://www.ultracare-dialysis.com/
Dialysis Stations: 21.

24668 ■ Fresenius Medical Care--West Louisville
Dialysis Facility
2600 W Broadway, Ste. 112
Louisville, KY 40211
Free: 866-434-2597
URL: http://www.ultracare-dialysis.com/
Dialysis Stations: 18.

24669 ■ Jewish Hospital Renal Dialysis--Acute Dialysis
200 Abraham Flexner Way
Louisville, KY 40202
Ph: (502)587-4688
URL: http://www.jhsmh.org/Locations/Jewish-Hospital.aspx
Dialysis Stations: 8.

24670 ■ Meadows East Dialysis
DaVita
2529 6 Mile Ln., Ste. B
Louisville, KY 40220
Free: 800-424-6589
URL: http://www.davita.com
Dialysis Stations: 10.

24671 ■ Springhurst Dialysis Center
DaVita
10201 Champion Farms Dr.
Louisville, KY 40241
Free: 800-424-6589
URL: http://www.davita.com
Dialysis Stations: 18.

24672 ■ University of Louisville
Kidney Disease Program
615 S Preston St.
Louisville, KY 40202
Ph: (502)852-5757
URL: http://www.kdp_baptist.louisville.edu/
Dialysis Stations: 31.

24673 ■ West Broadway Dialysis & At Home
DaVita
720 W Broadway
Louisville, KY 40202
Free: 800-424-6589
URL: http://www.davita.com
Dialysis Stations: 24.

24674 ■ West Broadway Dialysis
Fresenius Medical Care
Dialysis Facility
720 W Broadway St.
Louisville, KY 40202
Free: 866-434-2597
URL: http://www.ultracare-dialysis.com/
Dialysis Stations: 24.

Madisonville

24675 ■ Madisonville Dialysis Center
DaVita
435 N Kentucky Ave., Ste. B
Madisonville, KY 42431
Free: 800-424-6589
URL: http://www.davita.com
Dialysis Stations: 20. **Formerly:** Renal Dialysis Center.

Mayfield

24676 ■ Fresenius Medical Care--Mayfield
1029 Medical Center Cir., Ste. 301
Mayfield, KY 42066
Free: 866-434-2597
URL: http://www.ultracare-dialysis.com/
Dialysis Stations: 13. **Formerly:** NNA/Lourdes Dialysis of Mayfield.

Maysville

24677 ■ Dialysis Clinic, Inc.--Maysville
1210 Pope Dr.
Maysville, KY 41056
Ph: (606)759-7689
URL: http://www.dciinc.org
Dialysis Stations: 13.

24678 ■ Maysville At Home--Kentucky
DaVita
489 Tucker Dr.
Maysville, KY 41056
Free: 800-424-6589
URL: http://www.davita.com
Dialysis Stations: 12.

Mdisonville

24679 ■ Madisonville Dialysis
Fresenius Medical Care
1020 Waterfall Ct.
Mdisonville, KY 42431
Free: 866-434-2597
URL: http://www.ultracare-dialysis.com/
Dialysis Stations: 17.

Morehead

24680 ■ Fresenius Medical Care--Morehead
Dialysis Facility
250 Norman Wells Ln.
Morehead, KY 40351
Free: 866-434-2597
URL: http://www.ultracare-dialysis.com/
Dialysis Stations: 16.

Mount Sterling

24681 ■ Fresenius Medical Care--Mount Sterling
75 Sterling Way
Mount Sterling, KY 40353
Free: 866-434-2597
URL: http://www.ultracare-dialysis.com/
Dialysis Stations: 12.

Murray

24682 ■ Fresenius Medical Care--Murray
Dialysis Facility
609 S 12th St.
Murray, KY 42071
Free: 866-434-2597
URL: http://www.ultracare-dialysis.com/
Dialysis Stations: 13. **Formerly:** National Nephrology Associates - Lourdes Dialysis of Murray.

Nicholasville

24683 ■ Fresenius Medical Care--Nicholasville
115 Orchard Pl.
Nicholasville, KY 40355
Free: 866-434-2597
URL: http://www.ultracare-dialysis.com/
Dialysis Stations: 17.

Owensboro

24684 ■ Owensboro Dialysis Center
DaVita
1930 E Parrish Ave.
Owensboro, KY 42303
Free: 800-424-6589
URL: http://www.davita.com
Dialysis Stations: 25.

Paducah

24685 ■ Fresenius Medical Care----Paducah Dialysis Center
1532 Lone Oak Rd., Ste. G-15
Paducah, KY 42003
Free: 866-434-2597
URL: http://www.ultracare-dialysis.com
Dialysis Stations: 26. **Formerly:** National Nephrology Associates - Lourdes Dialysis of Paducah.

24686 ■ Fresenius Medical Care--Paducah South
1061 Husband Rd.
Paducah, KY 42003
Free: 866-434-2597
URL: http://www.ultracare-dialysis.com/
Dialysis Stations: 16. **Formerly:** Renal Care Group/ Lourdes Dialysis.

Paintsville

24687 ■ Fresenius Medical Care--Paintsville
620 Jefferson Ave.
Paintsville, KY 41240
Free: 866-434-2597
URL: http://www.ultracare-dialysis.com/
Dialysis Stations: 16.

Paris

24688 ■ Bourbon County Dialysis
DaVita
213 Letton Dr.
Paris, KY 40361
Free: 800-424-6589
URL: http://www.davita.com
Dialysis Stations: 8.

Pikeville

24689 ■ Eastern Kentucky Dialysis
DaVita
167 Weddington Branch Rd.
Pikeville, KY 41501
Free: 800-424-6589
URL: http://www.davita.com
Dialysis Stations: 12.

24690 ■ Fresenius Medical Care--Pikeville
146 Adams La.
Pikeville, KY 41501
Free: 866-434-2597
URL: http://www.ultracare-dialysis.com/
Dialysis Stations: 21.

Prestonsburg

24691 ■ Fresenius Medical Care--Prestonsburg
Dialysis Facility
61 Dewey St.
Prestonsburg, KY 41653
Free: 866-434-2597
URL: http://www.ultracare-dialysis.com/
Dialysis Stations: 15.

Princeton

24692 ■ Caldwell County Dialysis
Renal Advantage Inc.
401 S Jefferson
Princeton, KY 42445
Ph: (270)365-7588
URL: http://www.renaladvantage.com
Dialysis Stations: 16. **Formerly:** National Renal Alliance.

Richmond

24693 ■ Dialysis Clinic Inc.--Richmond
100 Keystone Dr.
Richmond, KY 40475
Ph: (859)625-0939
URL: http://www.dciinc.org
Dialysis Stations: 15.

24694 ■ Fresenius Medical Care--Central Richmond
Dialysis Facility
793 Eastern Bypass Medical Bldg. 3, Ste. G-04
Richmond, KY 40475
Free: 866-434-2597
URL: http://www.ultracare-dialysis.com/
Dialysis Stations: 14.

Shelbyville

24695 ■ Fresenius Medical Care--Shelbyville, Kentucky
Dialysis Facility
1900 Midland Trl.
Shelbyville, KY 40065
Free: 866-434-2597
URL: http://www.ultracare-dialysis.com/
Dialysis Stations: 12.

Shepherdsville

24696 ■ Fresenius Medical Care--Shepherdsville
421 Adam Shepherd Pkwy.
Shepherdsville, KY 40165
Free: 866-434-2597
URL: http://www.ultracare-dialysis.com/
Dialysis Stations: 12.

Somerset

24697 ■ Fresenius Medical Care--Somerset
119 Trade Park Dr.
Somerset, KY 42503
Free: 866-434-2597
URL: http://www.ultracare-dialysis.com/
Dialysis Stations: 20.

South Williamson

24698 ■ DaVita
South Williamson Dialysis
204 Appalachian Plz.
South Williamson, KY 41503
Free: 800-424-6589
URL: http://www.davita.com

Southgate

24699 ■ South Hill Dialysis
DaVita
Dialysis Facility
525 Alexandria Pike, Ste. 120
Southgate, KY 41071
Free: 800-424-6589
URL: http://www.davita.com
Dialysis Stations: 16. **Formerly:** Gambro Healthcare - South Hill.

Valley Station

24700 ■ Fresenius Medical Care--Rockford Lane
9616 Dixie Hwy.
Valley Station, KY 40272
Free: 866-434-2597
URL: http://www.ultracare-dialysis.com/
Dialysis Stations: 24.

Whitesburg

24701 ■ Whitesburg Dialysis
DaVita
2221 Hospital Rd., Ste. D
Whitesburg, KY 41858
Free: 800-424-6589
URL: http://www.davita.com
Dialysis Stations: 10.

Williamstown

24702 ■ Williamstown Dialysis
DaVita
103 Barnes Rd., Ste. A
Williamstown, KY 41097
Free: 800-424-6589
URL: http://www.davita.com
Dialysis Stations: 12.

Winchester

24703 ■ Fresenius Medical Care--Winchester, Kentucky
1145 W Lexington Ave.
Winchester, KY 40391
Free: 866-434-2597
URL: http://www.ultracare-dialysis.com/
Dialysis Stations: 16.

LOUISIANA

Abbeville

24704 ■ Fresenius Medical Care--Abbeville Dialysis Facility
904 N John Hardy Dr.
Abbeville, LA 70510
Free: 866-434-2597
URL: http://www.ultracare-dialysis.com/
Dialysis Stations: 12.

Alexandria

24705 ■ Fresenius Medical Care--Alexandria Dialysis Services
225 N Bolton Ave.
Alexandria, LA 71301
Free: 866-434-2597
URL: http://www.ultracare-dialysis.com/
Dialysis Stations: 23.

24706 ■ Fresenius Medical Care--South Alexandria
Dialysis Services
1915 Beatrice St.
Alexandria, LA 71301
Free: 866-434-2597
URL: http://www.ultracare-dialysis.com/
Dialysis Stations: 23.

Amite

24707 ■ Fresenius Medical Care--Amite Dialysis Services
110 N 1st St.
Amite, LA 70422
Free: 866-434-2597
URL: http://www.ultracare-dialysis.com/
Dialysis Stations: 13.

Avondale

24708 ■ Fresenius Medical Care--Avondale Dialysis Services
141 S Jamie Blvd.
Avondale, LA 70094
Free: 866-434-2597
URL: http://www.ultracare-dialysis.com/
Dialysis Stations: 16.

Bastrop

24709 ■ Morehouse Parish Dialysis Center, LLC
Fresenius Medical Care
530 Durham St.
Bastrop, LA 71220
Ph: (318)281-3725
URL: http://www.ultracare-dialysis.com/
Dialysis Stations: 20.

24710 ■ Morehouse Parish Dialysis
Fresenius Medical Care
530 Durham St.
Bastrop, LA 71220
Free: 866-434-2597
URL: http://www.ultracare-dialysis.com/

Baton Rouge

24711 ■ Baton Rouge Renal Center & At Home
DaVita
3888 North Blvd.
Baton Rouge, LA 70808
Free: 800-424-6589
URL: http://www.davita.com
Dialysis Stations: 16.

24712 ■ Diversified Specialty Institutes--Baton Rouge
Dialysis Facility
1333 O'Neal Ln.
Baton Rouge, LA 70816
Ph: (225)226-1440
Fax: (225)226-1450
URL: http://www.dsi-corp.com
Dialysis Stations: 16. **Formerly:** National Nephrology Associates.

24713 ■ Foster Drive Dialysis Services
Fresenius Medical Care--West Baton Rouge
1919 N Foster Dr.
Baton Rouge, LA 70806
Free: 866-434-2597
URL: http://www.ultracare-dialysis.com/
Dialysis Stations: 20.

24714 ■ Fresenius Medical Care--Airline
Dialysis Services
5948 Airline Hwy.
Baton Rouge, LA 70805
Free: 866-434-2597
URL: http://www.ultracare-dialysis.com/
Dialysis Stations: 29.

24715 ■ Fresenius Medical Care--Baton Rouge
Dialysis Services
524 Colonial Dr.
Baton Rouge, LA 70806
Free: 866-434-2597
URL: http://www.ultracare-dialysis.com/
Dialysis Stations: 20.

24716 ■ Fresenius Medical Care--Bon Carre
7656 Realtors Ave.
Baton Rouge, LA 70806
Free: 866-434-2597
URL: http://www.ultracare-dialysis.com/
Dialysis Stations: 20.

24717 ■ Fresenius Medical Care--Howell Place
7707 Howell Pl. Blvd.
Baton Rouge, LA 70807
Free: 866-434-2597
URL: http://www.ultracare-dialysis.com/
Dialysis Stations: 21.

24718 ■ Fresenius Medical Care--Mancuso
4848 Mancuso Ln., Ste. A
Baton Rouge, LA 70809
Free: 866-434-2597
URL: http://www.ultracare-dialysis.com/
Dialysis Stations: 22.

24719 ■ Fresenius Medical Care--North Baton Rouge--Airport
Dialysis Services
12230 Plank Rd.
Baton Rouge, LA 70811
Free: 866-434-2597
URL: http://www.ultracare-dialysis.com/
Dialysis Stations: 24.

24720 ■ Fresenius Medical Care--North Boulevard
Dialysis Services
2661 North Blvd.
Baton Rouge, LA 70806
Free: 866-434-2597
URL: http://www.ultracare-dialysis.com/
Dialysis Stations: 20.

24721 ■ Fresenius Medical Care--Picardy
7638 Picardy Ave., Ste. A
Baton Rouge, LA 70808
Free: 866-434-2597
URL: http://www.ultracare-dialysis.com/
Dialysis Stations: 20.

Bogalusa

24722 ■ DaVita--Bogalusa Kidney Care
2108 South Ave. F
Bogalusa, LA 70427
Free: 800-424-6589
URL: http://www.davita.com
Dialysis Stations: 15.

Bossier City

24723 ■ Bossier Regional Dialysis Center
Fresenius Medical Care
2907 Plantation Dr.
Bossier City, LA 71111
Free: 866-434-2597
URL: http://www.ultracare-dialysis.com/
Dialysis Stations: 20.

24724 ■ Fresenius Medical Care--South Bossier
3087 Stafford St.
Bossier City, LA 71112
Free: 866-434-2597
URL: http://www.ultracare-dialysis.com/
Dialysis Stations: 12.

Breaux Bridge

24725 ■ Fresenius Medical Care--Breaux Bridge
Bldg. A
100 Champagne Blvd., Bldg. A
Breaux Bridge, LA 70517
Free: 866-434-2597
URL: http://www.ultracare-dialysis.com/
Dialysis Stations: 12.

Bunkie

24726 ■ Fresenius Medical Care--Bunkie
Dialysis Services
102 Standard St.
Bunkie, LA 71322
Free: 866-434-2597
URL: http://www.ultracare-dialysis.com/
Dialysis Stations: 20.

Chalmette

24727 ■ Chalmette Dialysis Center
4020 Paris Rd.
Chalmette, LA 70043
Ph: (504)277-8423
Dialysis Stations: 10.

Columbia

24728 ■ Fresenius Medical Care--Caldwell Parish
Dialysis Services
7720 Hwy. 165, Ste. 3
Columbia, LA 71418
Free: 866-434-2597
URL: http://www.ultracare-dialysis.com/
Dialysis Stations: 8.

Coushatta

24729 ■ Fresenius Medical Care--Coushatta
501 Wilkinson St.
Coushatta, LA 71019
Free: 866-434-2597
URL: http://www.ultracare-dialysis.com/
Dialysis Stations: 16.

Covington

24730 ■ Dialysis Systems of Covington
DaVita
210 Greenbrier Blvd.
Covington, LA 70433
Free: 800-424-6589
URL: http://www.davita.com
Dialysis Stations: 12.

24731 ■ Fresenius Medical Care--Ponchartrain Kidney Center
170 Greenbriar Dr., Ste. A
Covington, LA 70433
Free: 866-434-2597
URL: http://www.ultracare-dialysis.com/
Dialysis Stations: 16.

Crowley

24732 ■ Dialysis Clinic Inc.--Crowley
1325 Wright Ave., Ste. B
Crowley, LA 70526
Ph: (337)788-1990
URL: http://www.dciinc.org
Dialysis Stations: 17.

24733 ■ Fresenius Medical Care--Crowley
Dialysis Center
625 E 8th St.
Crowley, LA 70526
Free: 866-434-2597
URL: http://www.ultracare-dialysis.com/
Dialysis Stations: 15.

Cut Off

24734 ■ Lady of the Sea Dialysis Center
Lady of the Sea General Hospital
17108 W Main Pl.
Cut Off, LA 70345
Ph: (985)632-4900
URL: http://www.losgh.org/services_renaldialysis.php
Dialysis Stations: 10.

DeRidder

24735 ■ DVA Renal Healthcare--DeRidder Dialysis
DaVita
239 E 1st St.
DeRidder, LA 70634
Free: 800-424-6589
URL: http://www.davita.com
Dialysis Stations: 11. **Formerly:** Gambro Healthcare.

Delhi

24736 ■ Fresenius Medical Care--Delhi Dialysis Center
307 Detroit St.
Delhi, LA 71232
Free: 866-434-2597
URL: http://www.ultracare-dialysis.com/
Dialysis Stations: 14.

Delta

24737 ■ Fresenius Medical Care--Delta Dialysis Facility
104 Railroad Ave.
Delta, LA 71233
Free: 866-434-2597
URL: http://www.ultracare-dialysis.com/
Dialysis Stations: 16. **Formerly:** National Nephrology Associates.

Denham Springs

24738 ■ DaVita--Denham Springs
26737 Hwy. 1032
Denham Springs, LA 70726
Free: 800-424-6589
URL: http://www.davita.com
Dialysis Stations: 12.

24739 ■ Fresenius Medical Care--Denham Springs
137 Veterans Blvd.
Denham Springs, LA 70726
Free: 866-434-2597
URL: http://www.ultracare-dialysis.com/
Dialysis Stations: 21.

Donaldsonville

24740 ■ DVA Renal Healthcare--Donaldsonville Dialysis
DaVita
101 Plimsol Dr.
Donaldsonville, LA 70346
Free: 800-424-6589
URL: http://www.davita.com
Dialysis Stations: 16. **Formerly:** Gambro Healthcare.

Eunice

24741 ■ Dialysis Clinic, Inc.--Eunice
2440 W Laurel Ave.
Eunice, LA 70535
Ph: (337)457-0005
URL: http://www.dciinc.org
Dialysis Stations: 16.

24742 ■ Fresenius Medical Care--Eunice Dialysis Facility
1101 Nile St.
Eunice, LA 70535
Free: 866-434-2597
URL: http://www.ultracare-dialysis.com/
Dialysis Stations: 12.

Farmerville

24743 ■ Fresenius Medical Care--Farmerville Dialysis Services
108 Hill St.
Farmerville, LA 71241
Free: 866-434-2597
URL: http://www.ultracare-dialysis.com/
Dialysis Stations: 12.

24744 ■ Fresenius Medical Care--Union Parish Dialysis Center
1012 Sterlington Hwy.
Farmerville, LA 71241
Ph: (318)368-1071
Dialysis Stations: 12. **Formerly:** Gambro Healthcare.

Ferriday

24745 ■ Fresenius Medical Care--Ferriday Dialysis Facility
1618 E Wallace Blvd.
Ferriday, LA 71334
Free: 866-434-2597
URL: http://www.ultracare-dialysis.com/
Dialysis Stations: 19. **Formerly:** Renal Care Group.

Franklin

24746 ■ Fresenius Medical Care--Franklin, Louisiana Dialysis Services
1604 Cynthia St.
Franklin, LA 70538
Free: 866-434-2597
URL: http://www.ultracare-dialysis.com/
Dialysis Stations: 12.

Franklinton

24747 ■ Fresenius Medical Care--Franklinton
806 B Riverside Dr.
Franklinton, LA 70438
Free: 866-434-2597
URL: http://www.ultracare-dialysis.com/
Dialysis Stations: 13. **Formerly:** Riverside Kidney Center.

24748 ■ Washington Parish Dialysis
DaVita
724 Washington St.
Franklinton, LA 70438
Free: 800-424-6589
URL: http://www.davita.com
Dialysis Stations: 14.

Gonzales

24749 ■ DaVita--Magnolia Dialysis Facility
210 E Spillman Rd.
Gonzales, LA 70737
Free: 800-424-6589
URL: http://www.davita.com
Dialysis Stations: 14. **Formerly:** Gambro Healthcare--Gonzales.

Gramercy

24750 ■ St. James Dialysis
1661 Hwy. 3125
Gramercy, LA 70052
Ph: (225)869-6681
Dialysis Stations: 10.

Gretna

24751 ■ Dialysis Clinic, Inc.--Westbank--Gretna
1010 Behrman Hwy.
Gretna, LA 70056
Ph: (504)391-9572
URL: http://www.dciinc.org
Dialysis Stations: 22.

24752 ■ Oakwood Dialysis & At Home
DaVita
148 Hector Ave.
Gretna, LA 70056
Free: 800-424-6589
URL: http://www.davita.com
Dialysis Stations: 12.

Hammond

24753 ■ Dialysis Systems of Hammond
DaVita
15799 Professional Plz.
Hammond, LA 70403
Free: 800-424-6589
URL: http://www.davita.com
Dialysis Stations: 13.

24754 ■ Florida Parish Kidney Center
Fresenius Medical Care Dialysis Services
16081 Doctors Blvd., Ste. A
Hammond, LA 70403
Free: 866-434-2597
URL: http://www.ultracare-dialysis.com/
Dialysis Stations: 23.

24755 ■ Quality Care Dialysis--Hammond
Fresenius Medical Care
1204 S Morrison Blvd., Ste. A
Hammond, LA 70403
Free: 866-434-2597
URL: http://www.ultracare-dialysis.com/
Dialysis Stations: 14.

Harvey

24756 ■ Marrero Dialysis
DaVita
1908 Jutland Dr.
Harvey, LA 70058
Free: 800-424-6589
URL: http://www.davita.com
Dialysis Stations: 17.

Homer

24757 ■ Fresenius Medical Care--Homer
3680 Hwy. 79
Homer, LA 71040
Free: 866-434-2597
URL: http://www.ultracare-dialysis.com/
Dialysis Stations: 12.

Houma

24758 ■ Diversified Specialty Institutes--Houma Dialysis Center
108 Picone Rd.
Houma, LA 70363
Ph: (985)868-8187
URL: http://www.dsi-corp.com
Dialysis Stations: 15. **Formerly:** National Nephrology Associates.

24759 ■ Fresenius Medical Care--Houma Dialysis Services
800 Point St.
Houma, LA 70360
Free: 866-434-2597
URL: http://www.ultracare-dialysis.com/
Dialysis Stations: 25.

Independence

24760 ■ Independence Renal Center
DaVita
12392 Hwy. 40
Independence, LA 70443
Free: 800-424-6589
URL: http://www.davita.com
Dialysis Stations: 12.

Jackson

24761 ■ Felicianas Dialysis Center
Fresenius Medical Care
2995 Race St.
Jackson, LA 70748
Free: 866-434-2597
URL: http://www.ultracare-dialysis.com/
Dialysis Stations: 17.

Jennings

24762 ■ Dialysis Clinic Inc.--Jennings
1322 Elton Rd., Ste. C
Jennings, LA 70546
Ph: (337)616-8232
URL: http://www.dciinc.org
Dialysis Stations: 16.

24763 ■ Fresenius Medical Care--Jennings Dialysis Services
1906 Johnson St.
Jennings, LA 70546
Free: 866-434-2597
URL: http://www.ultracare-dialysis.com/
Dialysis Stations: 12.

Kenner

24764 ■ Chateau Dialysis
DVA Renal Healthcare
DaVita
720 Village Rd.
Kenner, LA 70065
Free: 800-424-6589
URL: http://www.davita.com
Dialysis Stations: 16. **Formerly:** Gambro Healthcare--Kenner.

24765 ■ Fresenius Medical Care--Kenner Dialysis
2717 Decatur St.
Kenner, LA 20.
Free: 866-434-2597
URL: http://www.ultracare-dialysis.com/
Dialysis Stations: 20.

24766 ■ Kenner Regional Dialysis
DaVita
200 W Esplanade, Ste. 100
Kenner, LA 70065
Free: 800-424-6589
URL: http://www.davita.com
Dialysis Stations: 14.

Kentwood

24767 ■ Fresenius Medical Care--Kentwood
916 Ave. G
Kentwood, LA 70444
Free: 866-434-2597
URL: http://www.ultracare-dialysis.com/
Dialysis Stations: 12.

La Place

24768 ■ LaPlace Dialysis Center
2700 W Airline Hwy.
La Place, LA 70068
Ph: (985)536-7860
Dialysis Stations: 18.

24769 ■ River Parishes Dialysis
DaVita
2880 W Airline Hwy.
La Place, LA 70068
Free: 800-424-6589
URL: http://www.davita.com
Dialysis Stations: 12.

Lacombe

24770 ■ Fresenius Medical Care--Lacombe
64026 Hwy. 434, Ste. 100
Lacombe, LA 70445
Free: 866-434-2597
URL: http://www.ultracare-dialysis.com/
Dialysis Stations: 13.

Lafayette

24771 ■ Fresenius Medical Care--East Lafayette
1340 Surrey
Lafayette, LA 70501
Free: 866-434-2597
URL: http://www.ultracare-dialysis.com/
Dialysis Stations: 16.

24772 ■ Fresenius Medical Care--North Lafayette
Dialysis Services
910 Martin Luther King Jr. Dr.
Lafayette, LA 70501
Free: 866-434-2597
URL: http://www.ultracare-dialysis.com/
Dialysis Stations: 18.

24773 ■ Fresenius Medical Care--West Lafayette
2804 Ambassador Caffery Pkwy.
Lafayette, LA 70506
Free: 866-434-2597
URL: http://www.ultracare-dialysis.com/
Dialysis Stations: 25.

24774 ■ Kidney Care of Acadiana--Lafayette
224 St. Landry, Ste. 3C
Lafayette, LA 70506
Ph: (337)231-5511
Dialysis Stations: 10.

Lake Charles

24775 ■ Davita--Lake Charles Southwest Dialysis
Dialysis Center
433 Dr. Mmichael Debakey Dr.
Lake Charles, LA 70601
Free: 800-424-6589
URL: http://www.davita.com
Dialysis Stations: 17. **Formerly:** Gambro Healthcare.

24776 ■ DVA Renal Healthcare--Lake Charles Southwest
433 Dr. Michael DeBakey Dr.
Lake Charles, LA 70601
Ph: (337)494-1330
Dialysis Stations: 17. **Formerly:** Gambro Healthcare.

24777 ■ Lake Charles Dialysis Center
1801 Oak Park Blvd.
Lake Charles, LA 70601
Ph: (337)478-9585
Dialysis Stations: 15.

Leesville

24778 ■ Leesville Dialysis
Fresenius Medical Care
900 N 5th St., Ste. 5
Leesville, LA 71446
Free: 866-434-2597
URL: http://www.ultracare-dialysis.com/
Dialysis Stations: 12.

Luling

24779 ■ River Bend Dialysis
Saint Charles Parish Hospital
Dialysis Center
1057 Paul Maillard Rd.
Luling, LA 70070
Ph: (985)785-3688
URL: http://www.stch.net/in_patient_services.htm#dialysis
Dialysis Stations: 8.

Madisonville

24780 ■ Renal South of St. Tammany
397 Hwy. 21, Ste. 602
Madisonville, LA 70447
Ph: (985)792-5334
Dialysis Stations: 18.

Mamou

24781 ■ Fresenius Medical Care--Mamou
801 Poinciana Ave.
Mamou, LA 70554
Free: 866-434-2597
URL: http://www.ultracare-dialysis.com/
Dialysis Stations: 7.

Mansfield

24782 ■ Desoto Dialysis
Fresenius Medical Care
1410 McArthur Dr.
Mansfield, LA 71052
Free: 866-434-2597
URL: http://www.ultracare-dialysis.com/
Dialysis Stations: 24.

Many

24783 ■ Fresenius Medical Care--Many
100 Devera Dr.
Many, LA 71449
Free: 866-434-2597
URL: http://www.ultracare-dialysis.com/
Dialysis Stations: 16.

Marrero

24784 ■ Fresenius Medical Care--Barataria
1849 Baratoria Blvd., Ste. A
Marrero, LA 70072
Free: 866-434-2597
URL: http://www.ultracare-dialysis.com/
Dialysis Stations: 23.

24785 ■ Fresenius Medical Care--Marrero Dialysis Services
1111 Medical Center Blvd., Ste. S-150
Marrero, LA 70072
Free: 866-434-2597
URL: http://www.ultracare-dialysis.com/
Dialysis Stations: 23.

24786 ■ Fresenius Medical Care--Westbank
4899 Westbank Expy., Ste. B
Marrero, LA 70072
Free: 866-434-2597
URL: http://www.ultracare-dialysis.com/
Dialysis Stations: 12. **Formerly:** Renal Care Group.

Metairie

24787 ■ DaVita--Metairie
7100 Airline Dr.
Metairie, LA 70003
Free: 800-424-6589
URL: http://www.davita.com
Dialysis Stations: 12.

24788 ■ Fresenius Medical Care--Metairie Dialysis Services
4425 Utica St.
Metairie, LA 70006
Free: 866-434-2597
URL: http://www.ultracare-dialysis.com/
Dialysis Stations: 20.

24789 ■ Metairie Kidney Center
4424 Conlin St., Ste. 1A
Metairie, LA 70006
Ph: (504)887-8319
Dialysis Stations: 8.

Minden

24790 ■ Fresenius Medical Care--East Minden
10000 Industrial Rd.
Minden, LA 71055
Free: 866-434-2597
URL: http://www.ultracare-dialysis.com/
Dialysis Stations: 22.

24791 ■ Minden Dialysis
Fresenius Medical Care
610 Fleming Ln.
Minden, LA 71055
Free: 866-434-2597
URL: http://www.ultracare-dialysis.com/
Dialysis Stations: 20.

Monroe

24792 ■ Fresenius Medical Care--Monroe Dialysis Facility
1501 Southern Ave.
Monroe, LA 71202
Free: 866-434-2597
URL: http://www.ultracare-dialysis.com/
Dialysis Stations: 16.

24793 ■ Fresenius Medical Care--North Monroe Dialysis Center
2344 Sterlington Rd.
Monroe, LA 71203
Ph: (318)699-0001
URL: http://www.ultracare-dialysis.com/
Dialysis Stations: 16. **Formerly:** Gambro Healthcare.

24794 ■ Fresenius Medical Care Northeast Louisiana Dialysis Center
711 Wood St., Ste. B
Monroe, LA 71201
Free: 866-434-2597
URL: http://www.ultracare-dialysis.com/
Dialysis Stations: 25.

Morgan City

24795 ■ Fresenius Medical Care--Morgan City
7552-A Hwy. 182 E
Morgan City, LA 70380
Free: 866-434-2597
URL: http://www.ultracare-dialysis.com/
Dialysis Stations: 8.

24796 ■ Morgan City Dialysis Center
1224 David Dr.
Morgan City, LA 70380
Ph: (985)385-4213
Dialysis Stations: 12.

Natchitoches

24797 ■ FMCNA--Natchitoches DX Dialysis Facility
700 Keyser Rd.
Natchitoches, LA 71457
Free: 866-434-2597
URL: http://www.ultracare-dialysis.com/
Dialysis Stations: 16.

24798 ■ Fresenius Medical Care--East Natchitoches Dialysis Services
111 Masonic Dr.
Natchitoches, LA 71458
Free: 866-434-2597
URL: http://www.ultracare-dialysis.com/
Dialysis Stations: 22.

New Iberia

24799 ■ Fresenius Medical Care--New Iberia Dialysis Services
609 Rue de Brille
New Iberia, LA 70563
Free: 866-434-2597
URL: http://www.ultracare-dialysis.com/
Dialysis Stations: 32.

24800 ■ Kidney Care of Acadiana--New Iberia Dialysis Facility
902-A S Lewis Ave.
New Iberia, LA 70560
Ph: (337)367-3995
Dialysis Stations: 15.

New Orleans

24801 ■ Bienville Dialysis Center North
3333 Bienville St., Ste. 1B-C
New Orleans, LA 70119
Ph: (504)822-6336
Dialysis Stations: 12.

24802 ■ Children's Hospital Dialysis Center
200 Henry Clay Ave.
New Orleans, LA 70118
Ph: (504)896-2061
URL: http://www.chnola.org
Dialysis Stations: 8.

24803 ■ Crescent City Dialysis Center DaVita
3909 Bienville St., Ste. 1B
New Orleans, LA 70119
Free: 800-424-6589
URL: http://www.davita.com
Dialysis Stations: 17.

24804 ■ Dialysis Clinic Inc.--New Orleans
1400 Canal St.
New Orleans, LA 70112
Ph: (504)593-9895
Fax: (504)592-2393
URL: http://www.dciinc.org

24805 ■ Dialysis Clinic Inc.--New Orleans East
5571 Read Blvd.
New Orleans, LA 70128
Ph: (504)242-3770
Fax: (504)242-9937
URL: http://www.dciinc.org
Dialysis Stations: 16.

24806 ■ DVA Renal Healthcare--New Orleans Uptown Dialysis DaVita
1401 Foucher St., 4th Fl.
New Orleans, LA 70115
Free: 800-424-6589
URL: http://www.davita.com
Dialysis Stations: 20. **Formerly:** Gambro Healthcare.

24807 ■ Fleur de Lis Dialysis DaVita
5555 Bullard Ave., Ste. 110
New Orleans, LA 70128
Free: 800-424-6589
URL: http://www.davita.com
Dialysis Stations: 20.

24808 ■ Fresenius Medical Care--New Orleans Dialysis Center
1319 Jefferson Hwy., 2nd Fl.
New Orleans, LA 70121
Free: 866-434-2597
URL: http://www.ultracare-dialysis.com/
Dialysis Stations: 38. **Formerly:** RCG.

24809 ■ Fresenius Medical Care--New Orleans--Ferncrest
14500 Hayne Blvd., Ste. 100
New Orleans, LA 70128
Free: 866-434-2597
URL: http://www.ultracare-dialysis.com/
Dialysis Stations: 9.

24810 ■ Memorial Dialysis--New Orleans Davita
4427 S Robertson St.
New Orleans, LA 70115-6308
Free: 800-424-6589
URL: http://www.davita.com
Dialysis Stations: 213.

24811 ■ New Orleans Kidney Center
3434 Prytania St., Ste. 410
New Orleans, LA 70115
Ph: (504)899-8414
Dialysis Stations: 1. **Formerly:** Renal South of New Orleans.

24812 ■ Ochsner Multi-Organ Transplant
1514 Jefferson Hwy.
New Orleans, LA 70121
Ph: (504)842-3925
URL: http://www.ochsner.org/services/multi_organ_transplant/
Dialysis Stations: 0.

24813 ■ Renal South of New Orleans
2620 Jena
New Orleans, LA 70115
Ph: (504)269-6004
Dialysis Stations: 16.

24814 ■ Tulane University Hospital Transplant
Abdominal Transplant Institute Box TW35
New Orleans, LA 70112
Ph: (504)988-5344
URL: http://tulanehealthcare.com/
Dialysis Stations: 0.

24815 ■ Tulane University--New Orleans Dialysis Clinic Inc.
1415 Canal St., 7th Fl.
New Orleans, LA 70112
Ph: (504)988-6418
URL: http://tulane.edu
Dialysis Stations: 8.

24816 ■ Westbank Chronic Renal Ctr. DaVita Dialysis Facility
3631 Behrman Place
New Orleans, LA 70114
Free: 800-424-6589
URL: http://www.davita.com
Dialysis Stations: 20.

New Roads

24817 ■ Fresenius Medical Care--New Roads Dialysis Services
107 Fairfield Ave.
New Roads, LA 70760
Free: 866-434-2597
URL: http://www.ultracare-dialysis.com/
Dialysis Stations: 17.

Oak Grove

24818 ■ Fresenius Medical Care--Oak Grove Dialysis Center
711 E Jefferson Dr.
Oak Grove, LA 71263
Free: 866-434-2597
URL: http://www.ultracare-dialysis.com/
Dialysis Stations: 14.

Opelousas

24819 ■ Dialysis Clinic Inc.--Opelousas
927 E Prudhomme
Opelousas, LA 70570
Ph: (337)594-8535
URL: http://www.dciinc.org
Dialysis Stations: 24. **Formerly:** Kidney Treatment Options Center of Opelousas.

24820 ■ Fresenius Medical Care--Opelousas Dialysis Services
528 E Vine St.
Opelousas, LA 70570
Free: 866-434-2597
URL: http://www.ultracare-dialysis.com/
Dialysis Stations: 22.

Pineville

24821 ■ Fresenius Medical Care--Pineville Dialysis Services
151 Sandifer Ln.
Pineville, LA 71360

Free: 866 434 2597
URL: http://www.ultracare-dialysis.com/
Dialysis Stations: 14.

Plaquemine

24822 ■ Fresenius Medical Care--Plaquemine Dialysis Services
24660 Plaza Dr.
Plaquemine, LA 70764
Free: 866-434-2597
Fax: (225)687-9195
URL: http://www.ultracare-dialysis.com/
Dialysis Stations: 17.

Port Allen

24823 ■ Fresenius Medical Care--Westport Dialysis Facility
2500 Commercial Dr.
Port Allen, LA 70767
Free: 866-434-2597
URL: http://www.ultracare-dialysis.com/
Dialysis Stations: 14.

Prairieville

24824 ■ Fresenius Medical Care--Ascension
17392 Vallee Ct.
Prairieville, LA 70769
Free: 866-434-2597
URL: http://www.ultracare-dialysis.com/
Dialysis Stations: 17.

Raceland

24825 ■ Raceland Dialysis Center
4601 Hwy. 1
Raceland, LA 70394
Ph: (985)537-6962
Dialysis Stations: 8.

Rayville

24826 ■ Fresenius Medical Care--Richland Parish
230 Hwy. 3048
Rayville, LA 71269
Free: 866-434-2597
URL: http://www.ultracare-dialysis.com/
Dialysis Stations: 8. **Formerly:** Richardson Dialysis LLP.

Ruston

24827 ■ Fresenius Medical Care--Lincoln Kidney Center Dialysis Facility
219 Mills Ave.
Ruston, LA 71270
Free: 866-434-2597
URL: http://www.ultracare-dialysis.com/
Dialysis Stations: 20.

24828 ■ Fresenius Medical Care--Ruston
760 S Farmerville
Ruston, LA 71270
Free: 866-434-2597
URL: http://www.ultracare-dialysis.com/
Dialysis Stations: 21.

Saint Rose

24829 ■ Fresenius Medical Care--Saint Charles Parish
150 James Dr. E, Ste. 110
Saint Rose, LA 70087
Free: 866-434-2597
URL: http://www.ultracare-dialysis.com/
Dialysis Stations: 17. **Formerly:** Renal Care Group.

Shreveport

24830 ■ Dialysis Center of Shreveport Fresenius Medical Care
3949 Southern Ave.
Shreveport, LA 71106
Free: 866-434-2597
URL: http://www.ultracare-dialysis.com/
Dialysis Stations: 28.

24831 ■ Dialysis Clinic Inc.--East Shreveport
102 Ardmore Ave.
Shreveport, LA 71105
Ph: (318)861-5051
URL: http://www.dciinc.org
Dialysis Stations: 19.

24832 ■ Dialysis Clinic Inc.--North Shreveport
1515 N Hearne Ave.
Shreveport, LA 71107
Ph: (318)220-7012
URL: http://www.dciinc.org
Dialysis Stations: 20.

24833 ■ Dialysis Clinic, Inc.--Shreveport
1322 Kings Hwy.
Shreveport, LA 71103
Ph: (318)226-1020
URL: http://www.dciinc.org
Dialysis Stations: 30.

24834 ■ Fresenius Medical Care--Shreveport Regional
1800 Buckner St., Ste. A100
Shreveport, LA 71101
Free: 866-434-2597
URL: http://www.ultracare-dialysis.com/
Dialysis Stations: 26.

24835 ■ Fresenius Medical Care--South Shreveport
410 Ashley Ridge Blvd.
Shreveport, LA 71106
Free: 866-434-2597
URL: http://www.ultracare-dialysis.com/
Dialysis Stations: 22.

24836 ■ Fresenius Medical Care--Southwest Shreveport
9076 Kingston Rd.
Shreveport, LA 71118
Free: 866-434-2597
URL: http://www.ultracare-dialysis.com/
Dialysis Stations: 24.

24837 ■ Fresenius Medical Care--West Shreveport
4338 Pines Rd.
Shreveport, LA 71119
Free: 866-434-2597
URL: http://www.ultracare-dialysis.com/
Dialysis Stations: 19.

24838 ■ North Shreveport Dialysis Fresenius Medical Care
990 Aero Dr.
Shreveport, LA 71107
Free: 866-434-2597
URL: http://www.ultracare-dialysis.com/
Dialysis Stations: 28.

24839 ■ Shreveport Home Dialysis DaVita
1560 Irving Pl.
Shreveport, LA 71101
Free: 800-424-6589
URL: http://www.davita.com
Dialysis Stations: 4.

24840 ■ Willis Knighton Med Center--Transplant
2751 Albert Bicknell Dr., Ste. 4A
Shreveport, LA 71103
Ph: (318)212-4676
URL: http://www.wkhs.com/Home.aspx
Dialysis Stations: 0.

24841 ■ Willis Knighton Medical Center Dialysis Center
2600 Greenwood Rd.
Shreveport, LA 71103
Ph: (318)212-4849
URL: http://www.wkhs.com
Dialysis Stations: 13.

Shrevepport

24842 ■ Pierremonte Dialysis Fresenius Medical Care
2240 E Bert Kouns Industrial Loop
Shrevepport, LA 71105
Free: 866-434-2597
URL: http://www.ultracare-dialysis.com/
Dialysis Stations: 16.

Slidell

24843 ■ DaVita--Slidell Kidney Care Dialysis Center & At Home
1150 Robert Blvd., Ste. 240
Slidell, LA 70458
Free: 800-424-6589
URL: http://www.davita.com
Dialysis Stations: 20.

24844 ■ DaVita--Southeast--Northshore Kidney Center
106 Medical Center Dr., Ste. 101
Slidell, LA 70461
Free: 800-424-6589
URL: http://www.davita.com
Dialysis Stations: 8.

24845 ■ Fresenius Medical Care--Slidell
877 Brownswitch Rd.
Slidell, LA 70548
Free: 866-434-2597
URL: http://www.ultracare-dialysis.com/
Dialysis Stations: 16.

24846 ■ Fresenius Medical Care--Trinity
1400 Lindberg Dr., Ste. 101
Slidell, LA 70458
Free: 866-434-2597
URL: http://www.ultracare-dialysis.com/
Dialysis Stations: 8.

Sulphur

24847 ■ DVA Renal Healthcare--Sulphur DaVita
944 S Beglis Pkwy.
Sulphur, LA 70664
Free: 800-424-6589
URL: http://www.davita.com
Dialysis Stations: 12. **Formerly:** Gambro Health-care.

Sunset

24848 ■ Fresenius Medical Care--Sunset
115 Acorn St.
Sunset, LA 70584
Free: 866-434-2597
URL: http://www.ultracare-dialysis.com/
Dialysis Stations: 16.

Thibodaux

24849 ■ Fresenius Medical Care NA--Thibodaux Dialysis Services
694 S Acadia Rd.
Thibodaux, LA 70301

Free: 866-434-2597
URL: http://www.ultracare-dialysis.com
Dialysis Stations: 25. **Formerly:** Bayou LaFourche Artificial Kidney Center.

Vacherie

24850 ■ Vacherie Dialysis Center
2504 Hwy. 20
Vacherie, LA 70090
Ph: (225)265-9030
Dialysis Stations: 12.

Ville Platte

24851 ■ Fresenius Medical Care--Ville Platte Dialysis Services
616 Jack Miller Rd.
Ville Platte, LA 70586
Free: 866-434-2597
URL: http://www.ultracare-dialysis.com/
Dialysis Stations: 12.

West Monroe

24852 ■ Fresenius Medical Care--Ouachita Dialysis
102 Thomas Rd., Ste. 306
West Monroe, LA 71291
Free: 866-434-2597
URL: http://www.ultracare-dialysis.com/
Dialysis Stations: 25.

Winnfield

24853 ■ Fresenius Medical Care--Winnfield Dialysis Services
601 W Court St.
Winnfield, LA 71483
Free: 866-434-2597
URL: http://www.ultracare-dialysis.com/
Dialysis Stations: 14.

Winnsboro

24854 ■ Fresenius Medical Care--Winnsboro Dialysis Services
3982 Front St.
Winnsboro, LA 71295
Free: 866-434-2597
URL: http://www.ultracare-dialysis.com/
Dialysis Stations: 15.

Zachary

24855 ■ Fresenius Medical Care--Zachary Crossroad
Dialysis Facility
4709 Secretary Dr.
Zachary, LA 70791
Free: 866-434-2597
URL: http://www.ultracare-dialysis.com/
Dialysis Stations: 21.

MAINE

Auburn

24856 ■ Androscoggin Kidney Center
Fresenius Medical Care
Dialysis Facility
1100 Minot Ave.
Auburn, ME 04210
Free: 866-434-2597
URL: http://www.ultracare-dialysis.com/
Dialysis Stations: 19.

Augusta

24857 ■ Kennebec Kidney Center
Fresenius Medical Care
164 Civic Center Dr.
Augusta, ME 04330
Free: 866-434-2597
URL: http://www.ultracare-dialysis.com/
Dialysis Stations: 13.

Bangor

24858 ■ Eastern Maine Medical Center
Dialysis Unit
489 State St.
Bangor, ME 04401
Ph: (207)973-7467
URL: http://www.emmc.org
Dialysis Stations: 20.

Bath

24859 ■ Coastal Dialysis Center
Fresenius Medical Care
55 Congress Ave.
Bath, ME 04530
Free: 866-434-2597
URL: http://www.ultracare-dialysis.com/
Dialysis Stations: 15.

Belfast

24860 ■ Dialysis Clinic Inc.--Belfast
116 Northport Ave., Ste. 101
Belfast, ME 04915
Ph: (207)338-1170
URL: http://www.dciinc.org
Dialysis Stations: 6.

Biddeford

24861 ■ York County Dialysis Center
Fresenius Medical Care
20B W Cole Rd.
Biddeford, ME 04005
Free: 866-434-2597
URL: http://www.ultracare-dialysis.com/
Dialysis Stations: 18.

Damariscotta

24862 ■ Damariscotta Dialysis
Fresenius Medical Care
4 Edwards Ave.
Damariscotta, ME 04543
Free: 866-434-2597
URL: http://www.ultracare-dialysis.com/
Dialysis Stations: 12.

Eastport

24863 ■ Fresenius Medical Care
Sunrise County Dialysis
19 Vanasse Rd.
Eastport, ME 04631
Free: 866-434-2597
URL: http://www.ultracare-dialysis.com/
Dialysis Stations: 11.

Ellsworth

24864 ■ Eastern Maine Dialysis
ESRD Satellite Unit
11 Short St.
Ellsworth, ME 04605
Ph: (207)667-9294
Dialysis Stations: 12.

Lewiston

24865 ■ Lewiston Auburn Kidney Center
Fresenius Medical Care
710 Main St.
Lewiston, ME 04240
Free: 866-434-2597
URL: http://www.ultracare-dialysis.com/
Dialysis Stations: 15.

24866 ■ Lewiston--Auburn Kidney Center
Fresenius Medical Care
710 Main St.
Lewiston, ME 04240
Free: 866-434-2597
URL: http://www.ultracare-dialysis.com/
Dialysis Stations: 15.

Lincoln

24867 ■ Lincoln Lakes Regional Dialysis
250 Enfield Rd.
Lincoln, ME 04457
Ph: (207)794-6095
Dialysis Stations: 8.

Portland

24868 ■ Fresenius Medical Care
Southern Maine Dialysis Facility
1600 Congress St.
Portland, ME 04104
Free: 866-434-2597
URL: http://www.ultracare-dialysis.com/
Dialysis Stations: 21.

24869 ■ Maine Medical Center--Transplant
19 West St.
Portland, ME 04102
Ph: (207)662-7180
Free: 800-870-5230
URL: http://www.mmc.org/mmc_body.cfm?id=2006
Dialysis Stations: 0.

Presque Isle

24870 ■ County Dialysis Center
21 North St.
Presque Isle, ME 04769
Ph: (207)768-5863
Dialysis Stations: 9.

Skowhegan

24871 ■ Dialysis Clinic Inc.--Skowhegan
27 Research Dr.
Skowhegan, ME 04976
Ph: (207)474-6002
URL: http://www.dciinc.org
Dialysis Stations: 12.

Waterville

24872 ■ Maine General Medical Center
Thayer Campus
Dialysis Center
149 North St.
Waterville, ME 04901
Ph: (207)872-1290
URL: http://www.mainegeneral.org/body.cfm?id=98
Dialysis Stations: 13.

Westbrook

24873 ■ Casco Bay Dialysis Facility
Fresenius Medical Care
2 Chabot St.
Westbrook, ME 04092
Free: 866-434-2597
URL: http://www.ultracare-dialysis.com/
Dialysis Stations: 20.

Wilton

24874 ■ Umbagog Kidney Center
Fresenius Medical Care
Dialysis Services
73 Allen St.
Wilton, ME 04294
Free: 866-434-2597
URL: http://www.ultracare-dialysis.com/
Dialysis Stations: 12.

MARYLAND

Aberdeen

24875 ■ DaVita
Aberdeen Dialysis
780 W Bel Air Ave.
Aberdeen, MD 21001
Ph: (410)273-9333
Dialysis Stations: 15.

Adelphi

24876 ■ American Renal Associates--Adelphi
1801 Metzerott Rd.
Adelphi, MD 20783
Ph: (301)434-1884
URL: http://www.americanrenal.com
Dialysis Stations: 9.

Annapolis

24877 ■ Fresenius Medical Care--Anne Arundel
2032 Industrial Dr.
Annapolis, MD 21401
Free: 866-434-2597
URL: http://www.ultracare-dialysis.com/
Dialysis Stations: 19.

24878 ■ Fresenius Medical Care--South Annapolis Dialysis Facility
304 Harry S Truman Pkwy., Stes. H-K
Annapolis, MD 21401
Free: 866-434-2597
URL: http://www.ultracare-dialysis.com/
Dialysis Stations: 18.

Arnold

24879 ■ Dialysis Corporation of America--Chesapeake
305 College Pkwy.
Arnold, MD 21012
Ph: (410)431-5106
URL: http://www.dialysiscorporation.com
Dialysis Stations: 6. **Formerly:** Maryland Kidney Care--Chesapeake.

Baltimore

24880 ■ 25th Street Dialysis Inc. DaVita Dialysis Facility
920 E 25th St.
Baltimore, MD 21218
Free: 800-424-6589
URL: http://www.davita.com
Dialysis Stations: 21. **Formerly:** Gambro Healthcare - 25th Street.

24881 ■ Baltimore Geriatric DaVita
4940 Eastern Ave.
Baltimore, MD 21224
Free: 800-424-6589
URL: http://www.davita.com
Dialysis Stations: 3.

24882 ■ Bertha Sirk Dialysis Center DaVita
5820 York Rd.
Baltimore, MD 21212
Free: 800-424-6589
URL: http://www.davita.com
Dialysis Stations: 16.

24883 ■ Bon Secours Hospital Renal Dialysis Unit
2000 W Baltimore St.
Baltimore, MD 21223
Ph: (410)362-3094
URL: http://bonsecoursbaltimore.com
Dialysis Stations: 35.

24884 ■ Chestnut Square Dialysis Center Independent Dialysis Foundation
3303 Chestnut Ave.
Baltimore, MD 21214
Ph: (410)366-5400
URL: http://www.idfdn.org
Dialysis Stations: 21.

24885 ■ Community Dialysis Centers Inc.--Baltimore
2707 Rolling Rd., Ste. 104-105
Baltimore, MD 21244
Ph: (410)277-9101
Dialysis Stations: 18.

24886 ■ DaVita--Catonsville
1581 Sulphur Spring Rd., Ste. 112
Baltimore, MD 21227
Free: 800-424-6589
URL: http://www.davita.com
Dialysis Stations: 30.

24887 ■ DaVita--Harbor Park Dialysis Dialysis Facility
111 Cherry Hill Rd.
Baltimore, MD 21225
Free: 800-424-6589
URL: http://www.davita.com
Dialysis Stations: 21. **Formerly:** Gambro Healthcare - Harbor Park.

24888 ■ DaVita--J. B. Zachary Dialysis & At Home
333 Cassell Dr., Ste. 2300
Baltimore, MD 21224
Free: 800-424-6589
URL: http://www.davita.com
Dialysis Stations: 24. **Formerly:** Gambro Healthcare - J. B. Zachary Dialysis Center.

24889 ■ DaVita--Maryland Dialysis Center
409 N Caroline St.
Baltimore, MD 21231
Free: 800-424-6589
URL: http://www.davita.com
Dialysis Stations: 18. **Formerly:** Gambro Healthcare - Maryland.

24890 ■ DaVita--Mercy Dialysis Facility
315 N Calvert St., Ste. 300
Baltimore, MD 21202
Free: 800-424-6589
URL: http://www.davita.com
Dialysis Stations: 30. **Formerly:** Gambro Healthcare - Mercy.

24891 ■ DaVita--North Rolling Rd.
1108 N Rolling Rd.
Baltimore, MD 21228
Free: 800-424-6589
URL: http://www.davita.com
Dialysis Stations: 12. **Formerly:** Gambro Healthcare.

24892 ■ DaVita--White Square
1 Nashua Ct., Ste. E
Baltimore, MD 21221
Free: 800-424-6589
URL: http://www.davita.com
Dialysis Stations: 18. **Formerly:** Gambro Healthcare.

24893 ■ Dialysis Corporation of America--Baltimore
22 S Athol Ave.
Baltimore, MD 21229
Ph: (410)947-3227
URL: http://www.dialysiscorporation.com
Dialysis Stations: 15.

24894 ■ Dialysis Corporation of America--North Baltimore
2700 N Charles St., Ste. 102
Baltimore, MD 21218
Ph: (410)243-4193
URL: http://www.dialysiscorporation.com
Dialysis Stations: 12.

24895 ■ Downtown Dialysis Center DaVita
821 N Eutaw St., Ste. 401
Baltimore, MD 21201
Free: 800-424-6589
URL: http://www.davita.com
Dialysis Stations: 31.

24896 ■ Good Samaritan Hospital--Baltimore Lorien Frankford Dialysis Unit
5009 Frankford Ave.
Baltimore, MD 21209
Ph: (410)325-4000
URL: http://www.goodsam-md.org
Dialysis Stations: 6.

24897 ■ Good Samaritan Hospital--Baltimore Renal Dialysis Unit
5601 Loch Raven Blvd.
Baltimore, MD 21239
Ph: (410)532-4095
URL: http://www.goodsam-md.org
Dialysis Stations: 54.

24898 ■ Good Samaritan Hospital--Cromwell Center
8710 Emge Rd.
Baltimore, MD 21234
Ph: (410)661-0801
URL: http://www.goodsam-md.org
Dialysis Stations: 9.

24899 ■ Greenspring Dialysis Center DaVita
4701 Mt. Hope Dr., Ste. C
Baltimore, MD 21215
Free: 800-424-6589
URL: http://www.davita.com
Dialysis Stations: 28.

24900 ■ Greenspring Dialysis Center DaVita
4701 Mt. Hope Dr., Ste. C
Baltimore, MD 2215
Free: 800-424-6589
URL: http://www.davita.com
Dialysis Stations: 28.

24901 ■ Harford Road Dialysis Center DaVita
5800 Harford Rd.
Baltimore, MD 21214
Free: 800-424-6589
URL: http://www.davita.com
Dialysis Stations: 18.

24902 ■ Harford Road Dialysis DaVita
5800 Harford Rd.
Baltimore, MD 21214
Ph: (410)558-6000
Dialysis Stations: 18.

24903 ■ Independent Dialysis Foundation--Deaton Dialysis Center
611 S Charles St., 2nd Fl.
Baltimore, MD 21230
Ph: (410)752-8866
URL: http://www.idfdn.org
Dialysis Stations: 10.

24904 ■ Independent Dialysis Foundation--Parkview Center
840 Hollins St.
Baltimore, MD 21201
Ph: (410)468-0900
URL: http://www.idfdn.org
Dialysis Stations: 36.

24905 ■ Johns Hopkins Outpatient Care Dialysis Unit
Pediatric Nephrology
200 N Wolfe St.
Baltimore, MD 21287
Ph: (410)955-4427
URL: http://www.hopkinsmedicine.org
Dialysis Stations: 0.

24906 ■ Kidney Home Center DaVita
2245 Rolling Run Dr., Ste. 3
Baltimore, MD 21244
Free: 800-424-6589
URL: http://www.davita.com
Dialysis Stations: 8.

24907 ■ Kidney Home Center, Dialysis and At Home DaVita
2245 Rolling Run Dr.
Baltimore, MD 21244
Free: 800-424-6589
URL: http://www.davita.com
Dialysis Stations: 21.

24908 ■ Liberty Dialysis--Charring Cross
5730 Executive Dr.
Baltimore, MD 21228
Ph: (410)747-9356
URL: http://www.libertydialysis.com

24909 ■ Manor Care Dialysis Center
6600 Ridge Rd.
Baltimore, MD 21237
Ph: (410)780-7355
Dialysis Stations: 6.

24910 ■ Seton Drive Dialysis DaVita
4800 Seton Dr.
Baltimore, MD 21215
Free: 800-424-6589
URL: http://www.davita.com
Dialysis Stations: 12.

24911 ■ Union Memorial Hospital Dialysis Unit
201 E University Pkwy.
Baltimore, MD 21218
Ph: (410)554-0453
URL: http://www.unionmemorial.org/body.cfm?id=1190
Dialysis Stations: 18.

24912 ■ Union Memorial Hospital Dialysis Unit
Guilford Ave. Entrance
201 E University Pkwy.
Baltimore, MD 21218
Ph: (410)554-4535
URL: http://www.unionmemorial.org
Dialysis Stations: 18.

Bel Air

24913 ■ DaVita--Bel Air Dialysis Facility
2225 Old Emmorton Rd., Ste. 100
Bel Air, MD 21015
Free: 800-424-6589
URL: http://www.davita.com
Dialysis Stations: 24. **Formerly:** Gambro Healthcare - Bel Air.

Beltsville

24914 ■ Calverton Dialysis DaVita
4780 Corridor Pl.
Beltsville, MD 20705
Free: 800-424-6589
URL: http://www.davita.com
Dialysis Stations: 12.

24915 ■ Renal Advantage Inc.--Beltsville Dialysis Facility
10701 Baltimore Ave.
Beltsville, MD 20705
Ph: (301)595-0263
URL: http://www.renaladvantage.com
Dialysis Stations: 20. **Formerly:** Gambro Healthcare - Beltsville.

Berlin

24916 ■ DaVita--Berlin Dialysis Facility
314 Franklin Ave., Ste. 306
Berlin, MD 21811
Free: 800-424-6589
URL: http://www.davita.com
Dialysis Stations: 15. **Formerly:** Total Renal Care.

Bethesda

24917 ■ Dialysis Corp. of America--Chevy Chase
3 Bethesda Metro Center, Ste. B-005
Bethesda, MD 20814
Ph: (301)652-3434
URL: http://www.dialysiscorporation.com
Dialysis Stations: 12.

24918 ■ Fresenius Medical Care--Washington Dialysis Facility
6420 Rockledge Dr., Ste. 1100
Bethesda, MD 20817
Free: 866-434-2597
URL: http://www.ultracare-dialysis.com/
Dialysis Stations: 18.

Bowie

24919 ■ Renal Care of Bowie DaVita
4861 Telsa Dr., Ste. H
Bowie, MD 20715
Free: 800-424-6589
URL: http://www.davita.com
Dialysis Stations: 18.

Cambridge

24920 ■ Cambridge Dialysis Center DaVita
300 Byrn St.
Cambridge, MD 21613
Free: 800-424-6589
URL: http://www.davita.com
Dialysis Stations: 12.

Camp Springs

24921 ■ Quality Care Dialysis--Southern Maryland Fresenius Medical Care
6357 Old Branch Ave.
Camp Springs, MD 20748
Free: 866-434-2597
URL: http://www.ultracare-dialysis.com/
Dialysis Stations: 18.

Catonsville

24922 ■ Charing Cross Dialysis LLC
MIE Executive Park
5730 Executive Dr., Ste. 124-130
Catonsville, MD 21228
Ph: (410)747-9356
Dialysis Stations: 16.

Chestertown

24923 ■ DaVita--Chestertown Dialysis Facility
100 Brown St.
Chestertown, MD 21620
Free: 800-424-6589
URL: http://www.davita.com
Dialysis Stations: 9. **Formerly:** Total Renal Care.

Clinton

24924 ■ DaVita--Lakeside Dialysis Center
10401 Hospital Dr., Ste. G02
Clinton, MD 20735
Free: 800-424-6589
URL: http://www.davita.com
Dialysis Stations: 15. **Formerly:** Gambro Healthcare - Clinton.

24925 ■ DaVita--Southern Maryland Dialysis Facility
9211 Stuart Ln.
Clinton, MD 20735
Free: 800-424-6589
URL: http://www.davita.com
Dialysis Stations: 13. **Formerly:** Gambro Healthcare - Southern Maryland.

24926 ■ Renal Advantage Inc. Care Centers--Old Alexandria--Clinton
7201 Old Alexandria Ferry Rd.
Clinton, MD 20735
Ph: (301)877-3263
URL: http://www.renaladvantage.com
Dialysis Stations: 24.

Columbia

24927 ■ DaVita--Cedar Lane Dialysis Facility
6334 Cedar Ln.
Columbia, MD 21044
Free: 800-424-6589
URL: http://www.davita.com
Dialysis Stations: 13. **Formerly:** Gambro Healthcare - Cedar Lane.

24928 ■ DaVita--Howard County Dialysis Facility
5999 Harper's Farm Rd., Ste. E-110
Columbia, MD 21044
Free: 800-424-6589
URL: http://www.davita.com
Dialysis Stations: 15. **Formerly:** Gambro Healthcare - Howard County.

Cumberland

24929 ■ Independent Dialysis Foundation--Allegany Center
939 Frederick St.
Cumberland, MD 21502
Ph: (301)724-0351
URL: http://www.idfdn.org
Dialysis Stations: 12.

24930 ■ Independent Dialysis FoundationF--Lions Manor
Seton Dr. Ext.
Cumberland, MD 21502
Ph: (301)722-6299
URL: http://www.idfdn.org
Dialysis Stations: 6.

24931 ■ Western Maryland Health System Renal Dialysis Unit
12502 Willowbrook Rd., Ste. 250
Cumberland, MD 21502
Ph: (240)964-8600
URL: http://www.wmhs.com
Dialysis Stations: 35. **Formerly:** Memorial Hospital Medical Center.

District Heights

24932 ■ District Heights Dialysis DaVita
5701 Silver Hill Rd.
District Heights, MD 20747
Free: 800-424-6589
URL: http://www.davita.com
Dialysis Stations: 18.

24933 ■ District Heights Dialysis
DaVita
5701 Silver Hill Rd.
District Heights, MD 20747
Free: 800-424-6589
URL: http://www.davita.com
Dialysis Stations: 18.

24934 ■ Renal Advantage Inc.--Silver Hill Dialysis Facility
Penn Station Shopping Center
5652 Silver Hill Rd.
District Heights, MD 20747
Ph: (301)967-9891
URL: http://www.renaladvantage.com
Dialysis Stations: 24. **Formerly:** Gambro Healthcare - Silver Hill.

Dundalk

24935 ■ DaVita--Dundalk
14 Commerce St.
Dundalk, MD 21222
Free: 800-424-6589
URL: http://www.davita.com
Dialysis Stations: 12. **Formerly:** Gambro Healthcare.

24936 ■ Porter Dialysis--Dundalk
Fresenius Medical Care
1107 N Point Blvd., Ste. 201
Dundalk, MD 21224
Free: 866-434-2597
URL: http://www.ultracare-dialysis.com/
Dialysis Stations: 12.

Easton

24937 ■ Advanced Dialysis Center--Easton
610 Dutchman's Ln.
Easton, MD 21601
Ph: (410)820-9873
Dialysis Stations: 9.

24938 ■ DaVita--Easton
Dialysis Unit
402 Marvel Court
Easton, MD 21601
Free: 800-424-6589
URL: http://www.davita.com
Dialysis Stations: 15. **Formerly:** Total Renal Care - Easton.

Elkton

24939 ■ Fresenius Medical Care--Elkton
Elk River Kidney Center
216 S Bridge St.
Elkton, MD 21921
Free: 800-424-6589
URL: http://www.davita.com
Dialysis Stations: 18. **Formerly:** DaVita.

Ellicott City

24940 ■ Ellicott City Dialysis Center
3000 N Ridge Rd.
Ellicott City, MD 21043
Ph: (410)750-8426
Dialysis Stations: 12. **Formerly:** Independent Dialysis Foundation--Trinity Center Dialysis.

Fort Washington

24941 ■ Fresenius Medical Care--Fort Foote
8507 Oxon Hill Rd.
Fort Washington, MD 20744
Free: 866-434-2597
URL: http://www.ultracare-dialysis.com/
Dialysis Stations: 12.

24942 ■ Fresenius Medical Care--Fort Washington
Dialysis Facility
12780 Old Fort Rd.
Fort Washington, MD 20744
Free: 866-434-2597
URL: http://www.ultracare-dialysis.com/
Dialysis Stations: 12.

Frederick

24943 ■ DaVita - Frederick Dialysis & At Home
140 Thomas Johnson Dr.
Frederick, MD 21702
Free: 800-424-6589
URL: http://www.davita.com
Dialysis Stations: 27.

24944 ■ Frederick Renal Care
405 W 7th St.
Frederick, MD 21701
Ph: (301)696-2290
Dialysis Stations: 7.

24945 ■ Wellbound of Frederick LLC
Satellite Health
45 Thomas Johnson Dr., Ste. 211
Frederick, MD 21702
Ph: (301)624-1054
URL: http://www.satellitehealth.com/
Dialysis Stations: 4.

Germantown

24946 ■ Germantown Dialysis & At Home
DaVita
20111 Century Blvd., Ste. C
Germantown, MD 20874
Free: 800-424-6589
URL: http://www.davita.com
Dialysis Stations: 15.

24947 ■ Montgomery Renal Center, LLC
12401 Middlebrook Rd., Ste. 160
Germantown, MD 20874
Ph: (301)540-6020
Dialysis Stations: 20.

Glen Burnie

24948 ■ DaVita--Glen Burnie Dialysis
Dialysis Center
120 N Langley Rd.
Glen Burnie, MD 21060
Free: 800-424-6589
URL: http://www.davita.com
Dialysis Stations: 12. **Formerly:** Gambro Healthcare - Glen Burnie.

24949 ■ Independent Dialysis Foundation--Arundel Center
804 Landmark Dr., Ste. 112
Glen Burnie, MD 21061
Ph: (410)768-5722
URL: http://www.idfdn.org
Dialysis Stations: 24.

Hagerstown

24950 ■ Fresenius Medical Care--Hagerstown
12931 Oak Hill Ave.
Hagerstown, MD 21742
Free: 866-434-2597
URL: http://www.ultracare-dialysis.com/
Dialysis Stations: 29.

24951 ■ Robinwood Dialysis Facility
Fresenius Medical Care
11110 Medical Campus Rd., Ste. 149
Hagerstown, MD 21742
Free: 866-434-2597
URL: http://www.ultracare-dialysis.com/
Dialysis Stations: 13.

24952 ■ Western Maryland Center
Renal Division
1500 Pennsylvania Ave.
Hagerstown, MD 21740
Ph: (301)745-3748
Dialysis Stations: 12.

Hyattsville

24953 ■ Renal Advantage Inc.--Chillum--Hyattsville
Dialysis Center
2426 Chillum Rd.
Hyattsville, MD 20782
Ph: (301)927-8808
URL: http://www.renaladvantage.com
Dialysis Stations: 29. **Formerly:** Ultimate Renal Care.

24954 ■ Saint Thomas More Dialysis
Dialysis Corporation of America
4920 LaSalle Rd.
Hyattsville, MD 20782
Ph: (301)864-0490
URL: http://www.dialysiscorporation.com
Dialysis Stations: 18. **Formerly:** Fresenius Medical Care--Hyattsville.

24955 ■ Takoma Park Dialysis
DaVita
1502 University Blvd. E
Hyattsville, MD 20783
Free: 800-424-6589
URL: http://www.davita.com
Dialysis Stations: 21.

La Plata

24956 ■ Fresenius Medical Care--La Plata
Dialysis Facility
101 Catalpa Dr., Ste. 103
La Plata, MD 20646
Free: 866-434-2597
URL: http://www.ultracare-dialysis.com/
Dialysis Stations: 12.

Lanham

24957 ■ Prince Georges County Dialysis
Fresenius Medical Care
7558 Annapolis Rd., Ste. C-1
Lanham, MD 20784
Free: 866-434-2597
URL: http://www.ultracare-dialysis.com/
Dialysis Stations: 12.

24958 ■ Renal Care of Lanham & At Home
DaVita
Dialysis Facility
8855 Annapolis Rd., Ste. 200
Lanham, MD 20706
Free: 800-424-6589
URL: http://www.davita.com
Dialysis Stations: 33.

Largo

24959 ■ DaVita--Landover
1200 Mercantile Ln., Ste. 105
Largo, MD 20774
Free: 800-424-6589
URL: http://www.davita.com
Dialysis Stations: 22.

24960 ■ Kidney Care of Largo
DaVita
1300 Mercantile Ln.
Largo, MD 20774
Free: 800-424-6589
URL: http://www.davita.com
Dialysis Stations: 29.

Laurel

24961 ■ Kidney Care of Laurel
DaVita
14631 Laurel Bowie Rd., Ste. 100
Laurel, MD 20707
Free: 800-424-6589
URL: http://www.davita.com
Dialysis Stations: 18. **Formerly:** Kidney Care Center.

Leonardtown

24962 ■ Fresenius Medical Care--Leonardtown
Dialysis Facility
40865 Merchants Ln.
Leonardtown, MD 20650
Free: 866-434-2597
URL: http://www.ultracare-dialysis.com/
Dialysis Stations: 18.

Lutherville

24963 ■ DaVita--Falls Road
Dialysis Facility
10753 Falls Rd.
Lutherville, MD 21093
Free: 800-424-6589
URL: http://www.davita.com
Dialysis Stations: 12. **Formerly:** Gambro Healthcare - Greensprings.

Mitchellville

24964 ■ Holy Cross Dialysis Center--Woodmore
11721 Woodmore Rd., Ste. 190
Mitchellville, MD 20721
Ph: (302)390-7270
Dialysis Stations: 15.

Oakland

24965 ■ Independent Dialysis Foundation
Garrett Dialysis Center
888 Memorial Dr.
Oakland, MD 21550
Ph: (301)334-8955
URL: http://www.idfdn.org
Dialysis Stations: 12.

Owings Mills

24966 ■ DaVita--Owings Mills
Dialysis Facility
10 Crossroads Dr., Ste. 110
Owings Mills, MD 21117
Free: 800-424-6589
URL: http://www.davita.com
Dialysis Stations: 13.

Oxon Hill

24967 ■ Renal Advantage Inc.--Oxon Hill
Dialysis Facility
5410 Indian Head Hwy.
Oxon Hill, MD 20745
Ph: (301)749-9307
URL: http://www.renaladvantage.com
Dialysis Stations: 16. **Formerly:** Gambro Healthcare - Oxon Hill.

24968 ■ Rivertowne Dialysis Center
DaVita
6192 Oxon Hill Rd.
Oxon Hill, MD 20745
Free: 800-424-6589
URL: http://www.davita.com
Dialysis Stations: 16.

Pasadena

24969 ■ DaVita--Pasadena
8894 Fort Smallwood Rd., Ste. 15
Pasadena, MD 21122
Free: 800-424-6589
URL: http://www.davita.com
Dialysis Stations: 17. **Formerly:** Gambro Healthcare.

Pikesville

24970 ■ Pikesville Dialysis
DaVita
1500 Reisterstown Rd., Ste. 220
Pikesville, MD 21208
Free: 800-424-6589
URL: http://www.davita.com
Dialysis Stations: 6.

24971 ■ Porter Dialysis--Pikesville
Fresenius Medical Care
115 McHenry Ave., Ste. D
Pikesville, MD 21208
Free: 866-434-2597
URL: http://www.ultracare-dialysis.com/
Dialysis Stations: 12.

Prince Frederick

24972 ■ Independent Dialysis Foundation--Calvert Center
225 W Dares Beach Rd.
Prince Frederick, MD 20678
Ph: (410)535-6300
URL: http://www.idfdn.org
Dialysis Stations: 18.

24973 ■ Renal Carepartners--Prince Frederick
205 Steeple Chase Dr., Ste. 201
Prince Frederick, MD 20678
Ph: (410)414-8000
URL: http://www.renalcp.com
Dialysis Stations: 16.

Randallstown

24974 ■ Advanced Dialysis Center--Randallstown
9109 Liberty Rd.
Randallstown, MD 21133
Ph: (410)496-0077
Dialysis Stations: 9.

24975 ■ Baltimore County Dialysis Facility
DaVita
9635 Liberty Rd., Ste. A
Randallstown, MD 21133
Free: 800-424-6589
URL: http://www.davita.com
Dialysis Stations: 21.

Rockville

24976 ■ Advanced Dialysis Center--Rockville
299 Hurley Ave.
Rockville, MD 20850
Ph: (301)838-9119
Dialysis Stations: 9.

24977 ■ DaVita--Rockville
Dialysis Facility
14915 Broschart Rd., Ste. 100
Rockville, MD 20850
Free: 800-424-6589
URL: http://www.davita.com
Dialysis Stations: 17.

24978 ■ Dialysis Corporation of AmericaA--Rockville
11800A Nebel St.
Rockville, MD 20852
Ph: (301)468-3221
URL: http://www.dialysiscorporation.com
Dialysis Stations: 15.

24979 ■ Fresenius Medical Care--Rockville
Dialysis Facility
7524 Standish Pl., Ste. 100-B
Rockville, MD 20855
Free: 866-434-2597
URL: http://www.ultracare-dialysis.com/
Dialysis Stations: 16.

Rosedale

24980 ■ Porter Dialysis--Rosedale
Fresenius Medical Care
9411 Philadelphia Rd., Ste. A
Rosedale, MD 21237
Free: 866-434-2597
URL: http://www.ultracare-dialysis.com/
Dialysis Stations: 15.

Salisbury

24981 ■ Deers Head Center
Dialysis Center
351 Deers Head Hospital Rd.
Salisbury, MD 21801
Ph: (410)543-4085
Dialysis Stations: 24.

24982 ■ Fresenius Medical Care--North Salisbury
1314 Belmont Ave., Ste. 304
Salisbury, MD 21804
Free: 866-434-2597
URL: http://www.ultracare-dialysis.com/
Dialysis Stations: 24.

24983 ■ Fresenius Medical Care--Salisbury
1340 S Division St., Ste. 302
Salisbury, MD 21804
Free: 866-434-2597
URL: http://www.ultracare-dialysis.com/
Dialysis Stations: 21.

Seat Pleasant

24984 ■ Renal Care of Seat Pleasant
DaVita
6274 Central Ave.
Seat Pleasant, MD 20743
Free: 800-424-6589
URL: http://www.davita.com
Dialysis Stations: 21.

Silver Spring

24985 ■ Adventist Dialysis Services
Fresenius Medical Care
12325 New Hampshire Ave.
Silver Spring, MD 20904
Free: 866-434-2597
URL: http://www.ultracare-dialysis.com/
Dialysis Stations: 11. **Formerly:** Fresenius Medical Care-Springbrook.

24986 ■ DaVita--Silver Spring
Dialysis Facility
8412 Georgia Ave.
Silver Spring, MD 20910
Free: 800-424-6589
URL: http://www.davita.com
Dialysis Stations: 15. **Formerly:** Gambro Healthcare - Silver Spring.

24987 ■ Fresenius Medical Care--Silver Spring
12120 Plum Orchard Rd., Ste. 140
Silver Spring, MD 20904
Free: 866-434-2597
URL: http://www.ultracare-dialysis.com/
Dialysis Stations: 12.

24988 ■ Holy Cross Hospital
Renal Dialysis Unit
1500 Forest Glen Rd.
Silver Spring, MD 20910

Ph: (301)754-7560
URL: http://www.holycrosshealth.org
Dialysis Stations: 14.

24989 ■ KRU Medical Ventures
Silver Spring Artificial Kidney Center
Dialysis Facility
8630 Fenton St., Ste. 238
Silver Spring, MD 20910
Ph: (301)563-6808
URL: http://www.krumedicalventures.com
Dialysis Stations: 17.

Suitland

24990 ■ Fresenius Medical Care--Camp Springs
Dialysis Facility
3700 St. Barnabas Rd., Ste. A
Suitland, MD 20746
Free: 866-434-2597
URL: http://www.ultracare-dialysis.com/
Dialysis Stations: 18.

Timonium

24991 ■ Fresenius Medical Care--Greater Baltimore
Dialysis Facility
1840 York Rd., Ste. A1
Timonium, MD 21093
Free: 866-434-2597
URL: http://www.ultracare-dialysis.com/
Dialysis Stations: 12.

Towson

24992 ■ Dulaney Towson Dialysis Center
DaVita
113 West Rd., Ste. 201
Towson, MD 21204
Free: 800-424-6589
URL: http://www.davita.com
Dialysis Stations: 14.

Waldorf

24993 ■ Fresenius Medical Care--Waldorf
Dialysis Services
3510 Old Washington Rd., Ste. 300
Waldorf, MD 20603
Free: 866-434-2597
URL: http://www.ultracare-dialysis.com/
Dialysis Stations: 15.

Westminster

24994 ■ DaVita
Carroll County Dialysis Facility
412 Malcom Dr., Ste. 310
Westminster, MD 21157
Free: 800-424-6589
URL: http://www.davita.com
Dialysis Stations: 12.

Wheaton

24995 ■ Fresenius Medical Care--Wheaton
Dialysis Facility
Wheaton Plaza Shopping Center
11160 Viers Mill Rd.
Wheaton, MD 20902
Free: 866-434-2597
URL: http://www.ultracare-dialysis.com/
Dialysis Stations: 16.

24996 ■ Wheaton Dialysis Center
DaVita
Wheaton Park Shopping Center
11941 Georgia Ave.
Wheaton, MD 20902
Free: 800-424-6589
URL: http://www.davita.com
Dialysis Stations: 18.

White Marsh

24997 ■ Porter Dialysis--White Marsh
Fresenius Medical Care
Bldg. 3, Ste. 131
7939 Honeygo Blvd.
White Marsh, MD 21236
Free: 866-434-2597
URL: http://www.ultracare-dialysis.com/
Dialysis Stations: 12.

MASSACHUSETTS

Agawam

24998 ■ Heritage Dialysis Center LLC
67 Cooper St.
Agawam, MA 01001
Ph: (413)786-2022
Dialysis Stations: 13.

Amesbury

24999 ■ Amesbury Renal Center
Diversified Specialty Institutes
24 Morrill Pl.
Amesbury, MA 01913
Ph: (978)388-7100
URL: http://www.dsi-corp.com
Dialysis Stations: 17. **Formerly:** Renex Dialysis Clinic of Amesbury Inc.

Beverly

25000 ■ North Shore Regional Dialysis Center
Fresenius Medical Care
133 Brimbal Ave., Unit E
Beverly, MA 01915
Free: 866-434-2597
URL: http://www.ultracare-dialysis.com/
Dialysis Stations: 22.

Boston

25001 ■ Beth Israel Deaconess Medical Center--Transplant
330 Brookline Ave.
Boston, MA 02215
Ph: (617)632-9700
URL: http://www.bidmc.org/CentersandDepartments/Departments/TransplantInstitute
Dialysis Stations: 0.

25002 ■ Boston Dialysis
DaVita
660 Harrison Ave.
Boston, MA 02118
Free: 800-424-6589
URL: http://www.davita.com
Dialysis Stations: 30.

25003 ■ Boston Medical Center--Transplant Surgery
Boston University School of Medicine
720 Harrison Ave., Ste. 700
Boston, MA 02118
Ph: (617)638-8430
URL: http://www.bmc.org/findaphysician/departmentDet.php?dept=General%20Surgery%20Transplant%20Surgery
Dialysis Stations: 0.

25004 ■ Brigham and Women's Hospital
Dialysis Center
75 Francis St.
Boston, MA 02115
Ph: (617)732-6130
URL: http://www.brighamandwomens.com
Dialysis Stations: 6.

25005 ■ Brigham and Women's Hospital Dialysis Unit
715 Francis St.
Boston, MA 02115
Ph: (617)732-5951
URL: http://www.brighamandwomens.org/Departments_and_Services/medicine/services/ renal/
Dialysis Stations: 6.

25006 ■ Children's Hospital Boston
Dialysis Unit, Farley Four
300 Longwood Ave.
Boston, MA 02115
Ph: (617)355-7631
URL: http://www.childrenshospital.org
Dialysis Stations: 7.

25007 ■ Dialysis Clinic, Inc.--Boston
35 Kneeland St., 5th Fl.
Boston, MA 02111
Ph: (617)636-6389
URL: http://www.dciinc.org
Dialysis Stations: 21.

25008 ■ Massachusetts General Hospital
Dialysis Unit
32 Fruit St., Bigelow 10
Boston, MA 02114
Ph: (617)726-3700
Dialysis Stations: 8.

25009 ■ TKC--Babcock Artificial Kidney Center
Fresenius Medical Care
888 Commonwealth Ave.
Boston, MA 02215
Free: 866-434-2597
URL: http://www.ultracare-dialysis.com/
Dialysis Stations: 21.

25010 ■ Tufts Medical Center
Transplant
750 Washington St.
Boston, MA 02111
Ph: (617)636-5592
URL: http://www.tufts-nemc.org
Formerly: Tufts New England Medical Center.

Brighton

25011 ■ Saint Elizabeth's Medical Center of Boston
Dialysis Unit
736 Cambridge St., CCP7
Brighton, MA 02135
Ph: (617)789-2592
URL: http://www.caaritasstelizabeths.org
Dialysis Stations: 17.

Brockton

25012 ■ Brockton Dialysis Center
Fresenius Medical Care
375 Westgate Dr.
Brockton, MA 02301
Free: 866-434-2597
URL: http://www.ultracare-dialysis.com/
Dialysis Stations: 1.

25013 ■ Brockton Regional Kidney Center
76 Campanelli Industrial Dr.
Brockton, MA 02301
Ph: (508)427-5329
Dialysis Stations: 25.

Brookline

25014 ■ Brookline Dialysis
DaVita
Dialysis Center
322 Washington St.
Brookline, MA 02445

Free: 800-424-6589
URL: http://www.davita.com
Dialysis Stations: 27. **Formerly:** Gambro Healthcare - Brookline.

Burlington

25015 ■ Burlington Regional Dialysis
DaVita
31 Mall Rd., Ste. 1B
Burlington, MA 01803
Free: 800-424-6589
URL: http://www.davita.com
Dialysis Stations: 17. **Formerly:** Gambro Healthcare--Burlington.

25016 ■ Lahey Clinic-- Transplant
Tufts University School of Medicine
41 Mall Rd.
Burlington, MA 01805
Ph: (781)744-8974
URL: http://www.lahey.org/Transplantation/
Dialysis Stations: 0.

Cambridge

25017 ■ Northeast Cambridge Dialysis
DaVita
Dialysis Center
799 Concord Ave.
Cambridge, MA 02138
Free: 800-424-6589
URL: http://www.davita.com
Dialysis Stations: 18. **Formerly:** Gambro Healthcare - Cambridge.

Chicopee

25018 ■ Dialysis Center of Western Massachusetts
American Renal Associates
601 Memorial Dr., Ste. H
Chicopee, MA 01020
Ph: (303)403-1127
URL: http://www.americanrenal.com
Dialysis Stations: 15.

25019 ■ Fresenius Medical Care--Chicopee
1391 Industrial Pk.
Chicopee, MA 01013
Free: 866-434-2597
URL: http://www.ultracare-dialysis.com/

Concord

25020 ■ Dialysis Clinic, inc.--Walden Pond
56 B Winthrop St.
Concord, MA 01742
Ph: (978)369-1683
URL: http://www.dciinc.org
Dialysis Stations: 13.

Dartmouth

25021 ■ Southeastern Massachusetts Dialysis Clinic
237 State Rd., Rte. 6
Dartmouth, MA 02747
Ph: (508)994-9692
Dialysis Stations: 26.

Dorchester

25022 ■ Boston Dialysis Center
Fresenius Medical Care
Seton Medical Bldg., 1 S
2100 Dorchester Ave.
Dorchester, MA 02124
Free: 866-434-2597
URL: http://www.ultracare-dialysis.com/
Dialysis Stations: 21.

25023 ■ Fresenius Medical Care--Boston Carney
2100 Dorchester Ave., Ste. 1 S
Dorchester, MA 02124
Free: 866-434-2597
URL: http://www.ultracare-dialysis.com/
Dialysis Stations: 21.

Fall River

25024 ■ Dialysis Center of Fall River
American Renal Associates
221-223 Weaver St.
Fall River, MA 02720
Ph: (508)676-0112
URL: http://www.americanrenal.com
Dialysis Stations: 19.

25025 ■ Fresenius Medical Care--Fall River
48 Weaver St.
Fall River, MA 02720
Free: 866-434-2597
URL: http://www.ultracare-dialysis.com/
Dialysis Stations: 26.

Fitchburg

25026 ■ Physician's Dialysis--Fitchburg
DaVita
551 Electric Ave.
Fitchburg, MA 01420
Free: 800-424-6589
URL: http://www.davita.com
Dialysis Stations: 19. **Formerly:** North County Kidney Center.

Framingham

25027 ■ Fresenius Medical Care--Framingham
West Suburban Artificial Kidney Center
4 Vernon St.
Framingham, MA 01701
Free: 866-434-2597
URL: http://www.ultracare-dialysis.com/
Dialysis Stations: 17.

Great Barrington

25028 ■ Fairview Hospital Dialysis Center
10 Maple Ave., Ste. 200
Great Barrington, MA 01230
Ph: (413)854-9910
Dialysis Stations: 7.

Greenfield

25029 ■ Fresenius Medical Care
Yankee Family Dialysis Center
115 Wildwood Ave.
Greenfield, MA 01301
Free: 866-434-2597
URL: http://www.ultracare-dialysis.com/
Dialysis Stations: 12.

Hyde Park

25030 ■ Hyde Park Dialysis Center
Fresenius Medical Care
1628 Hyde Park Ave.
Hyde Park, MA 02136
Free: 866-434-2597
URL: http://www.ultracare-dialysis.com/
Dialysis Stations: 19.

Jamaica Plain

25031 ■ Dialysis Clinic Inc.--Brigham/Faulkner
Belkin House
1153 Centre St.
Jamaica Plain, MA 02130
Ph: (617)983-4470
URL: http://www.dciinc.org
Dialysis Stations: 21.

25032 ■ Lemuel Shattuck Hospital Dialysis Unit
170 Morton St.
Jamaica Plain, MA 02130
Ph: (617)971-3470
URL: http://www.shattuckhospital.org
Dialysis Stations: 14.

Lowell

25033 ■ Saints Medical Center Dialysis
847 Rogers St.
Lowell, MA 01854
Ph: (978)441-5100
URL: http://www.saintsmedicalcenter.com/
Dialysis Stations: 32. **Formerly:** Saints Memorial Medical Center--Merrimack Valley Dialysis Center, Lowell.

Marlborough

25034 ■ Fresenius Medical Care--Marlborough
360 Cedar Hill St.
Marlborough, MA 01752
Free: 866-434-2597
URL: http://www.ultracare-dialysis.com/
Dialysis Stations: 13.

Mashpee

25035 ■ Fresenius Medical Care of Mashpee
34 Bates Rd., Ste. 201
Mashpee, MA 02649
Free: 866-434-2597
URL: http://www.ultracare-dialysis.com/
Dialysis Stations: 16.

Medford

25036 ■ Medford Dialysis Center
Fresenius Medical Care
29 Forest St.
Medford, MA 02155
Free: 866-434-2597
URL: http://www.ultracare-dialysis.com/
Dialysis Stations: 12.

25037 ■ Wellington Circle Dialysis Center & At Home
DaVita
10 Cabot Rd., Ste. 103B
Medford, MA 02155
Free: 800-424-6589
URL: http://www.davita.com
Dialysis Stations: 17.

Methuen

25038 ■ Fresenius Medical Care of Methuen
421 Merrimack St.
Methuen, MA 01844
Free: 866-434-2597
URL: http://www.ultracare-dialysis.com/
Dialysis Stations: 21.

25039 ■ Saints Memorial Medical Center
Merrimack Valley Dialysis Center--Methuen
100 Milk St.
Methuen, MA 01844
Ph: (978)686-9900
URL: http://www.saintsmemorial.org
Dialysis Stations: 19.

Milford

25040 ■ Fresenius Medical Care--Blackstone Valley
42 Cape Rd.
Milford, MA 01757
Free: 866-434-2597
URL: http://www.ultracare-dialysis.com/
Dialysis Stations: 13.

Nantucket

25041 ■ Nantucket Cottage Hospital Dialysis Unit
57 Prospect St.
Nantucket, MA 02554
Ph: (508)228-1200
URL: http://www.nantuckethospital.org
Dialysis Stations: 2.

New Bedford

25042 ■ New Bedford Dialysis & At Home
DaVita
Dialysis Center
524 Union St.
New Bedford, MA 02740
Free: 800-424-6589
URL: http://www.davita.com
Dialysis Stations: 17. **Formerly:** Gambro Healthcare - New Bedford.

Newburyport

25043 ■ Fresenius Medical Care of Newburyport
Towle Bldg.
260 Merrimac St.
Newburyport, MA 01950
Free: 866-434-2597
URL: http://www.ultracare-dialysis.com/
Dialysis Stations: 13.

North Andover

25044 ■ North Andover Renal Center
Diversified Specialty Institutes
201 Sutton St.
North Andover, MA 01845
Ph: (978)975-1119
URL: http://www.dsi-corp.com
Dialysis Stations: 19. **Formerly:** NRI.

North Billerica

25045 ■ Dialysis Clinic Inc.--Billerica
267 Boston Rd., RT 3A, Ste. 8
North Billerica, MA 01862
Ph: (978)294-1000
URL: http://www.dciinc.org
Dialysis Stations: 16.

North Dartmouth

25046 ■ Southeastern Massachusetts Dialysis Clinic
Fresenius Medical Care
237 B State Rd., Ste. 6
North Dartmouth, MA 02747
Free: 866-434-2597
URL: http://www.ultracare-dialysis.com/
Dialysis Stations: 26.

Northampton

25047 ■ Hampshire County Dialysis Center
Fresenius Medical Care
84 Conz St.
Northampton, MA 01060
Free: 866-434-2597
URL: http://www.ultracare-dialysis.com/
Dialysis Stations: 13.

Norwood

25048 ■ Norwood Dialysis Center
101 Access Rd.
Norwood, MA 02062
Ph: (781)762-1544
Dialysis Stations: 12.

Oak Bluffs

25049 ■ Martha's Vineyard Hospital Dialysis Unit
1 Hospital Rd.
Oak Bluffs, MA 02557
Ph: (508)693-0410
URL: http://www.mvhospital.com
Dialysis Stations: 3.

Palmer

25050 ■ Dialysis Services of Palmer
Fresenius Medical Care
42 Wright St.
Palmer, MA 01069
Free: 866-434-2597
URL: http://www.ultracare-dialysis.com/
Dialysis Stations: 13.

Peabody

25051 ■ Peabody Dialysis Center
Fresenius Medical Care
19-A Centennial Dr.
Peabody, MA 01960
Free: 866-434-2597
URL: http://www.ultracare-dialysis.com/
Dialysis Stations: 16.

Pittsfield

25052 ■ Berkshire Medical Center Dialysis Unit
725 North St.
Pittsfield, MA 01201
Ph: (413)447-3066
URL: http://www.berkshirehealthsystems.com
Dialysis Stations: 25.

Plymouth

25053 ■ Fresenius Medical Care--Plymouth Cordage
10 Cordage Park Cir., Ste. 213
Plymouth, MA 02360
Free: 866-434-2597
URL: http://www.ultracare-dialysis.com/
Dialysis Stations: 16.

Quincy

25054 ■ South Suburban Dialysis Facility
Fresenius Medical Care
241 Parkingway
Quincy, MA 02169
Free: 866-434-2597
URL: http://www.ultracare-dialysis.com/
Dialysis Stations: 20.

Roxbury

25055 ■ Mary Eliza Mahoney Dialysis Center
Fresenius Medical Care
416 Warren St.
Roxbury, MA 02119
Free: 866-434-2597
URL: http://www.ultracare-dialysis.com/
Dialysis Stations: 24.

Salem

25056 ■ Salem Northeast Dialysis
DaVita
Dialysis Center
10 Colonial Rd., Ste. 205
Salem, MA 01970
Free: 800-424-6589
URL: http://www.davita.com
Dialysis Stations: 16. **Formerly:** Gambro Healthcare - Salem.

Saugus

25057 ■ North Suburban Dialysis Center
Fresenius Medical Care
Augustine Plz.
124 Broadway, Rte. 1 N
Saugus, MA 01906
Free: 866-434-2597
URL: http://www.ultracare-dialysis.com/
Dialysis Stations: 21.

Shrewsbury

25058 ■ University Dialysis Center--Shrewsbury
Fresenius Medical Care
239-243 Boston Turnpike Rd.
Shrewsbury, MA 01545
Free: 866-434-2597
URL: http://www.ultracare-dialysis.com/
Dialysis Stations: 13.

Somerville

25059 ■ Dialysis Clinic Inc.--Ball Square
634 Broadway
Somerville, MA 02145
Ph: (617)616-3600
Fax: (617)616-3699
URL: http://www.dciinc.org
Dialysis Stations: 16.

Springfield

25060 ■ Baystate Medical Center--Transplant
759 Chestnut St.
Springfield, MA 01199
Ph: (413)794-0000
URL: http://baystatehealth.com/Baystate/Main+Nav/Clinical+Services/Departments/S urgery/Transplant+Surgery
Dialysis Stations: 0.

25061 ■ East Springfield Dialysis Center
Fresenius Medical Care
435 Cottage St.
Springfield, MA 01104
Free: 866-434-2597
URL: http://www.ultracare-dialysis.com/
Dialysis Stations: 13.

25062 ■ Springfield Dialysis Center--Massachusetts
125 Liberty St., Ste. 101
Springfield, MA 01103
Ph: (413)736-9600
Dialysis Stations: 16.

25063 ■ Western Massachusetts Kidney Center
Fresenius Medical Care
2000 Main St.
Springfield, MA 01103
Free: 866-434-2597
URL: http://www.ultracare-dialysis.com/
Dialysis Stations: 33.

Stoneham

25064 ■ Fresenius Medical Care Services of Stoneham
Dialysis Facility
2 Main St., Ste. 100
Stoneham, MA 02180
Free: 866-434-2597
URL: http://www.ultracare-dialysis.com/
Dialysis Stations: 24.

Stoughton

25065 ■ Goddard Brockton Kidney Center
Medical Office Bldg., Ste. M107
907 Sumner St.
Stoughton, MA 02072
Ph: (781)341-8550
Dialysis Stations: 18.

Taunton

25066 ■ Taunton Kidney Center
Fresenius Medical Care
1 Washington St.
Taunton, MA 02780
Free: 866-434-2597
URL: http://www.ultracare-dialysis.com/
Dialysis Stations: 19.

25067 ■ Taunton Regional Dialysis Center
Mill River Place
Taunton, MA 02780
Ph: (508)828-5986
Dialysis Stations: 20.

Waltham

25068 ■ Dialysis Center at Waltham
American Renal Associates
135 Beaver St., Ste. 111
Waltham, MA 02452
Ph: (781)642-0331
URL: http://www.americanrenal.com
Dialysis Stations: 14.

Webster

25069 ■ South County Dialysis Center
Fresenius Medical Care
336 Thompson Rd., Ste. 1
Webster, MA 01570
Free: 866-434-2597
URL: http://www.ultracare-dialysis.com/
Dialysis Stations: 13.

Wellesley

25070 ■ Wellesley Dialysis
DaVita
Dialysis Center
195 Worcester St., Lower Level
Wellesley, MA 02481
Free: 800-424-6589
URL: http://www.davita.com
Dialysis Stations: 18. **Formerly:** Gambro Healthcare - Wellesley.

West Springfield

25071 ■ Pioneer Valley Dialysis Center
Fresenius Medical Care
208 Ashley Ave.
West Springfield, MA 01089
Free: 866-434-2597
URL: http://www.ultracare-dialysis.com/
Dialysis Stations: 29.

Westwood

25072 ■ Westwood Dialysis Center
Fresenius Medical Care
90 Glacier Dr.
Westwood, MA 02090
Free: 866-434-2597
URL: http://www.ultracare-dialysis.com/
Dialysis Stations: 18.

Weymouth

25073 ■ DaVita
North Shore Massachusetts Acutes
330 Libbey Industrial Pkwy.
Weymouth, MA 02189
Free: 800-424-6589
URL: http://www.davita.com

25074 ■ DaVita--Weymouth Dialysis & At Home
330 Libbey Industrial Pkwy., Ste. 900
Weymouth, MA 02189
Free: 800-424-6589
URL: http://www.davita.com
Dialysis Stations: 27. **Formerly:** Gambro Healthcare.

25075 ■ Quality Care Dialysis Center
Fresenius Medical Care
Stetson W Bldg., Unit 1
2 West St.
Weymouth, MA 02190
Free: 866-434-2597
URL: http://www.ultracare-dialysis.com/
Dialysis Stations: 15.

Woburn

25076 ■ Personal Dialysis Inc.
400 W Cummings Park
Woburn, MA 01801
Ph: (617)783-3800
Dialysis Stations: 1.

25077 ■ Woburn Dialysis
DaVita
Dialysis Center
23 Warren Ave.
Woburn, MA 01801
Free: 800-424-6589
URL: http://www.davita.com
Dialysis Stations: 17. **Formerly:** Gambro Healthcare - Woburn.

Worcester

25078 ■ DaVita
PDI--Worcester Dialysis & At Home
19 Glennie St., Ste. A
Worcester, MA 01605
Free: 800-424-6589
URL: http://www.davita.com
Dialysis Stations: 29.

25079 ■ Saint Vincent's Hospital
Hemodialysis Unit
123 Summer St.
Worcester, MA 01608
Ph: (508)363-9460
URL: http://www.stvincenthospital.com
Dialysis Stations: 12.

25080 ■ U-Mass Memorial Health Care Systems
Dialysis Unit
Worcester, MA 01655
Ph: (774)442-3814
URL: http://www.umassmemorial.org/MedicalCenterHP2.cfm?id=5645
Dialysis Stations: 8.

25081 ■ University of Massachusetts Memorial Healthcare System
Dialysis Unit
55 Lake Ave. N
Worcester, MA 01655
Ph: (508)856-3814
URL: http://www.umass.memorial.org
Dialysis Stations: 8.

Yarmouth Port

25082 ■ Cape Cod Artificial Kidney Center
Fresenius Medical Care
241 Willow St.
Yarmouth Port, MA 02675
Free: 866-434-2597
URL: http://www.ultracare-dialysis.com/
Dialysis Stations: 22.

MICHIGAN

Adrian

25083 ■ Fresenius Medical Care--Adrian
715 Lakeshire Trl.
Adrian, MI 49221
Free: 866-434-2597
URL: http://www.ultracare-dialysis.com/
Dialysis Stations: 18.

Allegan

25084 ■ Fresenius Medical Care--Allegan Dialysis Facility
730 Airway Dr.
Allegan, MI 49010
Free: 866-434-2597
URL: http://www.ultracare-dialysis.com
Dialysis Stations: 12. **Formerly:** Renal Care Group - Allegan.

Allen Park

25085 ■ DaVita/Downriver Kidney Center
5600 Allen Rd.
Allen Park, MI 48101
Free: 800-424-6589
URL: http://www.davita.com
Dialysis Stations: 24.

Alma

25086 ■ Great Lakes Renal Network--Alma Dialysis Center
330 E Warwick Dr.
Alma, MI 48801
Ph: (989)466-3330
Dialysis Stations: 17.

Alpena

25087 ■ Alpena Dialysis Services
301 Oxbow St.
Alpena, MI 49707
Ph: (989)356-3128
Free: 800-647-5303
URL: http://www.alpenaregionalmedicalcenter.org/index.php
Dialysis Stations: 19.

Ann Arbor

25088 ■ Fresenius Medical Care--Ann Arbor West
2355 W Stadium Blvd.
Ann Arbor, MI 48103
Free: 866-434-2597
URL: http://www.ultracare-dialysis.com/
Dialysis Stations: 10.

25089 ■ Saint Joseph Mercy Hospital Dialysis Center
5301 E Huron River Dr.
Ann Arbor, MI 48106
Ph: (734)712-3476
URL: http://www.sjmercyhealth.org/body.cfm?id=164
Dialysis Stations: 14. **Formerly:** Catherine McCauley Health System.

25090 ■ University of Michigan
Adult Dialysis
D7605 University Hospital
1500 E Medical Center Dr.
Ann Arbor, MI 48109
Ph: (734)936-5656
URL: http://www.med.umich.edu/intmed/nephrology/edu/adult.htm
Dialysis Stations: 4.

25091 ■ University of Michigan Dialysis
1500 E Medical Ctr. Dr.
Ann Arbor, MI 48109
Ph: (734)936-5656
URL: http://www.med.umich.edu/intmed/nephrology/patients/inpatient.htm
Dialysis Stations: 4.

25092 ■ University of Michigan
Dialysis Clinics Ann Arbor
2850 S Industrial Hwy., Ste. 100
Ann Arbor, MI 48104
Ph: (346)771-1490
URL: http://www.med.umich.edu/intmed/nephrology/
Dialysis Stations: 16.

Baldwin

25093 ■ Fresenius Medical Care--Baldwin
1101 Washington Ave.
Baldwin, MI 49304
Ph: (231)745-2020
Dialysis Stations: 6. **Formerly:** Renal Dialysis Center.

Battle Creek

25094 ■ DaVita Battle Creek Dialysis
220 E Goodale St., Ste. B
Battle Creek, MI 49017
Free: 800-424-6589
URL: http://www.davita.com
Dialysis Stations: 20.

25095 ■ Fresenius Medical Care--Battle Creek North
233 E Roosevelt Ave.
Battle Creek, MI 49017
Free: 866-434-2597
URL: http://www.ultracare-dialysis.com/
Dialysis Stations: 16. **Formerly:** Renal Care Group.

25096 ■ Fresenius Medical Care--Battle Creek South
2845 Capital Ave. SW, Ste. 102
Battle Creek, MI 49015
Free: 866-434-2597
URL: http://www.ultracare-dialysis.com/
Dialysis Stations: 18. **Formerly:** Michigan Nephrology Center.

Bay City

25097 ■ Regional Dialysis--Bay City
3170 S Professional Dr.
Bay City, MI 48706
Ph: (989)686-8782
Dialysis Stations: 16.

Berkley

25098 ■ Beaumont Dialysis Services--Berkley
2624 11 Mile Rd.
Berkley, MI 48072
Ph: (248)543-7005
URL: http://www.beaumonthospitals.com
Dialysis Stations: 28.

25099 ■ Southeast Michigan Kidney Center
Greenfield Health Systems
1695 W 12 Mile Rd., Ste. 250
Berkley, MI 48072
Ph: (248)414-5200
URL: http://www.ghsrenal.com
Dialysis Stations: 0.

Big Rapids

25100 ■ Fresenius Medical Care--Big Rapids
14307 Northland Dr.
Big Rapids, MI 49307
Ph: (231)527-1622
Dialysis Stations: 12. **Formerly:** Renal Dialysis Center.

Brighton

25101 ■ DaVita--Brighton Dialysis
7960 W Grand River Ave., Ste. 210
Brighton, MI 48114
Free: 800-424-6589
URL: http://www.davita.com
Dialysis Stations: 9. **Formerly:** Michigan Kidney Center.

25102 ■ Fresenius Medical Care--Brighton
315 W North St., Ste. C
Brighton, MI 48116
Free: 866-434-2597
URL: http://www.ultracare-dialysis.com/
Dialysis Stations: 8.

Cadillac

25103 ■ Fresenius Medical Care--Cadillac
203 Paluster St.
Cadillac, MI 49601
Ph: (231)779-8917
Dialysis Stations: 14. **Formerly:** Mercy Hospital Dialysis Facility.

Canton

25104 ■ Fresenius Medical Care--Sheldon Corners
6064 Sheldon Corners
Canton, MI 48187
Free: 866-434-2597
URL: http://www.ultracare-dialysis.com/
Dialysis Stations: 13.

Caro

25105 ■ Caro Dialysis
Fresenius Medical Care
95 Elmdor Dr.
Caro, MI 48723
Free: 866-434-2597
URL: http://www.ultracare-dialysis.com/
Dialysis Stations: 12.

Cass City

25106 ■ Thumb Area Dialysis Center
Great Lakes Regional Dialysis
6757 Main St.
Cass City, MI 48726
Ph: (989)872-5544
Dialysis Stations: 16.

Charlotte

25107 ■ Fresenius Medical Care--Lansing Road, Charlotte
111 Lansing Rd., Ste. 120
Charlotte, MI 48813
Free: 866-434-2597
URL: http://www.ultracare-dialysis.com/
Dialysis Stations: 12.

Chelsea

25108 ■ DaVita--Chelsea
1620 Commerce Park Dr., Ste. 200
Chelsea, MI 48118
Free: 800-424-6589
URL: http://www.davita.com
Dialysis Stations: 8.

Chesterfield Township

25109 ■ Fresenius Medical Care--Chesterfield
48565 Gratiot A
Chesterfield Township, MI 48051
Free: 866-434-2597
URL: http://www.ultracare-dialysis.com/
Dialysis Stations: 16.

Clarkston

25110 ■ Clarkston Dialysis
DaVita
6770 Dixie Hwy., Ste. 205
Clarkston, MI 48346
Free: 800-424-6589
URL: http://www.davita.com
Dialysis Stations: 20.

Clinton Township

25111 ■ Clinton Township Dialysis and At Home
DaVita
15918 19 Mile Rd.
Clinton Township, MI 48038
Free: 800-424-6589
URL: http://www.davita.com
Dialysis Stations: 16.

25112 ■ Fresenius Medical Care Dialysis--Clinton
35351-A Gratiot Ave.
Clinton Township, MI 48035
Free: 866-434-2597
URL: http://www.ultracare-dialysis.com/
Dialysis Stations: 32. **Formerly:** Clinton Dialysis Center.

Clinton Twp.

25113 ■ Macomb Regional Dialysis Center
Greenfield Health Systems
16151 Nineteen Mile Rd.
Clinton Twp., MI 48038
Ph: (586)263-8350
URL: http://www.ghsrenal.com/
Dialysis Stations: 15.

Coldwater

25114 ■ Fresenius Medical Care--Coldwater
360 E Chicago St., Ste. 112
Coldwater, MI 49036
Free: 866-434-2597
URL: http://www.ultracare-dialysis.com/
Dialysis Stations: 12.

Commerce Township

25115 ■ Commerce Township Dialysis
DaVita
120 W Commerce Rd.
Commerce Township, MI 48382
Free: 800-424-6589
URL: http://www.davita.com
Dialysis Stations: 12.

Crystal Falls

25116 ■ Northstar Health System--Dialysis
1328 US Hwy 2
Crystal Falls, MI 49920
Ph: (906)875-4746
URL: http://www.northstarhs.org/getpage.php?name=darling_homepage
Dialysis Stations: 6.

25117 ■ Northstar Health Systems--Crystal Falls
Dialysis Center
1328 US Hwy. 2
Crystal Falls, MI 49920
Ph: (906)875-4746
URL: http://www.northstarhs.org/getpage.php?name=hemodialysis&sub=Services
Dialysis Stations: 6.

Davison

25118 ■ Davison Dialysis
DaVita
1011 S State Rd.
Davison, MI 48423
Free: 800-424-6589
URL: http://www.davita.com
Dialysis Stations: 15.

25119 ■ RRC--Davison
2031 Fairway Dr.
Davison, MI 48423
Ph: (810)654-0138
URL: http://reliantrenalcare.com/
Dialysis Stations: 16. **Formerly:** Hemacare Dialysis Center.

Dearborn

25120 ■ DaVita--Dearborn
1185 Monroe
Dearborn, MI 48124
Free: 800-424-6589
URL: http://www.davita.com
Dialysis Stations: 24. **Formerly:** Gambro Healthcare - Dearborn.

25121 ■ Dearborn Home Dialysis and At Home
DaVita
22030 Park St.
Dearborn, MI 48124
Free: 800-424-6589
URL: http://www.davita.com
Dialysis Stations: 2.

25122 ■ East Dearborn Dialysis
DaVita
13200 W Warren
Dearborn, MI 48126
Free: 800-424-6589
URL: http://www.davita.com
Dialysis Stations: 16.

25123 ■ Greenfield Health Systems--Dearborn Dialysis Facility
19001 Hubbard Dr.
Dearborn, MI 48126
Ph: (313)441-1160
URL: http://www.ghsrenal.com
Dialysis Stations: 36.

Detroit

25124 ■ Children's Hospital of Michigan Transplant/Dialysis Center
3901 Beaubien Blvd.
Detroit, MI 48201
Ph: (313)745-5604
URL: http://www.childrensdmc.org/?id=928
Dialysis Stations: 7.

25125 ■ DaVita--Cadieux
6150 Cadieux
Detroit, MI 48224
Free: 800-424-6589
URL: http://www.davita.com
Dialysis Stations: 32.

25126 ■ DaVita--Detroit Dialysis
2674 E Jefferson Ave.
Detroit, MI 48207
Free: 800-424-6589
URL: http://www.davita.com
Dialysis Stations: 21.

25127 ■ DaVita of Detroit--Kresge Dialysis Facility
4145 Cass Ave.
Detroit, MI 48201
Free: 800-424-6589
URL: http://www.davita.com
Dialysis Stations: 32. **Formerly:** Gambro Healthcare - Detroit Kresge.

25128 ■ DaVita--Redford Dialysis Facility
22711 Grand River
Detroit, MI 48219
Free: 800-424-6589
URL: http://www.davita.com
Dialysis Stations: 32. **Formerly:** Gambro Healthcare - Redford.

25129 ■ DaVita--Schaefer Drive Dialysis Facility
18100 Schaefer Dr.
Detroit, MI 48235
Free: 800-424-6589
URL: http://www.davita.com
Dialysis Stations: 20. **Formerly:** Gambro Healthcare of Detroit.

25130 ■ Fresenius Medical Care--Bewick
10201 E Jefferson Ave., Ste. A
Detroit, MI 38214
Free: 866-434-2597
URL: http://www.ultracare-dialysis.com
Dialysis Stations: 32.

25131 ■ Fresenius Medical Care--Conner
5555 Conner Ave.
Detroit, MI 48213
Free: 866-434-2597
URL: http://www.ultracare-dialysis.com/
Dialysis Stations: 32.

25132 ■ Fresenius Medical Care--East Detroit
22151 Moross Rd., Prof. Bldg. 1
Detroit, MI 48236
Free: 866-434-2597
URL: http://www.ultracare-dialysis.com/
Dialysis Stations: 16.

25133 ■ Fresenius Medical Care--Northwest Detroit
18944 Grand River Ave.
Detroit, MI 48223
Free: 866-434-2597
URL: http://www.ultracare-dialysis.com/
Dialysis Stations: 26. **Formerly:** Bio-Medical Applications of Northwest Detroit.

25134 ■ Fresenius Medical Care--University
18430 Livernois St.
Detroit, MI 48221
Free: 866-434-2597
URL: http://www.ultracare-dialysis.com/
Dialysis Stations: 32.

25135 ■ Great Lakes Dialysis, LLC
14614 Kercheval St.
Detroit, MI 48215
Ph: (313)308-4200
URL: http://www.greatlakesdialysis.com/
Dialysis Stations: 24.

25136 ■ Greenfield Health Systems--Detroit West Pavilion Dialysis Facility
2799 W Grand Blvd.
Detroit, MI 48202
Ph: (313)916-7062
URL: http://www.ghsrenal.com
Dialysis Stations: 46.

25137 ■ Greenfield Health Systems--Northwest Detroit
7800 W Outer Dr.
Detroit, MI 48235
Ph: (313)653-2850
URL: http://www.ghsrenal.com
Dialysis Stations: 42.

25138 ■ Grosse Pointe Dialysis and At Home DaVita
18000 E Warren Ave.
Detroit, MI 48224
Free: 800-424-6589
URL: http://www.davita.com
Dialysis Stations: 25.

25139 ■ Henry Ford Hospital--Transplant
2799 W Grand Blvd., CFP2
Detroit, MI 48202
Ph: (313)916-3364
URL: http://www.henryfordhealth.org/body.cfm?id=45264
Dialysis Stations: 0.

25140 ■ Life--Alysis Kidney Center
5830 Conner St.
Detroit, MI 48213
Ph: (313)371-5433
Dialysis Stations: 13.

25141 ■ Motor City Dialysis DaVita
4727 Saint Antoine St.
Detroit, MI 48201
Free: 800-424-6589
URL: http://www.davita.com
Dialysis Stations: 2. **Formerly:** Gambro Healthcare - Motor City Dialysis.

25142 ■ New Center Dialysis DaVita
3011 W Grand Blvd., Ste. 650
Detroit, MI 48202
Free: 800-424-6589
URL: http://www.davita.com
Dialysis Stations: 37.

25143 ■ St. John Hospital--Transplant
22101 Moross, Ste. 480, PB2
Detroit, MI 48236
Ph: (313)343-3048
URL: http://www.stjohnprovidence.org/transplant/
Dialysis Stations: 0.

25144 ■ State Fair Dialysis Center
19800 Woodward Ave.
Detroit, MI 48203
Ph: (313)893-8610
Dialysis Stations: 21.

25145 ■ Wayne County Dialysis Nephrology Center of Detroit
20001 Livernois Ave., Ste. 500
Detroit, MI 48221
Ph: (313)861-0340
Dialysis Stations: 23.

Dundee

25146 ■ Fresenius Medical Care--Dundee
129 Helle Blvd.
Dundee, MI 48131
Free: 866-434-2597
URL: http://www.ultracare-dialysis.com/
Dialysis Stations: 14.

East Lansing

25147 ■ Fresenius Medical Care--East Lansing
2601 Coolidge Rd., Ste. A
East Lansing, MI 48823
Free: 866-434-2597
URL: http://www.ultracare-dialysis.com
Dialysis Stations: 32. **Formerly:** Renal Care Group - East Lansing.

25148 ■ Lansing Home Hemodialysis DaVita
1675 Watertower Pl.
East Lansing, MI 48823
Free: 800-424-6589
URL: http://www.davita.com
Dialysis Stations: 0.

East Tawas

25149 ■ Fresenius Medical Care--Tawas Bay
1698 E Huron
East Tawas, MI 48730
Ph: (989)362-5267
URL: http://www.ultracare-dialysis.com
Dialysis Stations: 12.

Eastpointe

25150 ■ Greenfield Health Systems--Eastpointe Dialysis Facility
21400 Kelly Rd.
Eastpointe, MI 48021
Ph: (586)779-8779
URL: http://www.ghsrenal.com
Dialysis Stations: 26.

Escanaba

25151 ■ Fresenius Medical Care--Escanaba Dialysis Facility
3501 Ludington St.
Escanaba, MI 49829
Free: 866-434-2597
URL: http://www.ultracare-dialysis.com/
Dialysis Stations: 13. **Formerly:** Renal Care Group - Escanaba.

Essexville

25152 ■ Bay Area Regional Dialysis--Essexville
Fresenius Medical Care
1536 Center Ave.
Essexville, MI 48732
Free: 866-434-2597
URL: http://www.ultracare-dialysis.com/
Dialysis Stations: 24.

Fenton

25153 ■ Fenton Dialysis
DaVita
17420 Silver Pkwy.
Fenton, MI 48430
Free: 800-424-6589
URL: http://www.davita.com
Dialysis Stations: 12.

Flint

25154 ■ DaVita--Ballenger Pointe Dialysis & At Home
2262 S Ballenger Hwy.
Flint, MI 48503
Free: 800-424-6589
URL: http://www.davita.com
Dialysis Stations: 20.

25155 ■ Flint Dialysis
DaVita
2 Hurley Plz., Ste. 115
Flint, MI 48503
Free: 800-424-6589
URL: http://www.davita.com
Dialysis Stations: 24.

25156 ■ Fresenius Medical Services Dialysis--Flint
2222 S Linden Rd., Ste. S
Flint, MI 48532
Free: 866-434-2597
URL: http://www.ultracare-dialysis.com/
Dialysis Stations: 21. **Formerly:** Bio-Medical Applications of Flint.

25157 ■ Hallwood Dialysis
DaVita
4929 Clio Rd., Ste. B
Flint, MI 48504
Free: 800-424-6589
URL: http://www.davita.com
Dialysis Stations: 16.

25158 ■ Park Plaza Dialysis
DaVita
G-1075 N Ballenger Hwy.
Flint, MI 48504
Free: 800-424-6589
URL: http://www.davita.com
Dialysis Stations: 12.

25159 ■ Reliant Renal Care--Flint
4007 Corunna Rd.
Flint, MI 48532
Ph: (810)877-6582
URL: http://reliantrenalcare.com/partnersandphysicians/flint.html
Dialysis Stations: 24.

Flushing

25160 ■ Flushing Dialysis
DaVita
3469 Pierson Pl., Ste. A
Flushing, MI 48433
Free: 800-424-6589
URL: http://www.davita.com
Dialysis Stations: 12.

Fremont

25161 ■ DaVita--Newaygo County
1317 W Main St.
Fremont, MI 49412
Free: 800-424-6589
URL: http://www.davita.com
Dialysis Stations: 14. **Formerly:** Gambro Healthcare.

Gaylord

25162 ■ Dialysis Services of Gaylord
Otsego Memomrial Hospital
1989 Walden Dr.
Gaylord, MI 49735
Ph: (989)731-6418
URL: http://www.myomh.org/dialysis-services-of-gaylord.php
Dialysis Stations: 9.

Gladwin

25163 ■ Regional Dialysis--Gladwin
673 Quarter St.
Gladwin, MI 48624
Ph: (989)246-6440
Dialysis Stations: 19.

Grand Blanc

25164 ■ Grand Blanc Dialysis
DaVita
3625 Genesys Pkwy.
Grand Blanc, MI 48439
Free: 800-424-6589
URL: http://www.davita.com
Dialysis Stations: 20.

Grand Haven

25165 ■ DaVita--PDI Grand Haven
16964 Robbins Rd.
Grand Haven, MI 49417
Free: 800-424-6589
URL: http://www.davita.com
Dialysis Stations: 12.

Grand Rapids

25166 ■ DaVita--Grand Rapids Dialysis & PDI
801 Cherry St. SE
Grand Rapids, MI 49506
Free: 800-424-6589
URL: http://www.davita.com
Dialysis Stations: 36.

25167 ■ DaVita--Grand Rapids East PDI
1230 Elkhart St. NE
Grand Rapids, MI 49503
Free: 800-424-6589
URL: http://www.davita.com
Dialysis Stations: 25.

25168 ■ Helen Devos Children's Hospital Dialysis Unit
221 Michigan St., NE, Ste. 406
Grand Rapids, MI 49503
Ph: (616)391-3788
URL: http://www.helendevoschildrens.org/
Dialysis Stations: 3. **Formerly:** Devos Children's Hospital.

25169 ■ St. Marys Healthcaretransportationnsplant
200 Jefferson St. SE
Grand Rapids, MI 49503
Ph: (616)685-6222
URL: http://www.smhealthcare.org/clinicalservices/kidney/
Dialysis Stations: 0.

Greenville

25170 ■ Great Lakes Renal Network--Greenville
Dialysis Facility
101 S Greenville W Dr.
Greenville, MI 48838
Ph: (616)225-9500
Dialysis Stations: 10.

Hamtramck

25171 ■ Fresenius Medical Care--Detroit
9300 Conant
Hamtramck, MI 48212
Free: 866-434-2597
URL: http://www.ultracare-dialysis.com/
Dialysis Stations: 22.

Hancock

25172 ■ Portage Health Dialysis
500 Campus Dr.
Hancock, MI 49930
Ph: (906)483-1720
Dialysis Stations: 12. **Formerly:** Western Upper Peninsula Dialysis Unit.

Harper Woods

25173 ■ Fresenius Medical Care--Harper Woods
19265 Vernier Rd.
Harper Woods, MI 48225
Free: 866-434-2597
URL: http://www.ultracare-dialysis.com/
Dialysis Stations: 25.

Hazel Park

25174 ■ Beaumont Hospital Dialysis--Hazel Park
23231 John R Rd.
Hazel Park, MI 48030
Ph: (248)545-0550
URL: http://www.beaumonthospitals.com
Dialysis Stations: 18.

Highland Park

25175 ■ DaVita--Highland Park PDI
64 Victor
Highland Park, MI 48203
Free: 800-424-6589
URL: http://www.davita.com
Dialysis Stations: 28. **Formerly:** PDI.

Holland

25176 ■ Renal Advantage Inc.--Holland
655 Hastings Ave.
Holland, MI 49423
Ph: (616)392-3263
URL: http://www.renaladvantage.com
Dialysis Stations: 18.

Ionia

25177 ■ Ionia Dialysis
DaVita
2622 Heartland Blvd.
Ionia, MI 48846
Free: 800-424-6589
URL: http://www.davita.com
Dialysis Stations: 12.

Iron Mountain

25178 ■ Fresenius Medical Care--Iron Mountain
1711 S Stephenson Ave.
Iron Mountain, MI 49801
Free: 866-434-2597
URL: http://www.ultracare-dialysis.com/
Dialysis Stations: 10.

Jackson

25179 ■ Fresenius Medical Care--Jackson Oaks
128 N Elm Ave.
Jackson, MI 49202
Free: 866-434-2597
URL: http://www.ultracare-dialysis.com/
Dialysis Stations: 17.

25180 ■ Jackson Dialysis DaVita
234 W Louis-Glick Hwy.
Jackson, MI 49202
Free: 800-424-6589
URL: http://www.davita.com
Dialysis Stations: 21.

25181 ■ Renal Advantage Inc.--Jackson Dialysis Center
200 S East Ave.
Jackson, MI 49201
Ph: (517)788-8727
URL: http://www.renaladvantage.com
Dialysis Stations: 23. **Formerly:** Gambro Healthcare of Jackson.

Kalamazoo

25182 ■ Fresenius Medical Care--Kalamazoo
521 E Michigan Ave.
Kalamazoo, MI 49007
Free: 866-434-2597
URL: http://www.ultracare-dialysis.com/
Dialysis Stations: 24. **Formerly:** Renal Care Group.

25183 ■ Fresenius Medical Care--Kalamazoo
5010 Gull Rd.
Kalamazoo, MI 49048
Free: 866-434-2597
URL: http://www.ultracare-dialysis.com/
Dialysis Stations: 12.

25184 ■ Fresenius Medical Care--Kalamazoo East
2901 E Kilgore Rd.
Kalamazoo, MI 49001
Free: 866-434-2597
URL: http://www.ultracare-dialysis.com/
Dialysis Stations: 17.

25185 ■ Fresenius Medical Care--Oshtemo Dialysis Facility
6739 Seeco Dr.
Kalamazoo, MI 49009
Free: 866-434-2597
URL: http://www.ultracare-dialysis.com/
Dialysis Stations: 24. **Formerly:** Renal Care Group - Oshtemo.

25186 ■ Kalamazoo Central Dialysis DaVita
535 S Burdick St., Ste. 110
Kalamazoo, MI 49007
Free: 800-424-6589
URL: http://www.davita.com
Dialysis Stations: 10.

25187 ■ Kalamazoo PD Unit Fresenius Medical Care
527 East Michigan Ave.
Kalamazoo, MI 49007
Free: 866-434-2597
URL: http://www.ultracare-dialysis.com/
Dialysis Stations: 2.

25188 ■ Kalamazoo West Dialysis and At Home DaVita
1040 N 10th St., Ste. 100
Kalamazoo, MI 49009
Free: 800-424-6589
URL: http://www.davita.com
Dialysis Stations: 6.

Kalkaska

25189 ■ Kalkaska Dialysis Center
415 2nd St.
Kalkaska, MI 49646
Ph: (231)258-3680
Dialysis Stations: 12.

Lansing

25190 ■ Fresenius Medical Care--Lansing
3960 Patient Care Dr., Ste. 112
Lansing, MI 48911
Free: 866-434-2597
URL: http://www.ultracare-dialysis.com/
Dialysis Stations: 25. **Formerly:** Renal Care Group.

25191 ■ Lansing Central Dialysis Fresenius Medical Care
2710 S Washington Ave., Ste. 100
Lansing, MI 48910
Free: 866-434-2597
URL: http://www.ultracare-dialysis.com/
Dialysis Stations: 25.

25192 ■ Sparrow Dialysis--Saint Lawrence Campus
1210 W Saginaw Hwy.
Lansing, MI 48915
Ph: (517)364-7373
URL: http://www.sparrow.org
Dialysis Stations: 18.

25193 ■ Sparrow Dialysis--Sparrow Campus
1215 E Michigan Ave.
Lansing, MI 48909
Ph: (517)364-7373
URL: http://www.sparrow.org
Dialysis Stations: 3.

Lapeer

25194 ■ RRC Lapeer
1375 N Main St.
Lapeer, MI 48446
Ph: (810)667-5940
URL: http://reliantrenalcare.com
Dialysis Stations: 12. **Formerly:** Hemacare Dialysis Center.

Livonia

25195 ■ Fresenius Medical Care--Botsford Park
28424 W 8 Mile Rd.
Livonia, MI 48152
Ph: (248)442-7901
URL: http://www.botsfordkidneycenter.com
Dialysis Stations: 29.

25196 ■ Fresenius Medical Care--Livonia
32423 Schoolcraft Rd.
Livonia, MI 48150
Free: 866-434-2597
URL: http://www.ultracare-dialysis.com/
Dialysis Stations: 20. **Formerly:** Bio-Medical Applications of Livonia.

25197 ■ Greenfield Health Systems--Livonia Dialysis Facility
14555 Levan Rd.
Livonia, MI 48154
Ph: (734)591-6409
URL: http://www.ghsrenal.com
Dialysis Stations: 13.

25198 ■ Renal Research Institute University of Michigan Dialysis Clinics--Livonia
19900 Haggerty Rd., Ste. 106
Livonia, MI 48152
Ph: (734)432-7870
URL: http://www.renalresearch.com
Dialysis Stations: 16.

Ludington

25199 ■ DaVita--Ludington Dialysis Facility
5 N Atkinson Dr., Ste. 101
Ludington, MI 49431
Free: 800-424-6589
URL: http://www.davita.com
Dialysis Stations: 9. **Formerly:** Gambro Healthcare of Ludington.

Macomb Township

25200 ■ Fresenius Medical Care--Romeo Plank
46591 Romeo Plank Rd., Ste. 101
Macomb Township, MI 48044
Free: 866-434-2597
URL: http://www.ultracare-dialysis.com/
Dialysis Stations: 16.

Madison Heights

25201 ■ Fresenius Medical Services Dialysis--Madison Heights
25780 Commerce Dr.
Madison Heights, MI 48071
Free: 866-434-2597
URL: http://www.ultracare-dialysis.com/
Dialysis Stations: 18.

Manistee

25202 ■ Fresenius Medical Care--Manistee
1293 E Parkdale Ave.
Manistee, MI 49660
Ph: (231)398-1790
Dialysis Stations: 8. **Formerly:** West Shore Mercy.

Marlette

25203 ■ Reliant Renal Care--Marlette
2898 Main St.
Marlette, MI 48453
Ph: (989)635-1111
URL: http://reliantrenalcare.com/partnersandphysicians/marlette.html
Dialysis Stations: 13.

Marquette

25204 ■ Marquette General Hospital Dialysis Center
580 W College Ave.
Marquette, MI 49855
Ph: (906)225-3266
URL: http://www.mgh.org
Dialysis Stations: 15.

Marshall

25205 ■ Oaklawn Dialysis Center Fresenius Medical Care
310 E Michigan Ave.
Marshall, MI 49068
Free: 866-434-2597
URL: http://www.ultracare-dialysis.com/
Dialysis Stations: 8.

Midland

25206 ■ Regional Dialysis--Midland
4901 Jefferson Ave.
Midland, MI 48640
Ph: (989)839-7770
Dialysis Stations: 24.

Monroe

25207 ■ Great Lakes Dialysis--Monroe Fresenius Medical Care
700 Stewart Rd., Ste. 103
Monroe, MI 48162
Free: 866-434-2597
URL: http://www.ultracare-dialysis.com/
Dialysis Stations: 16.

Mount Morris

25208 ■ RRC--Mt. Morris
G-7220 N Saginaw Rd.
Mount Morris, MI 48458
Ph: (810)687-6837
URL: http://reliantrenalcare.com
Dialysis Stations: 17. **Formerly:** Hemacare.

Mount Pleasant

25209 ■ Great Lakes Renal Network--Mount Pleasant
404 S Crapo St.
Mount Pleasant, MI 48858
Ph: (989)779-8724
Dialysis Stations: 15.

Muskegon

25210 ■ DaVita--Muskegon
Dialysis Facility & At Home
1277 Mercy Dr.
Muskegon, MI 49444
Free: 800-424-6589
URL: http://www.davita.com
Dialysis Stations: 28. **Formerly:** Gambro Healthcare - Muskegon.

25211 ■ Renal Advantage Inc.--West Norton
1080 W Norton Ave.
Muskegon, MI 49441
Ph: (231)780-5468
URL: http://www.renaladvantage.com
Dialysis Stations: 16. **Formerly:** DaVita--Roosevelt Park.

Niles

25212 ■ Liberty Dialysis at Lakeland
8 Longmeadow Village Dr.
Niles, MI 49120
Ph: (269)684-0116
Dialysis Stations: 25. **Formerly:** Lakeland Dialysis.

Novi

25213 ■ Novi Kidney Center
DaVita
Dialysis Facility
47250 W 10 Mile Rd.
Novi, MI 48375
Free: 800-424-6589
URL: http://www.davita.com
Dialysis Stations: 18.

Oak Park

25214 ■ Oak Park Dialysis
DaVita
Parkwoods Plaza
13481 W 10 Mile Rd.
Oak Park, MI 48237
Free: 800-424-6589
URL: http://www.davita.com
Dialysis Stations: 20.

Owosso

25215 ■ Fresenius Medical Care--Owosso
918 Corunna Ave.
Owosso, MI 48867
Free: 866-434-2597
URL: http://www.ultracare-dialysis.com/
Dialysis Stations: 13. **Formerly:** Bio-Medical Applications of Owosso.

Petoskey

25216 ■ Northern Michigan Regional Hospital Dialysis Center
416 Connable St.
Petoskey, MI 49770
Ph: (231)487-4685
URL: http://www.northernhealth.org
Dialysis Stations: 13.

Pontiac

25217 ■ Greenfield Health Systems--Pontiac Dialysis Facility
44200 Woodward Ave., Ste. 109
Pontiac, MI 48341
Ph: (248)858-6103
URL: http://www.ghsrenal.com
Dialysis Stations: 21.

25218 ■ North Oakland Kidney Center
DaVita
Dialysis Facility
450 N Telegraph
Pontiac, MI 48341
Free: 800-424-6589
Fax: (248)333-9589
URL: http://www.davita.com
Dialysis Stations: 36.

Port Huron

25219 ■ Fresenius Medical Care--Port Huron
2607 Electric Ave.
Port Huron, MI 48060
Free: 866-434-2597
URL: http://www.ultracare-dialysis.com/
Dialysis Stations: 25. **Formerly:** Saint John Dialysis Center.

Rochester Hills

25220 ■ Rochester Hills Dialysis
DaVita
1886 W Auburn Rd., Ste. 100
Rochester Hills, MI 48309
Free: 800-424-6589
URL: http://www.davita.com
Dialysis Stations: 20.

Rockford

25221 ■ Renal Advantage Inc.--Rockford Park
311 Rockford Park Dr. NE
Rockford, MI 49341
Ph: (616)863-6214
URL: http://www.renaladvantage.com
Dialysis Stations: 16. **Formerly:** Grambro Healthcare of Rockford.

Romulus

25222 ■ DaVita--Romulus
31470 Ecorse Rd.
Romulus, MI 48174
Free: 800-424-6589
URL: http://www.davita.com
Dialysis Stations: 12. **Formerly:** Gambro Healthcare of Romulus.

25223 ■ Fresenius Medical Care--Romulus
11200 Metro Airport Center Dr., Ste. 120
Romulus, MI 48174
Free: 866-434-2597
URL: http://www.ultracare-dialysis.com/
Dialysis Stations: 14. **Formerly:** Bio-Medical Applications of Romulus.

Royal Oak

25224 ■ William Beaumont Hospital--Royal Oak
Transplant Center
36535 W 13 Mile Rd., Ste. 644
Royal Oak, MI 48073
Ph: (248)551-1033
URL: http://www.beaumonthospitals.com
Dialysis Stations: 0.

Saginaw

25225 ■ Bay Area Regional Dialysis Center--Saginaw
Fresenius Medical Care
4800 E McLeod Dr. E
Saginaw, MI 48604
Free: 866-434-2597
URL: http://www.ultracare-dialysis.com/
Dialysis Stations: 27.

25226 ■ Bay Area Regional Dialysis Center--Saginaw Riverside
Fresenius Medical Care
920 N Niagara St.
Saginaw, MI 48602
Free: 866-434-2597
URL: http://www.ultracare-dialysis.com/
Dialysis Stations: 32.

25227 ■ Saginaw Dialysis Clinic
DaVita
1527 E Genesee
Saginaw, MI 48607
Free: 800-424-6589
URL: http://www.davita.com
Dialysis Stations: 10.

Saint Clair Shores

25228 ■ Quality Care Dialysis Center--Saintn Clair Shores
Fresenius Medical Care
26100 Harper Ave.
Saint Clair Shores, MI 48081
Free: 866-434-2597
URL: http://www.ultracare-dialysis.com/
Dialysis Stations: 21.

Saint Ignace

25229 ■ Moses Dialysis Unit
1140 N State St.
Saint Ignace, MI 49781
Ph: (906)643-0408
Dialysis Stations: 6.

Saint Joseph

25230 ■ Liberty Dialysis at Lakeland--Royalton
3772 Hollywood Rd.
Saint Joseph, MI 49085
Ph: (269)428-7474
URL: http://www.lakelandcare.com
Dialysis Stations: 21. **Formerly:** Lakeland Dialysis Center.

Sandusky

25231 ■ Fresenius Medical Care--Sandusky
47 Dawson St.
Sandusky, MI 48471
Free: 866-434-2597
URL: http://www.ultracare-dialysis.com/
Dialysis Stations: 12.

Sault Sainte Marie

25232 ■ Chippewa Dialysis Services
500 Osborne
Sault Sainte Marie, MI 49783
Ph: (906)635-4640
Dialysis Stations: 5.

Shelby Township

25233 ■ Fresenius Medical Care--Shelby
56065 Van Dyke
Shelby Township, MI 48316
Free: 866-434-2597
URL: http://www.ultracare-dialysis.com/
Dialysis Stations: 24.

South Haven

25234 ■ Fresenius Medical Care--South Haven
199 Veterans lvd.
South Haven, MI 49090
Free: 866-434-2597
URL: http://www.ultracare-dialysis.com/
Dialysis Stations: 16. **Formerly:** Renal Care Group.

Southfield

25235 ■ Cornerstone Dialysis
DaVita
23857 Greenfield Rd.
Southfield, MI 48075
Free: 800-424-6589
URL: http://www.davita.com
Dialysis Stations: 25. **Formerly:** Southfield Kidney Center of DaVita.

25236 ■ DaVita--Greenview
18544 Eight Mile Rd.
Southfield, MI 48075
Free: 800-424-6589
URL: http://www.davita.com
Dialysis Stations: 24.

25237 ■ Northwest Detroit Dialysis--Lahser Satellite
Greenfield Health Systems
25664 Lahser Rd.
Southfield, MI 48034
Ph: (248)358-7521
URL: http://www.ghsrenal.com
Dialysis Stations: 24.

25238 ■ Southfield West Dialysis
DaVita
21900 Melrose Ave.
Southfield, MI 48075
Free: 800-424-6589
URL: http://www.davita.com
Dialysis Stations: 18.

Southgate

25239 ■ DaVita--Southgate
Dialysis Center
14752 Northline Rd.
Southgate, MI 48195
Free: 800-424-6589
URL: http://www.davita.com
Dialysis Stations: 30. **Formerly:** Gambro Healthcare of Southgate.

Sterling Heights

25240 ■ William Beaumont Hospital--Sterling Heights
Dialysis Center
44300 Dequindre Rd.
Sterling Heights, MI 48314
Ph: (248)964-0100
URL: http://www.beaumonthospitals.com
Dialysis Stations: 18.

Sturgis

25241 ■ Fresenius Medical Care--Sturgis
1276 Kitson St.
Sturgis, MI 49091
Free: 866-434-2597
URL: http://www.ultracare-dialysis.com/
Dialysis Stations: 14.

Taylor

25242 ■ Fresenius Medical Care--Taylor
22970 Northline Rd., No. 100
Taylor, MI 48180
Free: 866-434-2597
URL: http://www.ultracare-dialysis.com/
Dialysis Stations: 12. **Formerly:** Taylor Dialysis Center.

25243 ■ Greenfield Health Systems--Taylor
Dialysis Facility
24565 Haig Rd.
Taylor, MI 48180
Ph: (313)291-7800
URL: http://www.ghsrenal.com
Dialysis Stations: 27.

Three Rivers

25244 ■ Fresenius Medical Care--Three Rivers
601 S Health Pkwy.
Three Rivers, MI 49093
Free: 866-434-2597
URL: http://www.ultracare-dialysis.com/
Dialysis Stations: 12. **Formerly:** Renal Care Group.

Traverse City

25245 ■ Munson Dialysis Center
4062 W Royal Dr.
Traverse City, MI 49684
Ph: (231)935-0447
Dialysis Stations: 18. **Formerly:** Traverse Bay Regional Dialysis Center.

Troy

25246 ■ Greenfield Health Systems--Troy
Dialysis Facility
2050 Livernois Rd., Ste. A
Troy, MI 48083
Ph: (248)524-1270
URL: http://www.ghsrenal.com
Dialysis Stations: 16.

Warren

25247 ■ Fresenius Medical Care--Warren, Michigan
30300 Hoover
Warren, MI 48093
Free: 866-434-2597
URL: http://www.ultracare-dialysis.com/
Dialysis Stations: 24.

25248 ■ Macomb Kidney Center
DaVita
Dialysis Facility
28295 Schoenherr Rd., Ste. A
Warren, MI 48088
Free: 800-424-6589
URL: http://www.davita.com
Dialysis Stations: 20.

Waterford

25249 ■ Tel Huron Waterford Dialysis
DaVita
225 Summit Dr.
Waterford, MI 48328
Free: 800-424-6589
URL: http://www.davita.com
Dialysis Stations: 20.

West Bloomfield

25250 ■ West Bloomfield Dialysis
DaVita
6010 W Maple Rd., Ste. 215
West Bloomfield, MI 48322
Free: 800-424-6589
URL: http://www.davita.com
Dialysis Stations: 9.

West Branch

25251 ■ Regional Dialysis--West Branch
599 Court St.
West Branch, MI 48661
Ph: (989)345-8422
Dialysis Stations: 14.

Westland

25252 ■ DaVita--Garden West
Dialysis Center
5715 Venoy
Westland, MI 48185
Free: 800-424-6589
URL: http://www.davita.com
Dialysis Stations: 24. **Formerly:** Gambro Healthcare of Westland.

25253 ■ Westland Dialysis
Davita
36588 Ford Rd.
Westland, MI 48185
Free: 800-424-6589
URL: http://www.davita.com
Dialysis Stations: 16.

Wyoming

25254 ■ Renal Advantage Inc.--Clyde Park
Dialysis Facility
4893 Clyde Park Ave.
Wyoming, MI 49509
Ph: (616)531-5353
URL: http://www.renaladvantage.com
Dialysis Stations: 36. **Formerly:** Gambro Healthcare - Clyde Park.

Ypsilanti

25255 ■ Fresenius Medical Care--Ann Arbor
5205 McAuley Dr.
Ypsilanti, MI 48197
Free: 866-434-2597
URL: http://www.ultracare-dialysis.com/
Dialysis Stations: 20. **Formerly:** Washtenaw Regional Dialysis Center.

25256 ■ Ypsilanti Dialysis & At Home
DaVita
2766 Washtenaw Rd.
Ypsilanti, MI 48197
Free: 800-424-6589
URL: http://www.davita.com
Dialysis Stations: 14.

Zeeland

25257 ■ Renal Advantage Inc. Care Centers--Zeeland
2 Royal Park Dr.
Zeeland, MI 49464
Ph: (616)748-0522
URL: http://www.renaladvantage.com
Dialysis Stations: 14.

25258 ■ Renal Advantage Inc. Royal Park--Zeeland
2 Royal Park Dr.
Zeeland, MI 49464
Ph: (616)748-0522
URL: http://www.renaladvantage.com
Dialysis Stations: 14. **Formerly:** Gambro Healthcare of Zeeland.

MINNESOTA

Albert Lea

25259 ■ Mayo Health System/Albert Lea Medical Center
Dialysis Facility
1705 SE Broadway
Albert Lea, MN 56007
Ph: (507)377-5920
URL: http://www.almedcenter.org
Dialysis Stations: 18.

Alexandria

25260 ■ Centracare Dialysis at Douglas County Hospital
111 17th Ave. S
Alexandria, MN 56308
Ph: (320)762-1226
URL: http://www.centracare.com/specialty_centers/dialysis/index.html
Dialysis Stations: 7.

Arden Hills

25261 ■ DaVita--Arden Hills Dialysis
3900 Northwood S, Ste. 110
Arden Hills, MN 55112
Free: 800-424-6589
URL: http://www.davita.com
Dialysis Stations: 12.

Bemidji

25262 ■ Sanford Dialysis--Bemidji
Sanford Health
1233 34th St. NW
Bemidji, MN 56601
Ph: (218)333-5640
URL: http://www.sanfordhealth.org/
Dialysis Stations: 12.

Big Lake

25263 ■ Centracare Kidney Program at Big Lake
16830 198th Ave. NW
Big Lake, MN 55309
Ph: (763)263-7320
URL: http://www.centracare.com/specialty_centers/dialysis/index.html
Dialysis Stations: 9.

Bloomington

25264 ■ DaVita--Bloomington Dialysis
8591 Lyndale Ave. S
Bloomington, MN 55420
Free: 800-424-6589
URL: http://www.davita.com
Dialysis Stations: 20.

25265 ■ Fresenius Medical Care--Southtown
7901 Xerxes Ave. S, Ste. 103
Bloomington, MN 55431
Free: 866-434-2597
URL: http://www.ultracare-dialysis.com/
Dialysis Stations: 12.

Brainerd

25266 ■ Centracare Dialysis--Brainerd
Business Hwy. 371
2024 S 6th St.
Brainerd, MN 56401
Ph: (218)825-8964
URL: http://www.centracare.com/specialty_centers/dialysis/index.html
Dialysis Stations: 15.

Buffalo

25267 ■ Fresenius Medical Care Dialysis--Buffalo
Buffalo Dialysis Center
104 Marty Dr., Ste. 2
Buffalo, MN 55313
Free: 866-434-2597
URL: http://www.ultracare-dialysis.com/
Dialysis Stations: 7.

Burnsville

25268 ■ DaVita--Burnsville Dialysis
501 E Nicollet Blvd., Ste. 150
Burnsville, MN 55337
Free: 800-424-6589
URL: http://www.davita.com
Dialysis Stations: 20.

Cambridge

25269 ■ Centracare Kidney Program--Cabridge
520 SW 11th Ave.
Cambridge, MN 55008
Ph: (763)263-7390
URL: http://www.centracare.com/specialty_centers/dialysis/index.html
Dialysis Stations: 15.

Canby

25270 ■ Sanford Dialysis--Canby
112 St. Olaf Ave. S
Canby, MN 56220
Ph: (507)223-7277
Dialysis Stations: 2. **Formerly:** Sioux Valley Canby Dialysis.

Cass Lake

25271 ■ Cass Lake Dialysis
DaVita
602 Grant Utley Ave.
Cass Lake, MN 56633
Free: 800-424-6589
Fax: (218)335-7752
URL: http://www.davita.com
Dialysis Stations: 8.

Champlin

25272 ■ Fresenius Medical Care--Champlin
12339 Champlin Dr.
Champlin, MN 55316
Free: 866-434-2597
URL: http://www.ultracare-dialysis.com/
Dialysis Stations: 24.

Coon Rapids

25273 ■ Coon Rapids Dialysis
DaVita
3960 Coon Rapids Blvd., Ste. 309
Coon Rapids, MN 55433
Free: 800-424-6589
URL: http://www.davita.com
Dialysis Stations: 16.

25274 ■ Fresenius Medical Care--Coon Rapids
3465 Northdale Blvd.
Coon Rapids, MN 55448
Free: 866-434-2597
URL: http://www.ultracare-dialysis.com/
Dialysis Stations: 12.

25275 ■ Fresenius Medical Care--North Suburban
Dialysis Facility
9144 Springbrook Dr.
Coon Rapids, MN 55433
Free: 866-434-2597
URL: http://www.ultracare-dialysis.com/
Dialysis Stations: 18. **Formerly:** North Suburban Dialysis Center--Lakeland.

Cottage Grove

25276 ■ DaVita--Cottage Grove
8800 E Point Douglas Dr.
Cottage Grove, MN 55016
Free: 800-424-6589
URL: http://www.davita.com
Dialysis Stations: 12.

Detroit Lakes

25277 ■ Sanford Dialysis Detroit Lakes
1027 Washington Ave.
Detroit Lakes, MN 56501
Ph: (218)847-0825
URL: http://www.sanfordhealth.org/
Dialysis Stations: 12.

Duluth

25278 ■ Fresenius Medical Care--Duluth
502 E 2nd St.
Duluth, MN 55805
Free: 866-434-2597
URL: http://www.ultracare-dialysis.com/
Dialysis Stations: 18. **Formerly:** Miller-Dawn Medical Center Duluth Dialysis Center.

25279 ■ Fresenius Medical Care--Spirit Valley Dialysis Center
4700 Mike Colalillo Dr.
Duluth, MN 55807
Free: 866-434-2597
URL: http://www.ultracare-dialysis.com/
Dialysis Stations: 22.

Eagan

25280 ■ Eagan Dialysis
DaVita
2750 Bluewater Rd., Ste. 300
Eagan, MN 55121
Free: 800-424-6589
URL: http://www.davita.com
Dialysis Stations: 16.

Eden Prairie

25281 ■ Eden Prairie Dialysis
DaVita
14852 Scenic Heights Rd., Ste. 255
Eden Prairie, MN 55344
Free: 800-424-6589
URL: http://www.davita.com
Dialysis Stations: 12.

Edina

25282 ■ Edina Dialysis
DaVita
6550 York Ave. S, Ste. 100
Edina, MN 55435
Free: 800-424-6589
URL: http://www.davita.com
Dialysis Stations: 16.

Eveleth

25283 ■ Fresenius Medical Care--Eveleth
227 McKinley Ave.
Eveleth, MN 55734
Free: 866-434-2597
URL: http://www.ultracare-dialysis.com/
Dialysis Stations: 10.

Fairmont

25284 ■ Mayo Dialysis--Fairmont
835 Johnson St.
Fairmont, MN 56031
Ph: (507)238-5060
Dialysis Stations: 12.

Faribault

25285 ■ Faribault Dialysis
DaVita
201 S Lyndale, Ste. F
Faribault, MN 55021
Free: 800-424-6589
URL: http://www.davita.com
Dialysis Stations: 10.

Fergus Falls

25286 ■ Fresenius Medical Care Dialysis--Fergus Falls
714 S Mill St.
Fergus Falls, MN 56537
Free: 866-434-2597
URL: http://www.ultracare-dialysis.com/
Dialysis Stations: 7. **Formerly:** Lake Region Hospital and Nursing Home Dialysis Facility.

Forest Lake

25287 ■ Forest Lake Dialysis
DaVita
1068 S Lake St., Ste. 110
Forest Lake, MN 55025
Free: 800-424-6589
URL: http://www.davita.com
Dialysis Stations: 7.

Fridley

25288 ■ Fridley Dialysis
DaVita
5301 E River Rd. NE
Fridley, MN 55421
Free: 800-424-6589
URL: http://www.davita.com
Dialysis Stations: 12.

Golden Valley

25289 ■ Fresenius Medical Care Dialysis--Golden Valley
6155 Duluth St.
Golden Valley, MN 55422
Free: 866-434-2597
URL: http://www.ultracare-dialysis.com/
Dialysis Stations: 18.

Grand Rapids

25290 ■ Fresenius Medical Care--Grand Rapids
410 SW 1st Ave.
Grand Rapids, MN 55744
Free: 866-434-2597
URL: http://www.ultracare-dialysis.com/
Dialysis Stations: 6.

Hibbing

25291 ■ Fresenius Medical Care of Hibbing Dialysis Facility
750 E 34th St., Ste. 3127
Hibbing, MN 55746
Free: 866-434-2597
URL: http://www.ultracare-dialysis.com/
Dialysis Stations: 12.

Hutchinson

25292 ■ Fresenius Medical Care--Hutchinson
1095 Hwy. 15 S
Hutchinson, MN 55350
Free: 866-434-2597
URL: http://www.ultracare-dialysis.com/
Dialysis Stations: 6.

Litchfield

25293 ■ Centracare Kidney Program--Litchfield
520 US Hwy. 12 E
Litchfield, MN 55355
Ph: (320)693-7777
URL: http://www.centracare.com/specialty_centers/dialysis/index.html
Dialysis Stations: 9.

Little Falls

25294 ■ Centracare Dialysis/Saint Gabriel's Hospital
808 3rd St. SE, No. 330
Little Falls, MN 56345
Ph: (320)632-1191
URL: http://www.centracare.com/specialty_centers/dialysis/index.html
Dialysis Stations: 9.

Mankato

25295 ■ Immanuel-Saint Joseph's Hospital Dialysis Unit
1025 Marsh St.
Mankato, MN 56002
Ph: (507)625-4031
URL: http://www.isj-mhs.org
Dialysis Stations: 16.

Maple Grove

25296 ■ Fresenius Medical Care--Maple Grove
7365 Kirkwood Ct., Ste. 135
Maple Grove, MN 55369
Free: 866-434-2597
URL: http://www.ultracare-dialysis.com/
Dialysis Stations: 12.

25297 ■ Maple Grove Dialysis Unit and At Home
DaVita
15655 Grove Cir. N
Maple Grove, MN 55369
Free: 800-424-6589
URL: http://www.davita.com
Dialysis Stations: 14.

Maplewood

25298 ■ Fresenius Medical Care--Maplewood Heights
2017 Woodlyn Ave.
Maplewood, MN 55109
Free: 866-434-2597
URL: http://www.ultracare-dialysis.com/
Dialysis Stations: 12.

25299 ■ Maplewood Dialysis
DaVita
2785 White Bear Ave., Ste. 201
Maplewood, MN 55109
Free: 800-424-6589
URL: http://www.davita.com
Dialysis Stations: 16.

Marshall

25300 ■ DaVita--Marshall Dialysis
300 S Bruce St.
Marshall, MN 56258
Free: 800-424-6589
URL: http://www.davita.com
Dialysis Stations: 7.

Minneapolis

25301 ■ Abbott Northwestern Transplant
Allina Hospitals & Clinics
800 E 28th St.
Minneapolis, MN 55407
Ph: (612)863-5638
URL: http://www.allina.com/ahs/anw.nsf/page/op_transplantation
Dialysis Stations: 0.

25302 ■ DaVita--Minneapolis Northeast Dialysis
1049 10th Ave. SE
Minneapolis, MN 55414
Free: 800-424-6589
URL: http://www.davita.com
Dialysis Stations: 12.

25303 ■ DaVita--Uptown Dialysis
3601 Lyndale Ave. S
Minneapolis, MN 55409
Free: 800-424-6589
URL: http://www.davita.com
Dialysis Stations: 12.

25304 ■ Fairview University Medical Center Dialysis Unit
420 Delaware St. SE
Minneapolis, MN 55455
Ph: (612)273-3999
URL: http://www.fairview-university.fairview.org
Dialysis Stations: 11.

25305 ■ Fresenius Medical Care Dialysis--South Minneapolis
4310 Nicollet Ave. S
Minneapolis, MN 55409
Free: 866-434-2597
URL: http://www.ultracare-dialysis.com/
Dialysis Stations: 12.

25306 ■ Hennepin County Medical Center Transplant
825 S 8th St.
Minneapolis, MN 55404
Ph: (612)347-5931
URL: http://www.hcmc.org/depts/transplant/transplantserv.htm
Dialysis Stations: 0.

25307 ■ Minneapolis Dialysis Unit
DaVita
825 S 8th St.
Minneapolis, MN 55404
Free: 800-424-6589
URL: http://www.davita.com
Dialysis Stations: 28.

25308 ■ Park Ave. Dialysis Center
Fresenius Medical Care Dialysis Dialysis Center
2637 Park Ave. S
Minneapolis, MN 55407
Free: 866-434-2597
URL: http://www.ultracare-dialysis.com/
Dialysis Stations: 14. **Formerly:** Abbott Northwestern Hospital.

25309 ■ U of MN Med Center--Fairview Dialysis Center
Harvard St. at E River Rd.
MMC 805
Minneapolis, MN 55455
Ph: (612)273-3999
Fax: (612)273-1166
URL: http://www.fairview-university.fairview.org
Dialysis Stations: 11.

Minnetonka

25310 ■ Minnetonka Dialysis
DaVita
17809 Hutchins Dr.
Minnetonka, MN 55345
Free: 800-424-6589
URL: http://www.davita.com
Dialysis Stations: 10.

Montevideo

25311 ■ Montevideo Dialysis
DaVita
824 N 11th St.
Montevideo, MN 56265
Free: 800-424-6589
URL: http://www.davita.com
Dialysis Stations: 6.

Monticello

25312 ■ Centracare Dialysis at Monticello
114 3rd St. W
Monticello, MN 55362
Ph: (763)295-2133
URL: http://www.centracare.com/specialty_centers/dialysis/index.html
Dialysis Stations: 6.

Mora

25313 ■ Fresenius Medical Care--Mora Dialysis Center
820 Howe Ave., Ste. 104
Mora, MN 55051
Free: 866-434-2597
URL: http://www.ultracare-dialysis.com/
Dialysis Stations: 6.

Morris

25314 ■ Meritcare Dialysis--Morris
400 E 1st St.
Morris, MN 56267
Ph: (320)589-2832
URL: http://www.meritcare.com/medicalservices/specialties/kidney/dialysis/index
Dialysis Stations: 5.

25315 ■ Sanford Dialysis Morris
Box 660
Morris, MN 56267
Ph: (320)589-2832
URL: http://www.sanfordhealth.org/
Dialysis Stations: 6.

New Brighton

25316 ■ Fresenius Medical Care Dialysis--New Brighton
550 County Rd. D, Ste. 7
New Brighton, MN 55112
Free: 866-434-2597
URL: http://www.ultracare-dialysis.com/
Dialysis Stations: 12.

New Hope

25317 ■ DaVita--New Hope
5640 International Pkwy.
New Hope, MN 55428
Free: 800-424-6589
URL: http://www.davita.com
Dialysis Stations: 12.

New Ulm

25318 ■ Immanuel-Saint Joseph's Hospital--New Ulm
Dialysis Center
1324 5th St. N
New Ulm, MN 56073
Ph: (507)233-1620
URL: http://www.isj-mhs.org
Dialysis Stations: 6.

Ortonville

25319 ■ Satellite Dialysis--Ortonville
450 Eastvold Ave.
Ortonville, MN 56278
Ph: (320)839-4070
URL: http://www.prairielakes.com/services/index.php?id=66
Dialysis Stations: 6.

Owatonna

25320 ■ Mayo Dialysis--Owatonna
2200 26th St.
Owatonna, MN 55060
Ph: (507)446-5112
URL: http://www.mayohealthsystem.org
Dialysis Stations: 12.

Pine City

25321 ■ Pine City Dialysis
DaVita
129 6th Ave. SE
Pine City, MN 55063
Free: 800-424-6589
URL: http://www.davita.com
Dialysis Stations: 8.

Pipestone

25322 ■ Pipestone Dialysis
DaVita
916 4th Ave. SW
Pipestone, MN 55164
Free: 800-424-6589
URL: http://www.davita.com
Dialysis Stations: 7.

Princeton

25323 ■ Centracare Dialysis at Princeton
112 S Rum River, Ste. 10
Princeton, MN 55371
Ph: (763)389-7969
URL: http://www.centracare.com/specialty_centers/dialysis/index.html
Dialysis Stations: 9.

25324 ■ Fresenius Medical Care Dialysis--Central Minnesota Regional Dialysis
124 Rum River Dr. N
Princeton, MN 55371
Free: 866-434-2597
URL: http://www.ultracare-dialysis.com/
Dialysis Stations: 8.

Red Lake

25325 ■ Meritcare Dialysis--Red Lake
Red Lake Hospital
Hwy. 1
Red Lake, MN 56671
Ph: (218)679-3117
URL: http://www.meritcare.com/medicalservices/specialties/kidney/dialysis/index
Dialysis Stations: 5.

25326 ■ Sanford Dialysis Red Lake
24760 Hospital Dr.
Red Lake, MN 56671
Ph: (218)679-3117
URL: http://www.sanfordhealth.org/Locations/City/Red%20Lake,MN
Dialysis Stations: 5.

Red Wing

25327 ■ Red Wing Dialysis
DaVita
3028 N Service Dr.
Red Wing, MN 55066-1921
Free: 800-424-6589
URL: http://www.davita.com
Dialysis Stations: 8.

Redwood Falls

25328 ■ Redwood Falls Dialysis
DaVita
100 Fallwood Rd.
Redwood Falls, MN 56283
Free: 800-424-6589
URL: http://www.davita.com
Dialysis Stations: 5.

Richfield

25329 ■ DaVita--Richfield
6601 Lyndale Ave. S, Ste. 150
Richfield, MN 55423
Free: 800-424-6589
URL: http://www.davita.com
Dialysis Stations: 12.

Rochester

25330 ■ Mayo Dialysis Rochester--Methodist Hosp.
Dialysis Center
201 W Center St., El-1G
Rochester, MN 55905
Ph: (507)266-1610
URL: http://www.mayo.edu
Dialysis Stations: 26.

25331 ■ Mayo Dialysis Rochester--NE Clinic
3041 Stonehedge Dr. NE
Rochester, MN 55906
Ph: (507)538-8580
URL: http://www.mayo.edu
Dialysis Stations: 24.

25332 ■ St. Marys Hospital Transplant
Mayo Clinic
200 1st St., SW, Charlton 9
Rochester, MN 55905
Ph: (507)266-3466
URL: http://www.mayoclinic.org/kidney-transplant/
Dialysis Stations: 0.

Roseville

25333 ■ Fresenius Medical Care Dialysis--Roseville
2045 Rice St.
Roseville, MN 55113
Free: 866-434-2597
Fax: (651)489-6982
URL: http://www.ultracare-dialysis.com/
Dialysis Stations: 15.

Saint Cloud

25334 ■ Centracare Kidney Program
Health Plaza Dialysis
Saint Cloud, MN 56303
Ph: (320)229-4921
URL: http://www.centracare.com/specialty_centers/dialysis/index.html
Dialysis Stations: 22.

25335 ■ Saint Cloud Hospital
Regional Centracare Dialysis
1406 6th Ave. N
Saint Cloud, MN 56303
Ph: (320)240-7808
URL: http://www.centracare.com/hospitals/sch/index.html
Dialysis Stations: 5.

Saint Louis Park

25336 ■ DaVita--Westwood Hills
7525 Wayzata Blvd.
Saint Louis Park, MN 55426
Free: 800-424-6589
URL: http://www.davita.com
Dialysis Stations: 12.

25337 ■ Fresenius Medical Care--Saint Louis Park
5680 36th St. W
Saint Louis Park, MN 55416
Free: 866-434-2597
URL: http://www.ultracare-dialysis.com/
Dialysis Stations: 12.

25338 ■ Saint Louis Park Dialysis
DaVita
3505 Louisiana Ave.
Saint Louis Park, MN 55426
Free: 800-424-6589
Dialysis Stations: 28.

Saint Paul

25339 ■ Capitol Home Program of DaVita--PD Unit
DaVita
555 Park St.
Saint Paul, MN 55103
Free: 800-424-6589
URL: http://www.davita.com
Dialysis Stations: 2.

25340 ■ DaVita
University Dialysis Unit and At Home Riverside
1045 Westgate Dr.
Saint Paul, MN 55114
Free: 800-424-6589
URL: http://www.davita.com
Dialysis Stations: 19.

25341 ■ Fresenius Medical Care--Midway Saint Paul
University Medical Bldg.
1690 University Ave. W, Ste. B100
Saint Paul, MN 55104
Free: 866-434-2597
URL: http://www.ultracare-dialysis.com/
Dialysis Stations: 22.

25342 ■ Fresenius Medical Care--Saint Paul
445 Etna St., Ste. 60
Saint Paul, MN 55106
Free: 866-434-2597
URL: http://www.ultracare-dialysis.com/
Dialysis Stations: 20.

25343 ■ Highland Park Dialysis
DaVita
1559 7th St. W
Saint Paul, MN 55102

Free: 800-424-6589
URL: http://www.davita.com
Dialysis Stations: 12.

25344 ■ Saint Paul Capital Dialysis, At Home & PD
DaVita
555 Park St., Ste. 230
Saint Paul, MN 55103
Free: 800-424-6589
URL: http://www.davita.com
Dialysis Stations: 16.

25345 ■ St. Paul Dialysis
DaVita
555 Park St., Ste. 180
Saint Paul, MN 55103
Free: 800-424-6589
URL: http://www.davita.com
Dialysis Stations: 16.

25346 ■ Sun Ray Dialysis
DaVita
1758 Old Hudson Rd.
Saint Paul, MN 55106
Free: 800-424-6589
URL: http://www.davita.com
Dialysis Stations: 12.

Savage

25347 ■ Scott County Dialysis
DaVita
7456 S Park Dr.
Savage, MN 55378
Free: 800-424-6589
URL: http://www.davita.com
Dialysis Stations: 12.

Shakopee

25348 ■ Fresenius Medical Care--Shakopee
1515 St. Francis Ave., Ste. 105
Shakopee, MN 55379
Free: 866-434-2597
URL: http://www.ultracare-dialysis.com/
Dialysis Stations: 6.

Staples

25349 ■ Centracare Dialysis at Lakewood Health System
403 E Prairie Ave.
Staples, MN 56479
Ph: (218)894-0026
URL: http://www.centracare.com/specialty_centers/dialysis/index.html
Dialysis Stations: 12.

Stillwater

25350 ■ River City Dialysis
DaVita
1970 Northwestern Ave. N
Stillwater, MN 55082
Free: 800-424-6589
URL: http://www.davita.com
Dialysis Stations: 12.

Thief River Falls

25351 ■ Sanford Dialysis--Thief River Falls
120 Labree Ave. S
Thief River Falls, MN 56701
Ph: (218)683-4246
URL: http://www.sanfordhealth.org/
Dialysis Stations: 6.

Wabasha

25352 ■ Mayo Dialysis--Wabasha
1200 5th Grant Blvd. W
Wabasha, MN 55981
Ph: (651)565-5995
URL: http://www.mayo.edu
Dialysis Stations: 6.

Waconia

25353 ■ Waconia Dialysis
Fresenius Medical Care
560 S Maple St., Ste. 6
Waconia, MN 55387
Free: 866-434-2597
URL: http://www.ultracare-dialysis.com/
Dialysis Stations: 10.

West Saint Paul

25354 ■ West Saint Paul Dialysis
DaVita
1555 Livingston Ave.
West Saint Paul, MN 55118
Free: 800-424-6589
URL: http://www.davita.com
Dialysis Stations: 20.

25355 ■ West St. Paul Dialysis
Fresenius Medical Care
1590 S Robert St., Ste. 102
West Saint Paul, MN 55118
Free: 866-434-2597
URL: http://www.ultracare-dialysis.com/
Dialysis Stations: 13.

Willmar

25356 ■ Rice Memorial Hospital Dialysis Facility
301 Becker Ave. SW
Willmar, MN 56201
Ph: (320)231-4253
URL: http://www.ricehospital.com
Dialysis Stations: 12.

Winona

25357 ■ Winona Health Services Dialysis Facility
855 Mankato St.
Winona, MN 55987
Ph: (507)454-3650
URL: http://www.winonahealth.org
Dialysis Stations: 8.

Woodbury

25358 ■ Woodbury Dialysis
DaVita
1850 3 Weir Dr., No. 3
Woodbury, MN 55125
Free: 800-424-6589
URL: http://www.davita.com
Dialysis Stations: 12.

Worthington

25359 ■ Sanford Regional Hospital--Worthington Dialysis Facility
1018 6th Ave.
Worthington, MN 56187
Ph: (507)372-3279
URL: http://www.worthingtonhospital.com
Dialysis Stations: 8.

MISSISSIPPI

Aberdeen

25360 ■ Fresenius Medical Care--Highway 8 W, Aberdeen
Dialysis Services
308 Hwy. 8 W
Aberdeen, MS 39730
Free: 866-434-2597
URL: http://www.ultracare-dialysis.com/
Dialysis Stations: 32. **Formerly:** Renal Care Group - Aberdeen.

Bay Springs

25361 ■ Bay Springs Dialysis Unit
14 Bay Ave.
Bay Springs, MS 39422
Ph: (601)764-6427
Dialysis Stations: 21.

Belzoni

25362 ■ Fresenius Medical Care--Belzoni
16451 US Hwy. 49
Belzoni, MS 39038
Free: 866-434-2597
URL: http://www.ultracare-dialysis.com/
Dialysis Stations: 9.

Biloxi

25363 ■ SMKC Biloxi Home Dialysis
Fresenius Medical Care
784 Vieux Marche Mall
Biloxi, MS 39530
Free: 866-434-2597
URL: http://www.ultracare-dialysis.com/
Dialysis Stations: 22.

Brandon

25364 ■ Diversified Specialty Institutes--Brandon Dialysis Facility
101 Christian Dr.
Brandon, MS 39042
Ph: (601)824-9700
URL: http://www.dsi-corp.com
Dialysis Stations: 20. **Formerly:** National Renal Institutes.

25365 ■ Fresenius Medical Care - Rankin County
141 Gateway Dr.
Brandon, MS 39042
Free: 866-434-2597
URL: http://www.ultracare-dialysis.com/
Dialysis Stations: 21.

Brookhaven

25366 ■ Fresenius Medical Care--Brookhaven Dialysis Facility
534 Irby Dr.
Brookhaven, MS 39601
Free: 866-434-2597
URL: http://www.ultracare-dialysis.com/
Dialysis Stations: 32. **Formerly:** Renal Care Group.

Canton

25367 ■ Diversified Specialty Institutes--Canton Dialysis Facility
620 E Peace St.
Canton, MS 39046
Ph: (601)859-3382
Fax: (601)859-8591
URL: http://www.dsi-corp.com
Dialysis Stations: 22. **Formerly:** Renal Care Group.

25368 ■ Fresenius Medical Care of Canton Dialysis Facility
1976 Hwy. 43, Ste. F
Canton, MS 39046
Free: 866-434-2597
URL: http://www.ultracare-dialysis.com/
Dialysis Stations: 18.

Carthage

25369 ■ Diversified Specialty Institutes--Carthage Dialysis Facility
312 Ellis St.
Carthage, MS 39051

Ph: (601)267-6856
URL: http://www.dsi-corp.com
Dialysis Stations: 15. **Formerly:** Fresenius Medical Care of Carthage.

Centreville

25370 ■ Fresenius Medical Care--Centreville Dialysis Facility
205 E Main St.
Centreville, MS 39631
Free: 866-434-2597
URL: http://www.ultracare-dialysis.com
Dialysis Stations: 17. **Formerly:** Renal Care Group - Centreville.

Clarksdale

25371 ■ Fresenius Medical Care--Clarksdale Dialysis Facility
2010 N State St.
Clarksdale, MS 38614
Free: 866-434-2597
URL: http://www.ultracare-dialysis.com
Dialysis Stations: 40. **Formerly:** Renal Care Group - Clarksdale.

Cleveland

25372 ■ Fresenius Medical Care--Cleveland Dialysis Facility
222 N Pearman Ave.
Cleveland, MS 38732
Free: 866-434-2597
URL: http://www.ultracare-dialysis.com
Dialysis Stations: 29. **Formerly:** Renal Care Group - Cleveland.

Columbia

25373 ■ Columbia Dialysis Hattiesburg Clinic
Highwaay 98 Bypass
Columbia, MS 39429
Ph: (601)731-1234
URL: http://www.hattiesburgclinic.com/
Dialysis Stations: 30.

Columbus

25374 ■ Fresenius Medical Care--Columbus Dialysis Facility
92 Brookmoore Dr.
Columbus, MS 39705
Free: 866-434-2597
URL: http://www.ultracare-dialysis.com
Dialysis Stations: 37. **Formerly:** Renal Care Group - Columbus.

Corinth

25375 ■ Fresenius Medical Care--Corinth
810 Alcorn Dr.
Corinth, MS 38834
Free: 866-434-2597
URL: http://www.ultracare-dialysis.com
Dialysis Stations: 23. **Formerly:** Renal Care Group - Corinth.

D'Iberville

25376 ■ Fresenius Medical Care--D'Iberville South Mississippi Kidney Center
10374 Lamey Bridge Rd.
D'Iberville, MS 39532
Free: 866-434-2597
URL: http://www.ultracare-dialysis.com/
Dialysis Stations: 12.

Diamondhead

25377 ■ Fresenius Medical Care--Diamondhead
4405 E Aloha Dr., Ste. 1
Diamondhead, MS 39525
Free: 866-434-2597
URL: http://www.ultracare-dialysis.com/
Dialysis Stations: 14.

Eupora

25378 ■ Fresenius Medical Care--Eupora
207 Meadowlane St.
Eupora, MS 39744
Free: 866-434-2597
URL: http://www.ultracare-dialysis.com
Dialysis Stations: 14. **Formerly:** Renal Care Group - Eupora.

Fayette

25379 ■ DRG Fayette
225 Community Dr.
Fayette, MS 39069
Ph: (601)488-6347
Dialysis Stations: 8.

Forest

25380 ■ Fresenius Medical Care of Forest Dialysis Center
1151 Hwy. 35 S
Forest, MS 39074
Free: 866-434-2597
URL: http://www.ultracare-dialysis.com/
Dialysis Stations: 14.

Greenville

25381 ■ Fresenius Medical Care--Greenville, Mississippi
2001 S Medical Park Dr.
Greenville, MS 38701
Free: 866-434-2597
URL: http://www.ultracare-dialysis.com/
Dialysis Stations: 38. **Formerly:** Renal Care Group.

25382 ■ Mid-Delta Kidney Center, Inc.
1409 E Union St.
Greenville, MS 38703
Ph: (662)332-7100
Dialysis Stations: 4.

Greenwood

25383 ■ Fresenius Medical Care--Greenwood Dialysis Facility
613 Tallahatchie St.
Greenwood, MS 38930
Free: 866-434-2597
URL: http://www.ultracare-dialysis.com
Dialysis Stations: 33. **Formerly:** Renal Care Group - Greenwood.

Grenada

25384 ■ Fresenius Medical Care--Grenada Dialysis Facility
35 W Monroe St.
Grenada, MS 38901
Free: 866-434-2597
URL: http://www.ultracare-dialysis.com/
Dialysis Stations: 29. **Formerly:** Renal Care Group - Grenada.

Gulfport

25385 ■ Fresenius Medical Care--Gulfport South Mississippi Kidney Center
4300A W Railroad St.
Gulfport, MS 39501
Ph: (228)864-0009
Dialysis Stations: 24.

25386 ■ Fresenius Medical Care--Orange Grove/South Mississippi Kidney Center
11531 Old Hwy. 49
Gulfport, MS 39503
Free: 866-434-2597
URL: http://www.ultracare-dialysis.com/
Dialysis Stations: 18.

25387 ■ South Mississippi Kidney Center North Gulfport Fresenius Medical Care South Mississippi Kidney Center Dialysis Facility
2525 33rd St.
Gulfport, MS 39501
Free: 866-434-2597
URL: http://www.ultracare-dialysis.com/
Dialysis Stations: 16.

Hattiesburg

25388 ■ Collins Dialysis Unit Hattiesburg Clinic Dialysis Unit
5909 Hwy. 49, Ste. 10
Hattiesburg, MS 39401
Ph: (601)296-5619
URL: http://www.hattiesburgclinic.com/
Dialysis Stations: 21.

25389 ■ Hattiesburg Clinic Dialysis
Cloverleaf Medical Plaza, Ste. 10
5909 US Hwy. 49
Hattiesburg, MS 39402
Ph: (601)296-5619
URL: http://www.hattiesburgclinic.com/index.cfm/fuseaction/site.locations/action /dtl/loc/5217.cfm
Dialysis Stations: 60.

25390 ■ Richton Dialysis
5909 Hwy. 49 S
Hattiesburg, MS 39402
Ph: (601)788-2555
URL: http://www.hattiesburgclinic.com/
Dialysis Stations: 20.

Hazlehurst

25391 ■ Diversified Specialty Institutes--Hazelhurst Dialysis Facility
201 N Haley St.
Hazlehurst, MS 39083
Ph: (601)894-5509
URL: http://www.dsi-corp.com
Dialysis Stations: 17. **Formerly:** Renal Care Group.

25392 ■ Fresenius Medical Care of Hazlehurst
232A N Caldwell Dr.
Hazlehurst, MS 39083
Free: 866-434-2597
URL: http://www.ultracare-dialysis.com
Dialysis Stations: 13.

Holly Springs

25393 ■ Fresenius Medical Care--Holly Springs
1325 Hwy. 4 E
Holly Springs, MS 38635
Free: 866-434-2597
URL: http://www.ultracare-dialysis.com/
Dialysis Stations: 20. **Formerly:** Renal Care Group - Holly Springs.

Indianola

25394 ■ Fresenius Medical Care--Indianola Dialysis Facility
627 Hwy. 82 W
Indianola, MS 38751
Free: 866-434-2597
URL: http://www.ultracare-dialysis.com
Dialysis Stations: 21. **Formerly:** Renal Care Group - Indianola.

Jackson

25395 ■ Diversified Specialty Institutes--Jackson North Dialysis Facility
571 Beasley Rd., Ste. A
Jackson, MS 39206

Ph: (601)957-1999
URL: http://www.dsi-corp.com
Dialysis Stations: 46. **Formerly:** Renal Care Group.

25396 ■ Diversified Specialty Institutes--Jackson South
Dialysis Facility
2460 Terry Rd., Ste. 27-J
Jackson, MS 39204
Ph: (601)373-9154
Fax: (601)373-0136
URL: http://www.dsi-corp.com
Dialysis Stations: 35. **Formerly:** Renal Care Group.

25397 ■ Diversified Specialty Institutes--Jackson Southwest
1828 Raymond Rd.
Jackson, MS 39204
Ph: (601)373-9154
URL: http://www.dsi-corp.com
Dialysis Stations: 18. **Formerly:** Renex Dialysis.

25398 ■ Fresenius Medical Care of Jackson
Dialysis Facility
381 Medical Dr.
Jackson, MS 39216
Free: 866-434-2597
URL: http://www.ultracare-dialysis.com
Dialysis Stations: 38.

25399 ■ Fresenius Medical Care of Southwest Jackson
Dialysis Facility
1856 Hospital Dr.
Jackson, MS 39204
Free: 866-434-2597
URL: http://www.ultracare-dialysis.com
Dialysis Stations: 29.

25400 ■ Medical Mall Dialysis
350 W Woodrow Wilson
Jackson, MS 39213
Ph: (601)815-3645
Dialysis Stations: 43.

25401 ■ University of Mississippi Medical Center
Department of Pediatric Nephrology
2500 N State St., R-116A
Jackson, MS 39216
Ph: (601)984-5972
URL: http://www.umc.edu
Dialysis Stations: 0.

Kosciusko

25402 ■ Fresenius Medical Care of Kosciusko
Dialysis Facility
107 Ridgewood Circle
Kosciusko, MS 39090
Free: 866-434-2597
URL: http://www.ultracare-dialysis.com
Dialysis Stations: 20.

Laurel

25403 ■ Laurel Dialysis Center
1527 Larry Dr.
Laurel, MS 39440
Ph: (601)425-1853
Dialysis Stations: 34. **Formerly:** Laurel Renal Dialysis Center.

Lexington

25404 ■ Diversified Specialty Institutes--Lexington
22579 Depot St.
Lexington, MS 39095
Ph: (662)834-3355
URL: http://www.dsi-corp.com
Dialysis Stations: 22. **Formerly:** Renal Care Group.

Louisville

25405 ■ Fresenius Medical Care--Louisville
562-A E Main St.
Louisville, MS 39339
Free: 866-434-2597
URL: http://www.ultracare-dialysis.com/
Dialysis Stations: 17. **Formerly:** Renal Care Group.

Lucedale

25406 ■ Lucedale Dialysis
DaVita
652 Manilla St.
Lucedale, MS 39452
Free: 800-424-6589
URL: http://www.davita.com
Dialysis Stations: 12.

Macon

25407 ■ Fresenius Medical Care--Macon
Dialysis Facility
703 N Washington St.
Macon, MS 39341
Free: 866-434-2597
URL: http://www.ultracare-dialysis.com
Dialysis Stations: 16. **Formerly:** Renal Care Group - Macon.

Magee

25408 ■ Fresenius Medical Care of Magee
Dialysis Facility
211 1st St. SE
Magee, MS 39111
Free: 866-434-2597
URL: http://www.ultracare-dialysis.com
Dialysis Stations: 18.

McComb

25409 ■ Fresenius Medical Care--McComb
Dialysis Facility
1404 White St.
McComb, MS 39648
Free: 866-434-2597
URL: http://www.ultracare-dialysis.com
Dialysis Stations: 28. **Formerly:** Renal Care Group - McComb.

Meridian

25410 ■ Fresenius Medical Care--Meridian
2205 Hwy. 39 N
Meridian, MS 39301
Free: 866-434-2597
URL: http://www.ultracare-dialysis.com/
Dialysis Stations: 54. **Formerly:** Renal Care Group.

Natchez

25411 ■ Fresenius Medical Care--Natchez
312 Highland Blvd.
Natchez, MS 39120
Free: 866-434-2597
URL: http://www.ultracare-dialysis.com
Dialysis Stations: 31. **Formerly:** Renal Care Group - Natchez.

Newton

25412 ■ Fresenius Medical Care--Newton, Mississippi
121 Old 15 Loop
Newton, MS 39345
Free: 866-434-2597
URL: http://www.ultracare-dialysis.com
Dialysis Stations: 16. **Formerly:** Renal Care Group - Newton.

Ocean Springs

25413 ■ DaVita
Ocean Springs Dialysis & At Home
13150 Ponce de Leon Rd.
Ocean Springs, MS 39564
Free: 800-424-6589
URL: http://www.davita.com
Dialysis Stations: 12. **Formerly:** Grambo Healthcare.

Oxford

25414 ■ Fresenius Medical Care--Oxford, Mississippi
1760 Barron St.
Oxford, MS 38655
Free: 866-434-2597
URL: http://www.ultracare-dialysis.com
Dialysis Stations: 28. **Formerly:** Renal Care Group - Oxford.

Pachuta

25415 ■ Pachuta Dialysis
PO Box 340
Pachuta, MS 39347
Ph: (601)776-0973
Dialysis Stations: 9.

Pascagoula

25416 ■ Singing River Dialysis
DaVita
Dialysis Center
4907 Telephone Rd.
Pascagoula, MS 39567
Free: 800-424-6589
URL: http://www.davita.com
Dialysis Stations: 28. **Formerly:** Gambro Healthcare - Pascagoula.

Philadelphia

25417 ■ Fresenius Medical Care--Philadelphia
105 Office Dr.
Philadelphia, MS 39350
Free: 866-434-2597
URL: http://www.ultracare-dialysis.com/
Dialysis Stations: 34. **Formerly:** Renal Care Group.

Picayune

25418 ■ Pearl River Dialysis
1835 Cooper Rd.
Picayune, MS 39466
Ph: (601)798-8951
Dialysis Stations: 20. **Formerly:** Pearl River Renal Dialysis Center.

Port Gibson

25419 ■ Fresenius Medical Care--Port Gibson
123-A McComb Ave.
Port Gibson, MS 39150
Free: 866-434-2597
URL: http://www.ultracare-dialysis.com/
Dialysis Stations: 10. **Formerly:** Renal Care Group.

Richton

25420 ■ Richton Dialysis Unit
Hattiesburg Clinic
507 Front St.
Richton, MS 39476
Ph: (601)788-2555
URL: http://www.hattiesburgclinic.com
Dialysis Stations: 20.

Rolling Ford

25421 ■ Fresenius Medical Care--Mayersville
20119 Hwy. 61 S
Rolling Ford, MS 39159
Free: 866-434-2597
URL: http://www.ultracare-dialysis.com/
Dialysis Stations: 10. **Formerly:** Renal Care Group.

Sardis

25422 ■ Fresenius Medical Care--Sardis
200 E Frontage Rd.
Sardis, MS 38666
Free: 866-434-2597
URL: http://www.ultracare-dialysis.com
Dialysis Stations: 24. **Formerly:** Renal Care Group - Sardis.

Silver Creek

25423 ■ Silver Creek Dialysis
21 Emu St.
Silver Creek, MS 39663
Ph: (601)886-0072
Dialysis Stations: 18.

Southaven

25424 ■ Fresenius Medical Care--Southaven Dialysis Facility
7318 Southcrest Pkwy.
Southaven, MS 38671
Free: 866-434-2597
URL: http://www.ultracare-dialysis.com
Dialysis Stations: 40. **Formerly:** Renal Care Group - Southaven.

Starkville

25425 ■ Fresenius Medical Care--Starkville Dialysis Facility
104 W Garrard Rd.
Starkville, MS 39759
Free: 866-434-2597
URL: http://www.ultracare-dialysis.com
Dialysis Stations: 21. **Formerly:** Renal Care Group - Starkville.

Tunica

25426 ■ Fresenius Medical Care--Tunica
1821 US Hwy. 61 N
Tunica, MS 38676
Free: 866-434-2597
URL: http://www.ultracare-dialysis.com/
Dialysis Stations: 12. **Formerly:** Renal Care Group.

Tupelo

25427 ■ Fresenius Medical Care--Tupelo
2978 Mattox St.
Tupelo, MS 38801
Free: 866-434-2597
URL: http://www.ultracare-dialysis.com
Dialysis Stations: 36. **Formerly:** Renal Care Group - Tupelo.

Tylertown

25428 ■ Tylertown Dialysis Unit
Hattiesburg Clinic
4820 Plaza Dr., No. 6
Tylertown, MS 39667
Ph: (601)222-0311
URL: http://www.hattiesburgclinic.com/
Dialysis Stations: 20.

Vicksburg

25429 ■ Fresenius Medical Care--Vicksburg
105 Keystone Circle
Vicksburg, MS 39180
Free: 866-434-2597
URL: http://www.ultracare-dialysis.com/
Dialysis Stations: 23. **Formerly:** Renal Care Group - Vicksburg.

Waynesboro

25430 ■ Waynesboro Dialysis Unit
Hattiesburg Clinic
953 Matthew Dr.
Waynesboro, MS 39367
Ph: (601)735-5858
URL: http://www.hattiesburgclinic.com
Dialysis Stations: 15.

Wiggins

25431 ■ Wiggins Dialysis Unit
503 1st St.
Wiggins, MS 39577
Ph: (601)928-2999
URL: http://www.hattiesburgclinic.com
Dialysis Stations: 12.

Winona

25432 ■ Fresenius Medical Care--Winona
410 Hwy. 82
Winona, MS 38967
Free: 866-434-2597
URL: http://www.ultracare-dialysis.com/
Dialysis Stations: 15. **Formerly:** Renal Care Group.

Yazoo City

25433 ■ Fresenius Medical Care of Yazoo City
Dialysis Facility
716 Grand Ave.
Yazoo City, MS 39194
Free: 866-434-2597
URL: http://www.ultracare-dialysis.com
Dialysis Stations: 21.

MISSOURI

Belton

25434 ■ Dialysis Clinic, Inc.--Belton
17045 S 71 Hwy.
Belton, MO 64012
Ph: (816)322-4034
URL: http://www.dciinc.org
Dialysis Stations: 12.

Blue Springs

25435 ■ Fresenius Medical Care
Blue Springs Dialysis Center
205 W Mize Rd., No. 205
Blue Springs, MO 64014
Free: 866-434-2597
URL: http://www.ultracare-dialysis.com/
Dialysis Stations: 15.

Bolivar

25436 ■ Fresenius Medical Care--Bolivar
1145 N Butterfield
Bolivar, MO 65613
Free: 866-434-2597
URL: http://www.ultracare-dialysis.com/
Dialysis Stations: 11. **Formerly:** Renal Care Group.

Boonville

25437 ■ Dialysis Clinic, Inc.--Boonville
16895 Rankin Mill Rd.
Boonville, MO 65233
Ph: (660)882-2466
URL: http://www.dciinc.org
Dialysis Stations: 12.

Branson

25438 ■ Branson Dialysis, LLC
101 Skaggs Rd., No. 301
Branson, MO 65616
Ph: (417)335-5797
Dialysis Stations: 11.

Bridgeton

25439 ■ Fresenius Medical Care--Bridgeton
12380 Natural Bridge Rd.
Bridgeton, MO 63044
Free: 866-434-2597
URL: http://www.ultracare-dialysis.com/
Dialysis Stations: 26. **Formerly:** Renal Care Group/ Renex Dialysis Clinic of Bridgeton.

25440 ■ Quality Care Dialysis Center--Saint Louis
Fresenius Medical Care
12484 St. Charles Rock Rd.
Bridgeton, MO 63044
Free: 866-434-2597
URL: http://www.ultracare-dialysis.com/
Dialysis Stations: 14.

Butler

25441 ■ Butler Renal Center
Diversified Specialty Institutes
601 W Nursery
Butler, MO 64730
Ph: (660)679-6513
URL: http://www.dsi-corp.com
Dialysis Stations: 10.

Cameron

25442 ■ Cameron Dialysis
DaVita
1003 W 4th
Cameron, MO 64429
Free: 800-424-6589
URL: http://www.davita.com
Dialysis Stations: 10. **Formerly:** Gambro Healthcare.

25443 ■ Cameron Regional Medical Center Renal Dialysis Center
1600 E Evergreen
Cameron, MO 64429
Ph: (816)649-3398
URL: http://www.cameronregional.org/
Dialysis Stations: 3.

Cape Girardeau

25444 ■ Fresenius Medical Care--Cape Girardeau
3250 Gordonville Rd.
Cape Girardeau, MO 63701
Free: 866-434-2597
URL: http://www.ultracare-dialysis.com/
Dialysis Stations: 24. **Formerly:** Cape County Regional Dialysis Center.

25445 ■ Fresenius Medical Care--Southeast Missouri
1723 Broadway, Ste. 105
Cape Girardeau, MO 63701
Free: 866-434-2597
URL: http://www.ultracare-dialysis.com/
Dialysis Stations: 21. **Formerly:** Renal Care Group.

Chesterfield

25446 ■ Premier Dialysis West County
13190 S Outer Forty Rd.
Chesterfield, MO 63017
Ph: (314)754-2101
URL: http://www.premierdialysiscenters.com/contact.html
Dialysis Stations: 9.

25447 ■ Saint Luke's Hospital--West Dialysis Unit
Saint Luke's Health System
232 S Woods Mill Rd.
Chesterfield, MO 63017
Ph: (314)205-6423
URL: http://www.slhn-lehighvalley.org/locations/dialysis-centers/index.aspx
Dialysis Stations: 5.

Chillicothe

25448 ■ Chillicothe Dialysis
DaVita
588 E Business 36
Chillicothe, MO 64601
Free: 800-424-6589
URL: http://www.davita.com
Dialysis Stations: 9. **Formerly:** Dialysis Center of Chillicothe.

Clinton

25449 ■ Dialysis Clinic, Inc.--Clinton
1669 N 2nd St.
Clinton, MO 64735
Ph: (660)890-0889
URL: http://www.dciinc.org
Dialysis Stations: 12.

Columbia

25450 ■ Dialysis Clinic, Inc.--Columbia
3300 Lemone Blvd.
Columbia, MO 65201
Ph: (573)443-1531
URL: http://www.dciinc.org
Dialysis Stations: 37.

25451 ■ RTC Columbia Dialysis & At Home
DaVita
1701 E Bradway, Ste. G-102
Columbia, MO 65201
Free: 800-424-6589
URL: http://www.davita.com
Dialysis Stations: 12.

25452 ■ University of Missouri Hospital and Clinics
Transplant/Dialysis Center
1 Hospital Dr.
Columbia, MO 65212
Ph: (573)882-1051
URL: http://www.muhealth.org
Dialysis Stations: 9.

Creve Coeur

25453 ■ Affiliated Hospital Dialysis Center--West County
St. John's Mercy Health Care
1009 Executive Pkwy., No. 100
Creve Coeur, MO 63141
Ph: (314)434-4770
URL: http://www.stjohnsmercy.org/services/dialysis/Default.asp
Dialysis Stations: 40.

25454 ■ Fresenius Medical Care--Creve Coeur
555 N New Ballas Rd.
Creve Coeur, MO 63141
Free: 866-434-2597
URL: http://www.ultracare-dialysis.com/
Dialysis Stations: 12. **Formerly:** Renal Care Group.

25455 ■ Saint Louis West PD Dialysis
DaVita
450 N Lindbergh Blvd., Ste. 100C
Creve Coeur, MO 63141
Free: 800-424-6589
URL: http://www.davita.com
Dialysis Stations: 2.

Crystal City

25456 ■ Crystal City Dialysis Center
DaVita
1400 Hwy. 61 and I-55 S
Crystal City, MO 63019
Free: 800-424-6589
URL: http://www.davita.com
Dialysis Stations: 12.

25457 ■ DaVita--Crystal City Dialysis Facility
Hwy. 61 S & I-55
Crystal City, MO 63019
Free: 800-424-6589
URL: http://www.davita.com
Dialysis Stations: 12.

Dexter

25458 ■ Dexter Dialysis
DaVita
2010 N Outer Rd.
Dexter, MO 63841
Free: 800-424-6589
URL: http://www.davita.com
Dialysis Stations: 8.

Ellisville

25459 ■ Ellisville Dialysis Center
257 Clarkson Rd.
Ellisville, MO 63011
Ph: (636)207-7401
Dialysis Stations: 18.

Eureka

25460 ■ Eureka Dialysis Center
DaVita
419 Meramec Blvd.
Eureka, MO 63025
Free: 800-424-6589
URL: http://www.davita.com
Dialysis Stations: 13.

Farmington

25461 ■ Farmington Dialysis Clinic
Renal Advantage Inc.
1370 W Liberty St.
Farmington, MO 63640
Ph: (573)760-1030
URL: http://www.renaladvantage.com
Dialysis Stations: 21.

25462 ■ Maple Valley Plaza Dialysis
DaVita
649 Maple Valley Dr.
Farmington, MO 63640
Free: 800-424-6589
URL: http://www.davita.com
Dialysis Stations: 12. **Formerly:** Total Renal Care.

Fenton

25463 ■ Fenton Dialysis Center
Affiliated Hospital Dialysis Center--Fenton
850 Horan Dr.
Fenton, MO 63026
Ph: (636)305-1144
URL: http://www.stjohnsmercy.org/services/dialysis/Default.asp
Dialysis Stations: 18.

Ferguson

25464 ■ Premier Dialysis North County
800 Chambers Rd.
Ferguson, MO 63135
Ph: (314)754-2101
URL: http://www.premierdialysiscenters.com/contact.html
Dialysis Stations: 9.

Festus

25465 ■ Jefferson County Dialysis Center
Fresenius Medical Care
1301 YMCA Dr., No. 200
Festus, MO 63028
Free: 866-434-2597
URL: http://www.ultracare-dialysis.com/
Dialysis Stations: 13.

Florissant

25466 ■ Florissant Dialysis
DaVita
Dialysis Facility
11687 W Florrisant Rd.
Florissant, MO 63033
Free: 800-424-6589
URL: http://www.davita.com
Dialysis Stations: 12. **Formerly:** Gambro Healthcare.

25467 ■ Fresenius Medical Care--Florissant
577 Hodershell Rd.
Florissant, MO 63031
Free: 866-434-2597
URL: http://www.ultracare-dialysis.com/
Dialysis Stations: 13.

25468 ■ Metro Dialysis Center--North
Fresenius Medical Care
2 Grandview Plaza
Florissant, MO 63033
Free: 866-434-2597
URL: http://www.ultracare-dialysis.com/
Dialysis Stations: 26.

25469 ■ North Saint Louis County Dialysis
DaVita
13119 New Halls Ferry Rd.
Florissant, MO 63033
Free: 800-424-6589
URL: http://www.davita.com
Dialysis Stations: 14.

25470 ■ Quality Care Dialysis Center--North County
Fresenius Medical Care
6865 Parker Rd.
Florissant, MO 63033
Free: 866-434-2597
URL: http://www.ultracare-dialysis.com/
Dialysis Stations: 25.

Fredericktown

25471 ■ Renal Advantage Inc.--Fredericktown
105 Armory St.
Fredericktown, MO 63645
Ph: (573)783-2089
URL: http://www.renaladvantage.com
Dialysis Stations: 18.

Frontenac

25472 ■ Renal Advantage Inc.--Frontenac
10435 Clayton Rd.
Frontenac, MO 63131
Ph: (314)567-0645
URL: http://www.renaladvantage
Dialysis Stations: 6.

Hannibal

25473 ■ Hannibal Dialysis
Fresenius Medical Care
3140 Palmyra Rd.
Hannibal, MO 63401
Free: 866-434-2597
URL: http://www.ultracare-dialysis.com/
Dialysis Stations: 15.

Harrisonville

25474 ■ Harrisonville Dialysis Center
Diversified Specialty Institutes
Galaxie Office Park
308 Galaxie Ave.
Harrisonville, MO 64701
Ph: (816)380-2004
URL: http://www.dsi-corp.com
Dialysis Stations: 12.

Hazelwood

25475 ■ DaVita--Hazelwood
637 Dunn Rd., No. 125
Hazelwood, MO 63042
Free: 800-424-6589
URL: http://www.davita.com
Dialysis Stations: 12. **Formerly:** Gambro Healthcare.

Independence

25476 ■ Eastland Dialysis and At Home DaVita
19101 E Valley View Pkwy., Ste. E
Independence, MO 64055
Free: 800-424-6589
URL: http://www.davita.com
Dialysis Stations: 22.

25477 ■ Fresenius Medical Care--Centerpoint
19401 E 37th Terrace Ct. S, Ste. 200
Independence, MO 64057
Free: 866-434-2597
URL: http://www.ultracare-dialysis.com/
Dialysis Stations: 12.

25478 ■ Fresenius Medical Care--Independence Dialysis Center
1135 S Claremont
Independence, MO 64054
Free: 866-434-2597
URL: http://www.ultracare-dialysis.com/
Dialysis Stations: 16.

Jefferson City

25479 ■ Dialysis Clinic, Inc.--Jefferson City East
1916 Boggs Creek Rd.
Jefferson City, MO 65101
Ph: (573)632-2633
URL: http://www.dciinc.org
Dialysis Stations: 12.

25480 ■ Dialysis Clinic, Inc.--Jefferson City West
144 Scott Station Rd.
Jefferson City, MO 65109
Ph: (573)893-5220
URL: http://www.dciinc.org
Dialysis Stations: 16.

Joplin

25481 ■ Freeman Nephrology and Dialysis Center
932 E 34th St.
Joplin, MO 64804
Ph: (417)347-8330
URL: http://www.freemanhealth.com/body.cfm?id=1102
Dialysis Stations: 17.

25482 ■ Fresenius Medical Care--Joplin East Dialysis Facility
2700 E 34th St.
Joplin, MO 64804
Free: 866-434-2597
URL: http://www.ultracare-dialysis.com
Dialysis Stations: 19. **Formerly:** Renal Care Group - Joplin East.

25483 ■ Fresenius Medical Care--Joplin West Dialysis Facility
1800 W 30th St., Ste. A
Joplin, MO 64804
Free: 866-434-2597
URL: http://www.ultracare-dialysis.com
Dialysis Stations: 13. **Formerly:** Renal Care Group - Joplin West.

Kansas City

25484 ■ Children's Mercy Hospital Transplant/Dialysis Center
2401 Gillham Rd.
Kansas City, MO 64108
Ph: (816)234-3100
URL: http://www.childrens-mercy.org/Content/view.aspx?id=575
Dialysis Stations: 10.

25485 ■ DaVita--Hospital Hill Dialysis Center
2250 Holmes St.
Kansas City, MO 64108
Free: 800-424-6589
Fax: (816)421-3820
URL: http://www.davita.com
Dialysis Stations: 16. **Formerly:** Gambro Healthcare.

25486 ■ Dialysis Clinic, Inc.--Baptist
6530 Troost Ave.
Kansas City, MO 64131
Ph: (816)363-8228
URL: http://www.dciinc.org
Dialysis Stations: 24.

25487 ■ Dialysis Clinic, Inc.--Saint Joseph
650 Carondelet Dr.
Kansas City, MO 64114
Ph: (816)363-8228
URL: http://www.dciinc.org
Dialysis Stations: 38.

25488 ■ Fresenius Medical Care Kansas City Dialysis and Transplant Center
6400 Prospect East Bldg., No., 100
Kansas City, MO 64132
Free: 866-434-2597
URL: http://www.ultracare-dialysis.com/
Dialysis Stations: 33.

25489 ■ Penn Valley Dialysis Clinic Fresenius Medical Care
2502 Summit
Kansas City, MO 64108
Free: 866-434-2597
URL: http://www.ultracare-dialysis.com/
Dialysis Stations: 20.

25490 ■ Platte Woods Dialysis DaVita
7667 NW Prairie View Rd.
Kansas City, MO 64151
Free: 800-424-6589
URL: http://www.davita.com
Dialysis Stations: 14. **Formerly:** Gambro Healthcare.

25491 ■ Research Medical Center Dialysis Unit
2316 E Meyer Blvd.
Kansas City, MO 64132
Ph: (816)276-4095
URL: http://www.researchmedicalcenter.com
Dialysis Stations: 12.

25492 ■ Research Medical Center Transplant Institute HCA Midwest Health System
2316 E Meyer Blvd.
Kansas City, MO 64132
Ph: (816)822-8257
URL: http://researchmedicalcenter.com/healthcare-services/transplant-institute/
Dialysis Stations: 0.

25493 ■ Saint Luke's Dialysis Center Diversified Specialty Institutes
4333 Madison Ave.
Kansas City, MO 64111
Ph: (816)756-0645
URL: http://www.dsi-corp.com
Dialysis Stations: 24.

25494 ■ Saint Luke's Hospital Kidney Transplant Unit Saint Luke's Health System
4401 Wornall
Kansas City, MO 64111
Ph: (816)932-2000
URL: https://www.saintlukeshealthsystem.org/featured-service/transplant-services
Dialysis Stations: 0.

25495 ■ Timberlake Dialysis DaVita
12110 Holmes Rd.
Kansas City, MO 64145
Free: 800-424-6589
URL: http://www.davita.com
Dialysis Stations: 6.

25496 ■ Westport Dialysis Center Diversified Specialty Institutes
3947 Broadway
Kansas City, MO 64111
Ph: (816)531-1181
URL: http://www.dsi-corp.com
Dialysis Stations: 15.

Kennett

25497 ■ Fresenius Medical Care----Kennett
715 Teaco Rd.
Kennett, MO 63857
Free: 866-434-2597
URL: http://www.ultracare-dialysis.com
Dialysis Stations: 15. **Formerly:** Renal Care Group.

25498 ■ Hope Again Dialysis Center DaVita
1207 State Rte. Vv
Kennett, MO 63857
Free: 800-424-6589
URL: http://www.davita.com
Dialysis Stations: 16.

Kirksville

25499 ■ Dialysis Clinics, Inc.--Kirksville
600 Rosewood Dr.
Kirksville, MO 63501
Ph: (660)665-8372
URL: http://www.dciinc.org
Dialysis Stations: 12.

Lake Saint Louis

25500 ■ Lake St. Louis Dialysis DaVita
200 Brevco Plaza
Lake Saint Louis, MO 63367
Free: 800-424-6589
URL: http://www.davita.com
Dialysis Stations: 14. **Formerly:** Gambro Healthcare.

Lebanon

25501 ■ Fresenius Medical Care--Lebanon Dialysis Facility
331 Hospital Dr., Ste. F
Lebanon, MO 65536
Free: 866-434-2597
URL: http://www.ultracare-dialysis.com
Dialysis Stations: 16. **Formerly:** Renal Care Group - Lebanon.

Lees Summit

25502 ■ Dialysis Clinic, Inc.--Lees Summit
219 NW Executive Way
Lees Summit, MO 64063
Ph: (816)554-2711
URL: http://www.dciinc.org
Dialysis Stations: 12.

25503 ■ Diversified Specialty Institutes--Lee's Summit Renal Center
100 NE Missouri Rd., Ste. 100
Lees Summit, MO 64086
Ph: (816)524-3312
URL: http://www.dsi-corp.com/
Dialysis Stations: 17.

25504 ■ Lee's Summit Dialysis Fresenius Medical Care
1831 SE Blue Pkwy.
Lees Summit, MO 64063
Free: 866-434-2597
URL: http://www.ultracare-dialysis.com/
Dialysis Stations: 12.

Liberty

25505 ■ Liberty Dialysis DaVita Dialysis Center
2525 Glenn Hendren Dr.
Liberty, MO 64068
Free: 800-424-6589
URL: http://www.davita.com
Dialysis Stations: 14. **Formerly:** Gambro Healthcare.

Louisiana

25506 ■ Dialysis Clinic, Inc.--Louisiana
2305 W Georgia St.
Louisiana, MO 63353
Ph: (573)754-6239
URL: http://www.dciinc.org
Dialysis Stations: 9.

Macon

25507 ■ Samaritan Memorial Hospital Dialysis Unit
1205 N Missouri St.
Macon, MO 63552
Ph: (660)385-8744
URL: http://www.samaritanhospital.net
Dialysis Stations: 9.

Marshall

25508 ■ Marshall Dialysis Center Diversified Specialty Institutes
359 W Morgan
Marshall, MO 65340
Ph: (660)886-9080
URL: http://www.dsi-corp.com
Dialysis Stations: 8.

Mexico

25509 ■ Dialysis Clinic, Inc.--Mexico
806 Medical Park Dr.
Mexico, MO 65265
Ph: (573)581-2638
URL: http://www.dciinc.org
Dialysis Stations: 16.

Moberly

25510 ■ Dialysis Clinic, Inc.--Moberly
1511 Union Ave.
Moberly, MO 65270
Ph: (660)263-1611
URL: http://www.dciinc.org
Dialysis Stations: 12.

Monett

25511 ■ Ozark Dialysis Services--Monett Cox Health
825 Hwy. 60, Ste. B
Monett, MO 65708
Ph: (417)354-1110
URL: http://www.coxhealth.com/body.cfm?id=1433
Dialysis Stations: 20.

Mountain Grove

25512 ■ Fresenius Medical Care--Mountain Grove
1200 N Main St., No. 2
Mountain Grove, MO 65711
Free: 866-434-2597
URL: http://www.ultracare-dialysis.com/
Dialysis Stations: 12. **Formerly:** Satellite Kidney Disease Center of the Ozarks.

Nixa

25513 ■ Fresenius Medical Care--Nixa
121 N Massey
Nixa, MO 65714
Free: 866-434-2597
URL: http://www.ultracare-dialysis.com/
Dialysis Stations: 12. **Formerly:** Renal Care Group.

Normandy

25514 ■ Fresenius Medical Care Metro Dialysis Center--Normandy
25 N Oaks Plz.
Normandy, MO 63121
Free: 866-434-2597
URL: http://www.ultracare-dialysis.com/
Dialysis Stations: 17.

North Kansas City

25515 ■ Northland Dialysis DaVita
2750 Clay Edwards Dr., No. 100
North Kansas City, MO 64116
Free: 800-424-6589
URL: http://www.davita.com
Dialysis Stations: 21. **Formerly:** Gambro Healthcare.

O'Fallon

25516 ■ Villa of Waterbury DaVita
929 Waterbury Falls Dr.
O'Fallon, MO 63368
Free: 800-424-6589
URL: http://www.davita.com
Dialysis Stations: 6.

Ofallon

25517 ■ Fresenius Medical Care--Fallon
4663 Hwy. K
Ofallon, MO 63368
Free: 866-434-2597
URL: http://www.ultracare-dialysis.com/
Dialysis Stations: 12.

Osage Beach

25518 ■ Dialysis Clinics, Inc.--Osage Beach
1027 Pallisades Blvd.
Osage Beach, MO 65065
Ph: (573)348-9406
URL: http://www.dciinc.org
Dialysis Stations: 16.

Perryville

25519 ■ Perry Dialysis Centers Fresenius Medical Care
12 N Kingshighway, No. 100
Perryville, MO 63775
Free: 866-434-2597
URL: http://www.ultracare-dialysis.com/
Dialysis Stations: 14.

Poplar Bluff

25520 ■ Bluff City Dialysis & At Home DaVita
2400 Lucy Lee Pkwy., Ste. E
Poplar Bluff, MO 63901
Free: 800-424-6589
URL: http://www.davita.com
Dialysis Stations: 12.

25521 ■ Fresenius Medical Care--Poplar Bluff
2311 Eugene Blvd.
Poplar Bluff, MO 63901
Free: 866-434-2597
URL: http://www.ultracare-dialysis.com/
Dialysis Stations: 16. **Formerly:** Poplar Bluff Dialysis Center.

Potosi

25522 ■ Renal Advantage Inc.--Potosi
828 High St., Ste. 2
Potosi, MO 63664
Ph: (573)436-8085
URL: http://www.renaladvantage.com
Dialysis Stations: 14. **Formerly:** Potosi Dialysis Centers.

Raytown

25523 ■ Fresenius Medical Care--Raytown
11503 E 63rd St.
Raytown, MO 64133
Free: 866-434-2597
URL: http://www.ultracare-dialysis.com/
Dialysis Stations: 20.

Richmond

25524 ■ Letholt Dialysis Center Fresenius Medical Care
906 Wollard Blvd.
Richmond, MO 64085
Free: 866-434-2597
URL: http://www.ultracare-dialysis.com/
Dialysis Stations: 8.

Rolla

25525 ■ DaVita--Rolla Dialysis Center
1503 E 10th St.
Rolla, MO 65401
Free: 800-424-6589
URL: http://www.davita.com
Dialysis Stations: 16. **Formerly:** Gambro Healthcare.

Saint Ann

25526 ■ Fresenius Medical Care--St. Louis
10951 St. Charles Rock Rd.
Saint Ann, MO 63074
Free: 866-434-2597
URL: http://www.ultracare-dialysis.com/
Dialysis Stations: 17.

Saint Charles

25527 ■ St. Charles Dialysis DaVita Dialysis Facility
2125 Bluestone Dr.
Saint Charles, MO 63303
Free: 800-424-6589
URL: http://www.davita.com
Dialysis Stations: 12. **Formerly:** Gambro Healthcare.

Saint Joseph

25528 ■ Saint Joseph Dialysis & At Home DaVita
5514 Corporate Dr., Ste. 100
Saint Joseph, MO 64507
Free: 800-424-6589
URL: http://www.davita.com
Dialysis Stations: 26. **Formerly:** Gambro Healthcare.

Saint Louis

25529 ■ Barnes Jewish Dialysis Center
4205 Forest Park Ave.
Saint Louis, MO 63108
Ph: (314)286-0800
Dialysis Stations: 32.

25530 ■ Barnes Jewish Hospital--Transplant
216 Kingshighway
Saint Louis, MO 63110
Ph: (314)362-5365
URL: http://www.barnesjewish.org/kidney-transplant
Dialysis Stations: 0.

25531 ■ Cardinal Glennon Children's Hospital
Renal Dialysis Unit
1465 S Grand Blvd., 2N
Saint Louis, MO 63104
Ph: (314)268-6423
URL: http://www.cardinalglennon.com
Dialysis Stations: 0.

25532 ■ Chromalloy American Kidney Center
Wohl Clinic Bldg.
4950 Children's Pl.
Saint Louis, MO 63110
Ph: (314)362-7209
Dialysis Stations: 30.

25533 ■ Crestwood Dialysis
DaVita
9901 Watson Rd., Ste. 125
Saint Louis, MO 63126
Free: 800-424-6589
URL: http://www.davita.com
Dialysis Stations: 12.

25534 ■ DaVita
Shrewsbury Dialysis
7435 Watson Rd., No. 119
Saint Louis, MO 63119
Free: 800-424-6589
URL: http://www.davita.com
Dialysis Stations: 12.

25535 ■ Fresenius Medical Care--Chouteau
4030 Chouteau Ave., 1st Fl.
Saint Louis, MO 63110
Free: 866-434-2597
URL: http://www.ultracare-dialysis.com/
Dialysis Stations: 20. **Formerly:** Renal Care Group/ Renex Dialysis Center of St. Louis.

25536 ■ Fresenius Medical Care--Drummond Hall, Saint Louis
3691 Rutger St.
Drummond Hall, Ste. 222
Saint Louis, MO 63110
Free: 866-434-2597
URL: http://www.ultracare-dialysis.com/
Dialysis Stations: 29. **Formerly:** Renal Care Group.

25537 ■ Fresenius Medical Care--Maplewood
6512 Manchester Rd.
Saint Louis, MO 63139
Free: 866-434-2597
URL: http://www.ultracare-dialysis.com/
Dialysis Stations: 16. **Formerly:** Renal Care Group.

25538 ■ Fresenius Medical Care--Rutger Street, Saint Louis
Dialysis Facility
Drummond Hall
3691 Rutger St., Ste. 222
Saint Louis, MO 63110
Free: 866-434-2597
URL: http://www.ultracare-dialysis.com/
Dialysis Stations: 29. **Formerly:** Renal Care Group.

25539 ■ Fresenius Medical Care--Saint Louis--Midtown
Dialysis Facility
5535 Delmar Blvd.
Saint Louis, MO 63112
Free: 866-434-2597
URL: http://www.ultracare-dialysis.com/
Dialysis Stations: 16. **Formerly:** Saint Louis Connect Care.

25540 ■ Fresenius Medical Care--Tesson Ferry Dialysis
13134 Tesson Ferry Rd.
Saint Louis, MO 63128
Free: 866-434-2597
URL: http://www.ultracare-dialysis.com/
Dialysis Stations: 16.

25541 ■ Hampton Avenue Dialysis
DaVita
1425 Hampton Ave.
Saint Louis, MO 63139
Free: 800-424-6589
URL: http://www.davita.com
Dialysis Stations: 12.

25542 ■ Lamplighter Plaza Dialysis
DaVita
12654 Lamplighter Sq.
Saint Louis, MO 63128
Free: 800-424-6589
URL: http://www.davita.com
Dialysis Stations: 16.

25543 ■ Metro Saint Louis Dialysis Center, LLC
10160 W Florissant
Saint Louis, MO 63136
Ph: (314)869-4978
Dialysis Stations: 16.

25544 ■ Renal Advantage Inc.--Hampton Ave.--St. Louis
2635 Hampton Ave.
Saint Louis, MO 63139
Ph: (314)646-1717
URL: http://www.renaladvantage.com
Dialysis Stations: 24. **Formerly:** National Renal Alliance.

25545 ■ Saint John's Mercy Medical Center
Dialysis Facility
615 New Ballas Rd.
Saint Louis, MO 63141
Ph: (314)251-6424
URL: http://www.stjohnsmercy.org
Dialysis Stations: 8.

25546 ■ Saint Louis Children's Hospital
Dialysis Center
1 Children's Pl., 2N80
Saint Louis, MO 63110
Ph: (314)454-6065
URL: http://www.stlouischildrens.org/content/greystone_1687.htm
Dialysis Stations: 6.

25547 ■ St. Louis Dialysis Center
DaVita
Dialysis Facility
2610 Clark Ave.
Saint Louis, MO 63103
Free: 800-424-6589
URL: http://www.davita.com
Dialysis Stations: 25.

25548 ■ St. Louis Dialysis
DaVita
Dialysis Center
324 De Baliviere Ave.
Saint Louis, MO 63112
Free: 800-424-6589
URL: http://www.davita.com
Dialysis Stations: 32. **Formerly:** Gambro Healthcare.

25549 ■ Saint Louis Renal Care--Des Peres
Dialysis Center
2325 Dougherty Ferry Rd., Ste. 103
Saint Louis, MO 63121
Ph: (314)822-8963
Dialysis Stations: 12. **Formerly:** Deaconess Hospital--West St. Louis.

25550 ■ St. Louis Renal Care--Forest Park
Fresenius Medical Care
1400 Strassner
Saint Louis, MO 63144
Free: 866-434-2597
URL: http://www.ultracare-dialysis.com/
Dialysis Stations: 20. **Formerly:** Renal Care Group.

25551 ■ Saint Louis University Hospital Transplant Unit
3635 Vista Blvd., 5th Fl., FDT
Saint Louis, MO 63110
Ph: (314)577-8867
URL: http://www.sluhospital.com/en-US/ourServices/medicalServices/Pages/OrganTra nsplantation.aspx
Dialysis Stations: 0.

25552 ■ Saint Louis West Dialysis
DaVita
400 N Lindberg Blvd.
Saint Louis, MO 63141
Free: 800-424-6589
URL: http://www.davita.com
Dialysis Stations: 21. **Formerly:** Gambro Healthcare.

25553 ■ South County Dialysis Center & At Home
DaVita
4145 Union Rd.
Saint Louis, MO 63129
Free: 800-424-6589
URL: http://www.davita.com
Dialysis Stations: 12.

25554 ■ South Towne Square Dialysis Clinic
Renal Advantage Inc.
11107 S Towne Sq.
Saint Louis, MO 63123
Ph: (314)894-3400
URL: http://www.renaladvantage.com
Dialysis Stations: 18. **Formerly:** National Renal Alliance.

25555 ■ Villa of St. John
DaVita
9030 St. Charles Rock Rd.
Saint Louis, MO 63114
Free: 800-424-6589
URL: http://www.davita.com
Dialysis Stations: 6.

Saint Peters

25556 ■ Saint Charles County Dialysis
Fresenius Medical Care
335 Mid Rivers Mall Dr.
Saint Peters, MO 63376
Free: 866-434-2597
URL: http://www.ultracare-dialysis.com/
Dialysis Stations: 21.

25557 ■ St. Peters Dialysis
DaVita
300 1st Executive Ave., Ste. A
Saint Peters, MO 63376
Free: 800-424-6589
URL: http://www.davita.com
Dialysis Stations: 12. **Formerly:** Gambro Healthcare.

Salem

25558 ■ Salem Memorial Hospital Dialysis Facility
Hwy. 72 N
Salem, MO 65560
Ph: (573)729-6626
Dialysis Stations: 7.

Sedalia

25559 ■ Dialysis Clinic, Inc.--Sedalia
1727 W 7th St.
Sedalia, MO 65301
Ph: (660)826-0566
URL: http://www.dciinc.org
Dialysis Stations: 18.

Sikeston

25560 ■ Sikeston Jaycee Regional Dialysis Center
135 Plaza Dr., No. 101
Sikeston, MO 63801
Ph: (573)472-7230
URL: http://www.missourldelta.com/renal.html
Dialysis Stations: 18.

Springfield

25561 ■ Fresenius Medical Care--Springfield, Missouri
1675 E Seminole, Ste. A
Springfield, MO 65804
Free: 866-434-2597
URL: http://www.ultracare-dialysis.com/
Dialysis Stations: 24. **Formerly:** Renal Care Group.

25562 ■ Ozark Dialysis Services--South Cox Health
3525 S National Ave., No. 102
Springfield, MO 65807
Ph: (417)269-7082
URL: http://www.coxhealth.com/body.cfm?id=1433
Dialysis Stations: 21.

25563 ■ Ozark Home Dialysis and PD Services--Primrose Cox Health
1001 E Primrose
Springfield, MO 65807
Ph: (417)875-3307
URL: http://www.coxhealth.com/body.cfm?id=1433
Dialysis Stations: 1.

Sullivan

25564 ■ Fresenius Medical Care--Sullivan
123 Progress Pkwy.
Sullivan, MO 63080
Free: 866-434-2597
URL: http://www.ultracare-dialysis.com/
Dialysis Stations: 12.

Troy

25565 ■ Dialysis Services of Lincoln County Fresenius Medical Care
9 Lincoln Center, Hwy. 47, Unit A
Troy, MO 63379
Free: 866-434-2597
URL: http://www.ultracare-dialysis.com/
Dialysis Stations: 17.

Union

25566 ■ Fresenius Medical Care--Union
1780 Old Hwy. 50 E, Ste. 111
Union, MO 63084
Free: 866-434-2597
URL: http://www.ultracare-dialysis.com/
Dialysis Stations: 14. **Formerly:** Renal Care Group/ Renex Dialysis Clinic of Union.

University City

25567 ■ Fresenius Medical Care--University City
6850 Olive Blvd.
University City, MO 63130
Free: 866-434-2597
URL: http://www.ultracare-dialysis.com/
Dialysis Stations: 22. **Formerly:** Renal Care Group/ Renex Dialysis Clinic of University City.

Warrensburg

25568 ■ Dialysis Clinic Inc.--Warrensburg
609 C East Young St.
Warrensburg, MO 64093
Ph: (660)429-1110
URL: http://www.dciinc.org
Dialysis Stations: 12.

Washington

25569 ■ Washington Square Dialysis DaVita Dialysis Facility
1112 Washington Sq.
Washington, MO 63090
Free: 800-424-6589
URL: http://www.davita.com
Dialysis Stations: 16. **Formerly:** Gambro Healthcare.

Wentzville

25570 ■ Fresenius Medical Care--Wentzville
1534 W Meyer Rd.
Wentzville, MO 63385
Free: 866-434-2597
URL: http://www.ultracare-dialysis.com/
Dialysis Stations: 21.

25571 ■ Villa of Wentzville DaVita
1126 W Pearce Blvd.
Wentzville, MO 63385
Free: 800-424-6589
URL: http://www.davita.com
Dialysis Stations: 6.

West Plains

25572 ■ Dialysis Clinic, Inc.--West Plains
205 Valley View Dr.
West Plains, MO 65775
Ph: (417)257-1683
URL: http://www.dciinc.org
Dialysis Stations: 12.

MONTANA

Billings

25573 ■ Billings Clinic Dialysis Center
2800 10th Ave. N
Billings, MT 59107
Ph: (406)657-4100
Dialysis Stations: 17. **Formerly:** Northern Rockies Kidney Center.

25574 ■ Dialysis Clinic, Inc.--Billings
2411 Village Ln.
Billings, MT 59102
Ph: (406)252-9270
URL: http://www.dciinc.org
Dialysis Stations: 19.

Bozeman

25575 ■ Bozeman Dialysis Center
931 Highland Blvd., Ste. 3105
Bozeman, MT 59715
Ph: (406)585-5090
Dialysis Stations: 6.

Browning

25576 ■ Dialysis Clinic Inc.--Blackfeet
Hospital Circle
Browning, MT 59417
Ph: (406)338-7472
URL: http://www.dciinc.org
Dialysis Stations: 8.

Butte

25577 ■ Saint Patrick--Butte Dialysis Center Saint James Community Hospital
400 S Clark St.
Butte, MT 59701
Ph: (406)723-2505
URL: http://www.stjameshealthcare.org
Dialysis Stations: 6.

Great Falls

25578 ■ Benefis Dialysis Center
Doctor's Plz., Ste. 22
2800 11th Ave. S
Great Falls, MT 59405
Ph: (406)455-3960
Dialysis Stations: 20.

Havre

25579 ■ Northern Montana Hospital Dialysis Unit
30 W 13th St.
Havre, MT 59501
Ph: (406)262-1470
URL: http://www.nmhcare.org
Dialysis Stations: 6.

Helena

25580 ■ Saint Peter's Hospital Dialysis Unit
2475 Broadway
Helena, MT 59601
Ph: (406)444-2280
URL: http://www.stpetes.org
Dialysis Stations: 13.

Kalispell

25581 ■ Dialysis Clinic Inc.--Kalispell
135 Commons Way
Kalispell, MT 59901
Ph: (406)756-5565
URL: http://www.dciinc.org
Dialysis Stations: 16.

Libby

25582 ■ Dialysis Clinic Inc.--Libby
308 Louisiana Ave., Ste. 2
Libby, MT 59923
Ph: (406)293-9913
URL: http://www.dciinc.org
Dialysis Stations: 4. **Formerly:** Glacier Regional Dialysis Center.

Missoula

25583 ■ Saint Patrick Hospital - Missoula Dialysis Center
615 W Alder
Missoula, MT 59802
Ph: (406)327-1750
URL: http://www.saintpatrick.org
Dialysis Stations: 24.

Poplar

25584 ■ Fort Peck Tribal Dialysis Unit
107 H St. E
Poplar, MT 59255
Ph: (406)768-5468
URL: http://www.fortpecktribes.org/fptdu/
Dialysis Stations: 10.

NEBRASKA

Alliance

25585 ■ Box Butte Dialysis Unit/Box Butte General Hospital
2101 Box Butte Ave.
Alliance, NE 69301
Ph: (308)762-6660
URL: http://www.bbgh.org
Dialysis Stations: 6.

Beatrice

25586 ■ Dialysis Center of Beatrice
1110 N 10th St.
Beatrice, NE 68310
Ph: (402)228-4722
E-mail: info@dialysisnebraska.org
URL: http://www.dialysisnebraska.org/beatrice.html
Dialysis Stations: 12.

Bellevue

25587 ■ Dialysis Clinic, Inc.
4112 Twin Creek Dr.
Bellevue, NE 68123
Ph: (402)934-9560
URL: http://www.dciinc.org
Dialysis Stations: 12.

Chadron

25588 ■ Chadron Community Hospital Dialysis
825 Centennial Dr.
Chadron, NE 69337
Ph: (308)432-5586
E-mail: ceo@chadronhospital.com
URL: http://www.chadronhospital.com/dialysis.html
Dialysis Stations: 4.

Columbus

25589 ■ Dialysis Center of Columbus
2452 39th Ave.
Columbus, NE 68601
Ph: (402)563-2139
URL: http://www.dialysisnebraska.org/satell.html
Dialysis Stations: 12.

Fremont

25590 ■ Dodge County Dialysis
DaVita
1949 E 23rd Ave. S
Fremont, NE 68025
Free: 800-424-6589
Fax: (402)721-7480
URL: http://www.davita.com
Dialysis Stations: 12. **Formerly:** Gambro Healthcare.

25591 ■ RAI Care Center--Fremont
Renal Advantage Inc.
Dialysis Facility
2340 N Health Way
Fremont, NE 68025
Ph: (402)753-9453
URL: http://www.renaladvantage.com
Dialysis Stations: 18. **Formerly:** Fremont Dialysis Center.

Grand Island

25592 ■ Fresenius Medical Care--Grand Island
3516 Richmond Cir.
Grand Island, NE 68803
Free: 866-434-2597
URL: http://www.ultracare-dialysis.com/
Dialysis Stations: 19. **Formerly:** Renal Care Group/Kidney Dialysis Center of Grand Island.

25593 ■ Grand Island Dialysis
DaVita
603 S Webb Rd.
Grand Island, NE 68803
Free: 800-424-6589
URL: http://www.davita.com
Dialysis Stations: 12. **Formerly:** Clarkson Kidney Center.

Hastings

25594 ■ Hasting Dialysis Center
DaVita
1900 N St. Joseph Ave.
Hastings, NE 68901
Free: 800-424-6589
URL: http://www.davita.com
Dialysis Stations: 12.

Kearney

25595 ■ Fresenius Medical Care--Overland Trails
5210 Parklane Dr.
Kearney, NE 68847
Free: 866-434-2597
URL: http://www.ultracare-dialysis.com/
Dialysis Stations: 17.

Lincoln

25596 ■ Capital City Dialysis & At Home
DaVita
307 N 46th St.
Lincoln, NE 68503
Free: 800-424-6589
URL: http://www.davita.com
Dialysis Stations: 12.

25597 ■ Dialysis Center of Lincoln
7910 'O' St.
Lincoln, NE 68510
Ph: (402)489-5339
E-mail: info@dialysisnebraska.org
URL: http://www.dialysisnebraska.org
Dialysis Stations: 22. **Remarks:** Three satellite locations in Beatrice, Columbus, and Lincoln.

25598 ■ Dialysis Center of Lincoln--Home
5355 S 16th St.
Lincoln, NE 68512
Ph: (402)742-8500
Dialysis Stations: 6.

25599 ■ Dialysis Center--Lincoln Northwest
4911 N 26th St., Ste. 106
Lincoln, NE 68521
Ph: (402)438-7330
E-mail: info@dialysisnebraska.org
URL: http://www.dialysisnebraska.org/north27.html
Dialysis Stations: 12.

25600 ■ Dialysis Center of Lincoln--Southwest
5355 S 16th St.
Lincoln, NE 68512
Ph: (402)742-8500
Dialysis Stations: 18.

25601 ■ South Lincoln Dialysis
DaVita
3401 Plantation Dr.
Lincoln, NE 68516
Free: 800-424-6589
URL: http://www.davita.com
Dialysis Stations: 8.

Macy

25602 ■ Carl T. Curtis Health Education Center Dialysis
100 Indian Hills Dr.
Macy, NE 68039
Ph: (402)837-4136
Dialysis Stations: 12.

McCook

25603 ■ McCook Dialysis Center
DaVita
801 W C St.
McCook, NE 69001
Free: 800-424-6589
URL: http://www.davita.com
Dialysis Stations: 8.

Norfolk

25604 ■ Northeast Nebraska Dialysis Center
1603 Prospect Ave.
Norfolk, NE 68701
Ph: (402)644-7592
Dialysis Stations: 12. **Formerly:** Lutheran Community Hospital.

North Platte

25605 ■ Fresenius Medical Care--North Platte
785 E Francis
North Platte, NE 69101
Free: 866-434-2597
URL: http://www.ultracare-dialysis.com/
Dialysis Stations: 17. **Formerly:** Renal Care Group.

O'Neill

25606 ■ Avera Saint Anthony's Hospital ESRD
223 Adams St.
O'Neill, NE 68763
Ph: (402)336-2611
URL: http://www.avera-sta.org
Dialysis Stations: 5.

Omaha

25607 ■ Dialysis Clinic, Inc.--Omaha
3316 Dodge St.
Omaha, NE 68131
Ph: (402)342-0190
URL: http://www.dciinc.org
Dialysis Stations: 30.

25608 ■ Dialysis Clinic, Inc.--West Omaha
3015 N 118th Circle
Omaha, NE 68164
Ph: (402)493-9331
URL: http://www.dciinc.org
Dialysis Stations: 24.

25609 ■ Omaha Central Dialysis
DaVita
144 S 40th St.
Omaha, NE 68131
Free: 800-424-6589
URL: http://www.davita.com
Dialysis Stations: 17. **Formerly:** Gambro HealthcareeaHe.

25610 ■ Omaha North Dialysis
DaVita
Dialysis Facility
6572 Ames Ave.
Omaha, NE 68104
Free: 800-424-6589
URL: http://www.davita.com
Dialysis Stations: 14. **Formerly:** Gambro Healthcare.

25611 ■ Omaha South Dialysis
DaVita
3427 L St., Ste. 16
Omaha, NE 68107
Free: 800-424-6589
URL: http://www.davita.com
Dialysis Stations: 16. **Formerly:** Gambro Healthcare.

25612 ■ Omaha West Dialysis
DaVita
13014 W Dodge Rd.
Omaha, NE 68154

Free: 800-424-6589
URL: http://www.davita.com
Dialysis Stations: 23. **Formerly:** Gambro Healthcare.

25613 ■ RAI Care Center--Ames Ave.
Renal Advantage Inc.
5084 Ames Ave.
Omaha, NE 68104
Ph: (402)451-7754
URL: http://www.renaladvantage.com
Dialysis Stations: 12. **Formerly:** Baker Place Dialysis.

25614 ■ RAI Care Center--Center Street
Renal Advantage Inc.
4411 Center, Ste. A
Omaha, NE 68105
Ph: (402)558-3284
URL: http://www.renaladvantage.com
Dialysis Stations: 22.

25615 ■ University Hospital Transplant ESRD
Nebraska Medical Center--Transplant Center
983285 Nebraska Medical Center
Omaha, NE 68198
Ph: (402)552-2440
URL: http://www.nebraskamed.com/transplant/kidney/
Dialysis Stations: 0.

Papillion

25616 ■ DaVita--Papillion
1502 S Washington St., No. 100
Papillion, NE 68046
Free: 800-424-6589
URL: http://www.davita.com
Dialysis Stations: 12. **Formerly:** Gambro Healthcare.

Scottsbluff

25617 ■ Scottsbluff Dialysis Center
DaVita
Dialysis Facility
3812 Ave. B
Scottsbluff, NE 69361
Free: 800-424-6589
URL: http://www.davita.com
Dialysis Stations: 16. **Formerly:** Renal Treatment Centers.

Valentine

25618 ■ Cherry County Hospital
Dialysis Unit
510 N Green St.
Valentine, NE 69201
Ph: (402)376-2525
Dialysis Stations: 4.

York

25619 ■ York General Dialysis Services
2319 N Lincoln Ave.
York, NE 68467
Ph: (402)363-6631
URL: http://www.yorkdevco.com/health.asp
Dialysis Stations: 8.

NEVADA

Carson City

25620 ■ Carson City Dialysis Center
Dvita
3310 Goni Rd.
Carson City, NV 89706
Ph: (775)886-6450
Dialysis Stations: 8.

25621 ■ Carson City Dialysis
Dialysis Clinic, Inc
778 Basque Way
Carson City, NV 89706
Ph: (775)883-5400
URL: http://www.dciinc.org
Dialysis Stations: 12.

25622 ■ Liberty Dialysis--Carson City
4500 S Carson St.
Carson City, NV 89701
Ph: (775)624-8055
URL: http://www.libertydialysis.com
Dialysis Stations: 20.

Elko

25623 ■ Elko Dilaysis
Dialysis Clinic Inc.
1995 Errecart Blvd., Ste. 100
Elko, NV 89801
Ph: (775)738-4090
URL: http://www.dciinc.org
Dialysis Stations: 9.

Fallon

25624 ■ DaVita
Fallon Dialysis
1103 New River Pkwy.
Fallon, NV 89406
Free: 800-424-6589
URL: http://www.davita.com
Dialysis Stations: 21.

Gardnerville

25625 ■ Gardnerville Dialysis
Dialysis Clinic Inc.
1281 Kimmerling Rd., Ste. A1
Gardnerville, NV 89460
Ph: (775)265-4706
URL: http://www.dciinc.org

Henderson

25626 ■ Anthem Village Dialysis
DaVita
2530 Anthem Village Dr., No. 100
Henderson, NV 89052
Free: 800-424-6589
URL: http://www.davita.com
Dialysis Stations: 18.

25627 ■ DaVita
Siena Henderson Dialysis Center
2865 Siena Hts. Dr., Ste. 141
Henderson, NV 89052
Free: 800-424-6589
URL: http://www.davita.com
Dialysis Stations: 17.

25628 ■ Green Valley Dialysis
Diversified Specialty Insitutes
1489 W Warm Springs Rd., Ste. 122
Henderson, NV 89014
Ph: (702)450-8877
URL: http://www.dsi-corp.com
Dialysis Stations: 18. **Formerly:** Renal Advantage Inc.

25629 ■ Nevada Dialysis Center
DaVita
1510 W Warm Springs Rd., Ste. 100
Henderson, NV 89014
Free: 800-424-6589
URL: http://www.davita.com
Dialysis Stations: 20.

Las Vegas

25630 ■ Centennial Dialysis
Fresenius Medical Care
7465 W Azure Dr., Ste. 1A
Las Vegas, NV 89130
Free: 866-434-2597
URL: http://www.ultracare-dialysis.com/
Dialysis Stations: 24.

25631 ■ Centennial Dilaysis Center
DaVita
8775 Deer Springs Way
Las Vegas, NV 89149
Free: 800-424-6589
URL: http://www.davita.com
Dialysis Stations: 20.

25632 ■ Desert Inn Dialysis
Fresenius Medical Care
1750 E Desert Inn Rd., Ste. 100
Las Vegas, NV 89169
Free: 866-434-2597
URL: http://www.ultracare-dialysis.com
Dialysis Stations: 27. **Formerly:** Renal Care Group - Las Vegas.

25633 ■ Desert Springs Dialysis Center
DaVita
2110 E Flamingo Rd., Ste. 108
Las Vegas, NV 89119
URL: http://www.davita.com
Dialysis Stations: 18.

25634 ■ Fire Mesa Dialysis
Fresenius Medical Care
2450 Fire Mesa St., Ste. 120
Las Vegas, NV 89128
Free: 866-434-2597
URL: http://www.ultracare-dialysis.com/
Dialysis Stations: 24.

25635 ■ Five Star Dialysis Center and At Home
DaVita
2400 Tech Center Ct.
Las Vegas, NV 89128
Free: 800-424-6589
URL: http://www.davita.com
Dialysis Stations: 28.

25636 ■ Green Valley Dialysis
Fresenius Medical Care
6330 S Pecos, Ste. 110
Las Vegas, NV 89120
Ph: (702)433-3079
Free: 866-434-2597
URL: http://www.ultracare-dialysis.com
Dialysis Stations: 24. **Formerly:** Renal Care Group - Green Valley.

25637 ■ Las Vegas Dialysis Center & At Home
DaVita
3100 W Charleston Blvd., Ste. 100
Las Vegas, NV 89102
Free: 800-424-6589
URL: http://www.davita.com
Dialysis Stations: 37. **Formerly:** Dialysis Systems West.

25638 ■ Las Vegas Dialysis
Diversified Specialty Institutes
2333 Renaissance Dr.
Las Vegas, NV 89119
Ph: (702)740-8580
URL: http://www.dsi-corp.com
Dialysis Stations: 14. **Formerly:** National Renal Institutes.

25639 ■ Las Vegas Pediatrics Dialysis Center
DaVita
7271 W Sahara Ave., Ste. 120
Las Vegas, NV 89117
Free: 800-424-6589
URL: http://www.davita.com
Dialysis Stations: 4.

25640 ■ Liberty Dialysis--Las Vegas
6970 W Patrick Ln., Ste. 100
Las Vegas, NV 89113
Ph: (702)247-6761
URL: http://www.libertydialysis.com
Dialysis Stations: 16.

25641 ■ Mountain View Dialysis
DaVita
Dialysis Facility
2881 Business Park Court, Ste. 150
Las Vegas, NV 89128
Free: 800-424-6589
URL: http://www.davita.com
Dialysis Stations: 20. **Formerly:** Grambo Healthcare.

25642 ■ Northwest Las Vegas Dialysis
Fresenius Medical Care
3150 N Tenaya, Ste. 110
Las Vegas, NV 89128
Free: 866-434-2597
URL: http://www.ultracare-dialysis.com
Dialysis Stations: 14. **Formerly:** Renal Care Group - Northwest Las Vegas.

25643 ■ Red Moon Dialysis
900 S Main St.
Las Vegas, NV 89101
Ph: (702)383-9741
URL: http://www.redmoondialysis.com/
Dialysis Stations: 16.

25644 ■ South Las Vegas Dialysis
DaVita
2250 S Rancho Dr., Ste. 115
Las Vegas, NV 89102
Free: 800-424-6589
URL: http://www.davita.com
Dialysis Stations: 22.

25645 ■ South Rainbow Dialysis
Fresenius Medical Care
7040 W Sunset Rd.
Las Vegas, NV 89113
Free: 866-434-2597
URL: http://www.ultracare-dialysis.com/
Dialysis Stations: 21.

25646 ■ Southern Hills Dialysis Center
DaVita
9280 W Sunset Rd., Ste. 110
Las Vegas, NV 89148
Free: 800-424-6589
URL: http://www.davita.com
Dialysis Stations: 23.

25647 ■ Summerlin Dialysis Center
DaVita
653 Town Center Dr., Ste. 70
Las Vegas, NV 89144
Free: 800-424-6589
URL: http://www.davita.com
Dialysis Stations: 20.

25648 ■ University Medical Center Transplantation Services
1120 Shadow Ln., Ste. D100
Las Vegas, NV 89102
Ph: (702)383-2224
URL: https://www.umcsn.com/Medical-Services-at-UMCSN/Transplant-Center.aspx?intMenuID=132&intPageID=226
Dialysis Stations: 0.

Mesquite

25649 ■ University of Utah Dialysis Program
350 Falcon Ridge Pkwy., Bldg. 700, Ste. 104
Mesquite, NV 89027
Ph: (702)345-4144
URL: http://healthcare.utah.edu/dialysis/facilities/desert%20valley.html
Dialysis Stations: 10.

North Las Vegas

25650 ■ Las Vegas Kidney Clinic
1905 Civic Center Dr., Ste. 201
North Las Vegas, NV 89030
Ph: (702)214-9516
Dialysis Stations: 11.

25651 ■ North Las Vegas Dialysis Center
DaVita
2300 McDaniel St.
North Las Vegas, NV 89030
Free: 800-424-6589
URL: http://www.davita.com
Dialysis Stations: 22. **Formerly:** Dialysis Systems North.

Pahrump

25652 ■ Pahrump Dialysis Center
DaVita
330 S Lola Ln., Ste. 100
Pahrump, NV 89048
Free: 800-424-6589
URL: http://www.davita.com
Dialysis Stations: 16.

Reno

25653 ■ Liberty Dialysis--Northwest Reno
6144 Mae Anne Dr.
Reno, NV 89523
Ph: (775)747-1100
URL: http://www.libertydialysis.com
Dialysis Stations: 20.

25654 ■ Liberty Dialysis--Reno Home
601 Sierra Rose Dr., Ste. 201
Reno, NV 89511
Ph: (775)829-9961
URL: http://www.libertydialysis.com

25655 ■ Reno Dialysis Center & At Home
DaVita
1500 E 2nd St., No. 101
Reno, NV 89502
Free: 800-424-6589
URL: http://www.davita.com
Dialysis Stations: 25. **Formerly:** Northern Sierra Dialysis Center.

25656 ■ Sierra Rose Dialysis Center
DaVita
685 Sierra Rose Dr.
Reno, NV 89511
Free: 800-424-6589
URL: http://www.davita.com
Dialysis Stations: 19.

25657 ■ South Meadows Dialysis Center
DaVita
10085 Doubler Blvd.
Reno, NV 89521
Free: 800-424-6589
URL: http://www.davita.com
Dialysis Stations: 25.

Sparks

25658 ■ Sparks Dialysis Facility
DaVita
4860 Vista Blvd., Ste. 100
Sparks, NV 89436
Free: 800-424-6589
URL: http://www.davita.com
Dialysis Stations: 21.

NEW HAMPSHIRE

Concord

25659 ■ New Hampshire Kidney Center
Fresenius Medical Care
Pillsbury Bldg., Ste. G400
248 Pleasant St.
Concord, NH 03301
Free: 866-434-2597
URL: http://www.ultracare-dialysis.com
Dialysis Stations: 16.

Exeter

25660 ■ Dialysis Services of Exeter
Fresenius Medical Care
1 Hampton Rd., Ste. 109
Exeter, NH 03833
Free: 866-434-2597
URL: http://www.ultracare-dialysis.com
Dialysis Stations: 13.

Keene

25661 ■ Monadnock Dialysis Center
Fresenius Medical Care
426B Winchester St.
Keene, NH 03431
Free: 866-434-2597
URL: http://www.ultracare-dialysis.com/
Dialysis Stations: 13.

Laconia

25662 ■ Central New Hampshire Kidney Center
87 Spring St.
Laconia, NH 03246
Ph: (603)528-3738
Dialysis Stations: 21.

Lancaster

25663 ■ Fresenius Medical Care--Lancaster
173 Middle St.
Lancaster, NH 03584
Free: 866-434-2597
URL: http://www.ultracare-dialysis.com
Dialysis Stations: 14. **Formerly:** North Country Kidney Center.

Lebanon

25664 ■ Dartmouth Hitchcock Medical Center--Transplant
One Medical Center Dr.
Lebanon, NH 03756
Ph: (603)653-3931
URL: http://www.dhmc.org/webpage.cfm?site_id=2&org_id=132&gsec_id=0&sec_id=0&item_id=3543
Dialysis Stations: 0.

25665 ■ Fresenius Medical Care of Lebanon
56 Etna Rd.
Lebanon, NH 03766
Free: 866-434-2597
URL: http://www.ultracare-dialysis.com/
Dialysis Stations: 27. **Formerly:** Dartmouth Hitchcock Medical Center, Section of Transplant Surgery.

Londonderry

25666 ■ Fresenius Medical Care--Londonderry
1F Common Dr.
Londonderry, NH 03053
Free: 866-434-2597
URL: http://www.ultracare-dialysis.com/
Dialysis Stations: 14.

25667 ■ Steam Dialysis
DaVita
1 Action Blvd., Ste. 2
Londonderry, NH 03053
Free: 800-424-6589
URL: http://www.davita.com
Dialysis Stations: 13.

Manchester

25668 ■ Manchester Kidney Center
Fresenius Medical Care
1050 Perimeter Rd., Ste. 502
Manchester, NH 03103
Free: 866-434-2597
URL: http://www.ultracare-dialysis.com/
Dialysis Stations: 20.

Nashua

25669 ■ Nashua Dialysis
DaVita
Dialysis Center & At Home
38 Tyler St.
Nashua, NH 03061
Free: 800-424-6589
URL: http://www.davita.com
Dialysis Stations: 22. **Formerly:** Gambro Healthcare.

Portsmouth

25670 ■ Seacoast Dialysis Center
Fresenius Medical Care
195 Commerce Way
Portsmouth, NH 03801
Free: 866-434-2597
URL: http://www.ultracare-dialysis.com/
Dialysis Stations: 18.

Rochester

25671 ■ Strafford County Dialysis
Fresenius Medical Care
27 Sterling Dr.
Rochester, NH 03867
Free: 866-434-2597
URL: http://www.ultracare-dialysis.com/
Dialysis Stations: 17.

NEW JERSEY

Atlantic City

25672 ■ Atlantic City Medical Center
Dialysis Unit
1925 Pacific Ave.
Atlantic City, NJ 08401
Ph: (609)441-8944
URL: http://www.atlanticare.org
Dialysis Stations: 12.

25673 ■ Fresenius Medical Care--Atlantic City
Dialysis Center
1501 Atlantic Ave.
Atlantic City, NJ 08401
Free: 866-434-2597
URL: http://www.ultracare-dialysis.com
Dialysis Stations: 20. **Formerly:** DaVita - Atlantic City.

Bayonne

25674 ■ Bayonne Hospital Renal Center
Dialysis Unit
29 E 29th St.
Bayonne, NJ 07002
Ph: (201)858-5358
URL: http://www.bayonnemedicalcare.org
Dialysis Stations: 12.

25675 ■ Renal Ventures Management--Bayonne
Dialysis Center
434-436 Broadway
Bayonne, NJ 07002
Ph: (201)436-1664
URL: http://www.renalventures.com/
Dialysis Stations: 21.

Belleville

25676 ■ Nutley Kidney Clinic
500 Cortland St.
Belleville, NJ 07109
Ph: (973)450-1560
URL: http://www.nutleykidneyclinic.com/
Dialysis Stations: 27.

Berlin

25677 ■ Liberty Dialysis--Berlin
30 Tansboro Rd.
Berlin, NJ 08009
Ph: (856)809-0036
URL: http://www.libertydialysis.com
Dialysis Stations: 15.

Bloomfield

25678 ■ Fresenius Medical Care--Bloomfield
206 Belleville Ave.
Bloomfield, NJ 07003
Free: 866-434-2597
URL: http://www.ultracare-dialysis.com
Dialysis Stations: 20. **Formerly:** Renal Care Group/ Renex Bloomfield Dialysis Clinic Bloomfield.

Bound Brook

25679 ■ Bridgewater Dialysis Center
DaVita
2121 Rte. 22 W
Bound Brook, NJ 08805-1546
Free: 800-424-6589
URL: http://www.davita.com
Dialysis Stations: 15.

Brick

25680 ■ Ocean County Medical Center--Brick
Dialysis Unit
Brick Medical Arts Bldg., Dialysis
1640 Rte. 88, Ste. 102
Brick, NJ 08724
Ph: (732)206-8200
URL: http://www.oceanmedicalcenter.com
Dialysis Stations: 21.

25681 ■ Renal Ventures Management--Brick
Renal Center
150 Brick Blvd.
Brick, NJ 08723
Ph: (732)477-2247
URL: http://www.renalventures.com/
Dialysis Stations: 20.

25682 ■ Shining Star DaVita Bricktown Dialysis Center
525 Jack Martin Blvd., Ste. 200
Brick, NJ 08724
Free: 800-424-6589
URL: http://www.davita.com
Dialysis Stations: 18. **Formerly:** DaVita.

Bridgeton

25683 ■ Bridgeton South Jersey Hospital
Dialysis Unit
333 Irving Ave.
Bridgeton, NJ 08302
Ph: (856)641-7800
URL: http://www.sjhealthcare.net
Dialysis Stations: 19.

Burlington

25684 ■ Burlington North Dialysis Center
DaVita
1164 Rte. 130 N
Burlington, NJ 08016
Free: 800-424-6589
URL: http://www.davita.com
Dialysis Stations: 13. **Formerly:** Gambro.

Camden

25685 ■ Our Lady of Lourdes Medical Center--Camden
Lourdes Health System
East Gate Park, Ste. 172
130 Gaither Dr.
Camden, NJ 08103
Ph: (856)222-3884
E-mail: info@lourdesnet.org
URL: http://www.lourdesnet.org/services/dialysis.php
Dialysis Stations: 22.

25686 ■ Our Lady of Lourdes Medical Center
Dialysis Unit
1601 Haddon Ave.
Camden, NJ 08103
Ph: (856)757-3770
URL: http://www.lourdesnet.org
Dialysis Stations: 22.

Cape May

25687 ■ Cape May Courthouse
Fresenius Medical Care
1259 Rte. 9 S
Cape May, NJ 08210
Ph: (609)465-3444
URL: http://www.ultracare-dialysis.com/
Dialysis Stations: 15. **Formerly:** Renal Care Group Cape May Dialysis Center.

Cherry Hill

25688 ■ Cherry Hill Dialysis Center
DaVita
1030 N Kings Hwy., Ste. 100
Cherry Hill, NJ 08034
Free: 800-424-6589
URL: http://www.davita.com
Dialysis Stations: 19. **Formerly:** Gambro.

25689 ■ Silver Dialysis--Cherry Hill
Fresenius Medical Care
1417 Brace Rd.
Cherry Hill, NJ 08034
Free: 866-434-2597
URL: http://www.silvercarecenter.com
Dialysis Stations: 35. **Formerly:** Silver Care Center.

Clifton

25690 ■ Renal Center of Passiac
Renal Ventures Management
10 Clifton Blvd.
Clifton, NJ 07011
Ph: (973)594-9100
URL: http://www.renalventures.com
Dialysis Stations: 20.

Colonia

25691 ■ Colonia Dilaysis Center
Fresenius Medical Care
1250 Rte. 27
Colonia, NJ 07067
Free: 866-434-2597
URL: http://www.ultracare-dialysis.com
Dialysis Stations: 16. **Formerly:** Bio-Medical Applications - Colonia.

Delran

25692 ■ DaVita--Delran
Dialysis Facility
8008 Rte. 130 N
Delran, NJ 08075
Free: 800-424-6589
URL: http://www.davita.com
Dialysis Stations: 13. **Formerly:** Gambro.

Deptford

25693 ■ Woodbury Dialysis Center
Fresenius Medical Care
571 Evergreen Ave.
Deptford, NJ 08096
Free: 866-434-2597
URL: http://www.ultracare-dialysis.com/
Dialysis Stations: 18. **Formerly:** RCG Renex Woodbury Dialysis Center.

East Orange

25694 ■ DaVita--East Orange Dialysis Facility
90 Washington St.
East Orange, NJ 07017
Free: 800-424-6589
URL: http://www.davita.com
Dialysis Stations: 21. **Formerly:** Gambro.

25695 ■ East Orange General Hospital Dialysis Unit
Medical Arts Bldg.
310 Central Ave.
East Orange, NJ 07017
Ph: (973)395-4035
URL: http://www.evh.org
Dialysis Stations: 24.

25696 ■ Fresenius Medical Care--East Orange Dialysis Center
110 S Grove St.
East Orange, NJ 07018
Free: 866-434-2597
URL: http://www.ultracare-dialysis.com/
Dialysis Stations: 20. **Formerly:** Renal Care Group.

Eatontown

25697 ■ Atlantic Kidney Center Dialysis Center & At Home
DaVita
6 Industrial Way W
Eatontown, NJ 07724
Free: 800-424-6589
URL: http://www.davita.com
Dialysis Stations: 27.

Edison

25698 ■ DaVita--Edison
29 Meridian Rd.
Edison, NJ 08820
Free: 800-424-6589
URL: http://www.davita.com
Dialysis Stations: 20. **Formerly:** Gambro.

Egg Harbor Twp.

25699 ■ Egg Harbor Dialysis Center
Fresenius Medical Care
6701 Black Horse Pike
Egg Harbor Twp., NJ 08234
Free: 866-434-2597
URL: http://www.ultracare-dialysis.com/
Dialysis Stations: 18. **Formerly:** Renal Care Group.

Elizabeth

25700 ■ Fresenius Medical Care--Elizabeth
595 Division St., Ste. B
Elizabeth, NJ 07201
Free: 866-434-2597
URL: http://www.ultracare-dialysis.com/
Dialysis Stations: 20. **Formerly:** RCG NNA Elizabeth Dialysis Center.

25701 ■ Trinitas Hospital Dialysis Unit
225 Williamson St.
Elizabeth, NJ 07207
Ph: (908)994-5203
URL: http://www.trinitashospital.org
Dialysis Stations: 14.

25702 ■ Trinitas Livingston Street Dialysis Unit
629 Livingston St.
Elizabeth, NJ 07206
Ph: (908)994-7011
URL: http://www.trinitashospital.org
Dialysis Stations: 14.

Englewood

25703 ■ Englewood Dialysis Center
Fresenius Medical Care
197 S Van Brunt St.
Englewood, NJ 07631
Free: 866-434-2597
URL: http://www.ultracare-dialysis.com/
Dialysis Stations: 20.

Ewing

25704 ■ Fresenius Medical Care--Ewing
1962 N Olden Ave.
Ewing, NJ 08638
Free: 866-434-2597
Dialysis Stations: 20.

Fair Lawn

25705 ■ Valley--Fairlawn Dialysis Center Outpatient Dialysis Facility
18-01 Pollitt Dr.
Fair Lawn, NJ 07410
Ph: (201)447-8587
URL: http://valleyhealth.com
Dialysis Stations: 20.

Fairview

25706 ■ Fresenius Medical Care--Fairview
1550161 Bergen Blvd.
Fairview, NJ 07022
Free: 866-434-2597
URL: http://www.ultracare-dialysis.com/
Dialysis Stations: 19.

Flemington

25707 ■ Kings Court Dialysis--Flemington
Fresenius Medical Care
2 Kings Court, Ste. 100
Flemington, NJ 08822
Free: 866-434-2597
URL: http://www.ultracare-dialysis.com
Dialysis Stations: 13. **Formerly:** Bio-Medical Applications - Kings Court - Flemington.

Freehold

25708 ■ Dialysis Clinic, Inc.--Central State--Freehold
901 W Main St.
Freehold, NJ 07728
Ph: (732)294-5200
URL: http://www.dciinc.org
Dialysis Stations: 9.

Hackensack

25709 ■ Hackensack Medical Center
30 Prospect Ave.
Hackensack, NJ 07601
Ph: (201)996-2800
URL: http://www.humc.com/kidneytransplant/
Dialysis Stations: 36.

25710 ■ Hackensack Medical Center Renal Unit
Johnson Hall
30 Prospect Ave.
Hackensack, NJ 07601
Ph: (201)996-2800
URL: http://www.humed.com
Dialysis Stations: 36.

Hacketstown

25711 ■ DaVita--Hackettstown
657 Willow Grove St., Ste. 202
Hacketstown, NJ 07840
Free: 800-424-6589
URL: http://www.davita.com
Dialysis Stations: 14.

Hamilton

25712 ■ Fresenius Medical Care--Hamilton Square
Two Hamilton Health Place
Hamilton, NJ 08690
Free: 866-434-2597
URL: http://www.ultracare-dialysis.com/
Dialysis Stations: 20.

25713 ■ Wellbound of Mercer Dialysis Center
Satellite Healthcare
3836 Quakerbridge Rd., Ste. 200
Hamilton, NJ 08619
Ph: (609)586-5001
Fax: (609)586-1862
URL: http://www.satellitehealth.com/
Dialysis Stations: 4.

Hammonton

25714 ■ Liberty Dialysis--Hammonton
392 N White Horse Pike, Ste. 1
Hammonton, NJ 08037
Ph: (609)561-0044
URL: http://www.libertydialysis.com
Dialysis Stations: 18.

Harrison

25715 ■ Fresenius Medical Care--Harrison
620 Essex St.
Harrison, NJ 07029
Free: 866-434-2597
URL: http://www.ultracare-dialysis.com/
Dialysis Stations: 20. **Formerly:** RCG Renex Harrison Dialysis Center.

Hillside

25716 ■ Hillside Dialysis Center
KRU Medical Ventures
1529 N Broad St.
Hillside, NJ 07205
Ph: (973)474-1199
Free: 866-836-7852
URL: http://www.krumed.com
Dialysis Stations: 20.

Hoboken

25717 ■ Hoboken Dialysis Center
Fresenius Medical Care
1600 Willow Ave.
Hoboken, NJ 07030
Free: 866-434-2597
URL: http://www.ultracare-dialysis.com
Dialysis Stations: 16. **Formerly:** Bio-Medical Applications of Hoboken.

Holmdel

25718 ■ Holmdel Dialysis Center
DaVita
668 N Beers St.
Holmdel, NJ 07733
Free: 800-424-6589
URL: http://www.davita.com
Dialysis Stations: 15. **Formerly:** Gambro Healthcare.

Irvington

25719 ■ Fresenius Medical Care--Irvington Dialysis Facility
10 Camptown Rd.
Irvington, NJ 07111

Free: 866-434-2597
URL: http://www.ultracare-dialysis.com/
Dialysis Stations: 27. **Formerly:** Bio-Medical Applications - Irvington.

Jersey City

25720 ■ Fresenius Medical Care--Jersey City
107-123 Pacific Ave.
Jersey City, NJ 07304
Free: 866-434-2597
URL: http://www.ultracare-dialysis.com/
Dialysis Stations: 32. **Formerly:** BMA Jersey City.

25721 ■ Hamilton Park Dialysis Center
328 9th St.
Jersey City, NJ 07302
Ph: (201)716-7708
Dialysis Stations: 21.

25722 ■ Jersey City Medical Center
Liberty Health
Division of Nephrology
355 Grand St.
Jersey City, NJ 07302
Ph: (201)946-6885
URL: http://www.libertyhealth.org/programs.aspx?id=692
Dialysis Stations: 3.

Kenilworth

25723 ■ Fresenius Medical Care--Kenilworth
131 S 31st St.
Kenilworth, NJ 07033
Free: 866-434-2597
URL: http://www.ultracare-dialysis.com/
Dialysis Stations: 21. **Formerly:** Renal Care Group.

Kenvil

25724 ■ Fresenius Medical Care--Kenvil
677 Rte. 46, Ste. C
Kenvil, NJ 07847
Free: 866-434-2597
URL: http://www.ultracare-dialysis.com/
Dialysis Stations: 20.

Lakewood

25725 ■ Fresenius Medical Care--Lakewood Dialysis Center
1328 River Ave., No. 16
Lakewood, NJ 08701
Free: 866-434-2597
URL: http://www.ultracare-dialysis.com/
Dialysis Stations: 18. **Formerly:** RCG Lakewood.

Lincoln Park

25726 ■ Renal Center of North Jersey, LLC
Renal Ventures Management LLC
6A Frassetto Way
Lincoln Park, NJ 07035
Ph: (973)872-0099
URL: http://www.renalventures.com/
Dialysis Stations: 20.

25727 ■ Renal Centers of North Jersey
Renal Ventures Management
6A Frassetto Way, No. A
Lincoln Park, NJ 07035
Ph: (973)872-0099
URL: http://www.renalventures.com
Dialysis Stations: 20.

Linden

25728 ■ Trinitas Satellite--Linden
10 N Wood Ave., Ste. G
Linden, NJ 07036
Ph: (908)862-7400
URL: http://www.trinitashospital.org
Dialysis Stations: 15.

Linwood

25729 ■ Liberty Dialysis--Linwood
1201 New Road, Ste. 170
Linwood, NJ 08221
Ph: (609)926-9090
URL: http://www.libertydialysis.com
Dialysis Stations: 18.

Livingston

25730 ■ Fresenius Medical Care--Livingston ACC
200 S Orange Ave.
Livingston, NJ 07039
Free: 866-434-2597
URL: http://www.ultracare-dialysis.com/
Dialysis Stations: 18. **Formerly:** RCG/Saint Barnabus-East Orange Avenue.

25731 ■ Fresenius Medical Care--St. Barnabas S Orange Ave.
Outpatient Hemodialysis
Livingston, NJ 07039
Free: 866-434-2597
URL: http://www.ultracare-dialysis.com/
Dialysis Stations: 18. **Formerly:** Renal Care Group.

25732 ■ St. Barnabas Medical Center--Transplant
St. Barnabas Health Care System
94 Old Short Hills Rd.
Livingston, NJ 07039
Ph: (888)409-4707
URL: http://www.saintbarnabas.com/services/renal/index.html
Dialysis Stations: 0.

Lumberton

25733 ■ Lumberton Dialysis Center
DaVita
668 Main St., Ste. 2
Lumberton, NJ 08048
Free: 800-424-6589
URL: http://www.davita.com
Dialysis Stations: 20.

Manahawkin

25734 ■ Dialysis Corporation of America of Manahawkin
675 State Hwy. 72, Ste. 1006-B
Manahawkin, NJ 08050
Ph: (609)978-6723
URL: http://www.dialysiscorporation.com
Dialysis Stations: 11.

25735 ■ Fresenius Medical Care--Southern Ocean County
Dialysis Center
1100 Rte. 72 W, Ste. 110
Manahawkin, NJ 08050
Free: 866-434-2597
URL: http://www.ultracare-dialysis.com
Dialysis Stations: 12. **Formerly:** Renal Care Group - Southern Ocean County.

Manalapan

25736 ■ DaVita--Freehold
Dialysis Facility
Century Office Park
300 Craig Rd.
Manalapan, NJ 07726
Free: 800-424-6589
URL: http://www.davita.com
Dialysis Stations: 15. **Formerly:** Gambro.

Maplewood

25737 ■ Maplewood Dialysis Center
Fresenius Medical Care
2130 Milburn Ave.
Maplewood, NJ 07040
Free: 866-434-2597
URL: http://www.ultracare-dialysis.com/
Dialysis Stations: 16. **Formerly:** Renal Care Group.

Marlton

25738 ■ Marlton Dialysis Center
Diversified Specialty Institutes
E Bldg. C
769 Rte. 70
Marlton, NJ 08053
Ph: (856)797-7044
URL: http://www.dsi-corp.com
Dialysis Stations: 15.

Matawan

25739 ■ Dialysis Clinic Inc.--Madison Center
625 Hwy. 34
Matawan, NJ 07747
Ph: (732)566-5050
URL: http://www.dciinc.org
Dialysis Stations: 9.

Milville

25740 ■ Kidney Center at Millville
South Jersey Healthcare
3 Elizabeth Ave.
Milville, NJ 08332
Ph: (856)739-7300
URL: http://www.sjhealthcare.net/content/dialysis-center.htm
Dialysis Stations: 18.

Monroe

25741 ■ Dialysis Clinic Inc.--Monroe
2 Research Way
Monroe, NJ 08831
Ph: (609)356-7200
URL: http://www.dciinc.org
Dialysis Stations: 12.

Montclair

25742 ■ Mountainside Hospital
Dialysis Unit
1 Bay Ave.
Montclair, NJ 07042
Ph: (973)429-6767
URL: http://www.mountainsidenow.org
Dialysis Stations: 20.

Morristown

25743 ■ Morristown Memorial Hospital
Hemodialysis Unit
Dialysis Center
100 Madison Ave.
Morristown, NJ 07962
Ph: (973)971-5128
URL: http://www.atlantichealth.org/Morristown
Dialysis Stations: 25.

Mount Laurel

25744 ■ Lourdes Dialysis at Innova, Inc.
Lourdes Health System
3716 Church Rd.
Mount Laurel, NJ 08054
Ph: (856)380-3980
URL: http://www.lourdesnet.org/news/news.php?id=296
Dialysis Stations: 24.

25745 ■ Mount Laurel Dialysis Center
130 Gaither Dr., Ste. 172
Mount Laurel, NJ 08054
Ph: (856)222-3880
Dialysis Stations: 20.

Mountainside

25746 ■ Summit Dialysis Center
DaVita
1139 Spruce Dr.
Mountainside, NJ 07092
Free: 800-424-6589
URL: http://www.davita.com
Dialysis Stations: 20. **Formerly:** Gambro.

Neptune

25747 ■ DaVita--Neptune Dialysis Facility
3297 Rte. 66
Neptune, NJ 07753
Free: 800-424-6589
URL: http://www.davita.com
Dialysis Stations: 17. **Formerly:** Gambro.

25748 ■ Jersey Shore Medical Center Dialysis Unit
1945 Rte. 33
Neptune, NJ 07754
Ph: (732)776-4274
Dialysis Stations: 18.

25749 ■ Neptune Dialysis Center
DaVita
2180 Bradley Ave.
Neptune, NJ 07753
Free: 800-424-6589
URL: http://www.davita.com
Dialysis Stations: 18.

Neptune City

25750 ■ Jane H. Booker Outpatient Dialysis Center
Jersey Shore University Medical Center
2441 State Hwy. 33 at Fortunato Pl.
Neptune City, NJ 07753
Ph: (732)776-4274
URL: http://www.jerseyshoreuniversitymedicalcenter.com/JSUMC/services/Dialysis.c fm
Dialysis Stations: 25.

25751 ■ Shining Star Neptune Dialysis Clinic
2180 Bradley Ave.
Neptune City, NJ 07753
Ph: (732)775-2725
Dialysis Stations: 18. **Formerly:** DaVita Neptune.

New Brunswick

25752 ■ Dialysis Clinic Inc./Saint Peter University Hospital
254 Easton Ave.
New Brunswick, NJ 08903
Ph: (732)565-5440
URL: http://www.dciinc.org
Dialysis Stations: 12.

25753 ■ Robert Wood Johnson University Hospital
Transplant Center
1 Robert Wood Johnson Pl.
New Brunswick, NJ 08903
Ph: (732)828-3000
URL: http://www.rwjuh.edu/medical_services/kidney_pancreas_center.html

Newark

25754 ■ Fresenius Medical Care--Ironbound
248 South St.
Newark, NJ 07114
Free: 866-434-2597
URL: http://www.ultracare-dialysis.com/
Dialysis Stations: 19.

25755 ■ Fresenius Medical Care--Newark Dialysis Facility
91-101 Hartford St.
Newark, NJ 07103
Free: 866-434-2597
URL: http://www.ultracare-dialysis.com/
Dialysis Stations: 18. **Formerly:** Bio-Medical Applications - Newark University Dialysis Center.

25756 ■ Fresenius Medical Care--Pinebrook
155 Berkeley Ave.
Newark, NJ 07107
Free: 866-434-2597
URL: http://www.ultracare-dialysis.com/
Dialysis Stations: 20. **Formerly:** BMA Pine Brook.

25757 ■ Newark Beth Israel Medical Center Dialysis Unit
201 Lyons Ave.
Newark, NJ 07112
Ph: (973)926-7600
URL: http://www.saintbarnabus.com/hospitals/newark_beth_israel
Dialysis Stations: 27.

25758 ■ Newark Dialysis Center
DaVita
571 Central Ave.
Newark, NJ 07107
Free: 800-424-6589
URL: http://www.davita.com
Dialysis Stations: 18.

25759 ■ Parkside Dialysis Center
KRU Medical Ventures
580 Frelinghuysen Ave.
Newark, NJ 07114
Ph: (973)624-2226
URL: http://www.krumed.com/
Dialysis Stations: 18.

25760 ■ Saint Michael's Medical Center Dialysis Unit
268 Martin LutherKing Blvd.
Newark, NJ 07102
Ph: (973)877-5091
URL: http://www.cathedralhealth.org
Dialysis Stations: 13.

Newton

25761 ■ Renal Center of Newton
Renal Ventures Management
7 E Clinton St.
Newton, NJ 07860
Ph: (973)940-0965
URL: http://www.renalventures.com
Dialysis Stations: 21.

North Bergen

25762 ■ Jersey City Artificial Kidney Center--North Bergen
KRU Medical Ventures
1310 5th St.
North Bergen, NJ 07047
Ph: (201)770-9220
URL: http://www.krumed.com/
Dialysis Stations: 18.

North Brunswick

25763 ■ Dialysis Clinic, Inc.--North Brunswick
Dialysis Center
117 N Center Dr.
North Brunswick, NJ 08902
Ph: (732)940-4460
URL: http://www.dciinc.org
Dialysis Stations: 34.

Old Bridge

25764 ■ Old Bridge Dialysis Center
DaVita
3 Hospital Plz., 1st Fl., Ste. 101
Old Bridge, NJ 08857
Free: 800-424-6589
URL: http://www.davita.com
Dialysis Stations: 9. **Formerly:** Gambro.

Orange

25765 ■ Fresenius Medical Care--Orange
151 Central Ave.
Orange, NJ 07050
Free: 866-434-2597
URL: http://www.ultracare-dialysis.com
Dialysis Stations: 20. **Formerly:** Renal Care Group Renex Orange Dialysis Center.

Parsippany

25766 ■ Dialysis Associates of Northern New Jersey
Fresenius Medical Care
2200 Rte. 10 W
Parsippany, NJ 07054
Free: 866-434-2597
URL: http://www.ultracare-dialysis.com
Dialysis Stations: 20.

Paterson

25767 ■ Saint Joseph Hospital Medical Center
Dialysis Unit
703 Main St.
Paterson, NJ 07503
Ph: (973)754-3570
URL: http://www.stjosephhealth.org
Dialysis Stations: 14.

25768 ■ Saint Joseph's Satellite--Paterson Outpatient Dialysis Center
275 Hospital Plz.
11 Getty Ave.
Paterson, NJ 07503
Ph: (973)569-6450
URL: http://www.stjosephhealth.org
Dialysis Stations: 60.

Pennsauken

25769 ■ Pennsauken Dialysis Center and At Home
DaVita
7024 Kaighns Ave.
Pennsauken, NJ 08109
Free: 800-424-6589
URL: http://www.davita.com
Dialysis Stations: 22.

Perth Amboy

25770 ■ Perth Amboy Dialysis Center
DaVita
Raritan Bay Medical Center Dialysis Unit
530 New Brunswick Ave.
Perth Amboy, NJ 08861
Free: 800-424-6589
URL: http://www.davita.com
Dialysis Stations: 24. **Formerly:** Gambro.

Phillipsburg

25771 ■ Phillipsburg Dialysis Center
Fresenius Medical Care
471 Center St.
Phillipsburg, NJ 08865
Free: 866-434-2597
URL: http://www.ultracare-dialysis.com
Dialysis Stations: 12. **Formerly:** Bio-Medical Applications - Phillipsburg.

Plainfield

25772 ■ Plainfield Dialysis Center & At Home
DaVita
Kenyon House
1200 Randolph Rd.
Plainfield, NJ 07060

Free: 800-424-6589
URL: http://www.davita.com
Dialysis Stations: 20.

Princeton

25773 ■ Fresenius Medical Care--Princeton Dialysis Facility
707 Alexander Rd., Bldg. 3, Ste. 301
Princeton, NJ 08540
Free: 866-434-2597
URL: http://www.ultracare-dialysis.com
Dialysis Stations: 15. **Formerly:** Bio-Medical Applications - Princeton.

Red Bank

25774 ■ Riverview Medical Center Dialysis Unit
Booker Outpatient Dialysis Center
1 Riverview Plz.
Red Bank, NJ 07701
Ph: (732)530-2200
URL: http://www.meridianhealth.com
Dialysis Stations: 9.

25775 ■ Shining Star DaVita Middletown Dialysis Center
Union Square Plz.
500 Rte. 35 S
Red Bank, NJ 07701
Free: 800-424-6589
URL: http://www.davita.com
Dialysis Stations: 15.

Ridgewood

25776 ■ Valley Hospital Renal Care Center
223 N Van Dien Ave.
Ridgewood, NJ 07450
Ph: (201)447-8159
URL: http://www.valleyhealth.com/Renal_Care.aspx?id=556
Dialysis Stations: 9.

Runnemede

25777 ■ Liberty Dialysis--Runnemede
170 9th Ave., Unit B
Runnemede, NJ 08078
Ph: (856)312-0101
URL: http://www.libertydialysis.com
Dialysis Stations: 18.

Salem

25778 ■ Salem Dialysis Center Fresenius Medical Care Dialysis Center
310 Woodstown Rd.
Salem, NJ 08079
Free: 866-434-2597
URL: http://www.ultracare-dialysis.com
Dialysis Stations: 9. **Formerly:** Renal Care Group/Renex - Salem.

Sewell

25779 ■ Kennedy Hospital--Washington Dialysis Unit
300 Medical Center Dr., Ste. A
Sewell, NJ 08080
Ph: (856)218-4990
URL: http://www.kennedyhealth.org
Dialysis Stations: 24.

25780 ■ Our Lady of Lourdes Dialysis Services Renal Center of Sewell Renal Ventures Management
660 Woodbury-Glassboro Rd., Ste. 29
Sewell, NJ 08080
Ph: (856)468-4095
URL: http://www.renalventures.com
Dialysis Stations: 21.

Sicklerville

25781 ■ Fresenius Medical Care--Winslow Twp.
510 Williamstown Rd., Unit 2A
Sicklerville, NJ 08081
Free: 866-434-2597
URL: http://www.idsdialysis.com
Dialysis Stations: 19. **Formerly:** Innovative Dialysis Centers.

Somerset

25782 ■ Shining Star DaVita Somerset Dialysis
240 Churchill Ave.
Somerset, NJ 08873
Free: 800-424-6589
URL: http://www.davita.com
Dialysis Stations: 18. **Formerly:** Shining Star Dialysis.

Somerville

25783 ■ RV Somerville Dialysis Center Renal Ventures Management
1 Rte. 206 N
Somerville, NJ 08876
Ph: (908)450-0396
URL: http://www.renalventures.com
Dialysis Stations: 16.

South Plainfield

25784 ■ Fresenius Medical Care--South Plainfield Dialysis Facility
2201 S Clinton Ave.
South Plainfield, NJ 07080
Free: 866-434-2597
URL: http://www.ultracare-dialysis.com
Dialysis Stations: 15. **Formerly:** Bio-Medical Applications - South Plainfield.

Succasunna

25785 ■ MMH DCNWJ Succasunna Dialysis Center of Northwest Jersey
175 Righter Rd.
Succasunna, NJ 07876
Ph: (973)584-1117
Dialysis Stations: 12.

Teaneck

25786 ■ Bergen RCC Dialysis Center
647 Cedar Ln.
Teaneck, NJ 07666
Ph: (201)692-1113
Dialysis Stations: 20.

25787 ■ Holy Name Home Dialysis Fresenius Medical Care
222 Cedar Ln., Ste. 103
Teaneck, NJ 07666
Free: 866-434-2597
URL: http://www.ultracare-dialysis.com
Dialysis Stations: 2.

25788 ■ Holy Name Hospital Dialysis Unit
718 Teaneck Rd.
Teaneck, NJ 07666
Ph: (201)833-3378
URL: http://www.holyname.org
Dialysis Stations: 37.

Toms River

25789 ■ Renal Institute of Central Jersey--Toms River Fresenius Medical Care
1 Plaza Dr.
Toms River, NJ 08757
Free: 866-434-2597
URL: http://www.ultracare-dialysis.com
Dialysis Stations: 36. **Formerly:** Renal Care Group/Renal Institute of Central Jersey - Toms River.

Trenton

25790 ■ Fresenius Medical Care--Trenton
40 Fuld St., 1st Fl.
Trenton, NJ 08638
Free: 866-434-2597
URL: http://www.ultracare-dialysis.com/
Dialysis Stations: 28.

25791 ■ Helene Fuld Capital Health Dialysis Unit
Capital Health Regional Medical Center
750 Brunswick Ave.
Trenton, NJ 08638
Ph: (609)394-6000
URL: http://www.capitalhealth.org
Dialysis Stations: 24.

25792 ■ Renal Center of Trenton Renal Ventures Management
601 Hamilton Ave., 1st Fl.
Trenton, NJ 08629
Ph: (609)393-2388
URL: http://www.renalventures.com
Dialysis Stations: 18.

Union

25793 ■ Hillside Dialysis Center Fresenius Medical Care
879 Rahway Ave.
Union, NJ 07083
Free: 866-434-2597
URL: http://www.ultracare-dialysis.com
Dialysis Stations: 18. **Formerly:** Bio-Medical Applications - Hillside.

Union City

25794 ■ Union City Renal Center
508 31st St.
Union City, NJ 07087
Ph: (201)902-9382
Dialysis Stations: 19.

Vineland

25795 ■ Dialysis Corporation of America--Vineland
1450 E Chestnut Ave., Ste. 2C
Vineland, NJ 08361
Ph: (856)692-9060
URL: http://www.dialysiscorporation.com
Dialysis Stations: 15.

25796 ■ Vineland RC Dialysis Center
1318 S Main Rd., Bldg. C
Vineland, NJ 08360
Ph: (856)692-1600
Dialysis Stations: 19.

Voorhees

25797 ■ Kennedy Hospital Dialysis Center--Stratford
201 Laurel Oak Rd., Ste. A
Voorhees, NJ 08043
Ph: (856)566-5460
URL: http://www.kennedyhealth.org
Dialysis Stations: 24.

Wayne

25798 ■ Willowbrook Dialysis Center--Wayne
57 Willowbrook Blvd.
Wayne, NJ 07470
Ph: (973)754-4048
Dialysis Stations: 20.

Westwood

25799 ■ Renal Center--Westwood
Renal Ventures Management
363 Old Hook Rd.
Westwood, NJ 07675
Ph: (201)664-6649
URL: http://www.renalventures.com
Dialysis Stations: 18.

Whiting

25800 ■ Whiting Dialysis Center
Fresenius Medical Care
400-430 Rte. 530
Pinewald-Keswick Rd.
Whiting, NJ 08759
Free: 866-434-2597
URL: http://www.ultracare-dialysis.com/
Dialysis Stations: 18. **Formerly:** Renal Care Group.

Willingboro

25801 ■ DaVita--Willingboro
230 Van Sciver Pkwy.
Willingboro, NJ 08046
Free: 800-424-6589
URL: http://www.davita.com
Dialysis Stations: 18.

NEW MEXICO

Alamogordo

25802 ■ Alamogordo Dialysis
Fresenius Medical Care
Dialysis Facility
2578 Medical Dr.
Alamogordo, NM 88310
Free: 866-434-2597
URL: http://www.ultracare-dialysis.com
Dialysis Stations: 17. **Formerly:** Renal Care Group - Alamogordo.

Albuquerque

25803 ■ Albuquerque Dialysis
Dialysis Clinic Inc.
1500 Indian School Rd. NE
Albuquerque, NM 87102
Ph: (505)724-1500
URL: http://www.dciinc.org
Dialysis Stations: 32.

25804 ■ Albuquerque Kidney Center
Fresenius Medical Care
11296 Lomas Blvd. NE
Albuquerque, NM 87112
Free: 866-434-2597
URL: http://www.ultracare-dialysis.com/
Dialysis Stations: 21.

25805 ■ Dialysis Clinic Inc.--Albuquerque East
905 Louisiana Blvd. NE
Albuquerque, NM 87110
Ph: (505)254-2800
URL: http://www.dciinc.org
Dialysis Stations: 24.

25806 ■ Gibson Dialysis Center
Fresenius Medical Care
5400 Gibson Blvd. SE
Albuquerque, NM 87108
Free: 866-434-2597
URL: http://www.ultracare-dialysis.com/
Dialysis Stations: 16. **Formerly:** Lovelace Dialysis Center.

25807 ■ New Mexico Artificial Kidney Center
Fresenius Medical Care
1600 Randolph SE, Ste. 100
Albuquerque, NM 87106
Free: 866-434-2597
URL: http://www.ultracare-dialysis.com/
Dialysis Stations: 21.

25808 ■ North Albuquerque Dialysis Center
Fresenius Medical Care
4700 Jefferson NE, Ste. 300
Albuquerque, NM 87109
Free: 866-434-2597
URL: http://www.ultracare-dialysis.com
Dialysis Stations: 24.

25809 ■ Presbyterian Healthcare Transplant
PO Box 26666
Albuquerque, NM 87125
Ph: (505)841-1434
URL: http://www.phs.org/PHS/hospitals/specialty/kidneytransplant/index.htm
Dialysis Stations: 0.

25810 ■ University of New Mexico Pediatric Dialysis
2211 Lomas Blvd. NE
5 West Dialysis Unit, Mailbox 273
Albuquerque, NM 87106
Ph: (505)925-4387
URL: http://hospitals.unm.edu/mds/unmch/featured_programs/pediatric_dialysis_tra nsplantation.shtml
Dialysis Stations: 4.

Artesia

25811 ■ Artesia Dialysis
DaVita
702 N 13th St.
Artesia, NM 88210
Free: 800-424-6589
URL: http://www.davita.com
Dialysis Stations: 7.

Carlsbad

25812 ■ Carlsbad Dialysis
Dialysis Clinic, Inc.
2319 Osborne Rd.
Carlsbad, NM 88220
Ph: (505)885-6998
URL: http://www.dciinc.org
Dialysis Stations: 22.

25813 ■ Fresenius Medical Care
Carlsbad Dialysis
902 W Pierce
Carlsbad, NM 88220
Free: 866-434-2597
URL: http://www.ultracare-dialysis.com/
Dialysis Stations: 12.

Clovis

25814 ■ Plains Regional Dialysis Center
Fresenius Medical Care
2117 N Thomas
Clovis, NM 88101
Free: 866-434-2597
URL: http://www.ultracare-dialysis.com
Dialysis Stations: 16.

Deming

25815 ■ Demming Dialysis
Fresenius Medical Care
Dialysis Facility
814 Adobe Dr.
Deming, NM 88030
Free: 866-434-2597
URL: http://www.ultracare-dialysis.com/
Dialysis Stations: 12. **Formerly:** Vivra Renal Care.

Espanola

25816 ■ Fresenius Medical Care--Espanola
Dialysis Services
1420 Calle de la Merced
Espanola, NM 87532
Free: 866-434-2597
URL: http://www.ultracare-dialysis.com/
Dialysis Stations: 12.

Farmington

25817 ■ Four Corners Dialysis Center
DaVita
801 W Broadway
Farmington, NM 87401
Free: 800-424-6589
URL: http://www.davita.com
Dialysis Stations: 36.

Gallup

25818 ■ Rehoboth McKinley Christian Hospital
Dialysis Center
1901 Red Rock Dr.
Gallup, NM 87301
Ph: (505)863-7250
Fax: (505)863-7300
URL: http://www.rmch.org
Dialysis Stations: 28.

Grants

25819 ■ Grants Dialysis
Dialysis Clinic, Inc.
1213 Bonita
Grants, NM 87020
Ph: (505)285-5200
URL: http://www.dciinc.org
Dialysis Stations: 12.

Hobbs

25820 ■ Hobbs Dialysis
Fresenius Medical Care
Dialysis Services
2827 N Dal Paso, Ste. 105
Hobbs, NM 88240
Free: 866-434-2597
URL: http://www.ultracare-dialysis.com
Dialysis Stations: 20.

Las Cruces

25821 ■ Fresenius Medical Care--Las Cruces
3875 Foothills Rd.
Las Cruces, NM 88011
Free: 866-434-2597
URL: http://www.ultracare-dialysis.com/
Dialysis Stations: 25. **Formerly:** RCG.

25822 ■ Las Cruces Renal Center
Diversified Specialty Institutes
3961 E Lohman Ave., Ste. 29
Las Cruces, NM 88011
Ph: (505)532-9437
URL: http://www.dsi-corp.com
Dialysis Stations: 20. **Formerly:** Fresenius Medical Care.

25823 ■ Las Cruces South Dialysis
Fresenius Medical Care
2525 S Telshor Blvd., Ste. B
Las Cruces, NM 88011
Free: 866-434-2597
URL: http://www.ultracare-dialysis.com/
Dialysis Stations: 16. **Formerly:** Renal Care Group.

Las Vegas

25824 ■ Las Vegas NM Dialysis Center
Fresenius Medical Care
246 Mills Ave.
Las Vegas, NM 87701
Free: 866-434-2597
URL: http://www.ultracare-dialysis.com
Dialysis Stations: 9.

Los Lunas

25825 ■ Central New Mexico Kidney Center
Fresenius Medical Care
2800 Palmilla Rd.
Los Lunas, NM 87031

Free: 866-434-2597
URL: http://www.ultracare-dialysis.com/
Dialysis Stations: 20.

Mescalero

25826 ■ Mescalero Care Center--Dialysis
454 Lipan Ave.
Mescalero, NM 88340
Ph: (505)464-4827
Dialysis Stations: 8.

Raton

25827 ■ Raton Dialysis
Dialysis Clinic Inc.
900 S 6th St.
Raton, NM 87740
Ph: (505)445-4300
URL: http://www.dciinc.org
Dialysis Stations: 9.

Rio Rancho

25828 ■ Fresenius Medical Care--North Rio Rancho
7555 Enchanted Hills Blvd. NE, Ste. 102
Rio Rancho, NM 87144
Free: 866-434-2597
URL: http://www.ultracare-dialysis.com/
Dialysis Stations: 25.

25829 ■ North Rio Rancho Dialysis
Fresenius Medical Care
7555 Enchanted Hills Blvd., Ste. 102
Rio Rancho, NM 87144
Free: 866-434-2597
URL: http://www.ultracare-dialysis.com/
Dialysis Stations: 30.

25830 ■ Rio Rancho dialysis
Dialysis Clinic, Inc.
4045 Jackie Rd. SE
Rio Rancho, NM 87124
Ph: (505)896-8861
URL: http://www.dciinc.org
Dialysis Stations: 24.

Roswell

25831 ■ Southeastern New Mexico Kidney Center Inc.
Fresenius Medical Care
Dialysis Center
2801 N Main, Ste. H
Roswell, NM 88201
Free: 866-434-2597
URL: http://www.ultracare-dialysis.com
Dialysis Stations: 22.

San Fidel

25832 ■ ACL Dialysis
Dialysis Clinic Inc.
I-40, Exit 102
San Fidel, NM 87049
Ph: (505)552-7292
URL: http://www.dciinc.org
Dialysis Stations: 6.

Santa Fe

25833 ■ Fresenius Medical Care--Santa Fe
Dialysis Facility
641 Harkle Rd.
Santa Fe, NM 87505
Free: 866-434-2597
URL: http://www.ultracare-dialysis.com
Dialysis Stations: 20.

Shiprock

25834 ■ Shiprock Dialysis
DaVita
US Hwy. 491 N
Shiprock, NM 87420
Free: 800-424-6589
URL: http://www.davita.com
Dialysis Stations: 20.

Silver City

25835 ■ Silver City Dialysis
Dialysis Clinic, Inc.
1310 Sunset Ln.
Silver City, NM 88061
Ph: (505)538-0208
URL: http://www.dciinc.org
Dialysis Stations: 16.

Taos

25836 ■ Taos Dialysis
Dialysis Clinic, Inc.
1335 Maestas Rd.
Taos, NM 87571
Ph: (505)751-4010
URL: http://www.dciinc.org
Dialysis Stations: 24.

Zuni

25837 ■ Rehoboth McKinley Christian Hospital
Dialysis Facility
301 N B St.
Zuni, NM 87327
Ph: (505)782-5663
Fax: (505)782-5612
URL: http://www.rmch.org
Dialysis Stations: 31.

NEW YORK

Albany

25838 ■ Albany Dialysis Center
64 Albany Shaker Rd.
Albany, NY 12204
Ph: (518)427-0473
Dialysis Stations: 24.

25839 ■ Albany Regional Kidney Center
2 Clara Barton Dr.
Albany, NY 12208
Ph: (518)434-6565
Dialysis Stations: 30.

Amherst

25840 ■ Suburban Dialysis Center
1542 Maple Rd.
Amherst, NY 14221
Ph: (716)636-3300
Dialysis Stations: 22.

Amsterdam

25841 ■ Amsterdam Dialysis Center
Fresenius Medical Care
1810 Riverfront Center
Amsterdam, NY 12010
Ph: (518)842-4360
URL: https://www.ultracare-dialysis.com/
Dialysis Stations: 17. **Formerly:** Renal Research Institute.

Arvene

25842 ■ Pola Tenenbaum Center for Renal Care
Dialysis Facility
430 Beach 68th St.
Arvene, NY 11692
Ph: (718)474-0357
Dialysis Stations: 10.

Astoria

25843 ■ Astoria Dialysis Center
34-01 35th Ave.
Astoria, NY 11106
Ph: (718)707-9988
Dialysis Stations: 24. **Formerly:** Western Queens Dialysis Management Corporation.

25844 ■ Newtown Dialysis Center Inc.
29-20 Newtown Ave.
Astoria, NY 11102
Ph: (718)728-2222
Dialysis Stations: 24.

Auburn

25845 ■ Dialysis Clinic Inc.--Auburn
21 Nelson St.
Auburn, NY 13021
Ph: (315)255-9004
URL: http://www.dciinc.org
Dialysis Stations: 13. **Formerly:** University Dialysis Center.

Batavia

25846 ■ Lake Plains Dialysis at Batavia
587 E Main St.
Batavia, NY 14020
Ph: (585)344-7098
Dialysis Stations: 16.

Bay Shore

25847 ■ Bay Shore Dialysis Center
Good Samaritan Hospital
Chronic Dialysis Center
929 Sunrise Hwy.
Bay Shore, NY 11706
Ph: (631)224-8500
URL: http://www.good-samaritan-hospital.org/index.php
Dialysis Stations: 26.

Bayside

25848 ■ Bayside Dialysis Center
201-10 Northern Blvd.
Bayside, NY 11361
Ph: (718)423-6638
Dialysis Stations: 20.

Bellmore

25849 ■ South Shore Dialysis Center II
250 Pettit Ave.
Bellmore, NY 11710
Ph: (516)679-3090
Dialysis Stations: 20.

Bethpage

25850 ■ Winthrop University Hospital
Dialysis Center at Bethpage
530 Hicksville Rd.
Bethpage, NY 11714
Ph: (516)663-4980
URL: http://www.winthrop.org/departments/specialty-centers/?id=12
Dialysis Stations: 12.

Binghamton

25851 ■ United Health Services
Dialysis Unit
10-42 Mitchell Ave.
Binghamton, NY 13903
Ph: (607)762-2225
URL: http://www.uhs.net/medical/dialysis.asp
Dialysis Stations: 24.

25852 ■ United Health Services Hospital, Inc.
Renal Care Center
65 Pennsylvania Ave.
Binghamton, NY 13903

Ph: (607)762-2015
URL: http://www.uhs.net/medical/dialysis.asp
Dialysis Stations: 15.

Bronx

25853 ■ Bedford Park Dialysis Center
DaVita
3119 Webster Ave.
Bronx, NY 10467
Free: 800-424-6589
URL: http://www.davita.com
Dialysis Stations: 21.

25854 ■ Bronx Dialysis Center & At Home
DaVita
1615 Eastchester Rd.
Bronx, NY 10461
Free: 800-424-6589
URL: http://www.davita.com
Dialysis Stations: 25. **Formerly:** IHS of New York Inc.

25855 ■ Bronx River Nephro Care Inc.
Dialysis Facility
1616 Bronxdale Ave.
Bronx, NY 10462
Ph: (718)430-9800
Dialysis Stations: 30.

25856 ■ Bronx River Nephrology Care/Jewish Home and Hospital Life Care System
100 W Kingsbridge Rd.
Bronx, NY 10468
Ph: (718)410-1374
Dialysis Stations: 6.

25857 ■ Daughters of Jacob
Dialysis Center
1160 Teller Ave.
Bronx, NY 10456
Ph: (718)293-1500
Dialysis Stations: 12.

25858 ■ DaVita
Boston Post Road Dialysis Center
4026 Boston Rd.
Bronx, NY 10475
Free: 800-424-6589
URL: http://www.davita.com
Dialysis Stations: 25. **Formerly:** Co-op City Dialysis Center.

25859 ■ Eastchester Road Dialysis Center
DaVita
1515 Jarrett Pl.
Bronx, NY 10461
Free: 800-424-6589
URL: http://www.davita.com
Dialysis Stations: 12.

25860 ■ Island Rehabilitative Services, Bronx
1780 Grand Concourse
Bronx, NY 10457
Ph: (718)583-1800
URL: http://www.islandrehabdialysis.com
Dialysis Stations: 24.

25861 ■ Kings Harbor Health Services LLC
2020 E Gun Hill Rd.
Bronx, NY 10469
Ph: (718)320-1335
URL: http://www.kingsharbor.com
Dialysis Stations: 8.

25862 ■ Lincoln Hospital
Hemodialysis Unit
234 E 149th St.
Bronx, NY 10451
Ph: (718)579-5548
URL: http://www.nyc.gov/html/hhc/lincoln/html/home/home.shtml
Dialysis Stations: 8.

25863 ■ Montefiore Dialysis Center--Unit III
1325 Morris Park Ave.
Bronx, NY 10461
Ph: (718)597-2255
Dialysis Stations: 24.

25864 ■ Montefiore Dialysis Center--Unit IV
1695 Eastchester Rd., 4th Fl.
Bronx, NY 10461
Ph: (718)792-0470
Dialysis Stations: 28.

25865 ■ Montefiore Hospital and Medical Center
111 E 210th St.
Bronx, NY 10467
Ph: (718)920-4974
URL: http://www.montefiore.org/services/pediatric-kidney-transplant/
Dialysis Stations: 11.

25866 ■ Montefiore Medical Center--North Division
Hemodialysis Unit
600 E 233rd St.
Bronx, NY 10466
Ph: (718)920-9041
URL: http://www.montefiore.org/services/nephrology/
Dialysis Stations: 8. **Formerly:** Our Lady of Mercy Medical Center.

25867 ■ New York Renal Associates
Dialysis Facility
3468 Park Ave.
Bronx, NY 10456
Ph: (718)401-2836
Dialysis Stations: 20.

25868 ■ Pelham Parkway Dialysis Center
DaVita
Bldg. 5
1400 Pelham Pkwy. S
Bronx, NY 01461
Free: 800-424-6589
URL: http://www.davita.com
Dialysis Stations: 25.

25869 ■ Riverdale Dialysis Center
DaVita
170 W 233rd St.
Bronx, NY 10463
Free: 800-424-6589
URL: http://www.davita.com
Dialysis Stations: 24. **Formerly:** Continental Dialysis Center.

25870 ■ Saint Barnabas Hospital
Dialysis Center
4451 Third Ave.
Bronx, NY 10457
Ph: (718)960-3860
URL: http://www.stbarnabashospital.org
Dialysis Stations: 23.

25871 ■ Soundview Dialysis Center
DaVita
1622-24 Bruckner Blvd.
Bronx, NY 10473
Free: 800-424-6589
URL: http://www.davita.com
Dialysis Stations: 18.

25872 ■ South Bronx Dialysis Center
DaVita
1940 Webster Ave.
Bronx, NY 10457
Free: 800-424-6589
URL: http://www.davita.com
Dialysis Stations: 20.

Brooklyn

25873 ■ Atlantic CAPD and Home Training
59-61 Atlantic Ave.
Brooklyn, NY 11201
Ph: (718)780-4686
Dialysis Stations: 0. **Formerly:** Atlantic Peritoneal Dialysis and Home Training Center.

25874 ■ Atlantic Hemodialysis Center
339 Hicks St.
Brooklyn, NY 11201
Ph: (718)780-1224
Dialysis Stations: 28. **Formerly:** Long Island College Hospital Dialysis Center.

25875 ■ Atlantic Hemodialysis at Cobble Hill Nursing Home
Dialysis Facility
380 Henry St.
Brooklyn, NY 11201
Ph: (718)625-4385
Dialysis Stations: 5.

25876 ■ Bayridge Sunset Park Dialysis Center
140 58th St., Bldg. B
Box 65
Brooklyn, NY 11220
Ph: (718)567-0255
Dialysis Stations: 26.

25877 ■ Brookdale Physicians Dialysis Associates Inc.
Renal Research Institute
Dialysis Facility
9701 Church Ave.
Brooklyn, NY 11212
Ph: (718)495-4680
URL: http://www.renalresearch.com
Dialysis Stations: 28. **Formerly:** Renal Research Institute.

25878 ■ Brookdale University Hospital and Medical Center
Dialysis Center
1 Brookdale Plz., Rm. 249
Brooklyn, NY 11212
Ph: (718)240-5727
URL: http://www.brookdale.edu
Dialysis Stations: 10.

25879 ■ Brooklyn Hospital Center
Dialysis Unit
121 DeKalb Ave., Unit 2W
Brooklyn, NY 11201
Ph: (718)250-8160
URL: http://www.tbh.org
Dialysis Stations: 6.

25880 ■ Brooklyn Hospital Center--II
Dialysis Unit
19 Rockwell Pl.
Brooklyn, NY 11217
Ph: (718)260-2710
URL: http://www.tbh.org
Dialysis Stations: 25.

25881 ■ Brooklyn Kidney Center
184 Sterling Pl.
Brooklyn, NY 11217
Ph: (718)780-4601
Dialysis Stations: 22.

25882 ■ Central Brooklyn Dialysis Center LLC
818 Sterling Pl.
Brooklyn, NY 11216
Ph: (718)735-6660
Dialysis Stations: 30.

25883 ■ Downstate Medical Center/State University of New York, Brooklyn
Dialysis Unit
450 Clarkson Ave.
Brooklyn, NY 11203
Ph: (718)270-2510
URL: http://www.downstate.edu
Dialysis Stations: 4.

25884 ■ Downstate Medical Center--SUNY
450 Clarkson Ave.
Brooklyn, NY 11203
Ph: (718)270-3168
URL: http://www.downstate.edu/
Dialysis Stations: 0.

25885 ■ Dyker Heights Dialysis Center
DaVita
1435 86th St.
Brooklyn, NY 11228
Free: 800-424-6589
URL: http://www.davita.com
Dialysis Stations: 20.

25886 ■ Gateway Dialysis Center
1170 E 98th St.
Brooklyn, NY 11236
Ph: (718)223-2100
Dialysis Stations: 20.

25887 ■ Kings County Hospital Center
Dialysis Unit
451 Clarkson Ave., Rm. C6210
Brooklyn, NY 11203
Ph: (718)613-8157
URL: http://www.nyc.gov/html/hhc/kchc/html/home/home.shtml
Dialysis Stations: 24.

25888 ■ Kingsbrook Jewish Medical Center
Dialysis Unit
585 Schenectady Ave.
Brooklyn, NY 11203
Ph: (718)604-5591
URL: http://www.kingsbrook.org
Dialysis Stations: 13.

25889 ■ Long Island College Hospital
Dialysis Center
339 Hicks St.
Brooklyn, NY 11201
Ph: (718)780-1224
URL: http://www.wehealny.org/patients/lich_description.html
Dialysis Stations: 28. **Formerly:** Renal Research Institute.

25890 ■ Midwood Chaim Aruchim
Dialysis Facility
1915 Ocean Ave.
Brooklyn, NY 11230
Ph: (718)258-7700
Dialysis Stations: 34.

25891 ■ Midwood Chayim Auchim Dialysis Site II
1408 Ocean Ave., 2nd Fl.
Brooklyn, NY 11230
Ph: (718)677-7600
Dialysis Stations: 20.

25892 ■ Narrows Kidney Center
Dialysis Clinic Inc.
6520 Fort Hamilton Pkwy.
Brooklyn, NY 11219
Ph: (718)836-8444
URL: http://www.dciinc.org
Dialysis Stations: 19.

25893 ■ Neomy Dialysis Center
1122 Coney Island Ave.
Brooklyn, NY 11230
Ph: (718)434-1444
URL: http://neomydialysis.com/
Dialysis Stations: 27.

25894 ■ Nephro Care Inc.--West
Fresenius Medical Care
358-362 Fourth Ave.
Brooklyn, NY 11215
Free: 866-434-2597
URL: https://www.ultracare-dialysis.com
Dialysis Stations: 20.

25895 ■ Nephrocare Inc.
Fresenius Medical Care
1402 Atlantic Ave.
Brooklyn, NY 11216
Ph: (866)434-2597
URL: https://www.ultracare-dialysis.com
Dialysis Stations: 24.

25896 ■ Nephrology Foundation of Brooklyn East
Dialysis Facility
63 Pennsylvania Ave.
Brooklyn, NY 11207
Ph: (718)345-9000
Dialysis Stations: 24.

25897 ■ Nephrology Foundation of Brooklyn North
342 Flatbush Ave.
Brooklyn, NY 11238
Ph: (718)857-3000
Dialysis Stations: 23.

25898 ■ Nephrology Foundation of Brooklyn South
1845 McDonald Ave.
Brooklyn, NY 11223
Ph: (718)336-9700
Dialysis Stations: 30.

25899 ■ New York AKC, Inc.
Dialysis Center
2651 E 14th St.
Brooklyn, NY 11235
Ph: (718)769-4100
Dialysis Stations: 24.

25900 ■ Rogosin Kidney Center--Brooklyn
Dialysis Unit
506 6th St.
Brooklyn, NY 11215
Ph: (718)780-5800
URL: http://www.rogosin.org/treatment-dialysis-centers.php
Dialysis Stations: 22.

25901 ■ Sheepshead Bay Renal Care Center
DaVita
26 Brighton 11th St.
Brooklyn, NY 11235
Free: 800-424-6589
URL: http://www.davita.com
Dialysis Stations: 16. **Formerly:** Coney Island Dialysis Center.

25902 ■ South Brooklyn Nephrology Center
DaVita
Dialysis Facility
3915 Ave. V
Brooklyn, NY 11234
Free: 800-424-6589
URL: http://www.davita.com
Dialysis Stations: 29.

25903 ■ SUNY Parkside Dialysis Center
710 Parkside Ave.
Brooklyn, NY 11226
Ph: (718)703-5900
URL: http://www.downstate.edu
Dialysis Stations: 24.

25904 ■ Utica Avenue Dialysis Clinic
DaVita
1305 Utica Ave.
Brooklyn, NY 11203
Free: 800-424-6589
URL: http://www.davita.com
Dialysis Stations: 30. **Formerly:** Gambro Healthcare/Empire State Dialysis Center.

Buffalo

25905 ■ Buffalo General Hospital
Transplant/Dialysis Center
100 High St., Ste. A-5
Buffalo, NY 14203
Ph: (716)859-2585
URL: http://bgh.kaleidahealth.org
Dialysis Stations: 22.

25906 ■ Buffalo General Hospital--Transplant
Kaleida Health
100 High St.
Buffalo, NY 14203
Ph: (716)859-1345
URL: http://bgh.kaleidahealth.org/
Dialysis Stations: 0.

25907 ■ Cleve-Hill Dialysis & At Home Dialysis Center
DaVita
1461 Kensington Ave.
Buffalo, NY 14215
Free: 800-424-6589
URL: http://www.davita.com
Dialysis Stations: 24. **Formerly:** Erie County Medical Center at Cleve-Hill.

25908 ■ Erie County Medical Center
Dialysis Unit
462 Grider St.
Buffalo, NY 14215
Ph: (716)898-4803
URL: http://www.ecmc.edu
Dialysis Stations: 14.

25909 ■ Gates Circle Dialysis Center
3 Gates Circle
Buffalo, NY 14209
Ph: (716)887-4736
Dialysis Stations: 14. **Formerly:** Millard Fillmore Hospital.

25910 ■ Western New York Artificial Kidney Center--Buffalo
237 Linwood Ave.
Buffalo, NY 14209
Ph: (716)885-6363
Dialysis Stations: 20.

25911 ■ Women and Children's Hospital of Buffalo
Transplant/Dialysis Center
219 Bryant St.
Buffalo, NY 14222
Ph: (716)878-7297
URL: http://www.wchob.org/services/service_dialysis.asp?SID=275&CID=9
Dialysis Stations: 4.

Camillus

25912 ■ Liberty Dialysis
Saint Joseph's Hospital--Camillus
Dialysis Unit
5101 W Genesee St.
Camillus, NY 13031

Ph: (315)448-2979
URL: http://www.libertydialysis.com
Dialysis Stations: 11.

Carmel

25913 ■ Celia Dill Dialysis Center
DaVita
667 Stoneleigh Ave.
Carmel, NY 10512
Free: 800-424-6589
URL: http://www.davita.com
Dialysis Stations: 17.

Catskill

25914 ■ Columbia Greene Dialysis Center
159 Jefferson Heights
Catskill, NY 12414
Ph: (518)943-1404
Dialysis Stations: 24. **Formerly:** Northern Hudson Valley Dialysis Center.

Clifton Park

25915 ■ Hortense & Louise Rubin Dialysis Center
21 Crossing Blvd.
Clifton Park, NY 12065
Ph: (518)831-6700
URL: http://www.rubindialysis.org
Dialysis Stations: 20.

Commack

25916 ■ Island Rehabilitative Servicescommitteemack
68 Hauppauge Rd.
Commack, NY 11725
Ph: (631)715-2740
Dialysis Stations: 12.

Cooperstown

25917 ■ Mary Imogene Bassett Hospital
Dialysis Center
1 Atwell Rd.
Cooperstown, NY 13326
Ph: (607)547-3350
URL: http://www.bassett.org
Dialysis Stations: 12.

Corning

25918 ■ Arnot Ogden Medical Center--Corning
Dialysis Unit
8 W Pultney St.
Corning, NY 14830
Ph: (607)962-2790
URL: http://www.aomc.org
Dialysis Stations: 6.

Cortland

25919 ■ Saint Joseph's Cortland
Liberty Dialysis
3993 West Rd.
Cortland, NY 13045
Ph: (315)662-0140
URL: http://www.libertydialysis.com
Dialysis Stations: 10.

Cortlandt Manor

25920 ■ Peekskill-Cortlandt Dialysis Center
DaVita
2050 E Main St., Ste. 15
Cortlandt Manor, NY 10567
Free: 800-424-6589
URL: http://www.davita.com
Dialysis Stations: 19.

Davis Park

25921 ■ Brookhaven Memorial Hospital
Dialysis Satellite
109 W Main St.
Davis Park, NY 11772
Ph: (631)687-2828
URL: http://www.brookhavenhospital.org
Dialysis Stations: 24.

Dunkirk

25922 ■ Brooks Memorial Hospital
Dialysis Unit
529 Central Ave.
Dunkirk, NY 14048
Ph: (716)366-3979
URL: http://www.brookshospital.org
Dialysis Stations: 14.

East Meadow

25923 ■ Nassau County Medical Center
Dialysis Center
2201 Hempstead Tpke.
East Meadow, NY 11554
Ph: (516)572-3351
URL: http://www.ncmc.edu
Dialysis Stations: 14.

East Setauket

25924 ■ Stony Brook Kidney Center
Dialysis Clinic, Inc.
26 Research Way
East Setauket, NY 11733
Ph: (631)444-0502
URL: http://www.dciinc.org
Dialysis Stations: 26.

Elizabethtown

25925 ■ Champlain Valley Physicians Hospital /Elizabethtown Community Hospital
Dialysis Facility
Park St., Rte. 9 N
Elizabethtown, NY 12932
Ph: (518)566-7043
URL: http://www.cvph.org
Dialysis Stations: 6.

Elmhurst

25926 ■ Elmhurst Hospital Center
Dialysis Unit
79-01 Broadway
Elmhurst, NY 11373
Ph: (718)334-3930
URL: http://www.nyc.gov/html/hhc/ehc/html/home/home.shtml
Dialysis Stations: 0.

25927 ■ Saint John's Queens Hospital
Dialysis Unit
90-02 Queens Blvd., 5th Fl.
Elmhurst, NY 11373
Ph: (718)558-1179
Dialysis Stations: 10.

Elmira

25928 ■ Arnot-Odgen Medical Center--Elmira
Hemodialysis Unit
602 Ivy St.
Elmira, NY 14905
Ph: (607)737-4186
URL: http://www.aomc.org
Dialysis Stations: 20.

25929 ■ St. Joseph's Kidney Center
200 Madison Ave.
Elmira, NY 14901
Ph: (607)271-3438
URL: http://www.stjosephs.org/getpage.php?name=Kidney_Center_Dedication
Dialysis Stations: 16.

Elmsford

25930 ■ Westchester Artificial Kidney Center
Dialysis Unit
234 Tarrytown Rd.
Elmsford, NY 10523
Ph: (914)592-5858
Dialysis Stations: 20.

Far Rockaway

25931 ■ Marjorie Basser Dialysis Center
Saint John's Episcopal Hospital
327 Beach 19th St.
Far Rockaway, NY 11691
Ph: (718)869-7637
URL: http://www.ehs.org/stjohnshospital
Dialysis Stations: 15.

Fayetteville

25932 ■ Saint Joseph's Northeast Dialysis Center
Liberty Dialysis
4105 Medical Center Dr.
Fayetteville, NY 13066
Ph: (315)329-7200
URL: http://www.libertydialysis.com
Dialysis Stations: 12.

Flushing

25933 ■ Broadway Dialysis Center
Elmhurst Hospital
79-01 Broadway, D-7 Wing
Flushing, NY 11373
Ph: (718)205-7772
URL: http://www.nyc.gov/html/hhc/ehc/html/home/home.shtml
Dialysis Stations: 20.

25934 ■ Cliffside Nursing Home
CRD Associates LLC
Dialysis Center
119-19 Graham Ct.
Flushing, NY 11354
Ph: (718)886-0700
Dialysis Stations: 6.

25935 ■ College Point Dialysis Center
23-14 College Point Blvd.
Flushing, NY 11356
Ph: (718)762-3330
Dialysis Stations: 24.

25936 ■ DaVita
Queens Dialysis & At Home
7112 Park Ave.
Flushing, NY 11365
Free: 800-424-6589
URL: http://www.davita.com
Dialysis Stations: 25.

25937 ■ Flushing Hospital Medical Center
Renal Services
Outpatient Dialysis Facility
4500 Parsons Blvd.
Flushing, NY 11355
Ph: (718)670-5950
URL: http://www.flushinghospital.org
Dialysis Stations: 14.

25938 ■ Flushing Manor Dialysis Center, LLC
36-17 Parsons Blvd.
Flushing, NY 11354
Ph: (718)888-5228
URL: http://www.flushingmanors.com/index.asp?pg=6
Dialysis Stations: 6.

25939 ■ The New York Hospital Medical Center of Queens
Hemodialysis Unit
56-45 Main St., 8th Fl.
Flushing, NY 11355

Ph: (718)670-1258
Dialysis Stations: 10.

Freeport

25940 ■ Freeport Kidney Center
DaVita
267 W Merrick Rd.
Freeport, NY 11520
Free: 800-424-6589
URL: http://www.davita.com
Dialysis Stations: 30. **Formerly:** Huntington Artificial Kidney Center.

Fresh Meadows

25941 ■ Trude Weishaupt Memorial Dialysis Center
59-28 174th St.
Fresh Meadows, NY 11365
Ph: (718)670-1276
URL: http://www.nyhq.org/oth/Page.asp?PageID=OTH000269
Dialysis Stations: 29. **Formerly:** Trude Weishaupt Satellite Dialysis Center.

Garden City

25942 ■ Garden City Dialysis Center
DaVita
1100 Stewart Ave.
Garden City, NY 11530
Free: 800-424-6589
URL: http://www.davita.com
Dialysis Stations: 19.

Geneseo

25943 ■ Noyes Center for Kidney Disease and Dialysis
Noyes Memorial Hospital
4616 Millennium Dr.
Geneseo, NY 14454
Ph: (585)991-5015
URL: http://www.noyes-health.org/orgMain.asp?orgid=79&storyTypeID=&sid=&
Dialysis Stations: 12.

Geneva

25944 ■ Geneva General Hospital
Finger Lakes Health
Dialysis Unit
196 North St.
Geneva, NY 14456
Ph: (315)787-4580
Fax: (315)787-4584
URL: http://www.FLHealth.org
Dialysis Stations: 13.

Ghent

25945 ■ Columbia Green Dialysis Centers--Ghent
30 Whitier Rd.
Ghent, NY 12075
Ph: (518)828-0717
Dialysis Stations: 15.

Glen Cove

25946 ■ Winthrop University Hospital
Dialysis Center at Glen Cove
Glen Gariff Health Care Center
Dosoris Ln.
Glen Cove, NY 11542
Ph: (516)676-1100
URL: http://www.winthrop.org
Dialysis Stations: 6.

Glens Falls

25947 ■ Glens Falls Hospital
Dialysis Unit
3 Broad St. Plz.
Glens Falls, NY 12801
Ph: (518)926-6720
URL: http://www.glensfallshospital.org
Dialysis Stations: 24.

Great Neck

25948 ■ North Shore University Hospital
Walbaum Dialysis Center
100 Community Dr.
Great Neck, NY 11021
Ph: (516)465-8250
URL: http://www.northshorelij.com/body.cfm?ID=51
Dialysis Stations: 34.

Hampton Bays

25949 ■ South Hampton Hospital
184 W Montauk Hwy.
Hampton Bays, NY 11946
Ph: (631)723-4200
URL: http://www.southhamptonhospital.org
Dialysis Stations: 17.

Harriman

25950 ■ Good Samaritan Hospital--Harriman Regional Kidney Center
Dialysis Facility
33-1 Rte. 17M
Harriman, NY 10926
Ph: (845)781-7100
URL: http://www.goodsamhosp.org
Dialysis Stations: 20.

Hauppauge

25951 ■ Suffolk Kidney Center
30 Central Ave.
Hauppauge, NY 11788
Ph: (631)761-6605
Dialysis Stations: 16.

Hawthorne

25952 ■ Dialysis Clinic Inc.--Bradhurst
19 Bradhurst Ave.
Hawthorne, NY 10532
Ph: (914)592-4366
URL: http://www.dciinc.org
Dialysis Stations: 24.

Hempstead

25953 ■ South Shore Dialysis Center
615 Peninsula Blvd.
Hempstead, NY 11550
Ph: (516)483-6702
Dialysis Stations: 20.

Herkimer

25954 ■ Faxton St. Luke's Healthcare--Herkimer Satellite
201 E State St.
Herkimer, NY 13350
Ph: (315)574-3025
Dialysis Stations: 8.

Hornell

25955 ■ Saint James Mercy Hospital
Dialysis Unit
1 Bethesda Dr.
Hornell, NY 14843
Ph: (607)324-6950
URL: http://www.stjamesmercy.org
Dialysis Stations: 10.

Huntington

25956 ■ Carillon Dialysis LLC
830 Park Ave.
Huntington, NY 11743
Ph: (631)630-0398
Dialysis Stations: 8.

25957 ■ Huntington Hospital
Dialysis Unit
270 Park Ave.
Huntington, NY 11743
Ph: (631)351-2471
URL: http://www.hunthospital.org
Dialysis Stations: 7.

Huntington Station

25958 ■ Huntington Artificial Kidney Center
DaVita
256 Broadway
Huntington Station, NY 11746
Free: 800-424-6589
URL: http://www.davita.com
Dialysis Stations: 18.

Ithaca

25959 ■ Ithaca Dialysis Clinic
DaVita
201 Dates Dr., Ste. 206
Ithaca, NY 14850
Free: 800-424-6589
URL: http://www.davita.com
Dialysis Stations: 7.

Jackson Heights

25960 ■ Queens Artificial Kidney Center
Renal Research Institute
34-35 70th St.
Jackson Heights, NY 11372
Ph: (718)651-9700
URL: http://www.renalresearch.org
Dialysis Stations: 52.

Jamaica

25961 ■ Queens Dialysis Center
DaVita
11801 Guy R. Brewer Blvd.
Jamaica, NY 11434
Free: 800-424-6589
URL: http://www.davita.com
Dialysis Stations: 21.

25962 ■ Saint Albans Dialysis Center
Renal Research Institute
172-70 Baisley Blvd.
Jamaica, NY 11434
Ph: (718)949-1600
URL: http://www.renalresearch.com
Dialysis Stations: 24.

25963 ■ South Queens Dialysis Center
Renal Research Institute
175-37 Liberty Ave.
Jamaica, NY 11433
Ph: (718)297-9100
URL: http://www.renalresearch.com
Dialysis Stations: 32.

25964 ■ Springfield Dialysis Center--New York
134-35 Springfield Blvd.
Jamaica, NY 11413
Ph: (718)978-1233
Dialysis Stations: 24.

Jamestown

25965 ■ Woman's Christian Association Hospital
Dialysis Unit
207 Foote Ave.
Jamestown, NY 14701
Ph: (716)487-0141
URL: http://www.wcahospital.org
Dialysis Stations: 18.

Kenmore

25966 ■ Western New York AKC Kenmore Unit
1508 Sheridan Dr.
Kenmore, NY 14217
Ph: (716)871-9988
Dialysis Stations: 15.

Kew Gardens

25967 ■ Island Rehabilitative Services--Queens
Dialysis Facility
120-46 Queens Blvd.
Kew Gardens, NY 11415
Ph: (718)793-3341
URL: http://www.islandrehabdialysis.com/
Dialysis Stations: 31.

Kingston

25968 ■ Kingston Hospital
Dialysis Center Satellite
37 Albany Ave.
Kingston, NY 12401
Ph: (845)334-2821
URL: http://www.kingstonhospital.org/index.html
Dialysis Stations: 30.

Lindenhurst

25969 ■ Good Samaritan Hospital--Lindenhurst
Dialysis Unit
185 S 10th St.
Lindenhurst, NY 11757
Ph: (631)956-6060
URL: http://www.goodsamhosp.org
Dialysis Stations: 18.

Liverpool

25970 ■ Liberty Dialysis
Saint Joseph's Hospital ESRD--Seneca Campus
Dialysis Facility
8136 Oswego Rd.
Liverpool, NY 13090
Ph: (315)652-8474
URL: http://www.libertydialysis.com
Dialysis Stations: 10.

Malone

25971 ■ Hastings Hemodialysis Center
22 4th St.
Malone, NY 12953
Ph: (518)481-2445
Dialysis Stations: 11.

Manhasset

25972 ■ North Shore University Hospital--Manhasset TC
1554 Northern Blvd., Transplant Center
Manhasset, NY 11030
Ph: (718)0.
URL: http://www.northshorelij.com/NSLIJ/nsuh

Massena

25973 ■ Massena Memorial Hospital
Dialysis Center
290 Main St.
Massena, NY 13662
Ph: (315)705-0101
URL: http://www.massenahospital.org
Dialysis Stations: 8.

Medford

25974 ■ Medford Kidney Center
DaVita
1725 N Ocean Ave.
Medford, NY 11763
Free: 800-424-6589
URL: http://www.davita.com
Dialysis Stations: 10. **Formerly:** Huntington Artificial Kidney Center.

Medina

25975 ■ Lake Plains Dialysis Center
11020 W Center St.
Medina, NY 14103
Ph: (585)798-3757
Dialysis Stations: 9.

Middletown

25976 ■ Middletown Dialysis Center
220 Crystal Run Rd.
Middletown, NY 10941
Ph: (845)695-1200
Dialysis Stations: 20.

Mineola

25977 ■ Winthrop University Hospital
Dialysis Center
200 Old Country Rd.
Mineola, NY 11501
Ph: (516)663-9000
URL: http://www.winthrop.org/departments/specialty-centers/?id=12
Dialysis Stations: 34.

Monticello

25978 ■ Catskill Dialysis Center
DaVita
139 Forestburgh Rd.
Monticello, NY 12701
Free: 800-424-6589
URL: http://www.davita.com
Dialysis Stations: 14.

Montour Falls

25979 ■ Arnot Health Schuyler Dialysis
Schuyler Dialysis
220 Steuben St.
Montour Falls, NY 14865
Ph: (607)210-1997
URL: http://www.schuylerhospital.org/
Dialysis Stations: 4.

Mount Vernon

25980 ■ Mount Vernon Dialysis, LLC
12 N 7th Ave.
Mount Vernon, NY 10550
Ph: (914)665-4343
Dialysis Stations: 24.

N Amityville

25981 ■ Long Island Renal Care, Inc.
3460 Great Neck Rd.
N Amityville, NY 11701
Ph: (631)532-6969
Dialysis Stations: 24.

New Hyde Park

25982 ■ Long Island Jewish Medical Center
Dialysis Unit
270-05 76th Ave., Rm. 223
New Hyde Park, NY 11040
Ph: (718)470-7820
URL: http://www.lij.edu/body.cfm?ID=60
Dialysis Stations: 6.

25983 ■ New Hyde Park Dialysis Center
1574 Hillside Ave.
New Hyde Park, NY 11040
Ph: (516)327-5555
Dialysis Stations: 24.

25984 ■ Queens-Long Island Renal Institute
271-11 76th Ave.
New Hyde Park, NY 11040
Ph: (718)289-2600
URL: http://www.qliri.org/
Dialysis Stations: 15.

New Rochelle

25985 ■ Sound Shore Dialysis Center
Renal Research Institute
16 Guion Pl.
New Rochelle, NY 10802
Ph: (914)235-6878
URL: http://www.renalresearch.com
Dialysis Stations: 24. **Formerly:** New Rochelle Hospital and Medical Center Dialysis Center.

New York

25986 ■ Bellevue Hospital
Dialysis Unit
462 1st Ave.
New York, NY 10016
Ph: (212)562-3212
URL: http://www.nyc.gov/html/hhc/html/facilities/bellevue.shtml
Dialysis Stations: 18.

25987 ■ Beth Israel Medical Center
Upper Manhattan Dialysis Center
Renal Research Institute
2465 Broadway, 3rd Fl.
New York, NY 10025
Ph: (212)501-8100
URL: http://www.renalresearch.com
Dialysis Stations: 25.

25988 ■ Chinatown Dialysis Center Inc.
150 Lafayette St.
New York, NY 10013
Ph: (212)925-0404
Dialysis Stations: 24.

25989 ■ City Dialysis Center Inc.
Renal Research Institute
105 E 106th St.
New York, NY 10029
Ph: (212)348-6637
URL: http://www.renalresearch.com
Dialysis Stations: 20.

25990 ■ Columbia Presbyterian Hospital
Dialysis Center
New York Presbyterian
622 W 168th St., PH 4 CTR.430
New York, NY 10032
Ph: (212)305-3394
URL: http://nyp.org/services/nephrology.html
Dialysis Stations: 6.

25991 ■ Columbia University Dialysis
DaVita
60 Haven Ave., Ste. B3
New York, NY 10032
Free: 800-424-6589
URL: http://www.davita.com
Dialysis Stations: 24.

25992 ■ DaVita
Life Care Dialysis Center
221 W 61 St.
New York, NY 10023
Free: 800-424-6589
URL: http://www.davita.com

25993 ■ Harlem Dialysis Center
2615-21 Frederick Douglas Blvd.
New York, NY 10030
Ph: (212)281-8200
Dialysis Stations: 19.

25994 ■ Harlem Hospital
Dialysis Unit
506 Lenox Ave., Rm. 18-107
New York, NY 10037
Ph: (212)939-4848
URL: http://www.nyc.gov/html/hhc/html/facilities/harlem.shtml
Dialysis Stations: 11.

25995 ■ Irving Place Dialysis
Beth Israel Medical Center
120 E 16th St., 6th Fl.
New York, NY 10003
Ph: (212)844-8611
URL: http://wehealny.org/patients/BI_home/Bi_index.html

25996 ■ Lenox Hill Hospital
Dialysis Unit
100 E 77th St.
New York, NY 10021
Ph: (212)434-3260
URL: http://www.lenoxhillhospital.org
Dialysis Stations: 12.

25997 ■ Lower Manhattan Dialysis Center
323 E 34th St.
New York, NY 10016
Ph: (212)889-1082
URL: http://lowermanhattandialysis.com/index.html
Dialysis Stations: 30.

25998 ■ Lower Manhattan Dialysis Center II
187 3rd Ave.
New York, NY 10003
Ph: (212)388-0095
URL: http://lowermanhattandialysis.com/index.html
Dialysis Stations: 14.

25999 ■ Metropolitan Hospital Center
Dialysis Unit
1901 1st Ave.
New York, NY 10029
Ph: (212)423-6086
URL: http://www.nyc.gov/html/hhc/html/facilities/metropolitan.shtml
Dialysis Stations: 8.

26000 ■ Mount Sinai Kidney Center
Dialysis Center
309 E 94th St.
New York, NY 10128
Ph: (212)987-7208
URL: http://www.mountsinai.org
Dialysis Stations: 24.

26001 ■ Mount Sinai Medical Center
Dialysis Center
1 Gustav Levy Pl.
New York, NY 10029
Ph: (212)241-8081
URL: http://www.mountsinai.org
Dialysis Stations: 0.

26002 ■ New York Downtown Hospital
Hemodialysis Unit
170 William St.
New York, NY 10038
Ph: (212)312-5245
URL: http://www.downtownhospital.org
Dialysis Stations: 7.

26003 ■ New York-Presbyterian Weill Cornell Medical Center
Hemodialysis Unit
525 E 68th St.
New York, NY 10065
Ph: (212)746-4430
URL: http://nyp.org/services/nephrology.html
Dialysis Stations: 10.

26004 ■ New York University Langone Medical Center
Dialysis Unit
530 1st Ave., Ste. 9N
New York, NY 10016
Ph: (212)263-5851
URL: http://medicine.med.nyu.edu/nephrology/about-us/nephrology-faculty-group-pr actice
Dialysis Stations: 5.

26005 ■ Renal Research Institute
Beth Israel Medical Center
Dialysis Center
281 1st St.
New York, NY 10003
Ph: (212)844-8611
URL: http://www.wehealny.org
Dialysis Stations: 7.

26006 ■ Renal Research Institute
Beth Israel Medical Center
Dialysis Unit
Hospital Satellite
Irving Pl.
120 E 16th St.
New York, NY 10003
Ph: (212)844-8611
URL: http://www.wehealny.org
Dialysis Stations: 24.

26007 ■ Rogosin Institute
Dialysis Center
505 E 70th St., Rm. 226
New York, NY 10021
Ph: (212)746-1566
URL: http://www.rogosin.org
Dialysis Stations: 43.

26008 ■ Saint Clare's Hospital
Dialysis Unit
415 W 51st St.
New York, NY 10019
Ph: (212)459-8560
URL: http://www.saintclares.org
Dialysis Stations: 8.

26009 ■ Saint Luke's Hospital Center New York City
Dialysis Center
1111 Amsterdam Ave.
New York, NY 10025
Ph: (212)523-3530
URL: http://www.slrsurgery.org/transplant-surgery/division-of-transplant-surgery .aspx

26010 ■ Southern Manhattan Dialysis Center
Fresenius Medical Care
510-526 Ave. of the Americas
Subcellar
New York, NY 10014
Ph: (212)675-6880
URL: https://www.ultracare-dialysis.com
Dialysis Stations: 26.

26011 ■ Terence Cardinal Cooke Health Center
Dialysis Unit
1249 5th Ave.
New York, NY 10029
Ph: (212)360-3860
URL: http://www.tcchcc.org
Dialysis Stations: 22.

26012 ■ Upper Eastside Dialysis Facility
210 E 86th St., 3rd Fl.
New York, NY 10028
Ph: (212)794-2850
Dialysis Stations: 27. **Formerly:** Island Rehabilitative Service Corporation.

26013 ■ Yorkville Dialysis Center
1555 3rd Ave., 2nd Fl.
New York, NY 10128
Ph: (212)870-9395
Dialysis Stations: 26.

Newburgh

26014 ■ Saint Luke's Cornwall Hospital--Newburgh
Dialysis Center
4 Corwin Court
Newburgh, NY 12550
Ph: (845)562-7711
URL: http://www.stlukescornwallhospital.org/
Dialysis Stations: 17.

Niagara Falls

26015 ■ Niagara Falls Memorial Medical Center Renal Center
621 Tenth St.
Niagara Falls, NY 14301
Ph: (716)278-4639
URL: http://www.nfmmc.org/News/RenalCenter
Dialysis Stations: 17.

26016 ■ Niagara Renal Center
Apollo Healthcare
3018 Military Rd.
Niagara Falls, NY 14304
Ph: (716)298-4195
E-mail: info@apollohealth.us
URL: http://www.apollohealth.us/
Dialysis Stations: 15.

Oceanside

26017 ■ South Nassau Community Hospital
Acute Dialysis Unit
1 Healthy Way
Oceanside, NY 11572
Ph: (516)632-3944
URL: http://www.southnassau.org
Dialysis Stations: 6.

26018 ■ South Nassau Outpatient Dialysis Center
3618 Oceanside Rd.
Oceanside, NY 11572
Ph: (516)255-8000
URL: http://www.southnassau.org
Dialysis Stations: 18.

Ogdensburg

26019 ■ Dr. Ravinder N. Agarwal Renal Center
124 Ford Ave.
Ogdensburg, NY 13669
Ph: (315)394-9718
Dialysis Stations: 24. **Formerly:** Barton Hepburn Hospital.

26020 ■ Ravinder N Agarwal Renal Center
Renal Center
124 Ford Ave.
Ogdensburg, NY 13669
Ph: (315)394-8718
Dialysis Stations: 24.

Olean

26021 ■ Marie Lorenz Dialysis Center
Olean General Hospital
Hemodialysis Unit
623 Main St.
Olean, NY 14760
Ph: (716)375-6901
URL: http://www.ogh.org/programs-and-services/dialysis/index.php
Dialysis Stations: 13.

Oneida

26022 ■ Faxton--Saint Lukes Healthcare
Oneida Dialysis Unit
221 Broad St.
Oneida, NY 13421
Ph: (315)361-9147
URL: http://www.mvnhealth.com
Dialysis Stations: 8.

Oneonta

26023 ■ Bassett Healthcare
Renal Dialysis Facility
1 Associate Dr.
Oneonta, NY 13820
Ph: (607)433-6360
URL: http://www.bassett.org
Dialysis Stations: 12.

Orchard Park

26024 ■ Orchard Park Dialysis Center
3801 Taylor Rd.
Orchard Park, NY 14127
Ph: (716)209-7200
Dialysis Stations: 24.

Oswego

26025 ■ University Dialysis Center at Oswego
Dialysis Clinic Inc.
Oswego Plz.
140 State Rte. 104
Oswego, NY 13126
Ph: (315)342-3045
URL: http://www.dciinc.org
Dialysis Stations: 13.

Patchogue

26026 ■ Brookhaven Memorial Hospital Acute Unit
101 Hospital Rd.
Patchogue, NY 11772
Ph: (631)687-2828
URL: http://www.brookhavenhospital.org
Dialysis Stations: 24.

Pittsford

26027 ■ Strong Health Dialysis--Highlands Living Center
Renal Research Institute
500 Hahnemann Trl.
Pittsford, NY 14534
Ph: (585)389-3080
URL: http://www.renalresearch.com
Dialysis Stations: 4.

Plattsburgh

26028 ■ Champlain Valley Physicians Hospital --Freedman Renal Center
Dialysis Center
91 Plaza Blvd.
Plattsburgh, NY 12901
Ph: (518)566-7043
URL: http://www.cvph.org
Dialysis Stations: 24.

26029 ■ Champlain Valley Physicians Hospital Medical Center
Renal Center
75 Beekman St.
Plattsburgh, NY 12901
Ph: (518)562-7780
URL: http://www.cvph.org
Dialysis Stations: 2.

Port Chester

26030 ■ Port Chester Dialysis and Renal Center
DaVita
38 Bulkley Ave.
Port Chester, NY 10573
Free: 800-424-6589
URL: http://www.davita.com
Dialysis Stations: 15.

Port Washington

26031 ■ Port Washington Dialysis Center
DaVita
50 Seaview Blvd.
Port Washington, NY 11050
Free: 800-424-6589
URL: http://www.davita.com
Dialysis Stations: 18.

Poughkeepsie

26032 ■ Dutchess Dialysis Center
Renal Research Institute
2585 South Rd.
Poughkeepsie, NY 12601
Ph: (845)471-6300
URL: http://www.renalresearch.com
Dialysis Stations: 24.

Pt. Jefferson Station

26033 ■ Central Suffolk AKC
5225 Nesconset Hwy.
Pt. Jefferson Station, NY 11776
Ph: (631)331-5600
Dialysis Stations: 24.

Queens Village

26034 ■ Queens Village Dialysis Center
Dialysis Facility
DaVita
22202 Hempstead Ave.
Queens Village, NY 11429
Free: 800-424-6589
URL: http://www.davita.com
Dialysis Stations: 25. **Formerly:** Long Island Jewish Satellite.

Ridgewood

26035 ■ Ridgewood Dialysis Center
385 Seneca Ave.
Ridgewood, NY 11385
Ph: (718)366-1111
Dialysis Stations: 43.

Riverhead

26036 ■ East End Dialysis Management LLC--Riverhead
762 Harrison Ave.
Riverhead, NY 11901
Ph: (631)369-2005
Dialysis Stations: 24.

Rochester

26037 ■ Monroe Community Dialysis
Fresenius Medical Care
435 E Henrietta Rd.
Rochester, NY 14620
Free: 866-434-2597
URL: http://www.ultracare-dialysis.com/
Dialysis Stations: 16.

26038 ■ Park Ridge Hospital
Dialysis Center
Unity Hospital of Rochester
1561 Long Pond Rd., Ste. 301
Rochester, NY 14626
Ph: (585)723-7760
URL: http://www.unityhealth.org
Dialysis Stations: 26.

26039 ■ Renal Research Institute
Strong Health Dialysis
Inpatient Unit
601 Elmwood Ave., 8th Fl.
Rochester, NY 14642
Ph: (585)275-2820
URL: http://www.renalresearch.com
Dialysis Stations: 8.

26040 ■ Rochester General Hospital
Dialysis Unit
370 Ridge Rd. E, Ste. 10
Rochester, NY 14621
Ph: (585)922-0300
URL: http://www.rochestergeneral.org/
Dialysis Stations: 46.

26041 ■ Strong Health Dialysis--Brighton
2613 W Henrietta Rd.
Rochester, NY 14623
Ph: (585)273-7600
Dialysis Stations: 36.

26042 ■ Strong Health Dialysis--Clinton Crossing
Renal Research Institute
2400 S Clinton Ave.
Rochester, NY 14618
Ph: (585)461-0770
URL: http://www.renalresearch.com
Dialysis Stations: 30.

26043 ■ Strong Memorial Hospital--Ambulatory Care
Dialysis Unit
601 Elmwood Ave.
Rochester, NY 14642
Ph: (585)461-0770
URL: http://www.stronghealth.com
Dialysis Stations: 12.

Rome

26044 ■ Saint Luke's Memorial Hospital
Rome Dialysis Clinic
Griffiss Park
91 Perimeter Rd.
Rome, NY 13441
Ph: (315)334-4786
URL: http://www.mvnhealth.com
Dialysis Stations: 8.

Roslyn Heights

26045 ■ Winthrop University Hospital at Sun Harbor
255 Warner Ave.
Roslyn Heights, NY 11577
Ph: (516)626-8355
URL: http://www.winthrop.org
Dialysis Stations: 3.

Saranac Lake

26046 ■ Adirondack Medical Center ESRD
Dialysis Center
2233 State Rte. 86
Saranac Lake, NY 12983
Ph: (518)897-2641
URL: http://www.amccares.org
Dialysis Stations: 7.

Saratoga Spring

26047 ■ Hortense & Louis Rubin Dialysis Center II
59-C Myrtle St.
Saratoga Spring, NY 12866
Ph: (518)587-1919
URL: http://www.rubindialysis.org
Dialysis Stations: 18.

Schenectady

26048 ■ Capital District Dialysis Center
650 McClellan St.
Schenectady, NY 12304
Ph: (518)382-0202
Dialysis Stations: 24.

Smithtown

26049 ■ Saint Catherine of Siena Medical Center
Dialysis Center
50 Rte. 25A
Smithtown, NY 11787
Ph: (631)862-3707
URL: http://stcatherines.chsli.org
Dialysis Stations: 18. **Formerly:** Saint John's Episcopal Hospital.

Spencerport

26050 ■ Unity Hospital Dialysis at Spencerport
5 Land-Re Way
Spencerport, NY 14559
Ph: (585)368-6610
URL: http://www.unityhealth.org/dialysis/
Dialysis Stations: 17.

Staten Island

26051 ■ Carol Molinaro Dialysis Center
Dialysis Clinic Inc.
800 Castleton Ave.
Staten Island, NY 10310
Ph: (718)816-6455
URL: http://www.dciinc.org
Dialysis Stations: 16.

26052 ■ Dialysis Clinic Inc.--Staten Island
1550 Richmond Ave.
Staten Island, NY 10314
Ph: (718)983-7000
URL: http://www.dciinc.org
Dialysis Stations: 26. **Formerly:** Staten Island Dialysis Clinic and Artificial Kidney Center.

26053 ■ Island Rehabilitative Service Inc.
Dialysis Unit
470 Seaview Ave.
Staten Island, NY 10305
Ph: (718)987-5942
URL: http://www.islandrehabdialysis.com
Dialysis Stations: 23.

26054 ■ Island Rehabilitative Services
Clove Lakes Extension
25 Fanning St.
Staten Island, NY 10314
Ph: (347)671-8399
URL: http://www.islandrehabdialysis.com
Dialysis Stations: 4.

26055 ■ Staten Island Dialysis Clinic--AKC
Dialysis Clinic Inc.
1550 Richmond Ave.
Staten Island, NY 10314
Ph: (718)983-7000
URL: http://www.dciinc.org
Dialysis Stations: 26.

Suffern

26056 ■ Weiss Renal Center
Dialysis Facility
Good Samaritan Hospital
255 Lafayette Ave.
Suffern, NY 10901
Ph: (845)368-5094
Fax: (845)368-5324
URL: http://www.goodsamhosp.org
Dialysis Stations: 23.

Syosset

26057 ■ DaVita
Kidney Center--Syosset
1 Locust Ln.
Syosset, NY 11791
Free: 800-424-6589
URL: http://www.davita.com
Dialysis Stations: 17. **Formerly:** Huntington Artificial Kidney Center.

Syracuse

26058 ■ Central New York Dialysis Center
910 Erie Blvd. E
Syracuse, NY 13210
Ph: (315)410-8040
Dialysis Stations: 31.

26059 ■ Dialysis Clinic Inc.--Syracuse
1127 E Genesee St.
Syracuse, NY 13210
Ph: (315)473-5100
URL: http://www.dciinc.org
Dialysis Stations: 30. **Formerly:** University Dialysis Center.

26060 ■ Liverpool Dialysis Center, LLC
1304 Buckley Rd.
Syracuse, NY 13212
Ph: (315)671-9950
URL: http://www.liverpooldialysis.com/
Dialysis Stations: 12.

26061 ■ Saint Joseph's Hospital
Regional Dialysis Center
Liberty Dialysis
973 James St.
Syracuse, NY 13203
Ph: (315)703-6700
URL: http://www.libertydialysis.com
Dialysis Stations: 30.

26062 ■ SUNY Health Science Center at Syracuse
750 E Adams St.
Syracuse, NY 13210
Ph: (315)464-5413
URL: http://www.upstate.edu/
Dialysis Stations: 0.

Tarrytown

26063 ■ DaVita
Hudson Valley Dialysis Center
155 White Plains Rd., Ste. 107
Tarrytown, NY 10591
Free: 800-424-6589
URL: http://www.davita.com
Dialysis Stations: 20.

Troy

26064 ■ Hortense & Louis Rubin Dialysis Center
1850 Peoples Ave.
Troy, NY 12180
Ph: (518)271-0702
URL: http://www.rubindialysis.org
Dialysis Stations: 17.

Uniondale

26065 ■ A. Holly Patterson Extended Care Facility
North Shore/LIJ Health System
875 Jerusalem Ave.
Uniondale, NY 11553
Ph: (516)572-1400
URL: http://www.nuhealth.net/about/centers-of-care.asp?page=ahp
Dialysis Stations: 29.

Utica

26066 ■ Faxton--Saint Luke's Healthcare
Masonic Dialysis Unit
1676 Sunset Ave.
Utica, NY 13502
Ph: (315)724-3897
URL: http://www.mvnhealth.com
Dialysis Stations: 8.

Valhalla

26067 ■ Westchester Medical Center
Dialysis Clinic Inc. Extension
95 Grasslandns Rd.
Valhalla, NY 10595
Ph: (914)493-1160
URL: http://www.dciinc.org
Dialysis Stations: 8.

26068 ■ Westchester Medical Center--Nephrology
Nephrology Dept. at Westchester Medical Center
100 Woods Rd.
Valhalla, NY 10595
Ph: (914)493-7701
URL: http://www.worldclassmedicine.com/body.cfm?id=82
Dialysis Stations: 0.

Valley Cottage

26069 ■ Renal Care of Rockland, Inc.
131 Rte. 303
Valley Cottage, NY 10989
Ph: (845)268-2777
URL: http://renalcareofrockland.com/
Dialysis Stations: 18.

Valley Stream

26070 ■ West Nassau Dialysis Center Inc.
75 Rockaway Ave.
Valley Stream, NY 11580
Ph: (516)823-4444
Dialysis Stations: 24.

Vestal

26071 ■ Liberty Dialysis--Vestal
116 N Jensen St.
Vestal, NY 13850
Ph: (607)798-1916
URL: http://www.libertydialysis.com
Dialysis Stations: 24.

Victor

26072 ■ Eastview Dialysis Inc.
120 Victor Heights Pkwy.
Victor, NY 14564
Ph: (585)742-1250
Dialysis Stations: 17.

26073 ■ Strong Health Dialysis--Fingerlakes
New York Dialysis Services
6385 Victor Manchester Rd.
Victor, NY 14564
Ph: (585)742-1370
Dialysis Stations: 12.

Watertown

26074 ■ Renal Care of Northern New York, LLC
19328 Washington St., Ste. A
Watertown, NY 13601
Ph: (315)779-2140
Dialysis Stations: 24.

West Islip

26075 ■ Good Samaritan Hospital--West Islip
Dialysis Unit
1000 Montauk Hwy., Annex 3
West Islip, NY 11795

Ph: (631)376-4128
URL: http://www.goodsamhosp.org
Dialysis Stations: 8.

West Seneca

26076 ■ Renal Care of Buffalo & At Home Dialysis Facility
DaVita
550 Orchard Park Rd.
West Seneca, NY 14224
Free: 800-424-6589
URL: http://www.davita.com
Dialysis Stations: 24.

White Plains

26077 ■ White Plains Dialysis & At Home
DaVita
200 Hamilton Ave., Ste. 13B
White Plains, NY 10601
Free: 800-424-6589
URL: http://www.davita.com
Dialysis Stations: 25. **Formerly:** White Plains Dialysis & Renal Center Inc.

Williamsville

26078 ■ Comprehensive Dialysis of Western New York
6010 Main St.
Williamsville, NY 14221
Ph: (716)631-4700
Dialysis Stations: 25.

Woodmere

26079 ■ Woodmere Dialysis LLC
Rehabilitation and Healthcare Center
121 Franklin Pl.
Woodmere, NY 11598
Ph: (516)791-5277
Dialysis Stations: 7. **Formerly:** Bronx River Nephro Care, Inc.--Woodmere.

Woodside

26080 ■ Rogosin Institute--Queens Dialysis Center
66-20 Queens Blvd.
Woodside, NY 11377
Ph: (718)457-3000
URL: http://www.rogosin.org
Dialysis Stations: 30.

Yonkers

26081 ■ Saint Joseph's Hospital and Health Center--Yonkers
Dialysis Unit
127 S Broadway
Yonkers, NY 10701
Ph: (914)378-7480
URL: http://www.saintjosephs.org/index2.html
Dialysis Stations: 5.

26082 ■ Southern Westchester Dialysis Center
Renal Research Institute
44 Vark St.
Yonkers, NY 10701
Ph: (914)965-0200
URL: http://www.renalresearch.com
Dialysis Stations: 31.

26083 ■ Yonkers Dialysis Center
DaVita
575 Yonkers Ave.
Yonkers, NY 10704
Free: 800-424-6589
URL: http://www.davita.com
Dialysis Stations: 21.

26084 ■ Yonkers East Dialysis Center
DaVita
5 Odell Plz.
Yonkers, NY 10701
Free: 800-424-6589
URL: http://www.davita.com
Dialysis Stations: 21.

Yorktown Heights

26085 ■ Yorktown Artificial Kidney Center Dialysis Facility
Dialysis Clinic, Inc.
2649 Strang Blvd.
Yorktown Heights, NY 10598
Ph: (914)962-4005
URL: http://www.dciinc.org
Dialysis Stations: 16.

NORTH CAROLINA

Ahoskie

26086 ■ Ahoskie Dialysis
DaVita
129 Hertford County High Rd.
Ahoskie, NC 27910
Free: 800-424-6589
URL: http://www.davita.com
Dialysis Stations: 27.

Albemarle

26087 ■ Fresenius Medical Care--Albemarle Dialysis Facility
203 NE Connector
Albemarle, NC 28001
Free: 866-434-2597
URL: http://www.ultracare-dialysis.com/
Dialysis Stations: 22.

Apex

26088 ■ Fresenius Medical Care--Apex
1000 American Way
Apex, NC 27523
Free: 866-434-2597
URL: http://www.ultracare-dialysis.com/
Dialysis Stations: 10.

Asheboro

26089 ■ Fresenius Medical Care of Asheboro Inc
Dialysis Facility
312 W Ward St.
Asheboro, NC 27205
Free: 866-434-2597
URL: http://www.ultracare-dialysis.com/
Dialysis Stations: 27.

Asheville

26090 ■ DaVita
Asheville Kidney Center & At Home
1600 Centre Park Dr.
Asheville, NC 28805
Free: 800-424-6589
URL: http://www.davita.com
Dialysis Stations: 36.

Ayden

26091 ■ Fresenius Medical Care of Ayden
3793 Lee St.
Ayden, NC 28513
Free: 866-434-2597
URL: http://www.ultracare-dialysis.com/
Dialysis Stations: 15.

Belmont

26092 ■ Belmont Dialysis Center
Fresenius Medical Care
5010 Medical Care Ct.
Belmont, NC 28012
Free: 866-434-2597
URL: http://www.ultracare-dialysis.com/
Dialysis Stations: 16.

Biscoe

26093 ■ Montgomery Dialysis Center
DaVita
323 W Main St.
Biscoe, NC 27209
Free: 800-424-6589
URL: http://www.davita.com
Dialysis Stations: 19.

Boone

26094 ■ Fresenius Medical Care--Watauga County
PO Box 2600
Boone, NC 28607
Free: 866-434-2597
URL: http://www.ultracare-dialysis.com/
Dialysis Stations: 14.

26095 ■ Watauga Kidney Dialysis Facility
Fresenius Medical Care
337 Deerfield Rd.
Boone, NC 28607
Ph: (828)265-5050
URL: https://www.ultracare-dialysis.com
Dialysis Stations: 14. **Formerly:** Scott Mallard Kidney Dialysis Center.

Burgaw

26096 ■ Southeastern Dialysis--Burgaw
DaVita
704 S Dickerson
Burgaw, NC 28425
Free: 800-424-6589
URL: http://www.davita.com
Dialysis Stations: 20.

Burlington

26097 ■ Burlington Dialysis
DaVita
873 Heather Rd.
Burlington, NC 27215
Free: 800-424-6589
URL: http://www.davita.com
Dialysis Stations: 27.

26098 ■ Fresenius Medical Care--Burlington
3325 Garden Rd.
Burlington, NC 27215
Free: 866-434-2597
URL: http://www.ultracare-dialysis.com/
Dialysis Stations: 49.

Carrboro

26099 ■ Carolina Dialysis--Carrboro Dialysis Center
Renal Research Institute
105 Renee Lynne Court
Carrboro, NC 27510
Ph: (919)966-4359
URL: http://www.renalresearch.com
Dialysis Stations: 36.

Cary

26100 ■ Cary Kidney Center Dialysis Facility
Fresenius Medical Care
5045 Old Raleigh Rd.
Cary, NC 27511
Free: 866-434-2597
URL: http://www.ultracare-dialysis.com/
Dialysis Stations: 27.

Chadbourn

26101 ■ DaVita Dialysis of Chadbourn
210 E Strawberry Blvd.
Chadbourn, NC 28431
Free: 800-424-6589
URL: http://www.davita.com
Dialysis Stations: 17.

Chapel Hill

26102 ■ UNC Comprehensive Transplant Center
North Carolina Children's Hospital
101 Manning Dr.
Chapel Hill, NC 27514
Ph: (919)966-6815
URL: http://www.ncchildrenshospital.org/ourservices/transplant
Dialysis Stations: 0.

Charlotte

26103 ■ Carolinas Medical Center Dialysis Unit
PO Box 32861
Charlotte, NC 28232
Ph: (704)381-7175
Dialysis Stations: 9.

26104 ■ Carolinas Medical Center
Dialysis Unit
1000 Blythe Blvd.
Charlotte, NC 28232
Ph: (704)355-2098
URL: http://www.carolinasmedicalcenter.org
Dialysis Stations: 1.

26105 ■ Charlotte Dialysis
DaVita
2321 W Moorehead St.
Charlotte, NC 28208
Free: 800-424-6589
URL: http://www.davita.com
Dialysis Stations: 26. **Formerly:** Gambro Healthcare.

26106 ■ Charlotte East Dialysis
DaVita
3204 N Sharon Amity Rd.
Charlotte, NC 28205
Free: 800-424-6589
URL: http://www.davita.com
Dialysis Stations: 16. **Formerly:** Gambro Healthcare.

26107 ■ Dialysis Care of Mecklenburg County Inc.
Renal Advantage Inc.
3515 Latrobe Dr.
Charlotte, NC 28211
Ph: (704)366-5299
URL: http://www.renaladvantage.com
Dialysis Stations: 24.

26108 ■ Fresenius Medical Care--Baxter Street, Charlotte
928 Baxter St.
Charlotte, NC 28204
Free: 866-434-2597
URL: http://www.ultracare-dialysis.com/
Dialysis Stations: 46. **Formerly:** Metrolina Kidney Center Charlotte.

26109 ■ Fresenius Medical Care--Beatties Ford
Dialysis Facility
1534 N Hoskins Rd.
Charlotte, NC 28216
Free: 866-434-2597
URL: http://www.ultracare-dialysis.com/
Dialysis Stations: 32.

26110 ■ Fresenius Medical Care--East Charlotte
1334 Central Ave.
Charlotte, NC 28205
Free: 866-434-2597
URL: http://www.ultracare-dialysis.com/
Dialysis Stations: 25.

26111 ■ Fresenius Medical Care--Nations Ford
Dialysis Facility
7901 England St.
Charlotte, NC 28273
Free: 866-434-2597
URL: http://www.ultracare-dialysis.com/
Dialysis Stations: 20.

26112 ■ Fresenius Medical Care--North Charlotte
5220 N Tryon St.
Charlotte, NC 28213
Free: 866-434-2597
URL: http://www.ultracare-dialysis.com/
Dialysis Stations: 28.

26113 ■ Fresenius Medical Care--West Charlotte
3057 Freedom Dr.
Charlotte, NC 28208
Free: 866-434-2597
URL: http://www.ultracare-dialysis.com/
Dialysis Stations: 29. **Formerly:** Metrolina Kidney Center West Charlotte.

26114 ■ Independent Nephrology Services--Charlotte
8430 University Executive Park Dr., Ste. 690
Charlotte, NC 28262
Ph: (704)717-2825
Fax: (704)717-2851

26115 ■ North Charlotte Dialysis Center
DaVita
6620 Old Statesville Rd.
Charlotte, NC 28269
Free: 800-424-6589
URL: http://www.davita.com

26116 ■ RAI Care Centers--Charlotte
Renal Advantage Inc.
9030 Glenwater Dr.
Charlotte, NC 28262
Ph: (704)503-6900
URL: http://www.renaladvantage.com
Dialysis Stations: 29. **Formerly:** Dialysis Care of North Mecklenburg University.

26117 ■ South Charlotte Dialysis
DaVita
6450 Bannington Rd.
Charlotte, NC 28226
Free: 800-424-6589
URL: http://www.davita.com
Dialysis Stations: 17. **Formerly:** Gambro Healthcare.

Cherokee

26118 ■ Cherokee Dialysis Center
DaVita
53 Echota Church Rd.
Cherokee, NC 28719
Free: 800-424-6589
URL: http://www.davita.com
Dialysis Stations: 20.

Clayton

26119 ■ Clayton Dialysis Center, Inc.
5420 Barber Mill Rd.
Clayton, NC 27520
Ph: (919)550-7456
Dialysis Stations: 10.

Clinton

26120 ■ Fresenius Medical Care--Clinton
Dialysis Facility
1740 Southeast Blvd.
Clinton, NC 28328
Free: 866-434-2597
URL: http://www.ultracare-dialysis.com/
Dialysis Stations: 39.

Clyde

26121 ■ Waynesville Dialysis Center
DaVita
11 Park Terrace Dr.
Clyde, NC 28721
Free: 800-424-6589
URL: http://www.davita.com
Dialysis Stations: 18.

Concord

26122 ■ Copperfield Dialysis
DaVita
1030 Vinehaven Dr.
Concord, NC 28025
Free: 800-424-6589
URL: http://www.davita.com
Dialysis Stations: 21.

26123 ■ Harrisburg Dialysis Center
DaVita
3310 Perry St.
Concord, NC 28027
Free: 800-424-6589
URL: http://www.davita.com
Dialysis Stations: 10.

Conover

26124 ■ Fresenius Medical Services of Catawba Valley
301 10th St. NW, Ste. C 101
Conover, NC 28613
Free: 866-434-2597
URL: http://www.ultracare-dialysis.com/
Dialysis Stations: 23.

Conway

26125 ■ Rich Square Dialysis Center
Fresenius Medical Care
121 N Church St.
Conway, NC 27820
Free: 866-434-2597
URL: http://www.ultracare-dialysis.com/
Dialysis Stations: 16.

Dunn

26126 ■ Dunn Kidney Center Inc.
Fresenius Medical Care
605 Tilghman Dr.
Dunn, NC 28334
Free: 866-434-2597
URL: http://www.ultracare-dialysis.com/
Dialysis Stations: 25.

Durham

26127 ■ Dialysis Services of Briggs Avenue
Fresenius Medical Care
1209 S Briggs Ave.
Durham, NC 27703
Free: 866-434-2597
URL: http://www.ultracare-dialysis.com/
Dialysis Stations: 27.

26128 ■ Duke University Medical Center
Dialysis Center
1306 Morreene Rd.
Durham, NC 27710
Ph: (919)684-3012
URL: http://medschool.duke.edu
Dialysis Stations: 15.

26129 ■ Duram Dialysis
DaVita
Dialysis Center
601 Fayetteville St.
Durham, NC 27701
Free: 800-424-6589
URL: http://www.davita.com
Dialysis Stations: 33. **Formerly:** Gambro Healthcare.

26130 ■ Durham West Dialysis & At Home
DaVita
4307 Western Park Pl., Ste. 8
Durham, NC 27705
Free: 800-424-6589
URL: http://www.davita.com
Dialysis Stations: 26. **Formerly:** Gambro Healthcare.

26131 ■ Freedom Lake Dialysis Center
Fresenius Medical Care
4016 Freedom Lake Dr.
Durham, NC 27704
Free: 866-434-2597
URL: http://www.ultracare-dialysis.com/
Dialysis Stations: 22.

26132 ■ West Pettigrew Dialysis Center
Fresenius Medical Care
1507 W Pettigrew St.
Durham, NC 27705
Free: 866-434-2597
URL: http://www.ultracare-dialysis.com/
Dialysis Stations: 20.

Eden

26133 ■ Dialysis Care of Rockingham County
DaVita
251 W Kings Hwy.
Eden, NC 27288
Free: 800-424-6589
URL: http://www.davita.com
Dialysis Stations: 23.

Edenton

26134 ■ Edenton Dialysis
DaVita
Dialysis Center
703 Luke St.
Edenton, NC 27932
Free: 800-424-6589
URL: http://www.davita.com
Dialysis Stations: 17. **Formerly:** Gambro Healthcare.

Elizabeth City

26135 ■ Elizabeth City
Dialysis Center
DaVita
1840 W City Dr.
Elizabeth City, NC 27909
Free: 800-424-6589
URL: http://www.davita.com
Dialysis Stations: 24. **Formerly:** Gambro Healthcare.

Elizabethtown

26136 ■ Southeastern Dialysis--Elizabethtown
DaVita
101 Dialysis Dr.
Elizabethtown, NC 28337
Free: 800-424-6589
URL: http://www.davita.com
Dialysis Stations: 21.

Elkin

26137 ■ Wake Forest University
Elkin Dialysis Center
941 Johnson Ridge. Rd.
Elkin, NC 28621
Ph: (336)527-4722
URL: http://www.wfubmc.edu/
Dialysis Stations: 19.

Fairmont

26138 ■ Fresenius Medical Care--Robeson County
704 S Walnut St.
Fairmont, NC 28340
Free: 866-434-2597
URL: http://www.ultracare-dialysis.com/
Dialysis Stations: 23.

Fayetteville

26139 ■ Dialysis Services--North Ramsey
Fresenius Medical Care
130 Longview Dr.
Fayetteville, NC 28311
Free: 866-434-2597
URL: http://www.ultracare-dialysis.com/
Dialysis Stations: 37.

26140 ■ Fayetteville Kidney Center
Fresenius Medical Care
1315 Avon St.
Fayetteville, NC 28304
Free: 866-434-2597
URL: http://www.ultracare-dialysis.com/
Dialysis Stations: 40.

26141 ■ Fresenius Medical Care Dialysis Services--South Ramsey
526 Ramsey St.
Fayetteville, NC 28301
Free: 866-434-2597
URL: http://www.ultracare-dialysis.com/
Dialysis Stations: 51.

26142 ■ Fresenius Medical Services of West Fayetteville
6959 Nexus Ct.
Fayetteville, NC 28304
Free: 866-434-2597
URL: http://www.ultracare-dialysis.com/
Dialysis Stations: 37.

Forest City

26143 ■ DaVita--Dialysis Care of Rutherford County Inc.
226 Commercial Dr.
Forest City, NC 28043
Free: 800-424-6589
URL: http://www.davita.com
Dialysis Stations: 30.

Four Oaks

26144 ■ Smithfield Kidney Center
Fresenius Medical Care
5815 Hwy. 301 S
Four Oaks, NC 27524
Free: 866-434-2597
URL: http://www.ultracare-dialysis.com/
Dialysis Stations: 19.

Fuquay Varina

26145 ■ Fuquay Varina Kidney Center
Fresenius Medical Care
916 S Main St.
Fuquay Varina, NC 27526
Free: 866-434-2597
URL: http://www.ultracare-dialysis.com/
Dialysis Stations: 23.

Gastonia

26146 ■ Fresenius Medical Care--Gastonia
348 Burtonwood Dr.
Gastonia, NC 28054
Free: 866-434-2597
URL: http://www.ultracare-dialysis.com/
Dialysis Stations: 39. **Formerly:** Metrolina Kidney Center.

26147 ■ South Gaston Dialysis
Fresenius Medical Care
710 W Hudson Blvd.
Gastonia, NC 28052
Free: 866-434-2597
URL: http://www.ultracare-dialysis.com/
Dialysis Stations: 17.

Goldsboro

26148 ■ Goldsboro Dialysis
Dialysis Center & At Home
Davita
2609 Hospital Rd.
Goldsboro, NC 27534
Free: 800-424-6589
URL: http://www.davita.com
Dialysis Stations: 25. **Formerly:** Gambro Healthcare.

26149 ■ Goldsboro South Dialysis
Davita
1704 Wayne Memorial Dr.
Goldsboro, NC 27530
Free: 800-424-6589
URL: http://www.davita.com
Dialysis Stations: 22. **Formerly:** Gambro Healthcare.

26150 ■ RAI Care Centers--Goldsboro
Renal Advantage Inc.
2403 Wayne Memorial Dr.
Goldsboro, NC 27530
Ph: (919)734-0044
URL: http://www.renaladvantage.com
Dialysis Stations: 16. **Formerly:** Dialysis Care of Wayne County Inc.

Greensboro

26151 ■ East Greensboro Kidney Center
Fresenius Medical Care
3839 Burlington Rd.
Greensboro, NC 27405
Free: 866-434-2597
URL: http://www.ultracare-dialysis.com/
Dialysis Stations: 37.

26152 ■ Fresenius Medical Care--South Greensboro
622 Industrial Ave.
Greensboro, NC 27405
Free: 866-434-2597
URL: http://www.ultracare-dialysis.com/
Dialysis Stations: 59.

26153 ■ Greensboro Kidney Center
Fresenius Medical Care
2700 Henry St.
Greensboro, NC 27405
Free: 866-434-2597
URL: http://www.ultracare-dialysis.com/
Dialysis Stations: 56.

26154 ■ Northwest Greensboro Kidney Center
Fresenius Medical Care
2837 Horsepen Creek
Greensboro, NC 27410
Free: 866-434-2597
URL: http://www.ultracare-dialysis.com/
Dialysis Stations: 25.

Greenville

26155 ■ Fresenius Medical Care--East Carolina
2355 W Arlington Blvd.
Greenville, NC 27834
Free: 866-434-2597
URL: http://www.ultracare-dialysis.com/
Dialysis Stations: 38.

26156 ■ Greenville Dialysis Center
Fresenius Medical Care
Dialysis Facility
510 Paladin Dr.
Greenville, NC 27834
Free: 866-434-2597
URL: http://www.ultracare-dialysis.com/
Dialysis Stations: 48.

26157 ■ Pitt County Memorial Hospital Transplant Program
University Health Systems
600 Moye Blvd.
Greenville, NC 27834
Ph: (252)744-2620
URL: http://www.uhseast.com/transplant/
Dialysis Stations: 0.

Hamlet

26158 ■ Dialysis Care of Richmond County
DaVita
771 Cheraw Rd.
Hamlet, NC 28345
Free: 800-424-6589
URL: http://www.davita.com
Dialysis Stations: 32.

Henderson

26159 ■ Vance County Dialysis
DaVita
Vance Medical Arts Bldg.
854 S Beckford Dr.
Henderson, NC 27536
Free: 800-424-6589
URL: http://www.davita.com
Dialysis Stations: 33. **Formerly:** Gambro Healthcare--Henderson.

Hendersonville

26160 ■ DaVita--Hendersonville Dialysis Center
500 Beverly Hanks Center
Hendersonville, NC 28792
Free: 800-424-6589
URL: http://www.davita.com
Dialysis Stations: 20.

Hickory

26161 ■ Fresenius Medical Care--Hickory
1899 Tate Blvd., Ste. 1103
Hickory, NC 28602
Free: 866-434-2597
URL: http://www.ultracare-dialysis.com/
Dialysis Stations: 33.

High Point

26162 ■ High Point Kidney Center Inc.
Wake Forest University
1900 Westchester Dr.
High Point, NC 27262
Ph: (336)889-9200
URL: http://www.wfopd.com/
Dialysis Stations: 42.

26163 ■ Triad Dialysis Center
Wake Forest University
4370 Regency Dr.
High Point, NC 27265
Ph: (336)454-0076
URL: http://www.wfopd.com/
Dialysis Stations: 20.

Huntersville

26164 ■ Independent Nephrology Services--Franklin County
9920 Kincey Ave., Ste. 140
Huntersville, NC 28078
Ph: (919)554-8534
Dialysis Stations: 0.

26165 ■ Independent Nephrology Services--Huntersville
9920 Kincey Ave., Ste. 140
Huntersville, NC 28078
Ph: (704)947-2341
Dialysis Stations: 10.

Jacksonville

26166 ■ Southeastern Dialysis Center & At Home--Jacksonville
DaVita
14 Office Park Dr.
Jacksonville, NC 28546
Free: 800-424-6589
URL: http://www.davita.com
Dialysis Stations: 35.

Jamestown

26167 ■ Fresenius Medical Care--Southwest Greensboro
Dialysis Facility
5020 Mackay Rd.
Jamestown, NC 27282
Free: 866-434-2597
URL: http://www.ultracare-dialysis.com/
Dialysis Stations: 31.

Kannapolis

26168 ■ Dialysis of Kannapolis & At Home
DaVita
1607 N Main St.
Kannapolis, NC 28081
Free: 800-424-6589
URL: http://www.davita.com
Dialysis Stations: 25.

Kenansville

26169 ■ Southeastern Dialysis Kenansville
DaVita
305 Beasley St.
Kenansville, NC 28349
Free: 800-424-6589
URL: http://www.davita.com
Dialysis Stations: 14.

King

26170 ■ Wake Forest University
King Dialysis Center
140 Moore Rd.
King, NC 27021
Ph: (336)985-3531
URL: http://www.wfopd.com
Dialysis Stations: 17.

Kings Mountain

26171 ■ Fresenius Medical Care--Kings Mountain
Dialysis Facility
508 Canterbury Rd.
Kings Mountain, NC 28086
Free: 866-434-2597
URL: http://www.ultracare-dialysis.com/
Dialysis Stations: 14.

Kinston

26172 ■ Fresenius Medical Care--Vernon Dialysis Unit
3101 W New Bern Rd.
Kinston, NC 28501
Free: 866-434-2597
URL: http://www.ultracare-dialysis.com/
Dialysis Stations: 24.

26173 ■ Kinston Dialysis Unit
Fresenius Medical Care
Dialysis Unit
604 Airport Rd.
Kinston, NC 28504
Free: 866-434-2597
URL: http://www.ultracare-dialysis.com
Dialysis Stations: 39.

Laurinburg

26174 ■ Laurinburg Dialysis Center
Fresenius Medical Care
701 Lauchwood Dr.
Laurinburg, NC 28352
Ph: (910)276-6669
URL: http://www.ultracare-dialysis.com
Dialysis Stations: 29.

26175 ■ Scotland County Dialysis
Fresenius Medical Care
1061 Aberdeen Rd.
Laurinburg, NC 28353
Free: 866-434-2597
URL: http://www.ultracare-dialysis.com/
Dialysis Stations: 12.

Lenoir

26176 ■ Fresenius Medical Care--Lenoir
Dialysis Facility
322 Mulberry St. SW
Lenoir, NC 28645
Free: 866-434-2597
URL: http://www.ultracare-dialysis.com/
Dialysis Stations: 34.

Lexington

26177 ■ Lexington Dialysis Center Inc.
Wake Forest University
233 Anna Lewis Dr.
Lexington, NC 27292
Ph: (336)248-6808
URL: http://www.wfopd.com
Dialysis Stations: 36.

Lillington

26178 ■ Fresenius Medical Care--Lillington
1605 S Main St.
Lillington, NC 27546
Free: 866-434-2597
URL: http://www.ultracare-dialysis.com/
Dialysis Stations: 15.

Lincolnton

26179 ■ Fresenius Medical Care--Lincolnton
1090 S Grove St. Ext.
Lincolnton, NC 28092
Free: 866-434-2597
URL: http://www.ultracare-dialysis.com
Dialysis Stations: 25. **Formerly:** Metrolina Kidney Care.

Louisburg

26180 ■ Dialysis Care of Franklin County
DaVita
1706 NC 39 Hwy. N
Louisburg, NC 27549
Free: 800-424-6589
URL: http://www.davita.com
Dialysis Stations: 23.

Lumberton

26181 ■ Lumberton Dialysis Unit
Fresenius Medical Care
720 Wesley Pines Rd.
Lumberton, NC 28358
Free: 866-434-2597
URL: http://www.ultracare-dialysis.com
Dialysis Stations: 32.

Madison

26182 ■ Madison Dialysis Center
DaVita
302 N Highway St., Ste. 105
Madison, NC 27025
Free: 800-424-6589
URL: http://www.davita.com
Dialysis Stations: 10.

Manteo

26183 ■ Fresenius Medical Care
Dare County Dialysis
115 Exeter St.
Manteo, NC 27954
Free: 866-434-2597
URL: http://www.ultracare-dialysis.com/
Dialysis Stations: 9.

Marion

26184 ■ McDowell County Dialysis
DaVita
100 Spaulding Rd., No. 2
Marion, NC 28752
Free: 800-424-6589
URL: http://www.davita.com
Dialysis Stations: 13.

Marshville

26185 ■ Marshville Dialysis Center
DaVita
7260 E Marshville Blvd.
Marshville, NC 28103
Free: 800-424-6589
URL: http://www.davita.com
Dialysis Stations: 10.

Monroe

26186 ■ Fresenius Medical Care--Monroe
1338 E Sunset Dr.
Monroe, NC 28112
Free: 866-434-2597
URL: http://www.ultracare-dialysis.com/
Dialysis Stations: 21. **Formerly:** Metrolina Kidney Care.

26187 ■ Union County Dialysis--North Carolina
DaVita
Dialysis Center
701 E Roosevelt Blvd., Bldg. 400
Monroe, NC 28112
Free: 800-424-6589
Fax: (704)283-3965
URL: http://www.davita.com
Dialysis Stations: 24. **Formerly:** Gambro Healthcare.

Mooresville

26188 ■ Independent Nephrology Services--Iredell County
124 Professional Park Dr., Ste. C
Mooresville, NC 28117
Ph: (704)663-3534
Dialysis Stations: 3.

26189 ■ Lake Norman Dialysis Center
Wake Forest University
164 Professional Park Dr.
Mooresville, NC 28117
Ph: (704)799-1860
URL: http://www.wfopd.com
Dialysis Stations: 27.

Morehead City

26190 ■ Fresenius Medical Care--Crystal Coast
Dialysis Facility
3332 Bridges St., Ste. 7
Morehead City, NC 28557
Free: 866-434-2597
URL: http://www.ultracare-dialysis.com/
Dialysis Stations: 20.

Morganton

26191 ■ Fresenius Medical Care--Burke County
Dialysis Facility
145 W Parker Rd.
Morganton, NC 28655
Free: 866-434-2597
URL: http://www.ultracare-dialysis.com/
Dialysis Stations: 25.

Mount Airy

26192 ■ Mount Airy Dialysis Center
Wake Forest University
1280 Newsome St.
Mount Airy, NC 27030
Ph: (336)789-4090
URL: http://www.wfopd.com
Dialysis Stations: 27.

Mount Olive

26193 ■ Mount Olive Dialysis
DaVita
105 Michael Martin Rd.
Mount Olive, NC 28365
Free: 800-424-6589
URL: http://www.davita.com
Dialysis Stations: 11.

Murphy

26194 ■ Smokey Mountain Dialysis
DaVita
1611 Andrews Rd.
Murphy, NC 28906
Free: 800-424-6589
URL: http://www.davita.com
Dialysis Stations: 10.

New Bern

26195 ■ Fresenius Medical Care Dialysis of Craven County
813 Kennedy Ave.
New Bern, NC 28560
Free: 866-434-2597
URL: http://www.ultracare-dialysis.com
Dialysis Stations: 29.

26196 ■ Fresenius Medical Care--New Bern Dialysis Unit
2113 Neuse Blvd.
New Bern, NC 28560
Free: 866-434-2597
URL: http://www.ultracare-dialysis.com/
Dialysis Stations: 37.

North Wilkesboro

26197 ■ Wilkes Regional Dialysis Center
1917-A West Park Dr.
North Wilkesboro, NC 28659
Ph: (336)667-3762
URL: http://www.wilkesregional.com/nodes/41.aspx
Dialysis Stations: 16.

Oxford

26198 ■ Fresenius Medical Care--Oxford, North Carolina
1620 Williamsboro St.
Oxford, NC 27565
Free: 866-434-2597
URL: http://www.ultracare-dialysis.com/
Dialysis Stations: 16.

26199 ■ Neuse River Dialysis Center
Fresenius Medical Care
625 Lewis St.
Oxford, NC 27565
Free: 866-434-2597
URL: http://www.ultracare-dialysis.com/
Dialysis Stations: 18.

Pinehurst

26200 ■ Dialysis Care of Moore County & At Home
DaVita
16 Regional Dr.
Pinehurst, NC 28374
Free: 800-424-6589
URL: http://www.davita.com
Dialysis Stations: 33.

Pittsboro

26201 ■ Carolina Dialysis--Pittsboro
Renal Research Institute
480 Hillsboro St., Ste. 300
Pittsboro, NC 27312
Ph: (919)545-0019
URL: http://www.renalresearch.com
Dialysis Stations: 10.

Plymouth

26202 ■ Plymouth Kidney Center
Fresenius Medical Care
734 US Hwy. 64 E
Plymouth, NC 27962
Free: 866-434-2597
URL: http://www.ultracare-dialysis.com/
Dialysis Stations: 12.

Raeford

26203 ■ Dialysis Care of Hoke County & At Home
DaVita
403 S Main St.
Raeford, NC 28376
Free: 800-424-6589
URL: http://www.davita.com
Dialysis Stations: 30.

Raleigh

26204 ■ New Hope Dialysis
Fresenius Medical Care
835 S New Hope Rd.
Raleigh, NC 27610
Free: 866-434-2597
URL: http://www.ultracare-dialysis.com/
Dialysis Stations: 24.

26205 ■ Raleigh Dialysis Clinic Inc.
Fresenius Medical Care
3943 New Bern Ave., Ste. 100
Raleigh, NC 27610
Free: 866-434-2597
URL: http://www.ultracare-dialysis.com/
Dialysis Stations: 48.

26206 ■ Six Forks Dialysis Clinic
Fresenius Medical Care
3411 W Millbrook Rd.
Raleigh, NC 27613
Free: 866-434-2597
URL: http://www.ultracare-dialysis.com/
Dialysis Stations: 16.

26207 ■ Southwest Wake Dialysis
Fresenius Medical Care
320 Gideon Creek Way
Raleigh, NC 27603
Free: 866-434-2597
URL: http://www.ultracare-dialysis.com/
Dialysis Stations: 23.

26208 ■ Wake Dialysis Clinic
Fresenius Medical Care
3604 Bush St.
Raleigh, NC 27609

Free: 866-434-2597
URL: http://www.ultracare-dialysis.com/
Dialysis Stations: 50.

26209 ■ Wake Forest Dialysis Center
DaVita
11001 Ingleside Pl.
Raleigh, NC 27614
Free: 800-424-6589
URL: http://www.davita.com
Dialysis Stations: 10.

Red Springs

26210 ■ Red Springs Dialysis Center
Fresenius Medical Care
1000 E 4th Ave.
Red Springs, NC 28377
Free: 866-434-2597
URL: http://www.ultracare-dialysis.com/
Dialysis Stations: 18

Reidsville

26211 ■ Reidsville Dialysis
DaVita
1307 Freeway Dr.
Reidsville, NC 27320
Free: 800-424-6589
URL: http://www.davita.com
Dialysis Stations: 19.

26212 ■ Rockingham Kidney Center
Fresenius Medical Care
2206 Barnes St.
Reidsville, NC 27320
Free: 866-434-2597
URL: http://www.ultracare-dialysis.com/
Dialysis Stations: 15.

Roanoke Rapids

26213 ■ Fresenius Medical Care--Roanoke Rapids
Dialysis Facility
260 Smith Church Rd.
Roanoke Rapids, NC 27870
Free: 866-434-2597
URL: http://www.ultracare-dialysis.com/
Dialysis Stations: 35. **Formerly:** Roanoke Rapids Dialysis Center.

Rocky Mount

26214 ■ Fresenius Medical Care--East Rocky Mount
Dialysis Facility
230 S Fairview Rd.
Rocky Mount, NC 27801
Free: 866-434-2597
URL: http://www.ultracare-dialysis.com/
Dialysis Stations: 30.

26215 ■ Fresenius Medical Care--Rocky Mount
Dialysis Facility
750 English Rd.
Rocky Mount, NC 27804
Free: 866-434-2597
URL: http://www.ultracare-dialysis.com/
Dialysis Stations: 42.

Rolesville

26216 ■ Fresenius Medical Care--Eastern Wake
670 Granite Vista Dr.
Rolesville, NC 27571
Free: 866-434-2597
URL: http://www.ultracare-dialysis.com/
Dialysis Stations: 14.

Roxboro

26217 ■ Roxboro Dialysis
DaVita
Dialysis Center
718 Ridge Rd.
Roxboro, NC 27573
Free: 800-424-6589
URL: http://www.davita.com
Dialysis Stations: 24. **Formerly:** Gambro Healthcare.

Saint Pauls

26218 ■ Saint Paul's Dialysis Center
DaVita
564 McLean St.
Saint Pauls, NC 28384
Free: 800-424-6589
URL: http://www.davita.com
Dialysis Stations: 10.

Salisbury

26219 ■ Dialysis Care of Rowan County
DaVita
111 Dorsett Dr.
Salisbury, NC 28144
Free: 800-424-6589
URL: http://www.davita.com
Dialysis Stations: 29.

Sanford

26220 ■ Carolina Dialysis--Sanford
Renal Research Institute
1922 KM Wicker Memorial Dr.
Sanford, NC 27330
Ph: (919)718-0680
URL: http://www.renalresearch.com
Dialysis Stations: 31.

Scotland Neck

26221 ■ Halifax County Dialysis Center
Fresenius Medical Care
612 Main St.
Scotland Neck, NC 27874
Free: 866-434-2597
URL: http://www.ultracare-dialysis.com/
Dialysis Stations: 11.

Shallotte

26222 ■ Southeastern Dialysis--Shallotte
DaVita
4770 Shallotte Ave.
Shallotte, NC 27874
Free: 800-424-6589
URL: http://www.davita.com
Dialysis Stations: 13.

Shelby

26223 ■ Dialysis Clinic Inc.--Kings Mountain
1016 N Lafayette St.
Shelby, NC 28150
Ph: (704)739-9342
URL: http://www.dciinc.org
Dialysis Stations: 12.

26224 ■ Dialysis Clinic, Inc.--Shelby
1016 N Lafayette St.
Shelby, NC 28150
Ph: (704)481-8405
URL: http://www.dciinc.org
Dialysis Stations: 34.

26225 ■ Dialysis Clinic Inc.--South Shelby
1530 S Lafayette St.
Shelby, NC 28152
Ph: (704)487-0399
URL: http://www.dciinc.org
Dialysis Stations: 10.

Siler City

26226 ■ Carolina Dialysis--Siler City
Renal Research Institute
806 W 4th St.
Siler City, NC 27344
Ph: (919)742-2140
URL: http://www.renalresearch.com
Dialysis Stations: 9.

Smithfield

26227 ■ Johnston Dialysis Center
Fresenius Medical Care
545 E Market St.
Smithfield, NC 27577
Free: 866-434-2597
URL: http://www.ultracare-dialysis.com/
Dialysis Stations: 25.

Snow Hill

26228 ■ Greene County Dialysis Center
DaVita
1025 Kingold Blvd.
Snow Hill, NC 28580
Free: 800-424-6589
URL: http://www.davita.com
Dialysis Stations: 13.

Southern Pines

26229 ■ Southern Pines Dialysis Center
DaVita
209 Windstar Pl.
Southern Pines, NC 28387
Free: 800-424-6589
URL: http://www.davita.com
Dialysis Stations: 12.

Southport

26230 ■ Southport Dialysis Center
DaVita
1513 N Howe St., Ste. 15
Southport, NC 28461
Free: 800-424-6589
URL: http://www.davita.com
Dialysis Stations: 10.

Spring Hope

26231 ■ Fresenius Medical Care of Spring Hope
102 Dodd St.
Spring Hope, NC 27882
Free: 866-434-2597
URL: http://www.ultracare-dialysis.com/
Dialysis Stations: 10.

Spruce Pine

26232 ■ Mayland Dialysis Center
DaVita
575 Altapass Hwy.
Spruce Pine, NC 28777
Free: 800-424-6589
URL: http://www.davita.com
Dialysis Stations: 9.

St. Pauls

26233 ■ Fresenius Medical Care--St. Pauls
153 E McLean St.
St. Pauls, NC 28358
Free: 866-434-2597
URL: http://www.ultracare-dialysis.com/
Dialysis Stations: 10.

Statesville

26234 ■ INS Statesville
2604 Davie Ave.
Statesville, NC 28625
Ph: (704)878-6590
Dialysis Stations: 6.

26235 ■ Wake Forest University Statesville Dialysis Center Inc.
627 Signal Hill Dr. Ext.
Statesville, NC 28625
Ph: (704)872-0148
URL: http://www.wfopd.com
Dialysis Stations: 26.

26236 ■ West Iredell Dialysis Center Wake Forest University
115 Westbrook Ln.
Statesville, NC 28625
Ph: (704)881-0336
URL: http://www.wfopd.com
Dialysis Stations: 20.

Swannanoa

26237 ■ Swannanoa Dialysis Center DaVita
2305 US Hwy. 70
Swannanoa, NC 28778
Free: 800-424-6589
URL: http://www.davita.com
Dialysis Stations: 10.

Sylva

26238 ■ Sylva Dialysis Center DaVita
655 Asheville Rd.
Sylva, NC 28779
Free: 800-424-6589
URL: http://www.davita.com
Dialysis Stations: 22.

Tarboro

26239 ■ Dialysis Care of Edgecombe County DaVita
3206 Western Blvd.
Tarboro, NC 27886
Free: 800-424-6589
URL: http://www.davita.com
Dialysis Stations: 25.

Thomasville

26240 ■ Thomasville Dialysis Center Wake Forest University
10 Laura Ln.
Thomasville, NC 27360
Ph: (336)472-4500
URL: http://www.wfopd.com
Dialysis Stations: 16.

Trenton

26241 ■ Dialysis Services of Jones County Fresenius Medical Care
110 Industrial Park Dr.
Trenton, NC 28585
Free: 866-434-2597
URL: http://www.ultracare-dialysis.com/
Dialysis Stations: 10.

Wadesboro

26242 ■ Dialysis Care of Anson County DaVita
923 E Caswell
Wadesboro, NC 28170
Free: 800-424-6589
URL: http://www.davita.com
Dialysis Stations: 15.

26243 ■ Fresenius Medical Care--Anson County
2349 US Hwy. 74 W
Wadesboro, NC 28170
Free: 866-434-2597
URL: http://www.ultracare-dialysis.com/
Dialysis Stations: 10.

Wallace

26244 ■ Wallace Dialysis DaVita
5650 S Old NC 41 Hwy.
Wallace, NC 28466
Free: 800-424-6589
URL: http://www.davita.com
Dialysis Stations: 12.

Warrenton

26245 ■ Warren Hills Dialysis Fresenius Medical Care
884 US Hwy. 158
Rte. 1, Box 480
Warrenton, NC 27589
Free: 866-434-2597
URL: http://www.ultracare-dialysis.com/
Dialysis Stations: 10.

Warsaw

26246 ■ Warsaw Dialysis Center Renal Advantage Inc.
213 W College St.
Warsaw, NC 28398
Ph: (910)293-9984
URL: http://www.renaladvantage.com
Dialysis Stations: 16. **Formerly:** DaVita.

Washington

26247 ■ Fresenius Medical Care--Pamlico Dialysis Facility
1983 W 5th St.
Washington, NC 27889
Free: 866-434-2597
URL: http://www.ultracare-dialysis.com/
Dialysis Stations: 25.

Weaverville

26248 ■ Weaverville Dialysis Center DaVita
329 Merrimon Ave.
Weaverville, NC 28787
Free: 800-424-6589
URL: http://www.davita.com
Dialysis Stations: 20.

Whiteville

26249 ■ Southeastern Dialysis DaVita DaVita
608 Pecan Ln.
Whiteville, NC 28472
Free: 800-424-6589
URL: http://www.davita.com
Dialysis Stations: 27.

Williamston

26250 ■ Dialysis Care of Martin County DaVita
100 Medical Dr.
Williamston, NC 27892
Free: 800-424-6589
URL: http://www.davita.com
Dialysis Stations: 23.

Wilmington

26251 ■ Southeastern Dialysis & At Home DaVita
2215 Yaupon Dr.
Wilmington, NC 28401
Free: 800-424-6589
URL: http://www.davita.com
Dialysis Stations: 49.

Wilson

26252 ■ Forest Hills Dialysis DaVita
2693 Forest Hills Rd.
Wilson, NC 27893
Free: 800-424-6589
URL: http://www.davita.com
Dialysis Stations: 21. **Formerly:** Gambro Healthcare.

26253 ■ Wilson Dialysis DaVita Dialysis Center & At Home
1605 Medical Park Dr.
Wilson, NC 27893
Free: 800-424-6589
URL: http://www.davita.com
Dialysis Stations: 29. **Formerly:** Gambro Healthcare.

Windsor

26254 ■ Fresenius Medical Care--Windsor Dialysis Facility
1421 S King St.
Windsor, NC 27983
Free: 866-434-2597
URL: http://www.ultracare-dialysis.com/
Dialysis Stations: 20.

Winston Salem

26255 ■ Baptist Medical Center Wake Forest University Dialysis Center
Medical Center Blvd., 8N Hemodialysis
Winston Salem, NC 27157
Ph: (336)716-3170
URL: http://www.wfopd.com
Dialysis Stations: 4.

26256 ■ Miller St. Dialysis Center
120 Miller St.
Winston Salem, NC 27103
Ph: (336)724-0468
Dialysis Stations: 36.

26257 ■ Northside Dialysis Center Wake Forest University
500 W Hanes Mill Rd.
Winston Salem, NC 27105
Ph: (336)744-0577
URL: http://www.wfopd.com
Dialysis Stations: 45.

26258 ■ Piedmont Dialysis Center Wake Forest University
655 Cotton St.
Winston Salem, NC 27101
Ph: (336)721-1360
URL: http://www.wfopd.com
Dialysis Stations: 62.

26259 ■ Salem Kidney Center Wake Forest University
2705 Boulder Park Court
Winston Salem, NC 27101
Ph: (336)761-8808
URL: http://www.wfopd.com
Dialysis Stations: 36.

26260 ■ Wake Forest University Baptist Medical Center Transplant Program
Dept. of Surgery
Winston Salem, NC 27157
Ph: (336)716-0548
URL: http://www.wfubmc.edu/General-Surgery/Transplant-Surgery.htm
Dialysis Stations: 0.

Yadkinville

26261 ■ Yadkin Dialysis Center Wake Forest University
225 Washington St.
Yadkinville, NC 27055
Ph: (336)677-1182
Dialysis Stations: 13.

Yanceyville

26262 ■ Fresenius Medical Care--Caswell
1702 Hwy. 86N
Yanceyville, NC 27379
Free: 866-434-2597
URL: http://www.ultracare-dialysis.com/
Dialysis Stations: 10. **Formerly:** Renal Care Group.

Zebulon

26263 ■ Fresenius Medical Care--Zebulon Dialysis Facility
465 Stratford Dr.
Zebulon, NC 27597
Free: 866-434-2597
URL: http://www.ultracare-dialysis.com/
Dialysis Stations: 30.

NORTH DAKOTA

Bismarck

26264 ■ Medcenter One Dialysis Unit
209 N 7th St.
Bismarck, ND 58501
Ph: (701)323-2800
URL: http://www.medcenterone.com
Dialysis Stations: 20.

26265 ■ Saint Alexius Medical Center Kidney Care Center Dialysis Center
900 E Broadway
Bismarck, ND 58501
Ph: (701)530-8350
URL: http://www.st.alexis.org
Dialysis Stations: 19.

Devils Lake

26266 ■ Altru Dialysis Satellite Mercy Hospital
1031 7th St.
Devils Lake, ND 58301
Ph: (701)662-9670
URL: http://www.mercyhospitaldl.com
Dialysis Stations: 5.

Dickinson

26267 ■ Dickinson Dialysis Facility Saint Joseph's Hospital
30 W 7th St.
Dickinson, ND 58601
Ph: (701)456-4615
URL: http://www.stjoeshospital.org
Dialysis Stations: 7.

Fargo

26268 ■ Fargo Dialysis and At Home DaVita
4474 23rd Ave. S
Fargo, ND 58104
Free: 800-424-6589
URL: http://www.davita.com

26269 ■ Sanford Dialysis--Fargo Sanford Health
PO Box MC-334
Fargo, ND 58122
Ph: (701)234-8400
URL: http://www.sanfordhealth.org/Locations/218312701
Dialysis Stations: 32.

26270 ■ Sanford Transplant--Fargo Sanford Health
801 Broadway Dr.
Fargo, ND 58122
Ph: (701)234-6715
URL: http://north.sanfordhealth.org/medicalservices/programs/transplant/index.as px
Dialysis Stations: 0.

Fort Yates

26271 ■ Medcenter One Satellite--Fort Yates Dialysis Facility
Standing Rock Hospital
River Rd.
Fort Yates, ND 58538
Ph: (701)854-7553
URL: http://www.medcenterone.com
Dialysis Stations: 8.

Grand Forks

26272 ■ Altru Hospital Renal Dialysis Center
1200 S Columbia Rd.
Grand Forks, ND 58201
Ph: (701)780-5870
URL: http://www.altru.org
Dialysis Stations: 13.

26273 ■ Kidney Institute of North Dakota Aurora Medical Park
1451 44th Ave. S, Ste. 104D
Grand Forks, ND 58201
Ph: (701)757-5700
Free: 877-732-2008
URL: http://auroramedicalpark.com/
Dialysis Stations: 0.

Jamestown

26274 ■ Medcenter One Satellite--Jamestown Dialysis Unit
419 5th St. NE
Jamestown, ND 58401
Ph: (701)952-4872
URL: http://www.medcenterone.com
Dialysis Stations: 8.

Minot

26275 ■ Trinity Hospital at Saint Joseph's Dialysis Center
407 3rd St. SE
Minot, ND 58701
Ph: (701)857-5404
URL: http://www.trinityhealth.org
Dialysis Stations: 10. **Formerly:** Trinity Health Center.

New Town

26276 ■ Three Affiliated Tribes Dialysis
9281 Hwy. 23
New Town, ND 58763
Ph: (701)627-4840
Dialysis Stations: 10.

Oakes

26277 ■ Oakes Dialysis DaVita
413 S 7th St.
Oakes, ND 58474
Free: 800-424-6589
URL: http://www.davita.com
Dialysis Stations: 8.

Williston

26278 ■ Mercy Hospital--Williston Dialysis Unit
1301 15th Ave. W
Williston, ND 58801
Ph: (701)774-4183
URL: http://www.mercy-williston.org
Dialysis Stations: 7.

OHIO

Akron

26279 ■ Akron City Hospital Hemodialysis Center
525 E Market St.
Akron, OH 44304
Ph: (330)375-3896
URL: http://www.summahealth.org
Dialysis Stations: 18.

26280 ■ Children's Hospital and Medical Center--Akron Dialysis Center
1 Perkins Sq.
Akron, OH 44308
Ph: (330)543-8773
URL: http://www.akronchildrens.org
Dialysis Stations: 4.

26281 ■ Diversified Specialty Institutes--White Pond
534 White Pond Dr., Ste. A
Akron, OH 44320
Ph: (330)873-1150
URL: http://www.dsi-corp.com
Dialysis Stations: 15. **Formerly:** National Renal Institutes.

26282 ■ Fresenius Medical Care--Akron East Dialysis Facility
199 Perkins St.
Akron, OH 44304
Free: 866-434-2597
URL: http://www.ultracare-dialysis.com
Dialysis Stations: 25.

26283 ■ Fresenius Medical Care--Akron West
3558 Ridgewood Rd.
Akron, OH 44333
Free: 866-434-2597
URL: http://www.ultracare-dialysis.com/
Dialysis Stations: 6.

26284 ■ Fresenius Medical Care--Greater Akron Dialysis Facility
345 Bishop St.
Akron, OH 44307
Free: 866-434-2597
URL: http://www.ultracare-dialysis.com
Dialysis Stations: 30.

26285 ■ Summit Renal Care Diversified Specialty Institutes
73 Massillon Rd.
Akron, OH 44312
Ph: (330)733-1861
URL: http://www.dsi-corp.com
Dialysis Stations: 15. **Formerly:** National Renal Institutes.

Alliance

26286 ■ Community Dialysis Unit--Alliance DaVita
270 E State St.
Alliance, OH 44601
Free: 800-424-6589
URL: http://www.davita.com
Dialysis Stations: 20.

Amelia

26287 ■ Ohio Pike Dialysis DaVita
1761 State Rte. 125, Ste. G
Amelia, OH 45102
Free: 800-424-6589
URL: http://www.davita.com
Dialysis Stations: 12.

Amherst

26288 ■ Elyria Renal Care--Amherst Fresenius Medical Care
1168 Cleveland Ave.
Amherst, OH 44001
Free: 866-434-2597
URL: http://www.ultracare-dialysis.com/
Dialysis Stations: 20. **Formerly:** Renal Care Group.

Anderson

26289 ■ Anderson Dialysis
DaVita
7502 State Rd., Ste. 1160
Anderson, OH 45255
Free: 800-424-6589
URL: http://www.davita.com
Dialysis Stations: 16.

Andover

26290 ■ Andover Dialysis
DaVita
488 S Main St.
Andover, OH 44003
Free: 800-424-6589
URL: http://www.davita.com
Dialysis Stations: 14.

Ashland

26291 ■ Fresenius Medical Care--Ashland County
1100 Redwood Dr.
Ashland, OH 44805
Free: 866-434-2597
URL: http://www.ultracare-dialysis.com/
Dialysis Stations: 12.

Ashtabula

26292 ■ Ashtabula Dialysis
DaVita
1614 W 19th St.
Ashtabula, OH 44004
Free: 800-424-6589
URL: http://www.davita.com
Dialysis Stations: 17. **Formerly:** Gambro Healthcare.

Athens

26293 ■ Rivers Edge Dialysis
DaVita
1006 E State St., Ste. B
Athens, OH 45701
Free: 800-424-6589
URL: http://www.davita.com
Dialysis Stations: 12.

Austintown

26294 ■ Fresenius Medical Care--Austintown
139 Javit Ct.
Austintown, OH 44515
Free: 866-434-2597
URL: http://www.ultracare-dialysis.com/
Dialysis Stations: 36. **Formerly:** Renal Care Group.

Batavia

26295 ■ Batavia Dialysis
DaVita
4000 Golden Age Dr.
Batavia, OH 45103
Free: 800-424-6589
URL: http://www.davita.com
Dialysis Stations: 12.

Beachwood

26296 ■ Centers for Dialysis Care--Harborside
3800 Park E Dr.
Beachwood, OH 44122
Ph: (216)593-1234
URL: http://www.cdcare.org
Dialysis Stations: 10.

Bellefontaine

26297 ■ Mad River Dialysis Center
Fresenius Medical Care
130 Dowell Ave.
Bellefontaine, OH 43311
Free: 866-434-2597
URL: http://www.ultracare-dialysis.com
Dialysis Stations: 16.

Belpre

26298 ■ Belpre Dialysis & At Home
DaVita
2906 Washington Blvd.
Belpre, OH 45714
Free: 800-424-6589
URL: http://www.davita.com
Dialysis Stations: 12.

26299 ■ Dialysis Services of Belpre
809 Farson St., Ste. 108
Belpre, OH 45714
Ph: (740)401-0880
Dialysis Stations: 8.

Boardman

26300 ■ Boardman Dialysis Center, LLC
7153 Tiffany Blvd.
Boardman, OH 44514
Ph: (330)729-1355
Dialysis Stations: 21.

26301 ■ Fresenius Medical Care--Boardman
257 Boardman-Canfield Rd.
Boardman, OH 44512
Free: 866-434-2597
URL: http://www.ultracare-dialysis.com/
Dialysis Stations: 18. **Formerly:** Renal Care Group.

Bowling Green

26302 ■ US Renal Care of Bowling Green
1037 Conneaut St., Ste. 101
Bowling Green, OH 43402
Ph: (419)353-1080
URL: http://www.usrenalcare.com/renal_care_contacts_centers_Ohio.htm
Dialysis Stations: 12.

Brook Park

26303 ■ Fresenius Medical Care--Cleveland Clinic Westside
Dialysis Facility
14670 Snow Rd.
Brook Park, OH 44142
Free: 866-434-2597
URL: http://www.ultracare-dialysis.com
Dialysis Stations: 24. **Formerly:** Renal Care Group/ Ohio Renal Care Group - West.

Bryan

26304 ■ Fresenius Medical Care--Bryan
537 W High St.
Bryan, OH 43506
Free: 866-434-2597
URL: http://www.ultracare-dialysis.com
Dialysis Stations: 13. **Formerly:** Renal Care Group - Regional Dialysis Center of Williams County.

Bucyrus

26305 ■ Crawford County Kidney Center
Fresenius Medical Care
701 Tiffin St.
Bucyrus, OH 44820
Free: 866-434-2597
URL: http://www.ultracare-dialysis.com
Dialysis Stations: 12.

Cambridge

26306 ■ Guernsey County Dialysis
DaVita
Dialysis Facility
1300 Clark St.
Cambridge, OH 43725
Free: 800-424-6589
URL: http://www.davita.com
Dialysis Stations: 8. **Formerly:** Gambro Healthcare.

Canfield

26307 ■ Center for Dialysis Care--Canfield
3695 Stutz Dr.
Canfield, OH 44406
Ph: (330)702-3040
URL: http://www.cdcare.org
Dialysis Stations: 20.

Canton

26308 ■ Aultman Dialysis Center of Canton
2912 W Tuscarwas St.
Canton, OH 44708
Ph: (330)458-0150
URL: http://www.aultman.com
Dialysis Stations: 27.

26309 ■ Aultman Hospital
Dialysis Unit
2600 6th St. SW
Canton, OH 44710
Ph: (330)363-5475
URL: http://www.aultman.com
Dialysis Stations: 9.

26310 ■ Belden Community Dialysis
DaVita
4685 Fulton Dr. NW
Canton, OH 44718
Free: 800-424-6589
URL: http://www.davita.com
Dialysis Stations: 42.

26311 ■ Mercy Canton
Dialysis Center
DaVita
1320 Mercy Dr. NW
Canton, OH 44708
Free: 800-424-6589
URL: http://www.davita.com
Dialysis Stations: 19. **Formerly:** Community Dialysis Unit--Mercy.

Celina

26312 ■ Kidney Services of West Central Ohio--Mercer County
801 Pro Dr., Ste. B
Celina, OH 45822
Ph: (419)586-1686
Dialysis Stations: 15.

Centerville

26313 ■ Dayton Regional Dialysis--South
7700 Washington Village Dr.
Centerville, OH 45459
Ph: (937)438-9595
URL: http://www.naod-drd.org/
Dialysis Stations: 20.

Chesapeake

26314 ■ Tristate Dialysis
Fresenius Medical Care
517 3rd Ave.
Chesapeake, OH 45619
Free: 866-434-2597
URL: http://www.ultracare-dialysis.com/
Dialysis Stations: 15.

Chillicothe

26315 ■ Chilicothe Regional Dialysis Center
American Renal Associates
465 Shawnee Ln.
Chillicothe, OH 45601
Ph: (740)774-4777
URL: http://www.americanrenal.com
Dialysis Stations: 20.

Cincinnati

26316 ■ Blue Ash Dialysis
Dialysis Center
DaVita
10600 McKinley Rd.
Cincinnati, OH 45242
Free: 800-424-6589
URL: http://www.davita.com
Dialysis Stations: 18. **Formerly:** Gambro Healthcare - Blue Ash.

26317 ■ Children's Hospital and Medical Center
Transplant Center
3333 Burnet Ave.
Cincinnati, OH 45229
Ph: (513)636-4443
URL: http://www.cincinnatichildrens.org
Dialysis Stations: 7.

26318 ■ Christ Hospital
Transplant/Dialysis Center
2139 Auburn Ave.
Cincinnati, OH 45219
Ph: (513)585-2431
URL: http://www.thechristhospital.com
Dialysis Stations: 28.

26319 ■ DCA of Eastgate
Dialysis Corporation of America
4600 Beechwood Rd., Ste. 900
Cincinnati, OH 45245
Ph: (513)528-3222
URL: http://www.dialysiscorporation.com/
Dialysis Stations: 15.

26320 ■ Delhi Dialysis
DaVita
5040 Delhi Ave.
Cincinnati, OH 45238
Free: 800-424-6589
URL: http://www.davita.com
Dialysis Stations: 16.

26321 ■ Dialysis Clinic, Inc.--Cincinnati
499 E McMillan St.
Cincinnati, OH 45206
Ph: (513)281-0091
URL: http://www.dciinc.org
Dialysis Stations: 41.

26322 ■ Dialysis Clinic Inc.--Western Hills
6432 Glenway Ave.
Cincinnati, OH 45211
Ph: (513)598-9050
URL: http://www.dciinc.org
Dialysis Stations: 13.

26323 ■ East Galbraith Dialysis
DaVita
3877 E Galbraith Rd.
Cincinnati, OH 45236
Free: 800-424-6589
URL: http://www.davita.com
Dialysis Stations: 10.

26324 ■ East Gate Dialysis and Home
DaVita
4435 Aicholtz Rd.
Cincinnati, OH 45245
Free: 800-424-6589
URL: http://www.davita.com
Dialysis Stations: 3.

26325 ■ Good Samaritan Hospital--Cincinnati
Dialysis Unit
375 Dixmyth Ave.
Cincinnati, OH 45220
Ph: (513)872-2448
URL: http://www.trihealth.com
Dialysis Stations: 20.

26326 ■ Mount Auburn Dialysis & Home
DaVita
2109 Reading Rd.
Cincinnati, OH 45202
Free: 800-424-6589
URL: http://www.davita.com
Dialysis Stations: 35. **Formerly:** Gambro Healthcare - Southwest Ohio.

26327 ■ Norwood Dialysis
2300 Wall St.
Cincinnati, OH 45211
Free: 800-424-6589
URL: http://www.davita.com
Dialysis Stations: 12.

26328 ■ Redbank Village Dialysis
DaVita
3960 Red Bank Rd.
Cincinnati, OH 45227
Free: 800-424-6589
URL: http://www.davita.com
Dialysis Stations: 12.

26329 ■ Silverton Dialysis & Home Training
DaVita
6929 Silverton Ave.
Cincinnati, OH 45236
Free: 800-424-6589
URL: http://www.davita.com
Dialysis Stations: 16.

26330 ■ University Hospital Cincinnati
Dialysis Center
234 Goodman Ave., ML 726C
Cincinnati, OH 45267
Ph: (513)584-5231
URL: http://www.universityhospitalcincinnati.com
Dialysis Stations: 10.

26331 ■ US Renal Care of Kenwood
5150 E Galbraith Rd., Ste. 101
Cincinnati, OH 45236
Ph: (513)791-2698
URL: http://www.usrenalcare.com/renal_care_contacts_centers_Ohio.htm
Dialysis Stations: 18.

26332 ■ US Renal Care of Norwood Dialysis
1721 Tennessee Ave.
Cincinnati, OH 45229
Ph: (513)242-6733
URL: http://www.usrenalcare.com/renal_care_contacts_centers_Ohio.htm
Dialysis Stations: 16.

26333 ■ Western Hills Southwest Dialysis
DaVita
3267 Westbourne Ave.
Cincinnati, OH 45248
Free: 800-424-6589
URL: http://www.davita.com
Dialysis Stations: 16.

26334 ■ White Oaks Dialysis, Home Training & At Home
DaVita
5520 Cheviot Rd., Ste. B
Cincinnati, OH 45247
Free: 800-424-6589
URL: http://www.davita.com
Dialysis Stations: 4.

26335 ■ Winton Road Dialysis
Dialysis Facility
DaVita
6550 Winton Rd.
Cincinnati, OH 45224
Free: 800-424-6589
URL: http://www.davita.com
Dialysis Stations: 24. **Formerly:** Gambro Healthcare - Winton Road.

Circleville

26336 ■ Fresenius Medical Care--Circleville
790 N Court St.
Circleville, OH 43113
Ph: (740)477-7225
URL: https://www.ultracare-dialysis.com
Dialysis Stations: 12. **Formerly:** Dialysis Services of Central Ohio.

26337 ■ Pickaway Dialysis Center
American Renal Associates
1180 N Court St.
Circleville, OH 43113
Ph: (303)403-1127
URL: http://www.americanrenal.com
Dialysis Stations: 12.

Cleveland

26338 ■ Center for Dialysis Care--Cityview
Dialysis Facility
6606 Carnegie Ave.
Cleveland, OH 44103
Ph: (216)426-2020
URL: http://www.cdcare.org
Dialysis Stations: 20.

26339 ■ Center for Dialysis Care--Cleveland East
11717 Euclid Ave.
Cleveland, OH 44106
Ph: (216)229-6170
URL: http://www.cdcare.org
Dialysis Stations: 80.

26340 ■ Center for Dialysis Care--Cleveland West
3330 W 25th
Cleveland, OH 44109
Ph: (216)741-5776
URL: http://www.cdcare.org
Dialysis Stations: 30.

26341 ■ Cleveland Clinic
Children's Hospital for Rehabilitation
2801 Martin Luther King Jr. Dr.
Cleveland, OH 44104
Ph: (216)721-1494
URL: http://childrens_hospital/departments/pediatric_dialysis_unit.aspx
Dialysis Stations: 8.

26342 ■ Cleveland Clinic Hospital
Transplant and Dialysis Center
9500 Euclid Ave., Q6-1
Cleveland, OH 44195
Ph: (216)444-5790
URL: http://childrens_hospital/departments/pediatric_dialysis_unit.aspx
Dialysis Stations: 8.

26343 ■ Detroit Road Dialysis
DaVita
7901 Detroit Ave.
Cleveland, OH 44102
Ph: (216)961-5666
URL: http://www.davita.com
Dialysis Stations: 24. **Formerly:** Saint John Dialysis Center.

26344 ■ Farnsworth Dialysis
Fresenius Medical Care
Farnsworth Bldg.
3764 Pearl Rd.
Cleveland, OH 44109
Free: 866-434-2597
URL: http://www.ultracare-dialysis.com/
Dialysis Stations: 24. **Formerly:** RCG/Ohio Renal Care Group - Cleveland.

26345 ■ Fresenius Medical Care--Cleveland Clinic Eastside
Dialysis Facility
11203 Stokes Blvd.
Cleveland, OH 44104
Free: 866-434-2597
URL: http://www.ultracare-dialysis.com/
Dialysis Stations: 50. **Formerly:** RCG/Ohio Renal Care Group - Cleveland East.

26346 ■ Parma Dialysis Center
DaVita
6735 Ames Rd.
Cleveland, OH 44129
Free: 800-424-6589
URL: http://www.davita.com
Dialysis Stations: 19.

26347 ■ Saint Vincent Quadrangle/St. John Dialysis Network
2302 Community College Ave.
Cleveland, OH 44115
Ph: (216)771-7365
Dialysis Stations: 13.

26348 ■ Shaker Square Dialysis
DaVita
12800 Shaker Blvd., Ste. 1
Cleveland, OH 44120
Free: 800-424-6589
URL: http://www.davita.com
Dialysis Stations: 20.

26349 ■ University Hospitals of Cleveland Dialysis Center
11100 Euclid Ave.
Cleveland, OH 44106
Ph: (216)844-1585
URL: http://www.uhhospitals.org
Dialysis Stations: 16.

Columbus

26350 ■ Clayton Taylor Dialysis Facility
Fresenius Medical Care--Ohio State University
730 Taylor Ave.
Columbus, OH 43219
Free: 866-434-2597
URL: http://www.ultracare-dialysis.com/
Dialysis Stations: 18.

26351 ■ Columbus Dialysis--Olentangy River Road
DaVita
Dialysis Facility
3830 Olentangy River Rd.
Columbus, OH 43214
Free: 800-424-6589
URL: http://www.davita.com
Dialysis Stations: 24. **Formerly:** Gambro Healthcare - Columbus.

26352 ■ Columbus Downtown Dialysis
DaVita
415 E Mound St.
Columbus, OH 43215
Free: 800-424-6589
URL: http://www.davita.com
Dialysis Stations: 24. **Formerly:** Gambro Healthcare - Columbus.

26353 ■ Columbus East Dialysis & At Home
DaVita
299 Outer Belt St.
Columbus, OH 43213
Free: 800-424-6589
URL: http://www.davita.com
Dialysis Stations: 24. **Formerly:** Gambro Healthcare - Columbus East.

26354 ■ Columbus East Dialysis
DaVita
299 Outerbelt St.
Columbus, OH 43213
Free: 800-424-6589
URL: http://www.davita.com
Dialysis Stations: 24.

26355 ■ Columbus West Home Dialysis and Training
DaVita
1391 Georgesville Rd.
Columbus, OH 43228
Free: 800-424-6589
URL: http://www.davita.com
Dialysis Stations: 13.

26356 ■ Dialysis Corporation of America of Columbus
2360 Citygate Dr.
Columbus, OH 43219
Ph: (614)428-4001
URL: http://www.dialysiscorporation.com
Dialysis Stations: 24. **Formerly:** Hood Dialysis Services--Citygate.

26357 ■ Dialysis Specialists of Columbus
Fresenius Medical Care
1299 Olentangy River Rd., Ste. 100
Columbus, OH 43212
Free: 866-434-2597
URL: http://www.ultracare-dialysis.com/
Dialysis Stations: 15.

26358 ■ Fresenius Medical Care--Central Ohio
Dialysis Center
4661 Karl Rd.
Columbus, OH 43229
Free: 866-434-2597
URL: http://www.ultracare-dialysis.com/
Dialysis Stations: 24.

26359 ■ Fresenius Medical Care--Central Ohio East
Dialysis Center
4039 E Broad St.
Columbus, OH 43213
Free: 866-434-2597
URL: http://www.ultracare-dialysis.com/
Dialysis Stations: 20.

26360 ■ Fresenius Medical Care
Columbus Southside Dialysis Center
3700 S High St., Ste. 163
Columbus, OH 43207
Free: 866-434-2597
URL: http://www.ultracare-dialysis.com/
Dialysis Stations: 17.

26361 ■ Fresenius Medical Care--Grant Park
Dialysis Facility
393 E Town St., Ste. 111
Columbus, OH 43215
Free: 866-434-2597
URL: http://www.ultracare-dialysis.com/
Dialysis Stations: 9.

26362 ■ Fresenius Medical Care--Mt. Carmel East
85 McNaughten Rd., Ste. 140
Columbus, OH 43213
Free: 866-434-2597
URL: http://www.ultracare-dialysis.com/
Dialysis Stations: 24.

26363 ■ Fresenius Medical Care--Mount Carmel West
745 W State St., Ste. 660
Columbus, OH 43222
Free: 866-434-2597
URL: http://www.ultra-dialysis.com
Dialysis Stations: 20. **Formerly:** Renal Care Group - Mount Carmel West.

26364 ■ Fresenius Medical Care--Ohio State University Campus
456 W 10th Ave.
University Clinic Building, Rm. 1410
Columbus, OH 43210
Free: 866-434-2597
URL: http://www.ultracare-dialysis.com/
Dialysis Stations: 14. **Formerly:** Ohio State University Hospital.

26365 ■ Fresenius Medical Care--Regency
2000 Regency Manor Circle, Ste. 100
Columbus, OH 43207
Free: 866-434-2597
URL: http://www.ultracare-dialysis.com/
Dialysis Stations: 12.

26366 ■ Greater Columbus Regional Dialysis LLC
Fresenius Medical Care
285 E State St., Ste. 170
Columbus, OH 43215
Ph: (614)228-9114
URL: https://www.ultracare-dialysis.com
Dialysis Stations: 30.

26367 ■ Kidney Center of Columbus East
American Renal Associates
1805 E Main St.
Columbus, OH 43205
Ph: (614)253-3300
URL: http://www.americanrenal.com
Dialysis Stations: 22.

26368 ■ Kidney Center of Columbus North
American Renal Associates
5700 Karl Rd.
Columbus, OH 43229
Ph: (614)846-9722
URL: http://www.americanrenal.com
Dialysis Stations: 7.

26369 ■ Kidney Center of Columbus South
American Renal Associates
2046 Lockbourne Rd.
Columbus, OH 43207
Ph: (614)449-7300
URL: http://www.americanrenal.com
Dialysis Stations: 20.

26370 ■ Mid--America Dialysis LLC
Liberty Dialysis
2355 S Hamilton Rd.
Columbus, OH 43227
Ph: (614)367-1679
URL: http://www.libertydialysis.com
Dialysis Stations: 24.

26371 ■ Nationwide Children's Hospital Transplant/Dialysis Center
700 Children's Dr.
Columbus, OH 43205
Ph: (614)722-4859
URL: http://www.nationwidechildrens.org
Dialysis Stations: 2. **Formerly:** Columbus Children's Hospital.

26372 ■ Ohio State University Transplant
70 Kinnear Rd.
Columbus, OH 43212
Ph: (614)293-7567
URL: http://medicalcenter.osu.edu/patientcare/healthcare_services/transplant/Pag es/index.aspx
Dialysis Stations: 0.

Cortland

26373 ■ Fresenius Medical Care--Warren, Ohio
2100 Millenium Blvd.
Cortland, OH 44410
Free: 866-434-2597
URL: http://www.ultracare-dialysis.com/
Dialysis Stations: 37.

Coshocton

26374 ■ Coshocton Dialysis
DaVita
1404 Chestnut St.
Coshocton, OH 43812
Free: 800-424-6589
URL: http://www.davita.com
Dialysis Stations: 8.

26375 ■ Dialysis Specialists of Coshocton
235 Kenwood Dr.
Coshocton, OH 43812
Ph: (740)622-6474
Dialysis Stations: 14.

Dayton

26376 ■ Dialysis Center of Dayton--North
455 Turner Rd.
Dayton, OH 45415
Ph: (937)208-7900
Dialysis Stations: 44

26377 ■ Dialysis Centers of Dayton East
1431 Business Center Ct., Ste. B
Dayton, OH 45410
Ph: (937)254-0083
Dialysis Stations: 2.

26378 ■ Miami Valley Hospital Dialysis Center
1 Wyoming St.
Dayton, OH 45409
Ph: (937)208-2531
URL: http://www.miamivalleyhospital.org
Dialysis Stations: 5.

26379 ■ PDCI/Home Dialysis of Dayton
627 Edwin C. Moses Blvd., Ste. 28
Dayton, OH 45408
Ph: (937)260-4506
Dialysis Stations: 4.

26380 ■ Peritoneal Dialysis Concepts Inc.
4700 Springboro Pike, Ste. 300
Dayton, OH 45439
Ph: (937)294-6030
Dialysis Stations: 0.

Defiance

26381 ■ Defiance Dialysis Center
Innovative Dialysis Centers
220 Stadium Dr.
Defiance, OH 43512
Ph: (419)784-2100
URL: http://www.idsdialysis.com
Dialysis Stations: 12.

26382 ■ Fresenius Medical Care--Defiance
1850 E 2nd St., Stes. 1850 & 1846
Defiance, OH 43512
Free: 866-434-2597
URL: http://www.ultracare-dialysis.com/
Dialysis Stations: 12. **Formerly:** Renal Care Group.

Delaware

26383 ■ Delaware Dialysis
Fresenius Medical Care
36 Troy Rd.
Delaware, OH 43015
Free: 866-434-2597
URL: http://www.ultracare-dialysis.com/
Dialysis Stations: 13.

26384 ■ Dialysis Corporation of America of Delaware County
1788 Columbus Pke.
Delaware, OH 43015
Ph: (740)369-4870
Fax: (740)369-4890
URL: http://www.dialysiscorporation.com
Dialysis Stations: 12.

Dublin

26385 ■ DaVita--Dublin
6770 Perimeter Dr.
Dublin, OH 43016
Free: 800-424-6589
URL: http://www.davita.com
Dialysis Stations: 12.

East Liverpool

26386 ■ Dialysis Clinic, Inc.--East Liverpool
325 W 6th St.
East Liverpool, OH 43920
Ph: (330)382-0835
URL: http://www.dciinc.org
Dialysis Stations: 22.

Eaton

26387 ■ Eaton Dialysis Center
DaVita
105 E Washington Jackson Rd.
Eaton, OH 45320
Free: 800-424-6589
URL: http://www.davita.com
Dialysis Stations: 12.

26388 ■ Preble County Regional Dialysis, Inc.
450 D. Washington-Jackson Rd.
Eaton, OH 45320
Ph: (937)456-0400
Dialysis Stations: 15.

Elyria

26389 ■ Elyria Renal Care Group
Fresenius Medical Care
5316 Hoag Dr.
Elyria, OH 44035
Free: 866-434-2597
URL: http://www.ultracare-dialysis.com/
Dialysis Stations: 20. **Formerly:** Renal Care Group - Elyria.

26390 ■ Fresenius Medical Care--Lorain County Elyria
1070 Abbe Rd. N
Elyria, OH 44035
Free: 866-434-2597
Fax: (440)365-6550
URL: http://www.ultracare-dialysis.com/
Dialysis Stations: 21. **Formerly:** Renal Care Group - Elyria.

26391 ■ Heritage Dialysis
Fresenius Medical Care
1160 E Broad St.
Elyria, OH 44035
Free: 866-434-2597
URL: http://www.ultracare-dialysis.com/
Dialysis Stations: 20. **Formerly:** Renal Care Group.

26392 ■ Lorain County Elyria Home
Fresenius Medical Care
1050 N Abbe Rd.
Elyria, OH 44035
Free: 866-434-2597
URL: http://www.ultracare-dialysis.com/
Dialysis Stations: 0. **Formerly:** Renal Care Group--Lorain County Elyria Home.

Euclid

26393 ■ Center for Dialysis Care--Euclid
25301 Euclid Ave.
Euclid, OH 44117
Ph: (216)732-3750
URL: http://www.cdcare.org
Dialysis Stations: 35.

Fairborn

26394 ■ Fairborn Dialysis
DaVita
3070 Presidential Dr., Ste. 120
Fairborn, OH 45324
Free: 800-424-6589
URL: http://www.davita.com
Dialysis Stations: 12.

26395 ■ Midwest Fairborn Dialysis
DaVita
1266 N Broad St.
Fairborn, OH 45324
Ph: (937)879-0433
URL: http://www.davita.com
Dialysis Stations: 19. **Formerly:** Community Physicians Dialysis Center--Fairborn.

Fairfield

26396 ■ Dialysis Specialists of Fairfield
Fresenius Medical Care
4750 Dixie Hwy.
Fairfield, OH 45014
Free: 866-434-2597
URL: http://www.ultracare-dialysis.com/
Dialysis Stations: 19.

26397 ■ Fairfield Home Dialysis Dialysis Facility
DaVita
1210 Hicks Blvd.
Fairfield, OH 45014
Free: 800-424-6589
URL: http://www.davita.com
Dialysis Stations: 14. **Formerly:** Gambro Healthcare - Fairfield.

Fairview Park

26398 ■ Villa of Fairview Park
DaVita
19050 Lorain Rd.
Fairview Park, OH 44126
Free: 800-424-6589
URL: http://www.davita.com
Dialysis Stations: 6.

26399 ■ Villa of Great Northern
DaVita
22710 Fairview Center Dr., Ste. 100
Fairview Park, OH 44126
Free: 800-424-6589
URL: http://www.davita.com
Dialysis Stations: 7.

Findlay

26400 ■ Blanchard Valley Dialysis Services
Innovative Dialysis Systems
1717 Medical Blvd., Ste. C
Findlay, OH 91770
Ph: (419)420-1633
URL: http://www.idsdialysis.com/facilities.html
Dialysis Stations: 21.

26401 ■ Creighton Dialysis Center
Blanchard Valley Health System
Riverview Suites Bldg.
1000 E Main Cross St.
Findlay, OH 45840
Ph: (419)423-5184
URL: http://www.bvhealthsystem.org/?id=376&sid=1
Dialysis Stations: 21.

Forest Park

26402 ■ Dialysis Clinic Inc.--Forest Park
1075 Kemper Meadow Dr.
Forest Park, OH 45240
Ph: (513)522-6200
Fax: (513)522-7144
URL: http://www.dciinc.org
Dialysis Stations: 15.

26403 ■ Forest Fair Dialysis
DaVita
1145 Kemper Meadow Dr.
Forest Park, OH 45240
Free: 800-424-6589
URL: http://www.davita.com
Dialysis Stations: 16.

Fostoria

26404 ■ Fostoria Community Dialysis Center
501 Van Buren St., Ste. 201
Fostoria, OH 44830
Ph: (419)436-6685
Dialysis Stations: 6.

Franklin

26405 ■ Butler County Southwest Ohio Dialysis
DaVita
3497 S Dixie Hwy.
Franklin, OH 45005
Free: 800-424-6589
URL: http://www.davita.com
Dialysis Stations: 20.

26406 ■ DaVita
Butler County Home Training Dialysis
3497 S Dixie Hwy.
Franklin, OH 45005
Free: 800-424-6589
URL: http://www.davita.com
Dialysis Stations: 2.

Fremont

26407 ■ Fremont Dialysis Center
Innovative Dialysis Centers
2400 Enterprise Dr.
Fremont, OH 43420
Ph: (419)332-9104
URL: http://www.idsdialysis.com
Dialysis Stations: 11.

Gallipolis

26408 ■ Fresenius Medical Care--Gallipolis
137 Pine St., Ste. 101
Gallipolis, OH 45631
Free: 866-434-2597
URL: http://www.ultracare-dialysis.com/
Dialysis Stations: 21.

Garfield Heights

26409 ■ Centers for Dialysis Care--Garfield
5595 Transportation Blvd., Ste. 110
Garfield Heights, OH 44125
Ph: (216)581-0801
URL: http://www.cdcare.org
Dialysis Stations: 15.

Georgetown

26410 ■ US Grant Dialysis
DaVita
458 Home St.
Georgetown, OH 45121
Free: 800-424-6589
URL: http://www.davita.com
Dialysis Stations: 12.

Glandorf

26411 ■ Putham County Ambulatory Care Dialysis Center
601 State Rte. 224
Glandorf, OH 45848
Ph: (419)226-4420
Dialysis Stations: 12.

Greenville

26412 ■ Dialysis Center of Darke County LLC
1111 Sweitzer St., Ste. B
Greenville, OH 45331
Ph: (937)548-7019
Dialysis Stations: 10.

Grove City

26413 ■ Grove City Dialysis
DaVita
4155 Kelnor Dr.
Grove City, OH 43123
Free: 800-424-6589
URL: http://www.davita.com
Dialysis Stations: 8.

Hamilton

26414 ■ Fresenius Medical Care--Hamilton, Ohio
3090 McBride C, Ste. A
Hamilton, OH 45011
Free: 866-434-2597
URL: http://www.ultracare-dialysis.com/
Dialysis Stations: 14.

Heather Hill

26415 ■ Center for Dialysis Carehealth:ther Hill
12340 Bass Lake Rd.
Heather Hill, OH 44024
Ph: (440)286-4103
Dialysis Stations: 12.

Hillsboro

26416 ■ Highland County Dialysis
DaVita
120 Roberts La., Ste. 4
Hillsboro, OH 45133
Free: 800-424-6589
URL: http://www.davita.com
Dialysis Stations: 10.

Hinckley

26417 ■ Brunswick Dialysis Center
Fresenius Medical Care
2583-2585 Center Rd.
Hinckley, OH 44233
Free: 866-434-2597
URL: http://www.ultracare-dialysis.com/
Dialysis Stations: 19.

Howland

26418 ■ Warren Dialysis Center
American Renal Associates
8720 E Market St., Ste. 1A
Howland, OH 44484
Ph: (303)403-1127
URL: http://www.americanrenal.com
Dialysis Stations: 25.

Huber Heights

26419 ■ Dayton Regional Dialysis--North
7211 Shull Rd.
Huber Heights, OH 45424
Ph: (937)237-2000
URL: http://www.naod-drd.org/
Dialysis Stations: 28.

Independence

26420 ■ Rockside Dialysis
DaVita
4801 Acorn Dr.
Independence, OH 44131
Free: 800-424-6589
URL: http://www.davita.com
Dialysis Stations: 16.

Jackson

26421 ■ Fresenius Medical Care--Indian Hills
820 Veterans Dr.
Jackson, OH 45640
Free: 866-434-2597
URL: http://www.ultracare-dialysis.com/
Dialysis Stations: 12.

26422 ■ Jackson Dialysis & Kidney Center
500 McCarty La.
Jackson, OH 45640
Ph: (740)286-1600
Dialysis Stations: 16.

Jefferson

26423 ■ Center for Dialysis Care--Jefferson Dialysis Center
222 E Beech St.
Jefferson, OH 44047
Ph: (440)576-7161
Free: 800-352-3647
URL: http://www.cdcare.org
Dialysis Stations: 10.

Kent

26424 ■ Portage County Kidney Center
Fresenius Medical Care
401 Devon Pl., Ste. 100
Kent, OH 44240
Free: 866-434-2597
Fax: (330)677-2385
URL: http://www.ultracare-dialysis.com/
Dialysis Stations: 16.

Kenwood

26425 ■ Liberty Dialysis--Kenwood
8251 Pine Road, Ste. 110
Kenwood, OH 45236
Ph: (513)745-0800
URL: http://www.libertydialysis.com
Dialysis Stations: 24.

Kettering

26426 ■ Kettering Dialysis & At Home
DaVita
5721 Bigger Rd.
Kettering, OH 45440
Free: 800-424-6589
URL: http://www.davita.com
Dialysis Stations: 16.

Kings Mills

26427 ■ Fresenius Medical Care--Kings Mills
1992 King Ave.
Kings Mills, OH 45034
Free: 866-434-2597
URL: http://www.ultracare-dialysis.com/
Dialysis Stations: 12.

Lancaster

26428 ■ American Renal Associates
Fairfield Kidney Center
618 Pleasantview Rd.
Lancaster, OH 43130
Ph: (740)687-6480
URL: http://www.americanrenal.com
Dialysis Stations: 15.

26429 ■ Hocking Hills Dialysis Center
Fresenius Medical Care
1550 Sheridan Dr., Ste. 206
Lancaster, OH 43130
Free: 866-434-2597
URL: http://www.ultracare-dialysis.com/
Dialysis Stations: 20.

Lebanon

26430 ■ Lebanon Dialysis, At Home and Home Training Center
DaVita
918B Columbus Ave., Ste. 1
Lebanon, OH 45036
Free: 800-424-6589
URL: http://www.davita.com
Dialysis Stations: 2.

Lima

26431 ■ Lima Memorial Hospital Dialysis Center
1001 Bellafontaine Ave.
Lima, OH 45804
Ph: (419)998-4574
URL: http://www.limamemorial.org
Dialysis Stations: 20.

26432 ■ St. Rita's Dialysis Center
Kidney Services of West Central Ohio
750 W High St., Ste. 100
Lima, OH 45801
Ph: (419)227-0918
URL: http://www.kidney-hypertension.com/srmc.htm
Dialysis Stations: 22.

26433 ■ St. Ritas Medical Center ESRD Unit
730 W Market St.
Lima, OH 45801
Ph: (419)227-0918
URL: http://www.ehealthconnection.com/regions/st_ritas/content/2349.asp
Dialysis Stations: 3.

Logan

26434 ■ Logan Dialysis
DaVita
12880 Grey St.
Logan, OH 43138
Free: 800-424-6589
URL: http://www.davita.com
Dialysis Stations: 12.

London

26435 ■ Dialysis Services of London
Fresenius Medical Care
306 Lafayette St., Ste. J
London, OH 43140
Free: 866-434-2597
URL: http://www.ultracare-dialysis.com/
Dialysis Stations: 13.

Madison

26436 ■ Lake County Dialysis
DaVita
1963 Hubbard Rd.
Madison, OH 44057
Free: 800-424-6589
URL: http://www.davita.com
Dialysis Stations: 12. **Formerly:** Gambro Healthcare - Lake County.

Mansfield

26437 ■ Fresenius Medical Care--Richland County
Dialysis Services
680 Bally Row
Mansfield, OH 44906
Free: 866-434-2597
URL: http://www.ultracare-dialysis.com/
Dialysis Stations: 24.

26438 ■ Mansfield Kidney Center
Fresenius Medical Care
647 Bally Row
Mansfield, OH 44906
Free: 866-434-2597
URL: http://www.ultracare-dialysis.com/
Dialysis Stations: 19. **Formerly:** Bio-Medical Applications of Mansfield.

Marietta

26439 ■ Dialysis Specialists of Marietta
Fresenius Medical Care
14-16 Acme St.
Marietta, OH 45750
Free: 866-434-2597
URL: http://www.ultracare-dialysis.com/
Dialysis Stations: 16.

26440 ■ Marietta Dialysis
Dialysis Facility
DaVita
1019 Pike St.
Marietta, OH 45750
Free: 800-424-6589
URL: http://www.davita.com
Dialysis Stations: 12. **Formerly:** Gambro Healthcare - Marietta.

Marion

26441 ■ Heart of Ohio Dialysis Center
Fresenius Medical Care
1730 Marion-Waldo Rd.
Marion, OH 43302
Free: 866-434-2597
URL: http://www.ultracare-dialysis.com/
Dialysis Stations: 24.

Massillon

26442 ■ Massillon Dialysis Center
Fresenius Medical Care
2474 Lincoln Way E
Massillon, OH 44646
Free: 866-434-2597
URL: http://www.ultracare-dialysis.com/
Dialysis Stations: 17.

Maumee

26443 ■ Arrowhead Dialysis Center
Fresenius Medical Care
322 W Dussel Dr.
Maumee, OH 43537
Free: 866-434-2597
URL: http://www.ultracare-dialysis.com/
Dialysis Stations: 24. **Formerly:** National Nephrology Associates.

Medina

26444 ■ Medina County Kidney Center
Fresenius Medical Care
970 E Washington St., Ste. B-3
Medina, OH 44256
Free: 866-434-2597
URL: http://www.ultracare-dialysis.com/
Dialysis Stations: 20.

26445 ■ Valley City Dialysis
Fresenius Medical Care
2400 Columbia Rd.
Medina, OH 44256
Free: 866-434-2597
URL: http://www.ultracare-dialysis.com/
Dialysis Stations: 6.

Mentor

26446 ■ Centers for Dialysis Care--Mentor
8900 Tyler Blvd.
Mentor, OH 44060
Ph: (440)951-3602
URL: http://www.cdcare.org
Dialysis Stations: 26.

Middleburg Heights

26447 ■ Middleburg Heights Dialysis Center
DaVita
7360 Engle Road
Middleburg Heights, OH 44130
Ph: (440)891-5645
Dialysis Stations: 24. **Formerly:** Hillmed Dialysis Center.

Middletown

26448 ■ Atrium Medical Center
Outpatient Dialysis Center
4421 Roosevelt Blvd., Ste. D
Middletown, OH 45044
Ph: (513)727-2700
URL: http://www.atriummedcenter.org
Dialysis Stations: 16. **Formerly:** Middletown Regional Hospital.

Milford

26449 ■ Clermont Inc.
DaVita
5901 Montclair Blvd., Ste. 100
Milford, OH 45150
Free: 800-424-6589
URL: http://www.davita.com
Dialysis Stations: 12.

Moraine

26450 ■ Dialysis Centers of Dayton--South
4700 Springboro Pike
Moraine, OH 45439
Ph: (937)294-7188
Dialysis Stations: 25.

Mount Healthy

26451 ■ Dialysis Corporation of America of Cincinnati
7600 Affinity Pl.
Mount Healthy, OH 45231
Ph: (513)931-7900
Fax: (513)931-0400
URL: http://www.dialysiscorporation.com
Dialysis Stations: 16.

Mount Vernon

26452 ■ Knox County Kidney Center
Fresenius Medical Care
Dialysis Facility
14 Wood Lake Trl.
Mount Vernon, OH 43050
Free: 866-434-2597
URL: http://www.ultracare-dialysis.com/
Dialysis Stations: 14.

Munroe Falls

26453 ■ Diversified Specialty Institutes--Munroe Falls
265 N Main St.
Munroe Falls, OH 44262
Ph: (330)689-1400
URL: http://www.dsi-corp.com
Dialysis Stations: 13. **Formerly:** National Renal Institutes.

New Philadelphia

26454 ■ Tuscarawas County Kidney Center
Fresenius Medical Care
Dialysis Facility
1260 Monroe Ave. NW, Ste. 41-T
New Philadelphia, OH 44663
Free: 866-434-2597
URL: http://www.ultracare-dialysis.com/
Dialysis Stations: 13.

Newark

26455 ■ Cherry Valley Dialysis
DaVita
1627 W Main St.
Newark, OH 43055
Free: 800-424-6589
URL: http://www.davita.com
Dialysis Stations: 25.

26456 ■ Choice One Renal Care of Newark
65 S Terrace Ave.
Newark, OH 43055
Ph: (740)522-2955
Dialysis Stations: 22.

North Lima

26457 ■ Fresenius Medical Care--North Lima
9174 Market St.
North Lima, OH 44452
Free: 866-434-2597
URL: http://www.ultracare-dialysis.com/
Dialysis Stations: 6. **Formerly:** Renal Care Group.

North Randall

26458 ■ Ohio Renal Care Group--North Randall
Fresenius Medical Care
Dialysis Facility
4750 Northfield Rd.
North Randall, OH 44128
Free: 866-434-2597
URL: http://www.ultracare-dialysis.com/
Dialysis Stations: 15. **Formerly:** Ohio Renal Group - North Randall.

Northwood

26459 ■ Northwood Dialysis
DaVita
611 Lemoyne Rd.
Northwood, OH 43619
Free: 800-424-6589
URL: http://www.davita.com
Dialysis Stations: 17.

Norwalk

26460 ■ Fresenius Medical Care--Norwalk Dialysis Facility
290 Benedict Ave.
Norwalk, OH 44857
Free: 866-434-2597
URL: http://www.ultracare-dialysis.com/
Dialysis Stations: 13.

Norwood

26461 ■ Liberty Dialysis--Norwood
2071 Sherman Ave.
Norwood, OH 45212
Ph: (513)841-1800
URL: http://www.libertydialysis.com
Dialysis Stations: 24.

Oakwood Village

26462 ■ Centers for Dialysis Care--Oakwood
7690 1st Place, Ste. E
Oakwood Village, OH 44146
URL: http://www.cdcare.org
Dialysis Stations: 20.

Oregon

26463 ■ Dialysis Partners--Maumee Bay
3310 Dustin Rd.
Oregon, OH 43616
Ph: (419)697-2191
Dialysis Stations: 18. **Formerly:** Maumee Bay Dialysis.

Oxford

26464 ■ Fresenius Medical Care--Talawanda
5148 College Corner Pike
Oxford, OH 45056
Free: 866-434-2597
URL: http://www.ultracare-dialysis.com/
Dialysis Stations: 12.

Parma Heights

26465 ■ Advanced Dialysis of Parma
9050 N Church Dr.
Parma Heights, OH 44130
Ph: (440)292-0231
Dialysis Stations: 19.

Pataskala

26466 ■ Pataskala Dialysis Center
DaVita
642 E Broad St.
Pataskala, OH 43062
Free: 800-424-6589
URL: http://www.davita.com
Dialysis Stations: 8.

Piketon

26467 ■ Piketon Regional Dialysis Center
American Renal Associates
7143 US Rt. 23
Piketon, OH 45661
Ph: (303)403-1127
URL: http://www.americanrenal.com
Dialysis Stations: 10.

Poland

26468 ■ Youngstown Home Care
Centers for Dialysis Care
807 Southwestern Run
Poland, OH 44514
Ph: (330)758-0995
URL: http://www.cdcare.org/
Dialysis Stations: 2.

Portsmouth

26469 ■ Dialysis Clinic Inc.--Portsmouth
1207 17th St.
Portsmouth, OH 45662
Ph: (740)351-0596
URL: http://www.dciinc.org
Dialysis Stations: 25.

26470 ■ Fresenius Medical Care--Portsmouth Dialysis Facility
1648 11th St.
Portsmouth, OH 45662
Free: 866-434-2597
URL: http://www.ultracare-dialysis.com/
Dialysis Stations: 12.

Rocky River

26471 ■ Advanced Dialysis LLC
19133 Hilliard Blvd.
Rocky River, OH 44116
Ph: (216)712-4700
Dialysis Stations: 18.

26472 ■ Rocky River Dialysis
DaVita
20220 Center Ridge Rd., Ste. 50
Rocky River, OH 44116
Free: 800-424-6589
URL: http://www.davita.com
Dialysis Stations: 20. **Formerly:** Hillmed Dialysis Center.

Saint Clairsville

26473 ■ Belmont Dialysis--Crestview
68639 Bannock Rd.
Saint Clairsville, OH 43950
Ph: (740)699-0220
Dialysis Stations: 10.

Saint Marys

26474 ■ LMH Satellite at Saint Mary's Dialysis Center
200 Saint Clair St.
Saint Marys, OH 45885
Ph: (419)394-6089
Dialysis Stations: 12.

26475 ■ LNHSatellite at St. Marys
200 St. Clair St.
Saint Marys, OH 45885
Ph: (419)394-6089
Dialysis Stations: 12.

Salem

26476 ■ Fresenius Medical Care--Salem South
2345 E Pershing St.
Salem, OH 44460
Free: 866-434-2597
URL: http://www.ultracare-dialysis.com/
Dialysis Stations: 22. **Formerly:** Renal Care Group.

Sandusky

26477 ■ Firelands Dialysis Center--South
Firelands Regional Medical Center
904 Pierce St.
Sandusky, OH 44870
Ph: (419)557-7228
URL: http://www.firelands.com
Dialysis Stations: 31. **Formerly:** Providence Hospital.

26478 ■ Home Dialysis Services of Sandusky, Inc.
2819 S Hayes Ave., Ste. 2
Sandusky, OH 44870
Ph: (419)627-8403
Dialysis Stations: 0. **Formerly:** Dialysis Associates of Northeast Ohio.

26479 ■ Sandusky Dialysis Center
DaVita
795 Bardshar Rd.
Sandusky, OH 44870
Free: 800-424-6589
URL: http://www.davita.com
Dialysis Stations: 8.

Seaman

26480 ■ Dialysis Clinic Inc.--Seaman
65 Commerce Dr.
Seaman, OH 45679
Ph: (937)386-0818
URL: http://www.dciinc.org
Dialysis Stations: 13.

Shaker Heights

26481 ■ Center for Dialysis Care--Shaker Heights
18720 Chagrin Blvd.
Shaker Heights, OH 44122
Ph: (216)295-7000
URL: http://www.cdcare.org
Dialysis Stations: 46.

Sidney

26482 ■ Fresenius Medical Care--Sidney Dialysis Facility
1015 Fair Rd.
Sidney, OH 45365

Free: 866-434-2597
URL: http://www.ultracare-dialysis.com/
Dialysis Stations: 14. **Formerly:** Shelby County Kidney Center.

Solon

26483 ■ Fresenius Medical Care--Solon
6020 Enterprise Pkwy.
Solon, OH 44139
Free: 866-434-2597
URL: http://www.ultracare-dialysis.com/
Dialysis Stations: 16. **Formerly:** Renal Care Group.

Springboro

26484 ■ Dialysis Centers of Warren County
90 Commercial Way
Springboro, OH 45066
Ph: (937)704-0589
Dialysis Stations: 10.

Springfield

26485 ■ Clark County Dialysis Facility
247 S Burnett Rd., Ste. 110
Springfield, OH 45505
Ph: (937)328-8921
Dialysis Stations: 18.

26486 ■ Midwest Springfield Dialysis
DaVita
2200 N Limestone St., Ste. 104
Springfield, OH 45503
Ph: (937)390-3125
URL: http://www.davita.com
Dialysis Stations: 21. **Formerly:** Community Physicians Dialysis Center--Springfield.

Steubenville

26487 ■ Dialysis Clinic Inc.--Steubenville
4227 Mall Dr.
Steubenville, OH 43952
Ph: (740)266-6687
URL: http://www.dciinc.org
Dialysis Stations: 12.

Streetsboro

26488 ■ Fresenius Medical Care--Streetsboro Kidney Center
Dialysis Facility
9200 Staples Dr., Ste. A
Streetsboro, OH 44241
Free: 866-434-2597
URL: http://www.ultracare-dialysis.com/
Dialysis Stations: 13.

Strongsville

26489 ■ Strongsville Dialysis & At Home
DaVita
17792 Pearl Rd.
Strongsville, OH 44136
Free: 800-424-6589
URL: http://www.davita.com
Dialysis Stations: 16.

Tiffin

26490 ■ Seneca County Dialysis
Davita
65 Saint Francis Ave.
Tiffin, OH 44883
Free: 800-424-6589
URL: http://www.davita.com
Dialysis Stations: 9.

Toledo

26491 ■ Alexis Dialysis Center
Innovative Dialysis Centers
5719 Jackman Rd.
Toledo, OH 43613
Ph: (419)471-1710
URL: http://www.idsdialysis.com
Dialysis Stations: 15.

26492 ■ DaVita--Point Place
4747 Suder Ave., Ste. 107
Toledo, OH 43611
Free: 800-424-6589
URL: http://www.davita.com
Dialysis Stations: 10.

26493 ■ Dialysis Partners of Northwest Ohio--Glendale
3401 Glendale Ave.
Toledo, OH 43614
Ph: (419)389-9681
Dialysis Stations: 28.

26494 ■ Innovative Dialysis of Toledo
3829 Woodley Rd., Ste. C-12
Toledo, OH 43606
Ph: (419)473-9900
URL: http://www.idsdialysis.com
Dialysis Stations: 15.

26495 ■ Medical College Hospital
Transplant/Dialysis Center
3000 Arlington Ave., Rm. 3101
Toledo, OH 43614
Ph: (419)383-4985
URL: http://utmc.utoledo.edu
Dialysis Stations: 4.

26496 ■ Peritoneal Dialysis Center of Northwest Ohio
Innovative Dialysis Systems
4447 Talmadge Rd., Ste. E
Toledo, OH 43623
Ph: (419)475-3000
URL: http://www.idsdialysis.com
Dialysis Stations: 2.

26497 ■ Saint Vincent Mercy Medical Center
Dialysis Unit
ACC Bldg.
2213 Cherry St.
Toledo, OH 43608
Ph: (419)251-4760
URL: http://www.mercyweb.org
Dialysis Stations: 6.

26498 ■ Toledo Central Dialysis
Fresenius Medical Care
Dialysis Center
3100 W Central Ave., Ste. 100
Toledo, OH 43606
Free: 866-434-2597
URL: http://www.ultracare-dialysis.com/
Dialysis Stations: 24. **Formerly:** National Nephrology Associates of Central Toledo.

26499 ■ Toledo Dialysis & At Home
Dialysis Center
DaVita
1614 S Byrne Rd., Ste. R
Toledo, OH 43614
Free: 800-424-6589
URL: http://www.davita.com
Dialysis Stations: 20. **Formerly:** Gambro Healthcare - Toledo.

26500 ■ The Toledo Hospital
Dialysis Unit
2142 N Cove Blvd.
Toledo, OH 43606
Ph: (419)291-8670
URL: http://www.promedica.org
Dialysis Stations: 4.

26501 ■ Toledo Wernerts Corner Dialysis
Fresenius Medical Care
2532 W Laskey Rd.
Toledo, OH 43613
Free: 866-434-2597
URL: http://www.ultracare-dialysis.com/
Dialysis Stations: 20.

26502 ■ Wildwood Dialysis Center
Innovative Dialysis Systems
2249 N Reynolds Rd.
Toledo, OH 43615
Ph: (419)535-7415
URL: http://www.idsdialysis.com
Dialysis Stations: 15.

Troy

26503 ■ UVMC Dialysis Services
Outpatient Dialysis Center
3130 N County Rd., Ste. 25-A
Troy, OH 45373
Ph: (937)440-4990
URL: http://www.uvmc.com
Dialysis Stations: 22.

Uniontown

26504 ■ Akron/Canton Kidney Center
Fresenius Medical Care
1575 Corporate Woods Pkwy., Ste. 100
Uniontown, OH 44685
Free: 866-434-2597
URL: http://www.ultracare-dialysis.com/
Dialysis Stations: 23.

Urbana

26505 ■ Midwest Urbana Dialysis
DaVita
1430 E US Hwy. 36
Urbana, OH 43078
Free: 800-424-6589
URL: http://www.davita.com
Dialysis Stations: 12.

Van Wert

26506 ■ Van Wert Dialysis
Fresenius Medical Care
140 Fox Rd., Ste. 405
Van Wert, OH 45891
Free: 866-434-2597
URL: http://www.ultracare-dialysis.com/
Dialysis Stations: 12. **Formerly:** Renal Care Group.

Wadsworth

26507 ■ Wadsworth Dialysis
DaVita
195 Wadsworth Rd.
Wadsworth, OH 44281
Free: 800-424-6589
URL: http://www.davita.com
Dialysis Stations: 12.

26508 ■ Wadsworth Dialysis
Fresenius Medical Care
1160 Williams Reserve Blvd.
Wadsworth, OH 44281
Free: 866-434-2597
URL: http://www.ultracare-dialysis.com/
Dialysis Stations: 13.

Warren

26509 ■ Centers for Dialysis Care--Warren
1950 Niles Cortland Rd.
Warren, OH 44484
Ph: (330)609-0370
URL: http://www.cdcare.org
Dialysis Stations: 16.

Warrensville Heights

26510 ■ Center for Dialysis Care--Warrensville Heights
4877 Galaxy Pkwy., Ste. A
Warrensville Heights, OH 44128
Ph: (216)378-5050
URL: http://www.cdcare.org
Dialysis Stations: 30.

26511 ■ Suburban Home Dialysis
Fresenius Medical Care
20050 Harvard Rd., Ste. 103
Warrensville Heights, OH 44122
Free: 866-434-2597
URL: http://www.ultracare-dialysis.com/
Dialysis Stations: 0.

26512 ■ Warrensville Heights PD Dialysis
DaVita
4200 Warrensville Center Rd.
Bldg. A, Ste. 210
Warrensville Heights, OH 44122
Free: 800-424-6589
URL: http://www.davita.com
Dialysis Stations: 2.

Washington Court House

26513 ■ Washington Courthouse
Fresenius Medical Care
Medical Office Bldg. 2
1510 Columbus Ave., Ste. 130
Washington Court House, OH 43160
Free: 866-434-2597
URL: http://www.ultracare-dialysis.com/
Dialysis Stations: 6. **Formerly:** Renal Care Group.

Wauseon

26514 ■ Wasueon Dialysis
DaVita
721 S Shoop Ave.
Wauseon, OH 43567
Free: 800-424-6589
URL: http://www.davita.com
Dialysis Stations: 13.

Westchester

26515 ■ Dialysis Clinic Inc.--Westchester
7625 University Dr.
Westchester, OH 45069
Ph: (513)777-0855
URL: http://www.dciinc.org
Dialysis Stations: 14.

Westerville

26516 ■ Fresenius Medical Care--Westerville Dialysis
477 Cooper Rd., Ste. 140
Westerville, OH 43081
Free: 866-434-2597
URL: http://www.ultracare-dialysis.com/
Dialysis Stations: 12.

Westlake

26517 ■ Saint John Westshore Dialysis Center
St. John Medical Center
29000 Center Ridge Rd.
Westlake, OH 44145
Ph: (440)827-5161
URL: http://www.sjws.net/health-services/renal-dialysis.htm
Dialysis Stations: 10.

26518 ■ Westlake Dialysis Center
Fresenius Medical Care
26024 Detroit Rd.
Westlake, OH 44145
Free: 866-434-2597
URL: http://www.ultracare-dialysis.com/
Dialysis Stations: 23. **Formerly:** Renal Care Group.

Willoughby

26519 ■ Fresenius Medical Care--Willoughby
5105 SOM Center Rd., 3rd Fl.
Willoughby, OH 44094
Free: 866-434-2597
URL: http://www.ultracare-dialysis.com/
Dialysis Stations: 16. **Formerly:** Renal Care Group.

Wilmington

26520 ■ Willow Dialysis Center
DaVita
1675 Alex Dr.
Wilmington, OH 45177
Free: 800-424-6589
URL: http://www.davita.com
Dialysis Stations: 18. **Formerly:** Dialysis Services of Southern Ohio.

Wooster

26521 ■ Wayne County Kidney Center
Fresenius Medical Care
387 W Milltown Rd.
Wooster, OH 44691
Free: 866-434-2597
URL: http://www.ultracare-dialysis.com/
Dialysis Stations: 17.

Wright Patterson AFP

26522 ■ Wright Patterson Medical Center Hemodialysis Department
4881 Sugar Maple Dr.
Wright Patterson AFP, OH 45433
Ph: (937)257-0957
URL: http://www.wpafb.af.mil/units/wpmc/
Dialysis Stations: 5.

Xenia

26523 ■ Southwest Ohio Dialysis
DaVita
215 S Allison Ave.
Xenia, OH 45385
Free: 800-424-6589
URL: http://www.davita.com
Dialysis Stations: 16.

Youngstown

26524 ■ Fresenius Medical Care--Youngstown
1340 Belmont Ave.
Youngstown, OH 44504
Free: 866-434-2597
URL: http://www.ultracare-dialysis.com/
Dialysis Stations: 26. **Formerly:** Renal Care Group.

26525 ■ St. Elizabeth Health Center
Humility of Mary Health Partners
1044 Belmont Ave.
Youngstown, OH 44501
Ph: (330)480-3642
URL: http://www.ehealthconnection.com/regions/youngstown/content/show_facility.a sp?facility_id=188
Dialysis Stations: 0.

Zanesville

26526 ■ Kidney Care Centers of Zanesville
American Renal Associates
3239 Maple Ave.
Zanesville, OH 43701
Ph: (303)403-1127
URL: http://www.americanrenal.com
Dialysis Stations: 25.

26527 ■ Zanesville Dialysis & At Home Dialysis Facility
DaVita
3120 Newark Rd.
Zanesville, OH 43701
Free: 800-424-6589
URL: http://www.davita.com
Dialysis Stations: 20. **Formerly:** Gambro Healthcare - Zanesville.

OKLAHOMA

Ada

26528 ■ Ada Dialysis Center
Renal Advantage Inc.
324 NW J A Richardson Loop
Ada, OK 74820
Ph: (580)421-9131
URL: http://www.renaladvantage.com
Dialysis Stations: 21. **Formerly:** National Renal Alliance.

Altus

26529 ■ DaVita--Altus Dialysis Center
205 S Park Ln., Ste. 130
Altus, OK 73521
Free: 800-424-6589
URL: http://www.davita.com
Dialysis Stations: 10.

Anadarko

26530 ■ DaVita--Anadarko
412 SE 11th St.
Anadarko, OK 73005
Free: 800-424-6589
URL: http://www.davita.com
Dialysis Stations: 10.

Ardmore

26531 ■ Fresenius Medical Care--Ardmore Dialysis Facility
1402 Brookview Dr.
Ardmore, OK 73401
Free: 866-434-2597
URL: http://www.ultracare-dialysis.com/
Dialysis Stations: 28. **Formerly:** RCG--Ardmore.

Bartlesville

26532 ■ Jane Phillips Dialysis Facility
3500 SE State St.
Bartlesville, OK 74006
Ph: (918)331-1770
Dialysis Stations: 18.

Bethany

26533 ■ DaVita--Northwest Bethany Dialysis Facility & At Home
7800 NW 23rd St., Ste. A
Bethany, OK 73008
Free: 800-424-6589
URL: http://www.davita.com
Dialysis Stations: 16.

Chickasha

26534 ■ Chickasha Dialysis Center
DaVita
228 S 29th St.
Chickasha, OK 73018
Free: 800-424-6589
URL: http://www.davita.com
Dialysis Stations: 8.

Claremore

26535 ■ DaVita--Claremore Dialysis Facility
202 E Blue Starr Dr.
Claremore, OK 74017
Free: 800-424-6589
URL: http://www.davita.com
Dialysis Stations: 16.

Clinton

26536 ■ DaVita--Clinton Dialysis Facility
150 S 31st St.
Clinton, OK 73601

Free: 800-424-6589
URL: http://www.davita.com
Dialysis Stations: 16.

Duncan

26537 ■ DaVita--Duncan
Dialysis Facility
2645 W Elk
Duncan, OK 73533
Free: 800-424-6589
URL: http://www.davita.com
Dialysis Stations: 10. **Formerly:** Renal Treatment Center.

Durant

26538 ■ Durant Dialysis
DaVita
411 Westside Dr.
Durant, OK 74701
Free: 800-424-6589
URL: http://www.davita.com
Dialysis Stations: 16.

Edmond

26539 ■ Edmond Dialysis Center
DaVita
Dialysis Facility
50 S Baumann Ave.
Edmond, OK 73034
Free: 800-424-6589
URL: http://www.davita.com
Dialysis Stations: 12.

El Reno

26540 ■ Fresenius Medical Care--El Reno
Dialysis Services
1629-B E Hwy. 66
El Reno, OK 73036
Free: 866-434-2597
URL: http://www.ultracare-dialysis.com/
Dialysis Stations: 17.

Elk City

26541 ■ Elk City Dialysis
DaVita
Dialysis Facility
1601 W 2nd St.
Elk City, OK 73644
Free: 800-424-6589
URL: http://www.davita.com
Dialysis Stations: 12.

Enid

26542 ■ Enid Dialysis Center
Fresenius Medical Care
121 W Owen K Garriott
Enid, OK 73701
Free: 866-434-2597
URL: http://www.ultracare-dialysis.com/
Dialysis Stations: 16.

Henryetta

26543 ■ Fresenius Medical Care--Henryetta
2405 W Main St., Ste. A
Henryetta, OK 74437
Free: 866-434-2597
URL: http://www.ultracare-dialysis.com/
Dialysis Stations: 12.

Lawton

26544 ■ Fresenius Medical Care--Lawton
Dialysis Facility
Eisenhower Sq., Ste. 1
5110-12 W Gore Blvd.
Lawton, OK 73505
Free: 866-434-2597
URL: http://www.ultracare-dialysis.com/
Dialysis Stations: 24. **Formerly:** Renal Care Group.

26545 ■ Fresenius Medical Care--Lawton East
4516 SE Lee Blvd., Ste. 108
Lawton, OK 73501
Free: 866-434-2597
URL: http://www.ultracare-dialysis.com/
Dialysis Stations: 23.

26546 ■ Sooner Dialysis--Lawton
Liberty Dialysis
924 SW 38th St.
Lawton, OK 73505
Ph: (580)351-1716
URL: http://www.libertydialysis.com
Dialysis Stations: 20.

McAlester

26547 ■ McAlester Regional Dialysis Center LLC
2 Clark Bass Blvd., Ste. 101
McAlester, OK 74501
Ph: (918)421-8373
URL: http://www.mrhcok.com
Dialysis Stations: 12.

Miami

26548 ■ Fresenius Medical Care--Miami Midwest
Dialysis Center
2111 Denver Harner Dr.
Miami, OK 74354
Free: 866-434-2597
URL: http://www.ultracare-dialysis.com/
Dialysis Stations: 12. **Formerly:** Renal Care Group.

26549 ■ Tri--State Dialysis
DaVita
2510 N Main
Miami, OK 74354
Free: 800-424-6589
URL: http://www.davita.com
Dialysis Stations: 18. **Formerly:** DaVita--Miami.

Midwest City

26550 ■ DaVita--Midwest City
Dialysis Center
7221 E Reno Ave.
Midwest City, OK 73110
Free: 800-424-6589
URL: http://www.davita.com
Dialysis Stations: 16.

26551 ■ Fresenius Medical Care--Heritage Park
Dialysis Services
310 S Highland Ave.
Midwest City, OK 73110
Free: 866-434-2597
URL: http://www.ultracare-dialysis.com/
Dialysis Stations: 20. **Formerly:** Mid-Del Regional Dialysis Center.

Muskogee

26552 ■ DaVita
Muskogee Community
Dialysis Center
2316 W Shawnee St.
Muskogee, OK 74401
Free: 800-424-6589
URL: http://www.davita.com
Dialysis Stations: 10. **Formerly:** DaVita.

26553 ■ Muskogee Dialysis Center
Fresenius Medical Care
3371 W Broadway
Muskogee, OK 74401
Free: 866-434-2597
URL: http://www.ultracare-dialysis.com/
Dialysis Stations: 21.

Norman

26554 ■ DaVita--Norman
Dialysis Facility
1818 W Lindsey, Bldg. B, Ste. 104
Norman, OK 73069
Free: 800-424-6589
URL: http://www.davita.com
Dialysis Stations: 12.

26555 ■ Sooner Dialysis Center--Norman
Fresenius Medical Care
1561 Porter Ave.
Norman, OK 73071
Free: 866-434-2597
URL: http://www.ultracare-dialysis.com/
Dialysis Stations: 20.

Oklahoma City

26556 ■ Cinema Dialysis
DaVita
3909 S Western Ave.
Oklahoma City, OK 73109
Free: 800-424-6589
URL: http://www.davita.com
Dialysis Stations: 12.

26557 ■ DaVita--Oklahoma City South
5730 S May Ave.
Oklahoma City, OK 73119
Free: 800-424-6589
URL: http://www.davita.com
Dialysis Stations: 16. **Formerly:** DVA Renal Healthcare.

26558 ■ Fresenius Medical Care--Morning Star
3806 N Barr
Oklahoma City, OK 73122
Free: 866-434-2597
URL: http://www.ultracare-dialysis.com/
Dialysis Stations: 7. **Formerly:** Bio-Medical Applications of Morning Star.

26559 ■ Fresenius Medical Care--North Central Oklahoma City
200 NE 50th St.
Oklahoma City, OK 73105
Free: 866-434-2597
URL: http://www.ultracare-dialysis.com/
Dialysis Stations: 17. **Formerly:** Dialysis Specialists--Central Oklahoma.

26560 ■ Fresenius Medical Care--Northwest Oklahoma City
3107 NW 50th St.
Oklahoma City, OK 73112
Free: 866-434-2597
URL: http://www.ultracare-dialysis.com/
Dialysis Stations: 12.

26561 ■ Fresenius Medical Care--Oklahoma City
Dialysis Services
1011 N Dewey, Ste. 300
Oklahoma City, OK 73102
Free: 866-434-2597
URL: http://www.ultracare-dialysis.com/
Dialysis Stations: 21.

26562 ■ Fresenius Medical Care--South OKC
5419 S Western
Oklahoma City, OK 73109
Free: 866-434-2597
URL: http://www.ultracare-dialysis.com/
Dialysis Stations: 18.

26563 ■ Fresenius Medical Care--Southwest Oklahoma City
10301 Greenbriar Pkwy.
Oklahoma City, OK 73139
Free: 866-434-2597
URL: http://www.ultracare-dialysis.com/
Dialysis Stations: 17.

26564 ■ Heartland Dialysis
Davita
Dialysis Facility & At Home
925 NE 8th St.
Oklahoma City, OK 73104
Free: 800-424-6589
URL: http://www.davita.com
Dialysis Stations: 32. **Formerly:** Gambro Healthcare - UNV.

26565 ■ Integris Baptist Medical Center--Transplant
Renal Transplant 100-3440
Oklahoma City, OK 73112
Ph: (405)949-3816
URL: http://integrisok.com/baptist
Dialysis Stations: 0.

26566 ■ Medical Plaza Dialysis
Fresenius Medical Care
Dialysis Services
3435 NW 56th St., Ste. 600
Oklahoma City, OK 73112
Free: 866-434-2597
URL: http://www.ultracare-dialysis.com/
Dialysis Stations: 20.

26567 ■ Oklahoma Kidney Care Dialysis LLC
13901 Mcauley Blvd., Ste. 102
Oklahoma City, OK 73134
Ph: (405)748-5812
Dialysis Stations: 16.

26568 ■ Oklahoma University Medical Center Children's Dialysis
1200 Everett Dr., Ste. 6015
Oklahoma City, OK 73104
Ph: (405)271-3302
URL: http://www.ouphysicians.com
Dialysis Stations: 6.

26569 ■ St. Anthony Hospital--Transplant
1000 N Lee
Oklahoma City, OK 73101
Ph: (405)272-7164
URL: http://www.ssmhc.com/internet/home/saintsok.nsf/documents/96922A77C9FE41838625751C004C183B
Dialysis Stations: 0.

Okmulgee

26570 ■ DaVita--Okmulgee
Dialysis Facility
201 S Delaware Ave.
Okmulgee, OK 74447
Free: 800-424-6589
URL: http://www.davita.com
Dialysis Stations: 16. **Formerly:** Hillcrest/Okmulgee Dialysis Facility.

Pauls Valley

26571 ■ Fresenius Medical Care--Pauls Valley
310 S Chickasaw
Pauls Valley, OK 73075
Free: 866-434-2597
URL: http://www.ultracare-dialysis.com/
Dialysis Stations: 10.

Ponca City

26572 ■ Fresenius Medical Care--Ponca City Dialysis Facility
1208 E Hartford
Ponca City, OK 74601
Free: 866-434-2597
URL: http://www.ultracare-dialysis.com/
Dialysis Stations: 12. **Formerly:** Renal Care Group.

Poteau

26573 ■ Poteau Dialysis Center
1200 Central St.
Poteau, OK 74953
Ph: (918)647-9373
Dialysis Stations: 12. **Formerly:** Hillcrest/Poteau Regional Dialysis Facility.

Pryor

26574 ■ DaVita--Pryor
Dialysis Center
309 E Graham Ave.
Pryor, OK 74361
Free: 800-424-6589
Dialysis Stations: 14. **Formerly:** Gambro Healthcare.

Sapulpa

26575 ■ Saint John--Sapulpa Dialysis
1013 Cleveland
Sapulpa, OK 74066
Ph: (918)227-3351
URL: http://www.sjmc.org
Dialysis Stations: 12.

Seminole

26576 ■ Dialysis Specialists of Seminole
12581 N S 3540 CR
Seminole, OK 74818
Ph: (405)382-9809
Dialysis Stations: 13.

Shawnee

26577 ■ DaVita--Shawnee
Dialysis Facility
4409 N Kickapoo Ave.
Shawnee, OK 74804
Free: 800-424-6589
URL: http://www.davita.com
Dialysis Stations: 16.

26578 ■ Fresenius Medical Care--Shawnee
Dialysis Services
3807 N Harrison
Shawnee, OK 74801
Free: 866-434-2597
URL: http://www.ultracare-dialysis.com/
Dialysis Stations: 25. **Formerly:** Bio-Medical Applications of Shawnee.

Stillwater

26579 ■ DaVita--Stillwater
Dialysis Facility
406 E Hall of Fame, Ste. 300
Stillwater, OK 74075
Free: 800-424-6589
URL: http://www.davita.com
Dialysis Stations: 12.

26580 ■ Fresenius Medical Care--Stillwater
Dialysis Center
1921 W 6th Ave., Bldg. B
Stillwater, OK 74074
Free: 866-434-2597
URL: http://www.ultracare-dialysis.com/
Dialysis Stations: 10. **Formerly:** Stillwater Medical Center.

Stilwell

26581 ■ Stilwell Dialysis Facility
DaVita
319 N 2nd St.
Stilwell, OK 74960
Free: 800-424-6589
URL: http://www.davita.com
Dialysis Stations: 10.

Tahlequah

26582 ■ DaVita--Tahlequah
Dialysis Facility
228 N Bliss Ave.
Tahlequah, OK 74464
Free: 800-424-6589
URL: http://www.davita.com
Dialysis Stations: 21.

Tulsa

26583 ■ DaVita--Central Tulsa
Dialysis Facility
1124 S St. Louis Ave.
Tulsa, OK 74120
Free: 800-424-6589
URL: http://www.davita.com
Dialysis Stations: 26. **Formerly:** Hillcrest Medical Center Dialysis Center.

26584 ■ DaVita--Southcrest
9001 S 101 East Ave., Ste. 110
Tulsa, OK 74133
Free: 800-424-6589
URL: http://www.davita.com
Dialysis Stations: 16.

26585 ■ DaVita--Tulsa
Dialysis Facility & At Home
4436 S Harvard Ave.
Tulsa, OK 74135
Free: 800-424-6589
URL: http://www.davita.com
Dialysis Stations: 20.

26586 ■ Fresenius Medical Care--East Tulsa
5147 S Garnett Rd., Ste. C
Tulsa, OK 74146
Free: 866-434-2597
URL: http://www.ultracare-dialysis.com/
Dialysis Stations: 12.

26587 ■ Fresenius Medical Care--North Tulsa
2309 W Edison Ste. A
Tulsa, OK 74127
Free: 866-434-2597
URL: http://www.ultracare-dialysis.com/
Dialysis Stations: 13.

26588 ■ Fresenius Medical Care--South Tulsa
8260 S Lewis
Tulsa, OK 74137
Free: 866-434-2597
URL: http://www.ultracare-dialysis.com/
Dialysis Stations: 23.

26589 ■ Greenwood Dialysis
DaVita
1345 N Lansing Ave.
Tulsa, OK 74106
Free: 800-424-6589
URL: http://www.davita.com
Dialysis Stations: 12.

26590 ■ Saint Francis Hospital
Dialysis Center
6161 S Yale Ave.
Tulsa, OK 74136
Ph: (918)494-5575
URL: http://www.saintfrancis.com
Dialysis Stations: 20.

26591 ■ Saint John Kidney Center--North Harvard
1515 N Harvard, Ste. D
Tulsa, OK 74115
Ph: (918)835-5599
URL: http://www.sjmc.org
Dialysis Stations: 28.

26592 ■ Saint John Kidney Center
Transplant and Dialysis Center
1923 E 21st St.
Tulsa, OK 74114

Ph: (918)744-3540
URL: http://www.sjmc.org
Dialysis Stations: 23.

26593 ■ Sapulpa Dialysis
DaVita
9647 Ridgeview St.
Tulsa, OK 74131
Free: 800-424-6589
URL: http://www.davita.com
Dialysis Stations: 16.

Woodward

26594 ■ Fresenius Medical Care--Woodward Dialysis Center
909 18th St.
Woodward, OK 73801
Free: 866-434-2597
URL: http://www.ultracare-dialysis.com/
Dialysis Stations: 12.

OREGON

Albany

26595 ■ Qualicenters Albany Dialysis Center
Fresenius Medical Care
1050 7th Ave. SW
Albany, OR 97321
Free: 866-434-2597
URL: http://www.ultracare-dialysis.com/
Dialysis Stations: 14.

Astoria

26596 ■ Fresenius Medical Care--Astoria
2120 Exchange St., Ste. 100
Astoria, OR 97103
Free: 866-434-2597
URL: http://www.ultracare-dialysis.com/
Dialysis Stations: 12. **Formerly:** Renal Care Group/Pacific Northwest Renal Services/North Coast Dialysis Clinic.

Beaverton

26597 ■ Fresenius Medical Care--Beaverton
271 SW 153rd Dr.
Beaverton, OR 97006
Free: 866-434-2597
URL: http://www.ultracare-dialysis.com/
Dialysis Stations: 21. **Formerly:** PNRS.

26598 ■ Fresenius Medical Care--Twin Oaks Dialysis Facility
1815 NW 169th Pl., Ste. 1000
Beaverton, OR 97006
Free: 866-434-2597
URL: http://www.ultracare-dialysis.com/
Dialysis Stations: 15. **Formerly:** Legacy Twin Oaks Dialysis Center.

Bend

26599 ■ Qualicenters Bend Dialysis Center
Fresenius Medical Care
2275 NE Doctors Dr., Ste. 1
Bend, OR 97701
Free: 866-434-2597
URL: http://www.ultracare-dialysis.com/
Dialysis Stations: 15.

Clackamas

26600 ■ Clackamas Kidney Center
Fresenius Medical Care
13560 SE 97th St.
Clackamas, OR 97015
Free: 866-434-2597
URL: http://www.ultracare-dialysis.com/
Dialysis Stations: 21. **Formerly:** Renal Care Group.

Coos Bay

26601 ■ Qualicenters Coos Bay Dialysis Center
Fresenius Medical Care
1971 Thompson Rd.
Coos Bay, OR 97420
Free: 866-434-2597
URL: http://www.ultracare-dialysis.com/
Dialysis Stations: 21.

Corvallis

26602 ■ Samaritan Dialysis--Corvallis
Good Samaritan Regional Medical Center
3580 NW Samaritan Dr.
Corvallis, OR 97330
Ph: (541)768-5182
URL: http://www.samhealth.org/shs_facilities/gsrmc/hospital_services/dialysisser vices.html
Dialysis Stations: 12.

Eugene

26603 ■ Oregon Dialysis Services
Fresenius Medical Care
201 River Ave.
Eugene, OR 97401
Free: 866-434-2597
URL: http://www.ultracare-dialysis.com/
Dialysis Stations: 25.

Forest Grove

26604 ■ Raines Dialysis
Fresenius Medical Care
Dialysis Center
1809 Maple St.
Forest Grove, OR 97116
Free: 866-434-2597
Dialysis Stations: 12. **Formerly:** Renal Care Group/Pacific Northwest Renal Services.

Grants Pass

26605 ■ Redwood Dialysis
DaVita
201 SW L St.
Grants Pass, OR 97526
Free: 800-424-6589
URL: http://www.davita.com
Dialysis Stations: 12.

Gresham

26606 ■ Dialysis Services of Mount Hood
Fresenius Medical Care
100 SE Cleveland
Gresham, OR 97080
Free: 866-434-2597
URL: http://www.ultracare-dialysis.com/
Dialysis Stations: 12.

26607 ■ Gresham Dialysis Center
Innovative Dialysis Systems
1360 E Powell Blvd.
Gresham, OR 97030
Ph: (503)465-1650
URL: http://www.idsdialysis.com
Dialysis Stations: 12.

Hermiston

26608 ■ Hermiston Community Dialysis Center & At Home
DaVita
1155 W Linda Ave., Ste. A
Hermiston, OR 97838
Free: 800-424-6589
URL: http://www.davita.com
Dialysis Stations: 13.

Hillsboro

26609 ■ Hillsboro Dialysis Center & At Home
DaVita
2500 NW 229th Ave., Bldg. E, Ste. 300
Hillsboro, OR 97124
Free: 800-424-6589
URL: http://www.davita.com
Dialysis Stations: 13.

Hood River

26610 ■ Providence Ray Yasui Dialysis Center
810 12th St.
Box 149
Hood River, OR 97031
Ph: (541)386-3911
Free: 800-955-3911
URL: http://www.providence.org/hoodriver/services/dialysis_center/default.htm
Dialysis Stations: 13. **Formerly:** Hood River Memorial Hospital.

Klamath Falls

26611 ■ Klamath Falls Dialysis
DaVita
Meale W Medical Center
2230 Eldorado Blvd.
Klamath Falls, OR 97601
Free: 800-424-6589
URL: http://www.davita.com
Dialysis Stations: 8. **Formerly:** West Dialysis Center.

La Grande

26612 ■ Eastern Oregon Dialysis Clinic
Fresenius Medical Care
710 Sunset Dr., Ste. A
La Grande, OR 97850
Free: 866-434-2597
URL: http://www.ultracare-dialysis.com/
Dialysis Stations: 9. **Formerly:** Renal Care Group/Pacific Northwest Renal Services.

Lebanon

26613 ■ Samaritan Dialysis--Lebanon Dialysis Facility
Good Samaritan Regional Medical Center
55 Twin Oak Ave., Ste. C2
Lebanon, OR 97355
Ph: (541)451-7865
URL: http://www.samhealth.org/shs_facilities/gsrmc/hospital_services/dialysisser vices.html
Dialysis Stations: 8.

McMinnville

26614 ■ Fresenius Medical Care--McMinnville Dialysis Facility
345 SE Norton Ln., Ste. B
McMinnville, OR 97128
Free: 866-434-2597
URL: http://www.ultracare-dialysis.com/
Dialysis Stations: 12. **Formerly:** Renal Care Group/Pacific Northwest Renal Services.

Medford

26615 ■ Rogue Valley Dialysis Services
DaVita
760 Golf View Dr.
Medford, OR 97504
Free: 800-424-6589
URL: http://www.davita.com
Dialysis Stations: 39.

Milwaukee

26616 ■ Sunnyside Renal Center
Diversified Specialty Institutes Dialysis Services
6902 SE Lake Rd., Ste. 100
Milwaukee, OR 97267

Ph: (503)794-1288
URL: http://www.dsi-corp.com
Dialysis Stations: 21. **Formerly:** Fresenius Medical Care--Lake Road.

Newberg

26617 ■ Newberg Dialysis Center
Fresenius Medical Care
3100 Haworth Ave.
Newberg, OR 97132
Free: 866-434-2597
URL: http://www.ultracare-dialysis.com/
Dialysis Stations: 12. **Formerly:** Renal Care Group.

Newport

26618 ■ Samaritan Pacific Dialysis
Samaritan Health Services
930 SW Abbey St.
Newport, OR 97365
Ph: (541)574-4870
URL: http://www.samhealth.org/Pages/default.aspx
Dialysis Stations: 12.

Ontario

26619 ■ Four Rivers Dialysis Center & At Home
DaVita
515 E Lane
Ontario, OR 97914
Free: 800-424-6589
URL: http://www.davita.com
Dialysis Stations: 13. **Formerly:** Saint Alphonsus Nephrology Center--Ontario.

Oregon City

26620 ■ Willamette Valley Kidney Center
Diversified Specialty Institutes
1510 Division St., Ste. 90
Oregon City, OR 97045
Ph: (503)557-1373
Fax: (503)557-1087
URL: http://www.dsi-corp.com
Dialysis Stations: 10. **Formerly:** National Renal Institutes.

Pendleton

26621 ■ Blue Mountain Kidney Center
DaVita
72556 Coyote Rd.
Pendleton, OR 97801
Free: 800-424-6589
URL: http://www.davita.com
Dialysis Stations: 13.

Portland

26622 ■ Emanuel Inpatient & Pediatric Dialysis
Fresenius Medical Care
2801 N Gantenbein Rm. 4400
Portland, OR 97227
Free: 866-434-2597
URL: http://www.ultracare-dialysis.com/
Dialysis Stations: 5.

26623 ■ Fresenius Medical Care--Hollywood Dialysis Center
2824 NE Wasco St.
Portland, OR 97232
Free: 866-434-2597
URL: http://www.ultracare-dialysis.com/
Dialysis Stations: 20. **Formerly:** Renal Care Group/ Pacific Northwest Renal Services.

26624 ■ Fresenius Medical Care--Pacific Northwest
Dialysis Facility
2300 SW 6th Ave., Ste. 101
Portland, OR 97201
Free: 866-434-2597
URL: http://www.ultracare-dialysis.com/
Dialysis Stations: 4. **Formerly:** Renal Care Group/ Northwest Renal Services Home Dialysis.

26625 ■ Fresenius Medical Care--Rose Quarter
Dialysis Center
3131 N Vancouver Ave., Ste. 200
Portland, OR 97227
Free: 866-434-2597
URL: http://www.ultracare-dialysis.com/
Dialysis Stations: 25. **Formerly:** Renal Care Group.

26626 ■ Legacy Transplant Services
Legacy Health
1040 NW 22nd Ave., Ste. 480
Portland, OR 97210
Ph: (503)413-6555
URL: http://www.legacyhealth.org/body.cfm?id=833&fr=true
Dialysis Stations: 0.

26627 ■ Northeast Oregon Renal Center
Diversified Specialty Institutes
Dialysis Services
5318 NE Irving
Portland, OR 97213
Ph: (503)284-1939
URL: http://www.dsi-corp.com
Dialysis Stations: 24. **Formerly:** National Renal Institutes.

26628 ■ Northeast Portland Renal Center
Diversified Specialty Institute
703 NE Hancock
Portland, OR 97212
Ph: (503)493-3322
URL: http://www.dsi-corp.com
Dialysis Stations: 15. **Formerly:** FMC Dialysis.

26629 ■ Oregon Health and Science Univ. Clinical Transplant Program
3505 SW US Veterans Hospital Rd. CB569
Portland, OR 97239
Ph: (503)494-8472
URL: http://www.ohsu.edu/transplant/
Dialysis Stations: 0.

26630 ■ Portland Dialysis Center
Innovative Dialysis Systems
10595 SE Stark St.
Portland, OR 97216
Ph: (503)252-0019
URL: http://www.idsdialysis.com
Dialysis Stations: 15.

26631 ■ Portland Home Dialysis Clinic
Peritoneal Dialysis Center
Innovative Dialysis Systems
11300 NE Halsey, Ste. 220
Portland, OR 97220
Ph: (503)254-4426
URL: http://www.idsdialysis.com
Dialysis Stations: 2.

26632 ■ Providence Portland Medical Center
Dialysis Unit
4805 NE Glisan
Portland, OR 97213
Ph: (503)215-6021
URL: http://www.providence.org/oregon/facilities/hospitals/providence_portland
Dialysis Stations: 12.

26633 ■ Providence--Saint Vincent Medical Center
Dialysis Center
9450 SW Barnes Rd., Ste. 125
Portland, OR 97225
Ph: (503)216-1234
URL: http://www.providence.org/oregon/facilities/hospitals/providence_st_vincent
Dialysis Stations: 21.

26634 ■ Rose Quarter Dialysis
Fresenius Medical Care
4905 NE Martin Luther King Blvd.
Portland, OR 97211
Free: 866-434-2597
URL: http://www.ultracare-dialysis.com/
Dialysis Stations: 25.

Redmond

26635 ■ Fresenius Medical Care--Redmond
916 SW 17th St., Ste. 100
Redmond, OR 97756
Free: 866-434-2597
URL: http://www.ultracare-dialysis.com/
Dialysis Stations: 16.

Roseburg

26636 ■ Roseburg/Mercy Dialysis & At Home
DaVita
2599 NW Edenbower Blvd.
Roseburg, OR 97471
Free: 800-424-6589
URL: http://www.davita.com
Dialysis Stations: 12. **Formerly:** Grambo Healthcare.

Saint Helens

26637 ■ St. Helens Dialysis
Fresenius Medical Care
500 N Columbia River Hwy., Ste. 510
Saint Helens, OR 97051
Free: 866-434-2597
URL: http://www.ultracare-dialysis.com/
Dialysis Stations: 13.

Salem

26638 ■ Fresenius Medical Care--West Salem
1060 2nd St. NW
Salem, OR 97304
Free: 866-434-2597
URL: http://www.ultracare-dialysis.com/
Dialysis Stations: 13.

26639 ■ Qualicenters Salem
Dialysis Center
Fresenius Medical Care
3878 Beverly Ave. NE, Bldg. H, Ste. 11
Salem, OR 97305
Free: 866-434-2597
URL: http://www.ultracare-dialysis.com/
Dialysis Stations: 29.

26640 ■ Salem Dialysis
Dialysis Center & At Home
DaVita
3550 Liberty Rd. S, Ste. 100
Salem, OR 97302
Free: 800-424-6589
Dialysis Stations: 25. **Formerly:** Grambo Healthcare.

26641 ■ Salem North Dialysis
DaVita
1220 Liberty St. NE
Salem, OR 97303
Free: 800-424-6589
URL: http://www.davita.com
Dialysis Stations: 12. **Formerly:** Grambo Healthcare.

Sherwood

26642 ■ Sherwood Dialysis Center
DaVita
21035 SW Pacific Hwy.
Sherwood, OR 97140
Free: 800-424-6589
URL: http://www.davita.com
Dialysis Stations: 13.

Springfield

26643 ■ Qualicenters Eugene/Springfield Dialysis Center
Fresenius Medical Care
304 Q St.
Springfield, OR 97477
Free: 866-434-2597
URL: http://www.ultracare-dialysis.com/
Dialysis Stations: 17.

Tillamook

26644 ■ Tillamook Dialysis Center
Innovative Dialysis Systems
1000 3rd St.
Tillamook, OR 97141
Ph: (503)842-0444
URL: http://www.idsdialysis.com
Dialysis Stations: 6.

Tualatin

26645 ■ Fresenius Medical Care--Tualatin
7780 SW Mohawk St.
Tualatin, OR 97062
Free: 866-434-2597
URL: http://www.ultracare-dialysis.com/
Dialysis Stations: 25. **Formerly:** Renal Care Group.

26646 ■ Meridian Park Dialysis Center & At Home
DaVita
19255 SW 65th Ave., Ste. 100
Tualatin, OR 97062
Free: 800-424-6589
URL: http://www.davita.com
Dialysis Stations: 14. **Formerly:** Lake Oswego Dialysis Center.

West Linn

26647 ■ West Linn Dialysis Center
DaVita
19056 Williamette Dr.
West Linn, OR 97068
Free: 800-424-6589
URL: http://www.davita.com
Dialysis Stations: 13.

Woodburn

26648 ■ DaVita--Woodburn Dialysis Center
1840 Newberg Hwy., Ste. 140
Woodburn, OR 97071
Free: 800-424-6589
URL: http://www.davita.com
Dialysis Stations: 12.

PENNSYLVANIA

Aliquippa

26649 ■ Liberty Dialysis--Hopewell
400 Corporation Dr.
Aliquippa, PA 15001
Ph: (724)378-6304
URL: http://www.libertydialysis.com
Dialysis Stations: 22.

Allentown

26650 ■ Fresenius Medical Care--Allentown Dialysis Services
3136 Hamilton St.
Allentown, PA 18103
Free: 866-434-2597
URL: http://www.ultracare-dialysis.com/
Dialysis Stations: 29.

26651 ■ Fresenius Medical Care--South Allentown
2820-2828 Mitchell Ave.
Allentown, PA 18103
Free: 866-434-2597
URL: http://www.ultracare-dialysis.com/
Dialysis Stations: 18.

26652 ■ Lehigh Valley Hospital Dialysis Center
Cedar Crest & D-78
Allentown, PA 18105
Ph: (610)402-1916
URL: http://www.lvh.com
Dialysis Stations: 15.

26653 ■ Lehigh Valley Hospital Transplant Center
Lehigh Valley Health Network
1250 S Cedar Crest Blvd.
Allentown, PA 18103
Ph: (610)402-8506
URL: http://www.lvhn.org/lvh/Your_LVH/Health_Care_Services/Transplant/Organ_Dona tion
Dialysis Stations: 0.

Altoona

26654 ■ Altoona Regional Health System Dialysis Center
620 Howard Ave.
Altoona, PA 16601
Ph: (814)946-2847
URL: http://www.altoonaregional.org
Dialysis Stations: 22.

26655 ■ Bon Secours Hospital Dialysis
Altoona Regional Health System
2500 Seventh Ave.
Altoona, PA 16602
Ph: (814)949-4212
E-mail: info@altoonaregional.org
URL: http://www.altoonaregional.org/contact.htm
Dialysis Stations: 2.

26656 ■ Fresenius Medical Care--Altoona Dialysis Facility
2525 9th Ave., Ste. 1C
Altoona, PA 16602
Free: 866-434-2597
URL: http://www.ultracare-dialysis.com/
Dialysis Stations: 10.

Armstrong

26657 ■ Dialysis Clinic Inc.--Parks Bend
1143 Industrial Park Rd.
Armstrong, PA 15690
Ph: (724)845-3313
URL: http://www.dciinc.org
Dialysis Stations: 19.

Baden

26658 ■ Liberty Dialysis--Baden
1682 State St.
Baden, PA 15005
Ph: (724)869-2830
URL: http://www.libertydialysis.com
Dialysis Stations: 18.

Beaver

26659 ■ Liberty Dialysis--Friendship Ridge
246 Friendship Cir.
Beaver, PA 15009
Ph: (724)728-4320
URL: http://www.libertydialysis.com
Dialysis Stations: 6.

Beaver Falls

26660 ■ Dialysis Clinic, Inc.--Beaver Falls/Chippewa
2562 Constitution Blvd.
Beaver Falls, PA 15010
Ph: (724)891-5044
URL: http://www.dciinc.org
Dialysis Stations: 33.

26661 ■ Liberty Dialysis--Chippewa
100 Pappan Business Dr.
Beaver Falls, PA 15010
Ph: (724)846-5030
URL: http://www.libertydialysis.com
Dialysis Stations: 26.

Bensalem

26662 ■ Belmont Court Dialysis--Torresdale Campus
1 Woodhaven Mall, Ste. 100
Bensalem, PA 19020
Ph: (215)633-1231
Dialysis Stations: 20.

26663 ■ Bensalem Dialysis Center
American Renal Associates
1336 Bristol Pike
Bensalem, PA 19020
Ph: (303)403-1127
URL: http://www.americanrenal.com
Dialysis Stations: 21.

26664 ■ Woodhaven Dialysis Center
1336 Bristol Pike, Ste. B
Bensalem, PA 19020
Ph: (215)639-1070
Dialysis Stations: 12.

Berwick

26665 ■ Fresenius Medical Care--Berwick
301 Market St.
Berwick, PA 18603
Free: 866-434-2597
URL: http://www.ultracare-dialysis.com/
Dialysis Stations: 13.

Bethel Park

26666 ■ Fresenius Medical Care of South Hills
Dialysis Facility
4651 Library Rd.
Bethel Park, PA 15102
Free: 866-434-2597
URL: http://www.ultracare-dialysis.com/
Dialysis Stations: 18.

Bethlehem

26667 ■ Fresenius Medical Care of Bethlehem
Dialysis Services
2014 City Line Rd., Ste. 200
Bethlehem, PA 18017
Free: 866-434-2597
URL: http://www.ultracare-dialysis.com/
Dialysis Stations: 25.

26668 ■ Saint Luke's Hospital Dialysis Center
801 Ostrum St.
Bethlehem, PA 18015
Ph: (610)954-4894
URL: http://www.mystlukesonline.org
Dialysis Stations: 23.

26669 ■ Saint Luke's North Dialysis Center, LP
89 S Commerce Way, Ste. 900
Bethlehem, PA 18017
Ph: (610)954-2888
URL: http://www.mystlukesonline.org
Dialysis Stations: 20.

Bradford

26670 ■ Bradford Dialysis
DaVita
Dialysis Center & At Home
665 E Main St.
Bradford, PA 16701
Free: 800-424-6589
URL: http://www.davita.com
Dialysis Stations: 13. **Formerly:** Gambro Healthcare.

Bristol

26671 ■ Dialysis Center of Bucks County
American Renal Associates
1900 Frost Rd.
Bristol, PA 19007
Ph: (215)785-0382
URL: http://www.americanrenal.com
Dialysis Stations: 20.

Brookville

26672 ■ Kidney Care Services of Brookville
477 Rte. 28
Brookville, PA 15825
Ph: (814)849-8894
Dialysis Stations: 9.

Brownsville

26673 ■ Fresenius Medical Care of Redstone
685 National Pke. E
Brownsville, PA 15417
Free: 866-434-2597
URL: http://www.ultracare-dialysis.com/
Dialysis Stations: 14.

Bryn Mawr

26674 ■ Bryn Mawr Dialysis Services
Fresenius Medical Care
The Clothier Bldg.
130 S Bryn Mawr Ave.
Bryn Mawr, PA 19010
Free: 866-434-2597
URL: http://www.ultracare-dialysis.com/
Dialysis Stations: 13. **Formerly:** Renal Care Group.

Butler

26675 ■ Butler County Dialysis Center
American Renal Associates
229 W Diamond St.
Butler, PA 16001
Ph: (724)431-2241
URL: http://www.americanrenal.com
Dialysis Stations: 21.

Camp Hill

26676 ■ Camp Hill Dialysis Center & At Home
DaVita
Plaza 21 Bldg., 1st Fl.
425 N 21st St.
Camp Hill, PA 17011
Free: 800-424-6589
URL: http://www.davita.com
Dialysis Stations: 25.

26677 ■ Dialysis Corporation of America of Camp Hill
158 S 32nd St., Ste. 19
Camp Hill, PA 17011
Ph: (717)731-0506
Fax: (717)731-0508
URL: http://www.dialysiscorporation.com
Dialysis Stations: 24.

26678 ■ Fresenius Medical Care--Camp Hill
240 Grandview Ave., Ste. 200
Camp Hill, PA 17011
Free: 866-434-2597
URL: http://www.ultracare-dialysis.com/
Dialysis Stations: 17.

Canonsburg

26679 ■ Dialysis Clinic Inc.--Hillpointe
131 Hillpointe Dr.
Canonsburg, PA 15317
Ph: (724)873-1242
URL: http://www.dciinc.org
Dialysis Stations: 23.

26680 ■ Liberty Dialysis--Southpointe
1200 Corporate Dr.
Canonsburg, PA 15317
Ph: (724)745-5565
URL: http://www.libertydialysis.com
Dialysis Stations: 22.

Carlisle

26681 ■ Dialysis Corporation of America of Carlisle
101 Noble Blvd., Ste. 103
Carlisle, PA 17013
Ph: (717)258-3099
URL: http://www.dialysiscorporation.com
Dialysis Stations: 14. **Formerly:** Dialysis Services of Pennsylvania, Inc.

26682 ■ Fresenius Medical Care--Cumberland County
Dialysis Services
254 E High St.
Carlisle, PA 17013
Free: 866-434-2597
URL: http://www.ultracare-dialysis.com/
Dialysis Stations: 16.

Carmichaels

26683 ■ Fresenius Medical Care--Greene County
Dialysis Services
11 Industrial Park Rd.
Carmichaels, PA 15320
Free: 866-434-2597
URL: http://www.ultracare-dialysis.com/
Dialysis Stations: 12.

Chambersburg

26684 ■ Dialysis Corporation of America--Chambersburg
Park Fifth Ave. Professional Center, Ste. A
765 Fifth Ave.
Chambersburg, PA 17201
Ph: (717)263-9300
URL: http://www.dialysiscorporation.com
Dialysis Stations: 21.

26685 ■ Fresenius Medical Care--Chabersburg
755 Norland Ave.
Chambersburg, PA 17201
Free: 866-434-2597
URL: http://www.ultracare-dialysis.com/
Dialysis Stations: 21.

Charleroi

26686 ■ Dialysis Services of Mon Valley
Fresenius Medical Care
Vista One Professional Center
17 Arentzen Blvd., Ste. 105
Charleroi, PA 15022
Free: 866-434-2597
URL: http://www.ultracare-dialysis.com/
Dialysis Stations: 13.

Cheswick

26687 ■ Dialysis Clinic Inc.--Harmar Village
725 Freeport Rd.
Cheswick, PA 15024
Ph: (724)275-7801
URL: http://www.dciinc.org
Dialysis Stations: 14.

Childs

26688 ■ Childs Dialysis
DaVita
101 S Main St.
Childs, PA 18407
Free: 800-424-6589
URL: http://www.davita.com
Dialysis Stations: 8. **Formerly:** Moses Taylor Regional Dialysis System.

Clairton

26689 ■ Fresenius Medical Care--Clairton
South Hills Medical Bldg., Ste. 262
575 Coal Valley Rd.
Clairton, PA 15025
Free: 866-434-2597
URL: http://www.ultracare-dialysis.com/
Dialysis Stations: 13. **Program(s):** In-Center Noctornal Program; Home Training & Home support. **Formerly:** Renal Care Group - Clairton.

Clarion

26690 ■ Dialysis Clinic, Inc. of Clarion
65 Dolby St.
Clarion, PA 16214
Ph: (814)227-2222
URL: http://www.dciinc.org
Dialysis Stations: 15.

26691 ■ Renal Care of Clarion
Dreiling Medical Management
825 Main St.
Clarion, PA 16214
Ph: (814)223-4655
Dialysis Stations: 28.

Clearfield

26692 ■ Clearfield Dialysis
DaVita
1033 Turnpike Ave., Ste. 100
Clearfield, PA 16830
Free: 800-424-6589
URL: http://www.davita.com
Dialysis Stations: 10.

Coraopolis

26693 ■ Thorn Run Dialysis
DaVita
1136 Thorn Run Rd.
Coraopolis, PA 15108
Free: 800-424-6589
URL: http://www.davita.com
Dialysis Stations: 15.

Corry

26694 ■ Corry Dialysis
DaVita
Dialysis Center
300 York St.
Corry, PA 16407
Free: 800-424-6589
URL: http://www.davita.com
Dialysis Stations: 12. **Formerly:** Gambro Healthcare.

Cranberry

26695 ■ Renal Care of Oil City Inc.
Dreiling Medical Management
Cranberry Mall, Ste. 640
6945 US Rte. 322
Cranberry, PA 16319
Ph: (814)677-7034
URL: http://www.dreilingmedical.com
Dialysis Stations: 16.

Cranberry Township

26696 ■ Fresenius Medical Care of Cranberry Township
Dialysis Facility
5 St. Francis Way
Cranberry Township, PA 16066
Free: 866-434-2597
URL: http://www.ultracare-dialysis.com/
Dialysis Stations: 7.

Danville

26697 ■ Geisinger Health System
100 N Academy Ave.
Danville, PA 17822-9800
Ph: (570)271-6211
Free: 800-275-6401
Fax: (570)271-7498
URL: http://www.geisinger.org
Glenn D. Steele MD, PhD., Jr., President
Dialysis Stations: 24. **Formerly:** Geisinger Medical Management Corp. (GMMC).

26698 ■ GMC Outpatient Dialysis Unit--Justin Drive
100 Justin Dr.
Danville, PA 17822
Ph: (570)271-6392
Dialysis Stations: 21.

Donora

26699 ■ Fresenius Medical Care--Donora
Dialysis Services
470 Galiffa Dr.
Donora, PA 15033
Free: 866-434-2597
URL: http://www.ultracare-dialysis.com/
Dialysis Stations: 13.

Doylestown

26700 ■ Belmont Court Dialysis Center Inc.
Doylestown Campus
252 Belmont Ave.
Doylestown, PA 18901
Ph: (215)348-7333
Dialysis Stations: 22.

26701 ■ Doylestown Dialysis Center
Fresenius Medical Care
708 Shady Retreat Rd., Ste. 5
Doylestown, PA 18901
Free: 866-434-2597
URL: http://www.ultracare-dialysis.com/
Dialysis Stations: 14. **Formerly:** Renal Care Group.

Du Bois

26702 ■ Dubois Dialysis
DaVita
Dialysis Center
5780 Shaffer Rd.
Du Bois, PA 15801
Free: 800-424-6589
Fax: (814)375-1263
URL: http://www.davita.com
Dialysis Stations: 16. **Formerly:** Gambro Healthcare.

DuBois

26703 ■ Kidney Care Services of DuBois
635 D Maple Ave.
DuBois, PA 15801
Ph: (814)375-6295
Dialysis Stations: 20.

Dunmore

26704 ■ Dunmore Dialysis
DaVita
1212 O'Neal Hwy.
Dunmore, PA 18512
Free: 800-424-6589
URL: http://www.davita.com
Dialysis Stations: 12.

26705 ■ Fresenius Medical Care--Dunmore
1416 Monroe Ave., 1st Fl.
Dunmore, PA 18509
Free: 866-434-2597
URL: http://www.ultracare-dialysis.com/
Dialysis Stations: 15.

East Stroudsburg

26706 ■ Fresenius Medical Care of East Stroudsburg
Dialysis Facility
125 S Courtland St.
East Stroudsburg, PA 18301
Free: 866-434-2597
URL: http://www.ultracare-dialysis.com/
Dialysis Stations: 14.

26707 ■ Pocono Dialysis Center
DaVita
100 Plaza Ct.
East Stroudsburg, PA 18301
Free: 800-424-6589
URL: http://www.davita.com
Dialysis Stations: 16.

Easton

26708 ■ Fresenius Medical Care of Easton
Dialysis Services
3501 Northwood Ave.
Easton, PA 18045
Free: 866-434-2597
URL: http://www.ultracare-dialysis.com/
Dialysis Stations: 30.

26709 ■ Palmer Dialysis Center
DaVita
30 Community Dr.
Easton, PA 18045
Free: 800-424-6589
URL: http://www.davita.com
Dialysis Stations: 20.

Ebensburg

26710 ■ DaVita--Ebensburg
236 Jamesway Rd.
Ebensburg, PA 15931
Free: 800-424-6589
URL: http://www.davita.com
Dialysis Stations: 6.

26711 ■ Prodigy Dialysis, LLC--Ebensburg
429 Manor Dr.
Ebensburg, PA 15931
Ph: (814)419-8107
URL: http://prodigydialysis.com/
Dialysis Stations: 9.

Elizabeth

26712 ■ Elizabeth Dialysis & At Home
DaVita
201 McKeesport Rd.
Elizabeth, PA 15037
Free: 800-424-6589
URL: http://www.davita.com
Dialysis Stations: 12.

26713 ■ Jefferson Dialysis
DaVita
201 McKeesport Rd.
Elizabeth, PA 15037
Free: 800-424-6589
URL: http://www.davita.com
Dialysis Stations: 16.

Elizabethtown

26714 ■ Elizabethtown Dialysis
DaVita
Dialysis Center
844 N Hanover St.
Elizabethtown, PA 17022
Free: 800-424-6589
URL: http://www.davita.com
Dialysis Stations: 12. **Formerly:** Gambro Healthcare.

Ellwood City

26715 ■ Fresenius Medical Care of Ellwood City
Dialysis Services
1407 Woodside Ave.
Ellwood City, PA 16117
Free: 866-434-2597
URL: http://www.ultracare-dialysis.com/
Dialysis Stations: 9.

Erie

26716 ■ Dialysis Center of Erie
DaVita
1641 Sassafras St.
Erie, PA 16502
Free: 800-424-6589
URL: http://www.davita.com
Dialysis Stations: 28.

26717 ■ Erie Dialysis
Dialysis Center & At Home
DaVita
350 E Bayfront Pkwy., Ste. A
Erie, PA 16507
Free: 800-424-6589
URL: http://www.davita.com
Dialysis Stations: 30. **Formerly:** Gambro Healthcare.

Everett

26718 ■ Dialysis Corporation of America of Bedford
141 Memorial Dr.
Everett, PA 15537
Ph: (814)623-2977
URL: http://www.dialysiscorporation.com
Dialysis Stations: 11. **Formerly:** Keystone Kidney Care Inc.

Export

26719 ■ Dialysis Service of Murrysville Inc.
Fresenius Medical Care
20 Wesco Ln.
Export, PA 15632
Free: 866-434-2597
URL: http://www.ultracare-dialysis.com/
Dialysis Stations: 13.

Exton

26720 ■ Exton Dialysis Center
DaVita
710 Springdale Dr.
Exton, PA 19341
Free: 800-424-6589
URL: http://www.davita.com
Dialysis Stations: 36.

Flourtown

26721 ■ Fresenius Medical Care--Harston Hall
350 Haws La.
Flourtown, PA 19031
Free: 866-434-2597
URL: http://www.ultracare-dialysis.com/
Dialysis Stations: 9.

Greensburg

26722 ■ Fresenius Medical Care of Greensburg Inc.
Dialysis Facility
Medical Arts Bldg., Ground Fl.
562 Shearer St.
Greensburg, PA 15601
Free: 866-434-2597
URL: http://www.ultracare-dialysis.com/
Dialysis Stations: 16.

Grove City

26723 ■ Dialysis Clinic, Inc. of Grove City
United Community Hospital
631 N Broad St. Ext.
Grove City, PA 16127
Ph: (724)458-0877
Fax: (724)458-4566
URL: http://www.dciinc.org
Dialysis Stations: 12.

Harrisburg

26724 ■ Cityline Dialysis
Fresenius Medical Care
2601 N 3rd St.
Harrisburg, PA 17110
Free: 866-434-2597
URL: http://www.ultracare-dialysis.com/
Dialysis Stations: 17. **Formerly:** Renal Care Group - Harrisburg.

26725 ■ Fresenius Medical Care Dialysis Services of the Capital Area
1300 Linglestown Rd., 1st Fl.
Harrisburg, PA 17110
Free: 866-434-2597
URL: http://www.ultracare-dialysis.com/
Dialysis Stations: 21.

26726 ■ Fresenius Medical Care of Harrisburg
Dialysis Services
Union Court
4343 Union Deposit Rd.
Harrisburg, PA 17111
Free: 866-434-2597
URL: http://www.ultracare-dialysis.com/
Dialysis Stations: 16. **Formerly:** Bio-Medical Applications of Harrisburg.

26727 ■ Pinnacle Health Transplant Unit at Harrisburg Hospital
111 S Front St.
Harrisburg, PA 17101
Ph: (717)231-8700
URL: http://www.pinnaclehealth.org/services/transplant
Dialysis Stations: 0.

Hastings

26728 ■ Dialysis Clinic Inc.--Hastings
264 Haida Ave., Ste. D
Hastings, PA 16646
Ph: (814)247-8075
URL: http://www.dciinc.org
Dialysis Stations: 8.

Hazleton

26729 ■ Fresenius Medical Care of Hazleton Inc.
Dialysis Facility
110 Butler Dr.
Hazleton, PA 18201
Free: 866-434-2597
URL: http://www.ultracare-dialysis.com/
Dialysis Stations: 12.

26730 ■ Kidney Center of Greater Hazelton
American Renal Associates
426 Airport Beltway
Hazleton, PA 18202
Ph: (570)450-0870
URL: http://www.americanrenal.com
Dialysis Stations: 21.

Hermitage

26731 ■ Dialysis Clinic, Inc.--Shenango Valley
737 Brookshire Dr.
Hermitage, PA 16148
Ph: (724)342-3040
URL: http://www.dciinc.org
Dialysis Stations: 19.

26732 ■ Fresenius Medical Care--Hermitage
2425 Garden Wy., Ste. 102
Hermitage, PA 16148
Free: 866-434-2597
URL: http://www.ultracare-dialysis.com/
Dialysis Stations: 20. **Formerly:** Renal Care Group.

Hershey

26733 ■ MS/Hershey Medical Center Transplant/Dialysis Center
1400 University Physicians Center, MC HU23
500 University Dr.
Hershey, PA 17033
Ph: (717)531-5033
URL: http://www.hmc.psu.edu
Dialysis Stations: 13.

Honesdale

26734 ■ Honesdale Dialysis Center
DaVita
RR 6, Box 6636
Honesdale, PA 18431
Free: 800-424-6589
URL: http://www.davita.com
Dialysis Stations: 12.

Huntingdon

26735 ■ Dialysis Corporation of America of Huntingdon
Dialysis Facility
820 Bryan St., Ste. 4
Huntingdon, PA 16652
Ph: (814)643-3600
URL: http://www.dialysiscorporation.com
Dialysis Stations: 13. **Formerly:** Keystone Kidney Care.

Huntingdon Valley

26736 ■ Huntingdon Valley Dialysis
DaVita
769 Huntingdon Pke.
Huntingdon Valley, PA 19006
Free: 800-424-6589
URL: http://www.davita.com
Dialysis Stations: 23.

Indiana

26737 ■ Dialysis Clinic, Inc. of Indiana
Indiana Ambulatory Surgical Center
841 Hospital Rd., Ste. 3500
Indiana, PA 15701
Ph: (724)465-7010
URL: http://www.dciinc.org
Dialysis Stations: 21.

Jeannette

26738 ■ Dialysis Clinic, Inc.--Jeannette
520 Jefferson Ave., Ste. 301
Jeannette, PA 15644
Ph: (724)523-6386
URL: http://www.dciinc.org
Dialysis Stations: 22.

Johnstown

26739 ■ DaVita--Johnstown Dialysis & At Home
344 Budfield St.
Johnstown, PA 15904
Free: 800-424-6589
URL: http://www.davita.com
Dialysis Stations: 21. **Formerly:** Physicians Dialysis Inc.

26740 ■ Prodigy Dialysis LLC--Franklin Street
1111 Franklin St., Ste. 220
Johnstown, PA 15905
Ph: (814)539-0798
Dialysis Stations: 1.

26741 ■ Prodigy Dialysis, LLC--Osborne St.
88 Osborne St.
Johnstown, PA 15905
Ph: (814)539-0798
URL: http://prodigydialysis.com/
Dialysis Stations: 11.

26742 ■ Prodigy Dialysis, LLC--Richland Square
Richland Square I
Johnstown, PA 15904
Ph: (814)262-7560
URL: http://prodigydialysis.com/
Dialysis Stations: 12.

Kittanning

26743 ■ Central Kittanning Dialysis Center, LLC
American Renal Associates
One Nolte Dr.
Kittanning, PA 16201
Ph: (303)403-1127
URL: http://www.americanrenal.com
Dialysis Stations: 19.

Kutztown

26744 ■ Fresenius Medical Care--Kutztown Dialysis Services
45 Constitution Blvd.
Kutztown, PA 19530
Free: 866-434-2597
URL: http://www.ultracare-dialysis.com/
Dialysis Stations: 11.

Lancaster

26745 ■ DaVita--PDL Annex--PD
2110 Harrisburg Pike
Lancaster, PA 17604
Free: 800-424-6589
Dialysis Stations: 42. **Formerly:** Lancaster General Health Campus Dialysis Facility.

26746 ■ Physicians Dialysis of Lancaster Dialysis Facility & At Home
DaVita
c/o Community Hospital of Lancaster
1412 E King St.
Lancaster, PA 17602
Free: 800-424-6589
URL: http://www.davita.com
Dialysis Stations: 18.

Langhorne

26747 ■ Belmont Court Dialysis Center Inc.
Fairless Hills Campus
183 Bristol-Oxford Valley Rd.
Langhorne, PA 19047
Ph: (215)269-6864
Dialysis Stations: 20.

26748 ■ Belmont Court Dialysis--Fairless Hills Campus
183B Bristol Oxford Valley Rd.
Langhorne, PA 19047
Ph: (215)269-6864
Dialysis Stations: 20.

26749 ■ Dialysis Center at Oxford Court
DaVita
930 Town Center Dr., Ste. G-100
Langhorne, PA 19047
Free: 800-424-6589
URL: http://www.davita.com
Dialysis Stations: 14.

26750 ■ Langhorne Dialysis Center
American Renal Associates
880 Town Center Dr.
Langhorne, PA 19047
Ph: (303)403-1127
URL: http://www.americanrenal.com
Dialysis Stations: 27.

Lansdale

26751 ■ Fresenius Medical Care--Landsdale
120 Medical Campus Dr.
Lansdale, PA 19446
Free: 866-434-2597
URL: http://www.ultracare-dialysis.com/
Dialysis Stations: 16. **Formerly:** Renal Care Group.

Latrobe

26752 ■ Fresenius Medical Care of Latrobe
Dialysis Facility
121 W 2nd St.
Latrobe, PA 15650
Free: 866-434-2597
URL: http://www.ultracare-dialysis.com/
Dialysis Stations: 14.

Lebanon

26753 ■ GSH Dialysis, Inc.
Dialysis Facility
440 Oak St.
Lebanon, PA 17042
Ph: (717)274-7552
Dialysis Stations: 16.

Lehighton

26754 ■ Fresenius Medical Care of Carbon County
Dialysis Facility
168 Sgt. Stanley Hoffman Blvd.
Lehighton, PA 18235
Free: 866-434-2597
URL: http://www.ultracare-dialysis.com/
Dialysis Stations: 14.

Lewistown

26755 ■ Lewistown Dialysis Center
DaVita
611 Electric Ave.
Lewistown, PA 17044
Free: 800-424-6589
URL: http://www.davita.com
Dialysis Stations: 14.

Limerick

26756 ■ Fresenius Medical Care--Limerick
420 W Linfield Trappe Rd.
Bldg. B, Ste. 100
Limerick, PA 19469
Free: 866-434-2597
URL: http://www.ultracare-dialysis.com/
Dialysis Stations: 20. **Formerly:** Renal Care Group.

Littlestown

26757 ■ Littlestown Dialysis Center
Wellspan Dialysis
43 Columbus Ave.
Littlestown, PA 17340
Ph: (717)359-8110
URL: http://www.wellspan.org/body.cfm?id=556
Dialysis Stations: 18.

Lock Haven

26758 ■ North Central Pennsylvania Dialysis Clinics
Lock Haven Dialysis Clinic
257 S Hanna St.
Lock Haven, PA 17745
Ph: (570)748-3800
Dialysis Stations: 10.

McKee Rocks

26759 ■ American Renal Associates--Ohio Valley Hospital
Medical Arts Bldg.
McKee Rocks, PA 15136
Ph: (303)403-1127
URL: http://www.americanrenal.com
Dialysis Stations: 14.

McKeesport

26760 ■ McKeesport West Dialysis
DaVita
101 9th St.
McKeesport, PA 15132
Free: 800-424-6589
URL: http://www.davita.com
Dialysis Stations: 16.

Meadville

26761 ■ Meadville Dialysis
DaVita
Dialysis Center & At Home
19050 Park Ave. Plz.
Meadville, PA 16335
Free: 800-424-6589
URL: http://www.davita.com
Dialysis Stations: 17. **Formerly:** Gambro Healthcare.

Mechanicsburg

26762 ■ Dialysis Corporation of America--Mechanicsburg
120 S Filbert St.
Mechanicsburg, PA 17055
Ph: (717)790-6080
URL: http://www.dialysiscorporation.com
Dialysis Stations: 15. **Description:** Offers in-center hemodialysis, staff-assisted peritoneal dialysis, and home training/home support hemodialysis/peritoneal dialysis.

Media

26763 ■ Riddle Dialysis Center
DaVita
100 Granite Dr.
Media, PA 19063
Free: 800-424-6589
URL: http://www.davita.com
Dialysis Stations: 16.

Meyersdale

26764 ■ Prodigy Dialysis, LLC--Meyersdale
312 Sherman St.
Meyersdale, PA 15552
Ph: (814)634-7032
URL: http://prodigydialysis.com/
Dialysis Stations: 7.

Milford

26765 ■ Delaware Valley Dialysis Center
DaVita
102 DaVita Dr.
Milford, PA 18337
Free: 800-424-6589
URL: http://www.davita.com
Dialysis Stations: 16.

Millersburg

26766 ■ Fresenius Medical Care--Millersburg
75 Evelyn Dr.
Millersburg, PA 17061
Free: 866-434-2597
URL: http://www.ultracare-dialysis.com/
Dialysis Stations: 9. **Formerly:** Renal Care Group - Millersburg.

Monroeville

26767 ■ Dialysis Clinic Inc. of Five Points
2534 Monroeville Blvd.
Monroeville, PA 15146
Ph: (412)823-5422
Dialysis Stations: 18.

26768 ■ Dialysis Clinic, Inc. of Monroeville
4445 Old William Penn Hwy.
Monroeville, PA 15146
Ph: (412)372-3455
URL: http://www.dciinc.org
Dialysis Stations: 19.

26769 ■ Monroeville Dialysis
DaVita
2690 Monroeville Blvd.
Monroeville, PA 15146
Free: 800-424-6589
URL: http://www.davita.com
Dialysis Stations: 22.

Montoursville

26770 ■ Williamsport Dialysis Clinic
North Central Pennsylvania Dialysis Clinics
1660 Sycamore Rd., Ste. B
Montoursville, PA 17754
Ph: (570)329-3300
Dialysis Stations: 25.

Morton

26771 ■ Waverly Dialysis
DaVita
Waverly Sq.
407 E Baltimore Pke.
Morton, PA 19070
Free: 800-424-6589
URL: http://www.davita.com
Dialysis Stations: 20.

Mount Carmel

26772 ■ Northumberland Dialysis
DaVita
103 W State Rte. 61
Mount Carmel, PA 17851
Free: 800-424-6589
URL: http://www.davita.com
Dialysis Stations: 13.

Mount Pleasant

26773 ■ Dialysis Clinic, Inc. of Mount Pleasant
20 E Main St.
Mount Pleasant, PA 15666
Ph: (724)547-6511
URL: http://www.dciinc.org
Dialysis Stations: 12.

26774 ■ Fresenius Medical Services of Mount Pleasant
Dialysis Facility
Crossroads Plaza, RD 7
Mount Pleasant, PA 15666
Free: 866-434-2597
URL: http://www.ultracare-dialysis.com/
Dialysis Stations: 11.

Nanticoke

26775 ■ Fresenius Medical Care Dialysis Services of Nanticoke
450 W Main St.
Nanticoke, PA 18634
Free: 866-434-2597
URL: http://www.ultracare-dialysis.com/
Dialysis Stations: 13.

Natrona Heights

26776 ■ Allegheny Valley Dialysis Center
Davita
Heights Plaza Shopping Center
1620 Pacific Ave.
Natrona Heights, PA 15065
Ph: (724)224-4382
URL: http://www.davita.com
Dialysis Stations: 11.

New Castle

26777 ■ Fresenius Medical Care of New Castle
Dialysis Facility
207 W Laurel Ave.
New Castle, PA 16101
Free: 866-434-2597
URL: http://www.ultracare-dialysis.com/
Dialysis Stations: 16.

26778 ■ New Castle Dialysis Center
American Renal Associates
100 S Jefferson St., Ste. 187
New Castle, PA 16101
Ph: (303)403-1127
URL: http://www.americanrenal.com
Dialysis Stations: 16.

New Kensington

26779 ■ Dialysis Clinic, Inc. of New Kensington
722 Fourth Ave.
New Kensington, PA 15068
Ph: (724)339-1772
URL: http://www.dciinc.org
Dialysis Stations: 20.

Newtown

26780 ■ NewTown Dialysis Center
DaVita
60 Blacksmith Rd.
Newtown, PA 18940
Free: 800-424-6589
URL: http://www.davita.com
Dialysis Stations: 18.

Norristown

26781 ■ East Norristown Dialysis
Fresenius Medical Care
2925 DeKalb Pkc.
Norristown, PA 19401
Free: 866-434-2597
URL: http://www.ultracare-dialysis.com/
Dialysis Stations: 25. **Formerly:** Renal Care Group.

26782 ■ Fresenius Medical Care--Montgomery East
1350 Powell St.
Norristown, PA 19401
Free: 866-434-2597
URL: http://www.ultracare-dialysis.com/
Dialysis Stations: 24. **Formerly:** Renal Care Group.

North Versailles

26783 ■ Dialysis Clinic Inc.--North Versailles
613 E Pittsburgh
North Versailles, PA 15137
Ph: (412)675-0960
URL: http://www.dciinc.org
Dialysis Stations: 19.

Old Forge

26784 ■ Old Forge Dialysis
DaVita
325 S Main St.
Old Forge, PA 18518
Free: 800-424-6589
URL: http://www.davita.com
Dialysis Stations: 12. **Formerly:** Moses Taylor Regional Dialysis System - Old Forge.

Palmerton

26785 ■ Palmerton Dialysis Center & At Home
DaVita
185-C Delaware Ave.
Palmerton, PA 18071
Free: 800-424-6589
URL: http://www.davita.com
Dialysis Stations: 10.

Palmyra

26786 ■ Fresenius Medical Care--Lebanon County
Dialysis Services
38-42 N Londonderry Sq.
Palmyra, PA 17078
Free: 866-434-2597
URL: http://www.ultracare-dialysis.com/
Dialysis Stations: 16.

Paris

26787 ■ Paris Dialysis
Dialysis Facility
DaVita
32 Steubenville Pike
Paris, PA 15021
Free: 800-424-6589
URL: http://www.davita.com
Dialysis Stations: 19. **Formerly:** Gambro Healthcare.

Philadelphia

26788 ■ Albert Einstein Medical Center
Transplant/Dialysis Center
Levy Ground Fl.
5501 Old York Rd.
Philadelphia, PA 19141
Ph: (215)456-6980
URL: http://www.einstein.edu
Dialysis Stations: 10.

26789 ■ Belmont Court Dialysis Center--Northeast Campus
Dialysis Facility
2200 Michener St., Ste. 20
Philadelphia, PA 19115
Ph: (215)676-8800
Dialysis Stations: 25.

26790 ■ Belmont Court Dialysis Center--Roosevelt Campus
6593 Roosevelt Blvd.
Philadelphia, PA 19149
Ph: (215)537-6000
Dialysis Stations: 21.

26791 ■ Callowhill Dialysis Center
DaVita
313 Callowhill St.
Philadelphia, PA 19123
Free: 800-424-6589
URL: http://www.davita.com
Dialysis Stations: 20.

26792 ■ Children's Hospital of Philadelphia
Dialysis Center
Main Bldg., 2nd Fl.
34th and Civic Center Blvd.
Philadelphia, PA 19104
Ph: (215)590-4600
URL: http://www.chop.edu
Dialysis Stations: 6.

26793 ■ Cobbs Creek Dialysis
DaVita
1700 S 60th St.
Philadelphia, PA 19142
Free: 800-424-6589
URL: http://www.davita.com
Dialysis Stations: 25.

26794 ■ Cottman Kidney Center
DaVita
7198 Caster Ave.
Philadelphia, PA 19149
Free: 800-424-6589
URL: http://www.davita.com
Dialysis Stations: 28.

26795 ■ DaVita--42nd Street
Dialysis Services
4126 Walnut St.
Philadelphia, PA 19104
Free: 800-424-6589
URL: http://www.davita.com
Dialysis Stations: 36. **Formerly:** Grambo Healthcare.

26796 ■ DaVita--Market Street
3701 Market St.
Philadelphia, PA 19104
Free: 800-424-6589
URL: http://www.davita.com
Dialysis Stations: 16.

26797 ■ DaVita
Northeast Philadelphia Dialysis Center
518 Knorr St.
Philadelphia, PA 19111
Free: 800-424-6589
URL: http://www.davita.com
Dialysis Stations: 16.

26798 ■ DaVita--PDI Walnut Towers
834 Walnut St.
Philadelphia, PA 19107
Free: 800-424-6589
URL: http://www.davita.com
Dialysis Stations: 20.

26799 ■ Dialysis Clinic, Inc.--East Falls
3300 Henry Ave.
Philadelphia, PA 19129
Ph: (412)341-7410
URL: http://www.dciinc.org
Dialysis Stations: 26.

26800 ■ Dialysis Services of Central Philadelphia
Fresenius Medical Care
417 N 8th St.
Philadelphia, PA 19123
Free: 866-434-2597
URL: http://www.ultracare-dialysis.com/
Dialysis Stations: 25.

26801 ■ Diversified Specialty Institutes--Northern Philadelphia
5933 N Broad St.
Philadelphia, PA 19141
Ph: (215)549-5000
URL: http://www.dsi-corp.com
Dialysis Stations: 31. **Formerly:** Fresenius Medical Care Dialysis Services of Northern Philadelphis Inc.

26802 ■ Diversified Specialty Institutes--Philadelphia
3310-24 Memphis St.
Philadelphia, PA 19134
Ph: (215)739-9558
URL: http://www.dsi-corp.com
Dialysis Stations: 18. **Formerly:** Renex Dialysis Clinic of Philadelphia.

26803 ■ Franklin Dialysis Centers & At Home DaVita
101 Public Ledger Bldg.
150 S Independence W 101
Philadelphia, PA 19106
Free: 800-424-6589
URL: http://www.davita.com
Dialysis Stations: 28.

26804 ■ Fresenius Medical Care--Cambria
2850 N 21st St.
Philadelphia, PA 19132
Free: 866-434-2597
URL: http://www.ultracare-dialysis.com/
Dialysis Stations: 16.

26805 ■ Fresenius Medical Care Dialysis Services--Graduate
1740 South St., Ste. 100
Philadelphia, PA 19146
Free: 866-434-2597
URL: http://www.ultracare-dialysis.com/
Dialysis Stations: 24.

26806 ■ Fresenius Medical Care Dialysis Services of Hahnemann
Broad & Vine Sts., 18th Fl.
Philadelphia, PA 19102
Free: 866-434-2597
URL: http://www.ultracare-dialysis.com/
Dialysis Stations: 7. **Formerly:** Hahnemann University Hospital Transplant and Dialysis Center.

26807 ■ Fresenius Medical Care Dialysis Services of Northwest Philadelphia
Rowland Hall, Ste. 124
4190 City Ave.
Philadelphia, PA 19131
Free: 866-434-2597
URL: http://www.ultracare-dialysis.com/
Dialysis Stations: 17.

26808 ■ Fresenius Medical Care Dialysis Services of Parkview
Medical Bldg.
1331 E Wyoming Ave., Ste. 1090
Philadelphia, PA 19124
Free: 866-434-2597
URL: http://www.ultracare-dialysis.com/
Dialysis Stations: 28.

26809 ■ Fresenius Medical Care Dialysis Services of Philadelphia
4216 Market St.
Philadelphia, PA 19104
Free: 866-434-2597
URL: http://www.ultracare-dialysis.com/
Dialysis Stations: 34.

26810 ■ Fresenius Medical Care--Fairmount
1241 N Taney St.
Philadelphia, PA 19121
Free: 866-434-2597
Fax: (215)236-6692
URL: http://www.ultracare-dialysis.com/
Dialysis Stations: 32.

26811 ■ Fresenius Medical Care--Mount Airy
6656-60 Germantown Ave.
Philadelphia, PA 19119
Free: 866-434-2597
URL: http://www.ultracare-dialysis.com/
Dialysis Stations: 31. **Formerly:** Renal Care Group.

26812 ■ Fresenius Medical Care--Nazareth
Marion Bldg., Gr. Fl.
2601 Holme Ave.
Philadelphia, PA 19152
Free: 866-434-2597
URL: http://www.ultracare-dialysis.com/
Dialysis Stations: 17.

26813 ■ Fresenius Medical Care of Northeast Philadelphia Dialysis Facility
900 E Howell St., Ste. A
Philadelphia, PA 19149
Free: 866-434-2597
Fax: (215)335-9757
URL: http://www.ultracare-dialysis.com/
Dialysis Stations: 23.

26814 ■ Fresenius Medical Care--Olney
2154-58 Stenton Ave.
Philadelphia, PA 19144
Free: 866-434-2597
URL: http://www.ultracare-dialysis.com/
Dialysis Stations: 20. **Formerly:** Renal Care Group - Germantown.

26815 ■ Fresenius Medical Care--Temple Episcopal
Medical Arts Bldg., Ste. L-7
100 E Lehigh Ave.
Philadelphia, PA 19125
Free: 866-434-2597
URL: http://www.ultracare-dialysis.com/
Dialysis Stations: 23.

26816 ■ Fresenius Medical Care--Temple Germantown
Bldg. 5
3401 Fox St.
Philadelphia, PA 19129
Free: 866-434-2597
URL: http://www.ultracare-dialysis.com/
Dialysis Stations: 32.

26817 ■ Fresenius Temple Dialysis Services--Germantown
Bldg.5
3401 Fox St., Ste. A
Philadelphia, PA 19140
Free: 866-434-2597
URL: http://www.ultracare-dialysis.com/
Dialysis Stations: 32. **Formerly:** North Philadelphia Dialysis Center.

26818 ■ Girard Dialysis Center
8th St. & Girard Ave.
Philadelphia, PA 19122
Ph: (215)787-2278
Dialysis Stations: 11.

26819 ■ Hospital of the University of Pennsylvania Transplant Unit
3400 Spruce St.
Philadelphia, PA 19104
Ph: (215)662-6200
URL: http://www.pennmedicine.org/transplant/
Dialysis Stations: 0.

26820 ■ Presbyterian Medical Center--Lombard Dialysis Services DaVita
51 N 39th St.
Philadelphia, PA 19104
Free: 800-424-6589
URL: http://www.davita.com
Dialysis Stations: 30. **Formerly:** Grambo Healthcare.

26821 ■ Renal Care Partners Inc.--Philadelphia
2910 S 70th St.
Philadelphia, PA 33028
Ph: (215)937-1673
URL: http://www.renalcp.com/
Dialysis Stations: 21.

26822 ■ Renal Center of Philadelphia Dialysis Facility
5630 Chestnut St., 2nd Fl.
Philadelphia, PA 19139
Ph: (215)476-8301
Dialysis Stations: 24.

26823 ■ Roxboro Dialysis--Philadephia DaVita
5003 Umbria St.
Philadelphia, PA 19128
Free: 800-424-6589
URL: http://www.davita.com
Dialysis Stations: 17.

26824 ■ Saint Christopher's Hospital for Children Transplant/Dialysis Center
Erie Ave. at Front St.
Philadelphia, PA 19134
Ph: (215)427-5118
URL: http://www.stchristopherhospital.com
Dialysis Stations: 7.

26825 ■ South Broad Street Dialysis DaVita
1172-74 S Broad St.
Philadelphia, PA 19146
Free: 800-424-6589
URL: http://www.davita.com
Dialysis Stations: 24.

26826 ■ South Philadelphia Dialysis Center DaVita
109 Dickinson St.
Philadelphia, PA 19147
Free: 800-424-6589
URL: http://www.davita.com
Dialysis Stations: 20.

26827 ■ Temple University Hospital Transplant Unit
3401 N Broad St.
Philadelphia, PA 19140
Ph: (215)707-8889
URL: http://kidney.templehealth.org/content/default.htm
Dialysis Stations: 0.

26828 ■ Thomas Jefferson University Hospital Transplant Unit
833 Chestnut St.
Philadelphia, PA 19107
Ph: (215)955-7625
URL: http://www.jeffersonhospital.org/departments-and-services/transplantation.a spx
Dialysis Stations: 0.

26829 ■ West Philadelphia Dialysis Dialysis Facility DaVita
7609 Lindbergh Blvd.
Philadelphia, PA 19153
Free: 800-424-6589
URL: http://www.davita.com
Dialysis Stations: 24. **Formerly:** Gambro Healthcare.

Philipsburg

26830 ■ Kidney Care Services of Philipsburg
1031 North Front St.
Philipsburg, PA 16866
Ph: (814)342-0280
Dialysis Stations: 12.

Pittsburgh

26831 ■ Allegheny General Hospital Transplant Services
320 E North Ave.
South Tower, 4th Fl.
Pittsburgh, PA 15212
Ph: (412)359-6800
URL: http://www.wpahs.org/agh

26832 ■ Bloomfield-Pittsburgh Dialysis DaVita
5171 Liberty Ave.
Pittsburgh, PA 15224
Free: 800-424-6589
URL: http://www.davita.com
Dialysis Stations: 24.

26833 ■ Center for Renal Care--Shadyside
440 S Fairmont St.
Pittsburgh, PA 15232
Ph: (412)661-8000
Dialysis Stations: 1.

26834 ■ Children's Hospital of Pittsburgh of UPMC Dialysis Unit
One Children's Hospital Dr.
Pittsburgh, PA 15224
Ph: (412)864-8717
URL: http://www.chp.edu/CHP/P03082
Dialysis Stations: 6.

26835 ■ Dialysis Clinic, Inc. of Banksville
2727 Banksville Rd.
Pittsburgh, PA 15216
Ph: (412)341-7410
URL: http://www.dciinc.org
Dialysis Stations: 29.

26836 ■ Dialysis Clinic, Inc.--North Borough
100 S Jackson Ave., 7th Central
Pittsburgh, PA 15202
Ph: (412)766-6590
URL: http://www.dciinc.org
Dialysis Stations: 8.

26837 ■ Dialysis Clinic, Inc. of North Hills
3412 Babcock Blvd.
Pittsburgh, PA 15237
Ph: (412)635-0211
URL: http://www.dciinc.org
Dialysis Stations: 18.

26838 ■ Dialysis Clinic, Inc. of Oakland
3260 Fifth Ave.
Pittsburgh, PA 15213
Ph: (412)647-3700
URL: http://www.dciinc.org
Dialysis Stations: 30.

26839 ■ Dialysis Clinic, Inc. of Wilkinsburg
7620 Meade St.
Pittsburgh, PA 15221
Ph: (412)247-5223
URL: http://www.dciinc.org
Dialysis Stations: 22.

26840 ■ East End Pittsburgh Dialysis DaVita
7714 Penn Ave. Park Plz.
Pittsburgh, PA 15221
Free: 800-424-6589
URL: http://www.davita.com
Dialysis Stations: 16.

26841 ■ Fresenius Medical Care Dialysis Services of Mount Oliver, Inc.
1630 Arlington Ave.
Pittsburgh, PA 15210
Free: 866-434-2597
URL: http://www.ultracare-dialysis.com/
Dialysis Stations: 14.

26842 ■ Fresenius Medical Care Dialysis Services--Ohio Valley
Robinson Plz. No. 3
Rte. 60, Ste. 110
Pittsburgh, PA 15205
Free: 866-434-2597
URL: http://www.ultracare-dialysis.com/
Dialysis Stations: 15.

26843 ■ Fresenius Medical Care Dialysis Services--Penn Hills
11624 Keleket Dr.
Pittsburgh, PA 15235
Free: 866-434-2597
URL: http://www.ultracare-dialysis.com/
Dialysis Stations: 13.

26844 ■ Fresenius Medical Care Dialysis Services--Three Rivers
1401 Forbes Ave.
Pittsburgh, PA 15219
Free: 866-434-2597
URL: http://www.ultracare-dialysis.com/
Dialysis Stations: 16.

26845 ■ Fresenius Medical Care--East Hills
10922 Frankstown Rd.
Pittsburgh, PA 15235
Free: 866-434-2597
URL: http://www.ultracare-dialysis.com/
Dialysis Stations: 8. **Formerly:** Renal Care Group/Renex Dialysis Clinic of Penn Hills.

26846 ■ Fresenius Medical Care--Pittsburgh
5301 Fifth Ave.
Pittsburgh, PA 15232
Free: 866-434-2597
URL: http://www.ultracare-dialysis.com/
Dialysis Stations: 13.

26847 ■ Fresenius Medical Care--Shadyside
4925 Baum Blvd.
Pittsburgh, PA 15213
Free: 866-434-2597
URL: http://www.ultracare-dialysis.com/
Dialysis Stations: 20. **Formerly:** Renal Care Group/Renex Dialysis Clinic.

26848 ■ Fresenius Medical Care--Shaler
Shaler Plz.
880 Butler St.
Pittsburgh, PA 15223
Free: 866-434-2597
URL: http://www.ultracare-dialysis.com/
Dialysis Stations: 17. **Formerly:** Renal Care Group/Renex Dialysis Clinic of Shaler.

26849 ■ Fresenius Medical Care--West Pennsylvania
5124 Liberty Ave.
Pittsburgh, PA 15224
Free: 866-434-2597
URL: http://www.ultracare-dialysis.com/
Dialysis Stations: 23.

26850 ■ Liberty Dialysis--Banksville
2875 Banksville Rd.
Pittsburgh, PA 15216
Ph: (412)343-3060
URL: http://www.libertydialysis.com
Dialysis Stations: 27.

26851 ■ Northside Dialysis DaVita
320 E North Ave.
Pittsburgh, PA 15212
Free: 800-424-6589
URL: http://www.davita.com
Dialysis Stations: 20.

26852 ■ Pittsburgh Dialysis & At Home DaVita
4312 Penn Ave.
Pittsburgh, PA 15224
Free: 800-424-6589
URL: http://www.davita.com
Dialysis Stations: 12.

26853 ■ UPMC Health System Presbyterian Renal Unit
200 Lothrop St.
Pittsburgh, PA 15213
Ph: (412)647-3114
URL: http://www.upmc.com
Dialysis Stations: 12.

26854 ■ UPMC Presbyterian--Transplant Thomas E Starzl Transplantation Institute
200 Lothrop St.
Pittsburgh, PA 15213
Ph: (412)647-5800
URL: http://www.upmc.com/Services/TransplantationServices/Pages/default.aspx
Dialysis Stations: 0.

26855 ■ Veterans Affairs Healthcare System of Pittsburgh Dialysis Center
University Dr. C
Pittsburgh, PA 15240
Ph: (412)688-6004
URL: http://www.pittsburgh.va.gov
Dialysis Stations: 14.

Pittston

26856 ■ Fresenius Medical Care Dialysis Services of Pittston
455 N Main St.
Pittston, PA 18640
Free: 866-434-2597
URL: http://www.ultracare-dialysis.com/
Dialysis Stations: 14.

Pottstown

26857 ■ Dialysis Corporation of America of Pottstown
5 S Sunnybrook Rd., Ste. 500
Pottstown, PA 19464
Ph: (610)718-1127
URL: http://www.dialysiscorporation.com
Dialysis Stations: 18.

26858 ■ Pottstown Memorial Medical Center
13 Armand Hammer Blvd.
Pottstown, PA 19464
Ph: (610)327-7700
URL: http://www.pottstownmemorial.com
Dialysis Stations: 15.

Pottsville

26859 ■ Fresenius Medical Care Dialysis Services--Pottsville
278 Industrial Park Rd.
Pottsville, PA 17901
Free: 866-434-2597
URL: http://www.ultracare-dialysis.com/
Dialysis Stations: 16.

Punxsutawney

26860 ■ Dialysis Clinic Inc.--Punxsutawney
158 Elmwood Dr.
Punxsutawney, PA 15767
Ph: (814)938-9045
URL: http://www.dciinc.org
Dialysis Stations: 16.

Quakertown

26861 ■ Saint Luke's Quakertown Hospital Dialysis Facility
1021 Park Ave.
Quakertown, PA 18951

Ph: (215)538-4665
URL: http://www.mystlukesonline.org/locations/stl-quakertown/index.aspx
Dialysis Stations: 12.

Radnor

26862 ■ Radnor Dialysis & At Home
DaVita
250 King of Prussia Rd.
Radnor, PA 19087
Free: 800-424-6589
URL: http://www.davita.com
Dialysis Stations: 12. **Formerly:** Gambro Healthcare.

Reading

26863 ■ Reading Dialysis Center
2201 Dengler St.
Reading, PA 19606
Ph: (610)370-5323
Dialysis Stations: 18.

Saint Marys

26864 ■ Saint Marys Dialysis Center
West Pennsylvania Allegheny Health System
Allegheny General Hospital
763 Johnsonburg Rd.
Saint Marys, PA 15857
Ph: (814)834-5181
URL: http://www.wpahs.org/agh/services/DialysisSt-Marys.html
Dialysis Stations: 9.

Sayre

26865 ■ Robert Packer Hospital
Dialysis Center
Guthrie Sq.
Sayre, PA 18840
Ph: (570)882-4431
URL: http://www.guthrie.org/AboutGuthrie/GuthrieFa-cilities/Packer
Dialysis Stations: 16.

Scranton

26866 ■ Moses Taylor Hospital
Renal Unit
DaVita
700 Quincy Ave.
Scranton, PA 18510
Free: 800-424-6589
URL: http://www.davita.com
Dialysis Stations: 12.

26867 ■ Scranton Dialysis
DaVita
475 Morgan Hwy.
Scranton, PA 18510
Free: 800-424-6589
URL: http://www.davita.com
Dialysis Stations: 14. **Formerly:** Moses Taylor Regional Dialysis Allied Services.

Selinsgrove

26868 ■ Dialysis Corporation of America--Selinsgrove
21 Susquehanna Valley Mall Dr., Ste. D
Selinsgrove, PA 17870
Ph: (570)374-5577
URL: http://www.dialysiscorporation.com
Dialysis Stations: 10.

26869 ■ Selinsgrove Dialysis
Dialysis Center & At Home
DaVita
1030 N Susquehanna Tr.
Selinsgrove, PA 17870
Free: 800-424-6589
URL: http://www.davita.com
Dialysis Stations: 14.

Sellersville

26870 ■ Sellersville Dialysis Center
DaVita
1112 Old Bethlehem Rd.
Sellersville, PA 18960
Ph: (215)257-0950
URL: http://www.davita.com
Dialysis Stations: 20. **Formerly:** Diversified Specialty Institutes.

Seven Fields

26871 ■ Dialysis Clinic, Inc. of Seven Fields
201 Highpointe Dr.
Seven Fields, PA 16046
Ph: (724)779-3930
URL: http://www.dciinc.org
Dialysis Stations: 19.

Somerset

26872 ■ Prodigy Dialysis, LLC--Somerset
211 Georgian Pl.
Somerset, PA 15501
Ph: (814)443-1600
URL: http://prodigydialysis.com/
Dialysis Stations: 9.

26873 ■ Somerset Dialysis Center
DaVita
229 S Kimberly Ave., Ste. 100
Somerset, PA 15501
Ph: (814)445-6127
URL: http://www.davita.com
Dialysis Stations: 8.

State College

26874 ■ Fresenius Medical Care--State College
3901 S Atherton St., Ste. 7
State College, PA 16801
Free: 866-434-2597
URL: http://www.ultracare-dialysis.com/
Dialysis Stations: 13. **Formerly:** Centre Community Hospital.

Stevens

26875 ■ PDI--Ephrata
DaVita
67 West Church St.
Stevens, PA 17578
Free: 800-424-6589
URL: http://www.davita.com
Dialysis Stations: 15. **Formerly:** Physicians Dialysis - Ephrata.

Swarthmore

26876 ■ Fresenius Medical Care--Swarthmore Dialysis Services
Rte. 320
709 S Chester Rd.
Swarthmore, PA 19081
Free: 866-434-2597
URL: http://www.ultracare-dialysis.com/
Dialysis Stations: 16.

Tamaqua

26877 ■ Fresenius Medical Care--Tamaqua Dialysis Services
1215 E Broad St.
Tamaqua, PA 18252
Free: 866-434-2597
URL: http://www.ultracare-dialysis.com/
Dialysis Stations: 8.

Tobyhanna

26878 ■ Mount Pocono Dialysis
DaVita
100 Community Ct., Ste. 106
Tobyhanna, PA 18466
Free: 800-424-6589
URL: http://www.davita.com
Dialysis Stations: 12.

Towanda

26879 ■ Robert Packer Hospital
Towanda Satellite Unit
603 Williams St.
Towanda, PA 18848
Ph: (570)265-2209
URL: http://www.guthrie.org/AboutGuthrie/GuthrieFa-cilities/Packer
Dialysis Stations: 9.

Tunkhannock

26880 ■ Tunkhannock Dialysis
DaVita
880 State Rte. 6W
Tunkhannock, PA 18657
Free: 800-424-6589
URL: http://www.davita.com
Dialysis Stations: 12. **Formerly:** Moses Taylor Regional Dialysis System - Tunkhannock.

Uniontown

26881 ■ Fresenius Medical Care--Uniontown Dialysis Facility
100 Woodlawn Ave., Ste. 175
Uniontown, PA 15401
Free: 866-434-2597
URL: http://www.ultracare-dialysis.com/
Dialysis Stations: 17.

Upland

26882 ■ Upland Dialysis Center
DaVita
Professional Office Bldg. 2, Ste. 120
Upland, PA 19013
Free: 800-424-6589
URL: http://www.davita.com
Dialysis Stations: 53.

Upper Darby

26883 ■ Fresenius Medical Care of Delco
1740 S State Rd.
Upper Darby, PA 19082
Free: 866-434-2597
URL: http://www.ultracare-dialysis.com/
Dialysis Stations: 16.

Warminster

26884 ■ Belmont Court Dialysis Center--Warminster Campus
225 Newtown Rd.
Warminster, PA 18974
Ph: (215)957-7990
Dialysis Stations: 14.

26885 ■ Franklin Commons Dialysis
DaVita
720 Johnsville Blvd., Ste. 800
Warminster, PA 18974
Free: 800-424-6589
URL: http://www.davita.com
Dialysis Stations: 16.

Warren

26886 ■ DaVita--Warren
Dialysis Facility
2 Crescent Park W
Warren, PA 16365
Free: 800-424-6589
URL: http://www.davita.com
Dialysis Stations: 12. **Formerly:** Renal Care of Warren.

Warrington

26887 ■ Liberty Dialysis--Doylestown
2800 Kelly Dr., Ste. 110
Warrington, PA 18976
Ph: (215)343-0483
URL: http://www.libertydialysis.com
Dialysis Stations: 20.

Washington

26888 ■ Dialysis Clinic, Inc. of Washington
280 North Ave.
Washington, PA 15301
Ph: (724)229-8834
URL: http://www.dciinc.org
Dialysis Stations: 23.

26889 ■ Liberty Dialysis--Washington
90 W Chestnut St., 100 E Wing
Washington, PA 15301
Ph: (724)228-7398
URL: http://www.libertydialysis.com
Dialysis Stations: 24.

26890 ■ Oak Springs Dialysis
DaVita
764 Locust Ave.
Washington, PA 15301
Free: 800-424-6589
Dialysis Stations: 15.

Waynesboro

26891 ■ Fresenius Medical Care--Waynesboro
27 Vista Dr.
Waynesboro, PA 17268
Free: 866-434-2597
URL: http://www.ultracare-dialysis.com/
Dialysis Stations: 12.

Waynesburg

26892 ■ Waynesburg Dialysis
DaVita
Dialysis Facility
248 Elm Dr.
Waynesburg, PA 15370
Free: 800-424-6589
URL: http://www.davita.com
Dialysis Stations: 12. **Formerly:** Gambro Healthcare.

Wellsboro

26893 ■ Dialysis Corporation of America of Wellsboro
223 Tioga St.
Wellsboro, PA 16901
Ph: (570)724-3188
URL: http://www.dialysiscorporation.com
Dialysis Stations: 11. **Formerly:** Dialysis Services of Pennsylvania.

West Grove

26894 ■ Jennersville Dialysis Center
DaVita
1011 W Baltimore Pike, Ste. 107
West Grove, PA 19390
Free: 800-424-6589
URL: http://www.davita.com
Dialysis Stations: 18.

West Homestead

26895 ■ Homestead Dialysis
DaVita
Dialysis Facility
207 W 7th Ave.
West Homestead, PA 15120
Free: 800-424-6589
URL: http://www.davita.com
Dialysis Stations: 16. **Formerly:** Gambro Healthcare.

White Oak

26896 ■ McKeesport Dialysis
Dialysis Center
DaVita
Oak Park Mall
2001 Lincoln Way
White Oak, PA 15131
Free: 800-424-6589
URL: http://www.davita.com
Dialysis Stations: 14. **Formerly:** Gambro Healthcare.

26897 ■ Renal Care of White Oak
Dreiling Medical Management
1303 Lincoln Way, Ste. A
White Oak, PA 15131
Ph: (412)673-1191
URL: http://www.dreilingmedical.com
Dialysis Stations: 14.

Whitehall

26898 ■ Fresenius Medical Care--Whitehall
1320 Mickley Rd.
Whitehall, PA 18052
Free: 866-434-2597
URL: http://www.ultracare-dialysis.com/
Dialysis Stations: 24.

Wilkes Barre

26899 ■ Fresenius Medical Care of Wilkes-Barre
307 Laird St., No. 1
Wilkes Barre, PA 18702
Free: 866-434-2597
URL: http://www.ultracare-dialysis.com/
Dialysis Stations: 33.

Willow Grove

26900 ■ Abington Dialysis
Dialysis Center & At Home
DaVita
3940A Commerce Ave.
Willow Grove, PA 19090
Free: 800-424-6589
URL: http://www.davita.com
Dialysis Stations: 22. **Formerly:** Gambro Healthcare.

26901 ■ Fresenius Medical Care--Abington Inc., Willow Grove
Dialysis Facility
1036 N Easton Rd.
Willow Grove, PA 19090
Free: 866-434-2597
URL: http://www.ultracare-dialysis.com/
Dialysis Stations: 22.

Wind Gap

26902 ■ Kidney Treatment Center of Slatebelt
Dialysis Facility
Fresenius Medical Care
525 East West St.
Wind Gap, PA 18091
Free: 866-434-2597
URL: http://www.ultracare-dialysis.com/
Dialysis Stations: 10.

Wyncote

26903 ■ DaVita--Wyncote
Cedarbrook Plaza
Wyncote, PA 19095
Free: 800-424-6589
URL: http://www.davita.com
Dialysis Stations: 18.

Wynnewood

26904 ■ Fresenius Medical Care--Wynnewood
Dialysis Unit
Lankenau Hospital Medical Office Bldg., Ste. 61
100 Lancaster Ave.
Wynnewood, PA 19096
Free: 866-434-2597
URL: http://www.ultracare-dialysis.com/
Dialysis Stations: 31.

26905 ■ Main Line Hospital Lankenau Transplant Center
Medical Science Bldg., Ste. 4405
Wynnewood, PA 19096
Ph: (610)645-8485
URL: http://www.mainlinehealth.org/oth/Page.asp?PageID=OTH000131
Dialysis Stations: 0.

Wyomissing

26906 ■ Pennsylvania Dialysis Clinic of Reading Inc.
625 Spring St.
Wyomissing, PA 19610
Ph: (610)375-1215
Dialysis Stations: 30.

York

26907 ■ Dialysis Corporation of America--York
1975 Kenneth Rd.
York, PA 17404
Ph: (717)764-8322
URL: http://www.dialysiscorporation.com
Dialysis Stations: 24.

26908 ■ Wellspan Dialysis--York
308 St. Charles Way
York, PA 17402
Ph: (717)851-6500
Dialysis Stations: 49.

PUERTO RICO

Aguadilla

26909 ■ Atlantis/Aguadilla
Dialysis Center
107 Ave. Kennedy, 4th Fl.
Aguadilla, PR 00605
Ph: (787)882-6110
URL: http://www.atlantishgi.com/
Dialysis Stations: 17. **Formerly:** Aguadilla Renal Services Group.

26910 ■ Fresenius Medical Care--Aguadilla
Dialysis Facility
0.7 bo. Camaseyis
Carr. 459, KM 0.7
Aguadilla, PR 00603
Free: 866-434-2597
URL: http://www.ultracare-dialysis.com/
Dialysis Stations: 25. **Formerly:** Bio-Medical Applications.

Arecibo

26911 ■ Arecibo Norte Dialicentro
Fresenius Medical Care
Carr. 129 Ave. San Luis Hospital
Cayetano Coll y Toste, Ste. 108
Arecibo, PR 00612
Free: 866-434-2597
URL: http://www.ultracare-dialysis.com/
Dialysis Stations: 19.

26912 ■ Fresenius Medical Care--Arecibo
Dialysis Facility
Carr. No. 2, Km. 78.5
1072 Miramar Ave.
Arecibo, PR 00612

Free: 866-434-2597
URL: http://www.ultracare-dialysis.com/
Dialysis Stations: 31. **Formerly:** Bio-Medical Applications.

Bayamon

26913 ■ Bayamon Dialysis Center Fresenius Medical Care
Carr No. 2, KM 11.2
Bayamon, PR 00960
Free: 866-434-2597
URL: http://www.ultracare-dialysis.com/
Dialysis Stations: 27. **Formerly:** Bio-Medical Applications.

26914 ■ Fresenius Medical Care--Santa Juanita
URB Santa Juanita
Bayamon, PR 00956
Free: 866-434-2597
URL: http://www.ultracare-dialysis.com/
Dialysis Stations: 24.

Caguas

26915 ■ Atlantis Caguas Dialysis Clinic
2 Ave. Luis Munoz Marin
URB Mariolga
Caguas, PR 00978
Ph: (787)292-7979
Dialysis Stations: 20.

26916 ■ Caguas Dialysis Center Fresenius Medical Care
PO Box 6659
Caguas, PR 00726
Free: 866-434-2597
URL: http://www.ultracare-dialysis.com/
Dialysis Stations: 33.

Canovanas

26917 ■ Fresenius Medical Care--Canovanas
East Professional Medical Center
BO Canovans Rd., No. 3 KM 19.9
Canovanas, PR 00729
Free: 787-957-7902
URL: http://www.ultracare-dialysis.com/engine/
Dialysis Stations: 29.

Carolina

26918 ■ Atlantis Carolina Dialysis Center
Paseo Del Prado Shopping Center
Carr PR 3 KM 8 HM 4
Carolina, PR 00988
Ph: (787)292-7979

26919 ■ Fresenius Medical Care--Carolina Dialysis Facility
Centro Commercial
Golden Tower
C-8 Pontzuela Ave.
Carolina, PR 00983
Free: 866-434-2597
URL: http://www.ultracare-dialysis.com/
Dialysis Stations: 36. **Formerly:** Bio-Medical Applications.

Fajardo

26920 ■ Atlantis Fajardo Renal Center
410 Ave. General Valero, Ste. 101
Torre San Pablo del Este
Fajardo, PR 00738
Ph: (787)292-7979
URL: http://www.atlantishgi.com/
Dialysis Stations: 30.

Guayama

26921 ■ Fresenius Medical Care--Guayama Dialysis Facility
Road NBR 3 KM 135.7
Avenida Los Veteranos NBR 5
Guayama, PR 00784
Free: 866-434-2597
Dialysis Stations: 12.

26922 ■ Fresenius Medical Care--Santa Rosa
Hospital Santa Rosa
Ave. Los Veteranos, Carr. 3, KM 13.7
Guayama, PR 00785
Free: 866-434-2597
URL: https://www.ultracare-dialysis.com
Dialysis Stations: 4.

Guaynabo

26923 ■ Atlantis HRG Guaynabo Dialysis Center
Guaynabo Medical Mall Bldg.
140 Ave. Las Cumbres, Ste. 107
Guaynabo, PR 00969
Ph: (787)790-6093
URL: http://www.atlantishgi.com/
Dialysis Stations: 21.

Humacao

26924 ■ Humacao Dialysis Center Fresenius Medical Care
Carr. 3 KM73.8
3 Blvd. Del Rio Corner
Humacao, PR 00792
Free: 866-434-2597
URL: http://www.ultracare-dialysis.com/engine/
Dialysis Stations: 37.

Isabela

26925 ■ Atlantis Isabela Dialysis Center
7227 Ave. Agustin Ramos Calero PMB 123
Isabela, PR 00662
Ph: (787)292-7979
URL: http://www.atlantishgi.com/
Dialysis Stations: 15.

Lares

26926 ■ Atlantis Lares Atlantis Healthcare Group of Puerto Rico Inc
Carr 129 Km. 25.6
Bo. Piletas Castro Borough
Lares, PR 00669
Ph: (787)897-6766
URL: http://www.atlantishgi.com/
Dialysis Stations: 15.

Levittown

26927 ■ Atlantis Toa Baja Dialysis Center
A La Orden Shopping Center
Ave. Comerio 600, Carr. 167
Levittown, PR 00949
Free: 787-795-8800
Dialysis Stations: 29.

Manati

26928 ■ Atlantis Manati Dialysis Center
Doctor's Center Hospital
Carr. 2 KM 47.7
Manati, PR 00674
Ph: (787)854-3322
URL: http://www.atlantishgi.com
Dialysis Stations: 17.

Mayaguez

26929 ■ Atlantis Mayaguez Dialysis Center
Hospital Ramon E. Betances Dialysis
1er. Piso Ave. Hostos 410
Mayaguez, PR 00680
Ph: (787)832-2100
URL: http://www.atlantishgi.com
Dialysis Stations: 18.

26930 ■ Fresenius Medical Care--Mayaguez Dialysis Facility
1050 Los Corazones Ave., Ste. 101
Mayaguez, PR 00680
Free: 866-434-2597
URL: http://www.ultracare-dialysis.com/
Dialysis Stations: 38. **Formerly:** Bio-Medical Applications.

26931 ■ Fresenius Medical Care--Mayaguez North
Rd. 64 KM 0.5 BO Sabanetas
Mayaguez, PR 00681
Free: 866-434-2597
URL: http://www.ultracare-dialysis.com/engine/
Dialysis Stations: 22.

Ponce

26932 ■ Atlantis Ponce CNDS
609 Ave. Tito Castro, Ste. 102
Ponce, PR 00716
Ph: (787)292-7979
Dialysis Stations: 25.

26933 ■ Fresenius Medical Care--Ponce Centro
7309 Calle Ramon Power
Ponce, PR 00717
Free: 866-434-2597
URL: http://www.ultracare-dialysis.com/
Dialysis Stations: 14.

26934 ■ Fresenius Medical Care--Ponce Dialysis Facility
Pass San Jorge Professional Bldg.
Carr. 2 km 23.8 bo. Canas
Ponce, PR 00730
Free: 866-434-2597
URL: http://www.ultracare-dialysis.com/
Dialysis Stations: 31. **Formerly:** Bio-Medical Applications.

26935 ■ Fresenius Medical Care--West Ponce Dialcentro Inc. Dialysis Facility
Urb Punto Oro
500 Ave. Punto Oro
Ponce, PR 00728-2063
Free: 866-434-2597
URL: http://www.ultracare-dialysis.com/
Dialysis Stations: 22. **Formerly:** Bio-Medical Applications.

26936 ■ Ponce Regional Hospital Dialysis Center
609 Ave. Tito Castro, Ste. 102
PMB 380
Ponce, PR 00716
Ph: (787)844-3315
Dialysis Stations: 1.

Rio Piedras

26937 ■ Fresenius Medical Care--Vieques
1535 Ponce de Leon Ave.
Rio Piedras, PR 00926
Free: 866-434-2597
URL: http://www.ultracare-dialysis.com/
Dialysis Stations: 4.

San German

26938 ■ Fresenius Medical Care--San German Dialysis Facility
Torre Medica San Vincente De Paul Rd.
2 km 173.4 bo. Cain Alto
San German, PR 00683

Free: 866-434-2597
URL: http://www.ultracare-dialysis.com/
Dialysis Stations: 25.

San Juan

26939 ■ Auxilio Mutuo Hospital TX Dialysis Center
PO Box 191227
San Juan, PR 00919
Ph: (787)765-7650

26940 ■ Caguas Dialysis & Nephrology Center
1357 Ave. Ashford PMB 460
San Juan, PR 00907
Ph: (787)653-2233
Dialysis Stations: 7.

26941 ■ Centro Renal Universitario
Caparra Heights Station
San Juan, PR 00922
Ph: (787)754-0101
Dialysis Stations: 31.

26942 ■ Fresenius Medical Care--Auxilio Mutuo Dialysis Center
Las Cumbres Ave. PR-199 KM.3
San Juan, PR 00936
Free: 866-434-2597
URL: http://www.ultracare-dialysis.com/
Dialysis Stations: 55.

26943 ■ Fresenius Medical Care--Rio Piedras Dialysis Facility
Sector El Cinco
1535 Ponce de Leon Ave., No. 102
San Juan, PR 00926
Free: 866-434-2597
URL: http://www.ultracare-dialysis.com/
Dialysis Stations: 38. **Formerly:** Bio-Medical Applications.

26944 ■ San Juan Dialysis Center Fresenius Medical Care
Antillas Warehouse
461 Calle Francia, Ste. A-101
San Juan, PR 00917
Ph: (787)764-5640
URL: http://www.ultracare-dialysis.com/engine/
Dialysis Stations: 27.

26945 ■ University Pediatric Hospital Pediatric Renal Center, Department de Salud Dialysis Center
PO Box 191079
San Juan, PR 00919
Ph: (787)777-3535
Dialysis Stations: 5.

San Sebastian

26946 ■ Atlantis San Sebastian Dialysis Center
120 Pavia Fernandez
San Sebastian, PR 00685
Ph: (787)280-6767
URL: http://www.atlantishgi.com
Dialysis Stations: 16.

Vega Baja

26947 ■ Fresenius Medical Care--Vega Baja
3945 Las Vegas Shopping Center
Rd. No. 2, Ste. 14
Vega Baja, PR 00693
Free: 866-434-2597
URL: http://www.ultracare-dialysis.com/
Dialysis Stations: 15. **Formerly:** Vega Baja Renal Dialysis Center.

Yauco

26948 ■ Yauco Dialysis Center Fresenius Medical Care
Prolongacion 25 de Julio St.
Condominio Torres Navel, Ste. 102
Yauco, PR 00698
Free: 866-434-2597
URL: http://www.ultracare-dialysis.com/
Dialysis Stations: 12. **Formerly:** Yauco Dialysis Center.

RHODE ISLAND

East Providence

26949 ■ Dialysis Center of East Providence American Renal Associates
318 Waterman Ave.
East Providence, RI 02914
Ph: (401)435-5200
E-mail: info@americanrenal.com
URL: http://www.americanrenal.com
Dialysis Stations: 21. **Formerly:** Artificial Kidney Center, Rhode Island.

Johnston

26950 ■ Dialysis Center of Johnston American Renal Associates
1526 Atwood Ave.
Johnston, RI 02919
Ph: (401)521-0400
E-mail: info@americanrenal.com
URL: http://www.americanrenal.com
Dialysis Stations: 21.

North Providence

26951 ■ North Providence Dialysis Center Diversified Specialty Institutes
1635 Mineral Spring Ave.
North Providence, RI 02904
Ph: (401)354-5340
URL: http://www.dsi-corp.com
Dialysis Stations: 21.

Pawtucket

26952 ■ Dialysis Center of Pawtucket American Renal Associates
201 Armistice Blvd.
Pawtucket, RI 02860
Ph: (401)722-3313
E-mail: info@americanrenal.com
URL: http://www.americanrenal.com
Dialysis Stations: 21.

26953 ■ Fresenius Medical Care--Pawtucket
79 Division St.
Pawtucket, RI 02860
Free: 866-434-2597
URL: http://www.ultracare-dialysis.com/
Dialysis Stations: 12. **Formerly:** Renal Care Group.

Providence

26954 ■ Dialysis Center of Providence American Renal Associates
9 Plenty St.
Providence, RI 02907
Ph: (401)273-4898
E-mail: info@americanrenal.com
URL: http://www.americanrenal.com
Dialysis Stations: 21.

26955 ■ Fresenius Medical Care--Providence Dialysis Center
125 Corliss St.
Providence, RI 02904
Free: 866-434-2597
URL: http://www.ultracare-dialysis.com/
Dialysis Stations: 22. **Formerly:** Gambro Healthcare.

26956 ■ Miriam Hospital Dialysis Unit
164 Summit Ave.
Providence, RI 02906
Ph: (401)793-3050
URL: http://www.lifespan.org/tmh/index.php
Dialysis Stations: 4.

26957 ■ Rhode Island Hospital Dialysis Unit
593 Eddy St.
Providence, RI 02903
Ph: (401)444-5252
URL: http://www.lifespan.org/rih/
Dialysis Stations: 9.

Tiverton

26958 ■ Dialysis Center of Tiverton American Renal Associates
22 Hurst Ln.
Tiverton, RI 02878
Ph: (401)624-4403
E-mail: info@americanrenal.com
URL: http://www.americanrenal.com
Dialysis Stations: 21.

Wakefield

26959 ■ Dialysis Center of Wakefield
Bacon House
140 Kenyon Ave.
Wakefield, RI 02879
Ph: (401)792-3450
E-mail: info@americanrenal.com
URL: http://www.americanrenal.com
Dialysis Stations: 19.

Warwick

26960 ■ Dialysis Center of Warwick American Renal Associates
1775 Bald Hill Rd.
Warwick, RI 02886
Ph: (401)823-8420
E-mail: info@americanrenal.com
URL: http://www.americanrenal.com
Dialysis Stations: 34.

26961 ■ Fresenius Medical Care--Warwick Dialysis Facility
2814 Post Rd.
Warwick, RI 02886
Free: 866-434-2597
URL: http://www.ultracare-dialysis.com/
Dialysis Stations: 22.

Westerly

26962 ■ Dialysis Center of Westerly American Renal Associates
1 Rhody Dr.
Westerly, RI 02891
Ph: (015)823-8420
E-mail: info@americanrenal.com
URL: http://www.americanrenal.com
Dialysis Stations: 11.

Woonsocket

26963 ■ Dialysis Center of Woonsocket American Renal Associates
2100 Diamond Hill Rd.
Woonsocket, RI 02895
Ph: (401)765-4995
E-mail: info@americanrenal.com
URL: http://www.americanrenal.com
Dialysis Stations: 17.

SOUTH CAROLINA

Aiken

26964 ■ Aiken Dialysis & At Home DaVita
775 Medical Park Dr.
Aiken, SC 29801

Free: 800-424-6589
URL: http://www.davita.com
Dialysis Stations: 22. **Formerly:** Gambro Healthcare.

26965 ■ Dialysis Corporation of America of Aiken II
169 Crepe Myrtle Dr.
Aiken, SC 29801
Ph: (803)644-8484
URL: http://www.dialysiscorporation.com
Dialysis Stations: 18.

Anderson

26966 ■ Fresenius Medical Care--Anderson Dialysis Clinic Inc.
416 E Calhoun St., Ste. A
Anderson, SC 29621
Free: 866-434-2597
URL: http://www.ultracare-dialysis.com/
Dialysis Stations: 47.

Andrews

26967 ■ Dialysis Services--Andrews Fresenius Medical Care
102 S County Line Rd.
Andrews, SC 29510
Free: 866-434-2597
URL: http://www.ultracare-dialysis.com/
Dialysis Stations: 12.

Bamberg

26968 ■ Bamberg Dialysis Renal Advantage Inc.
2046 Main Hwy.
Bamberg, SC 29003
Ph: (803)245-1775
URL: http://www.renaladvantage.com
Dialysis Stations: 16.

26969 ■ Central Bamberg Dialysis DaVita
67 Sunset Dr.
Bamberg, SC 29003
Free: 800-424-6589
URL: http://www.davita.com
Dialysis Stations: 20.

Barnwell

26970 ■ Dialysis Corporation of America of Barnwell
10708 Marlboro Ave.
Barnwell, SC 29812
Ph: (803)541-7225
Fax: (803)541-7228
URL: http://www.dialysiscorporation.com
Dialysis Stations: 15.

Beaufort

26971 ■ Dialysis Clinic Inc.--Port Royal
300 Midtown Dr.
Beaufort, SC 29906
Ph: (843)521-4300
URL: http://www.dciinc.org
Dialysis Stations: 17.

Bennettsville

26972 ■ Bennettsville Dialysis Center Fresenius Medical Care
1104 Frank W Evans Way
Bennettsville, SC 29512
Free: 866-434-2597
URL: http://www.ultracare-dialysis.com/
Dialysis Stations: 21.

Bishopville

26973 ■ Fresenius Medical Care of Lee County Dialysis Center
289 Fairview Ave.
Bishopville, SC 29010
Free: 866-434-2597
URL: http://www.ultracare-dialysis.com/
Dialysis Stations: 21.

Camden

26974 ■ Fresenius Medical Care--Camden Dialysis Facility
7 Haile Ln.
Camden, SC 29020
Free: 866-434-2597
URL: http://www.ultracare-dialysis.com/
Dialysis Stations: 21.

Charleston

26975 ■ Dialysis Clinic, Inc.--Azalea Place
2270 Technical Pkwy.
Charleston, SC 29406
Ph: (843)863-8974
URL: http://www.dciinc.org
Dialysis Stations: 10.

26976 ■ Dialysis Clinic, Inc.--James Island
959 Folly Rd.
Charleston, SC 29412
Ph: (843)795-8386
URL: http://www.dciinc.org
Dialysis Stations: 16.

26977 ■ Dialysis Clinic, Inc.--Magnolia Court
1427 King St.
Charleston, SC 29403
Ph: (843)853-3399
URL: http://www.dciinc.org
Dialysis Stations: 16.

26978 ■ Dialysis Clinic, Inc.--West Ashley
46-B Markfield Rd.
Charleston, SC 29407
Ph: (843)766-2317
URL: http://www.dciinc.org
Dialysis Stations: 23.

26979 ■ Faber Place Dialysis DaVita
3801 Faber Place Dr.
Charleston, SC 29405
Free: 800-424-6589
URL: http://www.davita.com
Dialysis Stations: 17.

26980 ■ Medical University of South Carolina--Transplant
PO Box 250586
Charleston, SC 29425
Ph: (843)792-4177
URL: http://www.muschealth.com/transplant
Dialysis Stations: 0.

26981 ■ North Charleston Dialysis DaVita
5900 Rivers Ave., Ste. E
Charleston, SC 29406
Free: 800-424-6589
URL: http://www.davita.com
Dialysis Stations: 17.

26982 ■ Renal Advantage Inc.--Charleston West Dialysis Facility
2080 Charlie Hall Blvd.
Charleston, SC 29414
Ph: (843)766-4655
URL: http://www.renaladvantage.com
Dialysis Stations: 26. **Formerly:** Gambro Healthcare.

26983 ■ Renal Advantage Inc. Medical Plaza North Charleston Dialysis Facility
9305 Medical Plaza Dr.
Charleston, SC 29406
Ph: (843)572-1660
URL: http://www.renaladvantage.com
Dialysis Stations: 20. **Formerly:** Gambro Healthcare.

Cheraw

26984 ■ Fresenius Medical Care--Care Cheraw
104 Grace La.
Cheraw, SC 29520
Free: 866-434-2597
URL: http://www.ultracare-dialysis.com/
Dialysis Stations: 16.

Chester

26985 ■ Fresenius Medical Care--Chester Dialysis Facility
501 Healthway Dr.
Chester, SC 29706
Free: 866-434-2597
URL: http://www.ultracare-dialysis.com/
Dialysis Stations: 17.

Clinton

26986 ■ Fresenius Medical Care--Palmetto Dialysis Facility
317 Professional Park Rd.
Clinton, SC 29325
Free: 866-434-2597
URL: http://www.ultracare-dialysis.com/
Dialysis Stations: 21. **Formerly:** Renal Care Group - Palmetto.

Columbia

26987 ■ Central Columbia Dialysis & At Home DaVita
3511 Medical Dr.
Columbia, SC 29203
Free: 800-424-6589
URL: http://www.davita.com
Dialysis Stations: 24.

26988 ■ Columbia Northeast Dialysis DaVita
10 Gateway Corners Pkwy., Ste. 200
Columbia, SC 29203
Free: 800-424-6589
URL: http://www.davita.com
Dialysis Stations: 12. **Formerly:** Grambo Healthcare.

26989 ■ DaVita Capitol Centre Dialysis
201 Columbia Mall Blvd.
Columbia, SC 29223
Free: 800-424-6589
URL: http://www.davita.com

26990 ■ Fresenius Medical Care--Lower Richland Dialysis Center
1840 Pineview Dr.
Columbia, SC 29209
Free: 866-434-2597
URL: http://www.ultracare-dialysis.com/
Dialysis Stations: 20.

26991 ■ Fresenius Medical Care--Midtown-South Carolina
1301 Taylor St., Ste. 4M
Columbia, SC 29201
Free: 866-434-2597
URL: http://www.ultracare-dialysis.com/
Dialysis Stations: 25.

26992 ■ Meadowlake Dialysis
Fresenius Medical Care
7631 Wilson Blvd.
Columbia, SC 29203
Free: 866-434-2597
URL: http://www.ultracare-dialysis.com/
Dialysis Stations: 21.

26993 ■ South Columbia Dialysis
Fresenius Medical Care
2139 Adams Grove Rd.
Columbia, SC 29203
Free: 866-434-2597
URL: http://www.ultracare-dialysis.com/
Dialysis Stations: 30.

Conway

26994 ■ Conway Dialysis Center
Fresenius Medical Care
838 Farrar Dr.
Conway, SC 29526
Free: 866-434-2597
URL: http://www.ultracare-dialysis.com/
Dialysis Stations: 15.

26995 ■ Fresenius Medical Care--West Conway
1702 Millpond Rd.
Conway, SC 29527
Free: 866-434-2597
URL: http://www.ultracare-dialysis.com/
Dialysis Stations: 16.

Darlington

26996 ■ Darlington Dialysis Center
Fresenius Medical Care
103 Saleeby Loop
Darlington, SC 29532
Free: 866-434-2597
URL: http://www.ultracare-dialysis.com/
Dialysis Stations: 30.

Dillon

26997 ■ Fresenius Medical Care--Dillon
1304 Hwy. 301 S
Dillon, SC 29536
Free: 866-434-2597
URL: http://www.ultracare-dialysis.com/
Dialysis Stations: 20.

Easley

26998 ■ Easley Dialysis Center
Diversified Specialty Institutes
125 Whitmire Rd.
Easley, SC 29640
Ph: (864)855-6208
URL: http://www.dsi-corp.com
Dialysis Stations: 28. **Formerly:** National Renal Institutes.

Edgefield

26999 ■ Dialysis Corporation of America--Edgefield
306 Main St.
Edgefield, SC 29824
Ph: (803)637-3225
URL: http://www.dialysiscorporation.com
Dialysis Stations: 15.

Fairfax

27000 ■ Allendale County Dialysis
DaVita
202 N Hampton Ave.
Fairfax, SC 29827
Free: 800-424-6589
URL: http://www.davita.com
Dialysis Stations: 10. **Formerly:** Gambro Healthcare.

Florence

27001 ■ Florence Dialysis Clinic
Fresenius Medical Care
435 N Cashua
Florence, SC 29506
Free: 866-434-2597
URL: http://www.ultracare-dialysis.com/
Dialysis Stations: 31.

27002 ■ Freedom Dialysis Center
Fresenius Medical Care
1520 Freedom Blvd.
Florence, SC 29505
Free: 866-434-2597
URL: http://www.ultracare-dialysis.com/
Dialysis Stations: 28.

27003 ■ Fresenius Medical Care--Church Street
406 S Church St.
Florence, SC 29501
Free: 866-434-2597
URL: http://www.ultracare-dialysis.com/
Dialysis Stations: 21.

Fort Lawn

27004 ■ Fresenius Medical Care--Fort Lawn
5707 Willowbrook St.
Fort Lawn, SC 29714
Free: 866-434-2597
URL: http://www.ultracare-dialysis.com/
Dialysis Stations: 17.

Fort Mill

27005 ■ Fort Mill Dialysis
DaVita
1975 Carolina Pl. Dr.
Fort Mill, SC 29708
Free: 800-424-6589
URL: http://www.davita.com
Dialysis Stations: 12.

27006 ■ Fresenius Medical Care--Fort Mill
535 Riverside Crossing Dr.
Fort Mill, SC 29715
Free: 866-434-2597
URL: http://www.ultracare-dialysis.com/
Dialysis Stations: 32.

Fountain Inn

27007 ■ Fresenius Medical Care--Gray Court
289 Chapman Rd.
Fountain Inn, SC 29644
Free: 866-434-2597
URL: http://www.ultracare-dialysis.com/
Dialysis Stations: 21.

Gaffney

27008 ■ Dialysis Clinic, Inc.--Gaffney
405 Tiffany Pk.
Gaffney, SC 29340
Ph: (864)487-1727
URL: http://www.dciinc.org
Dialysis Stations: 28.

Georgetown

27009 ■ Fresenius Medical Care--Georgetown Dialysis Facility
712 N Fraser St.
Georgetown, SC 29440
URL: http://www.ultracare-dialysis.com/
Dialysis Stations: 28.

27010 ■ Fresenius Medical Care--Winyah
2623 S Fraser St.
Georgetown, SC 29440
Free: 866-434-2597
URL: http://www.ultracare-dialysis.com/
Dialysis Stations: 15.

Goose Creek

27011 ■ Charleston Renal Care--Goose Creek
DaVita
109 Greenland Dr.
Goose Creek, SC 29445
Free: 800-424-6589
URL: http://www.davita.com
Dialysis Stations: 17.

27012 ■ Dialysis Clinic Inc.--Goose Creek
98 Hamlet Cir.
Goose Creek, SC 29445
Ph: (843)863-8633
URL: http://www.dciinc.org
Dialysis Stations: 17.

Greenville

27013 ■ Diversified Specialty Institutes--Greenville
3 Butternut Dr., Ste. A
Greenville, SC 29605
Ph: (864)242-4320
URL: http://www.dsi-corp.com/
Dialysis Stations: 30. **Formerly:** Twin Oaks Dialysis.

27014 ■ Fresenius Medical Care--Greenville, South Carolina
605 S Academy St.
Greenville, SC 29601
Free: 866-434-2597
URL: http://www.ultracare-dialysis.com/
Dialysis Stations: 39. **Formerly:** Renal Care Group - Greenville.

27015 ■ Upstate Dialysis Center & At Home
DaVita
308 Mills Ave.
Greenville, SC 29605
Free: 800-424-6589
URL: http://www.davita.com
Dialysis Stations: 52. **Program(s):** In-center Hemodialysis; Home Peritoneal.

Greenwood

27016 ■ DaVita--Greenwood Dialysis Center
109 Overland Dr.
Greenwood, SC 29646
Free: 800-424-6589
URL: http://www.davita.com
Dialysis Stations: 25. **Formerly:** Gambro Healthcare.

Greer

27017 ■ Fresenius Medical Care--Greer
3254 Brushy Creek Rd.
Greer, SC 29650
URL: http://www.ultracare-dialysis.com/
Dialysis Stations: 21. **Formerly:** Renal Care Group.

27018 ■ Greer Kidney Center Inc.
DaVita
211 Village Dr.
Greer, SC 29651
Free: 800-424-6589
URL: http://www.davita.com
Dialysis Stations: 35.

Hartsville

27019 ■ Dialysis Services of Hartsville
Fresenius Medical Care
1308 S 4th St.
Hartsville, SC 29550
Free: 866-434-2597
URL: http://www.ultracare-dialysis.com/
Dialysis Stations: 17.

Hilton Head Island

27020 ■ Hilton Head Dialysis Center
Fresenius Medical Care
Medical Pavilion, Ste. 108
25 Hospital Center Blvd.
Hilton Head Island, SC 29926
Free: 866-434-2597
URL: http://www.ultracare-dialysis.com/
Dialysis Stations: 9.

Holly Hill

27021 ■ Holly Hill Dialysis Center
Renal Advantage Inc.
8532 Old State Rd.
Holly Hill, SC 29059
Ph: (803)496-2800
URL: http://www.renaladvantage.com
Dialysis Stations: 16. **Formerly:** National Renal Alliance.

Honea Path

27022 ■ Fresenius Medical Care--Belton Honea Path
200 Church St.
Honea Path, SC 29654
Free: 866-434-2597
URL: http://www.ultracare-dialysis.com/
Dialysis Stations: 17.

Irmo

27023 ■ Fresenius Medical Care--Irmo
Dialysis Services
1012 Lykes Ln.
Irmo, SC 29063
Free: 866-434-2597
URL: http://www.ultracare-dialysis.com/
Dialysis Stations: 21.

Johnsonville

27024 ■ Fresenius Medical Care--Johnsonville
200 Stuckey St.
Johnsonville, SC 29555
Free: 866-434-2597
URL: http://www.ultracare-dialysis.com/
Dialysis Stations: 11.

Kingstree

27025 ■ Kingstree Dialysis
Fresenius Medical Care
215 N Brooks St.
Kingstree, SC 29556
Free: 866-434-2597
URL: http://www.ultracare-dialysis.com/
Dialysis Stations: 33.

Lake City

27026 ■ Pee Dee Dialysis Center
Fresenius Medical Care
331 Elizabeth Anne Court
Lake City, SC 29560
Free: 866-434-2597
URL: http://www.ultracare-dialysis.com/
Dialysis Stations: 18.

Lancaster

27027 ■ Lancaster Dialysis
DaVita
980 Woodland Dr., Ste. 100
Lancaster, SC 29720
Free: 800-424-6589
URL: http://www.davita.com
Dialysis Stations: 17. **Formerly:** Gambro Healthcare.

Landrum

27028 ■ Dialysis Clinic, Inc.--Landrum
110 Ashbury Dr.
Landrum, SC 29356
Ph: (864)457-2435
URL: http://www.dciinc.org
Dialysis Stations: 13.

Leesville

27029 ■ Fresenius Medical Care--Batesburg Leesville
303 Village Sq.
Leesville, SC 29070
Free: 866-434-2597
URL: http://www.ultracare-dialysis.com/
Dialysis Stations: 21.

Lexington

27030 ■ Fresenius Medical Care--Lexington
131 Whispering Winds Dr.
Lexington, SC 29073
Free: 866-434-2597
URL: http://www.ultracare-dialysis.com/
Dialysis Stations: 21.

Longs

27031 ■ Longs Dialysis
DaVita
90 Cloverleaf Dr.
Longs, SC 29568
Free: 800-424-6589
URL: http://www.davita.com
Dialysis Stations: 10.

Loris

27032 ■ Loris Dialysis Center
Fresenius Medical Care
3827 Bell St.
Loris, SC 29569
Free: 866-434-2597
URL: http://www.ultracare-dialysis.com/
Dialysis Stations: 11.

Lugoff

27033 ■ Fresenius Medical Care--Lugoff Elgin
909 Carolina Dr.
Lugoff, SC 29078
Free: 866-434-2597
URL: http://www.ultracare-dialysis.com/
Dialysis Stations: 21.

Manning

27034 ■ Fresenius Medical Care--Manning
3107 Sumter Hwy.
Manning, SC 29102
Free: 866-434-2597
URL: http://www.ultracare-dialysis.com/
Dialysis Stations: 21.

Marion

27035 ■ Marion Dialysis Center
Fresenius Medical Care
109 Merritt Ct.
Marion, SC 29571
Free: 866-434-2597
URL: http://www.ultracare-dialysis.com/
Dialysis Stations: 24.

Moncks Corner

27036 ■ Renal Advantage Inc.--Moncks Corner
Dialysis Facility
112 McCormick Cir.
Moncks Corner, SC 29461
Ph: (843)899-4953
URL: http://www.renaladvantage.com
Dialysis Stations: 22. **Formerly:** Vivra Renal Care.

Mount Pleasant

27037 ■ Dialysis Clinic, Inc.--East Cooper
1088 Johnnie Dodds Blvd.
Mount Pleasant, SC 29464
Ph: (843)881-8344
URL: http://www.dciinc.org
Dialysis Stations: 13.

27038 ■ Mt. Pleasant Dialysis Center
1028 E Wall St.
Mount Pleasant, SC 29464
Ph: (843)884-3115
Dialysis Stations: 16.

27039 ■ Renal Advantage Inc.
Mount Pleasant Dialysis Center
Bldg. A3
1028 Ewall St.
Mount Pleasant, SC 29464
Ph: (843)884-3115
URL: http://www.renaladvantage.com
Dialysis Stations: 16.

Murrells Inlet

27040 ■ Dialysis Services Murrells Inlet
Fresenius Medical Care
5011 Hwy. 17 Bypass
Murrells Inlet, SC 29576
Free: 866-434-2597
URL: http://www.ultracare-dialysis.com/
Dialysis Stations: 14.

Myrtle Beach

27041 ■ Fresenius Medical Care--Myrtle Beach
4592 Oleander Dr.
Myrtle Beach, SC 29577
Free: 866-434-2597
URL: http://www.ultracare-dialysis.com/
Dialysis Stations: 21.

27042 ■ Myrtle Beach Dialysis
DaVita
3919 Mayfair St.
Myrtle Beach, SC 29577
Free: 800-424-6589
URL: http://www.davita.com
Dialysis Stations: 16.

Newberry

27043 ■ Fresenius Medical Care of Newberry
Dialysis Facility
2041 Medical Park Dr.
Newberry, SC 29108
Free: 866-434-2597
URL: http://www.ultracare-dialysis.com/
Dialysis Stations: 16.

North Augusta

27044 ■ River View Kidney Center
Renal Advantage Inc.
540 Atomic Rd.
North Augusta, SC 29841
Ph: (803)279-3722
URL: http://www.renaladvantage.com
Dialysis Stations: 22.

North Myrtle Beach

27045 ■ Fresenius Medical Care Dialysis Services--North Myrtle Beach
710-A Hwy. 17 S
North Myrtle Beach, SC 29582
Free: 866-434-2597
URL: http://www.ultracare-dialysis.com/
Dialysis Stations: 15.

Orangeburg

27046 ■ DaVita--South Orangeburg Dialysis Facility
1080 Summers Ave.
Orangeburg, SC 29115
Free: 800-424-6589
URL: http://www.davita.com
Dialysis Stations: 21. **Formerly:** Gambro Healthcare.

27047 ■ North Orangeburg Dialysis Dialysis Facility & At Home
DaVita
3031 St. Matthews Rd.
Orangeburg, SC 29118
Free: 800-424-6589
URL: http://www.davita.com
Dialysis Stations: 21. **Formerly:** Gambro Healthcare.

27048 ■ Orangeburg Dialysis
Renal Advantage Inc.
1184 Orangeburg Mall Cir.
Orangeburg, SC 29115
Ph: (803)531-7501
URL: http://www.renaladvantage.com
Dialysis Stations: 16. **Formerly:** National Renal Alliance.

Pageland

27049 ■ Pageland Dialysis
DaVita
505A S Pearl St.
Pageland, SC 29728
Free: 800-424-6589
URL: http://www.davita.com
Dialysis Stations: 12. **Formerly:** Grambo Healthcare.

Pendleton

27050 ■ Fresenius Medical Services of Pendleton
908 S Mechanic St.
Pendleton, SC 29670
Free: 866-434-2597
URL: http://www.ultracare-dialysis.com/
Dialysis Stations: 11.

27051 ■ Pendleton Dialysis
DaVita
7703 Hwy. 76
Pendleton, SC 29670
Free: 800-424-6589
URL: http://www.davita.com
Dialysis Stations: 10.

Port Royal

27052 ■ Fresenius Medical Care--Low Country Dialysis
10 Johnny Morall Cir.
Two Professional Dr.
Port Royal, SC 29935
Free: 866-434-2597
URL: http://www.ultracare-dialysis.com/
Dialysis Stations: 22.

Ravenel

27053 ■ Renal Advantage Inc.--Jacobs Point Blvd.--Ravenel
5953 Jacobs Point Blvd.
Ravenel, SC 29470
Ph: (843)571-4025
URL: http://www.renaladvantage.com

Ridgeland

27054 ■ Fresenius Medical Care--The Marshlands
28 Rice Pond Rd.
Ridgeland, SC 29936
Free: 866-434-2597
URL: http://www.ultracare-dialysis.com/
Dialysis Stations: 18.

27055 ■ Ridgeland Dialysis
DaVita
112 Weathersby St.
Ridgeland, SC 29936
Free: 800-424-6589
URL: http://www.davita.com

Rock Hill

27056 ■ Fresenius Medical Care--York County
1560 Health Care Dr.
Rock Hill, SC 29732
Free: 866-434-2597
URL: http://www.ultracare-dialysis.com/
Dialysis Stations: 23.

Saluda

27057 ■ Dialysis Clinic Inc.--Saluda
301 W. Butler Ave.
Saluda, SC 29138
Ph: (864)445-7755
URL: http://www.dciinc.org
Dialysis Stations: 10.

Santee

27058 ■ Santee Dialysis
DaVita
228 Bradford Blvd.
Santee, SC 29142
Free: 800-424-6589
URL: http://www.davita.com
Dialysis Stations: 24.

Seneca

27059 ■ Oconee Dialysis Clinic Inc.
Fresenius Medical Care
685 S Oak St.
Seneca, SC 29678
Free: 866-434-2597
URL: http://www.ultracare-dialysis.com/
Dialysis Stations: 14.

Simpsonville

27060 ■ Diversified Specialty Institutes--Powderhorn
16 Powderhorn Rd.
Simpsonville, SC 29681
Ph: (866)962-2222
URL: http://www.dsi-corp.com/
Dialysis Stations: 21. **Formerly:** Renal Care Group.

27061 ■ Diversified Specialty Institutes--Simpsonville
209 N Maple St.
Simpsonville, SC 29681
Ph: (864)963-7275
URL: http://www.dsi-corp.com/
Dialysis Stations: 12. **Formerly:** National Renal Institutes.

Spartanburg

27062 ■ Carolina Dialysis LLC
American Renal Associates
115 Interstate Park
Spartanburg, SC 29303
Ph: (864)576-9999
E-mail: info@americanrenal.com
URL: http://www.americanrenal.com
Dialysis Stations: 20.

27063 ■ Dialysis Clinic, Inc.--East Spartanburg
155 Dillon Dr.
Spartanburg, SC 29307
Ph: (864)585-4840
URL: http://www.dciinc.org
Dialysis Stations: 35.

27064 ■ Dialysis Clinic, Inc.--Spartanburg
203 Freemont Ave.
Spartanburg, SC 29303
Ph: (864)585-2046
URL: http://www.dciinc.org
Dialysis Stations: 26.

27065 ■ Dialysis Clinic, Inc.--West Spartanburg
105 Tradd St.
Spartanburg, SC 29301
Ph: (864)574-8828
URL: http://www.dciinc.org
Dialysis Stations: 25.

Summerton

27066 ■ Fresenius Medical Care--Lake Marion
20 Buff Blvd.
Summerton, SC 29148
Free: 866-434-2597
URL: http://www.ultracare-dialysis.com/
Dialysis Stations: 13.

Summerville

27067 ■ Jedburg Dialysis and At Home
DaVita
2897 W 5th North St.
Summerville, SC 29483
Free: 800-424-6589
URL: http://www.davita.com
Dialysis Stations: 18.

27068 ■ Renal Advantage Inc.--Summerville
109 Burton Ave., Ste. A
Summerville, SC 29485
Ph: (843)875-9800
URL: http://www.renaladvantage
Dialysis Stations: 22.

Sumter

27069 ■ Fresenius Medical Care--Sumter Dialysis Center
615 W Wesmark Blvd.
Sumter, SC 29150
Free: 866-434-2597
URL: http://www.ultracare-dialysis.com/
Dialysis Stations: 54.

Union

27070 ■ Dialysis Clinic, Inc.--Union
315 Thompson Blvd.
Union, SC 29379
Ph: (864)429-2940
URL: http://www.dciinc.org
Dialysis Stations: 15.

Varnville

27071 ■ Hampton Dilaysis Clinic
Renal Advantage Inc.
Dialysis Center
593 W Carolina Ave.
Varnville, SC 29944
Ph: (803)943-4334
URL: http://www.renaladvantage.com
Dialysis Stations: 13. **Formerly:** NRA/Hampton Regional Medical Center.

Walterboro

27072 ■ Walterboro Dialysis
DaVita
302 Ruby St.
Walterboro, SC 29488
Free: 800-424-6589
URL: http://www.davita.com
Dialysis Stations: 25.

West Columbia

27073 ■ Fresenius Medical Care--West Columbia
Dialysis Facility
105 Sum-mor Dr.
West Columbia, SC 29169
Free: 866-434-2597
URL: http://www.ultracare-dialysis.com/
Dialysis Stations: 20. **Formerly:** North America West Columbia Dialysis Center.

Winnsboro

27074 ■ Fairfield County Dialysis
Fresenius Medical Care
1126 Hwy. 321 Business S, Ste. A
Winnsboro, SC 29180
Free: 866-434-2597
URL: http://www.ultracare-dialysis.com/
Dialysis Stations: 21.

York

27075 ■ Fresenius Medical Care--York
1440 E Alexander Love Hwy.
York, SC 29745
Free: 866-434-2597
URL: http://www.ultracare-dialysis.com/
Dialysis Stations: 16.

SOUTH DAKOTA

Aberdeen

27076 ■ Avera Saint Luke's Hospital
Dialysis Facility
305 S State St.
Aberdeen, SD 57401
Ph: (605)622-5550
URL: http://www.averastlukes.org
Dialysis Stations: 10.

Chamberlain

27077 ■ Sanford Chamberlain Dialysis Unit
300 S Byron Blvd.
Chamberlain, SD 57325
Ph: (605)234-7273
URL: http://www.sanfordhealth.org/Locations/904049232
Dialysis Stations: 7.

Eagle Butte

27078 ■ Black Hills Dialysis--Eagle Butte
Main St.
Eagle Butte, SD 57625
Ph: (605)964-2311
Dialysis Stations: 8.

Gregory

27079 ■ Avera Gregory Healthcare Dialysis Unit
400 Park St.
Gregory, SD 57533
Ph: (605)835-8394
URL: http://www.gregoryhealthcare.org
Dialysis Stations: 4. **Formerly:** Sacred Heart Health Services.

Hot Springs

27080 ■ VA Medical Center--Hot Springs
500 N 5th St.
Hot Springs, SD 57747
Ph: (605)745-2000
URL: http://www2.va.gov/directory/guide/facility.asp?id=60
Dialysis Stations: 5.

Huron

27081 ■ Huron Regional Medical Center
Dialysis Facility
172 4th St. SE
Huron, SD 57350
Ph: (605)353-6518
URL: http://www.huronregional.org
Dialysis Stations: 7.

Madison

27082 ■ Madison Dialysis of Sioux Valley Hospital
917 N Washington Ave.
Madison, SD 57042
Ph: (605)256-8870
URL: http://www.sanfordhealth.org
Dialysis Stations: 6.

Mitchell

27083 ■ Mitchell Community Dialysis
DaVita
525 N Foster St.
Mitchell, SD 57301
Free: 800-424-6589
URL: http://www.davita.com
Dialysis Stations: 6.

Pierre

27084 ■ Saint Mary's Healthcare Center
Dialysis Facility
800 E Sioux.
Pierre, SD 57501
Ph: (605)224-3100
URL: http://www.st-marys.com
Dialysis Stations: 6.

Pine Ridge

27085 ■ Black Hills Dialysis--Pine Ridge
100 Dialysis Dr.
Pine Ridge, SD 57770
Ph: (605)867-5983
Dialysis Stations: 12.

Rapid City

27086 ■ Regional Dialysis Center
640 Flormann St., Ste. 401
Rapid City, SD 57701
Ph: (605)719-6950
Dialysis Stations: 31.

Rosebud

27087 ■ Rosebud Dialysis
DaVita
1 Soldier Creek Rd.
Rosebud, SD 57570
Free: 800-424-6589
URL: http://www.davita.com
Dialysis Stations: 12.

Sioux

27088 ■ Sanford Dialysis--Sioux Falls
Sanford Health
1305 W 18th St.
Sioux, SD 57117
Ph: (218)333-5640
URL: http://www.sanfordhealth.org/
Dialysis Stations: 21.

Sioux Falls

27089 ■ Avera Transplant Institute
800 E 21st St.
Sioux Falls, SD 57105
Ph: (605)322-7350
Free: 888-909-1112
URL: http://www.avera.org/clinics/transplant-institute/index.aspx
Dialysis Stations: 0.

27090 ■ DaVita--Sioux Falls Dialysis
800 E 21st St., Ste. 4600
Sioux Falls, SD 57105
Free: 800-424-6589
URL: http://www.davita.com
Dialysis Stations: 18.

27091 ■ Sanford Health
Dialysis Center
1305 W 18th St.
Sioux Falls, SD 57117
Ph: (605)333-1000
URL: http://www.sanfordhealth.org
Dialysis Stations: 21. **Formerly:** Sioux Valley Hospital.

Spearfish

27092 ■ Regional Dialysis Center--Spearfish
132 Yankee St.
Spearfish, SD 57783
Ph: (605)644-9000
Dialysis Stations: 6. **Formerly:** Northern Hills Dialysis Facility.

Wagner

27093 ■ Wagner Dialysis of Sioux Valley Hospital
Dialysis Center
111 Washington Ave.
Wagner, SD 57380
Ph: (605)384-3731
URL: http://www.sanfordhealth.org
Dialysis Stations: 4. **Formerly:** Avera Sacred Heart.

Watertown

27094 ■ Prairie Lakes Healthcare System
Dialysis Facility
401 9th Ave. NW
Watertown, SD 57201
Ph: (605)882-7905
URL: http://www.prairielakes.com
Dialysis Stations: 8.

27095 ■ Satellite Dialysis--Ortonville
Satellite Health
401 9th Ave. NW
Watertown, SD 57201
Ph: (320)839-4070
URL: http://www.satellitehealth.com/
Dialysis Stations: 6.

Yankton

27096 ■ Avera Sacred Heart--Yankton
Dialysis Center
501 Summit Ave.
Yankton, SD 57078
Ph: (605)668-8627
Fax: (605)668-8621
URL: http://www.averasacredheart.com
Dialysis Stations: 7.

TENNESSEE

Athens

27097 ■ Fresenius Medical Care--Decatur Pike, Athens
Dialysis Facility
1303 Decatur Pike
Athens, TN 37303
Free: 866-434-2597
URL: http://www.ultracare-dialysis.com/
Dialysis Stations: 7.

Bartlett

27098 ■ Fresenius Medical Care--Bartlett
3348 N Germantown Rd.
Bartlett, TN 38113
Free: 866-434-2597
URL: http://www.ultracare-dialysis.com/
Dialysis Stations: 16.

Bolivar

27099 ■ Bolivar Dialysis
DaVita
515 Pecan Dr.
Bolivar, TN 38008
Free: 800-424-6589
URL: http://www.davita.com
Dialysis Stations: 16.

Bristol

27100 ■ Fresenius Medical Care--Bristol Dialysis Facility
1 Medical Park Blvd., Ste. 100E
Bristol, TN 37621
Free: 866-434-2597
URL: http://www.ultracare-dialysis.com/
Dialysis Stations: 16.

Brownsville

27101 ■ Brownsville Dialysis
DaVita
380 Dupree St.
Brownsville, TN 38012
Free: 800-424-6589
URL: http://www.davita.com
Dialysis Stations: 21. **Formerly:** Tennessee Kidney Clinic Inc.

Camden

27102 ■ Camden Dialysis
DaVita
168 A W Main St.
Camden, TN 38320
Free: 800-424-6589
URL: http://www.davita.com
Dialysis Stations: 13. **Formerly:** Camden Kidney Clinic.

Centerville

27103 ■ Fresenius Medical Care--Centerville
193 Brown Junction Rd.
Centerville, TN 37033
Free: 866-434-2597
URL: http://www.ultracare-dialysis.com/
Dialysis Stations: 13.

Chattanooga

27104 ■ Chattanooga Kidney Center
2118 Stein Dr.
Chattanooga, TN 37421
Ph: (423)648-4900
Dialysis Stations: 30.

27105 ■ Chattanooga Kidney Center North, LLC
649 Morrison Springs Rd.
Chattanooga, TN 37415
Ph: (423)468-1000
URL: http://www.ckcdialysis.com/
Dialysis Stations: 28.

27106 ■ Dialysis Clinic, Inc.--Chattanooga
1425 E 3rd St.
Chattanooga, TN 37404
Ph: (423)698-0927
URL: http://www.dciinc.org
Dialysis Stations: 29.

27107 ■ Dialysis Clinic, Inc.--Chattanooga
3555 Broad St.
Chattanooga, TN 37409
Ph: (423)756-8808
URL: http://www.dciinc.org
Dialysis Stations: 16.

27108 ■ Dialysis Clinic Inc.--Dayton
6104 N Mack Smith Rd.
Chattanooga, TN 37412
Ph: (423)775-3386
URL: http://www.dciinc.org
Dialysis Stations: 14.

27109 ■ Dialysis Clinic, Inc.--Lyerly
2300 E 3rd St., Ste. A
Chattanooga, TN 37404
Ph: (423)698-6422
URL: http://www.dciinc.org
Dialysis Stations: 26.

27110 ■ Erlanger Regional Kidney Dialysis and Renal Services
975 E 3rd St.
Chattanooga, TN 37403
Ph: (423)778-7583
Fax: (423)778-6674
Dialysis Stations: 4.

Clarksville

27111 ■ Clarksville Dialysis
DaVita
231 Hillcrest Dr.
Clarksville, TN 37043
Free: 800-424-6589
URL: http://www.davita.com
Dialysis Stations: 14. **Formerly:** Grambo Healthcare.

27112 ■ Clarksville North Dialysis
DaVita
3071 Clay Lewis Rd.
Clarksville, TN 37040
Free: 800-424-6589
URL: http://www.davita.com
Dialysis Stations: 13.

27113 ■ Cumberland Dialysis Center
Dialysis Clinic Inc.
312 Landrum Place
Clarksville, TN 37043
Ph: (931)645-1236
URL: http://www.dciinc.org
Dialysis Stations: 28.

Cleveland

27114 ■ Bradley Dialysis Clinic
Fresenius Medical Care
905 Clingan Ridge Rd.
Cleveland, TN 37312
Free: 866-434-2597
URL: http://www.ultracare-dialysis.com/
Dialysis Stations: 17.

Clinton

27115 ■ Clinton Dialysis Center
702 N Main St.
Clinton, TN 37716
Ph: (865)457-1114
Dialysis Stations: 16.

Collierville

27116 ■ Collierville Dialysis
DaVita
791 W Poplar Ave.
Collierville, TN 38017
Free: 800-424-6589
URL: http://www.davita.com
Dialysis Stations: 15.

27117 ■ Fresenius Medical Care--Collierville
155 Crescent Dr.
Collierville, TN 38017
Free: 866-434-2597
URL: http://www.ultracare-dialysis.com/
Dialysis Stations: 13.

Columbia

27118 ■ Columbia Dialysis--Grove Street
DaVita
1705 Grove St.
Columbia, TN 38401
Free: 800-424-6589
URL: http://www.davita.com
Dialysis Stations: 18. **Formerly:** Grambo Healthcare.

27119 ■ Fresenius Medical Care--Columbia
861 W James Campbell Blvd.
Columbia, TN 38401
Free: 866-434-2597
URL: http://www.ultracare-dialysis.com/
Dialysis Stations: 42. **Formerly:** Dialysis Associates of Columbia.

Cookeville

27120 ■ Cookeville Dialysis
DaVita
Dialysis Center & At Home
140 W 7th St.
Cookeville, TN 38501
Free: 800-424-6589
URL: http://www.davita.com
Dialysis Stations: 18. **Formerly:** Grambo Healthcare.

Covington

27121 ■ Fresenius Medical Care--Tipton County
Dialysis Facility
2047 Hwy. 51 S
Covington, TN 38019
Free: 866-434-2597
URL: http://www.ultracare-dialysis.com/
Dialysis Stations: 15.

27122 ■ Tipton County Dialysis
DaVita
Dialysis Center
107 Tennessee Ave.
Covington, TN 38019
Free: 800-424-6589
URL: http://www.davita.com
Dialysis Stations: 13. **Formerly:** Grambo Healthcare.

Crossville

27123 ■ Crossville Dialysis Clinic
Renal Advantage Inc.
121 Dooley St.
Crossville, TN 38555
Ph: (931)484-4500
URL: http://www.renaladvantage.com
Dialysis Stations: 16.

Dickson

27124 ■ Dialysis Clinic, Inc.--Dickson
100 Academy St.
Dickson, TN 37055
Ph: (615)446-0111
URL: http://www.dciinc.org
Dialysis Stations: 24.

27125 ■ Renal Advantage Inc.--Dickson Dialysis Clinic
254 Beasley Dr.
Dickson, TN 37055
Ph: (615)441-8886
URL: http://www.renaladvantage.com
Dialysis Stations: 21.

Dyersburg

27126 ■ Dyersburg Dialysis
DaVita
1575 Parr Ave.
Dyersburg, TN 38024

Free: 800-424-6589
URL: http://www.davita.com
Dialysis Stations: 20.

East Ridge

27127 ■ Dialysis Clinic, Inc.--East Ridge
6104 N Mack Smith Rd.
East Ridge, TN 37412
Ph: (423)894-8133
URL: http://www.dciinc.org
Dialysis Stations: 24.

Elizabethton

27128 ■ Fresenius Medical Care--Elizabethton
1210 Militia Court
Elizabethton, TN 37643
Free: 866-434-2597
URL: http://www.ultracare-dialysis.com/
Dialysis Stations: 13.

Etowah

27129 ■ Woods Memorial Regional Dialysis Center
886 Hwy. 411 N
Etowah, TN 37331
Ph: (423)263-3666
URL: http://www.woodshospital.org/aboutus.html
Dialysis Stations: 16.

Fayetteville

27130 ■ Fresenius Medical Care--Elk River Dialysis
501 Amana Ave.
Fayetteville, TN 37334
Free: 866-434-2597
URL: http://www.ultracare-dialysis.com/
Dialysis Stations: 12.

Franklin

27131 ■ Fresenius Medical Care--Franklin, Tennessee
1120 Lakeview Dr., Ste. 400
Franklin, TN 37067
Free: 866-434-2597
URL: http://www.ultracare-dialysis.com/
Dialysis Stations: 14. **Formerly:** Dialysis Associates.

27132 ■ Williamson County Dialysis
Dialysis Center
DaVita
3983 S Carothers Rd.
Franklin, TN 37064
Free: 800-424-6589
URL: http://www.davita.com
Dialysis Stations: 9. **Formerly:** Grambo Healthcare.

Gallatin

27133 ■ Fresenius Medical Care--Gallatin
561 S Water St.
Gallatin, TN 37066
Free: 866-434-2597
URL: http://www.ultracare-dialysis.com/
Dialysis Stations: 17. **Formerly:** Dialysis Associates.

27134 ■ Sumner Dialysis
DaVita
300 Steam Plant Rd., Ste. 270
Gallatin, TN 37066
Free: 800-424-6589
URL: http://www.davita.com
Dialysis Stations: 14. **Formerly:** Grambo Healthcare.

Germantown

27135 ■ Fresenius Medical Care--Memphis Germantown
7640 Wolf River Cir.
Germantown, TN 38138
Free: 866-434-2597
URL: http://www.ultracare-dialysis.com/
Dialysis Stations: 24. **Formerly:** Renal Care Group.

Greeneville

27136 ■ Fresenius Medical Care--Eastern Tennessee
180 Serral Dr.
Greeneville, TN 37745
Free: 866-434-2597
URL: http://www.ultracare-dialysis.com/
Dialysis Stations: 19.

Harriman

27137 ■ Fresenius Medical Care--Roane County
Dialysis Facility
527 Devonia St.
Harriman, TN 37748
Free: 866-434-2597
URL: http://www.ultracare-dialysis.com/
Dialysis Stations: 10.

Hermitage

27138 ■ Dialysis Clinic, Inc.--Summit
Medical Office Bldg., Ste. 334
5653 Frist Blvd.
Hermitage, TN 37076
Ph: (615)889-3444
URL: http://www.dciinc.org
Dialysis Stations: 12.

Hixson

27139 ■ Dialysis Clinic, Inc.--Hixson
1816 Hamill Rd.
Hixson, TN 37343
Ph: (423)875-0020
URL: http://www.dciinc.org
Dialysis Stations: 12.

Humboldt

27140 ■ Dialysis Clinic, Inc.--Humboldt
215 N 14th St.
Humboldt, TN 38343
Ph: (731)784-4384
URL: http://www.dciinc.org
Dialysis Stations: 12.

27141 ■ Humboldt Dialysis
DaVita
Dialysis Facility
2214 Osborne
Humboldt, TN 38343
Free: 800-424-6589
URL: http://www.davita.com
Dialysis Stations: 25. **Formerly:** Tennessee Kidney Clinic Inc.

Jackson

27142 ■ Carriage Dialysis
DaVita
37 Carriage House Dr.
Jackson, TN 38305
Free: 800-424-6589
URL: http://www.davita.com
Dialysis Stations: 8. **Formerly:** Fresenius Medical Care, Madison County.

27143 ■ DaVita
Stonegate PD Dialysis & At Home
16 Murray Guard Dr.
Jackson, TN 38305
Free: 800-424-6589
URL: http://www.davita.com
Dialysis Stations: 0.

27144 ■ Dialysis Clinic, Inc.--Jackson
31 Sandstone Circle
Jackson, TN 38305
Ph: (731)668-0800
URL: http://www.dciinc.org
Dialysis Stations: 20.

Jasper

27145 ■ Dialysis Clinic, Inc.--Jasper
300 Westfield Pl.
Jasper, TN 37347
Ph: (423)942-9977
URL: http://www.dciinc.org
Dialysis Stations: 18.

Johnson City

27146 ■ Fresenius Medical Care--Johnson City
Dialysis Facility
100 Technology Ln.
Johnson City, TN 37604
Free: 866-434-2597
URL: http://www.ultracare-dialysis.com/
Dialysis Stations: 32.

27147 ■ Smokie Mountain Dialysis Center
101 Med Tech Pkwy., Ste. 406
Johnson City, TN 37604
Ph: (423)232-8882
Dialysis Stations: 0.

27148 ■ Tennessee Valley Dialysis Center
DaVita
107 Woodlawn Dr., Ste. 2
Johnson City, TN 37604
Free: 800-424-6589
URL: http://www.davita.com
Dialysis Stations: 16.

Kingsport

27149 ■ Fresenius Medical Care--Kingsport
2002 Brookside Dr., Ste. 101
Kingsport, TN 37660
Free: 866-434-2597
URL: http://www.ultracare-dialysis.com/
Dialysis Stations: 23.

27150 ■ Fresenius Medical Care--West Kingsport
Dialysis Facility
3600 Netherland Inn Rd.
Kingsport, TN 37660
Free: 866-434-2597
URL: http://www.ultracare-dialysis.com/
Dialysis Stations: 18.

Knoxville

27151 ■ Dialysis Clinic, Inc.--Knoxville
3734 Martin Mill Pike
Knoxville, TN 37920
Ph: (865)573-3944
URL: http://www.dciinc.org
Dialysis Stations: 48.

27152 ■ Fort Sanders Dialysis
Fresenius Medical Care
1740 Western Ave.
Knoxville, TN 37921
Free: 866-434-2597
URL: http://www.ultracare-dialysis.com/
Dialysis Stations: 26.

27153 ■ Fresenius Medical Care--Powell
732 E Emory Rd.
Knoxville, TN 37938
Free: 866-434-2597
URL: http://www.ultracare-dialysis.com/
Dialysis Stations: 26.

27154 ■ Fresenius Medical Care--West Knoxville
Dialysis Facility
11305 Station W
Knoxville, TN 37922
Free: 866-434-2597
URL: http://www.ultracare-dialysis.com/
Dialysis Stations: 13.

27155 ■ Holston River Clinic
Dialysis Clinic Inc.
5811 E Gov. John Sevier Hwy.
Knoxville, TN 37924
Ph: (865)523-3755
URL: http://www.dciinc.org
Dialysis Stations: 24.

27156 ■ Knoxville Central Dialysis and At Home
DaVita
9141 Cross Park Dr.
Knoxville, TN 37923
Free: 800-424-6589
URL: http://www.davita.com
Dialysis Stations: 8.

27157 ■ North Knoxville Dialysis Center
Fresenius Medical Care
4440 Walker Blvd.
Knoxville, TN 37917
Free: 866-434-2597
URL: http://www.ultracare-dialysis.com/
Dialysis Stations: 24.

La Follette

27158 ■ La Follette Dialysis Center
Fresenius Medical Care
305 River Dr.
La Follette, TN 37766
Free: 866-434-2597
URL: http://www.ultracare-dialysis.com/
Dialysis Stations: 15.

Lakeland

27159 ■ Galleria Home Training Dialysis and Training At Home
DaVita
9045 Hwy. 64
Lakeland, TN 38002
Free: 800-424-6589
URL: http://www.davita.com
Dialysis Stations: 5.

27160 ■ Galleria Kidney Clinic
Dialysis Facility
DaVita
9160 Hwy. 64 E
Lakeland, TN 38002
Free: 800-424-6589
URL: http://www.davita.com
Dialysis Stations: 16.

Lawrenceburg

27161 ■ Fresenius Medical Care--Lawrenceburg
1311 S Locust Ave.
Lawrenceburg, TN 38464
Free: 866-434-2597
URL: http://www.ultracare-dialysis.com/
Dialysis Stations: 17.

Lebanon

27162 ■ Dialysis Clinic, Inc.--Lebanon
417 Harding Industrial Dr.
Lebanon, TN 37087
Ph: (615)444-7955
URL: http://www.dciinc.org
Dialysis Stations: 25.

Lenoir City

27163 ■ Loudon Dialysis
Fresenius Medical Care
200 Interchange Pk. Dr.
Lenoir City, TN 37772
Free: 866-434-2597
URL: http://www.ultracare-dialysis.com/
Dialysis Stations: 20.

Lewisburg

27164 ■ Fresenius Medical Care--Lewisburg
1030 War Eagle Dr.
Lewisburg, TN 37091
Free: 866-434-2597
URL: http://www.ultracare-dialysis.com/
Dialysis Stations: 13.

Lexington

27165 ■ Dialysis Clinic Inc.--Beech Lake
870 W Church St.
Lexington, TN 38351
Ph: (731)968-2513
URL: http://www.dciinc.org
Dialysis Stations: 7.

27166 ■ Lexington Kidney Clinic
Dialysis Facility
DaVita
317 Church W St.
Lexington, TN 38351
Free: 800-424-6589
URL: http://www.davita.com
Dialysis Stations: 13.

Livingston

27167 ■ Livingston Tennessee Dialysis
DaVita
308 Oak St.
Livingston, TN 38570
Free: 800-424-6589
URL: http://www.davita.com
Dialysis Stations: 8.

Madison

27168 ■ Cumberland Dialysis
Dialysis Facility
DaVita
Point Magan Professional Bldg., Ste. 5
312 Hospital Dr.
Madison, TN 37115
Free: 800-424-6589
URL: http://www.davita.com
Dialysis Stations: 12. **Formerly:** Gambro Healthcare - Cumberland.

27169 ■ Dialysis Clinic, Inc.--Madison
605 W Due West Ave.
Madison, TN 37115
Ph: (615)865-7310
URL: http://www.dciinc.org
Dialysis Stations: 26.

27170 ■ Fresenius Medical Care--Madison
1221 Briarville Rd.
Madison, TN 37115
Free: 866-434-2597
URL: http://www.ultracare-dialysis.com/
Dialysis Stations: 20. **Formerly:** Renal Care Group.

Manchester

27171 ■ Renal Advantage Inc.
Manchester Dialysis Clinic
367 Interstate Dr.
Manchester, TN 37355
Ph: (931)728-7733
URL: http://www.renaladvantage.com
Dialysis Stations: 16.

Martin

27172 ■ Fresenius Medical Care--Martin
113 E C Thurman Center
Martin, TN 38237
Free: 866-434-2597
URL: http://www.ultracare-dialysis.com/
Dialysis Stations: 16. **Formerly:** Martin Dialysis Center.

Maryville

27173 ■ Blount Dialysis Center
714 E Harper St.
Maryville, TN 37804
Ph: (865)379-1070
Dialysis Stations: 12.

27174 ■ Dialysis Clinic, Inc.--Maryville
1851 Crest Rd.
Maryville, TN 37804
Ph: (865)983-2212
URL: http://www.dciinc.org
Dialysis Stations: 24.

27175 ■ East Tennessee Dialysis Center Inc.
1605 E Broadway
Maryville, TN 37804
Ph: (865)681-2900
Dialysis Stations: 24.

McMinnville

27176 ■ Fresenius Medical Care--McMinnville
1428 Sparta St.
McMinnville, TN 37110
Free: 866-434-2597
URL: http://www.ultracare-dialysis.com/
Dialysis Stations: 16. **Formerly:** Renal Care Group.

Memphis

27177 ■ Capelville Dialysis Center
DaVita
7008 E Shelby Dr.
Memphis, TN 38125
Free: 800-424-6589
URL: http://www.davita.com
Dialysis Stations: 24.

27178 ■ Central Memphis Renal Center
Diversified Specialty Institutes
1331 Union Ave., Ste. 101
Memphis, TN 38104
Ph: (901)278-5400
URL: http://www.dsi-corp.com
Dialysis Stations: 40. **Formerly:** National Renal Institutes.

27179 ■ Diversified Specialty Institutes--Galleria
8592 Ricky Bell Cove
Memphis, TN 38133
Ph: (901)380-5755
URL: http://www.dsi-corp.com
Dialysis Stations: 20. **Formerly:** National Renal Institutes.

27180 ■ Fresenius Medical Care--East Memphis
6490 Mt. Moriah Ext.
Memphis, TN 38115
Free: 866-434-2597
URL: http://www.ultracare-dialysis.com/
Dialysis Stations: 31.

27181 ■ Fresenius Medical Care--Graceland Dialysis Facility
1200 Farrow St.
Memphis, TN 38116
Free: 866-434-2597
URL: http://www.ultracare-dialysis.com/
Dialysis Stations: 34.

27182 ■ Fresenius Medical Care--Memphis
1428 Monroe Ave.
Memphis, TN 38104
Free: 866-434-2597
URL: http://www.ultracare-dialysis.com/
Dialysis Stations: 33.

27183 ■ Fresenius Medical Care--Midtown-Tennessee
2225 Union Ave., Ste. 200
Memphis, TN 38104
Free: 866-434-2597
URL: http://www.ultracare-dialysis.com/
Dialysis Stations: 29. **Formerly:** Memphis Kidney & Dialysis Services.

27184 ■ Fresenius Medical Care--North Memphis Dialysis Facility
3850 Austin Peay Hwy.
Memphis, TN 38128
Free: 866-434-2597
URL: http://www.ultracare-dialysis.com/
Dialysis Stations: 25. **Formerly:** Memphis Kidney & Dialysis Services.

27185 ■ Fresenius Medical Care--Whitehaven
4115 S Plaza Dr.
Memphis, TN 38116
Free: 866-434-2597
URL: http://www.ultracare-dialysis.com/
Dialysis Stations: 33. **Formerly:** Memphis Kidney & Dialysis Services.

27186 ■ Le Bonheur Children's Hospital Transplant/Dialysis Center
50 N Dunlap
Memphis, TN 38103
Ph: (901)387-6133
Dialysis Stations: 6.

27187 ■ Memphis Central Dialysis Dialysis Center DaVita
889 Linden Ave.
Memphis, TN 38126
Free: 800-424-6589
URL: http://www.davita.com
Dialysis Stations: 26. **Formerly:** Gambro Healthcare - Memphis Central.

27188 ■ Memphis Downtown Dialysis and At Home DaVita
2076 Union Ave.
Memphis, TN 38104
Free: 800-424-6589
URL: http://www.davita.com
Dialysis Stations: 28.

27189 ■ Memphis East Dialysis, PD & At Home DaVita Dialysis Center
50 Humphrey Blvd., Ste. 42
Memphis, TN 38120
Free: 800-424-6589
URL: http://www.davita.com
Dialysis Stations: 34. **Formerly:** Gambro Healthcare - Memphis.

27190 ■ Memphis Graceland--South Diversified Specialty Institutes
4180 Auburn Rd.
Memphis, TN 38116
Ph: (901)332-8699
URL: http://www.dsi-corp.com
Dialysis Stations: 16. **Formerly:** National Renal Institutes.

27191 ■ Memphis Midtown--Central Diversified Specialty Institutes
1166 Monroe Ave.
Memphis, TN 38104
Ph: (901)722-2012
URL: http://www.dsi-corp.com
Dialysis Stations: 24. **Formerly:** National Renal Institutes.

27192 ■ Memphis North Renal Center Diversified Specialty Institutes
4913 Raleigh Commons, Ste. 100
Memphis, TN 38128
Ph: (901)937-0650
URL: http://www.dsi-corp.com
Dialysis Stations: 17. **Formerly:** National Renal Institutes.

27193 ■ Memphis South Dialysis DaVita
1205 Marlin Rd.
Memphis, TN 38116
Free: 800-424-6589
URL: http://www.davita.com
Dialysis Stations: 16. **Formerly:** Grambo Healthcare.

27194 ■ Memphis South Renal Center Diversified Specialty Institutes Dialysis Facility
3960 Knight Arnold Rd., No. 107
Memphis, TN 38118
Ph: (901)396-6012
URL: http://www.dsi-corp.com
Dialysis Stations: 25. **Formerly:** Renal Care Group.

27195 ■ Memphis Southeast Dialysis DaVita
1805 Moriah Woods Blvd.
Memphis, TN 38117
Free: 800-424-6589
URL: http://www.davita.com
Dialysis Stations: 24.

27196 ■ Whitehaven Renal Center Diversified Specialty Institutes
3420 Elvis Presley Blvd.
Memphis, TN 38116
Ph: (901)396-3794
URL: http://www.dsi-corp.com
Dialysis Stations: 25. **Formerly:** National Renal Institutes.

Millington

27197 ■ DaVita--Millington
8150 Wilkinsville Rd.
Millington, TN 38053
Free: 800-424-6589
URL: http://www.davita.com
Dialysis Stations: 12.

27198 ■ Fresenius Medical Care--Millington
7840 Church St.
Millington, TN 38053
Free: 866-434-2597
URL: http://www.ultracare-dialysis.com/
Dialysis Stations: 16.

Morristown

27199 ■ Fresenius Medical Care--Morristown Dialysis Services
420 W Morris Blvd., Ste. 110
Morristown, TN 37813
Free: 866-434-2597
URL: http://www.ultracare-dialysis.com/
Dialysis Stations: 15.

Mountain City

27200 ■ Fresenius Medical Care--Mountain City Dialysis Services
120 Pioneer Village Dr., No. 15
Mountain City, TN 37683
Free: 866-434-2597
URL: http://www.ultracare-dialysis.com/
Dialysis Stations: 13.

Murfreesboro

27201 ■ Dialysis Clinic, Inc.--Murfreesboro
1024 N Highland Ave.
Murfreesboro, TN 37130
Ph: (615)890-7741
URL: http://www.dciinc.org
Dialysis Stations: 30.

27202 ■ Fresenius Medical Care--Murfreesboro
1020 N Highland Ave., Ste. C1
Murfreesboro, TN 37130
Free: 866-434-2597
URL: http://www.ultracare-dialysis.com/
Dialysis Stations: 2. **Formerly:** Renal Care Group.

27203 ■ Murfreesboro Dialysis Dialysis Center DaVita
1346 Dow St.
Murfreesboro, TN 37130
Free: 800-424-6589
URL: http://www.davita.com
Dialysis Stations: 14. **Formerly:** Gambro Healthcare - Murfreesboro.

Nashville

27204 ■ Centennial Medical Center--Transplant
2300 Patterson St.
Nashville, TN 37203
Ph: (615)342-5626
URL: http://www.centennialmedicalcenter.com/CustomPage.asp?guidCustomContentID=7 F7DEE38-54F3-4F1A-9EC4-D425E107B531
Dialysis Stations: 0.

27205 ■ Dialysis Association of East Nashville Fresenius Medical Care
604 Gallatin Rd. E
Nashville, TN 37206
Free: 866-434-2597
Dialysis Stations: 12. **Formerly:** Renal Care Group.

27206 ■ Dialysis Association Home Training Fresenius Medical Care
28 White Bridge Rd., Ste. 300
Nashville, TN 37205
Free: 866-434-2597
URL: http://www.ultracare-dialysis.com/
Dialysis Stations: 5. **Formerly:** Renal Care Group.

27207 ■ Dialysis Clinic, Inc.--Clarksville Highway
3229 Clarksville Hwy.
Nashville, TN 37218
Ph: (615)742-3033
URL: http://www.dciinc.org
Dialysis Stations: 20.

27208 ■ Dialysis Clinic, Inc.--Medical Center
1600 Hayes St., Main Fl.
Nashville, TN 37203
Ph: (615)327-3302
URL: http://www.dciinc.org
Dialysis Stations: 32.

27209 ■ Dialysis Clinic, Inc.--Nashville
935 21st Ave. N
Nashville, TN 37208
Ph: (615)327-3984
URL: http://www.dciinc.org
Dialysis Stations: 48.

27210 ■ Dialysis Clinic, Inc.--Southern Hills
417 Harding Industrial Dr.
Nashville, TN 37211
Ph: (615)832-0761
URL: http://www.dciinc.org
Dialysis Stations: 18. **Formerly:** Dialysis Clinic, Inc.-Lebanon.

27211 ■ Fresenius Medical Care--West Nashville
242 Orlando Ave.
Nashville, TN 37209
Free: 866-434-2597
URL: http://www.ultracare-dialysis.com/
Dialysis Stations: 24. **Formerly:** Dialysis Associates.

27212 ■ Nashville Home Training Dialysis PD and At Home Training
DaVita
1919 Charlotte Ave.
Nashville, TN 37203
Free: 800-424-6589
URL: http://www.davita.com
Dialysis Stations: 7.

27213 ■ PD Dialysis Center of Middle Tennessee
Dialysis Clinic Inc.
1633 Church St., Ste. 160
Nashville, TN 37203
Ph: (615)329-1812
URL: http://www.dciinc.org
Dialysis Stations: 1.

27214 ■ Vanderbilt Dialysis Clinic East
Fresenius Medical Care
20 Rachel Dr.
Nashville, TN 37214
Free: 866-434-2597
URL: http://www.ultracare-dialysis.com/
Dialysis Stations: 17.

27215 ■ Vanderbilt Dialysis Clinic
Fresenius Medical Care
1500 21st Ave. S, Ste. 3600
Nashville, TN 37212
Free: 866-434-2597
URL: http://www.ultracare-dialysis.com/
Dialysis Stations: 30.

27216 ■ White Bridge Dialysis
Dialysis Center & At Home
DaVita
103 White Bridge Rd., Ste. 6
Nashville, TN 37209
Free: 800-424-6589
URL: http://www.davita.com
Dialysis Stations: 21. **Formerly:** Gambro Healthcare - White Bridge.

New Market

27217 ■ Fresenius Medical Care--New Market
1030 W US Hwy. 11E
New Market, TN 37820
Free: 866-434-2597
URL: http://www.ultracare-dialysis.com/
Dialysis Stations: 12.

New Tazewell

27218 ■ Appalachian Dialysis Center
503 Elm Ave.
New Tazewell, TN 37825
Ph: (423)626-1242
Dialysis Stations: 14.

Newport

27219 ■ Fresenius Medical Care--Newport
119 Hedrick St.
Newport, TN 37821
Free: 866-434-2597
URL: http://www.ultracare-dialysis.com/
Dialysis Stations: 16.

Oak Ridge

27220 ■ Fresenius Medical Care--Oak Ridge Dialysis Clinic
650 Briarcliff Ave.
Oak Ridge, TN 37830
Free: 866-434-2597
URL: http://www.ultracare-dialysis.com/
Dialysis Stations: 17.

Paris

27221 ■ Dialysis Clinic, Inc.--Paris
1101 Kelley Dr.
Paris, TN 38242
Ph: (731)644-0763
URL: http://www.dciinc.org
Dialysis Stations: 16.

Portland

27222 ■ Fresenius Medical Care--Portland
923 S Broadway
Portland, TN 37148
Free: 866-434-2597
URL: http://www.ultracare-dialysis.com/
Dialysis Stations: 12. **Formerly:** Renal Care Group.

Savannah

27223 ■ Pickwick Dialysis
Dialysis Facility
DaVita
121 N Pickwick Rd.
Savannah, TN 38372
Free: 800-424-6589
URL: http://www.davita.com
Dialysis Stations: 15. **Formerly:** Savannah Kidney Clinic.

Selmer

27224 ■ Selmer Dialysis
Dialysis Center
DaVita
251 Oak Grove Rd.
Selmer, TN 38375
Free: 800-424-6589
URL: http://www.davita.com
Dialysis Stations: 10. **Formerly:** Tennessee Kidney Clinic - Selmer.

Sevierville

27225 ■ Dialysis Clinic, Inc.--Sevierville
765 Sunrise Circle
Sevierville, TN 37862
Ph: (865)453-4068
URL: http://www.dciinc.org
Dialysis Stations: 16.

Shelbyville

27226 ■ Dialysis Clinic, Inc.--Shelbyville
1701 N Main St., Ste. G
Shelbyville, TN 37160
Ph: (931)684-3040
URL: http://www.dciinc.org
Dialysis Stations: 16.

Smyrna

27227 ■ DaVita--Smyrna
537 Stonecrest Pkwy.
Smyrna, TN 37167
Free: 800-424-6589
URL: http://www.davita.com
Dialysis Stations: 8.

27228 ■ Dialysis Association of Smyrna
Fresenius Medical Care
1100 Rock Springs Rd.
Smyrna, TN 37167
Free: 866-434-2597
URL: http://www.ultracare-dialysis.com/
Dialysis Stations: 16. **Formerly:** Renal Care Group.

Somerville

27229 ■ Somerville Dialysis
DaVita
12475 US Hwy. 64
Somerville, TN 38068
Free: 800-424-6589
URL: http://www.davita.com
Dialysis Stations: 14.

Springfield

27230 ■ Fresenius Medical Care--Springfield, Tennessee
106 Mooreland Dr.
Springfield, TN 37172
Free: 866-434-2597
URL: http://www.ultracare-dialysis.com/
Dialysis Stations: 16. **Formerly:** Dialysis Associates.

Tullahoma

27231 ■ Fresenius Medical Care--Tullahoma
144 Jack Farrar Ln.
Tullahoma, TN 37388
Free: 866-434-2597
URL: http://www.ultracare-dialysis.com/
Dialysis Stations: 16. **Formerly:** Dialysis Associates.

Union City

27232 ■ Fresenius Medical Care--Union City Dialysis Center
1117 S Miles Ave., Ste. 6
Union City, TN 38261
Free: 866-434-2597
URL: http://www.ultracare-dialysis.com/
Dialysis Stations: 16. **Formerly:** Gambro Healthcare Dialysis Center.

Winchester

27233 ■ Fresenius Medical Care--Winchester, Tennessee
359 Old Mill Rd.
Winchester, TN 37398
Free: 866-434-2597
URL: http://www.ultracare-dialysis.com/
Dialysis Stations: 16. **Formerly:** Renal Care Group.

TEXAS

Abilene

27234 ■ Dialysis Services of Abilene South
Fresenius Medical Care
2009 Hospital Pl.
Abilene, TX 79606
Free: 866-434-2597
URL: http://www.ultracare-dialysis.com/
Dialysis Stations: 26.

27235 ■ Fresenius Medical Care--Abilene
1802 Pine St.
Abilene, TX 79601
Free: 866-434-2597
URL: http://www.ultracare-dialysis.com/
Dialysis Stations: 33.

Alamo

27236 ■ Fresenius Medical Care--Tri-City
734 N Alamo Rd.
Alamo, TX 78516
Free: 866-434-2597
URL: http://www.ultracare-dialysis.com/
Dialysis Stations: 20.

Alice

27237 ■ Alice Renal Center
Diversified Specialty Institutes
2345 Alice Regional Blvd.
Alice, TX 78332
Ph: (361)664-1723
URL: http://www.dsi-corp.com
Dialysis Stations: 24. **Formerly:** South Texas Kidney Center.

27238 ■ Fresenius Medical Care--Alice
901 Medical Center Blvd.
Alice, TX 78332
Free: 866-434-2597
URL: http://www.ultracare-dialysis.com/
Dialysis Stations: 24. **Formerly:** Renal Care Group.

Allen

27239 ■ Fresenius Medical Care--Allen
925 Exchange Pkwy.
Allen, TX 75013
Free: 866-434-2597
URL: http://www.ultracare-dialysis.com/
Dialysis Stations: 16.

Alvin

27240 ■ Alvin Dialysis Center
Fresenius Medical Care
2625 S Loop 35, Ste. 154
Alvin, TX 77511
Free: 866-434-2597
URL: http://www.ultracare-dialysis.com/
Dialysis Stations: 12.

Amarillo

27241 ■ Amarillo Kidney Specialists, LLC
8604 S Coulter Rd.
Amarillo, TX 79121
Ph: (806)358-0051
URL: http://amarillokidney.com/
Dialysis Stations: 36. **Formerly:** Renal Ventures Management.

27242 ■ Crown of Texas Kidney Center
Fresenius Medical Care
3501 Soncy Rd., Ste. 130
Amarillo, TX 79119
Free: 866-434-2597
URL: http://www.ultracare-dialysis.com/
Dialysis Stations: 10.

27243 ■ Fresenius Medical Care--Amarillo
5920 Amarillo Blvd. W
Amarillo, TX 79106
Free: 866-434-2597
URL: http://www.ultracare-dialysis.com/
Dialysis Stations: 32.

27244 ■ Renal Carepartners--Amarillo
1915 S Coulter St., Ste. B
Amarillo, TX 79106
Ph: (806)355-3310
URL: http://www.renalcp.com
Dialysis Stations: 16.

Angleton

27245 ■ Angleton Kidney Center
102 E Hospital Dr.
Angleton, TX 77515
Ph: (979)864-4330
Dialysis Stations: 20.

Aransas Pass

27246 ■ Fresenius Medical Care--Aransas Pass
709 S Commercial, Ste. C-1
Aransas Pass, TX 78336
Free: 866-434-2597
URL: http://www.ultracare-dialysis.com/
Dialysis Stations: 16.

Arlington

27247 ■ Ameri-Tech Kidney Center
1138 S Bowen Rd.
Arlington, TX 76013
Ph: (817)265-7115
Dialysis Stations: 20.

27248 ■ Arlington Dialysis
DaVita
1250 E Pioneer Pkwy., Ste. 700
Arlington, TX 76010
Free: 800-424-6589
URL: http://www.davita.com
Dialysis Stations: 12.

27249 ■ South Arlington Dialysis Center
3295 S Cooper, Ste. 137
Arlington, TX 76015
Ph: (817)465-8585
URL: http://www.sadctx.com
Dialysis Stations: 30.

27250 ■ Tarrant Dialysis Center--Arlington
US Renal Care
203 W Randol Mill Rd.
Arlington, TX 76011
Ph: (817)275-7787
URL: http://www.usrenalcare.com
Dialysis Stations: 13.

Athens

27251 ■ Fresenius Medical Care--S Carroll Street, Athens
Dialysis Facility
425 S Carroll St., Ste. 3
Athens, TX 75751
Free: 866-434-2597
URL: http://www.ultracare-dialysis.com/
Dialysis Stations: 20. **Formerly:** Renal Care Group - Athens.

Atlanta

27252 ■ Northeast Texas Dialysis Center
606 Loop 59 N
Atlanta, TX 75551
Ph: (903)796-3311
Dialysis Stations: 8.

Austin

27253 ■ Austin Waterloo Dialysis
DaVita
5310 Burnet Rd., Ste. 122
Austin, TX 78756
Free: 800-424-6589
URL: http://www.davita.com
Dialysis Stations: 24.

27254 ■ Children's Dialysis Clinic of Central Texas
Dialysis Clinic Inc.
1301 Barbara Jordan Blvd., Ste. 103
Austin, TX 78723
Ph: (512)524-4213
URL: http://www.dciinc.org
Dialysis Stations: 7.

27255 ■ El Milagro Dialysis Center
DaVita
2800 S Interstate Hwy. 35, Ste. 120
Austin, TX 78704
Free: 800-424-6589
URL: http://www.davita.com
Dialysis Stations: 24.

27256 ■ Manor Clinic
Capital Nephrology Associates
3607 Manor Rd.
Austin, TX 78723
Ph: (512)927-0300
URL: http://www.capitalnephrology.com/
Dialysis Stations: 38. **Formerly:** Captial Dialysis of Texas Ltd.

27257 ■ Metric Clinic
Capital Nephrology Associates
10000 Metric Blvd., Ste. 100
Austin, TX 78758
Ph: (512)977-0300
URL: http://www.capitalnephrology.com
Dialysis Stations: 28. **Formerly:** Captial Dialysis of Texas Ltd.

27258 ■ Moncrief Dialysis Center
DaVita
800 W 34th St., Ste. 101
Austin, TX 78705
Free: 800-424-6589
URL: http://www.davita.com
Dialysis Stations: 24.

27259 ■ National Nephrology Associates--Central
2220 Hancock Dr.
Austin, TX 78756
Ph: (512)452-7881
Dialysis Stations: 22.

27260 ■ National Nephrology Associates--North
Dialysis Facility
12221 N Mopac Expy.
Austin, TX 78758
Ph: (512)901-4044
Dialysis Stations: 17.

27261 ■ National Nephrology Associates--South
Dialysis Facility
621 Radam Ln.
Austin, TX 78745
Ph: (512)707-7601
Dialysis Stations: 20.

27262 ■ North Austin Medical Center Transplant
1221 N Mopac Expy.
Austin, TX 78758
Ph: (512)901-2880
URL: http://www.stdavids.com/home.aspx
Dialysis Stations: 0.

27263 ■ South Austin Dialysis
DaVita
6114 S 1st St.
Austin, TX 78745
Free: 800-424-6589
URL: http://www.davita.com
Dialysis Stations: 20.

27264 ■ Southwood Clinic
Capital Nephrology Associates
1701 W Ben White Blvd., Ste. 180
Austin, TX 78704
Ph: (512)383-0300
URL: http://www.capitalnephrology.com
Dialysis Stations: 34. **Formerly:** Captial Dialysis of Texas Ltd.

27265 ■ Wellbound of Austin
Satellite Health
12176 N Mo Pac Expy., Ste. A
Austin, TX 78758
Ph: (512)833-6695
URL: http://www.satellitehealth.com/
Dialysis Stations: 4.

Bastrop

27266 ■ Fresenius Medical Care--Bastrop
423 Old Austin Hwy.
Bastrop, TX 78602
Free: 866-434-2597
URL: http://www.ultracare-dialysis.com/
Dialysis Stations: 20.

27267 ■ Fresenius Medical Care--North Bastrop
423 Old Austin Hwy.
Bastrop, TX 78602
Free: 866-434-2597
URL: https://www.ultracare-dialysis.com
Dialysis Stations: 20. **Formerly:** National Nephrology Associates.

Bay City

27268 ■ Matagorda Renal Dialysis Center
Renal Advantage Inc.
1105 Ave. H
Bay City, TX 77414
Ph: (979)245-0099
URL: http://www.renaladvantage.com
Dialysis Stations: 15. **Formerly:** Bay City Dialysis.

Baytown

27269 ■ Baytown Dialysis
DaVita
4665 Garth Rd., Ste. 900
Baytown, TX 77521
Free: 800-424-6589
URL: http://www.davita.com
Dialysis Stations: 12.

27270 ■ Baytown Dialysis Facility
Fresenius Medical Care
2202 Rollingbrook
Baytown, TX 77521
Free: 866-434-2597
URL: http://www.ultracare-dialysis.com/
Dialysis Stations: 38.

Beaumont

27271 ■ Beaumont Kidney Center
American Renal Associates
1085 S 23rd St.
Beaumont, TX 77707
Ph: (409)840-2020
URL: http://www.americanrenal.com
Dialysis Stations: 25.

27272 ■ Fresenius Medical Care--Beaumont
3740 Laurel St.
Beaumont, TX 77707
Free: 866-434-2597
URL: http://www.ultracare-dialysis.com/
Dialysis Stations: 16. **Formerly:** Renal Care Group.

27273 ■ Golden Triangle Dialysis Center
Fresenius Medical Care
3965 Phelan Blvd., Ste. 200
Beaumont, TX 77707
Free: 866-434-2597
URL: http://www.ultracare-dialysis.com/
Dialysis Stations: 30.

Bedford

27274 ■ Ameri-Tech Kidney Center--HEB
1600 Central Dr., Ste. 130
Bedford, TX 76022
Ph: (817)545-2044
Dialysis Stations: 20.

27275 ■ DaVita--Bedford
HEB Dialysis Center
1401 Brown Trail Rd., Ste. A
Bedford, TX 76022
Free: 800-424-6589
URL: http://www.davita.com
Dialysis Stations: 15. **Formerly:** Hurst-Euless-Bedford Dialysis Center.

Beeville

27276 ■ Beeville Dialysis & At Home DaVita
100 W Huntington
Beeville, TX 78102
Free: 800-424-6589
URL: http://www.davita.com
Dialysis Stations: 20.

27277 ■ Beeville Renal Center
Diversified Specialty Institutes
1905 NW Frontage Rd.
Beeville, TX 78102
Ph: (361)358-4175
URL: http://www.dsi-corp.com
Dialysis Stations: 21. **Formerly:** National Renal Institutes.

Bellmead

27278 ■ Bellmead Kidney Disease Center Dialysis Facility
Fresenius Medical Care
137 Eastgate Shopping Center
Bellmead, TX 76705
Free: 866-434-2597
URL: http://www.ultracare-dialysis.com/
Dialysis Stations: 28.

Big Spring

27279 ■ Fresenius Medical Care
West Texas Dialysis
501 Birdwell Ln., Ste. 10
Big Spring, TX 79720
Free: 866-434-2597
URL: http://www.ultracare-dialysis.com/
Dialysis Stations: 15.

Boerne

27280 ■ Boerne Dialysis Center
DaVita
1369 S Main St.
Boerne, TX 78006
Free: 800-424-6589
URL: http://www.davita.com
Dialysis Stations: 12.

27281 ■ US Renal Care Inc.--Boerne
1595 S Main, Ste. 107
Boerne, TX 78006
Ph: (830)816-3030
URL: http://www.usrenalcare.com
Dialysis Stations: 16.

Bonham

27282 ■ Bonham Dialysis
DaVita
201 W 5th St.
Bonham, TX 75418
Free: 800-424-6589
URL: http://www.davita.com
Dialysis Stations: 9.

Brenham

27283 ■ DaVita--Brenham Dialysis Center
2536 S Day St.
Brenham, TX 77833
Free: 800-424-6589
URL: http://www.davita.com
Dialysis Stations: 16.

27284 ■ Liberty Dialysis--Brenham
604 Medical Courts
Brenham, TX 77833
URL: http://www.libertydialysis.com
Dialysis Stations: 12.

Brownsville

27285 ■ Brownsville Kidney Center Dialysis Facility
Diversified Specialty Institutes
2945 Central Blvd.
Brownsville, TX 78520
Ph: (956)542-8094
URL: http://www.dsi-corp.com
Dialysis Stations: 20. **Formerly:** National Renal Institutes.

27286 ■ Dialysis Services of North Brownsville
Fresenius Medical Care
1900 N Expressway, Ste. E
Brownsville, TX 78521
Free: 866-434-2597
URL: http://www.ultracare-dialysis.com/
Dialysis Stations: 20.

27287 ■ Valley Hemodialysis Center
Fresenius Medical Care
2600 N Coria
Brownsville, TX 78520
Free: 866-434-2597
URL: http://www.ultracare-dialysis.com/
Dialysis Stations: 32.

Brownwood

27288 ■ Brownwood Renal Care Center Dialysis Facility
110 Southpark Dr.
Brownwood, TX 76801
Ph: (325)646-9510
Dialysis Stations: 24.

Bryan

27289 ■ Bryan Dialysis
Fresenius Medical Care
1612 N Texas
Bryan, TX 77803
Free: 866-434-2597
URL: http://www.ultracare-dialysis.com/
Dialysis Stations: 17.

27290 ■ Liberty Dialysis--Bryan
2390 E 29th St.
Bryan, TX 77802
URL: http://www.libertydialysis.com
Dialysis Stations: 21.

Burleson

27291 ■ US Renal Care
Tarrant Dialysis Center--South Fort Worth
11905 Med Park Dr.
Burleson, TX 76028
Ph: (817)293-1978
URL: http://www.usrenalcare.com
Dialysis Stations: 20.

Canton

27292 ■ US Renal Care--Canton HD and Home
400 E State Hwy. 243, Ste. 14
Canton, TX 75103
Ph: (903)567-2250
Fax: (903)567-2209
URL: http://www.usrenalcare.com
Dialysis Stations: 13.

Carrizo Springs

27293 ■ Carizzo Springs Kidney Disease Clinic
Fresenius Medical Care
409 S 7th St.
Carrizo Springs, TX 78834
Free: 866-434-2597
URL: http://www.ultracare-dialysis.com/
Dialysis Stations: 20.

Carrollton

27294 ■ Carrollton Dialysis
DaVita
1544 Valwood Pkwy.
Carrollton, TX 75006
Free: 800-424-6589
URL: http://www.davita.com
Dialysis Stations: 12.

27295 ■ Renal Center of Carrollton
Renal Ventures Management
4240 International Pkwy., Ste. 158
Carrollton, TX 75007
Ph: (972)306-8410
URL: http://www.renalventures.com
Dialysis Stations: 20.

Carthage

27296 ■ Carthage Dialysis Center
Fresenius Medical Care
1614 S Market St.
Carthage, TX 75633
Free: 866-434-2597
URL: http://www.ultracare-dialysis.com/
Dialysis Stations: 13.

Cedar Park

27297 ■ Cedar Park Dialysis Center and At Home
DaVita
1720 E Whitestone Blvd.
Cedar Park, TX 78613
Free: 800-424-6589
URL: http://www.davita.com
Dialysis Stations: 12.

27298 ■ Fresenius Medical Care--Cedar Park
1201 N Lakeline Blvd.
Cedar Park, TX 78613
Free: 866-434-2597
URL: http://www.ultracare-dialysis.com/
Dialysis Stations: 16.

Center

27299 ■ Center Dialysis
Fresenius Medical Care
457 Hwy. 7E
Center, TX 75935
Free: 866-434-2597
URL: http://www.ultracare-dialysis.com/
Dialysis Stations: 13. **Formerly:** Renal Care Group.

Channelview

27300 ■ Channelview Dialysis
DaVita
777 Sheldon Rd., Ste. C
Channelview, TX 77530
Free: 800-424-6589
URL: http://www.davita.com
Dialysis Stations: 20. **Formerly:** Grambo Healthcare.

Childress

27301 ■ Childress Regional Medical Center Dialysis
PO Box 1030
Childress, TX 79201
Ph: (940)937-7099
URL: http://www.childresshospital.com/
Dialysis Stations: 10.

Cleburne

27302 ■ Cleburne Dialysis Center
Fresenius Medical Care
160 Jack Burton Rd.
Cleburne, TX 76031
Free: 866-434-2597
URL: http://www.ultracare-dialysis.com/
Dialysis Stations: 20.

27303 ■ Tarrant Dialysis Cleburne
US Renal Care
1206 N Henderson
Cleburne, TX 76033
Ph: (817)641-5530
URL: http://www.usrenalcare.com/
Dialysis Stations: 13.

Cleveland

27304 ■ Cleveland Dialysis Center
DaVita
600 E Houston, Ste. 630
Cleveland, TX 77327
Free: 800-424-6589
URL: http://www.davita.com
Dialysis Stations: 14.

College Station

27305 ■ College Station Dialysis
DaVita
Dialysis Facility & At Home
701 University Dr. E, Ste. 401
College Station, TX 77840
Free: 800-424-6589
URL: http://www.davita.com
Dialysis Stations: 25. **Formerly:** Grambo Healthcare.

27306 ■ DaVita--Rock Prairie Road
1605 Rock Prairie Rd., Ste. 101
College Station, TX 77845
Free: 800-424-6589
URL: http://www.davita.com
Dialysis Stations: 20. **Formerly:** Grambo Healthcare.

27307 ■ Gambro Healthcare--Rock Prairie Rd.
1605 Rock Prairie Rd.
College Station, TX 77845
Ph: (979)764-6500
URL: http://www.gambro.com/en/global/
Dialysis Stations: 20.

27308 ■ Liberty Dialysis--College Station
3314 Longmire Dr.
College Station, TX 77845
URL: http://www.libertydialysis.com
Dialysis Stations: 16.

Colorado City

27309 ■ Colorado City Dialysis
AccessCare
1546 Chestnut St.
Colorado City, TX 79512
Ph: (325)728-8348
URL: http://accesscaredialysis.com/
Dialysis Stations: 8.

Conroe

27310 ■ DaVita--Conroe Dialysis Center
500 Medical Center Blvd., Ste. 175
Conroe, TX 77304
Free: 800-424-6589
URL: http://www.davita.com
Dialysis Stations: 20. **Formerly:** Total Renal Care.

27311 ■ River Park Dialysis
DaVita
2010 S Loop 336W, Ste. 200
Conroe, TX 77304
Free: 800-424-6589
URL: http://www.davita.com
Dialysis Stations: 12.

Corpus Christi

27312 ■ Corpus Christi Renal Center
Diversified Specialty Institutes
2733 Swantner Dr.
Corpus Christi, TX 78404
Ph: (361)855-4911
URL: http://www.dsi-corp.com
Dialysis Stations: 23. **Formerly:** National Renal Institutes.

27313 ■ Driscoll Children's Hospital Dialysis Unit
Sloan Bldg., 2nd Fl.
3533 Alameda
Corpus Christi, TX 78466
Ph: (361)694-6800
URL: http://www.driscollchildrens.org
Dialysis Stations: 5.

27314 ■ Fresenius Medical Care--Calallen
4147 Five Points Rd.
Corpus Christi, TX 78410
Free: 866-434-2597
URL: http://www.ultracare-dialysis.com/
Dialysis Stations: 14. **Formerly:** Renal Care Group - Riverside.

27315 ■ Fresenius Medical Care--Corpus Christi
1125 3rd St.
Corpus Christi, TX 78404
Free: 866-434-2597
URL: http://www.ultracare-dialysis.com/
Dialysis Stations: 22. **Formerly:** Renal Care Group.

27316 ■ Fresenius Medical Care--Saratoga
6017 Parkway Dr.
Corpus Christi, TX 78414
Free: 866-434-2597
URL: http://www.ultracare-dialysis.com/
Dialysis Stations: 16.

27317 ■ Fresenius Medical Care--Southside
4112 S Staples, Ste. A&B
Corpus Christi, TX 78411
Free: 866-434-2597
URL: http://www.ultracare-dialysis.com/
Dialysis Stations: 24. **Formerly:** Renal Care Group.

27318 ■ Greenwood Holly Renal Center
Diversified Specialty Institutes
1533 Holly Dr.
Corpus Christi, TX 78417
Free: 866-508-0079
URL: http://www.dsi-corp.com
Dialysis Stations: 24.

27319 ■ Riverside Renal Center
Diversified Specialty Institutes
13434 Leopard St., Ste. A-17
Corpus Christi, TX 78410
Ph: (361)241-4873
URL: http://www.dsi-corp.com
Dialysis Stations: 17. **Formerly:** Dialysis Specialists.

27320 ■ South Central Texas Renal Center
Diversified Specialty Institutes
2222 Morgan Ave., Ste. 104
Corpus Christi, TX 78405
Ph: (361)884-1113
URL: http://www.dsi-corp.com
Dialysis Stations: 20. **Formerly:** Dialysis Specialists.

27321 ■ South Texas Acute Dialysis Center
Diversified Specialty Institutes
4301 S Padre Island Dr., Ste. 2-2
Corpus Christi, TX 78404

Ph: (361)855-9469
URL: http://www.dsi-corp.com
Dialysis Stations: 20.

27322 ■ South Texas Renal Center
Diversified Specialty Institutes
43002-2 S Padre Island Dr.
Corpus Christi, TX 78411
Ph: (361)855-9469
URL: http://www.dsi-corp.com
Dialysis Stations: 20. **Formerly:** Dialysis Specialists.

Corsicana

27323 ■ Fresenius Medical Care--Corsicana Dialysis Facility
1321 W 2nd Ave.
Corsicana, TX 75110
Free: 866-434-2597
URL: http://www.ultracare-dialysis.com/
Dialysis Stations: 21.

Crockett

27324 ■ Fresenius Medical Care--Crockett Dialysis Facility
951 Loop 304 E, Ste. 100
Crockett, TX 75835
Free: 866-434-2597
URL: http://www.ultracare-dialysis.com/
Dialysis Stations: 16. **Formerly:** Renal Care Group - Crockett.

Crosby

27325 ■ Crosby Dialysis Facility
Fresenius Medical Care
6107 FM 2100
Crosby, TX 77532
Free: 866-434-2597
URL: http://www.ultracare-dialysis.com/
Dialysis Stations: 12.

Cuero

27326 ■ Cuero Lakeview Dialysis
DaVita
1105 E Broadway
Cuero, TX 77954
Free: 800-424-6589
URL: http://www.davita.com
Dialysis Stations: 13. **Formerly:** Cuero Lakeview Kidney Center.

Dallas

27327 ■ Baylor University Medical Center, ESRD Transplant
3500 Gaston Ave.
Dallas, TX 75246
Ph: (214)820-2050
URL: http://www.baylortransplant.com/
Dialysis Stations: 0.

27328 ■ Brookriver Dialysis & At Home
DaVita
8101 Brookriver Dr.
Dallas, TX 75247
Free: 800-424-6589
URL: http://www.davita.com
Dialysis Stations: 20.

27329 ■ Central Dallas Dialysis
DaVita
9500 N Central Expy.
Dallas, TX 75231
Free: 800-424-6589
URL: http://www.davita.com
Dialysis Stations: 16.

27330 ■ Children's Medical Center Transplant Services
Dialysis Center
1935 Medical District Dr.
Dallas, TX 75235
Ph: (214)456-2980
URL: http://www.childrens.com
Dialysis Stations: 6. **Program(s):** Hemodialysis; CAPD/CCPD; Transplants.

27331 ■ Dallas East Dialysis
DaVita
3312 N Buckner, Ste. 213
Dallas, TX 75228
URL: http://www.davita.com
Dialysis Stations: 17. **Formerly:** Grambo Healthcare.

27332 ■ Dallas North Dialysis Center & At Home
DaVita
11886 Greenville Ave., Ste. 100B
Dallas, TX 75243
Free: 800-424-6589
URL: http://www.davita.com
Dialysis Stations: 12.

27333 ■ DaVita
UT Southwestern--Oakcliff Dialysis
608-610 Wynnewood Village
Dallas, TX 75224
Free: 800-424-6589
URL: http://www.davita.com
Dialysis Stations: 36. **Formerly:** Grambo Healthcare.

27334 ■ Dialysis Services Southwestern
Fresenius Medical Care
6010 Forest Park, Ste. 200
Dallas, TX 75235
Free: 866-434-2597
URL: http://www.ultracare-dialysis.com/
Dialysis Stations: 7.

27335 ■ Downtown Dallas Dialysis
DaVita
3515 Swiss Ave., Ste. A
Dallas, TX 75204
Free: 800-424-6589
URL: http://www.davita.com
Dialysis Stations: 16.

27336 ■ Fresenius Medical Care--Dallas Central
7610 Military Pkwy.
Dallas, TX 75227
Free: 866-434-2597
URL: http://www.ultracare-dialysis.com/
Dialysis Stations: 30.

27337 ■ Fresenius Medical Care--Dallas South
Dialysis Facility
1150 N Bishop, Ste. 200
Dallas, TX 75208
Free: 866-434-2597
URL: http://www.ultracare-dialysis.com/
Dialysis Stations: 32.

27338 ■ Fresenius Medical Care--Forest Park
6010 Forest Park, Ste. 100
Dallas, TX 75235
Free: 866-434-2597
URL: http://www.ultracare-dialysis.com/
Dialysis Stations: 31.

27339 ■ Fresenius Medical Care--Kiest Station
5148 S Lancaster, Ste. B
Dallas, TX 75241
Free: 866-434-2597
URL: http://www.ultracare-dialysis.com/
Dialysis Stations: 16.

27340 ■ Fresenius Medical Care of South Dallas County
Dialysis Facility
1111 W Ledbetter St., Ste. 800
Dallas, TX 75224
Free: 866-434-2597
URL: http://www.ultracare-dialysis.com/
Dialysis Stations: 27.

27341 ■ Home Kidney Care
Real Ventures Management, LLC
6200 LBJ Fwy., Ste. 100
Dallas, TX 75230
Ph: (214)466-7233
Fax: (214)393-4738
URL: http://www.homekidneycare.net/
Dialysis Stations: 0.

27342 ■ Lake Cliff Dialysis Center
DaVita
805 N Beckley Ave.
Dallas, TX 75203
Free: 800-424-6589
URL: http://www.davita.com
Dialysis Stations: 20.

27343 ■ Medical City Dallas Renal Transplant
7777 Forest La.
Dallas, TX 75230
Ph: (972)566-6768
URL: http://www.medicalcityhospital.com/CustomPage.asp?guidCustomContentID=%7BAD 687797-CA06-4ED1-918D-4AD0008D43B7%7D
Dialysis Stations: 0.

27344 ■ Methodist Hospital Dallas Transplant Institute
PO Box 655999
Dallas, TX 75265
Ph: (214)947-1800
Dialysis Stations: 0.

27345 ■ Mockingbird Peritoneal Dialysis
Fresenius Medical Care
8700 N Stemmons, Ste. 133
Dallas, TX 75247
Free: 866-434-2597
URL: http://www.ultracare-dialysis.com/
Dialysis Stations: 0.

27346 ■ North Buckner Dialysis Center
Fresenius Medical Care
3650 N Buckner, Ste. 108
Dallas, TX 75228
Free: 866-434-2597
URL: http://www.ultracare-dialysis.com/
Dialysis Stations: 26.

27347 ■ Oak Cliff Dialysis
DaVita
2000 S Llewellyn
Dallas, TX 75224
Free: 800-424-6589
URL: http://www.davita.com
Dialysis Stations: 16.

27348 ■ Parkland Hospital ESRD Transplant Services
5201 Harry Hines
Dallas, TX 75235
Ph: (214)590-5656
URL: http://www.parklandhospital.com/other_services/organ_transplants.html
Dialysis Stations: 0.

27349 ■ Redbird Dialysis Center
Fresenius Medical Care
4111 Camp Wisdom Rd.
Dallas, TX 75237
Free: 866-434-2597
URL: http://www.ultracare-dialysis.com/
Dialysis Stations: 32.

27350 ■ South Oak Cliff Dialysis Center
Fresenius Medical Care
740 Wynnewood Shopping Center
Dallas, TX 75224
Free: 866-434-2597
URL: http://www.ultracare-dialysis.com/
Dialysis Stations: 40.

27351 ■ Swiss Avenue Dialysis Center
Fresenius Medical Care
2613 Swiss Ave.
Dallas, TX 75204
Free: 866-434-2597
URL: http://www.ultracare-dialysis.com/
Dialysis Stations: 28.

27352 ■ University of Texas Southwestern Medical Center
Transplant Services
5939 Harry Hines Blvd.
Dallas, TX 75390
Ph: (214)645-1919
URL: http://www.utsouthwestern.edu/patientcare/medicalservices/transplants/tissu e.html
Dialysis Stations: 0.

27353 ■ UT Southwestern--Dallas Dialysis
DaVita
8230 Elmbrook Dr.
Dallas, TX 75247
Free: 800-424-6589
URL: http://www.davita.com
Dialysis Stations: 33. **Formerly:** Grambo Healthcare.

27354 ■ Village II Dialysis Center
Fresenius Medical Care
6300 Samuel Blvd., Ste. 125
Dallas, TX 75228
Free: 866-434-2597
URL: http://www.ultracare-dialysis.com/
Dialysis Stations: 28.

27355 ■ Walnut Hill Dialysis Center
Fresenius Medical Care
9840 N Central Expy., Ste. 340
Dallas, TX 75231
Free: 866-434-2597
URL: http://www.ultracare-dialysis.com/
Dialysis Stations: 24.

De Soto

27356 ■ Pleasant Run Dialysis
Fresenius Medical Care
900 Polk St.
De Soto, TX 75115
Free: 866-434-2597
URL: http://www.ultracare-dialysis.com/
Dialysis Stations: 24.

Decatur

27357 ■ Wise Regional Health System Dialysis Center
2000 Ben Merritt, Ste. B
Decatur, TX 76234
Ph: (940)626-1700
URL: http://www.wiseregional.com
Dialysis Stations: 24.

Deer Park

27358 ■ Dialysis Services of Deer Park
Fresenius Medical Care
4621 Center
Deer Park, TX 77536
Free: 866-434-2597
URL: http://www.ultracare-dialysis.com/
Dialysis Stations: 12.

Del Rio

27359 ■ Fresenius Medical Care--Del Rio
2201 N Bedell, Ste. D
Del Rio, TX 78840
Free: 866-434-2597
URL: http://www.ultracare-dialysis.com/
Dialysis Stations: 24.

27360 ■ Val Verde Renal Care Center Dialysis Facility
608 Bedell Ave.
Del Rio, TX 78840
Ph: (830)774-3031
Dialysis Stations: 14.

Denison

27361 ■ Denison Dialysis Center & At Home
DaVita
1220 Reba McEntire Ln.
Denison, TX 75020
Free: 800-424-6589
URL: http://www.davita.com
Dialysis Stations: 21.

Denton

27362 ■ Renal Center of North Denton
Renal Ventures Management
4309 Mesa Dr.
Denton, TX 76207
Ph: (940)566-2701
URL: http://www.renalventures.com
Dialysis Stations: 25.

Denver City

27363 ■ Dialysis Services of West Texas
Yoakum County Hospital
500 W 5th St.
Denver City, TX 79323
Ph: (806)592-2090
URL: http://www.ych.us/dialysis.asp
Dialysis Stations: 12.

Dickinson

27364 ■ Fresenius Medical Care--Dickinson
3800 Hughes Ct.
Dickinson, TX 77539
Free: 866-434-2597
URL: http://www.ultracare-dialysis.com/
Dialysis Stations: 16.

Duncanville

27365 ■ Duncanville Dialysis
DaVita
270 E Hwy. 67, Ste. 100
Duncanville, TX 75137
Free: 800-424-6589
URL: http://www.davita.com
Dialysis Stations: 12.

27366 ■ Liberty Dialysis--Duncanville
1038 US Hwy. 67
Duncanville, TX 75137
Ph: (214)302-0238
URL: http://www.libertydialysis.com
Dialysis Stations: 20.

Eagle Pass

27367 ■ Eagle Pass Kidney Disease Clinic
Fresenius Medical Care
3065 Megan St.
Eagle Pass, TX 78852
Free: 866-434-2597
URL: http://www.ultracare-dialysis.com/
Dialysis Stations: 45.

27368 ■ Maverick County Dialysis Facility
US Renal Care
3420 Amy St.
Eagle Pass, TX 78852
Ph: (830)773-8878
URL: http://www.usrenalcare.com
Dialysis Stations: 36. **Formerly:** Rencare Ltd.

Edinburg

27369 ■ Diversified Specialty Institutes
Edinburg Dialysis Center
4302 S Sugar Rd., Ste. 105
Edinburg, TX 78538
Ph: (956)287-9810
URL: http://www.dsi-corp.com
Dialysis Stations: 24.

27370 ■ Edinburg Kidney Center
Fresenius Medical Care
5406 S Jackson
Edinburg, TX 78539
Free: 866-434-2597
Fax: (956)668-1130
URL: http://www.ultracare-dialysis.com/
Dialysis Stations: 20. **Formerly:** Renal Care Group.

27371 ■ US Renal Care--Edinburg
4001 S Sugar Rd., Ste. B
Edinburg, TX 78539
Ph: (956)383-8488
URL: http://www.usrenalcare.com
Dialysis Stations: 12.

Edna

27372 ■ Edna Dialysis Center
DaVita
1008 N Wells St.
Edna, TX 77957
Free: 800-424-6589
URL: http://www.davita.com
Dialysis Stations: 12.

El Campo

27373 ■ El Campo Dialysis
307 Sandy Corner Rd.
El Campo, TX 77437
Ph: (979)543-8200
Dialysis Stations: 18.

El Paso

27374 ■ Cielo Vista Dialysis
DaVita
7200 Gateway E, Ste. B
El Paso, TX 79915
Free: 800-424-6589
URL: http://www.davita.com
Dialysis Stations: 20.

27375 ■ DaVita--Central City Dialysis Center
1300 Murchison Dr., Ste. 320
El Paso, TX 79902
Free: 800-424-6589
URL: http://www.davita.com
Dialysis Stations: 20.

27376 ■ DaVita--East Dialysis
11989 Pellicano Dr.
El Paso, TX 79936
Free: 800-424-6589
URL: http://www.davita.com
Dialysis Stations: 20.

27377 ■ DaVita--West Texas Dialysis Center
1250 E Cliff Dr., Bldg. B
El Paso, TX 79902
Free: 800-424-6589
URL: http://www.davita.com
Dialysis Stations: 17.

27378 ■ El Paso Kidney Center--East
Diversified Specialty Institutes
10737 Gateway W, Ste. 100
El Paso, TX 79935

Ph: (915)590-8334
URL: http://www.dsi-corp.com
Dialysis Stations: 18.

27379 ■ El Paso Kidney Center--West Dialysis Facility
Diversified Specialty Institutes
3100 N Stanton
El Paso, TX 79902
Ph: (915)532-7007
URL: http://www.dsi-corp.com
Dialysis Stations: 16.

27380 ■ Fresenius Medical Care Dialysis Services--Vista Del Sol
10420 Vista Del Sol Dr., Ste. 201
El Paso, TX 79925
Free: 866-434-2597
URL: http://www.ultracare-dialysis.com/
Dialysis Stations: 17.

27381 ■ Fresenius Medical Care--El Paso/Cliff View
Dialysis Facility
1225 E Cliff, Ste. 1-A
El Paso, TX 79902
Free: 866-434-2597
URL: http://www.ultracare-dialysis.com/
Dialysis Stations: 21.

27382 ■ Fresenius Medical Care--El Paso/Gateway
Dialysis Facility
10767 Gateway W, Ste. 600
El Paso, TX 79935
Free: 866-434-2597
URL: http://www.ultracare-dialysis.com/
Dialysis Stations: 20.

27383 ■ Fresenius Medical Care--Horizon Dialysis
12245 Rojas Dr.
El Paso, TX 79936
Free: 866-434-2597
URL: http://www.ultracare-dialysis.com/
Dialysis Stations: 24.

27384 ■ Loma Vista Dialysis
DaVita
1382-A Lomaland Dr.
El Paso, TX 79935
Free: 800-424-6589
URL: http://www.davita.com
Dialysis Stations: 39.

27385 ■ Mesa Vista Dialysis Center
DaVita
2400 N Oregon, Ste. C
El Paso, TX 79902
Free: 800-424-6589
URL: http://www.davita.com
Dialysis Stations: 20.

27386 ■ Mission Hills Dialysis
DaVita
2700 N Stanton
El Paso, TX 79902
Free: 800-424-6589
URL: http://www.davita.com
Dialysis Stations: 20.

27387 ■ Sun City Dialysis Center
DaVita
600 Newman St.
El Paso, TX 79902
Free: 800-424-6589
URL: http://www.davita.com
Dialysis Stations: 20.

27388 ■ Transmountain Dialysis
DaVita
5255 Transmountain Rd.
El Paso, TX 79924
Free: 800-424-6589
URL: http://www.davita.com
Dialysis Stations: 20.

27389 ■ Upper Valley Dialysis
DaVita
7933 Mesa, Ste. H
El Paso, TX 79932
Free: 800-424-6589
URL: http://www.davita.com
Dialysis Stations: 16.

Elsa

27390 ■ US Renal Care--Delta
400 E Edinburg Blvd.
Elsa, TX 78543
Ph: (956)262-3400
URL: http://www.usrenalcare.com
Dialysis Stations: 15.

Ennis

27391 ■ Fresenius Medical Care--Ennis
711 S Clay St., Ste. B
Ennis, TX 75119
Free: 866-434-2597
URL: http://www.ultracare-dialysis.com/
Dialysis Stations: 12.

Falfurrias

27392 ■ Fresenius Medical Care--Falfurrias
720 N Saint Marys St.
Falfurrias, TX 78355
Free: 866-434-2597
URL: http://www.ultracare-dialysis.com/
Dialysis Stations: 16.

Farmers Branch

27393 ■ Farmers Branch Dialysis Center
Fresenius Medical Care
2280 Springlake Rd., Ste. 110
Farmers Branch, TX 75234
Free: 866-434-2597
URL: http://www.ultracare-dialysis.com/
Dialysis Stations: 24.

Floresville

27394 ■ Floresville Dialysis
DaVita
Dialysis Facility
543 10th St.
Floresville, TX 78114
Free: 800-424-6589
URL: http://www.davita.com
Dialysis Stations: 12. **Formerly:** Gambro Healthcare.

Fort Stockton

27395 ■ Fort Stockton Dialysis
AccessCare
387 W IH-10
Fort Stockton, TX 79735
Ph: (432)336-4859
URL: http://accesscaredialysis.com/
Dialysis Stations: 8.

Fort Worth

27396 ■ Baylor All Saints Medical Center Transplant Center
1400 Eighth Ave.
Fort Worth, TX 76104
Ph: (817)922-4650
URL: http://www.baylortransplant.com/
Dialysis Stations: 0.

27397 ■ Cook Children's Medical Center Transplant and Dialysis Center
801 7th Ave.
Fort Worth, TX 76104
Ph: (682)885-3944
URL: http://www.cookchildrens.org
Dialysis Stations: 4.

27398 ■ Fresenius Medical Care Central Fort Worth Dialysis Center
1210 Alston
Fort Worth, TX 76104
Free: 866-434-2597
URL: http://www.ultracare-dialysis.com/
Dialysis Stations: 28.

27399 ■ Fresenius Medical Care--Fort Worth Parkway
6551 Harris Pkwy.
Fort Worth, TX 76132
Free: 866-434-2597
URL: http://www.ultracare-dialysis.com/
Dialysis Stations: 24.

27400 ■ Fresenius Medical Care--North Fort Worth
2530 Jacksboro Hwy.
Fort Worth, TX 76119
Free: 866-434-2597
URL: http://www.ultracare-dialysis.com/
Dialysis Stations: 24.

27401 ■ Harris Methodist Ft. Worth Transplant
1301 Pennsylvania Ave.
Fort Worth, TX 76104
Ph: (817)250-2443
URL: http://www.texashealth.org/body.cfm?id=384
Dialysis Stations: 0.

27402 ■ Reliant Renal Care--East Fort Worth
1032 Sandy Ln.
Fort Worth, TX 76120
Ph: (817)429-1944
URL: http://www.reliantrenalcare.com/
Dialysis Stations: 19.

27403 ■ Southwest Fort Worth Dialysis Center
Fresenius Medical Care
4804 Bryant Irvin Ct.
Fort Worth, TX 76107
Free: 866-434-2597
URL: http://www.ultracare-dialysis.com/
Dialysis Stations: 24.

27404 ■ Tarrant County Campus Dialysis
Fresenius Medical Care
5000 Campus Dr.
Fort Worth, TX 76119
Free: 866-434-2597
URL: http://www.ultracare-dialysis.com/
Dialysis Stations: 30.

27405 ■ Tarrant Dialysis Center--Central
US Renal Care
4201 E Berry, Ste. 8
Fort Worth, TX 76105
Ph: (817)531-0326
URL: http://www.usrenalcare.com
Dialysis Stations: 30.

27406 ■ Tarrant Dialysis Center--Fort Worth
US Renal Care
1001 Pennsylvania Ave.
Fort Worth, TX 76104
Ph: (817)877-5907
URL: http://www.usrenalcare.com
Dialysis Stations: 30.

27407 ■ Tarrant Dialysis Center--Fort Worth
US Renal Care
5127 Old Granbury Rd.
Fort Worth, TX 76133
Ph: (817)370-7830
URL: http://www.usrenalcare.com
Dialysis Stations: 24.

27408 ■ Tarrant Dialysis Center--Tarrant County
US Renal Care
1009 Pennsylvania Ave.
Fort Worth, TX 76104
Ph: (817)877-1515
URL: http://www.usrenalcare.com
Dialysis Stations: 1. **Remarks:** Peritoneal dialysis only.

27409 ■ Texas Renal Ventures Dialysis Facility
Renal Ventures Management
1049 Clifton St.
Fort Worth, TX 76107
Ph: (817)870-5002
URL: http://www.renalventures.com
Dialysis Stations: 16.

27410 ■ US Renal Care
Tarrant Dialysis Center--North Fort Worth
1978 Ephriham Ave.
Fort Worth, TX 76106
Ph: (817)624-7811
URL: http://www.usrenalcare.com
Dialysis Stations: 24.

Friendswood

27411 ■ Friendswood Dialysis
US Renal Care
3324 E FM 528
Friendswood, TX 77546
Ph: (281)993-5067
Fax: (281)482-0360
URL: http://www.usrenalcare.com
Dialysis Stations: 12.

Frisco

27412 ■ Renal Ventures Management of Frisco
10850 Frisco St., Ste. 300
Frisco, TX 75034
Ph: (214)872-2421
Fax: (214)872-2426
URL: http://www.renalventures.com
Dialysis Stations: 21.

Gainesville

27413 ■ The Dialysis Cottage
1902 Hospital Blvd., Ste. D
Gainesville, TX 76240
Ph: (940)612-8800
URL: http://www.thedialysiscottage.com/
Dialysis Stations: 12. **Formerly:** Gainesville Memorial Hospital Dialysis Facility.

Galveston

27414 ■ Island Dialysis Center
DaVita
5920 Broadway
Galveston, TX 77551
Free: 800-424-6589
URL: http://www.davita.com
Dialysis Stations: 27.

27415 ■ University of Texas Medical Branch Transplant
301 University Blvd.
Galveston, TX 77555
Ph: (409)772-8643
Dialysis Stations: 0.

27416 ■ University of Texas Medical Branch Transplant/Dialysis Center
301 University Blvd., RT 0483
Galveston, TX 77555
Ph: (409)772-6731
URL: http://www.utmb.edu
Dialysis Stations: 12.

Garland

27417 ■ Fresenius Medical Care--North Garland
530 Clara Barton Dr., Ste. 105
Garland, TX 75042
Free: 866-434-2597
URL: http://www.ultracare-dialysis.com/
Dialysis Stations: 20.

27418 ■ Garland Dialysis
DaVita
776 E Centerville Rd.
Garland, TX 75041
Free: 800-424-6589
URL: http://www.davita.com
Dialysis Stations: 20.

27419 ■ Town Gate Dialysis Center
Fresenius Medical Care
1901 W Northwest Hwy., Ste. 210
Garland, TX 75041
Ph: (972)278-2014
Dialysis Stations: 36.

Gilmer

27420 ■ Fresenius Medical Care--Gilmer
Gilmer Plz.
1203 FM 49
Gilmer, TX 75644
Free: 866-434-2597
URL: http://www.ultracare-dialysis.com/
Dialysis Stations: 16. **Formerly:** Renal Care Group.

27421 ■ Gilmer Dialysis
DaVita
519 N Wood St.
Gilmer, TX 75644
Free: 800-424-6589
URL: http://www.davita.com
Dialysis Stations: 12.

Gonzales

27422 ■ DaVita--Gonzales Dialysis Facility
1406 N Sarah DeWitt
Gonzales, TX 78629
Free: 800-424-6589
URL: http://www.davita.com
Dialysis Stations: 16.

Granbury

27423 ■ Fresenius Medical Care--Granbury Dialysis Facility
950 Whitehead Rd.
Granbury, TX 76048
Free: 866-434-2597
URL: http://www.ultracare-dialysis.com/
Dialysis Stations: 12.

Grand Prairie

27424 ■ Fresenius Medical Care--Grand Prairie
825 Dalworth Ave.
Grand Prairie, TX 75050
Free: 866-434-2597
URL: http://www.ultracare-dialysis.com/
Dialysis Stations: 24.

27425 ■ Grand Prairie Dialysis Center Inc.
550 S Carrier Pkwy., Ste. 450
Grand Prairie, TX 75051
Ph: (972)237-2400
Dialysis Stations: 24.

27426 ■ Tarrant Dialysis Center--Grand Prairie
US Renal Care
1006 N Carrier Pkwy.
Grand Prairie, TX 75050
Ph: (972)263-7202
URL: http://www.usrenalcare.com
Dialysis Stations: 25.

Grapevine

27427 ■ Grapevine Dialysis & At Home
DaVita
1600 W Northwest Hwy., Ste. 100
Grapevine, TX 76051
Free: 800-424-6589
URL: http://www.davita.com
Dialysis Stations: 12.

Greenville

27428 ■ Greenville Dialysis
4309 Ridgecrest Rd., Ste. 100
Greenville, TX 75402
Ph: (903)455-9911
Dialysis Stations: 18.

27429 ■ North East Texas Dialysis Center
Diversified Specialty Institutes
4805 Wesley St.
Greenville, TX 75401
Ph: (903)454-9890
URL: http://www.dsi-corp.com
Dialysis Stations: 20. **Formerly:** National Renal Institutes.

Haltom City

27430 ■ Northeast Fort Worth Dialysis Center
Fresenius Medical Care
4121 Denton Hwy.
Haltom City, TX 76117
Free: 866-434-2597
URL: http://www.ultracare-dialysis.com/
Dialysis Stations: 24.

Harlingen

27431 ■ Fresenius Medical Care--Harlingen
1653 Treasure Hills Blvd.
Harlingen, TX 78552
Free: 866-434-2597
URL: http://www.ultracare-dialysis.com/
Dialysis Stations: 12.

27432 ■ Harlingen Dialysis
US Renal Care
4302 Sesame Dr.
Harlingen, TX 78550
Ph: (956)365-4103
URL: http://www.usrenalcare.com
Dialysis Stations: 30.

27433 ■ Valley Baptist Medical Center
2220 Haine Dr., Ste. 40
Harlingen, TX 78550
Ph: (956)389-2345
Dialysis Stations: 48. **Formerly:** Watson W. Wise Memorial Dialysis Center.

Hearne

27434 ■ Hearne Dialysis Center
DaVita
106 Cedar St.
Hearne, TX 77859
Free: 800-424-6589
URL: http://www.davita.com
Dialysis Stations: 12.

Henderson

27435 ■ Henderson Dialysis Center
DaVita
1002 Hwy. 79 N
Henderson, TX 75652
Free: 800-424-6589
URL: http://www.davita.com
Dialysis Stations: 12.

Hereford

27436 ■ Fresenius Medical Care--Hereford
533 N 25 Mile Ave., Ste. A
Hereford, TX 79045
Free: 866-434-2597
URL: http://www.ultracare-dialysis.com/
Dialysis Stations: 12.

Hillsboro

27437 ■ Fresenius Medical Care--Hillsboro
1507 Hillview
Hillsboro, TX 76645
Free: 866-434-2597
URL: http://www.ultracare-dialysis.com/
Dialysis Stations: 13.

Hondo

27438 ■ Medina Dialysis Facility
US Renal Care
3202 Ave. G
Hondo, TX 78861
Ph: (830)426-3843
URL: http://www.usrenalcare.com
Dialysis Stations: 16.

Houston

27439 ■ 1960 Dialysis Center
324 FM 1960 E
Houston, TX 77073
Ph: (281)443-2209
URL: http://1960dialysiscenter.com/
Dialysis Stations: 30.

27440 ■ Bayou City Dialysis
DaVita
10655 Eastex Fwy.
Houston, TX 77093
Free: 800-424-6589
URL: http://www.davita.com
Dialysis Stations: 16.

27441 ■ Bear Creek Dialysis
DaVita
4978 N Hwy. 6, Ste. 1
Houston, TX 77084
Free: 800-424-6589
URL: http://www.davita.com
Dialysis Stations: 12.

27442 ■ Beechnut Dialysis Center
8325 Beechnut
Houston, TX 77036
Ph: (713)772-5228
Dialysis Stations: 24.

27443 ■ Bissonnet Dialysis Center
8800 Bissonnet, Ste. A
Houston, TX 77074
Ph: (713)773-1717
Dialysis Stations: 18.

27444 ■ Brookhollow Dialysis
DaVita
4918 W 34th St.
Houston, TX 77092
Free: 800-424-6589
URL: http://www.davita.com
Dialysis Stations: 12.

27445 ■ Central Houston Dialysis
DaVita
610B S Wayside
Houston, TX 77011
Free: 800-424-6589
URL: http://www.davita.com
Dialysis Stations: 20. **Formerly:** Grambo Healthcare.

27446 ■ Cyfair Dialysis Center
DaVita
9110 Jones Rd., Ste. 110
Houston, TX 77065
Free: 800-424-6589
URL: http://www.davita.com
Dialysis Stations: 16.

27447 ■ DaVita
Cypress Woods Northwest Dialysis
20320 Northwest Fwy.
Houston, TX 77065
Free: 800-424-6589
URL: http://www.davita.com

27448 ■ DaVita
Houston Kidney Center--Southwest
Bldg. 100, Ste. 100
11111 Brooklet Dr., Ste. 100
Houston, TX 77099
Free: 800-424-6589
URL: http://www.davita.com
Dialysis Stations: 20.

27449 ■ Downtown Houston Dialysis Center
DaVita
2207 Crawford St.
Houston, TX 77002
Free: 800-424-6589
URL: http://www.davita.com
Dialysis Stations: 16.

27450 ■ Elik Dialysis Home Therapy
1445 N Loop W
Houston, TX 77008
Ph: (713)861-7500
URL: http://www.elikdialysis.com/
Dialysis Stations: 1.

27451 ■ Fresenius Medical Care--Downtown Houston
1914 Caroline St., Ste. 140
Houston, TX 77002
Free: 866-434-2597
URL: http://www.ultracare-dialysis.com/
Dialysis Stations: 30. **Formerly:** St. Joseph Dialysis Center.

27452 ■ Fresenius Medical Care--East Central Houston Dialysis Center
6830 Capitol St.
Houston, TX 77011
Free: 866-434-2597
URL: http://www.ultracare-dialysis.com/
Dialysis Stations: 15.

27453 ■ Fresenius Medical Care--Fifth Ward
2133 Lockwood
Houston, TX 77020
Free: 866-434-2597
URL: http://www.ultracare-dialysis.com/
Dialysis Stations: 12.

27454 ■ Fresenius Medical Care--Fondren
7435 SW Fwy.
Houston, TX 77074
Free: 866-434-2597
URL: http://www.ultracare-dialysis.com/
Dialysis Stations: 24.

27455 ■ Fresenius Medical Care--Meyerland
10311 S Post Oak
Houston, TX 77035
Free: 866-434-2597
URL: http://www.ultracare-dialysis.com/
Dialysis Stations: 16.

27456 ■ Fresenius Medical Care--Mission Bend
6886 Hwy. 6 S
Houston, TX 77083
Free: 866-434-2597
URL: http://www.ultracare-dialysis.com/
Dialysis Stations: 16.

27457 ■ Fresenius Medical Care--Museum District
4407 Yoakum Blvd.
Houston, TX 77006
Free: 866-434-2597
URL: http://www.ultracare-dialysis.com/
Dialysis Stations: 24.

27458 ■ Fresenius Medical Care--North Houston Dialysis
5435 Aldine Mail Rte.
Houston, TX 77039
Free: 866-434-2597
URL: http://www.ultracare-dialysis.com/
Dialysis Stations: 29. **Formerly:** North Houston Dialysis Center.

27459 ■ Fresenius Medical Care--Sunnyside
8340 Coffee
Houston, TX 77033
Free: 866-434-2597
URL: http://www.ultracare-dialysis.com/
Dialysis Stations: 20.

27460 ■ Gessner Dialysis and Kidney Center
8700 S Gessner
Houston, TX 77074
Ph: (713)774-4002
Dialysis Stations: 25.

27461 ■ Hillcroft Dialysis Center
6015 Hillcroft, Ste. 3000
Houston, TX 77081
Ph: (713)772-0992
Dialysis Stations: 20.

27462 ■ Houston Dialysis
DaVita
7543 S Freeway Rd.
Houston, TX 77021
Free: 800-424-6589
URL: http://www.davita.com
Dialysis Stations: 20. **Formerly:** Grambo Healthcare.

27463 ■ Houston Home Dialysis
9850 Drysdale La.
Houston, TX 77041
Ph: (713)690-2200
E-mail: email@houstonhomedialysis.com
URL: http://www.houstonhomedialysis.com/
Dialysis Stations: 2.

27464 ■ Houston Kidney Center--Cypress Dialysis Facility
DaVita
221 H FM 1960 W
Houston, TX 77090
Free: 800-424-6589
URL: http://www.davita.com
Dialysis Stations: 24. **Formerly:** Total Renal Care.

27465 ■ Houston Kidney Center Southwest
DaVita
11111 Brooklet Dr., Ste. 100, Bldg. 100
Houston, TX 77099
Free: 800-424-6589
URL: http://www.davita.com
Dialysis Stations: 20.

27466 ■ Innovative Renal Care--Webster Inc.
1700 Webster
Houston, TX 77003
Ph: (713)571-6674
Dialysis Stations: 25.

27467 ■ Lone Star Dialysis Center
DaVita
8560 Monroe
Houston, TX 77061
Free: 800-424-6589
URL: http://www.davita.com
Dialysis Stations: 48.

27468 ■ Med-Center At Home
DaVita
7580 Fannin St.
Houston, TX 77054
Free: 800-424-6589
URL: http://www.davita.com
Dialysis Stations: 4.

27469 ■ Med Center Dialysis
DaVita
5610 Almeda Rd.
Houston, TX 77004
Free: 800-424-6589
URL: http://www.davita.com
Dialysis Stations: 72.

27470 ■ Medical Center Kidney Clinic
Fresenius Medical Care
2254 Holcombe Blvd.
Houston, TX 77030
Free: 866-434-2597
URL: http://www.ultracare-dialysis.com/
Dialysis Stations: 32.

27471 ■ Memorial Dialysis Center & At Home
DaVita
11621 Katy Fwy.
Houston, TX 77079
Free: 800-424-6589
URL: http://www.davita.com
Dialysis Stations: 26.

27472 ■ Memorial Hermann Hospital Transplant/Dialysis Center
6411 Fannin St.
Houston, TX 77030
Ph: (713)704-0093
URL: http://www.memorialhermann.org
Dialysis Stations: 7.

27473 ■ Methodist Hospital ESRD Transplant Services
6565 Fannin Mail Station SM 1201
Houston, TX 77030
Ph: (713)441-5496
Dialysis Stations: 45.

27474 ■ Midtown Kidney Center
Fresenius Medical Care
2616 Blodgett
Houston, TX 77004
Free: 866-434-2597
URL: http://www.ultracare-dialysis.com/
Dialysis Stations: 26.

27475 ■ Moody Park Dialysis
Fresenius Medical Care
2920 Fulton St.
Houston, TX 77009
Free: 866-434-2597
URL: http://www.ultracare-dialysis.com/
Dialysis Stations: 16.

27476 ■ North Houston Dialysis Center
DaVita
129 Little York
Houston, TX 77076
Free: 800-424-6589
URL: http://www.davita.com
Dialysis Stations: 22.

27477 ■ North Loop East Dialysis Dialysis Center
Davita
7139 N Loop E
Houston, TX 77028
Free: 800-424-6589
URL: http://www.davita.com
Dialysis Stations: 16. **Formerly:** Grambo Healthcare.

27478 ■ North Shepherd Kidney Clinic
Fresenius Medical Care
7272 N Shepherd
Houston, TX 77091
Free: 866-434-2597
URL: http://www.ultracare-dialysis.com/
Dialysis Stations: 30.

27479 ■ North Star Dialysis Center
DaVita
380 W Little York
Houston, TX 77076
Free: 800-424-6589
URL: http://www.davita.com
Dialysis Stations: 49.

27480 ■ Northwest Houston Dialysis Center
Fresenius Medical Care
13312 FM, 1960 W
Houston, TX 77065
Free: 866-434-2597
URL: http://www.ultracare-dialysis.com/
Dialysis Stations: 16.

27481 ■ Northwest Kidney Center Dialysis Facility
DaVita
11029 Northwest Fwy.
Houston, TX 77092
Free: 800-424-6589
URL: http://www.davita.com
Dialysis Stations: 16.

27482 ■ Omni Dialysis Center
DaVita
9350 Kirby Dr., No. 110
Houston, TX 77054
Free: 800-424-6589
URL: http://www.davita.com
Dialysis Stations: 48.

27483 ■ Physicians Dialysis North Houston
DaVita
7115 N Loop E, North Port 2
Houston, TX 77028
Free: 800-424-6589
URL: http://www.davita.com
Dialysis Stations: 20.

27484 ■ Physicians Dialysis South Houston
DaVita
5989 S Loop East
Houston, TX 77033
Free: 800-424-6589
URL: http://www.davita.com
Dialysis Stations: 24.

27485 ■ Reliant Dialysis
DaVita
1335 La Concha Ln.
Houston, TX 77054
Free: 800-424-6589
URL: http://www.davita.com
Dialysis Stations: 24.

27486 ■ Renal Solutions Dialysis Services
2756 W TC Jester Blvd.
Houston, TX 77018
Ph: (713)680-9056
Dialysis Stations: 10.

27487 ■ Riverside Dialysis Center
3315 Delano St.
Houston, TX 77004
Ph: (713)566-3900
Dialysis Stations: 22.

27488 ■ Romano Woods Kidney Clinic
16910 Mathis Church Rd.
Houston, TX 77090
Ph: (281)893-6300
Dialysis Stations: 30.

27489 ■ Romano Woods Kidney Clinic
16910 Mathis Church Rd.
Houston, TX 77090
Ph: (281)893-6300
Dialysis Stations: 30.

27490 ■ Sagemont Dialysis
DaVita
Dialysis Center
10851 Scarsdale Blvd., Ste. 200
Houston, TX 77089
Free: 800-424-6589
URL: http://www.davita.com
Dialysis Stations: 12. **Formerly:** Grambo Healthcare.

27491 ■ Saint Luke's Episcopal Hospital Transplant Center
6720 Bertner Ave., Ste. P357
Mail Code 2-114
Houston, TX 77030
Ph: (832)355-3128
Fax: (832)355-6697
URL: http://www.sleh.com
Dialysis Stations: 0.

27492 ■ San Jacinto Dialysis
DaVita
Dialysis Center
11430 E Freeway, Ste. 330
Houston, TX 77029
Free: 800-424-6589
URL: http://www.davita.com
Dialysis Stations: 17. **Formerly:** Grambo Healthcare.

27493 ■ Southeast Houston Dialysis Center
7647 South Freeway
Houston, TX 77021
Ph: (713)842-1010
Dialysis Stations: 25.

27494 ■ Southeast Kidney Center
Fresenius Medical Care
8537 Gulf Fwy., Bldg. A
Houston, TX 77017
Free: 866-434-2597
URL: http://www.ultracare-dialysis.com/
Dialysis Stations: 28.

27495 ■ Southwest Houston Dialysis Facility
Fresenius Medical Care
8303 Creek Bend
Houston, TX 77071
Free: 866-434-2597
URL: http://www.ultracare-dialysis.com/
Dialysis Stations: 30.

27496 ■ Spring Branch Dialysis
DaVita
1425 Blalock, Ste. 100
Houston, TX 77055
Free: 800-424-6589
URL: http://www.davita.com
Dialysis Stations: 18.

27497 ■ Spring Dialysis Inc.
607 Timberdale Ln., Ste. 100
Houston, TX 77090
Ph: (281)880-7066
Dialysis Stations: 18.

27498 ■ Summit Dialysis
DaVita
3150 Polk St.
Houston, TX 77003

Free: 800-424-6589
URL: http://www.davita.com
Dialysis Stations: 12.

27499 ■ Texas Children's Hospital Transplant Services
6621 Fannin, WT 8-100
Houston, TX 77030
Ph: (832)826-0820
URL: http://www.texaschildrenshospital.org
Dialysis Stations: 8.

27500 ■ US Renal Care--Baylor Scott Street
6120 Scott St., Ste. F
Houston, TX 77021
Ph: (713)741-7059
Fax: (713)741-4320
URL: http://www.usrenalcare.com
Dialysis Stations: 24.

27501 ■ US Renal Care--Home Therapies
1313 La Concha
Houston, TX 77054
Ph: (713)668-2744
URL: http://www.usrenalcare.com
Dialysis Stations: 1. **Formerly:** Eumana Dialysis Center.

27502 ■ Wellbound/Satellite Dialysis Houston Dialysis Center
7505 S Main, Ste. 120
Houston, TX 77030
Ph: (713)799-9344
Fax: (713)795-0574
URL: http://www.satellitehealth.com/
Dialysis Stations: 4.

27503 ■ West Houston Dialysis Center
9623 Long Point Rd.
Houston, TX 77055
Ph: (713)932-6324
Dialysis Stations: 20.

27504 ■ West Mount Houston Dialysis Center
2506 W Mt. Houston Rd., Ste. A
Houston, TX 77038
Ph: (281)820-4880
Dialysis Stations: 17.

27505 ■ West Park Dialysis Care
6400 Southwest Fwy., Ste. G
Houston, TX 77074
Ph: (713)977-7877
URL: http://www.westparkdialysis.com/
Dialysis Stations: 20.

27506 ■ Westminster Dialysis Center Fresenius Medical Care
12121 Westheimer, Ste. 138
Houston, TX 77077
Free: 866-434-2597
URL: http://www.ultracare-dialysis.com/
Dialysis Stations: 24.

27507 ■ Willowbrook Dialysis--Houston DaVita
12120 Jones Rd., Ste. G
Houston, TX 77070
Free: 800-424-6589
URL: http://www.davita.com
Dialysis Stations: 12.

Humble

27508 ■ Deerbrook Dialysis DaVita
9660 FM 1960 Bypass
Humble, TX 77338
Free: 800-424-6589
URL: http://www.davita.com
Dialysis Stations: 12.

Huntsville

27509 ■ Huntsville Dialysis DaVita
521 IH 45S, Ste. 20
Huntsville, TX 77340
Free: 800-424-6589
URL: http://www.davita.com
Dialysis Stations: 24. **Formerly:** Grambo Healthcare.

Hurst

27510 ■ Mid Cities Dialysis Center and At Home DaVita
117 E Harwood Rd.
Hurst, TX 76054
Free: 800-424-6589
URL: http://www.davita.com
Dialysis Stations: 12.

Irving

27511 ■ Irving Dialysis Center Fresenius Medical Care
1625 N Story Rd., Ste. 140
Irving, TX 75061
Free: 866-434-2597
URL: http://www.ultracare-dialysis.com/
Dialysis Stations: 40.

Jacinto City

27512 ■ Jacinto Dialysis Center DaVita
11515 Market St.
Jacinto City, TX 77029
Free: 800-424-6589
URL: http://www.davita.com
Dialysis Stations: 16.

Jacksonville

27513 ■ Jacksonville Dialysis Center Fresenius Medical Care
908 East Loop 456
Jacksonville, TX 75766
Free: 866-434-2597
URL: http://www.ultracare-dialysis.com/
Dialysis Stations: 16. **Formerly:** Renal Care Group.

Jasper

27514 ■ Kidney Center of Jasper American Renal Associates
930 Marvin Hancock Dr.
Jasper, TX 75951
Ph: (409)384-4200
URL: http://www.americanrenal.com
Dialysis Stations: 21.

27515 ■ New Century Dialysis Center of Jasper
2014 S Wheeler St., Ste. 300
Jasper, TX 75951
Ph: (409)384-2711
Dialysis Stations: 10.

Jourdanton

27516 ■ Fresenius Medical Care--Jourdanton
1720 Hwy. 97 E
Jourdanton, TX 78026
Free: 866-434-2597
URL: http://www.ultracare-dialysis.com/
Dialysis Stations: 24. **Formerly:** Tri City Dialysis Clinic.

Katy

27517 ■ Katy Cinco Ranch Dialysis DaVita
1265 Rock Canyon Rd.
Katy, TX 77450
Free: 800-424-6589
URL: http://www.davita.com
Dialysis Stations: 12. **Formerly:** Grambo Healthcare.

27518 ■ Katy Dialysis Center DaVita
403 W Grand Pkwy. S
Katy, TX 77494
Free: 800-424-6589
URL: http://www.davita.com
Dialysis Stations: 12.

27519 ■ Pin Oak Dialysis DaVita
1302 Pin Oak Rd.
Katy, TX 77494
Free: 800-424-6589
URL: http://www.davita.com
Dialysis Stations: 12. **Formerly:** Total Renal Care.

Kaufman

27520 ■ Fresenius Medical Care--Kaufman
2213 Old Kemp Hwy.
Kaufman, TX 75142
Free: 866-434-2597
URL: http://www.ultracare-dialysis.com/
Dialysis Stations: 12.

27521 ■ Kaufman Dialysis DaVita
2851 Millenium Dr.
Kaufman, TX 75142
Free: 800-424-6589
URL: http://www.davita.com
Dialysis Stations: 12.

Kerrville

27522 ■ Kerrville Dialysis DaVita Dialysis Center & At Home
515-A Granada
Kerrville, TX 78028
Free: 800-424-6589
URL: http://www.davita.com
Dialysis Stations: 16. **Formerly:** Grambo Healthcare.

Kilgore

27523 ■ Kilgore Dialysis Center DaVita
209 Hwy. 42 North
Kilgore, TX 75662
Free: 800-424-6589
URL: http://www.davita.com
Dialysis Stations: 12. **Formerly:** Total Renal Care.

Killeen

27524 ■ Fresenius Medical Care--Killeen Dialysis Center
726 S Fort Hood St.
Killeen, TX 76541
Free: 866-434-2597
URL: http://www.ultracare-dialysis.com/
Dialysis Stations: 29.

27525 ■ Scott and White Memorial Hospital Killeen Dialysis Unit
3701 Scott & White Dr.
Killeen, TX 76541
Ph: (254)680-1371
URL: http://www.sw.org
Dialysis Stations: 18.

27526 ■ Scott and White Memorial Hospital Killeen Dialysis West
2201 S WS Young Dr., Ste. 101B
Killeen, TX 76543
Ph: (254)501-6467
URL: http://www.sw.org
Dialysis Stations: 12.

Kingsville

27527 ■ Fresenius Medical Care--Kingsville
1601 S Hwy. 77 Bypass, Ste. 3
Kingsville, TX 78363
Free: 866-434-2597
URL: http://www.ultracare-dialysis.com/
Dialysis Stations: 16. **Formerly:** Renal Care Group.

Kingwood

27528 ■ Kingwood Dialysis Center
DaVita
2300 Green Oak Dr., Ste. 500
Kingwood, TX 77339
Free: 800-424-6589
URL: http://www.davita.com
Dialysis Stations: 12.

27529 ■ US Renal Care--Kingwood
4006 Hwy. 59 N
Kingwood, TX 77339
Ph: (281)312-5562
Fax: (281)358-3115
URL: http://www.usrenalcare.com
Dialysis Stations: 20.

Kirby

27530 ■ Kirby Kidney Disease Center
Fresenius Medical Care
4653 Binz Engleman Rd., Ste. 2
Kirby, TX 78219
Free: 866-434-2597
URL: http://www.ultracare-dialysis.com/
Dialysis Stations: 20.

La Marque

27531 ■ Mainland Dialysis Facility
DaVita
2600 Gulf Fwy.
La Marque, TX 77568
Free: 800-424-6589
URL: http://www.davita.com
Dialysis Stations: 19. **Formerly:** Grambo Healthcare.

La Porte

27532 ■ La Porte Dialysis Facility
Fresenius Medical Care
1307 W Fairmont Pkwy., Ste. A
La Porte, TX 77571
Free: 866-434-2597
URL: http://www.ultracare-dialysis.com/
Dialysis Stations: 12.

27533 ■ Meridian Dialysis Center
DaVita
201 W Fairmont Pkwy., Ste. A
La Porte, TX 77571
Free: 800-424-6589
URL: http://www.davita.com
Dialysis Stations: 12.

Lake Jackson

27534 ■ Lake Jackson Dialysis and Kidney Center
405 This Way St.
Lake Jackson, TX 77566
Ph: (979)299-6565
Dialysis Stations: 24. **Formerly:** Brazoria Kidney Center.

Lampasas

27535 ■ Fresenius Medical Care--Lampasas
1202 Central Texas Expy.
Lampasas, TX 76550
Free: 866-434-2597
URL: http://www.ultracare-dialysis.com/
Dialysis Stations: 12.

Lancaster

27536 ■ Lancaster Dialysis
DaVita
2424 W Pleasant Run
Lancaster, TX 75146
Free: 800-424-6589
URL: http://www.davita.com
Dialysis Stations: 12.

27537 ■ Liberty Dialysis Lancaster
3250 W Pleasant Run Rd., No. 280
Lancaster, TX 75146
Ph: (972)230-7778
URL: http://www.libertydialysis.com
Dialysis Stations: 17.

Laredo

27538 ■ Dialysis Services of West Laredo
Fresenius Medical Care
4151 Bob Bullock Loop, Ste. 105
Laredo, TX 78046
Free: 866-434-2597
URL: http://www.ultracare-dialysis.com/
Dialysis Stations: 25.

27539 ■ Fresenius Medical Care--Laredo
5501 Springfield Ave.
Laredo, TX 78041
Free: 866-434-2597
URL: http://www.ultracare-dialysis.com/
Dialysis Stations: 24.

27540 ■ Fresenius Medical Care--South Laredo
802 Guadalupe St.
Laredo, TX 78040
Free: 866-434-2597
URL: http://www.ultracare-dialysis.com/
Dialysis Stations: 30.

27541 ■ Hope Kidney Clinic
Liberty Dialysis
2309 E Saunders St., Ste. 200
Laredo, TX 78041
Ph: (959)242-4810
URL: http://www.libertydialysis.com
Dialysis Stations: 20.

27542 ■ Laredo Dialysis Ltd.
US Renal Care
6801 McPherson Rd., Ste. 107
Laredo, TX 78041
Ph: (956)725-1202
URL: http://www.usrenalcare.com
Dialysis Stations: 25.

27543 ■ Laredo South Dialysis Center
US Renal Care
4602 Ben-Cha Rd.
Laredo, TX 78041
Ph: (956)753-2121
URL: http://www.usrenalcare.com
Dialysis Stations: 24.

League City

27544 ■ South Shore Dialysis & At Home
DaVita
212 Gulf Fwy. S
League City, TX 77573
Free: 800-424-6589
URL: http://www.davita.com
Dialysis Stations: 12.

Lewisville

27545 ■ Lewisville Dialysis Clinic
Renal Ventures Management
1600 Waters Ridge Dr., Ste. B
Lewisville, TX 75057
Ph: (972)436-7211
URL: http://www.renalventures.com
Dialysis Stations: 30.

Liberty

27546 ■ Liberty Dayton Dialysis FAC
Fresenius Medical Care
2331 N Main
Liberty, TX 77575
Free: 866-434-2597
URL: http://www.ultracare-dialysis.com/
Dialysis Stations: 12.

Live Oak

27547 ■ Live Oak Dialysis
DaVita
6700 Randolph Blvd., Ste. 101
Live Oak, TX 78233
Free: 800-424-6589
URL: http://www.davita.com
Dialysis Stations: 19.

27548 ■ Village Oaks Kidney Disease Clinic
Fresenius Medical Care
11701 Toepperwein Rd.
Live Oak, TX 78233
Free: 866-434-2597
URL: http://www.ultracare-dialysis.com/
Dialysis Stations: 28.

Livingston

27549 ■ DaVita--Livingston Dialysis Center
209 W Park
Livingston, TX 77351
Free: 800-424-6589
URL: http://www.davita.com
Dialysis Stations: 12.

Longview

27550 ■ Fourth Street Dialysis Center
DaVita
3101-B 4th St.
Longview, TX 75605
Free: 800-424-6589
URL: http://www.davita.com
Dialysis Stations: 13.

27551 ■ Longview Dialysis Center
DaVita
Dialysis Center & At Home
425 N Fredonia, Ste. 300
Longview, TX 75601
Free: 800-424-6589
URL: http://www.davita.com
Dialysis Stations: 35.

Lubbock

27552 ■ Brownfield Dialysis
AccessCare
5152 69th, Ste. 108
Lubbock, TX 79424
Ph: (806)637-6373
URL: http://accesscaredialysis.com/
Dialysis Stations: 8.

27553 ■ Dialysis Center of Lubbock
Fresenius Medical Care
6630 Quaker Ave., Ste. 102
Lubbock, TX 79413
Free: 866-434-2597
URL: http://www.ultracare-dialysis.com/
Dialysis Stations: 29.

27554 ■ Fresenius Medical Care--Lubbock
1607 W Loop 289
Lubbock, TX 79416
Free: 866-434-2597
URL: http://www.ultracare-dialysis.com/
Dialysis Stations: 30. **Formerly:** South Plains Kidney Disease Center.

27555 ■ Kidney Center of Lubbock
3801 21st St.
Lubbock, TX 79410
Ph: (806)771-9933
Dialysis Stations: 12.

27556 ■ Lubbock Dialysis Center--Redbud
Fresenius Medical Care
1126 Slide Rd., Ste. 4-A
Lubbock, TX 79416
Free: 866-434-2597
URL: http://www.ultracare-dialysis.com/
Dialysis Stations: 56.

27557 ■ Muleshoe Dialysis
AccessCare
5152 69th, Ste. 108
Lubbock, TX 79424
Ph: (806)272-3122
URL: http://accesscaredialysis.com/
Dialysis Stations: 8.

27558 ■ University Medical Center Transplant Services
602 Indiana Ave.
Lubbock, TX 79415
Ph: (806)761-0710
URL: https://www.umchealthsystem.com/
Dialysis Stations: 0.

Lufkin

27559 ■ Henderson Kidney Disease Center
1201 Ellis Ave.
Lufkin, TX 75901
Ph: (936)639-7711
Dialysis Stations: 10.

27560 ■ Lufkin Dialysis
DaVita
Dialysis Facility
700 S John Redditt Dr.
Lufkin, TX 75904
Free: 800-424-6589
URL: http://www.davita.com
Dialysis Stations: 36.

Lytle

27561 ■ Tri County Dialysis Facility
US Renal Care
14832 Main St.
Lytle, TX 78052
Ph: (830)772-5784
URL: http://www.usrenalcare.com
Dialysis Stations: 17. **Formerly:** Rencare Ltd.

Magnolia

27562 ■ Magnolia Dialysis Center and At Home
DaVita
17649 FM 1488 Rd.
Magnolia, TX 77354
Free: 800-424-6589
URL: http://www.davita.com
Dialysis Stations: 12.

Mansfield

27563 ■ Mansfield Dialysis Center
DaVita
987 N Walnut Creek Dr.
Mansfield, TX 76063
Free: 800-424-6589
URL: http://www.davita.com
Dialysis Stations: 12.

27564 ■ Tarrant Dialysis Center--Mansfield
US Renal Care
1800 Hwy. 157 N, Ste. 101
Mansfield, TX 76063
Ph: (682)518-0126
URL: http://www.usrenalcare.com
Dialysis Stations: 23.

Marble Falls

27565 ■ National Nephrology Associates--Marble Falls
802 Steve Hawkins Pkwy.
Marble Falls, TX 78654
Ph: (830)798-9575
Dialysis Stations: 16.

Marlin

27566 ■ Falls County Kidney Center
Dialysis Facility
602 Hwy. 6 S
Marlin, TX 76661
Free: 866-434-2597
Dialysis Stations: 11.

Marshall

27567 ■ DaVita--Marshall
Dialysis Facility
1301 S Washington
Marshall, TX 75670
Free: 800-424-6589
URL: http://www.davita.com
Dialysis Stations: 15.

27568 ■ Pinecrest Dialysis Center
DaVita
913 E Pinecrest Dr.
Marshall, TX 75670
Free: 800-424-6589
URL: http://www.davita.com
Dialysis Stations: 13.

McAllen

27569 ■ Fresenius Medical Care--McAllen
1325 E Quebec
McAllen, TX 78503
Free: 866-434-2597
URL: http://www.ultracare-dialysis.com/
Dialysis Stations: 37.

27570 ■ McAllen Dialysis Center
Diversified Specialty Institutes
411 Lindberg Ave.
McAllen, TX 78501
Ph: (956)687-6701
URL: http://www.dsi-corp.com
Dialysis Stations: 24.

27571 ■ McAllen Dialysis Ltd.
US Renal Care
1301 E Ridge Rd., Ste. C
McAllen, TX 78503
Ph: (956)668-8484
URL: http://www.usrenalcare.com
Dialysis Stations: 20. **Formerly:** Trucare Health Care.

27572 ■ South Texas Transplant Center
McAllen Medical Center
301 W Expy. 83
McAllen, TX 78503
Ph: (956)971-5726
Free: 800-321-3084
URL: http://www.southtexashealthsystem.com/Services-P-Z/Transplant-Center
Dialysis Stations: 0.

27573 ■ US Renal Care--McAllen
1301 E Ridge Rd., Ste. C
McAllen, TX 78503
Ph: (956)668-8484
URL: http://www.usrenalcare.com
Dialysis Stations: 22. **Formerly:** McAllen Dialysis Ltd.

McKinney

27574 ■ Fresenius Medical Care--McKinney
1831 Harroun
McKinney, TX 75069
Free: 866-434-2597
URL: http://www.ultracare-dialysis.com/
Dialysis Stations: 19.

Mesquite

27575 ■ Liberty Dialysis--Mesquite
3330 N Galloway, Ste. 160 & 165
Mesquite, TX 75150
Ph: (215)989-4110
URL: http://www.libertydialysis.com
Dialysis Stations: 20.

27576 ■ Metro East Dialysis Center
Fresenius Medical Care
909 Gross Rd., Ste. 200
Mesquite, TX 75149
Free: 866-434-2597
URL: http://www.ultracare-dialysis.com/
Dialysis Stations: 28.

Midland

27577 ■ Midland Dialysis Center
NorthPark Executive Center
731 W Wadley, Bldg. K, Ste. 130
Midland, TX 79705
Ph: (432)687-4044
E-mail: office@dsparkmd.com
URL: http://www.dsparkmd.com/
Dialysis Stations: 21.

27578 ■ Permian Basin Dialysis Center
Fresenius Medical Care
4200 W Illinois, Ste. 140
Midland, TX 79703
Free: 866-434-2597
URL: http://www.ultracare-dialysis.com/
Dialysis Stations: 16.

Mineola

27579 ■ Mineola Dialysis
Fresenius Medical Care
102 Maxine
Mineola, TX 75773
Free: 866-434-2597
URL: http://www.ultracare-dialysis.com/
Dialysis Stations: 16. **Formerly:** Renal Care Group.

Mission

27580 ■ Mission Dialysis
US Renal Care
1300 S Bryan Rd., Ste. 107
Mission, TX 78572
Ph: (956)581-8489
URL: http://www.usrenalcare.com
Dialysis Stations: 24.

27581 ■ Mission Kidney Center
Fresenius Medical Care
901 Plaza Dr.
Mission, TX 78572
Free: 866-434-2597
URL: http://www.ultracare-dialysis.com/
Dialysis Stations: 20. **Formerly:** Renal Care Group.

27582 ■ Mission Valley Dialysis
DaVita
1203 St. Clare Blvd., Ste. 9B
Mission, TX 78572
Free: 800-424-6589
URL: http://www.davita.com
Dialysis Stations: 13.

27583 ■ South Texas Dialysis Center
Fresenius Medical Care
1615 E Expy. 83
Mission, TX 78572

Free: 866-434-2597
URL: http://www.ultracare-dialysis.com/
Dialysis Stations: 25. **Formerly:** South Texas Dialysis Center.

Missouri City

27584 ■ Fort Bend Dialysis Center
Fresenius Medical Care
3819 Cartwright Rd.
Missouri City, TX 77459
Free: 866-434-2597
URL: http://www.ultracare-dialysis.com/
Dialysis Stations: 16. **Formerly:** Renal Care Group.

27585 ■ Missouri City Dialysis
Fresenius Medical Care
1673 Cartwright Rd.
Missouri City, TX 77459
Free: 866-434-2597
URL: http://www.ultracare-dialysis.com/
Dialysis Stations: 20.

Mount Pleasant

27586 ■ Mount Pleasant Dialysis Center Inc.
Fresenius Medical Care
628 S Jefferson Ave.
Mount Pleasant, TX 75455
Free: 866-434-2597
URL: http://www.ultracare-dialysis.com/
Dialysis Stations: 25. **Formerly:** Renal Care Group.

Nacogdoches

27587 ■ Dialysis Clinic, Inc.--Dialysis Care Services Inc.
4731 NE Stallings
Nacogdoches, TX 75965
Ph: (936)569-9900
URL: http://www.dciinc.org
Dialysis Stations: 21.

27588 ■ Fresenius Medical Care--Nacogdoches
3222 University Dr., Ste. 100
Nacogdoches, TX 75965
Free: 866-434-2597
URL: http://www.ultracare-dialysis.com/
Dialysis Stations: 16.

27589 ■ Nacogdoches Memorial Hospital Dialysis Facility
1204 Mound St.
Nacogdoches, TX 75961
Ph: (936)568-8511
URL: http://www.nacmem.org
Dialysis Stations: 19.

New Braunfels

27590 ■ New Braunfels Dialysis Center
DaVita
900 Loop 337
New Braunfels, TX 78130
Free: 800-424-6589
URL: http://www.davita.com
Dialysis Stations: 18. **Formerly:** New Braunfels Kidney Disease Center.

27591 ■ New Braunfels Kidney Disease Clinic
Dialysis Facility
Fresenius Medical Care
1561 Interstate Hwy. 35 N
New Braunfels, TX 78130
Free: 866-434-2597
URL: http://www.ultracare-dialysis.com/
Dialysis Stations: 18.

North Richland Hills

27592 ■ North Hills Dialysis
DaVita
7927 Blvd. 26
North Richland Hills, TX 76180
Free: 800-424-6589
URL: http://www.davita.com
Dialysis Stations: 15.

27593 ■ Renal Ventures Management of the Hills
6331 Grapevine Hwy., Ste. 200
North Richland Hills, TX 76180
Ph: (817)284-3343
Fax: (817)284-3448
URL: http://www.renalventures.com
Dialysis Stations: 25.

27594 ■ Tarrant Dialysis Center--North Richland Hills
US Renal Care Inc.
6455 Hilltop Dr., Ste. 112
North Richland Hills, TX 76180
Ph: (817)485-8700
URL: http://www.usrenalcare.com
Dialysis Stations: 15.

Odessa

27595 ■ Desert Milagro Dialysis Center
Fresenius Medical Care
230 N Washington Ave.
Odessa, TX 79761
Free: 866-434-2597
URL: http://www.ultracare-dialysis.com/
Dialysis Stations: 50.

27596 ■ Odessa Kidney Dialysis Center
6005 Eastridge Rd.
Odessa, TX 79762
Ph: (432)550-6012
Dialysis Stations: 12.

27597 ■ Renal Center of Midland--Odessa
Renal Ventures Management
4241 Tanglewood, Ste. 104
Odessa, TX 79762
Ph: (432)366-3940
URL: http://www.renalventures.com
Dialysis Stations: 16.

Orange

27598 ■ Biotronics Kidney Center of Orange
Dialysis Facility
1301 Martin Luther King Dr.
Orange, TX 77630
Ph: (409)886-7714
Dialysis Stations: 9.

27599 ■ Fresenius Medical Care--Orange County
Dialysis Center
280 Strickland Dr.
Orange, TX 77630
Free: 866-434-2597
URL: http://www.ultracare-dialysis.com/
Dialysis Stations: 13. **Formerly:** Renal Care Group - Orange.

Palestine

27600 ■ Palestine Dialysis Center
Fresenius Medical Care
2260 S Sycamore St.
Palestine, TX 75801
Free: 866-434-2597
URL: http://www.ultracare-dialysis.com/
Dialysis Stations: 24. **Formerly:** Renal Care Group.

Pampa

27601 ■ Fresenius Medical Care--Pampa
2545 Perryton Pkwy., Ste. E-1
Pampa, TX 79065
Free: 866-434-2597
URL: http://www.ultracare-dialysis.com/
Dialysis Stations: 12.

Paris

27602 ■ Fresenius Medical Care--Paris
110 S Collegiate
Paris, TX 75460
Free: 866-434-2597
URL: http://www.ultracare-dialysis.com/
Dialysis Stations: 28. **Formerly:** Renal Care Group.

Pasadena

27603 ■ Bayshore Dialysis Center
Fresenius Medical Care
4300 Fairmont Pkwy., Ste. 100
Pasadena, TX 77504
Free: 866-434-2597
URL: http://www.ultracare-dialysis.com/
Dialysis Stations: 24.

Pearland

27604 ■ Dialysis Services of Pearland
Fresenius Medical Care
1830 Broadway
Pearland, TX 77581
Free: 866-434-2597
URL: http://www.ultracare-dialysis.com/
Dialysis Stations: 12.

27605 ■ Pearland Dialysis
DaVita
6516 Broadway, Ste. 122
Pearland, TX 77581
Free: 800-424-6589
URL: http://www.davita.com
Dialysis Stations: 20. **Formerly:** TRC Texas LP.

Pearsall

27606 ■ DaVita--Pearsall
Dialysis Center
1305 N Oak St.
Pearsall, TX 78061
Free: 800-424-6589
URL: http://www.davita.com
Dialysis Stations: 12.

Pecos

27607 ■ Reeves County Hospital
Dialysis Center
2323 Texas St.
Pecos, TX 79772
Ph: (432)447-2221
URL: http://www.reevescountyhospital.com
Dialysis Stations: 15.

Plainview

27608 ■ Dialysis Services of Plainview
Fresenius Medical Care
3304 Olton Rd.
Plainview, TX 79072
Free: 866-434-2597
URL: http://www.ultracare-dialysis.com/
Dialysis Stations: 20.

Plano

27609 ■ Collin County Dialysis Center
Fresenius Medical Care
3420 Ave. K, Ste. 150
Plano, TX 75074
Free: 866-434-2597
URL: http://www.ultracare-dialysis.com/
Dialysis Stations: 25.

27610 ■ Fresenius Medical Care--West Plano
4405 Tradition Tr.
Plano, TX 75093
Free: 866-434-2597
URL: http://www.ultracare-dialysis.com/
Dialysis Stations: 20.

27611 ■ Plano Dialysis Center
DaVita
481 Shiloh Rd.
Plano, TX 75074
Free: 800-424-6589
URL: http://www.davita.com
Dialysis Stations: 12.

Port Arthur

27612 ■ Fresenius Medical Care--Nederland
8797 9th Ave.
Port Arthur, TX 77642
Free: 866-434-2597
URL: http://www.ultracare-dialysis.com/
Dialysis Stations: 16. **Formerly:** Renal Care Group.

27613 ■ Southeast Texas Kidney Center
Fresenius Medical Care
3730 Dryden Rd.
Port Arthur, TX 77642
Free: 866-434-2597
URL: http://www.ultracare-dialysis.com/
Dialysis Stations: 25. **Formerly:** Renal Care Group.

Port Lavaca

27614 ■ Port Lavaca Dialysis Facility
DaVita
1300 N Virginia St., Ste. 102
Port Lavaca, TX 77979
Free: 800-424-6589
URL: http://www.davita.com
Dialysis Stations: 10. **Formerly:** Memorial Medical Plaza Dialysis.

Raymondville

27615 ■ Valley Baptist
Raymondville Dialysis Center
894 FM 3168
Raymondville, TX 78580
Ph: (956)689-9084
Dialysis Stations: 16.

Rio Grande City

27616 ■ Fresenius Medical Care - Rio Grande City
2764 Pharmacy Rd.
Rio Grande City, TX 78582
Free: 866-434-2597
URL: http://www.ultracare-dialysis.com/
Dialysis Stations: 25.

27617 ■ Fresenius Medical Care--Rio Grande City
2533 Central Palm Dr.
Rio Grande City, TX 78582
Free: 866-434-2597
URL: http://www.ultracare-dialysis.com/
Dialysis Stations: 25.

27618 ■ US Renal Care--Rio Grande
2787 Pharmacy Rd.
Rio Grande City, TX 78582
Ph: (956)487-2929
URL: http://www.usrenalcare.com
Dialysis Stations: 15.

Robstown

27619 ■ Fresenius Medical Care--Robstown
902 Lincoln Ave.
Robstown, TX 78380
Free: 866-434-2597
URL: http://www.ultracare-dialysis.com/
Dialysis Stations: 16. **Formerly:** Renal Care Group.

Rockdale

27620 ■ Rockdale Kidney Center
Fresenius Medical Care
300 Josie La.
Rockdale, TX 76567
Free: 866-434-2597
URL: http://www.ultracare-dialysis.com/
Dialysis Stations: 12.

Rockport

27621 ■ Fresenius Medical Care--Rockport
1102 F.M. 3036
Rockport, TX 78382
Free: 866-434-2597
URL: http://www.ultracare-dialysis.com/
Dialysis Stations: 12.

27622 ■ Rockport Dialysis
DaVita
2102 FM 2165
Rockport, TX 78382
Free: 800-424-6589
URL: http://www.davita.com
Dialysis Stations: 12.

Rockwall

27623 ■ Liberty Dialysis--Rockwall
2850 Ridge Rd., Ste. 112
Rockwall, TX 75032
Ph: (972)961-4336
URL: http://www.libertydialysis.com
Dialysis Stations: 16.

27624 ■ Rockwall Dialysis Center
DaVita
2455 Ridge Rd., Ste. 101
Rockwall, TX 75087
Free: 800-424-6589
URL: http://www.davita.com
Dialysis Stations: 8.

Rosenberg

27625 ■ Brazos Dialysis Center
1730 B.F. Terry Blvd.
Rosenberg, TX 77471
Ph: (832)595-0003
URL: http://www.brazosdialysis.org/
Dialysis Stations: 20.

27626 ■ Rosenberg Dialysis Facility
Fresenius Medical Care
4519 Reading Rd., Ste. 18
Rosenberg, TX 77471
Free: 866-434-2597
URL: http://www.ultracare-dialysis.com/
Dialysis Stations: 28.

Round Rock

27627 ■ National Nephrology Associates--Round Rock
Dialysis Facility
1499 E Old Settlers Blvd.
Round Rock, TX 78664
Ph: (512)671-8012
Dialysis Stations: 21.

27628 ■ Round Rock Clinic
Capital Nephrology Associates
16010 Park Valley Dr., Ste. 100
Round Rock, TX 78681
Ph: (512)275-0100
URL: http://www.capitalnephrology.com/
Dialysis Stations: 24. **Formerly:** Capital Dialysis of Texas Ltd.

27629 ■ Scott and White Memorial Hospital
Round Rock Dialysis
2120 N Mays St., Ste. 230
Round Rock, TX 78664
Ph: (512)238-2900
URL: http://www.sw.org
Dialysis Stations: 18.

Rowlett

27630 ■ Fresenius Medical Care--Rowlett
3801 Lakeview Pkwy., Ste. 100
Rowlett, TX 75088
Free: 866-434-2597
URL: http://www.ultracare-dialysis.com/
Dialysis Stations: 12.

San Angelo

27631 ■ Angelo Kidney Connection
18 W College Ave.
San Angelo, TX 76904
Ph: (325)617-2496
Dialysis Stations: 12.

27632 ■ Shannon Medical Center Outpatient Dialysis Center
2018 Pulliam
San Angelo, TX 76905
Ph: (325)659-7360
Dialysis Stations: 24.

27633 ■ West Texas Renal Care Center
Dialysis Facility
3501 Executive Dr.
San Angelo, TX 76904
Ph: (325)949-5081
Dialysis Stations: 20.

San Antonio

27634 ■ Alamo City Dialysis
Fresenius Medical Care
805 Camden St.
San Antonio, TX 78215
Free: 866-434-2597
URL: http://www.ultracare-dialysis.com/
Dialysis Stations: 28.

27635 ■ Barlite Southwest Kidney Center
Innovative Dialysis Systems
7500 Barlite, Ste. 103
San Antonio, TX 78224
Ph: (210)922-3377
URL: http://www.idsdialysis.com
Dialysis Stations: 12.

27636 ■ Broadway Kidney Disease Center
Dialysis Center
Fresenius Medical Care
8840 Tradeway
San Antonio, TX 78217
Free: 866-434-2597
URL: http://www.ultracare-dialysis.com/
Dialysis Stations: 20.

27637 ■ Callaghan Road Dialysis
DaVita
Dialysis Center
4151 Callaghan Rd., Ste. 101
San Antonio, TX 78228
Free: 800-424-6589
URL: http://www.davita.com
Dialysis Stations: 16. **Formerly:** Gambro Healthcare.

27638 ■ Christus Children's Kidney Center
333 N Santa Rosa St.
San Antonio, TX 78207
Ph: (210)704-3705
Dialysis Stations: 8.

27639 ■ Christus Children's Kidney Center
333 N Santa Rosa St.
San Antonio, TX 78207
Ph: (210)704-3705
Dialysis Stations: 8.

27640 ■ DaVita
Northwest Medical Center Dialysis
5284 Medical Dr., Ste. 135
San Antonio, TX 78229
Free: 800-424-6589
URL: http://www.davita.com
Dialysis Stations: 24.

27641 ■ DaVita
San Antonio At Home
8132 Fredericksburg
San Antonio, TX 78229
Free: 800-424-6589
URL: http://www.davita.com

27642 ■ DaVita--Southwest San Antonio Dialysis Facility & At Home
7515 Barlite Ave.
San Antonio, TX 78224
Free: 800-424-6589
URL: http://www.davita.com
Dialysis Stations: 36.

27643 ■ Dialysis Services of Ingram
Fresenius Medical Care
6945 Alamo Downs Pkwy.
San Antonio, TX 78238
Free: 866-434-2597
URL: http://www.ultracare-dialysis.com/
Dialysis Stations: 24.

27644 ■ Dialysis Services of Southwest San Antonio
Fresenius Medical Care
134 Camino de Oro
San Antonio, TX 78224
Free: 866-434-2597
URL: http://www.ultracare-dialysis.com/
Dialysis Stations: 20.

27645 ■ Downtown San Antonio Dialysis & At Home
DaVita
615 E Quincy
San Antonio, TX 78215
Free: 800-424-6589
URL: http://www.davita.com
Dialysis Stations: 20.

27646 ■ Floyd Curl Dialysis
DaVita
9238 Floyd Curl Dr., Ste. 102
San Antonio, TX 78240
Free: 800-424-6589
URL: http://www.davita.com
Dialysis Stations: 20.

27647 ■ Fresenius Medical Care--Bexar County
1222 McCullough Ave.
San Antonio, TX 78212
Free: 866-434-2597
URL: http://www.ultracare-dialysis.com/
Dialysis Stations: 30.

27648 ■ Gateway Dialysis Facility
US Renal Care
7171 Hwy. 90 W, Ste. 101
San Antonio, TX 78227
Ph: (210)673-9200
URL: http://www.usrenalcare.com
Dialysis Stations: 25.

27649 ■ Guadalupe Kidney Disease Clinic
Fresenius Medical Care
626 Merida
San Antonio, TX 78207
Free: 866-434-2597
URL: http://www.ultracare-dialysis.com/
Dialysis Stations: 20.

27650 ■ Houston Street Dialysis and PD
US Renal Care
2011 E Houston, Ste. 102-D
San Antonio, TX 78202
Ph: (210)225-0004
URL: http://www.usrenalcare.com
Dialysis Stations: 28.

27651 ■ Kidney Disease Clinic--Central San Antonio
Dialysis Facility
Fresenius Medical Care
305 N Frio
San Antonio, TX 78207
Free: 866-434-2597
URL: http://www.ultracare-dialysis.com/
Dialysis Stations: 30.

27652 ■ Kidney Disease Clinic of San Antonio
Fresenius Medical Care
7434 Louis Pasteur Dr, Ste. 120
San Antonio, TX 78229
Free: 866-434-2597
URL: http://www.ultracare-dialysis.com/
Dialysis Stations: 22.

27653 ■ Kidney Treatment Center--East
Dialysis Facility
1608 S New Braunfels
San Antonio, TX 78210
Ph: (210)531-9693
Dialysis Stations: 24.

27654 ■ Kidney Treatment Center--Northwest PA
3939 Medical Dr., Ste. 110
San Antonio, TX 78229
Ph: (210)692-3075
Dialysis Stations: 24.

27655 ■ Kidney Treatment Center--San Antonio
803 Castroville Rd., Ste. 401
San Antonio, TX 78237
Ph: (210)435-4725
Dialysis Stations: 30.

27656 ■ Las Palmas Dialysis Center
DaVita
803 Castroville Rd., Ste. 415
San Antonio, TX 78237
Free: 800-424-6589
URL: http://www.davita.com
Dialysis Stations: 24.

27657 ■ Lockehill Kidney Disease Clinic
Dialysis Facility
Fresenius Medical Care
10134 Huebner Rd.
San Antonio, TX 78240
Free: 866-434-2597
URL: http://www.ultracare-dialysis.com/
Dialysis Stations: 15.

27658 ■ Marymount Dialysis Center
DaVita
2391 NE Loop 410, Ste. 211
San Antonio, TX 78217
Free: 800-424-6589
URL: http://www.davita.com
Dialysis Stations: 24.

27659 ■ North Central Kidney Disease Center
Dialysis Facility
Fresenius Medical Care
116 Gallery Circle, No. 102
San Antonio, TX 78258
Free: 866-434-2597
URL: http://www.ultracare-dialysis.com/
Dialysis Stations: 16.

27660 ■ Northwest San Antonio Dialysis Center
DaVita
8132 Fredericksburg Rd.
San Antonio, TX 78229
Free: 800-424-6589
URL: http://www.davita.com
Dialysis Stations: 15.

27661 ■ Pleasanton Road Dialysis Facility
US Renal Care
1515 Pleasanton Rd.
San Antonio, TX 78221
Ph: (210)922-6255
URL: http://www.usrenalcare.com
Dialysis Stations: 36. **Formerly:** Rencare Ltd.

27662 ■ Rivercenter Dialysis
DaVita
1123 N Main St., Ste. 150
San Antonio, TX 78215
Free: 800-424-6589
URL: http://www.davita.com
Dialysis Stations: 22.

27663 ■ Rosedale Kidney Disease Clinic
Dialysis Facility
Fresenius Medical Care
411 N General McMullen St.
San Antonio, TX 78237
Free: 866-434-2597
URL: http://www.ultracare-dialysis.com/
Dialysis Stations: 20.

27664 ■ San Saba Downtown Kidney Center
Innovative Dialysis Systems
315 N San Saba, Ste. 101
San Antonio, TX 78207
Ph: (210)798-1955
URL: http://www.idsdialysis.com
Dialysis Stations: 13.

27665 ■ South Antonio Dialysis Center
DaVita
1313 SE Military Dr., Ste. 111
San Antonio, TX 78214
Free: 800-424-6589
URL: http://www.davita.com
Dialysis Stations: 24.

27666 ■ Southcross Dialysis Center
DaVita
4602 E Southcross Blvd.
San Antonio, TX 78222
Free: 800-424-6589
URL: http://www.davita.com
Dialysis Stations: 24.

27667 ■ Southeast Kidney Disease Center
Dialysis Facility
Fresenius Medical Care
4626 E Southcross Blvd.
San Antonio, TX 78222
Free: 866-434-2597
URL: http://www.ultracare-dialysis.com/
Dialysis Stations: 40.

27668 ■ Southside Kidney Disease Clinic
Fresenius Medical Care
1335 SE Military Dr.
San Antonio, TX 78214
Free: 866-434-2597
URL: http://www.ultracare-dialysis.com/
Dialysis Stations: 15.

27669 ■ Southwest San Antonio Dialysis
DaVita
Dialysis Center
1620 Somerset Rd.
San Antonio, TX 78211
Free: 800-424-6589
URL: http://www.davita.com
Dialysis Stations: 16. **Formerly:** Gambro Healthcare.

27670 ■ University Dialysis Southeast
1407 Fair Ave.
San Antonio, TX 78223
Ph: (210)358-5780
Dialysis Stations: 16.

27671 ■ University Dialysis--West San Antonio
701 S Zarazmora
San Antonio, TX 78207
Ph: (210)358-7300
Dialysis Stations: 28.

27672 ■ University Hospital--San Antonio Renal Unit
4502 Medical Dr.
San Antonio, TX 78229
Ph: (210)358-2668
URL: http://www.universityhealthsystem.com
Dialysis Stations: 20.

27673 ■ US Renal Care--SA Bandera Bandera Road Dialysis Facility
7180 Bandera Rd.
San Antonio, TX 78238
Ph: (210)682-1300
URL: http://www.usrenalcare.com
Dialysis Stations: 25. **Formerly:** Rencare Ltd.

27674 ■ West Bexar County Kidney Disease Center
Fresenius Medical Care
803 Castroville Rd., Ste. 410
San Antonio, TX 78237
Free: 866-434-2597
Fax: (210)431-0031
URL: http://www.ultracare-dialysis.com/
Dialysis Stations: 30.

San Antonnio

27675 ■ University Hospital Renal Transplant Services
University of Texas Health Science Center
7703 Floyd Curl Dr., MC 7858
San Antonnio, TX 78229
Ph: (210)567-5777
URL: http://transplant.uthscsa.edu/adult/kidney.asp
Dialysis Stations: 20.

San Augustine

27676 ■ San Augustine Dialysis Clinic
403 N Milam St.
San Augustine, TX 75972
Ph: (936)275-3446
Dialysis Stations: 10.

San Benito

27677 ■ San Benito Dialysis
US Renal Care
295 N Sam Houston
San Benito, TX 78586
Ph: (956)399-4037
URL: http://www.usrenalcare.com
Dialysis Stations: 16.

San Marcos

27678 ■ Hill Country Dialysis Center of San Marcos
DaVita
Dialysis Facility
1820 Peter Garza Dr.
San Marcos, TX 78666
Free: 800-424-6589
URL: http://www.davita.com
Dialysis Stations: 17.

27679 ■ National Nephrology Associates--San Marcos
1340 Wonder World Dr.
San Marcos, TX 78666
Ph: (512)878-2420
Dialysis Stations: 24.

27680 ■ San Marcos Clinic
Capital Nephrology Associates
900 Bugg Ln., Ste. 220
San Marcos, TX 78666
Ph: (512)392-9199
URL: http://www.capitalnephrology.com
Dialysis Stations: 22. **Formerly:** Capital Dialysis of Texas.

Seguin

27681 ■ Fresenius Medical Care--West Seguin
757 W Court
Seguin, TX 78155
Free: 866-434-2597
URL: http://www.ultracare-dialysis.com/engine/
Dialysis Stations: 16.

27682 ■ Kidney Disease Clinic--Seguin
Fresenius Medical Care
128 S Moss, Ste. 500
Seguin, TX 78155
Free: 866-434-2597
URL: http://www.ultracare-dialysis.com/
Dialysis Stations: 20.

Shenandoah

27683 ■ The Woodlands Dialysis Center
DaVita
9301 Pinecroft Dr.
Shenandoah, TX 77380
Free: 800-424-6589
URL: http://www.davita.com

Sherman

27684 ■ DaVita--Sherman
Dialysis Facility
205 W Lamberth Rd.
Sherman, TX 75092
Free: 800-424-6589
URL: http://www.davita.com
Dialysis Stations: 19.

Shertz

27685 ■ RSA Schertz
5000 Baptist Health Dr.
Shertz, TX 78154
Ph: (210)659-6070
Dialysis Stations: 16.

Sinton

27686 ■ Fresenius Medical Care--Sinton
222 E Sinton Blvd.
Sinton, TX 78387
Free: 866-434-2597
URL: http://www.ultracare-dialysis.com/
Dialysis Stations: 16. **Formerly:** Renal Care Group/ Bay Area Dialysis Services.

Southlake

27687 ■ Dialysis Services of Grapevine
Fresenius Medical Care
1601 Hart Ct.
Southlake, TX 76092
Free: 866-434-2597
URL: http://www.ultracare-dialysis.com/
Dialysis Stations: 12.

Stafford

27688 ■ Quality Dialysis Two inc.
4007 Greenbriar, Ste. E
Stafford, TX 77477
Ph: (281)491-4009
Dialysis Stations: 2.

27689 ■ Stafford Dialysis
12220 Murphy Rd., Ste. R
Stafford, TX 77477
Ph: (281)568-9911
Dialysis Stations: 16.

Sugar Land

27690 ■ Sugar Land Dialysis
13855 Southwest Fwy.
Sugar Land, TX 77478
Ph: (281)240-5095
URL: http://www.sldialysis.com
Dialysis Stations: 12.

Sugarland

27691 ■ First Colony Dialysis Center and At Home
DaVita
1447 Hwy. 6, Ste. 140
Sugarland, TX 77478
Free: 800-424-6589
URL: http://www.davita.com
Dialysis Stations: 13.

Sulphur Springs

27692 ■ Fresenius Medical Care--Sulphur Springs
1401 Medical Dr.
Sulphur Springs, TX 75482
Free: 866-434-2597
URL: http://www.ultracare-dialysis.com/
Dialysis Stations: 16. **Formerly:** Renal Care Group.

Taylor

27693 ■ Taylor Dialysis
DaVita
3100 W 2nd St.
Taylor, TX 76574
Free: 800-424-6589
URL: http://www.davita.com
Dialysis Stations: 12.

Temple

27694 ■ Scott and White Artificial Kidney Unit
2401 S 31st St.
Temple, TX 76508
Ph: (254)724-2026
URL: http://www.sw.org
Dialysis Stations: 53.

27695 ■ Temple Kidney Center
Dialysis Facility
Fresenius Medical Care
2915 Saulsbury Dr.
Temple, TX 76504
Free: 866-434-2597
URL: http://www.ultracare-dialysis.com/
Dialysis Stations: 17.

Terrell

27696 ■ Fresenius Medical Care Dialysis Services--Terrell
351 S Virginia Ave., Ste. 300
Terrell, TX 75160
Free: 866-434-2597
URL: http://www.ultracare-dialysis.com/
Dialysis Stations: 24.

27697 ■ Terrell Dialysis Center
Fresenius Medical Care
301 S Virginia, Ste. 300
Terrell, TX 75160
Free: 866-434-2597
URL: http://www.ultracare-dialysis.com/
Dialysis Stations: 24.

Texarkana

27698 ■ Hempstead County Dialysis Unit
Texarkana Regional Dialysis Center
Texarkana, TX 75504
Ph: (870)777-4040
Dialysis Stations: 10.

27699 ■ Miller County Dialysis Unit
Texarkana Regional Dialysis Center
4800 Texas Blvd.
Texarkana, TX 75503
Ph: (903)614-3600
Dialysis Stations: 20.

Texas City

27700 ■ Sandcastle Dialysis LLC
8900 Emmett Lowry Expy., Ste. 201
Texas City, TX 77591
Ph: (409)933-0406
Dialysis Stations: 18.

27701 ■ Texas City Dialysis LLP
3557 Palmer Hwy.
Texas City, TX 77590
Ph: (409)948-9300
Dialysis Stations: 17.

The Woodlands

27702 ■ Cypress Creek Dialysis Center
Fresenius Medical Care
9449 Grogans Mill Rd.
The Woodlands, TX 77380
Free: 866-434-2597
URL: http://www.ultracare-dialysis.com/
Dialysis Stations: 15.

Tomball

27703 ■ Tomball Dialysis Center
DaVita
27720-A Tomball Pkwy.
Tomball, TX 77375
Free: 800-424-6589
URL: http://www.davita.com
Dialysis Stations: 25.

Tyler

27704 ■ East Texas Medical Center Transplant
1000 S Beckham
Tyler, TX 75701
Ph: (903)531-8126
URL: http://www.etmc.org/transplant.htm
Dialysis Stations: 0.

27705 ■ Fresenius Medical Care--Tyler
815 E 1st St.
Tyler, TX 75701
Free: 866-434-2597
URL: http://www.ultracare-dialysis.com/
Dialysis Stations: 42. **Formerly:** Watson W. Wise Dialysis - Tyler.

27706 ■ Fresenius Medical Care
Tyler Home Dialysis
38265 Troup Hwy., Ste. K
Tyler, TX 75703
Free: 866-434-2597
URL: http://www.ultracare-dialysis.com/
Dialysis Stations: 0. **Formerly:** Renal Care Group.

27707 ■ Renal Center of Tyler
Renal Ventures Managment
Dialysis Center
510 S SW Loop 323, Ste. 580
Tyler, TX 75702
Ph: (903)596-0102
URL: http://www.renalventures.com
Dialysis Stations: 20.

27708 ■ Renal Ventures Management of Waterton
2895 Shiloh Rd.
Tyler, TX 75703
Ph: (903)561-0292
Fax: (903)561-1896
URL: http://www.renalventures.com
Dialysis Stations: 20.

27709 ■ Tyler Home Dialysis
Fresenius Medical Care
3826 Troup Hwy., Ste. K
Tyler, TX 75703
Free: 866-434-2597
URL: http://www.ultracare-dialysis.com/
Dialysis Stations: 0. **Formerly:** Renal Care Group.

27710 ■ West Tyler Dialysis
Fresenius Medical Care
3600 W Erwin
Tyler, TX 75702
Free: 866-434-2597
URL: http://www.ultracare-dialysis.com/
Dialysis Stations: 20. **Formerly:** Renal Care Group.

Uvalde

27711 ■ Kidney Disease Clinic--Uvalde
Fresenius Medical Care
1819 Garner Field Rd.
Uvalde, TX 78801
Free: 866-434-2597
URL: http://www.ultracare-dialysis.com/
Dialysis Stations: 24.

Vernon

27712 ■ Wilbarger General Hospital Dialysis of Vernon
1000 Garland F. Johnston Dr.
Vernon, TX 76384
Ph: (940)552-9351
URL: http://www.wghospital.com
Dialysis Stations: 10.

Victoria

27713 ■ DaVita--Victoria
Dialysis Facility & At Home
1405 Victoria Station Dr.
Victoria, TX 77901
Free: 800-424-6589
URL: http://www.davita.com
Dialysis Stations: 29. **Formerly:** Total Renal Care.

Waco

27714 ■ Brazos Kidney Disease Center - Waco
Fresenius Medical Care
2329 N 39th St.
Waco, TX 76708
Free: 866-434-2597
URL: http://www.ultracare-dialysis.com/
Dialysis Stations: 28.

27715 ■ Dialysis Services--Waco West
Fresenius Medical Care
730 W Hwy. 6
Waco, TX 76712
Free: 866-434-2597
URL: http://www.ultracare-dialysis.com/
Dialysis Stations: 29.

Waxahachie

27716 ■ Dialysis Services Waxahachie
Fresenius Medical Care
1300 S Rogers St.
Waxahachie, TX 75165
Free: 866-434-2597
URL: http://www.ultracare-dialysis.com/
Dialysis Stations: 20.

Weatherford

27717 ■ Tarrant Dialysis Center--Weatherford
US Renal Care
504 Sante Fe
Weatherford, TX 76086
Ph: (817)594-2832
URL: http://www.usrenalcare.com
Dialysis Stations: 19.

27718 ■ Weatherford Dialysis Center
Fresenius Medical Care
128 College Park
Weatherford, TX 76086
Ph: (866)434-2597
URL: https://www.ultracare-dialysis.com
Dialysis Stations: 12.

Webster

27719 ■ Clear Lake Kidney Center
Fresenius Medical Care
1550 Live Oak
Webster, TX 77598
Free: 866-434-2597
URL: http://www.ultracare-dialysis.com/
Dialysis Stations: 20.

Weslaco

27720 ■ Mid Valley Weslaco Dialysis
US Renal Care
1005 S Airport Dr.
Weslaco, TX 78596
Ph: (956)968-5806
URL: http://www.usrenalcare.com
Dialysis Stations: 25. **Formerly:** Weslaco Kidney Center Ltd.

27721 ■ Weslaco Dialysis Center
Diversified Specialty Institutes
910 Utah
Weslaco, TX 78596
Ph: (956)968-1895
URL: http://www.dsi-corp.com
Dialysis Stations: 20.

27722 ■ Weslaco Dialysis Center
Fresenius Medical Care
1614 E Commercial Dr.
Weslaco, TX 78596
Free: 866-434-2597
URL: http://www.ultracare-dialysis.com/
Dialysis Stations: 29.

Wharton

27723 ■ Wharton Kidney Center
103 W Ahl Dag St.
Wharton, TX 77488
Ph: (979)282-8484
Dialysis Stations: 25.

Wichita Falls

27724 ■ Fresenius Medical Care--North Texas
1600 9th St.
Wichita Falls, TX 76301
Free: 866-434-2597
URL: http://www.ultracare-dialysis.com/
Dialysis Stations: 37.

Woodville

27725 ■ Woodville Dialysis Center
American Renal Associates
712 W Bluff St.
Woodville, TX 75979
Ph: (409)331-1500
URL: http://www.americanrenal.com
Dialysis Stations: 10.

UTAH

American Fork

27726 ■ American Fork Dialysis Center
120 N 1220 E, Ste. 14
American Fork, UT 84003
Ph: (801)763-0652
Dialysis Stations: 8.

27727 ■ Lone Peak Dialysis
DaVita
1175 E 50 S, Ste. 111
American Fork, UT 84003
Free: 800-424-6589
URL: http://www.davita.com
Dialysis Stations: 12.

Blanding

27728 ■ Blue Mountain Hospital Dialysis
802 S 200 W
Blanding, UT 84511
Ph: (435)678-4624
URL: http://bmhutah.com/Dialysis.php
Dialysis Stations: 8.

Bountiful

27729 ■ Lakeside Dialysis Center
532 South 500 West
Bountiful, UT 84010
Ph: (801)299-3470
Dialysis Stations: 12.

Cedar City

27730 ■ Iron Mission Dialysis Center
1277 N Northfield Rd., Ste. A-100
Cedar City, UT 84720
Ph: (435)867-8175
Dialysis Stations: 12.

Hurricane

27731 ■ Hurricane Dialysis Center
University Health Care
48 S 2500 W, Ste. 100
Hurricane, UT 84737
Ph: (435)635-0399
URL: http://healthcare.utah.edu/dialysis/facilities/hurricane.html
Dialysis Stations: 12.

Layton

27732 ■ Farmington Bay Dialysis Center
942 S Main St.
Layton, UT 84041
Ph: (801)593-9111
Dialysis Stations: 16.

27733 ■ Liberty Dialysis--Layton
2132 North 1700 W, Ste. 120
Layton, UT 84041
Ph: (801)779-6106
URL: http://www.libertydialysis.com
Dialysis Stations: 12.

Logan

27734 ■ Bridgerland Dialysis Facility
1400 North 500 East
Logan, UT 84341
Ph: (435)716-5314
Dialysis Stations: 12.

Marriott-Slaterville

27735 ■ Weber Valley Dialysis and At Home
DaVita
1920 W 250th N
Marriott-Slaterville, UT 84404
Free: 800-424-6589
URL: http://www.davita.com
Dialysis Stations: 12.

Ogden

27736 ■ Bonneville Dialysis Center
5575 South 500 East
Ogden, UT 84405
Ph: (801)479-0351
Dialysis Stations: 33.

27737 ■ Liberty Dialysis--Ogden
4780 Old Post Rd.
Ogden, UT 84403
Ph: (801)394-1230
URL: http://www.libertydialysis.com
Dialysis Stations: 16.

27738 ■ Pleasant View Dialysis
University Health Care
2715 N Hwy. 89
Ogden, UT 84414
Ph: (801)737-9555
URL: http://healthcare.utah.edu/dialysis/facilities/pleasant%20view.html
Dialysis Stations: 20.

Payson

27739 ■ Payson Regional Dialysis
155 1000 E, Ste. 50
Payson, UT 84651
Ph: (801)465-2060
Dialysis Stations: 12.

Price

27740 ■ Castleview Dialysis
230 N Hospital Dr., Ste. 1
Price, UT 84501
Ph: (435)637-8696
Dialysis Stations: 12.

Provo

27741 ■ DaVita/Utah Valley Regional Dialysis Center
1055 N 500W, Ste. 221
Provo, UT 84604
Free: 800-424-6589
URL: http://www.davita.com
Dialysis Stations: 25.

27742 ■ Timpanogos Dialysis Center & At Home
DaVita
1055 N 500 W, Ste. 222
Provo, UT 84604
Free: 800-424-6589
URL: http://www.davita.com
Dialysis Stations: 0.

27743 ■ University of Utah Provo Dialysis Center
Bldg. 15
1675 N Freedom Blvd.
Provo, UT 84604
Ph: (801)373-0169
URL: http://www.utah.edu
Dialysis Stations: 14.

Richfield

27744 ■ Sevier Valley Dialysis
1100 N Main
Richfield, UT 84701
Ph: (435)893-0358
Dialysis Stations: 10.

Roosevelt

27745 ■ Uintah Basin Dialysis Center
384 North 100 West, 74-6
Roosevelt, UT 84066
Ph: (435)722-5056
Dialysis Stations: 10.

Saint George

27746 ■ Dixie Dialysis Center
720 S River Rd., Ste. D-1100
Saint George, UT 84790
Ph: (435)656-0857
URL: http://www.med.utah.edu/dialysis
Dialysis Stations: 20.

27747 ■ Liberty Dialysis--Saint George
1173 South 250 W, Ste. 406
Saint George, UT 84770
Ph: (435)634-6600
URL: http://www.libertydialysis.com
Dialysis Stations: 19.

Salt Lake City

27748 ■ Central Valley Dialysis Center
880 East 3900 South
Salt Lake City, UT 84107
Ph: (801)408-2950
Dialysis Stations: 21.

27749 ■ Intermountain Transplant Center
5169 S Cottonwood St., Bldg. B, Ste. 320
Salt Lake City, UT 84107
Ph: (801)507-3380
URL: http://intermountainhealthcare.org/hospitals/imed/services/transplantnew/Pa ges/home.aspx
Dialysis Stations: 0.

27750 ■ Primary Children's Care Transplant
100 N Mario Capecchi Dr.
Salt Lake City, UT 84113
Ph: (801)662-6800
Dialysis Stations: 0.

27751 ■ University of Utah Dialysis Program
50 Medical Dr., ECCP R PA 220
Salt Lake City, UT 84132
Ph: (801)581-3212
URL: http://uuhsc.utah.edu/dialysis
Dialysis Stations: 4.

27752 ■ University of Utah--Kolff Dialysis Center
Kolff Dialysis Center
85 N Medical Dr. E, Rm. 201
Salt Lake City, UT 84112
Ph: (801)581-3981
URL: http://uuhsc.utah.edu/dialysis
Dialysis Stations: 13.

27753 ■ Utah Dialysis Lab
1000 S Main St., Ste. 105
Salt Lake City, UT 84101
Ph: (801)408-1400
Dialysis Stations: 19.

27754 ■ Wasatch Artificial Kidney Center
650 E 4500 South, No. 150
Salt Lake City, UT 84107
Ph: (801)747-0880
Dialysis Stations: 22.

Sandy

27755 ■ South Valley Dialysis Center
8750 S Sandy Pkwy.
Sandy, UT 84070
Ph: (801)233-8745
URL: http:/www.med.utah.edu/dialysis
Dialysis Stations: 17.

South Jordan

27756 ■ South Mountain Dialysis
Liberty Dialysis
10969 S Riverfront Pkwy., No. 100
South Jordan, UT 84095
Ph: (801)253-9696
URL: http://www.libertydialysis.com
Dialysis Stations: 16.

Taylorsville

27757 ■ Liberty Dialysis--Oquirrh
2496 W 4700 South
Taylorsville, UT 84118
Ph: (801)417-9900
URL: http://www.libertydialysis.com
Dialysis Stations: 20.

27758 ■ West Valley Dialysis Clinic
3854 W 5400 S
Taylorsville, UT 84118
Ph: (801)969-6801
Dialysis Stations: 16.

Tooele

27759 ■ Tooele Valley Dialysis Center
196 East 2000 North, Ste. 112
Tooele, UT 84074
Ph: (801)408-1430
Dialysis Stations: 7.

Vernal

27760 ■ Bessa, Inc.
Mountain View Dialysis Center
224 E 500 South, Ste. A
Vernal, UT 84078
Ph: (435)781-2335
Dialysis Stations: 6.

Weber

27761 ■ Mark Lindsay Dialysis
University Health Care
1154 E Country Hillside Dr.
Weber, UT 84405
Ph: (801)479-4460
URL: http://healthcare.utah.edu/dialysis/facilities/mark%20lindsay.html
Dialysis Stations: 21.

West Bountiful

27762 ■ DaVita--West Bountiful Dialysis & At Home
724 West 500 South, Ste. 300
West Bountiful, UT 84087
Free: 800-424-6589
URL: http://www.davita.com
Dialysis Stations: 12.

West Jordan

27763 ■ Liberty Dialysis--West Jordan
3823 W 9000 S, Ste. D
West Jordan, UT 84088
Ph: (801)280-4600
URL: http://www.libertydialysis.com
Dialysis Stations: 13.

Woods Cross

27764 ■ Liberty Dialysis--Woods Cross
572 West 750 S
Woods Cross, UT 84010
Ph: (801)292-2658
URL: http://www.libertydialysis.com
Dialysis Stations: 12.

VERMONT

Barre

27765 ■ Fletcher Allen Healthcare Satellite--Barre
Renal Dialysis Facility
Central Vermont Hospital
130 Fisher Rd., 3rd Fl.
Barre, VT 05641
Ph: (802)225-7033
URL: http://www.fahc.org
Dialysis Stations: 9.

Bennington

27766 ■ Southwestern Vermont Renal Center
Fletcher Allen Dialysis Services, LLC
SVMC 100 Hospital Dr.
Bennington, VT 05201
Ph: (802)440-6020
URL: http://www.fahc.org
Dialysis Stations: 6.

Burlington

27767 ■ Fletcher Allen Health Care
111 Colchester Ave.
Burlington, VT 05401
Ph: (802)847-3572
URL: http://www.fletcherallen.org/
Dialysis Stations: 10.

27768 ■ Medical Center Hospital of Vermont
Fletcher Allen Healthcare
Rehabilitation Bldg. 2321
1 S Prospect St.
Burlington, VT 05401
Ph: (802)847-3572
URL: http://www.fahc.org
Dialysis Stations: 10.

Newport

27769 ■ North Country Dialysis Unit
Fletcher Allen Healthcare
189 Prouty Dr.
Newport, VT 05855
Ph: (802)847-5411
URL: http://www.fahc.org
Dialysis Stations: 9.

Rutland

27770 ■ Fletcher Allen Healthcare--RRMC Satellite
Dialysis Unit
160 Allen St.
Rutland, VT 05701
Ph: (802)747-6239
URL: http://www.fahc.org
Dialysis Stations: 9.

Saint Albans

27771 ■ Fletcher Allen Healthcare Satellite--Saint Albans
Dialysis Unit
7 Crest Rd., Ste. 78
Saint Albans, VT 05478
Ph: (802)847-5008
URL: http://www.fahc.org
Dialysis Stations: 9.

Saint Johnsbury

27772 ■ St. Johnsbury Dialysis
Fresenius Medical Care
1080 Hospital Dr.
Saint Johnsbury, VT 05819
Free: 866-434-2597
URL: http://www.ultracare-dialysis.com/
Dialysis Stations: 13.

South Burlington

27773 ■ Fletcher Allen Healthcare--Chittenden County
Dialysis Unit
35 Joy Dr.
South Burlington, VT 05403
Ph: (802)847-3030
URL: http://www.fahc.org
Dialysis Stations: 19.

VIRGIN ISLANDS

Christiansted

27774 ■ Caribbean Kidney Center
5134 Sundial Park
Christiansted, VI 00820
Ph: (340)773-3227
URL: http://www.vikidneycenter.com/contact%20us.htm
Dialysis Stations: 18.

27775 ■ J Luis Hospital Saint Croix
Dialysis Center
4007 EST Diamond Ruby
Christiansted, VI 00820
Ph: (340)778-6311
Dialysis Stations: 12.

Saint Thomas

27776 ■ Schneider Hospital Saint Thomas
Dialysis Center
9048 Sugar Estate
Saint Thomas, VI 00802
Ph: (340)776-8311
Dialysis Stations: 8.

VIRGINIA

Abingdon

27777 ■ Fresenius Medical Care--Falls Drive, Abingdon
341 Falls Dr.
Abingdon, VA 24210
Free: 866-434-2597
URL: http://www.ultracare-dialysis.com/
Dialysis Stations: 12.

Alexandria

27778 ■ Alexandria Kidney Center
Fresenius Medical Care
4141 Duke St.
Alexandria, VA 22304
Free: 866-434-2597
URL: http://www.ultracare-dialysis.com/
Dialysis Stations: 27.

27779 ■ Continental Dialysis Center
DaVita
5999 Stevenson Ave., Ste. 100
Alexandria, VA 22304
Free: 800-424-6589
URL: http://www.davita.com
Dialysis Stations: 14.

27780 ■ DaVita--Alexandria
Dialysis Facility
5150 Duke St.
Alexandria, VA 22304
Free: 800-424-6589
URL: http://www.davita.com
Dialysis Stations: 20. **Formerly:** Gambro Healthcare - Alexandria.

27781 ■ Franconia Dialysis Center
DaVita
5695 King Center Dr.
Alexandria, VA 22315
Free: 800-424-6589
URL: http://www.davita.com
Dialysis Stations: 14.

27782 ■ Fresenius Medical Care--Fort Belvoir Dialysis Facility
8796-P Sacramento Dr.
Alexandria, VA 22309
Free: 866-434-2597
URL: http://www.ultracare-dialysis.com/
Dialysis Stations: 18.

Altavista

27783 ■ UVA Altavista Dialysis
University of Virginia Health System
701 5th St., Ste. 102
Altavista, VA 24517
Ph: (434)309-1128
URL: http://www.healthsystem.virginia.edu/internet/renal-services/locations/alta vista.cfm
Dialysis Stations: 15.

Amelia

27784 ■ DaVita--Amelia
Dialysis Facility & At Home
15151 Patrick Henry Hwy.
Amelia, VA 23002
Free: 800-424-6589
URL: http://www.davita.com
Dialysis Stations: 15. **Formerly:** Gambro Healthcare - Amelia.

Amherst

27785 ■ UVA Amherst Dialysis
143 Ambriar Plz.
Amherst, VA 24521
Ph: (434)946-0089
URL: http://www.healthsystem.virginia.edu/internet/renal-services/locations/amhe rst.cfm
Dialysis Stations: 26.

Arlington

27786 ■ Advanced Dialysis Center--Potomac
1785 S Hayes St.
Arlington, VA 22202
Ph: (703)521-1056
Dialysis Stations: 9.

27787 ■ DaVita--Arlington
Dialysis Facility
1701 N George Mason Dr.
Arlington, VA 22205
Free: 800-424-6589
URL: http://www.davita.com
Dialysis Stations: 5. **Formerly:** Gambro Healthcare - Arlington.

27788 ■ Renal CarePartners - Arlington/Alexandria
Dr. Anderson Bldg., 2nd Fl.
2445 Army Navy Dr.
Arlington, VA 22206
Ph: (703)892-0250
URL: http://www.renalcp.com
Dialysis Stations: 14.

Ashland

27789 ■ Dialysis Corporation of America--Ashland
113 N Washington Hwy.
Ashland, VA 23005
Ph: (804)752-3444
URL: http://www.dialysiscorporation.com
Dialysis Stations: 15.

Bedford

27790 ■ Fresenius Medical Care----Blue Ridge
Dialysis Facility
838 Ole Turnpike Dr.
Bedford, VA 24523
Free: 866-434-2597
URL: http://www.ultracare-dialysis.com/
Dialysis Stations: 16.

Blacksburg

27791 ■ Fresenius Medical Care--Montgomery County
Dialysis Services
106 Southpark Dr.
Blacksburg, VA 24060
Free: 866-434-2597
URL: http://www.ultracare-dialysis.com/
Dialysis Stations: 15.

Blairs

27792 ■ Blairs Dialysis
Fresenius Medical Care
9325 US Hwy. 29
Blairs, VA 24527
Free: 866-434-2597
URL: http://www.ultracare-dialysis.com/
Dialysis Stations: 25.

Bowling Green

27793 ■ Fresenius Medical Care--Bowling Green
Dialysis Facility
102 W Broaddus Ave.
Bowling Green, VA 22427
Free: 866-434-2597
URL: http://www.ultracare-dialysis.com/
Dialysis Stations: 12.

Charlottesville

27794 ■ Charlottesville North Dialysis & At Home
DaVita
1800 Timberwood Blvd., Ste. C
Charlottesville, VA 22911
Free: 800-424-6589
URL: http://www.davita.com
Dialysis Stations: 13.

27795 ■ DaVita--Charlottesville
Dialysis Facility
1460 Pantops Mountain Pl.
Charlottesville, VA 22911
Free: 800-424-6589
URL: http://www.davita.com
Dialysis Stations: 20. **Formerly:** Jefferson Nephrology.

27796 ■ University of Virginia Medical Center Renal Services
Transplant/Dialysis Center
1416 University Ave., 5th Fl.
Box 800265
Charlottesville, VA 22908
Ph: (434)924-5590
URL: http://www.healthsystem.virginia.edu
Dialysis Stations: 38.

Chesapeake

27797 ■ Dialysis Center
DaVita
Crossway II, Ste. 106
1400 Crossways Blvd.
Chesapeake, VA 23320
Free: 800-424-6589
URL: http://www.davita.com
Dialysis Stations: 24. **Formerly:** Total Renal Care.

27798 ■ Fresenius Medical Care
Dominion Dialysis Center
910 Great Bridge Blvd., Ste. 101
Chesapeake, VA 23320
Free: 866-434-2597
URL: http://www.ultracare-dialysis.com/
Dialysis Stations: 16.

27799 ■ Fresenius Medical Care--Eastern Virginia
111 Medical Pkwy., Ste. 100
Chesapeake, VA 23320
Free: 866-434-2597
URL: http://www.ultracare-dialysis.com/
Dialysis Stations: 13.

27800 ■ Great Bridge Dialysis Center
DaVita
745 N Battlefield Blvd.
Chesapeake, VA 23320
Free: 800-424-6589
URL: http://www.davita.com
Dialysis Stations: 26.

27801 ■ Renal Advantage Inc.--Churchland - Chesapeake
Dialysis Facility
3204 Churchland Blvd.
Chesapeake, VA 23321
Ph: (757)484-3628
URL: http://www.renaladvantage.com
Dialysis Stations: 12. **Formerly:** Gambro Healthcare - Chesapeake.

Chester

27802 ■ Chester Dialysis
DaVita
10360 Ironbridge Rd.
Chester, VA 23831
Free: 800-424-6589
URL: http://www.davita.com
Dialysis Stations: 17.

Covington

27803 ■ Covington Dialysis
Dialysis Facility
DaVita
2504 Valley Ridge Rd.
Covington, VA 24426
Free: 800-424-6589
URL: http://www.davita.com
Dialysis Stations: 14. **Formerly:** Vivra Renal Care.

Culpeper

27804 ■ DaVita--Culpeper
Dialysis Facility
430 Southridge Pkwy.
Culpeper, VA 22701
Free: 800-424-6589
URL: http://www.davita.com
Dialysis Stations: 17. **Formerly:** Gambro Healthcare - Culpeper.

Dale City

27805 ■ Fresenius Medical Care--Potomac Mills
3057 Golansky Blvd.
Dale City, VA 22192
Free: 866-434-2597
URL: http://www.ultracare-dialysis.com/
Dialysis Stations: 12.

Danville

27806 ■ Fresenius Medical Care--Danville
Dialysis Facility
129 Broad St., Ste. C
Danville, VA 24541
Free: 866-434-2597
URL: http://www.ultracare-dialysis.com/
Dialysis Stations: 36. **Formerly:** Danville Urologic Clinic.

Emporia

27807 ■ Meherrin Dialysis Center
DaVita
201 A Weaver Ave.
Emporia, VA 23847

Free: 800-424-6589
URL: http://www.davita.com
Dialysis Stations: 24.

Fairfax

27808 ■ Fair Oaks Dialysis & At Home
DaVita
3955 Pender Dr.
Fairfax, VA 22030
Free: 800-424-6589
URL: http://www.davita.com
Dialysis Stations: 13.

27809 ■ Fairfax Dialysis Center
Fresenius Medical Care
8316 Arlington Blvd., Ste. 108
Fairfax, VA 22031
Free: 866-434-2597
URL: http://www.ultracare-dialysis.com/
Dialysis Stations: 22.

27810 ■ Fairfax Hospital for Children
Pediatric Kidney Center
8505 Arlington Blvd., Ste. 100
Fairfax, VA 22031
Ph: (703)970-2600
URL: http://www.inova.org/ifh/
Dialysis Stations: 0.

27811 ■ Fairfax Hospital Inova Transplant Center
8503 Arlington Blvd., Ste. 200
Fairfax, VA 22031
Ph: (703)970-3200
URL: http://www.inova.org/healthcare-services/transplant/index.jsp
Dialysis Stations: 0.

27812 ■ Renal Carepartners--Fairfax
3930 Walnut St., Ste. 100
Fairfax, VA 22030
Ph: (703)691-7820
URL: http://www.renalcp.com
Dialysis Stations: 17.

27813 ■ Total Renal Care--Fairfax
Dialysis Center
DaVita
8501 Arlington Blvd., Ste. 100
Fairfax, VA 22031
Free: 800-424-6589
URL: http://www.davita.com
Dialysis Stations: 25.

Farmville

27814 ■ Fresenius Medical Care--Farmville
Dialysis Facility
1801 E 3rd St.
Farmville, VA 23901
Free: 866-434-2597
URL: http://www.ultracare-dialysis.com/
Dialysis Stations: 19.

Fishersville

27815 ■ UVA Augusta Dialysis
70 Medical Center Cir., Ste. 105
Fishersville, VA 22939
Ph: (540)332-5970
URL: http://uvahealth.com/directions-locations/clinics/augusta-dialysis-center
Dialysis Stations: 16.

Franklin

27816 ■ Southhampton Dialysis Center
Fresenius Medical Care
1333 Armory Dr.
Franklin, VA 23851
Free: 866-434-2597
URL: http://www.ultracare-dialysis.com/
Dialysis Stations: 14.

Fredericksburg

27817 ■ Fredericksburg Dialysis Center
Fresenius Medical Care
230 Executive Center Pkwy.
Fredericksburg, VA 22401
Free: 866-434-2597
URL: http://www.ultracare-dialysis.com/
Dialysis Stations: 25.

27818 ■ Fresenius Medical Care--Spotsylvania
10718 Ballantraye Dr.
Fredericksburg, VA 22407
Free: 866-434-2597
URL: http://www.ultracare-dialysis.com/
Dialysis Stations: 16.

Front Royal

27819 ■ Front Royal Dialysis Center
DaVita
1077-D N Shenandoah Ave.
Front Royal, VA 22630
Free: 800-424-6589
URL: http://www.davita.com
Dialysis Stations: 11.

Gainesville

27820 ■ Fresenius Medical Care--Heritage Hunt
7001 Heritage Village Plaza
Gainesville, VA 20155
Free: 866-434-2597
URL: http://www.ultracare-dialysis.com/
Dialysis Stations: 12.

27821 ■ Haymarket Dialysis
DaVita
14664 Gap Way, Ste. 2268
Gainesville, VA 20155
Free: 800-424-6589
URL: http://www.davita.com
Dialysis Stations: 13.

Galax

27822 ■ Twin County Dialysis Center
Fresenius Medical Care
1159 Glendale Rd.
Galax, VA 24333
Free: 866-434-2597
URL: http://www.ultracare-dialysis.com/
Dialysis Stations: 16.

Gloucester

27823 ■ Renal Advantage Inc.
Riverside Dialysis Center--Gloucester
7547 Medical Dr., Ste. 1400
Gloucester, VA 23061
Ph: (804)695-2904
URL: http://www.renaladvantage.com
Dialysis Stations: 12.

Goochland

27824 ■ Fresenius Medical Care--Goochland
2913 River Rd. W, Unit K
Goochland, VA 23063
Free: 866-434-2597
URL: http://www.ultracare-dialysis.com/
Dialysis Stations: 12.

Gordonsville

27825 ■ Zions Cross Road Dialysis
75 Circle Pointe Dr.
Gordonsville, VA 22942
Ph: (434)924-9009
Dialysis Stations: 12.

Grundy

27826 ■ Fresenius Medical Care--Southwest Virginia
Dialysis Facility
460 W Riverside Dr.
Grundy, VA 24614
Free: 866-434-2597
URL: http://www.ultracare-dialysis.com/
Dialysis Stations: 9.

Hampton

27827 ■ Butler Farm Dialysis Center & At Home
DaVita
501 Butler Farm Rd.
Hampton, VA 23666
Free: 800-424-6589
URL: http://www.davita.com
Dialysis Stations: 28.

27828 ■ Care Centers of Virginia
Renal Advantage Inc.
3319 W Mercury Blvd.
Hampton, VA 23666
Ph: (757)826-1795
URL: http://www.renaladvantage
Dialysis Stations: 24.

Harrisonburg

27829 ■ DaVita--Harrisonburg
Dialysis Facility
871 Cantrell Ave., Ste. 100
Harrisonburg, VA 22801
Free: 800-424-6589
URL: http://www.davita.com
Dialysis Stations: 35. **Formerly:** Gambro Healthcare - Harrisonburg.

Hopewell

27830 ■ DaVita--Hopewell
Dialysis Center
301 W Broadway
Hopewell, VA 23860
Free: 800-424-6589
URL: http://www.davita.com
Dialysis Stations: 16. **Formerly:** Tri-City Dialysis Center.

Jarrett

27831 ■ Peabody Dialysis
901 Corrections Way
Jarrett, VA 23870
Ph: (434)535-7000
Dialysis Stations: 16.

Lebanon

27832 ■ Fresenius Medical Care--Russell County
Dialysis Facility
150 E South Main St.
Lebanon, VA 24266
Free: 866-434-2597
URL: http://www.ultracare-dialysis.com/
Dialysis Stations: 10. **Formerly:** Russell County Dialysis Facility.

Leesburg

27833 ■ Leesburg Dialysis
DaVita
224D Cornwall St. NW, Ste. 100
Leesburg, VA 20176
Free: 800-424-6589
URL: http://www.davita.com
Dialysis Stations: 12.

Lexington

27834 ■ Lexington Dialysis
Dialysis Facility
DaVita
756 N Lee Hwy.
Lexington, VA 24450
Free: 800-424-6589
URL: http://www.davita.com
Dialysis Stations: 20. **Formerly:** Gambro Healthcare- Lexington.

Lorton

27835 ■ Fresenius Medical Care--Lorton
8986 Lorton Station Blvd., Ste. 100
Lorton, VA 22079
Free: 866-434-2597
URL: http://www.ultracare-dialysis.com/
Dialysis Stations: 12.

Manassas

27836 ■ DaVita
Continental Dialysis Center--Manassas
10655 Lomond Dr., Ste. 102
Manassas, VA 20109
Free: 800-424-6589
URL: http://www.davita.com
Dialysis Stations: 16.

27837 ■ Prince William County Dialysis
Dialysis Center
Fresenius Medical Care
9302 W Courthouse Rd.
Manassas, VA 20110
Free: 866-434-2597
URL: http://www.ultracare-dialysis.com/
Dialysis Stations: 16. **Formerly:** Prince William Hospital.

Martinsville

27838 ■ DaVita--Martinsville
Dialysis Facility
33 Bridge St.
Martinsville, VA 24112
Free: 800-424-6589
URL: http://www.davita.com
Dialysis Stations: 20. **Formerly:** Gambro Healthcare- Martinsville.

27839 ■ Fresenius Medical Care--Martinsville
500 Blue Ridge St.
Martinsville, VA 24112
Free: 866-434-2597
URL: http://www.ultracare-dialysis.com/
Dialysis Stations: 20. **Formerly:** Martinsville Dialysis Facility.

Mechanicsville

27840 ■ DaVita--Mechanicsville
8191 Atlee Rd.
Mechanicsville, VA 23116
Free: 800-424-6589
URL: http://www.davita.com
Dialysis Stations: 22.

27841 ■ Mechanicsville Dialysis
American Renal Associates
8400 N Run Medical Dr.
Mechanicsville, VA 23116
Ph: (804)569-6083
URL: http://www.americanrenal.com
Dialysis Stations: 24.

Midlothian

27842 ■ Charter Colony Dialysis Center
DaVita
2312 Colony Crossing Pl.
Midlothian, VA 23112
Free: 800-424-6589
URL: http://www.davita.com
Dialysis Stations: 20.

27843 ■ Midlothian Dialysis
DaVita
14281 Midlothian Trnpke.
Midlothian, VA 23113
Free: 800-424-6589
URL: http://www.davita.com
Dialysis Stations: 16.

Nassawadox

27844 ■ Fresenius Medical Care--Nassawadox
Dialysis Facility
9550 Hospital Ave.
Nassawadox, VA 23413
Free: 866-434-2597
URL: http://www.ultracare-dialysis.com/
Dialysis Stations: 27.

Newport News

27845 ■ DaVita--Newport News
Dialysis Facility
711 79th St.
Newport News, VA 23605
Free: 800-424-6589
URL: http://www.davita.com
Dialysis Stations: 32.

27846 ■ Jefferson Avenue Dialysis
DaVita
11234 Jefferson Ave.
Newport News, VA 23601
Free: 800-424-6589
URL: http://www.davita.com
Dialysis Stations: 12.

27847 ■ Peninsula Dialysis Center
Dialysis Unit
DaVita
716 Denhigh Blvd., Stes. D1 & D2
Newport News, VA 23602
Free: 800-424-6589
URL: http://www.davita.com
Dialysis Stations: 16.

27848 ■ Renal Advantage Inc.--Chesapeake Avenue
225 Chesapeake Ave.
Newport News, VA 23607
Ph: (757)247-4080
URL: http://www.renaladvantage.com
Dialysis Stations: 10.

27849 ■ Renal Advantage Inc.--Thimble Shoals
Dialysis Facility
739 Thimble Shoals Blvd., Ste. 600
Newport News, VA 23606
Ph: (757)873-1090
URL: http://www.renaladvantage.com
Dialysis Stations: 24. **Formerly:** Gambro Health-care - Newport News.

Norfolk

27850 ■ Children's Hospital of the King's Daughters
Pediatric Dialysis Center
601 Children's Ln.
Norfolk, VA 23507
Ph: (757)668-8151
URL: http://www.chkd.org
Dialysis Stations: 6.

27851 ■ Fresenius Medical Care--Greater Norfolk
Granby Dialysis Center
1902 Omohundro Ave., Ste. 100
Norfolk, VA 23517
Free: 866-434-2597
URL: http://www.ultracare-dialysis.com/
Dialysis Stations: 24.

27852 ■ Kempsville Dialysis Center
Fresenius Medical Care
Bldg. 15, Ste. 140
6320 N Center Dr.
Norfolk, VA 23502
Free: 866-434-2597
URL: http://www.ultracare-dialysis.com/
Dialysis Stations: 34.

27853 ■ Leigh Dialysis Center
DaVita
Bldg. 11, Ste. 128
420 N Center Dr.
Norfolk, VA 23502
Free: 800-424-6589
URL: http://www.davita.com
Dialysis Stations: 15.

27854 ■ Midtowne Norfolk Dialysis
DaVita
2201 Colonial Ave.
Norfolk, VA 23517
Free: 800-424-6589
URL: http://www.davita.com
Dialysis Stations: 17.

27855 ■ Norfolk Dialysis Center
DaVita
962 Norfolk Sq.
Norfolk, VA 23502
Free: 800-424-6589
URL: http://www.davita.com
Dialysis Stations: 41.

27856 ■ Sentara Norfolk General Hospital Transplant Program
600 Gresham Dr.
Norfolk, VA 23507
Ph: (757)388-3906
URL: http://www.sentara.com/Services/Transplant/Pages/Transplant.aspx
Dialysis Stations: 0.

27857 ■ Tidewater Renal Dialysis Center
Fresenius Medical Care
5623 Tidewater Dr.
Norfolk, VA 23509
Free: 866-434-2597
URL: http://www.ultracare-dialysis.com/
Dialysis Stations: 24.

Norton

27858 ■ Fresenius Medical Care--Mountain Empire
205 Virginia Ave. NW
Norton, VA 24273
Free: 866-434-2597
URL: http://www.ultracare-dialysis.com/
Dialysis Stations: 15.

Orange

27859 ■ Orange Dialysis Facility
661 University Ln.
Orange, VA 22960
Ph: (540)661-3011
Dialysis Stations: 12.

Pearisburg

27860 ■ Fresenius Medical Care--Giles
Dialysis Facility
1615 Wenonoah Ave.
Pearisburg, VA 24134
Free: 866-434-2597
URL: http://www.ultracare-dialysis.com/
Dialysis Stations: 8.

Petersburg

27861 ■ Appomattox Dialysis Center
DaVita
15 W Old St.
Petersburg, VA 23803

Free: 800-424-6589
URL: http://www.davita.com
Dialysis Stations: 12.

27862 ■ Liberty Dialysis--Petersburg
3400 S Crater Rd.
Petersburg, VA 23805
Ph: (804)732-8228
URL: http://www.libertydialysis.com
Dialysis Stations: 36.

27863 ■ Southside Regional Medical Center
Renal Dialysis Unit
3335 S Crater Rd.
Petersburg, VA 23805
Ph: (804)862-5261
URL: http://www.srmconline.com
Dialysis Stations: 30.

Portsmouth

27864 ■ DaVita--Greater Portsmouth Dialysis Unit
3516 Queen St.
Portsmouth, VA 23707
Free: 800-424-6589
URL: http://www.davita.com
Dialysis Stations: 18. **Formerly:** Portsmouth General Hospital.

27865 ■ Portsmouth Dialysis Center
DaVita
2000 High St.
Portsmouth, VA 23705
Free: 800-424-6589
URL: http://www.davita.com
Dialysis Stations: 15.

27866 ■ Renal Advantage Inc.--Airline Portsmouth
Dialysis Facility
2809 Airline Blvd.
Portsmouth, VA 23701
Ph: (757)465-5085
URL: http://www.renaladvantage.com
Dialysis Stations: 24. **Formerly:** Gambro Healthcare - Airline Boulevard.

27867 ■ Renal Advantage Inc.--Goode Way--Portsmouth
Dialysis Facility
311 Goode Way
Portsmouth, VA 23704
Ph: (757)393-6582
URL: http://www.renaladvantage.com
Dialysis Stations: 20. **Formerly:** Gambro Healthcare - Portsmouth.

Purcellville

27868 ■ Purcellville Dialysis Center & At Home
DaVita
280 N Hatcher Ave.
Purcellville, VA 20132
Free: 800-424-6589
URL: http://www.davita.com
Dialysis Stations: 16.

Radford

27869 ■ Fresenius Medical Care--New River Valley
Dialysis Facility
1200-A Tyler Ave.
Radford, VA 24141
Free: 866-434-2597
URL: http://www.ultracare-dialysis.com/
Dialysis Stations: 15.

27870 ■ Radford Dialysis & At Home
DaVita
600 E Main St., Ste. F
Radford, VA 24141
Free: 800-424-6589
URL: http://www.davita.com
Dialysis Stations: 17.

Reston

27871 ■ Renal Carepartners of Reston LLC
12330 Pinecrest Rd., Ste. 200
Reston, VA 20191
Ph: (703)476-0605
URL: http://www.renalcp.com
Dialysis Stations: 16.

27872 ■ Reston Dialysis Center
DaVita
1875 Campus Commons Dr., Ste. 110
Reston, VA 20191
Free: 800-424-6589
URL: http://www.davita.com
Dialysis Stations: 8.

Richmond

27873 ■ DaVita--East End
Dialysis Center
2201 E Main St.
Richmond, VA 23223
Free: 800-424-6589
URL: http://www.davita.com
Dialysis Stations: 24. **Formerly:** Total Renal Care.

27874 ■ DaVita--Henrico County
Dialysis & At Home
5270 Chamberlayne Rd.
Richmond, VA 23227
Free: 800-424-6589
URL: http://www.davita.com
Dialysis Stations: 26. **Formerly:** Gambro Healthcare - Henrico County.

27875 ■ DaVita--Richmond Community Hospital Dialysis
Dialysis Facility
1510 N 28th St., Ste. 110
Richmond, VA 23223
Free: 800-424-6589
URL: http://www.davita.com
Dialysis Stations: 16. **Formerly:** Total Renal Care.

27876 ■ Forest Park Dialysis Center
American Renal Associates
1603 Santa Rosa Rd.
Richmond, VA 23229
Ph: (804)288-2751
URL: http://www.americanrenal.com
Dialysis Stations: 16.

27877 ■ Fresenius Medical Care--West End
Dialysis Facility
1501 Santa Rosa Rd.
Richmond, VA 23229
Free: 866-434-2597
URL: http://www.ultracare-dialysis.com/
Dialysis Stations: 28. **Formerly:** Bio-Medical Applications - West End.

27878 ■ Henrico Doctors Hospital--Transplant
HCA Virginia Health System
1602 Skipwith Rd.
Richmond, VA 23229
Ph: (804)289-4941
URL: http://henricodoctors.com/CustomPage.asp?guidCustomContentID=467830FF-95D4-4BD3-87B6-05CF7E4A3B25
Dialysis Stations: 0.

27879 ■ Hioaks Dialysis, PD & At Home Dialysis Center
DaVita
681 Hioaks Rd., Ste. A
Richmond, VA 23225
Free: 800-424-6589
URL: http://www.davita.com
Dialysis Stations: 24. **Formerly:** Gambro Healthcare - South Richmond.

27880 ■ Hume-Lee Transplant Center
VCU Medical Center
1250 E Marshall St.
Richmond, VA 23298
Ph: (804)828-9224
URL: http://www.vcuhealth.org/transplant/
Dialysis Stations: 14.

27881 ■ Renal Advantage Inc.--MCV Turnpike Dialysis Center
2521 Mechanicsville Tpke.
Richmond, VA 23223
Ph: (804)644-0566
URL: http://www.renaladvantage.com
Dialysis Stations: 27. **Formerly:** Gambro Healthcare - MCV.

27882 ■ Renal Advantage Inc.--Richmond Dialysis Facility
800 W Leigh St.
Richmond, VA 23220
Ph: (804)649-8070
URL: http://www.renaladvantage.com
Dialysis Stations: 33. **Formerly:** Gambro Healthcare.

27883 ■ South Laburnum Dialysis
American Renal Associates
4817 S Laburnum Ave.
Richmond, VA 23231
Ph: (303)403-1127
URL: http://www.americanrenal.com
Dialysis Stations: 20.

27884 ■ Three Chopt Dialysis
DaVita
8813 Three Chopt Rd.
Richmond, VA 23229
Free: 800-424-6589
URL: http://www.davita.com
Dialysis Stations: 16.

27885 ■ Virginia Commonwealth University Medical Center
Renal Dialysis Unit
1200 E Marshall St.
Richmond, VA 23298
Ph: (804)828-9224
URL: http://www.vcu.edu/medcenter
Dialysis Stations: 14.

27886 ■ Westhampton Dialysis Center
American Renal Associates
5320 Patterson Ave.
Richmond, VA 23226
Ph: (804)285-3394
URL: http://www.americanrenal.com
Dialysis Stations: 17.

Roanoke

27887 ■ Fresenius Medical Care--North Roanoke
Dialysis Center
1326 7th St. NE
Roanoke, VA 24012
Free: 866-434-2597
URL: http://www.ultracare-dialysis.com/
Dialysis Stations: 25.

27888 ■ Friendship Manor Dialysis Unit
Fresenius Medical Care
331 Hershberger Rd.
Roanoke, VA 24012
Free: 866-434-2597
URL: http://www.ultracare-dialysis.com/
Dialysis Stations: 29.

Rocky Mount

27889 ■ Fresenius Medical Care--Franklin County Dialysis Facility
300 Technology Dr.
Rocky Mount, VA 24151
Free: 866-434-2597
URL: http://www.ultracare-dialysis.com/
Dialysis Stations: 16.

Salem

27890 ■ Fresenius Medical Care--Roanoke
2021 Apperson Dr.
Salem, VA 24153
Free: 866-434-2597
URL: http://www.ultracare-dialysis.com/
Dialysis Stations: 25.

Smithfield

27891 ■ Renal Advantage Inc.--South Church--Smithfield
1812-C S Church St.
Smithfield, VA 23430
Ph: (757)365-4293
URL: http://www.renaladvantage.com
Dialysis Stations: 15. **Formerly:** Riverside Dialysis Center--Smithfield.

South Boston

27892 ■ Fresenius Medical Care--South Boston Dialysis Facility
2043 Hamilton Blvd.
South Boston, VA 24592
Free: 866-434-2597
URL: http://www.ultracare-dialysis.com/
Dialysis Stations: 19. **Formerly:** RCG/ - South Boston.

South Hill

27893 ■ Community Memorial Health Center Dialysis Center
125 Buena Vista Circle
South Hill, VA 23970
Ph: (434)447-3151
URL: http://www.cmh-sh.org
Dialysis Stations: 12.

Springfield

27894 ■ Continental Dialysis Center--Springfield DaVita
8350-A Traford Ln.
Springfield, VA 22152
Free: 800-424-6589
URL: http://www.davita.com
Dialysis Stations: 11. **Formerly:** Continental Dialysis Center, Springfield/Fairfax.

Stafford

27895 ■ Fresenius Medical Care--Garrisonville Dialysis Facility
396 Garrisonville Rd.
Stafford, VA 22554
Free: 866-434-2597
URL: http://www.ultracare-dialysis.com/
Dialysis Stations: 10.

27896 ■ Garrisonville Dialysis Center DaVita
70 Doc Stone Rd., No. 101
Stafford, VA 22556
Free: 800-424-6589
URL: http://www.davita.com
Dialysis Stations: 13.

Stanley

27897 ■ UVA Page Dialysis
235 Medical Center Dr.
Stanley, VA 22851
Ph: (540)778-3484
URL: http://uvahealth.com/directions-locations/clinics/uva-dialysis-page
Dialysis Stations: 12.

Staunton

27898 ■ DaVita--Staunton
29 Idlewood Blvd.
Staunton, VA 24401
Free: 800-424-6589
URL: http://www.davita.com
Dialysis Stations: 17.

Sterling

27899 ■ Continental Dialysis Center DaVita
46396 Benedict Dr., Ste. 100
Sterling, VA 20164
Free: 800-424-6589
URL: http://www.davita.com
Dialysis Stations: 15.

Stuart

27900 ■ Fresenius Medical Care--Patrick County
221 Rich Creek Dr.
Stuart, VA 24171
Free: 866-434-2597
URL: http://www.ultracare-dialysis.com/
Dialysis Stations: 10. **Formerly:** Renal Care Croup.

Suffolk

27901 ■ Artificial Kidney Center--Suffolk Fresenius Medical Care
1005 Commercial Ln., Ste. 100
Suffolk, VA 23434
Free: 866-434-2597
URL: http://www.ultracare-dialysis.com/
Dialysis Stations: 28.

27902 ■ Harbor View Dialysis DaVita
1039 Champions Way
Suffolk, VA 23435
Free: 800-424-6589
URL: http://www.davita.com
Dialysis Stations: 13.

Tappahannock

27903 ■ Tappahannock Dialysis Center Fresenius Medical Care
1922 Tappahannock Blvd.
Tappahannock, VA 22560
Free: 866-434-2597
URL: http://www.ultracare-dialysis.com/
Dialysis Stations: 19.

Troy

27904 ■ Fluvanna Correctional Center for Women Dialysis Services
Rte. 250 W
Troy, VA 22974
Ph: (434)984-3700
URL: http://www.vadoc.state.va.us/facilities/central/fluvanna/
Dialysis Stations: 3.

Vienna

27905 ■ DaVita--Tysons Corner Dialysis Facility & At Home
8391 Old Courthouse Rd.
Vienna, VA 22182
Free: 800-424-6589
URL: http://www.davita.com
Dialysis Stations: 15. **Formerly:** Gambro Healthcare - Tysons Corner.

Virginia Beach

27906 ■ DaVita--Virginia Beach Dialysis Facility
740 Independence Circle
Virginia Beach, VA 23455
Free: 800-424-6589
URL: http://www.davita.com
Dialysis Stations: 20.

27907 ■ First Colonial--DaVita at Home DaVita
1157 1st Colonial Rd., Ste. 200
Virginia Beach, VA 23454
Free: 800-424-6589
URL: http://www.davita.com
Dialysis Stations: 4.

27908 ■ First Landing Dialysis Center DaVita
1745 Camelot Dr., Ste. 100
Virginia Beach, VA 23454
Free: 800-424-6589
URL: http://www.davita.com
Dialysis Stations: 14.

27909 ■ Fresenius Medical Care--Virginia Beach
525 S Independence Blvd., Ste. 150
Virginia Beach, VA 23452
Free: 866-434-2597
URL: http://www.ultracare-dialysis.com/
Dialysis Stations: 15.

27910 ■ Virginia Beach Dialysis Center DaVita
Camelot Professional Center
1800 Camelot Dr., Ste. 100
Virginia Beach, VA 23454
Free: 800-424-6589
URL: http://www.davita.com
Dialysis Stations: 25.

Warrenton

27911 ■ Fresenius Medical Care--Warrenton Dialysis Facility
170 W Shirley Ave., Ste. 100
Warrenton, VA 20186
Free: 866-434-2597
URL: http://www.ultracare-dialysis.com/
Dialysis Stations: 21.

Warsaw

27912 ■ Dialysis Corporation of America of Warsaw
4709 Richmond Rd.
Warsaw, VA 22572
Ph: (804)333-4444
Fax: (804)333-0400
URL: http://www.dialysiscorporation.com
Dialysis Stations: 15.

Williamsburg

27913 ■ Renal Advantage Inc.--John Tyler Highway Williamsburg
4511 John Tyler Hwy.
Williamsburg, VA 23185
Ph: (757)229-5701
URL: http://www.renaladvantage.com
Dialysis Stations: 12.

27914 ■ Williamsburg Dialysis and At Home DaVita
500 Sentara Cir.
Williamsburg, VA 23188

Free: 800-424-6589
URL: http://www.davita.com
Dialysis Stations: 16.

Winchester

27915 ■ Winchester Dialysis
DaVita
2301 Valor Dr.
Winchester, VA 22601
Free: 800-424-6589
URL: http://www.davita.com
Dialysis Stations: 25.

Woodbridge

27916 ■ Continental Dialysis Center--Woodbridge
Dialysis Facility
DaVita
2751 Killarney Dr.
Woodbridge, VA 22192
Free: 800-424-6589
URL: http://www.davita.com
Dialysis Stations: 24.

27917 ■ Renal Carepartners--Woodbridge
14000 Crown Ct., Ste. 110
Woodbridge, VA 22193
Ph: (703)680-3055
URL: http://www.renalcp.com
Dialysis Stations: 16.

Wytheville

27918 ■ Fresenius Medical Care--Wytheville
Dialysis Facility
340 Peppers Ferry Rd.
Wytheville, VA 24382
Free: 866-434-2597
URL: http://www.ultracare-dialysis.com/
Dialysis Stations: 13.

WASHINGTON

Aberdeen

27919 ■ Fresenius Medical Care--Industrial Parkway, Aberdeen
Dialysis Center
2012 Industrial Pkwy.
Aberdeen, WA 98520
Free: 866-434-2597
URL: http://www.ultracare-dialysis.com/
Dialysis Stations: 16. **Formerly:** Renal Care Group -Aberdeen.

Arlington

27920 ■ Puget Sound Kidney Center--Smokey Point
18828 Smokey Point Blvd.
Arlington, WA 98223
Ph: (360)454-5280
URL: http://www.pskc.net
Dialysis Stations: 28.

Auburn

27921 ■ Auburn Kidney Center
Northwest Kidney Center
1501 W Valley Hwy. N, Ste. 104
Auburn, WA 98001
Ph: (253)804-8323
URL: http://www.nwkidney.org
Dialysis Stations: 24.

Bellevue

27922 ■ Bellevue Dialysis Center
DaVita
3535 Factoria Blvd., Ste. 150
Bellevue, WA 98006
Free: 800-424-6589
URL: http://www.davita.com
Dialysis Stations: 10.

27923 ■ Lake Washington Kidney Center
Northwest Kidney Center
1474 112th Ave. NE, Ste. 100
Bellevue, WA 98004
Ph: (425)454-0067
URL: http://www.nwkidney.org
Dialysis Stations: 18.

Bellingham

27924 ■ Mount Baker Kidney Center
410 Birchwood Ave., Ste. 100
Bellingham, WA 98225
Ph: (360)734-4243
Dialysis Stations: 26. **Formerly:** Mount Baker Dialysis Training Unit.

Bothell

27925 ■ Mill Creek Dialysis Center
DaVita
18001 Bothell Everett Hwy., Ste. 112
Bothell, WA 98012
Free: 800-424-6589
URL: http://www.davita.com
Dialysis Stations: 9.

Bremerton

27926 ■ Olympic Peninsula Kidney Center
2613 Wheaton Way
Bremerton, WA 98310
Ph: (360)479-5908
Dialysis Stations: 16.

Chehalis

27927 ■ Fresenius Medical Care--Chehalis
505 SE Adams St.
Chehalis, WA 98532
Free: 866-434-2597
URL: http://www.ultracare-dialysis.com/
Dialysis Stations: 12.

Clarkston

27928 ■ Tri-State Tristate Memorial Hospital Inc.
Dialysis Unit
1221 Highland Ave.
Clarkston, WA 99403
Ph: (509)758-4656
URL: http://www.tristatehospital.org
Dialysis Stations: 12.

Colville

27929 ■ Fresenius Medical Care--Colville
147 Garden Homes Dr.
Colville, WA 99114
Free: 866-434-2597
URL: http://www.ultracare-dialysis.com/
Dialysis Stations: 10.

Ellensburg

27930 ■ Ellensburg Dialysis Center
DaVita
2101 W Dolarway Rd., Ste. 1
Ellensburg, WA 98926
Free: 800-424-6589
URL: http://www.davita.com
Dialysis Stations: 5.

Everett

27931 ■ Everett Dialysis Center
DaVita
8130 Evergreen Way, Ste. C
Everett, WA 98203
Free: 800-424-6589
URL: http://www.davita.com
Dialysis Stations: 21.

27932 ■ Puget Sound Kidney Center
Dialysis Facility
1005 Pacific Ave.
Everett, WA 98201
Ph: (425)259-5195
URL: http://www.pskc.net
Dialysis Stations: 37.

Federal Way

27933 ■ Federal Way Community Dialysis Center & At Home
DaVita
1015 S 348th St.
Federal Way, WA 98003
Free: 800-424-6589
URL: http://www.davita.com
Dialysis Stations: 25.

Gig Harbor

27934 ■ Saint Joseph Dialysis Center--Gig Harbor
Franciscan Health System West
4700 Point Fosdick Dr. NW, Ste. 101
Gig Harbor, WA 98335
Ph: (253)853-2965
URL: http://www.fhshealth.org/services/ns.asp
Dialysis Stations: 6.

Grahma

27935 ■ Graham Dialysis Center
DaVita
10219 196th Ct. E, Ste. C
Grahma, WA 98338
Free: 800-424-6589
URL: http://www.davita.com
Dialysis Stations: 8.

Kennewick

27936 ■ Fresenius Medical Care--Columbia Basin
Dialysis Facility
510 N Colorado, Ste. B
Kennewick, WA 99336
Free: 866-434-2597
URL: http://www.ultracare-dialysis.com/
Dialysis Stations: 13. **Formerly:** Tri-Cities Kidney Center.

Kent

27937 ■ Kent Dialysis Center
DaVita
21501 84th Ave. S
Kent, WA 98032
Free: 800-424-6589
URL: http://www.davita.com
Dialysis Stations: 13.

27938 ■ Kent Kidney Center
Northwest Kidney Center
25316 74th Ave. S, Ste. 101
Kent, WA 98032
Ph: (253)850-6810
Fax: (253)850-6815
URL: http://www.nwkidney.org
Dialysis Stations: 17.

Kirkland

27939 ■ Totem Lake Kidney Center
Northwest Kidney Center
12303 NE 130th Ln., Ste. 300
Kirkland, WA 98034
Ph: (425)821-8785
URL: http://www.nwkidney.org
Dialysis Stations: 15.

Lake Forest Park

27940 ■ Lake City Kidney Center
Northwest Kidney Centers
14524 Bothell Way NE
Lake Forest Park, WA 98155
Ph: (206)365-0775
URL: http://www.nwkidney.org
Dialysis Stations: 13.

Lakewood

27941 ■ Lakewood Community Dialysis Center & At Home
DaVita
5919 Lakewood Tower Center Blvd. SW, Ste. A
Lakewood, WA 98499
Free: 800-424-6589
URL: http://www.davita.com
Dialysis Stations: 21.

Long Beach

27942 ■ Seaview Dialysis Center
DaVita
101 18th St. S
Long Beach, WA 98631
Free: 800-424-6589
URL: http://www.davita.com
Dialysis Stations: 10.

Longview

27943 ■ Fresenius Medical Care--Longview
5616 Ocean Beach Hwy., Ste. 260
Longview, WA 98632
Free: 866-434-2597
URL: http://www.ultracare-dialysis.com/
Dialysis Stations: 6.

27944 ■ Peacehealth Dialysis Center
600 N Broadway
Longview, WA 98632
Ph: (360)414-2200
Dialysis Stations: 22. **Formerly:** St. John Medical Center.

Moses Lake

27945 ■ Fresenius Medical Care--Moses Lake
1545 S Pilgrim St.
Moses Lake, WA 98837
Free: 866-434-2597
URL: http://www.ultracare-dialysis.com/
Dialysis Stations: 20. **Formerly:** INFCG Moses Lake Dialysis Unit.

Mount Vernon

27946 ■ Skagit Valley Kidney Center
208 S 14th St.
Mount Vernon, WA 98273
Ph: (360)428-8260
URL: http://www.skagitvalleyhospital.org
Dialysis Stations: 27.

Mountlake Terrace

27947 ■ Puget Sound Kidney Center--South
21309 44th Ave. W
Mountlake Terrace, WA 98043
Ph: (425)744-1095
URL: http://www.pskc.net
Dialysis Stations: 27.

Oak Harbor

27948 ■ Puget Sound Kidney Center--Whidbey Island
430 SE Midway Blvd.
Oak Harbor, WA 98277
Ph: (360)679-6706
URL: http://www.pskc.net
Dialysis Stations: 6.

27949 ■ Whidbey Island Dialysis Center
DaVita
32650 State Rte. 20, Bldg. E
Oak Harbor, WA 98277
Free: 800-424-6589
URL: http://www.davita.com
Dialysis Stations: 5.

Olympia

27950 ■ Fresenius Medical Care--Lacey
719 Sleater-Kinney Rd. SE, Ste. 152
Olympia, WA 98503
Free: 866-434-2597
URL: http://www.ultracare-dialysis.com/
Dialysis Stations: 25. **Formerly:** Renal Care Group.

27951 ■ Olympia Dialysis Center
DaVita
335 Cooper Point Rd. NW
Olympia, WA 98502
Free: 800-424-6589
URL: http://www.davita.com
Dialysis Stations: 6.

Omak

27952 ■ Omak Dialysis Center
Fresenius Medical Care
800 Jasmine Ave., Ste. 1
Omak, WA 98841
Free: 866-434-2597
URL: http://www.ultracare-dialysis.com/
Dialysis Stations: 11. **Formerly:** Renal Care Group.

Othello

27953 ■ Leah Layne Dialysis Center
Fresenius Medical Care
530 S 1st Ave.
Othello, WA 99344
Free: 866-434-2597
URL: http://www.ultracare-dialysis.com/
Dialysis Stations: 5.

Pasco

27954 ■ Mid-Columbia Kidney Center Dialysis Facility & At Home
DaVita
6825 Burden Blvd., Ste. A
Pasco, WA 99301
Free: 800-424-6589
URL: http://www.davita.com
Dialysis Stations: 21.

Port Angeles

27955 ■ Port Angeles Kidney Center Dialysis Facility
Northwest Kidney Center
809 Georgiana St.
Port Angeles, WA 98362
Ph: (360)565-1435
URL: http://www.nwkidney.org
Dialysis Stations: 8.

Port Orchard

27956 ■ Olympic Peninsula Kidney Center--South Kitsap
Bldg. 1, Ste. 1400
450 S Kitsap Blvd.
Port Orchard, WA 98366
Ph: (360)895-7795
Dialysis Stations: 11.

Poulsbo

27957 ■ Olympic Peninsula Kidney Center--North
19472 Powder Hill Pl., Ste. 100
Poulsbo, WA 98370
Ph: (360)598-9712
Dialysis Stations: 8.

Puyallup

27958 ■ Greater Puyallup Dialysis Center
702 S Hill Park, Ste. 105
Puyallup, WA 98373
Ph: (253)445-7520
Dialysis Stations: 12.

27959 ■ Puyallup Dialysis Center
DaVita
716-C S Hill Park
Puyallup, WA 98373
Free: 800-424-6589
URL: http://www.davita.com
Dialysis Stations: 16.

Renton

27960 ■ Mount Rainier Kidney Center
Northwest Kidney Center
4242 E Valley Hwy.
Renton, WA 98055
Ph: (425)251-0647
URL: http://www.nwkidney.org
Dialysis Stations: 28.

Richland

27961 ■ Chinook Kidney Center
DaVita
1315 Aaron Dr.
Richland, WA 99352
Free: 800-424-6589
URL: http://www.davita.com
Dialysis Stations: 19.

SeaTac

27962 ■ SeaTac Kidney Center
Northwest Kidney Center
17900 International Blvd. S, Ste. 301
SeaTac, WA 98188
Ph: (206)292-2771
URL: http://www.nwkidney.org
Dialysis Stations: 25.

Seattle

27963 ■ Elliott Bay Kidney Center
Northwest Kidney Center
600 Broadway, Ste. 240
Seattle, WA 98122
Ph: (206)292-2515
URL: http://www.nwkidney.org
Dialysis Stations: 18.

27964 ■ Haviland Kidney Center
Northwest Kidney Center
700 Broadway
Seattle, WA 98122
Ph: (206)292-2771
URL: http://www.nwkidney.org
Dialysis Stations: 15.

27965 ■ Olympic View Dialysis Center & At Home
DaVita
125 16th Ave. E, CSB 5
Seattle, WA 98112
Free: 800-424-6589
URL: http://www.davita.com
Dialysis Stations: 25.

27966 ■ Scribner Kidney Center
Northwest Kidney Center
2150 N 107th St., Ste. 105
Seattle, WA 98133
Ph: (206)363-5090
URL: http://www.nwkidney.org
Dialysis Stations: 22.

27967 ■ Seattle Children's Hospital Division of Nephrology Dialysis Center
4800 Sand Point Way NE, A-7931
Seattle, WA 98105
Ph: (206)987-2524
Dialysis Stations: 5.

27968 ■ Seattle Kidney Center Northwest Kidney Center
548 15th Ave.
Seattle, WA 98122
Ph: (206)720-3940
URL: http://www.nwkidney.org
Dialysis Stations: 38.

27969 ■ Swedish Medical Center Transplant Services
1101 Madison St., Ste. 200
Seattle, WA 98104
Ph: (206)386-3660
URL: http://www.swedish.org/Services/Organ-Transplant
Dialysis Stations: 0.

27970 ■ University of Washington Medical Center Transplant Services
Box 356174
Seattle, WA 98195
Ph: (206)0.
URL: http://depts.washington.edu/surgery/divisions/transplant/index.html

27971 ■ Virginia Mason Medical Center Transplant
PO Box 900
Seattle, WA 98111
Ph: (206)341-0925
URL: https://www.virginiamason.org/home/dept.cfm?id=633
Dialysis Stations: 0.

27972 ■ West Seattle Kidney Center Dialysis Facility Northwest Kidney Center
4045 Delridge Way SW, Ste. 100
Seattle, WA 98106
Ph: (206)923-3562
URL: http://www.nwkidney.org
Dialysis Stations: 20.

27973 ■ Westwood Dialysis Center & At Home DaVita
2615 SW Trenton St.
Seattle, WA 98126
Free: 800-424-6589
URL: http://www.davita.com
Dialysis Stations: 7.

Shelton

27974 ■ Fresenius Medical Care--Shelton
1872 N 13th Loop Rd.
Shelton, WA 98584
Free: 866-434-2597
URL: http://www.ultracare-dialysis.com/
Dialysis Stations: 6. **Formerly:** Renal Care Group.

Snoqualmie

27975 ■ Snoqualmie Ridge Kidney Center Northwest Kidney Centers
35131 SE Douglas St., Ste. 113
Snoqualmie, WA 98065
Ph: (425)396-7090
URL: http://www.nwkidney.org
Dialysis Stations: 9.

Spokane

27976 ■ Diversified Specialty Institutes--Spokane Valley
12610 E Mirabeau Pkwy., Ste. 100
Spokane, WA 99216
Ph: (509)228-9933
URL: http://www.dsi-corp.com
Dialysis Stations: 10. **Formerly:** National Renal Institutes.

27977 ■ Downtown Spokane Renal Center Diversified Specialty Institutes
601 W 5th St., Ste. 101
Spokane, WA 99204
Ph: (509)363-0070
URL: http://www.dsi-corp.com
Dialysis Stations: 12. **Formerly:** Fresenius Medical Care.

27978 ■ Fresenius Medical Care--North Pines
1017 N Pines Rd.
Spokane, WA 99206
Free: 866-434-2597
Dialysis Stations: 20.

27979 ■ North Spokane Renal Center Diversified Specialty Institutes
7407 N Division, Ste. F
Spokane, WA 99208
Ph: (509)465-4779
URL: http://www.dsi-corp.com
Dialysis Stations: 12. **Formerly:** National Renal Institutes.

27980 ■ Northpointe Dialysis Unit Fresenius Medical Care--Northpointe
9651 N Nevada St.
Spokane, WA 99218
Free: 866-434-2597
URL: http://www.ultracare-dialysis.com/
Dialysis Stations: 24. **Formerly:** INRCG Northpointe Dialysis Unit.

27981 ■ Sacred Heart Medical Center Transplant
PO Box 2555
Spokane, WA 99220
Ph: (509)474-4500
URL: http://www2.providence.org/spokane/facilities/sacred-heart-medical-center/s ervices/kidney/Pages/kidney-transplant.aspx
Dialysis Stations: 0.

27982 ■ Spokane Kidney Center Fresenius Medical Care
610 S Sherman Ave., Ste. 101
Spokane, WA 99202
Free: 866-434-2597
URL: http://www.ultracare-dialysis.com/
Dialysis Stations: 24. **Formerly:** Renal Care Group.

Sunnyside

27983 ■ Mount Adams Kidney Center DaVita
3220 Picard Pl.
Sunnyside, WA 98944
Free: 800-424-6589
URL: http://www.davita.com
Dialysis Stations: 15.

Tacoma

27984 ■ Saint Joseph Medical Center Nephrology Services
1717 S J St.
Tacoma, WA 98401
Ph: (253)426-6688
URL: http://www.fhshealth.org/location/sjmc.asp
Dialysis Stations: 50.

27985 ■ Tacoma Dialysis and At Home DaVita
3401 S 19th St.
Tacoma, WA 98405
Free: 800-424-6589
URL: http://www.davita.com
Dialysis Stations: 10.

Union Gap

27986 ■ Union Gap Dialysis Center DaVita
1236 Ahtanum Ridge Dr.
Union Gap, WA 98903
Free: 800-424-6589
URL: http://www.davita.com
Dialysis Stations: 8.

Vancouver

27987 ■ Fresenius Medical Care----Fort Vancouver Dialysis Center
312 SE Stone Mill Dr., Ste. 150
Vancouver, WA 98684
Free: 866-434-2597
URL: http://www.ultracare-dialysis.com/
Dialysis Stations: 24. **Formerly:** Pacific Northwest Renal Services - Fort Vancouver.

27988 ■ Fresenius Medical Care--Salmon Creek Dialysis Facility
9105A Hwy. 99, Ste. 102
Vancouver, WA 98665
Free: 866-434-2597
URL: http://www.ultracare-dialysis.com/
Dialysis Stations: 16. **Formerly:** Pacific Northwest Renal Services - Salmon Creek.

27989 ■ Vancouver Dialysis Center DaVita
9120 NE Vancouver Mall Loop, Ste. 160
Vancouver, WA 98682
Free: 800-424-6589
URL: http://www.davita.com
Dialysis Stations: 12.

Wenatchee

27990 ■ Central Washington Hospital Dialysis Center
116 Olds Station Rd.
Wenatchee, WA 98801
Ph: (509)665-6149
URL: http://www.cwhs.com
Dialysis Stations: 22.

Yakima

27991 ■ Yakima Dialysis Center & At Home DaVita
1221 N 16th Ave.
Yakima, WA 98902
Free: 800-424-6589
URL: http://www.davita.com
Dialysis Stations: 21.

WEST VIRGINIA

Beckley

27992 ■ Fresenius Medical Care--Beckley
1737 Harper Rd.
Beckley, WV 25801
Free: 866-434-2597
URL: http://www.ultracare-dialysis.com/
Dialysis Stations: 25.

Bluefield

27993 ■ Fresenius Medical Care--Two Virginias Dialysis Services
400 Cherry St.
Bluefield, WV 24701

Free: 866-434-2597
URL: http://www.ultracare-dialysis.com/
Dialysis Stations: 17.

Bridgeport

27994 ■ Fresenius Medical Care--Clarksburg
No. 3 Hospital Plz., 4th Fl.
Rte. 19 S
Bridgeport, WV 26330
Free: 866-434-2597
URL: http://www.ultracare-dialysis.com/
Dialysis Stations: 20.

27995 ■ Gentle Dialysis Center
166 Thompson Dr., Ste. B
Bridgeport, WV 26330
Ph: (304)842-5668
Dialysis Stations: 0.

Bruceton Mills

27996 ■ Fresenius Medical Care--Bruceton Mills
RR 3, Box 300
Casteel Rd.
Bruceton Mills, WV 26525
Free: 866-434-2597
URL: http://www.ultracare-dialysis.com/
Dialysis Stations: 17.

Charleston

27997 ■ Charleston Area Medical Center
Kidney Dialysis Unit
501 Morris St.
Charleston, WV 25325
Ph: (304)388-7577
URL: http://www.camc.org
Dialysis Stations: 3.

27998 ■ Fresenius Medical Care--Charleston
2345 Chesterfield Ave.
Charleston, WV 25304
Free: 866-434-2597
URL: http://www.ultracare-dialysis.com/
Dialysis Stations: 32.

Danville

27999 ■ Greater Boone Dialysis LLC
PO Box 909
Danville, WV 25053
Ph: (304)307-6201
Dialysis Stations: 12.

Dunbar

28000 ■ Fresenius Medical Care--Kanawha County
951 Dunbar Village Plz., Ste. A07
Dunbar, WV 25064
Free: 866-434-2597
URL: http://www.ultracare-dialysis.com/
Dialysis Stations: 21.

Elkins

28001 ■ Fresenius Medical Care--Elkins
Dialysis Facility
100 Main St.
Elkins, WV 26241
Free: 866-434-2597
URL: http://www.ultracare-dialysis.com/
Dialysis Stations: 21.

Fairmont

28002 ■ Fresenius Medical Care--Fairmont
Dialysis Center
31 Landing Ln.
Fairmont, WV 26554
Free: 866-434-2597
URL: http://www.ultracare-dialysis.com/
Dialysis Stations: 21.

Fayetteville

28003 ■ Fresenius Medical Care--Oak Hill
185 Laurel Creek Rd.
Fayetteville, WV 25840
Free: 866-434-2597
URL: http://www.ultracare-dialysis.com/
Dialysis Stations: 12.

Huntington

28004 ■ Fresenius Medical Care--River Hills
5170 US Rte. 60 E
Huntington, WV 25705
Free: 866-434-2597
URL: http://www.ultracare-dialysis.com/
Dialysis Stations: 16.

28005 ■ J Robert Pritchard Dialysis Center
Cabell Huntington Hospital
1690 Medical Center Dr.
Huntington, WV 25701
Ph: (304)399-1290
URL: http://cabellhuntington.org/services/dialysis/
Dialysis Stations: 28.

Hurricane

28006 ■ Fresenius Medical Care--Hurricane
Dialysis Services
3768 Teays Valley Rd.
Hurricane, WV 25526
Free: 866-434-2597
URL: http://www.ultracare-dialysis.com/
Dialysis Stations: 15.

Kearneysville

28007 ■ Fresenius Medical Care--Charlestown
179 E Burr Blvd., Unit A
Kearneysville, WV 25430
Free: 866-434-2597
URL: http://www.ultracare-dialysis.com/
Dialysis Stations: 12.

Lewisburg

28008 ■ DaVita--Greenbrier
129 Seneca Trl.
Lewisburg, WV 24901
Free: 800-424-6589
URL: http://www.davita.com
Dialysis Stations: 16.

28009 ■ Fresenius Medical Care--Greenbriar County
1215 Maplewood Ave.
Lewisburg, WV 24902
Free: 866-434-2597
URL: http://www.ultracare-dialysis.com/
Dialysis Stations: 17.

Logan

28010 ■ West Virginia Dialysis
DaVita
167 Stollings Ave.
Logan, WV 25601
Free: 800-424-6589
URL: http://www.davita.com
Dialysis Stations: 13.

Martinsburg

28011 ■ Fresenius Medical Care--Martinsburg
Dialysis Facility
103 Marcley Dr.
Martinsburg, WV 25401
Free: 866-434-2597
URL: http://www.ultracare-dialysis.com/
Dialysis Stations: 24.

Moorefield

28012 ■ Renal Center of Moorefield LLC
Renal Ventures Management
8 Lee St., 2nd Fl.
Moorefield, WV 26836
Ph: (304)530-1200
URL: http://www.renalventures.com
Dialysis Stations: 12.

Morgantown

28013 ■ Fresenius Medical Care--Morgantown
Dialysis Facility
11 Commerce Dr., Ste. 102
Morgantown, WV 26501
Free: 866-434-2597
URL: http://www.ultracare-dialysis.com/
Dialysis Stations: 17.

28014 ■ West Virginia University Hospital
Renal Dialysis Center
PO Box 8043
Morgantown, WV 26506
Ph: (304)598-4108
URL: http://www.health.wvu.edu
Dialysis Stations: 10.

New Martinsville

28015 ■ New Martinsville Dialysis Facility
1 E Benjamin Dr.
New Martinsville, WV 26155
Ph: (304)455-2700
Dialysis Stations: 10.

Parkersburg

28016 ■ Parkersburg Dialysis
DaVita
1824 Murdoch Ave.
Parkersburg, WV 26101
Free: 800-424-6589
URL: http://www.davita.com
Dialysis Stations: 16. **Formerly:** Gambro Healthcare - Parkersburg.

Point Pleasant

28017 ■ Pleasant Valley Dialysis
PO Box 34
Point Pleasant, WV 25550
Ph: (304)675-1500
Dialysis Stations: 12.

Princeton

28018 ■ Fresenius Medical Care--Mercer County
Dialysis Services
160 Spring Haven Dr.
Princeton, WV 24740
Free: 866-434-2597
URL: http://www.ultracare-dialysis.com/
Dialysis Stations: 17.

Ripley

28019 ■ Fresenius Medical Care--Ripley
1000 New Stone Ridge Rd.
Ripley, WV 25271
Free: 866-434-2597
URL: http://www.ultracare-dialysis.com/
Dialysis Stations: 16.

South Charleston

28020 ■ Greater Charleston Dialysis LLC
24 MacCorkle Ave. SW
South Charleston, WV 25303
Ph: (304)720-2222
Dialysis Stations: 23.

Summersville

28021 ■ Mountain Ridge Dialysis
Liberty Dialysis
229 Merchants Walk
Summersville, WV 26651
Ph: (304)872-9206
URL: http://www.libertydialysis.com
Dialysis Stations: 12.

Welch

28022 ■ Fresenius Medical Care--Welch Dialysis Facility
394 McDowell St.
Welch, WV 24801
Free: 866-434-2597
URL: http://www.ultracare-dialysis.com/
Dialysis Stations: 12.

Weston

28023 ■ Fresenius Medical Care--Weston
Market Place Plz., Ste. 1C
Weston, WV 26452
Free: 866-434-2597
URL: http://www.ultracare-dialysis.com/
Dialysis Stations: 11.

Wheeling

28024 ■ Wheeling Dialysis Center
500 Medical Park, Ste. 100
Wheeling, WV 26003
Ph: (304)242-7770
Dialysis Stations: 17.

WISCONSIN

Amery

28025 ■ DaVita--Amery
970 Elden Ave.
Amery, WI 54001
Free: 800-424-6589
URL: http://www.davita.com
Dialysis Stations: 14.

Antigo

28026 ■ Langlade Memorial Dialysis
112 E 5th Ave.
Antigo, WI 54409
Ph: (715)623-9777
Dialysis Stations: 9.

Appleton

28027 ■ Fresenius Medical Care--Appleton Dialysis Care
2701 N Oneida St., Ste. E
Appleton, WI 54911
Free: 866-434-2597
URL: http://www.ultracare-dialysis.com/
Dialysis Stations: 19.

Ashland

28028 ■ Fresenius Medical Care Dialysis--Chequamegon Bay
1815 Beaser Ave.
Ashland, WI 54806
Free: 866-434-2597
URL: http://www.ultracare-dialysis.com/
Dialysis Stations: 12.

Baraboo

28029 ■ St. Clare Dialysis Center
1600 Jefferson St., Ste. 200
Baraboo, WI 53913
Ph: (608)355-1860
Dialysis Stations: 12.

Barron

28030 ■ Mayo Dialysis--Barron
1222 Woodland Ave.
Barron, WI 54812
Ph: (715)537-1345
URL: http://www.mayoclinic.com
Dialysis Stations: 5.

Beaver Dam

28031 ■ Beaver Dam Dialysis Center
110 Monroe St.
Beaver Dam, WI 53916
Ph: (920)887-3376
Dialysis Stations: 11.

Beloit

28032 ■ Beloit Memorial Hospital Dialysis Center
1969 W Hart Rd.
Beloit, WI 53511
Ph: (608)364-5580
URL: http://www.beloitmemorialhospital.org
Dialysis Stations: 18.

Black River Falls

28033 ■ Gundersen Lutheran Dialysis--Black River Falls
711 W Adams St.
Black River Falls, WI 54615
Ph: (715)284-3676
URL: http://www.gundluth.org/?id=312&sid=1
Dialysis Stations: 12.

Brookfield

28034 ■ DaVita--Capitol Drive Dialysis Facility & At Home
19395 W Capitol Dr., Ste. 100
Brookfield, WI 53045
Free: 800-424-6589
URL: http://www.davita.com
Dialysis Stations: 12. **Formerly:** Gambro Healthcare - Brookfield.

28035 ■ Purity Dialysis--Brookfield
18740 W Bluemound Rd.
Brookfield, WI 53045
Ph: (262)782-9856
URL: http://puritydialysis.com
Dialysis Stations: 8.

Cedarburg

28036 ■ DaVita--Cedarburg Dialysis Facility
N 54, W 6135 Mill St.
Cedarburg, WI 53012
Free: 800-424-6589
URL: http://www.davita.com
Dialysis Stations: 10. **Formerly:** Gambro Healthcare - Cedarburg.

Chippewa Falls

28037 ■ Sacred Heart Dialysis
Saint Joseph Hospital
2661 County Trunk I
Chippewa Falls, WI 54729
Ph: (715)726-3740
URL: http://minstryhealth.org/SJH/home.nws
Dialysis Stations: 8.

Darlington

28038 ■ Memorial Hospital of Lafayette County
Dialysis Unit
800 Clay St.
Darlington, WI 53530
Ph: (608)776-5751
URL: http://www.mhlc-mhf.org/hospital
Dialysis Stations: 6.

Dodgeville

28039 ■ Upland Hills Dialysis Center
800 Compassion Way
Dodgeville, WI 53533
Ph: (608)930-7176
Dialysis Stations: 12.

Eau Claire

28040 ■ Luther Hospital--Mayo Clinic Dialysis
1221 Whipple St.
Eau Claire, WI 54702
Ph: (715)838-3171
URL: http://www.luthermidelfort.org
Dialysis Stations: 12.

28041 ■ Mayo Clinic Dialysis--London Road
1221 Whipple St.
Eau Claire, WI 54701
Ph: (715)838-3006
URL: http://www.mayoclinic.com
Dialysis Stations: 24.

28042 ■ Sacred Heart Hospital Dialysis
900 W Clairemont Ave.
Eau Claire, WI 54701
URL: http://www.cdcare.org
Dialysis Stations: 11.

Fitchburg

28043 ■ Wisconsin Dialysis Inc.--Fitchburg Clinic
3034 Fish Hatchery Rd.
Fitchburg, WI 53713
Ph: (608)270-5600
URL: http://www.wisconsindialysis.org
Dialysis Stations: 30.

Fond du Lac

28044 ■ Aurora Medical Group Dialysis Unit
Aurora Health Care
210 Wisconsin American Dr., Hwy. 23 E
Fond du Lac, WI 54937
Ph: (920)907-7120
URL: http://www.aurorahealthcare.org/facilities/display.asp?id=0029
Dialysis Stations: 9.

28045 ■ Fond du Lac Dialysis Center
101 S Pioneer Rd.
Fond du Lac, WI 54935
Ph: (920)923-2333
Dialysis Stations: 12.

Fort Atkinson

28046 ■ Purity Dialysis--Fort Atkinson
525 Handeyside Ln.
Fort Atkinson, WI 53538
Ph: (920)563-8665
URL: http://puritydialysis.com
Dialysis Stations: 15.

Germantown

28047 ■ Purity Dialysis--Germantown
W175 N, 11056 Stonewood Dr.
Germantown, WI 53022
Ph: (262)251-3044
Dialysis Stations: 13.

Glendale

28048 ■ Bay Shore Dialysis
DaVita
5650 N Green Bay Rd., No. 150
Glendale, WI 53209
Free: 800-424-6589
URL: http://www.davita.com
Dialysis Stations: 28. **Formerly:** Kidney Institute of Wisonsin.

Green Bay

28049 ■ Aurora Medical Group Brown County Dialysis DaVita
1751 Deckner Ave.
Green Bay, WI 54302
Free: 800-424-6589
URL: http://www.davita.com
Dialysis Stations: 10.

28050 ■ DaVita--Fox River Dialysis & At Home
1910 Riverside Dr.
Green Bay, WI 54301
Free: 800-424-6589
URL: http://www.davita.com
Dialysis Stations: 28. **Formerly:** Royce C. Lin Memorial Dialysis Center - Green Bay.

28051 ■ DaVita--Titletown Dialysis Center
120 Siegler St.
Green Bay, WI 54303
Free: 800-424-6589
URL: http://www.davita.com
Dialysis Stations: 20. **Formerly:** Royce C. Lin Memorial - West.

28052 ■ Saint Vincent's Hospital Regional Dialysis Center
1920 Libal St.
Green Bay, WI 54301
Ph: (920)433-8448
URL: http://www.stvincenthospital.org
Dialysis Stations: 21.

Greenfield

28053 ■ DaVita--South Ridge Commonwealth Dialysis Center
4848 S 76th St., Ste. 100
Greenfield, WI 53220
Ph: (414)281-6806
URL: http://thekidneyinstitute.com
Dialysis Stations: 21.

28054 ■ Loomis Road Dialysis and At Home DaVita
4120 W Loomis Rd.
Greenfield, WI 53221
Free: 800-424-6589
URL: http://www.davita.com
Dialysis Stations: 21.

Janesville

28055 ■ DaVita--Janesville
1305 Woodman Rd.
Janesville, WI 53545
Free: 800-424-6589
URL: http://www.davita.com
Dialysis Stations: 12. **Formerly:** Janesville Dialysis Center.

28056 ■ Mercy Regional Dialysis Center
903 Mineral Point Ave.
Janesville, WI 53548
Ph: (608)741-3814
Dialysis Stations: 10.

Kaukauna

28057 ■ Fresenius Dialysis Services--Kaukauna
2259 Progress Way
Kaukauna, WI 54130
Free: 866-434-2597
URL: http://www.ultracare-dialysis.com/
Dialysis Stations: 12.

Kenosha

28058 ■ Kenosha Kidney Dialysis
6125 Green Bay Rd., Ste. 100
Kenosha, WI 53142
Ph: (262)521-1776
Dialysis Stations: 12. **Formerly:** Kidney Replacement Therapies.

28059 ■ Midwest Kidney Care--Kenosha
6804 Green Bay Rd.
Kenosha, WI 53142
Ph: (262)697-6323
Dialysis Stations: 13.

La Crosse

28060 ■ Gundersen Lutheran Medical Center--La Crosse Dialysis Center
1900 South Ave.
La Crosse, WI 54601
Ph: (608)775-3635
URL: http://www.gundluth.org
Dialysis Stations: 12.

Lake Geneva

28061 ■ DaVita Aurora Medical Group--Lake Geneva
146 Lake Geneva Sq.
Lake Geneva, WI 53147
Free: 800-424-6589
URL: http://www.davita.com
Dialysis Stations: 13.

Madison

28062 ■ SSM Dialysis--Madison Station
2840 Index Rd.
Madison, WI 53713
Ph: (608)229-7222
Dialysis Stations: 35.

28063 ■ Wisconsin Dialysis Inc.--East
4600 American Pkwy., Ste. 108
Madison, WI 53718
Ph: (608)243-3003
URL: http://www.wisconsindialysis.org
Dialysis Stations: 6.

Manitowoc

28064 ■ Aurora Medical Group - Manitowoc Dialysis DaVita
601 Reed Ave.
Manitowoc, WI 54220
Free: 800-424-6589
URL: http://www.davita.com
Dialysis Stations: 9.

28065 ■ Holy Family Memorial Dialysis Center
2300 Western Ave.
Manitowoc, WI 54220
Ph: (920)320-2011
Dialysis Stations: 9.

Marinette

28066 ■ Aurora Medical Group DaVita Marinette Dialysis
4061 Old Peshtigo Rd.
Marinette, WI 54143
Free: 800-424-6589
URL: http://www.davita.com
Dialysis Stations: 10.

28067 ■ Bay Area Medical Center Dialysis Facility
3100 Shore Dr.
Marinette, WI 54143
Ph: (715)735-4200
Dialysis Stations: 9.

Marshfield

28068 ■ Ministry Dialysis--Marshfield
611 St. Joseph Ave.
Marshfield, WI 54449
Ph: (715)387-7757
Dialysis Stations: 17.

Mauston

28069 ■ Hess Memorial Hospital Dialysis Facility
1050 Division St.
Mauston, WI 53948
Ph: (608)847-6161
Dialysis Stations: 9.

Medford

28070 ■ Memorial Health Center Dialysis
135 S Gibson St.
Medford, WI 54451
Ph: (715)748-7520
Dialysis Stations: 6.

Menomonee Falls

28071 ■ Purity Dialysis--Menomonee Falls Dialysis Center
W 173, N 9170 St. Francis Dr.
Menomonee Falls, WI 53051
Ph: (262)253-9768
URL: http://puritydialysis.com
Dialysis Stations: 15.

Menomonie

28072 ■ Mayo Dialysis--Menomonie
2321 Stout Rd.
Menomonie, WI 54751
Ph: (715)233-7646
URL: http://www.mayoclinic.com
Dialysis Stations: 6.

Merrill

28073 ■ Merrill Kidney Center
601 S Center Ave.
Merrill, WI 54452
Ph: (715)539-5190
Dialysis Stations: 6.

Milwaukee

28074 ■ Children's Hospital of Wisconsin Dialysis Center
9000 W Wisconsin Ave.
Milwaukee, WI 53201
Ph: (414)266-2840
URL: http://www.chw.org
Dialysis Stations: 5.

28075 ■ DaVita--Humboldt Ridge
2211 N Humboldt Blvd.
Milwaukee, WI 53212
Free: 800-424-6589
URL: http://www.davita.com
Dialysis Stations: 24.

28076 ■ DaVita--River Center Drive Dialysis Center
117 N Jefferson St.
Milwaukee, WI 53202
Free: 800-424-6589
URL: http://www.davita.com
Dialysis Stations: 20. **Formerly:** Gambro Healthcare - Rivercenter Drive.

28077 ■ DaVita--West Appleton
10130 W Appleton Ave., Ste. 500
Milwaukee, WI 53225
Free: 800-424-6589
URL: http://www.davita.com
Dialysis Stations: 26. **Formerly:** Kidney Institute of Wisconsin--Northwest.

28078 ■ DaVita--Wisconsin Avenue Dialysis Center
3801 W Wisconsin Ave.
Milwaukee, WI 53208
Free: 800-424-6589
URL: http://www.davita.com
Dialysis Stations: 24. **Formerly:** Gambro Healthcare - Wisconsin Avenue.

28079 ■ Fresenius Medical Services Dialysis--Milwaukee
200 W Pleasant St.
Milwaukee, WI 53212
Free: 866-434-2597
URL: http://www.ultracare-dialysis.com/
Dialysis Stations: 23.

28080 ■ Froedtert Memorial Hospital--Transplant
Froedtert & Medical College of Wisconsin
9200 W Wisconsin Ave
Milwaukee, WI 53226
Ph: (414)456-6920
URL: http://www.froedtert.com/SpecialtyAreas/TransplantCenter/
Dialysis Stations: 0.

28081 ■ Midwest Dialysis--27th Street Branch
3120 S 27th St.
Milwaukee, WI 53215
Ph: (414)672-1006
URL: http://www.mdcwi.com
Dialysis Stations: 16.

28082 ■ Midwest Dialysis--Appleton Avenue Branch
7793 W Appleton Ave.
Milwaukee, WI 53222
Ph: (414)393-9810
URL: http://www.mdcwi.com
Dialysis Stations: 19.

28083 ■ Midwest Dialysis--Capitol Branch
4021 N 52nd St.
Milwaukee, WI 53216
Ph: (414)873-3600
URL: http://www.mdcwi.com
Dialysis Stations: 17.

28084 ■ Midwest Dialysis--Glendale
400 W Estabrook Blvd.
Milwaukee, WI 53212
Ph: (414)332-9960
URL: http://www.mdcwi.com
Dialysis Stations: 17.

28085 ■ Midwest Dialysis--Good Hope Branch
Dialysis Center
7701 N Clinton Ave.
Milwaukee, WI 53223
Ph: (414)760-3090
URL: http://www.mdcwi.com
Dialysis Stations: 19.

28086 ■ Midwest Dialysis--South Milwaukee
3267 S 16th St., Ste. 203
Milwaukee, WI 53215
Ph: (414)672-8230
URL: http://www.mdcwi.com
Dialysis Stations: 16.

28087 ■ Milwaukee Dialysis Center
American Renal Associates
4775 N Green Bay Ave.
Milwaukee, WI 53209
Ph: (414)265-1700
URL: http://www.americanrenal.com
Dialysis Stations: 21.

28088 ■ St. Luke's Renal Transplant Center
5th Fl., Galleria Bldg.
Milwaukee, WI 53215
Ph: (414)646-2550
Dialysis Stations: 0.

28089 ■ University of Wisconsin Transplant
600 Highland Ave.
Milwaukee, WI 53792
Ph: (608)263-1385
URL: http://www.surgery.wisc.edu/divisions/transplantation/
Dialysis Stations: 0.

Monroe

28090 ■ Monroe Clinic Dialysis
Liberty Dialysis
515 22nd Ave.
Monroe, WI 53566
Ph: (608)324-1952
URL: http://www.libertydialysis.com
Dialysis Stations: 8.

Mukwonago

28091 ■ Purity Dialysis--Mukwonago
400 Bayview Rd., Ste. F
Mukwonago, WI 53149
Ph: (262)363-1925
URL: http://puritydialysis.com
Dialysis Stations: 10.

Neenah

28092 ■ Fresenius Dialysis Services--Neenah
300 N Commercial St.
Neenah, WI 54956
Free: 866-434-2597
URL: http://www.ultracare-dialysis.com/
Dialysis Stations: 19.

Oak Creek

28093 ■ Midwest Dialysis--Ryan Road
9420 S 22nd St.
Oak Creek, WI 53154
Ph: (414)761-8080
URL: http://www.mdcwi.com
Dialysis Stations: 19.

28094 ■ Oak Creek Dialysis
DaVita
8201 S Howell Ave.
Oak Creek, WI 53154
Free: 800-424-6589
URL: http://www.davita.com
Dialysis Stations: 12.

Oconomowoc

28095 ■ Purity Dialysis--Oconomowoc
1253 Corporate Center Dr.
Oconomowoc, WI 53066
Ph: (262)567-3199
URL: http://puritydialysis.com
Dialysis Stations: 15.

Onalaska

28096 ■ Gundersen Lutheran SAT--Onalaska
3075 S Kinney Coulee Rd.
Onalaska, WI 54650
Ph: (608)775-1360
URL: http://www.gundluth.org
Dialysis Stations: 30.

28097 ■ Mayo Clinic Dialysis--La Crosse
191 Theater Rd.
Onalaska, WI 54650
Ph: (608)392-5011
URL: http://www.mayoclinic.com
Dialysis Stations: 18.

Oshkosh

28098 ■ Aurora Medical Group--Oshkosh West
Dialysis Unit
DaVita
855 N Westhaven Dr.
Oshkosh, WI 54904
Free: 800-424-6589
URL: http://www.davita.com
Dialysis Stations: 10.

28099 ■ Fresenius Dialysis Services of Oshkosh
2700 W 9th Ave., Ste. 101A
Oshkosh, WI 54904
Free: 866-434-2597
URL: http://www.ultracare-dialysis.com/
Dialysis Stations: 10.

Platteville

28100 ■ Tri State Dialysis--Platteville
1250 E Business Hwy. 151, Ste. B
Platteville, WI 53818
Ph: (608)348-5064
Dialysis Stations: 12.

Pleasant Prairie

28101 ■ Saint Catherine's Kidney Center
United Hospital System
St. Catherine's Medical Center Campus
9555 76th St.
Pleasant Prairie, WI 53158
Ph: (262)577-8791
URL: http://www.uhsi.org
Dialysis Stations: 18.

Portage

28102 ■ Divine Savior Healthcare Dialysis
2817 New Pinery Rd.
Portage, WI 53901
Ph: (608)745-5160
URL: http://www.dshealthcare.com
Dialysis Stations: 6.

Prairie du Chien

28103 ■ Gundersen Lutheran Dialysis Satellite--Prairie du Chien
705 E Taylor St.
Prairie du Chien, WI 53821
Ph: (608)357-2000
URL: http://www.gundluth.org
Dialysis Stations: 5.

Racine

28104 ■ Midwest Kidney Care--Racine
5409 Durand Ave.
Racine, WI 53406
Ph: (262)598-8727
URL: http://www.mdcwi.com
Dialysis Stations: 17.

28105 ■ Wheaton Franciscan
All Saints Dialysis East
818 6th St.
Racine, WI 53403
Ph: (262)687-6363
URL: http://www.mywheaton.org
Dialysis Stations: 20.

28106 ■ Wheaton Franciscan
All Saints Dialysis West
1139 Warwick Way
Racine, WI 53406
Ph: (262)687-7551
URL: http://www.mywheaton.org
Dialysis Stations: 12.

Rhinelander

28107 ■ Rhinelander Dialysis Center
232 Courtney St., Ste. 2
Rhinelander, WI 54501
Ph: (715)365-8080
Dialysis Stations: 9.

Rice Lake

28108 ■ Lakeview Medical Center Dialysis Center
1100 N Main St.
Rice Lake, WI 54868
Ph: (715)236-6159
URL: http://www.lakeviewmedical.com
Dialysis Stations: 9.

Ripon

28109 ■ Fresenius Medical Care--Ripon South
37 Stoney Ridge Rd.
Ripon, WI 54971
Free: 866-434-2597
URL: http://www.ultracare-dialysis.com/
Dialysis Stations: 12. **Formerly:** Dialysis Care.

Saint Croix Falls

28110 ■ Saint Croix Falls Dialysis DaVita
744 E Louisiana Ave.
Saint Croix Falls, WI 54024
Free: 800-424-6589
URL: http://www.davita.com
Dialysis Stations: 9. **Formerly:** Saint Croix Falls Memorial Hospital Regional Kidney Disease Program.

Saint Francis

28111 ■ Midwest Dialysis--Lakeshore
2000 E Layton, Ste. 200
Saint Francis, WI 53235
Ph: (414)744-4343
URL: http://www.mdcwi.com
Dialysis Stations: 10.

Shawano

28112 ■ Green Bay Northwood Dialysis DaVita
W7305 Elm Ave.
Shawano, WI 54166
Free: 800-424-6589
URL: http://www.davita.com
Dialysis Stations: 15. **Formerly:** Royce C. Lin Memorial Dialysis - Shawano.

Sheboygan

28113 ■ Aurora Medical Group--Sheboygan DaVita
2414 Kohler Memorial Dr.
Sheboygan, WI 53081
Free: 800-424-6589
URL: http://www.davita.com
Dialysis Stations: 14. **Formerly:** Aurora Dialysis.

28114 ■ Saint Nicholas Hospital Dialysis Facility
3100 Superior Ave.
Sheboygan, WI 53081
Ph: (920)459-5163
URL: http://www.stnicholashospital.org/hospitalservices/hsdialysisservices.html
Dialysis Stations: 12.

Shorewood

28115 ■ Fresenius Medical Care--Shorewood
1409 E Capitol Dr.
Shorewood, WI 53211
Free: 866-434-2597
URL: http://www.ultracare-dialysis.com/
Dialysis Stations: 16.

Spooner

28116 ■ Lakeview Medical Center Satellite Dialysis
819 Ash St.
Spooner, WI 54801
Ph: (715)635-5303
URL: http://www.lakeviewmedical.com
Dialysis Stations: 6.

Stanley

28117 ■ Stanley Dialysis Center Saint Joseph's Hospital Ministry Dialysis
1120 Pine St.
Stanley, WI 54768
Ph: (715)644-6179
URL: http://ministryhealth.org/SJH/home.nws
Dialysis Stations: 6.

Stevens Point

28118 ■ Saint Michael's Hospital--Stevens Point Dialysis Center
900 Illinois Ave.
Stevens Point, WI 54481
Ph: (715)346-5680
URL: http://ministryhealth.org
Dialysis Stations: 9.

Sturgeon Bay

28119 ■ Aurora Medical Group Sturgeon Bay Dialysis DaVita
108 S 10th Ave.
Sturgeon Bay, WI 54235
Free: 800-424-6589
URL: http://www.davita.com
Dialysis Stations: 6.

Superior

28120 ■ Fresenius Medical Services Dialysis--Superior
3500 Tower Ave.
Superior, WI 54880
Free: 866-434-2597
URL: http://www.ultracare-dialysis.com/
Dialysis Stations: 8.

Tomah

28121 ■ Gundersen Lutheran Satellite--Tomah
321 Butts Ave.
Tomah, WI 54660
Ph: (608)374-0280
URL: http://www.gundhealth.org
Dialysis Stations: 6.

Viroqua

28122 ■ Gundersen Lutheran Satellite--Viroqua Dialysis Facility
407 S Main St.
Viroqua, WI 54665
Ph: (608)637-4376
URL: http://www.gundhealth.org
Dialysis Stations: 12.

Watertown

28123 ■ Purity Dialysis--Watertown
123 Hospital Dr., Ste. 1004
Watertown, WI 53098
Ph: (920)206-0666
URL: http://puritydialysis.com
Dialysis Stations: 11.

Waukesha

28124 ■ Midwest Kidney Care--Waukesha
111 Ann St.
Waukesha, WI 53188
Ph: (262)542-6179
Dialysis Stations: 13.

28125 ■ Purity Dialysis--Waukesha
721 American Ave., Ste. 204
Waukesha, WI 53188
Ph: (262)928-2575
URL: http://puritydialysis.com
Dialysis Stations: 23. **Formerly:** Waukesha Kidney Center.

28126 ■ Purity Dialysis--Waukesha South
1260 Sentry Dr.
Waukesha, WI 53186
Ph: (262)446-5100
Dialysis Stations: 12.

Waupaca

28127 ■ Fresenius Medical Care--Waupaca
102 Grand Seasons Dr.
Waupaca, WI 54981
Free: 866-434-2597
URL: http://www.ultracare-dialysis.com/
Dialysis Stations: 10. **Formerly:** Dialysis Care.

28128 ■ Waupaca Kidney Center Dialysis Facility
190 Grand Seasons Dr.
Waupaca, WI 54981
Ph: (715)258-3401
Dialysis Stations: 6.

Waupun

28129 ■ Waupun Regional Dialysis
620 W Brown St.
Waupun, WI 53963
Ph: (920)324-6531
Dialysis Stations: 12.

Wausau

28130 ■ Aspirus Hospital Dialysis Center
3000 Westhill Dr., Ste. 106
Wausau, WI 54401
Ph: (715)847-0019
URL: http://www.aspirus.org
Dialysis Stations: 12.

28131 ■ Wausau Kidney Center Dialysis Facility
2600 Stewart Ave., Ste. 144
Wausau, WI 54401
Ph: (715)845-8454
Dialysis Stations: 26.

Wautoma

28132 ■ Aurora Medical Group--Wautoma Dialysis DaVita
900 E Division St.
Wautoma, WI 54982
Free: 800-424-6589
URL: http://www.davita.com
Dialysis Stations: 8.

Wauwatosa

28133 ■ DaVita--Bluemound
601 N 99th St.
Wauwatosa, WI 53226
Free: 800-424-6589
URL: http://www.davita.com
Dialysis Stations: 23.

West Allis

28134 ■ Fresenius Medical Care--Centre Point
Dialysis Facility
11340 W Theodore Trecker Way
West Allis, WI 53214
Free: 866-434-2597
URL: http://www.ultracare-dialysis.com/
Dialysis Stations: 26. **Formerly:** Wisconsin Renal Care Group - Centre Point.

West Bend

28135 ■ Midwest Dialysis--West Bend
2050 Continental Dr.
West Bend, WI 53095
Ph: (262)306-2700
Dialysis Stations: 12.

Whitehall

28136 ■ Gundersen Lutheran Dialysis Satellite--Whitehall
18601 Lincoln St.
Whitehall, WI 54773
Ph: (715)538-4361
Fax: (715)538-2912
URL: http://www.gundluth.org
Dialysis Stations: 4.

Wisconsin Rapids

28137 ■ Saint Joseph's Hospital--Wisconsin Rapids
Dialysis Center
Riverview Hospital Campua
1041B Hill St.
Wisconsin Rapids, WI 54494
Ph: (715)422-0550
URL: http://ministryhealth.org/SJH/home.nws
Dialysis Stations: 18.

Woodruff

28138 ■ Howard Young Medical Center
Dialysis Center
240 Maple St.
Woodruff, WI 54568
Ph: (715)356-8881
URL: http://ministryhealth.org/HYMC/home.nws
Dialysis Stations: 24.

hayward

28139 ■ Fresenius Medical Care--Hayward
10342 Dyno Dr.
hayward, WI 54843
Free: 866-434-2597
URL: http://www.ultracare-dialysis.com/
Dialysis Stations: 12.

WYOMING

Casper

28140 ■ Wyoming Kidney Center
Dialysis Facility
1141 Wilkins Circle
Casper, WY 82601
Ph: (307)472-3700
URL: http://www.idsdialysis.com
Dialysis Stations: 10.

Cheyenne

28141 ■ Fresenius Medical Care--Cheyenne
Dialysis Center
1111 Logan Ave.
Cheyenne, WY 82001
Free: 866-434-2597
URL: http://www.ultracare-dialysis.com/
Dialysis Stations: 12.

Cody

28142 ■ Big Horn Regional Dialysis Center
707 Sheridan Ave.
Cody, WY 82414
Ph: (307)578-2223
Dialysis Stations: 6.

Evanston

28143 ■ Evanston Regional Hospital
Dialysis Center
112 Yellowcreek Rd.
Evanston, WY 82930
Ph: (307)444-8231
URL: http://www.evanstonregionalhospital.com
Dialysis Stations: 6.

Fort Washakie

28144 ■ Wind River Dialysis Center
140 Wyoming St.
Fort Washakie, WY 82514
Ph: (307)332-2998
Dialysis Stations: 13.

Gillette

28145 ■ Campbell County Memorial Hospital
Dialysis Unit
501 S Burma
Gillette, WY 82718
Ph: (307)688-1981
URL: http://www.ccmh.net
Dialysis Stations: 8.

Laramie

28146 ■ Ivinson Memorial Hospital
Dialysis Center
255 N 30th St.
Laramie, WY 82072
Ph: (307)742-2141
URL: http://www.ivinsonhospital.org
Dialysis Stations: 5.

Rock Springs

28147 ■ Memorial Hospital of Sweetwater County
Dialysis Facility
1200 College Dr.
Rock Springs, WY 82901
Ph: (307)352-8216
URL: http://minershospital.com
Dialysis Stations: 4.

Sheridan

28148 ■ Memorial Dialysis--Wyoming
1401 W 5th St., Rm. 205
Sheridan, WY 82801
Ph: (307)672-1191
Dialysis Stations: 8.

Chapter 23
Mental Health Services

This chapter includes three sections, each representing a different type of mental health service: (1) Multiservice Mental Health Organizations, (2) Psychiatric Hospitals, and (3) Residential Treatment Centers for Emotionally Disturbed Children. All sections are arranged geographically by states and cities, then alphabetically by organization names within cities. The "User's Guide" located at the front of this directory provides additional information.

MULTISERVICE MENTAL HEALTH ORGANIZATIONS

ALABAMA

Abbeville

28149 ■ Spectracare Henry County Clinic
219 Dothan Rd.
Abbeville, AL 36310
Ph: (334)585-6864
URL: http://www.spcare.com/html/henry_county.html

Albertville

28150 ■ Albertville Nursing Home
750 Alabama Hwy. 75 N
Albertville, AL 35951
Ph: (256)878-1398
Fax: (256)878-1706
URL: http://www.albertvillenursinghome.com/

28151 ■ Dogwood Place Apartments
99 Campbell St.
Albertville, AL 35950
Ph: (256)582-3203

Alexander City

28152 ■ Adams Nursing Home
1555 Hillabee St.
Alexander City, AL 35010
Ph: (256)329-0847

28153 ■ Chapman Nursing Home
3701 Dadeville Rd.
Alexander City, AL 35010
Ph: (256)234-6366
Fax: (256)234-2366
Formerly: Chapman Health Care Center.

28154 ■ East Alabama Mental Health Center
Brown Nursing Home
2334 Washington St.
Alexander City, AL 35010
Ph: (256)329-9061
URL: http://www.crownemanagement.com

28155 ■ Nan Coley Murphy Counseling Center
1508 Hwy. 22 W
Alexander City, AL 35010
Ph: (256)329-8463
URL: http://www.eastalabamamhc.org/locations.htm

Andalusia

28156 ■ South Central Alabama Community Mental Health Center
19815 Bay Branch Rd.
Andalusia, AL 36420-1220
Ph: (334)222-2525
URL: http://www.cityofandalusia.com
Formerly: South Central Alabama Mental Health Board.

28157 ■ South Central Alabama Community Mental Health Center
Andalusia Manor
670 Moore Rd.
Andalusia, AL 36420-5227
Ph: (334)222-2525

28158 ■ South Central Alabama Community Mental Health Center
Covington County Day Treatment
402 Academy Dr.
Andalusia, AL 36420-4102
Ph: (334)222-8411
Formerly: South Central Alabama Mental Health Board Covington County Adult Training Center.

28159 ■ South Central Alabama Community Mental Health Center
Early Intervention Program
400 Academy Dr.
Andalusia, AL 36420-4102
Ph: (334)222-0545
Formerly: South Central Alabama Mental Health Board.

28160 ■ South Central Alabama Community Mental Health Clinic
Covington Substance Abuse/Prevention
300 W Watson
Andalusia, AL 36420
Ph: (334)222-2868

Anniston

28161 ■ Calhoun Cleburne Mental Health Board
PO Box 2205
Anniston, AL 36207
Ph: (256)236-3403
Fax: (256)235-1952
URL: http://www.ccmhc.net/

28162 ■ Calhoun Cleburne Mental Health Center
331 E 8th St
Anniston, AL 36207
Ph: (256)236-3403
URL: http://www.ccmhc.net/

28163 ■ GrandView Behavioral Health Center--Anniston
1302 Noble St., Ste. 3D
Anniston, AL 36202
Ph: (256)237-4755
Free: 800-662-1002
URL: http://www.mtnviewhospital.com/Maps%20of%20Clinic%20Locations.htm
Formerly: Southern Behavioral Health Associates.

28164 ■ Northeast Alabama Regional Medical Center
Behavioral Health
400 E 10th St.
Anniston, AL 36207
Ph: (256)235-5121
URL: http://www.rmccares.org/

Ashford

28165 ■ SpectraCare--Dallas
1539 Sweetie Smith Rd.
Ashford, AL 36312
Ph: (334)691-8030
URL: http://www.spcare.com

Athens

28166 ■ Athens-Limestone Counseling Center
1307 E Elm St.
Athens, AL 35611
Ph: (256)232-3661

Attalla

28167 ■ Attalla Health Care, Inc.
915 Stewart Ave. SE
Attalla, AL 35954-3610
Ph: (256)538-7852

28168 ■ Cherokee Etowah Dekalb Community Mental Health Center
425 5th Ave. NW
Attalla, AL 35954
Ph: (256)492-7800
URL: http://www.cedmhc.org

Auburn

28169 ■ East Alabama Mental Health Woman's Center--SA
945 N Donahue Dr., Apt. 56
Auburn, AL 36832-2968
Ph: (334)887-8606

Bay Minette

28170 ■ Baldwin County Community Mental Health Center
Axalea Manor
2411 Hwy. 31 S
Bay Minette, AL 36507
Ph: (251)937-9708
URL: http://www.bcmhcal.com/

28171 ■ Baldwin County Community Mental Health Center--Medical Center Drive
2009 Medical Center Dr.
Bay Minette, AL 36507-4163
Ph: (251)937-2010
URL: http://www.bcmhcal.com/
Formerly: Baldwin County Mental Health Center.

Bessemer

28172 ■ Beverly Rehabilitation & Healthcare Center
820 Golf Course Rd.
Bessemer, AL 35023
Ph: (205)425-5241
URL: http://www.goldenlivingcenters.com/home.aspx
Formerly: Meadowood Rehabilitation & Healthcare Center.

28173 ■ UAB Medical West
995 9th Ave. SW
Bessemer, AL 35022
Ph: (205)481-7000
URL: http://www.medicalwesthospital.org

28174 ■ Vera House
1618 8th Ave. N
Bessemer, AL 35020
Ph: (205)426-6505
URL: http://www.goldenlivingcenters.com/home.aspx

Birmingham

28175 ■ Alabama Clinical Schools
1221 Alton Dr.
Birmingham, AL 35210
Ph: (205)836-9923
URL: http://alabamaclinicalschools.com

28176 ■ Alice Logan Home
JBS Mental Health Authority
1321 31st St. N
Birmingham, AL 35234-2928
Ph: (205)328-0276
URL: http://www.jbsmha.com/

28177 ■ Baptist Medical Center - Princeton Behavioral Health
701 Princeton Ave. SW
Birmingham, AL 35211-1318
Ph: (205)783-3000
URL: http://www.bhsala.com/body.cfm?id=7

28178 ■ Birmingham Veterans Affairs Medical Center
700 S 19th St.
Birmingham, AL 35233
Ph: (205)933-8101
URL: http://www.birmingham.va.gov/

28179 ■ Brief Intensive Treatment Home
JBS Mental Health Authority
3919 4th Ave. S
Birmingham, AL 35222-1920
Ph: (205)591-5488
URL: http://www.jbsmha.com/

28180 ■ Brookwood Medical Center
2010 Brookwood Medical Center Dr.
Birmingham, AL 35209
Ph: (205)877-1000
URL: http://www.bwmc.com/CWSContent/brookwood-medical

28181 ■ Carol K. Crider Home
JBS Health Authority
3218 Ave. E
Birmingham, AL 35218-2631
Ph: (205)780-6216
URL: http://www.jbsmha.com/

28182 ■ Charlie Major Foster Home
JBS Mental Health Authority
328 Albany St.
Birmingham, AL 35224-2035
Ph: (205)786-6714
URL: http://www.jbsmha.com/

28183 ■ Eastside Community Mental Health Center
129 E Park Cir.
Birmingham, AL 35235
Ph: (205)836-7311
Fax: (205)836-9594
URL: http://www.accmhb.org/eastside/
Remarks: Collect calls accepted.

28184 ■ Edwina Daniels Home
JBS Mental Health Authority
1216 28th St. N
Birmingham, AL 35234-3214
Ph: (205)251-2928
URL: http://www.jbsmha.com/

28185 ■ Estes Nursing Facility Civic Center
JBS Mental Health Authority
1201 22nd St. N
Birmingham, AL 35234-2726
Ph: (205)252-9169
URL: http://www.jbsmha.com/

28186 ■ Estes Nursing Facility Northway
1424 25th St. N
Birmingham, AL 35234
Ph: (205)328-5870

28187 ■ Fairview Nursing Home
JBS Mental Health Authority
1028 Bessemer Rd.
Birmingham, AL 35228-1199
Ph: (205)923-1777
URL: http://www.jbsmha.com/

28188 ■ Gateway--20th Street S, Birmingham
1401 20th St. S
Birmingham, AL 35205-4913
Ph: (205)510-2600

28189 ■ Gateway--Airport Highway, Birmingham
5201 Airport Hwy.
Birmingham, AL 35201
Ph: (205)259-2600
URL: http://www.gway.org

28190 ■ Glenwood, Inc.
Adult Day Habilitation
152 Glenwood Ln.
Birmingham, AL 35242-5700
Ph: (205)969-2880
Fax: (205)969-0611
URL: http://www.glenwood.org/

28191 ■ Glenwood Inc.
Adult Day Treatment
150 Glenwood Ln.
Birmingham, AL 35242
Ph: (205)969-2880
Fax: (205)967-1323
E-mail: information@glenwood.org
URL: http://www.glenwood.org

28192 ■ Glenwood Mental Health Services, Inc.
150 Glenwood Ln.
Birmingham, AL 35242-5700
Ph: (205)969-2880
Fax: (205)967-1323
E-mail: information@glenwood.org
URL: http://www.glenwood.org

28193 ■ Harrell Home
JBS Mental Health Authority
3923 9th Ct.
Birmingham, AL 35224-2096
Ph: (205)788-7792
Fax: (205)744-7566
URL: http://www.jbsmha.com/

28194 ■ JBS Mental Health Authority
940 Montclair Rd., Ste. 200
Birmingham, AL 35213
Ph: (205)595-4555
Fax: (205)592-3539
E-mail: lturley@jbsmha.com
URL: http://www.jbsmha.com

28195 ■ JBS Mental Health Authority Day Treatment Program
3600 4th Ave. S
Birmingham, AL 35222
Ph: (205)322-7335
URL: http://www.jbsmha.com

28196 ■ Joyce Fails Home
JBS Mental Health Authority
7715 4th Ave. S
Birmingham, AL 35206-4425
Ph: (205)833-2475
URL: http://www.jbsmha.com/

28197 ■ Lakewood Day Treatment
119 Glenwood Ln.
Birmingham, AL 35242-5701
Ph: (205)969-2880
URL: http://www.glenwood.org

28198 ■ Lucille Greene Home
JBS Mental Health Authority
2311 23rd St. N
Birmingham, AL 35234-1661
Ph: (205)788-4825
URL: http://www.jbsmha.com/

28199 ■ Mountain View Health Care Center
PO Box 28665
Birmingham, AL 35228-0007
Ph: (205)595-4555
Fax: (205)428-2683
URL: http://www.ballhealth.com/
Formerly: JBS Mental Health Authority.

28200 ■ Myrtle C. Robinson Home
JBS Mental Health Authority
4800 2nd Ave. N
Birmingham, AL 35212-3004
Ph: (205)592-2619
URL: http://www.jbsmha.com/

28201 ■ Naves Foster Home
JBS Mental Health Authority
3121 Naves Dr.
Birmingham, AL 35210-4226
Ph: (205)956-6641
URL: http://www.jbsmha.com/

28202 ■ Oasis Women's Counseling Center
1900 14th Ave. S
Birmingham, AL 35205
Ph: (205)933-0338
Fax: (205)933-0343
URL: http://www.oasiscounseling.org/

28203 ■ Parkland Place
2535 Highland Ave. S
Birmingham, AL 35205-2464
Ph: (205)251-2348
URL: http://www.glenwood.org/

28204 ■ Reliant Healthcare, LLC
2 Riverchase Office Plz., Ste. 214
Birmingham, AL 35244
Ph: (205)313-0445
Fax: (205)313-0446
E-mail: kglover@relianthealthcare.com
URL: http://www.relianthealthcare.com/

Black

28205 ■ Merle Wallace Purvis Center
1682 E County Rd. 4
Black, AL 36340
Ph: (334)684-2252

Brent

28206 ■ Indian Rivers Mental Health Center Bibb County Satellite
2439 Main St.
Brent, AL 35034-4012
Ph: (205)926-4681
URL: http://www.irmhc.org/

Brewton

28207 ■ Brewton Satellite Office
1321 McMillan Ave., Ste. A
Brewton, AL 36427-0086
Ph: (251)867-3242

28208 ■ Pine View Apartments
201 Oakwood St.
Brewton, AL 36426-5029
Ph: (205)867-6287

Butler

28209 ■ West Alabama Mental Health Center Choctaw County Office
401 Rogers Ave.
Butler, AL 36904
Ph: (205)459-2612
URL: http://www.wamhc.org/choctaw.htm

Calera

28210 ■ Hamilton Center
151 Hamilton Lane
Calera, AL 35040
Ph: (205)668-4308
URL: http://chiltonshelby.org

28211 ■ J Michael Horsley MI Residential Home
10072 Hwy. 31 S
Calera, AL 35040
Ph: (205)668-0940
Fax: (205)668-1150
URL: http://chiltonshelby.org

28212 ■ Richard L Parris MI Residential Home
10080 Hwy. 31 S
Calera, AL 35040
Ph: (205)668-1050
Fax: (205)668-1150
URL: http://chiltonshelby.org

Camden

28213 ■ Cahaba Center for Mental Health/Mental Retardation Services Wilcox County Satellite
45 Camden By-Pass
Camden, AL 36726-1751
Ph: (334)682-4499
URL: http://www.cahabamentalhealth.com/

Carrollton

28214 ■ Indian River Mental Health Center
140 Courthouse Sq. E
Carrollton, AL 35447
Ph: (205)367-8159
URL: http://www.irmhc.org/

Centre

28215 ■ CED Cherokee County Office
200 Dean Buttram Ave.
Centre, AL 35960-1026
Ph: (256)927-3601
Formerly: Mental Health.

28216 ■ Cherokee County Nursing Home
877 Cedar Bluff Rd.
Centre, AL 35960
Ph: (256)927-5778
Fax: (256)927-6294
URL: http://www.cherokeenursinghome.com/

Chatom

28217 ■ AltaPointe Health Systems, Inc. Washington County Mental Health
1812 Dixie Youth Dr.
Chatom, AL 36518
Ph: (251)847-2301
URL: http://www.altapointe.org/

Childersburg

28218 ■ Veterans Affairs Medical Center Childersburg Community Based Outpatient Clinic
151 9th Ave. NW
Childersburg, AL 35044
Ph: (256)378 9026
Fax: (256)378-3371
URL: http://www.birmingham.va.gov/visitors/Childersburg_CBOC.asp

Citronelle

28219 ■ Citronelle Convalescent Center Mobile Community Mental Health Center
108 N 4th St.
Citronelle, AL 36522
Ph: (251)866-5509

Clanton

28220 ■ Carrie Gray Home
783 County Rd. 418
Clanton, AL 35045
Ph: (205)755-3340
URL: http://chiltonshelby.org

28221 ■ Civitan Home
203 8th Ave. N
Clanton, AL 35045
Ph: (205)755-4313
URL: http://chiltonshelby.org

28222 ■ Katherine Vickery MI Residential Home
1105 Lay Dam Rd.
Clanton, AL 35045
Ph: (205)280-0825
Fax: (205)280-0825
URL: http://chiltonshelby.org

28223 ■ Pelham MI Outpatient
110 Medical Center Dr.
Clanton, AL 35045
Ph: (205)755-5933
Fax: (205)755-7060
URL: http://chiltonshelby.org

Collinsville

28224 ■ Collinsville Nursing Home, Inc.
685 N Valley Ave.
Collinsville, AL 35961
Ph: (256)524-2117

Cullman

28225 ■ Mental Healthcare of Cullman
1909 Commerce Ave. NW
Cullman, AL 35055
Ph: (256)734-4688
Fax: (256)734-4694
URL: http://www.mentalhealthcareofcullman.org/

Dadeville

28226 ■ Wilder Healthcare Center
345 E Lafayette St.
Dadeville, AL 36853
Ph: (256)825-7881

Decatur

28227 ■ The Albany Clinic
1316 13th Ave. SE
Decatur, AL 35601
Ph: (256)355-6105
Free: 800-365-6008
Fax: (256)355-6092
URL: http://www.mhcnca.org/albany/index.htm

28228 ■ Mental Health Center of North Central Alabama, Inc.
4110 Hwy. 31 S
Decatur, AL 35603
Ph: (256)355-6091
Free: 800-337-3162
Fax: (256)355-6092
E-mail: MentalHealth@mhcnca.org
URL: http://www.mhcnca.org

Demopolis

28229 ■ Springhill Home
1304 Old Springhill Rd.
Demopolis, AL 36732
Ph: (334)289-3270
Formerly: West Alabama Mental Health Center Springhill Home.

28230 ■ West Alabama Mental Health Center
1215 S Walnut Ave.
Demopolis, AL 36732
Ph: (334)289-2410
Fax: (334)289-2416
URL: http://www.wamhc.org/

Dothan

28231 ■ Houston County Clinic and Daycare Treatment
134 Prevatt Rd.
Dothan, AL 36301
Ph: (334)794-0731
URL: http://www.spcare.com

28232 ■ Laurel Oaks Behavioral Health Center
700 E Cottonwood Rd.
Dothan, AL 36301
Ph: (334)794-7373
URL: http://www.psysolutions.com/facilities/laureloaks/

28233 ■ Middleton Group Home
140 Prevatt Rd.
Dothan, AL 36301
Ph: (334)793-4020
URL: http://www.spcare.com

28234 ■ Southwest Alabama Medical Center Behavioral Medicine Center
1108 Ross Clark Circle
Dothan, AL 36301
Ph: (334)793-8858
URL: http://www.samc.org

28235 ■ Spectracare Mental Health System
2694 S Park Ave.
Dothan, AL 36301-4904
Ph: (334)712-2720
Fax: (334)712-2727
URL: http://www.spcare.com/

28236 ■ Spectracare Mental Health System Kornegay Street Foster Home
306 Kornegay St.
Dothan, AL 36301

Ph: (334)678-1886
URL: http://www.spcare.com/
Formerly: Regal Hearth.

28237 ■ Wiregrass Mental Health Board, Inc. dba SpectraCare
2694 S Park Ave.
Dothan, AL 36301
Ph: (334)712-2720
URL: http://www.spcare.com/

Dutton

28238 ■ Foster Home
4884 Alabama Hwy. 40
Dutton, AL 35744
Ph: (256)228-6514
URL: http://www.mlbhc.com

28239 ■ Residential Care Home
4886 Alabama Hwy. 40
Dutton, AL 35744
Ph: (256)228-3361
URL: http://www.mlbhc.com

Enterprise

28240 ■ Coffee County Day Mental Health Clinic
2861 Neal Metcalf Rd.
Enterprise, AL 36330-8003
Ph: (334)347-0212

28241 ■ South Central Alabama Community Mental Health Center
Coffee County Training Center
801 Aviation Blvd.
Enterprise, AL 36331
Ph: (334)393-1732
Formerly: South Central Alabama Mental Health Board.

Eutaw

28242 ■ West Alabama Mental Health Center
250 Prairie Ave., Ste. 106B
Eutaw, AL 35462-1175
Ph: (205)372-3106

Evergreen

28243 ■ Evergreen Satellite Office Outpatient Services
220 Magnolia Ave.
Evergreen, AL 36401
URL: http://store.samhsa.gov/mhlocator

Fairfield

28244 ■ JBS Mental Health Authority
Beverly Health Care Center - West
6825 Grasselli Rd.
Fairfield, AL 35064-1727
Ph: (205)780-3920
URL: http://www.jbsmha.com/

Fairhope

28245 ■ Baldwin County Community Mental Health Center--S Green Road
372 S Greeno Rd.
Fairhope, AL 36532-1905
Ph: (251)990-4211
Fax: (251)928-0126
URL: http://www.bcmhcal.com/

Fayette

28246 ■ Highlands Group Home
934 5th Terr. SW
Fayette, AL 35555
Ph: (205)932-3571

28247 ■ Northwest Alabama Mental Health Center
Fayette County Office
123 2nd Ave. NW
Fayette, AL 35555
Ph: (205)932-3216
URL: http://ww.nwamhc.com/

28248 ■ Residential Care Crossroads
402 2nd Ave. SE
Fayette, AL 35555
Ph: (205)932-5054

28249 ■ Spring Hill Apartments
5980 Hwy. 159
Fayette, AL 35555
Ph: (205)932-8769

Florence

28250 ■ Cedar Street Training Program
455 N Locust St.
Florence, AL 35630
Ph: (256)766-6929
URL: http://www.rcmh.org

28251 ■ Colebeck Lodge
120 Jones St.
Florence, AL 35630
Ph: (256)766-5155
URL: http://www.rcmh.org

28252 ■ Cypress Place
439 N Cypress St.
Florence, AL 35630
Ph: (256)766-6052
URL: http://www.rcmh.org

28253 ■ Eliza Coffee Memorial Hospital Behavioral Health Center
205 Marengo St.
Florence, AL 35630
Ph: (256)768-9128
URL: http://chgroup.org

28254 ■ Riverbend Center for Mental Health
635 W College St.
Florence, AL 35630
Ph: (256)764-3431
Fax: (256)582-4161
URL: http://www.rcmh.org/

28255 ■ Riverbend Center for Mental Health
Evergreen Place
106 S Cedar St.
Florence, AL 35630
Ph: (256)760-8629
URL: http://www.rcmh.org/

28256 ■ Riverbend Center for Mental Health
Franklin Street House
16 S Franklin St.
Florence, AL 35630
Ph: (256)764-3431
URL: http://www.rcmh.org/

28257 ■ Riverbend Center for Mental Health
Huntsville Road Home
3170 Huntsville Rd.
Florence, AL 35630
Ph: (256)764-3431
URL: http://www.rcmh.org/

28258 ■ Riverbend Community Mental Health Center
635 W College St.
Florence, AL 35630-5342
Ph: (256)764-3431
Fax: (256)766-4672
URL: http://www.rcmh.org
Formerly: Riverbend Center for Mental Health.

Foley

28259 ■ Baldwin County Community Mental Health Center--E Laurel Avenue
400 E Laurel Ave.
Foley, AL 36535
Ph: (251)943-6646
URL: http://www.bcmhcal.com/

28260 ■ Baldwin County Community Mental Health Center
Rockstall House
302 Alston St.
Foley, AL 36535
Ph: (251)943-2958
URL: http://www.bcmhcal.com/

Fort Payne

28261 ■ CED
Dekald County Office
301 14th St. NW
Fort Payne, AL 35967-3155
Ph: (256)845-4571
Formerly: CED Mental Health Center.

28262 ■ Crowne Healthcare
403 13th St. NW
Fort Payne, AL 35967
Ph: (256)845-5990
URL: http://www.crownemanagement.com/

28263 ■ DeKalb regional Medical Center
200 Medical Center Dr. SW
Fort Payne, AL 35968
Ph: (256)845-3150
URL: http://www.dekalbregional.com

28264 ■ Grandview Regional Medical Center--Fort Payne
701 Gault Ave. N, Ste. B
Fort Payne, AL 35967
Ph: (256)845-8227
URL: http://www.mtnviewhospital.com

Fyffe

28265 ■ Judy Haymon 3
Wigley Home
307 County Rd. 247
Fyffe, AL 35971-5229
Ph: (256)638-8479

Gadsden

28266 ■ Cherokee Etowah Dekalb Community Mental Health Center
Copeland/Matthews Home
1038 McDuffie St.
Gadsden, AL 35901-3049
Ph: (256)543-2883

28267 ■ Riverview Regional Medical Center
Behavioral Health
2013 Rainbow Dr.
Gadsden, AL 35901
Ph: (256)543-5200
URL: http://www.riverviewregional.com

28268 ■ Veterans Affairs Medical Center
Gadsden Clinic
206 Rescia Ave.
Gadsden, AL 35906
Ph: (256)413-7154
Fax: (256)413-7813
URL: http://www2.va.gov/directory/guide/facility.asp?ID=861&dnum=All

Geneva

28269 ■ Geneva County Clinic
1203 W Maple Ave.
Geneva, AL 36340-1641
Ph: (334)684-9615
URL: http://www.spcare.com/

Greensboro

28270 ■ West Alabama Mental Health Center Hale County Office
401 1st St.
Greensboro, AL 36744
Ph: (334)624-4905
URL: http://www.wamhc.org/hale.htm

Greenville

28271 ■ Butler Activity and Training Center
680 Hardscramble Rd.
Greenville, AL 36037
Ph: (334)382-2353

28272 ■ Butler County Mental Health Clinic
185 Industrial Pkwy.
Greenville, AL 36037-2421
Ph: (334)382-2018
Formerly: South Central Alabama Mental Health.

28273 ■ Crowne Health of Greenville
408 Country Club Dr.
Greenville, AL 36037-1310
Ph: (334)382-2693
URL: http://www.crownemanagement.com/
Formerly: South Central Mental Health.

Grove Hill

28274 ■ Clark Place
300 Carter Dr.
Grove Hill, AL 36451-0248
Ph: (251)275-4136

28275 ■ Grove Hill Satellite Office
129 Clark St.
Grove Hill, AL 36451
Ph: (205)275-4165

Guntersville

28276 ■ Marshall Manor Nursing Home
3120 North St.
Guntersville, AL 35976
Ph: (256)582-6561

28277 ■ Mountain Lakes Behavioral Healthcare
2409 Homer Clayton Dr.
Guntersville, AL 35976-2298
Ph: (256)582-4240
Free: 800-209-0049
Fax: (205)387-8270
URL: http://www.mlbhc.com/

28278 ■ Mountain Lakes Behavioral Healthcare Geriatric Services
2409 Homer Clayton Dr.
Guntersville, AL 35976
Ph: (256)582-3203
Free: 800-209-0049
URL: http://www.mlbhc.com/

Haleyville

28279 ■ Northwest Alabama Mental Health Center Winston County Office
71 Carraway Dr.
Haleyville, AL 35565
Ph: (205)486-4111
URL: http://www.nwamhc.com/

Hamilton

28280 ■ Northwest Alabama Mental Health Center Marion County Office
427 Smokey Bear Rd.
Hamilton, AL 35570
Ph: (205)921-2186
URL: http://www.nwamhc.com/

Hartselle

28281 ■ Hartselle Medical Center New Day Unit
201 Pine St. NW
Hartselle, AL 35640
Ph: (256)751-3033
URL: http://www.hartsellemedicalcenter.com

Hayneville

28282 ■ Montgomery Area Mental Health Authority Lowndes County Satellite Office
5 Academy Ln.
Hayneville, AL 36040-2617
Ph: (334)548-2578
Free: 877-279-7830
URL: http://www.mamha.org/

Heflin

28283 ■ Calhoun - Cleburne Mental Health Day Treatment Outpatient Satellite
150 Tompkins St.
Heflin, AL 36264-1836
Ph: (256)463-2969

Huntsville

28284 ■ Family Services Center
Bldg. 3
600 St. Clair
Huntsville, AL 35801-5057
Ph: (256)551-1610

28285 ■ Gateway--Huntsville
2707 Artie St., Bldg. 100, Ste. 13
Huntsville, AL 35805
Ph: (205)259-1320
URL: http://www.gatewaybhs.org

28286 ■ Mental Health Center of Madison County
4040 Memorial Pkwy. SW
Huntsville, AL 35802-4364
Ph: (256)533-1970
URL: http://www.mhcmc.org/
Formerly: Huntsville Madison County Mental Health.

28287 ■ Veterans Affairs Medical Center Huntsville Clinic
301 Governor's Dr. SW
Huntsville, AL 35801
Ph: (256)535-3100
Free: 866-847-4243
Fax: (256)534-1580
URL: http://www2.va.gov/directory/guide/facility.asp?ID=865&dnum=All

Irvington

28288 ■ Community Counseling Center South Mobile County
12701 Padgett Switch Rd.
Irvington, AL 36544
Ph: (251)824-2314
URL: http://www.altapointe.org

Jacksonville

28289 ■ Jacksonville Mental Health
614 Pelham Rd. S
Jacksonville, AL 36265-2732
Ph: (256)435-5502

Jasper

28290 ■ Faye Hogge Home
24827 Hwy. 69
Jasper, AL 35504
Ph: (205)384-3599

28291 ■ Lakeside Residential Care
9725 Smith Lake Dam Rd.
Jasper, AL 35504
Ph: (205)221-9798

28292 ■ Northwest Alabama Mental Health Center Adam Bishop (Wee Care) Day Treatment
1105 7th Ave.
Jasper, AL 35501
Ph: (205)302-9066
URL: http://www.nwamhc.com/

28293 ■ Northwest Alabama Mental Health Center Group Home
RR 10, Box 144-D
Jasper, AL 35504
Ph: (205)221-4129
URL: http://www.nwamhc.com/

28294 ■ Northwest Alabama Mental Health Center Jasper Apartments
1901 10th Ave.
Jasper, AL 35501
Ph: (205)387-9309
URL: http://www.nwamhc.com/

28295 ■ Northwest Alabama Mental Health Center Walker County Office
1100 7th Ave.
Jasper, AL 35501
Ph: (205)387-0541
URL: http://www.nwamhc.com/

28296 ■ Veterans Affairs Medical Center Jasper Clinic
3400 Hwy. 78 E, Ste. 215
Jasper, AL 35501
Ph: (205)221-7384
Fax: (205)221-7385
URL: http://www2.va.gov/directory/guide/facility.asp?ID=862&dnum=1

Lafayette

28297 ■ Chambers County Addictions Center
306 2nd Ave. NW
Lafayette, AL 36862-1629
Ph: (334)864-7999

Lanett

28298 ■ Lillian Smith Home
1827 32nd Dr. SW
Lanett, AL 36863
Ph: (334)576-2296

Livingston

28299 ■ Sumter County Office
1121 N Washington St.
Livingston, AL 35470
Ph: (205)652-6731
Formerly: West Alabama Mental Health Center; Greene County Satellite.

Lowndesboro

28300 ■ Montgomery Area Mental Health Authority Lowndesboro
7 Gardner Circle
Lowndesboro, AL 36752
Ph: (334)412-1418
URL: http://www.mamha.org

Luverne

28301 ■ Beacon Children's Hospital
150 Hospital Dr.
Luverne, AL 36049
Ph: (334)386-0343
URL: http://www.beaconchildrenshospital.com

28302 ■ Crenshaw Community Hospital
Special Services Unit
101 Hospital Circle
Luverne, AL 36049
Ph: (334)335-3374

28303 ■ Crenshaw County Mental Health Clinic
South Central Alabama CMHC
587 Bentley Ave.
Luverne, AL 36049
Ph: (334)335-5201

28304 ■ Luverne Nursing Facility
142 W 3rd St.
Luverne, AL 36049
Ph: (334)335-6528

Madison

28305 ■ Birmingham Veterans Affairs Medical Center
Madison/Decatur Clinic
8075 Madison Blvd., Ste. 101
Madison, AL 35758
Ph: (256)772-6220
Fax: (256)461-0030
URL: http://www2.va.gov/directory/guide/facility.asp?ID=386&dnum=1

28306 ■ Cahaba Center for Mental Health
Perry County Satellite
104 Edwards St.
Madison, AL 36756
Ph: (334)683-9957
URL: http://www.cahabamentalhealth.com

28307 ■ Huntsville Adult and Adolescent
Bradford Health Services
1600 Browns Ferry Rd.
Madison, AL 35758
Ph: (256)461-7272
URL: http://www.bradfordhealth.com

Minter

28308 ■ Safety Net Academy
80 Mel Bailey Dr.
Minter, AL 36761
Ph: (334)872-6196
Fax: (334)872-6117
URL: http://www.safetynetacademy.org

Mobile

28309 ■ Adult Outpatient
Alta Pointe Health Systems, Inc.
2400 Gordon Smith Sr.
Mobile, AL 36617
Ph: (251)473-4423
URL: http://www.altapointe.org

28310 ■ AltaPointe Health Systems, Inc.-BayPointe
5800 Southland Dr.
Mobile, AL 36693
Ph: (251)661-0153
E-mail: info@altapointe.org
URL: http://www.altapointe.org/aboutus_locations_BPHRS.asp

28311 ■ AltaPointe Health Systems, Inc.--Mobile
5750 Southland Dr., Ste. A
Mobile, AL 36693-3316
Ph: (251)450-5901
Fax: (251)666-7537
E-mail: info@altapointe.org
URL: http://www.altapointe.org/
Formerly: Mobile Community Mental Health Center.

28312 ■ Arbor Court
Mobile Community Mental Health Center
9650 Royal Woods Dr. N
Mobile, AL 36608-9206
Ph: (251)639-1822
URL: http://www.altapointe.org/

28313 ■ Bay Manor Health Care Center
Mobile Community Mental Health Center
7020 Bruns Dr.
Mobile, AL 36695-4399
Ph: (251)639-1588
URL: http://www.altapointe.org/

28314 ■ BayView Professional Associates
1110 Montlimar Dr.
Mobile, AL 36609
Ph: (251)450-2250
E-mail: info@altapointe.org
URL: http://www.altapointe.org/aboutus_locations_BVPA.asp

28315 ■ Gateway--Mobile
3103 Airport Rd., Ste. 453
Mobile, AL 36606
Ph: (251)545-4680
URL: http://www.gatewaybhs.org

28316 ■ Independent Living Facility
Mobile Community Mental Health Center
1704 Princess Helen Rd. W
Mobile, AL 36618-3042
Ph: (334)473-4423
URL: http://www.altapointe.org/

28317 ■ LeMoyne Center
501 Bishop Ln. N
Mobile, AL 36608-5821
Ph: (251)432-0233

28318 ■ Safehaven Community Homes
630 Zeigler Cir. E
Mobile, AL 36608-4828
Ph: (251)634-2329
Formerly: Zeigler Lodge Cottage.

28319 ■ Saint Mary's Home for Children
4350 Moffett Rd.
Mobile, AL 36618
Ph: (251)344-7733
URL: http://www.stmaryshomemobile.org

28320 ■ Spring Hill Manor Nursing Home
Mobile Community Mental Health Center
3900 Old Shell Rd.
Mobile, AL 36608
Ph: (251)342-5623
URL: http://www.altapointe.org/

28321 ■ Veterans Affairs Medical Center
Mobile Outpatient Clinic
1504 Springhill Ave.
Mobile, AL 36604
Ph: (251)219-3900
URL: http://www2.va.gov/directory/guide/facility.asp?ID=5583&dnum=1

28322 ■ Zeigler Outpatient
7280 Sellers Lane
Mobile, AL 36608
Ph: (251)776-1930
URL: http://www.altapointe.org

Monroeville

28323 ■ Monroe Nursing Facility
236 W Claiborne St.
Monroeville, AL 36460
Ph: (251)575-2645
URL: http://www.ballhealth.com/locations_list.asp?FacilityTypeID=1

28324 ■ Southwest Alabama Mental Health/Mental Retardation Board, Inc.
530 Hornady Dr.
Monroeville, AL 36461-8658
Ph: (251)575-4837
URL: http://www.swamh.com/

Montgomery

28325 ■ Betty Carter Home
704 Golden Gate Dr.
Montgomery, AL 36110
Ph: (334)263-3686
URL: http://www.mamha.org

28326 ■ Capitol Hill Health Care Center, Inc.
520 S Hull St.
Montgomery, AL 36104-4683
Ph: (334)834-2920

28327 ■ Child and Adolescent Center--Montgomery
101 Coliseum Blvd.
Montgomery, AL 36109
Ph: (334)279-7810
URL: http://www.wamha.org

28328 ■ Crowne Health Care of Montgomery
1837 Upper Wetumpka Rd.
Montgomery, AL 36107-1304
Ph: (334)264-8416
Fax: (334)264-1169
URL: http://www.crownehlthcre-montg.com/

28329 ■ Grandview Behavioral Health Center--Montgomery
315 Saint Luke's Dr.
Montgomery, AL 36117
Ph: (334)409-9263
URL: http://www.mtviewhospital.com

28330 ■ Hillview Terrace
100 Perry Hill Rd.
Montgomery, AL 36109
Ph: (334)272-0171
Fax: (334)396-5575
E-mail: hvt@hillviewterracehealthcarecenter.com
URL: http://www.hillviewterracehealthcarecenter.com/

28331 ■ James Quarles 1
404 S Holt St.
Montgomery, AL 36104-3917
Ph: (334)262-2813

28332 ■ James Quarles 2
412 S Holt St.
Montgomery, AL 36104-3917
Ph: (334)269-1673
URL: http://www.mamha.org/

28333 ■ Montgomery Area Mental Health Authority, Inc.
Montgomery
101 Coliseum Blvd.
Montgomery, AL 36109-2707
Ph: (334)279-7830
Fax: (334)277-8862
URL: http://www.mamha.org/

28334 ■ Montgomery Crisis Residential Facility
2140 A Upper Wetumpka Rd.
Montgomery, AL 36107
Ph: (334)262-0404
URL: http://www.montgomerycountymd.gov

28335 ■ SafetyNet Montgomery
5906 Carmichael Place
Montgomery, AL 36117
Ph: (334)277-1334

Moulton

28336 ■ Moulton-Lawrence Counseling Center
317 Hospital St.
Moulton, AL 35650
Ph: (256)974-6697
URL: http://www.mhcnca.org/moulton/index.htm

Oneonta

28337 ■ JBS Mental Health Authority
Crestline Home
907 Jones Ave.
Oneonta, AL 35121-1309
Ph: (205)274-7263
URL: http://www.jbsmha.com/

Opelika

28338 ■ East Alabama Mental Health
Brief Intensive Treatment
2500 Lambert Dr.
Opelika, AL 36801
Ph: (334)749-2871
Free: 800-815-0630
Fax: (334)742-2707
URL: http://www.eastalabamamhc.org/

28339 ■ East Alabama Mental Health Center
James I. Walter Main Center
2506 Lambert Dr.
Opelika, AL 36801-7237
Ph: (334)742-2700
Free: 800-815-0630
URL: http://www.eastalabamamhc.org/
Formerly: East Alabama Mental Health/Mental Retardation Board.

28340 ■ Family & Children's Services Center
2300 Center Hill Dr., Bldg. II
Opelika, AL 36801
Ph: (334)742-2112
URL: http://eastalabamamhc.org/
Formerly: Child Day Treatment; ABC Child Development Center.

28341 ■ Psychiatric Services
East Alabama Medical Center
2000 Pepperell Pkwy.
Opelika, AL 36801
Ph: (334)749-2996
URL: http://www.eastalabamamhc.org

28342 ■ Spring Villa Home--MR
590 Lee Rd. 148
Opelika, AL 36804-0991
Ph: (334)745-6224
URL: http://www.eastalabamamhc.org/locations.htm

28343 ■ Tall Oaks Apartments
2908 Birmingham Hwy., No. 108
Opelika, AL 36801-4611
Ph: (334)749-7115
Formerly: Tall Oaks Family Support Program.

Opp

28344 ■ Opp Nursing Facility
115 W Paulk Ave.
Opp, AL 36467-1695
Ph: (334)493-4558

Owens Cross Roads

28345 ■ Sequel Youth and Family Services
318 Hamer Rd.
Owens Cross Roads, AL 35763
Ph: (256)725-7170
URL: http://www.sequelyouthservices.com

Oxford

28346 ■ Veterans Affairs Medical Center
Anniston/Oxford Clinic
96 Ali Way Creekside S
Oxford, AL 36203
Ph: (256)832-4141
Fax: (256)832-4153
URL: http://www2.va.gov/directory/guide/facility.asp?ID=858&dnum=1

Ozark

28347 ■ Dale County Clinic
134 Katherine Ave.
Ozark, AL 36360-1973
Ph: (334)774-9112
URL: http://www.spcare.com

Pelham

28348 ■ Clinton Shelby CMHC
2100 County Service Dr.
Pelham, AL 35124
Ph: (205)668-4308
URL: http://www.clintonshelby.org

28349 ■ Family and Youth Intervention
2280 Hwy. 35
Pelham, AL 35124
Ph: (205)682-6186
Fax: (205)682-5855
URL: http://chiltonshelby.org

28350 ■ Gateway Family Counseling Services
Shelby County
333 Business Cir.
Pelham, AL 35124-1778
Ph: (205)664-5541
URL: http://www.gway.org

28351 ■ Pelham Mental Health Center
2100 County Services Dr.
Pelham, AL 35124
Ph: (205)663-1252
Fax: (205)663-3175
URL: http://chiltonshelby.org

Pell City

28352 ■ Crestline Home 2
JBS Mental Health Authority
2000 7th Ave. N
Pell City, AL 35125
Ph: (205)338-6338
URL: http://www.jnsmha.com

28353 ■ JBS Mental Health Authority
Greenwood Homes
508 15th St. N
Pell City, AL 35125
Ph: (205)338-0196
URL: http://www.jbsmha.com/

Phenix City

28354 ■ East Alabama Mental Health Center
Canterbury Health Care Facility
1720 Knowles Rd.
Phenix City, AL 36869
Ph: (334)291-0485
URL: http://eastalabamamhc.org/

28355 ■ East Alabama Mental Health Center
Hodges Home
1416 14th Ct.
Phenix City, AL 36867
Ph: (334)291-0897
URL: http://eastalabamamhc.org/

28356 ■ East Alabama Mental Health Center
Parkwood Health Care Facility
3301 Stadium Dr.
Phenix City, AL 36867
Ph: (334)297-0237
URL: http://eastalabamamhc.org/

28357 ■ Russell County Counseling Center
3170 MLK Pkwy
Phenix City, AL 36869-5359
Ph: (334)298-2405

28358 ■ Russell County Day Services
1011 8th Ave.
Phenix City, AL 36867
Ph: (334)298-2405
Formerly: Russell County Group Home.

Pleasant Grove

28359 ■ Pleasant Grove Health Care Center
30 7th St.
Pleasant Grove, AL 35127
Ph: (205)794-8226

Prattville

28360 ■ Montgomery Area Mental Health Authority
Autanga County Satellite Office
698 C commerce Court
Prattville, AL 36066
Ph: (334)365-2207
URL: http://www.mamha.org/

Roanoke

28361 ■ Randolph County Satellite Office
706 Main St.
Roanoke, AL 36274
Ph: (334)863-2518

28362 ■ Roanoke Health Care Center
680 Seymour Dr.
Roanoke, AL 36274-1522
Ph: (334)863-6151
URL: http://www.ballhealth.com/locations_list.asp?FacilityTypeID=1

Robertsdale

28363 ■ Baldwin County Community Mental Health Center
Bradford Place Therapeutic Group Home
23350-A N Chicago St.
Robertsdale, AL 36567
Ph: (251)947-3235

Russellville

28364 ■ Riverbend Russellville
205 Jackson Ave. S
Russellville, AL 35653-2233
Ph: (256)332-3971
URL: http://www.rcmh.org

Salem

28365 ■ East Alabama Mental Health Center
Salem House
5646 Lee Rd. 175
Salem, AL 36874
Ph: (334)742-9936
URL: http://www.eastalabamamhc.org/

28366 ■ Griffin Mill Residential Care Home
151 Lee Rd. 138
Salem, AL 36874-2553
Ph: (334)749-7169
Formerly: Freedom House.

Samson

28367 ■ Geneva County Day Treatment
10386 W State Hwy. 52
Samson, AL 36477-5786
Ph: (334)898-7423
URL: http://www.spcare.com

Scottsboro

28368 ■ Jackson County Mental Health Center--Scottsboro
508 Gregory St.
Scottsboro, AL 35768-4239
Ph: (256)259-1774
Formerly: Mountain Lakes Behavioral Health Center Jackson County Center.

Seale

28369 ■ Russell County Child Day Treatment Russell County Schools
91 Poorhouse Rd.
Seale, AL 36874
Ph: (334)855-0516

Section

28370 ■ Judy Haymon - Holiday Home
828 County Rd. 68
Section, AL 35771
Ph: (256)638-3102

Selma

28371 ■ Cahaba Center for Mental Health/Mental Retardation Services
417 Medical Center Pkwy.
Selma, AL 36701
Ph: (334)418-6500
Fax: (334)872-2084
URL: http://www.cahabamentalhealth.com/

28372 ■ Cahaba Center for Mental Health/Mental Retardation Services Cahaba Place
2990 Earl Goodwin Pkwy.
Selma, AL 36701
Ph: (334)418-6527
Fax: (334)875-3145
URL: http://www.cahabamentalhealth.com/

28373 ■ Cahaba Center for Mental Health/Mental Retardation Services Hilltop Home
418 Medical Center Pkwy.
Selma, AL 36701
Ph: (334)875-2100
URL: http://www.cahabamentalhealth.com/

28374 ■ Cahaba Center for Mental Health/Mental Retardation Services McDowell House
302 Franklin St.
Selma, AL 36703-4415
Ph: (334)418-6522
Fax: (334)875-0219
URL: http://www.cahabamentalhealth.com/

28375 ■ Cahaba Center for Mental Health/Mental Retardation Services Reynolds Building
1017 Medical Center Pkwy.
Selma, AL 36701-6780
Ph: (334)875-2100
Free: 800-291-1920
URL: http://www.cahabamentalhealth.com/

28376 ■ Lighthouse Convalescent Care, Inc.
2911 Earl Goodwin Pkwy.
Selma, AL 36701
Ph: (334)875-1868
URL: http://www.ballhealth.com/locations_list.asp?FacilityTypeID=1

Sheffield

28377 ■ Veterans Affairs Medical Center Shoals Area (Florence) Clinic
422 DD Cox Blvd.
Sheffield, AL 35660
Ph: (256)381-9055
Fax: (256)381-6101
URL: http://www2.va.gov/directory/guide/facility.asp?ID=864&dnum=1

Sulligent

28378 ■ Discovery Place Group Home
52285 Hwy. 17
Sulligent, AL 35586
Ph: (205)698-8325

Sylacauga

28379 ■ Cheaha Mental Health Center
351 W 3rd St.
Sylacauga, AL 35150
Ph: (256)245-1340
Fax: (256)245-1343

28380 ■ Coosa Valley Medical Center
315 W Hickory St.
Sylacauga, AL 35150
Ph: (256)401-4000
URL: http://www.cvhealth.net

28381 ■ Hillwood Home
210 Elm St.
Sylacauga, AL 35150
Ph: (256)245-6984

Talladega

28382 ■ Talladega Health Care Center
616 Chaffee St.
Talladega, AL 35160
Ph: (256)362-4197
Fax: (256)362-0726
URL: http://www.talladegahealthcarecenter.com/

28383 ■ Talladega Satellite Office
10 Bemiston Ave.
Talladega, AL 35160
Ph: (256)362-8600

Tallassee

28384 ■ Community Hospital, Tallassee, FL
805 Friendship Rd.
Tallassee, AL 36078
Ph: (334)283-6541
URL: http://www.chal.org

Theodore

28385 ■ Riverbend Center for Mental Health Franklin Street Home II
14 S Franklin St.
Theodore, AL 35360
Ph: (256)764-3431
URL: http://www.rcmh.org/

Troy

28386 ■ East Central Mental Health/Mental Retardation Board, Inc.
200 Cherry St.
Troy, AL 36081
Ph: (334)566-6022
Fax: (334)566-5346

Trussville

28387 ■ Trussville Health Care Center
119 Watterson Pkwy.
Trussville, AL 35173
Ph: (205)655-3226

Tuscaloosa

28388 ■ Goodwin Center
3701 Loop Rd, Bldg. 39
Tuscaloosa, AL 35404
Ph: (205)562-3700
URL: http://www.tuscaloosa.va.gov/

28389 ■ Indian Rivers Community Mental Health/Mental Retardation Administration
1914 7th St.
Tuscaloosa, AL 35403
Ph: (205)562-3700
Fax: (205)562-3769
URL: http://www.irmhc.org/

28390 ■ Mary Starke Harper Geriatric Psychiatry Center
200 University Blvd.
Tuscaloosa, AL 35401
Ph: (205)759-0900
URL: http://www.mh.alabama.gov/MI

Tuskegee

28391 ■ Macon County Satellite
103 E Oak St.
Tuskegee, AL 36083
Ph: (334)727-7001

28392 ■ Sequel TSI of Tuskegee
4280 US Hwy. 295
Tuskegee, AL 36083
Ph: (334)727-2216
URL: http://www.sequelyouthservices.com/html/secure-tuskegee.html

Union Springs

28393 ■ Bullock County Satellite
202 Abercrombie St.
Union Springs, AL 36089
Ph: (334)738-5279

Uniontown

28394 ■ Cahaba Center
314 James Ave.
Uniontown, AL 36786
Ph: (334)628-6515
URL: http://www.cahabamentalhealth.com/

Valley

28395 ■ O.D. Alsobrook Counseling Center
6376 Fairfax Bypass
Valley, AL 36854
Ph: (334)756-4117

Vernon

28396 ■ Lamar Community Reintegration Hope
245 Medical Center Dr.
Vernon, AL 35592
Ph: (205)695-7531

28397 ■ Northwest Alabama Mental Health Center Lamar County Office
141 2nd Ave. NW
Vernon, AL 35592
Ph: (205)695-9183

Warrior

28398 ■ Bradford Health Services
1189 Allbritton Rd.
Warrior, AL 35180
Ph: (205)244-3021

Wetumpka

28399 ■ Hillside Mental Health Center
8721 U.S Hwy. 231
Wetumpka, AL 36092-5342
Ph: (334)567-8408

28400 ■ Montgomery Area Mental Health Authority Wetumpka Nursing Facility
1825 Holtville Rd.
Wetumpka, AL 36092

Ph: (334)567-0322
URL: http://www.mamha.org/

Winfield

28401 ■ Northwest Medical Center Behavioral Health
1530 US Hwy 43
Winfield, AL 35594
Ph: (205)487-7000
URL: http://www.northwestmedcenter.net

greenville

28402 ■ L.V. Stabler Memorial Hospital Neuropsychiatric Care
29 L V Stabler Dr.
greenville, AL 36037
Ph: (334)382-2671
URL: http://www.lvstabler.com

huntsville

28403 ■ VOA Group Home Huntsville CMHC
3911 Triana Blvd. SW, Ste. A
huntsville, AL 35805
Ph: (256)830-2155
URL: http://voasoutheast.org

ALASKA

Anchorage

28404 ■ Alaska Veterans Affairs Healthcare System & Regional Office
2925 Debarr Rd.
Anchorage, AK 99508
Ph: (907)257-4700
Free: 888-353-7574
URL: http://www.visn20.med.va.gov/Alaska/

28405 ■ Anchorage Community Mental Health Services
4020 Folker St.
Anchorage, AK 99508
Ph: (907)563-1000
Fax: (907)563-2045
E-mail: info@acmhs.com
URL: http://www.acmhs.com/
Formerly: Southcentral Counseling Center.

28406 ■ Assets, Inc.
2330 Nichols St.
Anchorage, AK 99508
Ph: (907)279-6617
Fax: (907)274-0636
E-mail: matt_jones@assetsinc.org
URL: http://www.assetsinc.org
Matt Jones, Executive Director

28407 ■ Daybreak Adult Day Center
9210 Jupiter Dr.
Anchorage, AK 99507
Ph: (907)346-2234

28408 ■ Denali Family Services--Anchorage
1251 Muldoon Rd., Ste. 116
Anchorage, AK 99504
Ph: (907)274-8281
Fax: (907)274-4055
E-mail: info@denalfs.org
URL: http://www.denalifs.org/

28409 ■ Little Steps Preschool
545 5th Ave.
Anchorage, AK 99504
Ph: (907)274-8281
URL: http://www.deralifs.org

28410 ■ North Star Behavioral Health--Anchorage
1650 S Bragaw
Anchorage, AK 99508
Ph: (907)264-4321
URL: http://www.northstarbehavioral.com/

28411 ■ Providence Alaska Medical Center--Behavioral Health
3260 Providence Dr.
Anchorage, AK 99508
Ph: (907)562-2211
URL: http://www.providence.org/alaska/bhs/default.htm

Barrow

28412 ■ North Slope Borough Integrated Behavioral Health Services
5200 Karluk St.
Barrow, AK 99723
Ph: (907)852-0366

Bethel

28413 ■ Yukon Kuskokwim Health Corporation Behavioral Health Program
PO Box 528
Bethel, AK 99559
Ph: (907)543-6000
Fax: (907)543-6159
E-mail: info@ukhc.org
URL: http://www.ykhc.org

28414 ■ Yukon Kuskokwim Health Corporation Crisis Respite Center
PO Box 528
Bethel, AK 99559
Ph: (907)543-6100
Fax: (907)543-6159
E-mail: info@ukhc.org
URL: http://www.ykhc.org

28415 ■ Yukon Kuskokwim Health Corporation Transitional Living Program
PO Box 528
Bethel, AK 99559
Ph: (907)543-6100
Fax: (907)543-6159
E-mail: info@ukhc.org
URL: http://www.ykhc.org

Cordova

28416 ■ Sound Alternatives
602 Chase Ave.
Cordova, AK 99574
Ph: (907)424-8300

Craig

28417 ■ Communities Organized for Health Options
210 Coldstorage Rd.
Craig, AK 99921-0805
Ph: (907)826-3662

28418 ■ Community Connections--Craig
1800 CK Hwy., Ste. 241
Craig, AK 99921
Ph: (907)826-3891

Dillingham

28419 ■ Bristol Bay Counseling Center
6000 Kanakanak Rd.
Dillingham, AK 99576
Ph: (907)842-1230
URL: http://www.bbahc.org/mental.html

28420 ■ Bristol Bay Counseling Center Our House Crisis Respite Home
3820 Kanakonak Rd.
Dillingham, AK 99578
Ph: (907)842-4248
URL: http://www.bbahc.org/mental.html

Fairbanks

28421 ■ Boys and Girls Home of Alaska, Inc.
3101 Lathrop St.
Fairbanks, AK 99701
Ph: (907)459-4700
URL: http://www.boysandgirlshome.com

28422 ■ Fairbanks Community Behavior Health Center
122 1st Ave., 4th Fl.
Fairbanks, AK 99701
Ph: (907)452-1575
Fax: (907)456-9760
URL: http://www.fcbhc.org/
Formerly: Fairbanks Community Mental Health.

28423 ■ Family Centered Services of Alaska Residential Diagnostic Treatment Center
1423 Peger Rd.
Fairbanks, AK 99709
Ph: (907)456-7010
Formerly: Children's Services.

28424 ■ Presbyterian Hospitality House
209 Forty Mile Ave., Ste. 100
Fairbanks, AK 99701
Ph: (907)456-6445
URL: http://www.phhalaska.org

28425 ■ Tanana Chiefs Conference
122 1st Ave., Ste. 600
Fairbanks, AK 99701
Ph: (907)452-8251
Free: 800-770-8251
URL: http://www.tananachiefs.org

Galena

28426 ■ Yukon-Koyukuk Mental Health & Alcohol Program Edgar Nollner Health Center
17 Antoski Rd.
Galena, AK 99741
Ph: (907)656-1617

Haines

28427 ■ Lynn Canal Counseling Services--Haines
215 Willard St.
Haines, AK 99827-0090
Ph: (907)766-2177

Healy

28428 ■ Railbelt Mental Health & Addictions Healy Office
Dry Creek & Coal Sts.
Healy, AK 99743
Ph: (907)683-2743
Free: 800-478-2744
URL: http://railbelt.com/

Homer

28429 ■ South Peninsula Mental Health Association, Inc.
3948 Ben Walters Ln.
Homer, AK 99603-7708
Ph: (907)235-7701
Fax: (902)235-2290
URL: http://www.spbhs.org/
Formerly: South Peninsula Community Mental Health Center.

Huslia

28430 ■ Yukon- Koyukuk Mental Health Program
Huslia Counseling Center
PO Box 67
Huslia, AK 99746
Ph: (907)829-2268

Juneau

28431 ■ Bartlett Regional Hospital- Mental Health Unit
3260 Hospital Dr.
Juneau, AK 99801
Ph: (907)796-8430
URL: http://www.bartletthospital.org/patientServices/mentalHealth.html

28432 ■ Cornerstone
Juneau Youth Services, Inc.
9290 Hurlock Ave.
Juneau, AK 99801
Ph: (907)789-7654
URL: http://www.jys.org

28433 ■ Juneau Alliance for Mental Health, Inc.
3406 Glacier Hwy.
Juneau, AK 99801-9501
Ph: (907)463-3303
URL: http://www.jamhi.org/
Formerly: Juneau Alliance for the Mentally Ill.

28434 ■ Lighthouse--Juneau
Juneau Youth Services, Inc.
8460 Rainbow Row
Juneau, AK 99801
Ph: (907)523-6574
URL: http://www.jys,org

28435 ■ Miller House--Juneau
Juneau Youth Services, Inc.
10685 Mendenhall Loop Rd.
Juneau, AK 99801
Ph: (907)523-6555
URL: http://www.jys.org

28436 ■ Montana House
Juneau Youth Services, Inc.
10801 Black Bear Rd.
Juneau, AK 99801
Ph: (907)523-6576
URL: http://www.jys.org

28437 ■ Southeast Alaska Regional Health
3245 Hospital Dr.
Juneau, AK 99801
Ph: (907)463-4445
URL: http://www.searhc.org/common/pages/behavioralhealth/

Kaltag

28438 ■ Kaltag Counseling Center
PO Box 70
Kaltag, AK 99748-0070
Ph: (907)534-2209

Kenai

28439 ■ Alaska Veterans Affairs Health Care System
Kenai Veterans Affairs Community Based Outpatient Clinic
11312 Kenai Spur Hwy., Ste. 39
Kenai, AK 99669
Ph: (907)395-4100
Free: 877-797-8924
Fax: (907)283-4236
URL: http://www2.va.gov/directory/guide/facility.asp?ID=472&dnum=All

Ketchikan

28440 ■ Community Connections--Ketchikan
201 Deermount St.
Ketchikan, AK 99901
Ph: (907)225-7825
Free: 800-478-7825
Fax: (907)225-1541
URL: http://www.comconnections.org/

28441 ■ Gateway Center for Human Services
3056 5th Ave.
Ketchikan, AK 99901-5793
Ph: (907)225-4135
URL: http://www.city.ketchikan.ak.us/departments/gateway/index.html

28442 ■ Horizon House--Ketchikan
Gateway Center for Human Services
1356 Peyton Place
Ketchikan, AK 99901
Ph: (907)225-4135
URL: http://www.city.ketchikan.ak.us

Kodiak

28443 ■ Providence- Kodiak Island Counseling Center
717 E Rezanof Dr.
Kodiak, AK 99615-6416
Ph: (907)481-2400
URL: http://www.providence.org/Alaska/bhs/nkodiak-mhc.htm

Kotzebue

28444 ■ Maniilaq Counseling Services
733 2nd Ave.
Kotzebue, AK 99752
Ph: (907)442-7730
URL: http://www.maniilaq.org/behavioralServices.html

Nenana

28445 ■ Railbelt Mental Health & Addictions
Nenana Office
307 E 2nd St.
Nenana, AK 99760
Ph: (907)832-5557
URL: http://railbelt.com/

Nome

28446 ■ Norton Sound Health Corporation (NSHC)
Behavioral Health Services
305 W 5th Ave.
Nome, AK 99762
Ph: (907)443-3344
URL: http://nortonsoundhealth.org/

Nulato

28447 ■ Yukon- Koyukuk Mental Health Program
Nulato Counseling Center
PO Box 65110
Nulato, AK 99765-0110
Ph: (907)898-2335

Palmer

28448 ■ Denali Family Services--Palmer
Wasilla Hwy.
Palmer, AK 99645
Ph: (907)274-8281
URL: http://www.denalifs.org/

28449 ■ North Star Behavioral Health--Palmer Residential Treatment Center
3647 Clark-Wolverine Rd.
Palmer, AK 99645
Ph: (907)761-7400
URL: http://www.northstarbehavioral.com/

Petersburg

28450 ■ Petersburg Mental Health Services
201 N Nordic Dr.
Petersburg, AK 99833
Ph: (907)772-3332
URL: http://www.petersburg.org/community/medical.html

Providence

28451 ■ Providence Valdez Counseling Center
911 Meals Ave.
Providence, AK 99686
Ph: (907)835-2838
URL: http://www.providence.org/Alaska/Valdez/counseling.htm

Ruby

28452 ■ Yukon- Koyukuk Mental Health Program
Ruby Counseling Center
74 Titna St.
Ruby, AK 99768
Ph: (907)468-4433

Seward

28453 ■ Seaview Community Services
302 Railway Ave.
Seward, AK 99664
Ph: (907)224-5257
URL: http://www.seaviewseward.org/home.shtml

28454 ■ Seaview Community services
1400 Chamberlain Rd.
Seward, AK 99664
Ph: (907)224-5257
URL: http://www.seaviewseward.org

Sitka

28455 ■ Sitka Counseling and Prevention Services
701 Indian River Rd.
Sitka, AK 99835
Ph: (907)747-3636
URL: http://www.scpsak.org

28456 ■ Sitka Mental Health Clinic
514 Lake St., Ste. C
Sitka, AK 99835-7405
Ph: (907)747-8994

Skagway

28457 ■ Lynn Canal Counseling Services--Skagway
350 14th Ave.
Skagway, AK 99840
Ph: (907)983-2548
URL: http://www.lynncanalcounseling.org/

Soldotna

28458 ■ Central Peninsula Counseling Services
230 E Marydale Ave., Ste. 2
Soldotna, AK 99669
Ph: (907)260-3691
URL: http://www.pchsak.org/

Tok

28459 ■ Tok Area Counseling Center
W 1st St., Rm. 8
Tok, AK 99780
Ph: (907)883-5106

Wasilla

28460 ■ Mat-Su Health Services
1363 W Spruce Ave.
Wasilla, AK 99654-5327
Ph: (907)376-2411

Free: 800-478-2410
URL: http://www.bhs-mat-su.com/
Formerly: Life Quest.

28461 ■ Providence Alaska Medical Center Behavioral Medicine Group North
1700 E Bogard Rd., Ste. 201
Wasilla, AK 99654
Ph: (907)373-8080
URL: http://www.providence.org/alaska/bhs/default.htm

Wrangell

28462 ■ Alaska Island Community Services
333 Church St.
Wrangell, AK 99929
Ph: (907)874-2373
URL: http://akics.org/

Yakutat

28463 ■ Yakutat Tribal Social Servies
364 Ridge Rd.
Yakutat, AK 99689
Ph: (907)784-3639
URL: http://www.scpsak.org

ARIZONA

Anthem

28464 ■ Veterans Affairs Medical Center Anthem Community Based Outpatient Clinic
3618 W Anthem Way., Bldg. D, Ste. 120
Anthem, AZ 85086
Ph: (623)551-6092
Free: 800-949-1005
URL: http://www2.va.gov/directory/guide/facility.asp?ID=5335&dnum=1

Apache Junction

28465 ■ Superstition Mountain Mental Health Center
564 N Idaho Rd.
Apache Junction, AZ 85219-4001
Ph: (480)983-0065

Bellemont

28466 ■ Veterans Affairs Medical Center Bellemont Community Based Outpatient Clinic
Camp Navajo Army Depot
Bellemont, AZ 86015
Ph: (928)226-1056
Free: 800-949-1005
URL: http://www2.va.gov/directory/guide/facility.asp?ID=814&dnum=1

Benson

28467 ■ Southeastern Arizona Behavioral Health Services, Inc.
Benson Office
611 W Union
Benson, AZ 85602
Ph: (520)586-0800
URL: http://www.seabhs.org/

Bisbee

28468 ■ Southeastern Arizona Behavioral Health Services, Inc.
Bisbee Clinic
1326 Hwy. 92, Ste. J
Bisbee, AZ 85603
Ph: (520)432-7751
Fax: (520)432-7672
URL: http://www.seabhs.org/poc/view_doc.php?type=doc&id=1410

Bullhead City

28469 ■ Mohave Mental Health Clinic--Bullhead City
1145 Marina Blvd.
Bullhead City, AZ 86442
Ph: (928)758-5905

Casa Grande

28470 ■ Casa Grande Regional Medical Center
1800 E Florence Blvd.
Casa Grande, AZ 85122
Ph: (520)381-6300
URL: http://www.casagrandehospital.com

28471 ■ Horizon Human Services
Casa Grande Office, E Cottonwood Lane
210 E Cottonwood Ln.
Casa Grande, AZ 85222
Ph: (520)836-1688
Free: 866-836-1688

28472 ■ Horizon Human Services
Casa Grande Office, W Main Street
120 W Main St.
Casa Grande, AZ 85222
Ph: (520)836-1675
Formerly: Behavioral Health Agency.

Chandler

28473 ■ Harrison Clinic
6775 W Harrison St.
Chandler, AZ 85226
Ph: (480)785-4851

28474 ■ Pheasant Run
2141 N Evergreen St., Apt. 1049
Chandler, AZ 85225
Ph: (480)963-5108

Clifton

28475 ■ Southeastern Arizona Behavioral Health Services, Inc.
Clifton Clinic
430 N Coronado Blvd.
Clifton, AZ 85533
Ph: (928)865-4531
URL: http://www.seabhs.org/poc/view_doc.php?type=doc&id=1410

Cottonwood

28476 ■ Verde Valley Guidance Clinic
8 E Cottonwood St.
Cottonwood, AZ 86326
Ph: (928)634-2236

28477 ■ Verde Valley Medical Center
269 S Candy Lane
Cottonwood, AZ 86326
Ph: (928)634-2251
URL: http://www.verdevalleymedicalcenter.com

28478 ■ Veterans Affairs Medical Center Cottonwood Community Based Outpatient Clinic
203 S Candy Ln.
Cottonwood, AZ 86326
Ph: (928)649-1523
Free: 800-949-1005
URL: http://www2.va.gov/directory/guide/facility.asp?ID=5190&dnum=1

Dewey

28479 ■ Farrington House
Mingus Mountain Academy
100 S Dewey Rd.
Dewey, AZ 86327
Ph: (602)335-2000
URL: http://www.mmaaz.com

Douglas

28480 ■ Southeastern Arizona Behavioral Health Services, Inc.
Douglas Clinic
1701 N Douglas Ave.
Douglas, AZ 85607
Ph: (520)364-1286
Fax: (520)805-1221
URL: http://www.seabhs.org/poc/view_doc.php?type=doc&id=1410

Flagstaff

28481 ■ Flagstaff Medical Center Behavioral Health
1200 N Beaver St.
Flagstaff, AZ 86001
Ph: (028)779-3366
URL: http://www.flagstaffmedicalcenter.com

28482 ■ The Guidance Center--Flagstaff
2187 N Vickey St.
Flagstaff, AZ 86004-6106
Ph: (928)527-1899

28483 ■ Northern Arizona Regional Behavioral Health Authority
1300 S Yale St.
Flagstaff, AZ 86001
Ph: (928)774-7128
Free: 877-923-1400
Fax: (928)774-5665
URL: http://www.narbha.com

Fredonia

28484 ■ Community Behavioral Health Services--Fredonia
170 S Main St.
Fredonia, AZ 86022
Ph: (928)643-7230

Glendale

28485 ■ Aurora Behavioral Health System
6015 W. Peoria Ave.
Glendale, AZ 85302
Ph: (623)344-4444
URL: http://www.aurorabehavioral.com

28486 ■ Banner Thunderbird Medical Center
5555 W Thunderbird Rd.
Glendale, AZ 85306
Ph: (602)865-5555
URL: http://www.bannerhealth.com

28487 ■ Jewish Family and Children Services--Glendale
5701 W Talavi Blvd., Ste. 180
Glendale, AZ 85306
Ph: (623)486-8202
URL: http://www.jfcsaz.org

28488 ■ A New Leaf
Jag Center
7101 N 55th Ave.
Glendale, AZ 85301
Ph: (623)847-7040
URL: http://www.turnanewleaf.org/home.asp
Formerly: PREHAB of Arizona.

28489 ■ A New Leaf--N 61st Street, Glendale
8802 N 61st Ave.
Glendale, AZ 85302
Ph: (623)934-1991
URL: http://www.turnanewleaf.org/home.asp
Formerly: PREHAB of Arizona.

28490 ■ Touchstone Behavioral Health, Inc.
6153 W Olive Ave., Ste. 1
Glendale, AZ 85302-4564
Ph: (623)930-8705
URL: http://www.touchstonebh.org/

28491 ■ Triple R Behavioral Health, Inc.
Carol Ann
6009 W Carol Ann Way
Glendale, AZ 85306
Ph: (602)789-1730
URL: http://www.trbh.org/

28492 ■ Triple R Behavioral Health, Inc.
Tonopah
3710 W Tonopah Dr.
Glendale, AZ 85308
Ph: (623)780-1677
URL: http://www.trbh.org/

Globe

28493 ■ Horizon Human Services
Globe Office
415 W Baseline Spur
Globe, AZ 85501
Ph: (928)402-9297

Holbrook

28494 ■ Community Counseling Centers, Inc.--Holbrook
105 N 5th Ave.
Holbrook, AZ 86025-2817
Ph: (928)524-6126

Kingman

28495 ■ Mohave Mental Health Clinic--Sycamore Avenue, Kingman
1743 Sycamore Ave.
Kingman, AZ 86409
Ph: (928)757-8111

28496 ■ Mohave Mental Health Clinic--Western Avenue, Kingman
3505 Western Ave.
Kingman, AZ 86409
Ph: (928)757-8111
URL: http://www.mmhc-inc.org

28497 ■ Veterans Affairs Medical Center
Cottonwood Community Based Outpatient Clinic
1726 E Beverly Ave.
Kingman, AZ 86409
Ph: (928)692-0080
Free: 800-949-1005
URL: http://www2.va.gov/directory/guide/facility.asp?ID=813&dnum=1

Lake Havasu City

28498 ■ Mohave Mental Health Clinic--Lake Havasu City
2187 Swanson Ave.
Lake Havasu City, AZ 86403
Ph: (928)855-3432

Mesa

28499 ■ Family Service Agency
943 S Gilbert Rd., Ste. 204
Mesa, AZ 85204-4441
Ph: (480)507-8619

28500 ■ A New Leaf
Dorothy Mitchell Residence
3505 E University Dr.
Mesa, AZ 85213
Ph: (480)461-5073
URL: http://www.turnanewleaf.org/home.asp
Formerly: PREHAB of Arizona.

28501 ■ A New Leaf--E University Drive, Mesa
868 E University Dr.
Mesa, AZ 85203
Ph: (480)969-4024
URL: http://www.turnanewleaf.org/home.asp
Formerly: PREHAB of Arizona.

28502 ■ A New Leaf
Helaman House
2613 S Power Rd.
Mesa, AZ 85208
Ph: (480)461-5075
URL: http://www.turnanewleaf.org/home.asp
Formerly: PREHAB of Arizona.

28503 ■ A New Leaf
La Mesita Family Shelter
2254 W Main St.
Mesa, AZ 85201
Ph: (480)834-8723
URL: http://www.turnanewleaf.org/home.asp
Formerly: PREHAB of Arizona.

28504 ■ A New Leaf
Larry Simmons Residence
948 N Stapley Dr.
Mesa, AZ 85203
Ph: (480)969-4024
URL: http://www.turnanewleaf.org/home.asp
Formerly: PREHAB of Arizona.

28505 ■ A New Leaf
Mayfield Alternative Youth Center
217 W University Dr.
Mesa, AZ 85201
Ph: (480)464-7468
URL: http://www.turnanewleaf.org/home.asp
Formerly: PREHAB of Arizona.

28506 ■ PREHAB of Arizona
Center for Family Enrichment
1655 E University Dr., Ste. 100
Mesa, AZ 85203
Ph: (480)969-6955
URL: http://www.turnanewleaf.org/home.asp

28507 ■ Southwest Behavioral Health
Brookside Residential
653 W Guadalupe Rd.
Mesa, AZ 85210
Ph: (480)545-1782
URL: http://www.sbhservices.org/index.php?page=site_locations

28508 ■ Southwest Behavioral Health
Mesa Clinic
1255 W Baseline Rd.
Mesa, AZ 85202
Ph: (480)820-5422
URL: http://www.sbhservices.org/index.php?page=site_locations

Nogales

28509 ■ Horizon Human Services
Nogales Office
545 N Grand Ave., Ste. 2
Nogales, AZ 85621
Ph: (520)287-9678

28510 ■ Southeastern Arizona Behavioral Health Services, Inc.
Nogales Outpatient
32 Del Rey Blvd.
Nogales, AZ
Ph: (520)281-9189
Fax: (520)281-0916
URL: http://www.seabhs.org/poc/view_doc.php?type=doc&id=1410

Page

28511 ■ Community Behavioral Health Services--Page
463 S Lake Powell Blvd.
Page, AZ 86040
Ph: (928)645-5113

Payson

28512 ■ Rim Guidance Center
404 W Aero Dr.
Payson, AZ 85547
Ph: (928)474-3303
URL: http://www.sbhservices.org

28513 ■ Round Valley Residential
8985 W Stageline Rd.
Payson, AZ 85541
Ph: (928)468-2399
URL: http://www.sbhservices.org

Phoenix

28514 ■ Amber Ridge
3802 N 27th St., Ste. 112
Phoenix, AZ 85016-6753
Ph: (602)381-8416
URL: http://www.trbh.org

28515 ■ Carl T. Hayden Veterans Affairs Medical Center
Mental Hygiene
650 E Indian School Rd.
Phoenix, AZ 85012
Ph: (602)277-5551
Free: 800-554-7174
URL: http://www.phoenix.va.gov/

28516 ■ Jewish Family and Children's Services
Administrative Headquarters
4220 N 20th Ave.
Phoenix, AZ 85015-5101
Ph: (602)279-7655
URL: http://www.jfcsaz.org/

28517 ■ Marion Medical Center Behavioral Health Annex
2619 E Pierce St.
Phoenix, AZ 85008
Ph: (480)344-2000
URL: http://www.mihs.org

28518 ■ Palm Desert
8313 N 27th Ave., Ste. 165
Phoenix, AZ 85051
Ph: (602)347-0660

28519 ■ Presbyterian Service Agency
2001 W 3rd St., Ste. 104
Phoenix, AZ 85004
Ph: (602)340-1675

28520 ■ Southwest Behavioral Health
3450 N 3rd St.
Phoenix, AZ 85014
Ph: (602)265-8338
URL: http://www.sbhservices.org

28521 ■ Southwest Behavioral Health
Crisis Recovery Unit
1424 S 7th Ave., Bldg. A
Phoenix, AZ 85004
Ph: (602)257-1558
URL: http://www.sbhservices.org

28522 ■ Southwest Behavioral Health
Crisis Recovery Unit II
1424 S 7th Ave., Bldg. B
Phoenix, AZ 85007
Ph: (602)257-8970
URL: http://www.sbhservices.org

28523 ■ Southwest Behavioral Health
Harvard Independent Living
1708 E Harvard St.
Phoenix, AZ 85006-1857
Ph: (602)945-1156
URL: http://www.sbhservices.org
Formerly: Harvard Project.

28524 ■ Southwest Behavioral Health Northern Landing Transitional Living
8135 N 35th Ave., Apt. 1053
Phoenix, AZ 85051
Ph: (602)589-5598
URL: http://www.sbhservices.org

28525 ■ Southwest Behavioral Health Villa Agave
7439 S 7th St.
Phoenix, AZ 85040
Ph: (602)257-4889
URL: http://www.sbhservices.org

28526 ■ Triple R Behavioral Health, Inc.
40 E Mitchell Dr., Ste. 100
Phoenix, AZ 85012
Ph: (602)995-7474
URL: http://www.trbh.org/

28527 ■ Triple R Behavioral Health, Inc. Fairmount
3111 E Fairmount Ave., Apt. 2
Phoenix, AZ 85016
Ph: (602)381-0441
URL: http://www.trbh.org/

28528 ■ Triple R Behavioral Health, Inc. Greenway
2319 W Caribbean Ln.
Phoenix, AZ 85023
Ph: (602)863-2185
URL: http://www.trbh.org/

28529 ■ Triple R Behavioral Health, Inc. Palm Desert
8429 N 27th Ave., Apt. 120
Phoenix, AZ 85051
Ph: (602)995-5949
URL: http://www.trbh.org/

28530 ■ Triple R Behavioral Health, Inc. Palm Desert LTS
8313 N 27th Ave., Apt. 165
Phoenix, AZ 85051
Ph: (602)347-0660
URL: http://www.trbh.org/

28531 ■ Triple R Behavioral Health, Inc. Palm Lane
8531 W Palm Ln.
Phoenix, AZ 85037
Ph: (623)907-2327
URL: http://www.trbh.org/

28532 ■ Triple R Behavioral Health, Inc. Phoenix Clubhouse
755 E Willetta St.
Phoenix, AZ 85006
Ph: (602)262-2100
URL: http://www.trbh.org/

28533 ■ Triple R Behavioral Health, Inc. Raiven Gardens
4017 N 40th St., No. 2
Phoenix, AZ 85018
Ph: (602)955-3288
URL: http://www.trbh.org/

Prescott

28534 ■ Northern Arizona Veterans Affairs Healthcare System
500 Hwy. 89N
Prescott, AZ 86313
Ph: (928)445-4860
Free: 800-949-1005
URL: http://www.prescott.va.gov/

28535 ■ West Yavapai Guidance Clinic
642 Dameron Dr.
Prescott, AZ 86301
Ph: (928)445-5211

Rimrock

28536 ■ Copper Canyon Academy
3090 E Coronado Trail
Rimrock, AZ 86335
Ph: (928)567-1322
URL: http://www.coppercanyonacademy.com

Safford

28537 ■ Southeastern Arizona Behavioral Health Services, Inc. Safford Outpatient
1615 S 1st Ave.
Safford, AZ 85548
Ph: (928)428-4550
Fax: (928)428-4588
URL: http://www.seabhs.org/poc/view_doc.php?type=doc&id=1410

Saint Johns

28538 ■ Little Colorado Behavioral Health Centers
470 W Cleveland Ave.
Saint Johns, AZ 85936
Ph: (928)337-4301

Scottsdale

28539 ■ Devereux Arizona
11000 N Scottsdale Rd., Ste. 260
Scottsdale, AZ 85254
Ph: (480)998-2920
URL: http://www.devereux.org/site/PageServer

28540 ■ Devereux Sweetwater
6436 E Sweetwater Ave.
Scottsdale, AZ 85254
Ph: (480)998-2920
URL: http://www.devereux.org/site/PageServer?pagename=az_sweetwater_rtc

28541 ■ Southwest Behavioral Health Community Counseling Services
3200 N Hayden Rd., Ste. 285
Scottsdale, AZ 85251
Ph: (480)947-6353

Show Low

28542 ■ Community Counseling Centers, Inc.--Show Low
2500 Show Low Lake Rd.
Show Low, AZ 85901
Ph: (928)537-2951
Fax: (928)537-8520

28543 ■ Show Low Veterans Affairs Healthcare Clinic
2450 Show Low Lake Rd., Ste. 1
Show Low, AZ 85901
Ph: (928)532-1069
URL: http://www.phoenix.va.gov/CBOCs/show_low.asp

Sierra Vista

28544 ■ Southern Arizona Veterans Affairs Health Care System Sierra Vista Community Based Outpatient Clinic
101 N Coronado Dr., Ste. A
Sierra Vista, AZ 85653
Ph: (520)429-1529
URL: http://www.tucson.va.gov/CBOCs/SierraVista.asp

Sun City

28545 ■ Northwest Veterans Affairs Healthcare Clinic
10147 Grand Ave., Ste. C1
Sun City, AZ 85351
Ph: (602)222-2630
URL: http://www.phoenix.va.gov/CBOCs/sun_city.asp

Tempe

28546 ■ Presbyterian Service Agency
415 W Southern Ave., Ste. 101
Tempe, AZ 85282
Ph: (480)894-1568

28547 ■ Triple R Behavioral Health, Inc. Villages East
1701 E Don Carlos, Apt. 110
Tempe, AZ 85281
Ph: (480)377-8067
URL: http://www.trbh.org/

28548 ■ Villages West
1631 E Don Carlo, Ste. 108
Tempe, AZ 85281-4349
Ph: (480)967-2299
URL: http://www.trbh.org/

Tucson

28549 ■ CODAC Behavioral Health Services, Inc.
1650 E Fort Lowell, Ste. 202
Tucson, AZ 85719
Ph: (520)327-4505
E-mail: mail@codac.org
URL: http://www.codac.org

28550 ■ CODAC Outpatient
4901 E 5th St.
Tucson, AZ 85711-2201
Ph: (520)318-9222
URL: http://www.codac.org/

28551 ■ La Frontera Casa Alegre
1441 S No Le Hace
Tucson, AZ 85713-1120
Ph: (520)622-5805
URL: http://www.lafrontera.org

28552 ■ La Frontera Casa de Vida
1900 W Speedway Blvd.
Tucson, AZ 85745-2215
Ph: (520)792-0591
URL: http://www.lafrontera.org

28553 ■ La Frontera Center, Inc.
502 W 29th St.
Tucson, AZ 85713-3394
Ph: (520)884-9920
URL: http://www.lafrontera.org

28554 ■ La Frontera East Clinic
2222 N Craycroft Rd., Ste. 120
Tucson, AZ 85712-2898
Ph: (520)296-3296
URL: http://www.lafrontera.org

28555 ■ La Frontera Hope Center
260 S Scott Ave.
Tucson, AZ 85701-1998
Ph: (520)884-8470
URL: http://www.lafrontera.org

28556 ■ La Frontera La Pagosa
1909 E 7th St.
Tucson, AZ 85719
Ph: (520)791-9495
URL: http://www.lafrontera.org

28557 ■ La Frontera Main Clinic Child and Family Center
502 W 29th St.
Tucson, AZ 85713-3394
Ph: (520)884-9920
URL: http://www.lafrontera.org

28558 ■ La Frontera Pima House
4156 E Pima St.
Tucson, AZ 85712-3146
Ph: (520)325-2644
URL: http://www.lafrontera.org

28559 ■ La Frontera Psychiatric Health Facility
1601 E Apache Park Pl.
Tucson, AZ 85714-1775
Ph: (520)746-0260
URL: http://www.lafrontera.org

28560 ■ La Frontera Rapp Programs
748 N Stone Ave.
Tucson, AZ 85701
Ph: (520)882-8422
URL: http://www.lafrontera.org

28561 ■ Mountain Case Management
3620 N Mountain Ave.
Tucson, AZ 85719
Ph: (520)882-5145
URL: http://www.lafrontera.org

28562 ■ Sierra Tucson, Inc.
39580 S Lago Del Oro Pkwy.
Tucson, AZ 85739
Free: 800-624-9001
URL: http://www.sierratucson.com/

28563 ■ Sonora Behavioral Health Hospital
6050 N Corona Rd., Ste. 3
Tucson, AZ 85704
Ph: (520)469-8700
URL: http://www.sonorabehavioral.com/

28564 ■ Southeast Tucson Community Based Outpatient Clinic
7395 S Houghton Rd., Ste. 129
Tucson, AZ 85747
Ph: (520)792-1450
Free: 800-470-8262
URL: http://www.tucson.va.gov/CBOCs/SEClinic.asp

28565 ■ Veterans Affairs Northwest Tucson Clinic
2945 W Ina Rd.
Tucson, AZ 85741
Ph: (520)792-1450
Free: 800-470-8262
URL: http://www.tucson.va.gov/CBOCs/NWClinic.asp

Wickenburg

28566 ■ The Meadows
1655 N Tegner St.
Wickenburg, AZ 85390
Ph: (928)684-3926

28567 ■ A New Leaf--Wickenburg
255 N Washington
Wickenburg, AZ 85399
Ph: (520)684-7894
URL: http://www.turnanewleaf.org/
Formerly: PREHAB of Arizona.

28568 ■ Remuda Ranch Center for Anorexia & Bulimia
1 E Apache St.
Wickenburg, AZ 85390
Ph: (928)684-3913
Free: 800-445-1900
E-mail: info@remudaranch.com
URL: http://www.remudaranch.com/

Williams

28569 ■ The Guidance Center--Williams
220 W Grant St.
Williams, AZ 86046-2399
Ph: (928)635-4272

Winslow

28570 ■ Community Counseling Centers, Inc.--Winslow
1015 E 3rd St.
Winslow, AZ 86047
Ph: (928)289-4658

Yuma

28571 ■ Southern Arizona Veterans Affairs Healthcare System
Yuma Community Based Outpatient Clinic
2555 E Gila Ridge Rd.
Yuma, AZ 85365
Ph: (520)629-4952
Free: 800-470-8262
URL: http://www.tucson.va.gov/CBOCs/Yuma.asp

ARKANSAS

Alturas

28572 ■ Modoc County Mental Health Services
441 N Main St.
Alturas, AR 96101
Ph: (530)233-6312
URL: http://www.modoccohealthservices.com/

Arkadelphia

28573 ■ Ascent Children's Health Services, Arkadelphia
2410 Pine St.
Arkadelphia, AR 71923
Ph: (870)245-2210
Fax: (970)245-2225
URL: http://www.ascentchs.com

28574 ■ Community Counseling--Arkadelphia
201 N 26th St.
Arkadelphia, AR 71923
Ph: (870)246-4123

Ash Flat

28575 ■ Health Resources of Arkansas, Inc.
Ash Flat Behavioral Health Care
714A Ash Flat Dr.
Ash Flat, AR 72512
Ph: (870)994-2106
Free: 866-533-1761
URL: http://www.healthresourcesofarkansas.com/content/
Formerly: North Arkansas Human Services System Ash Flat Clinic.

Augusta

28576 ■ Health Resources of Arkansas, Inc.
Augusta Behavioral Health Care
623 N 9th St.
Augusta, AR 72006-2129
Ph: (870)347-3254
URL: http://www.healthresourcesofarkansas.com/content/
Formerly: North Arkansas Human Services System Augusta Clinic.

28577 ■ Pine Valley Rehabilitative Day Services
Augusta Inn
Hwy. 64 E
Augusta, AR 72006
Ph: (870)347-5906

Barling

28578 ■ Vista Health Services--Arkansas Psychiatric Care
10301 Mayo Dr.
Barling, AR 72923
Ph: (479)494-5700
Free: 866-813-HOPE
URL: http://www.vistahealthservices.com/locations

Batesville

28579 ■ Ascent Children's Health Services, Batesville
2040 Fitzhugh St.
Batesville, AR 72501
Ph: (870)793-3334
Fax: (870)793-3474
URL: http://www.ascentchs.com

28580 ■ Batesville Behavioral Health Clinic
1800 Myers St.
Batesville, AR 72501
Ph: (870)793-8925
URL: http://www.healthresourcesofarkansas.com/content/

28581 ■ White River Medical Center Behavioral Health
1710 Harrison St.
Batesville, AR 72501
Ph: (870)793-1000
URL: http://www.wrmc.com

Benton

28582 ■ Ascent children's Health Services, Benton
3214 Winchester
Benton, AR 72015
Ph: (501)326-6160
Fax: (501)326-6161
URL: http://www.ascentchs.com

28583 ■ Birch Tree Communities, Inc.
AHC Campus
6701 Hwy. 67 S, Bldg. 4
Benton, AR 72015
Ph: (501)315-3344
URL: http://www.birchtree.org/

28584 ■ Birch Tree Communities, Inc.
Benton
1718 Old Hot Springs Hwy.
Benton, AR 72015
Ph: (501)315-3344
URL: http://www.birchtree.org/

28585 ■ Birch Tree Communities, Inc.
Benton Town Center
1502 Mary Kaye Ave.
Benton, AR 72015
Ph: (501)315-3344
URL: http://www.birchtree.org/

28586 ■ Birch Tree Communities, Inc.
Hope House
6701 Hwy. 67 S, Bldg. 70
Benton, AR 72015
Ph: (501)315-3344
URL: http://www.birchtree.org/

28587 ■ Counseling Clinic, Inc.
307 E Sevier St.
Benton, AR 72015
Ph: (501)315-4224

Berryville

28588 ■ Ozark Guidance Center, Inc.--Berryville
208 Hwy. 62 W
Berryville, AR 72616
Ph: (870)423-2758
URL: http://www.ozarkguidance.org/

Blytheville

28589 ■ Ascent Children's Health Services, Blytheville
1510 Byrum Rd.
Blytheville, AR 72315
Ph: (870)532-2600
Fax: (870)532-9484
URL: http://www.ascentchs.com

Booneville

28590 ■ Western Arkansas Counseling and Guidance
174 N Welsh St.
Booneville, AR 72927-4130
Ph: (479)675-3909

Free: 800-542-1031
Fax: (479)452-5847
E-mail: wacgc@wacgc.org
URL: http://www.wacgc.org
Formerly: Logan County Clinic.

Cabot

28591 ■ Professional Counseling Associates - Cabot Clinic
405 N 2nd St.
Cabot, AR 72023
Ph: (501)843-3503
URL: http://www.pca-ar.org/

Camden

28592 ■ Ouachita County Medical Center Behavioral Health
638 California Ave. SW
Camden, AR 71701
Ph: (870)836-1200
URL: http://www.ouachitamedcenter.com

28593 ■ South Arkansas Regional Health Center
Camden Division
211 Jackson St. SW
Camden, AR 71701-3941
Ph: (479)836-5743
Free: 800-825-1554

Clarksville

28594 ■ Birch Tree Communities, Inc.
Clarksville
522 Mills Rd.
Clarksville, AR 72830
Ph: (501)315-3344
URL: http://www.birchtree.org/

28595 ■ Counseling Associates, Inc.
Clarksville Clinic
1021 Poplar St.
Clarksville, AR 72830-4428
Ph: (479)754-8610
URL: http://www.caiinc.org/
Formerly: Sycamore Point.

Clinton

28596 ■ Birch Tree Communities, Inc.
Clinton
1303 Hwy. 65 S
Clinton, AR 72031
Ph: (501)745-6644
Fax: (501)303-3177
URL: http://www.birchtree.org/

28597 ■ Health Resources of Arkansas, Inc.
Clinton Behavioral Health Clinic
1303 Hwy. 67 S
Clinton, AR 72031
Ph: (501)745-4584
Free: 866-533-1765
URL: http://www.healthresourcesofarkansas.com/content/

Conway

28598 ■ Birch Tree Communities, Inc.
Conway
704 4th Ave.
Conway, AR 72033
Ph: (501)315-3344
Fax: (501)303-3263
URL: http://www.birchtree.org/

28599 ■ Counseling Associates, Inc.
Park Place Clinic
350 Salem Rd., Ste. 1
Conway, AR 72034
Ph: (501)327-4889
Fax: (501)329-5508
URL: http://www.caiinc.org/faulkner.htm

28600 ■ Haven Children's Center
1701 Donaghey
Conway, AR 72032-4928
Ph: (501)327-1701

28601 ■ McCormack Place Apartments
855 S Salem Rd.
Conway, AR 72034
Ph: (479)968-1298
URL: http://www.caiinc.org/faulkner.htm

Crossett

28602 ■ Ashley County Medical Center Behavioral Health
1015 Unity Rd.
Crossett, AR 71635
Ph: (870)364-4111
URL: http://www.acmconline.org

28603 ■ Delta Counseling Associates--Crossett
1308 W 5th St.
Crossett, AR 71635
Ph: (870)364-6471
URL: http://www.deltacounseling.org/

Dardanelle

28604 ■ River Valley Medical Center
200 N 3rd St.
Dardanelle, AR 72834
Ph: (479)229-4677

El Dorado

28605 ■ South Arkansas Regional Health Center
715 N College St.
El Dorado, AR 71730
Ph: (870)862-7921
URL: http://www.sarhc.org/

28606 ■ South Arkansas Regional Health Center
Community Support Program
715 N College Ave.
El Dorado, AR 71730
Ph: (870)862-7921
URL: http://www.sarhc.org/

28607 ■ South Arkansas Regional Health Center
El Dorado Connections
824 Camp
El Dorado, AR 71730
Ph: (870)884-7080
URL: http://www.sarhc.org/page4.htm

28608 ■ South Arkansas Regional Health Center
Hope House
750 N Flenniken
El Dorado, AR 71730-4316
Ph: (870)862-2465
URL: http://www.sarhc.org/page4.htm

28609 ■ South Arkansas Regional Health Center
Recovery Center
710 W Grove St.
El Dorado, AR 71730-4481
Ph: (870)864-2475
URL: http://www.sarhc.org/page4.htm

Fayetteville

28610 ■ Fayetteville, Arkansas Veterans Affairs Medical Center
1100 N College Ave.
Fayetteville, AR 72703
Ph: (479)443-4301
Free: 800-691-8387
Fax: (479)444-5089
URL: http://www.fayettevillear.va.gov/contact/index.asp

28611 ■ Ozark Guidance Center, Inc.
Watson Street Apartments
215 Watson St.
Fayetteville, AR 72701
Ph: (479)442-9399
URL: http://www.ozarkguidance.org/

28612 ■ Springwoods Behavioral Health
1125 N North Hills Blvd.
Fayetteville, AR 72703
Ph: (479)973-6000
URL: http://www.springwoodsbehavioral.com

Forrest City

28613 ■ Forest City Medical Center Behavioral Health
1601 New Castle Rd.
Forrest City, AR 72335
Ph: (870)261-0000
URL: http://www.forestcitymedicalcenter.com

Fort Smith

28614 ■ Veterans Affairs Medical Center
Fort Smith Community Based Outpatient Clinic
1500 Dodson Ave., Sparks Medical Plz.
Fort Smith, AR 72917
Ph: (479)709-6850
Free: 877-604-0798
URL: http://www2.va.gov/directory/guide/facility.asp?ID=5402&dnum=1

28615 ■ Western Arkansas Counseling and Guidance Center, Inc.
3111 S 70th St.
Fort Smith, AR 72917
Ph: (479)452-6650
Free: 800-542-1031
Fax: (479)452-5847
E-mail: wacgc@wacgc.org
URL: http://www.wacgc.org

28616 ■ Western Arkansas Counseling and Guidance Center
NEW Clubhouse
3109 S 70th St.
Fort Smith, AR 72903-2771
Ph: (479)452-9490
URL: http://www.wacgc.org

28617 ■ Western Arkansas Counseling and Guidance Center
Therapeutic Children's Homes
7302 Rogers Ave.
Fort Smith, AR 72903-4164
Ph: (479)484-0059
Fax: (479)484-6749
E-mail: scarborough@wacqc.org
URL: http://www.wacqc.org

28618 ■ Western Arkansas Counseling and Guidance Center
Westark RSVP
401 N 13th St.
Fort Smith, AR 72901
Ph: (479)783-4155
URL: http://www.wacgc.org

Gassville

28619 ■ Baxter Regional Medical Center
Center for Individual and Family Development
7345 Hwy 62 W
Gassville, AR 72635
Ph: (870)435-5511
URL: http://www.baxterregional.org

Harris

28620 ■ Harris Hospital Behavioral Health
1205 McClain St.
Harris, AR 72112
Ph: (870)523-8911
URL: http://www.harrishospital.com

Harrison

28621 ■ Health Resources of Arkansas
724 W Spring Rd.
Harrison, AR 72602
Ph: (501)268-4181
URL: http://www.healthresourcesofarkansas.com

28622 ■ Ozark Counseling Services, Inc.
Maple Corner
308 S Pine St.
Harrison, AR 72601
Ph: (870)741-8219
Fax: (870)741-7064
URL: http://www.ozarkguidance.org/

28623 ■ Veterans Affairs Medical Center
Harrison Community Based Outpatient Clinic
707 N Main St.
Harrison, AR 72601
Ph: (870)741-3592
URL: http://www2.va.gov/directory/guide/facility.asp?ID=5403&dnum=1

Hazen

28624 ■ Professional Counseling Associates, Inc.--Hazen
109 N Hazen Ave.
Hazen, AR 72064
Ph: (870)255-3527
URL: http://www.pca-ar.org/contactus.html

Heber Springs

28625 ■ Health Resources of Arkansas, Inc.
Heber Springs Behavioral Health Center
1716 W Searcy
Heber Springs, AR 72543
Ph: (501)362-7595
Free: 866-533-1763
URL: http://www.healthresourcesofarkansas.com/
Formerly: North Arkansas Human Services System Heber Clinic.

Helena

28626 ■ Counseling Services of Eastern Arkansas
801 Newman Dr.
Helena, AR 72342
Ph: (870)338-3900
URL: http://www.csoea.org/

Hope

28627 ■ Hempstead County Clinic
300 E 20th St.
Hope, AR 71801-8217
Ph: (870)777-9051

Hot Springs

28628 ■ Community Counseling
Excel/Advantage Programs
505 W Grand Ave.
Hot Springs, AR 71901
Ph: (501)624-7111
URL: http://www.communitycounselingservices.com

28629 ■ Community Counseling Services, Inc.--Hot Springs
125 Dons Way
Hot Springs, AR 71913
Ph: (501)624-7111
Free: 800-264-2410
URL: http://www.communitycounselingservices.org/

28630 ■ Veterans Affairs Medical Center
Hot Springs Community Based Outpatient Clinic
1661 Airport Rd., Ste. E
Hot Springs, AR 71913
Ph: (501)881-4112
Fax: (501)767-6501
URL: http://www2.va.gov/directory/guide/facility.asp?ID=5404&dnum=1

Huntsville

28631 ■ Ozark Guidance Center, Inc.--Huntsville
1104 N College St.
Huntsville, AR 72740
Ph: (479)738-2878
URL: http://www.ozarkguidance.org/about_us/locations/

Jacksonville

28632 ■ Professional Counseling Associates--Jacksonville
1109 Burman
Jacksonville, AR 72076
Ph: (501)982-7515
URL: http://www.pca-ar.org/

28633 ■ Transitions
1400 Braden St.
Jacksonville, AR 72076
Ph: (501)985-7000
URL: http://www.northmetromed.com

Jonesboro

28634 ■ Ascent Children's Health Services, Glendale St.
806 Glendale St.
Jonesboro, AR 72401
Ph: (870)933-9528
Fax: (870)93-9778
URL: http://www.ascentchs.com

28635 ■ Ascent Children's Health Services, Turman Dr.
3012 Turman Dr.
Jonesboro, AR 72404
Ph: (870)819-0269
URL: http://www.ascentchs.com

28636 ■ Memphis Veterans Affairs Medical Center
Jonesboro Community Based Outpatient Clinic
1901 Woodsprings Rd.
Jonesboro, AR 72401
Ph: (870)268-6962
Fax: (870)268-1028
URL: http://www.memphis.va.gov/visitors/jonesboro.asp

28637 ■ Mid-South Health Systems, Inc.
Craighead County
2707 Browns Ln.
Jonesboro, AR 72401
Ph: (870)972-4000
Fax: (870)972-4968
URL: http://www.mshs.org/

28638 ■ Saint Bernards Counseling Center
615 A E Mathews
Jonesboro, AR 72401
Ph: (870)930-9090
URL: http://www.sbrmc.com/departments-services/clinical/behavior-health-unit/

Lake Village

28639 ■ Delta Counseling Associates--Lake Village
1127 2nd St.
Lake Village, AR 71653
Ph: (870)265-3808
URL: http://www.deltacounseling.org/

Little Rock

28640 ■ Baptist Health Medical Center
Behavioral Health
9601 Interstate 630, exit 7
Little Rock, AR 72205
Ph: (501)202-2000
URL: http://www.baptist-health.com

28641 ■ Center for Youth and Families
Therapeutic Independent Living
6425 W 12th
Little Rock, AR 72204
Ph: (501)666-7233
URL: http://www.centersforyouthandfamilies.org

28642 ■ John L. McClellan Memorial VAMC
Mental Hygiene Unit
4300 W 7th St.
Little Rock, AR 72205
Ph: (501)25-1000
URL: http://www.va.gov

28643 ■ Lawrence Schmidt Center
Vera Lloyd Presbyterian Home
1501 N University Home
Little Rock, AR 72207
Ph: (501)664-7777
URL: http://www.veralloyd.org

28644 ■ Little Rock Community Mental Health Center
4400 Shuffield Dr.
Little Rock, AR 72205-7100
Ph: (501)686-9300
URL: http://www.lrcmhc.org/content/index.php

28645 ■ Little Rock Community Mental Health Center
Mid-Arkansas Substance Abuse Center
4601 W 7th St.
Little Rock, AR 72205
Ph: (501)686-9393
URL: http://www.lrcmhc.org/content/index.php

28646 ■ Little Rock Community Mental Health Center
Pinnacle House
10201 W Daisy L. Gatson Bates Dr.
Little Rock, AR 72202
Ph: (501)371-9058
URL: http://www.lrcmhc.org/content/index.php

28647 ■ Little Rock Community Mental Health Center
Up and Up Rehabilitative Day Treatment
3601 W Roosevelt Rd.
Little Rock, AR 72204-5560
Ph: (501)666-8259
URL: http://www.lrcmhc.org/content/index.php
Formerly: Up and Up Day Program.

28648 ■ Professional Counseling Associates
Southwest Little Rock Clinic
9110 Geyer Springs Rd.
Little Rock, AR 72209
Ph: (501)568-4294
URL: http://www.pca-ar.org/Locations.htm

28649 ■ Saint Vincent Doctors Hospital
Behavioral Health Services
2 Saint Vincent Circle
Little Rock, AR 72205
Ph: (501)552-6000
URL: http://www.stvincenthealth.com

28650 ■ Treatment Homes, Inc.
700 W 4th St.
Little Rock, AR 72201
Ph: (501)372-5039
URL: http://treatmenthomes.org/

28651 ■ Youth Emergency Shelter
6425 W 12th St.
Little Rock, AR 72204
Ph: (501)666-7233
URL: http://www.centersforyouthandfamilies.org

28652 ■ Youth Home, Inc.
20400 Colonel Glenn Rd.
Little Rock, AR 72210
Ph: (501)821-5500
Free: 800-728-6452
URL: http://www.youthhome.org/

Lonoke

28653 ■ Professional Counseling Associates Lonoke Clinic
109 W 2nd St.
Lonoke, AR 72086
Ph: (501)676-3151
URL: http://www.pca-ar.org/Locations.htm

Magnolia

28654 ■ South Arkansas Regional Health Center Magnolia Division
412 N Vine St
Magnolia, AR 71753-2842
Ph: (479)234-7500

Malvern

28655 ■ Birch Tree Communities, Inc. Malvern
1400 E Page Ave.
Malvern, AR 72104
Ph: (501)315-3344
URL: http://www.birchtree.org

28656 ■ Community Counseling - Malvern
1615 Martin Luther King Blvd.
Malvern, AR 72104-2233
Ph: (501)332-5236
Free: 800-264-2410
URL: http://www.hsccs.org/poc/view_doc.php?type=doc&id=3914

28657 ■ HSC Medical Center Behavioral Health Services
1001 Schneider Dr.
Malvern, AR 72104
Ph: (501)337-4911
URL: http://www.hscmc.org

Marianna

28658 ■ Counseling Services of Eastern Arkansas Marianna Clinic
444 Atkins St.
Marianna, AR 72360-2110
Ph: (870)295-4050
Fax: (870)295-4054
URL: http://www.csoea.org/view/41

Marshall

28659 ■ Ozark Counseling Services, Inc.--Marshall
200 E Main St.
Marshall, AR 72650
Ph: (870)448-3724
URL: http://www.healthresourcesofarkansas.com/content/

McCrory

28660 ■ Pine Valley Day Treatment
900 W Poplar St.
McCrory, AR 72101
Free: 866-533-1757
URL: http://www.healthresourcesofarkansas.com

McGehee

28661 ■ Delta Counseling Associates--McGehee
2410 Hwy 65 N
McGehee, AR 71654
Ph: (870)222-3107
URL: http://www.deltacounseling.org

Melbourne

28662 ■ Birch Tree Communities, Inc., Melbourne, AR
102 Conniebrook Lane
Melbourne, AR 72556
Ph: (501)315-3344
URL: http://www.birchtree.org

28663 ■ Health Resources of Arkansas, Inc. Melbourne Behavioral Health Clinic
1109 E Main St.
Melbourne, AR 72556
Ph: (870)368-4397
Free: 866-533-1760
URL: http://www.healthresourcesofarkansas.com/content/

Mena

28664 ■ Mena Medical Center Senior Behavioral Health
311 Marrow St. N
Mena, AR 71953
Ph: (479)394-7400
Free: 888-394-7300
URL: http://www.menaregional.com/senior_health.html
Formerly: Behavioral Health.

28665 ■ Western Arkansas Counseling and Guidance Center Polk County Clinic
307 Cherry St.
Mena, AR 71953-4382
Ph: (479)394-5277
URL: http://www.wacgc.org

Monticello

28666 ■ Delta Counseling Associates, Inc.--Monticello
790 Roberts Dr.
Monticello, AR 71655
Ph: (870)367-2461
URL: http://www.deltacounseling.org/

Morrilton

28667 ■ Counseling Associates, Inc. Morrilton Clinic
8 Hospital Dr.
Morrilton, AR 72110
Ph: (501)354-1561
Fax: (501)354-1564
URL: http://www.caiinc.org/conway.htm

28668 ■ Saint Anthony's Healthcare Center of Morrilton
4 Hospital Dr.
Morrilton, AR 72110
Ph: (501)977-2300
URL: http://www.stanthonysmorrilton.com/

Mountain Home

28669 ■ Baxter Regional Medical Center Behavioral Health
624 Hospital Dr.
Mountain Home, AR 72653
Ph: (870)508-1000
URL: http://www.baxterregional.org/

Mountain View

28670 ■ Birch Tree Communities, Inc., Mountain View, AR
417 W Peabody Ave.
Mountain View, AR 72560
Ph: (501)315-3344
URL: http://www.birchtree.org

28671 ■ Health Resources of Arkansas, Inc. Mountain View Behavioral Health Clinic
211 Blanchard Ave.
Mountain View, AR 72560
Ph: (870)269-8100
URL: http://www.healthresourcesofarkansas.com/content/

Nashville

28672 ■ Nashville Clinic
508 N 2nd St.
Nashville, AR 71852-3925
Ph: (870)845-3110
Formerly: Howard County Clinic.

Newport

28673 ■ Birch Tree Communities, Inc. Newport
418 Beech St.
210 3rd St.
Newport, AR 72112
Ph: (501)315-3344
URL: http://www.birchtree.org/

28674 ■ Health Resources of Arkansas, Inc. Newport Behavioral Health Care
1507 N Pecan St.
Newport, AR 72112
Ph: (870)523-3643
Free: 866-533-1758
URL: http://www.healthresourcesofarkansas.com/content/behavior_health.php
Formerly: North Arkansas Human Services System Newport Clinic.

North Little Rock

28675 ■ Ascent Children's Health Services, North Little Rock
4107 Richards Rd.
North Little Rock, AR 72117
Ph: (501)955-2220
Fax: (501)955-5531
URL: http://www.ascentchs.com

28676 ■ Eugene J. Towbin Healthcare Center
2200 Ft. Roots Dr.
North Little Rock, AR 72114
Ph: (501)257-1000
URL: http://www.littlerock.va.gov/

28677 ■ Professional Counseling Associates--North Little Rock
4354 Stockton Dr.
North Little Rock, AR 72117
Ph: (501)955-7600
URL: http://www.pca-ar.org/contactus.html

Ozark

28678 ■ Western Arkansas Counseling and Guidance Center Franklin County Clinic
1600 N 18th St.
Ozark, AR 72949
Ph: (479)667-2497
URL: http://www.wacgc.org

Paragould

28679 ■ Ascent Children's Health Services, Paragould
1910 Rector Rd.
Paragould, AR 72450
Ph: (870)240-8500
Fax: (870)240-8505
URL: http://www.ascentchs.com

28680 ■ Mid-South Health Systems, Inc. Greene County
28 Southpointe Dr.
Paragould, AR 72450
Ph: (870)239-2244
Free: 800-356-3035
Fax: (870)236-1616
URL: http://www.mshs.org/view/42

28681 ■ Veterans Affairs Medical Center Paragould Clinic
1101 Morgan St.
Paragould, AR 72450
Ph: (870)236-9756
URL: http://www2.va.gov/directory/guide/facility.asp?ID=5257&dnum=1

Paris

28682 ■ Western Arkansas Counseling and Guidance Center Logan County Clinic
415 S 6th St.
Paris, AR 72855-4511
Ph: (479)963-2140
URL: http://www.wacgc.org/

Perryville

28683 ■ Counseling Associates, Inc. Perryville Clinic
112 S Pine St.
Perryville, AR 72126
Ph: (501)889-5185
URL: http://www.caiinc.org/

Pine Bluff

28684 ■ Jefferson Regional Medical Center Behavioral Health
1600 W 40th Ave.
Pine Bluff, AR 71603
Ph: (870)541-7100
URL: http://www.jrmc.org

Pocahontas

28685 ■ Inspirations Outpatient Counseling Center
2801 Medical Center Dr.
Pocahontas, AR 72455
Ph: (870)892-6000

Rose Bud

28686 ■ Cedar Mountain Rehabilitative Day Services
931 Hwy. 5
Rose Bud, AR 72137-9721
Ph: (501)556-4210
URL: http://www.healthresourcesofarkansas.com/content/

Russellville

28687 ■ Birch Tree Communities, Inc. Russellville
1000 Houston Ave.
Russellville, AR 72801
Ph: (501)315-3344
URL: http://www.birchtree.org/

28688 ■ Counseling Associates, Inc. Russellville Clinic
110 Skyline Dr.
Russellville, AR 72801
Ph: (479)968-1298
Fax: (479)968-6053
URL: http://www.caiinc.org/pope.htm

28689 ■ Houston Group Home
1000 S Houston Ave.
Russellville, AR 72801
Ph: (479)968-2263

28690 ■ Lighthouse--Russellville
1402 E 16th St.
Russellville, AR 72802
Ph: (479)890-3045
Fax: (479)967-9951
URL: http://www.caiinc.org/pope.htm

28691 ■ Russellville Transitional Crisis Unit
1404 E 16th St.
Russellville, AR 72802
Ph: (479)967-1397

Searcy

28692 ■ Searcy Behavioral
3302 E Moore Ave.
Searcy, AR 72143
Ph: (501)279-9220
URL: http://www.healthresourcesofarkansas.com

28693 ■ Searcy Outreach
403 Poplar St., Ste. A
Searcy, AR 72143
Ph: (501)279-9220
Fax: (501)279-9450
URL: http://rivendellofarkansas.com

28694 ■ Wilbur D. Mills Center Substance Abuse Treatment Center
3204 E Moore Ave.
Searcy, AR 72143
Ph: (501)268-7777

Sherwood

28695 ■ Professional Counseling Associates--Sherwood
7800 Hwy. 107
Sherwood, AR 72120
Ph: (501)835-4174
URL: http://www.pca-ar.org/contactus.html

Siloam Springs

28696 ■ Ozark Guidance Center, Inc.--Siloam Springs
710 Holly St.
Siloam Springs, AR 72761
Ph: (479)524-8618
URL: http://www.ozarkguidance.org/about_us/locations/

Springdale

28697 ■ Ozark Guidance Center, Inc.--Springdale
4960 Springhouse Dr.
Springdale, AR 72762
Ph: (479)750-0700
URL: http://www.ozarlguidance.org

28698 ■ Ozark Guidance Center, Inc. Williams Building
2400 S 48th St.
Springdale, AR 72762
Ph: (479)750-2020
Free: 800-234-7052
URL: http://www.ozarkguidance.org

Star City

28699 ■ Southeast Arkansas Behavioral Healthcare Star City Clinic
612 E Arkansas St.
Star City, AR 71667
Ph: (870)628-4181
URL: http://www.sabhs.org/

Stuttgart

28700 ■ Southeast Arkansas Behavioral Healthcare Stuttgart Clinic
121 Commercial Dr. B
Stuttgart, AR 72160
Ph: (870)673-1633
URL: http://www.sabhs.org/

Texarkana

28701 ■ Southwest Arkansas Counseling Mental Health Center
2904 Arkansas Blvd.
Texarkana, AR 71854
Ph: (870)773-4655

Van Buren

28702 ■ Western Arkansas Counseling and Guidance Center Crawford County Clinic
2705 Oak Ln.
Van Buren, AR 72956-4816
Ph: (479)474-8084
URL: http://www.wacgc.org

Waldron

28703 ■ Scott County Clinic
1045 Rice St.
Waldron, AR 72958
Ph: (479)637-2468
URL: http://www.wacgc.org

Walnut Ridge

28704 ■ Mid-South Health Systems, Inc.--Lawrence County
102 S Larkspur Ln.
Walnut Ridge, AR 72476
Ph: (870)886-7924
URL: http://www.mshs.org/

West Memphis

28705 ■ Ascent Children's Health Services, West Memphis
413 W Tyler Ave.
West Memphis, AR 72301
Ph: (870)733-1200
Fax: (870)733-3269
URL: http://www.ascentchs.com

28706 ■ Counseling Services of Eastern Arkansas/West Memphis Clinic Crittenden County
905 N 7th St.
West Memphis, AR 72301
Ph: (870)735-5118
Fax: (870)735-5260
URL: http://www.csoea.org/view/41

Yellville

28707 ■ Ozark Counseling Services, Inc.--Yellville
319 Hwy 14 S, Ste. 1
Yellville, AR 72687
Ph: (870)449-5177
Free: 866-308-9927
URL: http://www.usnodrugs.com

CALIFORNIA

Alameda

28708 ■ Alameda Community Support Center and Children's Outpatient Services
1429 Oak St.
Alameda, CA 94501
Ph: (510)522-4668
Formerly: Alameda Mental Health Services.

28709 ■ Alameda Family Services
2325 Clement Ave.
Alameda, CA 94501
Ph: (510)629-6300
URL: http://www.xanthos.org

28710 ■ Four Bridges Creative Living Center
1912 Central Ave.
Alameda, CA 94501-2623
Ph: (510)750-8810

Albany

28711 ■ New Bridge Foundation
979 San Pablo Ave.
Albany, CA 94706
Ph: (510)548-7270
Free: 800-785-2400
URL: http://www.new-bridge.org/

Altadena

28712 ■ El-Nido Residential
2933 El Nido Dr.
Altadena, CA 91001
Ph: (626)395-7100
URL: http://www.xznthos.org

Anaheim

28713 ■ Canyon Acres Children and Family Services--Anaheim
160 S Fairmont Blvd.
Anaheim, CA 92808
Ph: (714)998-3272
URL: http://www.canyonacres.org/main.asp

28714 ■ Veterans Affairs Medical Center
Anaheim Community Based Outpatient Clinic
Professional Ctr., 3rd Fl., Ste. 303
1801 W Romneya Dr.
Anaheim, CA 92801
Ph: (714)780-5400
URL: http://www2.va.gov/directory/guide/facility.asp?ID=5105&dnum=1

28715 ■ Western Medical Center, Anaheim
Behavioral Health Services
1025 S Anaheim Blvd.
Anaheim, CA 92805
Ph: (714)533-6220
URL: http://www.westernmedicalcenter.com

28716 ■ Western Youth Services--Anaheim
505 N Euclid, Ste. 300
Anaheim, CA 92801
Ph: (714)871-5646
URL: http://www.westernyouthservices.org/

Angwin

28717 ■ Crestwood Behavioral Health--Angwin
295 Pine Breeze Dr.
Angwin, CA 94508
Ph: (707)965-2461
URL: http://www.crestwoodbehavioralhealth.com/angwin.html

Antioch

28718 ■ East County Children's Mental Health
3501 Lone Tree Way, Ste. 200
Antioch, CA 94509
Ph: (925)427-8664
URL: http://cchealth.org

28719 ■ Family Stress Center
315 G St.
Antioch, CA 94509
Ph: (925)706-8477

28720 ■ Kaiser Permanente Mental Health
2213 Buchanan Rd., Ste. 203
Antioch, CA 94509
Ph: (925)779-5810
URL: http://www.wellness.com/antioch/Kaiserpermante

Arcadia

28721 ■ Arcadia Mental Health
330 E Live Oak Ave.
Arcadia, CA 91006-5617
Ph: (626)821-5858

28722 ■ Pacific Clinics
800 S Santa Anita Ave.
Arcadia, CA 91006-3555
Ph: (626)254-5000

Arcata

28723 ■ Humboldt Family Service Center
801 Crescent Way
Arcata, CA 95521
Ph: (707)443-7358
Fax: (707)443-1092
URL: http://www.humboldtfamilyservicecenter.org/

Arroyo Grande

28724 ■ Arroyo Grande Clinic
354 S Halcyon Rd., Ste. C
Arroyo Grande, CA 93420
Ph: (805)473-7060
URL: http://www.slocounty.ca.gov

Atascadero

28725 ■ San Luis Obispo County Mental Health
Atascadero Clinic
5575 Hospital Dr.
Atascadero, CA 93422
Ph: (805)461-6060
Free: 800-838-1381
Formerly: North County Mental Health Services.

Atwater

28726 ■ Veterans Affairs Central California Health Care Services
Veterans Affairs Castle OPC
3605 Hospital Rd., Ste. D
Atwater, CA 95301
Ph: (209)381-0105
URL: http://www2.va.gov/directory/guide/facility.asp?ID=5217&dnum=All

Auburn

28727 ■ Auburn Clinic
Sierra Family Services, Inc.
381 A Nevada St,
Auburn, CA 95603
Ph: (503)885-0441
URL: http://www.sierrafamily.org

28728 ■ Placer County Mental Health Services--Auburn
11512 B Ave.
Auburn, CA 95603-2605
Ph: (530)889-7240
URL: http://www.placer.ca.gov/Departments/hhs/adult/mental_health.aspx

Avalon

28729 ■ The Guidance Center- Avalon
125 Metropole Ave.
Avalon, CA 90704
Ph: (310)510-7500

Avenal

28730 ■ Kings View Counseling Services for King County
228 E Kings St.
Avenal, CA 93204
Ph: (559)386-4601
URL: http://www.countyofkings.com/

Bakersfield

28731 ■ Children's Outpatient
2621 Oswell St.
Bakersfield, CA 93306
Ph: (661)868-6750

28732 ■ Crestwood Behavioral Health, Inc.--Bakersfield
6700 Eucalyptus Dr., Ste. A
Bakersfield, CA 93306
Ph: (661)363-8127
URL: http://crestwoodbehavioralhealth.com

28733 ■ Greater Los Angeles Veterans Affairs Medical Center
Bakersfield Community Based Outpatient Clinic
1801 Westwind Dr.
Bakersfield, CA 93301
Ph: (661)632-1800
Fax: (661)632-1888
URL: http://www2.va.gov/directory/guide/facility.asp?ID=525

28734 ■ Henrietta Weill Memorial
Child Guidance Clinic
2001 N Chester
Bakersfield, CA 93308
Ph: (661)393-5836

28735 ■ Kern County Mental Health Services
Adult Outpatient Service-Rehab 3
3715 Columbus Ave.
Bakersfield, CA 93306
Ph: (661)868-7150
URL: http://www.co.kern.ca.us/kcmh/

28736 ■ Memorial Center, Inc.
5201 White Ln.
Bakersfield, CA 93309-6200
Ph: (661)398-1800

28737 ■ North Chester Clinic
Adult Outpatient
2525 N Chester Ave.
Bakersfield, CA 93308
Ph: (661)868-1840
URL: http://www.co.kern.ca.us

28738 ■ Sagebrush Center - Children's
1111 Columbus Ave.
Bakersfield, CA 93305-1921
Ph: (661)868-8300
Fax: (661)868-8317

Baldwin Park

28739 ■ Ettie Lee Youth and Family Services--Baldwin Park
5146 Maine Ave.
Baldwin Park, CA 91706
Ph: (626)960-4861
URL: http://www.ettielee.org

28740 ■ Hillsides Family Center
4600 Bogart Ave.
Baldwin Park, CA 91706
Ph: (626)813-2553
URL: http://hillsides.org

Banning

28741 ■ Banning Mental Health Services
1330 W Ramsey St., No. 100
Banning, CA 92220-4440
Ph: (951)849-7142

Barstow

28742 ■ Counseling and Mental Health Center
805 E Mountain View St.
Barstow, CA 92311-3033
Ph: (760)256-5026

28743 ■ Vista Guidance Centers of Barstow
309 E Mountain View St., Ste. 100
Barstow, CA 92311
Ph: (760)256-0376
URL: http://www.vgcenters.org/

Beaumont

28744 ■ Childhelp USA
14700 Manzanita Rd.
Beaumont, CA 92223
Ph: (951)845-3155
URL: http://www.childhelp.org

Bell Garden

28745 ■ Enki East Los Angeles Mental Health Services, Bell Garden
6001 Clara St.
Bell Garden, CA 90201
Ph: (562)806-5000
URL: http://losangeles.networkofcare.org

Bell Gardens

28746 ■ Somos Familia San Antonio Mental Health Services
6450 Garfield Ave.
Bell Gardens, CA 90201-1846
Ph: (562)806-4921

Berkeley

28747 ■ Berkeley City Mental Health--Adelene Street
Family, Youth, & Children's Clinic
3282 Adelene St.
Berkeley, CA 94704
Ph: (510)981-5280

28748 ■ Berkeley City Mental Health--Center Street
1947 Center St.
Berkeley, CA 94704
Ph: (510)981-5270

28749 ■ Berkeley Drop-In Center
3234 Adeline St.
Berkeley, CA 94703-2407
Ph: (510)653-3808

28750 ■ Bonita House--Berkeley
1410 Bonita Ave.
Berkeley, CA 94709-1909
Ph: (510)526-4765

28751 ■ Creative Living Center
2340 Durant Ave.
Berkeley, CA 94704-1607
Ph: (510)548-2269

Berkley

28752 ■ Alta Bates Medical Center, Ashby Ave.
Behavioral Health
2450 Ashby Ave.
Berkley, CA 94705
Ph: (510)204-4405
URL: http://www.altabatesmd.com

28753 ■ Alta Bates Medical Center, Dwight Way
Behavioral Health
2001 Dwight Way
Berkley, CA 94704
Ph: (510)204-4444
URL: http://www.altabatesmd.com

28754 ■ Reach Out
3238 Adeline St.
Berkley, CA 94703
Ph: (510)652-5891
URL: http://banmch.org/directory/ala_reachout.html

28755 ■ Turning Point, 8th St.
2418 8th St.
Berkley, CA 94710
Ph: (510)601-8961
URL: http://www.ci.berkley.ca.us

28756 ■ Turning Point, King St.
3404 King St.
Berkley, CA 94703
Ph: (510)601-8966
URL: http://www.ci.berkley.ca.us

Big Bear Lake

28757 ■ Bear Valley Family Counseling
41945 Big Bear Blvd., Ste. 222
Big Bear Lake, CA 92315
Ph: (909)866-5070

Bishop

28758 ■ Inyo County Mental Health
162 Grove St., Ste. J
Bishop, CA 93514-2696
Ph: (760)873-6533

28759 ■ Progressive Living Program
536 N 2nd St.
Bishop, CA 93514-2810
Ph: (760)873-5633

Blythe

28760 ■ Blythe Mental Health and Substance Abuse
1297 W Hobson Way
Blythe, CA 92225-1423
Ph: (760)921-5004

Brentwood

28761 ■ Familias Unidas
4510 O'Hara Ave., Ste. A
Brentwood, CA 94513
Ph: (925)240-2120
URL: http://www.familias-unidas.org

28762 ■ Familias Unidas Counseling Center
1191 Central Blvd., Ste. A
Brentwood, CA 94513
Ph: (925)634-4445
URL: http://www.familias-unidas.org

Buena Park

28763 ■ Child Guidance Center
6301 Beach Blvd., Ste. 245
Buena Park, CA 90621
Ph: (714)736-0231
URL: http://www.cgcoc.org

Burlingame

28764 ■ Peninsula Medical Center
Behavioral Health Services
1501 Trousdale Dr.
Burlingame, CA 94010
Ph: (650)696-5400
URL: http://www.mills-peninsula.org

Burney

28765 ■ Burney Satellite
37491 Enterprise Dr.
Burney, CA 96013
Ph: (530)335-2906

Canoga Park

28766 ■ El Centro de Amistad, Inc.
6800 Owensmouth Ave., Ste. 310
Canoga Park, CA 91303
Ph: (818)347-8565
URL: http://www.elcentrodeaminstad.com

28767 ■ West Valley Mental Health Center
7621 Canoga Ave.
Canoga Park, CA 91304
Ph: (818)598-6911

Carlsbad

28768 ■ Montecatini
2524 La Costa Ave.
Carlsbad, CA 92009
Ph: (760)436-8930
Free: 877-762-3753
URL: http://www.montecatinieatingdisorder.com/

Castro Valley

28769 ■ Eden Medical Center
Behavioral Health
20103 Lake Chabot Rd.
Castro Valley, CA 94546-5341
Ph: (510)889-5016

Cathedral City

28770 ■ Cathedral Canyon Mental Health and Substance Abuse Services
68615 Perez Rd., Ste. 2A
Cathedral City, CA 92234-7200
Ph: (760)770-2222

Ceres

28771 ■ Stanislaus County Behavioral Health
Health/Mental Health Team
1901 Richland Ave.
Ceres, CA 95350
Ph: (209)541-2121
URL: http://www.stanislausrecoverycenter.com/contact.shtm

Cerritos

28772 ■ Asian Pacific Counseling and Treatment Center
11050 Artesia Blvd., Ste. F
Cerritos, CA 90703
Ph: (562)860-8838
URL: http://www.apctc.org

28773 ■ Community Family Guidance Center
10929 South St., Ste. 208B
Cerritos, CA 90703
Ph: (562)924-5526

28774 ■ Rio Hondo Mental Health Services
17707 Studebaker Rd.
Cerritos, CA 90703-2640
Ph: (562)402-0688

Chico

28775 ■ Butte County Department of Behavioral Health
Special Services Division
109 Parmac Rd., Ste. 2
Chico, CA 95926-2218
Ph: (530)891-2784
Formerly: Butte County Mental Health Services.

28776 ■ Butte County Psychiatric Health
592 Rio Lindo Ave.
Chico, CA 95926
Ph: (530)891-2775

28777 ■ Sacramento Veterans Affairs Medical Center
Chico Outpatient Clinic
280 Cohasset Rd., Ste. 15
Chico, CA 95926
Ph: (530)891-2945
Free: 800-382-8387
Fax: (530)879-5025
URL: http://www2.va.gov/directory/guide/facility.asp?ID=795&dnum=All

28778 ■ Victor Community Support Services
7 Governors Ln.
Chico, CA 95926
Ph: (530)267-1700

28779 ■ Victor Treatment Centers, Inc.
North Valley Schools, Inc.
2561 California Park Dr.
Chico, CA 95928
Ph: (530)893-0758

Chino

28780 ■ Hillview Acres Children's Home
3683 Chino Ave.
Chino, CA 91710
Ph: (909)628-1272
URL: http://www.hillview.org

Chowchilla

28781 ■ Chowchilla Counseling Center
215 S 4th St.
Chowchilla, CA 93610
Ph: (559)665-2947

Chula Vista

28782 ■ Bayview Behavioral Health Campus
330 Moss St.
Chula Vista, CA 91911
Ph: (619)426-6310
URL: http://www.hospital-profiles.com/Bayview_Behavioral_Health_Campus

28783 ■ Chula Vista Clinic
VA San Diego Healthcare System
835 3rd Ave.
Chula Vista, CA 91910
Ph: (619)409-1600
URL: http://www.sandiego.va.gov/visitors/chulavista.asp

28784 ■ Nueva Vista Family Services
1161 Bay Blvd., Ste. B
Chula Vista, CA 91911
Ph: (619)585-7686
Fax: (619)585-7699
URL: http://www.comresearch.org/programs/sby/index.asp?id=23
Formerly: South Bay Youth and Family Services.

28785 ■ South Bay Guidance Center
835 3rd Ave., Ste. C
Chula Vista, CA 91911
Ph: (619)427-4661
Fax: (619)426-7849
URL: http://www.comresearch.org/programs/sba/index.asp?id=22

City of Commerce

28786 ■ Greater Los Angeles Veterans Affairs Medical Center
East Los Angeles Community Based Outpatient Center
5426 E Olympic Blvd.
City of Commerce, CA 90040
Ph: (323)725-7557
Fax: (323)725-7577
URL: http://www2.va.gov/directory/guide/facility.asp?ID=5110&dnum=All

28787 ■ Penny Lane Centers
2450 S Atlantic Blvd., Ste. 100
City of Commerce, CA 90040
Ph: (323)318-9960
URL: http://www.pennylane.org/contents/contact.html

Colusa

28788 ■ Colusa County Department of Behavioral Health
162 E Carson St., Ste. A
Colusa, CA 95932
Ph: (530)458-0520
URL: http://www.countyofcolusa.org

Commerce

28789 ■ Enki East Los Angeles Mental Health Services, Commerce
1436 Goodrich Blvd.
Commerce, CA 90022
Ph: (323)725-1337
URL: http://www.ehrs.com

Compton

28790 ■ Compton Mental Health Center
921 E Compton Blvd.
Compton, CA 90221
Ph: (310)668-6800

28791 ■ Step Out Transitional Age Youth Program
2010 E El Segundo Blvd.
Compton, CA 90222
Ph: (310)637-0917
URL: http://www.scharpla.org

Concord

28792 ■ Anderson House
1159 Everett Ct.
Concord, CA 94518
Ph: (925)933-2627
URL: http://www.manta.com/c/mm4qspr/youth-homes-incorporated

28793 ■ Anka Behavioral Health
Concord Day Treatment
3525 Chestnut Ave.
Concord, CA 94519
Ph: (925)680-0222
Free: 888-4-ANKABHI
URL: http://www.ankabhi.org/

28794 ■ Anka Behavioral Health
Nierika House
1959/1967 Solano Way
Concord, CA 94520
Ph: (925)676-9768
Free: 888-4-ANKABHI
URL: http://www.ankabhi.org/
Formerly: Phoenix Programs, Inc.

28795 ■ Anka Behavioral Health--Willow Pass Road
1875 Willow Pass Rd., Ste. 300, 3rd Fl.
Concord, CA 94520-2592
Ph: (925)825-4700
Free: 888-4-ANKABHI
URL: http://www.ankabhi.org/
Formerly: Phoenix Programs, Inc.

28796 ■ Grammercy House
4334 Grammercy Lane
Concord, CA 94521
Ph: (925)933-2627
URL: http://www.manta.com/c/mm4qspr/youth-homes-incorporated

28797 ■ Phoenix Center Day Treatment Center
1470 Enea Circle, Ste. 1500
Concord, CA 94520
Free: 888-678-7277
URL: http://www.ankabhi.org

28798 ■ Portia Bell Hume Behavioral Health
1333 Willow Pass Rd., Ste. 102
Concord, CA 94520
Ph: (925)825-1793
URL: http://www.humecenter.org

28799 ■ We Care Services for Children
1450 Enea Circle, Ste. 200
Concord, CA 94520
Ph: (925)671-0777
URL: http://www.wecarechildren.org

Corona

28800 ■ Corona Regional Medical Center Behavioral Health
730 Magnolia Ave.
Corona, CA 92879
Ph: (951)737-4343
URL: http://www.coronaregional.com

28801 ■ Loma Linda Veterans Affairs Medical Center
Corona Community Based Outpatient Clinic
800 Magnolia Ave., Ste. 101
Corona, CA 92879
Ph: (951)817-8820
URL: http://www2.va.gov/directory/guide/facility.asp?ID=5108&dnum=All

28802 ■ Riverside County Department of Mental Health
Substance Abuse Program
623 N Main St., Ste. D11
Corona, CA 92880
Ph: (951)737-2962

Costa Mesa

28803 ■ County of Orange Health Care Agency Mental Health Service
3115 Red Hill Ave.
Costa Mesa, CA 92626
Ph: (714)850-8463
URL: http://www.oc.ca.gov

Cotati

28804 ■ A Step Up
420 E Cotati Ave.
Cotati, CA 94931
Ph: (707)795-4336

Coulterville

28805 ■ Mariposa County Behavioral Health and Recovery Services
5026 Broadway
Coulterville, CA 95311
Ph: (209)878-0822
URL: http://www.mariposacounty.org/index.aspx-?NID=858

Covina

28806 ■ Aurora Charter Oak Hospital--Behavioral Health
1161 E Covina Blvd.
Covina, CA 91724
Ph: (626)966-1632
Free: 800-654-2673
URL: http://charteroak.aurorabehavioral.com/

28807 ■ Masonic Homes
1650 E Old Badillo St.
Covina, CA 91724
Ph: (626)251-2200
URL: http://www.masonichome.org/

28808 ■ Santa Anita Family Service
716 N Citrus Ave.
Covina, CA 91728
Ph: (626)966-1755
URL: http://www.santaanitafamilyservice.org

Culver City

28809 ■ Didi Hirsh Community Mental Health Center
c/o PMR Corporation
4760 S Sepulveda Blvd.
Culver City, CA 90230
Ph: (310)390-6612
URL: http://www.didihirsch.org/

Daly City

28810 ■ North County Mental Health Center
380 90th Ave.
Daly City, CA 94015
Ph: (650)994-3030

28811 ■ North County Mental Health Center
375 89th St.
Daly City, CA 94015
Ph: (650)301-8650
URL: http://www.mhasmc.org/prog/friendshipcenter.shtml

Danville

28812 ■ Discovery Counseling Center of the San Ramon Valley, Inc.
115A Town and Country Dr.
Danville, CA 94526-3960
Ph: (925)837-0505

Davis

28813 ■ EMQ Families First
2100 5th St.
Davis, CA 95618
Ph: (530)753-0220
URL: http://www.emqff.org

28814 ■ Yolo Community Care Continuum Farm House
24321 County Rd. 96
Davis, CA 95617
Ph: (530)753-1653
E-mail: main@y3c.org
URL: http://www.y3c.org

28815 ■ Yolo Community Care Continuum Supportive Housing/Vocational Services
1950 5th. St.
Davis, CA 95616
Ph: (530)758-2160
E-mail: main@y3c.org
URL: http://www.y3c.org

28816 ■ Yolo County Department of Alcohol, Drug, and Mental Health Services
600 A St.
Davis, CA 95616
Ph: (530)757-5530
E-mail: main@y3c.org
URL: http://www.y3c.org

28817 ■ Yolo Family Service Agency--Davis
1105 Kennedy Pl., Ste. 2
Davis, CA 95616
Ph: (530)753-8674
E-mail: main@y3c.org
URL: http://www.y3c.org

Delano

28818 ■ Child Guidance Clinic Henrietta Weill Memorial
1318 High St.
Delano, CA 93215
Ph: (661)725-1027
URL: http://www.hwmcg.org

Diamond Springs

28819 ■ Summitview Child and Family Servies
768 Pleasant Valley Rd., Ste. 304
Diamond Springs, CA 95619
Ph: (530)621-9800
URL: http://www.summitviewtreatment.org

Downey

28820 ■ Los Padrinos Juvenile Hall Mental Health Unit
7285 E Quill Dr.
Downey, CA 90242-2098
Ph: (562)940-8767
URL: http://www.topjuveniledefender.com/Los_Padrinos.html

Duarte

28821 ■ Foothills Family Service--Duarte
1801 Huntington Dr., Ste. 200
Duarte, CA 11010
Ph: (626)301-9700
URL: http://www.foothillfamily.org

El Cajon

28822 ■ Crossroads Family Center
1625 E Main St., Ste. 200
El Cajon, CA 92021
Ph: (619)441-1907
Fax: (619)441-1908
URL: http://www.comresearch.org

28823 ■ East Corner Clubhouse
1060 Estes St.
El Cajon, CA 92020-7411
Ph: (619)440-5133
Fax: (619)440-8522
URL: http://www.comresearch.org

28824 ■ Halcyon Center
1664 Broadway
El Cajon, CA 92021-5201
Ph: (619)579-8685
Fax: (619)579-1969
URL: http://www.comresearch.org

28825 ■ Heartland Center Dual Recovery Program
1060 Estes St.
El Cajon, CA 92020-7411
Ph: (619)440-5133
Fax: (619)440-8522
URL: http://www.comresearch.org

28826 ■ Professional Community Services Counseling Center
900 N Cuyamaca, Ste. 206
El Cajon, CA 92020
Ph: (619)449-8706
Fax: (619)449-4612
URL: http://www.comresearch.org

El Centro

28827 ■ Imperial County Mental Health
343 N 8th St.
El Centro, CA 92243
Ph: (760)339-6860

El Cerrito

28828 ■ West Coast Children's Center
545 Ashbury Ave.
El Cerrito, CA 94530-3220
Ph: (510)527-7249

El Monte

28829 ■ Enki Youth and Family Services, El Monte
3208 Rosemead Blvd., Ste. 100
El Monte, CA 91731
Ph: (626)227-7001
URL: http://www.ehrs.com/pages/services.html

28830 ■ Foothill Family Service--El Monte
11429 Valley Blvd.
El Monte, CA 91731
Ph: (626)442-8391
URL: http://www.foothillfamily.org/

Encino

28831 ■ Encino Hospital Medical Center
16237 Ventura Blvd.
Encino, CA 91436-2272
Ph: (818)995-5000
URL: http://www.encinomed.com/
Formerly: Tarzana Regional Medical Center.

Escondido

28832 ■ Escondido Clinic
815 E Pennsylvania Ave.
Escondido, CA 92025
Ph: (760)466-7020
URL: http://www.sandiego.va.gov

28833 ■ Palomar Medical Center Behavioral Health Services
555 E Valley Pkwy.
Escondido, CA 92025
Ph: (760)739-3000
URL: http://www.pph.org

Eureka

28834 ■ Crestwood Behavioral Health, Inc.--Eureka
2370 Buhne St.
Eureka, CA 95501
Ph: (707)443-7358
URL: http://crestwoodbehavioralhealth.com

28835 ■ Humboldt County Mental Health Services
720 Wood St.
Eureka, CA 95501-4413
Ph: (707)268-2900
URL: http://co.humboldt.ca.us/HHS/MHB/

28836 ■ Humboldt County Mental Health Services Children, Youth and Family Services
1711 3rd St.
Eureka, CA 95501
Ph: (707)268-2800
URL: http://co.humboldt.ca.us/HHS/MHB/
Formerly: Children, Youth and Family Services.

28837 ■ Redwood Family Institute
935 3rd St.
Eureka, CA 95501
Ph: (707)444-8895

Fairfield

28838 ■ Sacramento Veterans Affairs Medical Center Fairfield Outpatient Clinic
103 Bodin Cir.
Fairfield, CA 94535
Ph: (707)437-1800
Free: 800-382-8387
Fax: (707)437-1953
URL: http://www2.va.gov/directory/guide/facility.asp?ID=810&dnum=All

28839 ■ Solano County Mental Health Children's Mental Health Services
1745 Enterprise Dr., Bldg. 2
Fairfield, CA 94533
Ph: (707)399-4900
URL: http://www.scccmh.org

28840 ■ Youth and Family Services, Inc.--Fairfield
490 Chadbourne Rd., Ste. C
Fairfield, CA 94534
Ph: (707)427-6640
URL: http://www.youthandfamilyservices.org

Fillmore

28841 ■ Ventura County Behavioral Health Center--Fillmore
828 Ventura St., Ste. 240
Fillmore, CA 93015
Ph: (805)524-8660
URL: http://www.vchca.org/behavioral-health/behavioral.health.aspx

Fontana

28842 ■ Vista Counseling Center
17216 Slover Ave., Bldg. L
Fontana, CA 92337-7580
Ph: (909)854-3420

Fort Bragg

28843 ■ Mendocino County Mental Health
Coast Mental Health Center
790 S Franklin St.
Fort Bragg, CA 95437-5456
Ph: (707)964-4747

Fountain Valley

28844 ■ Western Youth Services--Fountain Valley
10101 Slater Ave., Ste. 241
Fountain Valley, CA 92708
Ph: (714)378-2620

Fremont

28845 ■ Crestwood Behavioral Health, Inc.
Crestwood Manor
4303 Stevenson Blvd.
Fremont, CA 94538
Ph: (510)651-1244
URL: http://www.crestwoodbehavioralhealth.com/fremont.html

28846 ■ Crestwood Behavioral Health, Inc.--Fremont
2171 Mowry Ave.
Fremont, CA 94538
Ph: (510)793-8383
URL: http://www.crestwoodbehavioralhealth.com/fremont.html

28847 ■ Family Paths, Inc.--Fremont
39155 Liberty St., Ste. F600
Fremont, CA 94536
Ph: (510)790-3803
Free: 800-829-3777
Fax: (510)790-3805
URL: http://www.familypaths.org/about.php

28848 ■ South County Creative Living Center
40965 Grimmer Blvd.
Fremont, CA 94538
Ph: (510)657-7425

Fresno

28849 ■ Fresno County Behavioral Health
Adult System of Care
4441 E Kings Canyon Rd.
Fresno, CA 93702-3604
Ph: (559)453-4099
Formerly: Fresno County Human Services System.

28850 ■ Fresno County Behavioral Health--Sanger
4441 E Kings Canyon Rd.
Fresno, CA 93702
Ph: (559)253-9180

28851 ■ Genesis Family Center
83 E Shaw St., Ste. 101
Fresno, CA 93726
Ph: (559)439-5437

28852 ■ Veterans Affairs Central California Health Care System
2615 E Clinton Ave.
Fresno, CA 93703
Ph: (559)225-6100
Free: 888-826-2838
Fax: (559)228-6903
URL: http://www2.va.gov/directory/guide/facility.asp?ID=53&dnum=All

Fullerton

28853 ■ Family Assessment, Counseling, and Education Services--Fullerton
505 E Commonwealth Ave., Ste. 200
Fullerton, CA 92832
Ph: (714)879-9616
Fax: (714)879-2041
E-mail: mail@facescal.org
URL: http://www.facescal.org

Garberville

28854 ■ Humboldt County Mental Health Services
Outpatient Clinic
727 Cedar St.
Garberville, CA 95542-3201
Ph: (707)923-2729

Gardena

28855 ■ Coastal Asian-Pacific Mental Health Services
14112 S Kingsley Dr.
Gardena, CA 90249-3018
Ph: (310)217-7312

28856 ■ Greater Los Angeles Veterans Affairs Medical Center
Gardena Clinic
1251 Redondo Beach Blvd., 3rd Fl.
Gardena, CA 90247
Ph: (310)851-4705
Fax: (310)851-4719
URL: http://www2.va.gov/directory/guide/facility.asp?ID=5112&dnum=All

Gilroy

28857 ■ Chamberlain's Mental Health Services
8352 Church St., Ste. C
Gilroy, CA 95020
Ph: (408)848-6511
URL: http://www.chamberlainsmhs.com

28858 ■ Community Solutions--Gilroy
6980 chestnut St.
Gilroy, CA 95020
Ph: (408)842-7138
URL: http://www.communitysolutions.org

28859 ■ Rebekah Children's Servies
290 F Ave.
Gilroy, CA 95020
Ph: (408)846-2100
URL: http://www.rcskids.org

28860 ■ Santa Clara County Mental Health Department
South County Community Mental Health Center
1215 1st St.
Gilroy, CA 95020
Ph: (408)686-2360
Free: 800-704-0900

Glendale

28861 ■ Glen Robert Child Study Center
1530 E Colorado St.
Glendale, CA 91205-1514
Ph: (818)244-0222

28862 ■ Glendale Adventist Medical Center--Psychiatric Institute
1509 Wilson Terr.
Glendale, CA 91206
Ph: (818)409-8000
URL: http://www.glendaleadventist.com/body.cfm?id=220

28863 ■ Stepping Stones
1812 Verdugo Blvd.
Glendale, CA 91208
Ph: (818)790-7100
URL: http://www.verdugohillshospital.org

Granada Hills

28864 ■ Penny Lane Centers
Satellite VI
11641 Balboa Blvd.
Granada Hills, CA 91344
Ph: (818)360-9342
URL: http://www.pennylane.org/

28865 ■ San Fernando Mental Health Services
10605 Balboa Blvd., Ste. 100
Granada Hills, CA 91344
Ph: (818)832-2400

Grass Valley

28866 ■ Nevada County Behavioral Health
500 Crown Point Circle, Ste. 120
Grass Valley, CA 95945
Ph: (530)265-1437
URL: http://mynevadacounty.com/bh

Greenbrae

28867 ■ County of Marin Community Mental Health Services
Community Client Services
250 Bon Air Rd.
Greenbrae, CA 94904
Ph: (415)499-6835

Gridley

28868 ■ Butte County Department of Behavioral Health--Gridley
995 Spruce St.
Gridley, CA 95948
Ph: (530)846-7305

Half Moon Bay

28869 ■ Coastside Mental Health
255 S Cabrillo Hwy.
Half Moon Bay, CA 94019
Ph: (650)726-6369

Hawthorne

28870 ■ South Bay Mental Health Services
2311 W El Segundo Blvd.
Hawthorne, CA 90250-3315
Ph: (323)241-6730
Remarks: Serves primarily persons with severe and chronic mental illnesses.

Hayward

28871 ■ Family Paths, Inc.--Hayward
22455 Maple Ct., Ste. 402
Hayward, CA 94541
Ph: (510)893-9230
Free: 800-829-3777
URL: http://www.familypaths.org/

28872 ■ Hedco Creative Living Center
590 B St.
Hayward, CA 94541-5004
Ph: (510)247-8235
URL: http://www.bayareacs.org/

28873 ■ Lincoln Child Center
Kinship Support Services
27287 Patrick Ave.
Hayward, CA 94544
Ph: (510)583-8026
Fax: (510)583-8060
URL: http://www.lincolncc.org/html/contact.html

28874 ■ Woodroe Place
22505 Woodroe Ave.
Hayward, CA 94541
Ph: (510)537-9223
URL: http://www.bayareacs.org/

Hemet

28875 ■ Anka Behavioral Health--SouthPoint
2190 S State St.
Hemet, CA 92543
Ph: (951)929-1968
URL: http://www.ankabhi.org/

28876 ■ Hemet Valley Medical Center
1117 E Devonshire Ave.
Hemet, CA 92543
Ph: (651)652-2811
URL: http://www.valleyhealthsystem.com/getpage.php?name=index

28877 ■ Riverside County Department of Mental Health
Hemet/San Jacinto Mental Health Services
650 N State St.
Hemet, CA 92543
Ph: (951)791-3300

Hollister

28878 ■ San Benito County Mental Health
1131 San Felipe Rd.
Hollister, CA 95023
Ph: (831)636-4020

Huntington Beach

28879 ■ Huntington Beach Partial Hospitalization Program
821 Newman St.
Huntington Beach, CA 92647
Ph: (714)375-5405
URL: http://www.hbhospital.com/hbstyle/shtm/services/medical.shtm

28880 ■ Huntington Beach Youth Shelter
7291 Talbert Ave.
Huntington Beach, CA 92648
Ph: (714)843-5020
URL: http://www.cspinc.org

Indio

28881 ■ Family Service of the Desert
81711 US Hwy. 111, Ste. 101
Indio, CA 92201
Ph: (760)347-2398

28882 ■ Riverside County Department of Mental Health
44199 Oasis St., Ste. C
Indio, CA 92201
Ph: (760)863-2578

28883 ■ Riverside County Department of Mental Health
Milestones Residential Facility
82485 Miles Ave.
Indio, CA 92201
Ph: (760)347-4347

28884 ■ Riverside County Department of Mental Health
Substance Abuse Program
83-912 Ave. 45, Ste. 9
Indio, CA 92201
Ph: (760)347-0754

28885 ■ STARS Behavioral Health Group
Oasis Rehabilitation Center
47915 Oasis St.
Indio, CA 92201
Ph: (760)863-8600

Inglewood

28886 ■ Didi Hirsch Community Mental Health Center
Inglewood Center
111 N LaBrea Ave., Ste. 500
Inglewood, CA 90301
Ph: (310)677-7808
Fax: (310)677-7205
URL: http://www.didihirsch.org/about/locations
Formerly: Centinela Family & Child Guidance Clinic.

28887 ■ Excelsior House
1007 Myrtle Ave.
Inglewood, CA 90301
Ph: (310)412-4191
Fax: (310)412-3942
URL: http://www.didihirsch.org/about/locations

Irwindale

28888 ■ Transitional Age Youth FSP Drop-In Center
13001 Ramona Blvd., Ste. H-I
Irwindale, CA 91706
Ph: (626)337-3828
URL: http://www.pacificclinic.org

Kerman

28889 ■ Fresno County Behavioral Health
West County Regional Clinic
275 S Madera Ave., Ste. 400
Kerman, CA 93630
Ph: (559)846-7500
Formerly: Fresno County Human Services System.

King City

28890 ■ Monterey County Mental Health
200 Broadway, Ste. 88
King City, CA 93930
Ph: (831)386-6868
Free: 888-258-6029
URL: http://www.mcsystemofcare.org/contact/

La Mesa

28891 ■ Alvarado Parkway Institute
Behavioral Health System
7050 Parkway Dr.
La Mesa, CA 91942
Ph: (619)465-4411
Free: 800-766-4272
URL: http://www.apibhs.com/

28892 ■ Hanbleceya Treatment Center
5520 Wellesley St., Ste. 107
La Mesa, CA 91942
Ph: (619)466-0547
URL: http://hanbleceya.com

28893 ■ Pegasus-East
Psychiatric Day Treatment
7841 El Cajon Blvd., Ste. C
La Mesa, CA 91942
Ph: (619)697-2388
URL: http://www.mhsinc.org/

La Puente

28894 ■ Enki Youth and Family Services, La Puenta
160 S 7th Ave.
La Puente, CA 90623
Ph: (714)670-7400
URL: http://www.ehrs.com

La Selva Beach

28895 ■ Youth Services--La Selva Beach
Tyler House
9C Marea Ave.
La Selva Beach, CA 95076
Ph: (831)688-6293

Lafayette

28896 ■ Cherry Lane House
1603 Pleasant Hill Rd.
Lafayette, CA 94549
Ph: (925)933-2627
URL: http://www.youthhomes.org

Laguna Beach

28897 ■ Child Mental Health Service
County of Orange Health Care Agency
21632 Wesley Dr.
Laguna Beach, CA 92563
Ph: (949)855-1556
URL: http://www.ochealthinfo.com/behavioral

28898 ■ South Coast Medical Center--Behavioral Health
31872 Coast Hwy.
Laguna Beach, CA 92651
Ph: (949)499-1311
URL: http://www.adventisthealth.org/healthservices/godocdocument.asp?cn=209

Laguna Hills

28899 ■ Western Youth Services, Laguna Hills
23461 S Pointe Dr., Ste. 220
Laguna Hills, CA 92653
Ph: (949)855-1556
URL: http://www.westernyouthservices.org

Lake Elsinore

28900 ■ Victor Community Support Services
31681 Riverside Dr., Ste. A
Lake Elsinore, CA 92530
Ph: (951)674-9243

Lancaster

28901 ■ Antelope Valley Mental Health
349 East Ave., K6
Lancaster, CA 93535
Ph: (661)723-4260

28902 ■ Tarzana Treatment Centers
Antelope Valley
44447 N 10th St. W
Lancaster, CA 93534
Ph: (661)726-2630
Free: 800-996-1051
URL: http://www.tarzanatc.org/

28903 ■ Tarzana Treatment Centers
Lancaster Boulevard, Lancaster
907 Lancaster Blvd.
Lancaster, CA 93534
Ph: (661)723-4829
Free: 800-996-1051
URL: http://www.tarzanatc.org/

28904 ■ Tarzana Treatment Centers
N 10th Street W, Lancaster
44443 N 10th St. W
Lancaster, CA 93534
Ph: (661)726-2630
Free: 800-996-1051
URL: http://www.tarzanatc.org/

Lawndale

28905 ■ Transitional Living Centers, Inc.
16119 Prairie Ave.
Lawndale, CA 90260
Ph: (310)542-4825

Livingston

28906 ■ Merced County Mental Health
Livingston Clinic
1471 B St.
Livingston, CA 95334
Ph: (209)394-4032

Loma Linda

28907 ■ Jerry L. Pettis Memorial Veterans Affairs Medical Center
11201 Benton St.
Loma Linda, CA 92357
Ph: (909)825-7084
Free: 800-741-8387
URL: http://www.lomalinda.va.gov/

Lompoc

28908 ■ Lompoc Mental Health Services
401 E Cyprus Ave.
Lompoc, CA 93436
Ph: (805)737-7715

28909 ■ Santa Barbara County Mental Health Services
Lompoc Clinic
117 N B St.
Lompoc, CA 93436-6901
Ph: (805)740-2100

Lone Pine

28910 ■ Inyo County Mental Health
South County Office
380 Mt. Whitney Dr.
Lone Pine, CA 93545
Ph: (760)876-5545

Long Beach

28911 ■ Children's Institute, Inc.--Long Beach
4300 Long Beach Blvd., Ste. 700
Long Beach, CA 90807
Ph: (213)385-5100
URL: http://www.childrensinstitute.org

28912 ■ The Guidance Center--Long Beach
4335 Atlantic Ave.
Long Beach, CA 90807
Ph: (562)485-3095

28913 ■ Hinchman House Outpatient Clinic
3711 long Beach Blvd., Ste. 600
Long Beach, CA 90807
Ph: (562)959-1159
URL: http://www.tgclb.org

28914 ■ Jewish Family and Children's Services--Long Beach
3801 E Willow St., Ste. 219
Long Beach, CA 90815
Ph: (562)427-7916
URL: http://www.jfcs.org

28915 ■ La Casa Psychiatric Health Facility
6060 Paramount Blvd.
Long Beach, CA 90805
Ph: (562)630-8672

28916 ■ Long Beach Adult Services
1975 Long Beach Blvd.
Long Beach, CA 90806-5501
Ph: (562)599-9280

28917 ■ Long Beach Asian Mental Health Services
1975 Long Beach Blvd.
Long Beach, CA 90806-5501
Ph: (562)599-9280

28918 ■ Long Beach Mental Health Services
Child and Adolescent
240 E 20th St.
Long Beach, CA 90806
Ph: (562)599-9271

28919 ■ Long Beach Veterans Affairs Medical Center
Villages at Cabrillo
2090 River Ave., Bldg. 28
Long Beach, CA 90810
Ph: (562)388-8000
Free: 888-769-8387
URL: http://www2.va.gov/directory/guide/facility.asp?ID=5420&dnum=All

28920 ■ Tarzana Treatment Centers
Atlantic Avenue, Long Beach
5190 Atlantic Ave.
Long Beach, CA 90805
Ph: (818)996-1051
Free: 800-996-1051
URL: http://www.tarzanatc.org/

28921 ■ Tarzana Treatment Centers
Magnolia Avenue, Long Beach
2101 Magnolia Ave.
Long Beach, CA 90806
Free: 800-996-1051
URL: http://www.tarzanatc.org/

Los Angeles

28922 ■ Alcott Center for Mental Health Services
14335 S Robertson Blvd.
Los Angeles, CA 90035
Ph: (310)785-2121
URL: http://www.alcottcenter.org

28923 ■ Asian Pacific Counseling and Treatment Center, Lafayette Park
520 S Lafayette Park Place, Ste. 300
Los Angeles, CA 90057
Ph: (213)252-2100
Fax: (213)252-2199
URL: http://www.apctc.org

28924 ■ Asian Pacific Counseling and Treatment Center, Wilshire
1310 Wilshire Blvd.
Los Angeles, CA 90017
Ph: (213)483-3000
Fax: (213)483-6529
URL: http://www.apctc.org

28925 ■ Augustus F. Hawkins Comprehensive Community Mental Health Center
1720 E 120th St.
Los Angeles, CA 90059
Ph: (323)668-4275

28926 ■ Aviva Family and Children's Services--Franklin Avenue
7120 Franklin Ave.
Los Angeles, CA 90046-3091
Ph: (323)876-0550
URL: http://www.avivacenter.org/

28927 ■ Aviva Family and Children's Services--Wilshire Boulevard
3580 Wilshire Blvd., Ste. 1024
Los Angeles, CA 90010
Ph: (213)637-5000
URL: http://www.avivacenter.org

28928 ■ California Mental Health Connection
3540 Wilshire Blvd., Ste. 1024
Los Angeles, CA 90010
Ph: (213)351-9406
URL: http://www.mentalhealthconnection.org

28929 ■ Central Juvenile Hall
1605 Eastlake Ave.
Los Angeles, CA 90033-1005
Ph: (323)226-8846

28930 ■ Central Los Angeles Continuing Care
2020 Zonal Ave.
Los Angeles, CA 90089-9520
Ph: (323)226-5726

28931 ■ Children's Institute, Inc.--Los Angeles
711 S New Hampshire Ave.
Los Angeles, CA 90005
Ph: (213)385-5100
Fax: (213)383-1820
URL: http://www.childrensinstitute.org/contact/

28932 ■ Didi Hirsch Community Mental Health Center
Mar Vista Center
12420 Venice Blvd.
Los Angeles, CA 90066
Ph: (310)751-1200
Fax: (310)398-0312
URL: http://www.didihirsch.org/about/locations

28933 ■ Didi Hirsch Community Mental Health Center
S. Mark Taper Foundation Center
1328 W Manchester Ave.
Los Angeles, CA 90044
Ph: (323)778-9593
Fax: (323)778-0028
URL: http://www.didihirsch.org/about/locations

28934 ■ Dorothy F. Kirby Mental Health Center
1500 S McDonnell Ave.
Los Angeles, CA 90040
Ph: (323)981-4301

28935 ■ Downtown Mental Health Center
529 S Maple Ave.
Los Angeles, CA 90013
Ph: (213)430-6700

28936 ■ Edelman Westside Mental Health Center
11080 W Olympic Blvd.
Los Angeles, CA 90064-1937
Ph: (310)966-6500

28937 ■ Hathaway-Sycamores Child and Family Services
1968 W Adams Blvd., Ste. 101
Los Angeles, CA 90018
Ph: (323)733-0322
URL: http://www.hathaway-sycamores.org/

28938 ■ Hathaway-Sycamores Child and Family Services
Family Resource Center
840 N Ave. 66
Los Angeles, CA 90004
Ph: (313)257-9600
URL: http://www.hathaway-sycamores.org/

28939 ■ Hollywood Mental Health Services
1224 N Vine St.
Los Angeles, CA 90038-1612
Ph: (323)769-6100

28940 ■ Jewish Family Service of Los Angeles
3580 Wilshire Blvd.
Ste. 700
Los Angeles, CA 90010
Ph: (323)761-8800
URL: http://www.jfsla.org/

28941 ■ Jump Street
1233 S La Cienega Blvd.
Los Angeles, CA 90035
Ph: (310)855-0031
Fax: (310)855-0138
URL: http://www.didihirsch.org/about/locations

28942 ■ Kedren Community Mental Health Center
4211 Avalon Blvd.
Los Angeles, CA 90011
Ph: (323)233-0425

28943 ■ LAMP Community
Frank Rice SafeHaven
627 San Julian St.
Los Angeles, CA 90014
Ph: (213)488-0031
URL: http://lampcommunity.org/?page_id=19

28944 ■ LAMP Day Center/Shelter
527 Crocker St.
Los Angeles, CA 90013
Ph: (213)488-9559
URL: http://lampcommunity.org/?page_id=19

28945 ■ LAMP Lodge
660 S Stanford Ave.
Los Angeles, CA 90021-1006
Ph: (213)688-2924
URL: http://lampcommunity.org/?page_id=19

28946 ■ LAMP Village
527 Crocker St.
Los Angeles, CA 90013-2116
Ph: (213)488-9559
Fax: (213)683-0969
URL: http://www.lampcommunity.org

28947 ■ Los Angeles Child Guidance Clinic
3787 S Vermont Ave.
Los Angeles, CA 90007
Ph: (323)766-2345
URL: http://www.lacgc.org/

28948 ■ Los Angeles County Mental Health
550 S Vermont Ave., 12th Fl.
Los Angeles, CA 90020-1998
Ph: (213)738-4601

28949 ■ Los Angeles Gay & Lesbian Center
Mental Health Services
1625 N Schrader Blvd.
Los Angeles, CA 90028
Ph: (323)993-7669
E-mail: mentalhealth@lagaycenter.org
URL: http://www.lagaycenter.org/site/PageServer?pagename=YH_Mental_Health_Counse ling

28950 ■ Northeast Family Mental Health Services
5321 Via Marisol
Los Angeles, CA 90042
Ph: (323)478-8200

28951 ■ Parole Outpatient Clinic--Region III
307 W 4th St., 2nd Fl.
Los Angeles, CA 90013
Ph: (213)620-2220

28952 ■ Portals House, Inc.
Corporate Headquarters
679 S New Hampshire Ave., 5th Fl.
Los Angeles, CA 90005-1355
Ph: (213)639-2500
Fax: (213)385-9246
E-mail: jballa@portalshouse.org
URL: http://www.portalshouse.org

28953 ■ Portals House, Inc.
Portals Mariposa Clubhouse
2500 Wilshire Blvd., Ste. 704
Los Angeles, CA 90057
Ph: (213)639-2660
URL: http://www.portalshouse.org/contactus/contactus.html

28954 ■ Portals Partners
679 S New Hampshire Ave., 5th Fl.
Los Angeles, CA 90005
Ph: (213)639-2500
Fax: (213)385-9246
URL: http://www.portalshouse.org/contactus/contactus.html

28955 ■ Portals Twin Peaks Transitional Residence
255 S Mariposa Ave.
Los Angeles, CA 90004
Ph: (213)639-2686
Fax: (213)380-6434
URL: http://www.portalshouse.org/contactus/contactus.html
Formerly: Portals Mariposa Transitional Residence.

28956 ■ Roybal Family Mental Health Services
4701 E Cesar Chavez Ave., 2nd Fl.
Los Angeles, CA 90022
Ph: (323)264-3400

28957 ■ South Central Health and Rehabilitation Program--Los Angeles
5201 S Vermont Ave.
Los Angeles, CA 90037-3527
Ph: (323)751-2677
URL: http://www.scharpla.org/service.htm

28958 ■ Southern California Counseling Center
5615 W Pico Blvd.
Los Angeles, CA 90019-3871
Ph: (323)937-1344
URL: http://www.sccc-la.org/

28959 ■ Veterans Affairs West Los Angeles Health Care Center
11301 Wilshire Blvd.
Los Angeles, CA 90073
Ph: (310)268-3526
Fax: (310)268-4730
URL: http://www2.va.gov/directory/guide/facility.asp?ID=735&dnum=All

28960 ■ West Central Family Mental Health Service
3751 Stocker St.
Los Angeles, CA 90008
Ph: (323)298-3680

Los Banos

28961 ■ Merced County Mental Health
Westside Community Counseling Center
40 W G St.
Los Banos, CA 93635
Ph: (209)710-6100

Lynwood

28962 ■ South Central Health and Rehabilitation Program (SHARP)--Lynwood
2610 Industrial Way, Ste. A
Lynwood, CA 90262
Ph: (310)631-8004
Fax: (310)631-5875
E-mail: info@scharpla.org
URL: http://www.scharpla.org/

Madera

28963 ■ Madera County Behavioral Health Services
14277 Rd. 28
Madera, CA 93638-5795
Ph: (559)675-7926
Formerly: Madera County Mental Health Clinic.

Malibu

28964 ■ The Canyon at Peace Park
2900 S Kanan Dume Rd.
Malibu, CA 90265
Ph: (310)457-3209

Martinez

28965 ■ Contra Costa County Mental Health
1340 Arnold Dr., Ste. 200
Martinez, CA 94553-4189
Ph: (925)957-5150
URL: http://www.co.contra-costa.ca.us

28966 ■ Sacramento Veterans Affairs Medical Center
Martinez Outpatient Clinic
150 Muir Rd.
Martinez, CA 94553
Ph: (925)372-2000
Free: 800-382-8387
Fax: (925)372-2851
URL: http://www2.va.gov/directory/guide/facility.asp?ID=528&dnum=All

Mather

28967 ■ Sacramento Veterans Affairs Medical Center
Mather Mental Health Clinic
10535 Hospital Way
Mather, CA 95655
Ph: (916)366-5420
Free: 800-382-8387
Fax: (916)366-5328
URL: http://www2.va.gov/directory/guide/facility.asp?ID=533&dnum=All

Merced

28968 ■ Merced County Mental Health--Administration Office
480 E 13th St.
Merced, CA 95341
Ph: (888)334-0163

28969 ■ Merced County Mental Health
Recovery Assistance for Teens
480 E 13th St., Bldg.2
Merced, CA 95341
Ph: (290)381-6830

Mission Viejo

28970 ■ Western Youth Services, Mission Viejo
26137 La Paz Rd., Ste. 230
Mission Viejo, CA 92691
Ph: (949)595-8610
URL: http://www.westernyouthservices.org

Modesto

28971 ■ Center for Human Services
1700 McHenry Village Way, Ste. 11
Modesto, CA 95350
Ph: (209)526-1440
URL: http://www.chs-nw.org

28972 ■ Children's System of Care
251 E Hackett Rd.
Modesto, CA 95358
Ph: (209)558-2411
URL: http://www.stancounty.com/bhrs

28973 ■ Josie's Place
1208 9th St.
Modesto, CA 95354
Ph: (209)558-4464
URL: http://www.stancounty.com/bhrs

28974 ■ Juvenile Justice
Stanislaus County Behavioral Health
2215 Blue Gum Ave.
Modesto, CA 95358

Ph: (209)525-5401
URL: http://www.co.stanislaus.ca.us/bhrs/

28975 ■ Stanislaus County Behavioral Health Garden Gate Respite--Turning Point
609 5th St.
Modesto, CA 95351
Ph: (209)341-0718
URL: http://www.co.stanislaus.ca.us/bhrs/

28976 ■ Stanislaus County Behavioral Health Integrated Forensics Team
500 N 9th St., Ste. C
Modesto, CA 95350
Ph: (209)558-4420
URL: http://www.co.stanislaus.ca.us/bhrs/

28977 ■ Stanislaus County Behavioral Health Kirk Baucher Day Treatment
140 Calaveras Ave.
Modesto, CA 95354
Ph: (209)550-5858
URL: http://www.co.stanislaus.ca.us/bhrs/

28978 ■ Stanislaus County Behavioral Health Leaps and Bounds Program
4640 Spyres Way, Bldg. B, Ste. 7
Modesto, CA 95356
Ph: (209)558-4595
URL: http://www.co.stanislaus.ca.us/bhrs/

28979 ■ Stanislaus County Behavioral Health & Recovery Services
800 Scenic Dr.
Modesto, CA 95350-6195
Ph: (209)525-6225
URL: http://www.co.stanislaus.ca.us/bhrs/

28980 ■ Telecare Recovery Access Center Homeless Outreach Program
500 N 9th St., Ste. B
Modesto, CA 95350
Ph: (209)341-1824
URL: http://www.stancounty.com/bhrs

28981 ■ Turning Point Community Programs Fifth Street Center
609 5th St.
Modesto, CA 95353
Ph: (916)364-8395
URL: http://www.tpcp.org/

28982 ■ Wellness Recovery Center
500 N 9th St., Ste. A
Modesto, CA 95350
Ph: (209)558-4610
URL: http://www.stancounty.com/bhrs

28983 ■ Wellness Recovery Center Stanislaus County Behavioral Health
500 N 9th St., Ste. C
Modesto, CA 95354-2320
Ph: (209)558-4610
URL: http://www.co.stanislaus.ca.us/bhrs/

28984 ■ Youth and Family Services, Modesto
800 Scenic Dr., Bldg. D
Modesto, CA 95354
Ph: (209)525-6070
URL: http://www.stancounty.com/bhrs

Monrovia

28985 ■ Santa Anita Family Services
605 S Myrtle Ave.
Monrovia, CA 91016
Ph: (626)359-9358
URL: http://www.santaanitafamilyservice.org

Monterey

28986 ■ Monterey County Mental Health--Monterey
1200 Aguajito Rd., Rm. 103
Monterey, CA 93940-4898
Ph: (831)647-7652

Moreno Valley

28987 ■ Incredible Kids Program
23119 Cottonwood Ave., Bldg. A, Ste. 110
Moreno Valley, CA 92553
Ph: (951)413-5678
Formerly: Children's Interagency Program.

Morgan Hill

28988 ■ Community Solutions La Casa Del Puente Treatment Center
17415 Depot St.
Morgan Hill, CA 95037-3618
Ph: (408)778-0555
URL: http://www.communitysolutions.org
Formerly: The Bridge Counseling Center.

28989 ■ Community Solutions--Morgan Hill
16264 Church St., Ste. 103
Morgan Hill, CA 95037
Ph: (408)779-2113
E-mail: cs@communitysolutions.org
URL: http://www.communitysolutions.org

Napa

28990 ■ Family Services of Napa Valley
709 Franklin St.
Napa, CA 94559-2920
Ph: (707)255-0966

28991 ■ Progress Foundation Laurel House
3133 Laurel St.
Napa, CA 94558-5628
Ph: (707)255-3711
URL: http://www.progressfoundation.org/

28992 ■ Progress Foundation Progress Place
1046 Bella Dr.
Napa, CA 94558
Ph: (707)257-7755
URL: http://www.progressfoundation.org/

Needles

28993 ■ Needles Counseling Center Child/Adolescent/Adult Outpatient Clinic
1300 Bailey Ave., Ste. E
Needles, CA 92363-3115
Ph: (760)326-9313

Nevada City

28994 ■ Milhous Children's Services, Inc
24077 State Hwy. 49
Nevada City, CA 95959
Ph: (530)265-9057
URL: http://www.milhous.org

28995 ■ Nevada County Mental Health
10433 Willow Valley Rd., Ste. A
Nevada City, CA 95959
Ph: (530)265-1437

Newhall

28996 ■ Child Family Center, Newhall
23504 Lyons Ave., Ste. 204
Newhall, CA 91321
Ph: (661)286-2550
URL: http://www.childfamilycenter.org

North Hills

28997 ■ Penny Lane Centers Doctor Rose Jenkins Memorial Clinic
15305 Rayen St.
North Hills, CA 91343
Ph: (818)892-3423
URL: http://www.pennylane.org/contents/contact.html

28998 ■ Penny Lane Centers Main Facility
15305 Rayen St.
North Hills, CA 91343
Ph: (818)892-3423
URL: http://www.pennylane.org/contents/contact.html

28999 ■ Penny Lane Centers Satellite I
9723 Burnet Ave.
North Hills, CA 91343
Ph: (818)893-9039
URL: http://www.pennylane.org/

29000 ■ Penny Lane Centers Satellite II
16656 Nordhoff St.
North Hills, CA 91343
Ph: (818)830-2720
URL: http://www.pennylane.org/

29001 ■ Penny Lane Centers Satellite V
8806 Haskell Ave.
North Hills, CA 91343
Ph: (818)894-2107
URL: http://www.pennylane.org/

North Hollywood

29002 ■ Jewish Family Service of Los Angeles--North Hollywood
12821 Victory Blvd.
North Hollywood, CA 91606-3098
Ph: (818)984-1380
URL: http://www.jfsla.org/

Northridge

29003 ■ Child and Family Guidance Center--Northridge
9650 Zelzah Ave.
Northridge, CA 91325
Ph: (818)993-9311
Fax: (818)739-5388
E-mail: info@childguidance.org
URL: http://www.childguidance.org/contact_us/contact_us2_1.htm

29004 ■ Penny Lane Centers Satellite VII
9630 Wilbur Ave.
Northridge, CA 91324
Ph: (818)772-0221
URL: http://www.pennylane.org/

29005 ■ Penny Lane Centers Satellite VIII
9845 Hayvenhurst Ave.
Northridge, CA 91343
Ph: (818)894-1360
URL: http://www.pennylane.org/

Novato

29006 ■ Sunny Hills Services Simmons Day Treatment
1097 Simmons Ln.
Novato, CA 94947
Ph: (415)457-3200
URL: http://www.sunnyhillsservices.org/

29007 ■ Sunny Hills Services Sutro Day Treatment
814 Sutro Ave.
Novato, CA 94947

Ph: (415)892-3200
URL: http://www.sunnyhillsservices.org/

29008 ■ Sunny Hills Services
Vivian Court Day Treatment
40 Vivian Ct.
Novato, CA 94947
Ph: (415)457-3200
URL: http://www.sunnyhillsservices.org/

Oakdale

29009 ■ Stanislaus County Behavioral Health
Eastside Regional Services
631 W F St.
Oakdale, CA 95361
Ph: (209)847-5927
URL: http://www.co.stanislaus.ca.us/bhrs/

29010 ■ Stanislaus County Behavioral Health
Oakdale Community Care Center for Children
145 N 2nd St.
Oakdale, CA 95361
Ph: (209)848-6018
URL: http://www.co.stanislaus.ca.us/bhrs/

Oakland

29011 ■ Alameda County Behavioral Health
Mental Health Division
2000 Embarcadero, Ste. 400
Oakland, CA 94606-5300
Ph: (510)567-8100
Formerly: Alameda County Health Care Services Mental Health Division.

29012 ■ Asian Pacific Psychological Services
255 International Blvd.
Oakland, CA 94606
Ph: (510)835-2777
URL: http://www.appsweb.org/

29013 ■ Bay Area Community Services, Inc.--Oakport Street
7901 Oakport St., Ste. 3400
Oakland, CA 94621-2038
Ph: (510)613-0330
URL: http://www.bayareacs.org/

29014 ■ Bay Area Community Services--Oakland Avenue
629 Oakland Ave.
Oakland, CA 94611
Ph: (510)658-9480
URL: http://www.bayareacs.org/

29015 ■ Bonita House--HOST
1422 Harrison St.
Oakland, CA 94612
Ph: (510)809-1780
Fax: (510)893-1642
E-mail: allegra@bonitahouse.org
URL: http://www.bonitahouse.org/

29016 ■ Bonita House--Oakland
6333 Telegraph Ave., Ste. 102
Oakland, CA 94609
Ph: (510)923-1099
E-mail: info@bonitahouse.org
URL: http://www.bonitahouse.org/

29017 ■ Center for Family Counseling
9925 International Blvd., Ste. 6
Oakland, CA 94603-2558
Ph: (510)562-3731
URL: http://cffc.biz/

29018 ■ East Bay Agency for Children
303 Van Buren Ave.
Oakland, CA 94610
Ph: (510)268-3770
Fax: (510)268-1073
URL: http://www.ebac.org/welcome.asp

29019 ■ East Bay Agency for Children--Hawthorne Family Resource Program
1700 28th Ave.
Oakland, CA 94601
Ph: (510)879-1642
URL: http://www.ebac.org/welcome.asp

29020 ■ East Bay Agency for Children--PALS
2540 Charleston St.
Oakland, CA 94602
Ph: (510)531-3666
URL: http://www.ebac.org/welcome.asp

29021 ■ East Bay Agency for Children--Sequioa Healthy Start Program
3730 Lincoln Ave.
Oakland, CA 94602
Ph: (510)879-2455
URL: http://www.ebac.org/welcome.asp

29022 ■ East Bay Agency for Children--Therapeutic Nursery School
6117 Martin Luther King Ave.
Oakland, CA 94609
Ph: (510)655-4896
URL: http://www.ebac.org/welcome.asp

29023 ■ Family Paths, Inc.--Oakland
1727 Martin Luther King Jr. Way, Ste. 109
Oakland, CA 94612
Ph: (510)893-9230
Free: 800-829-3777
URL: http://www.familypaths.org/about.php
Formerly: Parental Stress Service, Inc.

29024 ■ Lincoln Child Center
4368 Lincoln Ave.
Oakland, CA 94602
Ph: (510)531-3111
Fax: (510)530-8083
URL: http://www.lincolncc.org/html/contact.html

29025 ■ Oakland Center for Holistic Counseling
2501 Harrison St.
Oakland, CA 94612
Ph: (510)444-3344
URL: http://www.jfku.edu/locations/community-counseling-centers/oakland-centerho listic-counsel-ing.html

29026 ■ Sacramento Veterans Affairs Medical Center
Oakland Mental Health Clinic
2505 W 14th St.
Oakland, CA 94626
Ph: (510)587-3400
Free: 800-382-8387
Fax: (510)587-3420
URL: http://www2.va.gov/directory/guide/facility.asp?ID=808&dnum=All

29027 ■ STARS Behavioral Health Group
525 21st St.
Oakland, CA 94621
Ph: (510)635-9705
URL: http://www.starsinc.com/

29028 ■ Townhouse Creative Living Center
629 Oakland Ave.
Oakland, CA 94611-4567
Ph: (510)658-9480
URL: http://www.bayareacs.org/creative_living_centers.html

29029 ■ West Oakland Health Center--Mental Health Department
2730 Adeline St.
Oakland, CA 94607
Ph: (510)465-1800
URL: http://www.wohc.org/

Oceanside

29030 ■ Casa Pacifica
321 Cassidy St.
Oceanside, CA 92054
Ph: (760)721-2171
Free: 800-479-3339
Fax: (760)721-8582
E-mail: dhu@comresearch.org
URL: http://www.comresearch.org
Formerly: Pacific Quest.

29031 ■ North Coastal Mental Health Center
1701 Mission Ave., Ste. A
Oceanside, CA 92058
Ph: (760)967-4475
URL: http://www.mhsinc.org/

29032 ■ Turning Point Crisis Center
1738 S Tremont St.
Oceanside, CA 92054
Ph: (760)439-2800
Fax: (760)433-5031
URL: http://www.comresearch.org

Orange

29033 ■ Canyon Acres Children and Family Services--Orange
1845 W Orangewood Ave., Ste. 300
Orange, CA 92868
Ph: (714)383-9400
URL: http://www.canyonacres.org/main.asp

Orange Cove

29034 ■ Fresno County Human Services System
Orange Cove Community Clinic
445 S 11th St.
Orange Cove, CA 93646
Ph: (559)626-4031
Fax: (559)626-4963
URL: http://www.unitedhealthcenters.org
Formerly: Fresno County Health Services.

Oroville

29035 ■ Butte County Department of Behavioral Health--Oroville
18 County Center Dr., Ste. C
Oroville, CA 95965-3317
Ph: (530)538-7705

Palm Desert

29036 ■ Veterans Affairs Medical Center
Palm Desert Community Based Outpatient Clinic
41-990 Cook St., Bldg. F, Ste. 1004
Palm Desert, CA 92211
Ph: (760)341-5570
URL: http://www2.va.gov/directory/guide/facility.asp?ID=5118&dnum=1

Palo Alto

29037 ■ Achievekids
3860 Middlefield Rd.
Palo Alto, CA 94303
Ph: (650)494-1200
Fax: (650)494-1243
URL: http://www.achievekids.org/
Formerly: ACHIEVE.

29038 ■ Family & Children Services
Palo Alto Office
375 Cambridge Ave.
Palo Alto, CA 94306
Ph: (650)326-6576

Paradise

29039 ■ Butte County Department of Behavioral Health--Paradise
5910 Clark Rd. W
Paradise, CA 95969
Ph: (530)872-6328

29040 ■ Butte County Department of Behavioral Health
Paradise Treatment Center
805 Cedar St., Ste. A
Paradise, CA 95969-4602
Ph: (530)877-5845

Pasadena

29041 ■ Foothill Family Service--Pasadena
2500 E Foothill Blvd., Ste. 300
Pasadena, CA 91107-7102
Ph: (626)564-1613
URL: http://www.foothillfamily.org/

29042 ■ Fuller Psychological & Family Services
180 N Oakland Ave.
Pasadena, CA 91101-1714
Ph: (626)584-5515

29043 ■ Pacific Clinics Children's Services I
66 Hurlbut St.
Pasadena, CA 91105-3112
Ph: (877)722-2737
URL: http://www.pacificclinics.org/

29044 ■ Pacific Clinics Children's Services II
70 N Hudson Ave.
Pasadena, CA 91101-1808
Ph: (877)722-2737
URL: http://www.pacificclinics.org/

29045 ■ Pacific Clinics Passageways Program
1020 Arroyo Pkwy.
Pasadena, CA 91105
Ph: (626)403-4888
Free: 877-722-2737
URL: http://www.pacificclinics.org/

29046 ■ Youth Moving On
Hillsides Home for Children
650 N Oakland Ave.
Pasadena, CA 91101
Ph: (626)792-8717
URL: http://hillsides.org

Perris

29047 ■ Mid-County Mental Health Services
1688 N Perris Blvd., L7-11
Perris, CA 92571-4709
Ph: (909)443-2231
Fax: (909)443-2230
URL: http://mentalhealth.co.riverside.ca.us/opencms/
Formerly: Mid-County Mental Health Services Perris Mental Health.

Piedmont

29048 ■ Ann Martin Children's Center
1250 Grand Ave.
Piedmont, CA 94610
Ph: (510)655-7880
URL: http://www.annmartin.org

Placerville

29049 ■ El Dorado County Mental Health
344 Placerville Dr., Ste. 17
Placerville, CA 95667-3972
Ph: (530)621-6290
Formerly: El Dorado County Community Mental Health Services.

29050 ■ El Dorado County Mental Health Administrative Office
670 Placerville Dr., Ste. 1B
Placerville, CA 95667-3920
Ph: (530)621-6200
Formerly: El Dorado County Community Mental Health Services.

29051 ■ El Dorado County Mental Health Psychiatric Health Facility
935B Spring St.
Placerville, CA 95667-4543
Ph: (530)621-6210
Formerly: El Dorado County Community Mental Health Services.

29052 ■ El Dorado County Mental Health Western Slope Day Rehabilitation
2808 Mallard Land., Stes. A-D
Placerville, CA 95667
Ph: (530)621-6560

Pleasant Hill

29053 ■ Touchstone Counseling, Inc.
140 Mayhew Way, Ste. 606
Pleasant Hill, CA 94523
Ph: (925)932-0150
URL: http://www.touchstonecounseling.com/

Pleasanton

29054 ■ Valley Community Support Center & Children's Outpatient Services
3730 Hopyard Rd., Ste. 103
Pleasanton, CA 94588
Ph: (925)462-3010
Formerly: Valley Community Support Center.

29055 ■ Valley Creative Living Center
3900 Valley Ave., Ste. B
Pleasanton, CA 94566
Ph: (925)484-8457
Fax: (925)484-1075
URL: http://www.bayareacs.org

Point Reyes Station

29056 ■ Marin County Community Mental Health Services
West Marin Service Center
100 6th St.
Point Reyes Station, CA 94956
Ph: (415)473-3805

Pomona

29057 ■ Ettie Lee Youth and Family Services--Pomona
160 E Holt Ave., Ste. B
Pomona, CA 91767
Ph: (909)620-2521
URL: http://www.ettielee.org

29058 ■ Pacific Clinics--Bonita Family Center
790 E Bonita Ave.
Pomona, CA 91767
Ph: (909)625-7207
URL: http://www.pacificclinics.org/

29059 ■ Tri-City Mental Health Center
2008 N Garey Ave.
Pomona, CA 91767
Ph: (909)623-6131
URL: http://www.tricitymhs.org/

Redding

29060 ■ Sacramento Veterans Affairs Medical Center
Redding Outpatient Clinic
351 Hartnell Ave.
Redding, CA 96002
Ph: (530)226-7555
Free: 800-382-8387
Fax: (530)226-7505
URL: http://www2.va.gov/directory/guide/facility.asp?ID=532&dnum=All

29061 ■ Shasta County Mental Health Services
2640 Breslauer Way
Redding, CA 96001
Ph: (530)225-5200

29062 ■ Victor Community Support Services
3300 Churn Creek Rd.
Redding, CA 96002
Ph: (530)223-2822

29063 ■ Victor Treatment Centers, Inc.
Victor Youth Services
855 Canyon Rd.
Redding, CA 96001
Ph: (530)378-1855

Reedley

29064 ■ Fresno County Behavioral Health Reedley Regional Health Clinic
1131 I St.
Reedley, CA 93654
Ph: (559)638-8588
Formerly: Fresno County Human Services System; Reedley Community Clinic.

Reseda

29065 ■ Tarzana Treatment Centers Reseda
7101 Baird St.
Reseda, CA 91335
Ph: (818)342-5897
Free: 800-996-1051
URL: http://www.tarzanatc.org/who-are-we/locations.aspx

Rialto

29066 ■ San Bernardino County Department of Behavioral Health
850 E Foothill Blvd.
Rialto, CA 92376-5230
Ph: (909)421-9301
Formerly: San Bernardino County Department of Mental Health.

Richmond

29067 ■ Anka Behavioral Health--Nevin House
3221 Nevin Ave.
Richmond, CA 94804
Ph: (510)232-7633

Riverside

29068 ■ Continuing Community Care Central Services
1695 Spruce St.
Riverside, CA 92507-2426
Ph: (951)358-4801
Free: 800-706-7500
URL: http://mentalhealth.co.riverside.ca.us

29069 ■ Continuing Community Care South Services
6355 Riverside Ave.
Riverside, CA 92506-3163
Ph: (951)369-5714
Free: 800-706-7500
URL: http://mentalhealth.co.riverside.ca.us

29070 ■ Riverside County Department of Mental Health
4095 County Circle Dr.
Riverside, CA 92503
Ph: (951)358-4500
URL: http://mentalhealth.co.riverside.ca.us

29071 ■ Riverside County Regional Medical Center
Inpatient Treatment Facility
9990 County Farm Rd., Ste. 1
Riverside, CA 92503-3542
Ph: (951)358-4700
URL: http://mentalhealth.co.riverside.ca.us
Formerly: Riverside County Department of Mental Health Psychiatric Inpatient Unit.

29072 ■ Van Horn Counseling Center
10000 County Farm Rd.
Riverside, CA 92503-3529
Ph: (951)358-4390

Rosemead

29073 ■ BHC Alhambra Hospital
4619 Rosemead Blvd.
Rosemead, CA 91770
Ph: (626)286-1191
Free: 800-235-5570
URL: http://www.bhcalhambrahospital.net/

Roseville

29074 ■ Placer County Mental Health Services--Roseville
101 Cirby Hill Dr.
Roseville, CA 95678
Ph: (916)787-8814
URL: http://www.placer.ca.gov/Departments/hhs/adult/mental_health.aspx

Sacramento

29075 ■ Crestwood Behavioral Health, Inc.--Sacramento
2600 Stockton Blvd.
Sacramento, CA 95817
Ph: (916)452-1431
URL: http://www.crestwoodbehavioralhealth.com/sacramento.html

29076 ■ The Effort, Inc.
1820 J St.
Sacramento, CA 95811
Ph: (916)325-5556
Fax: (916)444-5620
E-mail: info@theeffort.org
URL: http://www.theeffort.org/

29077 ■ El Hogar Community Services, Inc.
930 G St.
Sacramento, CA 95814
Ph: (916)441-0226
URL: http://www.elhogarinc.org/

29078 ■ El Hogar Community Services, Inc.
Sierra Elder Wellness Program
9261 Folsom Blvd., Ste. 500
Sacramento, CA 95826
Ph: (916)363-1553
URL: http://www.elhogarinc.org/

29079 ■ FOCUS
7245 E Southgate Dr.
Sacramento, CA 95823
Ph: (916)427-7141

29080 ■ Mandy
Turning Point Community Programs, Inc.
7304 Mandy Dr.
Sacramento, CA 95823-2813
Ph: (916)364-8395
URL: http://www.tpcp.org

29081 ■ Millroy
Turning Point Community Programs, Inc.
7591 Millroy Way
Sacramento, CA 95823
Ph: (916)364-8395
URL: http://www.tpcp.org

29082 ■ Mossglen
Turning Point Community Programs, Inc.
128 Mossglen Cir.
Sacramento, CA 95826-1725
Ph: (916)364-8395
URL: http://www.tpcp.org

29083 ■ Turning Point Community Programs, Inc.
3440 Viking Dr., Ste. 114
Sacramento, CA 95827
Ph: (916)364-8395
URL: http://www.tpcp.org

Salinas

29084 ■ Monterey County Behavioral Health Services
1270 Natividad Rd., Rm. 200
Salinas, CA 93906
Ph: (831)755-4510
Fax: (831)755-4980
URL: http://000sweb.co.monterey.ca.us/health/Bo-havioralHealth/

29085 ■ Monterey County Mental Health--Salinas
1000 S Main St., Ste. 210B
Salinas, CA 93901
Ph: (831)796-1500

29086 ■ Salinas Day Treatment Center
1441 Constitution Blvd., Bldg. 400, Ste. 202
Salinas, CA 93906
Ph: (831)796-1710

San Anselmo

29087 ■ Sunny Hills Services
300 Sunny Hills Dr.
San Anselmo, CA 94960
Ph: (415)457-3200

San Bernardino

29088 ■ La Casa Ramona Counseling
1543 W 8th St.
San Bernardino, CA 92411
Ph: (909)386-5415

29089 ■ Shandin Hills Behavioral Therapy Center
4164 N 4th Ave.
San Bernardino, CA 92407
Ph: (909)886-6786

29090 ■ Valley Star Children and Family Services
1585 S D St., Ste. 101
San Bernardino, CA 92408
Ph: (909)388-2222
Fax: (909)388-2220
E-mail: sthorpe@starsinc.com
URL: http://www.starsinc.com/valley.php

29091 ■ Victor Community Support Services
1908 Business Center Dr., Ste. 220
San Bernardino, CA 92408
Ph: (909)890-5930

29092 ■ Victor Treatment Centers, Inc.
Victor Children's Services
1053 N D St.
San Bernardino, CA 92410
Ph: (909)886-1691

San Diego

29093 ■ Areta Crowell Center
1963 4th Ave.
San Diego, CA 92101
Ph: (619)233-3432
Fax: (619)233-7022
URL: http://www.comresearch.org/programs/groups.asp

29094 ■ Central Adult Mental Health and Vocational Services
2864 University Ave.
San Diego, CA 92104
Ph: (619)291-9611
URL: http://www.comresearch.org

29095 ■ Community Research Foundation
1202 Morena Blvd., Ste. 300
San Diego, CA 92110
Ph: (619)275-0822
Fax: (619)275-1422
URL: http://www.comresearch.org/programs/groups.asp

29096 ■ The Corner Clubhouse
2864 University Ave.
San Diego, CA 92104
Ph: (619)683-7423
Fax: (619)683-7248
URL: http://www.comresearch.org/programs/groups.asp

29097 ■ Douglas Young Clinic
10717 Camino Ruiz, Ste. 207
San Diego, CA 92126
Ph: (858)695-2211
Fax: (858)695-3521
URL: http://www.comresearch.org/programs/groups.asp

29098 ■ Douglas Young Youth and Family Services
10717 Camino Ruiz, Ste. 204
San Diego, CA 92126
Ph: (619)695-2211
E-mail: dyyfs@comresearch.org
URL: http://www.comresearch.org/programs/groups.asp

29099 ■ Isis Center
892 27th St.
San Diego, CA 92154
Ph: (619)575-4687
Fax: (619)575-1215
URL: http://www.comresearch.org/programs/groups.asp

29100 ■ Jary Barreto Crisis Center
2865 Logan Ave.
San Diego, CA 92113-2411
Ph: (619)232-4357
URL: http://www.comresearch.org/programs/groups.asp

29101 ■ Maria Sardinas Clinic
3025 Beyer Blvd., Ste. E-102
San Diego, CA 92154
Ph: (619)428-1000
Fax: (619)428-1091
URL: http://www.comresearch.org/programs/groups.asp

29102 ■ New Vistas
734 10th Ave.
San Diego, CA 92101
Ph: (619)239-4663
Fax: (619)239-3045
URL: http://www.comresearch.org/programs/groups.asp

29103 ■ San Diego County Mental Health Service
1700 Pacific Hwy.
San Diego, CA 92101
Ph: (619)563-2700
URL: http://www.co.san-diego.ca.us

29104 ■ San Diego County Mental Health Services
Central Regional Mental Health Services
1250 Morena Blvd.
San Diego, CA 92110

Ph: (619)692-8750
URL: http://www.co.san-diego.ca.us
Formerly: North Central Mental Health Center; Mental Health Social Services.

29105 ■ San Diego County Psychiatric Hospital
3853 Rosecrans St.
San Diego, CA 92110-3115
Ph: (619)692-8200
URL: http://www.co.san-diego.ca.us
Formerly: San Diego County Psychiatric Health Department.

29106 ■ Semi-Supervised Living Project
531 16th St.
San Diego, CA 92101
Ph: (619)233-7757
Fax: (619)233-7022
URL: http://www.comresearch.org/programs/groups.asp

29107 ■ Southeast County Mental Health Center
3177 Ocean View Blvd.
San Diego, CA 92113-1432
Ph: (619)595-4400

29108 ■ Vista Balboa
545 Laurel St.
San Diego, CA 92101
Ph: (619)233-4399
Fax: (619)233-0453
URL: http://www.comresearch.org/programs/groups.asp

San Francisco

29109 ■ Avenues Crisis Program
1443 7th Ave.
San Francisco, CA 94122
Ph: (415)242-8034
URL: http://www.progressfoundation.org

29110 ■ Progress Foundation
Administrative Office
368 Fell St.
San Francisco, CA 94102-5144
Ph: (415)861-0828
E-mail: mtolle@progressfoundation.org
URL: http://www.progressfoundation.org

29111 ■ Progress Foundation
Cortland House
77 Cortland Ave.
San Francisco, CA 94110-5435
Ph: (415)550-1881
URL: http://www.progressfoundation.org

29112 ■ Progress Foundation
Dorine Loso House Transitional Program
405 Baker St.
San Francisco, CA 94117
Ph: (415)346-7775
URL: http://www.progressfoundation.org

29113 ■ Progress Foundation
La Amistad
2481 Harrison St.
San Francisco, CA 94110-2710
Ph: (415)285-8100
URL: http://www.progressfoundation.org

29114 ■ Progress Foundation
La Posada
810 Capp St.
San Francisco, CA 94110-3225
Ph: (415)285-0810
URL: http://www.progressfoundation.org

29115 ■ Progress Foundation
Progress House
25 Beulah St.
San Francisco, CA 94117-3909
Ph: (415)668-1511
URL: http://www.progressfoundation.org

29116 ■ Progress Foundation
Shrader House
50 Shrader St.
San Francisco, CA 94117
Ph: (415)668-4166
URL: http://www.progressfoundation.org

29117 ■ Progress Foundation
Supported Living Program
711 Taraval St.
San Francisco, CA 94121-1622
Ph: (415)752-3416
E-mail: suppliv@concentric.net
URL: http://www.progressfoundation.org

29118 ■ Shrader House Crisis Program
50 Shrader St.
San Francisco, CA 94117
Ph: (415)668-4166
URL: http://www.progressfoundation.org

29119 ■ South of Market Mental Health Clinic
760 Harrison St.
San Francisco, CA 94107
Ph: (415)836-1700

29120 ■ Veterans Affairs Medical Center
San Francisco Clinic
4150 Clement St.
San Francisco, CA 94121
Ph: (415)221-4810
URL: http://www.sanfrancisco.va.gov/

San Jose

29121 ■ Alliance for Community Care
438 N White Rd.
San Jose, CA 95127
Ph: (408)254-6856
Fax: (408)254-6838

29122 ■ Goveia/Zeller Center
436 N White Rd.
San Jose, CA 95127
Ph: (408)259-0760

29123 ■ InnVision
974 Willow St.
San Jose, CA 95125
Ph: (408)292-4286
Fax: (408)271-0826
URL: http://www.innvision.org

29124 ■ InnVision
Julian Street Inn
546 W Julian St.
San Jose, CA 95110
Ph: (408)271-0820
URL: http://www.innvision.org

29125 ■ Momentum for Health
438 N White Rd.
San Jose, CA 95127
Ph: (408)254-6828
E-mail: info@momentummh.org
URL: http://www.momentumformentalhealth.org/

29126 ■ Santa Clara County Mental Health Department
Central Community Mental Health Center
2221 Enborg Ln.
San Jose, CA 95128
Ph: (800)704-0900

29127 ■ Santa Clara County Mental Health Department
Downtown Community Mental Health Center
1075 E Santa Clara St.
San Jose, CA 95116
Ph: (800)704-0900

29128 ■ Santa Clara County Mental Health Department
East Valley Community Mental Health Center
1993 McKee Rd.
San Jose, CA 95116
Ph: (408)926-7950

29129 ■ Santa Clara Valley Health and Hospital System
Mental Health Department
820 Enborg Ct.
San Jose, CA 95128
Ph: (408)885-6140

29130 ■ Starlight Community Services
1885 Lundy Ave., Ste. 223
San Jose, CA 95131
Ph: (408)284-9000
Fax: (408)284-9048
E-mail: mmcdonald@starsinc.ocm
URL: http://www.starsinc.com/starlight.php

San Juan Capistrano

29131 ■ Western Youth Services, San Juan Capistrano
31882 Camino Capistrano, Ste. 108
San Juan Capistrano, CA 92675
Ph: (949)487-6080
URL: http://www.westernyouthservices.org

San Leandro

29132 ■ Alameda County Behavioral Health Care Services
Guidance Clinic
2200 Fairmont Dr.
San Leandro, CA 94578-1003
Ph: (510)667-3000
Formerly: Alameda County Health Care Services Mental Health Division Guidance Clinic.

29133 ■ Seneca Center for Children and Families
2275 Arlington Dr.
San Leandro, CA 94578-1132
Ph: (510)317-1444
Fax: (510)276-6828
E-mail: HR@senecacenter.org
URL: http://www.senecacenter.org

29134 ■ STARS Community service
545 Estudillo Ave.
San Leandro, CA 94577
Ph: (510)352-9200
URL: http://starsinc.com

San Luis Obispo

29135 ■ San Luis Obispo County Mental Health Department
2178 Johnson Ave.
San Luis Obispo, CA 93401-4535
Ph: (805)781-4700
Formerly: San Luis Obispo Community Mental Health Services.

San Mateo

29136 ■ Jewish Family and Children Services
Eleanor Haas Koshland Center
2001 Winward Way, Ste. 200
San Mateo, CA 94404
Ph: (650)931-1800
Fax: (650)931-1814
E-mail: sanmateo@jfcs.org
URL: http://www.jfcs.org/contact-us/regional-offices

San Pedro

29137 ■ San Pedro Mental Health Services
150 W 7th St.
San Pedro, CA 90731
Ph: (310)519-6100

San Rafael

29138 ■ Jewish Family and Children Services--San Rafael
600 5th Ave.
San Rafael, CA 94901
Ph: (415)491-7960
Fax: (415)491-7958
E-mail: marin@jfcs.org
URL: http://www.jfcs.org/contact-us/regional-offices

29139 ■ Marin County Community Mental Health Services
20 N San Pedro Rd., Ste. 2028
San Rafael, CA 94903
Ph: (415)499-6769

29140 ■ Sunny Hills Services Braun Day Treatment
251 N San Pedro Rd.
San Rafael, CA 94903
Ph: (415)491-1645
URL: http://www.sunnyhillsservices.org/

Sanger

29141 ■ Fresno County Human Services System
East County Regional Clinic
225 Academy Ave.
Sanger, CA 93657
Ph: (559)875-7705

Santa Ana

29142 ■ Community Service Programs, Inc.
1821 E Dyer Rd., Ste. 200
Santa Ana, CA 92705
Ph: (949)250-0488
Fax: (949)251-1659
URL: http://www.cspinc.org

29143 ■ Family Assessment, Counseling, and Education Services--Santa Ana
1651 E 4th St., Ste. 128
Santa Ana, CA 92701
Ph: (714)547-7345
Fax: (714)835-6098
E-mail: mail@facescal.org
URL: http://www.facescal.org

29144 ■ The John Henry Foundation
403 N Susan St.
Santa Ana, CA 92703
Ph: (714)480-0025
Fax: (714)554-8770
E-mail: info@johnhenry.org
URL: http://www.johnhenry.org/

29145 ■ Santa Ana Veterans Affairs Medical Center
Bristol Medical Center
2740 S Bristol St., 1st Fl., Ste. 101
Santa Ana, CA 92704
Ph: (714)825-3500
URL: http://www2.va.gov/directory/guide/facility.asp?ID=5121&dnum=1

29146 ■ Western Youth Services, Santa Ana
1666 N Main St., Ste. 400
Santa Ana, CA 92701
Ph: (714)704-5900
URL: http://www.westernyouthservices.org

Santa Barbara

29147 ■ Calle Real Mental Health Clinic
4444 Calle Real
Santa Barbara, CA 93110-1002
Ph: (805)681-5190

29148 ■ Sanctuary Psychiatric Centers
Casa del Mural
222 W Valerio St.
Santa Barbara, CA 93101-2930
Ph: (805)569-2785
URL: http://www.spcsb.org

29149 ■ Santa Barbara County Mental Health Services
429 N San Antonio Rd., Bldg. 3
Santa Barbara, CA 93110-1370
Ph: (805)884-1600

29150 ■ Santa Barbara County Mental Health Services
Psychiatric Health Facility
315 Camino del Remedio
Santa Barbara, CA 93110-1332
Ph: (805)681-5244

29151 ■ Veterans Affairs Medical Center
Santa Barbara Community Based Outpatient Clinic
4440 Calle Real
Santa Barbara, CA 93110
Ph: (805)683-1491
URL: http://www2.va.gov/directory/guide/facility.asp?ID=535&dnum=1

Santa Cruz

29152 ■ Community Recovery Services
Alto Counseling Center
740 Front St., Ste. 130
Santa Cruz, CA 95060
Ph: (831)427-5290
E-mail: info@scccc.org
URL: http://www.scccc.org
Formerly: Alto Counseling Center.

29153 ■ Community Recovery Services
Santa Cruz Residential Recovery
125 Rigg St.
Santa Cruz, CA 95060-4297
Ph: (831)423-3890
URL: http://www.scccc.org
Formerly: Sunflower House.

29154 ■ Community Support Services
Pioneer House
290 Pioneer St.
Santa Cruz, CA 95060-2133
Ph: (831)459-0444
URL: http://www.scccc.org
Formerly: Community Support Services Stepping Out Pioneer House.

29155 ■ Community Support Services
The River Street Shelter
733 River St.
Santa Cruz, CA 95060-1735
Ph: (831)459-6644
URL: http://www.scccc.org

29156 ■ Community Support Services
Transition House
3035 Prather Ln.
Santa Cruz, CA 95065-1801
Ph: (831)476-4184
URL: http://www.scccc.org

29157 ■ Santa Cruz Community Counseling Center
195A Harvey West Blvd.
Santa Cruz, CA 95060-2126
Ph: (831)469-1700
E-mail: info@scccc.org
URL: http://www.scccc.org

29158 ■ Youth Services--Santa Cruz
709 Mission St.
Santa Cruz, CA 95060-3614
Ph: (831)429-8350
E-mail: ysnorth@sbcglobal.net
URL: http://www.scccc.org/youth-services/

Santa Fe Springs

29159 ■ Veterans Affairs Medical Center
Santa Fe Springs Community Clinic
10210 Orr Rd.
Santa Fe Springs, CA 90670
Ph: (562)826-8000
Free: 888-769-8387
URL: http://www2.va.gov/directory/guide/facility.asp?ID=5421&dnum=1

Santa Maria

29160 ■ Santa Barbara County Mental Health Services
Santa Maria Clinic
500 W Foster Rd.
Santa Maria, CA 93455-3620
Ph: (805)934-6380

Santa Rosa

29161 ■ Becker Program
913 Grand Ave.
Santa Rosa, CA 95404
Ph: (707)570-3646

29162 ■ Community Support Network
1410 Guerneville Rd., Ste. 15
Santa Rosa, CA 95403
Ph: (707)575-0979

29163 ■ Dutton House
15550 N Dutton Ave.
Santa Rosa, CA 95401
Ph: (707)573-6962

29164 ■ E Street House
201 S East St.
Santa Rosa, CA 95404
Ph: (707)573-6960

29165 ■ Veterans Affairs Medical Center
Santa Rosa Clinic
3841 Brickway Blvd.
Santa Rosa, CA 95403
Ph: (707)569-2300
URL: http://www.sanfrancisco.va.gov/cboc/santa-rosa.asp

29166 ■ Willow Creek Treatment Center
341 Irwin Rd.
Santa Rosa, CA 95401
Ph: (707)576-7218

Simi Valley

29167 ■ Simi Valley Mental Health Clinic
Ventura County Mental Health Center
3150 E Los Angeles Ave.
Simi Valley, CA 93065-3940
Ph: (805)577-0830

South Lake Tahoe

29168 ■ South Lake Tahoe Outpatient Clinic
1900 Lake Tahoe Blvd.
South Lake Tahoe, CA 96150
Ph: (530)573-3251

Stockton

29169 ■ Center for Positive Prevention Alternatives, Inc.
729 N California St.
Stockton, CA 95202
Ph: (209)929-6700
URL: http://www.cppainc.org
Remarks: Multi-service, community-based organization that provides shelter and transitional living services to homeless youth, county-certified intervention programs for domestic violence offenders and counseling services.

29170 ■ Crestwood Behavior Health, Inc.--Stockton
1130 Monaco Ct.
Stockton, CA 95207
Ph: (209)478-2060
URL: http://www.crestwoodbehavioralhealth.com/

29171 ■ San Joaquin County Behavioral Health Services
1212 N California St.
Stockton, CA 95202-1594
Ph: (209)468-8700
Formerly: San Joaquin County Mental Health Services.

29172 ■ Victor Community Support Services
2495 March Ln., Ste. 125
Stockton, CA 95207
Ph: (209)465-1080

Sun City

29173 ■ Loma Linda Veterans Affairs Medical Center
Sun City Outpatient Clinic
28125 Bradley Rd., Ste. 130
Sun City, CA
Ph: (951)672-1931
URL: http://www2.va.gov/directory/guide/facility.asp?ID=5122&dnum=All

Tarzana

29174 ■ Tarzana Treatment Centers
Tarzana
18646 Oxnard St.
Tarzana, CA 91356
Ph: (818)996-1051
URL: http://www.tarzanatc.org/

Thousand Oaks

29175 ■ Conejo Valley Clinic
72 Moody Ct.
Thousand Oaks, CA 91360
Ph: (805)777-3500

Torrance

29176 ■ STAR View Adolescent Center
4025 W 226th St.
Torrance, CA 90505
Ph: (310)373-4556
E-mail: boconnor@starsinc.com
URL: http://www.starsinc.com/viewad.php

Truckee

29177 ■ Truckee Clinic
10075 Levone Ave., Ste. 203
Truckee, CA 96161
Ph: (530)582-7803

Tulare

29178 ■ Fresno Veterans Affairs Medical Center
South Valley Outpatient Clinic
1050 N Cherry St.
Tulare, CA 93274
Ph: (559)684-8703
Free: 888-826-2838
URL: http://www2.va.gov/directory/guide/facility.asp?ID=5218&dnum=All

Turlock

29179 ■ Creative Alternatives, Inc.
2855 Geer Rd.
Turlock, CA 95382
Ph: (209)668-9361
URL: http://www.creative-alternatives.org/creative-alternatives.org/Home.html

29180 ■ Turlock Regional Services
2101 Geer Rd., Ste. 120
Turlock, CA 95382-2456
Fax: (209)644-8044

Ukiah

29181 ■ Mendocino County Mental Health
860 N Bush St.
Ukiah, CA 95482-3998
Ph: (707)463-4303

Upland

29182 ■ Loma Linda Veterans Affairs Medical Center
Upland Clinic
1238 E Arrow Hwy., Ste. 100
Upland, CA 91786
Ph: (909)946-5348
URL: http://www2.va.gov/directory/guide/facility.asp?ID=5123&dnum=All

29183 ■ Upland Community Counseling
934 N Mountain Ave., Ste. C
Upland, CA 91786-3659
Ph: (909)579-8100

Vallejo

29184 ■ Crestwood Behavioral Health, Inc.--Vallejo
2201 Tuolumne St.
Vallejo, CA 94589
Ph: (707)558-1777
URL: http://www.crestwoodbehavioralhealth.com/

Venice

29185 ■ Saint Joseph Center
204 Hampton Dr.
Venice, CA 90291
Ph: (310)396-6468

Ventura

29186 ■ Ventura County Behavioral Health Center--Ventura
4258 Telegraph Rd.
Ventura, CA 93003
Ph: (805)981-4200
Formerly: Ventura County Mental Health Center.

Victorville

29187 ■ Veterans Affairs Medical Center
Victorville Clinic
12138 Industrial Blvd., Ste. 120
Victorville, CA 92392
Ph: (760)951-2599
URL: http://www2.va.gov/directory/guide/facility.asp?ID=5124&dnum=1

29188 ■ Victor Community Support Services
15095 Amargosa Rd., Ste. 201
Victorville, CA 92395
Ph: (760)245-4695

Vista

29189 ■ Veterans Affairs Medical Center
Vista Clinic
1840 West Dr.
Vista, CA 92083
Ph: (760)643-2000
URL: http://www2.va.gov/directory/guide/facility.asp?ID=5125&dnum=1

Watsonville

29190 ■ Community Recovery Services
Alto Counseling Center
18 Alexander St.
Watsonville, CA 95075
Ph: (831)427-5290
E-mail: info@crs.org
URL: http://www.scccc.org/community-recovery-services/alto
Formerly: Alto Counseling Center.

29191 ■ Community Recovery Services
Si Se Puede
161A Miles Ln.
Watsonville, CA 95076-3127
Ph: (831)761-5422
URL: http://www.scccc.org/community-recovery-services/si-se-puede
Formerly: Si Se Puede.

29192 ■ Youth Services--Watsonville
241 E Lake Ave.
Watsonville, CA 95076
Ph: (831)688-8856

West Hills

29193 ■ Penny Lane Centers
Satellite IV
23310 Gilmore St.
West Hills, CA 91307
Ph: (818)992-1707
URL: http://www.pennylane.org/

29194 ■ Penny Lane Centers
Satellite IX
6564 Valley Circle Blvd.
West Hills, CA 91307
Ph: (818)715-0120
URL: http://www.pennylane.org/

West Sacramento

29195 ■ Yolo County Department of Alcohol, Drug and Mental Health
500 Jefferson Blvd., Ste. B
West Sacramento, CA 95605
Ph: (916)375-6350

29196 ■ Yolo Family Service Agency--West Sacramento
1600 Sacramento Ave., Ste. 3
West Sacramento, CA 95605
Ph: (530)375-1254

Woodland

29197 ■ Safe Harbor Crisis House
584 Kentucky Ave.
Woodland, CA 95695
Ph: (530)661-3213
E-mail: safe@y3c.org
URL: http://www.y3c.org

Yucca Valley

29198 ■ Pacific Clinics
58945 Business Center Dr., Ste. D
Yucca Valley, CA 92284
Ph: (760)228-9657
URL: http://www.pacificclinics.org/

COLORADO

Akron

29199 ■ Centennial Mental Health Center--Akron
871 E 1st St.
Akron, CO 80720
Ph: (970)345-2254
URL: http://www.centennialmhc.org

Aspen

29200 ■ Colorado West Mental Health, Inc.
Aspen Counseling Center
405 Castle Creek Rd., Ste. 9
Aspen, CO 81611-3125
Ph: (970)920-5555

Aurora

29201 ■ Aurora Community Mental Health Center
11059 E Bethany Dr., Ste. 200
Aurora, CO 80014-2637
Ph: (303)617-2300

29202 ■ Beeler Street House
1455 Beeler St.
Aurora, CO 80010-3027
Ph: (303)360-6014

29203 ■ Jefferson Hills II
1290 S Potomac St.
Aurora, CO 80012
Ph: (303)745-1281

29204 ■ University of Colorado at Denver Psychiatry Service
13001 E 17th Pl., Bldg. 500, 2nd Fl.
Aurora, CO 80045
Ph: (303)724-1000
URL: http://www.uchsc.edu/psychiatry/clinical/Outpatient.htm

Black Hawk

29205 ■ Jefferson Center for Mental Health Gilpin Mental Health Services
2960 Dory Hill Rd., Ste. 100
Black Hawk, CO 80403
Ph: (303)582-6033

Boulder

29206 ■ Boulder Community Hospital Behavioral Health
1100 Balsam Ave.
Boulder, CO 980304
Ph: (303)440-2273
URL: http://www.bch.org

29207 ■ The Chinook Clubhouse
1441 Broadway
Boulder, CO 80302
Ph: (303)440-4842
Fax: (303)415-0413
E-mail: clubhouse@mhcbc.org
URL: http://www.chinookclubhouse.org/

29208 ■ Community Support Systems Team Mental Health Center of Boulder County
1036 University Ave.
Boulder, CO 80302-6102
Ph: (303)443-6154
Formerly: Maslin House.

29209 ■ Mental Health Center of Boulder County Boulder Office
1333 Iris Ave.
Boulder, CO 80304
Ph: (303)443-8500
URL: http://www.mhcbc.org/

29210 ■ Mental Health Center of Boulder County, Inc. Halcyon Office
3100 Bucknell Ct.
Boulder, CO 80305-3465
Ph: (303)499-1121

29211 ■ Moving to End Sexual Assault
2885 E Aurora Ave., Ste. 10
Boulder, CO 80303-2251
Ph: (303)443-0400
URL: http://www.mhcbc.org/index.php?id=emergency_services
Formerly: Mental Health Center of Boulder County.

Brighton

29212 ■ Community Reach Center--Brighton Office
1850 E Egbert St.
Brighton, CO 80601
Ph: (303)853-3600

Broomfield

29213 ■ Mental Health Center of Boulder County Broomfield Office
899 Hwy. 287, Ste. 300
Broomfield, CO 80020
Ph: (303)466-3007

Burlington

29214 ■ Centennial Mental Health Center--Burlington
1251 Circle Dr.
Burlington, CO 80807
Ph: (719)346-8183
URL: http://www.centennialmhc.org

Canon City

29215 ■ West Central Mental Health Center, Inc.
3225 Independence Rd.
Canon City, CO 81212
Ph: (719)275-2351
URL: http://www.wcmhc.org/

Castle Rock

29216 ■ Arapahoe/Douglas Mental Health
1189 S Perry St., Ste. 150
Castle Rock, CO 80104
Ph: (303)688-6276
URL: http://www.admhn.org/Locations.aspx

Centennial

29217 ■ Arapahoe/Douglas Mental Health Network Administrative Office
6801 S Yosemite St., Ste. 200
Centennial, CO 80112
Ph: (303)779-9666
Fax: (303)779-6038
URL: http://www.admhn.org/Locations.aspx
Formerly: Arapahoe Mental Health Network.

Colorado Springs

29218 ■ Denver Veterans Affairs Medical Center Colorado Springs Clinic
25 N Spruce St.
Colorado Springs, CO 80905
Ph: (719)327-5660
Free: 800-278-3883
URL: http://www2.va.gov/directory/guide/facility.asp?ID=882&dnum=All

29219 ■ Pikes Peak Behavioral Health Group Administrative & Business Office
525 N Cascade Ave., Ste. 100
Colorado Springs, CO 80903
Ph: (719)572-6100
Free: 800-285-1204
Fax: (719)572-6199
URL: http://www.ppmhc.org

29220 ■ Pikes Peak Behavioral Health Group First Choice Counseling
2864 S Circle Dr., Ste. 600
Colorado Springs, CO 80906
Ph: (719)572-6190
Free: 800-285-1204
URL: http://www.ppmhc.org

29221 ■ Pikes Peak Mental Health Center Adult Services Network
875 W Moreno Ave.
Colorado Springs, CO 80905
Ph: (719)572-6200
Free: 800-285-1204
URL: http://www.ppmhc.org
Formerly: Community Support & Recovery Program.

29222 ■ Pikes Peak Mental Health Center Child and Family Center
179 Parkside Dr.
Colorado Springs, CO 80910-3130
Ph: (719)572-6300
Free: 800-285-1204
Fax: (719)572-6199
URL: http://www.ppmhc.org

Commerce City

29223 ■ Community Reach Center Commerce City Office
4371 E 72nd Ave.
Commerce City, CO 80022
Ph: (303)853-3456

Cortez

29224 ■ Cortez Counseling Center Southwest Colorado Mental Health Center, Inc.
215 W Arbecam Ave.
Cortez, CO 81321-2705
Ph: (970)565-7946

Craig

29225 ■ Colorado West Mental Health, Inc. Craig Mental Health
439 Breeze St., Ste. 200
Craig, CO 81625-2646
Ph: (970)824-6541
Fax: (970)824-0313

Delta

29226 ■ Midwestern Colorado Mental Health Center Center for Mental Health
107 W 111th St.
Delta, CO 81416-2298
Ph: (970)874-8981

Denver

29227 ■ Access Center
4353 E Colfax Ave.
Denver, CO 80220-1115
Ph: (303)504-1250

29228 ■ Capitol Hill ILT and CTT
555 Humboldt St.
Denver, CO 80218
Ph: (303)504-1800

29229 ■ Charg Resource Center
709 E 12th Ave.
Denver, CO 80203
Ph: (303)830-8805
Fax: (303)830-8918
E-mail: info@charg.org
URL: http://www.charg.org/about.html

29230 ■ Downing Community Treatment Team Mental Health Center of Denver
1634 Downing St.
Denver, CO 80218-1529
Ph: (303)504-1800
URL: http://www.mhcd.org/
Formerly: Mental Health Corporation of Denver.

29231 ■ Mental Health Center of Denver
4141 E Dickenson Pl.
Denver, CO 80222-6012
Ph: (303)504-6500
URL: http://www.mhcd.org/
Formerly: Mental Health Corporation of Denver.

29232 ■ Mental Health Center of Denver
Adult Outpatient
2925 E Colfax Ave.
Denver, CO 80206-1604
Ph: (303)504-1100
URL: http://www.mhcd.org/

29233 ■ Miller House--Denver
1920 E 13th Ave.
Denver, CO 80206
Ph: (303)321-2482

29234 ■ Monroe House
1425 Monroe St.
Denver, CO 80206-2708
Ph: (303)377-2586

29235 ■ NEW Visions
1810 S Hooker St.
Denver, CO 80219-4605
Ph: (303)936-8105
Formerly: South Hooker.

29236 ■ Second Street House
200 S Sherman
Denver, CO 80209
Ph: (303)765-2480

29237 ■ Shoshone House
3429 Shoshone
Denver, CO 80211
Ph: (303)458-5346

29238 ■ Third Way Center
50 W 5th Ave.
Denver, CO 80204
Ph: (303)780-9191
Fax: (303)780-9192
E-mail: info@thirdwaycenter.org
URL: http://www.thirdwaycenter.org/

29239 ■ Veterans Affairs Eastern Colorado Health Care System
1055 Clermont St.
Denver, CO 80220
Ph: (303)399-8020
Free: 888-336-8262
Fax: (303)393-2861
URL: http://www2.va.gov/directory/guide/facility.asp?ID=39&dnum=All

29240 ■ West Denver Child and Family Center
1405 N Federal Blvd.
Denver, CO 80204
Ph: (303)504-1500

29241 ■ Wishing Well Clubhouse
456 Bannock St.
Denver, CO 80203
Ph: (303)504-1700
URL: http://www.wishingwell.org/
Formerly: Wishing Well Enterprise.

29242 ■ Wishing Well Enterprises
2986 N Speer Blvd.
Denver, CO 80211-3793
Ph: (303)504-6800
URL: http://www.wishingwell.org/

Durango

29243 ■ Durango Counseling Center
Southwest Colorado Mental Health Center, Inc.
281 Sawyer Dr.
Durango, CO 81303
Ph: (970)259-2162
Fax: (970)247-5255
URL: http://www.swcmhc.org/

29244 ■ Southwest Colorado Mental Health Center, Inc.
Crossroads
1125 3 Springs Blvd.
Durango, CO 81301
Ph: (970)403-0180
Fax: (970)403-0190
URL: http://www.swcmhc.org/

Eagle

29245 ■ Colorado West Mental Health, Inc.
Eagle Valley
137 Howard St.
Eagle, CO 81631
Ph: (970)328-6969
Fax: (970)328-6329

Elizabeth

29246 ■ Centennial Mental Health Center--Elizabeth
650 E Walnut St.
Elizabeth, CO 80107
Ph: (303)646-4519
E-mail: elizabeth@centennialmhc.org
URL: http://www.centennialmhc.org

Englewood

29247 ■ Arapahoe Douglas Mental Health Network
Adolescent Day Resource Center
595 W Belleview Ave.
Englewood, CO 80110-6703
Ph: (303)761-7991

Estes Park

29248 ■ Larimer Center for Mental Health
1950 Red Tail Hawk Dr.
Estes Park, CO 80517
Ph: (970)586-9105

Evergreen

29249 ■ Jefferson Center for Mental Health
28577 Buffalo Rd., Ste 250
Evergreen, CO 80439
Ph: (303)432-5300

Fort Collins

29250 ■ Larimer Center for Mental Health
Adult Services
525 W Oak St.
Fort Collins, CO 80521
Ph: (970)494-4300
URL: http://www.larimercenter.org/
Formerly: Larimer County Mental Health Center.

29251 ■ Larimer Center for Mental Health
Children and Family Services
2001 S Shields, Bldg. K
Fort Collins, CO 80526
Ph: (970)494-4200
URL: http://www.larimercenter.org/

29252 ■ Larimer Center for Mental Health
Choice House
214 S Whitcomb St.
Fort Collins, CO 80521
Ph: (970)498-7610
URL: http://www.larimercenter.org/services.htm
Formerly: Larimer County Mental Health Center.

29253 ■ Larimer Center for Mental Health
Promise House
216 S Whitcomb St.
Fort Collins, CO 80521
Ph: (970)494-4300
URL: http://www.larimercenter.org/services.htm
Formerly: Larimer County Mental Health Center.

29254 ■ Mountain Crest Behavioral Healthcare System/PVHS
4601 Corbett Dr.
Fort Collins, CO 80528
Ph: (970)207-4800
Free: 800-523-1213
E-mail: pvhs@pvhs.org
URL: https://vic.pvhs.org/portal/page?_pageid=333,352947&_dad=portal&_schema=PORTAL

Fort Lupton

29255 ■ South County Clinic
120 1st St.
Fort Lupton, CO 80621
Ph: (303)857-2723
Formerly: North Range Behavioral Health South County Clinic.

Fort Morgan

29256 ■ Centennial Mental Health Center--Fort Morgan
910 E Railroad Ave.
Fort Morgan, CO 80701-3399
Ph: (970)867-4924
URL: http://www.centennialmhc.org

Frisco

29257 ■ Colorado West Mental Health, Inc.
Summit Center
360 Peak 1 Dr.
Frisco, CO 80443
Ph: (970)668-3478
Fax: (970)668-0632
URL: http://www.cwrmhc.org/frisco.htm

Glenwood Springs

29258 ■ Colorado West Regional Mental Health Center
Administrative Office & Garfield Service
6916 Hwy. 82
Glenwood Springs, CO 81601
Ph: (970)945-2583
Fax: (970)928-8852
URL: http://www.cwrmhc.org/garop.htm
Formerly: Colorado West Regional Mental Health.

29259 ■ Colorado West Regional Mental Health, Inc.
6916 Hwy. 82
Glenwood Springs, CO 81602
Ph: (970)945-2241
Fax: (970)945-5523
URL: http://www.cwrmhc.org/

Granby

29260 ■ Colorado West Mental Health, Inc.
Alpine Center
1023 Country Rd. 610
Granby, CO 80446-0726
Ph: (970)887-2179
Fax: (970)887-9311
URL: http://www.cwrmhc.org/granby.htm

Grand Junction

29261 ■ Colorado West Mental Health, Inc.
Child & Family Program
51528 3/4 Rd., Bldg. A
Grand Junction, CO 81506
Ph: (970)245-3270
Fax: (970)245-6660
URL: http://www.cwrmhc.org/gjcf.htm
Formerly: Colorado West Mental Health Rio Bianco Center.

29262 ■ Colorado West Mental Health, Inc. Grand Junction Adult Outpatient Cliic
Bldg. A
51528 3/4 Rd.
Grand Junction, CO 81501
Ph: (970)241-6023
URL: http://www.cwrmhc.org/gjadult.htm
Formerly: Colorado East Mental Health; Canyon View Center Adult Services.

Greeley

29263 ■ Acute Treatment Unit
1309 10th Ave.
Greeley, CO 80631-3832
Ph: (970)347-2127
URL: http://www.northrange.org/
Formerly: North Range Behavioral Unit Acute Treatment Center.

29264 ■ Cheyenne Veterans Affairs Medical Center Greeley Clinic
2001 70th Ave., Ste. 200
Greeley, CO 80631
Ph: (970)313-0027
URL: http://www2.va.gov/directory/guide/facility.asp?ID=871&dnum=All

29265 ■ North Range Behavioral Health
1300 N 17th Ave.
Greeley, CO 80631
Ph: (970)347-2120
URL: http://www.northrange.org/

29266 ■ North Range Behavioral Health Adult Services
1300 N 17th Ave.
Greeley, CO 80631
Ph: (970)347-2120
URL: http://www.northrange.org/programs.htm

Holyoke

29267 ■ Centennial Mental Health Center--Holyoke
127 E Denver St.
Holyoke, CO 80734-1513
Ph: (970)854-2114
URL: http://www.centennialmhc.org

Idaho Springs

29268 ■ Jefferson Center for Mental Health Clear Creek Community Service Center
1531 Colorado Blvd.
Idaho Springs, CO 80452
Ph: (303)567-3131

Julesburg

29269 ■ Centennial Mental Health Center--Julesburg
118 W 3rd St.
Julesburg, CO 80737-1680
Ph: (970)474-3769
URL: http://www.centennialmhc.org

La Junta

29270 ■ Denver Veterans Affairs Medical Center La Junta Clinic
1100 Carson Ave., Ste. 104
La Junta, CO
Ph: (719)383-5195
Free: 877-329-2625
URL: http://www2.va.gov/directory/guide/facility.asp?ID=5050&dnum=All

29271 ■ Southeast Mental Health Services
711 Barnes Ave.
La Junta, CO 81050-2100
Ph: (719)384-5446
Free: 800-511-5446
URL: http://www.semhs.org/
Formerly: Southeastern Colorado Family Guidance and Mental Health.

Lafayette

29272 ■ Mental Health Center of Boulder County, Inc. Lafayette Office
400 E Simpson St., Ste. 202
Lafayette, CO 80026
Ph: (303)665-2670
Fax: (303)661-0818
URL: http://www.mhcbc.org

Lakewood

29273 ■ Jefferson Center for Mental Health Carr Street Center and Older Adults
1675 Carr St.
Lakewood, CO 80215
Ph: (303)432-5700
URL: http://www.jeffersonmentalhealth.org/contact.cfm

29274 ■ Jefferson Center for Mental Health Fenton Place
5797 W 16th Ave.
Lakewood, CO 80214
Ph: (303)432-5000
URL: http://www.jeffersonmentalhealth.org/contact.cfm

29275 ■ Jefferson Center for Mental Health HAF House
8640 W Jewell Ave.
Lakewood, CO 80226
Ph: (303)988-8493
URL: http://www.jeffersonmentalhealth.org/contact.cfm

29276 ■ Jefferson Center for Mental Health Hilltop Residential Facility
10527 W 6th Pl.
Lakewood, CO 80215
Ph: (303)237-4799
URL: http://www.jeffersonmentalhealth.org/contact.cfm

29277 ■ Jefferson Center for Mental Health Jefferson Hills I
421 Zang St.
Lakewood, CO 80228
Ph: (303)989-4357
URL: http://www.jeffersonmentalhealth.org/contact.cfm

29278 ■ Jefferson Center for Mental Health Sobesky Academy Day Treatment
2001 Hoyt St.
Lakewood, CO 80215
Ph: (303)982-5995
URL: http://www.jeffersonmentalhealth.org/contact.cfm

29279 ■ Jefferson Center for Mental Health Teller Residential Facility
7290 W 14th Ave.
Lakewood, CO 80215
Ph: (303)232-8047
URL: http://www.jeffersonmentalhealth.org/contact.cfm

29280 ■ Jefferson Center for Mental Health Transitions in Community Living
9808 W Cedar Ave.
Lakewood, CO 80226
Ph: (303)432-5400
URL: http://www.jeffersonmentalhealth.org/contact.cfm

29281 ■ Jefferson Center for Mental Health Transitions Meadowlark Day Treatment
11025 W Glennon Dr.
Lakewood, CO 80226
Ph: (303)982-5997
URL: http://www.jeffersonmentalhealth.org/contact.cfm

29282 ■ Jefferson Center for Mental Health West Colfax Outpatient/Emergency Services
9485 W Colfax Ave.
Lakewood, CO 80215
Ph: (303)432-5200
URL: http://www.jeffersonmentalhealth.org/contact.cfm

Limon

29283 ■ Centennial Mental Health Center--Limon
606 Main St.
Limon, CO 80828
Ph: (719)775-2313
Fax: (719)775-2315
URL: http://www.centennialmhc.org

Littleton

29284 ■ Arapahoe/Douglas Mental Health Center Santa Fe House
6509 S Santa Fe Dr.
Littleton, CO 80120
Ph: (303)797-9343
Fax: (303)797-9345
URL: http://www.admhn.org/Locations.aspx
Formerly: Arapahoe Mental Health Center.

29285 ■ Arapahoe Douglas Mental Health Network
5500 S Sycamore St.
Littleton, CO 80120-8201
Ph: (303)797-9440
Fax: (303)797-9348
URL: http://www.admhn.org

Longmont

29286 ■ Mental Health Center of Boulder County, Inc. Saint Vrain ATP
834 S Sherman St.
Longmont, CO 80501
Ph: (303)776-7840
URL: http://www.mhcbc.org

29287 ■ Mental Health Center of Boulder County Longmont Office
529 Coffman Ave., Ste. 300
Longmont, CO 80501
Ph: (303)684-0555

Loveland

29288 ■ Larimer Center for Mental Health Loveland Branch
1250 N Wilson Ave.
Loveland, CO 80537
Ph: (970)494-9870

Monte Vista

29289 ■ San Luis Valley Comprehensive Community Mental Health Center
402 4th Ave.
Monte Vista, CO 81144-1120
Ph: (719)852-5186

Montrose

29290 ■ Grand Junction Veterans Affairs Medical Center Montrose Clinic
4 Hillcrest Plz. Way
Montrose, CO 81401

Ph: (970)249-7791
Free: 866-206-6415
URL: http://www2.va.gov/directory/guide/facility.asp?ID=874&dnum=All

Northglenn

29291 ■ Community Reach Center
Child and Family Services
11285 Highline Dr.
Northglenn, CO 80233
Ph: (303)853-3400

Pagosa Springs

29292 ■ Southwestern Colorado Mental Health Center, Inc.
Pagosa Springs Counseling Center
475 Lewis St., Ste. 104
Pagosa Springs, CO 81147
Ph: (970)264-2104

Parker

29293 ■ Arapahoe/Douglas Mental Health--Parker Office
19751 E Main St., Ste. 247
Parker, CO 80138
Ph: (303)805-4312
URL: http://www.admhn.org/Locations.aspx

Pueblo

29294 ■ Acute Treatment Unit
1302 Chinook Ln.
Pueblo, CO 81001-1851
Ph: (719)545-2746

29295 ■ Community Support Program
Psychosocial Rehabilitation
1012 W Abriendo Ave.
Pueblo, CO 81004-1128
Ph: (719)583-2207
Formerly: Community Support Program Psychosocial Rehabilitation Spanish Peaks Mental Health Center.

29296 ■ Denver Veterans Affairs Medical Center
Pueblo Clinic
4112 Outlook Blvd.
Pueblo, CO 81008
Ph: (719)553-1000
Free: 800-369-6748
URL: http://www2.va.gov/directory/guide/facility.asp?ID=884&dnum=All

29297 ■ Spanish Peaks Mental Health Center
1026 W Abriendo Ave.
Pueblo, CO 81004
Ph: (719)545-2746
Fax: (719)584-0110
E-mail: webmaster@spmhc.org
URL: http://www.spmhc.org

29298 ■ Spanish Peaks Mental Health Center
Chaurtard House
2109 Chaurtard
Pueblo, CO 81005
Ph: (719)545-8110
URL: http://www.spmhc.org

29299 ■ Spanish Peaks Mental Health Center
Community Support Program/Geriatrics
2003 E 4th St.
Pueblo, CO 81001-4196
Ph: (719)544-6373
URL: http://www.spmhc.org

29300 ■ Spanish Peaks Mental Health Center
Lavilla De Evans
1033 E Evans Ave.
Pueblo, CO 81004-2538
Ph: (719)545-0152
URL: http://www.spmhc.org

29301 ■ Spanish Peaks Mental Health Center
Spanish Peaks Apartments
621 W 10th St.
Pueblo, CO 81003-2255
Ph: (719)555-2746
URL: http://www.spmhc.org

Rangely

29302 ■ Colorado West Mental Health, Inc.
Rangely Outpatient Clinic
17497 Hwy. 64
Rangely, CO 81648
Ph: (970)675-8411
Fax: (970)675-2508
URL: http://www.cwrmhc.org/range.htm
Formerly: Rio Blanco Center.

San Luis

29303 ■ San Luis Valley Comprehensive
409 Trinchera St.
San Luis, CO 81152
Ph: (719)672-0331
E-mail: info@slvmhc.org
URL: http://www.slvmhc.org/locations2.htm

Springfield

29304 ■ Southeast Mental Health Services
1049 Kansas St.
Springfield, CO 81073
Ph: (719)384-5446

Steamboat Springs

29305 ■ Colorado West Mental Health, Inc.
Steamboat Center
407 S Lincoln Ave.
Steamboat Springs, CO 80477
Ph: (970)879-2141
Fax: (970)879-7912
URL: http://www.cwrmhc.org/sboat.htm

Sterling

29306 ■ Centennial Mental Health Center
Fourth Street House
114 N 4th St.
Sterling, CO 80751
Ph: (970)522-7657
URL: http://www.centennialmhc.org

29307 ■ Centennial Mental Health Center--Sterling
211 W Main St.
Sterling, CO 80751-3168
Ph: (970)522-4392
E-mail: webmaster@centennialmhc.org
URL: http://www.centennialmhc.org

Telluride

29308 ■ Midwestern Colorado Mental Health Center
Center for Mental Health
100 W Colorado Blvd., Ste. 225
Telluride, CO 81435
Ph: (970)728-6303

Trinidad

29309 ■ Spanish Peaks Mental Health Center
Trinidad Office
417 S Indiana Ave.
Trinidad, CO 81082-3198
Ph: (719)846-4416
Fax: (719)846-6408
URL: http://www.spmhc.org

Vail

29310 ■ Colorado West Mental Health, Inc.
Vail Outpatient Clinic
395 E Lionshead Cir.
Vail, CO 81657-5203
Ph: (970)476-0930
Formerly: Eagle Valley.

Walsenburg

29311 ■ Spanish Peaks Mental Health Center
Walsenburg Office
926 Russell Ave.
Walsenburg, CO 81089-2134
Ph: (719)738-2386
Fax: (719)738-2001
URL: http://www.spmhc.org

Westminster

29312 ■ Jefferson Center for Mental Health
Westminster Counseling Service
3031 W 76th Ave.
Westminster, CO 80030
Ph: (303)853-3661
URL: http://www.jeffersonmentalhealth.org/

29313 ■ Jefferson Center for Mental Health
Westminster Office
9101 Harlan St., Ste. 130
Westminster, CO 80031-2961
Ph: (303)432-5650
E-mail: info@jcmh.org
URL: http://www.jeffersonmentalhealth.org

Wheat Ridge

29314 ■ Jefferson Center for Mental Health
North Outpatient Office
4851 Independence St., Ste. 200
Wheat Ridge, CO 80033
Ph: (303)425-0300
Free: 800-201-5264
E-mail: info@jcmh.org
URL: http://www.jeffersonmentalhealth.org

29315 ■ Jefferson Center for Mental Health
The ROAD
6175 W 38th Ave.
Wheat Ridge, CO 80033
Ph: (303)233-0488
Free: 800-201-5264
E-mail: info@jcmh.org
URL: http://www.jeffersonmentalhealth.org

29316 ■ Jefferson Center for Mental Health
Summit Center
3810 Pierce St.
Wheat Ridge, CO 80033
Ph: (303)432-5800
Free: 800-201-5264
E-mail: info@jcmh.org
URL: http://www.jeffersonmentalhealth.org

29317 ■ Jefferson Center for Mental Health
Wellness on Wadsworth
4045 Wadsworth Blvd., Ste. 70
Wheat Ridge, CO 80033
Ph: (303)432-5032
Free: 800-201-5264
E-mail: info@jcmh.org
URL: http://www.jeffersonmentalhealth.org

Wray

29318 ■ Centennial Mental Health Center--Wray
340 S Birch St.
Wray, CO 80758-1840
Ph: (970)332-3133
URL: http://www.centennialmhc.org/

Yuma

29319 ■ Centennial Mental Health Center--Yuma
215 S Ash St.
Yuma, CO 80759-1903
Ph: (970)848-5412
Fax: (970)848-2414
URL: http://www.centennialmhc.org/

CONNECTICUT

Ansonia

29320 ■ Valley Mental Health Center--Ansonia
435 E Main St.
Ansonia, CT 06401
Ph: (203)736-2601
URL: http://www.bghealth.org/behavioral_health.htm

Bethlehem

29321 ■ Angelus House
158 Flanders Rd.
Bethlehem, CT 06751
Ph: (203)266-8080
URL: http://www.wellspring.org

29322 ■ Wellspring Foundation
21 Arch Bridge Rd.
Bethlehem, CT 06751-1612
Ph: (203)266-8002
Fax: (203)266-8030
URL: http://www.wellspring.org

Bozrah

29323 ■ Reliance House, Inc.
Bozrah House
36 Haughton Rd.
Bozrah, CT 06334
Ph: (860)892-5459
Fax: (860)823-1124
URL: http://www.reliancehouse.org/home_files/page0002.htm

Branford

29324 ■ Branford Counseling Center
342 Harbor St.
Branford, CT 06405-4540
Ph: (203)481-4248

29325 ■ Harbor Apartment and Respite Program
33 Briarwood Ln.
Branford, CT 06405
Ph: (203)483-2635

29326 ■ Harbor Health Services
14 Sycamore Way
Branford, CT 06405-6551
Ph: (203)483-2630
Fax: (203)483-2659
URL: http://www.harborhealthservices.org

29327 ■ Harbor House
79 Cedar St.
Branford, CT 06405-3605
Ph: (203)483-2662

Bridgeport

29328 ■ Child Guidance Center of Greater Bridgeport, Inc.
180 Fairfield Ave.
Bridgeport, CT 06604-3713
Ph: (203)367-5361

29329 ■ Saint Vincent's Medical Center
Behavioral Health
2800 Main St.
Bridgeport, CT 06606-4292
Ph: (203)576-6000

29330 ■ Southwest Connecticut Mental Health System
Greater Bridgeport Community Mental Health Center
1635 Central Ave.
Bridgeport, CT 06610-2700
Ph: (203)551-7400
Formerly: Greater Bridgeport Community Mental Health Center.

Bristol

29331 ■ Community Mental Health Affiliates, Inc.
81 N Main St.
Bristol, CT 06010
Ph: (860)583-9954
Fax: (860)585-6811
URL: http://www.cmhacc.org

Chester

29332 ■ Gateway Counseling Service, Inc.
86 Middlesex Ave.
Chester, CT 06412-1224
Ph: (860)526-2624

Columbia

29333 ■ United Services, Inc.--Columbia
233 Rte. 6
Columbia, CT 06237-1125
Ph: (860)228-4480
E-mail: mail@unitedservicesct.org
URL: http://www.unitedservicesct.org/

Danbury

29334 ■ Intensive Residential Support
29B Grand St.
Danbury, CT 06810-7928
Ph: (203)797-1201

29335 ■ Interlude
60 West St.
Danbury, CT 06810
Ph: (203)797-1210

29336 ■ Outreach Program
83 West St.
Danbury, CT 06810-5949
Ph: (203)748-3636

29337 ■ Recovery Program
19-1 Cleveland St.
Danbury, CT 06810
Ph: (203)743-1599

29338 ■ Veterans Affairs Connecticut Healthcare System
Danbury Clinic
7 Germantown Rd.
Danbury, CT 06810
Ph: (203)798-8422
URL: http://www2.va.gov/directory/guide/facility.asp?ID=5185&dnum=All

Darien

29339 ■ Family Centers, Inc.
590 Post Rd.
Darien, CT 06820
Ph: (203)655-4693

Dayville

29340 ■ United Services, Inc.--Dayville
1007 N Main St.
Dayville, CT 06241
Ph: (860)774-2020
E-mail: mail@unitedservicessct.org
URL: http://www.unitedservicesct.org

Derby

29341 ■ Griffin Hospital
130 Division St.
Derby, CT 06418-1326
Ph: (203)732-7580
URL: http://www.griffinhealth.org/

East Hartford

29342 ■ Intercommunity Mental Health Group
281 Main St.
East Hartford, CT 06118
Ph: (860)569-5900
URL: http://www.icmhg.org/

29343 ■ Town of East Hartford Department of Youth Services
50 Chapman Pl., Lower Level
East Hartford, CT 06108
Ph: (860)291-7179
URL: http://www.ci.east-hartford.ct.us/Public_Documents/EastHartfordCT_Youth/INDEX

East Haven

29344 ■ East Haven Counseling and Community Services
595 Thompson Ave.
East Haven, CT 06512-2934
Ph: (203)488-0105
Formerly: East Haven Counseling and Community Center.

Enfield

29345 ■ New Directions, Inc.--Enfield
113 Elm St., Ste. 204
Enfield, CT 06082
Ph: (860)741-3001
Fax: (860)741-8332
E-mail: cleary@newdirectionsct.org
URL: http://www.newdirectionsct.org/

29346 ■ Northfield Group Home
34 Prospect St.
Enfield, CT 06082
Ph: (860)253-5035
Fax: (860)253-5036

Fairfield

29347 ■ Child Guidance Center of Greater Bridgeport, Inc.
148 Beach Rd.
Fairfield, CT 06825
Ph: (203)255-2631
URL: http://www.cgcgb.org

Greenwich

29348 ■ Family Center, Inc.
20 Bridge St.
Greenwich, CT 06830
Ph: (203)629-2822
URL: http://www.familycenters.org/

29349 ■ Pathways, Inc.--Greenwich
175 Milbank Ave.
Greenwich, CT 06830
Ph: (203)869-5656
E-mail: info@pathways-greenwich,org
URL: http://pathways-greenwich.org/

Groton

29350 ■ Care Plus--Groton
1353 Gold Star Hwy.
Groton, CT 06340
Ph: (860)449-9947
URL: http://www.natchaug.org/locations.asp?loc=groton

29351 ■ Stonington Institute--Groton
428 Long Hill Rd.
Groton, CT 06340
Ph: (860)449-0611
URL: http://www.stoningtoninstitute.com/

Hamden

29352 ■ Yale Behavioral Health Services
95 Circular Ave.
Hamden, CT 06514
Ph: (203)288-6253
URL: http://www.med.yale.edu/psych/clinical_care/behavioral.html

Hartford

29353 ■ Center for Human Development, Inc.
Connecticut Outreach
237 Hamilton St., Ste. 107
Hartford, CT 06106-2977
Ph: (860)951-3325
URL: http://www.chd.org/
Formerly: Connecticut Outreach.

29354 ■ Hartford Behavioral Health
1 Main St.
Hartford, CT 06120-1806
Ph: (860)727-8703
URL: http://www.hartfordbehavioralhealth.org/

Jewett City

29355 ■ Reliance House, Inc.--Bridge Program
64 S Main St.
Jewett City, CT 06351
Ph: (860)376-5991
URL: http://www.reliancehouse.org/home.htm

Manchester

29356 ■ May Institute--Manchester
360 Tolland Tpke., Ste. 2D
Manchester, CT 06040
Ph: (860)643-9844
URL: http://www.mayinstitute.org/

Mansfield Center

29357 ■ Journey House
189 Storrs Rd.
Mansfield Center, CT 06250
Ph: (860)456-1311
Free: 800-426-7792
URL: http://www.natchaug.org/locations.asp

Meriden

29358 ■ MidState Medical Center--Behavioral Health
435 Lewis Ave.
Meriden, CT 06451
Ph: (203)694-8200
Free: 800-542-4791
URL: http://www.midstatemedical.org/ServiceProgram/Behavioral_Health.sdpx

Middletown

29359 ■ Gilead Community Services, Inc.
222 Main St.
Middletown, CT 06457
Ph: (860)343-5300
URL: http://www.gileadcs.org/index.php

29360 ■ Gilead Vocational & Social Center
31 DeJohn Dr.
Middletown, CT 06457
Ph: (860)343-5310
URL: http://www.gileadcs.org/index.php

29361 ■ Middlesex Hospital
Center for Behavioral Health
33 Pleasant St.
Middletown, CT 06457
Ph: (860)358-8800
URL: http://www.middlesexhealth.org/go/midHome

Milford

29362 ■ Boys Village Youth and Family Services
528 Wheelers Farm Rd.
Milford, CT 06461
Ph: (203)877-0300

29363 ■ Bridges--A Community Support System
949 Bridgeport Ave.
Milford, CT 06460
Ph: (203)878-6365

Montville

29364 ■ Reliance House, Inc.
Montville Home
1329 Rte. 163
Montville, CT 06382
Ph: (860)367-0535
Fax: (860)367-9045
E-mail: dwise@reliancehouse.org
URL: http://www.reliancehouse.org/home.htm

Moosup

29365 ■ Milner House
249 Main St.
Moosup, CT 06354
Ph: (860)564-4007
URL: http://www.unitedservicesct.org

New Britain

29366 ■ Adult Services Harvest House/ACT
5 Hart St.
New Britain, CT 06052
Ph: (860)229-4850
URL: http://www.cmhacc.org/index.php?option=com_content&view=article&id=83&Itemi d=83
Formerly: Adult Services Harvest House.

29367 ■ Catholic Family Services--New Britain
90 Franklin Sq.
New Britain, CT 06051-2607
Ph: (203)225-3561
Free: 800-547-1452
E-mail: pagenew@ccaoh.org
URL: http://www.ccaoh.org/

29368 ■ Child Guidance Clinic--New Britain
26 Russell St.
New Britain, CT 06052-1313
Ph: (860)223-2778
URL: http://www.cmhacc.org/index.php?option=com_content&view=article&id=66&Itemi d=77

29369 ■ Community Mental Health Affiliates, Inc.
Family Counseling Center
92 Vine St.
New Britain, CT 06052
Ph: (860)223-9291
URL: http://www.cmhacc.org/index.php?option=com_content&view=article&id=53&Itemi d=67

29370 ■ Community Mental Health Affiliates, Inc.
Intensive Assertive Community Treatment
235 Beaver St.
New Britain, CT 06051
Ph: (860)224-2044
URL: http://www.cmhacc.org/index.php?option=com_content&view=article&id=83&Itemi d=83

29371 ■ Transitional Youth Program
33 Elam St., Ste. 10
New Britain, CT 06053
Ph: (860)224-8880
URL: http://www.cmhacc.org/

New Haven

29372 ■ ALSO--Cornerstone, Inc.
Dwight House
282 Dwight St.
New Haven, CT 06511
Ph: (203)777-3216
URL: http://www.al-corn.org/

29373 ■ ALSO--Cornerstone, Inc.
Orange Street, New Haven
205 Orange St., Ste. 1
New Haven, CT 06510
Ph: (203)776-9900
URL: http://www.al-corn.org/

29374 ■ ALSO--Cornerstone, Inc.
West Village
52 Howe St.
New Haven, CT 06511
Ph: (203)776-9900
URL: http://www.al-corn.org/

29375 ■ Catholic Charities--New Haven Family Service Center
501 Lombard St.
New Haven, CT 06513
Ph: (203)787-2207
Fax: (203)773-3626
E-mail: newhaven@ccaoh.org
URL: http://www.ccaoh.org/location.html

29376 ■ Hill Health Corporation
400 Columbus Ave.
New Haven, CT 06519
Ph: (203)503-3250
URL: http://www.hillhealthcenter.com/

New London

29377 ■ Sound Community Services, Inc.
165 State St., Ste. 200
New London, CT 06320-6304
Ph: (860)443-0036
URL: http://www.soundcommunityservices.org/
Formerly: Integrated Behavioral Health, Inc.

New Milford

29378 ■ New Milford Supervised Apartment Program
11 S Main St.
New Milford, CT 06776
Ph: (860)355-0993

Newington

29379 ■ Veterans Affairs Connecticut Healthcare System
Newington Campus
555 Willard Ave.
Newington, CT 06111
Ph: (860)666-6951
Fax: (860)667-6764
URL: http://www2.va.gov/directory/guide/facility.asp?ID=914&dnum=All

Newton

29380 ■ Newton Youth and Family Services
121 Mount Pleasant Rd.
Newton, CT 06470
Ph: (203)426-8103
URL: http://www.newton.k12.ma.us/newtonpartnership/steeringcommittee.html

North Haven

29381 ■ North Haven Community Services
5 Linsley St.
North Haven, CT 06473-2518
Ph: (203)239-5321

North Stonington

29382 ■ Stonington Institute--North Stonington
75 Swantown Hill Rd.
North Stonington, CT 06359
Ph: (860)535-1010
URL: http://www.stoningtoninstitute.com/

Norwalk

29383 ■ Keystone House, Inc.
141 East Ave.
Norwalk, CT 06851
Ph: (203)855-7920
Fax: (203)855-7943
URL: http://www.keystonehouse.org/

29384 ■ Keystone House, Inc.
Group Home
4 Saint John St.
Norwalk, CT 06855
Ph: (203)831-6208
URL: http://www.keystonehouse.org/

29385 ■ Keystone House, Inc.
Halfway House and DBT
16 Elmcrest Terr.
Norwalk, CT 06850
Ph: (203)831-6206

Norwich

29386 ■ Artreach, Inc.
401 W Thames St., Unit 702
Norwich, CT 06360
Ph: (860)887-0014
Fax: (860)887-1915
URL: http://www.artreachheals.org/

29387 ■ Reliance House, Inc.
40 Broadway
Norwich, CT 06360
Ph: (860)887-6536
URL: http://www.reliancehouse.org/home.htm

29388 ■ Reliance House, Inc.
Community Apartment Program
90 North St.
Norwich, CT 06360
Ph: (860)886-4820
Fax: (860)889-5519
URL: http://www.reliancehouse.org/home.htm

29389 ■ Reliance House, Inc.
Penobscot Place
16 Penobscot St.
Norwich, CT 06360
Ph: (860)204-9094
Fax: (860)885-1970
URL: http://www.reliancehouse.org/home.htm

29390 ■ Reliance House, Inc.
Respite Program
117 Smith Ave., No. 1
Norwich, CT 06360
Ph: (860)887-6536
Fax: (860)887-2784
URL: http://www.reliancehouse.org/home.htm

29391 ■ Reliance House, Inc.
Teamworks Clubhouse
124 Laurel Hill Ave.
Norwich, CT 06360
Ph: (860)885-1908
Fax: (860)823-3029
URL: http://www.reliancehouse.org/home.htm

29392 ■ Reliance House, Inc.
TLC I and II
Uncas-on-Thames Cottages
401 W Thames St.
Norwich, CT 06360
Ph: (860)859-3511
Fax: (860)885-1781
URL: http://www.reliancehouse.org/home.htm

Orange

29393 ■ Bridges--Orange Family Counseling
605A Orange Center Rd.
Orange, CT 06477
Ph: (203)795-6698
Free: 866-573-4357
URL: http://www.orange-ct.gov/cominfo/family.htm

Plainville

29394 ■ Wheeler Clinic, Inc.
91 Northwest Dr.
Plainville, CT 06062-1552
Ph: (860)793-3500
Free: 888-793-3500
Fax: (860)793-3520
URL: http://www.wheelerclinic.org

Putnam

29395 ■ United Services, Inc.
Social Rehabilitation Services
79 Woodstock Ave.
Putnam, CT 06260
Ph: (860)928-6130
Fax: (860)928-6004
URL: http://www.unitedservicesct.org/

Stamford

29396 ■ F.S. DuBois Center
780 Summer St.
Stamford, CT 06901
Ph: (203)388-1600

Torrington

29397 ■ Catholic Family Services--Torrington
132 Grove St.
Torrington, CT 06790
Ph: (860)482-5558
Fax: (860)489-2984
URL: http://www.ccaoh.org/location.html

Wallingford

29398 ■ Masonic Geriatric Health Care
22 Masonic Ave.
Wallingford, CT 06492
Ph: (203)679-5900
Free: 888-679-9997
E-mail: info@masonicare.org
URL: http://www.masonicare.org

Waterbury

29399 ■ Catholic Family Services--Waterbury
56 Church St.
Waterbury, CT 06702-2103
Ph: (203)755-1196
URL: http://www.ccaoh.org/location.html

29400 ■ Family Intervention Center
1875 Thomaston Ave.
Waterbury, CT 06704
Ph: (203)753-2153

29401 ■ Saint Vincent De Paul Society of Waterbury, Inc.
173 Mark Ln., Ste. 6
Waterbury, CT 06704-2474
Ph: (203)757-0567
URL: http://svdpusa.org/

Wauregan

29402 ■ United Services, Inc.--Wauregan
303 Putnam Rd.
Wauregan, CT 06387
Ph: (860)564-6100
Fax: (860)564-6110
E-mail: mail@unitedservicessct.org
URL: http://www.unitedservicesct.org

Westport

29403 ■ Temenos Institute, Inc.
29 E Main St.
Westport, CT 06880
Ph: (203)227-4388
URL: http://www.temenosinstitute.com

Wethersfield

29404 ■ Inter-Community Mental Health Group
505 Silas Deane Hwy.
Wethersfield, CT 06109-2216
Ph: (860)659-3754
URL: http://www.icmhg.org/
Formerly: Central Connecticut Health District.

Willimantic

29405 ■ United Services, Inc.
The Lighthouse
47 Arnolds Ln.
Willimantic, CT 06226
Ph: (860)423-7791
URL: http://www.unitedservicesct.org/

29406 ■ United Services, Inc.
Passages
306-308 Pleasant St.
Willimantic, CT 06226
Ph: (860)450-7159
URL: http://www.unitedservicesct.org/

29407 ■ United Services, Inc.
Stepping Stones
26 Mansfield Ave.
Willimantic, CT 06226
Ph: (860)450-7387
URL: http://www.unitedservicesct.org/

29408 ■ United Services, Inc.--Willimantic
132 Mansfield Ave.
Willimantic, CT 06226
Ph: (860)456-2261
Fax: (860)450-1357
URL: http://www.unitedservicesct.org/

DELAWARE

Camden

29409 ■ Connections CSP, Inc.--Camden
124 West St.
Camden, DE 19934
Ph: (302)531-1103
Free: 866-477-5345
URL: http://www.connectionscsp.org/

Dover

29410 ■ Delaware Guidance Services
Dover Branch
103 Mont Blanc Blvd.
Dover, DE 19904-2758
Ph: (302)678-3020
Fax: (302)678-2458
URL: http://www.delawareguidance.org

29411 ■ Dover Behavioral Health System
725 Horespond Rd.
Dover, DE 19901
Ph: (302)741-0140
Fax: (302)741-8551
URL: http://www.doverbehavioral.com/

29412 ■ Psychotherapeutic Services, Inc.
630 W Division St., Ste. F
Dover, DE 19904
Ph: (302)674-3366
Fax: (302)674-3360
E-mail: psikent@ps-corp.net
URL: http://www.psychotherapeuticservices.com/programs/kentcccp.htm
Formerly: Psychotherapeutic Treatment Services, Inc.

29413 ■ Wilmington Veterans Affairs Medical Center
Dover Outpatient Clinic
Creek Stone Center, Bldg. A, 2nd Fl.
1198 Governors Ave.
Dover, DE 19901
Ph: (302)994-2511
Free: 800-461-8262
URL: http://www2.va.gov/directory/guide/facility.asp?ID=5632&dnum=All

Ellendale

29414 ■ Fellowship Health Resources, Inc.
Community Continuum of Care Program
12649 DuPont Blvd.
Ellendale, DE 19941
Ph: (302)422-1530
Fax: (302)422-2320
URL: http://www.fellowshiphr.org/

Felton

29415 ■ Psychotherapeutic Services, Inc.
Felton Group Home
1563 Paradise Alley Rd.
Felton, DE 19943
Ph: (302)284-8370
Fax: (302)284-8004
E-mail: psyfelton@ps-Corporationnet
URL: http://www.psychotherapeuticservices.com/programs/feltongrouphome.htm
Formerly: Psychotherapeutic Treatment Services, Inc.

Georgetown

29416 ■ Psychotherapeutic Services, Inc.
Georgetown Transitional Housing
18 W North St.
Georgetown, DE 19947
Ph: (302)854-6527
URL: http://www.psychotherapeuticservices.com/
Formerly: Psychotherapeutic Treatment Services, Inc.

29417 ■ Wilmington Veterans Affairs Medical Center
Georgetown Outpatient Clinic
15 Georgetown Plz.
Georgetown, DE 19947
Ph: (302)994-2511
Free: 800-461-8262
URL: http://www2.va.gov/directory/guide/facility.asp?ID=5633&dnum=All

Lewes

29418 ■ Delaware Guidance Services--Lewes
31168 Learning Ln.
Lewes, DE 19958
Ph: (302)645-5338
URL: http://www.delawareguidance.org/contact.htm

Milford

29419 ■ Fellowship Health Resources, Inc.
Hope House Group Home
7549 Wilkins Rd.
Milford, DE 19963
Ph: (302)422-6699
Fax: (302)422-1898
URL: http://www.fellowshiphr.org/delaware/

Milton

29420 ■ Fellowship Health Resources, Inc.
Taton House Group Home
18090 Harberson Rd.
Milton, DE 19968
Ph: (302)684-4400
URL: http://www.fellowshiphr.org/delaware/

New Castle

29421 ■ Connections CSP, Inc.--New Castle
600 Moores Ln.
New Castle, DE 19720
Ph: (302)322-9010
Free: 866-477-5345
URL: http://www.connectionscsp.org/

29422 ■ MeadowWood Behavioral Health System
575 S DuPont Hwy.
New Castle, DE 19720
Ph: (302)328-3330
Fax: (302)328-9336
URL: http://www.psysolutions.com/facilities/meadowwood/

Newark

29423 ■ Delaware Guidance Services
Newark Branch
1208 Drummond Plz., Bldg. 1
Newark, DE 19711-5705
Ph: (302)455-9333
URL: http://www.delawareguidance.org/contact.htm

29424 ■ Old Baltimore Pike Group Home
1000 Old Baltimore Pke.
Newark, DE 19702
Ph: (302)266-9711

Seaford

29425 ■ Delaware Guidance Services--Seaford
900 Health Services Dr.
Seaford, DE 19973
Ph: (302)262-3505
URL: http://www.delawareguidance.org/contact.htm

Wilmington

29426 ■ Connections CSP, Inc.--Supervised Apartments
816 N West St.
Wilmington, DE 19801
Ph: (302)654-9289
Free: 866-477-5345
URL: http://www.connectionscsp.org/

29427 ■ Connections CSP, Inc.--Wilmington
500 W 10th St.
Wilmington, DE 19801-1422
Ph: (302)984-3380
Free: 866-477-5345
URL: http://www.connectionscsp.org/
Formerly: Connections, Inc.

29428 ■ Delaware Guidance Services for Children and Youth
1213 Delaware Ave.
Wilmington, DE 19806
Ph: (302)652-3948
Fax: (302)652-8297
URL: http://www.delawareguidance.org

29429 ■ Horizon House of Delaware, Inc.
1902 Maryland Ave.
Wilmington, DE 19801
Ph: (302)655-7108
Fax: (302)655-0689
URL: http://www.hhinc.org

29430 ■ Horizon House, Inc.
Old Baltimore Pike Group Home
1020 Wilson Rd.
Wilmington, DE 19803
Ph: (302)477-1396
URL: http://www.hhinc.org
Formerly: Resource Management Service.

29431 ■ Washington Street Behavioral Health
917 Washington St.
Wilmington, DE 19720
Ph: (302)984-3380

29432 ■ Wilmington Hospital
501 W 14th St.
Wilmington, DE 19801
Ph: (302)428-2204
URL: http://www.christianacare.org/body.cfm?id=336

29433 ■ Wilmington Mental Health Center
809 Washington St.
Wilmington, DE 19801
Ph: (302)577-6490

DISTRICT OF COLUMBIA

Washington

29434 ■ Andromeda Transcultural Health Center
1400 Decatur St. NW
Washington, DC 20011
Ph: (202)291-4707
Fax: (202)723-4560
URL: http://www.andromedatransculturalhealth.org/default.aspx
Formerly: Andromeda Hispano Mental Health Center.

29435 ■ Centre Clinic
Georgetown University Hospital
2300 M St. NW, Ste. 910
Washington, DC 20037-1434
Ph: (202)496-6264

29436 ■ Child & Family Therapy Center
DC Department of Mental Health
51 N St. NE, Ste. 700A
Washington, DC 20002-3347
Ph: (202)724-5375

29437 ■ Community Connections, Inc.
801 Pennsylvania Ave. SE, Ste. 201
Washington, DC 20003
Ph: (202)546-1512
Fax: (202)544-5365
URL: http://www.communityconnectionsdc.org/

29438 ■ Community Connections, Inc.--Washington DC
Day Services Program
920 Rhode Island Ave. NE
Washington, DC 20018
Ph: (202)281-2900
URL: http://www.communityconnectionsdc.org/

29439 ■ DC Department of Mental Health
64 New York Ave. NE, 4th Fl.
Washington, DC 20002
Ph: (202)673-7440
Fax: (202)673-3433
URL: http://www.dc.gov/agencies/detail.asp?id=9

29440 ■ Green Door
1221 Taylor St. NW
Washington, DC 20011
Ph: (202)462-9200
URL: http://www.greendoor.org/

29441 ■ Hillcrest Children's Center
2570 Sherman Ave. NW
Washington, DC 20001
Ph: (202)232-6100
URL: http://www.hillcrestchildrenscenter.org/

29442 ■ House of Ruth
5 Thomas Cir. NW
Washington, DC 20005
Ph: (202)667-7001
Fax: (202)667-7047
E-mail: houseofruth@houseofruth.org
URL: http://www.houseofruth.org

29443 ■ House of Ruth Madison Program
651 10th St. NE
Washington, DC 20002-5396
Ph: (202)547-2600
E-mail: houseofruth@houseofruth.org
URL: http://www.houseofruth.org

29444 ■ House of Ruth Mothers' Program
700 6th St. NE
Washington, DC 20002-4324
Ph: (202)547-6173
E-mail: houseofruth@houseofruth.org
URL: http://www.houseofruth.org

29445 ■ House of Ruth Transitional/Unity
459 Massachusetts Ave. NW
Washington, DC 20001-2698
Ph: (202)347-2777
E-mail: houseofruth@houseofruth.org
URL: http://www.houseofruth.org

29446 ■ Institute for Life Enrichment
7852 16th St. NW
Washington, DC 20012
Ph: (202)291-5008

29447 ■ Lutheran Social Services of the National Capital Area
4406 Georgia Ave. NW
Washington, DC 20011
Ph: (202)723-3000
Fax: (202)723-3303
E-mail: gravesm@lssnca.org
URL: http://www.lssnca.org

29448 ■ Max Robinson Center
Whitman-Walker Clinic
2301 Martin Luther King, Jr. Ave. SE
Washington, DC 20020
Ph: (202)678-8877
Fax: (202)797-0178
E-mail: mrcwwc@wwc.org
URL: http://www.wwc.org

29449 ■ Meyer Treatment Center of the Washington School of Psychiatry
5028 Wisconsin Ave. NW, Ste. 400
Washington, DC 20016-4118
Ph: (202)537-6050
URL: http://www.wspdc.org/mTC.htm

29450 ■ Northwest Family Center
DC Department of Mental Health
1250 U St. NW, 2nd Fl.
Washington, DC 20009
Ph: (202)673-2042
Fax: (202)673-7642
URL: http://dmh.dc.gov/dmh/cwp/view,a,3,q,515889,dmhNav,%7C31250%7C.asp

29451 ■ Parent & Infant Development Program
DC Department of Mental Health
51 N St. NE, Ste. 700C
Washington, DC 20002
Ph: (202)724-5383
Fax: (202)724-5390
URL: http://dmh.dc.gov/dmh/cwp/view,A,3,Q,515924.asp

29452 ■ Progressive Life Center
1704 17th St. NE
Washington, DC 20002-1810
Ph: (202)842-4570
Fax: (202)842-1035
E-mail: info@ntuplc.org
URL: http://www.ntuplc.org/contact.htm

29453 ■ Southeast Family Center
DC Department of Mental Health
821 Howard Rd. SE, 1st Fl.
Washington, DC 20020
Ph: (202)698-1838
Fax: (202)698-2467
URL: http://dmh.dc.gov/dmh/cwp/view,a,3,q,515889,dmhNav,%7C31250%7C.asp

29454 ■ Washington DC Veterans Affairs Medical Center
Southeast Community Clinic
820 Chesapeake St. SE
Washington, DC 20032
Ph: (202)745-8685
Free: 888-553-0242
Fax: (202)562-8789
URL: http://www2.va.gov/directory/guide/facility.asp?ID=988&dnum=All

FLORIDA

Altamonte Springs

29455 ■ Grove Counseling Center, Inc.
Outpatient in Altamonte
1088 E Altamonte Dr.
Altamonte Springs, FL 32701
Ph: (407)327-1765
Free: 800-919-1765
Fax: (407)339-4624
URL: http://www.thegrove.org/locations.asp

Avon Park

29456 ■ Florida Center for Addictions and Dual Disorders
100 W College Dr.
Avon Park, FL 33825
Ph: (863)452-3858

Bartow

29457 ■ Crisis Stabilization Outpatient Office
1255 Golfview Ave.
Bartow, FL 33830
Ph: (863)519-0575
URL: http://www.peace-river.com

29458 ■ Peace River Center
Bartow Office
1239 E Main St.
Bartow, FL 33830
Ph: (863)519-0575
Fax: (863)534-7028
URL: http://www.peace-river.com
Formerly: Peace River Center for Personal Development.

Belle Glade

29459 ■ Oakwood Center of the Palm Beaches, Inc.--Belle Glade
406-408 SE Martin Luther King, Jr. Blvd.
Belle Glade, FL 33430
Ph: (561)993-8080
URL: http://www.oakwoodcenter.org/

Birmingham

29460 ■ Trinity Medical Center Behavioral Health
800 Montclair Rd.
Birmingham, FL 35213
Ph: (205)592-1650
URL: http://www.trinitymedicalonline.com

29461 ■ UBA Hospital Center for Psychiatric Medicine
619 19th St. S
Birmingham, FL 35249
Ph: (205)934-4011
URL: http://www.uabmedicine.org

29462 ■ Western Mental Health Center, Birmingham
1701 Ave. D
Birmingham, FL 35218
Ph: (205)788-7770
URL: http://www.westernmedicalhealth.com

Blountstown

29463 ■ Life Management Center
Calhoun County Facility
16869 NE Pear St.
Blountstown, FL 32424
Ph: (850)674-8790
E-mail: hrdept@lifemanagementcenter.org
URL: http://www.lifemanagementcenter.org/

Boca Raton

29464 ■ Boca Raton Community Based Outpatient Clinic
901 Meadows Rd.
Boca Raton, FL 33433
Ph: (561)416-8995
Fax: (561)416-9374
URL: http://www2.va.gov/directory/guide/facility.asp?ID=5064&dnum=All

29465 ■ Center for Group Counseling
22455 Boca Rio Rd.
Boca Raton, FL 33433
Ph: (561)483-5300
Fax: (561)483-5325
E-mail: center@groupcounseling.org
URL: http://www.groupcounseling.org/

29466 ■ North Star Centre
9033 Glades Rd.
Boca Raton, FL 33434
Ph: (561)361-0500
URL: http://northstar-centre.com/

Bonifay

29467 ■ Life Management Center
Holmes County
310 E Byrd Ave.
Bonifay, FL 32425
Ph: (850)547-2472
E-mail: hrdept@lifemanagementcenter.org
URL: http://www.lifemanagementcenter.org/

Bradenton

29468 ■ Camelot Community Care, Inc.--Bradenton
239 US 301 E, Ste. A
Bradenton, FL 34208
Ph: (941)708-9764
Fax: (941)708-9863
URL: http://www.camelotcommunitycare.org

29469 ■ Manatee Glens Corporation
391 6th Ave. W
Bradenton, FL 34205
Ph: (941)782-4299
Fax: (941)741-3132
E-mail: exeoffice@manateeglens.com
URL: http://www.manateeglens.org/

29470 ■ Manatee Glens Counseling Services
Youth Addiction Outpatient Services
5214 4th Ave.
Bradenton, FL 34208
Ph: (941)782-4840
URL: http://manateeglens.com
Formerly: Manatee Glens Adolescent Recovery Center.

29471 ■ Manatee Glens Hospital and Crisis Center
2020 26th Ave. E
Bradenton, FL 34208-7753
Ph: (941)782-4200
URL: http://www.manateeglens.org/

29472 ■ Manatee Glens West Counseling Services
379 6th Ave. W
Bradenton, FL 34205
Ph: (941)782-4100
Fax: (941)741-3196
URL: http://www.manateeglens.org/

Bronson

29473 ■ Levy County Clinic
100 NE 90th St.
Bronson, FL 32621
Ph: (352)439-0069

Brooksville

29474 ■ Eckerd Academy at Brooksville
397 Culbreath Rd.
Brooksville, FL 34602
Ph: (352)796-9493
Free: 800-822-4385
Fax: (352)754-6791
URL: http://www.eckerd.org
Formerly: Camp E-How-Kee.

Bunnell

29475 ■ ACT Corporation - Flagler Center
301 Justice Ln.
Bunnell, FL 32110-4436
Ph: (386)236-1810
Free: 800-539-4228

Clearwater

29476 ■ Camelot Community Care, Inc.--Clearwater
4910 Creekside Dr., Ste. D
Clearwater, FL 33760
Ph: (727)593-0003
Fax: (727)596-1713
URL: http://www.camelotcommunitycare.org/fl_locations.asp

29477 ■ Directions for Mental Health
1437 S Belcher Rd., Ste. 200
Clearwater, FL 33764
Ph: (727)524-4464
URL: http://www.healthehurt.com/

29478 ■ Fairwinds Treatment Center
1569 S Fort Harrison Ave.
Clearwater, FL 33756
Ph: (727)449-0300
Free: 800-226-0301
Fax: (727)446-1022
E-mail: fairwinds@fairwindstreatment.com
URL: http://www.fairwindstreatment.com

29479 ■ Gulf Coast Jewish Family Services
Icot Boulevard
14041 Icot Blvd.
Clearwater, FL 33760
Ph: (727)479-1800
Free: 800-888-5066
URL: http://www.gcjfs.org/
Formerly: Gulf Coast Jewish Family Guidance and Mental Health Services.

Clewiston

29480 ■ Hendry-Glades Mental Health Clinic
601 W Alverdez Ave.
Clewiston, FL 33440-3504
Ph: (863)983-1423

Coconut Groove

29481 ■ Miami Behavioral Health Center, Inc.
S Dixie Highway, Coconut Grove
17576 S Dixie Hwy.
Coconut Groove, FL 33157
Ph: (786)293-9544
URL: http://www.mbhc.org/

Crawfordville

29482 ■ Apalachee Center, Inc.
Wakulla County Clinic
85 High Dr.
Crawfordville, FL 32327
Ph: (850)926-5900
URL: http://www.apalacheecenter.org/

Crestview

29483 ■ B.C.I. Greenleaf Day Program
1007 Greenleaf Pl.
Crestview, FL 32536
Ph: (850)689-7840

29484 ■ Bridgeway Center, Inc.
351 N Ferdon Blvd.
Crestview, FL 32536
Ph: (850)833-7400
URL: http://bridgewaycenter.org

29485 ■ Bridgeway Center, Inc.
Geriatric Residential Treatment System
299 W Railroad Ave.
Crestview, FL 32536
Ph: (850)689-7810
URL: http://bridgewaycenter.org/

Cross City

29486 ■ Dixie County Clinic
Veterans' Rd.
Hwy. 419
Cross City, FL 32628
Ph: (352)471-0069
Free: 800-330-5615
URL: http://www.mbhci.org/index.php/services-locations.html

Dade City

29487 ■ Doris Cook Smith Counseling Center
14527 7th St.
Dade City, FL 33523
Ph: (352)521-1474

Davie

29488 ■ Bayview Center for Mental Health
Broward Case Management
3501 S University Dr.
Davie, FL 33328
Ph: (954)888-7977
URL: http://www.bayviewcenter.com/contactus.html

29489 ■ Nova Southeastern University, Inc.
Community Mental Health Center
3301 College Ave.
Davie, FL 33314
Ph: (954)262-5730

Daytona Beach

29490 ■ ACT Big Pine
207 San Juan Ave.
Daytona Beach, FL 32114-3227
Ph: (386)239-6129
URL: http://www.actcorp.org/

29491 ■ ACT Corporation
1220 Willis Ave.
Daytona Beach, FL 32114-2897
Ph: (386)947-3200
Free: 800-539-4228
Fax: (386)947-4238
URL: http://www.actcorp.org/

29492 ■ ACT Main Center
1220 Willis Ave.
Daytona Beach, FL 32114
Ph: (386)947-3200
URL: http://www.actcorp.org/Contact%20Us.htm

29493 ■ ACT Ocean Breeze
356 Roth St.
Daytona Beach, FL 32114-2750
Ph: (386)238-4716
URL: http://www.actcorp.org/Contact%20Us.htm

29494 ■ ACT Pine Grove Beach House
1150 Red John Rd.
Daytona Beach, FL 32124-1016
Ph: (386)236-3130
Free: 800-539-4228
Fax: (386)323-2326
URL: http://www.actcorp.org/Contact%20Us.htm
Formerly: beach House ACT.

29495 ■ Halifax Behavioral Health Services
841 Jimmy Ann Dr.
Daytona Beach, FL 32114
Ph: (386)274-5333
URL: http://www.halifaxhealth.org/locations/behavioralservices.aspx

29496 ■ Halifax Medical Center
303 N Clyde Morris Blvd.
Daytona Beach, FL 32114
Ph: (386)254-4000
URL: http://www.halifaxhealth.org/locations/medical-centerofdaytonabeach.aspx

29497 ■ Our Children First
517 S Ridgewood Ave.
Daytona Beach, FL 32114
Ph: (386)248-2771

DeFuniak Springs

29498 ■ COPE Center Beachside Counseling
3686 US Hwy. 331 S
DeFuniak Springs, FL 32435
Ph: (850)892-8035
Formerly: Cope Center.

Deerfield Beach

29499 ■ Miami Veterans Affairs Healthcare System
Deerfield Beach Clinic
2100 SW 10th St.
Deerfield Beach, FL 33442
Ph: (954)570-5572
URL: http://www2.va.gov/directory/guide/facility.asp?ID=5188&dnum=All

Deland

29500 ■ Devereux Volusia Counseling Center
Therapeutic Foster Care
120 E New York Ave., Ste. B1C
Deland, FL 32724
Ph: (386)738-5443
URL: http://www.devereux.org/site/PageServer?pagename=fl_fostercare

Delray Beach

29501 ■ Kids in Distress
Palm Beach County
1845 S Federal Hwy., 3rd Fl.
Delray Beach, FL 33483
Ph: (954)390-7620
E-mail: info@kidsindistress.org
URL: http://kidsindistress.org
Remarks: Specializes in child welfare, prevention and mental health services.

29502 ■ South County Mental Health Center
16158 S Military Trail
Delray Beach, FL 33484
Ph: (561)737-8400

29503 ■ Veterans Affairs Medical Center
Delray Beach Clinic
4800 Linton Blvd., Bldg. E, Ste. 300
Delray Beach, FL 33445
Ph: (561)495-1973
URL: http://www2.va.gov/directory/guide/facility.asp?ID=5066&dnum=1

Fern Park

29504 ■ Seminole Community Mental Health Center
237 Fernwood Blvd.
Fern Park, FL 32730
Ph: (407)831-2411

Fort Lauderdale

29505 ■ Avon Manor Group Home
1142 NE 5th Ave.
Fort Lauderdale, FL 33304
Ph: (954)763-2030

29506 ■ Broward County Elderly and Veteran Services
2995 N Dixie Hwy.
Fort Lauderdale, FL 33334
Ph: (954)537-2936
Fax: (954)537-2804
E-mail: bcevsd@broward.org
URL: http://www.broward.org/eldervets/Pages/Default.aspx

29507 ■ Children's Home Society
401 NE 4th St.
Fort Lauderdale, FL 33301
Ph: (954)763-6573
E-mail: info@chsfl.org
URL: http://www.chsfl.org

29508 ■ Henderson Mental Health Center Administrative Offices
4740 N State Rd. 7, Ste. 201
Fort Lauderdale, FL 33319
Ph: (954)486-4005
URL: http://www.hendersonmhc.org
Formerly: Henderson Mental Health Center.

29509 ■ Henderson Walk-In- Crisis Center
4720 N State Rd. 7, Bldg. B
Fort Lauderdale, FL 33319
Ph: (954)463-0911
URL: http://www.hendersonmhc.org

29510 ■ Youth and Family Services--Fort Lauderdale
4720 N State Rd. 7
Fort Lauderdale, FL 33319
Ph: (954)731-5100
Fax: (954)735-6624
URL: http://www.hendersonmhc.org

Fort Myers

29511 ■ Bay Pines Veterans Affairs Healthcare System Fort Myers Outpatient Clinic
3033 Winkler Ext.
Fort Myers, FL 33916
Ph: (239)939-3939
Fax: (239)931-6114
URL: http://www2.va.gov/directory/guide/facility.asp?ID=561&dnum=All

29512 ■ Coastal Behavioral Healthcare--Fort Myers
3677 Central Ave.
Fort Myers, FL 33901
Ph: (239)939-6111
URL: http://www.coastalbh.org/

29513 ■ JBL Behavioral Health Systems
12550 New Brittany Blvd.
Fort Myers, FL 33907
Ph: (239)936-1114
Fax: (239)936-5968
URL: http://www.jbhllc.com/

29514 ■ Ruth Cooper Center Campus
2789 Ortiz Ave.
Fort Myers, FL 33905
Ph: (239)275-3222
URL: http://www.rccbhc.org/

29515 ■ Vista Campus Behavioral Crisis Services
10140 Deer Run Farms Rd.
Fort Myers, FL 33966
Ph: (239)275-3222
URL: http://www.rccbhc.org/

Fort Pierce

29516 ■ New Horizon
709 S 5th St.
Fort Pierce, FL 34950
Ph: (772)468-5610
URL: http://www.nhtcinc.org

29517 ■ New Horizons of the Treasure Coast Fact Florida Assertive Community Treatment
709 S 5th St.
Fort Pierce, FL 34950
Ph: (772)467-3097
Fax: (772)468-5633
E-mail: nswanson@nhtcinc.org
URL: http://www.nhtcinc.org
Formerly: New Horizons of the Treasure Center.

29518 ■ New Horizons of the Treasure Coast--Fort Pierce
4500 W Midway Rd.
Fort Pierce, FL 34981
Ph: (772)468-5600
Free: 888-468-5600
Fax: (772)468-5606
E-mail: nswanson@nhtcinc.org
URL: http://www.nhtcinc.org

29519 ■ New Horizons of the Treasure Coast Saint Lucie County Outpatient Center
709 S 5th St.
Fort Pierce, FL 34950-8339
Ph: (772)468-5610
E-mail: nswanson@nhtcinc.org
URL: http://www.nhtcinc.org
Formerly: New Horizons of the Treasure Center St. Lucie County Outpatient Center.

Fort Walton Beach

29520 ■ B.C.I. Satellite Apartments
662 Anderson St.
Fort Walton Beach, FL 32547
Ph: (850)833-9208

29521 ■ B.C.I. Supervised Apartments
662 Reeves St., Apt. A
Fort Walton Beach, FL 32547
Ph: (850)833-9208

29522 ■ Bridgeway Center, Inc.--Day Services
333 Lewis St., Bldg. 2
Fort Walton Beach, FL 32548
Ph: (850)833-9206
URL: http://www.bridgewaycenter.org/

Gainesville

29523 ■ Meridian Behavioral Healthcare, Inc.
4300 SW 13th St.
Gainesville, FL 32608
Ph: (352)374-5600
Free: 800-330-5615
URL: http://www.mbhci.org/services_locations.cfm

29524 ■ Meridian Behavioral Healthcare, Inc. Alachua County Campus
4300 SW 13th St.
Gainesville, FL 32608
Ph: (352)374-5600
Free: 800-330-5615
URL: http://www.mbhci.org/services_locations.cfm

29525 ■ Meridian Behavioral Healthcare, Inc. Joyce House
3010 SW 35th Pl.
Gainesville, FL 32608
Ph: (352)372-9734
URL: http://www.mbhci.org/services_locations.cfm

29526 ■ Psychotherapeutic Services--Alachua County
2002 NW 13th St., Ste. 220
Gainesville, FL 32609
Ph: (352)271-8605
Fax: (352)271-8608
E-mail: psffact3@ps-corp.net
URL: http://www.psychotherapeuticservices.com/programs/floridafact.htm

Green Acres

29527 ■ Camelot Community Care--Green Acres
6416 Melaleuca Ln.
Green Acres, FL 33463
Ph: (561)649-0877
URL: http://www.camelotcommunitycare.org/fl_locations.asp

Hialeah

29528 ■ Citrus Health Network Kiva Outreach Team and Residential Program
1339 SE 9th Ave.
Hialeah, FL 33010
Ph: (305)884-1382
URL: http://www.citrushealth.org/citrushealth.htm

29529 ■ Citrus Health Network Lou Panci Alternative Education Center
106 W 9th St.
Hialeah, FL 33010
Ph: (305)883-7757
URL: http://www.citrushealth.org/citrushealth.htm

29530 ■ Citrus Health Network Partial Hospital Program
60 E 3rd St., Ste. 102C
Hialeah, FL 33010
Ph: (305)885-8222
URL: http://www.citrushealth.org/citrushealth.htm

29531 ■ Citrus Health Network Shaman Residential Program
302-308 E 9th St.
Hialeah, FL 33010
Ph: (305)887-5826
URL: http://www.citrushealth.org/citrushealth.htm

Holiday

29532 ■ Gulf Coast Jewish Family Services, Inc. Chatlin
2425 Chatlin Rd.
Holiday, FL 34691
Ph: (727)943-4847
URL: http://www.gcjfs.org/locations.htm

Hollywood

29533 ■ Henderson Mental Health Center South
1957 Jackson St.
Hollywood, FL 33021
Ph: (954)921-2600
Fax: (954)927-2393
URL: http://www.hendersonmhc.org

29534 ■ Kids in Distress--Hollywood
7261 Sheridan St.
Hollywood, FL 33024
Ph: (954)390-7620
E-mail: info@kidsindistress.org
URL: http://kidsindistress.org
Remarks: Specializes in child welfare, prevention and mental health services.

29535 ■ Miami Veterans Affairs Healthcare System Pembroke Pines/Hollywood Clinic
7369 W Sheridan St., Ste. 102
Hollywood, FL 33024

Ph: (954)894-1668
Fax: (954)894-6670
URL: http://www2.va.gov/directory/guide/facility.asp?ID=5059&dnum=All

Homestead

29536 ■ Miami Veterans Affairs Healthcare System
Homestead Clinic
950 Krome Ave., Ste. 401
Homestead, FL 33030
Ph: (305)248-0874
Fax: (305)248-1875
URL: http://www2.va.gov/directory/guide/facility.asp?ID=5055&dnum=All

Jacksonville

29537 ■ Daniel, Inc.
3725 Belfort Rd.
Jacksonville, FL 32216
Ph: (904)296-1055
URL: http://www.danielkids.org/sites/web/index.cfm

29538 ■ Jewish Family and Community Services
6261 Dupont Station Ct. E
Jacksonville, FL 32217
Ph: (904)448-1933
URL: http://www.jfcsjax.org/

29539 ■ Mental Health Center of Jacksonville
3333 W 20th St.
Jacksonville, FL 32254
Ph: (904)695-9145

29540 ■ Renaissance Center
900 University Blvd., Ste. 700
Jacksonville, FL 32211
Ph: (904)743-1883

29541 ■ Wekiva Springs Center for Women
3947 Salisbury Rd.
Jacksonville, FL 32216
Ph: (904)296-3533

Jasper

29542 ■ Hamilton County Clinic
406 10th Ave. NW
Jasper, FL 32052
Ph: (386)792-1338
Free: 800-330-5615
Formerly: Meridian Hamilton County Clinic.

Key Largo

29543 ■ Miami Veterans Affairs Healthcare System
Key Largo Clinic
105662 Overseas Hwy.
Key Largo, FL 33037
Ph: (305)451-0164
Fax: (305)451-4864
URL: http://www2.va.gov/directory/guide/facility.asp?ID=5056&dnum=All

Key West

29544 ■ Miami Veterans Affairs Healthcare System
Key West Clinic
1300 Douglas Cir., Bldg. L-15
Key West, FL 33040
Ph: (305)293-4609
Fax: (305)293-4813
URL: http://www2.va.gov/directory/guide/facility.asp?ID=5057&dnum=All

Kissimmee

29545 ■ Orlando Veterans Affairs Medical Center
Kissimmee Clinic
2285 N Central Ave.
Kissimmee, FL 34741
Ph: (407)518-5004
Fax: (407)518-6746
URL: http://www2.va.gov/directory/guide/facility.asp?ID=5063&dnum=All

29546 ■ Osceola Mental Health, inc.
DBA Park Place Behavioral Health Care
206 Park Place Blvd.
Kissimmee, FL 34741-2344
Ph: (407)846-0023
Formerly: Osceola Mental Health.

Lake Butler

29547 ■ Meridian Behavioral Healthcare Union County Office
395 W Main St.
Lake Butler, FL 32054
Ph: (386)496-2347
Free: 800-330-5615
URL: http://www.mbhci.org/index.php/services-locations.html
Formerly: Meridian Union County Clinic.

Lake City

29548 ■ Meridian Behavioral Healthcare
Gateway Acute Care/Recovery Center
950 W Michigan St.
Lake City, FL 32025
Ph: (386)487-0800
Free: 800-330-5615
URL: http://www.mbhci.org/index.php/services-locations.html
Formerly: North Florida Mental Health Center Gateway House.

Lake Mary

29549 ■ Grove Counseling Center, Inc.
Outpatient in Lake Mary
3525 W Lake Mary Blvd.
Lake Mary, FL 32746
Ph: (407)327-1765
Free: 800-919-1765
URL: http://www.thegrove.org/locations.asp

Lake Worth

29550 ■ Palm Beach Habilitation Center
4522 S Congress Ave.
Lake Worth, FL 33461
Ph: (561)965-8500
Fax: (561)433-8816
E-mail: postman@pbhab.com
URL: http://www.pbhab.org/

Lakeland

29551 ■ Peace River Center
Lakeland Office
715 N Lake Ave.
Lakeland, FL 33805
Ph: (863)248-3311
URL: http://www.peace-river.com/

Land O' Lakes

29552 ■ Adolescent Day Treatment West
Land O'Lakes High School
20325 Gator Ln.
Land O' Lakes, FL 34638-2825
Ph: (813)794-9400
Fax: (813)794-9491
URL: http://lolhs.pasco.k12.fl.us
Formerly: Adolescent Day Treatment Center.

Largo

29553 ■ Directions for Mental Health--Oakwoods Office
8823 115th Ave. N
Largo, FL 33773
Ph: (727)547-4566
URL: http://www.healthehurt.com/contactdirectionsformentalhealth.html

29554 ■ Wild Acres
12809 Wild Acres Rd.
Largo, FL 33773
Ph: (727)535-4423

Lauderhill

29555 ■ Henderson Mental Health Center Rainbow
5800 NW 27th Ct.
Lauderhill, FL 33313
Ph: (954)735-4331
URL: http://www.hendersonmhc.org
Formerly: Henderson Mental Health Center.

29556 ■ Henderson Village
5700 NW 27th Ct.
Lauderhill, FL 33313
Ph: (954)735-4331
URL: http://www.hendersonmhc.org/locations.html

Lecanto

29557 ■ Malcom Randall Veterans Affairs Medical Center
Lecanto Clinic
2804 W Marc Knighton Ct., Ste. A
Lecanto, FL 34461
Ph: (352)746-8000
Free: 800-324-8387
URL: http://www2.va.gov/directory/guide/facility.asp?ID=5033&dnum=All

29558 ■ Marion Citrus Mental Health Center
Citrus Outpatient Service
3238 S Lecanto Hwy.
Lecanto, FL 34461
Ph: (352)628-5020
URL: http://www.marion-citrusmhc.org

Leesburg

29559 ■ Orlando Veterans Affairs Medical Center
Leesburg Clinic
711 W Main St.
Leesburg, FL 34748
Ph: (352)435-4000
Fax: (352)435-4015
URL: http://www2.va.gov/directory/guide/facility.asp?ID=5052&dnum=All

Live Oak

29560 ■ Meridian Behavior Health Care
Suwannee County Office
920 NW Nobles Ferry Rd.
Live Oak, FL 32060
Ph: (386)362-4218
Free: 800-330-5615
Fax: (386)364-5606
URL: http://www.mbhci.org/index.php/services-locations.html
Formerly: Meridian Behavior Health Center.

Longwood

29561 ■ Grove Counseling Center, Inc.--Longwood
111 W Magnolia Ave.
Longwood, FL 32750
Ph: (407)327-1765
Free: 800-919-1765
URL: http://www.thegrove.org

Marathon

29562 ■ Guidance Clinic of the Middle Keys, Inc.
3000 41st St. Ocean
Marathon, FL 33050-2373
Ph: (305)434-9000
URL: http://www.gcmk.org/
Formerly: Guidance Clinic.

Marianna

29563 ■ Life Management Center
Jackson County Facility
4094 Lafayette St.
Marianna, FL 32446
Ph: (850)522-4485
URL: http://www.lifemanagementcenter.org/locations.htm

Melbourne

29564 ■ Circles of Care, Inc.
400 E Sheridan Rd.
Melbourne, FL 32901
Ph: (321)722-5257
URL: http://www.circlesofcare.org/current/index.html

Miami

29565 ■ Bayview Center for Mental Health
Crisis Stabilization Unit
0108 NW 8th Avo.
Miami, FL 33150
Ph: (305)691-4357
URL: http://www.bayviewcenter.com/

29566 ■ Family Counseling Services
7412 Sunset Dr.
Miami, FL 33143
Ph: (305)740-8998

29567 ■ Fellowship House--Miami
5711 S Dixie Hwy.
Miami, FL 33143
Ph: (305)667-1036
Fax: (305)667-4938
E-mail: fh-psr@shadow.net
URL: http://fellowshiphouse.org

29568 ■ Institute for Child & Family Health
15490 NW 7th Ave., Ste. 101
Miami, FL 33169
Ph: (305)685-0381
URL: http://www.icfhinc.org/
Formerly: Children's Psychiatric Center.

29569 ■ Institute for Child & Family Health
Sunset Clinic
9380 Sunset Dr., Ste. B120
Miami, FL 33173
Ph: (305)274-3172
URL: http://www.icfhinc.org/
Formerly: Children's Psychiatric Center.

29570 ■ Miami Behavioral Health Center, Inc.
Casa Nueva Vida
1560 SW 1st St.
Miami, FL 33135
Ph: (305)643-8000
Fax: (305)642-1184
URL: http://www.mbhc.org
Formerly: Miami Mental Health Center.

29571 ■ Miami Behavioral Health Center, Inc.
Coconut Grove
3750 S Dixie Hwy., Ste. 104
Miami, FL 33133-4309
Ph: (305)442-0748
URL: http://www.mbhc.org
Formerly: Miami Mental Health Center Coconut Grove.

29572 ■ Miami Behavioral Health Center, Inc.
W Flagler Street, Miami
3850 W Flagler St.
Miami, FL 33134
Ph: (305)774-3300
Fax: (305)774-6210
URL: http://www.mbhc.org/locations.html

29573 ■ Miami Behavioral Health Center, Inc.
Westchester
2826 SW 87th Ave., Ste. A111
Miami, FL 33165-2031
Ph: (305)421-2260
URL: http://www.mbhc.org/locations.html
Formerly: Miami Mental Health Center.

29574 ■ New Horizons Community Mental Health Center, Inc.
7505 NE 2nd Ave.
Miami, FL 33138
Ph: (305)635-0366

29575 ■ New Horizons Community Mental Health Center
NW 36th Street, Miami
1469 NW 36th St.
Miami, FL 33142
Ph: (305)635-0366
Fax: (305)635-6378
URL: http://www.nhcmhc.org/

29576 ■ Palmetto Place
1000 Park Centre Blvd., Ste. 138
Miami, FL 33169
Ph: (786)466-2900
Fax: (786)466-2922
URL: http://www.jhsmiami.org/body.cfm?id=9358

29577 ■ PsychSolutions, Inc.
701 SW 27th Ave., Ste. 500
Miami, FL 33135
Ph: (305)668-9000
URL: http://www.psychsolutionsinc.net/contacts.php

Miami Beach

29578 ■ Douglas Gardens Community Mental Health Center
701 Lincoln Rd., 2nd Fl.
Miami Beach, FL 33139
Ph: (305)531-5341

29579 ■ The Mayfair Residence
1980 Park Ave.
Miami Beach, FL 33139
Ph: (305)531-5341

29580 ■ Sandy Shores Crisis Residential
629 Lenox Ave.
Miami Beach, FL 33139
Ph: (305)538-7710

Miami Gardens

29581 ■ Bayview Center for Mental Health
111 NW 183rd St., Ste. 500
Miami Gardens, FL 33169
Ph: (305)892-4600
URL: http://www.bayviewcenter.com/

Monticello

29582 ■ Apalachee Center, Inc.--Monticello
1996 S Jefferson St.
Monticello, FL 32344
Ph: (850)997-3958
URL: http://www.apalacheecenter.org/

Naples

29583 ■ David Lawrence Center
6075 Bathey Ln.
Naples, FL 34116
Ph: (239)455-8500
Formerly: David Lawrence Mental Health Center.

29584 ■ Naples Veterans Affairs Primary Care Clinic
2685 Horseshoe Dr., Ste. 101
Naples, FL 34104
Ph: (239)659-9188
Fax: (239)659-0526
URL: http://www2.va.gov/directory/guide/facility.asp?ID=5027&dnum=All

New Port Richey

29585 ■ Adult Crisis Stabilization Unit
8132 King Helie Blvd.
New Port Richey, FL 34653
Ph: (727)841-4455
Formerly: Crisis Stabilization Unit.

29586 ■ Children's Crisis Stabilization Unit
8132 King Helie Blvd.
New Port Richey, FL 34653
Ph: (727)841-4455

29587 ■ Harbor Behavioral Health Care Institute
7809 Massachusetts Ave.
New Port Richey, FL 34653
Ph: (727)816-9851
Free: 866-762-1743
URL: http://www.baycare.org/body.cfm?id=761&fr=true

29588 ■ James A. Haley Veterans Affairs Medical Center
New Port Richey Clinic
9912 Little Rd.
New Port Richey, FL 34654
Ph: (727)869-4100
Fax: (727)861-4194
URL: http://www2.va.gov/directory/guide/facility.asp?ID=568&dnum=All

29589 ■ Outpatient Center West
8002 King Helie Blvd.
New Port Richey, FL 34653-1435
Ph: (727)841-4430
URL: http://www.baycare.org/body.cfm?id=761&fr=true

New Smyrna Beach

29590 ■ ACT
New Smyrna Beach Center
311 N Orange St.
New Smyrna Beach, FL 32168
Ph: (386)416-1023
Formerly: ACT.

North Fort Myers

29591 ■ Coastal Behavioral Healthcare--North Fort Myers
939 Pondella Rd.
North Fort Myers, FL 33903
Ph: (239)656-3461
URL: http://www.coastalbh.org/

North Miami

29592 ■ BayHouse
12690 NE 2nd Ave.
North Miami, FL 33161-4556
Ph: (305)769-1040

29593 ■ Biscayne Milieu Health Center Inc.
13499 Biscayne Blvd., Ste. 101
North Miami, FL 33181
Ph: (305)948-9000

29594 ■ FOCUS House
1585 NE 123rd St.
North Miami, FL 33161
Ph: (305)895-4800
URL: http://www.bayviewcenter.com/

North Port

29595 ■ Coastal Behavioral Healthcare--North Port
6919 Outreach Way
North Port, FL 34287
Ph: (941)429-3705
URL: http://www.coastalbh.org/

Ocala

29596 ■ Camelot Community Care--Ocala
1601 NE 25th Ave., Ste. 306
Ocala, FL 34470
Ph: (352)671-7884
URL: http://www.camelotcommunitycare.org/fl_locations.asp

29597 ■ The Centers
Martin Luther King Campus
717 SW Martin Luther King Jr. Ave.
Ocala, FL 34474
Ph: (352)351-6900
URL: http://www.marion-citrusmhc.org/CentersPages/CentersLocations.html

29598 ■ Malcom Randall Veterans Affairs Medical Center
Ocala Clinic
1515 Silver Springs Blvd.
Ocala, FL 34470
Ph: (352)369-3320
Fax: (352)369-3324
URL: http://www2.va.gov/directory/guide/facility.asp?ID=5053&dnum=All

29599 ■ Marion Citrus Mental Health Center
5694 SW 60th Ave.
Ocala, FL 34476
Ph: (352)732-1424
URL: http://www.marion-citrusmhc.org

29600 ■ Marion Citrus Mental Health Center
Northern Landing Transitional Program
5664 SW 60th Ave.
Ocala, FL 34474
Ph: (352)873-6500
Fax: (352)873-7921
URL: http://www.marion-citrusmhc.org

29601 ■ The Vines Hospital of Ocala
3130 SW 27th Ave.
Ocala, FL 34471
Ph: (352)671-3130
Free: 866-671-3130
URL: http://www.thevineshospital.com/

Okeechobee

29602 ■ New Horizons of the Treasure Coast--Okeechobee
1600 SW 2nd Ave.
Okeechobee, FL 34972
Ph: (863)462-0040
URL: http://www.nhtcinc.org/

29603 ■ West Palm Beach Veterans Affairs Medical Center
Okeechobee Clinic
1201 N Parrot Ave.
Okeechobee, FL 34972
Ph: (863)824-3232
Fax: (863)824-3379
URL: http://www2.va.gov/directory/guide/facility.asp?ID=5103&dnum=All

Opa Locka

29604 ■ Jackson North Community Mental Health Center
20201 NW 37th Ave.
Opa Locka, FL 33056
Ph: (786)466-2700

Opalocka

29605 ■ Miami Behavioral Health Center, Inc.
Opalocka
4469 NW 167th St.
Opalocka, FL 33055
Ph: (305)621-1455
URL: http://www.mbhc.org/locations.html

Orlando

29606 ■ Devereux Florida
6147 Christian Way
Orlando, FL 32808
Ph: (407)362-9210
Free: 800-338-3738
URL: http://www.devereux.org/site/PageServer?pagename=fl_residential_intensive

29607 ■ Pasadena Villa
119 Pasadena Pl.
Orlando, FL 32803
Ph: (407)246-0887

29608 ■ University Behavioral Center
2500 Discovery Dr.
Orlando, FL 32826
Ph: (407)281-7000
Fax: (407)282-7012
URL: http://www.psysolutions.com/facilities/universitybehavioralcenter/

Palm Coast

29609 ■ Stewart-Marchman-Act Behavioral Healthcare
1 Corporate Dr., Bldg. 3
Palm Coast, FL 32137
Ph: (386)446-6740
URL: http://www.smabehavioral.org/about-sma.html
Formerly: ACT Enrichment Flager.

Panama City

29610 ■ Life Management Center
Adult Day Program
525 E 15th St.
Panama City, FL 32405
Ph: (850)522-4474
Free: 888-785-8750
URL: http://www.lifemanagementcenter.org

29611 ■ Life Management Center of Northwest Florida, Inc.
525 E 15th St.
Panama City, FL 32405-1519
Ph: (850)769-9481
Free: 888-785-8750
URL: http://www.lifemanagementcenter.org
Formerly: Life Management Center of Northern Florida.

Pembroke Pines

29612 ■ Bayview Center for Mental Health--DART Program
1301 Poinciana Dr.
Pembroke Pines, FL 33025
Ph: (954)961-5985
URL: http://www.bayviewcenter.com/

29613 ■ Bayview Center for Mental Health--Fastrack
8445 S Palm Dr.
Pembroke Pines, FL 33025
Ph: (954)518-4072
URL: http://www.bayviewcenter.com/

29614 ■ Bayview Center for Mental Health--START Program
8113 S Palm Dr.
Pembroke Pines, FL 33025
Ph: (954)966-4442
URL: http://www.bayviewcenter.com/

Pensacola

29615 ■ Center for Personal & Family Development
9400 University Pkwy., Ste. 409
Pensacola, FL 32514
Ph: (850)208-6150

29616 ■ Lakeview Center
1221 W Lakeview Ave.
Pensacola, FL 32501
Ph: (850)432-1222
URL: http://www.elakeviewcenter.org/Lakeview-Center/

29617 ■ Veterans Affairs Gulf Coast Medical Center
Pensacola Clinic
790 Veterans Way
Pensacola, FL 32507
Ph: (850)912-2000
Free: 800-296-8872
URL: http://www2.va.gov/directory/guide/facility.asp?ID=5584&dnum=All

Perry

29618 ■ Taylor County Clinic
1421 Old Dixie Hwy.
Perry, FL 32348
Ph: (850)584-5613
URL: http://www.apalacheecenter.org/

Plant City

29619 ■ Mental Health Care, Inc.
Baylife Adult Center
301 N Palmer St.
Plant City, FL 33566
Ph: (813)237-3914
URL: http://www.mhcinc.org/

29620 ■ Mental Health Care, Inc.
East Panos Center
1403 W Reynolds St.
Plant City, FL 33566
Ph: (813)707-7044
URL: http://www.mhcinc.org/

Pompano Beach

29621 ■ Broward Adolescent Therapeutic Community
220 SW 2nd St.
Pompano Beach, FL 33060
Ph: (954)941-9828
URL: http://www.mbhc.org/locations.html

Port Charlotte

29622 ■ Port Charlotte Veterans Affairs Primary Care Clinic
4161 Tamiami Tr., Ste. 401
Port Charlotte, FL 33952
Ph: (941)235-2710
Fax: (941)235-2712
URL: http://www2.va.gov/directory/guide/facility.asp?ID=5026&dnum=All

Port Saint Joe

29623 ■ Life Management Center
Gulf County Facility
311 Williams Ave.
Port Saint Joe, FL 32456
Ph: (850)522-4485
URL: http://www.lifemanagementcenter.org

Punta Gorda

29624 ■ Charlotte Community Mental Health Services, Inc.
1700 Education Ave., Ste. A
Punta Gorda, FL 33950
Ph: (941)639-8300
URL: http://cbhcfl.org/

29625 ■ Charlotte Community Mental Health Services, Inc.
Crisis Stabilization Unit
1700 Education Ave., Ste. C
Punta Gorda, FL 33950

Ph: (941)575-0222
URL: http://cbhcfl.org/crisisstabilizationunit.aspx

29626 ■ Charlotte Community Mental Health Services, Inc.
Group Residential Treatment Systems
1700 Education Ave., Bldg. B
Punta Gorda, FL 33950
Ph: (941)637-6200
URL: http://cbhcfl.org/residentialtreatmentsystems.aspx

29627 ■ Charlotte Community Mental Health Services, Inc.
Therapeutic Family Care
1700 Education Ave., Bldg. B
Punta Gorda, FL 33950
Ph: (941)575-5104
URL: http://cbhcfl.org/therapeuticfamilycare.aspx

29628 ■ Coastal Behavioral Healthcare--Punta Gorda
2208 Castilla Ave.
Punta Gorda, FL 33950
Ph: (941)639-5535
URL: http://www.coastalbh.org/

Quincy

29629 ■ Apalachee Center, Inc.
Gadsden County Clinic
79 LaSalle Path
Quincy, FL 32351
Ph: (850)875-2422
URL: http://www.apalacheecenter.org

Saint Augustine

29630 ■ Malcom Randall Veterans Affairs Medical Center
Saint Augustine Clinic
1955 U.S. 1 S, Ste. 200
Saint Augustine, FL 32086
Ph: (904)829-0814
Free: 866-401-8387
Fax: (904)829-6174
URL: http://www2.va.gov/directory/guide/facility.asp?ID=5032&dnum=All

Saint Cloud

29631 ■ Sunnyside Village
84 Beehive Circle Dr.
Saint Cloud, FL 34769
Ph: (407)846-0023
URL: http://home.ppbh.org

Saint Petersburg

29632 ■ Boley Centers for Behavioral Healthcare, Inc.
445 31st St. N
Saint Petersburg, FL 33713
Ph: (727)821-4819
Fax: (727)822-6240
URL: http://www.boleycenters.org

29633 ■ Gulf Coast Jewish Family Services
66th Street Group Home
3200 66th St. N
Saint Petersburg, FL 33710-1511
Ph: (727)893-1661
URL: http://www.gcjfs.org

29634 ■ Markus Mittermeyer
4123 37th St. N
Saint Petersburg, FL 33714
Ph: (727)522-4717

29635 ■ Martin Lott Group Home
3537 5th Ave. N
Saint Petersburg, FL 33713
Ph: (727)824-5724

29636 ■ Mary Koening Center
Day Activity Center
647 34th Ave. S
Saint Petersburg, FL 33705
Ph: (727)824-5745
Formerly: Day Activity Center.

29637 ■ The Oaks Apartments
618 11th Ave. S
Saint Petersburg, FL 33701
Ph: (727)824-5738

29638 ■ Owl's Nest Apartments
1147 16th St. N, Ste. 1205
Saint Petersburg, FL 33705
Ph: (727)824-5735
URL: http://www.boleycenters.org

29639 ■ Saint Petersburg Veterans Affairs Primary Care Clinic
3420 8th Ave.
Saint Petersburg, FL 33711
Ph: (727)322-1304
Free: 888-820-0230
Fax: (727)322-1248
URL: http://www2.va.gov/directory/guide/facility.asp?ID=5030&dnum=All

29640 ■ Tyrone Apartments
8060 47th Ave. N, Ste. 8070
Saint Petersburg, FL 33709
Ph: (727)821-4819
URL: http://www.boleycenters.org

Sanford

29641 ■ Seminole Community Mental Health Center
Group Home
351 S Bay Ave.
Sanford, FL 32771
Ph: (407)831-2411
URL: http://www.seminolecares.org/

29642 ■ Seminole County Crisis Stabilization
300 S Bay Ave.
Sanford, FL 32771
Ph: (305)831-2411
URL: http://www.seminolecares.org/
Formerly: Seminole Community Crisis Stabilization Unit.

Sarasota

29643 ■ Coastal Behavioral Healthcare--Sarasota
1750 17th St.
Sarasota, FL 34234
Ph: (941)308-2936
URL: http://www.coastalbh.org/

29644 ■ Jewish Family and Children's Service of Sarasota-Manatee, Inc.
2688 Fruitville Rd.
Sarasota, FL 34237
Ph: (941)366-2224
Fax: (941)366-2982
URL: http://www.jfcs-cares.org/

29645 ■ Sarasota Veterans Affairs Primary Care Clinic
5682 Bee Ridge Rd., Ste. 100
Sarasota, FL 34233
Ph: (941)371-3349
Fax: (941)371-7749
URL: http://www2.va.gov/directory/guide/facility.asp?ID=5028&dnum=All

Sebring

29646 ■ Sebring Veterans Affairs Primary Care Clinic
3760 U.S. Hwy. 27 S
Sebring, FL 33870
Ph: (863)471-6227
Fax: (863)471-6510
URL: http://www2.va.gov/directory/guide/facility.asp?ID=5087&dnum=All

Starke

29647 ■ Bradford County Clinic
945 Grand St.
Starke, FL 32091-1821
Ph: (904)964-8382
URL: http://www.mbhci.org/
Formerly: Meridian Bradford County Clinic.

Stuart

29648 ■ New Horizons of the Treasure Coast
Martin County Outpatient Program
1111 SE Federal Hwy., Ste. 230
Stuart, FL 34994
Ph: (772)221-4088
URL: http://www.nhtcinc.org
Formerly: New Horizons of the Treasure Center Martin County Outpatient Program.

Sunrise

29649 ■ Alternate Family Care, Inc.
10001 W Oakland Park Blvd., Ste. 200
Sunrise, FL 33351
Ph: (954)746-5200
URL: http://www.altfam.com/

Tallahassee

29650 ■ Apalachee Center, Inc.--Tallahassee
2634 Capital Cir. NE, Ste. C
Tallahassee, FL 32308
Ph: (850)523-3289
Fax: (850)523-3434
URL: http://www.apalacheecenter.org
Formerly: Apalachee Center for Human Services.

29651 ■ Camelot Community Care--Tallahassee
1000 W Tharpe St., Ste. 7
Tallahassee, FL 32303
Ph: (850)561-8060
Fax: (850)561-1143
URL: http://www.camelotcommunitycare.org/fl_locations.asp

29652 ■ DISC Village, Inc.
3333 W Pensacola St., Ste. 300
Tallahassee, FL 32304
Ph: (850)575-4388
Free: 866-775-4960
Fax: (850)576-3317
E-mail: discinfo@discvilliage.com
URL: http://www.discvillage.com

29653 ■ Malcom Randall Veterans Affairs Medical Center
Tallahassee Clinic
1607 St. James Ct.
Tallahassee, FL 32308
Ph: (850)878-0191
Free: 800-541-8387
Fax: (850)878-8900
URL: http://www2.va.gov/directory/guide/facility.asp?ID=570&dnum=All

Tamarac

29654 ■ Henderson Dual Diagnosis Treatment Center
2900 W Prospect Rd.
Tamarac, FL 33309
Ph: (954)731-1000
Fax: (954)677-7555
URL: http://www.hendersonmhc.org

29655 ■ Henderson Mental Health Center New Vista
2900 W Prospect Rd.
Tamarac, FL 33309
Ph: (954)731-1000
URL: http://www.hendersonmhc.org

Tampa

29656 ■ Baylife Services
2313 W Violet St.
Tampa, FL 33603
Ph: (813)673-4622
URL: http://www.mhcinc.org/

29657 ■ Camelot Community Care--Tampa
1412 Tech Blvd.
Tampa, FL 33619
Ph: (813)635-9765
Fax: (813)635-9765
URL: http://www.camelotcommunitycare.org/fl_locations.asp

29658 ■ Children's Resource Center Mental Health Care
2905 E Henry Ave.
Tampa, FL 33610
Ph: (813)272-2888
URL: http://www.mhcinc.org/

29659 ■ The Garham Home and Transitional Living Community
2400 E Henry Ave.
Tampa, FL 33610
Ph: (813)272-2219
URL: http://www.mhcinc.org/

29660 ■ Gulf Coast Jewish Family Services N Florida Avenue
13542 N Florida Ave.
Tampa, FL 33613
Ph: (813)987-6700
Fax: (813)987-6588
URL: http://www.gcjfs.org
Formerly: Gulf Coast Jewish Family Guidance and Mental Health Services.

29661 ■ Northside Mental Health Center Access House
1109 E 139th Ave.
Tampa, FL 33613
Ph: (813)972-2289
Fax: (813)632-0923
URL: http://www.northsidemhc.org/
Formerly: Access House.

29662 ■ Northside Mental Health Center Access Manor
2220 E 138th Ave.
Tampa, FL 33612
Ph: (813)977-5241
URL: http://www.northsidemhc.org/
Formerly: Access Manor.

29663 ■ Northside Mental Health Center Satellite I Apartments
12707 N 15th St.
Tampa, FL 33612
Ph: (813)977-6900
URL: http://www.northsidemhc.org/
Formerly: Northside Mental Health Center.

29664 ■ Northside Mental Health Center Satellite II Apartments
1612 E 127th Ave.
Tampa, FL 33612
Ph: (813)977-6900
URL: http://www.northsidemhc.org/
Formerly: Northside Mental Health Center.

29665 ■ Northside Mental Health Center--Tampa
12512 Bruce B. Downs Blvd.
Tampa, FL 33612
Ph: (813)977-8700
URL: http://www.northsidemhc.org/

29666 ■ Tampa Crossroads
5120 N Nebraska Ave.
Tampa, FL 33603
Ph: (813)238-8557
URL: http://www.tampacrossroads.com/index.htm

29667 ■ Volunteers of America
1205 E 8th Ave.
Tampa, FL 33605-3503
Ph: (813)282-1525
URL: http://www.voa-fla.org

Temple Terrace

29668 ■ Northside Mental Health Center--Fasst
10630 N 56th St.
Temple Terrace, FL 33617
Ph: (813)980-1299
URL: http://www.northsidemhc.org/

The Villages

29669 ■ Malcom Randall Veterans Affairs Medical Center The Villages Clinic
1950 Laurel Manor Dr., Bldg. 240
The Villages, FL 32162
Ph: (352)205-8900
Fax: (352)205-8901
URL: http://www2.va.gov/directory/guide/facility.asp?ID=5338&dnum=All

Trenton

29670 ■ Gilchrist County Clinic
728 NE 7th St.
Trenton, FL 32693
Ph: (352)487-0064
URL: http://www.mbhci.org/
Formerly: Meridian Gilchrist County Clinic.

Venice

29671 ■ Coastal Behavioral Healthcare--Venice
7810 S Tamiami Trl.
Venice, FL 34292
Ph: (941)492-4300
URL: http://www.coastalbh.org/

Vero Beach

29672 ■ New Horizons of the Treasure Coast--Vero Beach
777 37th St., Ste. C101
Vero Beach, FL 32960
Ph: (772)778-7217
URL: http://www.nhtcinc.org/

29673 ■ West Palm Beach Veterans Affairs Medical Center Vero Beach Clinic
372 17th St.
Vero Beach, FL 32960
Ph: (772)299-4623
Fax: (772)299-4632
URL: http://www2.va.gov/directory/guide/facility.asp?ID=5102&dnum=All

Viera

29674 ■ Orlando Veterans Affairs Medical Center Viera Clinic
2900 Veterans Way
Viera, FL 32940
Ph: (321)637-3788
Free: 877-878-8387
URL: http://www2.va.gov/directory/guide/facility.asp?ID=800&dnum=All

Wauchula

29675 ■ Peace River Center Wauchula Office
213 E Orange St.
Wauchula, FL 33873
Ph: (863)519-0575

West Palm Beach

29676 ■ Oakwood Center of the Palm Beaches, Inc.--West Palm Beach
1041 45th St.
West Palm Beach, FL 33407
Ph: (561)383-8000
Free: 877-435-4740
Fax: (561)514-1995
URL: http://www.oakwoodcenter.org
Formerly: The 45th Street Mental Health Center.

29677 ■ Phoenix Residence I
2901 Broadway
West Palm Beach, FL 33401
Ph: (561)844-9741
URL: http://www.oakwoodcenter.org

29678 ■ Phoenix Residence II Oakwood Center of the Palm Beaches
Metcalf Ct., Ste. 1-12
West Palm Beach, FL 33401
Ph: (561)842-3145
Fax: (561)840-3360
URL: http://www.oakwoodcenter.org

29679 ■ West Palm Beach Veterans Affairs Medical Center
7305 N Military Tr.
West Palm Beach, FL 33410
Ph: (561)422-8262
Free: 800-972-8262
Fax: (561)422-8613
URL: http://www2.va.gov/directory/guide/facility.asp?ID=145&dnum=All

Wilton Manors

29680 ■ Kids in Distress--Wilton Manors
819 NE 26th St.
Wilton Manors, FL 33305-1239
Ph: (954)390-7620
Fax: (954)390-0145
E-mail: info@kidsindistress.org
URL: http://kidsindistress.org
Remarks: Specializes in child welfare, prevention and mental health services.

Winter Springs

29681 ■ Grove Counseling Center, Inc.--Winter Springs
580 Old Sanford Oveido Rd.
Winter Springs, FL 32708-2637
Ph: (407)327-1765
Free: 800-919-1765
E-mail: service@thegrove.org
URL: http://www.thegrove.org

Zephyrhills

29682 ■ James A. Haley Veterans Affairs Medical Center Zephyrhills Clinic
6937 Medical View Ln.
Zephyrhills, FL 33541
Ph: (813)780-2550
Fax: (813)780-3010
URL: http://www2.va.gov/directory/guide/facility.asp?ID=5414&dnum=All

GEORGIA

Adel

29683 ■ Behavioral Health Services of South Georgia Cook County Mental Health
1905 S Hutchinson Ave.
Adel, GA 31620

Ph: (229)896-4559
URL: http://www.bhsga.com

Albany

29684 ■ Albany Area Community Service Board--Albany
1120 W Broad Ave.
Albany, GA 31702
Ph: (229)430-4042
E-mail: info@albanycsb.org
URL: http://www.albanycsb.org

29685 ■ Dublin Veterans Affairs Medical Center
Albany Clinic
526 W Broad Ave.
Albany, GA 31701
Ph: (229)446-9000
Fax: (229)446-0404
URL: http://www2.va.gov/directory/guide/facility.asp?ID=851&dnum=All

29686 ■ Intensive Training Residence
PO Box 1988
Albany, GA 31707
Ph: (229)430-5103
URL: http://www.albanycsb.org

29687 ■ Mental Health/Substance Abuse Services
PO Box 1988
Albany, GA 31707
Ph: (229)430-4140
URL: http://www.albanycsb.org

29688 ■ Supportive Living Adaptive Group Residence
PO Box 1988
Albany, GA 31707
Ph: (229)430-4022
URL: http://www.albanycsb.org

29689 ■ Third Avenue Group Home
1205 W 3rd Ave.
Albany, GA 31707
Ph: (229)430-3949
URL: http://www.albanycsb.org

Americus

29690 ■ Middle Flint Behavioral HealthCare
415 N Jackson St.
Americus, GA 31709
Ph: (229)931-2470
URL: http://www.middleflintbhc.org/

29691 ■ Middle Flint Behavioral HealthCare
Alcohol/Drug Day Treatment
952 Anthony Dr.
Americus, GA 31709
Ph: (229)928-2201
URL: http://www.middleflintbhc.org/sa_day_services.htm

29692 ■ Middle Flint Behavioral HealthCare
Breezeway Adult Mental Health Day Services
523 US Hwy. 280 E
Americus, GA 31709
Ph: (229)931-2493
URL: http://www.middleflintbhc.org/adult_mh_day_services.htm

29693 ■ Middle Flint Behavioral HealthCare
Group Homes and Residences
103 Knollwood Dr.
Americus, GA 31709
Ph: (229)928-2897
URL: http://www.middleflintbhc.org/residential_services.htm

29694 ■ Middle Flint Behavioral HealthCare Residential Services
211 S Jackson St.
Americus, GA 31709
Ph: (229)931-2659
URL: http://www.middleflintbhc.org/residential_services.htm

Ashburn

29695 ■ Behavioral Health Services of South Georgia
Turner Alternative Service Center
391 County Farm Rd.
Ashburn, GA 31714-3413
Ph: (229)567-3496
URL: http://www.bhsga.com

Athens

29696 ■ Advantage Behavioral Health Systems
Child and Adolescent Services
165 Dougherty St.
Athens, GA 30606
Ph: (706)369-6363
URL: http://www.advantagebhs.org/

29697 ■ Advantage Behavioral Health Systems
Crisis Stabilization Program
195 Miles St.
Athens, GA 30601
Ph: (706)369-5745
URL: http://www.advantagebhs.org/

29698 ■ Advantage Behavioral Health Systems
Women's Day Service
115 Berlin St.
Athens, GA 30606
Ph: (706)227-5321
URL: http://www.advantagebhs.org/

29699 ■ Augusta Veterans Affairs Medical Center
Athens Clinic
9249 Hwy. 29 S, Ste. A
Athens, GA 30601
Ph: (706)227-4534
Fax: (706)227-4538
URL: http://www2.va.gov/directory/guide/facility.asp?ID=850&dnum=All

Atlanta

29700 ■ The Anxiety & Stress Management Institute
1640 Powers Ferry Rd., Bldg. 9, Ste. 100
Atlanta, GA 30067
Ph: (770)953-0080
Fax: (770)953-0031
URL: http://www.stressmgt.net/facility.htm

29701 ■ Atlanta Medical Center
Behavioral Health Services
303 Parkway Dr. NE
Atlanta, GA 30312
Ph: (404)265-4000
Fax: (404)265-3903
URL: http://www.atlantamedcenter.com

29702 ■ The Center for Health & Rehabilitation
265 Blvd. NE
Atlanta, GA 30312
Ph: (404)730-1650
URL: http://www.fultoncountyga.gov/departments/51-mental-health/1125

29703 ■ Child and Adolescent Outpatient Clinic
Piedmont Hall
22 Piedmont Ave. SE
Atlanta, GA 30303-3057
Ph: (404)616-2218
Formerly: Child and Adolescent Outpatient Clinic Grady Health System.

29704 ■ Emory University Hospital
1441 Clifton Rd. NW
Atlanta, GA 30329
Ph: (404)728-6222
URL: http://www.emoryhealthcare.org/psychiatry/index.html

29705 ■ Families First, Inc.
1105 W Peachtree St., NE
Atlanta, GA 30309
Ph: (404)853-2800
URL: http://www.familiesfirstinc.org/

29706 ■ Grady Central Fulton Mental Health Center
Florida Hall
60 Coca Cola Pl. SE
Atlanta, GA 30303
Ph: (404)616-4444

29707 ■ Hillside, Inc.
690 Courtenay Dr., NE
Atlanta, GA 30306
Ph: (404)875-4551
URL: http://www.hside.org/

29708 ■ Neighborhood Union Health Center
186 Sunset Ave.
Atlanta, GA 30314
Ph: (404)612-4665
URL: http://www.fultoncountyga.gov/departments/51-mental-health/1125

29709 ■ Northside Mental Health Center--Atlanta
1140 Hammond Dr., Ste. J1075
Atlanta, GA 30328
Ph: (404)851-8950
URL: http://www.northside.com

29710 ■ Peachford Hospital
2151 Peachford Rd.
Atlanta, GA 30338
Ph: (770)455-3200
URL: http://www.peachfordhospital.com/

29711 ■ Skyland Trail
1961 N Druid Hills Rd.
Atlanta, GA 30329
Ph: (404)315-8333
URL: http://www.skylandtrail.org/

29712 ■ South Central Fulton Community Mental Health Center
215 Lakewood Way SW, Rm. 205
Atlanta, GA 30315-6022
Ph: (404)762-3650
URL: http://www.fultoncountyga.gov/departments/51-mental-health/1125
Formerly: South Central Fulton County Mental Health Center.

29713 ■ Talbott Recovery Campus
5448 Yorktowne Dr.
Atlanta, GA 30349
Ph: (770)994-0185
Free: 800-445-4232
URL: http://www.talbottcampus.com/home.php

29714 ■ West Fulton County Mental Health Center
475 Fairburn Rd. SW
Atlanta, GA 30331
Ph: (404)691-9627
URL: http://www.fultoncountyga.gov/departments/51-mental-health/1125

Augusta

29715 ■ Adult Day Treatment
3421 Mike Padgett Hwy.
Augusta, GA 30906
Ph: (706)432-4800
URL: http://www.cmhc.us/locations/augusta/index.asp

29716 ■ Charlie Norwood Veterans Affairs Medical Center
1 Freedom Way
Augusta, GA 30904
Ph: (706)733-0188
Free: 800-836-5561
Fax: (706)823-3934
URL: http://www2.va.gov/directory/guide/facility.asp?ID=9&dnum=All

29717 ■ Child & Adolescent Services
3421 Mike Padgett Hwy.
Augusta, GA 30906-3815
Ph: (706)771-4750
URL: http://www.cmhc.us/locations/augusta/index.asp

Austell

29718 ■ Austell Day Supports and Peer Supports
6133 Love St.
Austell, GA 30168
Ph: (770)819-9229

29719 ■ Douglas County Day Services
6133 Love St.
Austell, GA 30168
Ph: (770)819-9229
URL: http://www.cobbcsb.com/contact.html

Bainbridge

29720 ■ Decatur County Mental Health Center
1005 Washington St.
Bainbridge, GA 39819
Ph: (229)248-2683

29721 ■ Decatur/Seminole Adult Day Support
503 Alice St.
Bainbridge, GA 39819
Ph: (229)248-2905

Barnesville

29722 ■ Pine Woods
Crisis Stabilization, Respite Care
700 Hwy. 341 S
Barnesville, GA 30204
Ph: (770)358-5252

Baxley

29723 ■ Pineland Area MH/MR/SA CSB
Appling Counseling Center
755 S Main St.
Baxley, GA 31515
Ph: (912)367-4614
URL: http://www.pinelandcsb.org/html/appling.html

29724 ■ Pineland Area MH/MR/SA CSB
Appling- Jeff Davis Service Center
100 Sunshine Dr.
Baxley, GA 31513
Ph: (912)367-3768
URL: http://www.pinelandcsb.org/html/appling.html

Blairsville

29725 ■ Union Mental Health/Substance Abuse Clinic
41 Hospital St., Ste. 100
Blairsville, GA 30512
Ph: (706)745-5911
URL: http://www.avitapartners.org/about/locations.php

Blakely

29726 ■ Albany Area Community Service Board
Early County Mental Health Center
12799 Magnolia St.
Blakely, GA 39823
Ph: (229)724-2206
URL: http://www.albanycsb.org/contact.htm

29727 ■ Albany Area Community Service Board
Early-Miller Mental Retardation Service Center
218 Damascus St.
Blakely, GA 39823
Ph: (229)723-4325
URL: http://www.albanycsb.org/contact.htm

Blue Ridge

29728 ■ Highland Rivers Community Service Board--Blue Ridge
990 E Main St.
Blue Ridge, GA 30513
Ph: (706)946-1175
URL: http://www.highlandrivers.org/sites/index.cfm?template=sites_gilmer_fannin

Bremen

29729 ■ Haralson County Center for MH/MR/SA
1449 Cashtown Rd.
Bremen, GA 30110
Ph: (770)537-2367

Brunswick

29730 ■ Gateway Behavioral Health Services
3441 Cypress Mill Rd., Ste. 102
Brunswick, GA 31520
Ph: (912)554-8500
URL: http://www.gatewaybhs.org/

Buena Vista

29731 ■ Americus Area Mental Health/Mental Retardation Program--Buena Vista, Georgia
111 Baker St., Ste. A
Buena Vista, GA 31803
Ph: (229)649-5664

Butler

29732 ■ Americus Area Mental Health/Mental Retardation Program
Taylor County Clinic
Hwy. 137 W
Butler, GA 31006
Ph: (478)862-5628

Cairo

29733 ■ Grady County Mental Health Center
1641 N Broad St.
Cairo, GA 39828
Ph: (229)377-5700

29734 ■ Grady County Mental Health Older Persons Day Treatment
631 1st Ave. NE
Cairo, GA 39828
Ph: (229)377-0007

Calhoun

29735 ■ Highland Rivers Community Service Board--Calhoun
320 N River St.
Calhoun, GA 30701
Ph: (706)625-8369
URL: http://www.highlandrivers.org/sites/index.cfm?template=sites_gordon

Camilla

29736 ■ Mitchell County Mental Health Children & Youth
108 S Harney St.
Camilla, GA 31730
Ph: (229)522-3565

Canton

29737 ■ Cherokee/Pickens Mental Health Center
191 Lamar Haley Pkwy.
Canton, GA 30114-8019
Ph: (770)704-1600
URL: http://www.highlandrivers.org/sites/index.cfm?template=sites_bartow
Formerly: Highland Rivers Center Cherokee/Pickens Counties.

Carrollton

29738 ■ Pathways Center
Carroll County Supportive Living Service
153 Independence Dr.
Carrollton, GA 30116
Ph: (770)836-6678
URL: http://www.pathwayscsb.org/

29739 ■ Pathways Center
IGR - Men
405 N Lake Dr.
Carrollton, GA 30117-1883
Ph: (706)832-7048
URL: http://www.pathwayscsb.org/
Formerly: Pathways Center.

29740 ■ Pathways Center
IGR--Women
403 N Lake Dr.
Carrollton, GA 30117
Ph: (770)836-0472
URL: http://www.pathwayscsb.org/

Cartersville

29741 ■ Highland Rivers Community Service Board
Bartow County Office
650 Joe Frank Harris Pkwy.
Cartersville, GA 30120
Ph: (770)387-3538
URL: http://www.highlandrivers.org/sites/index.cfm?template=sites_bartow
Formerly: Three Rivers Behavioral Health.

Cedartown

29742 ■ Highland Rivers Community Service Board
Polk County Office
180 Water Oak Dr.
Cedartown, GA 30125
Ph: (770)748-2225
Formerly: Three Rivers Behavioral Health.

29743 ■ Residential Treatment Unit
Highland Rivers Community Service Board
180 Water Oak Dr.
Cedartown, GA 30125-2095
Ph: (770)749-2390
URL: http://www.highlandrivers.org/sites/index.cfm?template=sites_polk

Chauncey

29744 ■ Community Service Board of Middle Georgia--Chauncey
4980 Hwy. 341
Chauncey, GA 31011
Ph: (229)868-6885

Chickamauga

29745 ■ Lookout Mountain Community Services
ANCOR- Chickamauga
1427 Lee Clarkson Rd.
Chickamauga, GA 30707
Ph: (706)375-2142
Free: 800-882-1552
URL: http://www.lmcs.org/

Cleveland

29746 ■ White County Mental Health/Substance Abuse Clinic
1241 Helen Hwy., Ste. 180
Cleveland, GA 30528
Ph: (706)865-7886

Colquitt

29747 ■ Miller County Mental Health Center
250 W Pine St.
Colquitt, GA 39837
Ph: (229)758-5090

Columbus

29748 ■ New Horizons Community Service Board
Adaptive Group Residence
9021 Veterans Pkwy.
Columbus, GA 31901
Ph: (706)660-9926
URL: http://www.newhorizonscsb.org/

29749 ■ New Horizons Community Service Board--Columbus
2100 Comer Ave.
Columbus, GA 31907
Ph: (706)596-5583
Free: 800-241-3659
URL: http://www.newhorizonscsb.org/

29750 ■ New Horizons Community Service Board
Family Enrichment Services
1230 2nd Ave.
Columbus, GA 31901
Ph: (706)321-9606
URL: http://www.newhorizonscsb.org/

29751 ■ New Horizons Community Service Board
Springlake Intensive Day Treatment
9055 Veterans Pkwy.
Columbus, GA 31901
Ph: (706)324-7074
URL: http://www.newhorizonscsb.org/

Commerce

29752 ■ Advantage Behavioral Health Systems
Jackson County Service Center
106 Industrial Pkwy.
Commerce, GA 30529
Ph: (706)335-5379
URL: http://www.advantagebhs.org/organizational-directory.html
Formerly: Jackson County Service Center; Solartech.

Conyers

29753 ■ Rockdale Center
GRN Community Services Board
977A Taylor St. SW
Conyers, GA 30012
Ph: (770)918-6677
Formerly: Rockdale Mental Health Center.

Cordele

29754 ■ Middle Flint Behavioral Healthcare
Adult Mental Health Day Treatment
110 E 4th Ave.
Cordele, GA 31015
Ph: (229)273-2091

Covington

29755 ■ Newton Center
GRN Community Services Board
8201 Hazelbrand Rd. NE
Covington, GA 30014
Ph: (770)787-3977

Crawford

29756 ■ Advantage Behavioral Health Systems
Oglethorpe Mental Health Clinic
29 Oglethorpe Dr.
Crawford, GA 30630
Ph: (706)743-7539
URL: http://www.advantagebhs.org/organizational-directory.html

Cumming

29757 ■ Forsyth County Mental Health/Substance Abuse Outpatient Clinic
125 N Corners Pkwy.
Cumming, GA 30040-2078
Ph: (678)341-3840
URL: http://www.avitapartners.org/about/locations.php
Formerly: Forsyth County Mental Health Substance Abuse and Mental Retardation.

Cuthbert

29758 ■ New Horizons Community Service Board
Substance Abuse/ Adult Day Services
201 Villa Nova St.
Cuthbert, GA 39840
Ph: (229)732-5276

Dalton

29759 ■ Highland Rivers Community Service Board--Dalton
1710 Whitehouse Dr., Ste. 204
Dalton, GA 30720
Ph: (706)270-5000
URL: http://www.highlandrivers.org/sites/index.cfm?template=sites_whitfield_murray

Danielsville

29760 ■ Advantage Behavioral Health System--Dainelsville
1430 Hwy. 98 W
Danielsville, GA 30633
Ph: (706)795-2141
URL: http://www.advantagebhs.org/organizational-directory.html
Formerly: Madison County Mental Health Center.

Dawson

29761 ■ Terrell County Mental Health Center
638 Forrester Dr. SE
Dawson, GA 39842-2009
Ph: (229)995-2701

Decatur

29762 ■ Clifton Springs Health Center
3110 Clifton Springs Rd.
Decatur, GA 30034
Ph: (404)243-9500

29763 ■ DeKalb Community Service
445 Winn Way
Decatur, GA 30030
Ph: (404)294-3836
URL: http://www.dekcsb.org

29764 ■ DeKalb Community Services Board
445 Winn Way, 4th Fl.
Decatur, GA 30031
Ph: (404)892-4646
URL: http://www.dekcsb.org

29765 ■ Newport Integrated Behavioral Healthcare
1810 Moseri Rd.
Decatur, GA 30032
Ph: (404)289-8223
E-mail: info@nibhinc.com
URL: http://www.nibhinc.com/

Demorest

29766 ■ Avita Community Partners
196 Scoggins Dr.
Demorest, GA 30535
Ph: (706)894-3700
URL: http://www.avitapartners.org/about/locations.php

Donalsonville

29767 ■ Seminole County Mental Health
904 N Wiley Ave.
Donalsonville, GA 39845
Ph: (229)225-4370

Douglas

29768 ■ Satilla Community Services
Coffee Behavioral Health
1005 Shirley Ave.
Douglas, GA 31533
Ph: (912)389-4188

Dublin

29769 ■ Child and Adolescent Mental Health
2121A Bellevue Rd., Bldg. 4
Dublin, GA 31021
Ph: (478)275-6811

29770 ■ Community Service Board of Middle Georgia
Middle Georgia Alcohol & Drug Clinic
600 N Jefferson St.
Dublin, GA 31021-6302
Ph: (478)275-6800

29771 ■ Dublin Day Treatment Services
2121A Bellevue Rd.
Dublin, GA 31021
Ph: (478)275-0825

29772 ■ Dublin Veterans Affairs Medical Center
1826 Veterans Blvd.
Dublin, GA 31021
Ph: (478)272-1210
URL: http://www.dublin.va.gov/

East Dublin

29773 ■ Community Service Board of Middle Georgia--East Dublin
1330 Hwy. 319 N
East Dublin, GA 31027
Ph: (478)275-5167

East Point

29774 ■ East Point Veterans Affairs Medical Center
1513 Cleveland Ave.
East Point, GA 30344
Ph: (404)321-6111
URL: http://www2.va.gov/directory/guide/facility.asp?ID=5367&dnum=1

Eastman

29775 ■ Eastman Day Treatment
Live Oak Day Treatment Center
733 Medical Center Dr.
Eastman, GA 31023
Ph: (478)374-6835

29776 ■ Eastman Mental Health Center
621 Plaza Ave.
Eastman, GA 31023
Ph: (478)448-1040
URL: http://www.csbmg.com/

Elberton

29777 ■ Elbert County Mental Health Center
50 Chestnut St.
Elberton, GA 30635
Ph: (706)213-2048
URL: http://www.advantagebhs.org/organizational-directory.html

Ellijay

29778 ■ Highland Rivers Center
Fannin/Gilmer Counties
18090 Hwy. 515 N
Ellijay, GA 30540
Ph: (706)635-2739
URL: http://www.highlandrivers.org/

Fayetteville

29779 ■ Fayette Counseling Center
715 Bradley Dr.
Fayetteville, GA 30214
Ph: (770)358-5252

Fitzgerald

29780 ■ Behavioral Health Services of South Georgia
Ben Hill Mental Health Center
124 S Grant St.
Fitzgerald, GA 31750-2901
Ph: (229)426-5213
URL: http://www.bhsga.com

Flowery Branch

29781 ■ Avita Community Partners
Adult Behavioral Health Services
4331 Thurmond Tanner Pkwy.
Flowery Branch, GA 30542
Ph: (678)513-5700
Free: 800-525-8751
URL: http://www.avitapartners.org/about/locations.php

Folkston

29782 ■ Satilla Community Services
Charlton Behavioral Health
3010 Homeland Park Rd.
Folkston, GA 31537
Ph: (912)496-7460

Forest Park

29783 ■ Adaptive Group Residence
5644 Sandhurst Dr.
Forest Park, GA 30297-2906
Ph: (404)363-8888

Forsyth

29784 ■ Monroe County Counseling Center
168 Old Brent Rd.
Forsyth, GA 31029
Ph: (478)994-7600

Fort Oglethorpe

29785 ■ Lookout Mountain Community Services- Horizons
1875 Fant Dr.
Fort Oglethorpe, GA 30742
Ph: (706)861-3387

Fort Valley

29786 ■ Phoenix Center
Peach County Office
410 E Church St.
Fort Valley, GA 31030
Ph: (478)825-6499

Franklin

29787 ■ Pathways Center
Heard County Mental Health/Substance Abuse Program
7690 Hwy. 27
Franklin, GA 30217
Ph: (706)675-6399

Gainesville

29788 ■ Avita Community Partners
Child & Adolescent Services
915 Interstate Ridge Dr., Ste. G
Gainesville, GA 30501
Ph: (678)207-2950
URL: http://www.avitapartners.org/about/locations.php

Georgetown

29789 ■ New Horizons Community Service Board--Georgetown
Harrison St.
Georgetown, GA 39854
Ph: (229)334-0900

Gordon

29790 ■ Oconee Community Service Board
Wilkinson County Service Center
113 Solomon St.
Gordon, GA 31031
Ph: (478)628-2777

Greensboro

29791 ■ Advantage Behavioral Health Systems
Greene County Mental Health Center
1040 Silver Rd.
Greensboro, GA 30642-2157
Ph: (706)453-2301
URL: http://www.advantagebhs.org/organizational-directory.html

Greenville

29792 ■ Pathways Center Merico
Opportunities Unlimited
756 Woodbury Rd.
Greenville, GA 30222
Ph: (706)672-1118

Griffin

29793 ■ McIntosh Trail Community Service Board
141 Solomon St.
Griffin, GA 30223
Ph: (770)229-3000

Hamilton

29794 ■ New Horizons Community Service Board
Harris County MH/SA Services
9989 Georgia Hwy. 116 E
Hamilton, GA 31811
Ph: (706)628-4740

Hartwell

29795 ■ Hart County Mental Health Center
228 N College Ave.
Hartwell, GA 30643
Ph: (706)376-4002
URL: http://www.avitapartners.org/about/locations.php

Hawkinsville

29796 ■ Pulaski County Mental Retardation Service Center
401 Progress Ave.
Hawkinsville, GA 31036
Ph: (478)783-3274

Hinesville

29797 ■ Liberty County Mental Health Center
1113 E Oglethorte Hwy.
Hinesville, GA 31313
Ph: (912)368-3502

Hiram

29798 ■ Highland Rivers Community Service Board
Paulding County Office
126 Enterprise Path, Ste. 206
Hiram, GA 30141
Ph: (678)567-0920
URL: http://www.highlandrivers.org/sites/index.cfm?template=sites paulding
Formerly: Three Rivers Behavioral Health.

Homerville

29799 ■ Satilla Community Services
Clinch Behavioral Health
551 Old Pearson Rd.
Homerville, GA 31634-1724
Ph: (912)487-5253

Jackson

29800 ■ Butts County Counseling Center
463B Ernest Biles Dr.
Jackson, GA 30233
Ph: (770)358-5252

Jasper

29801 ■ Highland Rivers Community Service Board--Jasper
323 Roland Rd.
Jasper, GA 30143-5336
Ph: (706)253-1112
URL: http://www.highlandrivers.org/sites/index.cfm?template=sites_pickens
Formerly: Highland Rivers MH Center.

Jefferson

29802 ■ Jackson County Mental Health Center--Jefferson
515 Darnell Rd.
Jefferson, GA 30549-2925
Ph: (706)367-5258
URL: http://www.advantagebhs.org/organizational-directory.html

Jessup

29803 ■ Pineland Area MH/MR/SA CSB
Wayne Service Center
244 Peachtree St.
Jessup, GA 31545
Ph: (912)427-9338

Jonesboro

29804 ■ Clayton Center Behavioral Health Services
112 Broad St.
Jonesboro, GA 30236
Ph: (770)478-2280
URL: http://www.claytoncenter.org/

29805 ■ Developmental Disabilities Clinic
217 Stockbridge Rd.
Jonesboro, GA 30236
Ph: (770)471-4617
URL: http://www.claytoncenter.org/

Kennesaw

29806 ■ Devereux Georgia
1291 Stanley Rd, NW
Kennesaw, GA 30152
Ph: (770)427-0147
URL: http://tfc.devereuxga.org/

La Fayette

29807 ■ Lookout Mountain Community Services
501 Mize St.
La Fayette, GA 30728
Ph: (706)638-5584
URL: http://www.lmcs.org/

29808 ■ Lookout Mountain Community Services
ANCOR - La Fayette
205 W Villanow St.
La Fayette, GA 30728
Ph: (706)639-2072
URL: http://www.lmcs.org/

29809 ■ Lookout Mountain Community Services
Cornerstone Psychosocial Rehabilitation Services
806 E Villanow St.
La Fayette, GA 30728
Ph: (706)639-2108
URL: http://www.lmcs.org/

LaGrange

29810 ■ Pathways Center for Behavioral and Developmental Growth
122 Gordon Commercial Dr., Ste. C
LaGrange, GA 30240
Ph: (706)845-4045
URL: http://www.pathways.org/

29811 ■ Pathways Center
Positive Options
122 Gordon Community Dr.
LaGrange, GA 30240
Ph: (706)845-4045
URL: http://www.pathways.org/

29812 ■ Pathways Center Second Season
124 Gordon Commercial Dr.
LaGrange, GA 30240
Ph: (706)298-7800
URL: http://www.pathways.org/

Lawrenceville

29813 ■ Atlanta Veterans Affairs Medical Center
Lawrenceville Clinic
1970 Riverside Pkwy.
Lawrenceville, GA 30043
Ph: (404)417-1750
Fax: (404)417-1708
URL: http://www2.va.gov/directory/guide/facility.asp?ID=5220&dnum=All

29814 ■ GRN Community Service Board
175 Gwinnett Dr.
Lawrenceville, GA 30045
Ph: (770)339-5019
URL: http://www.grncsb.com/

29815 ■ GRN Community Service Board
Beacon Place
595 Old Norcross Rd., Ste. B
Lawrenceville, GA 30045
Ph: (770)979-9379
URL: http://www.grncsb.com/

29816 ■ GRN Community Service Board
The Oaks Adaptive Group Residence
190 Oak St.
Lawrenceville, GA 30044
Ph: (404)963-8141
URL: http://www.grncsb.com/

Leesburg

29817 ■ Lee County Mental Health Center
112 Parks St.
Leesburg, GA 31763
Ph: (229)759-2600
URL: http://www.albanycsb.org/contact.htm

Lithonia

29818 ■ DeKalb Community Service Board--Choice Program
2277 S Stone Mountain-Lithonia Rd.
Lithonia, GA 30058
Ph: (404)294-3834
URL: http://www.dekcsb.org/

Louisville

29819 ■ Jefferson County Service Center
1114 Clarks Mill Rd.
Louisville, GA 30434
Ph: (478)625-7214

Lyons

29820 ■ Pineland Area MH/MR/SA CSB
Toombs Service Center
503 Reidsville Rd.
Lyons, GA 30436-3908
Ph: (912)526-3268

Macon

29821 ■ River Edge Behavioral Health Center
175 Emery Hwy.
Macon, GA 31217
Ph: (478)751-4519
URL: http://www.river-edge.org/

29822 ■ River Edge Behavioral Health Center
Forensic Services Division
668 Olgethorpe
Macon, GA 31201
Ph: (478)746-9446
URL: http://www.river-edge.org/

29823 ■ River Edge Behavioral Health Center
Peer Support
750 Baconsfield Dr.
Macon, GA 31211
Ph: (478)752-1240
URL: http://www.river-edge.org/

Marietta

29824 ■ Cobb Day and Residential Care
331 N Marietta Pkwy.
Marietta, GA 30060
Ph: (770)499-2422
URL: http://www.cobbcsb.com/contact.html

29825 ■ Cobb Douglas Community Services
361 North Marietta Pkwy.
Marietta, GA 30060
Ph: (770)429-5000
URL: http://www.cobbcsb.com

29826 ■ Cobb Outpatient Services
1650 County Services Pkwy.
Marietta, GA 30060
Ph: (770)514-2422

29827 ■ Wellstar Windy Hill Hospital
2540 Windy Hill Rd.
Marietta, GA 30067
Ph: (770)644-1000
URL: http://www.wellstar.org/ws_content/ws_hospitals.aspx?id=400&pic_id=1332

McDonough

29828 ■ Henry County Counseling Center
139 Henry Pkwy.
McDonough, GA 30253
Ph: (770)358-5252

Midland

29829 ■ Alchemy
9067 Veterans Pkwy.
Midland, GA 31820
Ph: (706)324-7241

Milledgeville

29830 ■ Baldwin County Service Center
1111 N Jefferson St. NE
Milledgeville, GA 31061
Ph: (478)453-5726

29831 ■ Oconee Adult Mental Health Clinic
430 N Jefferson St. NE
Milledgeville, GA 31061
Ph: (478)445-4721
URL: http://oconeecenter.com/contactus.php

29832 ■ Oconee Center
131 N Jefferson St. NE
Milledgeville, GA 31061
Ph: (478)445-4817
URL: http://oconeecenter.com/contactus.php
Formerly: Oconee Community Service Board.

29833 ■ Oconee Center Mental Retardation Services
830 W Charleton St.
Milledgeville, GA 31061
Ph: (478)445-3201
URL: http://oconeecenter.com/contactus.php

Monroe

29834 ■ The Alcove, Inc.
507 E Church St.
Monroe, GA 30655
Ph: (770)267-9156
URL: http://www.thealcoveshelter.com/

Morgan

29835 ■ Calhoun County Mental Health Center
Hwy. 45
Morgan, GA 39866
Ph: (229)849-5140

Moultrie

29836 ■ Colquitt County Mental Health Center
615 N Main St.
Moultrie, GA 31768
Ph: (229)891-7160

29837 ■ Turning Point Hospital
3015 Veterans Pkwy. S
Moultrie, GA 31788
Ph: (229)985-4815
Free: 800-342-1075
URL: http://www.turningpointcare.com/

Nahunta

29838 ■ Brantly Behavioral Health
RR 2, Box 23C
Nahunta, GA 31553
Ph: (912)462-5849

Nashville

29839 ■ Nashville Alternative Center
507 Laurel St.
Nashville, GA 31639
Ph: (229)686-2078
URL: http://www.bhsga.com/

Newton

29840 ■ Baker County Mental Health Center
100 Sunset Dr.
Newton, GA 39845
Ph: (229)734-5240

Norcross

29841 ■ Norcross Mental Health Clinic
GRN Community Services Board
5030 Georgia Belle Ct., Ste. 2036
Norcross, GA 30093
Ph: (770)638-5760
URL: http://www.grncsb.com/

Oakwood

29842 ■ Atlanta Veterans Affairs Medical Center
Oakwood Clinic
3931 Munday Mill Rd.
Oakwood, GA 30566
Ph: (404)728-8210
Fax: (404)728-8229
URL: http://www2.va.gov/directory/guide/facility.asp?ID=849&dnum=All

Pearson

29843 ■ Peachtree Place Group Home
104 W Austin St.
Pearson, GA 31642
Ph: (912)422-6309
URL: http://www.satilla.csb.state.ga.us/Peachtree/peachtree.htm

Reynolds

29844 ■ Morningstar Treatment Services, Inc.--Reynolds
14 Louisiana Ct.
Reynolds, GA 31076
Ph: (478)847-9879
URL: http://www.morningstartreatmentservices.com/

Riverdale

29845 ■ Flint River Center
6315 Garden Walk Blvd.
Riverdale, GA 30274
Ph: (404)991-7420

Rochelle

29846 ■ Wilcox County Mental Retardation Service Center
200 3rd Ave. NE
Rochelle, GA 31079
Ph: (229)365-7421

Rome

29847 ■ Highland Rivers Community Service Board
Adult Outpatient Services
43 Chateau Ct. SE
Rome, GA 30161-7238
Ph: (706)802-5606
URL: http://www.highlandrivers.org/
Formerly: Three Rivers Behavioral Health.

29848 ■ Morningstar Treatment Services, Inc.--Rome
1246 Cartersville Hwy.
Rome, GA 30161
Ph: (706)234-4355
URL: http://www.morningstartreatmentservices.com/

Sandersville

29849 ■ Washington County Service Center--Sandersville
522 Washington Ave.
Sandersville, GA 31082
Ph: (478)553-2424

Savannah

29850 ■ Charleston Veterans Affairs Medical Center
Savannah Clinic
325 W Montgomery Crossroads
Savannah, GA 31406
Ph: (912)920-0214
URL: http://www2.va.gov/directory/guide/facility.asp?ID=650&dnum=All

29851 ■ Coastal Harbor Treatment Center
1150 Cornell Ave.
Savannah, GA 31406-2797
Ph: (912)354-3911
URL: http://www.coastalharbor.com/

Swainsboro

29852 ■ Emanuel County Service Center
133 N Anderson Dr.
Swainsboro, GA 30401-4439
Ph: (478)289-2639

29853 ■ Ogeechee Behavioral Health Services
223 N Anderson Dr.
Swainsboro, GA 30401
Ph: (478)289-2522
Free: 800-715-4225
URL: http://www.obhs-ga.org/
Formerly: Ogeechee Mental Health/Mental Retardation/Substance Abuse Community Service Board.

Sylvania

29854 ■ Ogeechee Area Mental Health Clinic
302 E Ogeechee St.
Sylvania, GA 30467
Ph: (912)564-7825
URL: http://www.obhs-ga.org/sites/mentalhealth.html

Thomaston

29855 ■ Upson County Counseling Center
605 W Gordon St.
Thomaston, GA 30286
Ph: (770)358-8477

Thomasville

29856 ■ The Vashti Center, Inc.
1815 E Clay St.
Thomasville, GA 31792
Ph: (229)226-4634
URL: http://www.vashti.org/

Toccoa

29857 ■ Stephens County Mental Health/Substance Abuse Center
1763 Fernside Dr.
Toccoa, GA 30577
Ph: (706)282-4542
Fax: (706)282-4544
URL: http://www.avitapartners.org/about/locations.php

Valdosta

29858 ■ Malcom Randall Veterans Affairs Medical Center
Valdosta Clinic
2841 N Patterson St.
Valdosta, GA 31602
Ph: (229)293-0132
Fax: (229)293-0162
URL: http://www2.va.gov/directory/guide/facility.asp?ID=5054&dnum=All

Warner Robins

29859 ■ Phoenix Center
202 N Davis Dr.
Warner Robins, GA 31093-3348
Ph: (478)464-5200
URL: http://phoenixcenterbhs.com/default.aspx

29860 ■ Phoenix Center
Child and Family Counseling Center
940-A Hwy. 96
Warner Robins, GA 31088
Ph: (478)988-1222
URL: http://phoenixcenterbhs.com/default.aspx

29861 ■ Phoenix Center Crisis Stabilization
940C Hwy. 96
Warner Robins, GA 31088
Ph: (478)988-7100
URL: http://phoenixcenterbhs.com/default.aspx

29862 ■ Phoenix House Day Services
940 Georgia Hwy. 96
Warner Robins, GA 31088
Ph: (478)988-1002
URL: http://phoenixcenterbhs.com/default.aspx

Waycross

29863 ■ Morningstar Treatment Services, Inc.--Waycross
603 Mary St., Ste. A
Waycross, GA 31501
Ph: (912)283-5101
URL: http://www.morningstartreatmentservices.com/

Waynesboro

29864 ■ Ogeechee Behavioral Health Clinic
629 Shadrack St.
Waynesboro, GA 30830
Ph: (706)437-6863

29865 ■ Ogeechee Behavioral Health/Day Services
727 W 6th St.
Waynesboro, GA 30830
Ph: (706)437-6869

West Point

29866 ■ Morningstar Treatment Services, Inc.--West Point
809 Ave. C
West Point, GA 31833
Ph: (706)645-0398
URL: http://www.morningstartreatmentservices.com/

Winder

29867 ■ Barrow County Mental Health Center
98 Lanthier St.
Winder, GA 30680
Ph: (770)868-4150

GUAM

Agana Heights

29868 ■ Veterans Affairs
U.S. Naval Hospital Guam, Wing E-200
Agana Heights, GU 96919
Ph: (671)474-7250
URL: http://www2.va.gov/directory/guide/facility.asp?ID=5314&dnum=All

HAWAII

Ewa Beach

29869 ■ Kahi Mohala Behavioral Health
91-2301 Old Fort Weaver Rd.
Ewa Beach, HI 96706
Ph: (808)671-8511
URL: http://www.kahimohala.org/

Hilo

29870 ■ Hawaii Community Mental Health Center
37 Kekaulike St.
Hilo, HI 96720
Ph: (808)974-4300

29871 ■ Helping Hands Hawaii
120 Pauahi St., Ste. 207-208
Hilo, HI 96720
Ph: (808)934-9800

29872 ■ Hilo Veterans Center
126 Pu'uhonu Way, Ste. 2
Hilo, HI 96720
Ph: (808)969-3833
Fax: (808)969-2025
URL: http://www2.va.gov/directory/guide/facility.asp?ID=440&dnum=All

29873 ■ Mental Health Kokua--East Hawaii Office
208 Wainaku Ave.
Hilo, HI 96720
Ph: (808)935-7167
URL: http://www.mentalhealthkokua.org/locations.html

29874 ■ The Phoenix Center
169 Puueo St.
Hilo, HI 96720
Ph: (808)934-7355

29875 ■ Veterans Affairs Hilo Community Based Outpatient Clinic
1285 Waianuenue Ave., Ste. 211
Hilo, HI 96720
Ph: (808)935-3781
URL: http://www2.va.gov/directory/guide/facility.asp?ID=5310&dnum=All

Honokaa

29876 ■ Brantley Center, Inc.
Ohelo St.
Honokaa, HI 96727
Ph: (808)775-7245

Honolulu

29877 ■ Blueprint for Change
1500 S Beretania St., Ste. 314
Honolulu, HI 96826
Ph: (808)952-0488
Fax: (808)952-0487
E-mail: admin@blueprintforchange.org
URL: http://blueprintforchange.org/

29878 ■ Hale Kipa, Inc.
615 Pi'ikoi St., Ste. 203
Honolulu, HI 96814
Ph: (808)589-1829
Fax: (808)589-2610
URL: http://www.halekipa.org/

29879 ■ Honolulu Veterans Center
1680 Kapiolani Blvd., Ste. F-3
Honolulu, HI 96814
Ph: (808)973-8387
Fax: (808)973-5295
URL: http://www2.va.gov/directory/guide/facility.asp?ID=441&dnum=All

29880 ■ Mental Health Kokua--Main Office
1221 Kapiolani Blvd., Ste. 345
Honolulu, HI 96814
Ph: (808)737-2523
URL: http://www.mentalhealthkokua.org/locations.html

29881 ■ Oahu Community Mental Health Center
Diamond Head Treatment Services Section
3627 Kilauea Ave.
Honolulu, HI 96816
Ph: (808)733-9260

29882 ■ Queen's Medical Center
1301 Punchbowl St.
Honolulu, HI 96813
Ph: (808)547-4220
URL: http://www.queensmedicalcenter.net/

29883 ■ The Salvation Army Family Treatment Services
Kula-Kokua Pohai
845 22nd Ave.
Honolulu, HI 96816
Ph: (808)732-2802

29884 ■ Veterans Affairs Pacific Islands Health Care System
459 Patterson Rd.
Honolulu, HI 96819
Ph: (803)433-0600
Free: 800-214-1406
URL: http://www.hawaii.va.gov/

Kahului

29885 ■ Veterans Affairs Maui Community Based Outpatient Clinic
203 Ho'ohana St., Ste. 303
Kahului, HI 96732
Ph: (808)871-2454
URL: http://www2.va.gov/directory/guide/facility.asp?ID=5313&dnum=All

Kailua-Kona

29886 ■ Kailua-Kona Veterans Center
73-4976 Kamanu St., Ste. 207
Kailua-Kona, HI 96740
Ph: (808)329-0574
Fax: (808)329-2799
URL: http://www2.va.gov/directory/guide/facility.asp?ID=442&dnum=All

29887 ■ Mental Health Kokua--West Hawaii Office
75-166 Kalani St., Ste. 103
Kailua-Kona, HI 96740
Ph: (808)331-1468
URL: http://www.mentalhealthkokua.org/locations.html

29888 ■ Veterans Affairs Kona Community Based Outpatient Clinic
35-377 Hualalai Rd.
Kailua-Kona, HI 96740
Ph: (808)329-0774
URL: http://www2.va.gov/directory/guide/facility.asp?ID=5312&dnum=All

Kealakekua

29889 ■ Kona Community Hospital
Behavioral Health
79-1019 Haukapila St.
Kealakekua, HI 96750
Ph: (808)322-4429
URL: http://www.kch.hhsc.org/

Lihue

29890 ■ Mental Health Kokua--Kauai County Office
205 Akahi St.
Lihue, HI 96766
Ph: (808)632-0466
URL: http://www.mentalhealthkokua.org/locations.html

29891 ■ Veterans Affairs Kauai Community Based Outpatient Clinic
3367 Kuhio Hwy., Ste. 200
Lihue, HI 96766
Ph: (808)246-0497
URL: http://www2.va.gov/directory/guide/facility.asp?ID=5311&dnum=All

Pearl City

29892 ■ Mental Health Kokua--Duplex I
1186 Kuokoa St.
Pearl City, HI 96782
Ph: (808)456-9338
URL: http://www.mentalhealthkokua.org

29893 ■ Mental Health Kokua--Duplex II
1296 Hooli Cir.
Pearl City, HI 96782
Ph: (808)456-9338
URL: http://www.mentalhealthkokua.org

Wailuku

29894 ■ Maui Community Mental Health Center
121 Mahalani St.
Wailuku, HI 96793-2528
Ph: (808)984-2150

29895 ■ Mental Health Kokua
Maui County Services
220 Imi Kalai St.
Wailuku, HI 96793
Ph: (808)244-7405
URL: http://www.mentalhealthkokua.org/locations.html
Formerly: Maui Kokua Services.

IDAHO

Bellevue

29896 ■ Region V Mental Health Services
Department of Health and Welfare
621 N Main
Bellevue, ID 83313
Ph: (208)788-3584
Formerly: Region V Family & Children's Services; Child Mental Health Services.

Blackfoot

29897 ■ Idaho State Hospital South
700 E Alice St.
Blackfoot, ID 83221
Ph: (208)785-8402

Boise

29898 ■ Boise Veterans Affairs Medical Center
500 W Fort St.
Boise, ID 83702
Ph: (208)422-1000
Free: 866-437-5093
URL: http://www.visn20.med.va.gov/boise/index.asp

29899 ■ Boise Veterans Center
5440 Franklin Rd., Ste. 100
Boise, ID 83705
Ph: (208)342-3612
Fax: (208)342-0327
URL: http://www2.va.gov/directory/guide/facility.asp?ID=501&dnum=All

29900 ■ Saint Alphonsus Behavioral Health Services
6138 Emerald
Boise, ID 83706
Ph: (208)367-3553
URL: http://www.saintalphonsus.org/svc_behavioral.html

29901 ■ Warm Springs Counseling Center
740 Warm Springs Ave.
Boise, ID 83712
Ph: (208)343-7797
URL: http://www.childrenshomesociety.com/wscc/contact/

Caldwell

29902 ■ Caldwell Veterans Affairs Clinic
120 E Pine
Caldwell, ID 83605
Ph: (208)454-4820
URL: http://www2.va.gov/directory/guide/facility.asp?ID=5577&dnum=All

Coeur d'Alene

29903 ■ Coeur d'Alene Veterans Affairs Clinic
2177 N Ironwood Center Dr.
Coeur d'Alene, ID 83815
Ph: (208)665-1700
URL: http://www2.va.gov/directory/guide/facility.asp?ID=5674&dnum=All

Garden Valley

29904 ■ Project PATCH Ranch
25 Miracle Lane
Garden Valley, ID 83622
Ph: (208)462-3074
URL: http://projectpatch.org

Kellogg

29905 ■ Region I Mental Health Services
35 Wildcat Way, Ste. B
Kellogg, ID 83837
Ph: (208)784-1351

Lewiston

29906 ■ Lewiston Idaho Veterans Affairs Clinic
1630 23rd Ave., Bldg. 2
Lewiston, ID 83501
Ph: (208)746-7784
URL: http://www2.va.gov/directory/guide/facility.asp?ID=5372&dnum=All

Meridian

29907 ■ Warm Springs Counseling Center West
3023 E Copper Point Dr., Ste. 205
Meridian, ID 83642
Ph: (208)343-7797
Fax: (208)321-4142
URL: http://www.childrenshomesociety.com/wscc/contact/

Pocatello

29908 ■ Pocatello Veterans Affairs Clinic
444 Hospital Way, Ste. 801
Pocatello, ID 83201
Ph: (208)232-6214
URL: http://www2.va.gov/directory/guide/facility.asp?ID=989&dnum=All

29909 ■ Pocatello Veterans Center
1800 Garrett Way
Pocatello, ID 83201
Ph: (208)232-0316
Fax: (208)232-6258
URL: http://www2.va.gov/directory/guide/facility.asp?ID=5084&dnum=All

Rexburg

29910 ■ Upper Valley Resource and Counseling
36 N 2nd W
Rexburg, ID 83440
Ph: (208)359-0519

Twin Falls

29911 ■ Saint Luke's Canyon View Behavioral Health Services
228 Shoup Ave. W
Twin Falls, ID 83301
Ph: (208)734-6760
Free: 800-657-8000
URL: http://www.stlukesonline.org/magic_valley/specialties_and_services/mental_h ealth.php
Formerly: Canyon View Psychiatric & Addiction Services.

29912 ■ Twin Falls Veterans Affairs Clinic
260 2nd Ave. E
Twin Falls, ID 83301
Ph: (208)732-0959
URL: http://www2.va.gov/directory/guide/facility.asp?ID=5359&dnum=All

ILLINOIS

Addison

29913 ■ Du Page County Health Department North Office Mental Health
1111 W Lake St.
Addison, IL 60101
Ph: (630)682-7400

Albion

29914 ■ Southeastern Illinois Counseling Centers, Inc.--Albion
254 S 5th St.
Albion, IL 62806
Ph: (618)445-3559

Alsip

29915 ■ Sertoma Centre, Inc.
4343 W 123rd St.
Alsip, IL 60803
Ph: (708)371-9700
URL: http://www.chicagononprofit.org/profile/sertoma

Alton

29916 ■ Catholic Children's Home
1400 State St.
Alton, IL 62002
Ph: (618)465-3594
URL: http://www.catholicchildrenshome.com/

29917 ■ Community Counseling Center of North Madison
2615 Edwards St.
Alton, IL 62002-3915
Ph: (618)462-2331

Anna

29918 ■ Union County Counseling
204 South St.
Anna, IL 62906-1549
Ph: (618)833-8551

Arlington Heights

29919 ■ Alexian Center for Mental Health
3350 W Salt Creek Ln., Ste. 114
Arlington Heights, IL 60005
Ph: (847)952-7460
URL: http://www.alexianbrothershealth.org/services/acmh/index.aspx

29920 ■ Jewish Child and Family Services
1156 W Shure Dr., Ste. 181
Arlington Heights, IL 60004
Ph: (847)392-8970
URL: http://www.jfcschicago.org/con-main.cfm

Aurora

29921 ■ Association for Individual Development
309 W Indian Tr.
Aurora, IL 60506
Ph: (630)966-4000

29922 ■ Gateway Foundation
400 Mercy Ln.
Aurora, IL 60506
Ph: (630)966-7400
Free: 877-321-RECOVERY
URL: http://recovergateway.org/

Belleville

29923 ■ Belleville Veterans Affairs Clinic
6500 W Main St.
Belleville, IL 62223
Ph: (314)286-6988
Fax: (314)289-7660
URL: http://www2.va.gov/directory/guide/facility.asp?ID=5252&dnum=All

29924 ■ Chestnut Health Systems Psychosocial Rehabilitation
207 E Main St.
Belleville, IL 62226
Ph: (618)236-0435
URL: http://www.chestnut.org/About_CHS/locations.htm

Bloomington

29925 ■ McLean County Center for Human Services
108 W Market St.
Bloomington, IL 61701
Ph: (309)827-5351

Blue Island

29926 ■ The Thresholds--South Suburbs
12145 Western Ave.
Blue Island, IL 60406
Ph: (708)597-7997

Cairo

29927 ■ Delta Center, Inc.--Commercial Avenue
1400 Commercial Ave.
Cairo, IL 62914
Ph: (618)734-2665
URL: http://www.deltacenter.org/

29928 ■ Delta Center, Inc.--Washington Avenue
1702 Washington Ave.
Cairo, IL 62914
Ph: (618)734-9770
URL: http://www.deltacenter.org/

Carbondale

29929 ■ Southern Illinois Regional Social Service
604 E College St.
Carbondale, IL 62901
Ph: (618)457-6703
Fax: (618)457-8377
URL: http://www.sirss.org

Carlyle

29930 ■ Community Resource Center--Carlyle
580 8th St.
Carlyle, IL 62231
Ph: (618)594-4581

Centralia

29931 ■ Community Resource Center--Centralia
101 S Locust St.
Centralia, IL 62801
Ph: (618)533-1391

29932 ■ Horizon House--Centralia
8722 Jolliff Bridge Rd.
Centralia, IL 62801
Ph: (618)532-2517

Champaign

29933 ■ Mental Health Center of Champaign County
1801 Fox Dr.
Champaign, IL 61820
Ph: (217)398-8080
URL: http://www.mhcenter.org/
Formerly: Mental Health Center of Champaign Centerpoint; Provena Behavioral Health at Centerpoint.

29934 ■ The Pavilion Foundation
809 W Church St.
Champaign, IL 61820
Ph: (217)373-1700
Free: 800-373-1700
E-mail: info@pavilionhospital.com
URL: http://www.pavilionhospital.com

29935 ■ Respite Center
Provena Behavioral Health
502 N Market St.
Champaign, IL 61820-3634
Ph: (217)373-2428
URL: http://www.provena.org

Charleston

29936 ■ Supervised Group Homes
LifeLinks, Inc.
1504 20th St.
Charleston, IL 61920
Ph: (217)234-6405
URL: http://www.ccmhc.org/
Formerly: Coles County Mental Health Center.

Chicago

29937 ■ Abraham Lincoln Center
3858 S Cottage Grove
Chicago, IL 60653
Ph: (773)285-1390
URL: http://www.abelink.org

29938 ■ Ada S. McKinley Community Services, Inc.
725 S Wells St., Ste. 1A
Chicago, IL 60607
Ph: (312)554-0600
URL: http://www.adasmckinley.org

29939 ■ Adler School of Professional Psychology
65 E Wacker Pl., Ste. 2100
Chicago, IL 60601
Ph: (312)554-0600
URL: http://www.adler.edu

29940 ■ Anixter Center
2001 N Clybourn Ave., 3rd Fl.
Chicago, IL 60614
Ph: (773)973-7900
Fax: (773)973-5268
E-mail: askanixter@anixter.org
URL: http://www.anixter.org

29941 ■ Association House
1116 N Kedzie Ave.
Chicago, IL 60651
Ph: (773)772-7170
URL: http://www.associationhouse.org/

29942 ■ Auburn Gresham Veterans Affairs Clinic
7731 S Halsted St.
Chicago, IL 60620
Ph: (773)962-3700
Fax: (773)996-3703
URL: http://www2.va.gov/directory/guide/facility.asp?ID=782&dnum=All

29943 ■ Belle Plaine Group Home
4824 W Belle Plaine
Chicago, IL 60641
Ph: (773)685-3937
URL: http://www.lssi.org/SERVICE/GroupHomesForPersonswithMentalIllness.aspx

29944 ■ Bobby E. Wright Comprehensive Behavioral Health Center, Inc.
9 S Kedzie Ave.
Chicago, IL 60612
Ph: (773)722-7900
URL: http://www.bobbyewright.org/
Formerly: Bobby E. Wright Comprehensive Mental Health Center, Inc.

29945 ■ Circle Family Care Ministries
5002 Madison Ave.
Chicago, IL 60644
Ph: (773)379-1375
Fax: (773)379-1342
URL: http://www.circlefamilycare.org

29946 ■ Community Mental Health Council, Inc.
8704 S Constance Ave.
Chicago, IL 60617
Ph: (773)734-4033
E-mail: information@thecouncil-online.org
URL: http://www.thecouncil-online.org/

29947 ■ Department of Psychiatry
Northwestern Memorial Hospital
320 E Huron
Chicago, IL 60611
Ph: (312)926-8100
URL: http://www.nmh.org

29948 ■ Hands of Life Against AIDS Program
2319 S Damen Ave.
Chicago, IL 60608
Ph: (773)579-0832
E-mail: info@pilsenmh.org

29949 ■ Holbrook Counseling Center
641 W Lake St.
Chicago, IL 60661
Ph: (312)655-7719
URL: http://www.catholiccharities.net/holbrook/locations/

29950 ■ Holbrook Counseling Center--Chciago
16100 Seton Dr.
Chicago, IL 60473
Ph: (312)655-7719
URL: http://www.catholiccharities.net/holbrook/locations/

29951 ■ Jesse Brown Veterans Affairs Medical Center
820 S Damen Ave.
Chicago, IL 60612
Ph: (312)569-8387
Free: 800-591-4815
URL: http://www.chicago.va.gov/

29952 ■ McKinley Intervention Services
2715 W 63rd St.
Chicago, IL 60629
Ph: (773)434-5577
URL: http://www.adasmckinley.org

29953 ■ Outpatient Mental Health Program
1858 W Cermack Rd.
Chicago, IL 60608
Ph: (312)226-1120
Fax: (312)226-0135
URL: http://www.pilsenmh.org
Formerly: The Pilsen Little Village Community Mental Health Center.

29954 ■ Pilsen Inn Residential Program
Community Crisis Center
2635 W 23rd St.
Chicago, IL 60608
Ph: (773)927-1228
Fax: (773)927-0237
URL: http://www.pilsenmh.org
Formerly: Pilsen Little Village Community Mental Health Center.

29955 ■ Pilsen Little Village Community Mental Health Center, Inc.
2319 S Damen St.
Chicago, IL 60608
Ph: (773)579-0832
URL: http://www.pilsenmh.org

29956 ■ Pilsen Little Village Community Mental Health Center, Inc.
Vocational/Psychosocial Program
2015 W Cermack Rd.
Chicago, IL 60608-4115
Ph: (773)890-0045
URL: http://www.pilsenmh.org

29957 ■ South Central Community Services, Inc.
8545 S Cottage Grove Ave.
Chicago, IL 60619
Ph: (773)873-3000
URL: http://www.sccsinc.org/

29958 ■ The Thresholds--Bridge Southwest
3638 S Kedzie Ave.
Chicago, IL 60632
Ph: (773)927-7050
URL: http://www.thresholds.org/

29959 ■ The Thresholds--Bridge West
5000 W Roosevelt Rd.
Chicago, IL 60644
Ph: (773)287-0101
URL: http://www.thresholds.org/

29960 ■ Thresholds Psychiatric Rehabilitation Centers
4101 N Ravenswood
Chicago, IL 60613
Ph: (773)572-5500
Free: 888-99-REHAB
URL: http://www.thresholds.org/

29961 ■ Trilogy
1400 W Greenleaf
Chicago, IL 60626
Ph: (773)508-6100
Free: 800-322-8400
Fax: (773)262-4841
URL: http://www.trilogyinc.org/

29962 ■ Victor C. Neumann Association
5547 N Ravenswood
Chicago, IL 60640
Ph: (773)769-4313
Fax: (773)769-1476
E-mail: info@neumannfamilyservices.org
URL: http://www.neumannfamilyservices.org/

Cicero

29963 ■ Holbrook Counseling Center--Cicero
1400 S Austin Ave.
Cicero, IL 60804
Ph: (312)655-7719
URL: http://www.catholiccharities.net/holbrook/locations/

Danville

29964 ■ Center for Children's Services
702 N Logan Ave.
Danville, IL 61832
Ph: (217)446-1300

29965 ■ Crosspoint Day Treatment
213 Harrison
Danville, IL 61832
Ph: (217)431-1781

29966 ■ Crosspoint Human Services--Community Support
210 Ave. C
Danville, IL 61832
Ph: (217)442-3200
URL: http://www.co.vermilion.il.us/mental05.html

29967 ■ Veterans Affairs Illiana Health Care System
1900 E Main St.
Danville, IL 61832
Ph: (217)554-3000
Free: 888-838-6446
URL: http://www.danville.va.gov/

Decatur

29968 ■ Decatur Veterans Affairs Outpatient Clinic
3035 E Mound Rd.
Decatur, IL 62526
Ph: (217)875-2670
URL: http://www2.va.gov/directory/guide/facility.asp?ID=779&dnum=All

29969 ■ Heritage Behavioral Health Center
151 N Main St.
Decatur, IL 62523
Ph: (217)362-6262
Fax: (217)362-6290
E-mail: dknaebe@heritagenet.org
URL: http://www.heritagenet.org

29970 ■ Heritage Behavioral Health Child and Adolescent Services
151 N Main St.
Decatur, IL 62523
Ph: (217)877-8613
Fax: (217)362-6290
URL: http://www.heritagenet.org

Des Plaines

29971 ■ Holbrook Counseling Center--Des Plaines
1717 Rand Rd.
Des Plaines, IL 60016
Ph: (312)655-7725
URL: http://www.catholiccharities.net/holbrook/locations/

East Peoria

29972 ■ Valle Vista Counseling Center
100 N Main
East Peoria, IL 61611
Ph: (309)694-6462

East Saint Louis

29973 ■ Mental Health Center of Saint Clair County
4601 State St.
East Saint Louis, IL 62205
Ph: (618)482-7330
Formerly: Comprehensive Mental Health Center of St. Clair County, Inc.

Edgemont

29974 ■ Call for Help, Inc.
9400 Lebanon Rd.
Edgemont, IL 62203
Ph: (618)397-0968
Fax: (618)397-6836
E-mail: awilsing@callforhelpinc.org
URL: http://www.callforhelpinc.org

Effingham

29975 ■ Effingham Veterans Affairs Clinic
1901 S 4th St., Ste. 21
Effingham, IL 62401
Ph: (217)347-7600
URL: http://www2.va.gov/directory/guide/facility.asp?ID=5361&dnum=All

29976 ■ Heartland Human Services
1200 N 4th St.
Effingham, IL 62401
Ph: (217)347-7179
URL: http://www.heartlandhs.org/

Elgin

29977 ■ CILA
Ecker Center for Mental Health--CILA
1949 Mark Ave.
Elgin, IL 60123-1909
Ph: (847)931-9314
Fax: (847)931-7166
URL: http://www.eckercenter.org

29978 ■ Ecker Center for Mental Health--Elgin
1845 Grandstand Pl.
Elgin, IL 60123
Ph: (847)695-0484
URL: http://www.eckercenter.org

29979 ■ Ecker Center for Mental Health Psychiatric Emergency Program
934 Center St.
Elgin, IL 60120
Ph: (847)888-2211
URL: http://www.eckercenter.org

Elizabethtown

29980 ■ Family Counseling Center, Inc.--Elizabethtown
Hardin County Office
PO Box 242
Elizabethtown, IL 62931
Ph: (618)287-7010
URL: http://fccinconline.org/
Formerly: Elizabethtown Branch.

Evanston

29981 ■ Trilogy Evanston
1618 Orrington
Evanston, IL 60201
Ph: (847)733-0003
URL: http://www.trilogyinc.org/

Flora

29982 ■ Southeastern Illinois Counseling Centers, Inc.--Flora
901 W 3rd St.
Flora, IL 62839
Ph: (618)662-2871
URL: http://www.seicc.org/

Franklin Park

29983 ■ Leyden Family Service and Mental Health Center
10001 Grand Ave., Ste. 1
Franklin Park, IL 60131
Ph: (847)451-0330
Fax: (847)451-1652
URL: http://www.leydenfamilyservice.org

Galesburg

29984 ■ Bridgeway, Inc.--Galesburg
2323 Windish Dr.
Galesburg, IL 61401
Ph: (309)344-2323
Free: 800-344-2331
URL: http://www.bway.org

29985 ■ Bridgeway/The Lodge
1857 Knox Hwy. 40
Galesburg, IL 61401-8694
Ph: (309)342-5211
URL: http://www.bway.org

29986 ■ Galesburg Veterans Affairs Clinic
387 E Grove
Galesburg, IL 61401
Ph: (309)343-0311
URL: http://www2.va.gov/directory/guide/facility.asp?ID=5211&dnum=All

Geneva

29987 ■ Tri-City Family Services
1120 Randall Ct.
Geneva, IL 60134
Ph: (630)232-1070
E-mail: sjones@tricityfamilyservices.org
URL: http://www.tricityfamilyservices.org/

Golconda

29988 ■ Family Counseling Center, Inc.--Golconda
125 N Market
Golconda, IL 62938
Ph: (618)683-2461
URL: http://fccinconline.org/

Grayslake

29989 ■ College of Lake County Lake County Prevention Services Program
19361 W Washington St.
Grayslake, IL 60030
Ph: (847)543-2056
Fax: (847)223-8540
URL: http://www.clcillinois.edu/community/intouch.asp
Formerly: In Touch/Prevention Services.

Harvey

29990 ■ Emergency Mental Health Care Grand Prairie Services
Wyman Gordon Pavillion
1 Ingalls Dr.
Harvey, IL 60426
Ph: (708)331-0500
Free: 866-477-8632
URL: http://www.gpsbh.org

29991 ■ Grand Prairie Services Gloria McAfee Center
15406 Lexington Ave.
Harvey, IL 60426
Ph: (708)596-5900
Free: 866-477-8632
Fax: (708)596-4888
URL: http://www.gpsbh.org

Harwood Heights

29992 ■ Norwood Park Family Service
4600 N Harlem Ave.
Harwood Heights, IL 60706-4714
Ph: (708)867-6886
URL: http://www.leydenfamilyservice.org

Highland Park

29993 ■ Holbrook Counseling Center--Highland Park
777 Central Ave.
Highland Park, IL 60035
Ph: (312)655-7719
URL: http://www.catholiccharities.net/holbrook/locations/

Joliet

29994 ■ Cornerstone Services, Inc.
800 Black Rd.
Joliet, IL 60435
Ph: (815)727-6667
URL: http://www.cornerstoneservices.org

29995 ■ Trinity Services, Inc.--Joliet
100 N Gougar Rd.
Joliet, IL 60432
Ph: (815)485-6197
Fax: (815)485-5975
URL: http://www.trinity-services.org

Kankakee

29996 ■ Riverside Medical Center
350 N Wall St.
Kankakee, IL 60901
Ph: (815)933-1671
URL: http://www.riversidehealthcare.org/locations.html

La Salle

29997 ■ North Central Behavioral Health Systems
La Salle Office
2960 Chartres St.
La Salle, IL 61301
Ph: (815)223-0160
URL: http://www.ncbhs.org/

Lake Villa

29998 ■ Substance Abuse Program
121 E Grand Ave.
Lake Villa, IL 60046
Ph: (847)356-0058

Libertyville

29999 ■ Behavioral Health Service and Community Health Center
400 Winchester Rd.
Libertyville, IL 60048
Ph: (847)984-5090

Lockport

30000 ■ Lockport Center for Behavioral Health
900 S State St.
Lockport, IL 60441-3436
Ph: (815)838-0997

30001 ■ Trinity Services--Lockport
900 S State St.
Lockport, IL 60441
Ph: (815)838-0996
Fax: (815)838-1284
URL: http://www.trinity-services.org

Marion

30002 ■ Marion Veterans Affairs Medical Center
2401 W Main St.
Marion, IL 62959
Ph: (618)997-5311
URL: http://www.marion.va.gov/

Mattoon

30003 ■ LifeLinks, Inc.
750 Broadway Ave. E
Mattoon, IL 61938
Ph: (217)238-5700
URL: http://www.ccmhc.org/howhelp.htm

30004 ■ LifeLinks, Inc.
Psychosocial Rehabilitation Center
1221 Broadway Ave.
Mattoon, IL 61938
Ph: (217)238-5700
URL: http://www.ccmhc.org/howhelp.htm

30005 ■ LifeLinks, Inc.
Supervised Group Homes
1305 Wabash Ave.
Mattoon, IL 61938
Ph: (217)238-5700
URL: http://www.ccmhc.org/howhelp.htm

30006 ■ Veterans Affairs Medical Center
Mattoon Community Based Outpatient Clinic
501 Lakeland Blvd.
Mattoon, IL 61938
Ph: (217)258-3370
Fax: (217)258-3379
URL: http://www2.va.gov/directory/guide/facility.asp?ID=5900&dnum=1

McHenry

30007 ■ Family Service and Community Mental Health for McHenry County
4100 Veterans Hwy.
McHenry, IL 60050
Ph: (815)385-6400
Fax: (815)385-8127
E-mail: info@familyserviceonline.com
URL: http://www.familyserviceonline.org

30008 ■ Pioneer Center Clay Group Home
3941 W Dayton St.
McHenry, IL 60050
Ph: (815)344-1230

30009 ■ Pioneer Center of McHenry County
4001 W Dayton St.
McHenry, IL 60050
Ph: (815)344-1230

Moline

30010 ■ Robert Young Center
4600 3rd St.
Moline, IL 61265
Ph: (309)779-2031
URL: http://www.trinityqc.com/body.cfm?id=92

Monticello

30011 ■ Piatt County Mental Health Center
1921 N Market St.
Monticello, IL 61856
Ph: (217)762-5371

Morris

30012 ■ Grundy County Health Department
Mental Health Division
1320 Union St.
Morris, IL 60450
Ph: (815)941-3404

Mount Vernon

30013 ■ Mount Vernon Veterans Affairs Clinic
4105 N Water Tower Pl.
Mount Vernon, IL 62864
Ph: (618)246-2910
URL: http://www2.va.gov/directory/guide/facility.asp?ID=5254&dnum=All

Mundelein

30014 ■ Holbrook Counseling Center--Mundelein
998 E Maple St.
Mundelein, IL 60060
Ph: (312)655-7719
URL: http://www.catholiccharities.net/holbrook/locations/

Naperville

30015 ■ Long-Term Group Home Program
Naperville Group Home
408 Braemar Ave.
Naperville, IL 60563
Ph: (630)682-7400

North Chicago

30016 ■ North Chicago Veterans Affairs Medical Center
3001 Green Bay Rd.
North Chicago, IL 60064
Ph: (847)688-1900
Free: 800-393-0865
URL: http://www.northchicago.va.gov/

Northfield

30017 ■ Josselyn Center for Mental Health
405 Central Ave.
Northfield, IL 60093-3097
Ph: (847)441-5600

30018 ■ WilPower, Inc.
444 W Frontage Rd.
Northfield, IL 60093-3009
Ph: (847)501-2939
URL: http://www.wilpower.org/

Oak Park

30019 ■ The Thresholds--West Suburbs
1120 N Austin Blvd.
Oak Park, IL 60302
Ph: (708)386-0399
URL: http://www.thresholds.org/

Olney

30020 ■ Arbors Center--Olney
208 E Main
Olney, IL 62450
Ph: (618)392-3090
URL: http://www.seicc.org/

Pekin

30021 ■ Tazwood Mental Health Center
3248 Vandever Ave.
Pekin, IL 61554
Ph: (309)347-5522
URL: http://www.tazwoodmentalhealth.org/locations.html

Peoria

30022 ■ Bob Michel Veterans Affairs Outpatient Clinic
411 Dr. Martin Luther King Jr. Dr.
Peoria, IL 61605
Ph: (309)497-0790
Fax: (309)497-0796
URL: http://www2.va.gov/directory/guide/facility.asp?ID=640&dnum=All

30023 ■ Human Service Center--Peoria
600 Fayette St.
Peoria, IL 61603
Ph: (309)671-8000
URL: http://www.fayettecompanies.org/

30024 ■ Human Service Center--Peoria
Day Treatment Program
228 NE Jefferson Ave.
Peoria, IL 61603
Ph: (309)671-8000
URL: http://www.fayettecompanies.org/

30025 ■ Human Service Center--Peoria
Outpatient Services
229 NE Jefferson Ave.
Peoria, IL 61603
Ph: (309)671-8007
URL: http://www.fayettecompanies.org/

30026 ■ Human Service Center--Peoria Women at the Crossroads
3420 N Rochelle Ln.
Peoria, IL 61604
Ph: (309)671-8074
URL: http://www.fayettecompanies.org/

30027 ■ New Leaf Retreat for Women
3500 W New Leaf Ln.
Peoria, IL 61615
Ph: (309)689-3078
URL: http://www.fayettecompanies.org/contact%20us/aacontactus.html

30028 ■ White Oaks Knolls for Men
2101 W Willow Knolls Rd.
Peoria, IL 61614-1219
Ph: (309)689-3074
URL: http://www.fayettecompanies.org/contact%20us/aacontactus.html

30029 ■ White Oaks Outpatient Services Human Service Center
3400 W New Leaf Ln.
Peoria, IL 61614
Ph: (309)692-6900
URL: http://www.fayettecompanies.org/contact%20us/aacontactus.html
Formerly: White Oaks Companies of Illinois.

Princeton

30030 ■ North Central Behavioral Health Systems Princeton Area Office
526 S Bureau Valley Pkwy.
Princeton, IL 61356
Ph: (815)875-4458

Quincy

30031 ■ Quincy Veterans Affairs Clinic
721 Broadway
Quincy, IL 62301
Ph: (217)224-3366
Fax: (217)224-3311
URL: http://www2.va.gov/directory/guide/facility.asp?ID=5210&dnum=All

Red Bud

30032 ■ Human Service Center of South Metro East
10257 State Rte. 3
Red Bud, IL 62278
Ph: (618)282-6233

Robinson

30033 ■ Arbors North
204A W Highland
Robinson, IL 62454
Ph: (618)546-5232
URL: http://www.seicc.org/

Rockford

30034 ■ Janet Wattles Center
526 W State St.
Rockford, IL 61101
Ph: (815)968-9300
URL: http://www.janetwattles.org/
Formerly: Janet Wattles Mental Health Center.

Round Lake Park

30035 ■ Avon Township Offices
423 E Washington St.
Round Lake Park, IL 60073
Ph: (847)377-8855
Formerly: Branch Office of Behavioral Health Services and Community Health Center.

Saint Charles

30036 ■ Ecker Center for Mental Health--Saint Charles
309 Walnut St.
Saint Charles, IL 60174
Ph: (630)377-5200
URL: http://www.eckercenter.org

Salem

30037 ■ Community Resource Center--Salem
1325 W Whitaker St., Ste C
Salem, IL 62881
Ph: (618)548-2181

Shelbyville

30038 ■ Shelby County Community Services, Inc.
1810 W S 3rd St.
Shelbyville, IL 62565
Ph: (217)774-2113

Skokie

30039 ■ Turning Point Behavioral Health Center
8324 Skokie Blvd.
Skokie, IL 60077
Ph: (847)933-0051

Springfield

30040 ■ Springfield Veterans Affairs Outpatient Clinic
700 N 7th St., Ste. C
Springfield, IL 62702
Ph: (217)522-9730
URL: http://www2.va.gov/directory/guide/facility.asp?ID=5535&dnum=All

Streamwood

30041 ■ Ecker Center for Mental Health--Streamwood
1535 Burgundy Pkwy.
Streamwood, IL 60107
Ph: (630)837-6445
URL: http://www.eckercenter.org

Taylorville

30042 ■ Christian County Mental Health Association
730 N Pawnee
Taylorville, IL 62568
Ph: (217)824-4905

Tinley Park

30043 ■ Grand Prairie Services Administrative Center
17746 S Oak Park Ave.
Tinley Park, IL 60477-3936
Ph: (708)444-1012

Vandalia

30044 ■ Community Resource Center--Vandalia
421 W Main St.
Vandalia, IL 62471-2214
Ph: (618)283-4229

Vienna

30045 ■ Family Counseling Center, Inc.--Vienna
408 E Vine St.
Vienna, IL 62995
Ph: (618)658-2611
Fax: (618)658-2501
URL: http://fccinconline.org/locations/offices-outpatient-2/

Waterloo

30046 ■ Human Support Services
988 N Illinois Rte. 3
Waterloo, IL 62298-1059
Ph: (618)939-4444
Fax: (618)939-4181
E-mail: hss@htc.net
URL: http://www.hss1.org

Waukegan

30047 ■ Behavioral Health Services of the Lake County
2645 Washington St.
Waukegan, IL 60085
Ph: (847)377-8180
Formerly: Community Support Services.

Wood River

30048 ■ Behavioral Health Alternatives, Inc.
337 E Ferguson Ave.
Wood River, IL 62095
Ph: (618)251-4073

Worth

30049 ■ Holbrook Counseling Center--Worth
7000 W 111th St.
Worth, IL 60482
Ph: (312)655-7719
URL: http://www.catholiccharities.net/holbrook/locations/

INDIANA

Albion

30050 ■ Otis R. Bowen Center for Human Services
101 E Park St.
Albion, IN 46701
Ph: (260)636-6884

Anderson

30051 ■ The Center for Mental Health
2020 Brown St.
Anderson, IN 46016
Ph: (765)649-8161
URL: http://www.cfmh.org/

30052 ■ The Center for Mental Health, Inc.
1100 Broadway
Anderson, IN 46012-2576
Ph: (765)649-8161
URL: http://www.cfmh.org/

30053 ■ Center for Mental Health, Inc. Hudson Place
1933 Chase St.
Anderson, IN 46016-4238
Ph: (765)649-8161
URL: http://www.cfmh.org/

30054 ■ Center for Mental Health, Inc. McMahan House
245 W 12th St.
Anderson, IN 46016-1371
Ph: (765)649-8161
URL: http://www.cfmh.org/

30055 ■ Hartung Place
3115 Brown St.
Anderson, IN 46016
Ph: (765)649-8161

Angola

30056 ■ Northeastern Center, Inc. Steuben County Satellite/Community Support
200 Hoosier Dr., Ste. E
Angola, IN 46703

Ph: (260)665-9494
E-mail: necinfo@nec.org
URL: http://76.12.88.208/

Auburn

30057 ■ Northeastern Center, Inc.
Vision Quest Auburn
500 North St., Ste. B
Auburn, IN 46706-1622
Ph: (260)927-9211
E-mail: necinfo@nec.org
URL: http://www.nec.org

Avon

30058 ■ Cummins Mental Health Center, Inc.--Avon
6655 E US Hwy. 36
Avon, IN 46123
Ph: (317)272-3330
Free: 800-860-3330
URL: http://www.cumminsbhs.com/avon_in.htm

Batesville

30059 ■ Batesville Office
15 N Depot Amber Village
Batesville, IN 47006
Ph: (812)934-3245

Bedford

30060 ■ Centerstone--Bedford
1315 Hillcrest
Bedford, IN 47421
Ph: (812)279-3591
Free: 800-344-8802
Fax: (812)275-0787
URL: http://centerstone.org/indiana-facilities
Formerly: South Central Community Mental Health Centers, Inc.

Bloomington

30061 ■ Bloomington Veterans Affairs Outpatient Clinic
455 S Landmark Ave.
Bloomington, IN 47403
Ph: (812)336-5723
Free: 877-683-0865
Fax: (812)353-2405
URL: http://www2.va.gov/directory/guide/facility.asp?ID=919&dnum=All

30062 ■ Centerstone
Blair House
823 N Maple St.
Bloomington, IN 47401
Ph: (812)337-2420
Free: 800-344-8802
URL: http://centerstone.org/indiana-facilities
Formerly: South Central Community Mental Health Centers, Inc.

30063 ■ Centerstone
DBA Center for Behavioral Health
645 S Rogers St.
Bloomington, IN 47403
Ph: (812)339-1691
Free: 800-344-8802
URL: http://centerstone.org/indiana-facilities
Formerly: South Central Community Mental Health Centers, Inc.

30064 ■ Centerstone
Depression Treatment Clinic
645 S Rogers St.
Bloomington, IN 47403
Ph: (812)339-1691
Free: 800-344-8802
URL: http://centerstone.org/indiana-facilities
Formerly: Depression Treatment Clinic Center for Behavioral Health; South Central Community Mental Health Centers, Inc.

Bluffton

30065 ■ Park Center, Inc.--Bluffton
1115 S Main St.
Bluffton, IN 46714
Ph: (260)824-1071
Free: 866-654-1071
URL: http://www.parkcenter.org/

Carmel

30066 ■ Aspire Behavioral Health System
697 Pro-Med Ln.
Carmel, IN 46032
Ph: (317)587-0500
URL: http://www.behaviorcorp.com/

Clinton

30067 ■ Hamilton Center, Inc.
Vermillion County Center
510 S Main St.
Clinton, IN 47842-0406
Ph: (765)832-2436
URL: http://www.hamiltoncenter.org/

Columbia City

30068 ■ Otis R. Bowen Center for Human Services
Whitley County Office
119 W Market St.
Columbia City, IN 46725
Ph: (260)248-8176

Columbus

30069 ■ Caldwell House
1714 Cottage Ave.
Columbus, IN 47201
Ph: (812)376-4860

30070 ■ Quinco Behavioral Health Systems
720 N Marr Rd
Columbus, IN 47201
Ph: (812)348-7449
Formerly: Connections; Quinco Mental Health Provider.

30071 ■ Weinland House
2412 Indiana Ave.
Columbus, IN 47201
Ph: (812)348-7443
URL: http://centerstone.org/indiana-facilities

Corydon

30072 ■ LifeSpring Mental Health Services
Harrison County Office
535 Country Club Rd. SE
Corydon, IN 47112
Ph: (812)738-2114
URL: http://www.lifespr.com/

Crawfordsville

30073 ■ New Directions, Inc.--Crawfordsville
407 E Market St., Ste. 105B
Crawfordsville, IN 47933
Ph: (765)361-0230

30074 ■ Wabash Valley Hospital, Inc.
Outpatient Service
1480 Darlington Ave.
Crawfordsville, IN 47933
Ph: (765)362-2852
URL: http://www.wvhmhc.org

Danville

30075 ■ Veterans Illiana Health Care System
1900 E Main St.
Danville, IN 61832
Ph: (217)554-3000
Free: 888-838-6446
URL: http://www.danville.va.gov/

Delphi

30076 ■ Wabash Valley Hospital, Inc.
Outpatient Service
1265 N Bradford Ct.
Delphi, IN 46923
Ph: (765)564-2247
URL: http://www.wvhmhc.org

East Chicago

30077 ■ Tri-City Comprehensive Community Mental Health Center, Inc.--Geminus
3903 Indianapolis Blvd.
East Chicago, IN 46312
Ph: (219)398-7050

Elkhart

30078 ■ Oaklawn--Elkhart
2600 Oakland Ave.
Elkhart, IN 46517
Ph: (574)533-1234
URL: http://www.oaklawn.org/about/locations

Elwood

30079 ■ The Center for Mental Health
10731 N State Rd. 13
Elwood, IN 46036
Ph: (765)552-5009
URL: http://www.cfmh.org/

English

30080 ■ Crawford County Services
523 N Main St.
English, IN 47118
Ph: (812)338-2756
Formerly: Southern Hills Counseling Center Outreach Office.

Evansville

30081 ■ Evansville Veterans Affairs Outpatient Clinic
500 E Walnut St.
Evansville, IN 47713
Ph: (812)465-6202
URL: http://www2.va.gov/directory/guide/facility.asp?ID=5256&dnum=All

30082 ■ South Western Indiana Mental Health Center, Inc.
Chestnut Home
4615 E Chestnut
Evansville, IN 47714
Ph: (812)471-1753
URL: http://www.southwestern.org

30083 ■ Southwest Indiana Mental Health Center, Inc.
Chandler Home
19 E Chandler Ave.
Evansville, IN 47713
Ph: (812)425-8190
URL: http://www.southwestern.org

30084 ■ Southwestern Indiana Mental Health Center
415 Mulleberry St.
Evansville, IN 47713
Ph: (812)423-7791
URL: http://www.southwestern.org

30085 ■ Southwestern Indiana Mental Health Center, Inc.
Moulton Center
1 N Barker Ave.
Evansville, IN 47712-5601
Ph: (812)423-4418
URL: http://www.southwestern.org

30086 ■ Southwestern Indiana Mental Health Center, Inc.
Riverside Home
813 SE Riverside Dr.
Evansville, IN 47713-1128
Ph: (812)423-3616
URL: http://www.southwestern.org

30087 ■ Southwestern Indiana Mental Health Center, Inc.
Robert M. Spear Building
415 Mulberry St.
Evansville, IN 47713-1298
Ph: (812)423-7791
URL: http://www.southwestern.org

30088 ■ Southwestern Indiana Mental Health Center
Warrick Regional Center
415 Mulberry St.
Evansville, IN 47713
Ph: (812)423-7791
URL: http://www.southwestern.org

Fort Wayne

30089 ■ Park Center Carew
1909 Carew St.
Fort Wayne, IN 46805
Ph: (260)481-2800
URL: http://www.parkcenter.org/locations.htm

30090 ■ Park Center, Inc.--Fort Wayne
909 E State Blvd.
Fort Wayne, IN 46805
Ph: (260)481-2700
URL: http://www.parkcenter.org/locations.htm

30091 ■ Veterans Affairs Northern Indiana Health Care System
Fort Wayne Campus
2121 Lake Ave.
Fort Wayne, IN 46805
Ph: (260)426-5431
Free: 888-838-6446
URL: http://www.northernindiana.va.gov/

Franklin

30092 ■ Adult & Child Mental Health Center
86 Drake Rd.
Franklin, IN 46131
Ph: (317)736-7744
URL: http://www.adultandchild.org/

Gary

30093 ■ Edgewater Systems for Balanced Living
1100 W 6th Ave.
Gary, IN 46402
Ph: (219)885-4264
URL: http://www.edgewatersystems.org

30094 ■ Edgewater Systems for Balanced Living
New Life Center
1110 W 5th Ave.
Gary, IN 46402-1723
Ph: (219)885-4264
URL: http://www.edgewatersystems.org

Goshen

30095 ■ Goshen Veterans Affairs Outpatient Clinic
2014 Lincolnway E, Ste. 3
Goshen, IN 46526
Free: 888-683-3019
URL: http://www2.va.gov/directory/guide/facility.asp?ID=5699&dnum=All

30096 ■ Oaklawn--Goshen
330 Lakeview Dr.
Goshen, IN 46527
Ph: (574)533-1234
Free: 800-282-0809
URL: http://www.oaklawn.org/about/locations

Greencastle

30097 ■ Cummins Mental Health Center, Inc.
Greencastle Clinic
308 Medic Way
Greencastle, IN 46135
Ph: (765)653-2669
URL: http://www.cumminsbhs.com/

Greendale

30098 ■ Lawrenceburg Veterans Affairs Clinic
1600 Flossie Dr.
Greendale, IN 47205
Ph: (812)539-2313
Free: 888-267-7873
URL: http://www2.va.gov/directory/guide/facility.asp?ID=984&dnum=All

Greenfield

30099 ■ Gallahue Mental Health Services--Hancock County
145 W Green Meadows Dr.
Greenfield, IN 46140
Ph: (317)462-1481

Hammond

30100 ■ Elizabeth House
50 Elizabeth St.
Hammond, IN 46320
Ph: (219)398-7050

30101 ■ Rose Academy
5900 Hohman Ave.
Hammond, IN 46320
Ph: (219)931-0427

Hartford City

30102 ■ Grant Blackford Mental Health, Inc.
Hester Hollis Concern Center
118 E Washington St.
Hartford City, IN 47348
Ph: (765)348-1303

Highland

30103 ■ Lakeside Counseling Center
2600 Highway Ave.
Highland, IN 46322
Ph: (219)972-0131

Indianapolis

30104 ■ BehaviorCorp
2506 Willowbrook Pkwy., Ste. 300
Indianapolis, IN 46205
Ph: (317)257-3903
URL: http://www.behaviorcorp.com/locations.htm

30105 ■ BehaviorCorp Deaf Services
2506 Willowbrook Pkwy., Ste. 111
Indianapolis, IN 46205
Ph: (317)475-7270
URL: http://www.behaviorcorp.com/locations.htm

30106 ■ BehaviorCorp, Inc.
5525 Georgetown Rd., Ste. F-H
Indianapolis, IN 46254
Ph: (317)328-5800
URL: http://www.behaviorcorp.com/locations.htm

30107 ■ BehaviorCorp
Outpatient Services
2506 Willowbrook Pkwy.
Indianapolis, IN 46205
Ph: (317)257-3903
URL: http://www.behaviorcorp.com/locations.htm

30108 ■ Gallahue Mental Health Services--Indianapolis
6950 Hillsdale Ct.
Indianapolis, IN 46250-2040
Ph: (317)621-7740

30109 ■ Hamilton Center, Inc.--Indianapolis
2160 N Illinois St.
Indianapolis, IN 46202-1334
Ph: (317)937-3700
URL: http://www.hamiltoncenter.org

30110 ■ Richard L. Roudebush Veterans Affairs Medical Center
1481 W 10th St.
Indianapolis, IN 46202
Ph: (317)554-0000
Free: 888-878-6889
URL: http://www.indianapolis.va.gov/

Jasper

30111 ■ Southern Hills Counseling Center
480 Eversman Dr.
Jasper, IN 47546
Ph: (812)482-3020
URL: http://www.southernhills.org/

Jeffersonville

30112 ■ Lifespring
Center Place I
308 E Chestnut St.
Jeffersonville, IN 47130
Ph: (812)283-6041
Fax: (812)283-5710
URL: http://www.lifespr.com

30113 ■ Lifespring
Center Place II
521 John St.
Jeffersonville, IN 47130
Ph: (812)280-8680
Fax: (812)280-0393
URL: http://www.lifespr.com

30114 ■ LifeSpring, Inc.
207 W 13th St
Jeffersonville, IN 47130
Ph: (812)283-4491
URL: http://www.lifespr.com

30115 ■ LifeSpring, Inc.
460 Spring St.
Jeffersonville, IN 47130
Ph: (812)280-2080
URL: http://www.lifespr.com
Formerly: Lifespring Mental Health Services.

30116 ■ Lifespring
Substance Abuse Residential Services
1401 Mitchell Ave.
Jeffersonville, IN 47130
Ph: (812)280-6606
Fax: (812)280-6607
URL: http://www.lifespr.com
Formerly: Southern Indiana Mental Health and Guidance Center.

30117 ■ LifeSpring Turning Point Center
1060 Sharron Dr.
Jeffersonville, IN 47130
Ph: (812)283-7116
Fax: (812)283-7126
URL: http://www.lifespr.com

30118 ■ Manor House II
425 W Maple St.
Jeffersonville, IN 47130
Ph: (812)282-0107
Fax: (812)282-0563
URL: http://www.lifespr.com

30119 ■ Quinco Consulting Associates of Southern Indiana
335 Spring St.
Jeffersonville, IN 47130
Ph: (812)258-0310

Kendallville

30120 ■ Northeastern Center, Inc.
311 N Main St.
Kendallville, IN 46755-1424
Ph: (260)347-4442
URL: http://www.nec.org/
Formerly: Promise House.

30121 ■ Northeastern Center, Inc.
Noble County office/Administration
220 S Main St.
Kendallville, IN 46755-1718
Ph: (260)347-2453
URL: http://www.nec.org/
Formerly: Pioneer Lodge.

30122 ■ Northeastern Center
Kendallville Outpatient
1930 E Dowling St.
Kendallville, IN 46755
Ph: (260)347-4400
URL: http://www.nec.org/

Knox

30123 ■ Porter-Starke Services, Inc.--Knox
1003 S Edgewood Dr.
Knox, IN 46534-8226
Ph: (574)772-4040
URL: http://www.porterstarke.org/

La Porte

30124 ■ Swanson Center
1230 W State Rd. 2, Ste. B
La Porte, IN 46350
Ph: (219)362-2145

LaGrange

30125 ■ Northeastern Center, Inc.
La Grange County Office--OP
2155 N State Rd. 9
LaGrange, IN 46761-8707
Ph: (260)463-7144

Lafayette

30126 ■ Union Street Clubhouse
3415 Union St.
Lafayette, IN 47905-4447
Ph: (765)446-0142
URL: http://www.wvhmhc.org

30127 ■ Valley Enterprises
217 Farabee Dr. N
Lafayette, IN 47905
Ph: (765)447-1312
URL: http://www.wvhmhc.org1

30128 ■ Wabash Valley Hospital, Inc.
670 N 36th St.
Lafayette, IN 47905
Ph: (765)446-8412
URL: http://www.wvhmhc.org

30129 ■ Wabash Valley Hospital, Inc.
Elmwood House
2015 Meharry St.
Lafayette, IN 47904
Ph: (765)742-0183
URL: http://www.wvhmhc.org

30130 ■ Wabash Valley Hospital, Inc.
Gregory House
2304 Gregory St.
Lafayette, IN 47905-2213
Ph: (765)474-3223
Fax: (765)471-1284
URL: http://www.wvhmhc.org

Lawrenceburg

30131 ■ Dearborn Plaza
427 Eads Pkwy.
Lawrenceburg, IN 47025
Ph: (812)537-1302

Lebanon

30132 ■ BehaviorCorp
602 Ransdell Rd.
Lebanon, IN 46052-2349
Ph: (765)482-7100
URL: http://www.behaviorcorp.com/locations.htm

Ligonier

30133 ■ Northeastern Center, Inc.
Ligonier Outpatient
1150 Lincolnway S
Ligonier, IN 46767-1735
Ph: (260)894-7179
URL: http://www.nec.org/

Linton

30134 ■ Greene County Outreach
Lonetree Rd.
Linton, IN 47441
Ph: (812)847-4435
Formerly: Greene County General Home Health Care.

Logansport

30135 ■ Four County Counseling Center
Cass Satellite
1807 Smith St.
Logansport, IN 46947-1576
Ph: (574)732-1414
Free: 800-552-3106
URL: http://www.fourcounty.org

30136 ■ Four County Counseling Center
Center Cass County Office
1015 Michigan Ave.
Logansport, IN 46947-1597
Ph: (260)722-5151
Free: 800-552-3106
Fax: (260)732-9523
URL: http://www.fourcounty.org
Formerly: Four County Comprehensive Mental Health Center.

30137 ■ Four County Counseling Center
North Street Office
408 North St.
Logansport, IN 46947
Ph: (574)753-5540
Free: 800-552-3106
URL: http://www.fourcounty.org/info.htm

30138 ■ Four County Counseling Center
Residence
1115 E Broadway
Logansport, IN 46947-3253
Ph: (574)722-4910
Free: 800-552-3106
URL: http://www.fourcounty.org
Formerly: Four County Counseling Center Broadway St. Group Home.

30139 ■ Four County Counseling Center
Residence--Group Home
1402 E Market St.
Logansport, IN 46947-3224
Ph: (574)735-2009
URL: http://www.fourcounty.org

30140 ■ Four County Counseling Center
Spear Street Office
1120 Spear St.
Logansport, IN 46947
Ph: (574)732-0701
Free: 800-552-3106
URL: http://www.fourcounty.org/info.htm

30141 ■ Four County Counseling Center
Stepping Stones
1120 Spear St.
Logansport, IN 46947-3502
Ph: (574)732-0428
Free: 800-552-3106
Fax: (574)732-0428
URL: http://www.fourcounty.org

30142 ■ Four County Counseling Center
Supported Employment
408 North St.
Logansport, IN 46947-2732
Ph: (574)753-5540
Free: 800-552-3106
Fax: (574)753-8197
URL: http://www.fourcounty.org

Madison

30143 ■ LifeSpring
Jefferson County office
606 E Main St.
Madison, IN 47250-3741
Ph: (812)265-4513
URL: http://www.lifespr.com

Marion

30144 ■ Cornerstone Behavioral Health
Branson Club
206 W 8th St.
Marion, IN 46953-1921
Ph: (765)662-3971
URL: http://www.cornerstone.org/contact.aspx
Formerly: Grant Blackford Mental Health.

30145 ■ Cornerstone Behavioral Health--Marion
505 N Wabash Ave.
Marion, IN 46952-2680
Ph: (765)662-3971
URL: http://www.cornerstone.org/contact.aspx
Formerly: Grant Blackford Mental Health.

30146 ■ Veterans Affairs Northern Indiana Health Care System
Marion Campus
1700 E 38th St.
Marion, IN 46953
Ph: (765)674-3321
Free: 888-838-6446
URL: http://www.northernindiana.va.gov/

Michigan City

30147 ■ Swanson Center--Shorewood Place Residential
975 S Carroll Ave.
Michigan City, IN 46360
Ph: (219)872-2002
URL: http://www.swansoncenter.org/

30148 ■ Swanson Center--Ventures
301 E 8th St.
Michigan City, IN 46360
Ph: (219)873-2387
URL: http://www.swansoncenter.org/
Formerly: Community Service Center Site.

Monticello

30149 ■ Wabash Valley Hospital, Inc.
Outpatient Service
920 W Executive
Monticello, IN 47960
Ph: (574)583-9350
URL: http://www.wvhmhc.org

Mooresville

30150 ■ Mooresville Center
11370 N State Rd. 67
Mooresville, IN 46158
Ph: (317)834-8187

Mount Vernon

30151 ■ Southwestern Indiana Mental Health Center, Inc.
Posey Regional Office
100 Vista Dr.
Mount Vernon, IN 47620-1266
Ph: (812)838-6558
URL: http://www.southwestern.org/

Muncie

30152 ■ Meridian Services - Delaware County Services
240 N Tillotson Ave.
Muncie, IN 47304-3988
Ph: (765)288-1928
Formerly: Comprehensive Mental Health Services.

30153 ■ Muncie/Anderson Veterans Affairs Clinic
3500 W Purdue Ave.
Muncie, IN 47304
Ph: (765)284-6822
Fax: (765)284-6855
URL: http://www2.va.gov/directory/guide/facility.asp?ID=771&dnum=All

Munster

30154 ■ Frederick House
8130 Frederick St.
Munster, IN 46321
Ph: (219)398-7050

Nashville

30155 ■ Centerstone
Brown County Consulting Associates
91 W Mound St.
Nashville, IN 47448
Ph: (812)988-2258
URL: http://centerstone.org/indiana-facilities
Formerly: Quinco Behavioral Health Systems.

New Albany

30156 ■ LifeSpring
Floyd County Office
824 University Woods Dr., Ste. 6-10
New Albany, IN 47150
Ph: (812)981-2594
URL: http://www.lifespr.com

30157 ■ Manor House I
Life Spring
715 Scribner Dr.
New Albany, IN 47150
Ph: (812)949-0840
URL: http://www.lifespr.com

30158 ■ Veterans Affairs Healthcare Center--New Albany
811 Northgate Blvd.
New Albany, IN 47150
Ph: (502)287-4100
Free: 866-463-9838
URL: http://www.louisville.va.gov/visitors/newalbany.asp

New Castle

30159 ■ Henry County Services
930 N 14th St.
New Castle, IN 47362
Ph: (765)288-1928

Noblesville

30160 ■ BehaviorCorp--Noblesville
17840 Cumberland Rd.
Noblesville, IN 46060
Ph: (317)773-6864
URL: http://www.behaviorcorp.com/locations.htm

North Vernon

30161 ■ Aspen House
299 W Hayden Pke.
North Vernon, IN 47265
Ph: (812)346-7892

30162 ■ Centerstone--North Vernon
1260 Buckeye St.
North Vernon, IN 47265-8343
Ph: (812)346-4468
URL: http://centerstone.org/indiana-facilities
Formerly: Quinco Consulting of Jennings; Quinco Consulting Associates.

Osgood

30163 ■ Ripley County Counseling Center
240 W Craven St.
Osgood, IN 47037
Ph: (812)537-1302

Paoli

30164 ■ Orange County Services
488 W Hospital Rd.
Paoli, IN 47454
Ph: (812)723-4301

Peru

30165 ■ Four County Counseling Center
Miami County Satellite
655 E Main St.
Peru, IN 46970-2662
Ph: (765)472-1931
Free: 800-552-3106
Fax: (765)722-9523
URL: http://www.fourcounty.org
Formerly: Four County Comprehensive Mental Health Center.

Plainfield

30166 ■ Hamilton Center, Inc.--Hendricks County Center
900 Southfield Dr.
Plainfield, IN 46168
Ph: (317)837-9719

Plymouth

30167 ■ Otis R. Bowen Center for Human Services
990 Illinois St.
Plymouth, IN 46563
Ph: (574)936-9646
Free: 800-342-5653
URL: http://www.bowencenter.org/

30168 ■ Otis R. Bowen Center for Human Services
Russell House
1525 W Harrison St.
Plymouth, IN 46563
Ph: (574)936-6164
URL: http://www.bowencenter.org/

30169 ■ Otis R. Bowen Center for Human Services
Shady Rest Home
10924 Lincoln Hwy.
Plymouth, IN 46563
Ph: (574)936-2635
URL: http://www.bowencenter.org/

Portage

30170 ■ Porter-Starke Services, Inc.--Portage
3349 Willowcreek Rd.
Portage, IN 46368
Ph: (219)762-9557
URL: http://www.porterstarke.org/contact.php

Portland

30171 ■ Comprehensive Mental Health Services, Inc.
Jay County Services Department
931 W Water St.
Portland, IN 47371
Ph: (765)288-1928

Princeton

30172 ■ Southwestern Indiana Mental Health Center, Inc.
Gibson Regional Center
310 S 5th Ave.
Princeton, IN 47670
Ph: (812)385-5275
URL: http://www.southwestern.org/

Rensselaer

30173 ■ Wabash Valley Hospital, Inc.
Outpatient Service
131 W Drexel Pkwy.
Rensselaer, IN 47978-3248
Ph: (219)866-4194
Free: 800-859-5553
Fax: (219)866-4197
URL: http://www.wvhmhc.org

Richmond

30174 ■ Centerstone
Community Support Program
54 S 15th St.
Richmond, IN 47374-5606
Ph: (765)983-8105
Free: 888-983-8000
URL: http://centerstone.org/indiana-facilities
Formerly: Dunn Mental Health Center, Inc.

30175 ■ Centerstone
Samuel Gaar Resource Center
200 N 13th St.
Richmond, IN 47374
Ph: (765)983-8660
URL: http://centerstone.org/indiana-facilities

30176 ■ Centerstone
Wayne County OP
831 Dillon Dr.
Richmond, IN 47374
Ph: (765)983-8000
Free: 888-983-8000
URL: http://centerstone.org/indiana-facilities
Formerly: Dunn Mental Health Center, Inc.

30177 ■ Richmond Veterans Affairs Community Based Outpatient Clinic
4351 S A St.
Richmond, IN 47374
Ph: (765)973-6915
Fax: (765)965-6936
URL: http://www2.va.gov/directory/guide/facility.asp?ID=963&dnum=All

Rising Sun

30178 ■ Ohio County Office
315 Industrial Access Rd.
Rising Sun, IN 47040
Ph: (812)438-2711

Rochester

30179 ■ Four County Counseling Center
Fulton County Satellite
401 E 8th St., Ste. A
Rochester, IN 46975-1444
Ph: (574)223-8565
URL: http://www.fourcounty.org
Formerly: Four County Comprehensive Mental Health Center.

Rockport

30180 ■ Spencer County Services
107 N 2nd St.
Rockport, IN 47635-0201
Ph: (812)649-9168
Formerly: Southern Hills Counseling Center.

Salem

30181 ■ LifeSpring
Washington County Office
1321 Jackson St.
Salem, IN 47167
Ph: (812)883-3095
URL: http://www.lifespr.com

Scottsburg

30182 ■ LifeSpring
Scott County Office
75 N 1st Ave.
Scottsburg, IN 47170
Ph: (812)752-2837
URL: http://www.lifespr.com

Seymour

30183 ■ Centerstone--Seymour
1443 Corporate Way
Seymour, IN 47274
Ph: (812)522-4341
URL: http://centerstone.org/indiana-facilities
Formerly: Quinco Consulting Associates of Jackson County.

South Bend

30184 ■ South Bend Veterans Affairs Clinic
5735 S Ironwood Rd.
South Bend, IN 46614
Ph: (574)299-4847
Fax: (574)299-9073
URL: http://www2.va.gov/directory/guide/facility.asp?ID=5083&dnum=All

Spencer

30185 ■ Hamilton Center, Inc.--Spencer
51 S Main St.
Spencer, IN 47460-1729
Ph: (812)829-0037
URL: http://www.hamiltoncenter.org

Tell City

30186 ■ Perry County Services
1443 9th St.
Tell City, IN 47586
Ph: (812)547-7905
Formerly: Southern Hills Counseling Center Outreach Office.

Terre Haute

30187 ■ Hamilton Center, Inc.--Terre Haute
620 8th Ave.
Terre Haute, IN 47804-2771
Ph: (812)231-8323
URL: http://www.hamiltoncenter.org

30188 ■ Terre Haute Veterans Affairs Clinic
110 W Honeycreek Pkwy.
Terre Haute, IN 47802
Ph: (812)232-2890
Fax: (812)232-3506
URL: http://www2.va.gov/directory/guide/facility.asp?ID=777&dnum=All

30189 ■ Vigo County Adult Outpatient Addictions
1318 Ohio St.
Terre Haute, IN 47807-3926
Ph: (812)231-8171
Fax: (812)238-3871
URL: http://www.hamiltoncenter.org

Union City

30190 ■ Centerstone
Union City Children & Family Services
224 N Columbia St.
Union City, IN 47390
Ph: (765)964-3142
URL: http://centerstone.org/indiana-facilities

Valparaiso

30191 ■ Porter-Starke Services, Inc.
701 Wall St.
Valparaiso, IN 46383
Ph: (219)531-3500
URL: http://www.porterstarke.org/contact.php

Vevay

30192 ■ Community Mental Health Center, Inc.--Vevay
503 Pearl St.
Vevay, IN 47043-8420
Ph: (812)537-1302
URL: http://www.cmhcinc.org/

30193 ■ Switzerland County Counseling Center
205 W Main St.
Vevay, IN 47043
Ph: (812)537-1302

Vincennes

30194 ■ Vincennes Veterans Affairs Community Based Outpatient Clinic
1813 Willow St., Ste. 6A
Vincennes, IN 47591
Ph: (812)882-0894
Fax: (812)882-5031
URL: http://www2.va.gov/directory/guide/facility.asp?ID=5676&dnum=All

Wabash

30195 ■ Otis R. Bowen Center for Human Services
Wabash Office
255 N Miami St.
Wabash, IN 46992
Ph: (260)563-8446
URL: http://www.bowencenter.org/

Warsaw

30196 ■ Otis R. Bowen Center for Human Services
Warsaw Corporate Office
850 N Harrison St.
Warsaw, IN 46580-3199
Ph: (574)268-9748
Free: 800-342-5653
URL: http://www.bowencenter.org/
Formerly: Kosciusko County Office.

West Lafayette

30197 ■ Wabash Valley Hospital
2900 N River Rd.
West Lafayette, IN 47906-3766
Ph: (765)463-2555
URL: http://www.wvhmhc.org

30198 ■ Wabash Valley Hospital Riverside
2900 N River Rd.
West Lafayette, IN 47906
Ph: (765)463-2555
URL: http://www.wvhmhc.org

30199 ■ West Lafayette Veterans Affairs Clinic
3851 N River Rd.
West Lafayette, IN 47906
Ph: (765)464-2280
Fax: (765)464-2279
URL: http://www2.va.gov/directory/guide/facility.asp?ID=5080&dnum=All

Whiting

30200 ■ Phoenix House
2118 Indianapolis Blvd.
Whiting, IN 46394-1939
Ph: (219)473-1350

Winamac

30201 ■ Four County Counseling Center
Pulaski County Satellite
118 N Sally Dr.
Winamac, IN 46996
Ph: (574)946-4233
Fax: (574)946-4365
URL: http://www.fourcounty.org
Formerly: Four County Comprehensive Mental Health Center.

Winchester

30202 ■ Centerstone
Randolph County
325 S Oak St., Ste. 103
Winchester, IN 47394-2246
Ph: (765)584-1735
URL: http://centerstone.org/indiana-facilities
Formerly: Dunn Mental Health Center, Inc.

IOWA

Adel

30203 ■ West Central Mental Health Center
2111 W Green St.
Adel, IA 50003
Ph: (515)993-4535
Free: 800-622-2020

Algona

30204 ■ Kossuth Regional Health Center
1515 Phillips St.
Algona, IA 50511
Ph: (515)955-7171
URL: http://www.krhc.com/

Ames

30205 ■ The Richmond Center--Ames
1619 S High Ave.
Ames, IA 50010
Ph: (515)232-5811
Free: 800-830-7009
URL: http://www.richmondcenter.net/locations.cfm

Anamosa

30206 ■ Jones Regional Medical Center
104 Broadway Pl.
Anamosa, IA 52205
Ph: (319)462-6131
Fax: (319)462-4689
URL: http://www.jonesregional.org
Formerly: Anamosa Community Hospital.

Bettendorf

30207 ■ Bettendorf Veterans Affairs Clinic
2979 Victoria St.
Bettendorf, IA 52722
Ph: (563)332-8528
Fax: (563)332-9331
URL: http://www2.va.gov/directory/guide/facility.asp?ID=5206&dnum=All

Bloomfield

30208 ■ Davis Center
22425 Overland Ave.
Bloomfield, IA 52537
Ph: (641)664-3202

Boone

30209 ■ The Richmond Center--Boone
806 7th St.
Boone, IA 50036
Ph: (515)232-5811
Free: 800-830-7009
URL: http://www.richmondcenter.net/

Burlington

30210 ■ Touchstone Behavioral Counseling
407 N 4th St.
Burlington, IA 52601
Ph: (319)754-4618

Cedar Rapids

30211 ■ Abbe Center for Community Mental Health
520 11th St. NW
Cedar Rapids, IA 52405
Ph: (319)398-3562
URL: http://www.abbemhc.org/

30212 ■ Cedar Rapids Counseling & Psychotherapy Group
118 2nd St. SE, Ste. 220
Cedar Rapids, IA 52401
Ph: (319)362-0632
Fax: (319)362-5206
URL: http://www.crcounseling.net/

30213 ■ Four Oaks, Inc.--Cedar Rapids
1924 D St. SW
Cedar Rapids, IA 52404
Ph: (319)363-0636
URL: http://www.fouroaks.org/

Cherokee

30214 ■ Plains Area Mental Health Center
900 N 2nd St.
Cherokee, IA 51012
Ph: (712)225-2575

Council Bluffs

30215 ■ Alegent Health Behavioral Services
801 Harmony St., Ste. 302
Council Bluffs, IA 51503
Ph: (712)328-2609
URL: http://www.alegent.com/

Davenport

30216 ■ Frontier Community Support Program
311 E 2nd St.
Davenport, IA 52801
Ph: (563)322-5276

30217 ■ Vera French Community Mental Health Center
1441 W Central Park Ave.
Davenport, IA 52804
Ph: (563)383-1900

30218 ■ Vera French Community Mental Health Center
Pine Knoll Health Care Facility
2504 Telegraph Rd.
Davenport, IA 52804-4324
Ph: (563)322-6247

Des Moines

30219 ■ Eyerly Ball Community Mental Health Center
1301 Center St.
Des Moines, IA 50309
Ph: (515)243-5181

30220 ■ Four Oaks, Inc.--Des Moines
1211 Vine St., Ste. 2150
Des Moines, IA 50265
Ph: (515)261-3719
URL: http://www.fouroaks.org/

30221 ■ Golden Circle Behavioral Health
945 19th St.
Des Moines, IA 50314
Ph: (515)241-0982

30222 ■ Orchard Place--Child Guidance Center
808 5th Ave.
Des Moines, IA 50309
Ph: (515)244-2267
Fax: (515)244-1922
URL: http://www.orchardplace.org/

30223 ■ PACE Juvenile Center
620 8th St.
Des Moines, IA 50309
Ph: (515)697-5700
Fax: (515)697-5701
URL: http://www.orchardplace.org/

30224 ■ Polk County ResCare
602 E Grand Ave.
Des Moines, IA 50309
Ph: (515)283-1230

30225 ■ Veterans Medical Center-- Des Moines Division
3600 30th St.
Des Moines, IA 50310
Ph: (515)699-5999
Free: 800-294-8387
URL: http://www.centraliowa.va.gov/

30226 ■ Westminster House II
5631 Francis Ave.
Des Moines, IA 50310
Ph: (515)277-8108
Fax: (515)277-8709

30227 ■ Westminster House, Inc.
Behavioral Health Resources
940 Cummins Pkwy.
Des Moines, IA 50312-1100
Ph: (515)277-8108
Fax: (515)277-8137

Dubuque

30228 ■ Dubuque Veterans Affairs Clinic
250 Mercy Dr.
Dubuque, IA 52001
Ph: (563)589-8899
URL: http://www2.va.gov/directory/guide/facility.asp?ID=5212&dnum=All

30229 ■ Hillcrest Family Services
2005 Asbury Rd.
Dubuque, IA 52001
Ph: (563)583-7357
Free: 877-437-6333
URL: http://www.hillcrest-fs.org/

30230 ■ Hillcrest Family Services Clinic
220 W 7th St.
Dubuque, IA 52001
Ph: (563)583-6431
Free: 877-437-6333
URL: http://www.hillcrest-fs.org/

30231 ■ Hillcrest Family Services
Hillcrest Mental Health Center
200 Mercy Dr., Ste. 200
Dubuque, IA 52001
Ph: (563)582-0145
Free: 877-437-6333
URL: http://www.hillcrest-fs.org/

30232 ■ Hillcrest Family Services
Marywood Home
2671 Marywood Dr.
Dubuque, IA 52001
Ph: (563)557-4401
Free: 877-437-6333
URL: http://www.hillcrest-fs.org/

30233 ■ Hillcrest Family Services
Vizaleea Home
1785 Vizaleea Dr.
Dubuque, IA 52001
Ph: (563)588-1772
Free: 877-437-6333
URL: http://www.hillcrest-fs.org/

30234 ■ Julien Care Facility
13034 Seippel Rd.
Dubuque, IA 52002
Ph: (563)583-1791
E-mail: dsmith@juliencare.com
URL: http://www.dacincorp.com/juliencare.html

30235 ■ Mercy Medical Center
Behavioral Health
250 Mercy Dr.
Dubuque, IA 52001-7360
Ph: (563)589-9299
URL: http://www.mercydubuque.com/index.htm

Emmetsburg

30236 ■ Palo Alto County Office
717 Broadway St.
Emmetsburg, IA 50536
Ph: (712)262-2922
URL: http://www.seasonscenter.org/managed/locations.html

Estherville

30237 ■ Emmet County Office
103 S 6th St.
Estherville, IA 51334
Ph: (712)262-2922
URL: http://www.seasonscenter.org/managed/locations.html

Fairfield

30238 ■ Optimae Life Services
301 W Burlington Ave.
Fairfield, IA 52556-3242
Ph: (641)472-7236
Fax: (641)472-9241
URL: http://www.optimaelifeservices.com/
Description: Services to individuals with developmental disabilities, mental retardation, and brain injury. **Formerly:** ResCare, Inc.

Fort Dodge

30239 ■ Fort Dodge Veterans Affairs Clinic--2nd Avenue
2419 2nd Ave. N
Fort Dodge, IA 50501
Ph: (515)576-2235
Fax: (515)576-6863
URL: http://www2.va.gov/directory/guide/facility.asp?ID=5213&dnum=All

Grinnell

30240 ■ Poweshiek County Mental Health Center
200 4th Ave. W
Grinnell, IA 50112
Ph: (641)236-6137
URL: http://www.pcmentalhealth.org/

Indianola

30241 ■ Warren County Mental Health
1011 N Jefferson Way, Ste. 900
Indianola, IA 50125
Ph: (515)961-1068
Fax: (515)961-1142
E-mail: betsys@co.warren.ia.us
URL: http://www.co.warren.ia.us/Mental_Health/MentalH.html?Dept_Id=21&Page_Id=40 7

Iowa City

30242 ■ Birch House
745 Pepper Dr.
Iowa City, IA 52240
Ph: (319)341-9849

30243 ■ Hillcrest Family Services
449 Hwy. 1 W
Iowa City, IA 52246
Ph: (319)337-4204
Free: 877-437-6333
Fax: (319)341-3333
URL: http://www.hillcrest-fs.org

Jefferson

30244 ■ McFarland Clinic
1002 Lincolnway St.
Jefferson, IA 50129
Ph: (515)232-5811
Free: 800-830-7009
URL: http://www.richmondcenter.net/locations.cfm

Knoxville

30245 ■ Capstone Behavioral Healthcare, Inc.--Knoxville
1214 W Jackson St., Ste. 201
Knoxville, IA 50138
Ph: (641)842-4925
URL: http://www.capstonebh.com/

30246 ■ Veterans Medical Center--Knoxville Division
1515 W Pleasant St.
Knoxville, IA 50138
Ph: (641)842-3101
Free: 800-816-8878
URL: http://www.centraliowa.va.gov/

Maquoketa

30247 ■ DAC, Inc.
1710 E Maple St.
Maquoketa, IA 52060
Ph: (563)652-5252
URL: http://www.dacincorp.com/

Marshalltown

30248 ■ Mental Health Center of Mid-Iowa Center Associates
9 N 4th Ave.
Marshalltown, IA 50158
Ph: (641)752-1585

Mason City

30249 ■ Four Oaks, Inc.--Mason City
980 S Iowa Ave.
Mason City, IA 50402
Ph: (641)423-3222
URL: http://www.fouroaks.org/

30250 ■ Mason City Veterans Affairs Clinic
520 S Pierce, Ste. 150
Mason City, IA 50401
Ph: (641)421-8077
Fax: (641)421-5005
URL: http://www2.va.gov/directory/guide/facility.asp?ID=5205&dnum=All

30251 ■ Mental Health Center of North Iowa, Inc.
235 S Eisenhower Ave.
Mason City, IA 50401
Ph: (641)424-2075
Free: 800-700-IOWA
URL: http://www.mhconi.org/

Monticello

30252 ■ Four Oaks, Inc.--Monticello
818 W 1st St.
Monticello, IA 52310
Ph: (319)465-3727
URL: http://www.fouroaks.org/

Muscatine

30253 ■ Family Resources, Inc.
119 Sycamore St., Ste. 200
Muscatine, IA 52761
Ph: (563)263-0067
Fax: (563)263-0069
URL: http://www.famres.org/MAboutUs/

30254 ■ Houser Street Care Facility
810 Houser St.
Muscatine, IA 52761
Ph: (563)263-5585

Newton

30255 ■ Capstone Behavioral Healthcare, Inc.--Newton
306 N 3rd Ave. E
Newton, IA 50208
Ph: (641)792-4012
URL: http://www.capstonebh.com/

Okoboji

30256 ■ Oak Haven
2273 170th St.
Okoboji, IA 51355
Ph: (712)332-2932

Ottumwa

30257 ■ Southern Iowa Mental Health Center
110 E Main St.
Ottumwa, IA 52501
Ph: (641)682-8772

Rock Rapids

30258 ■ Seasons Center for Community Mental Health
Lyon County
315 1st Ave., Ste. 202
Rock Rapids, IA 51246
Ph: (712)472-9605
URL: http://www.seasonscenter.org/managed/locations.html

Sheldon

30259 ■ Seasons Center for Community Mental Health
O'Brien County
1022 3rd Ave.
Sheldon, IA 51201
Ph: (712)324-3263
URL: http://www.seasonscenter.org/managed/locations.html

Sibley

30260 ■ Seasons Center for Community Mental Health
Osceola County
600 N 9th Ave.
Sibley, IA 51249
Ph: (712)324-3263
URL: http://www.seasonscenter.org/managed/locations.html

Sioux City

30261 ■ Sioux City Veterans Affairs Clinic
1551 Indian Hills Dr., Ste. 214
Sioux City, IA 51104
Ph: (712)258-4700
Fax: (712)255-4777
URL: http://www2.va.gov/directory/guide/facility.asp?ID=5176&dnum=All

30262 ■ Siouxland Mental Health Center
625 Court St.
Sioux City, IA 51102
Ph: (712)252-3871
Free: 877-4-WECARE
URL: http://www.siouxlandmentalhealth.com/

30263 ■ Siouxland Mental Health Center
205 5th St.
Sioux City, IA 51101
Ph: (712)202-0173
URL: http://www.siouxlandmentalhealth.com/

Spencer

30264 ■ Seasons Center for Community Mental Health
Clay County
201 E 11th St.
Spencer, IA 51301
Ph: (712)262-2922
URL: http://www.seasonscenter.org/managed/locations.html

Spirit Lake

30265 ■ Seasons Center for Community Mental Health
Dickinson County
710 Lake St., Ste. 1
Spirit Lake, IA 51360
Ph: (712)336-4464
URL: http://www.seasonscenter.org/managed/locations.html

30266 ■ Spirit Lake Veterans Affairs Clinic
1310 Lake St.
Spirit Lake, IA 51360
Ph: (712)336-6400
Fax: (712)336-6439
URL: http://www2.va.gov/directory/guide/facility.asp?ID=5592&dnum=All

Storm Lake

30267 ■ Seasons Center for Community Mental Health
Buena Vista County
824 Flindt Dr., Ste. 103
Storm Lake, IA 50588
Ph: (712)732-3736
URL: http://www.seasonscenter.org/managed/locations.html

Washington

30268 ■ Orchard Hill ResCare
2175 Lexington Blvd.
Washington, IA 52353
Ph: (319)653-6571
Free: 888-472-1684
URL: http://www.iowarescare.com/services.htm

Waterloo

30269 ■ Black Hawk-Grundy Mental Health Center, Inc.
3251 W 9th St.
Waterloo, IA 50702
Ph: (319)234-2893
Free: 800-583-1526
URL: http://www.bhgmhc.com/

30270 ■ Waterloo Veterans Affairs Clinic
1015 S Hackett Rd.
Waterloo, IA 50701
Ph: (319)235-1230
Fax: (319)272-2348
URL: http://www2.va.gov/directory/guide/facility.asp?ID=5207&dnum=All

West Burlington

30271 ■ Gateway Care Facility
13702 Washington Rd.
West Burlington, IA 52655
Ph: (319)753-6262

KANSAS

Abilene

30272 ■ Central Kansas Mental Health Center
420 NE 10th St.
Abilene, KS 67410
Ph: (785)823-6322
URL: http://www.ckmhc.org/

Alma

30273 ■ Wabaunsee County Health Department
Mental Health Center of East Central Kansas
701 Missouri Ave.
Alma, KS 66401
Ph: (785)765-2425
Free: 800-279-3645

Andover

30274 ■ South Central Mental Health
217 Ira Ct.
Andover, KS 67002
Ph: (316)733-5047

Anthony

30275 ■ Horizons Mental Health Center
Harper County Area Office
123 Pennsylvania Ave.
Anthony, KS 67003
Ph: (620)842-3768

Atchison

30276 ■ The Guidance Center - Atchison County
1301 N 2nd St.
Atchison, KS 66002-1202
Ph: (913)367-1593
Fax: (913)367-1627
URL: http://www.theguidance-ctr.org/locations.shtml

Belleville

30277 ■ Pawnee Mental Health Services
Belleville Office--Republic Co. Hospital
1836 M St.
Belleville, KS 66935
Ph: (785)527-2549

Beloit

30278 ■ Pawnee Mental Health Services
Beloit Office
207 N Mill, No. 5
Beloit, KS 67420
Ph: (785)738-5363
Formerly: Mitchell County Community Hospital Pawnee Mental Health Services.

Burlington

30279 ■ Mental Health Center of East Central Kansas--Burlington
109 N 3rd St.
Burlington, KS 66839
Free: 800-279-3645

Chanute

30280 ■ Neosho Memorial Veterans Affairs Medical Center
629 S Plummer
Chanute, KS 66720
Ph: (620)431-4000
URL: http://www2.va.gov/directory/guide/facility.asp?ID=5385&dnum=All

Clay Center

30281 ■ Pawnee Mental Health Services
Clay Center Office
503 Grant Ave.
Clay Center, KS 67432
Ph: (785)632-2108

Coffeyville

30282 ■ Four County Mental Health Center--Coffeyville
1601 W 4th St.
Coffeyville, KS 67337
Ph: (620)251-8180
URL: http://www.fourcounty.org

Colby

30283 ■ High Plains Mental Health Center
Colby Branch Office
750 S Range Ave.
Colby, KS 67701
Ph: (785)462-6774
Fax: (785)462-3690
URL: http://www.highplainsmentalhealth.com

Dodge City

30284 ■ Area Mental Health Center
Community Support Services, Dodge City
3000 N 14th St.
Dodge City, KS 67801
Ph: (620)227-5040
URL: http://www.areamhc.org

30285 ■ Area Mental Health Center
Dodge City Branch Office
2101 W Hwy. 50
Dodge City, KS 67801
Ph: (620)227-8566
Fax: (620)225-5824
URL: http://www.areamhc.org

Emporia

30286 ■ Emporia Veterans Affairs Community Based Outpatient Clinic
919 W 12th Ave., Ste. D
Emporia, KS 66801
Free: 800-574-8387
URL: http://www2.va.gov/directory/guide/facility.asp?ID=5386&dnum=All

30287 ■ Mental Health Center of East Central Kansas--Emporia
1000 Lincoln St.
Emporia, KS 66801
Ph: (620)343-2211

Fort Dodge

30288 ■ Fort Dodge Veterans Affairs Clinic--Custer
300 Custer
Fort Dodge, KS 67801
Free: 888-878-6881
URL: http://www2.va.gov/directory/guide/facility.asp?ID=5232&dnum=All

Fort Scott

30289 ■ Choices Psychological Services
710 W 8th St.
Fort Scott, KS 66701
Ph: (620)223-8590

30290 ■ Fort Scott Veterans Affairs Community Based Outpatient Clinic
902 Horton St.
Fort Scott, KS 66701
Ph: (620)223-8655
URL: http://www2.va.gov/directory/guide/facility.asp?ID=5233&dnum=All

Garden City

30291 ■ Area Mental Health Center
Community Support Services, Garden City
531 Campus View St.
Garden City, KS 67846
Ph: (620)275-9434
URL: http://www.areamhc.org

30292 ■ Area Mental Health Center
Garden City Branch Office
1111 E Spruce St.
Garden City, KS 67846-5999
Ph: (620)276-7689
URL: http://www.areamhc.org

Garnett

30293 ■ Anderson County Veterans Affairs Hospital
421 S Maple
Garnett, KS 66032
Ph: (785)448-3131
URL: http://www2.va.gov/directory/guide/facility.asp?ID=5387&dnum=All

Goodland

30294 ■ High Plains Mental Health Center--Goodland
723 Main St.
Goodland, KS 67735
Ph: (785)899-5991
Fax: (785)899-2533
URL: http://www.highplainsmentalhealth.com

Great Bend

30295 ■ The Center for Counseling & Consultation
5815 Broadway
Great Bend, KS 67530
Ph: (620)792-2544
Free: 800-875-2544
E-mail: contact@thecentergb.org
URL: http://www.thecentergb.org/

Hays

30296 ■ Hays Veterans Affairs Clinic
207-B E 7th
Hays, KS 67601
Free: 888-878-6881
URL: http://www2.va.gov/directory/guide/facility.asp?ID=5234&dnum=All

30297 ■ High Plains Mental Health Center--Hays
208 E 7th St.
Hays, KS 67601
Ph: (785)628-2871
Fax: (785)628-1438
URL: http://www.highplainsmentalhealth.com

Hiawatha

30298 ■ Kanza Mental Health & Guidance Center
909 S 2nd St.
Hiawatha, KS 66434-2774
Ph: (785)742-7113
URL: http://www.kanzamhgc.org/

Holton

30299 ■ Holton Veterans Affairs Community Hospital
1110 Columbine Dr.
Holton, KS 66436
Free: 800-574-8387
URL: http://www2.va.gov/directory/guide/facility.asp?ID=5388&dnum=All

Hutchinson

30300 ■ Hutchinson Veterans Affairs Community Based Outpatient Clinic
1625 E 30th Ave.
Hutchinson, KS 67502
Free: 888-878-6881
URL: http://www2.va.gov/directory/guide/facility.asp?ID=5652&dnum=All

30301 ■ Prairie View, Inc.
35 N Washington, Ste. 260
Hutchinson, KS 67502-4864
Ph: (620)662-4700
Free: 800-992-6292
URL: http://www.prairieview.com/hutch-locations.html

Junction City

30302 ■ Junction City Veterans Affairs Clinic
715 Southwind Dr.
Junction City, KS 66441
Free: 800-574-8387
URL: http://www2.va.gov/directory/guide/facility.asp?ID=5390&dnum=All

30303 ■ Pawnee Mental Health Services Junction City Office
814 Caroline Ave.
Junction City, KS 66441
Ph: (785)762-5250
Free: 800-609-2002
URL: http://www.pawnee.org/locations.php

Kansas City

30304 ■ Wyandotte Veterans Affairs Community Based Outpatient Clinic
Bethany Medical Bldg., Ste. 110
21 N 12th St.
Kansas City, KS 66102
Free: 800-952-8387
URL: http://www2.va.gov/directory/guide/facility.asp?ID=5239&dnum=All

Lawrence

30305 ■ Lawrence Veterans Affairs Clinic
2200 Harvard Rd.
Lawrence, KS 66049
Free: 800-574-8387
URL: http://www2.va.gov/directory/guide/facility.asp?ID=5389&dnum=All

Leavenworth

30306 ■ Dwight D. Eisenhower Veterans Affairs Medical Center
4101 S 4th St.
Leavenworth, KS 66048
Ph: (913)682-2000
Free: 800-574-8387
URL: http://www.leavenworth.va.gov/

30307 ■ Guidance Center
500 Limit St.
Leavenworth, KS 66048-4435
Ph: (913)682-5118
URL: http://www.theguidance-ctr.org/

Liberal

30308 ■ Liberal Veterans Affairs Clinic
2 Rock Island Rd., Ste. 200
Liberal, KS 67901
Ph: (620)626-5574
URL: http://www2.va.gov/directory/guide/facility.asp?ID=5005&dnum=All

Manhattan

30309 ■ Pawnee Mental Health Services Community Mental Health Center
2001 Claflin Rd.
Manhattan, KS 66502
Ph: (785)587-4300
URL: http://www.pawnee.org/

Mankato

30310 ■ Pawnee Mental Health Services Mankato Office
114 E Main St.
Mankato, KS 66956
Ph: (785)378-3898
URL: http://www.pawnee.org/

Marysville

30311 ■ Pawnee Mental Health Services Marysville Office
406 N 3rd St., Ste. 3
Marysville, KS 66508
Ph: (785)562-3907
URL: http://www.pawnee.org/

McPherson

30312 ■ Prairie View at McPherson
1102 Hospital Dr.
McPherson, KS 67460
Ph: (620)245-5000
URL: http://www.prairieview.com/hutch-locations.html

Newton

30313 ■ Prairie View at Newton Harvey County Community Mental Health Center
1901 E 1st St.
Newton, KS 67114
Ph: (316)284-6400
Free: 800-362-0180
URL: http://www.prairieview.com/hutch-locations.html

Norton

30314 ■ High Plains Mental Health Center--Norton
211 S Norton
Norton, KS 67654
Ph: (785)877-5141
Fax: (785)877-5142
URL: http://www.highplainsmentalhealth.com/locations

Osborne

30315 ■ High Plains Mental Health Center Osborne Branch Office
209 W Harrison
Osborne, KS 67473
Ph: (785)346-2184
Fax: (785)346-2487
URL: http://www.highplainsmentalhealth.com

Oskaloosa

30316 ■ The Guidance Center - Jefferson County
1102 Walnut St.
Oskaloosa, KS 66002-1426
Ph: (785)863-2929
URL: http://www.theguidance-ctr.org/
Formerly: Oskaloosa.

Paola

30317 ■ Louisburg-Paola Veterans Affairs Clinic
510 S Hospital Dr.
Paola, KS 66071
Ph: (816)922-2160
URL: http://www2.va.gov/directory/guide/facility.asp?ID=5236&dnum=All

Parsons

30318 ■ Parsons Veterans Affairs Clinic
1907 Harding Dr.
Parsons, KS 67357
Free: 888-878-6881
URL: http://www2.va.gov/directory/guide/facility.asp?ID=5237&dnum=All

Phillipsburg

30319 ■ High Plains Mental Health Center Phillipsburg Branch Office
783 7th St.
Phillipsburg, KS 67661-1936
Ph: (785)543-5284
URL: http://www.highplainsmentalhealth.com

Salina

30320 ■ Salina Veterans Affairs Clinic
1410 E Iron, Ste. 1
Salina, KS 67401
Free: 888-878-6881
URL: http://www2.va.gov/directory/guide/facility.asp?ID=5238&dnum=All

Scott City

30321 ■ Area Mental Health Center Scott City Branch Office
210 W 4th St.
Scott City, KS 67871-1205
Ph: (620)872-5338
Fax: (620)872-2879
URL: http://www.areamhc.org

Seneca

30322 ■ Nemaha Valley Veterans Affairs Community Hospital
1600 Community Dr.
Seneca, KS 66538
Ph: (785)336-6181
URL: http://www2.va.gov/directory/guide/facility.asp?ID=5392&dnum=All

Shawnee

30323 ■ Community Support Services--Shawnee
6440 Nieman Rd.
Shawnee, KS 66203
Ph: (913)962-9955
Remarks: Serves adults over age 18 with severe, persistent mental illnesses.

Shawnee Mission

30324 ■ Shawnee Mission Medical Center Behavioral Health Unit
9100 W 74th St.
Shawnee Mission, KS 66204-4019
Ph: (913)676-2000
Formerly: Shawnee Mission Clinic.

Sublette

30325 ■ Southwest Guidance Center, Inc. Sublette Medical Clinic
301 Derby St.
Sublette, KS 67877
Ph: (620)675-2686
URL: http://www.swguidance.org/obtaining_services/index.html

Topeka

30326 ■ Topeka Veterans Affairs Medical Center
2200 Gage Blvd.
Topeka, KS 66622
Ph: (785)350-3111
Free: 800-574-8387
URL: http://www.topeka.va.gov/

Ulysses

30327 ■ Area Mental Health Center
Ulysses Branch Office
404 N Baughman
Ulysses, KS 67880-0757
Ph: (620)356-3198
Fax: (620)356-3101
URL: http://www.areamhc.org

Washington

30328 ■ Pawnee Mental Health Services
Washington Office
321 C St., Ste. 102
Washington, KS 66968
Ph: (785)325-3252
URL: http://www.pawnee.org/locations.php

Wichita

30329 ■ Prairie View at Legacy Park
9333 E 21st St. N
Wichita, KS 67206
Ph: (316)634-4700
URL: http://www.prairieview.com/hutch-locations.html

30330 ■ Prairie View at Reflection Ridge
7570 W 21st St. N, Ste. 1026-D
Wichita, KS 67205
Ph: (316)729-6555
URL: http://www.prairieview.com/hutch-locations.html

30331 ■ Robert J. Dole Veterans Affairs Medical Center
5500 E Kellogg Ave.
Wichita, KS 67218
Ph: (316)685-2221
Free: 888-878-6881
URL: http://www.wichita.va.gov/

KENTUCKY

Albany

30332 ■ Adanta Group - Clinton County Mental Health Center
101 Adanta Cir.
Albany, KY 42602-0115
Ph: (606)387-7635
Fax: (606)387-5638
URL: http://www.adanta.org
Formerly: Adanta Mental Health Services.

Ashland

30333 ■ Pathways, Inc.--22nd Street, Ashland
201 22nd St.
Ashland, KY 41101
Ph: (606)324-1141
Free: 800-562-8909
URL: http://ALERTRegionalPreventionCenter

30334 ■ Pathways, Inc.--Bath Avenue, Ashland
1212 Bath Ave., 9th Fl.
Ashland, KY 41105
Ph: (606)329-8588
Free: 800-562-8909
URL: http://www.pathways-ky.org/locations/index.html
Formerly: ALERT Regional Prevention Center.

Barbourville

30335 ■ Cumberland River Regional Mental Health/Mental Retardation Board--Barbourville
317 Cumberland Ave.
Barbourville, KY 40906
Ph: (606)546-3104
Fax: (606)546-3105
E-mail: crccc@cumberlandriver.com
URL: http://www.cumberlandriver.com

Bardstown

30336 ■ Bardstown Therapeutic Rehabilitation Programs
333 S 3rd St.
Bardstown, KY 40004
Ph: (502)349-6057
URL: http://www.communicare.org/nelson.asp

30337 ■ Communicare Outpatient Clinic--Bardstown
331 S 3rd St.
Bardstown, KY 40004
Ph: (502)348-9206
URL: http://www.communicare.org

30338 ■ Nelson County Industries
801 Allison Ave.
Bardstown, KY 40004
Ph: (502)348-2481
URL: http://www.communicare.org/nelson.asp

30339 ■ Tom McKay Group Home
329 S 3rd St.
Bardstown, KY 40004
Ph: (502)348-6090
URL: http://www.communicare.org/nelson.asp

Beattyville

30340 ■ Kentucky River Community Care, Inc.--Beattyville
Riverbend Treatment Center
15 Beech Ln.
Beattyville, KY 41311
Ph: (606)464-9790
URL: http://www.krccnet.com/

Beaver Dam

30341 ■ Ohio County Office
Ohio County Community Center
1269 Duvall Rd.
Beaver Dam, KY 42320
Ph: (270)274-0650
Formerly: River Valley Behavioral Health/ Ohio County Community Center.

Bellevue

30342 ■ Bellevue Veterans Affairs Community Based Outpatient Clinic
103 Landmark Dr., Ste. 300
Bellevue, KY 41073
Ph: (859)392-3840
URL: http://www2.va.gov/directory/guide/facility.asp?ID=932&dnum=All

Benham

30343 ■ Cumberland River Comprehensive Care Center--Benham
227 Main St.
Benham, KY 40807
Ph: (606)848-5444
Fax: (606)848-5918
URL: http://www.cumberlandriver.com/
Formerly: Cumberland River Regional Mental Health/ Mental Retardation Board.

Benton

30344 ■ Four Rivers Behavioral Health--Benton
1304 Main St.
Benton, KY 42025
Ph: (270)527-1434
Free: 800-592-3980
Fax: (270)527-1435
URL: http://www.4rbh.org
Formerly: Benton/Marshall County Mental Health/ Mental Retardation Services.

Berea

30345 ■ Berea Veterans Affairs Outpatient Clinic
209 Pauline Dr.
Berea, KY 40403
Ph: (859)986-1259
URL: http://www.lexington.va.gov/visitors/berea.asp

30346 ■ Marc Center
1315 Gabbardtown Rd.
Berea, KY 40403
Ph: (859)986-1687

Bowling Green

30347 ■ Bowling Green CORPCARE Veterans Affairs Clinic
Hartland Medical Plz.
1110 Wilkinson Trace Cir.
Bowling Green, KY 42103
Ph: (270)796-3590
URL: http://www.tennesseevalley.va.gov/visitors/Bowlinggreen_OPC.asp

30348 ■ Life Skills
Children's Crisis Stabilization Unit
501 Chestnut St.
Bowling Green, KY 42101
Ph: (270)901-5000
URL: http://www.lifeskills.com

30349 ■ LifeSkills Adult Crisis Stabilization
822 Woodway Dr.
Bowling Green, KY 42101
Ph: (270)901-5000
Free: 800-837-3954
Fax: (270)783-0609
URL: http://www.lifeskills.com/bhwarren.html

30350 ■ LifeSkills Service Center
380 Suwannee Trail St.
Bowling Green, KY 42103
Ph: (270)901-5000
Fax: (270)842-6553
URL: http://www.lifeskills.com/bhwarren.html

Brandenburg

30351 ■ Communicare Outpatient Clinic--Brandenburg
2025 Bypass Rd.
Brandenburg, KY 40108
Ph: (270)422-3971
Fax: (270)422-4886
URL: http://www.communicare.org/meade.asp

30352 ■ Meade County Industries
1895 Brandenburg Rd.
Brandenburg, KY 40108
Ph: (270)422-3412
URL: http://www.communicare.org/meade.asp
Formerly: Marc Industries.

Brownsville

30353 ■ Edmonson County Service Center
205 Mohawk Dr.
Brownsville, KY 42210
Ph: (270)597-2713
URL: http://www.lifeskills.com

Burkesville

30354 ■ Cumberland County Mental Health Center
390 Keen St.
Burkesville, KY 42717
Ph: (270)864-5631
URL: http://www.adanta.org
Formerly: Adanta Group.

Campbellsville

30355 ■ Taylor County Mental Health Center
3020 Old Lebanon Rd.
Campbellsville, KY 42718
Ph: (270)465-7424
URL: http://www.adanta.org
Formerly: Adanta.

Carlisle

30356 ■ Comprehensive Care Center--Carlisle
2330 Concrete Rd.
Carlisle, KY 40311
Ph: (859)289-7126
Fax: (859)289-7908

Carrollton

30357 ■ Carroll County Branch Office Northkey Community Care
1714 Highland Ave.
Carrollton, KY 41008-8775
Ph: (502)732-9331
URL: http://www.northkey.org/live/index.asp
Formerly: Northern Kentucky Mental Health/Mental Retardation Regional Center.

30358 ■ Carrollton Veterans Affairs Healthcare Center
1911 Hwy. 227
Carrollton, KY 41008
Ph: (502)287-6060
URL: http://www.louisville.va.gov/visitors/carrollton.asp

Cave City

30359 ■ Spectrum Care Academy, Inc.
6100 Jackson Hwy.
Cave City, KY 42127
Ph: (270)678-4706
URL: http://spectrumcareacademy.com/

Clarkson

30360 ■ Veterans Affairs Healthcare Center, Grayson
619 W Main St.
Clarkson, KY 42726
Free: 866-653-8232
URL: http://www.louisville.va.gov/visitors/grayson.asp

Clinton

30361 ■ Four Rivers Behavioral Health--Clinton
106 W Clay
Clinton, KY 42031
Ph: (270)653-6992
Fax: (270)653-4905
URL: http://www.4rbh.org
Formerly: Clinton/Hickman County Mental Health/Mental Retardation Services.

Columbia

30362 ■ Adair Eldercare
127 N Reed St.
Columbia, KY 42728-1356
Ph: (270)384-5351
E-mail: adairadh@adanta.org
URL: http://www.adanta.org

Corbin

30363 ■ Cumberland River Regional Mental Health/Mental Retardation Board--Corbin
1203 American Greeting Card Rd.
Corbin, KY 40701
Ph: (606)528-7010
Fax: (606)528-5401
URL: http://www.cumberlandriver.com
Formerly: Cumberland River Comprehensive Care Center.

Covington

30364 ■ North Key Community Care Employment Rehabilitation Program
722 Scott St.
Covington, KY 41011
Ph: (859)431-3052
Free: 877-331-3292
Fax: (859)431-7939
URL: http://www.northkey.org
Formerly: Northern Kentucky Mental Health/Mental Retardation Regional Center Partial Hospitalization Program and Therapeutic Rehabilitation Program.

30365 ■ NorthKey Community Care Children's Intensive Services
502 Farrell Dr.
Covington, KY 41011
Ph: (859)578-3202
Fax: (859)578-2874
URL: http://www.northkey.org
Formerly: Northern Kentucky Mental Health/Mental Retardation Regional Center; Northern Kentucky Mental Health/Mental Retardation Regional Center/Child/Adolescent Intensive Services.

30366 ■ NorthKey Community Care--Covington
503 Farrell Dr.
Covington, KY 41011
Ph: (859)578-3234
URL: http://www.northkey.org
Formerly: Northern Kentucky Mental Health/Mental Retardation Regional Center.

30367 ■ NorthKey Community Care Dixie Pike Family Health Center
1100 Pike St.
Covington, KY 41011-2135
Ph: (859)431-2079
URL: http://www.northkey.org
Formerly: Northern Kentucky Mental Health/Mental Retardation Regional Center; Family Health Center.

30368 ■ NorthKey Community Care Greenup Haus, Inc.
1122 Greenup St.
Covington, KY 41011-3269
Ph: (859)431-4496
URL: http://www.northkey.org
Formerly: Northern Kentucky Mental Health/Mental Retardation Regional Center.

Cynthiana

30369 ■ Harrison County Comprehensive Care
257 Parkland Hts.
Cynthiana, KY 41031
Ph: (859)234-6940

Danville

30370 ■ Comprehensive Care Center/Southwood Recovery
650 High St.
Danville, KY 40422
Ph: (859)236-2726

30371 ■ Ephraim McDowell Regional Medical Center
217 S 3rd St.
Danville, KY 40422
Ph: (859)239-1000
URL: http://www.emrmc.org/

Elizabethtown

30372 ■ Communicare, Inc.
1311 N Dixie Ave.
Elizabethtown, KY 42701
Ph: (270)769-1304
Free: 888-344-8066
Fax: (270)763-0512
URL: http://www.communicare.org/hardin.asp

30373 ■ Communicare, Inc. Adult and Children's Crisis Stabilization
100 Gray St.
Elizabethtown, KY 42701
Ph: (270)360-0419
Fax: (270)763-1609
URL: http://www.communicare.org/hardin.asp
Formerly: Children's Crisis Stabilization.

30374 ■ Communicare Inc.--Elizabethtown Regional Administration
1311 N Dixie Ave.
Elizabethtown, KY 42701
Ph: (270)765-2605
Free: 888-344-8066
Fax: (270)769-0836
URL: http://www.communicare.org/hardin.asp
Formerly: Elizabethtown Workshop.

30375 ■ Communicare Recovery Center
1311 N Dixie Ave.
Elizabethtown, KY 42701
Ph: (270)765-5145
Fax: (270)769-6581
URL: http://www.communicare.org/hardin.asp

30376 ■ Creekview Group Home
200 Diecks Dr.
Elizabethtown, KY 42701-2405
Ph: (270)737-2614
URL: http://www.communicare.org/hardin.asp

Eminence

30377 ■ Henry County Center
147 E Main St.
Eminence, KY 40019-0193
Ph: (502)845-2928

Falmouth

30378 ■ Pendleton County Office Northern Kentucky Community Care
318 Montjoy St.
Falmouth, KY 41040
Ph: (859)654-6988
URL: http://www.northkey.org
Formerly: Northern Kentucky Mental Health/Mental Retardation Regional Center.

Florence

30379 ■ Florence Veterans Affairs Clinic
7711 Ewing
Florence, KY 41042
Ph: (859)282-4480
URL: http://www2.va.gov/directory/guide/facility.asp?ID=5423&dnum=All

30380 ■ Northern Kentucky Mental Health/Mental Retardation Regional Center Boone County Adult Unit NorthKey Community Care
7459 Burlington Pke.
Florence, KY 41042
Ph: (859)525-6808
Fax: (859)524-6423
URL: http://www.northkey.org

30381 ■ Northern Kentucky Mental Health/Mental Retardation Regional Center Boone County Children's Unit
7459 Burlington Pke.
Florence, KY 41042-1553
Ph: (859)282-6585
Fax: (859)282-0532
URL: http://www.northkey.org

Fort Campbell

30382 ■ Fort Campbell Veterans Affairs Clinic
Desert Storm Ave., Bldg. 39
Fort Campbell, KY 42223
Ph: (270)798-4118
URL: http://www.tennesseevalley.va.gov/visitors/Fort-Campbell_OPC.asp

Fort Knox

30383 ■ Veterans Affairs Healthcare Center, Fort Knox
Ireland Army Community Hospital
821 Ireland Loop
Fort Knox, KY 40121
Ph: (502)624-9396
Fax: (502)624-9309
URL: http://www.louisville.va.gov/visitors/fortknox.asp

Fort Thomas

30384 ■ Campbell County Children's Unit NorthKey Community Care
1201 S Fort Thomas Ave.
Fort Thomas, KY 41075
Ph: (859)781-5596
URL: http://www.northkey.org

Frankfort

30385 ■ Bluegrass Impact--Frankfort
625 Leawood Dr., Ste. A
Frankfort, KY 40601
Ph: (502)875-3772
URL: http://www.bluegrass.org

30386 ■ Comprehensive Care Center--Frankfort
191 Doctors Dr.
Frankfort, KY 40601
Ph: (502)223-2182
URL: http://www.bluegrass.org

Frenchburg

30387 ■ Pathways, Inc.--Frenchburg
70 Main St.
Frenchburg, KY 40322
Ph: (606)768-2131
Free: 800-562-8909
Fax: (606)768-2134
URL: http://www.pathways-ky.org/

Fulton

30388 ■ Four Rivers Behavioral Health--Fulton
352 Browder St.
Fulton, KY 42041-1176
Ph: (270)472-1760
Fax: (270)472-6362
URL: http://www.4rbh.org

Georgetown

30389 ■ Comprehensive Care Center--Georgetown
110 Roach St.
Georgetown, KY 40324
Ph: (502)863-4734

Grayson

30390 ■ Pathways, Inc.--Grayson
840 Interstate Dr.
Grayson, KY 41143-1250
Ph: (606)474-5151
URL: http://www.pathways-ky.org/

Greensburg

30391 ■ Green County Mental Health Center
521 Old Hodgensville Rd.
Greensburg, KY 42743
Ph: (270)932-3226

Greenup

30392 ■ Pathways, Inc.--Greenup
57 Dora Ln.
Greenup, KY 41144
Ph: (606)473-7333
Free: 800-562-8909
Fax: (606)473-7335
URL: http://www.pathways-ky.org/

Hanson

30393 ■ Hanson Veterans Affairs Community Based Outpatient Clinic
926 Veterans Dr.
Hanson, KY 42413
Ph: (270)322-8019
Fax: (270)322-8957
URL: http://www2.va.gov/directory/guide/facility.asp?ID=435&dnum=All

Hardinsburg

30394 ■ Breckenridge County Industries
207 Fairgrounds Rd.
Hardinsburg, KY 40143
Ph: (270)756-5272
URL: http://www.communicare.org/breckinridge.asp
Formerly: Communicare Industries.

Harlan

30395 ■ Cumberland River Regional Mental Health/Mental Retardation Board--Harlan
134 Comprehensive Dr.
Harlan, KY 40831
Ph: (606)573-1624
Formerly: Cumberland River Comprehensive Care Center.

Harrodsburg

30396 ■ Alice G. Ransdell Community Mental Health Center
124 E Office St.
Harrodsburg, KY 40330
Ph: (859)734-5486

30397 ■ Rainbow House
710 Perryville Rd.
Harrodsburg, KY 40330
Ph: (859)734-7761

Hawesville

30398 ■ Hancock County Office
107 Harrison St.
Hawesville, KY 42348
Ph: (270)927-8659
Formerly: River Valley Behavioral Health.

Hazard

30399 ■ Hazard Veterans Affairs Community Based Outpatient Clinic
210 Black Gold Blvd.
Hazard, KY 41701
Ph: (606)436-2350
URL: http://www2.va.gov/directory/guide/facility.asp?ID=5697&dnum=All

30400 ■ Kentucky River Community Care, Inc.--Hazard
115 Rockwood Ln.
Hazard, KY 41701
Ph: (606)436-5761
URL: http://www.krccnet.com

Henderson

30401 ■ River Valley Behavioral Health Therapeutic Rehabilitation Program
205 US Hwy. 41 S
Henderson, KY 42420
Ph: (270)826-1979
URL: http://www.rvbh.com

Hopkinsville

30402 ■ Cumberland Hall
210 W 17th St.
Hopkinsville, KY 42240
Ph: (270)886-1919
URL: http://www.psysolutions.com/facilities/cumberlandhall/

30403 ■ Hopkinsville Clinic
735 North Dr.
Hopkinsville, KY 42240
Ph: (270)881-9551

Inez

30404 ■ Mountain Comprehensive Care Center--Inez
Rte. 3 Rock Castle Rd.
Inez, KY 41224
Ph: (606)298-7902
URL: http://www.mtcomp.org

Isom

30405 ■ Kentucky River Community Care, Inc.--Isom
75 Isom Plz.
Isom, KY 41824
Ph: (606)632-0405

Jackson

30406 ■ Kentucky River Community Care, Inc.--Jackson Breathitt County Outpatient Services
3770 Hwy. 15 S
Jackson, KY 41339
Ph: (606)666-9278

Jamestown

30407 ■ Adanta Group Russell County Mental Health Center
119 Herrifords Curve Rd.
Jamestown, KY 42629
Ph: (270)343-2551
URL: http://www.adanta.org/

La Grange

30408 ■ Oldham County Center
230 Yager Ave., No. 5
La Grange, KY 40031
Ph: (502)222-7210

Lancaster

30409 ■ Garrard Community Mental Health Center
322 Crab Orchard St., Ste. 1
Lancaster, KY 40444-1222
Ph: (859)792-2181

Lawrenceburg

30410 ■ Comprehensive Care Center--Lawrenceburg Rainbow House/Afterschool
1060 Glensboro Rd.
Lawrenceburg, KY 40342
Ph: (502)839-7203

Lebanon

30411 ■ Communicare Outpatient Clinic--Lebanon
65 Old Springfield Rd.
Lebanon, KY 40033
Ph: (270)692-2509
Free: 888-344-8066
Fax: (270)692-2592
URL: http://www.communicare.org/marion.asp

30412 ■ Lebanon Therapeutic Rehabilitation Programs
65 Old Springfield Rd., Ste. 2
Lebanon, KY 40033
Ph: (270)692-0437
URL: http://www.communicare.org/marion.asp

30413 ■ Marion County Industries
516 Workshop Ln.
Lebanon, KY 40143
Ph: (270)692-9237
URL: http://www.communicare.org/marion.asp

Leitchfield

30414 ■ Communicare Outpatient Clinic--Leitchfield
300 S Clinton St.
Leitchfield, KY 42754
Ph: (270)259-4652
Fax: (270)259-6655
URL: http://www.communicare.org/grayson.asp

30415 ■ Leitchfield Therapeutic Rehabilitation Program
106 W Main St.
Leitchfield, KY 42754
Ph: (270)259-5529
URL: http://www.communicare.org/grayson.asp

Lexington

30416 ■ Bluegrass Comprehensive Center
201 Mechanic St.
Lexington, KY 40507
Ph: (859)233-0444
Free: 800-928-8000
URL: http://www.bluegrass.org

30417 ■ Bluegrass Impact--Lexington
570 E Main St.
Lexington, KY 40508
Ph: (859)254-3106
URL: http://www.bluegrass.org/
Formerly: Bluegrass Impact Family Preservation.

30418 ■ Bluegrass Personal Care Home
627 W 4th St.
Lexington, KY 40508
Ph: (859)281-1394
URL: http://www.bluegrass.org/

30419 ■ Connections
3479 Buckhorn Dr., Ste. 106
Lexington, KY 40515
Ph: (859)271-3812

30420 ■ Eastern State Hospital Day Treatment Unit
627 W 4th St.
Lexington, KY 40508
Ph: (859)246-7004

30421 ■ Family Care Center
1135 Red Mile Cir.
Lexington, KY 40504-1172
Ph: (859)268-4292

30422 ■ Family Preservation Program
2311 Fortune, Ste. 295
Lexington, KY 40509
Ph: (859)299-0794
URL: http://www.bluegrass.org/

30423 ■ Forensic Services
177 N Upper St.
Lexington, KY 40507
Ph: (859)225-7147
URL: http://www.bluegrass.org/

30424 ■ Lexington Veterans Affairs Medical Center--Leestown Division
2250 Leestown Rd.
Lexington, KY 40511
Ph: (859)233-4511
Free: 888-824-3577
URL: http://www.lexington.va.gov/

30425 ■ Parents Place/The Children's Center
2220 Young Dr.
Lexington, KY 40505
Ph: (859)268-4292
URL: http://www.bluegrass.org/

Liberty

30426 ■ Casey County Mental Health Center
322 Middleburg St.
Liberty, KY 42539-3004
Ph: (606)787-6685
URL: http://www.adanta.org

London

30427 ■ Cumberland River Comprehensive Care Center--London
915 N Laurel Rd.
London, KY 40741
Ph: (606)864-2104
URL: http://www.cumberlandriver.com/

Louisa

30428 ■ Pathways, Inc.--Louisa
60 Professional Park Dr.
Louisa, KY 41230-0485
Ph: (606)638-4332
URL: http://www.pathways-ky.org/locations/index.html

Louisville

30429 ■ Center for Consulting Services--South
1512 Crums Ln.
Louisville, KY 40216
Ph: (502)589-8920

30430 ■ Center for Consulting Services--West
2225 W Broadway
Louisville, KY 40211
Ph: (502)589-8910

30431 ■ Center for Supported Living--Downtown
758 S 1st St.
Louisville, KY 40202
Ph: (502)589-8926

30432 ■ Center for Supported Living--East
4400 Breckenridge Ln., Ste. 115
Louisville, KY 40218
Ph: (502)495-7800

30433 ■ Center for Supported Living--South
2105 Crums Ln.
Louisville, KY 40216
Ph: (502)589-8915

30434 ■ Center for Supported Living--West
1912 W Broadway
Louisville, KY 40203
Ph: (502)776-0972

30435 ■ Dupont Veterans Affairs Healthcare Center
4010 Dupont Cir.
Louisville, KY 40207
Ph: (502)287-6187
URL: http://www.louisville.va.gov/visitors/dupont.asp

30436 ■ Louisville Veterans Affairs Medical Center
800 Zorn Ave.
Louisville, KY 40206
Ph: (502)287-4000
URL: http://www.louisville.va.gov/

30437 ■ Maryhurst
1015 Dorsey Ln.
Louisville, KY 40223
Ph: (502)245-1576
URL: http://www.maryhurst.org/

30438 ■ School Based Services
3717 Taylorsville Rd.
Louisville, KY 40220
Ph: (502)454-6343

30439 ■ Seven Counties Services, Inc.
101 W Muhammad Ali Blvd.
Louisville, KY 40202
Ph: (502)589-8600
URL: http://www.sevencounties.org/

30440 ■ Veterans Affairs Healthcare Center, Newburg
3430 Newburg Rd.
Louisville, KY 40218
Ph: (502)287-6223
URL: http://www.louisville.va.gov/visitors/newburg.asp

30441 ■ Veterans Affairs Healthcare Center, Shively
3934 N Dixie Hwy., Ste. 210
Louisville, KY 40216
Ph: (502)287-6000
URL: http://www.louisville.va.gov/visitors/shively.asp

Madisonville

30442 ■ Madisonville Clinic
1303 W Noel Ave.
Madisonville, KY 42431
Ph: (270)821-8874
URL: http://www.pennyroyalcenter.org/

Martin

30443 ■ Mountain Comprehensive Care Center--Martin
11206 Main St.
Martin, KY 41649
Ph: (606)285-3142
URL: http://www.mtcomp.org

Mayfield

30444 ■ Four Rivers Behavioral Health--Mayfield
1525 Cuba Rd.
Mayfield, KY 42066-6809
Ph: (270)247-2588
Free: 800-592-3980
Fax: (270)247-0142
URL: http://www.4rbh.org
Formerly: William H. Fuller Center.

30445 ■ Mayfield Veterans Affairs Clinic
1253 Paris Rd., Ste. A
Mayfield, KY 42066
Ph: (618)997-5311
Free: 866-289-3300
URL: http://www2.va.gov/directory/guide/facility.asp?ID=5702&dnum=All

Mc Kee

30446 ■ Cumberland River Comprehensive Care Center--McKee
101 Water St. W
Mc Kee, KY 40447-8900
Ph: (606)287-7137
URL: http://www.cumberlandriver.com/
Formerly: Cumberland River Regional Mental Health/Mental Retardation Board.

Middlesboro

30447 ■ Cumberland River Comprehensive Care Center--Middlesboro
324 1/2 N 19th St.
Middlesboro, KY 40965
Ph: (606)248-4949
URL: http://www.cumberlandriver.com/
Formerly: Cumberland River Regional Mental Health/Mental Retardation Board.

Monticello

30448 ■ Wayne County Mental Health Center
802 W Columbia Ave.
Monticello, KY 42633
Ph: (606)348-9319
Fax: (606)348-6932
URL: http://www.adanta.org
Formerly: Wayne County Mental Health Center and The Adanta Group, Behavioral Health Services.

30449 ■ Wayne Therapeutic Rehabilitation
802 Columbia Ave.
Monticello, KY 42633
Ph: (606)348-8935
URL: http://www.adanta.org

Morehead

30450 ■ Morehead Veterans Affairs Outpatient Clinic
333 Beacon Hill
Morehead, KY 40351
Free: 888-824-3577
URL: http://www.lexington.va.gov/visitors/morehead.asp

30451 ■ Pathways--Morehead
325 E Main St.
Morehead, KY 40351
Ph: (606)784-4161
URL: http://www.pathways-ky.org/locations/index.html

Morganfield

30452 ■ Union County Office
233 N Townsend
Morganfield, KY 42437
Ph: (270)389-3240
Formerly: River Valley Behavioral Health.

Morgantown

30453 ■ Life Skills Service Center, Morgantown
202 Industrial Dr. N
Morgantown, KY 42261
Ph: (270)526-3877
URL: http://www.lifeskills.com

Mount Sterling

30454 ■ Pathways--Mount Sterling
300 Foxglove Dr.
Mount Sterling, KY 40353
Ph: (859)498-2135
URL: http://www.pathways-ky.org/locations/index.html

Mount Vernon

30455 ■ Cumberland River Comprehensive Care Center--Mount Vernon
260 Valley View
Mount Vernon, KY 40456
Ph: (606)256-2129
URL: http://www.cumberlandriver.com/
Formerly: Cumberland River Regional Mental Health/Mental Retardation Board.

Murray

30456 ■ Four Rivers Behavioral Health--Murray
1051 N 16th St., Ste. B
Murray, KY 42071
Ph: (270)753-6622
Fax: (270)753-9669
URL: http://www.4rbh.org

Newport

30457 ■ Campbell County Adult Unit Northern Kentucky Community Care
718 Columbia St.
Newport, KY 41071
Ph: (859)491-6510
Free: 877-331-3292
Fax: (859)491-6589
URL: http://www.northkey.org
Formerly: Northern Kentucky Mental Health/Mental Retardation Regional Center.

Nicholasville

30458 ■ Jessamine Counseling & Education Center
324 Southview Dr.
Nicholasville, KY 40356
Ph: (859)885-6315

Owensboro

30459 ■ Hager Preschool
1701 W 7th St.
Owensboro, KY 42164
Ph: (270)237-4481
URL: http://www.owensboro.kyschools.us/hager

30460 ■ Owensboro Veterans Affairs Clinic
3400 New Hartford Rd.
Owensboro, KY 42301
Ph: (270)684-5034
URL: http://www2.va.gov/directory/guide/facility.asp?ID=5672&dnum=All

30461 ■ River Valley Behavioral Health Hospital
1000 Industrial Dr.
Owensboro, KY 42301
Ph: (270)689-6800
Free: 800-755-8477
Fax: (270)689-6809
E-mail: info@rvbh.com
URL: http://www.rvbh.com

30462 ■ River Valley Behavioral Health--Walnut Street, Owensboro
1100 Walnut St.
Owensboro, KY 42302
Ph: (270)689-6500
Free: 800-737-0696
E-mail: info@rvbh.com
URL: http://www.rvbh.com

Owenton

30463 ■ NorthKey Community Care Owen County Office
155 W Seminary
Owenton, KY 40359
Ph: (502)484-3464
URL: http://www.northkey.org/live/index.asp

Owingsville

30464 ■ Pathways--Owingsville
664 State Ave.
Owingsville, KY 40360
Ph: (606)674-6690
Free: 800-562-8909
Fax: (606)674-6903
URL: http://www.pathways-ky.org/locations/index.html

Paducah

30465 ■ Four Rivers Behavioral Health--Paducah
425 Broadway
Paducah, KY 42001
Ph: (270)442-7121
URL: http://www.4rbh.org

30466 ■ Paducah Veterans Affairs Community Based Outpatient Clinic
2620 Perkins Creek Dr.
Paducah, KY 42001
Ph: (270)444-8465
Fax: (270)443-8198
URL: http://www2.va.gov/directory/guide/facility.asp?ID=5253&dnum=All

Paintsville

30467 ■ Mountain Comprehensive Care Center--Paintsville
1110 S Mayo Trl.
Paintsville, KY 41240-1410
Ph: (606)789-3518
URL: http://www.mtcomp.org/

Pikeville

30468 ■ Mountain Comprehensive Care Center Community Support Program
118 River Dr.
Pikeville, KY 41653
Ph: (606)432-3143
URL: http://www.mtcomp.org/

30469 ■ Mountain Comprehensive Care Center Pikeville Clinic
98 River Dr.
Pikeville, KY 41501
Ph: (606)432-3143
URL: http://www.mtcomp.org/

Prestonburg

30470 ■ Auxiew Adult Day Habilitation Center
40 Greenhouse Ln.
Prestonburg, KY 41653
Ph: (606)886-6815
URL: http://www.mtcomp.org/

Prestonsburg

30471 ■ Mountain Comprehensive Care Center--Prestonburg
150 S Front St.
Prestonsburg, KY 41653
Ph: (606)886-8572
URL: http://www.mtcomp.org/

30472 ■ Prestonsburg Veterans Affairs Primary Care Clinic
5230 Kentucky Rte. 321, Ste. 8
Prestonsburg, KY 41653
Ph: (606)886-1970
URL: http://www.huntington.va.gov/visitors/prestonsburg.asp

Providence

30473 ■ River Valley Behavioral Health Webster County Office
606 1st St.
Providence, KY 42450
Ph: (270)667-7092
URL: http://www.rvbh.com
Formerly: River Valley.

Radcliff

30474 ■ Communicare Outpatient Clinic--Radcliff
1072 S Dixie Blvd.
Radcliff, KY 40160
Ph: (270)351-8166
Fax: (270)351-8322
URL: http://www.communicare.org/hardin.asp

Richmond

30475 ■ Cardinal House
407 Gibson Ln.
Richmond, KY 40475
Ph: (859)623-1328

30476 ■ Comprehensive Care Center--Richmond
415 Gibson Ln.
Richmond, KY 40475
Ph: (859)623-9367

30477 ■ Madison County Afterschool
409 Gibson Ln.
Richmond, KY 40475
Ph: (859)623-1910

30478 ■ Marc Center
Marc Graphics
1695 E Main St.
Richmond, KY 40475
Ph: (859)623-0308

Salyersville

30479 ■ Mountain Comprehensive Care Center--Salyersville
145 Allen Dr.
Salyersville, KY 41465
Ph: (606)349-3115
Fax: (606)349-5121
URL: http://www.mtcomp.org

Sandy Hook

30480 ■ Pathways, Inc.--Sandy Hook
Rte. 5 Box 800
Sandy Hook, KY 41171
Ph: (606)738-6163
Fax: (606)738-5030
URL: http://www.pathways-ky.org/locations/index.html

Scottsville

30481 ■ Life Skills Service Center, Scottsville
512 Bowling Green Rd.
Scottsville, KY 42164
Ph: (270)237-4481
URL: http://www.lifeskills.com

Smithland

30482 ■ Four Rivers Behavioral Health--Smithland
212 E Adair
Smithland, KY 42081
Ph: (270)928-2723
Fax: (270)928-4842
URL: http://www.4rbh.org

Somerset

30483 ■ Adanta Group
356 High Point Dr.
Somerset, KY 42501
Ph: (606)679-6251
URL: http://www.adanta.org

30484 ■ The Adanta Group
259 Parkers Mill Rd.
Somerset, KY 42501
Ph: (606)679-4782
Fax: (606)677-1746
URL: http://www.adanta.org
Formerly: Lake Cumberland Regional Mental Health/dba The Adanta Group.

30485 ■ Pulaski Child and Adolescence Services
113 Hardin Ln.
Somerset, KY 42503
Ph: (606)679-6251
URL: http://www.adanta.org

South Williamson

30486 ■ Mountain Comprehensive Care Center--South Williamson
140 Hospital Dr.
South Williamson, KY 41503
Ph: (606)237-9871
URL: http://www.mtcomp.org

Springfield

30487 ■ Washington County Industries
825 Walnut St.
Springfield, KY 40069
Ph: (859)336-7746
Free: 888-344-8066
Fax: (859)336-7746
URL: http://www.communicare.org/washington.asp

Stanford

30488 ■ Fort Logan Comprehensive Care
322 Frontier Blvd.
Stanford, KY 40484
Ph: (606)365-2197

30489 ■ Lincolnview
410 Anderson Hts.
Stanford, KY 40484
Ph: (606)365-3893

Tompkinsville

30490 ■ LifeSkills Service Center
800 N Main St.
Tompkinsville, KY 42167
Ph: (270)487-5655
Fax: (270)487-5948
URL: http://www.lifeskills.com/bhmonroe.html

West Liberty

30491 ■ Pathways, Inc.--West Liberty
767 Main St.
West Liberty, KY 41472
Ph: (606)743-3139
URL: http://www.pathways-ky.org/locations/index.html

Williamsburg

30492 ■ Cumberland River Comprehensive Care Center--Williamsburg
285 Cemetery Rd.
Williamsburg, KY 40769
Ph: (606)549-1440
URL: http://www.cumberlandriver.com/
Formerly: Cumberland River Regional Mental Health/Mental Retardation Board.

Williamstown

30493 ■ NorthKey Community Care--Williamstown
308 Barnes Rd.
Williamstown, KY 41097
Ph: (859)824-4442
Free: 877-331-3292
Fax: (859)824-4448
URL: http://www.northkey.org
Formerly: Northern Kentucky Mental Health/Mental Retardation Regional Center.

Winchester

30494 ■ Comprehensive Care Center--Winchester
26 N Highland
Winchester, KY 40391
Ph: (859)744-2562
Formerly: Clark County Comprehensive Care.

LOUISIANA

Abbeville

30495 ■ Abbeville Mental Health Clinic--E Vermilion Street
111 E Vermilion St.
Abbeville, LA 70510
Ph: (337)898-1290

Alexandria

30496 ■ Alexandria Wellness Center
2006 Gus Kaplan Dr., Ste. A
Alexandria, LA 71301
Ph: (318)473-0035
Fax: (318)443-0220
URL: http://www.compasshealthcare.com/site71.php

Baton Rouge

30497 ■ Baton Rouge Veterans Affairs Clinic
7968 Essen Park Ave.
Baton Rouge, LA 70809
Ph: (225)761-3400
URL: http://www2.va.gov/directory/guide/facility.asp?ID=636&dnum=1

30498 ■ Capital Area Center for Adult Behavioral Health Services
3455 Florida Blvd.
Baton Rouge, LA 70806
Ph: (225)925-1906
Free: 800-768-8824
URL: http://www.cahsd.org/02homeMHFrameset.html

30499 ■ Capital Area Human Services District Child/Adolescent Services
4615 Government St., Bldg. 1
Baton Rouge, LA 70806
Ph: (225)922-0445
Free: 800-590-2849
URL: http://www.cahsd.org/03homeMHCSFrameset.html

30500 ■ Margaret Dumas Mental Health Center
3843 Harding Blvd.
Baton Rouge, LA 70807
Ph: (225)359-9315
URL: http://www.cahsd.org/02homeMHFrameset.html

30501 ■ Med South Mental Health
3049 S Sherwood Forest, Ste. 250
Baton Rouge, LA 70816
Ph: (225)292-4117

30502 ■ Volunteers of America of Greater Baton Rouge
3949 North Blvd.
Baton Rouge, LA 70806
Ph: (225)387-0061
Fax: (225)381-7963
URL: http://www.voa-br.org

30503 ■ Wooddale Mental Health
1335-B Wooddale Blvd.
Baton Rouge, LA 70806
Ph: (225)928-4969

Bogalusa

30504 ■ Bogalusa Mental Health Center
619 Willis Ave.
Bogalusa, LA 70427
Ph: (985)732-6610
Fax: (985)732-6626
URL: http://www.dhh.louisiana.gov/offices/locations.asp?ID=62&Detail=18

Chalmette

30505 ■ Saint Bernard Mental Health Center
2712 Palmisano Blvd., Bldg. B
Chalmette, LA 70043
Ph: (504)278-7401
Fax: (504)278-7475
URL: http://www.dhh.louisiana.gov/offices/locations.asp?ID=62&Detail=133

Coushatta

30506 ■ Red River Mental Health Clinic
1313 Ringgold Ave.
Coushatta, LA 71019
Ph: (318)932-4029
Fax: (318)932-5914
URL: http://www.dhh.louisiana.gov/offices/locations.asp?ID=62&Detail=103

Crowley

30507 ■ Crowley Mental Health Center
1822 W 2nd St.
Crowley, LA 70527
Ph: (337)788-7511
Fax: (337)788-7588
URL: http://www.dhh.louisiana.gov/offices/locations.asp?ID=62&Detail=22

Deridder

30508 ■ Beauregard Mental Health Center
106 W Port
Deridder, LA 70634
Ph: (337)462-1641
URL: http://www.dhh.state.la.us/offices/page.asp?id=62&detail=3555

Gonzales

30509 ■ Gonzales Mental Health Center
1112 SE Ascension Comp. Ave.
Gonzales, LA 70707
Ph: (225)621-5775
URL: http://www.cahsd.org/02homeMHFrameset.html

Hammond

30510 ■ Hammond Veterans Affairs Clinic
1131 S Morrison Ave.
Hammond, LA 70403
Ph: (985)902-5026
Fax: (985)902-5030
URL: http://www2.va.gov/directory/guide/facility.asp?ID=5363&dnum=All

30511 ■ Rosenblum Mental Health Center
15785 Medical Arts Plz.
Hammond, LA 70403
Ph: (985)543-4080
Fax: (985)543-4090
URL: http://www.dhh.louisiana.gov/offices/locations.asp?ID=62&Detail=106

Houma

30512 ■ Houma Veterans Affairs Community Based Outpatient Clinic
1750 Martin Luther King Jr. Blvd., Ste. 107
Houma, LA 70360
Ph: (985)851-0188
Free: 800-310-5001
URL: http://www2.va.gov/directory/guide/facility.asp?ID=5560&dnum=All

30513 ■ Leonard J. Chabert Medical Center
1978 Industrial Blvd.
Houma, LA 70363
Ph: (985)873-2200
URL: http://www.lsuhospitals.org/hospitals/LJC/default.htm

30514 ■ Terrebonne Mental Health Center
500 Legion Ave.
Houma, LA 70364
Ph: (985)857-3615
Fax: (985)857-3706
URL: http://www.dhh.louisiana.gov/offices/locations.asp?ID=62&Detail=113

Jennings

30515 ■ Jennings Behavioral Health
619 N Main St.
Jennings, LA 70546
Ph: (337)824-4300
Fax: (337)824-4315

30516 ■ Jennings Veterans Affairs Clinic
1907 Johnson St.
Jennings, LA 70546
Ph: (337)824-1000
URL: http://www2.va.gov/directory/guide/facility.asp?ID=637&dnum=All

Jonesboro

30517 ■ Jonesboro Mental Health Clinic
4131 Hwy. 4
Jonesboro, LA 71251
Ph: (318)259-6624
Fax: (318)259-4840
URL: http://www.dhh.louisiana.gov/offices/locations.asp?ID=62&Detail=95

LaPlace

30518 ■ River Parishes Mental Health Center
1809 W Airline Hwy.
LaPlace, LA 70068
Ph: (985)652-8444
Fax: (985)652-2450
URL: http://www.dhh.louisiana.gov/offices/locations.asp?ID=62&Detail=105

Lafayette

30519 ■ Acadia Vermilion
2520 N University Ave.
Lafayette, LA 70507
Free: 800-821-2567
URL: http://www.acadiahealthcare.com/locations/vermillion-hospital

30520 ■ Lafayette Veterans Affairs Clinic
2100 Jefferson St.
Lafayette, LA 70501
Ph: (337)261-0734
Fax: (337)261-5471
URL: http://www2.va.gov/directory/guide/facility.asp?ID=5077&dnum=All

30521 ■ Lifecare Psychiatric Services--Lafayette
170 Industrial Pkwy.
Lafayette, LA 70508
Ph: (337)233-3880
URL: http://www.lifecarepsychiatricservices.com/

Lake Charles

30522 ■ Bridgeway Psychiatric Center
2827 4th Ave., Ste. 105
Lake Charles, LA 70601
Ph: (337)562-0211
Fax: (337)562-0212
URL: http://www.compasshealthcare.com/site82.php

30523 ■ Jennings Outreach
4105 Kirkman St.
Lake Charles, LA 70605
Ph: (337)475-8022
URL: http://www.dhh.louisiana.gov/offices/page.asp?id=62&detail=3555
Remarks: Jennings Outreach is based at the Lake Charles Mental Health Center and provides mental health services every other Wednesday at the First Presbyterian Church, 300 E Academy St., in Jennings, Louisiana.

30524 ■ Lake Charles Mental Health Center
4105 Kirkman St.
Lake Charles, LA 70605
Ph: (337)475-8022
Fax: (337)475-8054
URL: http://www.dhh.louisiana.gov/offices/locations.asp?ID=62&Detail=96

Leesville

30525 ■ Leesville Mental Health Center
105 Bellview Rd.
Leesville, LA 71446
Ph: (337)238-6431
Fax: (337)238-7070
URL: http://www.dhh.louisiana.gov/offices/locations.asp?ID=62&Detail=128

Mandeville

30526 ■ Lurline Smith Mental Health Center
900 Wilkinson St.
Mandeville, LA 70448
Ph: (985)624-4450
Fax: (985)624-4461
URL: http://www.dhh.louisiana.gov/offices/locations.asp?ID=62&Detail=97

Mansfield

30527 ■ Mansfield Mental Health Center
501 Louisiana Ave.
Mansfield, LA 71052
Ph: (318)872-5576
Fax: (318)872-9780
URL: http://www.dhh.louisiana.gov/offices/locations.asp?ID=62&Detail=907

Marksville

30528 ■ Avoyelles Mental Health Center
694 Government St.
Marksville, LA 71351
Ph: (318)253-9638

Marrero

30529 ■ West Jefferson Mental Health Center
5001 Westbank Expwy.
Marrero, LA 70072
Ph: (504)349-8708
URL: http://www.jphsa.org/

Metairie

30530 ■ East Jefferson Mental Health Center
3101 W Napoleon Ave., Ste. 1000
Metairie, LA 70001
Ph: (504)838-5257
Fax: (504)838-5414
URL: http://www.dhh.louisiana.gov/offices/locations.asp?ID=62&Detail=93

Monroe

30531 ■ Monroe Veterans Affairs Clinic
250 De Siard Plz. Dr.
Monroe, LA 71203
Ph: (318)343-6100
URL: http://www2.va.gov/directory/guide/facility.asp?ID=5519&dnum=All

Natchitoches

30532 ■ Natchitoches Mental Health Center
210 Medical Dr.
Natchitoches, LA 71457
Ph: (318)357-3122
Fax: (318)357-3240
URL: http://www.dhh.louisiana.gov/offices/locations.asp?ID=62&Detail=101

New Iberia

30533 ■ New Iberia Mental Health Center
611 W Admiral Doyle Dr.
New Iberia, LA 70560
Ph: (337)373-0002
Fax: (337)373-0129
URL: http://www.dhh.louisiana.gov/offices/locations.asp?ID=62&Detail=102

New Orleans

30534 ■ Central City Mental Health Center
2221 Philip St.
New Orleans, LA 70113
Ph: (504)568-6650
URL: http://www.dhh.louisiana.gov/offices/locations.asp?ID=62&Detail=19

30535 ■ Chartres Pontchartrain Behavioral Health Center
719 Elysian Fields Ave.
New Orleans, LA 70117
Ph: (504)942-8101
URL: http://www.dhh.louisiana.gov/offices/page.asp?id=62&detail=3551

30536 ■ New Orleans Mental Health Center
3100 General Degaulle Dr.
New Orleans, LA 70114-6699
Ph: (504)361-6211
Fax: (504)361-6451
URL: http://www.dhh.louisiana.gov/offices/locations.asp?ID=62&Detail=132

30537 ■ River Oaks Hospital
1525 River Oaks Rd. W
New Orleans, LA 70123
Ph: (504)734-1740
Free: 800-366-1740
Fax: (504)733-7020
URL: http://www.riveroakshospital.com/home.html

Oberlin

30538 ■ Allen Mental Health Center
402 Industrial Dr.
Oberlin, LA 70655
Ph: (337)639-3001
URL: http://www.dhh.state.la.us/offices/page.asp?id=62&detail=3555

Opelousas

30539 ■ Lifecare Psychiatric Services--Opelousas
216 Robin Ln.
Opelousas, LA 70570
Ph: (337)942-7475
URL: http://www.lifecarepsychiatricservices.com/

Pineville

30540 ■ Alexandria Veterans Affairs Medical Center
2495 Shreveport Hwy. 71 N
Pineville, LA 71360
Ph: (318)473-0010
Free: 800-375-8387
URL: http://www4.va.gov/502alexandria/

Raceland

30541 ■ Lafourche Mental Health Center
157 Twin Oaks Dr.
Raceland, LA 70394
Ph: (985)537-6823
Free: 800-840-7758
Fax: (985)537-5519
URL: http://www.dhh.louisiana.gov/offices/locations.asp?ID=62&Detail=127

Rayville

30542 ■ Richland Mental Health Center
115 Christian Dr.
Rayville, LA 71269
Ph: (318)728-6456
Fax: (318)728-4121
URL: http://www.dhh.louisiana.gov/offices/locations.asp?ID=62&Detail=104

Reserve

30543 ■ Saint John Veterans Affairs Outpatient Clinic
247 Veterans Blvd.
Reserve, LA 70084
Ph: (504)565-4705
URL: http://www2.va.gov/directory/guide/facility.asp?ID=5364&dnum=All

Shreveport

30544 ■ Overton Brooks Veterans Affairs Medical Center
510 E Stoner Ave.
Shreveport, LA 71101
Ph: (318)221-8411
Free: 800-863-7441
URL: http://www.shreveport.va.gov/

30545 ■ Shreveport Mental Health Center
1310 N Hearne Ave.
Shreveport, LA 71107-6548
Ph: (318)676-5111
URL: http://www.dhh.louisiana.gov/offices/locations.asp?ID=62&Detail=108

Slidell

30546 ■ Slidell Veterans Affairs Outpatient Clinic
60491 Doss Dr., Ste. B
Slidell, LA 70460
Ph: (985)690-2626
URL: http://www2.va.gov/directory/guide/facility.asp?ID=5365&dnum=All

Tallulah

30547 ■ Tallulah Mental Health Center
1012 Johnson St.
Tallulah, LA 71284
Ph: (318)574-1713
Fax: (318)574-2299
URL: http://www.dhh.louisiana.gov/offices/locations.asp?ID=62&Detail=112

Ville Platte

30548 ■ Ville Platte Mental Health Center
312 Court St.
Ville Platte, LA 70586
Ph: (337)363-5525
Fax: (337)363-1567
URL: http://www.dhh.louisiana.gov/offices/locations.asp?ID=62&Detail=114

Winnsboro

30549 ■ Winnsboro Mental Health Center
1301 B Landis St.
Winnsboro, LA 71295
Ph: (318)435-2146
Fax: (318)435-2134
URL: http://www.dhh.louisiana.gov/offices/locations.asp?ID=62&Detail=116

MAINE

Auburn

30550 ■ Spurwink Services, Inc.
Auburn Day Treatment Program
220 Danville Corner Rd.
Auburn, ME 04210
Ph: (207)782-0079
URL: http://www.spurwink.org/

Augusta

30551 ■ Capitol Clubhouse
37 Stone St.
Augusta, ME 04330
Ph: (207)629-9080
URL: http://www.kbhmaine.oeg

30552 ■ HealthReach Network
9 Green St.
Augusta, ME 04330
Ph: (207)626-3420
URL: http://www.mainegeneral.org/body.cfm?id=481

30553 ■ Kennebec Behavioral Health--Stone Street, Augusta
66 Stone St.
Augusta, ME 04330
Ph: (207)626-3455
Free: 888-322-2136
Fax: (207)626-3612
URL: http://www.kbhmaine.org/locations.html
Formerly: Kennebec Valley Mental Health.

30554 ■ Kennebec Behavioral Health--Western Avenue, Augusta
23 Western Ave.
Augusta, ME 04330
Ph: (207)621-6215
Free: 800-437-1220
URL: http://www.kbhmaine.org

30555 ■ Motivational Services, Inc.
14 Glenridge Dr.
Augusta, ME 04332
Ph: (207)626-3465
Fax: (207)626-3469
E-mail: rweiss@mocomaine.com
URL: http://www.mocomaine.com
Formerly: Clean Sweep/Motivational Services.

30556 ■ Motivational Services, Inc.
Augusta Supported Living Center
10 Noyes Pl.
Augusta, ME 04330
Ph: (207)621-6213
URL: http://www.mocomaine.com

30557 ■ Motivational Services, Inc.
Elm Street House
14 Elm St.
Augusta, ME 04330
Ph: (207)626-3475
URL: http://www.mocomaine.com

30558 ■ Motivational Services, Inc.
Sunrise House
2128 N Belfast Ave.
Augusta, ME 04332
Ph: (207)624-0530
Fax: (207)626-3417
URL: http://www.mocomaine.com

30559 ■ Motivational Services, Inc.
Transitional Intensive Residential
22 Green St.
Augusta, ME 04330
Ph: (207)626-7580
Fax: (207)621-2704
URL: http://www.mocomaine.com

30560 ■ Motivational Services, Inc.
Young Adult Housing and Support Services
22 Green St., Ste. 2
Augusta, ME 04330
Ph: (207)626-3444
Fax: (207)621-2852
URL: http://www.mocomaine.com
Formerly: Pathways to New Horizons.

30561 ■ Togus Veterans Affairs Medical Center
1 VA Center
Augusta, ME 04330
Ph: (207)623-8411
Free: 877-421-8263
URL: http://www.togus.va.gov/

30562 ■ Youth & Family Services--Augusta
72 Wintrop St.
Augusta, ME 04330
Ph: (207)626-3478

Bangor

30563 ■ Bangor Veterans Affairs Clinic
304 Hancock St., Ste. 3B
Bangor, ME 04401
Ph: (207)561-3600
Free: 877-421-8263
Fax: (207)947-1862
URL: http://www.togus.va.gov/visitors/togopc_bangor.asp

30564 ■ Community Health and Counseling Services--Bangor
42 Cedar St.
Bangor, ME 04401
Ph: (207)947-0366
E-mail: dnelson@chcs-me.org
URL: http://www.chcs-me.org

30565 ■ Community Health and Counseling Services
Big Red Redemption Center
12 Barker St.
Bangor, ME 04401-6408
Ph: (207)990-2267
URL: http://www.chcs-me.org

30566 ■ Dorothea Dix Psychiatric Center
656 State St.
Bangor, ME 04402
Ph: (207)941-4000

Belfast

30567 ■ Mid-Coast Mental Health Center
15 Mid Coast Dr.
Belfast, ME 04915
Ph: (207)338-2295
URL: http://www.penbayhealthcare.org/mcmental-health/

Biddeford

30568 ■ Counseling Services, Inc.
Sherry Sabo Center
2 Springbrook Dr.
Biddeford, ME 04005
Ph: (207)282-1500
Fax: (207)282-2581
URL: http://www.counselingservices.org/locations/

Bowdoinham

30569 ■ Perry's Place
336 Fisher Rd.
Bowdoinham, ME 04008
Ph: (207)666-3901

Brewer

30570 ■ Families United
731 Wilson St.
Brewer, ME 04412
Ph: (207)255-3000
E-mail: bfyi2@familiesunited-fyi.org
URL: http://www.familiesunited-fyi.org/

Bridgton

30571 ■ Tri-County Mental Health Services--Bridgton
41 N High St.
Bridgton, ME 04009
Ph: (207)647-5629
Free: 800-286-5629
URL: http://tcmhs.org/pages/ncumberland.php

Calais

30572 ■ Calais Veterans Affairs Clinic
50 Union St.
Calais, ME 04619
Ph: (207)904-3700
Free: 877-421-8263
Fax: (207)904-3778
URL: http://www.togus.va.gov/visitors/togopc_calais.asp

Caribou

30573 ■ AMHC-Crisis Stabilization Unit
43 Vickers Dr.
Caribou, ME 04736
Ph: (207)768-3304
Free: 800-432-7805
Fax: (207)464-6340
URL: http://www.amhc.org/
Formerly: AMHC-New Choices.

30574 ■ AMHC-Vickers Hope
43 Vickers Dr.
Caribou, ME 04736
Ph: (207)498-0922
Fax: (207)498-0922
URL: http://www.amhc.org

30575 ■ Aroostook Mental Health Center--Caribou
24 Sweden St., Ste. 201
Caribou, ME 04736
Ph: (207)493-3361
URL: http://www.amhc.org

Dexter

30576 ■ Northeast Occupational Exchange
51 High St.
Dexter, ME 04930
Ph: (207)924-7470
Free: 800-857-0500
URL: http://www.noemaine.org/

Dover Foxcroft

30577 ■ Charlotte White Administration
572 Bangor Rd.
Dover Foxcroft, ME 04426
Ph: (207)564-2464
Free: 888-440-4158
Fax: (207)564-2404
URL: http://www.charlottewhitecenter.com/

30578 ■ Community Health and Counseling Services--Dover Foxcroft
1093 W Main St.
Dover Foxcroft, ME 04426
Ph: (207)564-8175
URL: http://www.chcs-me.org/

Ellsworth

30579 ■ Community Health and Counseling Services
Adult Mental Health Services
1 High St.
Ellsworth, ME 04605
Ph: (207)667-5357
URL: http://www.chcs-me.org/
Formerly: Adult Mental Health Services.

30580 ■ Families United of Maine
11 Short St.
Ellsworth, ME 04605
Ph: (207)667-3239
Fax: (207)667-0701
URL: http://www.familiesunited-fyi.org/
Formerly: Families United of Washington County.

Falmouth

30581 ■ Girl's Transitional Program
137 Gray Rd.
Falmouth, ME 04102
Ph: (207)797-2933

Farmington

30582 ■ Tri-County Mental Health Services--Farmington
144 High St., Ste. 1
Farmington, ME 04938-1997
Ph: (207)778-2550
Free: 888-568-1112
URL: http://tcmhs.org/pages/franklin.php

Fort Kent

30583 ■ Aroostook Mental Health Center--Fort Kent
139 Market St., Ste. 109
Fort Kent, ME 04743
Ph: (207)834-3186
URL: http://www.amhc.org/

Gardiner

30584 ■ HealthReach Network--HomeCare and Hospice
150 Dresden Ave.
Gardiner, ME 04345
Ph: (207)861-3457
Free: 800-670-6959
URL: http://www.mainegeneral.org/body.cfm?id=481

Grand Isle

30585 ■ AMHC--Grand Isle Family Treatment
49 Cremerio St.
Grand Isle, ME 04746
Ph: (207)895-5290
URL: http://www.amhc.org/
Formerly: Bridge Home.

Houlton

30586 ■ Aroostook Mental Health Center--Houlton
11 Mill St.
Houlton, ME 04730
Ph: (207)532-6523
URL: http://www.amhc.org/

Kittery

30587 ■ Counseling Services, Inc.
CSI at Kittery
453 U.S. Rte. 1
Kittery, ME 03904
Ph: (207)439-8391
Fax: (207)439-4360
URL: http://www.counselingservices.org/locations/

Lewiston

30588 ■ KidsPeace--Lewiston
35 Westminster St., Ste. B
Lewiston, ME 04240
Ph: (207)786-8122
Free: 866-358-2400
Fax: (207)786-8164
URL: http://www.kidspeace.org

30589 ■ Saint Mary's Regional Medical Center
Behavioral Health Services
95 Campus Ave.
Lewiston, ME 04240-6055
Ph: (207)777-8700
URL: http://www.stmarysmaine.com/main-menu-behavioral.html

30590 ■ Spurwink Services, Lewiston
581 Sabattus St.
Lewiston, ME 04240
Ph: (207)795-0419
URL: http://spurwink.org

30591 ■ Tri-County Mental Health Services Crisis Intervention
230 Bartlett St.
Lewiston, ME 04240
Ph: (207)783-4695
Free: 888-304-4673
URL: http://www.tcmhs.org/

30592 ■ Tri-County Mental Health Services Group Home
306 Pine St.
Lewiston, ME 04240
Ph: (207)783-4658
URL: http://www.tcmhs.org/

30593 ■ Tri-County Mental Health Services--Lewiston
1155 Lisbon St.
Lewiston, ME 04210
Ph: (207)783-9141
Free: 888-304-4673
URL: http://www.tcmhs.org/

Limestone

30594 ■ Aroostook Mental Health Center--Limestone
Residential Treatment Facility
582 Main St.
Limestone, ME 04750
Ph: (207)325-4308
URL: http://www.amhc.org/

Lincoln

30595 ■ Community Health and Counseling Services--Lincoln
Rte. 155 Enfield Rd.
Lincoln, ME 04457
Ph: (207)794-3554
URL: http://www.chcs-me.org

30596 ■ Lincoln Veterans Affairs Clinic
99 River Rd.
Lincoln, ME 04457
Ph: (207)403-2000
Free: 877-421-8263
Fax: (207)403-2077
URL: http://www.togus.va.gov/visitors/togopc_Lincoln.asp

Machias

30597 ■ Families United
130 Upper Court St.
Machias, ME 04654
Ph: (207)255-3000
E-mail: execsecy@familiesunited-fyi.org
URL: http://www.familiesunited-fyi.org/

Madawaska

30598 ■ Aroostook Mental Health Center--Madawaska
88 Fox St.
Madawaska, ME 04756
Ph: (207)728-6341
URL: http://www.amhc.org/

30599 ■ Madawaska Group Home
704 Main St.
Madawaska, ME 04756
Ph: (207)728-6727
URL: http://www.amhc.org/

Oxford

30600 ■ Tri-County Mental Health Services Oxford Hills Clinic
143 Pottle Rd.
Oxford, ME 04270
Ph: (207)743-7911
Free: 800-750-7911
URL: http://tcmhs.org/pages/soxford.php

Portland

30601 ■ Shalom House Inc.
PO Box 560
Portland, ME 04112
Ph: (207)874-1080
Fax: (207)874-1077
URL: http://www.shalomhouseinc.org/

30602 ■ Stevens Avenue
824 Stevens Ave.
Portland, ME 04103
Ph: (207)874-1080
Fax: (207)773-2092
URL: http://www.shalomhouseinc.org
Formerly: Robertiello Inc.

30603 ■ Youth Alternatives Ingraham, Inc.
50 Lydia Lane
Portland, ME 04101
Ph: (207)523-5049
Free: 877-429-6884
Fax: (207)874-1181
URL: http://www.yimaine.org

Presque Isle

30604 ■ AMHC-Helpline/ACSU
162 Main St.
Presque Isle, ME 04769
Ph: (207)768-3304
URL: http://www.amhc.org/
Formerly: AMHC-Helpline/TRU.

30605 ■ AMHC Skyhaven
2 Airport Dr.
Presque Isle, ME 04769
Ph: (207)764-0759
URL: http://www.amhc.org/

Rockland

30606 ■ Mid-Coast Mental Health Center
12 Union St.
Rockland, ME 04841
Ph: (207)701-4400
URL: http://www.penbayhealthcare.org/mcmental-health/

Rumford

30607 ■ Oxford County Mental Health Services
150 Congress St.
Rumford, ME 04276
Ph: (207)364-3549
Fax: (207)364-2143
E-mail: info@ocmhs.org
URL: http://www.ocmhs.org/

30608 ■ Rumford Veterans Affairs Clinic
431 Franklin St.
Rumford, ME 04276
Ph: (207)369-3200
Free: 877-421-8263
Fax: (207)369-3277
URL: http://www.togus.va.gov/visitors/togopc_rumford.asp

30609 ■ Tri-County Mental Health Services--Rumford
49 Congress St.
Rumford, ME 04276
Ph: (207)364-7981
Free: 800-371-7981
Fax: (207)364-7983
URL: http://tcmhs.org/pages/noxford.php

Sabattus

30610 ■ Kelley Drive Home
46 Kelley Dr.
Sabattus, ME 04280
Ph: (207)375-8920
Free: 877-671-8038
Fax: (207)375-8924
URL: http://tcmhs.org/pages/housing.php

Saco

30611 ■ Counseling Services, Inc. CSI at Beach St.
31 Beach St.
Saco, ME 04072
Ph: (207)282-1500
Fax: (207)282-6606
URL: http://www.counselingservices.org/locations/

30612 ■ Sacro Veterans Affairs Clinic
655 Main St.
Saco, ME 04072
Ph: (207)294-3100
Free: 877-421-8263
Fax: (207)286-3709
URL: http://www.togus.va.gov/visitors/togopc_saco.asp

Skowhegan

30613 ■ Kennebec Behavioral Health--Skowhegan
30 High St.
Skowhegan, ME 04976
Ph: (207)474-8368
Free: 888-322-2136
URL: http://www.kbhmaine.org/locations.html
Formerly: Kennebec Valley Mental Health.

South Bend

30614 ■ Long Creek Youth Development Center
675 Westbrook St.
South Bend, ME 04106
Ph: (207)822-2600
Fax: (207)822-2775
URL: http://www.maine.gov/corrections/juvenile/Facilities/LCYDC/index.htm
Formerly: One Day--Long Creek Youth Development Center.

South Paris

30615 ■ Oxford County Mental Health Services
17 Gary St.
South Paris, ME 04281
Ph: (207)743-6161
Fax: (207)743-2999
E-mail: info@ocmhs.org
URL: http://www.ocmhs.org/

South Portland

30616 ■ Day One
525 Main St.
South Portland, ME 04106
Ph: (207)874-1045
Fax: (207)767-0995
E-mail: lisam@day-one.org
URL: http://www.day-one.org/

30617 ■ Heritage House--South Portland
677 Westbrook St.
South Portland, ME 04106
Ph: (207)842-6886

30618 ■ Spurwink Services, South Portland
341 Pine St.
South Portland, ME 04106
Ph: (207)871-1205
URL: http://spurwink.org

Springvale

30619 ■ Counseling Services, Inc. CSI at Springvale Square
474 Main St.
Springvale, ME 04083
Ph: (207)324-1500
Fax: (207)490-5263
URL: http://www.counselingservices.org/locations/

Waterville

30620 ■ Kennebec Behavioral Health--Waterville
67 Eustis Pkwy.
Waterville, ME 04901
Ph: (207)873-2136
Free: 888-322-2136
URL: http://www.kbhmaine.org/locations.html
Formerly: Kennebec Valley Mental Health.

Westbrook

30621 ■ Counseling Services, Inc. CSI at Westbrook
12 Westbrook Common
Westbrook, ME 04092
Ph: (207)282-6136
Fax: (207)856-1518
URL: http://www.counselingservices.org/locations/

Wilton

30622 ■ Care & Comfort
280 Main St., Ste. 190
Wilton, ME 04294
Ph: (207)645-5304
Free: 800-366-5302
Fax: (207)645-3277
URL: http://www.careandcomfort.com/

Windham

30623 ■ Tri County Mental Health Services
744 Roosevelt Trail
Windham, ME 04062
Ph: (207)892-4623
Fax: (207)892-5317
URL: http://tcmhs.org

MARYLAND

Aberdeen

30624 ■ Alliance, Inc.--Aberdeen
28 N Philadelphia Blvd.
Aberdeen, MD 21001
Ph: (410)273-1399
URL: http://www.allianceinc.org/

30625 ■ Key Point Health Services--Aberdeen
135 N Parke St.
Aberdeen, MD 21001
Ph: (443)625-1600
URL: http://www.keypoint.org/locations.asp

Annapolis

30626 ■ Psychotherapeutic Treatment Services
839 Bestgate Rd.
Annapolis, MD 21401
Ph: (410)224-1188
Fax: (410)571-6642
E-mail: pssmaaco@ps-corp.net
URL: http://www.psychotherapeuticservices.com/programs/pssomannapolis.htm

Baltimore

30627 ■ Alliance
234 S Broadway
Baltimore, MD 21231
Ph: (410)675-4704
Fax: (410)675-4996
URL: http://www.allianceinc.org

30628 ■ Baltimore Veterans Affairs Medical Center
10 N Greene St.
Baltimore, MD 21201
Ph: (410)605-7000
Free: 800-463-6295
URL: http://www.maryland.va.gov/facilities/Baltimore_VA_Medical_Center.asp
Remarks: Facility is home base for one of the VA's eight Mental Illness Research, Education and Clinical Centers dedicated to improving the provision of health care to veterans suffering from severe mental illness, with a special emphasis on the treatment of individuals with schizophrenia.

30629 ■ Bon Secours Community Institute of Behavioral Health
2000 W Baltimore St.
Baltimore, MD 21223
Ph: (410)362-3000
URL: http://bonsecoursbaltimore.com/
Formerly: Liberty Medical Center.

30630 ■ Fellowship House, Inc.--Baltimore
707 Saint Paul St.
Baltimore, MD 21202-2356
Ph: (410)752-6448
E-mail: fellowshiphouse@cbhhealth.com
URL: http://sites.google.com/site/cbhweb/home

30631 ■ Forbush School
407 Central Ave.
Baltimore, MD 21136
Ph: (410)517-5400
Fax: (410)517-5600
URL: http://www.sheppardpratt.org/sp_htmlcode/sp_locations/sp_loc_balt_forb.aspx

30632 ■ Harbor City Unlimited
1227 W Pratt St.
Baltimore, MD 21223
Ph: (410)328-8559
URL: http://www.umm.edu

30633 ■ Key Point Health Services--Baltimore
1012 N Point Rd.
Baltimore, MD 21222
Ph: (443)216-4800
URL: http://www.keypoint.org/locations.asp

30634 ■ Loch Raven Veterans Affairs Outpatient Clinic
3901 The Alameda
Baltimore, MD 21218
Ph: (410)605-7650
Free: 800-463-6295
URL: http://www.maryland.va.gov/facilities/Loch_Raven.asp

30635 ■ The North Baltimore Center Booker T. Middle School
1301 McCulloh St.
Baltimore, MD 21217-3044
Ph: (410)396-7734
URL: http://www.northbaltimorecenter.org/

30636 ■ The North Baltimore Center, Inc.
2225 N Charles St.
Baltimore, MD 21218
Ph: (410)366-4360
URL: http://www.northbaltimorecenter.org/

Bel Air

30637 ■ Alliance, Inc.--Bel Air
4 North Ave.
Bel Air, MD 21014
Ph: (410)420-7292
Fax: (410)420-7276
URL: http://www.allianceinc.org/index.php/Locations.html

Belcamp

30638 ■ Alliance, Inc.--Belcamp
4510 Wharf Point Ct.
Belcamp, MD 21017
Ph: (410)994-0600
Fax: (410)994-0274
URL: http://www.allianceinc.org/index.php/Locations.html

Bethesda

30639 ■ Saint Luke's House, Inc. Southport Residential
6036 6034 6032 Southport Dr.
Bethesda, MD 20814
Ph: (301)530-3643
URL: http://www.stlukeshouse.org/

Cambridge

30640 ■ Cambridge Veterans Affairs Outpatient Clinic
830 Chesapeake Dr.
Cambridge, MD 21613
Ph: (410)228-6243
Free: 877-864-9611
URL: http://www.maryland.va.gov/facilities/cambridge.asp

30641 ■ Channel Marker, Inc.--Cambridge
420 Dorchester Ave.
Cambridge, MD 21613
Ph: (410)288-8330
URL: http://www.channelmarker.org/

30642 ■ Crossroads Community, Inc.--Cambridge
404 LeCompte St.
Cambridge, MD 21613
Ph: (410)221-7540
URL: http://www.ccinconline.com/

Catonsville

30643 ■ The Children's Home
205 Bloomsbury Ave.
Catonsville, MD 21228
Ph: (410)744-7310

30644 ■ Key Point Health Services, Inc.--Catonsville Outpatient Clinic
500 N Rolling Rd.
Catonsville, MD 21228
Ph: (410)788-0300
Fax: (410)869-7244
URL: http://www.keypoint.org/locations.asp

Centreville

30645 ■ Crossroads Community, Inc.--Centreville
120 Banjo Ln.
Centreville, MD 21617
Ph: (410)758-3050
URL: http://www.ccinconline.com/

Chestertown

30646 ■ Psychotherapeutic Services
870-2 High St.
Chestertown, MD 21620
Ph: (410)778-1933
Fax: (410)778-9668
E-mail: mdcorp@ps-corp.net
URL: http://www.psychotherapeuticservices.com/mdcorp.htm

Columbia

30647 ■ Alliance, Inc.--Howard County
10632 Little Patuxent Pkwy.
Columbia, MD 21044
Ph: (410)992-4994
Fax: (410)992-0180
URL: http://www.allianceinc.org/index.php/Locations.html

30648 ■ Way Station, Inc.--Howard County
9030 Rte. 108, Ste. A
Columbia, MD 21044
Ph: (410)740-1901
URL: http://www.waystationinc.org/index.htm

Cumberland

30649 ■ Cumberland Veterans Affairs Clinic
200 Clenn St.
Cumberland, MD 21502
Ph: (301)724-0061
URL: http://www.martinsburg.va.gov/visitors/cumberland.asp

Denton

30650 ■ Channel Marker, Inc.--Denton
508 Kerr Ave.
Denton, MD 21629
Ph: (410)479-2318
URL: http://www.channelmarker.org/

Dundalk

30651 ■ Alliance, Inc.--Dundalk
7701 Wise Ave., Ste. 206
Dundalk, MD 21222-3228
Ph: (410)282-5900
Fax: (410)282-1788
URL: http://www.allianceinc.org/index.php/Locations.html

30652 ■ Key Point Health Services, Inc.--Dundalk
Outpatient Clinic
7701 Dunman Way
Dundalk, MD 21222-5437
Ph: (410)282-1792
URL: http://www.keypoint.org

Easton

30653 ■ Channel Marker, Inc.--Easton
222 Port St.
Easton, MD 21601
Ph: (410)822-4611
URL: http://www.channelmarker.org/

Elkton

30654 ■ Upper Bay Counseling and Support Services
200 Booth St.
Elkton, MD 21921
Ph: (410)996-5104
Free: 800-467-0304
URL: http://www.upperbay.org/index.htm

Forestville

30655 ■ Vesta
3900 Forestville Rd.
Forestville, MD 20747
Ph: (301)736-2636
Fax: (301)736-2405
URL: http://www.vesta.org

Fort Howard

30656 ■ Fort Howard Veterans Affairs Clinic
9600 N Point Rd.
Fort Howard, MD 21052
Ph: (410)477-1800
Free: 800-351-8387
URL: http://www.maryland.va.gov/facilities/Fort_Howard.asp

Frederick

30657 ■ Way Station, Inc.
230 W Patrick St.
Frederick, MD 21701
Ph: (301)662-0099
URL: http://www.waystationinc.org

30658 ■ Way Station, Inc.
Residential Crisis Program
1625 Shookstown Rd.
Frederick, MD 21702
Ph: (301)662-0099
URL: http://www.waystationinc.org

Gaithersburg

30659 ■ Family Services Agency, Inc.
610 E Diamond Ave., Ste. 100
Gaithersburg, MD 20877-5321
Ph: (301)840-2000
URL: http://www.familyservicesagency.org

Glen Burnie

30660 ■ Glen Burnie Veterans Affairs Clinic
808 Landmark Dr., Ste. 128
Glen Burnie, MD 21061
Ph: (410)590-4140
URL: http://www.maryland.va.gov/facilities/Glen_Burnie.asp

30661 ■ Omni House, Inc.
1421 Madison Park Dr.
Glen Burnie, MD 21060
Ph: (410)768-6777
URL: http://www.omnihouse.org/

30662 ■ Omni House, Inc.
Day Program
9 3rd Ave. SW
Glen Burnie, MD 21061
Ph: (410)768-6778
URL: http://www.omnihouse.org/

30663 ■ Omni House, Inc.
Omni Mental Health Clinic
1419 Madison Park Dr., 2nd Fl.
Glen Burnie, MD 21061
Ph: (410)768-2719
URL: http://www.omnihouse.org/

Hagerstown

30664 ■ Hagerstown Veterans Affairs Clinic
1101 Opal
Hagerstown, MD 21742
Ph: (301)665-1462
Fax: (301)665-1682
URL: http://www.martinsburg.va.gov/visitors/hagerstown.asp

30665 ■ The Mental Health Center
1180 Professional Ct.
Hagerstown, MD 21740
Ph: (301)791-3045
URL: http://www.thementalhealthcenter.net/

30666 ■ Turning Point of Washington County, Inc.
25 E North Ave.
Hagerstown, MD 21740
Ph: (301)733-6063
URL: http://www.waystationinc.org/index.htm

Kensington

30667 ■ Saint Luke's House, Inc.
Parkwood House
10615 Parkwood Dr.
Kensington, MD 20895
Ph: (301)897-5525
URL: http://www.stlukeshouse.org/

Landover

30668 ■ Psychiatric Rehabilitation Services
337 Brightseat Rd., Ste. 106
Landover, MD 20785
Ph: (301)499-6781
Fax: (301)499-1448
URL: http://www.psychotherapeuticservices.com/mdpgprp.htm

Lanham

30669 ■ Vesta, Inc. - Lenham Region
10123 Senate Dr.
Lanham, MD 20706-4367
Ph: (301)459-9840
Fax: (301)459-4856
URL: http://www.vesta.org

Mardela Springs

30670 ■ Maple Shade Youth & Family Services, Inc.
23704 Ocean Gateway
Mardela Springs, MD 21837
Ph: (410)742-7400
URL: http://www.maple-shade.org/

Newark

30671 ■ Go-Getters, Inc.
7033 Worcester Hwy.
Newark, MD 21841
Ph: (410)632-3737
URL: http://www.gogettersinc.org/newark.htm

North Bethesda

30672 ■ Saint Luke's House, Inc.
6040 Southport Dr.
North Bethesda, MD 20814
Ph: (301)493-4200
URL: http://www.stlukeshouse.org/contact_stlukes.html

Odenton

30673 ■ Vesta, Inc. - Odenton Region
1202 Annapolis Rd., Ste. F
Odenton, MD 21113-1387
Ph: (410)672-2862
URL: http://www.vesta.org

Oxon Hill

30674 ■ Vesta
Extended Care Facility
4615 Wheeler Hills Rd.
Oxon Hill, MD 20745-4202
Ph: (301)505-1700
Fax: (301)505-0030
URL: http://www.vesta.org

Perry Point

30675 ■ Perry Point Veterans Affairs Center
Broad St.
Perry Point, MD 21902
Ph: (410)642-2411
Free: 800-949-1003
URL: http://www.maryland.va.gov/facilities/Perry_Point_VA_Medical_Center.asp

Pikesville

30676 ■ Prologue, Inc.--Pikesville
3 Milford Mill Rd.
Pikesville, MD 21208
Ph: (410)653-6190
URL: http://www.prologueinc.org/

Pocomoke City

30677 ■ Pocomoke City Veterans Affairs Clinic
101 Market St.
Pocomoke City, MD 21851
Ph: (410)957-6718
Free: 866-441-0287
URL: http://www.maryland.va.gov/facilities/Pocomoke.asp

Princess Anne

30678 ■ Go-Getters, Inc.--Day Program
11559 Somerset Ave.
Princess Anne, MD 21853
Ph: (410)651-1547
URL: http://www.gogettersinc.org/princessanne.htm

Rockville

30679 ■ The Frost School
4915 Aspen Hill Rd.
Rockville, MD 20853
Ph: (301)933-3452
Fax: (301)933-0350
URL: http://www.frostcenter.com/index.html

Salisbury

30680 ■ Beacon Place
801 Johnson St.
Salisbury, MD 21804
Ph: (410)546-8125
URL: http://www.gogettersinc.org/beacon.htm

30681 ■ Go-Getters, Inc.--Lower Shore Clinic
505 E Main St.
Salisbury, MD 21804
Ph: (410)546-0381
URL: http://www.gogettersinc.org/lowershoreclinic.htm

30682 ■ Go-Getters, Inc.--Peer Connection
108 W Lehigh Ave.
Salisbury, MD 21801
Ph: (410)546-1822
URL: http://www.gogettersinc.org/peerconnection.htm

Silver Spring

30683 ■ Threshold Services, Inc.
1398 Lamberton Dr.
Silver Spring, MD 20902
Ph: (301)754-1102
Fax: (301)754-1690
URL: http://www.thresholdservices.org

Sykesville

30684 ■ Prologue, Inc.--Sykesville
6162 Timdan Ct.
Sykesville, MD 21784
Ph: (410)549-3508
Fax: (410)549-6510
URL: http://www.prologueinc.org/loca.html

Waldorf

30685 ■ Vesta, Inc.--Waldorf Region
22A Industrial Park Dr.
Waldorf, MD 20602
Ph: (301)638-7543
URL: http://www.vesta.org/

Westminster

30686 ■ Autumn Woods at Vesta, Inc.
2470 Collison Dr.
Westminster, MD 21157
Ph: (410)871-0967
URL: http://www.vesta.org/

MASSACHUSETTS

Acton

30687 ■ Advocates, Inc.--Acton
179 Great Rd., Ste. 220
Acton, MA 01720
Ph: (508)620-0024
URL: http://www.advocatesinc.org

30688 ■ Eliot Community Human Services Concord Road
27 Concord Rd.
Acton, MA 01720
Ph: (978)369-1113

30689 ■ Eliot Community Human Services Wright Terrace
2 Wright Terr.
Acton, MA 01720
Ph: (978)369-1113

Arlington

30690 ■ The Edinburg Center, Inc.--Arlington
742 Massachusetts Ave.
Arlington, MA 02476
Ph: (781)646-7301
Fax: (781)643-8726
URL: http://www.edinburgcenter.org/
Formerly: Center for Mental Health/Mental Retardation Services.

30691 ■ Eliot Community Human Services Willow Court
9 Willow Ct.
Arlington, MA 02476
Ph: (781)643-9944

30692 ■ Wild Acre Inns, Inc.
108 Pleasant St.
Arlington, MA 02476
Ph: (781)643-0643
Free: 800-750-0236
URL: http://www.wildacreinns.com/

Ashland

30693 ■ Advocates, Inc. Day Habilitation Services
250 Eliot St.
Ashland, MA 01721
Ph: (508)881-6494
URL: http://www.advocatesinc.org/locations.htm

Attleboro

30694 ■ Community Care Services Attleboro Clinic
140 Park St.
Attleboro, MA 02703
Ph: (508)226-6031
URL: http://www.communitycareservices.org/

30695 ■ Corner Clubhouse Community Care Services
247 Maple St.
Attleboro, MA 02703
Ph: (508)431-4100
URL: http://www.communitycareservices.org/

30696 ■ South Bay Mental Health Center
67 Mechanics St.
Attleboro, MA 02703
Ph: (508)223-4691
URL: http://www.southbaymentalhealth.com/

Ayer

30697 ■ Ayer Outreach Site
34 Main St., 2nd Fl.
Ayer, MA 01432
Ph: (508)628-6300
URL: http://www.advocatesinc.org/locations.htm

Bedford

30698 ■ The Edinburg Center, Inc.--Bedford
20 Railroad Ave., Ste. B
Bedford, MA 01730
Ph: (781)862-3600
URL: http://www.edinburgcenter.org/
Formerly: Center for Mental Health/Mental Retardation Services.

30699 ■ Edith Nourse Rogers Memorial Veterans Hospital
200 Springs Rd.
Bedford, MA 01730
Ph: (781)687-2000
Free: 800--VETMED1
URL: http://www.bedford.va.gov/

Bellingham

30700 ■ Advocates, Inc.--Bellingham
Maple St.
Bellingham, MA 02019
Ph: (508)966-4820
URL: http://www.advocatesinc.org

30701 ■ Riverside Community Care--Urgent Care Center
16 North St.
Bellingham, MA 02019
Ph: (508)883-1308
E-mail: Bellingham.outpatient@riversidecc.org
URL: http://www.riversidecc.org/soucent.html

Berkley

30702 ■ Lindencroft Program Community Care Services, Inc.
587 Berkley St.
Berkley, MA 02779
Ph: (508)880-0883
URL: http://www.communitycareservices.org/
Formerly: ComCare Services, Inc.

Beverly

30703 ■ Health and Education Services, Inc.
131 Rantoul St.
Beverly, MA 01915
Ph: (978)921-1293
Free: 877-255-1261
URL: http://www.hes-inc.org/

30704 ■ Health and Education Services, Inc. Adolescent Crisis Center for Evaluation
6 Echo Ave.
Beverly, MA 01915
Ph: (978)921-7907
URL: http://www.hes-inc.org/

30705 ■ Health and Education Services, Inc. Bridgeview Residential Home
11 Congress St.
Beverly, MA 01915
Ph: (978)922-3825
URL: http://www.hes-inc.org/

30706 ■ Health and Education Services, Inc. Cape Ann Adult Treatment Center
133 Rantoul St.
Beverly, MA 01915
Ph: (978)524-7133
URL: http://www.hes-inc.org/

30707 ■ Health and Education Services, Inc. The Center for Family Development
800 Cummings Center, Ste. 266T
Beverly, MA 01915
Ph: (978)921-1190
URL: http://www.hes-inc.org/

30708 ■ Health and Education Services, Inc. Harmony House
325 Rantoul St.
Beverly, MA 01915

Ph: (978)927-8437
URL: http://www.hes-inc.org/

30709 ■ Health and Education Services, Inc. Rantoul Garden
329 Rantoul St.
Beverly, MA 01915
Ph: (978)927-2890
URL: http://www.hes-inc.org/

Blackstone

30710 ■ Advocates, Inc.--Blackstone
29/31 Residential Ln.
Blackstone, MA 01504
Ph: (508)620-0024
URL: http://www.advocatesinc.org

Boston

30711 ■ Bay Cove Human Services, Inc.
66 Canal St.
Boston, MA 02114
Ph: (617)371-3000
Fax: (617)371-3100
E-mail: baycove@baycove.org
URL: http://www.baycove.org

30712 ■ Bay Cove Human Services, Inc. Center House
11 Bowker St
Boston, MA 02114
Ph: (617)371-3020
E-mail: baycove@baycove.org
URL: http://www.baycove.org
Formerly: Psychiatric Day Treatment Program.

30713 ■ Center for Health and Development, Inc.--Boston
10 Winter Pl., Ste. 3
Boston, MA 02108
Ph: (617)357-0224
Fax: (617)357-8161
URL: http://www.centerforhealth.org

30714 ■ Erich Lindemann Mental Health
25 Staniford St.
Boston, MA 02114
Ph: (617)626-8514

30715 ■ North Suffolk Mental Health Association Boston Emergency Service Team
25 Staniford St.
Boston, MA 02114
Ph: (617)912-7800
URL: http://www.northsuffolk.org/

30716 ■ North Suffolk Mental Health Association Harbor Area Early Childhood Services
530 Border St.
Boston, MA 02128
Ph: (617)569-6560
URL: http://www.northsuffolk.org/

30717 ■ Safe Home Program
15 Newbury St.
Boston, MA 02116
Ph: (617)236-8390

30718 ■ South End Community Health Center
1601 Washington St.
Boston, MA 02118
Ph: (617)425-2000
URL: http://www.sechc.org/

30719 ■ Veterans Affairs Boston Healthcare System Jamaica Plain Division
150 S Huntington Ave.
Boston, MA 02130
Ph: (617)232-9500
Free: 800-865-3384
URL: http://www.boston.va.gov/

Brewster

30720 ■ South Shore Mental Health--Bayview Associates
11 Baystate Ct.
Brewster, MA 02631
Ph: (508)247-3005
URL: http://www.bayviewassociates.org/

Brockton

30721 ■ Brockton Area Multi-Services
10 Christy's Dr.
Brockton, MA 02301
Ph: (508)580-8700
Fax: (508)580-3114
E-mail: services@bamsi.org
URL: http://www.bamsi.org

30722 ■ Brockton Multi-Service Center
165 Quincy St.
Brockton, MA 02302
Ph: (508)897-2000
URL: http://www.bamsi.org

30723 ■ South Bay Early Intervention
1115 W Chestnut St.
Brockton, MA 02301
Ph: (508)559-0473
URL: http://www.southbaymentalhealth.com/

30724 ■ Veterans Affairs Boston Healthcare System Brockton Division
940 Belmont St.
Brockton, MA 02301
Ph: (508)583-4500
Free: 800-865-3384
URL: http://www.boston.va.gov/

Brookline

30725 ■ Brookline Community Mental Health Center
41 Garrison Rd.
Brookline, MA 02445
Ph: (617)277-8107
URL: http://www.brooklinecenter.org/

Burlington

30726 ■ Eliot Community Human Services Northeastern Avenue
2 Northeastern Ave.
Burlington, MA 01803
Ph: (781)270-9196

Cambridge

30727 ■ North Suffolk Mental Health Association--PACT
23 East St., 3rd Fl.
Cambridge, MA 02141
Ph: (617)621-0090
URL: http://www.northsuffolk.org/

Cataumet

30728 ■ Gosnold Treatment Center
1140 Rte. 28A
Cataumet, MA 02534
Ph: (800)444-1554
URL: http://www.gosnold.org/

Chelmsford

30729 ■ Seven Hills Behavioral Health, Inc.--Chelmsford
7 Summer St., Ste. 19
Chelmsford, MA 01824
Ph: (978)256-1444
URL: http://www.sevenhills.org/aboutUs/direcLoc.php

Chelsea

30730 ■ Chelsea Counseling Center
301 Broadway
Chelsea, MA 02150
Ph: (617)889-4860
URL: http://www.northsuffolk.org

30731 ■ North Suffolk Mental Health Association, Inc.--Chelsea
297 Broadway
Chelsea, MA 02150-2807
Ph: (617)889-4860
Fax: (617)889-4635
URL: http://www.northsuffolk.org

Chicopee

30732 ■ Hawthorn Services, Inc.
93 Main St.
Chicopee, MA 01020
Ph: (413)592-5199
URL: http://www.hawthornservices.org/

Clinton

30733 ■ Clinton Outpatient Clinic
221 Greeley St.
Clinton, MA 01510
Ph: (978)368-0181
URL: http://www.communityhealthlink.org/

Concord

30734 ■ Eliot Community Human Services Old Concord Road
Old Concord Rd.
Concord, MA 01742
Ph: (978)369-1113
Fax: (978)369-0908
URL: http://www.eliotchs.org

Dedham

30735 ■ Riverside Community Care
450 Washington St.
Dedham, MA 02026
Ph: (781)329-0909
E-mail: administration@riversidecc.org
URL: http://www.riversidecc.org

30736 ■ Riverside Community Care Milton Street
307 Milton St.
Dedham, MA 02026
Ph: (781)326-1667
E-mail: administration@riversidecc.org
URL: http://www.riversidecc.org

Deham

30737 ■ Riverside Community Care Unity Place
525 Washington St.
Deham, MA 02026
Ph: (781)320-8480
E-mail: administration@riversidecc.org
URL: http://www.riversidecc.org

Dennisport

30738 ■ Clipper Lane Residence
150 Upper County Rd.
Dennisport, MA 02639
Ph: (508)760-1071

Dorchester

30739 ■ Dorchester House Multi-Service
1353 Dorchester Ave.
Dorchester, MA 02122
Ph: (617)288-3230
URL: http://www.dorchesterhouse.org/

Douglas

30740 ■ Riverside Community Care Family and Social Support
112 Vine St.
Douglas, MA 01516
Ph: (508)476-1787
URL: http://www.riversidecc.org/

East Boston

30741 ■ Meridian House
408 Meridian St.
East Boston, MA 02128
Ph: (617)569-6050
URL: http://www.northsuffolk.org/

Fall River

30742 ■ Doctor John C. Corrigan Mental Health Center
49 Hillside St.
Fall River, MA 02720
Ph: (508)235-7200

30743 ■ May Institute--Fall River Behavioral Health Services
37 Purchase St.
Fall River, MA 02720-3109
Ph: (508)675-5888
URL: http://www.mayinstitute.org/
Formerly: May Behavioral Health.

30744 ■ Seven Hills Foundation Mental Health Services
1402 Pleasant St.
Fall River, MA 02723
Ph: (508)679-0962
URL: http://www.sevenhills.org/about_dir.html

Falmouth

30745 ■ Bayberry House
61 Rose Morin Ln.
Falmouth, MA 02540
Ph: (508)540-1194

30746 ■ Cape Cod Human Services
270 Teaticket Hwy.
Falmouth, MA 02536
Ph: (508)862-7484

30747 ■ Gosnold, Inc.
200 Ter Heun Dr.
Falmouth, MA 02540
Ph: (508)540-6550
Free: 800-444-1554
URL: http://gosnold.org/

Feeding Hills

30748 ■ Agawam Counseling Center
30 Southwick St.
Feeding Hills, MA 01030
Ph: (413)786-6410
Formerly: Agawam Counseling Enter.

Fitchburg

30749 ■ Fitchburg Veterans Affairs Clinic
Burbank Hospital
275 Nichols Rd.
Fitchburg, MA 01420
Free: 800--VETMED1
Fax: (978)342-9521
URL: http://www.bedford.va.gov/bedopc_fitch.asp

30750 ■ LUK, Inc.
545 Westminster St.
Fitchburg, MA 01420
Ph: (978)345-0685
Fax: (978)345-3602
E-mail: info@luk.org
URL: http://www.luk.org

Framingham

30751 ■ Advocates, Inc. Advocates Community Counseling Center
345 Waverly St.
Framingham, MA 01702
Ph: (508)661-2020
Fax: (508)661-2024
URL: http://www.advocatesinc.org

30752 ■ Advocates, Inc.--Framingham
1 Clarks Hill, Ste. 305
Framingham, MA 01702
Ph: (508)628-6300
URL: http://www.advocatesinc.org

30753 ■ Framingham Veterans Affairs Clinic
61 Lincoln St., Ste. 112
Framingham, MA 01702
Ph: (508)628-0205
Fax: (508)628-8224
URL: http://www.boston.va.gov/bwropc_fram.asp

30754 ■ Harbinger House Wayside Youth and Family Support Network
85 Edgell Rd.
Framingham, MA 01701
Ph: (508)872-5665
URL: http://www.waysideyouth.org/joomla/

30755 ■ Key Program, Inc.--Framingham
670 Old Connecticut Path
Framingham, MA 01701
Ph: (508)877-3690
Fax: (508)366-9524
URL: http://www.key.org

30756 ■ South Middlesex Opportunity Council
300 Howard St.
Framingham, MA 01702
Ph: (508)620-2645
URL: http://www.smoc.org/

30757 ■ Wayside Metrowest Counseling Center
88 Lincoln St.
Framingham, MA 01702
Ph: (508)620-0010
URL: http://www.waysideyouth.org
Formerly: Wayside Family Counseling.

30758 ■ Wayside Youth and Family Support Network
75 Fountain St.
Framingham, MA 01702-6210
Ph: (508)879-9800
URL: http://www.waysideyouth.org

Franklin

30759 ■ Riverside Community Care Brook Street
192 Brook St.
Franklin, MA 02038
Ph: (508)541-6132
URL: http://www.riversidecc.org/

Gardner

30760 ■ North Central Human Services--Gardner
31 Lake Ave.
Gardner, MA 01440
Ph: (978)632-9400

Gloucester

30761 ■ Health & Education Services, Inc. Gloucester Clinic
298 Washington St., 2nd Fl.
Gloucester, MA 01930
Ph: (978)283-0296
URL: http://www.hes-inc.org/

Great Barrington

30762 ■ Main Street Human Resources The Brien Center
60 Cottage St.
Great Barrington, MA 01230
Ph: (413)528-9156
URL: http://www.briencenter.org/

Greenfield

30763 ■ Clinical Support and Options
13 Prospect St.
Greenfield, MA 01301
Ph: (413)774-1001
URL: http://www.csoinc.org/

30764 ■ ServiceNet, Inc. Greenfield Shelter
219 Silver St.
Greenfield, MA 01301
Ph: (413)584-7329
URL: http://www.servicenetinc.org
Formerly: Shelter.

Harwichport

30765 ■ Harwichport Clubhouse
383 Rte. 28
Harwichport, MA 02646
Ph: (508)984-4300

Haverhill

30766 ■ Haverhill Clinic
60 Merrimack St.
Haverhill, MA 01830
Ph: (978)373-1126

Holyoke

30767 ■ Center for Youth and Family Services
368 Maple St.
Holyoke, MA 01040
Ph: (413)536-2435
URL: http://www.chd.org/
Formerly: Center for Adolescent Resource.

30768 ■ CHD, Inc. Community Support Program
494 Appleton St.
Holyoke, MA 01040
Ph: (413)532-1456
Fax: (413)534-9044
URL: http://www.chd.org/program_details.asp?program=13&pf=6

30769 ■ Mount Tom Mental Health Center
40 Bobala Rd.
Holyoke, MA 01040
Ph: (413)536-5473
URL: http://www.bhninc.org/

Hyannis

30770 ■ Cape Cod and Islands Community Mental Health Center--Hyannis
77 High School Rd. Ext.
Hyannis, MA 02601
Ph: (508)957-0900

30771 ■ South Shore Mental Health Cape Services
310 Barnstable Rd.
Hyannis, MA 02601
Ph: (508)775-5814

Ipswich

30772 ■ Cornerstone Day School
35 Mitchell Rd.
Ipswich, MA 01938
Ph: (978)356-9321
URL: http://www.hes-inc.org/

30773 ■ Health & Education Services, Inc. Ipswich Clinic
25R Market St.
Ipswich, MA 01938
Ph: (978)356-1776
URL: http://www.hes-inc.org/

Jamaica Plain

30774 ■ Massachusetts Mental Health Center
180 Morton St.
Jamaica Plain, MA 02130
Ph: (617)626-9300

30775 ■ Michael J. Gill Rehabilitation Center
284 Amory St.
Jamaica Plain, MA 02130
Ph: (617)522-8110
Fax: (617)522-0070
URL: http://www.baycove.org

Lawrence

30776 ■ The Psychological Center
11 Union St.
Lawrence, MA 01840
Ph: (978)685-1337
Free: 888-522-1288
URL: http://www.tpc1.org/

Leeds

30777 ■ Northampton Veterans Affairs Medical Center
421 N Main St.
Leeds, MA 01053
Ph: (413)584-4040
Free: 800-893-1522
Fax: (413)582-3121
URL: http://www.northampton.va.gov/

Lexington

30778 ■ The Edinburg Center, Inc.--Lexington
1040 Waltham St.
Lexington, MA 02421
Ph: (781)862-3600
URL: http://www.edinburgcenter.org/
Formerly: The center for mental help and retardation.

30779 ■ Eliot Community Human Services Bedford Street
186 Bedford St.
Lexington, MA 02420
Ph: (781)861-0890
URL: http://www.eliotchs.org/

Lowell

30780 ■ Mental Health Association of Greater Lowell
99 Church St.
Lowell, MA 01852
Ph: (978)458-6282
URL: http://www.mhalowell.org/

30781 ■ Renaissance Club, Inc.
176 Walker St.
Lowell, MA 01854
Ph: (978)454-7944
E-mail: info@renclublowell.org
URL: http://www.renclublowell.org/

Lynn

30782 ■ Lynn Community Health Center
269 Union St.
Lynn, MA 01901
Ph: (781)581-3900
URL: http://www.lchcnet.org/

30783 ■ Tri-City Mental Health/Mental Retardation Center, Inc.
95 Pleasant St.
Lynn, MA 01901
Ph: (781)596-9200
Free: 800-988-1111
URL: http://www.eliotchs.org/
Remarks: Merged with Eliot Community Human Services.

Malden

30784 ■ Eliot Community Human Services Congregate Lodge
14 Clement St., Apt. 16
Malden, MA 02148-8223
Ph: (781)397-2131
URL: http://www.eliotchs.org/
Formerly: Tri-City Mental Health/Mental Retardation Center, Inc.

Marion

30785 ■ Seven Hills Behavioral Health, Inc.--Marion
345 Front St.
Marion, MA 02738
Ph: (508)748-3749
URL: http://www.sevenhills.org/aboutUs/direcLoc.php

Marlboro

30786 ■ Advocates, Inc. Windward Program
6 Warren Ave.
Marlboro, MA 01752
Ph: (508)303-2937
URL: http://www.advocatesinc.org/

Marlborough

30787 ■ Advocates, Inc. Community Counseling
340 Maple St., 4th Fl.
Marlborough, MA 01752
Ph: (508)485-9300
URL: http://www.advocatesinc.org/Directions-ACC-Marlboro.htm

30788 ■ Wayside Academy School
31 Main St.
Marlborough, MA 01752
Ph: (508)786-9424
URL: http://www.waysideyouth.org/joomla/

Mashpee

30789 ■ Park Place Residence
71 Park Place Way
Mashpee, MA 02649
Ph: (508)888-8443

Medford

30790 ■ Eliot Community Human Services Cabot Road
10 Cabot Rd.
Medford, MA 02155
Ph: (781)397-2100
URL: http://www.eliotchs.org/
Formerly: Tri-City Mental Health/Mental Retardation Center, Inc.

30791 ■ Eliot Community Human Services Satellite Residence
611 High St.
Medford, MA 02155
Ph: (781)397-2133
URL: http://www.eliotchs.org/
Formerly: Tri-City Mental Health/Mental Retardation Center, Inc.

Melrose

30792 ■ Hallmark Health System
585 Lebanon St.
Melrose, MA 02176
Ph: (781)979-3000
URL: http://www.hallmarkhealth.org/

Milford

30793 ■ Wayside Community Counseling
10 Asylum St.
Milford, MA 01757
Ph: (508)478-6888
URL: http://www.waysideyouth.org

Natick

30794 ■ Advocates, Inc.--Natick
18 Hill St.
Natick, MA 01760
Ph: (508)545-0933
URL: http://www.advocatesinc.org

30795 ■ Brandon Residential School and Treatment Center
27 Winter St.
Natick, MA 01760
Ph: (508)655-6400
URL: http://www.brandonschool.org/

Needham

30796 ■ Riverside Early Intervention
255 Highland Ave.
Needham, MA 02494
Ph: (781)449-1884
URL: http://www.riversidecc.org

New Bedford

30797 ■ Child and Family Service, Inc.
1061 Pleasant St.
New Bedford, MA 02740
Ph: (508)996-8572
Fax: (508)991-8618
URL: http://www.child-familyservices.org/

30798 ■ Luis E. Martinez House
101 Nye St.
New Bedford, MA 02746
Ph: (508)984-7514
URL: http://www.sevenhills.org/

30799 ■ Seven Hills Behavioral Health, Inc.--New Bedford
589 S 1st St.
New Bedford, MA 02740
Ph: (508)996-3147
URL: http://www.sevenhills.org/aboutUs/direcLoc.php

Newton

30800 ■ Advocates, Inc.--Newton
515 Walnut St.
Newton, MA 02460
Ph: (617)969-2315
URL: http://www.advocatesinc.org

30801 ■ Elliot House
23 Needham St.
Newton, MA 02461
Ph: (617)527-9500
URL: http://www.elliothouse.org

30802 ■ Riverside Community Care - Osborne Path
117 Osborne Path
Newton, MA 02459
Ph: (617)969-4180
E-mail: administration@riversidecc.org
URL: http://www.riversidecc.org

30803 ■ Riverside Outpatient Center at Newton
64 Eldredge St.
Newton, MA 02458
Ph: (617)969-4925
E-mail: administration@riversidecc.org
URL: http://www.riversidecc.org
Formerly: Newton Outpatient Center.

North Adams

30804 ■ Northern Berkshire Counseling Center
The Brien Center
25 Marshall St.
North Adams, MA 01247
Ph: (413)664-4541
Free: 800-252-0227
URL: http://www.briencenter.org/

North Attleboro

30805 ■ The Halcyon Center
55 Plain St., Ste. 2
North Attleboro, MA 02760
Ph: (508)699-2399
Free: 800-439-0183
Fax: (508)699-9475
E-mail: ghandel@halcyoncenter.org
URL: http://www.halcyoncenter.org/
Program(s): Provides day and residential programs for adults with autism and other developmental disorders, focusing on the development of job skills, social behavior, communication, and adaptive living skills.

Northampton

30806 ■ Community Enterprises, Inc.
441 Pleasant St.
Northampton, MA 01060
Ph: (413)584-1460
Fax: (413)586-1121
URL: http://www.communityenterprises.com

30807 ■ ServiceNet, Inc.
129 King St
Northampton, MA 01060
Ph: (413)585-1300
URL: http://www.servicenetinc.org

30808 ■ ServiceNet, Inc.
Emergency Services
131 King St.
Northampton, MA 01060
Ph: (413)585-1368
URL: http://www.servicenetinc.org

30809 ■ ServiceNet, Inc.
Outpatient Clinic
50 Pleasant St.
Northampton, MA 01060
Ph: (413)585-1302
URL: http://www.servicenetinc.org

Northborough

30810 ■ The Bridge of Central Massachusetts
Northborough Community Residence
59 Main St.
Northborough, MA 01532
Ph: (508)393-9074
E-mail: info@thebridgecm.org
URL: http://www.thebridgecm.org

Norwood

30811 ■ Riverside Community Care
Neponset River House
595 Pleasant St.
Norwood, MA 02062
Ph: (781)762-7075
Fax: (781)762-2409
URL: http://neponsetriverhouse.org/
Formerly: Neponset River House/ Foxwood Day Treatment.

30812 ■ Riverside Outpatient Center - Norwood
190 Lenox St.
Norwood, MA 02062
Ph: (781)551-8463
E-mail: norwood.outpatient@riversidecc.org
URL: http://www.riversidecc.org

30813 ■ Riverside Respite Program - Norwood
15 Beacon Ave.
Norwood, MA 02062
Ph: (781)769-1342
URL: http://www.riversidecc.org
Formerly: Respite Site.

Pittsfield

30814 ■ The Brien Center
741 North St.
Pittsfield, MA 01201
Ph: (413)447-2145
URL: http://www.briencenter.org/
Formerly: Mental Health and Substance Abuse Services of the Berkshires.

30815 ■ The Brien Center - Brenton Group Home
49 Brenton Ter.
Pittsfield, MA 01201
Ph: (413)499-0412
URL: http://www.briencenter.org/

30816 ■ The Brien Center - Central - Child and Adolescents
251 Fenn St.
Pittsfield, MA 01201
Ph: (413)496-9671
URL: http://www.briencenter.org/
Formerly: Options for Youth.

30817 ■ The Brien Center - Elm Group Home
15 Elm St.
Pittsfield, MA 01201
Ph: (413)499-0412
URL: http://www.briencenter.org/
Formerly: Elm House.

30818 ■ The Brien Center - Forensic Services
24 Wendell Ave.
Pittsfield, MA 01201
Ph: (413)499-1897
URL: http://www.briencenter.org/

30819 ■ The Brien Center - Transitions
59 Hamlin St.
Pittsfield, MA 01201
Ph: (413)443-4848
URL: http://www.briencenter.org/
Formerly: Westwoods.

30820 ■ Key Program, Inc.--Pittsfield
369 West St.
Pittsfield, MA 01201
Ph: (413)443-7379
URL: http://www.key.org/

30821 ■ Pomeroy Crisis Recovery House
The Brien Center
34 Pomeroy Ave.
Pittsfield, MA 01201-6304
Ph: (413)449-0412
URL: http://www.briencenter.org/

Plymouth

30822 ■ Bay State Community Services, Inc.
385 Court St.
Plymouth, MA 02360
Ph: (508)830-3444
URL: http://www.baystatecs.org/

Pocasset

30823 ■ Cape Cod and Islands Community Mental Health Center--Pocasset
830 County Rd.
Pocasset, MA 02559
Ph: (508)564-9600

Quincy

30824 ■ Center for Health and Development, Inc.
Atlantic Clubhouse
338 Washington St.
Quincy, MA 02169
Ph: (617)770-9660
URL: http://www.centerforhealth.org/clubhouse_atlantic.htm
Formerly: Atlantic House.

30825 ■ Quincy Mental Health Center
460 Quincy Ave.
Quincy, MA 02169-8117
Ph: (617)626-9000

30826 ■ South Shore Mental Health
500 Victory Rd., Ste. 19
Quincy, MA 02171
Ph: (617)847-1950
Free: 800-852-2844
URL: http://www.ssmh.org

30827 ■ South Shore Mental Health Center
460 Quincy Ave., 3rd Fl.
Quincy, MA 02169
Ph: (617)774-6047
Free: 800-852-2844
URL: http://www.ssmh.org
Formerly: Bayview Associates Evaluation and Counseling.

30828 ■ South Shore Mental Health Center
Community Support Program
460 Quincy Ave., 3rd Fl.
Quincy, MA 02169
Ph: (617)774-6047
URL: http://www.ssmh.org

30829 ■ South Shore Mental Health Center
Discovery Day/Evening Treatment Program
1431 Hancock St.
Quincy, MA 02169
Ph: (617)769-7200
URL: http://www.ssmh.org

Randolph

30830 ■ May Institute--Randolph
41 Pacella Park Dr.
Randolph, MA 02368
Ph: (781)440-0400
Fax: (781)440-0401
E-mail: info@mayinstitute.org
URL: http://www.mayinstitute.org

Rehoboth

30831 ■ Community Counseling of Bristol County
366 Winthrop St.
Rehoboth, MA 02769
Ph: (508)252-3383

Revere

30832 ■ Revere Counseling Center
265 Beach St.
Revere, MA 02151
Ph: (781)289-9331

Roxbury

30833 ■ Dimock Community Health Center, Inc.
Behavioral Health Services
55 Dimock St.
Roxbury, MA 02119
Ph: (617)442-8800
E-mail: contactinfo@dimock.org
URL: http://www.dimock.org

Rutland

30834 ■ Devereux Massachusetts
60 Miles Rd.
Rutland, MA 01543
Ph: (508)886-4746
Fax: (508)886-4773
URL: http://www.devereux.org/site/PageServer?pagename=ma_index

Salem

30835 ■ Health and Education Services, Inc.
Salem Clinic
162 Federal St.
Salem, MA 01970
Ph: (978)745-2440
URL: http://www.hes-inc.org/

Somerville

30836 ■ Somerville Mental Health Association
167 Holland St.
Somerville, MA 02144
Ph: (617)623-3278
E-mail: info@somervillementalhealth.org
URL: http://www.somervillementalhealth.org/about_us/contact.php

Springfield

30837 ■ Behavioral Health Network, Inc.
417 Liberty St.
Springfield, MA 01104
Ph: (413)747-0705
Free: 800-499-1123
Fax: (413)732-7075
URL: http://www.bhninc.org/

30838 ■ Center for Human Development, Inc.
332 Birnie Ave.
Springfield, MA 01107
Ph: (413)733-6624
Fax: (413)439-2109
E-mail: info@chd.org
URL: http://www.chd.org

30839 ■ Community Re-Entry Program
622 State St.
Springfield, MA 01109
Ph: (413)439-1200
URL: http://www.chd.org/

30840 ■ Gandara Mental Health Center
147 Norman St.
Springfield, MA 01089
Ph: (413)736-8329
Fax: (413)746-4270
URL: http://gandaracenter.org/

30841 ■ Key Program, Inc. - Western Key
576 State St.
Springfield, MA 01109-4104
Ph: (413)781-6485
Fax: (413)788-6925
URL: http://www.key.org

30842 ■ Main Street Center
2155 Main St.
Springfield, MA 01104
Ph: (413)736-0395
Fax: (413)734-1651
URL: http://gandaracenter.org/

30843 ■ Springfield Veterans Affairs Outpatient Clinic
25 Bond St.
Springfield, MA 01104
Ph: (413)731-6000
URL: http://www.northampton.va.gov/visitors/springfield.asp

Taunton

30844 ■ Community Care Services, Inc.--Taunton
70 Main St.
Taunton, MA 02780
Ph: (508)821-7777
Fax: (508)880-6155
URL: http://www.communitycareservices.org

30845 ■ Community Counseling of Bristol County
1 Washington St.
Taunton, MA 02780
Ph: (508)823-5400
URL: http://www.comcounseling.org/

Wakefield

30846 ■ Eliot Community Human Services
Princess Street
26 Princess St.
Wakefield, MA 01880
Ph: (781)338-8100
URL: http://www.eliotchs.org/

Walpole

30847 ■ Advocates, Inc.--Walpole
1 Lewis Park Ave.
Walpole, MA 02081
Ph: (508)620-0024
URL: http://www.advocatesinc.org/

Waltham

30848 ■ The Edinburg Center, Inc.--Waltham
634 Moody St.
Waltham, MA 02453
Ph: (781)862-3600
URL: http://www.edinburgcenter.org/
Formerly: Center for Mental Health/Mental Retardation Services.

West Boylston

30849 ■ Advocates, Inc.--West Goylston
85 Sterling Pl.
West Boylston, MA 01583
Ph: (508)723-4123
URL: http://www.advocatesinc.org

West Roxbury

30850 ■ Veterans Affairs Boston Healthcare System
West Roxbury Division
1400 VFW Pkwy.
West Roxbury, MA 02132
Ph: (617)323-7700
Free: 800-865-3384
URL: http://www.boston.va.gov/

Westfield

30851 ■ The Carson Center for Human Services, Inc.
Center for Children and Youth
20 Broad St.
Westfield, MA 01085
Ph: (413)568-1421
URL: http://www.carsoncenter.org/locations/westfieldlocations/
Formerly: Westfield Area Mental Health Clinic.

30852 ■ Carson Center for Human Services
Westfield Clinic
77 Mill St., Ste. 251
Westfield, MA 01085
Ph: (413)568-6141
URL: http://www.carsoncenter.org/locations/westfieldlocations/

30853 ■ Forensic Mental Health Services
27 Washington St.
Westfield, MA 01085-2879
Ph: (413)568-6451

Woburn

30854 ■ Eliot Community Human Services
Bennett Street
10 Bennett St
Woburn, MA 01801-5032
Ph: (781)938-0513
URL: http://www.eliotchs.org/

Worcester

30855 ■ Burncoat Family Center
Community Healthlink, Inc.
227 Burncoat St.
Worcester, MA 01606
Ph: (508)853-6988
URL: http://www.communityhealthlink.com

30856 ■ Community Healthlink, Inc.
72 Jacques Ave.
Worcester, MA 01610-2480
Ph: (508)860-1260
URL: http://www.communityhealthlink.com

30857 ■ Community Healthlink, Inc.
Outpatient Services
12 Queen St.
Worcester, MA 01610
Ph: (508)860-1260
Fax: (508)421-4350
URL: http://www.communityhealthlink.com

30858 ■ Gateway Resources
Community Healthlink, Inc.
162 Chandler St.
Worcester, MA 01609
Ph: (508)860-1101
URL: http://www.communityhealthlink.com

30859 ■ Ludlow Street
Community Healthlink, Inc.
10 Ludlow St.
Worcester, MA 01603
Ph: (508)756-7666
URL: http://www.communityhealthlink.com

30860 ■ McGowan House
Community Healthlink, Inc.
1030 Main St.
Worcester, MA 01603
Ph: (508)860-1185
URL: http://www.communityhealthlink.com

30861 ■ Oasis House
Community Healthlink, Inc.
9 Chadwick St.
Worcester, MA 01605-1236
Ph: (508)860-1175
URL: http://www.communityhealthlink.com

30862 ■ Santram House
Community Healthlink, Inc.
133 Paine St.
Worcester, MA 01605
Ph: (508)860-1169
URL: http://www.communityhealthlink.com

30863 ■ Second Street
Community Healthlink, Inc.
18 2nd St.
Worcester, MA 01602
Ph: (508)860-1181
URL: http://www.communityhealthlink.com

30864 ■ Sigourney House
Community Healthlink, Inc.
2 Sigourney St.
Worcester, MA 01605
Ph: (508)860-1172
URL: http://www.communityhealthlink.com

30865 ■ Unicorn Inn
Community Healthlink, Inc.
9 Granite St.
Worcester, MA 01604
Ph: (508)860-1166
URL: http://www.communityhealthlink.com

30866 ■ Windsor House
Community Healthlink, Inc.
66 Windsor St.
Worcester, MA 01605
Ph: (508)860-1190
URL: http://www.communityhealthlink.com

30867 ■ Worcester Youth Guidance Center
Community Healthlink, Inc.
275 Belmont St.
Worcester, MA 01604
Ph: (508)791-3261
URL: http://www.communityhealthlink.com

MICHIGAN

Adrian

30868 ■ Family Services and Children's Aid, Inc.
3266 N Adrian Hwy.
Adrian, MI 49221
Ph: (517)263-2625
Fax: (517)263-7369
URL: http://strong-families.org

30869 ■ Lenawee County Community Mental Health
1040 S Winter St., Ste. 1022
Adrian, MI 49221
Ph: (517)263-8905
Fax: (517)265-8237
URL: http://www.lcmha.org/

Albion

30870 ■ Starr Commonwealth
13725 Starr Commenwealth Rd.
Albion, MI 49224
Ph: (517)629-5591
Free: 800-837-5591
URL: http://www.starr.org/

Algonac

30871 ■ River District Counseling Center
555 Saint Clair River Dr.
Algonac, MI 48001
Ph: (810)794-7548
Free: 888-225-4447
URL: http://www.scccmh.org/aboutCMH/riverDistrict.cfm

Allegan

30872 ■ Adult Community Connections
Allegan County Community Mental Health Service Program
277 North St.
Allegan, MI 49010-1138
Ph: (269)673-5092
URL: http://www.allegancounty.org/Government/MH/Index.asp?pt=Government

30873 ■ Allegan County Community Mental Health Services
3283 122nd Ave.
Allegan, MI 49010
Ph: (269)673-0202
Free: 888-354-0596
URL: http://www.allegancounty.org/Government/MH/Index.asp?pt=Government

Alpena

30874 ■ Clement C. Van Wagoner Department of Veterans Affairs Clinic
180 N State Ave.
Alpena, MI 49707
Ph: (989)356-8720
Free: 800-406-5143
Fax: (989)356-8707
URL: http://www.saginaw.va.gov/

30875 ■ Northeast Michigan Community Mental Health Authority
Light of Hope Clubhouse
229 S 3rd St.
Alpena, MI 49707
Ph: (989)734-7223
Free: 800-968-1964
URL: http://www.nemcmh.org/index_files/page0003.htm

30876 ■ Northeast Michigan Community Mental Health Services Board--Alpena
400 Johnson St.
Alpena, MI 49707
Ph: (989)356-2161
Free: 800-968-1964
URL: http://www.nemcmh.org/

Ann Arbor

30877 ■ Ann Arbor Consultation Services, Inc.
5331 Plymouth Rd.
Ann Arbor, MI 48105
Ph: (734)996-9111
URL: http://www.a2consultation.com/

30878 ■ Judson Washtenaw Regional Center
4925 Packard Rd., Ste. 200
Ann Arbor, MI 48108
Ph: (734)528-1720
URL: http://www.judsoncenter.org/template.php?pid=39

30879 ■ Veterans Affairs Ann Arbor Healthcare System
2215 Fuller Rd.
Ann Arbor, MI 48105
Ph: (734)769-7100
Free: 800-361-8387
URL: http://www.annarbor.va.gov/

Bad Axe

30880 ■ Community Links
Huron Behavioral Health
1700 N Van Dyke Rd.
Bad Axe, MI 48413
Ph: (989)269-2962
URL: http://www.huroncmh.org/
Formerly: Center for Community Living.

30881 ■ Huron Behavioral Health
1108 S Van Dyke Rd.
Bad Axe, MI 48413
Ph: (989)269-9293
Free: 800-356-5568
URL: http://www.huroncmh.org/
Formerly: Huron County Community Mental Health.

Bangor

30882 ■ Van Buren County Community Mental Health Service Program
MTI
34276 52nd St.
Bangor, MI 49013
Ph: (269)427-5625
Free: 877-252-2133
URL: http://www.vbcmh.com/
Formerly: Van Buren Community Mental Health.

Battle Creek

30883 ■ Battle Creek Veterans Affairs Medical Center
5500 Armstrong Rd.
Battle Creek, MI 49037
Ph: (269)966-5600
Free: 888-214-1247
URL: http://www.battlecreek.va.gov/

30884 ■ Starr Battle Creek
155 Garfield Ave.
Battle Creek, MI 49037
Ph: (269)968-9287
Free: 800-225-7529
Fax: (269)966-4123
E-mail: info@starr.org
URL: http://www.starr.org/locations-starrbattlecreek

Bay City

30885 ■ Bay-Arenac Behavioral Health Authority
201 Mulholland St.
Bay City, MI 48708
Ph: (989)895-2300
Free: 800-327-4693
URL: http://www.babha.org/

Belding

30886 ■ Ionia County Community Mental Health, Belding
7441 Storey Rd.
Belding, MI 48809
Ph: (616)527-1790
URL: http://www.ioniacmhs.org/

Bellaire

30887 ■ Northern Country Community Mental Health--Bellaire
203 E Cayuga
Bellaire, MI 49615
Ph: (231)533-8619
URL: http://www.norcocmh.org/locations.html

Belleville

30888 ■ Community Care Services--Belleville
25 Owen St.
Belleville, MI 48111
Ph: (734)697-7880
URL: http://www.comcareserv.org/

Benton Harbor

30889 ■ Riverwood Center
Barrien Mental Health Authority
1485 M-139
Benton Harbor, MI 49022
Ph: (269)925-0585
Free: 800-336-0341
E-mail: info@riverwoodcenter.org
URL: http://www.riverwoodcenter.org
Formerly: Riverwood Community Mental Health.

Berkley

30890 ■ Oakland Family Services
Berkley Office
2351 W 12 Mile Rd.
Berkley, MI 48072
Ph: (248)544-4004
URL: http://www.oaklandfamilyservices.org

Brighton

30891 ■ Advanced Counseling Services, PC--Brighton
7600 Grand River, Ste. 290
Brighton, MI 48114
Ph: (810)220-2787
Fax: (810)220-2834
URL: http://www.advancedcounseling.org/

Cadillac

30892 ■ Northern Lakes Community Mental Health
Missaukee/Wexford County
527 Cobb St.
Cadillac, MI 49601
Ph: (231)775-3463
URL: http://www.northernlakescmh.org/

Calumet

30893 ■ Copper County Mental Health Services--Calumet Office
56938 Calumet Ave.
Calumet, MI 49913
Ph: (906)377-5810
URL: http://www.cccmh.org/home.html

Canton

30894 ■ Advanced Counseling Services, PC--Canton
5958 Canton Center Rd., Ste. 900
Canton, MI 48187
Ph: (734)737-1200
Fax: (734)737-1205
URL: http://www.advancedcounseling.org/locations.asp

30895 ■ Family Service, Inc.--Canton
50430 School House Rd.
Canton, MI 48187
Ph: (734)495-9526
URL: http://fsiwc.addanetwork.com/locations.htm

30896 ■ Saint Joseph Mercy Behavioral Services
2200 Canton Ctr. Rd., Ste. 200B
Canton, MI 48187
Ph: (734)981-3800
URL: http://www.sjmercyhealth.org/

Caro

30897 ■ Tuscola Behavioral Health Systems
323 N State St.
Caro, MI 48723
Ph: (989)673-6191
Free: 800-462-6814
URL: http://main.tbhsonline.com/

30898 ■ Tuscola Behavioral Health Systems Pineland Behavioral Home
135 Wire Line Rd.
Caro, MI 48723
Ph: (989)673-6191
URL: http://main.tbhsonline.com/

Cassopolis

30899 ■ Woodlands Behavioral Healthcare
960 E State St.
Cassopolis, MI 49031
Ph: (269)445-2451
Free: 800-323-0335
URL: http://www.woodlandsbhn.org/
Formerly: Cass County Community Mental Health Services.

30900 ■ Woodlands Behavioral Healthcare Work Activity Program
1124 Austin
Cassopolis, MI 49031
Ph: (269)445-2451
Free: 800-323-0335
URL: http://www.woodlandsbhn.org/
Formerly: Cass County Community Mental Health Services.

Charlevoix

30901 ■ Northern Country Community Mental Health--Charlevoix
6250 M-66 N
Charlevoix, MI 49720
Ph: (231)547-5885
URL: http://www.norcocmh.org/locations.html

Cheboygan

30902 ■ Doris E. Reid Center
825 S Huron St., Ste. 4
Cheboygan, MI 49721
Ph: (231)627-5627

Chelsea

30903 ■ Chelsea Community Hospital
775 S Main St., Ste. 1
Chelsea, MI 48118-1399
Ph: (734)475-4029
URL: http://www.cch.org/default.cfm

Clarkston

30904 ■ Advanced Counseling Services PC--Clarkston
6770 Dixie Hwy., Ste. 312
Clarkston, MI 48346
Ph: (248)922-2300
Fax: (248)922-2304
URL: http://www.advancedcounseling.org/

Clinton Township

30905 ■ First Resources and Treatment - North
43740 N Groesbeck Hwy.
Clinton Township, MI 48036
Ph: (586)469-7629

30906 ■ Ventures Assertive Community Treatment
38251 S Groesbeck Hwy.
Clinton Township, MI 48036
Ph: (586)469-6210

Coloma

30907 ■ Riverwood Center--Residential Home
5250 Becht Rd.
Coloma, MI 49038
Ph: (269)468-4009
Free: 800-336-0341
URL: http://www.riverwoodcenter.org/

Coopersville

30908 ■ Coopersville Community Based Services
259 Main St.
Coopersville, MI 49404
Ph: (616)837-6399
URL: http://www.co.ottawa.mi.us/HealthComm/CMH/cmhhome.htm

Dearborn

30909 ■ Family Services, Inc.
19855 W Outer Dr., Ste. 104
Dearborn, MI 48124
Ph: (313)274-5840
URL: http://fsiwc.addanetwork.com/

Deckerville

30910 ■ Sanco Industries
3680 Rangeline Rd.
Deckerville, MI 48427
Ph: (810)376-4268

Detroit

30911 ■ Adult Well-Being Services
1423 Field
Detroit, MI 48124
Ph: (313)825-2470
E-mail: info@awbs.org
URL: http://www.awbs.org/

30912 ■ Christ Child House
15751 Joy Rd.
Detroit, MI 48228
Ph: (313)548-6077
Fax: (313)584-6077
E-mail: info@christchildhouse.org
URL: http://www.christchildhouse.org

30913 ■ Detroit Central City Community Mental Health
10 Peterboro St.
Detroit, MI 48201
Ph: (313)831-3160
URL: http://www.dccmh.org/

30914 ■ Family Place
8726 Woodward
Detroit, MI 48202
Ph: (313)664-0700
URL: http://www.newcentercmhs.org/ncFacilities.aspx

30915 ■ Family Service, Inc.--Bagley, Detroit
220 Bagley, Ste. 700
Detroit, MI 48226
Ph: (313)965-2141
URL: http://fsiwc.addanetwork.com/locations.htm

30916 ■ Family Service, Inc.--Harper Avenue, Detroit
10900 Harper Ave.
Detroit, MI 48213
Ph: (313)579-5989
URL: http://fsiwc.addanetwork.com/locations.htm

30917 ■ John D. Dingell Veterans Affairs Medical Center
4646 John R St.
Detroit, MI 48201
Ph: (313)576-1000
Free: 888-838-6446
URL: http://www.detroit.va.gov/

30918 ■ Matrix Human Services
120 Parsons St.
Detroit, MI
Ph: (313)831-1000
E-mail: inquiries@matrixhs.org
URL: http://www.matrixhumanservices.org/

30919 ■ New Center Community Mental Health Services--Detroit
2051 W Grand Blvd.
Detroit, MI 48208-1105
Ph: (313)961-3200
URL: http://www.newcentercmhs.org/

30920 ■ New Center Community Mental Health Services--Highland Park
95 Victor
Detroit, MI 48203
Ph: (313)883-2400
URL: http://www.newcentercmhs.org/ncFacilities.aspx

30921 ■ New Center Community Mental Health Services--North Park
1001 Puritan
Detroit, MI 48238
Ph: (313)494-4000
URL: http://www.newcentercmhs.org/ncFacilities.aspx

Escanaba

30922 ■ Pathways
Delta County Site
2820 College Ave.
Escanaba, MI 49829
Ph: (906)786-6441
Free: 888-728-4929
URL: http://www.pathwaysup.org/
Formerly: Pathways.

30923 ■ Pathways
Touchstone Act
429 S 10th St.
Escanaba, MI 49829-3328
Ph: (906)786-9543
Free: 888-728-4929
URL: http://www.pathwaysup.org/

Farmington Hills

30924 ■ Pioneer Counseling Services--Farmington Hills
28511 Orchard Lake Rd., Ste. A
Farmington Hills, MI 48334
Ph: (248)489-1550
URL: http://www.pioneercounseling.com/about.asp

Flint

30925 ■ Child and Adolescent Center--Flint
1102 Mackin Rd.
Flint, MI 48503
Ph: (810)257-3676

30926 ■ Flint Veterans Affairs Outpatient Clinic
G3267 Beecher Rd.
Flint, MI 48532
Ph: (810)720-2913
Fax: (810)720-3296
URL: http://www2.va.gov/directory/guide/facility.asp?ID=5078&dnum=All

30927 ■ Genesee County Community Mental Health
420 W 5th Ave.
Flint, MI 48503
Ph: (810)257-3705
Free: 866-211-5455
URL: http://www.gencmh.org/

30928 ■ Taylor Psychological Clinic
1172 Robert T. Longway Blvd.
Flint, MI 48503
Ph: (810)232-8466
URL: http://taylorpsychologicalclinic.bzlnk.com/

Gaylord

30929 ■ Gaylord Veterans Affairs Clinic
806 S Otsego
Gaylord, MI 49735
Ph: (989)321-4530
Free: 888-838-6446
URL: http://www.saginaw.va.gov/visitors/gaylord.asp

30930 ■ Northern Country Community Mental Health--Gaylord
800 Livingston Blvd., Ste. A
Gaylord, MI 49735
Ph: (989)732-7558
URL: http://www.norcocmh.org/
Formerly: Northern Michigan Community Mental Health; Health Services Board.

Gladwin

30931 ■ Community Mental Health for Central Michigan
Gladwin County Mental Illness
655 E Cedar Ave.
Gladwin, MI 48624
Ph: (989)426-9295
URL: http://www.cmhcm.org/
Formerly: Midland Gladwin Community Mental Health.

Grand Haven

30932 ■ Community Mental Health of Ottawa County--Grand Haven
1111 Fulton St.
Grand Haven, MI 49417
Ph: (616)842-5350
URL: http://www.co.ottawa.mi.us/HealthComm/CMH/cmhhome.htm

Grand Rapids

30933 ■ Hope Network Behavioral Health Services
1256 Walker NW
Grand Rapids, MI 49504
Ph: (616)235-2910
Fax: (616)235-2066
URL: http://www.hopenetwork.org

30934 ■ Hope Network Leadership Center
755 36th St. SE
Grand Rapids, MI 49518
Ph: (616)301-8000
Free: 800-695-7273
Fax: (616)248-5161
URL: http://www.hopenetwork.org

Grayling

30935 ■ North Central Community Mental Health
Grayling Office
204 Meadows Dr.
Grayling, MI 49738
Ph: (989)348-8522

Hancock

30936 ■ Veterans Affairs Medical Center
Hancock Clinic
787 Market St.
Hancock, MI 49930
Ph: (906)482-7762
URL: http://www2.va.gov/directory/guide/facility.asp?ID=836&dnum=1

Harrisville

30937 ■ Northeast Michigan Community Mental Health Authority--Harrisville
311 Lake
Harrisville, MI 48740
Ph: (989)734-7223
Free: 800-968-1964
URL: http://www.nemcmh.org/index_files/page0003.htm

Hartford

30938 ■ Van Buren County CMHSP
Hartford Family Resource Center
57418 County Rd. 681, Ste. C
Hartford, MI 49057
Ph: (269)621-6251
URL: http://www.vbcmh.com/loc.htm
Formerly: Van Buren Community Mental Health.

30939 ■ Van Buren County CMHSP
Hope Center
57418 County Rd., 681, Ste. B
Hartford, MI 49057
Ph: (269)621-6261
Free: 888-516-4673
URL: http://www.vbcmh.com/loc.htm
Formerly: Van Buren Community Mental Health.

Highland Park

30940 ■ New Center Community Mental Health Services
95 Victor
Highland Park, MI 48203
Ph: (313)883-2400
URL: http://www.newcentercmhs.org/ncFacilities.aspx

Hillman

30941 ■ Northeast Michigan Community Mental Health Authority--Hillman
630 Caring St.
Hillman, MI 49746
Ph: (989)742-4549
Free: 800-968-1964
URL: http://www.nemcmh.org/index_files/page0003.htm

Holland

30942 ■ Community Mental Health of Ottawa County
12265 James St.
Holland, MI 49424
Ph: (616)392-8236
URL: http://www.co.ottawa.mi.us/HealthComm/CMH/cmhhome.htm

30943 ■ Community Mental Health of Ottawa County
Robert S. Brown Center
160 Manley St.
Holland, MI 49424
Ph: (616)396-0152
URL: http://www.co.ottawa.mi.us/HealthComm/CMH/cmhhome.htm

Holly

30944 ■ Rose Hill Center
5130 Rose Hill Blvd.
Holly, MI 48442
Ph: (248)634-5530
Free: 866-504-2259
Fax: (248)634-7754
URL: http://www.rosehillcenter.com/

Houghton

30945 ■ Copper Country Mental Community Mental Health Service Program
901 Memorial Rd.
Houghton, MI 49931
Ph: (906)482-9400
URL: http://www.cccmh.org/home.html
Formerly: Copper Country Mental Health Services.

Houghton Lake

30946 ■ North Central Community Mental Health
Houghton Lake Office
2715 S Townline Rd.
Houghton Lake, MI 48629
Ph: (989)366-8550
URL: http://www.northernlakescmh.org/about/?id=22

Hudsonville

30947 ■ Community Mental Health of Ottowa--Hudsonville
3100 Port Sheldon Rd.
Hudsonville, MI 49426
Ph: (616)669-6160
URL: http://www.co.ottawa.mi.us/HealthComm/CMH/cmhhome.htm

Inkster

30948 ■ Starfish Family Services
Lifespan Clinical Services
30000 Hiveley Rd.
Inkster, MI 48141

Ph: (734)728-3400
URL: http://www.sfish.org/

Ionia

30949 ■ Ionia County Community Mental Health, Ionia
375 Apple Tree Dr.
Ionia, MI 48846
Ph: (616)527-1790
URL: http://www.ioniacmhs.org

Iron Mountain

30950 ■ Oscar G. Johnson Veterans Affairs Medical Center
325 E H St.
Iron Mountain, MI 49801
Ph: (906)774-3300
URL: http://www.ironmountain.va.gov/

Iron River

30951 ■ Northpointe Behavioral Healthcare System--Iron River
703 2nd Ave.
Iron River, MI 49935
Ph: (906)265-5126
URL: http://www.nbhs.org/

Ironwood

30952 ■ Lutheran Social Services Branch Office
126 W Arch St.
Ironwood, MI 49938
Ph: (906)932-3902
URL: http://www.lssm.org/LSSM/Page.aspx?pid=442

Jackson

30953 ■ Allegiance Health Behavioral Health Services
205 N East Ave.
Jackson, MI 49201
Ph: (517)789-5971
Free: 800-531-3728
URL: http://www.allegiancehealth.org/

30954 ■ Family Service and Children's Aid
330 W Michigan Ave.
Jackson, MI 49201
Ph: (517)787-7920
Fax: (517)787-2440
URL: http://strong-families.org

Kalamazoo

30955 ■ The Elizabeth Upjohn Community Healing Center
2615 Stadium Dr.
Kalamazoo, MI 49008
Ph: (269)343-1651
Fax: (269)382-7078
URL: http://www.communityhealingcenter.org/our-locations.php

30956 ■ Jim Gilmore Jr. Community Healing Center
1910 Shaffer St.
Kalamazoo, MI 49048
Ph: (269)382-9820
URL: http://www.communityhealingcenter.org/our-locations.php

30957 ■ Kalamazoo Mental Health & Substance Abuse Services
418 W Kalamazoo Ave.
Kalamazoo, MI 49007
Ph: (269)373-6000
Free: 888-373-6200
Fax: (269)373-4951
URL: http://www.kazoocmh.org/

Kalkaska

30958 ■ Northern Country Community Mental Health--Kalkaska
625 Courthouse Dr.
Kalkaska, MI 49646
Ph: (231)258-5133
URL: http://www.norcocmh.org/locations.html

Kincheloe

30959 ■ Veterans Affairs Medical Center Sault Sainte Marie Clinic
16523 S Watertower Dr., Unit 1
Kincheloe, MI 49788
Ph: (906)495-4357
URL: http://www2.va.gov/directory/guide/facility.asp?ID=845&dnum=1

Kingsford

30960 ■ Northpointe Behavioral Healthcare System
715 Pyle Dr.
Kingsford, MI 49802
Ph: (906)774-0522
URL: http://www.nbhs.org/

Lansing

30961 ■ Clinton-Eaton-Ingham CMHSP
812 E Jolly Rd.
Lansing, MI 48910-6819
Ph: (517)346-8200
URL: http://www.ceicmh.org/
Formerly: Clinton, Eaton and Ingham Community Mental Health Services Board.

30962 ■ Sparrow Behavioral Health Services
1210 W Saginaw
Lansing, MI 48915
Ph: (517)364-7700
URL: http://www.sparrow.org/behavioralhealth/

30963 ■ Veterans Affairs Medical Center Lansing Clinic
2025 S Washington Ave.
Lansing, MI 48910
Ph: (517)267-3925
URL: http://www2.va.gov/directory/guide/facility.asp?ID=768

Lapeer

30964 ■ List Psychological Services, PLC
350 N Court St., Ste. 205
Lapeer, MI 48446
Ph: (810)667-4500
URL: http://www.listpsych.com/

Lawrence

30965 ■ Van Buren County CMHSP Center for Crisis Stabilization
430 Bangor Rd.
Lawrence, MI 49064
Ph: (269)674-4600
Formerly: Van Buren Community Mental Health Center for Crisis Stabilization.

Lincoln Park

30966 ■ Community Care Services--Lincoln Park
26184 Outer Dr.
Lincoln Park, MI 48146
Ph: (313)389-7525
Fax: (313)389-7515
URL: http://www.comcareserv.org

30967 ■ Turning Point
1736 Fort St.
Lincoln Park, MI 48146
Ph: (313)382-7861
URL: http://www.comcareserv.org

Livonia

30968 ■ Livonia Counseling Center
15370 Levan Rd., Ste. 2
Livonia, MI 48154
Ph: (734)744-0170

30969 ■ Psychiatric Intervention Center
33505 Schoolcraft, Ste. 3
Livonia, MI 48150
Ph: (734)721-0200
URL: http://www.hegira.net/locations.htm

30970 ■ Starfish Family Services
18316 Middlebelt Rd.
Livonia, MI 48152
Ph: (248)615-9730
URL: http://www.sfish.org/

Manistee

30971 ■ Manistee-Benzie Community Mental Health Services
395 3rd St.
Manistee, MI 49660
Ph: (231)723-6516
Free: 877-398-2013
Fax: (231)723-1735
URL: http://www.mbcmh.org/

Marquette

30972 ■ Fairweather Lodge--Marquette
135 W Ridge St.
Marquette, MI 49855
Ph: (906)225-1181
URL: http://www.pathwaysup.org

30973 ■ Pathways--Marquette
200 W Spring St., Ste. 1
Marquette, MI 49855
Ph: (906)225-7201
Fax: (906)225-7204
URL: http://www.pathwaysup.org

Menominee

30974 ■ Lutheran Social Services--Menominee
1309 14th St.
Menominee, MI 49858
Ph: (800)677-7410
URL: http://www.lsswis.org/

30975 ■ Northpointe Behavioral Healthcare System--Menominee
401 10th Ave.
Menominee, MI 49858
Ph: (906)863-7841
Free: 800-750-0522
URL: http://www.nbhs.org/

30976 ■ Veterans Affairs Medical Center Menominee Clinic
1110 10th Ave., Ste. 101
Menominee, MI 49858
Ph: (906)863-1286
URL: http://www2.va.gov/directory/guide/facility.asp?ID=841&dnum=1

Michigan Center

30977 ■ Jackson Veterans Affairs Clinic
4328 Page Ave.
Michigan Center, MI 49254
Ph: (517)764-3609
Fax: (517)764-3659
URL: http://www2.va.gov/directory/guide/facility.asp?ID=806&dnum=All

Midland

30978 ■ Community Mental Health for Central Michigan Midland County Branch
3611 N Saginaw Rd.
Midland, MI 48640

Ph: (989)631-2320
URL: http://www.cmhcm.org/
Formerly: Nursing Home/OBRA Treatment Services.

30979 ■ Community Mental Health for Central Michigan
Midland County/Developmentally Disabled
220 W Ellsworth St., 4th Fl.
Midland, MI 48640
Ph: (989)631-2323
URL: http://www.cmhcm.org/

30980 ■ Family & Children's Service of Midland
1714 Eastman Ave.
Midland, MI 48640-4216
Ph: (989)631-5390
URL: http://www.fcs-midland.org/

Monroe

30981 ■ Monroe County Community Mental Health Authority
1001 S Raisinville Rd.
Monroe, MI 48161
Ph: (734)243-7340
URL: http://www.monroecmha.org/

Montague

30982 ■ Indian Bay Services
Mouskegon County
8770 Indian Bay Rd.
Montague, MI 49437-9703
Ph: (231)894-6400

Munising

30983 ■ Pathways
Alger County Site
601 W Superior St.
Munising, MI 49862
Ph: (906)387-3611
Free: 888-728-4929
URL: http://www.pathwaysup.org/

Muskegon

30984 ■ Community Mental Health Center--Muskegon
125 E Southern Ave.
Muskegon, MI 49442
Ph: (231)724-3699

30985 ■ Muskegon County CMHSP
John Halmond Center
376 E Apple Ave.
Muskegon, MI 49442
Ph: (231)724-1111

30986 ■ Youth Services--Muskegon
173 E Apple Ave., Bldg. C
Muskegon, MI 49442
Ph: (231)724-6050

New Lothrop

30987 ■ Community Ties - South
17940 Lincoln Rd.
New Lothrop, MI 48460
Ph: (989)845-7336

Newberry

30988 ■ Pathways to Healthy Living - Luce County
14126 W County Rd. 428
Newberry, MI 49868-7762
Ph: (906)293-3284
Formerly: Superior Behavioral Health and Pathways.

Niles

30989 ■ Community Healing Center--Niles
1225 S 11th St.
Niles, MI 49120
Ph: (269)684-7741
URL: http://www.communityhealingcenter.org/our-locations.php

30990 ■ Riverwood Center
115 S St. Joseph Ave.
Niles, MI 49120
Ph: (269)684-4270
Free: 888-686-3670
URL: http://www.riverwoodcenter.org/

Northville

30991 ■ Northville Counseling Center
670 Griswold, Ste. 3
Northville, MI 48167
Ph: (248)347-3470
URL: http://www.hegira.net/locations.htm

Oscoda

30992 ■ Aleda E. Lutz Veterans Affairs Medical Center
Oscoda Clinic
5671 Skeel Ave., Ste. 4
Oscoda, MI 48750
Ph: (989)321-4530
Free: 888-838-6446
URL: http://www.saginaw.va.gov/visitors/oscoda.asp

Palmer

30993 ■ Palmer Program
Richmond Township Hall
Palmer, MI 49871
Ph: (906)475-5030

Paw Paw

30994 ■ Van Buren County CMHSP
801 Hazen St., Ste. C
Paw Paw, MI 49079
Ph: (269)657-5574
URL: http://www.vbcmh.com/loc.htm
Formerly: Van Buren Community Mental Health.

Petoskey

30995 ■ North Country Community Mental Health
1 MacDonald Dr., Ste. A
Petoskey, MI 49770
Ph: (231)347-6701
URL: http://www.norcocmh.org/
Formerly: Community Mental Health.

30996 ■ North Country Community Mental Health
Petoskey Club
555 W Mitchell St.
Petoskey, MI 49770
Ph: (231)347-1786
URL: http://www.norcocmh.org/

Plymouth

30997 ■ Access Behavioral Healthcare
42189 Ann Arbor Rd.
Plymouth, MI 48170
Ph: (734)453-5603
URL: http://www.mhweb.org/wayne/accessbehav.htm

Pontiac

30998 ■ Oakland Family Services
Pontiac Office
114 Orchard Lake Rd.
Pontiac, MI 48341
Ph: (248)858-7766
URL: http://www.oaklandfamilyservices.org

Rochester Hills

30999 ■ Oakland Family Services
Rochester Office
130 Hampton Cir., Ste. 100
Rochester Hills, MI 48307-4113
Ph: (248)853-0750
URL: http://www.oaklandfamilyservices.org

Rogers City

31000 ■ Northeast Michigan Community Mental Health Authority--Rogers City
156 N 4th St.
Rogers City, MI 49779
Ph: (989)734-7223
Free: 800-968-1964
URL: http://www.nemcmh.org/index_files/page0003.htm

Romeo

31001 ■ Macomb Family Services, Inc.
124 W Gates, Ste. 103
Romeo, MI 48065
Ph: (586)752-9696
URL: http://www.mfsonline.org/

Royal Oak

31002 ■ Judson Center
4410 W 13 Mile Rd.
Royal Oak, MI 48073
Ph: (248)549-4339
URL: http://www.judsoncenter.org

Saginaw

31003 ■ Aleda E. Lutz Veterans Affairs Medical Center--Saginaw
1500 Weiss St.
Saginaw, MI 48602
Ph: (989)497-2500
Free: 888-838-6446
URL: http://www.saginaw.va.gov/

31004 ■ Norman Westlund Child Guidance Clinic
3253 Congress Ave.
Saginaw, MI 48602
Ph: (989)793-4790
URL: http://www.svrcindustries.com/index.php/behavioral-health-services

31005 ■ Saginaw County Community Mental Health Authority
500 Hancock St.
Saginaw, MI 48602-4292
Ph: (989)797-3400
Free: 800-258-8678
Fax: (989)799-0206
Formerly: Saginaw County Mental Health.

Saint Clair Shores

31006 ■ Advanced Counseling Services, PC--Saint Clair Shores
24715 Little Mack, Ste. 200
Saint Clair Shores, MI 48080
Ph: (586)777-9000
Fax: (586)777-0823
URL: http://www.advancedcounseling.org/locations.asp

31007 ■ First Resources and Treatment - Southeast
25401 Harper Ave.
Saint Clair Shores, MI 48081
Ph: (586)466-6912

Saint Johns

31008 ■ Clinton County Counseling Center
1000 E Sturgis St., Ste. 3
Saint Johns, MI 48879
Ph: (989)224-6729

Sandusky

31009 ■ Assertive Community Treatment
190 N Delawar St.
Sandusky, MI 48471
Ph: (586)649-4450
URL: http://www.actassociation.org/

31010 ■ Sanilac County Community Mental Health Service Program
171 Dawson
Sandusky, MI 48471
Ph: (810)648-0330
Formerly: Sanilac Community Mental Health.

South Haven

31011 ■ Van Buren County Community Mental Health Service Program
South Haven Outpatient Clinic
1007 Wells St.
South Haven, MI 49090
Ph: (269)637-5297
URL: http://www.vbcmh.com/loc.htm
Formerly: Van Buren Community Mental Health.

Southfield

31012 ■ Advanced Counseling Services, PC--Southfield
29201 Telegraph Rd., Ste. 550
Southfield, MI 48034
Ph: (248)213-0501
Fax: (248)213-0521
URL: http://www.advancedcounseling.org/locations.asp

31013 ■ Family Service, Inc.--Southfield
15565 Northland Dr., Ste. 505
Southfield, MI 48075
Ph: (248)483-3100
URL: http://fsiwc.addanetwork.com/locations.htm

Southgate

31014 ■ Family Service, Inc.--Southgate
13331 Reeck Rd.
Southgate, MI 48195
Ph: (734)324-2801
URL: http://fsiwc.addanetwork.com/locations.htm

31015 ■ The Guidance Center--Southgate
13101 Allen Rd.
Southgate, MI 48195-2216
Ph: (734)785-7700
URL: http://www.guidance-center.org

Standish

31016 ■ Community Counseling Services
Arenac Center
1000 W Cedar St.
Standish, MI 48658
Ph: (989)846-4573
Free: 800-327-4693
URL: http://www.babha.org/MentalHealthTreatment-Services/CommunityCounselingServices.asp x

Stanton

31017 ■ Montcalm Center for Behavioral Health
611 N State St.
Stanton, MI 48888
Ph: (981)831-7520
Free: 800-377-0974
URL: http://www.montcalmcenter.org/

Sturgis

31018 ■ Community Healing Center--Sturgis
70050 M-66
Sturgis, MI 49091
Ph: (269)651-1212
URL: http://www.communityhealingcenter.org/our-locations.php

Taylor

31019 ■ Advanced Counseling Services, PC--Taylor
20600 Eureka Rd., Ste. 819
Taylor, MI 48180
Ph: (734)285-8282
Fax: (734)281-0402
URL: http://www.advancedcounseling.org/locations.asp

31020 ■ Community Care Services--Taylor
26650 Eureka Rd., Ste. A
Taylor, MI 48180
Ph: (734)955-3550
Fax: (734)389-7515
URL: http://www.comcareserv.org

Three Rivers

31021 ■ Community Healing Center--Three Rivers
1020 Millard St.
Three Rivers, MI 49093
Ph: (269)279-5187
Fax: (269)273-2083
URL: http://www.communityhealingcenter.org/our-locations.php

Traverse City

31022 ■ Northern Lakes Community Mental Health Service Program
105 Hall St., Unit A
Traverse City, MI 49684
Ph: (231)922-4850
URL: http://www.northernlakescmh.org

Troy

31023 ■ Michigan Behavioral Medicine
625 E Big Beaver Rd., Ste. 101
Troy, MI 48083
Ph: (248)740-9360

Vandalia

31024 ■ Woodlands Behavioral Healthcare
17321 M-60 E
Vandalia, MI 49095
Ph: (269)476-9781
Free: 800-323-0335
URL: http://www.woodlandsbhn.org/

Wakefield

31025 ■ Gogebic County Community Mental Health Services
103 W US Hwy. 2
Wakefield, MI 49968
Ph: (906)229-6100
URL: http://www.gccmh.org/gccmh/index.shtml

Walled Lake

31026 ■ Oakland Family Services
Walled Lake Office
2045 E Maple Rd., D-407
Walled Lake, MI 48390
Ph: (248)624-3812
URL: http://www.oaklandfamilyservices.org

Warren

31027 ■ Crossroads Clubhouse
27041 Schoenherr Rd.
Warren, MI 48088
Ph: (586)759-9100
URL: http://www.mhweb.org/macomb/maccmh2.htm
Remarks: A psychological rehabilitation program for adult Macomb County residents with serious mental illness.

31028 ■ First Resources and Treatment - Southwest
3701 E 13 Mile Rd., Ste. B
Warren, MI 48092
Ph: (586)274-0200

Westland

31029 ■ Hegira House
8623 N Wayne Rd., Ste. 325
Westland, MI 48185
Ph: (734)427-1144
Fax: (734)742-0608
URL: http://www.hegira.net/

31030 ■ Hegira Westland Counseling Center
8623 N Wayne Rd., Ste. 310
Westland, MI 48185
Ph: (734)425-0636
Fax: (734)425-4771
URL: http://www.hegira.net/

Yale

31031 ■ Yale Veterans Affairs Clinic
7470 Brockway Rd.
Yale, MI 48097
Ph: (810)387-3211
Fax: (810)387-2279
URL: http://www2.va.gov/directory/guide/facility.asp?ID=770&dnum=All

Ypsilanti

31032 ■ Assault Crisis Center
4009 Washtenaw St.
Ypsilanti, MI 48197
Ph: (734)484-6620

Zeeland

31033 ■ Pine Rest--Zeeland Clinic
8333 Felch St., Ste. 201
Zeeland, MI 49464
Ph: (616)741-3790
URL: http://www.pinerest.org/

MINNESOTA

Albert Lea

31034 ■ Hayward Group Home
Sheriffs Youth Programs of Minnesota
80880 County Rd. 46
Albert Lea, MN 56007
Ph: (507)373-8103
E-mail: pdhayward@sypmn.com
URL: http://www.minnesotahelp.info/public/details.aspx?AgencyID=13101302&LinkID= DAC2CDB2-0AB8-410D-97B2-B9AD581F50A1

Anoka

31035 ■ People Incorporated
2665 4th Ave. N, Ste. 108
Anoka, MN 55303
Ph: (763)422-0489
URL: http://www.peopleincorporated.org/contact/index.php

Atwater

31036 ■ Woodland Centers
Saint Francis Halfway House
202 S 3rd St.
Atwater, MN 56209-0075
Ph: (320)974-8850
URL: http://www.woodlandcenters.com

Bemidji

31037 ■ Bemidji Veterans Affairs Clinic
705 5th St. NW, Ste. B
Bemidji, MN 56601
Ph: (218)755-6360
URL: http://www2.va.gov/directory/guide/facility.asp?ID=5655&dnum=All

Benson

31038 ■ Woodland Centers
Benson Clinic
North Star Bldg.
1209 Pacific Ave.
Benson, MN 56215
Ph: (320)843-2061
URL: http://www.woodlandcenters.com

Big Lake

31039 ■ Family Prospective Resources, Inc.
101 Jefferson Blvd.
Big Lake, MN 55309
Ph: (763)263-7896
URL: http://familypros.com/

Brainerd

31040 ■ Brainerd Veterans Affairs Clinic
11800 State Hwy. 18
Brainerd, MN 56401
Ph: (218)855-1115
Fax: (218)855-1183
URL: http://www2.va.gov/directory/guide/facility.asp?ID=5138&dnum=All

Brooklyn Park

31041 ■ Scott House--People Incorporated
7573 Scott Ave. N
Brooklyn Park, MN 55443
Ph: (763)503-9343
URL: http://www.peopleincorporated.org/

Burnsville

31042 ■ LifeSpan of Minnesota, Inc.
12425 River Ridge Blvd., Ste. 200
Burnsville, MN 55337
Ph: (952)562-8500
URL: http://www.lifespanmn.com/

31043 ■ McAndrews House--People Incorporated
904 McAndrews Rd. W
Burnsville, MN 55337
Ph: (952)736-7802
URL: http://www.peopleincorporated.org/

31044 ■ River Hills House--People Incorporated
113066 W River Hills Dr.
Burnsville, MN 55337
Ph: (952)736-8452
URL: http://www.peopleincorporated.org/

Caledonia

31045 ■ Hiawatha Valley Mental Health--Caledonia
121 Marshall St., Ste. 100
Caledonia, MN 55921
Ph: (507)725-2022
URL: http://www.hvmhc.org/

Canby

31046 ■ Western Mental Health Clinic--Canby
Canby Community Hospital
112 Saint Olaf Ave. S
Canby, MN 56220
Ph: (507)223-7221
Formerly: Western Human Clinic.

Cloquet

31047 ■ Human Development Center--Cloquet
40 11th St.
Cloquet, MN 55720
Ph: (218)879-4559
Free: 800-634-8775
URL: http://www.humandevelopmentcenter.org/locations/carlton.aspx

Coon Rapids

31048 ■ Family Life Mental Health Center
1930 Coon Rapids Blvd. NW
Coon Rapids, MN 55433
Ph: (763)427-7964
URL: http://www.flmhc.org

Crookston

31049 ■ Northwestern Mental Health Center, Inc.
Crookston
603 Bruce St.
Crookston, MN 56716
Ph: (218)281-3940
URL: http://northwesternment.qwestoffice.net/
Formerly: Northwestern Mental Health Center, Main Office.

Duluth

31050 ■ Human Development Center--Duluth
1401 E 1st St.
Duluth, MN 55805
Ph: (218)728-4991
Free: 800-634-8775
URL: http://www.humandevelopmentcenter.org/

East Grand Forks

31051 ■ Northwestern Mental Health Center
East Grand Forks Branch Clinic
1424 Central Ave. NE, Ste. 142
East Grand Forks, MN 56721
Ph: (218)773-6102
URL: http://northwesternment.qwestoffice.net/

Eden Prairie

31052 ■ Pride Institute
14400 Martin Dr.
Eden Prairie, MN 55344
Ph: (952)934-7554
Free: 800-54-PRIDE
URL: http://www.pride-institute.com/

Fergus Falls

31053 ■ Fergus Falls Veterans Affairs Clinic
1821 N Park St.
Fergus Falls, MN 56537
Ph: (218)739-1400
Fax: (218)739-1401
URL: http://www2.va.gov/directory/guide/facility.asp?ID=5143&dnum=All

31054 ■ Lakeland Mental Health Center
126 E Alcott Ave.
Fergus Falls, MN 56537
Ph: (218)736-6987
Free: 800-223-4512
URL: http://www.lmhc.org/

Fosston

31055 ■ Northwestern Mental Health Center, Inc.
Fosston
102 Sather Dr.
Fosston, MN 56542
Ph: (218)435-1212
URL: http://northwesternment.qwestoffice.net/
Formerly: Fosston Clinic.

Grand Marais

31056 ■ Human Development Center--Grand Marais
1807 W Hwy. 61
Grand Marais, MN 55604
Ph: (218)387-9444
Free: 800-634-8775
URL: http://www.humandevelopmentcenter.org/locations/cook.aspx

Grand Rapids

31057 ■ Northland Counseling Center
215 SE 2nd Ave.
Grand Rapids, MN 55744
Ph: (218)326-1274
Formerly: Northland Mental Health Center.

Granite Falls

31058 ■ Western Mental Health Clinic--Granite Falls
818 Prentice St.
Granite Falls, MN 56241
Ph: (320)564-2238
Formerly: Western Human Development Center.

Hancock

31059 ■ Parkview Home
672 7th St.
Hancock, MN 56244
Ph: (320)392-5212
URL: http://www.pcs.sfhs.org/

Hibbing

31060 ■ Fairview University Medical Center - Mesabi
Behavioral Health Services
750 E 34th St.
Hibbing, MN 55746
Ph: (218)262-4881
URL: http://www.range.fairview.org/services/mental-health/
Formerly: Mesabi Regional Medical Center/ Range Mental Health Center; University Medical Center - Mesabi.

31061 ■ Hibbing Veterans Affairs Clinic
1101 E 37th St., Ste. 220
Hibbing, MN 55746
Ph: (218)263-9698
Fax: (218)262-1915
URL: http://www2.va.gov/directory/guide/facility.asp?ID=5145&dnum=All

31062 ■ Range Mental Health Center
3203 W 3rd Ave.
Hibbing, MN 55746
Ph: (218)263-9237
Free: 888-344-9237
URL: http://www.rangementalhealth.org/

Hopkins

31063 ■ Washburn Child Guidance Center
810 1st St. S, Ste. 210
Hopkins, MN 55343
Ph: (612)871-1454
URL: http://www.washburn.org/

International Falls

31064 ■ Koochiching Counseling Center
1404 Hwy. 11-71
International Falls, MN 56649
Ph: (218)283-3406
Formerly: Koochiching Counseling Center and Northland Counseling Center.

Ivanhoe

31065 ■ Western Mental Health Clinic--Ivanhoe
Divine Providence Hospital
336 E George St.
Ivanhoe, MN 56142
Ph: (507)694-1414
Formerly: Divine Providence Hospital/ Western Human Clinic.

Kasson

31066 ■ South Central Human Relations Center
13 W Main St.
Kasson, MN 55944
Ph: (507)634-4639

La Crescent

31067 ■ Hiawatha Valley Mental Health Center--La Crescent
306 Main St., Ste. 4
La Crescent, MN 55947
Ph: (507)895-2296

Litchfield

31068 ■ Woodland Centers
Litchfield Clinic
114 N Holcombe Ave., Ste. 230
Litchfield, MN 55355
Ph: (320)693-5300
Free: 888-281-0243
Fax: (320)693-7222
URL: http://www.woodlandcenters.com

Luverne

31069 ■ Southwestern Mental Health Center, Inc.--Luverne
216 E Luverne St.
Luverne, MN 56156
Ph: (507)283-9511

Maplewood

31070 ■ Maplewood Veterans Affairs Clinic
2785 White Bear Ave., Ste. 210
Maplewood, MN 55109
Ph: (651)290-3040
URL: http://www2.va.gov/directory/guide/facility.asp?ID=5149&dnum=All

Marshall

31071 ■ Western Mental Health Clinic--Marshall
1212 E College Dr.
Marshall, MN 56258
Ph: (507)532-3236
URL: http://www.whdcinc.com/
Formerly: Western Human Development Center.

Minneapolis

31072 ■ Anchor House--People Incorporated
1319 Girard Ave. N
Minneapolis, MN 55411
Ph: (612)529-2040
URL: http://www.peopleincorporated.org/

31073 ■ Epilepsy Services--People Incorporated
630 Cedar Ave. S, Ste. 204
Minneapolis, MN 55454
Ph: (612)338-9035
URL: http://www.peopleincorporated.org/

31074 ■ Hennepin House--People Incorporated
1622 Hillside Ave. N
Minneapolis, MN 55411
Ph: (612)588-0664
URL: http://www.peopleincorporated.org/

31075 ■ Huss Recovery--People Incorporated
1315 Girard Ave. N
Minneapolis, MN 55411
Ph: (612)287-2340
URL: http://www.peopleincorporated.org/

31076 ■ Minneapolis Veterans Affairs Medical Center
1 Veterans Dr.
Minneapolis, MN 55417
Ph: (612)725-2000
Free: 866-414-5058
URL: http://www1.va.gov/minneapolis/

31077 ■ Tasks Unlimited, Inc.
2411 Nicollet Ave.
Minneapolis, MN 55404
Ph: (612)871-3320
Fax: (612)871-0432
URL: http://www.tasksunlimited.org

Montevideo

31078 ■ Montevideo Veterans Affairs Clinic
1025 N 13th St.
Montevideo, MN 56265
Ph: (320)269-2222
Fax: (320)269-8929
URL: http://www2.va.gov/directory/guide/facility.asp?ID=5349&dnum=All

31079 ■ Woodland Centers
Montevideo Clinic
517 N 17th St.
Montevideo, MN 56265
Ph: (320)269-6581
Free: 800-992-1716
URL: http://www.woodlandcenters.com

Morris

31080 ■ Prairie Community Services
801 Nevada Ave., Ste. 301
Morris, MN 56267
Ph: (320)589-3077
URL: http://www.pcs.sfhs.org/

Oakdale

31081 ■ People Incorporated--Heather Ridge
7483 46th St. N
Oakdale, MN 55128
Ph: (651)748-8861
URL: http://www.peopleincorporated.org/

Olivia

31082 ■ Woodland Centers
Olivia Clinic
1635 W Lincoln Ave.
Olivia, MN 56277
Ph: (320)523-5526
URL: http://www.woodlandcenters.com

Owatonna

31083 ■ Safe Harbour
250 E Main St.
Owatonna, MN 55060
Ph: (507)455-8100

31084 ■ South Central Human Relations
610 Florence Ave.
Owatonna, MN 55060
Ph: (507)451-2630

Park Rapids

31085 ■ Upper Mississippi Mental Health Center
120 N Main St.
Park Rapids, MN 56470
Ph: (218)732-7266
URL: http://www.ummhcmn.org/

Pipestone

31086 ■ Southwestern Mental Health Center, Inc.--Pipestone
1016 8th Ave. SW
Pipestone, MN 56164
Ph: (507)825-5888

Redwood Falls

31087 ■ Western Mental Health Clinic--Redwood Falls
205 S Mill St.
Redwood Falls, MN 56283
Ph: (507)637-3340
URL: http://www.whdcinc.com/
Formerly: Western Human Development Center.

Richfield

31088 ■ People Incorporated
Upton House
7720 Upton Ave. S
Richfield, MN 55423
Ph: (612)866-5490
URL: http://www.peopleincorporated.org/

Rochester

31089 ■ Mayo Clinic
Mayo Foundation
200 1st St. SW
Rochester, MN 55905
Ph: (507)266-5100

31090 ■ Rochester Veterans Affairs Clinic
1617 Skyline Dr.
Rochester, MN 55902
Ph: (507)252-0885
URL: http://www2.va.gov/directory/guide/facility.asp?ID=5156&dnum=All

31091 ■ Zumbro Valley Mental Health Center
343 Wood Lake Dr. SE
Rochester, MN 55904
Ph: (507)289-2089
Free: 800-422-0670
URL: http://www.zumbromhc.org/

31092 ■ Zumbro Valley Mental Health Center
Community Support Program
47 13 1/2 St., NW
Rochester, MN 55901
Ph: (507)287-2274
Free: 800-422-0670
URL: http://www.zumbromhc.org/

31093 ■ Zumbro Valley Mental Health Center
Crisis Receiving Unit
2116 Campus Dr. SE, Ste. 105
Rochester, MN 55904
Ph: (507)281-6248
Free: 800-422-0670
URL: http://www.zumbromhc.org/

31094 ■ Zumbro Valley Mental Health Center
Thomas House
15 6th Ave. SE
Rochester, MN 55904-4671
Ph: (507)287-2026
Free: 800-422-0670
URL: http://www.zumbromhc.org/

Saint Cloud

31095 ■ Saint Cloud Veteran Affairs Medical Center
4801 Veterans Dr.
Saint Cloud, MN 56303
Ph: (320)252-1670
Free: 866-687-7382
URL: http://www.stcloud.va.gov/contact/index.asp

Saint James

31096 ■ South Central Veterans Affairs Clinic
St. James Medical Center
1101 Moultin Dr.
Saint James, MN 56081
Ph: (507)375-3391
URL: http://www2.va.gov/directory/guide/facility.asp?ID=5157&dnum=All

Saint Paul

31097 ■ APOLLO Resource Center--People Incorporated
313 Dale St. N, Apt. 337
Saint Paul, MN 55103
Ph: (651)227-6321
URL: http://www.peopleincorporated.org/

31098 ■ Edgebrook House--People Incorporated
2250 Edgebrook Ave.
Saint Paul, MN 55119
Ph: (651)731-0821
URL: http://www.peopleincorporated.org/

31099 ■ Hamm Memorial Clinic
408 Saint Peter St., No. 429
Saint Paul, MN 55102
Ph: (651)224-0614

31100 ■ Home Health--People Incorporated
317 York Ave.
Saint Paul, MN 55101
Ph: (651)774-0011
URL: http://www.peopleincorporated.org/

31101 ■ Londin Place--People Incorporated
384 Londin Pl.
Saint Paul, MN 55119
Ph: (651)731-0821
URL: http://www.peopleincorporated.org/

31102 ■ Maghakian Place--People Incorporated
1100 Hancock St.
Saint Paul, MN 55106
Ph: (651)793-6333
URL: http://www.peopleincorporated.org/

31103 ■ Ramsey House--People Incorporated
700 E 8th St.
Saint Paul, MN 55106
Ph: (651)774-2604
URL: http://www.peopleincorporated.org/

31104 ■ Ruth House--People Incorporated
246 Ruth St.
Saint Paul, MN 55119
Ph: (651)731-0821
URL: http://www.peopleincorporated.org/

Slayton

31105 ■ Western Mental Development Clinic
3001 Maple Rd.
Slayton, MN 56172
Ph: (507)836-6053
Formerly: Western Human Development Center.

Stillwater

31106 ■ Human Services, Inc.--Stillwater
375 E Orleans St.
Stillwater, MN 55082
Ph: (651)430-2720
URL: http://www.hsicares.org/

Two Harbors

31107 ■ Human Development Center--Two Harbors
629 1st Ave.
Two Harbors, MN 55616
Ph: (218)834-5520
Free: 800-634-8775
URL: http://www.humandevelopmentcenter.org/locations/lake.aspx

Virginia

31108 ■ Range Mental Health Center
624 S 13th St.
Virginia, MN 55792
Ph: (218)749-2881
Free: 800-450-2273
URL: http://www.rangementalhealth.org/

31109 ■ Range Mental Health Center, Inc.
504 1st St., N
Virginia, MN 55792
Ph: (218)741-4714
Free: 800-450-2273
URL: http://www.rangementalhealth.org/

Willmar

31110 ■ Woodland Centers--Willmar
1125 SE 6th St.
Willmar, MN 56201
Ph: (320)235-4613
Free: 800-992-1716
Fax: (320)231-9140
URL: http://www.woodlandcenters.com

Windom

31111 ■ Southwestern Mental Health Center, Inc.--Windom
Family Service Bldg.
9 4th St.
Windom, MN 56101
Ph: (507)831-2090

Winona

31112 ■ CBS House
73 W Broadway St.
Winona, MN 55987
Ph: (507)454-7155
URL: http://www.hvmhc.org/

31113 ■ Hiawatha Valley Mental Health Center--Winona
166 Main St.
Winona, MN 55987
Ph: (507)454-4341
Free: 800-657-6777
URL: http://www.hvmhc.org/

Worthington

31114 ■ Southwestern Mental Health Center, Inc.--Worthington
1024 7th Ave.
Worthington, MN 56187
Ph: (507)376-4141

31115 ■ Southwestern Mental Health Unity House
1224 4th Ave.
Worthington, MN 56187
Ph: (507)372-7671
Formerly: Unity House.

MISSISSIPPI

Ackerman

31116 ■ Region VII Community Counseling Services
100 Old Sturgis Rd.
Ackerman, MS 39735
Ph: (662)285-6225
URL: http://www.ccsms.org/

Amory

31117 ■ Region III Mental Health Center
Monroe County
317 Main St. N
Amory, MS 38821
Ph: (662)256-7416

Bay Saint Louis

31118 ■ Region XIII Gulf Coast Mental Health Center
Hancock County Office
819B Central Ave.
Bay Saint Louis, MS 39520-3913
Ph: (228)467-1881
URL: http://www.gcmhc.com/locations.html
Formerly: Cedar Point Group Home.

Bay Springs

31119 ■ Region X Weems Community Mental Health Center
Jasper County - Bay Springs
9 N 2nd St.
Bay Springs, MS 39422
Ph: (601)764-2201
URL: http://www.weemsmh.com

Belzoni

31120 ■ Life Help Region VI Mental Health
119 Jackson St.
Belzoni, MS 39038
Ph: (662)247-3256
URL: http://www.region6-lifehelp.org/

Biloxi

31121 ■ Gulf Oaks Hospital
Behavioral Health Services
180A DeBuys Rd.
Biloxi, MS 39531
Ph: (228)388-0600
URL: http://www.gulfcoastmedicalcenter.com

31122 ■ Veterans Affairs Gulf Coast Health Care System
400 Veterans Ave.
Biloxi, MS 39531
Ph: (228)523-5000
Free: 800-296-8872
URL: http://www.biloxi.va.gov/

Booneville

31123 ■ Region IV Timber Hills Mental Health Services
Rainbow Clubhouse
2100 E Chambers Dr.
Booneville, MS 38829
Ph: (662)728-3174
URL: http://www.timberhills.com/

Brandon

31124 ■ Region VIII Mental Health Services
613 Marquette Rd.
Brandon, MS 39042
Ph: (601)591-5553
URL: http://www.region8mhs.org/

Brookhaven

31125 ■ Region XI Southwest Mississippi
Lincoln County Mental Health Center
511 Brookman Dr.
Brookhaven, MS 39601
Ph: (601)833-5386
URL: http://www.swmmhc.org
Formerly: Region XI Southwest Lincoln County Mental Health Center.

31126 ■ Region XI Southwest Mississippi Mental Health
Lincoln County Life Skills Center
120 W Monticello St.
Brookhaven, MS 39601
Ph: (601)833-8605
Fax: (601)833-6067
URL: http://www.swmmhc.org

31127 ■ Region XI Southwest Mississippi
New Haven Recovery Center
310 Nalco Ln., NE
Brookhaven, MS 39601
Ph: (601)833-3698
URL: http://www.swmmhc.org

Collins

31128 ■ Region XII Pine Belt Mental Health Covington County
22 Westview Dr.
Collins, MS 39428
Ph: (601)765-4514
Fax: (601)765-8941
URL: http://www.pbmhr.com/offices.html

Columbia

31129 ■ Region XII Pine Belt Mental Health Marion County
217 Dewey St.
Columbia, MS 39429
Ph: (601)736-6799
Fax: (601)736-4809
URL: http://www.pbmhr.com/offices.html

Columbus

31130 ■ Columbus Veterans Affairs Clinic
824 Alabama St.
Columbus, MS 39702
Ph: (662)244-0391
URL: http://www2.va.gov/directory/guide/facility.asp?ID=5498&dnum=All

De Kalb

31131 ■ Region X Weems Community Mental Health Center Kemper County
110 Hopper Ave.
De Kalb, MS 39328
Ph: (601)743-5616
URL: http://www.weemsmh.com

Dublin

31132 ■ Fairland Institute
3000 Hwy. 49 S
Dublin, MS 38739
Ph: (662)624-2152
URL: http://www.regionone.org/

31133 ■ Fairland Institute--Adolescents
2900 Hwy. 49 S
Dublin, MS 38739
Ph: (662)624-4905
URL: http://www.regionone.org/

Eupora

31134 ■ Community Counseling Services--Eupora
203 Hwy. 9 S
Eupora, MS 39744
Ph: (662)258-8147
URL: http://www.ccsms.org/page.php?c=3

Fayette

31135 ■ Jefferson County Clubhouse
519 N Main St.
Fayette, MS 39069
Ph: (601)786-8091
URL: http://www.swmmhc.org

31136 ■ Region XI Southwest Mississippi Jefferson County Mental Health Center/New Hope
519 N Main St.
Fayette, MS 39069
Ph: (601)786-8091
Fax: (601)786-8023
URL: http://www.swmmhc.org
Formerly: Southwest Mississippi Mental Health.

Gautier

31137 ■ Region XIV Singing River Mental Health/Mental Retardation Services
3407 Shamrock Ct.
Gautier, MS 39553-5337
Ph: (228)497-0690
URL: http://www.dmh.state.ms.us/community_care.htm

Gloster

31138 ■ Region XI Southwest MS Train Clubhouse
136 N Captain Gloster Dr.
Gloster, MS 39638
Ph: (601)225-4866
Fax: (601)225-4868
URL: http://www.swmmhc.org/

Greenville

31139 ■ Greenville Veterans Affairs Clinic--S Colorado Street
1502 S Colorado St.
Greenville, MS 38703
Ph: (662)332-9872
URL: http://www2.va.gov/directory/guide/facility.asp?ID=5499&dnum=All

31140 ■ Region V Delta Community Mental Health Services Work Activity Center - Level 1
1654 E Union St.
Greenville, MS 38704
Ph: (662)335-5274
Fax: (662)378-3976
URL: http://www.dcmhs.com

Greenwood

31141 ■ Region VI Mental Health Center Life Help
2504 Browning Rd.
Greenwood, MS 38930
Ph: (662)453-6211
Fax: (662)455-8724
URL: http://www.region6-lifehelp.org/

Grenada

31142 ■ Life Help Mental Health Center - Region 6 Grenada County Office
965 Spring Hill Rd.
Grenada, MS 38901
Ph: (662)226-1112
URL: http://www.region6-lifehelp.org/
Formerly: Region VI Life Help Mental Health Center.

Gulfport

31143 ■ Region XIII Gulf Coast Mental Health Center
1600 Broad Ave.
Gulfport, MS 39501-3603
Ph: (228)863-1132
URL: http://www.gcmhc.com/locations.html

31144 ■ Region XIII Gulf Coast Mental Health Center Live Oaks
15094 County Barn Rd.
Gulfport, MS 39503
Ph: (228)248-0125
URL: http://www.gcmhc.com/locations.html
Formerly: Live Oaks Mental Health Center.

31145 ■ Region XIII Gulf Coast Mental Health Center New Hope House Group Home
554 Loposser Ave.
Gulfport, MS 39507
Ph: (228)896-9395
URL: http://www.gcmhc.com/locations.html
Formerly: Gulf Coast Mental Health Center.

Hattiesburg

31146 ■ Hattiesburg Veterans Affairs Clinic
231 Methodist Blvd.
Hattiesburg, MS 39401
Ph: (601)296-3530
URL: http://www2.va.gov/directory/guide/facility.asp?ID=5500&dnum=All

31147 ■ Pine Grove Life Focus
1611 S 28th Ave.
Hattiesburg, MS 34902
Ph: (601)288-4900
URL: http://www.pinegrovetreatment.com/

31148 ■ Pine Grove Recovery Center
2255 Broadway Dr.
Hattiesburg, MS 39402
Ph: (601)288-2273
Free: 888-574-4673
URL: http://www.pinegrovetreatment.com/

31149 ■ Region XII Pine Belt Mental Health Resources
103 S 19th Ave.
Hattiesburg, MS 39403
Ph: (601)544-4641
Fax: (601)582-1607
URL: http://www.pbmhr.com/

Hernando

31150 ■ Communicare - Hernando
185 W Center St.
Hernando, MS 38632-2268
Ph: (662)429-7875
URL: http://www.communicare.org/

Indianola

31151 ■ Life Help Mental Health Center-Region 6 Indianola Office-Sunflower County
200 E Baker St.
Indianola, MS 38751
Ph: (662)887-5441
URL: http://www.region6-lifehelp.org/
Formerly: Region VI Life Help Mental Health Center.

Iuka

31152 ■ Region IV Timber Hills Mental Health Services Children's Services
1213 Maria Ln.
Iuka, MS 38852
Ph: (662)423-3332
URL: http://www.timberhills.com/

Jackson

31153 ■ Cares Center
402 Wesley Ave.
Jackson, MS 39202
Ph: (601)360-0583
URL: http://www.mchscares.org/

31154 ■ G.V. Montgomery Veterans Affairs Medical Center
1500 E Woodrow Wilson Dr.
Jackson, MS 39216
Ph: (601)362-4471
Free: 800-949-1009
URL: http://www.jackson.va.gov/

Kosciusko

31155 ■ Kosciusko Veterans Affairs Clinic
332 Hwy. 12 W
Kosciusko, MS 39090
Ph: (662)289-1800
URL: http://www2.va.gov/directory/guide/facility.asp?ID=5502&dnum=All

Laurel

31156 ■ Pine Belt Mental Healthcare Resources
5192 Hwy. 11 N
Laurel, MS 39441
Ph: (601)649-7921
Fax: (601)649-7939
E-mail: info@pbmhr.com
URL: http://www.pbmhr.com

31157 ■ South Central Regional Medical Center
1220 Jefferson St.
Laurel, MS 39440-4355
Ph: (601)426-4000
URL: http://www.scrmc.com

Lexington

31158 ■ Region VI Life Help Mental Health Center
Lexington Office, Holmes County
328 Depot St.
Lexington, MS 39095
Ph: (662)834-1709
URL: http://www.region6-lifehelp.org/

Liberty

31159 ■ Region XI Southwest Mississippi Amite County Mental Health Center
315 E Main St.
Liberty, MS 39645
Ph: (601)657-4354
Fax: (601)657-4307
URL: http://www.swmmhc.org

Long Beach

31160 ■ Region XIII Gulf Coast Mental Health Center
Venture House
19049 Pineville Rd.
Long Beach, MS 39560
Ph: (228)822-1414
URL: http://www.gcmhc.com/locations.html

Louisville

31161 ■ Community Counseling Services--Louisville
504 W Main St.
Louisville, MS 39339
Ph: (662)773-9377
URL: http://www.ccsms.org/page.php?c=3

Lucedale

31162 ■ Region XIV Singing River Services Singing Pines Program
101B Industrial Park Rd.
Lucedale, MS 39452-6553
Ph: (601)947-4274

Macon

31163 ■ Community Counseling Services--Macon
200 W MLK Jr. St.
Macon, MS 39341
Ph: (662)726-5042
URL: http://www.ccsms.org/page.php?c=3

McComb

31164 ■ Region XI Southwest Mississippi Mental Health Complex
1701 White St.
McComb, MS 39648
Ph: (601)684-2173
URL: http://www.swmmhc.org

31165 ■ Region XI Southwest Mississippi Pike Country Lifeskills Center
651 S Broadway St.
McComb, MS 39648
Ph: (601)684-7543
Fax: (601)249-4233
URL: http://www.swmmhc.org

Meadville

31166 ■ Meadville Veterans Affairs Clinic
595 Main St. E
Meadville, MS 39653
Ph: (601)384-3650
URL: http://www2.va.gov/directory/guide/facility.asp?ID=5575&dnum=All

31167 ■ Region XI Southwest Mississippi Franklin County Mental Health Center
47 Maine St. E
Meadville, MS 39653
Ph: (601)384-2261
URL: http://www.swmmhc.org

Meridian

31168 ■ Alliance Health Center
5000 Hwy. 39 N
Meridian, MS 39307
Ph: (601)483-6211
URL: http://www.psysolutions.com/facilities/alliance/index.html

31169 ■ Meridian Veterans Affairs Clinic
2103 13th St.
Meridian, MS 39301
Ph: (601)482-7154
URL: http://www2.va.gov/directory/guide/facility.asp?ID=5503&dnum=All

31170 ■ Pine Grove Counseling Center of Meridian
2217 Highway 39 N, Ste. B
Meridian, MS 39301
Ph: (601)485-7094
URL: http://www.pinegrovetreatment.com

31171 ■ Region X Weems Community Mental Health Center
1415 College Dr.
Meridian, MS 39307
Ph: (601)483-4821
Fax: (601)485-0223
URL: http://www.weemsmh.com

31172 ■ Region X Weems Community Mental Health Center
Pinnacle House
633 22nd St., Ste. F
Meridian, MS 39301
Ph: (601)693-5051
URL: http://www.weemsmh.com

Monticello

31173 ■ Region XI Southwest Mississippi Lawrence County Mental Health Center
1230 Nola Rd.
Monticello, MS 39654
Ph: (601)587-4674
URL: http://www.swmmhc.org

Natchez

31174 ■ Natchez Veterans Affairs Clinic
46 Sgt. Prentiss Dr., Ste. 16
Natchez, MS 39120
Ph: (601)442-7141
URL: http://www2.va.gov/directory/guide/facility.asp?ID=5506&dnum=All

31175 ■ Region XI Southwest Mississippi Adams County Lifeskills Center
500 LaSalle St.
Natchez, MS 39120
Ph: (601)446-8649
URL: http://www.swmmhc.org

31176 ■ Region XI Southwest Mississippi Adams County Mental Health Center
200 S Wall St.
Natchez, MS 39120
Ph: (601)446-6634
Fax: (601)446-6898
URL: http://www.swmmhc.org

Oxford

31177 ■ Communicare--Oxford
152 Hwy. 7 S
Oxford, MS 38655-5392
Ph: (662)234-7521
URL: http://www.communicare.org/
Formerly: Region II Mental Health Center.

Pascagoula

31178 ■ Region XIV Singing River Services
903 11th St.
Pascagoula, MS 39567
Ph: (228)769-1511

31179 ■ Region XIV Singing River Services Eden House
2721 Eden St.
Pascagoula, MS 39581-3358
Ph: (228)769-1357

31180 ■ Region XIV Singing River Services Stevens Center
4905 Telephone Rd.
Pascagoula, MS 39567-1823
Ph: (228)769-1280

Picayune

31181 ■ Region XIII Gulf Coast Mental Health Center
Pearl River County Office
211 Hwy. 11 S
Picayune, MS 39466-4503
Ph: (601)798-7001
URL: http://www.gcmhc.com/locations.html

Port Gibson

31182 ■ Region XI Southwest Mississippi Claiborne County Mental Health and Pathway House
2090 Hwy. 61 N
Port Gibson, MS 39150
Ph: (601)437-8185
URL: http://www.swmmhc.org

Prentiss

31183 ■ Region XII Pine Belt Mental Health Jeff Davis County Mental Health Center
116 JE Johnson Rd.
Prentiss, MS 39474
Ph: (601)792-4872
Fax: (601)792-2643
URL: http://www.pbmhr.com
Formerly: Caring Hands House.

Purvis

31184 ■ Region XII Pine Belt Mental Health Work Activity Program
123 Front St.
Purvis, MS 39475
Ph: (601)794-8127
Fax: (601)794-2455
URL: http://www.pbmhr.com

Quitman

31185 ■ Region X Weems Community Mental Health Center
Clark County
100 Park Pl.
Quitman, MS 39355
Ph: (601)776-6051
URL: http://www.weemsmh.com

Richton

31186 ■ Region XII Pine Belt Mental Health--Richton
506 Oak St.
Richton, MS 39476
Ph: (601)788-6308
URL: http://www.pbmhr.com

Rolling Fork

31187 ■ Region V Delta Community Mental Health Services
418 W Race St.
Rolling Fork, MS 39159
Ph: (662)873-6228
URL: http://www.dcmhs.com/

Sardis

31188 ■ Communicare--Sardis
100 E Frontage
Sardis, MS 38666
Ph: (662)487-2746
URL: http://www.communicare.org/

Senatobia

31189 ■ Communicare--Senatobia
101 Preston McKay Dr.
Senatobia, MS 38668
Ph: (662)562 6216
URL: http://www.communicare.org/

Southaven

31190 ■ Parkwood Southaven
8829 Center St.
Southaven, MS 38671
Ph: (662)342-5591
URL: https://www.parkwoodbhs.com/

Summit

31191 ■ Region XI Southwest Mississippi Summit House
301 Robb St.
Summit, MS 39666-7053
Ph: (601)276-3040
URL: http://www.swmmhc.org

Tupelo

31192 ■ North Mississippi Medical Center
830 S Gloster St.
Tupelo, MS 38801-4934
Ph: (662)841-3000
Free: 800-843-3375
URL: http://www.nmhs.net/

31193 ■ Region III Mental Health Center
2434 S Eason Blvd.
Tupelo, MS 38804
Ph: (662)842-9217
URL: http://region3mh.com/

Tylertown

31194 ■ Region XI Southwest Mississippi Walthall County Mental Health Center
219 Ball Ave.
Tylertown, MS 39667
Ph: (601)876-4721
Fax: (601)876-0052
URL: http://www.swmmhc.org

Vicksburg

31195 ■ Region XV Warren-Yazoo Mental Health Service
3444 Wisconsin Ave.
Vicksburg, MS 39180
Ph: (601)638-0031
URL: http://www.warren-yazoo.org

31196 ■ Region XV Warren-Yazoo Mental Health Service Chemical Dependency Center
3442 Wisconsin Ave.
Vicksburg, MS 39180
Ph: (601)634-0181
Fax: (601)634-6291
URL: http://www.warren-yazoo.org

31197 ■ Region XV Warren-Yazoo Mental Health Service Warren County Group Home
3440 Wisconsin Ave.
Vicksburg, MS 39180
Ph: (601)636-1814
URL: http://www.warren-yazoo.org

Water Valley

31198 ■ Communicare--Water Valley
214 Frostland Dr.
Water Valley, MS 38965
Ph: (662)473-3693
URL: http://www.communicare.org/

Waveland

31199 ■ Region XIII Gulf Coast Mental Health Center Friendship House
919 St. Joseph St.
Waveland, MS 39576
Ph: (228)467-9904
URL: http://www.gcmhc.com/locations.html

Waynesboro

31200 ■ Region XII Pine Belt Mental Health--Waynesboro
1104B Cedar St/
Waynesboro, MS 39367
Ph: (601)735-3350
Fax: (601)735-9598
URL: http://www.pbmhr.com/offices.html

Wiggins

31201 ■ Region XIII Gulf Coast Mental Health Center Stone County Office
217 Parker St. N
Wiggins, MS 39577
Ph: (601)798-7001
URL: http://www.gcmhc.com/locations.html

Winona

31202 ■ Life Help Mental Heath Center-Region 6 Winona Office-Montgomery County
718 Alberta Dr.
Winona, MS 38967
Ph: (662)283-2529
URL: http://www.region6-lifehelp.org/

Woodville

31203 ■ Region XI Southwest Mississippi Wilkinson County Mental Health Center
1495 US Hwy. 61 S
Woodville, MS 39669
Ph: (601)888-3022
Fax: (601)888-7248
URL: http://www.swmmhc.org

Yazoo City

31204 ■ Region XV Warren-Yazoo Mental Health Service
2303 Gordon Ave.
Yazoo City, MS 39194-2067
Ph: (662)746-5712
Fax: (662)746-5723
URL: http://www.warren-yazoo.org

MISSOURI

Arnold

31205 ■ Comtrea Community Mental Health Center
21 Municipal Dr.
Arnold, MO 63010
Ph: (636)931-2700
Fax: (636)296-0102
E-mail: wecare@comtrea.org
URL: http://www.comtrea.org

Belton

31206 ■ Belton Veterans Affairs Clinic
17140 Bel-Ray Pl.
Belton, MO 64012
Ph: (816)922-2161
URL: http://www2.va.gov/directory/guide/facility.asp?ID=5240&dnum=All

31207 ■ Pathways Community Behavioral Healthcare Belton
201 Main
Belton, MO 64012
Ph: (816)322-4332
URL: http://www.pathwaysonline.org

Bolivar

31208 ■ Family Institute of the Ozarks
315 S Main Ave.
Bolivar, MO 65613
Ph: (417)326-2902
Fax: (417)326-4555
URL: http://happyfamilybolivar.com

Branson

31209 ■ Burrell Behavioral Health--Branson Outpatient Satellite
155 Corporate Pl.
Branson, MO 65616
Ph: (417)269-2476
URL: http://www.coxhealth.com
Formerly: urrell Branson Outpatient Satellite; Burrell Branson Outpatient Program.

Brookfield

31210 ■ North Central Missouri Mental Health Center--Brookfiled
1 Center Dr.
Brookfield, MO 64628
Ph: (660)258-7810
URL: http://www.mocmhc.org/memberagencies/north.htm

Buffalo

31211 ■ Burrell Behavioral Outpatient Satellite
119 N Ash St.
Buffalo, MO 65622
Ph: (417)345-8844
URL: http://www.coxhealth.com
Formerly: Burrell Behavioral Health Buffalo Office.

Camdenton

31212 ■ Lake of the Ozarks Veterans Affairs Clinic
246 E Hwy. 54
Camdenton, MO 65020
Ph: (573)317-1150
URL: http://www2.va.gov/directory/guide/facility.asp?ID=5246&dnum=All

Cameron

31213 ■ Cameron Veterans Affairs Clinic
1111 Euclid Dr.
Cameron, MO 64429
Ph: (816)922-2500
URL: http://www2.va.gov/directory/guide/facility.asp?ID=5352&dnum=All

Cape Girardeau

31214 ■ Cape Girardeau Veterans Affairs Clinic
3047 Williams St., Ste. 101
Cape Girardeau, MO 63701

Ph: (573)339-0909
URL: http://www2.va.gov/directory/guide/facility.asp?ID=5241&dnum=All

31215 ■ Community Counseling Center, Cape Girardeau
341 N Main St.
Cape Girardeau, MO 63701
Ph: (573)335-1424
URL: http://www.communitycounselingcenter.com

31216 ■ Community Counseling Center--Cape Girardeau
402 S Silver Springs Rd.
Cape Girardeau, MO 63703
Ph: (573)334-1100
Fax: (573)651-4345
URL: http://www.communitycounselingcenter.com

Carrollton

31217 ■ Burrell Behavioral Health--Carrollton
305 N Mason St.
Carrollton, MO 64633
Ph: (660)542-1403
URL: http://www.burrellcenter.com

Chillicothe

31218 ■ North Central Missouri Mental Health Center--Chillicothe
401 Youseef Dr.
Chillicothe, MO 64601
Ph: (660)646-6872
URL: http://www.mocmhc.org/memberagencies/north.htm

Clinton

31219 ■ Pathways Community Behavioral Healthcare, Inc.
Clinton
1800 Community Dr.
Clinton, MO 64735
Ph: (660)885-8131
Fax: (660)885-2393
URL: http://www.pathwaysonline.org

Columbia

31220 ■ Boys and Girls Town of Missouri
4304 S Bearfield Rd.
Columbia, MO 65201
Ph: (573)874-8686
Fax: (573)874-8608
E-mail: admissions@great-circle.org
URL: http://www.bgtm.org/aboutus/ourcampuses.htm#COL

31221 ■ Harry S. Truman Memorial Veterans Affairs Medical Center
800 Hospital Dr.
Columbia, MO 65201
Ph: (573)814-6000
URL: http://www.columbiamo.va.gov/

El Dorado Springs

31222 ■ Pathways Community Behavioral Healthcare
El Dorado Springs
107 W Broadway St.
El Dorado Springs, MO 64744
Ph: (417)876-5314
Fax: (417)876-5328
URL: http://www.pathwaysonline.org

Farmington

31223 ■ Farmington Veterans Affairs Clinic--W Columbia Street
1580 W Columbia St.
Farmington, MO 63640
Ph: (573)760-1365
URL: http://www2.va.gov/directory/guide/facility.asp?ID=5242&dnum=All

31224 ■ Pathways Community Behavioral Healthcare
Farmington
301 N Washington Sq., Ste. 1
Farmington, MO 63640
Ph: (573)756-6101
Fax: (573)756-6420
URL: http://www.pathwaysonline.org

Fort Leonard Wood

31225 ■ Fort Leonard Wood Veterans Affairs Clinic
126 Missouri Ave., Box 1239
Fort Leonard Wood, MO 65473
Ph: (573)329-8305
URL: http://www2.va.gov/directory/guide/facility.asp?ID=5244&dnum=All

Fredericktown

31226 ■ Community Counseling Center of Madison County
311 Garrett St.
Fredericktown, MO 63645
Ph: (573)783-4104
Fax: (573)783-4572
Formerly: Community Counseling Center at Fredericktown.

Hamilton

31227 ■ North Central Missouri Mental Health Center--Hamilton
1 Crossing St.
Hamilton, MO 64644
Ph: (816)583-2151
URL: http://www.mocmhc.org/memberagencies/north.htm

Hannibal

31228 ■ Mark Twain Area Counseling Center
917 Broadway
Hannibal, MO 63401
Ph: (573)221-2120
Fax: (573)221-4380

Harrisonville

31229 ■ Pathways Community Behavioral Healthcare--Harrisonville
300 Galaxie Ave.
Harrisonville, MO 64701
Ph: (816)380-5167
URL: http://www.pathwaysonline.org/

Hayti

31230 ■ Family Counseling Center, Inc.--Hayti
The Stapleton
Hwy. J
Hayti, MO 63851
Ph: (573)359-2600
Fax: (573)359-1103
E-mail: info@familycounselingcenter.org
URL: http://www.familycounselingcenter.org

Independence

31231 ■ Comprehensive Mental Health Services, Inc.--Independence
10901 E Winner Rd.
Independence, MO 64052
Ph: (816)254-3652
URL: http://www.thecmhs.com/

Jefferson City

31232 ■ Jefferson City Veterans Affairs Clinic
2707 W Edgewood
Jefferson City, MO 65109
Ph: (573)635-0233
URL: http://www2.va.gov/directory/guide/facility.asp?ID=5694&dnum=All

Joplin

31233 ■ Ozark Center - Community Placement Program
3010 McClelland Blvd.
Joplin, MO 64803
Ph: (417)347-7630
URL: http://www.freemanhealth.com/ozarkcenter

31234 ■ Ozark Center--Joplin
3006 McClelland Blvd.
Joplin, MO 64803
Ph: (417)347-7630
URL: http://www.freemanhealth.com/ozarkcenter

31235 ■ Ozark Center--Joplin
Turn Around Ranch
1949 S Snowberry Ln.
Joplin, MO 64804
Ph: (417)781-0821
URL: http://www.freemanhealth.com/ozarkcenter

31236 ■ Ozark Center/Ozark Oaks
3402 Schifferdecker Ave.
Joplin, MO 64804
Ph: (417)347-7760
URL: http://www.freemanhealth.com/ozarkcenter

Kansas City

31237 ■ Crittenton Children's Center
10918 Elm Ave.
Kansas City, MO 64134
Ph: (816)765-6600
URL: http://www.saintlukeshealthsystem.org/
Formerly: Crittenton Behavioral Health.

31238 ■ Imani House - Substance Abuse
3950 E 51st St.
Kansas City, MO 64130
Ph: (816)929-2600
URL: http://www.swopehealth.org/

31239 ■ Kansas City Veterans Affairs Medical Center
4801 Linwood Blvd.
Kansas City, MO 64128
Ph: (816)861-4700
Free: 800-525-1483
URL: http://www2.va.gov/directory/guide/facility.asp?ID=65&dnum=All

31240 ■ The Lodge
3860 E 60th St.
Kansas City, MO 64130
Ph: (816)349-3520
URL: http://www.swopehealth.org/

31241 ■ ReDiscover - South
6801 E 117th St.
Kansas City, MO 64134
Ph: (816)966-0903
URL: http://www.rediscovermh.org/
Formerly: Research Mental Health Services.

31242 ■ Swope Health Services
Behavioral Health Services
3801 Blue Pkwy.
Kansas City, MO 64130
Ph: (816)923-5800
Fax: (816)923-9210
URL: http://www.swopehealth.org
Formerly: Swope Parkway Health Community, Mental Health Center; Swope Parkway Health Center.

31243 ■ Western Missouri Mental Health Center
1000 E 24th St.
Kansas City, MO 64108
Ph: (816)512-7000
URL: http://dmh.mo.gov/wmmhc/

Kennett

31244 ■ Family Counseling Center, Inc.--Kennett
925 Hwy. VV
Kennett, MO 63857
Ph: (573)888-5925
Fax: (573)888-9365
URL: http://www.familycounselingcenter.org/kennett.html

Lees Summit

31245 ■ ReDiscover Mental Health Services
901 NE Independence Ave.
Lees Summit, MO 64086
Ph: (816)966-0900
URL: http://www.rediscovermh.org/
Formerly: Research Mental Health Services.

Marble Hill

31246 ■ Community Counseling Center of Bollinger County
208 Broadway
Marble Hill, MO 63764
Ph: (573)238-1027
Fax: (573)238-1171
URL: http://www.cccntr.com/

Marshall

31247 ■ East Ranch, Marshall
RR 1
Marshall, MO 65340
Ph: (660)886-3385
URL: http://www.bys-kids.org

31248 ■ North Ranch, Marshall
508 E Slater St.
Marshall, MO 65340
Ph: (660)886-6891
URL: http://www.bys-kids.org

31249 ■ Pathways Community Behavioral Healthcare Marshall
615 Cherokee Dr., Ste. 1
Marshall, MO 65340
Ph: (660)831-0908
URL: http://www.pathwaysonline.org

31250 ■ South Ranch, Marshall
1280 Hwy. W W
Marshall, MO 65340
Ph: (660)886-7481
URL: http://www.bys-kids.org

31251 ■ West Ranch, Marshall
1080 E Hwy. W W
Marshall, MO 65340
Ph: (660)886-2228
URL: http://www.bys-kids.org

Mexico

31252 ■ Arthur Center
321 W Promenade
Mexico, MO 65265
Ph: (573)582-1234

31253 ■ Mexico Veterans Affairs Clinic
1 Veterans Dr.
Mexico, MO 65265
Ph: (573)581-9630
URL: http://www2.va.gov/directory/guide/facility.asp?ID=5301&dnum=All

31254 ■ Options Unlimited of Mexico
400 E Liberty St.
Mexico, MO 65265
Ph: (573)581-7887
Free: 866-581-7887
Fax: (573)581-1026
URL: http://arthurcenter.com/contact-arthur-center/options-unlimited-of-mexico.h tml

Milan

31255 ■ North Central Missouri Mental Health Center--Milan
611 W 3rd St.
Milan, MO 63556
Ph: (660)265-3016
URL: http://www.mocmhc.org/memberagencies/north.htm

Monett

31256 ■ Burrell Monett Outpatient Satellite
801 N Lincoln
Monett, MO 65708
Ph: (417)269-1426
Formerly: Burrell Behavioral Health.

31257 ■ Clark Community Mental Health Center
1701 N Central Ave.
Monett, MO 65708
Ph: (417)235-6610
Fax: (417)236-0340
URL: http://www.clarkmentalhealth.com/

Mount Vernon

31258 ■ Gene Taylor Veterans Affairs Community Based Outpatient Clinic
600 N Main
Mount Vernon, MO 65712
Ph: (417)466-4000
URL: http://www2.va.gov/directory/guide/facility.asp?ID=5396&dnum=All

Neosho

31259 ■ Ozark Center--Neosho
336 S Jefferson St.
Neosho, MO 64850
Ph: (417)451-4565
URL: http://www.freemanhealth.com/ozarkcenter

Nevada

31260 ■ Nevada Veterans Affairs Clinic
322 S Prewitt
Nevada, MO 64772
Ph: (417)448-8905
URL: http://www2.va.gov/directory/guide/facility.asp?ID=5247&dnum=All

O'Fallon

31261 ■ Crider Center for Mental Health Services--O'Fallon
161 Pieper Pl.
O'Fallon, MO 63366
Ph: (636)978-3132
URL: http://www.cridercenter.org

Overland Park

31262 ■ Research Psychiatric Center Millcreek Outpatient Clinic
8787 Ballentine, Ste. 1200
Overland Park, MO 66214
Ph: (816)444-8161
URL: http://www.researchpsychiatriccenter.com/

Perryville

31263 ■ Community Counseling Center at Perryville
406 N Spring St., Ste. 2
Perryville, MO 63775
Ph: (573)547-8305
URL: http://www.cccntr.com/

Poplar Bluff

31264 ■ Poplar Bluff Mental Health Center
3001 Warrior Lane
Poplar Bluff, MO 63901
Ph: (573)686-1200
Fax: (573)686-1029
URL: http://www.familycounselingcenter.org/poplar_bluff.html

31265 ■ Poplar Bluff Veterans Affairs Medical Center
1500 N Westwood Blvd.
Poplar Bluff, MO 63901
Ph: (573)686-4151
Free: 888-557-8262
URL: http://www.poplarbluff.va.gov/

Raymore

31266 ■ Pathways Community Behavioral Healthcare Raymore
407 Laurus Dr.
Raymore, MO 64083
Ph: (816)318-4430
Fax: (816)318-8865
URL: http://www.pathwaysonline.org/contactUs.htm

Saint Charles

31267 ■ Crider Center for Mental Health Services--Saint Charles
300 Water St.
Saint Charles, MO 63301
Ph: (636)946-4000
URL: http://www.cridercenter.org

31268 ■ Saint Charles Veterans Affairs Clinic
7 Jason Ct.
Saint Charles, MO 63304
Ph: (314)286-6988
Free: 800-228-5459
Fax: (314)289-6360
URL: http://www2.va.gov/directory/guide/facility.asp?ID=5248&dnum=All

Saint James

31269 ■ Boys and Girls Town of Missouri, Saint James
13160 County Rd. 3610
Saint James, MO 65559
Ph: (573)265-3251
Fax: (573)265-5370
URL: http://www.bgtm.org

31270 ■ Saint James Veterans Affairs Clinic
620 N Jefferson St.
Saint James, MO 65559
Ph: (573)265-0448
URL: http://www2.va.gov/directory/guide/facility.asp?ID=5302&dnum=All

Saint Joseph

31271 ■ Saint Joseph Veterans Affairs Clinic
1314 N 36th St., Ste. A
Saint Joseph, MO 64506
Free: 800-852-8387
URL: http://www2.va.gov/directory/guide/facility.asp?ID=5249&dnum=All

Saint Louis

31272 ■ Adapt of Missouri, Inc.
2301 Hampton Ave.
Saint Louis, MO 63139
Ph: (888)657-3201
URL: http://www.adaptusa.com/services1.php

31273 ■ Boys and Girls Town of Missouri, Saint Louis
4485 Westminster Place
Saint Louis, MO 63108
Ph: (314)353-7911
URL: http://www.bgtm.org

31274 ■ Epworth Children & Family Services
110 N Elm Ave.
Saint Louis, MO 63119
Ph: (314)961-5718
URL: http://www.epworth.org/

31275 ■ Hopewell Center
1504 S Grand
Saint Louis, MO 63104
Ph: (314)531-1770
Fax: (314)531-3072
URL: http://www.hopewellcenter.com/

31276 ■ Hopewell Center, Saint Louis
4411 N Newstead Ave.
Saint Louis, MO 63115
Ph: (314)531-1770
URL: http://www.hopewellcenter.com/

31277 ■ Missouri Veterans Affairs Clinic
10600 Lewis and Clark Blvd.
Saint Louis, MO 63136
Ph: (314)286-6988
Fax: (314)868-2561
URL: http://www2.va.gov/directory/guide/facility.asp?ID=5334&dnum=All

31278 ■ Places for People, Inc.
4130 Lindell Blvd.
Saint Louis, MO 63108
Ph: (314)535-5600
Free: 800-584-3930
URL: http://www.placesforpeople.org/

31279 ■ Saint Louis Veterans Affairs Medical Center
Jefferson Barracks Division
1 Jefferson Barracks Dr.
Saint Louis, MO 63125
Ph: (314)652-4100
Free: 800-228-5459
URL: http://www.stlouis.va.gov/

31280 ■ Saint Louis Veterans Affairs Medical Center
John Cochran Division
915 N Grand Blvd.
Saint Louis, MO 63106
Ph: (314)652-4100
Free: 800-228-5459
URL: http://www.stlouis.va.gov/

Sainte Genevieve

31281 ■ Community Counseling Center Sainte Genevieve
748 Center Dr.
Sainte Genevieve, MO 63670
Ph: (573)883-7407
Fax: (573)883-7537
URL: http://www.cccntr.com/

Salem

31282 ■ Salem Veterans Affairs Clinic
Hwy. 72 N
Salem, MO 65560
Ph: (573)729-6626
Free: 888-557-8262
URL: http://www2.va.gov/directory/guide/facility.asp?ID=5354&dnum=All

Springfield

31283 ■ Burell - Cox North Center for Addictions
1423 N Jefferson
Springfield, MO 65802
Ph: (417)269-3748
URL: http://www.coxhealth.com/
Formerly: Inpatient Psychiatry Center.

31284 ■ Burrell Adult Crisis Stabilization Unit
930 S Robberson
Springfield, MO 65807
Ph: (417)862-6555

31285 ■ Burrell Behavioral Health--Springfield CSTAR Program
1300 E Bradford Pkwy.
Springfield, MO 65804
Ph: (417)269-5400

31286 ■ Burrell Behavioral Health - Wilkinson
904 S Campbell Ave.
Springfield, MO 65806
Ph: (417)831-7111
URL: http://www.coxhealth.com/body.cfm?id=1406

31287 ■ Burrell Transitions Program
323 E Grand St.
Springfield, MO 65807
Ph: (417)269-7300

Trenton

31288 ■ North Central Missouri Mental Health Center--Trenton
1601 E 28th St.
Trenton, MO 64683
Ph: (660)359-4487
Fax: (660)359-4129
E-mail: lori@mocmhc.org
URL: http://www.mocmhc.org/memberagencies/north.htm

Unionville

31289 ■ North Central Missouri Mental Health Center--Unionville
1926 Oak St.
Unionville, MO 63565
Ph: (660)947-7940
URL: http://www.mocmhc.org/memberagencies/north.htm

Warrensburg

31290 ■ Recovery Center--Warrensburg
703 N DeVasher
Warrensburg, MO 64093
Ph: (660)747-1355
Fax: (660)747-7925
URL: http://www.pathwaysonline.org/contactUs.htm

31291 ■ Warrensburg Veterans Affairs Clinic
1300 Veterans Dr.
Warrensburg, MO 64093
Ph: (816)922-2500
URL: http://www2.va.gov/directory/guide/facility.asp?ID=5353&dnum=All

Warsaw

31292 ■ Pathways Community Behavioral Healthcare Warsaw
1620 Hilltop Dr.
Warsaw, MO 65355
Ph: (660)428-1280
Fax: (660)428-1283
URL: http://www.pathwaysonline.org

Wentzville

31293 ■ Crider Center for Mental Health Services--Wentzville
1032 Crosswinds Ct.
Wentzville, MO 63385
Ph: (636)332-8000
Free: 800-574-2422
URL: http://www.cridercenter.org

West Plains

31294 ■ West Plains Veterans Affairs Clinic
1211 Missouri Ave.
West Plains, MO 65775
Ph: (417)257-2454
URL: http://www2.va.gov/directory/guide/facility.asp?ID=5250&dnum=All

MONTANA

Anaconda

31295 ■ Anaconda Veterans Affairs Clinic
118 E 7th St.
Anaconda, MT 59711
Ph: (406)563-6090
URL: http://www2.va.gov/directory/guide/facility.asp?ID=608&dnum=All

31296 ■ Western Montana Mental Health Center--Anaconda
307 E Park Ave., Ste. 211
Anaconda, MT 59711
Ph: (406)563-3413
Formerly: Anaconda Mental Health Center.

Baker

31297 ■ Baker Clincal Office
205 S 4th St. NW
Baker, MT 59313
Ph: (406)234-1687

Big Timber

31298 ■ Big Timber Mental Health Center
515 Hooper St.
Big Timber, MT 59011
Ph: (406)932-5924

Billings

31299 ■ Billings Clinic Behavioral Health Clinic
1020 N 27th St., 4th Fl.
Billings, MT 59107
Ph: (406)255-8550
URL: http://www.billingsclinic.com/body.cfm?id=28

31300 ■ Billings Veterans Affairs Clinic
2345 King Ave. W
Billings, MT 59102
Ph: (406)651-5670
URL: http://www2.va.gov/directory/guide/facility.asp?ID=616&dnum=All

31301 ■ Group Home Number 2
1212 Ave. C
Billings, MT 59102
Ph: (406)248-2925

31302 ■ Group Home Number 3
920 Parkhill Dr.
Billings, MT 59102
Ph: (406)252-5658

31303 ■ Mental Health Center
1245 N 29th St.
Billings, MT 59101
Ph: (406)252-5658
Free: 800-266-7198
E-mail: info@mhcbillings.org
URL: http://www.mhcbillings.org/

31304 ■ Mental Health Center--The Hub
515 N 27th St.
Billings, MT 59101
Ph: (406)248-4803
URL: http://www.mhcbillings.org/

31305 ■ Rainbow House
925 N 18th St.
Billings, MT 59101
Ph: (406)252-7851
URL: http://www.mhcbillings.org/

Bozeman

31306 ■ Bozeman Veterans Affairs Clinic
300 N Wilson, Ste. 703G
Bozeman, MT 59715
Ph: (406)522-8923
URL: http://www2.va.gov/directory/guide/facility.asp?ID=869&dnum=All

31307 ■ Hope House
316 N Tracy
Bozeman, MT 59715
Ph: (406)585-1130

Butte

31308 ■ Western Montana Mental Health Center
Silver House
106 W Broadway St.
Butte, MT 59701
Ph: (406)723-4033

Columbus

31309 ■ Columbus Mental Health Center
410 E Pike Ave.
Columbus, MT 59019
Ph: (406)322-4514

Cut Bank

31310 ■ Center for Mental Health
Cut Bank Center for Mental Health
1210 E Main St.
Cut Bank, MT 59427
Ph: (406)873-5538
URL: http://www.center4mh.org/
Formerly: Golden Triangle Community Mental Health Center ; Glacier County Clinic.

31311 ■ Glacier Veterans Affairs Community Health Center
519 E Main
Cut Bank, MT 59427
Ph: (406)873-9047
URL: http://www2.va.gov/directory/guide/facility.asp?ID=5666&dnum=All

Deer Lodge

31312 ■ Western Montana Mental Health Center--Addiction Services
304 Milwaukee Ave., Ste. 27
Deer Lodge, MT 59722
Ph: (406)846-3442

Dillon

31313 ■ Western Montana Mental Health Center
Beaverhead County Office
234 E Reeder St.
Dillon, MT 59725
Ph: (406)683-2200
Formerly: Anaconda Mental Health Center.

Fort Harrison

31314 ■ Veterans Affairs Montana Healthcare System
3687 Veterans Dr.
Fort Harrison, MT 59636
Ph: (406)265-4304
Free: 877-468-8387
URL: http://www.montana.va.gov/

Glasgow

31315 ■ Eastern Montana Community Mental Health Center
1009 6th Ave. N
Glasgow, MT 59230
Ph: (406)228-9349
URL: http://www.emcmhc.org/emcmhc_locations.htm

31316 ■ Glasgow Veterans Affairs Clinic
621 3rd St. S, Ste. 107
Glasgow, MT 59230
Ph: (406)228-3554
URL: http://www2.va.gov/directory/guide/facility.asp?ID=892&dnum=All

Glendive

31317 ■ Glendive Clinical Office
131 W Valontine
Glendive, MT 59330
Ph: (406)377-6075
URL: http://www.emcmhc.org/emcmhc_locations.htm

31318 ■ Glendive Veterans Affairs Clinic
2000 Montana Ave.
Glendive, MT 59330
Ph: (406)377-4755
URL: http://www2.va.gov/directory/guide/facility.asp?ID=889&dnum=All

Great Falls

31319 ■ Gateway--Great Falls
1220 Central Ave., Ste. 1A
Great Falls, MT 59403
Ph: (406)727-2512
URL: http://gatewayrecovery.org/

31320 ■ Great Falls Veterans Affairs Clinic
1417 9th St. S, Ste. 200
Great Falls, MT 59405
Ph: (877)468-8387
URL: http://www2.va.gov/directory/guide/facility.asp?ID=887&dnum=All

31321 ■ Langel House
1109 2nd Ave. N
Great Falls, MT 59401
Ph: (406)452-3354
URL: http://www.center4mh.org/

31322 ■ New Directions Center
621 1st Ave. S
Great Falls, MT 59401
Ph: (406)761-2104
URL: http://www.center4mh.org/

Hamilton

31323 ■ Western Montana Mental Health Center
Riverfront Counseling
209 N 10th St.
Hamilton, MT 59840
Ph: (406)532-9101

Hardin

31324 ■ Hardin Mental Health Center
809 N Custer Ave.
Hardin, MT 59034
Ph: (406)665-8730

Havre

31325 ■ Center for Mental Health
Havre Center for Mental Health
312 3rd St.
Havre, MT 59501
Ph: (406)265-9639
URL: http://www.center4mh.org/
Formerly: Golden Triangle Community Mental Health Center ; Hill County Clinic.

Helena

31326 ■ Hanniford House
925 N Hanniford St.
Helena, MT 59601
Ph: (406)449-5650
URL: http://www.center4mh.org/

31327 ■ Helena Center for Mental Health
900 N Jackson St.
Helena, MT 59601
Ph: (406)443-7151
URL: http://www.center4mh.org/
Formerly: Montana House; Golden Triangle Community Mental Health Center.

Kalispell

31328 ■ Kalispell Veterans Affairs Clinic
31 3 Mile Dr., Ste. 102
Kalispell, MT 59901
Ph: (406)751-5980
URL: http://www2.va.gov/directory/guide/facility.asp?ID=5093&dnum=All

31329 ■ Western Montana Mental Health Center
Sinopah House
420 Windward Way
Kalispell, MT 59901
Ph: (406)751-8375

31330 ■ Western Montana Mental Health Center
Stillwater Therapeutic Services
418 Windward Way
Kalispell, MT 59901
Ph: (406)752-6100

Lewistown

31331 ■ Harlowton Mental Health Center
PO Box 44
Lewistown, MT 59457
Ph: (406)632-4778

31332 ■ Lewistown Mental Health Center
212 Wendell Ave.
Lewistown, MT 59457
Ph: (406)538-7483
URL: http://www.center4mh.org/

Libby

31333 ■ Western Montana Mental Health Center
Lincoln County Office
1469 Hwy. 2 S
Libby, MT 59923
Ph: (406)293-8746

Miles City

31334 ■ Miles City Veterans Affairs Clinic and Nursing Home
210 S Winchester
Miles City, MT 59301
Ph: (406)874-5600
URL: http://www2.va.gov/directory/guide/facility.asp?ID=88&dnum=All

Missoula

31335 ■ Missoula Veterans Affairs Clinic
2687 Palmer St., Ste. C
Missoula, MT 59808
Ph: (406)442-6410
Free: 877-468-8387
URL: http://www2.va.gov/directory/guide/facility.asp?ID=886&dnum=All

31336 ■ Western Montana Mental Health Center
Child and Family Services Network
1305 Wyoming St.
Missoula, MT 59801
Ph: (406)532-9770

31337 ■ Western Montana Mental Health Center--Missoula
Fort Missoula, Bldg. T-9
Missoula, MT 59804
Ph: (406)532-8400

31338 ■ Western Montana Mental Health Center
Turning Point
1325 Wyoming St.
Missoula, MT 59801
Ph: (406)532-9800

Red Lodge

31339 ■ Red Lodge Mental Health Center
5 E 9th St.
Red Lodge, MT 59068
Ph: (406)446-2500

Ronan

31340 ■ Western Montana Mental Health Center
Lake County Office
8 2nd St. SW
Ronan, MT 59864
Ph: (406)532-9170

Roundup

31341 ■ Roundup Mental Health Center
26 Main St.
Roundup, MT 59072
Ph: (406)323-1142

Scobey

31342 ■ Eastern Montana Community Mental Health Clinic
Scobey Clinical Office
105 5th Ave. E
Scobey, MT 59263
Ph: (407)487-2296
URL: http://www.emcmhc.org/emcmhc_locations.htm

Shelby

31343 ■ Shelby Center for Mental Health
301 1st St.
Shelby, MT 59474-1964
Ph: (406)434-5285
URL: http://www.center4mh.org/
Formerly: Golden Triangle Community Mental Health Center.

Sidney

31344 ■ Eastern Montana Community Mental Health Clinic
Sidney Clinical Office
1201 W Holly St., Ste. 4
Sidney, MT 59270
Ph: (406)433-4635
URL: http://www.emcmhc.org/emcmhc_locations.htm

Terry

31345 ■ Eastern Montana Community Mental Health Clinic
Terry Clinical Office
409 Bowen
Terry, MT 59349
Ph: (406)234-1687
URL: http://www.emcmhc.org/emcmhc_locations.htm

Thompson Falls

31346 ■ Western Montana Mental Health Center
Sanders County Office
704 Malden Ln.
Thompson Falls, MT 59873
Ph: (406)532-9190

Townsend

31347 ■ Townsend Center for Mental Health
417 Broadway
Townsend, MT 59644
Ph: (406)266-3327
URL: http://www.center4mh.org/

Wibaux

31348 ■ Eastern Montana Community Mental Health Clinic
Wibaux Clinical Office
115 S Wibaux
Wibaux, MT 59353
Ph: (406)377-6075
URL: http://www.emcmhc.org/emcmhc_locations.htm

NEBRASKA

Alliance

31349 ■ Alliance Veterans Affairs Clinic
524 Box Butte Ave.
Alliance, NE 69301
Ph: (308)762-8814
URL: http://www2.va.gov/directory/guide/facility.asp?ID=5171&dnum=All

31350 ■ Panhandle Mental Health Center
221 Box Butte Ave.
Alliance, NE 69301
Ph: (308)762-2545
URL: http://www.pmhc.net/

Auburn

31351 ■ Blue Valley Behavioral Health--Auburn
820 Central Ave., Ste. 4
Auburn, NE 68305
Ph: (402)274-4373
URL: http://www.bvbh.net/
Formerly: Blue Valley Mental Health Center.

Beatrice

31352 ■ OMNI Behavioral Health--Beatrice
722 Court St., Ste. 101
Beatrice, NE 68310
Ph: (402)223-3843
URL: http://www.omnibehavioralhealth.com/

Bellevue

31353 ■ Lutheran Family Services
730 N Fort Crook Rd.
Bellevue, NE 68005
Ph: (402)292-9105
URL: http://www.lfsneb.org/

Broken Bow

31354 ■ Mid-Plains Center
225 S 10th St.
Broken Bow, NE 68822
Ph: (308)872-6705

Chadron

31355 ■ Panhandle Mental Health Center
Chadron Community Clinic
651 W 4th St.
Chadron, NE 69337
Ph: (308)432-6106
URL: http://www.pmhc.net/

Columbus

31356 ■ OMNI Behavioral Health--Columbus
2904 14th St., Ste. 3
Columbus, NE 68601
Ph: (402)562-7933
URL: http://www.omnibehavioralhealth.com/

31357 ■ Seekers of Serenity
4432 Sunrise Pl.
Columbus, NE 68601
Ph: (402)564-9994
URL: http://www.4bhs.org/
Formerly: Sunrise Place.

Crete

31358 ■ Blue Valley Behavioral Health--Crete
1212 Ivy St.
Crete, NE 68333
Ph: (402)826-2000
URL: http://bvbh.net/content/offices/crete.html

David City

31359 ■ Blue Valley Behavioral Health--David City
367 E St.
David City, NE 68632
Ph: (402)367-4216
URL: http://bvbh.net/content/offices/david_city.html

Fairbury

31360 ■ Blue Valley Behavioral Health--Fairbury
521 E St.
Fairbury, NE 68352
Ph: (402)729-2272
URL: http://bvbh.net/content/offices/fairbury.html

Falls City

31361 ■ Blue Valley Behavioral Health--Falls City
116 W 19th St.
Falls City, NE 68355
Ph: (402)245-4458
URL: http://bvbh.net/content/offices/falls_city.html

Geneva

31362 ■ Blue Valley Behavioral Health--Geneva
831 F St.
Geneva, NE 68361
Ph: (402)759-4761
URL: http://bvbh.net/content/offices/geneva.html

Grand Island

31363 ■ Mid-Plains Center for Behavioral Healthcare Services
615 N Elm St.
Grand Island, NE 68802
Ph: (308)385-5035
Fax: (308)395-1060
URL: http://www.midplainscenter.org/

31364 ■ Veterans Affairs Nebraska-Western Iowa Health Care System
Grand Island Division
2201 N Broadwell Ave.
Grand Island, NE 68803
Ph: (308)382-3660
Free: 866-580-1810
URL: http://www.nebraska.va.gov/visitors/grand_island.asp

Hastings

31365 ■ South Central Behavioral Services, Inc.
ACT Program
835 S Burlington, No. 107
Hastings, NE 68901

Ph: (402)462-4200
URL: http://www.scbsne.com/

31366 ■ South Central Behavioral Services, Inc.
Hastings Office
616 W 5th St.
Hastings, NE 68901
Ph: (402)463-5684
URL: http://www.scbsne.com/

31367 ■ South Central Behavioral Services, Inc.
Rehabilitation Services
724 S Burlington Ave.
Hastings, NE 68901
Ph: (402)463-7435
URL: http://www.scbsne.com/

Hebron

31368 ■ Blue Valley Behavioral Health--Hebron
141 N 4th St.
Hebron, NE 68370
Ph: (402)759-4761
URL: http://bvbh.net/content/offices/hebron.html

Holdrege

31369 ■ Holdrege Veterans Affairs Clinic
1118 Burlington St.
Holdrege, NE 68949
Ph: (308)995-3760
URL: http://www2.va.gov/directory/guide/facility.asp?ID=5700&dnum=All

31370 ■ South Central Behavioral Services, Inc.
701 4th Ave., Ste. 7
Holdrege, NE 68949
Ph: (308)237-5951
URL: http://www.scbsne.com/

Kearney

31371 ■ South Central Behavioral Services, Inc.
3810 Central Ave.
Kearney, NE 68847
Ph: (308)234-4017
URL: http://www.scbsne.com/

31372 ■ South Central Behavioral Services, Inc.
Unity House
4111 4th Ave., Ste. 12
Kearney, NE 68845
Ph: (308)698-0535
Fax: (308)698-0536
URL: http://www.scbsne.com/

Lincoln

31373 ■ Lancaster Child Guidance Residential Treatment
Lincoln
2444 O St.
Lincoln, NE 68510
Ph: (402)475-7666
Fax: (402)476-9623
E-mail: info@child-guidance.org
URL: http://www.child-guidance.org/

31374 ■ Lancaster County Community Mental Health Center
2201 S 17th St.
Lincoln, NE 68502
Ph: (402)441-7940
URL: http://www.lincoln.ne.gov/cnty/mental/

31375 ■ Lancaster County Community Mental Health Center
The Heather
2039 Q St., No. 202
Lincoln, NE 68503
Ph: (402)441-9101
URL: http://www.lincoln.ne.gov/cnty/mental/

31376 ■ Lancaster County Community Mental Health Center
Transitional Living Facility
2423 R St.
Lincoln, NE 68503
Ph: (402)441-8344
URL: http://www.lincoln.ne.gov/cnty/mental/

31377 ■ Midtown Center
2966 O St.
Lincoln, NE 68510
Ph: (402)441-8150
URL: http://www.lincoln.ne.gov/cnty/mental/
Formerly: Adams Street Center.

31378 ■ Veterans Affairs Nebraska-Western Iowa Health Care System
Lincoln Division
600 S 70th St.
Lincoln, NE 68510
Ph: (402)489-3802
URL: http://www.nebraska.va.gov/visitors/lincoln.asp

Nebraska City

31379 ■ Blue Valley Behavioral Health--Nebraska City
1903 4th Corso
Nebraska City, NE 68340
Ph: (402)873-5505
URL: http://bvbh.net/content/offices/nebraska_city.html

Norfolk

31380 ■ Behavioral Health Specialists, Inc.
900 W Norfolk Ave.
Norfolk, NE 68701
Ph: (402)370-3140
Fax: (402)370-3373
URL: http://www.4bhs.org/
Formerly: Monroe Mental Health Center.

31381 ■ Liberty Centre Services Inc.
900 E Norfolk Ave.
Norfolk, NE 68701
Ph: (402)370-3503
Fax: (402)370-3250
E-mail: libertycentre@cableone.net
URL: http://www.libertycentre.org

31382 ■ Norfolk Veterans Affairs Clinic
710 S 13th St., Ste. 1200
Norfolk, NE 68701
Ph: (402)370-4570
Free: 866-687-7382
URL: http://www.nebraska.va.gov/visitors/norfolk.asp

31383 ■ Park Place
808 Park Ave.
Norfolk, NE 68701
Ph: (402)370-4208
URL: http://www.libertycentre.org

31384 ■ Sunrise Place
923 E Norfolk Ave.
Norfolk, NE 68701
Ph: (402)379-0040
URL: http://www.4bhs.org/

North Platte

31385 ■ North Platte Veterans Affairs Clinic
600 E Francis, Ste. 3
North Platte, NE 69101
Ph: (308)532-6906
Free: 866-580-1810
URL: http://www.nebraska.va.gov/visitors/north_platte.asp

Omaha

31386 ■ Douglas County Hospital
Mental Health Unit
4102 Woolworth Ave.
Omaha, NE 68105
Ph: (402)444-7608

31387 ■ OMNI Behavioral Health--Omaha
5115 F St.
Omaha, NE 68117
Ph: (402)397-9866
URL: http://www.omnibehavioralhealth.com/

31388 ■ Veterans Affairs Nebraska-Western Iowa Health Care System
Omaha Division
4101 Woolworth Ave.
Omaha, NE 68105
Ph: (402)346-8800
Free: 800-451-5796
URL: http://www.nebraska.va.gov/

Pawnee City

31389 ■ Blue Valley Behavioral Health--Pawnee City
600 I St.
Pawnee City, NE 68420
Ph: (402)245-4458
URL: http://bvbh.net/content/offices/pawnee_city.html

Seward

31390 ■ Blue Valley Behavioral Health--Seward
459 S 6th St., Ste. 1
Seward, NE 68434
Ph: (402)643-3343
URL: http://bvbh.net/content/offices/seward.html

Tecumseh

31391 ■ Blue Valley Behavioral Health--Tecumseh
202 High St.
Tecumseh, NE 68450
Ph: (402)274-4373
URL: http://bvbh.net/content/offices/tecumseh.html

Wahoo

31392 ■ Blue Valley Behavioral Health--Wahoo
543 Linden St.
Wahoo, NE 68066
Ph: (402)443-4414
URL: http://bvbh.net/content/offices/wahoo.html

Wayne

31393 ■ Community Mental Health and Wellness Clinic
219 Main St.
Wayne, NE 68787
Ph: (402)375-2468

31394 ■ The Job Site
110 S Main St.
Wayne, NE 68787
Ph: (402)375-5741

31395 ■ Kirkwood House
514 E 6th St.
Wayne, NE 68787
Ph: (402)375-2515

York

31396 ■ Blue Valley Behavioral Health--York
722 S Lincoln Ave., Ste. 1
York, NE 68467
Ph: (402)362-6128
URL: http://bvbh.net/content/offices/york.html

NEVADA

Battle Mountain

31397 ■ Battle Mountain Mental Health Center
10 E 6th St.
Battle Mountain, NV 89820
Ph: (775)635-5753
Fax: (775)635-8028
URL: http://mhds.nv.gov/index.php?option=com_content&task=view&id=36&Itemid=208

Carson City

31398 ■ Carson Mental Health Center
1665 Old Hot Springs Rd., Ste. 150
Carson City, NV 89706
Ph: (775)687-4195
Fax: (775)687-5103
URL: http://mhds.nv.gov/index.php?option=com_content&task=view&id=38&Itemid=210

Elko

31399 ■ Elko Mental Health Center
1825 Pinion Rd., Ste. A
Elko, NV 89801
Ph: (775)738-8021
URL: http://mhds.nv.gov/index.php?option=com_content&task=view&id=41&Itemid=213

Ely

31400 ■ Ely Mental Health Center
1675 Ave. F
Ely, NV 89315
Ph: (775)289-1671
Fax: (775)289-1699
URL: http://mhds.nv.gov/index.php?option=com_content&task=view&id=42&Itemid=214

31401 ■ Ely Veterans Affairs Clinic
William Bee Ririe Rural Health Clinic
6 Steptoe Cir.
Ely, NV 89301
Ph: (775)289-3612
Fax: (801)584-5673
URL: http://www2.va.gov/directory/guide/facility.asp?ID=877&dnum=All

Fallon

31402 ■ Veterans Affairs Lahontan Valley Outpatient Clinic
345 W A St.
Fallon, NV 89406
Ph: (775)428-6161
URL: http://www2.va.gov/directory/guide/facility.asp?ID=5586&dnum=1

Gardnerville

31403 ■ Douglas Mental Health Center
1538 Hwy. 395 N
Gardnerville, NV 89410
Ph: (775)782-3671
Fax: (775)782-6639
URL: http://mhds.nv.gov/index.php?option=com_content&task=view&id=40&Itemid=212

Hawthorne

31404 ■ Rural Clinics Community Mental Health Center
100 C St.
Hawthorne, NV 89415
Ph: (775)945-3387
Fax: (775)945-2307
URL: http://mhds.nv.gov/index.php?option=com_content&view=article&id=12&Itemid=1 5

Henderson

31405 ■ Henderson Mental Health Office
1590 W Sunset Rd.
Henderson, NV 89014
Ph: (702)486-6700
URL: http://mhds.nv.gov/index.php?option=com_content&task=view&id=73&Itemid=82

31406 ■ Henderson Veterans Affairs Clinic
2920 N Greenvalley Pkwy., Ste. 215
Henderson, NV 89014
Ph: (702)636-6363
Fax: (702)456-6795
URL: http://www2.va.gov/directory/guide/facility.asp?ID=5113&dnum=All

31407 ■ South Neighborhood Family Service Center
522 E Lake Meade Pkwy., Ste. 5
Henderson, NV 89015
Ph: (702)455-7900

Las Vegas

31408 ■ Community Based Outreach Center for Homeless Veterans
926 W Owens Ave.
Las Vegas, NV 89106
Ph: (702)636-4077
URL: http://www2.va.gov/directory/guide/facility.asp?ID=5115&dnum=All

31409 ■ Las Vegas Veterans Affairs Medical Center
901 Rancho Ln.
Las Vegas, NV 89106
Ph: (702)636-6370
Free: 888-633-7554
URL: http://www.lasvegas.va.gov/

31410 ■ Mojave Mental Health Adult Services
4000 E Charleston, Ste. B-230
Las Vegas, NV 89104
Ph: (702)968-5000
Fax: (702)968-5050
E-mail: service@mojave.org
URL: http://www.mojave.org

31411 ■ Mojave Mental Health Children's Services
3171 S Jones Blvd.
Las Vegas, NV 89146
Ph: (702)253-0818
Fax: (702)253-9625
E-mail: service@mojave.org
URL: http://www.mojave.org

31412 ■ Southern Nevada Child and Adolescent Mental Health Services
6161 W Charleston Blvd.
Las Vegas, NV 89146-1126
Ph: (702)486-6100
URL: http://www.dcfs.state.nv.us/DCFS_ChildMental-Health.htm

31413 ■ Southern Nevada Division of Child & Family Services
3075 E Flamingo Rd., Ste. 108
Las Vegas, NV 89121-4300
Ph: (702)486-7500
Fax: (702)486-7522
URL: http://www.dcfs.state.nv.us/

31414 ■ Spring Mountain Treatment Center
7000 W Spring Mountain Rd.
Las Vegas, NV 89117
Ph: (702)873-2400
Free: 866-265-6117
URL: http://www.springmountaintreatmentcenter.com/

Laughlin

31415 ■ Laughlin Mental Health Center
3650 S Pointe Cir., Ste. 208
Laughlin, NV 89029
Ph: (702)298-5313
Fax: (702)298-0188
URL: http://mhds.nv.gov/index.php?option=com_content&task=view&id=46&Itemid=51

Lovelock

31416 ■ Lovelock Mental Health Center
775 Cornell Ave., Ste. A-1
Lovelock, NV 89419
Ph: (775)273-1036
Fax: (775)273-1109
URL: http://mhds.nv.gov/index.php?option=com_content&task=view&id=47&Itemid=220

Mesquite

31417 ■ Mesquite Mental Health Center
61 N Willow St., Ste. 4
Mesquite, NV 89024
Ph: (702)346-4696
URL: http://mhds.nv.gov/index.php?option=com_content&task=view&id=48&Itemid=221

Minden

31418 ■ Veterans Affairs Carson Valley Outpatient Clinic
925 Ironwood Dr., Ste. 2102
Minden, NV 89423
Ph: (775)786-7200
URL: http://www2.va.gov/directory/guide/facility.asp?ID=5561&dnum=All

Overton

31419 ■ Moapa Mental Health Center
320 N Moapa Valley Blvd.
Overton, NV 89040
Ph: (702)397-8900
Fax: (702)397-8920
URL: http://mhds.nv.gov/index.php?option=com_content&task=view&id=49&Itemid=222

Pahrump

31420 ■ Pahrump Mental Health Center
240 S Humahuaca St.
Pahrump, NV 89041
Ph: (775)751-7406
Fax: (775)751-7409
URL: http://mhds.nv.gov/index.php?option=com_content&task=view&id=50&Itemid=223

31421 ■ Pahrump Veterans Affairs Clinic
2100 E Calvada Blvd.
Pahrump, NV 89048
Ph: (775)727-7535
Fax: (775)751-6416
URL: http://www2.va.gov/directory/guide/facility.asp?ID=5119&dnum=All

Reno

31422 ■ Northern Nevada Child and Adolescent Services
2655 Enterprise Rd.
Reno, NV 89512
Ph: (775)688-1617
URL: http://www.dcfs.state.nv.us/

31423 ■ Veterans Affairs Sierra Nevada Health Care System
1000 Locust St.
Reno, NV 89502
Ph: (775)786-7200
URL: http://www.reno.va.gov/

Silver Springs

31424 ■ Silver Springs Mental Health Center
3595 Hwy. 50 E
Silver Springs, NV 89429
Ph: (775)577-0319
URL: http://mhds.nv.gov/index.php?option=com_content&task=view&id=51&Itemid=224

Wendover

31425 ■ Wendover Mental Health Center
935 N Wells, Unit B
Wendover, NV 89883
Ph: (775)738-8021
URL: http://mhds.nv.gov/index.php?option=com_content&task=view&id=54&Itemid=226

Winnemucca

31426 ■ Winnemucca Mental Health Center
3140 Traders Way
Winnemucca, NV 89445
Ph: (775)623-6580
Fax: (775)623-6584
URL: http://mhds.nv.gov/index.php?option=com_content&task=view&id=55&Itemid=227

Yerington

31427 ■ Yerington Mental Health Center
215 W Bridge St., Ste. 5
Yerington, NV 89447
Ph: (775)463-3191
Fax: (775)463-4641
URL: http://mhds.nv.gov/index.php?option=com_content&task=view&id=56&Itemid=228

NEW HAMPSHIRE

Berlin

31428 ■ Northern Human Services--Berlin
3 12th St.
Berlin, NH 03570
Ph: (603)752-7404
URL: http://www.northernhs.org/

31429 ■ Northern Human Services Mental Health Center
3 12th St.
Berlin, NH 03570
Ph: (603)752-7404
Fax: (603)752-5194
URL: http://www.northernhs.org

Claremont

31430 ■ Connecticut Valley House
7 Trinity St.
Claremont, NH 03743
Ph: (603)543-1182
Fax: (603)542-3683
URL: http://www.wcbh.org

31431 ■ West Central Behavioral Health Counseling Center of Claremont
140 North St.
Claremont, NH 03743
Ph: (603)542-2578
Free: 800-564-2578
URL: http://www.wcbh.org

Colebrook

31432 ■ Upper Connecticut Valley Mental Health and Developmental Services
55 Colby St.
Colebrook, NH 03576
Ph: (603)237-4955
URL: http://www.northernhs.org/colebrook-mental-health-center.html

31433 ■ Vershire Center
24 Depot St.
Colebrook, NH 03576
Ph: (603)237-5721
URL: http://www.northernhs.org/colebrook-vershire-center.html

Concord

31434 ■ Riverbend Children's Intervention Program
105 Loudon Rd., Bldg. 3
Concord, NH 03301
Ph: (603)228-0547
URL: http://www.riverbendcmhc.org/programs/chip.php

31435 ■ Riverbend Community Mental Health--Admissions
278 Pleasant St.
Concord, NH 03301
Ph: (603)226-0817
URL: http://www.riverbendcmhc.org/programs/counselingassoc.php

31436 ■ Riverbend Community Mental Health Inc.
PO Box 2032
Concord, NH 03302
Ph: (603)228-1551
URL: http://www.riverbendcmhc.org/

31437 ■ Riverbend Community Support Program--Pillar House
40 Pleasant St.
Concord, NH 03301
Ph: (603)225-0123
URL: http://www.riverbendcmhc.org/programs/pillar.php
Formerly: Pillar Health.

31438 ■ Riverbend Elders Program
105 Loudon Rd., Bldg. 4
Concord, NH 03302
Ph: (603)228-2101
URL: http://www.riverbendcmhc.org/programs/elderservices.php

31439 ■ Riverbend Emergency and Assessment Services
278 Pleasant St.
Concord, NH 03301
Ph: (603)226-0817
URL: http://www.riverbendcmhc.org/programs/eas.php

31440 ■ Riverbend Twitchell House
111 Pleasant St.
Concord, NH 03301
Ph: (603)226-7547
URL: http://www.riverbendcmhc.org/programs/twitchell.php

Conway

31441 ■ Carroll County Mental Health Services--Conway
25 W Main St.
Conway, NH 03818
Ph: (603)447-2111
URL: http://www.northernhs.org/conway-mhc.html

31442 ■ Conway Veterans Affairs Clinic
7 Greenwood Ave.
Conway, NH 03818
Ph: (603)447-3500
Fax: (603)447-5568
URL: http://www.manchester.va.gov/nhopc_con.asp

31443 ■ Northern Human Services--Conway
87 Washington St.
Conway, NH 03818
Ph: (603)447-3347
Fax: (603)447-8893
URL: http://www.northernhs.org/
Formerly: Northern New Hampshire Mental Health and Developmental Services.

Derry

31444 ■ Center for Life Management Beaver Lake Lodge
38 N Shore Rd.
Derry, NH 03038
Ph: (603)434-5200
URL: http://www.centerforlifemanagement.org/

31445 ■ Center for Life Management--Derry
10 Tsienneto Rd.
Derry, NH 03038
Ph: (603)434-1577
Fax: (603)434-3101
URL: http://www.centerforlifemanagement.org/

Dover

31446 ■ Behavioral Health and Developmental Services of Strafford County
113 Crosby Rd., Ste. 1
Dover, NH 03820
Ph: (603)516-9300
URL: http://www.dssc9.org/

Exeter

31447 ■ Seacoast Mental Health Center, Inc.--Exeter
30 Prospect Ave.
Exeter, NH 03833
Ph: (603)772-2710
URL: http://www.seacoastmentalhealth.org

Franklin

31448 ■ Twin Rivers Counseling Associates
53 Kendall St.
Franklin, NH 03235
Ph: (603)934-3400
Free: 800-852-3323
Fax: (603)934-3459
URL: http://www.riverbendcmhc.org/programs/twinrivers.php

Greenland

31449 ■ Fairweather Lodge--Greenland
463 Breakfast Hill Rd.
Greenland, NH 03840
Ph: (603)431-2250
URL: http://www.seacoastmentalhealth.org/

Henniker

31450 ■ Riverbend Contoocook Valley Counseling Center
7 Liberty Hill Rd.
Henniker, NH 03242
Ph: (603)428-3336
Free: 800-224-4844
URL: http://www.riverbendcmhc.org/
Formerly: Contoocook Valley Counseling Center.

Jaffrey

31451 ■ Monadnock Family Services Jaffrey District Office
15 North St.
Jaffrey, NH 03452
Ph: (603)532-4291
URL: http://www.mfs.org

Keene

31452 ■ Monadnock Family Services Administrative Office
17 93rd St.
Keene, NH 03431
Ph: (603)357-5270
URL: http://www.mfs.org

31453 ■ Monadnock Family Services Community Support Programs
17 93rd St.
Keene, NH 03431

Ph. (603)357-5270
URL: http://www.mfs.org

31454 ■ Mondanock Family Services/Emerald House
Momndanock Family
32 Emerald St.
Keene, NH 03431
Ph: (603)352-6649
URL: http://www.mfs.org

Laconia

31455 ■ Genesis Behavioral Health
111 Church St., Ste. 1
Laconia, NH 03246
Ph: (603)524-1100
Fax: (603)528-0760
E-mail: info@genesisbh.org
URL: http://www.genesisbh.org

31456 ■ Genesis Behavioral Health
Children's Center
771 N Main St.
Laconia, NH 03246
Ph: (603)524-1100
E-mail: info@genesisbh.org
URL: http://www.genesisbh.org

Lebanon

31457 ■ West Center Behavioral Health--Lebanon
85 Mechanic St., Ste. 360
Lebanon, NH 03766
Ph: (603)448-1101
URL: http://www.wcbh.org

Lincoln

31458 ■ White Mountain Mental Health Center
115 Main St.
Lincoln, NH 03251
Ph: (603)745-2090

Manchester

31459 ■ Manchester Veterans Affairs Medical Center
718 Smyth Rd.
Manchester, NH 03104
Ph: (603)624-4366
Free: 800-892-8384
URL: http://www.manchester.va.gov/

31460 ■ The Mental Health Center of Greater Manchester
401 Cypress St.
Manchester, NH 03103-3628
Ph: (603)668-4111
E-mail: info@mhcgm.org
URL: http://www.mhcgm.org

31461 ■ Pastoral Counseling Services, Inc.
2013 Elm St.
Manchester, NH 03104
Ph: (603)627-2702
URL: http://www.pcs-nh.org/

31462 ■ WestBridge Community Services
1361 Elm St., Ste. 207
Manchester, NH 03101
Ph: (603)634-4446
Free: 877-461-7711
URL: http://www.westbridge.org/

Nashua

31463 ■ Community Council of Nashua, New Hampshire Inc.
7 Prospect St.
Nashua, NH 03060-3990
Ph: (603)889-6147
URL: http://www.ccofnashua.org

31464 ■ Community Council of Nashua, New Hampshire, Inc.
Child and Adolescent Services
15 Prospect St.
Nashua, NH 03060
Ph: (603)889-6147
URL: http://www.ccofnashua.org

Newport

31465 ■ West Central Behavioral Health Counseling Center of Newport
167 Summer St., No. 3
Newport, NH 03773-1281
Ph: (603)863-1951
Free: 800-564-2578
URL: http://www.wcbh.org

Peterborough

31466 ■ Monadnock Community Hospital
454 Old St. Rd.
Peterborough, NH 03458
Ph: (603)924-7191
URL: http://www.monadnockhospital.org

31467 ■ Monadnock Family Services
Eastern Regional Office
9 Vose Farm Rd., Ste. 120
Peterborough, NH 03458
Ph: (603)924-7236
URL: http://www.mfs.org/

Portsmouth

31468 ■ Center for Learning & Attention Disorder
1149 Sagamore Ave.
Portsmouth, NH 03801
Ph: (603)436-4042
URL: http://www.smhc-nh.org/clad.asp

31469 ■ Portsmouth Veterans Affairs Clinic
302 Newmarket St.
Portsmouth, NH 03803
Ph: (603)624-4366
Fax: (603)431-8862
URL: http://www.manchester.va.gov/nhopc_ports.asp

31470 ■ Seacoast Mental Health Center, Inc.--Portsmouth
1145 Sagamore Ave.
Portsmouth, NH 03801
Ph: (603)431-6703
URL: http://www.seacoastmentalhealth.org

Rochester

31471 ■ Behavioral Health and Developmental Services
Rochester Clinic
25 Old Dover Rd., Ste. B
Rochester, NH 03867
Ph: (603)516-9300
Formerly: Strafford Guidance Center.

Salem

31472 ■ Center for Life Management
Behavioral Health
44 Stiles Rd.
Salem, NH 03079
Ph: (603)893-3548
URL: http://www.centerforlifemanagement.org/

Somersworth

31473 ■ Somersworth Veterans Affairs Clinic
200 Rte. 108
Somersworth, NH 03878
Ph: (603)624-4366
Free: 800-892-8384
Fax: (603)841-9038
URL: http://www.manchester.va.gov/nhopc_som.asp

Walpole

31474 ■ Fall Mountain Counseling Center
8 Westminster St.
Walpole, NH 03447
Ph: (603)756-4735
URL: http://www.mfs.org/

Winchester

31475 ■ Ashuelot Valley Counseling Center
20 Warwick Rd.
Winchester, NH 03470
Ph: (603)239-4376
URL: http://www.mfs.org/

Wolfeboro

31476 ■ Carroll County Mental Health Services--Wolfeboro
70 Bay St.
Wolfeboro, NH 03894
Ph: (603)569-1884
URL: http://www.northernhs.org/wolfeboro-mental-health-center.html

NEW JERSEY

Aberdeen

31477 ■ Aberdeen Counseling Center
1088 Hwy. 34
Aberdeen, NJ 07747
Ph: (732)290-1700
URL: http://www.cpcbehavioral.org/about-cpc/locations-maps.html

Absecon

31478 ■ Family Service Association
312 E White House Pike
Absecon, NJ 08201
Ph: (609)652-1600
Fax: (609)652-2226
URL: http://fsasj.org

Atlantic City

31479 ■ AtlantiCare Behavioral Health--Atlantic City
13 N Hartford Ave.
Atlantic City, NJ 08401
Ph: (609)348-1161
Free: 888-569-1000
URL: http://www.atlanticare.org/locations/behavior-health.php

Barnegat

31480 ■ Preferred Behavioral Health--Barnegat
848 W Bay Ave.
Barnegat, NJ 08005
Ph: (732)458-1700
URL: http://www.preferredbehavioral.org/

Berlin

31481 ■ Berlin House
4 Egg Harbor Rd.
Berlin, NJ 08009
Ph: (856)541-1700
URL: http://www.sjbhr.org/

31482 ■ Steininger Behavioral Care Services, Inc.
128 Cross Keys Rd., Ste. 300
Berlin, NJ 08009
Ph: (856)210-1500
URL: http://www.sbcs.us

Boonton

31483 ■ NewBridge Services, Inc.--Boonton
110 Cornelia St.
Boonton, NJ 07005
Ph: (973)335-0666
URL: http://www.newbridge.org

Brick

31484 ■ Preferred Behavioral Health--Brick
1500 Rte. 88
Brick, NJ 08724
Ph: (732)367-4700
URL: http://www.preferredbehavioral.org/contact.html

Bridgewater

31485 ■ Richard Hall Community Mental Health Center
500 N Bridge St.
Bridgewater, NJ 08807
Ph: (908)725-2800
Free: 888-744-4417
URL: http://www.co.somerset.nj.us/hservices/rhmhc/index.html

Budd Lake

31486 ■ Saint Clare's Behavioral Health Center
100 Rte. 46 N
Budd Lake, NJ 07828
Ph: (973)347-4300
Free: 888-626-2111
URL: http://www.saintclares.org/

Camden

31487 ■ Brimm Intensive Residential Program
6th & Cherry St.
Camden, NJ 08103
Ph: (856)541-1700
Free: 800-220-8081
URL: http://www.sjbhr.org/

31488 ■ Center for Family Services
584 Benson St.
Camden, NJ 08103
Ph: (856)964-1990
Fax: (856)964-0242
URL: http://www.centerffs.org/

31489 ■ Hispanic Family Center
2700 Westfield Ave.
Camden, NJ 08105
Ph: (856)365-7393
URL: http://hispanicfamilycenter.com

31490 ■ Spencer House
555 Spruce St.
Camden, NJ 08103
Ph: (856)541-1700
URL: http://www.sjbhr.org/Intensive.htm

Cape May

31491 ■ Cape May Veterans Affairs Clinic
1 Monroe Ave.
Cape May, NJ 08204
Free: 800-461-8262
Fax: (609)898-9400
URL: http://www2.va.gov/directory/guide/facility.asp?ID=5286&dnum=All

Cape May Court House

31492 ■ Cape Counseling Services
128 Crest Haven Rd.
Cape May Court House, NJ 08210
Ph: (609)465-4100
URL: http://www.capecounseling.org/

Carneys Point

31493 ■ Healthcare Commons Inc.
500 Pennsville-Auburn Rd.
Carneys Point, NJ 08069
Ph: (856)299-3200
E-mail: info@hcommons.com
URL: http://www.hcommons.com

Cherry Hill

31494 ■ Kennedy Memorial Hospital--University Medical Center
2201 Chapel Ave. W
Cherry Hill, NJ 08002
Ph: (856)488-6500
URL: http://www.kennedyhealth.org

31495 ■ Steininger Behavioral Care Services, Inc.
499 Cooper Landing Rd.
Cherry Hill, NJ 08002
Ph: (856)482-8747
Fax: (856)482-8420
URL: http://www.sbcs.us

31496 ■ University Behavioral Health Center--Cherry Hill
489 Marlboro Ave.
Cherry Hill, NJ 08002
Ph: (856)662-0955
Free: 800-969-5300
Fax: (856)662-1285
URL: http://ubhc.umdnj.edu

Clarksburg

31497 ■ CPC Behavioral Healthcare Men's Residence
417 Millstone Rd.
Clarksburg, NJ 08510
Ph: (732)935-2220
URL: http://www.cpcbhc.com/?sec=12

31498 ■ CPC Behavioral Healthcare Women's Residence
67 Red Valley Rd.
Clarksburg, NJ 08510
Ph: (732)935-2220
URL: http://www.cpcbhc.com/?sec=12

Collingswood

31499 ■ Volunteers of America--Delaware Valley
235 White Horse Pike, 2nd Fl.
Collingswood, NJ 08107
Ph: (856)854-4660
Fax: (856)854-0651
URL: http://www.voadv.org

Cranford

31500 ■ Catholic Community Services--Cranford
Mount Carmel Guild Behavioral Healthcare
505 South Ave. E
Cranford, NJ 07016
Ph: (908)497-3904
Free: 800-227-7705
URL: http://www.ccannj.com/

Dumont

31501 ■ Vantage Health System--Dumont
2 Park Ave.
Dumont, NJ 07628
Ph: (201)385-4400
Fax: (201)385-9689
URL: http://www.vantagenj.org/

East Orange

31502 ■ Veterans Affairs New Jersey Health Care System
East Orange Campus
385 Tremont Ave.
East Orange, NJ 07081
Ph: (973)676-1000
Fax: (973)676-4226
URL: http://www.eastorange.va.gov/

Eatontown

31503 ■ Heritage House--Eatontown
37 Throckmorton Ave.
Eatontown, NJ 07724
Ph: (732)935-2220
URL: http://www.cpcbehavioral.org/

Edison

31504 ■ Catholic Charities Mental Health Center--Edison
26 Safran Ave.
Edison, NJ 08837
Ph: (732)738-1323
URL: http://www.ccdom.org

Elizabeth

31505 ■ Bridgeway Rehabilitation Services, Inc.
567 Morris Ave.
Elizabeth, NJ 07208
Ph: (908)355-7200
URL: http://www.bridgewayrehab.com/

Englewood

31506 ■ Vantage Health System--Englewood
93 W Palisade Ave.
Englewood, NJ 07631-2611
Ph: (201)567-0500
URL: http://www.vantagenj.org/

Fairlawn

31507 ■ Care Plus New Jersey--Fairlawn
17-07 Romaine St.
Fairlawn, NJ 07410
Ph: (201)797-2660
URL: http://www.careplusnj.org/

Freehold

31508 ■ CPC Behavioral Healthcare Freehold Counseling Center
37 Court St.
Freehold, NJ 07728-1709
Ph: (732)780-7387
URL: http://www.cpcbhc.com/

Galloway

31509 ■ Atlanticare Behavioral Health--Galloway
400 Chris Gaupp
Galloway, NJ 08205
Ph: (609)404-1974
URL: http://www.atlanticare.org/locations/behavior-health.php

Garfield

31510 ■ Eldercare Garfield Senior Activity Center
480 Midland Ave.
Garfield, NJ 07026
Ph: (973)478-0502
URL: http://www.cafsnj.org/services/family/eldercare.html

Hackensack

31511 ■ ARC of Bergen and Passaic Counties
223 Moore St.
Hackensack, NJ 07601
Ph: (201)343-0322
Fax: (201)343-0401
URL: http://www.arcbergenpassaic.org

31512 ■ Comprehensive Behavioral Healthcare, Inc.--Hackensack
395 Main St.
Hackensack, NJ 07601

Ph: (201)646-0333
Fax: (201)646-0283
E-mail: staff@cbhcare.com
URL: http://www.cbhcare.com

31513 ■ Friendship House--Hackensack
125 Atlantic St.
Hackensack, NJ 07601
Ph: (201)488-2121

31514 ■ Veterans Affairs Medical Center Hackensack Clinic
385 Prospect Ave.
Hackensack, NJ 07601
Ph: (201)342-4536
URL: http://www2.va.gov/directory/guide/facility.asp?ID=701&dnum=1

Hainesport

31515 ■ Drenk Center Children's Mobile Response and Stabilization System
1289 Rte. 38, Ste. 202
Hainesport, NJ 08036-2730
Ph: (877)652-7624
URL: http://www.drenk.org/services_cmr.shtml

31516 ■ Lester A. Drenk Behavioral Health Center
1289 Rte. 38 W, Ste. 203
Hainesport, NJ 08036
Ph: (609)267-5656
URL: http://www.drenk.org

Hammonton

31517 ■ Atlanticare Behavioral Health--Hammonton
310 Bellevue Ave.
Hammonton, NJ 08037
Ph: (609)561-7911
URL: http://www.atlanticare.org/locations/behavior-health.php

Howell

31518 ■ Preferred Behavioral Health--Howell
450 Adelphia Rd.
Howell, NJ 07731
Ph: (732)458-1700
URL: http://www.preferredbehavioral.org/

Jersey City

31519 ■ Catholic Community Services--Jersey City Mount Carmel Guild Behavioral Healthcare
285 Magnolia Ave.
Jersey City, NJ 07304
Ph: (201)395-4800
Free: 800-227-7413
URL: http://www.ccannj.com/

31520 ■ Catholic Community Services--Jersey City Mount Carmel Guild Project Home
39 Gifford Ave.
Jersey City, NJ 07304
Ph: (201)332-4365
Free: 800-227-7413
URL: http://www.ccannj.com/

Lakewood

31521 ■ Preferred Behavioral Health--Lakewood
700 Airport Rd.
Lakewood, NJ 08701
Ph: (732)458-1700
URL: http://www.preferredbehavioral.org/

Livingston

31522 ■ Jewish Family Service of Metrowest
570 W Mt. Pleasant Ave.
Livingston, NJ 07039
Ph: (973)740-1233
URL: http://www.jfsmetrowest.org/

Lumberton

31523 ■ Drenk Center Gateway Group Home
691 Eayrestown Rd.
Lumberton, NJ 08048
Ph: (609)267-1224
URL: http://www.drenk.org

Lyndhurst

31524 ■ Comprehensive Behavioral Healthcare, Inc.--Lyndhurst
516 Valley Brook Ave.
Lyndhurst, NJ 07071
Ph: (201)935-3322
Fax: (201)460-3698
E-mail: staff@cbhcare.com
URL: http://www.cbhcare.com

Lyons

31525 ■ Veterans Affairs New Jersey Health Care System Lyons Campus
151 Knollcroft Rd.
Lyons, NJ 07019
Ph: (973)676-1000
Free: 800-315-7909
Fax: (973)676-4226
URL: http://www.lyons.va.gov/

Montville

31526 ■ NewBridge Services, Inc.--Montville
390 Main Rd.
Montville, NJ 07045-9785
Ph: (973)316-9333
E-mail: services@newbridge.org
URL: http://www.newbridge.org

31527 ■ NewBridge Services, Inc.--Montville Adult and Family Services
390 Main Rd.
Montville, NJ 07045
Ph: (973)316-9333
E-mail: services@newbridge.org
URL: http://www.newbridge.org

Morganville

31528 ■ CPC Behavioral Healthcare High Point Center
1 High Point Ctr. Way
Morganville, NJ 07751
Ph: (732)591-1750
URL: http://www.cpcbhc.com/

Morristown

31529 ■ Veterans Affairs Medical Center Morristown Clinic
340 W Hanover Ave.
Morristown, NJ 07960
Ph: (973)539-9791
URL: http://www2.va.gov/directory/guide/facility.asp?ID=940&dnum=1

Mount Holly

31530 ■ Drenk Center Crisis House
126 Spout Spring Ave.
Mount Holly, NJ 08060
Ph: (609)261-3034
URL: http://www.drenk.org

31531 ■ Drenk Center Outpatient Services
795 Woodlane Rd., Ste. 301
Mount Holly, NJ 08060
Ph: (609)267-1377
Free: 800-433-7365
URL: http://www.drenk.org

Mount Laurel

31532 ■ Family Service of Burlington County Florence Klemmer House
820 Union Mill Rd.
Mount Laurel, NJ 08054
Ph: (856)722-6726

New Brunswick

31533 ■ University Behavioral Health Center--New Brunswick
183 S Orange Ave.
New Brunswick, NJ 07103
Ph: (732)235-4594
URL: http://ubhc.umdnj.edu/

Newark

31534 ■ Mount Carmel Guild Behavioral Healthcare PACT
269 Oliver St.
Newark, NJ 07105
Ph: (973)466-1300
Free: 800-227-7705
URL: http://www.ccannj.com/PACT.php

31535 ■ Newark Beth Israel Medical Center
201 Lyons Ave.
Newark, NJ 07112
Ph: (973)926-7000
URL: http://www.saintbarnabas.com/hospitals/newark_beth_israel/index.html

Oakland

31536 ■ West Bergen Mental Healthcare--Oakland
3 Post Rd.
Oakland, NJ 07436
Ph: (201)651-1900
Fax: (201)651-9608
URL: http://www.westbergen.org/

Oaklyn

31537 ■ Parkview Apartments
540 Collings Ave.
Oaklyn, NJ 08107
Ph: (856)541-1700
Free: 800-220-8081
URL: http://www.sjbhr.org/

Paramus

31538 ■ Care Plus New Jersey, Inc.--Paramus
610 Valley Health Plz.
Paramus, NJ 07652-3607
Ph: (201)265-8200
E-mail: staff@careplusnj.org
URL: http://www.careplusnj.org
Formerly: Mid Bergen Center.

Park Ridge

31539 ■ Pascack Mental Health Center
114 Kinderkamack Rd.
Park Ridge, NJ 07656
Ph: (201)391-1355
URL: http://www.pascackmentalhealthctr.org/

Paterson

31540 ■ Veterans Affairs Medical Center Paterson Clinic
275 Getty Ave.
Paterson, NJ 07503

Ph: (973)247-1666
URL: http://www2.va.gov/directory/guide/facility.asp?ID=5327&dnum=1

Piscataway

31541 ■ University Behavioral Health Center--Piscataway
671 Hoes Ln.
Piscataway, NJ 08854
Ph: (732)235-5940
Free: 800-969-5300
URL: http://ubhc.umdnj.edu

Pompton Lakes

31542 ■ NewBridge Services, Inc.--Pompton Lakes
Adult and Family Services
105 Hamburg Tpke.
Pompton Lakes, NJ 07442
Ph: (973)831-0613
URL: http://www.newbridge.org

Pompton Plains

31543 ■ NewBridge Services, Inc.--Pompton Plains
640 Newark Pompton Tpke.
Pompton Plains, NJ 07444
Ph: (973)839-2520
URL: http://www.newbridge.org

Ramsey

31544 ■ West Bergen Center for Children and Youth
1 Cherry Ln.
Ramsey, NJ 07446-1848
Ph: (201)934-1160
URL: http://www.westbergen.org/

Red Bank

31545 ■ Helen Herrmann Counseling Center
270 Hwy. 35
Red Bank, NJ 07701
Ph: (732)842-2000
URL: http://www.cpcbhc.com/about-cpc/locations-maps.html

Ridgewood

31546 ■ West Bergen Mental Healthcare--Ridgewood
120 Chestnut St.
Ridgewood, NJ 07450
Ph: (201)444-3550
Fax: (201)652-1613
URL: http://www.westbergen.org/

Trenton

31547 ■ Greater Trenton Behavioral Healthcare
1001 Spruce St., Ste. 205
Trenton, NJ 08638
Ph: (609)396-6788
URL: http://www.gtbhc.org/

Union City

31548 ■ Catholic Community Services--Union City
Mount Carmel Guild Behavioral Healthcare
Hudson House
2201 Bergenline Ave.
Union City, NJ 07087
Ph: (201)558-3700
Free: 800-227-7705
URL: http://www.ccannj.com/hudson_house.php

Vineland

31549 ■ Vineland Veterans Affairs Clinic
1051 W Sherman Ave., Bldg. 3, Unit B
Vineland, NJ 08360
Ph: (302)994-2511
Fax: (856)690-0721
URL: http://www2.va.gov/directory/guide/facility.asp?ID=603&dnum=All

Wayne

31550 ■ NewBridge Services, Inc.--Wayne Visions
22 Riverview Dr., Ste. 202
Wayne, NJ 07470
Ph: (973)628-8530
E-mail: services@newbridge.org
URL: http://www.newbridge.org

West Milford

31551 ■ NewBridge Services, Inc.--West Milford
Adult and Family Services
1801 Greenwood Lake Tpke.
West Milford, NJ 07480
Ph: (973)728-3938
E-mail: services@newbridge.org
URL: http://www.newbridge.org

Westampton

31552 ■ Catholic Charities--Diocese of Trenton
Delaware House of Mental Health Services
25 Ikea Dr.
Westampton, NJ 08060
Ph: (609)267-9339
Free: 800-360-7711
URL: http://www.catholiccharitiestrenton.org/
Formerly: Psychiatric Rehabilitation Center.

31553 ■ Family Service of Burlington County
Young Adult Services
770 Woodlane Rd.
Westampton, NJ 08060
Ph: (609)267-5928
Free: 800-963-3377
URL: http://www.fam-serv.org/

31554 ■ Family Services of Burlington County
770 Woodlane Rd.
Westampton, NJ 08060
Ph: (609)267-5928
Free: 800-963-3377
URL: http://www.fam-serv.org/

Woodbury

31555 ■ Group Home
767 Washington Ave.
Woodbury, NJ 08096-3546
Ph: (856)848-8054
URL: http://www.njamha.org/

31556 ■ NewPoint Behavioral Healthcare
404 Tatum St.
Woodbury, NJ 08096-3497
Ph: (856)845-8050
URL: http://www.njamha.org/
Formerly: Community Mental Health Center--Gloucester County.

31557 ■ NewPoint Behavioral Healthcare
Emergency Screening Services
1 N Broad St.
Woodbury, NJ 08096
Ph: (856)845-8050
URL: http://www.njamha.org/
Formerly: Community Mental Health Center.

NEW MEXICO

Alamogordo

31558 ■ Alamogordo Veterans Affairs Clinic
1410 Aspen
Alamogordo, NM 88310
Ph: (505)437-7000
Fax: (505)434-6288
URL: http://www.albuquerque.va.gov/CBOCs/Alamogordo.asp

31559 ■ TeamBuilders Counseling Services, Inc.--Alamogordo
905 10th St., Ste. C
Alamogordo, NM 88310
Ph: (575)437-8964
URL: http://www.teambuilders-counseling.org/about/locations.html

Albuquerque

31560 ■ A New Day, Inc.
1330 San Pedro, Ste. 201-B
Albuquerque, NM 87110
Ph: (505)260-9912
Fax: (505)260-9934
URL: http://www.ndnm.org/

31561 ■ Raymond G. Murphy Veterans Affairs Medical Center
1501 San Pedro SE
Albuquerque, NM 87108
Ph: (505)265-1711
Free: 800-465-8262
URL: http://www.albuquerque.va.gov/

31562 ■ University of New Mexico Psychiatric Center
2600 Marble NE
Albuquerque, NM 87106
Ph: (505)272-2800
URL: http://hsc.unm.edu/

31563 ■ University of New Mexico Psychiatric Center
Psychosocial Rehabilitation Program
2001 Centro Familiar SW
Albuquerque, NM 87105
Ph: (505)272-5786
Fax: (505)873-5970
URL: http://hospitals.unm.edu/UNMPC/Psychosocial-Rehabilitation.shtml

Artesia

31564 ■ Artesia Counseling and Resource Center
1105 Memorial Dr.
Artesia, NM 88210
Ph: (505)746-9848
URL: http://quasar.pmsnet.org/hub/index.php

31565 ■ New Mexico Veterans Health Care System
Artesia Clinic
1700 W Main
Artesia, NM 88210
Ph: (505)746-8890
URL: http://www.albuquerque.va.gov/

Carlsbad

31566 ■ Carlsbad Mental Health Association
914 N Canal St.
Carlsbad, NM 88220
Ph: (505)885-4836
Fax: (505)628-0676
URL: http://www.carlsbadmh.com/

Clayton

31567 ■ TeamBuilders Counseling Services, Inc.--Clayton
15 Oak St.
Clayton, NM 88310
Ph: (505)375-8326
URL: http://www.teambuilders-counseling.org/about/locations.html

Clovis

31568 ■ TeamBuilders Counseling Services, Inc.--Clovis
121 Townsgate
Clovis, NM 88101
Ph: (505)742-2620
Free: 877-742-2620
URL: http://www.teambuilders-counseling.org/about/locations.html

Deming

31569 ■ Border Area Mental Health Services--Deming
901 W Hickory St.
Deming, NM 88030
Ph: (575)546-2174
URL: http://www.bamhs.org/

Espanola

31570 ■ Ayudantes, Inc.--Espanola
1206 N Riverside Dr.
Espanola, NM 87532
Ph: (505)747-0102
Fax: (505)753-9758
URL: http://www.ayudantes.org/

31571 ■ Espanola Veterans Affairs Clinic
620 Coronado St., Ste. B
Espanola, NM 87532
Ph: (505)747-5943
Fax: (505)753-8373
URL: http://www.albuquerque.va.gov/CBOCs/Espanola.asp

31572 ■ TeamBuilders Counseling Services, Inc.--Espanola
1302 Calle De La Merced
Espanola, NM 87532
Ph: (505)747-0081
URL: http://www.teambuilders-counseling.org/about/locations.html

Farmington

31573 ■ Farmington Veterans Affairs Clinic--C W Broadway
1001-C W Broadway
Farmington, NM 87401
Ph: (505)326-4383
Fax: (505)325-1925
URL: http://www.albuquerque.va.gov/CBOCs/Farmington.asp

31574 ■ Namaste, Inc.
501 Airport Dr., Ste. 253
Farmington, NM 87401
Ph: (505)325-2778
Free: 888-325-2729
URL: http://www.namasteinc.org/officesstaff.html

Fort Sumner

31575 ■ TeamBuilders Counseling Services, Inc.--Fort Sumner
678 Ave. C
Fort Sumner, NM 88119
Ph: (505)355-8326
URL: http://www.teambuilders-counseling.org/about/locations.html

Gallup

31576 ■ Western New Mexico Counseling
2025 E Aztec Ave.
Gallup, NM 87301
Ph: (505)863-3828
URL: http://quasar.pmsnet.org/portal/index.php

Hobbs

31577 ■ Guidance Center of Lea County Inc.
920 W Broadway St.
Hobbs, NM 88240
Ph: (505)393-3168

Las Cruces

31578 ■ Families and Youth Inc.
1320 S Solano Dr.
Las Cruces, NM 88001
Ph: (575)522-4004
URL: https://www.fyinm.org/default.aspx

31579 ■ Southwest Counseling Center--Downtown Mall, Las Cruces
118 S Downtown Mall
Las Cruces, NM 88001
Ph: (505)647-2860
URL: http://www.swccnm.com/

31580 ■ Southwest Counseling Center--S Main, Las Cruces
125 S Main
Las Cruces, NM 88001
Ph: (505)541-5000
URL: http://www.swccnm.com/

31581 ■ Southwest Counseling Center--W Griggs Avenue, Las Cruces
100 W Griggs Ave.
Las Cruces, NM 88001
Ph: (575)647-2800
URL: http://www.swccnm.com/

Las Vegas

31582 ■ Las Vegas Medical Center Community Mental Health Program
700 Friedman Ave.
Las Vegas, NM 87701
Ph: (505)454-5100

31583 ■ Namaste, Inc.
410 Thunderbird Dr.
Las Vegas, NM 87701
Ph: (505)425-2775
Free: 888-425-8775
URL: http://www.namasteinc.org/officesstaff.html

Lordsburg

31584 ■ Border Area Mental Health Services--Lordsburg
332 Motel Dr.
Lordsburg, NM 88045
Ph: (575)542-9477
URL: http://www.bamhs.org/

Los Alamos

31585 ■ Los Alamos Family Council
1505 15th St., Ste. A
Los Alamos, NM 87544
Ph: (505)662-3264
Free: 877-602-4060
URL: http://www.lafamilycouncil.com/

Los Lunas

31586 ■ Namaste Child and Family Development Center
40 Hob Rd.
Los Lunas, NM 87031
Ph: (505)865-3092
Free: 888-869-4118
Fax: (505)865-7721
URL: http://www.namasteinc.org/

Mescalero

31587 ■ TeamBuilders Counseling Services, Inc.--Mescalero
148 Cottonwood Dr.
Mescalero, NM 88340
Ph: (575)464-0016
URL: http://www.teambuilders-counseling.org/about/locations.html

Portales

31588 ■ Mental Health Resources, Inc.
300 E 1st St.
Portales, NM 88130
Ph: (575)359-1221

31589 ■ TeamBuilders Counseling Services, Inc.--Portales
220 W 2nd St.
Portales, NM 88130
Ph: (505)356-2222
Free: 866-356-2221
URL: http://www.teambuilders-counseling.org/about/locations.html

Raton

31590 ■ TeamBuilders Counseling Services, Inc.--Raton
130 N 2nd St.
Raton, NM 87740
Ph: (505)445-3557
URL: http://www.teambuilders-counseling.org/about/locations.html

Reserve

31591 ■ Border Area Mental Health Services--Reserve
1 Foster Ln.
Reserve, NM 87830
Ph: (575)533-6649
URL: http://www.bamhs.org/

Rio Rancho

31592 ■ TeamBuilders Counseling Services, Inc.--Rio Rancho
4359 Jager Dr. NE, Ste. E
Rio Rancho, NM 87144
Ph: (505)771-8299
URL: http://www.teambuilders-counseling.org/about/locations.html

Ruidoso

31593 ■ TeamBuilders Counseling Services, Inc.--Ruidoso
206 Porr Dr.
Ruidoso, NM 88345
Ph: (575)630-0571
URL: http://www.teambuilders-counseling.org/about/locations.html

Santa Fe

31594 ■ Presbyterian Medical Services--Santa Fe Community Guidance Center
820 Paseo de Peralta, Ste. 100
Santa Fe, NM 87501-2233
Ph: (505)986-9633
URL: http://quasar.pmsnet.org/portal/index.php

Santa Rosa

31595 ■ TeamBuilders Counseling Services, Inc.--Santa Rosa
501 S 4th St.
Santa Rosa, NM 88435
Ph: (505)472-0745
URL: http://www.teambuilders-counseling.org/about/locations.html

Sante Fe

31596 ■ Ayudantes, Inc.--Sante Fe
1316 Apache Ave.
Sante Fe, NM 87505
Ph: (505)438-0035
Fax: (505)438-0051
URL: http://www.ayudantes.org/

Silver City

31597 ■ Border Area Mental Health Services--E 32nd Street, Silver City Transitional Living
1720 E 32nd St.
Silver City, NM 88061
Ph: (575)574-4702
URL: http://www.bamhs.org/

31598 ■ Border Area Mental Health Services--N Silver Street, Silver City
2540 N Silver St.
Silver City, NM 88061
Ph: (575)538-3205
URL: http://www.bamhs.org/

31599 ■ Border Area Mental Health Services--S Hudson Street, Silver City
315 S Hudson St., Ste. 19
Silver City, NM 88061
Ph: (575)388-4497
URL: http://www.bamhs.org/

Taos

31600 ■ TeamBuilders Counseling Services, Inc.--Taos
118 Estes Rd.
Taos, NM 87529
Ph: (575)758-7263
URL: http://www.teambuilders-counseling.org/about/locations.html

Tucumcari

31601 ■ TeamBuilders Counseling Services, Inc.--Tucumcari
1110 E High St.
Tucumcari, NM 88401
Ph: (505)461-4411
Free: 888-961-4411
URL: http://www.teambuilders-counseling.org/about/locations.html

NEW YORK

Albany

31602 ■ Albany County Mental Health Center
175 Green St.
Albany, NY 12202
Ph: (518)447-4555
Fax: (518)447-4661
URL: http://www.albanycounty.com/departments/mentalhealth/default.asp?id=173

31603 ■ Albany Veterans Affairs Medical Center
113 Holland Ave.
Albany, NY 12208
Ph: (518)626-5000
Fax: (518)626-5500
URL: http://www.albany.va.gov/

31604 ■ ClearView Center Apartment & Program
543 Warren St.
Albany, NY 12208
Ph: (518)437-9015
URL: http://www.clearviewcenter.org/

31605 ■ ClearView Center, Inc.
500 Central Ave.
Albany, NY 12206
Ph: (518)435-9931
E-mail: clearview@clearviewcenter.com
URL: http://www.clearviewcenter.org/
Dorothy Cucinelli, Executive Director
Formerly: Mental Health Association of Albany.

31606 ■ ClearView Center, Inc. Outpatient Services
500 Central Ave.
Albany, NY 12206
Ph: (518)435-9931
E-mail: clearview@clearviewcenter.com
URL: http://www.clearviewcenter.org/
Michel T. Kimball, Executive Director
Program(s): Outpatient clinic; Outpatient program.

31607 ■ Holt House
222 Lancaster St.
Albany, NY 12210
Ph: (518)463-7866
URL: http://www.clearviewcenter.org/

31608 ■ Parsons Child and Family Center
60 Academy Rd.
Albany, NY 12208
Ph: (518)426-2600
URL: https://www.parsonscenter.org/index.asp

Auburn

31609 ■ Auburn Veterans Affairs Medical Center
17 Lansing St.
Auburn, NY 13021
Ph: (315)255-7002
Fax: (315)255-7143
URL: http://www.syracuse.va.gov/auburn.asp

31610 ■ Cayuga County Behavioral Health Unit
County House Rd.
Auburn, NY 13021
Ph: (315)253-1486

31611 ■ Cayuga County Mental Health Center
157 Genesee St., Ste. BSMT
Auburn, NY 13021
Ph: (315)253-0341

Bainbridge

31612 ■ Bainbridge Veterans Affairs Clinic
109 N Main St.
Bainbridge, NY 13733
Ph: (607)967-8590
URL: http://www.albany.va.gov/bainbridge.asp

Batavia

31613 ■ Batavia Veterans Affairs Medical Center
222 Richmond Ave.
Batavia, NY 14020
Ph: (585)297-1000
Free: 800-823-9656
URL: http://www.buffalo.va.gov/batavia.asp

Bath

31614 ■ Bath Veterans Affairs Medical Center
76 Veterans Ave.
Bath, NY 14810
Ph: (607)664-4000
Free: 877-845-3247
URL: http://www.bath.va.gov/

31615 ■ Steuben County Community Mental Health Center--Bath
115 Liberty St.
Bath, NY 14810
Ph: (607)776-6577
URL: http://www.steubencony.org/sccmhc.html

Bay Shore

31616 ■ Catholic Charities--Bay Shore Mental Health Clinic
9 4th Ave.
Bay Shore, NY 11706
Ph: (631)665-6707
URL: http://www.catholiccharities.cc

31617 ■ Family Service League Iovino South Shore Family Center
1444 5th Ave.
Bay Shore, NY 11706
Ph: (631)647-3100
URL: http://www.fsl-li.org/learn/locations.php

31618 ■ Siena Residence
12 Mechanicsville Rd.
Bay Shore, NY 11706-7370
Ph: (631)968-8007
Fax: (631)968-8009
URL: http://www.catholiccharities.cc/ourservices/mentalhealthin.html

Beacon

31619 ■ Beacon Community Residence
1 Wodenethe Dr.
Beacon, NY 12508
Ph: (845)831-6916
URL: http://www.gatewayindustries.org/beacon.html

Bellerose

31620 ■ Queens Children's Psychiatric Center
74-03 Commonwealth Blvd.
Bellerose, NY 11426
Ph: (718)264-4500
Fax: (718)740-0968
E-mail: queenscpc@omh.state.ny.us
URL: http://www.omh.state.ny.us/omhweb/facilities/qcpc/facility.htm

Bethpage

31621 ■ Haypath House
102 Haypath Rd.
Bethpage, NY 11714
Ph: (516)931-4534
E-mail: haypath@mhanc.org
URL: http://www.mhanc.org/default.aspx?PageID=577

Binghamton

31622 ■ Berkshire Farm Center and Services for Youth--Binghamton
2-8 Hawley St.
Binghamton, NY 13901
Ph: (607)772-3123
Fax: (607)772-2964
URL: http://www.berkshirefarm.org/

31623 ■ Binghamton Veterans Affairs Clinic
425 Robinson St.
Binghamton, NY 13901
Ph: (607)772-9100
URL: http://www.syracuse.va.gov/binghamton.asp

31624 ■ Catholic Charities of Broome County
232 Main St.
Binghamton, NY 13905-2699
Ph: (607)729-9166
URL: http://www.catholiccharitiesbc.org

Bronx

31625 ■ The Harry and Jeanette Weinberg Mental Health Center
3600 Jerome Ave.
Bronx, NY 10467
Ph: (718)741-5009
Fax: (718)231-5140
URL: http://www.fegs.org/
Formerly: Bronx Mental Health Clinic.

31626 ■ James J. Peters Veterans Affairs Medical Center
130 W Kingsbridge Rd.
Bronx, NY 10468
Ph: (718)584-9000

Free: 800-877-6976
Fax: (718)741-4269
URL: http://www.bronx.va.gov/

31627 ■ Jewish Board of Family and Children's Services--Bronx
55 Westchester Sq.
Bronx, NY 10461
Ph: (718)931-4045
Fax: (718)828-1329
URL: http://www.jbfcs.org/programs/index.php

31628 ■ Kelly Street Supervised Community Residence
932 Kelly St.
Bronx, NY 10459
Ph: (718)542-0880

31629 ■ Leake and Watts Services
1529-35 Williamsbridge Rd.
Bronx, NY 10461
Ph: (718)794-8200
URL: http://www.leakeandwatts.org/

31630 ■ MICA Community Residence
952 Anderson Ave.
Bronx, NY 10452
Ph: (718)588-4770
URL: http://www.omh.state.ny.us/omhweb/facilities/brpc/facility.htm

31631 ■ Riverdale Mental Health Association
5676 Riverdale Ave.
Bronx, NY 10471
Ph: (718)796-5300
Fax: (718)548-1161
E-mail: rmha@rmha.org
URL: http://www.rmha.org

31632 ■ Riverdale Mental Health Association Community Residence
640-642 W 232nd St.
Bronx, NY 10463
Ph: (718)884-2900
E-mail: rmha@rmha.org
URL: http://www.rmha.org/residence.htm

31633 ■ South Bronx Mental Health Council, Inc.
Adult Outpatient Services
781 E 142nd St.
Bronx, NY 10454
Ph: (718)993-1400
URL: http://www.sbmhc.org/

31634 ■ South Bronx Mental Health Council, Inc.
Community Mental Health Center
781 E 142nd St.
Bronx, NY 10454
Ph: (718)993-1400
URL: http://www.sbmhc.org
Remarks: Provides clinical and residential behavioral health services.

31635 ■ South Bronx Mental Health Council, Inc.
Community Support Systems
800 Barretto St.
Bronx, NY 10474
Ph: (718)378-6500
Fax: (718)842-3846
URL: http://www.sbmhc.org/

31636 ■ South Bronx Mental Health Council, Inc.
Triple Jeopardy Center
1241 Lafayette Ave.
Bronx, NY 10474
Ph: (718)378-6500
URL: http://www.sbmhc.org/

Brooklyn

31637 ■ Baltic Street Community Health Center
250 Baltic St.
Brooklyn, NY 11201
Ph: (718)855-3131
URL: http://www.omh.state.ny.us/omhweb/facilities/sbpc/facility.htm

31638 ■ Bensonhurst Community Mental Health Center
8620 18th Ave.
Brooklyn, NY 11214
Ph: (718)256-8818
URL: http://www.omh.state.ny.us/omhweb/facilities/sbpc/facility.htm

31639 ■ Catholic Charities--Brooklyn & Queens
Brooklyn West Family Center
191 Joralemon St.
Brooklyn, NY 11201
Ph: (718)722-6002
URL: http://www.ccbq.org

31640 ■ Circle of Hope--Brooklyn
2520 Flatbush Ave.
Brooklyn, NY 11234
Ph: (718)338-4716
Fax: (718)338-5383
URL: http://www.ccbq.org/mentalhealth.htm#residentialsvc

31641 ■ Emerson-Davis Family Development Center
2581 Atlantic Ave.
Brooklyn, NY 11207
Ph: (718)290-8100
URL: http://www.mhanys.org/programs/pwpd/pwpd_programs.htm

31642 ■ Flatlands Guidance and Psychosocial Center
2000 Flatbush Ave.
Brooklyn, NY 11234
Ph: (718)337-5755
Fax: (718)337-0752
URL: http://www.ccbq.org/mentalhealth.htm

31643 ■ Halsey House
1225 Halsey St.
Brooklyn, NY 11237
Ph: (718)386-9224
URL: http://iclinc.net/

31644 ■ Heights Hill Community Mental Health Center
25 Flatbush Ave.
Brooklyn, NY 11217
Ph: (718)875-1420
URL: http://www.omh.state.ny.us/omhweb/facilities/sbpc/facility.htm

31645 ■ Institute for Community Living Continuing Day Treatment Program
2384 Atlantic Ave.
Brooklyn, NY 11233
Ph: (718)272-6074
Free: 888-425-0501
URL: http://www.iclinc.net/

31646 ■ Jewish Board of Family and Children's Services
Kingsbrook ICF
5513 16th Ave.
Brooklyn, NY 11204
Ph: (718)756-1900
Free: 888-523-2769
Fax: (718)467-6532
URL: http://www.jbfcs.org

31647 ■ Kingsboro Psychiatric Center
681 Clarkson Ave.
Brooklyn, NY 11203
Ph: (718)221-7700
Fax: (718)221-7206
URL: http://www.omh.state.ny.us/omhweb/facilities/kbpc/facility.htm

31648 ■ Madeleine Borg Counseling Service--Boro Park
1276 47th St.
Brooklyn, NY 11219
Ph: (718)435-5700
Fax: (718)854-5495
URL: http://www.jbfcs.org/programs/index.php

31649 ■ Mapleton Community Mental Health Center
1083 McDonald Ave.
Brooklyn, NY 11219
Ph: (718)421-7444
URL: http://www.omh.state.ny.us/omhweb/facilities/sbpc/facility.htm

31650 ■ Park Slope Center for Mental Health, Inc.
348 13th St., Ste. 203
Brooklyn, NY 11215
Ph: (718)788-2461
Fax: (718)788-8274
E-mail: info@parkslopecenter.org
URL: http://www.parkslopecenter.org/

31651 ■ Partnership of Hope
715 Dean St.
Brooklyn, NY 11238
Ph: (718)398-0153
URL: http://www.ccbq.org/mentalhealth.htm

31652 ■ Paul J. Cooper Center for Human Services
519 Rockaway Ave.
Brooklyn, NY 11212
Ph: (718)346-5900
URL: http://pauljcooper.org/

31653 ■ Paul J. Cooper Center for Human Services
Mental Health Clinic
887A E New York Ave.
Brooklyn, NY 11203
Ph: (718)467-6441
URL: http://pauljcooper.org/

31654 ■ PSCH--48th Street Residence
323-325 E 48th St.
Brooklyn, NY 11203
Ph: (718)778-2844
URL: http://www.omh.state.ny.us/

31655 ■ PSCH--ACT Team
35 Bayridge Ave.
Brooklyn, NY 11220
Ph: (718)439-8972
URL: http://www.omh.state.ny.us/

31656 ■ PSCH--Bridger/ICM Program
681 Clarkson Ave., 2nd Fl.
Brooklyn, NY 11203
Ph: (718)771-1175
URL: http://www.omh.state.ny.us/

31657 ■ PSCH--Horizon I & II
1900 Sterling Pl.
Brooklyn, NY 11233
Ph: (718)342-4240
URL: http://www.omh.state.ny.us/

31658 ■ Rockwell Continuing Day Treatment Program
199 Jay St., 2nd Fl.
Brooklyn, NY 11201
Ph: (718)488-0100

31659 ■ State Street Clinic
415 State St., Ste. 417
Brooklyn, NY 11217
Ph: (718)625-4635
URL: http://iclinc.net/

31660 ■ Veterans Affairs Medical Center Brooklyn
800 Poly Pl.
Brooklyn, NY 11209
Ph: (718)836-6600
URL: http://www.brooklyn.va.gov/

Brushton

31661 ■ Brushton-Moira Central School
758 County Rte. 7
Brushton, NY 12916
Ph: (518)529-7342
URL: http://www.bmcsd.org/

Buffalo

31662 ■ Buffalo Federation of Neighborhood Centers, Inc.
97 Lemon St.
Buffalo, NY 14204
Ph: (716)856-0363
Fax: (716)856-1432
E-mail: jpeters@bfnc.org
URL: http://www.bfnc.org

31663 ■ Buffalo Psychiatric Center
400 Forest Ave.
Buffalo, NY 14213
Ph: (716)885-2261
Fax: (716)885-0937
E-mail: buffalopc@omh.state.ny.us
URL: http://www.omh.state.ny.us/omhweb/facilities/bupc/facility.htm

31664 ■ Buffalo Veterans Affairs Medical Center
3495 Bailey Ave.
Buffalo, NY 14215
Ph: (716)834-9200
Free: 800-532-8387
Fax: (716)862-8759
URL: http://www.buffalo.va.gov/

31665 ■ Child and Family Services--Buffalo
330 Delaware Ave.
Buffalo, NY 14202
Ph: (716)842-2750
URL: http://www.cfsbny.org/

31666 ■ Horizon Health Services
3020 Bailey Ave.
Buffalo, NY 14215
Ph: (716)831-0200
URL: http://www.horizon-health.org/

31667 ■ Lake Shore Behavioral Health
254 Franklin St.
Buffalo, NY 14202
Ph: (716)842-0440
URL: http://www.lake-shore.org/

31668 ■ Mid-Erie Counseling and Treatment Services
608 Williams St.
Buffalo, NY 14206
Ph: (716)855-1384
URL: http://www.mid-erie.org/

31669 ■ Recovery Plus--Del Nor Center
737 Delaware Ave.
Buffalo, NY 14209
Ph: (716)885-9894
URL: http://www.omh.state.ny.us/

31670 ■ Recovery Plus--Elmwood Wellness Center
400 Forest Ave.
Buffalo, NY 14213
Ph: (716)816-2911
URL: http://www.omh.state.ny.us/

31671 ■ Recovery Plus--Miller Broadway
1384 Broadway St.
Buffalo, NY 14212
Ph: (716)894-9672
URL: http://www.omh.state.ny.us/

31672 ■ Recovery Plus--North Buffalo
1547 Hertel Ave.
Buffalo, NY 14216
Ph: (716)837-5580
URL: http://www.omh.state.ny.us/

31673 ■ Spectrum Human Services--Buffalo
1280 Main St.
Buffalo, NY 14209
Ph: (716)842-6713
Fax: (716)842-0988
URL: http://www.spectrumhumanservices.com/

Cairo

31674 ■ Greene County Mental Health Center
905 Greene County Office Bldg.
Cairo, NY 12413
Ph: (518)622-9163
Fax: (518)622-8592
URL: http://www.greenegovernment.com/department/mentalhealth/index.htm

Canaan

31675 ■ Berkshire Farm Center and Services for Youth--Canaan
13640 Rte. 22
Canaan, NY 12029
Ph: (518)781-4567
E-mail: info@berkshirefarm.org
URL: http://www.berkshirefarm.org/

Canandaigua

31676 ■ Canandaigua Veterans Affairs Medical Center
400 Ft. Hill Ave.
Canandaigua, NY 14424
Ph: (585)394-2000
Free: 800-204-9917
Fax: (585)393-8328
URL: http://www.canandaigua.va.gov/

31677 ■ Lakeview Mental Health Services Community Residence
193 Parrish St.
Canandaigua, NY 14424
Ph: (585)394-7335
URL: http://www.lakeviewmhs.org

Canastota

31678 ■ Liberty Resources, Inc.--Canastota
110 N Main St.
Canastota, NY 13032
Ph: (315)697-5200
URL: http://www.liberty-resources.org/about/contact.cfm

Carmel

31679 ■ Arms Acres
75 Seminary Hill Rd.
Carmel, NY 10512
Ph: (845)225-3400
Free: 888-227-4641
URL: http://www.armsacres.com/

Carthage

31680 ■ Carthage Veterans Affairs Outpatient Clinic
3 Bridge St.
Carthage, NY 13619
Ph: (315)493-4180
Fax: (315)493-4188
URL: http://www.syracuse.va.gov/carthage.asp

Castle Point

31681 ■ Veterans Affairs Hudson Valley Healthcare System
Castle Point Campus
Rte. 9D
Castle Point, NY 12511
Ph: (845)831-2000
URL: http://www.hudsonvalley.va.gov/

Catskill

31682 ■ Catskill Veterans Affairs Clinic
159 Jefferson Heights, Ste. A102
Catskill, NY 12414
Ph: (518)943-7515
URL: http://www.albany.va.gov/catskill.asp

31683 ■ Mental Health Association of Columbia
Children and Families Division
377 Main St.
Catskill, NY 12414
Ph: (518)943-0349
URL: http://www.mhacg.org/

Clifton Park

31684 ■ Clifton Park Veterans Affairs Clinic
1673 Rte. 9
Clifton Park, NY 12065
Ph: (518)383-8506
Free: 888-838-7890
URL: http://www.albany.va.gov/cliftonpark.asp

Cohoes

31685 ■ Cohoes Community Residence
Clearview Center
30 Johnston Ave.
Cohoes, NY 12047
Ph: (518)237-1108
URL: http://www.clearviewcenter.com/

College Point

31686 ■ PSCH, Inc.
2244 119th St.
College Point, NY 11356
Ph: (718)445-4700
Fax: (718)762-6140
URL: http://www.psch.org/default.aspx

Collins

31687 ■ Recovery Plus--Zoar Valley
14308 Taylor Hollow Rd.
Collins, NY 14034
Ph: (716)532-2231
URL: http://www.omh.state.ny.us/

Corning

31688 ■ Steuben County Community Mental Health Center--Corning
114 Chestnut St.
Corning, NY 14830
Ph: (607)937-6201
URL: http://www.steubencony.org/sccmhc.html

Corona

31689 ■ Opportunities and Self Help Program
108-06 52nd Ave.
Corona, NY 11368-3316
Ph: (718)592-9497
URL: http://www.tsiny.org/

Cortland

31690 ■ Cortland Veterans Affairs Clinic
1129 Commons Ave.
Cortland, NY 13045
Ph: (607)662-1517
Fax: (607)756-7240
URL: http://www.syracuse.va.gov/cortland.asp

Dix Hills

31691 ■ SCO Family of Services--Dix Hills
151 Burrs Ln.
Dix Hills, NY 11746
Ph: (631)643-8800
URL: http://www.stchristopher-ottilie.org/

Dobbs Ferry

31692 ■ Saint Christopher's, Inc.
71 S Broadway
Dobbs Ferry, NY 10522
Ph: (914)693-3030
Fax: (914)693-8325
URL: http://www.sc1881.com/

Dunkirk

31693 ■ Dunkirk Veterans Affairs Clinic
166 E 4th St.
Dunkirk, NY 14048
Ph: (716)310-6474
Free: 800-310-5001
Fax: (716)363-1235
URL: http://www.buffalo.va.gov/dunkirk.asp

East Meadow

31694 ■ Garvey House
1727 N Jerusalem Rd.
East Meadow, NY 11554
Ph: (516)564-4715
E-mail: garvey@mhanc.org
URL: http://www.mhanc.org

Elizabethtown

31695 ■ Elizabethtown Veterans Affairs Clinic
Park St.
Elizabethtown, NY 12932
Ph: (518)873-3295
Fax: (518)873-2091
URL: http://www.albany.va.gov/elizabethtown.asp

Elmira

31696 ■ Elmira Veterans Affairs Clinic
200 Madison Ave., Ste. 2E
Elmira, NY 14901
Free: 877-845-3247
URL: http://www.bath.va.gov/elmira.asp

Elmsford

31697 ■ Mental Health Association of Westchester--Elmsford
2269 Saw Mill River Rd., Bldg. 1A
Elmsford, NY 10523
Ph: (914)345-5900
Fax: (914)347-8859
E-mail: help@mhawestchester.org
URL: http://www.mhawestchester.org

Far Rockaway

31698 ■ Freedom Village Psychosocial Club
1329 Beach Channel Dr.
Far Rockaway, NY 11691-3211
Ph: (718)337-0504
URL: http://www.ccbq.org/mentalhealth.htm

31699 ■ Rockaway Community Life Skills Center
13-29 Beach Channel Dr.
Far Rockaway, NY 11691
Ph: (718)337-6850
URL: http://www.ccbq.org/mentalhealth.htm

31700 ■ Rockaway CSS Screening
13-29 Beach Channel Dr.
Far Rockaway, NY 11691
Ph: (718)471-7586
URL: http://www.ccbq.org/mentalhealth.htm

31701 ■ Rockaway Mental Health Services
13-29 Beach Channel Dr.
Far Rockaway, NY 11691
Ph: (718)337-6800
Fax: (708)337-0940
URL: http://www.ccbq.org/mentalhealth.htm

31702 ■ Rockaway Outreach Mobile Crisis Team
13-29 Beach Channel Dr.
Far Rockaway, NY 11691-3211
Ph: (718)337-6800
URL: http://www.ccbq.org/mentalhealth.htm

Florida

31703 ■ Orange Intensive Day Treatment Program
Seward Memorial Bldg.
Florida, NY 10921
Ph: (845)651-9402

Fonda

31704 ■ Fonda Veterans Affairs Clinic
2623 State Hwy. 30A
Fonda, NY 12068
Ph: (518)853-1247
URL: http://www.albany.va.gov/fonda.asp

Forest Hills

31705 ■ Bleuler Psychotherapy Center
104-70 Queens Blvd., 2nd Fl.
Forest Hills, NY 11375
Ph: (718)275-6010
E-mail: info@bleulerpsychotherapycenter.org
URL: http://www.bleulerpsychotherapycenter.org/

Fort Covington

31706 ■ Salmon River Central School
637 Country Rte. 1
Fort Covington, NY 12937
Ph: (518)483-3261
URL: http://www.srk12.org/

Fredonia

31707 ■ Recovery Plus--Lakeside
355 Central Ave.
Fredonia, NY 14063-1125
Ph: (716)872-6117
URL: http://www.omh.state.ny.us/

Freeport

31708 ■ Catholic Charities Mental Health Services--Freeport
333 N Main St.
Freeport, NY 11520
Ph: (516)623-3322
URL: http://www.catholiccharities.cc/

Fulton

31709 ■ Liberty Resources, Inc.--Fulton
1850 County Rte. 57
Fulton, NY 13069
Ph: (315)598-4642
Fax: (315)592-7978
URL: http://www.liberty-resources.org/about/contact.cfm

Garnerville

31710 ■ Bernstein House
228 Ramapo Rd.
Garnerville, NY 10923
Ph: (845)429-3580

31711 ■ Community Support Center
230 E Ramapo Rd.
Garnerville, NY 10923
Ph: (845)429-1417

Geneva

31712 ■ Ontario Community Support Services
611 W Washington St.
Geneva, NY 14456-2119
Ph: (315)789-0550
URL: http://www.lakeviewmhs.org

31713 ■ Ontario County Mental Health Center
28 Seneca St., 2nd Fl.
Geneva, NY 14456
Ph: (315)789-6706
URL: http://www.co.ontario.ny.us/mental_health/patientinformation.html

31714 ■ Ontario Intensive/Supportive Apartments
199 Genesee St., No. 195
Geneva, NY 14456
Ph: (315)789-2356
URL: http://www.lakeviewmhs.org/

Glen Cove

31715 ■ Melillo Center for Mental Health
113 Glen Cove Ave.
Glen Cove, NY 11542
Ph: (516)676-2388
Fax: (516)759-5259
URL: http://melillo.org/document/18314

31716 ■ SCO Family Services--Glen Cove
1 Alexander Pl.
Glen Cove, NY 11542
Ph: (516)671-1253
URL: http://www.stchristopher-ottilie.org/

Glendale

31717 ■ Glendale Guidance Center
67-29 Myrtle Ave.
Glendale, NY 11385
Ph: (718)456-7001
URL: http://www.northshorelij.com/body.cfm?id=828

Glens Falls

31718 ■ Glens Falls Veterans Affairs Clinic
84 Broad St.
Glens Falls, NY 12801
Ph: (518)798-6066
Fax: (518)761-2097
URL: http://www.albany.va.gov/glensfalls.asp

Goshen

31719 ■ Orange Community Services
Gibson Rd.
Goshen, NY 10924
Ph: (845)294-7334
URL: http://www.omh.state.ny.us/

31720 ■ Orange Day Treatment Center
Gibson Rd.
Goshen, NY 10924
Ph: (845)294-7334
Fax: (845)294-5072
URL: http://www.omh.state.ny.us/

Gowanda

31721 ■ Alliance House Social Club
185 Buffalo St.
Gowanda, NY 14070
Ph: (716)532-9230
URL: http://www.omh.state.ny.us/

Guilderland

31722 ■ Rehabilitation Support Services, Inc.
2113 Western Ave., Ste. 3
Guilderland, NY 12084
Ph: (518)464-1511
Free: 888-824-4004
Fax: (518)464-9198
URL: http://www.rehab.org

Hamburg

31723 ■ Hamburg Counseling Service, Inc.
97 S Buffalo St.
Hamburg, NY 14075
Ph: (716)648-0650
Fax: (716)648-0666
URL: http://www.hamburgcounseling.org/

Haverstraw

31724 ■ North Rockland Mental Health Clinic
2 Main St.
Haverstraw, NY 10927
Ph: (845)429-4966

Hawthorne

31725 ■ Westchester Day Treatment Center
226 Linda Ave.
Hawthorne, NY 10532
Ph: (914)773-7478
URL: http://www.jbfcs.org/programs/index.php?sort1=WC

Hempstead

31726 ■ The Gathering Place
186 Clinton St.
Hempstead, NY 11550
Ph: (516)489-1120
E-mail: info@mhamc.org
URL: http://www.mhanc.org

31727 ■ Nassau County Mental Health Association
186 Clinton St.
Hempstead, NY 11550
Ph: (516)489-2322
E-mail: info@mhamc.org
URL: http://www.mhamc.org

Herkimer

31728 ■ Herkimer County Mental Health Services
301 N Washington St., Ste. 2470
Herkimer, NY 13350
Ph: (315)867-1465
URL: http://www.herkimercounty.org/content/Departments/View/14

Hicksville

31729 ■ Central Nassau Guidance and Counseling Services
950 S Oyster Bay Rd.
Hicksville, NY 11801
Ph: (516)822-6111
URL: http://www.centralnassau.org/

31730 ■ Community Residence
499 Jerusalem Ave.
Hicksville, NY 11801
Ph: (516)822-6111
URL: http://www.centralnassau.org/

Hornell

31731 ■ Steuben County Community Mental Health Center--Hornell
7454 Seneca Rd. N
Hornell, NY 14843
Ph: (607)324-2483
URL: http://www.steubencony.org/sccmhc.html

Hudson

31732 ■ Columbia Street Residence
900 Columbia St.
Hudson, NY 12534-2604
Ph: (518)828-8499
URL: http://www.mhacg.org/

31733 ■ Mental Health Association of Columbia/Greene Counties
713 Union St.
Hudson, NY 12534-3001
Ph: (518)828-4619
URL: http://www.mhacg.org/

Hudson Falls

31734 ■ Caleo Center
3043 State Rte. 4
Hudson Falls, NY 12839
Ph: (518)747-2282
URL: http://www.wwamh.org/programs.htm

31735 ■ Warren Washington Association for Mental Health, Inc.
3043 State Rte. 4
Hudson Falls, NY 12839-9632
Ph: (518)747-2284
Fax: (518)747-2253
URL: http://wwamh.org

Huntington

31736 ■ Family Service League
Olsten Family Center
790 Park Ave.
Huntington, NY 11743
Ph: (631)427-3700
URL: http://www.fsl-li.org/learn/locations.php

31737 ■ Pederson-Krag Center
55 Horizon Dr.
Huntington, NY 11743
Ph: (631)920-8000
URL: http://www.pederson-krag.org/

Ithaca

31738 ■ Family and Children's Services of Ithaca
127 W State St.
Ithaca, NY 14850
Ph: (607)273-7494
Fax: (607)273-7484
URL: http://www.fcsith.org/

31739 ■ Ithaca Veterans Affairs Clinic
10 Arrowwood Dr.
Ithaca, NY 14850
Ph: (607)274-4680
Fax: (607)252-3738
URL: http://www.syracuse.va.gov/ithaca.asp

Ithica

31740 ■ Elmshade
402 S Albany St.
Ithica, NY 14850
Ph: (607)645-0124
URL: http://www.lakeviewmhs.org/

31741 ■ Markham House
607 Cascadilla St.
Ithica, NY 14850
Ph: (607)277-0385
URL: http://www.lakeviewmhs.org/

Jackson Heights

31742 ■ Corona-Elmhurst Guidance Center
37-22 82nd St.
Jackson Heights, NY 11372
Ph: (718)779-1600
URL: https://a069-webapps3.nyc.gov/dsial/Agency_Detail.aspx?id=200

31743 ■ Queens Community Living Program
35-24 83rd St.
Jackson Heights, NY 11370
Ph: (718)639-0700
URL: http://www.ccbq.org/

Jamaica

31744 ■ Circle of Hope--Jamaica
90-50 Parsons Blvd., Ste. 207
Jamaica, NY 11432
Ph: (718)298-5790
URL: http://www.ccbq.org/

31745 ■ Hope House II
84-23 168th St.
Jamaica, NY 11432
Ph: (718)658-7122
URL: http://www.tsiny.org/

31746 ■ Jamaica Continuing Day Treatment
165-15 88th Ave.
Jamaica, NY 11432
Ph: (718)291-4848
URL: http://www.ccbq.org/

31747 ■ Jamaica Continuing Support System
165-15 88th Ave.
Jamaica, NY 11432
Ph: (718)291-4848
URL: http://www.ccbq.org/

31748 ■ Monica House
161-01 89th Ave.
Jamaica, NY 11432
Ph: (718)262-8190
URL: http://www.ccbq.org/

Jamestown

31749 ■ Jamestown Veterans Affairs Clinic--W 3rd Street
608 W 3rd St.
Jamestown, NY 14701
Ph: (716)338-1511
Fax: (716)338-1521
URL: http://www.buffalo.va.gov/jamestown.asp

Kenmore

31750 ■ Northwest Community Mental Health Center
Kenmore Center
2495 Kenmore Ave.
Kenmore, NY 14217
Ph: (716)877-6763
URL: http://www.erie.gov/health/mentalhealth/agencies_nw.asp

Kingston

31751 ■ Gateway Community Industries, Inc.--Kingston
1 Amy Kay Pkwy.
Kingston, NY 12401
Ph: (845)331-1261
Fax: (845)331-2112
E-mail: info@gatewayindustries.org
URL: http://www.gatewayindustries.org

31752 ■ Kingston Veterans Affairs Clinic
63 Hurley Ave.
Kingston, NY 12401
Ph: (845)331-8322
Fax: (845)331-0365
URL: http://www.albany.va.gov/kingston.asp

31753 ■ Vocational Transition Center
1 Amy Kay Pkwy.
Kingston, NY 12401-6444
Ph: (845)338-2110
E-mail: info@gatewayindustries.org
URL: http://www.gatewayindustries.org

Lackawanna

31754 ■ Baker Victory Services
780 Ridge Rd.
Lackawanna, NY 14218
Ph: (716)828-9500
Free: 888-287-1160
URL: http://www.bakervictoryservices.org/

31755 ■ Lackawanna Veterans Affairs Clinic
227 Ridge Rd.
Lackawanna, NY 14218
Ph: (716)822-5944
Fax: (716)822-3937
URL: http://www.buffalo.va.gov/lackawanna.asp

Lancaster

31756 ■ Child & Adolescent Treatment Services, Inc.
11 W Main St.
Lancaster, NY 14186-2123
Ph: (716)681-6611
URL: http://www.erie.gov/health/mentalhealth/agencies_cats.asp

31757 ■ Recovery Plus--Lancaster
525 Pavement Rd.
Lancaster, NY 14086-9718
Ph: (716)684-2662
URL: http://www.omh.state.ny.us/

Lawrence

31758 ■ Peninsula Counseling Center--Lawrence
270 Lawrence Ave.
Lawrence, NY 11559
Ph: (516)239-1945
URL: http://www.peninsulacounseling.org/

Lockport

31759 ■ Lockport Veterans Affairs Clinic
5883 Snyder Dr.
Lockport, NY 14094
Ph: (716)438-3890
Free: 888-838-7890
URL: http://www.buffalo.va.gov/lockport.asp

Long Island City

31760 ■ Steinway Child and Family Services, Inc.
25-15 43rd Ave.
Long Island City, NY 11101
Ph: (718)389-5100
URL: http://www.steinway.org/

Lyons

31761 ■ Wayne Behavioral Health Network
1519 Nye Rd.
Lyons, NY 14489
Ph: (315)946-5722
Fax: (315)946-5726
URL: http://www.co.wayne.ny.us/departments/WBHN/WBHN.htm

Malone

31762 ■ Crimson Phoenix Social Club
81 Fort Covington St.
Malone, NY 12953-1025
Ph: (518)483-1689

31763 ■ Malone Veterans Affairs Clinic
3372 State Rte. 11
Malone, NY 12953
Ph: (518)483-1529
Fax: (518)483-2468
URL: http://www.albany.va.gov/malone.asp

31764 ■ North Star Behavioral Health Services--Malone
24 4th St., Ste. 3
Malone, NY 12953
Ph: (518)483-3261
Fax: (518)483-3383
URL: http://www.nctrc.plattsburgh.edu/hrdirectory/agency.php?id=2019

Mamaroneck

31765 ■ Larchmont--Mamaroneck Branch Clinic
930 Mamaroneck Ave.
Mamaroneck, NY 10543
Ph: (914)381-6110

Marcy

31766 ■ Central New York Psychiatric Center
PO Box 300
Marcy, NY 13403
Ph: (315)765-3600
Fax: (315)765-3629
E-mail: cnypc@omh.state.ny.us
URL: http://www.omh.state.ny.us/omhweb/facilities/cnpc/facility.htm

Medford

31767 ■ Catholic Charities--Medford Mental Health Clinic
1727 N Ocean Ave.
Medford, NY 11763
Ph: (516)654-1919
Fax: (631)475-8407
URL: http://www.catholiccharities.cc

Merrick

31768 ■ Meroke House
2421 Babylon Tpke.
Merrick, NY 11566
Ph: (516)868-2050

Middletown

31769 ■ Occupations, Inc. Community Counseling
Union St. Professional Bldg.
16-24 Union St.
Middletown, NY 10940
Ph: (845)343-5556
Free: 888-750-2266
Fax: (845)343-1836
E-mail: mail@occupations.org
URL: http://www.occupations.org

31770 ■ Occupations, Inc. Community Counseling at Scotchtown
Amy Bull Crist Rehabilitation Center
15 Fortune Rd. W
Middletown, NY 10941
Ph: (845)692-4454
Free: 888-750-2266
Fax: (845)692-8887
URL: http://www.occupations.org

Millbrook

31771 ■ Millbrook Continuing Treatment Center
135 County House Rd.
Millbrook, NY 12545
Ph: (845)677-4060

Mineola

31772 ■ Catholic Charities--Mineola Mental Health Clinic
259 Mineola Blvd.
Mineola, NY 11501
Ph: (516)248-7100
URL: http://www.catholiccharities.cc

Mohegan Lake

31773 ■ Sunshine Social Club
1836 E Main St.
Mohegan Lake, NY 10547
Ph: (845)528-6995
URL: http://www.wjcs.com/contact.html

Montrose

31774 ■ Veterans Affairs Hudson Valley Healthcare System Montrose Campus
2094 Albany Post Rd.
Montrose, NY 12508
Ph: (914)737-4400
URL: http://www.hudsonvalley.va.gov/

Mount Kisco

31775 ■ Mental Health Association of Westchester--Mount Kisco
344 Main St., Ste. 301
Mount Kisco, NY 10549
Ph: (914)666-4646
E-mail: help@mhawestchester.org
URL: http://www.mhawestchester.org

Mount Vernon

31776 ■ Mount Vernon Community Service Center
100 E 1st St.
Mount Vernon, NY 10550
Ph: (914)813-6220
URL: http://mentalhealth.westchestergov.com/

31777 ■ Mount Vernon Girls Residence
152 E Prospect Ave.
Mount Vernon, NY 10550-2207
Ph: (914)668-9061
URL: http://www.jbfcs.org/programs/index.php?sort1=WC

Nanuet

31778 ■ Nanuet House Congregate Treatment Residence
357 S Middletown Rd.
Nanuet, NY 10954-3339
Ph: (845)623-9193
URL: http://www.mharockland.org/

New City

31779 ■ Mental Health Association of Rockland County
20 Squadron Blvd.
New City, NY 10956-5200
Ph: (845)639-7400
Fax: (845)639-7419
E-mail: info@mharockland.org
URL: http://www.mharockland.org

New Paltz

31780 ■ Gateway Community Industries, Inc.--New Paltz
137 N Chestnut St.
New Paltz, NY 12561
Ph: (845)255-6700
Fax: (845)255-6706
E-mail: info@gatewayindustries.org
URL: http://www.gatewayindustries.org

31781 ■ Gateway Manor
581 N Ohioville Rd.
New Paltz, NY 12561
Ph: (845)331-1261
URL: http://www.gatewayindustries.org

New Rochelle

31782 ■ The Guidance Center--New Rochelle
70 Grand St.
New Rochelle, NY 10801
Ph: (914)636-4440
URL: http://www.theguidancecenter.org

31783 ■ Lincoln Avenue Branch Clinic
95 Lincoln Ave.
New Rochelle, NY 10801
Ph: (914)632-6757

31784 ■ Search for Change, Inc.
1 Glencar Ave.
New Rochelle, NY 10801
Ph: (914)428-5600
URL: http://searchforchange.com

New Windsor

31785 ■ Occupations, Inc.
Arthur H. Daddazio Rehabilitation Center
67 Windsor Hwy.
New Windsor, NY 12553
Ph: (845)562-6850
Free: 888-750-2266
Fax: (845)562-1354
URL: http://www.occupations.org

New York

31786 ■ Ackerman Institute for the Family
149 E 78th St.
New York, NY 10075
Ph: (212)879-4900
URL: http://www.ackerman.org/

31787 ■ Assertive Community Treatment Team
1795 Lexington Ave.
New York, NY 10029
Ph: (212)289-1788

31788 ■ Bowery Residents Committee, Inc.
324 Lafayette St., 8th Fl.
New York, NY 10012
Ph: (212)803-5700
Fax: (212)533-1893
E-mail: info@brc.org
URL: http://www.brc.org/

31789 ■ The Children's Aid Society
East Harlem Center
130 E 101st St.
New York, NY 10029
Ph: (212)348-2343
Fax: (212)876-0711
URL: http://www.childrensaidsociety.org/eastharlem

31790 ■ Children's Aid Society, Inc.
Lord Memorial Building
105 E 22nd St.
New York, NY 10010
Ph: (212)949-4800
URL: http://www.childrensaidsociety.org/

31791 ■ Community Access
666 Broadway, 3rd Fl.
New York, NY 10012
Ph: (212)780-1400
Fax: (212)780-1412
URL: http://www.communityaccess.net

31792 ■ East 119th Street SRO
Veterans Residence
22 E 119th St.
New York, NY 10035
Ph: (212)423-2100
Fax: (212)423-2121

31793 ■ Fountain House
425 W 47th St.
New York, NY 10036
Ph: (212)307-6185
URL: http://www.fountainhouse.org/

31794 ■ Fountain House Inc.
19 W 100th St.
New York, NY 10025
Ph: (212)582-0340
URL: http://www.fountainhouse.org/

31795 ■ Fountain House North Supervised Residence
552 W 173rd St.
New York, NY 10036
Ph: (212)582-0340
URL: http://www.fountainhouse.org/

31796 ■ Hale House Center, Inc.
152 W 122nd St.
New York, NY 10027
Ph: (212)663-0700
URL: http://www.halehouse.org/

31797 ■ Hamilton--Madison House
50 Madison St.
New York, NY 10038
Ph: (212)349-3724

31798 ■ Karen Horney Clinic (KHC)
329 E 62nd St.
New York, NY 10065
Ph: (212)838-4333
URL: http://www.karenhorneyclinic.org
Dr. Henry Paul, Executive Director
Description: Promotes psychoanalytic and psychotherapeutic treatment of individuals and groups focusing on the special problems of children, adolescents, victims of violent crimes, adult survivors of childhood sexual abuse, and persons with psychoneurotic and emotional problems. Named for Karen Horney (1885-1952), German/American psychoanalyst and author of several books on neurosis, psychoanalysis, and related topics. Conducts children's services. **Formerly:** (1979) Karen Horney Psychoanalytic Clinic.

31799 ■ Institute for Community Living, Inc.
40 Rector St., 8th Fl.
New York, NY 10006
Ph: (212)385-3030
Free: 888-425-0501
Fax: (212)385-2380
URL: http://www.iclinc.net

31800 ■ Iyana House
168 107th St.
New York, NY 10029
Ph: (212)423-5733

31801 ■ Jewish Board of Family and Children's Services
Child Development Center
120 W 57th St.
New York, NY 10019
Ph: (212)582-9100
URL: http://www.jbfcs.org

31802 ■ Jewish Board of Family and Children's Services--New York
120 W 57th St.
New York, NY 10019
Ph: (212)582-9100
Free: 888-JBFCS-NY
E-mail: admin@jbfcs.org
URL: http://www.jbfcs.org

31803 ■ Jewish Board of Family and Children's ServicesManhattan North
Madeline Borg Counseling Service
549 W 180th St.
New York, NY 10033
Ph: (212)795-9888
Fax: (212)795-9899
URL: http://www.jbfcs.org

31804 ■ Madeline Borg Counseling Service--Manhattan West
120 W 57th St.
New York, NY 10019
Ph: (212)397-4550
URL: http://www.jbfcs.org/programs/index.php-?sort2=20

31805 ■ Northside Center for Child Development, Inc.
1301 5th Ave.
New York, NY 10029
Ph: (212)426-3400
URL: http://www.northsidecenter.org/

31806 ■ Postgraduate Center for Mental Health
344 W 36th St.
New York, NY 10018
Ph: (212)560-6757
URL: http://www.pgcmh.org/
Program(s): Continuing Day Treatment (CDT), CDT for dually-diagnosed persons (MICA), Adult Treatment Clinic, Intensive Psychiatric Rehabilitation Treatment (IPRT), Employment Services, and Project US Psychosocial Club.

31807 ■ Postgraduate Center for Mental Health--John Gutheil Residence
310 E 35th St.
New York, NY 10016
Ph: (212)889-2660
URL: http://www.pgcmh.org/

31808 ■ Postgraduate Center for Mental Health--Residence No. 1
516 W 50th St.
New York, NY 10019
Ph: (212)246-0898
URL: http://www.pgcmh.org/

31809 ■ Postgraduate Center for Mental Health--Residence No. 2
126 La Salle St.
New York, NY 10027
Ph: (212)866-5870
URL: http://www.pgcmh.org/

31810 ■ Postgraduate Center for Mental Health--Richard Dicker Residence
222 E 86th St.
New York, NY 10028
Ph: (212)678-3276
URL: http://www.pgcmh.org/

31811 ■ Rita and Stanley H. Kaplan House
74 Saint Mark's Pl.
New York, NY 10003
Ph: (212)477-1565
URL: http://www.jbfcs.org/programs/index.php?sort1=MN

31812 ■ Safe Space, Inc.
295 Lafayette St., Ste. 920
New York, NY 10012
Ph: (212)226-3536
URL: http://www.safespacenyc.org/

31813 ■ Safe Space, Inc.
Spa West
300 W 43rd St.
New York, NY 10036
Ph: (212)333-5302
URL: http://www.safespacenyc.org/

31814 ■ Saint Mark's Institute
57 Saint Marks Pl.
New York, NY 10003
Ph: (212)982-3470
URL: http://www.unitas-nyc.org/

31815 ■ Veterans Affairs Medical Center Manhattan
423 E 23 St.
New York, NY 10010
Ph: (212)686-7500
Free: 800-877-6976
URL: http://www.manhattan.va.gov/

Newburgh

31816 ■ Family Counseling of Occupations, Inc.
21 Grand St.
Newburgh, NY 12550
Ph: (845)562-7244
Free: 888-750-2266
Fax: (845)562-7635
URL: http://www.occupations.org

Niagara Falls

31817 ■ Community Missions of the Niagara Frontier Inc.
1570 Buffalo Ave.
Niagara Falls, NY 14303
Ph: (716)285-3403
URL: http://www.communitymissions.org/

31818 ■ Niagara Falls Outpatient Clinic
1001 11th St.
Niagara Falls, NY 14301
Ph: (716)278-1940
Fax: (716)278-1943

31819 ■ Niagara Falls Veterans Affairs Clinic
2201 Pine Ave.
Niagara Falls, NY 14301
Ph: (800)223-4810
Fax: (716)284-1702
URL: http://www.buffalo.va.gov/niagarafalls.asp

North Tonawanda

31820 ■ Recovery Plus--North Tonawanda
15 Webster St.
North Tonawanda, NY 14120-5816
Ph: (716)694-1225

Northport

31821 ■ Northport Veterans Affairs Medical Center
79 Middleville Rd.
Northport, NY 11768
Ph: (631)261-4400
Free: 800-877-6976
URL: http://www.northport.va.gov/

Oakdale

31822 ■ Skills Unlimited, Inc.
405 Locust Ave.
Oakdale, NY 11769
Ph: (631)567-3320
URL: http://www.skillsunlimited.org/

Olean

31823 ■ Olean Veterans Affairs Clinic
465 N Union St.
Olean, NY 14760
Ph: (716)373-7709
Fax: (716)373-8117
URL: http://www.buffalo.va.gov/olean.asp

Oneida

31824 ■ Liberty Resources, Inc.--Oneida Venture House
345 Main St.
Oneida, NY 13421
Ph: (315)363-1141
URL: http://www.liberty-resources.org/

Orangeburg

31825 ■ Rockland Children's Psychiatric Center
599 Convent Rd.
Orangeburg, NY 10962
Ph: (845)680-4000
Fax: (845)680-8905
E-mail: rocklandcpc@omh.state.ny.us
URL: http://www.omh.state.ny.us/omhweb/facilities/rcpc/facility.htm

Orchard Park

31826 ■ Spectrum Human Services--Orchard Park
227 Thorn Ave.
Orchard Park, NY 14127
Ph: (716)662-2040
Free: 800-466-2040
Fax: (716)662-0019
URL: http://www.spectrumhumanservices.com/pageDisplay.jsp?pageid=13622

Oswego

31827 ■ Oswego Veterans Affairs Clinic
105 County Rte. 45A, Ste. 400
Oswego, NY 13126
Ph: (315)343-0925
Fax: (315)343-1246
URL: http://www.syracuse.va.gov/oswego.asp

Ozone Park

31828 ■ New Horizon Counseling Center
108-19 Rockaway Blvd.
Ozone Park, NY 11420
Ph: (718)845-2620
URL: http://www.nhcc.us/home.html

Peekskill

31829 ■ Family Mental Health Clinic of Westchester Jewish Community Services
1101 Main St.
Peekskill, NY 10566
Ph: (914)737-7338
URL: http://www.wjcs.com/

Plattsburgh

31830 ■ Behavioral Health Services North, Inc.
22 US Oval, Ste. 218
Plattsburgh, NY 12903
Ph: (518)563-8206
URL: http://www.bhsn.org

31831 ■ Plattsburgh Veterans Affairs Clinic
80 Sharron Ave.
Plattsburgh, NY 12901
Ph: (518)561-6247
URL: http://www.albany.va.gov/plattsburgh.asp

Pomona

31832 ■ Crisis Services
Sanatorium Rd., Bldg. D
Pomona, NY 10970
Ph: (845)364-2200

31833 ■ Dr. Robert L. Yeager Health Center Rockland County Department of Mental Health
50 Sanatorium Rd., Bldg. A
Pomona, NY 10970
Ph: (845)364-2700
URL: http://www.co.rockland.ny.us/Hospitals/default.htm

31834 ■ J. Martin Carnell Residence
6 Tara Dr.
Pomona, NY 10970-3209
Ph: (845)362-4052
Fax: (845)362-2308
Formerly: VIP House; Congregate Treatment Residence.

31835 ■ Rockland County Department of Mental Health
Sanatorium Rd., Bldg. F
Pomona, NY 10970
Ph: (845)364-2378
Fax: (845)364-2381
E-mail: rcdmh@co.rockland.ny.us
URL: http://www.co.rockland.ny.us/MHealth/default.htm

Port Chester

31836 ■ Family Services of Westchester
1 Gateway Plz.
Port Chester, NY 10573
Ph: (914)937-2320
Fax: (914)937-4902
E-mail: fsw@fsw.org
URL: http://www.fsw.org/index.cfm?fuse=0,11

Port Ewen

31837 ■ Ulster Intensive Day Treatment Program
Rte. 9 W
Port Ewen, NY 12466
Ph: (845)339-8737

Port Jervis

31838 ■ Port Jervis Mental Health Clinic
146 Pike St.
Port Jervis, NY 12771
Ph: (845)858-1456
Fax: (845)858-1459
URL: http://www.co.orange.ny.us/orgMain.asp?storyID=518&sid=

Poughkeepsie

31839 ■ Dutchess Intensive Day Treatment Program
350 Dutchess Tpke.
Poughkeepsie, NY 12603
Ph: (845)486-4944

Queens Village

31840 ■ Creedmoor Psychiatric Center
79-25 Winchester Blvd.
Queens Village, NY 11427
Ph: (718)264-4000
URL: http://www.omh.state.ny.us/omhweb/facilities/crpc/facility.htm

31841 ■ Family Outreach Program
79-25 Winchester Blvd., Bldg. 40, Rm. 16-2A
Queens Village, NY 11427
Ph: (718)264-4188
URL: http://www.omh.state.ny.us/omhweb/facilities/crpc/outpatient_services.htm

31842 ■ Innovations Club
8045 Winchester Blvd.
Queens Village, NY 11427-2193
Ph: (718)464-5200
URL: http://www.omh.state.ny.us/omhweb/facilities/crpc/outpatient_services.htm

Ransomville

31843 ■ Recovery Plus--Ransomville
3509 Ransomville Rd.
Ransomville, NY 14131
Ph: (716)791-3571

Rego Park

31844 ■ Puerto Rican Family Institute Queens Mental Health Clinic
97-45 Queens Blvd., Ste. 503
Rego Park, NY 11374
Ph: (718)275-0983
URL: http://www.prfi.org/

Riverdale

31845 ■ Jewish Board of Family and Children's Services Older Adult Services
5625 Arlington Ave.
Riverdale, NY 10471
Ph: (718)601-2280
URL: http://www.jbfcs.org/programs/index.php

Riverhead

31846 ■ Family Service League
Riverhead Family Center
208 Roanoke Ave.
Riverhead, NY 11901
Ph: (631)369-0104
URL: http://www.fsl-li.org/learn/locations.php

31847 ■ Riverhead Mental Health Clinic
300 Center Dr., 2nd Fl.
Riverhead, NY 11901
Ph: (516)852-1440

Rochester

31848 ■ Rochester Veterans Affairs Clinic
465 Westfall Rd.
Rochester, NY 14620
Ph: (585)463-2600
Fax: (585)463-2649
URL: http://www.canandaigua.va.gov/rochester.asp

31849 ■ Unity Health System
Department of Psychiatry and Behavior
835 W Main St.
Rochester, NY 14611
Ph: (585)368-6500
Fax: (585)423-9523
URL: http://www.unityhealth.org/

Rome

31850 ■ Rome Veterans Affairs Clinic
125 Brookley Rd., Bldg. 510
Rome, NY 13441
Ph: (315)334-7100
Fax: (315)334-7171
URL: http://www.syracuse.va.gov/rome.asp

Saranac Lake

31851 ■ North Star Behavioral Health Services--Saranac Lake
10 Main St.
Saranac Lake, NY 12983
Ph: (518)891-2319
URL: http://www.nctrc.plattsburgh.edu/hrdirectory/agency.php?id=2112

31852 ■ North Star Substance Abuse Services
17 Main St.
Saranac Lake, NY 12983
Ph: (518)891-2467

Saratoga Springs

31853 ■ Saratoga Mental Health Center
211 Church St.
Saratoga Springs, NY 12866
Ph: (518)584-9030
Fax: (518)581-1709
URL: http://www.saratogacountyny.gov/departments.asp?did=196

Schenectady

31854 ■ Capital District Psychiatric Center
Schenectady County Clinic Treatment
426 Franklin St.
Schenectady, NY 12305
Ph: (518)374-3403
URL: http://www.omr.state.ny.us/ws/ws_capitaldist_resources.jsp

31855 ■ Schenectady Veterans Affairs Clinic
1322 Gerling St.
Schenectady, NY 12308
Ph: (518)346-3334
Fax: (518)346-4030
URL: http://www.albany.va.gov/schenectady.asp

Staten Island

31856 ■ Geller House
77 Chicago Ave.
Staten Island, NY 10305
Ph: (718)442-7828
URL: http://www.jbfcs.org/

31857 ■ Morris L. Black Community Counseling Center
2795 Richmond Ave.
Staten Island, NY 10314
Ph: (718)761-9800
URL: http://www.jbfcs.org/
Formerly: Madeleine Borg Counseling Service.

Suffern

31858 ■ Monsignor Patrick J. Frawley Mental Health Clinic
3 Campbell Ave.
Suffern, NY 10901
Ph: (845)368-5222
URL: http://www.goodsamhosp.org/html/mental_health_oupatient_clinic.html

Syracuse

31859 ■ Hutchings Psychiatric Center
620 Madison St.
Syracuse, NY 13210
Ph: (315)426-3600
Fax: (615)426-3603
E-mail: hutchingspc@omh.state.ny.us
URL: http://www.omh.state.ny.us/omhweb/facilities/hupc/facility.htm

31860 ■ Liberty Resources, Inc.--Syracuse
1065 James St., No. 200
Syracuse, NY 13203
Ph: (315)425-1004
URL: http://www.liberty-resources.org/

31861 ■ Syracuse Veterans Affairs Medical Center
800 Irving Ave.
Syracuse, NY 13210
Ph: (315)425-4400
Free: 800-792-4334
URL: http://www.syracuse.va.gov/

Troy

31862 ■ Troy Veterans Affairs Clinic
295 River St.
Troy, NY 12180
Ph: (518)274-7707
Fax: (518)266-0555
URL: http://www.albany.va.gov/troy.asp

Utica

31863 ■ Mohawk Valley Psychiatric Center
1400 Noyes St.
Utica, NY 13502
Ph: (315)738-3800
Fax: (315)738-4414
E-mail: mvpc@omh.state.ny.us
URL: http://www.omh.state.ny.us/omhweb/facilities/mvpc/facility.htm

Valatie

31864 ■ Berkshire Farm Center and Services for Youth--Valatie
3433 Rte. 203
Valatie, NY 12184
Ph: (518)758-1230
URL: http://www.berkshirefarm.org/contactus.aspx

Valhalla

31865 ■ Saint Christopher's, Inc.
1700 Old Orchard Rd.
Valhalla, NY 10595
Ph: (914)949-0665
Fax: (914)949-0130
URL: http://www.sc1881.com/

Valley Cottage

31866 ■ Elmwood Club Community Treatment Service
706 Executive Blvd., Ste. E
Valley Cottage, NY 10989
Ph: (845)267-2172
URL: http://www.mharockland.org/

Valley Stream

31867 ■ Peninsula Counseling Center--Valley Stream
50 W Hawthorne Ave.
Valley Stream, NY 11580
Ph: (516)569-6600
URL: http://www.peninsulacounseling.org/

Warsaw

31868 ■ Warsaw Veterans Affairs Clinic
400 N Main St.
Warsaw, NY 14569
Ph: (585)786-2233
Fax: (585)786-1208
URL: http://www.buffalo.va.gov/warsaw.asp

Waterloo

31869 ■ Seneca Community Residence
2722 Kingdom Rd.
Waterloo, NY 13165
Ph: (315)268-2963
URL: http://www.lakeviewmhs.org/

Wellsville

31870 ■ Wellsville Veterans Affairs Clinic
3458 Riverside Dr., Rte. 19
Wellsville, NY 14895
Ph: (607)664-4660
Free: 877-845-3247
Fax: (585)593-1087
URL: http://www.bath.va.gov/wellsville.asp

West Nyack

31871 ■ Rockland Intensive Day Treatment Program
61 Parrott Rd., Bldg. 6
West Nyack, NY 10994-1044
Ph: (845)623-0085

West Park

31872 ■ Saint Cabrini Home, Inc.
2085 Rte. 9 W
West Park, NY 12493
Ph: (845)384-6500
URL: http://www.cabrinihome.com/

White Plains

31873 ■ Central Westchester Community Mental Health Center
666 Old Orchard St.
White Plains, NY 10604
Ph: (914)328-0793

31874 ■ Search for Change, Inc.
95 Church St., Ste. 200
White Plains, NY 10601
Ph: (914)428-5600
Fax: (914)428-5642
URL: http://www.searchforchange.com/
Program(s): Vocational and rehabilitation residential programs in Putnam, Westchester, and Fairfield counties.

31875 ■ Search for Change, Inc.--Wyndover Woods
9 Wyndover Woods Ln.
White Plains, NY 10603
Ph: (914)428-5600
Fax: (914)428-5642
URL: http://www.searchforchange.com

Woodmere

31876 ■ Peninsula Counseling Center--Woodmere
124 Franklin Pl., Ste. 1
Woodmere, NY 11598
Ph: (516)569-6600
URL: http://www.peninsulacounseling.org/

Woodside

31877 ■ Woodside Guidance Center
61-20 Woodside Ave.
Woodside, NY 11377
Ph: (718)779-1234

Yaphank

31878 ■ Family Service League--Yaphank
1490 William Floyd Pkwy.
Yaphank, NY 11967
Ph: (631)924-3741
URL: http://www.fsl-li.org/learn/locations.php

Yonkers

31879 ■ Leake & Watts Services, Inc.
463 Hawthorne Ave.
Yonkers, NY 10705
Ph: (914)968-6304
URL: http://www.leakeandwatts.org/

NORTH CAROLINA

Aberdeen

31880 ■ Kids Peace--Aberdeen
604 Magnolia Dr.
Aberdeen, NC 28315
Ph: (910)944-2102
URL: http://www.kidspeace.org/

Albemarle

31881 ■ LifeSpan--Albermarle
2000 W Main St.
Albemarle, NC 28001
Ph: (704)986-6376
Fax: (704)986-0822
URL: http://www.lifespanservices.org/

31882 ■ Northeast Psychiatric Services--Albemarle
923 N 2nd St., Ste. 105
Albemarle, NC 28002
Ph: (704)403-1877
URL: http://www.northeastpsych.org/

Archdale

31883 ■ Sandhills Center for Mental Health/Developmental Disability/Substance Abuse
Randolph County Archdale Trinity Center
205 Balfour Dr.
Archdale, NC 27263
Ph: (336)431-0700
URL: http://www.sandhillscenter.org/
Formerly: Randolph County Mental Health Center; Archdale Trinity Center.

Asheboro

31884 ■ Sandhills Center for Mental Health/Developmental Disability/Substance Abuse
110 W Walker Ave.
Asheboro, NC 27203
Ph: (336)633-7000
URL: http://www.sandhillscenter.org/
Formerly: Randolph County Area Mental Health/ Developmental Disability/Substance Abuse Program.

Asheville

31885 ■ Veterans Affairs Medical Center Asheville
1100 Tunnel Rd.
Asheville, NC 28805
Ph: (828)298-7911
Free: 800-932-6408
URL: http://www.asheville.va.gov/

31886 ■ Western Highlands Network
356 Biltmore Ave.
Asheville, NC 28801
Ph: (828)225-2800
Free: 800-951-3792
URL: http://www.westernhighlands.org

Black Mountain

31887 ■ Julian F. Keith Alcohol and Drug Abuse Center
201 Tabernacle Rd.
Black Mountain, NC 28711
Ph: (828)257-6200
URL: http://www.jfkadatc.net/

Blowing Rock

31888 ■ New River Behavioral Healthcare/Serenity Farms
8043 US Hwy. 221 S
Blowing Rock, NC 28605-9464
Ph: (828)295-3113
URL: http://www.newriver.org/

Boone

31889 ■ New River Mental Health Program
132 Poplar Grove Connector, Ste. B
Boone, NC 28607
Ph: (828)264-8759
Fax: (828)262-5860
E-mail: hawkg@newriver.org
URL: http://www.wataugacounty.org/nrmh
Gail Hawkinson, Director

Burlington

31890 ■ Carolina Behavioral Care--Burlington
3119 A Lear Dr.
Burlington, NC 27215
Ph: (336)229-5905
URL: http://www.carolinabehavioralcare.com/burlingtonofficedetails.html

31891 ■ LifeSpan--Burlington
919 Stokes St.
Burlington, NC 27215
Ph: (336)513-4250
URL: http://www.lifespanservices.org/

31892 ■ Psychotherapeutic Treatment Services, Inc.
Mobile Crisis
1159 Huffman Mill Rd.
Burlington, NC 27215
Ph: (336)538-1220
Fax: (336)538-6991
URL: http://www.psychotherapeuticservices.com/programs/ncarolina2.htm

31893 ■ Psychotherapeutic Treatment Services, Inc.
Together House
405 Rudd St.
Burlington, NC 27217
Ph: (336)513-4429
URL: http://www.psychotherapeuticservices.com/programs/ncarolina2.htm

Camden

31894 ■ Albemarle Mental Health Center--Camden
160-A US Hwy. 158
Camden, NC 27921
Ph: (252)335-5158
Free: 877-388-8352
URL: http://www.albemarlemhc.org/

Candor

31895 ■ Eckerd Camp E-Ku-Sumee
500 E-Ku-Sumee Dr.
Candor, NC 27229
Ph: (910)974-4183
Free: 800-554-4357
E-mail: admisisons@eckerd.org
URL: http://www.eckerd.org

Chapel Hill

31896 ■ OPC Foundation
100 Europa Dr., Ste. 490
Chapel Hill, NC 27517
Ph: (919)913-4000
Free: 888-277-2303
URL: http://www.opcareaprogram.com
Debra Farrington, Director

Charlotte

31897 ■ Alexander Youth Network--Charlotte
6220 Thermal Rd.
Charlotte, NC 28211
Ph: (704)366-8712
URL: http://www.alexanderyouthnetwork.org/Page.aspx?pid=384

31898 ■ Alexander Youth Network Children and Family Services Center
601 E 5th St., Ste. 460
Charlotte, NC 28202
Ph: (704)335-0203
URL: http://www.alexanderyouthnetwork.org/Page.aspx?pid=384

31899 ■ Charlotte Veterans Affairs Clinic
8601 University E Dr.
Charlotte, NC 28213
Ph: (704)597-3500
URL: http://www2.va.gov/directory/guide/facility.asp?ID=5518&dnum=All

31900 ■ LifeSpan--Charlotte
2424 N Davidson St., Ste. 110
Charlotte, NC 28205
Ph: (704)363-4098
E-mail: thartzog@lifespanservices.org
URL: http://www.lifespanservices.org
Remarks: Provides education, enrichment and employment to persons who have developmental disabilities.

Concord

31901 ■ LifeSpan--Concord
56 McCachern Blvd.
Concord, NC 28025
Ph: (704)784-2845
URL: http://www.lifespanservices.org/

31902 ■ Northeast Psychiatric Services--Concord
380 Copperfield Blvd.
Concord, NC 28025
Ph: (704)403-1800
URL: http://www.northeastpsych.org/

Dobson

31903 ■ LifeSpan--Dobson
623 Rockford Rd.
Dobson, NC 27017
Ph: (336)374-4466
URL: http://www.lifespanservices.org/

Durham

31904 ■ Carolina Behavioral Care--Durham
725 Broad St.
Durham, NC 27705
Ph: (919)433-1491
URL: http://www.carolinabehavioralcare.com/durhamofficedetails.html

31905 ■ The Durham Center
501 Willard St.
Durham, NC 27701
Ph: (919)560-7100
Free: 800-510-9132
Fax: (919)560-7157
URL: http://durhamcenter.org

31906 ■ The Durham Center
Adult Services
501 Willard St.
Durham, NC 27701
Ph: (919)560-7500
Free: 800-510-9132
URL: http://durhamcenter.org

31907 ■ The Durham Center
Crisis & Access Services
309 Crutchfield St.
Durham, NC 27704
Ph: (919)560-7100
Free: 800-510-9132
Fax: (919)560-7240
URL: http://durhamcenter.org

31908 ■ Durham Veterans Affairs Medical Center
508 Fulton St.
Durham, NC 27705
Ph: (919)286-0411
Free: 888-878-6890
Fax: (919)286-6805
URL: http://www.durham.va.gov/

31909 ■ Hillandale Road Veterans Affairs Clinic
1824 Hillandale Rd.
Durham, NC 27705
Ph: (919)383-6107
Fax: (919)383-6128
URL: http://www.durham.va.gov/visitors/hillandale.asp

Edenton

31910 ■ Albemarle Adult Activity Center--Chowan County
202 W Hicks St.
Edenton, NC 27932
Ph: (252)482-7493

Elkin

31911 ■ New River Behavioral Health
Elkin Outpatient Office
189 Samaritan Ridge Rd.
Elkin, NC 28621
Ph: (336)526-8335
URL: http://www.newriver.org/

Fayetteville

31912 ■ Cumberland County Mental Health Center
Bradford Avenue Center
109 Bradford Ave.
Fayetteville, NC 28301
Ph: (910)323-0601
URL: http://www.ccmentalhealth.org/about_us/directions/directions_bradford.htm

31913 ■ Cumberland County Mental Health Center
Fuller Center
314 Jasper St.
Fayetteville, NC 28301
Ph: (910)822-5066
URL: http://www.ccmentalhealth.org

Franklin

31914 ■ Franklin Veterans Affairs Clinic
647 Wayah St.
Franklin, NC 28734
Ph: (828)369-1781
URL: http://www.asheville.va.gov/visitors/franklin.asp

Gastonia

31915 ■ Pathways--Gastonia
901 S New Hope Rd.
Gastonia, NC 28054
Ph: (704)884-2545
Free: 800-646-4518
URL: http://www.pathwayslme.org/

Grandy

31916 ■ Albemarle Mental Health Center
Currituck Unit
6644 Caratoke Hwy.
Grandy, NC 27939
Ph: (252)453-8886
Free: 877-338-8352
URL: http://www.albemarlemhc.org/

Greensboro

31917 ■ The Guilford Center
Edgeworth Bldg.
232 N Edgeworth St.
Greensboro, NC 27401
Ph: (336)641-4981
Free: 800-853-5163
URL: http://www.guilfordcenter.com

31918 ■ The Guilford Center/Bellemeade Center
201 N Eugene St.
Greensboro, NC 27401
Ph: (336)641-3630
URL: http://www.guilfordcenter.com

31919 ■ Guilford County Area Mental Health/Mental Retardation/Substance Abuse Services
201 N Eugene St.
Greensboro, NC 27401
Ph: (336)884-3630
Free: 800-853-5163
URL: http://www.guilfordcenter.com

31920 ■ LifeSpan--Greensboro
6 Dundas Cir.
Greensboro, NC 27407
Ph: (336)852-3845
Fax: (336)855-9908
URL: http://www.lifespanservices.org/

Greenville

31921 ■ Greenville Veterans Affairs Clinic--Moyle Boulevard
800 Moyle Blvd.
Greenville, NC 27858
Ph: (252)830-2149
Fax: (252)830-1106
URL: http://www.durham.va.gov/visitors/greenville.asp

31922 ■ Walter B. Jones Alcohol and Drug Treatment Center
2577 W 5th St.
Greenville, NC 27834
Ph: (252)830-3426
Fax: (252)830-8585
URL: http://www.dhhs.state.nc.us/MHDDSAS/jones.htm

Henderson

31923 ■ Carolina Behavioral Care--Henderson
510 Dabney Dr.
Henderson, NC 27536
Ph: (252)431-0072
URL: http://www.carolinabehavioralcare.com/hendersonofficedetails.html

31924 ■ Vance, Granville, Franklin, Warren Area Authority--HQ/Vance
134 S Garnett St.
Henderson, NC 27536
Ph: (252)430-1330
Free: 877-619-3761
URL: http://www.fivecountymha.org

Hickory

31925 ■ Catawba Valley Behavioral Healthcare
Main Center
3050 11th Ave. SE
Hickory, NC 28602
Ph: (828)695-6500
Free: 877-327-2593
Fax: (828)695-4256
URL: http://www.cvbh.org/

31926 ■ Hickory Veterans Affairs Clinic
1170 Fairgrove Church Rd.
Hickory, NC 28601
Ph: (828)431-5600
URL: http://www.salisbury.va.gov/visitors/hickory.asp

High Point

31927 ■ Guilford Center
211 S Centennial St.
High Point, NC 27260
Ph: (336)884-7946
URL: http://www.guilfordcenter.com/

31928 ■ LifeSpan--High Point
940 Beaumont St.
High Point, NC 27260
Ph: (336)883-0111
Fax: (336)883-0031
E-mail: contactus@lifespanservices.org
URL: http://www.lifespanservices.org
Formerly: St. Mark's Inc.

Hillsboro

31929 ■ Carolina Behavioral Care--Hillsboro
209 Millstone Dr., Ste. A
Hillsboro, NC 27278
Ph: (919)245-1056
URL: http://www.carolinabehavioralcare.com/hillsboroughofficedetails.html

Hillsborough

31930 ■ Orange County Department of Social Services
Adult Services Unit
300 W Tryon St.
Hillsborough, NC 27278
Ph: (919)968-4501
E-mail: ncoston@co.orange.nc.us
URL: http://www.co.orange.nc.us/socsvcs
Nancy Coston, Director

Hubert

31931 ■ Carobell, Inc.
198 Cinnamon Dr.
Hubert, NC 28539
Ph: (910)326-7600
Fax: (910)326-9988
URL: http://www.carobell.org/

Jacksonville

31932 ■ Jacksonville Veterans Affairs Clinic
1021 Hargett St.
Jacksonville, NC 28540
Ph: (910)219-1339
URL: http://www.fayettevillenc.va.gov/visitors/jacksonville.asp

31933 ■ Onslow Carteret Behavioral Healthcare Services
165 Center St.
Jacksonville, NC 28546
Ph: (910)219-8000
Free: 888-737-0327
URL: http://www.ocbhs.org

31934 ■ Onslow Carteret Behavioral Healthcare Services
Adult Development Activity Program
127 Center St.
Jacksonville, NC 28546
Ph: (910)353-1706
URL: http://www.ocbhs.org

31935 ■ Onslow Carteret Behavioral Healthcare Services
Developmental Disabilities Services
300 Western Blvd., Ste. C
Jacksonville, NC 28546
Ph: (252)353-5118
Free: 888-737-0327
Fax: (252)577-4245
URL: http://www.ocbhs.org

Lenoir

31936 ■ Alexander Youth Network--Lenoir Regional Office
140 Tremont Park Dr.
Lenoir, NC 28645
Ph: (828)758-1931
URL: http://www.alexanderyouthnetwork.org/

31937 ■ Repay, Inc.--Lenoir
201 1/2 Mulberry St.
Lenoir, NC 28645
Ph: (828)757-0902
URL: http://www.repayinc.org/

Louisburg

31938 ■ Carolina Behavioral Care--Louisburg
1683-B US Hwy. 401 S
Louisburg, NC 27549
Ph: (919)496-5827
URL: http://www.carolinabehavioralcare.com/louisburgofficedetails.html

Manteo

31939 ■ Albemarle Mental Health Center--Manteo
407 N Main St.
Manteo, NC 27954
Ph: (252)473-1135
URL: http://www.albemarlemhc.org/

Matthews

31940 ■ Thompson Child and Family Focus
6800 Saint Peters Lane
Matthews, NC 28105
Ph: (704)536-0375
Fax: (704)531-9266
URL: http://www.thompsoncff.org/

Mocksville

31941 ■ CenterPoint Human Services--Davie County
229 Hospital St.
Mocksville, NC 27028
Ph: (336)751-2195
Free: 888-581-9988
URL: http://www.cphs.org
Program(s): Mental health outpatient services; adult vocational program; substance abuse services (outpatient).

Monroe

31942 ■ LifeSpan--Monroe
2409-B Old Charlotte Hwy.
Monroe, NC 28110
Ph: (704)291-2332
URL: http://www.lifespanservices.org/

Morehead City

31943 ■ Morehead City Veterans Affairs Clinic
5420 U.S. Hwy. 70
Morehead City, NC 28557
Ph: (252)240-2349
Fax: (252)240-1840
URL: http://www.durham.va.gov/visitors/morehead.asp

Morganton

31944 ■ Catawba Valley Behavior Healthcare Burke County
350 E Parker Rd.
Morganton, NC 28655
Ph: (828)438-6226
Fax: (828)438-6225
URL: http://www.cvbh.org/location.asp

31945 ■ Repay, Inc.--Morganton
202 Bouchelle St.
Morganton, NC 28655
Ph: (828)437-6268
Fax: (828)437-6225
URL: http://www.repayinc.org/

31946 ■ Turning Point Services, Inc.
1001 S Sterling St.
Morganton, NC 28655
Ph: (828)433-4719
URL: http://www.turningpointservicesinc.com/

Mount Airy

31947 ■ Crossroads Behavioral Healthcare--Mount Airy
351 Riverside Dr.
Mount Airy, NC 27030
Ph: (336)719-3232
Free: 888-841-0408
URL: http://www.crossroadsbhc.org
David Swann, Chief Executive Officer

31948 ■ LifeSpan--Mount Airy
215 Jones School Rd.
Mount Airy, NC 27030
Ph: (336)786-7091
URL: http://www.lifespanservices.org/

Nags Head

31949 ■ Albemarle Mental Health Center--Nags Head
2514 S Croatan Hwy.
Nags Head, NC 27959
Ph: (252)441-9400
Fax: (252)441-3366
URL: http://www.albemarlemhc.org/

Nebo

31950 ■ Southmountain Children and Family Services
7330 Myrtle Dr.
Nebo, NC 28761
Ph: (828)584-1105
URL: http://www.southmountain.org/

New Bern

31951 ■ East Carolina Behavioral Health
405 Middle St.
New Bern, NC 28560
Ph: (252)636-1510
Free: 877-685-2415
Fax: (252)633-1237
URL: http://www.ecbhlme.org/
Formerly: Neuse Center for Mental Health/Developmental Disability/Substance Abuse.

31952 ■ Spencer's Place
201 9th St.
New Bern, NC 28560
Ph: (252)633-1118
URL: http://www.ecbhlme.org/

Newland

31953 ■ New River Behavioral Healthcare Avery Outpatient Center
360 Beech St.
Newland, NC 28657
Ph: (828)733-5889
URL: http://www.newriver.org/address.htm

Newport

31954 ■ Eckerd Camp E-Ma-Henwu
388 9 Mile Rd.
Newport, NC 28570
Ph: (252)726-9058
Free: 800-237-0302
Fax: (252)240-3245
E-mail: admisisons@eckerd.org
URL: http://www.eckerd.org

Newton

31955 ■ Repay, Inc.--Newton
PO Box 969
Newton, NC 28658
Ph: (828)466-6336
URL: http://www.repayinc.org/

Old Fort

31956 ■ SUWS of the Carolinas
363 Graphite Rd.
Old Fort, NC 28762
Ph: (828)668-7590
Free: 888-828-9770
Fax: (828)668-7959
URL: http://www.suwscarolinas.com/

Oxford

31957 ■ Five County Mental Health Authority--Granville
120-A Orange St.
Oxford, NC 27565
Ph: (919)693-2611
Free: 877-619-3761
URL: http://www.fivecountymha.org
Formerly: Jerry Hedrick Mental Health Clinic; Vance, Granville, Franklin, Warren Area Authority--Granville.

Pinehurst

31958 ■ Carolina Behavioral Care--Pinehurst
289 Olmsted Blvd.
Pinehurst, NC 28374
Ph: (910)295-6007
URL: http://www.carolinabehavioralcare.com/pinehurstofficedetails.html

31959 ■ Sandhills Mental Health Center Moore County Outpatient Unit
Hwy. 211 & Memorial Dr.
Pinehurst, NC 28370
Ph: (910)295-6853
Free: 800-256-2452
Fax: (910)295-9183
E-mail: robertg@sandhillscenter.org
URL: http://www.sandhillscenter.org

Plymouth

31960 ■ Albemarle Mental Health Center--Plymouth
716 Washington St.
Plymouth, NC 27962
Ph: (252)793-1154
Free: 877-338-8352
URL: http://www.albemarlemhc.org/
Formerly: Tideland Mental Health Center ; Washington County Office.

Raeford

31961 ■ Sandhills Mental Health Center Hoke County Outpatient Unit
121 E Elwood Ave.
Raeford, NC 28376
Ph: (910)875-8156
Free: 800-256-2452
Fax: (910)875-9560
URL: http://www.sandhillscenter.org

Raleigh

31962 ■ Carolina Behavioral Care--Raleigh
5505 Creedmoor Rd., Ste. 100
Raleigh, NC 27612
Ph: (919)852-5312
URL: http://www.carolinabehavioralcare.com/

31963 ■ Raleigh Veterans Affairs Clinic
3305 Sungate Blvd.
Raleigh, NC 27610
Ph: (919)212-0129
URL: http://www.durham.va.gov/visitors/raleigh.asp

31964 ■ Wellness Supports
8390 6 Forks Rd., Ste. 201
Raleigh, NC 27615
Ph: (919)782-8730
Fax: (919)782-8731
URL: http://www.wellnesssupports.com/

Roanoke Rapids

31965 ■ Carolina Behavioral Care--Roanoke Rapids
220 Smith Church Rd., Bldg. C
Roanoke Rapids, NC 27870
Ph: (252)537-6619
URL: http://www.carolinabehavioralcare.com/roanokerapidsofficedetails.html

Rockingham

31966 ■ Carolina Behavioral Care--Rockingham
109 Medical Cir., Ste. A
Rockingham, NC 28379
Ph: (910)895-0980
URL: http://www.carolinabehavioralcare.com/rockinghamofficedetails.html

31967 ■ Mallard Lane Center
142 Mallard Ln.
Rockingham, NC 28379
Ph: (910)895-3428
URL: http://www.arcofstanlync.org/

31968 ■ Sandhills Mental Health Center Richmond County Outpatient Unit
116 S Lawrence St.
Rockingham, NC 28379
Ph: (910)895-2462
Free: 800-256-2452
Fax: (910)895-9896
URL: http://www.sandhillscenter.org

Rocky Mount

31969 ■ Port Human Services
860 Tiffany Blvd.
Rocky Mount, NC 87804
Ph: (252)442-8100
URL: http://www.porthumanservices.org/

Roxboro

31970 ■ Carolina Behavioral Care--Roxboro
355 S Madison Blvd., Ste. C2
Roxboro, NC 27573
Ph: (336)597-2065
URL: http://www.carolinabehavioralcare.com/roxborofficedetails.html

Salisbury

31971 ■ W.G. (Bill) Hefner Veterans Affairs Medical Center
1601 Brenner Ave.
Salisbury, NC 28144
Ph: (704)638-9000
URL: http://www.salisbury.va.gov/

Shelby

31972 ■ Cleveland Center
917 1st St.
Shelby, NC 28150-3958
Ph: (704)480-6641
Free: 800-898-5898
URL: http://www.pathwaysime.org/

Smithfield

31973 ■ Johnston County Mental Health Center
521 N Brightleaf Blvd.
Smithfield, NC 27577
Ph: (919)989-5500
Free: 888-815-8934
Fax: (919)989-5532
URL: http://www.johnstonnc.com/mainpage.cfm?category_level_id=553&CFID=7755630&CFTOKEN=10078922

Sparta

31974 ■ New River Behavioral Health Care Sparta
1650 Highway 18 S
Sparta, NC 28675-0159
Ph: (336)372-4095
Fax: (336)372-2722
URL: http://www.wataugacounty.org/nrmh

Spruce Pine

31975 ■ Blue Ridge Community Mental Health Center Mitchell County Center
236 Hospital Dr.
Spruce Pine, NC 28777
Ph: (828)765-8808
Free: 800-951-3792
URL: http://www.westernhighlands.org

Statesville

31976 ■ Crossroads Behavioral Healthcare--Statesville
Hwy. 21 N
Statesville, NC 28677
Ph: (704)872-8916
Free: 866-841-0408
Fax: (704)872-2544
E-mail: dcrosby@crossroadsbhc.org
URL: http://www.crossroadsbhc.org

Swan Quarter

31977 ■ Albemarle Mental Health Center--Swan Quarter
1095 Main St.
Swan Quarter, NC 27885
Ph: (252)926-3751
Free: 877-338-8352
URL: http://www.albemarlemhc.org/
Formerly: Tideland Mental Health Center ; Hyde County Office.

Taylorsville

31978 ■ Alexander Group Home
220 1st St. NW
Taylorsville, NC 28681
Ph: (828)632-8733
Fax: (828)632-8743
URL: http://www.smokymountaincenter.com/

31979 ■ Alexander Opportunities
328 7th St. SW
Taylorsville, NC 28681
Ph: (828)632-7414
Fax: (828)632-7427
URL: http://www.turningpointservicesinc.com/

31980 ■ Alexander PSR Program
933 W Main St.
Taylorsville, NC 28681
Ph: (828)632-0790
URL: http://www.smokymountaincenter.com/

31981 ■ Foothills Mental Health Center of Alexander County
326 1st Ave. SW
Taylorsville, NC 28681-2402
Ph: (828)632-7005
Free: 800-849-6127
URL: http://www.smokymountaincenter.com/

Troutman

31982 ■ LifeSpan--Troutman
147 Iredell Ave.
Troutman, NC 28166
Ph: (704)872-1321
URL: http://www.lifespanservices.org/

Troy

31983 ■ Sandhills Mental Health Center Montgomery County Outpatient Unit
227 N Main St.
Troy, NC 27371
Ph: (910)572-3681
URL: http://www.sandhillscenter.org

Wadesboro

31984 ■ Sandhills Mental Health Center Anson County Outpatient Unit
704 Old Lilesville Rd.
Wadesboro, NC 28170
Ph: (704)694-6588
URL: http://www.sandhillscenter.org

Warrenton

31985 ■ Five County Mental Health Authority--Warren
548 Ridgeway St.
Warrenton, NC 27589
Ph: (252)257-2774
Free: 877-619-3761
URL: http://www.fivecountymha.org
Formerly: Vance, Granville, Franklin, Warren Area Authority.

Waynesville

31986 ■ The Balsam Center for Hope and Recovery
91 Timberlane Dr.
Waynesville, NC 28786
Ph: (828)454-1098
Free: 800-849-6127
Fax: (828)454-9242
URL: http://www.smokymountaincenter.com/about/centers.asp

31987 ■ Haywood County Center
1207 East St.
Waynesville, NC 28786
Ph: (828)456-9452
Fax: (828)456-4494
URL: http://www.smokymountaincenter.com/about/centers.asp

31988 ■ LifeSpan--Waynesville
627 N Main St., Ste. 1
Waynesville, NC 28786
Ph: (828)452-1720
URL: http://www.lifespanservices.org/

West End

31989 ■ Sandhills Center
1120 Seven Lakes Dr.
West End, NC 27376
Ph: (910)673-9111
URL: http://www.sandhillscenter.org

West Jefferson

31990 ■ New River Behavioral Healthcare Willow Place
603 Long St.
West Jefferson, NC 28694
Ph: (252)246-6504
URL: http://www.wataugacounty.org/nrmh

Williamston

31991 ■ Albemarle Mental Health Center Martin County Office Early Intervention Program
102 Medical Dr.
Williamston, NC 27892
Ph: (252)792-5151
Fax: (252)792-0802
URL: http://www.albemarlemhc.org/index.php?page=martin-county
Formerly: Tideland Mental Health Center.

Wilmington

31992 ■ Stepping Stone Manor
416 Walnut St.
Wilmington, NC 28401
Ph: (910)762-1743

31993 ■ Wilmington Veterans Affairs Clinic
1606 Physicians Dr., Ste. 104
Wilmington, NC 28401
Ph: (910)362-8811
URL: http://www.fayettevillenc.va.gov/visitors/wilmington.asp

Winston Salem

31994 ■ CenterPoint Human Services ADD Program
650 N Highland Ave.
Winston Salem, NC 27101
Ph: (336)725-7777
Free: 888-581-9988
URL: http://www.cphs.org

31995 ■ CenterPoint Human Services Partial Hospitalization Program
651 N Highland Ave.
Winston Salem, NC 27101
Ph: (336)607-8523
Free: 888-581-9988
URL: http://www.cphs.org

31996 ■ CenterPoint Human Services Services Office
4045 University Pkwy.
Winston Salem, NC 27106
Ph: (336)714-9100
Free: 888-581-9988
E-mail: cphs@cphs.org
URL: http://www.cphs.org

31997 ■ CenterPoint Human Services--Winston Salem
725 N Highland Ave.
Winston Salem, NC 27101
Ph: (336)725-7777
Free: 888-581-9988
Fax: (336)722-1567
URL: http://www.cphs.org

31998 ■ Club House Program/Friendship Center
726 N Cherry St.
Winston Salem, NC 27101
Ph: (336)748-5400
Free: 888-581-9988
URL: http://www.cphs.org/

31999 ■ Winston Salem Veterans Affairs Clinic
190 Kimel Park Dr.
Winston Salem, NC 27103
Ph: (336)768-3296
URL: http://www.salisbury.va.gov/visitors/winstonsalem.asp

Yadkinville

32000 ■ Crossroads Behavioral Healthcare--Yadkinville
320 E Lee St.
Yadkinville, NC 27055
Ph: (336)679-8805
Free: 866-841-0400
Fax: (336)679-3057
E-mail: srimm@crossroadsbhc.org
URL: http://www.crossroadsbhc.org
Sharon Rimm, Director

NORTH DAKOTA

Beulah

32001 ■ Region VII--West Central Human Service Center Satellite Office
1101 3rd Ave. NW
Beulah, ND 58523
Ph: (701)873-2399
Free: 888-616-1441
Fax: (701)873-2939
E-mail: dhswchsc@nd.gov
URL: http://www.nd.gov/dhs/locations/regionalhsc/westcentral/index.html

Bismarck

32002 ■ Bismarck Veterans Affairs Clinic
2700 State St.
Bismarck, ND 58503
Ph: (701)221-9152
Fax: (701)221-0918
URL: http://www.fargo.va.gov/visitors/bismarck.asp

32003 ■ Manchester House Residential Treatment Center
600 S 2nd St., Ste. 5
Bismarck, ND 58504
Ph: (701)223-5600
URL: http://www.prideinc.org/manchester-house.aspx

32004 ■ Region VII--West Central Human Service Center
1237 W Divide Ave., Ste. 5
Bismarck, ND 58501
Ph: (701)328-8888
Free: 888-328-2662
Fax: (701)328-8900
E-mail: dhswchsc@nd.gov
URL: http://www.nd.gov/dhs/locations/regionalhsc/westcentral/index.html

Devils Lake

32005 ■ Region III--Lake Region Human Service Center
200 Hwy. 2 SW
Box 650
Devils Lake, ND 58301
Ph: (701)665-2200
Free: 888-607-8610
Fax: (701)665-2300
E-mail: dhslrhsc@nd.gov
URL: http://www.nd.gov/dhs/locations/regionalhsc/lakeregion/

Dickinson

32006 ■ Dickinson Veterans Affairs Clinic
33 9th St. W
Dickinson, ND 58601
Ph: (701)483-6017
Free: 877-483-6017
URL: http://www.fargo.va.gov/visitors/dickinson.asp

32007 ■ Region VIII--Badlands Human Service Center
300 13th Ave. W, Ste. 1
Dickinson, ND 58601
Ph: (701)227-7500
Free: 888-227-7525
Fax: (701)227-7575
E-mail: dhsblhsc@nd.gov
URL: http://www.nd.gov/dhs/locations/regionalhsc/badlands/
Tim Sauter, Director

Fargo

32008 ■ Fargo Veterans Affairs Medical Center
2101 N Elm
Fargo, ND 58102
Ph: (800)410-9723
URL: http://www.fargo.va.gov/

32009 ■ Prairie Saint John's
510 S 4th St.
Fargo, ND 58103
Ph: (701)476-7208
Free: 877-333-9565
URL: http://www.prairie-stjohns.com/

32010 ■ Region V--Southeast Human Service Center
2624 9th Ave. SW
Fargo, ND 58103-2350
Ph: (701)298-4500
Free: 888-342-4900
Fax: (701)298-4400
E-mail: dhssehsc@nd.gov
URL: http://www.nd.gov/dhs/locations/regionalhsc/southeast/
Nancy McKenzie, Director

Grafton

32011 ■ Northeast Human Service Center--Grafton
5th & School Rd.
Grafton, ND 58237
Ph: (701)352-4334
Free: 888-845-2215
Fax: (701)352-4590
E-mail: dhsnehsc@nd.gov
URL: http://www.nd.gov/dhs/locations/regionalhsc/northeast/

Grand Forks

32012 ■ Duane R. Dornheim Transitional Living Facility
1407 S 10th Ave.
Grand Forks, ND 58201
Ph: (701)795-3889

32013 ■ Northeast Human Service Center--Grand Forks
151 S 4th St., Ste. 401
Grand Forks, ND 58201
Ph: (701)795-3000

Free: 888-256-6742
Fax: (701)795-3050
E-mail: dhsnehsc@nd.gov
URL: http://www.nd.gov/dhs/locations/regionalhsc/northeast/

32014 ■ Ruth Meiers Adolescent Center
770 S 14th St.
Grand Forks, ND 58201
Ph: (701)795-3870
Free: 888-823-5931
E-mail: ruthmeiers@nd.gov
URL: http://www.nd.gov/dhs/locations/regionalhsc/northeast/ruth-meiers.html

Jamestown

32015 ■ Jamestown Veterans Affairs Clinic--5th Street NE
419 5th St. NE
Jamestown, ND 58401
Ph: (701)052-4787
URL: http://www.fargo.va.gov/visitors/jamestown.asp

32016 ■ Region VI--South Central Human Service Center
520 3rd St. NW
Jamestown, ND 58402-2055
Ph: (701)253-6300
Free: 800-260-1310
Fax: (701)253-6400
E-mail: dhsschsc@nd.gov
URL: http://www.nd.gov/dhs/locations/regionalhsc/southcentral/
Candace Fuglesten, Director

Minot

32017 ■ Minot Veterans Affairs Clinic
10 Missile Ave.
Minot, ND 58705
Ph: (701)727-9800
Fax: (701)727-9804
URL: http://www.fargo.va.gov/visitors/minot.asp

32018 ■ Region II--North Central Human Service Center
1015 S Broadway, Ste. 18
Minot, ND 58701
Ph: (701)857-8500
Free: 888-470-6968
Fax: (701)857-8555
E-mail: dhsnchsc@nd.gov
URL: http://www.nd.gov/dhs/locations/regionalhsc/northcentral/index.html
Marilyn Rudolph, Director

Newtown

32019 ■ North Central Human Service Newtown Outreach Center
228 Eagle Dr.
Newtown, ND 58763
Ph: (701)627-2599
URL: http://www.nd.gov/dhs/locations/regionalhsc/northcentral/index.html

Rugby

32020 ■ North Central Human Service Rugby Outreach Center
210 S Main St.
Rugby, ND 58368
Ph: (701)228-5496
URL: http://www.nd.gov/dhs/locations/regionalhsc/northcentral/index.html

Stanley

32021 ■ North Central Human Service Stanley Outreach Center
War Memorial Bldg.
Stanley, ND 58701
Ph: (701)628-2877
URL: http://www.nd.gov/dhs/locations/regionalhsc/northcentral/index.html

Williston

32022 ■ Northwest Human Service
316 2nd Ave. W
Williston, ND 58802
Ph: (701)774-4600
Free: 800-231-7724
Fax: (701)774-4620
E-mail: dhsnwhsc@nd.gov
URL: http://www.nd.gov/dhs/locations/regionalhsc/northwest/

32023 ■ Williston Veterans Affairs Clinic
3 4th St. E, Ste. 104
Williston, ND 58802
Ph: (701)577-9838
URL: http://www.fargo.va.gov/visitors/williston.asp

OHIO

Akron

32024 ■ Akron Veterans Affairs Clinic
55 W Waterloo Rd.
Akron, OH 44319
Ph: (330)724-7715
Fax: (330)724-1029
URL: http://www.cleveland.va.gov/visitors/akron.asp

32025 ■ Blick Clinic
640 W Market St.
Akron, OH 44303
Ph: (330)762-5425
Fax: (330)762-4019
URL: http://www.blickclinic.org/

32026 ■ Child Guidance Center & Family Solutions
312 Locust St.
Akron, OH 44302
Ph: (330)762-0591
URL: http://www.cgfs.org/

32027 ■ Community Support Services, Inc.--Cross Street, Akron
150 Cross St.
Akron, OH 44311
Ph: (330)253-9388
E-mail: webadmin@cssbehavioral.org
URL: http://www.cssbehavioral.org

32028 ■ Community Support Services--Wolf Ledges Parkway, Akron
640 Wolf Ledges Pky.
Akron, OH 44311
Ph: (330)253-9675
E-mail: webadmin@cssbehavioral.org
URL: http://www.cssbehavioral.org

32029 ■ Kibler Hall
101 Ambassador Ct.
Akron, OH 44312-4410
Ph: (330)733-6203
URL: http://www.cssbehavioral.org/res.aspx

32030 ■ Portage Path Behavioral Health
340 S Broadway St.
Akron, OH 44308
Ph: (330)253-3100
URL: http://www.portagepath.org/locations.html

32031 ■ Portage Path Behavioral Health Psychiatric Emergency Services
10 Penfield Ave.
Akron, OH 44310
Ph: (330)762-6110
URL: http://www.portagepath.org/locations.html

Alliance

32032 ■ Child and Adolescent Service Center--Alliance
1207 W State St., Ste. G
Alliance, OH 44601
Ph: (330)823-5335
URL: http://www.casrv.org/

Amelia

32033 ■ Clermont Counseling Center--Amelia
43 E Main St.
Amelia, OH 45102
Ph: (513)947-7000
Free: 800-732-9805
Fax: (513)947-7001
URL: http://www.clermontcounseling.org

32034 ■ Phoenix Place
4 Cecelia Dr.
Amelia, OH 45102
Ph: (513)947-7025
Fax: (513)947-7055
URL: http://www.clermontcounseling.org/0103_home_location.html

Amherst

32035 ■ Firelands Counseling & Recovery Services of Erie County
315 N Leavitt Rd.
Amherst, OH 44001
Ph: (440)984-3882
URL: http://www.firelands.com/

Ashland

32036 ■ Appleseed Community Mental Health Center
2233 Rocky Ln.
Ashland, OH 44805
Ph: (419)281-3716
URL: http://www.appleseedmentalhealth.com/

Ashtabula

32037 ■ Community Counseling Center of Ashtabula County
2801 C Ct.
Ashtabula, OH 44004
Ph: (440)998-4210

Athens

32038 ■ Crisis Residential Center
7976 Dairy Ln.
Athens, OH 45701
Ph: (740)592-3091

32039 ■ Tri-County Mental Health & Counseling--Athens
90 Hospital Dr.
Athens, OH 45701
Ph: (740)592-3091
Free: 888-475-8484

Austintown

32040 ■ D&E Counseling Center--Austintown
142 Javit Ct.
Austintown, OH 44515
Ph: (330)793-2487
URL: http://www.dandecenter.com/locations.aspx

Barberton

32041 ■ Portage Path Behavioral Health
105 5th St. SE, Ste. 6
Barberton, OH 44203
Ph: (330)745-0081
URL: http://www.portagepath.org/locations.html

Beachwood

32042 ■ Jewish Family Service Association of Cleveland
Drost Family Center
24075 Commerce Park Rd.
Beachwood, OH 44122-5846
Ph: (216)292-3999
URL: http://www.jfsa-cleveland.org

Bellefontaine

32043 ■ Ben El Child and Family Center
1600 S Main St.
Bellefontaine, OH 43311
Ph: (937)599-2766
URL: http://www.crsi-oh.com/

32044 ■ Ben El Child and Family Center Day Treatment
468 County Rd. 11
Bellefontaine, OH 43311
Ph: (937)599-4644
URL: http://www.crsi-oh.com/

Bowling Green

32045 ■ Behavioral Connections of Wood County, Inc.--Gypsy Lane
320 W Gypsy Ln.
Bowling Green, OH 43402
Ph: (419)352-2551
URL: http://www.behavioralconnections.org/

32046 ■ Behavioral Connections of Wood County, Inc.--North Prospect
1010 N Prospect St.
Bowling Green, OH 43402
Ph: (419)352-5387
URL: http://www.behavioralconnections.org/

32047 ■ Family Service Counseling of Wood County
1616 E Wooster, Unit 24
Bowling Green, OH 43402
Ph: (419)352-4624

Brecksville

32048 ■ Cleveland Veterans Affairs Medical Center
Brecksville Campus
10000 Brecksville Rd.
Brecksville, OH 44141
Ph: (440)526-3030
Free: 888-838-6446
URL: http://www.cleveland.va.gov/

Bryan

32049 ■ Family Services of Northwest Ohio
228 S Main
Bryan, OH 43506
Ph: (419)335-3732
Free: 800-693-6000
Fax: (419)335-3462
URL: http://www.fsno.org/FourCounty.html

32050 ■ Maumee Valley Guidance Center--Bryan Office
203 N Lynn St.
Bryan, OH 43506
Ph: (419)636-2932
URL: http://www.maumeevalleyguidancecenter.org/

Bucyrus

32051 ■ Community Counseling Services, Inc.--Bucyrus
2458 Stetzer Rd.
Bucyrus, OH 44820
Ph: (419)562-2000
URL: http://www.communitycounseling.info/

Cadiz

32052 ■ Women's Tri-County Help Center, Inc.
109 W Warren St.
Cadiz, OH 43907
Ph: (740)942-1018
Free: 800-695-1639

Calcutta

32053 ■ Calcutta Veterans Affairs Clinic
15655 State Rte. 170
Calcutta, OH 43920
Ph: (330)386-4303
Fax: (330)386-4485
URL: http://www.cleveland.va.gov/visitors/calcutta.asp

Caldwell

32054 ■ Noble Counseling Center
44020 Marietta Rd.
Caldwell, OH 43724
Ph: (740)732-5233

Cambridge

32055 ■ Guernsey Counseling Center
2500 Glenn Hwy.
Cambridge, OH 43725
Ph: (740)439-4428

Canton

32056 ■ Canton Veterans Affairs Clinic
733 Market Ave. S
Canton, OH 44702
Ph: (330)489-4600
Fax: (330)489-4684
URL: http://www.cleveland.va.gov/visitors/canton.asp

32057 ■ Child and Adolescent Service Center--Belden
4641 Fulton Rd. NW
Canton, OH 44718
Ph: (330)433-6075
Free: 800-791-7917
URL: http://www.casrv.org/about/locations.htm

32058 ■ Child and Adolescent Service Center--Canton
919 2nd St. NE
Canton, OH 44704
Ph: (330)454-7917
URL: http://www.casrv.org/about/locations.htm

32059 ■ Crisis Intervention Center of Stark County
2421 13th St. NW, Ste. 100
Canton, OH 44708-3189
Ph: (330)452-9812
URL: http://www.starkmhrsb.org/info-services/search-for-information/crisis-inter vention-center/

Carrollton

32060 ■ Southeast, Inc.--Carrollton
783 Jones Ave. NW
Carrollton, OH 44615
Ph: (330)627-3954
Formerly: Cornerstone Support Services.

Celina

32061 ■ Foundations Behavioral Health Services
4761 State Rte. 29
Celina, OH 45822
Ph: (419)584-1000

Chardon

32062 ■ Ravenwood Mental Health Center
12557 Ravenwood Dr.
Chardon, OH 44024
Ph: (440)285-3568
Free: 877-285-3568
URL: http://www.ravenwoodmhc.org/

Chillicothe

32063 ■ Chillicothe Veterans Affairs Medical Center
17273 State Rte. 104
Chillicothe, OH 45601
Ph: (740)773-1141
Free: 800-358-8262
URL: http://www.chillicothe.va.gov/

32064 ■ Scioto-Paint Valley Mental Health Center--Chillicothe
312 E 2nd St.
Chillicothe, OH 45601
Ph: (740)775-1270
URL: http://www.spvmhc.org/

Cincinnati

32065 ■ Case Management Services
522 Maxwell Ave., Ste. 524
Cincinnati, OH 45219-2408
Ph: (513)559-2062

32066 ■ Centerpoint Health--College Hill
5837 Hamilton Ave.
Cincinnati, OH 45224
Ph: (513)541-7577
Fax: (513)541-5895
URL: http://www.centerpointhealth.org/locations.html
Formerly: Core Behavioral Health Center--Hamilton.

32067 ■ Centerpoint Health--Oakley
4760 Madison Rd.
Cincinnati, OH 45227
Ph: (513)321-8286
URL: http://www.centerpointhealth.org/locations.html

32068 ■ Centerpoint Health--Roselawn
7162 Reading Rd., Ste. 500
Cincinnati, OH 45237
Ph: (513)761-6222
URL: http://www.centerpointhealth.org/locations.html

32069 ■ Centerpoint Health--Victory Parkway, Cincinnati
2602 Victory Pkwy.
Cincinnati, OH 45206
Ph: (513)221-4673
URL: http://www.centerpointhealth.org/locations.html
Formerly: Norcen Behavioral Health System.

32070 ■ Centerpoint Health--Western Hills
4968 Glenway Ave.
Cincinnati, OH 45238
Ph: (513)541-7577
Fax: (513)471-8080
URL: http://www.centerpointhealth.org/locations.html
Formerly: Core Behavioral Health Center--Glenway.

32071 ■ Central Psychiatric Clinic
311 Albert Sabin Way
Cincinnati, OH 45229
Ph: (513)558-9015
URL: http://www.centralclinic.org/

32072 ■ Child Focus, Inc.
555 Cincinnati-Batavia Pke., No. 2
Cincinnati, OH 45244
Ph: (513)752-1555
URL: http://www.child-focus.org/

32073 ■ Elm Street Health Center
1525 Elm St.
Cincinnati, OH 45202
Ph: (513)352-3190

32074 ■ Geriatric Outreach Services
526 Maxwell Ave.
Cincinnati, OH 45219
Ph: (513)559-2060

32075 ■ Greater Cincinnati Behavioral Health Services--Madison Road
1501 Madison Rd.
Cincinnati, OH 45206
Ph: (513)354-7000
E-mail: info@gcbhs.com
URL: http://www.gcbhs.com/

32076 ■ Greater Cincinnati Behavioral Health Services--Reading Road
7162 Reading Rd., Ste. 1200
Cincinnati, OH 45237
Ph: (513)354-7200
Fax: (513)354-7115
E-mail: info@gcbhs.com
URL: http://www.gcbhs.com/

32077 ■ Marlowe House
1623 Marlowe Ave.
Cincinnati, OH 45224
Ph: (513)681-0326

32078 ■ Talbert House
2600 Victory Pkwy.
Cincinnati, OH 45206
Ph: (513)751-7747
Fax: (513)751-8107
URL: http://www.talberthouse.org

32079 ■ Veterans Affairs Medical Center Cincinnati
3200 Vine St.
Cincinnati, OH 45220
Ph: (513)861-3100
Free: 888-267-7873
URL: http://www.cincinnati.va.gov/

32080 ■ West End Health Center
1413 Linn St.
Cincinnati, OH 45214
Ph: (513)621-2727
URL: http://www.wehc.org/

Circleville

32081 ■ Scioto-Paint Valley Mental Health Center--Circleville
Pickaway County
145 Morris Rd.
Circleville, OH 43113
Ph: (740)474-8874
URL: http://www.spvmhc.org/

Cleveland

32082 ■ Applewood Centers Inc.--Children's Aid Society Campus
10427 Detroit Ave.
Cleveland, OH 44102
Ph: (216)521-6511
Fax: (216)521-6006
URL: http://www.applewoodcenters.org

32083 ■ Applewood Centers Inc.--Eleanor Gerson Alternative High School
1320 Sumner Ave.
Cleveland, OH 44115
Ph: (216)861-6015
Fax: (216)696-6986
URL: http://www.applewoodcenters.org

32084 ■ Applewood Centers Inc.--Jones Campus
3518 W 25th St.
Cleveland, OH 44109-1995
Ph: (216)741-2241
URL: http://www.applewoodcenters.org
Formerly: Applewood Centers Inc.--Cuyahoga County.

32085 ■ Applewood Centers inc.--Richard Paulson Center
2525 E 22nd St.
Cleveland, OH 44115-3266
Ph: (216)696-5800
Fax: (216)696-6592
URL: http://www.applewoodcenters.org

32086 ■ Bradley Manor
3234 West Blvd.
Cleveland, OH 44102
Ph: (216)476-0900
URL: http://www.bridgewayinc.org/

32087 ■ Bridgeway, Inc.
Administrative Office
3146 Scraton Rd.
Cleveland, OH 44109
Ph: (216)688-7202
URL: http://www.bridgewayinc.org

32088 ■ Bridgeway, Inc.--Cleveland
8301 Detroit Ave.
Cleveland, OH 44102
Ph: (216)631-1740
URL: http://www.bridgewayinc.org
Greg Uhland, Director

32089 ■ Bridgeway, Inc.--West Side
2103 Clark Ave.
Cleveland, OH 44109
Ph: (216)687-1350
URL: http://www.bridgewayinc.org

32090 ■ Carlos and Mary Jones Center
Shelter for Children
3518 W 25th St.
Cleveland, OH 44109
Ph: (216)741-2241
URL: http://www.applewoodcenters.org/

32091 ■ Center for Families and Children
4500 Euclid Ave.
Cleveland, OH 44105
Ph: (216)271-0095

32092 ■ Cleveland Free Clinic--Mental Health Services
12201 Euclid Ave.
Cleveland, OH 44106
Ph: (216)721-4010
URL: http://www.thefreeclinic.org/services.htm

32093 ■ Cleveland Veterans Affairs Medical Center
Wade Park Campus
10701 East Blvd.
Cleveland, OH 44106
Ph: (216)791-3800
Free: 888-838-6446
URL: http://www.cleveland.va.gov/

32094 ■ Clinton Lodge
3201 Clinton Ave.
Cleveland, OH 44113-2808
Ph: (216)281-0740
URL: http://www.spectrumsupport.org/

32095 ■ Diagnostic Assessment Service
3100 Euclid Ave.
Cleveland, OH 44115
Ph: (216)361-4400
Fax: (216)361-8600
URL: http://www.pepcleve.org

32096 ■ Euclid Lodge
13220 Euclid Ave.
Cleveland, OH 44112-4524
Ph: (216)681-4067

32097 ■ Fairhill Community Office
12200 Fairhill Rd.
Cleveland, OH 44120
Ph: (216)421-1350
Fax: (216)421-8874
URL: http://www.fairhillcenter.org/

32098 ■ McCafferty Veterans Affairs Clinic
4242 Lorain Ave.
Cleveland, OH 44113
Ph: (216)939-0699
Fax: (216)939-0789
URL: http://www.cleveland.va.gov/visitors/mccafferty.asp

32099 ■ Mental Health Services for Homeless Persons, Inc.
1744 Payne Ave.
Cleveland, OH 44114
Ph: (216)623-6555
URL: http://www.mhs-inc.org/

32100 ■ Murtis H. Taylor Multi-Service Center
13422 Kinsman Rd.
Cleveland, OH 44120
Ph: (216)283-4400
URL: http://www.murtistaylor.org/home/default.aspx

32101 ■ Near West Woodworks
1810 W 25th St.
Cleveland, OH 44113
Ph: (216)694-3767
URL: http://www.spectrumsupport.org/Fairweather.html

32102 ■ Positive Education Program
Main Office and DAS
3100 Euclid Ave.
Cleveland, OH 44115
Ph: (216)361-4400
Fax: (216)361-8600
URL: http://www.pepcleve.org/

32103 ■ Spectrum of Supportive Services
2900 Detroit Ave., 3rd Fl.
Cleveland, OH 44113
Ph: (216)939-2065
Fax: (216)939-2077
URL: http://www.spectrumsupport.org/

32104 ■ Tanaka House
8118 St. Claire Ave.
Cleveland, OH 44102
Ph: (216)431-4030
URL: http://www.bridgewayinc.org/

Columbus

32105 ■ Carpenter House
1699 S High St.
Columbus, OH 43207
Ph: (614)443-0141
URL: http://www.southeastinc.com/

32106 ■ Chalmers P. Wylie Veterans Clinic
420 N James Rd.
Columbus, OH 43219
Ph: (614)257-5631
Free: 888-838-6446
URL: http://www.columbus.va.gov/

32107 ■ Choices
PO Box 06157
Columbus, OH 43206
Ph: (614)224-4663
URL: http://www.choicesdvcols.org

32108 ■ Columbus Area Community Mental Health Center
1515 E Broad St.
Columbus, OH 43205
Ph: (614)252-0711
URL: http://www.columbus-area.com/

32109 ■ Columbus Area Community Mental Health Center
Intermediate Care
1203 E Broad St.
Columbus, OH 43205-1404
Ph: (614)251-7820
URL: http://www.columbus-area.com/

32110 ■ Columbus Area Halfway House
1515 E Broad St.
Columbus, OH 43205-1590
Ph: (614)252-0711
URL: http://www.columbus-area.com/

32111 ■ Huckleberry House, Inc.
1421 Hamlet St.
Columbus, OH 43201
Ph: (614)294-8097
URL: http://www.huckhouse.org/

32112 ■ Kendall Manor
1337 Bryden Rd.
Columbus, OH 43205
Ph: (614)251-7779
URL: http://www.columbus-area.com/

32113 ■ Madear's Kinship Village
1288 Brookcliff Ave.
Columbus, OH 43219
Ph: (614)258-5154
Remarks: Provides intergenerational housing and social services for grandparents that are caring for their grandchildren in order to ensure the physical and emotional health of these families. Organization also provides legal assistance through its case management services. **Formerly:** Kinship Village.

32114 ■ Maryhaven Adult Outpatient Services--Columbus
226 N 5th St., Ste. 218
Columbus, OH 43215
Ph: (614)917-2900
URL: http://www.maryhaven.com/

32115 ■ Maryhaven--Main Campus
1791 Alum Creek Dr.
Columbus, OH 43207
Ph: (614)445-8131
URL: http://www.maryhaven.com/

32116 ■ Net Care Access
741 E Broad St.
Columbus, OH 43205
Ph: (614)276-2273
Fax: (614)278-0210
URL: http://netcareaccess.org/

32117 ■ North Central Mental Health Services--Columbus
1301 N High St.
Columbus, OH 43201
Ph: (614)299-6600
URL: http://www.ncmhs.org/

32118 ■ North Central Mental Health Services
Family Focus
40 Spruce St.
Columbus, OH 43215
Ph: (614)227-6865
URL: http://www.ncmhs.org/

32119 ■ North Central Mental Health Services
Fowler House
422 E Lane Ave.
Columbus, OH 43201-6705
Ph: (614)421-3155
URL: http://www.ncmhs.org/

32120 ■ North Central Mental Health Services
Norwich House
431 E Norwich Ave.
Columbus, OH 43201-1326
Ph: (614)421-3158
URL: http://www.ncmhs.org/

32121 ■ North Central Mental Health Services
Soaring Sober
35 W 4th Ave.
Columbus, OH 43201
Ph: (614)421-3183
URL: http://www.ncmhs.org/

32122 ■ Pathway Clubhouse
1203 E Broad St.
Columbus, OH 43205
Ph: (614)251-7820
URL: http://www.columbus-area.com/aboutus.php-?contactus

32123 ■ Rosemont Center
2440 Dawnlight Ave.
Columbus, OH 43211
Ph: (614)471-2626
Free: 800-753-0424
Fax: (614)478-3234
URL: http://www.rosemont.org/

32124 ■ Southeast Counseling Services
1455 S 4th St.
Columbus, OH 43207
Ph: (614)444-0800
URL: http://www.southeastinc.com/contact_information.php#general

32125 ■ Southeast, Inc.--Columbus
16 W Long St.
Columbus, OH 43215
Ph: (614)225-0990
URL: http://www.southeastinc.com/contact_information.php#general

32126 ■ Southeast, Inc.--Columbus
Project Work
1705 S High St.
Columbus, OH 43207
Ph: (614)445-8441
URL: http://www.southeastinc.com/contact_information.php#general

Coshocton

32127 ■ Coshocton Counseling Center
710 Main St.
Coshocton, OH 43812
Ph: (740)622-3404

Cuyahoga Falls

32128 ■ Maggie Carroll Smith Group Home
1770 2nd St.
Cuyahoga Falls, OH 44221
Ph: (330)923-9957

32129 ■ North Summit Clinic
792 Graham Rd., Ste. C
Cuyahoga Falls, OH 44221
Ph: (330)928-2324
URL: http://www.portagepath.org/locations.html

Dayton

32130 ■ Dayton Veterans Affairs Medical Center
4100 W 3rd St.
Dayton, OH 45428
Ph: (937)268-6511
Free: 800-368-8262
URL: http://www.dayton.va.gov/

32131 ■ Eastway Corporation of Greater Dayton
Adult Outpatient Services
600 Wayne Ave.
Dayton, OH 45410
Ph: (937)222-6504
URL: http://www.eastway.org

32132 ■ Eastway Corporation
Marshall House
3417 Marshall Rd.
Dayton, OH 45429
Ph: (937)293-6400
Free: 800-496-2377
URL: http://www.eastway.org

32133 ■ Eastway Corporation/Springfield Plaza
Eastco Production and Employment Services
131 N Hedges St.
Dayton, OH 45403
Ph: (937)222-3274
URL: http://eastway.org

32134 ■ Eastway Corporation/Twin Towers Plaza
Crisis Residential
601 Xenia Ave.
Dayton, OH 45410-1825
Ph: (937)496-2027
URL: http://eastway.org

32135 ■ Eastway Corporation
Webster Street Academy and Family Center
1110 Webster St.
Dayton, OH 45404
Ph: (937)463-2955
URL: http://www.eastway.org
Formerly: Child and Adolescent Services Program.

Defiance

32136 ■ Center for Child & Family Advocacy, Inc.
511 Perry St.
Defiance, OH 43512
Ph: (419)782-1314

32137 ■ Four County Family Center--Defiance
118 Clinton St.
Defiance, OH 43512
Ph: (419)335-3732
Free: 800-693-6000
Fax: (419)335-3462
URL: http://www.fsno.org/FourCounty.html

32138 ■ Maumee Valley Guidance Center--Defiance
211 Biede Ave.
Defiance, OH 43512
Ph: (419)782-8856
URL: http://www.maumeevalleyguidancecenter.org/

Delaware

32139 ■ Maryhaven--Delaware
615 Sunbury Rd.
Delaware, OH 43015
Ph: (740)203-3800
URL: http://www.maryhaven.com/

Dover

32140 ■ Community Mental Healthcare
201 Hospital Dr.
Dover, OH 44622
Ph: (330)343-6631
URL: http://www.cmhdover.org/

Dublin

32141 ■ Dublin Counseling Center
299 Cramer Creek Ct.
Dublin, OH 43017
Ph: (614)889-5722
Fax: (614)889-9335
URL: http://www.dublincounselingcenter.org/

East Liverpool

32142 ■ Columbiana County Mental Health Center
East Liverpool Unit
518 Market St.
East Liverpool, OH 43920
Ph: (330)386-9004
URL: http://www.colmhc.org/WhoAreWe.htm

Elyria

32143 ■ Applewood Center
5255 N Abbe Rd., Ste. 1
Elyria, OH 44035
Ph: (440)934-9930
Fax: (440)934-9645
URL: http://www.applewoodcenters.org/locations.html

32144 ■ The Nord Center
Elyria Counseling Office
902 N Abbe Rd.
Elyria, OH 44035
Ph: (440)366-5262
Free: 866-888-6673
URL: http://www.nordcenter.org/Pages/contact.htm

32145 ■ Pathways Counseling Center
312 3rd St.
Elyria, OH 44035
Ph: (440)323-5707
URL: http://www.pathwayscounselingcenter.com/

Euclid

32146 ■ Eastwood Day Treatment Center Positive Education Program
1941 Sagamore Dr.
Euclid, OH 44117
Ph: (216)486-2999
URL: http://www.eastway.org/
Formerly: Eastwood Day Treatment Center Positive Education Program.

32147 ■ Flores Home
25540 Euclid Ave.
Euclid, OH 44107
Ph: (216)261-0948
URL: http://www.bridgewayinc.org/

Fairborn

32148 ■ TCN Behavioral Health Services, Inc.
600 Dayton-Yellow Springs Rd.
Fairborn, OH 45324
Ph: (937)376-8701
Free: 877-695-6333
URL: http://www.tcn-bhs.org/

Findlay

32149 ■ Century Health--Adult Treatment Center
1918 N Main St.
Findlay, OH 45840
Ph: (419)425-5050
URL: http://www.centuryhealth.net/

32150 ■ Family Resource Centers--Findlay
1941 Carlin St.
Findlay, OH 45840
Ph: (419)422-8616
Free: 888-422-7392
URL: http://www.frcohio.com/external/external.htm

Gahanna

32151 ■ North Central Counseling Associates
338 Granville St.
Gahanna, OH 43230
Ph: (614)475-7090
URL: http://www.ncmhs.org/
Formerly: NCC Associates.

Gallipolis

32152 ■ Woodland Center--Gallipolis
3086 State Rte. 160
Gallipolis, OH 45631
Ph: (740)446-5500
URL: http://woodlandcenters.org/

Georgetown

32153 ■ Brown County Counseling
75 Banting Dr.
Georgetown, OH 45121
Ph: (937)378-4811

Grafton

32154 ■ Willow Creek Day Treatment Center
11600 N Durkee Rd.
Grafton, OH 44044
Ph: (440)748-6120
URL: http://www.pepcleve.org/

Greenville

32155 ■ Darke County Mental Health Clinic
212 E Main St.
Greenville, OH 45331
Ph: (937)548-1635
URL: http://www.dcmhc.org/

Grove City

32156 ■ The Buckeye Ranch--Grove City
5665 Hoover Rd.
Grove City, OH 43123-9280
Ph: (614)875-2371
Free: 800-859-5665
Fax: (614)875-2366
URL: http://www.buckeyeranch.org

Hamilton

32157 ■ Pinecrest
2030 Princeton Rd.
Hamilton, OH 45011
Ph: (513)863-6383

32158 ■ Transitional Living, Inc.--Park Avenue, Hamilton
117 Park Ave.
Hamilton, OH 45013
Ph: (513)896-7269
Fax: (513)896-5320
URL: http://www.tliving.org/ContactUs.asp

32159 ■ Transitional Living, Inc.--Princeton Road, Hamilton
2052 Princeton Rd.
Hamilton, OH 45011
Ph: (513)863-6383
URL: http://www.tliving.org/

Hillsboro

32160 ■ Scioto Paint Valley Mental Health Center--Hillsboro
Highland County Satellite
108 Erin Ct.
Hillsboro, OH 45133-8591
Ph: (937)393-9946
URL: http://www.spvmhc.org/

Hopedale

32161 ■ Southeast, Inc.--Hopedale
306 Lahm Rd.
Hopedale, OH 43976
Ph: (740)937-2020
URL: http://www.southeastinc.com/contact_information.php#general
Formerly: Community Mental Health Services--Harrison County.

Jackson

32162 ■ Woodland Center--Jackson
1 Acy Ave., Ste. B
Jackson, OH 45640
Ph: (740)286-5075
URL: http://woodlandcenters.org/

Kent

32163 ■ Coleman Professional Services
Main Office
5982 Rhodes Rd.
Kent, OH 44240
Ph: (330)673-1347
URL: http://www.coleman-professional.com/

32164 ■ Coleman Professional Services
Rhodes Road House Group Home
5974 Rhodes Rd.
Kent, OH 44240
Ph: (330)673-1347
URL: http://www.coleman-professional.com/

32165 ■ Coleman Professional Services
Vocational Rehabilitation Services
277 Martinel Dr.
Kent, OH 44240
Ph: (330)678-2233
URL: http://www.coleman-professional.com/

32166 ■ Portage Area Senior Services
Day Treatment Program
Coleman Professional Services
1046 Lake St.
Kent, OH 44240
Ph: (330)673-6981
URL: http://www.coleman-professional.com/

Kenton

32167 ■ Family Resource Centers--Kenton
775 Eliza St.
Kenton, OH 43326
Ph: (419)675-2243
URL: http://www.frcohio.com/external/external.htm

Lancaster

32168 ■ Lighthouse--Lancaster
PO Box 215
Lancaster, OH 43130
Ph: (740)687-4423
Fax: (740)689-2616
URL: http://www.uwayfairfieldco.org/index.php?pr=Partner_Agencies

Lebanon

32169 ■ Mental Health Recovery Services of Warren & Clinton Counties
107 Oregonia Rd.
Lebanon, OH
Ph: (513)695-1695
URL: http://www.mhrsonline.org/

Lima

32170 ■ Champaign Residential Services, Inc.--Lima
2450 Mandolin Dr.
Lima, OH 45801
Ph: (419)229-3200
URL: http://www.crsi-oh.com/crsilocations.html

32171 ■ Lima Veterans Affairs Community Based Outpatient Clinic
1303 Bellefontaine Ave.
Lima, OH 45804
Ph: (419)222-5788
URL: http://www.dayton.va.gov/Lima_cboc.asp

32172 ■ Northwest Family Services
Family Resource Centers
530 S Main St.
Lima, OH 45804

Ph: (419)222-1168
Free: 800-472-5279
URL: http://www.frcohio.com/external/external.htm
Formerly: Renaissance Coed Group Home.

Lisbon

32173 ■ Columbiana County Mental Health Center--Lisbon
40722 State Rte. 154
Lisbon, OH 44432
Ph: (330)424-9573
URL: http://www.colmhc.org/WhoAreWe.htm

London

32174 ■ Champaign Residential Services, Inc.--London
117 W High St., Ste. 104
London, OH 43078
Ph: (740)852-3850
URL: http://www.crsi-oh.com/crsilocations.html

Lorain

32175 ■ Lorain Veterans Affairs Clinic
205 W 20th St.
Lorain, OH 44052
Ph: (440)244-3833
Fax: (440)244-3834
URL: http://www.cleveland.va.gov/visitors/lorain.asp

32176 ■ Nord Community Mental Health Center
6140 S Broadway
Lorain, OH 44053
Ph: (440)233-7232
Free: 866-888-6673
URL: http://www.nordcenter.org
Formerly: The Guidance Centers of Lorain.

32177 ■ Nord Community Mental Health Center
Group Home
3147 Toledo Ave.
Lorain, OH 44055-1431
Ph: (440)233-7232
Free: 800-888-6161
Fax: (440)233-5552
URL: http://www.nordcenter.org

32178 ■ Rehabilitation Center
3150 Clifton Ave.
Lorain, OH 44055
Ph: (440)244-4083
Free: 866-888-6673
Fax: (440)233-5552
URL: http://nordcenter.org
Remarks: Provides vocational evaluation, job training, job seeking skills training, and job placement services.

Mansfield

32179 ■ The Center for Individual and Family Services
741 Scholl Rd.
Mansfield, OH 44907
Ph: (419)756-1717
URL: http://www.richlandthecenter.com/

32180 ■ The Center for Individual and Family Services
Blymyer House
120 Blymyer Ave.
Mansfield, OH 44903
Ph: (419)522-5277
URL: http://www.richlandthecenter.com/

32181 ■ Mansfield Veterans Affairs Clinic
1456 Park Ave. W
Mansfield, OH 44906
Ph: (419)529-4602
Fax: (419)529-4664
URL: http://www.cleveland.va.gov/visitors/mansfield.asp

32182 ■ Park Avenue West Group Home
617 Park Ave. W
Mansfield, OH 44906
Ph: (419)526-2500
URL: http://www.richlandthecenter.com/

Marietta

32183 ■ Washington County Mental Health Services--Marietta
344 Muskingum Dr.
Marietta, OH 45750
Ph: (740)374-6900
URL: http://www.wcmhar.org/

Marion

32184 ■ Foundations Recovery Center
269 Rose Ave.
Marion, OH 43302
Ph: (740)382-9393
URL: http://www.maccsite.com/Locations.htm

32185 ■ Marion Area Counseling Center
320 Executive Dr.
Marion, OH 43302
Ph: (740)387-5210
URL: http://www.maccsite.com/Locations.htm

Mason

32186 ■ Mason Area Mental Health Center
201 Reading Rd.
Mason, OH 45040
Ph: (513)925-1695
URL: http://www.mhrsonline.org/

Medina

32187 ■ Alternative Paths, Inc.
246 Northland Dr., Ste. 200A
Medina, OH 44256
Ph: (330)725-9195
URL: http://www.alternativepaths.org/

Mentor

32188 ■ Pathways--Mentor
7350 Palisades Pkwy.
Mentor, OH 44060
Ph: (440)918-1000
Free: 888-854-0516
URL: http://www.pathwaysinc.com/

Middlefield

32189 ■ Ravenwood Mental Health Center
16030 E High St.
Middlefield, OH 44062
Ph: (440)632-5355
URL: http://www.ravenwoodmhc.org/

Middletown

32190 ■ Comprehensive Counseling Services
1659 S Breiel Blvd.
Middletown, OH 45044
Ph: (513)424-0921
URL: http://www.comprehensivecounselingservice.com/

32191 ■ Middletown Veterans Affairs Community Based Outpatient Clinic
675 N University Blvd.
Middletown, OH 45042
Ph: (513)423-8387
URL: http://www.dayton.va.gov/Midtwn_cboc.asp

32192 ■ Transitional Living, Inc.--Middletown
1131 Manchester Ave.
Middletown, OH 45042
Ph: (513)422-4004
Fax: (513)422-4807
URL: http://www.tliving.org/ContactUs.asp

Milford

32193 ■ Clermont Counseling Center--Milford
512 High St.
Milford, OH 45150
Ph: (513)947-7000
Free: 800-732-9805
Fax: (513)947-7001
URL: http://www.clermontcounseling.org/0103_home_location.html

Millersburg

32194 ■ Counseling Center of Wayne and Holmes Counties--Millersburg
212 N Washington St.
Millersburg, OH 44654
Ph: (330)674-6697
E-mail: info@ccwhc.org
URL: http://www.ccwhc.org

Montpelier

32195 ■ Four County Family Center--Montpelier
904 Snyder
Montpelier, OH 43543
Ph: (419)335-3732
Free: 800-693-6000
Fax: (419)335-3462
URL: http://www.fsno.org/FourCounty.html

Mount Gilead

32196 ■ Maryhaven--Mount Gilead
528 W Marion Rd.
Mount Gilead, OH 43338
Ph: (419)946-6734
URL: http://www.maryhaven.com/

Mount Vernon

32197 ■ Moundbuilders Guidance Center
8402 Blackjack Rd. Ext
Mount Vernon, OH 43050
Ph: (740)397-0442

Napoleon

32198 ■ Four County Family Center--Napoleon
600 Freedom Dr.
Napoleon, OH 43545
Ph: (419)335-3732
Free: 800-693-6000
Fax: (419)335-3462
URL: http://www.fsno.org/FourCounty.html

32199 ■ Maumee Valley Guidance Center--Napoleon
733 N Perry St.
Napoleon, OH 43545
Ph: (419)592-5981
Free: 800-569-3980
URL: http://www.maumeevalleyguidancecenter.org/Locations.htm

New Lexington

32200 ■ Perry Counseling Center
1375 Commerce Dr.
New Lexington, OH 43764
Ph: (740)342-5154
URL: http://www.sixcounty.org/

New Philadelphia

32201 ■ New Philadelphia Veterans Affairs Clinic
1260 Monroe Ave., Ste. 1A
New Philadelphia, OH 44663
Ph: (330)602-5339
Fax: (330)602-4388
URL: http://www.cleveland.va.gov/visitors/new_philadelphia.asp

32202 ■ Southeast, Inc.--New Philadelphia
344 W High Ave.
New Philadelphia, OH 44663-2152
Ph: (330)339-7850
URL: http://www.southeastinc.com/contact_information.php#general
Formerly: Cornerstone Support Services, Inc.

Newark

32203 ■ Moundbuilders Guidance Center
65 Messimer Dr.
Newark, OH 43055
Ph: (740)522-8477

Orrville

32204 ■ Counseling Center of Wayne and Holmes Counties--Orrville
345 S Crownhill Rd.
Orrville, OH 44667
Ph: (330)683-5106
E-mail: info@ccwhc.org
URL: http://www.ccwhc.org
Formerly: Counseling Center.

Painesville

32205 ■ Painesville Veterans Affairs Clinic
7 W Jackson St.
Painesville, OH 44077
Ph: (440)357-6740
Fax: (440)357-7906
URL: http://www.cleveland.va.gov/visitors/painesville.asp

Paulding

32206 ■ Westwood Behavioral Health Center, Inc.--Paulding
501 McDonald Pke.
Paulding, OH 45879
Ph: (419)399-3636
Free: 800-523-3978
URL: http://www.westwoodbehavioralhealth.com/

Pomeroy

32207 ■ Woodland Center--Pomeroy
112 E Memorial Dr.
Pomeroy, OH 45769
Ph: (740)992-2192
URL: http://woodlandcenters.org/

Portsmouth

32208 ■ Shawnee Mental Health Center, Inc.
901 Washington St.
Portsmouth, OH 45662
Ph: (740)354-7702
URL: http://www.shawneemhc.org/

Ravenna

32209 ■ Coleman Professional Services
The 227 Place
227 S Walnut St.
Ravenna, OH 44266-3155
Ph: (330)296-4506
URL: http://www.coleman-professional.com/

32210 ■ Ravenna Veterans Affairs Clinic
6751 N Chestnut St.
Ravenna, OH 44266
Ph: (330)296-3641
Fax: (330)296-5297
URL: http://www.cleveland.va.gov/visitors/ravenna.asp

Rittman

32211 ■ Counseling Center of Wayne and Holmes
Rittman Unit
8 N Main St.
Rittman, OH 44270-1482
Ph: (330)925-5466
E-mail: info@ccwhc.org
URL: http://www.ccwhc.org
Formerly: Counseling Center Rittman Unit.

Saint Marys

32212 ■ Family Resource Centers--Saint Marys
720 Armstrong St.
Saint Marys, OH 45885
Ph: (419)394-7451
Free: 888-394-6286
URL: http://www.frcohio.com/external/external.htm

Sandusky

32213 ■ Bayshore Counseling Services, Inc.
1218 Cleveland Rd., Ste. B
Sandusky, OH 44870
Ph: (419)626-9156

32214 ■ Firelands Counseling & Recovery Services of Erie County
2020 Hayes Ave.
Sandusky, OH 44870
Ph: (419)627-5094
Free: 800-342-1177
URL: http://www.firelands.com/

32215 ■ Sandusky Veterans Affairs Clinic
3416 Columbus Ave.
Sandusky, OH 44870
Ph: (419)625-7350
Fax: (419)625-6660
URL: http://www.cleveland.va.gov/visitors/sandusky.asp

Sidney

32216 ■ Eastway Corporation
Shelby County Counseling Center
500 E Court St.
Sidney, OH 45365
Ph: (937)492-8080
URL: http://www.eastway.org

Springfield

32217 ■ Champaign Residential Services, Inc.--Springfield
1711 W Main St.
Springfield, OH 45504
Ph: (937)324-3113
URL: http://www.crsi-oh.com/crsilocations.html

32218 ■ Mental Health Services for Clark County
1345 N Fountain Blvd.
Springfield, OH 45504
Ph: (937)399-9500
URL: http://www.mhscc.org/contactus.php

32219 ■ Mental Health Services for Clark County
Bridge House
104 E Ward St.
Springfield, OH 45504-2206
Ph: (937)399-9500
URL: http://www.mhscc.org/contactus.php

32220 ■ Mental Health Services for Clark County
Center for Community Support
1086 Mound St.
Springfield, OH 45504-1137
Ph: (937)390-7980
URL: http://www.mhscc.org/contactus.php

32221 ■ Mental Health Services for Clark County
Child, Adolescent and Family Center
1835 Miracle Mile
Springfield, OH 45503
Ph: (937)390-7960
URL: http://www.mhscc.org/contactus.php

32222 ■ Springfield Veterans Affairs Community Based Outpatient Clinic
512 S Burnett Rd.
Springfield, OH 45505
Ph: (937)328-3385
URL: http://www.dayton.va.gov/spgfld_cboc.asp

32223 ■ Youth Challenges
924 E Home Rd.
Springfield, OH 45503
Ph: (937)390-8004
URL: http://www.mhscc.org/contactus.php

Steubenville

32224 ■ Jefferson Behavioral Health System
3200 Johnson Rd.
Steubenville, OH 43952
Ph: (740)264-7751
Fax: (740)264-2422
URL: http://www.jcprb.org/jbhs_page.htm

Struthers

32225 ■ Turning Point Counseling Services
Struthers Office
420 Youngstown Poland Rd.
Struthers, OH 44471
Ph: (330)755-2147
URL: http://www.turningpointcs.com/
Formerly: Eastern Behavioral Health Center, Inc.

Toledo

32226 ■ Family Service of Northwest Ohio
701 Jefferson Ave., Ste. 301
Toledo, OH 43624
Ph: (419)321-6455
URL: http://www.fsno.org/

32227 ■ Unison Behavioral Health Group--E Woodruff, Toledo
544 E Woodruff
Toledo, OH 43604
Ph: (419)242-9577
URL: http://www.unisonbhg.org/

32228 ■ Unison Behavioral Health Group--Starr Avenue, Toledo
1425 Starr Ave.
Toledo, OH 43605
Ph: (419)936-0631
URL: http://www.unisonbhg.org/

32229 ■ Zepf Community Mental Health Center
6605 W Central Ave.
Toledo, OH 43617
Ph: (419)841-7701
URL: http://www.zepfcenter.org/

Troy

32230 ■ Champaign Residential Services, Inc.--Troy
405 Public Sq., Ste. 373
Troy, OH 45373
Ph: (937)335-6974
URL: http://www.crsi-oh.com/crsilocations.html

Urbana

32231 ■ Champaign Residential Services, Inc.--Urbana
1150 Scioto St.
Urbana, OH 43078
Ph: (937)653-1300
URL: http://www.crsi-oh.com/crsilocations.html

Van Wert

32232 ■ Westwood Behavioral Health Center, Inc.--Van Wert
1158 Westwood Dr.
Van Wert, OH 45891
Ph: (419)238-3434
Free: 800-523-3978
URL: http://www.westwoodbehavioralhealth.com/

Wapakoneta

32233 ■ Champaign Residential Services, Inc.--Wapakoneta
13101 Infirmary Rd.
Wapakoneta, OH 45895
Ph: (419)738-9511
URL: http://www.crsi-oh.com/crsilocations.html

Warren

32234 ■ Coleman Professional Services
552 N Park Ave.
Warren, OH 44481
Ph: (330)394-8831
URL: http://www.coleman-professional.com/

32235 ■ Valley Counseling Services--Warren
150 E Market St.
Warren, OH 44481
Ph: (330)394-6244
Fax: (330)394-6266
URL: http://www.vcsinc.org/

32236 ■ Valley Counseling Services--Warren Children's Office
318 Mahoning Ave.
Warren, OH 44483
Ph: (330)395-9563
URL: http://www.vcsinc.org/

Wauseon

32237 ■ Four County Family Center--Wauseon
7320 SH 108
Wauseon, OH 43567
Ph: (419)335-3732
Free: 800-693-6000
Fax: (419)335-3462
URL: http://www.fsno.org/FourCounty.html

32238 ■ Maumee Valley Guidance Center--Wauseon
222 Depot
Wauseon, OH 43567
Ph: (419)337-5941
Free: 800-569-3980
URL: http://www.maumeevalleyguidancecenter.org/Locations.htm

Waverly

32239 ■ Scioto Paint Valley Mental Health Center--Waverly
102 Dawn Ln.
Waverly, OH 45690
Ph: (740)947-7783
E-mail: pike@spvmhc.org
URL: http://www.spvmhc.org

West Union

32240 ■ Shawnee Mental Health Center, Inc. Adams County Clinic
192 Chestnut Ridge Rd.
West Union, OH 45693-9584
Ph: (937)544-3400
URL: http://www.shawneemhc.org/

Wooster

32241 ■ Counseling Center of Wayne and Holmes Counties--Wooster
2285 Benden Dr.
Wooster, OH 44691
Ph: (330)264-9029
E-mail: info@ccwhc.org
URL: http://www.ccwhc.org

32242 ■ Wooster Veterans Affairs Clinic
124 N Walnut St.
Wooster, OH 44691
Ph: (330)262-1001
URL: http://www.cleveland.va.gov/visitors/wooster.asp

Worthington

32243 ■ The Buckeye Ranch, Inc.--Worthington
445 E Dublin-Granville Rd.
Worthington, OH 43083
Ph: (614)543-1380
URL: http://www.buckeyeranch.org/

Youngstown

32244 ■ D&E Counseling Center--Youngstown
711 Belmont Ave.
Youngstown, OH 44502
Ph: (330)793-2487
URL: http://www.dandecenter.com/

32245 ■ Turning Point Counseling Services
611 Belmont Ave.
Youngstown, OH 44502
Ph: (330)744-2991
URL: http://www.turningpointcs.com/contact.html

32246 ■ Valley Counseling Services--Youngstown
4970 Belmont Ave.
Youngstown, OH 44505
Ph: (330)759-8237
URL: http://www.vcsinc.org/

Zanesville

32247 ■ Six County Core Enterprises
2845 Bell St.
Zanesville, OH 43701
Ph: (740)588-6427
URL: http://www.sixcounty.org/

OKLAHOMA

Ada

32248 ■ Mental Health Services of Southern Oklahoma--Ada
111 E 12th St.
Ada, OK 74820
Ph: (580)436-2690
URL: http://www.mhsso.org/

32249 ■ Mental Health Services of Southern Oklahoma Ada Clinic
111 E 12th St.
Ada, OK 74820-6501
Ph: (580)436-2690
URL: http://www.mhsso.org/

32250 ■ Rolling Hills Hospital
1000 Rolling Hills Ln.
Ada, OK 74820
Ph: (580)436-3600
URL: http://www.rollinghillshospital.com/

Afton

32251 ■ Grand Lake Mental Health Center, Inc.--Afton
138 S Main St.
Afton, OK 74331
Ph: (918)257-4244
URL: http://www.glmhc.net/

Altus

32252 ■ Jim Taliaferro Community Mental Health Center--Altus
215 W Commerence St.
Altus, OK 73522
Ph: (580)482-5954
Free: 866-818-5780

Alva

32253 ■ Northwest Center for Behavioral Health--Alva
604 Choctaw St.
Alva, OK 73717-1626
Ph: (580)327-1112

Anadarko

32254 ■ Jim Taliaferro Community Mental Health Center--Anadarko
110 SE 2nd St.
Anadarko, OK 73005
Ph: (405)247-2434
Free: 866-818-5780

Ardmore

32255 ■ Mental Health Services of Southern Oklahoma--Ardmore
2530 S Commerce St.
Ardmore, OK 73401-5519
Ph: (580)223-5070
URL: http://www.mhsso.org/

Bartlesville

32256 ■ Child Guidance Clinic Washington County Health Department
3838 State St.
Bartlesville, OK 74006
Ph: (918)335-3005

32257 ■ Grand Lake Mental Health Center
513 S Quapaw Ave.
Bartlesville, OK 74003-4331
Ph: (918)337-8080
URL: http://www.glmhc.net/

Blanchard

32258 ■ McClain County Health Department
107 S Main
Blanchard, OK 73010
Ph: (405)485-3319

Bristow

32259 ■ Creek County Guidance Clinic
408 W 4th Ave.
Bristow, OK 74010
Ph: (918)367-3341

Chandler

32260 ■ Red Rock Behavioral Health Services--Chandler
112 McKinley Ave.
Chandler, OK 74834
Ph: (405)258-3040
URL: http://www.red-rock.com

Chickasha

32261 ■ Red Rock Behavioral Health--Charles Allen
1710 Charles Allen
Chickasha, OK 73018
Ph: (405)222-4507
URL: http://www.red-rock.com/

32262 ■ Red Rock Behavioral Health--W Choctaw Avenue
804 W Choctaw Ave.
Chickasha, OK 73018
Ph: (405)222-0622
URL: http://www.red-rock.com/

Claremore

32263 ■ Grand Lake Mental Health Center, Inc. Rogers County Office
2000 W Blue Starr Dr.
Claremore, OK 74017-2021

Ph: (918)342-0770
URL: http://www.glmhc.net/

Clinton

32264 ■ Red Rock West Behavioral Health Services--Clinton
90 N 31st St.
Clinton, OK 73601
Ph: (580)323-6021
URL: http://www.red-rock.com/

Duncan

32265 ■ Jim Taliaferro Community Mental Health Center--Duncan
324 S Hwy. 81
Duncan, OK 73533
Ph: (580)252-0200
Free: 866-818-5780

Durant

32266 ■ Mental Health Services of Southern Oklahoma--Durant
1001 W Main St.
Durant, OK 74701
Ph: (580)924-7330
URL: http://www.mhsso.org/

Elk City

32267 ■ Red Rock West Behavioral Health Services--Elk City
3080 W 3rd St.
Elk City, OK 73648
Ph: (580)225-5136
URL: http://www.red-rock.com

Enid

32268 ■ Northwest Center for Behavioral Health--Enid
702 N Grand St.
Enid, OK 73701
Ph: (580)234-3791
Formerly: Wheatland Mental Health Center.

Fort Sill

32269 ■ Lawton/Fort Sill Veterans Affairs Clinic
4303 Pittman and Thomas Bldg.
Fort Sill, OK 73503
Ph: (580)585-5600
URL: http://www2.va.gov/directory/guide/facility.asp?ID=5514

Grove

32270 ■ Grand Lake Mental Health Center, Inc.
Delaware County Office
1115 Harber Rd.
Grove, OK 74344
Ph: (918)786-4434
URL: http://www.glmhc.net/

Guthrie

32271 ■ Northwest Center for Behavioral Health--Guthrie
1923 S Division St.
Guthrie, OK 73044
Ph: (405)282-1830
Formerly: Wheatland Mental Health Center.

Kingfisher

32272 ■ Northwest Center for Behavioral Health--Kingfisher
124 E Sheridan Ave., Rm. 200
Kingfisher, OK 73750-3200
Ph: (405)375-6377

Konawa

32273 ■ Veterans Affairs Medical Center Konawa Clinic
527 W 3rd t.
Konawa, OK 74849
Ph: (580)925-3286
URL: http://www2.va.gov/directory/guide/facility.asp?ID=5379&dnum=1

Lawton

32274 ■ Jim Taliaferro Community Mental Health Center--Lawton
602 SW 38th St.
Lawton, OK 73505
Ph: (580)248-5780

32275 ■ Jim Taliaferro Community Mental Health Center
Psychosocial Clubhouse
1 D Ave.
Lawton, OK 73501
Ph: (580)353-0162

Madill

32276 ■ Mental Health Services of Southern Oklahoma
Madill Clinic
603 S 1st St.
Madill, OK 73446
Ph: (580)795-7085
URL: http://www.mhsso.org/

McAlester

32277 ■ Pittsburg County Health Department
1400 E College Ave.
McAlester, OK 74501
Ph: (918)423-1267

Miami

32278 ■ Grand Lake Mental Health Center, Inc.
Ottawa County Office
120 S Treaty Rd.
Miami, OK 74354
Ph: (918)540-1511
URL: http://www.glmhc.net/

Muskogee

32279 ■ Green Country Behavioral Health Services, Inc.
619 N Main St.
Muskogee, OK 74401
Ph: (918)682-8407

32280 ■ Jack C. Montgomery Veterans Affairs Medical Center
1011 Honor Heights Dr.
Muskogee, OK 74401
Ph: (918)577-3000
Free: 866-397-8387
URL: http://www.muskogee.va.gov/

32281 ■ Muskogee County Health Department
530 S 34th St.
Muskogee, OK 74401
Ph: (918)683-0321
Free: 877-596-1596

Norman

32282 ■ Central Oklahoma Community Mental Health Center
909 Alameda St.
Norman, OK 73071
Ph: (405)360-5100
URL: http://www.cocmhc.org/

32283 ■ Central Oklahoma Community Mental Health Center
Youth Services
1120 E Main St.
Norman, OK 73071-5300
Ph: (405)360-5100
URL: http://www.cocmhc.org/

Nowata

32284 ■ Grand Lake Mental Health Center, Inc.
Administrative Office
114 W Delaware Ave.
Nowata, OK 74048
Ph: (918)273-1841
URL: http://www.glmhc.net/

32285 ■ Grand Lake Mental Health Center, Inc.
Nowata County Office
517 E Cherokee
Nowata, OK 74048-2717
Ph: (918)273-2671
URL: http://www.glmhc.net/

Okemah

32286 ■ Creoks Behavioral Mental Health Services--Okemah
209 W Broadway St.
Okemah, OK 74859
Ph: (918)623-2922
URL: http://www.creoks.org/

Oklahoma City

32287 ■ Hope Community Services
105 SE 45th St.
Oklahoma City, OK 73129
Ph: (405)634-4400
E-mail: hope@hopecls.org
URL: http://www.hopecsi.org/
Program(s): Outpatient mental health counseling; day treatment program; DUI assessment; medication clinic; psychosocial rehabilitation; community education; emergency; pre-vocational and job placement services; family support group; youth services.

32288 ■ North Care Adult Services
1140 N Hudson
Oklahoma City, OK 73103
Ph: (405)272-0660
URL: http://www.northcare.com/contact.html

32289 ■ North Care Center
4436 NW 50th St.
Oklahoma City, OK 73112
Ph: (405)858-2700
Fax: (405)858-2720
URL: http://www.northcare.com/

32290 ■ Oklahoma City Veterans Affairs Medical Center
921 NE 13th St.
Oklahoma City, OK 73104
Ph: (405)456-1000
Free: 866-835-5273
URL: http://www.oklahoma.va.gov/

32291 ■ Red Rock Behavioral Health Services--Oklahoma City
4400 N Lincoln Blvd.
Oklahoma City, OK 73105-5108
Ph: (405)424-7711
URL: http://www.red-rock.com/

32292 ■ Red Rock North
2401 W 44 Service Rd. Ste. 100
Oklahoma City, OK 73112-8739
Ph: (405)524-6500
URL: http://www.red-rock.com/

Okmulgee

32293 ■ Creoks Behavioral Mental Health Services--Okmulgee
114 N Grand, Ste. 418
Okmulgee, OK 74447
Ph: (918)756-9411
URL: http://www.creoks.org/locations.html

Pauls Valley

32294 ■ Mental Health Services of Southern Oklahoma
Pauls Valley Clinic
109 S Willow St.
Pauls Valley, OK 73075-3933
Ph: (405)238-7311
URL: http://www.mhsso.org/

Pawhuska

32295 ■ Edwin Fair Community Mental Health Center--Pawhuska
124 E 6th St.
Pawhuska, OK 74056
Ph: (918)287-1175
URL: http://www.efcmhc.com/

Perry

32296 ■ Edwin Fair Community Mental Health Center--Perry
102 E Fir
Perry, OK 73077
Ph: (580)336-5200
URL: http://www.efcmhc.com/locations.htm

Ponca City

32297 ■ Edwin Fair Community Mental Health Center--Ponca City
1500 N 6th St.
Ponca City, OK 74601
Ph: (580)762-7561
URL: http://www.efcmhc.com/

32298 ■ Edwin Fair Community Mental Health Center
Transitional Living Center
201 E Chestnut Ave.
Ponca City, OK 74601
Ph: (580)763-6017
URL: http://www.efcmhc.com/

Purcell

32299 ■ Purcell Clinic
129 N 3rd St., Ste. C
Purcell, OK 73080-4227
Ph: (405)360-5100
URL: http://www.cocmhc.org/

Sallisaw

32300 ■ Bill Willis Community Mental Health Center--Sallisaw
101 N Wheeler Ave.
Sallisaw, OK 74955-4617
Ph: (918)775-5513

Sand Springs

32301 ■ Associated Centers for Therapy
117 N Main St.
Sand Springs, OK 74063
Ph: (918)245-5565
Fax: (918)245-5564
E-mail: info@actcares.org
URL: http://www.actcares.org/

Sapulpa

32302 ■ Creoks Behavioral Mental Health Services--Sapulpa
15 E Dewey St.
Sapulpa, OK 74066
Ph: (918)227-2016
URL: http://www.creoks.org/locations.html

Seminole

32303 ■ Mental Health Services of Southern Oklahoma
Seminole Clinic
2010 Boren Blvd.
Seminole, OK 74818
Ph: (405)382-0059
URL: http://www.mhsso.org/

Stillwater

32304 ■ Edwin Fair Community Mental Health Center, Inc.--Stillwater
800 E 6th St., Ste. B
Stillwater, OK 74074
Ph: (405)372-1250
URL: http://www.efcmhc.com/locations.htm

Sulphur

32305 ■ Mental Health Services of Southern Oklahoma
Sulphur Clinic
414 W Muskogee Ave.
Sulphur, OK 73086
Ph: (580)622-6171
URL: http://www.mhsso.org/

Tahlequah

32306 ■ Bill Willis Community Mental Health Center--Tahlequah
1400 S Hensley Dr.
Tahlequah, OK 74464
Ph: (918)207-3000

Tulsa

32307 ■ Creoks Behavioral Mental Health Services--Tulsa
2725 E Skelly Dr., Ste. 200
Tulsa, OK 74105
Ph: (918)756-9411
URL: http://www.creoks.org/locations.html

32308 ■ Creoks Behavioral Mental Health Services--Tulsa
616 S Boston Ave.
Tulsa, OK 74119
Ph: (918)382-7300
URL: http://www.creoks.org/locations.html

32309 ■ Parkside Inc.
1620 E 12th St.
Tulsa, OK 74120
Ph: (918)582-2131
Free: 877-522-1959
URL: http://www.parksideinc.org/

32310 ■ Tulsa Center for Behavioral Health
2323 S Harvard Ave.
Tulsa, OK 74114
Ph: (918)745-2402

Vinita

32311 ■ Grand Lake Mental Health Center, Inc.--Vinita
405 E Excelsior Ave.
Vinita, OK 74301-4226
Ph: (918)256-6476
URL: http://www.glmhc.net

Wagoner

32312 ■ Bill Willis Community Mental Health Center--Wagoner
1202 W Cherokee, Ste. 6
Wagoner, OK 74467
Ph: (918)485-8404

Watonga

32313 ■ Red Rock West Behavioral Health Services--Watonga
204 W A St.
Watonga, OK 73772
Ph: (580)623-7199
URL: http://www.red-rock.com/

OREGON

Albany

32314 ■ Linn County Mental Health Division
445 3rd Ave. SW
Albany, OR 97321
Ph: (541)967-3866
Free: 800-304-7468
E-mail: linnmh@co.linn.or.us
URL: http://www.co.linn.or.us
Formerly: Linn County Mental Health Center.

Ashland

32315 ■ Southern Oregon Child Study & Treatment Center
1836 Fremont St.
Ashland, OR 97520
Ph: (541)482-5792
URL: http://www.socstc.org/

Astoria

32316 ■ Clatsop Behavioral Health Care
10 6th St., Ste. 103
Astoria, OR 97103
Ph: (503)325-5722
URL: http://www.clatsopbh.org/

Bandon

32317 ■ Bandon Veterans Affairs Clinic
1010 1st St. SE, Ste. 100
Bandon, OR 97411
Ph: (541)347-4736
Fax: (541)347-1098
URL: http://www2.va.gov/directory/guide/facility.asp?ID=594&dnum=All

Bend

32318 ■ Community Support Services--Bend
1128 NW Harriman St.
Bend, OR 97701
Ph: (541)330-4637

Boardman

32319 ■ Community Counseling Solutions
101 NW Boardman Ave.
Boardman, OR 97818
Ph: (541)481-2911
URL: http://www.morrowcountyoregon.com/behavioralhealth/index.html

Brookings

32320 ■ Veterans Affairs Medical Center
Brookings Clinic
555 5th St.
Brookings, OR 97415
Ph: (541)412-1152

Burns

32321 ■ Harney Behavioral Health
348 W Adams St.
Burns, OR 97720
Ph: (541)573-8376
Fax: (541)573-8378
URL: http://www.co.harney.or.us/hbh.html

Canyonville

32322 ■ Douglas County Mental Health Division--Canyonville
247 N Main St.
Canyonville, OR 97417

Ph: (541)839-4495
URL: http://www.co.douglas.or.us/health/SS/

Condon

32323 ■ Condon Center
422 N Main St.
Condon, OR 97823
Ph: (541)384-2666

Corvallis

32324 ■ New Beginnings
557 NW Monroe
Corvallis, OR 97330
Ph: (541)766-3540

32325 ■ Trillium Family Services
4455 NE Hwy. 20
Corvallis, OR 97330
Ph: (541)757-1852
URL: http://www.trilliumfamily.org/

Drain

32326 ■ Douglas County Mental Health Division--Drain
16 W A Ave.
Drain, OR 97435
Ph: (541)836-7311
URL: http://www.co.douglas.or.us/health/SS/

Eugene

32327 ■ Directions Services Counseling Center
576 Olive St., Ste. 307
Eugene, OR 97401
Ph: (541)344-7303
Fax: (541)686-6283
URL: http://www.directionservice.org/pg22.cfm

32328 ■ Laurel Hill Center
2145 Centennial Plz.
Eugene, OR 97401
Ph: (541)485-6340
URL: http://www.laurel.org/

Grants Pass

32329 ■ Josephine County Humane Services Department
714 NW A St.
Grants Pass, OR 97526-1802
Ph: (541)474-5365
Formerly: Josephine County Mental Health Center.

Hillsboro

32330 ■ Cascadia Behavioral Healthcare, Inc. Hillsboro Family Center
230 NE 2nd Ave., Ste. C
Hillsboro, OR 97124
Ph: (503)648-0753
URL: http://www.cascadiabhc.org/

32331 ■ LifeWorks Northwest--Hillsboro
971 SW Walnut St.
Hillsboro, OR 97123
Ph: (503)640-5297
Formerly: Tualatin Valley Centers - Hillsboro Site.

Hines

32332 ■ Independence Place
120 S Roanoke
Hines, OR 97738
Ph: (541)573-1786

Hood River

32333 ■ Mid-Columbia Center for Living Hood River Care Center
729 Henderson Rd.
Hood River, OR 97031-8772
Ph: (541)386-2688
Formerly: Hood River Care Center.

32334 ■ Mid-Columbia Center for Living Woods Court, Hood River
1610 Woods Ct.
Hood River, OR 97031
Ph: (541)386-2620

Jasper

32335 ■ Jasper Mountain Center
37875 Jasper-Lowell Rd.
Jasper, OR 97438
Ph: (541)747-1235
Fax: (541)747-4722
URL: http://www.scar-jaspermtn.org/

Lebanon

32336 ■ Linn County Health Services--Lebanon
1600 S Main St.
Lebanon, OR 97355-3143
Ph: (541)451-5932
Free: 888-451-2631
URL: http://www.co.linn.or.us/health/alcohol_drug/ad.htm

Madras

32337 ■ BestCare Treatment Services--Madras
125 SW C St.
Madras, OR 97741
Ph: (541)475-6675
URL: http://www.bestcaretreatment.org/

McMinnville

32338 ■ Yamhill County Mental Health and Human Services
614 NE Davis St.
McMinnville, OR 97128
Ph: (503)434-7523
URL: http://www.co.yamhill.or.us/hhs/

Medford

32339 ■ Jackson County Health and Human Services
1005 E Main St.
Medford, OR 97504
Ph: (541)774-8201
URL: http://www.jacksoncounty.org

Ontario

32340 ■ Lifeways, Inc.
702 Sunset Dr.
Ontario, OR 97914
Ph: (541)889-9167
Fax: (541)889-7873
URL: http://www.lifeways.org
Formerly: Leeways Behavioral Health.

Portland

32341 ■ Albertina Kerr Centers
424 NE 22nd Ave.
Portland, OR 97232
Ph: (503)239-8101
Fax: (503)239-8106
E-mail: info@albertinakerr.org
URL: http://www.albertinakerr.org/

32342 ■ Boys and Girls Aid Society of Oregon
018 SW Boundary Ct.
Portland, OR 97239
Ph: (503)222-9661
URL: http://www.boysandgirlsaid.org

32343 ■ Breakthrough
3390 SE Milwaukie Ave.
Portland, OR 97202
Ph: (503)736-6565
URL: http://www.morrisonkids.org/Locations.aspx

32344 ■ Cascadia Behavioral Healthcare, Inc.--Portland
847 NE 19th Ave., Ste. 100
Portland, OR 97232
Ph: (503)238-0769
E-mail: info@cascadiabhc.org
URL: http://www.cascadiabhc.org

32345 ■ Comet Club
5507 N Lombard St.
Portland, OR 97203
Ph: (503)283-2535
URL: http://www.co.multnomah.or.us/dchs/mhas/mh_dropin1.html

32346 ■ Counterpoint Outpatient Program
1718 NE 82nd Ave.
Portland, OR 97220-5602
Ph: (503)258-4636
Fax: (503)252-6234
URL: http://www.morrisonkids.org/Locations.aspx

32347 ■ Lifeworks Northwest Albina
4925 N Albina Ave.
Portland, OR 97217
Ph: (503)548-4922
URL: http://www.lifeworksnw.org/Locations/tabid/85/Default.aspx

32348 ■ Lutheran Community Services
605 SE 39th Ave.
Portland, OR 97214
Ph: (503)231-7480
URL: http://www.lcsnw.org/

32349 ■ Morrison Center
1500 NE Irving St., Ste. 250
Portland, OR 97232
Ph: (503)258-4200
Fax: (503)233-4359
URL: http://www.morrisonkids.org/Locations.aspx

32350 ■ Pacific University - Psychological Service Center
511 SW 10th Ave., Ste. 400
Portland, OR 97205
Ph: (503)352-2400
URL: http://www.pscpacific.org/

32351 ■ Plaza Rehabilitation Service
2415 SE 43rd Ave., Ste. 200
Portland, OR 97206
Ph: (503)239-5952
URL: http://www.cascadiabhc.org/

32352 ■ Portland Veterans Affairs Medical Center Portland Campus
3710 SW U.S. Veterans Hospital Rd.
Portland, OR 97239
Ph: (503)220-8262
Free: 800-949-1004
URL: http://www.visn20.med.va.gov/portland/

Redmond

32353 ■ BestCare Treatment Services--Redmond
676 NE Negus Way
Redmond, OR 97756
Ph: (541)504-9577
URL: http://www.bestcaretreatment.org/

32354 ■ Cascade Child Treatment Center
1379 SW 15th St.
Redmond, OR 97756
Ph: (541)548-6166
URL: http://www.cctc-inc.org/

Reedsport

32355 ■ Douglas County Mental Health Division--Reedsport
680 Fir St.
Reedsport, OR 97467-1497
Ph: (541)271-4835
URL: http://www.co.douglas.or.us/health/MH/default.asp

Roseburg

32356 ■ Douglas County Mental Health Department
Community Support Program
337 SE Fowler St.
Roseburg, OR 97470-4348
Ph: (541)440-4516
URL: http://www.co.douglas.or.us/health/MH/default.asp

32357 ■ Douglas County Mental Health Division--Roseburg
621 W Madrone St.
Roseburg, OR 97470
Ph: (541)440-3532
Free: 800-234-0985
URL: http://www.co.douglas.or.us/dch/

32358 ■ Roseburg Veterans Affairs Medical Center
913 NW Garden Valley Blvd.
Roseburg, OR 97470
Ph: (541)440-1000
Free: 800-549-8387
Fax: (541)440-1225
URL: http://www.visn20.med.va.gov/roseburg/index.asp

Saint Helens

32359 ■ Columbia Community Mental Health Center
58646 McNulty Way
Saint Helens, OR 97051
Ph: (503)397-5211
Fax: (503)397-5373
URL: http://www.ccmh1.com/

32360 ■ Pathways--Saint Helens
185 N 4th St.
Saint Helens, OR 97051-1535
Ph: (503)366-4540
URL: http://www.ccmh1.com/AD%20Dept/Residential/Pathways/pathways.html

Salem

32361 ■ Homeless Outreach and Advocacy Project (HOAP)
694 Church St. NE
Salem, OR 97301
Ph: (503)588-5827
URL: http://www.northwesthumanservices.org/NWHS_HOAP.php

32362 ■ Northwest Human Services
Administration and Connections Program
681 Center St. NE
Salem, OR 97301-3722
Ph: (503)588-5828
E-mail: info@nwhumanservices.org
URL: http://www.northwesthumanservices.org/

32363 ■ Salem Veterans Affairs Clinic
1660 Oak St. SE, Ste. 100
Salem, OR 97301
Ph: (503)220-8262
Free: 800-220-8262
URL: http://www2.va.gov/directory/guide/facility.asp?ID=5342&dnum=All

32364 ■ West Salem Clinic - Mental Health
Northwest Human Services
1233 Edgewater St. NW
Salem, OR 97304
Ph: (503)378-7526
Fax: (503)585-4278
URL: http://www.northwesthumanservices.org/NWHS_West_Salem.php

Sandy

32365 ■ Sandy Center
39084 Proctor Blvd.
Sandy, OR 97055
Ph: (503)826-8500

Seaside

32366 ■ Lifeworks Northwest Seaside
1000 S Holladay Dr.
Seaside, OR 97138
Ph: (503)738-4074
URL: http://www.lifeworksnw.org/Locations/tabid/85/Default.aspx

South Beach

32367 ■ South Beach Clinic
4909 S Coast Hwy. 101
South Beach, OR 97366
Ph: (541)574-5960

Springfield

32368 ■ Jasper Mountain SAFE Center
89124 Marcola Rd.
Springfield, OR 97478
Ph: (541)741-7402
URL: http://www.scar-jaspermtn.org/contact_us.html

Sweet Home

32369 ■ Linn County Health Services--Sweet Home
799 Long St.
Sweet Home, OR 97386-3304
Ph: (541)367-3888

The Dalles

32370 ■ Mid-Columbia Center for Living
419 E 7th St., Rm. 207
The Dalles, OR 97058
Ph: (541)296-5452
URL: http://www.mccfl.org/

Tigard

32371 ■ LifeWorks Northwest--Tigard
8770 SW Scoffins St.
Tigard, OR 97223
Ph: (503)684-1424
URL: http://www.lifeworksnw.org/

Tillamook

32372 ■ Tillamook Family Counseling Center
906 Main Ave.
Tillamook, OR 97141
Ph: (503)842-8201
Free: 800-962-2851
Fax: (503)815-1870
E-mail: frankhw@tfcc.org
URL: http://www.tfcc.org/index.html

PENNSYLVANIA

Allentown

32373 ■ Haven House--Allentown
1530 Hanover Ave.
Allentown, PA 18109-2360
Ph: (610)433-6181

32374 ■ Vitalistic Therapeutic Center
1406 W Hamilton St.
Allentown, PA 18102
Ph: (610)433-4383
Formerly: Children's Theapeutic Center.

Altoona

32375 ■ Blair House
230 6th Ave.
Altoona, PA 16602
Ph: (814)943-8254
Free: 800-445-6262
URL: http://www.homenursingagency.com/

32376 ■ James E. Van Zandt Veterans Affairs Medical Center
2907 Pleasant Valley Blvd.
Altoona, PA 16602
Ph: (877)626-2500
URL: http://www.altoona.va.gov/

32377 ■ Tantaglio Home
1912 12th Ave.
Altoona, PA 16601
Ph: (814)946-1885
Free: 800-445-6262
URL: http://www.homenursingagency.com/

Bellefonte

32378 ■ CSG Counsel House
205 W Curtin St.
Bellefonte, PA 16823
Ph: (814)353-8131
URL: http://www.csgonline.org/

32379 ■ The Meadows Psychiatric Center
206 W High St.
Bellefonte, PA 16823
Ph: (814)353-1487
URL: http://www.themeadows.net/locations.htm

Bentleyville

32380 ■ Bentleyville Clinic
100 Wilson Rd.
Bentleyville, PA 15022
Ph: (724)483-5482

Bethlehem

32381 ■ Solutions Counseling & Consultation Services
35 E Elizabeth Ave., Ste. 37
Bethlehem, PA 18018
Ph: (610)865-1303
Fax: (610)865-9632
E-mail: office@solutionscounseling.net
URL: http://www.solutionscounseling.net/

Braddock

32382 ■ Turtle Creek Valley Mental Health/Mental Retardation, Inc.--Braddock
723 Braddock Ave.
Braddock, PA 15104
Ph: (412)351-0222
URL: http://www.tcv.net/

Bradford

32383 ■ Bradford Family Center
1 Mechanic St.
Bradford, PA 16701
Ph: (814)362-1834
URL: http://www.penn.com/~guidance/FamCntr.htm

32384 ■ Dickinson Mental Health Center
Day Treatment Program
15 Kennedy St., No. 17
Bradford, PA 16701-2005
Ph: (814)362-7464
URL: http://www.dmhc.org/

32385 ■ The Guidance Center--Bradford
110 Campus Dr.
Bradford, PA 16701
Ph: (814)362-6535
URL: http://www.penn.com/~guidance/

Bridgeville

32386 ■ Chartiers Mental Health/Mental Retardation Center, Inc.
437 Railroad St.
Bridgeville, PA 15017
Ph: (412)221-3302
Fax: (412)221-5229
URL: http://www.chartierscenter.org/

Butler

32387 ■ Veterans Affairs Butler Healthcare
325 New Castle Rd.
Butler, PA 16001
Ph: (800)362-8262
URL: http://www.butler.va.gov/

Carlisle

32388 ■ The Stevens Center
33 State Ave.
Carlisle, PA 17013-4432
Ph: (717)243-6033
URL: http://www.nhsonline.org/locations.html

Chambersburg

32389 ■ The Meadows of Chambersburg
144 S 8th St.
Chambersburg, PA 17201
Ph: (717)263-8272
Fax: (717)263-8476
URL: http://www.themeadows.net/locations.htm

Clarion

32390 ■ Mental Health/Mental Retardation and Drug Abuse of Clarion County
214 S 7th Ave.
Clarion, PA 16214
Ph: (814)226-1080
Fax: (814)226-1085
Formerly: Clarion County Counseling Center.

Clearfield

32391 ■ Clearfield-Jefferson Community Mental Health Center
600 Leonard St.
Clearfield, PA 16830
Ph: (814)765-5337
Fax: (814)765-6273

Coatesville

32392 ■ Child Guidance Resource Centers--Coatesville
744 E Lincoln Hwy., Ste. 420
Coatesville, PA 19320
Ph: (610)383-5635
Free: 866-799-3325
URL: http://www.cgrc.org/locations.html

32393 ■ Coatesville Veterans Affairs Medical Center
1400 Black Horse Hill Rd.
Coatesville, PA 19320
Ph: (610)384-7711
Fax: (610)383-0207
URL: http://www.coatesville.va.gov/

Colmar

32394 ■ Hatfield House
110 Bethlehem Pke.
Colmar, PA 18915-9790
Ph: (215)822-9181

Crum Lynne

32395 ■ The Crumm Lynne Residence Carelink Community Support Services
338A Hollis Ave.
Crum Lynne, PA 19022
Ph: (610)833-5360
Fax: (610)833-1854
E-mail: dpaylor@carelinkservices.org
URL: http://www.carelink-svs.org/

Danville

32396 ■ CMSU Service System Behavioral Health Base Service Unit
217 Pine St., Ste. 1
Danville, PA 17821
Ph: (570)275-4962
Free: 800-676-4412
Fax: (570)275-5754
URL: http://www.cmsu.org/
Formerly: Danville Office.

32397 ■ Columbia, Montour, Snyder Union Counties of Central Pennsylvania Service System Mental Health & Drug & Alcohol Referral Service
PO Box 219
Danville, PA 17821
Ph: (570)275-5422
URL: http://www.cmsu.org

Downingtown

32398 ■ Human Services, Inc.--Downington
520 E Lancaster Ave.
Downingtown, PA 19335-2777
Ph: (610)873-1010

32399 ■ Marsh Creek Residence Carelink Community Support Services
630 Milford Rd.
Downingtown, PA 19335
Ph: (610)458-0685
URL: http://www.carelink-svs.org/

Doylestown

32400 ■ Foundations Behavioral Health
833 E Butler Ave.
Doylestown, PA 18901
Ph: (215)345-0444
Free: 800-445-4722
Fax: (215)345-7862
E-mail: admissions@fbh.com
URL: http://www.fbh.com/

Dubois

32401 ■ Clearfield Jefferson Community Mental Health Center, Inc.
100 Caldwell Dr.
Dubois, PA 15801-1152
Ph: (814)371-1105

Eagleville

32402 ■ Family Services of Montgomery County
3125 Ridge Pke.
Eagleville, PA 19403
Ph: (610)630-2111
Fax: (610)630-4003
URL: http://www.fsmontco.org/

Eddystone

32403 ■ Care Link Community Support Services
150 Chester Pke., Ste. 600
Eddystone, PA 19022
Ph: (610)874-1119
E-mail: admin@carelinkservices.org
URL: http://www.carelink-svs.org

Emporium

32404 ■ Dickinson Mental Health Center
112 S Cherry St.
Emporium, PA 15834
Ph: (814)486-0554
Fax: (814)486-1282
URL: http://www.dmhc.org

Erie

32405 ■ Erie Veterans Affairs Medical Center
135 E 38th St.
Erie, PA 16504
Ph: (814)868-8661
Free: 800-274-8387
URL: http://www.erie.va.gov/

32406 ■ Stairways Behavioral Health
2185 W 8th St.
Erie, PA 16505
Ph: (814)453-5806
Free: 888-453-5806
URL: http://www.stairwaysbh.org/

Greensburg

32407 ■ Family Services of Western Pennsylvania Family-Based Mental Health Services
211 Huff Ave., Ste. 1
Greensburg, PA 15601
Ph: (724)834-7830
Free: 888-222-4200
URL: http://www.fswp.org/
Formerly: Greensburg Office and Miller Square.

Greenville

32408 ■ Community Counseling Center Greenville Satellite Office
77 N Main St.
Greenville, PA 16125
Ph: (724)588-6490
URL: http://www.cccmer.org/

Hanover

32409 ■ Adams Hanover Counseling Services, Inc.
625 W Elm Ave.
Hanover, PA 17331-5141
Ph: (717)632-4900
URL: http://www.ahcsinc.com/

Harrisburg

32410 ■ Northwestern Human Services--Edgewater Partial Hospitalization Program
1801 N Front St.
Harrisburg, PA 17102
Ph: (717)238-8666
URL: http://www.nhsonline.org/locations.html

Haverford

32411 ■ Torrey House CareLink Community Support Services
3520 Darby Rd.
Haverford, PA 19041-1018
Ph: (610)527-7131
URL: http://www.carelink-svs.org/

Havertown

32412 ■ Child Guidance Resource Centers--Havertown
2000 Old W Chester Pke.
Havertown, PA 19083
Ph: (484)454-8700
URL: http://www.cgrc.org/

Hazleton

32413 ■ Northeast Counseling Services--Hazleton
750 E Broad St.
Hazleton, PA 18201
Ph: (570)455-6385
URL: http://www.northeastcounseling.org/

Hermitage

32414 ■ Community Counseling Center of Mercer County
2201 E State St.
Hermitage, PA 16148
Ph: (724)981-7141
URL: http://www.cccmer.org/

Homestead

32415 ■ Turtle Creek Valley Mental Health/Mental Retardation, Inc.--Maple Avenue, Homestead
1705 Maple Ave.
Homestead, PA 15120
Ph: (412)464-4781
URL: http://www.tcv.net/

32416 ■ Turtle Creek Valley Mental Health/Mental Retardation Services--E 18th Avenue, Homestead
201 E 18th Ave.
Homestead, PA 15120
Ph: (412)461-4100
URL: http://www.tcv.net/

Indiana

32417 ■ Family Counseling Center--Indiana, PA
155 N 10th St.
Indiana, PA 15701
Ph: (724)349-9448
URL: http://www.fccac.org/

Kane

32418 ■ The Guidance Center--Kane
2 Greeves St.
Kane, PA 16735
Ph: (814)837-5148
URL: http://www.penn.com/~guidance/FamCntr.htm

Lafayette Hill

32419 ■ Northwestern Human Services--Lafayette Hill
620 Germantown Pke.
Lafayette Hill, PA 19444
Ph: (610)260-4600
E-mail: contact@nhsonline.org
URL: http://www.nhsonline.org/

Lancaster

32420 ■ Lancaster Regional Medical Center Behavioral Health Unit
250 College Ave.
Lancaster, PA 17603-3378
Ph: (717)291-8211
URL: http://www.lancasterregional.com/Services/Default.aspx?Id=654

Lansdale

32421 ■ Northwestern Human Services of Montgomery County
400 N Broad St.
Lansdale, PA 19446
Ph: (215)368-2022
URL: http://www.nhsonline.org/

Lansdowne

32422 ■ Carelink Community Support Services
140 S Lansdowne Ave.
Lansdowne, PA 19050
Ph: (610)626-6400
URL: http://www.carelink-svs.org/

32423 ■ Carelink Community Support Services Mobile Psychiatric Rehabilitation
111 Lansdowne Ave.
Lansdowne, PA 19050
Ph: (610)284-1902
URL: http://www.carelink-svs.org/
Formerly: TFC -101.

Lebanon

32424 ■ Lebanon Veterans Affairs Medical Center
1700 S Lincoln Ave.
Lebanon, PA 17042
Ph: (717)272-6621
Free: 800-409-8771
URL: http://www.lebanon.va.gov/

Lewistown

32425 ■ Universal Community Behavioral Health
3 W Monument Sq.
Lewistown, PA 17044
Ph: (717)248-8197
Fax: (717)248-6449
URL: http://www.themeadows.net/locations.htm

Limeport

32426 ■ Tri-County Respite Newvitae, Inc. - Mount Trexler Manor
5201 Saint Joseph's Rd.
Limeport, PA 18060
Ph: (610)965-9021
Fax: (610)967-0451
E-mail: info@tcrespite.com
URL: http://www.tcrespite.com

Lock Haven

32427 ■ The Meadows Psychiatric Center
20 Woodward Ave.
Lock Haven, PA 17745
Ph: (570)748-4959
URL: http://www.themeadows.net/locations.htm

Mansfield

32428 ■ Northern Tier Counseling--Mansfield
10 S Main St., Ste. B
Mansfield, PA 16933
Ph: (570)662-7954
URL: http://www.northerntiercounseling.com/locations/index.php

Mar Lin

32429 ■ The Meadows Psychiatric Center
15 Maple Ave.
Mar Lin, PA 17951
Ph: (570)544-9392
URL: http://www.themeadows.net/locations.htm

McKeesport

32430 ■ Mon Yough Community Services, Inc.
500 Walnut St., 3rd FL.
McKeesport, PA 15132
Ph: (412)675-8530
Fax: (412)675-8888
E-mail: admin@mycs.org
URL: http://www.mycs.org

Media

32431 ■ Family and Community Service of Delaware County
600 N Olive St.
Media, PA 19063
Ph: (610)566-7540
Fax: (610)566-7677
URL: http://www.fcsdc.org/

Middletown

32432 ■ Child Guidance Resource Centers--Middletown
Bunker Hill Center II, Ste. 103
Middletown, PA 19709
Ph: (302)279-1010
Free: 866-799-3325
URL: http://www.cgrc.org/locations.html

Monessen

32433 ■ Diversified Human Services
8 Eastgate
Monessen, PA 15062
Ph: (724)684-0000
E-mail: postmaster@sphs.org
URL: http://www.sphs.org/dhshome.html
Formerly: Diversified Human Services and SPHS Behavioral Health.

Monroe Township

32434 ■ Northern Tier Counseling--Monroe Township
Rte. 414
Monroe Township, PA 18832
Ph: (570)265-5755
URL: http://www.northerntiercounseling.com/locations/index.php

Montrose

32435 ■ Tri-County Human Services Center
Lake Plz. 2, Rte. 706 E
Montrose, PA 18801
Ph: (570)278-3393
Fax: (570)278-1716
URL: http://www.che.org/behavioral/tri-county.php

Mountville

32436 ■ Community Services Group
320 Highland Dr.
Mountville, PA 17554
Ph: (717)285-7121
URL: http://www.csgonline.org/

Nanticoke

32437 ■ Mental Health Group Home Children's Service Center
137 E Noble St.
Nanticoke, PA 18634-2803
Ph: (570)735-7369
URL: http://www.cscwv.org/cscwv/CSCnanticoke.asp

32438 ■ Northeast Counseling Services--E Broad Street, Nanticoke
24 E Broad St., Ste. 26
Nanticoke, PA 18634
Ph: (570)735-7590
URL: http://www.northeastcounseling.org/

32439 ■ Northeast Counseling Services--W Washington Street, Nanticoke
130 W Washington St.
Nanticoke, PA 18634
Ph: (570)735-7590
URL: http://www.northeastcounseling.org/

New Castle

32440 ■ Horizon House--New Castle
24 E Grant St.
New Castle, PA 16101
Ph: (724)658-3578
E-mail: info@humanservicescenter.net
URL: http://www.humanservicescenter.net/

32441 ■ Human Services Center--New Castle
130 W North St.
New Castle, PA 16101
Ph: (724)658-3578
E-mail: info@humanservicescenter.net
URL: http://www.humanservicescenter.net/

32442 ■ Oakview Apartments
7 S Liberty St.
New Castle, PA 16102
Ph: (724)658-3578
E-mail: info@humanservicescenter.net
URL: http://www.humanservicescenter.net/

New Kensington

32443 ■ Family Services of Western Pennsylvania
310 Central City Plz.
New Kensington, PA 15068
Ph: (724)335-9883
Free: 888-222-4200
Fax: (724)335-2730
E-mail: fswp@fswp.org
URL: http://www.fswp.org

32444 ■ Family Services of Western Pennsylvania
Maverick Drop In Center
1005 5th Ave.
New Kensington, PA 15068
Ph: (724)334-2386
Free: 888-222-4200
E-mail: fswp@fswp.org
URL: http://www.fswp.org

32445 ■ Partial Hospital Program
310 Central City Plz.
New Kensington, PA 15068
Ph: (724)335-9883
Free: 888-222-4200
E-mail: fswp@fswp.org
URL: http://www.fswp.org

Norristown

32446 ■ Child Guidance Resource Centers--Norristown
705 General Washington Ave.
Norristown, PA 19403
Ph: (484)751-9691
Free: 866-799-3325
URL: http://www.cgrc.org/locations.html

32447 ■ Horizon House--Norristown
1001 Sterigere St., Bldg. 56
Norristown, PA 19401-5300
Ph: (610)278-6882
URL: http://www.hhinc.org/

32448 ■ Norristown State Hospital
1001 Sterigere St.
Norristown, PA 19401
Ph: (610)270-1000
URL: http://www.dpw.state.pa.us/PartnersProviders/MentalHealthSubstanceAbuse/Sta teHospitals/003670158.htm

Penndel

32449 ■ Penndel Mental Health Center
1517 Durham Rd.
Penndel, PA 19047
Ph: (215)752-1541
Fax: (215)752-2848
URL: http://www.penndelmhc.org/

Philadelphia

32450 ■ Centro de Servicios para Hispanos
2742-44 N 5th St.
Philadelphia, PA 19133
Ph: (215)427-3400
URL: http://www.jfkmhmr.org/locations.html

32451 ■ Citizens Acting Together Can Help, Inc.
Day Treatment
2401 Penrose Ave. 2nd Fl.
Philadelphia, PA 19145-5350
Ph: (215)465-5170
URL: http://www.catchinc.com/homepage.htm

32452 ■ Citizens Acting Together Can Help, Inc.
Elderly Day Treatment
1400 Reed St.
Philadelphia, PA 19146
Ph: (215)551-3150
URL: http://www.catchinc.com/homepage.htm

32453 ■ COMHAR
Community Living Room
121 N Broad St., 3rd Fl.
Philadelphia, PA 19107
Ph: (215)569-8414
URL: http://www.comhar.org

32454 ■ COMHAR, Inc.
100 W Lehigh Ave.
Philadelphia, PA 19133
Ph: (215)203-3000
Free: 800-654-5984
URL: http://www.comhar.org

32455 ■ COMHAR, Inc.
Intensive Care Residence/Mental Health Center
1319 E Wingohocking St.
Philadelphia, PA 19134
Ph: (215)324-8964
URL: http://www.comhar.org

32456 ■ COMHAR, Inc.
Latino Outpatient and HIV Program
166 W Lehigh Ave.
Philadelphia, PA 19133
Ph: (215)739-2669
URL: http://www.comhar.org

32457 ■ COMHAR, Inc.
Long-Term Structured Residence
Independence House
5116 Oxford St.
Philadelphia, PA 19124
Ph: (215)831-1569
URL: http://www.comhar.org

32458 ■ COMHAR, Inc.
Maximum Care Community Residence
3138 Frankford Ave.
Philadelphia, PA 19134
Ph: (215)427-5787
URL: http://www.comhar.org

32459 ■ COMHAR, Inc.
Outpatient Services
3201 Frankford Ave.
Philadelphia, PA 19134
Ph: (215)427-5800
Fax: (215)427-5767
URL: http://www.comhar.org

32460 ■ COMHAR, Inc.
PACTS - Outpatient/TRIAD
121 N Broad St.
Philadelphia, PA 19107
Ph: (215)569-8414
Fax: (215)569-2021
URL: http://www.comhar.org

32461 ■ COMHAR, Inc.
Supported Independent Living Program
105 E Lehigh Ave.
Philadelphia, PA 19125
Ph: (215)427-5899
URL: http://www.comhar.org

32462 ■ COMHAR
Open Door Clubhouse
1847 E Allegheny Ave.
Philadelphia, PA 19134
Ph: (215)427-5763
URL: http://www.comhar.org

32463 ■ COMHAR
Speakeasy
121 N Broad St.
Philadelphia, PA 19107
Ph: (215)569-8414
URL: http://www.comhar.org

32464 ■ Consortium, Inc.
3801 Market St., Ste. 201
Philadelphia, PA 19104
Ph: (215)596-8100
URL: http://www.consortium-inc.org/

32465 ■ Consortium, Inc.
University City Counseling Center
451 S University Ave.
Philadelphia, PA 19104
Ph: (215)596-8000
URL: http://www.consortium-inc.org/

32466 ■ Green Tree School
146 W Walnut Ln.
Philadelphia, PA 19144
Ph: (215)843-4528
URL: http://www.greentreeschool.org/

32467 ■ Hispanic Partial Hospitalization Program
JFK Center for Mental Health & Retardation
2742-44 N 5th St.
Philadelphia, PA 19133
Ph: (215)634-7060
URL: http://www.jfkmhmr.org/locations.html

32468 ■ Horizon House/First Step Shelter
4300 Monument Rd.
Philadelphia, PA 19131
Ph: (215)879-4350
URL: http://www.hhinc.org/

32469 ■ Horizon House, Inc.--Stokley Street, Philadelphia
3275 Stokley St.
Philadelphia, PA 19129
Ph: (215)386-3838
E-mail: horizon.house@hhinc.org
URL: http://www.hhinc.org/

32470 ■ Horizon House--S 30th Street, Philadelphia
120 S 30th St.
Philadelphia, PA 19104
Ph: (215)386-3838
URL: http://www.hhinc.org/

32471 ■ Intercommunity Action, Inc.
6012 Ridge Ave.
Philadelphia, PA 19128
Ph: (215)487-0914
URL: http://www.intercommunityaction.org/

32472 ■ Intercommunity Action, Inc.
Group Home 2
254 Kalos St.
Philadelphia, PA 19128-3832
Ph: (215)487-0906
URL: http://www.intercommunityaction.org/

32473 ■ Intercommunity Action, Inc.
Group Home 3
424 Ripka St.
Philadelphia, PA 19128
Ph: (215)487-0914
URL: http://www.intercommunityaction.org/

32474 ■ Intercommunity Action, Inc.
Group Home 4
4443 Mitchell St.
Philadelphia, PA 19128
Ph: (215)487-0914
URL: http://www.intercommunityaction.org/

32475 ■ Intercommunity Action, Inc.
Group Home 5
487-88 Green Ln.
Philadelphia, PA 19128
Ph: (215)487-0914
URL: http://www.intercommunityaction.org/

32476 ■ Intercommunity Action, Inc.
Outpatient Services
6122 Ridge Ave.
Philadelphia, PA 19128-1603
Ph: (215)487-1330
URL: http://www.intercommunityaction.org/

32477 ■ John F. Kennedy Community Mental Health/Mental Retardation Center
112 N Broad St.
Philadelphia, PA 19102
Ph: (215)568-0860
URL: http://www.jfkmhmr.org/

32478 ■ John F. Kennedy Community Mental Health/Mental Retardation Center
Life Acceptance Clinic--Partial Hospital
907 N Broad St.
Philadelphia, PA 19123
Ph: (215)684-2400
URL: http://www.jfkmhmr.org/

32479 ■ Northeast Community Center for Mental Health and Mental Retardation
4801 Roosevelt Blvd.
Philadelphia, PA 19124-2408
Ph: (215)831-2800

32480 ■ Northeast Community Center for Mental Health and Mental Retardation
Adult Adjustment Center
4371 Walnut St.
Philadelphia, PA 19124
Ph: (215)831-2950

32481 ■ Northeast Community Center for Mental Health and Mental Retardation
The Gathering Place
6726 Rising Sun Ave.
Philadelphia, PA 19111
Ph: (215)742-7800

32482 ■ Northwestern Human Services
Long Term Structured Program
305 W Chestnut Hill Ave.
Philadelphia, PA 19118
Ph: (215)247-1401
Fax: (215)247-1415
URL: http://www.nhsonline.org/
Formerly: Benjamin Rush Center for Mental Health/Mental Retardation.

32483 ■ Northwestern Human Services--Philadelphia
11082 Knights Rd.
Philadelphia, PA 19154
Ph: (215)632-9040
Fax: (215)632-1642
URL: http://www.nhsonline.org
Formerly: Benjamin Rush Center.

32484 ■ Northwestern Human Services
Specialized Supported Living
10929 Helmer Dr., 1st Fl.
Philadelphia, PA 19154
Ph: (215)632-6957
URL: http://www.nhsonline.org
Formerly: Benjamin Rush Center for Mental Health/Mental Retardation.

32485 ■ Path, Inc.
9215 Keystone St.
Philadelphia, PA 19114
Ph: (215)624-1862
URL: http://www.pathcenter.org/INDEX.HTM

32486 ■ Path, Inc. Community Mental Health Center
8220 Castor Ave.
Philadelphia, PA 19152
Ph: (215)728-4600
URL: http://www.pathcenter.org/INDEX.HTM
Formerly: Path Community Behavioral Health/Mental Retardation Center.

32487 ■ Philadelphia Elwyn
4040 Market St.
Philadelphia, PA 19104
Ph: (215)895-5500
URL: http://www.elwyn.org/

32488 ■ Philadelphia Veterans Affairs Medical Center
3900 Woodland Ave.
Philadelphia, PA 19104
Ph: (215)823-5800
Free: 800-949-1001
URL: http://www.philadelphia.va.gov/

32489 ■ Poplar Outpatient Clinic
321 W Girard Ave.
Philadelphia, PA 19123
Ph: (215)235-6250
URL: http://www.jfkmhmr.org/locations.html

32490 ■ Resources for Human Development
4700 Wissachickon Ave., Ste. 126
Philadelphia, PA 19144
Ph: (215)951-0300
Free: 800-894-9925
E-mail: info@rhd.org
URL: http://www.rhd.org

32491 ■ Southwest Counseling Center--Philadelphia
6408 Woodland Ave.
Philadelphia, PA 19142
Ph: (215)596-8163

32492 ■ University City Counseling Center
451 University Ave.
Philadelphia, PA 19104
Ph: (215)596-8000

Philipsburg

32493 ■ The Meadows Psychiatric Center
110 Walton St.
Philipsburg, PA 16866
Ph: (814)342-8090
URL: http://www.themeadows.net/locations.htm

Phoenixville

32494 ■ Horizon House--Phoenixville
1125 W Bridge St.
Phoenixville, PA 19460
Ph: (610)933-9040
URL: http://www.hhinc.org/AdminHome.asp?ArticleID=318

Pittsburgh

32495 ■ Family Services of Western Pennsylvania
Downtown Offices
3230 William Pitt Way
Pittsburgh, PA 15238
Ph: (412)820-2050
Free: 888-222-4200
Fax: (412)820-2060
E-mail: fswp@fswp.org
URL: http://www.fswp.org

32496 ■ Holy Family Institute
8235 Ohio River Blvd.
Pittsburgh, PA 15202
Ph: (412)766-4030
Fax: (412)766-5434
URL: http://www.hfi-pgh.org

32497 ■ Milestone Centers, Inc.
712 South Ave.
Pittsburgh, PA 15221
Ph: (412)243-3400
URL: http://www.milestonecentersinc.org/
Formerly: Allegheny East Mental Health/Mental Retardation Center.

32498 ■ Pace School
2432 Greensburg Pke.
Pittsburgh, PA 15221
Ph: (412)244-1900
URL: http://www.paceschool.org/

32499 ■ Veterans Affairs Pittsburgh Healthcare System
University Dr.
Pittsburgh, PA 15240
Ph: (412)688-6000
Free: 866-482-7488
URL: http://www.pittsburgh.va.gov/

Pottstown

32500 ■ Creative Health Services
11 Robinson St.
Pottstown, PA 19464
Ph: (610)941-0500
URL: http://www.creativehs.org/

Pottsville

32501 ■ Redco Group Behavioral Health Services--Pottsville
Turning Point
16 S Center St.
Pottsville, PA 17901
Ph: (570)628-5234
E-mail: turning@redcogrp.com
URL: http://www.redcogrp.com/

Punxsutawney

32502 ■ Clearfield Jefferson Community Mental Health Center
Punxsutawney Clinic
103 N Gilpin St
Punxsutawney, PA 15767
Ph: (814)938-8817
Free: 800-341-5040
Formerly: Community Mental Health Center Punxsutawney Clinic.

Rankin

32503 ■ Turtle Creek Valley Mental Health/Mental Retardation Services--Rankin
207 5th Ave.
Rankin, PA 15104
Ph: (412)271-2728
URL: http://www.tcv.net/

Reading

32504 ■ Family Guidance Center
501 Washington St.
Reading, PA 19601
Ph: (610)374-4963
URL: http://www.familyguidancecenter.com/

Ridgeway

32505 ■ Dickinson Mental Health Center
110 Lincoln St.
Ridgeway, PA 15853
Ph: (814)776-2145
URL: http://dmhc.org

Scranton

32506 ■ Scranton Counseling Center
326 Adams Ave.
Scranton, PA 18503
Ph: (570)348-6100
URL: http://www.scrantonscc.org/

Sharon

32507 ■ Community Counseling Center--Sharon
252 E State St.
Sharon, PA 16146
Ph: (724)981-6193
URL: http://www.cccmer.org/

32508 ■ Employment Resource Specialist
50 E State St.
Sharon, PA 16146
Ph: (724)981-6193
URL: http://www.merlink.org/mcjac/mh.htm

Shrewsbury

32509 ■ Crossroads Counseling and Education services
73 E Forrest Ave.
Shrewsbury, PA 17361
Ph: (717)235-0199
URL: http://www.ahcsinc.com/

Somerset

32510 ■ Bedford Somerset Mental Health/Mental Retardation Program
245 W Race St.
Somerset, PA 15501
Ph: (814)443-4891
Free: 877-814-4891
URL: http://www.besmhmr.dst.pa.us/

South Waverly

32511 ■ Northern Tier Counseling--South Waverly
356 Loder St.
South Waverly, PA 18840
Ph: (570)882-7414
Free: 888-322-1682
URL: http://www.northerntiercounseling.com/

Sunbury

32512 ■ Options
330A N 2nd St.
Sunbury, PA 17801
Ph: (570)286-2077
URL: http://www.csgonline.org/

Towanda

32513 ■ Northern Tier Counseling--Towanda
846 Main St.
Towanda, PA 18848
Ph: (570)265-0977
URL: http://www.northerntiercounseling.com/

Turtle Creek

32514 ■ Turtle Creek Valley Mental Health/Mental Retardation, Inc.--Turtle Creek
519 Penn Ave.
Turtle Creek, PA 15145
Ph: (412)824-8510
URL: http://www.tcv.net/

Uniontown

32515 ■ Chestnut Ridge Counseling Services, Inc.
100 New Salem Rd., Ste. 116
Uniontown, PA 15401
Ph: (724)437-0729
URL: http://www.crcsi.org/

Warren

32516 ■ Forest Warren Department of Human Services
People Place
311 Pann Ave.
Warren, PA 16365
Ph: (814)728-2671
URL: http://www.wc-hs.org/
Formerly: N.W. Human Development, Inc. People Place Drop In Center.

Wellsboro

32517 ■ Tioga County Department of Human Services
1873 Shumway Hill Rd.
Wellsboro, PA 16901
Ph: (570)724-5766
Fax: (570)724-6757
E-mail: tchsaad@epix.net
URL: http://www.tiogahsa.org/

West Chester

32518 ■ Human Services, Inc.--West Chester
1140 McDermott Dr., Ste. 100
West Chester, PA 19380
Ph: (610)873-1010

32519 ■ Human Services, Inc.
West Chester Office and Crisis Services
222 N Walnut St.
West Chester, PA 19380
Ph: (610)918-2100

Wilkes Barre

32520 ■ Children's Service Center of Wyoming Valley, Inc.
335 S Franklin St.
Wilkes Barre, PA 18702
Ph: (570)825-6425
Fax: (570)829-3337
URL: http://www.cscwv.org/

Wilkes-Barre

32521 ■ Veterans Affairs Medical Center Wilkes-Barre
1111 E End Blvd.
Wilkes-Barre, PA 18711
Ph: (570)824-3521
Free: 877-928-2621
URL: http://www.wilkes-barre.va.gov/

Wilmerding

32522 ■ Turtle Creek Valley Mental Health/Mental Retardation Services--Wilmerding
320 Airbrake Ave.
Wilmerding, PA 15148
Ph: (412)829-4044
URL: http://www.tcv.net/

York

32523 ■ Bell Socialization Services
160 S George St.
York, PA 17401
Ph: (717)848-5767
Fax: (717)854-2433
URL: http://www.bellsocialization.com/

32524 ■ The Meadows Psychiatric Center
2451 Kingston Ct.
York, PA 17402
Ph: (717)757-4229
URL: http://www.themeadows.net/locations.htm

PUERTO RICO

San Juan

32525 ■ Veterans Affairs Caribbean Healthcare System
10 Casia St.
San Juan, PR 00921
Ph: (787)641-7582
Free: 800-449-8729
Fax: (787)641-4557
URL: http://www.caribbean.va.gov/

RHODE ISLAND

Barrington

32526 ■ Barrington House
94 Old County Rd.
Barrington, RI 02806
Ph: (401)247-1420
URL: http://www.riverwoodmhs.org/

32527 ■ East Bay Center--Barrington
2 Old Country Rd.
Barrington, RI 02806
Ph: (401)246-1195
URL: http://www.eastbay.org/

Burrillville

32528 ■ The Providence Center--Burrillville
2198 Wallum Lake Rd.
Burrillville, RI 02904
Ph: (401)276-4020
URL: http://www.providencecenter.org/tabid/163/default.aspx

Central Falls

32529 ■ Hunt Street House
132 Hunt St.
Central Falls, RI 02863-1013
Ph: (401)726-1090
URL: http://www.gatewayhealth.org/

Charlestown

32530 ■ South Shore Mental Health Center-Addictions Program
4705A Old Post Rd.
Charlestown, RI 02813
Ph: (401)364-7705
URL: http://www.ssmhc.org/

Cranston

32531 ■ Wentworth Supervised Apartments
91 Wentworth St.
Cranston, RI 02905
Ph: (401)784-3606
URL: http://www.gatewayhealth.org/

Cumberland

32532 ■ NRI Community Services, Inc.
Chicoine House
712 Nate Whipple Hwy.
Cumberland, RI 02864
Ph: (401)334-2685
URL: http://www.nricommunityservices.org
Formerly: Chicoine House.

East Greenwich

32533 ■ The Kent Center - Cedar House
50 Cedar Ave.
East Greenwich, RI 02818
Ph: (401)884-3006
URL: http://www.thekentcenter.org/
Formerly: Cedar House.

East Providence

32534 ■ East Bay Center--East Providence
610 Wampanoag Trl.
East Providence, RI 02915
Ph: (401)431-9870
URL: http://www.eastbay.org/

32535 ■ East Bay Center, Inc.
Adams-Farley Counseling Center
610 Wampanoag Trl.
East Providence, RI 02915

Ph: (401)431-9870
URL: http://www.eastbay.org/locations-hours.htm

Johnston

32536 ■ Atwood House
1974 Atwood Ave.
Johnston, RI 02919
Ph: (401)861-8670

32537 ■ Mental Health Services Community Support Center
1443 Hartford Ave.
Johnston, RI 02919
Ph: (401)273-8100
URL: http://www.gatewayhealth.org/locations.asp

32538 ■ Mental Health Services--Johnston
1516 Atwood Ave.
Johnston, RI 02919
Ph: (401)553-1000
URL: http://www.gatewayhealth.org/locations.asp

32539 ■ Windsor House
36 N Long St.
Johnston, RI 02919
Ph: (401)861-8650
URL: http://www.gatewayhealth.org/

Lincoln

32540 ■ Lincoln House
34 Harris Ave.
Lincoln, RI 02865
Ph: (401)722-5573
URL: http://www.gatewayhealth.org/ch_resident.asp

Middletown

32541 ■ Anita Jackson House
316 Greene Ln.
Middletown, RI 02842
Ph: (401)848-5588
URL: http://www.nccmhc.org/
Formerly: Greene Lane Group Home.

32542 ■ Child and Family Services of Newport
31 John Clarke Rd.
Middletown, RI 02842
Ph: (401)849-2300
Fax: (401)841-8841
URL: http://www.cfsnewport.org/

32543 ■ Middletown Veterans Affairs Clinic
1 Corporate Pl.
Middletown, RI 02842
Ph: (401)847-6239
URL: http://www.providence.va.gov/riopc_mid.asp

32544 ■ Newport County Community Mental Health Center
Case Management
65 Valley Rd.
Middletown, RI 02842
Ph: (401)846-6620
URL: http://www.nccmhc.org/program.asp

32545 ■ Newport County Community Mental Health Center
Child and Adolescent Services
26 Valley Rd.
Middletown, RI 02842
Ph: (401)848-6363
URL: http://www.nccmhc.org/program.asp

32546 ■ Newport County Community Mental Health Center
Day Treatment
Phoenix One Club
Middletown, RI 02842
Ph: (401)846-3135
URL: http://www.nccmhc.org/program.asp

32547 ■ Newport County Community Mental Health Center Main Office
127 Johnny Cake Hill Rd.
Middletown, RI 02842
Ph: (401)846-1213
Fax: (401)848-9151
E-mail: info@nccmhc.org
URL: http://www.nccmhc.org/

North Kingstown

32548 ■ Labelle House
7233 Post Rd.
North Kingstown, RI 02852
Ph: (401)294-2645
URL: http://www.ssmhc.org/Contact.html

Pascoag

32549 ■ NRI Community Services, Inc.
Singleton House Group Home
2755 Wallum Lake Rd.
Pascoag, RI 02859
Ph: (401)568-0850
URL: http://www.nricommunityservices.org/
Formerly: Singleton House Group Home.

Pawtucket

32550 ■ Blackstone Adolescent Counseling Center
Community Counseling Center
575 Fountain St.
Pawtucket, RI 02860
Ph: (401)724-0535
URL: http://www.gatewayhealth.org/ch_resident.asp

32551 ■ Community Counseling Center
Gateway Healthcare
160 Beechwood Ave.
Pawtucket, RI 02860
Ph: (401)722-5573
URL: http://www.gatewayhealth.org/

32552 ■ Community Support Services
Community Counseling Center
101 Bacon St.
Pawtucket, RI 02860
Ph: (401)722-3560
URL: http://www.gatewayhealth.org/

32553 ■ NRI Community Services, Inc.
Robert J. Wilson House/Mabel Anderson
80 Summit St.
Pawtucket, RI 02860
Ph: (401)235-7432
URL: http://www.nricommunityservices.org/
Formerly: Robert J. Wilson House.

32554 ■ Rhode Island Youth Guidance Center, Inc.
82 Pond St.
Pawtucket, RI 02860
Ph: (401)725-0450
URL: http://www.gatewayhealth.org/locations.asp

Portsmouth

32555 ■ Portsmouth House
173 Locust Ave.
Portsmouth, RI 02871
Ph: (401)683-0804
URL: http://www.riverwoodmhs.org/

Providence

32556 ■ Child & Family
623 Atwells Ave., Ste. 201
Providence, RI 02909
Ph: (401)849-2300
Fax: (401)273-2021
URL: http://www.cfsnewport.org/

32557 ■ Community Support Services
The Providence Center
530 N Main St.
Providence, RI 02904
Ph: (401)274-2500
URL: http://www.providencecenter.org/

32558 ■ Counseling Services
The Providence Center
520 Hope St.
Providence, RI 02906
Ph: (401)861-6262
URL: http://www.providencecenter.org/

32559 ■ The COVE Center
610 Manton Ave.
Providence, RI 02909
Ph: (401)751-0459
Free: 800-745-5555
Fax: (401)434-7180
E-mail: grodencenter@grodencenter.org
URL: http://www.covecenter.org
Program(s): Provides individualized residential and day programs for adults with autism and other developmental disabilities. Focuses on the development of job skills, social behavior, communication, and adaptive living skills.

32560 ■ Eaton Street Center
The Providence Center
424 Eaton St.
Providence, RI 02908
Ph: (401)276-4050
URL: http://www.providencecenter.org/

32561 ■ Family Service of Rhode Island
55 Hope St.
Providence, RI 02906
Ph: (401)331-1350
E-mail: hugst@familyserviceri.org
URL: http://www.familyserviceri.org

32562 ■ Groden Center, Inc.
86 Mount Hope Ave.
Providence, RI 02906
Ph: (401)274-6310
E-mail: grodencenter@grodencenter.org
URL: http://www.grodencenter.org
Program(s): Provides day treatment for children ages 3-21 and residential treatment for children ages 12-21. Children served are those with autism and other developmental disabilities.

32563 ■ The Providence Center--Providence
951 N Main St.
Providence, RI 02904
Ph: (401)528-0123
URL: http://www.theprovidencecenter.org

32564 ■ Providence Veterans Affairs Medical Center
830 Chalkstone Ave.
Providence, RI 02908
Ph: (401)273-7100
Free: 866-363-4486
URL: http://www.providence.va.gov/

Smithfield

32565 ■ Cortland House
25 Cedar Swamp Rd.
Smithfield, RI 02825
Ph: (401)861-8655
URL: http://www.gatewayhealth.org/

Tiverton

32566 ■ Tiverton House
2698 Main Rd.
Tiverton, RI 02878
Ph: (401)624-2914
URL: http://www.riverwoodmhs.org/

Wakefield

32567 ■ South Shore Mental Health Center, Inc.
55 Cherry Ln.
Wakefield, RI 02879
Ph: (401)789-1367
URL: http://www.ssmhc.org/

32568 ■ South Shore Mental Health Center, Inc.
1157 South Rd.
Wakefield, RI 02879
Ph: (401)783-1150
URL: http://www.ssmhc.org/

Warren

32569 ■ East Bay Mental Health Center, Inc. Main Street House
945 Main St.
Warren, RI 02885
Ph: (401)245-5420
URL: http://www.eastbay.org/locations-hours.htm
Formerly: Main Street House.

32570 ■ Riverwood Mental Health Services
25 Railroad Ave.
Warren, RI 02885
Ph: (401)247-4278
URL: http://www.riverwoodmhs.org/
Program(s): Three group homes; vocational program; mobile treatment team. **Formerly:** Barrington House.

Warwick

32571 ■ Buttonwoods Group Home The Kent Center
116 Long St., Ste. A
Warwick, RI 02886-7726
Ph: (401)738-6060
URL: http://www.thekentcenter.org/

32572 ■ The Kent Center - Health Lane
50 Health Ln.
Warwick, RI 02886
Ph: (401)738-4300
URL: http://www.thekentcenter.org/
Remarks: Provides emergency, older adult, and community support services. **Formerly:** Kent County Mental Health Center.

32573 ■ The Kent Center - Hillsgrove House
70 Minnesota Ave.
Warwick, RI 02886
Ph: (401)732-0970
URL: http://www.thekentcenter.org/
Formerly: Hillsgrove House.

32574 ■ The Kent Center for Human and Organizational Development
2756 Post Rd., Ste. 104
Warwick, RI 02886
Ph: (401)732-5656
Free: 800-745-5555
URL: http://www.thekentcenter.org/
Remarks: Provides outpatient counseling and youth and family services. **Formerly:** Kent County Mental Health Center.

Woonsocket

32575 ■ NRI Community Services Northern Rhode Island Community Services, Inc. Administrative Offices
515 Cumberland St.
Woonsocket, RI 02895
Ph: (401)235-7000
Fax: (401)769-1810
E-mail: admin@nricommunityservices.com
URL: http://www.nricommunityservices.com/
Formerly: Northern Rhode Island Community Mental Health Center.

32576 ■ Viola M. Berard
181 Cumberland St.
Woonsocket, RI 02895
Ph: (401)235-7430
URL: http://www.nricommunityservices.org/

SOUTH CAROLINA

Abbeville

32577 ■ Abbeville Mental Health Clinic--Commercial Drive
101 Commercial Dr.
Abbeville, SC 29620
Ph: (864)459-9671
Fax: (864)459-2487
URL: http://www.beckmancenter.com/service-locations/abbeville-map

Anderson

32578 ■ New Foundations Children and Family Services, Inc.
2300 Standridge Rd.
Anderson, SC 29625
Ph: (864)225-1628
URL: http://nfcfs.com/

Bennettsville

32579 ■ Tri-County Community Mental Health Center
1035 Cheraw Hwy.
Bennettsville, SC 29512
Ph: (843)454-0841
Fax: (843)454-0635
URL: http://www.state.sc.us/dmh/cmhc.htm#tri

Charleston

32580 ■ Charleston Veterans Affairs Medical Center--Bee Street
109 Bee St.
Charleston, SC 29401
Ph: (843)577-5011
Free: 888-78-6884
URL: http://www.charleston.va.gov/

Chester

32581 ■ Catawba Community Mental Health Center--Chester
524 Doctors Ct.
Chester, SC 29706
Ph: (803)581-8311
Free: 800-475-1984
URL: http://www.state.sc.us/dmh/cmhc.htm

Chesterfield

32582 ■ Chesterfield Mental Health Clinic
207 Commerce Ave.
Chesterfield, SC 29709
Ph: (843)623-2229
Fax: (843)623-2553
URL: http://www.state.sc.us/dmh/cmhc.htm#tri

Clinton

32583 ■ Laurens Mental Health Center
442 Professional Park Rd.
Clinton, SC 29325
Ph: (864)938-0912
Fax: (864)938-0926
URL: http://www.beckmancenter.com/service-locations/laurens-map

Columbia

32584 ■ Columbia Area Mental Health Center--Columbia
2715 Colonial Dr.
Columbia, SC 29203
Ph: (803)898-4800
URL: http://www.state.sc.us/dmh/cmhc.htm#cola

32585 ■ Columbia Area Mental Health Center Independent House Clubhouse
1135 Carter St.
Columbia, SC 29204
Ph: (803)786-1183
URL: http://www.state.sc.us/dmh/cmhc.htm#cola

32586 ■ Columbia Area Mental Health Center Network Program
1800 Colonial Dr. A
Columbia, SC 29203
Ph: (803)898-1555
URL: http://www.state.sc.us/dmh/cmhc.htm#cola

32587 ■ Columbia Area Mental Health Center New Horizons Clubhouse
1850 Pineview Dr.
Columbia, SC 29209
Ph: (803)783-0303
URL: http://www.state.sc.us/dmh/cmhc.htm#cola

32588 ■ William Jennings Bryan Dorn Veterans Administration Hospital
6439 Garners Ferry Rd.
Columbia, SC 29209
Ph: (803)776-4000
Free: 800-293-8262
Fax: (803)695-6739
URL: http://www.va.gov/columbiasc/

Conway

32589 ■ Waccamaw Center for Mental Health--Conway
164 Waccamaw Medical Park Dr.
Conway, SC 29526
Ph: (843)347-4888
URL: http://www.waccamawmentalhealth.org/

Dillon

32590 ■ Dillon Mental Health Center
310 Commerce Rd.
Dillon, SC 29536
Ph: (843)774-3351
URL: http://www.state.sc.us/dmh/cmhc.htm#tri

Edgefield

32591 ■ Edgefield Mental Health Center
409 Simpkins St.
Edgefield, SC 29824
Ph: (803)637-5788
Fax: (803)637-0753
URL: http://www.beckmancenter.com/service-locations/edgefield-map

Florence

32592 ■ New Horizons
608 W Evans St.
Florence, SC 29501
Ph: (843)661-4870
URL: http://www.state.sc.us/dmh/peedee/

Greenwood

32593 ■ Greenwood Mental Health Clinic
1547 Parkway, Ste. 200
Greenwood, SC 29646
Ph: (864)223-8331
URL: http://www.beckmancenter.com/service-locations

Greer

32594 ■ Carolina Center for Behavioral Health
2700 E Phillips Rd.
Greer, SC 29650
Ph: (864)235-2335
Free: 800-866-4673
URL: https://www.thecarolinacenter.com/index.php

Hartsville

32595 ■ Darlington County Mental Health Center
217 E Carolina Ave.
Hartsville, SC 29550
Ph: (843)332-4141
URL: http://www.state.sc.us/dmh/peedee/

Holly Hill

32596 ■ Holly Hill Clinic
1375 Gilway Ext
Holly Hill, SC 29059
Ph: (803)496-3410

Kingstree

32597 ■ Waccamaw Center for Mental Health--Kingstree
501 Nelson Blvd.
Kingstree, SC 29556
Ph: (843)354-5453
URL: http://www.waccamawmentalhealth.org/

Lake City

32598 ■ New Dimensions
675 N Matthews Rd.
Lake City, SC 29560
Ph: (843)394-7600

McCormick

32599 ■ McCormick Mental Health Clinic
202 N Mine St.
McCormick, SC 29835
Ph: (864)465-2412
URL: http://www.beckmancenter.com/service-locations/mccormick-map

Newberry

32600 ■ Newberry Mental Health Center
2043 Medical Park Dr.
Newberry, SC 29108
Ph: (803)276-8000
Fax: (803)276-6669
URL: http://www.beckmancenter.com/service-locations/newberry-map

North Charleston

32601 ■ Palmetto Lowcountry Behavioral Health
2777 Speissegger Dr.
North Charleston, SC 29405
Ph: (843)747-5830
Free: 877-947-3223
URL: http://www.palmettobehavioralhealth.com/

Orangeburg

32602 ■ Orangeburg Area Mental Health Center
2319 St. Matthews Rd.
Orangeburg, SC 29118
Ph: (803)536-1571
Fax: (803)536-1463
URL: http://www.state.sc.us/dmh/cmhc.htm#oburg

Rock Hill

32603 ■ Catawba Community Mental Health Center
225 E Main St., Ste. 300
Rock Hill, SC 29730
Ph: (803)328-9600
Free: 800-475-1978
URL: http://www.state.sc.us/dmh/cmhc.htm#cat

32604 ■ Catawba Community Mental Health Center
York County Adult Services
166 Dotson St.
Rock Hill, SC 29732
Ph: (803)327-2012
Free: 800-252-2168
URL: http://www.state.sc.us/dmh/cmhc.htm#cat

Saluda

32605 ■ Saluda Mental Health Center
206 Travis Ave.
Saluda, SC 29138
Ph: (864)445-8122
Fax: (864)445-9546
URL: http://www.beckmancenter.com/service-locations/saluda-map

Union

32606 ■ Union Mental Health Center
130 Medical Sciences Dr.
Union, SC 29379
Ph: (864)429-0238
URL: http://www.state.sc.us/dmh/cmhc.htm

West Union

32607 ■ Lighthouse Care Center of Oconee
PO Box 1689
West Union, SC 29696
Ph: (864)944-9875
Fax: (864)944-6790
URL: http://www.psysolutions.com/facilities/index.html#SC

Winnsboro

32608 ■ Columbia Area Mental Health Center
Fairfield County Clinic
1073 US Hwy. 321, By-Pass S
Winnsboro, SC 29180
Ph: (803)737-3039
URL: http://www.state.sc.us/dmh/cmhc.htm#cola
Formerly: Fairfield County Mental Health Center.

SOUTH DAKOTA

Aberdeen

32609 ■ Northeastern Mental Health Center
Dakota House
723 SE 3rd Ave.
Aberdeen, SD 57401
Ph: (605)225-1013
URL: http://www.nemhc.org/

32610 ■ Northeastern Mental Health Center
Main Center
703 3rd Ave. SE
Aberdeen, SD 57401
Ph: (605)225-1014
URL: http://www.nemhc.org/

32611 ■ Northeastern Mental Health Center
Podoll Center
901 S Main St.
Aberdeen, SD 57402
Ph: (605)226-1988
URL: http://www.nemhc.org/

Black Hawk

32612 ■ Serenity Mental Health Services
6613 Eastridge Rd.
Black Hawk, SD 57718
Ph: (605)347-7560
Free: 888-347-7560
URL: http://www.serenitymentalhealth.com/

Canton

32613 ■ Southeastern Behavioral Healthcare
Canton Office
112 1/2 S Broadway
Canton, SD 57013-2225
Ph: (605)987-2561
URL: http://www.southeasternbh.org/

Desmet

32614 ■ Community Counseling Services
Outreach Program
901 3rd St. SW
Desmet, SD 57231
Ph: (605)854-3455
URL: http://www.ccs-sd.org/

Flandreau

32615 ■ Community Counseling Services
Outreach Program
220 N Prairie Ave.
Flandreau, SD 57028
Ph: (605)997-3771
URL: http://www.ccs-sd.org/

Fort Meade

32616 ■ Veterans Affairs Black Hills Health Care Systems
Fort Meade Campus
113 Comanche Rd.
Fort Meade, SD 57741
Ph: (605)347-2511
Free: 800-743-1070
URL: http://www.blackhills.va.gov/

Gregory

32617 ■ Southern Plains Behavioral Health Services--Gregory
811 Rice St.
Gregory, SD 57533
Ph: (605)835-8505

Hot Springs

32618 ■ Behavior Management Systems - Southern Hills
3 Canyon View Cir.
Hot Springs, SD 57747
Ph: (605)745-6222
Fax: (605)745-4930
E-mail: info@behaviormanagement.org
URL: http://www.behaviormanagement.org

32619 ■ Veterans Affairs Black Hills Health Care Systems
Hot Springs Campus
500 N 5th St.
Hot Springs, SD 57747
Ph: (605)745-2000
Free: 800-764-5370
URL: http://www.blackhills.va.gov/

Huron

32620 ■ Community Counseling Services
Bradfield Leary Center
317 Iowa Ave. SE
Huron, SD 57350-2515
Ph: (605)352-7072
URL: http://www.ccs-sd.org/

32621 ■ Community Counseling Services--Huron
357 Kansas Ave. SE
Huron, SD 57350
Ph: (605)352-8596
Fax: (605)352-7001
URL: http://www.ccs-sd.org/

Lake Andes

32622 ■ Lewis & Clark Behavioral Services, Inc.--Lake Andes
51 S 3rd St.
Lake Andes, SD 57356
Ph: (605)487-6082
URL: http://www.lcbhs.com/

Madison

32623 ■ Community Counseling Services Outreach Program
914 NE 3rd St.
Madison, SD 57042
Ph: (605)256-9656
URL: http://www.ccs-sd.org/

Milbank

32624 ■ Human Service Agency--Milbank
1303 E 4th Ave., Ste. 5C
Milbank, SD 57252
Ph: (605)432-4930
URL: http://www.humanserviceagency.org/locations.html

Miller

32625 ■ Community Counseling Services Outreach Services - Hand County Memorial
300 W 5th St.
Miller, SD 57362
Ph: (605)853-2421
URL: http://www.ccs-sd.org/
Formerly: Hand County Clinic.

Mission

32626 ■ Southern Plains Behavioral Health Services--Mission
132 N Main St.
Mission, SD 57555
Ph: (605)856-4631

Mitchell

32627 ■ Dakota Counseling Institute
910 W Havens St.
Mitchell, SD 57301
Ph: (605)996-9686
URL: http://www.dakotacounseling.com/

32628 ■ Dakota Counseling Institute--Pathway
900 W Havens St.
Mitchell, SD 57301
Ph: (605)996-9686
URL: http://www.dakotacounseling.com/

Mobridge

32629 ■ Northeastern Mental Health Center
210 E Grand Crossing
Mobridge, SD 57601
Ph: (605)845-2941
URL: http://www.nemhc.org/

Parker

32630 ■ Southeastern Behavioral Healthcare Parker Office
400 S Main St.
Parker, SD 57053
Ph: (605)297-3699
URL: http://www.southeasternbh.org/

Pierre

32631 ■ Capital Area Counseling Service
803 E Dakota Ave.
Pierre, SD 57501
Ph: (605)224-5811
URL: http://www.cacsnet.org

32632 ■ Capital Area Counseling Services Betty's Place
803 E Dakota Ave.
Pierre, SD 57501
Ph: (605)224-5811
Fax: (605)224-6921
URL: http://www.cacsnet.org

32633 ■ Capital Area Counseling Services Bridgeway
210 W Pleasant Ave.
Pierre, SD 57501
Ph: (605)224-8001
URL: http://www.cacsnet.org

32634 ■ Capital Area Counseling Services The Care Center
115 S Huron St.
Pierre, SD 57501
Ph: (605)224-4916
Fax: (605)224-0196
URL: http://www.cacsnet.org

Rapid City

32635 ■ Behavior Management Systems
350 Elk St.
Rapid City, SD 57701-7388
Ph: (605)343-7262
Free: 800-299-6023
Fax: (605)343-7293
E-mail: info@behaviormanagement.org
URL: http://www.behaviormanagement.org

32636 ■ Behavior Management Systems Mainstream and IMPACT West
111 N St.
Rapid City, SD 57701-1163
Ph: (605)343-0650
E-mail: info@behaviormanagement.org
URL: http://www.behaviormanagement.org

Redfield

32637 ■ Northeastern Mental Health Center Redfield
1005 1st St., Ste. 4B
Redfield, SD 57469
Ph: (605)472-3282
URL: http://www.nemhc.org/

Sioux Falls

32638 ■ Royal C. Johnson Veterans Affairs Medical Center
2501 W 22nd St.
Sioux Falls, SD 57105
Ph: (605)336-3230
Free: 800-316-8387
URL: http://www.siouxfalls.va.gov/

32639 ■ Southeastern Behavioral Healthcare Center House
3601 E 3rd
Sioux Falls, SD 57110
Ph: (605)333-9856
URL: http://www.southeasternbh.org/

32640 ■ Southeastern Behavioral Healthcare Community Support Services
100 W 5th St.
Sioux Falls, SD 57104
Ph: (605)336-0503
URL: http://www.southeasternbh.org/

32641 ■ Southeastern Behavioral Healthcare Judy House
3513 E 3rd St.
Sioux Falls, SD 57110
Ph: (605)988-9620
URL: http://www.southeasternbh.org/

32642 ■ Southeastern Behavioral Healthcare Klondike House
3511 E 3rd St.
Sioux Falls, SD 57110
Ph: (605)367-3499
URL: http://www.southeasternbh.org/

32643 ■ Southeastern Behavioral Healthcare Sioux Falls Office
2000 S Summit Ave.
Sioux Falls, SD 57105
Ph: (605)336-0510
E-mail: vickir@southeasternbh.org
URL: http://www.southeasternbh.org/

32644 ■ Southeastern Behavioral Healthcare Solar House
613 Solar Dr.
Sioux Falls, SD 57110
Ph: (605)335-6385
URL: http://www.southeasternbh.org/

32645 ■ Southeastern Behavioral Healthcare Solar House 2
610 Solar Dr.
Sioux Falls, SD 57110
Ph: (605)338-6450
URL: http://www.southeasternbh.org/

32646 ■ Southeastern Mental Health Center Wayne Dahl Transition House
334 W 8th St.
Sioux Falls, SD 57104
Ph: (605)336-0612
URL: http://www.southeasternbh.org/

Sisseton

32647 ■ HSA Behavioral Health Sisseton Outpatient Mental Health
309 2nd Ave. E
Sisseton, SD 57262
Ph: (605)698-7688
URL: http://www.humanserviceagency.org/sisseton.html
Formerly: Lake Region Mental Health Center and Human Service Agency.

Spearfish

32648 ■ Behavior Management Systems - Northern Hills
623 Dahl Rd.
Spearfish, SD 57783
Ph: (605)642-2777
Fax: (605)642-9356
URL: http://www.behaviormanagement.org

Sturgis

32649 ■ Serenity Mental Health Services
2315 Park Ave., Ste. 1 & 2
Sturgis, SD 57785
Ph: (888)347-7560
URL: http://www.serenitymentalhealth.com/staff.php

Vermillion

32650 ■ Lewis & Clark Behavioral Health Services, Inc.--Vermillion
28 E Cherry St.
Vermillion, SD 57069
Ph: (605)624-9148
URL: http://www.lcbhs.com/

Watertown

32651 ■ HSA Behavioral Health
123 19th St. NE
Watertown, SD 57201
Ph: (605)886-0123
Free: 800-444-3989
URL: http://www.humanserviceagency.org/locations.html

Webster

32652 ■ Northeastern Mental Health Center Webster Clinic
830 W Hwy. 12
Webster, SD 57274

Ph: (605)045-3146
URL: http://www.nemhc.org/

Wessington Springs

32653 ■ Community Counseling Services Outreach Program/Tri-County Clinic
602 1st St. NE
Wessington Springs, SD 57382
Ph: (605)539-1778
URL: http://www.ccs-sd.org/

Winner

32654 ■ Southern Plains Behavioral Health Services--Winner
500 E 9th St.
Winner, SD 57580
Ph: (605)886-0123

Yankton

32655 ■ Lewis & Clark Behavioral Health Services, Inc.--Yankton
1028 Walnut St.
Yankton, SD 57078
Ph: (605)665-4606
Free: 800-765-3382
URL: http://www.lcbhs.com/

TENNESSEE

Alcoa

32656 ■ Helen Ross McNabb Center, Inc. Blount County Mental Health Clinic
Midland Plz.
244 S Calderwood St.
Alcoa, TN 37701
Ph: (865)981-9429
URL: http://www.mcnabbcenter.org/locations/index.html

Ashland City

32657 ■ Centerstone - Cheatham County Harriett Cohn Center of Cheatham County
162 County Services Dr.
Ashland City, TN 37015
Ph: (615)463-6160
Fax: (615)463-6162
URL: http://www.centerstone.org

Athens

32658 ■ Hiwassee Mental Health Center
1805 Ingleside Ave.
Athens, TN 37303
Ph: (423)745-8802

Bean Station

32659 ■ Cherokee Health Systems Bean Station Office
1285 Hwy. 11 W
Bean Station, TN 37708
Ph: (865)993-4300
Fax: (865)993-4304
URL: http://www.cherokeehealth.com

Blaine

32660 ■ Cherokee Health Systems Blaine Office
180 Emory Rd.
Blaine, TN 37709
Ph: (865)933-4110
Fax: (865)933-4729
URL: http://www.cherokeehealth.com

Bluff City

32661 ■ Frontier Health - Crossing Point
321 Possum Creek Rd.
Bluff City, TN 37618
Ph: (423)391-4300
Fax: (423)391-4301
URL: http://www.frontierhealth.org/service_guide_detail.asp?80

Brentwood

32662 ■ Centerstone--Brentwood
1600 Westgate Cir.
Brentwood, TN 37027
Ph: (615)661-4443
Fax: (615)370-2408
URL: http://www.centerstone.org/tennessee-facilities

Bristol

32663 ■ Art Smart
26 Midway St.
Bristol, TN 37620
Ph: (423)989-4539
URL: http://www.frontierhealth.org/locations.htm

32664 ■ Bristol Regional Counseling Center
26 Midway St.
Bristol, TN 37620
Ph: (423)989-4500
URL: http://www.frontierhealth.org/locations.htm

32665 ■ Frontier Health--Bristol Tennessee Community Support
266 North St.
Bristol, TN 37620
Ph: (423)989-4558
Fax: (423)989-4570
URL: http://www.frontierhealth.org/service_guide_detail.asp?84

Brownsville

32666 ■ Pathways - Haywood County Office
1141 Tammbell St.
Brownsville, TN 38012
Ph: (731)772-4685
Free: 800-372-0693

Camden

32667 ■ Carey Counseling Center--Camden
300 Hwy. 641 N
Camden, TN 38320
Ph: (731)584-6999
Free: 800-611-7757
URL: http://www.bhillc.org/careyweb/www/index.htm

Centerville

32668 ■ Centerstone Hickman County Health Department
704 Hwy. 100, Ste. 101
Centerville, TN 37033
Ph: (931)729-3573
Fax: (931)729-9330
URL: http://www.centerstone.org

Chattanooga

32669 ■ Fortwood Center, Inc.
1028 E 3rd St.
Chattanooga, TN 37403
Ph: (423)266-6751
URL: http://www.fortwoodcenter.org/

32670 ■ Fortwood Center, Inc. Adult Services
601 Cumberland St.
Chattanooga, TN 37404
Ph: (423)266-6751
URL: http://www.fortwoodcenter.org/

32671 ■ Johnson Mental Health Center Main Center
420 Bell Ave.
Chattanooga, TN 37405
Ph: (423)634-8884
Fax: (423)634-0813
URL: http://www.vbhcs.org/poc/view_doc.php?type=doc&id=5723

32672 ■ Patton Peer-Support Center
509 S Highland Park Ave.
Chattanooga, TN 37404
Ph: (423)755-0825
URL: http://www.fortwoodcenter.org/fortwoodcenter_location.htm
Formerly: Patton House.

32673 ■ Volunteer Behavioral Health Care System
413 Spring St.
Chattanooga, TN 37405
Ph: (423)756-2740
Free: 877-567-6051
URL: http://www.vbhcs.org

Clarksville

32674 ■ Centerstone Associates Cumberland Associates
1820 Memorial Cir.
Clarksville, TN 37043
Ph: (931)920-7300
Fax: (931)920-7302
URL: http://www.centerstone.org
Formerly: Cumberland Associates.

32675 ■ Centerstone Cumberland Valley Group Home
404 Pageant Ln.
Clarksville, TN 37040
Ph: (931)920-2347
Fax: (931)553-8742
URL: http://www.centerstone.org

32676 ■ Centerstone Do Drop In--Drop-In Center-
1840 Memorial Dr.
Clarksville, TN 37043
Ph: (931)905-0933
Fax: (931)906-0355
URL: http://www.centerstone.org

32677 ■ Centerstone - Harriett Cohn Center Harriett Cohn Center--Craig Bldg.
201 Uffleman Dr.
Clarksville, TN 37040
Ph: (931)920-7330
Fax: (931)920-7332
URL: http://www.centerstone.org

32678 ■ Centerstone - Harriett Cohn Center Psychosocial Rehabilitation Enrichment Program
611 8th St.
Clarksville, TN 37040
Ph: (931)920-7210
Fax: (931)920-7212
URL: http://www.centerstone.org

32679 ■ Centerstone Harriett Cohn Center Regional Intervention Program
11 8th St.
Clarksville, TN 37040
Ph: (931)920-7200
Fax: (931)920-7202
URL: http://www.centerstone.org

32680 ■ Centerstone - Oak Hill Residential Oak Hill Residential
118 Union St.
Clarksville, TN 37040
Ph: (931)647-8257
Fax: (931)647-2978
URL: http://www.centerstone.org

32681 ■ Centerstone - The Lodge
The Lodge
901 Martin St.
Clarksville, TN 37040
Ph: (931)503-4600
Fax: (931)503-4620
URL: http://www.centerstone.org

32682 ■ Centerstone - Vivian House
Vivian House
125 Vivian Dr.
Clarksville, TN 37040
Ph: (931)920-7235
Fax: (931)920-7202
URL: http://www.centerstone.org

32683 ■ Centerstone
Weems Academy
812 Greenwood Ave.
Clarksville, TN 37040
Ph: (931)920-7370
Fax: (931)920-7372
URL: http://www.centerstone.org

32684 ■ Gateway Medical Center
Behavioral Health Unit
Crisis Walk-In Center
1771 Madison St.
Gateway Hospital, 1st Fl.
Clarksville, TN 37043
Ph: (931)502-2025
Fax: (931)502-2026
URL: http://www.centerstone.org
Formerly: Centerstone Centerstone at Gateway Medical Crisis Walk-In Center.

Cleveland

32685 ■ Hiwassee Mental Health Center
1855 Executive Park NW
Cleveland, TN 37312
Ph: (423)479-5454

Columbia

32686 ■ Centerston--LIFE Solutions Psychosocial
6011 B Trotwood Ave.
Columbia, TN 38401
Ph: (931)560-3050
Fax: (931)560-3052
URL: http://www.centerstone.org/tennessee-facilities

32687 ■ Centerstone - Columbia Area
321 W 7th St.
Columbia, TN 38401
Ph: (931)490-1400
Fax: (931)490-1402
URL: http://www.centerstone.org/tennessee-facilities
Formerly: Columbia Area Mental Health Center.

32688 ■ Centerstone
Cumberland Associates
801 School St.
Columbia, TN 38402-0598
Ph: (931)490-1460
Fax: (931)490-1462
URL: http://www.centerstone.org

32689 ■ Centerstone
Jackson Hall Residential Treatment
2122 Circle Dr.
Columbia, TN 38401
Ph: (931)490-1480
Fax: (931)490-1482
URL: http://www.centerstone.org/tennessee-facilities

32690 ■ Centerstone - Maury County Mental Health Center
Maury County Mental Health Center
1222 Medical Center Dr.
Columbia, TN 38401
Ph: (931)490-1500
Fax: (931)490-1502
URL: http://www.centerstone.org/tennessee-facilities

32691 ■ Centerstone at Maury Regional Hospital
Crisis Center
Maury Regional Hospital
Columbia, TN 38401
Ph: (931)540-4333
Fax: (931)540-4334
URL: http://www.centerstone.org/tennessee-facilities

Cookeville

32692 ■ Plateau Mental Health Center
1200 S Willow Ave.
Cookeville, TN 38506
Ph: (931)432-4123

Covington

32693 ■ Professional Care Services
1997 Hwy. 51 S
Covington, TN 38019
Ph: (901)476-8967
Fax: (901)476-2498
URL: http://www.pcswtn.org/
Formerly: Professional Counseling Services.

Dickson

32694 ■ Centerstone
Dickson Regional Intervention Program
Regional Intervention Program
805 N Charlotte St.
Dickson, TN 37055
Ph: (615)441-6074
Fax: (615)446-7250
URL: http://www.centerstone.org/tennessee-facilities
Formerly: Harriett Cohn Center of Dickson County Regional Intervention Program.

32695 ■ Centerstone - Southridge
Southridge Psychological Services
721 Hwy. 46 S
Dickson, TN 37055
Ph: (615)446-3797
Fax: (615)446-3760
URL: http://www.centerstone.org/tennessee-facilities
Formerly: S.ridge Psychological Services.

32696 ■ Centerstone
Stepping Stones Drop-In Center
15 Valley W Commercial Park, Bldg. 15
Dickson, TN 37055
Ph: (615)441-6178
Fax: (615)441-5829
URL: http://www.centerstone.org/tennessee-facilities

Dyersburg

32697 ■ Pathways - Dyer County Office
2035 Saint John Ave.
Dyersburg, TN 38024
Ph: (731)286-1589

Erwin

32698 ■ Erwin Mental Health Center
218 N Main St.
Erwin, TN 37650
Ph: (423)743-1470
URL: http://www.frontierhealth.org/locations.htm

32699 ■ Frontier Health--Erwin
218 N Main St.
Erwin, TN 37650
Ph: (423)743-1470
Fax: (423)743-1472
URL: http://www.frontierhealth.org

Estill Springs

32700 ■ Centerstone - Estill Springs
Highland Rim Mental Health Center
416 S Main St.
Estill Springs, TN 37330
Ph: (931)649-3408
Fax: (931)649-3409
URL: http://www.centerstone.org
Formerly: Centerstone Highland Rim Mental Health Center.

Fayetteville

32701 ■ Centerstone
Between Friends Drop-In Center
615 W Maple St.
Fayetteville, TN 37334
Ph: (931)438-4993
Fax: (931)438-4817
URL: http://www.centerstone.org

32702 ■ Centerstone - Fayetteville
Highland Rim Medical Center
2241 Thornton Taylor Pkwy.
Fayetteville, TN 37334
Ph: (931)433-6456
Fax: (931)433-8911
URL: http://www.centerstone.org
Formerly: Centerstone Highland Rim Medical Center.

Gallatin

32703 ■ Centerstone - Sumner County
Sumner County Family Services
332 Sumner Hall Dr.
Gallatin, TN 37066
Ph: (615)451-5190
Fax: (615)451-3345
URL: http://www.centerstone.org

Gray

32704 ■ Frontier Health--Gray
1167 Spratlin Park Dr.
Gray, TN 37615
Ph: (423)467-3600
URL: http://www.frontierhealth.org

Greeneville

32705 ■ Church Street Pavilion
616 E Church St., Ste. A
Greeneville, TN 37745
Ph: (423)639-3213
URL: http://www.frontierhealth.org/service_guide_detail.asp?19
Formerly: Frontier Health Services.

32706 ■ Frontier Health--Greenville
Continuous Treatment Team
401 Holston Dr.
Greeneville, TN 37744
Ph: (423)639-1104
URL: http://www.frontierhealth.org/locations.htm

32707 ■ Nolachuckey-Holston Area Mental Health Center
401 Holston Dr.
Greeneville, TN 37744
Ph: (423)639-1104
URL: http://www.frontierhealth.org/locations.htm

Hohenwald

32708 ■ Centerstone - Lewis County
912 Summertown Hwy.
Hohenwald, TN 38462
Ph: (931)796-5916
Fax: (931)796-1288
URL: http://www.centerstone.org/
Formerly: Lewis County Mental Health Center of Centerstone.

Huntington

32709 ■ Carey Counseling at Huntington
19410 W Main St.
Huntington, TN 38344
Ph: (731)986-4411
URL: http://www.bhillc.org/careyweb/www/index.htm

Jackson

32710 ■ Pathways of Tennessee, Inc.
238 Summer Dr.
Jackson, TN 38301
Ph: (731)935-8200
Free: 800-587-3854
URL: http://www.wth.net/body_pathways.cfm?id=1397

Jefferson City

32711 ■ Cherokee Health Systems Jefferson City Office
120 Hospital Dr. Ste. 230
Jefferson City, TN 37760
Ph: (865)471-0312
Fax: (865)475-2802
URL: http://www.cherokeehealth.com

Johnson City

32712 ■ Friendship House--Johnson City
301 W Watauga St.
Johnson City, TN 37604
Ph: (423)232-4264
URL: http://www.frontierhealth.org/locations.htm

32713 ■ Frontier Health--Johnson City
607 Baxter St.
Johnson City, TN 37604
Ph: (423)232-6760
URL: http://www.frontierhealth.org/locations.htm

32714 ■ Student Assistance Program
109 W Watauga Ave.
Johnson City, TN 37605
Ph: (432)232-2600
URL: http://www.frontierhealth.org/locations.htm

32715 ■ Victory Center
2243 Eddie Williams Rd.
Johnson City, TN 37601
Ph: (423)975-6000
URL: http://www.frontierhealth.org/locations.htm

32716 ■ Watauga Behavioral Health Services
109 W Watauga Ave.
Johnson City, TN 37604
Ph: (423)232-2600
URL: http://www.frontierhealth.org/locations.htm

Kingsport

32717 ■ Frontier Health - Supported Living
2017 Stonebrook Pl.
Kingsport, TN 37660
Ph: (423)224-1417
URL: http://www.frontierhealth.org/locations.htm
Formerly: Park Center.

32718 ■ Holston Children & Youth Services
2001 Stonebrook Pl.
Kingsport, TN 37660
Ph: (423)224-1000
URL: http://www.frontierhealth.org/locations.htm

32719 ■ Holston Counseling Center
1570 Waverly Rd.
Kingsport, TN 37664
Ph: (423)224-1300
Free: 800-332-7281
Fax: (423)224-1375
URL: http://www.frontierhealth.org/locations.htm
Formerly: Behavioral Health Services.

32720 ■ HOPE for Tennessee Frontier Health
1570 Waverly Rd.
Kingsport, TN 37664
Ph: (423)224-1300
URL: http://www.frontierhealth.org/
Formerly: Project HOPE.

32721 ■ Link House
433 New Beason Well Rd.
Kingsport, TN 37660
Ph: (423)288-1828
URL: http://www.frontierhealth.org

32722 ■ SAFE House
PO Box 3426
Kingsport, TN 37664
Ph: (423)246-2273
URL: http://www.frontierhealth.org/locations.htm

Knoxville

32723 ■ Cherokee Health Systems North Knox Office
7714 Conner Rd., No. 105
Knoxville, TN 37849
Ph: (865)947-6220
Fax: (865)512-1069
URL: http://www.cherokeehealth.com

32724 ■ Cherokee Health Systems West Knoxville Office
10263 Kingston Pke.
Knoxville, TN 37922
Ph: (865)670-9231
Fax: (865)531-3460
URL: http://www.cherokeehealth.com

32725 ■ The Florence Crittenton Agency, Inc.
1531 Dick Lonas Rd.
Knoxville, TN 37909
Ph: (865)602-2021
Fax: (865)602-2039
URL: http://www.fcaknox.org/

32726 ■ Friendship House--Knoxville
528 Lamar St.
Knoxville, TN 37917
Ph: (865)544-3841

32727 ■ Helen Ross McNabb Center Child and Youth Center
320 Arthur St.
Knoxville, TN 37920
Ph: (865)637-9711
Free: 800-255-9711
URL: http://www.mcnabbcenter.org

32728 ■ Helen Ross McNabb Center--Knoxville
201 W Springdale Ave.
Knoxville, TN 37917
Ph: (865)637-9711
Free: 800-255-9711
URL: http://www.mcnabbcenter.org

Lafayette

32729 ■ Valley Ridge Mental Health Center
907 Sycamore St.
Lafayette, TN 37083
Ph: (615)666-8070
Fax: (615)666-6933
URL: http://www.vbhcs.org/

Lawrenceburg

32730 ■ Centerstone Hand-In-Hand Drop-In Center
241 E Gaines St.
Lawrenceburg, TN 38464
Ph: (931)766-3711
Fax: (931)766-3712
URL: http://www.centerstone.org

32731 ■ Centerstone - Lawrence County Cumberland Associates
1090 Old Florence Rd.
Lawrenceburg, TN 38464
Ph: (931)762-6505
URL: http://www.centerstone.org
Formerly: Centerstone Cumberland Associates.

32732 ■ Centerstone - Lawrence County Lawrence County Counseling
1090 Old Florence Rd.
Lawrenceburg, TN 38464-8401
Ph: (931)762-6505
Fax: (931)762-3690
URL: http://www.centerstone.org

Lenoir City

32733 ■ Cherokee Health Systems Lenoir City Office
501 Adesa Dr. Ste. A150
Lenoir City, TN 37771-6719
Ph: (865)986-8082
URL: http://www.cherokeehealth.com

Lewisburg

32734 ■ Centerstone--Lewisburg
1481 New Columbia Hwy.
Lewisburg, TN 37091
Ph: (931)359-0307
Fax: (931)359-0307
URL: http://www.centerstone.org/tennessee-facilities

32735 ■ Centerstone - Marshall County Mental Health Center
1601 Nashville Hwy.
Lewisburg, TN 37091
Ph: (931)359-5802
Fax: (931)359-0148
URL: http://www.centerstone.org/

Lexington

32736 ■ Pathways - Henderson County Office
67C W Church St.
Lexington, TN 38351
Ph: (731)968-8197
URL: http://www.tennhelp.com/tennHelpView?th_id=5029

Livingston

32737 ■ Dale Hollow Mental Health Center
501 Spruce St.
Livingston, TN 38570
Ph: (931)823-5678

Madison

32738 ■ Centerstone - Adolescent Residential Dede Wallace Center--Adolescent Residential Treatment
315 Hospital Dr.
Madison, TN 37115-3050
Ph: (615)460-4260
Fax: (615)460-4262
URL: http://www.centerstone.org
Formerly: Dede Wallace Center--Adolescent Residential Treatment.

32739 ■ Centerstone - Adult A and D Services
620 Gallatin Rd. S
Madison, TN 37115-4013
Ph: (615)460-4300
Fax: (615)460-4302
URL: http://www.centerstone.org
Formerly: Dede Wallace Center.

Martin

32740 ■ Pathways
The Start Program
457 Hannings Ln.
Martin, TN 38237
Ph: (731)587-3854
Fax: (731)587-3850

Maryville

32741 ■ Cherokee Health Systems
Maryville Office
627 Smithview Dr.
Maryville, TN 37803
Ph: (865)380-4390
URL: http://www.cherokeehealth.com

32742 ■ Helen Ross McNabb Center, Inc.--Maryville
391 S Court St.
Maryville, TN 37804
Ph: (865)273-5942
URL: http://www.mcnabbcenter.org/locations/index.html

Maynardville

32743 ■ Cherokee Health Systems
Union Grainer Primary Care
4330 Maynardville Hwy.
Maynardville, TN 37807
Ph: (865)992-3849
URL: http://www.cherokeehealth.com

Memphis

32744 ■ Lakeside Behavioral Health System
2911 Brunswick Rd.
Memphis, TN 38133
Ph: (901)377-4700
URL: http://www.lakesidebhs.com

32745 ■ Memphis Veterans Affairs Medical Center
1030 Jefferson Ave.
Memphis, TN 38104
Ph: (901)523-8990
Free: 800-636-8262
URL: http://www.memphis.va.gov/

32746 ■ Midtown Counseling Center
1835 Union Ave., Ste. 101
Memphis, TN 38104
Ph: (901)726-4586

32747 ■ Midtown Mental Health Center
427 Linden Ave.
Memphis, TN 38126-2096
Ph: (901)577-0200

32748 ■ Southeast Mental Health Center, Inc.
3810 Winchester Rd.
Memphis, TN 38181
Ph: (901)369-1400
URL: http://www.semhcinc.com/default.aspx

32749 ■ Southeast Mental Health Center, Inc.
Orange Mound Location
2579 Douglass Ave.
Memphis, TN 38114
Ph: (901)369-1480
URL: http://www.semhcinc.com/default.aspx

32750 ■ Southeast Mental Health Center, Inc.
Pauline Location
135 N Pauline St.
Memphis, TN 38103
Ph: (901)577-9400
Formerly: Madison Location.

32751 ■ Southeast Mental Health Center, Inc.
Summer Location
3628 Summer Ave.
Memphis, TN 38122
Ph: (901)452-6941
URL: http://www.semhcinc.com/default.aspx

32752 ■ Southwest Mental Health Center, Inc.
Whitehaven
1087 Alice Ave.
Memphis, TN 38106
Ph: (901)259-1920
URL: http://www.wswmhc.net/

Morristown

32753 ■ Cherokee Health Systems
Morristown Office
815 W 5th North St.
Morristown, TN 37814
Ph: (423)586-5032
URL: http://www.cherokeehealth.com

Mountain City

32754 ■ Johnson County Counseling Center
318 Donnelly St.
Mountain City, TN 37683
Ph: (423)727-2100
URL: http://www.frontierhealth.org/service_guide_detail.asp?26

Mountain Home

32755 ■ James H. Quillen Veterans Affairs Medical Center
Lamont & Veterans Way
Mountain Home, TN 37684
Ph: (423)926-1171
Free: 877-291-5311
URL: http://www.mountainhome.va.gov/

Nashville

32756 ■ Centerstone - Child and Youth Services - East
230 Venture Cir.
Nashville, TN 37228
Ph: (615)460-4200
Fax: (615)460-4202
URL: http://www.centerstone.org
Formerly: Dede Wallace Center Child and Youth Services East.

32757 ■ Centerstone - Frank Luton Center
1921 Ransom Pl.
Nashville, TN 37217
Ph: (615)279-6700
Fax: (615)279-6702
URL: http://www.centerstone.org
Formerly: Luton Mental Health Services.

32758 ■ Centerstone - Harbor House
654 W Iris Dr.
Nashville, TN 37204
Ph: (615)269-5170
Fax: (615)269-8015
URL: http://www.centerstone.org

32759 ■ Centerstone--Nashville
1101 6th Ave. N
Nashville, TN 37208
Ph: (615)460-4100
Fax: (615)460-4104
URL: http://www.centerstone.org
Formerly: Dede Wallace Center.

32760 ■ Tennessee Valley Veterans Affairs Healthcare System
Nashville Campus
1310 24th Ave. S
Nashville, TN 37212
Ph: (615)327-4751
Free: 800-228-4973
URL: http://www.tennesseevalley.va.gov/

New Tazewell

32761 ■ Cherokee Health Systems
New Tazewell Office
1596 Hwy. 33 S
New Tazewell, TN 37825
Ph: (423)626-8271
URL: http://www.cherokeehealth.com

Newport

32762 ■ Cherokee Health Systems
Cocke County Office
215 Hedrick Dr.
Newport, TN 37821
Ph: (423)623-5301
URL: http://www.cherokeehealth.com

Paris

32763 ■ Carey Counseling Center--Paris
408 Virginia St.
Paris, TN 38242
Ph: (731)642-0521
URL: http://www.bhillc.org/bhi_main/html/template1/index.htm

Pulaski

32764 ■ Centerstone
Giles County Mental Health Center
1002 Brindley Dr.
Pulaski, TN 38478
Ph: (931)363-5438
Fax: (931)363-3564
URL: http://www.centerstone.org

Ripley

32765 ■ William F. Walker Professional Counseling Center
403 Commerce St.
Ripley, TN 38063
Ph: (731)635-3968
URL: http://www.pcswtn.org/

Seymour

32766 ■ Cherokee Health Systems
Seymour Office
10731 Chapman Hwy.
Seymour, TN 37865
Ph: (865)573-0698
URL: http://www.cherokeehealth.com

Shelbyville

32767 ■ Centerstone - Bedford County
604 S Wall St.
Shelbyville, TN 37160
Ph: (931)684-0522
Fax: (931)684-6238
URL: http://www.centerstone.org
Formerly: Highland Rim.

32768 ■ Centerstone - Bedford County
Highland Rim Mental Health Center
882 Union St.
Shelbyville, TN 37160
Ph: (931)685-9330
Fax: (931)685-9337
URL: http://www.centerstone.org
Formerly: Highland Rim Mental Health Center.

Sneedville

32769 ■ Hancock County Mental Health Clinic
333 Campbell Dr.
Sneedville, TN 37869
Ph: (423)733-2216
URL: http://www.frontierhealth.org/locations.htm

32770 ■ New Start Peer Support Center
119 Norah Alder Dr.
Sneedville, TN 37689
Ph: (423)733-1540
URL: http://www.frontierhealth.org/locations.htm

Somerville

32771 ■ J.B. Summers Center
12615 S Main St.
Somerville, TN 38068
Ph: (901)465-9831
URL: http://www.pcswtn.org/

Springfield

32772 ■ Centerstone - Robertson Harriett Cohn Center of Springfield
713 Cheatham St.
Springfield, TN 37172
Ph: (615)463-6200
Fax: (615)463-6202
URL: http://www.centerstone.org
Formerly: Harriott Cohn Center of Springfield.

32773 ■ Centerstone Silver Linings Drop-In Center
54 N Main St.
Springfield, TN 37172
Ph: (615)382-5260
Fax: (615)384-6490
URL: http://www.centerstone.org

Talbott

32774 ■ Cherokee Health Systems Talbott Office
6350 W Andrew Johnson Hwy.
Talbott, TN 37877
Ph: (423)587-7337
URL: http://www.cherokeehealth.com

Tazewell

32775 ■ Five Rivers Services, Inc.
1913 Cedar Dr.
Tazewell, TN 37879
Ph: (423)626-8308

Tennessee Ridge

32776 ■ Centerstone - Ridgeview Residential Ridgeview Residential
1330 N Main St.
Tennessee Ridge, TN 37178
Ph: (931)721-3312
Fax: (931)721-3308
URL: http://www.centerstone.org
Remarks: Mailing address: PO Box 428, Erin, TN 37061.

Tiptonville

32777 ■ Pathways - Lake County Office
223 S Court St.
Tiptonville, TN 38079
Ph: (731)253-7780

Trenton

32778 ■ Carey Counseling Center--Trenton
1263 Hwy. 45 Bypass N
Trenton, TN 38382
Ph: (731)855-2871

32779 ■ Pathways Pathways - The Turning Point Program
200 Hospital Dr.
Trenton, TN 38382
Ph: (731)855-7982

Tullahoma

32780 ■ Centerstone Community Living Center
207 W Blackwell St.
Tullahoma, TN 37388
Ph: (931)461-0290
Fax: (931)461-0209
URL: http://www.centerstone.org
Formerly: Highland Rim Residential Services.

32781 ■ Centerstone - Davidson Street Highland Rim Mental Health Center
709 N Davidson St.
Tullahoma, TN 37388
Ph: (931)393-5900
Fax: (931)393-5904
URL: http://www.centerstone.org
Formerly: Highland Rim Mental Health Center.

32782 ■ Centerstone - Jackson Street
1803 N Jackson St.
Tullahoma, TN 37388-2299
Ph: (931)461-1300
Fax: (931)461-1302
URL: http://www.centerstone.org

32783 ■ Centerstone My Place Drop-In Center
516 E Carroll St.
Tullahoma, TN 37388
Ph: (931)393-3255
Fax: (931)393-5204
URL: http://www.centerstone.org

Union City

32784 ■ Carey Counseling Center--Union City
201 W Main St., Ste. C
Union City, TN 38261
Ph: (731)885-8810
URL: http://www.bhillc.org/bhi_main/html/template1/index.htm

Washburn

32785 ■ Cherokee Health Systems Washburn Office
7719 Hwy. 131
Washburn, TN 37888
Ph: (865)497-2591
E-mail: april.clay@cherokeehealth.com
URL: http://www.cherokeehealth.com

Waverly

32786 ■ Centerstone - Waverly Harriett Cohn Center of Humphreys County
105 Waverly Plz.
Waverly, TN 37185
Ph: (931)296-4356
Fax: (931)296-4529
URL: http://www.centerstone.org
Formerly: Harriett Cohn Center of Humphreys County.

Waynesboro

32787 ■ Centerstone - Wayne County
418 S Main St.
Waynesboro, TN 38485
Ph: (931)722-3644
Fax: (931)722-7972
URL: http://www.centerstone.org
Formerly: Harriett Cohn Center of Humphreys County.

TEXAS

Abilene

32788 ■ Betty Hardwick Center Adult & Youth Outpatient/Crisis Services
2616 S Clack St.
Abilene, TX 79606
Ph: (325)690-5100
URL: http://www.bhcmhmr.org/

32789 ■ Hickory Street Center
744 Hickory St.
Abilene, TX 79601
Ph: (325)670-4860
URL: http://www.bhcmhmr.org/

Alvin

32790 ■ The Gulf Coast Center--Alvin Centralized Intake & Assessment
101 Brennan
Alvin, TX 77511
Ph: (281)331-4502
Free: 800-643-0967
URL: http://www.gcmhmr.com/

Amarillo

32791 ■ Texas Panhandle Mental Health/Mental Retardation
1501 S Polk
Amarillo, TX 79101
Ph: (806)337-1000
URL: http://www.tpmhmr.org/
Formerly: Texas Panhandle Mental Health Center.

32792 ■ Thomas E. Creek Veterans Affairs Medical Center
6010 Amarillo Blvd. W
Amarillo, TX 79106
Ph: (806)355-9703
Free: 800-687-8262
URL: http://www.amarillo.va.gov/

Andrews

32793 ■ Andrews County Mental Health Center
215 NW 1st St.
Andrews, TX 79714
Ph: (432)523-7340
URL: http://www.wtcmhmr.org/

Angleton

32794 ■ The Gulf Coast Center--Angleton
101 Tigner St.
Angleton, TX 77515
Ph: (979)848-0937
URL: http://www.gcmhmr.com/

Arlington

32795 ■ Lena Pope Home, Inc.
800 N Fielder Rd., Ste. 200
Arlington, TX 76012
Ph: (817)255-2652
URL: http://www.lenapopehome.org/Home.aspx

32796 ■ Millwood Hospital
1011 N Cooper St
Arlington, TX 76011
Ph: (817)261-3121
Fax: (817)404-2221
URL: http://www.psysolutions.com/facilities/millwood/

Athens

32797 ■ Andrews Center--Athens
S Hwy. 19 and FM 1615
Athens, TX 75751
Ph: (903)675-8541
Free: 800-374-6058
URL: http://www.andrewscenter.com

Austin

32798 ■ Austin-Travis County Integral Care Austin Clinic
1430 Collier St.
Austin, TX 78764

Ph: (512)447-4141
Fax: (512)440-4081
E-mail: help@atcmhmr.com
URL: http://www.integralcare.org/
Formerly: Austin-Travis County Mental Health/Mental Retardation Center.

32799 ■ Austin-Travis County Integral Care Autism Center
5225 N Lamar Blvd.
Austin, TX 78751
Ph: (512)483-5800
E-mail: help@atcmhmr.com
URL: http://www.atcmhmr.com
Formerly: Austin-Travis County Mental Health/Mental Retardation Center.

32800 ■ Austin-Travis County Integral Care Oak Springs Outpatient Clinic
3000 Oak Springs Dr.
Austin, TX 78702
Ph: (512)926-5301
E-mail: help@atcmhmr.com
URL: http://www.atcmhmr.com
Formerly: Austin-Travis County Mental Health/Mental Retardation Center.

32801 ■ Austin-Travis County Integral Care Oak Springs Outpatient Clinic
3000 Oak Springs Dr.
Austin, TX 78702
Ph: (512)926-5301
E-mail: help@atcmhmr.com
URL: http://www.atcmhmr.com
Formerly: Oak Springs Treatment Center; Austin-Travis County Mental Health/Mental Retardation Center.

32802 ■ Austin Veterans Affairs Clinic
2901 Montopolis Dr.
Austin, TX 78741
Ph: (512)389-1010
URL: http://www.centraltexas.va.gov/visitors/austin.asp

Baird

32803 ■ Callahan County Behavioral Health
100 W 4th St., Ste. 305
Baird, TX 79504
Ph: (325)854-5995
URL: http://www.bhcmhmr.org/

Baytown

32804 ■ Mental Health/Mental Retardation Authority of Harris County
Bayshore Mental Health/Mental Retardation Center
2001 Cedar Bayou
Baytown, TX 77522
Ph: (281)427-8544
Fax: (281)970-6080
URL: http://www.mhmraharris.org/

Beaumont

32805 ■ Spindletop Mental Health/Mental Retardation Services
2750 S 8th St.
Beaumont, TX 77701
Ph: (409)839-1000
URL: http://www.spindletopmhmr.org/
Formerly: Life Resource Administration.

32806 ■ Spindletop Mental Health/Mental Retardation Services
Community Psychiatric Center
2750 S 8th St.
Beaumont, TX 77701
Ph: (409)839-2291
Fax: (409)839-1090
URL: http://www.spindletopmhmr.org/

Big Spring

32807 ■ Howard County Mental Health Center
319 Runnels St.
Big Spring, TX 79720
Ph: (432)263-0027
URL: http://www.wtcmhmr.org/

32808 ■ West Texas Veterans Affairs Healthcare System
Big Spring
300 Veterans Blvd.
Big Spring, TX 79720
Ph: (432)263-7361
Free: 800-472-1365
URL: http://www.bigspring.va.gov/

Borger

32809 ■ Borger Family Service Center
412 N Main St.
Borger, TX 79007
Ph: (806)274-2297
URL: http://www.tpmhmr.org/

Brenham

32810 ■ Mental Health/Mental Retardation Authority of Brazos Valley
Washington County
609 E Blue Bell Rd.
Brenham, TX 77833
Ph: (979)830-0008
URL: http://www.mhmrabv.org/

Brownfield

32811 ■ Terry County Mental Health Center
502 W Broadway St.
Brownfield, TX 79316
Ph: (806)637-3206
URL: http://www.wtcmhmr.org/

Brownwood

32812 ■ Central Texas Mental Health/Mental Retardation Center
Brady Work Activity Center
408 Mulberry St
Brownwood, TX 76801
Ph: (915)646-9574
URL: http://www.cflr.us/locations.html

32813 ■ Central Texas Mental Health/Mental Retardation Center
The Center for Life Resources
408 Mulberry St.
Brownwood, TX 76801
Ph: (325)646-9574
URL: http://www.cflr.us/locations.html

32814 ■ Central Texas Mental Health/Mental Retardation Center
Respite Care
408 Mulberry St.
Brownwood, TX 76804
Ph: (915)646-9574
URL: http://www.cflr.us/locations.html

32815 ■ Central Texas Mental Health/Mental Retardation Center
Supported Housing Program
408 Mulberry Dr.
Brownwood, TX 76804
Ph: (915)646-9574
URL: http://www.cflr.us/locations.html

Bryan

32816 ■ Mental Health/Mental Retardation Authority of Brazos Valley--Bryan
1504 S Texas Ave.
Bryan, TX 77802
Ph: (979)822-6467
URL: http://www.mhmrabv.org/locations.shtml

Cameron

32817 ■ Central Counties Center for Mental Health/Mental Retardation Services
Milam County
206 S Central
Cameron, TX 76520
Ph: (254)697-6631
Free: 800-888-4036
URL: http://006bb0a.netsolhost.com/dnn494/

Canton

32818 ■ Andrews Center--Canton
575 W Hwy. 243
Canton, TX 75103
Ph: (903)567-4197
Free: 800-256-5861
URL: http://www.andrewscenter.com/canton.htm

Carthage

32819 ■ Sabine Valley Regional Mental Health/Mental Retardation Center
Panola County Family Services
1701-A S Adams
Carthage, TX 75633
Ph: (903)693-7811

Cleburne

32820 ■ Johnson/Ellis/Navarro Mental Health/Mental Retardation Services
1601 N Anglin St.
Cleburne, TX 76031
Ph: (817)648-7133

Cleveland

32821 ■ Tri County Mental Health/Mental Retardation Services
406 N Washington Ave.
Cleveland, TX 77327
Ph: (281)432-3000
Fax: (281)593-3879
URL: http://www.tcmhmrs.org/

Colorado City

32822 ■ Mitchell County Mental Health Center
505 Chestnut St.
Colorado City, TX 79512
Ph: (325)728-3611
URL: http://www.wtcmhmr.org/

Comanche

32823 ■ Central Texas Mental Health/Mental Retardation Center
Comanche County
1009 S Austin
Comanche, TX 76442
Ph: (325)356-5090
URL: http://www.cflr.us/

Conroe

32824 ■ Tri-County Mental Health/Mental Retardation Services
1020 Riverwood Ct., Ste. 3
Conroe, TX 77304
Ph: (936)521-6100
URL: http://www.tcmhmrs.org/

Corpus Christi

32825 ■ Nueces County Mental Health/Mental Retardation Brownlee Square
Mental Health Services
1546 S Brownlee Blvd.
Corpus Christi, TX 78404
Ph: (361)886-6970
URL: http://www.ncmhmr.org

32826 ■ Nueces County Mental Health/Mental Retardation Center
212 S Staples
Corpus Christi, TX 78404
Ph: (361)888-8982
URL: http://www.ncmhmr.org

32827 ■ Nueces County Mental Health/Mental Retardation Center
Haroldson Group Home
450 Haroldson
Corpus Christi, TX 78412
Ph: (512)993-4552
URL: http://www.ncmhmr.org

32828 ■ Nueces County Mental Health/Mental Retardation Center
Princess Group Home
501 Princess
Corpus Christi, TX 78410
Ph: (512)241-0346
URL: http://www.ncmhmr.org

32829 ■ Nueces County Mental Health/Mental Retardation Center
Youth Services
3733 S Port
Corpus Christi, TX 78415
Ph: (361)851-6726
Fax: (361)851-8874
URL: http://www.ncmhmr.org

Crockett

32830 ■ Burke Center
Houston County Mental Health Center
1401 W Austin
Crockett, TX 75835
Ph: (936)544-8627
Formerly: Burke Center for Mental Health.

Dallas

32831 ■ Dallas Metrocare Child and Adolescent Mental Health
OP Services - Eastside Family Center
4701 Samuell Blvd.
Dallas, TX 75228
Ph: (214)381-7070
URL: http://www.metrocareservices.org/
Formerly: Child and Adolescent Mental Health Outpatient Services.

32832 ■ Dallas Metrocare
Lancaster-Kiest Clinic
3330 S Lancaster Rd.
Dallas, TX 75216
Ph: (214)371-6639
URL: http://www.metrocareservices.org/
Formerly: Adult Outpatient Clinic.

32833 ■ Dallas Metrocare
Lancaster-Kiest Clinic
Special Needs Offender Program
3330 S Lancaster Rd.
Annex Bldg.
Dallas, TX 75216
Ph: (214)371-6639
URL: http://www.metrocareservices.org/
Formerly: Adult Mental Health Psychosocial Rehabilitation Services Special Needs Offender Program.

32834 ■ Dallas Metrocare Services
1380 River Bend Dr.
Dallas, TX 75247-4914
Ph: (214)743-1200
URL: http://www.metrocareservices.org/
Formerly: Dallas County Mental Health/Mental Retardation Center.

32835 ■ Dallas Metrocare
Westmoreland Clinic
1350 N Westmoreland Rd.
Dallas, TX 75211
Ph: (214)330-0036
Fax: (214)337-3905
URL: http://www.metrocareservices.org/
Formerly: Adult Mental Health Outpatient Program.

32836 ■ Dallas Veterans Affairs Medical Center
4500 S Lancaster Rd.
Dallas, TX 75216
Ph: (800)849-3597
URL: http://www.northtexas.va.gov/

32837 ■ Hillside Center
1353 N Westmoreland Rd.
Dallas, TX 75211
Ph: (214)330-4777
URL: http://www.metrocareservices.org/

32838 ■ Metrocare Services
Westside Family Center
1350 N Westmoreland Rd.
Dallas, TX 75211
Ph: (214)330-0036
URL: http://www.metrocareservices.org/
Formerly: Child and Adolescent Mental Health Outpatient Services.

Denton

32839 ■ Denton County Mental Health/Mental Retardation Center--Denton
PO Box 2346
Denton, TX 76202
Ph: (940)381-5000
URL: http://www.dentonmhmr.org/

32840 ■ University Behavioral Health of Denton
2026 W University Dr.
Denton, TX 76201
Ph: (940)320-8100
Free: 888-320-8101
URL: http://www.ubhdenton.net/

Denver City

32841 ■ Yoakum County Mental Health Center
412 W 5th St.
Denver City, TX 79323
Ph: (806)592-8226
URL: http://www.wtcmhmr.org/

Dimmitt

32842 ■ Central Plains Center
Dimmitt Outpatient Clinic
109 NE 2nd St.
Dimmitt, TX 79027
Ph: (806)647-0109

Dumas

32843 ■ Dumas Center
500 E 1st St., Ste. 203
Dumas, TX 79029
Ph: (806)935-5691
URL: http://www.tpmhmr.org/

Edinburg

32844 ■ Edinburg Regional Medical Center
1102 W Trenton Rd.
Edinburg, TX 78539
Ph: (956)388-1300
URL: http://www.southtexashealthsystem.com/Facilities/Edinburg-Regional-Medical-Center

32845 ■ Tropical Texas Center for Mental Health/Mental Retardation
1901 S 24th Ave.
Edinburg, TX 78539
Ph: (956)289-7000
Free: 877-289-7199
URL: http://www.ttbh.org/ContactList.html

El Paso

32846 ■ El Paso Community Mental Health/Mental Retardation Center
1600 Montana Ave.
El Paso, TX 79902
Ph: (915)887-3410
Free: 877-562-6467
URL: http://www.epmhmr.org/
Formerly: Life Management Center Service.

32847 ■ El Paso Mental Health/Mental Retardation
Assertive Community Treatment
8281 N Loop Dr.
El Paso, TX 79907
Ph: (915)633-0506
URL: http://www.epmhmr.org/

32848 ■ El Paso Mental Health/Mental Retardation
East Valley Outpatient Services
8375 Burnham Rd.
El Paso, TX 79936
Ph: (915)599-6735
URL: http://www.epmhmr.org/

32849 ■ El Paso Mental Health/Mental Retardation
Mental Retardation Services
6500 Boeing, Ste. L100
El Paso, TX 79925
Ph: (915)772-4446
URL: http://www.epmhmr.org/

32850 ■ El Paso Mental Health/Mental Retardation
Solana Outpatient Services
3410 Morenci St.
El Paso, TX 79903
Ph: (915)562-5898
URL: http://www.epmhmr.org/

32851 ■ El Paso Veterans Affairs Healthcare System
5001 N Piedras
El Paso, TX 79930
Ph: (915)564-6100
Free: 800-672-3782
URL: http://www.elpaso.va.gov/

32852 ■ Family Service of El Paso
6040 Surety Dr.
El Paso, TX 79930
Ph: (915)781-9900
Fax: (915)781-9930
URL: http://www.familyserviceofelpaso.com

Floydada

32853 ■ Floydada Outpatient Clinic
100 S Main St., Rm. 206
Floydada, TX 79235
Ph: (806)983-2584
URL: http://www.clplains.org/

Fort Worth

32854 ■ Child Study Center
1300 W Lancaster Ave.
Fort Worth, TX 76102
Ph: (817)336-8611
URL: http://www.cscfw.org/

32855 ■ Circle Drive Clinic
1200 Circle Dr., Ste. 400B
Fort Worth, TX 76119
Ph: (817)569-4750
Fax: (817)569-4796
URL: http://www.mhmrtc.org/LOC/Locations.aspx-?service=5

32856 ■ Fair West Clinic
1527 Hemphill
Fort Worth, TX 76104
Ph: (817)569-5900
Fax: (817)569-5998
URL: http://www.mhmrtc.org/LOC/Locations.aspx?service=5

32857 ■ Jennings Place
815 S Jennings Ave.
Fort Worth, TX 76104
Ph: (817)569-5500
Fax: (817)569-5515
URL: http://www.mhmrtc.org/LOC/Locations.aspx?service=5

32858 ■ Main Street Clinic
1400 S Main
Fort Worth, TX 76104
Ph: (817)569-4700
URL: http://www.mhmrtc.org/LOC/Locations.aspx?service=5

32859 ■ Northwest Clinic
2400 NW 24th St.
Fort Worth, TX 76106
Ph: (817)569-5000
URL: http://www.mhmrtc.org/LOC/Locations.aspx?service=5

32860 ■ Penn Square Clinic
300 Pennsylvania
Fort Worth, TX 76104
Ph: (817)569-4555
URL: http://www.mhmrtc.org/LOC/Locations.aspx?service=5

Friona

32861 ■ Friona Outpatient Clinic
715 Main St.
Friona, TX 79035
Ph: (806)250-3522
URL: http://www.clplains.org/

Frisco

32862 ■ LifePath Systems
ECI Frisco
2611 Internet Blvd., No. 107
Frisco, TX 75034
Ph: (972)377-7289
URL: http://www.lifepathsystems.org/Contact.aspx

Galveston

32863 ■ Gulf Coast Center
123 Rosenberg, Ste. 6
Galveston, TX 77553
Ph: (409)763-2373
Free: 866-729-3848
Fax: (409)763-5538
URL: http://www.gcmhmr.com/

Gilmer

32864 ■ Sabine Valley Regional Mental Health/Mental Retardation Center
Sabine Valley Counseling
101-103 Madison
Gilmer, TX 75644
Ph: (903)843-5518
Formerly: Sabine Valley Counseling.

Graham

32865 ■ Helen Farabee Mental Health/Mental Retardation Center--Graham
1720 4th St.
Graham, TX 76450-2926
Ph: (940)549-4896
E-mail: atkinsr@helenfarabee.org
URL: http://www.helenfarabee.org/

Granbury

32866 ■ Pecan Valley Mental Health and Mental Retardation Clinic--Granbury
104 Pirate Dr.
Granbury, TX 76048
Ph: (817)573-2662
URL: http://www.pvmhmr.org/

Hamilton

32867 ■ Central Counties Center for Mental Health/Mental Retardation
Hamilton
101 Park Hill Dr.
Hamilton, TX 76531
Ph: (254)386-8179
URL: http://006bb0a.netsolhost.com/dnn494/
Formerly: Hamilton Mental Health Center.

Harlingen

32868 ■ Rio Grande State Center
1401 S Rangerville Rd.
Harlingen, TX 78552
Ph: (956)364-8000
URL: http://www.dshs.state.tx.us/mhhospitals/RioGrandeSC/default.shtm

32869 ■ Tropical Texas Center for Mental Health/Mental Retardation
Harlingen
1242 N 77 Sunshine Strip
Harlingen, TX 78550
Ph: (856)423-8094
URL: http://www.ttbh.org/

Hearne

32870 ■ Mental Health/Mental Retardation Authority of Brazos Valley
Robertson County
1212 W Brown St.
Hearne, TX 77859
Ph: (979)279-5193
URL: http://www.mhmrabv.org/locations.shtml

Hebbronville

32871 ■ Border Region Mental Health/Mental Retardation Center
Hebbronville
517 W Viggie
Hebbronville, TX 78361
Ph: (361)527-5771
URL: http://www.borderregion.org/

Henderson

32872 ■ Sabine Valley Regional Mental Health/Mental Retardation Center
Rusk County
209 N Main St.
Henderson, TX 75652
Ph: (903)241-7642

Hillsboro

32873 ■ Heart of Texas Region Mental Health/Mental Retardation Center
Hill County Center
130 N Covington St.
Hillsboro, TX 76645-2026
Ph: (254)582-3444
Fax: (254)582-0035
URL: http://www.hotrmhmr.org/

Houston

32874 ■ Depelchin Children's Center
Main Campus
4950 Memorial Dr.
Houston, TX 77007
Ph: (713)730-2335
Free: 888-730-2335
Fax: (713)802-3801
E-mail: info@depelchin.org
URL: http://www.depelchin.org

32875 ■ Harris County Psychiatric Center
University of Texas
3610 Willowbend, Ste. 1000
Houston, TX 77054
Ph: (713)500-8800
Fax: (713)500-8831
URL: http://hcpc.uth.tmc.edu/

32876 ■ Menninger Clinic
2801 Gessner Dr.
Houston, TX 77080
Ph: (713)275-5000
Free: 800-351-9058
URL: http://www.menningerclinic.com/

32877 ■ Mental Health/Mental Retardation Authority of Harris County
5901 Long Dr.
Houston, TX 77087
Ph: (713)970-4300
URL: http://www.mhmraharris.org/

32878 ■ Mental Health/Mental Retardation Authority of Harris County
Behavioral Training Program
5518 Jackson St.
Houston, TX 77004
Ph: (713)524-6034
URL: http://www.mhmraharris.org/

32879 ■ Mental Health/Mental Retardation Authority of Harris County
Branard Street
612 Branard St.
Houston, TX 77006
Ph: (713)970-7526
URL: http://www.mhmraharris.org/

32880 ■ Mental Health/Mental Retardation Authority of Harris County
Early Childhood Intervention South Team
6032 Airline
Houston, TX 77076
Ph: (713)970-4900
URL: http://www.mhmraharris.org/

32881 ■ Mental Health/Mental Retardation Authority of Harris County
New Day Treatment Program
3630 W Dallas
Houston, TX 77019
Ph: (713)970-4407
URL: http://www.mhmraharris.org/

32882 ■ Mental Health/Mental Retardation Authority of Harris County
Ripley Clinic
340 N Sidney
Houston, TX 77003
Ph: (713)970-8100
URL: http://www.mhmraharris.org/

32883 ■ Mental Health/Mental Retardation Authority of Harris County
Safe Haven
1215 Dennis St.
Houston, TX 77004
Ph: (713)658-0972
URL: http://www.mhmraharris.org/

32884 ■ University of Texas Mental Sciences Institute
1300 Moursund Ave.
Houston, TX 77030
Ph: (713)500-2500
Fax: (713)500-2530
URL: http://www.uthouston.edu/

Jasper

32885 ■ Burke Center--Jasper
15546 FM 777
Jasper, TX 75951
Ph: (409)384-6864
URL: http://www.burke-center.org/

Kermit

32886 ■ Winkler County Mental Health Center
821 Jeffee Dr.
Kermit, TX 79745
Ph: (432)586-2016
URL: http://www.wtcmhmr.org/

Kerrville

32887 ■ Kerrville Veterans Affairs Hospital
3600 Memorial Blvd.
Kerrville, TX 78028
Ph: (830)896-2020
Free: 866-487-1653
URL: http://www.southtexas.va.gov/

Killeen

32888 ■ Central Counties Center for Mental Health/Mental Retardation
100 East Ave. A
Killeen, TX 76541
Ph: (254)526-4146
Free: 800-888-4036
URL: http://006bb0a.netsolhost.com/dnn494/
Formerly: Killeen Mental Health Center.

Lamesa

32889 ■ Dawson County Mental Health Center
211 N Main Ave.
Lamesa, TX 79331
Ph: (806)872-5987
URL: http://www.wtcmhmr.org/

Lampasas

32890 ■ Central Counties Center for Mental Health/Mental Retardation
1305 S Key Ave., Ste. 203
Lampasas, TX 76550
Ph: (512)556-6962
URL: http://006bb0a.netsolhost.com/dnn494/
Formerly: Lampasas Mental Health Center.

Lancaster

32891 ■ Medical Center at Lancaster
2600 W Pleasant Run Rd.
Lancaster, TX 75146-1199
Ph: (972)299-5241

Laredo

32892 ■ Border Region MHMR Community Center
Laredo
1500 Pappas St.
Laredo, TX 78041
Ph: (956)794-3000
Fax: (956)794-3575
URL: http://www.borderregion.org
Formerly: Laredo State Center.

32893 ■ Child, Adolescent & Parent Service
1500 Pappas St.
Laredo, TX 78041
Ph: (956)527-5771
URL: http://www.borderregion.org/

32894 ■ Laredo Veterans Affairs Outpatient Clinic
6551 Star Ct.
Laredo, TX 78041
Ph: (956)523-7850
Free: 877-527-3361
URL: http://www.southtexas.va.gov/scd/Laredo.asp

Lewisville

32895 ■ Denton County Mental Health/Mental Retardation Center--Lewisville
101 E Corporate Dr., Ste. 150
Lewisville, TX 75067
Ph: (940)381-5000
URL: http://www.dentonmhmr.org/

Livingston

32896 ■ Burke Center Family Counseling Center
1100 Ogletree Dr.
Livingston, TX 77351
Ph: (936)327-3786
URL: http://www.burke-center.org/
Formerly: Burke Center for Mental Health.

Longview

32897 ■ Sabine Valley Regional Mental Health/Mental Retardation Center
Sabine Valley Center
107 Woodbine Pl.
Longview, TX 75601
Ph: (903)758-2471

Lubbock

32898 ■ Lubbock Regional Mental Health/Mental Retardation Center
1602 W 10th
Lubbock, TX 79408-2828
Ph: (806)766-0310
Free: 800-687-7581
Fax: (806)741-0913
URL: http://www.lrl.mhmr.state.tx.us

Lufkin

32899 ■ Burke Center--Lufkin
4101 S Medford Dr.
Lufkin, TX 75901
Ph: (409)639-1141
Fax: (936)634-8601
URL: http://www.burke-center.org

32900 ■ Burke Center for Mental Health County Mental Health Center
4103 S Medford
Lufkin, TX 75901
Ph: (936)639-2384
URL: http://www.burke-center.org

32901 ■ Family Counseling Associates--Lufkin
2001 S Medford Dr.
Lufkin, TX 75901
Ph: (936)633-5600

32902 ■ Peavy Switch Programs and Substance Abuse Services
3884 FM 2497
Lufkin, TX 75904
Ph: (936)634-5010
Formerly: Peavy Switch Recovery Center.

Marlin

32903 ■ Heart of Texas Region Mental Health/Mental Retardation Center
Falls County Center
365 Coleman
Marlin, TX 76661
Ph: (254)803-5971
URL: http://www.hotrmhmr.org/

Marshall

32904 ■ Sabine Valley Regional Mental Health/Mental Retardation Center
Marshall Family Services
401 N Grove St.
Marshall, TX 75670
Ph: (903)938-7721

McCamey

32905 ■ Upton County Mental Health Center
Burleson Ave.
McCamey, TX 79752
Ph: (432)652-8973
URL: http://www.wtcmhmr.org/

McKinney

32906 ■ Life Path Systems
1416 N Church St.
McKinney, TX 75069
Ph: (972)562-0190
URL: http://www.lifepathsystems.org/

32907 ■ Medical Center of McKinney Behavioral Health
130 S Central Expressway
McKinney, TX 75070
Ph: (972)547-8888
URL: http://medicalcenterofmckinney.com/our-services/services-a-z/behavioral-med icine.dot

Meridian

32908 ■ Heart of Texas Region Mental Health/Mental Retardation Center
Bosque County Center
407 S Hill St
Meridian, TX 76665
Ph: (254)435-2211
URL: http://www.hotrmhmr.org/

Mesquite

32909 ■ Child and Family Guidance Center, Mesquite
120 W Main St., Ste. 220
Mesquite, TX 75149
Ph: (214)351-3490
URL: http://www.childrenandfamilies.info

Midland

32910 ■ Permian Basin Community Centers for Mental Health/Mental Retardation
1403 E Front St.
Midland, TX 79701
Ph: (432)570-3411
URL: http://www.pbmhmr.com/

Mineola

32911 ■ Andrews Center--Mineola
703 W Patten St.
Mineola, TX 75773
Ph: (903)569-5409
URL: http://www.andrewscenter.com/

Mineral Wells

32912 ■ Mineral Wells Clinic
244 Gorgas St.
Mineral Wells, TX 76067
Ph: (940)325-9541
URL: http://www.pvmhmr.org/

Monahans

32913 ■ Ward County Mental Health Center
1200 N Main Ave.
Monahans, TX 79756
Ph: (432)943-2875
URL: http://www.wtcmhmr.org/

Nacogdoches

32914 ■ Burke Center
Nacogdoches Mental Health Center
4632 NE Stalling, Ste. 100
Nacogdoches, TX 75961
Ph: (936)558-6200
URL: http://www.burke-center.org/

32915 ■ Family Counseling Associates--Nacogdoches
1329 N University Dr., Ste. E-5
Nacogdoches, TX 75961
Ph: (936)564-5777
URL: http://www.burke-center.org

Navasota

32916 ■ Mental Health/Mental Retardation Authority of Brazos Valley
Grimes County Outpatient Program
702 Lasalle St.
Navasota, TX 77868
Ph: (936)825-7969
URL: http://www.mhmrabv.org/locations.shtml

Odessa

32917 ■ Odessa Mental Health/Mental Retardation Center
1012 MacArthur Ave.
Odessa, TX 79763
Ph: (432)333-3265

Orange

32918 ■ Orange Outpatient Services
4305 N Tejas Pkwy.
Orange, TX 77630
Ph: (409)883-3864
URL: http://www.spindletopmhmr.org/

32919 ■ Spindletop Mental Health/Mental Retardation Services
Orange
4305 N Tejas Pkwy.
Orange, TX 77630
Ph: (409)883-2973
URL: http://www.spindletopmhmr.org/

Paris

32920 ■ Lakes Regional Mental Health/Mental Retardation Center--Paris
395 N Main
Paris, TX 75460
Ph: (903)737-2475
URL: http://www.lrmhmrc.org/

Pecos

32921 ■ Reeves County Mental Health Center
700 W Daggett St.
Pecos, TX 79772
Ph: (432)447-2628
URL: http://www.wtcmhmr.org/

Plainview

32922 ■ Central Plains Center for Mental Health/Mental Retardation
2700 Yonkers St.
Plainview, TX 79072-1826
Ph: (806)293-2636
URL: http://www.clplains.org/

32923 ■ Central Plains Center for Mental Health/Mental Retardation
Children's Development Center
631 Broadway
Plainview, TX 79072
Ph: (806)291-4416
URL: http://www.clplains.org/

32924 ■ Central Plains Center for Mental Health/Mental Retardation
New Horizons
602 W 6th
Plainview, TX 79072
Ph: (806)291-4425
URL: http://www.clplains.org/

32925 ■ Central Plains Center for Mental Health/Mental Retardation
Plainview Outpatient Clinic
715 Houston
Plainview, TX 79072-7905
Ph: (806)296-2726
URL: http://www.clplains.org/

Plano

32926 ■ Child and Family Guidance Center, Plano
4031 W Plano Pkwy., Ste. 211
Plano, TX 75093
Ph: (214)351-3490
URL: http://www.childrenandfamilies.info

32927 ■ Life Path Systems
3920 Alma Dr.
Plano, TX 75023
Ph: (972)422-5939
URL: http://www.lifepathsystems.org/

32928 ■ Presbyterian Hospital of Plano
Seay Behavioral Health Center
6110 W Parker Rd.
Plano, TX 75093
Ph: (972)981-8301
URL: http://www.texashealth.org/body.cfm?id=986

Port Arthur

32929 ■ Spindletop Mental Health/Mental Retardation Services
South County Outpatient Services
3407 57th St.
Port Arthur, TX 77640
Ph: (409)813-8300
Free: 800-317-5809
Fax: (409)983-6139
URL: http://www.spindletopmhmr.org/MHMR_Contacts.html

Post

32930 ■ Garza County Mental Health Center
E 7th & Ave. C
Post, TX 79356
Ph: (806)495-2813
URL: http://www.wtcmhmr.org/

Quanah

32931 ■ Helen Farabee Mental Health/Mental Retardation Center--Quanah
510 King St.
Quanah, TX 79252
Ph: (940)663-3566
URL: http://www.helenfarabee.org/

Richmond

32932 ■ DePelchin children's Center--Richmond
710 S 7th St.
Richmond, TX 77469
Ph: (281)342-4906
URL: http://www.depelchin.org/

Rio Grande City

32933 ■ Border Region Mental Health/Mental Retardation
Rio Grande
600 N Garza, Bldg C
Rio Grande City, TX 78582
Ph: (956)487-3748

Robstown

32934 ■ Nueces County Mental Health/Mental Retardation Services
Robstown Outpatient Clinic
102 N 4th St.
Robstown, TX 78380
Ph: (361)387-3588
URL: http://www.ncmhmr.org/

Rockwell

32935 ■ LifePath Systems
ECI Rockwell
1205 A Ridge Rd.
Rockwell, TX 75087
Ph: (972)722-7016
URL: http://www.lifepathsystems.org/Contact.aspx

Rosenberg

32936 ■ Texana Center
4910 Airport Ave.
Rosenberg, TX 77471
Ph: (281)239-1300
URL: http://www.texanacenter.com/

Round rock

32937 ■ Bluebonnet Trails Community Services
1009 N Georgetown St.
Round rock, TX 78664
Ph: (512)255-1720
Free: 800-841-1255
Fax: (512)244-8403
URL: http://www.bluebonnetmhmr.org

San Angelo

32938 ■ Mental Health/Mental Retardation Services for the Concho Valley
1501 W Beauregard Ave.
San Angelo, TX 76901
Ph: (325)658-7750
URL: http://www.mhmrcv.org/

San Antonio

32939 ■ Audie L. Murphy Veterans Affairs Hospital
7400 Merton Minter
San Antonio, TX 78229
Ph: (210)617-5300
Free: 877-469-5300
URL: http://www.southtexas.va.gov/

32940 ■ The Center for Health Care Services
3031 W Interstate 10
San Antonio, TX 78201
Ph: (210)731-1300
Fax: (210)731-1315
URL: http://www.chcsbc.org/

32941 ■ The Center for Health Care Services
Eastside Multiservice Unit
1920 Burnet St.
San Antonio, TX 78202
Ph: (210)227-3401
URL: http://www.chcsbc.org/

32942 ■ The Center for Health Care Services
Psychiatric Emergency Services/Multi Service Center
527 N Leona, Bldg. C
San Antonio, TX 78207
Ph: (210)225-5481
URL: http://www.chcsbc.org/

32943 ■ The Center for Health Care Services
Westside Multiservice Center
806 S Zarzamora
San Antonio, TX 78207
Ph: (210)434-7001
URL: http://www.chcsbc.org/

32944 ■ Southwest Mental Health Center
8535 Tom Slick Dr.
San Antonio, TX 78229
Ph: (210)616-0300
URL: http://www.smhc.org/

San Augustine

32945 ■ Burke Center
497 Brown St.
San Augustine, TX 75935
Ph: (936)598-6191
URL: http://www.burke-center.org/

San Saba

32946 ■ Central Texas Mental Health/Mental Retardation Center
San Saba/Mills
111 N Cherokee St.
San Saba, TX 76877
Ph: (325)372-5688

Seminole

32947 ■ Gaines County Mental Health Center
702 Hobbs Hwy.
Seminole, TX 79360
Ph: (432)758-4028
URL: http://www.wtcmhmr.org/

Snyder

32948 ■ Scurry County Mental Health Center
909 25th St.
Snyder, TX 79549
Ph: (325)573-4947
URL: http://www.wtcmhmr.org/

Stephenville

32949 ■ Pecan Valley Mental Health and Mental Retardation Center--Stephenville
650 W Green St.
Stephenville, TX 76401
Ph: (254)965-7806
URL: http://www.pvmhmr.org/

32950 ■ Stephenville Clinic
906 Lingleville Hwy.
Stephenville, TX 76401
Ph: (254)968-4181
URL: http://www.pvmhmr.org/

Sulphur Springs

32951 ■ Lakes Regional Mental Health/Mental Retardation Center--Sulphur Springs
1400 College St., Ste. 204
Sulphur Springs, TX 75482
Ph: (903)885-8611
URL: http://www.lrmhmrc.org/

Sweetwater

32952 ■ West Texas Centers for Mental Health/Mental Retardation
1401 Hailey St.
Sweetwater, TX 79556
Ph: (325)236-6619
URL: http://www.wtcmhmr.org/

Temple

32953 ■ Central Counties Center for Mental Health/Mental Retardation
304 S 22nd St.
Temple, TX 76501-4726
Ph: (254)298-7000
URL: http://006bb0a.netsolhost.com/dnn494/

32954 ■ Olin E. Teague Veterans Affairs Medical Center
1901 Veterans Memorial Dr.
Temple, TX 76504
Ph: (254)778-4811
Free: 800-423-2111
URL: http://www.centraltexas.va.gov/

Texarkana

32955 ■ Wadley Inspirations
1002 Texas Blvd., Ste. 320
Texarkana, TX 75501
Ph: (903)831-7585
URL: http://www.wadleyhealth.com/inspirations.asp

Texas City

32956 ■ The Gulf Coast Center--Texas City
7510 FM 1765
Texas City, TX 77591
Ph: (409)935-6083
URL: http://www.gcmhmr.com/

Tulia

32957 ■ Central Plains Center - Tulia Satellite
229 S Bowie Ave.
Tulia, TX 79088
Ph: (806)995-4337
URL: http://www.clplains.org/

Tyler

32958 ■ Andrews Center--Tyler
2323 W Front St.
Tyler, TX 75702
Ph: (903)597-1351
Free: 800-374-6058
URL: http://www.andrewscenter.com/

32959 ■ Tyler Veterans Affairs Primary Care Clinic
3414 Golden Rd.
Tyler, TX 75701
Ph: (903)590-3050
Free: 800-849-3597
URL: http://www2.va.gov/directory/guide/facility.asp?ID=5398&dnum=All

Victoria

32960 ■ Devereux Texas Treatment Network
120 David Wade Dr.
Victoria, TX 77902
Ph: (361)575-8271
Free: 800-383-5000
URL: http://www.devereux.org/

32961 ■ Gulf Bend Mental Health/Mental Retardation Center
6502 Nursery Dr., Ste. 100
Victoria, TX 77904
Ph: (361)575-0611
Free: 800-421-8825
URL: http://www.gulfbend.org

Waco

32962 ■ Heart of Texas Region Mental Health/Mental Retardation Center
Waco
110 S 12th St.
Waco, TX 76703-1810
Ph: (254)752-3451
URL: http://www.hotrmhmr.org/

32963 ■ Waco Veterans Affairs Medical Center
4800 Memorial Dr.
Waco, TX 76711
Ph: (254)752-6581
Free: 800-423-2111
URL: http://www.centraltexas.va.gov/

Waxahachie

32964 ■ Johnson/Ellis/Navarro Mental Health Mental Retardation
Ellis County Clinic
116 N Rogers St.
Waxahachie, TX 75164
Ph: (972)937-7660

Weatherford

32965 ■ Pecan Valley Mental Health and Mental Retardation Clinic--Weatherford
1715 Santa Fe Dr.
Weatherford, TX 76086
Ph: (817)599-9337
URL: http://www.pvmhmr.org/

Weslaco

32966 ■ Tropical Texas Behavioral Health Mid-Valley
601 W 6th St.
Weslaco, TX 78596
Ph: (956)968-8551
URL: http://www.ttbh.org/
Formerly: Mid-Valley Mental Health Center; Tropical Texas Center for Mental Health/Mental Retardation.

Wichita Falls

32967 ■ Helen Farabee Mental Health/Mental Retardation Center--Wichita Falls
1000 Brook St.
Wichita Falls, TX 76301
Ph: (940)397-3143
URL: http://www.helenfarabee.org/

Winters

32968 ■ Runnels County Mental Health Center
126 State St.
Winters, TX 79567
Ph: (325)754-5591
URL: http://www.wtcmhmr.org/

Zapata

32969 ■ Zapata Mental Health Center
101 1st St.
Zapata, TX 78076
Ph: (956)765-9664
URL: http://www.borderregion.org/

UTAH

Blanding

32970 ■ San Juan Mental Health
356 S Main St.
Blanding, UT 84511-2707
Ph: (435)678-2992
URL: http://www.sanjuancounty.org/

Bountiful

32971 ■ Davis County Mental Health Center
Bountiful Mental Health Clinic
470 E Medical Dr.
Bountiful, UT 84010-4928
Ph: (801)298-3446
URL: http://www.dbhutah.org/facilities.htm

Brigham City

32972 ■ Bear River Mental Health Center
Brigham City House
625 South 300 E
Brigham City, UT 84302-2910
Ph: (435)723-3176
URL: http://brmh.com/
Formerly: The Rainbow Club.

32973 ■ Bear River Mental Health Services--Brigham City
663 W 950 S
Brigham City, UT 84302
Ph: (435)734-9449
URL: http://brmh.com/

Castle Dale

32974 ■ Four Corners Community Behavioral Health--Castle Dale
45 E 100 South
Castle Dale, UT 84513
Ph: (435)381-2432
URL: http://www.fourcorners.ws/

Delta

32975 ■ Central Utah Counseling Center--Delta
51 N Center St.
Delta, UT 84624
Ph: (435)864-3073
Free: 888-343-3073
URL: http://www.cucc.us/

Draper

32976 ■ Youth Care, Inc.
PO Box 909
Draper, UT 84020
Ph: (801)572-6989
Free: 800-786-4924
URL: http://www.youthcare.com/

Duchesne

32977 ■ Northeastern Counseling Center--Duchesne
50 W 200 S St.
Duchesne, UT 84021
Ph: (435)738-5512

Eagle Mountain

32978 ■ Ark of Little Cottonwood
2590 Prairie View Dr.
Eagle Mountain, UT 84005
Ph: (801)733-0200
URL: http://arkrecovery.com

Ephraim

32979 ■ Central Utah Mental Health/Substance Abuse Center--Ephraim
390 W 100 North
Ephraim, UT 84627
Ph: (435)283-4065
Free: 877-283-4065
URL: http://www.cucc.us/

Escalante

32980 ■ Turn About Ranch
280 N 300 E
Escalante, UT 84726
Ph: (435)826-4240
Free: 800-842-1165
Fax: (435)826-4261
URL: http://www.turnaboutranch.com

Farmington

32981 ■ Davis Mental Health/A and D Services
Davis Behavioral Health
291 South 200 W
Farmington, UT 84025-2421
Ph: (801)451-7799
URL: http://www.dbhutah.org/

Junction

32982 ■ Central Utah Mental Health/Substance Abuse Center--Junction
Piute County Courthouse
550 N Main St.
Junction, UT 84740
Ph: (435)577-2055
Free: 800-742-9070
URL: http://www.cucc.us/junction.htm

Layton

32983 ■ Davis Behavioral Health
Layton Comprehensive Treatment Program
2250 Robins Dr.
Layton, UT 84041-1140
Ph: (801)773-7060
URL: http://www.dbhutah.org/

Logan

32984 ■ Bear River Mental Health Center Group Home
1115 N Main St.
Logan, UT 84321
Ph: (435)753-7053
URL: http://brmh.com/

32985 ■ Bear River Mental Health Services, Inc.--Logan
90 E 200 North
Logan, UT 84321
Ph: (435)752-0750
URL: http://brmh.com/

Midvale

32986 ■ Highland Ridge Hospital
7309 S 180 West
Midvale, UT 84047
Ph: (801)569-2153
URL: http://www.highlandridgehospital.com/

32987 ■ Oqirrh Ridge - East
6856 S 700 East
Midvale, UT 84047
Ph: (801)565-1267

32988 ■ Valley Mental Health Center
South Valley Unit
7434 S State St.
Midvale, UT 84047
Ph: (801)566-4423
URL: http://www.valleymentalhealth.org/

Moab

32989 ■ Four Corners Community Behavioral Health--Moab
198 E Center St.
Moab, UT 84532
Ph: (435)259-6131
URL: http://www.fourcorners.ws/

Mount Pleasant

32990 ■ Central Utah Mental Health Center--S State Street, Mount Pleasant
125 S State St.
Mount Pleasant, UT 84647
Ph: (435)462-2421
Free: 800-523-7412
URL: http://www.cucc.us/

32991 ■ Central Utah Mental Health Center--W Main Street, Mount Pleasant
255 W Main St.
Mount Pleasant, UT 84647
Ph: (435)462-2416
Free: 800-523-7412
URL: http://www.cucc.us/

Murray

32992 ■ Valley Mental Health - Community Treatment Program
3944 S 400 East
Murray, UT 84107
Ph: (801)261-1442
URL: http://www.valleymentalhealth.org/

Nephi

32993 ■ Central Utah Mental Health Center--Nephi
656 N Main St.
Nephi, UT 84648
Ph: (435)623-1456
Free: 888-859-3674
URL: http://www.cucc.us/

Ogden

32994 ■ South Ogden Veterans Affairs Clinic
982 Chambers St.
Ogden, UT 84403
Ph: (801)479-4105
URL: http://www2.va.gov/directory/guide/facility.asp?ID=876&dnum=1

32995 ■ Weber Human Services
237 26th St.
Ogden, UT 84401
Ph: (801)625-3700
URL: http://www.weberhs.org/home/

32996 ■ Weber Human Services
Day Treatment
238 27th St.
Ogden, UT 84401
Ph: (801)625-3625
URL: http://www.weberhs.org/home/

32997 ■ Weber Human Services
Men's Residential
2765 Madison Ave.
Ogden, UT 84403
Ph: (801)625-3749
URL: http://www.weberhs.org/home/

32998 ■ Weber Human Services
Women's Residential
2695 Childs Ave.
Ogden, UT 84401
Ph: (801)625-3600
URL: http://www.weberhs.org/home/

32999 ■ Weber Human Services
Youth Residential
210 27th St.
Ogden, UT 84401
Ph: (801)625-3767
URL: http://www.weberhs.org/home/

Orem

33000 ■ Orem Veterans Affairs Clinic
740 W 800 North, Ste. 440
Orem, UT 84057
Ph: (801)235-0953
URL: http://www.saltlakecity.va.gov/orem_cboc.asp

Paradise

33001 ■ Avalon Hills
8530 S 500 West
Paradise, UT 84328
Ph: (435)245-4537
Free: 800-330-0490
URL: http://www.avalonhills.org/

Park City

33002 ■ Valley Mental Health Center
Summit County Office
1753 Sidewinder Dr., Ste. 200
Park City, UT 84060
Ph: (435)649-9079
URL: http://www.valleymentalhealth.org/

Payson

33003 ■ Mountain View Hospital
1000 E 100 North
Payson, UT 84651
Ph: (801)465-7000
URL: http://www.mvhpayson.com/

Petersboro

33004 ■ Avalon Hills
7852 W 600 North
Petersboro, UT 84325
Ph: (435)753-3686
Free: 800-330-0490
URL: http://www.avalonhills.org/

Price

33005 ■ Four Corners Community Behavioral Health--Price
575 E 100 South
Price, UT 84501
Ph: (435)637-2358
URL: http://www.fourcorners.ws/

Provo

33006 ■ Wasatch Mental Health Center
750 N Freedom Blvd.
Provo, UT 84601
Ph: (801)373-4760
URL: http://www.wasatch.org

33007 ■ Wasatch Mental Health Youth Services
Park View School
1161 E 300 N
Provo, UT 84606
Ph: (801)373-4765
Fax: (801)375-4045
E-mail: watsatch.dwilliam@state.ut.us
URL: http://www.wasatch.org

Randolph

33008 ■ Bear River Mental Health Services--Randolph
275 N Main St.
Randolph, UT 84064
Free: 800-620-9949
URL: http://brmh.com/pages/locations.html

Richfield

33009 ■ Central Utah Counseling Center--Richfield
255 S Main
Richfield, UT 84701
Ph: (435)896-8236
Free: 800-742-9070
URL: http://www.cucc.us/richfield.htm

Roosevelt

33010 ■ Northeastern Counseling Center--Roosevelt
285 W 800 South
Roosevelt, UT 84066
Ph: (435)725-6300

Saint George

33011 ■ Dixie Regional Medical Center
544 S 400 East
Saint George, UT 84770
Ph: (435)688-4000
URL: http://intermountainhealthcare.org/hospitals/dixie/Pages/home.aspx

33012 ■ Saint George Veterans Affairs Clinic
1067 E Tabernacle, Ste. 7
Saint George, UT 84770
Ph: (435)634-7608
URL: http://www2.va.gov/directory/guide/facility.asp?ID=881&dnum=1

Salt Lake City

33013 ■ Alliance House
1724 S Main St.
Salt Lake City, UT 84115
Ph: (801)486-5012
E-mail: alliancehouselc@yahoo.com
URL: http://www.alliancehouse.org/homepage.asp

33014 ■ George E. Wahlen Veterans Affairs Medical Center
500 Foothill Dr.
Salt Lake City, UT 84148
Ph: (801)582-1565
URL: http://www.saltlakecity.va.gov/

33015 ■ University of Utah Neuropsychiatric Institute
501 Chipeta Way
Salt Lake City, UT 84108
Ph: (801)583-2500
URL: http://healthcare.utah.edu/UNI/

33016 ■ Valley Mental Health Center
Adolescent Day Care Program
4351 S Redwood Rd.
Salt Lake City, UT 84123
Ph: (801)263-6103
URL: http://www.valleymentalhealth.org/

33017 ■ Valley Mental Health Center
Adult Day Treatment Program
145 E 1300 South, Ste. 601
Salt Lake City, UT 84115
Ph: (801)536-6500
URL: http://www.valleymentalhealth.org/

33018 ■ Valley Mental Health Center
Children's Behavior Therapy Unit
780 S Guardsman Way
Salt Lake City, UT 84108
Ph: (801)581-0194
URL: http://www.valleymentalhealth.org/

33019 ■ Valley Mental Health Center
North Valley Unit
1020 S Main, Ste. 100
Salt Lake City, UT 84101
Ph: (801)539-7000
Fax: (801)539-7050
URL: http://www.valleymentalhealth.org/

33020 ■ Valley Mental Health Center--Salt Lake City
5965 S 900 East, Ste. 420
Salt Lake City, UT 84121-1794
Ph: (801)263-7100
URL: http://www.valleymentalhealth.org/

Sandy

33021 ■ The Ark of Little Cottonwood
2919 E Granite Hollow
Sandy, UT 84092
Ph: (801)733-0200
Free: 800-840-8098
URL: http://www.thearkoflittlecottonwood.com/

Syracuse

33022 ■ Aspen Institute for Behavioral Assessment
2732 W 2700 South
Syracuse, UT 84075
Ph: (801)825-5222
Free: 877-808-3088
URL: http://www.aspenassessment.com/

Tooele

33023 ■ Valley Mental Health--Tooele County Office
100 S 1000 West
Tooele, UT 84074
Ph: (435)843-3520
URL: http://www.valleymentalhealth.org/

Tremonton

33024 ■ Bear River Mental Health Center--Tremonton
18 N 200 East
Tremonton, UT 84337
Ph: (435)257-2168
URL: http://brmh.com/

Vernal

33025 ■ Northeastern Counseling Center--Vernal
1140 W 500 South
Vernal, UT 84078
Ph: (435)789-6300

Woods Cross

33026 ■ Benchmark Behavioral Health System
592 W 1350 South
Woods Cross, UT 84087
Ph: (801)299-5300
URL: http://www.psysolutions.com/facilities/benchmark/

VERMONT

Barre

33027 ■ South Main Street Group Home
285 S Main St.
Barre, VT 05641
Ph: (802)479-2949

33028 ■ Washington County Mental Health Center
Arioli Avenue Intermediate Care Program
15 Arioli Ave.
Barre, VT 05641
Ph: (802)479-1439
URL: http://www.wcmhs.org/

33029 ■ Washington County Mental Health Center
Kynock Street Intermediate Care
13 Kynock St.
Barre, VT 05641
Ph: (802)479-1339
URL: http://www.wcmhs.org/

Bellows Falls

33030 ■ Health Care and Rehabilitation Services of Southeastern Vermont--Bellows Falls
1 Hospital Ct., Ste. 410
Bellows Falls, VT 05101
Ph: (802)463-3947
Free: 800-622-4235
Fax: (802)463-1202
E-mail: bellowsfallsoffice@hcrs.org
URL: http://www.hcrs.org

Bennington

33031 ■ Autumn House
141 S Branch St.
Bennington, VT 05201
Ph: (802)442-1243
URL: http://www.ucsvt.org/

33032 ■ Mental Health Group Home
329 South St.
Bennington, VT 05201
Ph: (802)442-4679
URL: http://www.ucsvt.org/

33033 ■ Mental Retardation Group Home
215 Union St.
Bennington, VT 05201
Ph: (802)442-2233
URL: http://www.ucsvt.org/

33034 ■ Mental Retardation/ICF Group Home
348 Dewey St.
Bennington, VT 05201
Ph: (802)447-0860
URL: http://www.ucsvt.org/

33035 ■ United Counseling Service of Bennington County
100 Ledge Hill Dr.
Bennington, VT 05201
Ph: (802)442-5491
E-mail: ucs@ucsvt.org
URL: http://www.ucsvt.org

33036 ■ Veterans Affairs Bennington Community Based Outpatient Clinic
186 North St.
Bennington, VT 05201
Ph: (802)447-6913
Fax: (802)442-2137
URL: http://www.whiteriver.va.gov/visitors/bennington_cboc.asp

Berlin

33037 ■ Washington County Mental Health--Berlin
286 Hospital loop
Berlin, VT 05602
Ph: (802)229-0591
URL: http://www.wcmhs.org/

Bradford

33038 ■ Clara Martin Center--Bradford
1483 Lower Plain Rd.
Bradford, VT 05033
Ph: (802)222-4477
Free: 800-639-6360
URL: http://www.claramartin.org/

Brattleboro

33039 ■ Health Care and Rehabilitation Services
Community Rehabilitation Treatment
29 Elm St.
Brattleboro, VT 05301
Ph: (802)254-7511
E-mail: brattleborocrtoffice@hcrs.org
URL: http://www.hcrs.org/

33040 ■ Health Care and Rehabilitation Services of Southeastern Vermont--Brattleboro
51 Fairview St.
Brattleboro, VT 05301
Ph: (802)254-6028
URL: http://www.hcrs.org/

33041 ■ Retreat Healthcare
Anna Marsh Ln.
Brattleboro, VT 05302
Ph: (802)257-7785
Free: 800--RETREAT
URL: http://www.brattlebororetreat.org/

Bristol

33042 ■ Counseling Service of Addison County--Bristol
14 School St.
Bristol, VT 05443
Ph: (802)453-3009
URL: http://www.csac-vt.org/

Burlington

33043 ■ Baird Center for Children and Families
1138 Pine St.
Burlington, VT 05401
Ph: (802)488-6600
URL: http://www.howardcenter.org/

33044 ■ Howard Center for Human Services--Burlington
208 Flynn Ave., Ste. 3J
Burlington, VT 05401
Ph: (802)660-3678
Fax: (802)488-6901
URL: http://www.howardcenter.org/

33045 ■ Howard Center for Human Services
Howard Community Services
300 Flynn Ave.
Burlington, VT 05401
Ph: (802)488-6000

33046 ■ Howard Center for Human Services
Pine Street Counseling Center
855 Pine St.
Burlington, VT 05401
Ph: (802)658-0404
Fax: (802)865-6117
URL: http://www.howardcenter.org/

33047 ■ Howard Center for Human Services
Westview House
50 S Willard St.
Burlington, VT 05401
Ph: (802)658-3323
URL: http://www.howardcenter.org/

Chelsea

33048 ■ Chelsea Health Center
356 Vermont Rte. 110
Chelsea, VT 05038
Ph: (802)685-4859
Fax: (802)685-4869
URL: http://www.claramartin.org/contactus/service_locations

Colchester

33049 ■ Veterans Affairs Outpatient Clinic at Fort Ethan Allen
163 Hegeman Ave., Unit 100
Colchester, VT 05446
Ph: (802)655-1356
Fax: (802)655-1231
URL: http://www.whiteriver.va.gov/visitors/colchester_cboc.asp

Essex Junction

33050 ■ Howard Center for Human Services
Group Home
39 Lincoln St.
Essex Junction, VT 05452
Ph: (802)879-0832
URL: http://www.howardcenter.org/

Hardwick

33051 ■ Northeast Kingdom Human Services
144 Main St.
Hardwick, VT 05843
Ph: (802)472-6581
URL: http://www.nkhs.org/

Hartford

33052 ■ Health Care and Rehabilitation Services
Hartford Region Office
49 School St.
Hartford, VT 05047
Ph: (802)295-3031
E-mail: hartfordoffice@hcrs.org
URL: http://www.hcrs.org/

Middlebury

33053 ■ Counseling Service of Addison County
89 Main St.
Middlebury, VT 05753
Ph: (802)388-6751
Fax: (802)388-3108
URL: http://www.csac-vt.org/main.html

33054 ■ Counseling Service of Addison County
Community Support Services
89 Main St.
Middlebury, VT 05753
Ph: (802)388-6751
URL: http://www.csac-vt.org/

33055 ■ Counseling Service
Addison County Group Home
907 Foote St.
Middlebury, VT 05753
Ph: (802)388-3423
URL: http://www.csac-vt.org/

33056 ■ Counseling Service of Addison
Family Advocate Project
89 Main St.
Middlebury, VT 05753
Ph: (802)388-6751
URL: http://www.csac-vt.org/

33057 ■ Counseling Services of Addison County
Mental Health Services
89 Main St.
Middlebury, VT 05753
Ph: (802)388-6751
Fax: (802)388-8183
URL: http://www.csac-vt.org

33058 ■ Counseling Services of Addison
Outpatient Mental Health Services
89 Main St
Middlebury, VT 05753
Ph: (802)388-6751
Fax: (802)388-3108
URL: http://www.csac-vt.org

33059 ■ Men's Group Home
45 Seminary St.
Middlebury, VT 05753
Ph: (802)388-2091

33060 ■ Women's Group Home
15 Elm St.
Middlebury, VT 05753
Ph: (802)388-7706

Montpelier

33061 ■ Saint Paul Street Group Home
7 St. Paul St.
Montpelier, VT 05602
Ph: (802)229-5084

33062 ■ Sunrise House
157 Barre St.
Montpelier, VT 05602
Ph: (802)223-7544

33063 ■ Washington County Mental Health Center
Children and Youth Services
9 Heaton St.
Montpelier, VT 05602
Ph: (802)229-0586
URL: http://www.wcmhs.org/

33064 ■ Washington County Mental Health Center
Group Home
62 Barre St.
Montpelier, VT 05602
Ph: (802)229-4109
URL: http://www.wcmhs.org/

33065 ■ Washington County Mental Health Center--Montpelier
174 Hospital Loop
Montpelier, VT 05602
Ph: (802)229-0591
Fax: (802)223-8623
E-mail: kittyw@wcmhs.org
URL: http://www.wcmhs.org

Morrisville

33066 ■ Lamoille County Mental Health Service
520 Washington Hwy.
Morrisville, VT 05661
Ph: (802)888-4914

33067 ■ Lamoille County Mental Health Service
Day Treatment Program
275 Brooklyn St.
Morrisville, VT 05661
Ph: (802)888-5026

33068 ■ Lamoille County Mental Health Service
Intensive Family-Based Service
520 Washington Hwy.
Morrisville, VT 05661
Ph: (802)888-4914

Newport

33069 ■ Northeast Kingdom Mental Health Service--Newport
154 Duchess Ave.
Newport, VT 05855
Ph: (802)334-6744
Free: 800-696-4979
URL: http://www.nkhs.org

Randolph

33070 ■ Clara Martin Center--Randolph
11 N Main St.
Randolph, VT 05060
Ph: (802)728-4466
URL: http://www.claramartin.org/

Rutland

33071 ■ Community Access Program of Rutland
1 Scale Ave., Bldg. 18
Rutland, VT 05701
Ph: (802)775-0828
URL: http://www.rmhsccn.org/

33072 ■ Rutland Area Community Service
78 S Main St.
Rutland, VT 05701
Ph: (802)775-8224
URL: http://www.rmhsccn.org/

33073 ■ Rutland Area Community Service
Group Home
2 Westview Ct.
Rutland, VT 05701
Ph: (802)775-2381
URL: http://www.rmhsccn.org/

Saint Albans

33074 ■ Northwestern Counseling and Support Services
107 Fisher Pond Rd.
Saint Albans, VT 05478
Ph: (802)524-6554
Free: 800-834-7793
Fax: (802)527-7801
URL: http://www.ncssinc.org/default.asp?Key=1
Remarks: A HUD funded transitional house for homeless adults with severe and persistent mental illness.

33075 ■ Northwestern Counseling and Support Services
Group Home
22 Upper Weldon St.
Saint Albans, VT 05478
Ph: (802)524-0568
URL: http://www.ncssinc.org/default.asp?Key=1

Saint Johnsbury

33076 ■ Northeast Kingdom Mental Health Service--Saint Johnsbury
2225 Portland St.
Saint Johnsbury, VT 05819
Ph: (802)748-3181
Free: 800-649-0118
URL: http://www.nkhs.org/

South Burlington

33077 ■ Howard Center
1025 Airport Dr.
South Burlington, VT 05403
Ph: (802)488-7711
URL: http://www.howardcenter.org

Springfield

33078 ■ Health Care and Rehabilitation Service of Southeastern Vermont Programs--Union Street, Springfield
197 Union St.
Springfield, VT 05156
Ph: (802)885-4588
URL: http://www.hcrs.org/

33079 ■ Health Care and Rehabilitation Service of Southeastern Vermont--River Street, Springfield
390 River St.
Springfield, VT 05156
Ph: (802)886-4500
URL: http://www.hcrs.org/

Waterbury

33080 ■ Waterbury Day Treatment Center and Alternative Care
2 Moody Ct.
Waterbury, VT 05676-1508
Ph: (802)244-7866

White River Junction

33081 ■ Health Care and Rehabilitation Service of Southeastern Vermont--White River Junction
195 N Main St., Ste. 2
White River Junction, VT 05001
Ph: (802)295-3031
URL: http://www.hcrs.org/

33082 ■ Health Care and Rehabilitation Services of Southeastern Vermont
Mount Ascutney Hospital and Health Center
195 N Main St. Ste. 2
White River Junction, VT 05001
Ph: (802)295-3031
URL: http://www.hcrs.org/

33083 ■ White River Junction Veterans Affairs Medical Center
215 N Main St.
White River Junction, VT 05009
Ph: (802)295-9363
Free: 866-OUR-VETS
URL: http://www.whiteriver.va.gov/

Wilder

33084 ■ Clara Martin Center--Wilder
39 Fogg Farm Rd.
Wilder, VT 05088
Ph: (802)295-1311
URL: http://www.claramartin.org/contactus/service_locations

Windsor

33085 ■ Windsor County Community Services
14 River St.
Windsor, VT 05089
Ph: (802)674-2539
URL: http://www.hcrs.org/

Woodstock

33086 ■ Health Care and Rehabilitation Service of Southeastern Vermont--Woodstock
476 Woodstock Rd.
Woodstock, VT 05091
Ph: (802)457-1845
URL: http://www.hcrs.org/

VIRGIN ISLANDS

Kings Hill

33087 ■ Saint Croix Veterans Affairs Community Based Outpatient Clinic
The Village Mall, No. 113, Box 12
Kings Hill, VI 00850
Ph: (340)778-5553
Fax: (340)778-5554
URL: http://www2.va.gov/directory/guide/facility.asp?ID=5068&dnum=All

Saint Thomas

33088 ■ Saint Thomas Veterans Affairs Clinic
Havensight Mall, Bldg. III, Ste. 310
Saint Thomas, VI 00802
Ph: (340)774-6674
Fax: (340)774-2096
URL: http://www2.va.gov/directory/guide/facility.asp?ID=5069

VIRGINIA

Abingdon

33089 ■ Highlands Community Services Board
Counseling Center
610 Campus Dr., Ste. 110
Abingdon, VA 24210
Ph: (276)628-9504

Alexandria

33090 ■ Alexandria Community Services Board
720 N Saint Asaph St.
Alexandria, VA 22314-1941
Ph: (703)746-3400
URL: http://alexandriava.gov/mhmrsa/

33091 ■ Alexandria Detention Center
2003 Mill Rd.
Alexandria, VA 22314
Ph: (703)746-4114
Fax: (703)838-6307
URL: http://alexandriava.gov/sheriff/info/default.aspx?id=8460

33092 ■ Alexandria Mental Health Center
Community Support Program
4480 King St.
Alexandria, VA 22304
Ph: (703)838-4706

33093 ■ Center for Alexandria's Children
1900 N Beauregard St., Ste. 200
Alexandria, VA 22311
Ph: (703)746-6008
URL: http://centerforalexandriaschildren.org

33094 ■ Fairfax-Falls Church Community Services Board
Crisis Care Facility/Gregory House
8247 Gregory Dr.
Alexandria, VA 22309
Ph: (703)780-2713
URL: http://www.fairfaxcounty.gov/csb/

33095 ■ Fairfax-Falls Church Community Services Board
Mount Vernon Center
Comprehensive Treatment and Recovery Program
8850 Richmond Hwy.
Alexandria, VA 22306

Ph: (703)799-0300
URL: http://www.fairfaxcounty.gov/csb/

33096 ■ Mental Health Services Mount Vernon
8119 Holland Rd.
Alexandria, VA 22306
Ph: (703)360-6910
URL: http://www.fairfaxcounty.gov/csb/mhs/mhsites.htm

Altavista

33097 ■ Altavista Group Home
101 Avoca Ln.
Altavista, VA 24517
Ph: (434)369-7187
Fax: (434)369-4146
URL: http://www.cvcsb.org/

Amelia

33098 ■ Amelia Center
Washington & Church Sts.
Amelia, VA 23002
Ph: (804)561-5057
URL: http://www.crossroadscsb.org/index.htm

Amherst

33099 ■ Amherst Counseling Center
114 Lexington Tpke., Ste. 200
Amherst, VA 24521
Ph: (424)946-2316
URL: http://www.cvcsb.org/

33100 ■ Amherst Group Home
115 Robindale Cir.
Amherst, VA 24521
Ph: (424)929-4702
Fax: (434)929-1505
URL: http://www.cvcsb.org/

Annandale

33101 ■ Fairfax-Falls Church Community Service Board
Woodburn Center for Community Mental Health
3340 Woodburn Rd.
Annandale, VA 22003
Ph: (703)207-6960
URL: http://www.fairfaxcounty.gov/csb/

Arlington

33102 ■ Arlington County Community Services
Aging and Disability Services
3033 Wilson Blvd.
Arlington, VA 22201
Ph: (703)228-1700
URL: http://www.arlingtonva.us/Departments/human-services/services/aging/HumanSer vicesServic-esAgingAgingDisability.aspx

33103 ■ Clarendon House
3141 N 10th St.
Arlington, VA 22201
Ph: (703)228-5236
URL: http://www.arlingtonva.us/Departments/Human-Services/HumanServicesClarendonH ouse.aspx

Ashland

33104 ■ Hanover County Community Services
12300 Washington Hwy.
Ashland, VA 23005
Ph: (804)365-4221
URL: http://www.co.hanover.va.us/csb/default.htm

Bedford

33105 ■ Bedford Counseling Center
101-J Turnpike Rd.
Bedford, VA 24523
Ph: (540)586-5429
URL: http://www.cvcsb.org

Big Stone Gap

33106 ■ Independence House
2532 4th Ave. E
Big Stone Gap, VA 24219
Ph: (276)523-4357
Fax: (765)234-2527
URL: http://www.frontierhealth.org/service_guide_detail.asp?65

33107 ■ Wise County Behavioral Health
3169 2nd Ave. E
Big Stone Gap, VA 24219
Ph: (276)523-8300
Fax: (276)523-6964
URL: http://www.frontierhealth.org/service_guide_detail.asp?64

33108 ■ Wise County Children and Youth Services
3169 2nd Ave. E
Big Stone Gap, VA 24219
Ph: (276)523-8360
URL: http://www.frontierhealth.org/service_guide_detail.asp?64

Blacksburg

33109 ■ Mental Health Association of the New River Valley
303 Church St.
Blacksburg, VA 24060
Ph: (540)951-4990
Free: 800-559-2800
Fax: (540)951-5015
E-mail: mhainfo@mhanrv.org
URL: http://www.mhanrv.org/

33110 ■ New River Valley Community Services--Blacksburg
700 University City Blvd.
Blacksburg, VA 24060-2706
Ph: (540)961-8300
Fax: (540)961-8465
E-mail: info@nrvcs.state.va.us
URL: http://www.nrvcs.org

Bristol

33111 ■ Highlands Community Services Board
Behavior Intervention Services
102 Oakview Ave.
Bristol, VA 24201
Ph: (276)645-4780
URL: http://www.highlandscsb.org/pages/service_location.asp

33112 ■ Highlands Community Services Board
Bristol Community Support Services
1969 Lee Hwy., Ste. M-5
Bristol, VA 24201
Ph: (276)466-4292
URL: http://www.highlandscsb.org/

33113 ■ Highlands Community Services Board
Child and Adolescent Services
102 Oakview Ave.
Bristol, VA 24201-4359
Ph: (276)645-4700
URL: http://www.highlandscsb.org/pages/service_location.asp

Burke

33114 ■ Autumnleaf Group, Inc.
8983 Hersand Dr., Ste. 2
Burke, VA 22015
Ph: (703)658-7103
Fax: (703)426-7105
URL: http://www.autumnleafgroup.com/

Centreville

33115 ■ Fairfax/Falls Church Community Services Board
Crisis Care Facility/Leland House
13525 Leland Rd.
Centreville, VA 20120
Ph: (703)222-3556
URL: http://www.fairfaxcounty.gov/csb/

Charlottesville

33116 ■ Region X Community Services Board
502 Old Lynchburg Rd.
Charlottesville, VA 22903
Ph: (434)972-1800
URL: http://www.regionten.org/

33117 ■ Region X Community Services Board
Blue Ridge House
100 Burnett St.
Charlottesville, VA 22902
Ph: (434)972-1825
URL: http://www.regionten.org/

Chesapeake

33118 ■ Chesapeake Community Services Board
224 Great Bridge Blvd.
Chesapeake, VA 23320
Ph: (757)547-9334
Fax: (757)819-6292
URL: http://www.chesapeake.va.us/services/depart/com-ser/index.shtml

Colonial Heights

33119 ■ Colonial Heights Counseling Services
3660 Boulevard, Ste. A
Colonial Heights, VA 23834
Ph: (804)520-7210
URL: http://www.d19csb.com/mh/colonialheights.html

Courtland

33120 ■ Main Street Opportunities Day Support
22229 Main St.
Courtland, VA 23938
Ph: (757)653-0257
URL: http://www.wtcsb.org/

Danville

33121 ■ Danville Pittsylvania Community Services
Mental Health Division
245 Hairston St.
Danville, VA 24540
Ph: (434)799-0456
URL: http://www.dpcs.org

33122 ■ Danville Regional Medical Center Behavioral Health
142 S Main St.
Danville, VA 24541
Ph: (434)799-2100
URL: http://www.danvilleregional.org/

Dinwiddie

33123 ■ Dinwiddie Counseling Services
13900 Courthouse Rd., Ste. C
Dinwiddie, VA 23841-2285
Ph: (804)469-3746
URL: http://www.d19csb.com/mh/dinwiddie.html

Duffield

33124 ■ Hillcrest Group Home
579 Fraley Ave.
Duffield, VA 24244
Ph: (276)431-4760
Fax: (276)431-4506
URL: http://www.frontierhealth.org/service_guide_detail.asp?56

Emporia

33125 ■ Greensville Emporia Counseling Services
215 W Atlantic St.
Emporia, VA 23847
Ph: (434)634-5181
Fax: (434)634-4397
E-mail: singram@d19csb.com
URL: http://www.d19csb.com/mh/emporia.html

Fairfax

33126 ■ Fairfax/Falls Church Community Services Board
12011 Government Center Pkwy., Ste 800
Fairfax, VA 22035
Ph: (703)324-7000
URL: http://www.fairfaxcounty.gov/csb/

33127 ■ Kaiser Permanente Merrifield Mental Health Center
8550 Lee Hwy., Ste. 300
Fairfax, VA 22031
Ph: (703)207-2800
URL: http://members.kaiserpermanente.org/kpweb/facilitydir/facility.do?id=100417&rop=MR N

Falls Church

33128 ■ Fairfax/Falls Church Community Services Board
Woodburn Center for Community Mental Health
6245 Leesburg Pke., Ste 420
Falls Church, VA 22044
Ph: (703)573-0523
URL: http://www.fairfaxcounty.gov/csb/

Farmville

33129 ■ Farmville Center
214 Bush Dr.
Farmville, VA 23901
Ph: (434)392-3187
URL: http://www.crossroadscsb.org/

Floyd

33130 ■ New River Valley Community Services--Floyd
203 W Main St.
Floyd, VA 24091
Ph: (540)745-2047
URL: http://www.nrvcs.org/

Forest

33131 ■ Vista Park Center
1085 Vista Park Dr.
Forest, VA 24551
Ph: (434)455-0030
Fax: (434)455-2921
URL: http://www.cvcsb.org/

Front Royal

33132 ■ Northwestern Community Service Center
209 W Criser Rd., Ste. 300
Front Royal, VA 22630
Ph: (540)636-4250
Free: 800-342-1462
URL: http://www.nwcsb.com/

Galax

33133 ■ Fernwood Counseling Center
6999 Carrollton Pke., Ste. 1
Galax, VA 24333
Ph: (276)238-9700
URL: http://www.mtrogerscsb.com/Community_Counseling_Centers.aspx

33134 ■ Powerhouse
Mount Rogers Community Services Board
500 N Main St.
Galax, VA 24333
Ph: (276)236-8146
URL: http://www.mtrogerscsb.com/

Gate City

33135 ■ Scott County Mental Health Center
1006 US Hwy. 23 N
Gate City, VA 24251
Ph: (276)225-0976
Fax: (276)225-1241
URL: http://www.frontierhealth.org/service_guide_detail.asp?61

Glen Allen

33136 ■ Henrico Area Mental Health/Mental Retardation Services--Glen Allen
10299 Woodman Rd.
Glen Allen, VA 23060
Ph: (804)727-8500
Fax: (804)727-8580
URL: http://www.co.henrico.va.us/mhmr/

Goochland

33137 ■ Goochland Powhatan Community Services Board
3058 River Rd. W
Goochland, VA 23063
Ph: (804)556-5400
URL: http://www.gpcsb.org/

Grafton

33138 ■ Colonial Services Board
3804 George Washington Memorial Hwy.
Grafton, VA 23692
Ph: (757)220-3200
URL: http://www.colonialcsb.org/

Hampton

33139 ■ Comprehensive Outpatient Services--Hampton
200 Medical Dr.
Hampton, VA 23666
Ph: (757)825-1732
URL: http://www.hnncsb.org

33140 ■ Hampton Veterans Affairs Medical Center
100 Emancipation Dr.
Hampton, VA 23667
Ph: (757)722-9961
URL: http://www.hampton.va.gov/

33141 ■ Pathways--Hampton
2131 Cunningham Dr.
Hampton, VA 23666
Ph: (757)826-2949
URL: http://www.hnncsb.org

33142 ■ Riverside Behavioral Health Center
2244 Executive Dr.
Hampton, VA 23666
Ph: (757)827-1001
Free: 800-759-1001
URL: http://www.riversideonline.com/rbhc/

Harrisonburg

33143 ■ Harrisonburg Rockingham Community Services Board
1241 N Main St.
Harrisonburg, VA 22802
Ph: (540)434-1941
E-mail: info@hrcsb.org
URL: http://www.hrcsb.org

33144 ■ McNulty Center
463 E Washington St.
Harrisonburg, VA 22802
Ph: (540)433-3100
URL: http://www.hrcsb.org

Hopewell

33145 ■ District 19 Crisis Intervention
222 N Main St., Ste. 320
Hopewell, VA 23860
Ph: (804)862-8000
Free: 866-365-2130
E-mail: rtsiptsis@d19csb.com
URL: http://www.d19csb.com/ics/ics.html

Independence

33146 ■ Mount Rogers Community Service Board
Grayson County Mental Health Center
108 Bedwell St.
Independence, VA 24348
Ph: (276)773-3515
URL: http://www.mtrogerscsb.com/Community_Counseling_Centers.aspx
Formerly: Mount Rogers Community Mental Health/Mental Retardation Services.

Jonesville

33147 ■ Lee County Counseling Center
Rte. 3, Box 1700
Jonesville, VA 24263
Ph: (276)346-3590
URL: http://www.frontierhealth.org/locations.htm

Kilmarnock

33148 ■ Rappahannock General Hospital--Behavioral Health
101 Harris Dr.
Kilmarnock, VA 22482
Ph: (804)435-8000
URL: http://www.rgh-hospital.com/

Leesburg

33149 ■ Loudon County Mental Health Center
102 Heritage Way NE, Ste. 302
Leesburg, VA 20176
Ph: (703)771-5100
URL: http://www.loudoun.gov/Default.aspx?tabid=873

Louisa

33150 ■ Region Ten Community Services Board
107 McDonald St.
Louisa, VA 23093
Ph: (540)967-2880
URL: http://www.regionten.org/

Luray

33151 ■ Northwestern Community Service--Luray
23 W Main St.
Luray, VA 22835
Ph: (540)743-4548
URL: http://www.nwcsb.com/

Lynchburg

33152 ■ Arise Counseling Center
Courtland Center
620 Court St.
Lynchburg, VA 24504
Ph: (434)847-8035
URL: http://www.cvcsb.org/

33153 ■ Central Virginia Community Services Board
2241 Langhorne Rd.
Lynchburg, VA 24501
Ph: (434)847-8050
Fax: (434)847-6099
URL: http://www.cvcsb.org

33154 ■ Child and Family Center
2215 Longherne Rd., Ste. 102-B
Lynchburg, VA 24501
Ph: (434)948-4831
Fax: (434)948-4855
URL: http://www.cvcsb.org

33155 ■ Haley Center for Community Living
456 Rivermont Ave.
Lynchburg, VA 24503
Ph: (434)847-8030
URL: http://www.cvcsb.org/

33156 ■ Hudson House
2420 Woodrow St.
Lynchburg, VA 24501
Ph: (434)847-8031
URL: http://www.cvcsb.org/

33157 ■ Lynchburg Counseling Center
2235 Landover Pl.
Lynchburg, VA 24501
Ph: (434)847-8000
URL: http://www.cvcsb.org/
Formerly: Adult & Family Services CVCSB.

Manassas

33158 ■ Prince William County Community Services Board
8033 Ashton Ave., Ste. 105
Manassas, VA 20109
Ph: (703)792-7700
URL: http://www.pwcgov.org//default.aspx-?topic=010009000890000595

33159 ■ Prince William County Community Services Board
Adult Day Treatment Program
9208 Centerville Rd.
Manassas, VA 22109
Ph: (703)361-5256
URL: http://www.pwcgov.org//default.aspx-?topic=010009000890000595

Marion

33160 ■ Mount Rogers Community Service Board
Friendship House
506 E Main St.
Marion, VA 24354
Ph: (276)783-4131
URL: http://www.mtrogerscsb.com/
Formerly: Mount Rogers Community Mental Health/ Mental Retardation Services.

33161 ■ Mount Rogers Community Service Board
Smyth County Mental Health Center
416 E Main St.
Marion, VA 24354
Ph: (276)783-8185
URL: http://www.mtrogerscsb.com/
Formerly: Mount Rogers Community Mental Health/ Mental Retardation Services.

33162 ■ Mount Rogers Community Service Board
Transitions
115 N Church St.
Marion, VA 24354
Ph: (276)783-9005
URL: http://www.mtrogerscsb.com/
Formerly: Mount Rogers Community Mental Health/ Mental Retardation and Substance Abuse Services Board.

Martinsville

33163 ■ Horizons Day Treatment Programs--Martinsville
213 E Main St.
Martinsville, VA 24112
Ph: (276)632-9608
Fax: (276)632-6661
URL: http://www.piedmontcsb.org
Formerly: Horizons Unlimited.

33164 ■ Piedmont Community Services--Martinsville
24 Clay St.
Martinsville, VA 24112
Ph: (276)632-7128
URL: http://www.piedmontcsb.org/

Newport News

33165 ■ Comprehensive Outpatient Services--Newport News
11832 Canon Blvd., Ste. A
Newport News, VA 23606-2580
Ph: (757)595-6341
Fax: (757)873-3601
URL: http://www.hnncsb.org

Norfolk

33166 ■ Norfolk Community Services Board
225 W Olney Rd.
Norfolk, VA 23510
Ph: (757)823-1600
URL: http://www.norfolkcsb.org/

Orange

33167 ■ Family Guidance Services of Orange
458 Madison Rd.
Orange, VA 22960
Ph: (540)672-2718
URL: http://www.dbhds.virginia.gov/CFS-default.htm

Patrick Springs

33168 ■ Horizons Day Treatment--Patrick Springs
24141 Jeb Stuart Hwy.
Patrick Springs, VA 24133
Ph: (276)694-4361
URL: http://www.piedmontcsb.org/Locations.htm

Pearisburg

33169 ■ Mental Health Services of the New River Valley
601 Church St.
Pearisburg, VA 24134
Ph: (540)921-2238
URL: http://www.nrvcs.org/

Petersburg

33170 ■ District 19 Community Services
20 W Bank St., Ste. 6
Petersburg, VA 23803
Ph: (804)862-8002
E-mail: mberrey@d19csb.com
URL: http://www.d19csb.com

Portsmouth

33171 ■ Portsmouth Behavioral Healthcare Services
545 High St.
Portsmouth, VA 23704
Ph: (757)393-5357
URL: http://www.portsmouthva.gov/behaviorhealth-careservices/

Prince George

33172 ■ Hopewell/Prince George Counseling Services
4010 Prince George Dr.
Prince George, VA 23875
Ph: (804)541-8660
E-mail: jdawson@d19csb.com
URL: http://www.d19csb.com/mh/hpwlpg.html

Pulaski

33173 ■ Pulaski Center
1006 E Main St.
Pulaski, VA 24301
Ph: (540)994-5023
URL: http://www.nrvcs.org/

Reston

33174 ■ Fairfax-Falls Church Community Services Board
Northwest Center
1850 Cameron Glen Dr., Ste. 600
Reston, VA 20190
Ph: (703)481-4100
URL: http://www.fairfaxcounty.gov/csb/

Richmond

33175 ■ Henrico Area Mental Health/Mental Retardation Services--Richmond
4825 S Laburnum Ave.
Richmond, VA 23231-2713
Ph: (804)222-2607
URL: http://www.co.henrico.va.us/mhmr/

33176 ■ Hunter Holmes McGuire Veterans Affairs Medical Center
1201 Broad Rock Blvd.
Richmond, VA 23249
Ph: (804)675-5000
URL: http://www.richmond.va.gov/

33177 ■ Richmond Behavioral Health Authority
107 S 5th St.
Richmond, VA 23219
Ph: (804)819-4000
URL: http://www.rbha.org/

33178 ■ Richmond Community Hospital
1500 N 28th St.
Richmond, VA 23223
Ph: (804)225-1700
URL: http://www.bonsecours.com/hospitals/richmond/

Roanoke

33179 ■ Blue Ridge Behavioral Health Care
Assesment Center
1729 Patterson St.
Roanoke, VA 24016
Ph: (703)344-3287
URL: http://www.brbh.org/

33180 ■ Blue Ridge Community Services
301 Elm Ave. SW
Roanoke, VA 24016
Ph: (540)345-9841
URL: http://www.brbh.org/

33181 ■ Mountain House Clubhouse
317 Washington Ave. SW
Roanoke, VA 24016
Ph: (703)344-8386
URL: http://www.brbh.org/

Rocky Mount

33182 ■ Piedmont Community Services--Rocky Mount
30 Technology Dr.
Rocky Mount, VA 24151
Ph: (540)483-0582
Fax: (540)483-0583
URL: http://www.piedmontcsb.org/Locations.htm

Rustburg

33183 ■ Campbell County Counseling Center
37 Village Hwy.
Rustburg, VA 24588-4112
Ph: (434)332-5149
URL: http://www.cvcsb.org/

Salem

33184 ■ Salem Veterans Affairs Medical Center
1970 Roanoke Blvd.
Salem, VA 24153
Ph: (540)982-2463
Free: 888-982-2463
URL: http://www.salem.va.gov/

Saluda

33185 ■ Middle Peninsula Northern Neck Community Services Board
530 General Puller Hwy.
Saluda, VA 23149
Ph: (804)758-5314
Free: 800-639-9667
URL: http://www.mpnncsb.org/

Springfield

33186 ■ Fairfax-Falls Church Community Services Board
Springfield Outpatient Unit
8348 Traford Ln.
Springfield, VA 22150
Ph: (703)866-2100
URL: http://www.fairfaxcounty.gov/csb/

Stuart

33187 ■ Piedmont Community Services--Stuart
22280 Jeb Stuart Hwy.
Stuart, VA 24171
Ph: (276)694-4361
Fax: (276)694-3445
URL: http://www.piedmontcsb.org/Locations.htm

Suffolk

33188 ■ Pathways Day Support
1000 Commercial Ln.
Suffolk, VA 23434
Ph: (757)942-1069
URL: http://www.wtcsb.org/

33189 ■ Saratoga Street Mental Health Support Center
135 S Saratoga St.
Suffolk, VA 23434
Ph: (757)925-2222
URL: http://www.wtcsb.org/

33190 ■ Western Tidewater Mental Health Center
5268 Godwin Blvd.
Suffolk, VA 23434
Ph: (757)255-7133
URL: http://www.wtcsb.org/

Surry

33191 ■ Surry Counseling Services
474 Colonial Tr. W
Surry, VA 23883
Ph: (757)294-0037
URL: http://www.d19csb.com/

Warsaw

33192 ■ Middle Peninsula Northern Neck Community Services Board
Warsaw Counseling Center
414 Main St.
Warsaw, VA 22572
Ph: (804)333-3671
Free: 800-639-9882
URL: http://www.mpnncsb.org/

Waverly

33193 ■ Sussex Counseling Services
232 Coppahaunk Ave.
Waverly, VA 23890
Ph: (804)834-2205
Fax: (804)834-2625
E-mail: rsmith@d19csb.com
URL: http://www.d19csb.com/mh/sussex.html

Williamsburg

33194 ■ Colonial Services Board
1657 Merrimac Tr.
Williamsburg, VA 23185
Ph: (757)220-3200
URL: http://www.colonialcsb.org/

Winchester

33195 ■ Northwestern Community Service--Winchester
158 Front Royal Rd., Ste. 2
Winchester, VA 22602
Ph: (540)667-8888
Free: 800-342-1462
URL: http://www.nwcsb.com/

Wytheville

33196 ■ Mount Rogers Community Service Board
770 W Ridge Rd.
Wytheville, VA 24382
Ph: (276)223-3200
Fax: (276)223-3250
URL: http://www.mtrogerscsb.com
Formerly: Mount Rogers Community Mental Health/Mental Retardation Services.

33197 ■ Mount Rogers Community Service Board
Board Wytheville Clubhouse
410 W Main St.
Wytheville, VA 24382
Ph: (276)228-6659
URL: http://www.mtrogerscsb.com
Formerly: Mount Rogers Community Mental Health/Mental Retardation Services.

WASHINGTON

Aberdeen

33198 ■ Aberdeen Behavioral Health Clinic
1813 Sumner St.
Aberdeen, WA 98520
Ph: (360)538-1461
URL: http://www.seamar.org/locations/aberdeen_obh.htm

Arlington

33199 ■ Compass Health Family and Children Clinic
3320 173rd Pl. NE
Arlington, WA 98223
Ph: (425)349-8700
URL: http://www.compasshealth.org/

Auburn

33200 ■ Auburn Youth Resource
816 F St. SE
Auburn, WA 98002
Ph: (253)939-2202
URL: http://www.ayr4kids.org/

33201 ■ Sound Mental Health--Auburn Way N
4240 Auburn Way N
Auburn, WA 98002
Ph: (253)876-8900
URL: http://www.smh.org/locations.html

33202 ■ Valley Cities Counseling & Consultation
2704 I St. NE
Auburn, WA 98002
Ph: (253)833-7444
URL: http://www.valleycities.org/

Battle Ground

33203 ■ North County Family Resource Center
701 E Main St.
Battle Ground, WA 98604
Ph: (360)687-7126
Fax: (360)687-6794
URL: http://www.selfwa.org/

Bellevue

33204 ■ Bellevue Behavioral Health Clinic
Bldg. 100, Ste. 145
12835 Bell-Red Rd.
Bellevue, WA 98005
Ph: (425)460-7114
URL: http://www.seamar.org/locations/bellevue_obh.htm

33205 ■ Overlake Hospital Medical Center
2840 Northup Way
Bellevue, WA 98004
Ph: (425)688-5000
URL: http://www.overlakehospital.org/

33206 ■ Seattle Mental Health--Rainbow Creek
14270 NE 21st St.
Bellevue, WA 98007
Ph: (425)653-5000
Fax: (425)653-5010
URL: http://www.smh.org/locations.html
Formerly: Mental Health Northwest.

Bellingham

33207 ■ Bellingham Behavioral Health Clinic
4455 Cordata Pkwy.
Bellingham, WA 98226
Ph: (360)734-5458
URL: http://www.seamar.org/locations/bellingham_obh.htm

Bremerton

33208 ■ Kitsap Mental Health Services
5455 Almira Dr. SE
Bremerton, WA 98311
Ph: (360)405-4010
URL: http://www.kitsapmentalhealth.org/

33209 ■ Lutheran Community Services Northwest
645 4th St., Ste. 202
Bremerton, WA 98337
Ph: (360)377-5511
Free: 800-378-5771
URL: http://www.lcsnw.org/bremerton/index.html

Burien

33210 ■ Navos Outpatient Services--Burien Campus
1010 S 146th St.
Burien, WA 98168
Ph: (206)241-0990
Fax: (206)248-8232
URL: http://www.navos.org/

Centralia

33211 ■ Cascade Mental Health Care Child & Adolescent Program
2428 Reynolds Ave.
Centralia, WA 98356
Ph: (360)330-9044
Fax: (360)736-3139
URL: http://www4.localaccess.com/cascade071/

Chehalis

33212 ■ Cascade Mental Health Center
135 W Main St.
Chehalis, WA 98532
Ph: (360)748-6696
Fax: (360)748-0627
URL: http://www4.localaccess.com/cascade071/

Chewelah

33213 ■ NorthEast Washington Alliance Counseling Services--Chewelah
301 E Clay Ave., Rm. 201
Chewelah, WA 99109
Ph: (509)935-4808
URL: http://www.co.stevens.wa.us/counseling/index.htm

Clarkston

33214 ■ Rogers Counseling Center
900 7th St.
Clarkston, WA 99403
Ph: (509)758-3341
Fax: (509)758-8009
URL: http://www.qualitybehavioralhealth.com/

Colville

33215 ■ NorthEast Washington Alliance Counseling Services--Colville
165 E Hawthorne Ave.
Colville, WA 99114
Ph: (509)684-4597
URL: http://www.co.stevens.wa.us/counseling/index.htm
Formerly: Stevens County Counseling Services.

Coupeville

33216 ■ Island Mental Health Center
105 NW 1st St.
Coupeville, WA 98239
Ph: (360)678-5555
URL: http://www.compasshealth.org/dir_island_county.html#coupeville

Dayton

33217 ■ Inland Counseling Network
221 E Washington St.
Dayton, WA 99328
Ph: (509)382-2527

33218 ■ Inland Counseling Network Day Treatment Center
213 W Clay St.
Dayton, WA 99328
Ph: (509)382-2525

Eastsound

33219 ■ Compass Health Orcas Island Office
1286 Mt. Baker Rd.
Eastsound, WA 98245
Ph: (360)378-2669
URL: http://www.compasshealth.org/

Edmonds

33220 ■ The Aurora House
20903 70th Ave. W
Edmonds, WA 98026
Ph: (425)672-3333
URL: http://www.compasshealth.org

Ellensburg

33221 ■ Central Washington Comprehensive Services
220 W 4th Ave.
Ellensburg, WA 98926-3060
Ph: (509)925-9861
URL: http://www.cwcmh.org/

Everett

33222 ■ Compass Health--Broadway, Everett
3322 Broadway
Everett, WA 98201
Ph: (425)349-6800
URL: http://www.compasshealth.org/

33223 ■ Compass Health--Federal Avenue, Everett
4526 Federal Ave.
Everett, WA 98203
Ph: (425)349-6200
Free: 800-457-9303
Fax: (425)349-8411
URL: http://www.compasshealth.org
Formerly: Adult Extended Care Services.

33224 ■ Everett Behavioral Health Clinic
5007 Claremont Way
Everett, WA 98203
Ph: (425)609-5505
URL: http://www.seamar.org/locations/everett.obh.htm

33225 ■ Haven House--Everett
2613 W Marine View Dr.
Everett, WA 98201
Ph: (425)349-6700
URL: http://www.compasshealth.org/

Friday Harbor

33226 ■ Compass Health San Juan Island Office
520 Spring St.
Friday Harbor, WA 98250
Ph: (360)378-2669
URL: http://www.compasshealth.org/

Hoquiam

33227 ■ Evergreen Counseling Center
205 8th St.
Hoquiam, WA 98550
Ph: (360)532-8629
URL: http://karisable.com/ghc/mh.htm

33228 ■ Grays Harbor County Crisis Clinic
615 8th St.
Hoquiam, WA 98550
Ph: (360)532-4357
URL: http://karisable.com/ghc/mh.htm

Kennewick

33229 ■ Lutheran Community Service Northwest
3321 W Kennewick Ave., Ste. 150
Kennewick, WA 99336
Ph: (509)735-6446
Fax: (509)735-6449
URL: http://www.lcsnw.org

Lakewood

33230 ■ Greater Lakes Mental Health Care--Lakewood
9330 59th Ave SW
Lakewood, WA 98499
Ph: (253)581-7020
URL: http://www.glmhc.org

Lopez

33231 ■ Compass Health Lopez Island Office
Lopez Village
Lopez, WA 98261
Ph: (360)378-2669
URL: http://www.compasshealth.org/

Lynnwood

33232 ■ Compass Health--Lynnwood
4807 196th SW, Ste. 100
Lynnwood, WA 98036
Ph: (425)835-5850
URL: http://www.compasshealth.org/

33233 ■ Lynnwood Behavioral Health Clinic
19707 44th Ave. W, Ste. 101
Lynnwood, WA 98036
Ph: (425)977-2560
URL: http://www.seamar.org/locations/lynnwood_obh.htm

Marysville

33234 ■ Adult Extended Care Services
4308 76th St. NE
Marysville, WA 98270
Ph: (425)349-7352
URL: http://www.compasshealth.org/

Monroe

33235 ■ Monroe Behavioral Health Clinic
909 W Main St., Ste. 102A
Monroe, WA 98272
Ph: (360)805-3122
URL: http://www.seamar.org/locations/monroe_obh.htm

33236 ■ Primary Care Services
1022 W Main St.
Monroe, WA 98272
Ph: (425)349-8810
URL: http://www.compasshealth.org/

Morton

33237 ■ Cascade Mental Health Care Morton Site
123 Main St.
Morton, WA 98356
Ph: (360)748-6696
Fax: (360)748-0627
URL: http://www4.localaccess.com/cascade071/

Moses Lake

33238 ■ Grant Mental Healthcare
840 E Plum St.
Moses Lake, WA 98837
Ph: (509)765-9239
Free: 800-346-4529
URL: http://www.gmhealthcare.org/

Mount Vernon

33239 ■ Compass Health Second Street Building
1100 S 2nd St.
Mount Vernon, WA 98273
Ph: (360)419-3500
URL: http://www.compasshealth.org/

33240 ■ Compass Health Veteran's Services
209 S Milwaukee
Mount Vernon, WA 98273
Ph: (360)419-3500
URL: http://www.compasshealth.org/

33241 ■ Mount Vernon Behavioral Health Clinic
2500 E College Way, Ste. 100
Mount Vernon, WA 98273
Ph: (360)428-8912
URL: http://www.seamar.org/locations/mtvernon_obh.htm

Mukilteo

33242 ■ Mukilteo Evaluation and Treatment Program
10710 Mukilteo Speedway
Mukilteo, WA 98275
Ph: (425)349-8888
URL: http://www.compasshealth.org/dir_mukilteo.html

Port Angeles

33243 ■ Horizon Center
205 E 5th St.
Port Angeles, WA 98362
Ph: (360)457-3566
URL: http://www.pcmhc.org/

33244 ■ Peninsula Community Mental Health Center
118 E 8th St.
Port Angeles, WA 98362
Ph: (360)457-0431
E-mail: info@pcmhc.org
URL: http://www.pcmhc.org/

Puyallup

33245 ■ Good Samaritan Community Services
325 E Pioneer Ave.
Puyallup, WA 98372
Ph: (253)697-5571
URL: http://www.multicare.org/goodsam/

33246 ■ Puyallup Behavioral Health Clinic
10217 125th St., Ct. E, 1st Fl.
Puyallup, WA 98374
Ph: (253)864-4770
URL: http://www.seamar.org/locations/puyallup_obh.htm

Redmond

33247 ■ Sound Mental Health Counseling Services
16345 NE 87th, Ste. C-1
Redmond, WA 98052
Ph: (425)869-6634
Fax: (425)653-4961
URL: http://www.smh.org
Formerly: Mentor Health Northwest; Northwest Counseling Institute.

SeaTac

33248 ■ The Village at Angle Lake
4040 S 188th St.
SeaTac, WA 98188
Ph: (206)901-1685
Fax: (206)244-7547
URL: http://www.lcsnw.org/anglelake/index.html

Seattle

33249 ■ Community Psychiatric Clinic Bridge Way Program
3825 Bridge Way N
Seattle, WA 98103-7922
Ph: (206)632-5009
URL: http://www.cpcwa.org/

33250 ■ Community Psychiatric Clinic City Center
1008 James St., Ste. A
Seattle, WA 98104
Ph: (206)461-3209
URL: http://www.cpcwa.org/

33251 ■ Community Psychiatric Clinic Clean Start
2329 4th Ave.
Seattle, WA 98121
Ph: (206)461-8416
URL: http://www.cpcwa.org/

33252 ■ Community Psychiatric Clinic North Gate
10501 Meridian Ave. N, Ste. D
Seattle, WA 98133
Ph: (206)461-4544
Fax: (206)461-6939
URL: http://www.cpcwa.org

33253 ■ Community Psychiatric Clinic Stone Way
4120 Stone Way N
Seattle, WA 98103
Ph: (206)461-3707
URL: http://www.cpcwa.org/

33254 ■ Downtown Emergency Service Center
515 3rd Ave.
Seattle, WA 98104
Ph: (206)464-1570
Fax: (206)624-4196
E-mail: info@desc.org
URL: http://www.desc.org

33255 ■ Highline-West Seattle Mental Health Center
2600 SW Holden St.
Seattle, WA 98126
Ph: (206)933-7000
Fax: (206)933-7014
URL: http://www.navos.org/

33256 ■ Seattle Behavioral Health Clinic
10001 17th Pl. S, Lower Level
Seattle, WA 98168
Ph: (206)766-6976
URL: http://www.seamar.org/locations/seattle_obh.htm

33257 ■ Sound Mental Health--Seattle
1600 E Olive St.
Seattle, WA 98122
Ph: (206)302-2200
Fax: (206)302-2210
URL: http://www.smh.org/locations.html
Formerly: NWMHS Service Center North; Seattle Mental Health.

33258 ■ Veterans Affairs Puget Sound
1660 S Columbian Way
Seattle, WA 98108
Ph: (206)762-1010
Free: 800-329-8387
URL: http://www1.va.gov/pugetsound/

Sedro Woolley

33259 ■ North Sound Evaluation and Treatment Facility
7825 N Sound Dr.
Sedro Woolley, WA 98248-7675
Ph: (866)215-8233
URL: http://www.compasshealth.org/dir_skagit.html

Sequim

33260 ■ Peninsula Community Mental Health Center Community Resource Center
490 N 5th Ave.
Sequim, WA 98382
Ph: (360)681-0585
URL: http://www.pcmhc.org/

Snohomish

33261 ■ Compass Health--Snohomish
221 Ave. B
Snohomish, WA 98290
Ph: (425)349-7244
URL: http://www.compasshealth.org/

Spanaway

33262 ■ Greater Lakes Mental Health Center Independence Inn
113 S 170th St.
Spanaway, WA 98387
Ph: (253)535-1935
URL: http://www.glmhc.org/

Spokane

33263 ■ Spokane Mental Health
107 S Division St.
Spokane, WA 99202
Ph: (509)838-4651
URL: http://www.smhca.org/

33264 ■ Spokane Mental Health Elder Services
5125 N Market St.
Spokane, WA 99217
Ph: (509)458-7450
URL: http://www.smhca.org/

33265 ■ Spokane Veterans Affairs Medical Center
4815 N Assembly St.
Spokane, WA 99205
Ph: (509)434-7000
Free: 800-325-7940
URL: http://www.visn20.med.va.gov/spokane/index.asp

Sunnyside

33266 ■ Central Washington Comprehensive Center Lower Valley Center
1319 Saul Rd.
Sunnyside, WA 98944-2300
Ph: (509)837-2089
URL: http://www.cwcmh.org/

Tacoma

33267 ■ Chance Program
3834 S 19th St.
Tacoma, WA 98405
Ph: (253)396-5901
URL: http://www.compmh.org/index2.html

33268 ■ Comprehensive Mental Health Center Pearl Street Center
815 S Pearl St.
Tacoma, WA 98465
Ph: (253)396-5930
URL: http://www.compmh.org/index2.html

33269 ■ Comprehensive Mental Health Center Proctor Street Center
1201 S Proctor St., Ste. 1
Tacoma, WA 98405
Ph: (253)756-9960
URL: http://www.compmh.org/index2.html

33270 ■ Comprehensive Mental Health Services
Adult Services
514 S 13th St.
Tacoma, WA 98402
Ph: (253)396-5000
URL: http://www.compmh.org/index2.html

33271 ■ Greater Lakes Mental Health Center
Sunset Inn
4018 N Baltimore
Tacoma, WA 98407
Ph: (253)759-8326
URL: http://www.glmhc.org/

33272 ■ Tacoma Behavioral Health Clinic
1112 Cushman St.
Tacoma, WA 98405
Ph: (253)396-1634
URL: http://www.seamar.org/locations/tacoma_obh.htm

33273 ■ Veterans Affairs Puget Sound HCS American Lake Division
9600 Veterans Dr.
Tacoma, WA 98493
Ph: (253)582-8440
Free: 800-329-8387
URL: http://www2.va.gov/directory/guide/facility.asp?ID=5401&dnum=All

Tukwila

33274 ■ Sound Mental Health--S Center Boulevard
6100 S Center Blvd.
Tukwila, WA 98188
Ph: (206)444-7800
URL: http://www.smh.org/locations.html

Tumwater

33275 ■ Olympia Behavioral Health Clinic
409 Custer Way, Ste. D
Tumwater, WA 98501
Ph: (360)570-8258
URL: http://www.seamar.org/locations/olympia_obh.htm

Vancouver

33276 ■ Columbia River Mental Health Services
6926 NE 4th Plain Blvd.
Vancouver, WA 98666
Ph: (360)993-3000
E-mail: crmhs@crmhs.org
URL: http://www.crmhs.org

33277 ■ Portland Veterans Affairs Medical Center
Vancouver Campus
1601 E 4th Plain Blvd., Ste. C214
Vancouver, WA 98666
Ph: (360)397-2130
Fax: (360)397-6028
URL: http://www.visn20.med.va.gov/portland/MC/About/Vancouver.asp

33278 ■ Vancouver Behavioral Health Clinic
7410 Delaware Ln.
Vancouver, WA 98664
Ph: (360)566-4432
URL: http://www.seamar.org/locations/vancouver_obh.htm

Walla Walla

33279 ■ Jonathan M. Wainwright Memorial Veterans Affairs Medical Center
77 Wainwright Dr.
Walla Walla, WA 99362
Ph: (509)525-5200
Free: 888-687-8863
URL: http://www.visn20.med.va.gov/walla-walla/

Wenatchee

33280 ■ Chelan Douglas Behavioral Health Care
636 Valley Mall Pkwy., Ste. 200
Wenatchee, WA 98802
Ph: (509)886-6318
Free: 877-563-3678
URL: http://www.cdrsn.org/

Yakima

33281 ■ Central Washington Comprehensive Mental Health Services
402 S 4th Ave.
Yakima, WA 98902
Ph: (509)575-4084
URL: http://www.cwcmh.org

33282 ■ Yakima Veterans Affairs Mental Health Outreach Clinic
1111 N 1st St., Ste. 1
Yakima, WA 98902
Ph: (509)457-2736
Fax: (509)457-1822
URL: http://www2.va.gov/directory/guide/facility.asp?ID=538&dnum=All

WEST VIRGINIA

Beckley

33283 ■ Beckley Veterans Affairs Medical Center
200 Veterans Ave.
Beckley, WV 25801
Ph: (304)255-2121
Free: 877-902-5142
URL: http://www.beckley.va.gov/

33284 ■ F.M.R.S. Health System
101 S Eisenhower Dr.
Beckley, WV 25801
Ph: (304)256-7100
URL: http://www.fmrs.org/

Belington

33285 ■ Appalachian Community Health Center--Bellington
1410 Crim Ave.
Belington, WV 26416
Ph: (304)823-3873
URL: http://www.achcinc.org/other_facilities.htm

Berkeley Springs

33286 ■ EastRidge Health Systems
Morgan County
89 Sugar Hollow Rd.
Berkeley Springs, WV 25411
Ph: (304)258-2889
URL: http://www.eastridgehealthsystems.org/

Branchland

33287 ■ Prestera Center
Lincoln County Office
25 Lincoln Plz.
Branchland, WV 25506
Ph: (304)824-5790
Free: 800-642-3434
URL: http://www.prestera.org/

Buckhannon

33288 ■ Appalachian Mental Health Center--Buckhannon
27 S Kanawha St.
Buckhannon, WV 26201
Ph: (304)472-2022
URL: http://www.achcinc.org/

Charleston

33289 ■ Charleston Veterans Affairs Primary Care Clinic--Alex Lane
104 Alex Ln.
Charleston, WV 25304
Ph: (304)926-6001
URL: http://www.huntington.va.gov/visitors/charleston.asp

33290 ■ Mountain House Day Treatment
1514 Kanawha Blvd.
Charleston, WV 25312
Ph: (304)414-0099
URL: http://www.prestera.org/

33291 ■ Prestera Center - Kanawha County
511 Morris St.
Charleston, WV 25301
Ph: (304)341-0511
URL: http://www.prestera.org/
Formerly: Highland Community Behavorial Health And Prestera Center.

Clarksburg

33292 ■ Louis A. Johnson Veterans Affairs Medical Center
1 Med Center Dr.
Clarksburg, WV 26301
Ph: (304)623-3461
URL: http://www.clarksburg.va.gov/

Cross Lanes

33293 ■ Prestera Center - Viewpoint
5405 Alpine Dr.
Cross Lanes, WV 25313
Ph: (304)776-5726
URL: http://www.prestera.org/

Danville

33294 ■ Prestera Center - Boone Satellite Office
376 Kenmore Dr.
Danville, WV 25053
Ph: (304)369-1930
URL: http://www.prestera.org/

Dunbar

33295 ■ Prestera Center - Next Step
2305 Dunbar Ave.
Dunbar, WV 25064
Ph: (304)768-6119
URL: http://www.prestera.org/

Elkins

33296 ■ Appalachian Community Health Center--Elkins
725 Yokum St.
Elkins, WV 26241-3366
Ph: (304)636-3232
URL: http://www.achcinc.org/

33297 ■ Children's Regional Program
200 Wesse St.
Elkins, WV 26241
Ph: (304)636-2431
URL: http://www.achcinc.org/

33298 ■ Youth Crisis Shelter
200 Weese St.
Elkins, WV 26241
Ph: (304)636-2431
URL: http://www.achcinc.org/

Fairmont

33299 ■ Valley Health Care
448 Leonard Ave.
Fairmont, WV 26554
Ph: (304)366-7174
Fax: (304)366-7419
URL: http://www.valleyhealthcare.org/locations.php

Fayetteville

33300 ■ FMRS Health Systems, Inc.
209 W Maple Ave.
Fayetteville, WV 25840
Ph: (304)574-2100
URL: http://www.fmrs.org/
Formerly: Fayette-Monroe-Raleigh-Summers Mental Health Center.

Franklin

33301 ■ Potomac Highlands Mental Health Center--Franklin
100 Maple Ave.
Franklin, WV 26807
Ph: (304)358-2351
Fax: (304)358-3671
URL: http://thephg.org/

Grafton

33302 ■ Valley Comprehensive Community Mental Health Center, Inc.
501 N Pike St.
Grafton, WV 26354
Ph: (304)265-3947
URL: http://www.valleyhealthcare.org/

Harrisville

33303 ■ Westbrook Health Services--Harrisville
713 E Main St.
Harrisville, WV 26362
Ph: (304)643-2996
URL: http://www.westbrookhealth.com/sites.aspx

Huntington

33304 ■ Innerchange
1424 6th Ave.
Huntington, WV 25701
Ph: (304)526-9111
Free: 877-399-7776
URL: http://www.prestera.org/child-iop.html

33305 ■ Parc Place
1420 Washington Ave.
Huntington, WV 25704
Ph: (304)525-1522
Free: 877-399-7776
URL: http://www.prestera.org/

33306 ■ Parc West
1420 Washington Ave.
Huntington, WV 25701
Ph: (304)525-1522
Free: 877-399-7776
URL: http://www.prestera.org/

33307 ■ Prestera Center for Mental Health
3375 US Rte. 60 E
Huntington, WV 25705
Ph: (304)525-7851
Free: 877-399-7776
URL: http://www.prestera.org/

33308 ■ Prestera Center for Mental Health
Cornerstones
1853 8th Ave.
Huntington, WV 25703
Ph: (304)525-7851
Free: 877-399-7776
URL: http://www.prestera.org/

33309 ■ Prestera Center for Mental Health
Rehabilitation and Support Services
625 8th St.
Huntington, WV 25701
Ph: (304)697-2190
URL: http://www.prestera.org/

33310 ■ Veterans Affairs Medical Center Huntington
1540 Spring Valley Dr.
Huntington, WV 25704
Ph: (304)429-6741
URL: http://www.huntington.va.gov/

Kearneysville

33311 ■ EastRidge Health Systems
Jefferson County
340 Edmond Rd., Ste. D
Kearneysville, WV 25430
Ph: (304)725-7565
URL: http://www.eastridgehealthsystems.org/

Keyser

33312 ■ Potomac Highlands Guild
HC72 Box 369
Keyser, WV 26726
Ph: (304)788-2241
URL: http://thephg.org/

Kingwood

33313 ■ Valley Community Mental Health Center
Garden Towers
202 Tunnelton St.
Kingwood, WV 26537
Ph: (304)329-1059
URL: http://www.valleyhealthcare.org/

Lewisburg

33314 ■ Seneca Health Services, Inc.--Lewisburg
100 Church St.
Lewisburg, WV 24901
Ph: (304)645-3319
URL: http://www.shsinc.org/

Marlinton

33315 ■ Seneca Health Services, Inc.--Marlinton
704 3rd Ave., Ste. A
Marlinton, WV 24954-1196
Ph: (304)799-6865
URL: http://www.shsinc.org/

Martinsburg

33316 ■ EastRidge Health Systems--Martinsburg
235 S Water St.
Martinsburg, WV 25401
Ph: (304)263-8954
Fax: (304)264-0763
URL: http://www.eastridgehealthsystems.org/
Formerly: Eastern Panhandle Comprehensive Mental Health Center.

33317 ■ Martinsburg Veterans Affairs Medical Center
510 Butler Ave.
Martinsburg, WV 25405
Ph: (304)263-0811
URL: http://www.martinsburg.va.gov/

Morgantown

33318 ■ Valley Community Mental Health Center
301 Scott Ave.
Morgantown, WV 26505
Ph: (304)296-1731
Fax: (304)225-2288
URL: http://www.valleyhealthcare.org/

Moundsville

33319 ■ Northwood Health Systems
Ash Avenue Clinic
10 Ash Ave.
Moundsville, WV 26041
Ph: (304)845-3000

Mullens

33320 ■ Southern Highlands Community Mental Health Center--Mullens
102 Howard Ave.
Mullens, WV 25882
Ph: (304)294-5353
URL: http://shcmhc.com/
Formerly: Itmann Clinic.

New Creek

33321 ■ Potomac Highlands Mental Health Center--New Creek
PO Box 128
New Creek, WV 26743
Ph: (304)788-2241
URL: http://thephg.org/locations.htm

New Martinsville

33322 ■ Northwood Health Systems
Wetzel Outpatient Center
747 2nd St.
New Martinsville, WV 26155
Ph: (304)455-3622

Parkersburg

33323 ■ Amity Center
1011 Mission Dr.
Parkersburg, WV 26101-5561
Ph: (304)485-1781
URL: http://www.westbrookhealth.com/sites.aspx

33324 ■ Westbrook Health Services--Parkersburg
2121 E 7th St.
Parkersburg, WV 26101
Ph: (304)485-1721
URL: http://www.westbrookhealth.com

Parsons

33325 ■ Appalachian Mental Health Center--Parsons
601 Walnut St.
Parsons, WV 26287
Ph: (304)478-2764
URL: http://www.achcinc.org/

Petersburg

33326 ■ Potomac Highlands Mental Health Center
Cottage Highland House
32 Water St.
Petersburg, WV 26847
Ph: (304)257-9461
URL: http://thephg.org/

33327 ■ Potomac Highlands Mental Health Center--Petersburg
6 Park St.
Petersburg, WV 26847
Ph: (304)257-1155
URL: http://thephg.org/

Princeton

33328 ■ Southern Highlands Community Mental Health Center
Mental Health Council
200 12th St. Ext
Princeton, WV 24740
Ph: (304)425-9541
E-mail: info@shcmhc.com
URL: http://shcmhc.com/
Formerly: Mercer, McDowell, Wyoming.

33329 ■ Southern Highlands Mental Health Center--Princeton
200 12th Ext.
Princeton, WV 24740
Ph: (304)487-7000
E-mail: info@shcmhc.com
URL: http://shcmhc.com/

Rainelle

33330 ■ Rainelle Medical Center
645 Kanawha Ave.
Rainelle, WV 25962
Ph: (304)438-6188
URL: http://www.rmchealth.org/

Ravenswood

33331 ■ Westbrook Health Services, Inc.--Ravenswood
409 Professional Cir.
Ravenswood, WV 26164
Ph: (304)868-0112
Fax: (304)868-0114
URL: http://www.westbrookhealth.com/sites.aspx

Romney

33332 ■ Potomac Highlands Mental Health Center--Romney
850 N High St.
Romney, WV 26757
Ph: (304)822-3897
URL: http://thephg.org/

Saint Albans

33333 ■ Prestera Crisis Unit
Kanawha Street Center
7004 Kanawha St.
Saint Albans, WV 25177
Ph: (304)722-1795
Free: 877-399-7776
URL: http://www.prestera.org/

Saint Marys

33334 ■ Westbrook Health Services, Inc.--Saint Marys
210 2nd St.
Saint Marys, WV 26170
Ph: (304)684-2656
Fax: (304)684-2658
URL: http://www.westbrookhealth.com/sites.aspx

Spencer

33335 ■ Westbrook Health Services--Spencer
227 Clay Rd.
Spencer, WV 25276
Ph: (304)927-5200
URL: http://www.westbrookhealth.com/sites.aspx

Summersville

33336 ■ Seneca Health Services, Inc.--Summerville
1305 Webster Rd.
Summersville, WV 26651
Ph: (304)872-6503
URL: http://www.shsinc.org/

Union

33337 ■ FMRS Health Systems, Inc.
Middle St.
Union, WV 24983
Ph: (304)772-5452
URL: http://www.fmrs.org/
Formerly: Fayette-Monroe-Raleigh-Summers Mental Health Center.

Wayne

33338 ■ Prestera Center - Wayne
145 Kenova Ave.
Wayne, WV 25570
Ph: (304)272-3466
URL: http://www.prestera.org
Formerly: Wayne County Mental Health Service.

Webster Springs

33339 ■ Seneca Health Services, Inc.--Webster Springs
Conway House
70 Parcoal Rd.
Webster Springs, WV 26288
Ph: (304)847-5425
URL: http://www.shsinc.org/

Welch

33340 ■ Southern Highlands Community Mental Health Center
Welch Clinic
787 Virginia Ave.
Welch, WV 24801
Ph: (304)436-2106
URL: http://shcmhc.com/

Wheeling

33341 ■ Northwood Health Systems
2121 Eoff St.
Wheeling, WV 26003
Ph: (304)234-3570
Formerly: Northern Panhandle Behavioral Health Center.

WISCONSIN

Adams

33342 ■ Northland Community Services, Inc.--Adams
139 S Main St.
Adams, WI 53910
Ph: (608)339-4144

Antigo

33343 ■ Langlade Health Care Center
1225 Langlade Rd.
Antigo, WI 54409
Ph: (715)627-6694
URL: http://www.norcen.org/

Appleton

33344 ■ Fox Valley Pastoral Counseling Center
1260 W Valley Rd.
Appleton, WI 54915
Ph: (920)739-9319

33345 ■ Lutheran Social Services
Northeast Regional Office
3003 N Richmond St., No. A
Appleton, WI 54911-1148
Ph: (920)734-4326
URL: http://www.lsswis.org/

Ashland

33346 ■ New Horizons North
Community Support Services
514 Main St. W
Ashland, WI 54806
Ph: (715)682-7171
URL: http://www.newhorizonsnorth.com/

Athens

33347 ■ Athens Center
729 Pine St.
Athens, WI 54411
Ph: (715)257-7521
Free: 800-782-8581
URL: http://www.marshfieldclinic.org/patients/?page=centers

Baraboo

33348 ■ Pauquette Center--Baraboo
1002 Lincoln Ave.
Baraboo, WI 53913
Ph: (608)356-9055
URL: http://www.pauquette.com/

33349 ■ Sauk County Department of Human Services
505 Broadway St., Fl. 4
Baraboo, WI 53913
Ph: (608)355-4200
URL: http://www.co.sauk.wi.us/dept/hs/index.html

Belleville

33350 ■ American Family Institute, Inc.
6441 Sun Valley Pkwy.
Belleville, WI 53508
Ph: (608)424-6454

Beloit

33351 ■ Lutheran Social Services--Beloiot
749 Bluff St.
Beloit, WI 53511-5350
Ph: (608)362-6629
URL: http://www.lsswis.org/

Birchwood

33352 ■ Birchwood Center
101 W Loomis St., Ste. A
Birchwood, WI 54817
Ph: (715)354-7772
URL: http://www.marshfieldclinic.org/patients/?page=centers

Black River Falls

33353 ■ Lutheran Social Services
Wazee House
5488 N State Hwy. 54
Black River Falls, WI 54615
Ph: (715)284-4987
URL: http://www.lsswis.org/

Brookfield

33354 ■ Cornerstone Counseling Services--Brookfield
16535 W Bluemound Rd., Ste. 200
Brookfield, WI 53005
Ph: (262)789-1191
URL: http://www.cornerstonecounseling.com/

33355 ■ Elmbrook Family Counseling Center
12690 W North Ave.
Brookfield, WI 53005
Ph: (262)785-9188
URL: http://www.elmbrookfamilycounselingcenter.com/

Burlington

33356 ■ Genesis Behavioral Services--Burlington
256 E Chestnut St., Ste. B
Burlington, WI 53105
Ph: (262)342-0156

Chilton

33357 ■ Calumet County Department of Human Services
206 Court St.
Chilton, WI 53014
Ph: (920)849-1400
Fax: (920)849-1468
E-mail: humansvc@co.calumet.wi.us
URL: http://www.co.calumet.wi.us/departments2.iml?dept_id=8

Chippewa Falls

33358 ■ Chippewa Valley Veterans Affairs Clinic
2503 County Hwy. I
Chippewa Falls, WI 54729
Ph: (715)720-3780
URL: http://www2.va.gov/directory/guide/facility.asp?ID=5174&dnum=1

Cleveland

33359 ■ Cleveland Veterans Affairs Clinic
1205 North Ave.
Cleveland, WI 53015
Ph: (920)693-5600
URL: http://www.milwaukee.va.gov/visitors/cleveland.asp

Clintonville

33360 ■ Synergy Counseling Services
370 S Main
Clintonville, WI 54929
Ph: (715)526-5466

Columbus

33361 ■ Pauquette Center--Columbus
1511 Park Ave.
Columbus, WI 53925
Ph: (608)623-5578
URL: http://www.pauquette.com/

Crandon

33362 ■ Koller Behavioral Health Services
213 E Madison St.
Crandon, WI 54520
Ph: (715)478-3524
Free: 888-299-1188
URL: http://www.thehumanservicecenter.org/ISP%20and%20OWI.htm

Cudahy

33363 ■ Saint Luke's South Shore Behavioral Health
5900 S Lake Dr.
Cudahy, WI 53110
Ph: (414)489-9000
URL: http://www.aurorahealthcare.org/facilities/display.asp?ID=0002

Delafield

33364 ■ Acacia Clinic, Inc.
715B Oneida St.
Delafield, WI 53018
Ph: (262)646-2277

Eagle River

33365 ■ Northwoods Guidance Center
707 N Hwy. 45
Eagle River, WI 54521
Ph: (715)479-4585
URL: http://www.thehumanservicecenter.org/NGC.htm

Eau Claire

33366 ■ Eau Claire Behavioral Health
1128 Oak Ridge Dr.
Eau Claire, WI 54701
Ph: (715)858-4850
Free: 800-924-8515
URL: http://www.marshfieldclinic.org/patients/?page=centers

33367 ■ Eau Claire Psychiatry
2102 Craig Rd.
Eau Claire, WI 54701
Ph: (715)858-4850
Free: 800-924-8515
URL: http://www.marshfieldclinic.org/patients/?page=centers

33368 ■ Lutheran Social Services--Eau Claire
3136 Craig St.
Eau Claire, WI 54701
Ph: (715)834-2046
Fax: (715)834-7563
URL: http://www.lsswis.org

Fond du Lac

33369 ■ Aurora Behavioral Health Center
210 Wisconsin American Dr.
Fond du Lac, WI 54935
Ph: (920)907-7000
URL: http://www.aurorahealthcare.org/

Fort Atkinson

33370 ■ Catholic Charities, Inc.--Fort Atkinson
311 N Main St.
Fort Atkinson, WI 53538-1830
Ph: (920)563-9375
URL: http://www.catholiccharitiesofmadison.org/
Formerly: Lutheran Social Services.

Friendship

33371 ■ Adams County Health and Human Services
108 E North St.
Friendship, WI 53934
Ph: (608)339-4505
Free: 888-830-3454
URL: http://67.199.14.61/Departments/HealthHumanServices/tabid/75/Default.aspx

Germantown

33372 ■ Lutheran Social Services--Germantown
N122 W15568 Mequon Rd.
East Annex
Germantown, WI 53022
Ph: (262)255-6702
URL: http://www.lsswis.org

Glendale

33373 ■ Cornerstone Counseling Services--Glendale
5555 N Port Washington Rd., Ste. 200
Glendale, WI 53217
Ph: (262)789-1191
URL: http://www.cornerstonecounseling.com/

Green Bay

33374 ■ Family Services of Northeast Wisconsin
300 Crooks St.
Green Bay, WI 54305
Ph: (920)436-6800
E-mail: intake@familyservicenew.org
URL: http://www.familyservicesnew.org/

Greenfield

33375 ■ Cornerstone Counseling Services--Greenfield
4811 S 76th St., Ste. 208
Greenfield, WI 53220
Ph: (414)817-0441
URL: http://www.cornerstonecounseling.com/

Hudson

33376 ■ Lutheran Social Services--Hudson
920 3rd St.
Hudson, WI 54016-1696
Ph: (715)386-3581
URL: http://www.lsswis.org

Janesville

33377 ■ Janesville Veterans Affairs Clinic
2419 Morse St.
Janesville, WI 53545
Ph: (608)758-9300
URL: http://www2.va.gov/directory/guide/facility.asp?ID=833&dnum=1

33378 ■ Lutheran Social Services--Janesville
612 N Randall Ave., Ste. A
Janesville, WI 53545-1958
Ph: (608)752-7660
URL: http://www.lsswis.org

Jefferson

33379 ■ Cornerstone Counseling Services--Jefferson
120 S Main St., Ste. 102
Jefferson, WI 53549
Ph: (262)789-1191
URL: http://www.cornerstonecounseling.com/

La Crosse

33380 ■ Franciscan Skemp Healthcare
700 West Ave. S
La Crosse, WI 54601
Ph: (608)785-0940
URL: http://www.mayohealthsystem.org/mhs/live/page.cfm?pp=locations/locationhome.cfm&orgid=FSH

33381 ■ Gundersen Lutheran Medical Center Behavioral Health
1900 S Ave.
La Crosse, WI 54601
Ph: (608)782-7300
URL: http://www.gundluth.org/

Lake Geneva

33382 ■ Counseling Center of Lake Geneva
415 Broad St., Ste. 204A
Lake Geneva, WI 53147
Ph: (262)249-8828
URL: http://www.lake-geneva-counseling.com/default.html

Lancaster

33383 ■ Unified Community Services
200 W Alona Ln.
Lancaster, WI 53813
Ph: (608)723-6357
Fax: (608)723-4417
URL: http://www.co.grant.wi.gov/localgov_departments_details.asp?deptid=417&locid=147

Madison

33384 ■ Johnson Street Home
745 E Johnson St.
Madison, WI 53703-1532
Ph: (608)255-9662
URL: http://www.lsswis.org

33385 ■ Lutheran Social Services--Madison
5 Odana Ct.
Madison, WI 53719
Ph: (608)277-0610
URL: http://www.lsswis.org

33386 ■ Mendota Mental Health Institute
301 Troy Dr.
Madison, WI 53704
Ph: (608)301-1000
Fax: (608)301-1358
URL: http://dhs.wisconsin.gov/mh_mendota/

33387 ■ William S. Middleton Memorial Veterans Hospital
2500 Overlook Terr.
Madison, WI 53705
Ph: (608)256-1901

Free: 888-478-8321
URL: http://www.madison.va.gov/

Marshfield

33388 ■ Marshfield Clinic Psychiatry & Behavioral Health Department
1000 N Oak Ave.
Marshfield, WI 54449
Ph: (715)387-5511
Free: 800-782-8581
URL: http://www.marshfieldclinic.org/patients/?page=centers

33389 ■ Norwood Health Center
1600 N Chestnut Ave.
Marshfield, WI 54449
Ph: (715)384-2188
URL: http://www.co.wood.wi.us/Departments/Norwood/

Menasha

33390 ■ Samaritan Counseling Center--Menasha
1478 Kenwood Dr., Ste. 1
Menasha, WI 54952
Ph: (920)886-9319
Fax: (920)886-9357
URL: http://www.samaritan-counseling.com/

Milwaukee

33391 ■ Bell Therapy--North 35th Street
4065 N 35th St.
Milwaukee, WI 53216
Ph: (414)445-9180
URL: http://www.phoenixcaresystems.com/bell/index.php

33392 ■ Bell Therapy Silver Lawn
5554 W 57th St.
Milwaukee, WI 53218
Ph: (414)463-8006
URL: http://www.phoenixcaresystems.com/bell/index.php

33393 ■ Cornerstone Counseling Services--Milwaukee
10850 W Park Pl., Ste. 100
Milwaukee, WI 53224
Ph: (262)789-1191
URL: http://www.cornerstonecounseling.com/

33394 ■ Genesis Behavioral Services--Milwaukee
1218 W Highland Blvd.
Milwaukee, WI 53233
Ph: (414)342-6200
URL: http://www.genesishealth.com/

33395 ■ Lutheran Social Services of Wisconsin and Upper Michigan
647 W Virginia St., Ste. 300
Milwaukee, WI 53204
Ph: (414)281-4400
URL: http://www.lsswis.org/

33396 ■ Milwaukee Veterans Affairs Medical Center
5000 W National Ave.
Milwaukee, WI 53295
Ph: (414)384-2000
URL: http://www.milwaukee.va.gov/

Minocqua

33397 ■ Minocqua Behavioral Health Center
9792 Hwy. 70 W
Minocqua, WI 54548
Ph: (715)356-1793
Free: 800-347-0673
URL: http://www.marshfieldclinic.org/patients/?page=centers

Mukwonago

33398 ■ Cornerstone Counseling Services--Mukwonago
555 Bay View Rd., Ste. 4
Mukwonago, WI 53149
Ph: (262)363-7449
URL: http://www.cornerstonecounseling.com/

New London

33399 ■ Samaritan Counseling Center
709 W Pine St.
New London, WI 54961
Ph: (920)982-7863
URL: http://www.samaritan-counseling.com/

Niagara

33400 ■ ADAPT Clinic
1201 Jackson St.
Niagara, WI 54151
Ph: (715)251-4555
URL: http://www.marinettecounty.com/departments/?department=fdfaa9196972&subdepartment=947453e926ca

Oconomowoc

33401 ■ Cornerstone Counseling Service--Oconomowoc
888 Thackeray Tr., Ste. 105
Oconomowoc, WI 53066
Ph: (262)567-3232
URL: http://www.cornerstonecounseling.com/

Oshkosh

33402 ■ Samaritan Counseling Center--Oshkosh
110 Church Ave.
Oshkosh, WI 54901
Ph: (920)235-1678
URL: http://www.samaritan-counseling.com/about.asp
Formerly: Fox Valley Pastoral Counseling Center.

Platteville

33403 ■ Southwest Health Center--E Side Road, Platteville
1400 E Side Rd.
Platteville, WI 53818
Ph: (608)348-2331
URL: http://www.southwesthealth.org/

33404 ■ Southwest Health Center--N Elm Street, Platteville
1185 N Elm St.
Platteville, WI 53818
Ph: (608)744-3156
URL: http://www.southwesthealth.org/

Portage

33405 ■ Aspen Family Counseling
2639 New Pinery Rd., Ste. 1
Portage, WI 53901
Ph: (608)742-5020

33406 ■ Pauquette Center--Portage
2901 Hunters Trl.
Portage, WI 53901
Ph: (608)742-5518
URL: http://www.pauquette.com/

Racine

33407 ■ Catholic Charities--Racine
2711 19th St.
Racine, WI 53403
Ph: (262)637-8888
URL: http://www.catholiccharitiesusa.org/NetCommunity/Page.aspx?pid=1174
Formerly: Lutheran Social Services.

33408 ■ Genesis Behavioral Services--Racine
1654 Washington Ave.
Racine, WI 53403
Ph: (262)633-5001

Rhinelander

33409 ■ Ministry Behavioral Health--Rhinelander
2251 N Shore Dr.
Rhinelander, WI 54501
Ph: (715)361-2000
URL: http://ministryhealth.org/SHH/home.nws

33410 ■ Rhinelander Veterans Affairs Clinic
639 W Kemp St.
Rhinelander, WI 54501
Ph: (715)362-4080
URL: http://www2.va.gov/directory/guide/facility.asp?ID=843&dnum=1

Sheboygan

33411 ■ Aurora Sheboygan Memorial Medical Center
2629 N 7th St.
Sheboygan, WI 53083
Ph: (920)451-5000
URL: http://www.aurorahealthcare.org/facilities/display.asp?id=0011

Stevens Point

33412 ■ Saint Michael's Hospital
900 Illinois Ave.
Stevens Point, WI 54481
Ph: (715)346-5000
URL: http://ministryhealth.org/SMH/home.nws

Superior

33413 ■ HRC Mental Health Center
1500 N 34th St., No. 200
Superior, WI 54880
Ph: (715)392-8216
URL: http://www.humandevelopmentcenter.org/

33414 ■ Lutheran Social Services--Superior
2231 Catlin Ave., 4th Fl.
Superior, WI 54880
Ph: (715)394-4173
URL: http://www.lsswis.org/

Tomah

33415 ■ Tomah Veterans Affairs Medical Center
500 E Veterans St.
Tomah, WI 54660
Ph: (608)372-3971
URL: http://www.tomah.va.gov/

Waukesha

33416 ■ Cornerstone Counseling Services--Waukesha
741 N Grand Ave., Ste. 302
Waukesha, WI 53186
Ph: (262)542-3255
URL: http://www.cornerstonecounseling.com/

33417 ■ Human Services Center--Waukesha
500 Riverview Ave.
Waukesha, WI 53188
Ph: (262)548-7212
URL: http://www.waukeshacounty.gov/page.aspx?SetupMetaId=176&id=86

33418 ■ Lutheran Social Services Cephas Halfway House
548 W 28180 Saylesville Rd.
Waukesha, WI 53186
Ph: (262)549-9449
URL: http://www.lsswis.org/

33419 ■ Lutheran Social Services--Waukesha
W226 N 555 Eastmound Dr., Ste. A
Waukesha, WI 53186-0408
Ph: (262)896-3440
URL: http://www.lsswis.org/

33420 ■ Stress Management and Mental Health Clinic
2717 N Grandview Blvd., Ste. 303
Waukesha, WI 53188
Ph: (262)544-6486
URL: http://www.stressmanagementclinic.com/

Waupaca

33421 ■ ThedaCare Behavioral Health
902 Riverside Dr.
Waupaca, WI 54904
Ph: (715)256-1475

Wausau

33422 ■ Crossroads Mental Health Services
526 McClellan St.
Wausau, WI 54403
Ph: (715)845-5000
URL: http://www.doj.state.wi.us/cvs/referrals/rddetail.asp?rid=563&return=

West Bend

33423 ■ Cornerstone Counseling Services--West Bend
279 S 17th Ave., Ste. 10
West Bend, WI 53095
Ph: (262)306-8994
URL: http://www.cornerstonecounseling.com/

33424 ■ Saint Joseph's Community Hospital Washington County Mental Health Center
3200 Pleasant Valley Rd.
West Bend, WI 53095
Ph: (262)334-5533

33425 ■ Washington County Mental Health Center
Outpatient
333 E Washington St., Ste 2000
West Bend, WI 53095
Ph: (262)335-4545

Wisconsin Rapids

33426 ■ Ministry Behavioral Health--Wisconsin Rapids
4011 8th St. S
Wisconsin Rapids, WI 54494
Ph: (715)424-3933
Fax: (715)424-2452
URL: http://ministryhealth.org/MinistryHealth/Locations.nws

Wittenberg

33427 ■ Lutheran Social Services Homme Youth and Family Programs
W18105 Hemlock Rd.
Wittenberg, WI 54499-8647
Ph: (715)253-2116
URL: http://www.lsswis.org/Services/CYF/Homme

WYOMING

Afton

33428 ■ High Country Counseling abd Resource Centers--Afton
389 Adams St.
Afton, WY 83110
Ph: (307)885-9883
Fax: (307)885-5206
URL: http://www.highcountrycounseling.com/

Basin

33429 ■ Big Horn County Counseling Center
116 S 3rd St.
Basin, WY 82410
Ph: (307)568-2020
URL: http://www.wamhsac.org/bhcc.html

Buffalo

33430 ■ Northern Wyoming Mental Health Center
Johnson County Outpatient Office
521 W Lott St.
Buffalo, WY 82834
Ph: (307)684-5531
URL: http://www.wamhsac.org/nwmhc.html

Casper

33431 ■ Casper Veterans Affairs Clinic
4140 S Poplar St.
Casper, WY 82601
Ph: (307)235-4143
Free: 866-338-5168
URL: http://www.sheridan.va.gov/visitors/casper.asp

33432 ■ Wyoming Behavioral Institute
2521 E 15th St.
Casper, WY 82609
Ph: (307)237-7444
Free: 800-457-9312
URL: http://www.wbihelp.com/

Cheyenne

33433 ■ Cheyenne Veterans Affairs Medical Center
2360 E Pershing Blvd.
Cheyenne, WY 82001
Ph: (307)778-7550
Free: 888-483-9127
URL: http://www.cheyenne.va.gov/

33434 ■ Peak Wellness Center--Seymour Avenue, Cheyenne
2526 Seymour Ave.
Cheyenne, WY 82003
Ph: (307)634-9653
URL: http://www.peakwellnesscenter.org/PFlocations.html
Formerly: Southeast Wyoming Mental Health Center Inc.

33435 ■ Peak Wellness Center--W 29th Street, Cheyenne
510 W 29th St.
Cheyenne, WY 82001
Ph: (307)632-9362
URL: http://www.peakwellnesscenter.org/PFlocations.html
Formerly: Southeast Wyoming Mental Health Center.

Cody

33436 ■ Park County Mental Health Center
2538 Big Horn Ave.
Cody, WY 82414
Ph: (307)587-2197

Douglas

33437 ■ Eastern Wyoming Mental Health Center--Douglas
1841 Madora Ave.
Douglas, WY 82633
Ph: (307)358-2846
URL: http://www.wysfl.com/

Evanston

33438 ■ Pioneer Counseling Services--Evanston
350 City View Dr., Ste. 302
Evanston, WY 82930
Ph: (307)789-7915
URL: http://www.wamhsac.org/pcs.html

33439 ■ Wyoming State Hospital
830 Hwy. 150 S
Evanston, WY 82931
Ph: (307)789-3464

Gillette

33440 ■ Campbell County Memorial Hospital Behavioral Health
501 S Burma Ave.
Gillette, WY 82716
Ph: (307)682-8811
URL: http://www.ccmh.net/

33441 ■ Gillette Veterans Affairs Clinic
604 Express Dr.
Gillette, WY 82718
Ph: (307)685-0676
Free: 866-621-1887
URL: http://www.sheridan.va.gov/visitors/gillette.asp

33442 ■ Youth Emergency Services, Inc.
706 Longmont
Gillette, WY 82716
Ph: (307)686-0669
URL: http://youthemergencyservices.org/

Glenrock

33443 ■ Solutions for Life, Inc.
319 Birch St., Ste. 203
Glenrock, WY 82637
Ph: (307)436-8335
URL: http://www.wysfl.com/

Green River

33444 ■ Southwest Counseling Service--Green River
175 Riverview Dr.
Green River, WY 82935
Ph: (307)872-3205
URL: http://www.swcounseling.org/

Jackson

33445 ■ Jackson Hole Community Counseling Center
640 E Broadway
Jackson, WY 83001
Ph: (307)733-2046
Fax: (307)733-6289
E-mail: info@jhccc.org
URL: http://www.jhccc.org/

33446 ■ Mountain House
640 E Broadway
Jackson, WY 83001
Ph: (307)732-1161
URL: http://jhccc.org/MountainHouse.asp

33447 ■ Teton Youth & Family Services--Jackson
510 S Cache
Jackson, WY 83001
Ph: (307)733-6440
URL: http://www.redtopmeadows.org/

Kaycee

33448 ■ Northern Wyoming Mental Health Center
Kaycee Family Clinic
Holt St.
Kaycee, WY 82639
Ph: (307)283-2404
URL: http://wyomentalhealth.org/officelocations.htm

Kemmerer

33449 ■ High Country Counseling and Resource Center--Kemmerer
821 Sage St.
Kemmerer, WY 83101
Ph: (307)877-4466
Fax: (307)877-9832
URL: http://www.highcountrycounseling.com/index.cfm?ID=2

Lander

33450 ■ Fremont Counseling Service--Lander
748 W Main St.
Lander, WY 82520
Ph: (307)332-2231
URL: http://www.fremontcounseling.com/

33451 ■ Lander Regional Hospital
1320 Bishop Randall Dr.
Lander, WY 82520
Ph: (307)332-5700
URL: http://www.landerhospital.com/

Laramie

33452 ■ Peak Wellness Center--Laramie
1263 N 15th St.
Laramie, WY 82072
Ph: (307)745-8915
URL: http://www.peakwellnesscenter.org/
Formerly: Southeast Wyoming Mental Health Center.

Lovell

33453 ■ Big Horn Counseling Center
1114 Lane 12
Lovell, WY 82431
Ph: (307)548-6543

Lusk

33454 ■ Eastern Wyoming Mental Health Center--Lusk
905 S Main St.
Lusk, WY 82225
Ph: (307)334-3666
URL: http://www.wysfl.com/

Lyman

33455 ■ Pioneer Counseling Services--Lyman
303 S Main St.
Lyman, WY 82937
Ph: (307)786-2105
URL: http://www.pioneermhc.com/

Newcastle

33456 ■ Northern Wyoming Mental Health Center--Newcastle
420 Deanne Ave.
Newcastle, WY 82701
Ph: (307)746-4456

Pinedale

33457 ■ High Country Counseling and Resource Center--Pinedale
24 Country Club Ln.
Pinedale, WY 82941
Ph: (307)367-2111
Fax: (307)367-2166
URL: http://www.highcountrycounseling.com/index.cfm?ID=2

Powell

33458 ■ Park County Mental Health Center
627 Wyoming Ave.
Powell, WY 82435
Ph: (307)754-5687

33459 ■ Powell Veterans Affairs Clinic
777 Ave. H
Powell, WY 82435
Ph: (307)754-7257
Free: 888-284-9308
URL: http://www.sheridan.va.gov/visitors/powell.asp

Rawlins

33460 ■ Carbon County Counseling Center
721 W Maple St.
Rawlins, WY 82301
Ph: (307)324-7156

Riverton

33461 ■ Fremont Counseling Service--Riverton
1110 Major Ave.
Riverton, WY 82501
Ph: (307)856-6587
URL: http://www.fremontcounseling.com/

33462 ■ Riverton Veterans Affairs Clinic
2300 Rose Ln.
Riverton, WY 82501
Ph: (307)857-1439
Free: 866-338-2609
URL: http://www.sheridan.va.gov/visitors/riverton.asp

Rock Springs

33463 ■ Rock Springs Veterans Affairs Clinic
3000 College Dr.
Rock Springs, WY 82901
Ph: (307)362-6641
Free: 866-381-2830
URL: http://www.sheridan.va.gov/visitors/rocksprings.asp

33464 ■ Southwest Counseling Service--Rock Springs
1124 College Dr.
Rock Springs, WY 82901
Ph: (307)352-6677
Fax: (307)352-6676
URL: http://www.swcounseling.org/

Sheridan

33465 ■ Northern Wyoming Mental Health Center--W 5th Street, Sheridan
1221 W 5th St.
Sheridan, WY 82801
Ph: (307)674-4405
URL: http://wyomentalhealth.org/officelocations.htm

33466 ■ Northern Wyoming Mental Health Center--W Brundage, Sheridan
1133 W Brundage
Sheridan, WY 82801
Ph: (307)672-8958
URL: http://wyomentalhealth.org/officelocations.htm

33467 ■ Sheridan Veterans Affairs Medical Center
1898 Fort Rd.
Sheridan, WY 82801
Ph: (307)672-3473
Free: 800-370-0250
URL: http://www.sheridan.va.gov/

Sundance

33468 ■ Northern Wyoming Mental Health Center
Hulett Medical Clinic
122 Main St.
Sundance, WY 82720
Ph: (307)283-3636
URL: http://wyomentalhealth.org/officelocations.htm

33469 ■ Northern Wyoming Mental Health Center--Sundance
420 1/2 Main St.
Sundance, WY 82729
Ph: (307)283-3636
URL: http://wyomentalhealth.org/officelocations.htm

Thermopolis

33470 ■ Hot Springs County Counseling Center
121 S 4th St.
Thermopolis, WY 82443
Ph: (307)864-3138
URL: http://hsccs.com/

33471 ■ Hot Springs County Counseling Center
Common Ground
124 N 5th St.
Thermopolis, WY 82443
Ph: (307)864-3851
URL: http://hsccs.com/

Torrington

33472 ■ Peak Wellness Center--Torrington
501 Albany Ave.
Torrington, WY 82240
Ph: (307)532-4091
URL: http://www.peakwellnesscenter.org/
Formerly: Southeast Wyoming Mental Health Center.

Wheatland

33473 ■ Peak Wellness Center--Wheatland
1954 W Mariposa Pkwy.
Wheatland, WY 82201
Ph: (307)322-3190
URL: http://www.peakwellnesscenter.org/
Formerly: Southeast Wyoming Mental Health Center.

Wilson

33474 ■ Teton Youth & Family Services--Wilson
7905 Fall Creek Rd.
Wilson, WY 83014
Ph: (307)733-9098
URL: http://www.redtopmeadows.org/

Worland

33475 ■ Cloud Peak Counseling Center
206 S 7th St.
Worland, WY 82401
Ph: (307)347-6165
Fax: (307)347-6166

PSYCHIATRIC HOSPITALS

ALABAMA

Abbeville

33476 ■ Henry County Mental Retardation Day Training
1242 US Hwy. 431 S
Abbeville, AL 36310
Ph: (334)585-5136
URL: http://www.spcare.com/

33477 ■ Spectracare--Henry County Clinic
219 Dothan Rd.
Abbeville, AL 36310
Ph: (334)585-5331
URL: http://www.spcare.com/

Birmingham

33478 ■ Hill Crest Hospital
Hill Crest Behavioral Health Services
6869 5th Ave. S
Birmingham, AL 35212
Ph: (205)838-2050
Free: 800-292-8553
Fax: (205)838-2096
URL: http://hillcrestbhs.net/Hill_Crest_BHS/Welcome.html

Decatur

33479 ■ Decatur General Hospital
Behavioral Health Services
2205 Beltline Rd SW
Decatur, AL 35601
Ph: (256)306-4000
Free: 800-937-3873
URL: http://www.decaturgeneral.org/

33480 ■ North Alabama Regional Hospital
PO Box 2221
Decatur, AL 35609-2221
Ph: (256)560-2200
Fax: (256)350-3146
URL: http://www.mh.alabama.gov/MI/

Dothan

33481 ■ Dusy Street Group Home
802 Dusy St.
Dothan, AL 36301
Ph: (334)678-9356

33482 ■ The Haven
831 John D Odom Rd.
Dothan, AL 36303
Ph: (334)794-3771
Free: 866-506-2626
URL: http://www.stcare.com/

33483 ■ Kornegay Foster Home
306 Kornegay St.
Dothan, AL 36301
Ph: (334)678-1886

33484 ■ Lena Street Group Home
808 S Lena St.
Dothan, AL 36301
Ph: (334)678-0109

33485 ■ Wiregrass Mental Health Board Inc./dba Spectracare
2694 S Park Ave.
Dothan, AL 36301
Ph: (334)712-2720
URL: http://www.spcare.com/

Eufaula

33486 ■ Spectracare--Barbour County Clinic
133 N Orange Ave.
Eufaula, AL 36027
Ph: (334)687-2323
URL: http://www.spcare.com/

Gadsden

33487 ■ Mountain View Hospital
3001 Scenic Hwy.
Gadsden, AL 35904
Ph: (256)546-9265
Free: 800-662-1002
Fax: (256)547-3794
URL: http://www.mtnviewhospital.com/

Geneva

33488 ■ Spectracare--Geneva County
1203 W Maple Ave.
Geneva, AL 36340
Ph: (334)684-9615
URL: http://www.spcare.com/

Madison

33489 ■ Three Springs Inc.
Three Springs School of Medicine
1329 Browns Ferry Rd.
Madison, AL 35758
Ph: (256)895-0710
Free: 888-758-4356
URL: http://www.sequeltsi.com/programs/contract/madison

Montgomery

33490 ■ Greil Memorial Psychiatric Hospital
2140 Upper Wetumpka Rd.
Montgomery, AL 36107-1342
Ph: (334)262-0363
Fax: (334)834-4562
URL: http://www.mh.alabama.gov/MI/

Mount Vernon

33491 ■ Searcy Hospital
725 Coy Smith Hwy.
Mount Vernon, AL 36560
Ph: (251)662-6700

Owens Cross Roads

33492 ■ Three Springs Inc.
New Beginning and New Directions
318 Hamer Rd.
Owens Cross Roads, AL 35763
Ph: (256)725-7170
URL: http://www.threesprings.com/

Ozark

33493 ■ Dale County Coalition Prevention Services
126 Hospital Ave.
Ozark, AL 36360
Ph: (334)774-2601
URL: http://www.dalemedical.org

33494 ■ Spectracare--Dale County Clinic and Day Treatment
134 Katherine Ave.
Ozark, AL 36360
Ph: (334)774-9112
URL: http://www.spcare.com/

Samson

33495 ■ Geneva County Day Treatment
Our House--Specialized Residential Care
10386 W State Hwy. 52
Samson, AL 36477
Ph: (334)898-7423

Thomasville

33496 ■ Thomasville Mental Health Rehabilitation
2115 Bashi Rd.
Thomasville, AL 36784
Ph: (334)636-5421
Fax: (334)636-4422
E-mail: tmhrc@yahoo.com

Trenton

33497 ■ Three Springs Inc.
Paint Rock Valley Boys
3890 County Rd. 20
Trenton, AL 35774
Ph: (256)776-2503
Free: 888-758-4356
URL: http://www.threesprings.com/

33498 ■ Three Springs Inc.
Paint Rock Valley Girls
3850 County Rd. 20
Trenton, AL 35774
Ph: (256)776-2503
Free: 888-758-4356
URL: http://www.threesprings.com/

Tuscaloosa

33499 ■ Bryce Hospital
200 University Blvd.
Tuscaloosa, AL 35401
Ph: (205)759-0799
Fax: (205)759-0890
URL: http://www.mh.alabama.gov/MI/

33500 ■ Taylor Hardin Secure Medical Facility
1301 River Rd. NE
Tuscaloosa, AL 35404
Ph: (205)556-7060
Fax: (205)556-1198
URL: http://bama.ua.edu/~jhooper/thsmf.html

Webb

33501 ■ Spectracare--Houston County Rehabilitation Day Program
6154 Old Webb Rd.
Webb, AL 36376
Ph: (334)678-7162
URL: http://www.spcare.com/

33502 ■ Spectracare--Webb Group Home Number One
6150 Old Webb Rd.
Webb, AL 36376
Ph: (334)712-9191
URL: http://www.spcare.com/

33503 ■ Spectracare--Webb Group Home Number Two
6158 Old Webb Rd.
Webb, AL 36376
Ph: (334)702-0755
URL: http://www.spcare.com/

ALASKA

Anchorage

33504 ■ Alaska Psychiatric Institute
3700 Piper St.
Anchorage, AK 99508-4677
Ph: (907)269-7100
Fax: (907)269-7251
URL: http://www.hss.state.ak.us/DBH/API/default.htm

33505 ■ North Star Hospital
2530 Debarr Rd.
Anchorage, AK 99508
Ph: (907)258-7575
Free: 800-478-7575
URL: https://www.northstarbehavioral.com/

ARIZONA

Mesa

33506 ■ Desert Vista Behavioral Health Center
570 W Brown Rd.
Mesa, AZ 85201
Ph: (480)344-2000
URL: http://www.mihs.org/ourfacility/psych.html

Phoenix

33507 ■ Arizona State Hospital
2500 E Van Buren St.
Phoenix, AZ 85008
Ph: (602)244-1331
Fax: (602)220-6355
URL: http://www.azdhs.gov/azsh/

Scottsdale

33508 ■ Banner Behavioral Health Hospital Scottsdale
7575 E Earll Dr.
Scottsdale, AZ 85251-6915
Ph: (480)941-7500
Free: 800-254-HELP
Fax: (480)941-0890
E-mail: linda.buchanan@bannerhealth.com
URL: http://www.bannerhealth.com/
Formerly: Samaritan Health System Wendy Payne O'Brien Treatment Center.

Tucson

33509 ■ Palo Verde Hospital
Palo Verde Mental Health Services
5301 E Grant Rd.
Tucson, AZ 85712
Ph: (520)324-1282
URL: https://www.tmcaz.com/?q=PaloVerdeHospital

33510 ■ Sonora Behavioral Health Hospital
6050 N Corona Rd., Ste. 3
Tucson, AZ 85704
Ph: (520)469-8700
URL: http://www.havenbehavioral.com/

33511 ■ Tucson Medical Center
5301 E Grant Rd.
Tucson, AZ 85712
Ph: (520)327-5461
URL: https://www.tmcaz.com/

ARKANSAS

Barling

33512 ■ Vista Health--Fort Smith
10301 Mayo Dr.
Barling, AR 72923-1660
Ph: (479)494-5700
URL: http://www.vistahealthservices.com/
Formerly: Harbor View Mercy Psychiatric Hospital.

Batesville

33513 ■ Health Resources of Arkansas Inc. Batesville Behavioral Health Clinic
1800 Myers St.
Batesville, AR 72501
Ph: (870)793-8925
URL: http://www.healthresourcesofarkansas.com/content/

Benton

33514 ■ Rivendell Behavioral Health Services--Benton
100 Rivendell Dr.
Benton, AR 72019
Ph: (501)316-1255
URL: https://www.rivendellofarkansas.com/indexnew.htm
Formerly: Rivendell Psychiatric Center.

Bentonville

33515 ■ Ozark Guidance Center Inc. Miriam Enfield Center for Community Mental Health
2508 SE 20th St.
Bentonville, AR 72712
Ph: (479)273-9088
URL: http://www.ozarkguidance.org/

Berryville

33516 ■ Ozark Guidance Center Inc.--Berryville
208 Hwy. 62 W
Berryville, AR 72616
Ph: (870)423-2758
URL: http://www.ozarkguidance.org/

Eureka Springs

33517 ■ Ozark Guidance Center Inc. Club of the Ozarks
107 Whispering Pines
Eureka Springs, AR 72632
Ph: (479)253-5665
URL: http://www.ozarkguidance.org/

Fordyce

33518 ■ Millcreek of Arkansas
1810 Industrial Dr.
Fordyce, AR 71742
Ph: (870)352-8203
URL: http://www.millcreekofarkansas.com/

Hot Springs

33519 ■ Living Hope Texarkana
216 McAuley Ct.
Hot Springs, AR 71913
Ph: (501)623-9220

Huntsville

33520 ■ Ozark Guidance Center Inc.--Huntsville
702 Phillips Pl., Ste. 1
Huntsville, AR 72740
Ph: (479)738-2878
URL: http://www.ozarkguidance.org/

Jonesboro

33521 ■ Saint Bernard's Behavioral Health
2712 E Johnson Ave.
Jonesboro, AR 72401-1874
Ph: (870)932-2800

Little Rock

33522 ■ Arkansas State Hospital
305 S Palm St.
Little Rock, AR 72205
Ph: (501)686-9000
URL: http://www.arkansas.gov/dhs/dmhs/ar_state_hospital.htm

33523 ■ Pinnacle Pointe Hospital
11501 Financial Center Pkwy.
Little Rock, AR 72211
Ph: (501)223-3322
Free: 800-880-3322
URL: http://www.pinnaclepointehospital.com/

Maumelle

33524 ■ United Methodist Behavioral Hospital
1601 Murphy Dr.
Maumelle, AR 72113-6187
Ph: (501)803-3388
URL: https://www.methodistfamily.org/

North Little Rock

33525 ■ Bridgeway Hospital
21 Bridgeway Rd.
North Little Rock, AR 72113
Ph: (501)771-1500
Free: 800-245-0011
Fax: (501)771-0498
URL: http://www.thebridgeway.com

Siloam Springs

33526 ■ Opportunity House
302 N Maxwell
Siloam Springs, AR 72761
Ph: (479)524-5935
URL: http://www.ozarkguidance.org/about_us/locations/

Springdale

33527 ■ Ozark Guidance Center Inc. Hemingway House
2514 S 48th St.
Springdale, AR 72762
Ph: (479)750-7349
URL: http://www.ozarkguidance.org/about_us/locations/

CALIFORNIA

Atascadero

33528 ■ Atascadero State Hospital
10333 El Camino Real
Atascadero, CA 93422
Ph: (805)461-2000
URL: http://www.dmh.ca.gov/Services_and_Programs/State_Hospitals/Atascadero/Defa ult.asp

Auburn

33529 ■ Placer County Mental Health Services
11512 B Ave.
Auburn, CA 95603
Ph: (530)889-7240
Fax: (530)889-7293
URL: http://www.placer.ca.gov/Departments/hhs/adult/mental_health.aspx

Bakersfield

33530 ■ Memorial Center for Behavioral Health
5201 White Ln.
Bakersfield, CA 93309
Ph: (661)398-1800

Campbell

33531 ■ Families First Inc.--Campbell
1475 S Bascom Ave., Ste. 112
Campbell, CA 95008
Ph: (408)369-2220
Free: 800-400-4732
Fax: (408)369-2221
URL: http://www.familiesfirstinc.org/

Caruthers

33532 ■ Fresno County Department of Children and Family Services Elkhorn Facility--Mental Health
500 E Elkhorn St.
Caruthers, CA 93609
Ph: (559)864-5933
URL: http://www.co.fresno.ca.us/DepartmentPage.aspx?id=12923

Cerritos

33533 ■ College Hospital Cerritos
10802 College Pl.
Cerritos, CA 90703-1579
Ph: (562)924-9581
URL: http://www.collegehospitals.com/

Chino

33534 ■ Canyon Ridge Hospital
5353 G St.
Chino, CA 91710
Ph: (909)590-3700
URL: http://www.psysolutions.com/facilities/canyon-ridge/

Clovis

33535 ■ Clovis Elementary School--Based Fresno County Department of Children and Family Services
1100 Armstrong
Clovis, CA 93611
Ph: (559)327-1600
URL: http://www.co.fresno.ca.us/Departments.aspx?id=126

33536 ■ Gateway High School Youth Fresno County Department of Children and Family Services
1550 Herndon Ave.
Clovis, CA 93611
Ph: (559)327-1800
URL: http://www.co.fresno.ca.us/Departments.aspx?id=126

Coalinga

33537 ■ Coalinga Regional Center Fresno County Department of Children and Family Services
311 N 5th St.
Coalinga, CA 93210
Ph: (559)935-6355
URL: http://www.co.fresno.ca.us/Departments.aspx?id=126

Concord

33538 ■ Families First Inc.--Dlayton Road, Concord
3350 Clayton Rd., Ste. 100
Concord, CA 94519
Ph: (925)602-1750
Fax: (925)602-1754
URL: http://www.familiesfirstinc.org/

33539 ■ Families First Inc.--Mount Diablo High School, Concord
Mt. Diablo High School
2450 Grant St.
Concord, CA 94520
Ph: (925)827-3857
Fax: (925)827-4104
URL: http://www.familiesfirstinc.org/

Covina

33540 ■ Aurora Charter Oak Hospital
1161 E Covina Blvd.
Covina, CA 91724
Ph: (626)966-1632
Free: 800-654-2673
URL: http://charteroak.aurorabehavioral.com/

Downey

33541 ■ Downey Community Mental Health Center
8425 Iowa St.
Downey, CA 90241
Ph: (562)862-6506

El Cajon

33542 ■ East County Mental Health Center
1000 Broadway, Ste. 210
El Cajon, CA 92021
Ph: (619)441-6550
URL: http://www.sdcounty.ca.gov/hhsa/facilities/east/east_county_mental_health_clinic.h tml

Escondido

33543 ■ San Diego County Mental Health Services
North Inland Mental Health Center
125 W Mission Ave., Ste. 103
Escondido, CA 92025
Ph: (760)747-3424
URL: http://www.sdcounty.ca.gov/hhsa/facilities/north_inland/north_inland_mental_health _center.html

Fairfield

33544 ■ Families First Inc.--Fairfield
2420 Martin Rd., Ste. 200
Fairfield, CA 94534
Ph: (707)428-4198
Fax: (707)423-2020
URL: http://www.familiesfirstinc.org/

Fremont

33545 ■ Fremont Hospital
39001 Sundale Dr.
Fremont, CA 94538
Ph: (510)796-1100
URL: http://www.psysolutions.com/facilities/fremont/

Fresno

33546 ■ Fresno County Behavioral Health
Apollo Residential Treatment
205 N Blackstone Ave.
Fresno, CA 93701
Ph: (559)498-0241
URL: http://www.co.fresno.ca.us/Departments.aspx?id=120

33547 ■ Fresno County Behavioral Health
Southeast Asian Program
2211 N Fine Ave.
Fresno, CA 93727
Ph: (559)455-2175
URL: http://www.co.fresno.ca.us/Departments.aspx?id=120

33548 ■ Fresno County Mental Health
Intensive Services
4441 E Kings Canyon Rd.
Fresno, CA 93702
Ph: (559)253-9180
URL: http://www.co.fresno.ca.us/Departments.aspx?id=120

33549 ■ Fresno County
Pinedale Clinic
40 E Minarets Ave.
Fresno, CA 93650
Ph: (559)436-0482
URL: http://www.co.fresno.ca.us/Departments.aspx?id=120

33550 ■ In Care of Families First
7080 N Marks St., Ste. 104
Fresno, CA 93711
Ph: (559)248-8550
Free: 800-948-8550
Fax: (559)248-8555
URL: http://www.familiesfirstinc.org/

Hayward

33551 ■ Morton Bakar Center
494 Blossom Way
Hayward, CA 94541
Ph: (510)582-7676

Kerman

33552 ■ Fresno County Behavioral Health
West County Regional Clinic
275 S Madera Ave., Ste. 103
Kerman, CA 93630
Ph: (559)846-7500
URL: http://www.co.fresno.ca.us/Departments.aspx?id=120

La Mesa

33553 ■ Alvarado Parkway Institute Behavioral Health System
7050 Parkway Dr.
La Mesa, CA 91942
Ph: (619)465-4411
Free: 800-766-4274
URL: http://www.apibhs.com/

Long Beach

33554 ■ La Casa Psychiatric Health Facility
6060 Paramount Blvd.
Long Beach, CA 90805
Ph: (562)634-9534
Fax: (562)634-8560
URL: http://www.telecarecorp.com/programs/display.sd?iid=16

Los Angeles

33555 ■ Gateways Community Mental Health Center
Hoover Street Programs
437 N Hoover St.
Los Angeles, CA 90004-2306
Ph: (323)644-2030
Fax: (323)660-6866
URL: http://www.gatewayshospital.org/forensic.php

33556 ■ Gateways Forensic Community Treatment Program
621 S Virgil Ave., Ste. 300
Los Angeles, CA 90005
Ph: (213)368-5400
Fax: (213)368-5454
URL: http://www.gatewayshospital.org/forensic.php
Formerly: Forensic Community Treatment Program.

33557 ■ Gateways Homeless Services
340 N Madison Ave.
Los Angeles, CA 90004
Ph: (323)644-2026
URL: http://www.gatewayshospital.org/forensic.php

33558 ■ Gateways Hospital and Mental Health Center
Effie Street, Los Angeles
1891 Effie St.
Los Angeles, CA 90026
Ph: (323)644-2000
URL: http://www.gatewayshospital.org/

33559 ■ Gateways Hospital and Mental Health Center
N Mariposa Avenue, Los Angeles
225 N Mariposa Ave.
Los Angeles, CA 90004
Ph: (213)389-5820
URL: http://www.gatewayshospital.org/

33560 ■ Gateways Hospital and Mental Health Center
Percy Street, Los Angeles
3455 Percy St.
Los Angeles, CA 90023
Ph: (323)268-2100
URL: http://www.gatewayshospital.org/

33561 ■ Gateways Hospital and Mental Health Center
Percy Village Adult Residential Program
3455 Percy St.
Los Angeles, CA 90023
Ph: (323)268-2100
URL: http://www.gatewayshospital.org/

33562 ■ Kedren Community Mental Health Center
4211 Avalon Blvd.
Los Angeles, CA 90011
Ph: (323)233-0425

33563 ■ Residential Re-Entry Center
1801 Lake Shore Ave.
Los Angeles, CA 90026
Ph: (323)644-2020
URL: http://www.gatewayshospital.org/forensic.php

33564 ■ University of California, Los Angeles
Neuropsychiatric Hospital
760 Westwood Plz., MC 175919
Los Angeles, CA 90095
Ph: (310)825-6962
URL: http://www.semel.ucla.edu/

33565 ■ Vista Del Mar Boys Group Home
8546 Keokuk Ave.
Los Angeles, CA 91306
Ph: (818)700-9439

Mentone

33566 ■ ACTS for Children
2258 Mentone Blvd.
Mentone, CA 92359
Ph: (909)794-1975

Napa

33567 ■ Aldea Children and Family Services--Napa
1546 1st St.
Napa, CA 94559
Ph: (707)224-8266
Fax: (707)224-8628
URL: http://www.aldeainc.com/

33568 ■ Aldea Children and Family Services
Supported Living Program
1546 1st St.
Napa, CA 94559

Ph: (707)253-0850
Fax: (707)253-8118
URL: http://www.aldeainc.com/

33569 ■ Aldea Children and Family Services Wolfe Center
2310 1st St.
Napa, CA 94559
Ph: (707)255-1855
URL: http://www.aldeainc.com/

33570 ■ Napa State Hospital
2100 Napa Vallejo Hwy.
Napa, CA 94558
Ph: (707)253-5000
Fax: (707)253-5379
URL: http://www.dmh.ca.gov/Services_and_Programs/State_Hospitals/Napa/default.as p

Newport Beach

33571 ■ Newport Bay Hospital
1501 E 16th St.
Newport Beach, CA 92663
Ph: (949)650-9750
URL: http://www.newportbayhospital.com/

Norwalk

33572 ■ Metropolitan State Hospital
11401 Bloomfield Ave.
Norwalk, CA 90650
Ph: (562)863-7011
Fax: (562)929-3131
URL: http://www.dmh.ca.gov/Services_and_Programs/State_Hospitals/Metropolitan/de fault.asp

Oxnard

33573 ■ Pacific Shores Hospital
2130 N Ventura Rd.
Oxnard, CA 93036-2258
Ph: (805)604-1216
Free: 800-841-1515
URL: http://www.raderprograms.com/about-us/locations

Pasadena

33574 ■ Las Encinas Hospital
2900 E Del Mar Blvd.
Pasadena, CA 91107
Ph: (626)795-9901
Free: 800-792-2345
URL: http://www.lasencinashospital.com/

Patton

33575 ■ Patton State Hospital
3102 E Highland Ave.
Patton, CA 92369
Ph: (909)425-7000
Fax: (909)425-7520
URL: http://www.dmh.ca.gov/Services_and_Programs/State_Hospitals/Patton/defaulta sp

Redding

33576 ■ Crestwood Behavioral Health Inc. Crestwood Treatment Center
3062 Churn Creek Rd.
Redding, CA 96002
Ph: (530)221-0976
URL: http://www.crestwoodbehavioralhealth.com/redding.html

Redwood City

33577 ■ Cordilleras Mental Health Center
200 Edmonds Rd.
Redwood City, CA 94062
Ph: (650)367-1890

Riverside

33578 ■ Riverside Center for Behavioral Health
5900 Brockton Ave.
Riverside, CA 92506
Ph: (909)275-8400
Free: 800-992-0901
URL: http://www.rcbm.com/
Formerly: Knollwood Psychiatric and Chemical Dependency Center.

Rosemead

33579 ■ Alhambra Hospital
4619 N Rosemead Blvd.
Rosemead, CA 91770
Ph: (626)286-1191
Free: 800-235-5570
URL: http://www.bhcalhambrahospital.net/
Formerly: Alhambra Behavioral Health Center.

Roseville

33580 ■ Placer County Mental Health Services
101 Cirby Hills Dr.
Roseville, CA 95678
Ph: (916)787-8800
Fax: (916)787-8857
URL: http://www.placer.ca.gov/Departments/hhs/adult/mental_health.aspx

Sacramento

33581 ■ Crestwood Behavioral Health Inc. Crestwood Manor Sacramento
2600 Stockton Blvd.
Sacramento, CA 95817
Ph: (916)452-1431
URL: http://www.crestwoodbehavioralhealth.com/sacramento.html

33582 ■ Heritage Oaks Hospital
4250 Auburn Blvd.
Sacramento, CA 95841
Ph: (916)489-3336
URL: http://www.psysolutions.com/facilities/heritageoaks/

33583 ■ Sacramento County Mental Health Treatment Center
2150 Stockton Blvd.
Sacramento, CA 95817
Ph: (916)875-1000
URL: http://www.sacdhhs.com/default.asp?WOID=MEN
Formerly: Sacramento Mental Health Center.

33584 ■ Sierra Vista Hospital
8001 Bruceville Rd.
Sacramento, CA 95823
Ph: (916)288-0300
URL: http://www.sierravistahospital.com/

33585 ■ Sutter Center for Psychiatry
7700 Folsom Blvd.
Sacramento, CA 95826
Ph: (916)386-3000
Free: 800-801-3077
URL: http://suttermedicalcenter.org/psychiatry/

33586 ■ Sutter Counseling Center
855 Howe Ave., No. 1
Sacramento, CA 95825-3912
Ph: (916)929-0808
URL: http://suttermedicalcenter.org/psychiatry/counseling.cfm

San Bernardino

33587 ■ Shandin Hills Behavioral Therapy Center Shandin Hills Adolescent Center
4164 N 4th Ave.
San Bernardino, CA 92407
Ph: (909)886-6786

San Diego

33588 ■ Aurora Behavioral Healthcare/San Diego
11878 Ave. of Industry
San Diego, CA 92128
Ph: (858)487-3200
URL: http://www.aurorabehavioral.com
Formerly: Charter Behavioral Health System of San Diego.

33589 ■ San Diego County Psychiatric Hospital
3851 Rosecrans St.
San Diego, CA 92110
Ph: (619)692-8200
URL: http://www.sdcounty.ca.gov/hhsa/programs/bhs/mental_health_services_adult_older_ad ult/hospital_services.html

San Dimas

33590 ■ David and Margaret Home Inc. La Casa
125 S Gaffney Ave.
San Dimas, CA 91773
Ph: (909)592-0440
URL: http://www.dmhome.org/

San Francisco

33591 ■ Burt Center
940 Grove St.
San Francisco, CA 94117
Ph: (415)922-7700

33592 ■ Edgewood Cleveland Day Treatment
455 Athens St.
San Francisco, CA 94112
Ph: (415)469-4709
URL: http://www.edgewood.org/whatwedo/day-treatment.html

33593 ■ Langley Porter Psychiatric Hospital & Clinics
401 Parnassus Ave.
San Francisco, CA 94143
Ph: (415)476-7500
Fax: (415)502-6361
URL: http://psych.ucsf.edu/lpphc.aspx

San Jose

33594 ■ Crestwood Behavioral Health Inc. Crestwood Center San Jose
1425 Fruitdale Ave.
San Jose, CA 95128
Ph: (408)275-1010
URL: http://www.crestwoodbehavioralhealth.com/san_jose.html

San Rafael

33595 ■ Saint Vincent's School of Boys
1 St. Vincent's Dr.
San Rafael, CA 94903
Ph: (415)507-2000
URL: http://www.cccyo.org/programs/stvincents.php

Santa Ana

33596 ■ Olive Crest RTC--Rosemead
4619 N Rosemead Blvd.
Santa Ana, CA 92705
Ph: (626)285-2912
Free: 800-550-2445
URL: http://www.olivecrest.org/

Santa Monica

33597 ■ Family Service of Santa Monica
1533 Euclid St.
Santa Monica, CA 90404
Ph: (310)451-9747

Sebastopol

33598 ■ Plumfield Ranch
1767 Darby Ln.
Sebastopol, CA 95472
Ph: (707)823-4426

Stockton

33599 ■ Crestwood Behavioral Health Inc. Monaco Court, Stockton
1130 Monaco Ct.
Stockton, CA 95207
Ph: (209)478-2060
URL: http://www.crestwoodbehavioralhealth.com/stockton.html

33600 ■ Crestwood Behavioral Health Inc. Shoreline Drive, Stockton
7556 Shoreline Dr.
Stockton, CA 95219
Ph: (209)478-5291
URL: http://www.crestwoodbehavioralhealth.com/stockton.html

33601 ■ Saint Joseph's Behavioral Health Center
2510 N California St.
Stockton, CA 95204
Ph: (209)461-2000
URL: http://www.stjosephscanhelp.org/index.htm

Torrance

33602 ■ Del Amo Hospital
23700 Camino del Sol
Torrance, CA 90505
Ph: (310)530-1151
Free: 800-533-5266
URL: http://www.delamohospital.com/

Turlock

33603 ■ Berkeley Cottage
1601 N Berkeley Ave.
Turlock, CA 95382
Ph: (209)667-8481
URL: http://creative-alternatives.org/creative-alternatives.org/Home.html

33604 ■ Berkeley Lodge
2701 N Berkeley
Turlock, CA 95382
Ph: (209)667-6034
URL: http://creative-alternatives.org/creative-alternatives.org/Home.html

33605 ■ Greenway Orchard
1101 E Greenway Ave.
Turlock, CA 95380
Ph: (209)667-1421
URL: http://creative-alternatives.org/creative-alternatives.org/Home.html

33606 ■ Rochelle House
2201 Rochelle Ave.
Turlock, CA 95382
Ph: (209)634-6510
URL: http://creative-alternatives.org/creative-alternatives.org/Home.html

33607 ■ Tuolumme Inn
1195 E Tuolumme Rd.
Turlock, CA 95382
Ph: (209)632-9600
URL: http://creative-alternatives.org/creative-alternatives.org/Home.html

Ukiah

33608 ■ Trinity Children and Family Services--Ukiah
915 W Church St.
Ukiah, CA 95482
Ph: (707)462-8721

Vallejo

33609 ■ Aldea Children and Family Services--Vallejo
1000 Marin St.
Vallejo, CA 94590
Ph: (707)557-4560
URL: http://www.aldeainc.com/

33610 ■ California Specialty Hospital
525 Oregon St.
Vallejo, CA 94590
Ph: (707)648-2200
URL: http://www.sthelenahospital.org/Behavioral/

33611 ■ Crestwood Behavioral Health Inc. Crestwood Manor Vallejo
115 Oddstad Dr.
Vallejo, CA 94589
Ph: (707)552-0215
URL: http://www.crestwoodbehavioralhealth.com/vallejo.html

Van Nuys

33612 ■ San Fernando Valley Community Mental Health Center
6842 Van Nuys Blvd.
Van Nuys, CA 91405
Ph: (818)901-4830
URL: http://www.sfvcmhc.org/

Ventura

33613 ■ Aurora Vista del Mar Hospital
801 Seneca St.
Ventura, CA 93001
Ph: (805)653-6434
Free: 800-776-0040
URL: http://www.vistadelmarhospital.com/
Formerly: Vista del Mar Hospital.

White Water

33614 ■ Trinity Children and Family Services--White Water
55860 Verbenia Ave.
White Water, CA 92282
Ph: (760)325-1387

Woodland Hills

33615 ■ Pacific Lodge Youth Services
4900 Serrania Ave.
Woodland Hills, CA 91364
Ph: (818)347-1577
URL: http://plys.org/

COLORADO

Aspen

33616 ■ Colorado West Regional Mental Health Inc. Aspen Outpatient Clinic
405 Castle Creek Rd., No. 9
Aspen, CO 81611
Ph: (970)920-5555
URL: http://www.cwrmhc.org/

Broomfield

33617 ■ Devereux Colorado Westminster Campus
8405 Church Ranch Blvd.
Broomfield, CO 80021
Ph: (303)466-7391
URL: http://www.devereux.org/

Colorado Springs

33618 ■ Cedar Springs Hospital Cedar Springs Behavioral Health
2135 Southgate Rd.
Colorado Springs, CO 80906
Ph: (719)633-4114
URL: http://www.psysolutions.com/facilities/cedar-springs/site/
Formerly: Cedar Springs Hospital.

Craig

33619 ■ Colorado West Regional Mental Health Inc. Craig Outpatient Clinic
439 Breeze St., Ste. 200
Craig, CO 81625
Ph: (970)824-6541
URL: http://www.cwrmhc.org/

Denver

33620 ■ Colorado Mental Health Institute at Fort Logan
3520 W Oxford Ave.
Denver, CO 80236
Ph: (303)866-7066
URL: http://www.cdhs.state.co.us/cmhifl/

33621 ■ Third Way Center Inc.
PO Box 61385
Denver, CO 80206
Ph: (303)780-9191
Fax: (303)780-9192
URL: http://www.thirdwaycenter.org/

33622 ■ Third Way Center Inc.--Pontiac
1735 Pontiac St.
Denver, CO 80220
Ph: (303)388-3545
URL: http://www.thirdwaycenter.org/

Eagle

33623 ■ Colorado West Regional Mental Health Inc. Eagle Outpatient Clinic
137 Howard St.
Eagle, CO 81631
Ph: (970)328-6969
URL: http://www.cwrmhc.org/

Fort Collins

33624 ■ Mountain Crest Behavioral Healthcare System/PVHS
4601 Corbett Dr.
Fort Collins, CO 80528
Ph: (970)207-4800
Free: 800-523-1213
URL: https://vic.pvhs.org/portal/page?_pageid=333,429643&_dad=portal&_schema=PORTAL&pagid=107

Fort Lupton

33625 ■ North Range Behavioral Health South County Clinic
120 1st St.
Fort Lupton, CO 80621
Ph: (303)857-2723
URL: http://www.northrange.org/

Frisco

33626 ■ Colorado West Regional Mental Health Inc. Frisco Outpatient Clinic
360 Peak One Dr.
Frisco, CO 80443
Ph: (970)668-3478
URL: http://www.cwrmhc.org/

Glenwood Springs

33627 ■ Colorado West Regional Mental Health Inc. Garfield Outpatient Clinic
6916 Hwy. 82, Box A
Glenwood Springs, CO 81601

Ph: (970)945-2583
URL: http://www.cwrmhc.org/

Golden

33628 ■ CBR YouthConnect
Denver Office
1767 Denver W Blvd., Ste. A
Golden, CO 80401
Ph: (303)691-6095
E-mail: info@youthconnect.org
URL: http://www.coloradoboysranch.org/cbrweb/site/

Granby

33629 ■ Colorado West Regional Mental Health Inc.
Alpine Center
1023 County Rd. 610
Granby, CO 80446
Ph: (970)887-2179
URL: http://www.cwrmhc.org/

Grand Junction

33630 ■ Colorado West Regional Mental Health Inc.
Grand Junction Child and Adult Outpatient Clinic
Bldg. A
515 28 3/4 Rd.
Grand Junction, CO 81506
Ph: (970)245-3270
URL: http://www.cwrmhc.org/

Greeley

33631 ■ North Range Behavioral Health
ACT Program
515 13th Ave.
Greeley, CO 80631
Ph: (970)392-9939
URL: http://www.northrange.org/

33632 ■ North Range Behavioral Health
Acute Treatment Unit
1309 10th Ave.
Greeley, CO 80631
Ph: (970)347-2127
URL: http://www.northrange.org/

33633 ■ North Range Behavioral Health
Adult Recovery Program
510 13th Ave., Ste. 6
Greeley, CO 80631
Ph: (970)351-0200
URL: http://www.northrange.org/

33634 ■ North Range Behavioral Health
Children's Residential Treatment Center
2350 3rd St.
Greeley, CO 80631
Ph: (970)347-2127
URL: http://www.northrange.org/

33635 ■ North Range Behavioral Health
Monfort Children's and Clinic
100 N 11th Ave.
Greeley, CO 80631
Ph: (970)347-2384
URL: http://www.northrange.org/

33636 ■ North Range Behavioral Health
Outpatient Child and Family Services
710 11th Ave., Ste. 105
Greeley, CO 80631
Ph: (970)347-2124
URL: http://www.northrange.org/

Louisville

33637 ■ Centennial Peaks Hospital
2255 S 88th St.
Louisville, CO 80027
Ph: (303)673-9990
URL: http://www.centennialpeaks.com/

Meeker

33638 ■ Colorado West Regional Mental Health Inc.
Meeker Outpatient Clinic
267 6th St.
Meeker, CO 81641
Ph: (970)878-5112
URL: http://www.cwrmhc.org/

Pueblo

33639 ■ Colorado Mental Health Institute of Pueblo
1600 W 24th St.
Pueblo, CO 81003
Ph: (719)546-4000
URL: http://www.cdhs.state.co.us/cmhip/

Rangely

33640 ■ Colorado West Regional Mental Health Inc.
Rangely Outpatient Clinic
County Annex Bldg.
17497 Hwy. 64
Rangely, CO 81648
Ph: (970)675-8411
URL: http://www.cwrmhc.org/

Rifle

33641 ■ Colorado West Regional Mental Health Inc.
Rifle Outpatient Clinic
2128 Railroad Ave., Ste. 5
Rifle, CO 81650
Ph: (970)625-3582
URL: http://www.cwrmhc.org/

Steamboat Springs

33642 ■ Colorado West Regional Mental Health Inc.
Steamboat Springs Outpatient Clinic
407 S Lincoln Ave.
Steamboat Springs, CO 80477
Ph: (970)879-2141
URL: http://www.cwrmhc.org/

Vail

33643 ■ Colorado West Regional Mental Health Inc.
Vail Outpatient Clinic
395 E Lionshead Cir.
Vail, CO 81657
Ph: (970)476-0930
URL: http://www.cwrmhc.org/

Wheat Ridge

33644 ■ Exempla West Pines
3400 Lutheran Pkwy.
Wheat Ridge, CO 80033
Ph: (303)467-4000
URL: http://www.exempla.org/

CONNECTICUT

Brooklyn

33645 ■ Joshua Center of Brooklyn
7 Providence Rd.
Brooklyn, CT 06234
Ph: (860)779-2101
Free: 800-426-7792
URL: http://www.natchaug.org/

Enfield

33646 ■ Natchaug Hospital
Joshua Center--Enfield
151 Hazard Ave.
Enfield, CT 06082
Ph: (860)749-2243
Free: 800-426-7792
URL: http://www.natchaug.org/

Hamden

33647 ■ Children's Center of Hamden
1400 Whitney Ave.
Hamden, CT 06517
Ph: (203)248-2116
URL: http://www.childrenscenterhamden.org/

Hartford

33648 ■ The Blue Ridge PHP
500 Blue Hills Ave.
Hartford, CT 06112
Ph: (860)714-9200
Formerly: Adult Day Treatment Program at Mt. Sinai.

33649 ■ Klingberg Family Centers--Hartford
120 Holcomb St.
Hartford, CT 06112
Ph: (860)243-4416
URL: http://www.klingberg.org/

33650 ■ Saint Francis Care Behavioral Health
114 Woodland St.
Hartford, CT 06105
Ph: (860)342-0480
URL: http://www.stfranciscare.org/

33651 ■ Village for Family and Children Inc.--Albany Avenue, Hartford
1680 Albany Ave.
Hartford, CT 06105
Ph: (860)236-4511
URL: http://www.villageforchildren.org/

33652 ■ Village for Family and Children Inc.
Village North
2550 Main St., 3rd Fl.
Hartford, CT 06120
Ph: (860)527-4224
URL: http://www.villageforchildren.org/

33653 ■ Village for Family and Children Inc.--Wethersfield Avenue, Hartford
331 Wethersfield Ave.
Hartford, CT 06114
Ph: (860)296-5714
URL: http://www.villageforchildren.org/

Litchfield

33654 ■ Connecticut Junior Republic--Litchfield
550 Goshen Rd.
Litchfield, CT 06759
Ph: (860)567-9423
URL: http://www.ctjuniorrepublic.org/

Mansfield Center

33655 ■ Joshua Center Mansfield
189 Storrs Rd.
Mansfield Center, CT 06250
Ph: (860)456-1311
URL: http://www.natchaug.org/

33656 ■ Natchaug Hospital, Inc.
Joshua Center/Sachem House
189 Storrs Rd.
Mansfield Center, CT 06250-1683
Ph: (860)456-1311
URL: http://www.natchaug.org/
Formerly: Natchaug Hospital.

Middletown

33657 ■ Connecticut Valley Hospital
Page Hall
1000 Silver St.
Middletown, CT 06457

Ph: (860)262-5000
URL: http://www.ct.gov/dmhas/cwp/view.asp?a=2899&q=334102

33658 ■ Riverview Hospital for Children and Youth
915 River Rd.
Middletown, CT 06457-3921
Ph: (860)704-4000

New Britain

33659 ■ Klingberg Family Centers--New Britain
370 Linwood St.
New Britain, CT 06052
Ph: (860)224-9113
URL: http://www.klingberg.org/

New Canaan

33660 ■ Silver Hill Hospital
208 Valley Rd.
New Canaan, CT 06840
Ph: (203)966-3561
Free: 866-542-4455
E-mail: info@silverhillhospital.com
URL: http://www.silverhillhospital.org

New Haven

33661 ■ Assertive Community Treatment
235 Nicoll St.
New Haven, CT 06511
Ph: (203)789-6912
URL: http://www.med.yale.edu/psych/csn/casemgt.html

33662 ■ Connecticut Mental Health Center
34 Park St.
New Haven, CT 06519
Ph: (203)974-7300
Fax: (203)974-7295
URL: http://www.ct.gov/dmhas/cwp/view.asp?a=2906&q=334596

33663 ■ Hispanic Clinic
1 Long Wharf Dr.
New Haven, CT 06511
Ph: (203)974-5800
URL: http://medicine.yale.edu/psychiatry/

33664 ■ Substance Abuse Treatment Unit
1 Long Wharf Dr., Box 18
New Haven, CT 06511
Ph: (203)974-5707
URL: http://www.med.yale.edu/psych/satu/about/location.html

Newington

33665 ■ Cedarcrest Regional Hospital
525 Russell Rd
Newington, CT 06111
Ph: (860)666-7642
URL: http://www.ct.gov/DMHAS/cwp/view.asp?a=2899&q=334096

Norwalk

33666 ■ Norwalk Clinic
20 N Main St.
Norwalk, CT 06854
Ph: (203)838-6508
URL: http://www.ctcounseling.org/

Norwich

33667 ■ Thames Valley Programs
1 Ohio Ave., Ste. 1
Norwich, CT 06360
Ph: (860)886-4850

Putnam

33668 ■ Quinebaug Day Treatment Center
320 Pomfret St.
Putnam, CT 06260
Ph: (860)963-6416
URL: http://www.natchaug.org/locations.asp

Uncasville

33669 ■ Joshua Center of Montville
20 Maple Ave.
Uncasville, CT 06382
Ph: (860)848-3098
URL: http://www.natchaug.org/locations.asp

Vernon

33670 ■ Rivereast Day Hospital & Treatment Center
428 Hartford Tpke., Ste. 105
Vernon, CT 06066
Ph: (860)870-0119
URL: http://www.natchaug.org/

Waterbury

33671 ■ Connecticut Junior Republic--Waterbury
80 Prospect St.
Waterbury, CT 06702
Ph: (203)757-9939
URL: http://www.ctjuniorrepublic.org/

West Haven

33672 ■ West Haven Mental Health Clinic
270 Center St.
West Haven, CT 06516
Ph: (203)974-5900
URL: http://www.ct.gov/dmhas/cwp/view.asp?a=2906&q=334654

Westport

33673 ■ Hall-Brooke Behavioral Health Services
47 Long Lots Rd.
Westport, CT 06880-3828
Ph: (203)227-1251
URL: http://www.hallbrooke.org/
Formerly: Hall/Brooke Foundation.

Willimantic

33674 ■ Clinical Day Treatment Program
345 Jackson St.
Willimantic, CT 06226
Ph: (860)450-7373
URL: http://www.natchaug.org/

DELAWARE

Dover

33675 ■ Children and Families First--Dover
91 Wolf Creek Blvd., Ste. 1
Dover, DE 19901
Ph: (302)674-8384
URL: http://www.cffde.org

33676 ■ Pressley Ridge of Delaware
870 Forest Ave.
Dover, DE 19904
Ph: (302)677-1590
Fax: (302)677-0159
URL: http://www.pressleyridge.org/index.php?pID=76

33677 ■ Saint Jones Center for Behavioral Health
725 Horsepond Rd.
Dover, DE 19901
Ph: (302)744-7499
URL: http://www.bayhealth.org/

New Castle

33678 ■ Delaware Psychiatric Center
14 Central Ave.
New Castle, DE 19720
Ph: (302)577-2484
Free: 800-652-2929
URL: http://www.dhss.delaware.gov/dsamh/dpc.html

33679 ■ Meadow Wood Hospital
575 S Dupont Hwy.
New Castle, DE 19720
Ph: (302)328-3330
URL: http://www.psysolutions.com/facilities/meadow-wood/

Newark

33680 ■ Rockford Center
100 Rockford Dr.
Newark, DE 19713
Ph: (302)996-5480
URL: http://www.rockfordcenter.com/
Formerly: Charter Behavioral Health System - Rockford Center.

Seaford

33681 ■ Children and Families First--Seaford Seaford House Residential Treatment Center
400 N Market St. Ext.
Seaford, DE 19973
Ph: (302)629-6996
URL: http://www.cffde.org

Wilmington

33682 ■ Children and Families First--Baynard Boulevard, Wilmington
2001 Baynard Blvd.
Wilmington, DE 19802
Ph: (302)658-5177
URL: http://www.cffde.org

33683 ■ Children and Families First--Tatnall Street, Wilmington
715 Tatnall St.
Wilmington, DE 19801
Ph: (302)654-1088
URL: http://www.cffde.org

DISTRICT OF COLUMBIA

Washington

33684 ■ District of Columbia Department of Mental Health
ACT 4 Program
3849 Alabama Ave. SE
Washington, DC 20020
Ph: (202)645-7272
URL: http://dmh.dc.gov/dmh/site/default.asp

33685 ■ House of Ruth
Madison Program
651 10th St. NE
Washington, DC 20002
Ph: (202)547-2600
URL: http://www.houseofruth.org/

33686 ■ House of Ruth
Mother's Program
700 6th St. NE
Washington, DC 20002
Ph: (202)547-6173
URL: http://www.houseofruth.org/

33687 ■ House of Ruth
Transitional/Unity
459 Massachusetts Ave. NW
Washington, DC 20001
Ph: (202)347-2777
URL: http://www.houseofruth.org/

33688 ■ House of Ruth
Washington DC
5 Thomas Cir. NW
Washington, DC 20005
Ph: (202)667-7001
URL: http://www.houseofruth.org/

33689 ■ Psychiatric Institute of Washington
4228 Wisconsin Ave. NW
Washington, DC 20016
Ph: (202)885-9600
Free: 800-369-2273
URL: http://www.psychinstitute.com/

33690 ■ Riverside Hospital and Treatment Center
4460 MacArthur Blvd. NW
Washington, DC 20007
Ph: (202)333-9355

FLORIDA

Altoona

33691 ■ LifeStream Academy--Altoona
42630 State Rd. 19
Altoona, FL 32702
Ph: (352)669-0900
URL: http://www.lsbc.net/

Barberville

33692 ■ Florida Sheriffs Youth Ranches
Youth Camp
1170 Youth Camp Ln.
Barberville, FL 32105
Ph: (386)749-9999
Fax: (386)749-9020
URL: http://www.youthranches.org

Bartow

33693 ■ Florida Sheriffs Youth Ranches
Youth Villa--Bartow
3350 State Rd. 60 E
Bartow, FL 33830
Ph: (863)533-0371
Fax: (863)533-7006
URL: http://www.youthranches.org

Boys Ranch

33694 ■ Florida Sheriffs Youth Ranches
Boys Ranch
1813 Cecil Webb Pl.
Boys Ranch, FL 32060
Ph: (386)842-5555
Fax: (386)842-1012
URL: http://www.youthranches.org

Bradenton

33695 ■ Florida Assertive Community Treatment Team
5942 W 34th St.
Bradenton, FL 34210
Ph: (941)782-4860
URL: http://medinfo.ufl.edu/~compsych/fact.html

33696 ■ Florida Sheriffs Youth Ranches--Bradenton/Sarasota
751 Rye Wilderness Rd. NE
Bradenton, FL 34212
Ph: (941)776-1777
Fax: (941)776-2812
URL: http://www.youthranches.org

33697 ■ Manatee Glens Corporation
2020 26th Ave. E
Bradenton, FL 34208
Ph: (941)782-4600
URL: http://www.manateeglens.org/
Formerly: Manatee Palms Youth Service.

33698 ■ Manatee Palms Youth Services
4480 51st St. W
Bradenton, FL 34210
Ph: (941)792-2222
URL: http://www.psysolutions.com/facilities/manatee/

Brooksville

33699 ■ Springbrook Hospital
7007 Grove Rd.
Brooksville, FL 34609
Ph: (352)596-4306
Fax: (352)596-4336
URL: http://www.springbrookhospital.org/

Bushnell

33700 ■ LifeStream- Bushnell Outpatient
4416 Market St.
Bushnell, FL 33513
Ph: (352)793-4126
URL: http://www.lsbc.net/

Century

33701 ■ Century Clinic
6021A Industrial Blvd.
Century, FL 32535
Ph: (850)256-6280
URL: http://www.elakeviewcenter.org/Lakeview-Center/Facilities.aspx

Chattahoochee

33702 ■ Florida State Hospital
100 N Main St.
Chattahoochee, FL 32324
Ph: (850)663-7536
Fax: (850)663-7303
URL: http://www.dcf.state.fl.us/facilities/fsh/

Clearwater

33703 ■ Windmoor Healthcare
11300 US Hwy. 19 N
Clearwater, FL 33764-7451
Ph: (727)541-2646
Free: 800-288-4673
Fax: (727)544-5825
URL: http://www.windmoorhealthcare.com/

Clermont

33704 ■ LifeStream - Southlake Outpatient Center
655 W Hwy. 50
Clermont, FL 34711
Ph: (352)394-5922
URL: http://www.lsbc.net/LocationsInfo/Clermont.asp

Dade City

33705 ■ Harbor Behavioral Health Care Institute
Doris Cook Smith Counseling Center
14527 7th St.
Dade City, FL 33523
Ph: (352)521-1474
Free: 866-762-1743
URL: http://www.theharbor-bhci.org/

Eustis

33706 ■ LifeStream Behavioral Center
Crossroads II - Safer Communities
115 E Citrus Ave.
Eustis, FL 32726
Ph: (352)357-1550
URL: http://www.lsbc.net/LocationsInfo/Eustis.asp

Florida City

33707 ■ South Florida Evaluation and Treatment Center
18680 SW 376th St.
Florida City, FL 33034
Ph: (786)349-6000
Fax: (786)349-6028
URL: http://www.thegeogroupinc.com/geocarefacilities.asp?fid=82

Fort Lauderdale

33708 ■ Atlantic Shores Hospital
4545 N Federal Hwy.
Fort Lauderdale, FL 33308-5274
Ph: (954)771-2711
Free: 888-771-2711
Fax: (954)493-9998
URL: http://www.atlanticshoreshospital.com/

33709 ■ Fort Lauderdale Hospital
1601 E Las Olas Blvd.
Fort Lauderdale, FL 33301
Ph: (954)463-4321
Free: 800-585-7527
Fax: (954)453-5497
URL: http://www.psysolutions.com/facilities/ftlauderdale/

Gainesville

33710 ■ Shands at Vista
4101 NW 89th Blvd.
Gainesville, FL 32606
Ph: (352)265-5481
Free: 888-391-7181
URL: http://www.shands.org/hospitals/Vista/

Gulf Breeze

33711 ■ Center for Personal and Family Development--Gulf Breeze
1118 Gulf Breeze Pkwy.
Gulf Breeze, FL 32561
Ph: (850)916-3770
URL: http://www.elakeviewcenter.org/Lakeview-Center/

Hialeah

33712 ■ Citrus Health Network
Crisis, Foster Care, Child Substance Abuse
4175 W 20th Ave.
Hialeah, FL 33012
Ph: (305)825-0300
Free: 877-470-9617
Fax: (305)424-3184
URL: http://www.citrushealth.org
Formerly: Citrus Health Network.

33713 ■ Citrus Health Network
Outpatient & Case Management
4175 W 20th Ave.
Hialeah, FL 33012
Ph: (305)825-0300
Free: 877-408-3505
URL: http://www.citrushealth.org
Formerly: Citrus Health Network.

Hollywood

33714 ■ Hollywood Pavilion Hospital
1201 N 37th Ave.
Hollywood, FL 33021
Ph: (954)962-1355
Free: 800-403-4208
Fax: (954)981-5520
URL: http://www.hollywoodpavilion.com/

Immokalee

33715 ■ David Lawrence Center
Immokalee Satellite Center
425 N 1st St.
Immokalee, FL 34142
Ph: (239)657-4434
URL: http://www.davidlawrencecenter.org/

Indiantown

33716 ■ Treasure Coast Forensic Treatment Center
96 SW Allapattah Rd.
Indiantown, FL 34956
Ph: (772)597-9400

Inglis

33717 ■ Florida Sheriffs Youth Ranches Caruth Camp
14770 SE US Hwy. 19 H
Inglis, FL 34449
Ph: (352)447-2259
Fax: (352)447-0400
URL: http://www.youthranches.org

Jacksonville

33718 ■ Ten Broeck Hospital of Jacksonville
3599 University Blvd. S
Jacksonville, FL 32216
Ph: (904)724-9202
Free: 800-749-3967
Fax: (904)724-7395
Formerly: Ten Broeck Hospital.

Jupiter

33719 ■ Alternate Family Care Inc. Jupiter Office
6650 W Indiantown Rd., Ste. 210
Jupiter, FL 33458
Ph: (561)745-4154
URL: http://www.altfam.com/contact.htm

Lady Lake

33720 ■ Lady Lake Outpatient Center
314 Lagrande Blvd.
Lady Lake, FL 32159
Ph: (352)259-5762
URL: http://www.lsbc.net/

Leesburg

33721 ■ LifeStream Behavioral Center Crossroads
404 Webster St.
Leesburg, FL 34748
Ph: (352)360-6680
URL: http://www.lsbc.net/

33722 ■ LifeStream Behavioral Center Full Circle/Geriatric Residential Treatment
404 Childs St.
Leesburg, FL 34748
Ph: (352)360-6630
URL: http://www.lsbc.net/

33723 ■ LifeStream--Lake Region Homes
2016 Tally Rd.
Leesburg, FL 34748
Ph: (352)360-6622
URL: http://www.lsbc.net/

MacClenny

33724 ■ Northeast Florida State Hospital
7487 S State Rd. 121
MacClenny, FL 32063
Ph: (904)259-6211
Fax: (904)259-7101
E-mail: joseph_infantino@dcf.state.fl.us
URL: http://www.dcf.state.fl.us/facilities/nefsh/

Melbourne

33725 ■ Alternate Family Care Inc. Melbourne Office
1600 Sarno Rd., Ste. 115
Melbourne, FL 32935
Ph: (321)722-1992
URL: http://www.altfam.com/program.htm

33726 ■ Circles of Care--E Sheridan Road, Melbourne
400 E Sherdan Rd.
Melbourne, FL 32901
Ph: (321)722-5200
URL: http://www.circlesofcare.org/current/index.html

33727 ■ Circles of Care, Inc.--Commerce Drive, Melbourne
2020 Commerce Dr.
Melbourne, FL 32904
Ph: (321)952-6000
URL: http://www.circlesofcare.org

33728 ■ Devereux Melbourne Outpatient Center
1600 Sarno Rd., Ste. 214
Melbourne, FL 32935
Ph: (321)752-3111
Fax: (321)752-3114
URL: http://www.devereux.org/site/PageServer?pagename=fl_outpatient

33729 ■ Devereux Pine Grove Day School
2175 N Wickham Rd.
Melbourne, FL 32935
Ph: (321)751-9950
URL: http://www.devereux.org/site/PageServer?pagename=fl_index

33730 ■ Intensive Residential Treatment Center Center for Developmental Disabilities
8000 Devereux Dr.
Melbourne, FL 32940
Ph: (321)242-9100
URL: http://www.devereux.org/site/PageServer?pagename=fl_index

Miami

33731 ■ Alternative Family Care Inc.
8390 NW 53rd St., Ste. 300
Miami, FL 33166
Ph: (305)477-9055
URL: http://www.altfam.com/contact.htm

33732 ■ Devereux Therapeutic Foster Care--Dade Kroger Center
Savannah Bldg.
8525 NW 53rd Terr.
Miami, FL 33166
Ph: (305)463-9967
URL: http://www.devereux.org/site/PageServer?pagename=fl_index

Milton

33733 ■ Avalon Center of Lakeview
6024 Spikes Way
Milton, FL 32583
Ph: (850)437-8900
URL: http://www.elakeviewcenter.org/

33734 ■ West Florida Community Care Center
5500 Stewart
Milton, FL 32570
Ph: (850)983-5500
URL: http://www.elakeviewcenter.org/Lakeview-Center/

Naples

33735 ■ David Lawrence Center Adult Community Services
219 Airport Rd. S
Naples, FL 34104
Ph: (239)261-5148
URL: http://www.davidlawrencecenter.org/

33736 ■ David Lawrence Center Children's Community Services
239 Airport Rd. S
Naples, FL 34104
Ph: (239)263-4013
URL: http://www.davidlawrencecenter.org/

33737 ■ David Lawrence Center and Foundation
6075 Golden Gate Pkwy.
Naples, FL 34116
Ph: (239)455-1031
URL: http://www.davidlawrencecenter.org/

33738 ■ David Lawrence Center Naples
6075 Bathey Ln.
Naples, FL 34116
Ph: (239)455-1031
E-mail: info@dlcmhc.com
URL: http://www.davidlawrencecenter.org/

New Port Richey

33739 ■ Harbor Behavioral Health Care Institute
7809 Massachusetts Ave.
New Port Richey, FL 34653
Ph: (727)841-4200
Free: 866-762-1743
URL: http://www.baycare.org/body.cfm?id=761&fr=true

33740 ■ Harbor Behavioral Health Care Institute Assertive Resource Management Service
7619 Little Rd.
New Port Richey, FL 34654
Ph: (727)841-4430
Free: 866-762-1743
URL: http://www.baycare.org/body.cfm?id=761&fr=true

33741 ■ Harbor Behavioral Health Care Institute Children's Crisis Stabilization Unit
8132 King Helie Blvd.
New Port Richey, FL 34653
Ph: (727)834-3959
Free: 866-762-1743
URL: http://www.baycare.org/body.cfm?id=761&fr=true

33742 ■ Harbor Behavioral Health Care Institute Community Recovery Center
6040 Indiana Ave.
New Port Richey, FL 34653
Ph: (727)816-1836
Free: 866-762-1743
URL: http://www.baycare.org/body.cfm?id=761&fr=true

Orlando

33743 ■ Devereux Edgewater Outpatient Center
2626 Edgewater Dr.
Orlando, FL 32804
Ph: (407)425-4491
URL: http://www.devereux.org/site/PageServer

Oviedo

33744 ■ Devereux Transitional Living Center
2180 Snow Hill Rd.
Oviedo, FL 32766
Ph: (407)977-0336
URL: http://www.devereux.org/site/PageServer

33745 ■ Father Flanagan's Boys Town--Oviedo
950 N Central Ave.
Oviedo, FL 32765
Ph: (407)366-3667

Free: 800-448-3000
URL: http://www.boystown.org/Pages/default3.aspx

Pembroke Pines

33746 ■ South Florida State Hospital
800 E Cypress Dr.
Pembroke Pines, FL 33025
Ph: (954)392-3000
Fax: (954)392-3041

Pensacola

33747 ■ Center for Personal and Family Development--Pensacola
9400 University Pkwy., Ste. 409
Pensacola, FL 32514
Ph: (850)208-6150
URL: http://www.elakeviewcenter.org/Lakeview-Center/

33748 ■ Coppinger House
8590 Ashland Ave.
Pensacola, FL 32534
Ph: (850)475-5576
URL: http://www.elakeviewcenter.org/Lakeview-Center/

33749 ■ Crisis Stabilization Unit
1304 W Avery St.
Pensacola, FL 32501
Ph: (850)469-3500
URL: http://www.elakeviewcenter.org/Lakeview-Center/

33750 ■ FACT Team
600 University Office Blvd., Ste. 11
Pensacola, FL 32504
Ph: (850)202-0387
URL: http://www.elakeviewcenter.org/Lakeview-Center/

33751 ■ Lakeview Center
1221 W Lakeview Ave.
Pensacola, FL 32501
Ph: (850)469-3500
URL: http://www.elakeviewcenter.org/Lakeview-Center/

33752 ■ Lakeview Center
Southeast Vocational Services
2001 N E St.
Pensacola, FL 32501
Ph: (850)469-3500
URL: http://www.elakeviewcenter.org/Lakeview-Center/

33753 ■ Lakeview Lodges
2001 N H St.
Pensacola, FL 32501
Ph: (850)432-1222
URL: http://www.elakeviewcenter.org/Lakeview-Center/

33754 ■ Lakeview Place
1435 W Jordan St.
Pensacola, FL 32501
Ph: (850)469-3950
URL: http://www.elakeviewcenter.org/Lakeview-Center/

33755 ■ Lakeview Villas
1620 W Hernandez St.
Pensacola, FL 32501
Ph: (850)469-3464
URL: http://www.elakeviewcenter.org/Lakeview-Center/

33756 ■ Pathway
6425 N Pensacola Blvd.
Pensacola, FL 32501
Ph: (850)494-7376
URL: http://www.elakeviewcenter.org/Lakeview-Center/

33757 ■ Primary Care Service
1302 W Lakeview Ave.
Pensacola, FL 32501
Ph: (850)469-3500
URL: http://www.elakeviewcenter.org/Lakeview-Center/

33758 ■ STEP
1900 N Palafox
Pensacola, FL 32501
Ph: (850)469-3500
URL: http://www.elakeviewcenter.org/Lakeview-Center/

Pinellas Park

33759 ■ Personal Enrichment Through Mental Health Services
11254 58th St.
Pinellas Park, FL 33782
Ph: (727)545-6477
URL: http://www.pemhs.org/

Punta Gorda

33760 ■ Riverside Behavioral Center
733 E Olympia Ave.
Punta Gorda, FL 33950
Ph: (941)639-3131
URL: http://www.charlotteregional.com/getpage.php?name=riverside

Rockledge

33761 ■ Circles of Care--Rockledge
1770 Cedar st.
Rockledge, FL 32955
Ph: (321)634-6264
URL: http://www.circlesofcare.org

33762 ■ Devereux Rockledge Outpatient Center
500 Barton Blvd., Ste. 4
Rockledge, FL 32955
Ph: (407)631-6753
URL: http://www.devereux.org/site/PageServer

Saint Augustine

33763 ■ Saint Augustine Youth Services
Transitional Independent Living Program
3921 Barbara Terr.
Saint Augustine, FL 32086
Ph: (904)797-6869
URL: http://www.staugustineyouthservices.com/

Saint Petersburg

33764 ■ Personal Enrichment Through Mental Health
400 15th St. N
Saint Petersburg, FL 33705
Ph: (727)552-1053
URL: http://www.pemhs.org/

Sanford

33765 ■ Devereux Sanford Outpatient Center
2298 W Airport Blvd.
Sanford, FL 32771
Ph: (407)322-5500
URL: http://www.devereux.org/site/PageServer

Sumterville

33766 ■ LifeStream Behavioral Center
Phoenix House
411 S US Hwy. 301
Sumterville, FL 33585
Ph: (352)793-7002
URL: http://www.lsbc.net/

Tallahassee

33767 ■ Father Flanagan's Boys Town--Tallaahassee
2555 Commonwealth Blvd.
Tallahassee, FL 32303
Ph: (850)575-6422
URL: http://www.boystown.org/AboutUs/locations/Pages/BoysTownNorthFlorida.aspx

Titusville

33768 ■ Circles of Care, Inc.--Titusville
6700 S Washington Ave.
Titusville, FL 32780
Ph: (321)269-4590
URL: http://www.circlesofcare.org

33769 ■ Devereux Titusville Outpatient Center
524 S Hopkins Ave., Ste. 3
Titusville, FL 32796
Ph: (321)200-9102
URL: http://www.devereux.org/site/PageServer?pagename=homepage

33770 ■ Devereux Whispering Hills Day School
800 Lane Ave.
Titusville, FL 32780
Ph: (321)631-1911
URL: http://www.devereux.org/site/PageServer?pagename=homepage

West Palm Beach

33771 ■ Flagler Outpatient Center
Oakwood Center of the Palm Beaches
2707 N Flagler Dr.
West Palm Beach, FL 33401
Ph: (561)383-5743
URL: http://www.oakwoodcenter.org/

33772 ■ Girls and Boys Town of South Florida
3111 S Dixie Hwy., Ste. 200
West Palm Beach, FL 33405
Ph: (561)366-9400
URL: http://www.boystown.org/AboutUs/locations/Pages/BoysTownSouthFlorida.aspx

33773 ■ Oakwood Center of the Palm Beaches
1041 45th St.
West Palm Beach, FL 33407
Ph: (561)383-8000
URL: http://www.oakwoodcenter.org/

33774 ■ Oakwood Center of the Palm Beaches
Phoenix Residence II
Metcalf Ct. 1-12
West Palm Beach, FL 33401
Ph: (561)842-3145
URL: http://www.oakwoodcenter.org/

33775 ■ Oakwood Center of the Palm Beaches
Synergy
4393 Windsor Ave.
West Palm Beach, FL 33407
Ph: (561)383-7460
URL: http://www.oakwoodcenter.org/

33776 ■ Oakwood Center of the Palm Beaches
UMI Village
2720 Poinsettia Ave.
West Palm Beach, FL 33407
Ph: (561)383-5836
URL: http://www.oakwoodcenter.org/

33777 ■ Oakwood Center of the Palm Beaches
Waldon Arms
4333 Windsor Ave.
West Palm Beach, FL 33407
Ph: (561)383-8000
URL: http://www.oakwoodcenter.org/

Winter Haven

33778 ■ Devereux Therapeutic Foster Care--Polk
175 5th St., Ste. C
Winter Haven, FL 33880
Ph: (407)294-4523
URL: http://www.devereux.org/site/PageServer?pagename=homepage

GEORGIA

Atlanta

33779 ■ Anchor Hospital
5454 Yorktowne Dr.
Atlanta, GA 30349
Ph: (770)991-6044
Free: 866-667-8797
URL: http://www.anchorhospital.com
Formerly: Charter Anchor Hospital.

33780 ■ Peachford Behavioral Health System
2151 Peachford Rd.
Atlanta, GA 30338
Ph: (770)455-3200
Fax: (770)454-2376
URL: http://www.peachfordhospital.com/

Augusta

33781 ■ East Central Regional Hospital
3405 Mike Padgett Hwy.
Augusta, GA 30906
Ph: (706)792-7000
URL: http://www.ecrh.dhr.state.ga.us/

33782 ■ Lighthouse Care Center of Augusta
3100 Perimeter Pkwy.
Augusta, GA 30909
Ph: (706)651-0005
Fax: (706)650-7666
URL: http://www.psysolutions.com/facilities/lighthouseaugusta/

Blairsville

33783 ■ Avita Community Partners
Union Mental Health/Substance Abuse Clinic
41 Hospital St., Ste. 100
Blairsville, GA 30512
Ph: (706)745-5911
URL: http://www.gamtns.org/about/locations.php
Formerly: Georgia Mountains Community Services.

Columbus

33784 ■ West Central Georgia Regional Hospital
3000 Schatulga Rd.
Columbus, GA 31907
Ph: (706)568-5000
URL: http://www.wcgrh.org/

Cumming

33785 ■ Avita Community Partners
Forsyth County Mental Health/Substance Abuse and Psychiatric Rehabilitation
125 N Corners Pkwy.
Cumming, GA 30040
Ph: (678)341-3840
URL: http://www.gamtns.org/about/locations.php
Formerly: Georgia Mountains Community Services.

33786 ■ Avita Community Partners
Gateway ECS
5110 Piney Grove Rd.
Cumming, GA 30040
Ph: (770)887-4350
URL: http://www.gamtns.org/about/locations.php
Formerly: Georgia Mountains Community Services.

Dahlonega

33787 ■ Avita Community Partners
LARC--Lumpkin County
67 Ethan Allen Dr.
Dahlonega, GA 30533
Ph: (706)864-6183
URL: http://www.gamtns.org/about/locations.php
Formerly: Georgia Mountains Community Services.

33788 ■ Avita Community Partners
Lumpkin County Mental Health/Substance Abuse and Psychiatric Rehabilitation
150A Johnson St.
Dahlonega, GA 30533
Ph: (706)864-6822
URL: http://www.gamtns.org/about/locations.php
Formerly: Georgia Mountains Community Services.

Decatur

33789 ■ Georgia Regional Hospital of Atlanta
3073 Panthersville Rd.
Decatur, GA 30034
Ph: (404)243-2304
URL: http://www.atlantareg.dhr.state.ga.us/

Douglasville

33790 ■ Inner Harbour Hospitals
The Shoals
4685 Dorsett Shoals Rd.
Douglasville, GA 30135
Ph: (770)942-2391
Free: 800-255-8657
Fax: (770)489-0406
URL: http://www.youthvillages.org/IHcampus.aspx

33791 ■ Inner Harbour Outpatient Services
8657 Hospital Dr.
Douglasville, GA 30134-2263
Ph: (678)838-9336
URL: http://www.youthvillages.org/IHcampus.aspx

Flowery Branch

33792 ■ Avita Community Partners--Flowery Branch
4331 Thurmond Tanner Rd.
Flowery Branch, GA 30542
Ph: (678)513-5700
Free: 800-525-8751
URL: http://www.gamtns.org/about/locations.php
Formerly: Georgia Mountains Community Services.

Gainesville

33793 ■ Avita Community Partners
Child and Adolescent Day Services
915 Interstate Ridge, Ste. G
Gainesville, GA 30501
Ph: (678)207-1800
URL: http://www.gamtns.org/about/locations.php

33794 ■ Avita Community Partners--Gainesville
2318 Browns Bridge Rd.
Gainesville, GA 30504
Ph: (678)207-1180
URL: http://www.gamtns.org/about/locations.php
Formerly: Georgia Mountains Community Services.

33795 ■ Avita Community Partners
Gainesville Hub Child and Adolescent Programs
1314 W Ridge Rd.
Gainesville, GA 30501
Ph: (678)207-1800
URL: http://www.gamtns.org/about/locations.php
Formerly: Georgia Mountains Community Services.

33796 ■ Avita Community Partners
Hall County Supported Apartment Program
2354 Pine Cover Cir., Apt. D4
Gainesville, GA 30504
Ph: (770)536-7476
URL: http://www.gamtns.org/about/locations.php
Formerly: Georgia Mountains Community Services.

33797 ■ Avita Community Partners
Parkway Enterprises Hall/Banks ECS
3509 Mabry Rd.
Gainesville, GA 30504
Ph: (770)536-2310
URL: http://www.gamtns.org/about/locations.php
Formerly: Georgia Mountains Community Services.

Hartwell

33798 ■ Avita Community Partners
Hart County Mental Health/Substance Abuse and Psychiatric Rehabilitation
228 N College Ave.
Hartwell, GA 30643
Ph: (706)376-9001
URL: http://www.gamtns.org/about/locations.php
Formerly: Georgia Mountains Community Services.

Kennesaw

33799 ■ Devereux Georgia
1000 Cobb Place Blvd. NW, Ste. 360
Kennesaw, GA 30144
Ph: (770)422-2135
URL: http://www.devereux.org/site/PageServer

Macon

33800 ■ Macon Behavioral Health System
3500 Riverside Dr.
Macon, GA 31210
Ph: (478)477-3829
URL: http://www.psysolutions.com/facilities/macon/

Milledgeville

33801 ■ Central State Hospital--Milledgeville
620 Broad St.
Milledgeville, GA 31062
Ph: (478)445-4128
Fax: (478)445-6034
E-mail: info@centralstatehospital.org
URL: http://www.centralstatehospital.org/

Moultrie

33802 ■ Turning Point Hospital
3015 Veterans Pkwy.
Moultrie, GA 31788
Ph: (229)985-4815
Free: 800-342-1075
URL: http://turningpointcare.com/

Rome

33803 ■ Northwest Georgia Regional Hospital
705 N Division St.
Rome, GA 30165
Ph: (706)295-6011
URL: http://www.nwgrh.dhr.state.ga.us/

33804 ■ Windwood Psychiatric Hospital
Windwood Behavioral Health Services
306 Shorter Ave. NW
Rome, GA 30165
Ph: (706)295-6246
Formerly: Windwood.

Saint Simons Island

33805 ■ Saint Simons By-The-Sea Hospital
2927 Demere Rd.
Saint Simons Island, GA 31522
Ph: (912)638-1999
Free: 800-821-7224
Fax: (912)638-2112
URL: http://www.psysolutions.com/facilities/index.html#GA
Formerly: Charter by the Sea Behavioral Health Service; Focus Healthcare of Georgia.

Savannah

33806 ■ Coastal Harbor Treatment Center
1150 Cornell Ave.
Savannah, GA 31406
Ph: (912)354-3911
URL: http://www.coastalharbor.com/

33807 ■ Georgia Regional Hospital at Savannah
1915 Eisenhower Dr.
Savannah, GA 31406
Ph: (912)356-2011
Fax: (912)356-2691
URL: http://www.garegionalsavannah.com/

Smyrna

33808 ■ Ridgeview Institute
3995 S Cobb Dr.
Smyrna, GA 30080
Ph: (770)434-4567
Free: 800-329-9775
Fax: (770)434-7088
E-mail: dgay@ridgeviewinstitute.com
URL: http://www.ridgeviewinstitute.com

Thomasville

33809 ■ Southwestern State Hospital
400 S Pinetree Blvd.
Thomasville, GA 31799
Ph: (229)227-2883
URL: http://www.swsh.org/

Toccoa

33810 ■ Avita Community Partners
Stephens County Mental Health--North Star Ventures
1763 Fernside Dr.
Toccoa, GA 30577
Ph: (706)282-4542
URL: http://www.gamtns.org/
Formerly: Georgia Mountains Community Services.

HAWAII

Ewa Beach

33811 ■ Kahi Mohala Behavioral Health
91-2301 Fort Weaver Rd.
Ewa Beach, HI 96706
Ph: (808)671-8511
Fax: (808)677-2570
URL: http://www.kahimohala.org/

Hilo

33812 ■ Acadia Hawaii - Pu'ukamalu
440 Kapiolani St.
Hilo, HI 96720
Ph: (877)730-3466
URL: http://www.acadiahealthcare.com/locations/hawaii-treatment-center

Kaneohe

33813 ■ Hawaii State Hospital
45-710 Keaahala Rd.
Kaneohe, HI 96744
Ph: (808)247-2191

IDAHO

Blackfoot

33814 ■ Idaho State Hospital South
700 E Alice St.
Blackfoot, ID 83221
Ph: (208)785-8402

Boise

33815 ■ Idaho Youth Ranch Emancipation Home
1415 W Franklin St.
Boise, ID 83702
Ph: (208)343-5370
Free: 877-817-8141
URL: http://www.youthranch.org/

33816 ■ Intermountain Hospital
303 N Allumbaugh St.
Boise, ID 83704
Ph: (208)377-8400
Free: 800-321-5984
URL: http://intermountainhospital.com/

33817 ■ SunHealth Behavioral Health System for Boise
8050 Northview St.
Boise, ID 83704
Ph: (208)327-0504

Coeur d'Alene

33818 ■ Anchor House
1609 N Government Way
Coeur d'Alene, ID 83814
Ph: (208)667-3340
URL: http://www.youthranch.org/

Nampa

33819 ■ Nampa Group Home
4403 E Locust Ln.
Nampa, ID 83686
Ph: (208)467-1750
URL: http://www.youthranch.org/

Orofino

33820 ■ State Hospital North
300 Hospital Dr.
Orofino, ID 83544
Ph: (208)476-4511
URL: http://www.hospitalnorth.com/

Rupert

33821 ■ Idaho Youth Ranch
1275 N 400 E
Rupert, ID 83350
Ph: (208)532-4117
Free: 877-817-8141
URL: http://www.youthranch.org/

ILLINOIS

Alton

33822 ■ Alton Mental Health Center
4500 College Ave.
Alton, IL 62002
Ph: (618)474-3200
Fax: (618)474-3251
URL: http://www.dhs.state.il.us/page.aspx

Anna

33823 ■ Choate Mental Health Center
1000 N Main St.
Anna, IL 62906
Ph: (618)833-5161
Fax: (618)833-4191
URL: http://www.dhs.state.il.us/page.aspx?item=29728

Arlington Heights

33824 ■ Kids Hope United
Lake/Cook Behavioral Health Center
3285 N Arlington Heights Rd., Ste. 201
Arlington Heights, IL 60004
Ph: (847)577-1501
URL: http://www.kidshopeunited.org/

Centralia

33825 ■ One Hope United--Centralia
1400 E McCord St.
Centralia, IL 62801
Ph: (618)532-4311
URL: http://www.onehopeunited.org/
Formerly: Kids Hope United.

Champaign

33826 ■ Pavilion Behavioral Health System
809 W Church St.
Champaign, IL 61820-3999
Ph: (217)373-1700
Free: 800-373-1700
Fax: (217)373-1737
E-mail: info@pavilionhospital.com
URL: http://www.pavilionhospital.com
Formerly: The Pavilion.

Chester

33827 ■ Chester Mental Health Center
1315 Lehmen Dr.
Chester, IL 62233-2542
Ph: (618)826-4571

Chicago

33828 ■ Chicago Lakeshore Hospital
4840 N Marine Dr.
Chicago, IL 60640
Ph: (773)878-9700
Free: 800-888-0560
URL: http://www.chicagolakeshorehospital.com

33829 ■ Chicago--Read Mental Health Center
4200 N Oak Park Ave.
Chicago, IL 60634-1417
Ph: (773)794-4000
URL: http://www.dhs.state.il.us/page.aspx?item=29734

33830 ■ Children's Home and Aid Society
125 S Wacker Dr., 14th Fl.
Chicago, IL 60606
Ph: (312)424-0200
URL: http://www.childrenshomeandaid.org/

33831 ■ Hartgrove Hospital
5730 W Roosevelt Rd.
Chicago, IL 60644
Ph: (773)413-1700
URL: http://www.hartgrovehospital.com/

33832 ■ Mercy Home for Boys and Girls
Girls Campus
1140 W Jackson Blvd.
Chicago, IL 60607
Ph: (312)738-7560
Free: 877-637-2955
URL: http://www.mercyhome.org/

33833 ■ One Hope United--Chicago
514 W 31st St.
Chicago, IL 60601
Ph: (312)949-4000
URL: http://www.onehopeunited.org/
Formerly: Kids Hope United.

33834 ■ Uhlich Children's Advantage Network
Uhlich Children's Home
3737 N Mozart St.
Chicago, IL 60618

Ph: (773)588-0180
Fax: (773)588-7762
E-mail: info@ucanchicago.org
URL: http://www.ucanchicago.org/

33835 ■ University of Chicago Sonia Shankman Orthogenic School
1365 E 60th St.
Chicago, IL 60637
Ph: (773)702-1203
Fax: (773)702-1304
URL: http://orthogenicschool.uchicago.edu/

Chicago Heights

33836 ■ Aunt Martha's Youth Service Center
233 W Joe Orr Rd.
Chicago Heights, IL 60411
Ph: (708)754-1044
URL: http://www.auntmarthas.org/

Elgin

33837 ■ Elgin Mental Health Center
750 S State St.
Elgin, IL 60123-7692
Ph: (847)742-1040
URL: http://www.dhs.state.il.us/page.aspx

Forest Park

33838 ■ Riveredge Hospital
8311 Roosevelt Rd.
Forest Park, IL 60130
Ph: (708)771-7000
Fax: (708)209-2280
URL: http://www.psysolutions.com/facilities/riveredge/
Beds: 210.

Hoffman Estates

33839 ■ Alexian Brothers Behavioral Health Hospital
1650 Moon Lake Blvd.
Hoffman Estates, IL 60169
Ph: (847)882-1600
Free: 800-432-5005
Fax: (847)843-6575
URL: http://www.alexianbrothershealth.org/services/abbhh/index.aspx

Joliet

33840 ■ Highland Group Home
2259 Highland Park Dr.
Joliet, IL 60432
Ph: (815)722-2435

33841 ■ Trinity Services Inc.
100 Gougar Rd.
Joliet, IL 60432
Ph: (815)485-6197
URL: http://www.trinity-services.org/

Lockport

33842 ■ Caton Farm House
1133 Caton Farm Rd.
Lockport, IL 60441
Ph: (815)723-6782

33843 ■ Lockport Center for Behavioral Health
900 S State St.
Lockport, IL 60441
Ph: (815)838-0997

33844 ■ Oak Center for Behavioral Health
18100 S Oak Ave.
Lockport, IL 60441
Ph: (815)774-0327
URL: http://www.trinity-services.org/programs_services/Behavioral_Health.aspx

33845 ■ Pod House
18130 Oak Ave.
Lockport, IL 60441
Ph: (815)727-4608

33846 ■ Purdy Farm House
1733 Cougar Rd.
Lockport, IL 60441
Ph: (815)838-1101

33847 ■ State Street House
2002 S State St.
Lockport, IL 60441
Ph: (815)836-8355

Manhattan

33848 ■ Manhattan Cougar House
27655 Cougar Rd.
Manhattan, IL 60442
Ph: (815)478-7559

Maywood

33849 ■ Madden Mental Health Center
1200 S 1st Ave.
Maywood, IL 60153
Ph: (708)338-7202

Naperville

33850 ■ Linden Oaks Hospital
1250 N Mill St.
Naperville, IL 60540
Ph: (630)646-8000
URL: http://www.edward.org/body.cfm?id=106&oTopID=106

33851 ■ Linden Oaks Hospital--Edwards
801 S Washington St.
Naperville, IL 60540
Ph: (630)305-5500
URL: http://www.edward.org/body.cfm?id=106&oTopID=106

New Lenox

33852 ■ Spencer House
15544 W Spencer
New Lenox, IL 60451
Ph: (815)462-3449

Oak Lawn

33853 ■ Advocate Christ Medical Center
4440 W 95th St.
Oak Lawn, IL 60453-2699
Ph: (708)425-8000
URL: http://www.advocatehealth.com

Palatine

33854 ■ Camelot Schools LLC Palatine Campus
1502 W Northwest Hwy.
Palatine, IL 60067
Ph: (847)359-5600
URL: http://www.camelotforkids.org/

Park Ridge

33855 ■ Park Ridge Youth Campus
733 N Prospect Ave.
Park Ridge, IL 60068
Ph: (847)823-5161
URL: http://www.theyouthcampus.org/

Rockford

33856 ■ H. Douglas Singer Mental Health Center
4402 N Main St.
Rockford, IL 61103
Ph: (815)987-7096
Fax: (815)987-7581
Formerly: H. Douglas Singer Mental Health Development Center.

Springfield

33857 ■ Andrew McFarland Mental Health Center
901 Southwind Dr.
Springfield, IL 62703
Ph: (217)786-6900
Fax: (217)786-7167
URL: http://www.dhs.state.il.us/page.aspx

Streamwood

33858 ■ Streamwood at Saint Mary's
1400 E Irving Park Rd.
Streamwood, IL 60107
Ph: (312)837-9000
URL: http://www.psysolutions.com/facilities/streamwood/stmary.html

Tinley Park

33859 ■ Tinley Park Mental Health Center
7400 W 183rd St.
Tinley Park, IL 60477
Ph: (708)614-4000
URL: http://www.dhs.state.il.us/page.aspx

West Lafayette

33860 ■ Wabash Valley Hospital--West Lafayette
2900 N River Rd.
West Lafayette, IL 47906
Ph: (765)463-2555
Free: 800-859-5553
URL: http://www.wvhmhc.org/

Westchester

33861 ■ Resurrection Behavioral Health
9855 W Roosevelt Rd.
Westchester, IL 60154
Ph: (708)681-2324
URL: http://www.reshealth.org/rhcservices/behavioral/behavioral_health_servicesc fm

INDIANA

Auburn

33862 ■ Samara Hospital Northeastern Center Inc.
1850 Wesley Rd.
Auburn, IN 46706
Ph: (260)927-0726
URL: http://76.12.88.208/

Bloomington

33863 ■ Meadows Behavioral Healthcare
241 Winslow Rd.
Bloomington, IN 47401
Ph: (812)331-8000
Free: 800-972-4410
URL: http://www.psysolutions.com/facilities/meadows/

33864 ■ Meadows Hospital
3600 N Prow Rd.
Bloomington, IN 47404-1616
Ph: (812)331-8000
Free: 800-972-4410
URL: http://www.psysolutions.com/facilities/meadows/

Bluffton

33865 ■ Park Center, Inc.
1115 S Main St.
Bluffton, IN 46714
Ph: (260)824-1071
URL: http://www.parkcenter.org/

Columbus

33866 ■ Behavioral HealthCare Columbus
2223 Poshard Rd.
Columbus, IN 47203
Ph: (812)376-1711
Free: 800-562-5213
URL: http://www.psysolutions.com/facilities/columbus/

Crawfordsville

33867 ■ Wabash Valley Hospital--Crawfordsville
1480 Darlington Ave.
Crawfordsville, IN 47933
Ph: (765)362-2852
URL: http://www.wvhmhc.org/contact.htm

Delphi

33868 ■ Wabash Valley Hospital--Delphi
1265 N Bradford Ct.
Delphi, IN 46823
Ph: (765)564-2247
URL: http://www.wvhmhc.org/contact.htm

Elkhart

33869 ■ Madison Center Elkhart
56218 Parkway Ave.
Elkhart, IN 46516
Ph: (574)523-3750
Fax: (574)523-3770
URL: http://www.madison.org/index.php?MenuID=6

33870 ■ Oaklawn Center--Elkhart
2600 Oakland Ave.
Elkhart, IN 46517-1597
Ph: (574)533-1234
URL: http://www.oaklawn.org/

33871 ■ The Villages of Indiana--Elkhart
3132 Old US 20 W, Ste. A1
Elkhart, IN 46514
Ph: (574)294-5756
URL: http://www.villageskids.org/

Evansville

33872 ■ Deaconess Cross Pointe Center
7200 E Indiana St.
Evansville, IN 47715
Ph: (812)476-7200
Free: 800-947-6789
URL: http://www.deaconess.com/body.cfm?id=8

33873 ■ Evansville State Hospital
3400 Lincoln Ave.
Evansville, IN 47714-0146
Ph: (812)469-6800
URL: http://www.in.gov/fssa/dmha/4325.htm

33874 ■ Evansville State Psychiatric Treatment Center for Children
3300 E Morgan Ave.
Evansville, IN 47715-2232
Ph: (812)477-6436
URL: http://www.in.gov/fssa/dmha/4325.htm

33875 ■ The Villages of Indiana--Evansville
1522 SE Riverside Dr.
Evansville, IN 47713
Ph: (812)434-2956
URL: http://www.villageskids.org/

Fort Wayne

33876 ■ Park Center, Inc.
909 E State Blvd.
Fort Wayne, IN 46805
Ph: (260)481-2700
Free: 866-481-2717
URL: http://www.parkcenter.org

33877 ■ Park Center, Inc. Drop In Center
3020 S Calhoun St.
Fort Wayne, IN 46807
Ph: (260)456-1227
URL: http://www.parkcenter.org

33878 ■ Park Center, Inc. Harmony House
4929 Hoagland Ave.
Fort Wayne, IN 46807-3226
Ph: (260)745-0163
URL: http://www.parkcenter.org

33879 ■ Park Center, Inc. Haven House
2605 E State Blvd.
Fort Wayne, IN 46805-4729
Ph: (219)496-8625
URL: http://www.parkcenter.org

33880 ■ Park Center, Inc. Lee House
2714 N Clinton St.
Fort Wayne, IN 46805-1906
Ph: (260)483-0475
Fax: (260)483-0475
URL: http://www.parkcenter.org

33881 ■ Park Center, Inc. Leslie House
2827 Tilman Rd.
Fort Wayne, IN 46816
Ph: (260)447-3977
URL: http://www.parkcenter.org

33882 ■ Park Center, Inc. Noel House
2821 Elmdale Dr.
Fort Wayne, IN 46816-1411
Ph: (260)447-3378
URL: http://www.parkcenter.org

33883 ■ Park Center, Inc. Quinn House
1004 W Wayne St.
Fort Wayne, IN 46802-5933
Ph: (260)426-3219
URL: http://www.parkcenter.org

33884 ■ Park Center, Inc. Unity House
924 W Washington Blvd.
Fort Wayne, IN 46802-3955
Ph: (260)422-3202
URL: http://www.parkcenter.org

33885 ■ Park Center Lifeplan--Employee Assistance Program
3225 N Wells St.
Fort Wayne, IN 46808
Ph: (260)481-2888
Free: 800-677-4477
Fax: (260)969-4827
URL: http://www.parkcenter.org

Gary

33886 ■ Edgewater Systems for Balanced Living
1100 W 6th Ave.
Gary, IN 46402
Ph: (219)885-4264
URL: http://www.edgewatersystems.org/

33887 ■ The Villages of Indiana--Gary
3229 Broadway
Gary, IN 46409
Ph: (219)980-6185
URL: http://www.villageskids.org/

Goshen

33888 ■ Oaklawn
101 Marilyn Ave.
Goshen, IN 46526
Ph: (219)533-1234
URL: http://www.oaklawn.org

33889 ■ Oaklawn Center--Goshen
201 N Cottage Ave.
Goshen, IN 46528-3345
Ph: (574)533-9908
URL: http://www.oaklawn.org
Formerly: Oaklawn Work Release Addictions Program.

33890 ■ Oaklawn Psychiatric Center, Inc.
330 Lakeview Dr.
Goshen, IN 46528-7000
Ph: (574)533-1234
Free: 800-282-0809
Fax: (574)537-2673
E-mail: info@oaklawn.org
URL: http://www.oaklawn.org

Greenwood

33891 ■ Valle Vista Health System
898 E Main St.
Greenwood, IN 46143
Ph: (317)887-1348
URL: http://www.psysolutions.com/facilities/valle-vista/

Hutchinson

33892 ■ Prairie View Inc.--Hutchinson
335 N Washington St., Ste. 260
Hutchinson, IN 67502
Ph: (620)662-4700
Free: 800-992-6292
URL: http://www.prairieview.com/hutch-locations.html

Indianapolis

33893 ■ Larue D. Carter Memorial Hospital
2601 Cold Spring Rd.
Indianapolis, IN 46222
Ph: (317)941-4000
Fax: (317)941-4085

33894 ■ Options Treatment Center
5602 Caito Dr.
Indianapolis, IN 46226
Ph: (317)544-4340
Free: 800-431-1114
URL: http://www.optionstreatmentcenter.com/

33895 ■ The Villages of Indianapolis
3706 Washington Blvd.
Indianapolis, IN 46205
Ph: (317)927-7757
URL: http://www.villageskids.org/

Kendallville

33896 ■ Northeastern Center
1930 E Dowling St.
Kendallville, IN 46755
Ph: (260)347-4400
URL: http://76.12.88.208/

33897 ■ Northeastern Center
220 S Main St.
Kendallville, IN 46755
Ph: (260)347-2453
Free: 800-790-0118
URL: http://76.12.88.208/

Kokomo

33898 ■ The Villages of Indiana--Kokomo
608 E Blvd.
Kokomo, IN 46902
Ph: (765)455-8545
URL: http://www.villageskids.org/

Lafayette

33899 ■ Wabash Valley Hospital--Lafayette
610 Main St.
Lafayette, IN 47901
Ph: (765)423-2638
Free: 800-859-5553
URL: http://www.wvhmhc.org/contact.htm

Lexington

33900 ■ Three Springs Inc.
Three Springs Englishton Park
2426 S English Dr.
Lexington, IN 47138
Ph: (812)889-3992
URL: http://www.sequeltsi.com/

Logansport

33901 ■ Logansport State Hospital
1098 S State Rd. 25
Logansport, IN 46947
Ph: (574)722-4141
Fax: (574)735-3414
URL: http://www.in.gov/fssa/dmha/

Madison

33902 ■ Madison State Hospital
711 Green Rd.
Madison, IN 47250
Ph: (812)265-2611
URL: http://www.in.gov/fssa/dmha/

Mishawaka

33903 ■ Children's Campus, Inc.
1411 Lincoln Way W
Mishawaka, IN 46544
Ph: (574)259-5666
Free: 888-8-CAMPUS
URL: http://www.childrenscampus.org/

Monticello

33904 ■ Wabash Valley Hospital--Monticello
920 W Executive
Monticello, IN 47960
Ph: (574)583-9350
Free: 800-859-5553
URL: http://www.wvhmhc.org/contact.htm

Plymouth

33905 ■ Madison Center Plymouth
209 E Jefferson St.
Plymouth, IN 46563-1823
Ph: (574)935-3770
Fax: (574)935-3788
URL: http://www.madison.org/

33906 ■ Michiana Behavioral Health Center
1800 N Oak Rd.
Plymouth, IN 46563
Ph: (574)936-3784
Formerly: Northern Indiana Hospital, Behavioral Health Care Center.

Portage

33907 ■ The Villages of Indiana--Portage
1605 Adler Cir., Ste. A
Portage, IN 46368
Ph: (219)762-3465
URL: http://www.villageskids.org/

Rensselaer

33908 ■ Wabash Valley Hospital--Rensselaer
131 W Drexel Pkwy.
Rensselaer, IN 47978
Ph: (219)866-4194
URL: http://www.wvhmhc.org/contact.htm

Richmond

33909 ■ Richmond State Hospital
498 NW 18th St.
Richmond, IN 47374
Ph: (765)966-0511
URL: http://www.in.gov/fssa/dmha/6914.htm

South Bend

33910 ■ Madison Center for Children
701 N Niles Ave.
South Bend, IN 46617
Ph: (574)234-0061
Free: 877-234-0061
Fax: (574)283-1129
URL: http://www.madison.org/index.php?MenuID=6

33911 ■ Madison Center Harris House
1301 E Jackson Rd.
South Bend, IN 46614
Ph: (574)299-0840
URL: http://www.madison.org/

33912 ■ Madison Center and Hospital
403 E Madison St.
South Bend, IN 46617
Ph: (574)234-0061
URL: http://www.madison.org/

33913 ■ Madison Center Metcalfe House
801 Riverside Ct.
South Bend, IN 46616-1645
Ph: (574)232-7907
URL: http://www.madison.org/

33914 ■ Madison Center New Passages and Community Support Program
813 S Michigan St.
South Bend, IN 46601-3102
Ph: (574)282-8712
URL: http://www.madison.org/

33915 ■ Madison Center Portage Manor
3016 Portage Ave.
South Bend, IN 46628
Ph: (574)272-1266
URL: http://www.madison.org/

33916 ■ Madison Center Providence House
475 N Niles Ave.
South Bend, IN 46617
Ph: (574)246-4123
URL: http://www.madison.org/

33917 ■ Riverside Hospital and Madison Center QuietCare
533 N Niles Ave.
South Bend, IN 46617
Ph: (574)283-1751
Fax: (574)235-1965
URL: http://www.madison.org/

IOWA

Cherokee

33918 ■ Mental Health Institute Cherokee
1251 W Cedar Loop
Cherokee, IA 51012
Ph: (712)225-1698
E-mail: rmoller@dhs.state.ia.us
URL: http://www.dhs.state.ia.us/Consumers/Facilities/Cherokee.html

Clarinda

33919 ■ Clarinda Mental Health Institute
1800 N 16th St.
Clarinda, IA 51632
Ph: (712)542-2161
URL: http://www.dhs.state.ia.us/Consumers/Facilities/Clarinda.html
Formerly: Clarinda Treatment Complex.

Des Moines

33920 ■ Orchard Place
PACE Juvenile Center
620 8th St.
Des Moines, IA 50309
Ph: (515)697-5700
Fax: (515)697-5701
URL: http://www.orchardplace.org/

Independence

33921 ■ Mental Health Institute
2277 Iowa Ave.
Independence, IA 50644
Ph: (319)334-2583
Fax: (319)334-5252
URL: http://www.dhs.state.ia.us/Consumers/Facilities/Independence.html

Mason City

33922 ■ Gerard Treatment Programs
980 Iowa Ave.
Mason City, IA 50401
Ph: (641)423-3222

Mount Pleasant

33923 ■ Mount Pleasant Treatment Center Mental Health Institute
1200 E Washington St.
Mount Pleasant, IA 52641-1897
Ph: (319)385-7231
Fax: (319)385-8465
URL: http://www.dhs.state.ia.us/Consumers/Facilities/MtPleasant.html

Sioux City

33924 ■ Boys and Girls Home and Family Services
2101 Court St.
Sioux City, IA 51104
Ph: (712)293-4700
URL: http://www.boysandgirlshome.com/

Wallingford

33925 ■ Forest Ridge Youth and Family Resource Services
4502 230th St.
Wallingford, IA 51365
Ph: (712)867-4724
Fax: (712)867-4177
URL: http://www.yfrs.org/
Formerly: Forest Ridge Youth Services.

KANSAS

Kansas City

33926 ■ Kaw Valley Psychiatric Hospital
4300 Brenner Dr.
Kansas City, KS 66104
Ph: (913)334-0294
URL: http://www.kvc.org/

33927 ■ Rainbow Mental Health Facility
2205 W 36th Ave.
Kansas City, KS 66103-2198
Ph: (913)789-5800
URL: http://www.srskansas.org/hcp/MHSIP/MHSIPRainbowMHF.htm

Larned

33928 ■ Larned State Hospital
1301 KS Hwy. 264
Larned, KS 67550
Ph: (620)285-2131
URL: http://www.srskansas.org/LSH/default.html

McPherson

33929 ■ Prairie View Inc.--McPherson
1102 Hospital Dr.
McPherson, KS 67460
Ph: (620)245-5000
Free: 800-992-6292
URL: http://www.prairieview.org/marion-locations.html

Mission

33930 ■ Johnson County Mental Health Center
6000 Lamar Ave., Ste. 130
Mission, KS 66202
Ph: (913)831-2550
URL: http://mentalhealth.jocogov.org/contactus.htm

Newton

33931 ■ Prairie View, Inc.--Newton
1901 E 1st St.
Newton, KS 67114
Ph: (316)284-6400
Free: 800-362-0180
URL: http://www.prairieview.org

Olathe

33932 ■ KVC Behavioral Health Care
21350 W 153rd St.
Olathe, KS 66061
Ph: (913)621-5753
URL: http://www.kvc.org/

Osawatomie

33933 ■ Osawatomie State Hospital
500 State Hospital Dr.
Osawatomie, KS 66064
Ph: (913)755-7000
URL: http://www.srskansas.org/hcp/MHSIP/MHSI-POsawatomieStateMHHospital.htm

Overland Park

33934 ■ Marillac Center
8000 W 127th St.
Overland Park, KS 66213
Ph: (913)663-KIDS
URL: http://www.marillac.org/

Topeka

33935 ■ The Menninger Clinic
5800 SW 6th Ave.
Topeka, KS 66601-0829
Ph: (713)275-5000
Free: 800-351-9058
Fax: (713)275-5107
URL: http://www.menningerclinic.com

Wichita

33936 ■ Prairie View Inc.--Wichita
7570 W 21st St. N, Ste. 1026D
Wichita, KS 67205
Ph: (316)729-6555
URL: http://www.prairieview.com/hutch-locations.html

33937 ■ Prairie View Inc.--Wichita
9333 E 21st St. N
Wichita, KS 67206
Ph: (316)634-4700
URL: http://www.prairieview.com/hutch-locations.html

33938 ■ Via Christi Regional Medical Center
8901 E Orme St.
Wichita, KS 67207
Ph: (316)858-0333
URL: http://www.via-christi.org/

33939 ■ Youthville
8400 W Murdock St.
Wichita, KS 67212
Ph: (316)283-1950
URL: http://www.youthville.org/Default.aspx

KENTUCKY

Bowling Green

33940 ■ Rivendell Behavioral Health Service--Bowling Green
1035 Porter Pke.
Bowling Green, KY 42103
Ph: (270)843-1199
Free: 800-548-2621
URL: http://www.rivendellbehavioral.com/

Burlington

33941 ■ Children's Home of Northern Kentucky
Maplewood Campus
3261 Maplewood Dr.
Burlington, KY 41005
Ph: (859)334-3550
URL: http://www.chnk.org/

Henderson

33942 ■ River Valley Behavioral Health--Henderson
Therapeutic Rehabilitation Program
205 US Hwy. 41 S
Henderson, KY 42420
Ph: (270)826-1978
Free: 800-737-0696
E-mail: info@rvbh.com
URL: http://www.rvbh.com/

Hopkinsville

33943 ■ FHC Cumberland Hall - Hopkinsville
210 W 17th St.
Hopkinsville, KY 42240
Ph: (270)886-1919
URL: http://www.psysolutions.com/facilities/cumberlandhall/

33944 ■ Western State Hospital--Hopkinsville
2400 Russellville Rd.
Hopkinsville, KY 42240
Ph: (270)889-6025

La Grange

33945 ■ Kentucky Correctional Psychiatric Center
1612 Dawkins Rd.
La Grange, KY 40031
Ph: (502)222-7161

Lexington

33946 ■ Eastern State Hospital--Lexington
627 W 4th St.
Lexington, KY 40508
Ph: (859)246-7000
Fax: (859)246-7018

33947 ■ Ridge Behavioral Health System
3050 Rio Dosa Dr.
Lexington, KY 40509
Ph: (859)269-2325
Free: 800-753-4673
Fax: (859)268-6456
URL: https://www.ridgebhs.com/indexnew.html

Louisville

33948 ■ Central State Hospital--Louisville
10510 La Grange Rd.
Louisville, KY 40223
Ph: (502)253-7500
URL: http://www.centralstatehospital.org/

33949 ■ Our Lady of Peace
2020 Newburg Rd.
Louisville, KY 40205
Ph: (502)451-3330
URL: http://www.caritas.com/carecenters/mental-health.asp

33950 ■ Ten Broeck Hospital - Kentucky
8521 La Grange Rd.
Louisville, KY 40242
Ph: (502)426-6380
Free: 800-866-8876
Fax: (502)429-5787

33951 ■ Tenbroeck Hospital at KMI Campus
1405 Browns Ln.
Louisville, KY 40207
Ph: (502)896-0495

Owensboro

33952 ■ River Valley Behavioral Health Hospital
Psychiatric Residential Treatment
360 Rudy Rd.
Owensboro, KY 42301
Ph: (270)691-0786
Free: 800-769-4920
URL: http://www.rvbh.com/locations.html

33953 ■ River Valley Behavioral Health--Industrial Drive, Owensboro
1000 Industrial Dr.
Owensboro, KY 42301
Ph: (270)689-6800
Free: 800-755-8477
URL: http://www.rvbh.com/locations.html

33954 ■ River Valley Behavioral Health--Walnut Street, Owensboro
1100 Walnut St.
Owensboro, KY 42301
Ph: (270)689-6500
Free: 800-769-4920
URL: http://www.rvbh.com/locations.html

Radcliff

33955 ■ Lincoln Trail Hospital
Lincoln Trail Behavioral Health System
3909 S Wilson Rd.
Radcliff, KY 40160
Ph: (270)351-9444
E-mail: info@linlolnbehavioral.com
URL: http://www.lincolnbehavioral.com/

LOUISIANA

Alexandria

33956 ■ Crossroad Regional Hospital
110 Eskew Dr.
Alexandria, LA 71303
Ph: (318)445-5111
URL: http://www.crossroadshospital.com/

Covington

33957 ■ HSA Greenbrier Hospital
201 Greenbrier Blvd.
Covington, LA 70433
Ph: (985)893-2970
Formerly: Advance Care.

Greenwell Springs

33958 ■ Greenwell Springs Hospital
23260 Greenwell Springs Rd.
Greenwell Springs, LA 70739
Ph: (225)261-2730
URL: http://www.dhh.louisiana.gov/offices/locations.asp?ID=62&Detail=1015

Jackson

33959 ■ East Louisiana Mental Health System
4502 Hwy. 951
Jackson, LA 70748
Ph: (225)634-0100
E-mail: alord@dhh.la.gov
URL: http://www.dhh.louisiana.gov/offices/locations.asp?ID=62&Detail=126

33960 ■ Feliciana Forensic Facility
5226 Hwy. 951
Jackson, LA 70748
Ph: (225)634-2661
URL: http://www.dhh.louisiana.gov/offices/locations.asp?ID=62&Detail=126

Lafayette

33961 ■ Joseph H. Tyler Jr. Mental Health Center
University Medical Center
302 Dulles Dr.
Lafayette, LA 70506
Ph: (337)262-4100
Fax: (337)262-1146
URL: http://www.dhh.louisiana.gov/offices/locations.asp?ID=62&Detail=91

33962 ■ Vermilion Hospital
2520 N University Ave.
Lafayette, LA 70507
Ph: (337)234-5614
Free: 800-821-2567
Fax: (337)235-0696
URL: http://www.acadiahealthcare.com/

Mandeville

33963 ■ Southeast Louisiana Hospital
23515 Hwy. 190
Mandeville, LA 70470
Ph: (985)626-6300
Fax: (985)626-6559
URL: http://www.dhh.louisiana.gov/offices/locations.asp?ID=62&Detail=125

Monroe

33964 ■ Saint Patrick's Psychiatric Hospital
309 Jackson St.
Monroe, LA 71201
Ph: (318)327-4686
URL: http://www.stpatrickshospital.net/

New Orleans

33965 ■ DePaul Tulane Behavioral Health Center
1040 Calhoun St.
New Orleans, LA 70118
Ph: (504)897-5720
URL: http://www.depaultulane.com

33966 ■ New Orleans Adolescent Hospital
210 State St.
New Orleans, LA 70118
Ph: (504)897-3400
Fax: (504)896-4959
URL: http://www.dhh.louisiana.gov/offices/locations.asp?ID=62&Detail=130

33967 ■ River Oaks Psychiatric Hospital
1525 River Oaks Rd. W
New Orleans, LA 70123
Ph: (504)734-1740
Free: 800-366-1740
Fax: (504)733-7020
URL: http://www.riveroakshospital.com

Opelousas

33968 ■ Opelousas Mental Health Center
220 S Market St.
Opelousas, LA 70570
Ph: (337)948-0226
Fax: (337)948-0399
URL: http://www.dhh.louisiana.gov/offices/locations.asp?ID=62&Detail=906

Pineville

33969 ■ Central Louisiana State Hospital
242 W Shamrock St.
Pineville, LA 71361
Ph: (318)484-6200
Fax: (318)484-6501
E-mail: clshmail@dhh.state.la.us
URL: http://www.dhh.louisiana.gov/offices/locations.asp?ID=62&Detail=124

Shreveport

33970 ■ Brentwood Hospital--Shreveport
1006 Highland Ave.
Shreveport, LA 71101
Ph: (318)678-7500
Free: 877-678-7500
URL: http://www.psysolutions.com/facilities/brentwoodhospital/
Formerly: Charter Behavioral Health System of Shreveport and Brentwood--A Behavioral Health Co., L.L.C.

MAINE

Augusta

33971 ■ Augusta Mental Health Institute
67 Independence Dr.
Augusta, ME 04332
Ph: (207)287-7200
Fax: (207)287-7127

33972 ■ Riverview Psychiatric Center
250 Arsenal St.
Augusta, ME 04332
Ph: (207)624-4600
URL: http://www.maine.gov/dhhs/riverview/index.shtml

Bangor

33973 ■ The Acadia Hospital
268 Stillwater Ave.
Bangor, ME 04402
Ph: (207)973-6100
Free: 800-640-1211
URL: http://acadiahospital.org/
Formerly: Acadia Hospital Corp.

33974 ■ Dorthea Dix Psychiatric Center
656 State St.
Bangor, ME 04402
Ph: (207)941-4000
Free: 888-774-5290
E-mail: larry.larson@maine.gov
URL: http://www.maine.gov/dhhs/DDPC/index.shtml
Formerly: Bangor Mental Health Institute.

Blue Hill

33975 ■ Acadia Hospital Blue Hill Clinic
65 Water St.
Blue Hill, ME 04614
Ph: (207)374-5780
URL: http://acadiahospital.org/

Pittsfield

33976 ■ Acadia Hospital Pittsfield Clinic
169 N Main St.
Pittsfield, ME 04967
Ph: (207)487-3308
Fax: (207)487-4591
URL: http://acadiahospital.org/

Westbrook

33977 ■ Spring Harbor Hospital
123 Andover Rd.
Westbrook, ME 04092
Ph: (207)761-2200
Free: 888-524-0080
URL: http://www.springharbor.org/sphar_homepage.cfm?id=2432&SubDomain=true

MARYLAND

Baltimore

33978 ■ Sheppard Pratt Health System
6501 N Charles St.
Baltimore, MD 21204
Ph: (410)938-3000
URL: http://www.sheppardpratt.org

33979 ■ Walter P. Carter Center
630 W Fayette St.
Baltimore, MD 21201
Ph: (410)209-6200
Fax: (410)209-6020
URL: http://www.dhmh.state.md.us/carter/

Cambridge

33980 ■ Eastern Shore Hospital Center
5262 Woods Rd.
Cambridge, MD 21613
Ph: (410)221-2300
Free: 888-216-8110
URL: http://www.dhmh.state.md.us/eshc/index.htm

Catonsville

33981 ■ Spring Grove Hospital Center
55 Wade Ave.
Catonsville, MD 21228
Ph: (410)402-6000
URL: http://www.springgrove.com/
Beds: 440.

Chestertown

33982 ■ Upper Shore Community Mental Health Center
300 Scheeler Rd.
Chestertown, MD 21620
Ph: (410)778-6800

Cumberland

33983 ■ Thomas B. Finan Center
10102 Country Club Rd. SE
Cumberland, MD 21501
Ph: (301)777-2240
Free: 888-854-0035
Fax: (301)777-2364
URL: http://dhmh.state.md.us/finan/

Ellicott City

33984 ■ Sheppard Pratt at Ellicott City Taylor Manor Hospital
4100 College Ave.
Ellicott City, MD 21041
Ph: (410)465-3322
URL: http://www.sheppardpratt.org/sp_htmlcode/sp_locations/sp_loc_hc_tayresid.as px

Hagerstown

33985 ■ Brook Lane Health Services
13218 Brooklane Dr.
Hagerstown, MD 21742
Ph: (301)733-0330
Free: 800-342-2992
URL: http://www.brooklane.org/

33986 ■ Meadow Lane health Services Meadowbrook
18714 North Village Shopping Center
Hagerstown, MD 21740

Ph: (301)733-0330
URL: http://www.brooklane.org/
Formerly: Meadow Brook.

Jessup

33987 ■ Clifton T. Perkins Hospital Center
8450 Dorsey Run Rd.
Jessup, MD 20794
Ph: (410)724-3000
Free: 866-867-2027
Fax: (410)724-3249
URL: http://www.dhmh.state.md.us/perkins/

Randallstown

33988 ■ Mosaic Community Services
3525 Resource Dr.
Randallstown, MD 21133
Ph: (410)922-1900
Fax: (410)922-6288
URL: http://www.sheppardpratt.org/sp_htmlcode/sp_locations/sp_loc_balt_mosaic.as px
Formerly: Sheppard Pratt at Northwestern.

Rockville

33989 ■ Potomac Ridge Behavioral Health
14901 Broschart Rd.
Rockville, MD 20850
Ph: (301)251-4500
URL: http://www.potomacridge.com/PRBH/index.aspx
Formerly: Charter Behavioral Health System of Maryland at Potomac Ridge; Adventist Health at Potomac Ridge.

Sykesville

33990 ■ Springfield Hospital Center
6655 Sykesville Rd.
Sykesville, MD 21784
Ph: (410)970-7000
Free: 800-333-7564
URL: http://www.dhmh.state.md.us/springfield/

MASSACHUSETTS

Ashburnham

33991 ■ McLean Ambulatory Treatment Center, Naukeag
216 Lake Rd.
Ashburnham, MA 01430
Ph: (978)827-5115
Free: 800-230-8764
URL: http://www.mclean.harvard.edu/patient/adult/nauk.php

Attleboro

33992 ■ Arbour Fuller Hospital
200 May St.
Attleboro, MA 02703
Ph: (508)761-8500
URL: http://www.arbourhealth.com/

Belmont

33993 ■ McLean Hospital
115 Mill St.
Belmont, MA 02478
Ph: (617)855-2000
Free: 800-333-0338
Fax: (617)855-3299
E-mail: mcleaninfo@mclean.harvard.edu
URL: http://www.mclean.harvard.edu

Boston

33994 ■ Doctor Solomon Carter Fuller Mental Health Center
85 E Newton St.
Boston, MA 02118
Ph: (617)626-8800

Bridgewater

33995 ■ Bridgewater State Hospital
20 Administration Rd.
Bridgewater, MA 02324
Ph: (508)279-4500
URL: http://www.mass.gov/

Brockton

33996 ■ McLean Hospital Southeast
940 Belmont St., Bldg. 7, 2nd Fl.
Brockton, MA 02301
Ph: (508)894-8420
URL: http://www.mclean.harvard.edu/patient/child/mse.php

Brookline

33997 ■ Arbour - HRI Hospital
227 Babcock St.
Brookline, MA 02446
Ph: (617)731-3200
URL: http://www.arbourhealth.com/hri.htm

Chestnut Hill

33998 ■ Bournewood Health Systems Bournewood Hospital
300 South St.
Chestnut Hill, MA 02467
Ph: (617)469-0300
Free: 800-468-4358
URL: http://www.bournewood.com/

Georgetown

33999 ■ Baldpate Hospital
83 Baldpate Rd.
Georgetown, MA 01833-2399
Ph: (978)352-2131
E-mail: info@baldpateh.com
URL: http://www.baldpateh.com/

Jamaica Plain

34000 ■ Arbour Hospital
49 Robinwood Ave.
Jamaica Plain, MA 02130
Ph: (617)522-4400
URL: http://www.arbourhealth.com/

Palmer

34001 ■ Wing Memorial Hospital
40 Wright St.
Palmer, MA 01069
Ph: (413)283-7651
URL: http://www.umassmemorial.org/wingip.cfm?id=1795

Pembroke

34002 ■ Pembroke Hospital
199 Oak St.
Pembroke, MA 02359
Ph: (781)829-7000
Free: 800-222-2237
URL: http://www.arbourhealth.com/pembroke.htm

Quincy

34003 ■ Quincy Mental Health Center
460 Quincy Ave.
Quincy, MA 02169
Ph: (617)626-9025

Stockbridge

34004 ■ Austen Riggs Center
25 Main St.
Stockbridge, MA 01262
Ph: (413)298-5511
URL: http://www.austenriggs.org/

Taunton

34005 ■ Taunton State Hospital
60 Hodges Ave.
Taunton, MA 02780
Ph: (508)977-3000

Tewksbury

34006 ■ Tewksbury State Hospital
365 East St.
Tewksbury, MA 01876
Ph: (978)851-7321
URL: http://www.mass.gov/

Westborough

34007 ■ Westborough State Hospital
288 Lyman St.
Westborough, MA 01581
Ph: (508)616-2100

Westwood

34008 ■ Westwood Lodge Hospital
45 Clapboardtree St.
Westwood, MA 02090
Ph: (781)762-7764
Free: 800-222-2237
URL: http://www.arbourhealth.com

Worcester

34009 ■ Worcester State Hospital
305 Belmont St.
Worcester, MA 01604-1695
Ph: (508)334-2551

MICHIGAN

Auburn Hills

34010 ■ Havenwyck Hospital
1525 University Dr.
Auburn Hills, MI 48326
Ph: (248)373-9200
Free: 800-401-2727
URL: http://www.psysolutions.com/facilities/havenwyck/

Battle Creek

34011 ■ Fieldstone Center
Battle Creek Health Systems Department of Psychiatry and Behavioral Health
165 N Washington Ave.
Battle Creek, MI 49017
Ph: (269)964-7121
URL: http://www.bchealth.com/services/fieldstone/
Formerly: Battle Creek Health Systems/ Fieldstone Center.

Caro

34012 ■ Caro Center
2000 Chambers Rd.
Caro, MI 48723
Ph: (989)673-3191
URL: http://www.michigan.gov/mdch/0,1607,7-132-2941_4868_4896-14451--,00.html

Clinton Township

34013 ■ Henry Ford Behavioral Health--Clinton Township
42633 Garfield Rd., Ste. 314
Clinton Township, MI 48038
Ph: (586)226-7007
Free: 800-436-7936
URL: http://www.mhweb.org/macomb/hford.htm

Dearborn

34014 ■ Henry Ford Behavioral Health--Dearborn
5111 Auto Club Dr., Ste. 112
Dearborn, MI 48126
Ph: (313)317-2000

Free: 800-436-7936
URL: http://www.mhweb.org/

Detroit

34015 ■ Henry Ford Behavioral Health--Detroit
1 Ford Pl.
Detroit, MI 48202
Ph: (313)874-6677
Free: 800-436-7936
URL: http://www.mhweb.org/

Ferndale

34016 ■ Henry Ford Kingswood Hospital
10300 W 8 Mile Rd.
Ferndale, MI 48220
Ph: (248)398-3200
Free: 800-436-7936
URL: http://www.henryfordhealth.org/

Grand Rapids

34017 ■ Forest View Hospital
1055 Medical Park Dr. SE
Grand Rapids, MI 49546
Ph: (616)942-9610
URL: https://www.forestviewhospital.com/installflash.html

34018 ■ Pine Rest Christian Hospital
Health Services
300 68th St. SE
Grand Rapids, MI 49548-6995
Ph: (616)455-5000
Free: 800-678-5500
Fax: (616)455-5360
URL: http://www.pinerest.org

Kalamazoo

34019 ■ Kalamazoo Psychiatric Hospital
1312 Oakland Dr., Ste. A
Kalamazoo, MI 49008
Ph: (269)337-3000
Fax: (269)337-3350
URL: http://www.michigan.gov/mdch/0,1607,7-132-2941_4868_4896-14451--,00.html

34020 ■ Pine Rest Christian Mental Health Services
1530 Nicholas Rd.
Kalamazoo, MI 49006
Ph: (269)343-6700
Free: 800-678-5500
URL: http://www.pinerest.org/

New Baltimore

34021 ■ Harbor Oaks Hospital
35031 23 Mile Rd.
New Baltimore, MI 48047
Ph: (586)725-5777
Free: 800-537-7924
URL: http://www.harboroaks.com/

Northville

34022 ■ Hawthorn Center
18471 Haggerty Rd.
Northville, MI 48167
Ph: (248)349-3000
Fax: (248)349-9552
URL: http://www.michigan.gov/mdch/0,1607,7-132-2941_4868_4896-70281--,00.html

Troy

34023 ■ Henry Ford Behavioral Health--Troy
2825 Livernois Rd.
Troy, MI 48083
Ph: (248)680-2060
URL: http://www.mhweb.org/wayne/hford.htm

West Bloomfield

34024 ■ Henry Ford Behavioral Health--West Bloomfield
6773 W Maple Rd.
West Bloomfield, MI 48322
Ph: (248)661-6100
Free: 800-436-7936
URL: http://www.henryford.com/body_academic.cfm?id=48946

Westland

34025 ■ Walter Reuther Psychiatric Hospital
30901 Palmer Rd.
Westland, MI 48185
Ph: (734)367-8400
Fax: (734)722-5562
URL: http://www.michigan.gov/mdch/0,1607,7-132-2941_4868_4896-14451--,00.html
Formerly: Walter P. Reuther Psychiatric.

Wyoming

34026 ■ Pine Rest Christian Mental Health Services
2215 44th St. SW
Wyoming, MI 49509
Ph: (616)252-8371
Free: 800-678-5500
URL: http://www.pinerest.org/

MINNESOTA

Brainerd

34027 ■ Brainerd Regional Human Services Center
11800 State Hwy. 18
Brainerd, MN 56401
Ph: (218)828-2201

Fergus Falls

34028 ■ Fergus Falls Regional Treatment Center
1400 N Union Ave.
Fergus Falls, MN 56537
Ph: (218)739-7200
Fax: (218)739-7243
URL: http://www.ci.fergus-falls.mn.us/

Minnetonka

34029 ■ Prairie Saint John's Day Treatment
11610 Wayzata Blvd.
Minnetonka, MN 55305
Ph: (952)230-9110
Free: 877-333-9565
URL: http://prairie-stjohns.com/services/treatment-programs-available/

Moorhead

34030 ■ Prairie Saint John's
2925 20th St. S
Moorhead, MN 56560
Ph: (218)284-0300
Free: 877-333-9565
URL: http://prairie-stjohns.com/services/treatment-programs-available/

Saint Peter

34031 ■ Saint Peter's Regional Treatment
100 Freeman Dr.
Saint Peter, MN 56082
Ph: (507)931-5112
URL: http://www.dhs.state.mn.us/

Willmar

34032 ■ Willmar Regional Treatment Center
1550 N Hwy. 71
Willmar, MN 56201
Ph: (320)231-5330

Woodbury

34033 ■ Prairie Saint John's Day Treatment
7616 Currell Blvd., Ste. 100
Woodbury, MN 55125
Ph: (651)259-9700
Free: 888-9-PRAIRI
URL: http://prairie-stjohns.com/services/treatment-programs-available/

MISSISSIPPI

Flowood

34034 ■ Memorial Behavioral Health at Gulfport
Memorial Behavioral Health--Jackson
4 River Bend Pl., Ste. 205
Flowood, MS 39208
Ph: (601)939-8833
Free: 800-831-1700
URL: http://www.gulfportmemorial.com/

Gulfport

34035 ■ Memorial Behavioral Health
4500 13th St.
Gulfport, MS 39501
Ph: (228)831-1700
Free: 800-831-1700
URL: http://www.gulfportmemorial.com/

34036 ■ Memorial Behavioral Health at Gulfport
12266 Ashley Dr.
Gulfport, MS 39503
Ph: (228)831-1700
Free: 800-831-1700
URL: http://www.gulfportmemorial.com/

Hattiesburg

34037 ■ Memorial Behavioral Health at Gulfport--Hattiesburg
100 S 20th Ave.
Hattiesburg, MS 39401
Ph: (601)545-9301
Free: 800-831-1700
URL: http://www.gulfportmemorial.com/

Jackson

34038 ■ Brentwood Hospital--Jackson
Brentwood Behavioral Healthcare of Mississippi
3531 E Lakeland Dr.
Jackson, MS 39232
Ph: (601)936-2024
Free: 800-863-4004
URL: http://www.psysolutions.com/facilities/brentwoodjackson/physicians.html

34039 ■ Mississippi State Hospital
Claiborne House
539 Claiborne Ave.
Jackson, MS 39209
Ph: (601)368-9337
URL: http://www.msh.state.ms.us/

34040 ■ Mississippi State Hospital
Kitty Mitchell Group Home
1817 Wightman St.
Jackson, MS 39202
Ph: (601)352-3868
URL: http://www.msh.state.ms.us/

34041 ■ Mississippi State Hospital
Opportunity House
101 Rose St.
Jackson, MS 39203
Ph: (601)354-4469
URL: http://www.msh.state.ms.us/

34042 ■ Mississippi State Hospital Villa Hope Group Home
2631 St. Charles St.
Jackson, MS 39209
Ph: (601)969-5910
URL: http://www.msh.state.ms.us/
Formerly: Mississippi State Hospital Community Services.

Meridian

34043 ■ Alliance Health Center
5000 Hwy. 39 N
Meridian, MS 39307
Ph: (601)483-6211
URL: http://www.psysolutions.com/facilities/alliance

34044 ■ East End Manor
1601 17th Ave.
Meridian, MS 39301-3331
Ph: (601)693-0210

34045 ■ East Mississippi State Hospital
4555 Highland Park Dr.
Meridian, MS 39307
Ph: (601)581-7600
URL: http://www.emsh.state.ms.us

Olive Branch

34046 ■ Parkwood Behavioral Health System
8135 Goodman Rd.
Olive Branch, MS 38654
Ph: (662)895-4900
Free: 800-477-3422
E-mail: info@parkwoodbhs.com
URL: http://www.parkwoodbhs.com
Formerly: Charter Parkwood Behavioral Health System.

Pearl

34047 ■ Mississippi State Hospital
3550 Hwy. 468 W
Pearl, MS 39208
Ph: (601)351-8000
URL: http://www.msh.state.ms.us/

Purvis

34048 ■ South Mississippi State Hospital
823 Hwy. 589
Purvis, MS 39475
Ph: (601)794-0100
URL: http://www.smsh.state.ms.us/

Tupelo

34049 ■ North Mississippi State Hospital
1937 Briar Ridge Rd.
Tupelo, MS 38804
Ph: (662)690-4200
URL: http://www.nmsh.state.ms.us/

Whitfield

34050 ■ Mississippi State Hospital
3550 Hwy. 468 W
Whitfield, MS 39193
Ph: (601)351-8000
Fax: (601)939-0648
E-mail: info@msh.state.ms.us
URL: http://www.msh.state.ms.us

MISSOURI

Blue Springs

34051 ■ Blue Springs Behavioral Health Clinic
1932 NW Copper Oaks Cir.
Blue Springs, MO 64015
Ph: (816)228-9811

Farmington

34052 ■ Southeast Missouri Mental Health Center
1010 W Columbia St.
Farmington, MO 63640
Ph: (573)218-6792
URL: http://dmh.mo.gov/southeast/

Fulton

34053 ■ Fulton State Hospital
600 E 5th St.
Fulton, MO 65251-1798
Ph: (573)592-4100
URL: http://dmh.mo.gov/fulton/

Kansas City

34054 ■ Two Rivers Psychiatric Hospital
5121 Raytown Rd.
Kansas City, MO 64133
Ph: (816)382-6300
Fax: (816)358-5395
URL: http://www.tworivershospital.com

34055 ■ Western Missouri Mental Health Center
1000 E 24th St.
Kansas City, MO 64108-2776
Ph: (816)512-7000
URL: http://www.med.umkc.edu/admin/sections/hospitals/western_mo/western_mo.html

Nevada

34056 ■ Heartland Behavioral Health Services
1500 W Ashland St.
Nevada, MO 64772
Ph: (417)667-2666
Free: 800-654-9605
URL: http://www.psysolutions.com/facilities/heartland/

Saint Charles

34057 ■ Center Pointe of Saint Louis Hospital
5931 S Hwy. 94
Saint Charles, MO 63304
Ph: (636)441-7300
Free: 800-345-5407
Fax: (636)447-6001
URL: http://www.centerpointehospital.com/
Formerly: Spirit of Saint Louis Hospital.

Saint Joseph

34058 ■ Northwest Missouri Psychiatric Rehabilitation Center
3505 Frederick Ave.
Saint Joseph, MO 64506
Ph: (816)387-2300
URL: http://dmh.mo.gov/nmprc/

Saint Louis

34059 ■ Hawthorne Children's Psychiatric Hospital
1901 Pennsylvania Ave.
Saint Louis, MO 63133
Ph: (314)512-7800
URL: http://dmh.mo.gov/hcph/

34060 ■ Metropolitan Saint Louis Psychiatric Center
5351 Delmar Ave.
Saint Louis, MO 63112
Ph: (314)877-0500
Fax: (314)877-0553
URL: http://dmh.mo.gov/mpc/

34061 ■ Saint Louis Psychiatric Rehabilitation Center
5300 Arsenal St.
Saint Louis, MO 63137
Ph: (314)877-6500
E-mail: mfslprcinternetmail@dmh.mo.gov
URL: http://dmh.mo.gov/slprc/

Springfield

34062 ■ Lakeland Regional Hospital
440 S Market Ave.
Springfield, MO 65806
Ph: (417)865-5581
Free: 800-432-1210
URL: http://www.lakeland-hospital.com/

Windsor

34063 ■ Royal Oaks Hospital
307 N Main St.
Windsor, MO 65360
Ph: (660)647-2182
URL: http://www.royal-oaks-hospital.org/

MONTANA

Helena

34064 ■ Shodair Children's Hospital
2755 Colonial Dr.
Helena, MT 59604
Ph: (406)444-7500
Free: 800-447-6614
E-mail: ssavage@shodair.org
URL: http://www.shodairhospital.org

34065 ■ Shodair Residential Treatment Center
2755 Colonial Dr.
Helena, MT 59604
Ph: (406)444-7500
Free: 800-447-6614
E-mail: ssavage@shodair.org
URL: http://www.shodairhospital.org

Warm Springs

34066 ■ Montana State Hospital
PO Box 300
Warm Springs, MT 59756
Ph: (406)693-7000
Fax: (406)693-7069
E-mail: eamberg@mt.gov
URL: http://msh.mt.gov/

NEBRASKA

Hastings

34067 ■ Hastings Regional Center
4200 W 2nd St.
Hastings, NE 68902
Ph: (402)462-1971
E-mail: william.gibson@dhhs.ne.gov
URL: http://www.hhs.state.ne.us/beh/rc/hrcserv.htm
William Gibson, Director

Kearney

34068 ■ Richard H. Young Hospital
1755 Prairie View Pl.
Kearney, NE 68845-8300
Ph: (308)865-2000
URL: http://www.gshs.org/body.cfm?id=46

Lincoln

34069 ■ Lincoln Regional Center
801 W Prospector Pl.
Lincoln, NE 68522-2299
Ph: (402)479-5388
E-mail: william.gibson@dhhs.ne.gov
URL: http://www.hhs.state.ne.us/beh/rc/lrcserv.htm
William Gibson, Director

Norfolk

34070 ■ Norfolk Regional Center
1700 N Victory Rd.
Norfolk, NE 68701
Ph: (402)370-3400
Fax: (402)370-3551
E-mail: william.gibson@dhhs.ne.gov
URL: http://www.hhs.state.ne.us/beh/rc/nrcserv.htm
William Gibson, Director

NEVADA

Las Vegas

34071 ■ Montevista Hospital
5900 W Rochelle Ave.
Las Vegas, NV 89103
Ph: (702)364-1111
URL: http://www.psysolutions.com/facilities/montevista/

34072 ■ Southern Nevada Adult Mental Health Services
6161 W Charleston Blvd.
Las Vegas, NV 89146
Ph: (702)486-6000
URL: http://mhds.nv.gov/index.php?option=com_content&task=view&id=61&Itemid=69

Reno

34073 ■ West Hills Hospital
1240 E 9th St.
Reno, NV 89512
Ph: (775)323-0478
Free: 800-242-0478
URL: http://www.psysolutions.com/facilities/westhills/

NEW HAMPSHIRE

Claremont

34074 ■ Valley Regional Hospital
243 Elm St.
Claremont, NH 03743-2099
Ph: (603)542-7771
E-mail: info@vrh.org
URL: http://www.vrh.org/

Concord

34075 ■ New Hampshire Hospital
36 Clinton St.
Concord, NH 03301
Ph: (603)271-5300
Free: 800-852-3345
URL: http://www.dhhs.nh.gov/DHHS/NHH/default.htm

Hampstead

34076 ■ Hampstead Hospital
218 East Rd.
Hampstead, NH 03841
Ph: (603)329-5311
Fax: (603)329-4746
URL: http://www.hampsteadhospital.com

NEW JERSEY

Belle Mead

34077 ■ Carrier Clinic
252 Rte. 601
Belle Mead, NJ 08502
Free: 800-933-3579
URL: http://www.carrier.org

Berkeley Heights

34078 ■ Runnells Specialized Hospital of Union County
40 Watchung Way
Berkeley Heights, NJ 07922
Ph: (908)771-5700
E-mail: runnells@ucnj.org
URL: http://www.unioncountynj.org/runnells
Beds: 369.

Blackwood

34079 ■ Camden County Health Services Center
Psychiatric Division
20 N Woodbury-Turnersville Rd.
Blackwood, NJ 08012
Ph: (856)374-6600
E-mail: fmaestrale@cchsc.com
URL: http://www.cchsc.com

Cedar Grove

34080 ■ Essex County Hospital Center
125 Fairview Ave.
Cedar Grove, NJ 07009-1399
Ph: (973)228-8200
URL: http://www.essex-countynj.org/index.php?section=pr/print/122006

Glen Gardner

34081 ■ Senator Garrett W. Hagedorn Psychiatric Hospital
200 Sanatorium Rd.
Glen Gardner, NJ 08826
Ph: (908)537-2141
URL: http://www.state.nj.us/humanservices/dmhs/home/index.html

Hammonton

34082 ■ Ancora Psychiatric Hospital
202 Spring Garden Rd.
Hammonton, NJ 08037
Ph: (609)561-1700

Morris Plains

34083 ■ Greystone Park Psychiatric Hospital
59 Koch Ave.
Morris Plains, NJ 07950
Ph: (973)538-1800
Fax: (973)889-8947
E-mail: jerri.casazza@dhs.state.nj.us
URL: http://www.state.nj.us/humanservices/

Pemberton

34084 ■ Buttonwood Hospital of Burlington County
600 Pemberton-Browns Mills Rd.
Pemberton, NJ 08064
Ph: (609)726-7000
URL: http://www.co.burlington.nj.us/

Secaucus

34085 ■ Meadowview Psychiatric Hospital
595 County Ave.
Secaucus, NJ 07094-2605
Ph: (201)319-3660
URL: http://www.hudsoncountynj.org/

Summit

34086 ■ Summit Oaks Hospital
19 Prospect St.
Summit, NJ 07902
Ph: (908)522-7000
Free: 800-753-5223
URL: http://www.summitoakshospital.com/
Formerly: Charter Behavioral Health System of Summit.

Toms River

34087 ■ Saint Barnabas Behavioral Health Center
1691 US Hwy. 9, CN 2025
Toms River, NJ 08754
Ph: (732)914-1688
Free: 800-300-0628
URL: http://www.saintbarnabas.com/hospitals/psychiatric/facilities/shoreline/index.htm
Formerly: Shoreline Behavioral Health Center.

Trenton

34088 ■ Trenton Psychiatric Hospital
Sullivan Way
Trenton, NJ 08628
Ph: (609)633-1500
Fax: (609)292-1315
E-mail: mhs-tph-resume@dhs.state.nj.us
URL: http://www.state.nj.us/humanservices/

Westampton

34089 ■ Hampton Hospital
650 Rancocas Rd.
Westampton, NJ 08060
Ph: (609)267-7000
Free: 800-603-6767
Fax: (609)518-2193
URL: https://www.hamptonhospital.com/indexnew.html
Formerly: Hampton Behavioral Health Center.

Wyckoff

34090 ■ Ramapo Ridge Psychiatric Hospital
301 Sicomac Ave.
Wyckoff, NJ 07481
Ph: (201)848-5800
URL: http://www.christianhealthcare.org/

NEW MEXICO

Albuquerque

34091 ■ Memorial Psychiatric Hospital
806 Central Ave. SE
Albuquerque, NM 87102
Ph: (505)247-0220
Free: 800-448-9238

34092 ■ University of New Mexico Children's Psychiatric Center
1001 Yale Blvd. NE
Albuquerque, NM 87131
Ph: (505)272-2890
URL: http://hospitals.unm.edu/hospitals/unmcpc.shtml

34093 ■ University of New Mexico Psychiatric Center
2600 Marble NE
Albuquerque, NM 87131
Ph: (505)272-2800
URL: http://hospitals.unm.edu/hospitals/unmcpc.shtml

Las Cruces

34094 ■ Mesilla Valley Hospital
3751 Del Rey Blvd.
Las Cruces, NM 88012
Ph: (505)382-3500
Free: 800-877-3500
URL: http://www.psysolutions.com/facilities/mesillavalley/

Las Vegas

34095 ■ Las Vegas Medical Center
3695 Hot Springs Blvd.
Las Vegas, NM 87701
Ph: (505)454-2100

NEW YORK

Albany

34096 ■ Capital District Psychiatric Center
75 New Scotland Ave.
Albany, NY 12208-3474
Ph: (518)447-9611
Fax: (518)434-0041
URL: http://www.omh.state.ny.us/omhweb/facilities/cdpc/facility.htm

Amityville

34097 ■ Brunswick Hospital Center
366 Broadway
Amityville, NY 11701-2778
Ph: (631)789-7000
URL: http://www.brunswickhospital.com/

34098 ■ South Oaks Hospital
400 Sunrise Hwy.
Amityville, NY 11701
Ph: (631)608-5610
URL: http://www.south-oaks.org/

Astoria

34099 ■ Creedmoor Psychiatric Center--Astoria
Steinway Community Services
38-11 Broadway
Astoria, NY 11103
Ph: (718)726-5953
URL: http://www.omh.state.ny.us/omhweb/facilities/crpc/outpatient_services.htm

Bath

34100 ■ Steuben County Community Mental Health Center--Bath
Clinic & Continuing Treatment Center
115 Liberty St.
Bath, NY 14810
Ph: (607)776-9631
URL: http://www.steubencony.org/sccmhc.html
Formerly: Elmira Psychiatric Center.

Bellerose

34101 ■ Queens Children's Psychiatric Center
74-03 Commonwealth Blvd.
Bellerose, NY 11426
Ph: (718)264-4500
Fax: (718)740-0968
URL: http://www.omh.state.ny.us/omhweb/facilities/qcpc/facility.htm

Binghamton

34102 ■ Binghamton Psychiatric Center
Community Treatment and Rehabilitation Center
425 Robinson St.
Binghamton, NY 13904
Ph: (607)724-1391
Fax: (607)773-4387
E-mail: binghamton@omh.state.ny.us
URL: http://www.omh.state.ny.us/omhweb/facilities/bipc/facility.htm

34103 ■ Greater Binghamton Health Center
425 Robinson St.
Binghamton, NY 13901-4199
Ph: (607)724-1391
Fax: (607)773-4387
E-mail: binghamton@omh.state.ny.us
URL: http://www.omh.state.ny.us/omhweb/facilities/bipc/facility.htm

Bronx

34104 ■ Bronx Psychiatric Center
1500 Waters Pl.
Bronx, NY 10461
Ph: (718)862-3300
Fax: (718)862-4879
E-mail: bronxpc@omh.state.ny.us
URL: http://www.omh.state.ny.us/omhweb/facilities/brpc/facility.htm

34105 ■ Ginsburg Outpatient Clinic
1500 Waters Pl.
Bronx, NY 10461
Ph: (718)862-3300
URL: http://www.omh.state.ny.us/omhweb/facilities/brpc/facility.htm#ginsburg

Brooklyn

34106 ■ Brooklyn Children's Psychiatric Center
1819 Bergen St.
Brooklyn, NY 11233
Ph: (718)221-4500
Fax: (718)221-4581
URL: http://www.omh.state.ny.us/omhweb/facilities/bkpc/facility.htm

34107 ■ Kingsboro Psychiatric Center
681 Clarkson Ave.
Brooklyn, NY 11203
Ph: (718)221-7700
Fax: (718)221-7206
E-mail: kingsboro@omh.state.ny.us
URL: http://www.omh.state.ny.us/omhweb/facilities/kbpc/facility.htm

34108 ■ Kingsboro Psychiatric Center
Brooklyn Manor/CSS
2830 Pitkin Ave.
Brooklyn, NY 11208-3297
Ph: (718)827-8000
URL: http://www.omh.state.ny.us/omhweb/facilities/kbpc/facility.htm

34109 ■ Kingsboro Psychiatric Center
Canarsie Service
9502 Glenwood Rd.
Brooklyn, NY 11236
Ph: (718)257-7780
URL: http://www.omh.state.ny.us/omhweb/facilities/kbpc/facility.htm

34110 ■ South Beach Acute Day Treatment Program
Sheepshead Bay Day Hospital
532 Neptune Ave.
Brooklyn, NY 11224
Ph: (718)946-2600
Fax: (718)265-0430
URL: http://www.omh.state.ny.us/omhweb/facilities/sbpc/facility.htm

34111 ■ South Beach Psychiatric Center
Baltic Street Outpatient Clinic & Day Hospital
250 Baltic St.
Brooklyn, NY 11201
Ph: (718)855-3131
URL: http://www.omh.state.ny.us/omhweb/facilities/sbpc/facility.htm

34112 ■ South Beach Psychiatric Center
Bensonhurst Outpatient Clinic & Day Hospital
8620 18th Ave.
Brooklyn, NY 11214
Ph: (718)256-8818
Fax: (718)234-2314
URL: http://www.omh.state.ny.us/omhweb/facilities/sbpc/facility.htm

34113 ■ South Beach Psychiatric Center--Coney Island
Sheepshead Bay Day Hospital
532 Neptune Ave.
Brooklyn, NY 11224
Ph: (718)946-2600
URL: http://www.omh.state.ny.us/omhweb/facilities/sbpc/facility.htm

34114 ■ South Beach Psychiatric Center
Fort Hamilton Outpatient Clinic
8710 5th Ave.
Brooklyn, NY 11209
Ph: (718)680-0006
E-mail: sbcsmss@omh.state.ny.us
URL: https://www.omh.state.ny.us/omhweb/facilities/sbpc/facility.htm

34115 ■ South Beach Psychiatric Center--Heights
Heights Hill Outpatient Clinic
25 Flatbush Ave.
Brooklyn, NY 11217
Ph: (718)875-1420
URL: http://www.omh.state.ny.us/omhweb/facilities/sbpc/facility.htm

Buffalo

34116 ■ BryLin Hospital
1263 Delaware Ave.
Buffalo, NY 14209
Ph: (716)886-8200
E-mail: info@brylin.com
URL: http://www.brylin.com

34117 ■ Buffalo Psychiatric Center
Cudmore Heights Residence
400 Forest Ave.
Buffalo, NY 14213
Ph: (716)885-2261
URL: http://www.omh.state.ny.us/omhweb/facilities/bupc/facility.htm

Corning

34118 ■ Steuben County Community Mental Health Center--Corning
114 Chestnut St.
Corning, NY 14830
Ph: (607)937-6201
URL: http://www.steubencony.org/sccmhc.html
Formerly: Elmira Psychiatric Center, Outpatient Clinic & Continuing Treatment Program.

Dix Hills

34119 ■ Sagamore Children's Psychiatric Center--Dix Hills
197 Half Hollow Rd.
Dix Hills, NY 11746
Ph: (631)370-1700
Fax: (631)370-1714
E-mail: scisdcc@omh.state.ny.us
URL: http://www.omh.state.ny.us/omhweb/facilities/scpc/facility.htm

Elmira

34120 ■ Elmira Psychiatric Center
100 Washington St.
Elmira, NY 14902
Ph: (607)737-4711
Fax: (607)737-0158
E-mail: elmirapc@omh.state.ny.us
URL: http://www.omh.state.ny.us/omhweb/facilities/elpc/facility.htm

Elmsford

34121 ■ Stony Lodge Hospital--Elmsford
Partial Hospitalization Program
33 W Main St.
Elmsford, NY 10523
Ph: (914)345-5676
URL: http://www.stonylodgehospital.com/

Herkimer

34122 ■ Herkimer Clinic and Club
205 N Main St.
Herkimer, NY 13350
Ph: (315)866-0193

Holliswood

34123 ■ The Holliswood Hospital
87-37 Palermo St.
Holliswood, NY 11423
Ph: (718)776-8181
Free: 800-486-3005
Fax: (718)776-8572
URL: http://www.holliswoodhospital.com/

Jamaica

34124 ■ Jamaica Community Services
150-11 Hillside Ave.
Jamaica, NY 11432
Ph: (718)739-5778
URL: http://www.omh.state.ny.us/omhweb/facilities/crpc/outpatient_services.htm

Katonah

34125 ■ Four Winds Hospital--Westchester
800 Cross River Rd.
Katonah, NY 10536
Ph: (914)763-8151
Free: 800-528-6624
Fax: (914)763-9597
E-mail: info.westchester@fourwindshospital.com
URL: http://www.fourwindshospital.com

Kingston

34126 ■ Pine Grove
340 Aaron Ct.
Kingston, NY 12401
Ph: (845)339-4733

34127 ■ Tudor House
9 E Chestnut St., Ste. 11
Kingston, NY 12401-5105
Ph: (845)331-6230

Marcy

34128 ■ Central New York Psychiatric Center
9005 Old River Rd.
Marcy, NY 13403
Ph: (315)765-3600
E-mail: cnypc@omh.state.ny.us
URL: http://www.omh.state.ny.us/omhweb/facilities/cnpc/facility.htm

Monticello

34129 ■ Residential Services Mental Health Clinic
14 Pelton St.
Monticello, NY 12701
Ph: (845)794-3283

New Hampton

34130 ■ Mid-Hudson Forensic Psychiatric Center
2834 Rte. 17-M
New Hampton, NY 10958
Ph: (845)374-8700
Fax: (845)374-8861
E-mail: midhudsonfpc@omh.state.ny.us
URL: http://www.omh.state.ny.us/omhweb/facilities/mhpc/facility.htm

New York

34131 ■ Kirby Forensic Psychiatric Center Ward Island
600 E 125th St.
New York, NY 10035
Ph: (212)672-5800
URL: http://www.omh.state.ny.us/omhweb/facilities/krpc/facility.htm

34132 ■ Manhattan Psychiatric Center--125th Street Clinic
600 E 125th St.
New York, NY 10035-6098
Ph: (646)672-6767
Fax: (646)672-6446
E-mail: mpcinfo@omh.state.ny.us
URL: http://www.omh.state.ny.us/omhweb/facilities/mapc/facility.htm

34133 ■ Manhattan Psychiatric Center--Ward's Island
1 Wards Island
New York, NY 10035-6002
Ph: (212)369-0500
URL: http://www.omh.state.ny.us/omhweb/facilities/mapc/facility.htm

34134 ■ New York Psychiatric Institute
1051 Riverside Dr.
New York, NY 10032
Ph: (212)543-5000
URL: http://www.nyspi.org/
Formerly: Washington Heights Community Service.

34135 ■ New York State Psychiatric Institute
1051 Riverside Dr., Rm. 1501
New York, NY 10032
Ph: (212)543-5767
URL: http://www.nyspi.org

34136 ■ New York State Psychiatric Institute Washington Heights Community Service
26 Sherman Ave.
New York, NY 10040
Ph: (212)942-8500
URL: http://www.nyspi.org/

Newburgh

34137 ■ Middletown Psychiatric Center Newburgh Mental Health Clinic
280 Broadway
Newburgh, NY 12550
Ph: (845)562-7326

Ogdensburg

34138 ■ Saint Lawrence Psychiatric Center--Ogdensburg
1 Chimney Point Dr.
Ogdensburg, NY 13669
Ph: (315)541-2001
Fax: (315)541-2013
E-mail: slpcinfo@omh.state.ny.us
URL: http://www.omh.state.ny.us/omhweb/facilities/slpc/facility.htm

34139 ■ Saint Lawrence Psychiatric Center--Ogdensburg Hamilton Hall
1 Chimney Point Dr.
Ogdensburg, NY 13669
Ph: (315)393-1180
URL: http://www.omh.state.ny.us/omhweb/facilities/slpc/facility.htm

Orangeburg

34140 ■ Rockland Children's Psychiatric Center
599 Convent Rd.
Orangeburg, NY 10962
Ph: (845)680-4000
Fax: (845)680-8905
URL: http://www.omh.state.ny.us/omhweb/facilities/rcpc/facility.htm

34141 ■ Rockland Psychiatric Center
140 Old Orangeburg Rd.
Orangeburg, NY 10962
Ph: (845)359-1000
Fax: (845)359-3143
E-mail: rocklandpc@omh.state.ny.us
URL: http://www.omh.state.ny.us/omhweb/facilities/rppc/facility.htm

Ossining

34142 ■ Stony Lodge Hospital Inc.--Ossining
40 Croton Dam Rd.
Ossining, NY 10562
Ph: (914)941-7400
URL: http://www.stonylodgehospital.com/

Patchogue

34143 ■ Sagamore Children's Psychiatric Center Waverly Clinic
440 Waverly Ave.
Patchogue, NY 11772
Ph: (631)654-2077
URL: http://www.omh.state.ny.us/omhweb/facilities/scpc/facility.htm

Poughkeepsie

34144 ■ Hudson River Psychiatric Center
10 Ross Cir.
Poughkeepsie, NY 12601
Ph: (845)452-8000
Fax: (845)452-8040
URL: http://www.omh.state.ny.us/omhweb/facilities/hrpc/facility.htm

Queens Village

34145 ■ Creedmoor Psychiatric Center--Queens Village
79-25 Winchester Blvd.
Queens Village, NY 11427
Ph: (718)264-4000
Fax: (718)264-3627
URL: http://www.omh.state.ny.us/omhweb/facilities/crpc/facility.htm

Riverhead

34146 ■ Pilgrim Psychiatric Center Peconic Center
540 E Main St.
Riverhead, NY 11901
Ph: (631)369-1277
E-mail: pilgriminfo@omh.state.ny.us
URL: http://www.omh.state.ny.us/omhweb/facilities/pgpc/facility.htm
Formerly: King's Park Psychiatric Center.

Rochester

34147 ■ Rochester Psychiatric Center
1111 Elmwood Ave.
Rochester, NY 14620
Ph: (585)241-1200
Fax: (585)241-1424
E-mail: rochesterpc@omh.state.ny.us
URL: http://www.omh.state.ny.us/omhweb/facilities/ropc/facility.htm

34148 ■ Via Health--Genesee Mental Health Center
224 Alexander St.
Rochester, NY 14607
Ph: (585)922-7770
URL: http://www.rochestergeneral.org/

34149 ■ Via Health--Rochester Mental Health Center
490 E Ridge Rd.
Rochester, NY 14621
Ph: (585)922-2501
URL: http://www.rochestergeneral.org/

Rye

34150 ■ Rye Hospital Center
754 Boston Post Rd.
Rye, NY 10580
Ph: (914)967-4567
URL: http://www.ryehospitalcenter.org/

Saratoga Springs

34151 ■ Four Winds Hospital--Saratoga
30 Crescent Ave.
Saratoga Springs, NY 12866
Ph: (518)584-3600
Free: 800-888-5448
E-mail: info.saratoga@fourwindshospital.com
URL: http://www.fourwindshospital.com

Schenectady

34152 ■ Capital District Psychiatric Center Schenectady County Clinic Treatment
426 Franklin St.
Schenectady, NY 12305
Ph: (518)374-3403

34153 ■ Ellis Hospital Psychiatry
1101 Nott St.
Schenectady, NY 12308
Ph: (518)386-3300
URL: http://www.ellishospital.org/ellishospital/mental.aspx

Staten Island

34154 ■ South Beach Psychiatric Center
777 Seaview Ave.
Staten Island, NY 10305
Ph: (718)667-2300
Fax: (718)667-2344
E-mail: sbcsmss@omh.state.ny.us
URL: https://www.omh.state.ny.us/omhweb/facilities/sbpc/facility.htm

Syracuse

34155 ■ Hutchings Psychiatric Center Children and Youth Services
645 Madison St.
Syracuse, NY 13202
Ph: (315)473-4980
URL: http://www.omh.state.ny.us/omhweb/facilities/hupc/facility.htm

34156 ■ Hutchings Psychiatric Center Outpatient Services
620 Madison St.
Syracuse, NY 13210
Ph: (315)426-3600
Fax: (315)426-3603
E-mail: hutchingspc@omh.state.ny.us
URL: http://www.omh.state.ny.us/omhweb/facilities/hupc/facility.htm

Utica

34157 ■ Mohawk Valley Psychiatric Center
1400 Noyes St.
Utica, NY 13502
Ph: (315)738-3800
Fax: (315)738-4414
E-mail: mvpc@omh.state.ny.us
URL: http://www.omh.state.ny.us/omhweb/facilities/mvpc/facility.htm

West Brentwood

34158 ■ Pilgrim Psychiatric Center
998 Crooked Hill Rd.
West Brentwood, NY 11717
Ph: (631)761-3500
Fax: (631)761-2600
URL: http://www.omh.state.ny.us/omhweb/facilities/pgpc/facility.htm

34159 ■ Pilgrim Psychiatric Center Buckman Center
998 Crooked Hill Rd., Bldg. 47
West Brentwood, NY 11717
Ph: (631)761-2289
E-mail: pilgriminfo@omh.state.ny.us
URL: http://www.omh.state.ny.us/omhweb/facilities/pgpc/facility.htm

34160 ■ Pilgrim Psychiatric Center Progress House
998 Crooked Rd.
West Brentwood, NY 11717
Ph: (631)761-3500
Fax: (631)761-2600
E-mail: pilgriminfo@omh.state.ny.us
URL: http://www.omh.state.ny.us/omhweb/facilities/pgpc/facility.htm

34161 ■ Pilgrim Psychiatric Center Western Suffolk Center
998 Crooked Hill Rd., Bldg. 56
West Brentwood, NY 11717
Ph: (631)761-2282
URL: http://www.omh.state.ny.us/omhweb/facilities/pgpc/facility.htm

West Seneca

34162 ■ Western New York Children's Psychiatric Center
1010 East & West Rd.
West Seneca, NY 14224
Ph: (716)677-7000
Fax: (716)675-6455
E-mail: westernnewyorkcpc@omh.state.ny.us
URL: http://www.omh.state.ny.us/omhweb/facilities/wcpc/facility.htm

34163 ■ Western New York Children's Psychiatric Center Day Treatment Center
1010 East and West Rd.
West Seneca, NY 14224
Ph: (716)677-7000
Fax: (716)675-6455
E-mail: westernnewyorkcpc@omh.state.ny.us
URL: http://www.omh.state.ny.us/omhweb/facilities/wcpc/facility.htm

NORTH CAROLINA

Albemarle

34164 ■ Stanly Memorial Hospital
301 Yadkin St.
Albemarle, NC 28001
Ph: (704)984-4000
URL: http://www.stanly.org/

Butner

34165 ■ John Umstead Hospital
1003 12th St.
Butner, NC 27509
Ph: (919)575-7211
Fax: (919)575-7643
E-mail: patsy.christian@ncmail.net
URL: http://www.dhhs.state.nc.us/mhddsas/Umstead.htm

34166 ■ John Umstead Hospital Children's Psychiatric Institute
1003 12th St.
Butner, NC 27509
Ph: (919)575-7211
Fax: (919)575-7643
URL: http://www.dhhs.state.nc.us/mhddsas/Umstead.htm

Charlotte

34167 ■ Carolinas Health System Behavioral Health Center CMC--Randolph
501 Billingsley Rd.
Charlotte, NC 28211
Ph: (704)444-2400
Free: 800-418-2065
URL: http://www.carolinas.org/services/behavioral/Centers/Randolph.cfm

Goldsboro

34168 ■ Cherry Hospital
201 Stevens Mill Rd.
Goldsboro, NC 27530
Ph: (919)731-3326
Fax: (919)731-3793
URL: http://www.cherryhospital.org/

Greensboro

34169 ■ Moses Cone Health System Behavioral Health Center
700 Walter Reed Dr.
Greensboro, NC 27403
Ph: (336)832-9600
URL: http://www.mosescone.com/

Kernersville

34170 ■ Moses Cone Health System Behavioral Health Center
1617 Hwy. 66 S, Ste. 200
Kernersville, NC 27284
Ph: (336)993-6120
URL: http://www.mosescone.com/

Morganton

34171 ■ Broughton Hospital
1000 S Sterling St.
Morganton, NC 28655
Ph: (828)433-2111
E-mail: bh.information@ncmail.net

Raleigh

34172 ■ Dorothea Dix Hospital
820 S Boylan Ave.
Raleigh, NC 27603-2176
Ph: (919)733-5540
Fax: (919)733-9781
URL: http://www.dhhs.state.nc.us/mhddsas/DIX

Riedsville

34173 ■ Moses Cone Health System Behavioral Health Center
415 W Harrison St.
Riedsville, NC 27320
URL: http://www.mosescone.com/

Rocky Mount

34174 ■ Coastal Plain Hospital
2301 Medpark Dr.
Rocky Mount, NC 27804
Ph: (252)962-5000
Free: 800-234-0234
URL: http://www.nhcs.org/hospitals/coastal_plain

Wilmington

34175 ■ Oaks Behavioral Health Hospital
2131 S 17th St.
Wilmington, NC 28401
Ph: (910)343-7787
Free: 800-622-6257
URL: http://www.nhrmc.org/body.cfm?id=33

Winston Salem

34176 ■ Old Vineyard Youth Services
3637 Old Vineyard Rd.
Winston Salem, NC 27104
Ph: (336)794-3550
URL: http://www.oldvineyard.net/

NORTH DAKOTA

Fargo

34177 ■ Prairie Saint John's
510 S 4th St. S
Fargo, ND 58103
Ph: (701)476-7216
Free: 877-333-9565
URL: http://www.prairie-stjohns.com/

Grand Forks

34178 ■ Richard P. Stadter Psychiatric Center
1451 44th Ave. S
Grand Forks, ND 58201
Ph: (701)772-2500
Free: 866-772-2500
URL: http://www.stadtercenter.com/

Jamestown

34179 ■ North Dakota State Hospital
2605 Circle Dr.
Jamestown, ND 58401-6905
Ph: (701)253-3650
URL: http://www.nd.gov/dhs/locations/statehospital/

OHIO

Athens

34180 ■ Appalachian Psychiatric Healthcare System
Athens
100 Hospital Dr.
Athens, OH 45701
Ph: (740)594-5000
URL: http://www.seorf.ohiou.edu/~xx091/

Cambridge

34181 ■ Appalachian Psychiatric Healthcare System
Cambridge Campus
66737 Old Twenty One Rd.
Cambridge, OH 43725
Ph: (740)439-1371
URL: http://www.seorf.ohiou.edu/~xx091/

Chagrin Falls

34182 ■ Windsor Hospital
115 E Summit St.
Chagrin Falls, OH 44022
Ph: (440)247-5300

Cincinnati

34183 ■ Summit Behavioral Healthcare
1101 Summit Rd.
Cincinnati, OH 45237
Ph: (513)948-3717
URL: http://mentalhealth.ohio.gov/

Cleveland

34184 ■ Northcoast Behavioral Healthcare
Cleveland Campus
1708 Southpoint Dr.
Cleveland, OH 44109
Ph: (330)467-7131
URL: http://mentalhealth.ohio.gov/
Formerly: Cleveland Psychiatric Institute.

Columbus

34185 ■ Twin Valley Psychiatric System
Columbus Campus
2200 W Broad St.
Columbus, OH 43223
Ph: (614)752-0333
URL: http://mentalhealth.ohio.gov/

Dayton

34186 ■ Twin Valley Psychiatric System
Dayton Campus
2611 Wayne Ave.
Dayton, OH 45420
Ph: (937)258-0440
Fax: (937)258-0440
URL: http://mentalhealth.ohio.gov/
Formerly: Dayton Mental Health Center.

Massillon

34187 ■ Heartland Behavioral Healthcare
3000 Erie St. S
Massillon, OH 44648
Ph: (330)833-3135
URL: http://mentalhealth.ohio.gov/
Formerly: Massillon Psychiatric Center.

Northfield

34188 ■ Northcoast Behavioral Healthcare System
Northfield Campus
1756 Sagamore Rd.
Northfield, OH 44706
Ph: (330)467-7131
URL: http://mentalhealth.ohio.gov/
Formerly: Northcoast Behavioral Healthcare.

Saint Clairsville

34189 ■ Fox Run Hospital
67670 Traco Dr.
Saint Clairsville, OH 43950
Ph: (740)695-2131
URL: http://www.psysolutions.com/facilities/foxrun/

Toledo

34190 ■ North Coast Behavioral Healthcare System
West Campus
930 S Detroit Ave.
Toledo, OH 43614-0002
Ph: (419)381-1881
URL: http://mentalhealth.ohio.gov/
Formerly: N.W. Psychiatric Hospital.

Troy

34191 ■ Dettmer Behavioral Health Services
3130 N Dixie Hwy.
Troy, OH 45373
Ph: (937)440-4000
Formerly: Dettmer Hospital.

Willoughby

34192 ■ Laurelwood Hospital
35900 Euclid Ave.
Willoughby, OH 44094
Ph: (440)953-3000
Free: 800-438-4673
URL: http://www.windsorlaurelwood.com/

Youngstown

34193 ■ Belmont Pines Hospital
615 Churchill Hubbard Rd.
Youngstown, OH 44505
Ph: (330)759-2700
Free: 800-423-5666
URL: http://www.psysolutions.com/facilities/belmont-pines/

OKLAHOMA

Ada

34194 ■ Rolling Hills Hospital
1000 Rolling Hills Ln.
Ada, OK 74820
Ph: (580)436-3600
Free: 800-522-9505
URL: http://www.rollinghillshospital.com/

Alva

34195 ■ Northwest Center for Behavioral Health--Alva
604 Choctaw St.
Alva, OK 73717
Ph: (580)327-1112

Enid

34196 ■ Northwest Center for Behavioral Health--Enid
702 N Grand St.
Enid, OK 73701
Ph: (580)234-3791

Fairview

34197 ■ Northwest Center for Behavioral Health--Fairview
1425 N Main St.
Fairview, OK 73737
Ph: (580)227-2088
Formerly: Western State Psychiatric Center.

Fort Supply

34198 ■ Northwest Center for Behavioral Health--Fort Supply
Hwy. 270
Fort Supply, OK 73841
Ph: (580)766-2311

Guthrie

34199 ■ Northwest Center for Behavioral Health--Guthrie
1923 S Division St.
Guthrie, OK 73044
Ph: (405)282-1830

Guymon

34200 ■ Northwest Center for Behavioral Health--Guymon
1007 NE 4th St.
Guymon, OK 73942-5425
Ph: (580)338-5851
Formerly: Western State Psychiatric Center.

Heavener

34201 ■ Carl Albert Community Mental Health Center--Heavener
511 E 2nd St.
Heavener, OK 74937
Ph: (918)653-7718

Holdenville

34202 ■ Carl Albert Community Mental Health Center--Hughes County
711 N Bullitt St.
Holdenville, OK 74848
Ph: (405)379-6668

Hugo

34203 ■ Carl Albert Community Mental Health Center--Hugo
104 N 4th St.
Hugo, OK 74743
Ph: (580)326-7531

Idabel

34204 ■ Carl Albert Community Mental Health Center--McCurtain County
2000 E Lincoln Rd.
Idabel, OK 74745
Ph: (580)286-6639

Kingfisher

34205 ■ Northwest Center for Behavioral Health--Kingfisher
124 E Sheridan Ave., Rm. 200
Kingfisher, OK 73750
Ph: (405)375-6377

Lawton

34206 ■ Southwestern Behavioral Health Center
1602 SW 82nd St.
Lawton, OK 73505
Ph: (580)510-2715

McAlester

34207 ■ Carl Albert Community Mental Health Center--McAlester
1101 E Monroe St.
McAlester, OK 74501

Ph: (918)426-7800

Miami

34208 ■ Moccasin Bend Ranch
62410 E 105 Rd.
Miami, OK 74354
Ph: (918)540-1692
URL: http://www.willowcresthospital.com/

34209 ■ Willow Crest Hospital
130 A St. SW
Miami, OK 74354
Ph: (918)542-1836
Fax: (918)542-6060
URL: http://www.willowcresthospital.com/

Norman

34210 ■ Bridge Mental Health Continuum--Norman
2001 Venture Dr.
Norman, OK 73069
Ph: (405)447-1911

34211 ■ Griffin Memorial Hospital
900 E Main St.
Norman, OK 73071
Ph: (405)321-4880

Oklahoma City

34212 ■ Bridge Mental Health Continuum--Oklahoma City
5350 S Western Ave.
Oklahoma City, OK 73109
Ph: (405)631-4567
Formerly: The Brown Schools.

34213 ■ Integris Mental Health Center
4900 N Portland, Ste. 111
Oklahoma City, OK 73112
Ph: (405)330-1213
URL: http://www.integris-health.com/INTEGRIS/en-US/

34214 ■ Integris Mental Health Oklahoma City Campus
5100 N Brookline Ave., Ste. 800
Oklahoma City, OK 73112
Ph: (405)717-9800
URL: http://www.integris-health.com/INTEGRIS/en-US/

Spencer

34215 ■ Integris Mental Health Spencer Campus
2601 N Spencer Rd.
Spencer, OK 73084
Ph: (405)427-2441
URL: http://www.integris-health.com/INTEGRIS/en-US/

Stigler

34216 ■ Carl Albert Community Mental Health Center
205 N Broadway
Stigler, OK 74462
Ph: (918)967-8491

Tulsa

34217 ■ Brookhaven Hospital
201 S Garnett Rd.
Tulsa, OK 74128
Ph: (918)438-4257
Free: 888-298-HOPE
Fax: (918)438-8016
E-mail: wecanhelp@brookhavenhospital.com
URL: http://www.brookhavenhospital.com

34218 ■ Laureate Psychiatric Clinic and Hospital
6655 S Yale Ave.
Tulsa, OK 74136
Ph: (918)481-4000
URL: http://www.laureate.com/

34219 ■ Shadow Mountain Behavioral Health
6262 S Sheridan Rd.
Tulsa, OK 74133
Ph: (918)492-8200
URL: http://www.psysolutions.com/facilities/shadow-mtn/

34220 ■ Transitional Living Center
15323 E 13th St.
Tulsa, OK 74108
Ph: (918)439-0281

Vinita

34221 ■ Eastern State Hospital--Vinita
442104 E 250 Rd.
Vinita, OK 74301
Ph: (918)256-7841

Woodward

34222 ■ Northwest Center for Behavioral Health--Woodward
1222 10th St., Ste. 211
Woodward, OK 73801
Ph: (580)256-8615
Fax: (580)256-8609
Formerly: Western State Psychiatric Center.

OREGON

Pendleton

34223 ■ Eastern Oregon Psychiatric Center
2600 Westgate
Pendleton, OR 97801
Ph: (541)276-0810

Portland

34224 ■ Oregon State Hospital--Portland
1121 NE 2nd Ave.
Portland, OR 97232
Ph: (503)731-8620
URL: http://www.oregon.gov/DHS/mentalhealth/osh/index.shtml

Salem

34225 ■ Oregon State Hospital
2600 Center St. NE
Salem, OR 97301
Ph: (503)945-2800
Free: 800-544-7078
URL: http://www.oregon.gov/DHS/mentalhealth/osh/index.shtml

PENNSYLVANIA

Allentown

34226 ■ Allentown State Hospital
1600 Hanover Ave.
Allentown, PA 18109
Ph: (610)740-3200
Free: 800-692-7462
URL: http://www.dpw.state.pa.us/

Ambler

34227 ■ The Horsham Clinic
722 E Butler Pke.
Ambler, PA 19002
Ph: (215)643-7800
Free: 800-237-4447
Fax: (215)654-1256
URL: https://www.horshamclinic.com/indexnew.html

Bridgeville

34228 ■ Mayview State Hospital
1601 Mayview Rd.
Bridgeville, PA 15017-1599
Ph: (412)257-6700

Centre Hall

34229 ■ The Meadows Psychiatric Center
132 The Meadows Dr.
Centre Hall, PA 16828
Ph: (814)364-2161
Free: 800-641-7529
Fax: (814)364-9742
URL: http://www.themeadows.net

Chambersburg

34230 ■ Meadows Psychiatric Center
144 S 8th St.
Chambersburg, PA 17201
Ph: (717)263-8272
Free: 800-641-7529
Fax: (717)263-8476
URL: http://www.themeadows.net

Clarion

34231 ■ Clarion Psychiatric Center
2 Hospital Dr.
Clarion, PA 16214
Ph: (814)226-9545
Free: 800-253-4906
URL: http://www.clarioncenter.com/

Clarks Summit

34232 ■ Clark's Summit State Hospital
1451 Hillside Dr.
Clarks Summit, PA 18411-9505
Ph: (570)586-2011
URL: http://www.dpw.state.pa.us/

Danville

34233 ■ Danville State Hospital
200 State Hospital Dr.
Danville, PA 17821
Ph: (570)271-4500
Free: 800-692-7462
URL: http://www.dpw.state.pa.us/

Downingtown

34234 ■ Saint John Vianney Hospital
151 Woodbine Rd.
Downingtown, PA 19335
Ph: (610)269-2600
Free: 888-993-8885
URL: http://www.sjvcenter.org/

Doylestown

34235 ■ Foundations Behavioral Health
833 E Butler Ave.
Doylestown, PA 18901
Ph: (215)345-0444
Free: 800-445-4722
URL: http://www.fbh.com/

Elizabethtown

34236 ■ Philhaven--Elizabethtown
422 Cloverleaf Rd.
Elizabethtown, PA 17022
Ph: (717)653-9359
URL: http://www.philhaven.org/

Fort Washington

34237 ■ Brooke Glen Behavioral Hospital
7170 Lafayette Ave.
Fort Washington, PA 19034
Ph: (215)641-5300
URL: http://www.psysolutions.com/facilities/brookeglen/site/

Harrisburg

34238 ■ Philhaven--Harrisburg
2717 N Front St.
Harrisburg, PA 17110
Ph: (717)230-9622
Fax: (717)230-9627
E-mail: tah@philhaven.com
URL: http://www.philhaven.com

Kingston

34239 ■ First Hospital Wyoming Valley
562 Wyoming Ave
Kingston, PA 18704
Ph: (570)552-3900
Free: 800-624-9902

Lancaster

34240 ■ Philhaven--Lancaster
780 Eden Rd.
Lancaster, PA 17601
Ph: (717)735-7770
Fax: (717)569-3045
URL: http://www.philhaven.org/

Lebanon

34241 ■ Philhaven--Lebanon
204 Hathaway Park
Lebanon, PA 17042-6193
Ph: (717)274-9777
Fax: (717)274-9815
URL: http://www.philhaven.org/

Leola

34242 ■ Philhaven--Leola
352 E Main St.
Leola, PA 17540
Ph: (717)656-7036
URL: http://www.philhaven.org/

Mount Gretna

34243 ■ Philhaven Behavioral Health
283 S Butler Rd.
Mount Gretna, PA 17064
Ph: (717)273-8871
URL: http://www.philhaven.org

Norristown

34244 ■ Crisis Residential Program
12 Circle Dr.
Norristown, PA 19401
Ph: (610)631-2480
URL: http://www.mces.org/crp.html

34245 ■ Montgomery County Emergency Service Inc.
50 Beech Dr.
Norristown, PA 19403
Ph: (610)279-6100
URL: http://www.mces.org/

34246 ■ Norristown State Hospital
1001 Sterigere St.
Norristown, PA 19401
Ph: (610)313-5206
URL: http://www.dpw.state.pa.us/

North Warren

34247 ■ Warren State Hospital
33 Main Dr.
North Warren, PA 16365
Ph: (814)723-5500
URL: http://www.dpw.state.pa.us/

Philadelphia

34248 ■ Belmont Behavioral Health Center for Comprehensive Treatment
4200 Monument Rd.
Philadelphia, PA 19131
Ph: (215)877-2000
Fax: (215)879-2443
URL: http://www.einstein.edu/belmont
Formerly: Belmont Center.

34249 ■ Fairmount Behavioral Health System
561 Fairthorne Ave.
Philadelphia, PA 19128
Ph: (215)487-4000
Free: 800-235-0200
E-mail: gerald.kosmin@uhsinc.com
URL: http://www.fairmountbhs.com

34250 ■ Friends Hospital
4641 Roosevelt Blvd.
Philadelphia, PA 19124-2399
Ph: (215)831-4600
Free: 800-889-0548
URL: http://www.friendshospitalonline.org/

34251 ■ Philadelphia Center for Human Development
10360 Drummond Rd.
Philadelphia, PA 19154
Ph: (215)632-6400
URL: http://www.einstein.edu/facilities/belmont/article9085.html

Pittsburgh

34252 ■ Southwood Psychiatric Hospital Inc.
2575 Boyce Plz. Rd.
Pittsburgh, PA 15241
Ph: (412)257-2290
Free: 888-907-5437
Fax: (412)257-0374
E-mail: info.southwoodhospital@yfcs.com
URL: http://www.southwoodhospital.com/index.php

34253 ■ University of Pittsburgh Medical Center Health System
Western Psychiatric Institute and Clinic
3811 O'Hara St.
Pittsburgh, PA 15213
Ph: (412)624-2100
Free: 888-796-8226
URL: http://www.upmc.com/HospitalsFacilities/Hospitals/wpic/Pages/default.aspx

Torrance

34254 ■ Torrance State Hospital
PO Box 111
Torrance, PA 15779
Ph: (724)459-4444
URL: http://www.dpw.state.pa.us/

Villanova

34255 ■ Devereux Beneto Center
Devereux Foundation
444 Devereux
Villanova, PA 19085
Free: 800-345-1292
URL: http://www.devereux.org
Formerly: Mapleton Psychiatric Institute and Devereux Children's Behavioral Health Center.

Wernersville

34256 ■ Wernersville State Hospital
Sportsman Rd. & Rte. 422
Wernersville, PA 19565
Ph: (610)678-3411
URL: http://www.dpw.state.pa.us/

York

34257 ■ The Meadows of York
2451 Kingston Ct.
York, PA 17402
Ph: (717)757-4229
Fax: (717)757-6511
URL: http://www.themeadows.net/locations.htm
Formerly: Meadows Psychiatric Center.

RHODE ISLAND

Cranston

34258 ■ Eleanor Slater Hospital
Behavioral Health
111 Howard Ave.
Cranston, RI 02920
Ph: (401)462-3085
Fax: (401)462-5243
URL: http://www.mhrh.ri.gov/esh/

Providence

34259 ■ Butler Hospital
345 Blackstone Blvd.
Providence, RI 02906
Ph: (401)455-6200
E-mail: info@butler.org
URL: http://www.butler.org

34260 ■ Groden Center Inc.
86 Mt. Hope Ave.
Providence, RI 02906
Ph: (401)274-6310
URL: http://www.grodencenter.org/

34261 ■ Groden Center Inc.
Cove Center
610 Manton Ave.
Providence, RI 02909
Ph: (401)438-2459
URL: http://www.grodencenter.org/

34262 ■ Groden Center Inc.
Livingston Center for Early Childhood
30 Livingston St.
Providence, RI 02904
Ph: (401)421-1673
URL: http://www.grodencenter.org/

Riverside

34263 ■ Bradley Hospital
1011 Veterans Memorial Pkwy.
Riverside, RI 02915
Ph: (401)432-1000
URL: http://www.lifespan.org/bradley/

Smithfield

34264 ■ Groden Center Inc.
Branch Pike House
73 Branch Pke.
Smithfield, RI 02917
Ph: (401)233-2218
URL: http://www.grodencenter.org/

Warwick

34265 ■ Groden Center Inc.
Cowesett House
563 Cowesett St.
Warwick, RI 02886
Ph: (401)885-2706
URL: http://www.grodencenter.org/

SOUTH CAROLINA

Anderson

34266 ■ Patrick B. Harris Psychiatric Hospital
130 Hwy. 252
Anderson, SC 29621
Ph: (864)231-2600
URL: http://www.patrickbharrispsychiatrichospital.com/

Columbia

34267 ■ G. Werber Bryan Psychiatric Hospital
220 Faison Dr.
Columbia, SC 29203
Ph: (803)935-7140
URL: http://www.state.sc.us/dmh/bryan/

34268 ■ South Carolina State Hospital/William S. Hall Psychiatric Institute
18 Colonial Dr.
Columbia, SC 29203
Ph: (803)898-1725
URL: http://www.state.sc.us/dmh/directions_hall.htm

Greer

34269 ■ Carolina Center for Behavioral Health
2700 E Phillips Rd.
Greer, SC 29650
Ph: (864)235-2335
Free: 800-866-4673
URL: https://www.thecarolinacenter.com/index.php
Formerly: Charter Behavioral Health System of Greenville.

North Charleston

34270 ■ Palmetto Lowcountry Behavioral Health
2777 Speissegger Dr.
North Charleston, SC 29405
Ph: (843)747-5830
Free: 877-947-3223
URL: http://www.palmettobehavioralhealth.com/

Travelers Rest

34271 ■ SpringBrook Behavioral Health System
1 Havenwood Ln.
Travelers Rest, SC 29690
Ph: (864)834-8013
URL: http://www.springbrookbehavioral.com/

West Columbia

34272 ■ Three Rivers Behavioral Health
2900 Sunset Blvd.
West Columbia, SC 29169
Ph: (866)796-9911
URL: http://www.psysolutions.com/facilities/threerivers/site/

SOUTH DAKOTA

Yankton

34273 ■ South Dakota Human Services Center
State Psychiatric Hospital
3515 Broadway Ave.
Yankton, SD 57078
Ph: (605)668-3100
Fax: (605)668-3460
URL: http://dhs.sd.gov/hsc/

TENNESSEE

Bolivar

34274 ■ Western Mental Health Institute
11100 Old Hwy. 64
Bolivar, TN 38008
Ph: (731)228-2000
URL: http://www.tennessee.gov/mental/mhs/mhs2.html

Chattanooga

34275 ■ Columbia/HCA Valley Hospital
Parkridge Medical Center
2200 Morris Hill Rd.
Chattanooga, TN 37421
Ph: (423)894-4220
Free: 800-542-9600
URL: http://www.parkridgevalley.com
Formerly: Valley Behavioral Health System A Campus of Parkridge Health System.

34276 ■ FHC Cumberland Hall--Chattanooga
7351 Standifer Gap Rd.
Chattanooga, TN 37421
Ph: (423)499-9007
URL: http://www.psysolutions.com/facilities/chattanooga/

34277 ■ Moccasin Bend Mental Health Institute
100 Moccasin Bend Rd.
Chattanooga, TN 37405
Ph: (423)265-2271
URL: http://www.tn.gov/mental/mhs/mhs2.html

Jackson

34278 ■ West Tennessee Healthcare
Pathways Behavioral Health Services
238 Summar Dr.
Jackson, TN 38301
Ph: (731)541-8200
URL: http://www.wth.org/body.cfm?id=292

Johnson City

34279 ■ Woodridge Hospital
403 N State of Franklin Rd.
Johnson City, TN 37604
Ph: (423)928-7111
URL: http://www.woodridge-hospital.org/

Kingsport

34280 ■ Indian Path Pavilion
2300 Pavilion Dr.
Kingsport, TN 37660
Ph: (423)392-5500
URL: http://www.msha.com/facility_bh.cfm?id=51

Knoxville

34281 ■ Lakeshore Mental Health Institute
5908 Lyons View Dr.
Knoxville, TN 37919-7598
Ph: (865)584-1561
URL: http://www.tennessee.gov/mental/mhs/mhs2.html

LaFollette

34282 ■ La Follette Outpatient Clinic
Ridgeview Psychiatric Hospital and Center
110 N Tennesee Ave.
LaFollette, TN 37766-2425
Ph: (615)562-7426
URL: http://www.ridgevw.com/
Formerly: Ridgeview Outpatient Clinic.

34283 ■ Ridgeview Psychiatric Hospital and Center
101 E Central Ave.
LaFollette, TN 37766
Ph: (423)562-2637
URL: http://www.ridgevw.com/

Louisville

34284 ■ Peninsula Hospital
2347 Jones Bend Rd.
Louisville, TN 37777
Ph: (865)970-9800
URL: http://www.peninsulabehavioralhealth.org/?id=1645&sid=15

Memphis

34285 ■ Lakeside Behavioral Health System
2911 Brunswick Rd.
Memphis, TN 38133
Ph: (901)377-4700
Free: 800-232-LAKE
Fax: (901)373-0912
URL: http://www.lakesidebhs.com
Formerly: Charter Lakeside Behavioral Health.

34286 ■ Memphis Mental Health Institute
951 Court Ave.
Memphis, TN 38103
Ph: (901)577-1800
URL: http://www.tn.gov/mental/mhs/mhs2.html

Nashville

34287 ■ Middle Tennessee Mental Health Institute
221 Stewarts Ferry Pke.
Nashville, TN 37214
Ph: (615)902-7400
URL: http://www.tn.gov/mental/mhs/mhs2.html

34288 ■ Parthenon Pavilion
Centennial Medical Center
2401 Parman Pl.
Nashville, TN 37203-1579
Ph: (615)342-1400
URL: http://www.parthenonpavilion.com/

34289 ■ Psychiatric Hospital at Vanderbilt
1601 23rd Ave. S
Nashville, TN 37212
Ph: (615)320-7770
URL: http://www.vanderbilt.edu

Oak Ridge

34290 ■ Ridgeview
240 W Tyrone Rd.
Oak Ridge, TN 37830
Ph: (865)482-1076
URL: http://www.ridgeviewresources.com
Formerly: Ridgeview Psychiatric Hospital.

34291 ■ Ridgeview Psychiatric Hospital and Center
Stepping Stones Psychosocial Program
117A Flint Rd.
Oak Ridge, TN 37830
Ph: (865)482-1239
URL: http://www.ridgeviewresources.com

Oneida

34292 ■ Ridgeview Psychiatric Hospital and Center
Quest Psychosocial Program
341 Industrial Ln.
Oneida, TN 37841
Ph: (423)569-9797
URL: http://www.ridgeviewresources.com

34293 ■ Ridgeview Psychiatric Hospital and Center
Scott County Outpatient Clinic
133 W 2nd Ave.
Oneida, TN 37841
Ph: (423)569-7979
URL: http://www.ridgeviewresources.com

TEXAS

Arlington

34294 ■ Millwood Hospital
1011 N Cooper St.
Arlington, TX 76011
Ph: (817)261-3121
Fax: (817)404-2221
URL: http://www.psysolutions.com/facilities/millwood/

Austin

34295 ■ Austin State Hospital
4110 Guadalupe St.
Austin, TX 78751
Ph: (512)452-0381
URL: http://www.dshs.state.tx.us/mhhospitals/austinsh/default.shtm

34296 ■ Saint David's Pavilion
1025 E 32nd St.
Austin, TX 78705
Ph: (512)867-5800
URL: http://stdavids.com/

34297 ■ Seton Shoal Creek Hospital
3501 Mills Ave.
Austin, TX 78731
Ph: (512)324-2000
URL: http://www.seton.net/locations/shoal_creek/

34298 ■ Texas NeuroRehab Center
1106 W Dittmar Rd.
Austin, TX 78745
Ph: (512)444-4835
Free: 800-252-5151
Fax: (512)462-6749
URL: http://www.psysolutions.com/facilities/tx-neurorehab/

Belton

34299 ■ Cedar Crest Hospital & Residential Treatment Center
3500 S Interstate 35
Belton, TX 76513
Ph: (254)939-2100
URL: http://www.cedarcresthospital.com/

Big Spring

34300 ■ Big Spring State Hospital
1901 N Hwy. 87
Big Spring, TX 79720
Ph: (432)267-8216
URL: http://www.dshs.state.tx.us/mhhospitals/BigSpringSH/default.shtm

Dallas

34301 ■ Green Oaks Hospital
7808 Clodus Fields Dr.
Dallas, TX 75251
Ph: (972)991-9504
Free: 800-866-6554
Fax: (972)789-1865
URL: http://www.greenoakspsych.com

34302 ■ Timberlawn Mental Health System
4600 Samuell Blvd.
Dallas, TX 75228
Ph: (214)381-7181
Free: 800-426-4944
URL: http://www.timberlawn.com/

DeSoto

34303 ■ Cedars Hospital
2000 N Old Hickory Trail
DeSoto, TX 75115
Ph: (972)298-7323
URL: http://www.psysolutions.com/facilities/hickorytrail/

El Paso

34304 ■ NCED Mental Health Center
1900 Denver Ave.
El Paso, TX 79902
Ph: (915)351-0299
Formerly: Columbia Behavioral Center.

Greenville

34305 ■ Glen Oaks Hospital
301 Division St.
Greenville, TX 75402
Ph: (903)454-6000
Free: 800-443-1109
URL: https://www.glenoakshospital.com/indexnew.html

Harlingen

34306 ■ Rio Grande State Center South Texas Health Care System
1401 S Rangerville Rd.
Harlingen, TX 78552
Ph: (956)425-8900
URL: http://www.dshs.state.tx.us/mhhospitals/RioGrandeSC/default.shtm

Houston

34307 ■ Cypress Creek Hospital
17750 Cali Dr.
Houston, TX 77090
Ph: (281)586-7600
URL: http://www.psysolutions.com/facilities/cypress-creek/

34308 ■ Intercare North Hospital
1120 Cypress Sta. Dr.
Houston, TX 77090
Ph: (281)893-7200
URL: http://www.intracarehospital.com/

34309 ■ Menninger Clinic
2801 Gessner Dr.
Houston, TX 77080
Ph: (713)275-5000
Free: 800-351-9058
URL: http://www.menningerclinic.com/

34310 ■ University of Texas Harris County Psychiatric Center
2800 S MacGregor Way, Hwy. 288
Houston, TX 77021
Ph: (713)741-5000
URL: http://hcpc.uth.tmc.edu/

34311 ■ University of Texas, Harris County Psychiatric Center Behavioral Health Services
3610 Willowbend, Ste. 1000
Houston, TX 77054
Ph: (713)500-8800
URL: http://hcpc.uth.tmc.edu/

34312 ■ West Oaks Hospital
6500 Hornwood
Houston, TX 77074
Ph: (713)995-0909
Fax: (713)778-5253
URL: http://www.psysolutions.com/facilities/westoaks/

Kerrville

34313 ■ Kerrville State Hospital
721 Thompson Dr.
Kerrville, TX 78028-5199
Ph: (830)896-2211
URL: http://www.dshs.state.tx.us/mhhospitals/KerrvilleSH/default.shtm

Kingwood

34314 ■ Kingwood Health Center
2001 Ladbrook Dr.
Kingwood, TX 77339
Ph: (281)358-1495

League City

34315 ■ Devereux Texas Treatment Network
1150 Devereux Dr.
League City, TX 77573
Ph: (281)335-1000
URL: http://www.devereux.org/site/PageServer

Lubbock

34316 ■ Sunrise Canyon Hospital
1950 Aspen
Lubbock, TX 79408
Ph: (806)766-0310
Free: 800-687-7581
URL: http://www.lubbockmhmr.org/sch/

Plano

34317 ■ Green Oaks Behavioral Healthcare of Plano
4001 W 15th St., Ste. 465
Plano, TX 75093
Ph: (972)985-1599
URL: http://www.greenoakspsych.com/specsrvc.asp

Rusk

34318 ■ Rusk State Hospital
805 N Dickerson Dr.
Rusk, TX 75785
Ph: (903)683-3421
URL: http://www.dshs.state.tx.us/mhhospitals/RuskSH/default.shtm

San Angelo

34319 ■ River Crest Hospital
1636 Hunters Glen Rd.
San Angelo, TX 76901-5016
Ph: (325)949-5722
Free: 800-777-5722
Fax: (325)947-2054
E-mail: brandi.smith@uhsinc.com
URL: http://www.rivercresthospital.com

San Antonio

34320 ■ Laurel Ridge Psychiatric Hospital Treatment Center
17720 Corporate Woods Dr.
San Antonio, TX 78259
Ph: (210)491-9400
Free: 800-624-7975
URL: http://www.psysolutions.com/facilities/laurel-ridge/SITE/

34321 ■ Mission Vista Behavioral Health
14747 Jones Maltsberger Rd.
San Antonio, TX 78247
Ph: (210)497-0004
Fax: (210)572-1447
URL: http://www.psysolutions.com/facilities/mission-vista/

34322 ■ San Antonio State Hospital
6711 S New Braunfels Ave., Ste. 100
San Antonio, TX 78223
Ph: (210)532-8811
URL: http://www.dshs.state.tx.us/mhhospitals/SanAntonioSH/default.shtm

34323 ■ Southwest Mental Health Center
8535 Tom Slick
San Antonio, TX 78229-3363
Ph: (210)616-0300
Free: 877-676-5437
URL: http://www.smhc.org/

Terrell

34324 ■ Terrell State Hospital
1200 E Brin St.
Terrell, TX 75160
Ph: (972)563-6452
URL: http://www.dshs.state.tx.us/mhhospitals/TerrellSH/default.shtm

Vernon

34325 ■ North Texas State Hospital--Vernon Campus
4730 College Dr.
Vernon, TX 76384
Ph: (940)553-2500
URL: http://www.dshs.state.tx.us/mhhospitals/northtexassh/default.shtm

Victoria

34326 ■ Devereux Texas Treatment Network
120 Wade Dr
Victoria, TX 77904
Ph: (361)575-8271
Free: 800-383-5000
Fax: (361)575-6520
URL: http://www.devereux.org

Waco

34327 ■ DePaul Center
301 Londonberry Dr.
Waco, TX 76712
Ph: (254)776-5970
URL: http://www.providence.net/DePaul.htm

34328 ■ Providence Health Center
6901 Medical Pkwy.
Waco, TX 76712
Ph: (254)751-4000
URL: http://www.providence.net/ProvHealthCenter.htm

Wichita Falls

34329 ■ North Texas State Hospital Wichita Falls Campus
6515 Lake Rd.
Wichita Falls, TX 76308-5419
Ph: (940)692-1220
URL: http://www.dshs.state.tx.us/mhhospitals/northtexassh/default.shtm

34330 ■ Red River Hospital
1505 8th St.
Wichita Falls, TX 76301
Ph: (940)322-3171
URL: http://www.redriverhospital.com/

UTAH

Bountiful

34331 ■ Davis Behavioral Health Bountiful Clinic
470 E Medical Dr.
Bountiful, UT 84010
Ph: (801)298-3446
URL: http://www.dbhutah.org/

Clearfield

34332 ■ Davis Behavioral Health Clearfield
1190 E 1450 S
Clearfield, UT 84015
Ph: (801)776-4800
URL: http://www.dbhutah.org/

Farmington

34333 ■ Davis Behavioral Health Farmington
291 S 200 West
Farmington, UT 84025
Ph: (801)451-7799
URL: http://www.dbhutah.org/

Layton

34334 ■ Davis Behavioral Health Layton Clinic
2250 Robins Dr.
Layton, UT 84041
Ph: (801)773-7060
URL: http://www.dbhutah.org/

Midvale

34335 ■ Highland Ridge Hospital
7309 S 180 West
Midvale, UT 84047
Ph: (801)569-2153
URL: http://www.highlandridgehospital.com/

Provo

34336 ■ Utah State Hospital
1300 E Center St.
Provo, UT 84603
Ph: (801)344-4400
URL: http://www.ush.utah.gov/

VERMONT

Brattleboro

34337 ■ The Brattleboro Retreat
Anna Marsh Ln.
Brattleboro, VT 05301
Ph: (802)257-7785
Free: 800-RETREAT
Fax: (802)257-3791
URL: http://www.brattlebororetreat.org/

Waterbury

34338 ■ Vermont State Hospital
103 S Main St.
Waterbury, VT 05671
Ph: (802)241-1000

VIRGINIA

Burkeville

34339 ■ Piedmont Geriatric Hospital
5001 E Patrick Henry Hwy.
Burkeville, VA 23922
Ph: (434)767-4401
URL: http://www.pgh.dmhmrsas.virginia.gov/

Catawba

34340 ■ Catawba Hospital
5525 Catawba Hospital Dr.
Catawba, VA 24070
Ph: (540)375-4200
Free: 800-451-5544
URL: http://catawba.dmhmrsas.virginia.gov/

Christiansburg

34341 ■ Carilion Saint Alban's Psychiatric Hospital
2900 Lamb Cir.
Christiansburg, VA 24073
Ph: (540)731-2000
Free: 800-284-8898
URL: http://www.carilionclinic.org/Carilion/Saint+Albans+Hospital

Danville

34342 ■ Southern Virginia Mental Health Institute
382 Taylor Dr.
Danville, VA 24541
Ph: (434)799-6220
URL: http://www.svmhi.dmhmrsas.virginia.gov/

Falls Church

34343 ■ HCA Dominion Hospital
2960 Sleepy Hollow Rd.
Falls Church, VA 22044-2030
Ph: (703)538-2871
Fax: (703)533-9650
URL: http://www.dominionhospital.com
Formerly: Columbia Dominion Hospital.

34344 ■ Northern Virginia Mental Health Institute
3302 Gallows Rd.
Falls Church, VA 22042-3398
Ph: (703)207-7100
URL: http://www.nvmhi.dmhmrsas.virginia.gov/

Hampton

34345 ■ Riverside Behavioral Health Center
2244 Executive Dr.
Hampton, VA 23666
Ph: (757)827-1001
Fax: (757)827-3128
URL: http://www.riversideonline.com
Formerly: Peninsula Behavioral Center.

Marion

34346 ■ Southwestern Virginia Mental Health Institute
340 Begley Cir.
Marion, VA 24354-3390
Ph: (276)783-1200
URL: http://www.swvmhi.dmhmrsas.virginia.gov/

Petersburg

34347 ■ Central State Hospital--Petersburg
26317 W Washington St.
Petersburg, VA 23803
Ph: (804)524-7000
URL: http://www.csh.dmhmrsas.virginia.gov/

34348 ■ Poplar Springs Hospital
350 Poplar Dr.
Petersburg, VA 23805
Ph: (804)796-2100
Free: 866-546-2229
URL: http://poplarsprings.com/

Richmond

34349 ■ Virginia Treatment Center for Children
515 N 10th St.
Richmond, VA 23298
Ph: (804)828-8822
Fax: (804)828-9879
URL: http://www.vcuhealth.org/vtcc

Staunton

34350 ■ Commonwealth Center for Children and Adolescents
1355 Richmond Ave.
Staunton, VA 24401
Ph: (540)332-2100
URL: http://www.ccca.dmhmrsas.virginia.gov/
Formerly: DeJarnette Center.

34351 ■ Western State Hospital--Staunton
1301 Richmond Rd.
Staunton, VA 24401
Ph: (540)332-8000
Free: 877-618-1481
URL: http://www.wsh.dmhmrsas.virginia.gov/

Virginia Beach

34352 ■ Virginia Beach Psychiatric Center
1100 1st Colonial Rd.
Virginia Beach, VA 23454
Ph: (757)496-6000
Fax: (757)481-0484
URL: http://www.psysolutions.com/facilities/virginiabeach/

Williamsburg

34353 ■ Eastern State Hospital--Williamsburg
4601 Ironbound Rd.
Williamsburg, VA 23187-8791
Ph: (757)253-5161
URL: http://www.esh.dmhmrsas.virginia.gov/

WASHINGTON

Kirkland

34354 ■ BHC Fairfax Hospital
10200 NE 132nd St.
Kirkland, WA 98034
Ph: (425)821-2000

Free: 800-435-7221
URL: http://www.psysolutions.com/facilities/fairfax/

Medical Lake

34355 ■ Eastern State Hospital--Medical Lake
Maple St., MS B 32-23
Medical Lake, WA 99022
Ph: (509)565-4000
Fax: (509)565-4705
URL: http://www.dshs.wa.gov/mentalhealth/esh.shtml

Seattle

34356 ■ Highline Mental Health
2600 SW Holden St.
Seattle, WA 98126
Ph: (206)933-7299
URL: http://www.navos.org/index.php?option=content&task=section&id=2&Itemid=86
Formerly: West Seattle Psychiatric Hospital.

Tacoma

34357 ■ Western State Hospital--Tacoma
9601 Steilacoom Blvd. SW
Tacoma, WA 98498-7213
Ph: (253)582-8900
URL: http://www.dshs.wa.gov/mentalhealth/wsh.shtml

WEST VIRGINIA

Charleston

34358 ■ Highland Hospital
300 56th St.
Charleston, WV 25304
Ph: (304)926-1600
Free: 800-250-3806
URL: http://www.highlandhospital.net/

Huntington

34359 ■ Mildred Mitchell-Bateman Hospital
1530 Norway Ave.
Huntington, WV 25705-1336
Ph: (304)525-7801
Free: 800-644-9318
URL: http://www.batemanhospital.org/

34360 ■ River Park Hospital
1230 6th Ave.
Huntington, WV 25701
Ph: (304)526-9111
Fax: (304)526-9140
URL: http://www.riverparkhospital.net/
Formerly: Columbia River Park Hospital.

Morgantown

34361 ■ Chestnut Ridge Hospital
930 Chestnut Ridge Rd.
Morgantown, WV 26505
Ph: (304)598-6400
URL: http://www.health.wvu.edu/crh/

Weston

34362 ■ William R. Sharpe Jr. Hospital
936 Sharpe Hospital Rd.
Weston, WV 26452
Ph: (304)269-1210
URL: http://www.wvdhhr.org/sharpe/

WISCONSIN

Antigo

34363 ■ Langlade Health Care Center
1225 Langlade Rd.
Antigo, WI 54409
Ph: (715)627-6694
Fax: (715)627-4194
URL: http://www.norcen.org/

Burlington

34364 ■ Aurora Behavioral Health Center Behavioral Health Services
190 Gardner Ave., No. 3
Burlington, WI 53105
Ph: (262)763-7766
URL: http://www.aurorahealthcare.org

Delavan

34365 ■ Aurora Behavioral Health Center
1550 Hobbs Dr.
Delavan, WI 53115-2027
Ph: (262)740-4200
URL: http://www.aurorahealthcare.org

Elkhorn

34366 ■ Aurora Behavioral Health Center Behavioral Health Services
205 E Commerce St.
Elkhorn, WI 53121
Ph: (262)723-3100
URL: http://www.aurorahealthcare.org

Fond Du Lac

34367 ■ Aurora Behavioral Health Center--Fond Du Lac
210 Wisconsin American Dr.
Fond Du Lac, WI 54935
Ph: (920)907-7000
URL: http://www.aurorahealthcare.org

Franklin

34368 ■ Aurora Behavioral Health Center--Franklin
9200 W Loomis Rd., Ste. 103
Franklin, WI 53132
Ph: (414)425-1250
URL: http://www.aurorahealthcare.org

Germantown

34369 ■ Aurora Behavioral Health Center--Germantown
9830 Rivercrest Dr., Ste. 104
Germantown, WI 53022
Ph: (414)773-4312
URL: http://www.aurorahealthcare.org

Green Bay

34370 ■ Bellin Psychiatric Center
744 S Webster Ave.
Green Bay, WI 54305-3400
Ph: (920)433-3500
Free: 888-433-3111
URL: http://www.bellin.org

34371 ■ Brown County Human Services
2900 St. Anthony Dr.
Green Bay, WI 54311
Ph: (920)391-4700
URL: http://www.co.brown.wi.us/departments/?department=dd09bd30c78e

Kenosha

34372 ■ Aurora Behavioral Health Center Behavioral Health Services
10400 75th St., Ste. 307
Kenosha, WI 53142
Ph: (262)948-6770
URL: http://www.aurorahealthcare.org/

34373 ■ Rogers Memorial Hospital--Kenosha Child and Adolescent Day Treatment
9916 75th St.
Kenosha, WI 53142
Ph: (262)942-4000
URL: http://www.rogershospital.org/index2.php

Lake Geneva

34374 ■ Aurora Behavioral Health Center Behavioral Health Services
146 E Geneva Sq.
Lake Geneva, WI 53147
Ph: (262)249-4640
URL: http://www.aurorahealthcare.org/

Madison

34375 ■ Mendota Mental Health Institute
301 Troy Dr.
Madison, WI 53704
Ph: (608)301-1000
Fax: (608)301-1358
URL: http://dhs.wisconsin.gov/mh_mendota/

34376 ■ Program for Assertive Community Treatment
600 Williamson St., Ste. A
Madison, WI 53703
Ph: (608)266-0721
Fax: (608)261-8085
URL: http://dhs.wisconsin.gov/mh_mendota/programs/Outpatient/PACT/PACT.htm

Manitowoc

34377 ■ Aurora Behavioral Health Center--Manitowoc
1425 Memorial Dr.
Manitowoc, WI 54220
Ph: (920)683-9500
URL: http://www.aurorahealthcare.org/

Marshfield

34378 ■ Norwood Health Center
1600 N Chestnut Ave.
Marshfield, WI 54449
Ph: (715)384-2188
URL: http://www.co.wood.wi.us/Departments/Norwood/

Merrill

34379 ■ Lincoln Health Care Center
607 N Sales St.
Merrill, WI 54452
Ph: (715)536-9482
URL: http://www.norcen.org/

Milwaukee

34380 ■ Aurora Behavioral Health Center--North Shore
6980 N Port Washington Rd., Ste. 202
Milwaukee, WI 53217
Ph: (414)351-7100
URL: http://www.aurorahealthcare.org/

34381 ■ Milwaukee County Mental Health
9455 Watertown Plank Rd.
Milwaukee, WI 53226
Ph: (414)257-6995
URL: http://www.mhamilw.org/

34382 ■ Milwaukee County Mental Health Community Support Program
734 N 4th St.
Milwaukee, WI 53203
Ph: (414)226-4040

34383 ■ Milwaukee County Mental Health Day Hospital
9201 Watertown Plank Rd.
Milwaukee, WI 53226
Ph: (414)257-7356

34384 ■ Milwaukee County Mental Health Metro-North Community Clinic
2770 N 5th St.
Milwaukee, WI 53212
Ph: (414)286-8886

34385 ■ Milwaukee County Mental Health Southside Community Support Program
1201 W Historic Mitchell St.
Milwaukee, WI 53204
Ph: (414)649-4620

34386 ■ Psychiatric Crisis Services
9499 Watertown Plank Rd.
Milwaukee, WI 53226
Ph: (414)257-7260
URL: http://www.county.milwaukee.gov/Behavioral-HealthDivi7762/CrisisServices.htm

34387 ■ Rogers Memorial Hospital--Milwaukee
11101 W Lincoln Ave.
Milwaukee, WI 53227
Ph: (414)327-3000
URL: http://www.rogershospital.org/index2.php

New Berlin

34388 ■ Aurora Behavioral Health Center--New Berlin
14555 W National Ave., Ste. 193
New Berlin, WI 53151
Ph: (262)796-8426
Fax: (262)796-8437
URL: http://www.aurorahealthcare.org
Formerly: New Berlin Counseling Center.

Oconomowoc

34389 ■ Rogers Memorial Hospital--Oconomowoc
34700 Valley Rd.
Oconomowoc, WI 53066
Ph: (262)646-4411
Free: 800-767-4411
Fax: (262)646-3158
URL: http://www.rogershospital.org/index2.php

Oshkosh

34390 ■ Aurora Behavioral Health Center Aurora Medical Center Oshkosh
414 Doctors Ct.
Oshkosh, WI 54901
Ph: (920)303-8700
URL: http://www.aurorahealthcare.org/

Racine

34391 ■ Aurora Behavioral Health Center--Racine
6015 Durand Ave., Ste. 400
Racine, WI 53406
Ph: (262)554-0205
URL: http://www.aurorahealthcare.org/

Saint Francis

34392 ■ Aurora Behavioral Health Center--Airport
2000 Layton Ave., Ste. 250
Saint Francis, WI 53235
Ph: (414)482-7700
URL: http://www.aurorahealthcare.org/

Tomahawk

34393 ■ Lincoln Health Care Center
310 W Wisconsin Ave.
Tomahawk, WI 54487
Ph: (715)453-5381
URL: http://www.norcen.org/

Waukesha

34394 ■ Aurora Behavioral Health Center--Waukesha
W231N 1440 State Rd. 164, Ste. 310
Waukesha, WI 53186
Ph: (262)896-6186
URL: http://www.aurorahealthcare.org/

Wausau

34395 ■ North Central Health Care
1100 Lakeview Dr.
Wausau, WI 54403-6799
Ph: (715)848-4600
URL: http://www.norcen.org/

Wauwatosa

34396 ■ Aurora Psychiatric Hospital Inc.
1220 Dewey Ave.
Wauwatosa, WI 53213
Ph: (414)454-6600
URL: http://www.aurorahealthcare.org/facilities/display.asp?ID=0010

Winnebago

34397 ■ Winnebago Mental Health Institute
1300 South Dr.
Winnebago, WI 54985
Ph: (920)235-4910
URL: http://dhs.wisconsin.gov/mh_winnebago/

WYOMING

Casper

34398 ■ Wyoming Behavioral Institute
2521 E 15th St.
Casper, WY 82609
Ph: (307)237-7444
URL: http://www.wbihelp.com/

Evanston

34399 ■ Wyoming State Hospital
830 Hwy. 150 S
Evanston, WY 82931-5341
Ph: (307)789-3464
URL: http://wdh.state.wy.us/

RESIDENTIAL TREATMENT CENTERS FOR EMOTIONALLY DISTURBED CHILDREN

ALABAMA

Black

34400 ■ Johnson Mental Retardation Group Home
1630 E County Rd. 4
Black, AL 36340
Ph: (334)684-9899

34401 ■ Merle Wallace Purvis Center
1682 E County Rd. 4
Black, AL 36340
Ph: (334)684-2252

Courtland

34402 ■ Three Springs of Courtland Residential Treatment Center
PO Box 370
Courtland, AL 35618
Ph: (256)637-2199
Free: 888-758-4356
Fax: (256)637-8911
E-mail: info@threesprings.com
URL: http://www.threesprings.com

Double Springs

34403 ■ Hendrix Health Care
1000 Hwy. 33
Double Springs, AL 35553
Ph: (205)489-2136
Free: 800-489-1046
URL: http://www.northporthealth.com/

Huntsville

34404 ■ Three Springs, Inc.
1131 Eagletree Ln.
Huntsville, AL 35801
Ph: (256)880-3339
Free: 888-758-4356
Fax: (256)880-7026
E-mail: info@threesprings.com
URL: http://www.threesprings.com

Tuscaloosa

34405 ■ University of Alabama Brewer Porch Children's Center
2501 Woodland Ave.
Tuscaloosa, AL 35404
Ph: (205)348-7236
URL: http://bpcc.ua.edu/

ALASKA

Anchorage

34406 ■ Alaska Children's Services
4600 Abbott Rd.
Anchorage, AK 99507
Ph: (907)346-2101
Fax: (907)348-9230
E-mail: akchild@ak.net
URL: http://www.akchild.org/

34407 ■ Alaska Youth & Parent Foundation
6th Ave. & H St.
Anchorage, AK 99508
Ph: (907)929-2633
E-mail: aypf@ak.net
URL: http://www.aypfalaska.org/

34408 ■ Hope Community Resource, Inc.
540 W International Airport Rd., Ste. 100
Anchorage, AK 99518
Ph: (907)561-5335
Free: 800-478-0078
URL: http://www.hopealaska.org/

Fairbanks

34409 ■ Family-Centered Services of Alaska
1825 Marika Rd.
Fairbanks, AK 99701
Ph: (907)474-0890
Free: 800-478-2108
Fax: (907)451-8945
URL: http://www.familycenteredservices.com/

Juneau

34410 ■ Juneau Youth Services, inc.
2075 Jordan Ave.
Juneau, AK 99803-2839
Ph: (907)789-7610
Free: 877-JYS-HELP
Fax: (907)789-8443
E-mail: colleenm@jys.org
URL: http://www.jys.org

34411 ■ Juneau Youth Services, Inc. Wallington House
2461 Oday Dr.
Juneau, AK 99802
Ph: (907)523-6518
URL: http://www.jys.org

Kenai

34412 ■ Kenai Peninsula Community Care Center
320 S Spruce St.
Kenai, AK 99611-7939
Ph: (907)283-9635
URL: http://www.kpccc.com/

ARIZONA

Bisbee

34413 ■ Arizona Children's Association Bisbee Office
7 Bisbee Rd., Ste. 4
Bisbee, AZ 85603-0040
Ph: (520)432-2375
URL: http://www.arizonaschildren.org/

Mesa

34414 ■ Dorothy B. Mitchell Counseling Center
1655 E University Dr., Ste. 100
Mesa, AZ 85203
Ph: (480)969-6955
Fax: (480)898-0705
URL: http://www.turnanewleaf.org/counseling.asp
Formerly: Center for Family Enrichment.

34415 ■ Dorothy Mitchell Residence
3505 E University Dr.
Mesa, AZ 85213-8619
Ph: (480)461-5073
Fax: (480)641-5165
URL: http://www.turnanewleaf.org/counseling.asp

34416 ■ Mayfield Alternative Youth Center
615 E University Dr.
Mesa, AZ 85203-7926
Ph: (480)464-7468
Fax: (480)461-4219
URL: http://www.turnanewleaf.org/counseling.asp

34417 ■ A New Leaf
868 E University Dr.
Mesa, AZ 85203
Ph: (480)969-4024
Fax: (480)969-0039
E-mail: bnoble@prehab.org
URL: http://www.turnanewleaf.org/counseling.asp
Formerly: PREHAB of Arizona.

Phoenix

34418 ■ Arizona Baptist Children's Services
PO Box 35637
Phoenix, AZ 85069
Ph: (602)346-2300
Free: 877--HOPE4AZ
Fax: (602)346-2399
URL: http://www.abcs.org

34419 ■ Devereux Metro
2432 W Peoria Ave., Ste. 1047
Phoenix, AZ 85029
Ph: (602)944-6222
URL: http://www.devereux.org

Scottsdale

34420 ■ Devereux Arizona
11000 N Scottsdale Rd., Ste. 260
Scottsdale, AZ 85254
Ph: (480)998-2920
Fax: (480)443-5587
E-mail: svitali@devereux.org
URL: http://www.devereux.org

34421 ■ Devereux Sweetwater
6436 E Sweetwater Ave.
Scottsdale, AZ 85254-4581
Ph: (480)443-2920
URL: http://www.devereux.org
Formerly: Devereaux Arizona Treatment Center.

34422 ■ New Foundation
PO Box 3828
Scottsdale, AZ 85271-3828
Ph: (480)945-3302
Fax: (480)945-9308
E-mail: thenewfoundation@aol.com
URL: http://www.thenewfoundation.org

Tucson

34423 ■ Arizona Children's Association Regional Office
2700 S 8th Ave.
Tucson, AZ 85713
Ph: (520)622-7611
Free: 800-947-7611
Fax: (520)624-7042
URL: http://www.arizonaschildren.org

34424 ■ Devereux--Tucson
6141 E Grant Rd.
Tucson, AZ 85712
Ph: (520)296-5551
Fax: (520)296-8244
URL: http://www.Devereux.org

Yuma

34425 ■ Arizona Children' Association Yuma Office
3780 S 4th Ave., Ste. J
Yuma, AZ 85365
Ph: (928)344-8800
URL: http://www.arizonaschildren.org/

ARKANSAS

Bentonville

34426 ■ Ozark Guidance Center, Inc. Assertive Community Treatment
2205 Phyllis St.
Bentonville, AR 72712
Ph: (479)845-2107
URL: http://www.ozarkguidance.org/

Jacksonville

34427 ■ Centers for Youth & Families Jacksonville Branch Office
511 Stonewall Sq., No.8
Jacksonville, AR 72076
Ph: (501)666-8686
URL: http://centersforyouthandfamilies.org/

Little Rock

34428 ■ Centers For Youth & Families--Little Rock
5118 Stonewall Rd.
Little Rock, AR 72207
Ph: (501)666-8686
URL: http://centersforyouthandfamilies.org/

34429 ■ Centers for Youth & Families Elizabeth Mitchell Adolescent Center
6501 W 12th St.
Little Rock, AR 72204
Ph: (501)666-8686
E-mail: sjohns@aristotle.net
URL: http://centersforyouthandfamilies.org/

34430 ■ Centers for Youth & Families Parent Center Programs
5905 Forest Pl.
Little Rock, AR 72207
Ph: (501)666-6886
URL: http://centersforyouthandfamilies.org/

North Little Rock

34431 ■ Centers for Youth & Families Adolescent Day Treatment Program
200 W 20th St.
North Little Rock, AR 72114
Ph: (501)771-5511
URL: http://centersforyouthandfamilies.org/

CALIFORNIA

Anaheim

34432 ■ Canyon Acres
160 S Fairmont Blvd.
Anaheim, CA 92808-1336
Ph: (714)385-5270
E-mail: info@canyonacres.org
URL: http://www.canyonacres.org
Formerly: Canyon Acres Children's Services.

Camarillo

34433 ■ Casa Pacifica
975 Flynn Rd.
Camarillo, CA 93012
Ph: (805)445-7800
Fax: (805)987-7237
URL: http://www.casapacifica.org

Campbell

34434 ■ Eastfield Ming Quong Children's and Family Services
251 Llewellyn Ave.
Campbell, CA 95008-1940
Ph: (408)379-3790
URL: http://www.emqff.org/index.html

34435 ■ Families First--Campbell
1475 S Bascom Ave., Ste. 112
Campbell, CA 95008
Ph: (530)753-0220
Free: 800-698-4968
Fax: (530)753-3390
E-mail: info@familiesfirstinc.org
URL: http://www.familiesfirstinc.org

Colton

34436 ■ Trinity Children and Family Services--Colton
1460 E Cooley Rd.
Colton, CA 92324
Ph: (909)825-5588
Free: 800--KIDS730
Fax: (909)825-8004
URL: http://www.trinitychildrensfoundation.org/

Davis

34437 ■ Families First--Davis
1909 Galileo Ct.
Davis, CA 95616
Ph: (530)750-5470
Free: 800-698-4968
Fax: (530)753-3390
URL: http://www.familiesfirstinc.org/

Fresno

34438 ■ Families First Inc.--Fresno
7080 N Marks Ave. Ste. 104
Fresno, CA 93711
Ph: (559)248-8550
Free: 800-948-8550
Fax: (559)248-8555
URL: http://www.familiesfirst.org

Hollister

34439 ■ Chamberlain Children's Center
1850 San Benito St.
Hollister, CA 95023
Ph: (831)636-2121
URL: http://www.chamberlaincc.org/

34440 ■ Chamberlain's Acres
1850b San Benito St.
Hollister, CA 95024
Ph: (831)637-1677
URL: http://www.chamberlaincc.org/

La Verne

34441 ■ David and Margaret Home, Inc.
1350 3rd St.
La Verne, CA 91750
Ph: (909)596-5921
Fax: (909)596-3954
E-mail: information@dmhome.org
URL: http://www.dmhome.org

34442 ■ Wenwood House
1350 3rd St.
La Verne, CA 91750
Ph: (909)596-5921
Fax: (909)596-3954
E-mail: Information@DMHome.Org
URL: http://www.dmhome.org

Lake View Terrace

34443 ■ Hathaway Children's Services
8955 Gold Creek Rd.
Lake View Terrace, CA 91342
Ph: (818)896-2474
URL: http://www.hathaway-sycamores.org/

Los Angeles

34444 ■ Hathaway Children's and Family Services
840 N Ave.
Los Angeles, CA 90042
Ph: (323)257-9600
URL: http://www.hathaway-sycamores.org/

34445 ■ Optimist Youth and Family Services
6957 N Figueroa St.
Los Angeles, CA 90042
Ph: (323)443-3175
URL: http://www.oyhfs.org/

34446 ■ Reiss--Davis Child Study Center
3200 Motor Ave.
Los Angeles, CA 90034
Ph: (310)204-1666
URL: http://vistadelmar.org/

34447 ■ Vista Del Mar Child and Family Services
3200 Motor Ave.
Los Angeles, CA 90034
Ph: (310)836-1223
URL: http://vistadelmar.org/

34448 ■ Vista Del Mar Girls' Group Home
8546 Keokuk Ave.
Los Angeles, CA 91306
Ph: (818)700-9439
URL: http://vistadelmar.org/

Los Gatos

34449 ■ Eastfield Ming Quong
499 Loma Alta Ave.
Los Gatos, CA 95030
Ph: (408)354-6051
URL: http://www.emqff.org/index.html

34450 ■ Rolling Hills School-Based Day Treatment
1585 More Ave.
Los Gatos, CA 95032-1094
Ph: (408)341-7073

Martinez

34451 ■ Discovery House
4639 Pacheco Blvd.
Martinez, CA 95470
Ph: (925)229-4212

Modesto

34452 ■ Center for Human Services
1700 McHenry Village Way, Ste. 11
Modesto, CA 95350-4341
Ph: (209)526-1440
Fax: (209)526-0908
E-mail: kusiak@centerforhumanservices.org
URL: http://www.centerforhumanservices.org

34453 ■ Families First--Modesto
1620 N Carpenter Rd., Ste. C-23
Modesto, CA 95351
Ph: (209)523-3710
Free: 877-799-1699
Fax: (209)523-3725
URL: http://www.familiesfirstinc.org

34454 ■ Sierra Vista Children's Center
100 Poplar Ave., Ste. 1
Modesto, CA 95354
Ph: (209)523-4573
Free: 888-524-KIDS
Fax: (209)550-5866
URL: http://sierravistacares.org/

North Hills

34455 ■ Penny Lane Centers
Dr. Rose Jenkens Memorial Clinic
15305 Rayen St.
North Hills, CA 91343
Ph: (818)892-3423
URL: http://www.pennylane.org/
Formerly: National Foundation for the Treatment of the Emotionally Handicapped.

34456 ■ Penny Lane Centers
Main Facility
15302 Rayen St.
North Hills, CA 91343
Ph: (818)892-3423
Fax: (818)893-4509
URL: http://www.pennylane.org/
Formerly: National Foundation for the Treatment of the Emotionally Handicapped.

North Hollywood

34457 ■ Dubnoff Center for Child Development & Educational Therapy
10526 Dubnoff Way
North Hollywood, CA 91606
Ph: (818)755-4950
Fax: (818)752-0783
E-mail: sandrab@dubnoffcenter.org
URL: http://www.dubnoffcenter.org

Oakland

34458 ■ Families First--Oakland
7801 Edgewater, Ste. 1000
Oakland, CA 94621
Ph: (510)636-2000
Free: 877-799-2799
Fax: (510)439-4136
URL: http://www.familiesfirstinc.org

34459 ■ Lincoln Child Center
4368 Lincoln Ave.
Oakland, CA 94602-2529
Ph: (510)531-3111
Fax: (510)530-8083
E-mail: info@lincolncc.org
URL: http://www.lincolncc.org

34460 ■ Nicol Group Home
2841 Nicol Ave.
Oakland, CA 94602
Ph: (510)531-3111

Palo Alto

34461 ■ Caravan House
Adolescent Counseling Services
2361 High St.
Palo Alto, CA 94301
Ph: (650)321-0690
URL: http://www.acs-teens.org/programs/success_stories/warm_return_at_caravan.ph p

Pasadena

34462 ■ Bonnie House
63 N Bonnie Ave.
Pasadena, CA 91106
Ph: (626)795-1020

34463 ■ Group Home for Girls
873 N Hill
Pasadena, CA 91104
Ph: (323)254-2274

34464 ■ Hillside Home for Children
940 Ave. 64
Pasadena, CA 91105-2711
Ph: (323)255-9005

34465 ■ Solita Road Group Home
1236 Solita Rd.
Pasadena, CA 91103
Ph: (626)798-2234

34466 ■ The Sycamores
210 S De Lacey, Ste. 110
Pasadena, CA 91105
Ph: (626)395-7100
Fax: (626)395-7270
E-mail: info@sycamores.org
URL: http://www.hathaway-sycamores.org
Remarks: Mental Health Outpatient and Homebased Services.

Ramona

34467 ■ Broad Horizons
1236 H St.
Ramona, CA 92065
Ph: (760)789-7060
Fax: (760)797-4062

Sacramento

34468 ■ FamiliesFirst--Sacramento
2330 Glendale Ln., Ste. 100
Sacramento, CA 95825
Ph: (916)641-9599
Free: 800-495-9559
URL: http://www.familiesfirstinc.org

34469 ■ Milhous Center
9211 Gerber Rd.
Sacramento, CA 95829
Ph: (916)423-1157

34470 ■ River Oak Center for Children, Inc.
5445 Laurel Hills Dr.
Sacramento, CA 95841-3105
Ph: (916)344-2295
URL: http://www.riveroak.org/

34471 ■ Riverside Group Home
6675 Riverside Blvd.
Sacramento, CA 95831
Ph: (916)452-3981

34472 ■ Sacramento Children's Home
2750 Sutterville Rd.
Sacramento, CA 95820
Ph: (916)452-3981

San Anselmo

34473 ■ Sunny Hills Children's Garden
300 Sunny Hills Dr.
San Anselmo, CA 94960-1995
Ph: (415)256-1580
E-mail: contactus@SunnyHillsServices.org
URL: http://www.sunnyhillsservices.org
Formerly: Sunny Hills Children's Services.

San Diego

34474 ■ San Diego Center for Children
3002 Armstrong St.
San Diego, CA 92111
Ph: (858)277-9550
Free: 800-277-9550
URL: http://www.centerforchildren.org/

San Francisco

34475 ■ Edgewood Center for Children and Families
1801 Vicente St.
San Francisco, CA 94116
Ph: (415)681-3211
URL: http://www.edgewoodcenter.org/

San Jose

34476 ■ Giarretti Institute
232 E Gish Rd.
San Jose, CA 95112
Ph: (408)453-7616

San Rafael

34477 ■ Children's Garden of California
7 Mt. Lassen Dr.
San Rafael, CA 94903
Ph: (415)472-7620
Fax: (415)472-7635
URL: http://www.childrensgardenco.com/
Formerly: Sunny Hills Children's Garden.

34478 ■ Sunny Hills Children's Garden
7 Mount Lassen Dr., Ste. B256
San Rafael, CA 94903-1162
Ph: (415)472-7620
URL: http://www.sunnyhillsservices.org/
Remarks: Multiple locations serving children and adolescents.

Santa Ana

34479 ■ Olive Crest Treatment Centers, Inc.
2130 E 4th St., Ste. 200
Santa Ana, CA 92705-3818
Ph: (714)543-5437
URL: http://www.olivecrest.org

Sebastopol

34480 ■ Phoenix Home
3157 Frei Rd.
Sebastopol, CA 95472-2301
Ph: (707)823-1044
Fax: (707)823-0421
E-mail: information@tlc4kids.org
URL: http://www.tlc4kids.org

34481 ■ Plumfield Farm
5615 Hessel Ave.
Sebastopol, CA 95472
Ph: (707)823-4584

34482 ■ Plumfield, Inc.
Administrative Office
9360 Occidental Rd.
Sebastopol, CA 95472
Ph: (707)824-1414

34483 ■ Plumfield Ranch
10425 Mill Station Rd.
Sebastopol, CA 95472
Ph: (707)823-0214

34484 ■ Plumfield Villa
7620 Lynch Rd.
Sebastopol, CA 95472
Ph: (707)823-2327

34485 ■ True To Life Children's Services & Orchid House
1800 N Gravenstein Hwy.
Sebastopol, CA 95472-2607
Ph: (707)823-7300
Fax: (707)823-3410
E-mail: information@tlc4kids.org
URL: http://www.tlc4kids.org
Formerly: True to Life Children's Services.

Sherman Oaks

34486 ■ Help Group
13130 Burbank Blvd.
Sherman Oaks, CA 91401
Ph: (818)781-0360
Free: 877-943-5747
URL: http://www.thehelpgroup.org/index.php

Sonoma

34487 ■ Hanna Boys Center
17000 Arnold Dr.
Sonoma, CA 95476
Ph: (707)996-6767
Free: 877-994-2662
Fax: (707)996-8435
E-mail: Info@hannacenter.org
URL: http://www.hannacenter.org/HannaBoysCenter/default.aspx

Stockton

34488 ■ Children's Home of Stockton
430 N Pilgrim St.
Stockton, CA 95201
Ph: (209)466-0853
URL: http://www.chsstk.com/

34489 ■ Families First--Stockton
2291 W March Ln., Ste. C-101
Stockton, CA 95207
Ph: (209)954-3000
Free: 800-310-7799
Fax: (209)957-8876
URL: http://www.familiesfirstinc.org/

Sylmar

34490 ■ Hathaway--Sycamores Child and Family Services
8955 Goldcreek Rd
Sylmar, CA 91342-5900
Ph: (818)896-2474
URL: http://www.hathaway-sycamores.org/
Formerly: Hathaway Children's Services.

Turlock

34491 ■ Creative Alternatives
2855 Geer Rd., Ste. C
Turlock, CA 95382
Ph: (209)668-9361
URL: http://creative-alternatives.org/

Van Nuys

34492 ■ Center for Family Living
14545 Sherman Cir.
Van Nuys, CA 91405
Ph: (818)901-4854
URL: http://www.sfvcmhc.org/html/center_for_family_living.html

34493 ■ Doris Foster Independent Living Center
14803 Friar St.
Van Nuys, CA 91411-2254
Ph: (818)988-8050

Walnut Creek

34494 ■ Turning Points Counseling Center
1291 Oakland Blvd.
Walnut Creek, CA 94596-4374
Ph: (925)933-2627
Formerly: Youth Homes Inc.

Yucaipa

34495 ■ Trinity Children's and Family Services--Yucaipa
10776 Fremont St.
Yucaipa, CA 92399
Ph: (909)797-0114
Free: 800-KIDS-730
URL: http://www.trinitychildrensfoundation.org/

COLORADO

Aurora

34496 ■ Excelsior Youth Center
15001 E Oxford Ave.
Aurora, CO 80014
Ph: (303)693-1550
Fax: (303)693-8309
E-mail: paulinet@excelsioryc.org
URL: http://www.excelsioryc.org

Denver

34497 ■ Beacon Center
Daybreak Girls' Home
3804 W Princeton Cir.
Denver, CO 80236
Ph: (303)789-2987
URL: http://www.beaconcenter.org/

34498 ■ Beacon Center
Daybreak Girls' Home--Princeton
3640 W Princeton Cir.
Denver, CO 80236
Ph: (303)761-6773
URL: http://www.beaconcenter.org/

34499 ■ Beacon Center
Marilee Center
3874 W Princeton Cir.
Denver, CO 80236
Ph: (303)761-5229
URL: http://www.beaconcenter.org/

34500 ■ The Denver Children's Home
1501 Albion St.
Denver, CO 80220
Ph: (303)399-4890
E-mail: info@denverchildrenshome.org
URL: http://www.denverchildrenshome.org

34501 ■ Mount Saint Vincent Home
4159 Lowell Blvd.
Denver, CO 80211
Ph: (303)458-7220
URL: http://www.msvhome.org/

34502 ■ Third Way Center Inc.
1295 York St.
Denver, CO 80206
Ph: (303)780-9191
Fax: (303)780-9192
E-mail: info@thirdwaycenter.org
URL: http://www.thirdwaycenter.org

Englewood

34503 ■ Beacon Center
Englewood
333 W Hampden Ave., Ste. 305
Englewood, CO 80110-2333
Ph: (303)761-6756
URL: http://www.beaconcenter.org/

Evergreen

34504 ■ Forest Heights Lodge School
4761 Forest Hill Rd.
Evergreen, CO 80439
Ph: (303)674-6681
URL: http://www.forestheightslodge.org/

Greely

34505 ■ North Range Behavioral Health
Stanek Center
1103 5th St.
Greely, CO 80631-4610
Ph: (303)353-3686
URL: http://www.northrange.org/

La Junta

34506 ■ Colorado Boys Ranch
28071 State Hwy. 109
La Junta, CO 81050
Ph: (719)384-5981
Free: 800-790-4993
Fax: (719)384-8119
E-mail: Info@CBRyouthconnect.org
URL: http://www.coloradoboysranch.org/cbrweb/site/

Loveland

34507 ■ Namaqua Center
404 E 7th St.
Loveland, CO 80537
Ph: (970)669-7550
Fax: (970)663-2907
URL: http://www.namaqua.com/

Pueblo

34508 ■ El Pueblo Boys' and Girls' Ranch
1 El Pueblo Ranch Way
Pueblo, CO 81006-2103
Ph: (719)544-7496
URL: http://www.elpueblokids.org/

CONNECTICUT

Cromwell

34509 ■ The Children's Home--Cromwell
60 Hicksville Rd.
Cromwell, CT 06416
Ph: (860)635-6010
URL: http://www.childhome.org/
Formerly: The Children's Home of Cromwell.

Litchfield

34510 ■ Connecticut Junior Republic
550 Goshen Rd.
Litchfield, CT 06759
Ph: (860)567-9423
E-mail: info@ctjuniorrepublic.org
URL: http://www.ctjuniorrepublic.org/

Madison

34511 ■ Grove School, Inc.
Therapeutic School For Emotionally Fragile Teenagers
175 Copse Rd.
Madison, CT 06443
Ph: (203)245-2778
Fax: (203)245-6098
E-mail: info@groveschool.org
URL: http://groveschool.org

New Haven

34512 ■ Saint Frances Home for Children
651 Prospect St.
New Haven, CT 06511
Ph: (203)777-5513
URL: http://www.stfrancishome.com/
Formerly: Saint Francis Home for Children at Highland Heights.

Quaker Hill

34513 ■ Waterford Country School, Inc.
78 Hunts Brook Rd.
Quaker Hill, CT 06375-1000
Ph: (860)442-9454
URL: http://www.waterfordcountryschool.org/

Washington

34514 ■ Devereux Glenholme School
81 Sabbaday Ln.
Washington, CT 06793
Ph: (860)868-7377
Fax: (860)868-7894
E-mail: info@theglenholmeschool.org
URL: http://www.theglenholmeschool.org

DELAWARE

Dover

34515 ■ Brenford Place Residential Treatment Center
136 Waterview Ln.
Dover, DE 19904-1049
Ph: (302)653-6589

Georgetown

34516 ■ Children & Families First--Georgetown
410 S Bedford St.
Georgetown, DE 19947
Ph: (302)856-2388
URL: http://www.cffde.org

Middletown

34517 ■ Middletown Residential Treatment Center
495 E Main St.
Middletown, DE 19709
Ph: (302)378-5238

New Castle

34518 ■ Terry Children's Psychiatric Center
10 Central Ave.
New Castle, DE 19720
Ph: (302)577-4270
URL: http://dhss.delaware.gov/dhss/main/maps/holloway/terrycpc.htm

Wilmington

34519 ■ Children & Families First--Wilmington
2005 Baynard Blvd.
Wilmington, DE 19802
Ph: (302)658-5177
Free: 800-734-2388
Fax: (302)658-5170
E-mail: info@cffde.org
URL: http://www.cffde.org

DISTRICT OF COLUMBIA

Washington

34520 ■ Devereaux Children's Center of Washington, DC
3050 R St. NW
Washington, DC 20007
Ph: (202)282-1200
URL: http://www.devereux.org/site/PageServer

FLORIDA

Bradenton

34521 ■ Manatee Children's Services
The Flamiglio Center
453 Cortez Rd. W
Bradenton, FL 34207
Ph: (941)345-1200
URL: http://www.manateechildrensservices.com/

Bristol

34522 ■ Bristol Youth Academy Residential Treatment
12422 NW Gordon & Truett Revell Rd.
Bristol, FL 32321
Ph: (850)643-4600
Fax: (850)643-2061
URL: http://www.djj.state.fl.us/Residential/facilities/north_facilities/Bristol_ Youth_Academy.html

Bunnell

34523 ■ Devereux Flagler Day School
3265 E Hwy. 100
Bunnell, FL 32110
Ph: (386)586-3812
URL: http://www.devereux.org/site/PageServer

Coral Gables

34524 ■ CHARLEE Homes for Children
5915 Ponce de Leon Blvd., Ste. 26
Coral Gables, FL 33146
Ph: (305)665-7365
URL: http://www.charleeprogram.org/

Coral Springs

34525 ■ Brookwood Florida - East, Inc.
11461 NW 43rd St.
Coral Springs, FL 33065
Ph: (954)757-3833
URL: http://www.brookwoodflorida.org/

Deland

34526 ■ Devereux Deland Outpatient Center
120 E New York Ave.
Deland, FL 32724
Ph: (386)740-7110
URL: http://www.devereux.org/site/PageServer

34527 ■ Devereux Therapeutic Foster Care Volusia
120 E New York Ave., Ste. C
Deland, FL 32724
Ph: (386)738-5543
URL: http://www.devereux.org/site/PageServer
Formerly: Devereux Therapeutic Foster Care.

Fort Walton Beach

34528 ■ Gulf Coast Youth Services
1015 Mar Walt Dr.
Fort Walton Beach, FL 32547
Ph: (850)863-4160
Free: 800-537-5433
URL: http://www.gulfcoasttreatment.com/
Formerly: Gulf Coast Treatment Center.

Hialeah

34529 ■ Citrus Health Network
Center for Adolescent Treatment Services
4175 W 20th Ave.
Hialeah, FL 33021
Ph: (305)825-0300
Free: 877-470-9617
Fax: (305)424-3184
URL: http://www.citrushealth.org

Live Oak

34530 ■ Florida Sheriffs Boys Ranch
PO Box 2000
Live Oak, FL 32064
Ph: (386)842-5501
Free: 800-765-3797
Fax: (386)842-2429
E-mail: fsyr@youthranches.org
URL: http://www.youthranches.org

Maitland

34531 ■ LaAmistad Behavioral Health Services
LaAmistad Residential Treatment Center
1650 N Park Ave.
Maitland, FL 32751
Ph: (407)647-0660
Free: 800-433-1122
Fax: (407)647-3068
E-mail: lamistadintake@aol.com
URL: http://www.lamistad.com

Miami

34532 ■ Gladstone Center for Girls
7412 Sunset Dr.
Miami, FL 33143
Ph: (305)665-7356
URL: http://www.cdgfl.org/children.htm

Orlando

34533 ■ Devereux Florida
5850 T.G. Lee Blvd., Ste. 400
Orlando, FL 32822-4409
Ph: (407)812-4555
Fax: (407)816-6481
URL: http://www.devereux.org

34534 ■ Devereux Residential Treatment Center
6147 Christian Way
Orlando, FL 32808-1435
Ph: (407)296-5300
URL: http://www.devereux.org

34535 ■ Devereux Semoran Outpatient Center
1140 S Semoran Blvd., Ste. A
Orlando, FL 32807
Ph: (407)273-7117
URL: http://www.devereux.org

34536 ■ University Behavioral Center
2500 Discovery Dr.
Orlando, FL 32826
Ph: (407)281-7000
Fax: (407)282-7012
URL: http://www.psysolutions.com/facilities/universitybehavioralcenter/

Palm Bay

34537 ■ Devereux Aquarius Group Home
212 Aquarius Ave. SE
Palm Bay, FL 32909-3657
Ph: (321)726-9988
Fax: (321)724-5245
URL: http://www.devereux.org

Riverview

34538 ■ Tampa Bay Academy
12012 Boyette Rd.
Riverview, FL 33569-5631
Ph: (813)677-6700
Free: 800-678-3838
Fax: (813)671-3145
E-mail: james.merritt@tampa.yfcs.com
URL: http://www.TampaBay-academy.com

Rockledge

34539 ■ Devereux Therapeutic Foster Care--Brevard
500 Barton Blvd., Ste. 7
Rockledge, FL 32955-3172
Ph: (407)631-4865
URL: http://www.devereux.org
Formerly: Devereux Therapeutic Foster Care.

Safety Harbor

34540 ■ Florida Sheriffs Youth Ranch Safety Harbor
3180 Enterprise Rd E
Safety Harbor, FL 34695
Ph: (727)725-4761
E-mail: fsyr@youthranches.org
URL: http://www.youthranches.org

Saint Augustine

34541 ■ Saint Augustine Youth Services
50 Saragossa St.
Saint Augustine, FL 32084
Ph: (904)829-1770
URL: http://www.staugustineyouthservices.com/

Saint Petersburg

34542 ■ Brookwood Florida - Central, Inc.
901 7th Ave. S
Saint Petersburg, FL 33705
Ph: (727)822-4789
URL: http://www.brookwoodflorida.org/
Formerly: Brookwood.

Sunrise

34543 ■ Alternate Family Care, Inc.
10001 W Oakland Park Blvd.
Ste. 302
Sunrise, FL 33351
Ph: (954)746-5200
Fax: (954)746-5217
E-mail: sneilafc@aol.com
URL: http://www.altfam.com

Tampa

34544 ■ The Children's Home--Tampa
10909 Memorial Hwy.
Tampa, FL 33615
Ph: (813)855-4435
URL: http://www.thechildrenshomeinc.com

Tequesta

34545 ■ Sandy Pines Hospital
11301 SE Tequesta Terr.
Tequesta, FL 33469
Ph: (561)744-0211
Fax: (561)575-1445
URL: http://www.psysolutions.com/facilities/sandypines/

Viera

34546 ■ Devereux Florida Specialty Hospital
8000 Devereux Dr.
Viera, FL 32940
Ph: (321)242-9100
Free: 800-338-3738
Fax: (321)242-1573
URL: http://www.devereux.org

Winter Park

34547 ■ Devereux Therapeutic Foster Care
501 N Wymore Rd.
Winter Park, FL 32789
Ph: (407)975-2565
URL: http://www.devereux.org

GEORGIA

Atlanta

34548 ■ Hillside, Inc.
690 Courtenay Dr. NE
Atlanta, GA 30306
Ph: (404)875-4551
Fax: (404)875-1394
E-mail: residential@hside.org
URL: http://www.hside.org

34549 ■ Laurel Heights Hospital
934 Briarcliff Rd. NE
Atlanta, GA 30306
Ph: (404)888-7860
URL: http://www.laurelheightshospital.com/index.htm

Demorest

34550 ■ Avita Community Partners Habersham County Mental Health/Substance Abuse
196 Scroggins Dr.
Demorest, GA 30535-5354
Ph: (706)894-3700
URL: http://www.gamtns.org/
Formerly: Georgia Mountains Community Services.

Jessup

34551 ■ Three Springs Inc. Wayne County Girls' Program
236 Leadership Ln.
Jessup, GA 31545
Ph: (912)586-2511
URL: http://www.sequeltsi.com/

HAWAII

Hilo

34552 ■ Pu'ukama Kid Behavioral Health of Hawaii
440 Kapiolani St.
Hilo, HI 96720
Ph: (808)961-6635
URL: http://www.hibh.org/

IDAHO

Boise

34553 ■ Idaho Youth Ranch--Main Campus
5465 W Irving St.
Boise, ID 83704
Ph: (208)377-2613
Free: 877-817-8141
URL: http://www.youthranch.org/

Lewiston

34554 ■ Northwest Children's Home Residential Treatment--Main Campus
419 22nd Ave.
Lewiston, ID 83501
Ph: (208)743-9404
Fax: (208)746-4955
E-mail: rwilson@northwestchildrenshome.org
URL: http://www.northwestchildrenshome.org

Nampa

34555 ■ Northwest Children's Home Syringa House
1723 S Horton
Nampa, ID 83687-3074
Ph: (208)467-5223
E-mail: lindasyringa@velocitus.net
URL: http://www.northwestchildrenshome.org

ILLINOIS

Addison

34556 ■ Lutherbrook Children's Center Lutheran Child & Family Services
343 W Lake St.
Addison, IL 60101-2599
Ph: (630)543-6900
URL: http://www.lcfs.org/Page.aspx?pid=178

Broadview

34557 ■ Resurrection Behavioral Health--Broadview
1820 S 25th Ave.
Broadview, IL 60155
Ph: (708)681-2324
Fax: (708)681-1289
URL: http://www.reshealth.org/locations/complete_list.cfm
Formerly: Proviso Family Service and Mental Health Center.

Centreville

34558 ■ Children's Center for Behavioral Development
353 N 88th St.
Centreville, IL 62203
Ph: (618)398-1152

Chicago

34559 ■ Avers Group Home
5100 N Avers St.
Chicago, IL 60625-6015
Ph: (773)769-3500

34560 ■ Chase Group Home
1715 W Chase Ave.
Chicago, IL 60626-2413
Ph: (773)769-3500

34561 ■ Children's Home and Aid Society--Chicago
125 S Wacker Dr., 14th Fl.
Chicago, IL 60606-4475
Ph: (312)424-0200
E-mail: contact@chasi.org
URL: http://www.childrenshomeandaid.org/Page.aspx?pid=183

34562 ■ Lawrence Hall Youth Services
4833 N Francisco Ave.
Chicago, IL 60625
Ph: (773)769-3500
URL: http://www.lawrencehall.org/index.shtml

34563 ■ Mercy Home for Boys and Girls
Boys Campus
1140 W Jackson Blvd.
Chicago, IL 60607-2929
Ph: (312)738-7560
URL: http://www.mercyhome.org/

Elgin

34564 ■ College House Group Home
150 College St.
Elgin, IL 60120-5652
Ph: (847)608-2069

34565 ■ Highland Avenue Group Home
510 W Highland Ave.
Elgin, IL 60123
Ph: (847)608-2067

34566 ■ The Larkin Center
1212 Larkin Ave.
Elgin, IL 60123
Ph: (847)695-5656
E-mail: mpotter@larkincenter.org
URL: http://www.larkincenter.org

34567 ■ The Larkin Centers
Transitional Skills Center
518 W Highland Ave.
Elgin, IL 60123
Ph: (847)695-4290
E-mail: mpotter@larkincenter.org
URL: http://www.larkincenter.org
Formerly: Fox West Group Home.

34568 ■ Park Row Group Home
59 Park Row
Elgin, IL 60120-6525
Ph: (847)608-2066

Evanston

34569 ■ Children's Home and Aid Society--Evanston
Rice Child and Family Center
1101 Washington
Evanston, IL 60202
Ph: (847)866-3800
URL: http://www.childrenshomeandaid.org/Page.aspx?pid=183

Joliet

34570 ■ Guardian Angel Home
1550 Plainfield Rd.
Joliet, IL 60435
Ph: (815)729-0930
URL: http://www.guardianangelhome.org

Lake Villa

34571 ■ Allendale Association
600 E Grand Ave.
Lake Villa, IL 60046
Ph: (847)356-2351
Free: 888-255-3631
URL: http://www.allendale4kids.org/

34572 ■ Allendale Association
Bradley Outpatient Clinic
420 W Grand Ave.
Lake Villa, IL 60046
Ph: (847)356-3322
Free: 888-255-3631
URL: http://www.allendale4kids.org/

Lockport

34573 ■ Gaylord House
16830 S Gaylord Rd.
Lockport, IL 60441-6536
Ph: (815)730-9373

Melrose Park

34574 ■ Resurrection Behavioral Health--Melrose Park
1414 Main St.
Melrose Park, IL 60160
Ph: (708)343-2042
URL: http://www.reshealth.org/rhcservices/service_detail.cfm?rhcServiceID=93

Mundelein

34575 ■ Alternative Behavior Treatment Centers
27255 N Fairfield Rd.
Mundelein, IL 60060
Ph: (847)487-9455
Fax: (847)307-4140
E-mail: rmcginnis@abtc-centers.org
URL: http://www.abtc-centers.org

Park Ridge

34576 ■ Jeanine Schultz Memorial School
2101 W Oakton St.
Park Ridge, IL 60068
Ph: (847)696-3315
Fax: (847)696-3330
URL: http://jeanineschultzmemorialschool.org/
Formerly: Arthur E. Welby Hall.

Peoria

34577 ■ Children's Home Academy
404 NE Madison Ave.
Peoria, IL 61603-3720
Ph: (309)685-1047
URL: http://www.chail.org

34578 ■ Children's Home Association of Illinois
2130 N Knoxville Ave.
Peoria, IL 61603
Ph: (309)687-1047
Fax: (309)687-7299
URL: http://www.chail.org

34579 ■ Children's Home of Illinois
Boys Group Home
613 E Frye Ave.
Peoria, IL 61603
Ph: (309)685-2677
URL: http://www.chail.org

Quincy

34580 ■ Chaddock Center
205 S 24th St.
Quincy, IL 62301
Ph: (217)222-0034
Fax: (217)222-3865
URL: http://www.chaddock.org

Rockford

34581 ■ Children's Home and Aid Society--Rockford
Northern Regional Office
910 2nd Ave.
Rockford, IL 61104
Ph: (815)962-1043
URL: http://www.childrenshomeandaid.org/Page.aspx?pid=183

34582 ■ Motivating Individuals for Learning and Living
Mill School
2445 Elmwood Rd.
Rockford, IL 61101
Ph: (815)877-3440

Urbana

34583 ■ Cunningham Children's Home
1301 N Cunningham Ave.
Urbana, IL 61802-1893
Ph: (217)367-3728
Fax: (217)367-2896
E-mail: page@cunninghamhome.org
URL: http://www.cunninghamhome.org

INDIANA

Bloomington

34584 ■ The Villages of Indiana
2405 N Smith Pike
Bloomington, IN 47404
Ph: (812)332-1245
Free: 800-822-4888
Fax: (812)333-4717
URL: http://www.villages.org
Formerly: Tapestry Evansville/Indianapolis, Referral Office.

Decatur

34585 ■ Park Center, Inc.
809 High St.
Decatur, IN 46733
Ph: (260)724-9669
URL: http://www.parkcenter.org/

Fort Wayne

34586 ■ Crossroad
2525 Lake Ave.
Fort Wayne, IN 46805-5457
Ph: (260)484-4153
Free: 800-976-2306
Fax: (888)814-4521
URL: http://www.crossroad-fwch.org
Formerly: The Fort Wayne Children's Home.

Goshen

34587 ■ Bashor Children's Home
62226 County Rd. 15
Goshen, IN 46526
Ph: (574)875-5117
URL: http://www.bashor.org/
Formerly: Bashor Home of the United Methodist Church.

Indianapolis

34588 ■ Lutherwood Residential Treatment Center for Troubled Youth
1525 N Ritter Ave.
Indianapolis, IN 46219
Ph: (317)359-5467
URL: http://www.lutheranfamily.org/lutherwood.htm

34589 ■ Resource Treatment Center
1404 S State Ave.
Indianapolis, IN 46203
Ph: (317)783-4003
URL: http://www.yfcs.com/index.php

34590 ■ The Villages of Indiana, Inc.
652 N Girls School Rd., Ste. 240
Indianapolis, IN 46214
Ph: (317)273-7575
Free: 800-874-6880
Fax: (317)273-7565
URL: http://www.villageskids.org/

Kouts

34591 ■ Midwest Center for Youth and Families
1012 W Indiana St.
Kouts, IN 46347
Ph: (219)766-2999
Free: 888-629-3471
URL: http://www.midwest-center.com/

Lebanon

34592 ■ Indiana United Methodist Children's Home
Centenary Hall
916 W Camp St.
Lebanon, IN 46052-1681
Ph: (765)482-5900
URL: http://www.childrenshome.net/

34593 ■ Indiana United Methodist Children's Home, Inc.
515 W Camp St.
Lebanon, IN 46052-1682
Ph: (765)482-5900
E-mail: iumch@iumch.org
URL: http://www.childrenshome.net/home/

Richmond

34594 ■ Wernle Children's Home, Inc.
2000 Wernle Rd.
Richmond, IN 47374
Ph: (765)966-2506
URL: http://www.wernle.org/

IOWA

Ames

34595 ■ Lutheran Services in Iowa, Inc.--Ames
1323 Northwestern Ave.
Ames, IA 50010-5267
Ph: (515)232-7262
URL: http://www.lsiowa.org/

Burlington

34596 ■ Woodlands Treatment Center
4715 Sullivan Slough Rd.
Burlington, IA 52601
Ph: (319)753-0700
URL: http://www.younghouse.org/

34597 ■ Young House Family Services, Inc.
724 N 3rd St.
Burlington, IA 52601-0845
Ph: (319)752-4000
Fax: (319)752-6933
E-mail: info@younghouse.org
URL: http://www.younghouse.org

Cedar Rapids

34598 ■ Hillcrest Family Services
Cedar Rapids Office
4080 1st Ave. NE
Cedar Rapids, IA 52402
Ph: (563)362-3149
URL: http://www.hillcrest-fs.org/

34599 ■ Tanager Place
2309 C St. SW
Cedar Rapids, IA 52404-3707
Ph: (319)365-9164
Fax: (319)365-6411
URL: http://www.tanagerplace.org

Des Moines

34600 ■ Orchard Place
Child Guidance Center
808 5th Ave.
Des Moines, IA 50309
Ph: (515)244-2267
Fax: (515)244-1922
URL: http://www.orchardplace.org

Dubuque

34601 ■ Hillcrest Family Services
2005 Asbury Rd.
Dubuque, IA 52001-3000
Ph: (563)583-7357
Free: 877-437-6333
Fax: (563)583-7026
E-mail: jwoodyard@hillcrest-fs.org
URL: http://www.hillcrest-fs.org

Fort Dodge

34602 ■ Gerard Treatment Programs
104 S 17th St.
Fort Dodge, IA 50501-5028
Ph: (515)574-5492

Mount Pleasant

34603 ■ Christamore Family Treatment Center
905 S Iris St.
Mount Pleasant, IA 52641-1851
Ph: (319)385-2906
URL: http://www.younghouse.org/cftc.htm

Waverly

34604 ■ Lutheran Services in Iowa, Inc.--Waverly
106 16th St. SW
Waverly, IA 50677
Ph: (319)352-2630
URL: http://www.lsiowa.org/
Formerly: Bremwood Lutheran Services.

KANSAS

Dodge City

34605 ■ Youthville--Dodge City
11200 Lariat Way
Dodge City, KS 67801
Ph: (620)225-0276
URL: http://www.youthville.org/Default.aspx

Ellsworth

34606 ■ Saint Francis Academy
Ellsworth Campus
1655 Ave. K
Ellsworth, KS 67439
Ph: (785)472-4453
Fax: (785)472-5352
E-mail: dave.lang@st-francis.org
URL: http://www.st-francis.org

Newton

34607 ■ Youthville--Newton
900 W Broadway
Newton, KS 67114
Ph: (316)283-1950
URL: http://www.youthville.org/Default.aspx

Olathe

34608 ■ Johnson County Mental Health Center
Adolescent Center for Treatment
301 N Monroe St.
Olathe, KS 66061
Ph: (913)782-0283
URL: http://mentalhealth.jocogov.org/welcome.htm

Salina

34609 ■ Saint Francis at Salina, Inc.
509 E Elm St.
Salina, KS 67401
Ph: (785)825-0541
Free: 800-423-1342
Fax: (785)825-2502
E-mail: dave.lang@st-francis.org
URL: http://www.st-francis.org

KENTUCKY

Buckhorn

34610 ■ Presbyterian Child Welfare Agency
Buckhorn Children's Center
116 Buckhorn Ln.
Buckhorn, KY 41721
Ph: (606)398-7000
Free: 800-472-3678
URL: http://www.buckhorn.org/

California

34611 ■ Holly Hill Children's Services
9599 Summer Hill Rd.
California, KY 41007
Ph: (859)635-0500
Fax: (859)635-0504
E-mail: info@hollyhill-ky.org
URL: http://www.hollyhill-ky.org/

Covington

34612 ■ Children's Home of Northern Kentucky
200 Home Rd.
Covington, KY 41011
Ph: (859)261-8768
URL: http://www.chnk.org/

Elizabethtown

34613 ■ Brown Baptist Youth Ranch
854 Tunnel Hill Church Rd.
Elizabethtown, KY 42702
Ph: (270)737-3888
Formerly: Baptist Youth Ranch.

Louisville

34614 ■ Maryhurst
1015 Dorsey Ln.
Louisville, KY 40223
Ph: (502)245-1576
URL: http://www.maryhurst.org

34615 ■ Maryhurst In-Homes Programs
5227 Bardstown Rd.
Louisville, KY 40291
Ph: (502)499-1570
URL: http://www.maryhurst.org

34616 ■ Maryhurst Journey Place
5227 Bardstown Rd.
Louisville, KY 40291
Ph: (502)491-1570
Fax: (502)499-6466
E-mail: journey@maryhurst.org
URL: http://www.maryhurst.org

34617 ■ Maryhurst Rosehaven
2252 Payne St.
Louisville, KY 40206
Ph: (502)895-2950
URL: http://www.maryhurst.org

34618 ■ Maryhurst Treasure Home
132 Stoll Ave.
Louisville, KY 40206
Ph: (502)895-0190
Fax: (502)245-2550
E-mail: llmagre@maryhurst.org
URL: http://www.maryhurst.org

Rogers

34619 ■ Dessie Scott Children's Home
4640 Old Kentucky 15
Rogers, KY 41365
Ph: (606)668-6445

Versailles

34620 ■ Kentucky United Methodist Homes for Children and Youth
2050 Lexington Pke.
Versailles, KY 40383
Ph: (859)873-4481
Free: 877-887-4481
URL: http://www.kyumh.com/
Formerly: The Methodist Home of Kentucky.

LOUISIANA

Houma

34621 ■ MacDonell United Methodist Children's Services, Inc.
8326 Main St.
Houma, LA 70363
Ph: (985)868-8362
URL: http://www.macchildservices.com/

Slidell

34622 ■ Broadway, Inc. K Bar B Youth Ranch
31294 Hwy. 190
Slidell, LA 70458
Ph: (985)641-1425
URL: http://www.kbarb.com/about.html

MAINE

Casco

34623 ■ CASCO Program
1002 Meadon Rd.
Casco, ME 04015
Ph: (207)627-6915
URL: http://www.spurwink.org/

Chelsea

34624 ■ Chelsea Day Treatment
31 Spurwink Dr.
Chelsea, ME 04330
Ph: (207)582-7686
URL: http://www.spurwink.org/

Kennebunk

34625 ■ Kennebunk Community Residence Sweetser
19 Day St.
Kennebunk, ME 04043
Ph: (207)985-0345
Free: 800-434-3000

Portland

34626 ■ Child Abuse Program
17 Bishop St.
Portland, ME 04103-2600
Ph: (207)871-1235
URL: http://www.spurwink.org/

34627 ■ Portland Help Center
477 Congress St., Ste. 408
Portland, ME 04101-3431
Ph: (207)773-7811
URL: http://www.spurwink.org/

34628 ■ Public School Intensive Counseling Program
899 Riverside St.
Portland, ME 04103-1077
Ph: (207)871-1200
URL: http://www.spurwink.org

34629 ■ Spurwink Clinic
17 Bishop St.
Portland, ME 04103
Ph: (207)871-1235
URL: http://www.spurwink.org

34630 ■ Spurwink School
899 Riverside St.
Portland, ME 04103
Ph: (207)871-1200
URL: http://www.spurwink.org

34631 ■ Therapeutic Nursery Programs
17 Bishop St.
Portland, ME 04103
Ph: (207)871-1200
Fax: (207)871-1232
E-mail: lbutler@spurwink.org
URL: http://www.spurwink.org

Saco

34632 ■ Sweetser
50 Moody St.
Saco, ME 04072-0892
Free: 800-434-3000
E-mail: intake@sweetser.org
URL: http://www.sweetser.org

34633 ■ Sweetser Children's Home and Community Residence
50 Moody St
Saco, ME 04072
Ph: (207)294-4400
Free: 800-434-3000
Fax: (207)294-4529
E-mail: intake@sweetser.org
URL: http://www.sweetser.org

MARYLAND

Baltimore

34634 ■ Good Shepherd Center
4100 Maple Ave.
Baltimore, MD 21227
Ph: (410)247-2770
Fax: (410)247-3242
E-mail: info@goodshepherdcenter.org
URL: http://www.goodshepherdcenter.org

34635 ■ Regional Institute for Children and Adolescents - Baltimore
605 S Chapel Gate Ln.
Baltimore, MD 21229
Ph: (410)368-7954
Fax: (410)368-7989
URL: http://www.dhmh.state.md.us/volunteer/field_offices/thefacilities/RICABalth tm

34636 ■ Woodbourne Center
1301 Woodbourne Ave.
Baltimore, MD 21239
Ph: (410)433-1000
URL: http://www.woodbourne.org/

Bethesda

34637 ■ The National Center for Children and Families
6301 Greentree Rd.
Bethesda, MD 20817
Ph: (301)365-4480
Fax: (301)365-2536
E-mail: redwards@nccf-cares.org
URL: http://www.nccf-cares.org
Formerly: Baptist Home for Children & Families.

Cheltenham

34638 ■ Regional Institute for Children and Adolescents - Southern Maryland
9400 Surratts Rd.
Cheltenham, MD 20623
Ph: (301)372-1911
Fax: (301)372-1906

Oldtown

34639 ■ New Dominion School of Maryland, Inc.
20700 Wagner Cutoff Rd., SE
Oldtown, MD 21555
Ph: (301)478-5721
URL: http://www.nd.allconet.org/

Rockville

34640 ■ John L. Gildner Regional Institute for Children and Adolescents Rockville
15000 Broschart Rd.
Rockville, MD 20850
Ph: (301)251-6836
URL: http://www.dhmh.state.md.us/volunteer/field_offices/thefacilities/ricarockv ille.htm
Formerly: John L. Gildner Rica.

Timonium

34641 ■ Villa Maria Continuum
2300 Dulaney Valley Rd.
Timonium, MD 21093-2799
Ph: (410)252-4700
URL: http://www.cc-md.org/mental-health/villa-maria-continuum/
Formerly: Villa Maria Treatment Center.

MASSACHUSETTS

Amesbury

34642 ■ Harbor Schools--Amesbury
101 Pleasant Valley Rd.
Amesbury, MA 01913
Ph: (978)388-4131

Arlington

34643 ■ Germaine Lawrence Center, Inc.
18 Claremont Ave.
Arlington, MA 02476
Ph: (781)648-6200
URL: http://www.germainelawrence.org/
Formerly: Germaine Lawrence Diagnostic Center.

34644 ■ Germaine Lawrence Diagnostic Center
2 Claremont Ave.
Arlington, MA 02476
Ph: (781)648-1859
URL: http://www.germainelawrence.org/

Beverly

34645 ■ Northeast Health Systems Beverly Hospital
85 Herrick St.
Beverly, MA 01915
Ph: (978)922-3000
Fax: (978)921-7025
URL: http://www.beverlyhospital.org/

Boston

34646 ■ Justice Resource Institute, Inc.
545 Boylston St., Ste. 700
Boston, MA 02116
Ph: (617)450-0500
Fax: (617)450-0501
E-mail: jricorporate@jri.org
URL: http://www.jri.org

34647 ■ Robert F. Kennedy Children's Action Corps, Inc.
11 Beacon St., Ste. 200
Boston, MA 02108
Ph: (617)227-4183
Free: 877-735-3500
URL: http://www.rfkchildren.org/

Brighton

34648 ■ Children's Community Support Collaborative
77 Warren St., Bldg. 9
Brighton, MA 02135
Ph: (617)254-0964
Fax: (617)254-5539
URL: http://www.thehome.org/site/PageServer?pagename=programs_case_management

Danvers

34649 ■ North American Family Institute, Inc.--Danvers
67 Poplar St.
Danvers, MA 01923
Ph: (978)774-1511
Fax: (978)774-2531
E-mail: poplarpd@aol.com
URL: http://www.nafi.com
Formerly: Northeastern Family Institute Inc.

34650 ■ North American Family Institute, Inc.--Danvers
Emergency Placement Intervention Center
4 Riverside St.
Danvers, MA 01923
Ph: (978)774-0774
Fax: (978)774-8369
E-mail: yitzhakbakal@nafi.com
URL: http://www.nafi.com
Formerly: Northeastern Family Institute Inc.

34651 ■ North American Family Institute, Inc.--Danvers
Massachusetts
10 Harbor St.
Danvers, MA 01923
Ph: (978)774-0774
Fax: (978)774-8369
URL: http://www.nafi.com
Formerly: Northeastern Family Institute and NFI Massachusetts, Inc.

East Freetown

34652 ■ Whitney Academy
85 Dr. Braley Rd.
East Freetown, MA 02717
Ph: (508)763-3737
URL: http://www.whitneyacademy.org/

Fall River

34653 ■ De Paul Center
2425 Highland Ave.
Fall River, MA 02720
Ph: (508)679-8511
Fax: (508)672-2558
URL: http://www.stvincentshome.org
Formerly: De Paul Diagnostic Center and Saint Vincent's Home.

34654 ■ Saint Vincent's Group Home
2425 Highland Ave
Fall River, MA 02720
Ph: (508)679-8511
Fax: (508)672-2558
URL: http://www.stvincentshome.org

34655 ■ Saint Vincent's Home
2425 Highland Ave.
Fall River, MA 02720
Ph: (508)679-8511
Fax: (508)672-2558
URL: http://www.stvincentshome.org

34656 ■ Saint Vincent's Vinhaven
2425 Highland Ave
Fall River, MA 02720
Ph: (508)679-8511
Fax: (508)627-2558
URL: http://www.stvincents.org

34657 ■ Stevens Children's Home, Inc.
Transitional Living Program
84 Bigelow St.
Fall River, MA 02720
Ph: (508)678-9678

Framingham

34658 ■ Reed Academy
1 Winch St.
Framingham, MA 01701
Ph: (508)877-1222
URL: http://www.reedacademy.net/

Hancock

34659 ■ Intensive Treatment Unit
Rte. 43
Hancock, MA 01237
Ph: (413)738-5151
Fax: (413)738-5199
URL: http://www.hillcrestec.org

Hudson

34660 ■ The Bridge of Central Massachusetts
Southboro Program
164 Central St.
Hudson, MA 01749
Ph: (508)755-0333
Fax: (508)755-2191
E-mail: info@thebridgecm.org
URL: http://www.thebridgecm.org

Jamaica Plain

34661 ■ Italian Home for Children
1125 Centre St.
Jamaica Plain, MA 02130
Ph: (617)524-3116
URL: http://www.italianhome.org/site/PageServer

Lee

34662 ■ Kolburne School, Inc.
The Brigham Center
87 Summer St., Stes. C & D
Lee, MA 01238-1111
Ph: (413)243-1355
URL: http://www.kolburne.net

Leicester

34663 ■ Nazareth Home for Boys
77 Mulberry St.
Leicester, MA 01524
Ph: (508)892-4886
URL: http://www.nazareth-home.org/

Lenox

34664 ■ Valleyhead, Inc.
79 Reservoir Rd.
Lenox, MA 01240-2008
Ph: (413)637-3635

Methuen

34665 ■ Saint Ann's Home
100A Haverhill St.
Methuen, MA 01844
Ph: (978)682-5276
Fax: (978)688-4932
E-mail: info@st.annshome.org
URL: http://www.st.annshome.org/Site/

Natick

34666 ■ Brandon Residential Treatment Center, Inc.
27 Winter St.
Natick, MA 01760
Ph: (508)655-6400
URL: http://www.brandonschool.org/
Formerly: Brandon Residential Treatment Program.

Newburyport

34667 ■ Harbor Schools
Newburyport Youth Home
72 High St.
Newburyport, MA 01950-3050
Ph: (978)463-9504

Newton

34668 ■ Northeastern Family Institute, Inc.
Keystone
47 Park St.
Newton, MA 02458
Ph: (617)244-7424
URL: http://www.nafi.com/

34669 ■ Northeastern Family Institute
North Crossing
47 Park St.
Newton, MA 02458
Ph: (617)244-7424
URL: http://www.nafi.com/

Northampton

34670 ■ Cutchins Programs for Children and Families, Inc.
78 Pomeroy Ter.
Northampton, MA 01060
Ph: (413)584-1310
URL: http://www.cutchins.org/
Formerly: Northampton Center for Children & Families.

Norwood

34671 ■ The Community Living Program
103 Winter St.
Norwood, MA 02062
Ph: (781)769-9720

Peabody

34672 ■ North American Family Institute, Inc.--Peabody
349 Lowell St.
Peabody, MA 01960
Ph: (978)531-5443
Fax: (978)538-5477
E-mail: cmtnfi@aol.com
URL: http://www.nafi.com
Formerly: Northeastern Family Institute-Lowell Crossing.

34673 ■ Northeastern Family Institute, Inc.
Washington Manor
136 Washington St.
Peabody, MA 01960-5926
Ph: (978)532-8820
Fax: (978)532-8820
URL: http://www.nafi.com

Pittsfield

34674 ■ Hillcrest Educational Centers
788 South St.
Pittsfield, MA 01201
Ph: (413)499-7924
Fax: (413)443-1246
URL: http://www.hillcrestec.org

Plymouth

34675 ■ The Baird Center
900 Ship Pond Rd.
Plymouth, MA 02360
Ph: (508)224-8041

Rutland

34676 ■ Devereux Massachusetts
60 Miles Rd.
Rutland, MA 01543
Ph: (508)886-4746
URL: http://www.devereux.org/site/PageServer?pagename=ma_index

34677 ■ Devereux--Rutland
91 Maple Ave.
Rutland, MA 01546
Ph: (508)886-4748
URL: http://www.devereux.org/site/PageServer?pagename=ma_index

Springfield

34678 ■ Children's Study Home and Kathleen Thorton Day Treatment School
44 Sherman St.
Springfield, MA 01109
Ph: (413)739-5626
Fax: (413)732-5457
E-mail: smccafferty@studyhome.org
URL: http://www.studyhome.org
Formerly: Springfield Home for Friendless Youth.

34679 ■ Children's Study Home Sharp I
91 Old Acre Rd.
Springfield, MA 01129-1832
Ph: (413)782-5825
URL: http://www.studyhome.org/

Swansea

34680 ■ Meadowridge Behavioral Health Center
664 Stevens Rd.
Swansea, MA 02777
Ph: (508)677-0304
URL: http://www.jri.org/meadowridge/

34681 ■ Stevens Treatment Programs
24 Main St.
Swansea, MA 02777
Ph: (508)679-0183
Fax: (508)679-1950
E-mail: info@stevensprograms.org
URL: http://www.stevenshome.org

Wakefield

34682 ■ Northeastern Family Institute, Inc. Wakefield Lodging House
43 Avon St.
Wakefield, MA 01880-2310
Ph: (781)245-4539
URL: http://www.nafi.com/

Walpole

34683 ■ Home for Little Wanderers Longview Farm and Clifford School
399 Lincoln Rd.
Walpole, MA 02081
Ph: (508)668-7703
Free: 888--HOME321
URL: http://www.thehome.org/site/PageServer

MICHIGAN

Belleville

34684 ■ Girlstown Foundation
525 E Huron River Dr.
Belleville, MI 48111
Ph: (734)697-4804
URL: http://www.girlstownfoundation.org/

34685 ■ Girlstown Foundation Transitional Treatment Program
12001 Quirk Rd.
Belleville, MI 48111
Ph: (734)697-7242
URL: http://www.girlstownfoundation.org/

Dearborn Heights

34686 ■ Vista Maria
20651 W Warren Ave.
Dearborn Heights, MI 48127
Ph: (313)271-3050
Free: 800-7-VISTA6
Fax: (313)271-6250
E-mail: lbarclay@vistamaria.org
URL: http://www.vistamaria.org

Detroit

34687 ■ Methodist Children's Home Society
26645 W 6 Mile Rd.
Detroit, MI 48240
Ph: (313)531-4060
Fax: (313)531-1040
URL: http://www.themethodistchildrenshome.com//04/

Farmington Hills

34688 ■ Boys and Girls Republic
28000 W 9 Mile Rd.
Farmington Hills, MI 48336
Ph: (248)476-9550
URL: http://www.lcfsmi.org/page.asp?ID=38

34689 ■ Saint Vincent - Sarah Fisher Center
27400 W 12 Mile Rd.
Farmington Hills, MI 48334
Ph: (248)626-7527
URL: http://www.svsfcenter.org/

Flint

34690 ■ Whaley Children's Center
1201 N Grand Traverse St.
Flint, MI 48503-1394
Ph: (810)234-3603
URL: http://www.whaleychildren.org/
Formerly: Donald M. Whaley Children's Center.

Grand Rapids

34691 ■ Community Program Office Wedgwood Christian Services
3351-36th St., SE
Grand Rapids, MI 49512-2809
Ph: (616)942-7294
URL: http://www.wedgwood.org/

34692 ■ Saint John's Home
2355 Knapp St., NE
Grand Rapids, MI 49505
Ph: (616)361-5227
Fax: (616)361-9923
E-mail: mthomson@stjohnshome.org
URL: http://www.stjohnshome.org

34693 ■ Wedgwood Christian Services--Grand Rapids
3300 36th St., SE
Grand Rapids, MI 49512
Ph: (616)942-2110
URL: http://www.wedgwood.org
Formerly: Delta Home.

34694 ■ Wedgwood Christian Youth and Family Services
3300 36th St., SE
Grand Rapids, MI 49518
Ph: (616)942-2110
Fax: (616)942-0589
URL: http://www.wedgwood.org

34695 ■ Wedgwood Recovery Program Wedgwood Christian Services
300 68th St. SE
Grand Rapids, MI 49548-6927
Ph: (616)455-4611
URL: http://www.wedgwood.org

Grosse Pointe

34696 ■ Children's Home of Detroit--Grosse Pointe
900 Cook Rd.
Grosse Pointe, MI 48236-2799
Ph: (313)886-0800
URL: http://www.starr.org/chd

Jonesville

34697 ■ The Manor
115 East St.
Jonesville, MI 49250
Ph: (517)849-2151
Fax: (517)849-2880
URL: http://www.the-manor.org/

Kalamazoo

34698 ■ Lakeside Treatment and Learning
3921 Oakland Dr.
Kalamazoo, MI 49008
Ph: (269)381-4760

Lansing

34699 ■ Catholic Social Services of Lansing Saint Vincent's Home, Inc.
913 W Holmes Rd., Ste. 290
Lansing, MI 48910
Ph: (517)272-1524
Fax: (517)272-1562
URL: http://www.stvcc.org/

34700 ■ Saint Vincent's Home for Children
2800 W Willow St.
Lansing, MI 48917
Ph: (517)323-4734
URL: http://www.stvcc.org/

Traverse City

34701 ■ Town Hall Center Wedgwood Christian Services
3180 Racquet Club Dr.
Traverse City, MI 49684-4797
Ph: (231)922-2885
URL: http://www.wedgwood.org/
Formerly: Wedgwood Christian Youth & Families Program.

Warren

34702 ■ Children's Home of Detroit--Warren
6902 Chicago Rd.
Warren, MI 48092
Ph: (586)939-4940
Fax: (586)939-1567
URL: http://www.starr.org/chd

Wyoming

34703 ■ Wedgwood Christian Services--Wyoming
4045 Byron Ctr. Ave., SW
Wyoming, MI 49509-3673
Ph: (616)534-6270
URL: http://www.wedgwood.org/
Formerly: Brookside Home.

MINNESOTA

Austin

34704 ■ Gerard Academy
1111 28th St., NE
Austin, MN 55912
Ph: (507)433-1843
Fax: (507)433-7868
E-mail: brenth@nexustreatment.org
URL: http://www.nexustreatment.org

34705 ■ Sheriff's Youth Program of Austin
1918 4th St., SE
Austin, MN 55912
Ph: (507)433-0100
Fax: (507)433-6501
E-mail: sypaustin@sypmn.com
URL: http://www.sheriffs-youth-program.org
Formerly: Sheriffs Youth Ranch of Austin.

Bemidji

34706 ■ Episcopal Community Services Residential and Youth Services
1741 15th St. NW
Bemidji, MN 56601
Ph: (218)751-6553
URL: http://www.ecsmn.org/
Formerly: Archdeacon Gilfillan Center.

Duluth

34707 ■ Northwood Children Honors Home - Boys
714 W College St.
Duluth, MN 55812
Ph: (218)724-8815
Fax: (218)724-0251
E-mail: JEK@NWCH.com
URL: http://www.northwoodchildren.org/
Formerly: Northwood Children & Family Center.

34708 ■ Northwood Children Honors Home - Girls
Exceptional Children's Annex
1131 N 11th Ave., E
Duluth, MN 55805
Ph: (218)724-7953
URL: http://www.northwoodchildren.org/
Formerly: Northwood Children's Home Society Exceptional Children's Annex.

34709 ■ Northwood Children's Home
2401 E 4th St.
Duluth, MN 55812-1433
Ph: (218)724-8815
URL: http://www.northwoodchildren.org/

34710 ■ Northwood Children's Services and Little Learners Enrichment Center.
714 College St.
Duluth, MN 55811
Ph: (218)724-8815
Fax: (218)724-0251
E-mail: info@nwch.com
URL: http://www.northwoodchildren.org/

34711 ■ Northwood West and Merritt Creek Academy - IDT
4000 W 9th St.
Duluth, MN 55807
Ph: (218)628-0237
URL: http://www.northwoodchildren.org/
Formerly: Northwood Children's Services--West Campus.

34712 ■ Woodland Hills
4321 Allendale Ave.
Duluth, MN 55803
Ph: (218)728-7500
E-mail: mail@woodlandhills.org
URL: http://www.woodlandhills.org

34713 ■ Woodland Hills
Chisholm House - Community Transition Program
4321 Allendale Ave.
Duluth, MN 55803
Ph: (218)724-8528
E-mail: mail@woodlandhills.org
URL: http://www.woodlandhills.org
Formerly: Chisholm House.

34714 ■ Woodland Hills Neighborhood youth Services
310 N 1st Ave., W
Duluth, MN 55806
Ph: (218)723-3522
Fax: (218)723-3524
URL: http://www.woodlandhills.org
Formerly: Neighborhood Youth Services.

Hastings

34715 ■ Harbor Shelter and Counseling Center--Hastings
321 6th St. E
Hastings, MN 55033
Ph: (651)480-8377
URL: http://harborshelter.net/

Inver Grove Heights

34716 ■ Sheriffs Youth Programs of Minnesota
2925 Buckley Way
Inver Grove Heights, MN 55076
Ph: (651)552-9823
Free: 800-910-0104
Fax: (651)552-5741
E-mail: president@sypmn.com
URL: http://www.sheriffs-youth-program.org

Minneapolis

34717 ■ Saint Joseph's Home for Children
1121 E 46th St.
Minneapolis, MN 55407-3586
Ph: (612)827-6241
URL: http://www.ccspm.org/

Saint Cloud

34718 ■ Catholic Charities
Saint Cloud Children's Home
1726 S 7th Ave. S
Saint Cloud, MN 56301
Ph: (320)650-1500
Free: 800-830-8254
Fax: (320)650-1508
URL: http://www.ccstcloud.org/cc06/rp/scch1.htm

Saint Paul

34719 ■ Amerst H. Wilder Foundation
451 Lexington Pkwy. N
Saint Paul, MN 55104
Ph: (651)280-2000
URL: http://www.wilder.org/research.0.html
Formerly: Holcomb House.

34720 ■ Clues Saint Paul
797 E 7th St.
Saint Paul, MN 55106
Ph: (651)379-4200
Fax: (651)292-0347
URL: http://www.clues.org
Formerly: Clues/Partner in Consortium.

Saint Peter

34721 ■ Leo A. Hoffmann Center
1715 Sheppard Dr.
Saint Peter, MN 56082
Ph: (507)934-6122
URL: http://www.hoffmanncenter.org

South Saint Paul

34722 ■ Hearthstone of Minnesota
222 Grand Ave. W, Ste. 200
South Saint Paul, MN 55075
Ph: (651)457-2629
Fax: (651)457-2837
E-mail: info@hearthstonemn.org

Stillwater

34723 ■ Harbor Shelter and Counseling Center--Stillwater
310 W Myrtle St. W
Stillwater, MN 55082
Ph: (651)480-8377
Fax: (651)351-9172

Willmar

34724 ■ Kandiyohi County Boys Group Home
1013 Lakeland Dr., NE
Willmar, MN 56201
Ph: (320)235-6895
Fax: (320)231-3818

MISSISSIPPI

Jackson

34725 ■ Catholic Charities--Jackson
530 George St.
Jackson, MS 39202-3013
Ph: (601)355-8634
URL: http://www.catholiccharitiesjackson.org/

Macon

34726 ■ Region VII Community Counseling Services
Macon PSR
507 Lawrence St.
Macon, MS 39341-2009
Ph: (662)726-9174

Magee

34727 ■ Millcreek Behavioral Health Services
900 1st Ave. NE
Magee, MS 39111
Ph: (601)849-4221
URL: http://www.yfcs.com/view/47
Formerly: Millcreek Rehabilitation Center.

Picayune

34728 ■ Saint Francis Academy Inc.
Bacot Home for Youth
4021 Chicot St.
Picayune, MS 39466
Ph: (228)769-0477
URL: http://www.st-francis.org/index.php

MISSOURI

Cape Girardeau

34729 ■ Cottonwood Residential Treatment Center
1025 N Sprigg St.
Cape Girardeau, MO 63701
Ph: (573)290-5888
Fax: (573)290-5895
URL: http://www.dmh.missouri.gov/cottonwood/

Kansas City

34730 ■ Evangelical Children's Home
5100 Noland Rd.
Kansas City, MO 64133
Ph: (816)356-0187
URL: http://evangelicalchildrenshome.org/NetCommunity/Page.aspx?pid=309

34731 ■ Gillis
8150 Wornall Rd.
Kansas City, MO 64114
Ph: (816)508-3500
Fax: (816)508-3535
E-mail: geninfo@gillis.org
URL: http://www.gillis.org

34732 ■ Marillac Center
2826 Main St.
Kansas City, MO 64108
Ph: (816)508-3300
Fax: (816)508-3321
E-mail: marillac@marillac.org
URL: http://www.marillac.org

34733 ■ Niles Home for Children, Inc.
1911 E 23rd St.
Kansas City, MO 64127
Ph: (816)241-3448
Fax: (816)241-2797
URL: http://www.nhc-kc.org/

34734 ■ Ozanam
421 E 137th St.
Kansas City, MO 64145
Ph: (816)508-3600
Free: 816-508-3797
URL: http://www.ozanam.org

34735 ■ Ozanam Pathways
3632 Wyandotte St.
Kansas City, MO 64111
Ph: (816)561-2266
Fax: (816)756-2839
URL: http://www.ozanam.org
Formerly: Ozanam Pathways Transitional Living Program.

34736 ■ Spofford Home
9700 Grandview Rd.
Kansas City, MO 64134
Ph: (816)508-3400
Free: 877-806-3400
Fax: (816)508-3425
E-mail: info@spoffordhome.org
URL: http://www.spoffordhome.org
Formerly: The Spofford Home.

Marshall

34737 ■ Butterfield Youth Services Child and Family Therapy Center
1180 Hwy. W
Marshall, MO 65340
Ph: (660)886-2253
Fax: (660)886-6601
URL: http://www.bys-kids.org

Saint Louis

34738 ■ Evangelical Children's Home
8240 St. Charles Rock Rd.
Saint Louis, MO 63114
Ph: (314)427-3755
URL: http://evangelicalchildrenshome.org/NetCommunity/Page.aspx?pid=183

34739 ■ Lakeside Center
13044 Marine Ave.
Saint Louis, MO 63146
Ph: (314)434-4535
URL: http://www.stlouisco.com/dhs/lakeside.html

Webster Groves

34740 ■ Edgewood Children's Center
330 N Gore Ave.
Webster Groves, MO 63119
Ph: (314)968-2060
E-mail: info@eccstl.org
URL: http://www.eccstl.org/homepage.aspx

34741 ■ Epworth Children and Family Services
110 North Elm Ave.
Webster Groves, MO 63119
Ph: (314)961-5718
Free: 800-899-KIDS
Fax: (314)961-3503
URL: http://www.epworth.org

MONTANA

Billings

34742 ■ Dennis Wear Group Home
314 W 36th St.
Billings, MT 59102
Ph: (406)652-5545
Fax: (406)652-4419
URL: http://www.ybgr.org/
Beds: 4. **Remarks:** Intensive group home for girls age 8 to 18.

34743 ■ King Group Home
2120 Brentwood Ln.
Billings, MT 59102
Ph: (406)652-7140
Free: 800-726-6755
Fax: (406)651-0149
E-mail: kgh@ybgr.org
URL: http://www.ybgr.org

34744 ■ Yellowstone Boys and Girls Ranch
1732 S 72nd St. W
Billings, MT 59106
Ph: (406)655-2100
Free: 800-726-6755
Fax: (406)656-0021
E-mail: karig@ybgr.org
URL: http://www.ybgr.org

Butte

34745 ■ KIDS Behavioral Health of Montana
55 Basin Creek Rd.
Butte, MT 59701
Ph: (406)494-4183
Free: 800-477-1067
URL: http://www.acadiamontana.com/

Dillon

34746 ■ Pioneer Youth Home
740 Barnett Ave.
Dillon, MT 59725
Ph: (406)683-8293

Helena

34747 ■ Intermountain Children's Home & Services
500 S Lamborn St.
Helena, MT 59601
Ph: (406)442-7920
Free: 800-200-9112
Fax: (406)442-7949
URL: http://www.intermountain.org

NEBRASKA

Boystown

34748 ■ Boystown Treatment Group Home
14188 Mother Teresa Ln.
Boystown, NE 68010-7554
Ph: (402)498-3367
Free: 800-448-3000
URL: http://www.boystown.org/nebraska-iowa/programs

Grand Island

34749 ■ Kruse Group Home
2317 N Kruse Ave.
Grand Island, NE 68803-2038
Ph: (308)381-7445
URL: http://www.epworthvillage.org/treatmentprograms/traditionalgrouphome.php

Kearney

34750 ■ I Believe In Me Ranch Inc.
2041 E 56th St.
Kearney, NE 68847
Ph: (308)236-7145

Omaha

34751 ■ Cooper Village
8502 Mormon Bridge Rd.
Omaha, NE 68112
Ph: (402)451-3100
Fax: (402)451-2211
E-mail: pmahoney@utahalee-cooper.org
URL: http://www.utahalee-cooper.org

34752 ■ Uta Halee Girls Village
10625 Calhoun Rd.
Omaha, NE 68112
Ph: (402)453-0803
Fax: (402)453-1247
E-mail: pmahoney@utahalee-cooper.org
URL: http://www.utahalee-cooper.org

South Sioux City

34753 ■ Boys and Girls Home of Nebraska
100 Futures Dr.
South Sioux City, NE 68776
Ph: (402)494-4185
URL: http://www.boysandgirlshome.com/index.html

York

34754 ■ Epworth Village Inc.
2119 Division Ave.
York, NE 68467
Ph: (402)362-3353
Fax: (402)362-3248
E-mail: dianer@epworthvillage.org
URL: http://www.epworthvillage.org

34755 ■ Epworth Village Inc. Coleman Treatment Group Home
614 E 7th St.
York, NE 68467
Ph: (402)362-3353
URL: http://www.epworthvillage.org

34756 ■ Slife Treatment Group Home
605 E 9th St.
York, NE 68467-3109
Ph: (402)362-3353
URL: http://www.epworthvillage.org/treatmentprograms/treatmentgrouphome.php

NEVADA

Reno

34757 ■ Willow Springs Center
690 Edison Way
Reno, NV 89502
Ph: (775)858-3303
Free: 800-448-9454
URL: http://www.willowspringscenter.com/

NEW HAMPSHIRE

Allenstown

34758 ■ Pine Haven Boy's Center
133 River Rd.
Allenstown, NH 03275
Ph: (603)485-7141
Fax: (603)485-7142
URL: http://www.pinehaven.k12.nh.us/pine.htm
Remarks: Residential treatment center for boys with behavioral, emotional and academic problems. The program accepts sexually abused, sexually reactive children. Admission age: 6-12.

Manchester

34759 ■ Easter Seals Girls Group Home
55 Webster St.
Manchester, NH 03104
Ph: (603)627-9909
Free: 800-870-8728
URL: http://nh.easterseals.com/site/PageServer?pagename=NHDR_locations

34760 ■ Easter Seals Jolicolur School
1 Mammoth Rd.
Manchester, NH 03109
Ph: (603)623-8863
URL: http://nh.easterseals.com/site/PageServer?pagename=NHDR_locations

Rumney

34761 ■ New England Salem Children's Village
768 Doetown Rd.
Rumney, NH 03266
Ph: (603)786-9427
Fax: (603)786-2221
URL: http://www.salemchildrensvillage.org/

Tilton

34762 ■ Spaulding Youth Center
PO Box 189
Tilton, NH 03276
Ph: (603)286-8901
Fax: (603)286-8650
URL: http://www.spauldingyouthcenter.org

Windsor

34763 ■ Wediko Children's Services
11 Bobcat Blvd.
Windsor, NH 03244
Ph: (603)478-5236
Fax: (603)478-2049
E-mail: tdhamer@wediko.org
URL: http://www.wediko.org

NEW JERSEY

Avenel

34764 ■ Woodbridge Child & Diagnostic Treatment Center
15 Paddock St.
Avenel, NJ 07001
Ph: (732)499-5050
URL: http://www.state.nj.us/dcf/contact/residential.html

Bayville

34765 ■ Ocean Mental Health Services, Inc.--Bayville
160 Rte. 9
Bayville, NJ 08721
Ph: (732)349-5550
URL: http://www.oceanmentalhealth.org/

Ewing

34766 ■ Ewing Residential Center
1610 Stuyvesant Ave.
Ewing, NJ 08618-3299
Ph: (609)530-3350

Liberty Corner

34767 ■ Bonnie Brae Educational Center
3415 Valley Rd.
Liberty Corner, NJ 07938
Ph: (908)647-0800
Fax: (908)647-5021
E-mail: info@bonnie-brae.org
URL: http://www.bonnie-brae.org

Manahawkin

34768 ■ Ocean Mental Health Services, Inc.--Manahawkin
81 Nautilus Dr.
Manahawkin, NJ 08050
Ph: (609)597-5327
URL: http://www.oceanmentalhealth.org/

Mount Holly

34769 ■ The Children's Home--Mount Holly
243 Pine St.
Mount Holly, NJ 08060
Ph: (609)267-1550
Free: 877-TLC-KIDS
Fax: (609)261-5672
E-mail: kids@chbc.org
URL: http://www.childrens-home.org

NEW MEXICO

Albuquerque

34770 ■ Albuquerque Girls Community Residential Center
3409 Pan American Frwy.
Albuquerque, NM 87107
Ph: (505)841-8810

34771 ■ Amistad Crisis Shelter
1706 Centro Familiar SW
Albuquerque, NM 87105
Ph: (505)877-0371
E-mail: pit@ydinm.org
URL: http://www.ydinm.org/PIT/amistad.aspx

34772 ■ Desert Hills of New Mexico
5310 Sequoia NW
Albuquerque, NM 87120
Ph: (505)836-7330
Free: 800-765-7330
Fax: (505)836-7424
E-mail: info.deserthillsnm@yfcs.com
URL: http://www.yfcs.com/view/50

34773 ■ Hogares Casa--Casa Antigua
4620 9th St. NW
Albuquerque, NM 87107
Ph: (505)345-6209
E-mail: info@hogares.org
URL: http://www.nmjustice.net/nmsc/juvenile/program.php?id=490

34774 ■ Hogares, Inc.
1218 Griegos Rd. NW
Albuquerque, NM 87107
Ph: (505)345-8471
E-mail: info@hogares.org
URL: http://www.nmjustice.net/nmsc/juvenile/program.php?id=490

34775 ■ Sequoia Adolescent Treatment Center
3405 W Pan American Fwy. NE
Albuquerque, NM 87107
Ph: (505)222-0355
URL: http://www.nmhealth.org/nmsatc/index.shtml

Belen

34776 ■ Valencia Counseling Services Belen Office
325 S Main
Belen, NM 87002
Ph: (505)966-0151
URL: http://www.vcs-nm.com/contact.html

Cedar Crest

34777 ■ Villa Santa Maria
PO Box 156
Cedar Crest, NM 87008
Ph: (505)281-3609
Free: 800-453-5037
Fax: (505)281-0124
E-mail: info@villasantamaria.org
URL: http://www.villasantamaria.org

Grants

34778 ■ Cibola Counseling
906 N 1st St.
Grants, NM 87020
Ph: (505)287-7985

Las Vegas

34779 ■ Namaste Child & Family Development Center--Las Vegas
40 Thunderbird Dr.
Las Vegas, NM 87701
Ph: (505)425-2775
URL: http://www.namasteinc.org/

Los Lunas

34780 ■ Valencia Counseling Services, Inc. Casa Manzana
703 Don Pasqual Rd.
Los Lunas, NM 87031
Ph: (505)865-1408
URL: http://www.vcs-nm.com/contact.html

Roswell

34781 ■ Assurance Home
1000 E 18th St.
Roswell, NM 88201
Ph: (575)624-1780
Fax: (575)624-2033
E-mail: ron@assurancehome.org
URL: http://www.assurancehome.org
Ron Malone, Executive Director

34782 ■ Namaste Child & Family Development Center--Roswell
500 N Main St., Ste. 620
Roswell, NM 88201
Ph: (505)622-8826
URL: http://www.namasteinc.org/

Santa Fe

34783 ■ Namaste Child and Family Development Center--Santa Fe
1807 2nd St., Ste. 58
Santa Fe, NM 87505
Ph: (505)955-0091
URL: http://www.namasteinc.org/

Valmora

34784 ■ Rancho Valmora
HCR 50, Box 1
Valmora, NM 87750
Ph: (505)425-6057
Fax: (505)425-3522
E-mail: ranchovalmora@starband.net
URL: http://www.ranchovalmora.com
Dale Parker, Director

NEW YORK

Albany

34785 ■ Parsons Child and Family Center
60 Academy Rd.
Albany, NY 12208
Ph: (518)426-2600
Fax: (518)447-5234
E-mail: info@parsonscenter.org
URL: http://www.parsonscenter.org

34786 ■ Parsons Child & Family Center Group Home
490 Hudson Ave.
Albany, NY 12203
Ph: (518)426-2600
Fax: (518)447-5234
E-mail: development@parsonscenter.org
URL: http://www.parsonscenter.org

34787 ■ Parsons Child and Family Center Group Home
353 New Scotland Ave.
Albany, NY 12208
Ph: (518)426-2600
URL: http://www.parsonscenter.org

34788 ■ Saint Catherine's Center for Children
40 N Main Ave.
Albany, NY 12203
Ph: (518)453-6700
Fax: (518)453-6712
E-mail: bbell@st-cath.org
URL: http://www.st-cath.org

34789 ■ Saint Catherine's Center for Children Brady House
105 Delaware St.
Albany, NY 12202
Ph: (518)432-1624
URL: http://www.st-cath.org

34790 ■ Saint Catherine's Center for Children Group Residence
145 Sherman St.
Albany, NY 12206
Ph: (518)465-8433
URL: http://www.st-cath.org

34791 ■ Saint Catherine's Center for Children Hubbard House
56 N Pine Ave.
Albany, NY 12203
Ph: (518)482-1628
URL: http://www.st-cath.org

34792 ■ Saint Catherine's Center for Children Marrillac Shelter
195 Washington Ave. Ext.
Albany, NY 12205
Ph: (518)869-1960
URL: http://www.st-cath.org

Amityville

34793 ■ Hope for Youth
201 Dixon Ave.
Amityville, NY 11701
Ph: (631)691-5100
Fax: (631)691-5104
URL: http://www.hfyny.org/

Bayside

34794 ■ The Children's Village--Bayside
21133 45th Dr.
Bayside, NY 11361
Ph: (914)693-0600
URL: http://www.childrensvillage.org/

Brewster

34795 ■ Green Chimneys Children's Services, Inc.
400 Doansburg Rd.
Brewster, NY 10509
Ph: (845)279-2995
Fax: (845)279-3077
E-mail: lsignorini@greenchimneys.com
URL: http://www.greenchimneys.org

Bronx

34796 ■ The Astor Child Guidance Center
750 Tilden St.
Bronx, NY 10467
Ph: (718)231-3400
URL: http://www.astorservices.org

34797 ■ The Astor Day Treatment Program
4330 Byron Ave.
Bronx, NY 10466
Ph: (718)324-7526
URL: http://www.astorservices.org

34798 ■ West Side School
2555 Tratman Ave.
Bronx, NY 10461
Ph: (718)863-6903

Brooklyn

34799 ■ Ohel Children's Home and Family Services
4510 16th Ave.
Brooklyn, NY 11204
Ph: (718)851-6300
Free: 800-603-OHEL
Fax: (718)851-2772
E-mail: info@ohelfamily.org
URL: http://www.ohelfamily.org

34800 ■ Ohel Children's Home and Family Services Critical Care Residence
1402 Ave. I
Brooklyn, NY 11230
Ph: (718)377-2333
Free: 888-311-OHEL
Fax: (718)851-2772
E-mail: askohel@ohelfamily.org
URL: http://www.ohelfamily.org

34801 ■ Ohel Children's Home and Family Services Group Home
775 Westminster Rd.
Brooklyn, NY 11230
Ph: (718)859-8194
Free: 888-311-OHEL
Fax: (718)851-2772
E-mail: askohel@ohelfamily.org
URL: http://www.ohelfamily.org

34802 ■ Ohel Children's Home and Family Services Group Residence for Boys
1523 58th St.
Brooklyn, NY 11219
Ph: (718)851-6300
Free: 888-311-OHEL
Fax: (718)851-2772
E-mail: askohel@ohelfamily.org
URL: http://www.ohelfamily.org

Buffalo

34803 ■ Conners Children's Center
824 Delaware Ave.
Buffalo, NY 14209
Ph: (716)884-3802
URL: http://www.childfamilybny.org/

Canaan

34804 ■ Berkshire Farm Center & Services for Youth--Canaan
13640 State Rte. 22
Canaan, NY 12029
Ph: (518)781-4567
URL: http://www.berkshirefarm.org/

Dobbs Ferry

34805 ■ The Children's Village--Dobbs Ferry
Echo Hills
Dobbs Ferry, NY 10522
Ph: (914)693-0600
URL: http://www.childrensvillage.org/

34806 ■ Saint Christopher's Inc.
71 Broadway
Dobbs Ferry, NY 10522
Ph: (914)693-3030
URL: http://www.sc1881.com/direction.html

34807 ■ Saint Christopher's-Jenny Clarkson Child Care Services, Inc.
71 S Broadway
Dobbs Ferry, NY 10522
Ph: (914)693-3030
URL: http://www.watpa.org/sc/sc.html

Flushing

34808 ■ The Children's Village--Flushing
4722 Smart St.
Flushing, NY 11355
Ph: (914)693-0600
URL: http://www.childrensvillage.org/

Hamburg

34809 ■ Hopevale Inc.
3780 Howard Rd.
Hamburg, NY 14075
Ph: (716)648-1964
Fax: (716)648-5266
E-mail: info@hopevaleinc.org
URL: http://www.hopevaleinc.org
Program(s): Residential treatment program for girls.

Hawthorne

34810 ■ Hawthorne Cedar Knolls School
226 Linda Ave.
Hawthorne, NY 10532-2099
Ph: (914)749-2900
Fax: (914)749-2904
URL: http://www.hcks.org/home

34811 ■ Hawthorne Group Home
40 Bradford St.
Hawthorne, NY 10532
Ph: (914)372-7173
URL: http://www.hawthornecountryday.org/

Lackawanna

34812 ■ Baker Victory Services
780 Ridge Rd.
Lackawanna, NY 14218
Ph: (716)828-9500
Free: 888-287-1160
URL: http://www.bakervictoryservices.org/

Madison

34813 ■ Berkshire Farm Center and Services for Youth--Madison
3362 Frederick Rd.
Madison, NY 13402
Ph: (315)893-7290
URL: http://www.berkshirefarm.org/
Formerly: Madison County Group Home.

New Hartford

34814 ■ The House of The Good Shepherd--New Hartford
620 French Rd.
New Hartford, NY 13413
Ph: (315)235-7770
URL: http://www.hgs-utica.com/contact/

Ossining

34815 ■ Ossining Group Home
185 Cedar Ln.
Ossining, NY 10562
Ph: (914)762-7350

Plattsburgh

34816 ■ Berkshire Farm Center and Services for Youth--Plattsburgh
4766 Crete Blvd.
Plattsburgh, NY 12901
Ph: (518)561-2391
URL: http://www.berkshirefarm.org/
Formerly: Champlain Home for Children.

Poughkeepsie

34817 ■ The Astor Counseling Center
13 Mt. Carmel Pl.
Poughkeepsie, NY 12601
Ph: (845)452-6293
Fax: (845)452-6235
URL: http://www.astorservices.org

Randolph

34818 ■ Randolph Children's Home
356 Main St. ER
Randolph, NY 14772-9485
Ph: (716)358-2620
URL: http://www.ndyfs.org/

Rhinebeck

34819 ■ Astor Services for Children
6339 Mill St.
Rhinebeck, NY 12572
Ph: (845)871-1000
Fax: (845)876-2020
URL: http://www.astorservices.org

Rochester

34820 ■ Berkshire Farms Services for Youth--Rochester
17 Phelps Ave.
Rochester, NY 14608
Ph: (585)458-4900
URL: http://www.berkshirefarm.org/

34821 ■ Crestwood Children's Center
2075 Scottsville Rd.
Rochester, NY 14623
Ph: (585)429-2700
E-mail: info@hillside.com
URL: http://www.hillside.com
Formerly: Crestwood Child & Family Therapy of Honeoye Falls.

34822 ■ Crestwood Children's Center Group Home--Mills House
1048 South Ave.
Rochester, NY 14620
Ph: (585)436-4442
E-mail: info@hillside.com
URL: http://www.hillside.com

34823 ■ Saint Joseph's Villa of Rochester
3300 Dewey Ave.
Rochester, NY 14616
Ph: (585)865-1550
Fax: (585)865-5219
URL: http://www.stjosephsvilla.org

34824 ■ Saint Joseph's Villa of Rochester Group Home
115 Canterbury Rd.
Rochester, NY 14607
Ph: (716)865-1550
Fax: (716)865-5219
URL: http://www.stjosephsvilla.org

34825 ■ Saint Joseph's Villa of Rochester Group Home Program
Water Tower Park, Bldg. P
1099 Jay St.
Rochester, NY 14611
Fax: (585)328-0740
URL: http://www.stjosephsvilla.org

Schenectady

34826 ■ Berkshire Farm Center and Services for Youth--Schenectady Community Services Office
120 Rotterdam Industrial Park
Schenectady, NY 12306
Ph: (518)346-6201
URL: http://www.berkshirefarm.org/

Seaford

34827 ■ Seaford Group Home
1255 Alken Ave.
Seaford, NY 11783
Ph: (516)785-7487

Syracuse

34828 ■ Berkshire Farm Center & Services for Youth--Syracuse Community Service Office
5858 E Molloy Rd., Ste. 115
Syracuse, NY 13211
Ph: (315)454-4700
Fax: (315)454-4646
URL: http://www.berkshirefarm.org/

34829 ■ Elmcrest Children's Center, Inc.
960 Salt Springs Rd.
Syracuse, NY 13224
Ph: (315)446-6250
URL: http://www.elmcrest.org

Tully

34830 ■ Skeele Valley Group Home
6912 Jones Rd.
Tully, NY 13159-3231
Ph: (315)446-6250
Formerly: Skula Valley Group Home.

Utica

34831 ■ The House of The Good Shepherd--Utica
1550 Champlin Ave.
Utica, NY 13502
Ph: (315)733-0436
E-mail: info@hgs-utica.com
URL: http://www.hgs-utica.com

Valatie

34832 ■ Berkshire Farm Center and Services for Youth--Valatie
3433 Rte. 203
Valatie, NY 12184
Ph: (518)758-1230
URL: http://www.berkshirefarm.org/
Formerly: Columbia County Group Home.

West Park

34833 ■ Saint Cabrini Home, Inc.
Rte. 9W
West Park, NY 12493
Ph: (845)384-6500
Fax: (845)384-6004
E-mail: info@cabrinihome.com
URL: http://www.cabrinihome.com/

Williamson

34834 ■ Saint Joseph's Villa of Rochester Group Home
6228 Lake Ave.
Williamson, NY 14589
Ph: (585)865-1550
URL: https://www.stjosephsvilla.org/default.aspx

NORTH CAROLINA

Charlotte

34835 ■ Alexander Youth Network
6220 Thermal Rd.
Charlotte, NC 28212
Ph: (704)366-8712
Fax: (704)362-8464
E-mail: info@alexanderyouthnetwork.org
URL: http://www.alexanderyouthnetwork.org

Greensboro

34836 ■ Youth Focus Residential Treatment Center
1601 Huffine Mill Rd.
Greensboro, NC 27405
Ph: (336)375-8333
Fax: (336)621-0444
E-mail: vcatterall@youthfocus.org
URL: http://www.youthfocus.org

Lumberton

34837 ■ Southeastern Regional Mental Health Center
450 Country Club Rd.
Lumberton, NC 28360
Ph: (910)738-5261
Free: 800-670-6871
E-mail: info@srmhc.org
URL: http://www.srmhc.org

Pittsboro

34838 ■ Three Springs of North Carolina
2480 Hadley Mill Rd.
Pittsboro, NC 27312
Ph: (919)542-1104
URL: http://www.sequeltsi.com/

Raleigh

34839 ■ Haven House
706 Hillsborough St., Ste. 102
Raleigh, NC 27603
Ph: (919)833-3312
E-mail: hkasey@havenhousenc.org
URL: http://www.havenhousenc.org

34840 ■ Haven House for Boys
28 Shepherd St.
Raleigh, NC 27607
Ph: (919)832-7358
URL: http://www.havenhousenc.org

34841 ■ Haven House for Girls
101 Horne St.
Raleigh, NC 27607
Ph: (919)821-4924
URL: http://www.havenhousenc.org

NORTH DAKOTA

Fargo

34842 ■ Dakota Boys and Girls Ranch Fargo Youth Home
1641 31st Ave. S
Fargo, ND 58103
Ph: (701)237-3123
Free: 800-593-3098
Fax: (701)237-5711
URL: http://www.dakotaranch.org/

Minot

34843 ■ Dakota Boys and Girls Ranch--Minot
6301 19th Ave. NW
Minot, ND 58703
Ph: (701)852-3628
Free: 800-593-3098
Fax: (701)839-5541
URL: http://www.dakotaranch.org/

OHIO

Akron

34844 ■ The Village Network of Akron
3445 S Main St.
Akron, OH 44319
Ph: (330)245-1041
URL: http://www.thevillagenetwork.org/locations/

Bowling Green

34845 ■ Children's Resource Center
1045 Klotz Rd.
Bowling Green, OH 43402
Ph: (419)352-7588
Free: 888-466-KIDS
URL: http://www.wcnet.org/~crckids/

Chesterville

34846 ■ Buckhorn Children's Foundation--Ohio
7130 C.R. 121
Chesterville, OH 43317
Ph: (419)768-2225
Free: 800-472-3678
URL: http://www.buckhorn.org

Cleveland

34847 ■ Beech Brook--Cleveland
3737 Lander Rd.
Cleveland, OH 44124
Ph: (216)831-2255

Free: 877-546-1225
Fax: (216)831-0436
URL: http://www.beechbrook.org

34848 ■ Cleveland Christian Home Residential Treatment Center
11401 Lorain Ave.
Cleveland, OH 44111
Ph: (216)416-4277
URL: http://www.cchome.org

Columbus

34849 ■ Rosemont Center
2440 Dawnlight Ave.
Columbus, OH 43211
Ph: (614)471-2626
Free: 800-753-0424
Fax: (614)478-3234
E-mail: rjmarx@rosemont.org
URL: http://www.rosemont.org

34850 ■ Saint Vincent Family Centers Main Campus
1490 E Main St.
Columbus, OH 43205
Ph: (614)252-0731
E-mail: mandd@svfc.org
URL: http://www.svfc.org

34851 ■ Starr Columbus
301 Obetz Rd.
Columbus, OH 43207
Ph: (614)491-5784
Free: 866-289-9202
URL: http://www.starr.org/locations-starrcolumbus
Formerly: Hannah Neil Center/Wilson Clinic.

34852 ■ Starr My Place
1625 E Mound St.
Columbus, OH 43205
Ph: (614)491-5784
Free: 866-289-9202
Fax: (614)491-7246
URL: http://www.starr.org/locations-starrcolumbus

34853 ■ United Methodist Children's Home Treatment/Foster Care
526 N Cassingham Ave.
Columbus, OH 43209
Ph: (614)262-4260
URL: http://umchohio.org/
Formerly: Como House.

Mount Vernon

34854 ■ The Village Network of Mount Vernon/Knox County
17606 Coshocton Rd.
Mount Vernon, OH 43050
Ph: (740)397-7568
URL: http://www.thevillagenetwork.org/locations/

New Concord

34855 ■ Thompkins Child & Adolescent Services, Inc.
172 S Friendship Dr.
New Concord, OH 43762
Ph: (740)826-7650
Free: 800-844-4146
URL: http://www.tcasinc.org/
Formerly: Muskingum Area Adolescent Treatment Services.

Parma

34856 ■ Parmadale
6753 State Rd.
Parma, OH 44134
Ph: (440)845-7700
URL: http://www.clevelandcatholiccharities.org/
Formerly: CCSC/Parmadale.

Pepper Pike

34857 ■ Beech Brook--Pepper Pike
3737 Lander Rd.
Pepper Pike, OH 44124
Ph: (216)831-2255
Fax: (216)831-0436
URL: http://www.beechbrook.org

Shaker Heights

34858 ■ Bellefaire and Jewish Children's Bureau
22001 Fairmount Blvd.
Shaker Heights, OH 44118
Ph: (216)932-2800
URL: http://www.bellefairejcb.org

Smithville

34859 ■ The Village Network
PO Box 518
Smithville, OH 44677
Ph: (330)264-3232
URL: http://www.thevillagenetwork.org/
Formerly: Boys Village.

Springfield

34860 ■ Findlay Hall Group Home Oesterlen Services for Youth, Inc.
554 E Madison Ave.
Springfield, OH 45503
Ph: (937)399-6101
URL: http://www.oesterlen.org/

34861 ■ Oesterlen Services for Youth, Inc.
1918 Mechanicsburg Rd.
Springfield, OH 45503
Ph: (937)399-6101
Fax: (937)399-6609
E-mail: osfyi@oesterlen.org
URL: http://www.oesterlen.org

34862 ■ Osterlen Services for youth Robert Hall Group Home
854 Rodgers Dr.
Springfield, OH 45503
Ph: (937)399-6101
E-mail: osfyi@oesterlen.org
URL: http://www.oesterlen.org

Wooster

34863 ■ The Village Network of Wooster Boys' Village Campus
3011 Akron Rd.
Wooster, OH 44691
Ph: (330)264-3232
URL: http://www.thevillagenetwork.org/locations/

Worthington

34864 ■ The United Methodist Children's Home
1033 High St.
Worthington, OH 43085
Ph: (614)885-5020
Fax: (614)885-4058
URL: http://umchohio.org/

OREGON

Ashland

34865 ■ Lithia Springs Programs
695 Mistletoe Rd.
Ashland, OR 97520
Ph: (541)482-8906
Free: 888-609-HELP
URL: http://www.community-works.org/educationresidential.shtml
Formerly: Ashland Adolescent Center.

Beaverton

34866 ■ Saint Mary's Home for Boys
16535 SW Tualatin Valley Hwy.
Beaverton, OR 97006
Ph: (503)649-5651
Fax: (503)649-7405
URL: http://www.stmaryshomeforboys.org/

Corvallis

34867 ■ Trillium Family Services--Corvallis
4455 NE Hwy. 20
Corvallis, OR 97330
Ph: (541)758-5900
Free: 888-333-6177
URL: http://www.trilliumfamily.org/
Formerly: Children's Farm Home.

Eugene

34868 ■ Stepping Stone Program
2517 Centennial Loop
Eugene, OR 97401
Ph: (541)686-2688
Fax: (541)345-7605
URL: http://www.lookingglass.us/

Grants Pass

34869 ■ Southern Oregon Adolescent Study and Treatment Center
210 Tacoma St.
Grants Pass, OR 97526
Ph: (541)476-3302
URL: http://www.soastc.org/

Jasper

34870 ■ SCAR/Jasper Mountain
37875 Jasper Lowell Rd.
Jasper, OR 97438
Ph: (541)747-1235
Fax: (541)747-4722
E-mail: contact@scar-jaspermtn.org
URL: http://www.scar-jaspermtn.org/

McMinnville

34871 ■ Rainbow Lodge, Inc.
21250 Baker Creek Rd.
McMinnville, OR 97128
Ph: (503)435-1992

Medford

34872 ■ Community Works
900 E Main St.
Medford, OR 97504
Ph: (541)779-2393
Fax: (541)779-3317
E-mail: nwatson@community-works.org
URL: http://www.community-works.org

Oregon City

34873 ■ RiverBend Youth Center
15544 S Clackamas River Dr.
Oregon City, OR 97045-9490
Ph: (503)656-8005
Fax: (503)656-8929
URL: http://schools.privateschoolsreport.com/Oregon/OregonCity/RiverBendYouthCen terInc.html

Pendleton

34874 ■ Pendleton Academies
622 Airport Rd.
Pendleton, OR 97801-4598
Ph: (541)276-0057
Formerly: Eastern Oregon Adolescent/Children's Multi-Treatment Center.

Portland

34875 ■ Kerr Youth and Family Center
722 NE 162nd Ave.
Portland, OR 97230
Ph: (503)255-4205
URL: http://www.albertinakerr.org/

34876 ■ Parry Center for Children
3415 SE Powell Blvd.
Portland, OR 97202
Ph: (503)234-9591
URL: http://www.trilliumfamily.org/

34877 ■ Trillium Family Services--Portland
3415 SE Powell Blvd.
Portland, OR 97202
Ph: (503)234-9591
URL: http://www.trilliumfamily.org/

PENNSYLVANIA

Allentown

34878 ■ KidsPeace
531-535 Carldon St.
Allentown, PA 18103
Ph: (610)799-7879
Free: 800-25-PEACE
URL: http://www.kidspeace.org

Ambler

34879 ■ Saint Mary's Villa for Children and Families
701 S Bethlehem Pke.
Ambler, PA 19002
Ph: (215)643-7676
URL: http://www.smvcf.org/

Bensalem

34880 ■ Bensalem House
Saint Joseph Children's Home
1817 Hulmeville Rd.
Bensalem, PA 19020
Ph: (215)638-9310
URL: http://www.sfsj.org/

34881 ■ Saint Francis Saint Joseph Home for Children
3126-28 Bristol Pke.
Bensalem, PA 19020
Ph: (215)638-9310
URL: http://www.sfsj.org/

34882 ■ Saint Francis-Saint Joseph Homes for Boys
3400 Bristol Pike
Bensalem, PA 19020
Ph: (215)638-9310
Fax: (215)638-2498
URL: http://www.sfsj.org

Bethlehem

34883 ■ KidsPeace Broadway Campus
1650 Broadway
Bethlehem, PA 18015
Ph: (610)437-1790
Free: 800-346-7827
Fax: (610)799-8239
URL: http://www.kidspeace.org

Clarks Summit

34884 ■ Lourdesmont Good Shepherd Youth and Family Services
537 Venard Rd.
Clarks Summit, PA 18411
Ph: (570)587-4741
URL: http://www.lourdesmont.com/sys-tmpl/programsservices/

Danville

34885 ■ KidsPeace Montour County
3 Wesner Ln., Ste. 100
Danville, PA 17821
Ph: (570)271-0590
Free: 800-876-0590
URL: http://www.kidspeace.org

Erie

34886 ■ Sarah A. Reed Children's Center
2445 W 34th St.
Erie, PA 16506
Ph: (814)838-1954
E-mail: dwalsh@sarahreed.org
URL: http://www.sarahreed.org/

Gettysburg

34887 ■ Hoffman Homes
PO Box 4777
Gettysburg, PA 17325
Ph: (717)359-7148
Fax: (717)359-2600
E-mail: info@hoffmanhomes.com
URL: http://www.hoffmanhomes.com

Grove City

34888 ■ Zeta House
120 W Main St.
Grove City, PA 16127
Ph: (724)458-5315

Guys Mills

34889 ■ Omega House
28484 Guys Mills Rd.
Guys Mills, PA 16327
Ph: (814)789-4747

Honesdale

34890 ■ KidsPeace Wayne County
709 Church St.
Honesdale, PA 18431
Ph: (570)253-7910
URL: http://www.kidspeace.org

Kingston

34891 ■ KidsPeace Luzerne County
480 Pierce St., Ste. 320
Kingston, PA 18704
Ph: (570)287-5339
Free: 800-727-4482
URL: http://www.kidspeace.org

Meadville

34892 ■ Bethesda Children's Home
15667 State Hwy. 86
Meadville, PA 16335
Ph: (814)724-7510
Fax: (814)724-6237
URL: http://www.bethesda-home.org

New Cumberland

34893 ■ KidsPeace Cumberland County
764 Corporate Cir., Ste. 600
New Cumberland, PA 17070
Ph: (717)770-1364
URL: http://www.kidspeace.org

Orefield

34894 ■ KidsPeace Orchard Hills Campus
5300 KidsPeace Dr.
Orefield, PA 18069
Ph: (610)799-8000
Free: 800-8KID-123
URL: http://www.kidspeace.org

Philadelphia

34895 ■ Allegheny House
1424 W Allegheny Ave.
Philadelphia, PA 19132
Ph: (215)227-1549
Fax: (215)227-7435
E-mail: fhallegheny@friendshiphousepa.org
URL: http://www.friendshiphousepa.org/locations.html

34896 ■ Saint Francis--Saint Joseph Homes for Children
9600 State Rd.
Philadelphia, PA 19114-3022
Ph: (215)638-9310
URL: http://www.sfsj.org/
Formerly: Torresdale Group Home.

Plymouth Meeting

34897 ■ Silver Springs Martin Luther School
512 W Township Line Rd.
Plymouth Meeting, PA 19462
Ph: (610)825-4440
URL: http://www.silver-springs.org

Pottsville

34898 ■ Friendship House Cloud Home
351 S 2nd St.
Pottsville, PA 17901
Ph: (570)622-5015
Fax: (570)622-2967
E-mail: fhcloudhome@friendshiphousepa.org
URL: http://www.friendshiphousepa.org/locations.html

Rosemont

34899 ■ Presbyterian Children's Village Services
452 S Roberts Rd.
Rosemont, PA 19010
Ph: (610)525-5400
Fax: (610)525-8396
E-mail: village@pcv.org
URL: http://www.pcv.org

Schuylkill Haven

34900 ■ KidsPeace Schuylkill County
355 Saylor St.
Schuylkill Haven, PA 17972
Ph: (570)385-6821
URL: http://www.kidspeace.org

Scranton

34901 ■ Friendship House
1615 Elm St.
Scranton, PA 18505
Ph: (570)342-8305
Fax: (570)343-2041
URL: http://www.friendshiphousepa.org/locations.html

34902 ■ KidsPeace Lackawanna County
101 Pittston Ave., 1st Fl., Ste. 3
Scranton, PA 18505
Ph: (570)342-5444
Free: 800-551-2238
URL: http://www.kidspeace.org

Somerset

34903 ■ Children's Aid Home Programs of Somerset County, Inc.
1476 N Center Ave.
Somerset, PA 15501
Ph: (814)443-1637
Fax: (814)445-8481
URL: http://www.cahprogram.org

Vandergrift

34904 ■ George Junior Republic
Howard Walker
1114 Walker Ln.
Vandergrift, PA 15690
Ph: (724)458-9330
URL: http://www.georgejuniorrepublic.org/

Williamsport

34905 ■ KidsPeace Lycoming County
1000 Commerce Park Dr., Ste. 311
Williamsport, PA 17701
Ph: (570)326-7811
URL: http://www.kidspeace.org

RHODE ISLAND

Chepachet

34906 ■ Harmony Hill School
63 Harmony Hill Rd.
Chepachet, RI 02814
Ph: (401)949-0690
URL: http://www.harmonyhillschool.org/residential.htm

SOUTH CAROLINA

North Charleston

34907 ■ Carolina Youth Development Center
5055 Lackawanna Blvd.
North Charleston, SC 29405
Ph: (843)266-5200
Fax: (843)266-5201
E-mail: info@cydc.org
URL: http://www.cydc.org/

York

34908 ■ Episcopal Church Home for Children
234 Kings Mountain St.
York, SC 29745
Ph: (803)684-4011
Fax: (803)684-8002
URL: http://www.yorkplace.org/

SOUTH DAKOTA

Aberdeen

34909 ■ Lutheran Social Services--Aberdeen
202 S Main St., Ste. 228
Aberdeen, SD 57401
Ph: (605)229-1500
URL: http://www.lsssd.org/

Mitchell

34910 ■ Abbott House, inc.
909 Court Merrill St.
Mitchell, SD 57301
Ph: (605)996-2486
URL: http://www.abbotthouse.org/

Rapid City

34911 ■ Children's Home Society of South Dakota
Black Hills Children's Home
24100 S Rockerville Rd.
Rapid City, SD 57702
Ph: (605)343-5422
Fax: (605)343-1411
URL: http://www.chssd.org/

34912 ■ Lutheran Social Services--Rapid City
2920 Sheridan Lake Rd.
Rapid City, SD 57702
Ph: (605)348-0477
URL: http://www.lsssd.org/

Sioux Falls

34913 ■ Children's Home Society of South Dakota
Sioux Falls Children's Home
801 N Sycamore Ave.
Sioux Falls, SD 57110
Ph: (605)334-6004
URL: http://www.chssd.org/
Formerly: Children's Home Society.

34914 ■ Lutheran Social Services of South Dakota
Residential and Outpatient Services
705 E 41st St. Ste. 100
Sioux Falls, SD 57105-6047
Ph: (605)357-0131
Free: 800-568-2401
Fax: (605)357-0140
URL: http://www.lsssd.org

34915 ■ Summit Oaks Center
333 S Summit Ave
Sioux Falls, SD 57104
Ph: (605)336-9102
Fax: (605)336-9141
URL: http://www.lsssd.org/

Watertown

34916 ■ Lutheran Social Services of South Dakota
1424 9th Ave. SE, No. 7
Watertown, SD 57201
Ph: (605)882-2740
URL: http://www.lsssd.org/

TENNESSEE

Ashland City

34917 ■ Chad Youth Enhancement Center
1751 Oak Plains Rd.
Ashland City, TN 37015
Ph: (931)362-4723
URL: http://www.oakplainsacademy.com/

Clarksville

34918 ■ Centerstone - Harriet Cohn Center
511 8th St.
Clarksville, TN 37040
Ph: (931)920-7200
Fax: (931)920-7202
URL: http://www.centerstone.org
Formerly: Harriett Cohn Center.

TEXAS

Abilene

34919 ■ New Horizons, Inc.
500 Chestnut, Ste. 1101
Abilene, TX 79602
Ph: (325)437-1852
URL: http://www.newhorizonsinc.com/
Formerly: New Horizons Ranch & Center.

Austin

34920 ■ The Oaks Treatment Center
1407 W Stassney Ln.
Austin, TX 78745
Ph: (512)464-0200
Free: 800-843-6257
Fax: (512)464-0444
URL: http://www.theoakstc.com/
Formerly: The Oaks Psychiatric Health System.

34921 ■ Settlement Home for Children
1600 Peyton Gin Rd.
Austin, TX 78758
Ph: (512)836-2150
Fax: (512)836-2159
E-mail: info@settlementhome.org
URL: http://www.settlementhome.org

Belton

34922 ■ Cedar Crest Hospital and Residential Treatment Center
3500 S Interstate 35
Belton, TX 76513
Ph: (254)939-2100
Fax: (254)939-2335
URL: http://www.cedarcresthospital.com/
Formerly: HCA Cedar Crest Behavioral Health.

Corpus Christi

34923 ■ Pathfinders--Corpus Christi
3833 S Staples St., Ste. 73
Corpus Christi, TX 78411
Ph: (361)853-6700
E-mail: burkefound@sbcglobal.net
URL: http://www.burkefoundation.com/

Driftwood

34924 ■ Pathfinders--Driftwood
Burke Foundation Child Placing Agency
PO Box 40
Driftwood, TX 78619
Ph: (512)858-4258
Fax: (512)858-4960
URL: http://www.burkefoundation.com/

El Paso

34925 ■ El Paso Center for Children
220 N Stevens St.
El Paso, TX 79930
Ph: (915)565-8361
URL: http://www.epccinc.org/

Fort Davis

34926 ■ High Frontier, Inc.
PO Box 1325
Fort Davis, TX 79734
Ph: (432)364-2241
URL: http://www.thehighfrontier.org/

Laredo

34927 ■ Pathfinders--Laredo
608B W Calton Rd.
Laredo, TX 78041
Ph: (956)723-5886
E-mail: burkefoundation@sbcglobal.net
URL: http://www.burkefoundation.com/

Liberty Hill

34928 ■ Meridell Achievement Center
12550 W Hwy. 29
Liberty Hill, TX 78642
Ph: (512)528-2100
URL: http://www.meridell.com

San Marcos

34929 ■ San Marcos Treatment Center
120 Bert Brown Rd.
San Marcos, TX 78666
Ph: (512)396-8500
Fax: (512)754-3883
URL: http://www.psysolutions.com/facilities/sanmarcos/

Waco

34930 ■ Waco Center for Youth
3501 N 19th St.
Waco, TX 76708-2097
Ph: (254)756-2171
URL: http://www.dshs.state.tx.us/mhhospitals/wacocenterforyouth/default.shtm

UTAH

Castle Dale

34931 ■ Four Corners Community Mental Health Center
45 E 100 South
Castle Dale, UT 84513
Ph: (435)381-2432
URL: http://www.fourcorners.ws/

Draper

34932 ■ YouthCare Residential Treatment Center for Troubled Teens
12595 Minuteman Dr.
Draper, UT 84020
Ph: (801)572-6989
Free: 800-786-4924
URL: http://www.youthcare.com/

Kearns

34933 ■ The Children's Center--Kearns
5242 S 4820 West
Kearns, UT 84118
Ph: (801)966-4251
URL: http://www.tccslc.org/

Salt Lake City

34934 ■ The Children's Center--Salt Lake City
350 S 400 East
Salt Lake City, UT 84111
Ph: (801)582-5534
URL: http://www.tccslc.org/

VERMONT

Bennington

34935 ■ Bennington School
192 Fairview St.
Bennington, VT 05201
Ph: (802)447-1557
Free: 800-639-3156
URL: http://www.benningtonschoolinc.com/

Chelsea

34936 ■ Brookhaven Home for Boys Inc.
331 State Rte. 110
Chelsea, VT 05038
Ph: (802)685-4458
URL: http://www.brookhaventlc.org/
Formerly: Brookhaven Children and Family Services.

Johnson

34937 ■ Laraway Youth and Family Services
95 School St.
Johnson, VT 05656
Ph: (802)635-2805
URL: http://www.laraway.org/

Winooski

34938 ■ North American Family Institute--Winooski
486 Main St.
Winooski, VT 05404-1338
Ph: (802)655-8833
URL: http://nafi.com/program_detail.htm?ID=69

VIRGINIA

Portsmouth

34939 ■ The Pines Residential Treatment Center
825 Crawford Pkwy.
Portsmouth, VA 23704
Ph: (757)398-0061
Free: 877-227-7000
URL: http://www.psysolutions.com/facilities/pinesportsmouth/

Winchester

34940 ■ Leary Educational Foundation
PO Box 3160
Winchester, VA 22604
Ph: (540)888-3456
Free: 877-877-3004
E-mail: tnewbraugh@trschool.org
URL: http://www.timber-ridge-school.org

WASHINGTON

Burien

34941 ■ Ruth Dykeman Children's Center--Youth and Family Services
137 SW 154th St.
Burien, WA 98166
Ph: (206)243-5544
URL: http://www.rdcc.org

Burlington

34942 ■ Secret Harbor School
225 N Walnut St.
Burlington, WA 98233
Ph: (360)755-5700
Free: 888-812-5757
URL: http://www.secretharbor.org/

Seattle

34943 ■ Catholic Community Services of Seattle/King County
100 23rd Ave. S
Seattle, WA 98144
Ph: (206)328-5696
Fax: (206)328-5699
E-mail: info@ccsww.org
URL: http://www.ccsww.org

34944 ■ Children's Home Society of Washington--Seattle
3300 NE 65th St.
Seattle, WA 98115
Ph: (206)695-3200
Fax: (206)695-3201
E-mail: pr@chs-wa.org
URL: http://childrenshomesociety.org

34945 ■ Ruth Dykeman Children's Center
1033 SW 152nd St.
Seattle, WA 98166
Ph: (206)242-1698
URL: http://www.rdcc.org
Formerly: Ruth Dykeman Center.

34946 ■ Ryther Child Center
2400 NE 95th St.
Seattle, WA 98115
Ph: (206)525-5050
URL: http://www.ryther.org

34947 ■ Seattle Children's Home
2142 10th Ave. W
Seattle, WA 98119
Ph: (206)283-3300
Fax: (206)284-7843
E-mail: info@seattlechildrenshome.org
URL: http://www.seattlechildrenshome.org

Spokane

34948 ■ Children's Home Society of Washington--Spokane
2323 N Discovery Pl.
Spokane, WA 99216
Ph: (509)747-4174
URL: http://www.childrenshomesociety.org

34949 ■ Tamarack Center
W 2901 Ft. George Wright Dr.
Spokane, WA 99224
Ph: (509)326-8100
Free: 800-736-3410
E-mail: info@tamarack.org
URL: http://www.tamarack.org

Vancouver

34950 ■ Children's Home Society of Washington
309 W 12th St.
Vancouver, WA 98666
Ph: (360)695-1325
Fax: (360)695-9803
URL: http://www.childrenshomesociety.org

WEST VIRGINIA

Beckley

34951 ■ Burlington United Methodist Family Services--Beckley
4700 Robert C. Byrd Dr.
Beckley, WV 25801
Ph: (304)252-8508
Fax: (304)252-3670
URL: http://www.bumfs.org/

Burlington

34952 ■ Burlington United Methodist Family Services--Burlington
1 Rainbow Ln.
Burlington, WV 26710
Ph: (304)289-6010
Fax: (304)289-3903
URL: http://www.bumfs.org/

Grafton

34953 ■ Burlington United Methodist Family Services--Grafton
US Rte. 119 N
Grafton, WV 26354
Ph: (304)265-1338
Fax: (304)265-1575
URL: http://www.bumfs.org/

Huntington

34954 ■ Cammack Children's Center
64 W 6th Ave.
Huntington, WV 25701
Ph: (304)523-3497
Free: 800-244-3497
URL: http://www.cammack.org/

Keyser

34955 ■ Burlington United Methodist Family Services--Keyser
US Rte. 220 S
Keyser, WV 26726
Ph: (304)788-2342
Fax: (304)788-2409
URL: http://www.bumfs.org/

Morgantown

34956 ■ Burlington United Methodist Family Services--Morgantown
475 Baird St.
Morgantown, WV 26505
Ph: (304)296-0621
Fax: (304)296-9385
URL: http://www.bumfs.org/

WISCONSIN

Dousman

34957 ■ Lad Lake
W350 S1401 Waterville Rd.
Dousman, WI 53118
Ph: (262)965-2131
URL: http://www.ladlake.org/

Eau Claire

34958 ■ Eau Claire Academy
550 N Dewey St.
Eau Claire, WI 54701
Ph: (715)834-6681
URL: http://www.clinicarecorp.com/academy/eau-claire/eauclaire.html

La Crosse

34959 ■ Family & Children's Center
1707 Main St.
La Crosse, WI 54601
Ph: (608)788-6322
Fax: (608)785-0002

Milwaukee

34960 ■ Bell Therapy Florist House
7401 W Florist Ave.
Milwaukee, WI 53218
Ph: (414)438-1820
URL: http://www.phoenixcaresystems.com/bell/index.php

34961 ■ The Counseling Center of Milwaukee
2038 N Bartlett Ave.
Milwaukee, WI 53202
Ph: (414)271-2565
URL: http://pathfindersmke.org/

34962 ■ Pathfinders for Runaways
1614 E Kane Pl.
Milwaukee, WI 53202
Ph: (414)271-1560
URL: http://pathfindersmke.org/

34963 ■ Saint Aemilian-Lakeside
8901 W Capitol Dr.
Milwaukee, WI 53222
Ph: (414)463-1880
Fax: (414)463-2770
URL: http://www.st-al.org/

34964 ■ Willowglen Academy
5554 N 57th St.
Milwaukee, WI 53218
Ph: (414)342-2060
URL: http://www.phoenixcaresystems.com/wi/milwaukee.php

Mukwonago

34965 ■ Norris Adolescent Center
W247 S10395 Center Dr.
Mukwonago, WI 53149
Ph: (262)662-5900
URL: http://www.norriscenter.org/

Oconomowoc

34966 ■ Oconomowoc Developmental Training
36100 Genesee Lake Rd.
Oconomowoc, WI 53066
Ph: (262)569-5515
Fax: (262)569-5513
URL: http://www.odtc-wi.com/

Plymouth

34967 ■ Willowglen Academy North
1111 Reed St.
Plymouth, WI 53073
Ph: (920)565-2607
URL: http://www.phoenixcaresystems.com/wi/north.php

Prairie du Chien

34968 ■ Clincare Corporation/Wyalusing Academy
601 S Beaumont Rd.
Prairie du Chien, WI 53821
Ph: (608)326-6481
URL: http://www.clinicarecorp.com/academy/wyalusing/wyalusing.html

Sheboygan

34969 ■ Willowglen Academy Wilson
3603 S Business Ave.
Sheboygan, WI 53081
Ph: (920)565-2607
URL: http://www.phoenixcaresystems.com/wi/wilson.php

Wauwatosa

34970 ■ Carmelite Home for Boys
1214 Kavanaugh Pl.
Wauwatosa, WI 53213
Ph: (414)258-4791
URL: http://www.carmelitedcjnorth.org/

WYOMING

Casper

34971 ■ Central Wyoming Counseling Center
1430 Wilkins Cir.
Casper, WY 82601
Ph: (307)237-9583
Fax: (307)265-7277
URL: http://www.cwcc.us/

34972 ■ New Directions
1514 E 12th St., Ste. 101
Casper, WY 82601-7123
Ph: (307)237-6033
URL: http://www.wamhsac.org/cwcc.html

34973 ■ New Horizons Residential Treatment Facility
837 East C St.
Casper, WY 82601-2014
Ph: (307)237-7077
URL: http://www.wamhsac.org/cwcc.html

Jackson

34974 ■ Hirschfield Center for Children
PO Box 2631
Jackson, WY 83001
Ph: (307)733-7946
E-mail: cgmoll@tyfs.org
URL: http://www.redtopmeadows.org/hc-programs.html

34975 ■ Teton Youth and Family Services
510 S Cache Dr.
Jackson, WY 83001
Ph: (307)732-1829
URL: http://www.redtopmeadows.org/

34976 ■ Tri-County Group Home
510 S Cache Dr.
Jackson, WY 83001
Ph: (307)733-6482

34977 ■ Van Veck House
510 S Cache Dr.
Jackson, WY 83001
Ph: (307)733-6440
URL: http://www.redtopmeadows.org/vvh-programs.html

Laramie

34978 ■ Cathedral Home for Children
4989 N 3rd St.
Laramie, WY 82072
Ph: (307)745-8997
Free: 800-676-1909
URL: http://www.cathedralhome.org/

Torrington

34979 ■ Saint Joseph's Children's Home
1419 S Main St.
Torrington, WY 82240
Ph: (307)532-4197
Fax: (307)532-8405
URL: http://www.stjoseph-wy.org/
Formerly: Saint Joseph's Group Home.

Wilson

34980 ■ Red Top Meadows Residential Treatment Center
7905 S Fall Creek Rd.
Wilson, WY 83014
Ph: (307)733-9098
URL: http://www.redtopmeadows.org/

Chapter 24
Multiple Sclerosis Centers & Clinics

Listed below are MS care clinics and comprehensive care centers. Arrangement is geographical by states, then alphabetical by organization names within states. For additional information, consult the "User's Guide" located at the front of this directory.

ALABAMA

34981 ■ Tanner Center for Multiple Sclerosis
509 Brookwood Blvd.
Birmingham, AL 35209
Ph: (205)803-2210
Free: 866-803-2214
URL: http://www.tannercenterforms.com

34982 ■ University of Alabama, Birmingham Center for Pediatric-Onset Demyelinating Disease
CIRC 235A
1719 6th Ave. S
Birmingham, AL 35294
Ph: (205)996-7633
Fax: (205)996-7333
URL: http://www.uab.edu/cpodd
Dr. Jayne Ness, Director

34983 ■ University of Alabama, Birmingham Neurology Department
Sparks Center 440
1720 7th Ave. S
Birmingham, AL 35233
Ph: (205)934-2402
Fax: (205)975-6030
URL: http://www.main.uab.edu/neurology/

34984 ■ Veterans Affairs Medical Center, Birmingham
Multiple Sclerosis Center
700 S 19th St.
Birmingham, AL 35233
Ph: (205)933-8101
URL: http://www.va.gov/ms

34985 ■ Veterans Affairs Medical Center--Tuscaloosa
Multiple Sclerosis Center
3701 Loop Rd. E
Tuscaloosa, AL 35404
Ph: (205)554-2000
URL: http://www.tuscaloosa.va.gov

34986 ■ Veterans Affairs Medical Center, Tuskegee
Multiple Sclerosis Center
2400 Hospital Rd.
Tuskegee, AL 36083
Ph: (334)727-0550
Fax: (334)724-6857
URL: http://www.va.gov/ms

ALBERTA

34987 ■ University of Calgary
Multiple Sclerosis Center
Foothills Medical Center Bldg., Rm. C1223
1403 29 St. NW, 12th Fl.
Calgary, AB, Canada T2N 2T9
Ph: (403)944-4241
Fax: (403)944-3465
URL: http://www.mscare.org/cmsc/

ARIZONA

34988 ■ Barrow Neurology Clinic
Multiple Sclerosis and Related Diseases Clinic
500 W Thomas Rd., Ste. 300
Phoenix, AZ 85013
Ph: (602)406-3390
Fax: (602)406-7161
URL: http://www.thebarrow.com/

34989 ■ Bob Stump Northern Veterans Affairs Medical Center
Multiple Sclerosis Center
PM&R Service (117)
500 N Hwy. 89
Prescott, AZ 86313
Ph: (520)776-6087
Fax: (520)776-6172
URL: http://www.va.gov/ms

34990 ■ Carl T. Hayden Veterans Affairs Medical Center
Multiple Sclerosis Center
650 E Indian School Rd.
Phoenix, AZ 85012
Ph: (602)222-6401
Fax: (602)200-6021
URL: http://www.va.gov/ms

34991 ■ Phoenix Neurological Associates
Multiple Sclerosis Center
5090 N 40th St., Ste. 250
Phoenix, AZ 85018
Ph: (602)258-3354
Fax: (602)258-3368
URL: http://www.phoenixneurology.com

34992 ■ Southern Arizona Veterans Affairs Health Care System
Multiple Sclerosis Center
3601 S 6th Ave.
Tucson, AZ 85723
Ph: (520)792-1450
URL: http://www.va.gov/ms
Dr. Ronnie Bergen, Director

ARKANSAS

34993 ■ John L. McClellan Memorial VA Medical Center
Multiple Sclerosis Center
4300 W 7th St.
Little Rock, AR 72205
Ph: (501)660-2070
Fax: (501)671-2514
URL: http://www.va.gov/ms

BRITISH COLUMBIA

34994 ■ Burnaby Hospital
Multiple Sclerosis Center
Fraser Health
3935 Kincaid St.
Burnaby, BC, Canada V5G 2X6
Ph: (604)412-6405
Fax: (604)412-6407
URL: http://www.mscare.org/cmsc/

34995 ■ Kelowna General Hospital
Multiple Sclerosis Clinic
2268 Pandosy St.
Kelowna, BC, Canada V1Y 1T2
Ph: (250)862-4071
URL: http://www.mscare.org/cmsc/

34996 ■ Northern Health
Porch Multiple Sclerosis Clinic
1475 Edmonton St.
Prince George, BC, Canada V2M 1S2
Ph: (250)565-2304
Fax: (250)565-2662
URL: http://www.mscare.org/cmsc/

34997 ■ University of British Columbia
Multiple Sclerosis Clinic
S126-2211 Wesbrook Mall
Vancouver, BC, Canada V6T 2B5
Ph: (604)822-1728
Fax: (604)990-4626
URL: http://www.mscare.org/cmsc/

CALIFORNIA

34998 ■ Casa Colina Multiple Sclerosis Centers
255 E Bonita Ave.
Pomona, CA 91769
Ph: (909)596-7733
Fax: (909)450-0322
URL: http://www.casacolina.org/

34999 ■ Fullerton Neurology and Headache Center
Multiple Sclerosis Center
100 Laguna Rd., Ste. 208
Fullerton, CA 92835
Ph: (714)738-0800
Fax: (714)738-3758
URL: http://www.mscare.org/cmsc/

35000 ■ Jerry L. Pettis Memorial Veterans Affairs Medical Center
Multiple Sclerosis Center
11201 Benton St.
Loma Linda, CA 92357
Free: 800-741-8387
URL: http://www.va.gov/ms
Dr. Bradley Cole, Director

35001 ■ Mercy Multiple Sclerosis Center
6555 Coyle Ave., 3rd Fl.
Carmichael, CA 95608
Ph: (916)536-3670
Fax: (916)536-2480
URL: http://www.mercysacramento.org

35002 ■ Riverside Medical Center
Multiple Sclerosis Center
7117 Brockton Ave.
Riverside, CA 92506
Ph: (951)782-6215
Fax: (951)784-3266
URL: http://www.riversidemedicalclinic.com

35003 ■ San Francisco Veterans Affairs Medical Center
Multiple Sclerosis Center
4150 Clement St.
San Francisco, CA 94121
Ph: (415)221-4810
URL: http://www.va.gov/ms
Dr. Douglas Goodin, Director

35004 ■ Stanford Hospital
Multiple Sclerosis Center
300 Pasteur Dr.
Stanford, CA 94305
Ph: (650)723-6469
Fax: (650)723-7434
URL: http://www.stanfordhospital.com

35005 ■ Sutter East Bay Physicians Medical Group
Multiple Sclerosis Clinic
2850 Telegraph Ave., Ste. 110
Berkeley, CA 94705
Ph: (510)204-8140
URL: http://www.sebmf.org

35006 ■ University of California, Irvine
Multiple Sclerosis Clinic
Gottschalk Medical Plz.
1 Medical Plz. Dr.
Irvine, CA 92697
Ph: (714)456-7239
URL: http://www.uci.edu
Dr. Michael Demetriou, Director

35007 ■ University of California, San Francisco
Pediatric Center of Excellence
Pediatric Multiple Sclerosis Center
350 Parnassus Ave., Ste. 908
San Francisco, CA 94117
Ph: (415)514-1684
Fax: (415)514-2443
URL: http://www.ucsfhealth.org/pedsms

35008 ■ University of Southern California
Multiple Sclerosis Comprehensive Care Center
1520 San Pablo St., Ste. 3000
Los Angeles, CA 90033-4606
Ph: (323)442-5710
Fax: (323)442-5736
E-mail: mscare@usc.edu
URL: http://www.usc.edu/neurology/mscenter

35009 ■ Veterans Affairs Central California Health Care System
Multiple Sclerosis Center
Neurology - 127
2615 E Clinton Ave.
Fresno, CA 93703
Ph: (209)228-5328
Fax: (209)228-6943
URL: http://www.va.gov/ms

35010 ■ Veterans Affairs Greater Los Angeles Health Care System
Multiple Sclerosis Clinic
11301 Wilshire Blvd.
Los Angeles, CA 90073
Ph: (310)268-3013
Fax: (310)268-4611
URL: http://www.losangeles.va.gov

35011 ■ Veterans Affairs Long Beach Health Care System
Multiple Sclerosis Center
5901 E 7th St.
Long Beach, CA 90822
Free: 888-769-8387
URL: http://www.va.gov/ms
Dr. Paul Gutierrez, Director

35012 ■ Veterans Affairs Northern California Health Care System
Multiple Sclerosis Center
Sacramento Valley Division
10535 Hospital Way, MC 127
Sacramento, CA 95655
Ph: (916)366-5325
URL: http://www.va.gov/ms
Dr. Mark Agius, Director

35013 ■ Veterans Affairs Palo Alto Healthcare System
Multiple Sclerosis Center
Dept. of Neurology
3801 Miranda Ave.
Palo Alto, CA 94304
Ph: (650)493-5000
Fax: (650)852-3280
URL: http://www.va.gov/ms

35014 ■ Veterans Affairs San Diego Health Care System
Multiple Sclerosis Center
3350 La Jolla Village Dr., MC 9127
San Diego, CA 92161
Ph: (858)642-3470
URL: http://www.va.gov/ms
Dr. Jodi Corey-Bloom, Director

35015 ■ Veterans Affairs Sepulveda
Multiple Sclerosis Center
OPC & Nursing Home
16111 Plummer St.
Sepulveda, CA 91343
Ph: (818)895-9473
Fax: (818)895-5801
URL: http://www.va.gov/ms/

COLORADO

35016 ■ Can Do
Multiple Sclerosis Center
27 Main St., Ste. 303
Edwards, CO 81632
Ph: (970)926-1290
Fax: (970)926-1295
URL: http://www.mscando.org/

35017 ■ Colorado Neurological Institute
Multiple Sclerosis Services
701 E Hampden Ave., Ste. 320
Englewood, CO 80113
Ph: (303)788-7667
Fax: (303)409-6800
URL: http://www.thecni.org/
Formerly: Rocky Mountain Multiple Sclerosis Center.

35018 ■ Office of Patricia Fodor, MD, PC
Multiple Sclerosis Center
7606 N Union Blvd., Ste. G
Colorado Springs, CO 80920
Ph: (719)598-9991
Fax: (719)598-2044
URL: http://www.mscare.org/cmsc/

35019 ■ Rocky Mountain Multiple Sclerosis Center
8845 Wagner St.
Westminster, CO 80031
Ph: (303)788-4030
Fax: (303)788-8854
URL: http://www.mscenter.org

35020 ■ University of Colorado Anschutz Medical Campus
Multiple Sclerosis Center
1635 Aurora Ct.
Aurora, CO 80045
Ph: (303)724-2199
Fax: (303)724-2203
URL: http://www.ucdenver.edu

35021 ■ Veterans Affairs Medical Center, Denver
Multiple Sclerosis Center
1055 Clermont St., PMRS 117
Denver, CO 80220
Ph: (303)393-2819
Fax: (303)393-5164
URL: http://www.va.gov/ms

CONNECTICUT

35022 ■ Mandell Center for Comprehensive Multiple Sclerosis Care and Neuroscience Research
Mt. Sinai Rehab Hospital
490 Blue Hills Ave.
Hartford, CT 06112
Ph: (860)714-2149
Fax: (860)714-8933
URL: http://www.saintfrancisdoctors.com/ms

35023 ■ Multiple Sclerosis Care of Connecticut
1 Towne Park Plz.
Norwich, CT 06360
Ph: (860)886-1433
Fax: (860)886-4644
URL: http://www.mscarect.org
Dr. Derek R. Smith, Director

35024 ■ West Haven Veterans Affairs Medical Center
Multiple Sclerosis Program
Spinal Cord Clinic
950 Campbell Ave.
West Haven, CT 06516
Ph: (203)937-5711
Fax: (203)937-3457
URL: http://www.connecticut.va.gov/

35025 ■ Yale University School of Medicine
Multiple Sclerosis Clinic
40 Temple St., Ste. 6-C
New Haven, CT 06510-8018
Ph: (203)764-4280
Fax: (203)764-4288
URL: http://medicine.yale.edu
Dr. Jana Preiningerova, Director

DELAWARE

35026 ■ Wilmington Veterans Affairs Medical Center
Multiple Sclerosis Center
1601 Kirkwood Hwy. 127
Wilmington, DE 19805
Ph: (302)994-2511
Fax: (302)633-5582
URL: http://www.va.gov/ms

DISTRICT OF COLUMBIA

35027 ■ Georgetown University Hospital
Multiple Sclerosis Center
PHC Bldg., 7th Fl.
3800 Reservoir Rd. NW
Washington, DC 20007
Ph: (202)444-8525
Fax: (202)784-2261
URL: http://www.mscenter.georgetown.edu

35028 ■ Veterans Affairs Medical Center, Washington
Multiple Sclerosis Center
50 Irving St. NW, 3B West
Washington, DC 20422

Ph: (202)745-8148
Fax: (202)745-8231
URL: http://www.va.gov/ms

FLORIDA

35029 ■ Center of Neurological Services Orlando
Multiple Sclerosis Care Center
3849 Oakwater Cir.
Orlando, FL 32806
Ph: (407)240-1762
Fax: (407)812-5869
URL: http://www.orlandoneurological.com

35030 ■ James A. Haley Veterans Affairs Hospital, Tampa
Multiple Sclerosis Center
13000 Bruce B Downs Blvd.
Tampa, FL 33612
Ph: (813)972-7517
Fax: (813)978-5913
URL: http://www.va.gov/ms

35031 ■ Multiple Sclerosis Center of Greater Orlando
301 N Maitland Ave.
Maitland, FL 32751
Ph: (407)647-5996
Fax: (407)644-5967
URL: http://www.floridams.org

35032 ■ Multiple Sclerosis Comprehensive Care Center of Central Florida
6001 Vineland Rd., Ste. 116
Orlando, FL 32819
Ph: (407)352-5434
Fax: (407)345-9765
URL: http://www.mscentralfl.com

35033 ■ Neuroscience Consultants
Comprehensive Multiple Sclerosis Center
4601 Ponce de Leon Blvd., Ste. 100
Coral Gables, FL 33146
Ph: (786)219-3145
Fax: (786)219-3155
URL: http://www.mscare.org/cmsc

35034 ■ Shands Jacksonville Medical Center, Inc.
Comprehensive Multiple Sclerosis Center
580 W 8th St.
Tower 1, 9th Fl.
Jacksonville, FL 32209
Ph: (904)244-9538
Fax: (904)244-9798
URL: http://jax.shands.org/hs/neuro/multiplesclerosis.asp

35035 ■ University of Miami
Multiple Sclerosis Center
NPF Bldg., 2nd Fl.
1501 NW 9th Ave.
Miami, FL 33136
Ph: (305)243-1088
Fax: (305)243-1119
URL: http://www.miami.edu
June Halper, Executive Director

35036 ■ Veterans Affairs Medical Center, Bay Pines
Multiple Sclerosis Center
10000 Bay Pines Blvd.
Bay Pines, FL 33744
Ph: (727)398-9387
Fax: (727)398-9554
URL: http://www.va.gov/ms

35037 ■ Veterans Affairs Medical Center, Miami
Multiple Sclerosis Center
1201 NW 16th St.
Miami, FL 33125
Ph: (305)324-3151
Fax: (305)324-3210
URL: http://www.va.gov/ms

GEORGIA

35038 ■ Augusta Multiple Sclerosis Center
Department of Neurology
1120 15th St., 6 West
Augusta, GA 30912
Ph: (706)721-1411
Fax: (706)721-6950
URL: http://www.neuro.mcg.edu

35039 ■ Emory University
Multiple Sclerosis Clinic
1365 Clifton Rd.
Atlanta, GA 30322
Ph: (404)778-3444
Fax: (404)778-5150
URL: http://www.emoryhealthcare.org/neurology/specialties/multiple-sclerosis/ind ex.html

35040 ■ Multiple Sclerosis Center of Atlanta
3200 Downwood Cir. NW, Ste. 550
Atlanta, GA 30327
Ph: (404)351-0205
Fax: (404)351-0924
URL: http://www.mscatl.org
Dr. William Stuart, Director

35041 ■ Shepherd Center, Inc.
Multiple Sclerosis Center
2020 Peachtree Rd. NW
Atlanta, GA 30309
Ph: (404)352-2020
Fax: (404)350-7526
URL: http://www.shepherd.org

ILLINOIS

35042 ■ Consultants in Neurology Multiple Sclerosis Center, Northbrook
1535 Lake Cook Rd., Ste. 601
Northbrook, IL 60062
Ph: (847)509-0270
Fax: (847)509-0273
URL: http://www.cinltd.com

35043 ■ Edward Hines Jr. Veterans Affairs Hospital
Multiple Sclerosis Center
5th & Roosevelt Rd., MC 151
Hines, IL 60141
Ph: (708)202-8387
Fax: (708)202-2263
URL: http://www.va.gov/ms

35044 ■ Loyola University Medical Center
Multiple Sclerosis Clinic
2160 S 1st Ave., Rm. 4009
Maywood, IL 60153
Ph: (708)216-8408
URL: http://www.loyolamedicine.org

35045 ■ Northwest Neurology
Multiple Sclerosis Clinic
2260 W Higgins Rd., Ste. 201
Hoffman Estates, IL 60195
Ph: (847)882-6604
Fax: (847)882-6228
URL: http://www.northwestneuro.com
Dr. George Katsamakis, Director

35046 ■ Northwestern University Medical Center
Department of Neurology
Galter Outpatient Facility
Multiple Sclerosis Clinic
675 N St. Clair St., Ste. 20-100
Chicago, IL 60611
Ph: (312)695-7950
URL: http://www.nmh.org

35047 ■ Rush Presbyterian-Saint Luke's Medical Center
Multiple Sclerosis Center
1725 W Harrison St.
Professional Bldg., Ste. 309
Chicago, IL 60612
Ph: (312)942-8011
Fax: (312)942-2253
URL: http://www.rush.edu

35048 ■ University of Chicago
Multiple Sclerosis Clinic
5841 Maryland Ave., MC2030
Chicago, IL 60637
Ph: (773)702-6386
Fax: (773)702-9060
URL: http://www.uchospitals.edu

35049 ■ Veterans Affairs Medical Center, Chicago--Lakeside
Multiple Sclerosis Center
333 E Huron
Chicago, IL 60611
Ph: (312)943-6600
Fax: (312)640-2153
URL: http://www.va.gov/ms

35050 ■ Veterans Affairs Medical Center, Chicago--Westside
Multiple Sclerosis Center
Dept. of Physical Medicine
820 S Damen Ave.
Chicago, IL 60612
Ph: (312)666-6500
Fax: (312)455-5821
URL: http://www.va.gov/ms

35051 ■ Veterans Affairs Medical Center, North Chicago
Multiple Sclerosis Center
3001 Greenbay Rd.
North Chicago, IL 60064
Ph: (847)688-1900
Fax: (847)578-3863
URL: http://www.va.gov/ms

INDIANA

35052 ■ Fort Wayne Neurological Center
Multiple Sclerosis Center
2622 Lake Ave.
Fort Wayne, IN 46805
Ph: (260)460-3100
Fax: (260)460-3130
URL: http://www.fwnc.com
Formerly: Gaylor Nickel Medical Center, Multiple Sclerosis Clinic.

35053 ■ Indiana University Multiple Sclerosis Center
541 Clinical Dr., CL292
Indianapolis, IN 46202-0270
Ph: (317)278-0270
Free: 866-740-1941
Fax: (317)274-3619
URL: http://www.indiana.edu

35054 ■ Veterans Affairs Medical Center, Indianapolis
Multiple Sclerosis Center
Neurology (127)
1481 W 10th St.
Indianapolis, IN 46202
Ph: (317)554-0227
Fax: (317)554-0215
URL: http://www.va.gov/ms

IOWA

35055 ■ Iowa City Veterans Affairs Medical Center
Multiple Sclerosis Center
601 Hwy. 6 W, MC 11E
Iowa City, IA 52246

Free: 800-637-0128
URL: http://www.va.gov/ms
Terry Clark, Director

35056 ■ Ruan Neurology Multiple Sclerosis Center
East Tower, Ste. A 100
1111 6th Ave.
Des Moines, IA 50314
Ph: (515)643-4500
Fax: (515)643-4505
URL: http://www.mercydesmoines.org/ruanneurology/index.cfm

35057 ■ Veterans Affairs Central Iowa Health Care System
Multiple Sclerosis Center
3600 30th St., MC DSM,J9
Des Moines, IA 50310
Free: 800-294-8387
URL: http://www.va.gov/ms
Dr. Debra Benjamin, Director

KANSAS

35058 ■ MidAmerica Neuroscience Institute
Multiple Sclerosis Center
8550 Marshall Dr., Ste. 100
Lenexa, KS 66214
Ph: (913)894-1500
Fax: (913)894-1502
URL: http://www.neurokc.com

35059 ■ University of Kansas Medical Center
Multiple Sclerosis Clinic
Department of Neurology
3599 Rainbow Blvd., MS-2012
Kansas City, KS 66160
Ph: (913)588-6970
Fax: (913)588-6965
URL: http://www.kumc.edu

35060 ■ Veterans Affairs Medical Center, Topeka
Multiple Sclerosis Center
2200 Gage Blvd.
Topeka, KS 66622
Ph: (785)350-3111
Fax: (785)350-4429
URL: http://www.va.gov/ms

KENTUCKY

35061 ■ The Multiple Sclerosis Center
3991 Dutchmans Ln., Ste. 316
Louisville, KY 40207
Ph: (502)569-4183
URL: http://www.loumscenter.com

LOUISIANA

35062 ■ Alexandria Veterans Affairs Medical Center
Multiple Sclerosis Center
PO Box 69004
Alexandria, LA 71360
Free: 800-375-8387
URL: http://www.va.gov/ms

35063 ■ Our Lady of Lourdes
Multiple Sclerosis Center
Dept. of Neurology
601 W St. Mary's Blvd., Ste. 309
Lafayette, LA 70506
Ph: (337)289-4978
Fax: (337)289-4951
URL: http://www.mscares.org
Dr. Steven Snatic, Director

35064 ■ Veterans Affairs Medical Center, Alexandria
Multiple Sclerosis Center
Medical SVC III
2495 Shreveport, Hwy. 71 N
Pineville, LA 71360
Ph: (318)473-0010
Fax: (318)483-0065
URL: http://www.va.gov/ms

35065 ■ Veterans Affairs Medical Center, New Orleans
Multiple Sclerosis Center
Neurology Section HF 165
1601 Perdido St.
New Orleans, LA 70146
Ph: (504)589-5227
Fax: (504)589-5232
URL: http://www.va.gov/ms

MAINE

35066 ■ Maine Medical Partners Neurology
Multiple Sclerosis Clinic
49 Spring St.
Scarborough, ME 04074
Ph: (207)883-1414
Fax: (207)883-1010
URL: http://www.medicalpartners.org
Dr. Paul Muscat, Director
Remarks: Maine Neurology.

35067 ■ Togus Veterans Affairs Medical Center
Multiple Sclerosis Center
1 VA Center
Augusta, ME 04330
Ph: (207)623-8411
Fax: (207)621-4819
URL: http://www.va.gov/ms

MARYLAND

35068 ■ Johns Hopkins Hospital
School of Medicine
Johns Hopkins Outpatient Center
Multiple Sclerosis Center
Pathology 627
609 N Wolfe St.
Baltimore, MD 21287
Ph: (410)614-1522
Fax: (410)502-6736
URL: http://www.hopkinsneuro.org

35069 ■ University of Maryland Medical Center
Maryland Center for Multiple Sclerosis
Frenkil Bldg.
16 S Eutaw St., 3rd Fl.
Baltimore, MD 21201
Ph: (410)328-5605
Fax: (410)328-5425
URL: http://www.umm.edu/ms

35070 ■ Veterans Affairs Medical System--East
Multiple Sclerosis Center of Excellence
Neurology Services 127
10 N Green St.
Baltimore, MD 21201
Ph: (410)605-7061
Fax: (410)605-7929
URL: http://www.va.gov/ms/

MASSACHUSETTS

35071 ■ Lahey Clinic, Inc.
Multiple Sclerosis Clinical Center
16 Hayden Ave.
Lexington, MA 02421
Ph: (781)372-7194
URL: http://www.lahey.org
Dr. Claudia Chaves, Director

35072 ■ Massachusetts General Hospital for Children
Pediatric Center of Excellence
Partners Pediatric Multiple Sclerosis Center
Yawkey Center for Outpatient Care, Ste. 6B
55 Fruit St.
Boston, MA 02114
Ph: (617)726-2664
URL: http://partnersmscenter.org/index.php?id=62&mn=12
Dr. Tanuja Chitnis, Director

35073 ■ Mount Auburn Hospital
Multiple Sclerosis Care Center
300 Mt. Auburn St., Ste. 316
Cambridge, MA 02238
Ph: (617)499-5047
Fax: (617)499-5441
URL: http://www.mountauburnhospital.org/

35074 ■ Newton Wellesley Hospital
Multiple Sclerosis Clinic
Rehab Services Dept.
2014 Washington St.
Newton, MA 02462
Ph: (617)969-1723
Fax: (617)630-0860
URL: http://www.nwh.org
Dr. Richard Toran, Director

35075 ■ Partners Multiple Sclerosis Center
1 Brookline Pl., Ste. 225
Boston, MA 02445
Ph: (617)525-6550
Fax: (617)525-6554
URL: http://www.partnersmscenter.org/

35076 ■ Saint Elizabeth's Medical Center
Multiple Sclerosis Center
736 Cambridge St.
Boston, MA 02135
Ph: (617)789-2378
Fax: (617)789-5177
URL: http://www.cchcs.org
Dr. Ellen Lathi, Director

35077 ■ Springfield Neurology Associates
Multiple Sclerosis Center
300 Carew St., Ste. 2
Springfield, MA 01104
Ph: (413)781-5045
Fax: (413)781-2510
URL: http://www.mscare.org/cmsc/

35078 ■ UMASS Memorial Medical Center
Multiple Sclerosis Clinic
55 Lake Ave. N
Worcester, MA 01655
Ph: (508)793-6568
Fax: (508)856-6778
URL: http://www.umassmemorial.org/MedicalCenterIP.cfm?id=1725

35079 ■ Veterans Affairs Medical Center, West Roxbury
Multiple Sclerosis Center
1400 VFW Pkwy.
West Roxbury, MA 02132
Ph: (617)323-7700
URL: http://www.va.gov/ms/

MICHIGAN

35080 ■ Henry Ford Hospital
Department of Neurology
Multiple Sclerosis Clinic
2799 W Grand Blvd.
Detroit, MI 48202
Ph: (313)916-2585
Fax: (313)916-3014
URL: http://www.henryford.com

35081 ■ Michigan Institute for Neurological Disorders (MIND)
Multiple Sclerosis Center
28595 Orchard Lake Rd., Ste. 200
Farmington Hills, MI 48334
Ph: (248)553-0010
Fax: (248)553-5957
URL: http://www.mindonline.com

35082 ■ Michigan Neurology Associates
Multiple Sclerosis Center
19699 E 8 Mile Rd.
Saint Clair Shores, MI 48080
Ph: (586)445-9900
Fax: (586)445-2641
URL: http://www.mnapc.org

35083 ■ Wayne State University
The School of Medicine
Department of Neurology
Comprehensive Clinical and Research Multiple Sclerosis Center
University Health Center, 8D
4201 St. Antoine
Detroit, MI 48201
Free: 866-263-1257
Fax: (313)745-4216
URL: http://www.med.wayne.edu/neurology

MINNESOTA

35084 ■ Mayo Clinic
T. Denny Sanford Pediatric Outpatient Center
200 1st St. SW
Rochester, MN 55905
Ph: (507)293-0378
URL: http://www.mayoclinic.org/pediatric-center/
Dr. Marc A. Patterson, Director

35085 ■ Minneapolis Clinic of Neurology
Shapiro Center for Multiple Sclerosis
4225 Golden Valley Rd.
Golden Valley, MN 55422
Ph: (763)588-0661
Fax: (763)529-9018
URL: http://www.minneapolisclinic.com/

35086 ■ Multiple Sclerosis Treatment and Research Center
4225 Golden Valley Rd.
Golden Valley, MN 55422
Ph: (763)588-0661
Fax: (763)287-2310
URL: http://www.minneapolisclinic.com

35087 ■ Saint Mary's/Duluth Clinic
Comprehensive Multiple Sclerosis Program
Polinsky Medical Rehab Center
400 E 3rd St.
Duluth, MN 55805
Ph: (218)786-3925
Fax: (218)722-4302
URL: http://www.smdc.org/

35088 ■ University of Minnesota
Multiple Sclerosis Center
516 Delaware St. SE, Clinic 1A
Minneapolis, MN 55455
Ph: (612)626-6688
Fax: (612)624-6181
URL: http://www.umphysicians.umn.edu/Clinics/clinic_381.asp

35089 ■ Veterans Affairs Medical Center, Minneapolis
Multiple Sclerosis Center
1 Veterans Dr.
Minneapolis, MN 55417
Ph: (612)725-2047
Fax: (612)725-2068
URL: http://www.va.gov/ms

MISSISSIPPI

35090 ■ G.V. Sonny Montgomery Veterans Affairs Medical Center
Multiple Sclerosis Center
1500 E Woodrow Wilson Dr., MC 127
Jackson, MS 39216
Free: 800-949-1009
URL: http://www.va.gov/ms
Dr. Eric Undesser, Director

35091 ■ University of Mississippi
Multiple Sclerosis Center
Neurology L-407
2500 N State St.
Jackson, MS 39216
Ph: (601)984-5500
Fax: (601)984-5503
URL: http://www.umc.edu

MISSOURI

35092 ■ Harry S. Truman Memorial Veterans Hospital
Multiple Sclerosis Center
800 Hospital Dr., MC SC/MED
Columbia, MO 65201
Ph: (573)814-6000
URL: http://www.va.gov/ms

35093 ■ Missouri Baptist Medical Center
Multiple Sclerosis Center for Innovations in Care
3009 N Ballas Rd., Ste. 207B
Saint Louis, MO 63131
Ph: (314)872-7333
URL: http://www.missouribaptist.org
Dr. Barry A. Singer, Director

35094 ■ Saint John's Mercy Medical Center
Multiple Sclerosis Center
Tower B, Ste. 5018
621 S New Ballas Rd.
Saint Louis, MO 63141
Ph: (314)569-6507
URL: http://www.mercy.net/stlouismo
Dr. Barbara Green, Director

35095 ■ Saint Louis University
Multiple Sclerosis Center
Dept. of Neuro & Psych
3660 Vista Ave.
Saint Louis, MO 63110
Ph: (314)977-6082
URL: http://www.slu.edu
Dr. Florian Thomas, Director

35096 ■ Saint Louis Veterans Affairs Medical Center
Multiple Sclerosis Center
1 Jefferson Barracks Dr.
Saint Louis, MO 63125
Ph: (314)894-6677
Fax: (314)845-5039
URL: http://www.va.gov/ms/

35097 ■ Washington University
John L. Trotter Multiple Sclerosis Center
660 S Euclid
Box 8111
Saint Louis, MO 63110
Ph: (314)362-3293
Fax: (314)747-1345
URL: http://www.neuro.wustl.edu/

MONTANA

35098 ■ SVH Neuroscience Center
Multiple Sclerosis Center
2900 12th Ave. N, Ste. 400E
Billings, MT 59101
Ph: (406)237-4290
Fax: (406)237-4291
URL: http://www.svh-mt.org

35099 ■ Veterans Affairs Montana Health Care System
Multiple Sclerosis Center
Dept. of Neurology & Rehab
3687 Veterans Dr.
Fort Harrison, MT 59636
Free: 877-468-8387
URL: http://www.va.gov/ms
Dr. Mark Dietz, Director

NEBRASKA

35100 ■ University of Nebraska Medical Center
Multiple Sclerosis Clinic
Neurological Sciences
982045 Nebraska Medical Center
Omaha, NE 68198
Ph: (402)559-7857
Fax: (402)559-3545
URL: http://www.unmc.edu

NEVADA

35101 ■ Renown Institute for Neurosciences
Multiple Sclerosis Center
10085 Double R Blvd., Ste. 310
Reno, NV 89521
Ph: (775)982-7310
URL: http://www.renown.org

35102 ■ Veterans Affairs Sierra Nevada Health Care System
Multiple Sclerosis Center
1000 Locust St.
Reno, NV 89502
Ph: (775)328-1297
URL: http://www.va.gov/ms
Dr. John Peacock, Director

35103 ■ Veterans Affairs Southern Nevada Health Care System
Multiple Sclerosis Center
MC Neurology Services
North Las Vegas, NV 89036
Free: 877-252-4866
URL: http://www.va.gov/ms

NEW BRUNSWICK

35104 ■ Saint John Regional Hospital
Multiple Sclerosis Center
400 University Ave., 5DN
Saint John, NB, Canada E2L 4L2
Ph: (506)649-2718
Fax: (506)648-7765
URL: http://www.mscare.org/cmsc/

NEW HAMPSHIRE

35105 ■ Upper Valley Neurology Neurosurgery
Multiple Sclerosis Clinic of New Hampshire
106 Hanover St.
Lebanon, NH 03766
Ph: (603)448-0447
Free: 888-391-9737
Fax: (603)448-0019
URL: http://www.uvnn.com/

35106 ■ Veterans Affairs Medical Center, Manchester
Multiple Sclerosis Center
SCI-D Clinic (E02)
718 Smyth Rd.
Manchester, NH 03104
Ph: (603)624-4366
Fax: (603)314-1613
URL: http://www.va.gov/ms/

NEW JERSEY

35107 ■ CentraState
Linda E. Cardinale Multiple Sclerosis Center
901 W Main St.
Freehold, NJ 07728
Ph: (732)294-2505
Fax: (732)761-8084
URL: http://www.centrastate.com

35108 ■ Holy Name Hospital
Multiple Sclerosis Center
718 Teaneck Rd.
Teaneck, NJ 07666

Ph: (201)837-0727
Fax: (201)837-8504
URL: http://www.holyname.org/ms_center.asp

35109 ■ Kessler Foundation Research Center
Multiple Sclerosis Center
1199 Pleasant Valley Way
West Orange, NJ 07052
Ph: (973)530-3600
Fax: (973)736-7880
URL: http://www.kessler-rehab.com

35110 ■ Robert Wood Johnson Center for Multiple Sclerosis
Clinical Academic Bldg., 6th Fl.
125 Paterson St.
New Brunswick, NJ 08901
Ph: (732)235-7733
Fax: (732)235-7041
URL: http://www2.umdnj.edu/nurolweb

35111 ■ Saint Barnabas Hospital
Multiple Sclerosis Center
200 South Orange Ave.
Ste. 124A
Livingston, NJ 07039
Ph: (973)322-7478
Fax: (973)322-7802
URL: http://www.barnabashealth.org/hospitals/ambulatory_care_center/programs/ms/ index.html

35112 ■ University of Medicine and Dentistry of New Jersey
Multiple Sclerosis Diagnostic and Treatment Center
90 Bergen St., Ste. 8100
Newark, NJ 07103
Ph: (973)972-7998
URL: http://www.rwjms.umdnj.edu/neurology

35113 ■ Veterans Affairs Medical Center, East Orange
Multiple Sclerosis Center
385 Tremont Ave.
East Orange, NJ 07018
Ph: (973)676-1000
Fax: (973)676-1648
URL: http://www.va.gov/ms

NEW MEXICO

35114 ■ University of New Mexico
Health Sciences Center
Multiple Sclerosis Specialty Clinic
1101 Yale Blvd. NE
Albuquerque, NM 87131
Ph: (505)925-4531
Fax: (505)272-4056
URL: http://mic.health.unm.edu

35115 ■ Veterans Affairs Medical Center, Albuquerque
Multiple Sclerosis Center
1501 San Pedro Dr. SW
Albuquerque, NM 87108
Ph: (505)256-2752
Fax: (505)256-2870
URL: http://www.va.gov/ms

NEW YORK

35116 ■ Albany Medical College
Center for Multiple Sclerosis
Neurology MC-70
47 New Scotland Ave.
Albany, NY 12208
Ph: (518)262-6611
Fax: (518)262-6612
URL: http://www.amc.edu/neurosciences

35117 ■ Alpha Neurology PC
Comprehensive Multiple Sclerosis Center of Staten Island
27 New Dorp Ln.
Staten Island, NY 10306
Ph: (718)667-3800
Fax: (718)667-3590
URL: http://www.alphaneurology.com

35118 ■ Bronx--Lebanon Hospital
Multiple Sclerosis Center
1770 Grand Concourse, Ste. 2G
Bronx, NY 10457
Ph: (718)901-8142
URL: http://www.bronx-leb.org/InternalMedicine.html
Dr. Rene Elkin, Director

35119 ■ Capital Neurological Associates
Multiple Sclerosis Center
400 Patroon Creek Blvd., Ste. 210
Albany, NY 12206
Ph: (518)459-8106
Fax: (518)489-6441
URL: http://www.capitalneuro.com

35120 ■ Center for Disability Services
Multiple Sclerosis Clinic
Dept. of Neurology
314 S Manning Blvd.
Albany, NY 12208
Ph: (518)437-5535
Fax: (518)437-5965
URL: http://www.cfdsny.org

35121 ■ Jacobs Neurological Institute and William C. Baird Multiple Sclerosis Research Center
100 High St.
Buffalo, NY 14203
Ph: (716)859-7501
Fax: (716)859-2430
URL: http://www.thejni.com/treatment_centers/pediatric.html

35122 ■ Maimonides Medical Center
Linda Morgante Multiple Sclerosis Care Center
883 65th St.
Brooklyn, NY 11220
Ph: (718)283-7470
Fax: (718)635-6082
URL: http://www.maimonidesmed.org/

35123 ■ Mount Sinai Medical Center
Corrine Goldsmith Dickinson Center for Multiple Sclerosis
5 E 98th St.
New York, NY 10029
Ph: (212)241-6854
Fax: (212)423-0440
URL: http://www.mountsinai.org

35124 ■ Multiple Sclerosis Center of Northeastern New York
1205 Troy-Schenectady Rd., Ste. 105
Latham, NY 12110
Ph: (518)785-1000
Fax: (518)785-5000
URL: http://www.msneny.empireneuro.org

35125 ■ New York University Hospital for Joint Diseases
Multiple Sclerosis Comprehensive Care Center
301 E 17th St., Ste. 544
New York, NY 10003
Ph: (212)598-6305
Fax: (212)598-6214
URL: http://hjd.med.nyu.edu/ms

35126 ■ Rochester Multiple Sclerosis Center
601 Elmwood Ave., Box 605
Rochester, NY 14612
Ph: (585)273-1184
Fax: (585)275-9953
URL: http://www.rochesterms.org

35127 ■ South Shore Neurologic Associates, PC
Comprehensive Multiple Sclerosis Care Center
77 Medford Ave.
Patchogue, NY 11772
Ph: (631)758-1910
Fax: (631)758-5704
URL: http://www.southshoreneurologic.com

35128 ■ State University of New York
Jacobs Neurology Institute
Pediatric Center of Excellence
Pediatric Multiple Sclerosis Center
219 Bryan St.
Buffalo, NY 14222
Ph: (716)878-7367
Free: 877-878-7367
E-mail: PedMS@thejni.org
URL: http://www.pedms.com
Dr. Bianca Weinstock-Guttman, Director

35129 ■ State University of New York, Stony Brook
Department of Neurology
Comprehensive Multiple Sclerosis Care Center
Health Science Center, T-12, Rm. 020
Stony Brook, NY 11794-8121
Ph: (631)444-7802
Fax: (631)444-6438
E-mail: info@pediatricmscenter.org
URL: http://www.pediatricmscenter.org

35130 ■ SUNY Upstate Medical University
Department of Neurology
Multiple Sclerosis Center
90 Presidential Plaza
Syracuse, NY 13202
Ph: (315)464-4243
Fax: (315)464-7328
URL: http://www.upstate.edu/uh/

35131 ■ Veterans Affairs Medical Center, Albany
Multiple Sclerosis Center
113 Holland Ave., MC 111G
Albany, NY 12208
Ph: (518)626-6497
Fax: (518)626-6495
URL: http://www.va.gov/ms

35132 ■ Veterans Affairs Medical Center, Brooklyn
Multiple Sclerosis Center
800 Poly Pl.
Brooklyn, NY 11209
Ph: (718)630-3724
Fax: (718)439-3577
URL: http://www.va.gov/ms

35133 ■ Veterans Affairs Medical Center, Buffalo
Multiple Sclerosis Center
3495 Bailey Ave.
Buffalo, NY 14215
Ph: (716)862-3653
Fax: (716)862-3475
URL: http://www.va.gov/ms

35134 ■ Veterans Affairs Medical Center, New York
Multiple Sclerosis Center
423 E 23rd St.
New York, NY 10010

Ph: (212)951-3320
Fax: (212)951-3246
URL: http://www.va.gov/ms

35135 ■ Veterans Affairs Medical Center, Northport
Multiple Sclerosis Center
79 Middleville Rd.
Northport, NY 11768
Ph: (631)754-7962
URL: http://www.va.gov/ms

NEWFOUNDLAND AND LABRADOR

35136 ■ Saint John's Multiple Sclerosis Center
300 Prince Philip Dr.
Saint John's, NL, Canada A1B 3V6
Ph: (709)777-6594
Fax: (709)777-6656
URL: http://www.mscare.org/cmsc/

NORTH CAROLINA

35137 ■ Advance Neurology and Pain
Multiple Sclerosis Center
152 E Kinderton Way, Ste. 101
Advance, NC 27006
Ph: (336)940-2781
Fax: (336)940-2782
URL: http://www.cornerstonehealthcare.com

35138 ■ Carolinas Healthcare System
Multiple Sclerosis Center
1010 Edgehill Rd.
Charlotte, NC 28207
Ph: (704)446-1900
Free: 800-924-7620
Fax: (704)446-1289
URL: http://www.carolinashealthcare.org

35139 ■ Raleigh Neurology Associates
Multiple Sclerosis Center
1540 Sunday Dr.
Raleigh, NC 27607
Ph: (919)782-3456
Fax: (919)420-1688
URL: http://www.raleighneurology.com

35140 ■ Veterans Affairs Medical Center, Ashville
Multiple Sclerosis Center
15 S Oak Forest Dr.
Asheville, NC 28805
Ph: (828)687-9380
Fax: (828)299-5946
URL: http://www.va.gov/ms

35141 ■ Veterans Affairs Medical Center, Durham
Multiple Sclerosis Center
508 Fulton St., MC 117
Durham, NC 27705
Ph: (919)286-6874
Fax: (919)416-5913
URL: http://www.va.gov/ms

35142 ■ Wake Forest University
Multiple Sclerosis Center
Dept. of Neurology
Medical Center Blvd.
Winston Salem, NC 27157
Ph: (336)716-4101
Fax: (336)716-2810
URL: http://www.wakehealth.edu/neurology/multiple-sclerosis-program.htm

NORTH DAKOTA

35143 ■ Sanford NeuroScience
Multiple Sclerosis Center
700 1st Ave. S
Fargo, ND 58103
Ph: (701)234-4036
Fax: (701)234-4151
URL: http://www.sanfordhealth.org/MedicalServices/Specialties/Neurology
Remarks: MeritCare Neuroscience.

NOVA SCOTIA

35144 ■ Dalhousie University
Multiple Sclerosis Research Unit
1341 Summer St.
Halifax, NS, Canada B3H 4K4
Ph: (902)473-5734
Fax: (902)725-1512
URL: http://www.cdha.nshealth.ca

OHIO

35145 ■ Cleveland Clinic Foundation
Mellen Center for Multiple Sclerosis Treatment and Research
9500 Euclid Ave., U-10
Cleveland, OH 44195
Ph: (216)445-8600
Fax: (216)445-7013
URL: http://my.clevelandclinic.org

35146 ■ Louis Stokes Veterans Affairs Medical Center
Multiple Sclerosis Center
10701 East Blvd.
Cleveland, OH 44106
Ph: (216)421-3040
Fax: (216)421-3040
URL: http://www.va.gov/ms/

35147 ■ Neurological Associates
Mid--Ohio Multiple Sclerosis Center
931 Chatham Ln., Ste. 200
Columbus, OH 43221
Ph: (614)457-4880
Fax: (614)457-4890
URL: http://www.neuroassociates.com

35148 ■ Neurology Specialists Inc.
Multiple Sclerosis Center
West Medical Plz.
1 Elizabeth Pl., Ste. 210
Dayton, OH 45417
Ph: (937)495-0000
Fax: (937)853-1504

35149 ■ Oak Clinic for Multiple Sclerosis
3838 Massillon Rd.
Ste. 360
Uniontown, OH 44685
Ph: (330)896-9625
URL: http://www.oakclinic.com

35150 ■ Ohio State University Medical Center
Multiple Sclerosis Clinic
Dept. of Neurology
395 W 12th Ave., 7th Fl.
Columbus, OH 43210
Ph: (614)293-4969
Fax: (614)293-6111
URL: http://neurology.osu.edu

35151 ■ Veterans Affairs Medical Center, Dayton
Multiple Sclerosis Center
Neurology Services
4100 W 3rd St.
Dayton, OH 45428
Ph: (513)262-2161
Fax: (513)267-3983
URL: http://www.va.gov/ms/

35152 ■ Veterans Affairs Medical Center, Ohio
Multiple Sclerosis Center
PM&R 117
17273 State Rte. 104
Chillicothe, OH 45601
Ph: (740)773-1141
Fax: (740)772-7144
URL: http://www.va.gov/ms/

35153 ■ Waddell Center for Multiple Sclerosis
University Medical Arts Bldg.
222 Piedmont Ave., Ste. 3200
Cincinnati, OH 45219
Ph: (515)475-9235
Fax: (515)558-0412
URL: http://www.waddellcenterforMS.com

OKLAHOMA

35154 ■ Veterans Affairs Medical Center, Oklahoma City
Multiple Sclerosis Center
Neurosciences Center
921 NE 13th St.
Oklahoma City, OK 73104
Ph: (405)270-0501
Fax: (405)271-5723
URL: http://www.va.gov/ms/

ONTARIO

35155 ■ Hamilton Multiple Sclerosis Center
1200 Main St. W, Rm. 4 U3
Hamilton, ON, Canada L8N 3Z5
Ph: (905)521-2100
Fax: (905)521-2656
URL: http://www.mscare.org/cmsc/

35156 ■ Ottawa Hospital
Multiple Sclerosis Clinic
501 Smyth Rd., Box 606, Rm. 4128
Ottawa, ON, Canada K1H 8L6
Ph: (613)737-8532
Fax: (613)739-6631
URL: http://www.ottawahospital.on.ca

35157 ■ Saint Michael's Hospital
Multiple Sclerosis Center
Shuter Wing, No. 3-003
30 Bond St.
Toronto, ON, Canada M5B 1W8
Ph: (416)864-5377
Fax: (416)864-5378
URL: http://www.stmichaelshospital.com

OREGON

35158 ■ Oregon Health Science University
Multiple Sclerosis Center
3181 SW Sam Jackson Park Rd., CR 120
Portland, OR 97239
Ph: (503)494-7321
URL: http://www.ohsu.edu/ms

35159 ■ Portland Veterans Affairs Medical Center
3710 SW US Veterans Hospital Rd., 153
Portland, OR 97239
Ph: (503)220-8262
Fax: (503)220-3439
URL: http://www.va.gov/ms/
Dr. Dennis Bourdette, Director

35160 ■ Providence Multiple Sclerosis Center
9427 SW Barnes Rd., No. 595
Portland, OR 97225
Ph: (503)216-1060
Fax: (503)216-1066
URL: http://www.providence.org/oregon
Dr. Stanley Cohan, Director

PENNSYLVANIA

35161 ■ Allegheny University
Multiple Sclerosis Treatment Center
420 E North Ave., Ste. 206
Pittsburgh, PA 15212

Ph: (412)359-8850
Fax: (412)359-8878
URL: http://www.allegheny.edu

35162 ■ Associates in Neurology of Pittsburgh
Multiple Sclerosis Center
5750 Centre Ave., Ste. 100
Pittsburgh, PA 15206
Ph: (412)361-4576
Fax: (412)361-1014
URL: http://anpneuro.com

35163 ■ Drexel Multiple Sclerosis Center
219 N Broad St., 7th Fl.
Philadelphia, PA 19107
Ph: (215)762-6915
Fax: (215)762-6914
URL: http://www.drexelmed.edu

35164 ■ Geisinger Medical Center
Multiple Sclerosis Clinic
100 N Academy Ave.
Danville, PA 17822
Ph: (570)271-6419
Fax: (570)271-5874
URL: http://www.geisinger.org

35165 ■ Good Shepherd Rehabilitation Hospital
Multiple Sclerosis Center
MS Wellness Program & MS Day Hospital
850 S 5th St.
Allentown, PA 18103
Ph: (610)778-9303
Fax: (610)776-3225
URL: http://www.goodshepherdrehab.org/ms-wellness-program

35166 ■ Greenstein Neurology and Multiple Sclerosis Institute
1341 N Delaware Ave., Ste. 212
Philadelphia, PA 19125
Ph: (267)597-3830
Fax: (267)597-3831
URL: http://www.mscare.org/cmsc/

35167 ■ Lehigh Valley Hospital
Multiple Sclerosis Center of the Lehigh Valley
1250 S Cedar Crest Blvd., Ste. 405
Allentown, PA 18103
Ph: (610)402-8420
Fax: (610)402-1689
URL: http://www.lvh.org

35168 ■ Pennsylvania State University Hershey Medical Center
Multiple Sclerosis Diagnostic and Evaluation Center
Dept. of Neurology
30 Hope Dr.
Hershey, PA 17033
Ph: (717)531-1804
Fax: (717)531-0384
URL: http://www.hmc.psu.edu

35169 ■ Saint Luke's Hospital
Multiple Sclerosis Center
Integrated Health Campus
240 Cetronia Rd., Ste. 210A
Allentown, PA 18104
Ph: (610)366-9160
Fax: (610)336-4490
URL: http://www.mystlukesonline.org

35170 ■ Thomas Jefferson University
Comprehensive Multiple Sclerosis Center
Neurology Dept.
900 Walnut St., Ste. 200
Philadelphia, PA 19107
Ph: (215)955-7310
Fax: (215)503-2990
URL: http://www.jefferson.edu/neurology

35171 ■ University of Pennsylvania Hospital System
Comprehensive Multiple Sclerosis Care Center
3 W Gates Bldg.
3400 Spruce St.
Philadelphia, PA 19104
Ph: (215)349-8110
Fax: (215)349-5579
URL: http://medicine.com/neuro/services/ms/index.html

35172 ■ University of Pittsburgh Medical Center
Multiple Sclerosis Center
3471 5th Ave., Ste. 810
Pittsburgh, PA 15213
Ph: (412)692-4920
Fax: (412)692-4907
URL: http://www.upmc.com

35173 ■ Veterans Affairs Medical Center, Lebanon
Multiple Sclerosis Center
1700 S Lincoln Ave.
Lebanon, PA 17042
Ph: (717)228-5929
Fax: (717)228-5982
URL: http://www.va.gov/ms/

35174 ■ Veterans Affairs Medical Center, Philadelphia
Multiple Sclerosis Center
3900 Woodland Ave.
Philadelphia, PA 19104
Ph: (215)823-5850
Fax: (215)823-5969
URL: http://www.va.gov/ms/

35175 ■ Veterans Affairs Medical Center, Pittsburgh
Multiple Sclerosis Center
University Dr. C
Pittsburgh, PA 15240
Ph: (412)360-6185
URL: http://www.va.gov/ms/

35176 ■ Wellspan Multiple Sclerosis Center
290 St. Charles Way
York, PA 17402
Ph: (717)851-5503
Fax: (717)851-5507
URL: http://www.wellspan.org

QUEBEC

35177 ■ Montreal Neurological Hospital
Multiple Sclerosis Research Clinic
3801 University St., Rm. 267
Montreal, QC, Canada H3A 2B4
Ph: (514)398-1931
Fax: (514)398-7454
URL: http://www.msclinic.ca

35178 ■ Multiple Sclerosis Center for the Greater Quebec Area
IRDPQ
525 Blvd. Wilfrid-Hamel
Quebec City, QC, Canada G1M 2S8
Ph: (418)529-9141
Fax: (418)649-3703
URL: http://www.mscare.org/cmsc/

RHODE ISLAND

35179 ■ Rhode Island Hospital
Multiple Sclerosis Center
2 Dudley St., Ste. 555
Providence, RI 02905
Ph: (401)444-3032
URL: http://www.lifespan.org
Dr. Syed Rizvi, Director

SOUTH CAROLINA

35180 ■ Absher Neurology
Multiple Sclerosis Center
155 Halton Rd., Ste. B
Greenville, SC 29607
Ph: (864)286-8222
Fax: (864)286-3356
URL: http://www.absherneurology.com

35181 ■ Carolina Neurology
Multiple Sclerosis Center
541 Floyd Rd.
Spartanburg, SC 29307
Ph: (864)585-6179
Fax: (864)583-5403
URL: http://www.carolinaneurologyspartanburg.com

35182 ■ Ralph H. Johnson Veterans Affairs Medical Center
Multiple Sclerosis Center
109 Bee St.
Charleston, SC 29401
Ph: (843)793-3221
Fax: (843)793-8626
URL: http://www.va.gov/ms/

35183 ■ William Jennings Bryan Dorn Veterans Affairs Medical Center
Multiple Sclerosis Center
6439 Garners Ferry Rd.
Columbia, SC 29209
Ph: (803)776-4000
Fax: (803)695-7932
URL: http://www.va.gov/ms

SOUTH DAKOTA

35184 ■ Neurology Associates
Great Plains Multiple Sclerosis Center
1100 E 21 St., Ste. 506
Sioux Falls, SD 57105
Ph: (605)315-0844
Dr. Lisa Viola, Director

35185 ■ Royal C. Johnson Veterans Medical Center
Multiple Sclerosis Center
2501 W 22nd St.
Sioux Falls, SD 57105
Ph: (605)336-3230
URL: http://www.va.gov/ms
Dr. Xuesheng Feng, Director

35186 ■ Veterans Affairs Black Hills Health Care System
Fort Meade Veterans Affairs Medical Center
Multiple Sclerosis Center
113 Comanche Rd., MC GECR
Fort Meade, SD 57741
Free: 800-743-1070
URL: http://www.va.gov/ms
Dr. Laurie Weisensee, Director

TENNESSEE

35187 ■ Advanced Neurosciences Institute
Multiple Sclerosis Center
101 Forrest Crossing Blvd., Ste. 103
Franklin, TN 37064
Ph: (615)791-5470
URL: http://www.neurosci.us

35188 ■ Hope Neurology Clinic PLLC
10800 Parkside Dr., Ste. 202
Knoxville, TN 37934
Ph: (865)218-6222
Fax: (865)218-6220
URL: http://www.hopeneurology.com
Dr. Sibyl Wray, Director

35189 ■ Saint Thomas Neurosciences Institute
Center for Multiple Sclerosis Treatment
4230 Harding Rd., Ste. 501W
Nashville, TN 37205
Ph: (615)383-8575
Fax: (615)383-8190
URL: http://www.stthomas.org

TEXAS

35190 ■ Baylor College of Medicine/The Methodist Hospital
Multiple Sclerosis Center
6501 Fannin, NB 100
Houston, TX 77030
Ph: (713)798-7707
Fax: (713)798-6273
URL: http://www.bcm.edu/neurology/ms

35191 ■ El Paso Veterans Affairs Health Care System
Multiple Sclerosis Center
5001 N Piedras
El Paso, TX 79930
Free: 800-672-3782
URL: http://www.va.gov/ms
Dr. Viswanatha Kharidi, Director

35192 ■ Memorial Hermann Hospital
The Institute of Rehabilitation and Research (TIRR)
Multiple Sclerosis Center
1333 Moursund St.
Houston, TX 77030
Ph: (713)797-7500
Fax: (713)797-7564
URL: http://www.memorialhermanntirr.org

35193 ■ Multiple Sclerosis Center of South Texas
3603 Paesanos Way, Ste. 300
San Antonio, TX 78231
Ph: (210)853-3957
Fax: (210)692-9311
URL: http://www.mscenterofsouthtexas.org

35194 ■ University of Texas Health Science Center at Houston
Multiple Sclerosis Clinic
Dept. of Neurology
6410 Fannin St., Ste. 1014
Houston, TX 77030
Ph: (832)325-7082
Fax: (832)512-2239
URL: http://www.neurology.uth.tmc.edu
Dr. Raymond Martin, Director

35195 ■ University of Texas Southwestern Medical Center
Multiple Sclerosis Center
5323 Harry Hines Blvd.
Dallas, TX 75390
Ph: (214)645-0555
Fax: (214)645-0556
URL: http://www.utsouthwestern.edu

35196 ■ Veterans Affairs Medical Center/University of Texas Health Science Center
Multiple Sclerosis Center
7703 Floyd Curl Dr.
San Antonio, TX 78284
Ph: (210)617-5161
Fax: (210)567-4659
URL: http://www.va.gov/ms

35197 ■ Veterans Affairs North Texas Healthcare System
Multiple Sclerosis Center
Neurology Service
4500 S Lancaster Rd.
Dallas, TX 75216
Ph: (214)857-0114
Fax: (214)857-1759
URL: http://www.va.gov/ms/

UTAH

35198 ■ Rocky Mountain Multiple Sclerosis Clinic
370 E 9th Ave., Ste. 106
Salt Lake City, UT 84103
Ph: (801)408-5700
Fax: (801)408-5704
URL: http://www.mscare.org/cmsc

35199 ■ University of Utah School of Medicine
Multiple Sclerosis Center
729 Arapeen Way
Salt Lake City, UT 84108
Ph: (801)587-8127
URL: http://www.medicine.utah.edu/neurology

35200 ■ Veterans Affairs Medical Center, Salt Lake City
Multiple Sclerosis Center
500 Foothill Dr.
Salt Lake City, UT 84148
Ph: (801)584-1292
Fax: (801)582-6908
URL: http://www.va.gov/ms

35201 ■ Western Neurological Associates
Multiple Sclerosis Center
1151 East 3900 S St., B-150
Salt Lake City, UT 84124
Ph: (801)262-3441
Fax: (801)269-9005
URL: http://wna-pc.com

VERMONT

35202 ■ Comprehensive Multiple Sclerosis Center of Southern Vermont
160 Benmont Ave., Ste. 25
Bennington, VT 05201
Ph: (802)447-7577
Fax: (802)447-2676
URL: http://www.vtmscenter.com

35203 ■ Fletcher Allen Health Care
Multiple Sclerosis Center
UHC Campus
1 S Prospect St.
Burlington, VT 05401
Ph: (802)847-4589
Fax: (802)847-9489
URL: http://www.fletcherallen.org

VIRGINIA

35204 ■ Integrated Neurology Services
Multiple Sclerosis Center
6355 Walker Ln., Ste. 313
Alexandria, VA 22310
Ph: (703)313-9111
Fax: (703)313-4945
URL: http://www.integratedneurologyservices.com

35205 ■ Neurology Center of Fairfax
Multiple Sclerosis Center
3020 Hamaker Ct., Ste. 400
Fairfax, VA 22031
Ph: (703)876-0800
Fax: (703)876-0866
URL: http://www.neurologycenteroffairfax.com

35206 ■ University of Virginia Health System
James Q. Miller Consultative Multiple Sclerosis Clinic
500 Ray C. Hunt Dr.
Charlottesville, VA 22903
Ph: (434)243-5611
Fax: (434)982-3544
URL: http://www.medicine.virginia.edu

35207 ■ Veterans Affairs Medical Center, Salem
Multiple Sclerosis Center
1970 Roanoke Blvd.
Salem, VA 24153
Ph: (540)982-2463
Fax: (540)224-1963
URL: http://www.va.gov/ms

WASHINGTON

35208 ■ Cascadia Multiple Sclerosis Center
11 Bellwether Way, Ste. 210
Bellingham, WA 98225
Ph: (360)752-9919
Fax: (360)752-1647
URL: http://www.cascadiamultiplesclerosiscenter.net

35209 ■ Evergreen Neuroscience Institute
Multiple Sclerosis Center
12039 NE 128th St., Ste. 200
Kirkland, WA 98034
Ph: (425)899-5350
Fax: (425)899-5355
URL: http://www.evergreenhospital.org
Dr. Raymond Park, Director

35210 ■ Providence Holy Family Hospital
Multiple Sclerosis Center
5901 N Lidgerwood, Ste. 25
Spokane, WA 99208
Ph: (509)489-5019
URL: http://www2.providence.org/
Dr. Roger N. Cooke, Director

35211 ■ Rockwood Clinic
Rockwood Multiple Sclerosis Center
400 E 5th Ave.
Spokane, WA 99202
Ph: (509)838-2531
Fax: (509)459-1522
URL: http://www.rockwoodclinic.com

35212 ■ Spokane Veterans Affairs Medical Center
Multiple Sclerosis Center
MC Neurology
4815 N Assembly St.
Spokane, WA 99205
Free: 800-325-7940
URL: http://www.va.gov/ms
Dr. Heidi Heller, Director

35213 ■ University of Washington Medical Center
Western Multiple Sclerosis Center
Rehabilitation Unit
1959 NE Pacific St.
Seattle, WA 98195
Ph: (206)598-3344
Fax: (206)598-2813
URL: http://msrrtc.washington.edu

35214 ■ Veterans Affairs Puget Sound Health Care System
Multiple Sclerosis Center of Excellence, West
1660 S Columbian Way, 117-MSCOE
Seattle, WA 98108
Ph: (206)277-4688
Fax: (206)277-4827
URL: http://www.va.gov/ms

35215 ■ Virginia Mason Multiple Sclerosis Center
Mailstop: X7-NEU
1100 9th Ave.
Seattle, WA 98101
Ph: (206)223-6764
Fax: (206)625-7240
URL: http://www.virginiamason.org/body.cfm?id=708

WISCONSIN

35216 ■ Aurora Bay Care Medical Center
Multiple Sclerosis Center
2845 Greenbrier Rd., Ste. 140
Green Bay, WI 54308
Ph: (920)288-8100
URL: http://www.aurorabaycare.com
Dr. Merle Teetzen, Director

35217 ■ Clement J. Zablocki Veterans Affairs Medical Center
Multiple Sclerosis Center
5000 W National Ave.
Milwaukee, WI 53295
Ph: (414)384-2000
URL: http://www.va.gov/ms

35218 ■ Marshfield Clinic
Multiple Sclerosis Center
1000 N Oak Ave.
Marshfield, WI 54449
Ph: (715)387-5351
Fax: (715)387-5727
URL: http://www.marshfieldclinic.org/

35219 ■ Medical College of Wisconsin
Department of Neurology
Multiple Sclerosis Clinic
Lutheran Hospital
9200 W Wisconsin Ave.
Milwaukee, WI 53226
Ph: (414)805-5203
Fax: (414)259-0469
URL: http://www.mcw.edu

35220 ■ Pro Health Care Neuroscience Center
Multiple Sclerosis Center
725 American Ave.
Waukesha, WI 53188
Ph: (262)928-8668
URL: http://www.prohealthcare.org/services/NeuroscienceCenter/
Dr. Stanya Smith, Director

35221 ■ William S. Middleton Memorial Veterans Affairs Hospital
Multiple Sclerosis Center
2500 Overlook Terr.
Madison, WI 53705
Free: 888-478-8321
URL: http://www.va.gov/ms
Dr. Michael Carrithers, Director

WYOMING

35222 ■ Cheyenne Veterans Affairs Medical Center
Multiple Sclerosis Center
2360 E Pershing Blvd.
Cheyenne, WY 82001
Free: 888-483-9127
URL: http://www.va.gov/ms
Dr. Roy Kanter, Director

Chapter 25
Muscular Dystrophy Clinics

Listed below are hospital-affiliated clinics sponsored by the Muscular Dystrophy Association (MDA). Entries are arranged geographically by states, then alphabetically by organization names within states. See the "User's Guide" located at the front of this directory for additional information.

ALABAMA

35223 ■ Children's Hospital--Birmingham Neurology Office
MDA Clinic
1600 7th Ave. S, Clinic 11
Birmingham, AL 35233
Ph: (205)939-9588
Fax: (205)939-6184
URL: http://www.mda.org/
Dr. Charles R. Law, Director

35224 ■ Huntsville Hospital
MDA Clinic
725 Madison St.
Huntsville, AL 35801
URL: http://www.mda.org
Dr. Anjane Yula Alapati, Director

35225 ■ University of Alabama Birmingham Hospital
MDA Clinic
Kirklin Clinic, 5th Fl.
2000 6th Ave. S
Birmingham, AL 35233
URL: http://www.mda.org
Dr. Gwendoly C. Claussen, Director

ALASKA

35226 ■ Alaska Regional Hospital Neurology Center
3841 Piper St, Ste. T345
Anchorage, AK 99508
Ph: (907)565-6000
Fax: (877)800-1969
URL: http://akneurologycenter.com
Dr. Franklin Ellenson, Director

ARIZONA

35227 ■ Center at University of Arizona Health Sciences
MDA Center
1501 N Campbell Ave.
Tucson, AZ 85724
Ph: (520)626-6609
Fax: (520)626-6925
E-mail: lrstern@u.arizona.edu
URL: http://www.mda.org/
Dr. Lawrence Z. Stern, Director

35228 ■ Children's Clinics for Rehabilitative Services
MDA Clinic
2600 N Wyatt Dr.
Tucson, AZ 85712
URL: http://www.mda.org/
Dr. Timothy M. Miller, Director

35229 ■ Saint Joseph's Hospital and Medical Center
MDA/ALS Center
Barrow Neurological Institute
500 W Thomas Rd., Ste. 710
Phoenix, AZ 85013
Ph: (602)406-6262
Fax: (602)406-4608
E-mail: shafeeq.ladha@chw.edu
URL: http://www.mda.org/
Dr. Shafeeq Ladha, Director

35230 ■ University Physicians Healthcare Hospital
MDA/ALS Center
2800 E Ajo Way
Tucson, AZ 85713
Ph: (520)874-2747
Fax: (520)874-2742
E-mail: kscherer@uph.org
URL: http://www.mda.org/
Dr. Katalin Scherer, Director

ARKANSAS

35231 ■ University of Arkansas for Medical Sciences
MDA/ALS Clinic
4301 W Markham St., Slot 500
Little Rock, AR 72205
Ph: (502)686-5135
Fax: (501)686-8689
E-mail: rudnickistacya@uams.edu
URL: http://www.mda.org/
Dr. Stacy Rudnicki, Director

CALIFORNIA

35232 ■ California Pacific Medical Center
Forbes Norris MDA/ALS Research Center
2324 Sacramento St., Ste. 150
San Francisco, CA 94115
Ph: (415)600-3604
Fax: (415)923-6567
E-mail: katzjs@sutterhealth.org
URL: http://www.mda.org/
Dr. Jonathan Katz, Director

35233 ■ Center at the University of California, Irvine
MDA/ALS Center
200 S Manchester Ave., Ste. 110
Orange, CA 92868
Ph: (714)456-2332
Fax: (714)456-5997
E-mail: mozaffar@uci.edu
URL: http://www.mda.org/
Dr. Tahseen Mozaffar, Director

35234 ■ Children's Hospital of Orange County
MDA Clinic
455 S Main St.
Orange, CA 92868
Ph: (714)532-8736
Fax: (714)532-8754
URL: http://www.mda.org/
Dr. Samuel R. Rosenfeld, Director

35235 ■ Loma Linda University
MDA Clinic
Pediatric Neuroscience Center
2195 Club Center Dr., Ste. A
San Bernardino, CA 92408
URL: http://www.mda.org/

35236 ■ Rancho Los Amigos National Rehabilitation Center
MDA Clinic
7601 E Imperial Hwy.
Downey, CA 90242
URL: http://www.mda.org/
Dr. Luis Antonio Montes, Director

35237 ■ Sanford University
Pediatric Neurology
730 Welch Rd., 2nd Floor
Palo Alto, CA 94304
Free: 866-213-2727
URL: http://www.mda.org

35238 ■ Stanford University
Neurology Clinic
300 Pasteur Dr., Room A301
Stanford, CA 94305
Ph: (650)723-6469
Fax: (650)725-0390
URL: http://www.mda.org
Dr. Ching H. Wang, Director

35239 ■ University of California at Davis
Sacramento Medical Center
PM&R Muscular Dystrophy Clinic
4860 Y St., Ste. 1700
Sacramento, CA 95817
Ph: (916)734-7041
Fax: (916)734-6212
URL: http://www.mda.org/
Dr. Craig McDonald, Director

35240 ■ University of California, Los Angeles
Medical Center, Olive View
MDA Clinic
14445 Olive View Dr., No. 2C136
Sylmar, CA 91342
URL: http://www.mda.org/
Dr. K. Mishra, Director

35241 ■ University of California, Los Angeles
Neurological Services
MDA/ALS Center
300 UCLA Medical Plaza, Ste. B200
Los Angeles, CA 90095
Ph: (310)825-7266
Fax: (310)825-3995
E-mail: mcgraves@mednet.ucla.edu
URL: http://www.mda.org/
Dr. Michael C. Graves, Director

35242 ■ University of Southern California Hospital of the Good Samaritan Neuromuscular Center
616 S Witmer St.
Los Angeles, CA 90017
URL: http://www.mda.org/
Dr. Valerie Askansas, Director

35243 ■ University of Southern California School of Medicine USC Neuromuscular Center Jerry Lewis MDA/ALS Clinical and Research Center
637 S Lucas Ave.
Los Angeles, CA 90017
Ph: (213)743-1612
Fax: (213)743-1617
E-mail: kengel@usc.edu
URL: http://www.mda.org/
Dr. W. King Engel, Director

35244 ■ Valley Children's Hospital of Central California Pediatric Neurology MDA Clinic
9300 Valley Children's Pl.
Madera, CA 93638
Ph: (559)353-6500
Fax: (559)353-6555
URL: http://www.mda.org/
Dr. Raymund David, Director

COLORADO

35245 ■ Children's Hospital--Aurora MDA Clinic
13123 E 16th Ave.
Aurora, CO 80045
Ph: (303)861-8888
Fax: (303)861-6066
URL: http://www.mda.org/
Dr. Dennis J. Mathhews, Director

35246 ■ University of Colorado Health Sciences Center MDA/ALS Center
4200 E 9th Ave., Box B-185
Denver, CO 80262
Ph: (303)315-7221
Fax: (303)315-6796
E-mail: steven.ringel@uchsc.edu
URL: http://www.mda.org/
Dr. Stephen P. Ringel, Director

35247 ■ University of Colorado MDA Clinic
Anschutz Center for Advanced Medicine
1635 N Ursula
Aurora, CO 80010
URL: http://www.mda.org/
Dr. Steven P. Ringel, Director

CONNECTICUT

35248 ■ Hospital for Special Care MDA Clinic
2150 Corbin Ave.
New Britain, CT 06053
URL: http://www.mda.org/
Dr. Kevin J. Felice, Director

35249 ■ Yale University School of Medicine Department of Neurology MDA/ALS Center
40 Temple St., Ste. 6C
New Haven, CT 06519
Ph: (203)785-4867
Fax: (203)785-5694
E-mail: jonathan.goldstein@yale.edu
URL: http://info.med.yale.edu/neurol/
Dr. Jonathan M. Goldstein, Director

DISTRICT OF COLUMBIA

35250 ■ Children's Hospital National Medical Center MDA Clinic
111 Michigan Ave. NW
Washington, DC 20010
Ph: (202)884-5000
Fax: (202)884-4492
URL: http://www.mda.org/
Dr. Olga M. Morozova, Director

35251 ■ Georgetown University Hospital MDA Clinic
Department of Neurology
3800 Reservoir Rd. NW
Washington, DC 20007
Ph: (202)784-1748
Fax: (202)784-2261
URL: http://www.mda.org/
Dr. Michael Sirdofsky, Director

FLORIDA

35252 ■ Broward General Medical Center MDA Clinic
1600 S Andrews Ave.
Fort Lauderdale, FL 33316
URL: http://www.mda.org/
Dr. Harish D. Thaker, Director

35253 ■ Jupiter Medical Center
1210 S Old Dixie Hwy.
Jupiter, FL 33458
URL: http://www.mda.org/
Dr. Linda Pao, Director

35254 ■ Lee Memorial Hospital MDA Clinic
Medical Office Bldg.
2780 Cleveland Ave., 5th Fl.
Fort Myers, FL 33902
URL: http://www.mda.org/
Dr. Harris L. Bonnette, Director

35255 ■ Mayo Clinic--Jacksonville MDA Center
4500 San Pablo Rd.
Jacksonville, FL 32224
Ph: (904)953-2000
URL: http://www.mda.org/
Dr. Kevin B. Boylan, Director

35256 ■ Nemours Children's Clinic MDA Program
807 Children's Way
Jacksonville, FL 32207
URL: http://www.mda.org/
Dr. David N. Hammond, Director

35257 ■ Saint Joseph's Children's Hospital of Tampa MDA Clinic
3001 W Buffalo Ave.
Tampa, FL 33677
URL: http://www.mda.org/
Dr. Raymond J. Fernandez, Director

35258 ■ Shands Hospital MDA Clinic
UF Clinic, Health Science Center
Medical Plz.
2000 Archer Rd.
Gainesville, FL 32610
URL: http://www.mda.org/
Dr. S. H. Subramony, Director

35259 ■ Tallahassee Neurological Clinic MDA Clinic
1401 Centerville Rd., Ste. 300
Tallahassee, FL 32308
Ph: (850)878-8121
Fax: (850)878-4016
URL: http://www.mda.org/
Dr. Winston R. Ortiz, Director

35260 ■ University of Miami Kessenich Family MDA/ALS Center
1150 NW 14th St. Ste. 701
Miami, FL 33136
Ph: (305)243-7400
Free: 800-690-ALS1
Fax: (305)243-1249
E-mail: averma@med.miami.edu
URL: http://www.miami-als.org
Dr. Ashok Verma, Director

GEORGIA

35261 ■ Children's Healthcare of Atlanta at Scottish Rite MDA Clinic
5455 Meridian Mark Rd., Ste. 200
Atlanta, GA 30342
URL: http://www.mda.org/
Edward Goldstein, Director
Program(s): Neurology; Psychology; Genetics; Orthopaedics; Dentistry; Dermatology; Pulmonology; Rheumatology; Urology; Advocacy; Rehabilitation; Follow-Up.

35262 ■ Emory University School of Medicine Department of Neurology, MDA/ALS
1365A Clifton Rd. NE
Atlanta, GA 30322
Ph: (404)778-3754
Fax: (404)773-3495
E-mail: jglas03@emory.edu
URL: http://www.mda.org/
Dr. Jonathan Glass, Director

35263 ■ Medical College of Georgia Health MDA Clinic
ACC, 1120 15th St.
Augusta, GA 30912
URL: http://www.mda.org/
Dr. Jerry Ned Pruitt, Director

IDAHO

35264 ■ Idaho Elks Rehabilitation Hospital MDA Clinic
600 Robbins Rd.
Boise, ID 83702
URL: http://www.mda.org/
Dr. Robert H. Friedman, Director

ILLINOIS

35265 ■ Carle Clinic Association
602 W University Ave.
Urbana, IL 61801
Ph: (217)383-3311
URL: http://www.carle.com
Dr. Robert E. Cranston, Director

35266 ■ Memorial Medical Center MDA Clinic
Koke Mill Medical Center
3132 Old Jacksonville Rd.
Springfield, IL 62704
URL: http://www.mda.org/
Dr. Michael R. Pranzotelli, Director

35267 ■ Northwestern Memorial Hospital
675 N St. Clair, 20th Fl.
Chicago, IL 60611
URL: http://www.mda.org/
Dr. Robert Sufit, Director

35268 ■ OSF Saint Francis Medical Group Center MDA Clinic
OSF Neurology Group
100 NE Randolph St.
Peoria, IL 61606
URL: http://www.mda.org/
Dr. Greg Blume, Director

35269 ■ Rush University Medical Center
MDA Clinic
1725 W Harrison, Ste. 1118
Chicago, IL 60612
Ph: (312)942-6121
Fax: (312)942-2380
URL: http://www.mda.org/
Peter T. Heydemann, Director
Program(s): Therapy; Genetic Counseling; Support Groups, Flu Inoculations; Transportation; Camp Programs; Education; Neurologic Consultations; Orthopedic Orthotics. **Remarks:** The only requirement for receiving an evaluation at the MDA clinic is the written recommendation of a physician in whose judgment a person may have one of the neuromuscular diseases covered by the Association's medical services program.

35270 ■ University of Illinois, Chicago
MDA Clinic
1801 W Taylor St.
Chicago, IL 60612
Ph: (312)996-4780
Fax: (312)413-5780
E-mail: rowin@uic.edu
URL: http://www.mda.org/
Dr. Julie Rowin, Director

INDIANA

35271 ■ Elkhart Clinic
MDA Clinic
303 S Nappanee
Elkhart, IN 46514
Ph: (574)296-3200
Fax: (574)296-3921
URL: http://www.elkhartclinic.com
Dr. Thomas Vidic, Director

35272 ■ Lutheran Hospital of Indiana
MDA Clinic
7950 W Jefferson Blvd.
Fort Wayne, IN 46804
Ph: (260)435-7001
Free: 800-444-2001
Fax: (219)435-7642
URL: http://www.lutheranhealthnetwork.com/
Dr. C.J. Ottinger, Director

IOWA

35273 ■ University of Iowa Hospitals and Clinics
MDA Clinic
200 Hawkins Dr.
Iowa City, IA 52242
Ph: (319)356-1851
URL: http://www.mda.org/
Dr. Katherine Mathews, Director

KANSAS

35274 ■ Center at the University of Kansas Medical Center
MDA/ALS Center
39th and Rainbow Blvd.
Kansas City, KS 66103
Ph: (913)588-5000
Fax: (913)588-6965
E-mail: adick1@kumc.edu
URL: http://www.mda.org/
Dr. Arthur Dick, Director

35275 ■ Via Christi Medical Center--Saint Francis Campus
MDA Clinic
929 N St. Francis Ave.
Wichita, KS 67214
Ph: (316)268-5040
Fax: (316)291-7366
URL: http://www.mda.org/
Dr. Dilawer H. Abbas, Director

KENTUCKY

35276 ■ Baptist Hospital East
MDA Clinic
4000 Kresge Way
Louisville, KY 40207
Ph: (502)897-8100
E-mail: louisvilleservices@mdausa.org
URL: http://www.baptisteast.com
Dr. Gregory L. Pittman, Director

LOUISIANA

35277 ■ Baton Rouge Clinic, AMC
MDA Clinic
7373 Perkins Rd.
Baton Rouge, LA 70809
URL: http://www.mda.org/
Dr. Barbara Jean Golden, Director

35278 ■ Louisiana State University Health Science Center, Shreveport
MDA Clinic
1501 Kings Hwy.
Shreveport, LA 71130
URL: http://www.lsuhsc.edu
Dr. Robert Schwendimann, Director

35279 ■ The Neuro Medical Center
MDA Clinic
10101 Park Rowe Ave., 4th Fl, Ste. 200
Baton Rouge, LA 70810
Ph: (225)763-9900
Free: 800-468-8345
URL: http://www.theneuromedicalcenter.com
Dr. Carolyn C. Baker, Director

35280 ■ Saint Francis Medical Health Center
MDA Clinic
920 Oliver Rd., Ste. 1600B
Monroe, LA 71201
URL: http://www.mda.org/
Dr. Aristoteles Pena-Miches, Director

35281 ■ Women's and Children's Hospital Rapides Regional Medical Center
MDA Clinic
211 4th St., Box 30101
Alexandria, LA 71301
URL: http://www.mda.org/
Dr. Charles Ugokwe, Director

MAINE

35282 ■ Eastern Maine Medical Center
MDA Clinic
905 Unim St., Ste. 9
Bangor, ME 04401
Ph: (207)973-7559
Free: 877-366-3662
Fax: (207)973-7674
URL: http://www.mda.org/
Dr. Peter Keebler, Director

35283 ■ Maine Medical Center
MDA Clinic
Department of Rehabilitative Medicine
22 Bramhall St.
Portland, ME 04102
Ph: (207)871-0111
URL: http://www.mmc.org
Dr. Stephen D. Rioux, Director

MARYLAND

35284 ■ Johns Hopkins University School of Medicine
MDA/ALS Center
600 N Caroline St.
Baltimore, MD 21287-7519
Ph: (410)614-3846
Fax: (410)955-0672
E-mail: jrothste@jhmi.edu
URL: http://www.hopkinshospital.org/
Dr. Jeffrey D. Rothstein, Director

MASSACHUSETTS

35285 ■ Baystate Medical Center
MDA Clinic
140 High St.
Springfield, MA 01105
Ph: (413)794-4754
Fax: (413)794-7134
URL: http://www.mda.org
Dr. George Baquis, Director

35286 ■ Children's Hospital Boston
Neurology Department
300 Longwood Ave.
Boston, MA 02115
Ph: (617)355-6388
Fax: (617)738-0583
E-mail: basil.darras@tch.harvard.edu
URL: http://www.childrenshospital.org
Dr. Basil Darras, Director

35287 ■ Massachusetts General Hospital
MDA/ALS Center
CNY Bldg. 149
13th St., Rm. 2274
Charlestown, MA 02129
E-mail: mcudkowicz@partners.org
URL: http://neuro-www.mgh.harvard.edu/units/neuromuscular.html
Dr. Merit Cudkowicz, Director

35288 ■ University of Massachusetts Medical Center
MDA/ALS Clinic
55 Lake Ave. N
Worcester, MA 01655
Ph: (508)856-3664
Fax: (508)856-4485
E-mail: Robert.Brown@umassmed.edu
URL: http://www.mda.org/
Dr. Robert H. Brown, Director

MICHIGAN

35289 ■ Children's Hospital of Michigan Department of Neurology
MDA Clinic
3901 Beaubien
Detroit, MI 48201
Ph: (313)745-5788
Fax: (313)745-0955
URL: http://www.mda.org/
Dr. A. Edward Dabrowksi, Director

35290 ■ Mary Free Bed Rehabilitation Hospital
MDA/ALS Clinic
350 Lafayette St., Ste. 308
Grand Hapids, MI 49503
Ph: (616)752-5333
Fax: (616)752-5399
E-mail: gelinasd@trinity-health.org
URL: http://www.mda.org/
Dr. Deborah F. Gelinas, Director

35291 ■ Mary Free Bed Rehabilitation Hospital
MDA Clinic
350 Lafayette, Ste. 308
Grand Rapids, MI 49503
Ph: (616)752-5333
Fax: (616)752-5399
E-mail: gelinasd@trinity-health.org
URL: http://www.mda.org/
Dr. John F. Butzer, Director

35292 ■ Michigan Institute for Neurological Disorders
MDA Clinic
28595 Orchard Lake Rd., Ste. 200
Farmington Hills, MI 48334
Ph: (248)553-0010
Fax: (248)553-5957
URL: http://www.mda.org/
Dr. Martin Belkin, Director

35293 ■ Michigan State University Clinical Center
MDA/ALS Clinic
138 Service Rd. Ste A-117
East Lansing, MI 48824
Ph: (517)358-8122
Fax: (517)432-7390
E-mail: wchlphysician@msn.com
URL: http://www.mda.org/
Dr. David Simpson, Director

35294 ■ Michigan State University Kalamazoo Center for Medical Studies
MDA Clinic
1000 Oakland Dr.
Kalamazoo, MI 49008
URL: http://www.mda.org
Dr. Michelle Crooks, Director

35295 ■ University of Michigan
MDA Clinic
Burlington Bldg.
325 E Eisenhower Pkwy.
Ann Arbor, MI 48108
URL: http://www.mda.org/
Dr. James Dowling, Director

35296 ■ Wayne State University
Harper University Hospital
Adult MDA Clinic
4201 St. Antoine, Ste. 8A
Detroit, MI 48201
URL: http://www.mda.org/
Dr. Richard A. Lewis, Director

MINNESOTA

35297 ■ Duluth Clinic
MDA Clinic
400 E 3rd St.
Duluth, MN 55805
Ph: (218)786-8364
Free: 800-342-1388
Fax: (218)727-7258
URL: http://www.smdc.org
Dr. Wolcott S. Holt, Director

MISSISSIPPI

35298 ■ University of Mississippi Medical Center
MDA Clinic
Jackson Medical Mall
Department of Neurology
350 W Woodrow Wilson
Jackson, MS 39213
URL: http://www.mda.org/
Dr. V.V. Vedanarayanan, Director

MISSOURI

35299 ■ Saint John's Regional Health Center
MDA Clinic
1965 S Fremont
Springfield, MO 65804
E-mail: springfieldmoservices@mdausa.org
URL: http://www.mda.org
Dr. Michael Luzecky, Director

35300 ■ Saint John's Regional Medical Center
MDA Clinic
2727 McClelland Blvd.
Joplin, MO 64804
URL: http://www.mda.org/
Dr. Taylor Bear, Director

35301 ■ Washington University School of Medicine
MDA/ALS Center
4921 Parkview Place
Saint Louis, MO 63110
Ph: (314)362-6981
Fax: (314)362-2826
E-mail: pestronk@neuro.wustl.edu
URL: http://www.neuro.wustl.edu/neuromuscular/spinal/als.htm
Dr. Alan Pestronk, Director

NEBRASKA

35302 ■ University of Nebraska Medical Center
Physical & Occupational Therapy
600 S 42nd St.
Omaha, NE 68198
Ph: (402)559-6415
Free: 800-656-3937
Fax: (402)559-9263
E-mail: wstuberg@asunmc.edu
URL: http://www.mda.org/
Dr. Wayne Stuberg, Director

NEW JERSEY

35303 ■ University Hospital
MDA Clinic
Doctor's Office Center, 8th Fl.
90 Bergen St., Rm. 3100
Newark, NJ 07103
URL: http://www.mda.org/
Dr. John Bach, Director

35304 ■ University Medical Center
Kennedy Memorial Hospital
MDA Clinic
18 E Laurel Rd.
Stratford, NJ 08084
URL: http://www.mda.org
Dr. Donald A. Barone, Director

NEW MEXICO

35305 ■ Center at the University of New Mexico
Health Sciences Center
MDA/ALS Center
915 Camino de Salud, NE
Albuquerque, NM 87131
Ph: (505)272-3342
Fax: (505)272-6692
URL: http://www.mda.org/
Dr. Sarah Youssof, Director

35306 ■ University of New Mexico Hospital
MDA Clinic
2211 Lomas Blvd. NE
Albuquerque, NM 87106
URL: http://www.mda.org/
Dr. Leslie Morrison, Director

NEW YORK

35307 ■ Albany Medical Center Hospital
MDA Clinic
Department of Neurology, A-70
43 New Scotland Ave.
Albany, NY 12208
Ph: (518)262-5226
Fax: (518)262-5041
URL: http://www.mda.org/
Dr. Matthew Murnane, Director

35308 ■ Columbia University
College of Physicians and Surgeons
Eleanor and Lou Gehrig MDA/ALS Center
Neurological Institute
Department of Neurology
710 W 168th St., N19-016
New York, NY 10032
Ph: (212)305-1319
Fax: (212)305-8398
E-mail: alscenter@columbia.edu
URL: http://www.mda.org/
Hiroshi Mitsumoto, Director

35309 ■ Dent Neurologic Institute
MDA Clinic
3980 Sheridan Dr.
Amherst, NY 14226
URL: http://www.mda.org/
Dr. Tomas Holmlund, Director

35310 ■ Erie County Medical Center
MDA Clinic
ECMC
Department of Neurology
462 Grider St.
Buffalo, NY 14215
Ph: (716)898-4893
Fax: (716)898-5202
URL: http://www.mda.org/
Dr. Nicholas J. Silvestri, Director

35311 ■ Long Island Jewish Medical Center
MDA Clinic
270-05 76th Ave.
New Hyde Park, NY 11040
URL: http://www.mda.org/
Dr. Roger W. Kula, Director

35312 ■ Montefiore Medical Center
MDA Clinic
1515 Blondell Ave.
Bronx, NY 10461
URL: http://www.mda.org/
Dr. Emma C. Laureta, Director

35313 ■ Mount Sinai Hospital and Medical Center
MDA Clinic
1 Gustave Levy Pl.
Annenburg 14-94
New York, NY 10029
Ph: (212)241-7317
Fax: (212)987-7363
E-mail: dale.lange@mssm.edu
URL: http://www.mssm.edu/neurology/neuromuscular/als/index.shtml
Dr. Dale Lange, Director

35314 ■ New York University Medical Center
Institute of Rehabilitation Medicine
MDA Clinic
400 E 34th St., Rm. RG-29
New York, NY 10016
Ph: (212)263-6350
Fax: (212)263-5499
URL: http://www.mda.org/
Dr. Jeffrey M. Cohen, Director

35315 ■ Saint Charles Hospital and Rehabilitation Center
MDA Clinic
200 Belle Terre Rd.
Port Jefferson, NY 11777
Ph: (631)474-6300
Fax: (631)474-6161
URL: http://www.mda.org/
Dr. Scott McWilliams, Director

35316 ■ Saint Peters Hospital
Lewis Golub MDA/ALS Clinic
19 Warehouse Row
Albany, NY 12205
URL: http://www.mda.org
Dr. Roberta Miller, Director

35317 ■ State University of New York Health Sciences Center
Department of Neurology
MDA/ALS Center
750 E Adams St.
Syracuse, NY 13210
Ph: (315)464-2480
Fax: (315)464-7328
E-mail: shefnerj@upstate.edu
URL: http://www.hscsyr.edu/neurology/neuropat.htm
Dr. Jeremy M. Shefner, Director

35318 ■ SUNY Downstate Medical Center
MDA Clinic
450 Clarkson Ave.
Brooklyn, NY 11203
URL: http://www.mda.org/
Dr. Yaacov Anziska, Director

35319 ■ University of Rochester Medical Center
MDA Clinic
601 Elmwood Ave.
Rochester, NY 14642
Ph: (585)275-2559
Fax: (716)273-1255
E-mail: charles_thornton@urmc.rochester.edu
URL: http://www.mda.org/
Charles A. Thornton, Director

35320 ■ White Plains Hospital and Medical Center
MDA Clinic
Davis Ave. at E Post Rd.
White Plains, NY 10601
Ph: (914)681-0600
Fax: (914)345-5845
E-mail: hawthorneservices@mda.usa.org
URL: http://www.mda.org
Dr. Stanley B. Holstein, Director

NORTH CAROLINA

35321 ■ Carolinas Medical Center
Carolinas Neuromuscular/ALS-MDA Center
1010 N Edgehill Rd.
Charlotte, NC 28203
Ph: (704)446-4360
Fax: (704)446-6255
E-mail: Benjamin.Brooks@carolinashealthcare.org
URL: http://www.hscsyr.edu/neurology/neuropat.htm
Dr. Benjamin Brooks, Director

35322 ■ Duke University Medical Center
MDA Clinic
705 Broad St.
Durham, NC 27706
URL: http://www.mda.org/
Dr. E. Wayne Massey, Director

35323 ■ University of North Carolina Hospitals
School of Medicine
Department of Neurology
MDA Clinic
101 Manning Dr.
Chapel Hill, NC 27514
URL: http://www.mda.org/
Dr. James F. Howard, Director

NORTH DAKOTA

35324 ■ MeritCare Hospital
MDA Clinic
720 4th St. N
Fargo, ND 58122
Ph: (701)234-6000
Free: 800-828-2901
Fax: (701)234-7453
URL: http://www.meritcare.com
Samira H. El-Zind, Director

OHIO

35325 ■ Children's Hospital--Columbus
MDA Clinic
Outpatient Care Center
555 S 18th St.
Columbus, OH 43205
URL: http://www.mda.org/
Dr. John Kissel, Director

35326 ■ Children's Hospital Medical Center
MDA Clinic
3333 Burnet Ave.
Cincinnati, OH 45229-3039
URL: http://www.mda.org/
Dr. Brenda Wong, Director

35327 ■ Metrohealth Medical Center
MDA Clinic
2500 MetroHealth Dr.
Cleveland, OH 44109
Ph: (216)778-3958
Fax: (216)778-8865
URL: http://www.mda.org/
Dr. Mark David Winkelman, Director

35328 ■ Ohio State University Medical Center
MDA/ALS Clinic
1580 Dodd Dr.
Columbus, OH 43210
Ph: (614)293-7715
Fax: (614)293-4688
E-mail: nash.46@osu.edu
URL: http://www.mda.org/
Dr. John T. Kissel, Director

35329 ■ Saint Elizabeth Hospital Medical Center
Dean Martin Neuromuscular Clinic
MDA Clinic
Neurology Dept.
1044 Belmont Ave.
Youngstown, OH 44501
Ph: (330)480-3069
Free: 800-480-1876
Fax: (330)480-2946
URL: http://www.mda.org/
Dr. Donald J. Tamulonis, Director

35330 ■ University of Cincinnati Medical Center
231 Bethesda Ave., Pav-B1
Cincinnati, OH 45267
URL: http://med.uc.edu
Dr. John Quinlan, Director

OKLAHOMA

35331 ■ Integris Southwest Medical Center
MDA/ALS Center
4221 S Western, Ste. 5010
Oklahoma City, OK 73109
Ph: (405)644-5170
Fax: (405)644-6112
E-mail: brent.beson@integrisok.com
URL: http://www.mda.org/
Dr. Brent Benson, Director

OREGON

35332 ■ Oregon Health & Science University
MDA/ALS Clinic
3303 SW Bond
Portland, OR 97239-3098
Ph: (503)494-5236
Fax: (503)494-0966
E-mail: louja@ohsu.edu
URL: http://www.mda.org/
Dr. Jau-Shin Lou, Director
Formerly: Oregon Health Sciences University.

35333 ■ Providence Medford Medical Center
MDA Clinic
1111 Crater Lake Ave.
Medford, OR 97504
URL: http://www.mda.org/
Dr. Cornelia Byers, Director

35334 ■ Sacred Heart Medical Center
MDA Clinic
1255 Hilyard St.
Eugene, OR 97401
Ph: (541)686-7300
Fax: (541)686-8355
URL: http://www.peacehealth.org
Dr. Steven Goins, Director

PENNSYLVANIA

35335 ■ Children's Hospital of Pittsburgh
MDA Clinic
Faculty Pavilion, 6th Fl.
45th & Penn
Pittsburgh, PA 15201
Ph: (412)692-5520
Fax: (412)692-6787
URL: http://www.mda.org/
Dr. Mary Louise Russell, Director

35336 ■ Drexel University
Center of Hope
MDA Clinic
219 N Broad St.
Philadelphia, PA 19107
E-mail: heiman@drexel.edu
URL: http://www.mda.org
Dr. Terry D. Heiman-Patterson, Director

35337 ■ Drexel University College of Medicine
MDA/ALS Clinic
Dept. of Neurology
219 N Broad St.
Philadelphia, PA 19107
Ph: (215)762-5035
Fax: (215)762-3899
E-mail: heiman@drexel.edu
URL: http://www.mda.org/
Dr. Terry D. Heiman-Patterson, Director

35338 ■ Geisinger Medical Center
MDA Clinic
HealthSouth Bldg.
2 Rehab Ln.
Danville, PA 17822
URL: http://www.mda.org/
Dr. Scott M. Friedenberg, Director

35339 ■ Geisinger Wyoming Valley Medical Center
MDA Clinic
1010 E Mountain Dr.
Wilkes-Barre, PA 18702
Ph: (570)826-7300
Fax: (570)826-7943
URL: http://www.geisinger.edu
Dr. James F. Hora, Director

35340 ■ Good Shepherd Rehabilitation Hospital
MDA Clinic
850 S 5th St.
Allentown, PA 18103
Ph: (610)776-3499
Fax: (610)776-3542
URL: http://www.mda.org/
Terry D. Heiman-Patterson, Director

35341 ■ Hospital of the University of Pennsylvania
MDA Clinic
Dept. of Neurology
3400 Spruce St.
Philadelphia, PA 19104
URL: http://www.mda.org/
Dr. Shawn J. Bird, Director

35342 ■ Northshore Neurosciences
MDA Clinic
120 E 2nd St., 3rd Fl.
Erie, PA 16507
URL: http://www.mda.org/
Dr. Jeffrey J. Esper, Director
Formerly: Northshore Clinical Associates.

35343 ■ Pennsylvania State University
Milton S. Hershey Medical Center
Section of Neurology
MDA Clinic
500 University Dr.
Hershey, PA 17033
Ph: (717)531-8692
Free: 800-243-1455
Fax: (717)531-4694
URL: http://www.mda.org/
Dr. Zachary Simmons, Director

35344 ■ University of Pittsburgh Medical Center
MDA/ALS Center
200 Lothrop St., F878
Pittsburgh, PA 15213
Ph: (412)647-1706
Fax: (412)547-8398
E-mail: lacomis@upmc.edu
URL: http://www.mda.org/
Dr. David Lacomis, Director

35345 ■ University of Pittsburgh Medical Center
MDA/ALS Clinic
Falk Clinic
200 Lothrop St., 7th Fl.
Pittsburgh, PA 15213
Ph: (412)647-1706
Fax: (412)647-8398
E-mail: lacomis@np.awing.upmc.edu
URL: http://www.mda.org/
Dr. David Lacomis, Director

RHODE ISLAND

35346 ■ Rhode Island Hospital
Child Development Center
MDA Clinic
593 Eddy St.
Providence, RI 02903
Ph: (401)444-5685
Fax: (401)444-6115
URL: http://www.mda.org/
Dr. James Gilchrist, Director

SOUTH CAROLINA

35347 ■ Greenville Hospital System
University Medical Group
MDA Clinic
200 Patewood Dr., Ste. A200
Greenville, SC 29615
URL: http://www.mda.org
Dr. Addie S. Hunnicutt, Director

35348 ■ Medical University of South Carolina
MUSC Medical Center
MDA Clinic
171 Ashley Ave.
Charleston, SC 29425
Ph: (843)792-3221
Fax: (843)792-8626
URL: http://www.mda.org/
Dr. Mary Herring, Director

35349 ■ Spartanburg Neurological Services
362 N Pine St.
Spartanburg, SC 29302
URL: http://www.mda.org/
Dr. Bodgan P. Gheorghiu, Director

SOUTH DAKOTA

35350 ■ Neurology Associates
1100 E 21st St., Ste. 506
Sioux Falls, SD 57105
URL: http://www.mda.org/
Dr. Lisa C. Viola, Director

35351 ■ Regional Rehabilitation Institute
MDA Clinic
2908 5th St.
Rapid City, SD 57701
Ph: (605)719-1101
Fax: (605)719-1116
URL: http://www.rcrh.org
Dr. Matthew E. Simmons, Director

TENNESSEE

35352 ■ MDA/ALS Center of Memphis Mid-South
8095 Club Pkwy.
Cordova, TN 38016
Ph: (901)725-8920
Fax: (901)725-8934
E-mail: tbertorini@aol.com
URL: http://www.mda.org/
Dr. Tulio Bertorini, Director

35353 ■ Methodist Lebonheur Health Care
MDA Clinic
8095 Club Pkwy.
Cordova, TN 38017
URL: http://www.mda.org/
Dr. Tulio Dertorini, Director

35354 ■ University of Tennessee Medical Center
MDA Clinic
Cole Neuroscience Ctr.
Medical Bldg. B, Ste. 102
1928 Alcoa Hwy.
Knoxville, TN 37920
URL: http://www.mda.org/
Dr. Randall G. Trudell, Director

35355 ■ Vanderbilt University Medical Center
MDA/ALS Center
1301 22nd Ave., South No. 3603
Nashville, TN 37212
Ph: (615)936-0060
Fax: (615)936-1263
E-mail: peter.d.donofrio@vanderbilt.edu
URL: http://www.mda.org/

TEXAS

35356 ■ Center at the University of Texas at San Antonio
Health Science Center
MDA/ALS Center
HealthSouth Rehabilitation Institute of San Antonio
9119 Cinnamon Hill
San Antonio, TX 78240
Ph: (210)567-1945
Fax: (210)567-1948
E-mail: jacksonce@uthscsa.edu
URL: http://www.mda.org/
Dr. Carlayne E. Jackson, Director

35357 ■ Children's Medical Center of Dallas
1935 Medical District Dr.
Dallas, TX 75235
Ph: (214)456-7000
Fax: (214)456-6133
URL: http://www.childrens.com
Christopher Durovich, Chief Executive Officer

35358 ■ Cook--Fort Worth Children's Medical Center
MDA Clinic
901 7th Ave., Ste. 120
Fort Worth, TX 76104
Ph: (817)885-4000
Fax: (817)885-4118
URL: http://www.mda.org/
Dr. Warren A. Marks, Director

35359 ■ Methodist Hospital
Neurological Institute
MDA/ALS Center
6560 Fannin St., Ste. 802
Houston, TX 77030
Ph: (713)441-1141
E-mail: sappel@tmhs.edu
URL: http://www.mda.org/
Dr. Stanley H. Appel, Director

35360 ■ Neurological Clinic of Texas
MDA Clinic
Medical City Dallas Hospital
7777 Forest Ln., Ste. B-116
Dallas, TX 75230
Ph: (972)566-7684
Fax: (972)566-7023
E-mail: naards@aol.com
URL: http://www.mda.org/
Dr. Susan E. Hotz, Director

35361 ■ Neurology Associates of Arlington
MDA Clinic
811 W IH 20, Ste. 212
Arlington, TX 76012
Ph: (817)795-5566
Fax: (817)261-7315
URL: http://www.mda.org/
Dr. Robert E. McMichael, Director

35362 ■ Neurology Center
MDA Clinic
1600 7th St., Ste. B
Wichita Falls, TX 76301
URL: http://www.mda.org/
Dr. Stephen Farmer, Director

35363 ■ Providence Health Center
MDA Clinic
6901 Medical Pkwy.
Waco, TX 76712
URL: http://www.mda.org/
Dr. George Mark Schwartze, Director

35364 ■ Texas Neurology
MDA Clinic
6301 Gaston Ave., Ste. 200W
Dallas, TX 75214
URL: http://www.mda.org/
Dr. Daragh Heitzman, Director

35365 ■ Texas Tech University Health Sciences Center
MDA Clinic
4800 Alberta Ave.
El Paso, TX 79905
URL: http://www.mda.org/
Dr. Johanan Levine, Director

35366 ■ Texoma Neurology Associates
MDA Clinic
321 N Highland, Ste. 200
Sherman, TX 75092
URL: http://www.mda.org/
Dr. Easwar M. Sundaram, Director

35367 ■ University of Texas Health Science Center
MDA/ALS Clinic
HealthSouth Rehab Institute of San Antonio
9119 Cinnamon Hill
San Antonio, TX 78240
Ph: (210)567-1945
Fax: (210)567-1948
E-mail: jacksonce@uthscsa.edu
URL: http://www.mda.org/
Dr. Carlayne E. Jackson, Director

35368 ■ University of Texas
Southwest Medical Center at Dallas
MDA/ALS Center
5323 Harry Hines Blvd.
Dallas, TX 75235-8897
Ph: (214)648-2871
Fax: (214)648-7992
E-mail: jeffrey.elliott@utsouthwestern.edu
URL: http://www.mda.org/
Dr. Jeffrey L. Elliott, Director

35369 ■ Valley Baptist Medical Center
MDA Clinic
2101 Pease St.
Harlingen, TX 78550

Ph: (956)389-1100
URL: http://www.mda.org/
Dr. Cynthia A. Garcia, Director
Remarks: Held the third Monday of every month.

UTAH

35370 ■ University of Utah School of Medicine Department of Neurology MDA/ALS Center
50 N Medical Dr.
Salt Lake City, UT 84132
Ph: (801)585-5885
Fax: (801)585-2054
E-mail: mbromberg@hsc.utah.edu
URL: http://www.mda.org/
Dr. Mark B. Bromberg, Director

VERMONT

35371 ■ Fletcher Allen Health Care Center MDA Clinic
1 S Prospect St.
Burlington, VT 05401
URL: http://www.mda.org/
Dr. Rup Tandan, Director

VIRGINIA

35372 ■ Children's Hospital--Richmond MDA Clinic
2924 Brook Rd.
Richmond, VA 23220
Ph: (804)321-7474
Fax: (804)228-5857
URL: http://www.mda.org/
Dr. Eugenio A. Monasterio, Director

35373 ■ Kluge Children's Rehabilitation Center
2270 Ivy Rd., Box 232
Charlottesville, VA 22920
URL: http://www.mda.org/
Dr. Christine M. Houlihan, Director

35374 ■ Medical College of Virginia MDA Clinic
PO Box 980599, MCV Sta.
Richmond, VA 23298
URL: http://www.mda.org/
Dr. Scott A. Vota, Director

35375 ■ Roanoke Neurological Associates, Inc. MDA Clinic
4431 Starkey Rd.
Roanoke, VA 24018
URL: http://www.mda.org/
Dr. J. Gordan Burch, Director

35376 ■ University of Virginia Hospital MDA Clinic
Dept. of Neurology, Box 394
Charlottesville, VA 22908
URL: http://www.mda.org/
Dr. Ted M. Burns, Director

WASHINGTON

35377 ■ Physicians Health Center
1200 N 14th St., Ste. 275
Pasco, WA 99301
URL: http://www.mda.org/
Dr. Donald G. Dicken, Director

35378 ■ Providence/Saint Peter's Hospital MDA Clinic
410 Providence Ln.
Olympia, WA 98503
Ph: (360)491-9480
Free: 888-492-9480
Fax: (360)493-7977
URL: http://www.providence.org
Dr. Greg Carter, Director

35379 ■ Saint Lukes'Rehabilitation Institute MDA Clinic
Deaconess Medical Bldg.
801 W 5th Ave., Ste. 104
Spokane, WA 99204
URL: http://www.mda.org/
Dr. Vivan M. Moise, Director

35380 ■ Seattle Children's Hospital MDA Clinic
4800 Sand Point Way NE
Seattle, WA 98105
Ph: (206)987-2000
URL: http://www.seattlechildrens.org
Dr. Susan D. Apkon, Director

35381 ■ Shriners Hospital for Children
911 W 5th Ave.
Spokane, WA 99204
URL: http://www.mda.org/
Dr. Sharon Genung, Director

35382 ■ University of Washington Medical Center Rehabilitation Medical Clinic MDA/ALS Center
1959 NE Pacific St.
Seattle, WA 98195-6115
Ph: (206)598-4590
Fax: (206)598-2813
E-mail: gtcarter@u.washington.edu
URL: http://www.mda.org/
Dr. Greg Carter, Director

WEST VIRGINIA

35383 ■ West Virginia University Hospitals MDA Clinic
1 Stadium Dr., Neurology Suite
Morgantown, WV 26506
URL: http://www.mda.org/
Dr. Laurie Gutmann, Director

WISCONSIN

35384 ■ Children's Hospital of Wisconsin Medical College of Wisconsin MDA Clinic
9000 W Wisconsin Ave.
Milwaukee, WI 53201
Ph: (414)456-4090
Fax: (414)456-6538
E-mail: jacobson@mcw.edu
URL: http://www.chw.org/specialty/program.htm
Dr. Richard Jacobson, Director
Program(s): Pediatric Neuromuscular Clinic.

35385 ■ Froedtert Memorial Lutheran Hospital Medical College of Wisconsin Clinics MDA Clinic
9200 W Wisconsin Ave.
Milwaukee, WI 53226
Ph: (414)805-5200
Fax: (414)259-0469
E-mail: wlarson@mcw.edu
URL: http://www.neurology.mcw.edu
Dr. Wendy L. Peltier, Director

35386 ■ Marshfield Clinic MDA Clinic
1000 N Oak Ave.
Marshfield, WI 54440
Ph: (715)387-5351
Fax: (715)387-5727
URL: http://www.mda.org/
Dr. Rodney Sorensen, Director

35387 ■ Saint Vincent Hospital MDA Clinic
Prevea Clinic, Allouez Site
1821 S Webster
Green Bay, WI 54301
URL: http://www.mda.org/
Dr. Terrence S. Edgar, Director

35388 ■ University of Wisconsin--Madison MDA/ALS Clinical Research Center
600 Highland Ave. S, H4-622
Madison, WI 53792-5132
Ph: (608)263-6616
Fax: (608)265-0172
E-mail: lotz@neurology.wisc.edu
URL: http://www.mda.org/
Dr. Barend P. Lotz, Director

WYOMING

35389 ■ Central Wyoming Neurology Clinic MDA Clinic
5820 2nd St.
Casper, WY 82609
URL: http://www.mda.org/
Dr. Angelo M. Santiago, Director

Chapter 26
Organ and Tissue Banks

Listed below are eye, tissue, organ, and blood cord banks. The eye banks are members of the Eye Bank Association of America. Entry arrangement is geographical by states, then alphabetical by organization names within states. See the "User's Guide" located at the front of this directory for additional information.

ALABAMA

35390 ■ Alabama Eye Bank
500 Robert Jemison Rd.
Birmingham, AL 35209
Ph: (205)942-2120
Free: 800-423-7811
Fax: (205)942-2184
E-mail: info@alabamaeyebank.org
URL: http://www.alabamaeyebank.org

35391 ■ Alabama Organ Center
500 22nd St. S, Ste. 102
Birmingham, AL 35233
Free: 800-252-3677
Fax: (205)731-9332
E-mail: joe.captain@ccc.uab.org
URL: http://alabamaorgancenter.com

35392 ■ Southern Cord
303 Williams Ave. SW, Ste. 114
Huntsville, AL 35801
Ph: (256)564-7088
E-mail: info@southerncord.com
URL: http://www.southerncord.com

ALASKA

35393 ■ Life Alaska Donor Services, Inc.
235 E 8th Ave., Ste. 100
Anchorage, AK 99501
Ph: (907)652-5433
Free: 800-719-5433
Fax: (907)562-5333
URL: http://www.lifealaska.org

ALBERTA

35394 ■ Cells for Life Limited--Calgary
Quarry Park
160 Quarry Park Blvd. SE, Ste. 300
Calgary, AB, Canada 52C 3G3
Ph: (403)450-7890
Free: 877-235-1997
Fax: (403)451-9906
E-mail: calgary@cellsforlife.com
URL: http://www.cellsforlife.com

35395 ■ Lions Eye Bank, Alberta Society
Rockyview Hospital
7007 14th St. SW
Calgary, AB, Canada T2V 1P9
Ph: (403)943-3609
Fax: (403)943-3244
E-mail: mijana.ridic@albertahealthservices.ca
URL: http://www.act4sight.com

35396 ■ Southern Alberta Organ and Tissue Program
Foothills Medical Center
South Tower, Rm. 1002
1403 29th St. NW
Calgary, AB, Canada T2N 2T9
Ph: (403)944-1232
Fax: (403)944-3340
E-mail: Sharon.Havey@albertahealthservices.ca
URL: http://www.act4sight.com

35397 ■ University of Alberta Hospital Comprehensive Tissue Centre
Walter MacKenzie Bldg.
7415 Aberhart Center 1
11402 University Ave.
Edmonton, AB, Canada T6G 2J3
Ph: (780)407-1970
Free: 866-408-LINK
Fax: (780)407-7509
E-mail: ctc@albertahealthservices.ca
URL: http://www.albertahealthservices.ca/

ARIZONA

35398 ■ Donor Network of Arizona
201 Coolidge
Phoenix, AZ 85013
Ph: (602)222-2200
Free: 800-94-DONOR
Fax: (602)222-2201
E-mail: Alan@dnaz.org
URL: http://www.dnaz.org

35399 ■ International Biologics LLC
16701 N 90th St., Ste. 200
Scottsdale, AZ 85260
Ph: (480)563-0800
Free: 866-989-1919
Fax: (480)563-0810
E-mail: jerry@internationalbiologics.com
URL: http://www.internationalbiologics.com

35400 ■ LifeLegacy Foundation
6825 E Outlook Dr.
Tucson, AZ 85706
Ph: (520)881-0293
Free: 888-774-4438
Fax: (520)881-0335
E-mail: mburgess@lifelegacy.org
URL: http://www.lifelegacy.org
Remarks: Non-transplantable tissues.

35401 ■ ScienceCare Anatomical Body Donation Services
21410 N 19th Ave., Ste. 126
Phoenix, AZ 85080
Ph: (602)331-3641
Free: 800-417-3747
Fax: (602)288-0054
E-mail: james.rogers@sciencecare.com
URL: http://www.sciencecare.com
Remarks: Non-transplantable tissues.

35402 ■ University of Arizona Cord Blood Bank
University of Arizona Medical Center
Tucson, AZ
Ph: (520)626-5125
Free: 888-932-6568
URL: http://www.healthycordblood.com/university-of-arizona-cord-blood-bank

ARKANSAS

35403 ■ University of Arkansas for Medical Sciences
Arkansas Lions Eye Bank and Laboratory
4301 W Markham, Slot 523-1
Little Rock, AR 72205
Ph: (501)686-8388
Fax: (501)603-1463
E-mail: BrownGeoffreyC@uams.edu
URL: http://eye.uams.edu/

BRITISH COLUMBIA

35404 ■ Eye Bank of British Columbia
Centennial Pavilion, Rm. 380
855 W 12th Ave.
Vancouver, BC, Canada V5Z 1M9
Ph: (604)875-4567
E-mail: linda.dwong@vch.ca
URL: http://www.eyebankofbc.com

35405 ■ Lifebank Cryogenics Corporation
4475 Wayburne Dr., Ste. 200
Burnaby, BC, Canada V5G 4X4
Ph: (604)738-2722
Free: 888-888-7836
Fax: (604)738-2726
E-mail: life@lifebank.com
URL: http://www.lifebank.com

CALIFORNIA

35406 ■ Advanced Biohealing Inc.
10933 N Torrey Pines Rd., Ste. 200
La Jolla, CA 92037
Free: 877-422-4463
Fax: (858)754-3750
E-mail: sschaffer@abh.com
URL: http://www.abh.com

35407 ■ AlloSource--California
1700 N Chrisman Rd.
Englewood, CA 95304
Ph: (209)832-4373
Free: 888-873-8330
Fax: (209)832-4937
E-mail: questions@allosource.org
URL: http://www.allosource.org/

35408 ■ Allosource--San Diego
9323 Chesapeake Dr., Ste. C1
San Diego, CA 92123
Ph: (858)309-6831
Free: 800-345-8024
Fax: (858)309-6835
URL: http://www.allosource.org

35409 ■ Berkeley Advanced Biomaterials Inc.
901 Grayson St., Ste. 101
Berkeley, CA 94710
Ph: (510)883-0500
Fax: (510)883-0511
E-mail: fgenin@hydroxyapatite.com
URL: http://www.hydroxyapatite.com

35410 ■ BioBank USA
5 Lower Ragsdale Dr., Ste. 100
Monterey, CA 93940
Free: 888-246-2262
Fax: (831)646-2266
E-mail: info@biobancusa.com
URL: http://www.biobancusa.com

35411 ■ California Cryobank, Inc., Los Angeles
11915 LaGrange Ave.
Los Angeles, CA 90025
Ph: (310)443-5244
Free: 800-231-3373
Fax: (310)443-5258
E-mail: dschillinger@cryobank.com
URL: http://www.cryobank.com/

35412 ■ California Cryobank, Inc., Palo Alto
700 Welch Rd., Ste. 101
Palo Alto, CA 94304
Ph: (650)324-1900
Free: 800-231-3373
Fax: (650)324-1946
E-mail: kdamico@cryobank.com
URL: http://www.cryobank.com/

35413 ■ California Cryobank, Inc., Westwood
1019 Gayley Ave.
Los Angeles, CA 90024
Ph: (310)443-5245
Free: 866-927-9622
Fax: (310)443-0487
URL: http://www.cryobank.com/

35414 ■ California Transplant Services
5845 Owens Ave.
Carlsbad, CA 92008
Ph: (760)804-6890
Free: 800-928-4778
Fax: (760)804-6899
E-mail: info@catransplant.org
URL: http://www.catransplant.org/

35415 ■ Children's Hospital Orange County Cord Blood Bank
455 S Main St.
Orange, CA 92868
Ph: (714)516-4335
E-mail: caaguire@choc.org
URL: http://www.choc.org/services/cfm?id=P00191

35416 ■ Community Tissue Services, California
7100 New Financial Dr., Ste. 105
Fresno, CA 93720
Ph: (559)224-1168
Free: 800-201-8477
Fax: (559)229-7217
E-mail: fcordova@cbccts.org
URL: http://www.communitytissue.org/

35417 ■ Cord Blood Registry
1200 Bayhill Dr., Ste. 301
San Bruno, CA 94066
Free: 888-932-6568
Fax: (800)844-2202
URL: http://www.cordblood.com/
Formerly: CBR Systems Inc.

35418 ■ CordBanc USA
5 Lower Ragsdale Dr., Ste. 100
Monterey, CA 93940
Free: 888-273-7770
Fax: (831)646-4929
E-mail: service@cordbancusa.com
URL: http://www.cordbancusa.com

35419 ■ Doheny Eye and Tissue Transplant Bank
1127 Wilshire Blvd., Ste. 602
Los Angeles, CA 90017
Ph: (213)482-9355
Fax: (213)482-9343
E-mail: dettb@tbionline.org
URL: http://www.tbionline.org

35420 ■ Family Cord Blood Services
11915 La Grange Ave.
Los Angeles, CA 90025
Free: 800-490-2673
Fax: (310)315-0472
URL: http://www.familycord.com/

35421 ■ FamilyCord--Palo Alto
700 Welch Rd., Ste. 107
Palo Alto, CA 94304
Ph: (310)496-5651
Free: 800-490-2673
Fax: (310)315-0472
URL: http://www.familycord.com

35422 ■ Golden State Donor Services
1760 Creekside Oaks Dr., Ste. 220
Sacramento, CA 95816
Ph: (916)567-1600
Free: 800-762-8819
Fax: (916)569-0300
E-mail: info@gsds.org
URL: http://www.gsds.org
Formerly: Sierra Eye and Tissue Donor Services.

35423 ■ International Cornea Project
9246 Lightwave Ave.
San Diego, CA 92123
Ph: (858)694-0400
Free: 888-EYE-BANK
Fax: (858)565-7368
E-mail: icp@sdeb.org
URL: http://www.sdeb.org

35424 ■ Interpore Cross International
181 Technology Dr.
Irvine, CA 92618
Ph: (949)453-3200
Fax: (949)453-3225
E-mail: Kathleen.Ideo@biomet.com
URL: http://interpore.com/

35425 ■ IsoTis OrthoBiologics
2 Goodyear, Ste. A
Irvine, CA 92618
Ph: (949)595-8710
Free: 800-550-7155
Fax: (949)595-8711
E-mail: Irvine.cs@itegra-is.com
URL: http://www.integralife.com/

35426 ■ Lifesharing Tissue Services
3465 Camino del Rio S, Ste. 410
San Diego, CA 92108
Ph: (619)521-1983
Fax: (619)521-2833
E-mail: info@lifesharing.org
URL: http://www.lifesharing.org/

35427 ■ Musculoskeletal Transplant Foundation (MTF)--Costa Mesa, CA
3535 Hyland Ave.
Costa Mesa, CA 92626
Free: 800-272-5287
Fax: (714)708-1331
E-mail: joel_osborne@mft.org
URL: http://www.mtf.org

35428 ■ Musculoskeletal Transplant Foundation (MTF)--Redlands, CA
1795-A Orange Tree Ln.
Redlands, CA 92374
Ph: (909)792-7544
E-mail: bobbi_paritte@mtf.org
URL: http://www.mtf.org

35429 ■ OneLegacy
221 S Figueroa St., Ste. 500
Los Angeles, CA 90012
Ph: (213)229-5600
Fax: (213)633-1641
E-mail: pgarimella@onelegacy.org
URL: http://www.onelegacy.org
Formerly: Inland Eye and Tissue Bank.

35430 ■ PacifiCord
185 Technology Dr., Ste. 150
Irvine, CA 92618
Free: 888-379-2670
Fax: (949)789-0337
E-mail: info@PacifiCord.com
URL: http://www.pacificord.com

35431 ■ San Diego Blood Bank--El Cajon
776 Arnele Ave.
El Cajon, CA 92020
Ph: (619)441-1804
URL: http://www.sandiegobloodbank.org/

35432 ■ San Diego Blood Bank--El Centro Imperial Valley Blood Services
1575 W Main
El Centro, CA 92243
Ph: (760)482-0173
URL: http://www.sandiegobloodbank.org/

35433 ■ San Diego Blood Bank--Escondido
1340 W Valley Pkwy.
Escondido, CA 92029
Ph: (760)489-0621
URL: http://www.sandiegobloodbank.org/

35434 ■ San Diego Blood Bank--Murrieta Valley Blood Services
25115 Madison Ave., Ste. 105
Murrieta, CA 92562
Ph: (951)696-4067
URL: http://www.sandiegobloodbank.org/

35435 ■ San Diego Blood Bank--National City
1727 Sweetwater Rd., Ste. Z
National City, CA 91950
Ph: (616)336-4090
URL: http://www.sandiegobloodbank.org/

35436 ■ San Diego Blood Bank--San Diego
440 Upas St.
San Diego, CA 92103
Ph: (619)296-6393
URL: http://www.sandiegobloodbank.org/

35437 ■ San Diego Blood Bank--San Diego
3636 Gateway Center Ave., Ste. 100
San Diego, CA 92102
Free: 800-4MY-SDBB
URL: http://www.sandiegobloodbank.org/

35438 ■ San Diego Blood Bank--Vista
161 Thunder Dr.
Vista, CA 92083
Ph: (760)945-1906
URL: http://www.sandiegobloodbank.org/

35439 ■ San Diego Eye Bank
9246 Lightwave Ave., Ste. 120
San Diego, CA 92123
Ph: (858)694-0400
Free: 800-EYE-BANK
Fax: (858)565-7368
E-mail: sdeb@sdeb.org
URL: http://www.sandiegoeyebank.org

35440 ■ Stemcyte, Inc.
1589 W Industrial Park St.
Covina, CA 91722
Ph: (626)430-9042
Free: 866-389-4659
E-mail: info@stemcytefamily.com
URL: http://www.stemcyte.com/

35441 ■ Tissue Banks International--San Rafael
National Processing Center
2597 Kerner Blvd.
San Rafael, CA 94901
Ph: (415)455-9000
Free: 800-922-3100
Fax: (415)455-9335
URL: http://www.tbionline.org/

35442 ■ Tissue Banks International--Santa Ana
Orange County Eye and Tissue Bank
Santa Ana Tustin Medical Center
801 N Tustin Ave., Ste. 102
Santa Ana, CA 92705-3731
Ph: (714)550-1022
E-mail: ocetb@aol.com

35443 ■ University of California, Los Angeles School of Medicine
Jules Stein Eye Institute
100 Stein Plz.
Los Angeles, CA 90095
Ph: (310)825-5000
URL: http://www.jsei.org

35444 ■ University of California Medical Center, Davis
Transplant Center
2315 Stockton Blvd.
Sacramento, CA 95817
Ph: (916)734-2111
Free: 800-821-9912
E-mail: transplant@ucdavis.edu
URL: http://www.ucdmc.ucdavis.edu/transplant/

35445 ■ University of California, San Francisco
Tissue Bank
2340 Sutter St., Rm. N261
San Francisco, CA 94143
Ph: (415)502-0555
Fax: (415)353-9530
E-mail: Roshni.Ray@cc.ucsf.edu
URL: http://thoraciconcologylab.ucsf.edu

COLORADO

35446 ■ AlloSource--Colorado
6278 S Troy Cir.
Centennial, CO 80111
Ph: (720)873-0213
Free: 888-873-8330
Fax: (720)873-0212
E-mail: info@allosource.org
URL: http://www.allosource.org

35447 ■ Bonfils Blood Center
717 Yosemite St.
Denver, CO 80230
Ph: (303)341-4000
Free: 800-365-0006
URL: http://www.bonfils.org/

35448 ■ Donor Alliance, Inc.
720 S Colorado Blvd., Ste. 800-N
Denver, CO 80246
Ph: (303)329-4747
Free: 888-868-4747
Fax: (303)321-0366
E-mail: donoralliance@donoralliance.org
URL: http://www.donoralliance.org/

35449 ■ Rocky Mountain Lions Eye Bank
PO Box 6026
Aurora, CO 80045
Ph: (720)848-3937
Free: 800-444-7479
Fax: (720)848-3938
E-mail: info@corneas.org
URL: http://www.corneas.org

35450 ■ Rocky Mountain Tissue Bank
2993 S Peoria St., Ste. 390
Aurora, CO 80014
Ph: (303)337-3330
Free: 800-424-5136
Fax: (303)337-9383
E-mail: debspill@aol.com
URL: http://www.rmtb.org/

35451 ■ Science Care of Colorado
19301 E 23rd Ave.
Aurora, CO 80011
Ph: (303)373-0900
Free: 866-887-0900
Fax: (303)373-1919
E-mail: james.rogers@sciencecare.com
URL: http://www.sciencecare.com
Remarks: Non-transplantable tissues.

35452 ■ University of Colorado
Cord Blood Bank
ClinImmune Labs
Bioscience Park Center
12635 E Montview Blvd., Ste. 300
Aurora, CO 80045
Ph: (303)724-1300
E-mail: Stephanie.Warnell@ucdenver.edu
URL: http://www.clinimmune.com

CONNECTICUT

35453 ■ Connecticut Eye Bank and Visual Research Foundation
Research Foundation Inc.
234 Church St., 15th Fl.
New Haven, CT 06510
Ph: (203)404-4900
E-mail: rturkel@aol.com
URL: http://www.unitedforsight.org/news/eyebank.php

35454 ■ Lifeline Cryogenics, LLC
1275 Summer St., Ste. 204
Stamford, CT 06905-0000
Ph: (203)967-2796
Free: 866-967-2796
E-mail: info@lifelinecryogenics.com
URL: http://www.lifelinecryogenics.com

DISTRICT OF COLUMBIA

35455 ■ Eye Bank Association of America (EBAA)
1015 18th St. NW, Ste. 1010
Washington, DC 20036
Ph: (202)775-4999
Fax: (202)429-6036
E-mail: info@restoresight.org
URL: http://www.restoresight.org
David Korroch, Chairman
Description: Eye banks working to restore sight through the promotion and advancement of eye banking. Makes possible over 46,000 corneal transplants annually. Establishes standards for the procurement and distribution of eyes and corneal tissue. Offers training and certification programs for eye banking personnel. Compiles statistics; maintains speakers' bureau. Conducts research and educational programs.

FLORIDA

35456 ■ Allograft Innovations LLC
3542 NW 97th Blvd.
Gainesville, FL 32606
Ph: (352)333-0778
Free: 866-530-2669
Fax: (352)333-6925
E-mail: thomas@allograftinnovations.com
URL: http://www.allograftinnovations.com

35457 ■ AssureImmune LLC
1095 Broken Sound Pkwy. NW, Ste. 203
Boca Raton, FL 33487
Ph: (561)750-6030
Free: 888-346-6863
Fax: (561)750-6036
E-mail: info@assureimmune.com
URL: http://www.assureimmune.com

35458 ■ AxoGen Inc.
13859 Progress Blvd., Ste. 100
Aluchua, FL 32615
Ph: (386)462-6800
Fax: (386)462-6801
E-mail: mfriedman@axogeninc.com
URL: http://www.axogeninc.com

35459 ■ CORD:USE Cord Blood Bank
1991 Summit Park Dr., Ste. 2000
Orlando, FL 32810
Ph: (407)667-3000
Free: 888-267-3873
Fax: (407)667-3003
E-mail: contact@corduse.com
URL: http://www.corduse.com

35460 ■ Cryo-Cell International Inc.
700 Brooker Creek Blvd., Ste. 1800
Oldsmar, FL 34677-2905
Ph: (813)749-2100
Free: 800-786-7235
Fax: (813)855-4745
URL: http://www.cryo-cell.com
David I. Portnoy, Chief Executive Officer

35461 ■ Florida Blood Services, Inc.
10100 MLK Jr. St. N
Saint Petersburg, FL 33716
Ph: (727)568-5433
URL: http://www.fbsblood.org/

35462 ■ Florida Lions Eye Bank Inc.
900 NW 17th St., Ste. 347
Miami, FL 33136
Ph: (305)326-6359
Fax: (305)326-6394
E-mail: efcaraza@med.miami.edu
URL: http://www.fleb.org

35463 ■ Florida Tissue Services
12276 San Jose Blvd., Ste. 706
Jacksonville, FL 32223
Ph: (904)262-7711

35464 ■ GeneCell International--Clermont
1067 Glenraven
Clermont, FL 34711
Ph: (305)753-6754
Free: 888-994-3632
E-mail: equintero@genecell.com
URL: http://www.genecell.com

35465 ■ GeneCell International--Miami
8785 SW 165th Ave., Ste. 101
Miami, FL 33193
Ph: (305)382-6737
Free: 888-994-3632
Fax: (305)382-6062
URL: http://www.genecell.com

35466 ■ Gift of Life
800 Yamato Rd., Ste. 101
Boca Raton, FL 33431
Ph: (561)982-2900
Free: 800-9-MARROW
Fax: (561)982-2901
URL: http://www.giftoflife.org

35467 ■ International Sight Restoration Inc.
3808 Gunn Hwy.
Tampa, FL 33618
Ph: (813)264-6003
Fax: (813)264-6007
E-mail: contact@internationalsight.com
URL: http://www.internationalsight.com

35468 ■ Lifeforce Cryobanks
270 North Lake Blvd., Ste. 1012
Altamonte Springs, FL 32701-4335
Free: 800-869-8608
E-mail: info@lifeforcecryobanks.com
URL: http://www.cryo-intl.com
Formerly: Cryobanks International, Inc.

35469 ■ LifeLink Tissue Bank
9661 Delaney Creek Rd.
Tampa, FL 33619
Ph: (813)886-8111
Free: 800-683-2400
Fax: (813)888-9419
E-mail: dan.shires@lifelinkfound.org
URL: http://www.lifelinkfound.org/

35470 ■ LifeNet Health of Florida
3298 Summit Blvd., Ste. 29
Pensacola, FL 32503
E-mail: Michael_Plew@lifenethealth.org
URL: http://www.lifenethealth.org
Formerly: Florida Tissue Services.

35471 ■ LifeSouth Community Blood Center Headquarters
Civitan Regional Blood Center--Donor Testing Laboratory
4039 Newberry Rd.
Gainesville, FL 32607
Ph: (352)224-1610
Free: 888-795-2707
E-mail: info@lifesouth.org
URL: http://www.lifesouth.org

35472 ■ LifeSouth Community Blood Centers, Inc.
Civitan Region
1221 NW 13th St.
Gainesville, FL 32601
Ph: (352)334-1000
URL: http://www.lifesouth.org

35473 ■ LifeSouth
LifeCord
4039 Newberry Rd.
Gainesville, FL 32607
Ph: (352)224-1600
Free: 888-795-2707
URL: http://www.lifesouth.org/
Dr. John R. Wingard, Director

35474 ■ LifeTek OrthoBiologics, LLC
106 SW 140th Terr., Ste. 3
Gainesville, FL 32669
Free: 800-681-4953
Fax: (352)333-4953
E-mail: csimmons@lifetek.org

35475 ■ Lions Eye Institute for Transplant and Research
1410 N 21st St.
Tampa, FL 33605
Ph: (813)289-1200
Fax: (813)289-1800
E-mail: jwoody@lionseyeinstitute.org
URL: http://www.lionseyeinstitute.org
Program(s): Tissue and Eye Bank. **Remarks:** Dedicated to the recovery, evaluation and distribution of eye tissue for transplantation, research and education. **Formerly:** Central Florida Lions Eye and Tissue Bank Inc.

35476 ■ Medical Eye Bank of Florida
2177 E Michigan St., Ste. 2
Orlando, FL 32806
Ph: (407)422-2020
URL: http://ahca.myflorida.com

35477 ■ NeoCells
36430 US Hwy. 19N
Palm Harbor, FL 34684
Free: 888-502-3557
Fax: (888)402-3557
E-mail: Help@NeoCells.com
URL: http://www.neocells.com

35478 ■ New England Cord Blood Bank--Miami
1000 5th St., Ste. 200
Miami Beach, FL 33139
Ph: (305)704-3270
URL: http://www.cordbloodbank.com

35479 ■ New Hope Cord Blood Bank
2971 Northeast St., No. 1902
Aventura, FL 33180
Ph: (813)952-7736
Free: 888-7-STEMCELLS
Fax: (888)837-3767
URL: http://www.newhopecordbloodbank.com

35480 ■ ReproTech, Ltd., Fort Lauderdale
4661 Johnson Rd., Ste. 2
Coconut Creek, FL 33073
Free: 888-953-9669
Fax: (954)570-7696
E-mail: info@reprot.com
URL: http://www.reprot.com

35481 ■ RTI Biologics Inc.
11621 Research Cir.
Alachua, FL 32615
Ph: (386)418-8888
Free: 877-343-6832
Fax: (386)418-0342
URL: http://www.rtix.com/

35482 ■ RTI Donor Services--Alachua
11621 Research Cir.
Alachua, FL 32615
Ph: (386)418-8888
Free: 877-343-6832
Fax: (386)462-3821
E-mail: chartill@rtidonorservices.org
URL: http://www.rtidonorservices.org
Formerly: Regeneration Technologies, Inc.

35483 ■ Southeast Tissue Alliance, Inc.
6241 NW 23rd St., Ste. 400
Gainesville, FL 32653-7105
Ph: (352)248-2114
Free: 866-432-1164
Fax: (352)384-9323
E-mail: smccann@donorcare.org
URL: http://www.donorcare.org/

35484 ■ TissueNet
7022 TPC Dr., Ste. 400
Orlando, FL 32822
Ph: (407)380-2424
Free: 800-465-8800
Fax: (407)380-2660
E-mail: thuynh@tissuenet.com
URL: http://www.tissuenet.com

35485 ■ University of Miami Tissue Bank
1600 NW 10th Ave., RMSB, Rm. 8053
Miami, FL 33136
Free: 888-684-7738
Fax: (305)243-4622
E-mail: lposton@med.miami.edu
URL: http://www.umiamitb.org

GEORGIA

35486 ■ Alpha Cord Inc.
2200 Century Pkwy., Ste. 9
Atlanta, GA 30345
Ph: (404)315-6500
Free: 866-396-7283
Fax: (404)795-9126
E-mail: contact@alphacord.com
URL: http://www.alphacord.com

35487 ■ Cord Blood Solutions
Alpharetta, GA
Ph: (678)513-4656
Free: 866-584-7836
E-mail: aeinstein@cordbloodsolutions.com
URL: http://www.cordbloodsolutions.com

35488 ■ CryoLife Inc.
1655 Roberts Blvd. NW, Ste. 142
Kennesaw, GA 30144-3632
Ph: (770)419-3355
Free: 800-438-8285
Fax: (770)426-0031
E-mail: info@cryolife.com
URL: http://www.cryolife.com
Steven G. Anderson, President

35489 ■ Georgia Eye Bank
5605 Glenridge Dr. NE, Ste. 250
Atlanta, GA 30342
Ph: (404)264-1900
Free: 800-342-9812
Fax: (404)264-9111
E-mail: sight@georgiaeyebank.org
URL: http://www.georgiaeyebank.org

35490 ■ Stork Medical
Columbus, GA
Free: 866-65-STORK
URL: http://www.stork.md

35491 ■ Surgical Biologics
MiMedx Group
60 Chastain Center Blvd., Ste. 60
Kennesaw, GA 30144
Ph: (404)461-9265
Fax: (770)218-6195
E-mail: kchristie@surgicalbiologics.com
URL: http://www.surgicalbiologics.com

35492 ■ Xytex Cord Blood Bank
1100 Emmett St.
Augusta, GA 30904
Ph: (706)733-0130
Free: 877-505-4346
Fax: (706)736-9720
E-mail: tissues@xytex.com
URL: http://www.xytexcordblood.com

HAWAII

35493 ■ Hawaii Cord Blood Bank
1319 Punahou St.
Honolulu, HI 96826
Ph: (808)983-2265
Fax: (808)983-8719
E-mail: info@hcbb.org
URL: http://www.hcbb.org

35494 ■ Hawaii Lions Eye Bank & Makana Foundation
614 South St., Ste. 101
Honolulu, HI 96813
Ph: (808)536-7416
Fax: (808)528-5032
E-mail: shawn@hlebmf.org
URL: http://www.hlebmf.org

IDAHO

35495 ■ Community Tissue Services--Boise
390 Park Center, Ste. 120
Boise, ID 83706
Ph: (208)389-2194

Free: 866-284-7783
URL: http://www.communitytissue.org

35496 ■ Idaho Lions Eye Bank
1090 N Cole Rd.
Boise, ID 83704
Ph: (208)338-5466
Free: 800-546-6889
Fax: (208)338-6543
E-mail: jay@idahlions.org
URL: http://www.idaholions.org/

ILLINOIS

35497 ■ Allosource--Chicago
311 W Superior, Ste. 212
Chicago, IL 60654
Ph: (312)274-1401
Free: 800-762-4123
Fax: (312)274-1415
URL: http://www.allosource.org

35498 ■ Central Illinois Community Blood Bank--Edwardsville
5 Club Center Ct., Ste. B
Edwardsville, IL 62025
Ph: (618)659-0542
Free: 866-448-3253
Fax: (618)659-1014
E-mail: cicbb@justbusiness.net
URL: http://www.cicbc.org

35499 ■ Central Illinois Community Blood Bank--Springfield
1134 S 7th St.
Springfield, IL 62703
Ph: (217)753-1530
Free: 866-448-3253
Fax: (217)753-8116
E-mail: cicbb@justbusiness.net
URL: http://www.cicbc.org

35500 ■ Gift of Hope
425 Spring Lake Dr.
Itasca, IL 60143
Ph: (630)758-2600
Free: 888-307-3668
Fax: (630)758-2603
E-mail: alim@giftofhope.org
URL: http://www.giftofhope.org

35501 ■ Heartland Lions Eye Bank--Springfield, IL
800 E Carpenter
Springfield, IL 62769
Ph: (217)757-6050
Fax: (217)757-6055
URL: http://www.hleb.org

35502 ■ Illinois Eye-Bank, Chicago
547 W Jackson Blvd., Ste. 600
Chicago, IL 60661
Ph: (312)706-6750
Free: 800-548-4703
Fax: (312)706-6777
E-mail: info@illinoiseyebank.org
URL: http://www.illinoiseyebank.org

35503 ■ Illinois Eye-Bank, Watson Gailey
301 S Prospect, Ste. 2
Bloomington, IL 61704
Ph: (312)706-6770
Free: 800-548-4703
Fax: (312)706-6777
E-mail: info@illinoiseyebank.org
URL: http://www.illinoiseyebank.org

35504 ■ ITxM Clinical Services Cord Blood Services
Glenview, IL
Free: 800-627-7692
URL: http://www.givcord.org

35505 ■ Vascular Transplant Services--Schaumburg
2122 Palmer Dr.
Schaumburg, IL 60173
Ph: (847)925-0979
Fax: (847)303-5601
E-mail: tstevens@vtsrl.org
URL: http://www.vasculartransplantservices.org

INDIANA

35506 ■ Community Tissue Services, Indiana
7770 E 88th St.
Indianapolis, IN 46256
Ph: (317)842-0009
Free: 800-984-7783
Fax: (317)842-0243
E-mail: broe@cbccts.org
URL: http://www.communitytissue.org/

35507 ■ Donor Services of Indiana
6931 Quemetco Ct.
Fort Wayne, IN 46803
Ph: (260)749-9105
Free: 877-749-9105
Fax: (260)749-8304
E-mail: ttibbot@dsitissuebank.org
URL: http://www.dsitissuebank.org

35508 ■ Genesis Bank LLC
1102 Stadium Dr.
Indianapolis, IN 46202
Free: 800-265-0945
Fax: (317)917-3444
URL: http://www.thegenesisbank.com

35509 ■ Indiana Lions Eye and Tissue Transplant Bank
727 E 86th St.
Indianapolis, IN 46240
Ph: (317)808-5000
Free: 800-232-4384
Fax: (317)808-5026
E-mail: tfischer@ilettb.org
URL: http://www.indianalionseyebank.org
Formerly: Tissue Banks International.

35510 ■ Indiana Organ Procurement Organization--Indianapolis Eye and Tissue Bank
3760 Guion Rd.
Indianapolis, IN 46222
Ph: (317)685-0389
Free: 888-275-4676
Fax: (317)685-1687
E-mail: kellich@iopo.org
URL: http://www.iopo.org/

35511 ■ Indiana Organ Procurement Organization--Northeast Eye and Tissue Bank
7220 Engle Rd.
Fort Wayne, IN 46804
Free: 888-275-4676
Fax: (260)436-4275
E-mail: info@iopo.org
URL: http://www.iopo.org/

35512 ■ Indiana Organ Procurement Organization--Northwest Indiana Eye and Tissue Bank
326 W Plum St.
Argos, IN 46501
Free: 888-275-4676
E-mail: info@iopo.org
URL: http://www.iopo.org/

35513 ■ Indiana Organ Procurement Organization--Southern Indiana Eye and Tissue Bank
Deaconess Hospital, Rm. 3215
600 Mary St.
Evansville, IN 47747
Free: 888-275-4676
E-mail: info@iopo.org
URL: http://www.iopo.org/

35514 ■ Midwest Cord Blood Bank
1102 Indiana Ave.
Indianapolis, IN 46202
Free: 800-804-6703
Fax: (317)917-3444
URL: http://www.midwestcordbloodbank.org
Formerly: Indiana Cord Blood Bank.

35515 ■ New Life Generation Inc.
9755 West Point Dr.
Indianapolis, IN 46256
Free: 888-922-4483
Fax: (317)913-0500
E-mail: dzigler@newlifegen.org
URL: http://www.newlifegen.org

IOWA

35516 ■ Iowa Donor Network--Johnston
8191 Birchwood Ct., Ste. A
Johnston, IA 50131
Ph: (515)727-7897
Free: 800-831-4131
Fax: (515)727-7911
URL: http://www.iowadonornetwork.org/

35517 ■ Iowa Donor Network--North Liberty
550 Madison Ave.
North Liberty, IA 52317
Ph: (319)665-3787
Free: 800-831-4131
Fax: (319)665-3788
E-mail: sfewell@iadn.org
URL: http://www.iowadonornetwork.org/

35518 ■ Iowa Donor Network--Sioux City
801 5th St., Rm. 5182
Sioux City, IA 51101
Free: 800-831-4131
URL: http://www.iowadonornetwork.org/

35519 ■ Iowa Lions Eye Bank--Iowa City
2346 Mormon Trek Blvd., Ste. 1500
Iowa City, IA 52246
Ph: (319)356-2871
Fax: (319)384-9781
E-mail: Cynthia-Reed@uiowa.edu
URL: http://www.iowalionseyebank.org

35520 ■ University of Iowa Cord Blood Bank
Carver College of Medicine
Iowa City, IA
Ph: (319)384-8667
E-mail: cord-blood@uiowa.edu
URL: http://www.medicine.uiowa.edu/Programs/CordBlood/

KANSAS

35521 ■ Heartland Lions Eye Bank--Hays, KS
1111 E 30th St.
Hays, KS 67601
Ph: (785)650-0661
Fax: (785)650-0667
URL: http://www.hleb.org

35522 ■ Heartland Lions Eye Bank--Wichita, KS
9415 E Harry St., Ste. 106
Wichita, KS 67207
Ph: (316)613-2250
Fax: (316)613-2307
URL: http://www.hleb.org

35523 ■ Kansas Eye Bank and Cornea Research Center
625 N Carriage Pkwy., Ste. 190
Wichita, KS 67208
Ph: (316)260-8220

Free: 866-825-6516
Fax: (316)260-8225
URL: http://kansaseyebank.org
Formerly: Mid-Continent Eye Bank.

35524 ■ Midwest Transplant Network
1900 W 47th Pl., Ste. 400
Westwood, KS 66205
Ph: (913)262-1668
Fax: (913)261-6486
E-mail: info@mwtn.org
URL: http://www.mwtn.org

KENTUCKY

35525 ■ Kentucky Organ Donor Affiliates--Bowling Green
830 Fairview Ave.
Bowling Green, KY 42101
Ph: (270)793-9897
Free: 800-525-3456
Fax: (270)793-5658
URL: http://www.kyorgandonor.org/

35526 ■ Kentucky Organ Donor Affiliates--Lexington
2201 Regency Rd., Ste. 601
Lexington, KY 40503
Ph: (859)278-3492
Free: 800-525-3456
Fax: (859)278-0187
URL: http://www.kyorgandonor.org/

35527 ■ Kentucky Organ Donor Affiliates--Louisville
106 E Broadway
Louisville, KY 40202
Ph: (502)581-9511
Free: 800-525-3456
Fax: (502)589-5157
URL: http://www.kyorgandonor.org/

35528 ■ Kentucky Organ Donor Affiliates--Paducah
2320 Broadway
Paducah, KY 42001
Ph: (207)443-0658
Free: 800-525-3456
Fax: (207)443-3518
URL: http://www.kyorgandonor.org/

35529 ■ Norton Healthcare, Inc. Cord Blood Storage Program
200 E Chestnut St.
Louisville, KY 40202
Ph: (502)629-1234
Free: 800-852-1770
URL: http://www.nortonhealthcare.com/familylink-cordbloodstorageprogram

35530 ■ University of Kentucky Lions Eye Bank of Lexington
3290 Blazer Pkwy., Ste. 201
Lexington, KY 40509
Ph: (859)323-6740
Fax: (859)323-5927
E-mail: ragayh2@uky.edu
URL: http://www.mc.uky.edu/eyebank

35531 ■ University of Louisville Lions Eye Bank
301 E Muhammad Ali Blvd.
Louisville, KY 40202
Ph: (502)852-5457
Fax: (502)852-5471
E-mail: jrbill01@louisville.edu
URL: http://www.ulleb.org

LOUISIANA

35532 ■ Baton Rouge Regional Eye Bank
7777 Hennessy Blvd., Ste. 207
Baton Rouge, LA 70808
Ph: (225)766-8996
Fax: (225)765-4366
E-mail: info@eyebankbr.org
URL: http://www.eyebankbr.org
Formerly: Our Lady of Lake Regional Medical Center.

35533 ■ Children's Hospital Transfusion Service
200 Henry Clay Ave.
New Orleans, LA 70118
Ph: (504)896-9873
URL: http://www.chnola.org/PageDisplay.asp?p1=4348

35534 ■ LifeSource Cryobank LLC
101 E Fairway Dr., Ste. 502
Covington, LA 70433
Ph: (985)867-8902
Free: 866-400-7333
Fax: (985)867-8259
URL: http://www.lifesourcecryobank.com

35535 ■ Louisiana Organ Procurement Agency
3545 N-I-10 Service Rd. W, Ste. 300
Metairie, LA 70002
Free: 800-521-GIVE
Fax: (504)648-3448
E-mail: kranum@lopa.org
URL: http://www.lopa.org

35536 ■ Northwest Louisiana Lions Eye Bank
721 Boulevard St.
Shreveport, LA 71104
Ph: (318)222-7999
Fax: (318)222-8779
E-mail: Mike@lalionseyebank.org
URL: http://www.lalionseyebank.org

35537 ■ Southern Eye Bank
2701 Kingman St., Ste. 200
Metairie, LA 70006
Ph: (504)891-3937
Fax: (504)891-2401
URL: http://southerneyebank.com/eye

MANITOBA

35538 ■ Lions Eye Bank of Manitoba and Northwest Ontario Inc.
105-691 Wolseley Ave.
Winnipeg, MB, Canada R3G 1C3
Ph: (204)788-8507
Fax: (204)943-6823
E-mail: lfmnoi@mts.net
URL: http://www.eyebankmanitoba.com

MARYLAND

35539 ■ Living Legacy Foundation
1730 Twin Springs Rd., Ste. 200
Baltimore, MD 21227
Ph: (410)242-7000
Free: 800-641-4376
Fax: (410)242-1871
E-mail: communications@thellf.org
URL: http://www.thellf.org/
Formerly: Transplant Resource Center of Maryland.

35540 ■ Medical Eye Bank of Maryland
815 Park Ave.
Baltimore, MD 21201
Ph: (410)752-2020
Fax: (410)545-4455
URL: http://www.tbionline.org
Formerly: Doheny Eye & Tissue Transplant Bank.

35541 ■ Osiris Therapeutics Inc.
7015 Albert Einstein Dr.
Columbia, MD 21046
Ph: (443)545-1800
Free: 888-674-7471
Fax: (443)545-1701
E-mail: Osiris@Osiris.com
URL: http://www.osiristx.com/

35542 ■ Tissue Banks International--Baltimore
815 Park Ave.
Baltimore, MD 21201
Ph: (410)752-3800
Fax: (410)783-0183
URL: http://www.tbionline.org

MASSACHUSETTS

35543 ■ California Cryobank, Inc., Cambridge
950 Massachusetts Ave.
Cambridge, MA 02139
Ph: (617)497-8646
Fax: (617)497-6531
E-mail: dschillinger@cryobank.com
URL: http://www.cryobank.com/

35544 ■ ETEX Corporation
38 Sidney St.
Cambridge, MA 02139
Free: 877-383-9276
Fax: (617)577-7170
E-mail: egolovchenko@etexcorp.com
URL: http://etexcorp.com

35545 ■ FamilyCord--Cambridge
950 Massachusetts
Cambridge, MA 02139
Ph: (310)496-5651
Free: 800-490-2673
Fax: (310)315-0472
URL: http://www.familycord.com

35546 ■ New England Cord Blood Bank Inc.--Newton, MA
Bldg. 1
153 Needham St.
Newton, MA 02464
Ph: (617)244-3933
Free: 888-700-2673
Fax: (617)244-4483
E-mail: info@cordbloodbank.com
URL: http://www.cordbloodbank.com

35547 ■ New England Cryogenic Center, Inc.
153 Needham St.
Newton, MA 02464
Ph: (617)244-4447
Free: 800-991-4999
Fax: (617)244-6659
E-mail: info@necryogenic.com
URL: http://www.necryogenic.com

35548 ■ New England Eye & Tissue Transplant Bank
3 Longfellow Pl., Ste. 100
Boston, MA 02114
Ph: (617)523-3937
E-mail: neettb@tbionline.org

35549 ■ New England Organ Bank Tissue Banking Services
60 1st St.
Waltham, MA 02451
Free: 800-446-6362
Fax: (617)244-8755
E-mail: larry_sussman@newenglandeyebank.org
URL: http://www.newenglandeyebank.org/

35550 ■ Organogenesis Inc.
150 Dan Rd.
Canton, MA 02021
Free: 888-432-5232
Fax: (781)401-1288
E-mail: gabraham@organo.com
URL: http://www.organo.com

35551 ■ Viacord, Inc.
245 1st St., 15th Fl.
Cambridge, MA 02142
Ph: (617)914-3900

Free: 866-668-4895
Fax: (866)565-2243
E-mail: info@viacord.com
URL: http://www.viacord.com

MICHIGAN

35552 ■ Asterand
TechOne Ste. 501
440 Burroughs
Detroit, MI 48202-3420
Ph: (313)263-0960
Free: 866-3-TISSUE
Fax: (313)263-0961
URL: http://www.asterand.com

35553 ■ Barbara Ann Karmanos Cancer Institute
J.P. McCarthy Cord Stem Cell Bank
4100 John R, MC HW04HO
Detroit, MI 48201
Free: 800--KARMANOS
E-mail: cord@karmanos.org
URL: http://www.karmanos.org/app.asp?id=1142

35554 ■ Gift of Life Michigan
Eye Banking Division
3861 Research Park Dr.
Ann Arbor, MI 48108
Free: 800-482-4881
URL: http://www.giftoflifemichigan.org

35555 ■ Michigan Community Blood Centers
1036 Fuller Ave. NE
Grand Rapids, MI 49503
Ph: (616)233-8604
Free: 866-642-5663
E-mail: info@miblood.org
URL: http://www.miblood.org

35556 ■ Midwest Eye Banks
Michigan Eye Bank
4889 Venture Dr.
Ann Arbor, MI 48108
Ph: (734)780-2100
Free: 800-247-7250
Fax: (734)780-2111
E-mail: info@michiganeyebank.org
URL: http://www.michiganeyebank.org
Formerly: Midwest Eye Banks and Transplantation Center.

MINNESOTA

35557 ■ Allosource--Minneapolis
PO Box 19058
Minneapolis, MN 55419
Free: 800-558-5004
Fax: (513)246-4109
URL: http://www.allosource.org

35558 ■ American Donor Services
1285 Nininger Rd., Ste. 205
Hastings, MN 55033
Ph: (651)437-1018
Free: 877-365-3668
Fax: (651)437-1117
E-mail: rhaliburton@americandonorservices.org
URL: http://www.americandonorservices.org

35559 ■ Cryogenic Laboratories, Inc.
1944 Lexington Ave. N
Roseville, MN 55113
Free: 800-466-2796
Fax: (651)489-0340
E-mail: info@cryolab.com
URL: http://www.cryolab.com/

35560 ■ Fairview University Medical Center
Riverside Campus Clinical Laboratory/Blood Bank
2450 Riverside Ave.
Minneapolis, MN 55454
Ph: (612)672-4010
URL: http://pathology.umn.edu/clinical/home.html

35561 ■ Laboratory Services
WuXi AppTec Inc.
2450 Executive Dr.
Saint Paul, MN 55120
Ph: (651)675-2000
Free: 888-794-0077
Fax: (651)675-2005
E-mail: Sylvester.Williams@wuxiapptec.com
URL: http://www.wuxiapptec.com/

35562 ■ LifeSource
2550 University Ave. W, Ste. 315S
Saint Paul, MN 55114
Ph: (651)605-7800
Free: 888-536-6283
Fax: (651)603-7801
E-mail: kgeist@life-source.org
URL: http://www.life-source.org

35563 ■ Minnesota Lions Eye Bank
1000 Westgate Dr., Ste. 260
Saint Paul, MN 55114
Ph: (612)624-6446
Free: 866-887-4448
Fax: (612)625-4295
E-mail: mleb@umn.edu
URL: http://www.mnlionseyebank.org
Carol Engel, Director

35564 ■ ReproTech, Ltd.--Saint Paul, MN
550 Village Center Dr., Ste. 300
Saint Paul, MN 55127
Ph: (651)489-0827
Free: 888-489-8944
Fax: (651)489-0442
E-mail: rcbierbaum@reprot.com
URL: http://www.reprot.com

MISSISSIPPI

35565 ■ FamilyCord--Southeast Region
102C Rue de Grand Fromage
Starkville, MS 39759
Ph: (310)496-5651
Free: 800-490-2673
Fax: (310)315-0472
URL: http://www.familycord.com

35566 ■ Mississippi Lions Eye Bank
431 Katherine Dr.
Flowood, MS 39232
Ph: (601)420-5739
Fax: (601)420-5734
E-mail: lionsofms@aol.com
URL: http://www.mslionseyebank.org

MISSOURI

35567 ■ Allosource--Saint Louis
1110 Highlands Plaza Dr., Ste. 100
Saint Louis, MO 63110
Ph: (314)781-0246
Free: 800-477-8655
Fax: (314)781-0166
URL: http://www.allosource.org

35568 ■ Heartland Lions Eye Bank--Joplin, MO
1329 E 32nd St., Ste. 7
Joplin, MO 64804
Ph: (417)624-2494
Fax: (417)624-4131
URL: http://www.hleb.org

35569 ■ Heartland Lions Eye Bank--Kansas City, MO
10100 N Ambassador Dr., Ste. 200
Kansas City, MO 64153
Ph: (816)454-5454
Fax: (816)454-5446
URL: http://www.hleb.org/

35570 ■ Heartland Lions Eye Bank--Saint Louis, MO
10801 Pear Tree Ln., Ste. 170
Saint Louis, MO 63074
Ph: (314)428-4373
Fax: (314)428-3751
URL: http://www.hleb.org

35571 ■ Heartland Lions Eye Bank--Springfield, MO
3506 S Culpepper, Ste. D&F
Springfield, MO 65807
Ph: (417)887-0063
Fax: (417)882-8206
URL: http://www.hleb.org/

35572 ■ ISTO Technologies Inc.
1155 Olivette Exec. Pkwy., Ste. 200
Saint Louis, MO 63132
Ph: (314)995-6049
Fax: (407)432-6826
E-mail: jkrebs@istotech.com
URL: http://www.istotech.com

35573 ■ Mid-America Transplant Services
1110 Highlands Plz. Dr. E, Ste. 100
Saint Louis, MO 63110
Free: 888-376-4854
Fax: (314)754-1782
E-mail: lmartin@mts-stl.org
URL: http://www.mts-stl.org

35574 ■ Missouri Lions Eye Banks, Headquarters
Heartland Lions Eye Bank
404 Portland St.
Columbia, MO 65201
Ph: (573)443-1471
Free: 800-753-2265
Fax: (573)443-1657
E-mail: ron@mlerf.org
URL: http://www.hleb.org
Ronald J. Walkenbach, Director
Program(s): Eye Tissue Bank; Community Education; Research; Glaucoma Detection Screening; Eye Care Assistance; Eyeglass Recycling; Amblyopia Screening. **Remarks:** Delivers recycled eyeglasses to supplement visual care to persons in Third World countries.

35575 ■ Saint Louis Cord Blood Bank
3662 Park Ave.
Saint Louis, MO 63110
Ph: (314)268-2787
Free: 888-453-2673
Fax: (314)268-4197
URL: http://www.slcbb.org/

MONTANA

35576 ■ Bacterin International, Inc.
Biologics Division
600 Cruiser Ln.
Belgrade, MT 59714
Ph: (406)388-0480
Fax: (406)388-0422
E-mail: info@bacterin.com
URL: http://www.bacterin.com/biologics-division.php?category=biologics

35577 ■ Donate Life Today
2307 Stephens Ave., Unit B
Missoula, MT 59801
Free: 877-275-5269
Fax: (425)688-7641
E-mail: info@lcnw.org
URL: http://www.donatelifetoday.com/

35578 ■ Northwest Tissue Services--Missoula
5225 Hwy. 10 W
Missoula, MT 59802
Ph: (206)292-1879

Free: 888-266-4466
Fax: (206)343-5043
E-mail: info@nwts.org
URL: http://www.nwts.org

NEBRASKA

35579 ■ University of Nebraska Medical Center
Lions Eye Bank of Nebraska
985541 Nebraska Medical Center
Omaha, NE 68198
Ph: (402)559-4039
Fax: (402)559-7705
E-mail: LCKjar@yahoo.com
URL: http://www.eyebanksnebraska.org

NEVADA

35580 ■ CorCell
1857 Helm Dr.
Las Vegas, NV 89119
Ph: (702)914-7250
Free: 888-882-2673
Fax: (888)588-2673
E-mail: info@corcell.com
URL: http://www.corcell.com

35581 ■ Cord Blood America
1857 Helm Dr.
Las Vegas, NV 89119
Ph: (702)914-7250
Free: 888-326-7235
E-mail: info@cordblood-america.com
URL: http://www.cordblood-america.com

35582 ■ Fertility Center of Las Vegas
8851 W Sahara Ave., Ste. 100
Las Vegas, NV 89117
Ph: (702)524-1777
Free: 800-509-7174
Fax: (702)524-1213
E-mail: info@fertilitycenterlv.com
URL: http://www.fertilitycenterlv.com/

35583 ■ Fertility Center of Las Vegas
2769 Sunridge Heights Pkwy., Ste. 100
Henderson, NV 89052
Ph: (702)254-1777
Free: 800-509-7174
Fax: (702)254-1213
E-mail: info@fertilitycenterlv.com
URL: http://www.fertilitycenterlv.com

35584 ■ Nevada Donor Network, Inc.
2085 E Sahara
Las Vegas, NV 89104
Ph: (702)796-9600
Fax: (702)796-4225
E-mail: krichardson@nvdonor.org
URL: http://www.nvdonor.org

35585 ■ Northwestern Bone and Tissue
845 E 2nd St.
Reno, NV 89502
Ph: (775)786-3080
Free: 866-835-8623
Fax: (775)786-3438
E-mail: ghughes@pyramid.net

35586 ■ Regenerative Medicine Institute (RMI)
Las Vegas, NV
Free: 877-844-7379
URL: http://www.rmilabs.com

35587 ■ ReproTech, Ltd.--Reno, NV
110 Country Estates Cir., Ste. 2
Reno, NV 89511
Ph: (665)284-2795
Free: 888-831-2765
Fax: (775)284-2799
URL: http://www.reprotech.com

NEW BRUNSWICK

35588 ■ Doctor Donald MacLellan Tissue Bank
135 MacBeath Ave.
Moncton, NB, Canada E1C 6Z8
Ph: (506)870-2556
Fax: (506)857-5719
E-mail: mary.gatien2@horizonnb.ca
URL: http://www.serha.ca/moncton_hospital/subsections/surgery/htm/english/tissue _bank.htm

35589 ■ New Brunswick Eye and Tissue Bank
130 Bayard Dr.
Saint John, NB, Canada E2L 3L6
Ph: (506)632-5541
URL: http://www.eyesite.ca/english/public-information/eye-bank.htm

NEW JERSEY

35590 ■ BioGenetics Corp.
187 Mill Ln.
Mountainside, NJ 07092
Ph: (908)654-8836
Free: 800-637-7776
Fax: (908)232-2114
E-mail: director@sperm1.com
URL: http://www.sperm1.com/biogenetics/

35591 ■ Community Blood Services
970 Linwood Ave. W
Paramus, NJ 07653
Ph: (201)444-3900
Free: 866-728-2673
Fax: (201)670-6174
URL: http://www.communitybloodservices.org/

35592 ■ HemaStem Therapeutics--Paramus USA Lab
970 Linwood Ave. W
Paramus, NJ 07652
Free: 800-203-7349
URL: http://www.hemastem.com

35593 ■ LifeBank USA
45 Horsehill Rd.
Cedar Knolls, NJ 07927
Free: 877-543-3226
Fax: (877)801-2421
E-mail: info@lifebankusa.com
URL: http://www.lifebankusa.com/

35594 ■ LifeCell Corp.
1 Millennium Way
Branchburg, NJ 08876-3876
Ph: (908)947-1100
Free: 800-717-7427
Fax: (908)947-1200
E-mail: ggreenleaf@lifecell.com
URL: http://www.lifecell.com
Paul G. Thomas, President

35595 ■ Lions Eye Bank of New Jersey Midwest Eye Banks
77 Brant Ave.
Clark, NJ 07066
Ph: (732)382-3060
Fax: (732)499-0650
E-mail: info@lionseyebanknj.org
URL: http://www.lionseyebanknj.org

35596 ■ Medtronic Osteotech, Inc.
51 James Way
Eatontown, NJ 07724
Free: 800-542-2045
Fax: (732)389-8485
E-mail: smonte@medtronic.com
URL: http://www.osteotech.com/

35597 ■ Musculoskeletal Transplant Foundation--Edison, NJ
125 May St., Ste. 300
Edison, NJ 08837
Free: 800-248-9006
Fax: (732)661-2297
E-mail: joel.osborne@mtf.org
URL: http://www.mtf.org

35598 ■ NeoStem Family Stem Cell Banking
4 Pearl Ct., Ste. C
Allendale, NJ 07401
Free: 800-STEM-BANK
Fax: (616)514-7787
E-mail: info@neostem.com
URL: http://neostemcordblood.com

35599 ■ New Jersey Cord Blood Bank
Ellie Katz Umbilical Cord Blood Program
1 Pearl Ct., Unit C
Allendale, NJ 07401
Free: 866--SAVCORD
Fax: (201)251-3900
URL: http://www.communitybloodservices.org/

35600 ■ Sperm and Embryo Bank of New Jersey
187 Mill Ln.
Mountainside, NJ 07092
Ph: (908)654-8836
Free: 800-637-7776
Fax: (908)232-2114
E-mail: director@sperm1.com
URL: http://www.sperm1.com

NEW MEXICO

35601 ■ New Mexico Lions Eye Bank/Lions Eyebank of District 2T1
2501 Yale Blvd. SE, Ste. 100
Albuquerque, NM 87106
Ph: (505)266-3937
Fax: (505)266-5560
E-mail: lstampley@tbionline.org
URL: http://www.lionseyebank.org/

NEW YORK

35602 ■ Allosource--Buffalo
110 Broadway
Buffalo, NY 14203
Ph: (716)566-7199
Free: 888-704-8511
Fax: (716)852-2862
URL: http://www.allosource.org

35603 ■ Americord Registry LLC
244 Madison Ave., Ste. 2770
New York, NY 10016
Free: 866-503-6005
Fax: (646)304-7051
E-mail: info@cordadvantage.com
URL: http://www.cordadvantage.com

35604 ■ California Cryobank, Inc., New York
369 Lexington Ave., Ste. 401
New York, NY 10016
Ph: (212)779-1608
Free: 877-885-2796
Fax: (212)779-2054
URL: http://www.cryobank.com/

35605 ■ Center for Donation and Transplant
218 Great Oaks Blvd.
Albany, NY 12203
Ph: (518)262-5606
Free: 800-256-7811
E-mail: dfloeser@cdtny.org
URL: http://www.cdtny.org

35606 ■ Central New York Eye and Tissue Bank
517 E Washington St.
Syracuse, NY 13202
Ph: (315)476-0199

Free: 800-393-7487
Fax: (315)471-6060
E-mail: msimon@unyts.com
URL: http://www.cnyetb.com

35607 ■ Eye Bank for Sight Restoration
120 Wall St.
New York, NY 10005
Ph: (212)742-9000
Fax: (212)269-3139
E-mail: info@ebsr.org
URL: http://www.eyedonation.org
Program(s): Research. **Remarks:** Eyes donated to the Eye Bank that are medically unsuitable for transplant are used for medical research and education.

35608 ■ FamilyCord--New York
369 Lexington, Ste. 401
New York, NY 10017
Ph: (310)496-5651
Free: 800-490-2673
Fax: (310)315-0472
URL: http://www.familycord.com

35609 ■ Idant Laboratories
350 5th Ave., Ste. 7120
New York, NY 10118
Ph: (212)244-0555
E-mail: info@idant.com
URL: http://www.idant.com/

35610 ■ Lions Eye Bank at Albany
Sight Society of Northeastern New York
6 Executive Park Dr.
Albany, NY 12203
Ph: (518)489-7606
Fax: (518)489-7607
E-mail: vadler@lionseyebankalbany.com
URL: http://www.lionseyebankalbany.com
Formerly: Albany Medical College, Lions Eye Bank at Albany.

35611 ■ Lions Eye Bank for Long Island
North Shore University Hospital
350 Community Dr.
Manhasset, NY 11030
Ph: (516)465-8430
Fax: (516)465-8434
E-mail: kmanger@nshs.edu
URL: http://www.lebli.org

35612 ■ MAZE Cord Blood Laboratories
2975 Westchester Ave., G03
Purchase, NY 10577
Free: 877-629-3522
Fax: (914)683-0974
URL: http://www.mazecordblood.com

35613 ■ NeoStem
Adult Stem Cell Operations
420 Lexington Ave., Ste. 450
New York, NY 10170
Ph: (212)584-4180
Fax: (646)514-7787
URL: http://www.neostem.com

35614 ■ New York Blood Center
National Cord Blood Program
New York, NY
Free: 800-933-2566
E-mail: spraguecml@aol.com
URL: http://www.nybloodcenter.org

35615 ■ New York Cryo
900 Northern Blvd., Ste. 230
Great Neck, NY 10021
Ph: (516)487-2700
Free: 877-7NY-CRYO
Fax: (516)487-2007
E-mail: info@nycryo.com
URL: http://www.nycryo.com

35616 ■ New York Firefighter's Skin Bank
525 E 68th St., F23-11
New York, NY 10021
Ph: (212)746-7546
Fax: (212)746-8177
E-mail: ngallo@nyp.org

35617 ■ New York Organ Donor Network
460 W 34th St.
New York, NY 10001
Ph: (646)291-4444
Fax: (646)291-4600
E-mail: jlewis@nyodn.org
URL: http://www.donatelifeny.org

35618 ■ RMA of New York
635 Madison Ave., 10th Fl.
New York, NY 10022
Free: 866-477-3762
URL: http://www.cryobank.com/

35619 ■ Rochester/Finger Lakes Eye and Tissue Bank
524 White Spruce Blvd.
Rochester, NY 14623
Ph: (585)272-7890
Free: 800-568-4321
Fax: (585)272-7897
E-mail: info@rehpb.org
URL: http://www.rehpb.org

35620 ■ The Sperm Bank of New York Inc.
1090 Amsterdam Ave., 7G
New York, NY 10025
Ph: (212)531-0115
URL: http://donor.sperm1.com/

35621 ■ Upstate New York Transplant Services Inc.
110 Broadway
Buffalo, NY 14203
Ph: (716)853-6667
Free: 800-227-4771
Fax: (716)853-6674
E-mail: info@unyts.org
URL: http://www.unyts.org

NORTH CAROLINA

35622 ■ Carolinas Cord Blood Bank
Duke University Medical Center, Box 3350
Durham, NC 27710
Ph: (919)668-1119
Fax: (919)668-1183
URL: http://www.cancer.duke.edu/ccbb/

35623 ■ Lifeshare Eye Facility--Asheville
1200 Ridgefield Blvd., Ste. 150
Asheville, NC 28806
Ph: (828)665-0107
Free: 800-932-4483
Fax: (828)665-4729
URL: http://www.lifesharecarolinas.org

35624 ■ Lifeshare Eye Facility--Charlotte
5000-D Airport Ctr. Pkwy.
Charlotte, NC 28208
Ph: (704)512-3303
Free: 800-932-4483
Fax: (704)512-3056
URL: http://www.lifesharecarolinas.org
Description: Works to improve the quality of human life by providing organs and tissues for transplantation and helping hospitals and their communities through educational and support services.

35625 ■ The North Carolina Eye Bank
Vision Share
3900 Westpoint Blvd., Ste. F
Winston Salem, NC 27103
Ph: (336)765-0932
Free: 800-552-9956
Fax: (336)499-0123
E-mail: info@nceyebank.org
URL: http://www.nceyebank.org
Kurt Weber, Director

35626 ■ North Carolina Eye and Human Tissue Bank, Inc., Durham
Vision Share
3622 Lyckan Pkwy.
Durham, NC 27707
Ph: (919)489-5242

35627 ■ Vision Share
108 Acorn Hill Ln.
Apex, NC 27502
Ph: (919)303-2584
Free: 888-657-4448
E-mail: info@visionshare.org
URL: http://www.visionshare.org

NORTH DAKOTA

35628 ■ Lions Eye Bank of North Dakota
301 N 4th St.
Bismarck, ND 58501
Ph: (701)250-9390
Fax: (701)250-0805
E-mail: kthomas@tbionline.org
URL: http://www.lionseyebankofnd.org

NOVA SCOTIA

35629 ■ Multi--Organ Transplant Program, QEII Health Sciences
Victoria Bldg., Rm. 291
1278 Tower Rd.
Halifax, NS, Canada B3H 2Y9
Ph: (902)473-6193
Fax: (902)473-6640
URL: http://www.legacyoflife.ns.ca/about_us/partners.html

35630 ■ Regional Tissue Bank, QEII Health Sciences
McKenzie Bldg. Centre, Rm. 431
5788 University Ave.
Halifax, NS, Canada B3H 1V7
Ph: (902)473-4171
Free: 800-314-6515
Fax: (901)473-3665
E-mail: sean.margueratt@cdha.nshealth.ca
URL: http://www.legacyoflife.ns.ca/

OHIO

35631 ■ Allosource--Ohio
615 Elsinore Pl., Ste. 400
Cincinnati, OH 45202
Ph: (513)381-2630
Free: 800-558-5004
Fax: (513)246-4109
URL: http://www.allosource.org

35632 ■ Central Ohio Lions Eye Bank, Inc.
262 Neil Ave., Ste. 140
Columbus, OH 43215
Ph: (614)545-2057
Fax: (614)545-2067
E-mail: PMcNabb@coleb.org
URL: http://www.coleb.org

35633 ■ Cincinnati Eye Bank
4015 Executive Park Dr., Ste. 330
Cincinnati, OH 45241
Ph: (513)861-3716
Fax: (513)483-3984
E-mail: eyebank@cintieb.org
URL: http://www.cintieb.org

35634 ■ Cleveland Clinic Foundation
Andrology Laboratory and Sperm Bank
9500 Euclid Ave., Desk A19.1
Cleveland, OH 44195
Ph: (216)444-9485

Free: 866-922-6546
Fax: (216)445-6049
E-mail: agarwaa@ccf.org
URL: http://www.clevelandclinic.org/reproductiveresearchcenter/info/patientinfo3

35635 ■ Cleveland Eye Bank
Vision Share
Wearn Bldg., Ste. 615
11100 Euclid Ave., WRN 5068
Cleveland, OH 44106
Ph: (216)844-3937
Fax: (216)983-0069
E-mail: ceb@clevelandeyebank.org
URL: http://www.clevelandeyebank.org
Description: Dedicated to securing eyes for the purpose of transplanting corneas to those whose sight would be restored or improved by this procedure. Eyes that do not meet transplant criteria are used for education and research.

35636 ■ Community Tissue Services, Dayton
349 S Main St.
Dayton, OH 45402
Ph: (937)222-0228
Free: 800-684-7783
Fax: (937)586-6601
E-mail: kblair@cbccts.org
URL: http://www.communitytissue.org

35637 ■ Community Tissue Services--Kettering
Center for Tissues Innovation and Research
2900 College Dr.
Kettering, OH 45420
Ph: (937)222-0228
Free: 800-684-7783
E-mail: amoeder@cbccts.org
URL: http://www.communitytissue.org

35638 ■ Community Tissue Services, Toledo
2736 N Holland-Sylvania Rd.
Toledo, OH 43615
Ph: (419)536-4924
Free: 866-684-7783
Fax: (419)536-4973
E-mail: rdawson@cbccts.org
URL: http://www.communitytissue.org/
Formerly: Community Tissue Services, Northwest Ohio.

35639 ■ Cryobiology, Inc.
4830D Knightsbridge Blvd.
Columbus, OH 43214
Ph: (614)451-4375
Free: 800-359-4375
Fax: (614)451-5284
E-mail: info@cryobio.com
URL: http://www.cryobio.com

35640 ■ LifeBanc
4775 Richmond Rd.
Cleveland, OH 44128
Ph: (216)752-5433
Free: 888-558-5433
Fax: (216)751-4204
E-mail: debrac@lifebanc.org
URL: http://www.lifebanc.org/

35641 ■ LifeCenter Organ Donor Network
615 Elsinore Pl., Ste. 400
Cincinnati, OH 45202
Ph: (513)558-5000
Fax: (513)578-6800
E-mail: rwinter@lifepassiton.org
URL: http://www.lifepassiton.org

35642 ■ Lifeline of Ohio
770 Kinnear Rd., Ste. 200
Columbus, OH 43212
Ph: (614)291-5667
Free: 800-525-5667
Fax: (614)291-0660
E-mail: tsherman@lifelineofohio.org
URL: http://www.lifelineofohio.org

35643 ■ Lions Eye Bank of West Central Ohio
1945 Southtown Blvd., Ste. E
Dayton, OH 45439
Ph: (937)396-1000
Fax: (937)396-1880
E-mail: aburnham@tbionline.org
URL: http://www.lebwcoonline.org

35644 ■ Securacell Inc.
PO Box 35729
Canton, OH 44735
Free: 866-836-2355
Fax: (330)833-5230
E-mail: info@securacell.com
URL: http://www.securacell.com

OKLAHOMA

35645 ■ Advanced Nu Med Technologies, Inc.
7225 S 85th E Ave., Ste. 200
Tulsa, OK 74133
Ph: (918)249-2697
Free: 800-640-3131
Fax: (918)461-0682
E-mail: wcranford@numedtech.com
URL: http://www.numedtech.com

35646 ■ American Tissue Services Foundation
609 S Kelly, Ste. K-2
Edmond, OK 73003
Free: 866-497-7878
Fax: (405)562-1953
E-mail: rtturner@aol.com
URL: http://www.atsfoundation.org

35647 ■ LifeShare Transplant Services of Oklahoma
7200 Broadway Ext.
Oklahoma City, OK 73116
Free: 888-580-5680
Fax: (866)861-1436
E-mail: lbelcher@lifeshareok.org
URL: http://www.lifeshareoklahoma.org
Formerly: LifeNet Transplant Donor Services of Oklahoma.

35648 ■ Oklahoma Lions Eye Bank
3840 N Lincoln Blvd.
Oklahoma City, OK 73105
Ph: (405)557-1393
Fax: (405)557-0086
E-mail: jking@oleb.org
URL: http://www.oklionsfoundation.org/

ONTARIO

35649 ■ Cells for Life Limited--Markham
377 Church St., Ste. 201
Markham, ON, Canada L6B 1A1
Ph: (905)472-0060
Free: 877-235-1997
Fax: (905)472-2185
E-mail: info@cellsforlife.com
URL: http://www.cellsforlife.com

35650 ■ Cells for Life Limited--Toronto
Toronto General Hospital
585 University Ave., Ste. BC8131
Toronto, ON, Canada M5G 2N2
Ph: (416)260-0808
Free: 877-235-1997
Fax: (416)260-7151
E-mail: info@cellsforlife.com
URL: http://www.cellsforlife.com

35651 ■ Eye Bank of Canada--Ontario Division
1929 Bayview Ave., Ste. 203
Toronto, ON, Canada M4G 3E8
Ph: (416)978-7355
E-mail: eye.bank@utoronto.ca

35652 ■ HemaStem Therapeutics--Mississauga
4263 Sherwoodtowne Blvd., Ste. 303
Mississauga, ON, Canada L4Z 1Y5
Free: 800-203-7349
E-mail: info@hemastem.com
URL: http://www.hemastem.com

35653 ■ HemaStem Therapeutics--Toronto
Canadian Lab
14 Prince Arthur Ave.
Toronto, ON, Canada M5R 1A9
Free: 800-203-7349
E-mail: info@hemastem.com
URL: http://www.hemastem.com

35654 ■ Hospital for Sick Children
Tissue and Stem Cell Laboratory
555 University Ave., Rm. 3677
Toronto, ON, Canada M5G 1X8
Ph: (416)813-5423
Fax: (416)813-5433
E-mail: bienvenidosonny.lazaro@sickkids.ca
URL: http://www.sickkids.on.ca/Centres/Transplant-Centre/index.html

35655 ■ Mount Sinai Allograft Technologies
600 University Ave., Rm. 607
Toronto, ON, Canada M5G 1X5
Ph: (416)586-8870
Fax: (416)586-4458
E-mail: rbtb@mtsinai.on.ca
URL: http://www.mountsinai.on.ca/allograft/

35656 ■ Progenics Cord Blood Cryobank
Sheppard Medical Bldg.
701 Sheppard Ave. E, Ste. 310
Toronto, ON, Canada M2K 2Z3
Ph: (416)221-1666
Free: 866-921-1666
Fax: (416)221-9727
E-mail: info@progrenicscryobank.com
URL: http://www.progenicscryobank.com/
Dr. H. Yang, Director

OREGON

35657 ■ Community Tissue Services--Medford
329 Crater Lake Ave.
Medford, OR 97504
Ph: (541)773-6054
Free: 888-702-5662
URL: http://www.communitytissue.org

35658 ■ Community Tissue Services, Portland
16361 NE Cameron Blvd.
Portland, OR 97230
Ph: (503)408-9394
Free: 800-545-8668
Fax: (503)408-9395
E-mail: rboggs@cbccts.org
URL: http://www.communitytissue.org/

35659 ■ Lions Eye Bank of Oregon
Portland, OR 97214
Ph: (503)808-7020
Fax: (503)808-7021
E-mail: Barbara.Crow@orlions.org
URL: http://www.orlions.org
Barbara Crow, Executive Director

35660 ■ Lions Eye Bank of Oregon, Medford
Southern Oregon Laboratory
2201 SE 11th Ave.
Portland, OR 97214

Ph: (503)808-7070
Free: 800-843-7793
Fax: (503)808-7071
URL: http://eyebank.orlions.org

PENNSYLVANIA

35661 ■ Center for Organ Recovery and Education (CORE)
204 Sigma Dr.
RIDC Park
Pittsburgh, PA 15238
Free: 800-366-6777
Fax: (412)963-3563
E-mail: sstuart@core.org
URL: http://www.core.org
Susan A. Stuart, President
Description: Manages organ, tissue and eye donation activities. Offers families the opportunity to donate; coordinates the surgical recovery of the organs, tissue and eyes, and facilitates the computerized matching of donating organs and placement of corneas. Maintains permanent tribute to donors. Delivers continuing education programs for health professionals in regional hospitals and associations. Provides speakers for presentation to civic organizations and schools or corporations. **Formerly:** (1984) Transplant Organ Procurement Organization.

35662 ■ Community Tissue Services, Pennsylvania
3573 Bristol Pke., Ste. 201
Philadelphia, PA 19020
Ph: (215)245-4506
Free: 800-456-5445
Fax: (215)245-4358
E-mail: dwilson@cbccts.org
URL: http://www.communitytissue.org/

35663 ■ Gift of Life Donor Program Eye Bank
401 N 3rd St.
Philadelphia, PA 19123
Ph: (212)557-8090
Free: 800-366-6771
Fax: (212)557-0058
E-mail: rryan@donors1.org
URL: http://www.donors1.org

35664 ■ Globus Medical Inc.
2560 General Armistead Ave.
Audubon, PA 19403
Ph: (610)930-1800
Fax: (610)930-2042
E-mail: info@globusmedical.com
URL: http://www.globusmedical.com/

35665 ■ Lions Eye Bank of Delaware Valley
401 N 3rd St., Ste. 305
Philadelphia, PA 19123
Ph: (215)563-1679
Free: 800-743-6667
Fax: (215)563-3081
E-mail: pidgp@lebdv.org
URL: http://www.lebdv.org

35666 ■ Lions Eye Bank of Northwest Pennsylvania, Inc.
5105 Richmond St.
Erie, PA 16509
Ph: (814)866-3545
Fax: (814)864-1875
E-mail: sight@erieeyebank.org
URL: http://www.lionsclubs.org

35667 ■ Musculoskeletal Transplant Foundation (MTF)--Jessup, PA
1232 Mid Valley Rd.
Jessup, PA 18434
Ph: (570)496-3400
URL: http://www.mtf.org

35668 ■ National Disease Research Interchange
8 Penn Center, 8th Fl.
1628 John F. Kennedy Blvd.
Philadelphia, PA 19103
Free: 800-222-NDRI
E-mail: editor@ndri.com
URL: http://www.ndri.com

35669 ■ Northeast Pennsylvania Lions Eye Bank, Inc.
2346 Jacksonville Rd.
Bethlehem, PA 18017
Ph: (610)625-0360
Fax: (610)625-0367
E-mail: info@paeyebank.org
URL: http://www.PAEyeBank.org
Richard Rader, Chief Executive Officer

35670 ■ Pittsburgh Cryobank
4415 5th Ave., Ste. 161
Pittsburgh, PA 15213
Ph: (412)687-0335
Fax: (412)687-0358
E-mail: pittinfo@cryobio.com
URL: http://www.pittsburghcryobank.com

35671 ■ University of Pittsburgh Medical Center
Magee-Womens Hospital
Dan Berger Cord Blood Program
300 Halket St.
Pittsburgh, PA 15213-3180
Ph: (412)209-7479
E-mail: mwiegel@itxm.org
URL: http://www.upmc.com/HospitalsFacilities/Hospitals/Magee/ObGynServices/Pregn ancy/Pages/cordbloodprogram.aspx

PUERTO RICO

35672 ■ Lions Eye Bank of Puerto Rico
V-3, No. 22 Ave.
San Alfonso St.
Rio Piedras, PR 00921
Ph: (787)273-0597
Fax: (787)273-0974
E-mail: mvazquez@bolpr.org
URL: http://www.polpr.org

35673 ■ Safetycord Inc.
San Juan, PR
Ph: (305)432-2673
URL: http://www.safetycord.com

QUEBEC

35674 ■ Cells for Life Limited--Montreal
5858, chemin de la Cote-des-Neiges, Ste. 217
Montreal, QC, Canada H3T 1Y6
Ph: (514)739-9993
Free: 877-714-7007
Fax: (514)739-0681
E-mail: montreal@cellsforlife.com
URL: http://www.cellsforlife.com

35675 ■ Hema-Quebec--Sainte-Foy
1070 av des Sciences-de-la-Vie
Sainte-Foy, QC, Canada G1V 5C3
Ph: (418)780-4362
Free: 800-267-9711
Fax: (418)780-2097
E-mail: info@hema-quebec.qc.ca
URL: http://www.hema-quebec.qc.ca

35676 ■ Hema-Quebec, Tissue Services--Saint-Laurent
4045 Cote-Vertu Blvd.
Saint-Laurent, QC, Canada H4R 2W7
Ph: (514)832-5000
Free: 888-666-0882
Fax: (514)832-1025
E-mail: Suzanne.Remy@hema-quebec.qc.ca
URL: http://www.hema-quebec.qc.ca

SASKATCHEWAN

35677 ■ Lions Eye Bank of Saskatchewan
Saskatoon City Hospital
Eye Center
701 Queen St., 4th Fl.
Saskatoon, SK, Canada S7M 0M7
Ph: (306)655-5932
Fax: (306)655-5946
E-mail: Marla.Ewen@saskatoonhealthregion.ca
URL: http://www.eyebank.sklions.ca

SOUTH CAROLINA

35678 ■ Lifepoint Inc.--Charleston Vision Share
4200 Faber Pl. Dr.
Charleston, SC 29405
Ph: (843)763-7755
Fax: (843)745-2213
E-mail: simmonsp@lifepoint-sc.org
URL: http://www.lifepoint-sc.org

35679 ■ Lifepoint Inc.--Greenville Vision Share
1309 Grove Rd.
Greenville, SC 29605
Ph: (864)763-7755
Free: 800-462-0755
E-mail: info@lifepoint-sc.org
URL: http://www.lifepoint-sc.org

35680 ■ Lifepoint Inc.--West Columbia Vision Share
164 Lott Ct., Ste. B
West Columbia, SC 29169
Ph: (843)763-7755
Free: 800-462-0755
E-mail: info@lifepoint-sc.org
URL: http://www.lifepoint-sc.org

SOUTH DAKOTA

35681 ■ South Dakota Lions Eye Bank
4501 W 61st St. N
Sioux Falls, SD 57107
Ph: (605)373-1008
Free: 800-245-7846
Fax: (605)373-1261
E-mail: jens@sdleb.org
URL: http://www.sdleb.org

TENNESSEE

35682 ■ Community Tissue Services, Mid-South
1790 Kirby Pkwy., Ste. 130
Memphis, TN 38138
Ph: (901)683-6566
Free: 888-683-6566
Fax: (901)683-9910
E-mail: kward@cbccts.org
URL: http://www.communitytissue.org

35683 ■ DCI Donor Services
1714 Hayes St.
Nashville, TN 37203
Free: 888-234-4399
Fax: (615)234-5270
E-mail: ksnyder@dcids.org
URL: http://www.dcids.org

35684 ■ East Tennessee Lions Eye Bank
1924 Alcoa Hwy.
Box U-26
Knoxville, TN 37920
Ph: (865)305-9625
Fax: (865)523-4869
E-mail: etleb@mc.utmck.edu
URL: http://www.discoveret.org/eyebank/

35685 ■ Mid-South Eye Bank for Sight Restoration, Inc.
PO Box 40627
Memphis, TN 38174
Ph: (901)448-8264
E-mail: msebtn@aol.com
URL: http://www.msebtn.org

35686 ■ Mid-South Tissue Bank
5600 Pleasant View, Ste. 107
Memphis, TN 38134
Ph: (901)683-6566
Fax: (901)683-9910

35687 ■ National Eye Bank Center
1770 Moriah Woods Blvd.
Memphis, TN 38117
Ph: (901)202-6822
Fax: (901)202-6842

35688 ■ SpinalGraft Technologies, LLC
4340 Swinnea Rd., Ste. 39
Memphis, TN 38118
Ph: (901)344-0934
Free: 888-869-2435
Fax: (901)396-0933
E-mail: maris.m.garner@medtronic.com
URL: http://www.medtronic.com

35689 ■ Tennessee District 12-0 Lions Eye Bank and Sight Service
979 E 3rd St., Ste. A250
Chattanooga, TN 37403
Ph: (423)778-4000
Fax: (423)778-4050
E-mail: td120leb@aol.com
URL: http://www.lionsclubs.org

35690 ■ Tennessee Donor Services--Chattanooga
651 E 4th St., Ste. 402
Chattanooga, TN 37403
Ph: (423)756-5736
E-mail: dbenjamin@dcids.org
URL: http://www.donatelifetn.org

35691 ■ Tennessee Donor Services--Gray
110 KLM Dr., Ste. 2
Gray, TN 37615
Ph: (423)915-0808
Free: 888-562-3774
E-mail: jjenks@dcids.org
URL: http://www.donatelifetn.org

35692 ■ Tennessee Donor Services--Knoxville
7015 Middlebrook Pke.
Knoxville, TN 38909
Ph: (865)588-1031
E-mail: mmadden@dcids.org
URL: http://www.donatelifetn.org

35693 ■ Tennessee Donor Services--Nashville
1600 Hayes St., Ste. 300
Nashville, TN 37203
Ph: (615)234-5201
Free: 888-234-4440
Fax: (615)320-1655
E-mail: lclark@dcids.org
URL: http://www.donatelifetn.org

35694 ■ Vascular Transplant Services--Millington
8236 Hwy. 51N
Millington, TN 38053
Ph: (901)872-3799
Fax: (901)872-3788
E-mail: tstevesn@vtsrl.org
URL: http://www.vasculartransplantservices.org

35695 ■ Wright Medical Technology, Inc.
5677 Airline Rd.
Arlington, TN 38002
Free: 800-238-7188
Fax: (901)867-4788
E-mail: rwilliams@wmt.com
URL: http://www.wmt.com

TEXAS

35696 ■ Alamo Tissue Service, Ltd.
5844 Rocky Pte. Dr.
San Antonio, TX 78249
Ph: (210)738-2663
Free: 800-226-9091
Fax: (210)732-4263
E-mail: alamotissue@sbcglobal.net
URL: http://www.alamotissueservice.com/

35697 ■ Alcon Research Ltd.
6201 South Fwy.
Fort Worth, TX 76134
Ph: (817)293-0450
Free: 800-862-5266
URL: http://www.alcon.com/en/

35698 ■ Allotech LLC
Bldg. 78
4620 71st St.
Lubbock, TX 79424
Free: 888-796-1923
Fax: (806)796-0059
E-mail: shane.shuttlesworth@osteogenics.com
URL: http://www.osteogenics.com

35699 ■ Blood and Tissue Center of Central Texas--Austin
4300 N Lamar Blvd.
Austin, TX 78756
Free: 800-580-1121
Fax: (512)206-1386
URL: http://www.bloodandtissue.org/

35700 ■ Blood and Tissue Center of Central Texas--Bldg. L, Austin
Bldg. L, Ste. 800
9500 S IH-35
Austin, TX 78748
Ph: (512)206-1266
Free: 877-212-1266
Fax: (512)206-1129
URL: http://www.bloodandtissue.org/

35701 ■ Blood and Tissue Center of Central Texas--Cedar Park
920 N Vista Ridge Blvd., Ste. 560
Cedar Park, TX 78613
Ph: (512)206-1266
Fax: (512)206-1129
URL: http://www.bloodandtissue.org/

35702 ■ Blood and Tissue Center of Central Texas--Georgetown
1015 W University Ave., Ste. 340
Georgetown, TX 78628
Ph: (512)206-1266
Fax: (512)206-1129
URL: http://www.bloodandtissue.org/

35703 ■ Bone Bank Allografts
4808 Research Dr.
San Antonio, TX 78240
Ph: (210)696-7616
Free: 800-397-0088
Fax: (210)696-7609
E-mail: radams@bonebank.com
URL: http://www.bonebank.com

35704 ■ Community Tissue Services, Fort Worth
328 S Adams
Fort Worth, TX 76104
Ph: (817)332-1898
Free: 800-905-2556
Fax: (817)332-1958
E-mail: esombathy@cbccts.org
URL: http://www.communitytissue.org/

35705 ■ Great Plains Lions Eye Bank, Inc.
Health Sciences Ctr.
Texas Tech University
3601 4th St., Ste. BAB104-HSC
Lubbock, TX 79430
Ph: (806)743-2242
Fax: (806)743-1431
E-mail: greg.oliver@ttuhsc.edu
URL: http://www.ttuhsc.edu/eye

35706 ■ Legacy of Life Tissue Foundation
4804 Research Dr.
San Antonio, TX 78240
Ph: (210)696-7677
Free: 800-397-3077
Fax: (210)691-1472

35707 ■ LifoGift Organ Donation Center
2510 Westridge St.
Houston, TX 77054
Ph: (713)523-4438
Free: 800-633-6562
Fax: (713)737-8100
E-mail: sholtzman@lifegift.org
URL: http://www.lifegift.org

35708 ■ Lions Eye Bank of Texas
Baylor College of Medicine
Department of Ophthalmology
6565 Fannin
NC 205
Houston, TX 77030
Ph: (713)798-4951
Fax: (713)793-6864
E-mail: lebt@bcm.edu
URL: http://www.bayloreye.org/eyebank
Mary Beth Danneffel, Director

35709 ■ Lions Organ and Eye Bank of District 2-E2
PO Box 830
Fort Worth, TX 76101
Ph: (972)294-5916
E-mail: papa992000@yahoo.com
URL: http://www.loeb2e2.org
Remarks: Transplant Services Center contact: Ellen Heck, ellen.heck@utsouthwestern.edu, phone: (214) 648-2609 or (800) 433-6667, fax: (214) 631-5418.

35710 ■ Lions Sight and Tissue Foundation--District 2-X1
PO Box 191121
Dallas, TX 75219
Ph: (972)680-0943
Fax: (972)231-1630
E-mail: Harry_Katner@hotmail.com
URL: http://www.lstf.org
Remarks: Transplant Services Center contact: Ellen Heck, ellen.heck@utsouthwestern.edu, phone: (214) 648-2609 or (800) 433-6667, fax: (214) 631-5418.

35711 ■ Lions Tissue and Eye Bank Inc.--District 2-El
4317 S 6th St.
Abilene, TX 79605
Ph: (325)695-1226
Fax: (325)695-1226
E-mail: jhwjr25@sbcglobal.net
URL: http://www.lionsclubs.org

35712 ■ Lone Star Lions Eye Bank
PO Box 347
Manor, TX 78653
Ph: (512)457-0638
Fax: (512)457-0658
E-mail: info@lsleb.org
URL: http://www.lsleb.org

35713 ■ New England Cord Blood Bank--Dallas
3030 LBJ Fwy., Ste. 741
Dallas, TX 75234
Ph: (214)722-7575
Free: 888-799-2673
URL: http://www.cordbloodbank.com

35714 ■ New England Cord Blood Bank--Houston
410 Pierce St., Ste. 327
Houston, TX 77002
Ph: (713)357-9540
Free: 888-799-2673
Fax: (713)583-6304
URL: http://www.cordbloodbank.com

35715 ■ Precision Allograft Solutions
5844 Rocky Pte.
San Antonio, TX 78249
Free: 800-226-9091
Fax: (201)732-4263
E-mail: landrews@alamotissueservice.com
URL: http://www.alamotissueservice.com

35716 ■ RTI Donor Services, Texas Division/Corpus Christi
101 N Shoreline Blvd., Ste. 207
Corpus Christi, TX 78401
Ph: (361)904-0510
Fax: (361)904-0515
URL: http://www.rtidonorservices.org/en/default.aspx

35717 ■ RTI Donor Services, Texas Division/Dallas
5489 Blair Rd., Ste. 200
Dallas, TX 75231
Ph: (214)443-9279
Fax: (214)599-9386
URL: http://www.rtidonorservices.org/en/default.aspx

35718 ■ RTI Donor Services, Texas Division/El Paso
7618 Boeing Dr., Ste. B
El Paso, TX 79925
Ph: (915)775-1441
Fax: (915)774-0132
URL: http://www.rtidonorservices.org/en/default.aspx

35719 ■ San Antonio Eye Bank
8122 Datapoint Dr., Ste. 325
San Antonio, TX 78229
Ph: (210)614-1209
Free: 800-263-2078
URL: http://www.saeyebank.org

35720 ■ Shriners Hospital for Children Burns Institute, Galveston
815 Market St.
Galveston, TX 77550
Ph: (409)621-1366
Fax: (409)621-1390
URL: http://www.shriners.com/Hospitals/Galveston/

35721 ■ South Texas Blood and Tissue Center
6211 I-H 10 W at 1st Park Ten
San Antonio, TX 78201
Ph: (210)731-5565
Free: 800-292-5534
Fax: (210)731-5505
E-mail: mfisk@bloodntissue.org
URL: http://www.southtexasblood.org/

35722 ■ Texas Human Biologics
14805 Omicron Dr., Ste. 200
San Antonio, TX 78245
Ph: (210)798-8445
Free: 800-397-0088
Fax: (210)696-7609
E-mail: jmcdougal@bonebank.com
URL: http://www.bonebank.com

35723 ■ University of Texas Health Science Center
Allograft Resources, San Antonio
7703 Floyd Curl Dr., MC 7858
San Antonio, TX 78229
Ph: (210)567-6517
Fax: (210)567-6187
E-mail: Stutes@uthscsa.edu
URL: http://www.uthscsa.edu/allograft/

35724 ■ University of Texas
M.D. Anderson Cancer Center
Cord Blood Bank
1515 Holcombe Blvd.
Houston, TX 77030
Ph: (713)563-8000
Free: 866-869-5111
Fax: (713)792-8992
E-mail: cordbloodbank@mdanderson.org
URL: http://www.mdanderson.org/
Dr. Elizabeth Shpall, Director

35725 ■ University of Texas Transplant Services Center
5323 Harry Hines Blvd., MC 9074
Dallas, TX 75390-9074
Ph: (214)648-2609
Free: 800-433-6667
Fax: (214)648-2086
E-mail: Ellen.Heck@utsouthwestern.edu
URL: http://www.utsouthwestern.edu/utsw/home/research/transplantsvcs/index.html

35726 ■ Western Texas Lions Eye Bank Alliance
PO Box 2911
San Angelo, TX 76902
Ph: (325)653-8666
Fax: (325)655-2847
E-mail: wtleba@wcc.net
URL: http://www.wtleb.org

UTAH

35727 ■ Utah Cord Bank
UT
Free: 877-822-7836
E-mail: admin@utcb.us
URL: http://www.utahcordbank.com

35728 ■ Utah Lions Eye Bank
University of Utah Health Sciences Center
John A. Moran Eye Center
65 Mario Capecchi Dr.
Salt Lake City, UT 84132
Ph: (801)581-2039
Fax: (801)585-5703
E-mail: Chris.Hanna@hsc.uta.edu
URL: http://www.utaheyebank.org

VIRGINIA

35729 ■ Fairfax Cryobank
3015 Williams Dr., Ste. 110
Fairfax, VA 22031
Free: 800-338-8407
Fax: (703)698-3933
E-mail: info@fairfaxcryobank.com
URL: http://www.fairfaxcryobank.com

35730 ■ LifeNet Health--Virginia Beach
1864 Concert Dr.
Virginia Beach, VA 23453
Ph: (757)464-4761
Free: 800-847-7831
Fax: (757)464-5721
E-mail: Michael_Plew@lifenethealth.org
URL: http://www.lifenethealth.org

35731 ■ Lions Medical Eye Bank and Research Center of Eastern Virginia
600 Gresham Dr.
Norfolk, VA 23507
Ph: (757)388-2020
Fax: (757)388-3744
E-mail: drroch@lionseyebank.org
URL: http://www.lionseyebank.org
Formerly: Lions Medical Eye Bank and Research Foundation of Eastern Virginia, Inc.

35732 ■ Old Dominion Eye Bank
9200 Arboretum Pky., Ste. 104
Richmond, VA 23236
Ph: (804)560-7540
Free: 800-832-0728
Fax: (804)560-4752
E-mail: restoresight@odef.org
URL: http://www.odef.org

35733 ■ Washington Regional Transplant Community
7619 Little River Tpke., Ste. 900
Annandale, VA 22003
Ph: (703)641-0100
Free: 866-232-3666
Fax: (703)658-0711
E-mail: contactwrtc@wrtc.org
URL: http://www.beadonor.org

WASHINGTON

35734 ■ LifeCenter Northwest
11245 SE 6th St., Ste. 100
Bellevue, WA 98004
Free: 877-275-5269
Fax: (425)688-7641
E-mail: janh@lcnw.org
URL: http://www.lcnw.org
Formerly: Donate Life Today.

35735 ■ Northwest Tissue Services--Renton
501 SW 39th St.
Renton, WA 98057
Ph: (206)292-1879
Free: 800-858-2282
Fax: (206)343-5043
E-mail: info@nwts.org
URL: http://www.nwts.org

35736 ■ Northwest Tissue Services--Spokane
Gateway 6 Bldg.
901 E 2nd St.
Spokane, WA 99202
Free: 888-266-4466
E-mail: info@nwts.org
URL: http://www.nwts.org

35737 ■ Puget Sound Blood Center
Northwest Tissue Services
921 Terry Ave.
Seattle, WA 98104
Ph: (206)292-6500
Fax: (206)343-5043
E-mail: cordblood@psbc.org
URL: http://www.psbc.org/cordblood/

35738 ■ SightLife
221 Yale Ave. N, Ste. 450
Seattle, WA 98109
Ph: (206)682-8500
Free: 800-847-5786
Fax: (206)682-8504
E-mail: info@sightlife.org
URL: http://www.sightlife.org
Formerly: Northwest Lions Foundation for Sight & Hearing; Northwest Lions Eye Bank.

WEST VIRGINIA

35739 ■ Kentucky Organ Donor Affiliates--Huntington, WV
1448 10th Ave., Ste. 314
Huntington, WV 25701
Ph: (304)523-5775

Free: 800-525-3456
Fax: (304)523-7649
URL: http://www.kyorgandonor.org/

35740 ■ Medical Eye Bank of West Virginia Vision Share
3 Courtney Dr.
Charleston, WV 25304
Ph: (304)926-9200
E-mail: eyebank@wvdsl.net

WISCONSIN

35741 ■ La Crosse Cryobank
1202 State St., Ste. A
La Crosse, WI 54601
Ph: (608)782-2034
Fax: (608)782-2784
E-mail: michelle.skrede@cryobio.com
URL: http://www.lacrossecryobank.com

35742 ■ Lions Eye Bank of Wisconsin
2401 American Ln.
Madison, WI 53704
Ph: (608)233-2354
Fax: (608)233-2895
E-mail: info@lebw.com
URL: http://www.lebw.com

35743 ■ National Stem Cell Bank
WiCell Research Institute
614 Walnut St., 13th Fl.
Madison, WI 53707
Ph: (608)263-6297
Free: 888-204-1782
Fax: (608)263-1064
E-mail: info@wicell.org
URL: http://www.nationalstemcellbank.org

35744 ■ RTI Donor Services--Middleton
8120 Forsythia St.
Middleton, WI 53562
Ph: (608)231-9050
Fax: (608)231-9776
URL: http://www.rtidonorservices.org/

35745 ■ Wisconsin Tissue Bank
9000 W Chester St., Ste. 250
Milwaukee, WI 53214
Ph: (414)937-6999
Free: 800-722-8230
Fax: (414)937-6998
E-mail: Kathy.Simpson@bcw.edu
URL: http://www.bcw.edu

Chapter 27
Pain Management Programs

Listed below are institutions that provide chronic pain management services. Entries are geographical by states, then alphabetical by organization names within states. For additional information on these centers and clinics, see the "User's Guide" located at the front of this directory.

ALABAMA

35746 ■ Birmingham Pain Center
2057 Valleydale Rd., Ste. 100
Birmingham, AL 35244
Ph: (204)313-7246
URL: http://www.birminghampain.com

35747 ■ C. Paul Perry Pelvic Pain Center
Women's Medical Plaza
2006 Brookwood Medical Center Dr., Ste. 402
Birmingham, AL 35209
Ph: (205)877-2950
Free: 800-624-9676
Fax: (205)877-2973
E-mail: pelvicpain@aol.com
Linda Harman, Executive Director

35748 ■ DCH Regional Medical Center
Paincare Unit
809 University Blvd. E
Tuscaloosa, AL 35401
Ph: (205)759-7111
URL: http://www.dchsystem.com/body.cfm?id=36926

35749 ■ George H. Lanier Memorial Hospital
Pain Clinic
4800 48th St.
Valley, AL 36854
Ph: (334)756-1126
URL: http://www.lanierhospital.com

35750 ■ Huntsville Hospital East
Tennessee Valley Pain Consultants
Center for Pain Management and Rehabilitation
911 Big Cove Rd.
Huntsville, AL 35801
Ph: (256)265-7246
URL: http://www.huntsvillehospital.org

35751 ■ Painsouth
1600 Carraway Blvd., Ste. 402
Birmingham, AL 35234
Ph: (205)297-9801
URL: http://painsouth.com

35752 ■ University of Alabama Medical Center
Pain Management
845 Jefferson Tower
619 19th St. S
Birmingham, AL 35249
Ph: (205)934-6501
E-mail: kamara@uab.edu
URL: http://www.pain101.com/PainDoctors/Directory-ACGMEprogramsList.aspx

ALASKA

35753 ■ A.A. Pain Clinic
4100 Lake Otis Pkwy., Ste. 216
Anchorage, AK 99508
Ph: (907)563-2873
Fax: (907)563-5852
URL: http://www.aapain.com
Dr. Leon Chandler, Director

35754 ■ Juneau Urgent Care and Family Medical Clinic
Pain Clinic
8505 Old Dairy Rd.
Juneau, AK 99801
Ph: (907)790-3111
URL: http://www.juneauurgentcare.com

35755 ■ R.C. Goodman Institute for Pain Management
1500 Dodson Ave.
Fort Smith, AK 72901
Ph: (479)441-5475
Dr. Robert Fisher, Director

ALBERTA

35756 ■ LifeMark Health Center--Calgary
2121 29th St. NE
Calgary, AB, Canada T1Y 7H8
Ph: (403)297-9500
URL: http://www.pain101.com/paindoctors/directory-ofpaindoctorscarflist.aspx

35757 ■ LifeMark Health Institute
Meadowlark Health Centre
156th St. & 87th Ave., Ste. 154
Edmonton, AB, Canada T5R 5W9
Ph: (780)429-4761
URL: http://www.pain101.com/paindoctors/directory-ofpaindoctorscarflist.aspx

35758 ■ Millard Health
131 Airport Rd.
Edmonton, AB, Canada T5G 0W6
Ph: (780)498-3200
URL: http://www.pain101.com/paindoctors/directory-ofpaindoctorscarflist.aspx

35759 ■ Orion Health--Calgary
300 - 1010 1st Ave. NE
Calgary, AB, Canada T2E 7W7
Ph: (403)233-2415
URL: http://www.pain101.com/paindoctors/directory-ofpaindoctorscarflist.aspx

35760 ■ OrionHealth--Canmore
201 - 1205 Bow Valley Trl.
Canmore, AB, Canada T1W 1P5
Ph: (403)609-2228
URL: http://www.pain101.com/paindoctors/directory-ofpaindoctorscarflist.aspx

35761 ■ OrionHealth--Temple
202-5401 Temple Dr. NE
Calgary, AB, Canada T1Y 3R7
Ph: (403)285-5792
URL: http://www.pain101.com/paindoctors/directory-ofpaindoctorscarflist.aspx

ARIZONA

35762 ■ Accurate Care Pain Relief Center
100 Verde Valley School Rd., Ste. 110
Sedona, AZ 86531
Ph: (928)284-2228
URL: http://www.caringpainrelief.com

35763 ■ Banner Boswell Pain Center
13203 N 103rd Ave., Ste. H5
Sun City, AZ 85351
Ph: (623)875-7246
Fax: (623)972-0049
URL: http://www.bannerhealth.com

35764 ■ Barrow Neurological Institute
350 W Thomas Rd.
Phoenix, AZ 85013
Ph: (602)406-3000
URL: http://www.stjosephs-phx.org

35765 ■ Larry Savage, DC
Pain Clinic
4604 E Grant Rd.
Tucson, AZ 85712
Ph: (520)321-0331
URL: http://www.savagechiropractic.com

35766 ■ Maricopa Medical Center
Pain Clinic
2601 E Roosevelt, No. 7
Phoenix, AZ 85008
Ph: (602)344-5011
URL: http://www.mihs.org

35767 ■ Mayo Clinic, Arizona
Mayo School of Graduate Medical Education
Pain Management
5777 E Mayo Blvd.
Phoenix, AZ 85054
Ph: (480)342-1272
E-mail: rubin.cindy@mayo.edu
URL: http://www.pain101.com/PainDoctors/Directory-ACGMEprogramsList.aspx

35768 ■ Painnet Medical Group
Pain Clinic
7725 N 43rd Ave.
Phoenix, AZ 85051
Free: 800-206-7246
URL: http://www.painnetinc.com/arizona.html

35769 ■ Preferred Pain and Rehab Center
2813 E Camelback Rd., Ste. 430
Phoenix, AZ 85016
Ph: (602)507-6550
URL: http://www.preferredpaincenter.com

35770 ■ Scottsdale Pain Center
10200 N 92nd St. Ste. 200
Scottsdale, AZ 85258
Ph: (480)314-2288
URL: http://www.azpainmd.com

35771 ■ Sierra Tucson Pain Management Program
39580 S Lago Del Oro Pkwy.
Tucson, AZ 85739
Ph: (520)624-4000
Fax: (520)818-5897
URL: http://www.sierratucson.com/programs_pain.php

35772 ■ Southern Arizona Anesthesia Services
Pain Clinic
3390 N Campbell Ave., Ste. 110
Tucson, AZ 85719
Ph: (520)795-7650
URL: http://www.wouthernarizonaanesthesia.com

35773 ■ University of Arizona Pain Institute
PO Box 245114
Tucson, AZ 85725
Ph: (520)621-7246
Fax: (520)626-4593
E-mail: clinrsch@email.arizona.edu
URL: http://pain.medicine.arizona.edu/
Dr. Bennet Davis, Executive Director

35774 ■ Valley Therapy Services
Pain Clinic
9700 N 91st St., Ste. A-115
Scottsdale, AZ 85258
Ph: (480)922-1376
URL: http://www.valleytherapy.com

BRITISH COLUMBIA

35775 ■ Leslie R. Peterson Rehabilitation Center
13569 76 Ave., Ste. 203
Surrey, BC, Canada V3W 2W3
URL: http://rehabmaxphysio.com

35776 ■ LifeMark Health Center--Vancouver
181 Keefer Pl., Ste. 230
Vancouver, BC, Canada V6B 6C1
Ph: (604)687-5911
URL: http://www.pain101.com/paindoctors/directory-ofpaindoctorscarflist.aspx

35777 ■ OrionHealth--Vancouver
201 - 3150 E 54th Ave.
Vancouver, BC, Canada V5S 1Z1
Ph: (604)263-4998
URL: http://www.pain101.com/paindoctors/directory-ofpaindoctorscarflist.aspx

CALIFORNIA

35778 ■ Affordable Chiropractic
Pain Clinic
2309 K St., Ste. 100
Sacramento, CA 95816
Ph: (916)444-2308
URL: http://www.affordablechiropractic.us

35779 ■ Anaheim Memorial Medical Center
Pain Management Center
1182 N Euclid St.
Anaheim, CA 92801
Ph: (714)999-3994
URL: http://www.memorialcare.org/anaheim/services/pain_management.cfm

35780 ■ Arroyo Grande Community Hospital
Pain Management Clinic
345 S Halcyon Rd.
Arroyo Grande, CA 93420
Ph: (805)489-4261
URL: http://arroyograndehospital.org

35781 ■ AV Pain Medical Clinic
44215 15th St. W, Ste. 114
Lancaster, CA 93534
Ph: (661)945-4563
URL: http://www.avpain.com

35782 ■ Bay Area Pain and Wellness Center
15047 Los Gatos Blvd., Ste. 200
Los Gatos, CA 95032
Ph: (408)364-6799
Fax: (408)378-4510
E-mail: get_info@bapwc.com
URL: http://www.bapwc.com

35783 ■ Care Center Rehabilitation and Pain Management
16550 Ventura Blvd., 1st Fl.
Encino, CA 91436
Ph: (818)784-0990
URL: http://www.carectr.com

35784 ■ Cedars Sinai Medical Center
Pain Center
444 San Vincente, Ste. 1101
Los Angeles, CA 90048
Ph: (310)423-9600
URL: http://www.csmc.edu

35785 ■ Central Coast Pain Institute
21 Mandeville Ct., Ste. A
Monterey, CA 93940
Ph: (831)373-7246
URL: http://www.centralcoastpaininstitute.com

35786 ■ Chest Pain Clinic
303 E Buena Vista St.
Barstow, CA 92311
Ph: (760)256-4601
URL: http://www.mohanmallam.com

35787 ■ Community Hospital Monterey Peninsula
Pain Clinic
543 Cuesta Dr.
Aptos, CA 95003
Ph: (408)688-4830
URL: http://www.abpm.org/diplomates/california.html

35788 ■ Comprehensive Blood and Cancer Center
Pain Clinic
4100 Truxtun Ave.
Bakersfield, CA 93309
Ph: (661)322-2206
URL: http://cbccusa.com

35789 ■ Daniel Freeman Memorial Hospital Rehabilitation Centers
Pain Management Program
333 N Prairie Ave.
Inglewood, CA 90301
Ph: (310)674-7050
Fax: (310)674-3886
URL: http://www.centinelafreeman.com
Jane O. Bensussen, Vice President
Remarks: CLOSED.

35790 ■ Eisenhower Memorial Hospital
Pain Management Clinic
39000 Bob Hope Dr.
Rancho Mirage, CA 92270
Ph: (760)340-3911
URL: http://www.emc.org

35791 ■ Hill Park Clinic
Pain Center
616 Petaluma Blvd. N, Ste. C
Petaluma, CA 94952
Ph: (707)778-3171
URL: http://www.hillparkmedicalcenter.com

35792 ■ Innovative Pain Treatment Solutions
27412 Enterprise Cir. W, Ste. 100
Temecula, CA 92590
Ph: (951)694-6367
URL: http://www.innovativepaintreatment.com

35793 ■ Jacobs Family Chiropractic
Pain Clinic
2727 Roosevelt St.
Carlsbad, CA 92008
Ph: (760)434-9006
URL: http://www.jacobschiro.net

35794 ■ Kaiser Permanente--Bellflow
Pain Block Center
9400 E Rosecrans Ave., Ste. 4300
Bellflower, CA 90706
Ph: (562)461-3001
URL: http://www.kaiserpermanente.org

35795 ■ Loma Linda University Medical Center
Pain Management
11406 Loma Linda Dr., Ste. 516
Loma Linda, CA 92354
Ph: (909)558-6202
E-mail: lreynolds@llu.edu
URL: http://www.pain101.com/PainDoctors/Directory-ACGMEprogramsList.aspx

35796 ■ Metropolitan Pain Management Consultants
2288 Auburn Blvd., Ste. 106
Sacramento, CA 95821
Ph: (916)568-8338
URL: http://www.pain-mpmc.com

35797 ■ Neurology Center
Pain Clinic
11600 Wilshire Blvd.
West Los Angeles, CA 90025
Ph: (310)477-7201
URL: http://www.neurologycenter.org

35798 ■ O'Connor Hospital
Pain Clinic
2101 Forest Ave., Ste. 117
San Jose, CA 95128
Ph: (408)295-8628
URL: http://www.oconnorhospital.org/pages/default.aspx

35799 ■ Orange Coast Memorial Health Care
Coast Pain Management Center
9920 Talbert Ave.
Fountain Valley, CA 92708
Ph: (714)378-2243
URL: http://www.memorialcare.org

35800 ■ Pacific Pain Treatment Centers
2000 Van Ness Ave., Ste. 402
San Francisco, CA 94109
Ph: (415)567-1219
URL: http://www.pacpain.com

35801 ■ Pacifica Hospital of the Valley
Pain Clinic
9449 San Fernando Rd.
Sun Valley, CA 91352
Ph: (818)767-3310
URL: http://www.pacificahospital.com

35802 ■ Pain Management Institute of Santa Barbara
2420 Fletcher Ave.
Santa Barbara, CA 93105
Ph: (805)898-1111
URL: http://www.painmanagementsb.com/

35803 ■ Pain and Rehabilitation Medical Group
3445 Pacific Coast Hwy., Ste. 300
Torrance, CA 90505
Ph: (310)325-8054
URL: http://www.painrehabgroup.com/main.html

35804 ■ Pasadena Rehabilitation Institute
Pain Clinic
1017 S Fair Oaks Ave.
Pasadena, CA 91105
Ph: (626)403-6200
URL: http://www.thebigmd.com

35805 ■ Regional Pain Treatment Center
14350 Whittier Blvd., Ste. 210
Whittier, CA 90605
Ph: (562)698-9992
Free: 888-311-7246
URL: http://www.paindoc4u.com

35806 ■ Saint John's Regional Medical Center
Pain Clinic
1600 N Rose Ave.
Oxnard, CA 93030
Ph: (805)988-2500
URL: http://www.stjohnshealth.org

35807 ■ Saint Jude Medical Center
Chronic Pain Management Center
101 E Valencia Mesa Dr.
Fullerton, CA 92835
Ph: (714)992-3000
URL: http://www.stjudemedicalcenter.org/
Winkie Sonnefield, Director

35808 ■ San Francisco Medical Clinic for Treatment
Pain Clinic
1790 26th Ave.
San Francisco, CA 94122
Ph: (415)665-1800
URL: http://www.sfpain.com

35809 ■ Santa Clara Valley Medical Center
Pain Management Center
751 S Bascom Ave., 2nf Fl. New Wing, Rm. 2M106
San Jose, CA 95128
Ph: (408)885-5745
URL: http://www.scvmed.org

35810 ■ Scripps Memorial Hospital
Pain Center
9888 Genesee Ave.
La Jolla, CA 92037
Ph: (858)626-4123
URL: http://www.scripps.org

35811 ■ Spinecare Medical Group
Pain Clinic
1850 Sullivan Ave., Ste. 200
Daly City, CA 94015
Ph: (650)985-7500
URL: http://www.spinecare.com

35812 ■ Stanford University
Pain Management Center
300 Pasteur Dr., Rm. A408
Stanford, CA 94305
Ph: (650)723-6238
URL: http://paincenter.stanford.edu

35813 ■ Total Health and Fitness Chiropractic Clinic
Pain Center
4501 Mission Bay Dr., Ste. 2A
San Diego, CA 92109
Ph: (858)581-3568
URL: http://www.chirochar.com

35814 ■ University of California, Irvine Medical Center
Pain Management Center
101 The City Dr., S
Orange, CA 92868
Ph: (714)456-6754
URL: http://www.ucihealth.com/pmc.asp

35815 ■ University of California Medical Center, Davis
Pain Management
4860 Y St., Ste. 3020
Sacramento, CA 95817
Ph: (916)734-6824
E-mail: gmahajan@ucdavis.edu
URL: http://www.pain101.com/PainDoctors/Directory-ACGMEprogramsList.aspx

35816 ■ University of California Medical Center, La Jolla
Pain Management
Dept. of Anesthesiology
9300 Campus Point Dr., Ste. 7651
La Jolla, CA 92037
Ph: (858)657-7030
E-mail: painfellowship@ucsd.edu
URL: http://www.pain101.com/PainDoctors/Directory-ACGMEprogramsList.aspx

35817 ■ University of California Medical Center, Los Angeles
David Geffen School of Medicine
Pain Management
Center for the Health Sciences
10833 Le Conte Ave.
Los Angeles, CA 90095
Ph: (310)825-3316
E-mail: ccamargo@mednet.ucla.edu
URL: http://www.pain101.com/PainDoctors/Directory-ACGMEprogramsList.aspx

35818 ■ University of California Medical Center, San Francisco
Pain Management Center
2255 Post St.
San Francisco, CA 94143
Ph: (415)885-7347
E-mail: gouldc@anesthesia.ucsf.edu
URL: http://www.pain101.com/PainDoctors/Directory-ACGMEprogramsList.aspx

35819 ■ University of California San Diego
Pain Management Medical Group
200 W Arbor Dr.
San Diego, CA 92103
Ph: (619)543-6222
URL: http://health.ucsd.edu

35820 ■ University of Southern California
Pain Management
1520 San Pablo St., Ste. 3450
Los Angeles, CA 90033
Ph: (323)442-6202
E-mail: mdrodrig@usc.edu
URL: http://www.pain101.com/PainDoctors/Directory-ACGMEprogramsList.aspx

35821 ■ Veteran's Affairs Los Angeles Healthcare System
Pain Management
Dept. of PM & R (W117)
11301 Wilshire Blvd.
Los Angeles, CA 90073
Ph: (310)268-3342
E-mail: sanjog.pangarkar@med.va.gov
URL: http://www.pain101.com/PainDoctors/Directory-ACGMEprogramsList.aspx

COLORADO

35822 ■ Children's Hospital
Pain Clinic
1056 E 19th Ave.
Denver, CO 80218
Ph: (303)861-8888
URL: http://www.thechildrenshospital.org

35823 ■ Colorado Pain Specialists
7951 E Maplewood Ave., Ste. 1112
Greenwood, CO 80111
Ph: (303)268-4040
URL: http://www.coloradopainspecialists.com

35824 ■ Colorado Sports and Spine Centers
The Pain Center
1625 Medical Center Point, Ste. 100
Colorado Springs, CO 80907
Ph: (719)475-1404
Fax: (719)475-1409
URL: http://www.penrosestfrancis.org/
Dr. Dale P. Mann, Director

35825 ■ Colorado Springs Interventional Pain Management
3010 N Circle Dr., Ste. 202
Colorado Springs, CO 80909
Ph: (719)228-9440
URL: http://www.coloradopain.com

35826 ■ Craniofacial Diagnostic Center
1660 S Albion, Ste. 1008
Denver, CO 80222
Ph: (303)691-0267
Fax: (303)691-0268
URL: http://drsmwinber.com
Dr. Stephen M. Winber, Director

35827 ■ Denver Pain Management
7447 E Berry Ave., Ste. 150
Greenwood Village, CO 80111
Ph: (303)689-2300
URL: http://www.denverpainmanagement.com

35828 ■ Durango Orthopedic Associates
Pain Clinic
375 E Park Ave., Ste. 2A
Durango, CO 81301
Ph: (970)247-5362
URL: http://www.durangoorthopedics.com

35829 ■ Eagle's Gate Optimum Wellness and Physical Therapy
Pain Clinic
140 Oakwood Ct.
Milliken, CO 80543
Ph: (970)587-2494
URL: http://www.eaglesgate.info

35830 ■ Integrative Treatment Centers
10835 N Dover St., Ste. 800
Westminster, CO 80030
Ph: (303)487-0932
URL: http://www.integrativetreatmentcenters.com

35831 ■ Saint Mary--Corwin Medical Center
Pain Clinic
1008 Minnegua Ave.
Pueblo, CO 81004
Ph: (719)560-4000
URL: http://www.stmarycorwin.org

35832 ■ South Denver Anesthesiologists
Pain Clinic
333 W Hampden Ave., Ste. 600
Englewood, CO 80110
Ph: (303)761-5646
URL: http://www.sdapc.com

35833 ■ University of Colorado
Pain Management
Box 6511, MS F493
12631 E 17th Ave.
Aurora, CO 80045
Ph: (720)848-1980
E-mail: vy.malcik@uchsc.edu
URL: http://www.pain101.com/PainDoctors/Directory-ACGMEprogramsList.aspx

CONNECTICUT

35834 ■ Center for Pain Rehabilitation
105 Newtown Rd.
Danbury, CT 06810
Ph: (203)744-4343
URL: http://www.centerforpainrehab.com

35835 ■ Comprehensive Pain and Headache Treatment Centers
330 Orchard St., Ste. 207
New Haven, CT 06511
Ph: (203)782-0570
URL: http://www.painandheadache.com

35836 ■ Connecticut Pain Care--Bridgeport
4920 Main St., Ste. 308
Bridgeport, CT 06606
Ph: (203)372-7197
URL: http://www.ctpaincare.com

35837 ■ Connecticut Pain Care--Danbury
109 Newton Rd.
Danbury, CT 06851
Ph: (203)792-7246
Free: 800-361-4383
URL: http://www.ctpaincare.com

35838 ■ Connecticut Pain Care--Hartford
81 Gillott St., Ste. 3
Hartford, CT 06105
Ph: (860)247-0033
URL: http://www.ctpaincare.com

35839 ■ Connecticut Pain Care--Norwalk
148 East Ave., Ste. 3D
Norwalk, CT 06851
Ph: (203)372-7197
URL: http://www.ctpaincare.com

35840 ■ Connecticut Pain Care--Trumbull
5520 Park Ave., Ste. 303
Trumbull, CT 06611
Ph: (203)373-7330
URL: http://www.ctpaincare.com

35841 ■ Connecticut Pain Care--Waterbury
1389 W Main St., Ste. 123
Waterbury, CT 06708
Ph: (203)596-7302
URL: http://www.ctpaincare.com

35842 ■ Connecticut Spine and Pain Center
Brewster Rd.
Bristol, CT 06011-0977
Ph: (860)585-3040
Fax: (860)585-3040
E-mail: jbarret1@brishosp.chime.org
URL: http://www.ctspineandpain.org/
Dr. Jonathan Kost, Director

35843 ■ Orthopedic Specialty Group
Pain Clinic
75 Kings Hwy. Cutoff, Ste. 2
Fairfield, CT 06824
Ph: (203)337-2616
URL: http://www.osgpc.com

35844 ■ Pain and Neurologic Care Institute
27 Quinebaug Ave.
Putnam, CT 06260
Ph: (860)963-2242
URL: http://www.hellenkimmd.com

DELAWARE

35845 ■ Pain Management and Rehab Center
240 Beiser Blvd., Ste. 201
Dover, DE 19904
Ph: (302)734-7246
URL: http://painrehab.net

35846 ■ Pain Management and Rehabilitation Center--Lewes
33664 Bay View Medical Center
Lewes, DE 19958
Ph: (302)645-9066
Fax: (302)645-9088
URL: http://painrehab.net

35847 ■ Pain Management and Rehabilitation Center--Seaford
8957 Middleford Rd.
Seaford, DE 19973
Ph: (302)628-9100
Fax: (302)628-9199
URL: http://painrehab.net

35848 ■ Pain Management and Rehabilitation Center--Wilmington
390 Mitch Rd.
Wilmington, DE 19804
Ph: (302)992-9191
Fax: (302)992-9198
URL: http://painrehab.net

35849 ■ Saint Francis Hospital
Brandywine Pain Center
7 Clayton St.
Wilmington, DE 19805
Ph: (302)421-4330
URL: http://www.stfrancishealthcare.org

35850 ■ Temple University Hospital
Pain Management
139 E Chestnut Hill Rd.
Newark, DE 19713
Ph: (301)369-1700
E-mail: gkoch@midatlanticspine.com
URL: http://www.pain101.com/PainDoctors/Directory-ACGMEprogramsList.aspx

35851 ■ Wilmington Hospital
Center for Pain Management
PO Box 1668
Wilmington, DE 19899
URL: http://www.christianacare.org/PainManagement

DISTRICT OF COLUMBIA

35852 ■ George Washington University Hospital
Pain Management Center
2131 K St. NW
Washington, DC 20037
Ph: (202)715-4599
Fax: (202)715-4598
URL: http://www.gwhospital.com/Hospital-Services-O-Z/pain-management
Dr. May Lin Chin, Director

35853 ■ National Rehabilitation Hospital--Washington DC
Pain Program
102 Irving St. NW
Washington, DC 20007
Ph: (202)877-1760
URL: http://nrhrehab.org

35854 ■ Sibley Memorial Hospital
5255 Loughboro Rd. NW
Washington, DC 20016
Ph: (202)537-4589
Fax: (202)537-0921
URL: http://www.sibley.org/pain_center/default.aspx

35855 ■ Walter Reed Army Medical Center
National Capital Consortium Program
Pain Management
Bldg. 2, Ward 44
6900 Georgia Ave. NW
Washington, DC 20307
Ph: (202)782-2930
URL: http://www.pain101.com/PainDoctors/Directory-ACGMEprogramsList.aspx

35856 ■ Washington Hospital Center
National Rehabilitation Hospital Program
Pain Management
110 Irving St. NW
Washington, DC 20010
Ph: (202)877-3442
E-mail: pain.program@medstar.net
URL: http://www.pain101.com/PainDoctors/Directory-ACGMEprogramsList.aspx

FLORIDA

35857 ■ Brooks Rehabilitation at Healthcare Plaza--Outpatient 1
Pain and Spinal Rehabilitation Center
3901 University Blvd. S
Jacksonville, FL 32216
Ph: (904)858-7300
Fax: (904)858-7240
URL: http://www.brookshealth.org
Remarks: The Pain Program is an in- and outpatient program dedicated to the medical rehabilitation of those suffering as a result of injury or surgery. The program is bio-behavioral and patients are treated by psychologists specializing in the treatment of chronic pain and related disorders.

35858 ■ Brooks Rehabilitation Hospital
3599 University Blvd. S
Jacksonville, FL 32216
Ph: (904)858-7600
Fax: (904)858-7734
URL: http://www.brookshealth.org

35859 ■ Comprehensive Pain Medicine Inc.
Airport Medical Park
1549 Airport Blvd., Ste. 140
Pensacola, FL 32503
Ph: (850)969-9804
Fax: (850)475-2143
URL: http://comprehensivepainmedicine.com
Dr. Ruben Timmons, Director

35860 ■ Fawcett Memorial Hospital
Chest Pain Center
21298 Olean Blvd.
Port Charlotte, FL 33949
Ph: (941)629-1181
Fax: (941)624-7005
URL: http://www.fawcetthospital.com

35861 ■ HealthSouth Sunrise Rehabilitation Hospital
Comprehensive Pain Care Center
4399 Nob Hill Rd.
Sunrise, FL 33351
Ph: (954)742-7999
URL: http://www.healthsouthsunrise.com

35862 ■ Jackson Memorial Hospital
Pain Management
Dept. of Anesthesiology
Miami, FL 33101
Ph: (305)243-5201
E-mail: dpatin@med.miami.edu
URL: http://www.pain101.com/PainDoctors/Directory-ACGMEprogramsList.aspx

35863 ■ James A. Haley Veteran's Hospital
Physical Medicine and Rehabilitation Service
13000 Bruce B. Downs Blvd.
Tampa, FL 33612
Ph: (813)972-7606
Fax: (813)972-7673
URL: http://www.tampa.va.gov

35864 ■ Lee Memorial Health System, Cape Coral
Pain Management Center
708 Del Prado Blvd., Ste. 7
Cape Coral, FL 33990
Ph: (239)343-7200
Fax: (239)574-0213
URL: http://www.leememorial.org

35865 ■ Lee Memorial Health System, HealthPark
Pain Management Center
16281 Bass Rd., Ste. 300
Fort Myers, FL 33908
Ph: (239)985-3640
Fax: (239)983-3650
URL: http://www.leememorial.org

35866 ■ Mayo Clinic, Jacksonville
Mayo School of Graduate Medical Education
Pain Management
4500 San Pablo Rd.
Jacksonville, FL 32224
Ph: (904)296-5289
E-mail: paglia.melissa@mayo.edu
URL: http://www.pain101.com/PainDoctors/Directory-ACGMEprogramsList.aspx

35867 ■ National Pain Institute, Bradenton
3501 Cortez Rd. NW
Bradenton, FL 34210
Ph: (941)757-6300
URL: http://www.natpain.com

35868 ■ National Pain Institute--Delray Beach
5365 W Atlantic Ave., Ste. 504
Delray Beach, FL 33484
Ph: (561)495-6300
Fax: (561)495-8877
URL: http://www.natpain.com

35869 ■ National Pain Institute--Delray Beach
15127 Jog Rd., Ste. 106
Delray Beach, FL 33436
Ph: (561)495-6300
Fax: (561)495-8877
URL: http://www.natpain.com

35870 ■ National Pain Institute, Holiday
2435 US Hwy. 19, Ste. 100
Holiday, FL 34691
Ph: (727)939-2230
Fax: (727)939-5767
URL: http://www.natpain.com

35871 ■ National Pain Institute--Lady Lake
1501 N US Hwy. 441, Ste. 1302
Lady Lake, FL 32159
Ph: (352)277-3500
Fax: (352)277-3498
URL: http://www.natpain.com

35872 ■ National Pain Institute--Lake Mary
4106 W Lake Mary Blvd., Ste. 205
Lake Mary, FL 32746
Ph: (407)936-2070
Fax: (407)936-2071
URL: http://www.natpain.com

35873 ■ National Pain Institute--New Port Richey
4219 US Hwy. 19
New Port Richey, FL 34652
Ph: (727)939-2230
Fax: (727)847-5349
URL: http://www.natpain.com

35874 ■ National Pain Institute--Port Saint Lucie
150 Chamber Ct., Ste. 105
Port Saint Lucie, FL 34986
Ph: (772)807-9000
Fax: (772)807-9087
URL: http://www.natpain.com

35875 ■ National Pain Institute--Sand Lake
7364 Stonerock Cir., Ste. A
Orlando, FL 32819
Ph: (407)288-8080
Fax: (407)352-0104
URL: http://www.natpain.com

35876 ■ National Pain Institute, Winter Park
1201 S Orlando Ave., Ste. 200
Winter Park, FL 32789
Ph: (407)622-5766
URL: http://www.natpain.com

35877 ■ Tampa General Hospital Rehabilitation Center
Pain Management Clinic
6 Tampa General Cir.
Tampa, FL 33601
Ph: (813)844-7610
URL: http://www.tgh.org
Winnie Keller, Director

35878 ■ University of Florida Health Science Center
Pain Management
Box 100254
1600 Archer Rd.
Gainesville, FL 32610
Ph: (352)376-1611
E-mail: amt57@aol.com
URL: http://www.pain101.com/PainDoctors/Directory-ACGMEprogramsList.aspx

35879 ■ University of South Florida
College of Medicine
Pain Management
Dept of Neurology
12901 Bruce B. Downs Blvd., MDC 55
Tampa, FL 33612
Ph: (813)972-7633
E-mail: cbrock@health.usf.edu
URL: http://www.pain101.com/PainDoctors/Directory-ACGMEprogramsList.aspx

35880 ■ Wuesthoff Pain Management Center
2400 N Courtenay Pkwy.
Merritt Island, FL 32953
Ph: (321)637-2870
Fax: (321)453-8490
E-mail: marcia.guilford@wuesthoff.org
URL: http://www.wuesthoff.org/Services/painManagement.aspx

GEORGIA

35881 ■ Atlanta Back Pain Clinic
1287 Hwy. 138, Ste. 8
Jonesboro, GA 30236
Ph: (770)473-0038
URL: http://www.atlantabackpaincenter.com

35882 ■ Atlanta Pain Relief Center
110 Habersham Dr., Ste. 110
Fayetteville, GA 30214
Ph: (770)371-5182
URL: http://www.drgatell.com

35883 ■ Comprehensive Pain Care
840 Church St., Ste. B
Marietta, GA 30067
Ph: (770)421-8080
URL: http://www.dtaylor.yourmd.com

35884 ■ East--West Medical PC
Pain Clinic
4920 Roswell Rd., Ste. 35
Atlanta, GA 30342
Ph: (404)843-8880
URL: http://www.docbridges.com

35885 ■ Emory University Hospital
Pain Management
Dept. of Anesthesiology, 3 B South
1364 Clifton Rd. NE
Atlanta, GA 30322
Ph: (404)778-5582
URL: http://www.pain101.com/PainDoctors/Directory-ACGMEprogramsList.aspx

35886 ■ Floyd Medical Center
Pain Clinic
304 Turner McCall Blvd., Ste. 101
Rome, GA 30165
Ph: (706)509-6600
URL: http://www.floyd.org

35887 ■ Georgia Pain Specialists
2520 Windy Hill Rd., Ste. 204
Marietta, GA 30067
Ph: (770)955-7246
URL: http://www.georgiapain.com

35888 ■ Medical College of Georgia
Pain Management
1120 15th St.
Augusta, GA 30912
Ph: (706)721-7754
E-mail: sdawkins@mcg.edu
URL: http://www.pain101.com/PainDoctors/Directory-ACGMEprogramsList.aspx

35889 ■ Oconee Pain Clinic
1215 N Columbia Dr.
Milledgeville, GA 31061
Ph: (478)454-1977
URL: http://www.oconeepainclinic.com

35890 ■ Pain Control and Rehabilitation Institute of Georgia
2784 N Decatur Rd., No. 120
Decatur, GA 30033
Ph: (404)297-1400
Fax: (404)297-1427

35891 ■ Pain Evaluation and Treatment Center--Macon, GA
840 Pine St., Ste. 780
Macon, GA 31201
Ph: (478)745-2385
URL: http://www.hemlockpain.com

35892 ■ Pain Management Clinic
200 Parkbrooke Dr.
Woodstock, GA 30189
Ph: (770)591-8360
URL: http://www.thepainmanagementclinic.com

35893 ■ Physicians' Pain and Rehabilitation Specialists
993-C Johnson Ferry Rd., Ste. 305
Atlanta, GA 30342
Ph: (404)816-3000
URL: http://www.thephysicians.com

35894 ■ Royce Centers Pain Medicine
5400 Laurel Springs Pkwy., Ste. 1002
Suwanee, GA 30024
Ph: (770)888-8999
URL: http://www.roycecenters.com

35895 ■ Southeast Georgia Regional Medical Center
3003 Kemble Ave.
Brunswick, GA 31520
Ph: (912)466-5320
URL: http://www.sghs.org

35896 ■ Southeast Regional Pain Center
5669 Whitesville Rd.
Columbus, GA 31904
Ph: (706)571-7246
URL: http://www.thepaincenter.info

35897 ■ Southern Regional Medical Center
Pain Center
11 SW Upper Riverdale Rd.
Riverdale, GA 30274
Ph: (770)991-8094
URL: http://www.southernregional.com

35898 ■ Spine Care and Pain Management
1620 Prince Ave.
Athens, GA 30606
Ph: (706)549-8114
URL: http://www.tameyourpain.com

35899 ■ Walton Rehabilitation Hospital
1355 Independence Dr.
Augusta, GA 30901
Ph: (706)823-8502
Free: 866-724-7746
Fax: (706)724-5752
E-mail: postmaster@wrh.org
URL: http://www.wrh.org/programs_services/pain_management.html
Dennis B. Skelly, President

HAWAII

35900 ■ Pain Evaluation and Rehabilitation Center
1441 Kapiolani Blvd., Ste. 813
Honolulu, HI 96814
Ph: (808)955-7246

35901 ■ Rehabilitation Hospital of the Pacific
226 N Kuakini St.
Honolulu, HI 96817
Ph: (808)531-3511
URL: http://www.rehabhospital.org

IDAHO

35902 ■ Pain Care Boise
301 W Myrtle
Boise, ID 83702
Ph: (208)342-8200
URL: http://www.paincareboise.com

35903 ■ Saint Alphonsus Regional Medical Center
Pain Center
1055 N Curtis Rd.
Boise, ID 83704
Ph: (208)367-4343
URL: http://www.saintalphonsus.org/

35904 ■ Southern Idaho Pain Institute
236 Martin St.
Twin Falls, ID 83301
Ph: (208)733-3181
URL: http://www.thepaindoc.net

35905 ■ Sun Valley Pain Management
380 Washington Ave., Ste. 201
Ketchum, ID 83340
Ph: (208)726-0000
URL: http://www.kimvorsemd.com

ILLINOIS

35906 ■ Advanced Pain Management Institute
7309 N Knoxville Ave.
Peoria, IL 61614
Ph: (309)692-1539
Fax: (309)683-4208
URL: http://www.apmofillinois.com

35907 ■ Central Illinois Pain Center
OSF Center for Health
8600 N State, Rte. 91, No. 250
Peoria, IL 61615
Ph: (309)683-5094
Fax: (309)683-5095

35908 ■ Cook County Hospital
John H. Stroger Hospital
Pain Management
Dept. of Anesthesiology
1901 W Harrison St.
Chicago, IL 60612
Ph: (312)864-3221
URL: http://www.pain101.com/PainDoctors/Directory-ACGMEprogramsList.aspx

35909 ■ Head and Neck Pain Center
205 W Randolph, Ste. 1800
Chicago, IL 60602
Ph: (312)920-0505
Fax: (312)920-9020
E-mail: hnpc1800@aol.com
URL: http://www.headandneck.com
Formerly: Head and Neck Diagnostic Center.

35910 ■ Kishwaukee Community Hospital
Pain Management Program
1 Kish Hospital Dr.
DeKalb, IL 60115
Ph: (815)756-1521
Fax: (800)397-1521
URL: http://www.kishhospital.com/painclinic

35911 ■ Lake Forest Hospital
Center for Rehabilitation
660 N Westmoreland Rd.
Lake Forest, IL 60045
Ph: (847)234-6132
URL: http://www.lfh.org

35912 ■ Loyola University
Pain Center
2160 S 1st Ave.
Maywood, IL 60153
Ph: (708)216-7925
URL: http://www.pain101.com/PainDoctors/Directory-ACGMEprogramsList.aspx

35913 ■ Marianjoy, Oakbrook Terrace
Pain Management Program
17W682 Butterfield
Oakbrook Terrace, IL 60181
Ph: (630)268-1595
URL: http://www.marianjoy.org

35914 ■ Northwestern University
Feinberg School of Medicine
McGaw Medical Center
Pain Management
251 E Huron St., Ste. 5-704
Chicago, IL 60611
Ph: (312)926-8105
URL: http://www.pain101.com/PainDoctors/Directory-ACGMEprogramsList.aspx

35915 ■ Rehabilitation Institute of Chicago
345 E Superior St.
Chicago, IL 60611
Ph: (312)238-1000
Free: 800-354-7342
URL: http://www.ric.org

35916 ■ Rush University Medical Center
Pain Management
1653 W Congress Pkwy.
Chicago, IL 60612
Ph: (312)942-6504
E-mail: sherri_sachs@rush.edu
URL: http://www.pain101.com/PainDoctors/Directory-ACGMEprogramsList.aspx

35917 ■ Trinity Outpatient Rehabilitation Services
2701 17th St.
Rock Island, IL 61201
Ph: (309)779-2300
URL: http://www.trinityqc.com

35918 ■ Trinity Rehabilitation Services
500 John Deere Rd.
Moline, IL 61265
Ph: (309)779-5000
URL: http://www.trinityqc.com
Pamela J. Muehling, Director

35919 ■ University of Chicago Hospital
Pain Management
5841 S Maryland Ave.
Chicago, IL 60637
Ph: (773)834-3643
URL: http://www.pain101.com/PainDoctors/Directory-ACGMEprogramsList.aspx

35920 ■ University of Illinois
College of Medicine
Pain Management
835 S Wolcott Ave.
Chicago, IL 60612
Ph: (312)996-1128
E-mail: sharps@uic.edu
URL: http://www.pain101.com/PainDoctors/Directory-ACGMEprogramsList.aspx

INDIANA

35921 ■ Apac Centers for Pain Management
1205 S Main, Ste. 207
Crown Point, IN 46307
Ph: (219)226-0708
Free: 800-756-2110
URL: http://www.apacgroup.com

35922 ■ Center for Pain Management--Indianapolis, IN
8805 N Meridian St.
Indianapolis, IN 46260
Ph: (317)706-7246
URL: http://www.indypain.com

35923 ■ Indiana University
School of Medicine
Pain Management
Fesler Hall 204
1120 South Dr.
Indianapolis, IN 46202
Ph: (317)274-2866
E-mail: laronson@iupui.edu
URL: http://www.pain101.com/PainDoctors/Directory-ACGMEprogramsList.aspx

35924 ■ Indianapolis Neurosurgical Group
Pain Clinic
8333 Naab Rd., Ste. 250
Indianapolis, IN 46260
Free: 888-822-5546
URL: http://www.ing.md

35925 ■ Meridian Health Group
Pain Care Center
12772 Hamilton Crossing Blvd.
Carmel, IN 46032
Ph: (317)814-1000
Free: 866-814-6200
URL: http://www.meridianhealthgroup.com

35926 ■ Midwest Pain Management Centers
701 Superior Ave., Ste. C
Munster, IN 46321
Free: 877-934-7246
URL: http://www.midwestpain.org

35927 ■ Neurology and Pain Management--Lafayette
130 Professional Ct.
Lafayette, IN 47905
Ph: (766)446-8888
URL: http://www.drungar.com

35928 ■ Neurology and Pain Management--Rensselaer
123 S McKinley Ave.
Rensselaer, IN 47978
Ph: (219)866-7222
URL: http://www.drungar.com

35929 ■ Oliver Headache and Pain Clinic/Advanced Pain Care Clinic
1101 Professional Blvd.
Evansville, IN 47714
Ph: (812)477-7246
Fax: (812)477-7240
URL: http://oliverclinic.com

IOWA

35930 ■ Cedar Valley Medical Clinic
Pain Clinic
148 W Dale St.
Waterloo, IA 50703
Ph: (319)233-6448
URL: http://www.cedarvalleymedical.com

35931 ■ Mercy Center for Pain Management
250 Mercy Dr.
Dubuque, IA 52001
Ph: (563)589-8000
URL: http://www.mercydubuque.com

35932 ■ Pain Clinic
2180 Norcor Ave., Ste. B
Coralville, IA 52241
URL: http://www.pain-clinic.biz

35933 ■ University of Iowa Hospitals and Clinics
Pain Management
Dept. of Anesthesia
200 Hawkins Dr., 6 JCP
Iowa City, IA 52242
Ph: (319)353-7783
URL: http://www.pain101.com/PainDoctors/Directory-ACGMEprogramsList.aspx

KANSAS

35934 ■ Headache and Pain Center
11120 Tomahawk Creek Pkwy.
Leawood, KS 66211
Ph: (913)491-3999
URL: http://www.headacheandpaincenter.com

35935 ■ Midwest Rehabilitation Associates
Pain Center
634 SW Mulvane St., Ste. 401
Topeka, KS 66606
Ph: (785)357-6300
URL: http://midwestrehabilitation.com

35936 ■ Midwest Surgery Center
Pain Clinic
650 N Carriage Pkwy., Ste. 100
Wichita, KS 67208
Ph: (316)683-3937
URL: http://www.pain-spasticity.com

35937 ■ Olathe Medical Center
Pain Clinic
20375 W 151st St., Ste. 406
Olathe, KS 6061
Ph: (913)782-2292
URL: http://olathehealth.org

35938 ■ University of Kansas
Cancer Center
Pain Management Center
3901 Rainbow Blvd.
Kansas City, KS 66160
Ph: (913)588-5000
URL: http://www.kumed.com

KENTUCKY

35939 ■ Cardinal Hill Rehabilitation Hospital
2050 Versailles Rd.
Lexington, KY 40504
Ph: (606)254-5701
URL: http://www.cardinalhill.org/chrh

35940 ■ Ephraim McDowell Regional Medical Center
Pain Management Center
217 S 3rd St.
Danville, KY 40422
Ph: (859)239-2002
Fax: (859)239-6741
URL: http://www.emhealth.org

35941 ■ Kentuckiana Pain Specialists Inc.
2831 S Hurstbourne Pkwy., Ste. A
Louisville, KY 40220
Ph: (502)995-4004
URL: http://painstopshere.org

35942 ■ Kings Daughters Spine and Pain Center
Medical Plz. A
617 23rd St.
Ashland, KY 41101
Ph: (606)408-7246
Fax: (606)408-7230
URL: http://www.kdmc.com/rehabilitation/default.aspx?id=688

35943 ■ Murphy Pain Center
3020 Eastpoint Pkwy.
Louisville, KY 40223
Ph: (502)736-3636
Fax: (502)736-3637
URL: http://murphypain.com
Dr. James P. Murphy, Director

35944 ■ Spine and Brain Neurosurgical Center--Lexington
1721 Nicholasville Rd.
Lexington, KY 40503
Ph: (859)514-0145
Fax: (859)252-3073
URL: http://sbncmd.com

35945 ■ Spine and Brain Neurosurgical Center--London
189 W Hwy. 192 Bypass
London, KY 40741
Ph: (606)877-8776
Fax: (606)877-5454
URL: http://www.sbncmd.com

35946 ■ Spine and Brain Neurosurgical Center--Pikeville
7160 N Mayo Trl.
Pikeville, KY 41501
Ph: (606)478-7000
Fax: (606)478-7001
URL: http://sbncmd.com

35947 ■ University of Kentucky
College of Medicine
Pain Management
Dept. of Anesthesiology, Rm. N-202
800 Rose St.
Lexington, KY 40536
Ph: (859)323-5956
E-mail: jrhol2@email.uky.edu
URL: http://www.pain101.com/PainDoctors/Directory-ACGMEprogramsList.aspx

35948 ■ University of Louisville
School of Medicine
Pain Management
Dept. of Anesthesiology & Perioperative Medicine
530 S Jackson St.
Louisville, KY 40202
Ph: (502)852-1734
E-mail: anvina01@louisville.edu
URL: http://www.pain101.com/PainDoctors/Directory-ACGMEprogramsList.aspx

LOUISIANA

35949 ■ Louisiana State University Health Sciences Center, Shreveport
Pain Management
1501 Kings Hwy.
Shreveport, LA 71130
Ph: (318)675-4810
E-mail: thdosc49@yahoo.com
URL: http://www.pain101.com/PainDoctors/Directory-ACGMEprogramsList.aspx

35950 ■ Louisiana State University
Touro Infirmary
Pain Management
1401 Foucher St., Ste. 10012
New Orleans, LA 70115
Ph: (504)897-8948
E-mail: mniles@lsuhsc.edu
URL: http://www.pain101.com/PainDoctors/Directory-ACGMEprogramsList.aspx

35951 ■ Our Lady of Lourdes Rehabilitation Center
611 St. Landry St.
Lafayette, LA 70506
Ph: (337)289-2000
E-mail: info@lourdes.net
URL: http://www.lourdesnet.org

35952 ■ Pain Treatment Center of Baton Rouge
505 E Airport Dr.
Baton Rouge, LA 70806
Ph: (225)201-0950
URL: http://www.paintreatmentcenterinc.com

35953 ■ Touro Rehabilitation Center
Pain Management Center
1401 Foucher St.
New Orleans, LA 70115
Ph: (504)897-8560
URL: http://www.pain101.com/PainDoctors/Directory-ACGMEprogramsList.aspx

35954 ■ Touro Rehabilitation Center
Rehabilitation Services
1401 Foucher St.
New Orleans, LA 70115
Ph: (504)897-8560
URL: http://www.touro.com

MAINE

35955 ■ Brighton Medical Center
Paincare Center
335 Brighton Ave.
Portland, ME 04102
Ph: (207)879-8063
URL: http://www.mmc.org/mmc_body.cfm?id=1919

35956 ■ Medical Rehabilitation Associates--Augusta
55 Middle St., Ste. 1
Augusta, ME 04330
Ph: (207)629-9488
URL: http://mramaine.com/index.html

35957 ■ Medical Rehabilitation Associates--Brunswick
12 Industrial Pkwy.
Brunswick, ME 04011
Ph: (207)725-7854
URL: http://mramaine.com/index.html

35958 ■ Medical Rehabilitation Associates--Lewiston
77 Bates St., Ste. 102
Lewiston, ME 04240
Ph: (207)783-2300
URL: http://mramaine.com/index.html

MARYLAND

35959 ■ Georgetown University Hospital
Pain Clinic
7501 Surratts Rd., Ste. 206
Clinton, MD 20735
Ph: (301)856-2323
URL: http://www.georgetownuniversityhospital.org

35960 ■ Johns Hopkins Hospital
Department of Neurosurgery
4940 Eastern Ave.
Baltimore, MD 21224

Ph: (410)550-0100
Fax: (410)955-0626
URL: http://www.hopkinsmedicine.org/neuro

35961 ■ Johns Hopkins University Hospital
Pain Management
550 N Broadway, Ste. 301
Baltimore, MD 21205
Ph: (410)955-1818
E-mail: pchristo@jhmi.edu
URL: http://www.pain101.com/PainDoctors/Directory-ACGMEprogramsList.aspx

35962 ■ National Rehabilitation Hospital--Metro Center, Bethesda
Pain Clinic
3 Bethesda Metro Center, Ste. 950
Bethesda, MD 20814
Ph: (301)215-9100
URL: http://www.nrhrehab.org

35963 ■ National Rehabilitation Hospital--Rockledge Drive, Bethesda, MD
Pain Program
6410 Rockledge Dr., Ste. 600
Bethesda, MD 20817
Ph: (301)581-8030
Fax: (301)581-8031
URL: http://nrhrehab.org

35964 ■ Rehabilitation and Pain Management Associates
Ruxton Towers
8415 Bellona Ln., Ste. 201
Towson, MD 21204-2014
Ph: (410)821-7775
URL: http://www.rosen-hoffberg.com

35965 ■ Saint Joseph Medical Center
Pain Clinic
8525 Huntspring Dr.
Lutherville, MD 21093
Ph: (410)828-5863
URL: http://www.stjosephtowson.com

35966 ■ Sinai Hospital
Pain Center
Dept. of Anesthesiology
6124 Wooded Run Dr.
Columbia, MD 21044
URL: http://mountsinai.net

35967 ■ Union Hospital Cecil County
Pain Clinic
106 Bow St.
Elkton, MD 21921
Ph: (410)398-4000
URL: http://www.uhcc.com

35968 ■ University of Maryland Medical Center
Pain Management
22 S Greene St., Ste. S11C00
Baltimore, MD 21201
Ph: (410)448-6625
E-mail: mpurcell@anes.umm.edu
URL: http://www.pain101.com/PainDoctors/Directory-ACGMEprogramsList.aspx

MASSACHUSETTS

35969 ■ Beth Israel Deaconess Medical Center
Critical Care and Pain Medicine
Dept. of Anesthesia
330 Brookline Ave., E/St5
Boston, MA 02215
Ph: (617)667-5558
E-mail: cpeeters@bidmc.harvard.edu
URL: http://www.pain101.com/PainDoctors/Directory-ACGMEprogramsList.aspx

35970 ■ Brigham and Women's Hospital
Pain Management
Dept. of Anesthesiology
75 Francis St.
Boston, MA 02115
Ph: (617)732-9057
E-mail: hponde@partners.org
URL: http://www.pain101.com/PainDoctors/Directory-ACGMEprogramsList.aspx

35971 ■ Caritas Saint Elizabeth's Medical Center
Pain Management Center
736 Cambridge St., MMR-1
Boston, MA 02135
Ph: (617)789-2777
URL: http://www.pain101.com/PainDoctors/Directory-ACGMEprogramsList.aspx

35972 ■ Catholic Memorial Home
Pain Management Program
2446 Highland Ave.
Fall River, MA 02720
Ph: (508)679-0011
Fax: (508)672-5858

35973 ■ Harvard Medical School
Spaulding Rehabilitation Hospital
Pain Management
125 Nashua St.
Boston, MA 02114
Ph: (617)573-2178
URL: http://www.pain101.com/PainDoctors/Directory-ACGMEprogramsList.aspx

35974 ■ Madonna Manor Pain Program
85 N Washington St.
North Attleboro, MA 02760
Ph: (508)699-2740
Fax: (508)699-0481

35975 ■ Marian Manor Pain Management Program
33 Summer St.
Taunton, MA 02780-3491
Ph: (508)822-4885
Fax: (508)677-4361

35976 ■ Massachusetts General Hospital
Pain Management
MGH Pain Center, WAC 333
15 Parkman St.
Boston, MA 02114
Ph: (617)726-3332
E-mail: gjbrenner@partners.org
URL: http://www.pain101.com/PainDoctors/Directory-ACGMEprogramsList.aspx

35977 ■ Our Lady's Haven Pain Management Program
71 Center St.
Fairhaven, MA 02719
Ph: (508)999-4561
Fax: (508)997-0254

35978 ■ Sacred Heart Home Pain Management Program
359 Summer St.
New Bedford, MA 02740
Ph: (508)996-6751
Fax: (508)992-3145

35979 ■ Tufts University School of Medicine
Baystate Medical Center
Pain Management
Porter 2
759 Chestnut St.
Springfield, MA 01199
Ph: (413)794-4326
E-mail: maria.lopez@bhs.org
URL: http://www.pain101.com/PainDoctors/Directory-ACGMEprogramsList.aspx

MICHIGAN

35980 ■ Chelsea Community Hospital
Head Pain Treatment Program
775 S Main St.
Chelsea, MI 48118
Ph: (734)475-4051
URL: http://www.cch.org
Kathleen S. Griffiths, President

35981 ■ Great Lakes Pain Consultants
4121 Shrestha Dr.
Bay City, MI 48706
Free: 877-577-6227
URL: http://www.greatlakespain.com

35982 ■ Henry Ford Hospital
Anesthesiology Pain Fellowship Program
2799 W Grand Blvd.
Detroit, MI 48202
Ph: (313)916-8234
E-mail: jrobert1@hfhs.org
URL: http://www.pain101.com/PainDoctors/Directory-ACGMEprogramsList.aspx

35983 ■ Holland Hospital
Michigan Pain Consultants
Bldg. 1
844 S Washington, Ste. 100
Holland, MI 49423
Ph: (616)940-2662
Free: 800-281-3237
URL: http://www.michiganpain.com

35984 ■ Mary Free Bed Hospital and Rehabilitation Center
235 Wealthy St. SE
Grand Rapids, MI 49503
Ph: (616)242-0400
URL: http://www.maryfreebed.com

35985 ■ Michigan Head Pain and Neurological Institute
3120 Professional Dr.
Ann Arbor, MI 48104
Ph: (734)677-6000
Free: 800-518-3639
Fax: (734)677-2422
URL: http://www.mhni.com

35986 ■ Michigan Interventional Pain Center
19725 Allen Rd., Ste. 102
Brownstown, MI 48236
Ph: (734)479-7246
URL: http://www.mipaincenter.com

35987 ■ Michigan Pain Consultants
15044 220th Ave.
Big Rapids, MI 49307
Free: 800-281-3237
URL: http://www.michiganpain.com

35988 ■ Michigan Spine and Pain
2480 W Campus Dr., Ste. 500
Mount Pleasant, MI 48858
Ph: (989)772-1609
Free: 800-586-7992
URL: http://www.michiganspineandpain.com

35989 ■ Michigan State University
Rehabilitation Medicine Clinic
138 Service Rd., Ste. A-114
East Lansing, MI 48824-1313
Ph: (517)355-7648
URL: http://www.rehab.msu.edu

35990 ■ Pain Clinic of Michigan
710 Barkley Cir., Ste. 115
Rochester, MI 48307
Ph: (248)652-7558
URL: http://www.painguru.net

36001 ■ Pain Diagnostics Associates
Escanaba, MI
Free: 888-724-6377
URL: http://www.paindiagnostics.net

35992 ■ Pennock Hospital
Michigan Pain Consultants
1009 W Green St.
Hastings, MI 49058
Ph: (269)945-3451
URL: http://www.pennockhealth.com

35993 ■ Saint Joseph Mercy Ann Arbor
Pain Clinic
PO Box 995
Ann Arbor, MI 48106
Ph: (734)712-3456
URL: http://www.stjoesannarbor.com

35994 ■ Southern Michigan Pain Consultants
105 Winston
Marshall, MI 49068
Free: 877-377-6227
URL: http://www.southernmichiganpain.com

35995 ■ Sparrow Regional Pain Management Center
1215 E Michigan Ave.
Lansing, MI 48909-7980
Ph: (517)364-5330
Fax: (517)364-5335
E-mail: jennifer.isenhath@sparrow.org
URL: http://www.sparrow.org/painmanagement/

35996 ■ Spectrum Health
Michigan Pain Consultants
80 68th St., Ste. 202
Grand Rapids, MI 49548
Ph: (616)940-2662
Free: 800-281-3237
URL: http://www.michiganpain.com

35997 ■ Tri--County Pain Consultants
3055 Northwestern Hwy., Ste. L-50
Farmington Hills, MI 48334
Free: 800-319-3118
URL: http://www.tricountypain.com

35998 ■ University of Michigan
Pain Management
Dept. of Anesthesiology
C213 Med Inn Bldg.
Ann Arbor, MI 48109
Ph: (734)936-6585
E-mail: dosborn@umich.edu
URL: http://www.pain101.com/PainDoctors/Directory-ACGMEprogramsList.aspx

35999 ■ University Pain Clinic
4160 John R, Ste. 522
Detroit, MI 48201
Ph: (313)745-7246
URL: http://www.universitypainclinic.com

36000 ■ Wayne State University
Detroit Medical Center
Pain Management
Anesthesia Educ. Offices
3990 John R, Box 162, Rm. 2901
Detroit, MI 48201
Ph: (313)745-7233
E-mail: telininger@msn.com
URL: http://www.pain101.com/PainDoctors/Directory-ACGMEprogramsList.aspx

MINNESOTA

36001 ■ Mayo Clinic, Rochester
College of Medicine
Pain Management
200 1st St. SW
Rochester, MN 55905
Ph: (507)266-2077
E-mail: painfellowship@mayo.edu
URL: http://www.pain101.com/PainDoctors/Directory-ACGMEprogramsList.aspx

36002 ■ Medical Advanced Pain Specialists
2104 Northdale Blvd., Ste. 220
Coon Rapids, MN 55433
Ph: (763)537-6000
Free: 800-775-7246
URL: http://www.painphysicians.com

36003 ■ Minnesota Interventional Pain Associates
12203 Aberdeen St. NE, Ste. 100
Blaine, MN 55449
Ph: (763)390-1279
URL: http://www.mnpain.com

36004 ■ Twin Cities Pain Clinic
7601 France Ave. S, Ste. 270
Edina, MN 55435
Ph: (952)841-2345
URL: http://www.twincitiespainclinic.com

36005 ■ United Pain Center
280 N Smith Ave., Ste. 600
Saint Paul, MN 55102
Ph: (651)241-7246
Fax: (651)241-7272
E-mail: vicki.call@allina.com
URL: http://www.allina.com/ahs/united.nsf/page/pain_center

36006 ■ Wellspring Health Center
Pain Clinic
10903 Excelsior Blvd.
Hopkins, MN 55343
Ph: (952)930-3303
URL: http://www.wellspringhopkins.com

MISSISSIPPI

36007 ■ Pain Treatment Center
114 Jefferson Davis Blvd.
Natchez, MS 39120
Ph: (601)442-5382
URL: http://www.paintreatmentcenterinc.com

36008 ■ Rush Foundation Hospital
Pain Treatment Center
1314 19th Ave.
Meridian, MS 39301
Ph: (601)703-4362
Fax: (601)703-4363
E-mail: tonia.mckee@rushhealth.com
URL: http://www.rushhealthsystems.org/
Joey Daugherty, Director

36009 ■ University of Mississippi Medical Center
Pain Management
Dept. of Anesthesiology
2500 N State St.
Jackson, MS 39216
Ph: (601)984-5950
E-mail: ieriator@anesthesia.umsmed.edu
URL: http://www.pain101.com/PainDoctors/Directory-ACGMEprogramsList.aspx

MISSOURI

36010 ■ Headache Care Center
3805 S Kansas Expy.
Springfield, MO 65807
Ph: (417)890-7888
Free: 866-899-0745
Fax: (417)890-8827
E-mail: darnold@headachecare.com
URL: http://www.headachecare.com

36011 ■ Rusk Outpatient Services/Howard A. Rusk Rehabilitation Center
315 Business Loop
Columbia, MO 65203
Ph: (314)817-2703
URL: http://www.ruskrehab.com

36012 ■ Saint Francis Medical Center
Pain Management Center
211 St. Francis Dr.
Cape Girardeau, MO 63703
Ph: (573)331-5329
Fax: (573)331-5085
URL: http://www.sfmc.net
Sherry Hooe, Director

36013 ■ Saint Louise Behavioral Medicine Institute
Pain Clinic
1129 Macklind Ave.
Saint Louis, MO 63110
Ph: (314)534-0200
URL: http://www.slbmi.com

36014 ■ Saint Mary's Pain Center
210 NW Mize Rd.
Blue Springs, MO 64014
Ph: (816)655-5270
URL: http://www.carondelethealth.org/smbs/services/mpain.asp

36015 ■ Washington University
Pain Management
B-JH/SLCH Consortium Program
660 S Euclid St.
Saint Louis, MO 73110
Ph: (314)747-0202
E-mail: swarmr@msnotes.wustl.edu
URL: http://www.pain101.com/PainDoctors/Directory-ACGMEprogramsList.aspx

MONTANA

36016 ■ Benefis Health Care East
Pain Clinic
1101 26th St. S
Great Falls, MT 59405
Ph: (406)455-5000
URL: http://www.benefis.org

36017 ■ Frances Mahon Deaconess Hospital
Pain Management Program
621 3rd St. S
Glasgow, MT 59230
Ph: (406)228-3500
Fax: (406)228-3535
URL: http://www.fmdh.org

36018 ■ Northern Rockies Brain and Spine Center
Pain Clinic
2900 12th Ave. N, Ste. 340W
Billings, MT 59101
Ph: (406)237-5760
URL: http://www.montanaspine.com

36019 ■ Saint Peters Community Hospital
Pain Management Services
2475 Broadway
Helena, MT 59601
Ph: (406)444-2100
URL: http://www.stpetes.org

NEBRASKA

36020 ■ Comprehensive Pain Center
8031 W Center Rd., Ste. 226
Omaha, NE 68124
Ph: (402)391-8978

36021 ■ Health Services One
Central Pain Solutions
3500 Central Ave.
Kearney, NE 68847

36022 ■ Mary Lanning Memorial Healthcare Pain Clinic
715 N St. Joseph Ave.
Hastings, NE 68901
Ph: (402)463-4521
URL: http://www.mlmh.org

36023 ■ Medical Pain Center
7837 Chicago Plz.
Omaha, NE 68114
Ph: (402)390-6226

36024 ■ Medical Pain Relief Clinic
10020 Nicholas St., Ste. 106
Omaha, NE 68114
Ph: (402)894-9990
URL: http://www.drpains.com

36025 ■ Nebraska Spine and Pain Center
6940 Van Dorn, Ste. 201
Lincoln, NE 68506
Ph: (402)323-8484
Free: 866-672-4768
URL: http://www.nebpain.com

36026 ■ Northeast Spine and Pain Center
9850 Nicholas St., Ste. 310
Omaha, NE 68114
Ph: (402)502-9877
Free: 866-672-4768
URL: http://www.nebpain.com

36027 ■ University of Nebraska Medical Center
College of Medicine
Pain Management
984455 Nebraska Medical Center
Omaha, NE 68198
Ph: (402)559-7405
URL: http://www.pain101.com/PainDoctors/Directory-ACGMEprogramsList.aspx

NEVADA

36028 ■ Central Recovery Treatment Pain Clinic
3371 N Buffalo Dr.
Las Vegas, NV 89129
Ph: (702)515-1374
URL: http://www.centralrecovery.com

36029 ■ Las Vegas Pain Institute
2705 W Horizon Ridge, Ste. 120
Henderson, NV 89052
Ph: (702)880-4193

36030 ■ McKenna Pain Management
901 Rancho Ln., Ste. 135
Las Vegas, NV 89106
Ph: (702)307-7700
URL: http://www.mckennapainmanagement.com

36031 ■ NovaCare Outpatient Rehabilitation Injury Management Programs
2055 E Sahara Ave.
Las Vegas, NV 89106
Ph: (702)320-3370
URL: http://www.novacare.com/

36032 ■ Pain Management Association
4125 Hackamore Dr.
Reno, NV 89509
Ph: (775)747-2431

36033 ■ Tahoe Spine and Pain Care
889 Alder Ave., Ste. 303
Incline Village, NV 89451
Ph: (775)832-8288

NEW HAMPSHIRE

36034 ■ Cottage Hospital Pain Clinic
90 Stillwater Rd.
Woodsville, NH 03785
Ph: (603)747-9205
Fax: (603)747-0411
E-mail: mgeorgia@cottagehospital.org
URL: http://www.cottagehospital.org/services/category.php?CID=2

36035 ■ Dartmouth--Hitchcock Medical Center
Pain Management
1 Medical Center Dr.
Lebanon, NH 03766
Ph: (603)650-8391
URL: http://www.pain101.com/PainDoctors/Directory-ACGMEprogramsList.aspx

36036 ■ Elliot Hospital
Pain Management Center
1 Elliot Way
Manchester, NH 03103
Ph: (603)663-6730
URL: http://www.elliothospital.org/services/pain.html

36037 ■ North County Pain Clinic
262 Cottage St., Ste. 134
Littleton, NH 03561
Ph: (603)444-0083

36038 ■ Pain Solutions
21 Eastman Ave.
Bedford, NH 03110
Ph: (603)577-3003
Free: 877-889-0574
URL: http://www.painsolutionsusa.com

NEW JERSEY

36039 ■ Bacharach Institute for Rehabilitation
61 W Jimmie Leeds Rd.
Pomona, NJ 08240
Ph: (609)652-7000
URL: http://www.bacharach.org
Formerly: Bacharach Rehabilitation Hospital.

36040 ■ Back Rehabilitation Institute, Hamilton
1245 Whitehorse-Mercerville Rd.
Hamilton Township, NJ 08619
Ph: (609)581-2400
Fax: (609)581-2500
Formerly: Back Pain Institute, Hamilton.

36041 ■ Comprehensive Pain Management
2420 Hwy. 34
Manasquan, NJ 08736
Ph: (732)223-2873
URL: http://www.painknowmore.com

36042 ■ Kessler Institute for Rehabilitation
1199 Pleasant Valley Way
West Orange, NJ 07052
Ph: (973)731-3600
Free: 800-248-3221
Fax: (973)243-6819
URL: http://www.kessler-rehab.com/

36043 ■ Liberty Pain Relief
2333 Morris Ave., Ste. A-18
Union, NJ 07803
Ph: (908)206-9500
URL: http://www.paindoctor.com

36044 ■ Magaziner Center for Wellness Pain Clinic
1907 Greentree Rd.
Cherry Hill, NJ 08003
Ph: (856)424-8222
URL: http://www.drmagaziner.com

36045 ■ Medical One Pain Clinic
4248 Harbor Beach Blvd.
Brigantine, NJ 08203
Ph: (609)266-0400
URL: http://www.medicaloneonline.com

36046 ■ New Jersey Center for Pain Management
55-77 Schanck Rd., Ste. A-8
Freehold, NJ 07728
Ph: (732)431-9544

36047 ■ Pain Centers of America
1060 Clifton Ave.
Clifton, NJ 07012
Ph: (973)779-7246
URL: http://www.swarminteractive.com/paincenter.html

36048 ■ Pain Management Center at Hamilton
2271 Rte. 33, Ste. 103
Hamilton, NJ 08619
Ph: (609)890-4080
URL: http://www.painmanagementctr.com

36049 ■ Pain Management Center at Voorhees
1001 Laurel Oak Rd., Ste. A-2
Voorhees, NJ 08043
Ph: (856)566-8600
URL: http://www.painmanagementctr.com

36050 ■ Princeton Headache Clinic
11 State Rd., Ste. 300
Princeton, NJ 08540
Ph: (609)683-5404
URL: http://www.princetonheadache.com

36051 ■ Rehab Medicine Center of New Jersey
Pain Center
1350 Rte. 23 N
Wayne, NJ 07470
Ph: (973)709-9200
URL: http://www.rehabmd.com

36052 ■ Skylands Pain Relief Clinics
Rockaway Mall Convenience Center, Ste. 1015
Rockaway, NJ 07866
Ph: (973)989-2644
URL: http://www.paindoctor.com

36053 ■ University Headache Center
513 S Lenola Rd.
Moorestown, NJ 08057
Ph: (609)234-7421
URL: http://som.umdnj.edu/headweb/home.htm

36054 ■ University of Medicine and Dentistry of New Jersey
Robert Wood Johnson Medical School
Pain Management
CAB, Ste. 3100
125 Paterson St.
New Brunswick, NJ 08901
Ph: (732)235-6153
E-mail: douglael@umdnj.edu
URL: http://www.pain101.com/PainDoctors/Directory-ACGMEprogramsList.aspx

NEW MEXICO

36055 ■ Saint Vincent Hospital
Pain Center
455 St. Michaels Dr.
Santa Fe, NM 87505
Ph: (505)983-3361
URL: http://www.stvin.org

36056 ■ University of New Mexico
Carrie Tingley Hospital
Pain Management Center for Adults
1127 University Blvd. NE
Albuquerque, NM 87102
Ph: (505)272-5200
URL: http://www.hospitals.unm.edu

36057 ■ University of New Mexico School of Medicine
Pain Management
Surge Bldg., Rm. 110
2701 Frontier NE, MSC 11-6120
Albuquerque, NM 87131
Ph: (505)272-2610
URL: http://www.pain101.com/PainDoctors/Directory-ACGMEprogramsList.aspx

NEW YORK

36058 ■ Beth Israel Medical Center
Albert Einstein College of Medicine
Pain Management
Dept. of Pain Medicine & Palliative Care
1st Ave. at 16th St.
New York, NY 10003
Ph: (212)844-1479
URL: http://www.pain101.com/PainDoctors/Directory-ACGMEprogramsList.aspx

36059 ■ Healthworks of Staten Island
1428 Victory Blvd.
Staten Island, NY 10301
Ph: (718)698-3055
Fax: (718)698-2448
E-mail: lkopel123@aol.com
Dr. Larry Kopelman, Director

36060 ■ Kingston Hospital
Pain Management Service
358 Broadway
Kingston, NY 12401
Ph: (845)334-2755
URL: http://www.hahv.org/KingstonHospital

36061 ■ Memorial Sloan--Kettering Cancer Center
Pain Management
Pain & Palliative Care Service
1275 York Ave., Box 52
New York, NY 10021
Ph: (646)888-2680
URL: http://www.pain101.com/PainDoctors/Directory-ACGMEprogramsList.aspx

36062 ■ Mount Sinai School of Medicine
Pain Management
Box 1192
1 Gustave L. Levy Pl.
New York, NY 10029
Ph: (212)241-6372
URL: http://www.pain101.com/PainDoctors/Directory-ACGMEprogramsList.aspx

36063 ■ New York Presbyterian Hospital, Columbia Campus
Pain Management
622 W 168th St.
New York, NY 10032
Ph: (212)305-7114
E-mail: mlw45@columbia.edu
URL: http://www.pain101.com/PainDoctors/Directory-ACGMEprogramsList.aspx

36064 ■ New York Presbyterian Hospital, Cornell Campus
Pain Management
Anesthesiology Dept.
525 E 68th St., Box 124
New York, NY 10065
Ph: (212)746-2775
E-mail: sad2003@med.cornell.edu
URL: http://www.pain101.com/PainDoctors/Directory-ACGMEprogramsList.aspx

36065 ■ New York University Medical Center
School of Medicine
Pain Management
317 E 34th St., Ste. 902
New York, NY 10016
Ph: (212)201-1004
E-mail: zous01@med.nyu.edu
URL: http://www.pain101.com/PainDoctors/Directory-ACGMEprogramsList.aspx

36066 ■ Saint Luke's Medical Center
Roosevelt Hospital Center
Pain Management
Dept. of Anesthesiology
428 W 59th St.
New York, NY 10019
Ph: (212)523-6357
URL: http://www.pain101.com/PainDoctors/Directory-ACGMEprogramsList.aspx

36067 ■ Saint Vincent's Hospital and Medical Center
New York Medical College
Pain Management
153 W 11th St.
New York, NY 10011
Ph: (212)604-7566
URL: http://www.pain101.com/PainDoctors/Directory-ACGMEprogramsList.aspx

36068 ■ State University of New York at Stony Brook
Pain Management
Health Sciences Center L4-060
Stony Brook, NY 11794
Ph: (631)444-4234
URL: http://www.pain101.com/PainDoctors/Directory-ACGMEprogramsList.aspx

36069 ■ State University of New York Upstate Medical University
Pain Management
750 E Adams St.
Syracuse, NY 13210
Ph: (315)464-4891
URL: http://www.pain101.com/PainDoctors/Directory-ACGMEprogramsList.aspx

36070 ■ University of Buffalo
Pain Management
Bldg. 4, Hayes Annex A
3435 Main St.
Buffalo, NY 14214
Ph: (716)829-6102
URL: http://www.pain101.com/PainDoctors/Directory-ACGMEprogramsList.aspx

36071 ■ University of Rochester Medical Center
Pain Management
Dept. of Anesthesiology, Box 604
601 Elmwood Ave.
Rochester, NY 14642
Ph: (585)276-3770
URL: http://www.pain101.com/PainDoctors/Directory-ACGMEprogramsList.aspx

NORTH CAROLINA

36072 ■ Duke University Medical Center
Pain Clinic
932 Morreene Rd., Rm. 232
Durham, NC 27705
Ph: (919)684-3239
E-mail: scott002@mc.duke.edu
URL: http://www.pain101.com/PainDoctors/Directory-ACGMEprogramsList.aspx

36073 ■ Interventional Pain Services of Western North Carolina--Clyde
Haywood Regional Medical Center
262 Leroy George Dr.
Clyde, NC 28721
Ph: (828)454-1990
URL: http://www.ipswnc.medem.com

36074 ■ Interventional Pain Services of Western North Carolina--Franklin
190 Riverview St.
Franklin, NC 28734
Ph: (828)627-9998
URL: http://www.ipswnc.com

36075 ■ Lexington Memorial Hospital
Pain Center
250 Hospital Dr.
Lexington, NC 27292
Ph: (336)238-4090
URL: http://www.lexingtonmemorial.com/anexthesia.aspx

36076 ■ North Carolina Pain Management Services
1236 Huffman Mill Rd.
Burlington, NC 27215
Ph: (336)538-7180
URL: http://www.ncpainmanagement.com

36077 ■ Pitt County Memorial Hospital
Pain Management Center
2010 W Arlington Blvd.
Greenville, NC 27835
Ph: (252)847-0618
Fax: (252)847-0602
URL: http://www.pcmhcareers.com
Dr. Lynn R. Johnson, Director

36078 ■ Thoms Rehabilitation Hospital
68 Sweeten Creek Rd.
Asheville, NC 28813
Ph: (828)277-4800
URL: http://www.carepartners.org
Formerly: Thoms Rehabilitation Hospital.

36079 ■ University of North Carolina Hospitals
Anesthesiology and Pain Management Center
CB 7010, N2201
Chapel Hill, NC 27599
Ph: (919)966-4873
URL: http://www.unchealthcare.org

36080 ■ Wake Forest University
School of Medicine
Pain Management
Dept. of Anesthesiology & Pain Management
145 Kimel Park Dr., Ste. 330
Winston Salem, NC 27103
Ph: (336)714-6408
URL: http://www.pain101.com/PainDoctors/Directory-ACGMEprogramsList.aspx

NORTH DAKOTA

36081 ■ Altru Health System
Rehabilitation Center
1300 S Columbia Rd.
Grand Forks, ND 58201
Ph: (701)780-2439
URL: http://www.altru.org

36082 ■ Primecare Pain Clinic
Medical Arts Plz.
810 Rosser, 3rd Fl.
Bismarck, ND 58502
Ph: (701)530-7246

36083 ■ Spine and Pain Clinic
210 S 12th St.
Bismarck, ND 58504
Ph: (701)530-8500

36084 ■ Tri-Life Center, LLP
2401 Elk Dr.
Minot, ND 58702
Ph: (701)837-5433

Free: 888-323-5433
Fax: (701)837-5434
E-mail: trilife@minot.com
URL: http://www.tri-life.com

36085 ■ Trinity Pain Center
1 Burdick Expy. W
Minot, ND 58701
Ph: (701)857-5150

NOVA SCOTIA

36086 ■ LifeMark Health Center--Dartmouth
130 Eileen Stubbs Ave., Ste. 219N
Dartmouth, NS, Canada B3B 2C4
Ph: (902)404-3888
URL: http://www.pain101.com/paindoctors/directory-ofpaindoctorscarflist.aspx

OHIO

36087 ■ Cleveland Clinic Foundation
Pain Management
Dept. of Pain Management
9500 Euclid Ave.
Cleveland, OH 44195
Ph: (216)445-9421
E-mail: narouzs@ccf.org
URL: http://www.pain101.com/PainDoctors/Directory-ACGMEprogramsList.aspx

36088 ■ Doctors Pain Clinic--Youngstown
1011 Boardman-Canfield Rd.
Youngstown, OH 44512
Ph: (330)629-2888
Free: 888-784-4312
Fax: (330)629-8940
URL: http://www.doctorspainclinic.com
Tom Faloon, Director

36089 ■ Forum Health
Hillside Rehabilitation Hospital
8474 Squires Ln. NE
Warren, OH 44484
Ph: (330)841-3720
URL: http://www.hillsiderehabilitationhospital.net

36090 ■ Genesis HealthCare System
Rehabilitation Center
Pain Management Program
716 Adair Ave.
Zanesville, OH 43701
Ph: (740)454-5791
Free: 800-322-4762
Sharon Parker, Director

36091 ■ Grandview Hospital and Medical Center
Pain Management Center
405 Grand Ave.
Dayton, OH 45405
Ph: (937)723-3348
Fax: (937)723-3610
URL: http://www.grandviewfoundation.org

36092 ■ HIRE/ProWork
360 S Main St.
Dayton, OH 45402
Ph: (937)208-2065
URL: http://www.pain101.com

36093 ■ Lutheran Medical Center
Pain Management Center
1730 W 25th St.
Cleveland, OH 44113
Ph: (216)696-4300
URL: http://www.lutheranhospital.org

36094 ■ Marion Area Health Center
Industrial Rehabilitation
1050 Delaware
Marion, OH 43302
Ph: (740)383-8102
URL: http://www.marionareahealth.com

36095 ■ Meridia Center for Rehabilitation and Pain Management
18901 Lakeshore Blvd.
Euclid, OH 44119
Ph: (216)692-7543
URL: http://www.euclidhospital.org
Formerly: Cleveland Clinic Health System, Euclid Hospital.

36096 ■ Miami Valley Hospital
Pain Center
1 Wyoming St.
Dayton, OH 45409
Ph: (937)208-0723
Fax: (937)208-4534
URL: http://www.miamivalleyhospital.org
Mark Asnen, Director

36097 ■ Ohio State University Medical Center
Pain Management
N416 Doan Hall
410 W 10th Ave.
Columbus, OH 43210
Ph: (614)293-1070
E-mail: denise.mcmaster@osumc.edu
URL: http://www.pain101.com/PainDoctors/Directory-ACGMEprogramsList.aspx

36098 ■ OhioHealth
180 E Broad St.
Columbus, OH 43215-3707
Ph: (614)544-4455
Fax: (614)544-4450
URL: http://www.ohiohealth.com
Karen Connors, President
Formerly: (1997) U.S. Health Corp.

36099 ■ Saint Joseph Pain Management Center
1934 Niles-Courtland
Warren, OH 44484
Ph: (330)841-4032
Fax: (330)841-4381

36100 ■ Saint Rita's Medical Center
730 W Market St.
Lima, OH 45801
Ph: (419)227-3361
URL: http://www.ehealthconnection.com/regions/st_ritas/
Program(s): CARF Accredited Comprehensive Pain Management; Medical Management; Physical and Occupational Therapy; Pharmacological Interventions; Aquatic Therapy; Recreational Therapy; Relaxation Techniques; Stress Management; Social Services Intervention; Vocational Rehabilitation; Work Rehabilitation; Psychoeducational Classes.

36101 ■ University of Cincinnati Medical Center
University of Cincinnati College of Medicine
Pain Management
234 Goodman Ave., ML 0764
Cincinnati, OH 45267
Ph: (513)584-0909
E-mail: Christine.Veselsky@uc.edu
URL: http://www.pain101.com/PainDoctors/Directory-ACGMEprogramsList.aspx

36102 ■ University Hospitals of Cleveland
University Pain Center
11100 Euclid Ave.
Cleveland, OH 44106
Ph: (216)983-2085
Free: 877-844-8446
Fax: (216)983-2088
URL: http://www.uhhospitals.org
Dr. Thomas Chelimsky, Director

OKLAHOMA

36103 ■ Center for Pain Medicine
3811 W Gore Blvd., Ste. 1
Lawton, OK 73505

36104 ■ Neurology Neuro Pain Consulting
1533 Mountain Rd.
Bartlesville, OK 74003

36105 ■ Pain Care Associates of Oklahoma
6585 S Yale, Ste. 1110
Tulsa, OK 74136
Ph: (918)502-7246
URL: http://www.pcaoklahoma.com

36106 ■ Pain Center
630 24th Ave. SW
Norman, OK 73069
Ph: (405)364-2555

36107 ■ Pain Evaluation and Treatment Center--Tulsa, OK
5801 E 41st St., Ste. 100
Tulsa, OK 74135
Ph: (918)622-3888

36108 ■ Reynolds Army Community Hospital
Pain Clinic
3 NW Forest Ln.
Lawton, OK 73505
Ph: (580)458-3000
URL: http://www.rach.sill.amedd.army.mil

36109 ■ University of Oklahoma Health Sciences Center
University of Oklahoma Hospital
Pain Management
750 NE 13th St., Ste. 200
Oklahoma City, OK 73104
Ph: (405)271-4354
E-mail: Linda-Murphy@ouhsc.edu
URL: http://www.pain101.com/PainDoctors/Directory-ACGMEprogramsList.aspx

ONTARIO

36110 ■ Health Recovery Clinic--Mississauga
2155 Leanne Blvd., Ste. 118
Mississauga, ON, Canada L5K 2K8
Ph: (905)855-1807
Fax: (905)855-2825
URL: http://www.healthrecoverygroup.com

36111 ■ Health Recovery Clinic--Toronto
36 York Mills Rd., Ste. 110
Toronto, ON, Canada M2P 2E9
Ph: (416)226-4722
Fax: (416)226-9611
URL: http://www.healthrecoverygroup.com

36112 ■ Rehabilitation Solutions, Cambridge
405 Maple Grove Rd., Unit 1
Cambridge, ON, Canada N3E 1B6
Ph: (519)653-9203
URL: http://www.uhnrehabsolutions.com

36113 ■ Rehabilitation Solutions, Mississauga
989 Derry Rd. E, Ste. 200
Mississauga, ON, Canada L5T 2J8
Ph: (905)564-6872
URL: http://www.uhnrehabsolutions.com

36114 ■ Rehabilitation Solutions, Toronto
Fell Pavilion
399 Bathurst St., 4th Fl.
Toronto, ON, Canada M5T 2S8
Ph: (416)603-5800
URL: http://www.uhnrehabsolutions.com

OREGON

36115 ■ Integrated Spine Care
Pain Clinic
24076 SE Stark St., Ste. 320
Gresham, OR 97030
Ph: (503)512-1212
URL: http://www.integratedspinecare.net

36116 ■ Klamath Pain Clinic, PC
2301 Mountain View Blvd., Ste. B
Klamath Falls, OR 97601
Ph: (541)882-2023

36117 ■ Northwest Occupational Medicine Center, LLP
12250 SW Garden Pl.
Portland, OR 97223
Ph: (503)684-7246
Fax: (503)624-0724
URL: http://nwomc.com
Michael Leland, Director

36118 ■ Oregon Health and Science University
Comprehensive Pain Center
3303 SW Bond Ave., CH4P
Portland, OR 97239
Ph: (503)494-8399
E-mail: karlinge@ohsu.edu
URL: http://www.pain101.com/PainDoctors/Directory-ACGMEprogramsList.aspx

36119 ■ Oregon Pain Associates
527 SE 39th Ave.
Portland, OR 97214
Ph: (503)238-7246
Free: 866-785-7246
URL: http://www.oregonpainassociates.com

36120 ■ Pain Specialists of Southern Oregon
825 Bennett Ave.
Medford, OR 97504
Ph: (541)779-5228
URL: http://www.painspecialists.com

36121 ■ Progressive Rehabilitation Associates
1815 SW Marlow, Ste. 110
Portland, OR 97225
Ph: (503)292-0765
URL: http://www.progrehab.com

36122 ■ Willamette Orthopedic Group
Pain Clinic
1600 State St.
Salem, OR 97301
URL: http://www.oregonpainassociates.com

PENNSYLVANIA

36123 ■ Doctors Pain Clinic--Farrell
2120 Likens Ln.
Farrell, PA 16121
Ph: (724)983-7991
Fax: (724)981-4310
URL: http://www.doctorspainclinic.com

36124 ■ Excela Health
Latrobe Area Hospital
Pain Control Center
134 Industrial Park Rd., Ste. 100
Greensburg, PA 15650
Ph: (724)537-1557
Free: 877-771-1234
Fax: (724)532-6909
URL: http://www.lah.com

36125 ■ HEALTHSOUTH Rehabilitation of Mechanicsburg
175 Lancaster Blvd.
Mechanicsburg, PA 17055
Ph: (717)691-3831
URL: http://www.healthsouthpa.com

36126 ■ Jefferson Pain and Rehabilitation Center
4735 Clairton Blvd.
Pittsburgh, PA 15236
Ph: (412)885-5400
Free: 800-565-7246
Fax: (412)885-1773
URL: http://jeffersonpainclinic.com
Dennis Sabolcik, Director

36127 ■ Michael S. Melnick, DMD, MAGD
The Park Plz., No. 207
128 N Craig St.
Pittsburgh, PA 15213
Ph: (412)687-8888
Fax: (412)787-6453
E-mail: melnickdmd@aol.com
Dr. Michael S. Melnick, Director

36128 ■ Montgomery Surgery Center
1000 N Broad St., Ste. 2
Lansdale, PA 19446
Ph: (215)412-9115
Fax: (215)412-0488
E-mail: info@montgomerysurgerycenter.com
URL: http://www.montgomerysurgerycenter.com
Dr. Sofia Lam, Director

36129 ■ Oral and Maxillofacial Surgery and Pain Management
2606 Broad Ave.
Altoona, PA 16601
Ph: (814)944-6355
Fax: (814)941-7324

36130 ■ Penn State University
Milton Hershey Medical Center
Pain Management
Dept. of Anesthesiology, HU 32
500 University Dr.
Hershey, PA 17033
Ph: (717)531-5680
URL: http://www.pain101.com/PainDoctors/Directory-ACGMEprogramsList.aspx

36131 ■ Pinnacle Health Rehab Options
2501 N 3rd St., Landis 3
Harrisburg, PA 17110
Ph: (717)782-6858
Fax: (717)782-6859
URL: http://www.pinnaclehealth.org/rehab-options

36132 ■ Sarah and Benjamin Lincow Pain Foundation
7622 Ogontz Ave.
Philadelphia, PA 19150
Ph: (215)224-8980
Fax: (215)224-9342

36133 ■ Sinai Hospital of Baltimore
Center for Pain Management and Rehabilitation
Orthopaedic & Spine Specialists
1855 Powder Mill Rd.
York, PA 17402
Ph: (717)848-4800
E-mail: mbfurman@hotmail.com
URL: http://www.pain101.com/PainDoctors/Directory-ACGMEprogramsList.aspx

36134 ■ Temple University
Western Pennsylvania Hospital
Pain Management
4800 Friendship Ave., Ste. 459 MP
Pittsburgh, PA 15224
Ph: (412)578-5635
E-mail: jrandal@wpahs.org
URL: http://www.pain101.com/PainDoctors/Directory-ACGMEprogramsList.aspx

36135 ■ Thomas Jefferson University
Jefferson Pain Center
834 Chestnut St., Ste. T-150
Philadelphia, PA 19107
Ph: (215)955-2108
URL: http://www.pain101.com/PainDoctors/Directory-ACGMEprogramsList.aspx

36136 ■ University of Pennsylvania Hospital
Pain Management
Medical Office Bldg., Ste. 300
39th & Market Sts.
Philadelphia, PA 19104
Ph: (215)662-8816
E-mail: ashburnm@uphs.upenn.edu
URL: http://www.pain101.com/PainDoctors/Directory-ACGMEprogramsList.aspx

36137 ■ University of Pittsburgh Medical Center
Pain Management
200 Medical Arts Bldg.
200 Delafield Ave., Ste. 2070
Pittsburgh, PA 15215
Ph: (412)784-5343
URL: http://www.pain101.com/PainDoctors/Directory-ACGMEprogramsList.aspx

PUERTO RICO

36138 ■ Veteran's Affairs Caribbean Healthcare System
10 Casia St., 117
San Juan, PR 00921
Ph: (787)641-7582
URL: http://www.pain101.com/paindoctors/directory-ofpaindoctorscarflist.aspx

RHODE ISLAND

36139 ■ Naval Ambulatory Care Center
Chronic Pain Management Center
1 Riggs Rd.
Newport, RI 02841
Ph: (401)841-3771
URL: http://nhcne.med.navy.mil
Remarks: For active duty and retired military and family members only.

36140 ■ Rhode Island Hospital
Pain Clinic
2 Dudley St.
Providence, RI 02905
Ph: (401)444-3020
URL: http://www.rhodeislandhospital.org

36141 ■ Southern New England Anesthesia and Pain Associates
102 Smithfield Rd.
Pawtucket, RI 02860
Ph: (401)729-4985
URL: http://www.painri.com

36142 ■ University Anesthesiologists
Pain Care
164 Summit Ave.
Providence, RI 02906
Ph: (401)739-2500

SASKATCHEWAN

36143 ■ Chronic Pain Center
75 - 24th St. E, Ste. 204
Saskatoon, SK, Canada S7K 0K3
Ph: (306)655-4000
URL: http://www.pain101.com/paindoctors/directory-ofpaindoctorscarflist.aspx

SOUTH CAROLINA

36144 ■ Center for Pain Management--Columbia, SC
223 Stoneridge Dr.
Columbia, SC 29210
Ph: (803)296-5990

36145 ■ Coastal Interventional Pain Associates
210 Village Center Blvd., Ste. 150
Myrtle Beach, SC 29579
Ph: (843)903-9031
URL: http://www.freedomfrompaintoday.com

36146 ■ Intervenemd Pain Care Center
9231 Medical Plz. Dr. Ste. B
North Charleston, SC 29406
Ph: (843)216-4844
URL: http://www.intervenemd.com

36147 ■ Medical University of South Carolina Rehabilitation Unit
171 Ashley Ave.
Charleston, SC 29425
Ph: (803)792-1414
URL: http://www.muschealth.com

36148 ■ Pain Associates of Charleston
1341 Old Georgetown Rd., Ste. B
Mount Pleasant, SC 29464
Ph: (843)216-9870
URL: http://www.gainoverpain.com

36149 ■ Palmetto Pain and Rehabilitation Physicians
1060 N Church Pl.
Spartanburg, SC 29303
Ph: (864)278-6006
URL: http://www.palmettopain.com

36150 ■ Piedmont Physical Medicine and Rehabilitation Pain Clinic
317 St. Francis Dr., Ste. 350
Greenville, SC 29601
Ph: (864)235-1834
URL: http://piedmontpmr.com

SOUTH DAKOTA

36151 ■ Avera Saint Luke's Pain Management Center
815 1st Ave. SE
Aberdeen, SD 57401
Ph: (605)622-5123
URL: http://www.avera.org/st-lukes-hospital/index.aspx

36152 ■ Black Hills Chronic Spine Pain
614 E Boulevard
Rapid City, SD 57701
Ph: (605)343-5850

36153 ■ McKennan Hospital
1325 S Cliff Ave.
Sioux Falls, SD 57117
Ph: (605)322-8000
Free: 800-331-9929
Fax: (605)322-5120
URL: http://www.avera.org/mckennan/services/pain/index.aspx
LaVonne Gaspar, Director

36154 ■ Siouxland Pain Clinic
400 S Sycamore Ave.
Sioux Falls, SD 57110
Ph: (605)373-2083

TENNESSEE

36155 ■ Healthsouth--Chattanooga Center
400 N Holtzclaw Ave.
Chattanooga, TN 37404
Ph: (423)698-6871
URL: http://www.healthsouth.com

36156 ■ Marshall Medical Center Pain Clinic
1080 Ellington Pkwy., Ste. 1609
Lewisburg, TN 37091
Ph: (615)270-1705
URL: http://www.mauryregional.com/MMC.htm

36157 ■ Mays and Schnapp Pain Clinic and Rehabilitation Center
55 Humphreys Center Dr., Ste. 200
Memphis, TN 38120
Ph: (901)747-0040
URL: http://www.maysandschanapp.com

36158 ■ Nashville Pain Center
2001 Mallory Ln., Ste. 100
Franklin, TN 37067
Ph: (615)771-7772

36159 ■ Pain Institute of Tennessee
1510 Hatcher Ln., Ste. 1
Columbia, TN 38401
Ph: (931)840-4333
URL: http://www.pithq.com

36160 ■ Pain Management Group
8501 Crossings Blvd.
Antioch, TN 37013
Ph: (615)941-8501

36161 ■ Pelvic Pain and Reconstructive Surgery Center
1755 Gunbarrel Rd., Ste. 202
Chattanooga, TN 37421
Ph: (423)490-1136
Fax: (423)490-1137
URL: http://www.pprsc.net
Dr. Alfredo Nieves, Director

36162 ■ Primary Care and Pain Relief Center
1811 State St.
Nashville, TN 37203
Ph: (615)329-4357

TEXAS

36163 ■ Acute and Chronic Pain and Spine Center
24 Care Cir.
Amarillo, TX 79124
Ph: (806)353-6100
Fax: (806)353-8130
URL: http://www.acpsc.com
Dr. B. J. Daneshfar, Director

36164 ■ Alta Vista Healthcare, LP
1123 N Main Ave., Ste. 100
San Antonio, TX 78212
Ph: (210)822-6323

36165 ■ American College of Acupuncture and Oriental Medicine
9100 Park W Dr.
Houston, TX 77063
Ph: (713)780-9777
Fax: (713)781-5781
E-mail: scthomaswang@hotmail.com
URL: http://www.acaom.edu
Dr. Wen Huang, Director

36166 ■ Austin Pain Associates
2501 W William Cannon Dr., Ste. 401
Austin, TX 78745
Ph: (512)416-7240
Free: 888-299-9290
Fax: (512)416-6791
URL: http://www.austinpainassociates.com

36167 ■ Baylor Center for Pain Management Comprehensive Outpatient Program
3600 Gaston Ave.
Wadley Tower, Ste. 360
Dallas, TX 75246
Ph: (214)820-7526
Dr. Timothy S. Clark, Director

36168 ■ Buckner Family Medical Clinic/dba Family Physical Therapy and Rehabilitation
4801 S Buckner Blvd., Ste. 300
Dallas, TX 75227
Ph: (214)381-4800

36169 ■ Carefirst Medical Associates and Pain Rehabilitation
403 Hwy. 110 N
Whitehouse, TX 75791
Ph: (903)839-1000

36170 ■ Center for Pain Control
2692 W Walnut St., Ste. 105
Garland, TX 75042
Ph: (972)494-2676

36171 ■ Central Imaging of Arlington Pain Management Services
3100 Matlock Rd., Ste. 105
Arlington, TX 76012
Ph: (817)543-2412
Fax: (817)543-2663
URL: http://centralimagingofarlington.com

36172 ■ Chronic Pain Recovery Center
111 Vision Park Dr., Ste. 140
Shenandoah, TX 77384
Ph: (936)271-0221
URL: http://www.pain101.com/paindoctors/directory-ofpaindoctorscarflist.aspx

36173 ■ Dallas Spinal Rehabilitation Center, Inc.
6161 Harry Hines Blvd., Ste. 105
Dallas, TX 75235
Ph: (214)905-9555
Fax: (214)905-9556
E-mail: dsrc3@aol.com
URL: http://www.dallasspinalrehab.com
Greg Garland, Chief Executive Officer

36174 ■ Direct RehabMed
906 E Front St.
Tyler, TX 75702
Ph: (903)593-9999
E-mail: info@directrehabmed.com
URL: http://www.directrehabmed.com

36175 ■ Direct RehabMed--Longview
100 W Hawkins
Longview, TX 75605
Ph: (903)234-0999
URL: http://www.directrehabmed.com

36176 ■ Eugene McDermott Center for Pain Management
6236 Harry Hines Blvd.
Dallas, TX 75390
Ph: (214)645-8450
Fax: (214)645-8451
E-mail: Elizabeth.Bronstein@utsouthwestern.edu

36177 ■ Fit N Wise Rehabilitation Center
609 Medical Center Dr., Ste. 1100
Decatur, TX 76234
Ph: (940)627-2708

36178 ■ Functional Pain Center
1401 E Ridge Rd., Ste. D
McAllen, TX 78503
Ph: (956)683-0234
Fax: (956)683-0758
URL: http://www.functionalpaincenter.com

36179 ■ HighPoint Rehabilitation Institute
800 W Arbrook Blvd., Ste. 330
Arlington, TX 76015
Ph: (817)417-8782
Fax: (817)417-8766
URL: http://www.highpointrehab.com/

36180 ■ Injury 1 Treatment Center
185 Eastgate Plz.
Waco, TX 76705
Ph: (254)412-2667

36181 ■ Medical City Dallas Hospital Rehabilitation Services
7777 Forest Lane, Ste. C-240
Dallas, TX 75230
Ph: (972)566-7221
Fax: (972)566-5752
E-mail: medcity.main@hcahealthcare.com
URL: http://www.medicalcityhospital.com
Tim Lyons, Director

36182 ■ Monarch Pain Care and Rehabilitation Center, Inc.
5151 Katy Fwy., Ste. 305
Houston, TX 77007
Ph: (713)880-9500
URL: http://www.monarchpain.com

36183 ■ North Texas Pain Recovery Clinic
6702 W Poly Webb Rd.
Arlington, TX 76016
Ph: (817)478-0095
Fax: (817)478-7628
URL: http://www.painrecovery.net

36184 ■ North Texas Rehabilitation Center--Dallas
214 W Colorado Blvd.
Dallas, TX 75208
Ph: (214)377-4011
Fax: (214)234-8606
E-mail: info@ntrc.com
URL: http://www.ntrc.com

36185 ■ North Texas Rehabilitation Center--Fort Worth
1051 Haskel St., Ste. 200
Fort Worth, TX 76107
Ph: (817)941-4550
Fax: (817)234-8606
E-mail: info@ntrc.com
URL: http://www.ntrc.com

36186 ■ Pain Care Center Inc.
8925 Hwy. 6 N, Ste. B
Angleton, TX 77095
Ph: (281)463-0404

36187 ■ Pain Care Center Katy
611 S Mason Rd.
Katy, TX 77450
Ph: (713)457-0320
URL: http://www.paincarecenter.com

36188 ■ Pain Care Center Richmond
1106 Morton St., Ste. 5
Richmond, TX 77469
Ph: (281)344-8900
URL: http://www.paincarecenter.com

36189 ■ Pain and Rehab Services of the Southwest, LLC/Rehabilitative Pain Management
1000 1st St., Ste. A
Humble, TX 77338
Ph: (281)446-7246

36190 ■ Productive Rehabilitation Institute of Dallas for Ergonomics
5701 Maple Ave., Ste. 100
Dallas, TX 75235
Ph: (214)351-6600
Fax: (214)951-5046
E-mail: pride@airmail.net
URL: http://www.pridedallas.com
Susan Mayer, Executive Director

36191 ■ The Rehab Group
5201 S Westmoreland
Dallas, TX 75237
Ph: (214)339-2047
Free: 877-389-4335
Fax: (214)339-2049
E-mail: mail@therehabgroup.com
URL: http://www.therehabgroup.com
Janice Pettis Ingram, Director

36192 ■ Restore FX
2501 W William Cannon Dr., Ste. 302
Austin, TX 78745
Ph: (512)439-7360
URL: http://www.pain101.com/paindoctors/directory-ofpaindoctorscarflist.aspx

36193 ■ Rio Grande Health Center of El Paso, Inc. dba
Rio Grande Rehab Center
7230 Gateway E, Ste. E
El Paso, TX 79915
Ph: (915)599-1119
Fax: (915)592-9334

36194 ■ Source One Rehabilitation
514 S Hampton Rd.
Dallas, TX 75208
Ph: (817)457-9850
E-mail: info@s1rehab.com
URL: http://www.s1rehab.com

36195 ■ Source One Rehabilitation
5601 Bridge St., Ste. 500
Fort Worth, TX 76112
Ph: (817)457-9850
E-mail: info@s1rehab.com
URL: http://www.s1rehab.com

36196 ■ Southwest Dallas Family Medical Center/dba Family Physical Therapy and Rehabilitation
2815 S Hampton Rd.
Dallas, TX 75224
Ph: (214)333-7300

36197 ■ Syzygy Associates--Hampton Road, Dallas
516 S Hampton Rd.
Dallas, TX 75208
Ph: (214)948-1174
URL: http://www.pain101.com/paindoctors/directory-ofpaindoctorscarflist.aspx

36198 ■ Syzygy Associates LP--Fort Worth
5601 Bridge St., Ste. 500
Fort Worth, TX 76112
Ph: (817)457-9850

36199 ■ Syzygy Associates LP--North Central Expressway, Dallas
10300 N Central Expy., Se. 570
Dallas, TX 75231
Ph: (214)370-0404

36200 ■ Texas Back Institute--Arlington
400 W Arbrook, Ste. 320
Arlington, TX 76014
Ph: (682)518-1215
URL: http://www.texasback.com

36201 ■ Texas Back Institute--Denton
2817 S Mayhill Rd.
Denton, TX 76208
Ph: (940)382-2204
URL: http://www.texasback.com/

36202 ■ Texas Back Institute--Flower Mound
4401 Long Prairie Rd., Ste. 500
Flower Mound, TX 75028
Ph: (972)956-8181
URL: http://www.texasback.com

36203 ■ Texas Back Institute--Fort Worth
3600 W 7th St.
Fort Worth, TX 76107
Ph: (817)429-4545
URL: http://www.texasback.com/

36204 ■ Texas Back Institute--Mansfield
2800 E Broad St., Ste. 522
Mansfield, TX 76063
Ph: (682)518-1215
URL: http://www.texasback.com

36205 ■ Texas Back Institute--McKinney
6045 Alma Rd., Ste. 360
McKinney, TX 75070
Free: 800-247-BACK
URL: http://www.texasback.com

36206 ■ Texas Back Institute--McKinney North
6210 W Virginia Pkwy.
McKinney, TX 75071
Ph: (972)608-5000
URL: http://www.texasback.com

36207 ■ Texas Back Institute--North Denton
2535 W Oak St.
Denton, TX 76201
Ph: (940)382-2204
URL: http://www.texasback.com

36208 ■ Texas Back Institute--Odessa
801 N Grant Ave.
Odessa, TX 79760
Ph: (817)429-4545
URL: http://www.texasback.com

36209 ■ Texas Back Institute--Plano
6020 W Parker Rd., Ste. 200
Plano, TX 75093
Ph: (972)608-5000
URL: http://www.texasback.com

36210 ■ Texas Back Institute--Rockwall
1005 Ralph Hall Pkwy., Ste. 227
Rockwall, TX 75032
Ph: (972)772-8767
URL: http://www.texasback.com

36211 ■ Texas Back Institute--Trophy Club
2800 West Hwy. 114, Ste. 220
Trophy Club, TX 76262
Ph: (817)430-3900
URL: http://www.texasback.com

36212 ■ Texas Back Institute--Tyler
403 Hwy. 110 N
Whitehouse, TX 75791
Ph: (817)429-4545
URL: http://www.texasback.com

36213 ■ Texas Back Institute--Wichita Falls
501 Midwestern Pkwy. E
Wichita Falls, TX 76302
Free: 800-247-BACK
URL: http://www.texasback.com

36214 ■ Texas Tech University, Lubbock Pain Management
Dept. of Anesthesiology 1C282
3601 4th St.
Lubbock, TX 79430
Ph: (806)743-7246
E-mail: stacy.martin@ttuhsc.edu
URL: http://www.pain101.com/PainDoctors/Directory-ACGMEprogramsList.aspx

36215 ■ TexasHealth, LLC
5445 LaSierra, Ste. 204
Dallas, TX 75231-3444
Ph: (214)692-6666

36216 ■ TIRR Rehabilitation Centers
3440 Richmond Ave.
Houston, TX 77046
Ph: (713)521-0020
URL: http://www.memorialhermann.org/locations/tirr

36217 ■ Tri--County Pain Management Centre
200 N Arch St.
Royse City, TX 75189
Ph: (972)635-9577
Fax: (972)636-7048
E-mail: doctor@roysecitymedical.com
URL: http://www.roysecitymedical.com
Dr. R. W. Jones, Director

36218 ■ University of Texas Health Science Center, San Antonio
Pain Management
Dept. of Anesthesiology
7703 Floyd Curl Dr.
San Antonio, TX 78229
Ph: (210)567-4543
URL: http://www.pain101.com/PainDoctors/Directory-ACGMEprogramsList.aspx

36219 ■ University of Texas
MD Anderson Cancer Center
Pain Management
1400 Holcombe Blvd., Unit 409
Houston, TX 77030
Ph: (713)745-7246
URL: http://www.pain101.com/PainDoctors/Directory-ACGMEprogramsList.aspx

36220 ■ University of Texas Medical Branch Hospitals
Pain Clinic
301 University Blvd.
Galveston, TX 77555
Ph: (409)772-1221
URL: http://www.pain101.com/PainDoctors/Directory-ACGMEprogramsList.aspx

36221 ■ University of Texas Southwestern Medical School
John Peter Smith Hospital
Pain Management
1500 S Main St.
Fort Worth, TX 76104
Ph: (817)927-1200
URL: http://www.pain101.com/PainDoctors/Directory-ACGMEprogramsList.aspx

36222 ■ University of Texas Southwestern Medical School
Pain Management
5323 Harry Hines Blvd.
Dallas, TX 75390
Ph: (214)648-4751
E-mail: leslie.noe@utsouthwestern.edu
URL: http://www.pain101.com/PainDoctors/Directory-ACGMEprogramsList.aspx

36223 ■ WOL and MED Back and Neck Pain Center--Dallas
7125 Marvin D. Love Fwy., Ste. 107
Dallas, TX 75237
Ph: (972)572-5000
URL: http://wolmed.com

36224 ■ WOL and MED Back and Neck Pain Center--Denton
2436 I-35 East S, Ste. 336
Denton, TX 76205
Ph: (940)484-7000
Fax: (940)484-7888
URL: http://www.wolmed.com

UTAH

36225 ■ Bridge Health Recovery Center
Pain Center
991 West 230 S
Rockville, UT 84763
Ph: (435)772-0513
Free: 877-885-9567
URL: http://www.thebridgerecoverycenter.com

36226 ■ Nexus Pain Care
3585 N University Ave., Ste. 150
Provo, UT 84604
Ph: (801)356-6100
URL: http://www.nexuspaincare.com

36227 ■ Pain Research Institute
266 East 3200 N
Provo, UT 84604
Ph: (801)377-6900
URL: http://www.healpain.net

36228 ■ Summit Pain Management Clinic
5250 South 320 W, Ste. 305
Murray, UT 84107
Ph: (801)262-7246
Free: 866-366-7906
URL: http://www.summitpain.com

36229 ■ University of Utah Health Sciences Center
Pain Management
Dept. of Anesthesiology
30 North 1900 E, Ste. 3C444
Salt Lake City, UT 84132
Ph: (801)587-4802
E-mail: Patricia.Cook--Tippetts@hsc.utah.edu
URL: http://www.pain101.com/PainDoctors/Directory-ACGMEprogramsList.aspx

36230 ■ University of Utah
Pain Management Center
546 Chipeta Way, Ste. 220
Salt Lake City, UT 84108
Ph: (801)581-7246
Fax: (801)581-6243
URL: http://healthcare.utah.edu/paincenter
Dr. Michael Ashburn, Director

VERMONT

36231 ■ Mindbody Medicine Clinic
Pain Center
Bldg. 1
S Prospect St., 6th Fl
Burlington, VT 05401
Ph: (802)847-2673
URL: http://www.med.uvm.edu/mbmc

36232 ■ Springfield Hospital
Pain Management Center
25 Ridgewood Rd.
Springfield, VT 05156
Ph: (802)885-2151
URL: http://www.springfieldhospital.org

36233 ■ University of Vermont
Fletcher Allen Health Care
Pain Management
Dept. of Anesthesiology
111 Colchester Ave.
Burlington, VT 05401
Ph: (802)847-2415
URL: http://www.pain101.com/PainDoctors/Directory-ACGMEprogramsList.aspx

VIRGINIA

36234 ■ HEALTHSOUTH Rehabilitation Hospital of Virginia
5700 Fitzhugh Ave.
Richmond, VA 23226
Ph: (804)288-5700
URL: http://www.healthsouth.com

36235 ■ Maryview Medical Center
Neuroscience Center for Pain Management
3315 High St.
Portsmouth, VA 23707
Ph: (757)399-0759
Fax: (757)399-3892
URL: http://hamptonroads.bonsecours.com

36236 ■ Naval Medical Center
Naval Hospital Portsmouth
Pain Management
620 John Paul Jones Cir.
Portsmouth, VA 23708
Ph: (757)953-3158
URL: http://www.pain101.com/PainDoctors/Directory-ACGMEprogramsList.aspx

36237 ■ University of Virginia Health System
Pain Management
PO Box 801008
Charlottesville, VA 22908
Ph: (434)924-2283
E-mail: mw6r@virginia.edu
URL: http://www.pain101.com/PainDoctors/Directory-ACGMEprogramsList.aspx

36238 ■ Virginia Commonwealth University Health System
Pain Management
PO Box 980677
Richmond, VA 23298
Ph: (804)828-8693
E-mail: farichar@vcu.edu
URL: http://www.pain101.com/PainDoctors/Directory-ACGMEprogramsList.aspx

WASHINGTON

36239 ■ Northwest Center for Integrative Medicine, Inc.
2702 S 42nd St., Ste. 310
Tacoma, WA 98409-7315
Ph: (253)472-7844
Fax: (253)472-8474
URL: http://www.nwcim.com
Dr. Jeffrey L. Okey, Director
Program(s): Medical Evaluation and Treatment; Physical and Massage Therapy; Counseling; Reduction Services; Acupuncture; Case Management; Pain Management Program; Fibromyalgia Treatment Program; Stress Reduction Program.

36240 ■ Rehabilitation Institute of Washington
4300 Aurora Ave. N, Ste. 101
Seattle, WA 98103
Ph: (206)859-5030
URL: http://www.rehabwashington.com

36241 ■ Saint Joseph Medical Center
Tacoma Chronic Pain Management Program
1717 S J St.
Tacoma, WA 98405
Ph: (253)426-6992
URL: http://www.fhshealth.org
Claudia C. Lengenfelder, Director

36242 ■ Saint Luke's Rehabilitation Institute
711 S Cowley St.
Spokane, WA 99202
Ph: (509)838-4771
URL: http://www.st-lukes.org

36243 ■ United Backcare, Inc.--Everett
9617 7th Ave. SE
Everett, WA 98208
Ph: (425)513-8509
Fax: (425)290-9774
URL: http://unitedbackcare.com
Program(s): Return to Work Programs; Assessment Programs and Diagnostics; Specialty Programs and Prevention; Physical/Occupational Therapy; Support Services.

36244 ■ United Backcare, Inc.--Puyallup
126 15th St. SE
Puyallup, WA 98372
Ph: (253)445-8663
Fax: (253)445-8342
URL: http://unitedbackcare.com

36245 ■ United Backcare, Inc.--Redmond
15436 Bel-Red Rd., No. 100
Redmond, WA 98052
Ph: (425)644-4100
Fax: (425)644-4101
URL: http://unitedbackcare.com

36246 ■ University of Washington, Roosevelt Medical Center
4245 Roosevelt Way NE
Seattle, WA 98105
Ph: (206)598-5428
URL: http://uwmedicine.washington.edu

36247 ■ University of Washington School of Medicine
Center for Pain Medicine
1959 NE Pacific St., Box 356044
Seattle, WA 98195
Ph: (206)543-4070
E-mail: frantzl@u.washington.edu
URL: http://www.pain101.com/PainDoctors/Directory-ACGMEprogramsList.aspx

36248 ■ Virginia Mason Medical Center
Pain Management
925 Seneca St., H8-GME
Seattle, WA 98111
Ph: (206)583-6079
URL: http://www.pain101.com/PainDoctors/Directory-ACGMEprogramsList.aspx

36249 ■ Virginia Mason Medical Center
Pain Management Clinic
Health Resources Bldg.
1100 9th Ave.
Seattle, WA 98111
Ph: (206)223-7582
Free: 800-354-9527
Fax: (206)223-6959
E-mail: james.bevier@xmmc.org
URL: http://www.virginiamason.org
Tanya Seligman, Manager

36250 ■ Virginia Mason Medical Center
Physical Medicine and Rehabilitation
909 University St.
Seattle, WA 98101
Ph: (206)223-6746
URL: http://www.virginiamason.org
Dr. Deborah Abrams, Director

WEST VIRGINIA

36251 ■ Cabell Huntington Hospital
1340 Hal Greer Blvd.
Huntington, WV 25701
Ph: (304)526-2243
URL: http://www.paincenter.chhi.org

36252 ■ Center for Pain Relief
94 Hunting Hills Dr.
Charleston, WV 25311

36253 ■ HEALTHSOUTH Mountainview Regional Rehabilitation Hospital, Fairmont
1160 Van Voorhis Rd.
Morgantown, WV 26554
Ph: (304)598-1100
URL: http://www.healthsouthmountainview.com

36254 ■ HEALTHSOUTH Rehabilitation Hospital of Huntington
6900 W Country Club Dr.
Huntington, WV 25705
Ph: (304)733-1060
URL: http://www.healthsouthhuntington.com

36255 ■ HEALTHSOUTH/Southern Hills Rehabilitation Hospital
120 12th St.
Princeton, WV 24740
Ph: (304)487-8000
URL: http://www.healthsouth.com

36256 ■ Weirton Medical Center
Pain Clinic
601 Colliers Way
Weirton, WV 26062
Ph: (304)797-6614
URL: http://www.weirtonmedical.com

WISCONSIN

36257 ■ Columbia Hospital
Pain Center
2301 N Lake Dr.
Milwaukee, WI 53211
Ph: (414)291-1075
URL: http://www.columbia-stmarys.com/Pain_Management
Gerri Staffileno, Director

36258 ■ Elmbrook Memorial Hospital
Pain Rehabilitation Center
19333 W North Ave.
Brookfield, WI 53045
Ph: (414)785-2272
URL: http://www.myheaton.org

36259 ■ Medical College of Wisconsin
Pain Management
9200 W Wisconsin Ave.
Milwaukee, WI 53226
Ph: (414)805-6124
E-mail: sabram@mcw.edu
URL: http://www.pain101.com/PainDoctors/Directory-ACGMEprogramsList.aspx

36260 ■ Saint Nicholas Hospital
Comprehensive Rehabilitation Inpatient Unit
Center for Pain and Work Rehabilitation
3100 Superior Ave.
Sheboygan, WI 53081
Ph: (920)459-8300
Fax: (920)459-7497
URL: http://www.stnicholashospital.org
Cathleen Kelling, Director

36261 ■ Waukesha Memorial Hospital
Pain Rehabilitation Program
725 American Ave.
Waukesha, WI 53188-5099
Ph: (262)928-2244
Free: 800-544-2745
URL: http://www.prohealth.org

WYOMING

36262 ■ Pain Consultants of the Rockies
903A S Greeley Hwy.
Cheyenne, WY 82007
Ph: (307)633-8100
URL: http://www.painconsultants.org

Chapter 28
Runaway & Homeless Youth Centers

Listed below are organizations and agencies that provide services for runaway and homeless youth. Entry arrangement is geographical by states, then alphabetical by organization names within states. Refer to the "User's Guide" located at the front of this directory for additional information.

ALABAMA

36263 ■ Children's Aid Society
Runaway and Homeless Youth Program
181 W Valley Ave., Ste. 300
Birmingham, AL 35209
Ph: (205)943-5325
E-mail: cas@childrensaid.org
URL: http://www.childrensaid.org
Program(s): Transitional Program/Maternity Group Home.

36264 ■ Group Homes for Children, Inc.
Runaway and Homeless Youth Program
1905 S Court St.
Montgomery, AL 36104
Ph: (334)265-6720
Rick Vest, Director
Program(s): Basic Center Program; Transitional Living Program.

36265 ■ Morgan County System of Services
Runaway and Homeless Youth Program
Decatur, AL
Ph: (256)350-8434
E-mail: sara.hall@alacourt.gov
URL: http://www.alacourt.gov
Program(s): Basic Center Program.

36266 ■ New Life Center for Change/Teen University
Runaway and Homeless Youth Program
707 Dillingham St.
Phenix City, AL 36867
Ph: (334)298-0000
E-mail: alsmith1@bellsouth.net
Program(s): Transitional Living Program.

36267 ■ Tennessee Valley Family Services
Runaway and Homeless Youth Program
PO Box 952
Guntersville, AL 35976
Ph: (256)582-0377
Free: 800-753-4269
Fax: (256)582-4315
E-mail: ahome@hiwaay.net
URL: http://www.tvfsahome.net/
Alice Henderson, Executive Director
Program(s): Basic Center Program; Street Outreach Program.

36268 ■ Thirteenth Place, Youth and Family Services Inc.
Runaway and Homeless Youth Program
405 S 12th St.
Gadsden, AL 35906
Ph: (256)547-8971
Fax: (256)547-6814
URL: http://www.thirteenthplace.com/
Janice Fox, Director
Program(s): Basic Center Program; Street Outreach Program.

ALASKA

36269 ■ Alaska Youth and Parent Foundation
Runaway and Homeless Youth Program
700 W 6th Ave.
Anchorage, AK 99501
Ph: (907)929-2633
Fax: (907)279-2633
E-mail: aypfdir@aypfalaska.org
URL: http://aypfalaska.org/
Barbara Berner, President
Program(s): Teen Clinic: (907)563-8336. Street Outreach Program.

36270 ■ Covenant House Alaska
Runaway and Homeless Youth Program
609 F St.
Anchorage, AK 99510
Ph: (907)272-1255
Fax: (907)272-1466
E-mail: cmorgan@covenanthouseak.org
URL: http://www.covenanthouseak.org/
Deidre Cronin, Director
Program(s): Basic Center and Street Outreach Programs; Maternity Group Home.

36271 ■ Fairbanks Counseling and Adoption
Runaway and Homeless Youth Program
912 Barnette St.
Fairbanks, AK 99701
Ph: (907)456-4729
Fax: (907)456-4623
E-mail: fca@fcaalaska.org
URL: http://www.fcaalaska.org/
Program(s): Street Outreach and Pregnancy Programs. **Formerly:** Fairbanks Native Association.

36272 ■ Juneau Youth Services
Runaway and Homeless Youth Program
PO Box 32839
Juneau, AK 99803
Ph: (907)789-7610
Free: 877-597-4357
Fax: (907)789-2106
URL: http://www.jys.org/
Jordan Nigro, Director
Program(s): Basic Center Program; Transitional Living Program; Street Outreach Program.

36273 ■ Kids Are People, Inc.
Runaway and Homeless Youth Program
851 E Westpoint Dr., Ste. 104
Wasilla, AK 99654
Ph: (907)376-6016
Free: 866-376-7233
Fax: (907)373-4959
John Stein, Director
Program(s): Transitional Living Program.

36274 ■ Presbyterian Hospitality House
209 40 Mile Rd.
Fairbanks, AK 99701
Ph: (907)456-6445
Fax: (907)456-6402
E-mail: info@phhalaska.org
URL: http://www.phhalaska.org
Ty Tigner, Director
Program(s): Basic Center Program; Transitional Living Program.

36275 ■ Southcentral Foundation
Runaway and Homeless Youth Program
SCF Admin. Bldg.
4501 Diplomacy Dr.
Anchorage, AK 99508
Ph: (907)729-4955
Free: 800-478-3343
URL: http://www.southcentralfoundation.com/
Katherine Gottlieb, President
Program(s): Transitional Living Program.

36276 ■ Youth Advocates of Sitka
Runaway and Homeless Youth Program
Hanson House
216 Lance Dr.
Sitka, AK 99835
Ph: (907)747-3682
Fax: (907)747-8099
E-mail: ryan.haug@sitkayouth.org
URL: http://www.hss.state.ak.us/ocs/
Program(s): Transitional Living Program.

ARIZONA

36277 ■ Arizona Youth Partnership
Runaway and Homeless Youth Program
3275 W Ina Rd., Ste. 135
Tucson, AZ 85741
Ph: (520)744-9595
Fax: (520)744-2127
URL: http://www.azyp.org
Program(s): Basic Center Program.

36278 ■ La Paloma Family Services
Runaway and Homeless Youth Program
870 W Miracle Mile
Tucson, AZ 85705
Ph: (520)750-9667
URL: http://www.lapalomakids.org
Program(s): Basic Center Program; Maternity Group Home.

36279 ■ Northland Family Help Center
Runaway and Homeless Youth Program
2532 N 4th St., No. 506
Flagstaff, AZ 86004
Ph: (928)774-4503

Free: 877-634-2723
Fax: (928)774-5809
E-mail: nfhc@northlandfamily.org
URL: http://www.northlandfamily.org/
Sonja Burkhalter, Executive Director
Program(s): Basic Center Program.

36280 ■ Open-Inn
Runaway and Homeless Youth Program
PO Box 5766
Tucson, AZ 85703
Ph: (520)670-9040
Fax: (520)318-1609
E-mail: info@openinn.org
URL: http://openinn.org/
Nancy L. Panico, Executive Director
Program(s): Transitional Living Program.

36281 ■ Our Town Family Center
Runaway and Homeless Youth Services
3830 E Belleview St.
Tucson, AZ 85716
Ph: (520)323-1708
Free: 800-537-8696
Fax: (520)323-9077
E-mail: info@ourfamilyservices.org
URL: http://www.ourfamilyservices.org
Susan Krahe-Eggleston, Executive Director
Program(s): Basic Center Program; Transitional Living Program; Street Outreach Program; Maternity Group Home and TLP.

36282 ■ Tumbleweed Center for Youth Development
Runaway and Homeless Youth Program
1419 N 3rd St., Ste. 102
Phoenix, AZ 85004
Ph: (602)271-9904
Free: 866-SAFE-703
Fax: (602)271-0240
E-mail: info@tumbleweed.org
URL: http://www.tumbleweed.org/
Dick Geasland, Executive Director
Program(s): Provides emergency shelter. Basic Center Program; Transitional Living Program; Street Outreach Program. **Formerly:** Center for Youth Development.

36283 ■ WestCare Arizona
821 Hancock Rd., Ste. 2
Bullhead City, AZ 86439
Ph: (928)763-1945
Fax: (928)763-8809
E-mail: tstevens@westcare.com
URL: http://www.westcare.com/slarizona.jsp
Program(s): Transitional Living Program; Maternity Group Home.

ARKANSAS

36284 ■ Centers for Youth and Families/Stepping Stones Shelter
Runaway and Homeless Youth Program
5905 Forest Pl., Ste. 200
Little Rock, AR 72204
Ph: (501)666-8686
Free: 888-868-0023
Fax: (501)660-6834
URL: http://centersforyouthandfamilies.org/
Doug Stadter, President
Program(s): Transitional Living Program.

36285 ■ Comprehensive Juvenile Services
Runaway and Homeless Youth Program
1606 S J St.
Fort Smith, AR 72901
Ph: (479)785-4031
Fax: (479)785-5354
E-mail: cjsdirector@sbcglobal.net
URL: http://www.cjsinc.org
John Furness, Executive Director
Program(s): Basic Center Program.

36286 ■ Consolidated Youth Services
Runaway and Homeless Youth Program
PO Box 878
Jonesboro, AR 72403
Ph: (870)972-1110
Fax: (870)972-5433
E-mail: jamesgena@yahoo.com
URL: http://www.jajonesboro.org/view/20
Bonnie Smith, Executive Director
Program(s): Basic Center Program.

36287 ■ Youth Bridge
Runaway and Homeless Youth Program
3715 Business Dr., Ste. 104
Fayetteville, AR 72703
Ph: (479)521-1532
Free: 800-628-2260
Fax: (479)521-4971
E-mail: mjohnson@youthbridge.com
URL: http://youthbridge.com
Scott Linebaugh, Executive Director
Program(s): Transitional Living Program.

CALIFORNIA

36288 ■ 1736 Family Crisis Center
Runaway and Homeless Youth Program
2116 Arlington Ave., No. 200
Los Angeles, CA 90018
Ph: (323)737-3900
URL: http://www.1736fcc.org
Carol A. Adelkoff, Director
Program(s): Basic Center Program.

36289 ■ Alameda Family Services
2325 Clement Ave.
Alameda, CA 94501
Ph: (510)629-6300
Fax: (510)865-1930
E-mail: info@alamedafs.org
URL: http://www.alamedafs.org/
Kathy Moehring, President
Program(s): Basic Center Program.

36290 ■ Bill Wilson Counseling Center
Runaway and Homeless Youth Services
3490 The Alameda
Santa Clara, CA 95050
Ph: (408)243-0222
Fax: (408)246-5752
E-mail: bwcmail@billwilsoncenter.org
URL: http://www.billwilsoncenter.org
Sparky Harlan, Director
Program(s): Basic Center Program; Transitional Living Program; Maternity Group Home.

36291 ■ Butte County Behavioral Health Department
Runaway and Homeless Youth Program
107 Parmac Rd., Ste. 4
Chico, CA 95926
Ph: (530)891-2850
URL: http://www.buttecounty.net
Program(s): Basic Center Program.

36292 ■ Casa Youth Shelter
Runaway and Homeless Youth Program
10911 Reagan St.
Los Alamitos, CA 90720
Ph: (562)594-6825
Free: 800-914-2272
Fax: (562)594-9185
E-mail: agency@casayouthshelter.org
URL: http://www.casayouthshelter.org
Luciann Maulhardt, Director
Program(s): Basic Center Program.

36293 ■ Catholic Charities
Angels' Flight
Runaway and Homeless Youth Program
1531 James M. Wood Blvd.
Los Angeles, CA 90015
Ph: (213)251-3400
Free: 800-833-2499
Fax: (213)380-4603
E-mail: info@catholiccharitiesla.org
URL: http://www.catholiccharitiesla.org/index.php?view=article&id=81
Program(s): Basic Center Program; Street Outreach Program.

36294 ■ Center for Human Services
Runaway and Homeless Youth Program
1700 McHenry Village Way, Ste. 11
Modesto, CA 95350
Ph: (209)526-1476
Fax: (209)526-0908
E-mail: kusiak@centerforhumanservices.org
URL: http://www.centerforhumanservices.org
Program(s): Basic Center Program; Transitional Living Program.

36295 ■ Center for Positive Prevention Alternatives
Runaway and Homeless Youth Program
729 N California St.
Stockton, CA 95202
Ph: (209)948-4357
Program(s): Transitional Living Program. **Formerly:** Center for Positive Prevention Alternatives.

36296 ■ Children In Need of Hugs
Runaway and Homeless Youth Program
274 E Sunset Ave., Ste. 201
Suisun City, CA 94585
Ph: (707)428-3912
Free: 866-483-3666
Fax: (707)402-6369
E-mail: Hargrave@cinoh.org
URL: http://www.cinoh.org/
Lorraine Hargrave, Chief Executive Officer
Program(s): Basic Center Program; Maternity Group Home.

36297 ■ Coffee House Teen Shelter
Runaway and Homeless Youth Program
1243 Ripley St.
Santa Rosa, CA 95401
URL: http://www.saysc.org
Program(s): Basic Center Program.

36298 ■ Community Human Services
Runaway and Homeless Youth Program
PO Box 3076
Monterey, CA 93942
Ph: (831)658-3811
Fax: (831)658-3815
E-mail: info@chservices.org
URL: http://www.chservices.org
Robin McCrae, Executive Director
Program(s): Basic Center Program. **Remarks:** Program fees are determined by a sliding scale based on the client's ability to pay. Services will not be denied due to the inability to pay.

36299 ■ Community Service Programs, Inc.
Runaway and Homeless Youth Program
1821 E Dyer Rd., Ste. 200
Santa Ana, CA 92705
Ph: (949)250-0488
Fax: (949)251-1659
E-mail: generalinfo@cspinc.org
URL: http://www.cspinc.org
Margot R. Carlson, Executive Director
Program(s): Basic Center Program.

36300 ■ Contra Costa County Health Services
50 Douglas Dr.
Martinez, CA 94553
Ph: (925)313-5140
Free: 888-215-5555
Fax: (925)313-6708
URL: http://www.cchealth.org/
Program(s): Basic Center Program; Transitional Living Program.

36301 ■ Covenant House California
Runaway and Homeless Youth Program
200 Harrison St.
Oakland, CA 94607
Ph: (510)379-1010
Free: 866-268-3683
Fax: (510)985-0935
E-mail: info@covenanthousecalifornia.org
URL: http://www.covenanthousecalifornia.org
George Lozano, Director
Program(s): Street Outreach Program.

36302 ■ Covenant House California
Runaway and Homeless Youth Program
1325 N Western Ave.
Hollywood, CA 90027
Ph: (323)461-3131
Free: 866-268-3683
Fax: (323)461-6491
E-mail: info@covenanthousecalifornia.org
URL: http://www.covenanthousecalifornia.org
Julie Maxon, Director
Program(s): Street Outreach Program.

36303 ■ Diogenes Youth Services
Runaway and Homeless Youth Program
9719 Lincoln Village Dr., Ste. 502
Sacramento, CA 95827
Ph: (916)369-5447
Fax: (916)369-5389
URL: http://www.diogenesyouthservices.org/
Dieter Wittenberg, President
Program(s): Basic Center Program; Street Outreach Program.

36304 ■ Emergency Housing Consortium
507 Valley Way
Milpitas, CA 95035
Ph: (408)539-2100
Fax: (408)957-0253
E-mail: info@ehclifebuilders.org
URL: http://www.ehclifebuilders.org
Program(s): Basic Center Program; Transitional Living Program; Street Outreach Program.

36305 ■ Fresno County Economic Opportunities Commission
Runaway and Homeless Youth Program
1920 Mariposa Mall, Ste. 300
Fresno, CA 93721
Ph: (559)263-1000
Fax: (559)263-1286
E-mail: executiveoffice@fresnoeoc.org
URL: http://www.fresnoeoc.org/
Roger Palomino, Executive Director
Program(s): Transitional Living Program. **Formerly:** Fresno County Economic Opportunity Commission.

36306 ■ Girls and Boys Town of Southern California
Runaway and Homeless Youth Program
2740 N Grand Ave., 2nd Fl.
Santa Ana, CA 92705
Ph: (714)532-2399
Fax: (714)532-6692
URL: http://www.boystown.org/california
Keith Diederich, Director
Formerly: Boys Town of Southern California.

36307 ■ Homeless Emergency Runaway Effort
500 Cohasset Rd., No. 27
Chico, CA 95926
Ph: (530)895-6524
E-mail: bluz@buttecounty.net
URL: http://www.butte-dbh.org/HERE/here.htm
Program(s): Basic Center Program.

36308 ■ Huckleberry Youth Programs
Huckleberry House and Nine Grove
Runaway and Homeless Youth Program
1292 Page St.
San Francisco, CA 94117
Ph: (415)621-2929
Free: 800-735-2929
Fax: (415)621-4758
E-mail: bfisher@huckleberryouth.org
URL: http://www.huckleberryyouth.org/home.html
Bruce Fisher, Executive Director
Program(s): Basic Center Program.

36309 ■ Interface Children and Family Services
Runaway and Homeless Youth Program
1305 Del Norte Rd., Ste. 130
Camarillo, CA 93010
Ph: (805)485-6114
E-mail: esternad@icfs.org
URL: http://www.icfs.org/
Erik Sternad, Executive Director
Program(s): Basic Center Program. **Formerly:** Interface Community.

36310 ■ Larkin Street Youth Center
Runaway and Homeless Youth Program
701 Sutter St.
San Francisco, CA 94109
Ph: (415)673-0911
Fax: (415)749-3838
E-mail: mail@larkinstreetyouth.org
URL: http://www.larkinstreetyouth.org
Sherilyn Adams, Executive Director
Program(s): Transitional Living Program. **Formerly:** Larkin Street Youth Services.

36311 ■ Los Angeles Conservation Corps
605 W Olympic Blvd., Ste. 450
Los Angeles, CA 90015
Ph: (213)362-9000
Free: 877-9LA-CORPS
Fax: (213)362-7957
E-mail: info@lacorps.org
URL: http://www.lacorps.org
Bruce Saito, Executive Director
Program(s): Transitional Living Program.

36312 ■ Los Angeles Gay and Lesbian Youth Services
Runaway and Homeless Youth Program
1625 N Schrader Blvd.
Los Angeles, CA 90028
Ph: (323)993-7400
URL: http://laglc.convio-net/site/PageServer
Lorri Jean, Executive Director
Program(s): Street Outreach Program.

36313 ■ Los Angeles Youth Network
Runaway and Homeless Youth Program
1680 N Vine St., Ste. 1005
Los Angeles, CA 90028
Ph: (323)957-7757
Fax: (323)464-4357
E-mail: info@layn.org
URL: http://www.layn.org
Matt Kamin, Executive Director
Program(s): Basic Center Program; Transitional Living Program. **Remarks:** Provides shelter for youth ages 12 to 17.

36314 ■ Main Street Transitional Living Program
Runaway and Homeless Youth Program
4509/4539 Main St.
Riverside, CA 92501
Ph: (951)369-4921
URL: http://www.operationsafehouse.org/transitional-living-program
Ann Miller, Executive Director
Program(s): Transitional Living Program.

36315 ■ Mendocino County Youth Project
Runaway and Homeless Youth Program
Plaza del Sol
776 S State St., Ste. 107
Ukiah, CA 95482
Ph: (707)463-4915
Free: 800-575-4346
Fax: (707)463-4917
E-mail: kwandrei@mcyp.org
URL: http://www.mcyp.org
Karin Wandrei, Executive Director
Program(s): Transitional Living Program.

36316 ■ New Morning Youth and Family Services
Runaway and Homeless Youth Program
6765 Green Valley Rd.
Placerville, CA 95667
Ph: (530)622-5551
Fax: (530)622-5800
E-mail: mail@newmorningyfs.org
URL: http://www.newmorningyfs.org
David Ashby, Executive Director
Program(s): Basic Center Program.

36317 ■ Noah's Anchorages YMCA
Runaway and Homeless Youth Program
301 W Figerora St.
Santa Barbara, CA 93101
Ph: (805)963-8775
E-mail: Mark.Watson@ciymca.org
URL: http://www.ciymca.org/youthandfamilyservices/YouthFamilyServices-NoahsAnchorage.ht ml
Program(s): Basic Center Program.

36318 ■ Northern California Family Center
Runaway and Homeless Youth Program
2244 Pacheco Blvd.
Martinez, CA 94553
Ph: (925)370-1990
Program(s): Basic Center Program.

36319 ■ Operation Safehouse, Inc.
Runaway and Homeless Youth Program
9685 Hayes St.
Riverside, CA 92503
Ph: (951)351-4418
Free: 800-561-6944
Fax: (951)351-4265
E-mail: safehouse9@aol.com
URL: http://www.operationsafehouse.org
Kathy McAdara, Director
Program(s): Basic Center Program; Transitional Living Program; Street Outreach Program.

36320 ■ Redwood Community Action Agency
Runaway and Homeless Youth Program
904 G St.
Eureka, CA 95501
Ph: (707)443-8322
Fax: (707)445-1445
E-mail: ysb@northcoast.com
URL: http://www.rcaa.org/ysb
Program(s): Transitional Living Program. **Remarks:** Provides emergency shelter.

36321 ■ Safe Passage
Runaway and Homeless Youth Program
544 Pearl St.
Monterey, CA 93940
Ph: (831)717-4126
Fax: (831)717-4126
E-mail: vlara@chservices.org
URL: http://www.chservices.org
Program(s): Basic Center Program.

36322 ■ SafeHouse of the Desert
Runaway and Homeless Youth Program
72-710 E Lynn St.
Thousand Palms, CA 92276
Ph: (760)343-3211
URL: http://www.operationsafehouse.org/desert-safehouse
Program(s): Basic Center Program; Street Outreach Program; Transitional Living Program.

36323 ■ Saint Vincent de Paul Village
Runaway and Homeless Youth Program
1501 Imperial Ave.
San Diego, CA 92101

Ph: (619)233-8500
Fax: (619)235-9707
URL: http://www.svdpv.org/
Program(s): Transitional Living Program.

36324 ■ The Salvation Army, Hollywood CA
Runaway and Homeless Youth Program
5941 Hollywood Blvd.
Hollywood, CA 90028
Ph: (323)960-0640
URL: http://www.salvationarmysocal.org/
Program(s): Transitional Living Program.

36325 ■ San Diego Youth and Community Services
Runaway and Homeless Youth Program
3255 Wing St.
San Diego, CA 92110
Ph: (619)221-8600
Fax: (619)221-8611
E-mail: msantos@sdyouthservices.org
URL: http://www.sdyouthservices.org
Walter Phillips, Executive Director
Program(s): Transitional Living Program.

36326 ■ Santa Cruz Community Counseling Center
Runaway and Homeless Youth Services
195 Harvey W Blvd.
Santa Cruz, CA 95060
Ph: (831)469-1700
Fax: (831)425-1905
E-mail: info@scccc.org
URL: http://www.scccc.org
Paul O'Brien, Executive Director
Program(s): Basic Center Program.

36327 ■ Social Advocates for Youth
Runaway and Homeless Youth Program
3440 Airway Dr., Ste. E
Santa Rosa, CA 95403
Ph: (707)544-3299
Free: 800-544-3299
Fax: (707)544-6837
E-mail: saymain@saysc.org
URL: http://www.socialadvocatesforyouth.org
James E. Coffee, Executive Director
Program(s): Basic Center Program; Street Outreach Program. **Formerly:** Social Advocates for Youth.

36328 ■ South Bay Community Services
Runaway and Homeless Youth Program
1124 Bay Blvd., Ste. D
Chula Vista, CA 91911
Ph: (619)420-3620
Fax: (619)420-8722
E-mail: info@csbcs.org
URL: http://www.southbaycommunityservices.org
Kathryn Lembo, Director
Program(s): Basic Center Program; Transitional Living Program.

36329 ■ StarVista
Runaway and Homeless Youth Program
610 Elm St., Ste. 212
San Carlos, CA 94070
Ph: (650)591-9623
URL: http://www.starvista.org
Pete Nannarone, Executive Director
Program(s): Basic Center Program; Transitional Living Program. **Formerly:** Youth and Family Enrichment Services.

36330 ■ Tahoe Youth and Family Services
Runaway and Homeless Youth Program
1021 Fremont Ave.
South Lake Tahoe, CA 96150
Ph: (530)541-2445
Fax: (530)541-0517
E-mail: admin@tahoeyouth.org
URL: http://www.tahoeyouth.org
Nichole Loftis, Director
Program(s): Basic Center Program; Street Outreach Program.

36331 ■ Tamayo House
Runaway and Homeless Youth Program
1700 Yulupa Ave.
Santa Rosa, CA 95405
Ph: (707)528-7500
URL: http://www.saysc.org
Program(s): Basic Center Program.

36332 ■ Toby's House
Runaway and Homeless Youth Program
92 Argonaut, Ste. 205
Santa Ana, CA 92656
Ph: (949)916-8868
E-mail: director@tobyshouse.org
URL: http://www.tobyshouse.org/
Kathleen Eaton, Chief Executive Officer
Program(s): Transitional Living Program.

36333 ■ Waking the Village
PO Box 160085
Sacramento, CA 95816
Ph: (916)372-6272
E-mail: admin@wakingthevillage.org
URL: http://www.wakingthevillage.org/
Bill Alston, President
Program(s): Maternity Group Home.

36334 ■ WIND Youth Center
Runaway and Homeless Youth Program
701 Dixieanne Ave.
Sacramento, CA 95815
Ph: (916)561-2424
Fax: (916)641-5571
E-mail: info@windyouth.org
URL: http://www.windyouth.org
Bob Ekstrom, Director
Program(s): Basic Center Program.

36335 ■ YMCA of San Diego County--Youth Center
Runaway and Homeless Youth Program
2929 Meade Ave.
San Diego, CA 92116
Ph: (619)543-9850
E-mail: kmorgan@yfs.ymca.org
URL: http://www.yfs.ymca.org/
Kim Morgan, Executive Director
Program(s): Pryde; Juvenile Crisis Response Program; Safe Paths; Family Stress Counseling Services; OZ San Diego/OZ North Coast; Basic Center Program; Transitional Living Program. **Formerly:** YMCA Youth & Family Services.

COLORADO

36336 ■ Colorado Department of Human Services
Runaway and Homeless Youth Program
Denver, CO
Ph: (303)866-4706
E-mail: cdhs.communications@state.co.us
URL: http://www.colorado.gov
Program(s): Transitional Living Program; Support System for Rural Homeless Youth.

36337 ■ Comitis Crisis Center
Runaway and Homeless Youth Program
2178 Victor St.
Aurora, CO 80040
Ph: (303)341-9160
Fax: (303)341-0623
E-mail: management@comitis.org
URL: http://www.comitis.org/
Richard Barnhill, Executive Director
Program(s): Basic Center Program. **Remarks:** Offers emergency housing. No fee is charged for counseling but donations are requested.

36338 ■ Family Tree, Inc.--Gemini House
Runaway and Homeless Youth Program
Gemini House
1629 Sims St.
Lakewood, CO 80215
Ph: (303)235-0630
Fax: (303)235-0633
E-mail: info@thefamilytree.org
URL: http://www.thefamilytree.org/
Dennis Desparrois, Chief Executive Officer
Program(s): Basic Center Program.

36339 ■ Family Tree, Inc.
Runaway and Homeless Youth Program
3805 Marshall St.
Wheat Ridge, CO 80033
Ph: (303)422-2133
Fax: (303)422-5707
E-mail: info@thefamilytree.org
URL: http://www.thefamilytree.org
Scott Shields, Chief Executive Officer
Program(s): Basic Center Program.

36340 ■ Hilltop Special Services
Runaway and Homeless Youth Program
1331 Hermosa Ave.
Grand Junction, CO 81506
Ph: (970)242-4400
Fax: (970)243-4646
E-mail: corpinfo@htop.org
URL: http://www.htop.org/
Program(s): Basic Center Program.

36341 ■ Urban Peak--Colorado Springs
Runaway and Homeless Youth Program
423 E Cucharras St.
Colorado Springs, CO 80903
Ph: (719)630-3223
Fax: (719)630-3250
E-mail: coloradosprings@urbanpeak.org
URL: http://www.urbanpeak.org/locations.html
Program(s): Basic Center Program; Transitional Living Program.

36342 ■ Urban Peak--Denver
Runaway and Homeless Youth Program
730 21st St.
Denver, CO 80205
Ph: (303)974-2900
Fax: (303)295-6116
E-mail: urbanpeak@urbanpeak.org
URL: http://www.urbanpeak.org/locations.html
Jason Newcomer, Executive Director
Program(s): Basic Center Program; Transitional Living Program.

36343 ■ Urban Peak--Denver Shelter
Runaway and Homeless Youth Program
1630 S Acoma
Denver, CO 80223
Ph: (303)974-2908
Fax: (303)777-9438
E-mail: urbanpeak@urbanpeak.org
URL: http://www.urbanpeak.org
Kay Ramachandran, Chief Executive Officer
Program(s): Basic Center Program; Transitional Living Program.

36344 ■ Ute Mountain
Ute Tribe
Sunrise Youth Shelter
Runaway and Homeless Youth Program
332 Dry Creek Rd.
Towaoc, CO 81334
Ph: (970)565-9634
Fax: (970)565-2619
URL: http://www.utemountainute.com/
Program(s): Basic Center Program.

36345 ■ Volunteers of America--Denver, CO
Runaway and Homeless Youth Services
2660 Larimer St.
Denver, CO 80205

Ph: (303)297-0408
Fax: (303)297-3306
E-mail: info@voacolorado.org
URL: http://www.voacolorado.org
Dianna Kunz, President
Program(s): Basic Center Program; Transitional Living Program; Street Outreach Program.

CONNECTICUT

36346 ■ The Bridge Family Center, Inc.
Runaway and Homeless Youth Program
1022 Farmington Ave.
West Hartford, CT 06107
Ph: (860)521-8035
Fax: (860)521-8036
E-mail: info@bridgefamilycenter.org
URL: http://www.bridgefamilycenter.org
Margaret Hann, Executive Director
Program(s): Basic Center Program; Transitional Living Program.

36347 ■ Council of Churches of Greater Bridgeport
Runaway and Homeless Youth Program
Bldg. 5A
1100 Boston Ave.
Bridgeport, CT 06610
Ph: (203)334-1121
E-mail: info@ccgb.org
URL: http://www.ccgb.org
Dr. Brian Schofield-Bodt, President
Beds: 12. **Program(s):** Basic Center Program. **Remarks:** Operates Janus House Emergency Youth Shelter. Bilingual staffing.

36348 ■ Kids in Crisis
Runaway and Homeless Youth Program
1 Salem St.
Cos Cob, CT 06807
Ph: (203)327-KIDS
E-mail: sshapiro@kidsincrisis.org
URL: http://www.kidsincrisis.org
Shari Shapiro, Executive Director
Program(s): Basic Center Program.

36349 ■ United Services
Runaway and Homeless Youth Program
303 Putnam Rd.
Wauregan, CT 06387
Ph: (860)564-6100
Fax: (860)564-6110
E-mail: mail@unitedservicesct.org
URL: http://www.unitedservicesct.org
Diane L. Manning, President
Program(s): Basic Center Program. **Remarks:** Provides emergency shelter. Services are free.

36350 ■ Women and Families Center
169 Colony St.
Meriden, CT 06451
Ph: (203)235-9297
Fax: (203)237-7571
URL: http://www.womenfamilies.org/
Pat Ladner, Director
Program(s): Drop-in Center; Street Outreach Program.

36351 ■ Youth Continuum
Douglas House Shelter
Runaway and Homeless Youth Program
24 River St.
New Haven, CT 06513
Ph: (203)562-3396
Fax: (203)867-5888
E-mail: info@youthcontinuum.org
URL: http://www.youthcontinuum.org
Carole Shomo, Executive Director
Program(s): Transitional Living Program; Street Outreach Program.

DELAWARE

36352 ■ Aid in Dover
Runaway and Homeless Youth Program
Dover, DE 19904
Ph: (302)734-7610
Fax: (302)734-7714
E-mail: aidindover@aidindover.org
URL: http://www.aidindover.org
Beverly Williams, Director
Program(s): Transitional Living Program.

36353 ■ Child, Inc.
Runaway and Homeless Youth Program
507 Philadelphia Pke.
Wilmington, DE 19809
Ph: (302)762-8989
URL: http://www.childinc.com
Joseph Dell'Olio, Director
Program(s): Basic Center Program.

DISTRICT OF COLUMBIA

36354 ■ Boys Town Washington DC Assessment and Short-Term Residential Program
Runaway and Homeless Youth Program
4801 Sargent Rd. NE
Washington, DC 20017
Ph: (202)832-7343
Fax: (202)832-9807
E-mail: petersonj@boystown.org
URL: http://www.boystownwashingtondc.org/
Jeff Peterson, Executive Director
Program(s): Basic Center Program.

36355 ■ Covenant House Washington
Runaway and Homeless Youth Program
2001 Mississippi Ave. SE
Washington, DC 20020
Ph: (202)610-9600
Fax: (202)610-9610
URL: http://www.covenanthousedc.org
Judith Dobbins, Executive Director
Program(s): Transitional Living Program; Street Outreach Program.

36356 ■ Latin American Youth Center
Runaway and Homeless Youth Program
1419 Columbia Rd. NW
Washington, DC 20009
Ph: (202)319-2225
Fax: (202)462-5696
E-mail: info@layc-dc.org
URL: http://www.layc-dc.org
Lori Kaplan, Executive Director
Program(s): Basic Center Program; Transitional Living Program; Street Outreach Program.

36357 ■ Sasha Bruce Youthwork
Runaway and Homeless Youth Services
741 8th St. SE
Washington, DC 20003
Ph: (202)675-9340
E-mail: admin@sashabruce.org
URL: http://www.sashabruce.org
Deborah Shore, Executive Director
Program(s): Basic Center Program; Transitional Living Program.

FLORIDA

36358 ■ Anchorage Children's Home
Runaway and Homeless Youth Program
2121 Lisenby Ave.
Panama City, FL 32405
Ph: (850)763-7102
URL: http://www.anchoragechildrenshome.org
Tim Putman, Executive Director
Program(s): Transitional Living Program; Maternity Group Home.

36359 ■ Arnette House
Runaway and Homeless Youth Program
2310 NE 24th St.
Ocala, FL 34470
Ph: (352)622-6135
Fax: (352)622-2830
E-mail: info@arnettehouse.org
URL: http://www.arnettehouse.org
Kevin Priest, Chief Executive Officer
Program(s): Basic Center Program; Transitional Living Program.

36360 ■ Boys Town Broward County
Runaway and Homeless Youth Program
Bldg. 2, Ste. 8-B
2301 W Sample Rd.
Pompano Beach, FL 33073
Ph: (954)590-2503
Fax: (954)590-2504
URL: http://www.boystown.org/south-florida
Program(s): Basic Center Program.

36361 ■ Boys Town Central Florida
Runaway and Homeless Youth Program
975 Oklahoma St.
Oviedo, FL 32765
Ph: (407)588-2170
Fax: (407)588-2171
URL: http://www.boystown.org/central-florida
Program(s): Basic Center Program.

36362 ■ Boys Town North Florida Intervention and Assessment Services
Runaway and Homeless Youth Program
3555 Commonwealth Blvd.
Tallahassee, FL 32303
Ph: (850)575-6422
Fax: (850)575-7225
URL: http://www.boystown.org/north-florida
Program(s): Basic Center Program.

36363 ■ Boys Town South Florida Intervention and Assessment Services
Runaway and Homeless Youth Program
3111 S Dixie Hwy., Ste. 200
West Palm Beach, FL 33405
Ph: (561)366-9400
Fax: (561)366-1133
URL: http://www.boystown.org/south-florida/
Program(s): Basic Center Program.

36364 ■ Capital City Youth Services
Runaway and Homeless Youth Program
2407 Roberts Ave.
Tallahassee, FL 32310
Ph: (850)576-6000
Fax: (850)576-2580
E-mail: information@ccys.org
URL: http://www.ccys.org
Stacy Gromatski, Executive Director
Program(s): Basic Center Program.

36365 ■ CDS Family and Behavioral Health Services
1300 NW 6th St.
Gainesville, FL 32601
Ph: (352)244-0628
E-mail: Jim_Pearce@cornerdrugstore.org
Jim Pearce, Chief Executive Officer
Program(s): Basic Center Program. **Formerly:** Corner Drugstore.

36366 ■ Children's Home Society of Florida Brevard Division
Runaway and Homeless Youth Program
326 Croton Rd.
Melbourne, FL 32935
Ph: (321)752-3170
Fax: (321)752-3179
E-mail: Teresa.Miles@chsfl.org
URL: http://www.chsfl.org
Program(s): Transitional Living Program.

36367 ■ Children's Home Society of Florida Clair's House
Runaway and Homeless Youth Program
914 Harrison Ave.
Panama City, FL 32401

Ph: (850)747-5411
Fax: (850)872-7345
E-mail: William.Coleman@chsfl.org
URL: http://www.chsfl.org
William Coleman, Executive Director
Program(s): Transitional Living Program.

36368 ■ Children's Home Society of Florida Haven House
Runaway and Homeless Youth Program
711 NW 1st St.
Gainesville, FL 32601
Ph: (352)334-0955
Fax: (352)334-0957
E-mail: Jennifer.Anchors@chsfl.org
URL: http://www.chsfl.org
Jennifer Anchors, Executive Director
Program(s): Transitional Living Program.

36369 ■ Children's Home Society of Florida North Central Division
Runaway and Homeless Youth Program
Tree House
1801 Miccosukee Commons Dr.
Tallahassee, FL 32308
Ph: (850)921-0772
Fax: (850)921-0726
E-mail: Dixie.Casford@chsfl.org
URL: http://www.chsfl.org
Dixie Casford, Executive Director
Program(s): Basic Center Program.

36370 ■ Children's Home Society of Florida North Coastal Division
Runaway and Homeless Youth Program--South Daytona
2400 S Ridgewood Ave., Ste. 32
South Daytona, FL 32119
Ph: (386)304-7600
Fax: (386)304-7620
E-mail: Christine.Davenport@chsfl.org
URL: http://www.chsfl.org
Christine Davenport, Executive Director
Program(s): Basic Center Program; Transitional Living Program.

36371 ■ Children's Home Society of Florida South Coastal Division
Runaway and Homeless Youth Program--West Palm Beach
3333 Forest Hill Blvd.
West Palm Beach, FL 33406
Ph: (561)868-4300
Fax: (561)868-4499
E-mail: Stephen.Bardy@chsfl.org
URL: http://www.chsfl.org
Stephen Bardy, Executive Director
Program(s): Basic Center Program; Transitional Living Program.

36372 ■ Children's Home Society of Florida Treasure Coast Division
Runaway and Homeless Youth Program--Port Saint Lucie
590 NW Peacock Blvd., Ste. 9
Port Saint Lucie, FL 34986
Ph: (772)344-4020
Fax: (772)344-4038
E-mail: Jan.Huffert@chsfl.org
URL: http://www.chsfl.org
Jan Swink-Huffert, Executive Director
Program(s): Transitional Living Program.

36373 ■ Covenant House Florida
Runaway and Homeless Youth Program
733 Breakers Ave.
Fort Lauderdale, FL 33304
Ph: (954)561-5559
Free: 800-683-8338
Fax: (954)565-6551
E-mail: mission@covenanthousefl.org
URL: http://www.covenanthousefl.org
Program(s): Transitional Living Program; Street Outreach Program.

36374 ■ Covenant House--Orlando
Runaway and Homeless Youth Program
5931 E Colonial Dr.
Orlando, FL 32807
Ph: (407)482-0404
Free: 800-441-4478
Fax: (407)482-0657
E-mail: mission@covenanthousefl.org
URL: http://www.covenanthousefl.org
Program(s): Transitional Living Program; Street Outreach Program.

36375 ■ Crosswinds Youth Services, Inc.
Runaway and Homeless Youth Program
1407 Dixon Blvd.
Cocoa, FL 32922
Ph: (321)452-0800
Fax: (321)394-0385
E-mail: info@crosswindsyouthservices.org
URL: http://www.crosswindsyouthservices.org
Jan Lokay, Executive Director
Program(s): Basic Center Program; Transitional Living Program.

36376 ■ Family Resources, Inc.
Runaway and Homeless Youth Program
361 6th Ave. W
Bradenton, FL 34205
Ph: (941)741-3575
Fax: (941)741-3578
URL: http://www.family-resources.org
Program(s): Basic Center Program; Maternity Group Home. **Formerly:** Helpline.

36377 ■ Florida Keys Children's Shelter
Runaway and Homeless Youth Program
73 High Point Rd.
Tavernier, FL 33070
Ph: (305)852-4246
Fax: (305)852-6902
E-mail: fkcs@fkcs.org
URL: http://www.fkcs.org
Kathy Tuell, Executive Director
Program(s): Basic Center Program.

36378 ■ Hope Center for Teens, Inc.
Runaway and Homeless Youth Program
PO Box 19024
Pensacola, FL 32523
Ph: (850)434-1340
E-mail: hope@hc4t.org
URL: http://www.hopecenter4teens.org
Jennifer Young, Executive Director
Program(s): Maternity Group Home.

36379 ■ Lutheran Services Florida--Pensacola
Runaway and Homeless Youth Program
4610 W Fairfield Dr.
Pensacola, FL 32506
Ph: (850)453-2772
URL: http://www.lsfnet.org
Program(s): Basic Center Program.

36380 ■ Lutheran Services Florida--Tampa
Runaway and Homeless Youth Program
3627A W Waters Ave.
Tampa, FL 33614
Ph: (813)875-1408
Free: 800-651-1853
Fax: (813)875-1302
E-mail: ssipes@lsfnet.org
URL: http://www.lsfnet.org
Program(s): Basic Center Program.

36381 ■ Miami Bridge
Runaway and Homeless Youth Program
2810 NW S River Dr.
Miami, FL 33125
Ph: (305)635-8953
E-mail: info@miamibridge.org
URL: http://www.miamibridge.org
Mary Andrews, Executive Director
Program(s): Basic Center Program.

36382 ■ Orange County Board of County Commissioners
Runaway and Homeless Youth Program
1800 E Michigan St.
Orlando, FL 32806
Ph: (407)836-7626
Fax: (407)836-7469
E-mail: tracy.salem@ocfl.net
URL: http://www.onetgov.net/Dept/hfs/yfs
Program(s): Basic Center Program.

36383 ■ Sarasota Family YMCA
Youth and Family Services
Runaway and Homeless Youth Program
1106 S Briggs Ave.
Sarasota, FL 34237
Ph: (941)955-5596
Fax: (941)955-7195
E-mail: nhartsock@TheSarasotaY.org
URL: http://www.sarasota-ymca.org/socialServices/youthShelter.cfm
Program(s): Basic Center Program; Transitional Living Program.

36384 ■ Youth Crisis Center
Runaway and Homeless Youth Program
3015 Parental Home Rd.
Jacksonville, FL 32216
Ph: (904)720-0002
Free: 877-720-0007
E-mail: info@ycc.org
URL: http://www.youthcrisiscenter.org/
Program(s): Basic Center Program.

36385 ■ Youth and Family Alternatives Administration
Runaway and Homeless Youth Program
7524 Plathe Rd.
Newport Richey, FL 34653
Ph: (727)835-4166
Fax: (727)835-3942
E-mail: info@yfainc.org
URL: http://www.yfainc.org
Program(s): Street Outreach Program.

36386 ■ Youth and Family Alternatives--Bartow
George W. Harris, Jr. Runaway and Youth Crisis Shelter
1060 US Hwy. 17 S
Bartow, FL 33830
Ph: (863)595-0220
Free: 800-786-8614
URL: http://www.yfainc.org/
Program(s): Street Outreach Program.

36387 ■ Youth and Family Alternatives--Brooksville
Runaway and Homeless Youth Program
New Beginnings
18377 Clinton Blvd.
Brooksville, FL 34601
Ph: (352)797-6199
Fax: (352)799-6142
URL: http://www.yfainc.org
George Magrill, President
Program(s): Street Outreach Program.

GEORGIA

36388 ■ Advocates for Bartow's Children
Runaway and Homeless Youth Program
49 Monroe Crossing
Cartersville, GA 30120
Ph: (770)387-1143
Fax: (770)606-0732
E-mail: channel@advochild.org
URL: http://www.advochild.org/
Steve Yarish, Director
Program(s): Basic Center Program.

36389 ■ The Alcove
Runaway and Homeless Youth Program
507 E Church St.
Monroe, GA 30655
Ph: (770)267-9156
Fax: (770)207-9162
URL: http://www.thealcoveshelter.com/
Dorothy Morrow, Executive Director
Program(s): Basic Center Program.

36390 ■ Georgia Campaign for Adolescent Pregnancy Prevention
Runaway and Homeless Youth Program
1450 W Peachtree St. NW, Ste. 200
Atlanta, GA 30309
Ph: (404)524-2277
Fax: (404)523-7753
URL: http://www.gcapp.org
Program(s): Maternity Group Home.

36391 ■ Greenbriar Children's Center
Runaway and Homeless Youth Program
3709 Hopkins St.
Savannah, GA 31405
Ph: (912)234-3431
Fax: (912)238-9149
URL: http://www.greenbriarchildrenscenter.org
Gena P. Taylor, Executive Director
Program(s): Basic Center Program.

36392 ■ Gwinnett Children's Shelter
Runaway and Homeless Youth Program
PO Box 527
Buford, GA 30515
Ph: (678)546-8770
Fax: (678)546-8775
E-mail: opbount@gwinnettchildrenshelter.org
URL: http://www.gwinnettchildrenshelter.org
Nancy Friauf, Director
Program(s): Basic Center Program.

36393 ■ Open Arms
The Bridge
Runaway and Homeless Youth Program
420 Pine Ave.
Albany, GA 31702
Ph: (229)431-1121
Fonda Strong, Executive Director
Program(s): Basic Center Program; Transitional Living Program; Street Outreach Program.

36394 ■ Park Place Outreach Inc.
Runaway and Homeless Youth Program
514 E Henry St.
Savannah, GA 31401
Ph: (912)234-4048
Fax: (912)651-3621
E-mail: srh_admin@comcast.net
URL: http://www.parkplaceyes.org/
Linda Hilts, Executive Director
Program(s): Basic Center Program; Street Outreach Program.

36395 ■ Rainbow House
PO Box 871013
Morrow, GA 30287
Ph: (770)478-6905
Fax: (770)473-3849
URL: http://www.rainbowhouseinc.org/
Program(s): Basic Center Program.

36396 ■ Safe Harbor Children's Shelter
Runaway and Homeless Youth Program
2215 Gloucester St.
Brunswick, GA 31521
Ph: (912)267-6000
Fax: (912)267-0872
E-mail: admin@safeharborshelter.org
URL: http://www.safeharborshelter.org
Cindy Baas, Executive Director
Program(s): Basic Center Program.

36397 ■ WestCare--Atlanta GA
2818 Lakewood Ave.
Atlanta, GA 30315
Ph: (404)761-7485
Fax: (404)761-8427
URL: http://www.westcare.com/slgeorgia.jsp
Program(s): Basic Center Program.

36398 ■ Young Adult Guidance Center Inc.
Runaway and Homeless Youth Program
Emergency Shelter
1230 Hightower Rd. NW
Atlanta, GA 30377
Ph: (404)792-7616
Fax: (404)792-0151
URL: http://www.yagc.net/Youth_Guidance_Center/Emergency_Shelter.html
Marion Simpson, Executive Director
Program(s): Basic Center Program; Transitional Living Program.

36399 ■ Young People Matter
Runaway and Homeless Youth Program
5051 Snapfinger Woods Dr.
Decatur, GA 30035
Ph: (770)744-4050
E-mail: info@ypmatlanta.org
URL: http://www.ypmatlanta.org
Program(s): Basic Center Program.

GUAM

36400 ■ Sanctuary, Inc.
Runaway and Homeless Youth Program
406 Mai Mai Rd.
Chalan Pago, GU 96910
Ph: (671)475-7101
Fax: (671)477-3117
E-mail: info@sanctuaryguam.org
URL: http://www.sanctuaryguam.org
Program(s): Basic Center Program.

HAWAII

36401 ■ Hawaii Youth Services Network
Runaway and Homeless Youth Program
677 Ala Moana Blvd., Ste. 702
Honolulu, HI 96813
Ph: (808)531-2198
Fax: (808)534-1199
URL: http://www.hysn.org
Judith F. Clark, Executive Director
Program(s): Transitional Living Program.

36402 ■ Salvation Army Hawaiian and Pacific Islands Division
Runaway and Homeless Youth Program
2950 Manoa Rd.
Honolulu, HI 96822
Ph: (808)988-2136
URL: http://www1.usw.salvationarmy.org/usw/www_usw_hawaii.nsf
Program(s): Street Outreach Program.

IDAHO

36403 ■ Bannock Youth Foundation
Runaway and Homeless Youth Program
620 W Fremont
Pocatello, ID 83204
Ph: (208)234-1122
Fax: (208)234-1253
URL: http://www.byfhome.com/index.php
Program(s): Transitional Living Program.

36404 ■ Hays Shelter Home
Runaway and Homeless Youth Program
7221 W Poplar St.
Boise, ID 83704
Ph: (208)322-6687
Free: 877-817-8141
Fax: (208)322-3905
E-mail: sfields@youthranch.org
URL: http://www.youthranch.org/HaysHouse.aspx
Robert Ball, Vice President
Program(s): Basic Center Program.

36405 ■ Idaho Youth Ranch
Runaway and Homeless Youth Program
5465 W Irving St.
Boise, ID 83706
Ph: (208)377-2613
Free: 877-817-8141
Fax: (208)377-2819
E-mail: info@youthranch.org
URL: http://www.youthranch.org/
Steve Woodworth, President
Program(s): Basic Center Program.

ILLINOIS

36406 ■ Aunt Martha's Youth Service Center, Inc.
Runaway and Homeless Youth Program
19990 Governors Hwy
Olympia Fields, IL 60461
Ph: (708)747-7100
URL: http://www.auntmarthas.org
Program(s): Transitional Living Program.

36407 ■ Bethany for Children & Families
Runaway and Homeless Youth Program
1830 6th Ave.
Moline, IL 61265
Ph: (309)797-7700
Fax: (309)797-2386
E-mail: info@bethany-qc.org
URL: http://www.bethany-qc.org/
Lynn Lohman, Executive Director
Program(s): Transitional Living Program.

36408 ■ Boys Town Chicago
Intervention and Assessment Homes
Runaway and Homeless Youth Program
4538 S Hermitage
Chicago, IL 60609
Ph: (773)247-7725
Fax: (773)247-7794
URL: http://www.boystown.org/chicago
Fr. Bruce Wellems, Executive Director
Program(s): Basic Center Program.

36409 ■ Call for Help, Inc.
Runaway and Homeless Youth Program
9400 Lebannon Rd.
East Saint Louis, IL 62203
Ph: (618)397-0968
Free: 800-397-8707
Fax: (618)397-6836
E-mail: info@callforhelpinc.org
URL: http://www.callforhelpinc.org/
Carlyn Brooks, Executive Director
Program(s): Transitional Living Program.

36410 ■ Delta Center Inc.
Runaway and Homeless Youth Program
1400 Commercial Ave.
Cairo, IL 62914
Ph: (618)734-2665
Fax: (618)734-1999
E-mail: delta1@midwest.net
URL: http://www.deltacenter.org/
Program(s): Street Outreach Program.

36411 ■ The H Group
Runaway and Homeless Youth Program
902 W Main
West Frankfort, IL 62896
Ph: (618)937-6483
Fax: (618)937-1440
URL: http://www.buildingbettertomorrows.org/
Program(s): Transitional Living Program; Street Outreach. **Formerly:** Franklin-Williamson Human Services.

36412 ■ The Harbour Inc.
Runaway and Homeless Youth Program
1440 Renaissance Dr., Ste. 240
Park Ridge, IL 60068
Ph: (847)297-8540
Fax: (847)297-8562
E-mail: theharbour@theharbour.org
URL: http://www.theharbour.org/
Randi Gurian, Executive Director
Program(s): Basic Center Program; Transitional Living Program.

36413 ■ Hoyleton Youth and Family Services/Children First
Runaway and Homeless Youth Program
350 N Main St.
Hoyleton, IL 62803
Ph: (618)493-7382
Fax: (618)493-6390
E-mail: info@hoyleton.org
URL: http://www.hoyleton.org
Anne King, Director
Program(s): Basic Center Program; Transitional Living Program.

36414 ■ Le Penseur Youth and Family Services
Runaway and Homeless Youth Program
8550 S Manistee
Chicago, IL 60617
Ph: (773)375-8637
Fax: (773)375-8653
E-mail: lepenseur@att.net
URL: http://www.lepenseur.org/
Reginald Summerrise, Director
Program(s): Transitional Living Program.

36415 ■ McHenry County Youth Service
Runaway and Homeless Youth Program
101 S Jefferson St.
Woodstock, IL 60098
Ph: (815)338-7360
Fax: (815)337-5510
E-mail: info@ysb4kids.org
URL: http://www.ysb4kids.org/
Susan Krause, Executive Director
Program(s): Basic Center Program.

36416 ■ Mental Health Center of Champaign County
Community Elements
Runaway and Homeless Youth Program
1801 Fox Dr.
Champaign, IL 61820
Ph: (217)398-8080
Fax: (217)398-0172
URL: http://www.communityelements.org/
Sheila Ferguson, Chief Executive Officer
Program(s): Basic Center Program.

36417 ■ Midwest Youth Services
Runaway and Homeless Youth Program
2001 W Lafayette Ave.
Jacksonville, IL 62650
Ph: (217)245-6000
Free: 800-513-4357
Fax: (217)245-7000
E-mail: mys.exdir@mchsi.com
Program(s): Basic Center Program.

36418 ■ NCO Youth and Family Services
Runaway and Homeless Youth Program
1305 W Oswego Rd.
Naperville, IL 60540
Ph: (630)961-2992
Fax: (630)961-7251
URL: http://www.ncoyouth.org/
Debbie Carr, Director
Program(s): Transitional Living Program.

36419 ■ The Night Ministry
Runaway and Homeless Youth Program
4711 N Ravenswood Ave.
Chicago, IL 60640
Ph: (773)784-9000
Fax: (773)784-5865
E-mail: info@thenightministry.org
URL: http://www.thenightministry.org
Paul W. Hamann, President
Program(s): Basic Center Program; Transitional Living Program; Street Outreach Program.

36420 ■ Omni Youth Services
Runaway and Homeless Youth Program
1111 Lake Cook Rd.
Buffalo Grove, IL 60089
Ph: (847)353-1500
Fax: (847)465-1964
E-mail: info@omniyouth.org
URL: http://www.omniyouth.org
James Meyer, Executive Director
Program(s): Basic Center Program.

36421 ■ Project Oz
Runaway and Homeless Youth Services
1105 W Front St.
Bloomington, IL 61701
Ph: (309)827-0377
Fax: (309)829-8877
E-mail: projectoz@projectoz.org
URL: http://www.projectoz.org
Peter Rankaitis, Executive Director
Program(s): Maternity Group Home; Transitional Living Program.

36422 ■ Rockford Meld, Inc.
Runaway and Homeless Youth Program
3703 N Main St., Ste. 107
Rockford, IL 61104
Ph: (815)633-6353
Fax: (815)633-8709
E-mail: meld@rockfordmeld.org
URL: http://www.rockfordmeld.org/
Gene Maule, Executive Director
Program(s): Transitional Living Program.

36423 ■ Southern Illinois Regional Social Services, Inc.
Runaway and Homeless Youth Program
604 E College
Carbondale, IL 62901
Ph: (618)457-6703
Fax: (618)549-3734
E-mail: ys@sirss.org
URL: http://www.sirss.org
Karen Freitag, Director

36424 ■ Teen Living Programs, Inc.
Foundation House
Runaway and Homeless Youth Program
162 W Hubbard St., Ste. 400
Chicago, IL 60654
Ph: (312)568-5700
Free: 866-803-8336
Fax: (312)568-5701
E-mail: info@teenliving.org
URL: http://www.teenliving.org
David L. Myers, Executive Director
Program(s): Basic Center Program; Transitional Living Program. **Remarks:** Provides emergency shelter.

36425 ■ Youth Network Council
Runaway and Homeless Youth Program
111 E Wacker Dr., Ste. 325
Chicago, IL 60601
Ph: (312)861-6600
Fax: (312)861-6601
E-mail: secowen@youthnetworkcouncil.org
URL: http://youthnetworkcouncil.org/
Susan Cowen, Executive Director
Program(s): Basic Center Program; Street Outreach Program.

36426 ■ Youth Organizations Umbrella
Runaway and Homeless Youth Program
1027 Sherman Ave.
Evanston, IL 60202
Ph: (847)866-1200
Fax: (847)866-9143
E-mail: info@youevanston.org
URL: http://www.youevanston.org
Program(s): Basic Center Program.

36427 ■ Youth Outreach Services
Runaway and Homeless Youth Program
2411 W Congress Pkwy.
Chicago, IL 60612
Ph: (773)777-7112
Fax: (773)777-7611
URL: http://www.yos.org
Rick Velasquez, Executive Director
Program(s): Transitional Living Program.

36428 ■ Youth Service Bureau of Illinois Valley
Runaway and Homeless Youth Program
424 W Madison St.
Ottawa, IL 61350
Ph: (815)431-3026
E-mail: dmc@ysbiv.org
URL: http://www.ysbiv.org/
Dave McClure, Director
Program(s): Basic Center Program; Transitional Living Program.

36429 ■ Youth Service Bureau
Runaway and Homeless Youth Program
2901 Normandy Rd.
Springfield, IL 62703
Ph: (217)529-8300
Free: 866-529-8300
Fax: (217)529-8314
E-mail: ysb@ysbi.com
URL: http://www.ysbi.com
Kathleen Wright, Executive Director
Program(s): Basic Center Program; Transitional Living Program.

36430 ■ Youth Services Network
Runaway and Homeless Youth Program
3703 N Main St.
Rockford, IL 61103
Ph: (815)986-1947
Fax: (815)986-1954
Program(s): Transitional Living Program.

INDIANA

36431 ■ Children's Bureau
Runaway and Homeless Youth Program
1575 Dr. Martin Luther King Jr. St.
Indianapolis, IN 46202
Ph: (317)264-2700
Fax: (317)264-2714
E-mail: info@childrensbureau.org
URL: http://www.childrensbureau.org
Program(s): Basic Center Program; Transitional Living Program.

36432 ■ Crisis Center, Inc. Alternative House
Runaway and Homeless Youth Program
101 N Montgomery
Gary, IN 46403
Ph: (219)938-7070
Fax: (219)938-7502
E-mail: crisis@crisiscenterysb.org
URL: http://www.crisiscenterysb.org/
Shirley Caylor, Executive Director
Program(s): Basic Center Program.

36433 ■ Family and Children's Center
The Children's Campus, Inc.
Runaway and Homeless Youth Program
1411 Lincoln Way W
Mishawaka, IN 46544
Ph: (574)256-6179
Free: 888-8-CAMPUS
Fax: (574)255-6179
E-mail: infotcc@childrenscampus.org
URL: http://www.childrenscampus.org/
Patricia McLemore, Director
Program(s): Transitional Living Program.

36434 ■ Indiana Juvenile Justice Task Force Runaway and Homeless Youth Services
1800 N Meridian St., Ste. 402
Indianapolis, IN 46202
Ph: (317)926-6100
Free: 800-926-4661
Fax: (317)926-6165
URL: http://www.ijjtf.org/
Bill Glick, Executive Director
Program(s): Basic Center Program.

36435 ■ Promising Futures of Central Indiana Runaway and Homeless Youth Program
294 S 9th St.
Noblesville, IN 46060
Ph: (317)773-6342
Fax: (317)773-3340
E-mail: slyons@promisingfutures.org
URL: http://www.promisingfutures.org/
Stephanie Lyons, Executive Director
Program(s): Basic Center Program; Maternity Group Home. **Formerly:** Hamilton Centers Youth Services Bureau.

36436 ■ Stopover
Runaway and Homeless Youth Program
2236 E 10th St.
Indianapolis, IN 46201-2099
Ph: (317)633-8210
Fax: (317)633-8608
URL: http://www.jhbcc.org/
Elizabeth Malone, Director
Program(s): Basic Center Program; Transitional Living Program.

36437 ■ Youth Service Bureau of Monroe County
Runaway and Homeless Youth Program
615 S Adams St.
Bloomington, IN 47403
Ph: (812)349-2506
Fax: (812)349-2892
E-mail: yshelter@co.monroe.in.us
URL: http://www.youthservicesbureau.net/
Program(s): Basic Center Program.

36438 ■ Youth Service Bureau of Saint Joseph County, Inc.
Runaway and Homeless Youth Program
2222 Lincoln Way W
South Bend, IN 46628
Ph: (574)235-9231
Fax: (574)235-5578
URL: http://www.ysbsjc.org
Bonnie Strycker, Executive Director
Program(s): Basic Center Program.

IOWA

36439 ■ Foundation II
Youth Shelter
Runaway and Homeless Youth Program
1714 Johnson Ave. NW
Cedar Rapids, IA 52405
Ph: (319)362-1170
Fax: (319)297-7406
E-mail: dpeddycoart@foundation2.org
URL: http://www.foundation2.org/
Deb Peddycoart, Director
Program(s): Transitional Living Program. **Remarks:** Provides emergency shelter. Services are free.

36440 ■ Iowa Department of Human Services, Des Moines
Runaway and Homeless Youth Program
River Place
2309 Euclid Ave.
Des Moines, IA 50310
Ph: (515)725-2600
Fax: (515)725-2899
E-mail: CPolk01@dhs.state.ia.us
URL: http://www.dhs.state.ia.us
Program(s): Transitional Living Program; Support System for Rural Homeless Youth.

36441 ■ John Lewis Coffee Shop
Runaway and Homeless Youth Program
1016 W 5th St.
Davenport, IA 52808
Ph: (563)823-0508
Fax: (563)323-3782
URL: http://www.jlcs.org
Cody Smith, Director
Program(s): Basic Center Program; Street Outreach Program.

36442 ■ United Action for Youth
Runaway and Homeless Youth Program
355 Iowa Ave.
Iowa City, IA 52244
Ph: (319)338-7518
Fax: (319)337-7999
E-mail: jim.swain@unitedactionforyouth.org
URL: http://www.unitedactionforyouth.org/
Jim Swaim, Executive Director
Program(s): Basic Center Program; Transitional Living Program; Street Outreach Program.

36443 ■ Youth Emergency Services
Runaway and Homeless Youth Program
1219 Buchanan St.
Des Moines, IA 50316
Ph: (515)265-1222
Fax: (515)266-8377
E-mail: info@yessiowa.org
URL: http://www.yessiowa.org/
Michael Fritz, Executive Director
Program(s): Transitional Living Program.

36444 ■ Youth and Shelter Services
Runaway and Homeless Youth Program
420 Kellogg Ave.
Ames, IA 50010-1628
Ph: (515)233-3141
Free: 800-600-2330
Fax: (515)233-2440
URL: http://www.yss.ames.ia.us
George Belitsos, Chief Executive Officer
Program(s): Basic Center Program.

KANSAS

36445 ■ Kansas Children's Service League
Runaway and Homeless Youth Program
Oasis I
PO Box 303
Deerfield, KS 67838
Ph: (620)426-2180
Free: 877-530-5275
URL: https://www.kcsl.org/
Janet Schalansky, President
Program(s): Basic Center Program.

36446 ■ Kaw Valley Center
Runaway and Homeless Youth Services
4300 Brenner Dr.
Kansas City, KS 66104
Ph: (913)312-9024
Free: 888-566-5500
Fax: (913)312-9025
URL: http://www.kvc.org
Erin Stucky, President
Program(s): Basic Center Program.

36447 ■ Temporary Lodging for Children
Runaway and Homeless Youth Program
480 S Rogers Rd.
Olathe, KS 66062
Ph: (913)764-2887
Fax: (913)780-3387
E-mail: info@kidstlc.org
URL: http://www.kidstlc.org
Robert Brummond, Chief Executive Officer
Program(s): Basic Center Program.

36448 ■ Wichita Children's Home
Runaway and Homeless Youth Program
810 N Holyoke
Wichita, KS 67208
Ph: (316)684-6581
Fax: (316)684-7249
E-mail: sarah@wch.org
URL: http://www.wch.org
Sarah Robinson, Executive Director
Program(s): Transitional Living Program.

KENTUCKY

36449 ■ Brighton Center, Inc.
Runaway and Homeless Youth Program
741 Central Ave.
Newport, KY 41072
Ph: (859)491-8303
Fax: (859)491-8702
E-mail: brighton@brightoncenter.com
URL: http://www.brightoncenter.com/
Bob Brewster, Director
Program(s): Basic Center Program; Transitional Living Program; Street Outreach Program.

36450 ■ Buckhorn Children and Family Services
Runaway and Homeless Youth Program
116 Buckhorn Ln.
Buckhorn, KY 41721
Ph: (606)398-7000
Free: 800-472-3678
Fax: (606)398-7912
E-mail: tony.cecil@buckhorn.org
URL: http://www.buckhorn.org/
Program(s): Transitional Living Program. **Formerly:** Presbyterian Child Welfare Agency.

36451 ■ Family Connection, Inc.
Runaway and Homeless Youth Program
PO Box 257
Mount Sterling, KY 40353
E-mail: info@familyconnectioninc.com
URL: http://www.familyconnectioninc.com
Program(s): Basic Center Program; Street Outreach Program.

36452 ■ Lexington-Fayette Urban County Government
Division of Youth Services
Runaway and Homeless Youth Program
1177 Red Mile Pl.
Lexington, KY 40504
Ph: (859)246-4370
Fax: (859)231-1213
E-mail: shong@lexingtonky.gov
URL: http://www.lexingtonky.gov/index.aspx?page=317
Stephanie Hong, Director
Program(s): Basic Center Program.

36453 ■ Volunteers of America, Kentucky
Runaway and Homeless Youth Program
933 Goss Ave.
Louisville, KY 40217
Ph: (502)636-0771
Fax: (502)637-8111
E-mail: info@voaky.org
URL: http://www.volunteersofamericankentucky.org/
Jane Burks, President
Program(s): Transitional Living Program; Maternity Group Home.

36454 ■ YMCA Safeplace Services
Runaway and Homeless Youth Program
2400 Crittenden Dr.
Louisville, KY 40217
Ph: (502)635-5233
Fax: (502)635-1443
E-mail: safeplaceservices@ymcalouisville.org
URL: http://www.ymcalouisville.org
Matt Reed, Executive Director
Program(s): Basic Center Program; Street Outreach Program.

LOUISIANA

36455 ■ Educational and Treatment Council Inc.
Educational and Treatment Center
Runaway and Homeless Youth Program
PO Box 864
Lake Charles, LA 70602
Ph: (337)433-1062
Fax: (337)439-1094
URL: http://www.etc-youth.org
Program(s): Basic Center Program; Transitional Living Program.

36456 ■ Father Flanagan's Boys Home of New Orleans
Runaway and Homeless Youth Program
700 Frenchmen St.
New Orleans, LA 70116
Ph: (504)949-9248
Fax: (504)949-5735
URL: http://www.boystown.org/louisiana
Dennis Dillon, Executive Director
Program(s): Basic Center Program.

36457 ■ Gulf Coast Teaching Family Service
Runaway and Homeless Youth Program
2509 Petroleum Dr.
Houma, LA 70363
Ph: (985)853-1445
Free: 800-831-2630
Fax: (985)853-0709
E-mail: info@gctfs.org
URL: http://www.gctfs.org/houma.php
Willie Green, Director
Program(s): Transitional Living Program.

36458 ■ Healing Place Church
Runaway and Homeless Youth Program
19202 Highland Rd.
Baton Rouge, LA
Ph: (225)753-2273
E-mail: info@healingplacechurch.org
URL: http://www.healingplacechurch.org
Program(s): Basic Center Program.

36459 ■ New Horizons Youth Service Bureau
Runaway and Homeless Youth Program
47257 River Rd.
Hammond, LA 70401
Ph: (985)345-1171
Fax: (985)542-9878
URL: http://www.youthservicebureau.org
Jeanne Voorhees, Executive Director
Program(s): Basic Center Program.

36460 ■ Our House, Inc.
Runaway and Homeless Youth Program
205 Smith Ave.
Monroe, LA 71211
Ph: (318)345-5556
Fax: (318)345-5550
E-mail: ourhouse@bayou.com
URL: http://www.teen-help.com/
Carol Christopher, Executive Director
Program(s): Transitional Living Program.

36461 ■ Volunteers of America--North Louisiana
Runaway and Homeless Youth Program
360 Jordan St.
Shreveport, LA 71101
Ph: (318)221-2669
URL: http://www.voanorthla.org
Program(s): Transitional Living Program.

36462 ■ Youth Oasis
Runaway and Homeless Youth Program
260 S Acadian Thruway
Baton Rouge, LA 70806
Ph: (225)343-6300
Fax: (225)343-6303
URL: http://www.youthoasis.org/
Alvin Smith, Executive Director
Program(s): Basic Center Program; Transitional Living Program.

MAINE

36463 ■ Community Health and Counseling Services
Runaway and Homeless Youth Program
PO Box 425
Bangor, ME 04402-0425
Ph: (207)947-0366
Free: 800-924-0366
Fax: (207)947-3896
E-mail: info@chcs-me.org
URL: http://www.chcs-me.org/
Wayne Walker, Director
Program(s): Transitional Living Program.

36464 ■ Good Will Home Association
Runaway and Homeless Youth Program
16 Prescott Dr.
Hinckley, ME 04944
Ph: (207)238-4280
Fax: (207)238-4007
E-mail: info@gwh.org
URL: http://www.gwh.org/
Greg Dowty, Executive Director
Program(s): Transitional Living Program.

36465 ■ Home Counselors, Inc.
Runaway and Homeless Youth Program
375 Main St.
Rockland, ME 04841
Ph: (207)596-0359
Fax: (207)596-0350
URL: http://www.homecounselorsinc.org/
Program(s): Basic Center Program.

36466 ■ MAPS/Stepping Stones
Runaway and Homeless Youth Program
58 Pleasant St.
Houlton, ME 04730
Ph: (207)532-9358
Free: 800-287-9358
Fax: (207)532-5506
E-mail: contact@stepstones4youth.org
URL: http://www.stepstones4youth.org/
Program(s): Transitional Living Program.

36467 ■ New Beginnings
Runaway and Homeless Youth Program
436 Main St.
Lewiston, ME 04240
Ph: (207)795-4077
Fax: (207)795-4080
E-mail: newbegin@verizon.net
URL: http://www.newbeginmaine.org
Program(s): Transitional Living Program.

36468 ■ Penquis
Runaway and Homeless Youth Program
262 Harlow St.
Bangor, ME 04402
Ph: (207)973-3699
Free: 800-215-4942
Fax: (207)973-3699
E-mail: info@penquis.org
URL: http://www.penquis.org
Program(s): Transitional Living Program; Maternity Group Home.

36469 ■ Preble Street Resource Center
Runaway and Homeless Youth Program
18 Portland St.
Portland, ME 04104
Ph: (207)775-0026
Fax: (207)842-3614
E-mail: info@preblestreet.org
URL: http://www.preblestreet.org
James Sterling, President
Program(s): Basic Center Program; Street Outreach Program.

36470 ■ Rumford Group Homes
Runaway and Homeless Youth Program
160 Lincoln Ave.
Rumford, ME 04276
Ph: (207)364-3551
Fax: (207)364-3544
E-mail: rghinc@rumfordgrouphomes.org
URL: http://www.rumfordgrouphomes.org
Program(s): Basic Center Program.

36471 ■ Shaw House
Runaway and Homeless Youth Program
136 Union St.
Bangor, ME 04401
Ph: (207)941-2874
Free: 866-561-SHAW
Fax: (207)941-2875
E-mail: info@theshawhouse.org
URL: http://www.theshawhouse.org
Program(s): Street Outreach Program.

36472 ■ Volunteers of America Northern New England
Runaway and Homeless Youth Program
14 Maine St., Ste. 301
Brunswick, ME 04011
Ph: (207)373-1140
Fax: (207)373-1160
E-mail: help@voanne.org
URL: http://www.voanne.org/
June Koegel, President
Program(s): Transitional Living Program.

36473 ■ Youth Alternatives Ingraham
Runaway and Homeless Youth Program
50 Lydia Ln.
South Portland, ME 04106
Ph: (207)874-1175
Free: 877-429-6884
Fax: (207)874-1181
E-mail: info@yimaine.org
URL: http://www.yimaine.org
Mike Tarpinian, President
Program(s): Basic Center Program; Transitional Living Program.

36474 ■ Youth and Family Services, Skowhegan
Runaway and Homeless Youth Program
5 Commerce Dr.
Skowhegan, ME 04976
Ph: (207)474-8311
Free: 888-420-9605
Fax: (207)474-5148
E-mail: yfsinc@yfsinc.org
URL: http://www.yfsinc.org
Lynn Duby, Director
Program(s): Basic Center Program.

MARYLAND

36475 ■ AIRS/Empire Homes of Maryland
Runaway and Homeless Youth Program
1800 N Charles St., Ste. 700
Baltimore, MD 21201
Ph: (410)576-5070
Fax: (410)576-5074
E-mail: ft@airshome.org
URL: http://www.airshome.org
F.T. Burden, President

36476 ■ Fellowship of Lights, Inc.
Runaway and Homeless Youth Program
1300 N Calvert St.
Baltimore, MD 21202

Ph: (410)385-1200
Ross Pologe, Executive Director
Program(s): Basic Center Program.

36477 ■ Hearts & Homes for Youth
Runaway and Homeless Youth Program
1320 Fenwick Ln., Ste. 800
Silver Spring, MD 20910
Ph: (301)589-8444
Fax: (301)495-0923
E-mail: hhyinfo@heartsandhomes.org
URL: http://www.hh4y.org/
Rex Smith, President
Program(s): Transitional Living Program. **Remarks:** Second Mile House and Open Door Runaway Program offer 15 days of emergency refuge for runaway or homeless youths. Caithness Shelter Home gives emergency overnight, weekend, or extended shelter to boys or girls. Long-term group homes are offered for boys and girls. **Formerly:** Boys and Girls Homes and Community Services.

36478 ■ Rose Street Community Center
Runaway and Homeless Youth Program
821 N Rose St.
Baltimore, MD 21205
Ph: (410)675-1207
Fax: (410)675-1207
E-mail: civillife1@aol.com
URL: http://www.jhsph.edu/source/volunteeragencies/commdev/rosestreet.html
Program(s): Basic Center Program.

36479 ■ Worchester County Health Department, Berlin
Runaway and Homeless Youth Program
6040 Public Landing Rd.
Snow Hill, MD 21863
Ph: (410)629-0164
Fax: (410)629-0185
E-mail: jbaum@dhmh.state.md.us
URL: http://worcesterhealth.org/runaway-youth-menu
Joyce Baum, Director
Program(s): Basic Center Program. **Formerly:** Worchester County Health Department, Snow Hill.

MASSACHUSETTS

36480 ■ The Bridge Over Troubled Waters, Inc.
Runaway and Homeless Youth Program
47 West St.
Boston, MA 02111
Ph: (617)423-9575
Fax: (617)482-5459
E-mail: bridgc@bridgeotw.org
URL: http://www.bridgeotw.org/
Sheila Moore, Executive Director
Program(s): Basic Center Program; Transitional Living Program.

36481 ■ Brookline Community Mental Health Center
Runaway and Homeless Youth Program
41 Garrison Rd.
Brookline, MA 02445
Ph: (617)277-8107
Fax: (617)734-6385
URL: http://www.brooklinecenter.org
Dr. Cynthia Price, Executive Director
Program(s): Basic Center Program; Street Outreach Program.

36482 ■ Catholic Charities Archdiocese of Boston
Runaway and Homeless Youth Program
51 Sleeper St.
Boston, MA 02210
Ph: (617)482-5440
Fax: (617)451-0337
URL: http://www.ccab.org/cc_boston.html
Program(s): Transitional Living Program.

36483 ■ Center for Human Development
Runaway and Homeless Youth Program
332 Birnie Ave.
Springfield, MA 01107
Ph: (413)733-6624
Fax: (413)439-2109
E-mail: chdinfo@chd.org
URL: http://www.chd.org
James Williams, Director
Program(s): Basic Center Program.

36484 ■ Dial/Self
Runaway and Homeless Youth Program
21 Abbott St.
Greenfield, MA 01301
Ph: (413)774-7054
E-mail: kallen@dialself.org
URL: http://www.dialself.org/
Kate Allen, Director
Program(s): Basic Center Program; Transitional Living Program; Street Outreach Program.

36485 ■ The GRIP Project, Justice Research Institute: Growing Responsibility and Independence in People
Runaway and Homeless Youth Program
545 Boylston St., Ste. 700
Boston, MA 02116
Ph: (617)450-0500
URL: http://www.jri.org
Andrew Pond, President
Program(s): Basic Center Program; Transitional Living Program.

36486 ■ L.U.K. Crisis Center, Inc.
Runaway and Homeless Youth Program
545 Westminster St.
Fitchburg, MA 01420
Ph: (978)345-0685
Fax: (978)345-3602
E-mail: info@luk.org
URL: http://www.luk.org
Lois Barry, Executive Director
Program(s): Basic Center Program; Transitional Living Program; Street Outreach Program.

36487 ■ ServiceNet, Inc.
Runaway and Homeless Youth Program
129 King St.
Northampton, MA 01060
Ph: (413)585-1300
Fax: (413)582-4252
E-mail: info@servicenetinc.org
URL: http://www.servicenetinc.org
Susan Stubbs, Chief Executive Officer
Program(s): Basic Center Program.

36488 ■ United Teen Equality Center
Runaway and Homeless Youth Program
34 Hurd St.
Lowell, MA 01852
Ph: (978)441-9949
Fax: (978)654-6727
E-mail: info@utec-lowell.org
URL: http://www.utec-lowell.org/
Gregg Croteau, Executive Director
Program(s): Street Outreach Program.

36489 ■ Wayside Youth and Family Support Network
Runaway and Homeless Youth Program
1 Frederick Abbott Way
Framingham, MA 01701
Ph: (508)879-9800
Fax: (508)875-1348
E-mail: wayside_info@waysideyouth.org
URL: http://www.waysideyouth.org/joomla/
Eric L. Masi, Executive Director
Program(s): Basic Center Program; Transitional Living Program.

MICHIGAN

36490 ■ Alternatives for Girls
Runaway and Homeless Youth Program
903 W Grand Blvd.
Detroit, MI 48208
Ph: (313)361-4000
Fax: (313)361-8938
E-mail: mlawson@alternativesforgirls.org
URL: http://www.alternativesforgirls.org
Mashell Lawson, Executive Director
Program(s): Basic Center Program; Transitional Living Program; Maternity Group Home.

36491 ■ Arbor Circle Corporation
The Bridge for Runaways
Runaway and Homeless Youth Program
1115 Ball Ave. NE
Grand Rapids, MI 49505
Ph: (616)456-6571
E-mail: info@arborcircle.org
URL: http://www.arborcircle.org/
Susan Conrad, Director
Program(s): Basic Center Program; Transitional Living Program.

36492 ■ Bethany Christian Services
Runaway and Homeless Youth Program
6995 W 48th St.
Fremont, MI 49412
Ph: (231)924-3390
Fax: (231)924-2848
E-mail: info@bethany.org
URL: http://www.bethany.org/fremont
David Glerum, Director
Program(s): Basic Center Program.

36493 ■ Catholic Family Services, Kalamazoo
Runaway and Homeless Youth Program
1819 Gull Rd.
Kalamazoo, MI 49048
Ph: (269)381-9800
Fax: (616)381-2932
E-mail: info@catholicfamilyservices.org
URL: http://www.catholicfamilyservices.org/
Frances Denny, Director
Program(s): Basic Center Program; Transitional Living Program.

36494 ■ Child and Family Services of Southwestern Michigan
Runaway and Homeless Youth Program
2450 M-139
Benton Harbor, MI 49022
Ph: (269)925-1725
Free: 888-237-1891
Fax: (269)925-1730
URL: http://www.cfsswmi.org
Program(s): Basic Center Program.

36495 ■ Common Ground
Runaway and Homeless Youth Program
1410 S Telegraph
Bloomfield Hills, MI 48302
Ph: (248)456-8150
Fax: (248)456-8147
URL: http://www.commongroundsanctuary.org/
Tony Rothschild, Director
Program(s): Basic Center Program; Transitional Living Program.

36496 ■ Comprehensive Youth Services, Mount Clemens
Family Youth Interventions
Runaway and Homeless Youth Program
418 Cass Ave.
Mount Clemens, MI 48043
Ph: (586)465-1212
Fax: (586)465-4504
E-mail: familyyouth03@yahoo.com
URL: http://www.familyyouth.com
Jolyne Baarck, Director
Program(s): Basic Center Program; Transitional Living Program; Street Outreach Program.

36497 ■ The Connection Youth Services Livingston Family Center
Runaway and Homeless Youth Program
810 E Grand River
Howell, MI
Free: 866-440-7233
E-mail: theconnection.LFC@gmail.com
URL: http://www.theconnectionyouthservices.org
Program(s): Basic Center Program; Transitional Living Program.

36498 ■ Cory Place
Runaway and Homeless Youth Program
581 N Sheuermann Rd.
Bay City, MI 48708
Ph: (989)895-5563
Free: 888-895-5563
Fax: (989)895-7312
Jheri McAfee, Executive Director
Program(s): Basic Center Program. **Remarks:** Provides crisis intervention services to youth, 10-17 years old, and to their parents.

36499 ■ Covenant House Michigan
Runaway and Homeless Youth Program
2959 Martin Luther King Jr. Blvd.
Detroit, MI 48208
Ph: (313)463-2000
Fax: (313)463-2001
URL: http://www.covenanthousemi.org
Program(s): Street Outreach Program.

36500 ■ Every Woman's Place
Runaway and Homeless Youth Services
175 W Apple Ave.
Muskegon, MI 49440
Ph: (231)759-7909
Fax: (231)759-8618
E-mail: websitec@everywomansplace.org
URL: http://www.everywomansplace.org/
Susan Johnson, Director
Program(s): Basic Center Program; Transitional Living Program; Street Outreach Program.

36501 ■ Gateway Community Services
Runaway and Homeless Youth Services
2875 Northwind Dr., Ste. 105
East Lansing, MI 48823
Ph: (517)351-4000
Fax: (517)351-4094
E-mail: info@gatewayservices.org
URL: http://www.gatewayservices.org
Stephanie Vin, Director
Program(s): Transitional Living Program. **Remarks:** Program services are provided at no cost to clients or their parents/guardians.

36502 ■ Genesee County Youth Corporation Reach
Runaway and Homeless Youth Program
914 Church St.
Flint, MI 48502
Ph: (810)233-8700
Fax: (810)233-0263
E-mail: gcyc@intouchmi.org
Program(s): Transitional Living Program.

36503 ■ Listening Ear Crisis Center
Runaway and Homeless Youth Program
107 E Illinois St.
Mount Pleasant, MI 48804-0800
Ph: (989)772-2918
Fax: (989)772-5339
E-mail: nwanek@listeningear.com
URL: http://www.listeningear.com
Program(s): Basic Center Program; Transitional Living Program.

36504 ■ Livingston Family Center
Runaway and Homeless Youth Program
4736 East M-36
Pinckney, MI 48169
Ph: (810)231-9591
Fax: (810)231-9522
URL: http://www.livingstonfamilycenter.org
Program(s): Basic Center Program.

36505 ■ Lutheran Social Services of Wisconsin and Upper Michigan--Marquette, MI
Runaway and Homeless Youth Program
1029 N 3rd St.
Marquette, MI 49855
Ph: (906)225-5437
Fax: (906)226-9800
E-mail: marqvfy@lsswis.org
URL: http://www.lsswis.org
William Bundy, Director
Program(s): Basic Center Program; Transitional Living Program; Street Outreach Program. **Formerly:** Lutheran Social Services of Wisconsin and Upper Michigan.

36506 ■ Matrix Human Services
Runaway and Homeless Youth Program
120 Parsons St.
Detroit, MI 48201
Ph: (313)831-1000
Fax: (313)831-4634
E-mail: inquiries@matrixhs.org
URL: http://www.matrixhumanservices.org
Marcella Wilson, President
Program(s): Basic Center Program.

36507 ■ Ozone House
Runaway and Homeless Youth Program
1705 Washtenaw Ave.
Ann Arbor, MI 48104
Ph: (734)662-2265
Fax: (734)662-9724
E-mail: info@ozonehouse.org
URL: http://ozonehouse.org
Mary Jo Callan, Executive Director
Program(s): Basic Center Program; Transitional Living Program; Street Outreach Program. **Remarks:** Provides emergency shelter. Services are free.

36508 ■ Ruth Ellis Center
Runaway and Homeless Youth Program
77 Victor St.
Highland Park, MI 48203
Ph: (313)252-1950
Fax: (313)865-3372
E-mail: info@ruthelliscenter.com
URL: http://www.ruthelliscenter.com/
Program(s): Transitional Living Program.

36509 ■ Saginaw County Youth Council/Innerlink Transitional Living and Emergency Shelter
Runaway and Homeless Youth Program
1110 Howard
Saginaw, MI 48605
Ph: (989)753-3431
Fax: (989)752-5178
E-mail: epartlow@scypc.ldmi.net
URL: http://www.scypc.org/
Program(s): Transitional Living Program.

36510 ■ Starfish Family Services
Runaway and Homeless Youth Program
30000 Hiveley Rd.
Inkster, MI 48141
Ph: (734)728-3400
Fax: (734)728-3500
E-mail: pbrown@fish.org
URL: http://www.starfishonline.org
Program(s): Basic Center Program.

36511 ■ Third Level Crisis Intervention Center
Youth and Family Services
Runaway and Homeless Youth Program
1022 E Front St.
Traverse City, MI 49685
Ph: (231)922-4800
Free: 800-442-7315
Fax: (231)941-5786
E-mail: info@thirdlevel.org
URL: http://www.thirdlevel.org
Steve Hampton, Executive Director
Program(s): Transitional Living Program.

36512 ■ Wayne Metropolitan Community Action Agency
Runaway and Homeless Youth Program
2121 Biddle Ave., Ste. 102
Wyandotte, MI 48192
Ph: (734)246-2280
Fax: (734)246-2288
E-mail: info@waynemetro.org
URL: http://www.waynemetro.org
Program(s): Basic Center Program.

MINNESOTA

36513 ■ Ain Dah Yung Shelter
Runaway and Homeless Youth Program
1089 Portland Ave.
Saint Paul, MN 55104
Ph: (651)227-4184
Fax: (651)224-5136
E-mail: susan@aindahyung.com
URL: http://www.adycenter.org
Susan Jacobson, Executive Director
Program(s): Culturally specific emergency shelter and group home services provided to American Indian youth between the ages of five through seventeen. Basic Center Program; Transitional Living Program; Crisis Intervention; Information and Referral; Counseling; Case Management; Community Education; Family Support Program; Youth Lodge; Our Children Program.

36514 ■ Avenues for Homeless Youth
Runaway and Homeless Youth Program
1708 Oak Park Ave. N
Minneapolis, MN 55411
Ph: (612)522-1690
Fax: (612)522-1633
E-mail: info@avenuesforyouth.org
URL: http://www.avenuesforyouth.org
Dr. Lois Hall, President
Program(s): Basic Center Program.

36515 ■ Bridge for Runaway Youth
Runaway and Homeless Youth Program
1111 W 22nd St.
Minneapolis, MN 55405
Ph: (612)377-8800
Fax: (612)377-6426
E-mail: info@bridgeforyouth.org
URL: http://www.bridgeforyouth.org
Ed Murphy, Executive Director
Program(s): Basic Center Program; Transitional Living Program; Street Outreach Program. **Formerly:** The Bridge.

36516 ■ Catholic Charities of Saint Paul and Minneapolis
Hope Street Shelter
Runaway and Homeless Youth Program
1121 E 46th St.
Minneapolis, MN 55407
Ph: (612)204-8211
Fax: (612)827-9343
URL: http://www.cctwincities.org/hope_street.aspx
Program(s): Basic Center Program; Transitional Living Program; Street Outreach Program.

36517 ■ Evergreen House
Runaway and Homeless Youth Program
PO Box 662
Bemidji, MN 56619
Ph: (218)751-8223
Fax: (218)751-8070
URL: http://www.evergreenhouse.org/
Rebecca Scheuller, Director
Program(s): Transitional Living Program.

36518 ■ Face to Face Health and Counseling Services
Runaway and Homeless Youth Program
1165 Arcade St.
Saint Paul, MN 55106
Ph: (651)772-5555
Fax: (651)772-5566
E-mail: admin@face2face.org
URL: http://www.face2face.org/
Mary Planton-Krell, Executive Director

36519 ■ Freeport West, Inc.
Project Solo
Runaway and Homeless Youth Program
2222 Park Ave.
Minneapolis, MN 55404
Ph: (612)824-3040
Fax: (612)824-0379
URL: http://www.freeportwest.org/
Repa Mekha, Director
Program(s): Basic Center Program; Street Outreach Program. **Formerly:** Freeport West, Inc.

36520 ■ Greater Minneapolis Council of Churches
Runaway and Homeless Youth Program
1001 E Lake St.
Minneapolis, MN 55407
Ph: (612)721-8687
Fax: (612)276-1534
URL: http://www.gmcc.org/
Program(s): Transitional Living Program; Maternity Group Home.

36521 ■ Lower Sioux Community Center
Runaway and Homeless Youth Program
39527 Res. Hwy. 1
Morton, MN 56270
Ph: (507)697-6185
Fax: (507)697-8617
E-mail: gprescott@lowersioux.com
URL: http://www.lowersioux.com/
Gabe Prescott, President
Program(s): Basic Center Program.

36522 ■ Lutheran Social Services
Bethany Crisis Shelter
Runaway and Homeless Youth Program
2485 Como Ave.
Saint Paul, MN 55108
Ph: (541)642-5990
Free: 800-582-5260
URL: http://www.lssmn.org/
Program(s): Basic Center Program; Street Outreach Program.

36523 ■ Lutheran Social Services
Runaway and Homeless Youth Program
551 Birch Dr. S
Baxter, MN 56425
Ph: (218)828-4383
URL: http://www.lssmn.org/
Program(s): Transitional Living Program.

36524 ■ Youth Link
Runaway and Homeless Youth Program
41 N 12th St.
Minneapolis, MN 55403
Ph: (612)252-1200
URL: http://www.youthlinkmn.org
Heather Huseby, Executive Director
Program(s): Street Outreach Program.

MISSISSIPPI

36525 ■ Catholic Charities, Jackson
Runaway and Homeless Youth Program
200 N Congress, Ste. 100
Jackson, MS 39201
Ph: (601)355-8634
Fax: (601)960-8493
URL: http://www.catholiccharitiesjackson.org/
Linda Raff, Director
Program(s): Basic Center Program. **Remarks:** Provides emergency shelter for youth ages 12-17. Provides clothing and personal hygiene supplies.

36526 ■ Mississippi Children's Home Society
Runaway and Homeless Youth Program
1900 N West St., Ste. A
Jackson, MS 39212
Ph: (601)352-7784
Free: 800-388-6247
Fax: (601)968-0028
E-mail: info@mchscares.org
URL: http://www.mchscares.org
Christopher Cherney, Chief Executive Officer
Program(s): Basic Center Program. **Remarks:** Operates the Powers Group Home for adolescent girls, Rowland Home for adolescent boys. **Formerly:** Mississippi Children's Home Society and Family Services Association.

36527 ■ Mississippi Children's Home/Warren County Children's Shelter
Runaway and Homeless Youth Program
PO Box 820174
Vicksburg, MS 39182
Ph: (601)634-0640
Free: 866-969-4079
Fax: (601)969-6433
E-mail: admissions@mchscares.org
URL: http://www.mchscares.org/
Peggy Thomas, Director
Program(s): Basic Center Program.

36528 ■ Southern Christian Services
Runaway and Homeless Youth Program
PO Box 5235
Jackson, MS 39202
Ph: (601)354-0983
Fax: (601)352-8638
E-mail: scscyinfo@bellsouth.net
URL: http://www.scscy.org/
Susannah Cherney, Director
Program(s): Transitional Living Program.

MISSOURI

36529 ■ Boys and Girls Town of Missouri Columbia Center
Runaway and Homeless Youth Program
4304 Bearfield Rd.
Columbia, MO 65205
Ph: (573)874-8686
Fax: (573)874-8608
E-mail: admission@great-circle.org
URL: http://www.bgtm.org
Program(s): Basic Center Program; Transitional Living Program; Street Outreach Program.

36530 ■ Boys and Girls Town of Missouri Edgewood Children's Center
Runaway and Homeless Youth Program
330 N Gore Ave.
Saint Louis, MO 63119
Ph: (314)968-2060
Fax: (314)968-8308
E-mail: admission@great-circle.org
URL: http://www.bgtm.org
Program(s): Basic Center Program; Transitional Living Program; Street Outreach Program.

36531 ■ Boys and Girls Town of Missouri Great Circle
Runaway and Homeless Youth Program
4485 Westminster Pl.
Saint Louis, MO 63108
Ph: (314)535-7911
Fax: (314)535-6632
E-mail: admission@great-circle.org
URL: http://www.bgtm.org
Program(s): Basic Center Program; Transitional Living Program; Street Outreach Program.

36532 ■ Boys and Girls Town of Missouri
Runaway and Homeless Youth Program
13160 County Rd. 3610
Saint James, MO 65559
Ph: (573)265-3251
Fax: (573)265-5370
E-mail: admissions@great-circle.org
URL: http://www.bgtm.org/
Vince Hillyer, President
Program(s): Basic Center Program.

36533 ■ Boys and Girls Town of Missouri Springfield Center
Runaway and Homeless Youth Program
1212 W Lombard
Springfield, MO 65806
Ph: (417)865-1646
Fax: (417)866-1483
E-mail: admission@great-circle.org
URL: http://www.bgtm.org
Program(s): Basic Center Program; Transitional Living Program; Street Outreach Program.

36534 ■ Covenant House Community Services Center
Runaway and Homeless Youth Program
2727 N Kingshighway Blvd.
Saint Louis, MO 63113
Ph: (314)533-2241
Fax: (314)772-4996
URL: http://www.covenanthousemo.org/
Tammie Crumble-Belk, Director
Program(s): Basic Center Program.

36535 ■ Covenant House Missouri
Runaway and Homeless Youth Program
11 S Newstead Ave.
Saint Louis, MO 63108-2213
Ph: (314)450-7661
Free: 800-999-9999
Fax: (314)533-2215
URL: http://www.covenanthousemo.org/
Suzanne Wagener, Executive Director
Program(s): Transitional Living Program.

36536 ■ Epworth Children and Family Services
Runaway and Homeless Youth Program
110 N Elm Ave.
Saint Louis, MO 63119
Ph: (314)961-5718
Fax: (314)961-3503
E-mail: admissions@epworth.org
URL: http://www.epworth.org/
Kevin Drollinger, Director
Program(s): Basic Center Program; Transitional Living Program.

36537 ■ Evangelical Children's Home/Stepping Stones
Runaway and Homeless Youth Program
5100 Noland Rd.
Kansas City, MO 64133
Ph: (816)356-0187
URL: http://everychildshope.org/
Program(s): Transitional Living Program.

36538 ■ Faith House/Dream House
Runaway and Homeless Youth Program
5355 Page St.
Saint Louis, MO 63112
Ph: (314)367-5400
Fax: (314)367-3101
E-mail: mjamison@faithvillage.org
URL: http://www.faithvillage.org
Mildred Jamison, Director
Program(s): Transitional Living Program.

36539 ■ The Kitchen, Inc.
Runaway and Homeless Youth Program
1630 N Jefferson Ave.
Springfield, MO 65803

Ph: (417)837-1500
Fax: (417)831-6709
E-mail: rarebreed@thekitcheninc.org
URL: http://www.thekitcheninc.org/
Bill Stainaker, Director
Program(s): Transitional Living Program.

36540 ■ Marian Hall Emergency Shelter
Runaway and Homeless Youth Program
1340 Partridge Ave.
Saint Louis, MO 63130
Ph: (314)531-7233
Program(s): Basic Center Program; Transitional Living Program. **Remarks:** Provides emergency shelter.

36541 ■ Rainbow House Columbia
Runaway and Homeless Youth Program
1611 Towne Dr.
Columbia, MO 65203
Ph: (573)474-6600
Fax: (573)474-5992
E-mail: jstock@rainbowhousecolumbia.org
URL: http://www.rainbowhousecolumbia.org
Jan Stock, Executive Director
Program(s): Transitional Living Program.

36542 ■ reStart, Inc.
Runaway and Homeless Youth Program
918 E 9th St.
Kansas City, MO 64106
Ph: (816)472-5664
Fax: (816)472-6127
URL: http://www.restartinc.org/
Evelyn Craig, Executive Director
Program(s): Transitional Living Program.

36543 ■ Synergy Services
Runaway and Homeless Youth Program
400 E 6th St.
Parkville, MO 64152
Ph: (816)587-4100
Free: 800-491-1114
Fax: (816)587-6691
E-mail: info@synergyservices.org
URL: http://www.synergyservices.org
Robin Winner, Executive Director
Program(s): Basic Center Program; Transitional Living Program; Street Outreach Program. **Remarks:** Provides emergency shelter. Services are provided on a sliding scale fee basis.

36544 ■ Youth in Need, Inc.
Runaway and Homeless Youth Program
1815 Boone's Lick Rd.
Saint Charles, MO 63301
Ph: (636)946-5600
Fax: (636)925-0116
URL: http://www.youthinneed.org
Program(s): Basic Center Program; Transitional Living Program; Street Outreach Program. **Formerly:** Youth in Need Services.

MONTANA

36545 ■ HRDC District 7
Runaway and Homeless Youth Program
7 N 31st St.
Billings, MT 59103
Ph: (406)247-4700
URL: http://hrdc7.truebroadcast.com/
Program(s): Transitional Living Program.

36546 ■ Human Resources Development Council, District IX
Runaway and Homeless Youth Program
32 S Tracy
Bozeman, MT 59715
Ph: (406)587-4486
Free: 800-289-0896
Fax: (406)585-3538
E-mail: hello@thehrdc.org
URL: http://www.thehrdc.org/
Jeffrey Rupp, Chief Executive Officer
Program(s): Transitional Living Program.

36547 ■ Tumbleweed Runaway
Runaway and Homeless Youth Program
505 N 24th St.
Billings, MT 59101
Ph: (406)259-2558
Free: 888-816-4702
URL: http://www.tumbleweedprogram.org/
Sally Leep, Director
Program(s): Basic Center Program; Transitional Living Program; Street Outreach Program.

NEBRASKA

36548 ■ Boys Town Home Campus
Runaway and Homeless Youth Program
14100 Crawford St.
Boys Town, NE 68010
Ph: (402)498-1300
Free: 800-448-1111
Fax: (402)498-1348
E-mail: admissions@boystown.org
URL: http://www.boystown.org/nebraska-iowa
Robert Pick, Executive Director
Program(s): Basic Center Program.

36549 ■ Cedars Youth Service
Runaway and Homeless Youth Program
6601 Pioneers Blvd., Ste. 1
Lincoln, NE 68506
Ph: (402)434-5437
Fax: (402)437-8833
E-mail: info@cedars-kids.org
URL: http://www.cedars-kids.org
James Blue, President
Program(s): Basic Center Program; Transitional Living Program; Maternity Group Home; System Support for Rural Homeless Youth. **Remarks:** Provides emergency shelter. Fees based on family income.

36550 ■ Panhandle Community Services
Runaway and Homeless Youth Program
975 Crescent Dr.
Gering, NE 69341
Ph: (308)635-3089
Fax: (308)635-0264
URL: http://www.capwn.org
Brent Anderson, Director
Program(s): Basic Center Program; Transitional Living Program; Maternity Group Home. **Remarks:** Provides emergency shelter.

36551 ■ Youth Emergency Services, Omaha
Runaway and Homeless Youth Program
2679 Farnam St., Ste. 205
Omaha, NE 68131
Ph: (402)345-5187
E-mail: info@yesomaha.org
URL: http://www.yesomaha.org/
Robert Storey, Executive Director
Program(s): Basic Center Program; Transitional Living Program; Maternity Group Home.

NEVADA

36552 ■ Boys Town Nevada Assessment and Short-Term Residential Program
Runaway and Homeless Youth Program
821 N Mojave Rd.
Las Vegas, NV 89101
Ph: (702)642-7070
Fax: (702)649-3906
E-mail: singerc@boystown.org
URL: http://www.boystown.org/nevada
Chris Singer, Director
Program(s): Basic Center Program.

36553 ■ Children's Cabinet, Inc.
Runaway and Homeless Youth Program
1090 S Rock Blvd.
Reno, NV 89502
Ph: (775)856-6200
Fax: (775)856-6208
E-mail: mail@childrenscabinet.org
URL: http://www.childrenscabinet.org/
Program(s): Basic Center Program.

36554 ■ WestCare Foundation
Runaway and Homeless Youth Program
900 Grier Dr.
Las Vegas, NV 89119
Ph: (702)385-2090
E-mail: westcare@westcare.com
URL: http://www.westcare.com
Program(s): Transitional Living Program; Maternity Group Home.

36555 ■ WestCare, Inc.
Runaway and Homeless Youth Program
5659 Duncan Dr.
Las Vegas, NV 89130
Ph: (702)385-2020
Fax: (702)658-0480
E-mail: westcare@westcare.com
URL: http://www.westcare.com/slnevada.jsp
Richard Steinburg, President
Program(s): Basic Center Program; Street Outreach Program.

NEW HAMPSHIRE

36556 ■ Child and Family Services of New Hampshire
Runaway and Homeless Youth Program
464 Chestnut St.
Manchester, NH 03105
Ph: (603)518-4000
Free: 800-640-6486
Fax: (603)668-6260
E-mail: info@cfsnh.org
URL: http://www.cfsnh.org/
Michael Osterowski, President
Program(s): Transitional Living Program; Street Outreach Program.

NEW JERSEY

36557 ■ Anchor House
Runaway and Homeless Youth Services
482 Centre St.
Trenton, NJ 08611
Ph: (609)396-8329
Fax: (609)396-1239
E-mail: info@anchorhousenj.org
URL: http://www.anchorhousenj.org
Brian Rottkamp, Executive Director
Program(s): Street Outreach Program.

36558 ■ Atlantic County Division of Intergenerational Youth Shelter
Runaway and Homeless Youth Shelter
201 S Shore Rd.
Northfield, NJ 08225
Ph: (609)645-7700
Fax: (609)645-5847
URL: http://www.aclink.org
Program(s): Basic Center Program; Transitional Living Program. **Formerly:** Atlantic County Division of Intergenerational Services.

36559 ■ Center for Family Services
Runaway and Homeless Youth Program
584 Benson St.
Camden, NJ 08103
Ph: (856)964-1990
Fax: (856)964-0242
E-mail: access@centerffs.org
URL: http://www.centerffs.org/
Merilee Rutolo, Vice Pres.
Program(s): Basic Center Program; Transitional Living Program; Street Outreach Program.

36560 ■ Community Access Unlimited
Runaway and Homeless Youth Program
80 W Grand St.
Elizabeth, NJ 07202

Ph: (908)354-3040
Fax: (908)354-2665
URL: http://www.caunj.org
Program(s): Basic Center Program; Transitional Living Program.

36561 ■ Covenant House New Jersey Rights of Passage Program
Runaway and Homeless Youth Program
929 Atlantic Ave.
Atlantic City, NJ 08401
Ph: (609)348-4070
Fax: (609)348-1122
E-mail: chnj@covenanthouse.org
URL: http://www.covenanthousenj.org/
Jill Rottmann, Executive Director
Program(s): Transitional Living Program; Street Outreach Program.

36562 ■ Covenant House New Jersey
Runaway and Homeless Youth Program
330 Washington St.
Newark, NJ 07102
Ph: (973)621-8705
Fax: (973)286-0190
E-mail: chnj@covenanthouse.org
URL: http://www.covenanthousenj.org/
Jill Rottmann, Executive Director

36563 ■ Crossroads
Runaway and Homeless Youth Services
610 Beverly-Rancocas Rd.
Willingboro, NJ 08046
Ph: (609)880-0210
Fax: (609)880-0230
E-mail: julie@crossroadsprograms.org
URL: http://www.crossroadsprograms.org/
Cheryl Conway, Chief Executive Officer
Program(s): Basic Center Program.

36564 ■ New Community Corporation
Runaway and Homeless Youth Program
233 W Market St.
Newark, NJ 07103
Ph: (973)623-2800
URL: http://www2.newcommunity.org/
Program(s): Transitional Living Program; Maternity Group Home.

36565 ■ Ocean's Harbor House
Runaway and Homeless Youth Program
2445 Windsor Ave.
Toms River, NJ 08754
Ph: (732)929-0660
Fax: (732)929-3094
URL: http://www.oceansharborhouse.org/
Linda Gyimoty, Executive Director
Program(s): Basic Center Program; Transitional Living Program; Street Outreach Program.

36566 ■ Somerset Home for Temporarily Displaced Children
Runaway and Homeless Youth Program
49 Brahma Ave.
Bridgewater, NJ 08807
Ph: (908)526-6605
Fax: (908)526-4433
URL: http://www.somersethome.org
Jeffrey Fetzko, Executive Director
Program(s): Basic Center Program; Street Transitional Living Program; Outreach Program. **Formerly:** Somerset Youth Shelter.

36567 ■ Tri-County Youth Services, Paterson
Runaway and Homeless Youth Program
435 Main St.
Paterson, NJ 07501
Ph: (973)881-0280
Fax: (973)881-0126
E-mail: admin@fatherenglish.org
URL: http://www.fatherenglish.org
Program(s): Basic Center Program.

NEW MEXICO

36568 ■ The Dream Tree Project
Runaway and Homeless Youth Program
128 La Posta Rd.
Taos, NM 87571
Ph: (505)758-9595
Fax: (505)758-2045
E-mail: dtp@laplaza.org
URL: http://www.dreamtreeproject.org/
Barbara Jones, President
Program(s): Basic Center Program; Transitional Living Program.

36569 ■ Families and Youth, Inc.
Runaway and Homeless Youth Program
1320 S Solano
Las Cruces, NM 88001
Ph: (505)522-4004
Fax: (505)522-9017
E-mail: omorales@fyinm.org
URL: http://www.fyinm.org/
Jose Frietz, Director
Program(s): Basic Center Program; Transitional Living Program

36570 ■ Newday Youth and Family Services Safe Home
Runaway and Homeless Youth Program
2820 Ridgecrest SE
Albuquerque, NM 87108
Ph: (505)938-1060
Fax: (505)938-1064
E-mail: sjohnson@ndnm.org
URL: http://www.ndnm.org
Program(s): Basic Center Program; Transitional Living Program; Street Outreach Program.

36571 ■ Youth Development, Albuquerque
Runaway and Homeless Youth Program
6301 Central NW
Albuquerque, NM 87105
Ph: (505)352-3440
Fax: (505)352-3400
E-mail: pit@ydinm.org
URL: http://www.ydinm.org/
Program(s): Basic Center Program; Transitional Living Program.

36572 ■ Youth Shelters and Family Services, Santa Fe
Runaway and Homeless Youth Program
5686 Agua Fria
Santa Fe, NM 87592
Ph: (505)983-0586
Fax: (505)424-0949
E-mail: info@youthshelters.org
URL: http://www.youthshelters.org/
Mary Stelletello, Executive Director
Program(s): Basic Center Program; Transitional Living Program; Street Outreach Program.

NEW YORK

36573 ■ Berkshire Farm Center and Services for Youth
Runaway and Homeless Youth Program
13640 Rte. 22
Canaan, NY 12029
Ph: (518)781-4567
Fax: (518)781-4577
E-mail: info@berkshirefarm.org
URL: http://www.berkshirefarm.org/
Rose W. Washington, Director
Program(s): Basic Center Program; Transitional Living Program.

36574 ■ Boys Town New York Assessment and Short-Term Residential Program
Runaway and Homeless Youth Program
444 Park Ave. S, Ste. 801
New York, NY 10016
Ph: (212)725-4260
Fax: (212)725-4385
URL: http://www.boystown.org/new-york
Program(s): Basic Center Program.

36575 ■ Captain of Shenendehow, Inc.
Runaway and Homeless Youth Program
5 Municipal Plz., Ste. 3
Clifton Park, NY 12065
Ph: (518)371-1185
Free: 877-627-TALK
Fax: (518)383-7997
URL: http://www.captainyfs.org
Bill Casey, Executive Director
Program(s): Basic Center Program; Street Outreach Program.

36576 ■ Catholic Charities of the Diocese of Albany
Runaway and Homeless Youth Program
40 N Main Ave.
Albany, NY 12203
Ph: (518)453-6650
Fax: (518)453-6792
E-mail: Catholic.Charities@rcda.org
URL: http://www.ccrcda.org
Program(s): Basic Center Program.

36577 ■ The Center for Youth Services
Runaway and Homeless Youth Program
905 Monroe Ave.
Rochester, NY 14620
Ph: (585)473-2464
Free: 888-617-KIDS
URL: http://www.centerforyouth.net
Elaine Spaull, Director
Program(s): Basic Center Program; Transitional Living Program.

36578 ■ Chautauqua Opportunities
Runaway and Homeless Youth Program
17 W Courtney St.
Dunkirk, NY 14048
Ph: (716)366-3333
Fax: (716)366-7366
URL: http://www.chautauquaopportunities.com
William Vogt, Director
Program(s): Basic Center Program; Transitional Living Program; Street Outreach Program.

36579 ■ The Children's Village, Inc.
Dobbs Ferry, NY 10522
Ph: (914)693-0600
URL: http://www.childrensvillage.org
Jeremy Kohomban, President
Program(s): Transitional Living Program.

36580 ■ Compass House
Runaway and Homeless Youth Program
370 Linwood Ave.
Buffalo, NY 14209
Ph: (716)886-0935
Fax: (716)886-8386
E-mail: sylviahnadler@oradrunner.com
URL: http://www.compasshouse.org
Sylvia Nadler, Executive Director
Program(s): Basic Center Program. **Remarks:** Provides short-term emergency shelter and non-residential resource center. All services are free.

36581 ■ Covenant House New York/Bronx Resource Center
Runaway and Homeless Youth Program
81C Featherbed Ln.
Bronx, NY 10452
Ph: (718)294-7812
Fax: (718)294-4550
URL: http://www.covenanthouseny.org/services_programs.asp
Program(s): Basic Center Program; Transitional Living Program; Street Outreach Program.

36582 ■ Covenant House New York/Brooklyn Resource Center
Runaway and Homeless Youth Program
75 Lewis Ave.
Brooklyn, NY 11206
Ph: (718)452-6730
URL: http://www.covenanthouseny.org/services_programs.asp
Program(s): Basic Center Program; Street Outreach Program; Transitional Living Program.

36583 ■ Covenant House New York/Queens Resource Center
Runaway and Homeless Youth Program
159-17 Hillside Ave.
Queens, NY 11432
Ph: (718)725-9851
Fax: (718)725-9856
URL: http://www.covenanthouseny.org/services_programs.asp
Sharon Greer-Mboulou, Director
Program(s): Basic Center Program; Transitional Living Program; Street Outreach Program.

36584 ■ Covenant House of New York
Runaway and Homeless Youth Program
460 W 41st St.
New York, NY 10036
Ph: (212)613-0300
URL: http://www.covenanthouseny.org
Bruce J. Henry, Executive Director
Program(s): Basic Center Program; Transitional Living Program; Street Outreach Program.

36585 ■ Covenant House New York/Staten Island Resource Center
Runaway and Homeless Youth Program
70 Bay St.
Staten Island, NY 10301
Ph: (718)876-9810
Free: 800-999-9999
Fax: (718)876-5338
URL: http://www.covenanthouseny.org/services_programs.asp
Program(s): Basic Center Program; Transitional Living Program; Street Outreach Program.

36586 ■ Diaspora Community Services
Runaway and Homeless Youth Program
182 4th Ave.
Brooklyn, NY 11217
Ph: (718)399-0200
Fax: (718)399-0360
E-mail: info@diasporacs.org
URL: http://www.diasporacs.org
Program(s): Transitional Living Program; Maternity Group Home.

36587 ■ The Door
Runaway and Homeless Youth Program
121 Ave. of the Americas
New York, NY 10013
Ph: (212)941-9090
E-mail: info@door.org
URL: http://www.door.org
Program(s): Street Outreach Program.

36588 ■ Emergency Housing Group
Runaway and Homeless Youth Program
38 Seward Ave., Bldg. 14.
Middletown, NY 10940
Ph: (845)343-0970
Fax: (845)343-1831
URL: http://www.emergencyhousinggroup.org/AFriendsHouse.htm
John Harper, Director
Program(s): Basic Center Program.

36589 ■ Equinox
Runaway and Homeless Youth Services
95 Central Ave.
Albany, NY 12206
Ph: (518)434-6135
Fax: (518)434-4502
URL: http://www.equinoxinc.org
Mary Seeley, Executive Director
Program(s): Basic Center Program; Transitional Living Program; Street Outreach Program.

36590 ■ Family and Children's Association, Mineola
Runaway and Homeless Youth Program
100 E Old Country Rd.
Mineola, NY 11501
Ph: (516)746-0350
Fax: (516)294-0198
E-mail: info@familyandchildrens.org
URL: http://www.familyandchildrens.org
Richard P. Dina, President
Program(s): Transitional Living Program.

36591 ■ Family and Children's Service of Niagara
Runaway and Homeless Youth Program
1522 Main St.
Niagara Falls, NY 14305
Ph: (716)285-6984
Fax: (716)285-0831
URL: http://www.niagarafamily.org/
Kim Proch, Director
Program(s): Basic Center Program.

36592 ■ Family of Woodstock
Runaway and Homeless Youth Program
39 John St.
Kingston, NY 12402
Ph: (845)331-7080
Fax: (845)331-0526
E-mail: info@familyofwoodstockinc.org
URL: http://www.familyofwoodstockinc.org/
Carol Ricken, Secretary
Program(s): Basic Center Program; Transitional Living Program; Street Outreach Program.

36593 ■ Green Chimneys Children's Services
Runaway and Homeless Youth Program
400 Doansburg Rd.
Caller Box 719
Brewster, NY 10509
Ph: (845)279-2995
Fax: (845)279-3077
URL: http://www.greenchimneys.org/
Joseph Whalen, Executive Director
Program(s): Basic Center Program; Transitional Living Program; Street Outreach Program. **Formerly:** Green Chimneys Children's Services Arbor House.

36594 ■ Hillside Children's Center
Runaway and Homeless Youth Services
1183 Monroe Ave.
Rochester, NY 14620
Ph: (585)256-7500
E-mail: info@hillside.com
URL: http://www.hillside.com/
Dennis Richardson, President
Program(s): Transitional Living Program.

36595 ■ Hudson River Housing, Inc.
Runaway and Homeless Youth Program
313 Mill St.
Poughkeepsie, NY 12601
Ph: (845)454-5176
Fax: (845)485-1641
E-mail: gwebster@hudsonriverhousing.org
URL: http://www.hudsonriverhousing.org/
Gail V. Webster, Director
Program(s): Basic Center Program; Transitional Living Program.

36596 ■ Huntington Youth Bureau Sanctuary
Runaway and Homeless Youth Program
423 Park Ave.
Huntington, NY 11743
Ph: (631)351-3061
Fax: (631)271-1360
E-mail: hybydri@optonline.net
URL: http://www.hybydri.org/
Maria Georgiou, Executive Director
Program(s): Basic Center Program; Transitional Living Program; Street Outreach Program. **Formerly:** Town of Huntington Youth Bureau.

36597 ■ Learning Web
Runaway and Homeless Youth Program
515 W Seneca St.
Ithaca, NY 14850
Ph: (607)275-0122
Fax: (607)275-0312
E-mail: info@learning-web.org
URL: http://www.learning-web.org
Program(s): Transitional Living Program.

36598 ■ Long Island Crisis Center
Runaway and Homeless Youth Program
2740 Martin Ave.
Bellmore, NY 11710
Ph: (516)826-0244
Fax: (516)781-8306
URL: http://www.longislandcrisiscenter.org
Linda Leonard, Director
Program(s): Street Outreach Program.

36599 ■ Lower East Side Drop-In Center
Runaway and Homeless Youth Program
25 Allen St.
New York, NY 10002
Ph: (212)226-6333
URL: http://www.leshrc.org
Program(s): Basic Center Program; Street Outreach Program.

36600 ■ Mercy Residential Services
Runaway and Homeless Youth Program
198 Oriole St.
Rochester, NY 14613
Ph: (585)254-2175
Fax: (585)254-2229
URL: http://www.mercyresidential.org
Program(s): Basic Center Program; Street Outreach Program; Transitional Living Program; Maternity Group Home.

36601 ■ Mowhawk Valley Community Action Agency
Runaway and Homeless Youth Program
1721 Black River Rd.
Rome, NY 13440
Ph: (315)336-0749
Fax: (315)339-2981
E-mail: info@mvcaa.com
URL: http://www.mvcaa.com/
Amy Turner, Executive Director
Program(s): Basic Center Program; Transitional Living Program.

36602 ■ Oswego County Opportunities
Runaway and Homeless Youth Program
239 Oneida St.
Fulton, NY 13069
Ph: (315)598-4717
Fax: (315)592-7533
E-mail: youthservices@oco.org
URL: http://www.oco.org
Program(s): Transitional Living Program.

36603 ■ Safe Horizon
Runaway and Homeless Youth Program
33 Essex St.
New York, NY 10007
Ph: (646)602-6404
Free: 800-621-4673
E-mail: help@safehorizon.org
URL: http://www.safehorizon.org
Program(s): Basic Center Program.

36604 ■ SAFE Inc. of Schenectady
Runaway and Homeless Youth Program
1344 Albany St.
Schenectady, NY 12304
Ph: (518)374-0166
E-mail: safeinc@nycap.rr.com
URL: http://safeincofschenectady.org/
Program(s): Basic Center Program. **Formerly:** Schenectady Inner City Ministry.

36605 ■ Saint Agatha Home
Runaway and Homeless Youth Program
135 Convent Rd.
Nanuet, NY 10954
Ph: (845)623-3462
URL: http://www.stagathahome.org
Program(s): Basic Center Program.

36606 ■ The Salvation Army, Rochester NY Genesis House
Runaway and Homeless Youth Program
10 Franklin St.
Rochester, NY 14604
Ph: (585)987-9500
Fax: (585)987-9599
E-mail: ras.admin@use.salvationarmy.org
URL: http://www.rochestersalvationarmy.org/
Ron Provenzan, Director
Program(s): Basic Center Program.

36607 ■ The Salvation Army, Syracuse NY
Runaway and Homeless Youth Program
677 S Salina St.
Syracuse, NY 13202
Ph: (315)475-1688
Fax: (315)475-6307
URL: http://www.sasyr.org/
Linda Wright, Executive Director
Program(s): Basic Center Program; Transitional Living Program.

36608 ■ Streetwork Harlem Drop-In Center
Runaway and Homeless Youth Program
209 W 125th St.
New York, NY 10027
Ph: (212)695-2220
URL: http://www.safehorizon.org/
Program(s): Basic Center Program; Street Outreach Program; Transitional Living Program.

36609 ■ Volunteers of America - Greater New York
Runaway and Homeless Youth Program
340 W 85th St.
New York, NY 10024
Ph: (212)873-2600
E-mail: rweinstein@voa-gny.org
URL: http://www.voa-gny.org/
Program(s): Street Outreach Program.

36610 ■ Westchester Youth Services/Children's Village
Runaway and Homeless Youth Program
Echo Hills
Dobbs Ferry, NY 10522
Ph: (914)693-0600
URL: http://www.childrensvillage.org/youth.html
Program(s): Basic Center Program; Transitional Living Program; Street Outreach Program.

36611 ■ Westhab, Inc.
Runaway and Homeless Youth Program
85 Executive Blvd.
Elmsford, NY 10523
Ph: (914)345-2800
Fax: (914)345-3139
E-mail: mail@wethab.org
URL: http://www.westhab.org/
Program(s): Transitional Living Program.

NORTH CAROLINA

36612 ■ Alexander Youth Network, Charlotte
Runaway and Homeless Youth Services
6220 Thermal Rd.
Charlotte, NC 28211
Ph: (704)336-8712
Fax: (704)362-8464
E-mail: info@alexanderyouthnetwork.org
URL: http://www.alexanderyouthnetwork.org/
Dave Hoppe, Executive Director
Program(s): Basic Center Program. **Formerly:** The Relatives; Youth Network, Charlotte.

36613 ■ Born2Win Ministries
Runaway and Homeless Youth Program
308 Pennsylvania Ave.
Greenville, NC 27834
Ph: (252)752-3987
Program(s): Basic Center Program.

36614 ■ Caring for Children Trinity Place
Runaway and Homeless Youth Program
50 Roddick Rd.
Asheville, NC 28815
Ph: (828)298-0186
Fax: (828)298-4870
E-mail: info@caring4children.org
URL: http://www.caring4children.org/
John Lautherbach, Executive Director
Program(s): Basic Center Program; Transitional Living Program. **Formerly:** Buncombe Shelter, Inc.

36615 ■ Catholic Social Services Diocese of Charlotte
Runaway and Homeless Youth Program
1123 S Church St.
Charlotte, NC 28203
Ph: (704)370-3262
Fax: (704)370-3377
E-mail: mmsheppard@charlottediocese.org
URL: http://www.cssnc.org
Program(s): Basic Center Program.

36616 ■ The Children's Home
Runaway and Homeless Youth Program
1001 Reynolda Rd.
Winston Salem, NC 27104
Ph: (336)721-7625
E-mail: npearman@tchome.org
URL: http://www.tchome.org/
Program(s): Transitional Living Program; Maternity Group Home.

36617 ■ Coastal Horizons Center
Runaway and Homeless Youth Program
Willie Stargell Office Park
615 Shipyard Blvd.
Wilmington, NC 28412
Ph: (910)790-0187
Free: 800-672-2903
Fax: (910)790-0189
URL: http://www.coastalhorizons.org
Program(s): Basic Center Program.

36618 ■ Haven House
Runaway and Homeless Youth Program
706 Hillsborough St., Ste. 200
Raleigh, NC 27603
Ph: (919)833-3312
Fax: (919)833-3512
E-mail: jboyler@havenhousenc.org
URL: http://www.havenhousenc.org
Michael Rieder, Executive Director
Program(s): Basic Center Program; Transitional Living Program; Street Outreach Program.

36619 ■ Lee County Youth and Family Services
Runaway and Homeless Youth Program
112 Hillcrest Dr.
Sanford, NC 27331
Ph: (919)718-4650
E-mail: bpotts@leecountync.com
URL: http://leecountync.gov/Departments/YouthFamilyServices.aspx
Program(s): Basic Center Program.

36620 ■ Mountain Youth Resources
Runaway and Homeless Youth Program
PO Box 99
Webster, NC 28788
Ph: (828)586-8958
Free: 866-586-6739
Fax: (828)586-0649
E-mail: info@mountainyouthresources.org
URL: http://www.mountainyouthresources.org/
J. Keith Henry, Executive Director
Program(s): Basic Center Program. **Remarks:** Services are provided at no direct cost to youth or family.

36621 ■ With Friends, Inc.
Runaway and Homeless Youth Program
2098 Keith Dr.
Gastonia, NC 28053
Ph: (704)691-7116
Fax: (704)691-7315
E-mail: info@withfriendsyouthshelter.org
URL: http://www.withfriendsyouthshelter.org/
Patricia Krikorian, Executive Director
Program(s): Basic Center Program; Transitional Living Program; Maternity Group Home.

36622 ■ Youth Focus, Inc.
Runaway and Homeless Youth Program
715 N Eugene St.
Greensboro, NC 27401
Ph: (336)274-5909
Fax: (336)274-3622
E-mail: chodierne@youthfocus.org
URL: http://www.youthfocus.org
Charles Hodierne, Executive Director
Program(s): Basic Center Program; Transitional Living Program.

NORTH DAKOTA

36623 ■ Mountain Plains Network For Youth
Runaway and Homeless Youth Program
410 E Thayer Ave., Ste. 2
Bismarck, ND 58501
Ph: (701)355-0721
Free: 800-665-8682
Fax: (701)255-0848
E-mail: mtnplains@aol.com
URL: http://www.nrcyd.ou.edu/resources/fysb_providers.php
Linda Garding, Executive Director
Program(s): Transitional Living Program; Maternity Group Home.

OHIO

36624 ■ Bellefaire JCB
Runaway and Homeless Youth Program
22001 Fairmount Blvd.
Shaker Heights, OH 44118
Ph: (216)932-2800
Free: 800-879-2522
Fax: (216)932-6704
E-mail: info@bellefairejcb.org
URL: http://www.bellefairejcb.org
Adam G. Jacobs, Director
Program(s): Basic Center Program; Transitional Living Program.

36625 ■ Connecting Point
Runaway and Homeless Youth Program
1212 Cherry St.
Toledo, OH 43608
Ph: (419)243-6326
Fax: (419)321-6802
E-mail: skrieger@connectingpoint.org
URL: http://www.co.lucas.oh.us/facilities.aspx?pagenum=2&RID=7&Page=detail
Program(s): Basic Center Program.

36626 ■ Council on Rural Services Programs
Runaway and Homeless Youth Services
201 RM Davis Pkwy., Ste. B
Piqua, OH 45356
Ph: (937)778-5220
Fax: (937)778-8970
E-mail: info@councilonruralservices.org
URL: http://www.councilonruralservices.org/
Shirley Hathaway, Executive Director
Program(s): Basic Center Program. **Remarks:** Provides emergency shelter.

36627 ■ Daybreak
Runaway and Homeless Youth Program
605 S Patterson Blvd.
Dayton, OH 45402
Ph: (937)395-4600
Fax: (937)395-4610
URL: http://www.daybreakdayton.org/
Linda Kramer, Executive Director
Program(s): Basic Center Program; Transitional Living Program; Street Outreach Program.

36628 ■ Family Service Agency
Runaway and Homeless Youth Program
535 Marmion Ave.
Youngstown, OH 44502
Ph: (330)782-5664
Fax: (330)782-1614
E-mail: info@familyserviceagency.com
URL: http://www.familyserviceagency.com
David Arnold, Chief Executive Officer
Program(s): Transitional Living Program. **Formerly:** Children's and Family Service, Youngstown.

36629 ■ Huckleberry House
Runaway and Homeless Youth Program
1421 Hamlet St.
Columbus, OH 43201
Ph: (614)294-8097
Fax: (614)294-6109
URL: http://www.huckhouse.org/
John Monaghan, President
Program(s): Basic Center Program; Transitional Living Program; Street Outreach Program.

36630 ■ Lighthouse Youth Services
Runaway and Homeless Youth Program
401 E McMillan
Cincinnati, OH 45206
Ph: (513)221-3350
Free: 800-474-4138
Fax: (513)221-3665
E-mail: bmecum@lys.org
URL: http://www.lys.org
Bob Mecum, President
Program(s): Basic Center Program; Transitional Living Program; Street Outreach Program.

36631 ■ Lutheran Metro Ministry
Runaway and Homeless Youth Program
1468 W 25th St.
Cleveland, OH 44113
Ph: (216)696-2715
Fax: (216)696-3317
E-mail: mail@lutheranmetro.org
URL: http://www.lutheranmetro.org
Mark Brauer, Director
Program(s): Basic Center Program.

36632 ■ PAL Mission
Runaway and Homeless Youth Program
PO Box 14
New Philadelphia, OH 44663
Ph: (330)232-9959
E-mail: palmissionstore@gmail.com
URL: http://www.palmission.org/
Jill Miller, Director
Program(s): Transitional Living Program.

36633 ■ Shelter Care, Inc.
Safe Landing Youth Shelter
Runaway and Homeless Youth Program
32 South Ave.
Tallmadge, OH 44278
Ph: (330)630-5600
URL: http://www.sheltercareinc.org
Wesley Fair, Director
Program(s): Basic Center Program; Maternity Group Home.

36634 ■ Sojourners Care Network
Runaway and Homeless Youth Program
605 W Main St.
McArthur, OH 45651
Ph: (740)596-1117
Free: 800-237-5277
Fax: (740)596-7134
E-mail: tlp@sojournerscare.net
URL: http://www.sojournerscare.net/
Richard Games, Executive Director
Program(s): Basic Center Program; Transitional Living Program.

36635 ■ Southern Consortium for Children
Runaway and Homeless Youth Program
20 E Circle Dr., Unit 37026
Athens, OH 45701-0956
Ph: (740)593-8293
Fax: (740)592-4170
URL: http://317board.org/file/scc.html
Steve Trout, Executive Director
Program(s): Basic Center Program. **Remarks:** Due to budgetary reasons, the SCC has been forced to cease operations effective June 30, 2009. The new Web address gives the detailed explanation. **Formerly:** Southern Consortium for Behavioral Healthcare.

36636 ■ Specialized Alternatives for Youth
Runaway and Homeless Youth Program
6465 Frank Ave.
North Canton, OH 44720
Ph: (330)305-1668
Free: 800-787-7239
Fax: (330)305-1696
E-mail: safy@safy.org
URL: http://www.safy.org/
Dru Whitaker, Director
Program(s): Basic Center Program; Transitional Living Program. **Remarks:** Operates Safe Harbor, a runaway and homeless youth shelter. **Formerly:** Specialized Alternatives for Families and Youth.

OKLAHOMA

36637 ■ Cherokee Nation Youth Services
Runaway and Homeless Youth Program
PO Box 948
Tahlequah, OK 74465
Ph: (918)453-5000
Free: 800-256-0671
Fax: (918)458-7655
E-mail: icw@cherokee.org
URL: http://www.cherokee.org/Services/Default.aspx
Linda Vann, Director
Program(s): Basic Center Program; Transitional Living Program. **Remarks:** Provides emergency shelter. Services are free. **Formerly:** Cherokee Nation Youth Shelter.

36638 ■ The Chicsaw Nation
Runaway and Homeless Youth Program
231 Seabrook Rd.
Ada, OK 74820
Ph: (580)310-6620
URL: http://www.chickasaw.net/
Chris Redman, Director
Program(s): Transitional Living Program.

36639 ■ Marie Detty Youth and Family Service Center
Runaway and Homeless Youth Program
317 C Ave.
Lawton, OK 73507
Ph: (580)250-1123
Fax: (580)248-6486
URL: http://www.mariedetty.com
Program(s): Basic Center Program.

36640 ■ Northwest Family Services, Inc.
Runaway and Homeless Youth Program
620 Flynn St.
Alva, OK 73717
Ph: (580)327-2900
Fax: (580)327-1337
URL: http://www.northwestfamily.net/
John Jones, Executive Director
Program(s): Basic Center Program.

36641 ■ Oklahoma Department of Human Services
Runaway and Homeless Youth Program
2400 N Lincoln Blvd.
Oklahoma City, OK 73105
Ph: (405)521-3646
URL: http://okdhs.org
Program(s): Support System for Rural Homeless Youth.

36642 ■ Payne County Youth Services
Runaway and Homeless Youth Program
2224 W 12th St.
Stillwater, OK 74076
Ph: (405)377-1452
Free: 866-377-3380
Fax: (405)377-3499
E-mail: kimberlyc@pcys.org
URL: http://www.pcys.org/
Program(s): Transitional Living Program. **Remarks:** Provides a temporary shelter for youth who are experiencing serious problems at home or in other placements. Services are provided at no cost.

36643 ■ Southwest Youth and Family Services
Runaway and Homeless Youth Program
198 E Almar Dr.
Chickasha, OK 73023
Ph: (405)222-5437
Free: 800-998-1827
URL: http://www.swyouthandfamily.com/
Program(s): Basic Center Program; Transitional Living Program.

36644 ■ Southwestern Youth Services
Runaway and Homeless Youth Program
1313 N Forrest
Altus, OK 73522
Ph: (580)482-2809
Fax: (580)482-2820
E-mail: info@swys.org
URL: http://www.swys.org/
Judie M. Hanes, Director
Program(s): Transitional Living Program.

36645 ■ Youth and Family Services of Canadian County
Runaway and Homeless Youth Program
PO Box 1207
El Reno, OK 73036
Ph: (405)262-6555
Fax: (405)262-6557
E-mail: dab333@wans.net
Program(s): Basic Center Program; Transitional Living Program. **Remarks:** Emergency Youth Shelter.

36646 ■ Youth and Family Services of North Central Oklahoma
Runaway and Homeless Youth Program
605 W Oxford
Enid, OK 73701
Ph: (580)233-7220
Free: 888-720-1204
Fax: (580)237-7550
URL: http://www.yfsenid.org/
Justin Simmons, Executive Director
Program(s): Basic Center Program.

36647 ■ Youth Services for Oklahoma County
Runaway and Homeless Youth Program
201 NE 50th St.
Oklahoma City, OK 73105
Ph: (405)235-7537
Fax: (405)528-5754
E-mail: kids@ysoc.org
URL: http://ysoc3.publishpath.com
Debra G. Forshee, President
Program(s): Basic Center Program.

36648 ■ Youth Services for Stephens County
Runaway and Homeless Youth Program
16 S 7th St.
Duncan, OK 73534
Ph: (580)255-8800
Fax: (580)255-8842
E-mail: ythsvc@sbcglobal.net
Program(s): Basic Center Program. **Remarks:** Operates Children's Shelter.

36649 ■ Youth Services of Tulsa
Runaway and Homeless Youth Program
311 S Madison
Tulsa, OK 74120
Ph: (918)582-0061
Fax: (918)382-3400
E-mail: jwalker@yst.org
URL: http://www.yst.org
James Walker, Executive Director
Program(s): Basic Center Program; Transitional Living Program; Street Outreach Program.

OREGON

36650 ■ The Boys and Girls Aid Society, Portland
Runaway and Homeless Youth Program
018 SW Boundary Ct.
Portland, OR 97239
Ph: (503)222-9661
Free: 877-932-2734
Fax: (503)224-5960
URL: http://boysandgirlsaid.org
Michael Balter, Director
Program(s): Transitional Living Program.

36651 ■ Community Works
Runaway and Homeless Youth Program
201 W Main St., Ste. B
Medford, OR 97501
Ph: (541)779-2393
Fax: (541)779-3317
E-mail: info@community-works.org
URL: http://www.community-works.org
Stephanie Atkinson, Director
Program(s): Transitional Living Program. **Remarks:** Provides emergency shelter. Operates Youth Diagnostic Shelter for boys ages 12-14 and girls ages 10-18.

36652 ■ Integral Youth Services
Runaway and Homeless Youth Program
115 N 10th St.
Klamath Falls, OR 97601
Ph: (541)882-2053
Fax: (541)885-6809
E-mail: iys@iyskfalls.org
URL: http://www.iyskfalls.org
Bruce Beeson, Executive Director
Program(s): Basic Center Program. **Formerly:** Exodus House.

36653 ■ J Bar J Ranch
Runaway and Homeless Youth Program
62895 Hamby Rd.
Bend, OR 97701
Ph: (541)389-1409
Fax: (541)389-9348
E-mail: salvstad@jbarj.org
URL: http://www.jbarj.org/
Stephanie Alstad, Director
Program(s): Basic Center Program.

36654 ■ Janus Youth Programs Inc.
Runaway and Homeless Youth Program
707 NE Couch St.
Portland, OR 97232
Ph: (503)233-6090
Fax: (503)233-6093
E-mail: feedback@janusyouth.org
URL: http://www.janusyouth.org/
Dennis Morrow, Executive Director
Program(s): Transitional Living Program; Street Outreach Program.

36655 ■ Looking Glass Youth Family Services, Inc.
Runaway and Homeless Youth Program
1790 W 11th Ave., Ste. 200
Eugene, OR 97402
Ph: (541)686-2688
Fax: (541)345-7605
E-mail: lisa.gunter@lookingglass.us
URL: http://www.lookingglass.us
Craig Operman, Executive Director
Program(s): Basic Center Program; Transitional Living Program.

36656 ■ Northwest Human Services, Inc. Host Youth & Family Center
Runaway and Homeless Youth Program
681 Center St. NE
Salem, OR 97301
Ph: (503)588-5825
Fax: (503)362-5852
E-mail: info@nwhumanservices.org
URL: http://www.northwesthumanservices.org/
Paul Logan, Executive Director
Program(s): Transitional Living Program; Street Outreach Program.

36657 ■ Outside In
Runaway and Homeless Youth Program
1132 SW 13th Ave.
Portland, OR 97205
Ph: (503)535-3800
Fax: (503)223-6837
E-mail: info@outsidein.org
URL: http://www.outsidein.org/
Kathy Oliver, Executive Director
Program(s): Transitional Living Program.

36658 ■ Yamhill Community Action Partnership
Runaway and Homeless Youth Program
800 NE 2nd St.
Newberg, OR 97128
Ph: (503)472-0457
Free: 800-945-9992
URL: http://www.yamhillcap.org/
Program(s): Basic Center Program; Street Outreach Program. **Formerly:** Community Action Agency of Yamhill County.

36659 ■ Youth Shelter Jacksonstreet
Runaway and Homeless Youth Program
555 NW Jackson Ave.
Corvallis, OR 97339
Ph: (541)223-8844
Fax: (541)754-2405
URL: http://www.jacksonstreet.org
Program(s): Basic Center Program; Transitional Living Program.

PENNSYLVANIA

36660 ■ Baptist Children's Services, Collegeville
Runaway and Homeless Youth Program
57 E Armat St.
Philadelphia, PA 19144
Ph: (215)842-4800
URL: http://www.baptistchildrensservices.org/
Ken Campbell, President
Program(s): Basic Center Program. **Remarks:** Provides emergency shelter.

36661 ■ Catholic Social Services of the Diocese of Scranton
Runaway and Homeless Youth Program
516 Fig St.
Scranton, PA 18505
Ph: (570)207-2283
Fax: (570)207-2206
URL: http://www.cssdioceseofscranton.org
Program(s): Basic Center Program.

36662 ■ Centre County Youth Service - Stormbreak
Runaway and Homeless Youth Program
325 W Aaron Dr.
State College, PA 16801
Ph: (814)237-5731
Fax: (814)237-2228
E-mail: info@ccysb.com
URL: http://www.ccysb.com
Norma Keller, Executive Director
Description: Offers a safe, temporary environment where runaway, homeless, and other troubled youth can get help with individual and family problems. **Program(s):** Basic Center Program; Transitional Living Program; Street Outreach Program. **Remarks:** All services are free. **Formerly:** Centre County Youth Service.

36663 ■ Covenant House Pennsylvania Crisis Center and Outreach
Runaway and Homeless Youth Program
31 E Armat St.
Philadelphia, PA 19144
Ph: (215)951-5411
Free: 888-829-1249
Fax: (215)951-5412
E-mail: development@covenanthousepa.org
URL: http://www.covenanthousepa.org/
Cordella Hill, Executive Director
Program(s): Basic Center Program; Transitional Living Program; Street Outreach Program.

36664 ■ Family & Children's Service, Altoona
Runaway and Homeless Youth Program
2022 Broad Ave.
Altoona, PA 16601
Ph: (814)944-3583
Fax: (814)944-8701
E-mail: info@familyservicesinc.net
URL: http://www.familyservicesinc.net/
Mahlon Fiscel, Director
Program(s): Basic Center Program; Street Outreach Program.

36665 ■ Family Links
Runaway and Homeless Youth Program
2644 Banksville Rd.
Pittsburgh, PA 15216
Ph: (412)343-7166
Free: 866-583-6003
URL: http://www.familylinks.org
Program(s): Transitional Living Program.

36666 ■ Pathways PA
Runaway and Homeless Youth Program
310 Amosland Rd.
Holmes, PA 19043
Ph: (610)543-5022
Fax: (610)543-1549
URL: http://www.pathwayspa.org/
Program(s): Transitional Living Program; Maternity Group Home.

36667 ■ Persad
Runaway and Homeless Youth Program
5150 Penn Ave.
Pittsburgh, PA 15223
Ph: (412)441-9786
Free: 888-873-7723
URL: http://www.persadcenter.org
Program(s): Basic Center Program for LGBTQ Community.

36668 ■ Three Rivers Youth
Runaway and Homeless Youth Services
6117 Broad St.
Pittsburgh, PA 15206
Ph: (412)441-5020
Fax: (412)441-5021
E-mail: Gordon.Hill@threeriversyouth.org
URL: http://www.threeriversyouth.org/
Program(s): Transitional Living Program; Street Outreach Program.

36669 ■ Valley Youth House
8th Avenue Shelter
Runaway and Homeless Youth Program
539 8th Ave.
Bethlehem, PA 18018
Ph: (610)691-1200
Fax: (610)882-1068
URL: http://www.valleyyouthhouse.org
Program(s): Maternity Group Home.

36670 ■ Valley Youth House Committee
Runaway and Homeless Youth Program
827-829 Linden St.
Allentown, PA 18101
Ph: (610)820-0166
Fax: (610)820-5907
URL: http://www.valleyyouthhouse.org
David Gilgoff, President
Program(s): Basic Center Program; Transitional Living Program; Street Outreach Program.

36671 ■ Youth Services Inc.
Runaway and Homeless Youth Program
410 N 34th St.
Philadelphia, PA 19104
Ph: (215)222-3262
Fax: (215)222-2352
E-mail: gbailey@ysiphila.org
URL: http://www.ysiphila.org
Gwendolyn Bailey, Executive Director
Program(s): Basic Center Program; Street Outreach Program.

PUERTO RICO

36672 ■ Centro de Servicios a la Juventud
Runaway and Homeless Youth Program
Box 9368 Cotto Station
Arecibo, PR 00613
Ph: (787)878-6776
Fax: (787)878-6890
E-mail: centrocjs@prtc.net
Nidra Torres-Martinez, Director
Program(s): Transitional Living Program; Street Outreach Program.

36673 ■ Centros Sor Isolina Ferre
Runaway and Homeless Youth Program
PO Box 213
Ponce, PR 00731
Ph: (787)842-0000
Fax: (787)840-5020
URL: http://www.nlci.org/States/puertorico.htm#Centro
Program(s): Basic Center Program.

RHODE ISLAND

36674 ■ Boys Town New England
Runaway and Homeless Youth Program
Bazarsky Campus
58 Flanagan Rd.
Portsmouth, RI 02871
Ph: (401)845-2250
Fax: (401)845-2258
URL: http://www.boystown.org/new-england
Program(s): Basic Center Program.

36675 ■ Stopover Services of Newport County
Runaway and Homeless Youth Program
299 W Main Rd.
Middletown, RI 02842
Ph: (401)848-0758
Fax: (401)848-7435
Keller DiLugia, Executive Director
Program(s): Basic Center Program.

36676 ■ Urban League of Rhode Island
Runaway and Homeless Youth Program
246 Prairie Ave.
Providence, RI 02905
Ph: (401)351-5000
Fax: (401)454-1946
URL: http://www.ulri.org
Dennis Langley, President
Program(s): Basic Center Program; Transitional Living Program.

SOUTH CAROLINA

36677 ■ Charleston Orphan House
Runaway and Homeless Youth Program
5055 Lackawanna Blvd.
North Charleston, SC 29405
Ph: (843)266-5200
Fax: (843)266-5201
E-mail: info@cydc.org
URL: http://www.cydc.org/
Barbara Kelley Duncan, Chief Executive Officer
Program(s): Basic Center Program.

36678 ■ Greenhouse Runaway Shelter
Runaway and Homeless Youth Program
529 N Wise Dr.
Sumter, SC 29153
Ph: (803)775-3311
Fax: (803)934-0691
Program(s): Basic Center Program. **Formerly:** South Carolina Department of Youth Services; Department of Juvenile Justice.

36679 ■ Project Lighthouse
Runaway and Homeless Youth Program
505 9th Ave. N
Myrtle Beach, SC 29582
Ph: (843)626-1446
E-mail: oldzenlunatic@hotmail.com
URL: http://www.seahaveninc.com/lighthouse.html
David Palinski, Director
Program(s): Street Outreach Program.

36680 ■ Sea Haven, Inc.
Runaway and Homeless Youth Program
PO Box 600
North Myrtle Beach, SC 29597
Ph: (843)399-4045
Fax: (843)399-4881
E-mail: cbjack@sccoast.net
URL: http://www.seahaveninc.com/
Christina Jackson, Executive Director
Program(s): Basic Center Program; Transitional Living Program; Street Outreach Program.

36681 ■ Sea Haven, Inc.--Transitional Living
Runaway and Homeless Youth Program
710 C 21st Ave. N
Myrtle Beach, SC 29579
Ph: (843)213-1133
E-mail: seahavenyouth@sc.rr.com
URL: http://www.seahaveninc.com/projectlive.html
Melissa McGrath, Director
Program(s): Basic Center Program; Transitional Living Program.

SOUTH DAKOTA

36682 ■ Lutheran Social Services of South Dakota
Runaway and Homeless Youth Program
705 E 41st St., Ste. 200
Sioux Falls, SD 57105
Ph: (605)357-0100
Free: 800-568-2401
Fax: (605)357-0140
E-mail: info@isssd.org
URL: http://www.lsssd.org
Program(s): Transitional Living Program.

36683 ■ Oglala Sioux Tribe
Runaway and Homeless Youth Program
PO Box 2070
Pine Ridge, SD 57770
Ph: (605)867-5821
URL: http://home.comcast.net/~zebrec
Program(s): Basic Center Program; Transitional Living Program.

36684 ■ Rosebud Sioux Tribe
Indian Child Welfare Office
Runaway and Homeless Youth Program
11 Legron Ave.
Rosebud, SD 57570
Ph: (605)747-2381
Fax: (605)747-2905
URL: http://www.rosebudsiouxtribe-nsn.gov
Program(s): Basic Center Program.

36685 ■ Volunteers of America--Aberdeen SD
Runaway and Homeless Youth Program
112 N Main St.
Aberdeen, SD 57401
Ph: (605)262-1007
URL: http://www.voa-dakotas.org
Program(s): Basic Center Program.

36686 ■ Volunteers of America, Dakotas
Runaway and Homeless Youth Program
24 E New York St.
Rapid City, SD 57701
Ph: (605)341-8336
Free: 800-365-8336
URL: http://www.voa-dakotas.org/
Program(s): Basic Center Program; Transitional Living Program; Street Outreach Program.

36687 ■ Volunteers of America--Sioux Falls, SD
Street Outreach Services
Runaway and Homeless Youth Program
430 W 11th St.
Sioux Falls, SD 57109
Ph: (605)334-1414
Free: 800-365-8336
Fax: (605)336-7759
E-mail: j.neilan@voa-dakotas.org
URL: http://www.voa-dakotas.org/
Program(s): Street Outreach Program.

TENNESSEE

36688 ■ Child and Family Services, Knoxville
Runaway and Homeless Youth Program
901 E Summit Hill Dr.
Knoxville, TN 37915
Ph: (865)524-7483
Fax: (865)524-4790
URL: http://www.child-family.org
Kate O'Day, Executive Director
Program(s): Basic Center Program; Transitional Living Program.

36689 ■ Frontier Health
Safeplace Program
Runaway and Homeless Youth Program
1167 Spratlin Park Dr.
Gray, TN 37615
Ph: (423)467-3600
Free: 877-928-9062
Fax: (423)467-3710
URL: http://www.frontierhealth.org/
E. Douglas Varney, President
Program(s): Basic Center Program.

36690 ■ Oasis Center
Runaway and Homeless Youth Program
1704 Charlotte Ave., Ste. 200
Nashville, TN 37203

Ph: (615)327-4455
Fax: (615)329-1444
E-mail: info@oasiscenter.org
URL: http://www.oasiscenter.org/
Hal Cato, Executive Director
Program(s): Basic Center Program; Transitional Living Program; Street Outreach Program. **Remarks:** Provides emergency shelter.

36691 ■ Porter-Leath Children's Center
Runaway and Homeless Youth Program
868 N Manassas St.
Memphis, TN 38107
Ph: (901)577-2500
Fax: (901)577-2506
E-mail: porterleath@porter-leath.org
URL: http://www.porter-leath.org/
Sean M. Lee, President
Program(s): Basic Center Program.

36692 ■ Youth Villages
Runaway and Homeless Youth Program
3320 Brother Blvd.
Memphis, TN 38133
Ph: (901)251-5000
Fax: (901)725-4889
URL: http://www.youthvillages.org/
Program(s): Basic Center Program. **Formerly:** The Family Link.

TEXAS

36693 ■ ACH Child and Family Services
Runaway and Homeless Youth Program
1424 Summit Ave.
Fort Worth, TX 76102
Ph: (817)335-4673
Free: 888-296-8099
Fax: (817)335-4043
E-mail: wcarson@achservices.org
URL: http://www.achservices.org/
Wayne Carson, Chief Executive Officer
Program(s): Basic Center Program. **Formerly:** All Church Home for Children.

36694 ■ Big Springs Ranch for Children
Runaway and Homeless Youth Program
10664 US Hwy. 83 N
Leakey, TX 78873
Ph: (830)232-4121
Fax: (830)232-4256
E-mail: bsinfo@hctc.net
URL: http://www.youth-ranch.org
Program(s): Transitional Living Program.

36695 ■ Boys Town Texas
Runaway and Homeless Youth Program
503 Urban Loop
San Antonio, TX 78204
Ph: (210)271-1010
Fax: (210)271-3333
URL: http://www.boystown.org/texas/
Program(s): Basic Center Program.

36696 ■ Catholic Family Service
Runaway and Homeless Youth Program
102 Ave. J
Lubbock, TX 79401
Ph: (806)765-8475
Fax: (806)763-8630
URL: http://www.cfslubbock.org
Cynthia Quintanilla, Chief Executive Officer
Program(s): Basic Center Program.

36697 ■ Central Texas Youth Services Bureau
Runaway and Homeless Youth Program
PO Box 92
Belton, TX 76513
Ph: (254)939-3466
E-mail: ctysbtx@swbell.net
URL: http://www.centraltexasyouthservices.org
Program(s): Basic Center Program.

36698 ■ Children's Aid Society, Wichita Falls
Runaway and Homeless Youth Program
1101 30th St.
Wichita Falls, TX 76302
Ph: (940)322-3141
Free: 800-821-5762
Fax: (940)322-7672
E-mail: caswf@nts-online.net
URL: http://www.caswf.com
Program(s): Basic Center Program. **Remarks:** Provides emergency shelter. A sliding scale fee determines the cost. No one will be turned away due to inability to pay.

36699 ■ The Children's Center, Galveston Youth Shelter
Runaway and Homeless Youth Program
PO Box 2600
Galveston, TX 77553
Ph: (409)765-5212
Fax: (409)765-6094
E-mail: jamestkeel@thechildrenscenterinc.org
URL: http://www.thechildrenscenterinc.org/
James T. Keel, President
Program(s): Basic Center Program; Transitional Living Program.

36700 ■ Collin Intervention to Youth
Runaway and Homeless Youth Services
902 E 16th St.
Plano, TX 75074
Ph: (972)424-4626
Fax: (972)423-1681
E-mail: lgoodman@cityhouse.org
URL: http://www.cityhouse.org/
Linda Goodman, Director
Beds: 15. **Program(s):** Basic Center Program; Transitional Living Program.

36701 ■ Connections Individual and Family Services
Runaway and Homeless Youth Program
1414 W San Antonio St.
New Braunfels, TX 78131-1268
Ph: (830)629-6571
Fax: (830)608-1262
URL: http://www.connectionsnonprofit.org/
Kelly Stallings, Executive Director
Program(s): Basic Center Program. **Formerly:** Comal County Residential Supervision and Treatment Center.

36702 ■ Covenant House Texas
Runaway and Homeless Youth Program
1111 Lovett Blvd.
Houston, TX 77006
Ph: (713)523-2231
Free: 800-999-9999
Fax: (713)523-6904
URL: http://www.covenanthousetx.org/
Kathy Henderson, Director
Program(s): Basic Center Program; Street Outreach Program.

36703 ■ Crossroads Youth and Family Services
Runaway and Homeless Youth Program
PO Box 436
Victoria, TX 77902
Ph: (361)578-3686
Free: 800-369-7512
Fax: (361)578-6950
E-mail: sh-cyfs@suddenlinkmail.com
URL: http://crossroadsfs.org
Program(s): Basic Center Program; Transitional Living Program.

36704 ■ DePelchin Children's Center
Runaway and Homeless Youth Program
4950 Memorial Dr.
Houston, TX 77007
Ph: (713)730-2335
Free: 888-730-2335
Fax: (713)802-3801
E-mail: info@depelchin.org
URL: http://www.depelchin.org
Program(s): Basic Center Program.

36705 ■ El Paso Center for Children
Runaway and Homeless Youth Services
2200 N Stevens St.
El Paso, TX 79930
Ph: (915)565-8631
Fax: (915)565-0621
E-mail: info@epccinc.org
URL: http://www.epccinc.org
Program(s): Basic Center Program; Transitional Living Program.

36706 ■ George Gervin Youth Center, Inc.
Runaway and Homeless Youth Program
6903 Sunbelt Dr. S
San Antonio, TX 78218
Ph: (210)804-1786
Fax: (210)804-1469
URL: http://www.gervin-school.org/
Barbara Hawkins, Executive Director
Program(s): Basic Center Program; Transitional Living Program.

36707 ■ Harris County Children's Protective Services
Chimney Rock Center
Runaway and Homeless Youth Program
6300 Chimney Rock Rd.
Houston, TX 77081
Ph: (713)295-2500
URL: http://www.hc-ps.org
Program(s): Basic Center Program.

36708 ■ Hill Country Youth Ranch
Runaway and Homeless Youth Program
PO Box 67
Ingram, TX 78025
Ph: (830)367-2131
Fax: (830)367-6108
E-mail: response@youth-ranch.org
URL: http://www.youth-ranch.org
Program(s): Transitional Living Program.

36709 ■ KSTAR, Inc.
Runaway and Homeless Youth Program
PO Box 290962
Kerrville, TX 78029
Ph: (830)896-5437
Free: 800-381-4617
Fax: (830)257-6505
E-mail: kim.vogel@kstar.org
URL: http://www.kstar.org/
Kim Vogol, Director
Program(s): Basic Center Program.

36710 ■ Lifeworks Alliance of Youth and Family Services
Runaway and Homeless Youth Services
3700 S 1st St.
Austin, TX 78704
Ph: (512)735-2400
Fax: (512)735-2452
E-mail: info@lifeworksweb.org
URL: http://www.lifeworksweb.org
Susan McDowell, Executive Director
Program(s): Basic Center Program; Transitional Living Program; Street Outreach Program; Maternity Group Home. **Formerly:** (1998) Middle Earth Unlimited, Runaway and Homeless Youth Services.

36711 ■ Marywood
Runaway and Homeless Youth Program
818 E 53rd St.
Austin, TX 78705
Ph: (512)451-7361
Free: 800-222-4051
URL: http://www.childinc.org/
Jean Henry, Director
Program(s): Transitional Living Program.

36712 ■ Montgomery County Youth Services
Runaway and Homeless Youth Services
105 W Lewis St.
Conroe, TX 77301
Ph: (936)756-8682
Fax: (936)756-8877
E-mail: laurie.oliver@youthmc.org
URL: http://www.youthmc.org/
Program(s): Transitional Living Program.

36713 ■ North Texas Youth Connection
Runaway and Homeless Youth Services
PO Box 1625
Sherman, TX 75091
Ph: (903)893-4717
Fax: (903)868-2260
E-mail: gcja@cableone.net
URL: http://www.ntxyouthconnection.org/
Gene Perkins, Executive Director
Program(s): Basic Center Program; Transitional Living Program. **Formerly:** Grayson County Juvenile Alternatives.

36714 ■ Promise House
Runaway and Homeless Youth Program
224 W Page Ave.
Dallas, TX 75208
Ph: (214)941-8578
Free: 866-941-8578
Fax: (214)941-8670
E-mail: executivedirector@promisehouse.org
URL: http://www.promisehouse.org
Harriet Boorhem, Executive Director
Program(s): Basic Center Program; Transitional Living Program; Street Outreach Program.

36715 ■ Roy Maas' Youth Alternatives
The Bridge
Runaway and Homeless Youth Program
3103 West Ave.
San Antonio, TX 78213
Ph: (210)340-8077
Fax: (210)340-2232
E-mail: rmya@rmya.org
URL: http://www.rmya.org
Gloria Kelly, Chief Executive Officer
Program(s): Basic Center Program; Transitional Living Program. **Remarks:** Center operates The Bridge, an emergency shelter that provides care for children who need a safe place to stay for a short period of time; Girlsville, a long-term facility for girls aged 6-17; The Junction, a long term facility for boys aged 6-17; and the Meadows, a residential treatment center for young people aged 6-17 who have more specialized needs.

36716 ■ SCAN Emergency Youth Shelter
Runaway and Homeless Youth Program
2387 E Saunders St.
Laredo, TX 78041
Ph: (956)724-5111
Free: 800-355-7226
Fax: (956)724-4861
URL: http://www.scan-inc.org
Program(s): Transitional Living Program.

36717 ■ Starry: A Children at Heart Ministry
Runaway and Homeless Youth Program
1300 N Mays
Round Rock, TX 78664
Ph: (512)246-4288
Fax: (512)255-1250
E-mail: info@starryonline.org
URL: http://www.childrenattheartministries.org
Don Forrester, President
Program(s): Basic Center Program.

36718 ■ YMCA of Dallas, Community Services
Urban Outreach
Runaway and Homeless Youth Program
601 N Akard St., 4th fl.
Dallas, TX 75201
Ph: (214)880-9622
Fax: (214)871-3014
URL: http://www.ymcadallas.org
Gordon Echtenkamp, President
Program(s): Basic Center Program. **Remarks:** Provides emergency shelter. Fees for services are charged on a sliding scale. No one is refused service due to inability to pay.

36719 ■ Youth and Family Counseling
Runaway and Homeless Youth Program
PO Box 1611
Angleton, TX 77516
Ph: (979)864-1577
Free: 800-392-3352
Fax: (979)848-8628
E-mail: yfcs@yfcs.org
URL: http://www.yfcs.org/
Diana Fleming, Director
Program(s): Basic Center Program.

UTAH

36720 ■ Archway Youth Service Center
Runaway and Homeless Youth Program
2660 Lincoln Ave.
Ogden, UT 84401
Ph: (801)778-6500
Free: 888-442-6520
E-mail: kkashiwa@utah.gov
URL: http://www.medicalhomeportal.org/resources/services/provider/11687
Lana Dean, Director
Program(s): Basic Center Program.

36721 ■ Salt Lake County Youth Services
Runaway and Homeless Youth Program
177 W Price Ave.
South Salt Lake City, UT 84115
Ph: (385)468-4500
Fax: (385)468-4498
URL: http://www.youth.slco.org/
Pat Berckman, Director
Program(s): Basic Center Program.

36722 ■ Volunteers of America, Utah
Homeless Youth Resource Center
Runaway and Homeless Youth Program
511 West 200 S, Ste. 160
Salt Lake City, UT 84101
Ph: (801)363-9414
Fax: (801)355-3546
URL: http://www.voaut.org
Jeff St. Romain, President
Program(s): Basic Center Program; Transitional Living Program.

VERMONT

36723 ■ New England Network
Runaway and Homeless Youth Program
156 College St., Ste. 301
Burlington, VT 05445
Ph: (802)425-3006
Fax: (802)425-3007
E-mail: mgoodman@nenetwork.org
URL: http://www.nenetwork.org
Melanie Goodman, Executive Director
Program(s): Basic Center Program.

36724 ■ Spectrum Youth and Family Services
Runaway and Homeless Youth Program
31 Elmwood Ave.
Burlington, VT 05401
Ph: (802)864-7423
Fax: (802)660-0576
E-mail: info@spectrumvt.org
URL: http://www.spectrumvt.org/
Mark Redmond, Executive Director
Program(s): Transitional Living Program; Street Outreach Program.

36725 ■ Washington County Youth Service Bureau
Runaway and Homeless Youth Program
38 Elm St.
Montpelier, VT 05601
Ph: (802)229-9151
Fax: (802)229-2508
E-mail: wcysb@youthservicebureau.info
URL: http://www.youthservicebureau.info/
Thomas Howard, Executive Director
Program(s): Basic Center Program; Transitional Living Program; Street Outreach Program. **Remarks:** Provides emergency shelter. Services are offered free of charge and on a sliding-scale basis when appropriate.

VIRGINIA

36726 ■ Alternative House
Runaway and Homeless Youth Program
PO Box 694
Dunn Loring, VA 22027
Ph: (703)506-9191
Fax: (703)506-8949
E-mail: ah@thealternativehouse.org
URL: http://www.thealternativehouse.org
Program(s): Transitional Living Program; Maternity Group Home.

36727 ■ Chances For Youth
Runaway and Homeless Youth Program
13321 Occoquan Rd.
Woodbridge, VA 22191
Ph: (703)491-2053
Free: 800-491-2053
Fax: (703)842-6132
E-mail: info@chancesforyouth.org
URL: http://www.chancesforyouth.org
Program(s): Basic Center Program.

36728 ■ Children, Youth and Family Services
Runaway and Homeless Youth Program
1000 E High St.
Charlottesville, VA 22902
Ph: (434)296-4118
Fax: (434)295-2638
E-mail: info@cyfs.org
URL: http://www.cyfs.org/
Dominic Felix, Executive Director
Program(s): Basic Center Program.

36729 ■ Family Lifeline
Oasis House
Runaway and Homeless Youth Program
2325 W Broad St.
Richmond, VA 23220
Ph: (804)282-4255
Fax: (804)285-3701
E-mail: info@familylifeline.org
URL: http://www.family-lifeline.org
Reed Henderson, President
Program(s): Basic Center Program; Transitional Living Program; Street Outreach Program.

36730 ■ Residential Youth Services, Inc., Alexandria
Runaway and Homeless Youth Program
4820 Welford St.
Alexandria, VA 22309
Ph: (703)347-6423
E-mail: rys@tidalwave.net
URL: http://www.rysva.org
Cesar Adigwe, Director

36731 ■ Seton House, Inc.
Runaway and Homeless Youth Program
3333-28 Virginia Beach Blvd.
Virginia Beach, VA 23452
Ph: (757)335-2121
Fax: (757)340-5768
E-mail: kjeffries@setonyouthshelters.org
URL: http://www.setonyouthshelters.org
Kathy Jeffries, Executive Director
Program(s): Basic Center Program.

36732 ■ Volunteer Emergency Families for Children
Runaway and Homeless Youth Program
4915 Radford Ave., Ste. 100A
Richmond, VA 23230
Ph: (804)379-7767
Free: 800-756-6167
Fax: (804)379-7933
E-mail: centraloffice@volunteerfamilies.org
URL: http://www.volunteerfamilies.org
Karen Martinez, Executive Director
Program(s): Basic Center Program.

WASHINGTON

36733 ■ Auburn Youth Resources
Runaway and Homeless Youth Program
816 F St. SE
Auburn, WA 98002
Ph: (253)939-2202
Fax: (253)735-1894
E-mail: ayrcounseling@ayr4kids.org
URL: http://www.ayr4kids.org/
Jim Blanchard, Director
Program(s): Basic Center Program. **Formerly:** Auburn Youth Resources, South Kent County Youth Program.

36734 ■ Cocoon House
Runaway and Homeless Youth Program
2929 Pine St.
Everett, WA 98201
Ph: (425)259-5802
Free: 800-259-6042
Fax: (425)317-9632
E-mail: info@cocoonhouse.org
URL: http://www.cocoonhouse.org/
Lee Trevithick, Executive Director
Program(s): Transitional Living Program; Street Outreach Program.

36735 ■ Community Youth Services, Olympia
Runaway and Homeless Youth Program
711 State St. NE, 3rd Fl.
Olympia, WA 98506
Ph: (360)943-0780
Free: 888-698-1816
Fax: (360)943-0785
URL: http://www.communityyouthservices.org
Charles Shelan, Director
Program(s): Basic Center Program; Transitional Living Program; Street Outreach Program.

36736 ■ Friends of Youth
Runaway and Homeless Youth Services
16225 NE 87th St., Ste. A-6
Redmond, WA 98052
Ph: (425)869-6490
Fax: (425)869-6666
E-mail: terry@friendsofyouth.org
URL: http://www.friendsofyouth.org/
Terry Pottmeyer, President
Program(s): Basic Center Program; Transitional Living Program. **Remarks:** Provides emergency shelter. Fees are based on a sliding scale.

36737 ■ Lummi Indian Nation
Runaway and Homeless Youth Program
2530 Kwina Rd.
Bellingham, WA 98226
Ph: (360)384-2373
Fax: (360)384-0844
URL: http://www.lummi-nsn.org
Program(s): Transitional Living Program.

36738 ■ Northwest Youth Services
Runaway and Homeless Youth Program
1020 N State St.
Bellingham, WA 98225
Ph: (360)734-9862
Fax: (360)734-4720
E-mail: annel@nwys.org
URL: http://www.nwys.org/
Pat Britain, President
Program(s): Basic Center Program; Transitional Living Program.

36739 ■ Northwest Youth Services
Runaway and Homeless Youth Program
1111 Cleveland Ave., Ste. 102
Mount Vernon, WA 98273
Ph: (360)336-1988
Fax: (360)404-2082
URL: http://www.nwys.org/
Riannon Bardsley, Executive Director
Program(s): Transitional Living Program.

36740 ■ Rural Resources Community Action Agency
Youth.Dot.Com
Runaway and Homeless Youth Program
956 S Main, Ste. A
Colville, WA 99114
Ph: (509)684-8421
Free: 877-988-4266
Fax: (509)684-4740
E-mail: info@ruralresources.org
URL: http://www.ruralresources.org/
Barry Lamont, Executive Director
Program(s): Basic Center Program.

36741 ■ Serenity House of Clallam County
Runaway and Homeless Youth Program
2203 W 18th St.
Port Angeles, WA 98363
Ph: (360)452-7224
Fax: (360)452-0806
E-mail: serenity@olypen.com
URL: http://www.serenityhouseclallam.org/
Program(s): Transitional Living Program; Street Outreach Program.

36742 ■ Volunteers of America, Spokane
Runaway and Homeless Youth Program
525 W 2nd Ave.
Spokane, WA 99201
Ph: (509)624-2378
Fax: (509)624-2275
E-mail: voaspokane@voaspokane.org
URL: http://www.voaspokane.org/
Marilee K. Roloff, Director
Program(s): Basic Center Program; Transitional Living Program.

36743 ■ Youth-Family-Adult Connections
Runaway and Homeless Youth Program
22 S Thor
Spokane, WA 99220
Ph: (509)532-2000
Fax: (509)532-2005
E-mail: info@yfaconnections.org
URL: http://www.yfaconnections.org/
Peggy Larson, Executive Director
Program(s): Basic Center Program.

36744 ■ YouthCare
Runaway and Homeless Youth Program
2500 NE 54th St., Ste. 100
Seattle, WA 98105
Ph: (206)694-4500
Free: 800-495-7802
Fax: (206)694-4509
E-mail: Melinda.Giovento@youthcare.org
URL: http://www.YouthCare.org/
Melinda Giovengo, Executive Director
Program(s): Basic Center Program; Transitional Living Program; Street Outreach Program.

WEST VIRGINIA

36745 ■ Children's Home Society of West Virginia
Runaway and Homeless Youth Program
1422 Kanawha Blvd. E
Charleston, WV 25330
Ph: (304)346-0795
Fax: (304)346-1062
URL: http://www.childhswv.org
Program(s): Basic Center Program.

36746 ■ Daymark
Runaway and Homeless Youth Program
1592 Washington St. E, Ste. 2
Charleston, WV 25311
Ph: (304)340-3675
Fax: (304)340-3595
URL: http://www.daymark.org
Dennis Pease, Executive Director
Program(s): Basic Center Program.

36747 ■ New Connections
Runaway and Homeless Youth Program
1598C Washington St.
Charleston, WV 25311
Ph: (304)340-3690
URL: http://www.daymark.org/teens.htm
Program(s): Basic Center Program; Transitional Living Program.

36748 ■ Youth Services System, Inc.
Runaway and Homeless Youth Program
1000 Chapline St.
Wheeling, WV 26003
Ph: (304)233-9627
E-mail: ysswv@aol.com
URL: http://youthservicessystem.org/
Program(s): Basic Center Program; Transitional Living Program.

WISCONSIN

36749 ■ Counseling Center of Milwaukee
Pathfinders
Runaway and Homeless Youth Program
4200 N Holton St., Ste. 400
Milwaukee, WI 53212
Ph: (414)964-2565
Fax: (414)964-0102
E-mail: info@pathfindersmke.org
URL: http://pathfindersmke.org/
Dan Magnuson, Executive Director
Program(s): Basic Center Program.

36750 ■ Family Services of Northeast Wisconsin, Inc.
Runaway and Homeless Youth Program
300 Crooks St.
Green Bay, WI 53405
Ph: (920)436-6800
Free: 800-998-9609
E-mail: intake@familyservicesnew.org
URL: http://www.familyservicesnew.org/
Thomas Martin, President
Program(s): Transitional Living Program.

36751 ■ Kenosha Human Development Services Inc.
Runaway and Homeless Youth Program
5407 8th Ave.
Kenosha, WI 53140
Ph: (262)657-7188
URL: http://www.khds.org/
Program(s): Transitional Living Program.

36752 ■ Lutheran Social Services of Wisconsin and Upper Michigan--Appleton, WI
Runaway and Homeless Youth Program
3003-A N Richmond St.
Appleton, WI 54911

Ph: (920)734-1326
Fax: (920)734-2824
E-mail: info@lsswis.org
URL: http://www.lsswis.org/
Program(s): Basic Center Program; Transitional Living Program.

36753 ■ Pathfinders--Youth Shelter
Runaway and Homeless Youth Program
1614 E Kane Pl.
Milwaukee, WI 53202
Ph: (414)271-1560
Fax: (414)271-1831
E-mail: info@pathfindersmke.org
URL: http://pathfindersmke.org/
Program(s): Basic Center Program.

36754 ■ Positive Alternatives, Inc.
Teen Care Crisis Intervention
Runaway and Homeless Youth Program
603 Terril Rd.
Monomonic, WI 54751
Ph: (715)235-9552
Fax: (715)235-1075
E-mail: kedwards@positive-alternatives.org
URL: http://www.positive-alternatives.org/teencare.htm
Kimberly Edwards, Executive Director
Program(s): Basic Center Program; Street Outreach Program.

36755 ■ PSC for Safe Babies
Runaway and Homeless Youth Program
434 Madison St.
Waukesha, WI 53188
Ph: (262)524-4120
Fax: (262)548-0789
URL: http://www.pregnancy-support.org/
Theresa Leben, Executive Director
Program(s): Transitional Living Program. **Formerly:** Up Connections, Inc./Second Chance Home.

36756 ■ Safe Haven of Racine, Inc.
Runaway and Homeless Youth Program
1030 Washington Ave.
Racine, WI 53403
Ph: (262)637-9559
Fax: (262)632-8758
E-mail: safehaven@safehavenofracine.org
URL: http://www.safehavenofracine.org
James D. Huycke, Executive Director
Program(s): Basic Center Program; Transitional Living Program; Street Outreach Program. **Formerly:** Innovative Youth Services.

36757 ■ Walker's Point Youth and Family Center
Runaway and Homeless Youth Program
2030 W National Ave.
Milwaukee, WI 53204
Ph: (414)672-5300
Fax: (414)672-5340
E-mail: walkersp@sbcglobal.net
URL: http://www.walkerspoint.org/
Program(s): Basic Center Program; Transitional Living Program.

36758 ■ Wisconsin Association for Homeless and Runaway Services
Runaway and Homeless Youth Program
2318 E Dayton St.
Madison, WI 53704
Ph: (608)241-2649
Fax: (608)241-2649
E-mail: pbalke@sbcglobal.net
URL: http://www.wahrs.org
Patricia Balke, Director
Program(s): Basic Center Program; Street Outreach Program.

36759 ■ Youth and Family Project Runaway Program
Crossroad
630 Elm St.
West Bend, WI 53095
Ph: (262)338-1661
Fax: (262)338-7761
E-mail: yfpwash@excel.net
URL: http://www.youthandfamilyproject.org/
Program(s): Basic Center Program.

36760 ■ Youth Services of Southern Wisconsin
Briarpatch
Runaway and Homeless Youth Program
1955 Atwood Ave.
Madison, WI 53704
Ph: (608)245-2550
URL: http://www.youthsos.org
Program(s): Basic Center Program; Street Outreach Program.

36761 ■ Youth Services of Southern Wisconsin
Runaway and Homeless Youth Program
1955 Atwood Ave.
Madison, WI 53704
Ph: (608)245-2550
Free: 800-798-1126
Fax: (608)245-2551
E-mail: james.adams@youthsos.org
URL: http://www.youthsos.org
Casey Behrend, President

WYOMING

36762 ■ Attention Homes
Runaway and Homeless Youth Program
714 W Fox Farm Rd.
Cheyenne, WY 82007
Ph: (307)778-7832
Fax: (307)778-2576
Dr. Cherri Lester, Executive Director
Program(s): Basic Center Program.

36763 ■ Fremont County Group Homes
Runaway and Homeless Youth Program
11 Minter Ln.
Riverton, WY 82501
Ph: (307)856-2643
E-mail: sdoerr@bresnan.net
Program(s): Basic Center Program.

36764 ■ Laramie Youth Crisis Center
Runaway and Homeless Youth Program
PO Box 520
Laramie, WY 82073
Ph: (307)742-5936
URL: http://www.cathedralhome.org/lycc.html
Program(s): Basic Center Program.

36765 ■ Teton Youth & Family Services
Runaway and Homeless Youth Program
510 S Cache
Jackson, WY 83001
Ph: (307)733-6440
E-mail: bruce@tyfs.org
URL: http://www.redtopmeadows.org/
Program(s): Basic Center Program; Street Outreach Program; Transitional Living Program.

36766 ■ Volunteers of America--Sheridan WY
Runaway and Homeless Youth Program
1876 S Sheridan Rd.
Sheridan, WY 82801
Ph: (307)672-0475
URL: http://www.voanr.org/Youth-Services-Programs
Program(s): Basic Center Program; Street Outreach Program.

36767 ■ Youth Alternative Home Association
Runaway and Homeless Youth Program
395 City View Dr.
Evanston, WY 82930
Ph: (307)789-1477
Program(s): Transitional Living Program.

36768 ■ Youth Development Services
Runaway and Homeless Youth Program
800 Jackson St.
Douglas, WY 82633
Ph: (307)358-4352
Program(s): Basic Center Program; Street Outreach Program.

36769 ■ Youth Emergency Services
Runaway and Homeless Youth Program
905 N Gurley
Gillette, WY 82716
Ph: (307)686-0669
Fax: (307)686-2121
E-mail: sengland@ccsd.k12.wy.us
URL: http://www.youthemergencyservices.org/
Sheri England, Executive Director
Program(s): Transitional Living Program.

CPSIA information can be obtained
at www.ICGtesting.com
Printed in the USA
FFOW032226100613
1264FF

9 781414 478883